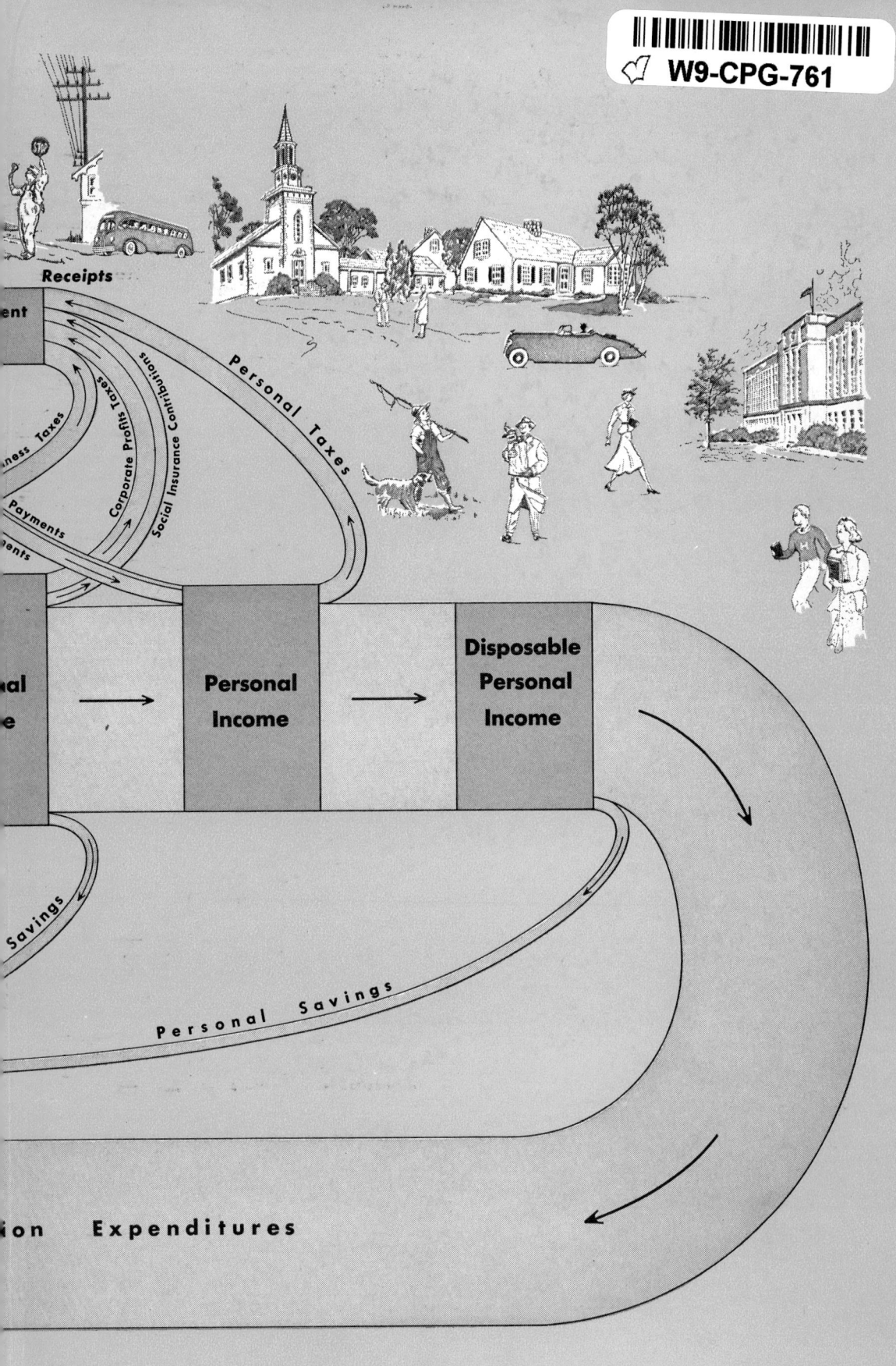

Receipts

Personal Taxes

Corporate Profits Taxes

Social Insurance Contributions

ness Taxes

Payments

ents

nal
e

**Personal
Income**

**Disposable
Personal
Income**

Savings

Personal Savings

ion   Expenditures

AMERICA'S NEEDS AND RESOURCES

A NEW SURVEY

STAFF OF THE SURVEY

J. FREDERIC DEWHURST
Research Director

THOMAS C. FICHANDLER
Associate Research Director

RESEARCH ASSOCIATES

LOUIS H. BEAN

ELIZABETH BLACKERT

LAWRENCE N. BLOOMBERG

HOWARD G. BRUNSMAN

WILLIAM G. CARR

ROBERT F. DRURY

LEAH L. FEINGOLD

WILBERT G. FRITZ

OWEN C. GRETTON

A. BENJAMIN HANDLER

ROBERT W. HARTLEY

HELEN HOLLINGSWORTH

HELEN M. HUMES

HYMAN B. KAITZ

WYLIE KILPATRICK

FRANCES KLAFTER

MARGARET C. KLEM

BENSON Y. LANDIS

JOHN W. MCCONNELL

WILFRED OWEN

MARGARET G. REID

C. A. R. WARDWELL

JOHN A. WARING, JR.

GERTRUDE S. WEISS

HERBERT K. ZASSENHAUS

AMERICA'S NEEDS AND RESOURCES

A NEW SURVEY

BY

J. Frederic Dewhurst and Associates

NEW YORK · The Twentieth Century Fund · 1955

MANUFACTURED IN THE UNITED STATES OF AMERICA
BY AMERICAN BOOK–STRATFORD PRESS, INC., NEW YORK

FOREWORD

Between the end of World War I and the end of World War II most of the world experienced a revolution, though the form of that revolution varied from country to country. When history is written, it may well prove to have been the most far-reaching in the annals of mankind. The Communist revolution in Russia — dramatic and violent though it was — was merely one phase (and in some ways not the most important phase) of a world-wide change.

In the United States, the revolution was primarily economic. It could hardly have been otherwise. The United States in previous generations had achieved a higher measure of political participation, civil liberty and mass education than any other great power. Consequently, political objectives elsewhere struggled for with anguish were commonplace here. Economically, nonetheless, the United States was struggling with the problem of so increasing its production that means for an adequate life might be available to substantially everyone, and distributing its income so that the fruits of increased production should be distributed through all the population. Included in the congeries of problems was that of accumulating and setting aside capital funds to exploit the ever greater capabilities created by the headlong progress of technology.

It was apparent a decade ago that the United States had in large measure achieved the first objective of this revolution. Some audit of its new position was needed. Partly with this in mind, the trustees of the Twentieth Century Fund commissioned J. Frederic Dewhurst, then Economist of the Fund and now Executive Director, to attempt the huge task. But we also asked of him something more difficult and more hazardous — a forecast, or at least a projection, of the trends his research might reveal.

Projection of trends can never be safe or accurate prediction in any case. It does, however, give some base for intelligent estimate of future developments. The result, *America's Needs and Resources,* published by the Fund in the year 1947, received wide recognition as a massive contribution to the understanding of the America produced by the twentieth century revolution.

Dr. Dewhurst as director of the study, and the trustees of the Fund, felt that none of us could rest even on this major accomplishment. Some of us felt that the forecasts based on projected historical experience, optimistic as they were, would be proved underestimates by the continuing onrush of the technical and economic American revolution. In consequence, and in large measure at Dr. Dewhurst's initiative, the Fund's trustees commissioned this second volume, a second audit which carries forward the record of experience into the year 1954.

The new volume accomplishes two purposes. It gives the present position of American economic resources, production and consumption. It establishes a basis of comparison with earlier figures and thus makes it possible to see with some clarity the extent of progress made. Actually, the progress has been enormous, and suggests (as some of us had felt) that the United States has not merely climbed to a new plateau, but is ascending heights whose upper limit is not yet measurable, and at an accelerated rate of speed.

The twentieth century has been a time of turbulence and terror. Yet it is endowing its children, at least in the United States, with resources beyond the dreams of past generations, and distributing its benefits well enough to give an overwhelming majority of Americans at once the highest standard of living ever achieved by a great population and the promise that this standard will continue to rise.

Thoughtful perusal of the data contained in this book suggests some fascinating and bewildering problems ahead.

When an entire population struggles for subsistence from one day to the next, its problems of economic philosophy are relatively few. Its choices and decisions are limited. No great spiritual question is raised about the desirability of obtaining for a half-fed population enough food to quell hunger, or creating shelter so that families are at least tolerably housed, or assuring clothes enough to satisfy moderate needs. Once this point is passed, however, each member of the population is faced with a new question: not "Can I live?" but "What kind of life do I wish to lead?" In this America a man may literally choose between a mean house with a good motor car and a good house with a poor motor car.

Men may (and do) choose to live in slums with television sets rather than in humble but decent houses without. Men can decide, within limits, whether or not they prefer to support churches and schools handsomely and skimp on movies and tobacco. Each man, whether he knows it or not, makes these choices according to his picture of "the good life."

This new volume, like the first, records, in quiet figures, the aggregate results of these personal decisions. We know now, approximately, the sum total of the results of these choices. We know that the area of choice and the capacity to choose have been increasing as the national income and individual buying power increase. We have solid reason to believe, from the record today, that the ability to choose and the range of choice will increase vastly in the next generation. Americans, on a scale never before known, are reaching a point where each can get what he really wants. Then, the real problem is that of orderly decision as to what he does want, or at least what he wants most.

This brief introduction barely suggests the wealth and implications of the material painstakingly gathered together in this book. It is more than a mine of facts, more even than an accurate economic audit. It is a starting point from which the twentieth century American may do some thinking about himself and the kind of man or woman he or she wishes to be. This is perhaps one of the most important tasks which face our great and fecund democracy.

ADOLF A. BERLE, JR., *Chairman, Board of Trustees*
The Twentieth Century Fund

NEW YORK, NEW YORK
FEBRUARY 10, 1955

PREFACE

THIS VOLUME is a new and more comprehensive survey of the demands and needs, the resources and capacities of the American economy. The original *America's Needs and Resources*, begun during World War II and published eight years ago, gave primary attention to the swift transition from a subnormal prewar economy to full-scale war production, the growing civilian shortages, and effects of these developments on the postwar economy. The present survey finds its major focus in the phenomenal postwar boom, in the long-range upsurge of the economy which this latest boom accentuated, and in the significance of our expanding economy for the future well-being of our nation.

Authors of the present study also give special attention to the impact in various fields of the many new products and techniques developed during the postwar period. In addition to this review of important technological developments in the topical chapters, the report includes as an innovation two chapters on technological change and its effects in increasing American productivity. The new report also adds a special chapter on Welfare, a subject treated only briefly in the original volume. In addition to these new chapters, the topical chapters corresponding to those in the first report have been completely rewritten and are longer and more comprehensive. In terms of tabular and graphic material, as well as in words and pages, the new book is substantially bigger than the original one.

The manuscript of this report was delivered to the printer in the fall of 1954, and for that reason the most recent data included cover the year 1953 and, in some cases, the early part of 1954. This means that the discussion of recent economic changes in Chapter 1 and elsewhere in the report takes account of the increase in unemployment and moderate decline in business activity during late 1953 and early 1954, but not of more recent developments. However, certain preliminary key data for the year 1954 are presented in a special appendix on page 1118. This appendix also presents basic data on income and expenditures, as well as the survey's basic 1960 projections, expressed in terms of the 1954 price level.

This volume as a whole — as well as almost every individual chapter — is in a very real sense the result of cooperative effort. The basic data on population, employment and working hours, on productivity, and on income, consumption and expenditure patterns, presented in Chapters 2, 3 and 4 and summarized in Chapter 26, are the responsibility of members of the central staff of the study. The contributing authors of chapters on various classes of consumption goods and services, on capital goods, on government and foreign transactions, and on resources and capacities, were asked to develop their own analyses within this consistent statistical frame of reference. The authors of these chapters, therefore, have no responsibility for any errors of fact or judgment in the basic data and projections.

The central staff also participated in the review and criticism of the drafts of the contributed chapters and in varying degrees aided in revising, reorganizing and editing and in the reconciliation of statistical data. It is difficult to recognize adequately the loyal and highly efficient services of this central staff and to express my gratitude to those who were so closely associated with me in this undertaking. In addition to personal responsibility for certain chapters, Thomas C. Fichandler bore the major share of administrative responsibility in supervising the basic statistical work of the study and in the coordination and revision of the work of individual contributors. Leah L. Feingold served with conscientious skill in preparing and revising an enormous volume of basic statistics. Frances Klafter collaborated in authorship of one chapter of the report, carried through a vast amount of checking and cross-checking, and discharged with competence the exacting task of preparing the index. Elizabeth Blackert edited the manuscript with meticulous care and great ability. My secretaries, J. Dart Morgan and Dorothy Williamson, displayed great capacity for handling administrative details and much patience in deciphering almost illegible script, and in typing manuscript.

On behalf of the Fund, I wish also to express deep appreciation to those research associates, not members of the central staff, who were the authors and co-authors of most of the individual chapters of this report. Without their specialized knowledge of particular fields and their diligence and patience in preparing and revising their chapters, this report could not have been prepared. The names of the authors of individual chapters, as well as of other persons, including members of the central staff of the study, who contributed substantively to this report as co-authors, collaborators or editors, or in the preparation of material on which the report is based, are listed opposite the title page of this volume. Specific responsibility for authorship of individual chapters is also shown on the first page of each chapter.

Although all of the chapters in the present report that appeared in the original book have been rewritten — in nine cases by different authors — all authors were requested to present their findings in the general pattern of the original report. They were informed that certain background material might be used from the original report, in the same wording where this seemed desirable, without specific credit. In most instances little or none of the original text appears in the chapter as revised, but in a few cases some repeated material has been used. Acknowledgment of indebtedness to earlier authors for this use of their material is hereby made.

The staff and contributors of the survey and the Fund are also indebted to many individuals and private and public organizations for generous aid in assembling material used in the report and for reviewing and criticizing portions of the manuscript. Among the organizations whose publications and personnel were drawn on extensively were the Bureau of the Census and Office of Business Economics of the Department of Commerce, the Bureau of Agricultural Economics, the Bureau of Labor Statistics, the Office of Education, the Bureau of Vital Statistics, the Board of Governors of the Federal Reserve System, the Public Housing Administration, the Social Security Administration, the Federal Power Commission, the Bureau of Mines, the Machinery and Allied Products Institute, the National City Bank, the National Industrial Conference Board, the National Bureau of Economic Research, The Brookings Institution and the National Planning Association. Milton Abelson reviewed with great care Chapter 19 on foreign trade and finance.

I am personally indebted to a number of persons for help in preparing chapters for which I am responsible and for reviewing portions of the manuscript. Evans Clark, who retired as Executive Director of the Fund as the manuscript of this report was nearing completion, carefully reviewed most of my chapters. Joseph Davis, of the Stanford Food Research Institute, gave me valuable comments on the population chapter. Lawrence Jennings of the Federal Power Commission aided greatly in the preparation of estimates of energy output presented in Chapter 25, and the advice of Walter Slifer of the Bituminous Coal Association, of Richard Josephson of the Forestry Service and of others on these questions was also very helpful. I am grateful to Philip Swain of *Power* magazine for his wise counsel on power production and use and on other technological questions.

In addition to his assistance in preparing certain chapters, John A. Waring, Jr., reviewed the chapters on productivity and technology. For reviewing the latter chapter, I am also indebted to John R. Dewhurst, of the Sperry Corporation, while generous aid in preparation of this chapter was extended by various technicians of a number of corporations and associations, including the Corning Glass Works, American Can Company, Owens-Illinois Glass Company, Dow Corning Corporation, General Electric Company, E. I. du Pont de Nemours Corporation, Consolidated Edison Company of N. Y., Western Union Telegraph Company, American Machine and Foundry Company, American Steel Dredge Company, General Motors Corporation, McGraw-Hill Publishing Company, Westinghouse Electric Corporation, Bell Telephone Laboratories, Portland Cement Association, Radio Corporation of America, Monsanto Chemical Company and The Studebaker Corporation. While I am very grateful for the help obtained from these and other experts, it is hardly necessary to say that they are in no degree responsible for any of the findings.

The enormously complex task of designing and planning the actual volume was in the competent hands of Elizabeth Mann, Chief of the Fund's Publishing Department. Her sudden death on October 27, when the book was in the final stages of manufacture, was a grievous loss to the Fund and to all of her associates in this undertaking. Sara Love deserves great credit for the imagination and professional skill she brought to the drafting of the end papers and the numerous charts which illustrate the volume. The styling of the manuscript for the printer was ably done by Ruth Rocker.

To all these and many others who have contributed to the completion of this work, I want to express my warm personal appreciation.

J. Frederic Dewhurst

CONTENTS

PART I. BASIC TRENDS

TABLES

FIGURES

## CHAPTER I

WAR AND AFTERMATH

Since the summer of 1940 the American economy has been in large measure a war economy. Never before during a period of equal length has our economic system been so stimulated and distorted by war — preparation for war, war itself, postwar readjustment, and then renewal of hostilities and rearmament. The economic expansion of World War II began slowly after the collapse of France, rapidly increased in speed after Pearl Harbor, and came to a climax in 1944. In that year one out of every four adult males less than 65 years old was under arms, nearly half of the nation's entire labor force was engaged in war-related activities, and more than 40 per cent of the gross national product was devoted to winning the war.

Demobilization and reconversion, which began after V-E Day, moved ahead swiftly after V-J Day, when military spending was sharply curtailed. But even after the postwar military budget had been "cut to the bone," it remained much larger than in prewar years. The $13 billion spent for defense in 1947 was a larger dollar total than we paid out for war purposes in the peak year of World War I and constituted a larger share of the gross national product than did military expenditures in any peacetime year before World War II.

Since the Communist attack on South Korea in the summer of 1950, national security expenditures have again risen steeply, reaching a volume of nearly $52 billion in 1953. Such an expenditure amounted to almost three fifths of the 1944 outlay, which was the largest of any World War II year, but it represented a much smaller share of the gross national product — 14 per cent as compared with 42 per cent in 1944. Security expenditures have been decreasing since the second quarter of 1953 (when they reached an annual rate of $53.5 billion) and by the first quarter of 1954

had fallen well below an annual rate of $50 billion.

Economic Effects of War

The economic effects of war are pervasive and long-continued, and cannot be measured simply in terms of the money outlay or the share of the national product involved. World War II spending, following a decade of unemployment and depression, merely took up the slack at first but soon brought prosperity and full employment. So much of our production "went to war," however, that consumers were unable to buy the things they wanted and had money to pay for. This concentration on war production and consequent accumulation of demand for other kinds of goods virtually guaranteed a postwar boom, while the great expansion of our money supply caused by meeting so much of the cost of the war out of loans rather than taxes also ensured a postwar inflation.

The Korean crisis, though it broke no more unexpectedly than the events ten years earlier that eventually led to our entrance into World War II, came under different economic and psychological circumstances. With the shortages of World War II fresh in mind, people rushed to buy in anticipation of future personal and business needs. Because there was little slack in the economy this time, the rush of buying sent prices, wages and costs into a steep climb. Thus the Korean inflation, instead of lagging after the developments which might have been expected to set it in motion, "came ahead of time."

Production Records

Whether because of war and inflation, or in spite of it, the 1940s and the years since the end of that decade have been a period of unexampled activity and prosperity. Production of all basic agricultural products, minerals and other raw materials during the war decade far exceeded the output of these products during the 1930s and surpassed that of the prosperous 1920s. This was also true of the output of steel, copper, zinc, lead,

By J. Frederic Dewhurst, Executive Director of the Twentieth Century Fund and Research Director of this study, and Charles A. R. Wardwell, Office of Business Economics, U.S. Department of Commerce. Opinions and judgments expressed in this chapter are those of the authors and should not be attributed to the organizations with which they are associated.

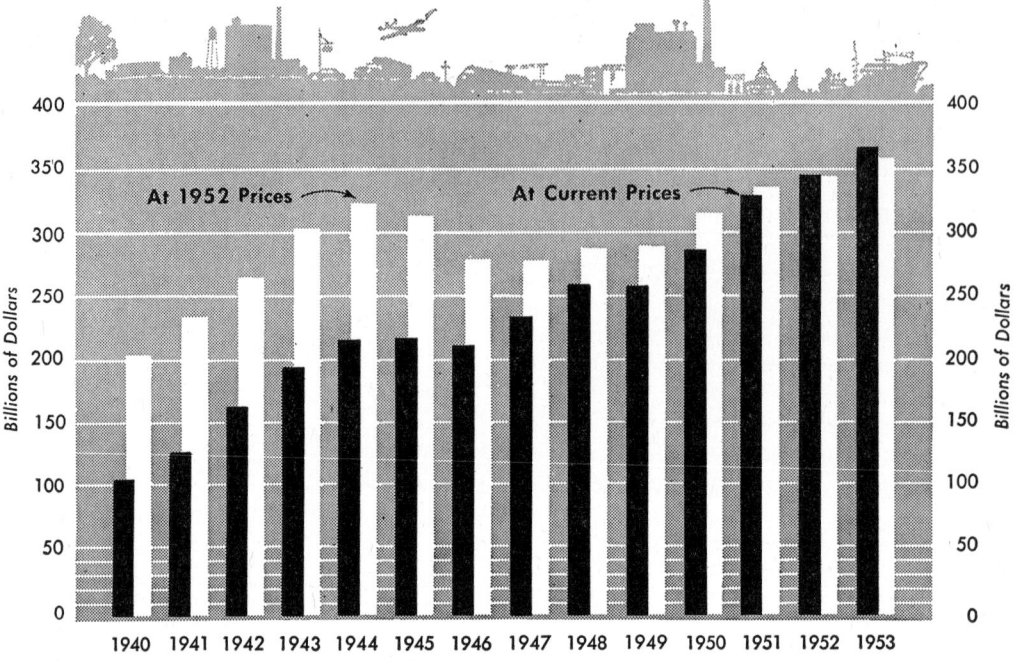

FIGURE 1. GROSS NATIONAL PRODUCT AT CURRENT AND AT 1952 PRICES, 1940–1953

Source: Based on Appendix 4–2.

aluminum and other industrial metals; of petroleum, natural gas and coal; of lumber and other forest products; of cement and most structural materials; and of phosphates, nitrates and a host of other chemicals. Production of consumers' durable goods — automobiles, household refrigerators, vacuum cleaners, radios, oil burners, etc. — even though virtually suspended from 1942 to 1944, was heavy enough during the postwar years to bring the total for the decade above that of any earlier ten-year period.

Gross national product and national income — the best over-all measures of output and material welfare — soared to heights never before approached. Even when adjustment is made for the price rise during the decade, it appears that the national economy turned out during 1941–1950 a gross total of more than $2.9 trillion worth of goods and services (in dollars of 1952 purchasing power), or 81 per cent more than the $1.6 trillion produced in the preceding decade. By the end of the decade the physical volume of the gross national product was approaching the World War II record of 1944, and the 1953 total of $361 billion exceeded it by 14 per cent. (See Figure 1.)

National income (in 1952 dollars) on a per capita basis amounted roughly to $1,740 in 1950 and to $1,870 in 1953, compared with $1,220 in 1940, $1,060 in 1930, and $950 in 1920. Thus per capita real income has increased 50 per cent since 1940 and has doubled in a generation.

Three Stages of Expansion

The long-continued expansion since 1940 has had three distinct phases. Beginning in 1940, and culminating in 1944 and early 1945, the American economy increasingly devoted itself to the task of producing what was needed to win the war, which meant the deferral of demand for many kinds of business and consumer goods.

The years after 1946 brought swift reconversion and a mounting postwar boom. This catching-up period approached an end in 1948 and 1949, by which time the war-deferred demand for most kinds of goods — with the notable exception of housing — had been satisfied. In any event, the minor slackening of business in 1949 apparently marked the termination of the most dynamic phase of the postwar boom.

The modest recovery in the early months of 1950 was greatly stimulated by the Korean crisis,

TABLE 1. GROSS NATIONAL PRODUCT AND WAR EXPENDITURES, 1940–1945
(*Billions*)

	1940	1941	1942	1943	1944	1945
Gross national product	$101.4	$126.4	$161.6	$194.3	$213.7	$215.2
Personal consumption expenditures	72.1	82.3	91.2	102.2	111.6	123.1
Durable goods	7.9	9.8	7.1	6.8	7.1	8.5
Nondurable goods	37.6	44.0	52.9	61.0	67.1	74.9
Services	26.6	28.5	31.2	34.5	37.4	39.7
Gross private domestic investment	13.9	18.3	10.9	5.7	7.7	10.7
Residential construction	3.1	3.7	1.9	1.0	.9	1.2
Nonresidential construction	1.9	2.5	1.6	1.0	1.3	2.0
Producers' durable equipment	6.1	7.7	4.9	4.1	5.7	7.5
Other [a]	2.8	4.4	2.5	—.4	—.2	—
Government purchases of goods and services	13.9	24.7	59.7	88.6	96.5	82.8
Nonwar—federal, state and local	11.7	11.0	10.4	8.9	9.1	9.1
War—federal	2.2	13.8	49.6	80.4	88.6	75.9
Less federal government sales	—	—	.2	.6	1.2	2.2
Net foreign investment	1.5	1.1	—.2	—2.2	—2.1	—1.4

Source: National Income and Product of the United States, 1929–1950 (1951 National Income Supplement to the *Survey of Current Business*), Table 2, p. 150, and Tables 30 and 31, p. 199.

a. Includes changes in business inventories, construction expenditures for crude petroleum and natural gas drilling; and minor differences between latest construction estimates included in Table 31 of the source and earlier estimates included in Table 2 of the source.

which ushered in the third phase of the long expansion that began in 1940. Since 1950, as in each of the earlier periods, there has again been a sharp gain in production, accompanied by an inflationary spurt in the price level. Defense expenditures, which provided the stimulus for this latest surge of activity as they did for the first, reached a peak in 1953 and during the early part of 1954 declined slowly and moderately.

THE WAR POTENTIAL

World War II showed what the American economy could do when working under forced draft. Within four years we were producing more than twice the dollar volume, and more than one and a half times the physical volume, of goods and services that we were turning out when the defense program got under way.

As the "arsenal of democracy" in the peak year of the war effort, 1944, the United States not only outproduced the Axis in combat munitions by more than 50 per cent, but accounted for nearly 45 per cent of the armament output of all belligerent nations together. We were devoting nearly one fourth of our total productive power

to the manufacture of combat armaments alone, more than 40 per cent to meeting all our war needs, and close to half to supplying total government requirements.

Even the vast war output of 1944 could probably have been surpassed had military necessity demanded it. We could have diverted a larger portion of total output to war purposes by further curtailing civilian consumption. Beyond this, we could have expanded the total output itself by further lengthening hours of work and by bringing a still larger proportion of our population into the labor force. In other words, by working harder we could have produced more, and by getting along on less we could have devoted more of what we produced to war needs.

With the ending of the European war, however, it was already clear that 1944 had represented the high-water mark of the war production effort. Following Japan's defeat, drastic cutbacks in the munitions program were made and, although production of civilian durable goods expanded rapidly, employment and production fell substantially below 1944 levels. With emergency workers withdrawing from the labor force and working hours curtailed, *the productive achievements of*

TABLE 2. PRODUCTION OF SELECTED MUNITIONS ITEMS, 1940–1945
(*Billions*)

	July 1, 1940 through 1941	*1942*	*1943*	*1944*	*January through June 30, 1945*
Munitions plus war construction	$16.2	$43.4	$62.7	$62.2	$33.2
Munitions	10.3	30.7	54.2	59.2	31.6
Aircraft	2.1	6.1	12.5	16.0	7.7
Ships	2.2	7.0	12.5	13.4	5.6
Guns and fire control	.5	2.0	3.6	3.1	1.5
Ammunition	.5	2.9	5.5	6.4	4.3
Combat and motor vehicles	1.6	4.9	6.5	5.4	3.1
Communication and electric					
equipment	.3	1.5	3.0	3.7	2.1
Other equipment and supplies	3.1	6.3	10.5	11.1	7.2
War construction	5.9	12.7	8.5	3.0	1.6
War facilities expansion	24.3	22.3	15.3	9.7	4.5
Federally financed	5.7	13.6	9.4	3.2	1.2
Privately financed	18.6	8.7	5.9	6.0	3.2

Sources: Munitions production from *Production, Wartime Achievements and the Reconstruction Outlook*, War Production Board, October 9, 1945, p. 29; war construction and war facilities expansion from *Facilities Expansion, July 1940 through June 1945*, Industrial Statistics Division, Civilian Production Administration, Tables A, B, C.

1944 and early 1945 were not surpassed until six years after the end of the war, when a new defense program was well under way. It is worth while considering these achievements, therefore, in terms of their possible relevance to production probabilities under abnormally high levels of employment in the future.

WAR PRODUCTION

The nation produced $101.4 billion of goods and services in 1940 and well over twice as much, $213.7 billion, in 1944. This is merely a measure of the dollar volume of goods and services, however, and not of the physical volume. Much of the 111 per cent increase in the gross national product was due to increased prices and costs. What remains after "deflating" the 1944 gross national product by the estimated increase in the price level constitutes a fair measure of the physical expansion of goods and services. On this basis, gross physical output probably increased by 57 per cent in the four-year period.

Of the $112.3 billion increase in the dollar volume of the gross national product, all but $29 billion came about through the expansion of government expenditures for goods and services. Government expenditures increased by $83 billion between 1940 and 1944 — from $14 billion to $97 billion. (See Table 1.)

War Outlays

War outlays, chiefly for combat armament and other munitions, were by far the largest factor accounting for the great increase in government expenditures and gross national product. The most spectacular gain was in munitions production, the outlay for which rose from less than $500 million monthly in the early months of the defense program to nearly $5 billion a month when the program reached flood tide after the middle of 1943. More than two thirds of the record annual volume of $59 billion in 1944 consisted of actual combat munitions, i.e., guns, ammunition, fighting and bombing planes, tanks, warships, etc. Expenditures for aircraft and ships, both combat and noncombat types, accounted for about half the outlay for munitions — aircraft for more than 27 per cent and ships for almost 23 per cent. Nearly 16 per cent was spent for guns, ammunition and fire control apparatus, almost 9 per cent for combat and motor vehicles, and the remainder for other equipment and supplies.[1] (See Table 2.)

Physical Output

The physical record of 1944 munitions production makes an even more impressive picture than the dollar totals. During the year, 96,359 planes, including 16,048 heavy bombers, were produced. This was four times the number, and ten times the air-frame weight, of all the planes produced during the eighteen-month period from July 1940 to December 1941.

The record of ship production was equally striking: 30,889 ships of all types produced, and eight times the number and displacement tonnage of combat ships that had been delivered between July 1940 and December 1941. Almost 16.5 million tons of Maritime Commission vessels were delivered in 1944, raising the total output of the three full wartime years to almost 44 million tons — the equivalent of a fleet four times the size of that controlled by the United States when it entered the war. With this wartime tonnage the American merchant marine at the end of the war constituted well over half of the world's shipping afloat.[2] The Navy, with more than 46,000 ships (excluding smaller craft) at the end of 1944, was 32 times its 1939 size and had more ships than were in all the merchant fleets of the world in that year.[3]

Among other types of munitions produced in 1944 were: 17,565 tanks, 595,330 Army Service Forces trucks, 3,284 heavy field guns and howitzers, 7,454 light guns, 152,000 army aircraft rocket launchers, 215,177 bazookas and 1,416,774 short tons of ground artillery ammunition. Output of all of these was negligible in 1940.

CONSTRUCTION AND FACILITIES

The tremendous output of munitions was made possible in part by a large-scale conversion of prewar plants from civilian to military products, especially in the automotive and durable-goods industries. But it also necessitated a vast program of construction of new plants and facilities, about half of which was financed by the federal government. This program reached its height in 1942, when $22 billion of new facilities, of which $14 billion were financed by the federal government, were added to the nation's productive plant. By 1944 most of the needed new facilities were already in use, and new additions of $10 billion in that year represented a return to nearly the 1940 level. In all, more than $75 billion of new war facilities were added under the program. (See Table 2.) New manufacturing facilities alone amounted to well over half the value of all the manufacturing plant in existence at the time the defense program began.

The trend of gross private domestic investment reflects the development of the war plant and equipment expansion program. Rising from less than $14 billion in 1940 to more than $18 billion in 1941, private domestic investment fell to about $11 billion in 1942 and sharply to less than $6 billion in 1943. This decline was due to the elimination of all nonessential construction, to federal financing of most facilities expansion after 1941, and to the tapering off of plant expansion after 1942. Also responsible was the steady decline in private residential construction from nearly $3.7 billion in 1941 to about $900 million in 1944. (See Table 1.)

CONSUMER GOODS AND SERVICES

During this vast war production program, American consumers continued to be well supplied with most of the necessities and many of the luxuries of life. After 1941, it is true, automobiles and other durable goods could not be replaced as they wore out, but the rising prosperity of 1940–1941 meant that consumers' "capital plant" was in good condition when the war came. It is also true that shortages of food and other products had become acute by 1944, black markets were flourishing, and the quality of many kinds of apparel and household furnishings had deteriorated. In spite of these annoyances and difficulties, however, the volume of goods and services consumed by civilians during the three following years remained above the record high levels of prosperous 1941.

Measured in dollars, consumer expenditures for goods and services rose from $72 billion in 1940 to $82 billion in 1941 and then advanced steadily to nearly $112 billion in 1944. (See Table 1.)

---

1. *War Production in 1944,* Report of the Chairman of the War Production Board, June 1945, pp. 14, 135.
2. Data in this section from *War Production in 1944,* pp. 9–10.
3. *The Road to Tokyo & Beyond,* Third Report by the Director of War Mobilization and Reconversion, July 1, 1945, p. 5.

Advancing prices reduced these gains. When expressed in constant dollars, personal consumption expenditures declined slightly in 1942 and increased thereafter; purchases of many kinds of consumers' durable goods, on the other hand, declined sharply after 1941.

This change in the *composition* of wartime consumption — aside from the problem of measuring the rise in prices and the lowered quality of goods — makes it difficult if not impossible to decide to what extent we were able to have both "guns and butter" during World War II. A family unable to obtain a new refrigerator might have spent the same amount of money for liquor and theater tickets, and thus "consumed as much" as if they had been able to get what they wanted. Only in a narrow statistical sense, however, can it be said that their standard of living, or consumption level, was just as high as if they had been able to exercise free choice. Although civilians were actually able to buy more goods and services at the height of the war than in the best prewar year, they were not nearly so "well off" in terms of the kinds of goods they wanted. Perhaps the best evidence that we had to forego butter during the war in order to get guns is the fact that even a full year after V-J Day consumers were still faced with a wide range of acute shortages — from white shirts to automobiles.

FOOD AND AGRICULTURE

World War II productive accomplishments were nowhere more spectacular than in agriculture. Civilian food consumption was the highest in history in 1944, yet almost one fourth of our total food output went to the armed forces and to our allies through lend-lease. Civilian per capita consumption in 1944 was 9 per cent above the 1935–1939 average, a gain accompanied by an improvement in the nutritive quality of the diet and, because of higher incomes and rationing, in the dietary level of the lower income classes. Although consumption of sugar, canned fruits, butter and cheese dropped below prewar averages, consumption of such protective foods as milk and cream, eggs, meats, chickens and turkeys in 1944 showed larger increases over prewar averages than the over-all gain in food consumption.

This remarkable achievement, involving new production records year after year and a 25 per cent rise in total farm output between 1939 and 1944, was accomplished in spite of an actual decline in farm employment and an increase in crop acreage of only 6 per cent. It was due to a number of factors, perhaps the most important of which was fortuitous: a long run of unusually favorable weather. Government planning and price policies helped stimulate maximum agricultural effort, while greatly increased use of fertilizer, more intensive cultivation and rapid extension of farm mechanization brought marked gains in efficiency. Taken together, all of these factors were responsible for an increase of more than one third in output per farm worker between 1939 and 1944, and of one sixth in average crop yields per harvested acre.[4]

TRANSPORTATION AND SHIPPING

Successful prosecution of the war on both the military and economic fronts would have been impossible without a fabulous expansion of freight and passenger transportation. This great task was accomplished in the face of such war-created difficulties as submarine warfare on Atlantic coastal shipping and a shortage of rubber and motor fuel, and in spite of serious shortages of manpower and equipment.

Railroads [5]

The railroads bore the brunt of the burden of domestic transportation. With the total volume of domestic freight movement rising from some 375 billion ton-miles in 1940 to nearly 741 billion in 1944, the railroads almost doubled their load. This they accomplished with only 7 per cent more freight cars and 4 per cent more locomotives than in 1940. At the same time, railroad passenger traffic of 96 billion passenger-miles in 1944 was nearly four times the 1940 total.

The brilliant record of the railroads in World War II showed the importance of large traffic volume in ensuring high efficiency and low unit costs and was also evidence of the lessons learned in World War I by both management and government. The Office of Defense Transportation, with the cooperation of management and workers, in-

---

4. *Survey of Current Business*, February 1945, pp. 10–12.

5. Data on railroads from *Historical Statistics of the United States, 1789–1945*, U.S. Bureau of the Census, 1949, pp. 202–203, and *Problems of Mobilization and Reconversion*, First Report by the Director of War Mobilization and Reconversion, January 1, 1945, p. 39; *War Production and VE-Day*, Second Report, April 1, 1945, p. 24.

stituted measures to penalize shippers for holding freight cars, to prevent freight congestion at the ports (which caused such serious tie-ups in World War I), and to compel maximum loading of freight cars and ensure maximum utilization of equipment. As a result of these measures the equivalent of 141,000 freight cars was added to the existing supply, movement of cars on line and through terminals increased from 39 miles a day in 1940 to 52 miles in 1944, and the average haul per ton of freight increased from 351 to 471 miles during the same period.

Although the railroads carried the great bulk of wartime traffic, most other common carriers were also called upon to shoulder greater burdens. The motor-carrier industry, handicapped though it was, increased its loads year by year. With replacements and expansions far below normal, and with the number of trucks and buses in use actually declining, intercity buses handled more than twice as many passenger-miles in 1944 as in 1940, and local and intercity trucks hauled about the same tonnage as before the war.

Water and Air Transport

Water-borne domestic commerce totaled 452 million tons in 1944 compared with nearly 497 million in 1940. Although Great Lakes tonnage greatly exceeded prewar volume, coastwise tonnage declined sharply. Our great wartime shipbuilding program made the United States more than self-sufficient in transportation of ocean cargo on a peacetime basis. United States ocean-going ships carried 54 million long tons of cargo (exclusive of Army and Navy cargo) in 1944 — more than two thirds of all our ocean shipping in that year. During the 1930s American ocean-going and Great Lakes ships carried an average of 24 million tons, or less than a third of all cargoes. By the end of the war the American merchant fleet numbered 5,700 vessels, of which 2,500 were efficient C-type and Victory dry-cargo ships and tankers. In 1939 only about 1,100 ocean ships flew the American flag.[6]

Although still a small factor in commodity movement, airplanes accounted for 68 million ton-miles of domestic mail and freight in 1944 — up from 11 million ton-miles in 1939. With the return of nearly all the planes that had been borrowed by the army, the airlines also experienced their largest percentage gain in passenger traffic in 1944.[7]

DISPOSITION OF WAR INCOME

It became fashionable during World War II to say that finance loses all importance when a country goes to war. Taken to mean that a self-sufficient nation need not lose a war for want of money, the statement cannot be gainsaid. But money still had to be used to make the wheels go round. Not only were the accomplishments and costs of the war — at least in its economic phases — measured in monetary terms, but financial incentives provided the most powerful motivation to maximum effort. Along with the phenomenal growth in the physical output of goods and services came great increases and profound changes in the receipt and disposition of money income by farmers, workers and business firms.

With gross national product and national income more than doubling between 1940 and 1944, marked expansion occurred in all classes of corporate and individual income. Wages and salaries paid to workers showed the largest gain. Total compensation of employees, because of higher wage rates, more workers and longer hours, more than doubled between 1940 and 1944 and accounted for more than two thirds of the total rise of $103 billion in national income.

Income of proprietors was more than twice as large in 1944 as in 1940, owing mainly to a very substantial rise in the income of farm operators. Corporate profits before taxes rose by 161 per cent over the four-year period; after taxes the increase was only 67 per cent. Interest and rents advanced by 25 per cent. (See Table 3.)

Changes in the disposition of income received by business firms and individuals also reflected the necessities of war. Business taxes more than doubled, rising from $13 billion in 1940 to nearly $28 billion in 1944, while personal tax payments of $19 billion in 1944 were seven times as large as the amount collected from individuals in 1940. Government expenditures, however, rose almost twice as fast as revenues, with the result that a government deficit (for federal, state and local

---

6. *Historical Statistics of the United States, 1789–1945,* p. 214; *Statistical Abstract of the United States, 1948,* U.S. Bureau of the Census, Table 621, p. 565; and *Problems of Mobilization and Reconversion,* pp. 41, 42.

7. *Historical Statistics of the United States, 1789–1945,* p. 224, and *Problems of Mobilization and Reconversion,* pp. 39–40; *Survey of Current Business,* February 1945, pp. 16–17.

TABLE 3. NATIONAL INCOME, GOVERNMENT FINANCE, SAVINGS AND PRICES, 1940-1945
(Dollar Figures in Billions)

	1940	1941	1942	1943	1944	1945
National income	$81.3	$103.8	$137.1	$169.7	$183.8	$182.7
Compensation of employees	51.8	64.3	84.9	109.2	121.2	123.0
Income of unincorporated enterprises [a]	12.7	16.5	23.0	26.7	29.0	31.2
Interest and rents	7.7	8.4	9.3	9.5	9.6	9.3
Corporate profits [a]	9.2	14.6	19.9	24.3	24.0	19.2
Government receipts and expenditures [b]						
Total receipts	17.8	25.2	32.9	49.5	51.8	53.7
Business taxes	12.9	19.1	23.4	27.1	27.7	26.7
Personal taxes	2.6	3.3	6.0	17.8	18.9	20.9
Social insurance contributions	2.3	2.8	3.5	4.5	5.2	6.1
Total expenditures [c]	18.3	28.7	64.0	93.4	103.1	93.0
Surplus (+) or deficit (−)	−.5	−3.5	−31.2	−43.9	−51.4	−39.2
Private savings and investment						
Gross private saving	16.0	23.0	41.8	47.4	57.0	48.5
Personal saving	3.7	9.8	25.6	30.2	35.4	28.0
Corporate saving	2.4	4.9	5.1	6.2	6.1	3.8
Capital consumption allowances by private business	8.4	9.3	10.0	10.7	11.9	12.4
Miscellaneous [d]	1.5	−1.0	1.1	.4	3.6	4.3
Gross investment	15.5	19.5	10.7	3.5	5.6	9.3
Gross private domestic investment	13.9	18.3	10.9	5.7	7.7	10.7
Net foreign investment	1.5	1.1	−.2	−2.2	−2.1	−1.4
Private saving minus investment	.5	3.5	31.2	43.9	51.4	39.2
Gross federal debt, end of year [e]	53.6	69.0	123.2	186.72	253.7	292.6
Net federal debt, end of year [e]	44.8	56.3	101.7	154.4	211.9	252.7
Price level index [f]	55.3	59.6	67.9	72.7	74.2	76.4

Sources: National Income and Product of the United States, 1929-1950 (1951 National Income Supplement to the *Survey of Current Business*), Tables 5, 7, 8, 9, pp. 153-155; gross and net federal debt from *Survey of Current Business*, September 1953, Table 3, p. 16; price level index from Appendix 4-2, Table B.

a. Includes inventory valuation adjustment.

b. Includes federal, state and local revenues and expenditures; receipts include business tax and nontax liabilities, personal tax and nontax payments and contributions to social insurance funds.

c. Includes expenditures for goods and services, transfer payments, net interest paid, and subsidies less current surplus of government enterprises.

d. Includes inventory valuation adjustment, excess of wage accruals over disbursements, and statistical discrepancy.

e. Includes debt of federal agencies such as TVA, RFC, HOLC, etc., which issue their own securities.

f. Price level indexes are the implicit price indexes for gross national product in *National Income and Product of the United States, 1929-1950*, Table B, p. 146, shifted to a 1950 base. (See Appendix 4-2, Table B.)

Note: Slight discrepancies in addition are due to rounding.

governments combined) of more than $51 billion was incurred in 1944.

Consumer Income

Despite the sevenfold increase in personal taxes, the vast rise in the dollar income of individuals left a much larger "disposable income" in the hands of consumers. Thus personal income rose from $78 billion in 1940 to $166 billion in 1944, and the increase in personal taxes absorbed only $16 billion of this $88 billion rise. This meant that consumers had cash incomes after taxes,

which they were free to spend or save as they pleased, amounting to more than $147 billion in 1944 compared with $76 billion in 1940. If all of this money had entered consumer markets without restraint, it would have had a disastrous effect on prices because of the diversion of nearly half the gross national product to war purposes and the consequent curtailment in the supply of consumer goods and services.

Actually, government price controls prevented runaway prices, rationing ensured an equitable distribution of essential foods, and Treasury war loan campaigns diverted a large proportion of consumer incomes into bond purchases. As a result of these measures and the general public awareness of the dangers of inflation, individuals probably spent a smaller proportion of their incomes for consumption purposes in 1944 than in any previous year in history. Consumer expenditures in 1944 amounted to about $112 billion, and even this $40 billion increase over the 1940 total of $72 billion largely reflected higher prices. Taking into account an increase of about one third in prices between 1940 and 1944, consumer purchases, measured in 1940 dollars, rose by only $10 billion, to a 1944 total of $82 billion. This 14 per cent increase would appear even smaller on a per capita basis, for population expanded by 5 per cent from 1940 to 1944.

Heavy Savings

That the wartime price increase was held to such modest proportions — much less than half the rise during the corresponding period in World War I — was due to the efficacy of price controls and to the fact that consumers saved such a large proportion of their increased incomes. Individuals saved over $35 billion in 1944 — more than nine times as much as in 1940 — and the total amount of savings in the hands of consumers at the end of 1945 was more than $129 billion *greater* than it was five years earlier. Corporate savings also increased, though on a much more modest scale, so that total savings of individuals and corporations amounted to about $42 billion for the year 1944, as compared with $6 billion for 1940. (See Table 3.)

Since private capital formation, which normally absorbs the bulk of savings, fell sharply from its peak in 1941, a very large part of the increased savings of both corporations and individuals was held in the form of government securities and other liquid assets.

While state and local governments were retiring obligations and accumulating surpluses during the war, the federal debt rose steadily and substantially. The gross federal debt stood at $254 billion at the end of 1944 — up $200 billion in four years.

FACTORS ACCOUNTING FOR WARTIME OUTPUT

The "miracle of production" achieved during the war was often cited as evidence of vast and hitherto unsuspected potentialities of production

and of tremendous technological gains that greatly increased our productive efficiency. The extraordinary accomplishments of American industry and labor during World War II are undeniable. But the great symbol of these accomplishments is to be found, not in statistics of wartime national income and gross national product, but in the brilliant successes of American arms throughout the world and in the fact that a vast plenitude of the weapons of war helped save American lives.

What this impressive war production record really meant, in terms of normal peacetime production, is hard to judge because wartime output cannot readily be compared with peacetime needs. The composition of the national output at the peak of the war effort was far different from what it was before the war and from what it has been since the end of the war. Although the volume of civilian consumption during World War II held above prewar levels, there was virtually no production of the most important types of consumers' durable goods, while some nondurable goods also became unavailable. Other kinds of consumer goods deteriorated in quality, and consumers' services of all kinds were limited in amount and changed in character.

Nearly half of the gross national product in 1944 was accounted for by government purchases, of which more than half went for combat munitions destined for destruction. What our ability to produce $10 billion worth of bombers, naval vessels and ammunition at government contract prices in 1944 meant in terms of refrigerators and oil burners at competitive market prices in 1950 is impossible to determine. Placing a dollar value on the priceless services of a division fighting in Normandy or in Korea is absurd enough — though necessary in estimating wartime national product — but it would be compounding an absurdity to try to evaluate the peacetime equivalent of such wartime services.

In spite of these difficulties, however, it is of some help in assessing wartime productive achievements to examine the factors responsible for more than doubling the dollar volume of output during the war. By what means was the 1940 gross national product of $101.4 billion raised to $213.7 billion in 1944?

Higher Prices

In the first place, a considerable part of this gain of more than $112 billion was not really an increase in the amount of goods and services produced, but merely a reflection of a substantial rise of prices. How much the prices of all the goods and services entering the gross national product rose during World War II will probably never be known with anything like the same degree of certainty with which price movements of civilian goods can be measured under normal conditions. However, the Department of Commerce has made a careful study of price changes which indicates an average rise of 34.2 per cent between 1940 and 1944.

On the basis of this price increase, the $101.4 billion gross national product for 1940 would have been valued at $136.1 billion in terms of 1944 purchasing power. Thus $34.7 billion of the total dollar increase of $112 billion in gross national product between 1940 and 1944, or close to a third, was due solely to higher prices.

More Workers and Longer Hours [8]

A large part of the expansion in the physical volume of output between 1940 and 1944 resulted from employment of several million additional workers and lengthening of hours of work. In 1940, unemployment was heavy, with 8.1 million members of the labor force out of work during the year. By the last half of 1944 unemployment had dropped to less than 700,000, so that 7.4 million of those out of work in 1940 had found jobs.

Employment gained another 2.4 million between 1940 and 1944 through the normal expansion of the labor force, which grew from an actual average of 56 million in 1940 to an estimated "normal" of 58.4 million in 1944. This resulted from the entrance of young people into their first jobs.

In addition to these normal new entrants, the labor force was further augmented by several million emergency and temporary workers. These included boys and girls below normal working age, wives of servicemen and other married women, and older workers who had retired. There were 65.9 million persons (including those in uniform), on the average, in the actual labor force in 1944, or 7.5 million more than the estimated normal of 58.4 million.

Taking into account the re-employment of unemployed workers, the normal additions to the labor force, and the employment of emergency

workers, employment increased from an average of 47.9 million in 1940 to 65.2 million in 1944, or by more than 36 per cent. If we assume that those at work in 1944 were as efficient and productive as those employed in 1940, the 36 per cent increase in employment would account for a corresponding expansion of the gross national product.

If the 47.9 million workers employed in 1940 produced a gross national product of $101.4 billion by working the 1940 average of 43.8 hours a week, their aggregate output would obviously have been larger if they had worked the 1944 average of 46.2 hours a week. Without allowing for any reduction in average output per man-hour because of the greater fatigue accompanying longer working hours, this increase of 5.5 per cent in the length of the work week would have accounted for an equivalent further rise in output over that attributable to higher prices and increased employment.

Combined Effect of Prices, Employment and Hours

The combined effect on gross national product of the increases in prices, employment and hours, therefore, would be the product of the separate percentages attributed to each of the three factors taken separately; viz., 134.2 per cent (prices), 136.1 per cent (employment), and 105.5 per cent (hours); or 192.7 per cent. A 92.7 per cent increase in 1940 gross national product of $101.4 billion would result in a total of $195.4 billion. (See Figure 2.)

Productivity Changes

Between 1940 and 1944, however, gross national product actually increased from $101.4 billion to $213.7 billion, or by 110 per cent. About $94 billion of the total increase is thus attributable to the factors discussed above. The remaining $18 billion of the $112 billion total increase remains unaccounted for by changes in prices, employment and hours. This residual difference could be explained by an annual increase of some 3 or 4 per cent in average productivity, and there is some evidence that productivity [9] did increase at approximately that rate during the defense and war periods.

This analysis, however, is only a very crude

---

8. For data used in this section, see Appendix 20–1 and Chapter 20.

9. See Chapter 2 and Chapter 20 for discussion of productivity changes.

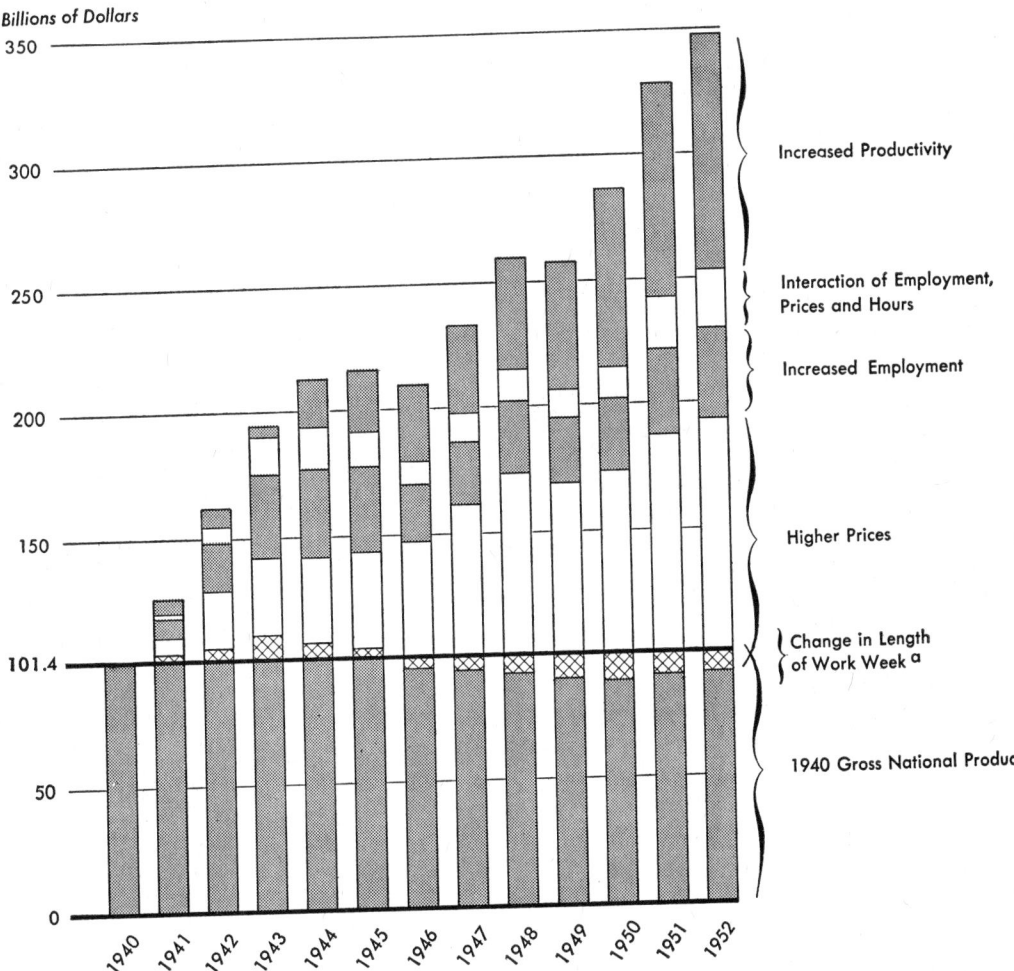

FIGURE 2. FACTORS CONTRIBUTING TO INCREASE IN GROSS NATIONAL PRODUCT ABOVE 1940 LEVEL, 1941–1952

Source: Appendix 1–1.

a. Decreases in the length of the work week below the 1940 level in the years 1946–1952 tended to decrease the national product.

hypothetical reconstruction and provides an unsatisfactory basis for computing anything as difficult to measure as productivity. It does not purport to explain how the actual 1944 gross national product *was in fact achieved,* but merely what dollar volume of output would have been attained on the basis of 1940 experience by reason of the increases in prices, employment and working hours that occurred after 1940. Some of the errors in this reconstruction, moreover, probably fall in the same direction. By 1943, for example, we had passed the normal "full employment" level, and many of the unemployed, and emergency workers, who found jobs at the peak of the war effort

were less efficient than the regular members of the labor force. The average output per worker of those added to the labor force after 1942 was therefore probably lower than the output of the persons at work in 1940.

Furthermore, the longer *average* work week of 1944 was due partly to the increase of overtime work. Many employees in such war industries as shipbuilding, aircraft and machine tools had to work a 56- or 60-hour week over considerable periods of time. This meant greater fatigue and, in the absence of offsetting influences, lower efficiency and a smaller output per man-hour than if these people had been working a normal work week. To what extent this lowered the average hourly output of the entire working force is impossible to determine, but the effect was probably not large, as only a small proportion of the entire labor force was working excessively long hours. Nevertheless, the assumption that a 5.5 per cent increase in average working time between 1940 and 1944 resulted in a corresponding increase in total output probably involved at least a slight overstatement.

Thus, while the $214 billion output at the height of the war effort was a remarkable tribute to American genius in mobilizing our unused material and human resources, it was by no means a "miraculous" accomplishment in the sense of involving extraordinary technological progress or vast increases in productive efficiency. On the contrary, the great productive achievements of the war were due very largely to the fact that many more people were at work, and were working longer hours than before the defense program got under way.

THE POSTWAR BOOM

During the later stages of the war there was a widespread belief in many quarters that the hurried demobilization and abrupt cessation of government spending accompanying a sudden end of the war would plunge the country into another severe depression. This "mature-economy thinking," a survival of the fears generated by the long depression of the 1930s, was especially noticeable among government officials. As late as August 1945 the Director of War Mobilization and Reconversion warned that unemployment three or four months later would rise to 5 million or more and that it might reach 8 million by the following spring.[10]

Such a view was widely held, and it was advocated by many that demobilization of the armed forces be slowed down so as to permit the more "orderly" absorption of discharged servicemen into the peacetime economy. Reconversion of industry, it was feared, would take place so slowly that heavy unemployment would be inevitable.

"BACK TO NORMAL"

These dire expectations proved ill-founded. In spite of prompt cancellation of government war

contracts, a precipitous decline in government war spending, and an extremely rapid demobilization of the armed forces, unemployment during the period of demobilization and reconversion never rose to a point that would have been considered normal even for a period of prosperity.

During the year and a half between the summer of 1945, when the strength of the armed forces had reached a peak of 12,130,000, and the end of 1946, more than 10 million service men and women were discharged and returned to civilian life. Government spending for war purposes, which reached its highest annual rate of over $90 billion in the first quarter of 1945, dropped to a rate of less than $28 billion a year later, and fell further to an annual rate of about $16 billion by the end of 1946.[11]

In the first quarter of 1945 and for the two years preceding, war expenditures represented more than 40 per cent of the total gross national product; by the end of 1946 they had dropped to little more than 7 per cent. These drastic cutbacks meant that in addition to the return of the 10 million service personnel to civilian pursuits, several million munitions workers had to find new jobs or withdraw from the labor force.

Even with this sudden and severe curtailment of government spending, however, the dollar value of the total gross national product showed a maximum decline of only 11 per cent — from an annual rate of $225 billion in the second quarter of 1945 to $200 billion in the first quarter of 1946. Thereafter there was a slow recovery, and for 1946 as a whole gross national product was only 2 per cent less than for 1945. Measured in dollars of constant purchasing power, the decline was somewhat larger because prices were rising, but it was still only 10 per cent for the entire year 1946 compared with 1945. Even this decline, moreover, could hardly be attributed to the difficulties of reconversion; it was more in the nature of a permanent adjustment to postwar conditions.

Perhaps the best evidence that we were operating under forced draft during the war is the trend of employment and unemployment. Total employment (including the armed forces) dropped from nearly 67 million in the middle of 1945 to 58 million by the end of 1946; yet unemployment rose little more than a million. This apparent anomaly was accounted for by the fact that some 6 million emergency workers dropped

---

10. *From War to Peace,* Office of War Mobilization and Reconversion, August 1945.

11. *Markets after the Defense Expansion,* U.S. Department of Commerce, 1952, p. 27.

out of the labor force when they were no longer needed. Wives returned to housekeeping, youngsters to school, oldsters to retirement.

The return to "normalcy" was thus easier done than said; it was accomplished without advance planning, without government intervention, and without confusion or distress. By the end of 1946, and earlier in some cases, most of industry had been reconverted to civilian production and was busy not only supplying consumer needs, but expanding capacity and building new plants. The postwar boom was well under way.

SPECIAL CHARACTERISTICS OF THE BOOM

The period since the end of World War II has been unique from an economic standpoint. Every other major war in American history was closely followed by a collapse of the wartime inflation bubble, but this time no such debacle took place. On the contrary, there was a relatively small advance in the price level *during* World War II, but a relatively high degree of inflation *after* the fighting stopped and controls were removed. This appears to be one reason we escaped an immediate postwar collapse.

The World War I inflation occurred in two stages: two thirds of the price rise during actual hostilities and one third in the immediate postwar period after removal of controls. In World War II, on the other hand, little more than one third of the entire inflationary rise took place before the fighting ended, while nearly two thirds occurred in the first three postwar years. This difference stemmed largely from the fact that during the actual hostilities inflationary pressures were less, and also were better controlled, in the second world war than in the first.

Two factors largely accounted for the relatively small price rise between 1939 and 1945. First was the large amount of idle productive resources available in 1939 to be put to work expanding output when the war broke out. Hence supply expanded almost as fast as demand at first, especially for nonagricultural products. The second factor was the imposition in 1942 of controls over the prices of goods and services, salaries and wages, and the distribution of available supplies. Imperfect as they were, these controls prevented inflationary pressures from making much headway during and for almost a year after the end of World War II.

Inflationary Explosion

Following the expiration of control legislation on June 30, 1946, however, prices shot upward in runaway markets. In July alone, wholesale prices rose 10 per cent. Notwithstanding the reimposition of limited controls at the end of that month, the rise continued more or less steadily as one control after another was relaxed or removed. When the Price Control Extension Act of 1946 finally expired on June 30, 1947, the wholesale price level was more than a third higher than at the war's end, most of this rise having occurred in the preceding twelve months.

Freed from all controls, the upward spiral continued for another year under pressure of increasing demand and rising costs. By August 1948, however, this first phase of the postwar inflation reached an end as quotations turned downward in wholesale markets under the weight of large and increasing inventories, particularly of agricultural products.

Inflation Renewed

Respite from inflation was brief, however, lasting little more than a year. Early in 1950, wholesale prices ceased to decline and began to rise gradually as demand firmed with the end of inventory liquidation. When at midyear the Communists invaded South Korea, the public reacted very much as if in expectation of a World War III. With the shortages, controls and rationing of the recent war fresh in mind, businessmen and consumers bid prices steeply upward in an explosive but short-lived burst of inflation. Between June 1950 and March 1951, the wholesale price level rose by one sixth. Never before in American history had the inflation of one major war been so quickly succeeded by that of a new war — if that word can be used to describe the three years of hostilities in which our armed forces were heavily engaged in Korea.

Broad economic controls over prices, wages, credit and materials were imposed in January 1951. These, powerfully aided by strong upward trends in supplies of raw materials and fabricated products, stopped the general wholesale price rise at the March 1951 level, although consumer prices continued to move slightly higher during 1952 and 1953. As output continued to rise, increased supplies made it possible once more to eliminate virtually all economic controls by stages during

1952 and 1953. With prices of most nonagricultural commodities at the end of 1953 still hovering not far from the 1951 inflation peak, the fourteen-year period from 1939 to 1953 constitutes perhaps the longest period of strong and almost uninterrupted price rise in American economic annals.

Spurt in Output

Regrettable as were the effects of this long period of inflation in reducing the purchasing power of each dollar of 1939 income and savings by one half or more, and of 1945 income and savings by one third, the price rise did have its usual effect of stimulating producers to their utmost efforts. Not only were the effects substantial during the war, but the national product increased tremendously once the transition to a peacetime economy had been completed. By 1953, with the gross national product aggregating $328 billion (measured in dollars of 1950 purchasing power), the wartime peak of production had been exceeded by one seventh. Output of civilian goods and services of 252 billion "1950 dollars" showed the far greater increase of 77 per cent.

Large as was the increased output of goods and services during this period, the fact that the price level nevertheless became so inflated indicates that the flow of purchasing power was even larger.

Veterans' Care

Another feature of the period following World War II which helped to ease the transition from a wartime to a peacetime economy and contributed to the developing boom was the unprecedented care provided for millions of veterans and their families, after their return to civilian life. This program, expressing the nation's gratitude for priceless services rendered, restricted the growth of unemployment during the demobilization period and at the same time added substantially to personal income and consumer demand. Since the veterans program got under way at the time of a precipitous decline in government demand for goods and services, it helped to forestall a postwar economic crisis by stimulating civilian demand.

Postwar payments by the federal government through the fiscal year 1953 to or for the benefit of more than 15 million veterans of World War II and of Korea totaled over $39 billion, or more than the entire direct cost of World War I. The heaviest payments were concentrated in the immediate postwar years. The program was broad and varied, beginning with the mustering-out and terminal leave pay averaging around $400 for each demobilized veteran. Approximately $9 billion was paid out in disability compensation and pensions, not counting payments to veterans of earlier wars.

The biggest outlays were for education and training. Nearly 8 million veterans received schooling and job training at an average cost of about $1,800 each, many attending institutions of higher learning. Other benefits included vocational rehabilitation for the disabled, readjustment allowances during unemployment or while establishing self-employment, national service life insurance dividends, and the guarantee or insurance of about $21 billion of loans for the purchase of homes, farms and businesses.

Veterans in the Labor Force

Demobilization released 11 million men and women from the armed forces in the first fifteen months after V-J Day. The demand for labor was so strong, however, that most of the veterans seeking work, as well as the people newly entering the labor force, were readily absorbed. A contributing factor was the shortening of the work week from the 45-hour average that prevailed during the latter part of the war to about 40 hours thereafter.

Accelerated Population Growth

A further characteristic of this boom that helped set it apart from other postwar periods was the sharply accelerated growth of population beginning shortly after the cessation of hostilities. This population spurt made an important contribution to the dynamic character of the boom. A major factor was the sharp rise in the marriage rate following demobilization of the armed forces, and the ensuing jump in the birth rate. Minor factors were the resumption of net immigration and the continued gradual decline in the death rate.

The jump in population, coming at a time of rising incomes, stimulated the demand for goods and services. An important part of this boost was largely independent of the increased number of people but came instead from the changing characteristics of the population. Even with no increase in the number of persons, more families are formed if the marriage rate increases and more households are established if incomes are high enough to permit both the newly married couples and families living doubled-up to set up housekeeping for themselves. Income permitting, therefore, the demand for dwelling units and certain consumer durables, such as automobiles, household appliances and furniture, is more closely allied to changes in the number of households than to changes in the number of people.

Economic Effects of the Population Spurt

The high level of personal income and savings at the end of the war and the marked increase in the marriage rate thus led to the formation of many new families and households, each requiring shelter, furniture, furnishings and household appliances, transportation, fuel, light and other utilities and services. The annual increase in the number of households, which averaged 500,000 in the fifteen years ending with 1945, reached 1.5 million between 1947 and 1948, and remained not far below that level over the next four years.

The growing excess of births over deaths and rising net immigration meant additional demands for food, clothing and other goods and services for which the individual is the consuming unit. The annual increment of population jumped from an average of 900,000 a year during the 1930s and 1.6 million between 1940 and 1945 to 2.7 million between 1946 and 1947 and has remained at approximately that level since then.

Thus the size of the consumer market has been expanding three times as fast since the end of World War II as it was during the depressed 1930s.

Associated with this increased demand for all types of consumer goods and services was a derived demand for additional business investment to supply these needs. Hence a rapid growth in the number of new businesses occurred, together with a marked expansion of old, established firms. The total number of business firms in operation, which had shrunk somewhat during the war, rose from 3.2 million when the fighting stopped to nearly 4 million in 1948. Growth occurred in all lines, but was relatively largest in contract construction, transportation (chiefly highway), durable-goods manufacturing and wholesale trade.

New Materials and Products

A factor of special significance in the postwar boom was the rapid advance in applied technol-

ogy.[12] Its immediate impact was transmitted through the marketing of new materials and products, which led to the establishment of new industries, and through new methods of producing goods and services, which contributed greatly to the rising productivity of the nation's resources.

A multitude of new materials and products, most of which were still in the laboratory during the 1930s, came to fruition during the war period and were placed on the market in the early postwar years. Many of these had the benefit of widespread publicity because of their use by the armed forces during the war, and having captured the public's imagination, enjoyed a wide market acceptance. Among the many new materials not previously available in commercial quantities or at prices competitive with alternative materials, which were offered to producers after the war, were synthetic rubber, a variety of synthetic fibers, plastics and many other new chemicals, glass fibers, magnesium metal, powdered metals and the radioactive by-products of uranium.

The availability of new materials with unique properties and the many inventions and discoveries involving the use of familiar materials led to an increasing flow of new products to market. Prominent among these were the "miracle" drugs and many other new chemical products such as insecticides, fungicides and weed-killers, synthetic detergents, waterproofing compounds and paints; new and improved building materials; television receivers and other new electronic products; and electrical appliances such as home freezers and air conditioners.

New and Fast-Growing Industries

The producers of these new materials and products constituted a whole group of new industries, if "industry" is defined broadly to mean either a new firm or a new establishment operated by an old firm but making a new material or product. The establishment of these industries stimulated the national economy in several ways. First was the added demand for producers' capital of all kinds, including construction of durable equipment; second was the additional demand for labor and the strengthening of the upward trend of wages and salaries; and third was the increase in the over-all demand for consumer goods and services as families began to incorporate the new prod-

---

12. See Chapter 24 for discussion of technological developments.

ucts in their normal pattern of consumption. To the extent that the new articles merely replaced the old familiar ones, the curtailed demand for the latter somewhat reduced the net gain, but on balance the new industries resulted in a substantial addition to the aggregate demand for goods and services rather than a mere change in its composition.

Some of these new industries showed extremely rapid annual growth rates, especially from 1946 to 1953. Although the older industries, with which the newcomers are competing, grew more slowly, some of the fast-growing industries are not new but are, so to speak, still in their youth. This is true, for example, of aluminum, rayon and acetate fibers, and natural gas — all of which are growing faster than the average. (See Table 4.)

Productivity Accelerated

A different but equally dynamic application of technology took the form of new and improved equipment and new and improved methods of management in virtually all segments of the national economy. As a general rule, these developments were a continuation of well-established long-term trends, notably the direct or indirect use of increasing amounts of inanimate energy by the individual worker in all lines of endeavor. Hence the per capita consumption of energy resources continued to rise during the postwar boom. Moreover, because of the greater efficiency with which fuels and water power were converted into heat, light or mechanical energy, the amount of delivered energy available to each worker rose even faster.[13]

Not only did the average worker have at his command in this period increasing amounts of energy, he also had faster and more accurate equipment capable of performing operations previously done entirely or largely by human effort. A special feature of this new and better equipment was its high degree of automaticity.

Hence, after a dip caused by the change-over from war to peace production, productivity scored impressive gains in virtually all fields. For the economy as a whole, output per man-hour rose 3 per cent a year from the postwar low in 1947 through 1952. This compares with an average annual gain of 2.8 per cent during the post-World War I boom from 1920 through 1929, of 2.1 per

cent over the period from 1909 through 1952, and of 2.3 per cent as the medium assumption of the present study for the 1950 decade.

HOW POSTWAR·DEMAND WAS MADE EFFECTIVE

The boom after World War II was activated by a tremendous volume of spending. All major groups participated: private individuals and families, business firms and government. Each group had plenty of funds and spent freely. The result was that the strong rise in the dollar volume of national income, which began in 1938 and accelerated during the war, was maintained throughout the postwar years. In examining the sources of postwar spending it is important to remember that since one person's expenditures become another's income, we shall at the same time be observing the sources of the rise in the national income.

Consumers' Liquid Assets

The funds available to consumers for spending in a given period consist of their accumulated liquid savings at the beginning of the period, their disposable income during the period, and the net additional funds they borrow.

The end of World War II left consumers with an unprecedentedly large volume of accumulated liquid savings. Wartime incomes had been high. Shortages of many consumer goods, especially durables, coupled with rationing and price controls, during the war meant that many consumers were unable to spend as much of their wartime incomes as they would ordinarily have done. This restriction on spending, in combination with patriotic purchases of savings bonds, accounted for the unusually high proportion of personal disposable income that was saved in liquid form during the war.

During 1941–1945 inclusive, disposable personal income, including unincorporated business income, totaled $639 billion, of which $129 billion, or 20 per cent, was saved, largely in liquid form. This saving rate dwarfed the 2.5 per cent average of the preceding decade and even the relatively high rate of 4.5 per cent reached in 1929.

In the closing months of 1945, personal ownership of liquid assets amounted to $188 billion,[14]

---

13. See Chapter 25 for discussion of trends in energy use and productivity.

14. Components of the $188 billion, as reported by the Securities and Exchange Commission, were currency and bank deposits, savings and loan shares, and U.S. government securities.

TABLE 4. ANNUAL GROWTH RATES FROM PREWAR TO POSTWAR OF SELECTED FASTER- AND SLOWER-GROWING INDUSTRIES

	Unit	Output			Average Percentage Growth Rate to 1953 or Highest Recent Year from:	
		1939	1946	1953 or Highest Recent Year	1939	1946
Gross national private product	Billions of 1950 dollars	153	229	300	4.9	3.9
Industrial production	Federal Reserve Board indexes, 1947–1949 = 100					
Total		58	90	134	6.2	5.9
Mining		68	91	116	3.9	3.5
Manufacturing		57	90	136	6.4	6.1
Selected industries						
Metals						
Magnesium	Thousands of short tons	3	5	106 [a]	31.5	66.4
Aluminum	Thousands of short tons	164	410	1,252	15.6	17.3
Titanium (dioxide)	Thousands of short tons	12 [b]	138	275 [a]	29.8 [b]	12.2
Steel ingots and steel for castings	Millions of short tons	53	67	112	5.5	7.6
Copper, recoverable, mine production	Thousands of short tons	728	609	928 [e]	2.0	8.8
Fibers						
Rayon and acetate	Millions of pounds	411	842	1,254 [d]	10.7	10.5
Other synthetics	Millions of pounds	5 [b]	56	301	37.1 [b]	27.2
Cotton consumption	Millions of pounds	3,538	4,720	4,818 [e]	2.6	0.4
Wool consumption, apparel and carpet	Millions of pounds	396	738	635 [d]	4.4	−3.7
Fuels						
Natural gas	Billions of cubic feet	2,477	4,031	8,425	9.1	11.1
Petroleum	Millions of barrels	1,265	1,734	2,360	4.6	4.5
Coal, anthracite	Millions of short tons	52	61	44 [d]	−1.5	−7.8
bituminous	Millions of short tons	395	534	534 [e]	2.5	0
Other materials						
Plastics and resin materials	Millions of pounds	213	1,025	2,770	20.1	15.3
Rubber, synthetic	Thousands of long tons	2	740	898	54.7	2.8
natural	Thousands of long tons	592	278	720 [d]	1.8	26.9
Plywood, softwood	Millions of sq. ft.	1,032	1,436	3,178 [a]	9.0	14.2
Lumber	Billions of bd. ft.	25	34	39	3.2	2.0
Products and services						
Antibiotics	Thousands of pounds	[e]	47	1,600	—	65.5
Air conditioning units, room	Thousands	9	30	1,075	40.7	66.7
Television sets	Thousands	[e]	6	7,464 [d]	—	493.9
Frozen foods	Millions of pounds	325	1,317	3,300	18.0	14.0
Home freezers	Thousands	[e]	210	1,200	—	28.3
Synthetic detergents	Index, 1940 = 100	100 [b]	1,000	6,300	37.5 [b]	30.1
Disposals, waste, food	Thousands	[e]	100 [f]	350	—	23.2 [f]
Electric power production	Billions of kilowatt-hours	161	270	514	8.6	9.6
Air traffic, passenger	Millions of passenger-miles	683	5,903	14,288	24.2	13.4
Air traffic, freight, express, mail	Millions of ton-miles	11	71	246	24.9	19.4
Railroad traffic, freight	Billions of ton-miles	333	595	650 [e]	4.9	1.2
Railroad traffic, passengers	Billions of passenger-miles	23	65	35 [e]	3.6	−11.6

Source: Production data from various trade associations and government agencies.

a. 1952.
b. 1940.
c. 1951.
d. 1950.
e. Prewar production insignificant.
f. 1947.

TABLE 5. PERSONAL DEBT AND DISPOSABLE INCOME, 1929–1952
(*Dollar Figures in Billions*)

| Year | Personal Debt, Year End [a] | | | Disposable Personal Income | Ratio (Per Cent) of Debt to Disposable Income |
	Total	Mortgage	Nonmortgage		
1929	$ 72.3	$40.8	$31.5	$ 82.5	87.6
1933	50.6	34.0	16.6	45.2	111.9
1939	50.8	31.6	19.2	70.2	72.4
1945	54.7	31.8	23.0	151.1	36.2
1952	135.3	81.9	53.4	235.0	57.6

Source: Survey of Current Business—personal debt from the September 1953 issue, disposable income from the July 1953 issue.

a. Personal debt includes debt of farms and other unincorporated businesses and therefore differs from consumer debt figures shown in Figure 18.

equal to 110 per cent of personal income, a proportion one-third higher than in 1939. This huge volume of spendable funds which consumers could — and to an extent, did — commit to market at their pleasure, was a major reason why personal consumption expenditures got off to such a fast postwar start.

In the spending boom covering the next seven years, consumers drew down the ratio of their liquid assets to their income until at the end of 1953 it was almost back to the prewar level again. This was achieved both by cashing in liquid assets (i.e., chiefly United States securities) and spending the proceeds, and by reducing the portions saved annually in liquid form out of the income of the postwar years. Even so, personal holdings of liquid savings at the end of 1953 aggregated approximately $238 billion, or 84 per cent of that year's personal income.

Increased Income and Borrowing of Consumers

In addition to the freer use of their accumulated liquid assets, consumers — including unincorporated business enterprises — gave another big boost to their postwar spending by borrowing on a grand scale. In the seven years following 1945, private noncorporate net debt expanded by $80 billion to a total of $135 billion at the end of 1952. Of the total postwar additional borrowing, $50 billion consisted of mortgage debt covering the purchase of fixed assets, while the remaining $30 billion represented shorter-term debt covering chiefly the purchase of durable goods or other assets but also including some outright consumption expenditures. (See Table 5.)

Notwithstanding the large expansion of borrowing, the rise of personal income during the postwar boom was so rapid that the debt burden relative to income was still considerably less at the end of 1952 than at the close of 1929 or 1939 and much less than at the end of 1933. The fact remains, however, that during the postwar years, consumers augmented their spending ability to an important extent by drawing against their accumulated liquid assets and by increasing their debt obligations relative to their disposable income.

The rise of personal income was itself largely a reflection of the intense demand for goods and services of all types following the wartime shortages. This scramble to buy resulted in turn in an intense demand for labor, and of course for capital also. Not only was the civilian labor force fully employed but because of the competitive demand for labor, pay rates rose rapidly. In manufacturing, for example, the average hourly earnings of production workers increased more or less steadily from $1.02 in 1945 to $1.77 in 1953. All of the other income streams composing personal income [15] also rose substantially, so that the total of $284.5 billion in 1953 was 65 per cent higher than 1945 personal income. Notwithstanding the rise of personal taxes resulting from the Korean outbreak, disposable personal income (i.e., after taxes) of $248 billion in 1953 was 64 per cent higher than in 1945.

15. The major types of personal income, other than wages and salaries, in order of magnitude, are income of unincorporated enterprises and rental income, transfer payments (which include the payments to veterans discussed earlier), personal interest income, and dividends.

The overwhelming mass of personal income recipients decided to spend larger portions of their rising postwar disposable incomes, and save smaller portions, than they had during the war. This increase in the "propensity to consume" gave a decisive stimulus to consumer spending. In normal times, consumer demand absorbs by far the major portion of the national product. Hence, since the expenditures of one person become the income of another, consumer spending normally gives rise to the largest share of disposable personal income. The efforts of consumers (including unincorporated enterprises) to spend more freely during the postwar period — by saving less from current income, by using accumulated savings, and by borrowing more heavily — therefore resulted in their being largely responsible for the rapid growth of their own income.

Sources of Business Investment Outlays

However, free spending by corporate businesses for investment purposes and large expenditures at all levels of government were also major factors in the expansion of the national income after World War II.

Corporate enterprises, like consumers, accumulated large holdings of liquid assets during the war. Liquid assets of nonfinancial corporations at the end of 1945 amounted to $40 billion — an increase of $29 billion over corporate holdings at the close of 1939. During the war period, corporations piled up liquid assets faster than sales rose. The ratio of liquid assets to sales mounted from 9 per cent at the 1939 year-end to 17 per cent on December 31, 1945. In the postwar period of free investment, corporations drew liberally against these holdings, with the result that liquid assets [16] as a percentage of sales were back to 9 per cent by the end of 1952.

The accumulation of liquid assets during World War II was largely due to the policy of retaining an unusually large portion of the profits after taxes instead of paying out more in dividends. Computations based on the national income and product data compiled by the Office of Business Economics, U. S. Department of Commerce, reveal that nonfinancial corporations retained the

following percentages of their earnings after payment of taxes:

	Per Cent
1929	34
1939	28
1940	38
1941–1945 average	55

Like consumers, business corporations also expanded their borrowing freely after 1945, in order to obtain additional funds to increase investment outlays. In the seven years following the end of the war, the total corporate net debt nearly doubled, with $82 billion of additional borrowing raising the total of debt outstanding at the end of 1952 to $167 billion.

During this period, nonfinancial corporations raised a total of $211 billion of new funds. Undistributed profits and net new borrowing (including trade receivables) accounted for 62 per cent of this total. Among other sources tapped, depreciation contributed $50 billion, or 24 per cent of all the new funds raised. New stock financing provided only 6 per cent of the total. The larger amounts raised by borrowing were chiefly attributable to the low interest rates prevailing during most of the period compared with the cost of equity funds.

Sources of Government Spending

The sharp decline in federal government expenditures after the war's end made possible some reduction in tax rates from wartime levels. However, various objectives — some irreducible and others deemed essential — maintained federal expenditures far above prewar levels, while outlays of state and local governments, no longer held in check by wartime controls, soon doubled. Because the need for revenues was pressing, their postwar tax rates remained considerably higher than those in effect prior to 1941. This tax structure applied to rising personal and corporate incomes lifted the annual receipts of federal, state and local governments to more than 60 per cent above even their high wartime level. (See Table 6.)

The federal Treasury entered the postwar period with the unusually large cash balance of $26 billion in its general fund on December 31, 1945. By reducing the size of this balance in succeeding years the Treasury freed approximately $20 billion of cash, which was used largely for debt reduction.

---

16. Corporate liquid assets data are compiled by the Board of Governors of the Federal Reserve System and consist of currency, demand and time bank deposits, United States government securities and a small quantity of savings and loan shares.

TABLE 6. GOVERNMENT RECEIPTS, 1929–1952
(*Billions*)

	1929	1939	1940	Average, 1941–1945 Inclusive	Average, 1946–1952 Inclusive
Total [a]	$11.3	$15.4	$17.8	$42.6	$67.8
Federal	3.8	6.7	8.7	32.6	50.3
Personal tax and nontax receipts	1.3	1.2	1.4	12.0	21.1
Corporate profit tax accruals	1.2	1.3	2.7	11.3	14.7
Indirect business tax and nontax accruals	1.2	2.3	2.6	5.2	8.7
Contributions to social insurance	0.1	1.9	2.0	4.1	5.8
State and local	7.6	9.7	10.0	10.9	19.5
Personal tax and nontax receipts	1.4	1.2	1.2	1.4	2.5
Corporate profit tax accruals	0.2	0.2	0.2	0.4	0.7
Indirect business tax and nontax accruals	5.8	7.0	7.4	7.9	13.5
Contributions to social insurance	0.1	0.3	0.3	0.3	0.8
Federal grants-in-aid	0.1	1.0	0.9	0.9	2.0

Sources: National Income and Product of the United States, 1929–1950 (1951 National Income Supplement to the *Survey of Current Business*), and *Survey of Current Business*, July 1953.

a. Excludes federal grants-in-aid to avoid duplication.

MAKING UP WARTIME SHORTAGES AND REBUILDING
DEFENSES: 1945–1953

For four years, wartime shortages and restrictions on civilian consumption had resulted in the accumulation of a great backlog of deferred wants on the part of all consuming groups. During this same period, as shown in the preceding pages, a large volume of liquid funds was piling up in consumer, business and government holdings. With the lifting of wartime controls, these liquid holdings poured into the nation's markets. Since the funds flowed to market faster than the goods and services they sought to buy, the result was the marked inflation of the price level discussed earlier.

The postwar boom has occurred in two phases. The first period, from 1945 to 1949, was marked by an effort to make up wartime shortages as rapidly as possible, but also by a decline in the physical quantity of the gross national product below wartime levels. This was entirely due to the shrinking quantity of goods and services purchased by the federal government after the fighting stopped and the armed services were demobilized. The volume of private gross product destined for civilian use, notwithstanding the problems involved in reconverting from wartime to peacetime production, grew steadily, but not as much as the decline in purchases of goods and services by the federal government. The quantity of output for civilian use expanded approximately 39 per cent in this period, while quantities purchased by government dropped more than 60 per cent. (See Table 7.) With total gross national product in 1949 about 6 per cent lower in quantity than in 1945, the price level [17] had been forced up by roughly 30 per cent in those four years by the pressure of demand effectuated by liquid funds and rising income. This phase of the boom was terminated toward the end of 1948 by a corrective price adjustment largely associated with a liquidation of business inventories.

The second phase of the boom, from 1949 to 1953, was characterized by the nation's rearmament effort to meet Communist aggression and the invasion of South Korea. During this second phase of the boom the quantity of the national product expanded by about one fourth, with the private economy and government each taking about half of the increased output. Despite the augmented flow of goods and services, demand by

17. Represented in Table 7 by the implicit price deflator of the gross national product.

TABLE 7. GROSS NATIONAL PRODUCT: VALUE AND QUANTITY, 1945, 1949 AND 1953

	1945	1949	Ratio: 1949 to 1945	1953	Ratio: 1953 to 1945
Gross national product, total					
Value: billions of current dollars	215.2	258.2	1.20	367.2	1.71
Quantity: billions of 1950 dollars	281.7	264.4	.94	327.9	1.16
Implicit price deflator: index,					
1950 = 100	76.4	97.7	1.28	112.0	1.47
Private product destined largely for civilian use					
Value: billions of current dollars	132.4	214.6	1.62	282.3	2.13
Quantity: billions of 1950 dollars	157.6	219.1	1.39	251.6	1.60
Implicit price deflator: index,					
1950 = 100	84.0	97.9	1.17	112.2	1.34
Government purchases of goods and services					
Value: billions of current dollars	82.8	43.6	.53	84.9	1.03
Quantity: billions of 1950 dollars	124.1	45.3	.37	76.4	.62
Implicit price deflator: index,					
1950 = 100	66.7	96.2	1.44	111.1	1.67

Sources: Survey of Current Business, July 1953 and February 1954. Quantity data were published in the source in 1939 constant dollars and the implicit price deflator was on the base 1939 = 100.

all major consuming groups again rose even faster, with the result that the price level moved up 15 per cent more from 1949 to 1953. Comparison of the quantity ratios in Table 7 with the implicit price deflator ratios will show the relative contributions of the quantity and price changes to the change in value of the national product during this period.

The basic vital statistic of the entire postwar boom period is this: the physical quantity of gross national product was one sixth larger in 1953 than in 1945, when war output was only a trifle down from its peak. This gain was achieved, however, at the cost of an inflation of roughly 47 per cent in the price level. It will be helpful at this point to examine more closely the productive effort of the national economy in both phases of the boom.

CATCHING UP WITH CONSUMER DEMAND

Consumer requirements absorb much the largest part of the nation's productive capacity. The output of this sector of the economy, as measured by personal consumption expenditures, increased sharply in the years following the war. Consumption demand during the boom can best be characterized by the fact that out of their steadily rising disposable incomes consumers spent much more, and saved less, than during the war. They were more than willing to trade their cash for things they had gone without in the wartime emergency. (See Table 8.)

The rise in consumer goods prices was a powerful incentive to producers to strive to catch up with deferred demand. The number of operating businesses increased rapidly, both because of strong markets and because many veterans started their own firms. Output of consumer goods and services, as measured by consumer expenditures, increased one fifth in volume during the first four years of the postwar boom. Since prices rose by about the same proportion, total dollar outlays of consumers went up by nearly one half between 1945 and 1949. Durable-goods supplies registered the largest increases, with 1949 volume nearly two and a half times the 1945 rate, as former war plants converted from munitions to civilian goods. Partly because their output expanded so fast during this phase of the boom, the average prices of consumers' durable goods rose less than those charged for either nondurables or services. (See Table 9.)

In the case of nondurable goods, the rise in personal consumption expenditures was occasioned chiefly by higher prices and only to a much

TABLE 8. DISPOSABLE PERSONAL INCOME AND EXPENDITURES, 1941–1953

Year	Disposable Personal Income	Personal Consumption Expenditures	Per Cent of Disposable Income	
			Spent	Saved
	(Billions)			
1941–1945 average	$127.8	$102.1	79.8	20.2
1946	158.9	146.9	92.4	7.6
1947	169.5	165.6	97.7	2.3
1948	188.4	177.9	94.4	5.6
1949	187.2	180.6	96.5	3.5
1950	205.8	194.6	94.5	5.5
1951	225.0	208.1	92.5	7.5
1952	235.0	218.1	92.8	7.2
1953	247.9	229.8	92.7	7.3

Sources: Personal disposable income and expenditure data from *Survey of Current Business,* July 1953, p. 13, and February 1954.

smaller extent by expanded volume. The relatively small increase in output is ascribable to both demand and supply factors. As for demand, it is clear that many nondurables, such as food, medicines and fuels, permit only a limited accumulation of deferred demand. For such goods, production during the war period was not unusually depressed and hence not in need of a sharp upswing after the fighting ended. On the supply side, the inelasticity of output was due largely to the fact that many nondurable goods are made from agricultural raw materials, whose supplies cannot readily be increased over short periods; furthermore, the domestic market had to compete with strong foreign demand for farm products.

Rising consumer expenditures for services were due almost equally to higher prices and larger quantities, each of which moved up roughly one fifth in this part of the boom. One reason for the moderate rise of service prices was the continuation of rent controls in many areas and the lag in the upward adjustment of the prices of utility services which are publicly controlled.

During the second phase of the boom, encompassing the period of Korean hostilities, personal consumption expenditure again expanded sharply — up one fourth from 1949 to 1953. Most of the increase was concentrated in 1950 and 1951, when many consumers bought in fear of a large-scale war. Consumption in 1952, however, would almost certainly have been larger than it was except for the widespread industrial curtailment due to the prolonged steel strike that summer. As in the first phase, higher prices accounted for a

slightly larger share of the increased consumption outlay than did expanded output. In this four-year period, the output of durable and nondurable goods and services increased by roughly the same magnitudes: durables, up 11 per cent; nondurables, 10 per cent; and services, 15 per cent. But with personal disposable income higher — up one third by 1953 — the pressure of demand added to rising costs boosted prices somewhat ahead of output.

Changing Consumption Pattern

Notwithstanding the rapid growth in population and in the number of households during the postwar years, the volume of consumer goods and services poured out by the nation's producers increased even faster. As a result consumption per capita and per household increased considerably. No simple way exists to determine to what extent the expanded output of consumer goods and services had by 1953 caught up with the war-deferred demand plus the subsequent growth of demand stemming from rising incomes. There is some evidence, however, that supplies of some goods had overtaken demand by the end of that year, while others had not.

With consumers in a better position to indulge their desires than ever before, because of their higher incomes, the postwar pattern of personal consumption showed some interesting changes from that of prewar years. One such difference was the larger portion of income devoted to the purchase of consumer durables in all postwar

TABLE 9. PERSONAL CONSUMPTION EXPENDITURES, 1945, 1949 AND 1953

	1945	1949	Ratio: 1949 to 1945	1953	Ratio: 1953 to 1945
Total					
Value: billions of current dollars	123.1	180.6	1.47	229.8	1.87
Quantity: billions of 1950 dollars [a]	155.0	184.5	1.19	206.5	1.33
Implicit price deflator: index, 1950 = 100 [a]	79.4	97.9	1.23	111.3	1.40
Durable goods					
Value: billions of current dollars	8.5	23.8	2.80	30.1	3.54
Quantity: billions of 1950 dollars	10.0	24.3	2.43	27.1	2.71
Implicit price deflator: index, 1950 = 100	85.0	97.9	1.15	111.1	1.31
Nondurable goods					
Value: billions of current dollars	74.9	99.2	1.32	121.2	1.62
Quantity: billions of 1950 dollars	95.1	100.6	1.06	110.8	1.17
Implicit price deflator: index, 1950 = 100	78.8	98.6	1.25	109.4	1.39
Services					
Value: billions of current dollars	39.7	57.5	1.45	78.4	1.97
Quantity: billions of 1950 dollars	50.0	59.6	1.19	68.6	1.37
Implicit price deflator: index, 1950 = 100	79.4	96.5	1.22	114.3	1.44

Sources: Survey of Current Business, July 1953, pp. 26–27 and February 1954, p. 5. Quantity data were published in the source in 1939 constant dollars and the implicit price deflator was on the base 1939 = 100.

a. Figures differ slightly from those shown in Appendix 4–2 because of differences in method of computation and rounding.

years not marked by supply difficulties. Another was the smaller share spent for apparel after demobilized veterans had bought their civilian wardrobes in 1945 and 1946. Still another difference was the larger slice of income expended for foods, as rising incomes brought better nourishment within reach of more people.

Finally, the portion of income spent for services was distinctly smaller than in prewar years. A considerable part of the shrinkage was accounted for by the lag in rents, which remained under control longer than any other consumer item. Some of the shifts, however, such as the decline in outlays for movies and organized baseball in favor of larger expenditures for television sets, appeared to reflect real changes in consumer preferences.

The automobile industry was one of the busiest of all during the boom. At the end of the war, the pent-up demand for better cars was so great that prices of one- or two-year-old models were bid up higher than the list prices of new cars. At that time the demand backlog consisting of several million cars was based largely on the following factors: (1) the increased number of households without cars, (2) the higher levels of income and accumulated savings, and (3) the higher average age per car — nearly double the prewar figure — and the more advanced state of deterioration, with many cars at the "jalopy" stage.

For the first year or so after the war, disposable personal income and new household formation increased so fast that only a minor dent was made in the backlog demand for automobiles. Not until the end of 1948 was the ratio of cars to households back to the 1941 figure, and even then the average car on the road was still far below prewar standards, as measured by the age distribution of registered cars. Faced with this seemingly insatiable demand, the nation's automobile plants turned out 35 million passenger cars in the eight years 1946–1953, the highest total for any comparable period in history. By comparison the output was 28 million cars for the eight years ending with 1929.

By 1953, largely because of rising incomes, the ratio of cars to households was up to 96 per cent

TABLE 10. PERSONAL CONSUMPTION EXPENDITURES FOR DURABLE GOODS OTHER THAN AUTOMOBILES AND ACCESSORIES, 1941–1952

Year	Total	Furniture [a]	Floor Covering	Major Appliances [b]	Musical Instruments, Radios and Television [c]	China, Glassware, Tableware and Utensils	All Other
			Total Expenditures (*Millions*)				
1941	$ 6,408	$1,295	$ 513	$1,165	$ 636	$ 633	$2,166
1945	7,385	1,541	543	317	399	841	3,744
1946	12,365	2,319	844	1,587	1,326	1,339	4,950
1947	14,809	2,700	1,049	2,791	1,724	1,442	5,103
1948	15,368	2,934	1,131	2,927	1,753	1,504	5,119
1949	14,451	2,820	964	2,403	1,992	1,422	4,850
1950	16,885	3,286	1,128	3,021	2,848	1,500	5,102
1951	16,391	3,350	1,140	2,516	2,421	1,548	5,416
1952	16,278	3,461	1,071	2,433	2,324	1,484	5,505
			Expenditures per Household				
1941	$179	$36	$14	$32	$18	$18	$ 60
1945	197	41	15	8	11	22	100
1946	323	61	22	41	35	35	129
1947	375	68	27	71	44	36	129
1948	375	72	28	71	43	37	125
1949	340	66	23	57	47	33	114
1950	385	75	26	69	65	34	116
1951	365	75	25	56	54	34	121
1952	355	75	23	53	51	32	120

Sources: Expenditures data from *National Income and Product of the United States, 1929–1950* (1951 National Income Supplement to the *Survey of Current Business*), pp. 192–199, and *Survey of Current Business,* July 1953, pp. 22–23; household data from U.S. Bureau of the Census.

a. New furniture only.
b. Other than for entertainment.
c. Includes phonographs, parts and records.

— far above the prewar 82 per cent. This does not mean that the car market is within 4 per cent of saturation, of course, as roughly 30 per cent of all private passenger cars are owned by business firms, while it is estimated that over 10 per cent of car-owning families have more than one car. Estimates based on consumer surveys indicate that about one third of the nation's families still did not own cars in early 1953, although by then the wartime demand backlog had virtually disappeared. Furthermore, the quality of the cars on the road in 1953 had been restored to approximately the prewar level; about three fourths of them were postwar models and only one sixth were 1939 or earlier models.

Other Consumer Durables

Production and sale of household durables also expanded sharply after World War II restrictions were removed. For all durables other than automobiles and accessories, consumers spent more than twice as much in 1947 and succeeding years as in 1945. Here, too, rising incomes, and the free use of accumulated savings and borrowed funds, were largely responsible for the leap in outlays, although the increased number of households was also important.

Consumer buying of radios, television sets and musical instruments, along with the major household appliances, shot up sixfold or more from 1945 levels, while purchases of furniture and floor coverings more than doubled. By 1947, expenditures for most of these items on a per household basis had virtually reached their peak. Thereafter the increased sales volume was largely accounted for by the continued expansion in the number of households.

The unusually high level of outlays per household in 1947 and other early postwar years was,

TABLE 11. PERSONAL CONSUMPTION EXPENDITURES FOR NONDURABLE
GOODS AND SERVICES, 1941–1953

(*At 1950 Prices*)

Year	Nondurable Goods		Services	
	Total	Per Capita	Total	Per Capita
	(*Billions*)		(*Billions*)	
1941	$ 79.6	$597	$41.5	$311
1945	95.1	679	50.0	357
1946	99.6	705	53.0	374
1947	98.2	682	54.8	380
1948	98.6	673	57.2	390
1949	100.6	675	59.6	399
1950	102.6	677	62.7	414
1951	104.0	674	64.1	415
1952	108.2	689	66.2	422
1953	110.8	694	68.6	430

Sources: Consumption expenditure data from *Survey of Current Business,* July 1953, p. 27, and February 1954, p. 5; computation of per capita figures based on population data from U.S. Bureau of the Census. In the source, the data were published in 1939 dollars.

of course, chiefly due to efforts to catch up with the most pressing of wartime shortages. The declining trend since 1950 indicates that the backlog of demand deferred during World War II had been largely eliminated as a market factor well before the end of 1952. (See Table 10.)

Nondurable Goods and Services

The nation's farms, factories, utilities and service enterprises turned out a steadily rising volume of nondurable goods and services over the postwar years. However, since output of nondurable goods had been less restricted by controls during the war period, it grew less rapidly than durable-goods output after the war. The volume of nondurable goods flowing to consumers, as measured by consumer expenditures in dollars of 1950 purchasing power, increased sharply in 1946 but thereafter barely kept pace with population growth. (See Table 11.) The volume of food, gasoline and oil continued to rise, but most other product groups, and particularly apparel, declined on a per capita basis.

Consumer services have grown steadily in volume, both in total and per capita. The major factor in this growth was the service of shelter afforded by the rapidly increasing number of occupied dwelling units. However, many other types of consumer services also expanded, particularly radio and television repair, which grew fastest of all. Other rapidly growing services expanding at substantially higher than average rates were the use of hotels and tourist courts, electricity, gas and telephone, interest on personal debt, auto insurance, private education and research, and foreign travel. On the other hand, some consumer services grew at substantially slower than average rates, such as barber and beauty shops, the brokerage and investment counsel businesses, and purchased local and intercity transportation. Some services actually declined, notably consumer purchases of movie theater entertainment, which declined by one quarter between 1946 and 1952, legitimate theater and opera entertainment, off 4 per cent, and professional baseball, down 6 per cent.

PRIVATE CAPITAL FORMATION

As an outstanding feature of these postwar years, private enterprises added the largest increment in the nation's history to their stock of private capital. Housing, farm and nonfarm plant and equipment were built on an unparalleled scale as the proportion of private civilian goods output diverted to capital formation rose to high levels in comparison with any former period.

The new private domestic capital took the form of housing, nonresidential construction, producers' durable equipment and business inventory.

TABLE 12. NEW PRIVATE NONFARM RESIDENTIAL CONSTRUCTION
AND NEW HOUSEHOLD FORMATION, 1920–1953

Period (Inclusive Dates)	New Private Nonfarm Dwelling Units Started	New Households Formed	New Dwelling Units per 100 New Households
	(Millions)	(Millions)	
1920–1929	7.0	5.5	127
1930–1941	3.8	6.5	58
1920–1941	10.8	12.0	90
1942–1945	0.8	1.6	50
1946–1953	7.9	9.3	85
1942–1953	8.8	10.9	81

Sources: New dwelling unit data, 1920–1952, from *Construction and Building Materials,* May 1953 Statistical Supplement, p. 47, published by National Production Authority, U.S. Department of Commerce; 1953 from U.S. Department of Labor, Bureau of Labor Statistics; household formation data from U.S. Bureau of the Census.

Residential Building

One of the largest backlogs of deferred demand that developed during World War II was for new private dwellings. It arose because the number of new households formed in the years 1942 to 1945 inclusive was about twice the number of new nonfarm dwellings built during those years — 1,600,000 as compared with 800,000. The deficit, however, was not actually as large as the difference between the two figures. A portion — estimated at roughly one tenth or more — of total new family formation has in the past been provided for by additions to existing dwellings or by remodeling them to make two or more dwellings out of one.[18]

The experience of the twenty-two years 1920–1941 seems to indicate that about 90 new private nonfarm dwelling units were required in prewar years for each 100 new households formed. During the first half of that period, the construction industry was catching up with any deficit accumulated during World War I and perhaps also piling up some surplus. In the second half of the period, however, any such surplus was absorbed;

hence the period as a whole may reasonably serve as a guide. If the round figure of 90 new nonfarm dwellings needed for 100 new households is used as a rough criterion, it would appear that the recent building boom was not overdone in relation to the growth in the number of new households. In fact, the construction of 8 million new nonfarm dwelling units in the first eight postwar years did not, according to that criterion, even take care of the 9 million new households formed in those years, nor did it make any dent in the wartime deficit. (See Table 12.) When such additional factors as the currently higher level of real income per household, the recently increasing size of families with children, the smaller size of modern dwelling units, which makes conversion into multiple dwellings more difficult, and the additional housing requirements arising from widespread internal migration are taken into account, it seems likely that residential builders will still have plenty to do in the years that lie ahead.

Nonresidential Building

The new private capital formation embodied in buildings or other types of improvements on land during the postwar period was almost evenly divided between residential nonfarm and nonresidential construction. Expansion of this nonresidential construction began immediately after the war and remained high throughout the ensuing eight years ending with 1953. It reached its highest activity, however, in the years following

---

18. Furthermore, new farm dwellings and those built by public authorities, although both these magnitudes are relatively small, are excluded from the new dwelling construction total. But if the figures overstate the deficit for the foregoing reasons, they understate it from a different standpoint; namely, they make no allowance for the new shelter requirements arising from the disappearance of existing dwellings either through destruction by fire or by other means or through converting them to business uses.

the outbreak of Korean hostilities as a result of the government's policy of stimulating expansion of the basic capacity of industries making goods for the defense establishment and of the associated service industries, such as electric power.

Despite the extraordinarily large amount of nonresidential construction put in place in the postwar period, it is doubtful whether the deferred demands of the war period and the requirements of the large new population increment of subsequent years were in all cases fully satisfied by the end of 1953. The unsatisfied requirements for new commercial and institutional construction stem from the restrictions placed on this type of building during World War II and again during the Korean hostilities in order to favor more essential construction. Hence many stores and other types of commercial buildings and the churches, private school and college buildings, private hospitals and social and recreational buildings needed to keep pace with population growth and to serve the new residential communities springing up throughout the country have been provided only after a lag. Some, apparently, are still to be built.

Producers' Durable Equipment

The business capital formed during the postwar boom consisted chiefly of producers' durable goods. Great as was plant building activity, the purchase of new equipment to install in the plant was even more concentrated. In these postwar years, roughly $2 has been spent for producers' durable equipment for every dollar invested in plant (other than residential building). Aggregate purchases of this type of capital in the years 1946 through 1953 amounted to $167 billion and constituted the largest addition to the stock of producers' durables in the nation's history.

Of course not all this new capital is a net addition to the stock of business durable equipment, because much capital — estimated on the basis of current depreciation at roughly 60 per cent of the total new capital purchased — was used up in the productive process. Nevertheless, it is estimated that between the end of 1941 and December 1952 the nation's total stock of producers' durable equipment was enlarged by about 110 per cent, after allowing for the depreciation during the interval. Alternatively measured, the stock increased by about seven eighths, after deducting all the equipment discarded.[19] Furthermore, as in the

19. *Survey of Current Business*, June 1953.

case of the country's stock of passenger cars, the quality of the capital stock was enhanced by lowering its average age through the addition of new equipment and the retirement of the older machines.

The unprecedented intensity of postwar investment stands out when measured against population growth and the national product. Investment in new producers' durable equipment on a physical units basis (i.e., measured in dollars of constant purchasing power) in the years 1946 through 1952 relative to each person added to the population in that period was one half larger than comparable investment in the prewar generation from 1920 through 1941. In 1929, new investment in producers' durable equipment constituted 7 per cent of the national physical product, whereas in the entire postwar period an average of 8 per cent of the national physical product was channeled into such investment.

The investment boom was especially intense in farm and industrial machinery, but not so pronounced in transportation equipment. After full allowance is made for price increases, investment in nonfarm machinery in the first seven postwar years exceeded by 10 per cent the total invested in the twenty-two-year period 1920–1941. Farmers more than kept pace with industry. They too went to town in the postwar era and came back with 15 per cent more farm machinery and tractors (measured in dollars of constant purchasing power) to add to their stock of capital goods than they had bought in the entire 1920–1941 generation.

Inventory Investment

As almost always happens in a boom, businessmen invested substantial sums in stocks of goods in the years following the war. Much of the increase was necessary to build working inventories up to a proper relationship to sales, which were rising under pressure of active demand. Furthermore, stocks had become unbalanced during the war and it became necessary to add to holdings of items formerly in short supply. But some of the additions to inventory were speculative in nature in anticipation of rising prices.

In 1947, demand increased more than output, so businessmen were unable to add to their stocks of goods. In 1948, a substantial amount was added to inventory. In 1949, however, business prospects were sufficiently clouded by a downward price

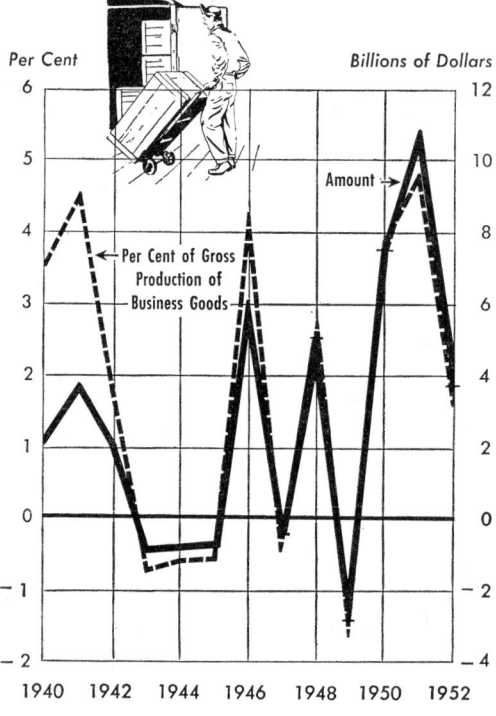

FIGURE 3. CHANGE IN BUSINESS INVENTORIES, 1940–1952

Sources: Based on *National Income and Product of the United States 1929–1950* (1951 National Income Supplement to the *Survey of Current Business*), Table 2, p. 150, and Table 7, p. 153, for years 1940–1948; for years 1949–1952, based on *Survey of Current Business,* July 1953, Table 2, p. 11, and Table 7, p. 14. Gross production of business goods equals business gross product minus personal consumption expenditures for services.

adjustment that output was cut back somewhat more than demand and moderate inventory liquidation occurred. The outbreak of Korean hostilities so altered the outlook in 1950 that inventory accumulation was again resumed on a generous scale. During the entire eight-year period from 1946 through 1953, $32 billion of goods were added to business inventories. This was 2.1 per cent of all the goods, totaling $1,554 billion, produced by the national economy during that postwar period. (See Figure 3.)

FOREIGN DEMAND

Superimposed upon the large demands for goods and services from private domestic sources were sizable demands upon the national product from the outside world, especially just after the war. In the four years 1946–1949, nearly 4 per cent of the gross national product available for civilian use, valued at $32 billion, went abroad as a net export surplus. In the following three years, the annual net export surpluses shrank considerably, although they continued large enough to bring the total for the whole postwar period 1946 through 1952 to $45 billion, or 2.8 per cent of the entire national product for civilian use.

The strength of foreign demand for our products was due to various factors arising out of the war. On the supply side, foreign productive capacity had either failed to grow in pace with demand or else had been reduced by wartime destruction. On the demand side, as in the case of the domestic economy, a backlog of deferred demand had been built up in foreign countries during the hostilities. Furthermore, inflationary fiscal policies had provided foreign individuals with large sums of liquid assets in terms of local currencies. In cases where dollar exchange was lacking, and particularly for the benefit of our wartime allies, the United States government and many private citizens contributed funds to pay for American goods and services to be given away free for the sake of maintaining a healthy postwar world safe from Communist encroachment.

Over two thirds of our postwar export surplus of $45 billion, or $31 billion, was given away in the form of government grants or private gifts. The remaining $14 billion, or 31 per cent of the total, was covered by a corresponding increase in our holdings of foreign assets: $10 billion took the form of foreign debt obligations payable to the United States government or to such agencies as the Export-Import Bank, the International Bank and the International Monetary Fund; $6 billion gave rise to increased private holdings of foreign investments; and the balance was settled by transferring ownership of gold or dollar reserves between nations. The impact of this foreign demand served to increase the inflationary postwar price rise in the United States. (See Table 13.)

Two developments appear as highlights of the recent investment capital flow. One is the decline of Europe and the rise of Latin America and other areas as the chief destinations of American private foreign investment. The other is the extent to which the recent new American foreign investment has been concentrated in the petroleum industry abroad.

TABLE 13. GROSS NATIONAL PRODUCT FOR CIVILIAN USE AND NET EXPORT SURPLUS
OF GOODS AND SERVICES, 1946–1952
(*Billions*)

	1946	*1947*	*1948*	*1949*	*1950*	*1951*	*1952*
Gross national product destined for civilian use	$180.19	$204.65	$222.45	$214.58	$244.79	$266.94	$270.44
Net export surplus of goods and services [a]	7.70	11.48	6.70	6.37	2.30	5.16	4.86
Total, per cent of national product for civilian use	4.3%	5.6%	3.0%	3.0%	0.9%	1.9%	1.8%
Portion given away as private gifts or government grants	2.89	2.58	4.84	5.84	4.60	4.91	5.09
Portion becoming net foreign investment	4.81	8.90	1.86	0.53	−2.30	0.25	−0.23
Method of financing: Loans by U.S. government or international agencies	2.69	4.66	1.26	0.78	0.18	0.22	0.48 [b]
Private capital	0.37	0.76	0.86	0.59	1.32	0.92	1.07 [b]
Acquisition of foreign gold or dollar assets	1.93	4.46	0.78	−0.06	−3.64	−0.36	−1.18 [b]
Errors and omissions	−0.18	−0.98	−1.04	−0.78	−0.16	−0.54	−0.60

Sources: Balance of Payments of the United States, 1949–1951, U.S. Department of Commerce, 1952, Appendix Tables 1 and 3; *Survey of Current Business,* June 1953, p. 4.

a. The figures in this table differ from figures shown in Chapter 19 because of a difference in treatment of private international donations. See Table 277, footnote c.

b. Beginning with 1952, international agencies are treated as foreign entities.

GOVERNMENT PURCHASES OF GOODS AND SERVICES

Requirements for goods and services by all governments — federal, state and local — were third in order of magnitude before the depression of the 1930s, being exceeded by consumer purchases and by business investment. In those days, expenditures of state and local governments overshadowed federal outlays and they continued to exceed them until 1941, when the nation began to arm for the approaching conflict.

During the four war years, purchases by federal, state and local governments pre-empted nearly 40 per cent of the entire gross national product; in that period, net government purchases from business — largely of goods — absorbed nearly 30 per cent of the private gross product.

Fortunately, in the first two years of the postwar boom when consumers and business investors were bidding against each other for scarce commodities, total government spending was shrinking drastically; otherwise the inflation would have been much worse. The shrinkage, which was entirely ascribable to plummeting expenditures for national security, was strongly deflationary, but was partly offset by state and local government outlays, which were on the increase. In the years 1946–1949, government purchases of goods and services called, on the average, for only 15 per cent of the gross national product, as compared with 39 per cent during the war, and for only 7 per cent of the private gross product as against 29 per cent in the war. (See Figure 4.)

Beginning in 1948, however, the growing threat of Communist aggression forced rearmament upon the nation once again. National security expenditures began their postwar rise and were an important factor both in halting the 1949 inventory recession which brought to an end the first phase of the postwar boom and in turning aggregate demand upward again.

Although private demand reached its low point in the final quarter of 1949 and had begun to rise in the first half of 1950, the Communist invasion of Korea at the end of June really pulled the trigger on the second phase of the postwar boom. In this phase, government purchases of goods and services played a much more dynamic part than

Per Cent

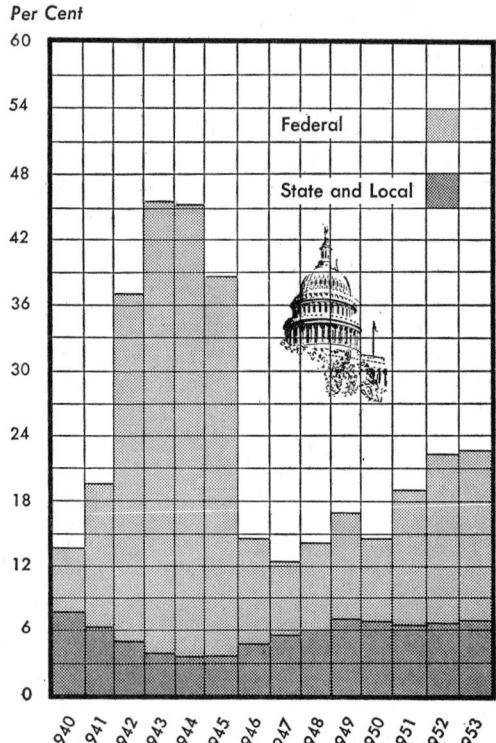

FIGURE 4. GOVERNMENT PURCHASES AS PER CENT
OF GROSS NATIONAL PRODUCT, 1940–1953

Sources: Basic data from *Markets after the Defense Expansion*, U.S. Department of Commerce, 1952, p. 26; for
years 1952–1953, from *Survey of Current Business*, February 1954, p. 12.

in the first. Government requirements accounted
for 20 per cent of the gross national product —
half as much as in the all-out emergency of World
War II — while net purchases from business absorbed more than one tenth of the entire private
gross product. In no previous postwar boom was
the government ever in the market on such a
scale. In this phase, lasting from 1950 through
1953, federal government purchases of goods and
services again far exceeded those of state and local
governments, with national security outlays accounting for 88 per cent of all federal purchases.

State and Local Government Purchases

Purchases of goods and services by state and
local governments increased steadily in the postwar years from the relatively low levels of World
War II. During the first phase of the boom, they
absorbed smaller portions of the gross national
product than is usual in periods of very active

business. From 1946 through 1949, state and local
government purchases required approximately 6
per cent of the gross national product instead of
the 7 or 8 per cent often registered in prosperous
years.

In the following period, 1950–1953 inclusive,
purchases by these governments had risen substantially more and accounted for almost 7 per
cent of the gross product. The higher level of expenditures was necessary to enable state and local
governments not only to meet higher operating
costs but also to keep up with population
growth [20] and to catch up with necessary projects
deferred during the war. The biggest backlog of
deferred needs was in public construction, especially schools, other public institutions and roads.
Construction outlays were the group that increased most after the war.

END OF THE BOOM

The great postwar boom, featured by unprecedented capital formation, by the defense
build-up and the Korean hostilities, finally
reached its crest in 1953. By mid-1954, economic
activity had flattened out on a level appreciably
below maximum capacity. The slower pace was
partly ascribable to the fact that the military
establishment took a somewhat smaller share of
the national product than during the period of
rapid rearmament, and partly to the diminished
requirements of business investment. Personal
consumption demand also abated a little once
stocks of automobiles and other durable goods in
consumer possession had been built up to a level
commensurate with high personal incomes and
large holdings of liquid assets.

Key Aspects of the Recession

The decline in demand for the national product
from the highest point reached in 1953 resulted
in unemployed productive resources. Industrial
production, as measured by the Federal Reserve
index, was relatively firm during the spring
quarter of 1954 at about 124 per cent of the
1947–1949 average and approximately one tenth
below the 1953 spring peak. Activity at that
lower level was accompanied by a substantial
rise in unemployment from about one and a

20. The functions of these governments are primarily
of a service type, such as public education, police and
fire protection, and hence are closely related to population
growth.

half million in the spring of 1953 to around three and a half million a year later. Considerable plant capacity was left idle, with the steel industry operating at little more than 70 per cent of capacity during the second quarter of 1954.

At the height of the boom in 1953, the gross national product, valued at $371 billion, consisted of $286 billion of goods and services destined for private consumption and $85 billion for government. By mid-1954 the national product was down to $356 billion. Goods and services purchased by consumers and business dropped to $276 billion, very largely because of a contraction in business investment, chiefly in inventories. Government outlays, primarily because of the decline in national security expenditures for goods and services, which was only partially offset by rising outlays of state and local governments, were cut to $80 billion. Federal budgetary plans call for a further shrinkage to about $79 billion by mid-1955. In order to bring total output back to the 1953 peak level, therefore, private demand must take up the slack left by reduced government purchases and must rise to $292 billion, compared with an aggregate of approximately $276 billion in mid-1954.

Adjustment Incomplete in Early 1954

The adjustment to the lessening of demand since the crest of the boom in 1953 has been almost entirely through lower production, reduced employment and smaller payrolls. Notwithstanding the evidence that supplies have finally caught up with and surpassed demand, the level of wholesale prices, especially those quoted for commodities of nonagricultural origin, remained relatively stable with prices of nonagricultural manufactures holding very close to the highs of the post-Korean inflation.

The existence of unemployed resources coupled with commodity prices at close to peak levels indicates a somewhat unusual situation. The increased demand needed to absorb the flow of goods which our economy can produce must come either through expanded disposable income or through lower prices, which would permit increased unit purchases without any increase of incomes.

Requisites for Revival

Just how promptly full-scale activity will be resumed is uncertain, though it is clear that revival will come eventually either as a result of normal recovery factors or because of special measures taken by the government — unless, of course, a new threat of hostilities should speed recovery as the outbreak of warfare in Korea did.

Normal recovery factors are of two types: those which are primarily normal business adjustments to cyclical changes and those which are primarily due to growth. Important among normal business adjustments is reduction of costs and selling prices as a means of stimulating demand. Another is the adjustment of business inventories; when in a period of recession inventory liquidation ends, it is necessarily followed by an upturn in industrial output as business purchases are lifted up to the level of actual materials consumption. A third cyclical recovery factor is the cessation of the net reduction of consumer debt, which began in January 1954. This puts consumers in a position where they have more income available for current expenditures and can augment their current income by a renewed expansion of borrowing.

A fourth factor is the using up, through wear or obsolescence, of goods in the hands of consumers. Nondurable goods usually need replacement first, and where their purchases had previously been appreciably "bunched up," as in the case of the well-established two- or three-year textile apparel cycle, consumers tend to re-enter the market for replacements at about the same time. Inasmuch as the latest peak of personal expenditures for apparel occurred in the final quarter of 1952, replacement demand could be substantial by 1955. In the case of automobiles, purchases of which reached a peak in 1953, the next substantial wave of replacement buying could be deferred somewhat longer.

Finally, the normal wearing out of producers' capital equipment, or its premature obsolescence through competition with more efficient new models, ultimately brings a renewal of buying for fixed investment purposes. Because of the longer life cycle of producers' durable equipment, replacement buying ordinarily comes after a longer lapse of time than in the case of consumer goods. But funds made available through normal and accelerated depreciation meanwhile pile up at a rapid rate. Moreover, it seems probable that the current high rate of technical progress will result in unusually rapid obsolescence. Hence the necessity of meeting competition and the desirability of making maximum

possible cost reductions seem capable of bringing another rise of fixed capital investment earlier
than might be expected under ordinary circumstances.

Influence of Growth Factors

Should normal business processes and adjustments to cyclical changes fail to bring full
recovery, it seems likely that growth factors will
ultimately do so. Basic among these is continued
population growth, which seems likely to add at
least 2.5 million persons to be fed and clothed and
some 800,000 new households to be equipped
each year during the next half decade. With this
growth, productive capacity, which in mid-1954
is somewhat in excess of demands, should not
remain excessive very long. The same applies to
stocks of dwelling units, automobiles and other
consumers' durable goods, the demand for which
is related to the growth of population and households.

Another basic growth factor is the stream of
new materials, new final products and new methods and processes that flow from the progress of
science and applied technology. Exploitation of
these developments brings new firms into the
field and leads to the expansion of established
firms. This growth factor could prove to be
unusually stimulating in the years ahead because
of the rapidly broadening horizons in plastics,
electronics and atomic energy.

If the above-mentioned factors fail to result
in full-scale recovery and a resumption of larger
output within a year or so, if not sooner, then it
seems quite certain that the federal government
will take appropriate action. Among the possible
governmental steps to stimulate recovery are:
further tax cuts to increase disposable income as
a means of promoting consumer buying and
business investment; increased aid to state and
local governments to stimulate state and local
public works projects; the easing of credit terms
on mortgages insured or guaranteed by federal
agencies as a means of aiding residential construction, and other measures to promote the
use of credit. Finally, if necessary to ensure recovery, the federal government can increase its
own purchases of goods and services, including
federal public works, civil defense projects, and
particularly goods and services needed for various aspects of national security.

Factors of Strength

Appraisal of the economic situation in mid-
1954 reveals that the decline from the 1953 peak
has been unique among recessions following
major American booms for a number of reasons.
Almost without exception, major boom periods
in the past in this country have been accompanied
by widespread and excessive speculation. This
time the national economy has been relatively
free from this weakness, and possesses unusually
strong resources compared to any probable financial strain.

Another unique feature of the recession is the
extent to which the economy is buttressed against
a severe downward spiral by the existence of a
large aggregate of demand of various types. The
largest component of this backlog of demand
consists of potential consumer expenditures. It
seems probable that these should be maintained
at a high level by the continued flow of personal
disposable income at close to its current volume.
Among the factors that have helped to keep personal disposable income from declining in
measure with the fall in the national output are
the reduction in personal taxes, the expansion of
unemployment compensation payments, and
some further rise in wage rates. Moreover, consumers are in possession of unprecedentedly
large holdings of liquid assets, which they could
use if necessary to support their standard of living.

Another major component of the demand
backlog consists of the requirements for goods
and services of federal, state and local governments, which, even under the strictest economy,
would be large enough to underwrite a very
substantial volume of business. With respect to
federal expenditures, there is the dismal but
stubborn fact that little or no relaxation in the
threat of external aggression seems probable in
the foreseeable future. Purchases of goods and
services for national security purposes, therefore,
can hardly be cut much below the $45 billion
level which is expected to be reached in the 1955
fiscal year. Hence, with state and local government spending on the uptrend, it seems unlikely
that total government expenditures for goods and
services can fall below a range of $75 to $79 billion annually in the next several years. This
would be only $6–$10 billion below the peak
attained in 1953.

Finally, the current recession is unique in that

the federal government is committed as never before to take all necessary measures to prevent a serious or prolonged setback. In addition to the commitment embodied in the Employment Act of 1946, President Eisenhower put his Administration squarely on record in his January 1954 Economic Report to the Congress as to his intention to use all available means to prevent a severe depression. In previous recessions following major booms, the government has planned no immediate positive action except to the extent necessary to defend the solvency of the federal Treasury against the threat of inability to redeem its obligations in gold. This time, the government has promised to take an active part, if necessary, in restoring and maintaining prosperity.

## CHAPTER 2

TRENDS AND PROJECTIONS

THE DIFFICULTIES THAT BESET any attempt to project the past into the future are great enough under "normal" circumstances. They are much greater when the functioning of the private economy is disturbed by abnormally heavy government expenditures, as in time of war. Uncertainties about the future are in some ways even greater during a period of "cold war" of indefinite duration than in the midst of a "hot war," which must end sometime. Under the latter circumstances it may be possible to make reasonable assumptions as to when that time will arrive.

Assumptions in First Edition

When the original survey of needs and resources was undertaken early in 1943, the authors of individual chapters were asked to assume that "the war will end in 1945, with Japan's defeat coming after Germany's, and with the peak of our industrial war effort being attained at some time in the 1944–1945 period." A further assumption was that "the transition from war to peace would be completed by the end of the decade," with war-deferred demands (except for housing) satisfied and demobilization and reconversion of industry completed.

Such an assumption about the future can never be more than a guess — which the dictionary defines as "an opinion formed from evidence admittedly uncertain" — even if it turns out to be correct. The fact that this particular assumption proved to be reasonably close to what actually happened does not, except in retrospect, mean that it was either a more or less intelligent guess than the assumption that population would increase during the decade by less than 13 million, which missed the mark by 6 million.

All assumptions about the future are based on uncertain evidence, and the uncertainties of a cold war are in some respects even greater than those of a full-scale shooting war. However, with the

end of active hostilities in Korea the defense build-up reached a peak in 1953 from which a moderate decline has already occurred. Barring the outbreak of new hostilities, it is possible to make some assumptions as to what the maintenance level of preparedness will mean in terms of the cost of meeting long-continued needs for manpower and material.

Commerce Department Estimates

The Department of Commerce reported that expenditures for national security in the last quarter of 1952 were running at an annual rate of around $50 billion. This total included over $45 billion of spending by the Defense Department for all purposes, including foreign military aid, and about $5 billion for atomic energy, foreign economic aid and other defense purposes. By the second quarter of 1953 security expenditures had risen to an annual rate of $53.5 billion, from which level they declined to a $50 billion annual rate in the last quarter of the year, and to $47 billion on an annual basis in the first quarter of 1954. A further decline is expected which will continue into 1955. What maintenance level will ultimately be reached is difficult to estimate, but an annual average of $40 to $45 billion to maintain an armed force of 3 to 3.5 million might well continue until such time as the present international tension may relax.

The sudden collapse of France and Hitler's rush to the sea catapulted us into our defense program in the summer of 1940 just as the outbreak of the Korean War almost exactly ten years later turned us from sharp retrenchment to sudden expansion of military expenditures. By late 1943, we approached our peak industrial effort, which continued at high levels through 1944 and then was curtailed in 1945 and cut sharply thereafter. Our present defense program appears to be following a similar pattern. The tempo is much slower of course, and the cutback from the 1953 peak to the maintenance level of the later years of the decade will be much smaller than the demobilization of the 1940s — barring a favorable change in the international outlook.

BY J. FREDERIC DEWHURST AND THOMAS C. FICHANDLER, Associate Research Director of this study. Opinions and judgments expressed in this chapter are those of the authors and should not be attributed to the organization with which they are associated.

PAST AND FUTURE TRENDS [1]

Contributors have prepared their estimates and analyses of demands and needs in 1960 on the basis of such output of goods and services as might be expected under conditions of stable prosperity and high levels of employment. This is not analogous to the "full employment" of World War II, when the economy was working under forced draft and the normal labor force had been expanded by the addition of millions of surplus workers, most of whom promptly withdrew when the emergency passed. Rather, it contemplates a situation somewhat like that of 1925–1929, when employment was high and rising but unemployment at no time disappeared, or 1949 and early 1950, when the postwar boom had slackened somewhat. This kind of assumption involves no implication that a merely *high* level of employment is preferable to *full* employment, but only that such is more likely to be the state of affairs in the absence of abnormally heavy government spending or active inflation.

How large a volume of goods and services we can turn out at high levels of employment and production in 1960 will depend upon (a) the number of persons in the labor force in that year, (b) the average number actually at work, after deducting the probable number of unemployed, (c) the average hours of work, and (d) the productivity of the working force as measured by average output per man-hour. Finally, inasmuch as dollars are the only common unit for measuring the great variety of goods and services produced by the economic system, changes in the price level also will be a determinant of the dollar total of the gross national product and national income in 1960. Since the future trend of prices seems even more uncertain than the trend of employment and production, no assumption has been made about the 1960 price level. Instead, projections of the dollar volume of output and income are presented in terms of 1950 prices.

SIZE OF THE LABOR FORCE

The size and composition of the labor force display considerable stability under normal circumstances. The size of the labor force varies seasonally, of course, and it shows some tendency to

expand under the stress of a severe depression, when many people not normally in the labor force may look for jobs, and at the peak of a boom, when jobs are plentiful and pay attractive. Aside from these changes, the labor force appears to grow and change in character only gradually, in response to long-term trends in the age and sex composition of the population. In 1950 the labor force averaged 64.6 million workers, or about eight and one half times as many as the number of persons with gainful occupations in 1850, five times as many as in 1870, and more than twice as many as in 1900.

Not only did the population grow rapidly during this whole period, but the proportion in the working force also increased steadily up to 1910. Two persons out of every five were in the labor market in 1910 — as compared with less than one out of three in 1870 and before. The proportion remained at about 40 per cent of the total population until the 1930s, when it again rose slightly. In 1940, and again in 1950, about 42 per cent of the population was in the labor force. (See Table 306.)

Projection of past trends of "participation in the labor force" by sex and age groups indicates an average total labor force of 72.5 million for 1960. Until the census of 1960 has been taken, of course, this estimate, like other projections, is wholly conjectural. A labor force of this size would mean again that about 42 per cent of the 1960 population would be in the labor market. The average number of workers per family would be as great as or greater than at any time in the past, with the exception of periods of war or abnormal boom.

EMPLOYMENT AND UNEMPLOYMENT

The volume of goods and services our economy would be able to produce with a labor force of 72.5 million in 1960 depends, first of all, on the extent to which the labor force would be utilized with the economy operating at a high level of activity. "Full employment" is of course never completely achieved in the sense that every member of the labor force is actually at work at the same moment of time. By the summer of 1942 the war boom had been under way for two years and prices and wages were rising so fast as to necessitate drastic measures of control. Yet, although more than 3 million emergency workers had already been attracted into the labor market, nearly

---

1. See Chapter 20 for fuller discussion of trends in the size of the labor force, in employment and unemployment, hours of work and productivity.

as large a number, or about 5 per cent of the civilian labor force, were still out of work. Even when the peak war effort had drawn some 8 million emergency workers into the labor market, there were still between half a million and a million workers unemployed. (See Appendix 20–1.)

During the boom years after the war, unemployment never dropped as low as 1.5 million and rarely fell below 2 million; at one time during the minor recession of 1949–1950, it rose well above 4 million. Throughout most of this period, however, one million or more emergency workers remained in the labor force.

Such records as exist for earlier periods confirm the conclusion that a good deal of unemployment continues even in periods of prosperity. During the long depression of the 1930s heavy unemployment persisted, and only in the minor boom of 1937 did the number of unemployed drop below 7 million — about 12 per cent of the labor force. In contrast with the 1930s, the 1920 decade was one of prosperity and high employment, except for 1921–1922. Yet Leo Wolman's estimates of the "average minimum volume of unemployment" in nonagricultural pursuits during 1920–1927 ranged from a little less than 4 per cent of the labor force in the active years 1920 and 1923 to more than 5 per cent in 1924, when a mild recession occurred. Unemployment was much higher in 1921 and 1922, and over the entire eight-year period an average of 5.5 per cent of the working force were out of work.

In the light of past experience, a decade economically comparable to the last half of the 1920s would probably involve unemployment amounting on the average to nearly 5 per cent of the labor force. Such an assumption is not a statement of an ideal, but merely sets up the optimum accomplishments of the past as a reasonable "par" for the future. A practical minimum of 5 per cent of the labor force does not of course imply a hard core of unemployed workers who never find jobs, but rather a shifting group, most of them out of work for short spells between jobs.

Average unemployment of close to 5 per cent would mean about 3.5 million unemployed out of the 72.5 million labor force in 1960. At a high level of activity in 1960, therefore, about 69 million would be employed. This compares with 61.5 million employed and 3.1 unemployed in 1950, and with 47.9 million and 8.1 million in 1940.

As explained below, government employees, including members of the armed forces, are expected to number 10.5 million in 1960. This would mean 58.5 million working in private [2] occupations in 1960, compared with 54.1 million in 1950.

Precise information on hours of work is available only for recent years, but it is clear that the average work week has been shrinking steadily for several decades. "During the 40-year period from 1870 to 1910, there was . . . a rapid decrease in the length of the work period. The 72-hour week, the 60-hour week, and, to some extent, the 54-hour week successively passed into history; the 12-hour day gave place to the 10-hour day, and the 10-hour day, in some measure, gave place to the 8-hour day." [3] This downtrend, which undoubtedly began before 1870, continued even more rapidly after 1910, with the result that the 40-hour week had become a reality by 1950.

Trends in Working Hours

An attempt has been made to estimate average hours of work for private nonagricultural pursuits and for agriculture in 1850 and in every tenth year thereafter. According to these estimates, the average agricultural work week declined from 72 hours in 1850 to 67 hours in 1900; in 1950 the average was 47 hours. The sharpest curtailment has come since 1940, when the agricultural work week was more than 54 hours. Working time in private nonagricultural activities declined by more than a third between 1850 and 1930 — from an average of 65.7 hours a week to 43.2. A further drop of more than 4 hours had occurred by 1950. The average decline in the nonagricultural work week since 1900 has been more than 3 hours per decade. (See Appendix 20–4.)

Average working time for all occupations, weighted in accordance with the numbers employed in agriculture and in nonagriculture, declined from 69.8 hours in 1850 to 44 hours in 1940 and to 40 hours in 1950. This steep downward trend has meant a drop in the average length of the work week of about 3 hours per decade over the entire century. Since 1900 the

2. The term "private" as used in this survey denotes exclusion of government enterprises as well as general government activities.

3. *Comparative Occupation Statistics for the United States, 1870–1940,* U.S. Bureau of the Census, 1940, p. 91.

average decline per decade has been about 4 hours. (See Table 14.)

The 10 per cent decline in the length of the work week during the 1940s was temporarily reversed by World War II. By 1943 working time averaged 47.6 hours a week, but hours declined before the end of the war and sharply after 1945. The Korean crisis brought a slight increase, but this pressure had slackened even before the peak of rearmament activity and by early 1954 the average work week had dropped below 40 hours.

Future Working Hours

Unless there is a marked quickening of the defense effort, it now seems reasonable to expect the long-term downtrend to continue, at least over the next decade or so. There is every reason to believe that we shall want to continue accepting the fruits of rising productivity partly in the form of more goods and services and partly in the form of more leisure.

Past trends and current tendencies provide some basis for surmise as to what a continuance of this long-term trend would mean in terms of working hours under conditions of high activity in 1960. The steady decline of working time in nonagricultural pursuits over the past several decades makes it seem reasonable to assume that the average nonagricultural work week will fall from 38.8 hours in 1950 to 36.5 in 1960. This decline is somewhat less than the average drop per decade since 1900. Hours in agriculture could easily drop from slightly more than 47 in 1950 to 44 in 1960, which would be appreciably less than the average decline of about 4 hours per decade since 1900.

The weighted average work week for the entire private labor force (i.e., excluding average working hours of government employees, for which no estimates are made) would be roughly 37.5 hours long in 1960, compared with 40 hours in 1950. This would represent a drop of 2.5 hours during the present decade, compared with a decline of 4 hours in the 1940s and an average decline of 4 hours per decade since 1900. It is expected that workers will continue to shift from agriculture, where the work week is relatively long, to nonagricultural pursuits, where it is much shorter. This accounts for the larger decline in average working time for the two fields combined than for the nonagricultural field alone.

Vacations and Lost Time

These are estimates of average weekly hours for the *year as a whole*. In other words, they take account of working time lost because of holidays, temporary plant shutdowns, part-time operation and occasional days off. Because of such losses the actual work week is always shorter than the standard work week — often by two or three hours or more. Another factor that tends to reduce the average number of hours worked per week for the year as a whole is the growing practice of including paid vacations in labor contracts. A two-week vacation with a standard 40-hour week means a loss of 80 work hours during the year — an average of about 1.6 hours a week, or about 4 per cent of the standard 40-hour work week.

In estimating actual hours for 1960, it was assumed that the two-week annual vacation, estimated to apply to about one quarter of the working force in 1940 and to about half the employed labor force in 1950, would become virtually universal by 1960. This again is an "average" assumption. It does not mean that every employed person will have a two-week vacation in 1960. Some will take longer and some shorter vacations; and there will be many, notably among the "petty capitalists" operating their own newsstands or delicatessens, who will get no vacation at all.

PRODUCTIVITY

How large a volume of goods and services 69 million persons working 37.5 hours a week would be able to produce in 1960 is a question that cannot be answered without assumptions about labor productivity in that year. In 1950 there were 54 million persons working an average of 40 hours a week in private employment. This resulted in 112.3 billion man-hours of labor effort, or labor input, in that year. Since national income produced by the private sector of the economy in 1950 amounted to $217.3 billion, net output (i.e., private national income) per man-hour came to about $1.93.[4]

In 1940, private employment averaged 43.3

---

4. No attempt is made to estimate productivity of government workers, who numbered 7.5 million, including the armed forces, in 1950.

TABLE 14. ESTIMATED EMPLOYMENT, HOURS AND PRODUCTIVITY, 1850–1960

Year	Total				Private [a]						
			National Income						National Income [b]		Productivity: National Income per Man-Hour in 1950 Prices
	Employed Workers	Annual Man-Hours	Current Prices	1950 Prices	Employed Workers	Average Weekly Hours	Annual Man-Hours	Price Level Index	Current Prices	1950 Prices	
	(1)	(2)	(3)	(4)	(5)	(6)	(7)	(8)	(9)	(10)	(11)
	(Millions)	(Billions)	(Billions)		(Millions)		(Billions)	(1950 = 100)	(Billions)		(Cents)
1850	7.4	26.8	$ 2.4	$ 9.4	7.2	69.8	26.1	26.0	$ 2.3	$ 8.8	33.7
1860	10.1	35.7	3.9	14.4	9.8	68.0	34.7	27.0	3.8	14.1	40.6
1870	12.4	42.0	7.2	18.6	12.0	65.4	40.8	39.0	6.8	17.4	42.6
1880	16.7	55.4	8.0	25.6	16.1	64.0	53.6	32.0	7.6	23.8	44.4
1890	21.9	70.3	13.1	44.3	21.0	61.9	67.6	30.0	12.4	41.3	61.1
1900	26.7	83.3	19.0	63.3	25.4	60.2	79.5	30.0	18.0	60.0	75.5
1910	34.0	97.0	31.9	86.4	32.1	55.1	92.0	37.0	30.5	82.4	89.6
1920	39.7	102.0	72.9	94.7	36.8	49.7	95.1	78.3	69.4	88.6	93.2
1929	47.8	116.4	87.4	132.8	44.4	47.0	108.5	66.9	82.2	122.9	113.3
1930	45.8	108.8	75.0	118.5	42.4	45.9	101.2	64.4	69.7	108.2	106.9
1940	47.9	108.9	81.3	147.0	43.3	44.0	99.1	55.7	72.6	130.3	131.5
1941	51.8	118.9	103.8	174.2	45.7	44.4	105.5	60.4	93.4	154.6	146.5
1942	57.6	134.7	137.1	201.9	48.4	45.4	114.3	68.8	120.7	175.4	153.5
1943	63.3	154.7	169.7	233.4	48.4	47.6	119.8	73.7	142.4	193.2	161.3
1944	65.2	155.7	183.8	247.7	47.9	46.4	115.6	74.6	149.6	200.5	173.4
1945	64.1	147.1	182.7	239.1	46.8	44.5	108.3	75.8	145.3	191.7	177.0
1946	58.5	128.9	180.3	217.0	49.6	42.6	109.9	83.1	157.6	189.7	172.6
1947	59.5	128.8	198.7	216.7	52.6	41.8	114.3	92.4	180.2	195.0	170.6
1948	60.7	128.6	223.5	227.1	53.8	40.9	114.4	99.1	203.9	205.8	179.9
1949	60.2	125.7	216.3	221.4	52.9	40.3	110.9	97.9	194.5	198.7	179.2
1950	61.5	127.4	240.6	240.6	54.0	40.0	112.3	100.0	217.3	217.3	193.5
1951	63.9	134.0	278.4	258.7	54.7	40.5	115.2	107.7	248.3	230.5	200.1
1952	64.7	135.8	291.6	264.6	54.7	40.5	115.2	110.1	257.6	234.0	203.1
1960	69.0	134.0	—	312.5	58.5	37.5	114.1	—	—	275.0	240.0

Sources: Col. 1: Appendix 20-4.

Col. 2: Col. 7, plus annual man-hours of government employees (Col. 1 minus Col. 5 times average weekly hours of nonagricultural workers, shown in Col. 6 of Appendix 20-4, times 52).

Col. 3: 1850–1900, carried back from 1910 on basis of estimates in Simon Kuznets, *Uses of National Income in Peace and War*, Occasional Paper No. 6, National Bureau of Economic Research, March 1942, Table 9, p. 38; 1910–1920, carried back from 1929 on basis of estimates in Appendix 4–2, Table A; 1929–1952, *Survey of Current Business*, July 1953, Table 1, pp. 10–11.

Col. 4: Based on price level index derived as follows: 1850–1910, carried back from 1913 on basis of the Carl Snyder–Rufus S. Tucker general price index as published in *Historical Statistics of the United States, 1789–1945*, U.S. Bureau of the Census, 1949, p. 231; 1913–1920, carried back from 1929 on basis of BLS consumers' price index, *Handbook of Labor Statistics, 1950*, Bureau of Labor Statistics, 1951, Table D–1, p. 100; 1929–1952, based on implicit price deflators for gross national product in *Survey of Current Business*, July 1953, Table B, pp. 26–27, shifted to 1950 base.

Col. 5 and Col. 6: Appendix 20-4.

Col. 7: Col. 5 times Col. 6 times 52.

Col. 8: Derived in same manner as price level index for Col. 4 except that indexes for 1929–1952 were based on implicit price deflators for gross *private* product.

Col. 9: Col. 3 minus wages and salaries (including supplements) of government employees. Wages and salaries (including supplements) of government employees: 1850–1900, estimates of Willford I. King, *Wealth and Income of the People of the United States*, Macmillan, New York, 1915, Table XXX A, p. 290, raised by 3 per cent—the percentage that supplements were of government wages and salaries in 1929 (*Survey of Current Business*, July 1950, Table 13, p. 15 and Table 14, p. 27); 1910, estimates of King, *The National Income and Its Purchasing Power*, National Bureau of Economic Research, New York, 1930, Table CXVII, p. 364, raised by 3 per cent; 1920, estimates of Kuznets, *National Income and Its Composition*, National Bureau of Economic Research, New York, 1941, Vol. II, Table G 1, p. 811, raised by 3 per cent; 1929–1952, *National Income and Product of the United States, 1929–1950* (1951 National Income Supplement to the *Survey of Current Business*), Table 13, p. 158, and *Survey of Current Business*, July 1953, Table 13, p. 16.

Col. 10: Col. 9 divided by Col. 8.

Col. 11: Col. 10 divided by Col. 7.

For 1960 estimates, see text.

a. The term "private" in this table and elsewhere in this survey denotes exclusion of government enterprises as well as general government activities.

b. Estimates for 1850–1920 have been adjusted upward to the 1929 level shown in more recent Department of Commerce estimates and hence are not consistent with those for total national income in Appendix 4–2.

million and total private labor input amounted to 99.1 billion man-hours. Private national income in 1940 amounted to $72.6 billion, but if this output had been valued at the much higher prices prevailing in 1950 it would have equaled $130.3 billion. Thus net output per man-hour in 1940 amounted to $1.31 at 1950 prices. (See Table 14.)

This means that productivity, as measured by private national income per man-hour expressed in constant prices, increased by about 47 per cent between 1940 and 1950. Year-to-year changes during the decade varied widely. Productivity increased more than 10 per cent from 1940 to 1941 and another 10 per cent by 1943. Not until 1948, however, did it rise a further 10 per cent above 1943. In fact, in each of the years 1946, 1947 and 1949 output per man-hour dropped below the level of the preceding year.

The decade-to-decade changes of the past century confirm the existence of wide variations in the rate of change in productivity, in contrast to the steady, persistent trends in the length of the work week and the size of the labor force. Not only does productivity change unevenly and irregularly, but the statistical devices for measuring it are at best quite crude.

In spite of difficulties and uncertainties, however, an estimate of future changes in productivity is necessary in order to arrive at an approximation of what our economy can produce under favorable conditions in 1960. On the whole, it appears reasonable to rely on over-all measures of productivity in projecting past trends rather than on indexes of productivity in specific industries or occupations, none of which can be considered representative of the entire economy.

Estimates of private national income (i.e., value of net output of goods and services exclusive of indirect business taxes) can be made at ten-year intervals back to 1850. These dollar estimates provide a rough measure of changes in the physical output of goods and services when converted by means of a price level index into "constant dollars" of 1950 purchasing power.

Thus expressed in dollars of constant purchasing power, private national income increased from $8.8 billion in 1850 to $60.0 billion in 1900 and to $217.3 billion in 1950. The century thus witnessed a 25-fold increase in the net output of the American economy — while population multiplied less than seven times.

Private labor input in the same period increased from an estimated 26.1 billion man-hours in 1850 to 112.3 billion in 1950, or a little more than four times. These estimates of private man-hours of labor effort divided into the corresponding estimates of private national income provide a measure of output per man-hour in 1850 and at ten-year intervals to 1950.[5]

The resulting series shows a rise from an estimated output per man-hour of 33.7 cents in 1850 to $1.93 in 1950. Thus, the productivity of labor was multiplied nearly six times during the century. Although the average increase per decade was about 18.4 per cent, the change from one decade to the next varied greatly. Generally speaking, the gains since 1900 have been greater than those during the last half of the nineteenth century. Between 1850 and 1900, productivity little more than doubled; between 1900 and 1950, it almost trebled.

How much productivity will increase during the 1950s nobody knows, but Figure 5 strengthens the judgment that the percentage increase from decade to decade has been showing a tendency to rise slightly. Projecting this slightly rising trend line [6] to 1960 suggests that it would be reasonable to expect an increase of about 25 per cent during the decade, or approximately 2.3 per cent a year.

ESTIMATED OUTPUT IN 1960

The private national income that would be produced at a high level of activity in 1960, on the basis of the assumptions stated above, can now be determined by simple arithmetic. If net output (national income) per man-hour increases at the average rate of 2.3 per cent a year, it will rise by about 47 cents between 1950 and 1960 — from $1.93 to $2.40.

PRIVATE NATIONAL INCOME

With 58.5 million persons working in private employment in 1960 and an average work week of 37.5 hours, total "labor input" would amount to 114 billion man-hours for a 52-week year. At

5. See Table 14 and Appendix 20–4 for data and estimates of unemployment and employment, working hours, national income and output per man-hour.

6. The curve fitted to the estimates for decade years has the following algebraic form: $\log y = 1.837 + .071x + .002x^2$. All the decade years fall within 12 per cent of the values along the trend curve.

gain in the form of shorter working hours and more leisure time. There is every reason to expect that further advances in productivity will mean a continuance of this trend toward more leisure as well as more goods.

TOTAL NATIONAL INCOME

Total national income in 1960 will exceed private national income by the amount of the government contribution to the national income stream. The value of the "government product," unlike the value of the goods and services produced by the private economy, cannot be established by its selling price in the market place. Nor can its value be estimated on this basis, or readily on any other basis. How much, for example, would the services of the police department, the use of city streets, or the protection afforded by the Lighthouse Service be worth in a competitive market? What is it worth to settle a strike, to win a war, or to prevent one? Because such questions cannot be answered, the value of the government product is usually considered to be equal to the total payments for the services of government employees. (Goods purchased by the government and purchased services, other than those of government employees, are of course produced by the private economy.)

Government employment has fluctuated widely in recent years. At the peak of World War II, about 17 million were on government payrolls, including more than 11 million in the armed forces. The average number of government employees in 1950 was approximately 7.5 million and total payments for services of government employees amounted to about $21 billion. About 1.5 million were in the armed forces.

By 1951 government employment, including the armed forces, had risen to an average of slightly over 9 million. We were then midway in the build-up of the defense program and at a lower level of rearmament than will be required for a maintenance program during the later years of the decade after the decline from the 1953 peak has "leveled off."

The strength of the armed services rose to 3.5 million in 1953, and it is expected that approximately this level will be maintained for the indefinite future. Our estimate for 1960 contemplates about 10.5 million employees at all levels of government. With the armed forces at their present strength, this will mean approximately 7.0 million civilian employees.

On the basis of past relationships between government employment and total employment and between government product and total national income it appears that with 10.5 million employees, government would account for about 12 per cent of total national income in 1960. On this basis, total national income would amount to $312.5 billion and the government share to $37.5 billion.

GROSS NATIONAL PRODUCT

To estimate gross national product requires assumptions as to the amount of indirect taxes payable in 1960 and the amount of "capital consumption," or the cost of replacing capital goods used up in the productive process in that year. Indirect business taxes, which came to $24 billion out of a $287 billion gross national product in 1950, are estimated at $29.5 billion for 1960. Adding this to the $312.5 billion national income yields a net national product of $342 billion in that year.[7]

Capital consumption has amounted to about 7.5 per cent of gross national product in recent years of fairly full employment, such as 1929, 1948 and 1949. If this same percentage relationship is assumed for 1960, capital consumption would amount to $28 billion and gross national product to approximately $370 billion, at 1950 prices. This would mean that our economy would be turning out about 29 per cent more goods and services than in 1950 and 28 per cent more than in 1944, the peak year of World War II.

The computations described above are shown as the "medium projections" in Table 15.

COMPARISON WITH OTHER ESTIMATES

Estimating what the postwar economy would be able to produce under conditions of full employment became one of the most popular of intellectual exercises during World War II. It produced a flood of widely varied estimates of

---

7. In addition to indirect business taxes, business transfer payments plus statistical discrepancy plus current surplus of government enterprises minus subsidies are to be added to national income to derive the net national product. The net effect of these miscellaneous items generally is small and they have been assumed to be in balance for 1960.

TABLE 15. NATIONAL INCOME AND GROSS NATIONAL PRODUCT IN 1950 AND
HIGH, MEDIUM AND LOW PROJECTIONS FOR 1960

(Dollar Amounts at 1950 Prices)

		1960		
	1950	*High*	*Medium*	*Low*
Labor force (*millions*)	64.6	74.0	72.5	71.0
Unemployment (*millions*)	3.1	3.0	3.5	4.0
Employment (*millions*)	61.5	71.0	69.0	67.0
Government (*millions*)	7.5	11.0	10.5	10.0
Private (*millions*)	54.1	60.0	58.5	57.0
Private sector of economy				
Average work week (*hours*)	40.0	40.0	37.5	36.0
Total man-hours (*billions*)	112.5	124.8	114.1	106.7
Productivity increase during decade (*per cent*)	47	35	25	15
National income per man-hour	$1.93	$2.60	$2.40	$2.20
National income (billions)	$217.3	$325.0	$275.0	$235.0
Government share of total national income (*per cent*)	10.0	12.2	12.0	11.8
Total national income (*billions*)	$240.6	$370.0	$312.5	$265.0
Indirect business taxes (*billions*)	$23.7	$35.0	$29.5	$25.0
Net national product (*billions*) [a]	$265.2	$405.0	$342.0	$290.0
Gross national product (*billions*)	$286.8	$440.0 [b]	$370.0 [b]	$315.0 [b]

Source: See text for estimates and analysis.

a. Net national product equals national income plus indirect business taxes plus a miscellaneous group of items (business transfer payments, statistical discrepancy and current surplus of government enterprises minus subsidies). This miscellaneous group was assumed equal to zero for 1960.

b. Net national product + capital consumption = gross national product. Capital consumption assumed to equal 7.5 per cent of gross national product for 1960 estimates.

future gross national product and a growing literature devoted to explaining, defending and criticizing them.

EARLIER ESTIMATES OF 1950 GROSS PRODUCT

The first edition of the present report, published in 1947, listed eleven such estimates of employment, unemployment and output in 1950, and of the productivity trend during the 1940-1950 decade.[8] The lowest of these estimates, all of which were made before the end of the war, placed the size of the 1950 labor force at 58.3 million, and the highest at 62.8 million; the actual labor force (including the armed forces), as shown by Census monthly reports, numbered 64.6 million in that year.

8. The various estimates were prepared by the National Planning Association; Jacob L. Mosak; E. E. Hagen and N. B. Kirkpatrick; Arno Johnson; S. Morris Livingston; Sumner H. Slichter; *Fortune* Magazine; W. S. Woytinsky; David Prince; Joseph Mayer; and Rufus S. Tucker. See Edwin B. George, "Gross National Product Projections for Full Employment," *Dun's Review*, May 1945.

Unemployment, estimates of which ranged from 1.5 million to 4 million, turned out to be 3.1 million in 1950. The lowest estimate of what employment would be in 1950 was 55.3 million and the highest was 61.3 million, whereas total employment actually averaged about 61.5 million in 1950. Assumptions as to what the length of the average work week would be in 1950 varied from less than 40 hours to more than 43. Actual working time appears to have been about 40 hours.

The widest differences were in the assumptions as to increases in output per worker, which ranged from less than one per cent a year to 2.6 per cent. The actual increase in output (i.e., private national income at constant prices) per worker appears to have been about 33 per cent during the decade, or an average of about 2.9 per cent a year cumulative.

As a result of these widely varying assumptions, the eleven estimates of 1950 gross national product (expressed in dollars of 1943 purchasing power) ranged from $157 billion to $207 billion. The projection worked out by the staff of the 1947 survey and presented in the first edition of this report was $173 billion. Gross national product in 1950, consistent with these projections, turned out to be roughly $185 billion,[9] in 1943 dollars. Thus the actual total exceeded the lowest estimate by 18 per cent and the projection used in the 1947 survey by 7 per cent, while it fell short of the highest estimate by approximately 11 per cent.

Wide as was the $50 billion range between highest and lowest estimates, it would have been even wider, and the errors larger, if the extreme projections had been based on a combination of the most optimistic and least optimistic of the assumptions as to each of the separate factors that together determine the size of the gross national product. A combination of the maximum assumptions as to employment, working hours and productivity would have yielded an estimate of gross national product in 1950 about half again as large as an estimate based on the minimum assumptions.

It is obvious that all such projections into the future are valid within the limits of their assumptions. Given the assumptions, estimating future national income or gross product is a simple matter of arithmetic. It is the assumptions that should be questioned rather than the projections themselves.

POSSIBLE RANGE OF 1960 ESTIMATES

The experience of the past makes it clear not only that the assumptions underlying the estimate of $312.5 billion national income and $370 billion gross national product in 1960 *can* be wrong, but that they are almost *sure* to be wrong in some respects. If the economy should be operating in 1960 under the pressure of a much heavier armament program than has been assumed — even though far short of the forced draft of war — the assumptions would prove to be incorrect. More people would probably be drawn into the labor force, fewer would be unemployed, a larger proportion would be working for the government, and the work week would be longer. The productivity increase under such pressure might also be greater, although this is by no means certain.

On the other hand, if the armament program should develop less intensively and if greater slack should appear in the economy than is contemplated in the assumptions on which the above estimates are based, these assumptions would again prove to be incorrect. Such conditions, though by no means implying a full-scale recession, would probably mean fewer people in the labor force and in government service, a larger number of unemployed, a shorter work week, and possibly a smaller increase in productivity.

Employment, Hours and Productivity

How much such divergent conditions might affect employment, working time and productivity is of course also a matter of surmise. It seems reasonable, however, that the labor force could easily be larger or smaller by 1.5 million than the assumed total of 72.5 million. Unemployment might be 4 million, or 3 million, instead of the assumed 3.5 million. Total employment could therefore be as low as 67 million or as high as 71 million. Depending on the size of the defense program and other considerations, government employment in 1960, assumed to be 10.5 million, could easily deviate from this figure by as much as 500,000 in either direction. Private employment under these circumstances would vary from 57 million to 60 million, or by 5 per cent. (See Table 15.)

Under the maximum assumptions for 1960, working time might remain at the 40-hour average prevailing in 1950 instead of declining to 37.5 hours. On the other hand, a slack economy would mean less overtime, some spreading of work, and quite possibly an average work week as low as 36 hours, or 10 per cent less than in 1950.

Under the maximum assumptions, therefore, total labor input of the private sector of the national economy would amount to nearly 125 billion man-hours for the year 1960, or not far from one fifth more than the 107 billion man-hours that would result from the minimum assumptions.

How large total private national income

<hr>

9. Since preparation of the first edition of this survey the Commerce Department has completely revised its estimates of gross national product, introducing changes in both concepts and methods of measurement. In 1946, the last year for which estimates on the old basis were published, the new series exceeded the old by about 8 per cent. For 1950, we estimated the difference would have been about 10 per cent and reduced the current Commerce estimates accordingly in arriving at the $185 billion estimate.

would be on the basis of these hypothetical labor inputs depends on the rise of productivity during the decade. As indicated earlier, the long-term trend of productivity over the past century appeared to justify a 25 per cent increase as a reasonable expectation for the 1950–1960 decade. This was the basis for the medium estimate of private national income.

Great uncertainty surrounds any such assumption, however, for productivity gains in the past have varied widely, and they will probably continue to do so in the future. The apparent 47 per cent increase in private national income per man-hour from 1940 to 1950 was larger than that of any previous decade. During the preceding decade the productivity gain amounted to about 23 per cent, but in some earlier decades the increase was less than 10 per cent, and indeed it fell as low as 4 per cent in the 1870s. An increase as small as this or as large as the 47 per cent of the 1940s seems hardly within the range of likely possibilities. Past experience suggests, however, that a range about half as great might constitute a reasonable statement of possibilities. In other words, the 1950–1960 increase might easily be as low as 15 per cent, or as high as 35 per cent, instead of the assumed 25 per cent.

National Income and Gross Product

Under the maximum assumption, therefore, net output (private national income) per man-hour would rise from $1.93 in 1950 to $2.60 in 1960, and, under the minimum assumptions, to only $2.20. The minimum assumptions as to productivity and total man-hours of labor input would lead to a total private national income of only $235 billion, while the maximum assumptions would indicate about $325 billion, compared with the medium projection of $275 billion.

With government employment, under the ⸱imum assumptions, at 11 million, past rela- ⸱⸱ suggest that the "government product" ⸱⸱te 12.2 per cent of total national inco⸱⸱ ⸱ indicate a government product of $4⸱ ⸱otal national income of about $370 ⸱ ⸱ minimum assumptions, with gov⸱ ⸱yment at 10 mil-

lion, the government share of total national income is estimated at 11.8 per cent. This would mean a government product of only $30 billion out of a total national income of $265 billion.

Since indirect business taxes would tend to be roughly proportional to the dollar volume of business, or of national income, they have been estimated at about $35 billion under maximum assumptions and at $25 billion under the minimum. Net national product under these conditions would show a range from $290 billion to $405 billion.

With capital consumption normally accounting for 7.5 per cent of gross national product, gross national product might be as high as $440 billion under maximum assumptions, and as low as $315 billion under the minimum. The medium assumptions, which appeared most reasonable for this survey, yielded $370 billion. Thus the gross national product resulting from a combination of maximum assumptions would be about $70 billion, or 19 per cent, above the medium figure, while that resulting from a combination of minimum assumptions would be about $55 billion, or 15 per cent, below the medium.

VALIDITY OF MEDIUM ASSUMPTIONS

Clearly, the medium projection of $370 billion gross national product (at 1950 prices; about $415 billion at 1953 prices) in 1960 and the assumptions on which it is based possess only limited validity. About all that one can say is that it seemed more reasonable than any other single figure in the light of all the uncertainties that surround any attempt to look several years into the future. In any event, it is these medium projections that provide the bases for further assumptions as to savings, taxes, government revenues and expenditures, capital formation, and consumption expenditures shown in Chapter 4.

These latter assumptions in turn serve as the foundation for the detailed breakdown of consumer and capital expenditures in 1960 as developed in subsequent chapters. Any errors in these basic estimates are solely the responsibility of the central staff of this survey and not of those responsible for authorship of the separate chapters.

## CHAPTER 3

POPULATION GROWTH

AMONG THE MOST STRIKING and unexpected developments of the war decade were a surprisingly large increase in the number of marriages and a sharp and sustained rise in the birth rate. With death rates continuing to decline, the consequent growth of population, particularly during the postwar years, went far beyond the maximum expectations of population experts. During the 1940–1950 decade more people got married — and more got divorced — and more babies were born than in any previous ten-year period. Our population in July 1950 numbered 152 million; it had grown during the preceding ten years by almost 20 million, of which some 12 million were added after the war's end. A year later the total had risen to 155 million, and by July 1953 to 160 million.[1] The growth since before World War II has been much larger numerically than in any previous period of equal length, though a comparatively modest percentage gain. These developments have already powerfully affected the postwar economy, and population changes will continue to play a large part in determining future needs and resources.

GROWTH TRENDS

The population of the United States has grown with extraordinary rapidity throughout our entire history as a nation. This rapid growth has resulted from a high birth rate and a substantial surplus of births over deaths throughout most of our history, together with a heavy volume of immigration during the latter part of the nineteenth century and the early part of the twentieth. During the first half of the nineteenth century, population quadrupled; it more than trebled during the last half and has doubled again since 1900. There are about seven times as many Americans today as there were in 1850, a little more than a century ago. (See Table 16 and Figure 7.)

Until the past two decades, the Negro population grew less rapidly than the white, chiefly because the natural increase of the native white population was augmented by a heavy flow of white immigrants from Europe. As a result, less than 10 per cent of our 1950 population were Negroes, compared with nearly 16 per cent a century earlier. Since 1930, however, immigration has declined sharply and the Negro population has increased somewhat more rapidly than the white.

The foreign-born have always been an important element of the American population. During the second half of the nineteenth century the increase of foreign-born from 2.2 million to 10.2 million far exceeded the rate of growth of the native-born. The foreign-born population reached its percentage peak (nearly 15 per cent of the total population) in 1910, after the heaviest decade of immigration, and its numerical peak (14 million) in 1930. Since then the population has become much more homogeneous, with sharp declines in the number and proportion of foreign-born as well as in those of foreign parentage.[2]

Uneven Growth

Population growth during the past century has been far from steady, owing chiefly to variations in the amount of immigration in the earlier decades and, more recently, to unusual fluctuations in marriage and birth rates. However, there has been a generally upward trend in the

---

1. Reference is to total population, including armed forces overseas and corrected for underenumeration. This total for 1950 is shown in Tables 27 and 28 and Appendix 3–6. The population reported by the 1950 Census, 150.7 million (shown in Tables 16, 21, 26 and Appendix 3–4), has not been adjusted for underenumeration and is for continental United States only and thus excludes armed forces overseas. The 1951 and 1953 figures represent the population increase from July 1950 to July 1951 and from July 1950 to July 1953 reported in *Current Population Reports: Population Estimates*, Series P–25, No. 79, September 16, 1953, added to the 1950 adjusted total of 152.5 million.

2. Except where otherwise stated, data throughout this chapter are from U.S. Bureau of the Census: *Historical Statistics of the United States, 1789–1945*, 1949; *Statistical Abstract of the United States*, various years; and reports of the Seventeenth Census (1950).

By J. FREDERIC DEWHURST. Opinions and judgments expressed in this chapter are those of the author and should not be attributed to the organization with which he is associated.

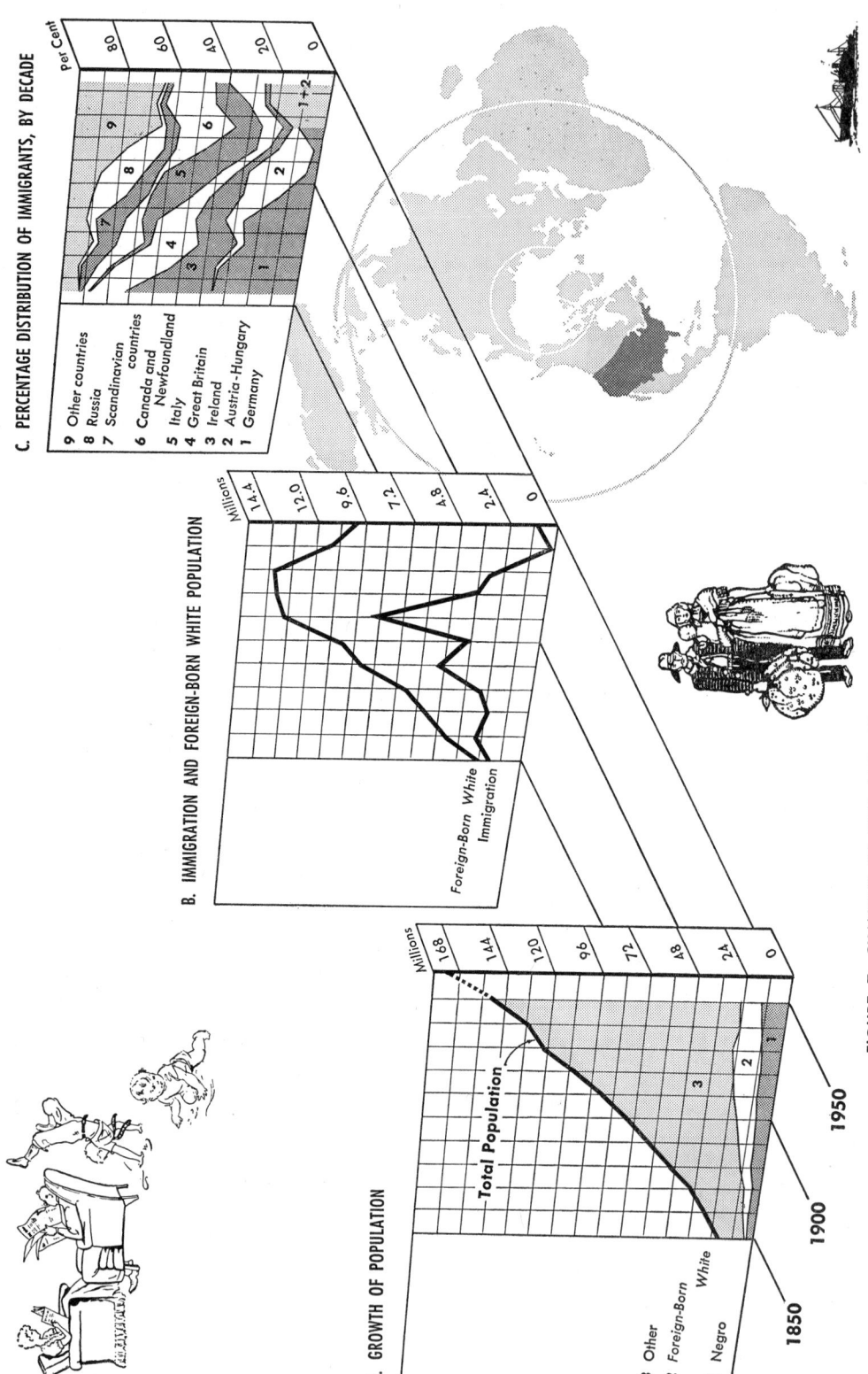

C. PERCENTAGE DISTRIBUTION OF IMMIGRANTS, BY DECADE

Per Cent

80
60
40
20
0

9 Other countries
8 Russia
7 Scandinavian
    countries
6 Canada and
    Newfoundland
5 Italy
4 Great Britain
3 Ireland
2 Austria-Hungary
1 Germany

B. IMMIGRATION AND FOREIGN-BORN WHITE POPULATION

Millions

14.4
12.0
9.6
7.2
4.8
2.4
0

Foreign-Born White
Immigration

A. GROWTH OF POPULATION

Millions

168
144
120
96
72
48
24
0

Total Population

3 Other
2 Foreign-Born
1 Negro
White

1850   1900   1950

FIGURE 7. CHANGES IN SIZE AND COMPOSITION OF POPULATION, 1850–1950

Sources: Table 16 and Appendix 3–1.

50

TABLE 16. GROWTH OF POPULATION AND IMMIGRATION IN CONTINENTAL UNITED STATES, 1850–1950

(Number in Millions)

Census Year	Population as Reported by Census	Population Increase over Preceding Census		Immigration in Preceding Decade		Foreign-Born White Population	Negro Population
		Amount	Per Cent	Amount [a]	Per Cent of Population Increase		
1850	23.2	6.1	35.9	1.7	27.9	2.2	3.6
1860	31.4	8.3	35.6	2.6	31.3	4.1	4.4
1870	39.8	8.4	26.6	2.3	27.4	5.5	4.9
1880	50.2	10.3	26.0	2.8	27.2	6.6	6.6
1890	62.9	12.8	25.5	5.2	40.6	9.1	7.5
1900	76.0	13.0	20.7	3.7	28.5	10.2	8.8
1910	92.0	16.0	21.1	8.8	55.0	13.3	9.8
1920	105.7	13.7	14.9	3.6	26.3	13.7	10.5
1930	122.8	17.1	16.1	3.1	18.1	14.0	11.9
1940	131.7	8.9	7.2	.07	0.8	11.4	12.9
1950	150.7	19.0	14.5	.9	4.7	10.2	15.0

Sources: Statistical Abstract of the United States, 1953, U.S. Bureau of the Census, Tables 2, 101, 102; *Historical Statistics of the United States, 1789–1945,* 1949, p. 25; Seventeenth Census of Population (1950), Vol. II, *Characteristics of the Population,* Table 35.

a. Up to 1867, alien passengers arriving; 1868–1891 and 1895–1897, immigrant alien arrivals; 1892–1894 and 1898–1910, immigrant aliens admitted; since 1910, net immigration. Only net immigration shows the actual contribution of immigration to population increase; no statistics of net immigration are available for the period before 1910.

Note: Slight discrepancies between the first and second columns are due to rounding.

size of the numerical increases by decades, accompanied by a downward trend in percentage gains.

Until World War I, immigration contributed heavily to these gains. In the 1920s, however, immigration was sharply curtailed and in the 1930s it virtually ceased, while the birth rate dropped to record low levels. The 1930–1940 population gain was smaller than that in any similar period since the 1860s, and the percentage increase was the lowest on record. By the end of the depression decade there was widespread acceptance of the idea that a period of stable if not declining population was not far off.

Rapid Recent Growth

Prospects began to change when the defense period got under way. Marriage and birth rates rose sharply in the early years of the war, and population in the first half of the decade grew almost 8 million, or only one million less than the entire increase during the 1930s. This gain was more or less in line with what might have been expected to result from the combined effects of a sharp recovery from prolonged depression and American entrance into large-scale war.

A further temporary rise in marriage and birth rates was anticipated immediately after demobilization, but the continuance of rapid population growth to the end of the decade and beyond was contrary to the predictions of most population experts. Population grew during the last half of the war decade by almost 12 million and over the whole 1940–1950 period by almost 20 million. This record gain was achieved despite the fact that net immigration contributed less than 900,000 during the decade.

The further gain of 8 million during the three years following the 1950 Census represents about the same annual percentage growth as occurred in the 1945–1950 period.

IMMIGRATION TRENDS

Throughout most of our history the United States has been a melting pot for many races and nationalities, with the great bulk of the immigrants coming from Europe. Not only has the number of immigrants been large in relation to our natural population growth, but the vast majority of immigrants have been of child-bearing ages. Thus immigration has augmented population both in itself and by contributing to the high birth rates prevailing throughout most of our history.

The number of immigrants admitted each decade from 1850 to 1920 never amounted to less than one fourth of the total population increase during the decade. The proportion rose above 40 per cent in the 1880s, and to 55 per cent in 1901–1910. During the 35-year period of heaviest immigration, from 1880 to 1915, more than 22 million aliens were admitted, while total population increased from about 50 million to 100 million.[3] The all-time peak of immigration came in the decade before World War I, when the number of immigrants averaged almost a million annually. (See Table 16.)

Geographic Shifts

Changing business conditions in the United States and economic and political pressures in Europe have caused marked shifts in the national composition of immigration as well as in the volume of the total inflow. The first sizable non-British groups to migrate to this country were the Germans and Irish, who began to arrive in large numbers in the early 1850s and accounted for three fourths of the total immigration in that decade. Germans, Irish and British together accounted for more than half of the total until the 1890s. By 1901–1910, entrances from western Europe, although still heavy, constituted a much smaller proportion of a much larger total. (See Figure 7 and Appendix 3–1.)

Scandinavians, Austro-Hungarians, Italians and Russians arrived for the first time in large numbers in the 1880s, and in the next decade immigrants from Russia, Italy and Austria-Hungary accounted for nearly half of the total. These three countries of southern and eastern Europe accounted for 5.7 million of the record 8.8 million admissions in the prosperous 1901–1910 decade and for more than half of the gross

immigration in the next decade. The years 1911–1920 also witnessed the peak of entrances from Greece and a heavy inflow from Canada and Newfoundland.

European immigration dropped sharply after the outbreak of World War I, and there was also a heavy return flow to Europe, so that *net* immigration from 1911 to 1920 amounted to only 3.6 million. (See Table 16.)

Racial Fusion

World War I marked the end of the liberal immigration policy that had prevailed since the nation was founded. This policy had always limited the entry of Orientals, but the inflow of white immigrants, chiefly from Europe, had been almost unrestricted for a century and a quarter. This heavy and heterogeneous immigration has made the United States uniquely a hybrid nation. No other nation has ever been created in so short a time from the intermingling and fusion of so many racial strains and national cultures.

One geneticist suggests that this mixing of racial stocks is producing the same heterosis, or "hybrid vigor," that has resulted from crossing different strains of agricultural plants and animals.[4] If this hypothesis is valid the favorable results of hybridization have not yet been fully felt, for the melting pot has not yet completed its task. Intermarriage has already erased or blurred the racial differences among descendants of the earlier western European immigrants, but such admixture may not take place before another generation or two among the more recently arrived groups from southern and eastern Europe.

Aside from the possible biological benefits of racial mixture, the character and diversity of immigration have undoubtedly contributed to American cultural and technological vigor. Even though the heavy immigration from Europe was free and unrestricted, the immigrants were in fact a highly selected group. Since they came on their own initiative, they were self-selected on a basis that ensured a larger-than-average proportion of risk-takers, of nonconformists and innovators, of those dissatisfied with things as they were and anxious to welcome change if it promised improvement. Coming to the United States,

---

3. These figures exaggerate to some (but an unknown) extent the direct contribution of immigration to our population growth, since they measure gross rather than net immigration, i.e., they take no account of the number of immigrants returning to their home countries. The volume of emigration was not measured statistically until after 1910, but it may have been substantial in periods when heavy immigration coincided with or followed closely after economic depression in the United States.

4. George D. Snell, "Hybrids and History, The Role of Race and Ethnic Crossing in Individual and National Achievements," *Quarterly Review of Biology,* December 1951, pp. 331–347.

as they did, from varied backgrounds, they brought with them many different occupational skills and a knowledge of various industrial techniques. Interchange of ideas in a highly favorable environment and within a society that had not acquired fixed industrial traditions helped to create a dynamic technology. Yankee ingenuity is a hybrid product.

Immigration Restricted

After World War I labor leaders and others strongly opposed the resumption of mass immigration on the ground that it threatened labor standards. As a result rigorous control was imposed on the volume of immigration, its national composition, and the economic status of immigrants. Congress in 1921 limited the total number of immigrants to 360,000 a year. This total was allocated among emigration countries in proportion to the distribution by national origin of the foreign-born population of the United States in 1910. Subsequent legislation has drastically reduced the total to its present level of about 155,000, but has retained the quota system of the original act.[5] This "national origin plan" results in the allocation of more than three fourths of total immigration to western and northern Europe. Great Britain and Northern Ireland are permitted about 65,400 entrances annually, Germany 25,800, Eire nearly 17,800 and Scandinavian countries 6,800.[6] Immigrants from Canada, Newfoundland and most of North and South America are not subject to quota restrictions.

Largely because of these restrictions, immigration in 1921–1930 dropped to 4.1 million, of which more than a third came from nonquota countries, chiefly Canada, Newfoundland and Mexico. Moreover, about one million emigrants left the United States during the decade, so that net immigration amounted to only 3.1 million.

The deep depression of the 1930s brought a further drop to record low levels. In fact, there were more emigrants than immigrants during the first half of the decade and, in spite of the recovery in the second half, a net immigration of only 69,000 for 1931–1940 as a whole.

Effects of World War II

Because of World War II, immigration, especially from the quota countries, fell to very low levels during 1941–1945. The end of the war, however, brought a sharp increase from both quota and nonquota countries. Of the 864,000 immigrants arriving during 1946–1950, about 245,000 came from Canada and other parts of the American hemisphere and 569,000 from Europe. Allowing for emigration, the net inflow during the last half of the war decade amounted to 752,000, compared with 129,000 in the first half. (See Appendix 3–2.)

Heavy immigration continued in the early 1950s, reaching a postwar peak of 266,000 in 1952. From 1951 to 1953 *net* immigration totaled 570,000. By 1953, however, the proportion of immigrants from Europe had declined to less than 50 per cent.

Immigration from northern and western Europe was well below quota levels, but the Displaced Persons Act of 1948 greatly stimulated admission of persons born in countries now behind the Iron Curtain. This act permits the "mortgaging" of 50 per cent of quotas for future years when necessary. As a result admission of quota immigrants from Poland, the Soviet Union, Latvia, Lithuania, Estonia, Hungary, Romania and Yugoslavia in 1950 — and in some cases in 1949 — amounted to several times the normal annual quotas assigned these countries. Nearly 150,000 were admitted from these countries in the two years, whereas the regular quotas allowed for less than 25,000. The flow continued in 1951 and 1952, with total admissions of former residents of these eight countries amounting to 190,000. America's doors were again open to the victims of political persecution.

This inflow from behind the Iron Curtain is likely to be short-lived, however, and immigration from countries having the largest quotas shows no tendency to approach permitted levels. Whether Congress will make changes in the act favorable to countries now having small quotas is uncertain. During the 1952 presidential cam-

5. The Act of 1924 reduced the permitted total to 165,000 and based allocations on the foreign-born population in 1890. It further provided that after July 1, 1929 the quota of any nationality be computed by applying to 150,000 the ratio between the calculated number of inhabitants in the continental United States in 1920 owing their origin to the nationality concerned and the total inhabitants in the United States of all nationalities subject to the quota law. The 150,000 total was increased slightly by subsequent special acts. The McCarran-Walter Immigration Act of 1952 adhered to the 1924 formula, but increased the total by adding some areas previously excluded.

6. *Federal Register*, July 4, 1952.

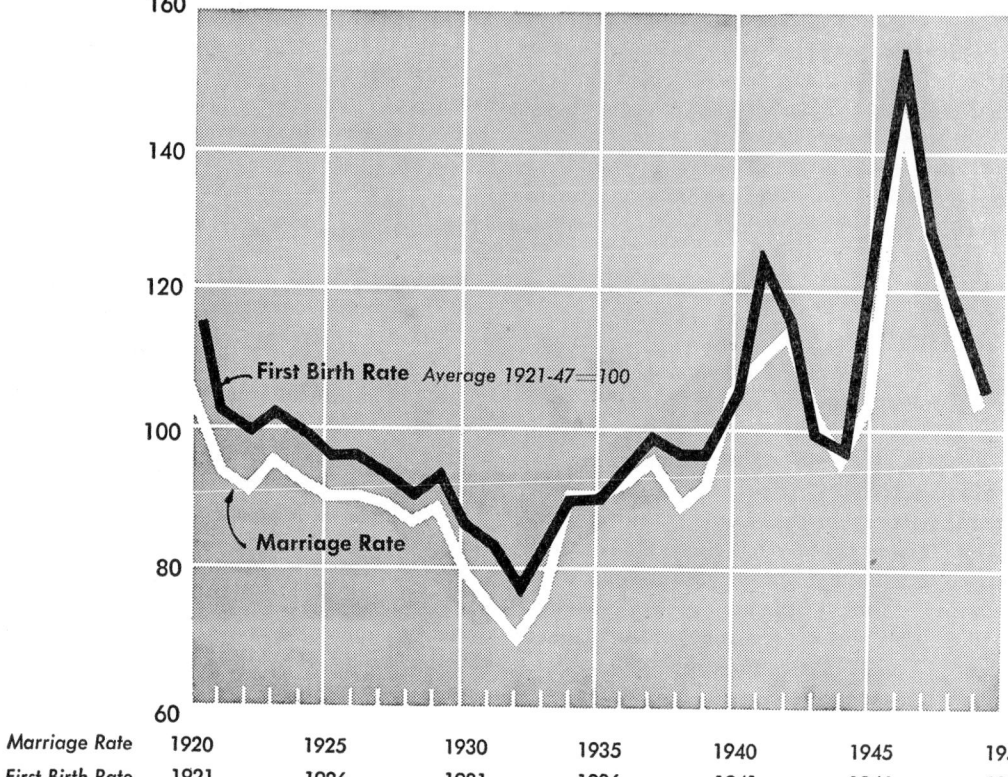

FIGURE 8. MARRIAGE RATE PER 1,000 WOMEN AGED 17–29, 1920–1949, AND FIRST-BIRTH RATE PER 1,000 NATIVE WHITE WOMEN AGED 15–44, 1921–1950

Source: Table 17.

paign, however, charges were made which appeared to imply that the quota system reflected a "master race" philosophy. Both candidates advocated changes in the act to eliminate "discrimination" among European countries. Such changes might involve either abandonment of the quota system altogether, or its application in such a way as to permit immigration from foreign countries in proportion to their own populations. Whether or not the quota system is changed, however, it seems unlikely that the limit on total immigration will be increased much, if at all. For these reasons immigration will probably not contribute much more to our population growth in the foreseeable future than it has in the past few years.

MARRIAGE AND DIVORCE RATES

The heavy increase in the number of marriages since the 1930s has been the chief cause of

the sharp jump in the birth rate and the rapid growth of population. Inasmuch as most married couples have their first-born children soon after marriage and first-born generally account for a third or more of the annual number of births,[7] changes in the rate of first births tend to reflect the marriage rate of the preceding year. (See Figure 8.)

While recent changes have been the greatest on record, the marriage rate has always been sensitive to war and the economic climate. Our entrance into World War I brought a sharp rise in the marriage rate to 96 per thousand women aged 17–29 [8] in 1917, compared with 85 at the

7. Currently about half of married couples have a child within two years after marriage. See *Statistical Bulletin,* Metropolitan Life Insurance Company, February 1951, p. 1, and *Births and Birth Rates in the Entire United States, 1909–1948,* National Office of Vital Statistics, September 29, 1950, p. 144.

8. The marriage rate is usually expressed in terms of the number of marriages per thousand of the population; for many purposes, however, it is more significant to relate

beginning of the decade. This jump was followed by a drop in 1918, when most of our troops were away from home, and by another sharp gain after the war. The record high of 104 per thousand in 1920 was followed during the prosperous 1920s by an irregular decline to a rate of 89 per thousand in 1929. (See Table 17.)

Depression Marriage Deficit

Warren S. Thompson and P. K. Whelpton estimated that the subnormal marriage rate during the 1930–1933 depression resulted in a "deficit" of some 800,000 marriages below the number that might have been expected on the basis of the 1925–1929 normal rate of 89.1 per thousand women aged 17 to 29. The marriage rate recovered to predepression levels in 1934 and when war broke out in Europe, followed by the draft at home, it rose to a new high of 110 per thousand in 1941. About 300,000 more marriages took place that year than would have been expected at the predepression normal rate;[9] for the entire 1934–1941 period the excess amounted to 700,000. Hence all but 100,000 of the "depression deficit" in marriages had been wiped out by the time the United States entered World War II.

In 1942 the marriage rate jumped to another record high (115 per thousand), and although it declined somewhat during the next three years it remained well above the 1925–1929 average throughout the decade. By the end of 1945, shortly after V-E Day, when the rate turned up again, there was an estimated net surplus of about 800,000 marriages.[10]

The Marriage Boom

A marriage boom was expected to follow the war, but when it came it exceeded all expectations, reaching a record peak in 1946 of nearly 2.3 million marriages, or 148 per thousand

women aged 17 to 29. Although a decline occurred in the next three years, the rate remained far above the predepression normal. The outbreak of the Korean War and the resumption of the draft brought another marriage upsurge. During the 1946–1950 period as a whole, some 9 million marriages took place — an annual average of 121 per thousand women aged 17 to 29. (See Table 17 and Appendix 3–3.)

Measured against the average marriage rate of 1925–1929, the war decade ended with a net surplus of more than 3 million marriages, compared with the net deficit of 100,000 when we entered the war. By the end of the decade there were more married couples and a larger proportion of our population married than ever before. Less than one fifth of the women over 14 years of age in 1950 had never been married, compared with more than a third in 1890. Slightly more than one fourth of the men were single, compared with nearly 44 per cent in 1890. (See Table 18.)

Although it is doubtful whether the marriage rate prevailing twenty years ago can still be considered as the normal rate, it is nevertheless clear that the number of marriages during the war decade was abnormally large for a number of reasons not likely to prevail during the next several years. The 1940s were a period of large-scale war and great prosperity following a long depression and an abnormally low rate of marriage. Some of the people who married in the early 1940s would probably have married earlier if they had been financially able to do so. And many of the marriages in the latter part of the decade would in all likelihood have been deferred for a few years had it not been for high wages and plenty of jobs for young people — plus the GI Bill of Rights. More young people were getting married than ever before. The median age at first marriage declined for both brides and grooms to a record low point in 1949. Brides in that year, with a median age of 20.3 years, were more than a year younger than the brides of 1940 and nearly two years younger than those of 1890. Grooms, at 22.7 years, were three and a half years younger than those of 1890. (See Table 18.)

The number of births during the 1920s, when most of the people who married in the 1940s were born, contributed to the record-breaking number of marriages in the latter decade. Births numbered 28.6 million in the 1920–1929 decade, while nearly 17.5 million marriages took place in 1941–1950. (The two periods are separated by an

marriages to the number of women aged 17 to 29, which is the age range when more than 75 per cent of first marriages take place. In the following discussion of marriage trends this latter ratio is used except when otherwise indicated.

9. Warren S. Thompson and P. K. Whelpton, *Estimates of Future Population of the United States, 1940–2000*, National Resources Planning Board, 1943, p. 19.

10. Based on an extension of the Thompson-Whelpton analysis. Estimates used in this section of the number of women aged 17–29 for the years 1942–1950 are from the Bureau of the Census; estimates of annual number of marriages for the same years, from the National Office of Vital Statistics.

TABLE 17. MARRIAGE, BIRTH AND DEATH RATES, 1910–1952

Year	Marriages per 1,000 Women Aged 17–29 [a]	Births per 1,000 Population	First Births per 1,000 Women Aged 15–44 [b]	Deaths per 1,000 Population [c]
1910	85	30.1	[d]	14.7
1911	85	29.9	[d]	13.9
1912	88	29.8	[d]	13.6
1913	89	29.5	[d]	13.8
1914	89	29.9	[d]	13.3
1915	86	29.5	[d]	13.2
1916	91	29.1	[d]	13.8
1917	96	28.5	[d]	14.0
1918	83	28.6	[d]	18.1
1919	95	26.2	[d]	12.9
1920	104	27.7	35	13.0
1921	94	28.1	36	11.5
1922	90	26.2	32	11.7
1923	96	26.0	31	12.1
1924	92	26.1	32	11.6
1925	90	25.1	31	11.7
1926	90	24.2	30	12.1
1927	89	23.5	30	11.3
1928	86	22.2	29	12.0
1929	89	21.2	28	11.9
1930	80	21.3	29	11.3
1931	75	20.2	27	11.1
1932	69	19.5	26	10.9
1933	76	18.4	24	10.7
1934	90	19.0	26	11.1
1935	90	18.7	28	10.9
1936	92	18.4	28	11.6
1937	96	18.7	29	11.3
1938	88	19.2	31	10.6
1939	91	18.8	30	10.6
1940	105	19.4	30	10.7
1941	110	20.3	33	10.5
1942	115	22.2	39	10.4
1943	102	22.7	36	10.9
1944	94	21.2	31	10.6
1945	104	20.4	30	10.6
1946	148	24.1	40	10.0
1947	128	26.6	48	10.1
1948	117	24.9	40	9.9
1949	103	24.6	37	9.7
1950	110	24.0	33	9.6
1951	105	24.5	[d]	9.7
1952	103	24.6	[d]	9.6

Sources: Warren S. Thompson and P. K. Whelpton, *Estimates of Future Population of the United States, 1940–2000*, National Resources Planning Board, 1943; P. K. Whelpton, *Forecasts of the Population of the United States, 1945–1975*, U.S. Bureau of the Census, 1947; *Historical Statistics of the United States, 1789–1945*, U.S. Bureau of the Census, 1949; *Statistical Abstract of the United States, 1951*, U.S. Bureau of the Census; *Monthly Vital Statistics Bulletin*, Office of Vital Statistics, Federal Security Agency, Vol. 13, No. 13, April 24, 1951 and Vol. 14, No. 13, September 17, 1952; *Births and Birth Rates in the Entire United States, 1909–1948*, National Office of Vital Statistics, September 29, 1950; *Vital Statistics of the United States*, Vol. I, 1950; *Monthly Vital Statistics Report*, Vol. I, No. 13, June 8, 1953; *Vital Statistics — Special Reports, National Summaries*, Vol. 38, No. 10, 1954.

a. 1940–1952, based on Bureau of the Census estimates of number of women aged 17–29 on July 1 of each year, and on number of marriages for each year as estimated by Office of Vital Statistics, Federal Security Agency (the same method as that used by Whelpton for marriage rate estimates for earlier years). See Appendix 3–3.

b. Native white women only. c. 1940–1950, excludes armed forces overseas. d. Not available.

TABLE 18. MARITAL STATUS OF POPULATION AND MEDIAN AGE AT FIRST MARRIAGE, 1890–1950

Year	Median Age at First Marriage		Per Cent of Population 14 Years Old and Over [a]			
			Married		Single	
	Male	Female	Male	Female	Male	Female
1890	26.1	22.0	52.1	54.8	43.6	34.1
1900	25.9	21.9	52.8	55.2	42.0	33.3
1910	25.1	21.6	54.2	57.1	40.4	31.8
1920	24.6	21.2	57.6	58.9	36.9	29.4
1930	24.3	21.3	58.4	59.5	35.8	28.4
1940	24.3	21.5	59.7	59.5	34.8	27.6
1950	22.7 [b]	20.3 [b]	68.2	66.1	26.2	19.6

Source: *Current Population Reports: Population Characteristics*, U.S. Bureau of the Census, Series P–20, No. 38, p. 3, and No. 35, p. 3.

a. The categories not shown which make up the remainder of the adult population are "widowed" and "divorced."

b. 1949; 1950 not available.

interval of 21 years — the approximate median age at first marriage.) In the 1930s the number of births fell to 24.4 million, or 15 per cent under the number in the 1920s. On this basis alone, therefore, we might expect 15 per cent fewer marriages in 1951–1960 than in 1941–1950, or no more than 15 million.

However, the marriage boom was making up for past "deficits" and borrowing from the future to some extent, so that the rate of the 1950s can probably be expected to fall appreciably below the average of the preceding decade. On the other hand, it is doubtful whether the estimated "surplus" of 3 million marriages as of the end of 1950 can be taken as a realistic measure of the extent to which the 1940s "borrowed" from the 1950s. Quite probably the normal marriage rate today is somewhat higher than it was in the 1920s, reflecting the lower average age at marriage, as well as the higher level of divorces, which are normally followed by remarriage.

Allowing for all these considerations, however, it is hard to see how the number of marriages in 1951–1960 can much exceed 14 million, which would be 20 per cent less than in the 1940s and only 10 per cent more than in the 1930s.

Marriages in 1951 totaled about 1,594,900, or 4 per cent less than in 1950. A further decline of about 4 per cent to about 1,531,000 occurred in 1952. There was a very slight upturn in 1953 to an estimated 1,533,000. However, in the first quarter of 1954 the trend was again downward

with about 4 per cent fewer marriages than in the first quarter of 1953.

Higher Divorce Rate

Another factor contributing to the high marriage rate of the war decade was the high and rising divorce rate, which reached a peak in 1946 almost three times as high as the peak rate in 1920, after World War I. Marriages reached an all-time record of nearly 2.3 million in 1946, but divorces numbered some 600,000, so that more than one fourth as many people were divorced as got married in that year. There is of course both a cause and effect relation between marriage and divorce rates. Many of the hasty war marriages ended in early divorce, but most of those who were divorced remarried promptly, thus adding to the number of marriages and increasing the marriage rate. Although more than 4 million marriages were legally dissolved during the decade, the total number of divorced persons 14 years old and over increased by only 651,000.[11] This is in line with a 1948 survey, which indicated that three fourths of those divorced in the preceding five years had remarried.[12]

The divorce rate, along with the marriage rate, has declined sharply from the postwar peak, as both did after World War I. However, the 1950 divorce rate of 2.6 per thousand of the population, compared with a marriage rate of 11.1, and the 1951 rate of 2.5 per thousand, compared with a marriage rate of 10.4,[13] were both much higher than the rates in any year before World War II.

Over the long run, divorce rates in the United States have risen from about 5 per cent of the number of marriages in the 1880s to approximately 10 per cent in the 1911–1920 decade and to around 25 per cent during the past few years. Evidently more people are marrying in haste and repenting at leisure and more are marrying more than once than was true even a few years ago.

11. *Current Population Reports: Population Characteristics*, U.S. Bureau of the Census, Series P–20, No. 35, p. 3; *Vital Statistics — Special Reports*, National Office of Vital Statistics, Vol. 36, No. 2, June 5, 1951.

12. See Paul C. Glick, "First Marriages and Remarriages," *American Sociological Review*, December 1949, pp. 726–734, and *Current Population Reports: Population Characteristics*, U.S. Bureau of the Census, Series P–20, No. 23, p. 2.

13. *Vital Statistics — Special Reports, National Summaries*, National Office of Vital Statistics, Vol. 38, No. 7, June 3, 1954.

This upward trend in divorce rates has not been limited to the United States, and there is little reason to believe that it has reached an end.

The birth rate, which had been declining for several decades, reached a record low point of 18.4 per thousand population at the bottom of the depression in 1933 — and again in 1936. In ten years it had dropped by almost one third and in a generation by almost one half.

Between 1910 and 1929, while the birth rate was declining almost uninterruptedly from 30 per thousand to about 21 per thousand, the marriage rate showed little change except for the temporary effects of World War I. Evidently the knowledge and practice of birth control was spreading rapidly during this period. After the onset of the depression, however, the continued decline in births was accompanied by a sharp drop in marriages. In fact, the drop in the marriage rate from 1929 to the depression low point in 1932 was greater than the decline in births from 1930 to 1933 — 23 per cent compared with 13 per cent. After 1932, in spite of the rise in marriages, the birth rate remained low until the end of the decade. (See Table 17.)

The defense and war period brought 1942 and 1943 birth rates back to the levels of the late 1920s. After a decline in 1944 and 1945, reflecting the absence of husbands in the armed forces, there was another spurt. From 20.4 per thousand in 1945 the rate rose to 26.6 per thousand in 1947, the year following the peak year for marriages. Thereafter a decline occurred, but the birth rate remained high to the end of the decade and beyond.

The 1950 birth rate of 24 per thousand was about 10 per cent below the postwar peak, but the rate rose to almost 25 per thousand in 1951 and continued at this level during 1952 and 1953. In the first quarter of 1954 it dropped to less than 24.

The effects of World War II on marriage and birth rates were similar to, but more pronounced than, the effects of World War I. The postwar marriage boom in the earlier period led to a rise in the birth rate from 26.2 per thousand in 1919 to 28.1 in 1921. Thus the increase in births was much more moderate after World War I, although the 1921 peak was slightly above that of 1947.

It is still too early to know to what extent this recent "baby boom" is due to such transitory factors as the abnormal increase in the marriage rate and the drop in the average age of marriage, or perhaps to a tendency to have children closer together, and to what extent it may reflect a fundamental change in the ideas of married couples about family size.

Age of Mother

Some light may be thrown on the question by comparing birth rates by age of mother and by order of birth (i.e., whether first child, second, third, etc.) in the two postwar peak years of births, 1921 and 1947. These two years, separated by a quarter century, are of course not strictly comparable although each followed a year of postwar business prosperity and peak marriage rates. For a period of several years before 1921, birth rates had remained substantially higher than they were in the years just before 1947. Furthermore, a smaller proportion of the population was married in 1921 than in 1947, and the median age at first marriage declined in the interval. (See Table 19.)

These last two factors, unless offset by other influences, would tend to cause an increase in the lower orders of births and in the birth rates for younger mothers that might well prove to be temporary. The birth rate for all fertile age classes (15–44 years) was less than 3 per cent higher in 1947 than in 1921 — a very small gain when it is considered that 64 per cent of the female population over 14 years of age was married in April 1947, compared with about 59 per cent in 1921.[14]

Furthermore, age groups under 30 were solely responsible for the gain. The birth rate for mothers between 15 and 24 — the most popular "marrying ages" — was about 20 per cent higher in 1947 than in 1921. The 25-to-29 age group showed a somewhat smaller fertility increase. Here again it seems quite probable that the higher birth rates for these younger women are due largely, or perhaps solely, to the fact that a much larger proportion were married in the later period than in the earlier. There is no clear evi-

14. *Current Population Reports: Population Characteristics,* U.S. Bureau of the Census, Series P–20, No. 35, November 25, 1951, p. 3. Figure for 1921 is not available. In January 1920, 58.9 per cent of the adult female population was married.

TABLE 19. BIRTH RATES BY AGE OF MOTHER AND ORDER OF BIRTH,
1921, 1947, 1950 AND 1951 [a]

Age of Mother or Order of Birth	1921	Lowest Rate between 1921 and 1947	1947	1950	1951
Age of mother					
15–44 years [b]	112	74	114	103	108
15–19	60	41	73 [c]	70	76
20–24	170	118	211	190	208
25–29	163	114	180	164	173
30–34	124	79	114	102	106
35–39	88	46	58	51	53
40–44	35	14	17	15	16
Order of birth					
First	36	24	48	33	36
Second	23	17	31	32	33
Third	16	10	16	18	20
Fourth	11	6	8	9	9
Fifth	8	4	4	4	4
Sixth	6	2	2	2	2
Seventh	4	2	2	1	1
Eighth and higher	8	3	3	3	2

Sources: National Office of Vital Statistics: *Births and Birth Rates in the Entire United States, 1909–1948,* September 29, 1950, pp. 143, 145; *Vital Statistics — Special Reports, National Summaries,* Vol. 37, No. 13, 1953 and Vol. 38, No. 10, 1954; and unpublished tabulations.

a. Data are for birth rates adjusted for underregistration for native white women only, since this is the only series for which comparable data are available for all the years shown.

Rates by age of mother are based on live births per 1,000 native white female population in each specified age group, estimated as of July 1 for 1921 and April 1 for 1947 and 1951, and enumerated as of April 1 for 1950. Rates by order of birth per 1,000 native white women aged 15–44 years.

b. Rates for age group 15–44 years computed by relating total births, regardless of age of mother, to female population 15–44 years.

Births to women reported as younger than 15 or older than 44 are combined with those to women 15–19 and 40–44, respectively. Births to women of unreported age are distributed proportionally.

c. 1948, which was peak year for this age class; for other categories 1947 was peak year.

dence that the birth rate per thousand *married women,* even among the younger groups, was any higher — or as high — immediately after World War II than after World War I.

For women over 30 years of age, moreover, the birth rate in 1947 was lower than in 1921. It was 10 per cent less for those from 30 to 34 years old, 32 per cent less for the 35-to-39 age group, and 50 per cent less for the 40-to-44-year-olds. It is also significant that all age groups except the youngest and the oldest showed a marked drop in fertility immediately after 1947. Evidently the return of the over-all birth rate to a level close to the peak after World War I is a phenomenon attributable to a substantial rise of

fertility at the younger ages, where the marriage rate has been abnormally high. Mothers from 15 to 29 years old had 73 per cent of the babies born in 1947, but only 68 per cent of those born in 1921.[15]

By 1950 the over-all birth rate had dropped to a point about 10 per cent below 1947 and 8 per cent below 1921. The birth rates for age groups over 30 continued to decline below 1921 and 1947 levels. The 15-to-29-year-old mothers were less fertile in 1950 than the similar group in 1947, but their birth rates were as high as those of the 1921 group. Apparently there was a continued

15. *Births and Birth Rates in the Entire United States, 1909–1948,* p. 142.

"concentration" of births at the younger ages.
(See Table 19.)

Order of Birth

Inasmuch as the younger women are responsible for most of the first and second births, it is not surprising to find these lower orders of birth showing the largest gains. The 1947 birth rates of 48 per thousand for first-born children and 31 per thousand for second-born were more than one third above the 1921 rates and close to twice the depression low points reached in 1933. First and second births accounted for 70 per cent of the babies born in 1947, compared with 53 per cent in 1921.[16]

The rate for third births, after falling from 16 per thousand in 1921 to 10 per thousand in 1935–1939, returned to 16 per thousand in 1947. For none of the higher orders of birth did the 1947 rate even approach the 1921 level. For the fifth and higher orders, in fact, there was no reversal of the persistent decline that had carried these rates by the end of the 1930s to small fractions of the 1921 level. By 1950 the first-birth rate, reflecting the decline in the marriage rate, had dropped off sharply, but it rose again in 1951. ·The rates for second and third births in both 1950 and 1951 were above the 1947 level and well above the 1921 rate. Evidently many of the war brides are having two or three children and having them close together.

These figures do not permit final conclusions, for not enough time has passed to demonstrate whether the war brides of a few years ago who have already had two or three children will want to have still larger families. The evidence to date, however, does not indicate a return to the very large family. On the other hand, perhaps fewer of the newly married couples will remain childless and more of those who do have children will want to have more than one. If recent tendencies may be taken as a clue to the future, it appears likely that family size will be more uniform, with the typical family having two or three children born fairly close together and early in marriage. This outlook would of course be radically altered by a severe depression. Such an economic calamity would, as in the 1930s, lead not only to a postponement of many marriages but, with birth control as widely practiced as it is today, to a deferment of births as well.

---

16. *Ibid.*, p. 144.

MORTALITY AND LIFE EXPECTANCY

Another factor helping to account for the doubling of population since 1900, and especially for the rapid recent growth, has been a steady and substantial decline in death rates. The average death rate for the population as a whole fell from 17.2 per thousand in 1900 to 9.6 per thousand in 1950 — a decline of 44 per cent. After adjustment for changes in the age composition of the population, the decline in average death rates computed for the "standard population" has been even greater — from 17.8 to 8.6 per thousand.[17] Although the sharpest drop occurred before 1925, the downward trend continued through the war decade. The 1950 rate was 10 per cent below the 1940 rate of 10.7 per thousand.

The death rates for 1951, 1952 and 1953, fluctuating between 9.6 and 9.7 per thousand, showed little change from 1950.

Considerable differences in mortality experience exist between whites and nonwhites and between males and females. Although the average death rate is still substantially lower for the white population than for the nonwhite — chiefly Negro — population, the disparity is much less today than it was at the turn of the century. The death rate of nonwhites fell during the half century from 25 per thousand to 10.9, or by 56 per cent, compared with a 44 per cent decline among the white population. (See Table 20.)

In both groups the death rate has declined more for females than for males, so that the disparity in mortality and life expectancy between the sexes has increased. The rate for nonwhite females fell by 61 per cent between 1900 and 1950, and for white by 50 per cent — in each case a much greater improvement than the male group showed.

Although all age groups have benefited from the advances in medical knowledge and public health and sanitation since 1900, the younger age groups have made the most spectacular gains. Infant mortality has been greatly reduced, and the communicable diseases of childhood have been virtually conquered. As a result, only one out of thirty-one babies died before reaching his first birthday in 1950, compared with one out of six in 1900. Even this great improvement was

---

17. National Office of Vital Statistics: *Vital Statistics of the United States, 1949*, Part I, Table BN; *Current Mortality Analysis*, Vol. IX, No. 13, October 15, 1952.

TABLE 20. DEATH RATES AND LIFE EXPECTANCY, 1900, 1925, 1950 AND 1951

Race, Age and Sex Group	1900	1925	1950	1951	Percentage Change, 1900–1950
Race and sex groups	Number of Deaths per Thousand				
All races	17.2	11.7	9.6	9.7	— 44.2
White	17.0	11.1	9.5	9.5	— 44.1
Male	17.7	11.8	10.9	11.0	— 38.4
Female	16.3	10.4	8.0	8.0	— 50.3
Nonwhite	25.0	17.4	11.2	11.1	— 56.4
Male	25.7	18.2	12.5	12.5	— 52.1
Female	24.4	16.6	9.9	9.8	— 61.1
Age groups					
Under one year	162.4	75.4	33.0	32.5	— 80.4
1– 4 years	19.8	6.4	1.4	1.4	— 92.4
5–14	3.9	2.0	0.6	0.6	— 84.6
15–24	5.9	3.8	1.3	1.3	— 78.0
25–34	8.2	4.8	1.8	1.8	— 78.0
35–44	10.2	7.2	3.6	3.5	— 63.7
45–54	15.0	12.2	8.5	8.4	— 44.0
55–64	27.2	23.3	19.1	18.9	— 31.6
65–74	56.4	51.7	40.7	40.1	— 23.2
75–84	123.3	119.3	93.3	93.1	— 22.2
85 years and over	260.9	272.3	202.0	192.6	— 6.9
Male	Years of Life Expectancy [a]				
At birth	48.2	57.9	66.6	66.6	17.3
Age 20	42.2	45.8	49.7	49.7	6.8
Age 40	27.7	29.4	31.4	31.4	3.0
Age 60	14.4	14.8	15.9	16.0	1.0
Female					
At birth	51.1	60.6	72.4	72.6	19.9
Age 20	43.8	47.5	54.9	55.1	10.0
Age 40	29.2	31.0	36.0	36.1	5.8
Age 60	15.2	15.7	19.0	19.1	2.9

Sources: Historical Statistics of the United States, 1789–1945, U.S. Bureau of the Census, 1949, pp. 45, 47 and 49; National Office of Vital Statistics: *Current Mortality Analysis*, Vol. VIII, No. 13, May 9, 1952, and *Vital Statistics of the United States*, 1950, Vol. I and 1951, Vol. I; *Statistical Abstract of the United States, 1951*, U.S. Bureau of the Census, pp. 76 and 913.

a. Whites only.

surpassed by the 92 per cent decline in mortality for the 1-to-4-year-olds and the 85 per cent decline for those from 5 to 14 years of age. Indeed, for each age group through 44 years of age the decrease in death rates was well over 50 per cent. For the higher age groups, however, the gains drop steadily to less than 7 per cent for people over 85 years of age.

Life Expectancy

The steady decline in the death rate during the past half century has greatly increased the av-erage length of life. A white male child born in 1900 could expect, on the average, to reach his forty-eighth birthday. Today his life expectancy is almost 67 years. For females life expectancy at birth has gained even more — from 51 years in 1900 to 72.6 in 1951.

Most of the gain, however, has been in infant and child mortality. Thus life expectancy for a young man of 20 has increased by little more than seven years since 1900; for a young woman of the same age, only 11 years. And the man of 60 today can expect to live less than two years longer than such a man in 1900, although women of this age have gained nearly four years in life expectancy. At ages above 60 the gains are even less; above age 85 they disappear entirely. What this means, of course, is that many more people reach old age today, not that older people live much longer than in 1900.

How much further the decline in death rates can continue before it stabilizes or turns upward is an unanswerable question. Progress in overcoming the degenerative diseases of middle and old age may radically change the mortality experience of the upper age groups. Unless old age itself is conquered, however, the average death rate for the population as a whole cannot fall indefinitely. How far it will decline, and when it will turn upward, are impossible to predict.

POPULATION CHARACTERISTICS

The uneven growth of population in recent decades, and especially the sharp rise in marriage and birth rates since the early 1940s, have brought marked shifts in the number and size of households, in the age composition of the population and in its geographic distribution. These changes may have more significant effects on the needs and resources of the United States than the mere increase of numbers.

AGE COMPOSITION

For more than a century the population of the United States has been steadily aging, in the sense that the number of older people has been increasing more rapidly than the number of younger people. A century ago the median age of the population was slightly less than 19 years, that is, about half of the people of the country were under 19 years of age and half were over. A slow advance brought the median age to 23 years by 1900, and a more rapid rise thereafter brought it to slightly over 30 years in 1950. This advance of nearly 60 per cent in the age of the population during the past century, and of more than 30 per cent since 1900, reflects pronounced changes at both ends of the age scale.

Increased Number of Aged

In 1850 only 600,000 persons, or 2.6 per cent of the population, were 65 years of age or older. Each census year since 1860 has recorded an increasing proportion in this age group, and the trend has accelerated since 1900. In that year 3.1 million people, or slightly over 4 per cent of the population, were 65 or over. By 1950 the proportion had doubled to more than 8 per cent and the number had quadrupled to 12.3 million. (See Table 21 and Figure 9.) A continuation of this trend brought the estimated total as of July 1953 to 14.3 million, or 9 per cent of the population.

This rapid increase in the number and proportion of older people is partly due to the high birth rates of the last half of the nineteenth century and the declining rates during the first four decades of the present century. Another important influence was the large number of immigrants who entered the country during the last part of the nineteenth century and the early years of the twentieth and who now make up a sizable portion of our aged population. But most important has been the persistent decline in death rates during the lifetime of people now in the older age groups. The present composition of the population indicates that the number of aged people, as well as the proportion they constitute of the total population, will continue to rise over the next two or three decades.

Shifting Proportion of Children

During most of the past century — until the unexpected "baby boom" of the 1940s — the proportion of children and youths in the population declined steadily. More than 41 per cent of the 1850 population were less than 15 years old; by 1900 the proportion had dropped to about 35 per cent; and by 1940, to a low point of 25 per cent.

The greatest change occurred among children under 5 years of age, who comprised more than 15 per cent of the 1850 population but only 8 per cent of the total in 1940. So steep was the decline that the actual number in this age class decreased after 1920 in spite of a continuing rise in total population.

The upsurge in births during the war decade brought a sharp reversal of this downward trend. By 1950 nearly one person out of nine in the population was less than 5 years old, and there were more than one and one half times as many children in this age class as there had been in 1940. Forty-one million, or 27 per cent of the population, were less than 15 years of age in 1950, compared with 33 million ten years earlier. All but 2 million of this 8 million increase in the

TABLE 21. AGE DISTRIBUTION OF THE POPULATION, CONTINENTAL UNITED STATES,
RATIO OF DEPENDENT TO WORKING AGES, AND MEDIAN AGE, 1850–1953

(Number in Millions)

Year	Under 5 Number	Under 5 Per Cent	5–14 Number	5–14 Per Cent	15–64 Number	15–64 Per Cent	65 and Over Number	65 and Over Per Cent	Ratio of Number in Working Age Group (15–64) to Number in Dependent Age Groups	Median Age
1850	3.5	15.1	6.1	26.3	13.0	56.0	.6	2.6	1.3	18.9
1860	4.8	15.3	7.9	25.1	17.9	57.1	.8	2.5	1.3	19.4
1870	5.5	14.2	9.6	24.9	22.3	57.8	1.2	3.1	1.4	20.2
1880	6.9	13.8	12.2	24.3	29.3	58.5	1.7	3.4	1.4	20.9
1890	7.6	12.2	14.6	23.4	37.8	60.6	2.4	3.8	1.5	22.0
1900	9.2	12.1	17.0	22.4	46.6	61.4	3.1	4.1	1.6	22.9
1910	10.6	11.5	18.9	20.6	58.4	63.7	3.9	4.2	1.7	24.1
1920	11.6	11.0	22.0	20.8	67.0	63.6	4.9	4.6	1.7	25.3
1930	11.4	9.3	24.6	20.1	80.0	65.2	6.6	5.4	1.9	26.5
1940 [a]	10.5	8.0	22.4	17.0	89.7	68.2	9.0	6.8	2.1	29.0
1950 [a]	16.2	10.7	24.3	16.2	97.9	65.0	12.3	8.1	1.8	30.2
1953 [b]	17.4	11.0	28.0	17.7	98.6	62.3	14.3	9.0	1.7	30.3

Sources: Historical Statistics of the United States, 1789–1945, U.S. Bureau of the Census, 1949, pp. 27 and 28; Seventeenth Census of Population (1950), Vol. II, *Characteristics of the Population,* p. 1–93; *Current Population Reports: Population Estimates,* U.S. Bureau of the Census, Series P–25, No. 93, April 26, 1954.

a. Figures differ from those shown in Appendix 3–6 because the 1940 and 1950 figures in that table have been adjusted for underenumeration and 1950 figures include armed forces overseas.

b. Estimates as of July 1.

number of young people, however, was accounted for by children under 5, i.e., those born during the postwar baby boom. By 1953, it was estimated, children under 5 comprised 11 per cent of the population, and 45 million, or 28 per cent of the population, were under 15 years of age.

These drastic shifts in the younger age groups have had a marked effect on demands for consumer goods and on educational, recreational and health services. The unprecedented need for school facilities has created a particularly acute problem in rural areas, with smaller resources than the urban but with a far larger proportion of their population of school age. In 1950 about one third of the population of rural areas were under 15 years of age, compared with less than one fourth in urban areas.[18]

Dependent and Working Ages

Although age provides no exact indication of employability, it seems probable that young people under 15 and older people over 65 are predominantly dependents who are supported by those of the working ages, 15 to 64. The latter include not only those in the labor force working for pay, but also wives and mothers and other family members who are not paid for their services in the household. These working age groups have always included a majority of the population, rising from 56 per cent in 1850 to nearly two thirds since 1910.

A more significant comparison, perhaps, is the relative size of the working and dependent groups. In 1850 there were 13 million in the working age groups and 10.2 million, or about 78 per cent as many, in the dependent age groups. The ratio declined steadily and steeply in succeeding decades, falling below 47 per cent in 1940. Thus, for each dependent in 1940 there were more than two persons of working age, compared with 1.3 in 1850. (See Table 21 and Figure 9.)

The sharp increase in the number of children after World War II, coupled with the continued rise in the population over 65 years of age, brought an abrupt change in the 1940s. There were nearly 54 per cent as many in the dependent

18. Seventeenth Census of Population (1950), Vol. II, *Characteristics of the Population,* p. 1–90.

Per Cent and Number

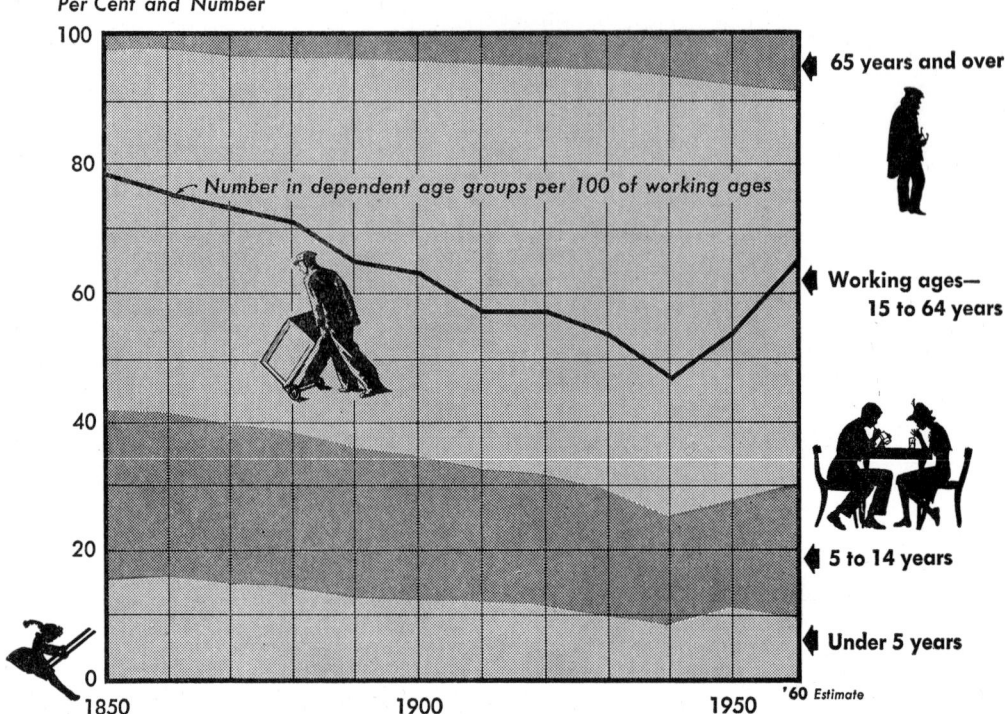

FIGURE 9. PERCENTAGE DISTRIBUTION OF POPULATION BY DEPENDENT AND WORKING AGE GROUPS, 1850–1950, WITH ESTIMATES FOR 1960

Sources: 1850–1950, Table 21; 1960, *Current Population Reports: Population Estimates,* U.S. Bureau of the Census, Series P–25, No. 28, August 21, 1953, p. 5, Table 1, Series C, adjusted from July to April and to exclude estimated armed forces overseas.

age groups as in the working ages in 1950, which means a ratio of 1.8 workers for each dependent. By 1953 the ratio was about 1.7 workers for each dependent. This reversal of the long-continued downward trend in the proportion of dependents is of considerable economic significance.

For a century or more prior to 1940 the number of workers — those producing the goods and services to be consumed by the entire population — had been increasing more rapidly than the number of nonproducing consumers. This was one of a number of causes of the substantial rise in real income per capita. This is more than an arithmetic truism. The steady decline in the proportion of school children in the population for many years before World War II, for example, meant lower real costs per capita (but not per student) for elementary schools and, in some places, surplus school capacity. For the individual family, few children, or none at all, meant more money for automobiles and theater tickets.

The recent upturn in the number of younger children is already being felt in crowding and heavier costs in the lower school grades. For the young married couple, having more children, or having them earlier, means more spending for food, medical care and baby sitters, and less for adult luxuries. At the other end of the age scale the rise in the dependency ratio is manifest in a larger proportion of old-age pensioners, and heavier costs, to be borne by those of working ages.

To say that these trends mean a smaller rise in average per capita income than would otherwise occur is not to imply their undesirability. As a matter of fact, the increasing "burden" of dependency is very largely the result of conscious choice: at the private level of decision, to marry and raise a family; at the public level, to provide adequate child care and school facilities and to care more generously for the nation's senior citizens.

TABLE 22. ESTIMATED POPULATION IN HOUSEHOLDS AND QUASI-HOUSEHOLDS, AND CONSUMER UNITS, BY TYPE AND RESIDENCE, MARCH 1950

	Number	Percentage Distribution [a]			
		Total	Urban	Rural Nonfarm	Rural Farm
	(Thousands)				
Population in households and quasi-households [b]	150,193	100.0	63.0	21.1	15.8
Members of households (including lodgers and servants)	147,309	100.0	63.2	20.7	16.1
Heads of households and relatives	138,609	100.0	62.2	21.1	16.7
Not related to head of household	8,700	100.0	78.7	14.2	7.1
Members of quasi-households	2,884	100.0	53.8	46.0	0.1
In hotels and rooming houses [c]	1,434	100.0	74.5	25.3	0.3
Inmates of institutions	1,450	100.0	33.3	66.7	—
Consumer units, total	50,397	100.0	67.2	19.5	13.3
Households	43,468	100.0	66.1	19.9	14.0
Primary families	38,732	100.0	64.8	20.4	14.9
One-person households	3,946	100.0	75.2	17.1	7.8
Other households of unrelated individuals	791	100.0	84.1	12.4	3.4
Subfamilies (family units of relatives of household heads)	2,369	100.0	66.8	18.5	14.7
Lodgers and resident employees [d]	4,560	100.0	78.0	16.6	5.4
Secondary families	462	100.0	86.8	11.5	1.7
Secondary individuals, 14 and over	4,098	100.0	77.1	17.1	5.8

Sources: Current Population Reports, Population Characteristics, U.S. Bureau of the Census, Series P–20, No. 33, February 12, 1951, Tables 3, 4, 5 and 9, and unpublished tabulations.

a. The urban, rural nonfarm and rural farm classification used is very similar to that used in the 1950 Census. (See *Population Characteristics,* No. 33, p. 5.)

b. Includes only 547,000 members of the armed forces living off post or with their families on post.

c. Also includes convents and monasteries, nurses' homes, workers' dormitories and the like.

d. In households and quasi-households.

Note: Slight discrepancies in addition are due to rounding.

HOUSEHOLDS AND CONSUMER UNITS

For many purposes the number and size of families, households and consumer units are more significant indicators of needs and demand than the actual size of the population. This is particularly true in times like the present, when sharp increases in marriage and birth rates have radically altered living patterns and the age composition of the population. The 23 per cent increase in the number of households between 1940 and 1950 (and the further estimated increase of 7 per cent from 1950 to 1953) is a more important measure of the expanding market for housing, furniture and furnishings, and kitchen equipment than the 15 per cent growth of population between 1940 and 1950 (followed by an estimated growth of slightly more than 5 per cent from 1950 to 1953).[19] The household, rather than the individual, is the buying unit for these kinds of goods. The market for food, on the other hand, is more closely related to the "number of mouths to feed," or the total population. For automobiles and vacation trips, perhaps, the extent of the market is determined by the number of consumer units, which includes, in addition to households, "independent adults" not maintaining their own living establishments.

In 1950 there were 43.5 million households in

19. Percentage increase in total population, 1940–1950, used here and elsewhere in the chapter, unless otherwise indicated, refers to population corrected for underenumeration and including armed forces overseas, as shown in Table 27 and Appendix 3–6. Percentage increase as reported by the Census, which is based on population for continental United States only and has not been adjusted for underenumeration, is 14.5.

the United States, of which 38.7 million were primary (or genuine) families and the remainder one-person households and establishments in which two or more unrelated individuals were living together. In addition to the households, individuals such as lodgers and servants and families not maintaining separate living establishments numbered 6.9 million, making a total of 50.4 million consumer units in 1950. The households, of course, are of most importance. They comprised 86 per cent of all consumer units; and members of households (exclusive of lodgers and servants, each of whom is a separate consumer unit) numbered 138.6 million, or 92 per cent of the total civilian population, including some members of the armed forces. (See Table 22.)

Household Size

For many decades the number of households has been increasing much faster than the population, while the average size of the household has steadily declined. This has been true for each decade since 1890. For the entire sixty-year period population increased 139 per cent and the number of households 237 per cent. Average household size, as roughly measured by population per household, decreased from 4.9 persons in 1890 to 3.5 in 1950. (See Table 23.) During the three years from 1950 to 1953 the number of households increased by an average of 950,000

TABLE 23. POPULATION, NUMBER OF HOUSEHOLDS, AND RATIO OF POPULATION TO HOUSEHOLDS, 1890–1950

Year	Population	Households [a]	Population per Household
	(Thousands)		
1890	62,948	12,690	4.9
1900	75,995	15,964	4.8
1910	91,972	20,256	4.5
1920	105,711	24,352	4.3
1930	122,775	29,905	4.1
1940	131,669	34,855 [b]	3.8
1950	150,697	42,826 [c]	3.5

Source: U.S. Bureau of the Census.

a. Or occupied dwelling units.

b. Based on complete 1940 Census returns; total differs from that shown in Table 24, where 1940 figures are based on sample of 1940 Census returns.

c. Disagrees with figure shown in Tables 22 and 27, which is based on a sample for March 1950; figure used in this table is based on complete count for the 1950 Housing Census.

a year while the average size of households declined further to 3.3 persons per household.

The decline in average household size results from a marked increase in the proportion of one- and two-person households during the past two decades, a smaller gain in the percentage of three-person establishments, and a sharp drop in the proportion of five-person and larger households. Households consisting of four persons — typically two parents and two children — have remained almost unchanged since 1930, at close to 18 per cent of the total. (See Table 24.)

These trends reflect a number of significant influences affecting family size and formation. Among the most important are the long-term downward trend in the median age at first marriage, which has contributed to a steady increase in the number and proportion of newlywed couples; a general decline in the birth rate until the 1940s, especially for the higher birth orders; and a sharp upturn in marriage rates during the late 1940s, which brought a rise in the proportion of two-person households.

The increase in the percentage of one-person households during the 20-year period emphasizes the importance of factors other than marriage and birth rates in determining household size. Increasing numbers of young people seek jobs away from their home communities, and even when they do not, the long-run rise of incomes has enabled older children to leave home and set up their own establishments. Old-age pensions and retirement plans are more prevalent today, so that more old people can live alone if they choose, rather than move in with younger members of the family.

The sharp decline in the relative importance of the very large household also probably reflects both social and economic influences. In 1930 nearly 19 per cent of all households consisted of six or more persons; by 1950 only 11 per cent were of this size. By April 1953 the percentage had declined to less than 10. These are large families — normally with four or more children and often with parents and married children living in the same dwelling. In spite of the sharp rise in birth rates since World War II, there is no evidence of a return to the very-large-family pattern,[20] and, as pointed out above, economic changes today make it less necessary for families to "double up" or for older children to live at home.

20. See p. 60.

TABLE 24. DISTRIBUTION OF HOUSEHOLDS BY SIZE, 1930, 1940 AND 1950

Size of Household	Number of Households			Percentage Distribution		
	1930 [a]	1940 [b]	1950	1930	1940	1950
	(Thousands)					
All households	29,905	35,087	42,826 [c]	100.0	100.0	100.0
Number of persons in household [d]						
1	2,357	3,497	3,993	7.9	10.0	9.3
2	6,983	9,013	12,023	23.4	25.7	28.1
3	6,227	7,710	9,763	20.8	22.0	22.8
4	5,235	6,164	7,878	17.5	17.6	18.4
5	3,574	3,749	4,466	12.0	10.7	10.4
6	2,273	2,172	2,258	7.6	6.2	5.3
7 or more	3,255	2,783	2,445	10.9	7.9	5.8

Sources: 1930, Sixteenth Census (1940), *Population and Housing, Families, General Characteristics,* 1943, p. 24; 1940, *Current Population Reports: Population Characteristics,* U.S. Bureau of the Census, Series P–20, No. 33, February 12, 1951, Table 6, p. 15; 1950, *1950 Census of Housing,* Vol. 1, *General Characteristics,* 1953, p. 1–8.

a. 1930 figure is number of families.
b. Based on sample of 1940 Census returns; total differs from that shown in Table 23 where 1940 figures are based on complete Census returns.
c. Disagrees with figure shown in Tables 22 and 27, which is based on a sample for March 1950; figure used in this table is based on complete count for the 1950 Housing Census.
d. Only related persons, excluding lodgers and boarders, resident servants, guests, and foster children or wards.

Urban-Rural Differences

Consumer units and households are concentrated more heavily in urban communities than is population as a whole. Although only 63 per cent of the 1950 civilian population [21] lived in urban centers, 67 per cent of the total number of consumer units and 66 per cent of the households were found in such communities. As might be expected, the concentration was especially marked in three groups: one-person households; households of two or more unrelated persons living together; and lodgers and resident employees not maintaining separate living establishments. Approximately six out of seven of the second of these groups, and three out of four of the other two, lived in urban communities. (See Table 22.)

The high concentration of resident servants in city households is indicated by the fact that 79 per cent of household members "not related to head of household" are found in urban communities. On the other hand, the fact that 46 per

cent of the "members of quasi-households," compared with 21 per cent of the population, live in rural nonfarm territory reflects the fact that many health and welfare establishments and penal institutions (both of which are classified as quasi-households) are located in country districts.

GEOGRAPHIC TRENDS

The United States has always had a mobile population, characterized for more than a century by a steady westward movement and a trend away from farms and rural communities to the great urban centers. More recently, people have been moving away from the centers of the large cities to the urban fringes and suburbs.

These three long-term trends were greatly accelerated during the 1940s, when war production and postwar prosperity created hundreds of thousands of new jobs in plants, factories and shipping centers. Internal migration during the war decade was of unprecedented magnitude. On April 1, 1947, the Census showed 12 million persons living in a different state from that in which they had lived on April 1, 1940, while an-

21. Population in households and quasi-households shown in Table 22, referred to for convenience as civilian population, although some members of the armed forces are included. See footnote b to Table 22.

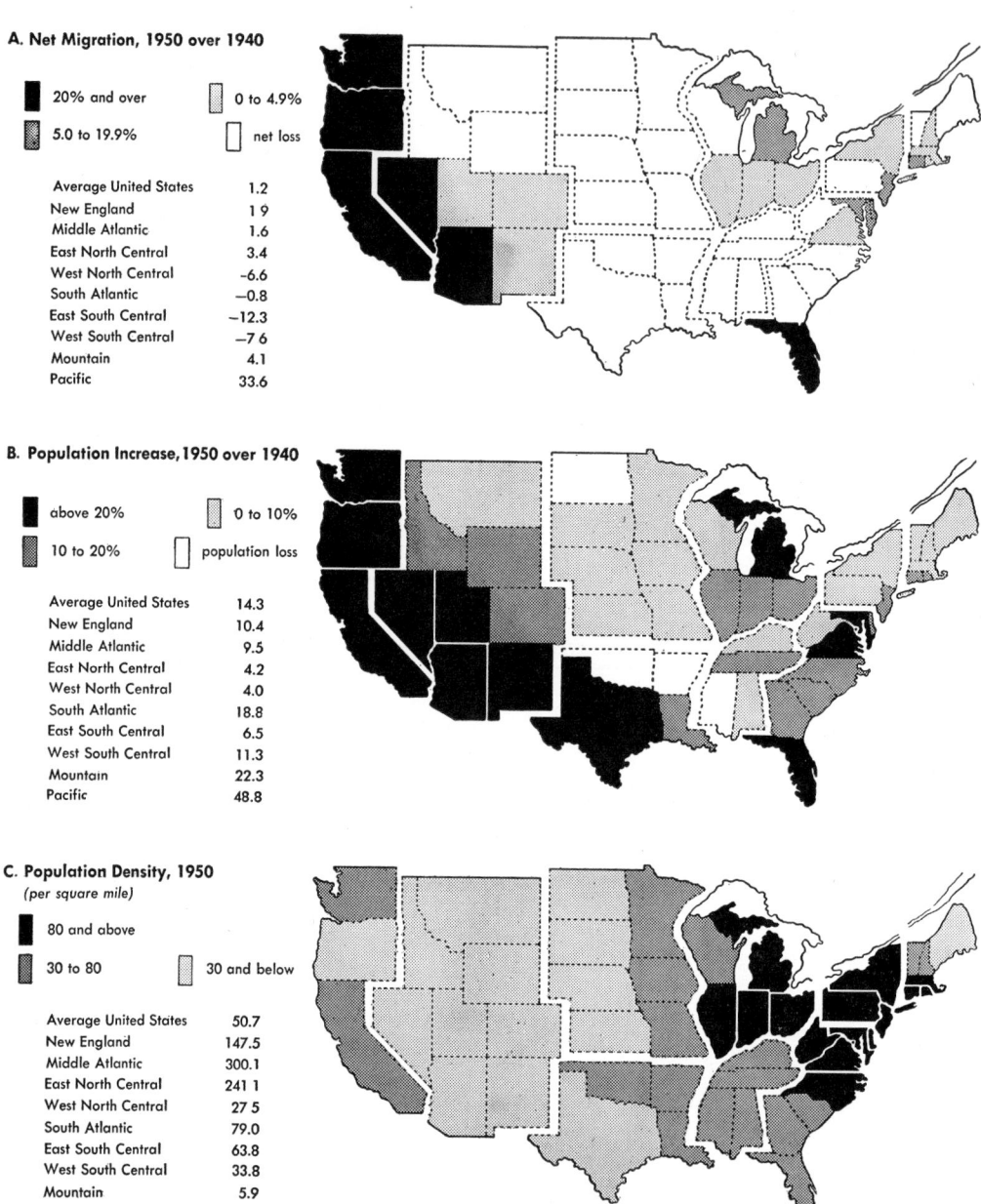

A. Net Migration, 1950 over 1940

■ 20% and over	░ 0 to 4.9%
▨ 5.0 to 19.9%	□ net loss

Average United States	1.2
New England	1 9
Middle Atlantic	1.6
East North Central	3.4
West North Central	−6.6
South Atlantic	−0.8
East South Central	−12.3
West South Central	−7 6
Mountain	4.1
Pacific	33.6

B. Population Increase, 1950 over 1940

■ above 20%	░ 0 to 10%
▨ 10 to 20%	□ population loss

Average United States	14.3
New England	10.4
Middle Atlantic	9.5
East North Central	4.2
West North Central	4.0
South Atlantic	18.8
East South Central	6.5
West South Central	11.3
Mountain	22.3
Pacific	48.8

C. Population Density, 1950
(per square mile)

■ 80 and above	
▨ 30 to 80	░ 30 and below

Average United States	50.7
New England	147.5
Middle Atlantic	300.1
East North Central	241 1
West North Central	27 5
South Atlantic	79.0
East South Central	63.8
West South Central	33.8
Mountain	5.9
Pacific	45.3

FIGURE 10. POPULATION TRENDS, 1940–1950, AND POPULATION DENSITY, 1950, BY STATE

Sources: Table 28 and Appendix 3–5.

other 13 million had changed counties within the same state.[22]

A sudden migration of such proportions greatly accentuated the problems created by the steady redistribution of the population that had been taking place for over a century. Unprecedented demands were made on public facilities and services — schools, housing, hospitals, transportation — in areas where hundreds of thousands of new residents settled overnight. Besides the immediate effects on areas undergoing heavy inward or outward movements of people, the geographic shifting of the population has had important long-term economic and social consequences.

WESTWARD AND REGIONAL SHIFTS

The center of population — a concept borrowed from physics and defined as "the center of population gravity of the United States" — has moved steadily westward roughly along the thirty-ninth parallel since 1790. By 1950 it had shifted to a point in eastern Illinois about 686 miles west and 30 miles south of its original location east of Baltimore. (See Figure 10.)

This steady westward movement has been the most important current of internal migration throughout our history, except for the period of World War I and immediately thereafter, when there was a heavy flow of population from the South to the North. This resulted from the sharp curtailment of immigration, accompanied by a rising demand for factory workers in the northern industrial areas.[23]

The depression of the early 1930s checked the northward movement. California and other West Coast states became the mecca for hundreds of thousands of migrants — particularly for those from the "dust bowl" of the Plains states.

Defense Migration

Scarcely had the West Coast had time to adjust itself to this new influx of residents when the defense program and World War II brought another wave of migrants, who came to work in the new war plants and the greatly expanded

shipping centers or to be near naval and military installations. From April 1, 1940 to November 1, 1943 the three Pacific Coast states had a net migratory gain of one and three quarter million persons.[24] The movement to these states continued after the war, though at a somewhat slower pace. Total net gains from migration for the war decade as a whole amounted to three and a quarter million. This influx into the Pacific states accounted for most of the westward migration during the 1940s, although there was substantial movement into the southern Mountain states. In the East, only Florida showed comparable growth from migration. (See Appendix 3–4 and Figure 10.)

Regional Shifts

Although the rate of population growth in different regions during the 1940s largely reflected wartime migration, these regional shifts were generally in line with the trends of the past half century. The Pacific and Mountain states continued their heavy relative growth, rising to 12.9 per cent of the total from 10.5 in 1940 and 5.4 in 1900. These gains in the West were accompanied by a continued downtrend in the proportion of the national population living in New England, and in the West North Central and East South Central states. Other regions have maintained relatively stable shares of the total population during the past few decades, although the Middle Atlantic and West South Central states experienced slight declines during the 1940s and the South Atlantic states a slight increase. (See Table 25 and Figure 10.)

In general, population shifts during the war decade involved a pronounced movement out of the thinly populated farming states west of the Mississippi River and the southern agricultural areas of low economic opportunity and high birth rates into industrial regions offering greater economic advantages.

The already heavily urbanized and industrialized northern and eastern states also received a substantial inflow of migrants. These fifteen states (all with a population density of 80 or more, as shown in Figure 10), with a combined area of 430,000 square miles and a 1950 population of almost 77 million, had a population density of 178 per square mile, compared with the

22. "Internal Migration in the United States: April 1940 to April 1947," *Current Population Reports: Population Characteristics*, Series P–20, No. 14, April 15, 1948, p. 1.

23. T. Lynn Smith, *Population Analysis*, McGraw-Hill, New York, 1948, p. 342.

24. *Population: Special Reports*, U.S. Bureau of the Census, Series P–44, No. 17, August 28, 1944, pp. 3–4.

TABLE 25. PERCENTAGE DISTRIBUTION OF THE POPULATION, BY MAJOR GEOGRAPHIC DIVISIONS, 1900–1940 AND ESTIMATES FOR JULY 1950 AND JULY 1960 [a]

Geographic Division	1900	1910	1920	1930	1940	July 1950	July 1960
United States	100.0	100.0	100.0	100.0	100.0	100.0	100.0
New England	7.36	7.13	7.00	6.65	6.41	6.19	5.97
Middle Atlantic	20.34	21.00	21.06	21.39	20.92	20.12	19.46
East North Central	21.03	19.84	20.32	20.60	20.22	20.23	20.14
West North Central	13.62	12.65	11.87	10.83	10.27	9.40	8.76
South Atlantic	13.74	13.26	13.23	12.86	13.54	13.96	14.29
East South Central	9.93	9.15	8.41	8.05	8.19	7.62	7.34
West South Central	8.60	9.55	9.69	9.92	9.92	9.61	9.43
Mountain	2.20	2.86	3.16	3.02	3.15	3.37	3.53
Pacific	3.18	4.56	5.27	6.67	7.39	9.50	11.08

Sources: 1900–1910, decennial censuses; 1920–1960, *Current Population Reports: Population Estimates*, U.S. Bureau of the Census, Series P–25, No. 56, January 27, 1952, pp. 5 and 6.

a. Percentages from 1900 to 1940 are based directly on data from the decennial censuses; those for July 1950 and July 1960 are based on estimated figures adjusted to include members of the armed forces residing in the area at the time of entry into the armed forces and to exclude all other members of the armed forces stationed in the area.

national average of less than 51. Although this area has been growing less rapidly than other parts of the country, particularly the West, it continues to be the urban-industrial heartland of the United States. With little more than 14 per cent of the country's total land area, it contains 51 per cent of the population, accounts for more than 70 per cent of the total value added by manufacture, and receives nearly 56 per cent of the total income payments to individuals.[25]

MOVEMENT FROM COUNTRY TO CITY

The urbanization of our population, like the westward movement, has been going on for more than a century. In 1850 close to 20 million persons, or about 85 per cent of the total population of 23.2 million, lived on farms and in other rural territory. Hardly more than 5 per cent of the American people at that time resided in cities of 100,000 population or more. (See Figure 11.)

Under the drive of industrialization during the last half of the nineteenth century, the cities grew even faster than the rapidly increasing total population. By the end of the century, rural territory accounted for only 60 per cent of the 76

million total, and the big cities[26] for nearly 19 per cent. The urban trend continued after 1900, until it was slowed by the depression of the 1930s. The ratio of urban to rural population remained virtually unchanged during that decade, although the actual number of people living in urban territory increased slightly. The big cities grew somewhat, but the proportion of the population in those cities dropped slightly to less than 29 per cent.

The urban trend was again very marked in the 1940s, when economic opportunities in industrial areas attracted large numbers of farm workers. By 1950 the rural population had dropped to 41 per cent of the total population, from 43.5 per cent in 1940,[27] and the percentage of the population living in big cities was almost back to the 1930 level. Cities with 250,000 to 500,000 inhabitants and those with over a million showed a continued decline in relative size during the twenty-year period from 1930 to 1950. Towns with population below 5,000 remained almost stationary. (See Appendix 3–5.)

25. *Annual Survey of Manufactures: 1952*, U.S. Bureau of the Census, 1953, p. 17; *Survey of Current Business*, August 1952, p. 11.

26. Those with population over 100,000.

27. For comparability, the old Census definitions of "urban" and "rural nonfarm" are used here. Under the definition used in the 1950 Census, which much more realistically depicts the actual character of residence of suburban residents, the urban population is increased by 7.5 million at the expense of the rural nonfarm. Thus, under the new definition, the rural population constitutes only 36 per cent of the total.

Farm Population Losses

Farm population in the United States has shown a net loss since 1920, not only in relation to the total population, but also in actual count. Although almost 30 million people migrated *to* farms between 1920 and 1945, the movement away from farms was sufficient to cause a net loss of farm population in every one of those twenty-six years except 1932. During the quarter century as a whole, farms contributed a net total of almost 17 million persons to the population of the nation's towns and cities.[28]

The most rapid decline in farm population occurred during the war decade. Between 1940 and 1945 the decrease was almost 5 million. When many war veterans and war workers returned to farms in 1946 and 1947, the trend was temporarily reversed. Thereafter, however, the downward trend was resumed and by April 1950 the farm population was about the same as at the end of the war — about 25 million. The downward trend continued during 1951, when the farm population dropped to about 24 million.[29]

The movement from the farm varied between regions. The South contributed almost half of the migrants leaving farms between 1920 and 1945 and because of the smaller number returning to farms during this period suffered a larger net loss than any other region.[30] Particularly marked was the emigration of Negro farm families. From 1940 to 1947 the southern states lost more than one third of their Negro farm families, for the most part to northern cities. The farm population of the New England and Pacific states, on the other hand, actually increased during the sharp nationwide decline of the 1940s.[31]

Rural Nonfarm Population

The rural population, of course, includes not only people living on farms, but also the nonfarm population living in the open country and in rural villages.

The rural nonfarm population, unlike the farm population, increased from 1920 to 1950 — and at a higher rate than the urban population. It almost doubled; from 19 per cent of the total population in 1920 it rose steadily to nearly 26

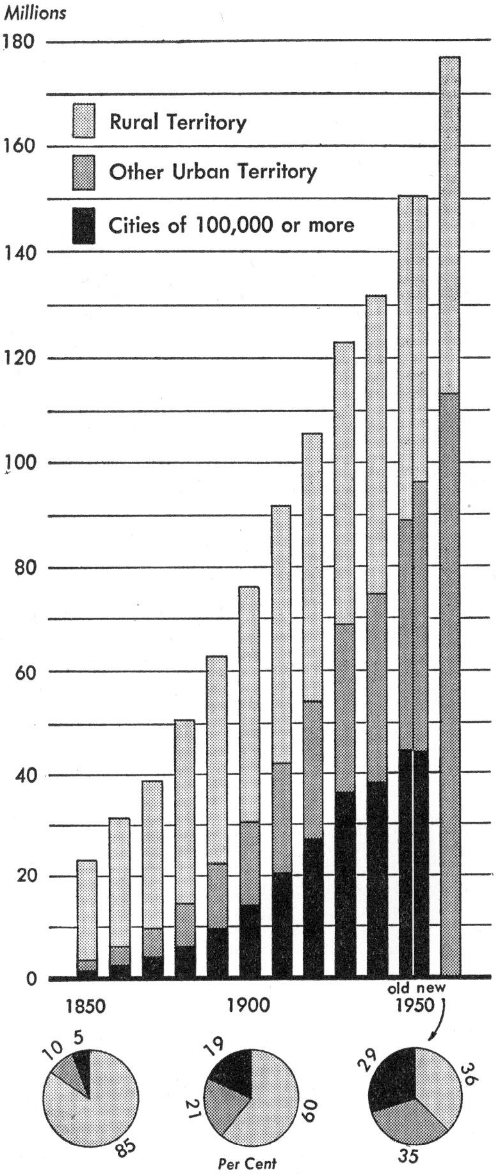

FIGURE 11. URBAN AND RURAL POPULATION GROWTH, 1850–1950, WITH ESTIMATES FOR 1960

Source: Seventeenth Census of Population (1950), Vol. 1, Number of Inhabitants, pp. 1–7.

Note: No breakdown of urban population is shown for 1960. The dark grey area in this bar represents all urban territory.

per cent in 1950.[32] The increase was due largely to the growth of suburban areas, however, and much of the population classed as "rural non-

28. Smith, *op. cit.*, pp. 326–327.
29. *Agricultural Statistics, 1953*, U.S. Department of Agriculture, p. 563.
30. Smith, *op. cit.*, p. 327.
31. *U.S. News and World Report*, February 25, 1949, and *Dun's Review*, April 1951.

32. On the basis of the old Census definition of rural nonfarm population.

TABLE 26. POPULATION OF CONTINENTAL UNITED STATES, URBAN, RURAL NONFARM
AND RURAL FARM, 1920–1950

	1920	1930	1940 [a]	1950 [a] Old Urban Definition	1950 [a] New Urban Definition
		Number (*Thousands*)			
Total population	105,711	122,775	131,669	150,697	150,697
Urban	54,158	68,955	74,424	88,927	96,468
Rural nonfarm	20,159	23,663	27,029	38,722	31,181
Rural farm	31,393	30,158	30,216	23,048	23,048
		Percentage Distribution			
Total population	100.0	100.0	100.0	100.0	100.0
Urban	51.2	56.2	56.5	59.0	64.0
Rural nonfarm	19.1	19.3	20.5	25.7	20.7
Rural farm	29.7	24.6	22.9	15.3	15.3

Sources: 1920, *Historical Statistics of the United States, 1789–1945,* U.S. Bureau of the Census, 1949; 1930 and 1940, *Statistical Abstract of the United States, 1949,* U.S. Bureau of the Census; 1950, *1950 Census of Population: Advance Reports,* Series PC–14, No. 6, December 1, 1952, *1950 Census of Population: Preliminary Counts,* Series PC–3, No. 10, February 11, 1951, p. 3, and Seventeenth Census of Population (1950), Vol. I, *Number of Inhabitants,* p. 1–6.

a. Figures for 1940 and 1950 differ from population figures shown in Table 27 because figures in that table have been adjusted for underenumeration for 1940 and 1950 and 1950 figures include armed forces overseas.

farm" lived in areas that were really urban in character.

It was for this reason that the Census Bureau changed its urban classification in 1950 to include the population of urban fringe areas and other areas formerly classed as rural nonfarm. According to the new classification, the rural nonfarm population in 1950 amounted to only 31.2 million, compared with 38.7 million under the old classification. The old figure compares with 27.0 million in these areas in 1940 — a much larger percentage increase than that for the population as a whole. (See Table 26.)

Urban Population Growth

The migration of farm workers to urban areas has, of course, resulted in an enormous increase in the urban population — from 54 million in 1920 to 89 million in 1950,[33] and from 51.2 per cent of the total population to 59.0 per cent.

The urban population increased during the 1940s by almost 15 million — or by 19.5 per cent,

compared with a growth of 14.5 per cent for the population as a whole. Each of the four broad geographic regions (Northeast, North Central, South and West) experienced an increase in urban population, ranging from 7.2 per cent for the already heavily urban Northeast to 42.5 per cent for the West.[34]

CITIES AND SUBURBS

As the urban population has increased, city populations have overflowed into surrounding areas. This process of suburbanization was particularly marked during the 1940s. Comparative figures for the population of central cities and their outlying areas are not available for the total urban population, but the Census Bureau has compiled data for 168 "standard metropolitan areas," which include all cities of 50,000 or more in the United States plus the county in which the central city of the area is located and any other contiguous counties closely linked economically with the urban center.[35]

33. On the basis of the old Census definition of urban population.

34. Seventeenth Census of Population (1950), Vol. I, *Number of Inhabitants,* p. 1–17.
35. *Ibid.,* p. xxxi.

The aggregate population of these metropolitan areas amounted to 84.5 million in 1950, over 56 per cent of the total population of the United States. As shown below, more than half of the 84.5 million were found in the fourteen largest metropolitan areas (population in millions):

		Population
14 areas of 1,000,000 or more		44.4
19 " " 500,000 to 1,000,000		12.4
44 " " 250,000 to 500,000		14.6
74 " " 100,000 to 250,000		11.6
17 " " under 100,000		1.4

Of the total population increase during the 1940s more than four fifths took place within these standard metropolitan areas. Their population increased by 22.0 per cent, compared with 15.5 per cent for the country as a whole and with 5.7 per cent for the population outside these areas.

The outlying parts of these metropolitan areas, which in 1950 contained nearly 42 per cent of their total population, had grown more rapidly from 1940 to 1950 than the central cities or the country as a whole. The population of the central cities increased by less than 14 per cent, compared with a gain of nearly 36 per cent in the outlying sections. More than 9 million, or nearly half, of the country's total population gain took place in the suburbs and outlying parts of these 168 standard metropolitan areas.[36]

FUTURE POPULATION CHANGES

Any attempt to project past population trends into the future should begin on a note of humility and confession. In the first edition of this report the author of the chapter on population [37] quoted estimates of future population prepared by two outstanding population experts and published in 1943 by the National Resources Planning Board.[38] These estimates were based on natality and mortality experience through 1940, but not extending into the war period. Of this series of six projections, the highest, based on assumptions of "high" fertility and "low" mortality, put the expected 1950 population at 145 million.

The estimate that was chosen for use in the first edition was based on "high" fertility and "medium" mortality. It indicated a 1950 population of 144.7 million. By the time the book was published, in 1947, however, the population of the United States had already risen to within one million of this estimate, and within three years it increased by another 8 million. Thus the estimate of the 1950 population was in error by more than 5 per cent — but this meant a 41 per cent error in the estimated *increase* during the decade.

There is scant satisfaction in the knowledge that many people had thought the forecast too optimistic and that all other official and unofficial forecasts published during the 1940s also fell wide of the mark.[39] And there is no satisfaction at all in the realization that all forecasts would have been much closer to reality had it not been for the sudden and sustained upsurge in births in the 1940s. Failure of forecasters to anticipate the sharp rise in the birth rate can hardly be excused by blaming those responsible for the upturn.

The experience of the past few years shows, as J. S. Davis points out, that the birth rate is subject to wide and unpredictable fluctuations. The same thing applies, but probably much less so, to the other "ingredients" of population change, immigration and the death rate. For these reasons, the projections for 1960 shown below, though stated in terms of a single figure, really encompass a wide range of possibilities.

POPULATION AND HOUSEHOLDS

The sobering effect of the past decade's experience is apparent in the increased caution displayed by estimators of future population. Projections of the Bureau of the Census published in 1952, for example, show a range of nearly 15 million between the "high" estimate for the

---

36. *Ibid.,* pp. xxxi, xxxii. The largest city of a standard metropolitan area is always a central city. Also counted as a central city is any other city within the area that has a population of 25,000 or more and one third or more of the population of the principal city. However, no more than three cities have been defined as central cities in any standard metropolitan area.

37. "Population Trends," Chapter 3, by W. S. Woytinsky, at that time Principal Economic Consultant, Bureau of Employment Security, Social Security Administration.

38. Warren S. Thompson and P. K. Whelpton, *Estimates of Future Population of the United States, 1940–2000.*

39. See "Our Changed Population Outlook and Its Significance," by J. S. Davis, in the *American Economic Review,* June 1952, for a thoughtful appraisal of recent population forecasts.

TABLE 27. POPULATION, URBAN, RURAL NONFARM
AND RURAL FARM, AND CONSUMER UNITS, 1940–1950
AND PROJECTIONS FOR 1960

(Millions)

| | | 1950 | | |
| | | Old Urban | New Urban | |
	1940	Definition	Definition	1960
Total popula-				
tion	132.5	152.5	152.5	177
Urban	74.8	90.0	97.6	113
Rural nonfarm	27.2	39.2	31.6	43
Rural farm	30.4	23.3	23.3	21
Consumer units [a]	[b]	50.4	—	58
Households	34.9 [c]	43.5	—	51
Primary				
families	31.6	38.7	—	44
Other [d]	3.4	4.7	—	7
Lodgers and				
resident				
employees [e]	[b]	6.9	—	7

Sources: Population: total, Appendix 3–6; urban and
rural nonfarm and farm, percentage distribution for 1940
and 1950 shown in Table 26 applied to adjusted totals
— for 1960 see discussion in text. Consumer units: *Current Population Reports: Population Characteristics,* U.S.
Bureau of the Census, Series P–20, variously as follows:
for 1940, No. 17, Table 3, p. 10; No. 33, Table 3, p. 12,
Table 5, p. 14, and p. 2; for 1950, No. 33, Table 3, p. 12,
Table 4, p. 13, Table 5, p. 14, and p. 2; for 1960, see
discussion in text.

a. These estimates relate primarily to the civilian
population but some members of the armed forces living
off post or with their families on post are included. In
1950, the number totaled 547,000. For 1960, on the
assumption of an armed forces total of 3.5 million, one
million were assumed to be living off post or with their
families on post and were included with the civilian
population.

b. Not available.

c. Based on complete 1940 Census returns; figure differs from that shown in Table 24 where 1940 figures
are based on sample of 1940 Census returns.

d. Includes one-person households and households of
unrelated individuals.

e. In households and quasi-households; includes subfamilies and excludes inmates of institutions.

Note: Population figures for 1950 and 1960 relate to
July; all other figures relate to March or April.

1960 population, 179.8 million, and the "low"
estimate, 165.2 million.[40] In the estimates of the
1950 population published by the National
Resources Planning Board in 1943, the range be-

tween lowest and highest had been only 2 million: 143 million vs. 145 million.

Total Population

The estimate of the 1960 population used in
this survey is 177 million. It is based on a Census projection of 176.1 million, adjusted for
underenumeration of children.[41] (See Table 27
and Appendix 3–6.)

If this estimate should prove to be closely accurate (and past experience indicates this is not
very likely), it would mean a population increase
during the present decade of about 24 million, or
16.0 per cent over 1950. This would be larger
than both the 1940–1950 numerical increase (19.9
million) and percentage increase (15.1).

Households and Families

The abnormally high marriage rate during the
last half of the war decade makes it very probable that the rate of family formation will slow
down somewhat in the 1950s. For this reason,
primary families are expected to increase from
38.7 million in 1950 to 44 million in 1960, or by
13.7 per cent during the decade. The gain from
1940 to 1950 was 22.5 per cent.

With continued prosperity, the number of oneperson households and those made up of two or
more unrelated individuals should continue to
increase more rapidly than the population. It is
estimated that they will increase to 7 million by
1960, and that this rise will be accompanied by
a slight increase in the number of lodgers and
resident employees to 7 million.

Under these assumptions the total number of
consumer units would increase from 50.4 million
to 58 million. This growth of 15 per cent is
about the same as that estimated for the total
population. (See Table 27.)

CHANGING AGE DISTRIBUTION

Widely varying rates of change between 1950
and 1960 can be expected for different age
groups, as well as marked variations from the
changes that occurred in the 1940s. (See Figure
12 and Appendix 3–6.)

Because of the expected moderate decline in the
birth rate after 1953, for example, it seems likely

40. *Current Population Reports: Population Estimates,*
Series P–25, No. 58, April 17, 1952. In 1953 the Bureau
of the Census published a new set of projections which
narrowed the range to less than 4 million. However, it
warned that its highest and lowest projections were "not
intended to define the range of reasonable possibility."
(Series P–25, No. 78, August 21, 1953.)

41. One of three Census projections for 1960; the one
used here was based on the assumption that 1950–1953
fertility rates would decline linearly from 1953 to about
the 1940 level by 1975.

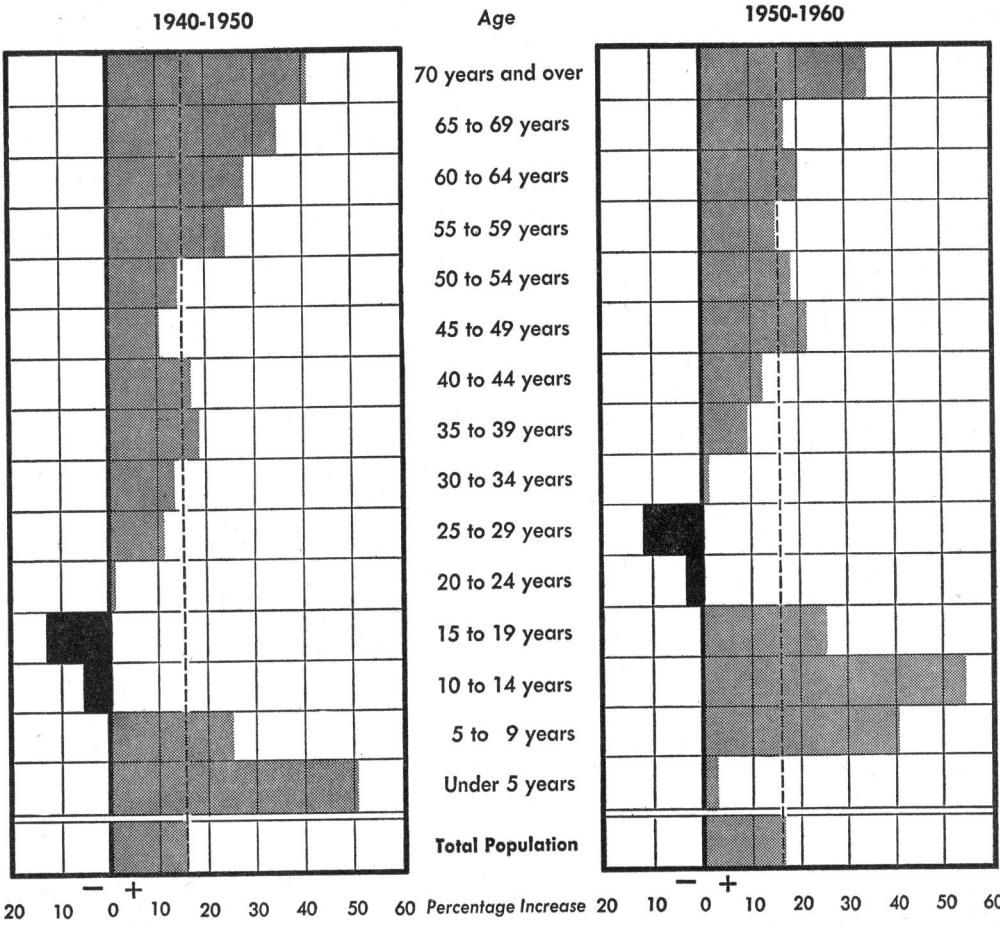

FIGURE 12. PERCENTAGE INCREASES IN POPULATION, BY AGE CLASS, 1940–1950, WITH ESTIMATES FOR 1950–1960

Source: Appendix 3–6.

that there will be only a slight increase in the number of children under 5 years of age in 1960 compared with 1950. The 5-to-9 and 10-to-14 age groups of 1960, on the other hand, will be made up of the children born during the prolific late 1940s and early 1950s. These groups are therefore sure to increase much more rapidly than they did before. The number of 15-to-19-year-olds actually declined by 13.4 per cent from 1940 to 1950, reflecting the low birth rates of the 1930s. With the rise of marriages and births in the 1940s, the size of this group can be expected to increase substantially by 1960.

There will probably be a sharp drop in the number in the "marrying ages" of 20 to 29 between 1950 and 1960, however. According to the Census medium projections, only 22.2 million of

the population will be in this age group in 1960, compared with 23.9 million in 1950 and 22.7 million in 1940. Thus, these fertile ages will show an actual decline in numbers over a twenty-year period when total population will have increased 33.5 per cent. The 30-to-34 group will show virtually no change in size during the 1950s. The failure of the 20-to-34 age groups to grow in number between 1950 and 1960 reflects the subnormal birth rates during 1926–1940.

The middle and upper age groups, on the whole, will probably grow somewhat more rapidly during the 1950s than the total population, reflecting the gradual "aging" of the population. The rise in the median age, however, has been markedly slowed since 1940 by the sharp increase in the number of children. According to the

TABLE 28. POPULATION ESTIMATES FOR JULY 1950 AND 1960 AND PERCENTAGE CHANGES IN POPULATION FROM 1940 TO 1950 AND 1950 TO 1960, BY STATE [a]

Division and State	July 1950	July 1960	Percentage Change [b]	
			1940 to 1950	1950 to 1960
	(Thousands)			
United States, total	152,479	176,928	14.5	16.0
New England	9,438	10,563	10.4	11.9
Maine	934	1,036	7.9	10.9
New Hampshire	544	604	8.5	11.0
Vermont	387	413	5.2	6.7
Massachusetts	4,751	5,261	8.7	10.7
Rhode Island	787	876	11.0	11.3
Connecticut	2,036	2,372	17.4	16.5
Middle Atlantic	30,679	34,430	9.5	12.2
New York	15,079	17,015	10.0	12.8
New Jersey	4,896	5,647	16.2	15.3
Pennsylvania	10,704	11,772	6.0	10.0
East North Central	30,847	35,633	14.2	15.5
Ohio	8,057	9,311	15.0	15.6
Indiana	4,004	4,636	14.8	15.8
Illinois	8,816	9,977	10.3	13.2
Michigan	6,469	7,757	21.2	19.9
Wisconsin	3,498	3,955	9.5	13.1
West North Central	14,333	15,499	4.0	8.1
Minnesota	3,043	3,369	6.8	10.7
Iowa	2,675	2,880	3.3	7.7
Missouri	4,030	4,377	4.5	8.6
North Dakota	635	654	− 3.5	3.0
South Dakota	666	702	1.5	5.4
Nebraska	1,353	1,420	0.7	5.0
Kansas	1,932	2,099	5.8	8.6
South Atlantic	21,286	25,283	18.8	18.8
Delaware	324	384	19.4	18.5
Maryland	2,350	2,872	28.6	22.2
District of Columbia	771	905	21.0	17.4
Virginia	3,282	3,929	23.9	19.7
West Virginia	2,050	2,283	5.4	11.4
North Carolina	4,100	4,748	13.7	15.8
South Carolina	2,139	2,422	11.4	13.2
Georgia	3,476	3,886	10.3	11.8
Florida	2,797	3,851	46.1	37.7

(Continued on page 77)

Census medium estimate of population growth, the median age will rise to 31 years by 1960, or about one year above the 1950 median.[42]

The number of persons over 65 will increase by an estimated 27 per cent between 1950 and

42. See Table 21 and *Current Population Reports: Population Estimates,* Series P–25, No. 43, August 10, 1950, p. 11; and P–25, No. 78, August 21, 1953.

1960, although both the actual increase and the percentage gain will be smaller than in the preceding decade. However, this upper age group will include 9 per cent of the population in 1960, compared with 8 per cent in 1950.

The number of people in the working age groups (15 to 64) is expected to increase by 9.3 million; the increase in the "dependent" groups

TABLE 28 (continued)

Division and State	July 1950	July 1960	Percentage Change [b] 1940 to 1950	Percentage Change [b] 1950 to 1960
		(Thousands)		
East South Central	11,619	12,987	6.5	11.8
Kentucky	2,970	3,266	3.5	10.0
Tennessee	3,338	3,832	12.9	14.8
Alabama	3,108	3,503	8.1	12.7
Mississippi	2,203	2,386	− 0.2	8.3
West South Central	14,653	16,684	11.3	13.9
Arkansas	1,946	2,064	− 2.0	6.1
Louisiana	2,718	3,137	13.5	15.4
Oklahoma	2,264	2,371	− 4.4	4.7
Texas	7,725	9,111	20.2	17.9
Mountain	5,139	6,246	22.3	21.5
Montana	605	666	5.6	10.1
Idaho	601	704	12.1	17.1
Wyoming	288	337	15.9	17.0
Colorado	1,340	1,588	18.0	18.5
New Mexico	688	862	28.1	25.3
Arizona	757	1,017	50.1	34.3
Utah	700	861	25.2	23.0
Nevada	159	210	45.2	32.1
Pacific	14,486	19,604	48.8	35.3
Washington	2,360	2,964	37.0	25.6
Oregon	1,544	2,004	39.6	29.8
California	10,582	14,638	53.3	38.3

Sources: Total population from Appendix 3–6; regional and state estimates based on percentage distribution in *Current Population Reports: Population Estimates,* U.S. Bureau of the Census, Series P–25, No. 56, January 27, 1952, p. 6; percentage change 1940 to 1950 from Seventeenth Census of Population (1950), Vol. I, *Number of Inhabitants,* p. 1–10.

a. The estimates are adjusted to include members of the armed forces residing in the area at the time of entry into the armed forces and to exclude all other members of the armed forces stationed in the area.

b. Since figures for 1940 comparable with the July 1950 estimates are not available, the 1940 and 1950 decennial census figures have been used as a basis for computing percentage changes from 1940 to 1950. These figures include members of the armed forces stationed in each state at the time of enumeration. The projected percentage increases from 1950 to 1960 are based on figures shown in the table.

Note: Discrepancies in addition are due to rounding.

(under 15 and over 65) will be 15.1 million. The ratio of "workers" to "dependents," which had been rising for more than a century, was sharply reversed after 1940. It dropped from 2.1 to 1 in 1940 to 1.8 in 1950 and will apparently decline further to about 1.6 to 1 in 1960.

GEOGRAPHIC SHIFTS

Whether or not the estimate of a 24 million increase in total population between 1950 and 1960 proves to be close to what really happens, the long-term geographic movements of the past will probably continue during the decade.

Urban-Rural Changes

It seems likely, for example, that the long-range downward trend of farm population will persist, though probably not so rapidly as in the 1940s. Farm population in 1960 is therefore estimated at 21 million, or 11 per cent below the

1950 total. This decline of about 2.5 million compares with a drop of over 7 million, or 23 per cent, from 1940 to 1950.

Largely because of the expected continuance of a strong growth trend in the outlying parts of metropolitan areas, it is estimated that the rural nonfarm population will increase to 43 million in 1960 from 31.6 million in 1950 — a rise of more than one third, but considerably less than the 44 per cent gain during the preceding decade.

Urban population is expected to increase by more than 15 million, about the same as the numerical increase during the 1940s. The percentage rise would be smaller in the 1950 decade and slightly less than the rate of growth for the population as a whole. (See Table 27.)

If these changes take place, the percentage of the population classified as urban in 1960 will be the same as in 1950 — 64 per cent. Rural nonfarm population will increase from 21 to 24 per cent of the total, while farm population will drop from 15 per cent of the total to 12 per cent.

Regional Trends

The westward movement of the population, and the drift away from sparsely settled farm states to urban-industrial regions, both of which were accelerated during the war, also seem likely to continue. This means that the Pacific and Mountain divisions will grow more rapidly than the rest of the country during the 1950s, and will have a larger proportion of the total population in 1960. (See Tables 25 and 28.)

The agricultural West North Central states will grow much more slowly than the rest of the country; they are expected to show an increase of 8.1 per cent, compared with 16.0 per cent for the United States as a whole. Likewise, New England and the Middle Atlantic and East South Central states will have a smaller proportion of

the country's population in 1960 than in 1950. The growth trends of most other sections will more closely correspond to the expected rate of increase for the entire population.

Among individual states there will undoubtedly be wide differences in population growth, as there were during the 1940s. According to the Census Bureau's medium projection,[43] California in the West and Florida in the East, each with an expected growth of about 38 per cent, will lead all other states. If this happens, California will be the second state of the Union in 1960, and its population will be close to that of New York.

All of the Mountain and Pacific states, except Montana, Idaho, Wyoming and Colorado, are expected to experience a growth of 20 per cent or more — a much larger increase than in any of the more easterly states except Florida and Maryland. The lowest growth rates — all less than 6 per cent — are expected in North Dakota, South Dakota, Nebraska and Oklahoma.

East of the Mississippi, the District of Columbia and the near-by states of Delaware, Maryland and Virginia will show the largest advance in the South Atlantic division, except for Florida's big gain. In New England, only Connecticut, and among the Middle Atlantic states, only New Jersey, are expected to grow about as rapidly as the country as a whole. Michigan alone among the East North Central states will substantially exceed the national average, but Ohio and Indiana will be close to it.

Texas will also grow more rapidly than the country as a whole; of the other southern states, Louisiana, Tennessee and North Carolina will approach the growth rate of the population as a whole.

---

43. See Table 28 for explanation of method used in estimating 1960 state population.

## CHAPTER 4

OUTPUT, INCOME AND EXPENDITURES

GROSS NATIONAL PRODUCT, net national product and national income are concepts designed to measure the continuing flow of goods and services into consumption and use, and the reverse flow and disposition of payments for their production and distribution. These concepts can therefore be looked at from different points of view.

MEASURES OF QUANTITIES AND PAYMENTS

In the first place, they are measures of *output.* Gross national product represents the gross value of all the goods and services produced by business enterprises (including farmers, professional persons and other self-employed individuals) and by government agencies. The term thus measures the market value of the nation's total annual output of goods and services. This is a gross figure because, though it excludes the value of raw materials and semifinished products "consumed" in the productive process, it does not exclude the value of the physical capital used up or worn out in that process.

Net national product, on the other hand, measures net output, because it represents the market value of the goods and services produced by the economy after deducting the value of the physical capital consumed in the process of turning them out. Since the net national product is measured at market prices, it includes the amount of indirect business taxes (such as sales and excise taxes) collected from buyers by business firms and turned over to the government. Subtracting these amounts and certain other minor transfer payments from the value of net national product yields the national income. National income, therefore, is the net national product measured not at market prices but at cost, i.e., the amounts paid in the form of wages, rent, interest, etc., to workers, investors and other "factors of production."

Second, these concepts measure the receipt and

By J. FREDERIC DEWHURST. Opinions and judgments expressed in this chapter are those of the author and should not be attributed to the organization with which he is associated.

allocation of *income* resulting from productive activities. Thus the total amount received in payment for the gross national product, or the "gross receipts from production," could equally well be described as "gross national income produced," as Arthur O. Dahlberg, President of the U.S. Economics Corporation, has suggested. Part of this total is set aside by business in the form of depreciation and depletion reserves to be spent for replacement of the machinery and equipment worn out in the productive process. The amount received in payment for the net national product remaining could properly be described as the "net national income produced." Another portion of the gross receipts goes to the government in the form of business taxes. This may be regarded as the value of government services "consumed" in the productive process, in the same way as depreciation and other reserves represent the value of the plant and equipment used up in that process.

The great bulk of the gross receipts from production, however, is either received directly by individuals, as in the case of farmers, professional people and other self-employed, or, after its receipt by business and government, is promptly paid out to individuals in the form of wages and salaries, interest and dividends, rents and royalties. These payments to individuals, plus a small fraction of gross receipts retained by business in the form of undistributed corporate profits, constitute the national income.

Finally, to complete the circle, these concepts measure *expenditures,* or the way in which the income recipients — consumers, business and government — budget and dispose of their income. Thus the gross national product, from this point of view, becomes the "gross national expenditure," since the total amount we spend for goods and services — including, of course, what we invest — is equal to the gross receipts from production, or the gross national income, and represents the value of the gross national product. Obviously, this does not mean that every pair of shoes, every automobile and every machine tool turned out at the factory in the course of a year is bought and paid for in the same year, or that every dollar of income is promptly spent or invested. Under national income accounting, "production" becomes complete only when the finished product or service has passed through the channels of distribution and is delivered to the ultimate buyer, and gross national product is valued in terms of the price paid by that buyer. For that reason, and because net additions to business inventories are accounted for as "purchases," it is axiomatic that gross national product must be equal to gross national expenditure, to gross national income, and to gross receipts from production. (See end-paper chart.)

It must be remembered that many billions of dollars of expenditures made each year for other than currently produced goods and services constitute no part of gross national expenditure, as the term is used here. These include a multitude of transactions in commodities, real estate and securities, which may bring speculative profits or losses to individuals but do not add to total national income or to the volume of goods and services produced.

Of a somewhat different nature is the chain of dollar transactions involved in the sale and resale of raw materials, semifinished products and finished goods in the long series of exchanges between their origin and their final distribution as finished articles ready for use. To include all these intermediate transactions would result in endless duplication, for the net costs incurred and the "values added" at succeeding steps in the production-distribution process are all included in the price paid for the final product.

Another kind of money transaction that does not enter into gross national expenditure or affect the size of the national income is the so-called "transfer payments." These involve the mere transfer of income from one person to another without any reverse transfer of goods or services. Sometimes this is effected directly, as with gifts or charitable contributions, or the repayment of debts. A large volume of such transfer payments is made through government in the form of old-age and veterans pensions, or subsidy payments of various kinds not made in exchange for currently produced goods and services. On the whole, the total volume of money transactions in the course of a year is several times larger than the national income or the gross national expenditure, as these terms are used in income analysis.[1]

This brief discussion of the composition and relationships of gross national product, net national product and national income makes no pretense of completeness or precision. It is an oversimplification of an extremely complex — and controversial — subject, about which many volumes have been written. A general picture of these relationships, and of the magnitudes involved, however, is essential for estimating the total volume of future consumption, private capital and government expenditures to be expected on the basis of the assumptions underlying this survey.

INCOME-EXPENDITURE RELATIONSHIPS

The gross national product comprises every variety of economic goods and services produced during the year except the above-mentioned intermediate goods and services used up in producing finished products. Included in the gross product at one extreme are such intangibles as shoeshines, haircuts, surgical operations, theatrical performances, police and fire protection, investment advice, and other services provided by individuals, business firms and government agencies. At the other extreme are tangible consumption goods ranging from radishes to radios, business capital goods such as typewriters, turbines and factory buildings, and such government items as highways and bridges, mail trucks and trash cans, stationery and submarines.

Viewed from the standpoint of the flow of money, personal consumption expenditures normally account for more than two thirds of total gross national expenditure, or for about twice as much as the combined amount spent for private construction and capital equipment and for government purchases of goods and services. However, these relationships, as well as the distribution of income, have varied widely among the prewar, war and postwar periods. Examination of these trends and relationships can furnish some basis for judgments as to the future.

Satisfactory detailed data on the components and sources of national income and gross national product (according to the Commerce Department concepts) are available only since 1929.

1. See *The Townsend Crusade*, Twentieth Century Fund, New York, 1936, Appendix F. The total volume of money transactions in 1929, for example, was estimated at $638 billion, or more than six times the gross national expenditure of $104 billion in that year.

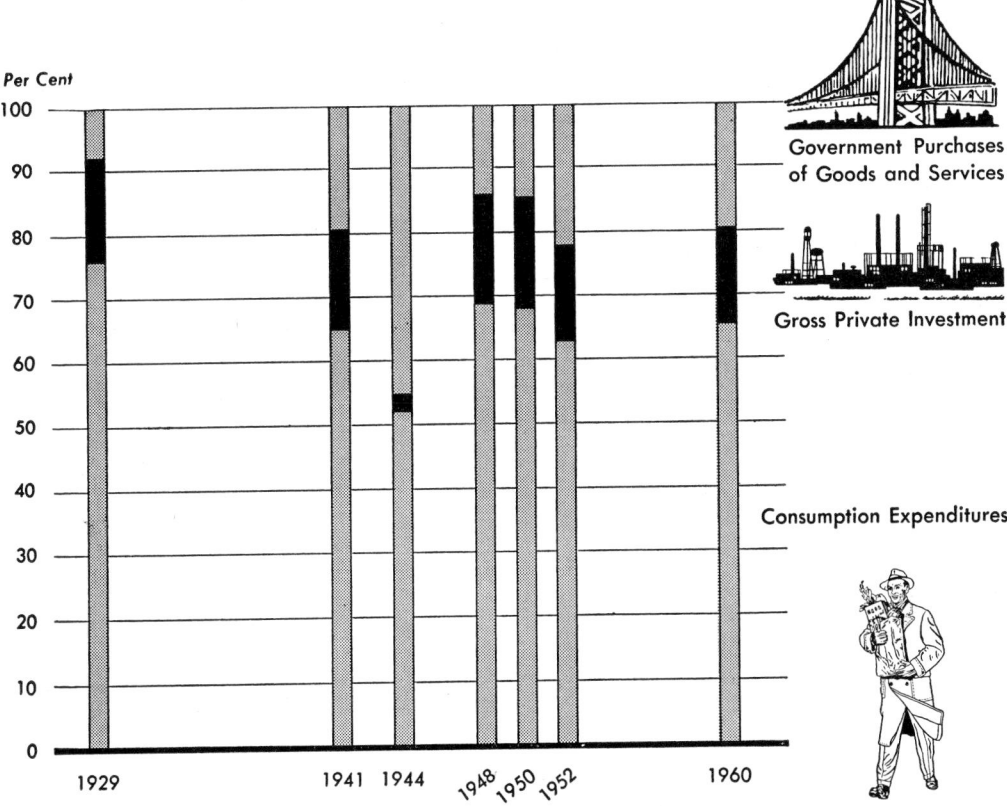

FIGURE 13. CONSUMPTION EXPENDITURES, GOVERNMENT PURCHASES AND GROSS INVESTMENT AS PER CENT OF GROSS NATIONAL PRODUCT, SELECTED YEARS, 1929–1952, WITH PROJECTIONS TO 1960

Source: Table 29.

Many of the years since then have been too abnormal — because of depression or war, or the postwar boom — to furnish a dependable guide as to what might be expected under a normal high level of peacetime activity in the future. The year 1929, when we enjoyed full employment under peacetime conditions, and the year 1941, when we were again approaching "full employment," with gross output more than one-fifth higher than in 1929, provide the only satisfactory pictures of income-expenditure relationships under fairly active peacetime conditions prior to World War II.

During that war normal relationships were drastically distorted by heavier taxes, price and production controls, and rationing. The year 1944 represents the peak of the war effort and provides the best picture of the effects of war on income distribution and expenditures. Immediately after the end of World War II these relationships were further distorted by a sharp price inflation and a rush by consumers to turn their unprecedented accumulation of cash into the goods they wanted but could not buy during the war, and by business firms to build up inventories and purchase new plant and equipment.

By 1948, however, the postwar price rise first slackened and then halted temporarily, marking the satisfaction of the bulk of the war-deferred demand for consumption goods. A moderate rise after 1949 was sharply accelerated by the outbreak of the Korean War in the middle of 1950. This marked the beginning of a new defense build-up, and a new burst of inflation, which continued for about two years. Defense spending began to level off and prices to stabilize on a new plateau during 1952, while both the price level and the volume of national production reached all-time peak levels in 1953 from which moderate declines occurred in 1954.

TABLE 29. INCOME AND EXPENDITURE RELATIONSHIPS FOR SELECTED PAST YEARS
AND ASSUMPTIONS FOR 1960

(Billions)

	1929	1941	1944	1948	1950	1952	1960
							(In 1950 Dollars)
Gross National Product, National Income and Consumption Expenditures							
Gross national product	$103.8	$126.4	$213.7	$259.0	$286.8	$348.0	$370.0
Less capital consumption	8.8	9.3	11.9	17.6	21.6	27.0	28.0
Net national product	95.0	117.1	201.8	241.4	265.2	321.0	342.0
Less indirect business taxes	7.0	11.3	14.1	20.4	23.7	28.1	29.5
Less miscellaneous[a]	.7	2.0	3.8	−2.4	.9	1.3	—
National income	87.4	103.8	183.8	223.5	240.6	291.6	312.5
Less corporate savings	2.6	4.9	6.1	13.5	13.6	9.5	14.0
Less corporate profits taxes	1.4	7.8	13.5	13.0	18.2	20.6	24.0
Less social insurance contributions	.2	2.8	5.2	5.2	6.9	8.6	14.5
Plus net interest paid by government	1.0	1.3	2.8	4.5	4.7	4.9	5.0
Plus government transfer payments	.9	2.6	3.1	10.5	14.3	12.0	17.0
Plus miscellaneous[b]	.1	3.1	1.0	2.8	5.8	—	—
Personal income	85.1	95.3	165.9	209.5	226.7	269.7	282.0
Less personal taxes	2.6	3.3	18.9	21.1	20.9	34.6	26.5
Disposable personal income	82.5	92.0	147.0	188.4	205.8	235.0	255.5
Less personal consumption expenditures	78.8[c]	82.3	111.6	177.9	194.6	218.1	241.5
Personal saving	3.7	9.8	35.4	10.5	11.3	16.9	14.0
Government Receipts and Expenditures							
Government receipts, total	11.3	25.2	51.8	59.8	69.7	92.0	94.5
Business taxes	8.4	19.1	27.7	33.4	42.0	48.7	53.5
Personal taxes	2.6	3.3	18.9	21.1	20.9	34.6	26.5
Social insurance contributions	.2	2.8	5.2	5.2	6.9	8.6	14.5
Government expenditures, total	10.2	28.7	103.1	51.6	61.4	94.4	94.5
Purchases of goods and services	8.5	24.7	96.5	36.6	42.0	77.5	72.5
Construction and capital equipment (civilian)[d]	2.6	4.3	2.3	5.1	7.3	10.1	10.5
Other goods and services	5.9	20.4	94.2	31.5	34.7	67.4	62.0
Transfer payments	.9	2.6	3.1	10.5	14.3	12.0	17.0
Net interest paid	1.0	1.3	2.8	4.5	4.7	4.9	5.0
Subsidies less current surplus of government enterprises	−.1	.1	.7	—	.4	.1	—
Government surplus (+) or deficit (−)	1.1	−3.5	−51.4	8.2	8.3	−2.4	—
Private Savings and Capital Formation							
Gross private savings	15.5	23.0	57.0	36.4	42.0	54.7	56.0
Personal saving	3.7	9.8	35.4	10.5	11.3	16.9	14.0
Corporate saving	2.6	4.9	6.1	13.5	13.6	9.5	14.0
Capital consumption allowances	8.8	9.3	11.9	17.6	21.6	27.0	28.0
Miscellaneous[e]	.4	−1.0	3.6	−5.2	−4.5	1.4	—
Gross investment[f, g]	16.6	19.5	5.6	44.6	50.2	52.3	56.0
Construction and capital equipment[f]	14.3	14.5	8.5	37.7	45.0	48.8	56.0
Inventory change and net foreign investment[g]	2.3	5.0	−2.9	6.9	5.2	3.5	—
Savings minus investment	−1.1	3.5	51.4	−8.2	−8.3	2.4	—

TABLE 29 (continued)

	1929	1941	1944	1948	1950	1952	1960
							(In 1950 Dollars)
Private and Public Expenditures for Construction and Capital Equipment [h]							
Total [d, f]	$16.9	$18.8	$10.8	$42.8	$52.3	$58.9	$66.5
Private capital facilities [f]	14.3	14.5	8.5	37.7	45.0	48.8	56.0
Government capital facilities (civilian) [d]	2.6	4.3	2.3	5.1	7.3	10.1	10.5

Sources: For 1929–1952, Appendix 4–1; for 1960, see text.

a. Business transfer payments, statistical discrepancy and current surplus of government enterprise minus subsidies.

b. Business transfer payments minus corporate inventory valuation adjustment minus excess of wage accruals over disbursements.

c. Differs from figure shown in Appendix 4–4, which includes estimate for alcoholic beverages during prohibition.

d. Excludes expenditures for publicly owned military and naval plant and equipment and expenditures by state governments for equipment; these expenditures are included with government purchases of "other goods and services."

e. Miscellaneous includes corporate inventory valuation adjustment, excess of wage accruals over disbursements and statistical discrepancy.

f. 1940 and later includes expenditures for oil and natural gas well drilling.

g. Includes government net foreign investment.

h. Slight differences between these data and the estimates in Appendix 4–8 are due to use of different sources and rounding.

Note: Slight discrepancies in addition are due to rounding.

Prewar Prosperity Years: 1929 and 1941

The 1929 gross national product, measured in current dollars, was not surpassed until 1941, which, in spite of persistent unemployment, was unquestionably our most prosperous prewar year. The $104 billion gross national product of 1929, after deducting capital consumption and indirect business taxes, yielded a national income of $87 billion. Subtracting the savings, profits taxes and social insurance payments of corporations, aggregating $4.2 billion, and adding the interest paid on government obligations, government transfer payments (insurance, pensions, etc.), and miscellaneous items, aggregating $2 billion, individuals were left with personal income of $85 billion in 1929. Payment of what now seems a modest $2.6 billion of personal taxes left them with $82.5 billion of disposable income. Out of this amount consumers saved $3.7 billion and spent nearly $79 billion for consumption goods and services. Thus by far the largest fraction — more than three fourths — of gross national product in that year consisted of the goods and services bought by consumers for their own consumption or use. (See Table 29 and Figure 13.)

Government receipts from personal and business taxes amounted to a paltry $11.3 billion, of which only $10.2 billion was spent by government, and out of that sum $8.5 billion was paid for goods and services purchased or produced by government. The remainder consisted chiefly of interest and pensions and other transfer payments. Thus the government share of goods and services accounted for little more than 8 per cent of gross national product in 1929.

"Gross investment" (which includes not only new construction and capital equipment but also additions to, or subtractions from, business inventories, and foreign investment) in that year accounted for the remainder of the gross national product. It amounted to $16.6 billion, or about 16 per cent of gross national product. Gross investment exceeded gross private savings (corporate savings and capital consumption plus personal savings) by $1.1 billion, which was the amount of the government surplus in that year.[2]

The magnitudes and relationships of 1929 (satisfactory as they seemed at the time!) seem unlikely to recur in the foreseeable future. The new trends, which have since brought such great changes in production, expenditures and income, and notably in the importance of government in the national economy, were beginning to show

2. In national income analysis the net government (federal, state and local) surplus, if any, must (if there is no borrowing from abroad) equal the amount by which gross investment exceeds gross private savings; while the net government deficit equals the amount by which gross private savings exceed gross investment.

themselves in 1941 on the eve of American participation in World War II.

Gross national product in 1941 exceeded $126 billion — some 22 per cent more than the 1929 dollar total. (Allowing for the higher prices of 1929 the increase in "real" national product was more than 34 per cent above 1929.) Largely because of the sharp increase in indirect business taxes, however, 1941 national income of nearly $104 billion was only 18 per cent larger than in 1929. Corporate profits taxes and social insurance contributions and, to a lesser extent, corporate savings increased steeply over 1929, so that 1941 personal income of $95 billion was only 11 per cent larger than in the earlier year. Finally — whether intentionally or not — consumers saved $9.8 billion in 1941, or nearly three times as much as in 1929. The result was that consumption expenditures of a little more than $82 billion were only 4 per cent larger than in 1929.

Government receipts of $25 billion in 1941 were more than twice the 1929 total, while government expenditures for goods and services — largely because of federal defense spending — amounted to nearly $25 billion, or almost three times the 1929 total. Gross investment increased to $19.5 billion, or by a somewhat smaller percentage rise than gross national product, while gross private savings exceeded investment by $3.5 billion, the amount of the federal deficit. (See Table 29.)

The Peak War Year: 1944

By 1944 the transformation of the economy to a war status was complete. Gross national product reached a peak of nearly $214 billion, which was far above any previous year, and the physical volume of production in 1944 *was not thereafter exceeded until 1951*. National income rose to nearly $184 billion and personal income to a record high of $166 billion. Because of wartime tax levies and restrictions on spending, personal taxes and personal saving together amounted to over $54 billion, or more than four times the 1941 total. The result was that individuals in 1944 bought less than $112 billion worth of consumption goods and services, representing little more than half of the gross national product.

This consumer share of the total volume of goods and services produced in that year was a much smaller proportion of the total than in any previous or subsequent year, just as the $97 billion of government purchases was by far the largest amount and the largest share of gross national expenditure in history. Total government expenditures in 1944, which also include interest and transfer payments, amounted to $103 billion, of which about half was financed by business and personal taxes and social insurance contributions. The record-breaking total of $57 billion of gross private savings exceeded gross investment by $51.4 billion, the amount of the government deficit in that year.

Postwar Boom Years: 1948, 1950 and 1952

By 1948 the postwar price inflation and the most intensive phase of the "catching-up period" were coming to an end. The rise of gross national product to $259 billion, or about $45 billion above the 1944 total, was entirely the result of higher prices, for the physical volume of production (gross national product in constant dollars) was more than 8 per cent below 1944.[3] The increase in the dollar total was accompanied by a sharp drop in the government share of gross national product and by marked increases in personal consumption expenditures and gross investment. Government expenditures for goods and services of $36.6 billion were $60 billion under the wartime peak and accounted for only 14 per cent of gross national product in 1948, compared with over 45 per cent in 1944. Consumption expenditures rose by $66 billion to $178 billion in 1948, when they accounted for nearly 69 per cent of gross national product, compared with only 52 per cent at the peak of the war effort. (See Table 29.)

Gross national product rose to a new high of $287 billion in 1950, although the physical volume of output was still slightly below 1944. The relative importance of the various components showed a stable relationship with 1948 and, with certain conspicuous exceptions, was similar to prewar years of prosperity. Gross private savings and gross investment, after the distortions of the war years, returned to a volume of not far from one sixth of gross national product, or about the same as in 1929. Personal income and saving, and capital consumption, were also of about the same relative importance as in 1929.

---

3. *National Income and Product of the United States, 1929–1950* (1951 National Income Supplement to the *Survey of Current Business*), p. 146.

However, with personal taxes in 1950 eight times as large as in 1929 and taking nearly three times as much of income, disposable personal income and consumption expenditures were both relatively smaller than in 1929 and other prewar years. With a sixfold rise in the share of gross national product represented by corporate income taxes and a substantial increase in the relative size of indirect business taxes, government receipts and disbursements were, relatively, more than twice as large, while the government share of gross national product was nearly twice as large, in 1950 as in 1929.

This expanded role of the government in the national economy, though greatly accelerated by the war and its aftermath, is obviously no transitory phenomenon. It is the result of a long-run trend which seems unlikely to be substantially reversed in the foreseeable future.

The outbreak of Korean hostilities brought a sharp upsurge in prices and production. In 1951, for the first time, the physical volume of the nation's production passed the 1944 wartime peak, and the 1952 gross national product of $348 billion was $61 billion larger than the total for 1950. More than half of this increase, however, is attributable to higher prices, for the gain measured in "1950 dollars" was only $29 billion, or about 10 per cent. (See Appendix 4–2.)

Changes in the relative importance of the components of 1952 gross national product largely reflected the new defense program. Net national product and national income remained at almost exactly the same proportion of gross national product as in 1950, but personal income dropped slightly in relative size. With personal taxes taking a larger proportion of income than even at the peak of the war, disposable personal income in 1952, though a record-breaking $235 billion, was about the same in relation to gross national product as in 1944, while consumption expenditures of $218 billion amounted to less than 63 per cent of gross national product. Gross investment dropped from more than 17 per cent of gross national product in 1948–1950 to about 15 per cent. Government purchases of goods and services showed the largest increase, rising from $42 billion in 1950 to more than $77 billion in 1952, and from 14.6 per cent of gross national product to 22.2 per cent. As we were in 1952 approaching a peak in a new defense program from which some decline has already occurred, it seems unlikely that the rela-

tionship among the components of gross national product in that year can be considered entirely typical of normal conditions in 1960.

INCOME–EXPENDITURE PROJECTIONS

The uncertainties which surround an attempt to project the total "normal" volume of gross national product into the future become even greater when an attempt is made to project the separate components of gross product. For that reason any estimates of the future can be no more than opinions, and all that can be hoped for is that they will be honest opinions and not expressions of hopes or fears. The 1960 estimates shown in Table 29 and Figure 14, though presented in precise terms, make no pretense at exactness but represent only approximate judgments of the disposition of income and expenditures, under the basic assumptions about population, labor force, working hours and productivity which underlie this survey.

On the whole the relative size of the various components of the estimated $370 billion gross national product of 1960 is not far different from what it actually was for the much smaller totals of the prosperous years 1948 and 1950 (but different in important respects from 1952); many components indeed are estimated to be roughly comparable with the relative magnitudes of 1929, when gross national product was only $104 billion. With capital consumption and indirect business taxes estimated to aggregate 15 per cent of gross national product, or about as much as in earlier prosperous peacetime years, the estimated 1960 national income of $312.5 billion would be 85 per cent of gross national product.[4]

---

4. Key assumptions as to magnitude in 1960 of various components of gross national product and national income shown in Table 29 based on examination of past relationships and judgment as to future trends are as follows: capital consumption assumed equal to 7.5 per cent of gross national product; corporate savings assumed equal to 4.5 per cent of national income and personal savings to 5 per cent of personal income; taxes were assumed to be distributed among indirect business taxes, corporate profits taxes and personal taxes as they were in 1950; government budgets assumed to balance and export balance and inventory change each equal to zero; government expenditures assumed to total $94.5 billion (at 1950 prices) with $40 billion for federal military expenditures, $20 billion for federal nonmilitary and $34.5 billion for state and local outlays; public capital expenditures just over one sixth the size of private capital outlays; social insurance contributions estimated at $14.5 billion on basis of increased coverage and size of payroll; government transfer payments estimated at $17 billion on basis of estimates from various government agencies.

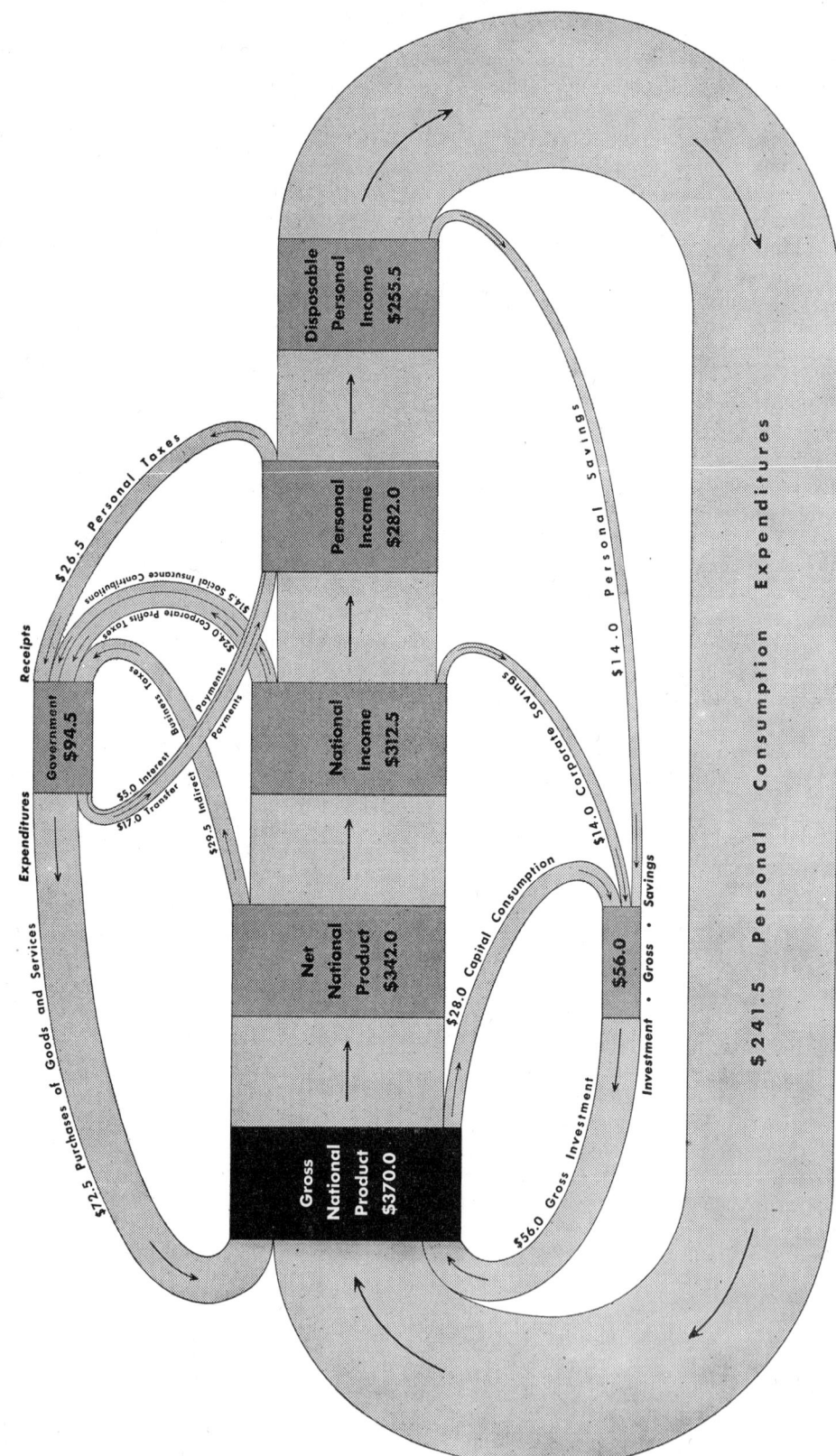

FIGURE 14. ESTIMATED FLOW OF INCOME AND EXPENDITURES IN 1960 (Billions at 1950 Prices)

Source: Table 29.

Chiefly because of an expected rise in the relative size of social insurance contributions in 1960 compared with 1950, and a decline in government transfer payments (with the completion of special payments to veterans), personal income is estimated at $282 billion in 1960, or 76 per cent of gross national product. This is smaller than the 79 per cent of 1950, the 81 per cent of 1948, and the 82 per cent of 1929 — and slightly below the 1952 percentage.

Although personal taxes in 1960 are estimated at a smaller proportion of gross national product than in war or other postwar years, their deduction leaves individuals with a disposable personal income of only 69 per cent of gross national product, or about $255.5 billion.

Consumption expenditures in 1960 on the basis of these assumptions will amount to slightly more than $241 billion (in dollars of 1950 purchasing power), or two thirds of gross national product — slightly less than in 1948 and 1950 and a much smaller proportion than the 76 per cent of 1929, but considerably more than in 1952. The actual dollar total of such spending would be about 25 per cent more than in 1950, however, and more than double the price-adjusted 1929 figure.

With personal consumption expenditures accounting for roughly two thirds of gross national product, compared with three fourths in prewar years, government purchases and private investment together will account for the remaining third in 1960, as compared with one fourth in 1929. Here the significant change is of course the greatly expanded economic role of government. This is manifested not only by government's larger share of gross national product, but also by its new and growing function as a funnel for transfer payments, i.e., by the collection of taxes and social insurance contributions and the disbursement of such funds in the form of pensions, subsidies and other unrequited payments.

Government receipts and expenditures — federal, state and local — are estimated at $94.5 billion, on the assumption of an over-all balanced government budget in 1960. This would be roughly eight times as many dollars as were collected and disbursed by American governments in 1929, and nearly two and one half times as large a sum in relation to the gross national product in each year. Government expenditures were less than 10 per cent *as large as* gross na-

tional product[5] in 1929, but are estimated at about 25 per cent in 1960 — more than in 1948 or 1950, about half the proportion in the peak war year 1944, and slightly less than in 1952. Government purchases of goods and services, estimated at $72.5 billion in 1960, would be more than three fourths of the dollar outlay of $96.5 billion in the peak year of World War II, but less than 20 per cent of gross national product, as compared with more than 45 per cent in that year. The 1960 proportion would be substantially higher than the 14 to 15 per cent of 1948 and 1950 and more than twice the 8.2 per cent of 1929, but substantially smaller than the 1952 percentage.

Because government budgets are assumed to be in balance in 1960, gross private savings would equal gross investment. The estimate of gross savings of $56 billion is composed of personal savings of $14 billion and corporate savings of the same amount — somewhat more than in 1950 — and capital consumption of $28 billion. The latter figure is larger than in earlier years because of the great expansion of the nation's capital plant. These assumptions therefore imply that about half of the $56 billion gross investment in 1960 represents replacement of worn-out and outmoded plant and equipment financed out of corporate depreciation accounts, and about half constitutes new facilities which expand our productive capacity and are financed by corporate and personal savings.

With gross investment in new private capital facilities (and gross private savings) thus accounting for 15.2 per cent of gross national product, the nation would be devoting about as much relatively to these purposes as in previous prosperous peacetime years.

Out of the $72.5 billion total estimated government expenditure for goods and services in 1960, about $10.5 billion, or 2.8 per cent of gross national product, will consist of expenditures for government civilian construction and capital facilities (i.e., roads, bridges, etc.). On the basis of these assumptions, the 1960 market for the products of the construction and capital equipment industries would amount to nearly $67 billion, or nearly 18 per cent of the gross national product in that year.

---

5. Government expenditures contain a large element of "transfer payments," which do not enter into and cannot be considered as part of gross national product or gross national expenditure, as these terms are used in national income analysis.

These projections of the main components of 1960 gross national product, as explained above, are expressed in terms of dollars of the purchasing power of 1950, when the price level was substantially lower than it is at the time this volume goes to press. In dollars of 1953 purchasing power, which is not far from the current level, the approximate values are roughly as follows (in billions):

	1950	1953	1960
Gross national product	$321	$367	$415
Consumption expenditures	216	230	268
Gross private investment	56	54	62
Government purchases	47	85	81

PERSONAL INCOME TRENDS

Personal income under assumptions of high-level activity in 1960 would amount to $282 billion at 1950 prices. This would be substantially above any previous annual total. It would exceed the dollar income of individuals in 1946, the first postwar year, by over $100 billion and would be six times the $47 billion received by individuals in 1933, the worst depression year. Even in the boom year 1953, from which some decline has already occurred, personal income (in 1950 dollars) was less than the assumed 1960 total by 10 per cent.

Income in 1950 Dollars

Obviously the above comparisons of recent dollar totals with those of earlier years give a greatly exaggerated impression of the real change in the material status of the American people, for they fail to take into account the drastically lower purchasing power of the dollar in postwar compared with prewar years, as well as the larger number of individuals, families and households among which personal income is distributed.[6] "Correcting" the annual dollar totals by means of an index of consumer goods prices makes it

6. There is of course the further fact that income and other direct taxes will take a much larger share of personal income — and thus leave a smaller proportion of "disposable income" — than in prewar years. If all the money taken from individuals in the form of direct personal taxes were considered as a net reduction in their standard of living, it would clearly be proper to make comparisons between different years in terms of disposable income, rather than personal income. However, increased government costs, to a considerable extent, measure expanded government services, which add to consumer well-being and therefore constitute a part of the goods and services consumed by individuals.

possible to express them in dollars of 1950 purchasing power, while computing personal income on a per capita or per household basis provides a better measure of changes in consumers' well-being. Expressed in 1950 dollars, the $282 billion personal income in 1960 would be more than three times the $92 billion total at the depression low point in 1933, about $66 billion more than the World War II peak in 1944 (which was not surpassed until 1950), $55 billion above 1950, and $28 billion above 1953.

Because income and other direct taxes on individuals have been increasing much more rapidly than personal income, however, disposable income provides a better measure of the expansion in consumer purchasing power for goods and services. Disposable personal income in 1960 (measured in 1950 dollars) is estimated in excess of $255 billion. This represents an increase over the depression low point of less than 190 per cent, while personal income is estimated to increase more than 200 per cent. Compared with the war years, however, when personal taxes took a larger bite than they are likely to take in 1960, the gain in disposable income would be somewhat greater than the rise in personal income. The $255 billion total for 1960 would exceed 1944 by $64 billion, or 33 per cent (compared with 30 per cent for personal income), and 1953 by $34 billion, or 15 per cent.

If these 1960 totals are achieved, American business can look forward to a consumer market with a total purchasing power for goods and services nearly three times as large as in the worst year of the depression, one third larger than in the peak year of World War II, and nearly one fourth larger than in prosperous 1950. (See Table 30.)

Average Personal Income

Because the number of people and the number of families and households has been increasing with extraordinary rapidity during recent years, average income has grown more slowly than total income. With an estimated population of 177 million and total personal income of $282 billion in 1960, per capita personal income would be $1,590 (in 1950 dollars). This would be one third more than in 1941, which was the most prosperous year before World War II, but only slightly ahead of the $1,560 per capita income of 1944, the most prosperous World War II year.

TABLE 30. PERSONAL INCOME AND DISPOSABLE INCOME PER CAPITA AND PER HOUSEHOLD AT CURRENT AND 1950 PRICES, 1929–1960

Year	Personal Income (Billions) Current Prices	Personal Income (Billions) 1950 Prices	Disposable Personal Income (Billions) Current Prices	Disposable Personal Income (Billions) 1950 Prices	Per Capita Personal Income Current Prices	Per Capita Personal Income 1950 Prices	Per Capita Disposable Personal Income Current Prices	Per Capita Disposable Personal Income 1950 Prices	Personal Income per Household Current Prices	Personal Income per Household 1950 Prices	Disposable Personal Income per Household Current Prices	Disposable Personal Income per Household 1950 Prices
1929	$ 85.1	$120.2	$ 82.5	$116.9	$ 700	$ 990	$ 680	$ 960	$2,550	$3,780	$2,470	$3,650
1930	76.2	112.9	73.7	109.2	620	920	600	890	—	—	—	—
1931	64.8	107.3	63.0	104.3	520	870	510	840	—	—	—	—
1932	49.3	92.8	47.8	90.0	400	740	380	720	—	—	—	—
1933	46.6	91.9	45.2	89.2	370	730	360	710	—	—	—	—
1934	53.2	99.1	51.6	96.1	420	780	410	760	—	—	—	—
1935	59.9	108.9	58.0	105.5	470	860	460	830	—	—	—	—
1936	68.4	122.8	66.1	118.7	530	960	520	930	—	—	—	—
1937	74.0	128.0	71.1	123.0	570	990	555	950	—	—	—	—
1938	68.3	120.9	65.5	115.9	530	930	500	890	—	—	—	—
1939	72.6	129.6	70.2	125.4	550	990	540	960	—	—	—	—
1940	78.3	138.3	75.7	133.7	590	1,050	570	1,010	2,240	3,960	2,170	3,830
1941	95.3	158.6	92.0	153.1	710	1,190	690	1,150	—	—	—	—
1942	122.7	182.3	116.7	173.4	910	1,350	870	1,290	—	—	—	—
1943	150.3	204.8	132.4	180.4	1,100	1,500	970	1,320	—	—	—	—
1944	165.9	215.7	147.0	191.2	1,200	1,560	1,060	1,380	—	—	—	—
1945	171.9	215.4	151.1	189.3	1,230	1,540	1,080	1,350	—	—	—	—
1946	177.7	206.9	158.9	185.0	1,260	1,460	1,120	1,310	—	—	—	—
1947	191.0	202.8	169.5	179.9	1,330	1,410	1,180	1,250	4,890	5,190	4,340	4,600
1948	209.5	211.0	188.4	189.7	1,430	1,440	1,290	1,290	5,150	5,180	4,630	4,660
1949	205.9	210.1	187.2	191.0	1,380	1,410	1,260	1,280	4,890	4,990	4,450	4,540
1950	226.7	226.9	205.8	205.8	1,490	1,490	1,360	1,360	5,210	5,210	4,730	4,730
1951	254.3	237.0	225.0	209.7	1,650	1,530	1,460	1,360	5,700	5,310	5,050	4,700
1952	269.7	246.1	235.0	214.4	1,720	1,570	1,500	1,370	5,930	5,410	5,170	4,710
1953	284.5	254.0	247.9	221.3	1,780	1,590	1,550	1,390	6,130	5,480	5,340	4,770
1960	—	282.0	—	255.5	—	1,590	—	1,440	—	5,530	—	5,010

Sources: Personal income and disposable personal income, in current and 1950 dollars, from Appendix 4–2, Tables A and B; projected income in 1960 from Table 29. Per capita income obtained by dividing income figures by population figures in *Statistical Abstract of the United States, 1952*, U.S. Bureau of the Census, Tables No. 8 and 9, p. 10, and *Current Population Reports*, Series P–25, No. 86, December 15, 1953; they are not corrected for underenumeration. The population figure used to obtain the 1960 per capita income is from Table 37. Number of households, 1930–1952, *Current Population Reports*, Series P–20, No. 42; 1953 Table 29. Per capita income based on Series P–20, No. 48 with downward adjustment of 450,000 households to achieve consistency with estimates for earlier years. Number of 1960 households from Table 37.

Note: Per capita income and per household figures are rounded to nearest $10.

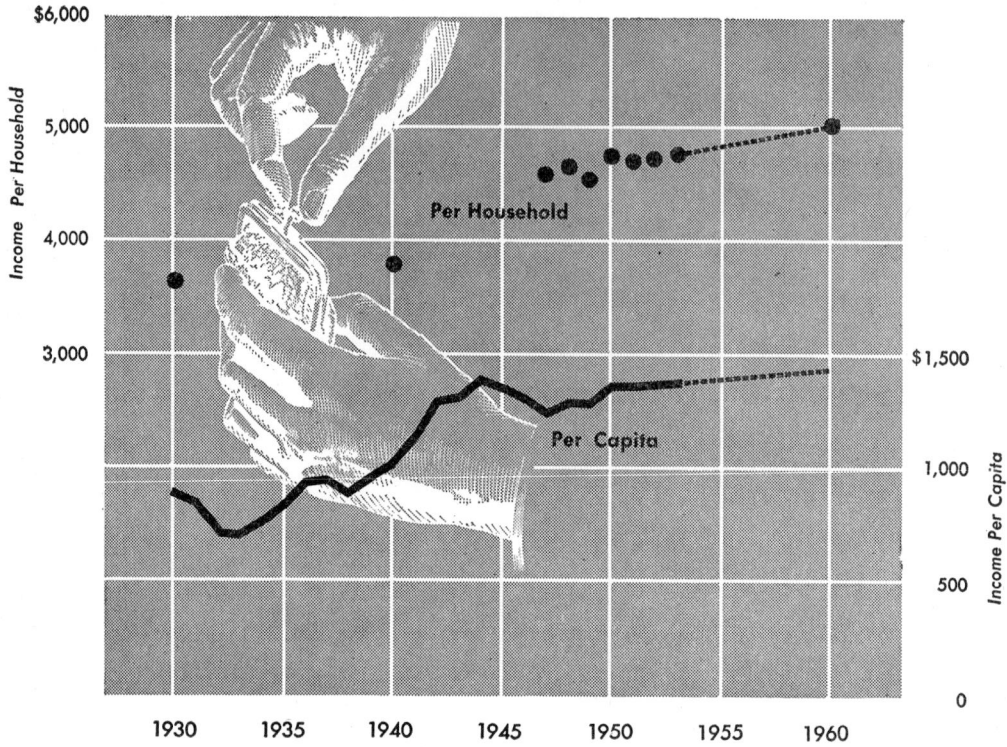

FIGURE 15. ESTIMATED DISPOSABLE PERSONAL INCOME PER CAPITA AND PER HOUSEHOLD, AT 1950 PRICES, 1930–1953, WITH PROJECTIONS TO 1960

Source: Table 30.

It would exceed 1952 per capita income by only $20 and would be no larger than in 1953. Compared with the worst years of the depression, however, estimated per capita income in 1960 would have more than doubled. (See Table 30.)

For many purposes — notably in assessing demand for housing and household furniture and equipment — the family, or the household, is a more significant unit than the individual. Households consist predominantly of families of two or more, but also include single individuals maintaining their own establishments and unrelated single individuals living together. The number of households in 1960 is estimated at 51 million. With personal income of $282 billion in that year, average income per household would amount to $5,530. This would be about *$1,500 more* per household than in 1940, *$120 above* the 1952 average and *$50 more* than the average in 1953 — all measured in dollars of 1950 purchasing power.

Between 1930 and 1960 per capita personal income (measured in 1950 dollars), according to

these estimates, would show an increase of about 73 per cent, while personal income per household would rise about 46 per cent. The difference between the two rates of gain reflects the fact that families were being formed and new households set up during this thirty-year period at a more rapid rate than population was increasing.

Average Disposable Income

Because of the marked rise in taxes since 1930, disposable personal income has been increasing less rapidly than personal income. Thus while it is estimated that per capita personal income will increase from $920 in 1930 to $1,590 in 1960, or by 73 per cent, per capita disposable income is expected to rise only from $890 to $1,440, or by 62 per cent.

Similarly, average personal income per household would increase from $3,780 in 1930 to $5,530 in 1960, or by 46 per cent, but the estimated gain in disposable income per household during the same period is only 37 per cent —

from $3,650 in 1930 to $5,010 in 1960. However, in spite of the great increase in personal taxes since the 1930s, the members of the average American household had nearly $400 a month to spend or save as they pleased in 1953, and will have well over $400 a month in 1960 — compared with only $300 a month in 1930.

Most of this advance in real income occurred during World War II, and the gain in the purchasing power of disposable income per capita and per household has not been large since the early postwar years. Indeed, per capita disposable income was actually higher in 1944 than in 1952, although below 1953 and the level projected for 1960. In 1948, disposable income per household amounted to $4,660 — only $110 less than in 1953. (See Figure 15.) What this means, of course, is that the rapid gain in total disposable income since the early postwar years has barely kept pace with increases in marriages and births and the consequent growth in number of households and in population.

DISTRIBUTION OF PERSONAL INCOME

Average income, on a per capita or per household basis, is useful in measuring trends but provides no indication of how income is distributed among families and individuals. Under certain circumstances, indeed, average income, like other averages, could give a misleading impression. An average family income of $5,000 a year might result from the existence of a substantial number of families with very high incomes, together with a heavy concentration of families at very low income levels; or it might reflect the concentration of a great majority of families at levels not far from the average. Hence the pattern of income distribution by income classes and between urban and rural consumer units, as well as the average level of income, will be an important determinant of the nature and "quality" of future consumer markets for different kinds of goods and services.

DISTRIBUTION OF CONSUMER UNITS

A comparison of the distribution of "consumer" or "spending" units by income classes in the middle of the 1930s with the distribution in recent years, it must be remembered, reflects not only a real gain in the welfare of consumers, but also a substantial rise in the general level of

prices and wages, i.e., a decline in the dollar's purchasing power.

In 1935–1936 more than two out of every five consumer units had annual incomes of less than $1,000 — in dollars of then current purchasing power — and only 3 per cent had incomes of $5,000 or over. By 1941 the proportion under $1,000 had dropped to 29 per cent, while those with more than $5,000 income had risen to 5 per cent. The proportion in the "middle class" — from $2,000 to $5,000 income — also nearly doubled during the same period. These changes chiefly reflect substantial gains in well-being, for prices had not increased much by 1941. (See Table 31.)

By 1944, only 10.7 per cent of consumer units received less than $1,000 income, while 48 per cent — compared with about 19 per cent in 1941 — had incomes in excess of $3,000. This change was attributable to a 27 per cent advance in the price level, as well as to a rise in employment and real earnings. A comparison of consumer income at the peak year of the war with more normal periods, however, lacks reality. A large proportion of the younger men were under arms, and therefore not included in this computation; prices had risen unevenly and lacked their usual significance under rationing; while many kinds of goods were wholly unavailable.

Chiefly because of continued increases in wages and prices in the postwar period, income distribution shifted further upward in 1947 and 1950. By 1947 only 8.4 per cent, and by 1950 only 7.6 per cent, of consumer units were receiving less than $1,000 annual income. The gains at the upper end of the income scale were even more striking. Almost one quarter of all consumer units had more than $5,000 income in 1947 and the proportion was nearly 30 per cent in 1950.

The outbreak of the Korean War in 1950 brought another upward surge in prices and wages, as well as a rise in employment and business activity, which were reflected in a further upward shift of income distribution. Although data that are strictly comparable with those cited above on "family personal income," which includes income in kind, are not available, the annual surveys of the *money income* of "spending units" conducted by the Federal Reserve System show closely enough what happened after 1950. By 1953 the proportions of spending units in money income categories below $4,000 declined

TABLE 31. PERCENTAGE DISTRIBUTION OF CONSUMER UNITS BY FAMILY PERSONAL INCOME CLASSES, 1935-1936, 1941, 1944, 1947 AND 1950

Income Class	Current Dollars					1950 Dollars		
	1935–1936	1941	1944	1947	1950	1935–1936	1941	1944
Total	100.0	100.0	100.0	100.0	100.0	100.0	100.0	100.0
Under $1,000	43.5	29.0	10.7	8.4	7.6	19.5	15.1	7.3
1,000–1,999	34.2	29.9	19.8	16.5	15.1	29.2	19.9	13.7
2,000–2,999	13.1	22.3	21.4	18.9	16.5	20.7	18.5	15.5
3,000–3,999	4.5	9.8	18.9	19.3	17.4	12.3	15.7	17.6
4,000–4,999	1.6	4.0	11.1	12.8	14.4	7.3	12.3	14.7
5,000–7,499	1.6	2.8	11.7	14.8	17.5	6.7	12.0	18.4
7,500–9,999	0.6	0.9	3.4	4.8	5.9	1.8	3.2	7.0
10,000 and over	0.9	1.3	3.0	4.5	5.6	2.5	3.4	5.8

Source: Selma Goldsmith, George Jaszi, Hyman Kaitz and Maurice Liebenberg, "Size Distribution of Income since the Mid-Thirties," *Review of Economics and Statistics*, February 1954, Tables 2 and 3.

without exception, while those at higher levels advanced, as the following percentage distributions indicate:

	1950	1953
Under $1,000	13	10
1,000–1,999	17	13
2,000–2,999	19	14
3,000–3,999	19	16
4,000–4,999	12	16
5,000–7,499	14	20
7,500–9,999	3	6
10,000 and over	3	5

The upward shift in the income distribution of consumer units since the mid-1930s reflects a tremendous improvement in the material well-being of American families and individuals, but part of the apparent gain is due to the fact that the dollar in 1936 bought almost twice as much as the 1950 dollar, which in turn had a somewhat smaller purchasing power than the 1953 dollar.

Income in 1950 Dollars

Even measured in dollars of constant purchasing power, however, the upward shift of income distribution has been substantial. In 1935–1936, when 43.5 per cent of all consumer units had incomes of less than $1,000 (measured in "1935–1936 dollars"), only 19.5 per cent had incomes of less than 1,000 "1950 dollars." By 1950 the proportion in the lowest income class had dropped to 7.6 per cent — and it was slightly less than this in 1944. Proportions in all income classes below $3,000 showed marked declines, while those in the upper income groups increased sharply. (See Figure 16.)

In 1950, twice as large a percentage had incomes of $3,000 and above as in 1935–1936 — 61 per cent compared with 31 per cent. Even in 1941 only 47 per cent of all consumer units enjoyed incomes with a 1950 purchasing power of $3,000 or more. By 1953, as pointed out above, there was a further gain in average income and another upward shift in income distribution, measured in current dollars. Although prices had advanced about 12 per cent above the mid-1950 level, there was probably also a slight further upward shift in the income distribution of consumer units measured in 1950 dollars.

Income in Kind

Certain considerations should be kept in mind in appraising the position of those at the lowest, as well as at the upper, income levels. The tabulation in Table 31 includes income in kind: the imputed rent of farmhouses, food and fuel produced by farmers for their own consumption, board and lodging received by farm workers and domestic servants, etc. The value of such income in kind is often understated, and rarely overstated, and this form of income is particularly important in the case of those at lower income levels. The result is to understate somewhat the actual income received by the low income groups and their purchasing power for other kinds of goods than housing, food and

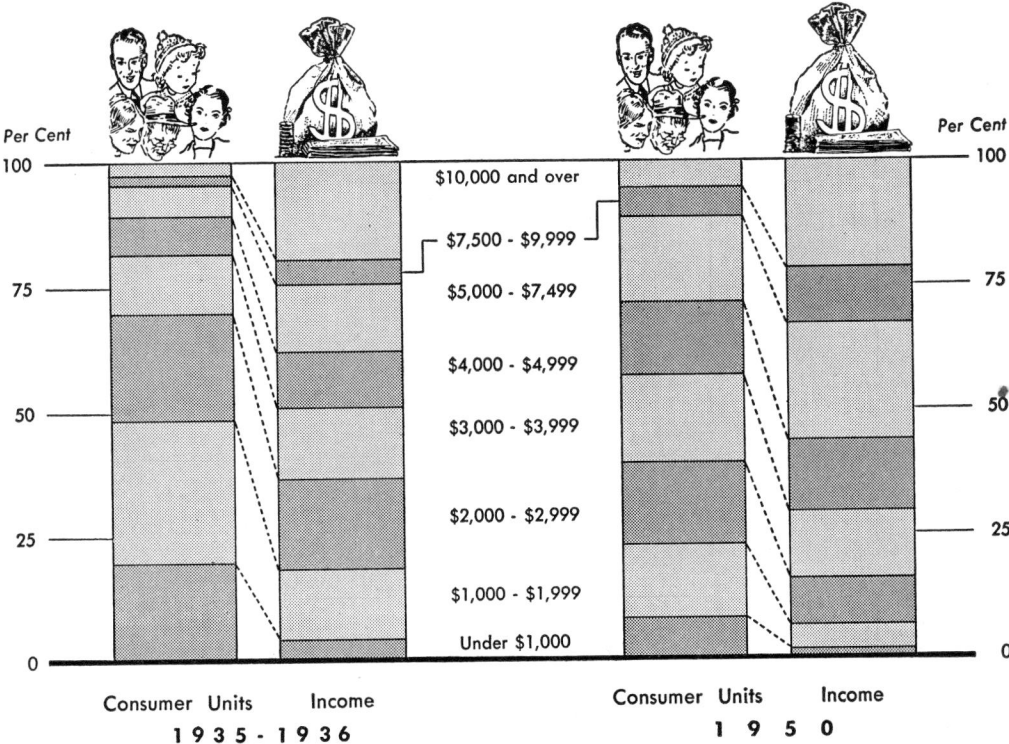

FIGURE 16. DISTRIBUTION OF CONSUMER UNITS AND FAMILY PERSONAL INCOME AT 1950 PRICES, BY FAMILY
PERSONAL INCOME LEVEL, 1935–1936 AND 1950

Source: Selma Goldsmith, George Jaszi, Hyman Kaitz and Maurice Liebenberg, "Size Distribution of Income since
the Mid-Thirties," *Review of Economics and Statistics,* February 1954, Table 2, p. 4.

fuel. Furthermore, these groups include a larger proportion of young people just graduating from school and others not employed for the entire year, who are, however, classified on the basis of their earnings for only part of the year.

Effects of Taxes

At the other extreme, progressive income taxes and other personal taxes cut most heavily into the incomes of those in the higher income classes. For example, consumer units with less than $4,000 of personal income in 1950 received 29 per cent of all personal income but paid less than 14 per cent of aggregate federal individual income taxes collected in that year, while consumer units in the $10,000-and-over personal income group received less than 22 per cent of total personal income but paid about 48 per cent of federal income taxes paid by individuals.[7]

7. See *Income Distribution in the United States,* U.S. Department of Commerce, 1953, Exhibit 21, p. 76; and

This means, of course, that the distribution of consumer units on the basis of "income after federal income taxes" will show a larger proportion at the lower levels and a smaller percentage at the upper levels. Thus, 60 per cent of all consumer units had less than $4,000 income after taxes in 1950, compared with less than 57 per cent before taxes, while 11.5 per cent had incomes of $7,500 or more before paying taxes and only 9.3 per cent had incomes of this size after taxes.[8]

"Size Distribution of Income since the Mid-Thirties," by Selma Goldsmith, George Jaszi, Hyman Kaitz and Maurice Liebenberg, *Review of Economics and Statistics,* February 1954. The figures cited above are not strictly comparable, since the tax percentages are computed on the basis of family *money* income levels and the income distribution is on the basis of *total* family personal income. The contrast between income tax burdens at upper and lower income levels would be even greater if data were available on a strictly comparable basis.

8. See *Income Distribution in the United States,* Tables 19 and 20, p. 85, for income distribution of consumer units after taxes.

TABLE 32. ESTIMATED DISTRIBUTION OF URBAN AND RURAL CONSUMER
UNITS [a] BY MONEY INCOME AFTER TAXES,[b] 1950 AND 1960

(At 1950 Prices)

Income Class	Urban 1950	Urban 1960	Rural Nonfarm 1950	Rural Nonfarm 1960	Rural Farm 1950	Rural Farm 1960
	Per Cent of Consumer Units					
Total	100.0	100.0	100.0	100.0	100.0	100.0
Under $1,000	8.9	8.5	13.2	12.5	22.7	19.4
1,000–1,999	14.2	13.3	17.3	16.1	24.4	21.0
2,000–2,999	16.5	15.3	19.2	18.0	19.2	18.5
3,000–3,999	18.3	17.6	17.8	17.6	14.6	15.1
4,000–4,999	15.2	15.4	12.5	13.2	7.7	10.2
5,000–5,999	9.5	10.0	7.3	7.6	3.6	5.3
6,000–7,499	7.7	9.2	5.8	7.1	2.9	4.0
7,500–9,999	5.6	6.1	4.0	4.5	2.6	3.2
10,000 and over	4.0	4.7	2.9	3.5	2.3	3.3
	Per Cent of Money Income after Taxes					
Total	100.0	100.0	100.0	100.0	100.0	100.0
Under $1,000	.9	.8	1.4	1.3	2.3	1.4
1,000–1,999	5.2	4.6	7.3	6.5	13.4	9.9
2,000–2,999	10.0	8.8	13.5	12.0	17.4	14.6
3,000–3,999	15.4	14.1	17.4	16.2	18.5	16.6
4,000–4,999	16.4	15.8	15.6	15.6	12.6	14.4
5,000–5,999	12.4	12.4	11.1	11.0	7.2	9.1
6,000–7,499	12.4	14.0	10.8	12.4	7.1	8.4
7,500–9,999	11.5	11.8	9.5	10.0	8.0	8.6
10,000 and over	15.7	17.6	13.3	15.1	13.5	17.0

Source: Derived from Appendix 4–3.

a. "Consumer units" as used here differs slightly from the term as used in Tables 22 and 27; here, subfamilies (i.e., family units related to the head of the main family in multi-family households) are not counted as separate consumer units but are included with the main family.

b. Money income excludes noncash items such as the imputed rent of owner-occupied homes and food and lodging received as wages. The taxes deducted are personal taxes such as federal and state income taxes and state and local personal property (not real estate) and poll taxes.

MONEY INCOME DISTRIBUTION IN 1950 AND 1960

Although the distribution of consumer units on the basis of *total* family personal income provides a satisfactory indication of the diffusion of material welfare, a distribution in terms of disposable income, or money income after taxes, provides a better measure of consumer spending power for goods and services bought in the market place.

Income distributions in terms of all consumer or spending units conceal important differences between families and single individuals, and between city dwellers and those living in the country and on farms. These differences are clear from Table 32, which shows the percentage of urban, rural nonfarm and farm consumer units in each money-income-after-taxes class and the percentage of money income after taxes received by each of these classes. Data for 1950 are supplemented by estimates for 1960, on assumptions of high-level employment and business activity in that year. (See Appendix 4–3.)

Less than 9 per cent of all urban families and individuals had money incomes after taxes in 1950 of less than $1,000, compared with more than 13 per cent of rural nonfarm consumer units, and nearly 23 per cent of farm units. This is money income only; a comparison that took into account income in kind would be more favorable to the rural nonfarm and farm groups.

At the upper end of the income range, nearly 27 per cent of the urban units had more than $5,000 left after taxes, and nearly 10 per cent had $7,500 or more. These proportions dropped to 20 per cent and 6.9 per cent for rural nonfarm consumer units and to 11.4 per cent and 4.9 per cent for rural farm consumer units. The heaviest concentration of urban consumer units was in the $3,000–$3,999 income class, which accounted for 18.3 per cent of the total; in the case of rural nonfarm units the $2,000–$2,999 class accounted for the largest proportion, 19.2 per cent; while the largest group of farm units, 24.4 per cent, was in the $1,000–$1,999 class.

The larger total of money income assumed in this study for 1960 results in a further upward shift of consumer units among income classes. Thus the proportion of urban consumer units in the "under $4,000" income classes declines and the proportion above that level increases. The same is true of rural nonfarm consumer units, while for the rural farm consumer units the dividing line would be $3,000 instead of $4,000. Particularly heavy increases occur for those at the upper income levels. The proportion of urban units with more than $5,000 money income left after taxes would increase from 26.8 per cent in 1950 to 30 per cent in 1960; of rural nonfarm units from 20 per cent to 22.7 per cent; and of farm units from 11.4 to 15.8 per cent.

CONSUMER MARKETS IN 1950 AND 1960

The urban market for consumption goods and services will obviously continue to be far more important than the rural market, not only because there are many more urban than rural consumers, but also because their money incomes are much higher. Of all consumer units — numbering 48.8 million in 1950 and 54.9 million in 1960 — slightly over two thirds are urban, and less than one third live on farms or in other rural territory. (There is a slight difference in timing and concept between consumer units here and in Table 37, as explained in Appendix 4–3, footnote a.) Urban families of two or more persons alone account for more than 50 per cent of all consumer units, both in 1950 and in the projections for 1960. (See Appendix 4–3.)

In terms of aggregate spending power, moreover, the urban preponderance is much greater than in numbers. The urban consumer units had an average disposable income of $4,150 in 1950 and would have $4,370 in 1960 according to the assumptions of this survey. These amounts compare with $3,570 in 1950 and $3,775 in 1960

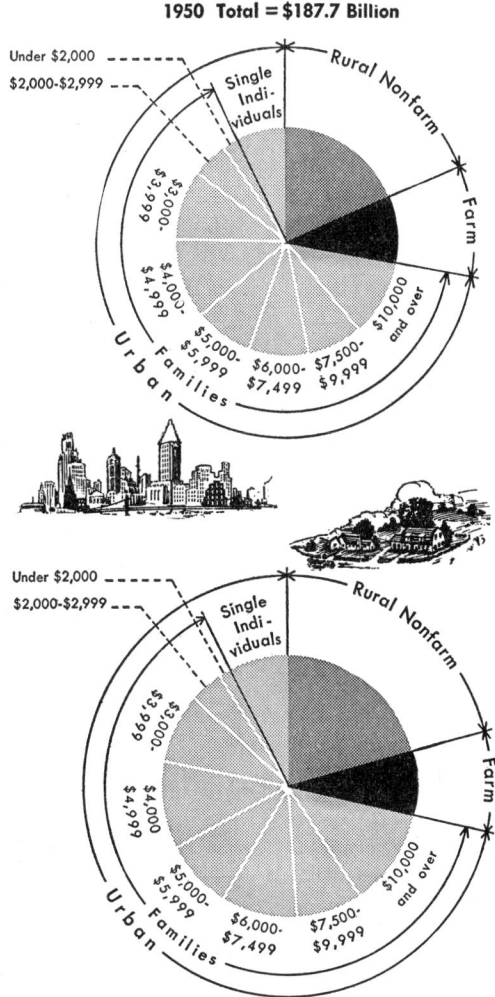

FIGURE 17. DISTRIBUTION OF ESTIMATED CASH INCOME AFTER TAXES OF URBAN AND RURAL CONSUMER UNITS, AT 1950 PRICES, 1950 AND 1960

Source: Appendix 4–3.

for rural nonfarm units, and with $2,731 and $3,161, respectively, for farm consumer units. Thus not only do urban consumer units outnumber rural by more than two to one, but their average purchasing power for goods and services is considerably greater.

Of total income after taxes, estimated at about $226 billion in 1960, urban consumers will receive $162 billion, or about 72 per cent. The proportion was about the same in 1950. (See Figure 17.) Single individuals in urban communities will receive only $16.5 billion, or 10 per cent of

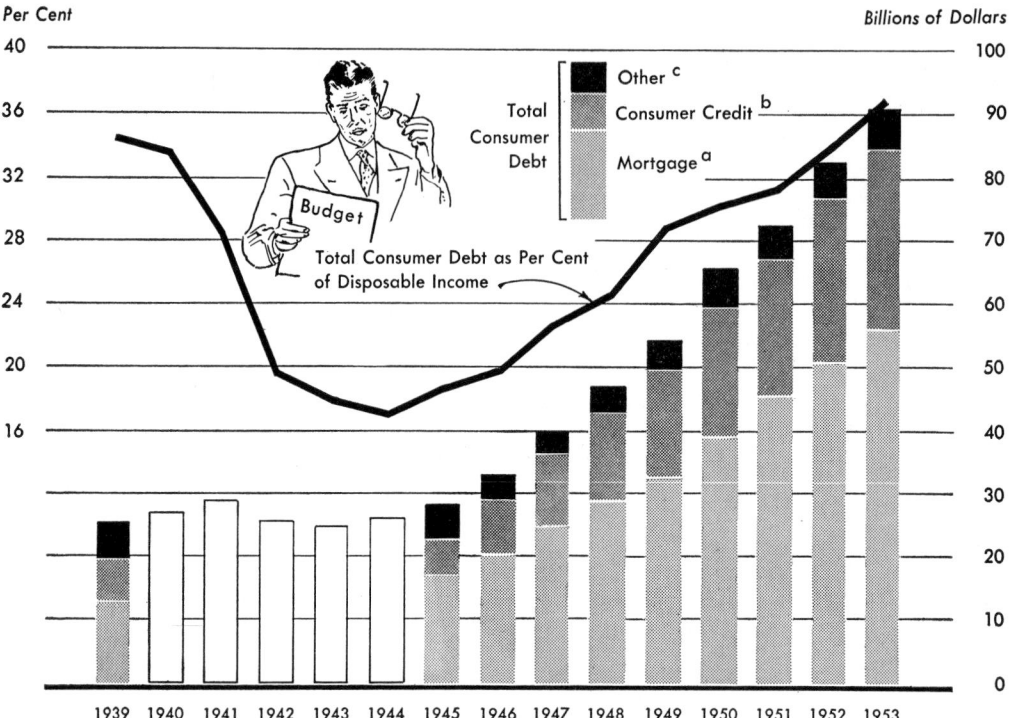

FIGURE 18. CONSUMER DEBT AND RATIO OF CONSUMER DEBT TO DISPOSABLE PERSONAL INCOME, 1939–1953

Source: Unpublished memorandum from Board of Governors of the Federal Reserve System.

a. Estimated debt on owner-occupied properties only; excludes real estate debt owed by landlords and builders.
b. Includes instalment credit, charge accounts, single-payment loans and service credit.
c. Includes security loans to banks, brokers and dealers, and policy loans.

total urban income in 1960, while the $145 billion of disposable income to be received by families of two or more alone accounts for nearly two thirds of the total disposable income of all consumer units in the nation.

The predominance of urban income, especially at upper income levels, is illustrated by the fact that the 7.2 million urban families with disposable incomes of $6,000 or more will have an aggregate income after taxes in 1960 in excess of $68 billion, which is several billion dollars more than the estimated total disposable income of all rural farm and nonfarm consumer units. The richest consumer market of the future, even more than today, will be the urban market of middle and upper incomes. Yesterday's luxury market is today's and tomorrow's mass market.

CONSUMER SAVINGS AND DEBT

By the end of World War II consumers had accumulated an unprecedented amount of liquid savings which were a powerful influence in translating the "backlog of shortages" that had been built up during the war into market demand during the postwar years. In addition consumer instalment debt had declined sharply during the war years, chiefly because of the virtual disappearance from the market of costly household durable goods usually bought on credit. Total consumer indebtedness also declined somewhat after 1941, while the ratio of consumer debt to disposable personal income had, by 1944, fallen to less than half what it was just before the war. (See Figure 18.)

Savings

For the same reasons that caused the decline in the use of consumer credit, personal savings rose to an unprecedented volume, both in terms of the dollar total saved and in relation to the disposable income of individuals. In the year

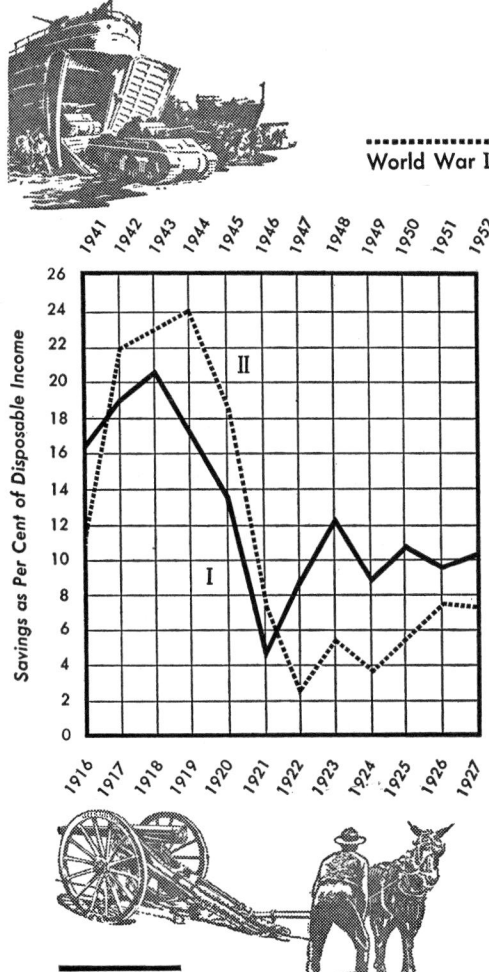

FIGURE 19. PERSONAL SAVINGS AS PER CENT OF
DISPOSABLE PERSONAL INCOME DURING AND AFTER
WORLD WARS I AND II

Source: Appendix 4–2, Table A.

The situation is far different today. Personal savings dropped steeply from $28 billion in 1945 to less than $4 billion in 1947. In that year they constituted only 2.3 per cent of disposable income, compared with 24 per cent in 1944. Since 1947 the volume of personal savings has risen irregularly until it amounted to $18.1 billion, or 7.6 per cent of disposable income, in 1953. The rise and decline in the proportion of income that consumers saved was similar in the World War I and World War II periods, although much more pronounced in the second war, which cost much more and lasted longer than the first. (See Figure 19.)

While savings were dropping off from the record levels of World War II, consumer indebtedness, especially instalment debt, was increasing markedly. By the end of 1952 total consumer debt exceeded $82 billion — three times what it was at the end of 1945, which in turn was above the low point of $24.5 billion reached in 1943. Instalment debt increased from $2.5 billion at the end of 1945 to $21.8 billion at the end of 1953 — more than eightfold; while mortgage debt, which normally accounts for almost two thirds of all consumer indebtedness, increased from $16.7 billion to $55.9 billion. Total consumer indebtedness at the end of 1953 reached the record high of $91.3 billion, which was well over three times what it was at the end of World War II. (See Figure 18.)

Although disposable personal income has increased steadily and rapidly during the postwar years, the increase in consumer debt has been even greater. At the end of 1944 the $26 billion of consumer debt outstanding was about one sixth as large as that year's disposable income. By the end of 1953 disposable income had increased about 70 per cent, but total consumer indebtedness was about three and a half times as large. Thus the ratio of consumer debt to disposable income was more than twice as high — 36.6 per cent against 17.1 per cent. Even after this spectacular rise, however, the 1953 percentage was not far above the prewar ratio of 34.4 per cent at the end of 1939. In other words, in spite of substantially larger indebtedness, consumer incomes had increased so rapidly that consumers were not much more heavily committed than on the eve of World War II.

1944 alone, for example, individuals laid aside more than $35 billion — almost one dollar out of every four they had left after paying direct taxes. (See Table 29.) As a result of this abnormally heavy wartime saving, consumers came to the end of World War II with more than $90 billion of *surplus savings* accumulated during the 1941–1945 period alone.[9]

---

9. See Appendix 4–2. Personal savings aggregated $129 billion during 1941–1945. On the assumption that personal savings normally amount to 5 per cent of personal income as assumed in this survey, "normal" personal savings for the 1941–1945 period would aggregate only $35 billion.

Liquidity

Although the "burden" of consumers' debts is most appropriately measured by comparing them with disposable income, the liquid position of individuals can best be indicated by comparing their liquid assets with their debts. Consumers have of course continued to save in the years since the end of World War II — though at a much lower rate than during the war — and their assets have continued to grow. Since 1945, however, the liquid assets of individuals have increased much less rapidly than debts have increased, and since 1946 the rise in liquid assets has failed to keep pace with the gain in disposable income.

The ratio of the liquid assets of individuals to the sum of mortgage and consumer credit and to personal disposable income in selected years since 1929 has been as follows: [10]

Year	Credit	Income
1929	2.05	66.4
1933	2.36	98.9
1937	2.46	75.6
1940	2.40	78.8
1945	7.86	115.4
1946	6.33	122.5
1947	5.12	118.8
1948	4.27	108.1
1949	3.75	109.2
1950	3.18	100.9
1951	2.96	94.9
1952	2.70	94.7

These comparisons show that the liquid position of individuals has slipped sharply from what was obviously an abnormal degree of liquidity immediately after the end of World War II. In spite of this decline, however, individuals at the end of 1952 were in a more liquid position in relation to debt than in the years before the war, while the ratio of liquid assets to disposable income was higher than in any of the prewar years shown above except at the pit of the depression in 1933.

The trends in consumers' savings and indebtedness in relation to the rising volume of disposable income and in the relation of their liquid assets to their indebtedness and income make it clear that the position of consumers at the end of 1953 was far different from what it was at the end of World War II. With the ratio of con-sumer debt to income at a record low, with individuals having larger savings and in a more liquid position than ever before, and with a vast amount of unfilled needs for durable and other goods, consumers were then in a position to underwrite and virtually guarantee the postwar boom that has since occurred. Today the "catching-up period" is certainly over, and the financial position of consumers as measured by the relation of their assets and debts to each other and to income is much closer to a historical "normal" than at any time since World War II began.

CONSUMPTION EXPENDITURES

Average income and income distribution, and the liquid assets and borrowing capacity of consumers, are perhaps the most important determinants of how they have spent their money in the past and how they will do so in the future. However, other factors, such as population growth, price fluctuations, the introduction of new products and the decline of old ones, changes in technology and in styles and tastes, consumers' expectations about the future, have a powerful influence on the pattern of consumption expenditure. Some of these influences, such as the growth in the size of the total population, are obviously slowly changing long-term trends. The effects of other factors, such as the successful introduction of a new product like the personal helicopter, or sudden price changes, must be highly speculative and unpredictable.

INCOME-ELASTICITY OF DEMAND

One factor of pervasive significance in determining changing consumption patterns is the varying sensitivity of different classes of expenditure to changes in consumer income. It is common knowledge, of course, that when a family moves from a lower to a higher income level it will spend less of the increase on necessities with which it was already well supplied, and more on luxuries that it could not previously afford. This was recognized a century ago by the German statistician Ernst Engel. On the basis of a study of Belgian family budgets he observed that "as the income of a family increases, a smaller percentage is spent for food," and "a constantly increasing percentage is expended for education, health, recreations, amusements and so forth." [11]

---

10. Figures for 1929–1949 based largely on data in R. W. Goldsmith, *A Study of Saving in the United States,* Vol. I, Princeton University Press, 1954; later estimates are unpublished data from the Federal Reserve Board.

11. Quoted from William A. Berridge, Emma A. Winslow and Richard A. Flinn, *Purchasing Power of the Consumer,* A. W. Shaw Company, New York, 1925, p. 168.

Thus many of the goods and services bought by consumers, particularly staple articles of food and clothing, fuel and household necessities, meet with a fairly steady demand in good times and bad. At the other extreme, the demand for automobiles and other costly durable goods, expensive fur coats and vacation trips abroad is extremely sensitive to changes in consumer income.

The Department of Commerce has made interesting studies of the sensitivity of a large number of separate items of consumption expenditure to changes in disposable personal income over the 1929–1940 period. This analysis classified all expenditure items into three "income-elasticity groups," according to the percentage increase in expenditure associated with a given percentage increase in disposable income — "all other factors affecting the expenditure assumed to remain constant."

For consumption expenditures *as a whole* it was found that a change of 8 per cent accompanied a change of 10 per cent in disposable income. Items of expenditure that rose or fell less than 8 per cent with a 10 per cent rise or fall in disposable income were classified as "insensitive." Expenditures that changed more than 8 per cent but less than 12 per cent with a 10 per cent change in disposable income were classified as "somewhat sensitive," and those changing more than 12 per cent were classified in the "sensitive" group. (The detailed data on which this section is based are shown in Appendix 4–6.)

About one third of the $218 billion spent by consumers in 1952 was paid for items which, on the basis of 1929–1940 experience, were insensitive to changes in disposable income. Less than half as much — or under one sixth of the total — was spent for sensitive items, while one half of the total expenditure went for goods and services in the "somewhat sensitive" class. (See Figure 20.)

There have been striking differences in the behavior of these three groups during the years of deflation, depression, recovery and boom since 1929. Expenditures for the sensitive items dropped by 64 per cent from 1929 to 1933, as compared with a drop of 44 per cent for the somewhat sensitive group and only 27 per cent for the insensitive items. During the years of irregular recovery from 1933 to 1941 the gain for the sensitive group was 146 per cent, for the somewhat sensitive items 102 per cent, and for the

the insensitive expenditures only 41 per cent. The tremendous advance in dollar totals during the war and postwar boom reflected steeply rising prices as well as an expanding volume of consumer buying. By 1952, expenditures for items sensitive to income changes had risen 178 per cent above the 1941 level. The gain for the somewhat sensitive group was almost as large — 176 per cent. The insensitive group increased 143 per cent. These changes, it must be remembered, are measured in current dollars and therefore reflect variations in price as well as in quantities purchased.

As might be expected, expenditures that are insensitive to income changes represent the more compelling needs — housing, fuel and household utilities, drugs and hospital care, education and the like; while the sensitive expenditures are more largely for deferrable and luxury purchases such as household mechanical appliances, automobiles and recreation. This relationship is by no means consistent, however, for virtually all of the ten major categories of consumption expenditures include some items at each of the three levels of sensitivity.

Thus the food, liquor and tobacco group consists predominantly of the "middle group" of items which are somewhat sensitive to income changes, but tobacco products and smoking supplies — though not necessary to life — are insensitive. Meals served in clubs and in dining cars account for the very small proportion of sensitive items in this group.

The clothing, accessories and personal care group also shows a wide distribution, although more than 80 per cent of these expenditures are somewhat sensitive to income changes. In the insensitive class, however, are shoe repair and the services of barber shops and beauty parlors. Purchases of jewelry and watches, as might be expected, are sensitive to income changes, as is the cleaning, repair and storage of garments and furs.

Because of the necessitous nature of housing expenditures, as well as the relative inflexibility of rents and of other housing costs such as fuel, ice, electricity, gas and water, nearly all of the expenditures for items in this category were insensitive to income changes. Indeed, housing and utilities were responsible for about 40 per cent of the $75 billion total of insensitive consumption expenditures.

The household equipment and operation

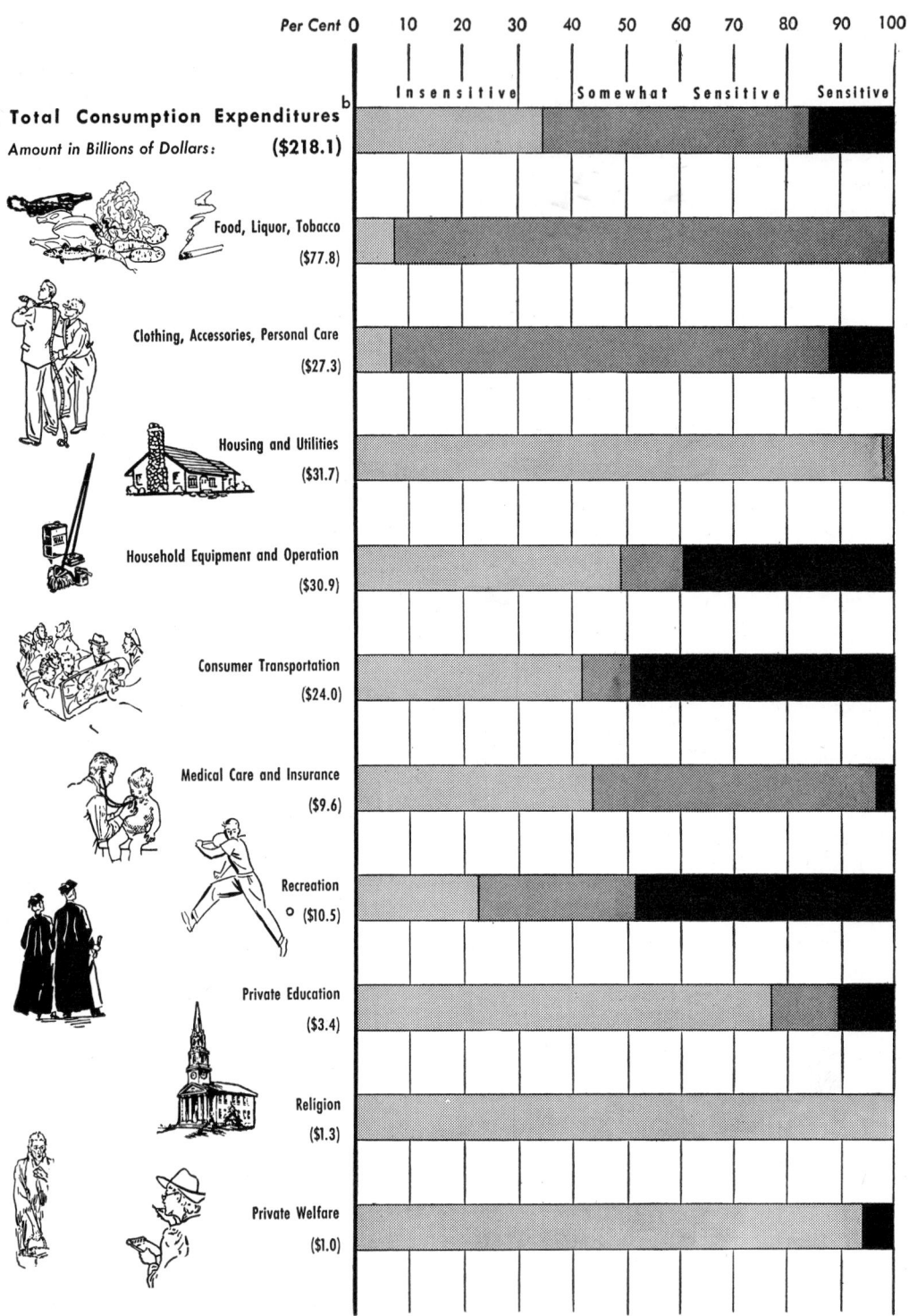

FIGURE 20. PERCENTAGE DISTRIBUTION OF CONSUMPTION EXPENDITURES IN 1952 ACCORDING TO SENSITIVITY TO CHANGES IN DISPOSABLE PERSONAL INCOME [a]

Source: Appendix 4–6.

a. Sensitivity based on relationship of expenditures to disposable personal income during the period 1929–1940.
b. Total includes Occupational and Miscellaneous Expenses, not shown separately in the chart.

group includes a wide range of items at each level of sensitivity, but with nearly one half in the insensitive category and almost 40 per cent at the sensitive level. Purchases of china, glassware and utensils, and payments for interest, for financial and legal services, for telephone services and for insurance and burial and cemetery services are insensitive to income changes. At the other extreme, consumer expenditures for furniture and floor coverings, for refrigerators, household electrical appliances and heating equipment, and also for domestic service, are sensitive to income changes.

Among the insensitive items in the consumer transportation group are such "inescapable" costs as local and commutation fares on railroads, ferries and local and intercity buses, bridge and tunnel tolls, and expenditures for gasoline and oil. Also included among insensitive expenditures are expenditures for foreign travel. Somewhat sensitive are expenditures for repair, storage and rental of automobiles and for airline travel. Most important of the sensitive items — more than one half of the total — are purchases of new and used cars, of automobile parts and accessories and of tires and tubes. Spending for railroad travel (other than commutation), for taxicab hire and for luggage is also sensitive to income changes.

The most important items in the medical care and health insurance group are in the somewhat sensitive and insensitive classes, which together account for nearly 96 per cent of total expenditures in this group. Only a few items, such as employment of practical nurses and group hospital and health payments, are sensitive. Insensitive to income changes are purchases of drug preparations and payments for the services of hospitals and trained nurses.

The distribution of expenditures in the recreation group offers little comfort to the moralist, for many items which might appear to be readily dispensable luxuries are found — as are tobacco and beauty parlor services — in the insensitive category. Admissions to motion-picture theaters, to college and professional football games and to horse and dog racetracks are all insensitive to income changes. Expenditures for magazines, newspapers and sheet music, and fees to camps and organizations are also insensitive.

Among the more important sensitive expenditures in the recreation group are purchases of radios, phonographs and musical instruments, of toys and sports equipment, of flowers and potted plants, of books and maps, and gambling expenditures on coin machines and for pari-mutuel betting. Somewhat sensitive to income changes are expenditures at photographic studios, dues and fees of athletic and social clubs, and expenditures for miscellaneous commercial amusements and for golf course fees.

Most of the expenditures for private education are insensitive to income changes. These include fees paid for higher education and to secondary and elementary schools, expenditures for periodicals and for museums and libraries, and foundation expenditure for education and research.

All of the consumer expenditures for religion and more than 94 per cent of private welfare expenditures are insensitive to income changes. The largest welfare items are contributions to social welfare and foreign-relief agencies, accounting for nearly three fourths of the total, and personal remittances to foreign countries, accounting for about one fifth of the total. None of the private welfare expenditures is in the somewhat sensitive class and only one — contributions to political organizations — is classified as sensitive to income changes.

CONSUMPTION EXPENDITURE TRENDS

Study of the actual trends in consumption expenditures over the past generation tends to confirm in a general way the results of the foregoing analysis of the sensitivity of demand for various consumption goods to changes in disposable income.

Consumption expenditure trends appear to support the conclusion that as consumers' incomes increase they tend to spend a smaller proportion on traditional necessities and a larger share on new products and luxuries. Since 1909, the first year for which reliable estimates are available, total consumption expenditures have increased from $28.8 billion to $218 billion (in 1952); on a per capita basis they increased from roughly $320 to $1,400. Two major price inflations occurred during this 43-year period, however, so that the actual increase in the physical volume of goods and services purchased by consumers was much smaller than the gain in dollar expenditures. Measured in dollars of 1950 purchasing power, total consumption expenditures in 1909 amounted to $75.8 billion instead of $28.8 billion. This means that the "real increase"

TABLE 33. CONSUMPTION EXPENDITURES BY MAJOR GROUPS, 1909–1952

Year	Total[a]	Food, Liquor and Tobacco	Clothing, Accessories and Personal Care	Housing and Utilities	Household Equipment and Operation	Consumer Transportation	Medical Care and Insurance	Recreation	Education (Private)	Religion	Welfare (Private)
					Amount (Billions, at Current Prices)						
1909	$ 28.8	$ 9.8	$ 4.3	$ 6.9	$ 3.4	$ 1.5	$ .8	$ .9	$ .4	$ .3	$ .5
1914	33.4	11.7	4.7	7.9	3.7	2.1	.9	1.0	.5	.3	.5
1919	60.6	22.0	9.6	10.2	7.3	4.9	2.1	2.2	.8	.6	.8
1921	55.8	16.8	9.3	12.3	6.7	4.8	1.5	2.1	.7	.6	.8
1923	66.6	19.1	11.1	13.8	9.0	6.5	2.2	2.6	.8	.7	.6
1925	71.8	21.1	11.0	14.2	10.0	7.6	2.5	2.8	.9	.8	.5
1927	74.6	21.7	11.8	14.4	11.0	7.2	2.7	3.1	1.0	.8	.6
1929	80.8	23.4	11.9	14.5	13.3	8.0	3.0	3.8	1.2	.9	.6
1930	72.4	21.1	10.4	14.1	11.0	6.6	2.9	3.5	1.1	.9	.6
1931	62.5	17.6	8.9	13.1	9.5	5.3	2.6	2.9	1.1	.8	.5
1932	50.1	13.6	6.6	11.6	7.6	4.2	2.2	2.1	.9	.7	.4
1933	46.3	12.8	5.9	10.5	7.3	4.1	2.0	1.9	.8	.7	.4
1934	51.9	15.6	7.1	10.3	7.8	4.7	2.2	2.1	.8	.6	.3
1935	56.2	17.7	7.6	10.4	8.5	5.4	2.3	2.3	.9	.6	.4
1936	62.5	20.0	8.3	10.9	9.7	6.3	2.5	2.6	1.0	.6	.4
1937	67.1	21.6	8.8	11.5	10.5	6.7	2.7	2.9	1.1	.6	.4
1938	64.5	20.7	8.7	11.7	9.8	5.8	2.7	2.8	1.1	.7	.4
1939	67.5	21.1	9.2	12.1	10.4	6.5	2.9	3.0	1.1	.7	.4
1940	72.1	22.6	9.7	12.7	11.1	7.1	3.1	3.3	1.1	.7	.5
1941	82.3	26.5	11.5	13.5	12.6	8.4	3.4	3.7	1.2	.7	.4
1942	91.1	32.8	14.3	14.6	12.7	5.6	3.9	4.2	1.4	.7	.6
1943	102.2	37.9	17.8	15.4	13.0	6.1	4.4	4.2	1.7	.7	.8
1944	111.6	41.5	19.7	16.1	14.1	6.7	4.9	4.8	1.7	.8	1.0
1945	123.1	45.9	22.0	16.8	15.7	8.2	5.1	5.4	1.8	.8	.9
1946	146.9	53.7	24.3	18.0	20.3	12.1	6.2	7.9	2.1	.8	1.0
1947	165.6	60.5	25.0	20.4	24.0	15.5	6.9	8.7	2.4	.9	1.0
1948	177.9	63.9	26.0	22.9	25.9	17.6	7.5	8.9	2.6	1.0	1.0
1949	180.6	63.1	24.8	24.4	25.7	20.2	7.8	9.2	2.8	1.1	.9

1950	194.6	65.6	25.0	27.2	29.1	23.5	8.4	10.2	3.0	1.1	.9
1951	208.1	73.7	26.6	29.3	30.0	23.3	9.0	10.2	3.2	1.2	.9
1952	218.1	77.8	27.3	31.7	30.9	24.0	9.6	10.5	3.4	1.3	1.0
Percentage Distribution											
1909	100.0	34.0	14.9	24.0	11.8	5.2	2.8	3.0	1.4	1.0	1.8
1914	100.0	35.0	14.1	23.6	11.1	6.4	2.7	3.0	1.5	.9	1.6
1919	100.0	36.3	15.8	16.9	12.1	8.1	3.4	3.6	1.2	1.0	1.4
1921	100.0	30.1	16.7	22.1	12.1	8.6	2.8	3.7	1.3	1.1	1.4
1923	100.0	28.7	16.7	20.7	13.5	9.8	3.3	3.9	1.2	1.0	.9
1925	100.0	29.5	15.4	19.8	14.0	10.6	3.5	4.0	1.3	1.1	.7
1927	100.0	29.2	15.8	19.4	14.7	9.6	3.6	4.2	1.4	1.1	.8
1929	100.0	28.9	14.8	18.0	16.4	9.9	3.7	4.8	1.5	1.1	.7
1930	100.0	29.2	14.4	19.5	15.2	9.1	4.0	4.9	1.6	1.2	.8
1931	100.0	28.1	14.3	21.0	15.2	8.5	4.2	4.6	1.8	1.3	.8
1932	100.0	27.2	13.3	23.2	15.2	8.4	4.3	4.2	1.8	1.5	.8
1933	100.0	27.6	12.8	22.6	15.7	8.9	4.4	4.0	1.8	1.4	.7
1934	100.0	30.1	13.7	19.9	15.1	9.1	4.3	4.0	1.6	1.2	.6
1935	100.0	31.5	13.5	18.6	15.1	9.6	4.1	4.0	1.6	1.1	.7
1936	100.0	32.0	13.3	17.5	15.5	10.1	4.1	4.2	1.5	1.0	.6
1937	100.0	32.2	13.1	17.1	15.7	10.1	4.1	4.4	1.6	1.0	.6
1938	100.0	32.0	13.5	18.2	15.1	9.0	4.2	4.4	1.6	1.0	.6
1939	100.0	31.2	13.6	17.9	15.4	9.6	4.3	4.4	1.6	1.0	.6
1940	100.0	31.4	13.5	17.6	15.4	9.9	4.3	4.5	1.6	.9	.6
1941	100.0	32.2	14.0	16.5	15.3	10.2	4.1	4.5	1.5	.8	.5
1942	100.0	36.0	15.7	16.1	14.0	6.2	4.3	4.6	1.5	.7	.6
1943	100.0	37.1	17.4	15.0	12.8	5.9	4.3	4.1	1.7	.7	.8
1944	100.0	37.2	17.6	14.4	12.7	6.0	4.4	4.3	1.5	.7	.9
1945	100.0	37.3	17.9	13.7	12.7	6.6	4.2	4.4	1.4	.6	.8
1946	100.0	36.6	16.5	12.3	13.9	8.3	4.2	5.4	1.4	.6	.7
1947	100.0	36.5	15.1	12.3	14.5	9.4	4.2	5.2	1.5	.5	.5
1948	100.0	35.9	14.6	12.9	14.6	9.9	4.2	5.0	1.5	.6	.5
1949	100.0	35.0	13.7	13.5	14.2	11.2	4.3	5.1	1.6	.6	.5
1950	100.0	33.7	12.8	14.0	14.9	12.1	4.3	5.2	1.5	.6	.5
1951	100.0	35.4	12.8	14.1	14.4	11.2	4.3	4.9	1.5	.6	.5
1952	100.0	35.6	12.5	14.6	14.2	11.0	4.4	4.8	1.6	.6	.5

Sources: Appendices 4–4 and 4–5. See Appendix 4–4 for subgroups and individual expenditure items; minor differences in individual items between this summary table and tables appearing elsewhere are due to problems of rounding.

a. Includes occupational and miscellaneous expenses, not shown separately.

in purchases between 1909 and 1952 was 163 per cent instead of 650 per cent. On a per capita basis the increase was from $840 in 1909 to $1,400 in 1952, or 66 per cent.

All of the ten major groups of consumption goods and services, each of which is discussed separately in a subsequent chapter of this report, shared in this broad advance. Relative gains varied widely, however, as can be seen from the following tabulation showing percentage gains (measured in current dollars) between 1909 and 1952:

Food, liquor and tobacco	695
Clothing, accessories and personal care	535
Housing and utilities	360
Household equipment and operation	810
Consumer transportation	1,500
Medical care and insurance	1,100
Recreation	1,060
Education (private)	750
Religion	330
Welfare (private)	100

At one extreme, expenditures for consumer transportation — predominantly for the family automobile — increased more than 1,500 per cent; at the other, private welfare expenditures were only 100 per cent larger in 1952 than in 1909. Although appropriate price indexes for the deflation of each of these groups are not available, it is clear that in every case, with the possible exception of welfare, dollar expenditures increased much more than prices. Since the general price level approximately trebled during this period, it appears that expenditures for private welfare failed to hold their own in terms of purchasing power. The obvious reason is that government has been assuming an increasing share of a vastly increased total welfare load. Of the eight remaining groups, medical care and recreation showed the largest percentage gain and housing and religion the smallest.

The varying rates of growth of different classes of consumption expenditures are also measured in terms of the share of total consumption expenditures which each represents. (See Table 33.) In all of the years for which records are available since 1909, food, liquor and tobacco has been by far the most important group, accounting for more than a third of the total in the early years, for a somewhat smaller proportion in the 1920s and 1930s, and again for more than a third during the past decade. Over the long run there appears to be no marked trend in the

proportion of consumption expenditures used for products in this group — a reflection perhaps of the fact that most of the items are somewhat sensitive, rather than sensitive or insensitive, to income changes. As for the intermediate fluctuation, price changes may have been more important than income changes. With the sharp decline in personal incomes and in total consumption expenditures from 1929 to 1933, the proportion spent for food might be expected to increase. Actually it declined, not because food consumption was markedly reduced during the depression but because food prices fell much more sharply than most other prices or the dollar total of consumption expenditures. A sharp rise in the relative importance of this group during the war years was again partly due to the fact that food prices advanced more rapidly than prices of most other commodities. It is also true that food purchases took a larger share of the consumer dollar because some products such as durable goods virtually disappeared from the market.

Expenditures for clothing, accessories and personal care have maintained a fairly stable proportion of the total with a very slight long-run tendency to decline. There was a rise due to exceptionally high prices immediately after World War I, and again during World War II, but the proportion dropped to a record low after 1950. The steadiness of this group of expenditures, which might be expected to decline with rising incomes, appears to reflect a minor decline in demand for staple articles of clothing coupled with a relative rise in spending for such "luxuries" as sports clothes, cosmetics and beauty parlor services.

The proportion of expenditures for housing and utilities shows a marked downward trend over the period as a whole — from nearly a fourth of the total in 1909 and 1914 to about one seventh since 1950. This is in accord with the insensitivity of these expenditures to income changes. Fluctuations in housing expenditures during the intervening years reflect the special influence of price movements. A sharp rise in the early depression years resulted not only from the necessitous nature of these expenditures but also from the tendency of rents — in contrast to the price of food — to lag behind the general deflation of prices and income. During World War II and in the immediate postwar period, while rent controls were in effect, housing expenditures dropped to a record low proportion of the total. In 1946 and 1947, housing accounted for only one eighth of the consumer's dollar — little more than half as much as in 1914 and again in 1932.

Consumers' outlays for household equipment and operation show an opposite trend to that of housing and household utilities. Here the strong upward trend from 11 per cent in 1914 to more than 15 per cent in the late 1930s and over 14 per cent today appears to be due to a mixture of influences, chiefly the great expansion in the purchase of many once new mechanical and electrical appliances which are now household necessities.

Among the remaining six expenditure groups shown in Table 33, consumer transportation is by far the most important, accounting for $24 billion in 1952, or for 11 per cent of all consumer expenditures, compared with 5 per cent in 1909. Medical care and insurance and recreation, and to a lesser extent education, also experienced a relative increase, while consumers devoted a much smaller proportion of their total expenditures to religion and private welfare at the end of the period than at the beginning.

Automotive and recreational expenditures have grown rapidly with the shortening of the work week and the rising standard of living. Higher living standards, coupled with the growing awareness of the need for more adequate medical and other protective service, also account for the substantial increase in expenditures for medical care and insurance. The declining share of expenditures for religion and social welfare reflects in large part a diminished willingness to support religious activities as generously as in the past and a growing acceptance of government responsibility for social welfare — and to some extent also the decline in personal remittances to foreign countries, which are included in this general expenditure group.

DEMAND VS. NEEDS IN 1950 AND 1960

None of these ten major groups of consumption goods and services is homogeneous in the sense that it responds as a unit to the varying influences that account for its importance in the consumer's budget. Each includes subgroups and individual expenditure items (shown in Appendix 4–4) that differ in their sensitivity to income changes and are affected to a varying extent by population changes and other long-term trends.

For these reasons, the estimates of 1960 expenditures for each of the ten major groups of consumption goods and services were arrived at on the basis of a separate analysis for each of the subgroups or individual expenditure items that showed a consistent past relationship to changes in disposable income and other influences or exhibited a definite upward or downward growth trend. From these estimates for the components the group estimates were obtained. In a few cases past experience provided an unsatisfactory basis for estimating future expenditures. In these instances future expenditures were estimated on the basis of the judgment of experts in the field.

Estimated Expenditures

On the whole, it is believed that these estimates of demand in 1960, or of the probable expenditures by consumers under the assumptions of this study for the ten major groups of commodities and services that consumers will purchase, are as dependable as such estimates can be at this time. The data presented in Table 34 and in greater detail in Appendix 4–7 provide the basic framework for the estimates of demand shown in Chapters 5 to 14.

In 1960, as in 1950, food, liquor and tobacco expenditures will be the most important items in consumers' budgets. They accounted for $65.6 billion, or 33.7 per cent, of all 1950 consumption expenditures, and it is estimated that they will account for a slightly larger proportion in 1960 — $81.8 billion out of $241.5 billion.

Outlays for clothing, accessories and personal care, it is estimated, will rise from $25 billion in 1950 to $32 billion in 1960, which would be 13.3 per cent of total expenditures in that year, a slightly larger proportion than in 1950.

Consumption expenditures for housing and utilities, being less sensitive to rising consumer incomes, will continue a long-term downtrend in relative importance. In 1950, housing expenditures of $27.2 billion amounted to 14 per cent of total consumer spending; in 1960, estimated expenditures of $33.2 billion will constitute 13.8 per cent of the total.

Although their long-term trend has been upward, it is estimated that expenditures for household equipment and operation, because of unusually heavy buying in 1950, will fall slightly in relative importance — from 14.9 per cent of the total in that year to 14.6 per cent in 1960. The actual total, however, is expected to rise from $29 billion to more than $35 billion.

For similar reasons, it is estimated that consumer transportation expenditures, though rising from $23.5 billion in 1950 to $28.5 billion in 1960, will decline from 12.1 per cent of the total to 11.8 per cent.

Medical care and insurance, which has shown a long-term upward trend with rising incomes over the past several decades, is estimated as increasing from $8.4 billion in 1950 to $10.7 billion in 1960, or from 4.3 per cent of total consumption expenditures to 4.4 per cent.

Recreation expenditures, which have increased steeply with rising incomes and shorter work hours, are estimated to increased from $10.2 billion in 1950 to $12.7 billion in 1960, although the proportion of total consumption expenditures will remain a little above 5 per cent.

The remaining three fields of consumption expenditures — private education, religion and private welfare — in the aggregate accounted for less than $5 billion in 1950. It is estimated that private education will account for a slightly larger proportion of total expenditures in 1960 than in 1950 — 1.7 per cent compared with 1.5 per cent. Although actual expenditures for religion and for private welfare are expected to increase in 1960 over 1950, it is estimated that the share of the total will decrease slightly in the case of religion and will remain unchanged in the case of private welfare. This is in accord with the long-range insensitivity of these expenditures to changes in consumer income. (See Appendix 4–7, Table A.)

Estimated Needs

In the aggregate and on the average, American consumers were "better off" in 1950 than in any previous year. Although average consumer income, measured in dollars of constant purchasing power, was lower than at the peak of the war, consumption expenditures were much larger than in any other year. Under assumed conditions in 1960, total consumption expenditures will be 24 per cent larger than in 1950, while per capita expenditures are expected to rise from $1,270 in 1950 to $1,360 in 1960, or by 7 per cent.

Even at these high levels of prosperity, however, there were in 1950 and will be in 1960 some consumers not living at a "minimum level of health and decency" — whether because of inadequate income or for other reasons. How large such deficiencies may be cannot be ascertained merely from statistics of income distribution. For the reasons mentioned earlier in this chapter, and also because the cost of living in different communities and the requirements of different individuals and families vary widely, it is clearly impossible to establish a single monetary standard of need or to determine the exact amount of income required to meet that need.

A more fruitful approach to the problem of determining the extent to which estimated consumption expenditures (i.e., demand) fail to provide an adequate standard of living is in terms of the specific necessities of life, such as food, clothing, housing, household equipment and medical care. This is the method followed in succeeding chapters of this report. It involves first the establishment of a "standard of minimum need for the maintenance of health and decency" for each of these groups of necessities; second, determination of the per capita (or per household) cost of supplying these needs; and, third, estimating the cost of making up the deficiencies for those consumers with incomes too small in 1950 and 1960 to meet such minimum needs.

Such a task is beset with uncertainties, the most perplexing being that of establishing a reasonable minimum consumption standard. In the case of food, it is true, we have generally accepted nutritional requirements that can be expressed quantitatively and measured in terms of the amounts of various available foodstuffs needed to provide an adequate diet. Even here, however, the wide gap between "bare subsistence" and "health and decency" is appallingly evident when we see millions of people throughout the world managing to survive on a fraction of what Americans would rightly consider a starvation diet.

As for clothing, housing and furniture, as well as education and recreation, the essential determinants of need are psychological and social and not merely physiological. Most of us could survive with one outfit of clothing, patched indefinitely, or with no clothes at all in the summertime; by sleeping on the floor instead of in bed; by sitting on appleboxes rather than chairs. And as for education and recreation, neither is essential to mere existence.

TABLE 34. ESTIMATED EXPENDITURES AND NEEDS FOR CONSUMPTION GOODS AND SERVICES
IN 1950 AND 1960

(*Dollar Amounts in Millions at 1950 Prices*)

| | Estimated Expenditures | | | | Estimated Needs | |
| | Amount | | Percentage Distribution | | | |
	1950	1960	1950	1960	1950	1960
Total [a]	$194,550	$241,500	100.0	100.0	$206,386	$251,870
Food, liquor and tobacco	65,606	81,800	33.7	33.9	66,365	82,300
Clothing, accessories and personal care	24,961	32,050	12.8	13.3	27,420	34,410
Housing and utilities	27,184	33,220	14.0	13.8	30,700	34,400
Household equipment and operation	29,060	35,350	14.9	14.6	29,253	35,540
Consumer transportation	23,546	28,510	12.1	11.8	23,546	28,510
Medical care and insurance	8,441	10,740	4.3	4.4	12,500	16,000
Recreation	10,211	12,670	5.2	5.2	10,211	12,670
Private education	2,950	4,030	1.5	1.7	3,525	4,610
Religion	1,125	1,300	.6	.5	1,400	1,600
Private welfare	901	1,140	.5	.5	901	1,140

Sources: Appendix 4–7 and Chapters 5–14.

a. Includes occupational and miscellaneous expenses, not shown separately.

A "minimum standard of living" in this twentieth-century world is thus primarily a social and psychological concept. This being so, the content of such a standard in terms of required kinds and quantities of goods cannot be "scientifically" established, but must in the last analysis be an expression of someone's judgment as to what people need.

The research associates whose findings are presented in succeeding chapters of this report were asked to estimate the quantities of, and the costs of supplying, the additional goods and services that would be needed to provide the entire population with a "health and decency" consumption standard. The estimates of costs were based on the assumption that the consumption expenditures of those consumers — who are the vast majority — whose estimated 1950 and 1960 incomes are more than enough to maintain adequate living standards would not be modified in any way. In other words, the contributors have estimated the cost of establishing a "floor" for consumption without disturbing the "ceiling." These analyses are presented in Chapters 5 to 14 of this report and the results are summarized in Table 34.

The cost of meeting the aggregate of estimated needs for consumption goods and services amounted to $206.4 billion in 1950, or about 6 per cent more than the $194.6 billion of actual expenditures in that year. By 1960, on the basis of the assumptions and projections of this study, the spread between needs and demand would diminish. The aggregate cost of meeting needs in that year is estimated at $251.9 billion, or roughly 4 per cent more than expenditures of $241.5 billion.

Medical care and insurance shows the largest gap between needs and demand in both years and accounts for 34 per cent of the total "deficiency" of $11.8 billion in 1950 and for 50 per cent of the 1960 deficiency, which amounts to $10.4 billion. Disparity between needs and demand is also especially large in the case of clothing, accessories and personal care; housing and utilities; and private education.

It is small in the case of the food group, and no attempt was made to estimate need for consumer transportation, recreation and private welfare. In other words, it has been assumed in such cases that "need" and "demand" are identical. Within all of the major groups of consumption goods, moreover, there are subgroups for which the same assumption was made, e.g., liquor and tobacco within the food group, and beauty parlor services within the clothing and accessories group.

INVESTMENT IN CAPITAL GOODS

Capital goods, in contrast to consumption goods and services, include, with certain somewhat arbitrary exceptions,[12] all kinds of durable and long-lived structures and equipment, whether purchased and owned by individuals, business firms or government agencies.[13] The distinguishing characteristic of capital goods is that they are not "consumed" at all, except in an indirect way and at a very slow rate, but that they produce a "flow" of other goods and services, most of which are consumed or used promptly. Railroads and trucks and highways and bridges are not consumed, but they supply transportation service, which is. Houses and hotels provide shelter; telephone, telegraph and radio installations supply communication service; factory buildings and machinery transform raw materials into consumable commodities. Pipelines, pumping stations and reservoirs provide city people with a steady and plentiful supply of water, and without this public investment and the large additional capital in the form of fire-fighting equipment and sewage facilities, our large cities would be uninhabitable.

Wheat on the farm is of no more direct use to the consumer than the capital goods — threshing machines, grain elevators and flour mills — which transmute it into his daily bread. Petroleum deep in the earth is an inaccessible and therefore useless substance. But an intricate and costly complex of drilling and pumping equipment, pipelines and storage facilities, and refineries, tankers and trucks, extracts it from the earth, converts it into hundreds of useful products, and then delivers them where they are wanted.

Some capital goods, such as houses, are owned and used by individual consumers; bridges and highways are examples of public capital goods; while factories and railway facilities are owned and administered by private enterprise. In considering the purchase and use of capital goods, however, it is convenient to classify them into three groups according to the functions they perform.

Private productive facilities is by far the most important category. It includes factories, office and other commercial buildings and warehouses, nonresidential farm structures and equipment, installations for transportation, communication, electricity and gas service — the whole range of structures and equipment used to produce, transport and deliver other goods and services. Some productive facilities, such as stores, hotels, theaters and transit lines, supply consumer services directly, but most do so only indirectly, i.e., by producing intermediate goods and services which often go through further stages of production and distribution before they reach the consumer. A very small share of the nation's total productive facilities is publicly owned and operated, but it is more convenient to classify them separately. The great bulk of the productive plant of the United States is in the possession of corporate and other private enterprises.

Consumer construction consists predominantly of houses — the principal type of capital goods bought and owned by consumers — and other kinds of residential structures, as well as religious, educational, recreational and hospital buildings.[14] This latter class, whether privately or publicly owned, provides services directly to consumers, often on a nonprofit basis.

Developmental and public enterprise construction, in magnitude the smallest of the three categories, includes as its most important component street and highway construction. Also included are bridges and tunnels, sewer and water supply systems, irrigation, soil erosion, flood control, conservation and river valley development, and a very small amount of publicly owned productive facilities. This general class of capital goods, which contributes directly and

---

12. Two important kinds of durable facilities not included in "capital goods," as the term is used here, are consumers' durable goods, such as refrigerators and automobiles, and publicly owned military and naval installations and equipment. The former are classified with other consumption goods and services discussed in Chapters 5 to 14 and the latter with other government goods and services, except in Chapter 18.

13. The term "capital goods" is not exactly identical with "capital formation" or "gross investment," as these terms are used in Table 29. Capital goods exclude "inventory change" and "net foreign investment," but include the important item of "civilian capital facilities" purchased by government.

---

14. Consumer construction also includes fixed types of residential equipment, but it is necessary, because of the nature of the data, to classify the equipment used in religious, educational, recreational and hospital buildings as productive facilities.

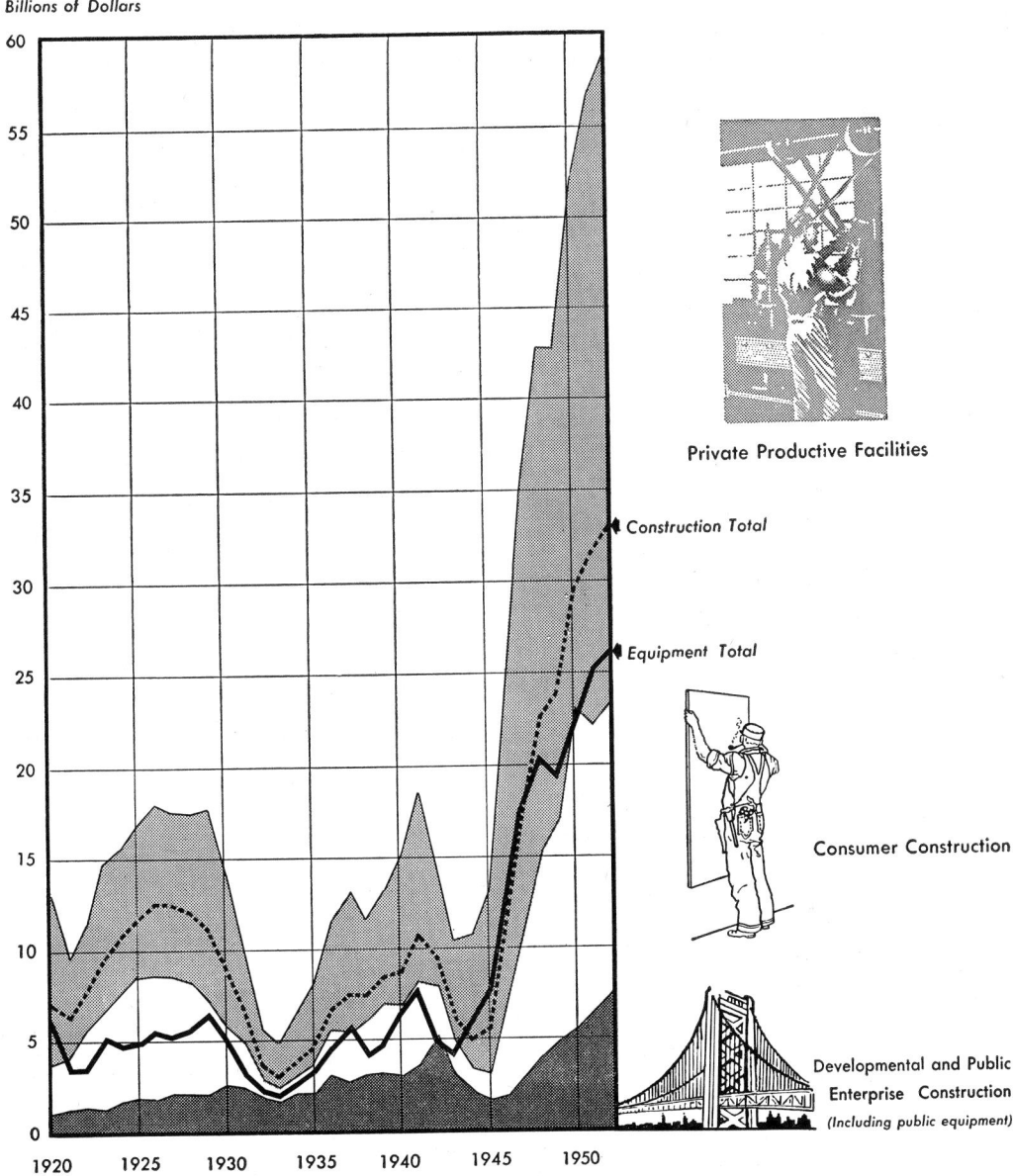

Billions of Dollars

FIGURE 21. EXPENDITURES FOR CAPITAL GOODS, BY TYPE, 1920–1952

Source: Appendix 4–8.

indirectly to general community welfare in many ways, is almost without exception provided and operated by government agencies.

Because capital goods are durable and costly, their purchase is thought of as an "investment," often financed by borrowing, and normally to be paid for out of past, current or future savings. There are exceptions to this generalization,

of course, notably in the case of public capital goods, which are often financed not out of borrowing but out of current tax receipts — which may be regarded as "forced savings" of taxpayers. Aside from tax revenues — which in the long run must always pay for public capital facilities, whether borrowing is involved initially or not — the principal sources of funds for purchases of

TABLE 35. DISTRIBUTION OF CAPITAL GOODS EXPENDITURES BY TYPES, 1920–1952

Year	All Capital Goods Expenditures	Private Productive Facilities	Developmental and Public Enterprise Construction	Consumer Construction	Public Equipment [a]
	(Millions)		(Per Cent of Total)		
1920	$13,042	71.00	7.95	20.91	.14
1921	9,637	57.68	13.08	29.02	.20
1922	11,364	50.47	11.72	37.35	.45
1923	14,718	54.40	8.76	36.34	.50
1924	15,327	49.57	10.27	39.43	.74
1925	16,712	48.76	10.44	40.12	.68
1926	17,898	51.42	9.68	38.41	.49
1927	17,396	50.46	11.66	37.12	.76
1928	17,395	52.63	11.75	34.84	.78
1929	17,748	60.43	11.51	27.29	.77
1930	14,096	59.11	17.05	22.72	1.12
1931	9,886	51.22	22.92	24.47	1.39
1932	5,588	49.59	29.33	19.24	1.85
1933	4,895	52.89	31.64	14.05	1.41
1934	6,479	53.50	30.30	15.05	1.16
1935	7,960	56.05	25.09	17.42	1.43
1936	11,445	52.44	25.75	20.53	1.27
1937	13,048	58.64	20.13	20.14	1.09
1938	11,415	49.17	25.37	24.39	1.07
1939	13,182	47.81	22.71	28.24	1.25
1940	15,009	54.55	18.92	25.15	1.37
1941	18,587	55.65	18.89	24.65	.81
1942	14,427	45.71	34.28	18.58	1.42
1943	10,342	51.87	28.28	18.27	1.57
1944	10,753	68.99	17.96	12.14	.92
1945	13,190	76.09	11.34	11.78	.79
1946	25,001	70.93	6.62	21.61	.83
1947	34,589	68.05	7.83	23.39	.73
1948	42,897	64.37	8.55	26.19	.88
1949	42,828	60.75	10.43	27.86	.96
1950	52,355	57.80	9.21	32.03	.96
1951	56,756	60.83	10.16	27.96	1.06
1952	58,959	60.41	11.41	27.00	1.19

Sources: Appendix 4–8 and Appendix 4–9.
a. Excludes expenditures by state governments for equipment.
Note: Discrepancies in addition are due to rounding.

capital goods are personal and corporate savings and "capital consumption allowances," or the amounts set aside by business firms in depreciation and depletion accounts. Whether capital goods are financed out of taxes, savings, borrowing or current income, however, any addition to our total stock of such goods constitutes a surplus over current consumption and therefore in "real" terms, savings.

CAPITAL EXPENDITURE TRENDS

Cyclical Changes

Because of the cost and character of capital goods, and the "residual" nature of the funds needed to pay for them, the volume purchased fluctuates widely between depression and boom. For example, expenditures for capital goods amounted to nearly $59 billion in 1952, or about

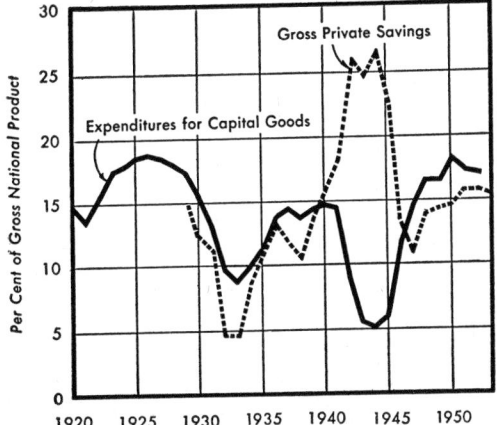

FIGURE 22. CAPITAL EXPENDITURES AND GROSS SAVINGS AS PER CENT OF GROSS NATIONAL PRODUCT, 1920–1953

Sources: Gross national product based on Appendix 4–2, Table A; expenditures for capital goods from Appendix 4–8; gross private savings from *Economic Report of the President,* January 1954, Table G 13, p. 180.

17 per cent of the $348 billion gross national product in that year. This was twelve times the $4.9 billion spent for capital goods at the bottom of the depression in 1933, whereas gross national product increased little more than six times during that period. In other words capital goods constituted almost twice as large a share of gross national product in boom year 1952 as at the depression low point.

Until the recent postwar boom, the most active period of capital investment was the last half of the 1920s. Total expenditures for that five-year period aggregated $87 billion. This was close to 19 per cent of aggregate gross national product for the period as a whole, a proportion that has not since been achieved for any comparable length of time. Nor was the dollar total of the last half of the 1920s, when construction and equipment costs were much lower than after World War II, surpassed until after World War II. (See Table 35 and Figure 21.)

The rough correspondence between gross private savings and capital expenditures is evident from Figure 22, which shows both series in relation to gross national product. The relationship was broken during the World War II period, when civilian capital investment was held to a minimum and large government deficits accounted for the disparity between gross savings

and expenditures for capital goods. (See p. 83, footnote 2.)

Whether the fluctuations in total expenditures for capital goods over the past quarter century can be regarded as due predominantly to cyclical influences or not there is some evidence that, over the long run, capital goods have constituted a slowly declining proportion of the total production of goods and services. Estimates by Simon Kuznets [15] published several years ago showed that capital goods constituted 19.6 per cent of gross national product in the 1890s, dropped below 17 per cent in the decade of the 1920s as a whole, and fell to almost 14 per cent in the 1930s. Even during the boom since World War II capital goods have accounted for a smaller share of gross national product than in the early decades of the century, although for a larger share than in the 1920s and 1930s.

Construction vs. Equipment

Cyclical fluctuations and trends in total expenditures for capital goods conceal somewhat different movements for the various classes of such goods. During the period covered by the Kuznets analysis, for example, the portion of total expenditures represented by construction was wholly responsible for the long-term decline in the total. Construction fell from more than 15 per cent of total gross national product in the 1890s to not far above 8 per cent in the 1930s, while the share of productive equipment rose from 4.5 per cent to more than 6 per cent during the same period. In other words about 77 per cent of capital goods expenditures consisted of payments for construction and only 23 per cent for equipment; by the 1930s these proportions had shifted to 57 per cent and 43 per cent respectively. During the past few years the proportions have remained about as they were in the 1930s. (See Appendix 4–8 and Figure 21.)

The cyclical drop from the last half of the 1920s and the subsequent long recovery were also much more pronounced in the case of construction than equipment. Construction expenditures dropped from a peak of $12.5 billion in 1926 to $3 billion in 1933 and then experienced an 11-

---

15. "Uses of National Income in Peace and War," Occasional Paper No. 6, National Bureau of Economic Research, New York, March 1942, Tables 1 and 4. These data do not correspond precisely to Department of Commerce data for the same periods, but the differences are slight.

fold rise to $33 billion in 1952. Nearly $6.6 billion was spent for equipment in the peak year 1929; less than $1.9 billion at the bottom of the depression in 1933; and $26.1 billion in 1952.

Types of Capital Goods

Of the three major classes of capital goods, developmental and public works showed the smallest cyclical fluctuations from prosperity to depression, apparently because they were publicly financed and suitable for work relief projects. Indeed, in spite of the drastic decline for capital expenditures as a whole, spending for developmental projects actually increased during the depressed 1930s above the average level of the prosperous 1920s. There was also a sharp increase in the early years of the defense and war periods. In recent years these expenditures have been more than twice as high as in the highest prewar year — a reflection primarily of increased costs rather than larger volume. Even at their peak in 1952, however, this class of capital goods accounted for only $6.7 billion of expenditures, or 11 per cent of total expenditures for capital goods.

Consumer construction has shown the most violent fluctuations since the last half of the 1920s, when it averaged nearly 36 per cent of total expenditures for capital goods. From a peak of nearly $6.9 billion in 1926, expenditures declined by 90 per cent to $690 million in 1933. In that year they accounted for only 14 per cent of total capital expenditures. During the last half of the 1930s a sharp recovery occurred in residential building, which normally accounts for some 80 per cent of expenditures for this class, but only in prosperous 1941 did expenditures again approach the 1929 volume. Moreover it was not until 1947, when consumer construction expenditures rose above $8 billion, that the 1926 peak was surpassed. Since 1948, however, with a further rise of prices the annual volume of consumer construction has exceeded $11 billion in every year and reached a peak of $16.8 billion in 1950. In 1952 consumer construction accounted for 27 per cent of all expenditures for capital goods.

Private productive facilities have always been the most important component of capital goods, averaging close to 53 per cent of total expenditures for such goods in the last half of the 1920s, and 60 per cent in 1952. During the economic collapse in the early years of the depression, expenditures for productive facilities were cut sharply from a peak of $10.7 billion in 1929 to $2.6 billion in 1933. The recovery thereafter was slow and uncertain, and in relatively prosperous 1941 expenditures of $10.3 billion were still smaller than in 1929.

During World War II, expenditures for commercial and miscellaneous facilities, for communication and other utility facilities and for mining were sharply curtailed, while expenditures for manufacturing were well maintained, and for agriculture sharply increased.

Outlays for private productive facilities as a whole dropped from $10.3 billion in 1941 to $7.4 billion in 1944. After the end of World War II, an immediate and substantial increase occurred, sending the total to $27.6 billion in 1948. With the stimulus to industrial expansion following the outbreak of Korean hostilities, expenditures for productive facilities jumped again to $35.6 billion in 1952.

DEMAND VS. NEEDS IN 1950 AND 1960

The difficulties of discovering stable or dependable trends and relationships for specific capital goods are much more serious than for most consumption goods and services. This is especially true because the available data cover a period of years during which cyclical fluctuations due to war and depression were especially severe. For this reason, and because long-term trends are hard to measure during such a disturbed period, estimates of future capital goods expenditures are subject to large possibilities of error.

Estimated Expenditures

Although there is some evidence, as indicated above, of a long-run decline in the proportion of gross national product represented by capital goods, this downward trend is not clearly established; it appears to have been sharply accentuated in the 1930s and abruptly reversed during the postwar period. In 1950 the more than $52 billion spent for public and private capital goods represented 18.3 per cent of gross national product — a somewhat larger proportion than in the years of prewar prosperity, 1929 and 1941. The present survey assumes that, under conditions of stable prosperity in 1960, capital goods expenditures will increase to $66.5 billion (in 1950 dollars), but will decline slightly to 18 per cent of the estimated $370 billion gross national product in that year.

None of these three major groups of capital goods is homogeneous; each contains individual items that have had, and will probably continue to have, different growth trends. Estimates of probable expenditures for each of these categories under high levels of employment and activity in 1960 are based on an examination of past trends in their *relative* importance within the total of all capital goods and in ratios to gross national product. (See Appendix 4–9.)

According to these projections the increase of some $14 billion in total expenditures for capital goods between 1950 and 1960 is attributable predominantly to an increase in expenditures for private productive facilities from $30.3 billion in 1950 to $42.3 billion in 1960. This would mean a rise in the relative importance of this group from 58 to 64 per cent of total capital expenditures. (See Table 36.) All of the separate items in this category, except mining, would show substantial gains, both absolute and relative. Detailed analysis of the expected gains in expenditures for private productive facilities is given in Chapter 15.

Consumer construction expenditures are estimated as declining slightly in dollar amount between 1950 and 1960 and as falling from 32 per cent of total capital goods expenditures to 24.4 per cent. The decline in the importance of this group is due chiefly to an expected shrinkage in residential construction from the high level of 1950, which is discussed in Chapter 7. Other types of consumer construction, which in 1950 together accounted for only 20 per cent of this group, are expected to increase substantially.

Developmental and public enterprise construction, which is the least important of the three groups, will increase in relative importance from 9.2 per cent of the total in 1950 to 11 per cent in 1960. This rise will be due primarily to an expected large increase in highway construction, which accounts for nearly half of the total expenditures for this group and for nearly half of the expected increase.

Estimated Needs

"Need" as a measure of the amount of goods and services required to maintain minimum standards of health and decency is obviously not applicable to most kinds of capital goods. They help to meet such needs only indirectly. About all that can be said is that if minimum consumption needs are to be met, productive facilities, such as factories, farm machinery and railroad equipment, must be of adequate quantity and quality to provide the required goods and services. Much the same relationship exists between such consumer structures as hospitals and schools and such public facilities as water supply and sewer systems and streets and highways, on the one hand, and the ultimate services such capital goods are designed to deliver, on the other. The minimum need for capital facilities, moreover, is much more elastic than the need for the goods and services they turn out. Needs for food and clothing must be met promptly but freight cars and machinery, hospitals and highways, can be made to "do" for a while longer without frustrating consumer wants.

To be sure, the concept of need can be applied directly in the case of the most important kind of residential construction, residential structures, and, with less precision, to the household utilities such as water, sewer facilities, gas and electricity. Also, generally accepted standards can be developed for school buildings and for hospitals.[16]

Because the need for factories, machinery and other productive facilities can be measured only in terms of the need for the goods and services they provide, it has been assumed that the total need for such facilities exceeds probable expenditures (or estimated demand) for them to the same extent as total need for other goods and services [17] exceeds the estimated demand for such

16. Definitions of, and estimates of outlays required to meet, needs for specific types of capital goods in 1950 and 1960 are presented as follows: For consumer construction: residential, Chapter 7; hospital, Chapter 10; recreational, Chapter 11; educational, Chapter 12; religious, Chapter 13. For private productive facilities, Chapter 15; highways, Chapter 9; conservation and development, and sewage disposal and water supply, Chapter 17; urban redevelopment, Chapter 16. All dollar figures are at 1950 prices.

17. "Other goods and services" for which estimated needs and demand are used include: (1) consumption goods and services (see Table 34); (2) capital goods for which separate estimates of need were made, i.e., developmental and public enterprise construction and residential, religious, educational, recreational and hospital construction (see Table 36); and government noncapital goods and services. In determining the gap between demand and needs for private productive facilities, the gap for other goods and services was weighted more heavily for goods than for services. (See Appendix 15–1.)

TABLE 36. ESTIMATED EXPENDITURES AND NEEDS FOR CAPITAL GOODS IN 1950 AND 1960 [a]

(Millions of 1950 Dollars)

	1950		1960	
	Demand	Needs	Demand	Needs
Total [a]	$52,355	$66,719	$66,500	$78,280
Private	45,032	51,713	56,000	62,100
Public [b]	7,323	15,006	10,500	16,180
Private productive facilities	30,263	34,800	42,310	44,800
Developmental and public enterprise construction	4,821	10,672	7,300	11,410
Private	112	762	150	800
Public	4,709	9,910	7,150	10,610
Highways (public only)	2,272	5,500	3,500	5,500
Conservation and development (public only)	881	1,760	1,250	1,760
Sewage disposal (public only)	383	500 [c]	500	500 [c]
Water supply (public only)	276	300 [c]	300	300 [c]
Urban redevelopment	[d]	1,300	[d]	1,300
Other [e]	1,009	1,312	1,750	2,050
Consumer construction	16,771	20,747	16,240	21,420
Private	14,657	16,151	13,540	16,500
Public	2,114	4,596	2,700	4,920
Residential	13,708	14,600	12,000	14,600
Private	13,363	14,250	11,650	14,250
Public	345	350	350	350
Religious (private only)	409	600	550	600
Educational	1,427	3,770	1,970	3,770
Private	294	710	400	710
Public	1,133	3,060	1,570	3,060
Recreational	387	477	520	650
Private	247	247	340	340
Public	140	230	180	310
Hospital	840	1,300	1,200	1,800
Private	344	344	600	600
Public	496	956	600	1,200

Sources: Appendices 4–7 and 4–8, and Chapters 7, 9–13 and 15–17.

a. These estimates cover all expenditures for plant and equipment except expenditures for publicly owned military and naval plant and equipment and expenditures by state governments for equipment.

b. Includes expenditures for public equipment (except by state governments); these expenditures are not distributed in body of table.

c. Based on assumption that program would be completed in 20 years instead of 25 years as assumed in Chapter 17.

d. Demand estimates included in other consumer and developmental items. Needs estimates equal sum of additional dwelling replacement, site improvements and nonresidential facilities under the two-thirds-centralized program in Chapter 16; the program was assumed to require 15 years for completion and to be split evenly between private and public funds.

e. Includes (a) private sewer, water, road and bridge construction and miscellaneous items such as parks and playgrounds and (b) public industrial and commercial and public administration construction and public construction not elsewhere classified. Needs assumed equal to demand, except for airways, airports, waterways and harbors, for which needs were estimated separately in Chapter 9.

goods and services. On this basis, to meet the need for private productive facilities in 1950 would have required expenditures of $34.8 billion, compared with actual expenditures of $30.3 billion in that year. In 1960 estimated needs would come to $44.8 billion, against estimated likely expenditures of $42.3 billion. Thus, on the basis of these assumptions, spending for productive plant in 1950 was 15 per cent short and in 1960 would fall short by 6 per cent of the requisite amount to meet the final needs for goods and services. Needs for each of the components of productive facilities were estimated on the basis of the ratio of the demand for each to the estimated total demand — or expenditures — for productive facilities in 1950 and 1960. (See Table 216.)

A program to bring housing — the most important component of consumer construction — up to a satisfactory standard would cost $14.6 billion, or $900 million more than actual expenditures in 1950, and the same amount, or $2.6 billion more than estimated expenditures, in 1960. This would replace or rehabilitate substandard housing over a 15-year period, provide satisfactory dwelling for new families and enable "doubled-up" families to separate. For education, needed outlays come to $3.8 billion in 1950 and the same amount in 1960. This would provide for increased enrollments and replace substandard buildings. Annual expenditures of $1.3 billion in 1950 and $1.8 billion in 1960 would be required to meet estimated needs for hospitals and health centers. These and other estimates of consumer construction needs are shown in Table 36.

To meet estimated needs for developmental works and public enterprise construction in 1950 would have required expenditures of $10.7 billion instead of the $4.8 billion actually spent for this class of capital goods in that year. In 1960, estimated needs come to $11.4 billion and estimated expenditures to $7.3 billion. The most pressing need, and the most costly, is for highway construction and improvement. Expenditures to fill estimated needs for highways, amounting to $5.5 billion in both 1950 and 1960, would provide an interregional highway system, rebuild almost all of the principal state highways and increase the mileage of rural highways. To meet estimated conservation and developmental needs would involve expenditures of $1.8 billion in 1950, compared with $881 million actually spent, and $1.8 billion in 1960, compared

with probable expenditures of $1.3 billion in that year. The larger amounts would finance an adequate soil conservation program, increase agricultural productivity by irrigating, draining and clearing to the extent economically feasible, improve watersheds, provide protection to our forests from fire, insects and disease, provide adequate parks and in other ways bring our rural areas into satisfactory condition.

For capital goods as a whole, aggregate needs are estimated at $66.7 billion in 1950, compared with actual expenditures of $52.4 billion; in 1960 estimated needs amount to $78.3 billion, compared with estimated actual expenditures of $66.5 billion. Thus, it is estimated that the normal operation of the economy at high levels in 1950 supplied 79 per cent of estimated needs, while at the higher level of activity in 1960 estimated actual expenditures may amount to 85 per cent of needs.

About 14 per cent of total capital expenditures in 1950 and nearly 16 per cent of the estimated total for 1960 consist of purchases by the government. Largest objects of government capital expenditures are highways, schools, conservation development, and "other," which includes among other things the atomic energy program. Estimated "needs" for government civilian capital goods were almost twice as large as actual expenditures in 1950 and about half again as large as estimated expenditures for 1960. The largest deficiencies, as indicated in Table 36, are in highways, schools, conservation development and urban redevelopment.

Government Expenditures

Total government expenditures include, in addition to (1) the purchase or construction of capital goods, discussed above, (2) expenditures for other goods and personal services, and (3) a variety of transfer payments, such as social security benefits and interest on government obligations. The last-named forms no part of gross national product, since transfer payments involve no *quid pro quo* in the form of currently produced goods and services.

Total government expenditures, and that part of the total represented by goods and services, have both risen steeply over the past quarter century. In 1929, the last year of prosperity before the great depression, federal, state and local governments in the United States spent a total of

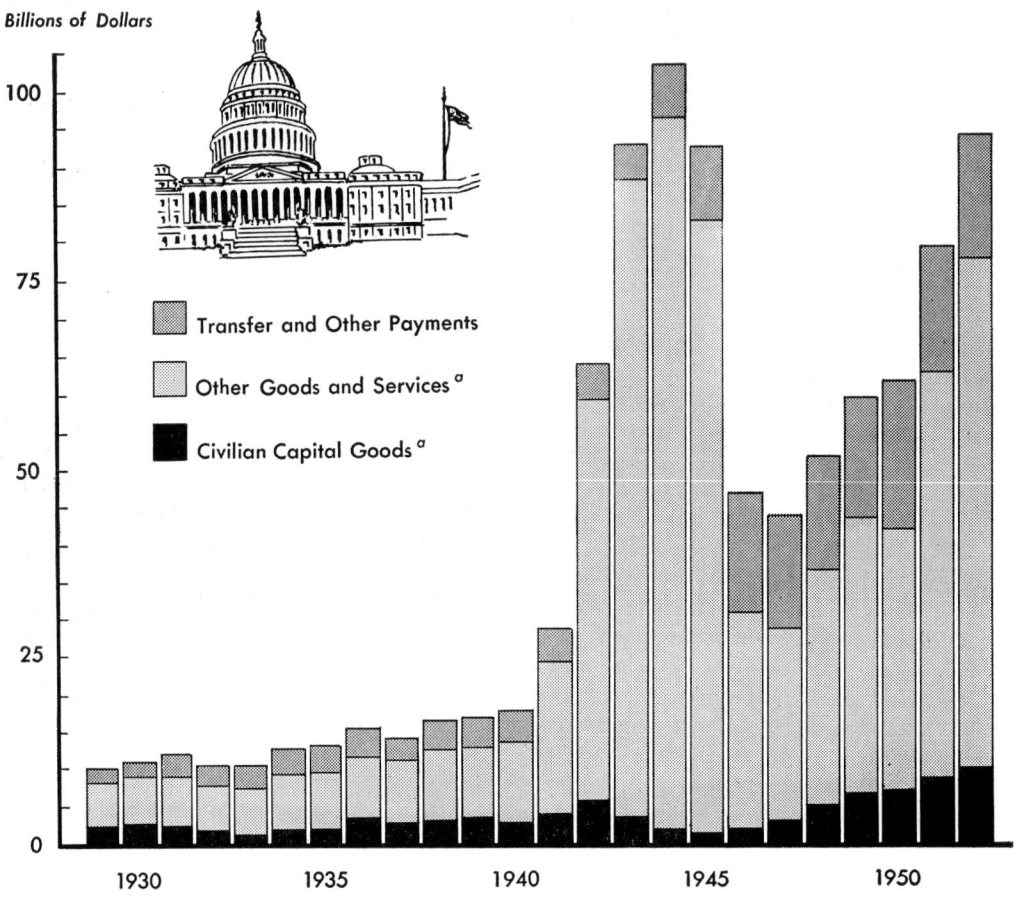

Billions of Dollars

Transfer and Other Payments

Other Goods and Services [a]

Civilian Capital Goods [a]

FIGURE 23. GOVERNMENT EXPENDITURES, 1929–1952

Source: Appendix 4–1.

a. "Other goods and services" includes and "civilian capital goods" excludes all government expenditures for publicly owned military and naval plant and equipment and state expenditures for equipment.

$10.2 billion for all purposes. By 1952 there had been a ninefold increase to $94.4 billion. Gross national product during the same period experienced a little more than a threefold increase, rising from $103.8 billion to $348 billion. (See Figure 23.)

Expenditure Trends

Close to 20 per cent of government spending — $1.9 billion in 1929 and $16.9 billion in 1952 — consisted of interest and transfer payments. Government expenditures for goods and services, therefore, rose from $8.5 billion in 1929 to $77.5 billion in 1952. The rise in the relative importance of government in the American economy is measured by the fact that government purchases of goods and services accounted for only 8.2 per cent of gross national product in 1929, but for more than 22 per cent by 1952.

The rise in government purchases since 1920 has been steep but irregular; they rose to a record peak of over $96 billion, or more than 44 per cent of gross national product, in 1944. After a sharp decline following the end of World War II to $29 billion in 1947, there was another rise, sharply accelerated after Korea, which reached at least a temporary postwar peak in 1953. In that year government purchases of goods and services amounted to $85 billion, or 23 per cent of gross national product, but a slight decline has taken place since the second quarter of that year.

Expenditures vs. Needs

Total government expenditures in 1950 amounted to $61.4 billion while estimated "needs" for the same year amounted to $96.6 billion, or 57 per cent more than the amount actually spent. Differences between actual expenditures and the estimated cost of meeting needs in 1950 are shown below (in billions):

	Expenditures	Needs
Total	$61.4	$96.6
Capital goods	7.3	15.0
Other goods and services	34.7	57.8
Other expenditures	19.4	23.8

About two thirds of the $35 billion "deficiency" for 1950 is accounted for by "other goods and services" and this is due almost exclusively to the assumption that the federal government was spending far too little on national defense in that year — as evidenced by the expenditures which proved to be necessary as soon as the true nature of the international situation became known when the Communists invaded South Korea. This deficiency, as well as that in "other goods and services," is discussed in Chapter 18; the disparity between needs and expenditures in the case of capital goods is discussed in the preceding section of the present chapter.

In 1960 the estimated gap between probable expenditures and needs will shrink to about $11.9 billion, chiefly because probable expenditures for defense purposes in that year are estimated as equal to needs. Estimates of government expenditures and needs in 1960 are shown below (in billions):

	Expenditures	Needs
Total	$94.5	$106.4
Capital goods	10.5	16.2
Other goods and services	62.0	66.2
Other expenditures	22.0	24.0

These estimated expenditures in 1960 will fall only 12 per cent short of meeting estimated needs.

BASIC ASSUMPTIONS

It is now possible to summarize briefly the basic assumptions and the statistical estimates and projections that provide the quantitative framework for succeeding chapters of this survey of needs and resources. The fundamental determinants of what the nation might produce and consume under relatively active conditions in 1960 are the number of persons at work; average hours of work; and productivity, or average output per man-hour. On the basis of different assumptions regarding these factors, Chapter 2 presented three different projections of gross national product in 1960. The lowest estimate was $315 billion and the highest was $440 billion, expressed in 1950 prices, as compared with an actual gross national product of $286.8 billion in 1950. It is the medium estimate of $370 billion which for reasons of convenience has been used as the basic "control" within which all other estimates presented in this and subsequent chapters have been made. Estimates of "probable expenditures" within this framework have also provided the base line for computation of "needs" in succeeding chapters of this report, which have been summarized in preceding sections of this chapter.

Population data and projections are presented in Chapter 3, while Chapter 20 gives the basis for estimates of future employment and working hours. The total number of consumers, or the population, is expected to increase by approximately 25 million to an estimated total of 177 million in 1960. As in other recent decades the farm population will continue to decline and the urban, and especially the rural nonfarm (largely suburban), populations will show marked gains. The numbers of households and of primary families, which are expected to rise to 51 million and 44 million respectively, will show smaller percentage gains than in the war decade ending in 1950. (See Table 37.)

According to the medium assumptions, the labor force will increase during the 1950–1960 decade by about 8 million — approximately the same numerical increase as in the 1940s — to a total of 72.5 million in 1960. With an assumed normal unemployment of about 5 per cent of the labor force, or 3.5 million, an average of 69 million would be actually at work in 1960, of whom it is estimated that 58.5 million would be in private, and 10.5 million in public, activities. With the likelihood of some further decline in working hours and the further extension of annual vacations, it is estimated that the average length of the work week will continue its long-term decline from 40 hours in 1950 to 37.5 hours in 1960. If these changes actually take place the total "labor input" in private activities in 1960

TABLE 37. BASIC ASSUMPTIONS FOR 1960 COMPARED WITH 1940 AND 1950

		1940	1950		1960
1.	Population (*millions*)	132.5	152.5		177.0
			Comparable with		
			1940	1960	
2.	Urban	74.8	90.0	97.6	113.0
3.	Rural nonfarm	27.2	39.2	31.6	43.0
4.	Rural farm	30.4	23.3	23.3	21.0
5.	Consumer units (*millions*)	a	50.4		58.0
6.	Households	34.9	43.5		51.0
7.	Primary families	31.6	38.7		44.0
8.	One-person households and households of unrelated individuals	3.4	4.7		7.0
9.	Lodgers and resident employees	a	6.9		7.0
10.	Labor force (*millions*)	56.0	64.6		72.5
11.	Unemployed	8.1	3.1		3.5
12.	Employed, total	47.9	61.5		69.0
13.	Private	43.3	54.1		58.5
14.	Average weekly hours	44.0	40.0		37.5
15.	Private man-hours per year (*billions*)	99.3	112.5		114.1
16.	Private national income per man-hour (1950 prices)	131.2¢	193.2¢		240.0¢
		(Billions at 1950 Prices)			
17.	Private national income	$130.3	$217.3		$275.0
18.	Total national income	147.0	240.6		312.5
19.	Gross national product or expenditure	183.4	286.8		370.0
20.	Consumption expenditures	127.4	194.6		241.5
21.	Government expenditures for goods and services	28.3	42.0		72.5
22.	Private gross capital formation [b]	27.7	50.2		56.0
23.	Construction and capital equipment expenditure (civilian) [c]	29.6	52.3		66.5
24.	Private	22.9	45.0		56.0
25.	Public (civilian) [c]	6.7	7.3		10.5

Sources: Lines 1–9: for 1940 and 1950, Table 27; for 1960, see discussion in Chapter 3.
    10–13: Appendix 20–4.
    14–17: Table 14.
    18–20: for 1940 and 1950, Appendix 4–2, Table B; for 1960, Table 29.
    21: Table 29 (1940 figure shifted to 1950 prices by use of price index in *Survey of Current Business,* July 1953, Table B, p. 26).
    22: subtraction.
    23–25: same as line 21, using price indexes for gross private domestic investment.
  a. Not available.
  b. Includes government net foreign investment.
  c. Excludes expenditures for publicly owned military and naval plant and equipment and expenditures by state governments for equipment.

will amount to 114.1 billion man-hours — only 1.4 per cent more than in 1950.

What this labor input will mean in terms of total output will depend on productivity, as measured by average output per man-hour. On the basis of past trends it is estimated that average private national income per man-hour will rise from $1.93 in 1950 to $2.40 (at 1950 prices)

in 1960. This would mean total private national income of $275 billion in 1960 and gross national product of $370 billion.

How the gross total of production and expenditures was distributed in 1950 and might be distributed in 1960 as among consumption expenditures, government purchases of goods and services, and capital goods has also been summarized in Table 37. Consumption expenditures account for about twice as much as the other two components in both 1950 and 1960 and government expenditures show the largest increase between the two years.

These projections, of course, do not purport to predict what employment, gross output, and expenditures by consumers, government and investors will actually be in the year 1960. These statistics merely represent a judgment as to what might reasonably be expected from an economy operating at a relatively high level in that year, as it was, for example, during the last half of the 1920s, or in 1949 and 1950. This does not mean an economy under forced draft, as in 1944, or at the peak of a boom, as in 1953, or with "all-out" use of all our human and material resources. Such a measurement of maximum possible output has important uses, but for the purposes of this study it has seemed more reasonable to assume a level of activity more in accord with past experience.

PART II

CONSUMPTION REQUIREMENTS

## CHAPTER 5

FOOD, LIQUOR AND TOBACCO

ONE THIRD OF THE FAMILY budget goes for food,[1] liquor[2] and tobacco. This exceeds the share for the family dwelling together with its operation and furnishings, which accounts for about one fourth of total family expenditures in a year. The importance of food, liquor and tobacco to consumers is matched by their importance to producers as a source of income.

ECONOMIC IMPORTANCE

Production and marketing of food, liquor and tobacco account for a major part of the nation's economy, measured in labor and resources engaged. Consumption expenditures for these items also reflect their economic importance.

WORKERS ENGAGED

In 1950, for every 100 persons 14 years of age and over in the labor force there were 54 women 14 years of age and over who reported no occupation other than housework for their own families.[3] The purchase, preparation and care of food and related activities took one third to one half of their average working day, which was probably as long as that of paid workers.[4]

Thirteen per cent of all employed persons worked in agriculture in 1950.[5] About 10 per cent of all manufacturing workers in that year were at work on food and kindred products and 0.7 per cent on tobacco products. Together, agriculture and the manufacture of food and kindred products occupied 17 per cent of the employed labor force. In addition, others were indirectly engaged in supplying consumers with food, liquor and tobacco; for example, factory workers making farm machinery and supplies, and many of the workers employed in transporting and storing and selling products.

A large share of total advertising man-hours also is devoted to the sale of food, alcoholic beverages, tobacco and smoking supplies. During 1950 these products accounted for about one third of all advertising in newspapers and magazines and on the radio.[6]

CONSUMPTION EXPENDITURES [7]

In 1949 and 1950, outlays for food and nonalcoholic beverages accounted for about 28 per cent of all consumption expenditures; alcoholic beverages accounted for 4 per cent and tobacco for 2 per cent. Between 1909 and 1950 the proportion devoted to food and nonalcoholic beverages varied from 25 to 31 per cent, and the proportion

---

1. Consumption categories are not always completely logical. For example, consumer outlays for bread are classed as food expenditures, but the synthetic vitamins contained in bread are classed as drugs if purchased in pill form. Although beer, wine and whiskey are classed as alcoholic beverages, patent medicines with a relatively high alcoholic content, which for some people serve the same purpose, are classed as drugs.

A large and increasing part of family food costs goes for processing. This increase may be partly or wholly counterbalanced by decreased costs of household operation because of reduced home preparation of food. Thus the purchase of bakery products and ready-to-serve cereals has cut fuel needs. The decrease in domestic servants is likely to bring greater expenditures for processed foods and meals away from home.

2. Liquor, like other beverages, is a food. Some of the consumption data do not provide a separate estimate for it apart from food in general. In this chapter, unless otherwise indicated, food includes alcoholic beverages.

3. See "Employment and Income in the United States, by Regions: 1950," *1950 Census of Population: Preliminary Reports,* Series PC–7, No. 2, April 11, 1951.

4. For discussion of the economic significance of housework see M. G. Reid, "The Economic Contribution of Homemakers," *Annals of the American Academy of Political and Social Science,* May 1947, pp. 61–69.

5. Based on monthly average, with armed forces excluded. See *Business Statistics, Statistical Supplement to the Survey of Current Business,* 1951.

6. *Statistical Abstract of the United States, 1951,* U.S. Bureau of the Census, p. 906.

7. "Consumption expenditures" as the term is used in annual estimates of the U.S. Department of Commerce includes not only money expenditures but also the value of selected types of consumption in kind, chiefly the imputed value of home-produced food of farm families and the net rental value of owner-occupied dwellings. (Principal payments on owner-occupied dwellings are classed as savings.) The Department of Commerce series includes consumption expenditures of private institutions, such as hospitals, schools, libraries, but excludes those of public institutions.

BY MARGARET G. REID, Professor of Economics and Home Economics, University of Chicago. Opinions and judgments expressed in this chapter are those of the author and should not be attributed to the organization with which she is associated.

TABLE 38. PER CENT OF TOTAL CONSUMPTION EXPENDITURES DEVOTED
TO FOOD, LIQUOR AND TOBACCO, 1909–1952

Period	Combined Groups	Food, Including Nonalcoholic Beverages	Alcoholic Beverages	Tobacco [a]
1909	34.0	25.6	6.25	2.18
1914	35.0	26.8	5.99	2.19
1919	36.3	30.6	3.30	2.36
1921, 1923	29.3	24.6	2.37	2.42
1925, 1927, 1929	29.2	24.6	2.42	2.13
1930–1934	28.5	23.7	2.27	2.43
1935–1939	31.8	24.3	4.98	2.56
1940–1944	35.1	26.9	5.68	2.49
1945–1946	36.9	28.5	6.09	2.36
1947–1948	36.2	28.9	4.96	2.34
1949–1950	34.3	27.7	4.27	2.31
1951–1952	35.5	29.2	4.06	2.31

Source: Appendix 4–5.
a. Includes smoking supplies.

going for tobacco fluctuated between 2.2 and 2.6 per cent. There was no apparent trend in the importance of tobacco in the total budget during that period despite the marked increase in the percentage of women smoking.[8] (See Table 38.)

The data for this period provide no evidence that a rise in real income tends to be associated with a decline in the importance of food and tobacco relative to total consumption expenditures. Of course, many influences other than changes in real income were at work during these years.

The importance of alcoholic beverages in consumption expenditures has varied a good deal. From 1909 to 1919 their share dropped from 6.3 to 3.3 per cent, partly as a result of the Webb-Kenyon Act of 1913, in which the federal government took steps to aid in state prohibition programs. During the 1920s and early 1930s, expenditures for alcoholic beverages accounted for about 2.3 per cent of all consumption expenditures. Since the repeal of prohibition the proportion has risen; by 1945–1946 it had reached 6.1 per cent — about the same level as in 1913 — and in 1949–1950 it was 4.3 per cent; in 1951–1952 it was 4.1 per cent.

Place in Family Budget

Only two nationwide surveys have been made of consumption of food, liquor and tobacco by

families and single consumers, one in 1935–1936 and the other in 1941.[9] Outlays for food, liquor and tobacco in these years accounted for about one third of total family expenditures. This proportion was the same as the share of total national consumption expenditures going for these products as estimated by the U.S. Department of Commerce.[10] (See Appendix 4–5.) The family data provide a means of examining differences in consumption among various groups within the nation.

9. There are also national data for the first quarter of 1942.
10. Data from national family consumption surveys are usually checked against the Department of Commerce estimates to test their validity. There are differences, however, in the coverage of items and the treatment of data. For example, while the annual estimates of the Department of Commerce include outlays of private institutions, family studies exclude these. The Department of Commerce does not include outlays by family members for goods and services provided by public institutions, such as school lunches under the management of a tax-supported school, but these are included in surveys of family expenditures. Some of the family studies include the home-produced food of all families irrespective of place of residence, whereas the Department of Commerce includes only that of farm families. The home production included in the Department of Commerce estimates is valued on the basis of farm sale prices, whereas family studies have used retail prices. The family studies are known to underreport alcoholic beverages, while the Department of Commerce has excellent data on which to base its estimate. Of the family data for 1941 the investigators state: "There can be little doubt that the . . . expenditures on alcoholic beverages have been seriously underreported, possibly by as much as two thirds." *Family Spending and Saving in Wartime*, Bulletin No. 822, U.S. Bureau of Labor Statistics, 1945, p. 78.

8. Data are not available to measure the increase in the use of tobacco by women.

TABLE 39. PER CENT OF FAMILY EXPENDITURES AND OF VALUE OF LIVING [a]
DEVOTED TO FOOD (INCLUDING LIQUOR) AND TOBACCO, FAMILIES OF TWO OR
MORE PERSONS,[b] BY TYPE OF COMMUNITY, 1935–1936 AND 1941

Period and Type of Community	Average Number of Persons per Family	Food and Tobacco	Food	Tobacco
		Per Cent of Family Expenditures [c]		
1935–1936				
Urban	3.7	33.2	31.3	1.96
Rural nonfarm	3.9	32.6	30.6	1.99
Farm	4.5	31.4	29.1	2.34
1941				
Urban	3.4	31.4	29.4	2.00
Rural nonfarm	3.7	32.3	30.3	2.02
Farm	4.2	30.7	28.8	1.93
		Per Cent of Value of Living [d]		
1935–1936				
Urban [e]	3.7	32.9	30.9	1.94
Rural nonfarm	3.9	33.0	31.1	1.93
Farm	4.5	38.1	36.4	1.66
1941				
Urban	3.4	31.4	29.5	1.95
Rural nonfarm	3.7	34.4	32.6	1.83
Farm	4.2	37.2	35.8	1.41

Sources: Family Expenditures in the United States, National Resources Planning Board, 1941, pp. 7, 29–30; and Family Spending and Saving in Wartime, Bulletin No. 822, U.S. Bureau of Labor Statistics, 1945, pp. 70, 73, 76 and 78.

a. "Value of living" means expenditures for family living plus consumer goods and services received without direct expenditures.

b. The importance of food tends to differ with family size and composition. Since there are relatively few one-person consuming units in farm communities, this comparison is confined to families of two or more persons.

c. Family expenditures include gifts and contributions made by the family. These are not included in value of living, which does, however, include some gifts in kind received.

d. In the initial reports of these surveys, retail prices or prices at "most likely place of purchase" were used in imputing a value to "food in kind." Such prices are likely to overstate the cost of food insofar as this is determined by income forgone because the food is used rather than sold. Because it seems probable that the quantity of food consumed by farm families is more nearly determined by the sale prices than by retail prices, in this analysis the value of food as reported in these surveys was reduced by one half. (The value of food as gift or pay was used as reported; but such food was of minor importance.) It was assumed that farm sale prices were on the average 50 per cent of the retail prices used in the initial evaluation. See Family Food Consumption in the United States, Spring 1942, Miscellaneous Publication No. 550, U.S. Department of Agriculture, 1944, p. 41, for the basis of this estimate.

e. In estimating income and consumption for 1935–1936 the National Resources Planning Board omitted food in kind for urban families. Its inclusion would probably have increased the percentage of value of living going for food by about one per cent.

Farm vs. Nonfarm Consumption

According to the two national surveys, farm families devote about the same percentage of their money expenditures to food as nonfarm families. During 1935–1936, 29 per cent of farm families' expenditures and 31 per cent of both rural nonfarm and urban families' expenditures went for food. In 1941 the proportions were 29 per cent for farm families and 30 and 29 per cent for rural nonfarm and urban families, respectively.[11] (See Table 39.)

11. Farm families in two Mississippi counties in 1945 used 35 per cent of their total expenditures for food, and rural nonfarm families 36 per cent. See Rural Levels of Living in Lee and Jones Counties, Mississippi, 1945, Agri-

TABLE 40. PER CENT OF NONFARM FAMILY EXPENDITURES DEVOTED TO FOOD AND TOBACCO, BY OCCUPATION OF FAMILY HEAD AND FAMILY TYPE, NORTH CENTRAL AND MIDDLE ATLANTIC REGIONS, 1935–1936 [a]

Occupation of Family Head	Family Types Combined [b]	Husband-Wife Families Plus:				At Least One Adult V	At Least One Adult and One Child VI
		No Others I	Children under 16 Years				
			One II	Two III	Three or Four IV		
		Per Cent of Total Expenditures Devoted to Food					
Total, 3 occupations	—	27.7	29.4	31.8	[c]	32.2	35.5
Wage-earner	32.8	29.4	30.6	33.1	35.8	34.2	36.6
Clerical	31.2	26.9	29.5	32.2	[c]	31.5	35.8
Business or professional [d]	30.1	26.8	28.1	30.3	[c]	30.8	34.2
		Per Cent of Total Expenditures Devoted to Tobacco					
Total, 3 occupations	—	2.28	2.08	1.99	[c]	2.03	1.96
Wage-earner	2.15	2.27	2.04	2.08	1.87	2.35	2.04
Clerical	2.11	2.33	2.15	2.00	[c]	1.91	2.07
Business or professional	1.94	2.24	2.04	1.80	[c]	1.84	1.79

Sources: U.S. Bureau of Labor Statistics (*Study of Consumer Purchases, Urban Series*): *Family Income and Expenditures in Chicago, 1935–36*, Bulletin No. 642, Vol. II, pp. 183–199, and *Family Income and Expenditures in Nine Cities of the East Central Region, 1935–36*, Bulletin No. 644, Vol. II, pp. 301–327; and *Consumer Purchases Study, Urban and Village Series: Family Income and Expenditures, Five Regions, Part 2, Family Expenditures*, Miscellaneous Publication No. 396, U.S. Department of Agriculture, 1940, pp. 229–247. The families are urban white families living in the East and North Central regions and village families in the Middle Atlantic and North Central regions.

a. Data for each occupation and family type are standardized as to income and city of residence.

b. Designation of family types differs from that in the original reports; one family type is omitted since data were available only for wage-earner families. The approximate number of persons per family for each type is as follows: I, 2.0; II, 3.0; III, 4.0; IV, 5.5; V, 3.5; VI, 5.5.

c. Not available.

d. For some sets of data the business and professional group is subdivided. Such data as exist indicate that the percentage of total expenditures going for food and tobacco is slightly higher for the independent business and professional groups than for the salaried groups.

When consumption is measured as "value of living," that is, when consumer goods and services received without direct expenditures [12] are taken into account along with direct monetary outlays, food is appreciably more important for farm than for nonfarm families.[13] During 1935–1936, food accounted for 36 per cent of the value of living of farm families and for 31 per cent among rural nonfarm and urban families. In 1941 the proportions were similar: 36 per cent for the farm group and 33 and 30 per cent for the rural nonfarm and urban groups.[14]

Tobacco shared about equally in expenditures and in value of living of both rural nonfarm and urban families, and the share — about 2.0 per cent — remained the same between 1935–1936 and 1941. Among farm families, however, tobacco decreased in importance during this period and accounted for a larger share of expenditures than of value of living. Tobacco took 2.3 per cent of the total money outlays of farm families in 1935–1936, a higher proportion than in the case of nonfarm families, and 1.9 per cent in 1941; it

culture Information Bulletin No. 41, U.S. Department of Agriculture, 1951.

12. Those included in the family studies are, for the most part, home-produced food at gross value and the imputed net rental value of owner-occupied dwellings. For tenant farm families, rent for the dwelling is included in rent for the farm, which is treated as a farm expense; to offset this, an imputed rent as nonmoney income and consumption in kind is included.

13. This difference with degree of urbanization may be partly due to the nature of the measurement. The consumption in kind included in the measure of total value of living is confined mainly to food and housing, and does not include other types, such as mutual assistance among neighbors, which may be more important for farm than for nonfarm families. The total value of living may therefore be understated more for farm than for nonfarm families.

14. In the Mississippi study food accounted for 43 per cent of the value of living of farm families and 35 per cent among rural nonfarm families.

TABLE 41. PER CENT OF FAMILY EXPENDITURES AND TOTAL VALUE OF LIVING
DEVOTED TO FOOD AND TOBACCO, PENNSYLVANIA AND OHIO FARM
FAMILIES OF DIFFERENT COMPOSITION, 1935–1936 [a]

Family Type (Family Members in Addition to Husband and Wife)	Approximate Number of Persons per Family	Per Cent of Total Expenditures		Per Cent of Total Value of Living	
		Food	Tobacco	Food	Tobacco
No others	2.0	24.0	3.22	35.8	1.74
One or more children					
One child	3.0	25.6	2.53	38.2	1.38
Two children	4.0	25.4	2.22	39.3	1.18
Three or four children	5.5	28.0	1.22	43.0	.62
Other adults and perhaps children					
One adult and perhaps another person	3.5	24.4	2.35	38.7	1.36
One adult, one child and perhaps two others	5.5	28.1	2.51	43.6	1.41

Source: Consumer Purchases Study, Farm Series: Family Income and Expenditures, Five Regions, Part 2, Family Expenditures, Miscellaneous Publication No. 465, U.S. Department of Agriculture, 1941, pp. 246–249.

a. The Pennsylvania and Ohio data are the only set in which family types were separated; in the other regions they were combined, so that the effect of the additional children was lost. The data are standardized for income level.

accounted for only 1.7 per cent of the total value of living of farm families in 1935–1936 and for even less (1.4 per cent) in 1941.[15] (See Table 39.)

Alcoholic beverages appear to increase in importance with urbanization. Urban families reported using about 1.5 per cent of their expenditures for alcoholic beverages in 1941; whereas rural nonfarm and farm families reported 0.7 and 0.6 per cent, respectively.[16]

Occupational Differences

Food consumption may be expected to vary among broad occupational groups because of differences in the physical exertion required in their work. Among nonfarm families in 1935–1936 the wage-earner group led in the percentage of expenditures going for food, the clerical group came second, and the business and professional group third. In a comparison limited to families of the same size and composition and with the same current annual income, wage-earner families were found to use 33 per cent of their expenditures for food, the clerical group 31 per cent, and the business and professional group 30 per cent. (See Table 40.)

Tobacco also appears to account for a larger share of expenditures among wage-earner families than among other occupational groups.

Food Budget and Family Size

During the spring of 1948, urban families without children under 16 years of age spent 27 per cent of their income for food (including alcoholic beverages), while families with children under age 16 spent 36 per cent. The families without children were smaller than the others, however. They averaged 2.3 persons while those with children averaged 4.2 persons.[17]

The percentage of family expenditures used for food rises steadily as family size increases. The pattern is much the same for farm and nonfarm families and for different occupational groups.

15. The lesser importance of tobacco for farm families in value of living terms than in expenditure terms is due to the greater importance of consumption in kind among farm than nonfarm families.

16. See Family Spending and Saving in Wartime, p. 78.

17. Food Consumption of Urban Families with Children and of Families with No Children, United States, Spring 1948, 1948 Food Consumption Surveys, Preliminary Report No. 14, U.S. Department of Agriculture, January 1950. This survey did not include data on total family expenditures.

TABLE 42. EXPENDITURES FOR FOOD BY URBAN HOUSEKEEPING FAMILIES
OF TWO OR MORE PERSONS IN SPRING OF 1948,[a] BY 1947 INCOME

1947 Income after Taxes	Average Number of Persons per Family	Average Weekly Income before Federal Taxes [b]	Amount	Per Cent of Weekly Income
All families	3.29	$ 80.34	$25.57	31.8
Under $1,000	2.51	18.60	13.76	74.0
1,000–2,000	2.90	38.00	17.12	45.1
2,000–3,000	3.28	54.94	22.35	40.7
3,000–4,000	3.52	77.52	27.06	34.9
4,000–5,000	3.49	94.36	30.07	31.9
5,000–7,500	3.40	128.52	31.36	24.4
7,500 and over	3.82	269.22	44.08	16.4
Not classified	2.98	79.44	26.80	33.7

Source: *Food Consumption of Urban Families (68 Cities) in the U.S., Spring 1948,* 1948 Food Consumption Surveys, Preliminary Report No. 5, U.S. Department of Agriculture, May 1949, p. 6.

a. Based on survey of expenditures during one week.
b. During the week of the survey.

(See Tables 40 and 41.) In 1941, families of two persons used 31 per cent of their total expenditures for food, and families of five or more persons at the same income level used 37 per cent. In actual dollars two-person families spent 8 per cent less than three-person families and families of five or more spent 28 per cent more than families of three persons.[18]

Tobacco Budget and Family Size

The share of tobacco in family expenditures declines slightly with the addition of children, partly because total expenditures are higher at the peak of family size. (See Tables 40 and 41.) But dollar expenditures for tobacco decline as well, and this decline is more marked for farm than for nonfarm families.[19] In the farm group,

families without children under 16 years of age spent 15 per cent more for tobacco than families with one child under age 16 and 24 per cent more than those with two children under age 16. Among nonfarm families the presence of one young child reduced the average expenditure for tobacco by one per cent and the presence of two young children reduced it by 3 per cent.

Expenditures for tobacco and smoking supplies among urban families in 1941 were much the same at all family sizes, but this comparison took no account of age.

The importance of tobacco in the family budget tends to be greater among young families than among older families. For example, during 1935–1936, among a group of nonfarm married couples, the proportion of family expenditures going for tobacco was 2.2 per cent when the wife was under 30 years of age and decreased gradually as the wife's age increased until, in the age group 60 years and over, it reached 1.1 per cent.[20]

18. *Family Spending and Saving in Wartime.* Families with incomes below $500 and those with incomes of $5,000 and over were omitted. A similar expenditure pattern by family size was found among urban families in 1944. See *Monthly Labor Review,* January 1946. Dorothy S. Brady has made a systematic examination of the published data on expenditures of urban families classified by both income and family size. She found that, when income is held constant, food expenditures tend to increase with family size at about the rate of the cube root of family sizes. See Dorothy S. Brady and Helen Barber, "The Pattern of Food Expenditures," *Review of Economics and Statistics,* August 1948, pp. 196–206.

19. Two methodological aspects of the farm data may account for the greater decline in the farm group. The families were classified by net total income, that is, net money income plus income in kind. Income in kind is much greater for farm than for nonfarm families, and

tends to increase appreciably with family size. Consequently, with a given net total income, the larger families had a smaller amount of money income available for the purchase of tobacco. In addition, the data cover only farm families in Ohio and in Lancaster County, Pennsylvania; the latter, being predominantly Amish and of similar religious groups, are relatively large families and have a strong taboo against smoking even by the men.

20. *Family Spending and Saving as Related to Age of Wife and Age and Number of Children,* Miscellaneous Publication No. 489, U.S. Department of Agriculture, 1942, pp. 53, 55, 60 and 63. These data are for small cities in the North Central region and villages in the Middle Atlantic and North Central regions. The data are

TABLE 43. EXPENDITURES FOR FOOD AND TOBACCO IN RELATION TO INCOME AND TO TOTAL EXPENDITURES,[a] FAMILIES OF TWO OR MORE PERSONS, BY TYPE OF COMMUNITY AND MONEY INCOME, 1941

Money Income Class	Average Number of Persons per Family	Per Cent of Disposable Money Income		Per Cent of Total Expenditures	
		Food	Tobacco	Food	Tobacco
Urban Families					
All	3.44	28.2	2.0	30.1	2.1
Below $500	2.64	56.8	2.8	38.8	1.9
500–1,000	3.17	44.1	2.0	40.6	1.9
1,000–1,500	3.05	37.2	2.7	35.5	2.6
1,500–2,000	3.39	32.8	2.3	33.5	2.3
2,000–3,000	3.48	31.3	2.1	30.7	2.1
3,000–5,000	3.71	25.7	1.9	27.9	2.1
5,000 and over	4.48	18.4	1.3	23.9	1.7
Rural Nonfarm Families					
All	3.66	28.0	1.9	30.3	2.0
Below $500	3.02	46.9	2.8	41.7	2.5
500–1,000	3.84	38.1	2.6	34.5	2.3
1,000–1,500	3.56	32.3	2.0	32.7	2.0
1,500–2,000	4.01	28.6	2.1	30.7	2.2
2,000–3,000	3.94	25.0	1.9	27.8	2.1
3,000–5,000	4.06	20.0	1.1	24.6	1.3
5,000 and over	3.51	13.0	0.9	20.6	1.4
Farm Families					
All	4.15	21.9	1.5	28.8	1.9
Below $500	3.94	59.8	5.0	32.8	2.8
500–1,000	4.13	30.3	2.0	30.5	2.1
1,000–1,500	4.74	24.1	1.4	30.3	1.7
1,500–2,000	4.39	20.0	1.3	26.9	1.7
2,000–3,000	3.56	18.3	1.1	27.1	1.6
3,000–5,000	4.54	12.4	0.6	23.9	1.2
5,000 and over	4.29	7.7	0.5	23.9	1.5

Sources: Family Spending and Saving in Wartime, Bulletin No. 822, U.S. Bureau of Labor Statistics, 1945, pp. 33, 70, 102 and 109, and Rural Family Spending and Saving in Wartime, Miscellaneous Publication No. 520, U.S. Department of Agriculture, June 1943, pp. 156–160. Unpublished data for rural families in lowest and highest income classes were provided by the Bureau of Human Nutrition and Home Economics.

a. Expenditures include outlays for gifts and contributions as well as purchases for family use.

Income and Consumption

Family spending in any one year is determined by current income, by assets available from savings and inheritance, and by willingness and ability to incur debts. In general high-income families spend less of their current income for food than low-income families.

Expenditures for food (including alcoholic beverages) in the spring of 1948 ranged from 74 per cent of current income for families with less than $1,000 income during 1947 to 16 per cent for those with incomes over $7,500. (See Table 42.) Earlier studies showed a similar drop. For example, among urban families in 1941, 57 per cent of incomes under $500 and 18 per cent of incomes of $5,000 and more went for food. Rural nonfarm families in these two income classes spent 47 and 13 per cent of income for food; and farm families, 60 and 8 per cent. (See Table 43.)

standardized for community size and income. Five income classes in the two types of communities were combined.

Such data, however, greatly overstate the importance of food at low income levels and understate its importance somewhat at high income levels. Family incomes fluctuate from year to year, and families do not always adjust their expenditures accordingly. Thus a family reporting low income for the survey year may be accustomed to higher returns and may therefore maintain expenditures by reducing savings, drawing upon assets, or incurring debts. Retired families, whose incomes are usually relatively low, often draw systematically on their assets and so spend more in relation to current income than other families at the same income level. The importance of food and other consumer goods at different economic levels is therefore probably judged better by the percentage of total expenditures, rather than of total income, used for different items.

Higher-income families use a smaller share of their total expenditures for food than do low-income families, but the range between income groups is narrower than when food expenditures are measured as a percentage of income. From income levels of below $500 to those of $5,000 or more, the share of food in family expenditures in 1941 dropped from 39 per cent to 24 per cent among urban families; from 42 per cent to 21 per cent among rural nonfarm families; and from 33 per cent to 24 per cent among farm families. (See Table 43.)

Trends in Consumption

American eating habits have altered radically over the past fifty years.[21] The shift to fruits and vegetables and away from cereals and potatoes has brought a virtual revolution in customary menus. Housewives no longer insist that their families eat meat and potatoes for dinner and porridge for breakfast. Salads and juices, especially fruit juices, help vary the diet and improve its nutritive content.

---

21. The changing food consumption pattern since the middle 1930s has been recognized in the revision of the consumers' price index. Until recently, the food weights for this index were based on consumption of wage-earner and clerical families during 1934-1936. In the spring of 1951 the U.S. Bureau of Labor Statistics made an interim adjustment pending the results of a large-scale urban study in 1950. Frozen food was introduced into the index; increased weight was given to vanilla cookies and layer cake, hamburger, poultry, fresh milk, shortening and margarine; and decreased weight to corn meal, rolled oats, rib roast, veal cutlet, butter, apples, canned tomatoes, coffee, sugar, lard and salad dressing. See "Interim Adjustment of the CPI," *Monthly Labor Review*, April 1951, p. 427.

The rise in real incomes has increased the relative consumption of more expensive foods. Changing technology has shifted the relative prices of foods, improved the quality of some and lengthened the season of others. Education has undoubtedly also influenced eating habits, since the shifts for the most part have been in the direction of improved nutrition.

Shifts have also occurred in consumption of alcoholic beverages and tobacco. Per capita consumption of alcoholic beverages mounted steadily after the repeal of prohibition, but, except for wines, never reached peak pre-prohibition levels. Per capita consumption of tobacco has greatly increased since the late 1930s, owing to the sharp increase in cigarette consumption.

FOOD [22]

The amount of food consumed per capita, measured in pounds without regard to type of food, has been remarkably constant during the entire period for which national data are available. In 1945-1946, a peak period, it was 10 per cent higher than in 1930-1934. The price-weighted index of per capita food consumption, on the other hand, between the same periods increased 15 per cent, and from 1910-1914 to 1949-1950 increased 12 per cent. A rise in real incomes undoubtedly played a part in these increases. Consumers demanded more of the high-priced foods such as eggs, meat, citrus fruits, and leafy, green and yellow vegetables. (See Table 44.)

Per capita consumption of total food, measured in pounds, actually decreased by 3 per cent between 1910-1914 and 1949-1950, but the shift in demand varied markedly by type of food. Per capita consumption of potatoes and grain products declined by 41 per cent during this period, while for all other foods combined it increased by 13 per cent. (See Figure 24 and Table 44.) The shift in demand was due partly to higher real incomes and partly to a reduction in the relative size of the farm population, in which con-

---

22. See *Consumption of Food in the United States, 1909-1952*, Agriculture Handbook No. 62, U.S. Department of Agriculture, 1953. These data measure apparent consumption or the disappearance of food from retail stores and the movement of food stocks on farms into the farm family kitchen, rather than actual consumption. A weakness of the measure is that the building up and liquidation of consumer inventories may vary somewhat from time to time. In addition, there are appreciable losses for some foods, notably fresh fruits and vegetables, through trimming and spoilage, and bread, because of staleness.

TABLE 44. ANNUAL PER CAPITA CONSUMPTION OF MAJOR FOOD GROUPS, 1910–1952

Food Group	1910–1914	1915–1919	1920–1924	1925–1929	1930–1934	1935–1939	1940–1944	1945–1946	1947–1948	1949–1950	1951–1952
					Amount (*Pounds*)						
Total food	1,580	1,537	1,552	1,562	1,519	1,527	1,598	1,668	1,575	1,529	1,528
Potatoes and grain products	473	442	405	392	363	342	334	326	290	278	270
Other foods	1,107	1,095	1,147	1,170	1,156	1,185	1,264	1,342	1,285	1,251	1,254
Dairy products (excluding butter)	370	373	378	375	375	376	409	452	420	411	412
Eggs	37	35	38	40	37	36	39	46	46	47	50
Meat, poultry and fish (excluding bacon and fatback)	148	141	142	138	134	131	150	159	155	153	154
Fats and oils (including butter, bacon and fatback)	59	60	61	65	66	64	67	62	64	66	65
Dry beans and peas, nuts and soya products	16	16	15	16	17	18	20	19	16	17	18
Potatoes (including sweet potatoes)	190	178	169	158	147	141	138	132	120	111	106
Citrus fruits and tomatoes	61	64	67	71	79	96	114	130	119	104	109
Leafy, green and yellow vegetables	63	72	89	97	102	106	118	126	110	105	102
Other fruits and vegetables	253	231	237	237	221	231	224	238	227	222	220
Grain products (flour and cereals)	283	264	236	234	216	201	196	194	170	167	164
Sugar and sirups	89	91	108	117	112	110	107	92	108	107	107
Coffee, tea and cocoa	10	12	13	13	13	16	16	18	18	18	17
					Index (*1935–1939 = 100*)						
Total food (unweighted)	103	100	102	102	99	100	105	109	103	100	100
Potatoes and grain products	138	129	118	115	106	100	98	95	85	81	79
Other foods	93	92	97	99	98	100	107	113	108	106	106
Total food (weighted with prices in a base year)	97	95	98	100	98	100	108	113	110	109	110
Dairy products (excluding butter)	98	99	101	100	100	100	109	120	112	109	110
Eggs	103	97	106	111	103	100	108	128	128	131	139
Meat, poultry and fish (excluding bacon and fatback)	113	108	108	105	102	100	115	121	118	117	118
Fats and oils (including butter, bacon and fatback)	92	94	95	102	103	100	105	97	100	103	102
Dry beans and peas, nuts and soya products	89	89	83	89	94	100	111	106	89	94	100
Potatoes (including sweet potatoes)	135	126	120	112	104	100	98	94	85	79	75
Citrus fruits and tomatoes	64	67	70	74	82	100	119	135	124	108	114
Leafy, green and yellow vegetables	59	68	84	92	96	100	111	119	104	99	96
Other fruits and vegetables	110	100	103	103	96	100	97	103	98	96	95
Grain products (flour and cereals)	141	131	117	116	107	100	98	97	85	83	82
Sugar and sirups	81	83	98	106	102	100	97	84	98	97	97
Coffee, tea and cocoa	63	75	81	81	81	100	100	113	113	113	106

Source: Consumption of Food in the United States, 1909–1952, Agriculture Handbook No. 62, U.S. Department of Agriculture, September 1953, Tables 38 and 39. Foods used in the production of alcoholic beverages are excluded. Meat, poultry and fish are on an eviscerated basis.

Note: Discrepancies in addition are due to rounding.

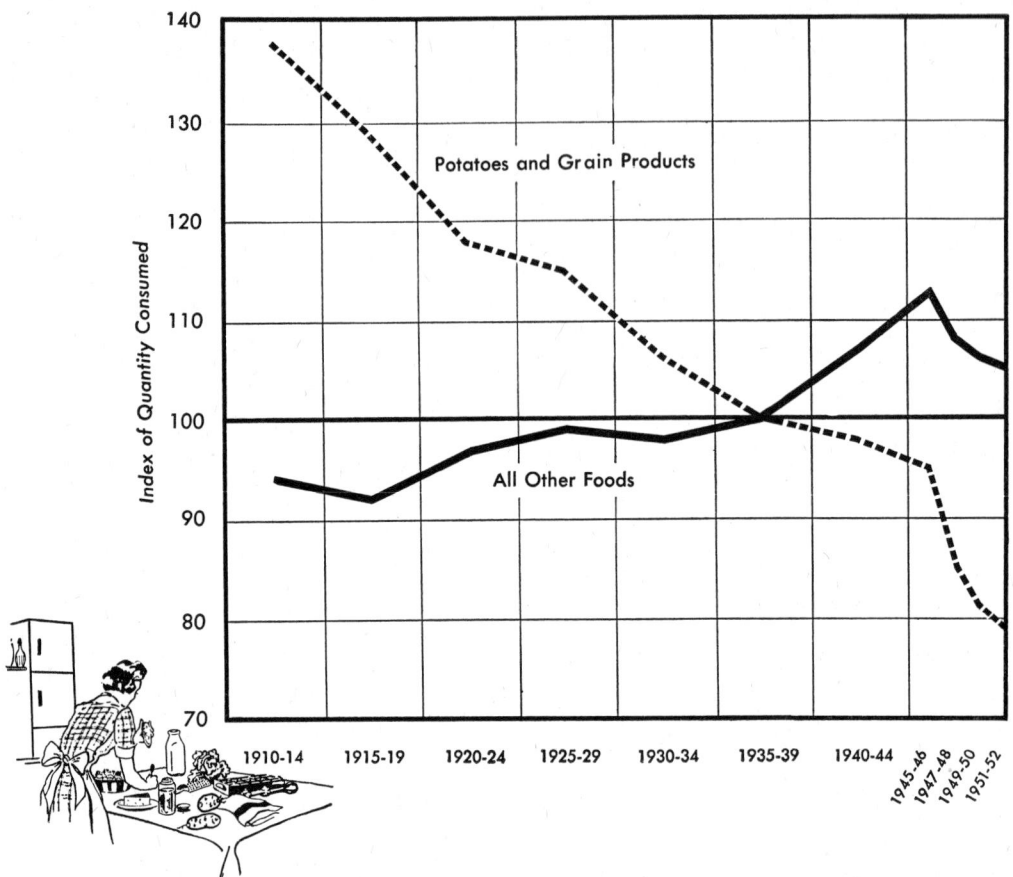

FIGURE 24. INDEXES OF PER CAPITA CONSUMPTION OF POTATOES AND GRAIN PRODUCTS
AND OF ALL OTHER FOODS, 1910–1952
(1935–1939 = 100)

Source: Table 44.

sumption of potatoes and grain products is high. Relative prices also changed: for example, from 1913–1914 to 1935–1939, per capita consumption in pounds of potatoes and grain products fell 26 per cent and that of "other" food rose 13 per cent. At the same time the price of bread and potatoes increased somewhat more than the prices of all foods; the price of bread went up 41 per cent and the price of potatoes 42 per cent, while the average price of all foods increased by 26 per cent.[23]

The rate and regularity of change has varied among the different food groups whose consumption has increased. Some groups have moved steadily upward while others have moved down and then up. For example, per capita consumption

23. Publications of the U.S. Bureau of Labor Statistics: *Retail Prices, 1890 to 1928*, No. 495, 1929, and *Retail Prices of Food, 1923–36*, No. 635, 1937.

of meat, poultry and fish declined from 148 pounds in 1910–1914 to 123 pounds in 1935 and then rose gradually to 159 pounds in 1945–1946. Consumption of citrus fruit and tomatoes increased spectacularly; in 1945–1946 the amount consumed per capita was 113 per cent higher than in 1910–1914. By 1949–1950 the level was somewhat lower. The increase for leafy, green and yellow vegetables was somewhat less. Per capita consumption of dairy products (apart from butter) showed only a slight upward trend from 1910–1940; but from 1935–1939 to 1945–1946 it increased 20 per cent. (Table 44 and Figure 25.)

Dairy Products

Despite the upward trend in consumption of dairy products, some items within this group

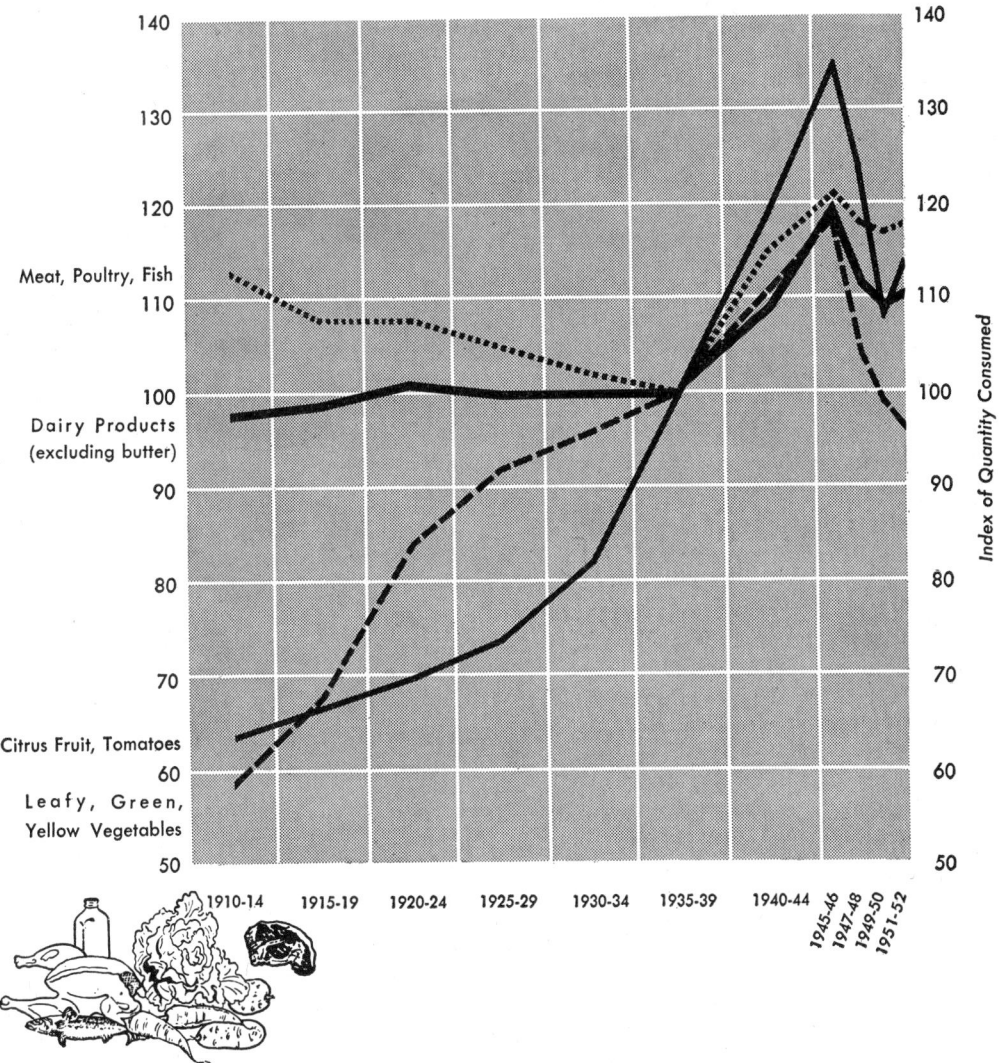

FIGURE 25. INDEXES OF PER CAPITA CONSUMPTION OF FOUR MAJOR FOODS, 1910–1950
(1935–1939 = 100)

Source: Table 44.

showed a decline. For example, per capita consumption of condensed milk fell from 5 pounds in 1910–1914 to 2 pounds in 1945–1946, a peak period for consumption of all dairy products. This drop may have been partly due to better refrigeration, which enabled people to substitute cream or fresh milk for condensed milk. Consumption of fresh skim milk and natural buttermilk declined from 84 pounds per capita to 48 pounds, probably because of the relative decline in the farm population.

During 1910–1914, skim milk for the most part was used in its natural form. A very large part is now used as dried skim milk or in chocolate-flavored drinks. From 1925–1929 to 1945–1946, consumption of dried skim milk per capita increased from 0.7 to 2.6 pounds, while per capita consumption of skim milk in chocolate drinks increased from 0.9 to 5.9 pounds.

Other changes in food marketing and consumer habits have caused varying rates of increase in the use of dairy products. For example, between 1910–1914 and 1945–1946, the per capita amount of milk and cream going into ice cream increased eightfold, whereas the per capita increase for fluid whole milk was only 26 per cent. In the same period per capita consumption of cultured buttermilk increased fivefold — from 1.3 to 6.7 pounds. By 1950 it was 8.3 pounds.

Meat

In the meat, poultry and fish group, veal and poultry have increased slightly in importance. They constituted 8 per cent of the total pounds consumed during 1910–1914 and 22 per cent during 1945–1949.

Fats and Oils

There has been a pronounced shift from butter to margarine. During 1920–1924, 13 pounds of margarine were consumed for every 100 pounds of butter; during 1945–1949, 47 pounds. Between the spring of 1942 and the spring of 1948 the proportion of urban families using some margarine during a week increased from 16 per cent to 51 per cent. The proportion using both butter and margarine increased from 3 per cent to 18 per cent in that period.[24]

Among the other fats and oils, lard has been decreasing in importance and vegetable shortening and shortening compounds have been gaining ground. Annual consumption of edible oils, important in salad dressings, increased from 3.6 pounds per capita in 1920–1924 to 6.8 pounds in 1945–1949. The popularity of salads probably accounts for some of this increase, and some of it may be due to the use of mayonnaise as a spread for sandwiches.

Fresh Fruits and Vegetables

Per capita consumption of lettuce and celery doubled between 1920–1924 and 1945–1949. However, these products accounted for only one sixth of all fresh vegetables consumed in 1945–1949 with potatoes excluded; cabbage and tomatoes sold in larger volume.

Consumer demand for fresh fruits has changed markedly. Per capita consumption of apples, for example, fell from 60 pounds in 1910–1914 to 27 pounds in 1945–1949, while that of citrus fruit rose from 18 pounds to 54 pounds. During that period, moreover, oranges became cheaper and apples dearer. The average wholesale price of

oranges in ten principal auctions was 7 per cent less in 1945–1948 than in 1927–1929, and the price received by farmers for apples was up 71 per cent.[25]

Frozen orange juice has increased rapidly in favor since its introduction in 1946. By 1951 about one fourth of the Florida crop was made into frozen concentrate. Between April–June 1950 and 1951, consumption of concentrated frozen orange juice increased 48 per cent, while that of canned single-strength orange juice declined 18 per cent.[26] One writer estimated that the civilian population in 1951 consumed slightly more frozen orange concentrate than canned orange juice, and anticipated that the consumption of the fresh fruit would drop to about half of the total consumption of oranges.[27]

Beverages

Urban families increased their home consumption of soft drinks by two thirds between the spring of 1942 and the spring of 1948 — from 0.58 to 0.97 pounds per capita per week.[28] Market data indicate, however, that soft drinks have decreased in importance relative to malt beverages such as beer and ale. For every $100 of malt beverages manufactured (excluding excise tax), the value of soft drinks manufactured was $71 in 1939 and only $58 in 1947.[29]

ALCOHOLIC BEVERAGES

Americans drank an average of about 17 gallons of beer and other malt drinks per capita in 1950, about 4 quarts of hard liquor and 4 quarts of wine.[30] Consumption in that year was a little

24. *Fats and Oils Consumed by City Families*, 1948 Food Consumption Surveys, Commodity Summary No. 2, U.S. Department of Agriculture, August 1948.

25. *Agricultural Statistics, 1941*, U.S. Department of Agriculture, p. 185; *1949*, p. 174; and *1950*, pp. 176 and 199.

26. *Consumer Purchases of Selected Fresh Fruits, Canned and Frozen Juice, and Dried Fruits, during August 1951*, U.S. Department of Agriculture, September 1951 (mimeographed).

27. B. H. Pubols, "Juices Play Increasing Part in Total Orange Consumption," *Agricultural Situation*, November 1951, p. 11.

28. U.S. Department of Agriculture: *Family Food Consumption in the United States, Spring 1942*, Miscellaneous Publication No. 550, 1944, and *Food Consumption of Urban Families (68 Cities) in the U.S., Spring 1948*, 1948 Food Consumption Surveys, Preliminary Report No. 5, May 1949.

29. *1947 Census of Manufactures: Product Supplement*, U.S. Bureau of the Census, 1950, pp. 16–17.

30. *Statistical Abstract of the United States, 1951*, p. 775. This is apparent consumption, that is, disappearance from the market. The U.S. gallon is used except for distilled spirits, where the measure is the tax gallon.

below the level of 1945–1949, when the per capita average for beer and other malt drinks was 18 gallons; for hard liquor, 5 quarts; and for wine, 3 quarts.

These are over-all averages. Many people, however, use little or no alcoholic beverages. Children, of course, share little in the consumption, and a Gallup poll made during 1949 reported 42 per cent of all adults as total abstainers. Since two thirds of the population in 1949 were 20 years of age or over, the consumption of alcoholic beverages is probably confined to about 38 per cent [31] of the population. In 1950, therefore, the average user of alcoholic beverages may have consumed about 45 gallons of malt beverages and 20 quarts of distilled spirits and wine.

For every 100 pounds of grain products used in flour or cereals in 1949–1950, 29 pounds went into alcoholic beverages; and for every 100 pounds of fresh, frozen and canned fruit and fruit juice consumed, 6 pounds of grapes were used in making wine.[32] The per capita amount of grain products and grapes used annually in producing alcoholic beverages has increased somewhat since prewar years. In 1936–1939, 42 pounds of grain per capita were used for this purpose and (in 1939) 7 pounds of grapes. In 1949–1950, the annual average for grain was 49 pounds per capita, and for grapes, 8.6 pounds.[33]

TOBACCO

From 1910 to the middle 1930s annual per capita consumption of tobacco was fairly stable, rising slightly from 5.9 pounds in 1911–1915 to 6.3 pounds in 1926–1930. Early depression years brought a slight drop; in 1932 consumption was at a low of 5.5 pounds. Thereafter the use of tobacco increased sharply. In 1945, and again in 1949, per capita consumption was 9.2 pounds — 67 per cent above the 1932 low.[34]

Cigarette smoking has accounted for all of the increased use of tobacco. Since 1910, consumption of cigarettes has risen rapidly, with only a slight leveling off during the early 1930s. On the other hand, per capita consumption of cigars fell until the 1930s, and has leveled off since that time. Per capita consumption of tobacco in other forms has been decreasing steadily, although it fell less rapidly during depression years than during other years. (See Figure 26.)

During 1949 Americans consumed a per capita average of 128 packs of cigarettes, 37 cigars, and 1.6 pounds of other tobacco and snuff.[35] However, as with alcoholic beverages, per capita consumption for the population as a whole takes no account of the large and changing block of abstainers. The sharp increase in tobacco consumption since the middle 1930s may be due chiefly to an increase in the percentage of women smoking. Data are not available to trace this change, but smoking is undoubtedly more prevalent among women today than it was twenty years ago.

A Gallup poll in 1949 [36] reported that 44 per cent of all adults smoked cigarettes — one third of the women and one half of the men. On this basis, and assuming that the percentage of smokers is as high among 15-to-20-year-olds as among adults, 1949 cigarette production provided each cigarette smoker with 22 cigarettes a day. In the poll, the average cigarette smoker said he consumed 17 cigarettes a day. The poll did not attempt to measure use of tobacco in other forms.

Food in the Market Economy

Americans tend more and more to purchase the food they consume; only farm families continue to produce an appreciable amount for themselves, and relatively few families receive food in return for work. Moreover, foods are now reaching the home more nearly ready for the table, and the practice of "eating out" is growing.

PURCHASED FOOD VS. FOOD IN KIND

Although food in kind — food produced by families for their own use or received without

---

31. The Gallup poll included only persons 21 years of age and over. This estimate assumes that inclusion of 20-year-olds would not change the rate.

32. Consumption of cereals and fruits reported in Table 44 excludes use for alcoholic beverages.

33. Data supplied by M. Burk, U.S. Bureau of Agricultural Economics. Per capita figures were derived from Department of Agriculture estimates of the population using civilian food supplies. Grain sorghums are not included.

34. *Statistical Abstract of the United States, 1951*, p. 776. Per capita consumption is based on population as of July 1 as shown in Supplement of September 1950 to Miscellaneous Publication No. 691, U.S. Department of Agriculture, p. 41.

35. Based on production data in *Statistical Abstract of the United States, 1951*. The per capita figures are for the total population as of July 1. The source reports number of cigarettes and cigars and pounds of tobacco and snuff; it was assumed that there are on the average 20 cigarettes to a pack.

36. Public Opinion News Service, release of December 17, 1949.

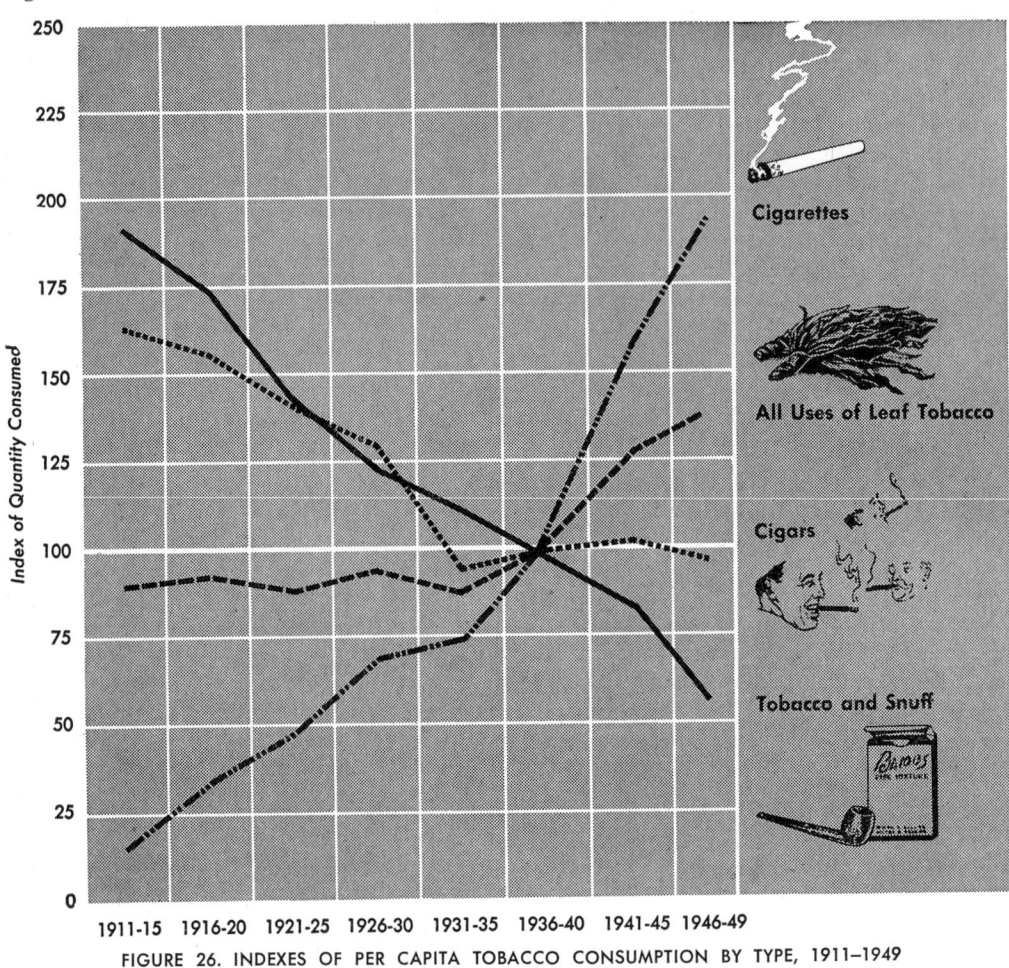

FIGURE 26. INDEXES OF PER CAPITA TOBACCO CONSUMPTION BY TYPE, 1911–1949

(1936–1940 = 100)

Sources: Statistical Abstract of the United States, 1951, U.S. Bureau of the Census, p. 776. Per capita consumption is based on population as of July 1 as shown in Supplement for 1949 to Consumption of Food in the United States, 1909–48, Supplement to Miscellaneous Publication No. 691, U.S. Department of Agriculture, September 1950, p. 41.

direct payment, as gifts, pay or relief — has declined in importance relative to purchased food, it continues to be of significance in the measurement of total annual consumption.

From 1930 to 1950 the value of food produced and consumed on farms fell from 8 per cent of total food expenditures to 4 per cent. (See Table 45.) This decline was partly due to the fact that the farm population decreased in that period from one quarter of the total population to under one sixth. In addition, farm families have tended to purchase a larger percentage of their total food. Their consumption of home-produced food, valued at retail prices, dropped from $163 for

every $100 of their food expenditures in 1935–1936 to $131 in 1942.[37]

Servants, nurses and other nonfarm workers sometimes receive meals as part of their pay. The value of meals received by domestic servants and nurses declined from 1.5 per cent of total food expenditures in 1930 to 0.6 per cent in 1950, partly because of the decrease in domestic employment. The value of food provided commercial and

---

37. Family Expenditures in the United States, National Resources Planning Board, 1941, p. 30; and Rural Family Spending and Saving in Wartime, Miscellaneous Publication No. 520, U.S. Department of Agriculture, June 1943, p. 32.

TABLE 45. VALUE OF FOOD IN KIND [a] AS PER CENT OF TOTAL FOOD EXPENDITURES, 1930–1950

| Year | Total | Food in Kind to Employees | | Food Produced and Consumed on Farms |
		Government and Commercial [b]	Domestic Servants and Nurses	
1930	10.8	1.4	1.5	7.9
1935	9.9	1.3	1.1	7.5
1940	7.8	1.4	1.0	5.4
1945	11.9	6.4	0.5	5.0
1950	6.4	1.9	0.6	3.9

Source: National Income and Product of the United States, 1929–1950 (1951 National Income Supplement to the Survey of Current Business), pp. 192, 193 and 203.

a. Excludes value of food received as gifts or relief.

b. The series does not differentiate between military and nonmilitary personnel. The sharp increase in 1945 appears to be due wholly to the military group.

government employees amounted to 1.4 per cent of all food outlays in 1940, 6.4 per cent in 1945 and 1.9 per cent in 1950. No trend is thus apparent. The peak level of 1945 appears to have been largely a war phenomenon, since food for military personnel was included. (See Table 45.)

Home production and receipts of food as pay are much less important for nonfarm families than for farm families. Among families of two or more, the retail value of food in kind for every $100 of food expenditures in 1941 was $137, $32 and $3 for farm, rural nonfarm and urban respectively. For each type of community the relative value of food in kind fell as family income rose. (See Table 46.) The drop was most marked

TABLE 46. VALUE OF FOOD IN KIND FOR EVERY $100 OF FOOD EXPENDITURES, FAMILIES OF TWO OR MORE, BY TYPE OF COMMUNITY AND MONEY INCOME, 1941 [a]

Money Income Class	Urban	Rural Nonfarm	Farm
All	$ 3	$32	$137
Under $500	39	80	217
500–1,000	11	56	163
1,000–1,500	5	25	124
1,500–2,000	4	25	112
2,000–3,000	2	20	75
3,000–5,000	2	19	88
5,000 and over	1	5	63

Sources: Rural Family Spending and Saving in Wartime, Miscellaneous Publication No. 520, U.S. Department of Agriculture, June 1943; and Family Spending and Saving in Wartime, Bulletin No. 822, U.S. Bureau of Labor Statistics, 1945.

a. Imputed value of home-produced food based on purchase prices.

for urban families, probably because income in this group rises with size of community and only in the smaller places, and therefore at the lower income levels, are urban families likely to have gardens or keep chickens.

During the fall of 1944 nearly 33 per cent of urban families consumed their own garden-grown fruits and vegetables; their average consumption of these products amounted to 4 pounds a week.[38] The percentage of families consuming home-grown produce and the amount consumed per family tended to increase somewhat with income and markedly with family size. Gardening was more important as a source of food in the Mountain and Pacific than in the other regions; it was least important in the South. (See Table 47.)

The source of food in kind varies among farm, rural nonfarm and urban families. In 1941, 98 per cent of the food in kind reported by farm families was home-produced. Rural nonfarm families (including families of hired farm workers, whether or not they lived on farms) produced 82 per cent of their total food in kind and received about 10 per cent as pay. The remaining 8 per cent was gifts or relief. Urban families received about half of their food in kind as pay. Even though the rural nonfarm group included families of farm laborers living on farms, the dollar value of food received as pay during 1941 was slightly less for rural nonfarm than for urban families — $11 compared with $13 annually.[39] The somewhat larger average for the city group may be due to their greater employment in hotels and restaurants.

38. The figures were probably unusually large in that year because of the Victory Garden campaign.

39. Family Spending and Saving in Wartime, p. 78.

TABLE 47. CONSUMPTION OF HOME-GROWN FRUIT AND VEGETABLES BY CITY HOUSEKEEPING FAMILIES [a] DURING ONE WEEK IN SEPTEMBER–OCTOBER 1944

	Per Cent Reporting Some Consumption [b]	Average Pounds Consumed per Family	
		Fruit	Vegetables
All families	32.9	1.27	3.05
Income class			
Under $1,000	23.7	.45	1.88
1,000–2,000	30.1	.72	2.08
2,000–3,000	32.3	1.28	3.05
3,000–4,000	43.8	2.07	4.89
4,000 and over	33.9	1.71	3.31
Family size			
1 person	21.0	.26	.81
2 and 3 persons	32.0	.98	2.38
4 or more persons	37.5	1.98	4.66
Region			
Northeast	31.6	1.25	2.86
South	18.4	.82	1.27
North Central	39.0	1.40	4.33
Mountain and Pacific	47.9	1.80	3.93

Source: "City Gardens in Wartime," Monthly Labor Review, October 1945, Table 1, p. 646.

a. Housekeeping families are those who eat a major portion of their meals at home. In this instance some one-person consuming units are included.

b. Includes consumption of fruits and vegetables raised in own gardens and of those raised or gathered by friends and given to the family.

There may be a growing tendency for other urban employers to provide meals at work.

HOME VS. PURCHASED MEALS

Purchases of restaurant and lunchroom meals and snacks have been increasing relative to other food purchases. Outlays for food eaten away from home for every $100 spent for food eaten at home increased from $24 in 1930–1932 to $27 in 1948–1950, dropping to a low of $22 in 1933–1935 and rising to a high of $33 in the war and immediate postwar years.[40]

The share of purchased meals in total food expenditures increases with degree of urbanization and with family income, but decreases as family size increases, especially if the additional family members are children. In 1941 for every $100 spent for food eaten at home or in boarding houses, urban, rural nonfarm and farm consumers (both families and individuals) spent $21, $9

and $8, respectively, for food eaten away from home — restaurant meals, meals bought at work or school or while traveling, board for children at school, ice cream, candy and soft drinks consumed away from home.[41] If the trend toward urbanization continues, therefore, meals away from home are likely to take a larger share of the family food dollar in the future.

Urban families consisting only of husband and wife spent 21 per cent of their food budgets for meals away from home in 1935–1936. Those with one child under age 16 spent 13 per cent; the addition of another child under 16 years of age cut the proportion spent for food away from home to 11 per cent.[42] The higher birth rate of recent years

40. National Income and Product of the United States, 1929–1950 (1951 National Income Supplement to the Survey of Current Business), Table 30. Alcoholic beverages are included, but food in kind is excluded.

41. These figures are based on family studies whose chief value lies in revealing differences within the nation as a whole that give clues on factors affecting change. In such surveys there seems to be a tendency to underreport consumption. The underreporting is especially marked for alcoholic beverages, perhaps because housewives who provide most of the data are likely to have only a vague notion about the consumption of alcoholic beverages, most of which may be consumed outside the home.

42. Bureau of Labor Statistics: Family Income and Expenditures in Chicago, 1935–36, Bulletin No. 642, Vol. II,

TABLE 48. HOME PRESERVATION OF FRUITS AND VEGETABLES BY CITY FAMILIES
OF TWO OR MORE PERSONS, BY INCOME AND BY SIZE OF CITY, 1947

	Average Number of Persons per Family	Canning [a]		Freezing	
		Per Cent of Families Reporting	Average Number of Quarts Canned by Those Reporting	Per Cent of Families Reporting	Average Number of Pounds Frozen by Those Reporting
All urban families of two or more	3.29	44.0	85.1	2.3	69.3
1947 income [b]					
Under $2,000	2.82	45.1	67.9	0.8 [c]	56.6 [c]
2,000–3,000	3.28	52.0	81.3	2.2	65.7
3,000–4,000	3.52	48.1	97.3	3.1	91.0
4,000–5,000	3.49	46.7	114.0	3.6	61.5
5,000 and over	3.53	43.8	73.4	3.5 [c]	61.2
Size of city					
2,500–10,000	[d]	60.7	107.3	4.4	73.5
10,000–50,000	[d]	52.6	84.3	4.9	76.3
50,000–250,000	[d]	50.2	86.2	0.6 [c]	13.5 [c]
250,000–1,000,000	[d]	38.7	68.4	0.7 [c]	57.0 [c]
1,000,000 and over	[d]	20.0	65.4	0.6 [c]	38.8 [c]

Source: Food Preservation by City Families, 1947, 1948
Food Consumption Surveys, Preliminary Report No. 15,
U.S. Department of Agriculture, November 1950, Tables
1 and 2.

a. Includes pickles, jellies and jams.
b. Money income after federal income tax.
c. Three or fewer families reporting.
d. Not reported.

may therefore reduce somewhat the proportion of food expenditures going for meals away from home.

For every $100 spent for food eaten at home in the spring of 1948 the following amounts were spent for food away from home by urban families in different income brackets: [43]

1947 Income	Amount
All families	$18
Under $1,000	11
1,000–2,000	9
2,000–3,000	13
3,000–4,000	15
4,000–5,000	21
5,000–6,000	29
7,500 and over	35
Not classified	25

The highest income class spent relatively three times as much as the lowest on food away from

and *Family Income and Expenditures in Nine Cities of the East Central Region, 1935–36*, Bulletin No. 644, Vol. II, Table 3; and *Consumer Purchases Study, Urban and Village Series: Family Income and Expenditures, Five Regions, Part 2, Family Expenditures*, Miscellaneous Publication No. 396, U.S. Department of Agriculture, 1940, Table 55.

43. *Food Consumption of Urban Families (68 Cities) in the U.S., Spring 1948.*

home. As national per capita income increases, therefore, expenditures for food away from home are likely to account for a larger portion of total food expenditures.

HOME VS. COMMERCIAL PROCESSING

Expansion of commercial food processing has been cutting down the work of food preparation in the home. Housewives can buy trimmed meats ready for the oven, sliced bread, sorted and cleaned spinach. They can obtain orange juice of nearly natural flavor without squeezing the fruit. Easy-to-serve foods are gaining popularity despite the increase of labor-saving kitchen equipment such as electric mixers and squeezers.

More and more of the fruits and vegetables purchased by consumers are canned or frozen. In 1910–1919, 6 pounds of canned fruits and juices were purchased for every 100 pounds of fresh; in 1950, 33 pounds plus 4 pounds of frozen fruits and juices. In 1920–1929, 17 pounds of canned and frozen vegetables (excluding potatoes) were purchased for every 100 pounds of fresh; in 1950, 31 pounds. The increase has been steady and the current decade will probably see a further rise.[44]

Trends in the consumption of canned soup and canned baby foods also illustrate the shift from home to commercial processing. Annual per capita consumption of canned soup rose from 3.7 pounds in 1930–1939 to 7.7 pounds in 1940–1949. In 1935–1939, 0.2 pounds of canned baby foods were consumed per capita; in 1940, 0.5 pounds; and in 1950, 3.4 pounds.[45]

Reports on foods consumed by urban families during a week in the spring of 1942 and 1948 suggest that some shifts from home to commercial processing have reached a plateau. Little increase occurred in the importance of ready-to-eat cereals compared with uncooked cereals, or in the purchase of bread in relation to flour. The introduction of prepared flour mixes apparently caused a decline in the purchase of cake. While the proportion of families reporting the use of prepared mixes increased from 2 per cent [46] to 28 per cent between 1942 and 1948, the proportion of families reporting purchases of "store" cake dropped from 40 per cent to 33 per cent.[47]

Moreover, canning and freezing are still important in city as well as farm homes. Nearly half the nation's urban housekeeping families of two or more persons reported some canning of fruits and vegetables during 1947 and 2.3 per cent reported some freezing. Those who did some canning averaged 85 quarts. The quantity was appreciably greater in towns and small cities than in large cities. Both home canning and freezing were more important at middle than at low or high incomes, but the drop from middle to high incomes was partly due to the greater concentration of high-income families in large cities. (See Table 48.)

DIFFERENCES IN FOOD CHOICES

There are important differences in the types of foods consumed by various groups within the population. Diets vary according to income

groups. Farm families eat somewhat different foods from nonfarm families, even when incomes are about the same. There are also regional differences in food choices, partly because of variations in incomes and prices but even more because of long-established food habits.

FOOD PATTERNS IN FOUR "TYPICAL" CITIES

Regional differences in food choices are illustrated by surveys of family food consumption during 1948 in Birmingham, Buffalo, Minneapolis-St. Paul and San Francisco. In the "high" city per capita consumption of most major foods was more than 25 per cent above that in the "low" city. Only four food groups — eggs; fresh fruits; meat, poultry and fish; and dairy products exclusive of butter — showed less than this variation. (See Table 49.)

Birmingham led in consumption of buttermilk, evaporated milk, American cheese, pork, chicken, white flour, margarine, lard, other shortening, eggs, sirup and other sweets, peanut butter and sweet potatoes. Poor home refrigeration may explain the relatively high consumption of buttermilk and evaporated milk. The high consumption of flour, shortening and sugar was due partly to home baking, especially of hot breads. Local preference was probably a major reason for the large use of lard, pork, sirup and sweet potatoes.

San Francisco held first place in consumption of beef, fresh fruits and vegetables other than potatoes, canned fruits and juices, frozen fruits and vegetables, rice, prepared flour mix, coffee and alcoholic beverages. Relatively low prices and high quality probably accounted in part for the high consumption of fruits and vegetables other than potatoes. Families in San Francisco used 12 pounds of these per capita per week, one and a half times as much as Birmingham families at the same income level. Two items in which San Francisco led — frozen fruits and vegetables and prepared cake mix — are the leading examples of technological changes in food processing.

Minneapolis-St. Paul led in the consumption of whole milk and butter and Buffalo in Irish potatoes and such prepared foods as bakery products, ready-to-eat cereals, canned vegetables and soft drinks.

FARM VS. NONFARM TASTES

Differences in occupation, in family type and income level, in economy of home production,

---

44. For data on food trends see *Consumption of Food in the United States, 1909–52*, Agriculture Handbook No. 62, U.S. Department of Agriculture, September 1953.

45. Some of the increase was probably due to the increase in the ratio of infants to adults in the population.

46. Prepared flour mix was not identified as such in 1942. It has been assumed that "other" flour reported in that year was wholly flour mix. See *Family Food Consumption in the United States, Spring 1942*, Miscellaneous Publication No. 550, U.S. Department of Agriculture, 1944, p. 94.

47. *Ibid.*; and *Food Consumption of Urban Families (68 Cities) in the U.S., Spring 1948*.

TABLE 49. WEEKLY PER CAPITA CONSUMPTION OF SELECTED FOODS BY FAMILIES
OF TWO ADULTS AND ONE OR TWO CHILDREN, AT THE SAME FAMILY
INCOME, IN FOUR CITIES, 1948
(*Pounds, unless otherwise indicated*)

Foods [a]	Birmingham, Alabama	Buffalo, New York	Minneapolis-St. Paul, Minnesota	San Francisco, California
Dairy products exclusive of butter [b] (qts.)	4.73	5.30	5.30	5.69
Whole milk (qts.)	1.99	3.48	3.91	3.34
Buttermilk (qts.)	.73	.05	.06	.07
Evaporated milk	.95	.36	.07	.35
American cheese	.22	.16	.16	.17
Fats and oils	1.31	.89	.85	.85
Butter	.10	.32	.42	.23
Margarine	.34	.15	.09	.21
Lard	.28	.08	.04	.02
Eggs (dozs.)	.67	.55	.60	.62
Flour, meal and bakery products [c]	3.62	2.51	2.16	2.06
White flour, plain and self-rising [d]	1.12	.41	.45	.23
Prepared flour mix	.10	.12	.12	.13
Bakery products	2.30	2.93	2.37	2.48
Cereals	.57	.53	.44	.67
Rice	.13	.06	.03	.19
Ready-to-eat breakfast	.12	.15	.13	.11
Meat, poultry and fish	3.34	3.84	3.22	3.89
Beef	.88	1.08	1.11	1.24
Pork	1.49	.82	1.00	.55
Chicken	.61	.52	.33	.52
Potatoes	1.79	2.73	2.34	1.86
Irish	1.34	2.64	2.29	1.78
Sweet	.45	.09	.05	.08
Fresh fruit	3.64	4.06	4.30	4.53
Other fresh vegetables	3.00	3.63	2.64	4.61
Frozen fruits and vegetables	.01	.10	.08	.14
Canned fruits and juices	.94	1.29	1.29	1.45
Canned vegetables	.75	1.23	1.04	1.08
Dried fruit and vegetables and nuts	.46	.37	.25	.27
Peanuts, including peanut butter	.12	.06	.09	.06
Sugar and sweets	1.75	1.39	1.20	.99
Sirup	.32	.09	.08	.10
Beverages Coffee	.37	.35	.33	.44
Soft drinks	.97	1.10	.42	.55

Sources: 1948 Food Consumption Surveys, Preliminary Reports Nos. 8, 9, 10 and 11, U.S. Department of Agriculture, August 15, September 30, October 3 and November 15, 1949; plus some unpublished data supplied by the U.S. Bureau of Human Nutrition and Home Economics. These data relate to purchased food only; family-produced food is unimportant in cities of this size. The per capita consumption of two income classes, $2,000–$3,000 and $3,000–$4,000, was averaged. The average household size for these two income classes was 2.9, 2.7, 2.6 and 2.5 persons, respectively, for the four cities. Data cover only three seasons of the year.

a. All foods apart from spices and some specialty foods are included.

b. This is in terms of milk equivalent.

c. Two thirds of the weight of bakery products was added to the weight of flour and meal reported.

d. For the cities other than Birmingham plain white flour only is included; in these cities self-rising flour was unimportant.

and in the quality and the relative prices of foods in retail stores probably all contribute to differences in the kinds and quantities of foods consumed by farm and nonfarm families. With the development of hard-surfaced roads and trucking, however, the kinds, quality and prices of foods available in rural and urban stores have approached the same level. At present, the variation in quality between city and country stores tends to be most pronounced for perishable products such as fresh fruits and vegetables and bakery products, which farm families produce and process for themselves to a great extent.

Rural stores probably also lag behind urban stores in introducing new products. In August 1951 the percentage of food stores handling canned orange juice and fresh oranges was about the same in small and in large cities, but only 34 per cent of stores in places of under 10,000 handled frozen orange juice, compared with 56 per cent of stores in places of 500,000 or more.[48]

This difference is reflected in family purchases. In six months of 1950, 27 per cent of families in cities of under 10,000 purchased frozen orange juice compared with 52 per cent in places of 500,000 or more. Only 11 per cent of farm families purchased frozen orange juice. In contrast, purchase of canned orange juice varied little with type of community. Families purchasing fresh oranges increased with degree of urbanization, ranging from 73 per cent in farm areas to 90 per cent in cities of 500,000 and over. (See Table 50.)

The amount of food consumed per capita generally decreases with degree of urbanization when other factors are held constant. Among northern families of the same income, size and composition in 1935–1936, for example, per capita consumption of fluid milk in villages and small cities was 67 and 58 per cent, respectively, of that on farms. Compared with farm families, nonfarm families consumed about 6 per cent less meat, 20 per cent less flour equivalent (i.e., flour purchased as such or in bakery products), over 40 per cent less potatoes, and about 20 per cent less of other vegetables. Only for fruit was nonfarm consumption greater than farm; families in small cities consumed about 10 per cent more fresh and canned fruit than either farm or village families.[49]

TABLE 50. PER CENT OF FARM AND CITY FAMILIES PURCHASING FROZEN AND CANNED ORANGE JUICE AND FRESH ORANGES, APRIL–SEPTEMBER 1950

	Frozen	Canned	Fresh
Farm	11	36	73
City			
Under 10,000 population	27	46	79
10,000–100,000	37	44	88
100,000–500,000	43	46	87
500,000 and over	52	41	90

Source: Consumer Buying Practices for Selected Fresh Fruits, Canned and Frozen Juices, and Dried Fruits, Related to Family Characteristics, Region and City Size, U.S. Department of Agriculture, August 1951.

Heavy manual work may cause a greater food consumption among farm families. Relatively low costs of most foods may also lead farm families to eat more.

FAMILY SIZE AND FOOD CHOICES

The importance of various foods differs with the number and age of family members. During the spring of 1948 fluid milk took 12 per cent of food expenditures (exclusive of purchased meals) of urban households with children and 8 per cent for those without children. Similarly, families with children spent 13 per cent of their food money for potatoes, flour, cereal and bakery products, whereas families without children spent 11 per cent for these foods. For meat, poultry and fish the difference was reversed; families with children spent 28 per cent and those without children spent 32 per cent of their food money for

---

48. *Fruits and Juices, Availability in Retail Stores, August 1951,* U.S. Department of Agriculture, October 1951.

49. Data are given in U.S. Department of Agriculture: *Consumer Purchases Study, Farm Series: Family Food*

Consumption and Dietary Levels, Five Regions, Miscellaneous Publication No. 405, 1941, Tables 47–53, and *Consumer Purchases Study, Urban and Village Series: Family Food Consumption and Dietary Levels, Five Regions,* Miscellaneous Publication No. 452, 1941, Tables 28, 30–34. The data permit a comparison of northern farm and village families in New England, the Middle Atlantic and the North Central states and families in small cities in the North Central states; and of farm and village white families in the Southeast. Food consumption for one week was averaged without weighting for five income classes and four family types. Since the number of persons of the various family types differed among communities in terms of meals per household during the survey week, differences among communities have been measured by per capita figures.

Families were classified by total net income, which included income in kind, chiefly in the form of housing and food (valued at retail prices). The use of such income narrows the difference between farm and nonfarm families as against a classification by money income. No attempt has been made to adjust the income figures for differences in purchasing power of incomes.

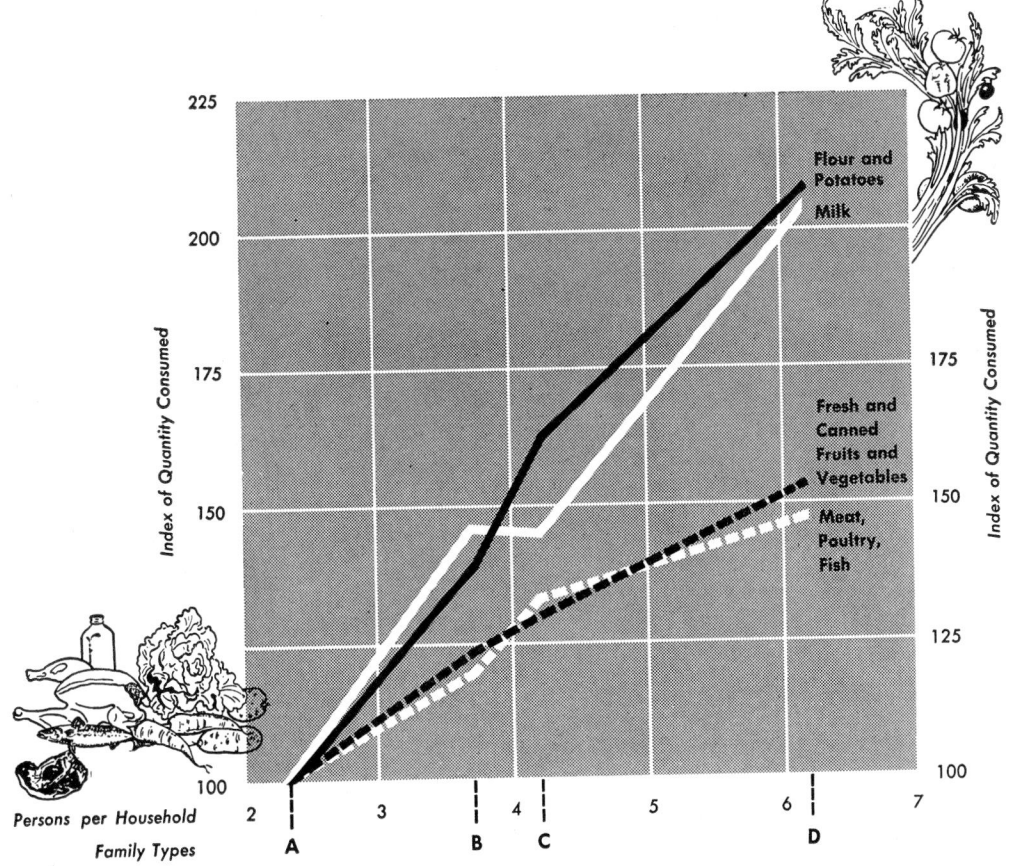

FIGURE 27. CONSUMPTION OF SELECTED FOODS [a] BY FOUR FAMILY TYPES,[b] 1935–1936
(Consumption of Type A Families = 100)

Sources: U.S. Department of Agriculture: *Consumer Purchases Study, Farm Series: Family Food Consumption and Dietary Levels, Five Regions,* Miscellaneous Publication No. 405, 1941, Tables 47–53; and *Consumer Purchases Study, Urban and Village Series: Family Food Consumption and Dietary Levels, Five Regions,* Miscellaneous Publication No. 452, 1941, Tables 28, 30–34. These data pertain to farm, village and small-city families in the New England, Middle Atlantic and North Central areas. Data for five income classes and for the three types of communities were combined without weighting.

a. "Flour" includes the flour equivalent of both bread and cereals. "Milk" includes the milk equivalent of cheese and dairy products other than butter. Vegetables and fruits are fresh and canned only.

b. Family types are as follows: A. Families of husband and wife only. B. Families of husband and wife and one or two children. C. Families with at least one adult in addition to husband and wife and one to three other persons. D. Families with three children and one to three other persons in addition to husband and wife.

The families are classified by family composition during the year to which the family income relates. The number of persons per household is the number who ate in the household during the week (21 meals equals one person). Hired help and guests as well as family members are included. Families of Type A therefore average more than two persons per household.

these.[50] Some of this difference was due to the number as well as the age of individuals in the family. Households with children averaged 4.26 persons, while those with no children averaged 2.50 persons.[51]

The study of food expenditures in 1935–1936

50. *Food Consumption of Urban Families with Children and of Families with No Children, United States, Spring 1948,* U.S. Department of Agriculture, January 1950.

51. Household sizes were measured in terms of the number of meals eaten at home during the week of the survey.

gives a more complete picture of the effect of family size and type. An increase in the number of persons to be fed out of a fixed money income brought some increase in the total amount of all major foods consumed. Flour and related foods and potatoes increased most; milk was next; fruits, vegetables and meat increased moderately. (See Figure 27.)

The need to feed more persons from the same income resulted in a shift to less expensive foods. Even for these foods, however, there was a drop in per capita consumption, or at least in the quantity purchased. Fruits and vegetables, which are doubtless regarded as more expensive and less "filling" than other foods, increased only slightly with family size.

The presence of children pushed up per capita consumption of milk and depressed that of bread, flour and cereals, potatoes and meat, poultry and fish. Per capita consumption of fruits and vegetables seemed to be unrelated to the age of family members.

These variations were much the same whether the families lived in small cities and villages or on the farm. There were some minor differences between farm and nonfarm families, however. For example, consumption of potatoes and vegetables increased more with family size among farm families; consumption of bread and flour and fruits, on the other hand, rose more among nonfarm families.

The presence of children under 12 years of age has a tendency to increase the family consumption of fresh oranges and canned and frozen orange juice. Among families with no children, 69 per cent bought fresh oranges during April–September 1950, 37 per cent bought canned orange juice, and 31 per cent bought frozen orange juice. Among families with children under 6 years of age, 72 per cent bought fresh oranges, 39 per cent bought canned orange juice, and 37 per cent bought frozen orange juice.[52]

INCOME AND FOOD CHOICES

Consumption of high-protein and vitamin-supplying foods, such as milk, meat, and fresh fruits and vegetables, generally increases with family income. On the other hand, consumption of pota-

toes and flour decreases as incomes rise. In the spring of 1948, urban families of all income classes reported about the same purchase of fats and sugar per capita. However, consumption of bakery products and of canned and frozen fruits, which contain fat and sugar, increased with income. If these additional sources are included, total consumption of fats and sugar apparently rose somewhat with income.[53] Total per capita consumption of grain products decreased at the higher income levels, largely because of a decline in the use of flour and meal in home baking, the amount of which dropped from 1.54 pounds per person in the lowest income class to 0.55 pounds per person at the highest. Per capita consumption of cereal foods such as breakfast cereal and macaroni was much the same at all income levels. (See Table 51.)

Many things other than income affect these food consumption data, but no method of isolating the influence of income in a national sample has yet been developed. Thus differences in opportunity to buy account for some of the variation in purchases among income groups. For example, low-income families bought much less frozen fruits and vegetables than high-income families, but this may have been because more of them lived in the smaller communities, where these products were less likely to be available at the time of survey.[54]

For some foods the effect of income is clearer if families with and without children are separated. Milk consumption, particularly, increases more with income among families with children than among those without children. At low income levels families with children consumed less milk per capita than those without children, whereas in the high income class they consumed more. (See Figure 28.)

Regional differences in food preferences may also obscure the true effect of income on consumption, since the various geographic divisions of the country are not equally represented in each income class. Thus the drop in per capita consumption of flour, meal and bakery products with rising income was due largely to the heavy concentration of southern families in the low-income

---

52. *Consumer Buying Practices for Selected Fresh Fruits, Canned and Frozen Juices and Dried Fruits Related to Family Characteristics, Region and City Size,* U.S. Department of Agriculture, August 1951.

53. An analysis of the sugar content of the 1948 diets described in Table 51 shows sugar increasing with income up to the income class $3,000–$4,000 and then declining. See *Sugars and Sweets in City Diets,* 1948 Food Consumption Surveys, Commodity Summary No. 5, U.S. Department of Agriculture, November 1949.

54. See p. 142.

TABLE 51. CONSUMPTION OF PURCHASED[a] FOODS PER PERSON,[b] URBAN HOUSEKEEPING FAMILIES OF TWO OR MORE PERSONS, BY 1947 INCOME, ONE WEEK DURING SPRING 1948

(Milk in Quarts, Eggs in Dozens, Other Foods in Pounds)

Foods	Family Income Class[c]								
	All Classes	Under $1,000	$1,000–$2,000	$2,000–$3,000	$3,000–$4,000	$4,000–$5,000	$5,000–$7,500	$7,500 and Over	Not Classified
Number of persons per household[b]	3.42	2.81	3.23	3.49	3.65	3.50	3.31	3.84	2.93
Milk and milk equivalent[d]	4.56	3.41	3.76	4.39	4.83	4.87	5.17	5.12	4.56
Fats and oils	0.85	0.88	0.88	0.84	0.88	0.82	0.81	0.80	0.87
Flour, meal, bakery products and other grain products[e]	2.72	3.15	3.17	2.75	2.76	2.63	2.34	2.23	2.57
Flour and meal	0.83	1.54	1.26	0.85	0.79	0.67	0.54	0.55	0.70
Bakery products	2.40	1.96	2.27	2.35	2.61	2.53	2.35	2.21	2.32
Other cereals	0.51	0.50	0.62	0.53	0.47	0.49	0.45	0.42	0.53
Eggs	0.52	0.45	0.45	0.49	0.54	0.56	0.56	0.61	0.59
Meat, poultry, fish	3.07	2.68	2.70	2.83	3.14	3.25	3.43	3.61	3.38
Sugars, sweets	1.20	1.14	1.27	1.18	1.31	1.17	1.06	0.99	1.22
Fresh fruits	3.44	2.08	2.63	2.98	3.37	3.81	4.59	4.64	4.23
Potatoes	2.05	1.68	1.94	2.15	2.23	2.13	1.73	1.70	1.96
Other fresh vegetables	2.70	2.68	2.29	2.42	2.58	3.10	3.11	3.59	3.13
Dried fruits, vegetables, nuts	0.29	0.36	0.35	0.29	0.29	0.26	0.26	0.26	0.30
Frozen fruits and vegetables	0.09	0.04	0.04	0.05	0.08	0.11	0.15	0.27	0.12
Canned fruits, vegetables, juices	2.09	1.29	1.65	1.99	2.22	2.40	2.26	2.14	2.37
Prepared, or partially prepared dishes, soups	0.34	0.21	0.26	0.35	0.38	0.33	0.37	0.30	0.37

Source: Food Consumption of Urban Families (68 Cities) in the U.S., Spring 1948, 1948 Food Consumption Surveys, Preliminary Report No. 5, U.S. Department of Agriculture, May 1949, pp. 8 and 12–14.

a. Data on total foods consumed are reported in Preliminary Report No. 12. Because of the season, home production of fresh fruits and vegetables was relatively unimportant. Total consumption of milk equivalent was one per cent higher than purchases; potatoes, 2 per cent higher; and eggs and poultry, 10 per cent higher.

b. 21 meals at home during the week equals one person.

c. By income in 1947 after federal income tax.

d. Includes dairy products except butter.

e. Includes 57 per cent of the weight of bakery products.

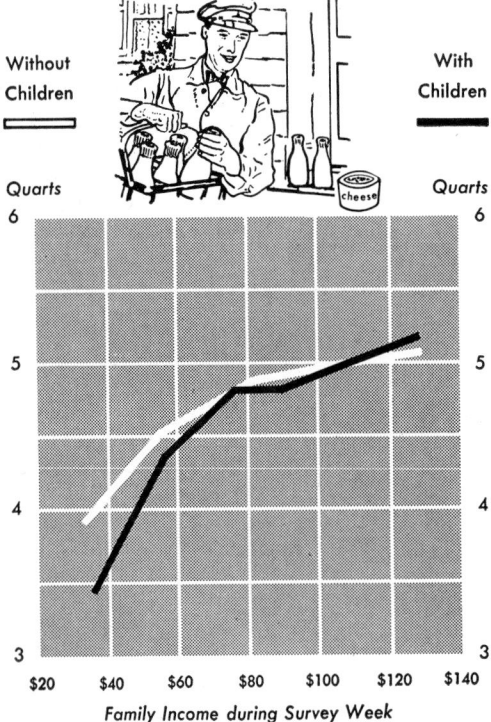

Without Children

With Children

FIGURE 28. PER CAPITA CONSUMPTION OF MILK,[a] URBAN FAMILIES WITH AND WITHOUT CHILDREN, BY INCOME LEVEL, ONE WEEK, SPRING 1948 [b]

Source: Food Consumption of Urban Families with Children and of Families with No Children, United States, Spring 1948, 1948 Food Consumption Surveys, Preliminary Report No. 14, U.S. Department of Agriculture, January 1950, pp. 5 and 9. The greater consumption of families without children at low income levels may be due to some extent to the concentration of retired families in this group. By drawing on assets accumulated for old age, such families are frequently able to live better than other families with the same current income.

a. "Milk" includes the milk equivalent of all dairy products except butter.

b. The families were classified by their income in 1947. The incomes shown in this chart are the average incomes during the week of the survey.

classes. As figures for Birmingham show, the South leads other regions in consumption of these products. Per capita consumption of flour, meal and bakery products in Minneapolis-St. Paul did not follow income consistently, but first rose slightly and then dropped slightly.[55] (See Table 49.)

55. The pattern was much the same in Buffalo and San Francisco and in winter and fall, as well as spring.

TECHNOLOGICAL DEVELOPMENTS

Scientific advances have brought an abundance undreamed of fifty years ago, and further advances are foreseen. At the International Congress of Pure and Applied Chemistry in September 1951, Professor Artturi Virtanen, a Nobel prize winner, expressed the opinion that the world could feed nearly twice its present population if modern agricultural methods were universally adopted. Dr. Conant, former President of Harvard University, speaking at a meeting of the American Chemical Society in the same month, predicted that within the next half century we will learn to harness the inexhaustible energy of the sun and will turn deserts into gardens.

The list of recent technological changes in food production is very long. Geneticists, chemists, engineers and many other scientists have contributed a great variety of new products and methods — from hybrid corn and more effective pesticides to better refrigeration and new modes of packaging. The *1950–51 Yearbook of Agriculture, Crops in Peace and War*, is devoted largely to the technological contributions of the U.S. Department of Agriculture and runs to nearly a thousand pages. A similar volume could be written on developments in animal products.

The Food Protection Committee of the National Research Council, in a 1951 report, summed up the results of increased agricultural efficiency as follows:

When this country was settled, nine farm workers produced enough food for themselves and one city dweller. By 1940, one farm worker could produce enough for himself and nine others. Today the ratio has further increased; 14 urban dwellers now depend on each farm laborer. This efficiency has been achieved even though there have been increasing difficulties from disease and insect pests and the depletion of three-quarter million acres of fertile land by soil erosion.[56]

Technological developments in distribution have not been so spectacular, but some important changes have occurred. Among the most impressive is the rise of the supermarket.

NEW FOODS

New foods for the most part are modifications of old foods. Changes in form, in type of processing and in combination of ingredients have been

56. *Use of Chemical Additives in Food*, November 1951, p. 3.

numerous. Many foods are now sold in smaller units to accommodate small families with little storage space. Lighter-weight turkeys and smaller cuts of beef pass across the butcher's counter; "small-family" loaves of bread, half-pound cans of coffee, dwarf watermelons and similar products have appeared on the market. Some new products — flour mixes, partially baked bread and rolls, tenderized meats, etc. — appeal to the consumer's desire to save time and effort. Others, such as breakfast food made from sweet potatoes, merely provide greater variety. New methods of processing and changes in ingredients may also improve the nutritive content of foods or reduce their cost.

Frozen and Concentrated Foods

The development of frozen foods has had widespread effects on marketing methods and on food preparation in the home. At first, frozen-food stores were established to handle these products, but now they are sold in grocery stores, delicatessens and supermarkets. Purchasers of home freezing units may contract with distributors for stocks of frozen foods. Refrigerator manufacturers are providing frozen-food compartments in new models. New methods of packaging have also been devised, and new items, such as baked goods and packaged meals, have been added to dealers' stocks.

Low-temperature evaporation, which makes it possible to concentrate foods with little loss of flavor, promises to revolutionize the marketing of liquids. Concentrated milk, now being offered for sale in a few cities, may narrow the price margin between producers and consumers, according to a U.S. Senate committee.[57] A variety of concentrated fruit juices are available, and it is said that the method may even be applied to wine and beer.

Enrichment of Foods

A major innovation of the past two decades has been the addition of nutrients to foods. Enrichment of basic foods is a quick and easy way of improving nutrition, for it means that many consumers get better diets without changing their eating habits.

Food enrichment has been an outgrowth of technological changes. Advances in nutritional science and food chemistry have made it possible to detect dietary deficiencies and find ways to correct them, while some of the need to improve the quality of foods is due to losses of nutrients in modern processing techniques, particularly in the milling of grains.

Synthetic vitamins or minerals are now added to a number of foods, notably bread, flour, other cereals, milk, margarine, and some canned fruits and salt. Experiments in enrichment continue. In 1951, for example, a large milk company put on the market a fresh homogenized milk, one quart of which was said to supply the daily minimum needs of an adult for thiamine, riboflavin, niacin, vitamins A and D, iron and iodine.

From 1943 to 1946 the addition of vitamins and minerals to bread was mandatory and their addition to flour for home use was optional. By 1944 about three quarters of all flour was enriched. Although the mandatory federal ruling lapsed at the end of the war, a large percentage of bread and flour continues to be enriched, partly because of state laws and partly because of consumer preference. It is estimated that about two thirds of all white flour used reaches the consumer in enriched products.[58] Early in 1951, 26 states required the enrichment of all bread and flour. In addition, many of the southern states require the enrichment of corn meal and grits.

It is generally agreed that enrichment of grain products with synthetic vitamins has increased the percentage of persons in the United States with adequate diets. Debate continues, however, as to whether it is better to add synthetic minerals and vitamins or to try to retain the original nutrients. Some people maintain that, while the extensive use of synthetic vitamins during the early 1940s may have had certain short-run advantages, greater benefits would accrue in the long run from reliance on natural foods.

Because bread is so important in the diet, and because it is a relatively low-cost food, a great deal of attention has been given to its improvement. Experimenters have been trying to develop a natural product high in "important" nutrients, acceptable in flavor, color and texture, and relatively low in cost. Nutritionists at Cornell University have proposed a formula with 6 to 8 per cent dried skim milk solids, 6 per cent soya flour and 2 per cent wheat germ.[59]

---

57. *Final Report of the Committee on Agriculture and Forestry*, U.S. Senate Report No. 604, 82d Cong., 1st sess., August 1951, p. 25.

58. Esther F. Phipard, "Changes in the Bread You Buy," *1950–51 Yearbook of Agriculture*, 1951, p. 118.

59. C. M. McCay, "Federal Bread Standards Discussed," *Journal of Home Economics*, March 1951, p. 181.

Chemical Bread-Softeners

In the late 1940s, nonfat emulsifiers were widely used to make bread soft and keep it fresh, but in 1950 the Food and Drug Administration issued a tentative standard of identity for bread barring their use. The notice cited these reasons for the action:

Although the use of surface-active agents in bread may enable consumers to keep such bread longer before it becomes unpalatable, it is doubtful that any substantial number of consumers have benefited by the use in bread of the substances. . . . Apart from their possible toxicity, the record as a whole [hearings held by the Food and Drug Administration] will not support a finding that it would promote honesty and fair dealing in the interests of consumers to recognize sorbitan esters of fatty acids and poly-oxyethylene esters of fatty acids as optional ingredients in bread, rolls and buns.[60]

Producing firms have challenged the Food and Drug Administration order on the grounds that the emulsifiers had not been proved toxic.[61]

Use of Dried Skim Milk

New processing techniques have brought an increase in the use of dried skim milk in foods. Two decades ago only about half the available nonfat milk solids were used for food; by 1950 the proportion had risen to 70 per cent. One authority believes that, with further technological advances, the 30 per cent being utilized for feed could be made available for human use.[62] Much of the dried skim milk consumed as food goes into bread, ice cream, candy and other processed foods. National per capita consumption in 1948 was 3.3 pounds, but skim milk purchased by families, as dried skim milk, amounted to 2 per cent of this quantity.[63]

LABELING FOODS

A fairly recent development in food marketing is the labeling of products so that consumers may base their choices on fact rather than fancy.

The Food, Drug and Cosmetic Act of 1938 required that labels on food mixtures list the ingredients in the order of their importance. How-

ever, this information does not permit consumers to differentiate between, say, bread with one per cent milk solids and bread with 6 per cent. The Food and Drug Administration's proposed standard of identity for white bread and the hearings of the Congressional Committee on Chemicals in Food[64] have intensified interest in requiring that the amounts of various ingredients used be listed on the labels, as on the labels of animal feeds. Such information would enable consumers to differentiate better among foods and might increase the effectiveness of consumer education.

The act of 1938 also required grade labels on canned fruits and vegetables if they were below a reasonable standard of quality. Only a very small part of the total pack falls in this class, but many firms voluntarily label their products according to the standard grades developed by the U.S. Department of Agriculture in cooperation with the industry. By December 1951 the Department of Agriculture had established standard grades for 65 canned and 28 frozen fruits and vegetables.

MAINTAINING A SAFE AND SANITARY FOOD SUPPLY

Better sanitation in the production and handling of food and improved methods of processing have greatly reduced hazards to health from polluted and spoiled food. Botulism, the severest type of food poisoning, is rare today, and when it occurs is usually traced to faulty home processing. American consumers can safely eat most raw fruits and vegetables if they take minor precautions. A large percentage of families, at least in towns and cities, can get pasteurized milk and have access to a safe water supply.

Death rates from typhoid and paratyphoid dropped from 31.3 per 100,000 population in 1900 to 0.1 per 100,000 in 1950.[65] Outbreaks of milk-borne disease have been reduced greatly over the past three decades. As against a high of 68 outbreaks in 1926, with 3,363 cases of illness and 95 deaths, there were 17 outbreaks in 1948, with 613 cases of illness and only 2 deaths.[66] Nevertheless, food-borne and water-borne diseases accounted for 1.6 per cent of reportable diseases in 1948, when 43,322 cases of dysentery, 3,962 of typhoid and paratyphoid, and 48,816 cases of undulant fever were reported.

---

60. *Federal Register,* August 8, 1950, p. 5107.

61. For proposed standards to govern the use of chemicals in food, see pp. 149 and 152.

62. Herbert C. Kriesel, "Our Hidden Milk Reserves," *Agricultural Situation,* June 1951, pp. 3–4.

63. See *Consumption of Food in the United States, 1909–52* and *Food Consumption of Urban Families (68 Cities) in the U.S., Spring 1948.*

64. See p. 149.

65. Table 132.

66. *Final Report of the Committee on Agriculture and Forestry,* U.S. Senate Report No. 604, 82d Cong., 1st sess., August 1951.

The food industries have made great advances in sanitation. A considerable portion of each year's canned food is processed under continuous inspection of the U.S. Department of Agriculture. In 1951, 59 million cases of canned and 501 million pounds of frozen fruits and vegetables were processed under the Department's inspection.[67] The U.S. Food and Drug Administration, in its 1950 annual report, said:

. . . the organized food industries are becoming increasingly conscious of sanitation. . . . National and local baking, milling, canning, dairy and confectionery associations have attacked the problem of plant sanitation, directly and favorably . . . long-range sanitation programs are showing results in clean food for consumers.[68]

Continued supervision is essential, however. In more than 80 per cent of food seizures by the Food and Drug Administration in 1950, the basic violation was filth or decomposition.[69]

Harmful Chemicals

The use of new and often superficially tested chemicals in foods and on growing crops has created new public health problems. Various standards have been proposed to govern the addition of chemicals to foods. The Food and Nutrition Board as of 1941 favored "appropriate enrichment of flour and bread (and perhaps cornmeal), the fortification of milk with vitamin D, the suitable addition of vitamin A to table fats and of iodine to salt for dietary use." It maintained, however, that "there is no information available . . . at the present time which indicates that it will be desirable to recommend the addition of vitamins and minerals to foods other than those named." [70] Hazel Stiebeling, Chief of the U.S. Bureau of Human Nutrition and Home Economics, has asserted that "no ingredient or chemical should be added to food unless it can be clearly demonstrated that (1) the added ingredient is nontoxic; (2) it does not have an adverse effect on nutritive value of diets; and (3) it measurably improves the consumer quality of the product." [71] A Senate committee recommended in 1951 that "the Food, Drug and Cosmetic Act be amended to provide that nonnutrient ingredients shall not be added to bread or other food products unless their addition shall serve some useful purpose to the consumers, and they have first been certified by the Food and Drug Administration to be noninjurious," and added that careful consideration should be given to "requiring a minimum fat content for bread," and to "requiring the labeling of bread or rolls." [72]

A congressional committee set up to investigate the use of food chemicals, with special reference to the existing powers of the Food and Drug Administration to bar harmful or potentially harmful foods from the market, said in its initial report: [73]

The evidence so far presented indicates that existing laws dealing with the use of chemicals in food are not adequate to protect the public against the addition of unsafe chemicals. It is important, of course, that unnecessary obstacles to technological improvements in food production and processing be not created. . . . Most witnesses before the committee testified strongly that a chemical or synthetic should not be permitted to be used in the production, processing, preparation, or packaging of food products until its safety for such use be established, and that the food chapter of the Federal Food, Drug and Cosmetic Act should be amended to include a section generally similar to the New Drug Section of that act.[74] In view of the far-reaching consequences of such an amendment the committee is of the opinion that the individuals or groups who would be affected by such legislation should be given further opportunity to present their views and to comment on proposed legislation before any specific recommendations are made to Congress.

The disclosures of these hearings led the National Research Council to establish a Food Protection Committee. Its report, issued in November 1951, also expressed the opinion that "chemical additives should not be permitted in a food until their safety for a given food use has been

---

67. *The Canning Trade Almanac*, Baltimore, 1951.
68. *Loc. cit.*, p. 2.
69. *Ibid.*
70. See Russell M. Wilder and Robert M. Williams, *Enrichment of Flour in Bread: A History of the Movement*, Bulletin No. 110, National Research Council, 1944, p. 90.
71. See *Utilization of Farm Crops*, Hearings before a Subcommittee of the Committee on Agriculture and Forestry, U.S. Senate, 81st Cong., 1st sess., Part 2, 1949, p. 583.
72. *Final Report of the Committee on Agriculture and Forestry*, U.S. Senate Report No. 604, 82d Cong., 1st sess., August 1951, p. 15.
73. *Investigation of the Use of Chemicals in Food*, Hearings before the House Select Committee to Investigate the Use of Chemicals in Food, Report No. 3254, 81st Cong., 2d sess., 1951.
74. New drugs must be certified as safe prior to being put on the market. The Food and Drug Administration can bar the use of chemicals in food only if it can prove that they are harmful and if the food moves in interstate trade.

TABLE 52. DAILY DIETARY ALLOWANCES RECOMMENDED BY FOOD AND NUTRITION BOARD OF NATIONAL RESEARCH COUNCIL [a]

Family Member	Calories	Protein (Grams)	Calcium (Grams)	Iron (Mg.)	Vitamin A[b] (I.U.)	Thiamine B_1[c] (Mg.)	Riboflavin[c] (Mg.)	Niacin (Nicotinic Acid)[c] (Mg.)	Ascorbic Acid (Mg.)	Vitamin D (I.U.)
Man (154 lb., 70 kg.)										
Sedentary	2,400					1.2	1.8	12	75	d
Physically active	3,000	70	1.0	12	5,000	1.5	1.8	15	75	d
With heavy work	4,500					1.8	1.8	18	75	d
Woman (123 lb., 56 kg.)										
Sedentary	2,000					1.0	1.5	10	70	d
Moderately active	2,400	60	1.0	12	5,000	1.2	1.5	12	70	d
Very active	3,000					1.5	1.5	15	70	d
Pregnancy (latter half)	2,400	85	1.5	15	6,000	1.5	2.5	15	100	400
Lactation	3,000	100	2.0	15	8,000	1.5	3.0	15	150	400
Children up to 12 years										
Under 1 year[e]	100[f]	35[f]	1.0	6	1,500	0.4	0.6	4	30	400
1–3 (27 lb., 12 kg.)	1,200	40	1.0	7	2,000	0.6	0.9	6	35	400
4–6 (42 lb., 19 kg.)	1,600	50	1.0	8	2,500	0.8	1.2	8	50	400
7–9 (58 lb., 26 kg.)	2,000	60	1.0	10	3,500	1.0	1.5	10	60	400
10–12 (78 lb., 35 kg.)	2,500	70	1.2	12	4,500	1.2	1.8	12	75	400
Children over 12 years										
Girls, 13–15 (108 lb., 49 kg.)	2,600	80	1.3	15	5,000	1.3	2.0	13	80	400
Girls, 16–20 (122 lb., 55 kg.)	2,400	75	1.0	15	5,000	1.2	1.8	12	80	400
Boys, 13–15 (108 lb., 49 kg.)	3,200	85	1.4	15	5,000	1.5	2.0	15	90	400
Boys, 16–20 (141 lb., 64 kg.)	3,800	100	1.4	15	6,000	1.7	2.5	17	100	400

Source: Recommended Dietary Allowances (Revised 1948), Reprint and Circular Series, No. 129, National Research Council, Washington, 1948, p. 16.

a. Objectives toward which to aim in planning practical dietaries can be met with a good variety of common foods. Such a diet will also provide other minerals and vitamins, the requirements for which are less well known. These allowances were released in 1948. They were revised in 1953, but not released in full in time to be tabulated here. The calcium allowance for adults was reduced from 1.0 to 0.8 grams. A downward revision was also made in the assumed average weight of men and women, which resulted in a lowering of the allowance for protein for adults — from 70 to 65 grams for men and from 60 to 55 grams for women. The allowance for riboflavin was also reduced slightly. For further details see official release of the National Research Council. (The revisions described do not apply to pregnant or lactating women.)

b. Allowance depends on the relative amounts of vitamin A and carotene. Allowances shown are based on the premise that approximately two thirds of the vitamin A value of the average diet is contributed by carotene and that carotene has half or less than half of the value of vitamin A.

c. For adults (except pregnant and lactating women) receiving diets supplying 2,000 calories or less, such as reducing diets, the allowances of thiamine and niacin may be 1 mg. and 10 mg. respectively. Riboflavin allowances are based on body weight rather than caloric levels. Other B vitamins also are required, but no values can be given. Foods supplying adequate thiamine, riboflavin and niacin tend to supply enough of the remaining B vitamins as well.

d. Adults leading a normal life seem to need a minimum of supplemental vitamin D. For persons working at night and elderly persons, small amounts are desirable.

e. Needs of infants increase from month to month. Amounts shown are for infants of approximately 6–8 months. Smaller amounts of protein and calcium are needed if derived from human milk.

f. Per kilogram of body weight.

established beyond reasonable doubt." The Committee did state, however, that:

Actually the quality and sanitary characteristics of our foods have been improving. Likewise, there is no evidence that consumption of foods resulting from the use of the new materials in crop production or in the production and processing of foods has created mysterious disease epidemics or endangered the health of people.[75]

NUTRITIONAL AND FOOD NEEDS

As knowledge of nutrition has advanced, the concept of an adequate diet has changed. In the beginning the major emphasis was on combating such deficiency diseases as scurvy, beriberi, pellagra and rickets. As the means of eliminating these diseases became known, attention shifted to the development of a diet which would be sufficient to maintain a high level of health and vitality. Consequently, an adequate diet has come to mean something close to an optimum diet, that is, one which is most conducive to physical well-being.

RECOMMENDED DIETARY ALLOWANCES OF THE NATIONAL RESEARCH COUNCIL

The "recommended dietary allowances" of the Food and Nutrition Board of the National Research Council are the most widely used yardstick of dietary adequacy in the United States. Originally released in 1941, they were revised in 1945, 1948 and 1953, and probably will be revised as research progresses. The NRC allowances of 1948, the latest available,[76] provide quantitative guides for ten nutrients: calories, protein, calcium, iron, vitamin A, thiamine, riboflavin, niacin, ascorbic acid and vitamin D. (See Table 52.) The Food and Nutrition Board felt that other essentials, such as fat and fatty acids, iodine, water, salt, phosphorous, copper, vitamin K and folic acid, would be provided if the NRC allowances of the ten nutrients were obtained from a good variety of common foods.

The Board describes these "recommended dietary allowances" as designed to maintain good nutrition for the population in general, rather than for any deficiency group:

The recommendations are not called "requirements" because they are intended to represent not merely the literal (minimal) requirements of average individuals, but levels enough higher to cover substantially all individual variations in the requirements of normal people.

The figures . . . recommended are, therefore, generally higher than average requirements but generally lower than the doses used to meet needs created by pathological states or certain environmental conditions or in compensating for an earlier period of depletion.[77]

The Board says, however, that the allowances are liberal enough to provide for the requirements of normal people who use nutrients less efficiently than the average:

. . . Experience has shown that the biological normal consists of a range of values. An allowance based on the need of the average of a group would be greater than the need of many and less than the need of many others. Many normal adult males require only 2,200 calories or less and many can subsist in health with half the stated protein allowance. Many children need no supplement of vitamin D, while others require the amount stated. In order to meet the needs of the whole population it is necessary to satisfy the requirements of those with less efficient usage. Because the allowances take into consideration the requirements of those of the upper level of the normal range of requirement, they allow a factor of safety for persons who have an average or less than average requirement. In most categories this factor of safety for the average person is estimated to be approximately 30 per cent. . . . Inasmuch as some persons who receive less than the recommended allowances of one or another nutrient may remain in good health through long periods, it becomes apparent that these allowances are not to be used as the sole criteria for judging the nutrition of any population. . . .[78]

Even though the NRC allowances are looked upon as meeting the needs of people who use nutrients rather inefficiently,[79] nevertheless, it is known that some nutrients may be taken in greater quantity than recommended with beneficial effects. According to the Food and Nutrition Board:

---

75. *Use of Chemical Additives in Food*, p. 13; see also report on *Safe Use of Chemical Additives in Foods*, December 1952.

76. The 1953 revisions, which were largely downward, were not released in full in time to be included here, but some details are given in Table 52, footnote a.

77. *Recommended Dietary Allowances* (Revised 1948), Reprint and Circular Series, No. 129, National Research Council, Washington, 1948, pp. 4–5.

78. *Ibid.*, pp. 23–24.

79. The official dietary allowances of Canada and the United Kingdom are in general lower than the NRC allowances. The greatest difference is in vitamin C. In Canada the standard is 40 per cent, and in the United Kingdom 27 per cent, of the NRC allowance. The allowances of the United Kingdom and Canada are to a greater extent based on estimates of average need with a smaller margin of safety. See L. B. Pett, "Limitations on the Use of Dietary Standards," *Journal of the American Dietetic Association*, January 1951, p. 29.

TABLE 53. AMOUNTS OF FOOD RECOMMENDED FOR LOW- AND MODERATE-COST MEALS [a]
PER FAMILY MEMBER PER WEEK

(*Milk in Quarts, Eggs in Units, All Others in Pounds*)

Food	Man, Sedentary		Infant, 9–12 Months		Girl, 13–15 Years	
	Low	Moderate	Low	Moderate	Low	Moderate
Milk [b]	5.0	5.0	6.0	6.0	6.5	7.0
Leafy, green and yellow vegetables	2.3	3.5	1.5	1.5	2.3	3.5
Citrus fruit, tomatoes	2.0	2.5	1.7	1.7	2.3	2.7
Potatoes, including sweet potatoes	3.0	2.5	.5	.5	3.3	2.5
Other vegetables and fruits	1.7	3.5	1.0	1.0	1.7	3.5
Meat, poultry and fish	2.0	2.7	.3	.3	2.0	2.7
Eggs	5.0	7.0	5.0	5.0	4.0	7.0
Dry beans, peas, nuts	.3	.1	.1	.1	.3	.1
Flour and cereals [c]	3.3	2.5	.6	.6	3.5	2.7
Fats and oils	.7	.9	.1	.1	.7	.9
Sugar, sirups and preserves	.7	.9	.1	.1	.7	.9

Source: Helping Families Plan Food Budgets, Miscellaneous Publication No. 662, U.S. Department of Agriculture, revised February 1950, Tables 4 and 5. These diets were based on the National Research Council dietary allowances as revised in 1948. The lowered calcium and protein allowances for adults in the 1953 revisions (see Table 52) might involve a reduction of as much as 20 per cent in the amount of milk recommended for adults (except pregnant and lactating women).

a. Does not provide for cod-liver oil or other source of vitamin D for children or other persons with special need or not exposed to the sun. The source reports amounts for the other age, sex and activity groups in addition to those shown here.
b. Whole milk or its equivalent in cheese, evaporated milk or dry milk.
c. Count one and a half pounds of bread as one pound of flour. As much as possible should be in the form of whole-grain, enriched or "restored" products.

. . . The nutrient factors differ in respect to the desirability of surplus intake. . . . Of a few nutrients . . . there is evidence from long-term (animal) experimentation that one may in the course of a lifetime derive increased benefit from increased intake up to levels considerably above those of ordinarily accepted adequacy. (Ascorbic acid, vitamin A and calcium are perhaps the best-established cases of this kind.) Conversely, it may be true of some other nutrient factors that surplus intakes should be held within bounds if undesirable consequences are to be avoided. The outstanding and undisputed example of the latter is the energy value or calories of the diet. . . .[80]

The NRC allowances are widely used in nutritional education, in planning diets in many public institutions, and for gauging the adequacy of diets of families or single consumers.[81]

FOODS TO PROVIDE THE NRC ALLOWANCES

Since people eat foods rather than nutrients, a program of nutritional education must translate dietary standards into food plans. In deciding what foods to recommend, four factors must be coordinated: physical needs, the nutrients in foods,[82] food preferences and cost. The foods recommended must not only meet nutritional needs but also be acceptable. How much consideration needs to be given to cost depends on its importance to the group addressed.

With these objectives in mind, the Bureau of Human Nutrition and Home Economics of the U.S. Department of Agriculture has designed two master food plans, one at low and the other at moderate cost, and has also given suggestions for a "low-low" cost plan.[83] The moderate-cost diet is relatively high in fruits and vegetables other than

80. National Research Council, *op. cit.,* pp. 5–6.
81. The U.S. Department of the Army has also formulated dietary allowances. For calcium and ascorbic acid the minimum standard is markedly lower than the NRC allowances. See *Nutrition,* Technical Manual 8–501, Department of the Army, 1949, p. 18.
82. See B. K. Watt and A. L. Merrill, "Composition of Foods," Agriculture Handbook No. 8, U.S. Department of Agriculture, 1950.
83. *Helping Families Plan Food Budgets,* Miscellaneous Publication No. 662, U.S. Department of Agriculture, revised February 1950. A simpler guide to an adequate diet is provided by *The National Food Guide,* U.S. Department of Agriculture, A15–53, August 1946.

potatoes, and in meat and eggs, while the low-cost diet is relatively high in potatoes and flour and cereals. The moderate-cost diet recommends 2.7 pounds of meat, poultry and fish for a sedentary man; the low-cost diet, 2 pounds; and the "low-low" cost diet only one pound. In addition, the moderate-cost diet recommends 2.5 pounds of citrus fruits and tomatoes; the low-cost diet, 2 pounds; and the "low-low" cost diet, 1.5 pounds. There is very little difference among the diets in the quantity of milk recommended. (See Table 53 for low- and moderate-cost diets.)

These food budgets, although intended mainly as guides in choosing foods, are at times used as a crude yardstick of adequacy — crude because an adequate diet can be achieved with many different food combinations.

At prices prevailing in large cities as of September 15, 1952, the moderate-cost food plan cost $26 to $27 a week and the low-cost food plan $18 to $20 a week for a family of four persons — husband and wife moderately active, a boy of 14 years and a girl of 8.[84]

ADEQUACY OF DIETS

Nutritional health is the ultimate test of dietary adequacy. It seems highly probable that better nutrition has played a part in the increase in life expectancy in the United States. But data relating to the nutritional health of the population are incomplete in coverage and otherwise unsatisfactory.

Pellagra is the only deficiency disease included in the morbidity statistics of the U.S. Public Health Service, and it is not a major problem. In 1946, 3,891 cases were reported; in 1947, 1,555 cases; and in 1948, 1,001 cases.[85]

Measurement of Malnutrition

Two methods apart from appraisal of diets are used to determine the occurrence of malnutrition:

(1) clinical examination to detect physical symptoms of specific nutritional deficiencies, for example, an abnormal gum condition associated with a deficiency of ascorbic acid; and
(2) biochemical examination of the blood to determine the concentration of specific nutrients, such as vitamin A and ascorbic acid.

The symptoms of deficiency diseases such as scurvy, pellagra and rickets are easily recognized. Between these and optimum nutrition, however, are all gradations of malnutrition or undernutrition, not so readily detected. Lists of symptoms associated with minor dietary deficiencies have been prepared,[86] but two difficulties arise in their use. Some of the symptoms are not specific but may be due to other conditions; and examiners may differ as to the significance of some conditions, for example, discoloration of the tongue. Biochemical tests have the advantage of being objective, but "normal" blood conditions cover a wide range and so far criteria of abnormal concentrations due to nutritional deficiency have not been established.

Techniques of both physical examinations and biochemical tests have been improved, but widespread scepticism persists concerning the interpretation of findings. W. J. Darby, writing in 1950, argued for caution. Of vitamin A he said:

> In my opinion, the only manner in which one may arrive at reasonable estimates of vitamin A deficiency within a population is by the combined application of the clinical, biochemical and physiological study coupled with observations on the therapeutic response of a subject judged deficient by these tests.[87]

In spite of the imperfections of the measures, many nutritional surveys were made during the 1940s involving clinical examinations and biochemical analyses. Some surveys of this type also secured dietary data. These provide scattered snapshots rather than a composite picture of the entire population.

Nutritional Surveys and Therapeutic Tests

An investigation in Newfoundland illustrates the effect of dietary changes on the level of nutritional health of an entire community. The food supply of the island was extremely low in vitamin A, riboflavin, ascorbic acid and calcium when physical and biochemical examinations of 868 persons were made in 1944. A close correspondence was found between food deficiencies for the country as a whole and signs of undernutrition.[88]

---

84. *Rural Family Living,* Bureau of Human Nutrition and Home Economics, U.S. Department of Agriculture, November 1952, p. 18.

85. Most of the cases were reported from Texas and South Carolina. In 1948, for example, 193 cases were reported from Texas and 602 from South Carolina.

86. See, for example, the list of signs and symptoms of vitamin deficiency prepared by the Council of Food and Nutrition of the American Medical Association, *Journal of the American Medical Association,* June 22, 1946.

87. W. J. Darby, "Evaluation of Symptoms," *Proceedings of the Federation of American Society of Experimental Biology,* September 1950, p. 595.

88. J. E. Adamson and others, "Medical Survey of Nutrition in Newfoundland," *Canadian Medical Association Journal,* March 1945, p. 227.

Beginning in that year, enrichment of all flour and margarine added appreciably to the supply of vitamin A, thiamine, niacin and riboflavin. When another series of examinations was made in 1948, including one fourth of the persons examined earlier, the investigators found that:

Not all the outward signs of malnutrition had decreased in prevalence. Only those had decreased which could have been affected by addition of vitamin A to the margarine and of riboflavin, niacin, and thiamine to the flour. There was no improvement and indeed a worsening with respect to . . . lesions relatable to deficiency of . . . ascorbic acid.[89]

Another study of the effects of dietary changes involved the administration of supplementary nutrients to school children. The investigators selected 124 out of 908 grade school children as showing signs of malnutrition and placed them in three groups to study the effects of supplements of vitamin A, ascorbic acid and niacin. Half the children in each group received a vitamin supplement, four times the NRC allowance, and the other half served as a control group, receiving a pill similar in appearance but without active ingredients in order to eliminate any psychological difference between the groups. A statistically significant reduction in symptoms was found in all groups getting the supplement.[90]

The U.S. Public Health Service in 1945 launched a "nutritional appraisal and demonstration program" which was largely carried out through public schools. More than one fourth of the white school children examined in this program showed signs of vitamin A deficiency, 16 per cent had signs of rickets caused by a deficiency of vitamin D, and 9 per cent had signs of goiter caused by deficiency of iodine.[91]

The nutritional status and diets of children with and without school lunches were studied in two Maryland schools, in the spring of 1947 and the spring of 1948. According to the investigators, "the percentage of children's diets meeting the recommended allowances of the National Research Council for vitamin A, ascorbic acid, and calcium was higher in the group having a school lunch than in the group with no school lunch."

Yet the clinical findings showed no consistent differences between the two groups. The children in general appeared to be in good physical condition. "For the most part only mild, if any, physical signs suggestive of malnutrition were seen." [92]

Physical examinations and dietary records of a representative sample of the population of a New York township in 1948 and 1949 revealed so few signs of malnutrition that the investigators concluded that they had happened to study a well-nourished population.[93]

Trends in Dietary Adequacy

Changes in the nutrients available in the national food supply reveal a long-run improvement in the quality of diets since 1910. From 1910–1914 to 1945–1946 steady increases occurred in per capita supplies of both calcium and ascorbic acid, the one associated with increased consumption of milk and the other with increased consumption of green and leafy vegetables. From 1935–1939 to 1945–1946 increased supplies of milk, meat, fruits and vegetables and the enrichment of grain products contributed to a systematic upward trend in the per capita intake of minerals and vitamins. The per capita supply of calories has been fairly stable, although during 1949–1950 it was 7 per cent below the 1910–1914 levels. The supply of protein dropped steadily between 1910–1914 and 1935–1939; by 1945–1946 it had risen above the 1910–1914 level, but by 1950 it was somewhat below. (See Table 54.)

An appreciable decline in the per capita supply of some nutrients between 1945–1946 and 1949–1950, most notably in vitamin A and ascorbic acid, was due partly to a decrease in consumption of milk, green and leafy vegetables, citrus fruit, tomatoes and potatoes. (See Table 44.)

Family studies over almost two decades show a general improvement in diets. The Food and Nutrition Board of the National Research Council reported in 1943 that "Every nutritional survey in the past decade has revealed that the consumption of diets below the recommended standards is widespread in the United States." [94]

89. G. R. Cowgill and W. A. Krehl, "Newfoundland Surveys in Human Nutrition," *Scientific Monthly*, October 1950, p. 234.

90. J. G. Browe and H. B. Pierce, "A Survey of Nutritional Status among School Children," *Nutrition in Relation to Health and Disease*, Conference of the Milbank Memorial Fund, November 1949, pp. 9–23.

91. *American Journal of Public Health*, March 1948, p. 365.

92. See C. Velat and others, *Evaluating School Lunches and Nutritional Status of Children*, Circular No. 859, U.S. Department of Agriculture, 1951, p. 2.

93. For further information on this study see p. 163.

94. "Inadequate Diets and Nutritional Deficiencies in the United States," *Bulletin of the National Research Council*, No. 109, November 1943.

TABLE 54. NUTRIENTS AVAILABLE PER DAY IN PER CAPITA FOOD SUPPLY, 1910-1952

Period	Calories[a]	Protein (Grams)	Calcium[b] (Grams)	Iron (Mg.)	Vitamin A (I.U.)	Thiamine (Mg.)	Riboflavin (Mg.)	Niacin (Mg.)	Ascorbic Acid (Mg.)
					Amount				
1910–1914	3,468	100	.85	15	6,820	1.6	1.9	17	128
1915–1919	3,386	96	.85	15	7,080	1.6	1.8	17	126
1920–1924	3,362	93	.88	15	7,480	1.5	1.9	16	126
1925–1929	3,466	94	.89	15	7,680	1.6	1.9	16	133
1930–1934	3,342	91	.90	14	7,980	1.5	1.9	16	131
1935–1939	3,268	89	.93	14	8,180	1.4	1.9	16	132
1940–1944	3,362	96	1.00	16	8,720	1.8	2.1	18	144
1945–1946	3,315	102	1.11	19	9,400	2.2	2.5	21	149
1947–1948	3,240	95	1.04	17	8,350	1.9	2.3	19	134
1949–1950	3,225	94	1.03	17	8,150	1.9	2.3	19	133
1951–1952	3,225	95	1.04	17	7,750	1.9	2.3	19	132
					Index (1935–1939 = 100)				
1910–1914	106	112	91	107	83	114	100	106	97
1915–1919	104	108	91	107	87	114	95	106	95
1920–1924	103	104	95	107	91	107	100	100	95
1925–1929	106	106	96	107	94	114	100	100	101
1930–1934	102	102	97	100	98	107	100	100	99
1935–1939	100	100	100	100	100	100	100	100	100
1940–1944	103	108	108	114	107	129	111	112	109
1945–1946	101	115	119	136	115	157	132	131	113
1947–1948	99	107	112	121	102	136	121	119	102
1949–1950	99	106	111	121	100	136	121	119	101
1951–1952	99	107	112	121	95	136	121	119	100

Source: Consumption of Food in the United States, 1909–1952, Agriculture Handbook No. 62, U.S. Department of Agriculture, 1953, Table 44. These estimates are based on foods as they leave the retail store or as they enter the home, without allowance for losses of minerals and vitamins in cooking or for spoilage or waste. Alcoholic beverages are not included.

a. Omission of alcoholic beverages may result in some understatement of the caloric value of the per capita food supply. Ralph Gerard points out, for example, that "An underestimate, based only on the amount of whiskey, rum, brandy, and beer produced in the United States per capita in 1940, indicates that these beverages provided about 3 per cent of the calories consumed or about 90 calories [per person] per day . . . These estimates are low because they omit wines, alcohol worked into drinks, and imported beverages." *Food for Life,* University of Chicago Press, 1952, p. 272.

b. No account is taken of calcium in the water supply. Moreover, no estimates have yet been made of the amount of self-rising flour used, and as this type of flour contains calcium in the form of calcium phosphate, there may be some understatement on this account.

156

TABLE 55. PERCENTAGE INCREASE IN AVERAGE NUTRIENTS PER NUTRITION UNIT[a]. SUPPLIED BY FOOD CONSUMED AT HOME, URBAN FAMILIES, BY INCOME, 1942 TO 1948[b]

Nutrient	All Incomes	Income Group		
		Lowest Third	Middle Third	Highest Third
Calories	8	14	5	6
Protein	11	16	7	11
Calcium	16	20	12	17
Iron	21	25	17	19
Vitamin A	4	9	0	6
Thiamine	25	33	18	21
Riboflavin	21	28	18	20
Niacin	20	35	12	15
Ascorbic acid	2	16	—5	—3

Source: *Nutritive Content of City Diets*, 1948–1949 Food Consumption Surveys, Special Report No. 2, U.S. Department of Agriculture, October 1950, p. 6.

a. The quantity of various nutrients needed differs with age and sex. (See Table 52.) In order to obtain a single meaningful measure of nutritional need for the various nutrients by families included in the survey, the need of a moderately active adult male was counted as one nutrition unit and the needs of other family members were expressed in terms of this unit. For example, a family of a moderately active husband and wife, a child of 4 years and a boy of 15 years would represent 3.4 nutrition units for calories and 4.4 nutrition units for calcium. The total nutrients of various kinds in the family diets were determined and divided by the nutrition units in the families to yield average nutrients per nutrition unit.

b. Comparison is for spring of both years.

The Consumer Purchases Survey, a major source of information at that time, revealed that

> . . . fewer than one-fifth of the families in this country had food supplies in 1936 that meet the Council's recommendations with respect to the seven nutrients studied. About one-fourth of the farm families were in this category, but only about one seventh of the nonfarm families. At least 60 per cent of the village and city families fell short of the Council's allowances for calcium, thiamine, ascorbic acid and/or riboflavin, and 30 per cent with respect to vitamin A.[95]

An example of the improvement that has occurred since the 1930s is the trend in dietary adequacy among urban families for two nutrients — calcium and ascorbic acid — often poorly supplied in family diets. According to Hazel Stiebeling:

> In the spring of 1948 almost three fourths of the urban families had diets that met recommended calcium levels, compared with about half in the spring of 1942, and only about one third in 1936. As for ascorbic acid 80 per cent of the city families had diets that met recommended levels in the spring of

1948 as compared with only 40 per cent twelve years earlier.[96]

Between the spring of 1942 and the spring of 1948 important increases occurred in the intake of many nutrients. The content of iron, thiamine, riboflavin and niacin in urban family diets increased by more than one fifth. (See Table 55.) Much of the increase was due to enrichment of bread and flour. Without enrichment, urban family diets in 1948 would have been 11 per cent lower in iron and niacin, 14 per cent lower in thiamine and 3 per cent lower in riboflavin.

Calcium intake also increased appreciably, owing largely to increased consumption of dairy products apart from butter. Per capita consumption of these in terms of milk equivalent increased by 4 per cent from 1942 to 1948.

The improvement in nutrient intake was somewhat greater in low than in high income groups, especially for thiamine and niacin, both of which are provided in enriched flour, bread and cereals. As Table 51 shows, cereal consumption tends to be more important at low than at high income levels.

95. *Ibid.*, pp. 3–4. The calcium standard used in this appraisal was 0.8 grams per adult male. This was below the NRC dietary allowance of 1948 (see Table 52) but much the same as the 1953 allowance.

96. Hazel K. Stiebeling, "Trends in Family Food Consumption," *Journal of the American Dietetic Association*, August 1950, pp. 597–598.

TABLE 56. PER CENT OF URBAN FAMILIES WHOSE DIETS PROVIDED AT LEAST THE
NATIONAL RESEARCH COUNCIL ALLOWANCES [a] OF VARIOUS NUTRIENTS, ONE WEEK IN 1948

Nutrient	All Urban Communities, Spring of 1948	Four Cities in Winter of 1948			
		Birmingham	Buffalo	Minneapolis-St. Paul	San Francisco
Average for nine nutrients [b]–dietary rating	80	87	88	84	87
Calories	79	90	88	81	83
Protein [c]	89	92	97	94	96
Calcium [d]	58 [e]	63	62	64	66
Iron	87	96	94	90	93
Vitamin A	86	92	93	94	97
Thiamine	78	94	89	79	79
Riboflavin [f]	84	90	93	90	89
Niacin	80	88	91	83	91
Ascorbic acid	79	75	89	84	87
Persons per household [g]	3.4	3.3	3.6	3.5	3.0
Per capita family income during week [h]	$24	$18	$20	$23	$30
Per capita expenditures for food during week [i]	$6.79	$6.16	$6.90	$6.16	$8.42

Sources: U.S. Department of Agriculture: 1948 Food Consumption Surveys, Preliminary Reports Nos. 1, 2, 3, 4, and 5; and *Nutritive Content of City Diets,* Special Report No. 2, October 1950, Tables 1 and 3. Data are for housekeeping families of two or more persons.

a. As released in 1948. Data are adjusted for average cooking losses of vitamins.

b. The NRC allowance of calcium for adults was lowered in 1953. If the 1953 allowance were used instead of the 1948 allowance, it is estimated that the average for the nine nutrients for each of the five groups of families would be raised by one percentage point. The other revisions that were made in the NRC allowances in 1953 might raise the level of adequacy somewhat further, but taken together they probably would not raise it by as much as one percentage point. (See Appendix 5–1.)

c. In terms of the 1953 NRC standard the percentages on the average would be one point higher. (See Appendix 5–1.)

d. If the 1953 NRC allowance had been used, it is estimated that 69 per cent of all urban families, 73 per cent of Birmingham families, 74 per cent of Buffalo families

and 76 per cent of Minneapolis-St. Paul and San Francisco families would have had adequate calcium in their diets. (See Appendix 5–1.)

e. If an allowance is made for calcium in drinking water and baking powder, this figure becomes approximately 70 per cent. The diets in the four cities might be affected somewhat differently depending on the composition of the local water supply and baking practices. Estimates taking these factors into account are not available.

f. If the 1953 allowance were used, the percentage for all urban families would be one point higher. (See Appendix 5–1 and 1948 Food Consumption Surveys, Preliminary Report No. 12, Table 18.) A similar estimate cannot be made for the four cities since the data made no separation among families with diets that provided less than the NRC allowance for riboflavin as of 1948.

g. Family size determined by number of meals eaten at home during week. Twenty-one meals equals one person.

h. Income before taxes.

i. Expenditures for food eaten at home divided by number of persons per household.

City Diets

Nearly four fifths of all city families during 1948 had weekly diets providing all nutrients except calcium in amounts equal to the NRC allowances.[97] Calcium was more frequently inadequate

than any other nutrient in each of the four large cities covered during the winter of 1948 as well as in the diets of urban families as a whole during the spring of 1948.[98] (See Table 56.)

---

97. *Nutritive Content of City Diets,* 1948–1949 Food Consumption Surveys, Special Report No. 2, U.S. Department of Agriculture, October 1950. The report gives only the percentage of families whose diets provided various quantities of nine nutrients. No over-all rating of the separate family diets is given. The NRC allowances used were those published in 1948.

98. Diets in the four large cities in the winter were more frequently adequate than those in urban communities in the United States as a whole in the spring. Data available for two of the cities show that diets were somewhat poorer in the spring than in the winter. (See *Nutritive Content of City Diets,* Table 4.) It is not possible to estimate the level of dietary adequacy for the four cities in the spring, but the seasonal differences do not appear to be great enough to account for the difference found between the four cities and all urban communities. Nor

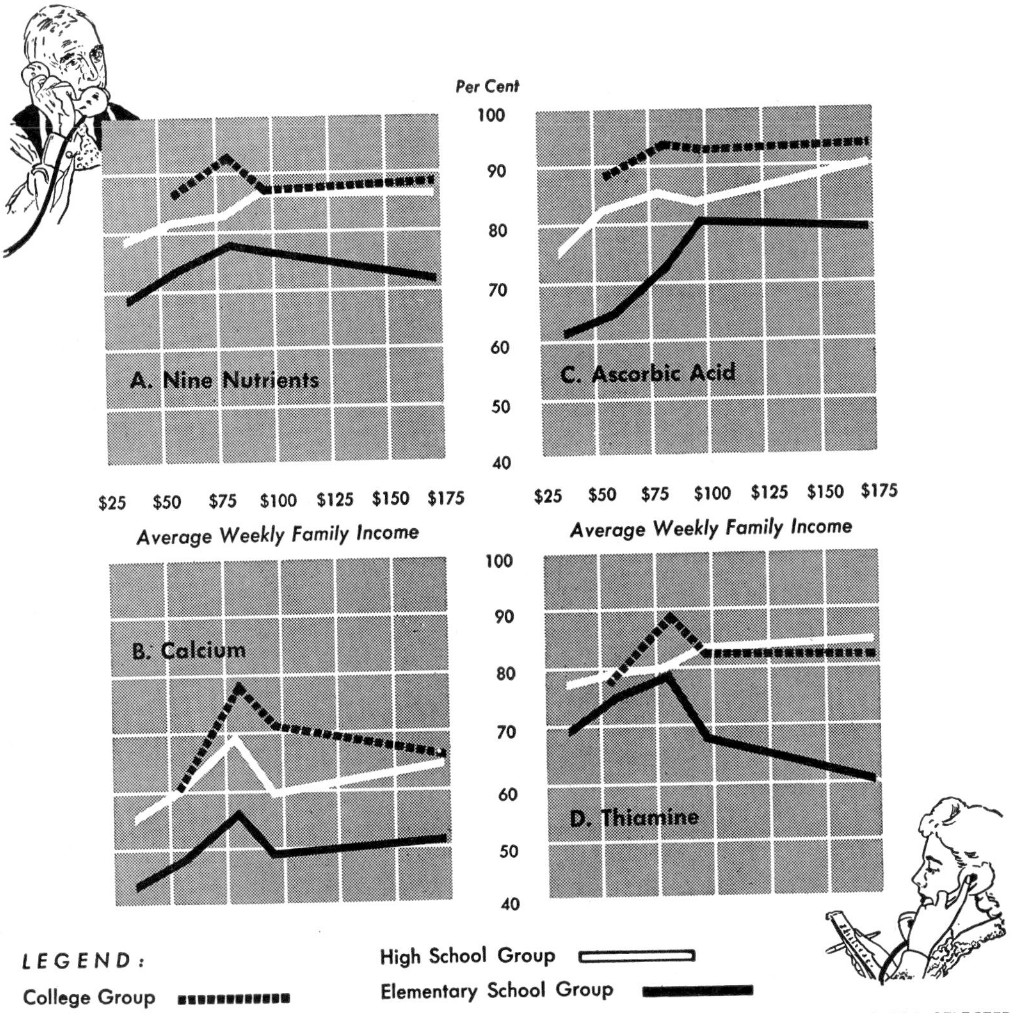

Per Cent

A. Nine Nutrients

$25 $50 $75 $100 $125 $150 $175
Average Weekly Family Income

B. Calcium

C. Ascorbic Acid

$25 $50 $75 $100 $125 $150 $175
Average Weekly Family Income

D. Thiamine

LEGEND: High School Group ▭

College Group ▪▪▪▪▪▪▪▪▪   Elementary School Group ▬▬▬

FIGURE 29. PER CENT OF URBAN FAMILIES WITH WEEKLY DIETS PROVIDING NRC ALLOWANCES FOR SELECTED NUTRIENTS, BY EDUCATION OF HOMEMAKER AND INCOME, 1948

Sources: U.S. Department of Agriculture, 1948 Food Consumption Surveys: *Nutritive Content of City Diets,* Special Report No. 2; and *Food Consumption of Urban Families (68 Cities) in the U.S., Spring 1948,* Preliminary Report No. 5, p. 6. In these reports families were classified by their 1947 disposable income. Income was not reported for the three educational groups separately. It was assumed that within each income class the average weekly income was the same for all groups.

Diet deficiencies in calcium, however, are not nearly as bad as these figures would imply. In the first place, if allowance is made for calcium in drinking water and baking powder, the proportion of all urban families whose diets meet at least

do differences in income appear to be a factor. One of the four cities had an appreciably higher income than the urban group as a whole, two were close to the national average and one was appreciably below it. Differences in markets may be important, since some small urban communities provide only a limited selection of fresh fruits and vegetables. Differences in the education of the homemaker may also be a factor. (See Table 57.)

the 1948 NRC standard rises from 58 to 70 per cent. Secondly, if allowance is made for the downward revision of the NRC calcium standard in May 1953 (see Table 52, footnote a), it seems likely that the diets of about 80 per cent of all urban families would prove adequate in calcium. In that case, calcium would be just about as well supplied as most other nutrients.

Thiamine and ascorbic acid were the nutrients most affected by differences in food habits among the four cities. Birmingham, which rates low

TABLE 57. PER CENT OF URBAN FAMILIES WHOSE DIETS PROVIDED AT LEAST THE NATIONAL RESEARCH COUNCIL ALLOWANCES [a] FOR VARIOUS NUTRIENTS, BY EDUCATION OF HOMEMAKER, PRESENCE OF CHILDREN, NUMBER OF PERSONS AND INCOME,[b] ONE WEEK, SPRING 1948

	Number of Persons per Household	Average for Nine Nutrients– Dietary Rating	Calcium [c]	Ascorbic Acid	Thiamine [d]	Niacin
All families	3.4	80	58 [e]	79	78	80
Education of Homemaker						
All incomes						
Elementary	3.6	73	50	69	73	76
High school	3.4	82	59	83	80	81
College	3.1	88	68	91	82	88
$2,000 to $3,000 [f]						
Elementary	3.6	73	49	65	75	75
High school	3.5	81	60	82	79	80
College	3.1	87	61	89	78	80
$3,000 to $4,000 [f]						
Elementary	3.8	79	57	73	80	76
High school	3.7	82	60	85	80	80
College	3.2	93	79	94	90	92
Number of Persons in Family						
All incomes						
2 persons	—	83	63	83	81	85
3 persons	—	82	64	82	77	81
4 persons	—	80	57	83	78	78
5 or more persons	—	72	42	66	73	76
$2,000 to $3,000 [f]						
2 persons	—	82	59	78	82	84
3 persons	—	83	65	80	80	80
4 persons	—	80	59	84	76	76
5 or more persons	—	67	39	60	71	69
$3,000 to $4,000 [f]						
2 persons	—	88	73	91	86	89
3 persons	—	85	67	84	80	80
4 persons	—	84	60	84	88	77
5 or more persons	—	76	51	71	75	78
Presence of Children						
All incomes						
With no children	2.5	79	57	80	76	80
With children	4.3	81	58	79	80	81
$2,000 to $3,000 [f]						
With no children	2.5	79	55	75	80	79
With children	4.3	82	57	77	77	77
$3,000 to $4,000 [f]						
With no children	2.5	82	62	86	80	81
With children	4.3	84	63	80	83	80

Sources: U.S. Department of Agriculture: *Nutritive Content of City Diets,* Food Consumption Surveys of 1948–1949, Special Report No. 2, October 1950, Tables 1, 5, 6 and 7; and *Food Consumption of Urban Families (68 Cities) in the U.S., Spring 1948,* 1948 Food Consumption Surveys, Preliminary Report No. 14, May 1949, Table 3.

a. As released in 1948. In evaluating the diets, cooking losses were deducted.

b. Disposable money income in 1947.

c. Were the 1953 NRC dietary allowance for calcium used instead of the 1948 allowance to appraise the diets, the proportion of families found to have adequate diets would be higher, since the calcium allowance for adults was reduced in the 1953 revision. (See Tables 52 and 56.) In addition, some of the relationships would be altered, and perhaps appreciably. The increase in the proportion of families with adequate diets would be greater for the small than for the large families since small families have a higher percentage of adults than large families. Accordingly, one would expect the increase to be relatively greater also for the "college" than for the "elementary school" group, merely because on the average the "college" group has fewer persons per family. Similarly, the difference between two-person families and families of five or more would be increased and families with no children would probably score higher, instead of lower, than families with children. The effect of the 1953 revision in the calcium allowance can be illustrated using data for families of two and of four persons in the income bracket relatively in consumption of fresh fruits and vegetables, had the lowest percentage of families with diets meeting the NRC ascorbic acid allowance — 75 per cent, compared with 84 per cent in Minneapolis-St. Paul, 87 per cent in San Francisco, and 89 per cent in Buffalo. San Francisco and Minneapolis-St. Paul, which rate relatively low in consumption of grain products, were lowest in percentage of family diets providing the NRC thiamine allowance — 79 per cent, as against over 89 per cent in Buffalo and 94 per cent in Birmingham.

Factors Affecting Adequacy of Urban Diets

The higher the formal education of the homemaker, the higher the family income and the smaller the family, the more likely is the family to have an adequate diet, according to family dietary surveys made by the U.S. Department of Agriculture in 1948. However, families with children tended to have better diets than those without children even though their average income was no higher and they had more persons to feed.[99] (See Table 57.)

The dietary rating of urban families whose homemakers had a high school education was 9 percentage points above, and that of families whose homemakers had a college education 15 percentage points above, the rating of families with homemakers having only elementary school education.[100] (Table 57.)

---

99. If the diets of individual family members were appraised instead of the average diet of the family as a whole, the difference between families with and without children might be narrowed. Although families with children consume more milk per capita, for example, it may be that adults in such families drink no more milk than other adults. Thus adults in families with children may be assumed to be getting more calcium than they actually do.

100. *Nutritive Content of City Diets.* In evaluating diets, cooking losses were deducted. The dietary rating is based on the average percentage of families in income classes $2,000–$3,000, $3,000–$4,000 and $4,000–$5,000 whose diets provided the NRC allowances for nine nu-

Moreover, homemakers with a higher education provided better diets at a lower cost. Average expenditures per person per week by three-person families with incomes of $3,000–$4,000 decreased from $7.95 in the "elementary school" group to $7.52 in the "high school" group and $7.12 in the "college" group. Similarly, among four-person families, the "college" group spent least per person per week — $5.87, compared with $6.38 in the "elementary school" and $6.78 in the "high school" groups.[101]

The percentage of families whose diets provided the NRC allowances increased only slightly with income,[102] and the effect of income differed among the various nutrients.[103] The increase with income is relatively great for ascorbic acid, which is largely provided by fresh fruits and vegetables, and is least for thiamine, which is provided chiefly by grain products.[104] (See Figure 29.)

---

trients. In the classification an interaction with other factors affecting the nutritive level of diets may have occurred. Family size, for example, was inversely related to the education of the homemaker. This may have been responsible for some of the difference in diets, but probably for not more than one point. There may also have been some differences in income between the groups. The income classes are broad, and mean incomes for the various educational groups are not reported. Furthermore, even though current income was the same, average income was probably higher for the "high school" and "college" groups than for the "elementary school" group.

101. *Ibid.,* p. 19.

102. In the four cities for which data are reported in Table 56 there was no relationship between dietary rating and per capita income. Furthermore, the similarity in dietary ratings among the cities probably cannot be explained in terms of the education of the homemakers. A high level of adequacy may be achieved in one city because of education and in another by the accident of local food habits.

103. Family size tends to increase a little with income, but such analysis as is possible does not indicate that this factor is important in the relationship shown. It might, of course, become important if the NRC calcium allowance of 1953 were used in appraising the diets. (See Table 57, footnote c.)

104. The pattern of nutrient supply by income class shown in Figure 29 is affected by differences in food habits among regions. In the South, consumption of thiamine is high and consumption of calcium and ascorbic

---

TABLE 57 (continued)

$3,000–$4,000. (See Special Report No. 2, Table 3.) If the two-person families consisted of two adults with no pregnant or lactating women, then use of the 1953 allowance would probably increase the proportion having adequate diets from 73 per cent to around 84 per cent; and if the families of four consisted of husband and wife, a child under 9 years and a girl of 15 years, use of the 1953 allowance would increase the proportion with adequate diets from 60 to 68 per cent. (See Appendix 5–1 for discussion of methodology.)

d. Differences with family size are much the same for riboflavin and niacin as for thiamine.

e. When allowance is made for calcium in the water

supply and in baking powder, the proportion is close to 70 per cent for all families. Probably the intake of calcium from the water supply does not vary with the education of the homemaker.

f. These two income levels were selected because of the large number of families in them. Data for other income levels show much the same pattern. Within each income class the average household size declines with higher education of the homemaker. This in itself contributes a little to a higher quality of diet. A tabulation in Special Report No. 2 for three- and four-person families in one income group shows the same pattern by education of the homemaker as the data in this table.

TABLE 58. PER CENT OF FARM AND RURAL NONFARM FAMILIES WHOSE DIETS PROVIDED AT LEAST THE
NATIONAL RESEARCH COUNCIL ALLOWANCES [a] OF VARIOUS NUTRIENTS, TWO MISSISSIPPI
COUNTIES, ONE WEEK IN SUMMER OF 1946

| | Farm Families [b] | | Rural Nonfarm Families | |
Nutrient	Income of $200 or More from Sale of Farm Products in 1945	All Others [c]	County A	County B
Average for nine nutrients–dietary rating	81	86	71	79
Calories	80	83	75	79
Protein	85	88	77	85
Calcium [d]	75	79	59	58
Iron	90	92	77	91
Vitamin A	72	78	51	73
Thiamine	93	97	81	91
Riboflavin	89	90	76	82
Niacin	80	84	72	83
Ascorbic acid	68	79	69	71
Average number of persons per family	4.4	4.0	3.1	2.8
Average total net income per capita [e]	$460	$564	$714	$849

Source: *Rural Levels of Living in Lee and Jones Counties, Mississippi, 1946*, Agriculture Information Bulletin
No. 41, U.S. Department of Agriculture, 1951, pp. 14, 21 and 55. The study includes a representative sample in
the two counties.

a. As released in 1948. Average cooking losses of thiamine, riboflavin, niacin and ascorbic acid have been
taken into account.

b. Farm families included all families living on farms, a farm being defined as a tract of land of three acres
or more, or one of less than three acres but occupied by a family having a cow or raising farm produce worth as
much as $250. The produce might be exclusively for family use.

c. Farm families whose income from the sale of farm products only was less than $200 in 1945.

d. No allowance is made for calcium in the water supply or in baking powder. Moreover, the percentages
would be greater if the lower NRC dietary allowance for calcium for adults in 1953 were used instead of the
1948 standard. Estimates in terms of the 1953 allowance for the four groups of families in the order listed in
the table are 79, 84, 68 and 67 per cent. The increase is somewhat greater for the rural nonfarm than for the
farm groups because of the smaller proportion of children in nonfarm families. (See Appendix 5–1 for description of estimating method. The adjustment factors for these estimates were developed using as weights rural
nonfarm and rural farm population in Mississippi as reported in *1950 Census of Population*, Series P-B 24, 1952,
Tables 15 and 32.)

e. Includes cash income from all sources and income in kind, including home-produced food and rental value
of houses occupied without direct cost during the year.

Diets of families with five or more members
were markedly poorer than those of smaller families. Families of five or more were 13 per cent
below two-person families in their average dietary
rating for nine nutrients, while four-person families and three-person families rated only 4 per cent
and one per cent, respectively, below two-person
families. (See Table 57.)

acid is low. Since the southern population is relatively
heavily represented in the lower income classes, the percentage of families having diets adequate in calcium and
ascorbic acid rises with income within the nation and the
percentage with diets adequate in thiamine at first rises
with income and then falls.

Rural Diets

Such surveys as have been made indicate that
farm families are more likely to have adequate
diets than village and city families of the same
size and income.

The latest dietary survey of rural families in
the United States as a whole, made in the spring
of 1942, showed considerable improvement over
1935–1936. Since 1942, further improvement has
probably occurred similar to that in urban diets
because of enrichment of flour and bread, higher
real incomes and nutritional education.

A survey of rural families in two Mississippi

TABLE 59. PER CENT OF FARM, RURAL NONFARM AND VILLAGE FAMILIES IN A NEW YORK TOWNSHIP WHOSE DIETS PROVIDED AT LEAST THE NATIONAL RESEARCH COUNCIL ALLOWANCES [a] OF VARIOUS NUTRIENTS, ONE WEEK IN FALL OF 1948 AND SPRING OF 1949

Nutrient	Farm	Rural Nonfarm [b]	Village [c]
		Fall of 1948	
Average of nine nutrients– dietary rating	89	82	73
		Spring of 1949	
Average of nine nutrients– dietary rating	85	80	72
Calories	60	64	58
Protein	91	92	83
Calcium [d]	71	46	31
Iron	91	85	80
Vitamin A	83	71	61
Thiamine	94	92	83
Riboflavin	94	90	83
Niacin	94	93	85
Ascorbic acid	89	90	85

Source: C. M. Young and others, "Nutritional Status Survey, Groton Township, New York," Journal of the American Dietetic Association, October 1950, p. 778.

a. As released in 1948. Data are adjusted for cooking losses of vitamins.

b. Nonfarm families living in the open country.

c. Nonfarm families not living in the open country but in built-up areas.

d. See Table 56 for an indication of the differences in percentages that would result from using the 1953 instead of the 1948 NRC calcium allowance. It was not possible to estimate the adequacy of diets in this study in terms of the 1953 standard since the distribution of families by level of calcium consumption was not reported.

counties in the summer of 1946 showed that two groups of farm families had average dietary ratings of 81 and 86, and two groups of nonfarm families had ratings of 71 and 79. The greatest deficiencies among these families were in ascorbic acid, vitamin A and calcium. Nonfarm families were low in calories as well. (See Table 58.)

In a New York township in 1948–1949, the average dietary rating in the fall of 1948 and the spring of 1949 was 87 for farm families, 81 for rural nonfarm families and 73 for village families. (See Table 59.)

Dietary ratings of the New York nonfarm families in the surveys in 1948 and 1949 were about the same as those of all urban families in the spring of 1948. The ratings of Mississippi non-

farm families in 1946 were lower than those of urban families two years later.[105] The dietary rating of the New York families is of special interest because physical examinations showed them to be a "well-nourished population." This finding gives some basis for assuming that dietary deficiencies reported in other recent surveys are minor.

Among rural as among urban families, dietary adequacy increases somewhat with income. The average dietary rating of farm families in Mississippi is estimated at 83 for those with current income under $1,000 and 89 for those with incomes of $2,000 to $5,000. The average for rural nonfarm families in Mississippi is estimated at

105. The total net per capita income of the Mississippi nonfarm families reporting was $782; whereas that of all nonfarm families in the United States in 1945 was $1,279. See U.S. Department of Agriculture: Rural Levels of Living in Lee and Jones Counties, Mississippi, 1945, Agriculture Information Bulletin No. 41, 1951, pp. 21, 55, and

94; and National Farm Income, July 1947, p. 2. Exact income data for the New York families are not given. The report gives the opinion, however, that the average per capita income of the families was almost 10 per cent below the national average in the year of the survey. See Journal of the American Dietetic Association, October 1950, p. 775.

75 in the lower income group and 80 in the higher income group.[106]

Open-country families in a Georgia and an Ohio county during the summer of 1945 had dietary ratings of 71 and 78 respectively.[107] The Georgia diets were poorest in vitamin A, calcium and riboflavin; the Ohio diets, in calcium, vitamin A and ascorbic acid. The counties were selected, however, for the purpose of investigating dietary adequacy where incomes were thought to be relatively low. The Ohio families had appreciably higher incomes and appreciably better diets than the Georgia families, and may also have had greater nutritional knowledge.[108]

Adequacy of Diets in 1950

Recent family surveys for the most part indicate diets of high quality, although some shortcomings persist. The most important shortages are in calcium, ascorbic acid, vitamin A and, to a much lesser extent, the B vitamins. Physical examinations have shown that in some geographic areas vitamin D and iodine are not consumed in sufficient quantities to prevent rickets and goiter, and have confirmed everyday observations that the calorie consumption of many adults tends to be too high. Dr. W. H. Sebrell, of the U.S. Public Health Service, speaking at the National Food and Nutrition Institute in 1952, said that "Obesity has replaced the vitamin deficiency diseases as the Number One nutrition problem in the United States. An estimated one fourth of the adults in this country are obese — that is, sufficiently overweight to result in appreciable damage to health; and the incidence may reach 60 per cent in older women." [109] Experimental evidence points to the life-shortening effects of obesity: [110]

Animal research has confirmed the observations of the physician concerning the injurious effects of a fat body. Experimental white rats . . . have longer spans of life when forced to keep thin by diets that are low in calories but high in other essentials. Their lives have been extended by as much as a year, which would be the equivalent, on the human scale, to the addition of thirty-five years of a life time.

The dietary studies, however, do not give a definitive report on the frequency of inadequate diets.[111] Many conditions make for crudity of measurement, for example, the roughness of the estimates of foods consumed. Moreover, the percentage of families with diets below NRC allowances probably would be less if two-week or three-week diets were examined instead of one-week diets. The studies take no account of consumption of nutrients above the allowances. Some families whose diets are below standard in a particular week are likely to exceed the standard sufficiently in the following week to offset the earlier deficiency. Some families, of course, may have adequate diets during a survey week and inadequate diets the next week. But in general the percentage of adequate diets will be greater in the longer than in the shorter period since evaluation of a single week's diet tends to understate the adequacy of all nutrients which are stored; and experiments indicate that most nutrients are stored when taken in excess of current need.[112]

Some data are available which permit a direct comparison of dietary ratings in one-week and three-week periods. Family dietary surveys made in four cities in three seasons of 1948 showed that the proportion of families with diets meeting the NRC allowances was greater in the three-week period than in the one-week period. In Birmingham, with 48 families reporting, the dietary rating of "one-week" diets was 90 while the rating of "three-week" diets was 94. In Buffalo, Minneapolis-St. Paul and San Francisco, with 76 families reporting, the dietary ratings were very similar: 89 for the "one-week" diets and 94 for the "three-week" diets.[113]

The intake of nutrients in a group of families also gives some clue to the likelihood that foods

---

106. *Rural Levels of Living in Lee and Jones Counties, Mississippi, 1945*, pp. 62–66 and 94. Family size increased with income. This may be the major reason for such a small increase in dietary rating with income.

107. See *Diets of Families in the Open Country — A Georgia and an Ohio County, Summer 1945*, Miscellaneous Publication No. 704, U.S. Department of Agriculture, April 1950. These are average percentages of families whose diets provided the 1945 NRC allowances for nine nutrients. The 1945 allowance for calcium was 0.8 grams, as compared with a 1948 allowance of 1.0 grams. In addition, the appraisal of these diets did not take cooking losses into account.

108. Per capita money income of these families was $524 in the Ohio county and $304 in the Georgia county.

109. *Nutrition Committee News*, January 1953, p. 1.

110. Ralph Gerard, *Food for Life*, University of Chicago Press, 1952, p. 279.

111. For extended discussion of the interpretation of dietary data see *Nutrition Surveys: Their Technique and Value*, Bulletin No. 117, National Research Council, 1949.

112. Uncertainty exists about the extent to which vitamin C is stored.

113. Unpublished data provided by the Bureau of Human Nutrition and Home Economics of the U.S. Department of Agriculture. For the one-week diets, three separate ratings, one in each season, were averaged. The estimate of adequacy made allowance for cooking losses.

consumed during other weeks make up for deficiencies in the one-week diet. In the spring of 1948
among urban households of two or more persons
with incomes of $1,000 to $2,000, the proportion
of families with diets below the NRC allowances
amounted to 22 per cent for vitamin A and 20
per cent for ascorbic acid.[114] But the median consumption per nutrition unit exceeded the allowances by 70 and 81 per cent respectively. Thus it
seems possible that over the longer period of time
many more families had diets meeting NRC allowances for vitamin A and ascorbic acid than
the survey indicated. One cannot be so optimistic,
however, concerning calcium. Consumption of
calcium per nutrition unit provided little excess
over the NRC allowance — only 7 per cent.[115]

Even more important in judging the adequacy
of diets in the population at large is the fact that
need varies appreciably among individuals. The
NRC allowances are to provide for the need of all
but a small fraction of the population. Some individuals do not need the full NRC allowances.
Thus many persons whose diets do not meet the
NRC allowances are nevertheless eating adequately. For example, even without taking into
account the calcium in the water consumed, 87
per cent of the nation's urban households in 1948
had diets providing at least 0.7 grams of calcium
a day — the average need for this nutrient.[116]

114. *Nutritive Value of Diets of Urban Families,
United States, Spring 1948, and Comparison with Diets
in 1942*, 1948 Food Consumption Surveys, Preliminary
Report No. 12, U.S. Department of Agriculture, p. 23.
115. *Ibid.*, p. 22. This measure does not take account
of the lowering of the NRC allowance for calcium in
1953 or the calcium in the water consumed.
116. *Ibid.* If the diets were similarly appraised using
the 1953 NRC calcium allowance, it is estimated that 91
per cent of the households would have been found to have
diets adequate in calcium. In measuring the frequency of
adequate diets by a yardstick based on the average need,
it is assumed that for everyone whose need is greater than
the average there is someone whose need is less.
This estimate of the frequency of adequate diets differs
from the one on p. 159. There the yardstick was the
recommended dietary allowance. Here the yardstick is
the estimated average need, which is less than the allowance. The recommended dietary allowance of the National Research Council as of 1948 was 1.0 gram per
adult male per day. (See Table 52.) The National Research Council in describing its allowances points out that
they tend to exceed average need by about 30 per cent.
(See the passage quoted on p. 152 above.) When differences in age and sex shown in Table 52 are taken into
account, 0.7 gram per day per nutrition unit is found to
provide a suitable measure of average need for calcium.
This 0.7 should not be confused with the ratio of .88
described in Appendix 5-1. It was developed to take
account of the difference in the 1953 revision of dietary
allowances for the various age and sex groups. If the
adequacy of the separate family diets had been recom-

The evidence supports the conclusion that the
nation as a whole is fairly well fed. Existing inadequacies should not be ignored, however, especially in view of the decline in the supply of
nutrients since 1948, the year to which most of
the dietary data relate.

NEEDS AND CONSUMPTION

Food satisfies psychological and social needs as
well as physiological requirements, and these
themselves cover a broad range from mere sus-
tenance of life to optimum nutrition. The concept
of need therefore varies with time and place,
depending on nutritional knowledge, amount
and variety of foods available, level of income, and
cultural setting. The measures of physiological
need most generally accepted in the United States
today assume that the diet should provide not
merely the minimum nutrients necessary for protection against actual deficiency disease but also a
fair margin to ensure good nutrition and protection of all body tissues. It is largely in this sense
that need beyond actual consumption is considered here.

GAPS BETWEEN CONSUMPTION AND NEED IN 1950

The per capita food supply of 1950, even though
lower than that of 1946, a peak year, would have
provided the entire population with adequate
diets as measured by the National Research Council nutritional allowances, had it been equally
shared. In fact, most nutrients were available in
sizable excess of the amounts recommended by
the NRC. The protein content of the 1950 per
capita food supply was around 50 per cent above
the NRC allowance; the vitamin A content,
around 90 per cent above it. Even for calcium
some excess existed on the average. In foods apart
from water, the per capita supply of calcium in
1950 amounted to 1.03 grams.[117] This exceeded
by 11 per cent the per capita NRC allowance as
of 1953, which has been estimated at .93 grams.[118]
If the 1953 allowance provides a margin of safety
to take into account those with needs above the
average without at the same time taking into
account those with below-average needs, as did
the allowance described on p. 152, then the quan-

puted using the revised allowances, this ratio .88 would
have been unnecessary.
117. *Consumption of Food in the United States, 1909–
1952*, p. 162.
118. See Appendix 5-1.

tity of calcium in the 1950 food supply exceeded average need by about 50 per cent.[119]

In spite of these surpluses in the total supply of various nutrients, studies of family diets over one-week periods show that some of them provide appreciably less than the NRC allowances. Some of the deficiency is due to the ups-and-downs common in weekly diets of families and does not exist in diets covering longer periods of time, say two or three weeks. Nevertheless, diets providing less than the NRC allowances over long periods do occur and, consequently, gaps between consumption and "need" do exist. Recent evidence of the undesirability of excess calories in diets, on the other hand, points to considerable consumption in excess of some "needs."

The nutrients whose intake falls most frequently below the NRC allowances are calcium and ascorbic acid, the major sources of which are milk, and fruits and vegetables, respectively. In 1948, 66 per cent of the total calcium in the diets of urban housekeeping families came from milk products other than butter, quite apart from the milk products in processed foods purchased, such as bread, and 94 per cent of the total ascorbic acid came from fruits and vegetables, including potatoes.[120] Need for calcium and ascorbic acid could be met by increased consumption of these foods. The required increase in their consumption may be estimated on the basis of the amounts recommended in the low-cost adequate diet developed by the U.S. Bureau of Human Nutrition and Home Economics.[121]

The purchase of milk products, apart from butter and milk in processed foods such as bread, would have been 7 per cent greater in 1950 if everyone had had at least as much of these products as recommended in the low-cost food budget. The amount purchased annually per person would have increased by 17 quarts, sufficient to furnish 7 per cent of the NRC calcium allowance

for a man.[122] Similarly, it is estimated that 1950 consumption of citrus fruits and tomatoes would have been 15 per cent higher and of leafy, green and yellow vegetables 11 per cent higher if everyone had had at least the amounts recommended in the low-cost food budget. This would have meant an annual per capita increase in consumption of 16 pounds of citrus fruits and tomatoes and 17 pounds of leafy, green and yellow vegetables. These quantities would have contributed 7 per cent of the NRC dietary allowance of ascorbic acid for a man.[123]

The gap between need and consumption of nutrients could be closed in other ways. For example, to make up the calcium deficiency calcium salts might be added to flour and bread. These salts are now an optional enrichment ingredient in flour and bread but are important only in "self-rising" flour, which is used in considerable amounts only in the southern states.

Many people consume more vitamins and minerals than the NRC recommends. Consumption of these beyond the allowances is beneficial to health and vigor. Excessive consumption of calories is undesirable, however, and studies of family diets show them to be high in caloric value. In every income class, average family consumption of sugar and sweets — apart from amounts purchased in processed foods such as bakery products and canned fruits — exceeds the level recommended in the low-cost food budget. Among urban housekeeping families in 1948, sugar and sweets purchased as such ranked fifth among the major food groups in their contribution to calories, trailing behind grain products, fats and oils, dairy products, and meat, poultry and fish. Since these other food groups provide appreciable amounts of nutrients other than calories, a cut in their consumption would seriously lower the quality of the diet. Sugar and sweets, on the other hand, contribute very little apart from calories. If their consumption had been cut to the level recommended, purchased sugar and sweets would have been 41 per cent below the levels reported by families in 1948. This reduction would amount to 27 pounds per person per year, the equivalent

---

119. In this estimate average per capita need of .93 grams was multiplied by .70.

120. See *Nutritive Value of Family Diets, Four Cities, Part II, Distribution of Families Classified by Nutritive Content of Diets,* 1948 Food Consumption Surveys, Preliminary Report No. 13, Table 13. Dried fruits and vegetables are not included. Their contribution to the total supply of ascorbic acid in diets is very small.

121. See *Helping Families Plan Food Budgets,* Miscellaneous Publication No. 662, U.S. Department of Agriculture, December 1948. The quantities of foods recommended for a moderate-cost diet are shown in Table 53, and the NRC dietary allowances in Table 52. For basis of estimates given below see Appendix 5–2.

122. For nutritive value of milk see *Composition of Foods,* Agriculture Handbook No. 8, U.S. Department of Agriculture, June 1950, p. 122.

123. The ascorbic acid per pound for the two food groups is that of the mixture of foods reported to have been purchased by urban families during the spring of 1948. No account is taken of cooking losses. See *1948 Food Consumption Surveys,* Preliminary Report No. 12, 1949, Tables 1, 3 and 13.

TABLE 60. PER CAPITA DEMAND FOR MAJOR FOODS, 1950, AND ESTIMATES FOR 1960

Food	1950	1960	1960 as Per Cent of 1950
		(Pounds)	
Dairy products (excluding butter)	410	431	105
Eggs	48	50	104
Meat, poultry and fish	154	165	107
Fats and oils (including fat cuts and butter)	68	66	97
Dry beans and peas, nuts and soya products	18	16	89
Potatoes (sweet and other)	108	107	99
Citrus fruit and tomatoes	101	111	110
Leafy, green and yellow vegetables	105	111	106
Other vegetables and fruits	220	239	109
Grain products	166	158	95
Sugars and sirups	107	107	100
Coffee, tea and cocoa	17	17	100

Sources: *Consumption of Food in the United States, 1909–1952*, Agriculture Handbook No. 62, U.S. Department of Agriculture, 1953, Table 38; for method of estimating 1960 demand see Appendix 5–3.

of 132 calories a day, or about 5 per cent of the calorie needs of a sedentary male.

DEMAND IN 1960

Americans will consume more food, liquor and tobacco in the years ahead. Between 1950 and 1960, consumption expenditures per capita are expected to increase as follows: [124]

	Percentage Increase
All consumption items	7
Food, liquor and tobacco	7
Food and beverages	7
Consumed inside the home	7
Consumed outside the home	10
Food and nonalcoholic beverages	7
Alcoholic beverages	11
Tobacco products and smoking supplies	7

The somewhat greater proportional increase in expenditures for food consumed away from home than in expenditures for food consumed at home, and in outlays for alcoholic beverages compared with those for other food, reflects the tendency

124. See Appendix 4–7 and Appendix 3–6. The 7 per cent increase in expenditures for food and beverages implies a coefficient of elasticity of expenditures in relation to income of 1.0. This is higher than the coefficient indicated by family studies: the coefficient of elasticity of expenditures for food including beverages in relation to average family expenditures for families classified by annual income tends to be around 0.7.

of these types of consumption to rise with increasing income and increasing concentration of the population in urban places. Higher income per capita, increased urbanization and the spread of nutritional education may also bring about important changes in the demand for individual foods.

Informed guesses can be made about the change in demand for various foods from 1950 to 1960. It seems probable that the increase will be greatest for citrus fruits and tomatoes (10 per cent) with "other vegetables and fruits" next (9 per cent). A decline in demand probably will occur for some foods. The sharpest drop, about 11 per cent, seems likely for dry beans and peas, nuts and soya products, with grain products following with 5 per cent. A slight decline in the consumption of fats and oils and potatoes also seems likely. (See Table 60.)

"NEED" IN RELATION TO DEMAND IN 1960

The increase in demand for milk anticipated by 1960 is almost as great as the "deficiency" noted in 1950, and the increase in demand for fruits and vegetables is even greater. Hence, if increased supplies of these foods went wholly to those who needed them most, then by 1960 the gaps between "need" and consumption would be practically eliminated. The increased supplies

TABLE 61. ESTIMATED NEEDS AND DEMAND FOR FOOD, LIQUOR AND TOBACCO,
1950 AND 1960
(*Millions at 1950 Prices*)

Item	1950		1960	
	Demand	Needs	Demand	Needs
Food, liquor and tobacco	$65,606	$66,365	$81,800	$82,300
Food and beverages	61,208	61,967	76,300	76,800
Food and nonalcoholic beverages	53,108	53,867	65,900	66,400
Alcoholic beverages	8,100	8,100	10,400	10,400
Tobacco products and smoking supplies	4,398	4,398	5,500	5,500

Sources: Appendix 4–7 and discussion in text.

will not be distributed in this way, however, so that they will tend merely to narrow the gaps noted in 1950 rather than eliminate them.

Deficiencies in milk consumption in 1960 probably would call for an increase in milk consumption of 6 per cent above the estimated demand in that year.[125] Further increases in consumption of citrus fruit and tomatoes and of leafy, green and yellow vegetables would also be needed in 1960, amounting to 2 per cent in each case.

COST OF MEETING DIETARY NEEDS

The cost of the additional amounts of milk products, citrus fruits and tomatoes, and leafy, green and yellow vegetables needed to bring average consumption of these foods up to recommended dietary levels would have been about $4.98 per person in 1950. The average cost of the excess sugar and sweets consumed was about $2.62 per person. Thus, if the needed foods were added and the excess of sugar and sweets over the amount in the low-cost diet removed, the additional cost of food per person would have been $2.36 above 1950 outlays.[126] In 1960, as a result

125. Data and methods used are described in Appendix 5–2.
126. The prices used are those in the *Statistical Abstract, 1951*, p. 287. It was assumed that the extra milk was in the form of whole milk purchased in stores, and that the store price was 2 cents per quart less than the delivered price quoted in the *Statistical Abstract*. The division between citrus fruits and tomatoes was made on the basis of consumption reported by families with in-

of the projected changes in per capita demand (Table 60), the cost of the needed additional amounts of milk products, citrus fruits and tomatoes and leafy, green and yellow vegetables would be $2.82 per person in 1950 prices; the cost of excess sugar and sweets would be $2.62 per person; and the net additional cost would be $0.21 per person.

Bringing food consumption to this dietary level would have added $360 million to the nation's 1950 food bill and would add about $37 million (in 1950 prices) to its probable 1960 expenditure.

However, the basic premise that the role of experts is to point out deficiencies and to ignore excesses calls for no reduction in outlays due to the purchase of excess sugar. Under this concept of need, some $759 million would have been added to the nation's 1950 food bill and $500 million (at 1950 prices) would be added to probable 1960 outlays. (See Table 61.)

come of less than $1,000 in the urban survey of the spring of 1948 as recorded in *1948 Food Consumption Surveys*, Preliminary Report No. 5. It was assumed that for both citrus fruits and tomatoes increased consumption was in the form of fresh products. An assumption that some of the increased milk was in the form of dried skim milk and that some of the increased consumption of citrus fruits and tomatoes was in the form of canned and frozen products would have resulted in a lower estimate of additional costs. Cabbage prices were assumed to represent adequately the cost of the increase in the consumption of leafy, green and yellow vegetables. This assumption probably led to an underestimate of increased cost which to some extent offset the excess cost that was probably introduced by the assumption relating to the other foods.

## CHAPTER 6

CLOTHING, ACCESSORIES AND PERSONAL CARE

CLOTHING IN ITS dual role as a necessity and a luxury has always played an important part in consumer budgets and in the whole economic structure of the nation. Even before the manufacture of apparel passed from the home to the factory, the production and distribution of textiles and leather were among the country's most important industries. Of the three essentials of life — food, housing and clothing — clothing expenditures are the most flexible, and therefore are more sensitive to changes in the consumer's economic status and subject to greater competition from other consumer goods and services. In the mid-twentieth century, mass production and distribution of cosmetics and emphasis on personal appearance through the media of radio, television, movies and printed advertising have made personal care goods and services "big business" also.

In the seven-year period following World War II, expenditures for personal care, clothing, accessories, shoes, jewelry and luggage, and for their cleaning, storage and repair averaged $25.6 billion a year, or about 14 per cent of the total spent for all consumption goods and services. In 1952, expenditures for clothing and related products amounted to $24.8 billion and expenditures for personal care to $2.5 billion. The total of $27.3 billion was higher than the average for the seven postwar years, but because of price increases during the period, it represented some reduction in volume. The 1952 expenditures for clothing and related products constituted only 11.4 per cent of total consumption expenditures, the lowest proportion since 1937, and cause of concern within the industry. (See Appendix 4-4 and Figure 30.)

Establishments and Workers Engaged

The myriad activities required to produce the raw materials for these items, to convert the raw materials to finished products, to distribute them

to the nation's 160 million consumers, and to provide for their maintenance and care, make it impossible to measure precisely the importance of clothing, personal care and related goods industries. Some idea of their general magnitude, however, can be gained by evaluating the importance of industries dealing directly with these goods and services. Such industries will, of course, be concerned also with products outside the field of clothing and personal care. And some activities, such as agriculture, which produces raw materials for clothing and cosmetics, will not enter into the accounting at all.

In 1947–1948, there were more than 45,000 establishments manufacturing clothing, articles for personal care and related goods. These represented about one fifth of all manufacturing establishments and hired about 2.5 million wage earners, or one fifth of all persons employed in manufacturing. Almost 29,000 wholesale establishments, with nearly 183,000 employees, and 227,000 retail stores, with more than 1.1 million employees, were engaged in distributing the products of these manufacturing establishments. These wholesale establishments represented about one ninth of all wholesale trades, and the retail establishments about one eighth of all retail trades. More than one half of all service establishments, almost 329,000, were connected with personal care and the care of clothing. In all, about 629,000 establishments, hiring 4.5 million employees, were engaged in meeting the clothing and personal care demands of the American people. (See Table 62.)

CONSUMPTION EXPENDITURES

Many complex and interrelated factors determine how much consumers spend for clothing and personal care, and the effect of changes in their spending patterns for these items may be far-reaching. A writer in *Harper's Weekly* in January 1860 remarked that "the amount of dry goods sold during the festive season is a pretty good criterion of the state of the money market. It is safe to infer, therefore, that New York

BY HELEN M. HUMES, Assistant Chief, Branch of Cost of Living, Bureau of Labor Statistics, U.S. Department of Labor. Opinions and judgments expressed in this chapter are those of the author and should not be attributed to the organization with which she is associated.

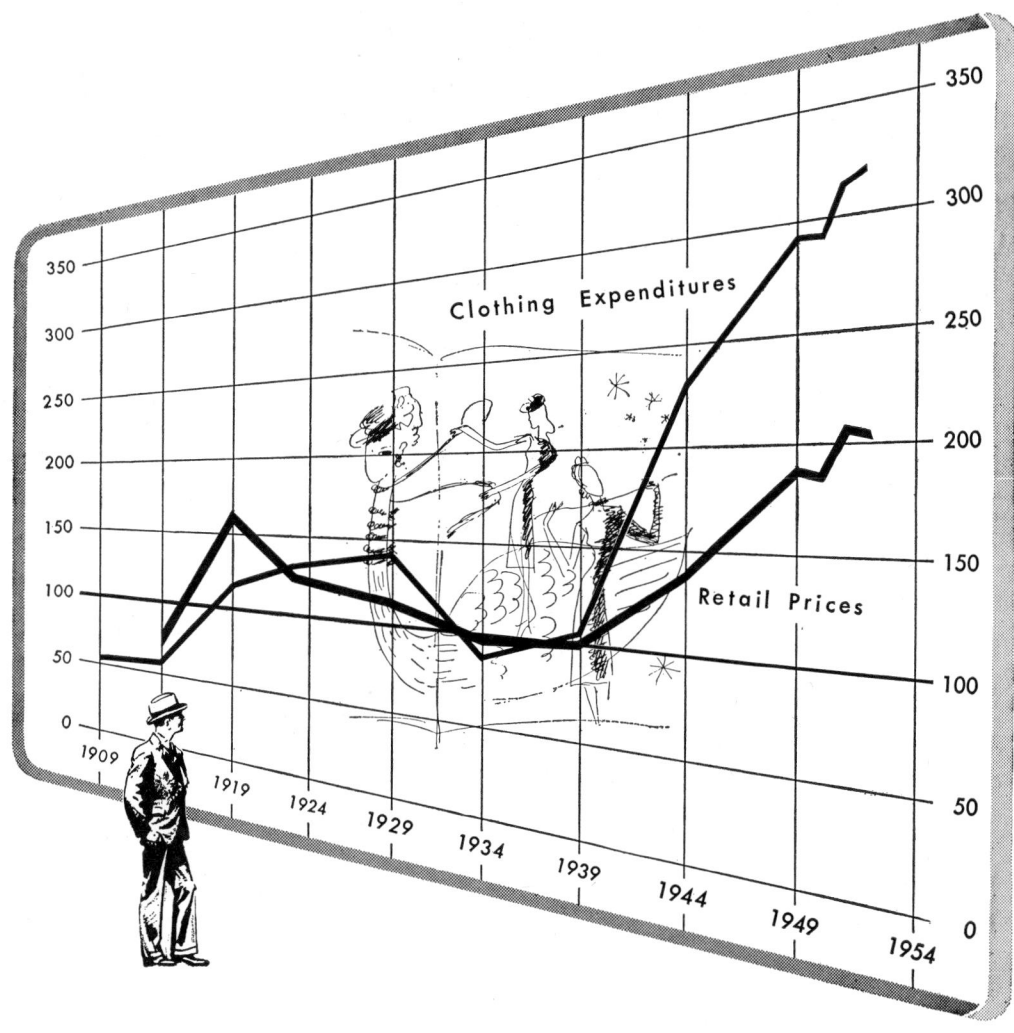

FIGURE 30. TRENDS IN CLOTHING EXPENDITURES AND RETAIL PRICES, 1909–1952
(1935–1939 = 100)

Sources: Consumption expenditures taken from Appendix 4–4; consumers' price index — apparel — from U.S. Department of Labor.

coffers are well furnished, for our ladies have been allowed more for dress from the 10th ult. to the present date than at any corresponding period since 1851." Expenditures for clothing in the twentieth century are a somewhat less reliable barometer. Although the level and distribution of income have a marked influence on the amount spent for clothing and personal care, the trend of expenditures for these items over the past four decades demonstrates that other factors are important as well.

TRENDS

Prior to 1930, rising incomes, increasing production of factory-made clothing, migration from rural to urban areas, and increasing employment of women outside the home all worked together to sustain a high expenditure for clothing and personal care in relation to total expenditures. During the period from 1909 to 1930, more than 14 per cent of total consumption expenditures were allocated to these items, with expenditures for clothing — including footwear, accessories,

TABLE 62. CLOTHING, ACCESSORIES AND PERSONAL CARE: INDUSTRIES, TRADES AND
BUSINESSES, BY GROUPS, 1947–1948

Kind of Business	Number of Establishments	Number of Wage Earners [a]	Value of Products, Sales or Receipts
			(Thousands)
Manufacturing—1947	45,143	2,501,814	$25,922,945
Textiles and fibers	7,603	1,074,811	10,296,403
Apparel and other finished products	29,730	959,734	9,632,411
Leather and rubber products	4,606	360,553	3,753,661
Jewelry	2,237	69,136	782,789
Soap, perfumes, cosmetics, etc.	967	37,580	1,457,681
Wholesale trade—1948	28,489	182,755	22,908,096
Clothing and furnishings	7,485	42,676	4,051,885
Dry goods and piece goods converters	8,569	67,153	10,148,630
Raw materials	3,689	17,010	5,407,334
Jewelry	3,853	18,226	1,016,911
Leather, textile and other products [b]	4,893	37,690	2,283,336
Retail trade—1948	226,984	1,119,633	17,972,091
Apparel stores	115,246	585,703	9,803,218
Drugstores	55,796	282,891	4,013,231
Dry goods and general merchandise stores	29,754	175,029	2,823,869
Jewelry stores	21,269	68,898	1,224,878
Other retail stores [c]	4,919	7,112	106,895
Service establishments—1948	328,655	742,867	3,467,323
Laundries, hand and power [d]	26,529	300,230	1,085,193
Barber and beauty shops, etc. [e]	170,704	159,202	856,205
Apparel cleaning, dyeing, repair, etc. [f]	116,056	268,660	1,392,134
Other service establishments [g]	15,366	14,775	133,791

Source: Appendix 6–1.

a. Includes employees in wholesale and retail trade, and service establishments; excludes self-employed.

b. Includes leather and shoe findings; leather goods; textiles and materials; yarns; barber and beauty shop supplies; laundry and dry cleaning supplies; and toiletries.

c. Includes second-hand clothing and shoe stores; and luggage stores.

d. Includes diaper services and self-service laundries.

e. Includes barber shops; beauty parlors; barber and beauty shops; and baths and electrolysis establishments.

f. Includes cleaning, dyeing, pressing, alteration and repair shops; cleaning and dyeing plants; cleaning and renovating hats; fur repair and storage; shoe repair and shoeshine parlors.

g. Includes watch, clock and jewelry repair; costume and dress suit rental; and other personal services not elsewhere classified.

cleaning, repair and maintenance — accounting for more than 12 per cent. (See Table 63 and Figure 30.)

Even before the decreased incomes of the early 1930s were reflected in smaller relative expenditures for the whole group, the proportion spent for clothing started to decline. From a peak of 14.7 per cent in 1921, the proportion of total expenditures used for clothing and related goods decreased steadily to a low of 11.0 per cent in 1933. It did not again exceed 12 per cent until 1942. During the two decades before World War II, the competition of other goods and services for the clothing dollar was being felt. Mass production and purchase of automobiles, radios, improved household electrical equipment and other durables, and increased emphasis on movies and recreation of all types, claimed many dollars which might otherwise have been spent for clothing.

Expenditures for personal care, on the other hand, advanced steadily from less than one per cent of total expenditures before World War I to 1.7 per cent in 1943. The multiplication of goods and services available to the consumer stimulated rather than reduced the expenditure for personal care. Automobile travel and movies made women and girls in the most remote communities conscious of the latest fashions in hairdress and cosmetics, and manufacturers of beauty preparations turned out an ever-increasing variety of new products.

TABLE 63. TRENDS IN CONSUMPTION EXPENDITURES FOR CLOTHING, JEWELRY
AND PERSONAL CARE, 1909–1952

| Year | Annual Expenditures | | | | Per Cent of Total Consumption Expenditures | | | |
	Total	Clothing [a]	Jewelry [b]	Personal Care [c]	Total	Clothing [a]	Jewelry [b]	Personal Care [c]
	(Millions)							
1909	$ 4,277	$ 3,774	$ 242	$ 261	14.9	13.1	.8	.9
1914	4,708	4,144	259	305	14.1	12.4	.8	.9
1919	9,567	8,284	668	615	15.8	13.7	1.1	1.0
1921	9,336	8,203	531	602	16.7	14.7	1.0	1.1
1923	11,120	9,698	549	873	16.7	14.6	.8	1.3
1925	11,059	9,581	575	903	15.4	13.3	.8	1.3
1927	11,787	10,175	570	1,042	15.8	13.6	.8	1.4
1929	11,913	10,237	560	1,116	14.8	12.7	.7	1.4
1930	10,400	8,848	513	1,039	14.4	12.2	.7	1.4
1931	8,911	7,604	328	979	14.3	12.2	.5	1.6
1932	6,646	5,577	252	817	13.3	11.1	.5	1.6
1933	5,908	5,076	172	660	12.8	11.0	.4	1.4
1934	7,117	6,159	198	760	13.7	11.9	.4	1.5
1935	7,603	6,568	233	802	13.5	11.7	.4	1.4
1936	8,279	7,150	265	864	13.3	11.4	.4	1.4
1937	8,773	7,479	333	961	13.1	11.1	.5	1.4
1938	8,684	7,410	323	951	13.5	11.5	.5	1.5
1939	9,159	7,800	355	1,004	13.6	11.6	.5	1.5
1940	9,746	8,233	406	1,107	13.5	11.4	.6	1.5
1941	11,518	9,763	547	1,208	14.0	11.9	.7	1.5
1942	14,327	12,211	715	1,401	15.7	13.4	.8	1.5
1943	17,753	15,120	931	1,702	17.4	14.8	.9	1.7
1944	19,676	16,789	1,010	1,877	17.6	15.1	.9	1.7
1945	22,039	18,759	1,203	2,077	17.9	15.2	1.0	1.7
1946	24,259	20,654	1,419	2,186	16.5	14.1	1.0	1.5
1947	25,000	21,391	1,348	2,261	15.1	12.9	.8	1.4
1948	26,043	22,474	1,324	2,245	14.6	12.6	.7	1.3
1949	24,823	21,334	1,273	2,216	13.7	11.8	.7	1.2
1950	24,961	21,346	1,312	2,303	12.8	11.0	.7	1.2
1951	26,631	22,825	1,385	2,421	12.8	11.0	.7	1.2
1952	27,301	23,362	1,424	2,515	12.5	10.7	.7	1.2

Sources: Appendices 4–4 and 4–5.

a. Includes clothes and accessories, footwear, cleaning, repair and maintenance.

b. Includes watches.

c. Comprises toilet articles and preparations, and beauty parlor and barber shop services.

Note: Slight discrepancies in addition are due to problems of rounding.

World War II and After

The rapid rise in incomes, increased employment of women in all types of work, migration from rural areas and small communities to large urban centers, and sharp reductions in the production of automobiles and other durables which followed the outbreak of World War II greatly increased the amount of money spent for cloth-ing and, to a lesser extent, for personal care. From 1940 to 1945, the amount spent for clothing, jewelry and personal care increased from 13.5 to 17.9 per cent of total expenditures. Increased expenditures for clothing and related goods accounted for most of this rise. In 1945, expenditures for clothing — including footwear, cleaning, repair and maintenance — reached 15.2

TABLE 64. ANNUAL CLOTHING PURCHASES AT TWO DIFFERENT INCOME LEVELS, 1941

| | Money Income per Family | |
| | Under $500 | $3,000–$5,000 |
Clothing Items	Average Expenditure per Person	Average Expenditure per Person
Men and Boys over 16 Years of Age		
Total	$20.29	$107.62
Headwear	1.20	4.47
Coats, jackets, sweaters	2.02	14.26
Suits, trousers, overalls	5.50	34.81
Shirts	2.47	8.99
Underwear, nightwear, robes	1.65	6.76
Hosiery	1.04	4.32
Footwear	4.91	15.51
Gloves, handkerchiefs, accessories	1.03	9.78
Upkeep, cleaning, pressing	.47	8.72
Women and Girls over 16 Years of Age		
Total	$18.89	$140.15
Headwear	1.05	6.88
Coats, raincoats, jackets, sweaters, furs	2.77	34.54
Dresses, suits, skirts, blouses, aprons	4.17	33.49
Underwear, nightwear, robes	2.26	14.79
Hosiery	2.10	13.93
Footwear	4.30	16.38
Accessories	.61	9.21
Home sewing	1.27	3.37
Upkeep, cleaning	.36	7.56

Source: U.S. Bureau of Labor Statistics. For information on number of specific articles of clothing purchased see *Family Spending and Saving in Wartime,* Bulletin No. 822, U.S. Bureau of Labor Statistics, 1945, Table 10, p. 80.

per cent of total expenditures, the highest level on record.

The increased importance of clothing expenditures relative to total expenditures resulted in part from the fact that clothing prices increased more during the late war years than did the prices of many other commodities and services. (See Figure 30.) However, during the war, production of women's apparel, except shoes, also increased enormously. There were no radical innovations in styles, largely because of wartime limitations, and the industry followed its conventional price policy as far as possible. From early 1942 until 1946, direct price increases were limited by price regulations and, except for a few items such as hosiery and girdles, no serious shortages developed, although complaints of a reduction in quality were rather widespread.

Production of clothing for men in civilian life declined sharply during the war years and important items, such as shirts, underwear and suits, became scarce. In spite of this, expenditures increased. Menswear retailing during the war period has been referred to as a "miracle of substitution." When conventional business shirts and suits were not available, sport shirts and slacks crossed the counter instead. Accessories also enjoyed a boom during the war years. In children's apparel low-priced lines disappeared and quality was reduced.

In spite of continued increases in incomes and high levels of employment in the postwar years, the share of total expenditures going for clothing, jewelry and personal care fell steadily after 1945. During this period deferred expenditures for automobiles and household equipment, which had not been available during the war, were claiming increasing proportions of the consumer's income. The pressures of housing shortages and rapid family formation greatly increased the purchases of homes in the postwar period, providing another strong competitor for the budget dollar previously used for clothing. Sharp rises in clothing prices followed the removal of controls at the end of the war.

By 1948 the backlog of demand caused by wartime shortages and the return of the military forces to civilian life had been satisfied, and resistance to high prices was felt in the clothing markets even though both the quality of garments and their variety were improving rapidly.[1] Increases in the prices of food, housing and other important items in the budget also contributed to the reduction in expenditures for clothing and personal care.

VARIATIONS IN EXPENDITURES

Family spending for clothing and personal care is influenced by a wide variety of factors, of which the most important are income, family size and composition, climate and place of residence, employment status of family members and the kind of work they do, and the range of choice in the quantity and price of clothing items in available markets.

Income Level

Of all these factors, income is probably the most important single determinant of the family's expenditures for clothing, accessories and personal care. As income increases, the amount spent for clothing and accessories increases, and, until a very high income level is reached, the importance of these items in the family budget also increases.

The contrast in average expenditure per person in families of very low and very high income is striking. In 1941, among men and boys, clothing expenditures per person at the $3,000-$5,000 family income level were more than five times those at the lowest income level (under $500). Among women and girls, the ratio was over seven to one.[2] (See Table 64.)

Differences in patterns of spending for cloth-

ing and personal care among urban families at different income levels in the postwar years are illustrated by the average expenditures per family in 1948 in three cities — Denver, Detroit and Houston.[3]

These averages reflect not only differences resulting from income, but also differences in age, size and composition of families, and differences in occupation and climate among the cities. Nevertheless, the average family expenditure for clothing and personal care is consistently larger at the higher levels of income. (See Table 65.) Clearly, income plays a major role in deciding what part of the budget will go for clothing the family.

Variations in average expenditures of families at different income levels arise in part from differences in the number of families buying various items, in part from the varying quantities bought, and in part from variations in the unit prices paid for their purchases. Changes in these three expenditure components, however, do not occur in the same way for all clothing items when incomes change. Purchases of families in Minneapolis-St. Paul, Minnesota, in 1948-1949 indicate that about the same proportion of women in each income group bought certain items, such as women's "heavy coats with no fur," but the average unit price paid per garment increased markedly as income increased. For other items, such as hosiery, there was little difference in the unit price or in the proportion of women buying, but the number of pairs bought per woman increased by about 30 per cent from the lower income level ($2,000-$2,999) to the higher ($4,000-$5,999). Less essential items and those bought largely for display — for example, accessories and jewelry — show the most marked increase in expenditures per woman with increased family incomes.[4]

Personal care expenditures, while, of course, increasing in amount as incomes increase, tend to remain remarkably stable with respect to total family spending. This has been observed both in comparisons from time to time and among families and communities at a given time. In-

1. See Louise J. Mack, "Postwar Changes in the Quality of Apparel," Monthly Labor Review, July 1948.

2. These data are based on 1941 expenditures per person 16 years of age and over. This is the latest date for which a detailed family expenditure survey covering both urban and rural United States has been made. Subsequent surveys relate to urban areas only or to selected rural areas and do not give valid estimates for the nation as a whole.

3. For a complete report on the findings in these and seven other cities, see Family Income, Expenditures, and Savings in 10 Cities, Bulletin No. 1065, U.S. Bureau of Labor Statistics, January 1952.

4. Studies of Family Clothing Supplies, Preliminary Report No. 2, Family Clothing Purchases by Income, Minneapolis-St. Paul, 1948–1949, U.S. Department of Agriculture.

TABLE 65. EXPENDITURES FOR CLOTHING AND PERSONAL CARE AT
SELECTED INCOME LEVELS IN THREE CITIES, 1948

	Money Income per Family					
	$1,000 to $2,000		$3,000 to $4,000		$5,000 to $6,000	
City	Expenditure per Family	Per Cent of Total Expenditure	Expenditure per Family	Per Cent of Total Expenditure	Expenditure per Family	Per Cent of Total Expenditure
	Clothing [a]					
Denver, Colo.	$139	7.1	$368	11.1	$573	12.2
Detroit, Mich.	173	8.2	408	11.8	713	13.3
Houston, Texas	291	13.0	490	14.0	882	15.5
	Personal Care					
Denver, Colo.	$ 47	2.4	$ 75	2.3	$107	2.3
Detroit, Mich.	44	2.1	73	2.1	104	1.9
Houston, Texas	53	2.4	98	2.8	159	2.8

Source: Family Income, Expenditures and Savings in 10 Cities, Bulletin No. 1065, U.S. Bureau of Labor Statistics, January 1952.
a. Includes cleaning and repair.

dexes of the sensitivity of changes in personal consumption expenditures to change over time in total disposable personal income show that personal care goods and services have only average sensitivity to such change.[5]

Family Size

Generally, both the amount and the proportion of total expenditures allocated to clothing the family increase as family size increases. Although recent studies are based on small samples and therefore do not permit precise measurements, the characteristic differences are discernible. In 1948, families of five persons in Denver, Detroit and Houston used 13 to 15 per cent of their total expenditures for clothing, while families of two persons used 10 to 13 per cent. In each city the larger families spent more for clothing than the smaller families. (See Table 66.)

Although the total clothing expenditure generally increases with family size, the expenditure per person decreases quite sharply. This, of course, is partly because additional family members are usually children, and average clothing expenditures for children are less than those for adults.

5. See Appendix 4–6.

TABLE 66. EXPENDITURES FOR CLOTHING IN THREE CITIES BY FAMILIES OF VARYING SIZE WITH MONEY INCOME OF $3,000–$4,000, 1948

Family Size	Average Expenditure per Family	Per Cent of Total Expenditure
	Denver, Colo.	
All families	$368	11.1
2-person families	297	10.4
3-person families	387	10.4
4-person families	394	10.7
5-person families	479	15.2
	Detroit, Mich.	
All families	$408	11.8
2-person families	342	10.4
3-person families	399	11.6
4-person families	561	14.3
5-person families	478	13.0
	Houston, Texas	
All families	$490	14.0
2-person families	458	13.5
3-person families	471	13.7
4-person families	565	14.8
5-person families	470	14.8

Source: "Consumer Spending, Denver, Detroit and Houston, 1948," *Monthly Labor Review,* December 1949.

The averages given in Table 66 for Houston, which are consistently higher than those for the other two cities, illustrate differences in clothing spending patterns due to differences in nationality and cultural backgrounds. Studies in the mid-1930s showed that families of Mexican origin in Houston, whose total expenditure for current consumption averaged $954, spent 13.3 per cent for clothing, while white families, other than Spanish-American, averaging $1,572 for total expenditures, spent only 10.6 per cent for clothing. This was in part due to the larger size of the Spanish-American families, which averaged 4.9 persons per family while the other white families averaged 3.4 persons.[6] However, in the data for 1948 in Table 66, where both income and family size are held constant, the high percentage of families of Mexican origin in Houston probably accounts for the consistently higher clothing expenditures there.

Age and Occupation

Age and occupation of family members also contribute to differences in expenditures for clothing among American families, although probably less than in other countries and at earlier times in our own history. Detailed analyses of the clothing expenditure reports of wage-earner and clerical-worker families in 42 cities in the mid-1930s, which eliminated the effect of differences in income and family size, showed that women under 30 years of age spent about twice as much for clothing as women who were over 50. Among the younger women, those employed outside the home spent about one and one half times as much for clothing as those who did not work outside the home. Clerical workers and wage earners in this age group spent roughly equal amounts. Among the older women also, those employed outside the home spent about 50 per cent more than those at home, but in this age group the clerical workers spent substantially more than the wage workers.[7]

More recent data which clearly measure the effect of age and occupation are not available, but changes in expenditures for clothing during the war, and comparisons of cities with different types of occupations prevailing, indicate that age and occupation are still important determinants of clothing expenditures. For example, the smaller

average expenditure shown in Table 66 for two-person families in Denver as compared with those in Houston is in part due to the higher average age of the Denver families.

Residence

The effect of place of residence on clothing expenditures is best illustrated by comparing the spending patterns of city and farm families. Before factory production of clothing standardized style, and before the time of cheap automobile transportation and easy mail-order buying, there were marked differences in what farm and city families wore and in the amount they spent for their clothing. Many of these differences have disappeared, especially in the postwar years when the gap between urban and rural incomes has narrowed. Today city and farm families buy much the same kind of clothing, yet the traditionally lower average clothing expenditure of farm families persists. The reason for this seems to be that farm families buy smaller quantities of the more expensive types of dress clothing.

In 1948–1949, farm husbands in two Minnesota counties spent less than two thirds as much as city husbands in Minneapolis-St. Paul and farm wives less than one half as much as city wives in the same areas for ready-to-wear clothing.[8] Farm families paid lower average prices for dress or street clothing than city families and, as is to be expected because of differences in occupation, farm husbands bought fewer of these garments. On the other hand, farm families bought more of the less expensive types of work clothing and footwear.

In the past, lower clothing expenditures by farm families reflected the large amounts of home sewing done in farm households. Home sewing seems to have little influence on current spending patterns. Very little clothing was made at home for the farm husbands and boys included in the Minnesota study, and home sewing for women was important only for housedresses and aprons. About three fourths of the aprons and about half of the housedresses added to the wardrobes of the farm wives during the year were homemade. The net effect of this home sewing on the average clothing expenditures of the farm families was not important.

6. *Money Disbursements in Southern Region, 1934–36,* Bulletin No. 640, U.S. Bureau of Labor Statistics, Table 3, p. 198.

7. *Money Disbursements of Wage Earners and Clerical Workers, 1934–36,* Bulletin No. 638, U.S. Bureau of Labor Statistics, Appendix C, Table B–3, p. 364.

8. Margaret L. Brew, *Family Clothing Practices, Minnesota,* 29th Annual Agricultural Outlook Conference, Washington, D.C., October 31, 1951.

TRENDS IN PRODUCTION AND TASTE

The vast majority of Americans dress in up-to-date styles and wear clothes that are whole and clean. As a people we think personal appearance is important, and an increase in income for a large part of the population has made the whole nation more fashion conscious.

The American clothing standard has long aroused favorable comment by visitors from abroad, although fashion critics contend that the rapid pace of American life is not conducive to fashion as a creative art. In the mid-1800s, many of the studies of living standards of working-men's families in the United States paid particular attention to the quality and diversity of clothing considered necessary here, as compared with that required by workers in other countries. Events of the twentieth century have accentuated this emphasis on good grooming, regardless of occupation or economic status, and American industry has produced a wide variety of apparel and cosmetics to meet this demand.

The American clothing standard is the result of three interacting long-term trends. One of these, the shift from home and custom to factory fabrication, is a process that has been substantially completed. Another development, the change in taste toward lighter, functional and more uniform styles, appears to be at its height. The third is a shift in the utilization of materials, and the emergence of new types of materials with changes in the fibers utilized and in methods of processing. Future possibilities in this direction are very great.

FACTORY PRODUCTION [9]

Factory-made clothing had very largely replaced home sewing by 1940. Though it is not possible to measure this shift, we know that output of manufactured textile products and clothing almost trebled during the first four decades of the century, and that per capita production increased by about two thirds. By the mid-1920s, the men's clothing industry, which got its start in the Civil War, was competing successfully with even the best custom tailors.

More important than the shift of men's clothing production into the factory was the move-

9. This section is based in part on Solomon Fabricant, *The Output of Manufacturing Industries, 1899–1937*, National Bureau of Economic Research, New York, 1940, pp. 60, 66, 92, 184–190.

TABLE 67. INDEXES OF THE PHYSICAL VOLUME OF PRODUCTION OF TEXTILES AND APPAREL, 1899–1947

(*1939 = 100*)

Year	Index	Year	Index
1899	32	1927	79
1904	40	1929	84
1909	51	1931	73
1914	60	1933	72
1919	57	1935	83
1921	54	1937	89
1923	69	1939	100
1925	72	1947	125

Source: U.S. Bureau of the Census; based on data contained in the Censuses of Manufactures over this period.

ment away from home and custom dressmaking to factory production. Particularly significant is the increasing importance of the knit goods industry, including hosiery. The rise in knit goods and the relative decline in woven products undoubtedly reflects a transfer to factory production.

Mass production of apparel has brought changes in both the amount and kind of fibers consumed and tremendous advances in the development of new fibers and new manufacturing techniques. Between 1919 and 1947, the physical volume of production of textiles and apparel increased about 120 per cent. (See Table 67.)

This increase in production of textiles reflected varying changes in the consumption of textile fibers. Cotton consumption in 1920 amounted to 2.8 billion pounds; in 1947 and in 1950 it was 4.7 billion pounds, and in 1952, 4.5 billion pounds. Wool consumption also increased, from 314 million pounds in 1920 to 708 and 647 million pounds in 1947 and 1950 respectively, but declined to 474 million pounds in 1952. Use of man-made fibers increased from 9 million pounds in 1920 to 1.0 billion pounds in 1947 and 1.5 billion pounds in 1950 and 1952. Silk consumption rose steadily through the 1920s and maintained its place through the 1930s in the underwear and hosiery markets. But silk was a casualty of World War II. Unavailable during the war, it now has only a small place in fiber consumption. (See Table 68.)

Between 1919 and 1937, production of woolen goods increased 16 per cent, cotton goods 27 per cent and leather shoes 26 per cent, while production of linen and worsted goods declined. Rapid increases in the production of silk, rayon

TABLE 68. U.S. MILL CONSUMPTION OF CERTAIN FIBERS, 1920–1952

(*Millions of Pounds*)

| Year | Total | Cotton | Wool | Man-Made | | Silk |
				Rayon + Acetate	Other	
1920	3,180.2	2,828.1	314.2	8.7		29.2
1921	3,000.8	2,595.3	343.4	19.8		42.3
1922	3,389.1	2,909.8	406.5	24.7		48.1
1923	3,622.5	3,120.5	422.4	32.5		47.1
1924	3,068.8	2,636.6	342.2	42.2		47.8
1925	3,548.8	3,074.7	349.9	58.2		66.0
1926	3,683.7	3,214.8	342.7	60.6		65.6
1927	4,113.4	3,587.7	354.1	100.0		71.6
1928	3,692.3	3,184.2	333.2	100.5		74.4
1929	4,005.0	3,422.7	368.1	133.4		80.8
1930	3,068.5	2,610.9	263.2	118.8		75.6
1931	3,203.3	2,656.6	311.0	158.9		76.8
1932	2,919.2	2,463.3	230.1	155.3		70.5
1933	3,646.3	3,052.5	317.1	217.2		59.5
1934	3,140.2	2,655.4	229.7	196.9		58.2
1935	3,493.6	2,754.7	417.5	259.1		62.3
1936	4,256.5	3,470.2	406.1	322.4		57.8
1937	4,396.2	3,657.1	380.8	304.7		53.6
1938	3,584.3	2,918.7	284.5	329.4		51.7
1939	4,532.3	3,629.7	396.5	458.8		47.3
1940	4,884.3	3,953.6	407.9	482.0	5.0	35.8
1941	6,462.5	5,187.3	648.0	591.8	12.0	23.4
1942	6,902.7	5,636.7	616.2	620.8	24.0	5.0
1943	6,600.7	5,269.0	636.2	656.1	38.0	1.4
1944	6,168.6	4,792.4	622.8	704.8	48.0	0.6
1945	5,977.8	4,511.3	645.1	769.9	51.0	0.5
1946	6,478.8	4,803.3	737.5	875.5	56.0	6.5
1947	6,416.3	4,668.1	708.3	987.9	50.0	2.0
1948	6,394.7	4,461.2	704.5	1,149.6	72.0	7.4
1949	5,439.0	3,838.2	511.0	993.4	92.0	4.4
1950	6,827.9	4,680.1	647.0	1,351.4	141.0	8.4
1951	6,889.7	4,908.0	495.0	1,276.1	205.0	5.6
1952	6,432.1	4,479.0	473.7	1,212.5	260.0	6.9

Source: Textile Organon, March 1953.

and knit goods followed the shift of women's apparel production from the home to the factory.[10] (See Appendix 6–2.)

Although apparel production in general has been increasing during the postwar years, several categories have decreased as a result of changes in preferences. For example, a decrease in the production of men's neckwear and a decrease or less than average increase in felt hats reflect the

shift to casual and sport attire. The increased use of paper cleansing tissue is reflected in a decreased production of handkerchiefs, and the inroads which the synthetics have made in the leather goods field are indicated by a decline in the production of leather handbags and purses. (See Table 69.)

TASTE AND STYLE

The trends in style and clothing preferences during the first half of this century are the result of fundamental changes in our way of life.

---

10. Not all textiles are used for clothing, and the proportions used for this purpose may have changed over the period.

TABLE 69. INDEXES OF PRODUCTION OF SELECTED
TEXTILE AND LEATHER PRODUCTS, 1947

(*1939 = 100*)

Industry Group	Index
Textiles and apparel	125
Textile mill products	128
Woolen and worsted	140
Cotton broad-woven fabrics	125
Rayon and related broad-woven fabrics	145
Full-fashioned hosiery	91
Seamless hosiery	102
Knit outerwear	138
Knit underwear	128
Knit fabrics	187
Fur-felt hats	84
Wool-felt hats	105
Apparel	121
Men's and boys':	
Suits, coats and separate trousers	120
Dress shirts and nightwear	114
Underwear	100
Neckwear	97
Cloth hats and caps	139
Work shirts	91
Miscellaneous clothing not elsewhere classified	106
Women's and misses':	
Dresses	107
Suits, coats and skirts	164
Women's and children's underwear	125
Fur goods	97
Fabric and combination work gloves	128
Suspenders and garters	51
Robes and dressing gowns	118
Leather and sheep-lined clothing	70
Belts	165
Handkerchiefs	79
Leather and leather products	115
Leather tanning and finishing	125
Footwear cut stock	103
Footwear, except rubber	111
Leather dress gloves	101
Leather work gloves	115
Luggage	143
Handbags and purses	88
Watches and clocks	208
Watch cases	214

Source: U.S. Bureau of the Census–Federal Reserve Board indexes calculated from data obtained from the Census of Manufactures. For indexes derived from earlier Census of Manufactures data see Appendix 6–2.

There have been three main stylistic tendencies: first, a steady trend toward uniformity, with the clothing worn by people of moderate income coming to approximate the appearance and materials of the clothing worn by people of high income; second, a decline in the number of frills, reflecting a movement in the direction of greater simplicity; third, and most recent, an "accent on youth." [11]

These trends reflect the rapid technological advances in all phases of the economy and the economics of mass production. The automobile, airplane, central heating, movies, radio and television, as well as factory production of clothing and man-made fibers, have all affected our manner of dress. It has been said that while the automobile wiped out local variations in clothing standards and gave people everywhere a chance to dress up and go visiting, television put people back in the home and encouraged the already growing tendency to casual dress.

Trend to Simplicity

The two world wars, directly and indirectly, have left their imprint on our tastes and preferences in clothing. In both, the influx of women into all types of occupations produced radical changes in their clothing needs, with emphasis on simplicity and ease of maintenance and care. The change in women's clothing over the past century has been a revolutionary one.

In the early 1850s "a typical outfit for women consisted of long drawers trimmed with lace, a flannel petticoat, another under-petticoat, then a wadded petticoat, wadded from the waist to the knee with frequent additions of whalebone and horsehair cloth to secure extra stiffness and extension. This garment was followed by still another white starched petticoat, and then two muslin petticoats and finally the outer dress." By 1921 the winter costume of most women had been reduced to merely a union suit, bone corset, camisole, bloomers, petticoat, heavy lined wool dress, lisle or heavy silk stockings, and high shoes. By 1931 further cuts had reduced the total to an all-in-one girdle-and-chemise combination, a slip, light wool dress, chiffon stockings, and pumps. The total yardage of everyday wear must in this period have dwindled from roughly fifty to five.[12]

The trend to simplicity and informality, well under way in the 1930s, has reached a peak in the postwar years. Skirts and sweaters, slacks

---

11. David L. Cohn, *The Good Old Days,* Simon & Schuster, New York, 1940, p. 308.

12. Walton Hamilton and Associates, *Price and Price Policies,* McGraw-Hill, New York, 1938, p. 306.

and simple suits have been the order of the day for women in recent years. Men, too, have taken to simplicity in dress. Sport shirts and slacks have become accepted in almost all leisure-time activities and, in summer, even in offices and in all except the most formal of social gatherings.[13] Children's clothing has become the essence of simplicity. "Jeans" and sweater or shirt are currently almost the standard everyday garb of boys in all levels of society.

The most important postwar development in the apparel field, however, is perhaps the special attention being given to teen-agers. In the fashion world and the retail markets this group, long overlooked, has become important.

TECHNOLOGICAL DEVELOPMENTS

For centuries man has relied on animal or vegetable raw materials for fibers from which to make his clothing textiles, while chemists have dreamed of creating such fibers from the basic elements. Medieval armor, metallic cloth for ceremonial occasions, and Cinderella's glass slipper were about all that came of these dreams before the end of the nineteenth century.

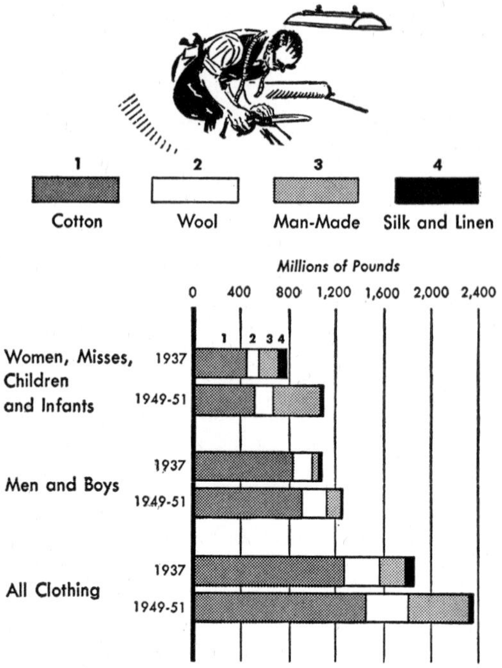

NEW MATERIALS AND METHODS

Rayon

In France, in 1884, synthetic or man-made textiles became a reality with the first commercial production of rayon. In the United States continous commercial production of rayon began in 1911, and output has increased substantially in most years since that time.

In common usage the term "rayon" has been applied to all types of synthetic fibers for which cellulose is the basic raw material. In the United States, wood pulp and cotton linters have been used almost exclusively in the commercial production of rayon.[14]

Consumption of man-made fibers in the United States has exceeded silk consumption since 1927

FIGURE 31. USE OF DIFFERENT TEXTILE FIBERS FOR CLOTHING, 1937 AND 1949–1951 AVERAGE

Source: Table 71.

and wool consumption since 1941.[15] (See Table 68.)

In recent years about 40 per cent of all textile fiber has been used for apparel. Civilian per capita consumption of man-made textile fibers, which averaged less than 2 per cent of the total in the years 1922–1925, increased steadily through the 1930s and the war years, until in 1952 it accounted for more than one fourth of the total consumption and was more than twice as much as wool consumption. (See Table 70 and Figure 31.) Much of this increase in the use of synthetic fiber has resulted from end uses other than apparel, but there has also been a spectacular increase in the use for apparel, especially for women's and misses' wear.

In 1937, 183 million pounds, or 23.2 per cent, of the fiber used in women's, misses' and children's apparel was man-made; in the period 1949–1951 the amount had risen to 385 million pounds and the proportion to 35.3 per cent. In women's and misses' apparel, 44 per cent of the fiber used in 1949 to 1951 was man-made; cotton accounted

13. See Fessenden S. Blanchard, "Revolution in Clothes," *Harper's Magazine,* March 1953, pp. 59–64.

14. For a detailed description of the various processes used in the manufacture of man-made fibers, and a bibliography on the development of man-made fibers prior to 1944, see Robert B. Evans, *Survey of Development and Use of Rayon and Other Synthetic Fibers,* Bureau of Agricultural and Industrial Chemistry, U.S. Department of Agriculture, October 1944.

15. This consumption covers all types of end uses: household textiles, rugs and upholstery, as well as apparel, and all types of users, including the military.

TABLE 70. CIVILIAN PER CAPITA CONSUMPTION OF CERTAIN TEXTILE FIBERS, 1922–1952
(Pounds)

Year or Annual Average	Total	Man-Made	Wool	Cotton
1922–1925	25.3	0.4	3.4	21.5
1926–1930	25.8	0.9	2.8	22.1
1931–1935	22.7	1.7	2.4	18.6
1936–1940	28.9	3.0	2.8	23.1
1941	39.6	4.4	3.9	31.3
1942	29.3	4.5	2.3	22.5
1943	26.8	4.5	2.5	19.8
1944	23.9	4.7	3.5	15.7
1945	27.9	5.0	3.1	19.8
1946	40.5	6.5	5.4	28.6
1947	35.8	6.6	4.8	24.4
1948	37.2	8.0	4.9	24.3
1949	30.9	6.7	3.5	20.7
1950	40.1	9.4	4.4	26.3
1951	35.4	8.6	2.6	24.2
1952	33.8	8.5	3.2	22.1

Source: *Textile Organon,* March 1953.

for 38 per cent, wool for 18 per cent, and silk and linen for less than one per cent.

Although the average amount of synthetic fiber used in men's and boys' apparel in 1949 to 1951 was about one third that used in women's and misses' clothing, the proportion used more than tripled in the twelve-year period. In 1937, 3.2 per cent of the total fiber used for men's and boys' apparel was man-made; in 1949 these fibers accounted for 10.6 per cent of the total. This increase resulted from about equal decreases in the proportions accounted for by cotton and wool. Cotton is still the most important textile for men's and boys' and for children's and infants' apparel, representing about three fourths of the total in each class. (See Table 71 and Figure 31.)

Although rayon and acetate made up more than 90 per cent of the total production of man-made fibers in 1950, the phenomenal development of the other synthetics in the postwar years may be the clue to a revolution in clothing and related industries, in apparel fashions and apparel care, and in consumer spending patterns.

Nylon

Nylon was the first of the miracle fibers. It has been said that "the real importance of nylon was simply that for the first time man had gone back to the elements and created a molecule that was meant to be a fiber. For the first time man had quit trying to imitate a worm, a plant or a tree and had struck out with his own intelligence to create a fiber that was meant to make a stocking instead of a cocoon. For the first time man was free from the capriciousness of animal and vegetable raw materials for his textiles." [16]

Inspired by this freedom and by the commercial success of nylon, chemists have since made several thousand types of fibers. About fifty of these fibers have been studied extensively for possible commercial production.

The successful research development of nylon was announced in late 1938, but it was not until early 1940 that production reached commercial proportions. About 4 million pounds were produced the first year, and capacity increased rapidly to about 20 million pounds in 1942. World War II interrupted the production of nylon for civilian use.

Some of the properties of nylon fiber which make it unusually good for textiles are: a dry tensile strength considerably higher than that of rayon and, unlike rayon, little loss of tensile strength when wet; elasticity, surpassing natural

16. J. B. Quig, "What's Ahead for the Chemical Fibers?," *Rayon and Synthetic Textiles,* October 1950, p. 67.

TABLE 71. USE OF DIFFERENT TEXTILE FIBERS FOR CLOTHING, 1937 AND 1949–1951 AVERAGE

| | 1937 | | | 1949–1951 Average | | | | |
| | | | Women, Misses, Children and Infants | | | | Women, Misses, Children and Infants | |
Fiber	Total	Men and Boys	Women, Misses, Children and Infants	Total	Men and Boys	Total	Women and Misses	Children and Infants
				Quantity (Millions of Pounds)				
All fibers	1,845	1,057	788	2,353	1,262	1,091	819	272
Cotton	1,256	808	448	1,448	925	523	309	214
Wool	319	210	109	379	201	178	145	33
Silk	51	4	47	4	1	3	3	—
Linen	2	1	1	3	1	2	2	—
Man-made	217	34	183	519	134	385	360	25
				Percentage Distribution				
All fibers	100.0	100.0	100.0	100.0	100.0	100.0	100.0	100.0
Cotton	68.1	76.4	56.9	61.5	73.3	47.9	37.7	78.7
Wool	17.3	19.9	13.8	16.1	15.9	16.3	17.7	12.1
Silk	2.8	0.4	6.0	0.2	0.1	0.3	0.4	—
Linen	0.1	0.1	0.1	0.1	0.1	0.2	0.2	—
Man-made	11.8	3.2	23.2	22.1	10.6	35.3	44.0	9.2

Source: Textile Organon, August 1953 Supplement (based on study by E. I. du Pont de Nemours & Co., Inc.).

fibers and rayon; ability to take a permanent set or shape when heated; a melting point higher than other thermo-plastic textile fibers; resistance to alkalies, and to mildew and soil micro-organisms; and, for hosiery, sheerness and speed of drying.

Twentieth-century fashions in women's hosiery, whether they arose from choice or from wartime necessity, tell a story of radical shifts in use of fibers. From the cotton and wool era of World War I and earlier, when silk was still in the luxury class, we moved to the silk era of the late 1920s and the 1930s. The year 1941 proved to be a forewarning of things to come, with nylon making big inroads on silk, and rayon

TABLE 72. SHIPMENTS OF WOMEN'S HOSIERY BY FIBER CONTENT, SELECTED YEARS, 1937–1952

| | Amount Shipped | | | | Percentage Distribution | | | |
Year	Total	Nylon [a]	Rayon	Silk	Cotton, Wool and Other	Total	Nylon [a]	Rayon	Silk	Cotton, Wool and Other
	(Million Dozen Pairs)									
1937	52.7	—	3.3	45.9	3.5	100.0	—	6.2	87.2	6.6
1939	56.9	—	3.6	49.9	3.4	100.0	—	6.3	87.7	6.0
1941	56.7	8.4	5.5	36.6	6.2	100.0	14.8	9.7	64.6	10.9
1943	51.4	.1	42.6	.1	8.5	100.0	.3	82.9	.3	16.5
1949	53.1	48.3	1.6	.3	2.8	100.0	91.1	3.0	.6	5.2
1950	60.2	56.2	1.4	.3	2.3	100.0	93.4	2.3	.5	3.8
1951	57.2	54.0	1.1	.2	1.9	100.0	94.4	2.0	.3	3.3
1952	60.1	57.1	1.0	.1	1.9	100.0	95.0	1.6	.3	3.2

Source: National Association of Hosiery Manufacturers, 468 Fourth Ave., New York 16, N.Y.
a. Introduced commercially May 1940.

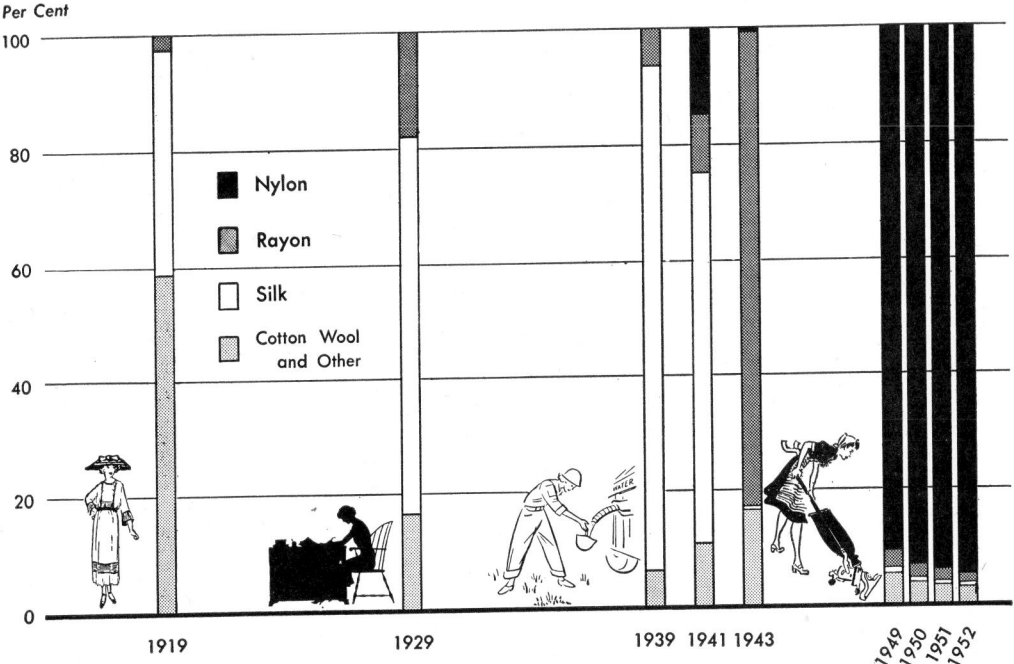

FIGURE 32. PERCENTAGE DISTRIBUTION OF FIBER CONTENT OF WOMEN'S HOSIERY, SELECTED YEARS, 1919–1952

Sources: 1919 and 1929 estimates from *Survey of Development and Use of Rayon and Other Synthetic Fibers,* by Robert B. Evans, Bureau of Agricultural and Industrial Chemistry, U.S. Department of Agriculture, October 1944; 1939–1952, Table 72.

approaching its late 1920s importance. By 1943 silk and nylon had practically vanished from the hosiery scene. Silk hosiery has not reappeared since the war in any appreciable volume, but nylon, since wartime restrictions were lifted, has almost completely won the field, going into 95 per cent of all women's hosiery in 1952. (See Table 72 and Figure 32.)

In the postwar years the use of nylon spread rapidly to other items of women's apparel, especially underwear, nightwear and blouses; to men's and children's hosiery; men's shirts and accessories; and, to a considerably less extent, men's and children's underwear and nightwear.

Other Man-Made Fibers

Some of the properties which have made nylon excellent for women's hosiery have made it unsuitable for other uses. Fortunately, the possibilities of developing chemical fibers whose properties can be tailor-made for specific applications appear to be limitless, and are rapidly being explored. The fibers which have so far appeared commercially, or for which immediate commercial production has been planned, are of five general types.

The *acrylic fibers,* the best-known of which are Orlon, Dynel, Acrilan and a fiber called in research X–51, have properties which will give them an advantage over nylon for some apparel, particularly where unusual resistance to sunlight and chemicals is important and warmth and wrinkle-resistance are desirable. Some of these fibers are resistant to fire and can be disinfected, and are therefore especially adaptable for special-purpose clothing. These acrylic fibers also show promise as the basis for blends with nylon, rayon and the natural fibers, to increase their durability or enhance their quality.

The *polyester fiber,* Dacron, has resilience and dimensional stability under both wet and dry conditions. Its light weight and resistance to wrinkles make it especially adaptable as a one hundred per cent fiber for sheer fabrics, men's lightweight suits, lightweight outerwear, and as a blend with wool for heavy apparel.

The *protein fibers,* represented in the prewar

years by Aralac, derived from casein, are at present being developed primarily for blending with other fibers, especially wool and nylon. Vicara, the leading product, is advertised as "the fiber that improves the blend." It is said to improve the quality and value of knit goods, hosiery, suits, dresses and sport clothes, as well as non-apparel textiles.

Fibers from vinyl resins and vinylidene chloride, such as Vinyon, Velon and Saran, have found their principal uses in upholstery fabrics, carpets and drapes, but tests are being made of civilian and military clothing made of Saran and wool blends.

Fibers from glass, of which Fiberglas is the best known, have also been used primarily for nonapparel textiles, but their resistance to fire makes them a possibility for special-purpose industrial clothing.

The ease of laundering most garments made of the synthetics has been a strong selling point, and, as their use increases, this advantage is likely to be reflected in reduced expenditures for cleaning services. It remains to be seen whether the increased durability of garments made from these new fabrics will reduce clothing expenditures also or whether it will lead to an increase in the variety of garments in the family wardrobe.

"Test Tube" Leather and Other Plastics

Recent increases in the use of synthetic leather in footwear and luggage have been almost as spectacular as the invasion of man-made fabrics in the apparel field. The first basic patents to make "artificial leather" date back to 1855, and "leatherette" has enjoyed a long-time popularity for such things as baby buggies, book bindings and inexpensive handbags. But extensive use of synthetic leather in footwear has resulted from the rapid technological advances following World War II. At first, these synthetics were used only in soles, linings or trimmings and, to a limited extent, for women's play or novelty shoes. Their inflexibility and lack of porosity raised serious objections to their use for the whole shoe. By late 1951, however, these obstacles were sufficiently overcome so that an all-synthetic-leather shoe for men appeared on the market.

Three main types of materials are included in the general term "synthetic leather," and they have found a wide variety of uses in addition to footwear. The one which is best known in shoes is a styrene plastic, Neolite, introduced by the Goodyear Tire and Rubber Company in 1945. Used extensively for soles, it has now been developed for uppers. Another synthetic leather is vinyl or pyroxylin plastic-coated fabric, and the third is plastic film from vinyl.

The plastic-coated fabrics are used widely in housefurnishings, particularly upholstering, and have been especially adaptable for use in women's handbags, billfolds, luggage and shoes. Colorful rainwear of vinyl film bears little resemblance to the fishoil-waterproofed or vulcanized-rubber raincoats of the past. The plastic films are also used in upholstery, draperies and even for wallpaper.

Not only have the plastics become an important basic material in fields previously dominated by natural textiles and leather, they have almost completely monopolized certain other areas. It is estimated that about 70 per cent of all small buttons are made from molded urea. The phenolics, acrylics or protein plastics are used extensively in buckles, buttons, beads and costume jewelry. Natural bristles for brushes of all types — toothbrushes, hairbrushes, etc. — have almost entirely disappeared and have been replaced by nylon monofilament bristles in plastic backs and handles.

The Plastic Coatings and Film Association has estimated that the industry's sales were $125 million in 1950, as compared with $90 million in 1949 and $33 million in 1941. Even with generous allowance for price increases, this indicates a substantial increase in volume. Most of this increase resulted from uses other than footwear; but with prices of leather remaining high, the synthetics, which are cheaper both as raw material and in processing, appear to have a good chance to become established in the footwear industry.

DEVELOPMENTS IN PERSONAL CARE

The care and dressing of hair has long been the mainstay of the beauty parlor and barber shop industry, and generally the biggest item of expense in a family's personal care budget. The invention of the permanent wave marked the beginning of the beauty parlor as big business and gave rise to many allied industries, producing a variety of products ranging all the way from special hair pins to beauty parlor furniture.

In the period between World Wars I and II, continual improvements were made in the permanent waving technique. Special lotions and shampoos were developed to combat the drying effect of the waving. Machineless and cold waves were introduced. But the process was still largely one to be performed by the professional in the beauty parlor.

In the 1940s, and particularly in the postwar years, the home permanent became a success. Using extravagant advertising by printed word, radio and television, several companies introduced home waving kits. By 1950 the industry had reached the $50 million-a-year mark, and improved types of plastic curlers, methods of winding, special lotions and equipment for children's hair were being introduced.

Encouraged by the success of the home permanent, the cosmetic companies turned to quick and easy home dyeing through "color rinses." Sales of the first of these, introduced in 1950, are said to have numbered over 10 million units during its first year.

The improved plastics have been used effectively not only for hair curlers and brushes but also for other toilet articles. Unbreakable, lightweight, inexpensive and colorful plastic bottles have been used extensively for toilet water, hand lotions and liquid deodorants. One flexible type of bottle works as an atomizer when squeezed. Plastic containers and lids have almost completely replaced glass and metal for some products.

Consumption in Early 1950s

In the early 1950s the physical volume of consumption of clothing and accessories was at a high level, even though it was less than in the early postwar years, 1946 and 1947. Consumption of these items cannot be measured directly, but there are several clues to its general level and to changes from year to year. Mill consumption of fibers and factory output of textiles are among such clues.

Consumption of Fibers

In both 1950 and 1951, United States mills consumed more than 6.8 billion pounds of cotton, wool, silk and man-made fibers, more than in any year since 1942 and 1.4 billion pounds over the 1949 figure. Consumption dropped to 6.4 billion pounds in 1952, but was still 1 billion pounds over the 1949 figure. (See Table 68.) This consumption reflected the increased use of fibers for military purposes which followed the outbreak of the war in Korea, but also marked an increase in textile fibers for civilian use. Civilian per capita consumption of wool, cotton and man-made textile fibers in 1950 was 40.1 pounds, the highest level since the peak year of 1946. Although the civilian per capita consumption had dropped to 33.8 pounds by 1952, this was still higher than the 1949 level. Another indication of the large consumption of clothing in 1950 was the 82 per cent rise over 1935–1939 in the physical volume of textiles and products manufactured.

These figures represent the consumption of textiles for all purposes — household textiles, upholstery for automobiles, etc. — and therefore can give only an approximation of what was happening to clothing consumption. It has been estimated, however, that about 40 per cent of all cotton (still the most important fiber for apparel) consumed in the postwar years has been used for clothing. Civilian consumption of cotton in 1950 amounted to 26.3 pounds per capita, almost 6 pounds more than in the previous year and about 5 pounds less than in the peak year, 1941. Per capita consumption of cotton in 1952 was 22.1 pounds, still 1.2 pounds above the 1949 level.

Indexes of the production of various types of apparel in 1947 as compared with 1939 (see Table 69) indicate that for all important groups postwar production exceeded that of prewar years. Retail sales in all types of apparel stores in 1950, when adjusted to eliminate the effects of price changes, furnish more evidence that clothing consumption in that year was higher than in 1949, only slightly less than in 1948, and substantially higher than before World War II.

Family Expenditures for Clothing

Family expenditures for clothing in 1950 reflected this high level of purchases and the high level of prices. Apparel prices in 1950, as measured by the consumers' price index of the United States Bureau of Labor Statistics, were 88 per cent above their 1935–1939 average. This represented a slight decline from the 1949 level but was a little higher than the average for the postwar years 1946–1950.

In a survey of more than 10,000 families in 91 cities, the Bureau of Labor Statistics found that average family expenditures for clothing and clothing upkeep in 1950 ranged from $303 in Salina, Kansas, to $608 and $609 in New York City and Chicago respectively. The proportion of total spending used for clothing ranged from about 9 to 14 per cent.[17]

Influence of City Size

The variations in these expenditures, while small, were characteristic of some of the trends in clothing expenditures in past years, and may be a clue to future spending patterns. Clothing expenditures in the large urban areas were generally higher than those in small cities and claimed a larger part of the total family budget. Among the largest metropolitan centers (places with over a million population), average family clothing expenditures exceeded $430 in all cities and accounted for more than 11 per cent of the total budget. There were several small cities (population under 30,500) at about the same income level where less than 11 per cent of the family spending went for clothing.

Cities in the Mountain and Pacific regions usually had smaller clothing expenditures, both in absolute amounts and in relation to other expenditures, than cities of the same income level and size in the East and South. This lends support to the belief that the growing preference for casual attire, which had its origin in the West, can have an appreciable effect on total clothing expenditures.

Some of the influence of city size was evident in the way clothing expenditures were distributed among various family members. In the large cities about 55 per cent of the family clothing dollar was spent for the women and girls, while the men and boys used a little over 40 per cent, and infants under 2 years and clothing materials and services accounted for the remainder. In the smaller cities about 50 per cent of the clothing dollar was allocated to the women and girls.

Among the broad types of clothing — outerwear, underwear and nightwear, hosiery, footwear, and hats and accessories — there was very little difference from city to city in the way the total expenditures were distributed. Within these groups, city size, climate and occupation deter-

mined what proportion was used for dress clothing and what for sport or work garments, or whether the outerwear dollar was used for coats and heavy outerwear or for dresses. The following percentage distributions of the men's and women's clothing dollars by type of garment are characteristic of the 1950 pattern:

	Men and Boys	Women and Girls
Total	100	100
Outerwear (coats, suits, jackets, dresses, etc.)	47	50
Shirts	11	—
Underwear and nightwear	8	14
Hosiery	5	10
Footwear	17	14
Hats, gloves and accessories	12	12

Personal Care

Personal care expenditures in 1950 accounted for about the same proportion of total spending as in previous years, averaging about 2.3 per cent in all urban areas. In cities of a million or more population these expenditures ranged from $91 to $107 per family and from 2.0 to 2.4 per cent of total spending. In cities of a quarter of a million to a million population the average amount spent for personal care goods and services ranged from $72 to $115 and from 1.9 to 2.9 per cent of total expenditures. In smaller cities the average expenditure ranged from $55 to $113, the wider spread being partly due to the greater variation of income among these cities. The proportion of total spending used for personal care in these smaller cities ranged from 1.7 to 2.9 per cent, but a majority of the cities reported that personal care expenditures were about 2 per cent of total spending.

CLOTHING NEEDS

In contrast to the substantial volume of information available on production of clothing and on clothing prices and expenditures, there has been relatively little analysis of the needs of the population for clothing and personal care items or of the adequacy of incomes to meet defined standards of need.

CLOTHING STANDARDS

Criteria of adequacy for clothing are peculiarly difficult to establish. In planning standards

---

17. See "Survey of Consumer Expenditures in 1950," *Monthly Labor Review*, August 1952; also *Family Income, Expenditures and Savings in 1950*, Bulletin No. 1097A (revised), U.S. Bureau of Labor Statistics.

for food, it is possible to use objective measurements of the diets required for growth and health in children and for health and physical efficiency in adults. In planning standard expenditures for clothing, however, it is generally conceded that psychological and social needs must be taken into account. Protection from heat and cold is not enough; the wearer wants to feel that his clothing conforms with that of his associates.

Lack of an objective measure of these psychological and social needs has been the stumbling block in the development of clothing standards. What should be spent has generally been approached through an analysis of what actually is spent. Until very recent years, the selection of a distribution of expenditures which might serve as a standard has involved considerable subjective judgment.

Developments in Family Budgeting

During the last quarter of the nineteenth century in the United States, there was some discussion of budgeting for family expenditures in relation to wage levels. In 1899, Ellen H. Richards, in *The Cost of Living as Modified by Sanitary Science,* suggested how to divide expenditures among five categories of consumption at four different income levels. Her recommendations were based primarily on her own household accounts and those of other professional families.

Beginning in 1906, social workers in certain northern cities, facing the practical problems of planning adequate allowances for dependent families, prepared much more detailed budget plans for all categories of family expenditure, including clothing. In almost every large city today, there are social agencies which periodically prepare budget manuals with detailed clothing allowances for the use of case workers in calculating over-all allowances for families in need of aid.[18]

Several states have prepared budgets for working women for use in minimum-wage determinations. Each of these lists in detail the minimum amounts of clothing considered to be required by a self-supporting employed woman.[19]

Between World Wars I and II, three different sets of family budgets with detailed clothing standards were published. During the period June 1918 to June 1920, the War Labor Board and the Bureau of Labor Statistics published three family budgets at different levels of comfort. All these budgets included detailed plans for clothing purchases.[20] Changes in clothing standards since that time have been so great, however, that these budgets are entirely outmoded.

Heller Committee and WPA Budgets

Since November 1933, the Heller Committee for Research in Social Economics has been publishing from time to time family budgets at three different standards of living — executive, white-collar worker and wage earner. The plan of these budgets has been described as follows: "These budgets were designed to show the items and quantities necessary to maintain the type of 'health and decency' standard generally accepted in the local community for each income level, and the cost of such a standard each year." [21]

In 1935, the Division of Social Research of the Works Progress Administration prepared two budgets for a workingman's family of four, one at the maintenance and one at the emergency, or minimum, level. The first of these budgets lists the goods and services estimated to be needed

18. Two outstanding studies have attempted to evaluate allowances, by objective criteria, in comparison with customary expenditures of families of wage earners. In 1907 a committee of the New York State Conference of Charities and Correction sponsored a study of the standard of living in New York City. This study was financed by the Russell Sage Foundation and issued as one of its regular publications. Appearing under the title *The Standard of Living Among Workingmen's Families in New York City* (R. C. Chapin, Charities Publication Committee, 1909), the study compares living costs, housing, clothing expenditures, food expenditures and the nutritional content of diets in New York City with social workers' budgets both in that city and in nine cities and towns outside Greater New York. In 1924, Professor Leila Houghteling of Chicago Univer-

sity, in *The Income and Standard of Living of Unskilled Laborers in Chicago,* checked the budget allowances of the Chicago Council of Social Agencies in much the same way. For a more detailed description of budgets prepared during this period, see: *Standards of Living, A Compilation of Budgetary Studies,* Vol. II, Bureau of Applied Economics, Washington, D.C., 1932.

19. For a summary of these budgets see *Working Women's Budgets in Thirteen States,* Bulletin No. 226, Women's Bureau, U.S. Department of Labor, revised 1951.

20. In each case they were based on actual family expenditures with certain adjustments. In the 1920 budget, which listed the goods and services necessary to maintain a worker's family of five in health and decency, the clothing provided was based on the purchases of 850 families, each with three children under 16 years of age, surveyed in a study made by the Bureau in 1917–1919. The actual clothing expenditures were modified in making the budget to take account of the serious curtailment of clothing purchases during the war period to which the survey applied.

21. "Cost of Living Studies Compiled under Heller Committee for Research in Social Economics," University of California, mimeographed.

by a four-person family of an unskilled manual worker living at the maintenance level. The "maintenance level" is described as above the "minimum of subsistence level" or "emergency level" of relief budgets, but below the standard of the skilled worker. It is stated that this budget does not "approach the content of what may be considered a satisfactory American standard of living." The clothing included is described as representative of that purchased by the families of industrial, service or other manual workers of small means. [22]

Budget in First Edition

In the first edition of the present report, Faith M. Williams and Louis Weiner used studies of actual family clothing expenditures as a basis for choosing standards which might legitimately be regarded as meeting social needs and, at the same time, as being so conservative that they could not be questioned as a reasonable minimum national goal.[23] They followed this approach because, at the time they were preparing their estimates, there were no clothing budgets which had been tested against the clothing expenditures of American families whose health, social adjustments and community relationships measured up to generally accepted physical and social criteria.

Thus, for nonfarm consumers the standard was based, with some modification, on the 1934–1936 consumption habits of families of employed wage earners and clerical workers with a family income of $1,486, or somewhat lower than the average income of $1,524 for all such families.[24] For farm families, the standard was developed from expenditures of families with an average money income in 1941 of $1,000 to $1,500 and a total income of $1,782 when food, housing and fuel furnished by the farm were valued and in-

cluded.[25] Both sets of expenditure data were converted to the 1940 price level.

The suggested over-all standard expenditures per year for five age and sex groups were as follows (at 1940 prices):

	Nonfarm	Farm
Men and boys, 16 years and older	$57.50	$46.50
Boys, 2 to 15 years	33.50	21.50
Women and girls, 16 years and older	61.00	48.00
Girls, 2 to 15 years	34.00	22.00
Infants, under 2	12.50	8.50

Detailed clothing allowances for the first and third of these groups appear in Appendix 6–4. The differences in the cost of the standard for men and women and for farm and nonfarm families represented customary differences in clothing expenditures.

These standards had the advantage of being related to a well-defined segment of the population. They could therefore be evaluated in relation to the actual consumption of other groups in the population. Even though the standards were based on the quantities of clothing actually purchased at a selected income level, and did not clearly represent the quantities necessary to meet some objectively described standard of need, they are in general agreement with subsequently developed standards.

No attempt was made to define a standard for personal care items.

City Worker's Family Budget Standard

In 1947, the United States Bureau of Labor Statistics published the City Worker's Family Budget, which was designed to provide a "modest but adequate" standard of living for a workingman's family of four persons — husband, wife (not employed outside the home), a boy of 13 and a girl of 8. The amounts of clothing and personal care items specified in this budget were defined as those necessary for "health, efficiency, the nurture of children and for participation in community activities," i.e., those which met social and psychological as well as physical needs. The budget provided a level of living which was

---

22. Margaret Loomis Stecker, *Intercity Differences in Costs of Living in March 1935, 59 Cities*, Research Monograph No. 12, Works Progress Administration, 1937.

23. See Chapter 7, "Clothing, Accessories and Personal Care," *America's Needs and Resources*, 1947 edition, pp. 132–137.

24. See Faith M. Williams and Alice C. Hanson, *Money Disbursements of Wage Earners and Clerical Workers, 1934–36*, Bulletin No. 638, U.S. Bureau of Labor Statistics. More precisely, the families upon whose expenditures the standard was based were those with an average expenditure of $400 to $500 per consumption unit. This concept took into account differences in family composition and size.

---

25. See *Rural Family Spending and Saving in Wartime*, Miscellaneous Publication No. 520, U.S. Department of Agriculture, June 1943. A few of the suggested prices were higher than prices calculated from this source.

adequate in relation to standards prevailing in large cities in prewar years.[26]

In preparing this budget, the Bureau analyzed expenditure data for families at successive income levels, obtained in surveys in the mid-1930s and in 1941–1942, in order to find out what quantities of clothing and personal care items the families themselves considered necessary. The procedure departed from the earlier method of selecting an income level which the budget maker judged to be adequate at a given point in time, and setting clothing standards in terms of actual purchases at the given income level. Instead, the method was to examine the relative change in the quantities of clothing purchased as incomes increased, i.e., the income elasticity of apparel purchases.

It was found that while clothing purchases increased successively from the lowest income level to the highest, the rate of increase reached a maximum at some point in the income scale and then declined. Thus, by studying the income elasticities of various groups of clothing and personal care items, it was possible to determine the point at which the consumers' demand for "more and more" gave way to a desire for better quality, for some other commodity or service, or for savings. The point where families started to buy in decreasing proportion to income determined the level of adequacy for the clothing and personal care budget. The types and quantities of clothing purchased by families at this indicated income level were those priced to determine the budget costs. [27]

In families consisting of husband, wife and two children under 15 years of age, the maximum elasticity for the husband's clothing was reached at a 1941 income of about $2,750. For the wife's and daughter's clothing the critical point was about $2,200, just above the median family income in that year; and for the boy's, about $1,840. The maximum elasticity for personal care items was reached at about $1,300.

The number of items of men's clothing purchased in a year ranged from an average of 30 at the lowest income level to 60 at the highest, with about 50 at the budget level. For the wives, the range was 25 to 55, with 40 articles at the

budget standard; for the girl, the range was 25 to 55 with the budget standard at 40; and for the boy, 20 to 60 with 35 determined as adequate. The quantities of specific clothing items for each family member provided by this budget are shown in Table 73, together with the quantities required to provide a comparable level of living for an elderly couple and for a farm family.[28]

Budgets for Elderly Couple and Farm Family

The elderly couple's budget was developed by the Federal Security Agency in cooperation with the Bureau of Labor Statistics. As is to be expected, the wardrobe considered adequate requires substantially fewer purchases each year than that for the younger city worker and his wife. The elderly man's budget calls for the purchase of about 16 apparel items a year, compared with 50 for the younger man; about 14 items are included for the elderly woman, compared with 40 for the younger woman.

The farm family standard was derived in the Department of Agriculture from data on farm family expenditures in 1941 in the same manner as the City Worker's Family Budget. The point of maximum elasticity for both the farm husband and wife was about $1,400, which was above the income of about 70 per cent of the farm families of this type in 1941. The farm standard determined by the use of income elasticities requires an annual purchase of about 45 articles for the husband, 35 for the wife, 32 for the farm boy and 30 for the girl.

Differences in the clothing needs of farm and city families are largely explained by differences in the occupation of the husband and in family activities. The city husband's clothing standard requires more coats, suits, underclothing, nightwear, socks and handkerchiefs than the farm husband's, while the farm husband's budget list includes more overalls, rubbers, overshoes, work gloves, hats and caps. The list for the city wife includes more hats, sport clothes and hosiery than that for the farm wife, while the farm wife's list provides for more aprons, rubbers and overshoes.

26. *Workers' Budgets in the United States,* Bulletin No. 927, U.S. Bureau of Labor Statistics, 1948.

27. For a more detailed description of the procedure see Dorothy S. Brady, "Statistical Procedures in the Derivation of Family Budgets," *Social Service Review,* June 1949, pp. 141–157.

28. This basic clothing standard is the average for large cities in the United States. For each city the quantities of clothing items classified as "heavy" and "light" are adjusted by a percentage factor which measures variation in clothing needs resulting from differences in climate. For a description of the climatic adjustment see *Workers' Budgets in the United States,* p. 36, footnote.

TABLE 73. CLOTHING STANDARDS FOR URBAN AND FARM FAMILIES

	Man			Boy	
	Urban		Farm	Urban	Farm
Clothing Item	City Worker's Family Budget	Elderly Couple's Budget	Farm Family Clothing Budget	City Worker's Family Budget	Farm Family Clothing Budget
Coats	.33	.16	.10	.29	.09
Overcoat and topcoat	.25	.12	.06	.21	.05
Raincoat	.08	.04	.04	.08	.04
Sweaters, jackets	.64	.24	.90	1.23	1.13
Sweaters	.35	.12	.30	.83	.55
Jackets	.29	.12	.60	.40	.58
Suits	.89	.32	.38	.44	.28
Wool, heavy	.44	.22	.22	.19	.11
Other	.45	.10	.16	.25	.17
Trousers, slacks, overalls	1.82	.94	4.06	2.59	4.00
Wool trousers or slacks	.35	.15	.30	.89	.55
Other trousers or slacks	.64	.27	.60	1.70	.97
Overalls or coveralls	.83	.52	3.16	—	2.48
Shirts	5.12	2.30	5.04	3.68	3.85
Cotton work (boy's polo)	2.21	.96	3.36	1.00	1.84
Other	2.91	1.34	1.68	2.68	2.01
Sportswear	.47	.09	.30	1.05	.38
Slack suit	.29	.04	.29	.54	.20
Shorts, bathing suit or trunks	.18	.05	.01	.51	.18
Underwear	7.52	2.15	4.99	5.99	5.13
Undershirts	3.24	.40	1.90	2.36	2.00
Underdrawers	3.56	.40	1.80	2.91	1.91
Union suits	.72	1.35	1.29	.72	1.22
Nightwear	.92	.24	.20	.67	.27
Pajamas	.84	.24	.20	.67	.25
Bathrobe	.08	—	—	—	.02
Socks	13.52	4.20	10.76	10.47	7.29
Shoes	2.30	1.10	2.40	3.18	2.66
Shoes, work and street	2.03	.89	1.96	2.87	2.16
Boots, house slippers, fabric shoes and special sport shoes	.27	.21	.44	.31	.50
Rubbers and arctics	.37	.20	.67	.44	.33
Hats and caps	1.26	.75	2.15	.69	1.08
Accessories	15.03	3.11	12.92	6.33	5.23
Gloves	4.56	1.10	7.96	.74	1.82
Handkerchiefs	6.42	.92	3.91	3.23	2.57
Ties	3.05	1.09	.51	1.36	.39
Belt, suspenders	1.00	} 8½% of annual cost of all other items of clothing	.54 } 3% of total clothing cost	1.00	.45 } 4% of total clothing cost
Shoe repairs	1.70			2.00	
Dry cleaning	9.0			—	
Miscellaneous accessories and cleaning supplies	3% of total clothing cost			3% of total clothing cost	

Sources: Workers' Budgets in the United States, Bulletin No. 927, U.S. Bureau of Labor Statistics, March 1948; "A Budget for an Elderly Couple," *Social Security Bulletin,* February 1948; Mollie Orshansky, "Use of

(Number or Pairs of Garments to Be Purchased Each Year)

	Woman			Girl	
	Urban			Urban	
Clothing Item	City Worker's Family Budget	Elderly Couple's Budget	Farm Family Clothing Budget	City Worker's Family Budget	Farm Family Clothing Budget
Coats	.52	.20	.45	1.16	.70
Heavy	.28	.12	.25	.32	.47
Light	.23	.08	.20	.33	—
Snow suit	—	—	—	.37	.23
Raincoat	.01	—	—	.14	—
Sweaters	.37	.18	.37	.63	.60
Jackets	.04	—	.02	.13	.40
Suits	.11	.03	.14	—	.06
Dresses	4.17	1.50	4.21	3.45	2.40
Skirts	.22	—	.16	.48	.20
Blouses	.48	.10	.38	.95	.51
Housewear or sportswear	1.30	.45	1.39	1.67	.58
Underwear	7.44	2.90	7.16	8.60	6.30
Slips	2.11	.75	1.76	1.56	.94
Panties	2.99	1.10	2.93	4.90	4.40
Underwaists	.25	.35	.39	1.63	—
Union suits	.16	.33	.32	.51	.96
Brassiere, girdle, corset	1.93	.37	1.76	—	—
Nightwear	1.39	.64	1.17	1.02	.80
Nightgown, pajamas	1.34	.56	1.09	.94	—
Bathrobe	.05	.08	.08	.08	—
Hosiery	12.88	4.50	9.65	12.54	10.19
Shoes	3.02	1.28	2.82	3.68	2.80
Shoes	2.56	1.07	2.52	3.39	2.55
House slippers	.46	.21	.30	.29	.25
Rubbers, arctics	.22	.10	.53	.54	.63
Hats	2.03	.90	1.40	1.20	1.09
Accessories	5.37	1.42	5.58	3.06	2.69
Gloves	.93	.31	.97	.81	.83
Handbag	.86	.21	.60	.24	.26
Handkerchiefs	3.44	.85	4.00	1.95	1.60
Umbrella	.14	.05	.01	.06	—
Yard goods, findings, etc.	3.00 yds.	1.80 yds.	6% of total clothing cost	3.00 yds.	8% of total clothing cost
Shoe repairs	3.00			1.50	
Dry cleaning, pressing	8.00	3½% of total clothing cost	5% of total clothing cost	—	2% of total clothing cost
Other accessories and cleaning supplies	3% of total clothing cost			2% of total clothing cost	

Income Elasticity for Farm-Urban Comparison," Paper for Allerton Park Conference on Research in Income and Wealth, National Bureau of Economic Research in cooperation with the University of Illinois, June 9–11, 1950.

TABLE 74. ESTIMATED COST OF CLOTHING BUDGETS FOR URBAN AND FARM FAMILIES
(*Annual Replacement Cost at 1947–1949 Prices*)

	Urban						Farm
	City Worker's Family				Elderly Couple 8 Cities June 1947		
	34 Cities June 1947		10 Cities October 1949				
Family Member	Range	Median	Range	Median	Range	Median	Winter 1947
All members	$392–$477	$426	$430–$470	$451	$92–$108	$98	$376
Husband	128– 159	140	149– 162	155	52– 63	58	123
Wife	111– 139	127	113– 135	128	39– 46	42	129
Boy	77– 92	86	74– 93	86	—	—	70
Girl	66– 97	80	75– 92	83	—	—	54

Sources: Workers' Budgets in the United States, Bulletin No. 927, U.S. Bureau of Labor Statistics, March 1948; "A Budget for an Elderly Couple," *Social Security Bulletin,* February 1948; Mollie Orshansky, "Use of Income Elasticity for Farm-Urban Comparison," Paper for Allerton Park Conference on Research in Income and Wealth, National Bureau of Economic Research in co-operation with the University of Illinois, June 9–11, 1950.

Comparison with Earlier Standards

The clothing allowances in these budgets differ from previously published standards principally in the larger number of suits, socks and underwear in the city man's budget and the smaller amounts of work clothing, nightwear and gloves in both the city man's and the farm man's lists. These lists include more shoes for the women, both city and farm, than earlier standards but fewer undergarments and blouses. There are also minor differences in the allowances for the various types of garments within the major clothing categories.[29]

ESTIMATED COST OF CLOTHING STANDARDS

Because of the greater quantities specified, the annual clothing budget for the city worker and his wife cost, in 1947, more than two and one half times that for the elderly urban couple. The farm families' clothing budget cost less than that for city families — $376 compared with $426. (See Table 74.) This lower cost is in part due to the fewer items of relatively expensive clothing — coats, suits, etc. — required by the farm husband, but it also reflects lower prices paid per garment. The differences in cost for farm and city families, however, are not as great as commonly imagined,

29. For a comparison of the city worker and farm family allowances and those of the WPA maintenance budget, the Heller Committee budget, and the standard used in the first edition of this survey, see Appendix 6–4.

and there is increasing evidence that clothing purchases of farm families do not differ radically in quality or style from those of city families in the same income range.

No information is available on the cost of these standards at 1950 prices. The City Worker's Family Budget was priced in 10 cities in October 1949. At that time the annual cost of the family's clothing needs ranged from $430 to $470, with the median at $451. Between October 1949 and October 1950, apparel prices as measured by the consumers' price index increased 3.3 per cent on the average in large cities, and by October 1951 they were 11.9 per cent over their October 1949 average.

Standards for items of personal care were established in the City Worker's Family Budget and in the budget for an elderly couple. No similar standards have been developed for farm families. The cost of the annual personal care budget for a city family was estimated to range from $51 to $66 in 1947 and from $59 to $71 in 1949. The more limited budget for an elderly couple was estimated to cost from $26 to $36 in 1947. (See Table 75.) Using these cost and price data, it has been estimated that an average of about $358 would be required (at 1950 prices) to clothe an urban family of two or more persons, whose head is less than 65 years of age, $100 to clothe an elderly couple, and $50 an elderly single person. Clothing budget costs (at 1950 prices) for a younger single person were estimated from

TABLE 75. PERSONAL CARE STANDARDS FOR URBAN FAMILIES

Group and Family Member Item	Unit	Quantity per Year	
		City Worker's Family Budget	Elderly Couple
Services			
Husband			
Haircut		14.6	14.5
Shave		1.7	—
Wife			
Haircut		4.2 ⎫	
Finger wave		2.9 ⎬	4.2
Shampoo		.8 ⎭	
Permanent wave		.6	.4
Children			
Haircut, boy		9.5	—
Haircut, girl		4.7	—
Commodities			
Husband			
Shaving cream	5-ounce tube	2.2	3.0
Razor		.2 ⎫	Included in
Razor blades	Package of 5	7.7	allowance
Shaving brush		.2 ⎬	for misc.
Shaving soap	Cake	3.2	toilet
Shaving lotion	5-ounce bottle	.2 ⎭	articles
Wife			
Face powder	2.5-ounce box	1.0 ⎫	
Cold cream	3.5-ounce jar	1.0	Allowance
Rouge compact	Large size	.5	of $1.05
Lipstick	Small	1.0	adjusted
Hand lotion	13½ ounce bottle	.2 ⎬	for price
Nail polish	Small size	1.0	change
Deodorant	1¼ ounce jar	1.5	from
Sanitary supplies	Box of 12	10.0	1941
Cleansing tissues	Box of 200	4.0 ⎭	
All family members			
Toilet soap	Cake	67.1	40.0
Toothpaste	3-ounce tube	10.2	5.0
Tooth powder	4.5-ounce can	1.0	1.0
			Allowance for
Mouth wash	14-ounce bottle	1.4 ⎫	misc. toilet
Toothbrush		6.0	articles is
Hairbrush		.5 ⎬	7% of annual
Comb		1.0	cost of other
			items

		34 Cities	8 Cities
Estimated annual cost at 1947 prices:			
Range		$51–$66	$26–$36
Median		$59	$29
		10 Cities	
Estimated annual cost at 1949 prices:			
Range		$59–$71	
Median		$64	

Sources: Workers' Budgets in the United States, Bulletin No. 927, U.S. Bureau of Labor Statistics, March 1948; "A Budget for an Elderly Couple," *Social Security Bulletin,* February 1948.

the budgets prepared by state agencies to be about $279 (see p. 187).[30]

These standards have all been developed on an annual replacement basis and therefore involve some implicit assumptions regarding the clothing inventories of the families. Nothing was known, however, about the clothing inventories of the families whose expenditure reports were used to develop the budget standards, and very little analysis has been done to determine standards of adequacy for clothing inventories.

Clothing Inventories

However, there have been from time to time limited studies of family clothing inventories which can be compared with purchases in a given year. One such study was made by the United States Department of Agriculture in Minneapolis-St. Paul in 1948–1949. (See Table 76 and Appendix 6–3.) Comparable studies of the clothing inventories of a sample of farm families in Meeker-Wright Counties, Minnesota, and families in Birmingham, Alabama, provide the most recent data on differences in clothing habits between cities, between city and farm families, and at different age and income levels.

These studies show that there is little difference in the kinds of clothing included in the wardrobes of city and farm families. The most significant differences are in the quantities of the various garments owned. It has been estimated that the farm husbands and wives included in these surveys owned about two thirds to three fourths as much clothing as the city husbands and wives.[31]

That younger men and women own substantially larger amounts of almost all items of apparel is clearly indicated by these reports. They also point up the preference of younger men and women for sportswear and casual clothes, and of older men and women for more formal attire. For example, in Minneapolis, men 50 to 59 years of age owned an average of 2.5 dress hats, whereas men under 30 owned about one apiece.

Differences found in clothing inventories between Minneapolis and Birmingham were mainly the result of differences in climate and in the occupational characteristics of the two cities. There was evidence, however, of a real preference among Birmingham men for business suits rather than the slacks and jackets owned by men in Minneapolis.[32]

Inventory Compared with Budget

Because the families covered by the Minneapolis-St. Paul study differ in age and composition from the family for which the City Worker's Family Budget was designed, their clothing purchases cannot be closely compared with the budget specifications. The results of the expenditure study do, however, point up the general reasonableness of the budget standard in light of actual practice and give some idea of the size of clothing inventories associated with this level of expenditure.

The median income of the families who reported their clothing inventories and purchases was about $3,000 after taxes, which is approximately the income required to buy the goods and services specified in the City Worker's Family Budget in Minneapolis in June 1947. The average 1948 expenditure per man for clothing was $129, while the estimated cost of the budget standard for the husband's clothing was about $145 (after adjustment for clothing services not included in the expenditure survey). The average expenditure per woman was $182, compared with an estimated cost of the wife's clothing budget of about $130. The average expenditure per boy was $80 and per girl $84, compared with estimated budget costs of $87 and $93 respectively.

NEEDS AND DEMAND IN 1950 AND 1960

In 1950, about 7 million, or 28 per cent, of the city families in the United States were spending less than the amount considered necessary to maintain an adequate clothing standard — $100 for elderly couples and $358 for other families of two or more persons. About 6 million urban individuals not in families were spending less than standard amounts — $50 for persons over 65 years

---

30. The average of $358 for urban families of two or more persons was obtained by applying family-size cost differentials to an estimated average cost of $433 for a four-person family, as derived from the City Worker's Family Budget. The estimated costs for each family size were then weighted together by the distribution of families by size, as reported in the 1950 Census.

31. For detailed analysis of the results of these studies, see *Studies of Family Clothing Supplies*, Preliminary Reports Nos. 1, 2, 3, 4, 5, Bureau of Human Nutrition and Home Economics, 1950–1951.

32. Margaret L. Brew, *Family Clothing Practices, Minnesota*, 29th Annual Agricultural Outlook Conference, U.S. Department of Agriculture, 1951.

TABLE 76. SELECTED ITEMS IN CLOTHING INVENTORY OF FAMILIES IN MINNEAPOLIS-ST. PAUL, MINNESOTA, 1948–1949

(Families without Children or with One or Two Children Aged 2-15 Years)

Item	Number or Pairs Owned	
	Husbands	*Boys*
Outercoats and jackets and snow suits	5.1	4.1
Suits and suit equivalents	5.1	—
Shirts and sweaters	20.9	17.2
Overalls and work trousers	3.7	—
Shoes and boots	4.5	2.5
Socks	18.2	11.6
	Wives	*Girls*
Outercoats and jackets	4.1	4.1
Dresses and suits	12.5	9.6
Blouses and sweaters	6.7	9.8
Skirts, slacks and jeans	3.2	7.6
Shoes and boots	5.8	3.0
Hosiery	9.4	12.3

Source: Appendix 6–3.

of age and $279 for younger individuals. For rural farm and rural nonfarm families and individuals, the cost of the clothing standard was estimated to be about 90 per cent of that for city families. On this basis, about 7.9 million families and individuals living outside urban areas were spending less than the amount required to clothe themselves adequately.

Total spending for clothing and related products was $22.7 billion in 1950. It is estimated that an additional expenditure of $2.1 billion would have been needed to bring all 21 million families and individuals who spent less than the standard up to that level.[33] This additional cost has been estimated only in terms of the annual replacement cost necessary to maintain the inventory implicit in the standard. The initial cost of providing adequate inventories of clothing would be substan-

33. The method of deriving these estimates is described in Appendix 6–5.

tially greater than the annual cost of maintaining them.

About one third of the families and individuals in the United States in 1950 spent less than the amount required to provide an adequate standard for personal care. From data obtained from the budgets previously described, it has been estimated that in urban areas an adequate budget in 1950 for personal care for a family of two or more persons would have cost $55; for an elderly couple, $31; and for a single person, $56. As in the case of clothing, the cost for persons living outside urban areas was estimated at 90 per cent of the city cost. If all families and individuals who spent less than the standard amount in 1950 increased their outlays to the budget level, an expenditure of about $317 million would have been required, in addition to the total of $2,303 million reported for that year.

The total demand for clothing, accessories and clothing care in 1960, estimated on the basis of the changes in population and income assumed for this study and the trends in the relation of clothing expenditures to disposable income, is expected to reach $29.3 billion (at 1950 prices). To raise the clothing expenditures of those below the specified standards to an adequate level would require an additional $2.0 billion in 1960.

For personal care the 1960 demand is estimated at $2.8 billion, with an additional $360 million needed to provide an adequate budget for those below the standard.

Estimated needs and demand for clothing, accessories and personal care in 1950 and 1960 may be summarized as follows (figures in millions at 1950 prices):

	1950		1960	
	Demand	*Needs*	*Demand*	*Needs*
Clothing, accessories and personal care	$24,961	$27,420	$32,050	$34,410
Clothing and related products	22,658	24,800	29,300	31,300
Personal care	2,303	2,620	2,750	3,110

## CHAPTER 7

HOUSING

To MOST PEOPLE in this country today housing implies not only shelter but also some, at least, of the utilities which are essential to the operation of a modern dwelling. Consequently, expenditures for "housing" are generally considered to include outlays for fuel, electricity, gas and water. Except for the period 1943–1951, housing and household utilities has consistently been the second largest item in the consumer's budget, only less important than food. In the 1920s it accounted for about one fifth of all consumer expenditures. By 1952, however, it comprised only about one seventh — not much more than the cost of household equipment and operation.

If the consumer is a tenant, he pays for the use of the dwelling and such fixed equipment as is part of the structure (and sometimes for one or more of the utility items) in the form of rent. If he owns his home, the services provided by the dwelling and its fixed equipment still have a rental value — the homeowner's "imputed rent."

Whether the consumer's housing costs take the form of rent or imputed rent, they must still cover the same items. Tenant and owner-occupier alike must pay for maintaining and repairing the structure, for services provided by the local government, for insurance protection against destruction or damage to the property by fire or other hazard. Each must also pay a return on the amount invested in the property. For the owner-occupier this cost takes the form of a forfeit of the return he would have received had he invested his money elsewhere; or if he has borrowed money, he has to pay interest on the loan. The renter pays interest on the landlord's investment and borrowings — and perhaps also a further sum as profit. Finally, each must pay for the capital cost of land and structure. This often takes the form of periodic repayments of money borrowed.

Even if no money has been borrowed to pay for capital cost, every owner seeks to maintain his capital. To this end he sets aside periodic depreciation allowances designed to equal the losses in value resulting from obsolescence, time and use — that is, to offset capital consumption.

Rental payments have to cover all these costs, and owners incur them whether or not they set aside a sum to cover them.

Capital outlays for housing are of special significance. Averaging more than one fifth of our total capital expenditures, they have been an important source of addition to our stock of capital goods. Housing is by far the largest single functional item in our national wealth. Our national living standard depends to a significant degree upon the quantity and quality of our housing stock. Since our past capital outlays for housing have not been large enough to provide for both the increase in population and the capital consumption of housing, through the years serious inadequacies have developed in our housing supply. These inadequacies are more apparent in urban than in rural communities, because dwellings cover so much of the land area of cities.[1]

HOUSING TRENDS

We had 46 million dwelling units in the United States in 1950. In 1940 we had 37.3 million, or just about four fifths as many; in 1900, only 17.9 million. Because the average size of families declined steadily in this period, the rate of increase in the number of dwelling units was considerably greater than the population growth, and the average number of occupants per dwelling unit decreased. By 1950 our homes contained 1.3 fewer persons on the average than in 1900 — 3.5 persons compared with 4.8. (See Table 77 and Figure 33.)

The greatest increase in our housing supply occurred in nonfarm areas. There were almost three and a half times as many dwelling units in

By A. BENJAMIN HANDLER, Associate Professor of Planning, University of Michigan; LAWRENCE N. BLOOMBERG, Chief Economist, Public Housing Administration; and HOWARD G. BRUNSMAN, Chief, Population and Housing Division, U.S. Bureau of the Census. Opinions and judgments expressed in this chapter are those of the authors and should not be attributed to the organizations with which they are associated.

1. The nature and condition of the housing stock has a profound effect on the livability of our cities. See Chapter 16.

TABLE 77. POPULATION, HOUSEHOLDS AND DWELLING UNITS, 1900–1950

Year	Population	Households or Occupied Dwelling Units	All Dwelling Units				Population per Occupied Unit
			Total	Urban	Rural Nonfarm	Rural Farm	
	(*Thousands*)			(*Thousands*)			
1900	75,995	15,964	17,850	8,420	3,377	6,053	4.8
1910	91,972	20,256	22,047	10,736	4,797	6,514	4.5
1920	105,711	24,352	26,294	13,456	5,656	7,182	4.3
1930	122,775	29,905	32,786	18,720	6,972	7,094	4.1
1940	131,669	34,855	37,325	21,616	8,067	7,642	3.8
1950	150,697	42,826	45,983	27,270	12,046	6,667	3.5

Sources: Figures on total population, households or occupied dwelling units and average number of persons per occupied dwelling unit for 1900 to 1950 and urban and rural dwelling units for 1940 are from the U.S. Bureau of the Census. Urban and rural nonfarm housing data were calculated from Miles L. Colean, *American Housing: Problems and Prospects,* Twentieth Century Fund, New York, 1944, Appendix C, Table 11, p. 366, and Appendix F, Table 35, p. 410, and from "Housing and the Increase in Population," *Monthly Labor Review,* April 1942, in the following manner: the combined total of urban and rural nonfarm dwelling units in 1900 to 1930 was obtained by projecting backwards on the number reported in the 1940 Census of Housing. Thus, 29,706,000 units were standing in 1940. According to the Bureau of Labor Statistics, a total of 3,459,000 new and converted units were built from 1930 to 1939, and according to the same report, 952,000 makeshift units were added, and 397,000 units were demolished. The total standing in 1930 was thus 25,692,000. For earlier decades the same procedure was followed. The distribution between urban and rural nonfarm of the nonfarm total for the 1900–1930 period was obtained by assuming that the increase during each decade was distributed the same as the distribution of dwelling units built during the decade. The urban-rural distribution of dwelling units in 1950 represents the distribution according to the old urban and farm definitions and was obtained by adjusting the Census data on the distribution according to the new definition by assuming that the same proportion of dwelling units as of population were shifted from rural to urban by the revision in the urban-rural definition and that 300,000 dwelling units were shifted from rural farm to rural nonfarm by the change in the farm definition.

nonfarm areas in 1950 as in 1900, while the increase in rural farm areas was only a little over 10 per cent. The movement of population from farms and rural areas into the city has been taking place for many decades. In recent decades the movement of population into metropolitan areas has become a major trend.[2]

While this shift to metropolitan areas has been in progress, an outward movement from central cities to suburbs has also taken place. Seeking an escape from overcrowding, lack of fresh air and of play and recreation space, while wishing still to retain the advantages of city life, families have moved from central cities toward the outlying parts of metropolitan areas. This has resulted in a high rate of population increase in the suburban areas against a small increase, or even a net loss, within the central cities and severe losses in the cores of many central cities.

Each of these movements — from country to city and from city to suburb — has had an important effect on the location of our housing. As the population became increasingly urbanized, construction of farmhouses tended to cease, and with the outward movement of city populations in recent decades, most new construction of nonfarm housing has occurred in suburban areas.

STATUS OF HOUSING IN 1950 [3]

American homes reflect differences in climate, local housebuilding materials, family income, tradition, taste and other factors. The Cape Cod cottage differs as much from the Park Avenue apartment as that, in turn, differs from the Georgian mansion of the South or the adobe house of the Southwest. Farm housing is differently equipped from urban housing. The dwelling places of the poor bear little resemblance to those of the rich.

Although the average family showed a marked

2. A standard metropolitan area includes all of the territory in counties containing cities of 50,000 or more and contiguous counties which are economically integrated with the central cities. In New England the standard metropolitan areas are composed of towns and cities instead of entire counties.

3. Unless otherwise indicated, data for this section are from *1950 Census of Housing,* Vol. I, *General Characteristics,* Chapter 1.

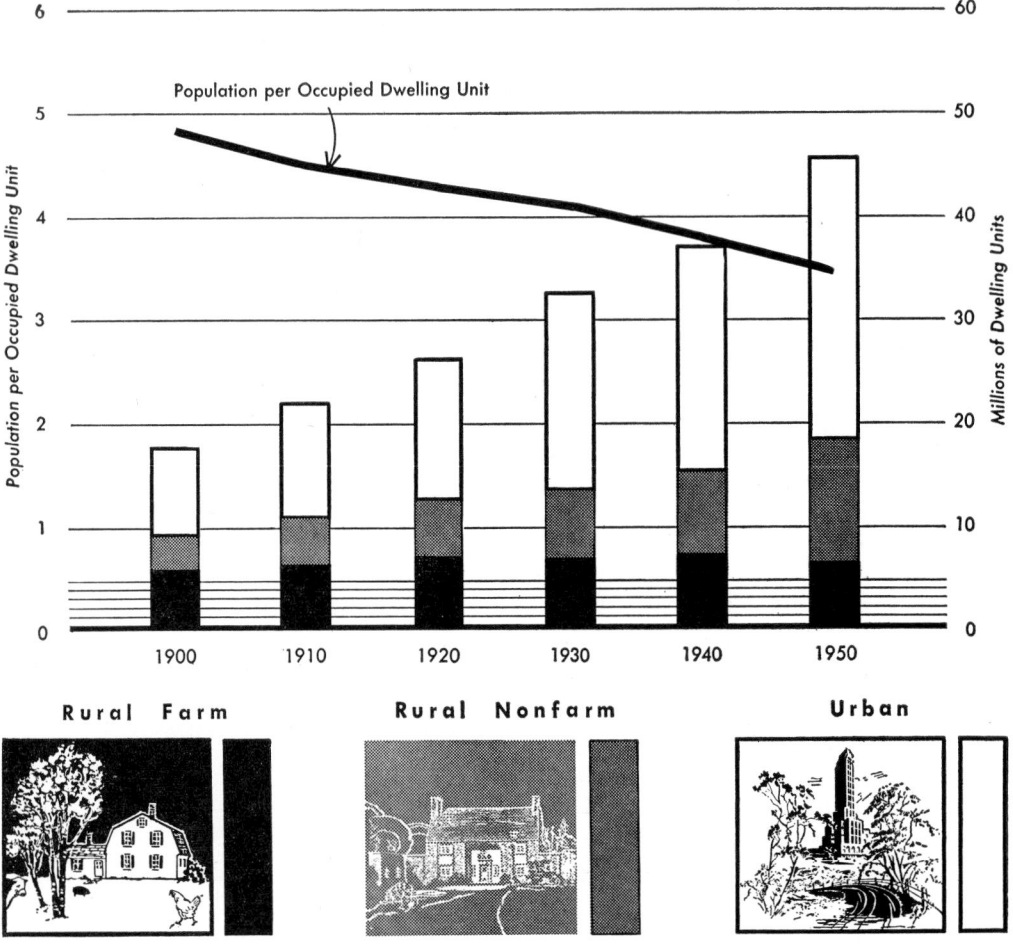

FIGURE 33. NUMBER OF DWELLING UNITS BY TYPE OF PLACE, AND POPULATION PER OCCUPIED UNIT, 1900–1950

Source: Table 77.

improvement in its housing during the ten-year period after 1940, conditions were still far from satisfactory in 1950. (See Figure 34.) About 10 per cent, or 4.5 million, of our 46 million homes were dilapidated; 17 per cent had no running water in the structure; 29 per cent had no private flush toilet; and 31 per cent had no private bathtub or shower. (See Tables 78 and 79.)

Home ownership has increased tremendously since 1940. There were 8 million more homeowners in 1950 than in 1940, an increase of 55 per cent. In contrast, the number of renters decreased by 0.4 million, so that rented structures declined from 56 per cent of all occupied dwelling units in 1940 to 45 per cent in 1950.

In 1950, 63 per cent of all dwelling units were single-family detached houses. Of the rest,

about 25 per cent were in other structures containing one to four dwelling units, and the remainder were in larger apartment houses.

Between 1940 and 1950 the number of persons per dwelling unit declined slightly more than the number of rooms. Thus, the number of homes containing seven or more persons decreased by one fifth, while those with one or two persons increased by more than two fifths. The number of units with an average of more than 1.5 persons per room decreased by one sixth, while the number with an average of no more than .75 person per room increased by one third.

Variations in Nonfarm Housing

Although nonfarm housing is in better condition than farm housing, it improved less be-

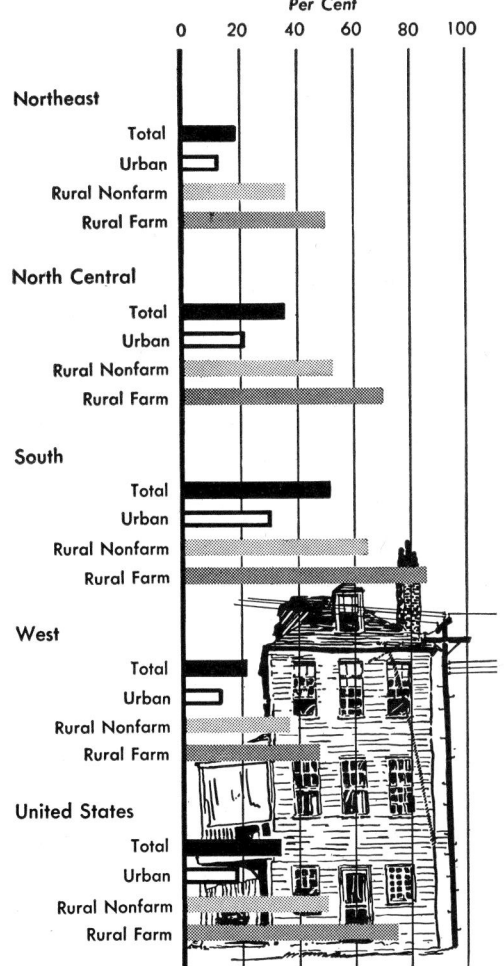

Per Cent

0   20   40   60   80   100

Northeast
Total
Urban
Rural Nonfarm
Rural Farm

North Central
Total
Urban
Rural Nonfarm
Rural Farm

South
Total
Urban
Rural Nonfarm
Rural Farm

West
Total
Urban
Rural Nonfarm
Rural Farm

United States
Total
Urban
Rural Nonfarm
Rural Farm

FIGURE 34. PER CENT OF HOUSING DILAPIDATED OR LACKING PRIVATE BATH OR TOILET, BY REGION AND TYPE, 1950

Source: Table 79.

tween 1940 and 1950 than farm housing and therefore less than all housing, including farm. About 8 per cent, or 3.1 million, of the 39.6 million nonfarm dwelling units (urban and rural nonfarm) were dilapidated in 1950. Nonfarm units without running water declined to 12 per cent of the total in 1950 from 17 per cent in 1940,[4] a decrease of two thirds of a million in

the number of such units. At the same time, however, the number of nonfarm units with running water increased by more than 10 million, or 42 per cent. (See Table 78 and Appendix 7-1.)

Nonfarm dwelling units without private flush toilet declined from 28 per cent to 22 per cent of the number reporting, but the number of such units increased by a quarter of a million. In contrast, nonfarm dwelling units with private flush toilet increased by 9.5 million, or nearly 45 per cent. The number of nonfarm units without private bath showed no change from 1940 while units with private bath increased by nearly 9.5 million, or 48 per cent.

Home ownership in nonfarm areas showed substantially the same type of change as in farm areas. Nearly nine tenths of the increase in number of occupied units was among owner-occupied units. The increase in number of nonfarm occupied dwelling units was about equally divided between units with one or two persons and those with three to six persons. Since there were fewer of the smaller households to start with, however, their number increased about 50 per cent whereas the number of three-to-six-person households rose only 30 per cent. The decline of one quarter of a million among households with seven or more persons represents a 12 per cent drop for this group. The number of nonfarm units with an average of more than 1.5 persons per room increased slightly, while those with an average of no more than .75 person per room increased by 43 per cent.

Variations in Farm Housing

The best housing is found in the cities of the North and the West. The worst is found on the farms of the South.[5] Urban housing in general is superior to rural nonfarm housing, and rural nonfarm housing is superior to farm housing.

In 1950 almost seven eighths of the southern farm homes were dilapidated or lacked private bath, private flush toilet, or running water in

4. The 1940 figures are based on statistics for dwelling units with no running water inside the dwelling unit, while those for 1950 are based on lack of running water in the structure for use of the occupants of the unit. It is unlikely, however, that this difference in definition accounts for as much as one half of the decline in the number of units without running water.

5. The states comprising the regions used here and below are as follows: Northeast — New York, Pennsylvania, New Jersey and the New England states; North Central region — Ohio, Michigan, Indiana, Illinois, Wisconsin, Minnesota, Iowa, Missouri, Kansas, Nebraska, South Dakota, and North Dakota; South — Texas, Oklahoma, Arkansas, Kentucky, West Virginia, Maryland, Delaware, and all of the area east and south of these states; West — Montana, Wyoming, Colorado, New Mexico, and all of the area west of these states.

TABLE 78. CHARACTERISTICS OF HOUSING
(Number in

	All Housing			
	1940		1950	
Item	Number of Dwelling Units	Per Cent of Number Reporting [a]	Number of Dwelling Units	Per Cent of Number Reporting [a]
All dwelling units	37,325	—	45,983	—
In one-dwelling-unit detached structure	24,909	66.8	29,116	63.3
In other structure	12,416	33.2	16,867	36.7
With running water in structure	25,796	69.9	37,505	82.8
No running water in structure	11,105	30.1	7,784	17.2
With private flush toilet	21,967	59.7	32,335	71.4
No private flush toilet	14,803	40.3	12,926	28.6
With private bath	20,606	56.2	31,022	69.3
No private bath	16,043	43.8	13,754	30.7
With electric lighting	28,915	78.7	42,359	94.0
No electric lighting .	7,831	21.3	2,687	6.0
Occupied dwelling units	34,855	—	42,827	—
Owner-occupied	15,196	43.6	23,560	55.0
Renter-occupied	19,659	56.4	19,266	45.0
With one or two persons in unit	11,308	32.5	16,016	37.4
With three to six persons in unit	20,493	58.7	24,365	56.9
With seven or more persons in unit	3,054	8.8	2,445	5.7
With .75 or fewer persons per room	18,910	54.9	25,357	60.2
With .76 to 1.50 persons per room	12,451	36.1	14,190	33.6
With 1.51 or more persons per room	3,086	9.0	2,608	6.2
With radio	28,048	82.8	40,411	95.7
No radio	5,842	17.2	1,823	4.3
With mechanical refrigerator	15,093	44.1	33,720	80.2
With ice refrigerator	9,253	27.1	4,445	10.6
Without mechanical or ice refrigerator	9,859	28.8	3,894	9.3
Cooking with gas	16,776	48.8	25,070	59.5
Cooking with electricity	1,838	5.4	6,295	15.0
Cooking with other	15,729	45.8	10,735	25.5
With central heat	14,347	42.0	21,191	50.4
No central heat	19,802	58.0	20,865	49.6
With mortgage-owner	[b]	[b]	[b]	[b]
No mortgage-owner	[b]	[b]	[b]	[b]

the structure, as compared with only one eighth of the urban homes of the Northeast. While three fourths of the farm homes of the Northeast had running water inside the structure and more than half had private flush toilet, these conveniences were found in less than 30 per cent and about 15 per cent, respectively, of the southern farm homes. Electric lighting was available to all except 7 per cent of the northeastern farm homes, but was lacking in 31 per cent of the southern ones. The proportion of farm homes without a mechanical refrigerator was more than twice as great in the South as in the Northeast. (See Table 79.)

The typical farm home of the Northeast is a single-family detached house with six or seven rooms, occupied and owned by a household of two to four persons. It was built before 1920, and the chances are about one in ten that it is dilapidated. It has electric lights, a mechanical refrigerator and a radio. It also has running water. There is a better than 50–50 chance that it has a bathtub or shower and a flush toilet for the exclusive use of the household, but slightly less than an even chance that it has central heating or that gas or electricity is used as cooking fuel.

The most common kind of farm housing in

IN THE UNITED STATES, 1940 AND 1950

Thousands)

Change, 1940 to 1950		Urban and Rural Nonfarm Housing					
		1940		1950		Change, 1940 to 1950	
Number	Per Cent	Number of Dwelling Units	Per Cent of Number Reporting[a]	Number of Dwelling Units	Per Cent of Number Reporting[a]	Number	Per Cent
8,658	23.2	29,683	—	39,625	—	9,942	33.5
4,207	21.8	16,394	59.1	23,038	58.1	6,644	40.5
4,451	35.8	11,354	40.9	14,067	41.9	2,713	23.9
11,709	45.4	24,456	83.3	34,834	89.2	10,378	42.4
−3,321	−29.9	4,897	16.7	4,206	11.8	−691	−14.1
10,368	47.2	21,124	72.2	30,603	78.5	9,479	44.9
−1,877	−12.7	8,120	27.8	8,404	21.5	284	3.5
10,416	50.5	19,726	67.6	29,178	69.3	9,452	47.9
−2,289	−14.3	9,471	32.4	9,412	30.7	−59	−0.6
13,444	46.5	26,564	90.9	37,541	96.6	10,977	41.3
−5,144	−65.7	2,670	9.1	1,303	3.4	−1,367	−51.2
7,972	22.9	27,748	—	37,105	—	9,357	33.7
8,364	55.0	11,413	41.1	19,802	53.4	8,389	73.5
−393	−2.0	16,335	58.9	17,304	46.6	969	5.9
4,708	41.6	9,559	34.4	14,393	38.8	4,834	50.6
3,872	18.9	16,215	58.4	20,968	56.5	4,753	29.3
−609	−19.9	1,974	7.1	1,744	4.7	−230	−11.7
6,447	34.1	15,499	56.5	22,140	60.2	6,641	42.8
1,739	14.0	9,973	36.4	12,373	34.2	2,400	24.1
−478	−15.5	1,957	7.1	2,036	5.6	79	4.0
12,363	44.1	23,889	88.5	35,212	96.3	11,323	47.4
−4,019	−68.8	6,969	11.5	1,369	3.7	−5,600	−80.4
18,627	123.4	14,058	51.6	30,194	82.9	16,136	114.8
−4,808	−52.0	8,009	29.4	3,783	10.4	−4,226	−52.8
−5,965	−60.5	5,202	19.0	2,461	6.8	−2,741	−52.7
8,294	49.4	16,510	60.4	23,791	65.2	7,281	44.1
4,457	242.5	1,651	6.0	5,395	14.8	3,744	226.8
−4,994	−31.8	9,179	33.6	7,277	20.0	−1,902	−20.7
6,844	47.7	13,643	50.2	20,178	55.3	6,535	47.9
1,063	5.4	13,552	49.8	16,290	44.7	2,738	20.2
b	b	4,805	45.3	7,825	44.0	3,020	62.9
b	b	5,806	54.7	9,971	56.0	4,165	71.7

Source: 1950 Census of Housing.

a. Number reporting with (or without) particular item divided by total number answering question about that item; total answering varies from item to item.

b. Not available.

the South is also a single-family detached structure and is owned by its occupant. It is much more crowded than the northeastern farmhouse, since it has only four rooms and is occupied by somewhat more persons. Built in the 1920s, it is a little newer than the typical farmhouse of the Northeast, but there are three chances in ten that it is dilapidated. It has electric lights and a radio, but there is only a 50–50 chance that it has a mechanical refrigerator. It does not have running water, a flush toilet, or a bathtub or shower. It does not have central heating but has a heating stove with an outside flue. Wood is used as fuel in heating and cooking.

Variations in Urban Housing

Our urban housing is far better than our farm housing, but it leaves much to be desired. The best city houses are found in the Northeast, the

Item	Total					Urban				
	United States	North-east	North Central	South	West	United States	North-east	North Central	South	West
Total dwelling units (*thousands*)	45,983	12,051	13,746	13,654	6,532	29,569	9,352	8,674	6,963	4,580
Total occupied dwelling units (*thousands*)	42,826	11,228	12,972	12,633	5,994	28,492	9,052	8,469	6,618	4,353
Owner-occupied units as per cent of all occupied units	55.0	48.4	60.7	53.7	57.8	50.5	43.0	55.7	50.8	55.4
Characteristics										
Average (Median)										
Number of rooms per unit	4.7	5.0	5.2	4.3	4.3	4.6	4.9	4.8	4.3	4.3
Number of persons per unit	3.1	3.1	3.0	3.2	2.8	3.0	3.1	2.9	3.0	2.7
Monthly rent of nonfarm renter-occupied units	$35.50	$36.67	$37.05	$28.12	$39.04	$37.54	$37.58	$38.98	$32.85	$40.39
Value of nonfarm owner-occupied 1-dwelling-unit structures	$7,354	$8,702	$7,280	$5,737	$8,421	$8,380	$9,361	$8,343	$6,825	$9,052
Condition										
Per cent of all reporting units										
Over 30 years old	45.8	58.3	56.1	33.2	27.6	46.4	58.8	53.8	32.6	28.3
Dilapidated	9.8	5.0	6.8	18.2	7.0	6.4	4.3	5.4	11.9	4.7
Dilapidated or lacking flush toilet or private bath for exclusive use	33.6	18.2	35.3	51.7	20.8	18.7	12.4	20.5	30.0	12.6
With bathtub or shower for exclusive use	69.3	84.5	67.4	51.6	82.3	83.6	90.3	81.6	73.0	89.7
With flush toilet for exclusive use	71.4	88.0	70.3	52.8	82.4	86.8	93.7	85.7	76.6	90.5
With running water inside structure	82.8	95.8	83.0	66.4	92.9	96.3	99.6	96.9	90.0	98.3
With electric lighting	94.0	98.6	95.9	86.6	97.0	98.8	99.6	99.5	96.1	99.6
Per cent of reporting occupied units										
With mechanical refrigeration	80.2	89.2	83.9	67.3	82.4	86.1	90.7	88.2	77.3	85.5
With ice refrigeration	10.6	7.5	7.7	17.7	7.5	10.0	7.6	7.9	17.4	7.8
With gas or electric cooking fuel	74.5	79.6	81.4	58.4	84.0	86.2	84.4	91.3	78.2	92.2
With central heating	50.4	76.2	61.0	20.0	42.1	62.6	80.7	73.6	31.2	50.8
With radio	95.7	98.1	97.1	91.7	96.3	97.2	98.5	97.9	94.4	97.4
With television	12.0	22.3	11.4	4.6	9.1	15.7	24.8	15.0	6.8	11.5

Item	Rural Nonfarm					Farm				
	United States	North-east	North Central	South	West	United States	North-east	North Central	South	West
Total dwelling units (*thousands*)	10,056	2,175	2,920	3,618	1,344	6,358	524	2,152	3,072	609
Total occupied dwelling units (*thousands*)	8,613	1,720	2,524	3,347	1,123	5,721	456	1,979	2,767	518
Owner-occupied units as per cent of all occupied units	63.0	69.1	70.4	54.7	60.8	65.7	79.4	69.9	59.4	71.2
Average (Median) Characteristics										
Number of rooms per unit	4.6	5.3	4.8	4.1	3.9	5.2	6.8	6.0	4.4	4.5
Number of persons per unit	3.1	3.1	2.9	3.2	3.0	3.6	3.5	3.4	3.8	3.3
Monthly rent of nonfarm renter-occupied units	$21.67	$23.84	$24.39	$16.16	$31.02	—	—	—	—	—
Value of nonfarm owner-occupied 1-dwelling-unit structures	$4,878	$6,528	$4,906	$3,491	$5,479	—	—	—	—	—
Condition										
Per cent of all reporting units										
Over 30 years old	39.0	51.0	51.2	28.4	21.8	53.4	78.6	71.6	40.0	35.0
Dilapidated	13.4	6.9	8.6	21.6	12.1	19.5	9.8	9.9	28.9	14.1
Dilapidated or lacking flush toilet or private bath for exclusive use	50.0	35.9	52.9	64.4	37.2	74.6	50.0	71.4	86.3	47.9
With bathtub or shower for exclusive use	51.8	66.5	49.9	39.2	67.3	29.8	53.5	33.5	17.7	58.3
With flush toilet for exclusive use	53.5	70.7	53.0	38.7	66.9	27.7	54.9	31.2	15.3	54.9
With running water inside structure	68.0	84.3	67.2	53.5	83.1	42.7	75.5	47.8	27.8	72.8
With electric lighting	90.3	95.5	94.2	83.2	93.0	77.7	92.7	83.9	69.0	86.9
Per cent of reporting occupied units										
With mechanical refrigeration	72.3	83.9	77.5	61.8	73.1	62.7	78.4	73.7	49.8	75.5
With ice refrigeration	11.7	7.2	8.4	18.0	7.5	11.8	5.8	6.3	18.1	4.5
With gas or electric cooking fuel	59.6	63.6	70.7	47.0	64.8	38.7	44.5	52.8	24.3	55.8
With central heating	31.1	60.5	41.4	10.9	20.4	18.1	46.9	32.1	3.7	15.8
With radio	93.1	96.8	95.8	89.1	93.3	92.0	95.6	95.8	88.3	93.5
With television	5.9	13.3	6.1	2.7	3.0	2.7	8.5	3.2	1.6	2.2

Source: 1950 Census of Housing, Vol. I, General Characteristics.

Note: Discrepancies in addition are due to rounding.

worst in the South. Even in the Northeast, however, 4 per cent of the dwelling units were dilapidated in 1950. More than 6 per cent of the urban dwelling units in the Northeast, 10 per cent in the West, and 14 per cent in the North Central region lacked a private flush toilet in 1950, although the water closet began to be installed in American houses around 1810.[6] (See Table 79 and Figure 34.)

The "gospel of the bathtub" started before the Civil War, but even now 10 per cent of the urban dwelling units in the Northeast and in the West, and 18 per cent in the North Central region, have no private bath. On the other hand, electricity, which was introduced for home use in 1856, but was not widely available until after the turn of the century, is now in almost universal use in the cities of the United States. The mechanical refrigerator did not come into household use until after World War I, but today 86 per cent of urban homes have this equipment.

About 29 per cent of the urban dwelling units in the Northeast are single-family detached houses; 45 per cent are in other one-to-four-dwelling-unit structures. The urban home of the Northeast may have four, five or six rooms, and it is occupied by two or three persons. It was built before 1920 and is in much better condition than the typical farmhouse: only 4 per cent of the urban units are dilapidated, compared with 10 per cent of all farm units. It has running water, private flush toilet and a private bath. It also has central heating, a mechanical refrigerator, gas or electric cooking equipment, and a radio. Even as early as April 1950, there was one chance in four that it had a television set. The unit was rented by its occupants, who were being charged a monthly rental of $38.

The typical urban dwelling unit in the South is a single-family detached house. It has three to five rooms and is occupied by two or three persons. It is somewhat newer than its northeastern counterpart, since it was built in the 1920s, but the chances are almost three times as great that it is dilapidated. It is slightly less likely than the northeastern home to have the various plumbing, cooking and refrigeration equipment or a radio. There are equal chances that it has central heating, a heating stove with an outside flue, or a

heating stove without a flue. Gas is used as heating and cooking fuel. There is a 50-50 chance that the house is owned by its occupants. The typical owner-occupied home has a value of $6,800; the typical rented one rents for $33.

These generalizations do not tell the whole story, being limited by the inadequacy of data. Many houses which are not dilapidated and have reasonably adequate equipment are still undesirable places in which to live. These statistics tell us nothing about the units with insufficient light and air, or those which are improperly drained, or those within range of intolerable industrial smoke or odors, or those subjected to constant noise.

Comparisons with Other Countries

Comparisons of United States housing with that of other countries are difficult to make, for the available figures are seldom comparable. Rough international comparisons made about twenty years ago [7] showed this country to be far ahead of others in frequency of bathrooms, central heating and electricity. There is every reason to believe that we are still well in the lead in most items of housing equipment. In Sweden, for instance, 7 per cent of rural dwellings have bathtubs, whereas in the United States 30 per cent of rural farm and 52 per cent of rural nonfarm units have a private bathtub or shower. Central heating is found in only 25 per cent of Swedish rural homes, while in the northern part of the United States it is found in 34 per cent of farm homes and 50 per cent of rural nonfarm homes.[8]

Whether our houses are in a better state of repair than those of other countries is not too clear. If we count only those dwelling units defined by our Census as "dilapidated," about 10 per cent of our units are unhealthful and unsafe. Roughly half the countries for which information is available have smaller proportions of unhealthful and unsafe units and half greater proportions. If we were to add to our "dilapidated" units those houses which are so surrounded by substandard units as to be incapable of rehabilitation, our proportion of unhealthful and unsafe dwelling units would be 21 per cent, considerably above the percentage reported for most European countries. (See Table 80.) Although we have no

---

6. According to A. F. Bemis and John Burchard, "It became popular almost at once." See *The Evolving House,* Massachusetts Institute of Technology, Technology Press, Cambridge, 1933, Vol. I, p. 298.

7. *Ibid.,* Vol. II, pp. 79–82.
8. Unpublished data of the U.S. Housing and Home Finance Agency and the U.S. Bureau of the Census.

TABLE 80. COMPARISON OF HOUSING CONDITIONS IN SELECTED COUNTRIES, 1949–1950
(Number in Thousands)

Country	Total Dwelling Units	Overcrowded [a] Number	Overcrowded [a] Per Cent	Unhealthful and Unsafe [b] Number	Unhealthful and Unsafe [b] Per Cent
Austria	1,933.1	218.5	11	123.4	6
Australia	1,873.6	[e]	—	100.0	5
Belgium	2,438.2	115.0	5	66.0	3
Denmark	1,220.0	45.0	4	140.0	11
Greece	1,482.0	173.0	12	337.0	23
Italy	10,215.6	952.0	9	1,218.2	12
Netherlands	2,068.4	175.0	8	70.0	3
Norway	738.0	50.0	7	35.0	5
United Kingdom	13,104.3	1,010.1	8	1,387.4	11
United States	45,983.0	2,608.0	6	4,495.0–9,590.0	10–21

Sources: Australia — Commonwealth Statistics and Commonwealth Ministry of National Development; United States — Appendix 7–1 and Tables 78 and 88; all other countries — *The European Housing Problem, a Preliminary Review*, United Nations Economic Commission for Europe, Geneva, October 1949, Appendix I, Table 19.

a. For the United States the criterion is 1.5 persons per room; for all other countries it is the definition given in the English overcrowding law of 1936, which works out to almost 2 persons per room.

b. Australia — substandard. United States — the first figure is dilapidated units; the second figure includes also those so surrounded by substandard housing (defined as dilapidated or lacking hot water, private toilet or bath) as to be incapable of rehabilitation. All other countries—unhealthful dwellings incapable of being rendered satisfactory by the carrying out of repairs, plus unsafe dwellings.

c. Not available.

reliable information about relative standards of health and safety, they are very probably higher in the United States than in Europe.

Overcrowding has never been a continuing widespread problem in this country, but in Europe it has long been the crux of the housing problem. This is partly a result of the greater concentration of European population in cities, but the long cessation of housebuilding during World War I was a contributing cause. The devastation wrought during World War II, which halted the attempt begun in the period between wars to alleviate shortages, aggravated the problem more than ever. In 1949–1950 about 6 per cent of dwelling units in the United States were overcrowded; only Belgium and Denmark, among the European countries for which information is available, had less overcrowding. For the others, the proportion of overcrowded units ranged from 7 to 12 per cent.[9] (See Table 80.)

The International Labor Office has brought together estimates made in various countries of the number of new dwelling units required during the first postwar decade or two. The numbers of units needed annually per 10,000 people were set at the following levels: [10]

Australia	114
Argentina	113
United States	76–115
Sweden	71
Canada	62
New Zealand	59
Finland	56

Our needs apparently are greater than those of most other countries covered. These estimates, however, are based on shortages, qualitative inadequacies and population growth, and reflect national standards. Our needs, therefore, may be, and undoubtedly are, greater because we have been able to pitch our sights higher.

EXPENDITURES FOR HOUSING

Expenditures for housing are of two types: capital outlays to create shelter, that is, to construct new dwelling units and to make major additions and alterations to old ones; and con-

9. The standard of overcrowding was more stringent in the United States than in the other countries. (See Table 80, footnote *a*.)

10. *Housing Policy*, International Labor Office, Montreal, 1945, p. 23.

TABLE 81. CONSUMPTION EXPENDITURES FOR HOUSING, 1909–1952

	Amount (Millions)						Per Cent of Total Consumption Expenditures					
Year	Total Housing Expenditures	Rent and Imputed Rent	Fuel, Ice and Lighting Supplies	Electricity	Gas	Water	Total Housing Expenditures	Rent and Imputed Rent	Fuel, Ice and Lighting Supplies	Electricity	Gas	Water
1909	$ 6,910	$ 5,563	$ 985	$ 83	$ 139	$140	23.98	19.31	3.42	.29	.48	.48
1914	7,872	6,222	1,190	132	173	155	23.57	18.63	3.56	.40	.52	.46
1919	10,244	8,045	1,492	265	272	170	16.91	13.28	2.46	.44	.45	.28
1921	12,327	9,682	1,817	306	342	180	22.10	17.36	3.26	.55	.61	.32
1923	13,777	10,613	2,160	389	425	190	20.69	15.94	3.24	.58	.64	.29
1925	14,237	11,454	1,646	462	470	205	19.84	15.96	2.30	.64	.66	.28
1927	14,431	11,319	1,882	509	506	215	19.35	15.18	2.52	.68	.68	.29
1929	14,512	11,421	1,694	616	548	233	17.97	14.14	2.10	.76	.68	.29
1930	14,085	10,992	1,618	660	567	248	19.46	15.18	2.24	.91	.79	.34
1931	13,108	10,235	1,389	674	562	248	20.99	16.39	2.22	1.08	.90	.40
1932	11,611	8,964	1,208	662	544	233	23.17	17.89	2.41	1.32	1.09	.46
1933	10,451	7,849	1,228	645	504	225	22.55	16.94	2.65	1.39	1.09	.48
1934	10,314	7,538	1,349	671	504	252	19.88	14.53	2.60	1.29	.97	.49
1935	10,439	7,597	1,374	697	511	260	18.57	13.52	2.44	1.24	.91	.46
1936	10,910	7,882	1,509	726	520	273	17.45	12.61	2.41	1.16	.83	.44
1937	11,466	8,378	1,514	766	531	277	17.08	12.48	2.26	1.14	.79	.41
1938	11,736	8,733	1,391	810	528	274	18.19	13.54	2.15	1.26	.82	.42
1939	12,104	8,940	1,484	849	544	287	17.94	13.25	2.20	1.26	.81	.42
1940	12,652	9,217	1,650	910	584	291	17.56	12.79	2.29	1.26	.81	.41
1941	13,544	9,863	1,830	965	587	299	16.47	11.99	2.23	1.18	.71	.36
1942	14,631	10,594	2,075	1,017	633	312	16.05	11.62	2.28	1.12	.69	.34
1943	15,383	11,125	2,236	1,045	656	321	15.04	10.88	2.18	1.02	.64	.32
1944	16,092	11,702	2,256	1,125	673	336	14.43	10.49	2.02	1.01	.61	.30
1945	16,835	12,205	2,376	1,194	713	347	13.68	9.92	1.93	.97	.58	.28
1946	18,003	13,047	2,559	1,270	767	360	12.26	8.89	1.74	.86	.52	.25
1947	20,401	14,603	3,136	1,406	869	387	12.32	8.82	1.89	.85	.53	.23
1948	22,892	16,466	3,500	1,564	958	404	12.87	9.26	1.97	.88	.54	.22
1949	24,413	18,080	3,133	1,746	1,031	423	13.52	10.01	1.74	.97	.57	.23
1950	27,184	20,210	3,392	1,955	1,177	450	13.97	10.39	1.74	1.01	.60	.23
1951	29,335	21,874	3,465	2,190	1,336	470	14.10	10.51	1.67	1.05	.64	.23
1952	31,732	24,014	3,350	2,418	1,448	502	14.55	11.01	1.54	1.11	.66	.23

Sources: Appendices 4–4 and 4–5.

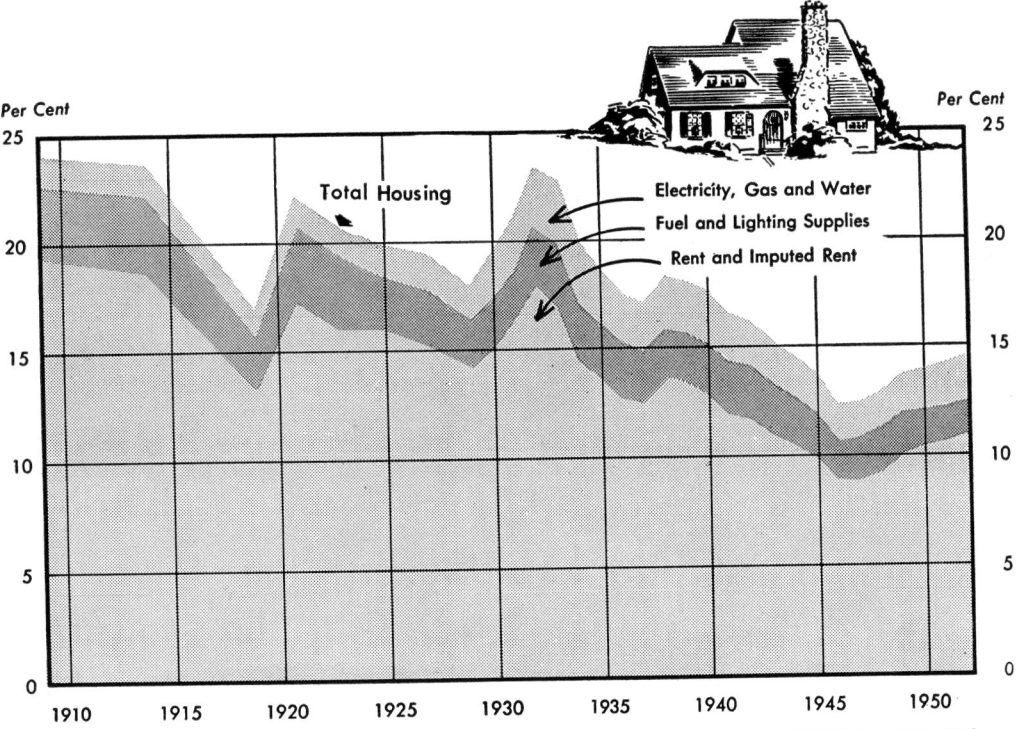

FIGURE 35. PER CENT OF TOTAL CONSUMPTION EXPENDITURES DEVOTED TO HOUSING, 1909–1952

Source: Table 81.

sumer expenditures for the service of shelter and for accompanying fuel and household utilities. During the 1920s, combined consumer and capital expenditures for housing amounted to somewhat over 20 per cent of the gross national product. In other words, over one fifth of our total production of finished goods and services was for the purpose of housing the population. During the 1930s this ratio declined to less than one sixth, and since World War II it has been around one seventh. We have thus been devoting progressively less of our resources to housing. In recent years the ratio of residential construction expenditures to gross national product was at least as high as ever, except for the mid-1920s. The consumption expenditures ratio, on the other hand, has shown a persistent long-term declining trend.

CONSUMPTION EXPENDITURES

During the years 1909–1952, shelter expenditures (rent and imputed rent) constituted about 14 per cent of the amount spent by consumers for all purposes, while utilities accounted for almost an additional 5 per cent. (See Table 81.) The share of consumption expenditures devoted to shelter declined sharply from more than 19 per cent in 1909 to 11 per cent in 1952, while utility, fuel and lighting expenditures declined from 4.7 per cent to 3.5 per cent. (See Figure 35.)

Trends

Consumer expenditures for shelter rose from less than $6 billion a year just before World War I to $11.5 billion in 1925, a figure which was not surpassed until 1944; thereafter the outlay increased rapidly to $24 billion in 1952. Fuel and utilities expenditures by consumers rose from $1.3 billion in 1909 to an average of $3 billion during the interwar period, and climbed steadily thereafter to a level of $7.7 billion in 1952. Thus, the total consumer housing bill rose from $6.9 billion in 1909 to $14.5 billion in 1929 and $31.7 billion in 1952. During most of this period the cost of fuel and utilities fluctuated at between 4 and 5 per cent of the total amount spent by consumers for all purposes, but it has remained below 4 per cent since 1944. On the other hand, shelter expenditures (rent and imputed rent) showed a marked downward trend from almost one fifth of the total before World War I to about one sixth in the 1920s, one eighth in the 1930s, and about one tenth in recent years.

This long-run tendency for shelter expenditures alone to become less important in the consumer's budget is a reflection of our rising standard of living. Once the most urgent food, clothing and shelter needs are met, it becomes increasingly possible to satisfy other wants. Consequently, as real income rises, a smaller portion of each successive addition to income goes for necessities. With the long-run rise in the American standard of living, therefore, an increasing share of consumer expenditures has been diverted to leisure-time activities — recreation and pleasure travel, sports clothes and the like — and a decreasing share has been devoted to shelter and other necessities.

The relatively high proportion of expenditures going for shelter during 1931–1933 was mainly the result of declines in income during the depression. Similarly, the low proportion in recent years resulted from high levels of employment and income. Rent control accentuated the decline in the ratio during and after the war.

Although the percentage of consumer expenditures going for fuel and utilities combined has also declined, it is doubtful whether this decline represents a long-run shift in the consumption pattern. The drop since 1944 may be the result of smaller increases in the prices of fuel and utilities than in prices of other consumer items.[11] This may well have led to newly established price relationships, which will maintain the existing ratios for a time.

Of the utility components, the consumer water bill has grown at a slow but steady pace, somewhat similar to population growth, but at a lesser rate than total consumer expenditures. The ratio of fuel expenditures to total consumer expenditures has shown a slow long-term decline. The proportion of consumer expenditures going for electricity rose steadily until 1940, fell during the 1940s and began a slight upward trend in 1950. Gas has followed a similar course. While electricity has been substituted for gas in lighting,

gas has been substituted for other fuels in heating. What happens in the future will depend largely on energy resources and on the degree to which increasingly costly sources of supply will have to be tapped. In this respect electricity is in the most favorable position since it is produced from coal and water power, while fuel oil is in the least favorable situation because of the rapidity with which low-cost deposits are being used up.

Variations with Income

The lowest income groups spend a very large proportion of their income for housing; the proportion decreases as the income level rises. In 1935–1936, rent and imputed rent constituted almost one third of money and imputed income in the "under $500" income group, dropped to about one fifth in the $500–$750 income group, and then declined more slowly to less than one tenth in the "over $15,000" group.[12] Data for 1941, relating to money income and money expenditures only, show the same general picture. Rent, fuel and utilities combined constituted about one fifth of income in the case of the "under $500" money-income class in 1941, and were less than one tenth in the "over $5,000" class.[13] A similar pattern prevailed during the war and again in the postwar period; the ratios in metropolitan areas in 1949 were two fifths for families with incomes under $3,000, about one fourth for the $3,000–$5,000 income range, and one fifth for the $5,000–$10,000 income bracket.[14]

The ratio of rent and imputed rent to total consumer expenditures does not vary with income to the same extent as does the rent-income ratio. This is of course due to the fact that savings increase steadily as income increases. In 1935–

11. The consumers' price index for all items rose 37 per cent between 1944 and 1950, while the index for utilities and fuel went up only 28 per cent.

12. *Consumer Expenditures in the United States*, National Resources Committee, 1939, Appendix A, Tables 6A and 21A, pp. 78 and 84.

13. *Spending and Saving of the Nation's Families in Wartime*, Bulletin No. 723, U.S. Bureau of Labor Statistics, 1942, Table 8A, p. 20. The proportion of income devoted to shelter as shown by the 1941 data is much smaller than that shown by the 1935–1936 data because nonmonetary income is so important to low income groups and because imputed rent is important to all income groups. For the same reasons the proportions used for shelter did not decline so precipitously with increased income in 1941 as in 1935–1936.

14. "Expenditures and Savings of City Families in 1944," *Monthly Labor Review*, January 1946; "Family Spending for Housing in Three Cities, 1947," *ibid.*, October 1949; "Family Income and New Rental Housing," *ibid.*, July 1951; and *Fourth Annual Report, 1950*, U.S. Housing and Home Finance Agency, pp. 274 and 277.

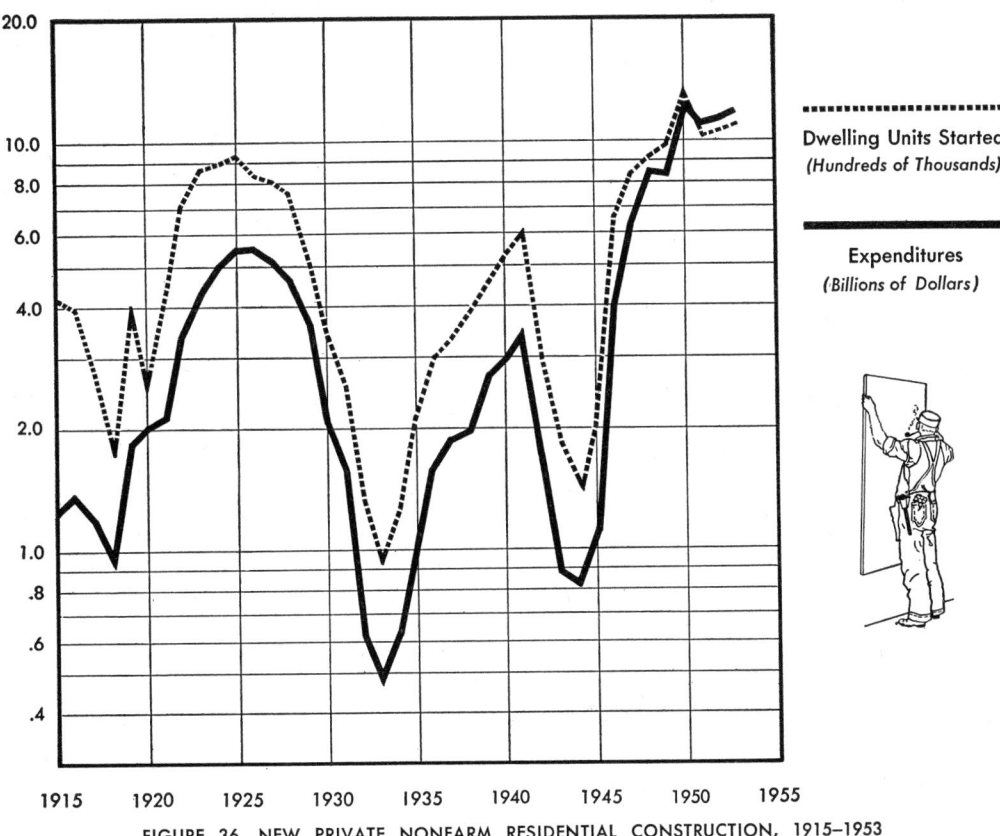

FIGURE 36. NEW PRIVATE NONFARM RESIDENTIAL CONSTRUCTION, 1915–1953

Sources: Tables 82 and 83 and U.S. Departments of Commerce and Labor.

1936 the lower third of the population devoted 21 per cent of total expenditures to housing and the upper third 18 per cent.[15] In 1944 the variation was wider, but not nearly so wide as it was for the rent-income ratio.[16]

Urban families spend a larger proportion of their incomes for housing than do rural nonfarm families, and these in turn spend a larger proportion than farm families.[17] Differences in land costs and in standards are chiefly responsible for these variations.

Rent and imputed rent represents a smaller proportion of total income for Negro families than for white ones in the South. However, in large northern cities the situation is reversed because of the shortage of dwellings available for Negro occupancy.[18]

CAPITAL EXPENDITURES

For the three decades beginning with 1920, residental construction expenditures averaged 22 per cent of all expenditures for capital goods and 38 per cent of all construction expenditures.

Capital expenditures for residential construction have varied enormously from year to year — from peaks of $5.7 billion, $9.5 billion and $13.7 billion in 1926, 1948 and 1950 to a low of $0.5 billion in 1933. Maintenance and repair expenditures have not fluctuated so markedly, but have shown a far more definite upward trend. From $0.6 billion in 1915 they rose to a peak of $1.4 billion in 1929, and after a depression low of

---

15. *Consumer Expenditures in the United States*, pp. 78, 79 and 84.
16. "Expenditures and Savings of City Families in 1944."
17. *Income and Spending and Saving of City Families in Wartime*, Bulletin No. 724, U.S. Bureau of Labor Statistics, 1942, Table 10, p. 14; *Spending and Saving of the Nation's Families in Wartime*; and *Consumer Expenditures in the United States*.

18. *Family Expenditures in the United States*, National Resources Planning Board, June 1941, Table 28, p. 10, and Tables 58 and 59, p. 19.

TABLE 82. RESIDENTIAL CONSTRUCTION EXPENDITURES, 1915–1952
(*Millions*)

Year	Total	New Construction					Maintenance and Repairs	
		Private Nonfarm			Private Farm	Public	Nonfarm	Farm
		Dwelling Units	Additions and Alterations	Nonhouse-keeping				
1915	$1,329	$1,040	$140	$ 40	$109	—	$ 506	$ 86
1916	1,529	1,170	145	60	154	—	521	91
1917	1,389	1,000	125	65	199	—	551	101
1918	1,146	760	110	45	203	$28	565	107
1919	2,137	1,645	130	75	273	14	595	122
1920	2,281	1,710	175	130	266	—	625	89
1921	2,203	1,795	185	125	98	—	670	72
1922	3,479	2,955	200	205	119	—	714	83
1923	4,542	3,960	210	230	142	—	759	130
1924	5,193	4,575	230	255	133	—	833	126
1925	5,656	4,910	250	355	141	—	908	121
1926	5,737	4,920	270	410	137	—	982	117
1927	5,320	4,540	290	330	160	—	1,056	127
1928	4,926	4,195	315	260	156	—	1,131	122
1929	3,772	3,040	340	245	147	—	1,222	136
1930	2,182	1,570	305	200	107	—	1,111	92
1931	1,624	1,320	175	70	59	—	959	69
1932	654	485	105	40	24	—	752	45
1933	499	290	145	35	29	—	728	66
1934	662	380	200	45	36	1	837	84
1935	1,080	710	250	50	61	9	909	114
1936	1,702	1,210	295	60	76	61	1,066	114
1937	2,068	1,475	320	80	100	93	1,154	123
1938	2,104	1,620	295	75	79	35	1,068	118
1939	2,851	2,270	320	90	106	65	1,154	129
1940	3,330	2,560	335	90	145	200	1,256	140
1941	4,122	3,040	375	95	182	430	1,333	175
1942	2,395	1,440	225	50	135	545	1,232	165
1943	1,745	710	160	15	121	739	1,111	182
1944	1,134	570	220	25	108	211	1,105	162
1945	1,280	720	340	40	100	80	1,188	151
1946	4,798	3,300	570	145	409	374	1,960	286
1947	7,193	5,450	735	125	683	200	2,850	184
1948	9,474	7,500	925	155	738	156	3,360	200
1949	9,321	7,257	825	185	695	359	3,460	188
1950	13,708	11,525	900	175	763	345	3,700	208
1951	12,339	9,849	934	190	771	595	3,840	200
1952	12,504	9,870	1,045	185	750	654	3,990	200

Source: Construction and Building Materials, U.S. Department of Commerce, May 1953.

$0.8 billion in 1933 they rose again to $1.5 billion in 1941 and $3.9 billion in 1950. To some extent expenditures for maintenance and repair have compensated for the wider fluctuations in total capital outlays, as have expenditures for additions and alterations, which also showed a definite upward trend over the entire period. (See Table 82 and Figure 36.)

Sufficiency of Housing Units

It is difficult to judge the adequacy of these expenditures for the fulfillment of housing needs.

TABLE 83. NEW PERMANENT NONFARM DWELLING UNITS STARTED, 1900–1952
(*Thousands*)

Year	Total	Urban	Rural Nonfarm	Private	Public [a]
1900	204	149	55	204	—
1901	303	191	112	303	—
1902	327	176	151	327	—
1903	411	191	220	411	—
1904	416	256	160	416	—
1905	459	288	171	459	—
1906	464	302	162	464	—
1907	433	284	149	433	—
1908	438	277	161	438	—
1909	573	380	193	573	—
1910	505	382	123	505	—
1911	501	376	125	501	—
1912	476	350	126	476	—
1913	435	318	117	435	—
1914	414	323	91	414	—
1915	414	364	50	414	—
1916	394	364	30	394	—
1917	277	180	97	277	—
1918	174	79	95	174	—
1919	405	303	102	405	—
1920	247	196	51	247	—
1921	449	359	90	449	—
1922	716	574	142	716	—
1923	871	698	173	871	—
1924	893	716	177	893	—
1925	937	752	185	937	—
1926	849	681	168	849	—
1927	810	643	167	810	—
1928	753	594	159	753	—
1929	509	400	109	509	—
1930	330	236	94	330	—
1931	254	174	80	254	—
1932	134	64	70	134	—
1933	93	45	48	93	—
1934	126	49	77	126	—
1935	221	106	115	216	5
1936	319	211	108	304	15
1937	336	218	118	332	4
1938	406	262	144	399	7
1939	515	359	156	459	56
1940	603	397	206	530	73
1941	706	434	272	619	87
1942	356	227	129	301	55
1943	191	124	67	184	7
1944	142	96	46	139	3
1945	209	134	75	208	1
1946	671	404	267	663	8
1947	849	480	369	846	3
1948	932	525	407	914	18
1949	1,025	589	436	989	36
1950	1,396	828	568	1,353	44
1951	1,091	595	496	1,020	71
1952	1,127	610	517	1,069	59

Sources: 1900–1919, Miles L. Colean, *American Housing: Problems and Prospects,* Twentieth Century Fund, New York, 1944, p. 364; 1920–1950, *Construction, Annual Review, 1950,* Bulletin No. 1047, U.S. Bureau of Labor Statistics, Table 1, p. 3; 1951–1952, *Monthly Labor Review,* November 1953, Table F–5.

a. Excludes 5,998 permanent dwelling units completed during 1918–1919 by the U.S. Housing Corporation and 182,138 units built by the federal government during World War II.

TABLE 84. INCREASE IN NONFARM DWELLING UNITS COMPARED WITH INCREASE
IN NONFARM HOUSEHOLDS AND POPULATION, 1900–1949
(*Thousands*)

	1900–1909	1910–1919	1920–1929	1930–1939	1940–1949
1. Permanent units started	4,028	3,995	7,034	2,734	5,683
2. Increase in dwelling unit inventory	3,736	3,579	6,580	4,014	9,633
3. Additions to households	3,858	3,469	5,700	4,448	9,079
4. Additions to population	14,454	14,201	18,300	8,836	25,083
Ratios:					
1 ÷ 3	1.04	1.15	1.23	.61	.63
2 ÷ 3	.97	1.03	1.15	.90	1.06
4 ÷ 1	3.58	3.55	2.60	3.23	4.41
4 ÷ 2	3.87	3.97	2.78	2.20	2.60

Sources:

1. Table 83.
2. Table 77.
3. *1950 Census of Housing*, Vol. I, *General Charac-teristics*, Chapter 1, Table J, p. 28, 1953, with adjustment in 1950 figures for change in urban and farm definitions.
4. 1910 to 1940 from *Historical Statistics of the United States, 1789–1945*, U.S. Bureau of the Cen-

sus, 1949, Series B 166 and 168; 1950 from *1950 Census of Population*, Part 1, Vol. II, Table 34, with adjustment for change in urban and farm definitions; 1900–1909 based on a rough estimate for 1900. Urban farms are included in figures for 1920–1949; excluded from figures for earlier years. Exclusion of urban farms uniformly in all years would not change the derived ratios significantly.

As might be expected, the number of new dwelling units has fluctuated just as violently as the outlays — from 937,000 nonfarm units started in 1925, a peak which was not surpassed until 1949, to a low point of 93,000 in 1933 and a new peak of 1.4 million in 1950. (See Table 83 and Figure 36.)

Permanent dwelling units added to the supply of nonfarm housing probably just about kept pace with the increase in the number of nonfarm households during the first two decades of the century, undoubtedly exceeded the increase in the number of households in the third decade by a comfortable margin, and fell a bit short thereafter. (See Table 84.) By definition, however, the term "household" tends to be equated with "occupied dwelling unit." When the number of permanent dwelling units started is compared with the increase in population instead, it appears that our nonfarm housing supply became increasingly more adequate during the first three decades of this century and less adequate thereafter. For each new permanent nonfarm unit started, the nonfarm population increased by 3.58 persons in the 1900–1909 decade, by 3.55 persons in the 1910–1919 decade, and by 2.60 persons in the 1920–1929 decade. The ratio of population growth to new units added then

rose to 3.23 in 1930–1939 and 4.41 in 1940–1949. (See Table 84.) Although the size of families decreased during the first three decades, so that more housing was required per person, the increase in housing supply was more than large enough to allow for this factor.

On a purely numerical basis (i.e., units started plus converted and makeshift units less demolitions), the relationship of our housing supply to population continued to improve through the 1930–1939 decade. The ratio of population growth to the increase in inventory dropped from 3.87 persons per unit in the years 1900–1909 and 3.97 in the next decade to 2.20 in the 1930–1939 decade. Moreover, this ratio during the 1940–1949 period was lower than in the first three decades of the century. A large part of the numerical increase, however, consisted of makeshift units which add nothing to our real housing supply. Their inclusion in the inventory gives an overly optimistic picture. In the 1930–1939 decade almost one fourth of the net additions consisted of makeshift units. During the 1940–1949 decade a substantial volume of temporary war housing was built, and much of it is still in existence. If these temporary units are excluded, our needs, as measured by the ratio of population additions to new permanent units started, were most ade-

TABLE 85. VALUE OF NONFARM HOUSING INVENTORY AND EXPENDITURES FOR
ADDITIONS AND ALTERATIONS AND FOR MAINTENANCE AND REPAIRS,
SELECTED YEARS, 1915–1949
(*Dollar Amounts in Millions*)

| Year | Value of Structures | Expenditures | | | |
| | | Additions and Alterations | | Maintenance and Repairs | |
		Amount	Per Cent of Value	Amount	Per Cent of Value
Average, 1915–1949	—	—	.33	—	1.29
1915	$ 29,100	$140	.48	$ 506	1.74
1920	60,400	175	.29	625	1.03
1925	72,600	250	.34	908	1.25
1930	85,100	305	.36	1,111	1.30
1935	70,200	250	.36	909	1.29
1940	92,500	335	.36	1,256	1.36
1945	124,600	340	.29	1,188	.95
1946	147,000	570	.39	1,960	1.33
1947	174,500	735	.42	2,850	1.63
1948	187,600	925	.49	3,360	1.79
1949	195,100	825	.42	3,460	1.77

Sources: Raymond W. Goldsmith, *A Study of Saving in the United States*, Princeton University Press, 1954, Vol. 3, Table W–1; and Table 82.

quately met during the 1920–1929 decade and least adequately met during the years 1940–1949. (Table 84.)

While the number of dwelling units started and expenditures for their construction both rose considerably, following much the same wide cyclical swings, between 1915 and 1952, the rise in outlays greatly exceeded the rise in number of units started. Expenditures for new private nonfarm residential construction in 1952 were nine times as high as in 1915, whereas the number of units started was only two and a half times as great. (See Figure 36.)

Condition of Housing

Even if our capital expenditures were sufficient to provide enough accommodations for the increase in population, the question still remains: Have we spent enough on our existing housing supply to offset depreciation and to keep it in good condition?

The average dwelling unit may be assumed to have a forty-year life span, or an annual depreciation rate of 2.5 per cent on original cost.[19] On the

further assumption that the average house in existence is twenty years old and therefore has lost half its value, the depreciation rate applicable to the current value is 5 per cent. This is the expenditure rate necessary if obsolete facilities are to be replaced or modernized. During the period 1915–1949, however, we spent for additions and alterations an average of only 0.3 per cent of the current value of existing nonfarm housing — clearly not enough to offset obsolescence. Moreover, only part of these expenditures went for modernization; the rest were used to add to the housing supply through conversions. (See Table 85.)

Maintenance and repair expenditures averaged 1.3 per cent of the current value of our nonfarm housing for the period 1915–1949. An average of one per cent of original cost probably needs to be spent annually to keep our housing in good shape; [20] hence if the existing housing is at any given time worth half its original cost, maintenance and repair outlays of 2 per cent of current value are required. Thus we have done a far better job of maintaining than of modernizing our housing, but our expenditures for this purpose also have been insufficient.

19. This is in line with the rates allowed by the U.S. Bureau of Internal Revenue in *Bulletin "F," Income Tax Depreciation and Obsolescence, Estimated Useful Lives and Depreciation Rates* (revised January 1942).

20. This figure is a common rule of thumb.

TECHNOLOGICAL CHANGES

Technological changes in housing are of two kinds: changes in the character and design of structures, and changes in the methods of their production. The first are attempts to find the technical means for meeting people's needs as they are modified by changes in the physical, social and economic environment. The objective of the second is to produce these technical means as efficiently and cheaply as possible.

The environment, housing needs, the house and methods of construction are in a continuous process of change, one acting upon the other. Thus the industrial revolution resulted in an ever-increasing concentration of population in urban areas, and with congestion, effective sanitation became imperative if epidemics were to be controlled. Techniques of water supply and sewage disposal were developed, and as the wealth resulting from industrial expansion made it economically feasible to apply them on a wide scale, the invention of indoor sanitary installations followed. Rising incomes led to a widespread demand for plumbing equipment and this in turn to its mass production. The water closet, the bath, the washing machine and the dishwasher were added to homes as people recognized their importance for health, cleanliness and the avoidance of household drudgery. Today plumbing is an integral part of the house, comprising perhaps 12 per cent of its total construction cost.

EQUIPMENT

Plumbing, heating and electrical installation and equipment together account for over 20 per cent of the construction cost of today's house.[21] The addition of this equipment is the great change that has occurred in the character of the house over the decades.

The bathtub, once portable, for some time now has been standard fixed equipment, progressively becoming less expensive and easier to clean and maintain. It has been complemented by the shower, either as a separate installation or combined with the bathtub. In some instances it has been displaced by the shower. These and other devices for personal cleanliness have gradually been improved in design, and will probably be still further improved for greater sanitation and convenience.[22]

Temperature Control

In the nineteenth century the wood-burning fireplace was replaced by the coal grate and that in turn by the stove. Finally, with the furnace, homes became centrally heated. At first massive and difficult to operate, the furnace has been gradually reduced in size, improved in efficiency and equipped with automatic controls. Recently other heating devices have been developed, such as the heat pump, which utilizes heat from the earth or the outside air, and electrically heated radiant panels. Both eliminate the problem not only of fuel storage but also of smoke, soot and fumes. Insulation of walls and roofs has helped considerably in controlling temperature, and air conditioning has been a boon in summer.

We are still far from being able to create a really satisfactory thermal environment for the human body, but collaboration between the physiologist and the engineer has greatly increased our understanding of the problem. Gradually their research will be translated into new and better devices for controlling humidity and temperature so that our houses may be healthier and more comfortable in both summer and winter.

Electrification

Household illumination progressed from candles to kerosene, to gas and finally to electricity. Electric lamps are still being improved to provide more and better light. Here, too, collaboration between physiologist and engineer is leading to significant results.

Electricity and, to a lesser extent, gas have made possible the development of all the mechanical equipment which in a few decades has gone far toward revolutionizing kitchen, laundry and housecleaning activities. In recent years the kitchen and its equipment have undergone a scientific redesign which is reminiscent of the early work of efficiency engineers in industry. For the housewife this has meant a better utilization of space and a smoother sequence of operations.

21. *High Cost of Housing*, Joint Committee on Housing, 80th Cong., 1st sess., 1948, pp. 47–53, especially Tables 21 and 22.

22. For possibilities along these lines see James Marston Fitch, *American Building*, Houghton Mifflin, Boston, 1948, pp. 283–286.

Packaged Units

All this added equipment has made the house more costly to produce. But as the various appliances became necessities and mass markets for them developed, mass-production techniques were used in their manufacture, their costs and selling prices were reduced and their use increased. The result has been lighter, more compact and more efficient equipment. Lately some manufacturers have created "packaged" bathroom and kitchen units, produced in the factory and ready for installation with a minimum of site labor. The best-known of these is Buckminster Fuller's one-piece stamped bathroom, which weighs only 535 pounds. So far, however, manufacturers of packaged units have not been able to secure a strong position in the equipment market.

Gains of the Last Decade

Despite the disruption in home building caused by World War II, tremendous strides were made in the equipment of the American home during the 1940s. While the great era of plumbing installation occurred some decades ago, the number of dwelling units with running water increased by 45 per cent between 1940 and 1950, the number with private flush toilet by 47 per cent and the number with private bath by 51 per cent, though the total number of dwelling units increased by only 23 per cent. The percentages of dwelling units lacking each of these items of equipment declined by about one third during the decade. In spite of an increase of 8.7 million in the total number of dwelling units, there was an actual decrease in the number that lacked running water, private flush toilet or private bath. (See Table 78.)

The gain in plumbing equipment occurred almost solely in rural farm areas. While the number of dwellings lacking a private indoor flush toilet declined by 1.9 million for the United States as a whole, there was a decrease of 2.2 million among rural farm dwellings and an increase of 300,000 nonfarm dwellings lacking this facility. All but 59,000 of the 2.3-million-unit decline in dwellings lacking a private bath or shower occurred among rural farm dwellings. (See Table 78.)

The proportion of occupied dwelling units with central heating increased from 42 per cent to 50 per cent during the decade. The increase in automatic heating was even more impressive. In 1940 little more than one fifth of all dwelling units with central heating used gas or liquid fuel; by 1950 the proportion had risen to more than one half. In 1950 nearly 6 million units burned gas in central heating — more than five times as many as in 1940.

Electric lighting and electric equipment also made tremendous gains during the decade. The number of dwelling units without electric lighting decreased by two thirds, as did the number without a radio. In 1950 only 6 per cent of all dwelling units lacked electric lighting and only 4.3 per cent of occupied dwelling units lacked a radio. Electric refrigerators, which were introduced only about thirty years ago, were in 15.1 million homes, or 44 per cent of the total, by 1940, and in 33.7 million homes, or 80 per cent of the total, by 1950. Electricity was used as cooking fuel in 6.3 million homes in 1950 — more than three times the number using it in 1940.

FUNCTIONAL DESIGN

Equipment has not only increased the cost of the house directly; it has also done so indirectly by requiring its own additional space. To keep down construction costs (which include costs of equipment and its installation), the over-all space within the dwelling has been reduced. This space reduction has been a major reason for attempts at optimum utilization of total dwelling space in architectural design. At the same time the increasing efficiency of equipment has made such attempts successful.

At first, space was simply traded for equipment. Rooms were made smaller and were reduced in number. The parlor and the pantry were eliminated. The dining room became a breakfast nook. The spacious hallway was pared down to a mere passageway or eliminated altogether. Storage space was reduced to a minimum. Ultimately the space-savers evolved the "efficiency apartment," a dwelling conceived merely as a headquarters and not as the center of the main activities of life.

This concept hardly constituted an adequate basis for family life, but the hard fact of space costs remained. The architect therefore turned his attention to the rational organization of minimum space so as to achieve compactness and a smooth relationship among the various functions of the dwelling without sacrificing comfort.

Our postwar housing construction has succeeded admirably in compressing the essentials into a minimum of space, but much (if not the bulk) of that construction has failed to organize the space properly. Even where the space-rationalizers have been at work, the results have seldom been really satisfactory, except perhaps in the more expensive housing. One of the few investigations into the adequacy of our housing for family living found two major fallacies in space planning:

(1) The failure to realize that family possessions are not of minimum sizes and cannot be accommodated in minimum spaces; and
(2) that the equipment requirements for household operations are far greater than the storage spaces provided. Inventories of family possessions with dimension specifications are guides only and some flexibility in space provided is necessary for the occasional extra item needed.[23]

Effective rationalization of dwelling space cannot be achieved without more space than is now being provided. The Housing and Home Finance Agency of the federal government, well aware of this, is promoting more spacious home planning.[24]

CONTROL OF THE ENVIRONMENT

The modern home designer is interested not only in the interrelation of space within the dwelling but also in the orientation of the structure and its parts with respect to prevailing winds, sun, view, noise, privacy, access and the like. He is paying more attention to adapting the house to its site and taking advantage of favorable site features. The physical setting is becoming an increasingly significant part of the whole. Houses are more and more opening themselves up to the outside and bringing it inside so that the line of demarcation between them is breaking down. This trend is an excellent example of the interaction of technical developments and changes in design.

The movement to the suburbs marked the beginning of a revolution in land-planning techniques. At first the suburbs merely reproduced the urban gridiron street pattern and crowding

of land. But later, and during the 1930s especially, more open methods of land utilization appeared with increasing frequency. The federal government played an important role in this development, particularly through the Federal Housing Administration, which has paid considerable attention to location and site planning. Its practices have spread and greatly influenced the character of new housing financed by mortgage-lending institutions. Public housing projects with their low land coverage are impressive demonstrations of the feasibility of providing adequate light, air, comfort and community facilities in large housing developments. Moreover, the apartment building, which has been built upward because of high land costs and scarcity of close-in land, began to move to the suburbs in the 1930s and to flatten out into the garden type of multiple dwelling.

As long as the suburb is merely a dormitory extension of the central city, a premium is placed on land nearest that center and crowding merely pushes outward. Lately, however, the tendency toward urban sprawl has begun to give way to a definite urban decentralization. Commercial and industrial functions of the city have accompanied and even led the residential movement outward. Large department stores have established branches in satellite communities. Shopping centers providing a wide variety of consumer goods and services have sprung up or been planned in conjunction with new communities. Industry, too, has fled the urban land congestion which increases costs, reduces efficiency and fails to attract labor. People living in or moving to outlying areas are finding opportunities for employment, shopping and recreation nearer their homes. There is less need to live within easy commuting distance of the central city.

The incentive to crowd the land is greatly reduced where acreage is plentiful and cheap. As a result, it has become economically possible to plan communities with large lots and adequate open space for other than the highest income groups.

The tendency toward decentralization is bound to become increasingly significant. It can bring about a reversal of the age-long trend toward greater and greater land congestion, and in so doing can recreate the conditions for community life.

23. *The Livability Problems of 1,000 Families,* Bulletin No. 28, Federal Public Housing Authority, October 1, 1945, p. 67.
24. See *Greater Livability at Small Additional Cost,* Technical Bulletin No. 16, November 1950.

Since the early 1930s the housebuilding industry has been continually criticized as lagging behind the rest of American industry in its technical achievements. During the 1920s, however, builders of large apartment houses made significant progress in the integration of operations, in the efficient handling of materials, and in the use of mechanical equipment and even assembly line methods. Today the so-called operative builder who constructs a number of houses on one site, the producer of garden apartments and the builder of large public housing projects are all able to use mass-production techniques. No one can doubt the progress made toward mechanization and job specialization, expansion of new markets and fabrication of new equipment. Yet the complaint that today's houses are put together largely by hand is still well founded, for the bulk of our housing is still erected by small builders who put up only one or two dwelling units a year.

Technological change in the industry has followed a familiar path. Before the Civil War the contractor supplied only the labor and the owner organized the work. But with the expansion of markets, a new pattern emerged which by and large still prevails — division and specialization of labor, with contractors and independent subcontractors supplying materials as well as labor, and the former in the role of small producers making a custom-made product. The emergence of large-scale construction (both for speculation and sale rather than on order, and for rental) has begun to displace the subcontractor or to subordinate him to the builder, who preplans and organizes a highly rationalized system of closely integrated operations, instead of trying to dovetail a number of separate isolated steps under different supervision.

Large-scale housing construction is an assembly line process which may take two forms — factory prefabrication of more or less complete dwelling units ready for trucking to the site and quick erection, or fabrication on the site of parts and components which are then put together by specialized crews who move from house to house according to a precise order and timing. A housebuilding industry completely mechanized in this manner, however, is still a thing of the future. Much of the industry is still small in scale, utilizing highly skilled labor performing handicraft operations.

Standardization

The degree to which mass production is feasible depends upon the extent to which standardization has occurred. Standardization of parts is a first step in this direction. During the 1920s the federal government's National Bureau of Standards promoted reduction of the number and sizes of various types of building materials from brick to roofing slate and metal laths. Correlation of shapes and sizes of building materials followed. These movements have cut down waste and labor time and have made possible a better product.

The standardized dwelling unit has been a more recent development. Repeated use of similar plans has enabled builders to cut down the cost of design, estimate materials more accurately, and take advantage of bulk buying. Labor efficiency has been improved as well, through repetitive operations.

Standardization has permitted factory production of stairways, doors and door frames, windows and window frames, and many other items. Development of new building materials such as pressed boards, which can be made into large panels, has also facilitated factory production. Prefabrication of parts has reached the point where factories produce packages of precut and partly assembled materials sufficient to erect the shell of a house without further cutting or subassembly. Some factories produce a package so complete it includes everything but land and foundations — in short, a prefabricated house.

The Prefabricated House

Prefabrication had been talked about for years, but a prefabricated dwelling comparable to the traditional house did not become economically feasible until lightweight, weather-resistant structural panels were invented. The earliest precut houses were summer cottages, mere shells without equipment. The first true factory-produced houses, requiring less skill and time to erect than site-built structures, began to appear on the market in the late 1930s. By the end of the 1930s the crucial technical problems connected with prefabrication were well on the way to solution, but hardly more than the first faint glimmering of a prefabricated-housing market was in view.

When the defense program in 1940 made it necessary for houses to be erected quickly and cheaply in centers of war industry, the conditions were created for the extensive utilization of mass-production techniques, including factory production, assembly line methods and field fabrication. The housebuilding industry seemed about to be revolutionized.

But during 1942 these high hopes were somewhat dimmed. The prefabricators had overestimated their capacity and ability. In addition, scarcities of materials began to develop, resulting in a lowering of quality and an increase in costs. With the limitation of materials and the necessity of reducing the size of developments, assembly line methods and prefabrication on the site also suffered setbacks.

A vicious circle thus prevented full realization of the advantages of mass production. Costs could not be reduced until volume was attained; volume could not be attained until costs were brought within the reach of the mass market. Yet the war advanced the idea of simplification and standardization of housebuilding. The elimination of high-priced building and the scarcity of materials taught builders a new economy of means and of operations. Builders who were unable to gear their activities to the production of inexpensive houses were forced out of the housebuilding field.

The prefabricated house, however, is not yet any cheaper than the conventionally built one. At its present stage of development, it still involves a good deal of site labor. At best, erection costs still constitute about 25 per cent of total costs, exclusive of land. Technically it is possible to reduce this percentage and to cut down total costs.

Cost, however, is not the main problem facing the prefabricated-house industry. The real difficulty is distribution. Building code restrictions are part of the problem, as is also the effective opposition of producers of conventional housing and associated products. Another aspect is the failure of the prefabricator adequately to finance his operations and develop effective marketing techniques.

The large-scale builder has been more successful in lowering housebuilding costs. Combining land development with building, he has the cost advantage of large-scale buying and the ability effectively to utilize techniques of mechanized production. Since volume and continuity are necessary to his success, his activities are confined to the larger urban areas.

Great technological advances have been and are being made in housebuilding. Only their diffusion through the industry has been slow; there is a sizable gap between knowledge and practice. Thus the direction of change seems clear, but its timing is uncertain.

HOUSING NEEDS

Much of our housing is inadequate. A large amount ought to be torn down and replaced, while a substantial proportion ought to be rehabilitated. But it is far from clear exactly how much should go, how much should be refurbished and how much could be left untouched. We need much more comprehensive and precise information about the condition of the country's housing. Moreover, we still are far from being able to arrive at a scientific and objective statement of what constitutes "adequacy" in a house. It is possible, however, to establish tentative standards on the basis of which an estimate of our housing needs may be made.

STANDARDS

A housing standard must be set in terms of human needs. Without a clear knowledge of these needs, it may be possible to establish standards, but not to judge their validity. No completely satisfactory calculation of housing needs can therefore be made unless we first have a quantitative measurement of the extent to which existing housing meets human needs. Thus human needs should set standards, and they in turn will determine the kinds and amounts of housing needed. Not all measurements of housing adequacy, however, can be stated in definite quantitative terms. Qualitative criteria such as provision for admission of direct sunlight or for aesthetic satisfaction must be utilized because so far we have been unable to formulate precise standards about these and numerous other matters.

Ideally, to arrive at housing needs we should:

(1) set forth the basic human physical, social, health and psychological needs which housing can take care of, in as comprehensive and objective a manner as possible

(2) translate these basic needs into more precise and detailed requirements

(3) scientifically determine the housing means, i.e., housing standards, most conducive to these requirements; and

(4) apply these standards to the existing housing stock to determine in what ways and to what extent it falls short of the standards.

In practice, we cannot come very close to this ideal at present. No analysis of the basic human needs has been made. Only a beginning on determining detailed requirements has been made by the Committee on the Hygiene of Housing of the American Public Health Association. While there is no dearth of standards of various types, it is extremely difficult to judge their validity in the absence of real knowledge of human requirements. Estimates of housing needs are also common, but they have only a remote connection to the standards which they are supposed to satisfy. We do not have the information about our housing stock necessary for applying standards. We are faced, therefore, with a real dilemma: Unless we apply standards to the existing stock, no estimate of need is well grounded; but the cost of gathering sufficient information to apply such standards on any scale has so far been prohibitive.

Despite the obstacles, more attention has been paid to standards in housing than in any other field of human consumption, with the exception of food. Standards of nutrition are more scientific than those of housing, largely because the problem is less complex.

Legal Standards

Housing standards were first established when inadequate housing came to be regarded as a social problem, and are embodied in legislation designed to correct the deficiencies for the benefit of both the inhabitants of the dwellings and the community as a whole. The earliest legislation dealt with the safety of structures. In the nineteenth century the emphasis shifted to sewage disposal and water supply in the interest of public health. All legislation in this field is justified on grounds of health, safety and public welfare, with the latter meaning in effect the same as the first two. The legal concepts of health and safety have been gradually broadened and extended and made more precise. The administrative practices of federal agencies concerned with financing housing have gone farthest in this direction.

Opinion of Experts

The second major source of standards is the analysis and opinion of experts. It is significant that the American Public Health Association has taken a leading role in this work, bringing together a variety of talents from medicine, engineering, sociology, architecture, city planning and other fields. A variety of methods have been utilized by public and private agencies in establishing standards, including engineering and medical analysis of heating and light requirements and possibilities, motion studies, attitude and opinion surveys. The basic human needs which determine standards are seldom stated, however, and are never subjected to analysis for the purpose of determining whether they are real or imaginary, or whether they are the most important.

The publications of the Federal Housing Administration, *Minimum Property Requirements,* and the Public Housing Administration, *Minimum Physical Standards and Criteria,* enumerate the following human needs: health, safety and well-being (or general welfare); economy and a proper degree of livability; privacy, convenience, comfort, efficiency and harmony of appearance.

The Committee on the Hygiene of Housing of the American Public Health Association regards the primary objective of housing to be health, understanding that term to include

safety from physical hazards and those qualities of comfort and convenience and esthetic satisfaction essential for emotional and social well being. . . . The problems of safety and of the physical, emotional and social health of the individual, in relation to the conduct of the individual life and the joint performance of family and community functions — these must be the fundamental aims of housing. . . . The mere elimination of specific hazards in poor neighborhoods falls short of the real goal of planning an environment which will foster a healthy and normal family life. . . . Under modern conditions of American living, a sense of inferiority due to living in a substandard home may often be a more serious health menace than any insanitary condition associated with housing. . . . Mental and emotional health is quite as important as physical health. . . . The frustration which results from overcrowding, conflict between the desires and needs of various members of the family, fatigue due to the performance of household duties under unfavorable conditions — these are health menaces quite as serious as (if less obvious than) poorly heated rooms or stairs without railings. . . . The home, if it is to be a setting for healthful living, must provide a physiological environment which regulates illumination, moisture, sound, temperature and ventilation and, also, a social environment which promotes emotional security and ensures privacy for the family and for the individual. . . . Space allotments that ensure a reasonable modicum of self-respect and satisfaction are essential for healthful living.[25]

In 1939 the Committee broke down these goals into physiological needs, psychological needs, protection against contagion, and protection against accidents.[26] Each of these was then further spelled out in detail. The Committee regarded all these taken together as basic principles. It translated each into specific requirements and set forth the most important means for meeting these requirements.

This classification of housing needs was in terms of human requirements. Deeming it necessary to move further into *design* requirements, in its postwar studies the Committee treats the problem as one of planning external areas and internal spaces and equipment. These studies set up standards for site selection, land development, placement of dwellings, provision of neighborhood community facilities, layout of pedestrian and vehicular routes; and for the dwelling itself, such as provision of space for the various home activities, temperature, light and ventilation, sanitation, noise control and safety features. All this is set forth in as precise and quantitative terms as possible.

Index of Substandardness

Such specifications do not help us in a statistical segregation of good from bad housing, for we do not have the detailed information about our housing supply that would permit us to apply them. All that we can do is to choose from among the particulars about which there are data the few important criteria which provide the most accurate practical index of general housing conditions. A house proving inadequate on these grounds will in all likelihood be inadequate on many other counts. Thus, if it does not meet the particular requirements, it is probably substandard. Merely to remedy these deficiencies, however, will not necessarily take a house out of the substandard class, for these particular deficiencies are only circumstantial evidence of its general deterioration.

The Housing Census of 1950 is the most recent, detailed and comprehensive body of information about our housing supply on a country-wide basis. The data from the Census that are important for our purposes fall into six main categories: age, rent, degree of crowding, state of repair, plumbing and equipment. (See Table 79.)

Of these criteria, state of repair and plumbing probably afford the best available circumstantial evidence of the condition of our housing. The Census gives information on the number of houses that are dilapidated, and on the number without private bath, flush toilet or hot and cold running water. Dilapidation stands out as a clear reflection of inadequacy. Running water, flush toilets and baths have become an integral part of our standard of living, and because their absence, especially in cities, is generally associated with bad housing conditions, plumbing has therefore been selected to supplement state of repair as a test of the quality of our housing supply.

Although rent is probably the best single index of housing quality, it was not chosen as one of the critical criteria because there are great regional as well as urban-rural and even purely local variations in the rent level that would indicate whether a house is substandard. Nevertheless, since in all places the worst houses are found in the lowest rent groups, it is possible to use rent as a rough check on the results obtained with the other criteria chosen.

Overcrowding as a criterion was discarded because it indicates shortage, not condition. Moreover, most overcrowding occurs in houses that are in a poor state of repair and lack adequate plumbing. Equipment was not used as a special measure of adequacy because of the same overlapping with the chosen criteria.

ESTIMATED REBUILDING NEEDS, 1950

How many dwelling units were substandard in 1950? How much would it cost to bring our entire housing supply up to standard? [27]

To provide the American people with adequate shelter, all existing dwellings that fail to come up to the standard of adequacy would have to be replaced or, if possible, rehabilitated. In estimating the number of these substandard units we must apply the criteria of dilapidation and plumb-

---

25. *Planning the Neighborhood,* 1948, Foreword, *passim; Planning the Home for Occupancy,* 1950, Foreword and Chapter 1, *passim; Construction and Equipment of the Home,* 1951, Foreword.

26. *Basic Principles of Healthful Housing,* 2d edition, New York, 1939.

---

27. Since 1950 is the latest date for which detailed housing data are available, throughout this section references to current housing conditions and needs are as of that date.

ing facilities in a different manner in urban than in rural areas.[28]

Urban Housing

In urban places (including rural nonfarm and farm units inside standard metropolitan areas) dilapidation of the dwelling and lack of running water, flush toilet and bathtub or shower for exclusive use of the occupants appear to offer the best clue to substandard housing. If a house is dilapidated, it is a potential threat to health and safety. An urban family that today shares a flush toilet with another family or is without access to any flush toilet lacks one of the sanitary facilities essential to health and decency in an area of concentrated population. Access to running water in the structure is also essential to proper health standards. Even if the houses without adequate plumbing are not dilapidated and even if those which are dilapidated are equipped with plumbing facilities, they are likely to be substandard in other ways — in design, surroundings, and general lack of equipment and amenities. In short, an urban dwelling unit which is dilapidated or, if not dilapidated, is without running water, private flush toilet or bath will also tend to have enough other faults to make it fall below standard.

According to the Census, 6.8 per cent of all dwelling units in urban places were dilapidated in 1950. Another 14.4 per cent were not dilapidated but lacked essential plumbing: 3.4 per cent were without running water and 11.0 per cent were without private flush toilet or bath. Thus, roughly one in five, or 6,938,000 of the total of 32,691,000,[29] dwelling units in urban places were dilapidated or lacked essential plumbing. Of these substandard units, 2,217,000 were dilapidated and 4,721,000, although not dilapidated, had no private toilet or bath or lacked running water. (See Table 86.)

These, however, were not the only substandard urban units. Deteriorated houses are found in clusters; the conditions which lead to deterioration — encroaching business districts, heavy traffic, shifting of work opportunities, and the

TABLE 86. STATE OF REPAIR AND PLUMBING EQUIPMENT OF DWELLING UNITS IN URBAN PLACES,[a] 1950

(*Thousands*)

Condition of Unit	Number	Per Cent
Total	32,691	100.0
Not dilapidated	30,474	93.2
With hot water, private toilet and bath	24,668	75.5
With private toilet and bath but no hot water	1,085	3.3
With running water, but no private toilet or bath	3,602	11.0
No running water	1,119	3.4
Dilapidated	2,217	6.8
With hot water, private toilet and bath	557	1.7
Without hot water, private toilet or bath	1,660	5.1

Source: Appendix 7–1.

a. Includes all urban units plus rural nonfarm and farm units inside standard metropolitan areas.

like — infect all, not only one or two, houses in a given area. Blocks and neighborhoods tend to rise and fall as a unit, for the houses usually are similar in age, design and equipment and possess the same original faults. If one house is not kept up, repaired and modernized, the rest of the block or neighborhood is likely to deteriorate as well. Therefore, if the Census records several houses in an area as dilapidated or lacking private toilet, bath or hot water, the surrounding dwellings, though they may have adequate plumbing and may not yet have reached the stage of dilapidation, probably are substandard for other reasons.

In order to discover these other substandard units it was assumed that if more than half of the units in a block were substandard, then the whole block was substandard.[30] This assumption added 1,993,000 dwelling units, including 423,000 lacking hot running water, to the number estimated as requiring rehabilitation or replacement. These plus the 6,938,000 classified as dilapidated or lacking running water, private toilet or bath gave a total of 8,931,000 substandard dwelling units, or 27 per cent of all units in urban areas in 1950. (See Table 87.)

---

28. In this section all units in standard metropolitan areas are included with urban dwelling units and the same housing standards apply. See Appendix 7–1 for detailed data on which this analysis is based.

29. The total of 32,691,000 is higher than the 29,-569,000 urban units in Table 79 and Appendix 7–1, since it includes 3,122,000 rural nonfarm and farm units that are inside standard metropolitan areas but which the Census classifies as rural.

30. Dwelling units classified by the Census as being dilapidated or without specified plumbing equipment averaged 72 per cent of the total number of units in these blocks; for the purpose of discovering substandard blocks, dwellings without hot running water were considered substandard.

TABLE 87. ESTIMATED NUMBER OF DWELLING UNITS IN URBAN PLACES [a]
NEEDING REHABILITATION OR REPLACEMENT, 1950
(*Thousands*)

			Needing Replacement		
Condition of Unit	*Total*	*Needing Rehabilitation (Scattered)*	*Total*	*In Substandard Blocks* [b]	*Scattered*
Total substandard units	8,931	1,996	6,935	5,566	1,369
Dilapidated or without running water	3,336	—	3,336	1,967	1,369
Not dilapidated and with running water	5,595	1,996	3,599	3,599	—
Without private toilet or bath	3,602	1,996	1,606	1,606	—
With private toilet and bath	1,993	—	1,993	1,993	—

Source: Appendix 7–2.

a. Includes all urban units plus rural nonfarm and farm units inside standard metropolitan areas.
b. Substandard block defined as one in which more than half the dwelling units are substandard.

Replacement vs. Rehabilitation

Some of these dwelling units must be completely demolished and replaced by new ones; others can be rehabilitated. Very few houses cannot be rehabilitated; but when the reconditioning has to be so extensive and the cost so high as to make it tantamount to new housing, then rehabilitation is a misnomer. If a substandard block or neighborhood is to be brought up to standard, a piecemeal attack, house by house, is never satisfactory. The whole area must be redeveloped as a unit if every house is to have adequate light and air, and if a satisfactory environment is to be created and maintained. Of the 8,931,000 substandard dwelling units in urban places, 5,566,-000, or about 62 per cent, are in substandard blocks and consequently should be replaced.

The remaining 3,365,000 substandard dwelling units are not in great clusters but are scattered over the urban area, either singly or in small groups of two or more. Many of these units could be rehabilitated and made into acceptable living places at comparatively low expense. Scattered houses lacking private toilet or bath but not dilapidated are on the whole in better condition than those that are dilapidated.

On the assumption that all units that are dilapidated or lack running water must be replaced, two fifths of the scattered substandard housing, or 1,369,000 units, should be replaced. When these are added to the number in concentrated substandard areas, the total number of urban dwelling units that need to be replaced becomes 6,935,000. The remaining 1,996,000 substandard units are not dilapidated and have running water but lack private toilet or bath; it is assumed that they could be rehabilitated.[31] (See Table 87.)

The remaining 23,760,000 dwelling units in urban areas are presumed to be satisfactory, although 662,000 of them lack hot running water. Hot running water certainly should be part of an acceptable minimum standard today. In many cases its lack will be associated with other substandard features. However, the absence of hot water, when occurring outside concentrations of bad housing, does not in itself furnish a significant enough index to warrant the inclusion of such units in an over-all estimate of housing need.

Cost Estimates

The cost of replacing 6,935,000 urban dwelling units and rehabilitating 1,996,000 would depend upon how cheaply we could produce a minimum-

---

31. For present purposes it is not necessary that exactly those dwelling units designated be treated in the way indicated. It is sufficient to show the magnitude of replacement and rehabilitation needs both together and singly. Doubtless many adequate units in bad neighborhoods have been classified as substandard; but there are also many substandard scattered houses which are neither dilapidated nor without essential plumbing. Similarly, there are substandard units in bad neighborhoods and scattered dilapidated units which could be rehabilitated while there are other scattered units without essential plumbing which should be replaced. Thus, errors in one direction tend to offset errors in another.

standard house. Using Bureau of Labor Statistics data on average construction cost as a guide, it is estimated that it would have cost around $6,500 in 1950, excluding land and nonfixed equipment cost, to build an urban house that would fulfill our minimum standards.[32] The total replacement program would therefore involve an expenditure of $45 billion in terms of 1950 costs.

There would have to be a further outlay for rehabilitating the scattered houses classified as without private flush toilet or bath. The rehabilitation of these units would require more than the addition of plumbing equipment, for this criterion is merely symptomatic of a general state of deterioration and indicates a need for extensive reconditioning. Experience with similar types of property indicates an average rehabilitation cost per dwelling unit of $2,000 to $2,500 at 1950 prices. At the lower figure the rehabilitation of the 1,996,000 scattered units lacking private flush toilet or private bath would cost about $4 billion.

Thus, the total cost of bringing our 1950 stock of urban houses up to standard would be $49 billion in 1950 prices. This figure, however, is artificial and incomplete. It covers only that part of our neighborhood redevelopment needs chargeable to the residential structures themselves. If substandard neighborhoods are to be brought up to standard, additional expenditures will have to be made for nonresidential neighborhood facilities and improvements, such as streets, parks and play spaces.[33] An analysis of the cost of such a program will be found in Chapter 16.

Rural Housing

The criteria used to discover the amount of substandard urban housing cannot be used in the same manner for rural housing. Lack of sewage disposal facilities does not create the same hazards to health in rural areas. Running water, flush toilets and baths are highly desirable in all dwellings, but it is doubtful if we have yet reached a sufficiently high standard of living to classify rural houses without them as substandard. Dilapidation, however, is just as symptomatic of general deterioration in rural as in urban housing.

Farm Housing

Of the 5,622,000 farmhouses (outside standard metropolitan areas) in 1950, 1,147,000, or 20 per cent, were dilapidated. (See Appendix 7–1.) In a survey of farm housing and construction in 1950, 36 per cent of farmhouses were classified as having a serious deficiency and 25 per cent as having an intermediate deficiency.[34] If the proportion of farmhouses with serious deficiencies is taken as representative of the proportion needing replacement, then 2,024,000 farmhouses should be replaced. If it is further assumed that increased productivity of farms would have permitted the abandonment of the 500,000 worst farmhouses, the number of farmhouses to be replaced would have been reduced to 1,524,000.

Available figures suggest $5,000 as a reasonable average cost of replacing a farmhouse at 1950 prices.[35] Thus, the cost of replacing 1,524,000 farmhouses will total $7.6 billion.

On the basis of the proportion of farm homes with intermediate deficiencies, the number to be rehabilitated is 1,405,000. It is estimated that the

---

32. In *Construction, Annual Review, 1950* (Bulletin No. 1047, Table 5, p. 9) the Bureau of Labor Statistics shows that the average construction cost of new permanent privately owned nonfarm dwelling units started in 1950 was $8,445. This figure excludes sales profits and the cost of land. It is assumed that site improvement, architectural and engineering fees not already included in construction cost amount to 4 per cent of the basic cost; allowance for this factor raises the average unit cost to $8,780. It is further assumed that the cost of the minimum-standard unit is three fourths the cost of the average unit. This brings the average cost of the minimum-standard unit to $6,585.

33. In fact, a program of urban redevelopment would involve the replacement of some additional houses, not because of any structural defects but because their replacement is necessary in a large-scale clearance and rebuilding program. See Chapter 16.

34. See *Farm Housing and Construction*, Bureau of Agricultural Economics, U.S. Department of Agriculture, February 1952. In this survey a house was rated as having a serious deficiency if it was not weather-tight, had an inadequate foundation, had major faults in the walls, roof or chimney, or contained less than 200 square feet of floor area. A house was rated as having an intermediate deficiency if it had wooden foundation posts, if the foundation required minor repairs, if windows or doors required major repairs, if parts of the steps were in hazardous condition, or if the house had similar deficiencies or contained 200 to 299 square feet of floor area.

35. The average estimated cost of construction of new farmhouses completed in 1949 was $3,946, according to the Bureau of Agricultural Economics survey of farm housing and construction. This figure includes the value of farm-produced materials and farm labor. It relates to new houses below minimum acceptable standards, as well as adequate houses. The average planned cost of new farm homes on which loans were made by the Farmers Home Administration, according to its annual report for 1951, was $5,384 in 1950 and $6,073 in 1951. All of these homes were required to meet minimum standards, which included adequate space, sanitary water supply, and bathroom or space where a bathroom could be installed later.

TABLE 88. ESTIMATED NUMBER OF DWELLING UNITS NEEDING REPLACEMENT
OR REHABILITATION, AND COST, 1950

| Location | Number of Units | | | Cost | | |
	Total	Needing Replacement	Needing Rehabilitation	Total	Replacement	Rehabilitation
	(Thousands)			(Millions)		
Total	14,832	9,590	5,242	$67,076	$58,918	$8,158
In urban places [a]	8,931	6,935	1,996	49,070	45,078	3,992
Rural nonfarm [b]	2,972	1,131	1,841	8,981	6,220	2,761
Rural farm [b]	2,929	1,524	1,405	9,025	7,620	1,405

Source: See discussion in text.
a. Includes all urban units plus rural nonfarm and farm units inside standard metropolitan areas.
b. Excludes rural units inside standard metropolitan areas.

cost of rehabilitation would average $1,000,[36] making a total of $1.4 billion. Needed replacement and rehabilitation of our farm housing, therefore, would have cost a total of $9 billion in 1950.

Rural Nonfarm Housing

Rural nonfarm housing is generally intermediate in condition between urban and farm housing. The proportion that is dilapidated or lacks running water is roughly midway between the urban and farm proportions in similar condition. While relatively few farmhouses have baths, flush toilets and running water and relatively few urban dwellings lack these amenities, about half of the rural nonfarm units have baths and flush toilets and about two thirds have running water.

If dilapidation or lack of running water is used as a criterion, some 2,972,000 rural nonfarm dwelling units, or 39 per cent of the total of 7,670,000 such units, were substandard in 1950. The 1,131,000 dilapidated rural nonfarm dwellings may be taken as an approximation of the number of units to be replaced and the additional 1,841,000 units without running water as an approximation of the number to be rehabilitated. (See Appendix 7–1.)

If we assume a unit cost for rural nonfarm dwellings about five sixths as great as for an urban unit, the average cost of replacing a rural nonfarm unit at 1950 prices would be $5,500.

Rehabilitation would cost $1,500 per unit, if the average is assumed to be midway between the urban and rural farm cost. Such a rural nonfarm program would require $6.2 billion for replacement and $2.8 billion for rehabilitation, or a total of $9.0 billion.

Thus, the total cost of bringing our 1950 rural housing supply — farm and nonfarm — up to standard would be $18.0 billion.

Total Rebuilding Costs

In summary, nearly 15 million dwelling units in use in 1950 did not provide reasonably adequate living quarters and needed to be replaced or rehabilitated. The total cost of bringing them up to a minimum standard would be $67 billion at 1950 prices. (See Table 88.)

ESTIMATED CONSUMPTION NEEDS, 1950

These rebuilding needs can readily be translated into annual housing consumption expenditures. The precise relation of rental value to capital value will vary with financial terms, property taxes, insurance, maintenance and repair expenses, the rate of return on investments in other sectors of the economy, and the durability and rate of obsolescence of the property. Longer amortization periods under FHA financing for cheaper housing is a factor tending to lower the ratio of rental to capital value for such housing. However, this is more than offset by the possibility of lower down payment ratios, less durability, higher rate of obsolescence, and the likeli-

---

36. The average cost of additions or remodeling and installation of facilities in farmhouses was $1,474 in 1949, according to the survey of farm housing and construction.

hood of relatively higher maintenance and repair expenses for cheaper as compared with more expensive housing.

In 1950 the estimated annual rental value of new FHA-insured single-family nonfarm homes ranged from 9.8 per cent to 10.3 per cent of property valuation in the price classes specified for minimum-standard housing in the last section, the ratio declining as value increased.[37] The more expensive urban housing will thus tend to be at the bottom of the range, and the cheaper rural nonfarm structures at the top. Farm housing, however, even when low in value, is likely to have a rent-capital ratio at the lower end of the range because of lower property taxes, the relatively low rate of return on agricultural investments, and the possibly slower rate of obsolescence. All the above considerations apply equally to new housing and to housing which is modernized or rehabilitated.

Eliminating Substandard Units

The application of the lower of the above rent-capital ratios, 9.8 per cent, to the estimated $67.1 billion cost of replacing and rehabilitating our substandard housing (Table 88) would translate our capital housing needs into an annual rental value of $6.6 billion.[38] This does not mean that bringing all substandard units in the United States up to a satisfactory level would add as much as $6.6 billion to our consumption expenditures. The additional expenditures for rent and imputed rent would be only the difference between what is being paid for substandard housing and what would have to be paid for adequate shelter. No direct information is available on the rent paid for substandard dwelling units. If, however, it is assumed that the lowest-rent housing is substandard, then existing data will permit an approximation of the difference between consumption expenditures for substandard housing and what would be needed for adequate shelter.

Of the estimated 14,832,000 substandard dwelling units in 1950, 7,603,000 were in urban, 3,913,000 in rural nonfarm and 3,316,000 in farm areas.[39] The estimated average annual rent or rental value of these substandard units was $327 for urban, $243 for rural nonfarm and $209 for farm.[40] Hence, the rental value of the country's substandard housing was $2.5 billion for the urban, $1.0 billion for the rural nonfarm and $0.7 billion for the farm units, or a total of $4.2 billion.

Since the cost in rental terms of bringing our total 1950 stock of substandard housing up to standard has been estimated at $6.6 billion, and the amount actually paid in rent and imputed rent for the substandard stock was $4.2 billion, the gap between need and demand in terms of rental value was $2.4 billion. This is the amount by which rent and imputed rent would have to be raised to substitute an adequate dwelling for every substandard one. Or to put it more accurately: this is what the increase in rental value would be if enough housing could be built and rehabilitated to eliminate all substandard housing. A housing program designed to accomplish this end, however, would of necessity have to be spread over a reasonable period of time. If we set as our objective elimination of all substandard housing over a period of fifteen years, then about two thirds should be accomplished during the 1950–1960 decade. If we accept as our needs objective the elimination of two thirds of all substandard housing during the 1950–1960 decade, and apply that standard to 1950 rents, the gap between needs and demand would be reduced to $1.6 billion.

Undoubling

However, even if all our substandard housing were replaced or rehabilitated so that the entire stock was adequate, our housing needs would still not be fully met. For a substantial number of families who should have their own living quarters would still be living with other families. In 1950, there were 462,000 secondary families and 6,467,000 subfamilies and secondary individuals living with primary families as lodgers or resident employees.[41]

Not all of these need separate dwelling units for an adequate family or individual life. Many

37. *Fourth Annual Report, 1950,* U.S. Housing and Home Finance Agency, Tables 21 and 28, pp. 264 and 274.

38. The rent-capital ratio of 10.3 per cent would yield an annual rental value of $6.9 billion.

39. Derived from Table 88 adjusted on the basis of data in Appendix 7–1 so as to shift rural nonfarm units and farm units inside metropolitan areas out of the urban classification. Urban standards were applied to rural non-farm and rural farm units inside standard metropolitan areas; thus, all such units which were dilapidated or lacked running water, private toilet or bath were classified as substandard.

40. For method of estimation and computations see Appendix 7–3.

41. See Chapter 3, Table 22.

subfamilies are so closely tied to the family with whom they live, either psychologically, economically, or by birth or marriage, that it is best for all concerned that they continue to share the same dwelling unit. Many older couples, also, are happier with lodgers, and many lodgers prefer not to live alone.

Probably all the secondary families, and perhaps one third of the subfamilies and secondary individuals, would be better off if they established separate households,[42] and by doing so would improve the family life of those with whom they lodge. On a rough estimate, this "undoubling" would add about 2 million households to the number in existence in 1950. If the distribution of the new dwelling units among urban and rural areas were the same as for substandard housing and if they were built at the minimum standard of adequacy, their average cost at 1950 prices would be in the neighborhood of $6,000 per unit.[43] Their total cost would then be about $12 billion.

At an average rent-capital ratio of 9.8 per cent, these additional units would raise the cost in rental terms of our 1950 stock of housing by $1.2 billion. This, added to the $1.6 billion additional cost in rental terms of bringing two thirds of our substandard housing up to standard, would increase the gap between need and demand to $2.8 billion.

Fuel and Utilities

This figure does not include unmet needs for fuel and utilities. For water, the need was probably adequately met. By 1950, inside running water was almost universally available in urban areas. The provision of private bathing facilities in every urban dwelling unit would increase water consumption somewhat, but hardly enough to affect consumption expenditures appreciably. In rural areas, for the most part, water cannot be supplied as a public utility, and each house has to rely on its own pump. The cost of the pump should be charged to capital and is usually included in the cost of building the house. Operating costs are largely covered by the electricity bill. Hence it is assumed that there was no difference between need and demand in expenditures for water in 1950.

Six per cent of our dwelling units had no electricity in 1950. (See Table 80.) Assuming that every house should have electric service, the needed consumption expenditure for electricity in 1950 was 6 per cent greater than the actual expenditure. However, dwelling units already supplied with electricity would increase their use of it if nearly all our housing were brought up to standard. If private bathing facilities and adequate refrigeration and cooking facilities were installed more widely, the average consumption of electricity or gas per dwelling unit would increase. If electricity had been used for all these additional needs, then total consumer expenditures for this form of energy might well have been more than 12 per cent above the $2 billion actually spent in 1950, or approximately $2.3 billion. Then no additional expenditures would have been needed for gas for cooking and refrigeration.

Additional expenditures for fuel were needed in 1950, since a substantial number of urban as well as rural dwelling units in the northern part of the country were still without central heating. (See Table 80.) Assuming the same percentage increase as for electricity, the actual expenditures of $3.4 billion for fuel[44] would have had to be increased to $3.8 billion. Then no additional expenditures would have been needed for gas for heating.

The gap between the need and demand for fuel and utilities in 1950 was thus $0.7 billion as against a gap of $2.8 billion for shelter. Total needed consumption expenditures for housing in 1950 were therefore $30.7 billion, compared with actual expenditures of $27.2 billion.

ESTIMATED DEMAND, 1960

The total demand for housing in 1960 is estimated at $45 billion in 1950 prices. One fourth of this amount is estimated to go for capital outlays — replacement and rehabilitation of existing structures and erection of additional units — and three fourths is projected in the form of consumption expenditures.

Consumption Demand

On the basis of past trends and relationships to income, total consumption expenditures for

---

42. The secondary individuals would not necessarily live alone, but to a considerable extent in groups of two, three or more.

43. From replacement cost estimates in Table 88.

44. A nominal amount of this was for ice and lighting supplies.

TABLE 89. CONSUMPTION EXPENDITURES FOR HOUSING, 1950 AND 1960

	Expenditures		Per Cent of Total Consumption Expenditures	
	1950	1960	1950	1960
	(Millions at 1950 Prices)			
Total housing	$27,184	$33,220	14.0	13.8
Rent and imputed rent	20,210	24,700	10.4	10.2
Fuel, ice and lighting supplies	3,392	4,280	1.7	1.8
Household utilities	3,582	4,240	1.8	1.8

Source: Appendix 4–7.

housing in 1960 have been projected at $33.2 billion (at 1950 prices), 22 per cent above the 1950 level. This total consists of $24.7 billion for rent and imputed rent, $4.3 billion for fuel, ice and lighting supplies, and $4.2 billion for household utilities. (See Table 89.)

Capital Demand

The annual rental value of new single-family, nonfarm residential construction of minimum adequacy was approximately 9.8 per cent of its capital value in 1950. (See p. 225.) There is no guarantee that the rent-capital ratio applicable to the existing stock of a like character of housing will be precisely this percentage, but it cannot be very different.[45] In 1950 the ratio of rental to capital value of the entire stock of nonfarm housing was estimated to be 8.4 per cent,[46] a decline from the ratios which prevailed during 1930–1945 and equal to the ratio of 1949. (See Table 90.) These ratios may be taken as representative of our entire stock of housing, farm as well as nonfarm, with little risk of error. Farm housing constitutes only a small part of our total stock: in the 1930s the number of farm dwelling units in existence was about a quarter the number of nonfarm units, and by 1950 it had declined to about a sixth. (See Table 77.) Moreover, there appears to be no particular reason why the rent-capital ratio of farm housing should deviate markedly from the nonfarm ratio. (See discussion on p. 225.)

45. Common market conditions tie old and new housing into a close interdependence with respect to both their capital and rental values.
46. Derived from rough projection of capital value based on construction outlays and depreciation allowance and rental value as shown in Appendix 4–4.

TABLE 90. RENTAL VALUE AS PER CENT OF CAPITAL VALUE, NONFARM HOUSING, 1930–1949

Year	Per Cent	Year	Per Cent
1930	11.6	1940	9.1
1931	12.4	1941	9.0
1932	11.9	1942	9.2
1933	10.2	1943	9.2
1934	9.6	1944	9.1
1935	9.7	1945	8.8
1936	9.3	1946	8.0
1937	9.2	1947	7.4
1938	9.5	1948	7.8
1939	9.4	1949	8.4

Sources: Raymond W. Goldsmith, A Study of Saving in the United States, Princeton University Press, 1954, Vol. 3, Table W–1, and Appendix 4–4.

What is likely to happen to this ratio in the future? The decline after 1931 accompanied the lowering of interest rates on residential mortgages and the lengthening of the amortization period, which reduced the financial charges on housing. With the general decline in interest rates, the reduction in financial charges was reflected in reduced rental values relative to capital values. Since the war, rent control reduced the ratio even further. But with the virtual elimination of rent control and the tendency toward higher mortgage and other interest rates, the ratio climbed back to slightly over 8.5 per cent by 1952.[47] In view of the more recent reduction in mortgage and interest rates the 1960 rent-capital ratio should be just about 8.5 per cent.

Assuming, then, a rent-capital ratio of 8.5 per cent in 1950, the $20.2 billion rental value of housing in that year would be equivalent to a capital

47. See footnote 46.

value of $238 billion. By 1960, on the basis of the projected rental value of $24.7 billion, the capital value of our housing would be $291 billion, a *net* increase of $53 billion over 1950. Under the assumption that there will be no change in the ratio of capital value to rental value during the decade, the net increase in capital value would average $5.3 billion a year.

Probable Gross Capital Outlay

In order to find what gross outlays for residential construction are implied by this net addition to capital value, replacement expenditures must be added to them to compensate for the loss in value of existing housing due to aging, use and obsolescence. According to the Bureau of Internal Revenue, dwellings and their equipment combined depreciate at an average rate of 2.5 per cent a year, while for dwellings without their equipment the rate could go down to 1.7 per cent.[48] Since equipment is so important in housing today, the first is the more realistic rate for present purposes.

Since our stock of housing in 1950 has been valued at $238 billion, the loss in value during that year was $6.0 billion, at a depreciation rate of 2.5 per cent. For 1960 the loss in value would be $7.3 billion. The average for the decade would then be $6.7 billion a year. The cost of replacing this annual loss plus the net increase in capital value of $5.3 billion a year yields a total of $12 billion (at 1950 prices) as the average annual *gross* outlay for residential construction likely to occur between 1950 and 1960. This estimate follows from and is consistent with the projected consumption expenditures for housing.

In 1950, residential construction expenditures amounted to $13.7 billion, by far the greatest portion of which was for new dwelling units; the remainder was for additions and alterations. If expenditures during 1950–1960 are distributed among new nonfarm dwellings, farm dwellings, and nonfarm additions and alterations as they were in 1950, then the estimated average annual outlay of $12 billion should yield about 1.2 million new dwelling units a year, costing $10.7 billion, with the remaining $1.3 billion going for additions and alterations.[49]

ESTIMATED CAPITAL NEEDS, 1950–1960

By 1960 the number of consumer units is expected to total about 58 million, consisting of 51 million households together with 7 million secondary families, subfamilies and secondary individuals.[50]

If all secondary families (estimated at about 500,000) and one third of the subfamilies (estimated at 6.5 million) and secondary individuals were to establish separate households,[51] then a little over 53 million dwelling units would be required in 1960. Some vacant units would be needed, however, to provide for the mobility of the population and to give families sufficient choice to meet their individual requirements. A long-standing rule of thumb has been a vacancy rate of 5 per cent. However, recent surveys have shown that a large proportion of vacancies are either dilapidated or not available for rent or sale.[52] On the assumption that two thirds of all substandard housing will be eliminated by 1960, a vacancy rate of 3 per cent appears to be sufficient. On the basis of this rate and the desirable increase in the number of households, a total of 54.7 million dwelling units will be needed in 1960, or an increase of 8.7 million over the 1950 housing stock.

The 8.7 million new units would (1) provide for the increase in families, (2) eliminate undesirable doubling-up, and (3) restore vacancies to a satisfactory level. In addition, about 400,000 units would be needed to replace losses during the decade by fire, flood, wind, earthquake or other disaster, the removal of temporary war housing, and other demolitions.[53] On the assumption that about two thirds of the 9.6 million substandard dwellings existing in 1950 were replaced by 1960, an additional 6.4 million units would be needed. Existing housing will continue to deteriorate during the decade, of course, but if estimated needs for replacement and rehabilitation in 1950 are taken care of, ordinary maintenance and repair expenditures should be sufficient to prevent further units from becoming substandard.

48. *Bulletin "F," Income Tax Depreciation and Obsolescence, Estimated Useful Lives and Depreciation Rates,* p. 17.

49. Tables 82 and 83; *Farm Housing and Construction,* Table 1.

50. See Chapter 3, especially Table 27.

51. It is assumed that households of secondary individuals would average approximately two per household.

52. *1950 Census of Housing,* Vol. I, Part 1, Table H. The number of vacant units was 6.6 per cent of the total in 1950, but only 1.6 per cent were nonseasonal, not dilapidated, and were for rent or sale.

53. "Housing and the Increase in Population," *Monthly Labor Review,* April 1942, shows 342,000 urban and 55,000 rural nonfarm units demolished during the 1930s.

In all, therefore, 15.5 million new dwelling units will have to be constructed during the decade, an average of 1.55 million a year. This annual need contrasts with a building rate during 1950–1952 of 1.3 million [54] units a year and with a probable demand during the decade of about 1.2 million units a year. Demand, therefore, would fall short of needs by about 350,000 units a year.

The cost of the 6.4 million units which would be needed to replace substandard units would be $39.3 billion. On the assumption of construction at the minimum standard of adequacy, an average expenditure of $6,120 would apply to the remaining 9.1 million units (all nonfarm) to be put up during the 1950–1960 decade, and their construction would cost $55.7 billion in 1950 prices.

However, given the national product and employment assumptions of this survey, a substantial portion of our housing needs will be filled between 1950 and 1960 by above-standard housing through the operations of the market. Of the 15.5 million new dwelling units needed during the decade, it has been estimated that 12.0 million are likely to be built at a cost of $107 billion (see p. 228), leaving a deficit of 3.5 million units. If the remaining units needed were built at an average cost of $6,120 (which would provide houses at a minimum standard of adequacy), their total cost would be $21 billion. Under our definition of need, which assumes that anyone spending at a level above the minimum standard remains at the higher level and that those spending less than the standard are brought up to it, the total cost of filling our need for new houses during the 1950 decade would be $128 billion.

An additional $5.4 billion will be needed if two thirds of the dwellings needing rehabilitation in 1950 are brought up to standard during the decade (see Table 88), and some $13 billion is likely to be spent on additions and alterations (see p. 228). In all, gross additions valued at $146 billion would be required.

These gross additions would add only a net of $65 billion to the stock of housing, for $67 billion would go toward offsetting depreciation occurring during the decade (see p. 228), and the value of the 1950 housing stock would be reduced by about $14 billion worth of substandard housing demolished.[55] The value of the 1960 stock of housing would then be approximately $303 billion. Total outlays needed to offset depreciation on this growing stock of housing would average $6.6 billion a year,[56] just about equal to the amount estimated as likely to be spent for this purpose.[57] The capital outlays necessary during the present decade to fulfill our housing needs by 1960 would thus be as follows (in billions):

New housing demanded	$107
Additions and alterations demanded	13
Unfilled new housing needs	21
Rehabilitation needs	5
Total	$146

Since total demand is likely to be $12 billion a year or $120 billion for the decade, needs unfilled by the ordinary processes of the market would amount to $26 billion for the decade, or an annual average of $2.6 billion.

All the above estimates of capital need and demand are brought together in consolidated Table 91.

ESTIMATED CONSUMPTION NEEDS, 1960

At a rent-capital ratio of 8.5 per cent, the 1960 stock of housing of $303 billion necessary under the standards of need as applied above would have a rental value of $25.7 billion. Since it is estimated that $24.7 billion is likely to be paid in rent and imputed rent in 1960 (Table 92), the gap between need and demand would be $1.0 billion.

---

54. Including about 100,000 farm units; estimated number of nonfarm units from *Construction and Building Materials,* U.S. Department of Commerce, May 1953, Table 18, p. 47.

55. The annual rental value of the 1950 stock of substandard housing was estimated to be $4.2 billion (p. 225). The rent-capital ratio for housing of a minimum standard of adequacy ranged from 9.8 per cent to 10.3 per cent, with the ratio increasing as value declined (p. 225). A ratio of 10.5 per cent is, therefore, not unlikely for substandard housing. On this basis, the capital value of these substandard units would be $40 billion. But only 65 per cent of all substandard units need replacing. (See Table 88.) Assuming that their average capital value is lower than the average for substandard units that can be rehabilitated, the capital value of all units needing replacement would be about $20 billion. If two thirds of the job is done by 1960, about $14 billion of housing would be demolished, and its value should be subtracted from the gross value of its replacements in order to arrive at the net value added by these replacements.

56. Average of estimated depreciation loss on the undemolished $224 billion housing stock of $5.6 billion during 1950 and $7.6 billion during 1960.

57. See p. 228.

TABLE 91. RELATION OF CAPITAL HOUSING NEEDS TO DEMAND, 1950–1960

(Dollar Figures at 1950 Prices)

Program	Rehabilitation and Replacement Needs as of 1950		Needs Program and Demand Projections, 1950–1960 — Decade Total		Annual Average	
	Units (Thousands)	Cost (Millions)	Units (Thousands)	Cost (Millions)	Units (Thousands)	Cost (Millions)
Rehabilitation of substandard housing[a]	5,242	$ 8,158	3,500	$ 5,400	350	$ 540
Urban[b]	1,996	3,992	1,300	2,600	130	260
Rural nonfarm	1,841	2,761	1,200	1,800	120	180
Farm	1,405	1,405	1,000	1,000	100	100
Replacement of substandard and obsolete housing	9,590	58,918	6,400	39,300	640	3,930
Urban[b]	6,935	45,078	4,600	30,100	460	3,010
Rural nonfarm	1,131	6,220	800	4,100	80	410
Farm	1,524	7,620	1,000	5,100	100	510
Replacement of demolished housing[a]	—	—	400	2,500	40	250
Net additions to housing supply[a]	—	—	8,700	53,200	870	5,320
Urban[b]	—	—	5,400	35,100	540	3,510
Rural nonfarm	—	—	3,300	18,100	330	1,810
Totals:						
Demand				120,000		12,000
New dwelling units[a]			12,000	107,000	1,200	10,700
Additions and alterations				13,000		1,300
Unfilled needs[a]				26,400		2,640
New dwelling units			3,500	21,000	350	2,100
Rehabilitation				5,400		540
Total needs[c]				146,400		14,640
New dwelling units			15,500	128,000	1,550	12,800
Additions, alterations and rehabilitation				18,400		1,840

Source: Table 88 and discussion in text.

a. Unit costs at minimum standards of adequacy.

b. Including all units in metropolitan districts.

c. Sum of demand and unfilled needs.

TABLE 92. SUMMARY OF HOUSING NEEDS AND DEMAND, 1950 AND 1960
(*Millions at 1950 Prices*)

	1950		1960	
	Demand	*Needs*	*Demand*	*Needs*
Capital outlays	$13,708	$14,600 [a]	$12,000 [a]	$14,600 [a]
Consumption expenditures	27,184	30,700	33,220	34,400
Rent and imputed rent	20,210	23,000	24,700	25,700
Fuel, ice and lighting supplies	3,392	3,800	4,280	4,400
Household utilities	3,582	3,900	4,240	4,300

Source: See text discussion and Tables 81 and 91.

a. Ten per cent of estimated 1950–1960 decade total.

Fuel and Household Utilities

For fuel and household utilities, needed consumption expenditures would not be much greater than probable expenditures. The reasoning applicable in 1950 for water and gas would, of course, apply even more strongly in 1960 to eliminate any gap between need and demand. As to electricity, it is likely that the 6 per cent of dwelling units without it will have been electrified by 1960. Of the remaining 6 per cent gap between need and demand that existed in 1950 due to insufficient private bathing facilities, refrigeration and cooking facilities, about two thirds is likely to be eliminated through the substitution of adequate for substandard housing.

The resulting inadequacy might then equal 2.0 per cent of the spending level of 1960, or under $0.1 billion. Assuming the same percentage inadequacy for fuel, the gap would in this instance also amount to just under $0.1 billion.

Total Consumption Needs

The resulting $0.2 billion gap between the need and demand for fuel and utilities plus the $1.0 billion gap for shelter yields an over-all gap of $1.2 billion. Needed consumption expenditures for housing in 1960 (at 1950 prices) would therefore be $34.4 billion, compared with projected expenditures of $33.2 billion. (See Table 92.)

## CHAPTER 8

HOUSEHOLD OPERATION

AMERICAN CONSUMERS SPENT $29 billion for household equipment and operation in 1950 and $31 billion in 1952. This was about one seventh of the total sum spent for consumption goods and services in those years. Of the major categories of consumer expenditures, only the food, liquor and tobacco group accounted for a larger sum. Expenditures for clothing, accessories and personal care, for housing and utilities, and for consumer transportation, were of the same general magnitude in 1952 spending by consumers.

Household equipment and operation, as defined for purposes of this survey, includes a wide variety of different kinds of goods and services ranging from the most durable of consumer goods to the most ephemeral of services. At one extreme it includes furniture, furnishings and floor coverings, refrigerators, washing machines and other household mechanical appliances, tableware and kitchen utensils; at the other extreme are moving and storage expenses, legal and financial charges, interest on personal debt, payments for domestic service, and consumer payments for postage and for telephone and telegraph service. Each of these and the other groups included in "household equipment and operation" consists of a multitude of widely varying individual products. (See Appendix 4–4 for detailed expenditures for household equipment and operation from 1909 to 1952.)

Distribution of Expenditures

Of the total sum spent by consumers for household equipment and operation in 1950–1952, about 60 per cent was spent for services, and most of the remainder for durable commodities, except for the small share spent for semidurable commodities. The expenditures for these goods and services and their relative importance in

By GERTRUDE S. WEISS, Assistant Chief, Home Economics Research Branch, Agricultural Research Service, U.S. Department of Agriculture. Opinions and judgments expressed in this chapter are those of the author and should not be attributed to the organization with which she is associated.

total consumption expenditures in 1950 were as follows:[1]

	Expenditures (Millions)	Per Cent of All Consumption Expenditures
Total household equipment and operation	$29,060	14.94
Furniture and furnishings	9,513	4.89
Mechanical appliances	3,021	1.55
Domestic service	2,525	1.30
Cleaning, repair and maintenance	1,844*	.95*
Communication	2,892	1.49
Financial, legal, insurance and death expenses	9,265	4.76

* For descriptive purposes the laundry expense classified under clothing in Chapter 6 could be added here. It amounted to $427 million, .22 per cent of total consumer expenditures.

The first four of these represent the expenses of housekeeping, as the term is usually understood. Changes in taste affect the kind of furnishings selected, providing a more or less elaborate scale of living and more or less work for the housewife, other family members or household employees in maintaining cleanliness and order.

The most important change in the equipment and operation of the household during the past century has been the increased ownership of mechanical equipment. Widespread use of such equipment has raised standards of housekeeping, particularly of cleanliness. In addition, it has changed the nature of the housewife's job and has decreased her dependence on domestic servants, laundries and other services sold outside the home.

Thus, shifts within the larger group of expenditures devoted to equipping and servicing the home reflect changes in the manner of living and in generally accepted standards of home equipment and maintenance.

Enterprises and Workers Engaged

Lack of data makes it impossible to measure precisely the employment and volume of business

1. For more detailed breakdowns see Table 102.

TABLE 93. SELECTED HOUSEHOLD EQUIPMENT INDUSTRIES AND TRADES, 1947 AND 1948
(*Dollar Figures in Thousands*)

Industry or Trade	Number of Establishments	Wage Earners	Wages	Value of Products Shipped
Manufacturing, 1947				
Furniture and furnishings				
Carpets, rugs and other floor coverings	296	50,883	$131,340	$ 230,295 [a]
Wool carpets, rugs and carpet yarn	95	35,560	92,656	
Carpets and rugs, not elsewhere classified	182	6,444	11,556	55,559
Linoleum, etc.	19	8,879	27,128	174,736
Curtains, draperies	397	6,928	11,702	109,640
Other textile housefurnishing products (inc. bedspreads)	1,233	36,384	63,053	504,065
Household furniture	4,880	204,020	450,772	1,821,703
Mattresses and bedsprings	879	25,460	60,824	331,079
Upholstered household furniture	1,391	39,786	92,908	381,053
Other than upholstered household furniture	2,610	138,774	297,040	1,109,571
Screens, shades and Venetian blinds	1,058	21,541	46,606	256,351
Mirror and picture frames	246	3,293	7,742	25,555 [b]
Mirrors, etc.	1,054	19,298	43,739	199,828
Earthenware food utensils	76	15,742	37,175	72,054
Vitreous enameled products	49	11,061	22,917	74,382
Glass tableware	126	37,474	86,853	234,795
Silverware and plated ware	235	18,542	55,804	219,131
Cutlery other than silver, plate and aluminum	195	17,579	42,530	142,571
Lamp shades	291	4,100	7,043	27,499
Mechanical appliances				
Electrical appliances	326	37,271	96,654	466,009
Domestic laundry equipment	65	23,651	65,596	442,297
Sewing machines	70	12,647	37,926	97,011
Mechanical refrigerators, etc.	561	108,316	299,175	[a]
Wholesale trade, 1948				
Household furniture	605	5,606	21,847	245,026
Floor coverings	649	6,715	28,357	416,112
China, glassware, crockery	537	3,784	13,214	116,884
Antiques	271	423	1,423	13,208
Miscellaneous home furnishings	1,183	9,718	32,208	389,011
Electrical appliances (general line)	365	14,407	55,162	769,714
Refrigerators, equipment (household)	239	6,661	24,185	443,158
Miscellaneous appliances, specialties	704	7,767	27,382	333,933
Retail stores, 1948				
Furniture	29,031	163,389	441,968	3,427,168
Floor coverings	4,568	19,348	55,745	358,953
Draperies, curtains, upholstery	3,178	10,350	22,479	141,403
China, glassware and metalware	1,626	13,793	21,191	146,916
Antique shops	4,963	2,004	4,013	53,062
Other home furnishings	5,288	34,852	79,046	273,318
Household appliances	29,700	118,176	277,897	2,159,302

Source: U.S. Bureau of the Census, volumes on *Manufactures,* 1947, *Wholesale Trade* and *Retail Trade,* 1948.
a. Omitted because of excessive duplication.   b. Contains some duplication.

involved in the wide range of industrial and commercial activities that supply consumers with the goods and services required for household equipment and operation. The 1947 Census of Manufactures and the 1948 Census of Trade list the manufacturing industries and the wholesale and retail establishments devoted principally to furniture, furnishings and mechanical appliances. However, many of these goods are made in factories that also produce goods not purchased by households. For example, furniture, furnishings and household mechanical appliances are used in offices, hotels and restaurants as well as in households. In addition, reports of manufactures include production for export, which was especially large for some of these products in 1947.

Among the most important of the manufacturing industries are household furniture, which employed 204,000 wage earners in 1947, and carpets and rugs, glass tableware, mechanical refrigerators, electrical appliances and household textiles other than carpets and curtains, each of which employed more than 30,000 workers. (See Table 93.)

Taken as a whole, the manufacturing industries listed in Table 93 employed nearly 883,000 wage earners in 1947. However, the table is too incomplete in some respects and too inclusive in others to give a very accurate picture. Most of these industries produce goods for hotels and for commercial and institutional use as well as for households. Certain other industries making heating, cooking and plumbing equipment are not included, although some of their products come within the scope of this chapter. However, many of these products are used for other than household purposes, and insofar as they are a fixed and integral part of the house, their cost is more properly allocated to "housing and utilities" than to "household equipment and operation."

The branches of wholesale trade listed in the table had 55,000 employees in 1948, and the retail trades 362,000. Here again the picture is incomplete, for very substantial proportions of furniture, furnishings and appliances are sold in types of stores not included in the table, such as general merchandise, department and hardware stores.

Moreover, Table 93 is confined to tangible goods and does not include important items such as domestic service in private households, furniture repair, furniture moving, telephoning and legal expenses. The table excludes also the manufacture of such commodities as cleaning and polishing preparations and writing supplies, since they are widely used outside the home and are sold at retail chiefly in grocery and drug stores.

So important are these household services and the miscellaneous household supplies not included in the table that the four excluded groups — domestic service, communication, financial and legal expenses, and cleaning, repair and maintenance — accounted for 57 per cent of total consumption expenditures for household equipment and operation in 1950, and for 61 per cent by 1952.

Added to all these employees supplying household equipment or products and engaged in household operation, maintenance or financing, is a veritable army of unpaid household workers. Many of the services performed by the nation's homemakers are productive services, in the sense that they could be, and sometimes are, performed by industry or by paid workers. But putting a value on them, in terms of either the cost of services that could be purchased or the alternative earning opportunities open to homemakers, presents so many difficulties that it is not attempted here.[2]

TRENDS IN PRODUCTION AND TASTE

Technological developments and shifts in consumer tastes and habits have produced great changes in the ways in which homes are equipped and run. The design and character of furniture and furnishings have changed radically in recent decades. New appliances and commercial services have mechanized and simplified housework. The job of housekeeping has changed, both as to the tools and methods used and as to the standards of how it should be done.

FURNITURE AND FURNISHINGS

Travelers and novelists have given us their impressions of the way the homes they observed were furnished. As tangible evidence of home life in the past we have historical monuments — from Mount Vernon to the cabins of the frontier. Museums have furnished period rooms, and there are many histories of American furniture. It has never seemed worth while, however, to take an inventory of the stocks of furniture and furnishings in a large enough sample of American homes to provide statistical data about the equipment that families of different periods, at different

2. See Margaret Gilpin Reid, *Economics of Household Production,* Wiley, New York, 1934, pp. 3–16, 165–169, and *Income in the United States,* National Bureau of Economic Research, New York, 1921, p. 59.

economic levels and in different parts of our country have used in cooking, eating, cleaning, sleeping, and playing.

Writing in the 1940s, Edgar W. Martin summed up the trend since 1860 as follows:

[In 1860] the furniture was well made, the floor coverings serviceable, and the wall paper decorative. Really good china, glassware and silver were too expensive for any except the very well-to-do, but probably no one regarded this as a very important matter. What have the eighty years since that time contributed toward making houses better places to live? . . . The only fundamental change in housing is the result of a changed set of values; we now prefer small rooms or even apartments, while in 1860, we were willing to sacrifice other enjoyments to have big, roomy houses. The other changes have been mostly additions to the number of conveniences — and the long list of labor saving devices. Much though these improvements added to our ease and comfort, it seems to me that the real progress in housing since 1860 has been not so much the raising of the level of consumption of the well-to-do as making it possible for a greatly increased proportion of the population to approach that level.[3]

The first extensive survey of family expenditures in the United States was made by the Federal Commissioner of Labor Statistics among families of factory workers in 1888. The report on this study gives a little information on the condition of the 7,000 homes covered in the survey. The things fieldworkers were told to observe about the condition and the furnishings of the houses they visited may be judged from the following typical entries:

House plainly furnished, have one carpet
House plainly furnished, bare floors, have a sewing machine
House poorly furnished, have carpets, organ music box and sewing machine
Frame house, neat, have a melodeon and a sewing machine
Handsome new house, well furnished, have a guitar and sewing machine
House dirty and uncomfortable, have a sewing machine and garden
Frame house neatly kept, have a violin and sewing machine
New house, good furniture, all rooms carpeted

Later studies of family expenditures presented details on purchases of furniture and housefurnishings. Few covered more than a year, however, or obtained data on the total amount of furniture and housefurnishings owned by the families surveyed. Accordingly, few data are available, either to describe the furnishings and equipment of households in this country today, or to serve as a basis for estimating either probable or needed expenditures.

It is a safe assumption, however, that relatively few homes in the country are furnished as well as the families who live in them would like. Women's magazines, movies, mail-order catalogs and advertisements in the daily papers have combined to make American families singularly conscious of the kinds of housefurnishings currently being produced by American industry and of current fashions in interior decoration. Judged by the amount of space that current magazines give to the subject, fashions in home decorating are of as much or more interest to women readers as fashions in dress.

In a book deploring the popularity of antique furniture in this country,[4] the author, an English architect, remarks, "There is a young generation of Americans to whom it seems as natural to find antique and reproduction furniture in the living room as it does to find an electric refrigerator in the kitchen." He believes that with research into the needs of American families we could produce very much more satisfactory furniture than we have today. The furniture and housefurnishings of our ancestors were far superior to the devices they had for washing their clothes, cleaning their houses, storing and cooking their food. The mechanics of housekeeping have changed much more than furniture and housefurnishings.

Utilitarian Trend

Nevertheless, furniture and furnishings have changed substantially since the 1890s. In spite of the popularity of antiques, there is a large demand for simpler styles in furniture, both "colonial" and "modern." The heavy draperies which shrouded the homes of the middle and upper income groups at the turn of the century have generally been discarded in favor of lighter fabrics that let in more light and air and are easier to keep clean. Perhaps the most striking change has been in floor coverings. Tacked-down carpets are losing favor to varnished and waxed floors, and to coverings that are easier to clean.

3. Edgar W. Martin, *The Standard of Living in 1860*, University of Chicago Press, Chicago, 1942, pp. 104–105.

4. T. H. Robsjohn-Gibbings, *Good-bye, Mr. Chippendale*, Knopf, New York, 1944.

TABLE 94. VALUE OF SELECTED HOUSEHOLD FURNITURE PRODUCED, 1939 AND 1947

Product	Value 1939[a]	1947[b]	Ratio: 1947 to 1939
	(Thousands)		
Wood house furniture, except upholstered	$279,165	$892,276	3.20
Living room, library, sunroom, and hall furniture	64,802	269,136	4.15
Dining room and junior dining room furniture	34,507	112,568	3.26
Bedroom furniture	102,177	345,028	3.38
Infants' and children's furniture	8,303	49,672	5.98
Kitchen furniture	26,216	54,186	2.07
Porch and lawn furniture, including beach furniture and steamer chairs	2,292	8,026	3.50
Unpainted furniture	560	15,399	27.50
Other and not specified	40,308	38,261	.95
Wood house furniture, upholstered	151,358	419,126	2.77
Reed and rattan house furniture	2,821	8,123	2.88
Metal house furniture, except upholstered	41,999	218,223	5.20
Living room, dining room, bedroom, and infants' and children's furniture	14,509	31,089	2.14
Kitchen furniture	14,147	144,130	10.19
Other metal house furniture	13,343	43,004	3.22

Source: 1947 Census of Manufactures, Household Furniture Release MC 25A, pp. 7, 8.
a. Value of production.
b. Value f.o.b. plant of total shipments and interplant transfers.

An entire complex of forces has operated to make the conventional unused parlor a real *living* room. Among these factors are the trend toward smaller houses and apartments and the need to make the most of existing space. Space consciousness also has contributed heavily to the popularity of dinette suites, fewer and more useful pieces of living room furniture, and the day bed in all its manifestations. But furniture and furnishings are far less standardized than, say, mechanical appliances or automobiles, and almost any sort of personal taste can still be gratified.

The shift toward furnishings that are easy to care for was especially marked in the past decade. Illustrative is the large increase in the production of unpainted furniture — from under $1 million in 1939 to over $15 million in 1947 — in contrast to the more moderate increase for upholstered furniture — from $151 million to $419 million. Increased production of metal furniture, especially metal kitchen furniture, which jumped tenfold between 1939 and 1947, is another indication of a growing emphasis on efficiency in housekeeping. (See Table 94.)

The popularity of furnishings that are inex-pensive and easy to care for is shown also in floor coverings. Although wool carpets and rugs continue to lead the field, production data suggest a trend toward greater use of other floor coverings. In 1939 and 1947 about 60 per cent (a little more in 1939 and a little less in 1947) of the total value of product of the floor-covering industry was accounted for by wool carpets and rugs. Next most important in 1947, by value of product, was asphalt-felt-base floor covering, a popular and relatively inexpensive hard-surface material. The largest increase (more than tenfold) from 1939 to 1947 took place in the value of production of asphalt floor tile, a comparatively new product, often used without rugs or other covering. (See Table 95.)

During this period there was a tendency to cover floors that were not covered before, as in apartment houses, public and office buildings and basements of homes. Accordingly, not all of the increase in production of hard-surface floor coverings from 1939 to 1947 was at the expense of wool carpets and rugs.

Hard-surface floor coverings undoubtedly make housekeeping easier. Asphalt-felt-base prod-

TABLE 95. VALUE AND QUANTITY OF FLOOR COVERINGS PRODUCED, 1939 AND 1947
(*Thousands*)

Type of Covering	Value		Square Yards[b]	
	1939	*1947*[a]	*1939*	*1947*
Wool carpets and rugs, woven	$142,301[c]	$340,975	58,371[d]	77,787[d]
Carpets, rugs, mats from fiber (not wool)	13,760[b]	52,801		
Linoleum	29,432[b]	67,683	36,004	65,808
Asphalt-felt-base floor and wall covering[e]	37,880[b]	86,231	166,567	236,028
Asphalt floor tile	3,633[f]	37,825	4,933	41,479

Sources: 1947 Census of Manufactures, MC 22D, "Carpets, Rugs and Other Floor Covering," Table 6; and MC 32E, "Abrasive, Asbestos, and Miscellaneous Nonmetallic Mineral Products," Table 6.

a. Net shipments.
b. Total production.
c. Gross sales, less returns.
d. Not available.
e. Including piece goods, wall covering, rugs and mats, but excluding "other"; 1947 value of net shipments $7,221,000.
f. Shipments and interplant transfers.

Note: Data for square yards on net shipment, on total production and on gross sales less returns indicate that differences are not large enough to affect the comparisons made.

ucts have long been popular as a low-cost substitute for carpets, rugs or inlaid linoleum, and have continued to be inexpensive. Over the period from 1940 to 1950 prices of asphalt-felt-base floor covering have increased much less than prices of wool rugs or the average of all housefurnishings items included in the consumers' price index. (See Table 96.)

Use of Man-Made Fibers

The use of man-made fibers — rayon, acetate, nylon, etc. — has changed the nature of some

TABLE 96. INDEXES OF CONSUMER PRICES FOR SELECTED ITEMS OF HOUSEFURNISHINGS
AND HOUSEHOLD OPERATION, 1940–1950
(*1935–1939 = 100*)

Item	*1940*[a]	*1947*[a]	*1950*[a]
All goods and services	100.2	159.6	171.9
All housefurnishings[b]	100.5	184.4	190.2
Bath towels	96.0	235.3	248.7
Muslin sheets	93.5	242.3	235.5
Wool Axminster rugs	115.0	165.4	211.4
Felt-base floor covering	90.1	127.7	128.8
All furniture and bedding	104.1	206.7	222.8
Household operation[b]	99.2	144.4	150.2
Laundry bundle service	100.5	144.2	165.9
Residential telephone service	99.4	115.6	136.5
Domestic service	102.8	278.5	284.2

Sources: Consumers' Prices in the United States, 1942–48, Bulletin No. 966, U.S. Bureau of Labor Statistics, 1949, pp. 44, 72–76; *Indexes of Retail Prices of Apparel, Housefurnishings and Services and Miscellaneous Goods to Moderate-Income Families in Large Cities of the United States, March 1951–September 1951,* November 1951, pp. 6 and 7 (mimeographed); and *Monthly Labor Review,* July 1952, p. 111.

a. Average for year.
b. Includes items in addition to those listed.

TABLE 97. USE OF SELECTED FIBERS IN HOUSEHOLD TEXTILES, 1937 AND 1949

(Millions of Pounds)

End Use [a]	1937					1949				
	Total	Cotton	Wool	Silk & Linen	Man-Made	Total	Cotton	Wool	Silk & Linen	Man-Made
Total	1,014.8	816.7	162.4	7.0	28.7	1,267.6	970.7	219.7	1.0	76.2
Bedding and blankets										
Mattresses, pillows, pads	53.0	53.0	0	0	0	49.7	48.8	0	0	0.9
Blankets and blanketing	136.1	109.6	26.3	0	0.2	80.8	42.8	28.0	0	10.0
Bedspreads	23.6	20.6	0	0.1	2.9	97.3	94.8	0	0	2.5
Comforters and quilts	10.2	7.6	0.3	0	2.3	6.1	3.1	0.5	0	2.5
Household linens										
Sheets and pillow cases	198.3	198.3	0	0	0	254.9	254.9	0	0	0
Towels and toweling	114.5	114.0	0	0.5	0	119.8	118.8	0	1.0	0
Tablecloths, napkins, lace	31.3	22.9	0	6.1	2.3	34.2	31.6	0	b	2.6
Floor coverings										
Carpets and rugs	162.1	31.3	130.0	0	0.8	219.6	34.9	179.1	0	5.6 b
Bath mats, scatter rugs	26.6	26.6	0	0	0	51.9	51.9	0	0	0
Window covering and miscellaneous										
Curtains	50.3	46.6	0	b	3.7	58.7	43.6	0	0	15.1
Upholstery and draperies	163.9	141.3	5.8	0.3	16.5	250.8	203.9	11.4	0	35.5
Other [c]	44.9	44.9	0	0	0	43.8	41.6	0.7	b	1.5

Source: "Textile Interfiber Competition 1937 and 1949," Rayon Organon (now Textile Organon), Supplement for May 1951, p. 93.

a. Use in homes, offices, hotels, buses, trains, but not automobiles.

b. Less than 50,000 pounds.

c. Window shades, piece goods, oil cloth, vacuum cleaner bags.

household textiles. Before 1940, man-made fibers accounted for very little of the total fiber used for all purposes in this country.[5] Their use has increased during the past decade, but these new fibers are still of less importance for housefurnishings than for clothing. Sheets still account for a large share of the fiber used in household textiles, and they are made almost entirely of cotton. In 1949, rugs were primarily of wool, and, secondarily, of cotton. Man-made fibers were most important in window curtains, accounting for one quarter of the fiber used, and in upholstery and draperies, for which they provided one seventh of the fiber used in 1949. (See Table 97.)

Increases from 1937 to 1949 in the share of man-made fibers in household textiles suggest that these fibers are gaining importance in household use. While the total amount of cotton, wool, silk and linen and man-made fibers used for household articles increased by about one fifth, the use of man-made fibers increased more than two and a half times. But man-made fibers provided only 6 per cent of the total used in household textiles in 1949 and 11 per cent in 1951.[6]

Paper and plastics have also been substituted to some extent for textiles. However, no measure is available of their importance relative to fabrics. Their place in housefurnishings, especially at low cost levels, is shown in a recent survey in Mississippi.[7]

Easier Housekeeping

The shift toward simpler furniture and furnishings appears to have eased the work of housekeeping. The demand for simplicity is not surprising, in view of the relatively large number of young families, resulting from the tendency since 1940 toward marriage at a younger age. Moreover, the frequent moves of the war and postwar period have meant less emphasis on setting up housekeeping with a stock of furniture and textiles that is expected to last for many years.

5. Barkley Meadows, *Trends in the Consumption of Fibers in the United States, 1892–1948,* Statistical Bulletin No. 89, Bureau of Agricultural and Industrial Chemistry, Agricultural Research Administration, U.S. Department of Agriculture, 1950, p. 3.

6. "Textile Interfiber Competition 1951," *Textile Organon,* Supplement for August 1953, p. 132.

7. Dorothy Dickins, *The Use of Cotton in Housefurnishings,* Technical Bulletin 34, Mississippi Agricultural Experiment Station, 1952, pp. 4 and 14.

Some of these recent changes also are in the direction of less costly first purchases and more frequent replacements. Unfinished furniture, feltbase floor coverings, and some of the cotton rugs, paper and plastic products are examples. On the other hand, some of the newer man-made fabrics used in curtains and other household textiles may prove to be more durable and hence will need less frequent replacement.

MECHANICAL APPLIANCES

During the century since the first mechanical laborsaving devices were invented to lighten the work of the housewife, many tasks that had been part of household operation throughout recorded history have been transferred from the home to the factory.

Among the many laborsaving devices commonly found in American homes today, the sewing machine, which was patented in 1846, is the oldest. Hand-operated washing machines, patented in 1872, came next. Vacuum cleaners and electric washing machines came into production well after the turn of the century. The electric range and the electric refrigerator were just coming into use before World War I, but a very small proportion of American families owned either one by 1925. Gas stoves and kerosene stoves were widely used in the last half of the nineteenth century, and about 1890, gas-producing companies began a campaign to increase gas sales. In the 1920s gas stoves were considerably improved in design to meet the competition of electric ranges.

Recent Developments

Since 1920, progress in equipping homes with mechanical appliances has been especially great. In 1925, for example, less than one per cent of wired homes had mechanical refrigerators; in 1935, 34 per cent were so equipped; in 1950, 86 per cent; and in 1952, 89 per cent. (See Figure 37 and Appendix 8–1.)

Because new dwelling units have been added and existing dwelling units have been newly provided with electricity, the amount of equipment added is even greater than these percentages suggest. The number of dwelling units increased by about 8 million from 1940 to 1950, and those with the electricity needed to make use of electrical equipment increased by 13 million. (See Figure 38.) The number of households with

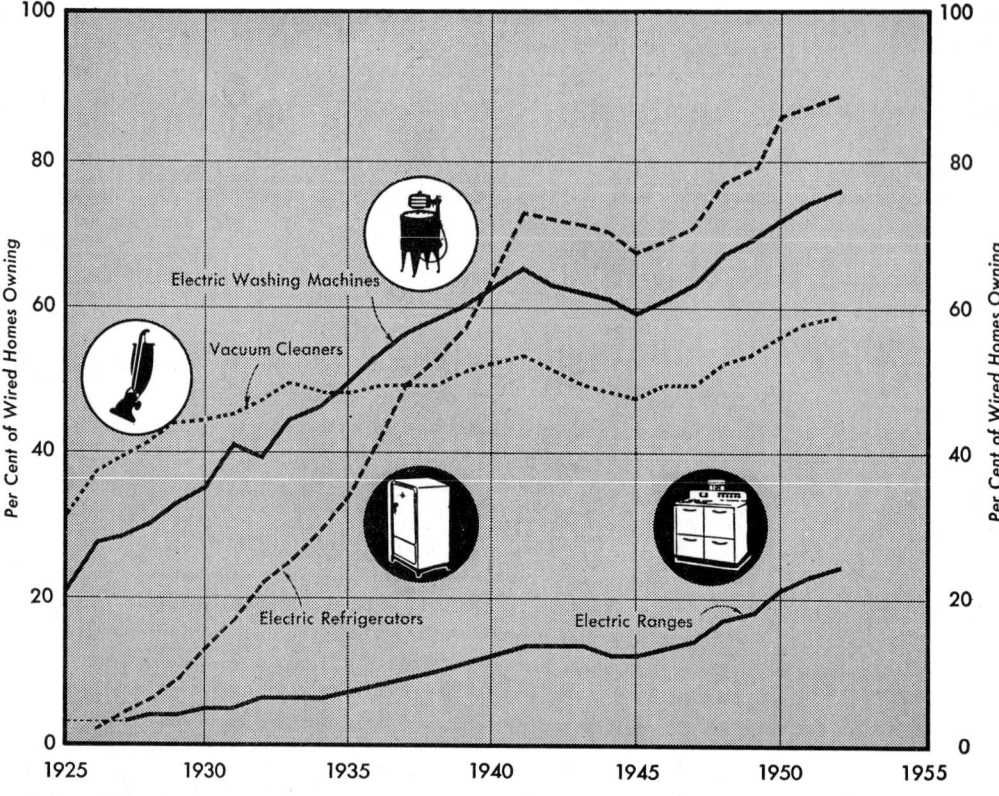

FIGURE 37. DOMESTIC UTILIZATION OF SELECTED ELECTRICAL APPLIANCES, 1925–1952

Source: Appendix 8–1.

mechanical refrigerators was 18 million larger in 1950 than in 1940. Modern cookstoves and washing machines also have been added in large numbers.

Four pieces of equipment are now so widely owned as to be almost standard. As of 1950, an electric iron was found in nearly nine out of ten homes; a mechanical refrigerator in eight out of ten; a gas or electric cookstove in more than seven out of ten; and a washing machine in nearly seven out of ten. (See Figure 39.) If the users of self-service laundries (estimated at 12 per cent) are counted in, the washing machine attains almost an equal place with the refrigerator in housekeeping.[8]

In addition to these basic pieces of equipment a great variety of new kinds of equipment has been offered to tempt the consumer dollar. Some,

such as electric ironers, freezers, dishwashers, food disposal units and clothes dryers, were owned by relatively few families in 1950. Sales of electric ranges, freezers, clothes dryers, dishwashers and room air-conditioning units have been especially large since 1950.[9]

Recent decades have also seen changes in efficiency and style in the older appliances so great as to make them almost new in their sales appeal. Refrigerators are larger than before 1940, and the space for storing frozen foods has been increased. More vacuum cleaners of the tank type are being produced. By far the greatest innovation has been the automatic washing machine. It is estimated that in 1950, 38 per cent, and in 1951, 46 per cent of the washing machines produced were of the automatic or semiautomatic type.[10] But even the nonautomatic washing machine

8. *The 1949 National Survey of the Family Laundry Market,* Special Report 184, made by the Psychological Corporation for the American Institute of Laundering and the Procter & Gamble Company, Joliet, Illinois, 1949, p. 22.

9. L. Jay Atkinson, "Consumer Markets for Durable Goods," *Survey of Current Business,* April 1952, p. 22.

10. Report of the American Washer and Ironer Manufacturers Association to the U.S. Department of Commerce.

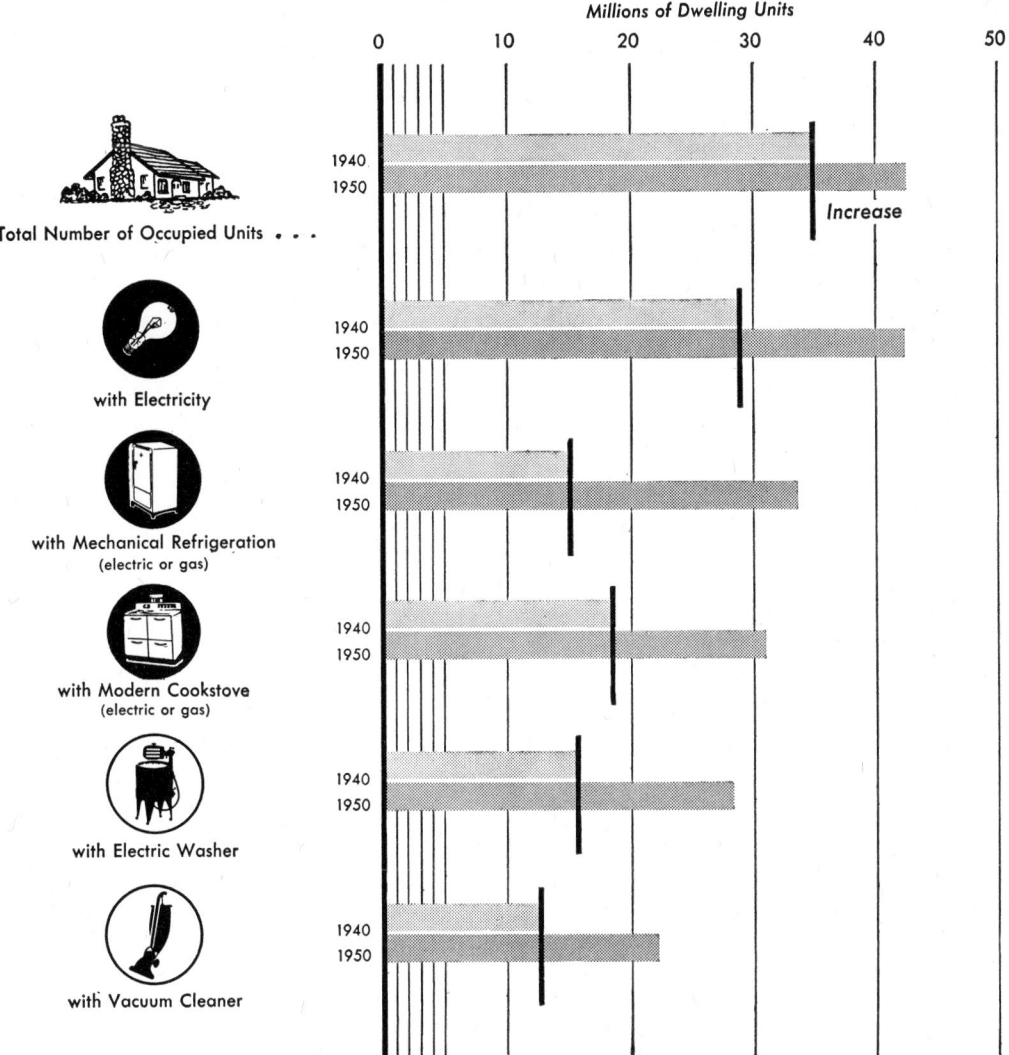

Total Number of Occupied Units . . .

with Electricity

with Mechanical Refrigeration
(electric or gas)

with Modern Cookstove
(electric or gas)

with Electric Washer

with Vacuum Cleaner

FIGURE 38. INCREASE IN NUMBER OF DWELLING UNITS AND IN NUMBER EQUIPPED WITH ELECTRICITY AND
SELECTED MECHANICAL APPLIANCES, 1940–1950

Sources: Figures for electric washers and vacuum cleaners taken from *Electrical Merchandising*, January 1941, p. 16; January 1951, p. 74. Other figures taken from U.S. Bureau of the Census, Series HC–5, No. 2, "Year Built, Household Equipment, and Cooking and Heating Fuel, for Dwelling Units in the United States: April 1, 1950," June 10, 1951, p. 7.

now has larger capacity, safer wringer installations, and is more likely to have a pump.

Savings in Time and Effort

The work load of homemakers has not been lightened as much as might be inferred from the amount of household machinery in use. A saving in physical labor can be credited to the washing machine, the modern cookstove and the vacuum cleaner. But at the same time, standards of household cleanliness have become more exacting. A saving in time of doing certain tasks, notably washing, can also be demonstrated. But for women whose primary job is homemaking, and especially for those with young children to care for, the use of mechanical appliances probably does not appreciably shorten the working

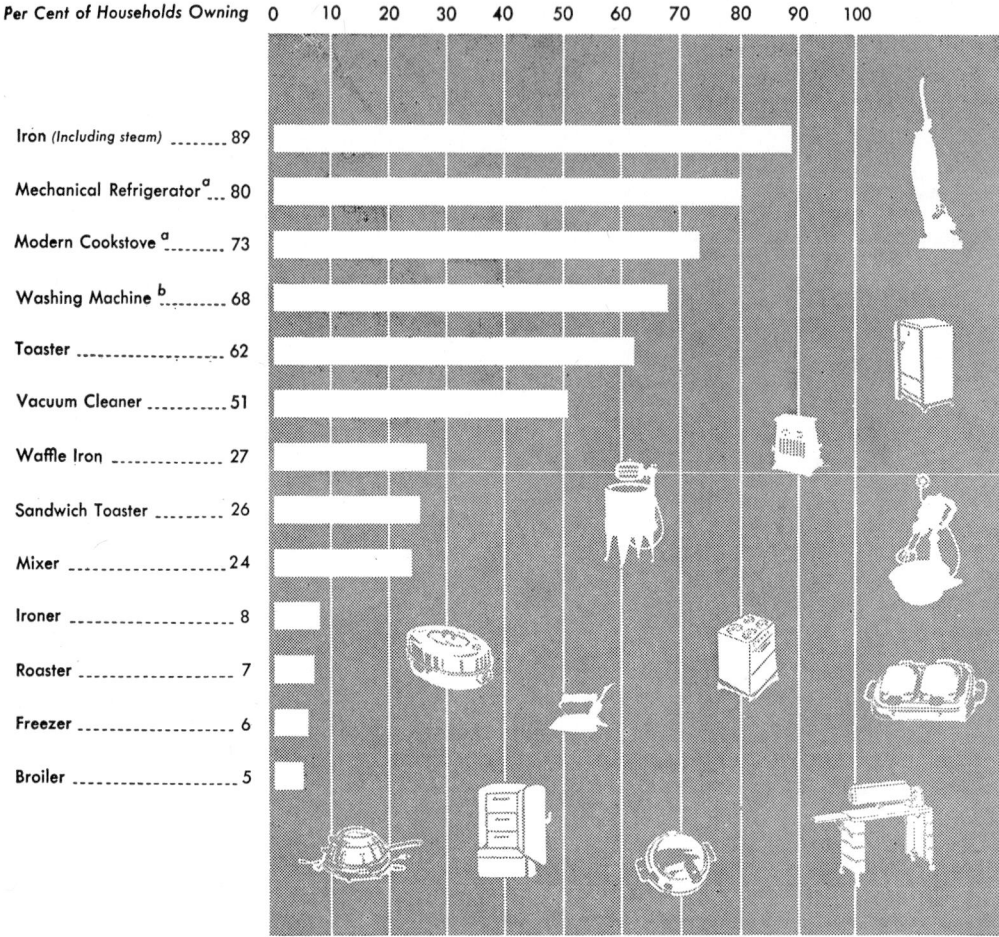

FIGURE 39. PER CENT OF HOUSEHOLDS EQUIPPED WITH SPECIFIED MECHANICAL APPLIANCES, 1950

Sources: Figures for mechanical refrigerators and modern cookstoves taken from U.S. Bureau of the Census, Series HC–5, No. 2, "Year Built, Household Equipment, and Cooking and Heating Fuel, for Dwelling Units in the United States: April 1, 1950," June 10, 1951, p. 7; figures for other items taken from *Electrical Merchandising*, January 1951, p. 74.

a. Electric or gas.
b. Electric, 65 per cent; gas engine, 3 per cent.

Note: Electric dishwashers, blenders, food waste units and clothes dryers were owned by less than 2 per cent of all households.

day. Some of the time released by improved housekeeping equipment probably has been used for the care of children, especially in cities where supervision is needed for young children's play out of doors. Moreover, standards of child care may well have become more demanding in recent years.

The mechanical refrigerator probably has improved the way the job is done as much as or more than it has saved time and effort. While the refrigerator might be credited with some saving of work for the homemaker, the great improvement in sanitary food storage is its major contribution to the operation of American homes.

DOMESTIC SERVICE

Domestic service contributes little to housekeeping in this country today. In 1950, 1.9 million women were employed in domestic service in private households. This amounted to only one worker for about twenty-five households.[11]

During World War I, and again during and after World War II, the number of women in domestic service in private households dropped sharply. With the long-run trend toward more households, the supply of domestics has progressively fallen behind the number of potential employers. In 1900, for example, there was one woman domestic for every thirteen households.[12]

Domestic employees are now very scarce indeed, whether viewed in relation to the number of households or to the situation at the beginning of the century. But, even in 1900, the household with domestic service was unusual.

Transfer of Services from the Home

Service in hotels, restaurants and institutions has to some extent been substituted for domestic service in households. In recent decades, jobs in public places have occupied from a fourth to a third of all women employed in service occupations, such as cooks, housekeepers, hostesses, servants and waitresses. Accordingly, the contribution of all such service to the total housekeeping task has decreased less than the contribution of servants to private housekeeping. Moreover, when measured against the population, rather than against the number of households, the change is less dramatic. Even in these terms, however, there are more people to be served for each woman employed in recent years than before 1900. The ratios of population to women service workers in private or public housekeeping are as follows: [13]

1870	44.1	1920	77.9*
1880	51.7	1930	57.2
1890	48.7	1940	46.5
1900	53.1	1950	55.6
1910	57.7		

* This high ratio for 1920 probably results from the fact that at that time women had not yet moved into public housekeeping jobs in great numbers and relatively few would accept domestic service positions because of the availability of preferable jobs during a period of extreme labor shortage.

11. Frieda Miller, "Household Employment in the United States," *International Labor Review*, October 1952, p. 5.

12. *Ibid.*, p. 5.

13. Janet M. Hooks, *Women's Occupations through Seven Decades*, Women's Bureau Bulletin No. 218, U.S. Department of Labor, 1951, p. 139. Preliminary estimate for 1950 supplied by the Women's Bureau.

As other occupations have opened to women, and especially at times when jobs were plentiful, domestic service has become less attractive. Since World War II, 10 per cent or less of all employed women have been working as domestics.

Competition from other occupations has made domestic service more costly to consumers. As an item in the consumers' price index, for example, domestic service in 1950 stood at 284 per cent of its 1935–1939 level, compared with the 172 per cent registered by the index for all goods and services. (See Table 96.) Nevertheless, private household workers have not fared so well in earnings over the past decade as have other workers.[14] Apparently domestic service in private households is still not as advantageous an occupation as others, while at the same time, such service is costly to consumers.

Mechanical household equipment has in part compensated for the lack of domestic workers. Housewives also have come to depend on industry for a number of services. Garment production, sewing of home furnishings, baking of bread, and canning and preserving have largely shifted from home to factory. More recently the growing practice of eating lunch in restaurants and in factory or school lunchrooms has further reduced the amount of work to be done at home. Especially during the last decade, more foods have been bought in work-saving forms — frozen and packaged vegetables, cooked foods, lunch meats, cookies, cakes, etc.

Effect on Work Load

Whether the net effect of these forces is a decrease in the work of housekeeping cannot be proved conclusively. Mechanical appliances and the transfer of much home production to industry have made housekeeping easier. But the decrease in domestic service and the more exacting standards of cleanliness and child care have added to the work expected of the homemaker. Moreover, young families who today set up their own households less often have parents or other relatives living with them who can help with the housework than did earlier generations.

The substitutes that industry has provided for domestic service are available to, and used by, the majority of families. Even in 1900 there were

14. Miller, *op. cit.*, p. 8.

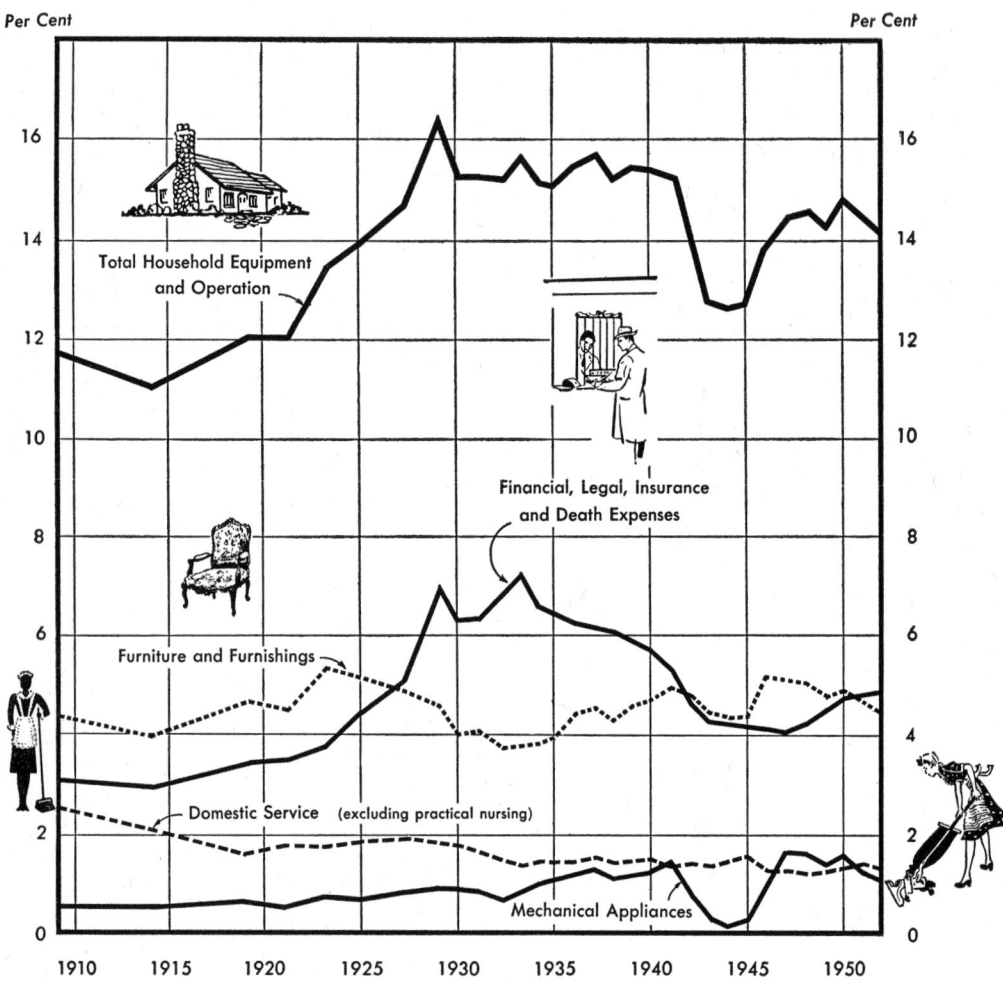

FIGURE 40. PER CENT OF TOTAL CONSUMPTION EXPENDITURES USED FOR SELECTED ITEMS OF HOUSEHOLD EQUIPMENT AND OPERATION, 1909–1952

Source: Appendix 4–5.

not enough domestics to serve more than a small fraction of the population. It could be argued, but not proved, that the present custom of employing day workers has increased the proportion of families obtaining some domestic service. There is no doubt, however, that appliances and commercial services are used by large numbers of families that, even fifty years ago, would not have employed domestic workers. Therefore, although domestic service, in the aggregate, has decreased in importance, the substitutes for such service are available to far more people than domestic service ever was.

If the number of working wives were interpreted as proof of less work to be done at home,

it could be said that a great deal of time had been released from housework. A century ago the married woman with paid employment was exceptional. In 1900, 6 per cent, and in 1940, 15 per cent of all married women were estimated to have employment outside the home.[15] By the early 1950s the employment of married women had so increased that one wife out of four either had or was seeking a job.[16]

Time released by use of commercial services and mechanical equipment is undoubtedly one condition that has made it possible for these

15. Hooks, *op. cit.*, p. 40.
16. *Current Population Reports*, U.S. Bureau of the Census, Series P–50, No. 29, 1951, and No. 50, 1953.

TABLE 98. CONSUMPTION EXPENDITURES FOR HOUSEHOLD EQUIPMENT AND
OPERATION, 1909, 1929, 1940, 1950, 1952

Class	Annual Expenditure					Percentage Distribution				
	1909	1929	1940	1950	1952	1909	1929	1940	1950	1952
	(Millions)									
Total	$3,389	$13,277	$11,089	$29,060	$30,875	100.0	100.0	100.0	100.0	100.0
Furniture and furnishings	1,229	3,698	3,369	9,513	9,667	36.3	27.9	30.4	32.7	31.3
Furniture—new and second-hand	294	1,201	1,062	3,311	3,487	8.7	9.0	9.6	11.4	11.3
Floor coverings	173	485	417	1,128	1,071	5.1	3.7	3.8	3.9	3.5
China, glassware, tableware and utensils	233	628	517	1,500	1,484	6.9	4.7	4.7	5.2	4.8
Miscellaneous furnishings	529	1,384	1,373	3,574	3,625	15.6	10.4	12.4	12.3	11.7
Mechanical appliances	145	768	884	3,021	2,433	4.3	5.8	8.0	10.4	7.9
Domestic service	712	1,501	1,081	2,525	2,734	21.0	11.3	9.7	8.7	8.9
Communication	174	860	913	2,892	3,459	5.1	6.5	8.2	10.0	11.2
Stationery, writing supplies and postage	92	301	332	821	924	2.7	2.3	3.0	2.8	3.0
Telephone, telegraph, cable and wireless	82	559	581	2,071	2,535	2.4	4.2	5.2	7.1	8.2
Cleaning, repair and maintenance	259	805	750	1,844	1,946	7.6	6.1	6.8	6.3	6.3
Financial, legal, insurance and death expenses	870	5,645	4,092	9,265	10,636	25.7	42.5	36.9	31.9	34.4

Source: Appendix 4–4.

Note: Slight discrepancies in addition are due to problems of rounding.

women to do work outside the home. But many also do a great deal of work at home. Thus, it cannot be said that machines and industry have released the working wife from all household tasks.

More Home Equipment

There is one counter trend to the transfer of services out of the home. A growing consumer investment in mechanical appliances means that households are increasingly equipped to perform these services. For example, since 1930, consumer expenditures for laundering outside the home have increased much less than has disposable income. Even though prices of laundry services have increased, they have risen far less than the cost of domestic service and a little less than the average of all consumer prices. (See Table 96.) Hence, it cannot be said that consumers have turned to doing their own laundry because the rise in cost of having it done is out of line with increases in other costs.

Expenditures for dry cleaning have to some extent been substituted for expenditures for laundry service as people have purchased more of the kind of clothing suitable for office work, sometimes made of fabrics that cannot be washed. Nevertheless, as more families own equipment, purchased services become less important.

Considering the difficulties of getting errands done when homemakers have paid employment and in view of the work-saving contribution of good equipment, families may find reason for increasing, rather than decreasing, the amount of work done in the home.

TRENDS IN CONSUMPTION EXPENDITURES

With the exception of a few years of unusual circumstances, expenditures for household equipment and operation have continued at about one seventh of the total sum spent by consumers over the past twenty-five years. (See Figure 40.) The share was smaller before 1925 when financial and legal expenses, which are a major segment of

TABLE 99. FAMILY EXPENDITURES FOR FURNISHINGS AND EQUIPMENT, BY INCOME,[a] DETROIT, DENVER, AND HOUSTON, 1948, AND MEMPHIS, 1949

(Families of Two or More, Incomes under $10,000)

	Under $10,000	Under $1,000	$1,000– 1,999	$2,000– 2,999	$3,000– 3,999	$4,000– 4,999	$5,000– 5,999	$6,000– 7,499	$7,500– 9,999
						Disposable Money Income Class [a]			
Detroit									
Average expenditure	$259	b	$34	$154	$201	$250	$396	$581	$564
Average income	$4,063	b	$1,428	$2,602	$3,482	$4,441	$5,471	$6,666	$8,595
Number of families	346	5	20	62	104	76	34	31	14
Denver									
Average expenditure	$270	b	$96	$175	$266	$266	$379	b	$405
Average income	$4,107	b	$1,621	$2,632	$3,471	$4,378	$5,415	b	$8,509
Number of families	156	4	14	29	36	31	20	9	13
Houston									
Average expenditure	$301	b	$176	$207	$254	$292	$486	$559	$713
Average income	$3,807	b	$1,614	$2,551	$3,471	$4,489	$5,367	$6,694	$8,631
Number of families	202	5	25	43	53	36	16	12	12
Memphis									
Average expenditure	$276	$13	$119	$207	$238	$345	$436	$750	$393
Average income	$3,583	$820	$1,534	$2,534	$3,484	$4,471	$5,438	$6,555	$8,536
Number of families	342	14	48	86	74	51	37	19	13

a. Net cash family income after personal taxes and occupational expenses.
b. Data not shown for fewer than ten families.

Source: Family Income, Expenditures, and Savings in Ten Cities, 1952, Bulletin No. 1065, U.S. Bureau of Labor Statistics, Table 2.

TABLE 100. FARM FAMILY EXPENDITURES FOR FURNISHINGS AND EQUIPMENT, BY INCOME,[a]
ILLINOIS, 1946 AND MONTANA, 1949
(*Farm-Operator Families and Single Farm Operators*)

Income Class[a]	Number of Consumer Units	Average Income[a]	Expenditures				
			Total	Furniture	Floor Coverings	Major Equipment[b]	Other[c]
Illinois, 1946							
All consumer units	454[d]	$ 3,957	$178	$35	$13	$ 54	$ 76
Under $1,000	47	578	97	20	13	21	43
$1,000–1,999	72	1,549	118	18	11	41	48
2,000–2,999	90	2,560	158	39	8	39	72
3,000–3,999	61	3,485	196	32	21	62	81
4,000–4,999	53	4,520	222	39	12	73	98
5,000–7,499	59	6,102	240	48	13	88	91
7,500 and over	51	11,765	271	66	15	76	114
Montana, 1949							
All consumer units	506[e]	8,189	304	42	22	107	133
$200– 2,499	114	2,360	178	15	20	79	64
2,500– 4,999	127	4,539	241	24	15	93	109
5,000– 9,999	125	7,671	336	58	31	119	128
10,000–24,999	87	16,195	537	81	28	170	258

Source: Unpublished data from Bureau of Human Nutrition and Home Economics, U.S. Department of Agriculture.

a. For Illinois, classification and average are both net cash family income (farm income adjusted for inventory change) after personal taxes. For Montana, classification is by gross farm income (not adjusted for inventory change); nonfarm income is added in the average income.

b. Mechanical refrigerator, home freezer, electric or gas cookstove, vacuum cleaner, washing machine, ironer.

c. Includes household textiles, glass, china, silverware, pots and pans, equipment not specified in footnote *b*, insurance on furnishings, and repairs to and cleaning of furniture and equipment.

d. Includes consumer units not reporting income and with negative incomes.

e. Includes consumer units not reporting income, and with gross cash income of less than $200 and of $25,000 or more.

household operation outlays, were less. Financial and legal expenses were especially large in 1929 and the years immediately following, with the result that a somewhat larger share of consumer expenditures was devoted to household operation.

FURNITURE AND FURNISHINGS

Expenditures for furniture and furnishings amounted to $9.5 billion during 1950, 5 per cent of total consumer expenditures. These have increased greatly over recent decades — for example, from $1.2 billion in 1909 to $3.4 billion in 1940 and $9.7 billion in 1952. (See Table 98.) But their share in total consumer expenditures has usually remained somewhat under 5 per cent, although it was larger, but only slightly larger, in 1923–1925 and in 1946–1948.

About half of the sum spent for furniture and furnishings in 1950 and 1952 was devoted to the purchase of furniture and floor coverings. These expenditures, being for the most part for durable goods, are especially affected by differences in disposable personal income.

Purchases Related to Income

Major items of furniture are purchased infrequently by families, and are not often replaced. Furniture purchases are far more postponable than, say, those of food or clothing. Families with high incomes spend much larger sums for furnishings and equipment than families with lower incomes. (See Tables 99 and 100.) In other words, family expenditures for furniture and floor coverings are highly "income elastic." [17]

17. Tables 99 and 100 summarize recent available data on family expenditures for furnishings and equipment by income class. See also H. Gregg Lewis and Paul H. Douglas, *Studies in Consumer Expenditures* (1901, 1918–1919, 1922–1924), University of Chicago Press, Chicago, 1947.

Since these expenditures are found to vary among families of different income, it is logical to assume that they will vary with the general level of incomes. Investigators of the relationship of aggregate consumer spending and aggregate disposable personal income have found that this is true.[18]

The direction in which family income is changing, as well as its present level, also affects the amounts spent for furniture and furnishings. A family survey, for example, that took account of the previous as well as the current year's income showed a larger share of family living expenditures devoted to furniture by those whose incomes had risen than by those with little change in income from the year before. The smallest purchases were reported by those with decreased incomes.[19]

Rate of Family Formation

A third factor in family purchases of furniture is the age of the family, often described as its stage in the family life cycle. Age and income are related, but an analysis of family data in which income was held constant shows clearly the relationship of age and furniture expenditures. Young couples, for example, were found to spend nearly four times as much for furniture as did couples in which the wife was sixty or older. Moreover, among families with children, those with only one child under five spent more than twice as much as those at a later stage in the family life cycle.[20] Accordingly, in a period in which the rate of family formation is high, high consumer expenditures for furniture would be expected. Since the level of income affects both the marriage rate and the extent to which

new households are set up, its impact on the amount of furniture expenditures is further intensified.[21]

Recent Trends

Looking back over several decades, the depression years 1932–1935 ranked lowest in the percentage of total consumer expenditures devoted to furniture and furnishings. (See Figure 40.) During World War II, consumer expenditures for furniture were below the level that would be expected in relation to disposable income because supplies were restricted. After 1946, war-induced scarcities were overcome and furniture expenditures increased. By 1949, the backlog demand appeared to have been met.

While 1951 expenditures for furniture and furnishings of $9.8 billion were the highest on record dollar-wise, they were in line with prewar experience as a share of the total sum spent by consumers. This sum could, then, be described as representing consumer expenditures for furniture in a year when markets were well stocked, personal disposable income had been at a high level for several years, and new families were a relatively large group in the population.

MECHANICAL APPLIANCES

Expenditures for mechanical appliances in 1950 amounted to $3.0 billion, and in 1952 to $2.4 billion. Mechanical appliances have taken an increasing share of the total sum spent by consumers. In 1909, for example, they accounted for 0.5 per cent of total consumer expenditures. By 1940 this share had increased to 1.2 per cent. In 1950 it had reached 1.6 per cent, but in 1952 it had dropped back to 1.1 per cent.

In 1950 over 6 million refrigerators were sold and over 4 million washing machines. (See Table 101.) The large sales and consequent high level of consumer expenditures for mechanical appliances were, in part, a response to the unfulfilled demand of the war period. By 1949, this war-deferred demand appeared to have been met. But in 1950, consumer expenditures were still high, doubtless stimulated by fear of shortages of consumer durable goods in the event of war. During 1951–1953, sales of washing machines and refrigerators were less, but still substantial.

18. Walter Jacobs and Clement Wilson, "The Post-war Furniture Market and the Factors Affecting Demand," *Survey of Current Business,* May 1950, p. 9, and Clement Wilson and Mabel A. Smith, "Income Sensitivity of Consumption Expenditures," *Survey of Current Business,* January 1950, p. 18.

19. Jean L. Pennock and Elisabeth L. Speer, "Changes in Rural Family Income and Spending in Tennessee, 1943–1944," Miscellaneous Publication No. 66, U.S. Department of Agriculture, pp. 7–11.

20. "How Families Use Their Incomes," Miscellaneous Publication No. 653, U.S. Department of Agriculture, 1948, pp. 14 and 15. Similar conclusions are drawn from the Survey of Consumer Finances in which families were sorted by the amount spent for durable goods (including automobiles as well as household durables) and the number of years married. See "1950 Survey of Consumer Finances," Part II, *Federal Reserve Bulletin,* July 1950, p. 21.

21. S. Morris Livingston, "Family Formation and the Demand for Residential Construction," *Survey of Current Business,* March 1950, p. 10.

TABLE 101. MANUFACTURERS' SALES OF SELECTED MECHANICAL APPLIANCES,
1940, 1941 AND 1946–1953
(*Thousands*)

	1940	1941	1946	1947	1948	1949	1950	1951	1952	1953
Refrigerators, electric	2,700	3,500	2,100	3,400	4,766	4,450	6,200	4,075	3,570	3,775
Washing machines, power	1,553	2,014	2,124	4,281	4,616	3,200	4,406	3,488	3,274	3,506
Vacuum cleaners	1,699	2,053	2,370	3,987	3,651	3,080	3,760	2,905	2,997	2,948
Toasters	2,307	2,641	3,500	5,019	4,850	4,200	4,525	3,725	2,975	3,165
Air conditioners, room	11	33	30	43	76	96	195	238	365	1,075
Dryers, clothes	a	a	a	58	92	106	318	492	635	685
Freezers, home	a	a	210	607	690	485	890	1,050	1,140	1,200
Ironing machines	176	259	175	599	477	307	409	284	211	170

Source: *Electrical Merchandising,* January 1954, pp. 82-84. Includes exports.
a. Not available.

Income and Other Influences

Some of the recent consumer spending for mechanical equipment is due to the high level of consumer disposable income.

The more important appliances, like major household furnishings, are purchases that families make infrequently. They are more readily postponable than many other consumer expenditures, and once acquired, these items are used over a long period. Hence, as with furniture, sales of mechanical equipment are sensitive to the level of consumer disposable income, and to the direction in which it is changing. In recent years, however, many kinds of mechanical equipment have become so widely owned that they have become increasingly a part of the American standard of living, and differentials in expenditures between income classes are not so great as formerly.

Widespread use of credit to finance the purchase of consumer durable goods began before World War I and developed rapidly during the 1920s and 1930s. So much of the furniture and mechanical appliances that consumers purchase is now bought on credit, that the availability and terms of credit are a factor in the level of spending for these goods. Judged by reports from 1949 and 1951, the proportion using consumer credit is a little over one half, and some increase since 1946 is indicated.[22]

DOMESTIC SERVICE

Before World War I, between 2.0 and 2.5 per cent of total consumer expenditures went for domestic service. In the late 1920s just under 2.0 per cent was spent for this purpose. In 1950 and 1952, however, domestic service took only a little more than one cent of the average consumer dollar.

Purchases of mechanical appliances exceeded expenditures for domestic service for the first time in 1941. Since then consumer expenditures for service and mechanical housekeeping aids have been close; in some years consumers have spent more for domestic service, in others, more for mechanical appliances.

MISCELLANEOUS HOUSEHOLD OPERATION

A variety of goods and services are covered by three categories of household operation and equipment: (1) communication, which comprises telephone and telegraph service, postage, and writing supplies; (2) cleaning, repair and maintenance, which includes laundering, cleaning and repairs, cleaning and polishing preparations, moving expenses, and insurance against fire and theft; and (3) financial and legal expenses, which are mainly for legal services, interest on personal debt, brokerage and bank charges.

Communication expenditures in 1950 amounted

22. Surveys of Consumer Finances, 1950 and 1952, *Federal Reserve Bulletin,* June 1947, p. 17; July 1950, p. 17; and August 1952, p. 4. The percentages using credit and/or other borrowing for selected durable goods

were: 1946, 35; 1947, 42; 1948, 41; 1949, 54; 1950, 50; 1951, 52. For trends in the aggregate amount of consumer credit outstanding, see "Revision of Consumer Credit Statistics," *Federal Reserve Bulletin,* April 1953, pp. 336-354.

to $2.9 billion and to $3.5 billion in 1952, above 1.5 per cent of total expenditures in both years. Since the turn of the century, by far the most striking development in this area has been the increase in the general use of the telephone. In 1907 there were 6.1 million telephone instruments in use; by 1917 the number was 11.7 million; in 1929, 19.3 million; in 1940, 20.8 million; and in 1953, 48.1 million.[23] These figures, however, include business telephones as well as those for private family use.

The total sum of $1.8 billion spent by consumers in 1950 and $1.9 billion in 1952 for cleaning, repair and maintenance amounted to slightly less than one per cent of all consumer expenditures. Over the years this share has remained about the same. Purchases of cleaning and polishing preparations accounted for a little more than one third of the expenditure. The remainder was for services.

Detergents, which have come into wide use in recent years, have had only slight effect on consumer expenditures for cleaning preparations, but have been very important to the popularity of the automatic washing machine and the dishwasher. Part of the early dissatisfaction with the cleansing efficiency of automatic washers and dishwashers, for example, has been overcome by the use of detergents.

Consumer expenditures for financial, legal, insurance and death expenses came to $9.3 billion in 1950 and to $10.6 billion in 1952. This was about one third of the total spent for household equipment and operation. Brokerage charges and interest and investment counseling fees were highest in 1929 and have not since reached that level. Bank service charges, on the other hand, have to some extent been substituted to make financial expenses still the largest item in this group of consumer expenditures. Life insurance handling expense, although included in the total, is more closely related to life insurance than to the process of equipping and operating the household.

Although financial and legal expenses take a sizable slice of the household budget, most of the items in this category bear no relation to changes in tastes in housekeeping, which are the major concern of this chapter.

---

23. Figure for 1907 is from *Census of Electrical Industries*, 1922, U.S. Bureau of the Census, p. 23. Data for other years relate to January 1 of each year and are from *Bell Telephone Magazine*.

URBAN-RURAL DIFFERENCES

Developments of the past twenty years have caused a narrowing of the difference between the urban and rural population in the way in which homes are equipped and operated, and in expenditures for household furnishings and equipment. Increased farm income has made it possible for farm families to purchase the equipment needed for efficient housekeeping and has stimulated the modernizing of farm homes. In addition, electric service, a necessary condition for the widespread use of mechanical equipment, is now far more generally available on farms.

Electric Service

In 1920 only 2 per cent of all farms were supplied with electricity from central power stations. In 1935, when the Rural Electrification Administration was established, 11 per cent of farms were electrified. By 1951 the proportion had risen to 84 per cent and in 1953 to 91 per cent. Some parts of the country, chiefly those where distances between farms are great, have lagged in the electrification program. (See Figure 41 and Appendix 8–2.)

The increased availability of electric service has opened a large market for electrical equipment in rural areas. It has meant improved living conditions for farm families and has been particularly helpful to farm housewives in processing food for family use. Even so, rural households are still not so well equipped as urban households. In 1950, when 99 per cent of urban households had electric lighting, 90 per cent of rural nonfarm homes and only 78 per cent of farm homes had this convenience. In the same year 86 per cent of urban households were equipped with mechanical refrigerators, but only 72 per cent of rural nonfarm homes and 63 per cent of farm homes. Gas or electricity was used for cooking in 86 per cent of urban households in 1950, but in only 60 per cent of rural nonfarm households and in a mere 39 per cent of farm households.[24]

Family Expenditures

Large-scale surveys of family expenditures in 1935–1936 and again in 1941 indicated that farm families spent less for furnishings and equipment

---

24. *1950 Census of Housing*, Volume I, *General Characteristics*.

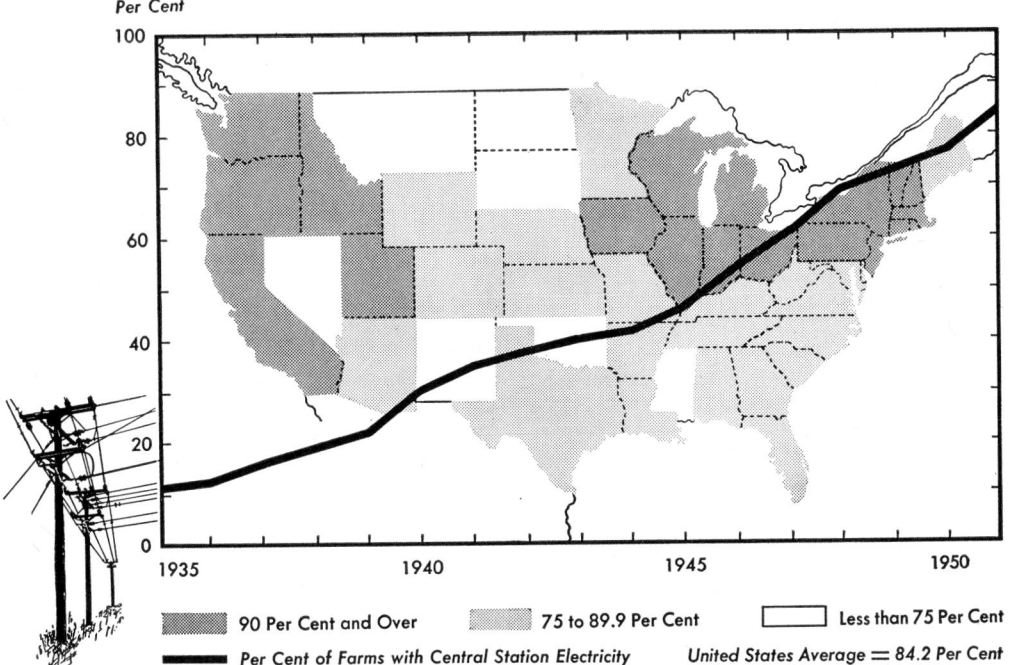

FIGURE 41. PER CENT OF NATION'S FARMS RECEIVING CENTRAL STATION ELECTRIC SERVICE, 1935–1951, AND BY STATE, JUNE 30, 1951

Source: Appendix 8–2.

than did nonfarm families. Comparable data are not available for more recent years. However, all evidence suggests that the gap between consumption expenditures of farm and nonfarm people has been narrowing since World War II and this seems to be especially true of expenditures for furnishing and equipping the home.

Trend data for recent years for selected groups of account-keeping farm families show large increases in their outlays for furnishings and equipment, especially in 1947 and 1948.[25] Moreover, in two recent state-wide surveys of farm family spending, relatively large expenditures for furnishings and equipment were reported, despite the fact that the data for one state (Illinois) related to 1946, when war-induced shortages were not completely overcome.

Illinois farm families with incomes between $1,000 and $2,000, for example, spent more for furniture and furnishings in 1946 than Detroit or Denver families with similar incomes spent

in 1949, and about the same as Memphis families. At the $2,000–$3,000 income level, the Illinois farm families spent more than Detroit families, about 90 per cent of the amount spent by Denver families and nearly three fourths of the amount laid out by Houston and Memphis families. In higher income groups the farm families spent less than the families in each of the four cities — but not always very much less: from 2 to 26 per cent less among families with incomes between $3,000 and $4,000, and from 11 to 36 per cent less among families earning between $4,000 and $5,000.[26] (See Tables 99 and 100.)

Increased expenditures for equipment by farm families are attributable to several factors. The war years when equipment was not available coincided with years of increased farm income

---

25. *Rural Family Living Charts*, Bureau of Human Nutrition and Home Economics, U.S. Department of Agriculture, October 1951, p. 57. (Prepared for 1952 Outlook Conference.)

26. Among the reasons comparisons of farm and nonfarm spending for furnishings and equipment are difficult to make are: (1) the fact that equipment is furnished in rented dwellings (and hence does not appear as family expenditure for equipment) more often for nonfarm than farm families; and (2) problems in selecting equivalent income levels for comparison, in order to avoid interpreting differences in income levels as differences in the propensity to spend.

TABLE 102. PROJECTED EXPENDITURES FOR HOUSEHOLD EQUIPMENT AND
OPERATION IN 1960 COMPARED WITH 1950

Class	Expenditures		Per Cent of Total Consumption Expenditures	
	1950	1960	1950	1960
	(Millions at 1950 Prices)			
Total	$29,060	$35,350	14.94	14.64
Furniture and furnishings	9,513	11,850	4.89	4.91
Furniture—new and secondhand	3,311	4,090	1.70	1.69
Floor coverings	1,128	1,300	.58	.54
China, glassware, tableware and utensils	1,500	1,920	.77	.80
Miscellaneous furnishings	3,574	4,540	1.84	1.88
Mechanical appliances	3,021	3,830	1.55	1.59
Domestic service	2,525	2,910	1.30	1.20
Communication	2,892	3,610	1.49	1.50
Cleaning, repair and maintenance	1,844	2,330	.95	.96
Cleaning and polishing preparations	718	890	.37	.36
Services	1,126	1,440	.58	.60
Financial, legal, insurance and death expenses	9,265	10,820	4.76	4.48

Source: Appendix 4–7.

and followed a period when many farms had been electrified. Thus, the deferred demand was especially large for the farm group. In addition, farm incomes have continued above prewar levels and electrification of farm homes has been carried forward.[27]

ESTIMATED DEMAND IN 1960

Total expenditures for household equipment and operation in 1960 are projected at $35.4 billion, at 1950 prices. The group as a whole would continue to account for nearly 15 per cent of the total sum spent by consumers. (See Table 102.)

Basic to this projection are the assumptions that the real disposable income of the population will continue to increase and that the relationships between consumer expenditures for each group of items and disposable income will continue to follow the patterns of the past. Some adjustments have been made to take account of current trends that seem especially significant, as the increasing importance of mechanical appliances, and the decreasing importance of domestic service and wool rugs.

With these adjustments, the basic assumptions

27. *Rural Family Living Charts*, p. 4.

should yield reasonably reliable projections. This is particularly true because many of the influences other than income on spending for household furnishings and equipment are themselves related to the level of income and the direction in which it is changing. For example, an increase in the number of households stimulates demand for many of the goods and services used in operating households. New dwellings are built and separate households are set up for different generations only as the level of income permits. An increase in employment opportunities, also, in addition to its effect on income, is likely to continue to cause families to move from one place to another and thus to intensify demand for household goods and services. Continued full employment, with large numbers of women holding jobs and keeping house, should also support the demand for laborsaving equipment in the home.

FURNITURE AND FURNISHINGS

Consumer expenditures for furniture and furnishings in 1960 are estimated at $11.9 billion. Continued growth in expenditures, especially for furniture and floor coverings, depends on an increase in consumer disposable income. Many kinds of furniture and floor coverings are purchased to last over a period of years, and both new purchases and replacements can be delayed from years of low income to a time of increased income.

Changes in the number of households also affect purchases of furniture and floor coverings. An increase by 1960 to 51 million households will mean a large number of new households to be equipped. A continued high rate of employment is likely to mean, also, continued migration of families. When families move in response to better employment opportunities and when young families begin housekeeping away from their parents' homes, they often choose to buy new furniture rather than pay the cost of moving some of the old. Both of these influences, the increase in the number of households and in the mobility of the population, depend on the general economic situation and add to the reasons why the level of purchases of these goods is so closely related to consumer income.

Changes in taste show a continued shift toward furniture and floor coverings that are easy to care for. The market for unpainted wood furniture and for special-purpose furniture, such as kitchen cabinets and children's furniture, has increased in the past decade and is likely to continue to expand. Some of this furniture requires a smaller initial investment than the conventional type but has, conversely, a shorter life. It is especially suited to young families and to families that do not expect to maintain a residence long in one place.

The same leaning toward kinds of furnishings that cost less originally, have a shorter life and are easy to care for is seen in the shift away from wool rugs. This shift is accentuated by the tendency to use more composition floor coverings and linoleum in houses and by price increases of wool rugs. Since both trends are likely to continue, consumer expenditures for floor coverings are not likely to increase as much as those for furniture, despite projected increases in consumer income.

MECHANICAL APPLIANCES

In 1950, consumer expenditures for mechanical appliances were unusually high, in terms of both the sum spent, $3.0 billion, and the percentage of consumer income devoted to these goods. A projection based on earlier years, but omitting the unusually low and high years during and immediately after World War II, indicates a 1960 expenditure of $3.8 billion (at 1950 prices) for mechanical appliances. Thus, continued large sales of these goods as a group are suggested, based on a continued increase in disposable income.

It could be argued that consumer expenditures for equipment have been so abnormally high in recent years that they are bound to decline. However, Americans have developed a taste for household laborsaving equipment and gadgets, and it seems fairly certain that, given the income to spend, large groups in the population will expect to own a variety of such equipment.

Since 1930, sales of refrigerators have been especially important in increasing consumer expenditures for mechanical appliances. With 80 per cent of all dwelling units equipped with mechanical refrigerators as of 1950, it is unlikely that output of this one piece of equipment will continue as high as it was in 1950. (See Figure 39.) Some demand will continue, and the factors affecting it illustrate the situation of other widely owned appliances, such as gas and electric stoves and washing machines.

Replacement Demand

Replacement of equipment should help to sustain demand for pieces now so widely used that a continued rapid growth is not likely. It will probably depend as much on the level of consumer income and on the change in products offered as on the actual wearing out of equipment. Whether the life expectancy of refrigerators is estimated at ten or fifteen years, for example, depends more on consumers' ability to buy new models and on the new designs offered than on the actual service life of the machines. The size of refrigerators has increased in the past decade and new ones may be purchased as much because the old ones are small as because they are worn out. More space for frozen foods and other new features also speed the obsolescence of older models.

Washing Machines

The replacement of old equipment by new models is well illustrated by the washing machine. It is estimated that as of 1949 only about one out of five of the washing machines in use was nonautomatic.[28] Automatic machines were

28. Psychological Corporation, *op. cit.*, p. 24.

manufactured even before 1940, but were not sold in large numbers until after World War II. Not until 1951 did their production equal that of the nonautomatic models.[29] Nonautomatic machines, therefore, probably will be replaced more rapidly than they would ordinarily wear out, as housewives shift to automatic models.

Some of the disadvantages of earlier models have been overcome. For example, many of the new machines do not need to be bolted to the floor. Some questions were at first raised about the washing ability of automatics, but recent laboratory experiments show the satisfactory performance of automatic machines.[30]

Judged by the work saved and the washing action of automatic machines, it seems likely that they will increasingly replace nonautomatic models. Where water supply is a problem, some homemakers will choose nonautomatic machines or other means of laundering that use less water. The price difference between the two kinds of machines still favors the nonautomatic, but with the projected conditions of increasing income, this price differential will probably be no more of a deterrent to the sale of automatic machines than it was in 1949 and 1950. Replacement of nonautomatic machines will help to sustain consumer expenditures at a high level, if consumer income is available.

Stoves and Vacuum Cleaners

Obsolescence of widely owned equipment speeded by the introduction of new models applies also, but to a lesser extent, to cookstoves and vacuum cleaners. Some of the sales of electric stoves in recent years reflect the popularity of electricity for cooking, as well as the equipping of rural and small-town houses to which central gas service is not available. In vacuum cleaners, the tank type is increasingly preferred. Shifts of this kind add to the expectation of increasing consumer expenditures for mechanical equipment.

New Types of Equipment

If consumer expenditures for mechanical appliances were, in the next decade, to depend

wholly on the purchase of basic equipment, such as refrigerators, cookstoves, washing machines and vacuum cleaners, by newly formed households, by households not yet equipped, or by those that buy to replace worn-out or obsolescent equipment, 1960 consumer expenditures probably would not be as high as projected. The demand for new kinds of equipment, however, is likely to be more than enough to compensate any slackening demand for the older kinds, assuming that consumer income increases. Most important among these new products are mechanical clothes dryers, ironers, dishwashers, home freezers, and room air-conditioning units.

In terms of labor saving for the housewife, the mechanical clothes dryer probably has the greatest possibility of future development. Research on home laundry methods shows that a great deal of lifting and carrying can be saved by use of the mechanical dryer. It also has demonstrated that, properly used, the mechanical dryer is at least as satisfactory as outdoor drying of laundry, if not more so.

With the concentration of population in coastal cities with damp climates, many households lack good outdoor drying conditions. The tendency to build smaller houses, without basement or attic space for drying laundry, should further stimulate the demand for dryers. Ownership of washing machines has increased greatly in the past decade, and, while it is not expected that every owner of a washing machine will eventually own a dryer, the tendency for more laundry to be done at home should greatly stimulate demand for dryers.

Home freezers are likely also to be purchased by large numbers of families. Because of the original cost, the expense of upkeep, and the materials needed for packaging food, it is unlikely that a large saving in food costs results, under present conditions of marketing foods.[31] Households that use the freezer to capacity, or that have large amounts of home produce, may show a gain in lowered food costs, but as freezers are now used in urban homes, a saving in cost cannot be proved.

In assessing future demand for home freezers, the convenience they afford is probably the more important factor. Shopping for food is one of the time-consuming tasks of housekeeping, and if

29. Unpublished data made available by the American Washer and Ironer Manufacturers Association to the Department of Commerce.

30. *Washing Machines, Selection and Use,* Home and Garden Bulletin No. 32, U.S. Department of Agriculture, 1953, p. 2.

31. *Home Freezers — Their Selection and Use,* Miscellaneous Publication No. 687, U.S. Department of Agriculture, 1949, p. 3.

more convenient ways of marketing food could be developed around the home freezer, a need for household service would be met. Whether consumers will continue to invest in freezers will depend in large part on the level of income, as well as on improvements in methods of food marketing. Homemakers will also need to know more about the most effective ways of using freezers if these appliances are to be as satisfactory and as popular as refrigerators. If freezers become established as effective time savers, demand will also depend on whether many homemakers set a high value on their time because they have the alternative of paid employment.

Electric ironers have been available for several decades, and their work-saving potentialities have been endorsed by experts in the household equipment field. Nevertheless, they have not been widely accepted. In 1950, for example, only 407,-000 were produced. Apparently many homemakers believe they are difficult to operate. Another deterrent is the trend toward simpler housekeeping and use of textiles that do not require ironing.

Electric dishwashers and room air-conditioning units are the next most important items of household equipment, in terms of recent growth. In 1953, 1.1 million room air conditioners were sold. Sales of dishwashers were generally smaller, 180,000.[32] Because the dishwasher provides help with a time-consuming and unpleasant task, sales are likely to increase. The popularity of air conditioning in theaters, restaurants, offices and factories has provided a basis for popular acceptance of home air conditioning.

Both electric dishwashers and room air conditioners illustrate the kinds of appliances that could be sold to large numbers of households if income and price relationships permit. Their present popularity indicates the appeal of mechanical equipment to American homemakers.

New Demand

New appliances will be needed to equip households not now supplied. Continued full employment, therefore, would mean that each year many families could add refrigerators, modern stoves and washing machines to their household equipment for the first time. Potential markets of this kind are especially important in rural areas. Increased farm income and use of the rural labor force in small-city industries or in industry located in the country should make it possible for rural homes to be better supplied with these basic pieces of equipment.

Electrification of farm homes will continue to open new rural markets for household equipment. The increase in rural electrification will not be as great in the next decade as in the last, simply because so large a share of the job has been done. Nevertheless, the impact of recent farm electrification probably has not yet been fully felt. Many farm families have had electric service for only a few years and have not yet completed their stock of basic equipment.

Great progress was made from 1940 to 1950 in installing pressure water systems in farmhouses. But even in 1950 fewer than half of the farmhouses (42 per cent) had installed running water. Farmhouses newly equipped with running water have provided a market for automatic washing machines and dishwashers, and there is still a potential market for this equipment on farms.

As new dwelling units are built, nearly all will be equipped with mechanical refrigerators and modern cookstoves. The addition during the 1950–1960 decade of approximately 12 million new dwelling units [33] would help sustain the market for this equipment. Some will have other kinds of equipment as well, such as washing machines and dishwashers, but the installation of refrigerators and modern cookstoves seems most assured.

DOMESTIC SERVICE

A continued decline in the proportion of consumer expenditures going for domestic service is likely. As long as other kinds of employment are readily available to women — and a projection of 69 million employed persons in 1960 would suggest that women will not be discriminated against because jobs are scarce — it is not likely that there will be a large supply of women available for domestic service. This implies competition for the workers available. The resulting high wages will mean that consumer expenditures for domestic service probably will drop less sharply than the number of employees.

If, as seems likely, households are increasingly well supplied with mechanical equipment and

---

32. *Electrical Merchandising*, January 1954, p. 83.

33. Table 91.

with services purchased with food and clothing, the lack of domestics will be partly made up by other kinds of service. The practice of family sharing in housework, which grew more prevalent after World War II, when many young men learned to help their wives run the household, is likely also to compensate increasingly for the lack of domestic service.

Current interest in amateur carpentry, home repairing, painting and remodeling is illustrative of family sharing of household tasks and the lessening distinction between men's and women's work in the home. Its impact on the market is shown by rising sales of household tools and materials.

OTHER HOUSEHOLD EQUIPMENT AND OPERATION

Consumer expenditures in 1960 for the remainder of the household equipment and operation group have been estimated on the basis of past relationships to consumer disposable income. These estimates are: $3.6 billion for communication, $2.3 billion for cleaning, repair and maintenance, and $10.8 billion for financial, legal, insurance and death expenses.

Such evidence as is available supports these conclusions. Continued expansion of telephone service is likely. The rural telephone program of the United States Department of Agriculture should give some of the same impetus to the equipping of rural homes with telephones as was provided for electricity by the electrification program. (See Appendix 8–2.)

In other household services, commercial laundering probably will be of decreasing importance, but dry cleaning and other housekeeping services are used more widely when consumer income is high.

Consumer expenditures for financial and legal services probably will continue to decline in relation to the total sum spent by consumers, as they have since 1933.

NEEDS FOR HOUSEHOLD EQUIPMENT AND OPERATION

Although over-all consumer expenditures for household equipment and operation have been relatively high in recent years and are expected to be higher still in 1960, total outlays would have to be increased in order to bring all groups in our population up to a reasonably adequate standard.

The first problem in deciding how much more needs to be spent is to select a minimum adequate standard for equipping and running the American home.

THE STANDARD

An adequate standard for household equipment and operation should provide not only for the minimum, simple physical needs, but for the far more complicated psychological and social ones as well. It is not enough to have only the physical equipment for sleeping and resting, for storing, preserving and preparing food, for washing and ironing clothes, for sweeping floors, etc. Such equipment must not be far from what is conventionally expected. Other kinds of home furnishings, especially living room furniture, rugs and curtains, are judged even more by social standards than by their usefulness in the mechanics of housekeeping.

Standards for household equipment and operation required for "decency" have much in common with standards for clothing; they are in large part a function of income level, of the distribution of families by income, of the technical competence and the culture of the community. For example, for health and comfort, shades would be a sufficient protection at windows, but curtains or Venetian blinds are necessary in most cases to meet American social standards.

The kinds of furniture, furnishings and equipment in a home affect the time required to operate the household efficiently, that is, to meet the standards of cleanliness necessary for health. If the dwelling is equipped with a mechanical refrigerator, a washing machine and a vacuum cleaner, much less time is required to provide sanitary food storage, clean clothes and a clean house than if this equipment is lacking. If the furniture and furnishings owned by a family are simply designed and easy to clean, they may provide a more adequate level of living than more elaborate and expensive furnishings that hold dust more tenaciously. But the standards of convention are not determined chiefly by ease and efficiency in housekeeping.

City Worker's Family Budget

The City Worker's Family Budget, developed by the Bureau of Labor Statistics, expresses the concept of a satisfactory standard as follows:

"This is not a 'subsistence' budget, nor is it a 'luxury' budget; it is an attempt to describe and measure a modest but adequate American standard of living." The standards of home furnishings and equipment for this budget specify a gas or electric cookstove, a mechanical refrigerator and a washing machine. These are "considered so essential that city families of moderate means possess them and families with low incomes make considerable sacrifice to obtain them."[34] Data presented earlier in this chapter on the extent to which households are equipped with these appliances also show that they should be specified in the standard.

Application of this standard in estimating the cost of meeting needs would require knowledge of the stocks of furnishings and equipment held by families. Some information on equipment ownership is supplied by the 1950 Census of Population and Housing and the 1950 Census of Agriculture. But surveys of household stocks of furniture and furnishings are too limited to serve as a basis for estimating inventories held by the total population.[35]

For lack of inventory data, the City Worker's Family Budget expresses needs for furnishings and equipment as replacement rates, based on surveys of family expenditures. The replacement rate is not necessarily the rate at which furnishings "wear out," since it is customary to replace long-lasting pieces before that time, especially when consumer incomes are high.

The needed rate of replacement, therefore, is more ambiguous, as a concept, than the needed level of expenditures for items such as food and services which are currently consumed. For these goods there is no problem of inventory. For equipment and furnishings, where inventories are important, the replacement rate of the City Worker's Family Budget at best can provide only a crude measure of need. Nevertheless, it is the best available base for an estimate of the cost of meeting needs for household furnishings and operation. (See Appendix 8–3.)

1950 COST OF MEETING NEEDS

Furnishings and Equipment

Cost estimates for the budget list of furnishings and equipment have been made for various dates, the most recent being for ten large cities of the United States in October 1949.[36]

Adjustments have been made for family size (the budget was based on a four-person family, while the national average family size is two or more persons) and for addition of replacement costs of stoves and refrigerators, which in the budget are included in housing costs. The resulting estimate for 1950 is $88 per family,[37] as the cost of replacing the items listed in the Family Budget of the City Worker for household furnishings and equipment.

Budget estimates of this kind have not been made for small-city or rural families. But since differences in spending for furnishings and equipment between farm and city families, which formerly were large, have decreased so much during the past decade, it seems reasonable to use the figure of $88 per family as a rough estimate for the total population. To the extent that standards are influenced by mass media, and that rural and urban families buy in the same markets, the cost of maintaining an acceptable standard tends to be uniform.

For the 38.7 million families in 1950, an average expenditure of $88 per family would come to $3.4 billion, about one fourth of the total sum spent for furnishings and household equipment in that year. Thus, if the total expenditure in 1950 were divided equally among all families, it would provide many times over the current average replacement cost of furnishings and equipment in the City Worker's Budget. It is obvious that the aggregate is not spent equally by all families, and some means is needed of identifying the group with average expenditures below the estimated budget cost.

---

34. *Workers' Budgets in the United States: City Families and Single Persons, 1946 and 1947*, Bulletin No. 927, U.S. Bureau of Labor Statistics, pp. 3 and 33.

35. See Calla Van Syckle, *Consumer Use and Purchase of Furniture in Flint, Michigan, 1951*, Technical Bulletin 233, Agricultural Experiment Station, Michigan State College, October 1952; and Dorothy Dickins, *The Use of Cotton in Housefurnishings*, Technical Bulletin 34, Agricultural Experiment Station, Mississippi State College, October 1952.

---

36. *Monthly Labor Review*, February 1951, p. 154.

37. The estimate for families of two or more, based on the City Worker's Budget, is $74. An annual replacement rate of .06 is used for refrigerators and stoves, which, when applied to 1950 mail-order catalogue prices for the low-priced family-size items, yields an addition of $14 to the budget cost. This replacement rate is often used, for example, in the City Worker's Budget. If these pieces of equipment were kept until they were entirely "worn out," the replacement rate would undoubtedly be lower. But since it is not customary to use equipment that long, this rate probably is close enough to the concept of adequacy used here.

TABLE 103. ESTIMATED NEEDS AND DEMAND FOR HOUSEHOLD EQUIPMENT
AND OPERATION IN 1950 AND 1960
(*Millions at 1950 Prices*)

| | 1950 | | 1960 | |
Class	Demand	Needs[a]	Demand	Needs[a]
Total	$29,060	$29,253	$35,350	$35,540
Furniture, furnishings, equipment and appliances	12,534	12,699	15,680	15,840
Domestic service	2,525	2,525	2,910	2,910
Communication	2,892	2,892	3,610	3,610
Cleaning, repair and maintenance	1,844	1,872	2,330	2,360
Financial and legal expenses	9,265	9,265	10,820	10,820

Sources: Demand estimates from Appendix 4–7; for estimates of needs, see accompanying text.

a. Needs exceed demand by the amount deemed necessary to bring replacement expenditures of all families up to the desired level; expenditures for new equipment by families not owning such equipment previously are included in the needs estimates only to the extent they are already in the demand figures.

Families Spending below Budget Level

From a review of recent published and unpublished data on family expenditures, it is evident that only in the income class below $1,000 were average expenditures for furnishings and equipment less than the estimated replacement cost. Average 1950 expenditures of families in that income class are estimated at $30,[38] or $58 under the needed level. For the 2,840,000 families[39] with incomes below $1,000 in 1950, the aggregate deficit is thus estimated at $165 million.

It does not necessarily follow that the furnishings and equipment owned by all these low-income families were inadequate. This income group includes many older families, whose stock of household goods would require less replacement than would that of the average family. Other families in this low income group may have had higher incomes in earlier years, and thus may also have had more than minimum stocks. Compensating for these would be the families with incomes over $1,000 that probably had furnishings and equipment below the standard specified.

Unmet needs can be estimated by this method for such items as soaps, other supplies for clean-ing and laundry, matches and household paper. The budget cost for these items is estimated at $37; average expenditures of families with incomes under $1,000, at $27. The 1950 deficit, for 2,840,000 families, is thus estimated at $28 million for "cleaning, repair and maintenance." (See Table 103.)

While it is reasonable to assert that there are unmet needs for domestic service, cleaning and repair of home furnishings, telephone and telegraph service, or the services of bankers, lawyers and life insurance agents, it is not feasible to estimate the extent of these needs or the cost of meeting them.

The estimated additional expenditure for meeting needs is less than 1 per cent of total consumer expenditures for all items of household operation. This is understandable in view of the importance of services, for which it is almost impossible to specify a minimum or adequate list. Moreover, furniture, furnishings, equipment and appliances have in this calculation been handled on a replacement basis, resulting in a lower figure than if the cost of equipping households not now supplied with basic equipment had been included.

1960 COST OF MEETING NEEDS

It is assumed, in the absence of factual material, that the difference between expenditures for the income class under $1,000 and the budget cost of furnishings, equipment and cleaning supplies would be the same in 1960 as for 1950. Since the

38. Estimates of expenditures were first derived from data on family expenditures and then adjusted upward to take account of the fact that stoves and refrigerators are often furnished with rented dwellings, especially in larger cities.

39. See Appendix 4–3 for a general description of the method followed in deriving estimates of the number of families at different income levels.

estimated number of families in that income class in 1960 is only a little smaller, the cost of meeting needs in 1960 is not much different from the 1950 estimate: $160 million for furnishings and equipment and, when rounded, to $30 million for cleaning, repair and maintenance.

UNMET NEEDS FOR DURABLE HOUSEHOLD EQUIPMENT

The estimated replacement cost derived from the Family Budget of the City Worker is expected to cover the average cost of keeping an established inventory of furnishings and equipment in condition. For major pieces of furnishings and mechanical appliances, replacement allows for new purchases when pieces are worn out or otherwise deemed to need replacing, but it does not allow for the purchase of equipment by the many families that do not have the minimum specified by the standard. These purchases are, in a sense, investments, because of their durability. Moreover, while there is no doubt that they are "needed," it would not be reasonable to require that all of this need be met in any one year. On the other hand, in the projections of 1960 expenditures, it has been assumed that large numbers of families not now supplied will purchase some equipment, and these purchases have thus been considered as consumer expenditures, rather than as investment.

Four pieces of equipment which can be considered part of the American standard of living and for which 1950 ownership is known — electric irons, mechanical refrigerators, modern cookstoves and washing machines — show how large a sum this kind of potential expenditure might be. Providing one of each of these items, except the washing machine, for each family of two or more persons would seem a reasonable goal to meet present needs. Since 10 per cent of families report that they are "regular" users of laundries, and 12 per cent use coin-operated machines either in self-service laundries or in apartment houses, the standard of having laundry

done by mechanical means could be met without providing a washing machine for each family.[40] How much of the regular use of self-service and commercial laundries is because the "need" for equipment at home is not met can be only a matter of conjecture. However, it seems reasonable to assume that 80 per cent of families should own washing machines.

On this basis, unmet needs in 1950 for these four pieces of equipment are estimated as follows: electric irons, 4.3 million; mechanical refrigerators, 7.7 million; gas or electric stoves, 10.4 million; washing machines, 7.7 million. On the basis of 1950 prices, meeting these needs alone would cost $2.6 billion. If allowance is made for 5.3 million new families added between 1950 and 1960,[41] an additional $0.2 billion might be spent, or a total of $2.8 billion during the decade, to fully satisfy the need for these appliances.[42] As explained in the footnote to Table 103, however, no special allowances were made in the "needs" estimates for this equipment, mainly because of the nebulousness of needs standards for new equipment. Instead, actual and projected demand were taken as the best measures of need, and expenditures for such equipment are included in the needs estimates only to the extent that they are already in the demand figures.

SUMMARY

In summary, adequate annual replacement of existing inventories and addition of appliances as demanded would have brought needed expenditures for "household operation" to $29.3 billion in 1950 and would bring them to $35.5 billion in 1960 (at 1950 prices).

---

40. Psychological Corporation, op. cit., pp. 9 and 22.
41. See Table 37.
42. Computed on the basis of the lowest prices for family-size items in 1950 Spring-Summer mail-order catalogues. Using prices more representative of what people pay (supplied by the Bureau of Labor Statistics and the Bureau of Agricultural Economics), the estimated investment would be $4.3 billion in 1950 and $4.6 billion if allowance is made for new families added between 1950 and 1960.

## CHAPTER 9

TRANSPORTATION

DEVELOPMENTS IN TRANSPORTATION in the United States have closely paralleled economic progress and social change. That the nation's growth and its mobility are related in this way is understandable, for, in the first place, an efficient and productive society is one in which obstacles of time and distance have to a large extent been overcome. Second, an economically advanced society in its specialization of activities causes regions and people to be closely dependent on one another for their daily needs, and this dependence is reflected in the volume of travel and commerce. Thus, high levels of industrial activity and employment mean more people traveling to and from work, more raw materials transported to the factory, and more finished goods delivered to consumers. Expansion of home ownership and development of suburban living increase the need for the family car. Consolidation of schools creates a need for more school buses. A growing population increasingly occupied in nonagricultural activities means more hauling of food from rural producing areas to metropolitan districts.

There is another reason to expect a close relationship between economic and social phenomena and the art of getting people and goods from one place to another. As rising levels of economic activity create more traffic, more resources must be allocated to the provision of transportation facilities and services. The freedom of movement which characterizes America today is achieved only through the efforts of millions of its people and the application of a large portion of its material resources — coal, steel, petroleum, rubber and countless other things — to the construction and operation of railroads and highways, motor vehicles, ships and aircraft.

Continuing growth of the national product will mean a sustained upward trend in the de-

mand for transportation. National defense requirements have accelerated the tempo of transport development and have promoted technological innovations in transport methods. The expansion of air power; developments in metals, power plants and fuels; and the commercial application of atomic energy are among the many factors that provide a continuing basis for revolutionary advances in transportation.

THE TRANSPORTATION SYSTEM

In 1953 the American people traveled over half a trillion miles, and their freight transportation system carried more than one trillion ton-miles of intercity traffic. The bill paid for all forms of passenger and freight facilities and services during the year, including capital outlay and expenditures for water, rail, pipeline, highway and air transport, is estimated at no less than $50 billion.

During the past three decades, transportation by highway has emerged as one of the dominant features of American life, and the use of automobiles, buses and trucks continues to expand. An extensive network of pipelines has provided a major distribution system, and water transportation has been stimulated by expansion of the merchant marine in wartime and by improvement of harbors and waterways. Air travel, both domestic and international, has developed very rapidly, and air freight provides a further addition to the transportation system. The railroads during this time have lost passenger business, but have carried a record volume of freight and have continued to move a major share of the goods in intercity commerce.

Facilities, Equipment and Employment

The United States possesses a substantial part of the world's transportation facilities and equipment. It owns 30 per cent of the world's rail mileage, one third of the highways and nearly eight out of every ten motor vehicles. Its pipe-

By WILFRED OWEN, The Brookings Institution. Opinions and judgments expressed in this chapter are those of the author and should not be attributed to the organization with which he is associated.

TABLE 104. PASSENGER TRANSPORTATION, 1916–1952

Type of Transport	Passenger-Miles				Percentage Distribution			
	1916	1940	1950	1952	1916	1940	1950	1952
	(Billions)							
Common carriers	42.9	37.7	61.9	69.3	100	100	100	100
Railways [a]	42.0	23.8	31.8	34.2	98	63	51	50
Buses	—	11.6	20.9	21.1	—	31	34	31
Inland waterways	0.9	1.3	1.2	1.4	2	3	2	1
Air carriers	—	1.0	8.0	12.6	—	3	13	18
Automobiles	18.0	496.0	540.0	600.0	—	—	—	—
Local public carriers [b]	14.5	13.1	17.2	15.1	—	—	—	—

Source: Interstate Commerce Commission Annual Reports.

a. Includes approximately 4 billion passenger-miles of railroad commuter traffic in 1940 and 5 billion in 1950 and 1952.

b. Billions of passengers.

line and air transport systems far exceed those of any other nation. The millions of miles of basic transportation routes over which the traffic of the nation moves, and the millions of units of equipment in which traffic is carried, present an imposing picture: [1]

Basic Transport Facilities	Miles
Highways—surfaced	2,070,387
Railways	224,732
Airways—domestic	65,940
Pipelines—petroleum	173,000
Inland waterways	28,383
Airports (number of units)	5,500*

Transportation Equipment	Number of Units
Railway locomotives	37,343
Railway passenger cars	34,767
Electric surface and rapid transit cars	19,176
Railway freight cars	1,776,741*
Passenger automobiles	45,035,000*
Trucks	9,460,000*
Buses—transit, school, intercity	250,000*
Aircraft—scheduled airline †	1,420*
Aircraft—private	54,000
Inland waterway vessels	14,400
Merchant fleet vessels	1,469

* 1953 data.   † Domestic and international.

1. Air Transport Facts and Figures, 1953, Air Transport Association of America; Civil Aeronautics Administration; Transit Fact Book, 1953, American Transit Association; Automobile Facts and Figures, 1953, and Motor Truck Facts, 1953, Automobile Manufacturers Association; Statistics of Railways of Class I, United States, Calendar Years 1939 to 1952, Association of American Railroads; The Inland Waterways and Mass Production, American Waterways Operators, Inc., 1952; Bureau of Public Roads, Table M–2; Competitive Transportation Review, December 1953. Except where otherwise indicated, data are for 1952.

More than 11 million persons were employed in 1953 in the construction, maintenance and operation of these transport facilities and in the provision of the many services directly related to their use. It is estimated that 9.5 million persons were employed in motor vehicle manufacture, petroleum refining, vehicle sales and servicing, highway work, and truck and bus operation.[2] Over a million persons were employed directly by the railroads, and thousands of others worked in supporting industries.[3]

Traffic Patterns, Past and Present

Technological innovations and the expansion of transport facilities and services during the past quarter century have brought about marked changes in traffic movement. Decades ago the railroads were responsible for practically all intercity passenger transportation by public carriers. By 1952 their share had declined to less than half the total, with buses carrying a third of the traffic and the airlines nearly a fifth. Passenger transportation by intercity public carriers and railroad commuter service increased moderately between 1916 and 1952, from 43 billion passenger-miles to 69 billion. Urban transit passengers were only slightly more numerous in 1952 than in 1916. Private automobile transportation, however, grew from a negligible volume to 600 billion passenger-miles, half in rural and half in urban areas. (See Table 104.) The motor

2. Automobile Facts and Figures, 1953, Automobile Manufacturers Association, p. 62.

3. Railway Age, January 11, 1954, p. 115.

TABLE 105. INTERCITY FREIGHT TRAFFIC, 1926, 1950 AND 1952

Type of Transport	Ton-Miles			Percentage Distribution		
	1926	1950	1952	1926	1950	1952
	(Billions)					
Total	586.7	1,017.0	1,133.9	100.0	100.0	100.0
Railroads	450.6	596.9	623.5	76.8	58.7	54.9
Great Lakes, rivers and canals	92.5	164.6	168.4	15.7	16.2	15.0
Trucks	16.2	126.0	184.1	2.8	12.4	16.2
Oil pipelines	25.9	129.2	157.5	4.4	12.7	13.9
Electric railroads	1.5	—	—	0.3	—	—
Air carriers	—	0.3	0.4	—	—	—

Source: Interstate Commerce Commission Annual Reports; 1952 data from Interstate Commerce Commission, *Monthly Comment on Transportation Statistics*, April 12, 1954, p. 14.

vehicle had become the principal passenger carrier, accounting for six out of every seven passenger-miles of travel outside of cities and for three out of every four passengers transported within urban areas.

Mainly because of increased use of the motor vehicle, American mobility has been growing enormously, both within urban areas and outside them. Per capita travel outside of cities increased from about 500 miles in 1916 to nearly 2,200 miles in 1950. Total travel per capita is now about 4,300 miles a year.

Freight movement has not grown as much as passenger travel, although in 1952 the volume was about double the 1926 figure. Most notable has been the increase in the share of the burden carried by motor trucks and pipelines. In 1926, 587 billion ton-miles of freight, or approximately 5,000 ton-miles per capita, were carried by rail, highway, water and pipeline. In 1952 the total was one trillion ton-miles, or over 6,700 per capita. The proportion of total ton-miles accounted for by railroads fell from 77 per cent in 1926 to 55 per cent in 1952, as truck traffic multiplied eleven times and oil pipeline business six times. (See Table 105.)

TRENDS IN TRAVEL [4]

The total of 61 billion passenger-miles of intercity travel by common carrier in 1953 rep-resented a much heavier peacetime traffic than the prewar average. Passenger transportation by common carrier declined after World War II as the wartime dislocations (and particularly the difficulty of buying new automobiles) disappeared. The downward trend would presumably have continued had it not been for the Korean conflict and the sharp increase in industrial activity resulting from defense mobilization. These developments reversed the downward trend in bus and rail traffic for a short period and caused sharp increases in air travel. In recent months rail and bus travel have continued to decline, and air travel has continued to rise.

In the prewar years, common carrier travel was about at its peak in 1929, 1937 and 1940, when between 31 and 33 billion passenger-miles of travel were recorded. These years were the best years for the economy as a whole during the 1929–1940 period. The low point in common carrier traffic was reached in the depression of 1932 and 1933, when intercity travel ranged from 18 to 19 billion passenger-miles. In relation to population also, travel was heaviest during good years and lightest during bad years. In 1929, 1937 and 1940, per capita travel ranged from 246 miles to 255 miles; in 1932 and 1933, the per capita rate fell to 149 and 154 miles.

A much more uniform relationship between

4. Attention is directed primarily to passenger transportation because consumption expenditures, with which this chapter is particularly concerned, involve only expenditures by the final consumer and therefore exclude expenditures for freight, and also travel expenditures charged to business. (Amounts spent for business travel and freight are included in the prices paid by consumers for goods and services.)

TABLE 106. INTERCITY TRAVEL BY COMMON CARRIER, 1929–1953[a]

Year	Passenger-Miles		
	Total	Per Capita	Per $100 Billion of Gross National Product[b]
	(Billions)		(Billions)
1929	31.0	255	19.6
1930	27.3	222	19.0
1931	22.7	183	17.1
1932	18.6	149	16.4
1933	19.3	154	17.1
1934	22.2	176	17.8
1935	24.0	189	17.7
1936	29.1	227	18.9
1937	32.4	251	20.1
1938	28.8	222	18.7
1939	30.5	233	18.2
1940	32.4	246	17.7
1941	40.3	303	19.0
1942	71.7	536	30.1
1943	111.6	833	41.8
1944	118.9	897	41.3
1945	116.6	882	41.4
1946	90.3	646	35.6
1947	69.4	484	27.3
1948	64.3	440	24.4
1949	57.6	388	21.8
1950	55.7	370	19.4
1951	62.6	405	20.4
1952	63.0	404	19.9
1953[c]	60.8	380	18.5

Sources: Interstate Commerce Commission Annual Reports. Economic data based on Appendix 4–2, Table B.

a. Excludes railroad commuter service and inland waterways.
b. In 1950 dollars.
c. Preliminary.

traffic volume and economic activity is observed when intercity travel is related to the national product, expressed in constant dollars. During the entire period from 1929 through 1940, common carrier business varied within a range of 16 to 20 billion passenger-miles for each $100 billion of gross national product expressed in 1950 dollars. (See Table 106.)

The war period upset these relationships. Per capita intercity travel by public carrier in 1944 rose to nearly 900 miles, or three to four times prewar figures; and in relation to a fixed unit of gross national product, intercity travel doubled. Abnormal demands were responsible for this distortion: troop movements, capacity operation of the economy, and long hauls to and from the West Coast due to the war in the Pacific. A major added factor was the shift to public carriers of traffic which would normally have moved by private automobile.

Over the years, intercity traffic has shifted significantly to the newer types of carriers. Railroad patronage has declined, air travel has increased markedly and buses have captured a substantial part of the market. From 1929 to 1953 the railroads' share of intercity common carrier traffic fell from 78 per cent to 46 per cent, while scheduled airline travel increased from one tenth of one per cent of the total volume to 24 per cent. Buses, which already accounted for 22 per cent of the total in 1929, had increased their share to 30 per cent by 1953. (See Appendix 9–1.)

TABLE 107. RAILROAD PASSENGER TRAVEL, 1900–1953

Passenger Travel	1900	1929	1933	1940	1950	1952	1953
Passengers carried (*millions*)	577.0	780.0	433.0	453.0	488.0	469.6	456.8
Passenger-miles (*billions*)	16.0	31.0	16.0	23.8	31.8	34.2	31.7
Commuter service	—	6.9	—	4.0	5.0	4.9	4.8
Other than commuter	—	24.1	12.1	19.8	26.8	29.3	26.9
Coach	—	11.3	6.8	12.5	17.4	19.8	19.0
Pullman	—	12.8	5.3	7.3	9.3	9.5	7.9

Source: *Statistics of Railways in the United States, 1950,* Interstate Commerce Commission. 1952 and 1953 data from I.C.C., *Monthly Comment on Transportation Statistics,* May 15, 1953 and March 16, 1954.

RAILROAD TRAVEL

Inroads of the automobile and bus, and later the airplane, have sharply reduced passenger travel by rail. This long-range trend has fluctuated in recent years in accordance with economic conditions. A low level of industrial activity reduced railroad travel in the middle 1930s to a level below that of almost a generation earlier. Far fewer passengers were carried in 1933 than in 1900, and there was no change in passenger-miles traveled. By 1940 there was substantial recovery from the lean years of the depression, and during the war period rail patronage increased to record heights.

The war placed heavy burdens on the railroads. Troop movements required the services of half of all Pullman equipment and one out of every six coaches. A tremendous volume of civilian traffic was generated by peak industrial activity and by the shift of intercity and commuter traffic from the automobile. In 1944 railroad traffic swelled to an all-time record of 98 billion passenger-miles, as contrasted with the prewar high of 47 billion passenger-miles in 1920. By 1953 railroad travel had fallen off sharply. Total rail passenger travel was only slightly above the 1929 figure. Pullman travel was about 27 per cent less than in 1929, with a heavier loss in parlor car than in sleeper service, while coach patronage was up 68 per cent. (See Table 107.)

INTERCITY BUS

Approximately 18,000 intercity buses, operating on 300,000 miles of highways, were handling 12.0 billion passenger-miles of intercity traffic in 1940. By 1953 the traffic volume was

TABLE 108. INTERCITY BUS TRAVEL, 1929–1953

(Billions)

Year	Passenger-Miles	Year	Passenger-Miles
1929	6.8	1941	14.0
1930	7.1	1942	22.0
1931	6.7	1943	27.8
1932	6.3	1944	26.9
1933	6.4	1945	27.3
1934	7.1	1946	26.1
1935	7.6	1947	24.5
1936	9.2	1948	24.2
1937	12.7	1949	23.2
1938	10.1	1950	21.7[a]
1939	11.6	1951	23.2
1940	12.0[a]	1952	21.5[a]
		1953	19.7

Sources: *Bus Facts,* National Association of Motor Bus Operators, 1952, p. 7. 1952 figure from National Association of Motor Bus Operators; 1953 figure from *Air Transport Facts and Figures, 1954,* Air Transport Association, p. 19.

a. Figures differ slightly from those shown in Table 104 because different sources are used.

19.7 billion passenger-miles, 8 billion less than in the peak World War II year, 1943. (See Table 108.)

Reduction of private automobile transportation during the war shifted a large volume of traffic to the intercity bus. In 1942 buses carried 692 million passengers, compared with 361 million in 1940. Passenger-miles of travel by bus in 1943 totaled 27.8 billion, more than double the figure of three years before.

The bus has assumed a major role in passenger transportation because it can provide frequent and inexpensive service and is adapted to short

TABLE 109. EXPANSION OF DOMESTIC AIR TRANSPORT, 1935–1953

Year	Passengers[a]	Change from Previous Year	Passenger-Miles[a]	Change from Previous Year
	(Thousands)	(Per Cent)	(Millions)	(Per Cent)
1935	679	64.0	316	72.1
1936	932	37.3	439	38.9
1937	985	5.7	412	−6.2
1938	1,197	21.5	480	16.5
1939	1,705	42.2	683	42.3
1940	2,803	64.4	1,052	54.0
1941	3,849	37.3	1,385	31.7
1942	3,129	−18.7	1,418	2.4
1943	3,036	−3.0	1,634	15.2
1944	4,046	33.3	2,178	33.3
1945	6,377	57.6	3,336	47.3
1946	11,890	86.6	5,903	76.9
1947	12,279	3.3	6,016	1.9
1948	12,324	0.4	5,840	−2.9
1949	14,021	13.8	6,563	12.4
1950	15,978	14.0	7,766	18.3
1951	20,621	29.1	10,211	31.5
1952	22,768	10.5	12,121	18.7
1953	25,958	14.0	14,228	17.4

Sources: Data for 1935–1940 from *Statistical Handbook of Civil Aviation*, 1948 and 1950, Civil Aeronautics Association; data for 1941–1943 from *Air Transport Facts and Figures, 1953*, Air Transport Association of America, p. 14; data for 1944–1953 from *ibid., 1954*, p. 13. Figures before 1945 include territorial lines.

a. Excludes local service carriers, which accounted for 2 million passengers and 391 million passenger-miles in 1953.

trips. Bus trips under 20 miles in length constitute 48 per cent of all bus passenger movement, and 75 per cent of all trips are under 50 miles.[5] The bus is nevertheless a significant factor in long-distance hauling, the small proportion of trips over 500 miles accounting for 25 per cent of total bus traffic. Besides the common carrier bus in intercity service, there were in 1953 a total of 135,000 school buses operating on 2 million miles of rural highways and serving 45,000 schools. It is estimated that these buses carried nearly 6 million children every day.[6]

DOMESTIC AIRLINE TRANSPORTATION

In 1952 domestic airlines carried 26 million passengers — more than nine times the 1940 number. Passenger-miles of domestic air travel increased almost 14-fold during the same period. (See Table 109.) Local feeder service carried over two million passengers in 1953 compared with some 25,000 only seven years earlier. In addition to the scheduled airlines, large irregular carriers, or nonscheduled airlines, accounted for over one billion passenger-miles in 1953.[7]

Airlines in 1940 accounted for only 3 per cent of all passenger-miles of intercity carrier travel. By 1953 they were doing nearly one fourth of the intercity business. (See Appendix 9–1.)

The airlines' share of the combined rail-air travel from the major traffic-generating cities in the nation increased from 2.6 per cent in 1933 to 57 per cent in 1953. By 1952 more first-class travel was accounted for by the air carriers than by rail Pullman. Total air travel, including coach service, was nearly double the volume of Pullman service in 1953. (See Tables 109 and 110 and Figure 42.)

5. Exhibit E, Docket No. ME-c-550, Interstate Commerce Commission.

6. *Automobile Facts and Figures, 1951*, Automobile Manufacturers Association, p. 32; *Mass Transportation*, January 1954, p. 89.

7. *Air Transport Facts and Figures, 1954*, Air Transport Association, p. 13; and *American Aviation*, April 26, 1954.

TABLE 110. AIRLINE TRAVEL AS PER CENT OF TOTAL
AIR-RAIL TRAVEL,[a] 1946–1953
(*Millions of Passenger-Miles*)

Year	Rail Parlor and Sleeping Car	Air Regular Flights	Air as Per Cent of Rail and Air Combined
1946	19,801	5,903	23.0
1947	12,261	6,011	32.9
1948	11,015	5,822	34.6
1949	9,349	6,322	40.3
1950	9,338	6,710	41.8
1951	10,226	8,939	46.6
1952	9,504	9,775	50.7
1953	7,950	10,698	53.1

Sources: Interstate Commerce Commission, *Monthly Comment on Transportation Statistics,* May 15, 1953, p. 14; *Air Transport Facts and Figures, 1954,* Air Transport Association, p. 14.

a. First class only. Air coach travel in 1953 (3,530 million passenger-miles) represented 15.6 per cent of coach rail and air travel combined.

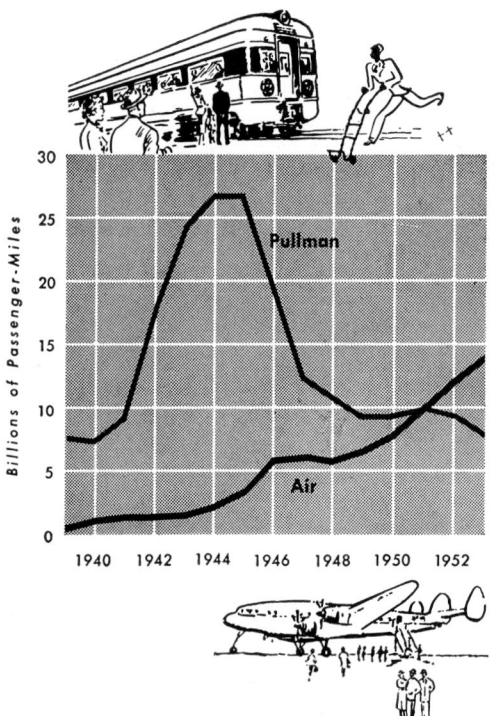

FIGURE 42. TRAVEL BY AIR AND PULLMAN, 1939–1953
Sources: Table 109 and Association of American Railroads.

PRIVATE FLYING

Private plane ownership before the war rose continuously from 8,600 planes in 1935 to 16,900 in 1940 and 24,000 in 1941. During the war, private flying was almost eliminated, but in the immediate postwar period total registration rose sharply to nearly 100,000 planes. The number of private aircraft had fallen to some 89,000 by 1952, as pleasure and instructional flying declined with the decrease in training under the G.I. Bill. Other factors in the decline of aircraft ownership include the high cost of operating war surplus planes and the expansion of military aviation as a result of the defense program. Executive-type aircraft owned by business firms and aircraft used in agriculture and industry are two notable commercial adaptations of the private plane.

DOMESTIC WATER TRAVEL

The 13 million passengers of domestic water carriers in 1940, including coastal, river and Great Lakes vessels, accounted for less than half of one per cent of all intercity travel in that year. Nevertheless, water carriers were providing more passenger-miles of travel in 1940 than the airlines. Most of these passengers were carried on Atlantic Coast runs. The outbreak of war resulted in some increase in the total volume of water traffic, but the increase was predominantly in the form of short-haul river traffic. In contrast, the former heavy volume of long-haul coastwise service was drastically reduced because of the submarine threat. In 1952 domestic water traffic totaled 1 billion passenger-miles, considerably below the 1940 volume.

INTERNATIONAL TRAVEL

In 1938, the last year in which war conditions did not restrict overseas travel, about half a million persons departed from this country for overseas destinations. International travel by United States citizens stepped up immediately after the war, and in the late 1940s made all-time records. In 1943 a low of 151,000 United States citizens moved to and from the United States and points outside the country (other than Canada, Mexico, and United States territories). By 1952 the total had risen to 773,000. Airlines alone now carry more overseas passengers than both ships and planes together carried before the war. In 1940 six times as many persons traveled to foreign countries by sea as by air; but in 1952, 300,000 more international passengers went by air than by sea.

TABLE 111. TRANSIT PASSENGERS AND RIDES PER CAPITA, 1940–1953

Year	Total Passengers [a]	Rides Per Capita [b]
	(Millions)	
1940	13,098	176
1941	14,085	188
1942	18,000	239
1943	22,000	291
1944	23,017	309
1945	23,254	312
1946	23,372	282
1947	22,540	269
1948	21,368	252
1949	19,008	219
1950	17,246	195
1951	16,125	184
1952	15,119	167
1953	13,902	150

Sources: Transit Fact Book, 1953, American Transit Association, p. 7; *Mass Transportation,* January 1954, p. 98.

a. As distinguished from revenue passengers.
b. Based on urban population according to the 1940 Census definition.

TABLE 112. AUTOMOBILE REGISTRATIONS, 1930–1953

Year	Cars Registered (End of Year)	Persons per Car	Cars per 100 Persons Employed
	(Millions)		
1930	23.0	5.4	48.4
1931	22.3	5.5	50.5
1932	20.8	6.0	52.6
1933	20.6	6.1	53.5
1934	21.5	5.9	53.1
1935	22.5	5.7	52.5
1936	24.1	5.3	53.2
1937	25.4	5.1	54.3
1938	25.2	5.1	54.8
1939	26.1	4.9	56.9
1940	27.4	4.8	57.1
1941	29.5	4.5	57.6
1942	27.9	4.8	58.6
1943	25.9	5.3	51.8
1944	25.5	5.4	47.6
1945	25.7	5.4	47.2
1946	25.1	5.0	48.6
1947	30.7	4.7	50.9
1948	33.2	4.4	52.9
1949	36.3	4.1	56.0
1950	40.2	3.8	61.8
1951	42.5	3.6	69.9
1952	43.6	3.6	71.1
1953	45.0	3.6	72.5

Sources: Automobile Facts and Figures, 1953, Automobile Manufacturers Association, p. 21; *Report of the Council of Economic Advisers,* January 1954, pp. 178, 182.

LOCAL TRANSIT

Transit patronage (bus, streetcar, rapid transit) declined gradually in the two decades preceding the war, despite population growth and the expansion of urban areas, as people moved about in cities more and more by private automobile. In 1922 the transit industry carried nearly 16 billion passengers; in 1926 and 1927, over 17 billion passengers, the prewar record number. A depression low point of 11.3 billion riders was reached in 1933, after which there was some recovery to 13 billion in 1940.

With the advent of war, however, streetcars, rapid transit and city buses were taxed to capacity by an increase in patronage. Between 1940 and 1945 the number of riders increased by 10 billion, to a record total of 23 billion. To handle the new customers the transit industry considerably expanded its use of motor vehicles — three out of every four new riders were accommodated by bus. The passenger load decreased after the war and by 1953 was only slightly above the 1940 level. (See Table 111.)

Local transit passengers are being carried more and more by trolley coaches and motor buses. Between 1940 and 1953 the number of streetcar riders declined from 6 billion to about 1.4 billion, and rapid transit patronage remained about the same. Trolley coach traffic, on the other hand, increased from 0.4 billion to over 1.5 billion passengers, and the passenger load of motor buses grew from 3.6 billion to over 8 billion.

AUTOMOBILE TRANSPORTATION

During the past decade, phenomenal changes have taken place in the ownership and operation of private automobiles. For the country as a whole, registrations increased from approximately 25.7 million in 1945 to 45 million in 1953. There were 15.5 million more cars on the road in 1953 than in 1941, the peak prewar year. Automobile ownership has been increasing more rapidly than population; in 1953 there was one car for every 3.6 persons in the United States, compared with one for every 4.5 persons in 1941. (See Table 112.) Approximately two thirds of all households own at least one car, and 8 per cent own two or more.

Automobile ownership, like population, is

TABLE 113. TEN STATES HAVING LARGEST NUMBER OF AUTOMOBILES IN 1952 AND
GREATEST INCREASES FROM 1941 TO 1952

Cars Registered in 1952			Increase in Car Registrations, 1941–1952					
Rank	State	Number	Rank	State	Number	Rank	State	Per Cent
		(Millions)			(Millions)			
1.	California	4.4	1.	California	1.8	1.	Arizona	112.2
2.	New York	3.5	2.	Texas	1.0	2.	Florida	111.4
3.	Pennsylvania	2.8	3.	New York	1.0	3.	New Mexico	102.1
4.	Ohio	2.6	4.	Pennsylvania	0.7	4.	Nevada	82.8
5.	Illinois	2.5	5.	Ohio	0.7	5.	Alabama	80.2
6.	Texas	2.5	6.	Michigan	0.7	6.	Oregon	77.3
7.	Michigan	2.2	7.	Illinois	0.6	7.	Georgia	73.3
8.	New Jersey	1.5	8.	Florida	0.5	8.	Utah	72.1
9.	Indiana	1.3	9.	New Jersey	0.5	9.	Virginia	72.0
10.	Massachusetts	1.2	10.	North Carolina	0.4	10.	Texas	69.9

Source: Automobile Facts and Figures, 1953, Automobile Manufacturers Association, p. 32.

heavily concentrated in a few large states. California, with nearly 4.4 million cars registered in 1952, had more than any other state, and the ten states having one million cars or more — California, New York, Pennsylvania, Ohio, Illinois, Texas, Michigan, New Jersey, Indiana and Massachusetts — accounted for 56 per cent of the nation's passenger cars.

California had 1.8 million more cars in 1952 than in 1940, while Texas gained a million cars. The ten states with the largest increases in car ownership during the decade, most of them also leaders in number of registrations, were responsible for approximately two thirds of the total national increase. On a percentage basis, however, the pattern of state increases was quite different. Gains of over 100 per cent were recorded in Arizona, Florida and New Mexico. (See Table 113.)

Population Factors Influencing Growth

Several factors account for the great expansion of automobile ownership and use. The most obvious one is that there were 24 million more people in 1952 than in 1940. The recent disproportionate growth in the number of individual households also accounts in part for the increased demand for the family car, since the number of households reflects the need for transportation from home to work and for shopping or other household duties. While the total population grew about 15 per cent between 1940

and 1950 (from 131.7 million persons to 150.7 million), the number of households increased by 25 per cent (from 34.9 million to 43.5 million).

During the 1940s, also, there was a disproportionate increase of population in the states which are most dependent on the automobile, particularly the western states, where distances and sparse population make public transport unfeasible, and where the speed and ready availability of the automobile are particular assets. Nearly 20 per cent of the total increase of population in the United States from 1940 to 1950 was accounted for by California, which has more cars in relation to population than any other state.

Another population factor influencing the growth of automobile registrations has been the development of suburban living. The 168 metropolitan areas in the United States accounted for four fifths of the nation's population increase from 1940 to 1950, gaining 15.2 million persons. Most of this growth occurred in the outlying areas, which are most dependent on the automobile. Population in the outlying parts of these metropolitan areas increased more than 9 million between 1940 and 1950, or almost 36 per cent, while the increase in the central cities was only 6 million, or 14 per cent. (See Table 114.)

Income and the Demand for Automobiles

Car registrations have increased also because of a growing demand for more than one car per

TABLE 114. GROWTH OF METROPOLITAN AREAS AND THEIR SUBURBS, 1940–1950

Location	Population in 1950	Increase, 1940–1950	
		Amount	Per Cent
	(Millions)	*(Millions)*	
Total	150.7	19.0	14.5
Outside metropolitan areas	66.2	3.8	6.1
Metropolitan areas	84.5	15.2	22.0
Central cities	49.4	6.0	13.9
Suburbs	35.1	9.2	35.5

Source: Seventeenth Census (1950), *Population*, Vol. I, *Number of Inhabitants*, pp. xxxi-xxxii.

household. Several years ago multiple car ownership was limited to a relatively few families. In recent years the growth of suburban living and rising incomes have made it both desirable and possible for many families to have two cars, one for home-to-work transportation and the other for shopping, transportation to school and other household use. In 1951, 8 per cent of all house-

TABLE 115. INDEXES OF AUTOMOBILE REGISTRATIONS AND NATIONAL ECONOMIC TRENDS, 1929–1953

(1940 = 100)

Year	Automobile Registrations	Population	Gross National Product [a]	Employment
1929	84.2	92.3	85.9	100.2
1930	83.9	93.3	78.1	95.7
1931	81.6	94.0	72.3	89.2
1932	76.1	94.6	61.9	81.9
1933	75.2	95.2	61.5	81.6
1934	78.4	95.8	67.9	86.0
1935	82.2	96.4	73.9	88.9
1936	88.1	97.0	83.9	93.5
1937	92.8	97.6	87.9	97.4
1938	91.9	98.4	84.0	93.1
1939	95.5	99.2	91.3	96.3
1940	100.0	100.0	100.0	100.0
1941	107.9	100.8	115.5	106.0
1942	101.8	101.4	129.7	113.1
1943	94.7	101.5	145.7	114.6
1944	93.0	100.5	156.9	113.6
1945	93.9	100.0	153.4	111.2
1946	102.7	106.0	138.4	116.3
1947	112.2	108.7	138.4	122.1
1948	121.5	110.7	143.5	125.0
1949	132.6	112.7	144.0	123.5
1950	146.7	113.6	156.2	126.2
1951	155.1	116.6	167.0	128.9
1952	159.1	118.9	172.0	129.0
1953	164.2	120.1	178.3	130.3

Sources: Automobile registrations from *Automobile Facts and Figures, 1953*, Automobile Manufacturers Association, p. 21; later data from Bureau of Public Roads, Tables MV–1. Population from *Economic Report of the President*, January 1954, p. 178. Gross national product from *Report of the Council of Economic Advisers*, January 1954, p. 170; employment from *ibid.*, p. 182.

a. Index derived from series expressed in constant (1939) dollars.

TABLE 116. PERCENTAGE CHANGES IN AUTOMOBILE OWNERSHIP AND IN
UNDERLYING FACTORS, 1940–1950, BY REGION

Region	Number of Cars	Total Population [a]	Suburban Population [a]	Per Capita Income [b]
National average	45.0	14.0	34.7	131
New England	36.9	9.7	23.9	92
Middle East	34.5	10.2	23.9	108
Southeast	70.4	11.8	43.4	174
Southwest	61.0	15.8	42.3	192
Central	35.9	11.2	33.4	134
Northwest	36.7	7.1	38.1	181
Far West	60.5	47.5	86.4	116

Source: "Automobile Transportation in Defense or War," Brookings Institution, Report to the Defense Transport Administration, U.S. Government Printing Office, 1951.

a. Figures differ from those shown in Table 114 and in Chapter 3, because they are based on preliminary 1950 Census figures.

b. Based on national income and population figures for 1940–1949.

holds in the United States owned more than one car, and in the West, where 80 per cent of all households owned at least one car, 16 per cent owned two or more.

The growth of automobile ownership has kept fairly close pace with the trend of the gross national product. From 1940 to 1953, for example, the index of automobile registrations increased

TABLE 117. PER CENT OF FAMILIES OWNING AUTOMOBILES, 1951

Description or Location of Household	No Car	At Least One	Only One	Two Cars or More
All households	33.5	66.5	58.1	8.4
Farm	29.4	70.6	59.9	10.7
Nonfarm	34.6	65.4	57.5	7.9
Geographical area				
Northeast	39.7	60.3	55.0	5.3
North Central	24.5	75.5	65.9	9.6
South	42.8	57.2	50.5	6.7
West	20.1	79.9	63.7	16.2
Metropolitan area				
500,000 population and over	45.9	54.1	48.6	5.5
50,000–499,999	37.0	63.0	56.4	6.6
Under 50,000	22.8	77.2	66.1	11.1
Outside metropolitan area				
2,500–49,999 population	27.1	72.9	62.7	10.2
Under 2,500	33.7	66.3	57.6	8.7
Income				
Under $2,000	55.3	44.7	42.7	1.9
2,000–2,999	35.5	64.5	57.5	7.0
3,000–4,999	23.2	76.8	69.1	7.7
5,000 and over	14.9	85.1	60.9	24.2

Source: "The Automobile in the Daily Life of the American Population," Alfred Politz Research, Inc., April 1951 (unpublished). See "Automobile Transportation in Defense or War," Brookings Institution, Report to the Defense Transport Administration, U.S. Government Printing Office, 1951.

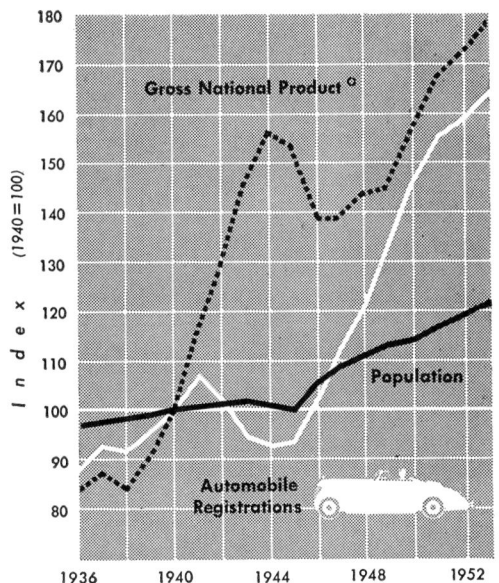

FIGURE 43. RELATION OF AUTOMOBILE REGISTRA-
TIONS TO POPULATION AND GROSS NATIONAL
PRODUCT, 1936–1953

Source: Table 115.

a. Index derived from series expressed in constant
(1939) dollars.

from 100 to 164 while the index of gross national
product increased from 100 to 178. (See Table
115 and Figure 43.)

The importance of income as a factor in automobile ownership is apparent from regional differences in the trend of auto registrations. Income per capita for the country as a whole increased 131 per cent from 1940 to 1950, but much
greater increases occurred in some areas: 192 per
cent in the Southwest, 181 per cent in the Northwest, and 174 per cent in the Southeast. In contrast, New England, the Middle East and the
Far West, where income per capita before the war
was already the highest in the nation, registered
below-average increases from 1940 to 1950. This
improvement in income position of the southern
and northwestern states largely accounts for the
marked increases in automobile registrations in
those regions. (See Table 116.)

Changes in the proportion of the population in
various income groups have also affected car
ownership. In 1941 only 5 per cent of all spending
units were receiving annual incomes of $5,000
or more. By 1954, 31 per cent were receiving
such income. Families with incomes under
$2,000 a year before taxes comprised 65 per cent

of the total in 1941; but in 1954, only 23 per
cent of all families were in this income bracket.
Although these data do not reflect taxes and
changes in the value of the dollar, the general
trend is significant. According to one study, 85
per cent of all families with incomes of $5,000
or more had cars in 1951 and 24 per cent had
two or more cars, but only 45 per cent of families with incomes under $2,000 a year were car
owners. (See Table 117.)

Automobile Production

With automobile production at a standstill
after the spring of 1942, the normal supply of
new automobiles was reduced from a ten-year
average of approximately 2,750,000 cars a year
to 250,000 rationed for each of the years 1942 and
1943, and practically none in 1944. As a result,
total registrations decreased from 29.5 million
passenger cars in 1941 to 25.7 million in 1945,
and the average age of automobiles on the road
increased from 5.3 years in 1941 to 9 years in
1947. By 1952 the average age of passenger cars
had declined to 6.8 years.[8]

Consumers in the postwar period made rapid
strides to overcome the deficiencies in private
transportation created by the wartime stoppage
of automobile production. From 1946 to mid-
1951, 22 million passenger cars were produced
for the domestic market. In 1950 a record 6.5
million new cars were produced and 1953 production was nearly as high:[9]

	Passenger Cars
1940	3,608,042
1941	3,681,558
1942	215,779
1943	121
1944	308
1945	68,093
1946	1,997,417
1947	3,272,028
1948	3,641,198
1949	4,947,920
1950	6,496,494
1951	4,809,175
1952	4,147,046
1953	6,121,787

The Auto in Intercity Travel

In recent years passenger traffic by auto on rural
highways has been five to seven times the volume

8. *Automobile Facts and Figures* (various years), Automobile Manufacturers Association.

9. *Automobile Facts and Figures, 1953*, Automobile
Manufacturers Association, p. 6.

TABLE 118. CONSUMER TRANSPORTATION EXPENDITURES, 1909–1952

(*Billions*)

Year	Total[a]	Private Automobile	Local Public Carriers	Intercity Public Carriers
1909	$ 1.5	$ 0.7[b]	$0.5	$0.3
1914	2.1	1.1[b]	0.6	0.3
1919	4.9	3.5[b]	0.8	0.6
1921	4.8	3.1	0.9	0.6
1923	6.5	4.7	1.0	0.6
1925	7.6	5.6	1.1	0.6
1927	7.2	5.1	1.1	0.6
1929	8.0	5.8	1.1	0.6
1931	5.3	3.6	0.9	0.4
1933	4.1	2.9	0.7	0.3
1935	5.4	4.1	0.8	0.3
1937	6.7	5.2	0.9	0.4
1939	6.5	5.0	0.9	0.4
1940	7.1	5.7	0.9	0.4
1941	8.4	6.8	1.0	0.5
1942	5.6	3.4	1.3	0.7
1943	6.1	2.9	1.7	1.1
1944	6.7	3.1	1.7	1.1
1945	8.2	3.8	1.8	1.2
1946	12.1	8.5	2.0	1.2
1947	15.5	11.8	2.0	1.1
1948	17.6	13.6	2.1	1.2
1949	20.2	16.1	2.1	1.1
1950	23.5	19.5	2.1	1.0
1951	23.3	18.8	2.1	1.2
1952	24.0	19.0	2.2	1.3

Source: Appendix 4–4.

a. Includes foreign travel; therefore total exceeds sum of items shown in all years except 1909 and 1919, when foreign travel was less than $0.1 billion.

b. Includes horse-drawn vehicles.

of traffic by intercity public carrier. The importance of the automobile in intercity travel is also apparent from the preponderance of consumer transportation expenditures devoted to it. Of the $24 billion spent by consumers for transportation services in 1952, $19 billion was disbursed for automobile ownership and use compared to $1.3 billion for intercity travel by public carriers.

The automobile took some intercity traffic away from the railroads, but to a much larger extent it created new traffic. Estimated passenger-miles of travel by automobile on rural highways in 1929 totaled four times the railroad traffic of 1916.

Although the automobile is used primarily for short trips, a substantial percentage of rural highway trips are for long distances. Before the war, about 22 per cent of all vehicle-miles traveled by passenger cars on rural highways represented trips of more than 100 miles one way; and in view of the tremendous mileage driven in private cars, this meant a heavy volume of traffic — perhaps in excess of 50 billion passenger-miles. Even trips of more than 250 miles one way accounted at that time for at least 20 billion passenger-miles. The importance of the private automobile in long-distance travel is demonstrated by the methods of transportation used by people traveling to New York from distant points in 1948. Of all trips to New York from places over 1,500 miles away, 43 per cent were made by auto, 35 per cent by air, 19 per cent by rail and 3 per cent by boat.[10]

10. Data from Market Research, Inc., New York, 1949, for the Port of New York Authority.

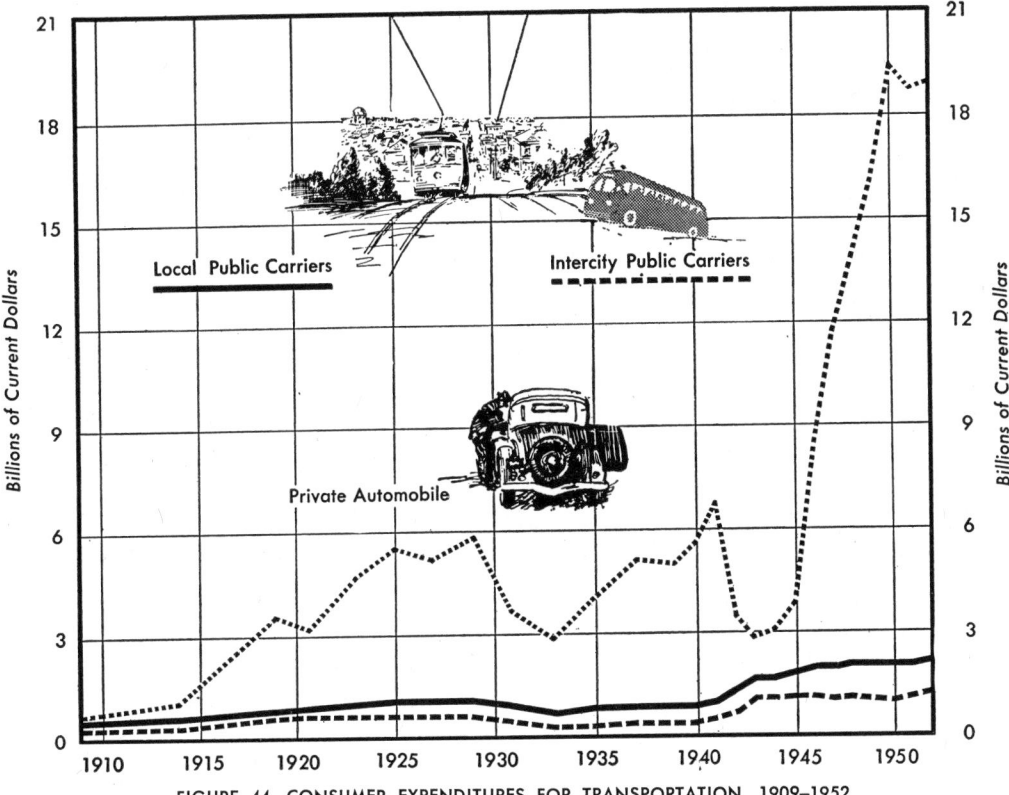

FIGURE 44. CONSUMER EXPENDITURES FOR TRANSPORTATION, 1909–1952

Source: Table 118.

TRENDS IN EXPENDITURES

CONSUMER EXPENDITURES

In the years of relative prosperity following World War I, consumer outlays for transportation comprised a fairly uniform proportion of total consumption expenditures, and in years of depression a smaller proportion. Transportation expenditures amounted to $8.0 billion, or 9.9 per cent of all consumption outlays, in 1929; $4.1 billion, or 8.9 per cent, in 1933; and $7.1 billion, or 9.9 per cent, in 1940. In 1952 the dollar outlay was $24 billion, a record high accounted for in part by the unprecedented sales of new cars during that year. Transportation expenditures constituted 11 per cent of all consumption expenditures in 1952. (See Table 118 and Appendix 4–5.)

The proportion of the total consumption outlay which has gone into the several types of transportation over a long period of time provides a valuable clue to probable future trends. The percentages accounted for by local and intercity public carrier service have changed very little since 1929. The share of local public carriers dropped slightly from 1.4 per cent in 1929 to 1.1 per cent in 1950, and at no time in that period did it go above 1.6 per cent or below 1.1. Similarly, the proportion spent for intercity travel by public carrier fell from 0.7 per cent in 1929 to 0.5 per cent in 1950, and except in the war years, varied within the narrow range of 0.5 to 0.8 per cent. The great change in transportation spending has resulted from the private automobile. Private transportation in 1909, largely by horse, cost $700 million — 2.3 per cent of all consumer expenditures. By 1952, $19 billion was spent for the automobile and its operation. (See Figure 44.)

The growing importance of private transportation is even more apparent when total expenditures for transportation are broken down according to type of transport. In 1909 private transportation accounted for 44.3 per cent of consumption expenditures for transportation. By 1952 the proportion had risen to 79.5 per cent. The

TABLE 119. PERCENTAGE DISTRIBUTION OF CONSUMER EXPENDITURES FOR TRANSPORTATION, 1909-1952

Type of Transportation	1909	1919	1923	1929	1937	1940	1949	1950	1952
All transportation	100.0	100.0	100.0	100.0	100.0	100.0	100.0	100.0	100.0
Private	44.3	71.1	72.1	72.5	76.5	80.1	79.5	82.6	79.5
Public carrier	55.7	28.9	27.9	27.5	23.5	19.9	20.5	17.4	20.5
Local	31.1	16.6	15.4	14.1	13.1	12.9	10.3	8.9	9.1
Intercity	18.1	11.6	9.0	7.0	5.8	5.7	5.3	4.4	5.3
Railway	—	—	—	5.2	3.4	3.0	2.5	1.9	2.2
Bus	—	—	—	0.6	1.2	1.4	1.6	1.3	1.4
Airline	—	—	—	—	0.1	0.3	0.7	0.7	1.1
Other	—	—	—	1.2	1.2	1.0	0.5	0.4	0.5
Foreign travel	6.5	0.6	3.5	6.4	4.6	1.3	4.8	4.2	6.1

Source: Based on Appendix 4-4.

TABLE 120. CAPITAL EXPENDITURES FOR TRANSPORTATION, 1930-1952[a]

(*Millions*)

Year	Total[a]	Private				Public			
		Railroad	Transit	Oil Pipeline	Other Private[b]	Highway Construction	Airway	Airport[c]	Waterway
1930	—	$ 865	$124	$ 26	[d]	$1,516	$ 0.2	—	$ 51
1931	—	360	132	66	[d]	1,355	0.2	—	57
1932	—	164	61	32	[d]	958	0.1	—	58
1933	$1,090	101	46	6	[d]	847	0.1	$ 34.1	56
1934	1,428	218	78	10	[d]	1,000	0.3	34.1	88
1935	1,318	168	117	17	[d]	845	2.2	34.1	135
1936	1,921	308	109	35	[d]	1,362	0.3	34.1	73
1937	2,045	524	101	57	[d]	1,226	0.8	34.1	103
1938	1,900	240	83	18	[d]	1,421	2.7	34.1	101
1939	2,155	280	107	30	$ 228	1,381	4.5	34.1	90
1940	2,400	439	113	26	398	1,302	5.0	34.1	83
1941	2,212	559	105	51	339	1,066	5.0	34.1	53
1942	1,897	539	91	68	258	734	6.3	152.0	49
1943	1,463	458	40	66	248	446	12.6	152.0	40
1944	1,624	577	65	61	369	362	7.7	152.0	30
1945	1,690	548	83	36	455	398	5.0	152.0	13
1946	2,521	583	144	54	725	895	13.7	80.0	26
1947	3,768	889	281	103	914	1,451	14.0	80.0	36
1948	4,520	1,319	236	128	921	1,774	13.6	80.0	48
1949	4,497	1,352	179	134	532	2,131	12.1	80.0	77
1950	4,794	1,111	168	141	888	2,272	17.5	80.0	116
1951	5,610	1,474	[e]	149	1,341	2,518	16.1	60.0	52
1952	5,737	1,391	[e]	196	1,167	2,860	8.4	60.0	55

Sources: Appendix 4-8. Airways from "A Program of Changes for the Federal Airways System," Civil Aeronautics Administration, 1953, p. 36. Waterways from *Public Aids to Domestic Transportation,* Board of Investigation and Research, H.Doc. 159, 79th Cong., 1st sess., September 19, 1944, p. 335; later figures from Annual Reports of the Chief of Engineers, U.S. Army; Bureau of Public Roads, Table HF-2.

a. Excludes private capital expenditures for transportation by industries outside the transportation field, such as outlays by manufacturing industries for business motor vehicles.

b. Motor carrier (including intercity bus), air and water transportation, and transit (for 1951 and 1952).

c. Annual averages computed from C.A.A. estimates of total outlays for various periods.

d. Not available.

e. Included in "Other private."

share of public carriers in consumer transportation expenditures fell from 55.7 per cent in 1909 to 20.5 per cent in 1952. The outlay for local public carrier transportation has been consistently higher than the outlay for intercity travel, and fluctuates less in relation to general economic conditions than expenditures for intercity movement. (See Table 119.)

CAPITAL EXPENDITURES

Capital expenditures for transportation include expenditures for equipment (ships, business motor vehicles, railroad rolling stock and planes) and basic facilities (highways, railroad tracks and roadbeds, pipelines, airports and airways, and waterways). Excluding business motor vehicles, the total of these expenditures in 1950 was approximately $4.8 billion. The high point was $5.7 billion in 1952. The other extreme was a low of a little over $1 billion in 1933.

During the past two decades the principal outlays have been for three purposes: railroads, highways and business motor vehicles. There has been a fairly even division of total capital outlays between public expenditures (highways, airways, airports and waterways) and private expenditures (rail and pipeline and equipment outlays). In 1940, for example, private capital expenditures amounted to $1 billion and public capital expenditures to $1.4 billion. During depression years private expenditures have fallen off more rapidly than public. Thus in 1933 they totaled less than $200 million compared with public outlays of over $900 million. In 1952 the private expenditure was $2.8 billion and the public approximately $3.0 billion. (See Table 120.)

Private Capital Outlays

In 1948, for the first time, the demand for motor trucks and buses exceeded one million. Production for domestic civilian purposes reached a low of 23,420 units during the war year 1943, and only 188,000 units were produced for domestic use in the depression year 1932.

The demand for motor trucks since the end of the war has increased greatly as improvements in speed and flexibility have created new markets for trucking services. In 1940 there were 4.8

TABLE 121. MOTOR TRUCK AND BUS SALES AND REGISTRATIONS, 1942–1953 [a]

(Thousands)

Year	Factory Sales of Vehicles (for Domestic Use)		Vehicles in Use	
	Motor Trucks	Buses	Motor Trucks	Buses
1942		164	4,887	139
1943		23	4,727	152
1944		102	4,760	153
1945		254	5,080	162
1946	736	6	5,986	174
1947	958	14	6,809	187
1948	1,145	10	7,538	197
1949	980	4	8,028	209
1950	1,141	4	8,638	224
1951	1,050	6	9,036	230
1952	871	3	9,244	240
1953	1,063	4	9,460	250

Sources: Motor Truck Facts, 1953 and *Automobile Facts and Figures, 1953,* Automobile Manufacturers Association.

a. Excludes military vehicles from 1942 to 1945. 1946–1953 excludes factory sales to all federal government agencies.

million registered motor trucks. By 1953 the number was 9.5 million. (See Table 121.) As more trucks appeared on the road the number of larger and heavier trucks increased rapidly. In the prewar decade only three out of every thousand trucks weighed over 50,000 pounds (gross); soon after the war the number was fifteen out of every thousand. The number of 30,000-pound trucks increased from forty per thousand in 1940 to one hundred forty per thousand in 1947.[11]

Since 1921 the railroads of the United States have invested $20.9 billion of capital in roadbeds, tracks, yards, shops, terminals, structures and rolling stock.[12] Approximately $9 billion of this outlay was spent during the years 1946–1953. (See Table 122.)

The number of commercial transport aircraft in use by the airlines of the United States has increased from 499 in 1945 to 1,420 in 1953. During the first three postwar years, over 150 transports were purchased annually; in 1953 the number was 160. (See Table 123.)

11. *Toll Roads and the Problem of Highway Modernization,* Brookings Institution, Washington, 1951, p. 36.
12. Association of American Railroads.

TABLE 122. NUMBER OF LOCOMOTIVES AND FREIGHT CARS INSTALLED AND
EXPENDITURES FOR NEW RAILROAD PLANT AND EQUIPMENT, 1945-1953

Year	Steam Locomotives Installed	Diesel-Electric Locomotives Installed	Freight Cars Installed	Expenditures on New Plant and Equipment
				(Millions)
1945	115	786	37,132	$ 563
1946	86	626	38,823	562
1947	69	1,328	55,543	865
1948	86	2,262	95,979	1,273
1949	57	2,827	80,815	1,312
1950	12	3,203	40,032	1,066
1951	18	3,496	86,627	1,414
1952	19	3,037	64,347	1,333
1953	14	—	64,407	1,251

Sources: Statistics of Railways of Class I, United States, Calendar Years 1939 to 1952, Association of American Railroads, Bureau of Railway Economics, October 1953. 1953 data from Railway Age, January 11, 1954, p. 120. Expenditures differ from those in Table 120 because of source differences.

TABLE 123. AIRLINE AIRCRAFT IN USE, AND
DELIVERIES, 1945-1953

	Planes in Use		
Year	Domestic Airlines	International Airlines[a]	Plane Deliveries
1945	402	97	10
1946	638	147	157
1947	748	313	172
1948	790	323	196
1949	784	379	114
1950	796	373	90
1951	804	379	78
1952	903	388	221
1953	1,420		160

Sources: American Aviation, April 28, 1952, p. 18; and Air Transport Facts and Figures, 1953, Air Transport Association, p. 10. 1953 data from Civil Aeronautics Administration Release 53-45, December 27, 1953.

a. The following aircraft operated in both foreign and domestic trunk service are listed in international as well as domestic: 1946 — 16; 1947 — 148; 1948 — 156; 1949 — 193; 1950 — 210; 1951 — 233; 1952 — 235.

Since the end of the war, American manufacturers of aircraft have produced 1,200 multiengine planes for airline use, valued at over $1 billion. Most of these were purchased by United States airlines. Engines, propellers and aircraft accessories bring the total output to $1.5 billion for seven years.

Aircraft production for personal use has fallen off sharply since the war, from 34,568 in 1946 and 15,339 in 1947 to 3,391 in 1950 and 3,200 in 1952.

The oil pipeline system increased from 90,000 miles in 1926 to 173,000 miles in 1953,[13] while capital expenditures rose from $31 million to $196 million.[14] There were also 314,000 miles of natural gas lines operating in 1950.[15]

By 1952 total private capital outlays for transportation had risen to over four times what they were in 1939. The trend by years has been as follows (in millions): [16]

1939	$ 645
1945	1,122
1946	1,506
1947	2,187
1948	2,604
1949	2,197
1950	2,308
1951	2,964
1952	2,754

Public Capital Outlays

The major share of public capital outlays for transportation goes for roadbuilding. In 1950 expenditures for this purpose were almost twice as much as a decade earlier. Large sums were also being spent for toll roads. Highway construction expenditures, excluding toll facilities, and total expenditures, including maintenance

13. Traffic World, January 2, 1954, p. 21.
14. In 1952. These figures exclude some capital outlays for pipelines made by refineries and included as part of capital investment of the manufacturing industry.
15. Gas Facts, American Gas Association, New York, 1951, p. 66.
16. Appendix 4-8.

and operation, have been as follows (in billions): [17]

	Highway Construction Expenditures	Total Highway Expenditures *
1940	$1.3	$2.3
1945	0.4	1.4
1946	0.9	2.1
1947	1.5	2.8
1948	1.8	3.4
1949	2.1	3.9
1950	2.3	4.3
1951	2.5	4.5
1952	2.9	5.0
1953	3.2	5.5

* Total expenditures include maintenance, administration, debt service.

Airway capital expenditures have risen sharply with the postwar expansion of air carrier operations and the recent installation of a new all-weather navigation and landing aids program. From $4.5 million in 1939 the outlays increased to $17.5 million in 1950, with reductions since that year.[18]

Airport capital expenditures up to 1944 totaled $1 billion, of which all but $83 million was made available by federal, state and municipal governments.[19] Since 1947 the Federal Aid Airport Program has provided some further assistance to airport development, involving approximately $40 million a year of federal funds and a nearly equal amount supplied by sponsoring local governments.

Trends in airport and airway capital expenditures have been as follows (in millions): [20]

	Airports	Airways
Before 1933	$146.3	$ 9.1
1933–1940	272.8	15.9
1941–1944	490.1	31.6
1945–1952	672.0	100.4

Construction expenditures for waterways and harbor facilities declined sharply after the peak of $135 million spent in 1935, and the $100 million outlays of 1937 and 1938. Recovery from a low of $13 million in 1945 brought outlays to a total of $116 million in 1950, but expenditures since 1950 have been at approximately half that

rate. Since 1922 the federal government has made total capital outlays of approximately $1.5 billion for rivers and harbors.[21]

TECHNOLOGICAL DEVELOPMENTS

The recent history of transportation is based to a large degree on the succession of technological innovations which have occurred during the past three decades. One of the most significant of these was the successful mass production of a reliable all-weather automobile. It was this development that enabled private transportation facilities to surpass the volume of services provided by public carriers. The motor bus, because it offered a low-cost method of travel, meanwhile became the most widely used public carrier. The airplane provided another new means of transportation, at speeds far greater than ever before possible. These innovations emancipated the passenger from a choice between horse and rail and stimulated a tremendous new volume of passenger movement.

In freight movement the march of technological progress has been no less spectacular. The railroad monopoly of long-distance freight movement disappeared quickly with advances in motor truck operation. The development of a vast new system of pipelines added a means of low-cost bulk distribution, and recently air freight has provided a promising specialized service.

Meanwhile, the introduction of diesel power on the railroads as a substitute for steam locomotion opened the way to fast streamliner passenger service and greater power and economy of freight movement. Truck and water transportation have also benefited by the use of diesel engines.

The volume of transportation in future years, and how it is distributed among the several methods of transportation, will depend importantly on future technological developments. Some judgment of the main directions of further change is therefore necessary to any estimate of future transportation outlays.

THE OUTLOOK FOR AVIATION

The most spectacular developments in transportation have occurred in aviation, and it is aviation which promises to exert the greatest in-

17. Bureau of Public Roads, Table HF–2; and Appendix 4–8.

18. Table 120.

19. L. I. Bollinger and Arthur Tully, Jr., *Personal Aircraft Business at Airports,* Harvard University Press, Cambridge, 1948, p. 225.

20. Table 120 and *National Transportation Policy,* Brookings Institution, Washington, 1949, pp. 21 and 31.

21. *Public Aids to Domestic Transportation,* Board of Investigation and Research, H.Doc. 159, 79th Cong., 1st sess., September 19, 1944, p. 335.

fluence on the transportation system during the years immediately ahead — partly because of the helicopter and partly because of the opportunities for further increasing airplane speed. The progress already made has been tremendous, but the possibilities now in sight through jet propulsion, rocket power, and the application of atomic energy overshadow past achievements. Jet aircraft capable of cutting long-distance travel time in half will be available for regular service in the foreseeable future. In the near future jet power applied to the propellers of commercial aircraft will introduce a new type of air travel in the United States. The turbo-prop airplane combines long range with substantially higher speeds than present-day reciprocating engines, and provides substantially greater economy on short hops than the turbo-jet. Turbo-jets have already been operated by foreign airlines, and in the United States Boeing's new jet transport will soon be furnishing commercial service at cruising speeds in excess of 500 miles an hour.

The helicopter has been one of the most important recent aviation developments. The importance of the helicopter lies in its ability to overcome the loss of passenger time in traveling to and from airports. Most passenger travel outside urban areas is relatively short haul. Approximately one fourth of all airline passengers now move less than 200 miles. And a very high proportion of bus and railroad patrons also travel short distances. Rail passengers other than commuters travel an average of 113 miles. On short trips the airplane loses much of its advantage of speed because of the inconvenient location of airports. For fixed-wing aircraft, airport sites must be large enough to provide unobstructed approaches and runways of sufficient length for long take-off runs and landing under adverse weather conditions. The helicopter, by reason of its vertical take-off and landing, and its ability to hover, may carry its load into the heart of a city. In addition, it is better adapted to operate when visibility is poor.

Widespread use of the helicopter in the Korean war theater has shown the possibilities of this newest air vehicle, and continuing experimentation and procurement by the military services indicate that marked progress can be expected in the years immediately ahead.[22] In the future,

helicopters might be used in several ways: from downtown to airport, from airport to airport, for intercity trips under 300 miles and for metropolitan area transportation.

Over what distances this vehicle might serve as a convenient and economical means of transport remains to be seen, but for trips of 200 miles a helicopter capable of making only 100 miles an hour provides speedier service from downtown area to downtown area than a plane traveling at 170 miles an hour.[23] Average over-all speed for the helicopter, including a five-minute ground trip at each terminal, would be 89.6 miles an hour for such trips, compared with an over-all speed of 86.3 miles an hour for the airplane, assuming a thirty-minute ground trip at each terminal. Helicopters flying at an average speed of 100 miles an hour would take the following percentages of the over-all time required to travel different distances by conventional planes:[24]

		Helicopter at 100 Mph
25	miles	38
50		51
75		62
100		72
150		86
200		97
300		111

The much higher speeds now attainable by helicopter indicate the competitive advantage that this new air vehicle can be expected to have over conventional aircraft for considerable distances.

Thus far commercial helicopter service in the United States has been confined primarily to the mail and cargo operations of Los Angeles Airways, Chicago Helicopter Air Service and New York Airways, which serve 96 communities. The latter is also certificated to carry passengers. Los Angeles Airways has flown 1.5 million miles and carried 15 million pounds of cargo. Chicago Helicopter Service has covered a million miles without an accident. National Airlines is the first airline to operate helicopter service, but availability of the twin-engine helicopter for commercial use will lead to the replacement of fixed-wing aircraft on many airlines in the near future. Sabena Belgian Airways is

22. "Federal Policy Regarding the Development of Commercial Transport Helicopters," Air Coordinating Committee, July 19, 1951.

23. *Ibid.*
24. *Ibid.*, p. 34.

operating the world's first international helicopter service with Sikorsky S-55's, from Belgium to Germany, France and the Netherlands. Applications for local helicopter service in the United States, involving some 40 carriers, would provide service to metropolitan areas virtually blanketing the country.

Both Piasecki and Sikorsky twin-engine helicopters carrying 40 to 50 passengers are now flying. Speeds in excess of 160 miles an hour are now feasible, and jet models will achieve higher speeds. It is estimated by the Port of New York Authority that New York City will be accommodating 2 million helicopter passengers in 1960.[25] Total helicopter passengers for the nation as a whole are estimated at 6.1 million passengers in 1960.[26]

If the helicopter principle can be applied successfully to fixed-wing aircraft to combine the advantages of both, it may be possible to realize the high point-to-point speed of conventional craft and the terminal advantages of vertical lift. In the so-called convertiplane, therefore, may lie the greatest potential for all-weather navigation, speed and safety in the air.

Revolutionary progress in aviation may come about within the foreseeable future through the atomic powering of aircraft, which would enormously increase the range of flights and the size of pay loads. Research and development in the field of nuclear energy for aircraft have been under way for several years.

Extensive improvements in the airways system may be expected to increase greatly the safety, efficiency and regularity of air travel by 1960. A radically different omnirange system of traffic control now being placed in operation offers point-to-point navigation far superior to what was possible with the radio ranges used for air navigation in the past. The present cumbersome landing system will have been replaced by new electronic aids to all-weather flying. Still more advanced types of navigation aids will be introduced to complete the new airways network.[27]

RAILROADS

Only about 13 per cent of railroad passenger service is now provided by coal-burning steam engines; and the preponderance of diesel-electric orders for new equipment indicates that the rapid trend away from coal-burning steam locomotives will continue. In freight service only one fourth of the traffic in 1952 was still moved by coal-burning steam engines. The rapidity with which Class I line-haul railways have adopted diesel-electric motive power since the end of the war is indicated by the following distribution of service by type of power in 1946 and 1952:[28]

	Freight Service		Passenger Service	
	1946	1952	1946	1952
	(Per Cent of Ton-Miles)		(Per Cent of Car-Miles)	
Coal-burning steam	70	26	52	13
Oil-burning steam	19	7	26	9
Diesel-electric	10	66	15	72
Electric	2	2	6	7

What this revolution in motive power has meant in fuel savings is indicated by the fact that the railroads now move a ton one mile with about two ounces of coal. With oil-burning steam engines it takes two tablespoons of oil to move a ton of freight a mile; and a diesel accomplishes the work with no more than two teaspoons of oil. The feasibility of jet propulsion and nuclear power for locomotives will continue the march of progress in railroad engines.

First-class train travel has now become a luxury, for the railroads have maintained their competitive position by improving the accommodations offered rather than the speed of travel. Coach accommodations have been improved on many roads to a quality comparable to first-class service on daytime runs. New lightweight streamliners have played a major role in the modernization of passenger service, and today there are 655 "named" passenger trains in the United States providing deluxe services. Altogether there are 2,764 passenger trains with runs of a mile a minute or faster, covering 152,000 route miles.[29]

MOTOR VEHICLES

At the beginning of the twentieth century, the automobile was not only expensive but un-

25. Port of New York Authority, "Helicopter Estimate, 1953."

26. *National Airport Program*, H.Doc. 95, 83d Cong., 2d sess., 1954, p. 39.

27. *National Transportation Policy*, pp. 23–24. The omnidirection system blankets the entire country with navigation aids, in contrast to the four-course radio ranges, which channelized traffic along a narrow path similar to the beam of a searchlight.

28. Interstate Commerce Commission, *Monthly Comment on Transportation Statistics*, March 16, 1953, pp. 10–11.

29. *Quiz on Railroads and Railroading*, Association of American Railroads, 1952.

reliable. One observer wrote, "There is no one kind of motor vehicle which is the best . . . [but] many which may be grouped as the worst." Yet nearly all automobiles then cost at least $2,000, and many cost three times that much. Most models on the road were patterned after the horse-drawn buggy. Only a few expensive models were able to do better than fifteen miles an hour, and speed laws were enforced by policemen on bicycles. One company advertised its product as "the trotting horse of automobiles"; another offered an automobile "as easily controlled as the best-mannered horse, and safer because it cannot scare." [30]

The combination of continually lower prices and increasing quality in subsequent years was a major factor in the expansion of automotive transportation. The evolution of the automobile in terms of durability alone was such that while the total distance driven by cars scrapped in 1925 averaged less than 22,000 miles, in 1945 the average was 81,000 miles. Automobiles scrapped in 1925 had cost their owners 4.4 cents a mile, compared with a cost of 0.9 cents a mile for vehicles retired in 1945; that is, the car purchaser received 23 miles of service for each dollar in the earlier period and 112 miles in the later period.[31] Today the average mileage traveled per vehicle at time of scrapping has increased to 121,000 miles, or 50 per cent above the 1945 figure.

Possibilities for further improvement of the automobile lie in the development of a lightweight vehicle of good riding quality and durability, designed for economy of operation. In recent years the weight of automobiles has increased with the greater horsepower required for improved performance, and costs have risen in almost direct proportion. The typical postwar car was 150 pounds heavier than the car of 1941, and 500 pounds heavier than the 1937 car. Today the average car contains nearly 3,500 pounds of materials. Yet it is recognized that weight saving and a good relationship between empty and loaded weight are basic to economical operation.

If no progress had been made in design and materials, cars would now weigh twice as much as they did thirty years ago and be correspondingly more expensive to run. Use of strong and relatively lightweight metals, together with the

development of smaller power plants and adequate vehicle suspension, may make the automobile — and the motor truck — still more economical to operate. These possibilities, already demonstrated by vehicles of European design, may become more attractive to the American consumer as high operating costs and multiple-car ownership suggest the need for lighter and more economical cars. With improvement of road surfaces, refinements in automobile design become more feasible.

Body weight might be considerably reduced by using materials such as aluminum and plastics, provided costs can be brought in line. In the average car, use of 500 pounds of aluminum can bring about a weight reduction of 500 pounds — since every pound of aluminum supplants two pounds of other materials.

In truck bodies, also, reduction of weight is a principal consideration. One company has saved 1,240 pounds per truck with bodies built of magnesium alloy and extruded magnesium shapes, thereby cutting gasoline consumption some three to four gallons on a run of 125 miles and reducing wear on tires and chassis.

Possibilities of more economical motor transportation lie also in the development of power plants and fuel. In over-the-road trucking the shift to diesel power has made possible significant economies. It is said that for a truck driven about 60,000 miles a year the extra cost of a diesel-powered unit can be paid for by fuel savings in fifteen months. In addition, there are substantial savings in maintenance, since twice as much mileage can be driven with diesels before an overhaul is necessary. The next step in power plants may be the use of turbo-jet propulsion, for both trucks and passenger cars.

Greater speed, safety and economy of operation may be expected from highway improvements. In the past most of the consumer expenditure for motor transport has been for vehicles and their operation, and only a small fraction for roads. This has been false economy, since highways of inadequate design and capacity are costly in terms of gasoline consumption, wasted time and accident frequency. Greater emphasis on road design and terminal facilities would result in substantial progress toward economical highway transportation.

The current development of an extensive network of toll highways in congested traffic areas points to a period of much greater emphasis on

---

30. *Automotive Transportation: Trends and Problems,* Brookings Institution, Washington, 1949.
31. *Ibid.*

modern roads to accommodate the modern vehicle. The toll road movement, which began before World War II with the 160-mile Pennsylvania Turnpike, has spread rapidly and widely since the war. In 1947 the Maine Turnpike was opened to traffic, followed by the New Hampshire Turnpike and extension of the Pennsylvania highway to a total length of 320 miles. New Jersey joined the toll road movement in 1951 with a 130-mile superhighway, which cost as much as $8 million a mile in the heavily traveled northern section. In 1954 the 500-mile New York thruway was nearing completion and work was proceeding on the 241-mile east-west road in Ohio. Toll roads were operating in Colorado and Oklahoma, and others were under way in West Virginia, Pennsylvania, Massachusetts, Connecticut, New Jersey and Indiana. As of 1954 it appeared that an extensive system of major toll express roads would soon be financed, and that by 1960 a total of some 7,000 miles of these superhighways would be in operation to speed long-distance motor travel and freight movement. The cost (in millions) is estimated as follows: [32]

	Miles	Estimated Cost
Toll roads in service	840	$ 674
Toll roads under construction	1,081	1,497
Authorized toll roads	3,056	3,573
Other projected toll roads	1,927	2,075
Totals as of January, 1954	6,904	$7,819

Transportation Needs and Demand

It is impossible to establish definite minimum standards of transportation needs for the average individual like those which can be established for food and housing. The location, occupation and living habits of the consumer strongly influence his need for transportation. Moreover, consumer requirements change as transportation techniques develop. A need for automobiles arose, for example, as the availability of the vehicle permitted cities to decentralize and workers to live farther from their jobs and changed recreation habits and community mobility. Similarly, the need for school buses is increasing with the consolidation of rural schools, which in the first instance was made possible by the bus.

That the "need" for transportation is a relative and indefinable term has been illustrated by war-

32. *Engineering News-Record,* January 7, 1954.

time experience. Prewar road-use surveys determined that the average car was used approximately 50 per cent of the time for "necessity" driving. Under wartime gasoline rationing, however, the basic allowance for necessary driving was established at only a fraction of so-called normal car use. Every motorist learned that much of the driving he once considered essential was not truly so.

OBJECTIVES AND STANDARDS

Minimum transportation needs, then, differ both in point of time and according to particular conditions. Probably the most satisfactory approach to the concept of need, therefore, is to describe the lines along which authorities believe passenger transportation should be developed in order to provide the maximum volume of travel with the highest degree of efficiency. Transportation efficiency may be measured in terms of speed, safety, economy and convenience or comfort.

Safety

Substantial progress toward greater safety of transportation has been made over a period of years. The total automobile death rate (including pedestrians) has been cut by more than half since 1932, to approximately 7 deaths for every 100 million vehicle-miles; and the passenger fatality rate for automobiles in 1953 had been reduced to 2.8. Passenger fatalities on scheduled airlines decreased from 3.7 per 100 million passenger-miles in 1942 to 0.5 in 1953. Buses had a record of 0.16 passenger fatalities for every 100 million passenger-miles in 1953.

Despite declining death rates, however, accidents remain a major problem, and the improved facilities and equipment needed to reduce the hazards of travel call for heavy investment. One million persons have thus far been killed in motor vehicle accidents on the streets and highways of the United States. Motor vehicle accidents in 1953 resulted in 38,000 deaths and 2,140,000 nonfatal injuries. Automobile owners paid out nearly $3 billion in insurance premiums that year. There were 88 deaths in scheduled airline accidents in 1953 on domestic and international flights; 100 in motor buses; and 126 on railroads.

Speed

Every new method of transportation has owed its success in part to its ability to provide faster service than its predecessors. The railroads superseded water transport on competitive routes wherever speed was important. The automobile increased the radius of daily travel far beyond the limits that could be reached by horse. Even when trucking is more costly than railroad freight, shippers may prefer the truck because of the time saved.

The airplane has left all other means of transport behind in the race to conquer time and distance. Cruising rates of commercial carriers progressed spectacularly from approximately 180 miles an hour during the war to more than 400 miles in 1954. With the inauguration of jet airlines service speeds of 550 to 600 miles an hour will be possible in the near future.

On the railroads the average speed of passenger trains was only 37 miles an hour in 1951 — just one mile faster than the 1941 average. The fastest train run in the United States was recorded in 1905, when the train now known as the Broadway Limited covered 3 miles in 85 seconds, traveling at a rate of 127 miles an hour. Although the over-all speed of today's passenger trains is surprisingly low, the average speed of modern streamliners is much higher. The fastest scheduled run of more than 50 miles is the Burlington Zephyr's 86 miles an hour, and several other streamliners exceed 80 miles an hour.

Time saved on the highway, on trains or in the air is often lost in terminal areas, however. Delays in terminal areas are the major obstacle to economy and service in both freight and passenger transportation. Motor vehicles averaging approximately 50 to 60 miles an hour on the open road can move at only 5 to 7 miles an hour during rush periods in some cities — less than the pace of the horse and buggy. Airplane speed is often nullified by the remoteness of airports, the inadequacy of transport from airport to city, and, in bad weather, by landing difficulties.

Cost

Rates for public carrier service have declined over a period of years. Railroad revenue per passenger-mile was 3.1 cents in 1921, reached a low of 1.9 cents during the war, and had risen again

TABLE 124. AVERAGE COST OF PASSENGER TRANSPORTATION, 1921–1953

(Average Revenue in Cents per Passenger-Mile)

Year	Rail	Air Domestic	Air International	Bus
1921	3.09	—	—	—
1941	1.75	—	—	1.46
1942	1.92	5.28	8.85	1.65
1943	1.88	5.35	7.91	1.69
1944	1.87	5.14	7.82	1.65
1945	1.87	4.95	8.67	1.64
1946	1.95	4.63	8.30	1.66
1947	2.10	5.05	7.77	1.68
1948	2.34	5.73	8.01	1.74
1949	2.45	5.68	7.72	1.84
1950	2.56	5.55	7.28	1.84
1951	2.59	5.56	7.14	1.94
1952	2.66	5.55	7.04	2.03
1953	2.65	5.42	6.96	—

Sources: Railroad figures from *Railway Age*, January 14, 1953, p. 152; air from *Air Transport Facts and Figures, 1954*, Air Transport Association, p. 12; bus from Interstate Commerce Commission, Docket No. MC–C–550, Exhibit 915, and *Bus Facts*, National Association of Motor Bus Operators, 1951, p. 12.

to 2.6 cents by 1953. (See Table 124.) Freight revenue of 1.3 cents a ton-mile in 1951 was approximately the same as in 1921, and during the war the rate was slightly below 1 cent a ton-mile. Domestic airline fares were 5.3 cents a mile in 1942 and 5.4 cents in 1953, while rates for international air travel declined from 8.9 to 7.0 cents a mile. Rates for the movement of goods by air have declined from 60 cents to an average of 16 cents a ton-mile, and recently air freight has been carried in full plane loads on transcontinental hauls for as little as 11 cents a ton-mile, or 2 cents below the rail express rate.

The cost of automobile transportation, which averaged about 4 cents a mile before the war, including the cost of the vehicle as well as its operation, was over double this amount in 1954 for a comparable vehicle and similar conditions of use.

NEEDS VS. DEMAND FOR SERVICES

The probability of rapid population growth and continued expansion of economic activity over the long run, combined with the promise of further technological advances, indicates ever-expanding needs and demand for transportation facilities and services. But in an age of scientific discovery on the scale witnessed in recent years, those who presume to foretell the transportation future are exposing themselves to considerable hazard. Much of the technological revolution of recent times has had and will continue to have special impact on methods of transportation: the development of the automobile, bus, truck and airplane; diesel power, jet propulsion and nuclear energy for ships and planes and locomotives; the helicopter and the convertiplane.

It would be presumptuous indeed, therefore, to proceed with the task at hand without first acknowledging that the odds are against victory, and without calling to mind how inconsiderate history has been of prognosticators who trifle with the future of transportation. In 1909, one of the deterrents to automobile ownership was thought to be the need for every motorist to keep his car in a costly "automobile house" equipped with complete repair facilities, drainage pits, washing apparatus and turntable.[33] It was widely conceded to be "nothing less than feeble-mindedness to expect anything to come of the horseless carriage movement." [34] As late as 1912, a proposal for a 50,000-mile national system of highways was attacked as a frivolous expenditure of public funds "for the benefit of a few wealthy pleasure seekers," and the possibility of today's 10 million trucks was not foreseen. "It should be understood in the first place that these highways are intended for . . . automobile touring traffic, since for long-distance freight transportation it is impossible for haulage over any road surface to compete with the low cost of hauling on a railway." [35]

The steam locomotive fared little better at the hands of the prophets, partly because they thought man would be unable to endure its speed. And as early as 1905 it was said of the airplane that "the limits of success have been reached with this type of flying machine." [36]

Lack of imagination has characterized most predictions concerning the future of transportation, and forecasts that ultimately proved reasonable were met with universal incredulity. At best, then, the estimator has the difficult choice of being considered feeble-minded now or later.

Nevertheless, transportation history has repeated itself often enough to furnish the crystal-gazer with something to look into — with caution.

VOLUME OF TRAFFIC IN 1960

As in the past, the general level of passenger and freight traffic in the future will depend to a major degree upon the nature of total needs in other fields and on the extent to which those needs are met. The assumptions of a high level of activity on which this study is based, however, indicate a very much heavier volume of total traffic than in the decade prior to the war.

Although the prospects for a substantial per capita increase in passenger traffic seem fairly certain, expectations for freight traffic are of a lesser magnitude. Intercity common carrier passenger transportation per capita increased about 50 per cent over the past quarter century, and when automobile transportation is added to the total the increase is several times as great. Intercity freight traffic on a per capita basis rose only from 4,700 ton-miles in 1916 to 6,800 ton-miles in 1953.

Changes in manufacturing techniques and in the location and organization of industry suggest a continuation of this trend, and increases in population and economic activity and reduction of low-income families will mean greater total volumes of passenger and freight movement. The growing urbanization of the country will likewise mean increasing specialization and interdependence of people and businesses in metropolitan areas.

While per capita freight traffic in the long run is more likely to register moderate gains, passenger travel per capita may be expected to rise to much higher levels. Among the reasons for this are an increase in leisure time and recreation, improvement of transportation facilities and equipment as a result of technological advances, the construction of an extensive network of express highways, and the much greater radius of travel provided by the airplane. Reduction in the real cost of transportation to the consumer may also be expected to increase domestic and foreign travel.

CONSUMER EXPENDITURES IN 1960

Largely because of air transport expansion, consumption expenditures for travel should con-

---

33. H. P. Maxim, *Horseless Carriage Days*, Harper, New York, 1937, p. 103.

34. *Motor*, May 1909, p. 33.

35. Editorial, *Engineering News-Record*, May 16, 1912, p. 937.

36. *Motor*, October 1905, p. 37.

TABLE 125. TRANSPORTATION EXPENDITURES AS PER
CENT OF TOTAL CONSUMPTION EXPENDITURES,
1909–1960

Year	Per Cent	Year	Per Cent
1909	5.2	1938	9.0
1914	6.4	1939	9.6
1919	8.1	1940	9.9
1921	8.6	1941	10.2
1923	9.8	1942	6.2
1925	10.6	1943	5.9
1927	9.6	1944	6.0
1929	9.9	1945	6.6
1930	9.1	1946	8.3
1931	8.5	1947	9.4
1932	8.4	1948	9.9
1933	8.9	1949	11.2
1934	9.1	1950	12.1
1935	9.6	1951	11.2
1936	10.1	1952	11.0
1937	10.1	1960 (est.)	11.8

Sources: 1909–1952 from Appendix 4–5; 1960 from
Appendix 4–7, Table A.

stitute a higher percentage of total consumer
outlays than in the past. These expenditures were
more than 12 per cent of total consumption outlays in 1950, and although the proportion was
high in that year because of a heavy backlog
demand for automobiles, it is expected to be nearly
as high in 1960. This contrasts with transportation outlays totaling 9.9 to 10.2 per cent of consumption expenditures in relatively prosperous
prewar years. (See Table 125.) Consumers are
likely to spend about $28.5 billion (at 1950
prices) for transportation in 1960, or $161 per
capita, compared with $23.5 billion, or $154
per capita, in 1950.

Private Transportation

The pre-eminence of the automobile in the
passenger transportation system may be explained
in several ways. In local service it is often the only
means of travel, and with the growth of suburban living, the dependence of the average family on this form of transport is bound to increase.
But when it comes to intercity movement the
automobile has certain cost advantages which
assure its continuing leadership despite any foreseeable competitive advantage developed by other
transport media.

To illustrate, the "average" new car may
operate at a total cost of approximately 8 cents
a mile. With only the driver being transported,

the cost of transportation is 8 cents a mile per
passenger, which is equivalent to, or in many
cases higher than, the cost of first-class travel by
public carrier. For two persons, however, the cost
is only 4 cents per passenger-mile; for three it
is less than 3 cents; and for four persons, 2 cents.
These figures include the entire cost from point
of origin to destination, while local transportation is generally an extra requirement if a public
carrier is used.

A cost of 8 cents per passenger-mile is high
for most automobile operators, however. Those
who do not purchase a new car are able to avoid
the full impact of high automobile prices, and
their operating costs may be as low as 4 cents per
vehicle-mile. Thus the cost for a family of four
may be only 1 cent per passenger-mile.

But even more significant is the fact that
the direct costs of a given automobile trip are
much lower than the total economic costs stated
above. Once a car has been purchased, registered
and insured, transportation cost may be and generally is considered by the owner as marginal
cost only: the extra cost incurred to make the
specific trip possible. This marginal cost generally
includes only gas and oil, and may amount to
only 3 cents a mile even for a new automobile.

Although these economic advantages of the
automobile are impressive, they are not the only
factors that place the family car at a competitive advantage. For example, from a strictly cost
standpoint, automobile ownership and operation
is an extravagance for many persons. It would
be cheaper for them to use taxis for local travel
and to patronize intercity public carriers for
longer trips. But convenience often weighs
heavier than economy in determining one's
choice. Emancipation from fixed routes and
time schedules makes use of a car not only convenient but in many situations the only way to
travel.

The tourist or vacationist prefers the automobile because it is available at his destination to provide local transportation. And
the capacity and convenience of the automobile for luggage, babies, and miscellaneous family belongings cannot be approached
by other forms of transportation. Similarly, the
commercial traveler prefers the automobile because it enables him to go any place in his territory where a sale may be made; and it furnishes
the space required for goods and samples at no

extra cost. Finally, driving an automobile is still for many persons a source of pleasure, and owning a car, however unwise economically, is often considered a matter of social prestige.

Technological developments in both the automobile and the highway will probably bring about an even wider use of this form of transportation in the future. Since the war, automotive design and performance have not been altered appreciably. It may be expected, however, that in the future there will be substantial improvements in the design of cars, and greater attention to safety, comfort and economy. At the same time changes in public policy are certain to bring improvements in the design of highways to permit better transportation by motor vehicle.

It is expected, then, that the factors which have made the ownership and operation of the automobile so widespread in the United States will continue to make this the most common means of passenger transportation in the years ahead. In 1960, with an estimated population of 177 million, and with further improvement of both the vehicle and the highway, it is estimated that there will be 59 million passenger cars, compared with 40 million in 1950. This level of registrations will mean one car for every 3 persons in the United States, compared with one for every 3.8 in 1950 and every 3.6 in 1953. Passenger car production is estimated at 6 million in 1960, 5.5 million for domestic use.

This expected growth of automobile ownership and operation will be made possible in part by some reduction in average automobile prices from the peaks reached in the postwar sellers' market. Thus it is believed that consumer expenditures for automobile transportation will increase by a more moderate 18 per cent, from $19.5 billion in 1950 to $22.9 billion in 1960. This increase in total outlays for the automobile will nevertheless mean a reduction in the proportion of the consumer's dollar going for this form of transportation — from 10.0 per cent in 1950 to 9.5 per cent in 1960. (See Table 127.)

Taking a longer-range view, the President's Materials Policy Commission has come to the conclusion that there will be 65 million cars by 1975. At the beginning of 1950 there was one car for every three persons 14 years of age or over. By 1975, it was estimated, there would be one car for every two to two and a half persons

in that age group. Replacement demand for cars in 1975, assuming a ten-year average life, would be 5.5 to 6 million cars a year; and new demands arising from expanding population and economic growth would be 1 million to 1.5 million cars. In total, then, 6.5 to 7.5 million cars a year would be demanded by 1975.[37]

Another recent study concludes that 1960 should see a total of 54 million passenger cars, and that average annual production for the period 1951–1960 will be 5.1 million passenger cars and 1.3 million trucks.[38]

Public Carriers

Transit

The trend at the present time continues away from public carriers in local service despite the difficulties and costs of using the family car in downtown areas. This downward trend in local transit patronage has also persisted in the face of record highs in the number of persons employed.

The future of mass transportation will depend on the extent of cost and service competition with the automobile. On the cost side, transit fares have been mounting with higher wage costs and the higher cost of new equipment. Although fares are generally lower than the out-of-pocket costs of using the family car, especially when parking fees are added, there is generally insufficient saving to persuade the motorist to forgo the greater comfort, speed and flexibility of his car. If municipal governments were to weigh more closely the economic advantages of encouraging mass movement of passengers in downtown areas, however, it might be that subsidized modern transit would compete for a larger number of patrons than at present.

Over a period of years the number of transit rides per person employed in nonagricultural activities has declined, and it is possible that any move in the direction of promoting rapid transit and bus travel may fall short of reversing

37. *Resources for Freedom*, A Report to the President by the President's Materials Policy Commission, June 1952, Vol. II, "The Outlook for Key Commodities," p. 114. In this study it is estimated that trucks will number 20 million by 1975, and that annual demand will be 2.6 million vehicles by that time — 2 million replacements and a growth of some 600,000 a year.

38. "Trends and Prospects in the Automotive, Rubber and Allied Industries, 1950–1960," B. F. Goodrich Company, February 1952.

this per capita trend. The possibilities of new mass transportation techniques, however, still offer hopes of rescuing the central cities from the plight of traffic congestion. It is estimated on the basis of growing urban population and rising public carrier fares that consumers will increase their total outlays for local transit from $1.4 billion in 1950 to $1.8 billion in 1960. Increased use of taxis will also result from growing demands for urban mobility. No rise in railroad commutation in the principal metropolitan areas can be expected despite the fact that dispersal of the population and the problems of automobile commuting might suggest the desirability of utilizing rail commutation services.

Intercity Transportation

In 1949, intercity public transportation accounted for only 5.3 per cent of consumer transportation expenditures, compared with 5.7 per cent in 1940. Even in 1909, when the horse and buggy were in common use, the public carriers in intercity service accounted for only 18 per cent of total expenditures. (See Table 119.)

From 1940 to 1950, consumer expenditures (measured in 1950 dollars) increased from $127 billion to $195 billion, or by 53 per cent. Population increased 15 per cent. During that period the number of passenger-miles of intercity common carrier travel increased 72 per cent. (See Table 106.)

If intercity travel per capita remains close to the 1950 figure of 370 miles, there will be some 65 billion passenger-miles of intercity travel by public carrier in 1960. In 1941, when the level of economic activity was not as high as in any of the postwar years, and when air transport was not significant, per capita travel was as high as 303 miles. With the growth of air travel, and the assumption of continued economic growth, it appears that a figure of at least 370 miles of intercity common carrier transportation per capita is warranted for 1960.

With respect to the division of the traffic among carriers, the least promising future is that of rail passenger service off the main high-density routes. Over an extended period of time the railroads have given ground consistently to the automobile and the bus, and in recent years the airlines have taken much of the longer-haul traffic. Traffic moving by rail is now predominantly overnight service or coach traffic on high-density routes where short hauls are predominant. This two-way squeeze on rail patronage seems destined to gain strength with the growing speed and reliability of the airlines, the possibilities of the helicopter, and continuing expansion of automobile ownership. The principal deterrents to a more rapid shift from rail to air at present are cost and safety factors, lack of capacity to handle air traffic expeditiously at the airports, inability to meet the problem of ground travel to and from the airport, and the ability of the railroads in many cases to provide modern equipment for luxury travel.

It appears that for short-haul passengers the helicopter will overcome the problem of getting to the airport, and that will help to overcome the congested conditions at the large airports. It seems probable that the influence of the helicopter will be substantial before 1960, and that rotary wing and jet aircraft will have added to the competitive advantages of air travel. These considerations, together with the expectation that express highways connecting major centers of population will encourage the use of buses and private cars, lead to a pessimistic view of the future growth of rail passenger transportation. Rail traffic may be expected to decline from 27 billion passenger-miles in 1953 to 22 billion in 1960.

The Civil Aeronautics Administration in 1951 estimated that domestic scheduled airline travelers in 1960 will total 40.2 million, compared with 20.6 million in 1951, and that passenger-miles of travel on the domestic airlines will be 18.1 billion, compared with 10.2 billion in 1951.[39] The record of 14.2 billion passenger-miles of air travel in 1953, combined with the potentials of direct-lift air vehicles and turbo-jets for long-distance movement, now indicate a much higher level of air travel by 1960. With reliable all-weather operations attainable it is probable that the volume of domestic air traffic will by that time reach a total of 25 billion passenger-miles, including local service airlines and irregular carriers.

Although express highway development should promote the use of intercity buses, it is expected that increased automobile ownership and the advent of helicopter service will together mean a fairly stationary level of bus travel.

In summary it is estimated that the volume of

39. *Airline Passengers,* Civil Aeronautics Administration, December 1931.

intercity travel in 1960 will reach 66 billion passenger-miles: 25 billion by air, 22 billion by rail, and 19 billion by bus. The total of 66 billion passenger-miles compares with 56 billion in 1950 and 61 billion in 1953. The share of this total accounted for by consumers as distinguished from business users will be about 70 per cent, or 46 billion passenger-miles.

Foreign Travel

Foreign travel has increased sharply with high levels of economic activity and the development of international air service. After record numbers of passengers had traveled between this country and foreign nations in 1929–1930, depression and war reduced the market drastically. By 1950, however, 2.1 million passengers traveled to and from overseas countries, 54 per cent of them by air; in 1953 the total had risen to 2.9 million, 60 per cent moving by plane. High national income and growing population, together with improved overseas transport services, indicate that by 1960, 4 million passengers will be transported, approximately two thirds by air. In 1952 United States residents spent $822 million in foreign countries, more than half of which ($448 million) was spent in Canada and Mexico. (See Table 126.)

Net expenditures for foreign travel by American consumers in 1960 are expected to show an increase of 54 per cent over 1950.

TABLE 126. ESTIMATED NUMBERS AND EXPENDITURES OF UNITED STATES RESIDENTS TRAVELING IN FOREIGN COUNTRIES, 1952

	Number	Expenditures
	(Thousands)	(Millions)
All countries	a	$822[b]
Canada	a	268
Mexico	a	180
Total oversea areas	773	374
Europe and Mediterranean	332	256
West Indies and Central America	382	78
South America	40	25
Other oversea countries	19	15

Source: Survey of Current Business, June 1953, p. 11.
a. Not available.
b. Excludes expenditures by United States government personnel (military and civilian) and payments to United States and foreign carriers for international fares, which are included in foreign travel in Table 127.

In summary, 1960 will see nearly $29 billion of transportation expenditures by consumers, or a 21 per cent increase over 1950. Out of every dollar spent by consumers, 11.8 cents will go for transportation, and of this amount private transportation alone will account for nearly 9.6 cents. (See Table 127.)

NEED FOR BASIC FACILITIES

From time to time, engineering studies have provided an indication of what it would cost to achieve the safety, speed and economy of transport service technically possible under existing conditions. Thus, for example, estimates have been made for the federal government and the states of the cost of modernizing the highway system and the airports.

Highways

Despite an expenditure of $70 billion for highways during the past thirty years, the nation's road network is inadequate to meet the needs of today's 55 million motor vehicles. Main roads and city streets are heavily congested, thousands of miles of rural roads lack year-round surfacing, and motor vehicle accidents occur at a shocking rate.

Although motor traffic is heaviest in and around cities, highway construction has been concentrated on rural roads. As a result, urban congestion and delays have become critical. A major objective in future transportation development must therefore be the construction of adequate urban arterials, as well as main intercity highways.

Improvements in the design of highways are also necessary, one of the greatest needs being for roads with control of access to prevent undesirable development of adjacent lands and restrict vehicle entrance to a relatively few points. Traffic can flow without interruption on such highways and without the hazards and congestion that result when commercial and residential properties abut on the highway. More widespread adoption of dual highways, highway grade separations and other "superhighway" features is also required.

The urban motorist has almost as much difficulty in parking as in moving. Off-street parking facilities are an essential part of any successful attack on the problem of providing the necessary highway capacity for urban mobility.

TABLE 127. ESTIMATED CONSUMER TRANSPORTATION EXPENDITURES, 1950 AND 1960

Item	Amount		Percentage Distribution		Percentage Increase over 1950
	1950	1960	1950	1960	
	(Millions at 1950 Prices)				
Total consumption	$194,550	$241,500	100.00	100.00	24.1
Consumer transportation	23,546	28,510	12.10	11.80	21.1
Private transportation	19,456	22,950	10.00	9.50	18.0
New cars and net purchases of used cars	10,285	10,760	5.29	4.46	4.6
Auto parts, repair and maintenance	4,070	5,070	2.09	2.10	24.6
Gasoline and oil	4,928	6,900	2.53	2.86	29.5
Luggage	173	220	.09	.09	27.2
Public carrier transportation	4,090	5,560	2.10	2.30	35.9
Local	2,084	2,650	1.07	1.10	27.2
Street car, electric railway and bus	1,390	1,760	.72	.73	26.6
Taxicabs—fares and tips	608	815	.31	.34	34.0
Steam railways (commutation) and ferries (foot passengers)	86	75	.04	.03	—12.8
Intercity	1,030	1,410	.53	.58	36.9
Railway	446	440	.23	.18	—1.3
Bus	310	350	.16	.14	12.9
Airline	174	500	.09	.21	187.4
Other intercity	100	120	.05	.05	20.0
Foreign travel (net) [a]	976	1,500	.50	.62	53.7

Source: Appendix 4–7, Table A.

a. Expenditures by United States residents abroad less expenditures by foreigners in the United States.

Neither the volume nor the speed of traffic in earlier days required basic departures from the ancient road. The automobile was able to use for some time, with minor surface improvement, the network of streets and highways it inherited from the horse. For many years it was necessary only to provide all-weather surfaces in rural areas; in the cities some type of surface was often already available. In carrying out this rural road program, width and alignment were secondary considerations. The main objective was to make the road passable. The engineer built for the traffic at hand, and neither the funds available nor public policy would have permitted any other course. While this approach had the merit of providing a million miles of surfaced highways in the course of the two decades from 1920 to 1940, it unfortunately preserved with more or less permanent surfaces and structures a system of horse-and-buggy roads wholly inadequate for the traffic which was soon to flood them.[40]

In recent years it has become evident that the highway problem can no longer be solved by improvisation — by adapting ancient roads to the new vehicle. Roads of substantially different design are required to handle heavy volumes of fast-moving traffic. The roads and streets of the United States must now handle three times as much automobile travel as they did in 1935. Travel by truck is nearly three times the 1935 volume, and in ton-mileage, which takes loads into account, there was a fivefold increase between 1935 and 1951.[41]

A committee of Congress estimated, on the

40. *Automotive Transportation: Trends and Problems.*
41. Thomas H. MacDonald, Statement before the Senate and House Committees on Public Works, 82d Cong., 2d sess., February 1952.

basis of information obtained from state governors and highway departments, that it would cost $41 billion to correct the deficiencies in the roads and streets of the nation in 1949.[42] New requirements equal to 35 per cent of these needs, it was estimated, would accumulate during the ten years after 1949, thus bringing total construction needs to about $55 billion by 1960.

The kinds of construction needed are illustrated by a report on the so-called Interstate Highway System, that is, the nearly 38,000 miles of national roads selected by the states and the federal government as representing the most important routes in the United States that demand priority attention. [43] The following work was considered to be required on this 38,000-mile network: construction of 4,893 bridges and improvement of 5,925; relocation and construction of 11,891 miles of road; complete reconstruction of 14,283 miles of road; and improvement, mostly widening, of 8,687 miles of road. The cost, on the basis of prices prevailing in 1948, was estimated at $11.3 billion, with $6 billion of this amount allocated to rural sections and $5.3 billion to sections within urban areas.[44]

The need for highway construction outlays in the 1950s, if backlog and new requirements were to be met by 1960, would be in the neighborhood of $5.5 billion annually. A large further investment would be required to provide off-street garages in urban areas, and truck and bus terminals.

Airways and Airports

The entire system of air navigation has been undergoing change in recent years to take advantage of new techniques of instrument landing, electronic traffic control, very high frequency communications, and easier and vastly superior point-to-point navigation. The new aids are applicable not only to commercial and military aircraft, but to private planes as well. An even more advanced air navigation system is scheduled for completion by the mid-1960s.

The first step toward an efficient all-weather airways system has been an interim program of installing presently available electronic aids. It is estimated that the long-range "target" program, based on radar, will eventually involve a minimum expenditure of $1,113 million.

The new facilities introduce an entirely new concept of air navigation. The use of omnidirectional ranges makes it possible to abandon the existing "airways," which are, in effect, highways in the air, delineated by radio beams. The new ranges provide instead for navigation aids blanketing the entire country, permitting navigation between any points in the continental United States. These facilities also provide static-free communication and other advantages.[45]

Information on airport needs is now kept current in the form of a National Airport Plan, which the Civil Aeronautics Administration is responsible for maintaining in accordance with the Federal Airport Act of 1946. The plan provides a comprehensive guide to the development of new airports and the improvement of existing facilities, based on estimates of the country's aeronautical needs for the following three years. Changes in the plan from year to year reflect current appraisal of the adequacy of the nation's airports and the changing requirements for safe and efficient air transport.

In 1951, 2,657 airports were scheduled for improvement under the National Airport Plan. The construction of 2,288 new airports was also planned. Most of the airports to be constructed or improved were of the smaller types, primarily for private flyers, but airports to accommodate airline operations accounted for a substantial proportion of the contemplated outlays. Total costs of the National Airport Plan were estimated at $662 million for land and construction, excluding the cost of buildings and hangars. (See Table 128.)

The introduction of jet aircraft may hasten the obsolescence of terminals, and expansion of passenger and freight traffic will intensify the need for buildings and other facilities. Altogether, an estimated $100 million a year will be required to meet foreseeable needs, including heliports.

Railroads

Some individual railroads estimate their future requirements for capital expenditures, but estimates are not available for the railroad industry as a whole. However, some estimates for

42. *Highways and the Nation's Economy*, Joint Committee on the Economic Report, 81st Cong., 2d sess., 1950.
43. See "Highway Needs of the National Defense," a report submitted to the Congress by the President, H.Doc. 249, June 30, 1949.
44. MacDonald, *op. cit.*

45. *National Transportation Policy*, pp. 23–25.

TABLE 128. NATIONAL AIRPORT PLAN

Type of Airport	Total Number to Be Constructed or Improved	To Be Constructed	To Be Improved	Total Cost
				(Millions)
Total	4,945	2,288	2,657	$662.0
Personal	2,310	1,524	786	109.0
Secondary	1,148	350	798	108.5
Feeder	656	75	581	115.5
Trunk	303	12	291	79.6
Express	77	3	74	43.6
Continental and up	64	5	59	194.7
Seaplane	304	257	47	8.8
Heliport	83	62	21	2.3

Source: National Airport Plan, Civil Aeronautics Administration, 1951, p. 4. The 1953 revision of the Plan calls for only 2,235 airports to be constructed or improved as federal projects.

equipment and classification yard facilities have been computed for the industry in connection with studies of national defense preparedness.[46] For motive power, some 19,000 units, involving costs of $2.7 billion at 1947 prices, would be needed to place the railroads on a preparedness basis.

The Interstate Commerce Commission has estimated that under conditions of full employment the nation's railroads could expect a sufficient volume of traffic to require the acquisition of 10,000 freight cars a month during the decade 1949–1958. Worn-out cars must be replaced at the rate of 68,000 a year in order to maintain the average age of cars at 30 years, but with full employment plus the threat of war, it is estimated that approximately 300,000 cars will have to be added to railroad rolling stock by 1955.

Waterways and Harbors

To fill in the broad outlines of a national water transportation plan would require substantial expenditures on inland waterways, Great Lakes harbors and channels, and commercial harbors on the coasts of the United States and its territories. The federal government spent approximately $4.1 billion for river and harbor projects from 1910 to mid-1952. Projects operating or under construction involved a further expendi-

46. "The Capacity and Capital Requirements of the Railroad Industry," Interstate Commerce Commission, June 1952 (study sponsored by the Department of the Air Force).

ture of $2.5 billion, and the backlog of needs at that time included some 369 separate projects estimated to call for an additional $3.2 billion. (See Table 129.)

TABLE 129. RIVER AND HARBOR IMPROVEMENT PROGRAM, 1952
(Millions)

Status	Estimated Federal Cost	Funds Appropriated Through Fiscal 1952	Required to Complete
Under construction			
In operation	$1,367.8	$1,052.9	$ 314.9
Not yet in operation	1,171.4	271.1	900.3
Subtotal	$2,539.2	$1,324.0	$1,215.2
Authorized—not yet started	3,174.1	12.2	3,161.9
Total	$5,713.3	$1,336.2	$4,337.1

Source: Department of the Army, *Annual Report of the Chief of Engineers*, 1951, Part 1, Vol. 3, p. 288.

NEEDS VS. DEMAND FOR FACILITIES

The estimated need for expansion, replacement and modernization of basic transportation facilities indicates that satisfactory standards of transportation service can be provided only after a period of years. Backlog highway construction requirements for accommodating today's traffic

TABLE 130. NEEDS VS. DEMAND FOR CAPITAL OUTLAYS FOR TRANSPORTATION, 1950 AND 1960

(*Millions of 1950 Dollars*)

Type of Facility	1950		1960	
	Demand	Needs	Demand	Needs
Total [a]	$4,794	$8,670	$6,900	$9,370
Highway construction	2,272	5,500	3,500 [b]	5,500
Airways	17.5	30	25	50
Airports	80 [c]	220	125	220
Waterways and harbors	116	270	100	270
Transit	168	190	250	260
Railroads	1,111	1,280	1,500	1,590
Oil pipelines	141	160	200	210
Other transportation [d]	888	1,020	1,200	1,270

Source: Appendix 4–7, Table B, and discussion in text.

a. Includes private outlays only by transportation industries. Excluded are outlays by other industries for transportation equipment — for example, manufacturing industry expenditures for business motor vehicles.

b. The President's recently proposed $50 billion program may increase this figure to $4.5 billion (at 1950 prices).

c. Estimate based on Civil Aeronautics Administration data.

d. Includes outlays by transportation industries other than the transit, railroad and oil pipeline industries — for example, airlines, shipping lines and intercity bus lines.

are estimated to amount to at least $40 billion, whereas construction outlays in 1953 were only $3.2 billion. A modern airways system based on the latest electronic aids, necessitating outlays for ground and aircraft equipment exceeding a billion dollars, is far from realization. The ultimate program begun in 1950 is not expected to be accomplished for several years. Waterway and harbor improvements add further billions to the backlog of proposed transportation projects.

Railroad modernization requires extensive redesign and relocation of terminals. Off-street parking space, including parking garages, are needed for urban highway transportation. Truck, bus and marine terminals are also needed. The modernization of motive power, new rail and transit equipment, new aircraft and motor trucks, would involve heavy outlays above basic facility requirements.

It is probable that the biggest outlays in the future will have to be made in the urban areas of the nation, where 100 million people are now living. Traffic congestion in these areas represents the most urgent transportation problem facing the nation; and it is here that the costs of accomplishing any noticeable relief are highest. Nearly every large city has under way or in the planning

stage ambitious schemes for the construction of express highways to carry traffic into and out of downtown areas, and for enlarging off-street parking capacity to accommodate traffic after it has arrived. Many cities are modernizing or extending their transit systems, inaugurating new rail commuter services, and building new airport capacity, underground parking garages, truck, bus and water terminals, and other costly facilities.

The various deficiencies in basic transportation facilities together represent a minimum backlog of some $50 billion, compared with an annual capital outlay of $5.7 billion in 1952. In the equipment field there is a further gap between needs and the 1952 rate of about $2 billion of expenditures.[47]

It is anticipated on the basis of expanding traffic in 1960 that capital expenditures for transportation will increase from less than $5 billion in 1950 to nearly $7 billion in 1960. The largest part of the increase will be for highways, with capital outlays for this purpose rising more

47. Estimated equal to the 1952 outlays by the transit, oil pipeline and "other transportation" industries plus about half the outlays of the railroad industry. (See Table 120.)

than 50 per cent as the growth of traffic continues to demand new highway capacity and modernization of road design, and as the desirability of adequate highways is demonstrated by the current development of expressways. Public transportation outlays for cities are expected to increase as the demand for better service becomes more pressing and the relative economy of good public transportation more evident. New motive power and rolling stock and terminal developments will call for increased investment in railroad facilities. The further expansion of aviation will likewise require expansion of existing facilities and the development of heliports.

Needed capital outlays in 1950 and 1960 in the case of highways were computed on the basis of how much would have to be spent annually for 10 years to overcome the accumulated deficiencies in 1950 ($40 billion) and the new deficiencies arising during the subsequent decade ($15 billion). The same method was followed for airport needs, using the requirements set forth in the National Airport Plan. Airway needs are based on the estimate of the all-weather system requirements. Waterway needs were based on a 10-year realization of the program of the Corps of Engineers. In the case of private transportation facilities, needs were assumed to exceed demand by the same percentage as for all private productive facilities. (See Chapter 15.) These estimates indicate that transportation facility and equipment needs in 1950 were almost $4 billion higher than actual expenditures. For 1960 it is estimated that needs will increase to over $9 billion a year, and that actual outlays will be approximately $7 billion. (See Table 130.)

Summary

The assumptions on which the estimates in this study are based include a 16 per cent increase in population from 1950 to 1960, and a 30 per cent increase in real national income. It is assumed that employment will be relatively high in 1960, that the decade will be free of major war or major depression, and that more leisure time and a somewhat lighter tax burden will provide additional incentive for consumer expenditures.

In the light of these assumptions, three developments will dominate the transportation picture in 1960. First will be the continued growth of private transportation through expanded auto-

mobile ownership and a nationwide acceleration of highway improvement. Second will be the growth of airline travel as flight safety and dependability and innovations such as the helicopter and turbo-jet combine with new aids to navigation to triple the volume of air traffic in the course of a decade. Third, it may be expected that our cities, where the need for transport modernization has long been neglected, will awaken to the necessity for extensive capital investment for all forms of transportation.

Transportation expenditures by consumers will increase less rapidly than consumer expenditures as a whole. Total consumption expenditures in 1960 are expected to be slightly more than 24 per cent above the 1950 level, while a 21 per cent rise is estimated for transportation. This is accounted for by a declining rate of increase in automobile ownership. Despite the rise in passenger car registrations to 59 million in 1960, car purchases in that year will be only 5 per cent above the very high sales of 1950. Gasoline sales, on the other hand, are expected to be up 30 per cent.

In the public carrier field, local transportation patronage in cities, by bus and rapid transit, is expected to expand as the traffic congestion of urban areas brings renewed pressure for the operation of more satisfactory mass methods of downtown movement, and as the growth of automobile ownership continues to outrun efforts to provide parking space in central business districts.

The greatest increase in public carrier expenditures, however, is expected in intercity service. An estimated rise of 37 per cent in this category from 1950 to 1960 is accounted for largely by expansion of consumer spending for air carrier service. Highway bus patronage is expected to rise by 13 per cent. It is believed that the railroads will continue to furnish profitable passenger service on heavy-density lines for both short trips and overnight distances, but that automobile and air competition will force a net decline in spending for railroad travel.

In the field of foreign travel, high levels of income and the expansion of ship and air services are expected to continue the upward trend in pleasure trips abroad. A 54 per cent increase in foreign travel expenditures by consumers is forecast.

In total, it is estimated that consumers in 1960 will be spending $28.5 billion (expressed in 1950 dollars) for the mobility that has become so important a characteristic of the American economy. Personal transportation will be taking nearly 12 cents out of every dollar spent by consumers for all purposes.

These mounting outlays for transportation will call for additional outlays for equipment and basic facilities. The magnitude of these expenditures will depend also on levels of freight traffic. Total capital outlays for transportation in 1960 are expected to approach $7 billion, compared with $4.8 billion in 1950.

## CHAPTER 10

HEALTH AND MEDICAL CARE

IN 1950 AN ESTIMATED $12.7 billion was spent in the United States for health and medical services and facilities for civilians. This sum represents the amount individuals spent for health and medical services (including insurance against the costs of such services); the amount spent by the government in health services for veterans and in medical services for recipients of public assistance; the costs of hospital construction; and expenditures of philanthropic agencies and industry for medical services and research. Comparable expenditures in 1951 were $13.6 billion; in 1952, $14.4 billion.

Consumers paid about two thirds of the total — or $8.4 billion in 1950, $9.0 billion in 1951 and $9.6 billion in 1952. These outlays are small in comparison with total consumer expenditures, but the costs of health and medical services are unevenly distributed and for a few families with expensive or chronic illnesses they may be one of the major items of family expense during the year.

Progress in medical science over the past fifty years has resulted in higher standards of medical care, and therefore in higher costs. Vast improvements in the techniques of preventive and curative medicine have brought a remarkable decline in death rates with a resulting increase in the average length of life, while the recent development of the so-called miracle drugs has greatly reduced the toll taken by certain diseases. Probably the greatest advance, however, is the fuller realization of the distinction between optimum health and absence of illness, and the concentration of interest upon the total health of the individual, including his environment and his attitudes, rather than upon a particular symptom or disease.

DEVELOPMENT OF MEDICAL CARE IN THE UNITED STATES

We take it for granted today that the doctor or dentist we visit has learned his profession in an

Revised on the basis of the chapter on "Medical Care" by MARGARET C. KLEM and HELEN HOLLINGSWORTH which appeared in the first edition of *America's Needs and Resources.*

accredited medical school and has passed rigid public examinations, that the nurses who assist him also have had professional training and that, if necessary, we can go to a hospital for special treatment. But less than fifty years ago some states still did not require physicians to be licensed, most granted licenses without examination to applicants who had graduated from dental schools — good or bad — and exploitation of medical education primarily for profit by commercially minded schools was widespread. The United States had no trained nurses when the Civil War began and no hospitals as we know them today.

Medical Science

In Colonial America, the art of medicine combined folklore and superstition with such primitive procedures as bloodletting and purging. Until the middle of the nineteenth century, activities to preserve health were directed largely toward control of communicable disease, environmental sanitation and vaccination against smallpox. After the Civil War, research in medical bacteriology and vastly improved bacteriological techniques led to discoveries in the origin and cause of infectious disease. Advances in methods of prevention and therapy followed. Progress was also made against noninfectious diseases as new precision instruments and X-rays made diagnosis easier and more accurate.

Even before 1900, progress in preventive medicine, surgery and therapy, and in public health measures, was reflected in declining mortality rates. The over-all decline resulted chiefly from decreases in infant mortality and from a sharp drop in deaths from certain diseases, notably tuberculosis, diphtheria, typhoid fever and diarrheal diseases. With the drop in the death rate, life expectancy increased.

World War I created a demand for immediate remedies for infectious diseases, for improved surgical techniques, for effective treatment of wounds and burns, and for clinical research in psychiatry. Research and wartime experience resulted in certain technical improvements — particularly in the use of antiseptics and anesthetics and in orthopedic and plastic surgery.

After 1930, rapid advances were made in prevention and prophylaxis and even more spectacular successes were achieved in therapy. During this period also, science came to grips with the viruses, chemotherapy contributed the well-known sulfonamides and penicillin, and the electron microscope opened a new world in biology and medicine.

The threat of a second world war brought a widespread realization that science would be the key to national defense. Through military laboratories and field installations and through contracts with civilian institutions, intensive studies were made of the diagnosis, treatment and prevention of such infectious diseases as typhoid and typhus; of the effects of gases, dusts, temperature and fatigue; and of other medical problems more closely related to civilian interests, such as blood derivatives, dysentery, encephalitis, atypical pneumonia, influenza and venereal disease. As a result of this research and earlier progress in medical science, mortality rates in the armed forces in World War II — both from disease and wounds — were considerably lower than in World War I.

While the civilian population benefited from the results of wartime medical research, a growing civilian problem — that of the chronic and degenerative diseases — was necessarily neglected. Not until well after the war's close was medical attention turned to the diseases of the older age groups.

Physicians

Most medical schools at the start of World War I were "Grade A," providing four years' training following a college education. Nearly all states required hospital internship of at least one year (arranged in cooperation with the American Hospital Association). By 1928 only six of the nation's eighty medical schools appeared on the "not approved" list of the American Medical Association.

As the medical profession gained in prestige, the number wanting to enter it increased and standards for admission were raised. Even in the depression of the 1930s, medical schools had far more applicants than they were prepared to accept. In World War II they accelerated their training periods under the pressure of a vastly increased demand. By 1944 approximately 60,000 physicians — 40 per cent of the active medical profession — were serving in the armed forces.

While nine out of ten practicing physicians at the start of World War II were in private practice, there was a growing trend toward salaried work — in hospitals, public health service, industry, teaching, research and administration. Between 1928 and 1942 the number of full-time salaried physicians increased 53 per cent — from 13,000 to 20,000.

With the expansion in the scope of medicine, it became more and more difficult for a physician to become expert in every field and many practitioners began to turn to the care of specific conditions. Specialization was on its way. In 1928 slightly over one fourth of the more than 152,000 licensed physicians in the country reported themselves as full-time or part-time specialists. At the start of World War II, when the profession included 175,000 physicians, specialists outnumbered general practitioners.

With specialization came a trend toward group practice. Pooling their skills and specialties, groups of physicians would share office space and equipment, employ a single staff of auxiliary personnel, and, usually, apportion the income.

Nursing

The establishment of training schools in 1873 in three outstanding hospitals — Bellevue, New Haven and Massachusetts General — marked the beginning of formal nursing education in this country. By the early years of the twentieth century the nursing profession was expanding at a rapid rate — too rapidly to maintain proper standards, as many members of the profession recognized. Studies sponsored by the National League of Nursing Education in 1919 were instrumental in bringing about reforms. Gradually, the poorer schools were weeded out and more collegiate schools of nursing were established. From a total of 2,155 in 1926 the number of nursing schools dropped to 1,780 by 1932.

At the onset of the depression the majority of nurses were in private-duty service and therefore suffered severe unemployment as job opportunities shrank. Those who were able to find and keep jobs had poor pay and long hours. The national defense and wartime periods changed the situation from one of apparently adequate supply — even surplus — to one of acute shortage.

Nurses were recruited from all fields to meet the heavy needs of the armed forces, with the result that too few nurses remained to give needed care to civilians.

Training programs were accelerated, and in 1943 the U.S. Cadet Nurse Corps was founded through authority of the Bolton Act, which provided federal funds for the training of student nurses and for refresher and postgraduate courses. Each student enrolled under the program had to agree to remain in essential nursing service, military or civilian, for the duration of the war. From the start of the program to its formal closing in 1948, the Corps enrolled 169,443 student nurses in 1,125 of the nation's 1,300 nursing schools and graduated 124,065. Experience with the program indicated the changes and improvements possible in nursing education as well as the increased responsibilities that could be assigned to student nurses.

By the end of World War II, 317,800 professional registered nurses were available for or employed in nursing work. It was estimated, however, that at least 360,000 were needed at that time.

Dentistry

The first world war brought home to the public the importance of dental health to general health. Because of dental defects, large numbers of young men were rejected for military service or accepted only for limited service. Consequently, demand for dental care increased, and more and more young men were encouraged to enter the dental field.

During the middle 1930s, however, two circumstances combined to cause a drop in enrollments in dental schools. First, the depression prevented many young men from taking the dental course. Second, in 1935, dental schools increased their admission requirements to two years of approved work in an accredited academic college. An upswing in enrollment came during the 1938–1939 school year, when 7,407 students were enrolled in the 39 approved schools.

By 1940, 70,121 dentists were in active practice in the United States. Only 5 per cent of all dentists were listed as full specialists in that year, but some 30 to 35 per cent combined their general practice with some type of specialty work.

World War II brought an acute demand for dentists. Publicity given to rejections among the first three million Selective Service registrants (tooth defects were the leading cause of rejection and accounted for 16.5 per cent of all rejections) made the public more than ever aware of the values of dental care. Dental health began to be included in all health discussion; dental health education programs were initiated; dental examinations were added to industrial health programs; and dental health services were added in state and local health units.

Hospitals

In 1873, when the first census of hospitals was taken, the United States had only 178 hospitals of all types, with a total capacity of less than 35,000 beds. Between then and World War I, many church hospitals were founded, municipal hospitals grew with the development of cities, and a start was made toward building hospitals for the care of specific diseases. With advances in medicine and nursing, hospitals underwent radical changes and began to provide skilled medical and surgical attention and nursing care to all types of patients. Every advance in medical science has created a need for special hospital services in addition to the usual medical, surgical and nursing care. Special departments became necessary as diagnostic and therapeutic services, social service, dietary service, medical records, physical and occupational therapy, and other services became increasingly important to the proper care of the sick.

By 1914, 5,037 hospitals with a total capacity of 532,000 beds were registered by the American Medical Association. Between the end of World War I and the beginning of the depression of the 1930s, hospital construction continued at a rapid pace. By 1928 there were 6,852 hospitals in operation — the largest number ever registered. The depression years, however, halted construction and closed more than 700 facilities. The financial difficulties of hospitals during the depression came in part from their haphazard location. Most of the building during the boom of the 1920s had been financed by private contributions; as a result there was overbuilding and duplication in some areas while great deficiencies remained in others. From 1929 to 1939, because of sharply reduced private incomes and increasing taxes, hospital construction at private expense was practically at a standstill. The limited construction that went on consisted largely of additions to existing hospitals, mainly among public facilities.

With the onset of World War II came a need for hospitals near defense plants, which were usually in nonmetropolitan areas. Through the wartime Lanham Act, 874 emergency facilities — hospitals, nurses' homes and public health centers — were constructed at a cost of nearly $100 million to the federal government and nearly $22 million to local governments.

Between 1944 and 1946, the Commission on Hospital Care, appointed by the American Hospital Association and assisted by funds from private foundations, studied the nation's hospital problems and made recommendations for their solution. In August 1946, Congress passed the Hospital Survey and Construction (Hill-Burton) Act, embodying the recommendations of the Commission and the principles set forth by the House of Delegates of the American Hospital Association. For the first time in its history the nation undertook a systematic, country-wide hospital program with financial aid from the federal government.

Voluntary Health Agencies

Voluntary efforts to combat health hazards began a rapid growth late in the nineteenth century. A notable example of private leadership in public health was the founding of the National Tuberculosis Association in 1904. Local groups organized to help meet other problems — those of venereal disease, mental hygiene, cancer, blindness, and maternal and infant mortality — expanded into national organizations by 1915.

The organization of voluntary health agencies gained impetus after World War I. For the most part these agencies have concentrated on a single disease, promoting research and carrying on extensive educational campaigns. Their pioneer work has frequently become in time partly or wholly the responsibility of public agencies. Not only the funds but also the services of great numbers of laymen have been enlisted in voluntary programs.

By the close of World War II some 20,000 voluntary health agencies (including national organizations and their state and local components) were active in various phases of health work. Examples of national organizations that have developed through voluntary efforts are the American Red Cross (1881), the National Tuberculosis Association (1904), the National Committee for Mental Hygiene (1908), the American Cancer Society (1913), Community Chests and Councils of America (1918), the National Society for Crippled Children and Adults (1921), the American Heart Association (1924), the National Foundation for Infantile Paralysis (1938), the National Multiple Sclerosis Society (1946), and the Commission on Chronic Illness (1949).

Government Activities

Government activity in the field of health and medical care was at first limited chiefly to city boards of health. In 1869, Massachusetts established a state board of health; other states took similar action in fairly rapid order. After 1905, county health boards were gradually established. Growing interest in the health of mothers and children resulted, during the 1890s and early 1900s, in the establishment of milk stations for infants in large cities and in the organization of hygiene bureaus in city departments of health and child hygiene divisions in state departments of health. Federal activities in behalf of child and maternal health were marked by the establishment, in 1912, of the federal Children's Bureau. The federal government through its Army Medical Corps and the Marine Hospital Service (later the United States Public Health Service) also carried on outstanding work in medical research and public hygiene.

Paralleling the developments in medical science after World War I, governmental units were placing increased emphasis on public health programs. Health departments were organized in all states, with responsibilities for control of acute communicable diseases, sanitation, collection of vital statistics, maternal and child hygiene, industrial hygiene, public health nursing, health education, laboratory service, inspection of public buildings, inspection of food and drugs, and similar functions. County health units, which had been spreading slowly, began a period of rapid growth. By 1935, 561 full-time local health units were serving 762 counties, and by 1947, 1,284 were serving 1,874 of the 3,070 counties in the United States.

Meanwhile, the federal government through the Public Health Service was developing its role as guide for state and local public health activities. The economic crisis beginning in 1929 accelerated the expansion of federal functions in public health, and in 1935 the Social Security Act authorized federal grants-in-aid to the states for certain programs, notably maternal and child health services and services for crippled children.

Federal interest in another field — rehabilitation of disabled adults — developed soon after World War I. Federal legislation in 1918 for the rehabilitation of disabled veterans of World War I was followed in 1920 by the first federal Vocational Rehabilitation Act, which authorized a four-year program of grants-in-aid to the states for vocational rehabilitation of disabled civilians. This act was later extended through 1936, and the Social Security Act made the program a permanent federal-state activity. In 1943 the Barden-LaFollette Act provided a substantial increase in federal participation, added physical restoration services, and made provision for rehabilitation of the mentally disabled.

The federal government's program of medical care for veterans also had its origins in the first world war. Until that time, federal responsibility for disabled war veterans was limited to care incidental to domiciliary care. In 1917, however, the federal government was given responsibility (Public Law 90, Sixty-fifth Congress) for providing medical and hospital care, not incidental to domiciliary care, to World War I veterans with disabilities or injuries incurred in or aggravated by military service. Succeeding laws extended coverage to veterans of any war, and expanded hospital benefits to include not only the service-connected disability for which hospitalization was required but concurrent disabilities as well. For veterans with non-service-connected disability and unable to pay the costs of care, hospitalization or domiciliary care was authorized in veterans' facilities, if beds were available.

Industrial Health Programs

Concern over occupational health hazards in the early years of this century resulted in passage of state workmen's compensation laws, which placed liability for industrial injuries and certain illnesses directly upon employers. These laws, first enacted in 1911, spread rapidly during World War I and the years immediately following.

Studies of lead poisoning — the first intensive studies of occupational disease — were conducted just prior to World War I. In the years following, industrial hygiene agencies were established by many states, and studies of industrial health hazards were undertaken. As factories grew in size, employers became increasingly conscious of the costs of absenteeism resulting from illness or injury, and many large plants established their own health services. War emergencies gave increasing momentum to the development of these services through the introduction of new toxic materials, the need to conserve manpower, and the use of cost-plus war contracts.

Prepayment Hospital and Medical Care Plans

Experiments in prepaid hospital care were made as early as 1880, when some hospitals in Minnesota arranged to provide lumberjacks with services on a prepayment basis. Some industries also initiated prepaid programs for their employees and sometimes their dependents. The spark to the present-day hospital service plan movement, however, is credited to the Baylor University Hospital plan, formed in Dallas, Texas, in 1929. From its beginning, growth of the Blue Cross movement was remarkable and rapid. By the end of World War II, 87 plans were in existence with a total enrollment of 20 million.

Medical society prepayment plans, first formed about 1917, also spread throughout the country, though less rapidly than Blue Cross. For the most part, their development has been through medical societies with affiliations with Blue Cross.

HEALTH AND MEDICAL CARE IN THE EARLY 1950S

Medical achievements and social advances in combination have brought about a striking decline in communicable disease. Chiefly for this reason, death rates have fallen sharply and life expectancy has increased. Over-all illness rates have probably not declined appreciably, however, and with the increase in medical knowledge and resources the demand for medical services has grown steadily.

STATE OF THE NATION'S HEALTH

Today the American people are closer to a full appreciation of the values of health than ever before in the nation's history. Modern medical science and technology have brought about great accomplishments in the diagnosis, control, prevention and treatment of disease, while health education of the public has stimulated an increas-

TABLE 131. AVERAGE LIFE EXPECTANCY AT BIRTH AND AT AGE 65, 1900–1950

(*Years*)

Race and Period	At Birth		Age 65	
	Males	*Females*	*Males*	*Females*
White				
1900–1902	48.2	51.1	11.5	12.2
1909–1911	50.2	53.6	11.3	12.0
1919–1921	56.3	58.5	12.2	12.8
1929–1931	59.1	62.7	11.8	12.8
1939–1941	62.8	67.3	12.1	13.6
1949	66.2	71.9	13.0	15.2
1950	66.6	72.4	13.0	15.3
Nonwhite				
1900–1902	32.5	35.0	10.4	11.4
1909–1911	34.1	37.7	9.7	10.8
1919–1921	47.1	46.9	12.1	12.4
1929–1931	47.6	49.5	10.9	12.2
1939–1941	52.3	55.5	12.2	14.0
1949	58.9	62.7	13.7	15.7
1950	59.2	63.2	13.3	15.6

Source: Abridged Life Tables: United States, 1950, National Office of Vital Statistics, U.S. Public Health Service, November 16, 1953, pp. 341–342.

ing awareness of the need for the prevention and proper care of sickness.

Death Rates

Some indication of how far we have traveled along the road to good health is given by the decline in death rates since the turn of the century. Between 1900 and 1950 the death rate dropped about 45 per cent — from 17.2 per 1,000 persons to 9.6 per 1,000. Most of this great saving in life has been accomplished among children and young adults — largely through the control of infectious diseases.

Life Expectancy

An infant born today can expect to live more than twenty years longer, on the average, than one born in 1900. The gains in life expectancy of females have been particularly impressive, and nonwhites of both sexes have gained more than whites. Between 1900 and 1950, life expectancy at birth among white males increased from 48.2 years to 66.6 years; among white females, from 51.1 years to 72.4; among nonwhite males, from 32.5 years to 59.2; and among nonwhite females,

from 35.0 years to 63.2. There has been no such dramatic change, however, in the average lifetime remaining to those who have reached the ages of 65 or 70. (See Table 131.)

Cause of Death

There are, today, more than four times as many persons 65 years of age and over in the United States as there were in 1900. With this growth in the number of the aged has come an increase in the chronic and degenerative diseases. At the beginning of the century, the three leading causes of death were influenza and pneumonia, tuberculosis, and diarrhea and enteritis. By 1950 the three leading causes of death were diseases of the heart, cancer or malignant tumors, and intracranial lesions of vascular origin — diseases primarily associated with the older age groups. (See Table 132.)

Maternal Mortality

Maternal mortality rates have decreased steadily since the early 1900s. The drop has been particularly rapid since 1936, when the rate was 56.8 per 10,000 live births. Nevertheless, in 1950,

TABLE 132. DEATH RATES FOR SPECIFIED CAUSES OF DEATH, SELECTED YEARS, 1900–1950

(*Per 100,000 Population*)

Cause of Death	1900	1910	1920	1930	1940	1950
All causes	1,719.1	1,468.0	1,298.9	1,132.1	1,076.4	963.8
Major cardiovascular-renal diseases	345.2	371.9	364.9	414.4	485.7	510.8
Diseases of the heart	137.4	158.9	159.6	214.2	292.5	355.5
Vascular lesions affecting central nervous system	106.9	95.8	93.0	89.0	90.8	104.0
Chronic and unspecified nephritis and other renal sclerosis	81.0	84.6	82.4	86.7	79.0	16.4
Malignant neoplasms including neoplasms of lymphatic and hematopoietic tissues	64.0	76.2	83.4	97.4	120.3	139.8
Influenza and pneumonia, except pneumonia of newborn	202.2	155.9	207.3	102.5	70.3	31.3
Motor vehicle accidents	—	1.8	10.3	26.7	26.2	23.1
Tuberculosis, all forms	194.4	153.8	113.1	71.1	45.9	22.5
Diabetes mellitus	11.0	15.3	16.1	19.1	26.6	16.2
Symptoms, senility and ill-defined conditions	117.5	47.5	31.8	30.4	23.7	14.9
Gastritis, duodenitis, enteritis and colitis, except diarrhea of newborn	142.7	115.4	53.7	26.0	10.3	5.1
Syphilis and its sequelae	12.0	13.5	16.5	15.7	14.4	5.0
Deliveries and complications of pregnancy, childbirth, and the puerperium	13.4	15.3	19.0	12.7	6.7	2.0
Whooping cough	12.2	11.6	12.5	4.8	2.2	.7
Measles	13.3	12.4	8.8	3.2	.5	.3
Diphtheria	40.3	21.1	15.3	4.9	1.1	.3
Typhoid fever	31.3	22.5	7.6	4.7	1.0	.1

Sources: National Office of Vital Statistics, U.S. Public Health Service: *United States: Summary of Vital Statistics, 1949,* September 10, 1952, p. 499, and *Deaths and Death Rates for 64 Selected Causes, by Age, Race and Sex: United States, 1950,* November 2, 1953, pp. 283–329.

according to the National Office of Vital Statistics, 2,960 women died from conditions directly related to pregnancy and childbirth — 8.3 for every 10,000 live births. The maternal mortality rate for nonwhite women — 22.2 per 10,000 live births — was three and one half times the rate among white women. (See Table 133.) For both race groups the rate was higher in rural areas than in urban communities.

Although every state has shown a marked reduction in maternal mortality, wide variations are found in the state-by-state rates. In Mississippi, for example, the rate in 1949–1950 was 23.5 maternal deaths for each 10,000 live births; in Utah, the rate was only 2.4 per 10,000.

Infant Mortality

The infant mortality rate declined almost steadily from 99.9 per 1,000 live births in 1915, when the system of birth-registration areas was established, to 29.2 per 1,000 in 1950 and 28.4 in

TABLE 133. MATERNAL MORTALITY RATE, BY RACE, 1936–1950

(*Per 10,000 Live Births*)

Year	All Races	White	Nonwhite
1936	56.8	51.2	97.2
1937	48.9	43.6	85.8
1938	43.5	37.7	84.9
1939	40.4	35.3	76.2
1940	37.6	32.0	77.3
1941	31.7	26.6	67.8
1942	25.9	22.2	54.4
1943	24.5	21.1	51.0
1944	22.8	18.9	50.6
1945	20.7	17.2	45.5
1946	15.7	13.1	35.9
1947	13.5	10.9	33.5
1948	11.7	8.9	30.1
1949	9.0	6.8	23.5
1950	8.3	6.1	22.2

Source: Maternal Mortality Statistics, United States, 1950, National Office of Vital Statistics, U.S. Public Health Service, December 3, 1953, p. 368.

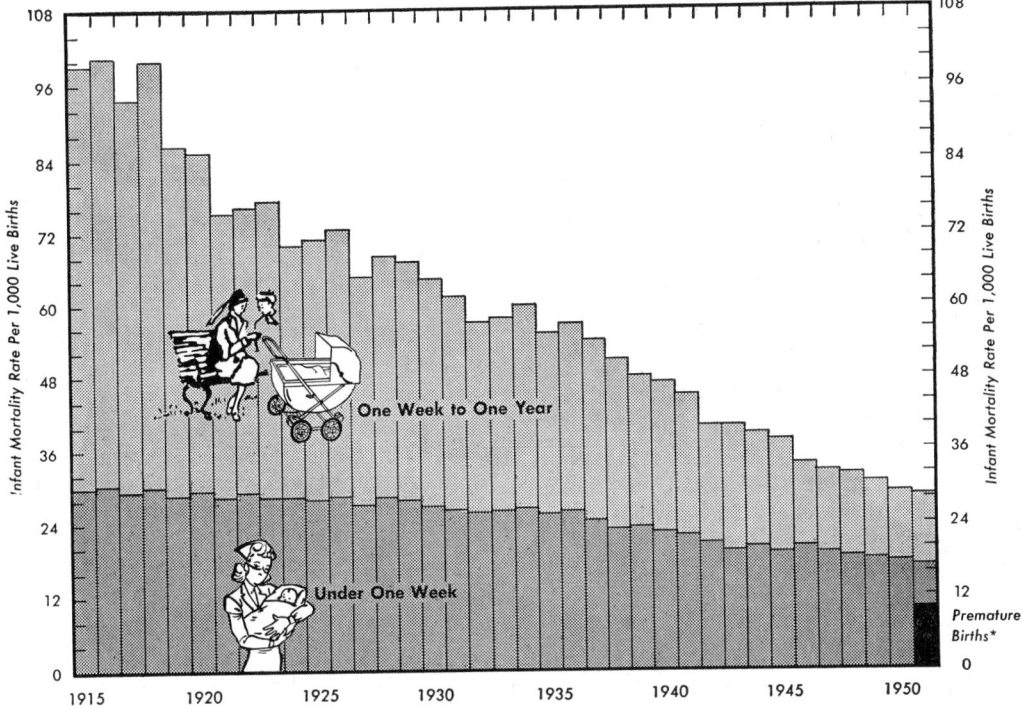

FIGURE 45. INFANT MORTALITY, 1915–1951
(Rate per 1,000 Live Births)

Source: National Office of Vital Statistics, U.S. Public Health Service.

1951. (See Figure 45.) Infant deaths in recent years have become increasingly a problem of mortality in the first four weeks of life. About seven out of every ten infant deaths in 1950 occurred within the first 28 days after birth. More than three out of ten occurred among infants under one day of age.[1]

Deaths among nonwhite infants have always been substantially above those among white infants. In 1950 the rate for nonwhite infants was 44.5 per 1,000 live births compared with 26.8 for white infants. The risk of death is also somewhat greater for infants in rural areas than in urban places — and there is reason to believe that infant deaths are underreported in rural areas. The rural rate for all races in 1950 was 30.4 for each 1,000 live births compared with 28.4 in urban areas. Among the states the rates varied from a low of 21.8 in Connecticut to a high of 54.8 in New Mexico.[2]

1. *Infant Mortality Statistics, United States, 1950,* National Office of Vital Statistics, U.S. Public Health Service, February 9, 1954, pp. 452, 462.
2. *Ibid.,* pp. 456–460.

Attendance at Birth

Important factors in the steady decline in maternal and infant mortality rates have been the increases in births in hospitals and in births attended by physicians. The proportion of births delivered in hospitals increased from 36.9 per cent in 1935, when data on attendance at birth were first tabulated by the National Office of Vital Statistics, to 88.0 per cent in 1950, with a particularly rapid rise occurring during World War II and the immediate postwar years. In round numbers, the percentage for 1950 represents over three million births in hospitals — almost four times the number in 1935. The proportion of births attended by physicians (in or out of hospitals) reached 95.1 per cent in 1950. In recent years, only about one in twenty births has not been attended by a physician. (See Table 134.)

The proportion of nonwhite births attended by physicians has always been substantially below that for white births, but it has increased rapidly since 1935, when it was only 44.6 per cent com-

TABLE 134. ATTENDANCE AT BIRTH, 1935–1950

Year	Per Cent of Births Attended by:		
	Physicians in Hospital[a]	Physicians Not in Hospital	Midwives and Other Non-physicians
1935	36.9	50.6	12.5
1940	55.8	35.0	9.3
1942	67.9	24.7	7.4
1945	78.8	14.7	6.5
1947	84.8	10.1	5.1
1949	86.7	8.1	5.1
1950	88.0	7.1	4.9

Source: National Office of Vital Statistics, U.S. Public Health Service: *Births by Person in Attendance: United States, Each Division and State, 1949,* July 2, 1951, p. 63; and *Vital Statistics of the United States, 1950,* Vol. II, p. 36.

a. It is assumed that all births in hospitals are attended by physicians.

pared with a rate of 93.6 per cent for white births. In 1950 the proportions were much closer — 72.2 per cent for nonwhite and 98.7 per cent for white.

A few states still report comparatively small proportions of births attended by physicians. In 1950, when at least 99 per cent of births were physician-attended in 29 states and the District of Columbia, the percentages in four of the southern states ranged from only 66 to 79.

Illness Surveys

Some health experts believe that the over-all sickness rates for the general population have changed little over the past fifteen to twenty years, despite changes in the incidence of specific diseases. If this assumption is valid, we then may still accept the findings of the 1935–1936 National Health Survey — the most extensive survey of the prevalence of illness ever made in this country — that, over a year's time, among every 1,000 persons there are 171 illnesses that disable for a week or more. Days of disability caused by these illnesses average 9.9 per person.[3] An earlier comprehensive nationwide study — by the Committee on the Costs of Medical Care in 1928–1931 — indicated that there are an average of 3.8 illnesses a year per family.[4]

A more recent study, conducted over the period 1938–1943 but limited to the Eastern Health District of Baltimore, Maryland, revealed 1,261.4 acute illnesses among each 1,000 persons during an average twelve-month period. This study indicated an annual rate of 238.2 chronic illnesses (75.5 disabling and 162.7 nondisabling) per 1,000 persons.[5]

Illness among the Aged

The National Health Survey found that all disabling illnesses, including both acute and chronic conditions, occurred more often among persons aged 65 and over than in the population as a whole. The number of illnesses lasting at least seven consecutive days per 1,000 persons was 279 in the old-age group in contrast to 171 for all ages. The Baltimore study revealed a higher rate of disability lasting seven or more days — 382 per 1,000 aged persons and 305 per 1,000 persons of all ages.[6] This difference probably is due to the fact that the Baltimore families were visited each month over a five-year period while in the National Health Survey only one visit was made and the persons reporting may have forgotten many illnesses of relatively short duration.[7]

In both studies the total days of disability per person per year were more than three times as great in the old-age group as in the general population, and the length of disability from chronic illness more than four times as great.

The old-age group had relatively fewer cases confining them to the house, bed or hospital than the population as a whole, but when they became bed cases they remained there about twice as long as did bed cases in the general population, according to the Baltimore study. A chronic disease was the cause of hospitalization three times more often in the old-age group than in the general population. (See Table 135.)

Representative Families, Publication No. 26, Committee on the Costs of Medical Care, University of Chicago Press, Chicago, 1933, p. 48.

5. Elizabeth H. Jackson, "Morbidity Among Males and Females at Specific Ages — Eastern Health District of Baltimore," *Milbank Memorial Fund Quarterly,* October 1950, pp. 437–441.

6. The Baltimore study included all disabling illness regardless of duration. Both studies included hospital cases or deaths occurring within the study period, regardless of duration of illness.

7. G. St. J. Perrott, Marcus S. Goldstein and Selwyn D. Collins, "Health Status and Health Requirements of an Aging Population," in *Illness and Health Services in an Aging Population,* Publication No. 170, U.S. Public Health Service, 1952, pp. 1–25.

3. Rollo H. Britten, Selwyn D. Collins and James S. Fitzgerald, "The National Health Survey: Some General Findings as to Disease, Accidents, and Impairments in Urban Areas," *Public Health Reports,* March 15, 1940, p. 450.

4. I. S. Falk, Margaret C. Klem and Nathan Sinai, *The Incidence of Illness and the Costs of Medical Care among*

TABLE 135. ILLNESSES CONFINING TO HOUSE, BED OR HOSPITAL, PER YEAR, AMONG PERSONS
OF ALL AGES AND THOSE 65 AND OVER, AS FOUND IN THE EASTERN
HEALTH DISTRICT OF BALTIMORE, 1938–1943

Item	All Ages	65 Years and Over
Illness confining to house		
House cases per 1,000 persons observed	595	482
Days confined to house per person observed	9.4	29.9
House days per house case	15.7	62.0
Per cent of disabling cases confined to house [a]	91.5	88.3
Bed illness (includes hospitalized illnesses)		
Bed cases per 1,000 persons observed	365	321
Days in bed per person observed	4.95	8.52
Days in bed per bed case	13.5	26.6
Per cent of disabling cases in bed [a]	56.2	58.7
Hospitalized illness [b]		
Hospital cases per 1,000 persons observed	70.6	57.4
Hospital days per person observed	2.60	2.45
Hospital days per hospitalized case	36.9	42.7
Per cent of disabling cases hospitalized [a]	10.9	10.5
Chronic diseases		
Individuals with one or more chronic illnesses per 1,000 persons observed:		
All chronic illnesses	68.7	211.3
Disabling chronic illnesses	41.6	157.1
Nondisabling chronic illnesses	27.1	54.2
Per cent of hospitalized cases that were chronic	23.8	70.8

Source: G. St. J. Perrott, Marcus S. Goldstein and Selwyn D. Collins, "Health Status and
Health Requirements of an Aging Population," in *Illness and Health Services in an Aging
Population,* Publication No. 170, U.S. Public Health Service, 1952, p. 6.

a. A disabling illness represents a disability lasting one day or longer.
b. All types of hospitalization are included, regardless of duration.

The volume of medical services received by the old-age group in contrast to the population as a whole is of particular note. Most studies show that older persons receive more than the average amount of physicians' services and hospital care for chronic illness but about the same number of calls by physicians for nondisabling cases. In fact, in the Baltimore survey population, fewer cases of nonchronic illness were attended by a physician per 1,000 persons observed among the older people than in the whole population covered. The average number of days of hospitalization per hospitalized case, however, was definitely greater in the old-age group.

Chronic Illness

Although chronic illness is of particular importance among people 65 or older, it affects all ages. More than half of the chronically ill are under age 45; more than three fourths are between 15 and 64 years of age.

In the 1940s a number of states initiated programs to control chronic disease, and in 1946 a national movement was started that resulted three years later in the establishment of the Commission on Chronic Illness, which is attempting "to stimulate in every state and locality a well-rounded plan for the prevention and control of chronic disease and for the care and rehabilitation of the chronically ill." In the same year, the Public Health Service established a division to develop public health methods for the control of chronic disease and to assist state and local health departments in their work in this field.

There is a trend to incorporate the provision of care for the chronically ill with general medical care and to wipe out the disparity between facilities and services for acute and chronic illness. The development of home care programs makes it possible for the patient to move easily between home and hospital and for the coordinated services of a medical team to be brought to the home. It has been estimated that about 70 per cent of those afflicted with a long-term illness can best be cared for in their own homes, provided adequate supervision is available and the home is suitable for such care.

Many of the chronically ill could be restored to normal, useful living, but only a few agencies, outside of the military services, the state-federal vocational rehabilitation programs and the Veterans Administration, are equipped to provide the retraining in physical skills that is a prerequisite to vocational training. Startling results have been obtained in both veterans and civilian hospitals in improving the condition of chronically ill patients who have been hospitalized for long periods. One veterans hospital through a medical rehabilitation program of only nine months' duration and limited to 130 chronic neurologic patients, many of whom had not been out of bed for ten years, saved the government a sum estimated to exceed $1,250,000. A similar program for civilians might be expected to yield comparable savings.[8]

Mental Illness

Mental illness has been called the nation's number one health problem. While there are no reliable statistics to show the full extent of mental sickness in this country, some scattered data suggest the severity of the problem.

On an average day in 1952 more than 700,000 persons — a number equivalent to the combined populations of Nevada and New Hampshire — were patients in nervous and mental hospitals. Nearly half of the hospital beds throughout the country were occupied by the mentally ill.[9] Care of those in tax-supported institutions was costing well over $600 million in 1952 — more than double the operating expenditures of such institutions in 1946.[10]

In World War II approximately 12 per cent of the men between the ages of 18 and 37 were rejected by Selective Service because of mental and personality disorders, not including mental deficiency or neurological defects.[11] Between 40 and 45 per cent of the medical discharges from the Army were for psychiatric disabilities. The Metropolitan Life Insurance Company has estimated that out of every twenty children born alive in the United States, one will at some time be hospitalized for a mental illness and one will suffer an emotional disturbance that will interfere with his well-being and general adjustment. Furthermore, from 30 to 60 per cent of all patients consulting doctors have symptoms related to emotional disorders.[12] Millions in our population have minor emotional illnesses which, while not necessarily incapacitating, are medically significant.

Traditionally the states have assumed major responsibility for the care of severe cases of mental illness. In 1946, however, the National Mental Health Act authorized federal grants to the states to assist them in developing state and local preventive mental health services. Grants for research and for training professional personnel in the mental health field were also authorized by this act. In 1951 all states had mental health programs and were spending almost $2 for every $1 contributed by the federal government. Public Health Service grants to the states of $3.5 million in that year were only half the amount — $7.3 million — expended from state and local funds. These public funds of almost $11 million plus $1 million of private funds were spent for community clinic services and for educational and consultant services.[13] Consultant service is provided to the states by the National Institute of Mental Health, and close working relationships are maintained on various phases of the mental health problem, such as alcoholism and drug addiction.

HEALTH PERSONNEL

In response to a steadily growing demand for more medical care, a vast health army has grown

8. Mary E. Switzer and Howard A. Rusk, "Keeping Older People Fit for Participation," *Annals of the American Academy of Political and Social Science,* January 1952, pp. 146–153.

9. F. H. Arestad and Mary A. McGovern, "Hospital Service in the United States: The 1952 Census of Hospitals," reprinted from *Journal of the American Medical Association,* May 9, 1953, p. 5.

10. *Hospitals,* Administrator's Guide Issue, June 1953, Part II, p. 23.

11. *Psychiatric Information for the Rehabilitation Worker,* Office of Vocational Rehabilitation, Federal Security Agency, 1950, p. 2.

12. "The National Mental Health Act and Your Community," Mental Health Series, No. 3, U.S. Public Health Service, June 1948.

13. *Annual Report of the Federal Security Agency, Public Health Service,* 1952, pp. 20–23.

TABLE 136. HEALTH PERSONNEL, 1940 AND 1950

Occupation	1940	1950	Percentage Increase 1940–1950
Physicians, active nonfederal	160,480	179,041[a]	12
Dentists, active	70,121	82,575	18
Nurses, active professional registered	270,630	318,880	18
Auxiliary nursing personnel	186,656	368,735	98
Dental hygienists	5,000	7,000	40
Medical laboratory technicians	20,000	30,000	50
X-ray technicians	15,000	25,600	71
Physical therapists	3,100	5,700	84
Occupational therapists	2,200	3,400	55
Medical social workers	2,480	3,000	21
Psychiatric social workers	500	2,250	350
Psychologists	2,739	7,273	166
Dietitians and nutritionists	11,250	16,000	42
Pharmacists	79,347	100,102	26
Optometrists	10,237	17,470	71
Osteopathic physicians	6,007	10,595	76
Chiropractors	10,629	15,000	41
Chiropodists	6,106	6,962	14
Veterinarians	10,717	15,305	43
Sanitary engineers	1,960	4,496	129
Sanitarians	[b]	4,940	—
Medical record librarians	[b]	5,300	—
Public health educators	[b]	500	—

Sources: George W. Bachman and Associates, *Health Resources in the United States,* Brookings Institution, Washington, 1952, p. 58; data on physicians from Maryland Y. Pennell and Marion E. Altenderfer, *Health Manpower Source Book, I: Physicians,* U.S. Public Health Service, May 1952 (preliminary), p. 19.

a. Figure applies to the year 1949.
b. Not available.

up in this country — an army of well over a million workers. The three major professional groups — physicians, dentists and registered nurses — account for roughly half this force, with nurses standing first in numbers and doctors second. In addition to these three groups, a wide variety of other specialized workers, professional and lay, are engaged directly or indirectly in furnishing medical service to the American people.

Auxiliary nursing personnel — practical nurses, nurses' aides, attendants, ward maids and orderlies — make up the largest single group of health workers, having increased in number from almost 187,000 in 1940 to almost 369,000 in 1950.

Of these, about 300,000 in 1950 were hospital employees, and some 150,000 were practical nurses.

Important roles in modern medicine, particularly in hospitals, are also played by medical technologists and technicians, who numbered, in 1950, about 30,000; by X-ray technicians — about 25,600; by physical therapists — 5,700; and by occupational therapists — some 3,400. The growth in numbers of physical and occupational therapists has been particularly rapid in recent years, stimulated to a considerable extent by interest in the growing field of rehabilitation of the mentally and physically disabled.

Medical and psychiatric social workers, for the most part employed in hospitals and clinics, are another expanding group. In 1950, about 3,000 social workers were in the field of medical care and 2,250 in mental hygiene.

Pharmacists, in 1950, totaled 100,102. About 90 per cent were working in retail pharmacies. The others were manufacturers' and wholesalers' representatives (4 per cent of the total), worked in hospital pharmacies or in manufacturing and wholesale establishments, or were in teaching or government positions.

The health corps includes also such diverse groups as psychologists, dietitians and nutritionists, osteopathic physicians, sanitary engineers and medical record librarians. (See Table 136.) To these numbers might be added still others such as administrative and clerical personnel and those engaged in the manufacture and distribution of health supplies.

Physicians

In July 1949, according to the latest American Medical Directory, there were 201,277 licensed physicians in the continental United States.[14] By the end of 1952, allowing for new licentiates and deaths in the intervening years, the number had increased to 214,667 — a net gain of 2,987 during 1952.[15]

Not all licensed physicians are engaged in the actual practice of medicine for the civilian population, or in such related work as medical research, teaching or administration. A significant number are retired or are partially or completely disabled,[16] and many are in federal service — in the armed forces, the U.S. Public Health Service, the Veterans Administration and other federal agencies. If only active, nonfederal physicians are counted, the number available at the end of 1952 totaled 186,406. Of these, about 151,400 were in private practice, 28,400 in hospital service, and nearly 6,700 in nonprivate practice, that is, employed full-time in research, in medical schools, by industrial and other organizations, by insurance companies and by state and local health departments. (See Table 137.)

There were 121 active nonfederal physicians

TABLE 137. NUMBER OF LICENSED PHYSICIANS, BY TYPE OF PRACTICE, DECEMBER 31, 1952

Type of Practice	Number
Total	214,667
Federal government service	20,095
Retired, not in practice	8,166
Active nonfederal	186,406
Private practice	151,363
Internship, residency, hospital administration	28,366
Research, teaching and other	6,677

Source: Donald G. Anderson and Anne Tipner, "Medical Licensure Statistics for 1952," Journal of the American Medical Association, May 30, 1953, p. 430.

for every 100,000 civilians in 1949, compared with 122 in 1940. In general, the wealthier and more heavily populated areas have relatively more physicians than poorer and sparsely settled areas. For example, in 1949 Mississippi had only 64 active nonfederal physicians for each 100,000 of its civilian population, while New York State had 196. There were twice as many active nonfederal physicians in metropolitan areas as in isolated counties, and 62 counties — 56 of them in isolated semirural or rural areas — had none.

Of the 201,277 licensed physicians listed for 1949 in the American Medical Directory, nearly one third (62,688) reported themselves as full-time specialists. In 1923, only 11 per cent were so reported and in 1940, 21 per cent. Internal medicine, surgery, ophthalmology-otorhinolaryngology and obstetrics-gynecology accounted for 62 per cent of all specialists in 1949.

During the academic year ending June 1953, 6,688 physicians were graduated from the 72 four-year schools approved by the American Medical Association. Only during the period of the accelerated wartime training program was this number of graduates exceeded. Enrollment in the 72 four-year schools and in the seven schools of basic science (two-year schools) totaled 27,688; 1,463 of these students were women and 715 were Negroes.

Physicians' Incomes

Physicians' incomes vary widely. Salaried physicians earn substantially less than physicians in independent practice; in 1949 their average net earnings were $8,272 as against $11,858 for independent physicians. Fifteen per cent of inde-

14. *American Medical Directory, 1950*, American Medical Association, Chicago.

15. Donald G. Anderson and Anne Tipner, "Medical Licensure Statistics for 1952," *Journal of the American Medical Association*, May 30, 1953, p. 430.

16. Estimated at 23,300 physicians in 1949, according to the Health Resources Advisory Committee, Office of Defense Mobilization; only 9,700 so designated in the American Medical Directory.

pendent physicians reported net incomes of $20,000 or more in 1949. However, one out of every 100 reported a net loss; about 8 per cent reported net incomes of less than $2,000; and 24 per cent reported less than $5,000.

Financial rewards are greater in larger cities and wealthier areas than in smaller, poorer places — although, of course, the greater earnings in larger communities may be partly offset by higher living costs. In 1949 the mean net income of physicians in independent practice rose gradually with size of community from a low of $7,109 in places of less than 1,000 population to a high of $14,276 in cities of 250,000 to 500,000. In cities of 500,000 and over, however, the average dropped considerably, perhaps because many very young physicians begin practice in such communities. (See Table 138.)

TABLE 138. NET INCOME OF PHYSICIANS WHOSE MAJOR SOURCE OF MEDICAL INCOME WAS FROM INDEPENDENT PRACTICE, BY SIZE OF COMMUNITY, 1949

Size of Community	Mean	Median
All communities	$11,858	$ 9,668
Less than 1,000	7,109	5,699
1,000–2,499	8,732	7,667
2,500–4,999	11,228	10,110
5,000–9,999	11,624	10,149
10,000–24,999	12,134	10,621
25,000–49,999	12,812	11,037
50,000–99,999	13,186	10,921
100,000–249,999	13,110	10,690
250,000–499,999	14,276	11,970
500,000–999,999	13,161	10,546
1,000,000 and over	10,661	7,988

Source: William Weinfeld, "Incomes of Physicians, 1929–49," *Survey of Current Business*, July 1951, p. 21.

Incomes increase, also, with degree of specialization. In 1949, among independent physicians, the mean net income of general practitioners was $8,835; that of part-time specialists was one-third higher — $11,758 — while the average for full-time specialists was $15,014, or more than two-thirds greater than the mean for general practitioners.

Nurses

The 1951 Inventory of Nurses, conducted by the American Nurses Association, showed 334,733 professional registered nurses in active service and 221,884 inactive.[17] For the United States as a whole, there were about 218 active nurses for each 100,000 persons in 1951, but the ratios varied widely among the states. The District of Columbia had 377 per 100,000 and Connecticut 361 per 100,000, while Arkansas had only 84 per 100,000.

Hospitals and other institutions employed nearly half of all active professional registered nurses. The next largest group (21 per cent) was engaged in private-duty service. Nearly 9 per cent were reported in some phase of public health service. (See Table 139.)

TABLE 139. ACTIVE PROFESSIONAL REGISTERED NURSES, BY FIELD OF NURSING, 1951

Field of Nursing	Number	Per Cent
Total	334,733	100.0
Hospitals and other institutions	163,026	48.7
Schools of nursing	7,701	2.3
Hospital and school of nursing	4,292	1.3
Public health	29,650	8.8
Public health and school of nursing	233	.1
Private duty	69,883	20.9
Industrial	14,323	4.3
Office	28,191	8.4
Other	1,794	.5
Unknown or unclassified	15,640	4.7

Source: *Inventory of Professional Registered Nurses, 1951*, American Nurses Association, New York.

Nursing students must not be overlooked in any consideration of the health manpower strength of the country, since from the start of their training they are directly involved in providing health service. In 1953 about 101,000 students were enrolled in 1,135 state-accredited schools of nursing. The number of graduates in 1952 reached 29,000 — far below the number at the peak of the Cadet Nurse Corps program but somewhat higher than in 1948 or 1949.

Nurses' Salaries

Nursing, regardless of the field of practice, has long been known to be low paid compared with other occupations requiring comparable training and experience. In recent years, however, nurses' salaries have been rising. The average monthly salary of the institutional staff nurse living outside hospital quarters increased from $172 in

17. *Inventory of Professional Registered Nurses, 1951*, American Nurses Association, New York, p. 6.

1946 to $205 in 1949. In 1946, public health nurses earned, on the average, $184 a month; in 1949, $238. Over the three-year period, average monthly salaries of nurse educators rose from $207 to $256.[18]

Private-duty nurses, unlike those in other nursing fields, are usually paid by the day. In 1949 the most frequent daily rate paid in most regions of the country was $10 for 8 hours of work, a rate which probably does not compare favorably with earnings of other nurses, since private-duty nurses do not work on every workday of the month nor do they receive paid vacations, sick leave or holidays. In September 1949, for example, they worked an average of only 13.9 days.

Improving Nursing Services

An important development in the field of nursing service is the growing trend toward evaluative studies of all aspects of nursing care. In 1948 a joint board of the six national nursing organizations [19] created the National Committee for the Improvement of Nursing Services. Supported by these organizations with assistance from two philanthropic agencies, the Committee is endeavoring to improve nursing education facilities, to coordinate research in nursing service, and to stimulate experimentation and sharing of findings by all groups actively engaged in or concerned with nursing in any form.

In 1950 the American Nurses Association initiated a five-year plan, providing for special funds to be used in research in nursing. The research studies, in which professional nurses and related experts — physicians, hospital or health administrators, social scientists, statisticians, anthropologists, industrial management engineers and others — are cooperating, are designed to find "practical ways of relating nursing to the increasing complexity of health services and of utilizing most effectively and economically the available nurse supply in the face of increasing demands."

Several of the studies already were under way in 1952.[20]

Dentists

Steadily increasing numbers have entered the dental profession. By 1950 there were 86,876 dentists in the United States, of whom 82,575, or nearly 95 per cent, were in active dental practice.[21] Ten years earlier, in 1940, the Bureau of the Census listed only 70,601 dentists.

The great majority of dentists are in independent private practice. In 1950, 92 per cent were in this type of practice, 2 per cent were in partnership practice, 1 per cent were in group practice, and 5 per cent were in salaried practice (mostly in federal service).

The 80,000 in active nonfederal practice in 1950 represented a ratio of 53 dentists per 100,000 population. As with physicians and nurses, the ratios varied widely among the states — from 19 per 100,000 in South Carolina to 88 in New York State and 90 in the District of Columbia.[22]

Although there is a growing trend toward specialization, specialty practice has developed to a far lesser extent than among physicians. In 1948 the great majority of dentists (88 per cent) limited their work to general practice; 6 per cent reported themselves as part specialists and 6 per cent as full specialists. The American Dental Association recognizes seven specialties — oral pathology, oral surgery, orthodontia, pedodontia, periodontia, prosthodontia and public health dentistry.

Dentists' Incomes

Dentists' incomes, on the average, have been substantially below those of physicians. Moreover, the rate of increase over the past years has not been as rapid as for physicians. In 1951 the average gross income of dentists was $14,085 and their average net income was $7,820, while the

---

18. *The Economic Status of Registered Professional Nurses, 1946–47,* Bulletin No. 931, U.S. Bureau of Labor Statistics, 1947; and "Salaries of Professional Registered Nurses," *American Journal of Nursing,* June 1950, pp. 329–330.

19. American Nurses Association; National League of Nursing Education (now the National League for Nursing); National Organization for Public Health Nursing; American Association of Industrial Nurses; Association of Collegiate Schools of Nursing; National Association of Colored Graduate Nurses.

20. Lucile Petry, Margaret Arnstein and Pearl McIver, "Research for Improved Nursing Practice," *Public Health Reports,* February 1952, pp. 183–188.

21. George W. Bachman and Associates, *Health Resources in the United States,* Brookings Institution, Washington, 1952, pp. 69–72. Data based on the *American Dental Directory,* 1950, of the American Dental Association.

22. *Distribution of Dentists in the United States by State, Region, District and County,* a 1953 report by the Bureau of Economic Research and Statistics of the American Dental Association, shows a total of 84,215 active and inactive nonfederal dentists, a ratio of 55.4 per 100,000 population. The ratio varied among states from 18 per 100,000 in South Carolina to 88 in New York State and 91 in the District of Columbia.

TABLE 140. AVERAGE INCOME OF PHYSICIANS AND DENTISTS, 1929-1951

Years	Physicians		Dentists	
	Gross	Net	Gross	Net
1929	$ 8,567	$ 5,224	$ 7,112	$4,267
1940	7,632	4,441	6,592	3,314
1947	17,742	10,726	12,032	6,610
1951	22,298	13,432	14,085	7,820
Percentage Increase				
1929-1951	160	157	98	83
1940-1951	192	202	114	136
1947-1951	26	25	17	18

Source: "Incomes of Physicians, Dentists, and Lawyers, 1949–51," Survey of Current Business, July 1952, p. 7.

averages for physicians were $22,298 and $13,432 respectively. Dentists have gained 83 per cent in net income over 1929; physicians, 157 per cent. (See Table 140.)

In 1952, when over 90 per cent of the dentists in active civilian practice were primarily in independent practice, independent dentists had a mean income of $10,873 compared with $6,920 for salaried dentists. In terms of median income, the figure was $9,961 for independent dentists compared with $6,525 for salaried dentists. Almost one in every six dentists had a net income below $5,000 in 1952. Nearly one in five had a net income of $15,000 or more. Net earnings of specialized dentists were, on the average, substantially above those of general practitioners — $13,-138 as compared with $10,293.[23]

As in the case of physicians, the size of community in which dentists practice has a definite effect on the amount earned. Average net incomes in 1952 (regardless of specialty or type of practice) varied from $7,600 in communities of less than 1,000 population to about $12,400 in cities of 250,000 to 500,000. There was also considerable variation of income according to region. The highest was in the Far West — an average net income of $12,867; the lowest was in the middle eastern states — $9,707.

HOSPITALS

Present-day hospitals not only provide care for the sick but also serve as a training ground for

23. "The 1953 Survey of Dental Practice," Journal of the American Dental Association, January 1954, pp. 68–74; February 1954, pp. 194–199.

medical personnel, as a laboratory for clinical research, and as a means for extending preventive care to the apparently well. They vary widely in size, type of ownership, range of services provided, and types of patients treated.

General Characteristics

According to data collected by the American Medical Association, the nation's hospital resources in 1952 consisted of 6,665 facilities with a capacity of 1.5 million beds. General hospitals and those handling allied specialties made up 82 per cent of the total number; nervous and mental facilities, 9 per cent; tuberculosis hospitals, 6 per cent; and hospital departments of other institutions accounted for the remainder. General and allied special hospitals, however, accounted for only 45 per cent of the total bed capacity, while nervous and mental facilities accounted for 48 per cent and tuberculosis facilities for 6 per cent.

Government provides a substantial part of the nation's hospital beds, particularly in the nervous and mental and the tuberculosis groups. Seventy-one per cent of all hospital beds in the country in 1952 were operated by government units — 44 per cent by state governments, 14 per cent by the federal government, and 13 per cent by city and county governments. Church-sponsored and other voluntary nonprofit institutions maintained only about one fourth of all beds although they accounted for 49 per cent of all hospitals. Proprietary (private profit-making) facilities — about 20 per cent of all hospitals — provided less than 4 per cent of all beds. (See Appendix 10-1.)

TABLE 141. NUMBER OF HOSPITALS, BY SIZE AND TYPE, 1952

Bed Capacity	All Hospitals	General	Nervous and Mental	Tubercu- losis	Other
Total	6,665	4,924	585	428	728
25 and under	1,183	988	29	16	150
26–50	1,575	1,230	80	59	206
51–100	1,395	1,013	76	107	199
101–200	1,126	874	48	105	99
201–300	503	386	26	55	36
301 and over	883	433	326	86	38

Source: F. H. Arestad and Mary A. McGovern, "Hospital Service in the United States: The 1952 Census of Hospitals," reprinted from *Journal of the American Medical Association*, May 9, 1953, p. 5.

Over 40 per cent of the nation's hospitals in 1952 had 50 or fewer beds. (See Table 141.) Institutions of this size are generally situated in small cities and towns, and in some cases two or more may be operating where one large facility would better serve the community's needs.

Utilization

About 19 million persons — one out of every eight in the population — entered a hospital at some time during 1952.[24] In no preceding year had hospital admissions reached this figure. These patients received a total of 479 million days of care.

General hospitals, with 42 per cent of all hospital beds, had 94 per cent of all admissions in 1952. On an average day, 475,000 persons were receiving general hospital care. This means, in terms of bed occupancy, that normally during the year 74.1 per cent of the general hospital beds were occupied. (An average occupancy of 80–85 per cent is usually considered the maximum limit of operating efficiency in general hospital facilities.) Nearly 174 million days of general hospital care were provided during 1952 — an average of 9.8 days for each patient admitted, compared with 14 days in 1935 and 15.1 days in 1931. The year-after-year decline in the average length of stay is striking evidence of the effects of medical advances, the use of modern drugs and techniques.

Although more patients are admitted to general hospitals than to any other type, mental facilities are first in the number of days of care given annually. In 1952, total days of patient care provided in mental hospitals reached 258 million. Days of care in tuberculosis institutions totaled 27 million.

Finances

In 1952, according to the American Hospital Association,[25] the assets of all hospitals totaled more than $9.4 billion. This represents an investment of about $60 for each person in the United States or nearly $6,000 for each hospital bed.

To maintain this hospital system required $4.5 billion — an average of $9.14 for each patient day of care. Nearly three fifths of this total amount ($2.6 billion) was needed to operate nonfederal general and special short-term facilities. The remaining two fifths went to operate the following facilities (figures in millions):

Federal	$925
Tuberculosis	177
Mental	636
General and special long-term	141

Operating expenses more than doubled between 1946 and 1952, although total hospital admissions increased only 25 per cent and the number of persons served on an average day increased 17 per cent. Salaries of hospital personnel are an important item of total expense; in nonprofit short-term hospitals in 1952, for example, they

24. F. H. Arestad and Mary A. McGovern, "Hospital Service in the United States: The 1952 Census of Hospitals," reprinted from *Journal of the American Medical Association*, May 9, 1953, pp. 5–12.

25. *Hospitals*, Administrator's Guide Issue, June 1953, Part II, pp. 13–23.

TABLE 142. VALUE OF HOSPITAL CONSTRUCTION PUT IN PLACE, 1939–1952

Year	Value of Construction in Current Prices	Index of Construction Costs	Value of Construction in 1939 Prices
	(Millions)	(1939 = 100)	(Millions)
1939	$158	100.0	$158
1942	64	120.2	53
1946	170	160.6	106
1949	679	244.4	278
1950	840	249.8	336
1951	947	265.5	357
1952	867	276.3	314

Sources: Louis S. Reed, "Hospital Construction Trends," *Modern Hospital*, March 1952, pp. 72–76; "Construction Volume and Costs, 1915–1952," *Construction and Building Materials, Statistical Supplement*, U.S. Department of Commerce, May 1953, pp. 7, 11, 32.

represented 57 per cent of the total per diem expense.

In 1952, nonprofit general and special short-term hospitals obtained 90 per cent of their total income from patients. The remainder came from voluntary contributions, endowments and governmental payments. Insurance plans have provided an increasing share of general hospital income in recent years. In 1952, Blue Cross and Blue Shield plans paid $548 million to hospitals for the care of members.[26]

Hospital Construction

The dollar volume of hospital construction in 1951 reached an all-time high of $947 million, more than five times the 1946 figure. Much of this increase can be accounted for by the decline in the purchasing power of the dollar, but even when allowance is made for this change, 1951 remains the peak year. Valued in constant (1939) prices, hospital construction in 1951 was more than three times the 1946 volume. The value of construction in current prices dropped to $867 million in 1952, the equivalent of $314 million in constant (1939) prices. (See Table 142.)

Private hospital construction has increased more than public since the end of World War II and is now nearly equal to it in volume after trailing behind for many years. In 1952, 45 per cent of the dollar value of hospital construction was for hospitals owned by private organizations — nonprofit or proprietary — and individuals; 55 per cent was for publicly owned facilities. (See Table 143.)

Hill-Burton Program

More than one fourth of all hospital construction in 1952 was carried out under the Hill-Burton program. The Hospital Survey and Construction (Hill-Burton) Act of 1946 authorized federal funds of $3 million to be paid to the states to defray one third of the costs of surveying their over-all needs for hospital and health centers and planning appropriate construction. In addition, $75 million was authorized for each of five years to help build the needed facilities.

Projects to which these funds were to be applied might be for additions or alterations to existing facilities, for replacement of old facilities or for construction of completely new facilities. One third of the total construction costs could be met from federal funds. In October 1949, amendments to the act doubled the total authorized construction funds and liberalized the terms of state aid to permit federal assistance for as much as two thirds of the construction costs in the poorer states and communities. At the same time, the program was extended through 1955.

In the seven years through December 1953, 2,192 project applications had been approved.[27]

26. *Annual Survey, Accident and Health Coverage in the United States as of December 31, 1952*, Health Insurance Council, New York, September 1953, p. 22.

27. "Hospital Construction under the Hill-Burton Program: Analysis of Projects Approved for Federal Aid," Division of Hospital Facilities, U.S. Public Health Service, December 31, 1953.

TABLE 143. VALUE OF PRIVATE AND PUBLIC HOSPITAL CONSTRUCTION
PUT IN PLACE, 1920–1952

(Dollar Amounts in Millions)

Period	Total	Private		Public	
		Amount	Per Cent	Amount	Per Cent
1920–1924	$ 495	$247	49.9	$248	50.1
1935–1939	533	124	23.3	409	76.7
1940–1944	378	145	38.4	233	61.6
1945–1949	1,515	560	37.0	955	63.0
1950	840	344	41.0	496	59.0
1951	947	419	44.2	528	55.8
1952	867	394	45.4	473	54.6

Sources: Louis S. Reed, "Hospital Construction Trends," *Modern Hospital,* March 1952, pp. 72–76; *Construction and Building Materials, Statistical Supplement,* U.S. Department of Commerce, May 1953, pp. 7–11.

Construction costs for these projects totaled $1.8 billion, with federal assistance amounting to over $600 million. In all, 1,395 projects had been completed and were in operation, 662 were under construction, and 135 were in the preconstruction stages. Nearly 75 per cent of the approved projects were for general hospital construction (including a few that combined general hospital construction with public health centers). Public health centers accounted for 12 per cent, mental hospitals 4 per cent, tuberculosis hospitals 3 per cent, and hospitals for chronic diseases 2 per cent, while auxiliary health centers and state health department laboratories made up the remainder. When completed, these approved projects will add 105,-702 hospital beds to the nation's supply — about four fifths of them in general hospitals.

Small towns and rural areas have clearly benefited from the Hill-Burton program. More than half (56 per cent) of the completely new hospital projects are located in communities with populations under 5,000. Of the 859 completely new general hospital projects, 57 per cent are in areas which previously had no hospitals and 20 per cent in areas where existing facilities were considered unacceptable for hospital use.

HEALTH AND DISABILITY PROGRAMS

Development of civilian health programs has been, in a sense, a joint activity of governmental and voluntary health agencies. Initial action in encouraging and sponsoring medical and related research, in applying new scientific knowledge, and in demonstrating new methods and techniques of sickness prevention and health care has generally been assumed by voluntary organizations or philanthropic foundations. Continuation and extension of these activities has frequently become the responsibility of government.

Governmental Programs

Traditionally, governmental activities in the field of health have been limited to public health services and care of the poor. Through grants-in-aid to the states, the federal government helps support state and local public health activities, as well as their programs of maternal and child health and crippled children's services, venereal disease control and tuberculosis control, and the vocational rehabilitation of the disabled. In addition, the federal government aids in providing medical care for the indigent and furnishes direct medical care to certain nonindigent groups, such as war veterans, seamen, Indians, inmates of federal prisons, and members of the armed forces.

State and Local Health Activities

The health departments are the official channels of the states for delivering health services or for seeing that they are made available, but many other agencies of the state governments have responsibility for certain specific health activities. Departments of education, welfare, labor, agriculture and public safety, for example, have important functions in improvement or conservation of health, while health-related activities are also performed, in many states, by industrial accident commissions, commissions for the blind, state universities and the like. Within the past ten years the kinds and volume of state health services have grown tremendously, and the responsibility for health functions has become increasingly divided. In 1950 as many as 32 agencies in at least one state were participating in some health activity in contrast to the top figure of 18 agencies with health responsibilities in a single state ten years earlier.[28]

An indication of the increase in health services can be obtained through analysis of the funds expended and the personnel employed. All state agencies together spent $945 million for health activities in the fiscal year 1948–1949, an increase of about 250 per cent over 1940 expenditures in terms of current dollars. In terms of 1935–1939 dollars, expenditures doubled over the period.[29] State funds represented 73.4 per cent of the total in 1948–1949, federal funds 15.3 per cent, local funds 1.4 per cent, and other sources 9.9 per cent.

The total expenditure in that year represented an average outlay of $6.30 per capita. States in the northeastern section of the country tended to have the highest expenditures, while those in the South were more often found in the bottom half of the scale, although Louisiana, with a per capita expenditure of $11.11, was second only to Washington, which had a per capita average of $13.58. Four states spent over $10.00 per person and 19 exceeded the $6.30 average.[30]

State agencies employed more than 38,000 persons[31] for health work in 1950, more than twice as many as in 1940. About 63 per cent of the total in 1940 were employed by health departments as contrasted with 58 per cent in 1950.[32]

The $945 million spent for health activities by state agencies in the fiscal year 1948–1949 was distributed among official agencies as follows:[33]

	Per Cent
Department of health	16.9
Department of welfare	20.3
Department of education	10.3
Special boards or commissions	36.2
Independent state hospitals	4.0
State universities or colleges	4.8
Other state agencies	7.5

State health departments expended $159 million[34] — more than three times as much as they spent ten years earlier in terms of current dollars and twice as much in terms of 1935–1939 dollars. Their per capita annual expenditure was $1.06 in 1948–1949 as against 35 cents in 1940. During this ten-year period, the share of the total derived from federal funds decreased slightly, from 36 per cent to 30 per cent.

State appropriations to state health departments ranged in 1951–1952 from $1.58 per capita in New York to 14 cents in Missouri; half the states appropriated less than 49 cents per capita.[35] There has been a considerable increase in appropriations over the past few years, and in some states the increase has been allocated specifically for grants to local health units.[36]

Full-time local health units multiplied rapidly during the decade 1940–1950, as they had in the preceding decade. By July 1952 there were 1,333 such units of one of the following types: county units, city-county units, and district units comprising two or more counties or townships. These units covered 53 per cent of the counties and served 78 per cent of the population of the United States.[37]

Expenditures during 1950–1951 by local health units in the 48 states amounted to $151 million, including funds raised through local taxation

---

28. Joseph W. Mountin, Evelyn Flook and Edward E. Minty, *Distribution of Health Services in the Structure of State Government, 1950, Part One, Administrative Provisions for State Health Services,* Publication No. 184, U.S. Public Health Service, 1952, pp. 5-17.

29. This sum includes expenditures of state agencies for both preventive services and hospital and other medical care, including payments made into the state treasuries by the federal government, by local governments and by private agencies. It does not include expenditures for hospital construction or expenditures of local governments for local health services, but it does include state contributions for local health services as shown in Table 144. It should be stressed that expenditure data are, in many instances, underreported. This is especially true for agencies whose main function is not health, since it is sometimes impossible to separate expenditures for health from those for other purposes.

30. *Ibid.,* p. 43.

31. Includes full-time and full-time equivalent staff in the 48 states and the other jurisdictions but excludes institutional personnel.

32. *Ibid.,* p. 51.

33. *Ibid.,* p. 40.

34. Includes grants to local units and reimbursements for hospital services.

35. These amounts exclude appropriations for hospital care and for construction of hospitals.

36. As reported to the Public Health Service by the states on P.H.S. Form 970.

37. Clifford H. Greve and Josephine R. Campbell, *Report of Local Public Health Resources, 1951,* Publication No. 278, U.S. Public Health Service, 1953, p. 1.

Table 144. Amounts Expended for Local Health Services, by Source of Funds, for Selected Fiscal Years, 1941–1951[a]

(Dollar Amounts in Thousands)

Source of Funds	1940–1941		1945–1946		1948–1949		1950–1951	
	Amount	Per Cent	Amount	Per Cent	Amount	Per Cent	Amount	Per Cent
All sources	$28,678	100.0	$71,600	100.0	$114,122	100.0	$150,992	100.0
State	4,340	15.1	7,248	10.1	23,644	20.7	27,101	17.9
Local	15,782	55.1	49,544	69.2	75,132	65.8	107,320	71.1
U.S. Public Health Service	6,548	22.8	11,526	16.1	10,777	9.4	10,660	7.1
U.S. Children's Bureau	[b]	—	[b]	—	3,381	3.0	3,671	2.4
Other sources	2,008[c]	7.0[c]	3,282[c]	4.6[c]	1,188[d]	1.1	2,239[d]	1.5

Source: Annual expenditure reports submitted by the 48 state health departments to the Division of State Grants, U.S. Public Health Service.

a. Reported data do not reflect a complete picture of funds expended for local health services; in earlier years, particularly, reports failed to include expenditures not involving federal funds.

b. Children's Bureau funds for maternal and child health services and services for crippled children were not compiled separately for these particular years but were combined with expenditures of private agency funds and included under "other sources."

c. For the most part, funds allocated by the Children's Bureau under Title V of the Social Security Act; private agency funds reported expended during these years are also included.

d. Private agency funds only.

and amounts allocated by the states (including federal grants to states) and by private agencies, as contrasted to $72 million available five years earlier. State financial support increased in the five-year period from $7.2 million to $27.1 million, and local support from $49.5 million to $107.3 million. In general, the federal share has declined over the past several years while the share supplied by state and local funds has increased markedly. (See Table 144.)

Federal Program for Veterans

The veterans medical care program is, today, the largest federal undertaking in the field of direct medical care to civilians — in terms of facilities operated, personnel employed, persons served and amounts expended. As of June 30, 1951, there were 151 veterans hospital facilities with an available bed capacity of 108,231.[38] More than 10,000 additional veterans beds were not available for use at that time — over one third of them, it was estimated, because of lack of personnel. In addition to beds in veterans facilities, 7,100 beds in other hospitals were used for Veterans Administration patients. Outpatient clinics were maintained in 55 regional offices and 15 centers.

About 120,000 full-time employees were staffing veterans facilities of all kinds — hospitals, outpatient clinics and domiciliary facilities. More than half of this full-time staff, which included 4,014 physicians, 903 dentists and 13,734 nurses, were directly connected with the provision of medical and auxiliary service.

On an average day in 1951, more than 96,000 veterans were receiving care in Veterans Administration hospitals and 8,000 were being cared for in other facilities. Most of these patients were hospitalized for disabilities not incurred in military service. War veterans with non-service-connected disabilities are eligible for hospital care under the veterans program, if beds are available, upon affirmation of their inability to pay for treatment. As of June 30, 1951, the ratio of hospitalized veterans with non-service-connected disabilities to those with service-connected disabilities was about two to one. However, a substantial number of these patients are admitted for tuberculosis, mental disorders or long-term illness, conditions

for which they might in any case be treated at public expense.

Well over half of the patients in Veterans Administration hospitals in 1951 had psychotic disabilities. Care of the psychotic has been a great problem, principally because of the lack of trained personnel. The Veterans Administration conducts a training program for psychiatrists and neurologists and also participates in training programs for psychiatric social workers and clinical psychologists.

In 1946 the Veterans Administration initiated an extensive "home-town" program,[39] through which veterans with service-connected disabilities may receive needed examinations and treatment from local physicians and dentists, and needed drugs and medicines. By June 30, 1951 this program was operating in 37 states and territories, with about 100,000 local physicians participating.

In March 1943, Congress authorized vocational rehabilitation for veterans who are disabled from an injury or disease incurred in World War II and whose handicap can be overcome by training. In addition to the necessary physical restoration services, provided through Veterans Administration hospitals, these veterans are offered education and occupational training, guidance in selecting a suitable vocational objective and assistance in job placement. During the 1951 fiscal year 8.1 million veterans received vocational training through the program, and at the end of the year 1.7 million were in training, nearly one fourth of them in institutions of higher learning. Expenditures amounted to $2.1 billion.[40]

The cost of operating all Veterans Administration hospitals in the fiscal year 1950–1951 totaled $410 million. The home-town medical program cost an additional $13 million, while the home-town dental program cost $26 million. Operation of domiciliary homes cost approximately $20 million.

Other Special Federal Beneficiaries

Direct medical care benefits are provided through Public Health Service facilities to seamen and certain other beneficiaries of the federal government, including personnel of the United States Coast Guard, officers and crews of Coast and Geodetic Survey vessels, and federal employees injured while at work. Benefits include

---

38. *Administrator of Veterans Affairs, Annual Report for Fiscal Year Ending June 30, 1951*, Veterans Administration, 1952, pp. 12–13.

39. *Ibid.*, p. 46.
40. *Ibid.*, pp. 3, 83–94.

hospitalization, general medical and dental care, and preventive health service.

During the fiscal year ending June 30, 1950, admissions to Public Health Service hospitals totaled 72,000. On any one day during the year, 7,470 patients were receiving care in these hospitals. Somewhat more than one million visits were made to outpatient stations during the year.

A program of medical care for Indians is operated by the Bureau of Indian Affairs, Department of the Interior, under the direction of a medical officer detailed to the Bureau by the Public Health Service. Those eligible for care through the program are medically indigent Indians living on reservations in the continental United States, and Indians, Aleuts and Eskimos in Alaska. For the most part the services are available through hospitals and field clinics operated by the Bureau of Indian Affairs. In 1951 the Bureau operated 62 hospitals (including four tuberculosis sanatoria) with a total bed capacity of 4,098.[41]

Maternal and Child Health Services

Through grants-in-aid the federal government shares with state and local governments the responsibility for maintaining community health services that children need if they are to have a good start in life. Two types of services are provided — maternal and child health services, and services for crippled children.

The state maternal and child health programs are usually concerned with the health supervision of expectant mothers, infants, and preschool and school children, and provide a limited amount of medical and dental treatment. An important part of their work is the continuing battle against infant mortality. Because premature birth is the leading cause of infant deaths, the states are giving special attention to this problem.

All state programs for crippled children provide diagnostic services for children with physically handicapping conditions, and skilled treatment within the limits of their funds. An estimated 500,000 children have handicaps that require orthopedic or plastic treatment; 500,000 have or have had rheumatic fever; 175,000 have cerebral palsy; 200,000 have epilepsy; 100,000 aged ten or younger have congenital syphilis; 1

million are deaf or hard of hearing; and 4 million are blind or have poor eyesight.[42]

Under the 1950 amendments to the Social Security Act, the maximum amount that can be authorized in federal grants is $16.5 million for maternal and child health services and $15 million for services for crippled children. The states receive flat grants for each program, plus other federal funds in variable amounts depending upon their population and financial resources and needs in rural areas. To qualify for grants the states must match half of the federal funds dollar for dollar. Actually they are spending much more than the required matching amount. Some of the federal funds that do not have to be matched are used for special pioneering projects and demonstrations.

Public Assistance

The federal, state and local governments share the cost of providing medical services to special groups of needy persons: the aged, the blind, children who lack parental support or care, and permanently and totally disabled persons. State and local funds, without federal participation, are used to help other needy persons through the general assistance programs.

An estimated $225 million was spent for medical care for the 6 million persons receiving assistance in 1951. This expenditure does not represent the cost of all the medical service they received, because additional unknown amounts of care were provided without charge to the assistance agencies by public hospitals and clinics, private health agencies, county doctors and private practitioners. As would be expected, the group receiving assistance because of permanent and total disability had the highest average medical expenses, an estimated $100 per person for all eligible cases for the year, while about $60 was spent for the average old-age assistance case. Hospital costs accounted for 20 to 30 per cent of the total amount expended for each category of assistance except general assistance, in which group they accounted for 40 per cent of the total. (See Table 145.)

A study of medical care received by assistance cases during six months in 1946 showed sharp differences in the extent to which medical services were provided in the 20 states participating in the study. The range in the proportion of old-age as-

41. Helen Hollingsworth, Helen L. Johnston and Anna Mae Baney, *Health Programs Digest: An Outline of Selected Plans, Programs, and Proposals in the United States*, Publication No. 191, U.S. Public Health Service, 1952, pp. 36–37.

42. "Services for Crippled Children," Children's Bureau Folder No. 38, 1952, pp. 10–11.

TABLE 145. ESTIMATED EXPENDITURES FROM PUBLIC ASSISTANCE FUNDS FOR MEDICAL CARE OF RECIPIENTS OF ASSISTANCE, BY PROGRAM, FISCAL YEAR ENDED JUNE 30, 1951 [a]

Program	Number of Persons Included in Assistance Caseloads in December 1950	Expenditures for Medical Care			Average Expenditure per Person Receiving Assistance
		Total	Hospitalization	All Other	
	(Thousands)		*(Millions)*		
Total	6,051	$225.0	$60.0	$165.0	$ 37
Old-age assistance	2,786	167.7	40.5	127.2	60
Aid to dependent children	2,233	19.4	5.9	13.5	9
Aid to the blind	97	2.9	6	2.3	30
Aid to the permanently and totally disabled	69	7.0	1.8	5.2	101
General assistance	866 [b]	28.0	11.2	16.8	c

Source: Based on unpublished data from Bureau of Public Assistance, Social Security Administration, Federal Security Agency, August 1952.

a. Estimated expenditures for each program include funds appropriated specifically for the program and expenditures from other assistance funds for services supplied to recipients of the specified program.

b. Does not include cases receiving medical care only.

c. Not computed.

sistance cases receiving care was from 84 per cent to 6 per cent. One state supplied care for 82 per cent of the families receiving aid to dependent children while, at the other extreme, one state provided care to only 10 per cent of such families. Among recipients of aid to the blind, the proportion of cases receiving care varied from 77 to 6 per cent; among general assistance cases, from 60 to 4 per cent. These variations in medical care provided by the states are due in large measure to differences in funds available rather than in need for service.

Vocational Rehabilitation

The federal-state program of vocational rehabilitation, which has now been serving the disabled of the nation for thirty-two years, was generally limited until 1943 to vocational guidance, training and job placement, and to the provision of prosthetic appliances. In that year the Barden-LaFollette Act provided for the use of federal funds for any medical or allied services which would eliminate or substantially reduce an individual's disability as an employment handicap; liberalized federal financial participation; extended services to the mentally disabled; and made specific provision for the blind.[43]

43. *Annual Reports of the Office of Vocational Rehabilitation, 1944–1951,* Federal Security Agency, 1945–1952.

The federal Office of Vocational Rehabilitation provides leadership and guidance to the states in carrying out their programs and administers the federal grants-in-aid. All told, 88 state agencies participate, including 36 agencies in states with special boards or commissions serving the blind only.

The services of the program are available to any man or woman of working age who has a substantial job handicap resulting from physical or mental impairment, and who has a reasonable chance of becoming employable. The services provided include medical, psychiatric and psychological evaluation to determine the extent of disability, the person's work capacity and his eligibility; counseling to select a suitable job; training; and placement and follow-up on the job — all at no cost to the disabled individual. In addition, the individual receives medical, surgical, psychiatric treatment; dental, hospital and nursing care; physical and occupational therapy; prosthetic appliances; living expenses and transportation during rehabilitation; occupational tools, equipment and licenses. For these services, he pays what he can.

A continuing program policy has been to utilize existing public and private facilities and resources wherever possible. Training is obtained from public and private schools, from vocational training courses and through in-service training on the job. Medical and surgical services are secured from practicing physicians and hospital care from public and voluntary hospitals.

Great progress has been made since the scope of the program was broadened in 1943. More than 466,000 men and women were rehabilitated and placed in self-supporting jobs in the nine years 1944–1952.[44] In the preceding twenty-three years, when legislative authority was limited, only 210,000 had been rehabilitated. In the fiscal year 1952 alone, 63,632 handicapped men and women were rehabilitated, out of a total of 228,000 who received rehabilitation services during the year.

Three fourths of those rehabilitated in 1951–1952 were unemployed when they were accepted for service,[45] and the others had been in jobs that were unsuitable, temporary or unsafe. After approximately one year of preparation, on the average, these men and women were satisfactorily placed in a wide variety of jobs in each of the major occupational groups. The experience of the program has proved that practically every kind of job can be performed by some handicapped person. Studies in industry have shown that handicapped workers work as regularly as unimpaired workers, stay on the job as long, have as good safety records, and have as good production records.[46]

The cost of operating the entire program in the 1951–1952 fiscal year was $32.6 million — $22.1 million in federal funds and $10.5 million in state funds. If their present earning rate continues, it is estimated that within three years the persons rehabilitated in 1951–1952 will return to the federal Treasury in income taxes alone the entire $22.1 million spent by the federal government.

Occupational Health Programs

Originally, health programs in industry were confined solely to the control of the working environment and the treatment of occupational disabilities. Today, they embrace the total health of the worker and provide broad preventive health services. This expanded concept is largely the result of a growing recognition of the cost of nonoccupational disabilities. Disability of nonoccupational origin causes about 90 per cent of the time lost from work because of illness, a loss that adds up to 400 to 500 million man-days a year or the equivalent of about 2 million workers being off the job each day.

In-Plant Programs

In-plant services were provided in 1950 by 2,000 physicians working full time or giving special attention to practice in the industrial health field. About half of these physicians limited their practice to industrial medicine. In addition, a large but unknown number of physicians devoted some time to industrial practice. About 11,300 registered professional nurses worked full time in industry in 1950, more than half of them having been in industrial nursing for five years or more. By 1951 the number of full-time nurses had increased to 12,600 and by 1952 to over 13,250.

More than 45 per cent of the companies with 2,500 or more employees had one or more full-time physicians during 1950, according to a recent study by the National Association of Manufacturers.[47] Sixty-two per cent of the companies of this size employed part-time physicians, who served alone or in cooperation with other part-time or full-time physicians. Of the companies with 1,000 to 2,500 employees, slightly over half had part-time and 9 per cent had full-time physicians. The proportions decreased with company size. Among firms with fewer than 250 employees, less than 4 per cent had part-time physicians and 0.5 per cent had full-time physicians. Many companies of all sizes had one or more physicians on call to care for emergency cases and in some instances to make pre-employment examinations also.

A rough estimate may be made of the number of employees to whom in-plant services by a full-time nurse are available (with or without the services of a full-time or part-time physician) by assuming that each full-time nurse serves on the average 760 employees, the ratio that existed in 1942.[48] On this assumption, nursing services were

44. *Annual Caseload Statistics of the State Rehabilitation Agencies, Fiscal Year 1952*, Rehabilitation Service Series, No. 299, Office of Vocational Rehabilitation, Federal Security Agency.

45. Unpublished data from the Office of Vocational Rehabilitation, Division of Research and Statistics.

46. *Vocational Rehabilitation for Civilians*, Office of Vocational Rehabilitation, Federal Security Agency, July 1952.

47. George W. Bachman and Associates, *Health Resources in the United States*, Brookings Institution, Washington, 1952, pp. 79–95.

48. Olive M. Whitlock, Victoria M. Trasko and F. Ruth Kahl, *Nursing Practices in Industry*, Public Health Bulletin No. 283, 1944, p. 37.

available to about 8.6 million employees in 1950, and to about 9.6 million in 1951 and 10.1 million in 1952.

The reported costs of in-plant health programs vary considerably, depending on the extent of the program, the number, age and sex of the employees, the type of industry, and the items of expense included. An average annual cost of $14.53 per employee was reported in a study of 569 plants with 1.7 million employees, made by the American College of Surgeons in 1949. In this group of plants, costs generally declined as the size of the plant increased, ranging from $26.43 in those having less than 500 employees to $9.48 in those with 7,500 to 15,000 employees. However, the ten largest plants in the study, with 15,000 to 35,000 employees, reported an average of $21.51.

Workmen's Compensation [49]

All states now have workmen's compensation laws, but there are vast differences among the states in the types and extent of protection afforded. No state law covers all employment. Five provide no compensation for occupational diseases, while 19 limit the number of diseases for which compensation will be paid. The laws in 17 states limit the amount of medical benefits.[50]

During 1951, of the $710 million spent for workmen's compensation payments, an estimated $233 million represented payment for medical care and hospitalization. Of the $787 million spent in 1952 for workmen's compensation cases, about $260 million was for medical care and hospitalization,[51] more than two and a half times the amount paid out in 1940 for these services.

REGIONAL COORDINATION OF HEALTH PROGRAMS

The value of coordinating the resources of a medical teaching center with other medical and hospital resources in the surrounding area is gaining recognition in various parts of the world. In the United States the principle of regional organization was applied as early as 1931 in New England by the Bingham Associates Program of Boston. This program was designed to break down the isolation of rural practitioners in Maine by establishing close working relationships between community hospitals and physicians in the area and the New England Medical Center in Boston. Other regional programs are now in operation in various parts of this country.

Important elements in regional programs are a medical teaching center, a system of general and special hospitals and health centers, and integration of medical and allied general and specialized services. A regional pattern for hospital construction was recommended as an organizational device by the Commission on Hospital Care in 1946 and adopted by the Seventy-ninth Congress as a guiding principle for the Hill-Burton Act. Later, an amendment authorized funds for grants for studies and demonstrations of the coordinated use of hospital facilities and services.[52]

A preliminary report of a study of ten selected regional programs shows that, except for the Bingham project, all were started soon after World War II.[53] The programs have been most interested in problems of rural areas, principally the need to attract physicians to these areas and to provide them with good training and facilities. In eight of the ten programs, the medical school is the administrative authority; in the other two, the medical school participates in the activities but a nonprofit agency, organized for the purpose, carries administrative responsibility.

In general the activities of the ten programs may be classified as educational, clinical, advisory and auxiliary services, and the improvement of facilities. The plans differ in the range of services they have so far developed, but most of them have put primary emphasis on graduate and postgraduate medical education. About half have arrangements for assigning interns and residents (both general practitioners and specialists) from the teaching center to affiliated hospitals that meet professional and educational standards. In some

---

49. Cf. Chapter 14.

50. Bruce A. Greene, "State Workmen's Compensation Legislation in 1951," *Monthly Labor Review*, January 1952, p. 18.

51. "Workmen's Compensation Payments, 1952," *Social Security Bulletin*, December 1953, p. 22.

---

52. See J. R. McGibony, M.D., and Louis Block, Dr.P.H., "Better Patient Care through Coordination," *Public Health Reports*, November 1949; and J. R. McGibony, M.D., "Coordination for Better Patient Care," *Official Journal of American Association of Hospital Accountants*, September 1951.

53. Leonard S. Rosenfeld, M.D., Nathan Kramer and Ruth Wadman, *Survey of Regional Organization of Health Services — Preliminary Report*, Division of Public Health Methods, U.S. Public Health Service, 1952. Plans included those at the University of Colorado, Emory University, Buffalo University, University of Kansas, New York University, University of Michigan, Tulane University, and the Medical College–University of Virginia plan, Bingham Associates Program, and Rochester Regional Hospital Council.

plans, also, the residents at affiliated hospitals may have a period of training at the center, but the shortage of physicians has hampered this type of activity.

Extramural postgraduate medical education is a major activity in all the programs. Several have also developed educational services for other types of health personnel, such as nurses, hospital administrators and laboratory technicians. At least two provide services for individual patients in addition to the clinical consultation services given as part of medical education. Two programs have advisory services for participating hospitals, on various aspects of hospital organization. One has extensive arrangements for pooling activities and for developing a central purchasing system and uniform accounting and record systems. It also cooperates actively with the Red Cross in maintaining a regional blood bank. Two of the programs have made funds available for improving physical facilities.

Initially nine of the ten programs received substantial support from philanthropic agencies; the tenth was aided by the Public Health Service. The programs that are administered by state-supported medical schools also receive substantial support from the state government. Local support has been limited. As outside support has diminished, the programs have requested and received some financial participation by affiliated hospitals, voluntary agencies and physicians. In one area, the local Blue Cross hospital plan is contributing toward the program's support.

The plans mentioned above by no means exhaust the list of what is being done to further interhospital cooperation and coordination. Many of the smaller hospitals are attempting to help one another through joint purchasing; sharing of specialized personnel (such as pathologists, radiologists, physical therapists and technicians); cooperation in performing unusual diagnostic tests and examinations; lending of specimens, films, books and other educational aids; mutual arrangements for sharing the patient-load in accidents and other disasters; interhospital blood banks; exchange of medical, social service, administrative and other information; and the pooling of specialized equipment and apparatus. These cooperative efforts are rarely publicized in the hospital literature or in the public press because they are generally informal arrangements. The work of the W. K. Kellogg Foundation in promoting the sharing of part-time consultants

TABLE 146. EXPENDITURES FOR MEDICAL RESEARCH, BY SOURCE OF FUNDS, 1951

Source of Funds	Amount	Per Cent
	(Millions)	
Total	$181.2	100.0
Government	76.2	42.1
Public Health Service	35.2	19.4
Atomic Energy Commission	18.0	9.9
Department of Defense		
Army	6.8	3.8
Navy	6.0	3.3
Air Force	4.7	2.6
Veterans Administration	4.5	2.5
Other	1.0	0.6
Industry	60.0	33.1
Pharmaceutical and proprietary	52.5	29.0
Industrial foundations	5.0	2.7
Other	2.5	1.4
Philanthropy	25.0	13.8
Philanthropic foundations	10.0	5.5
Voluntary health associations	10.0	5.5
Personal donations	5.0	2.8
Profession	20.0	11.0
Hospitals	15.0	8.3
Medical schools	5.0	2.7

Source: Justus J. Schifferes, "Who Pays for Medical Research?" *Medical Economics,* July 1951, p. 66.

and diagnostic services among the small hospitals in Michigan is an outstanding example of this type of approach.

MEDICAL RESEARCH AND MEDICAL ADVANCES

More than $181 million was spent in 1951 for medical research, according to estimates prepared for *Medical Economics.* Federal funds represented 42 per cent of the total; industry spent 33 per cent, chiefly through pharmaceutical and proprietary groups; philanthropy supplied 14 per cent; hospitals and medical schools, 11 per cent. Of the $76 million expended by government agencies, nearly half was used by the Public Health Service for research conducted by its own personnel and for grants to nonfederal research institutions and investigations; the Atomic Energy Commission and the Department of Defense each spent about $18 million, or a combined sum about equal to that of the Public Health Service.[54] (See Table 146.)

54. A total of $173 million was spent on medical research in 1952, the decrease from $181 million estimated to have been spent in 1951 being accounted for primarily

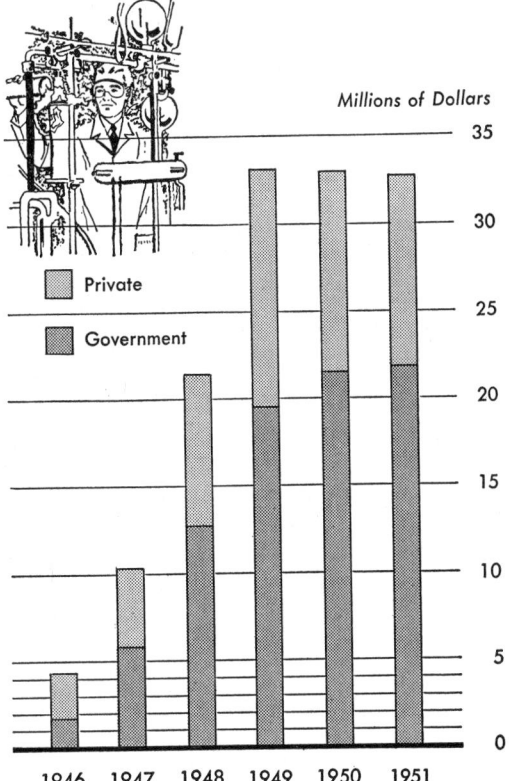

Millions of Dollars

— Private

— Government

FIGURE 46. RESEARCH GRANTS OR CONTRACTS
AWARDED BY GOVERNMENT AND PRIVATE SOURCES
IN MEDICAL AND ALLIED FIELDS, FISCAL YEARS
1946–1951

Source: Stella Leche Deignan and Esther Miller, "The
Support of Research in Medical and Allied Fields for the
Period 1946 through 1951," reprinted from *Science*,
March 28, 1952.

The John R. Steelman report, *The Nation's
Medical Research*,[55] shows a considerably smaller
total of $110–$115 million expended for medical
research in the fiscal year 1946–1947. The major
difference between the figures in these two reports is in expenditures by the federal government. The difference of $48 million in this item
is accounted for in part by the increases from
1946–1947 to 1951 in the amounts expended by

the Atomic Energy Commission as well as in federal grants for research.

Federal support of research in medical schools
and other research organizations increased from
$5.8 million in the fiscal year 1946–1947 to $21.3
million in 1949–1950, or nearly 270 per cent. During the same period the contributions of the
major foundations increased more than 160 per
cent — from $4.4 million to $11.7 million. (See
Figure 46.)

Of the total governmental and philanthropic
funds expended in 1946–1951, the largest share
(about 20 per cent) went for cancer investigations. Cancer research received nearly 15 per cent
of all funds contributed by the federal government and about 27 per cent of the funds contributed by foundations. Investigations in the
field of infectious diseases received 17 per cent
of governmental funds and 18 per cent of foundation funds. Studies of the cardiovascular system, general medical problems, and metabolism
and nutrition were the only other fields that received as much as 5 per cent of the total research
funds.

The relationship among illnesses differs if
funds available for research are translated into
dollars spent per estimated patient under treatment for the illness. In 1951, for example, almost
$45 was available for research for each polio pa-
tient, $26.60 for each patient with cancer, $15.13
for each tuberculous patient, and $4.75 for each
patient with a mental disorder.[56]

Progress in Medical Science

According to one writer, "It can be strongly
argued that greater progress has been made in
medical science in the past fifty years than in the
previous five thousand. Even though this may
be an exaggeration, it is almost certainly true
that, before another fifty years have elapsed, the
necessary knowledge and skills will have been
acquired to deal effectively with most, if not all,
of the principal problems of disease and health
not presently understood."[57]

This rapid progress is due in large measure to
the contributions of other fields of scientific inquiry. The work of psychiatrists and psycholo-

by the fact that all of the Atomic Energy Commission
expenditures for biological studies were credited in 1951
to contributions for medical research. Sources of funds in
1952 were as follows: government, $73 million; industry,
$60 million; philanthrophy, $25 million; schools, $15
million. (Irving Ladimer, "Trends in Support and Expenditures for Medical Research, 1941–52," *Public Health
Reports*, February 1954, p. 116.)

55. Vol. 5 of *Science and Public Policy*, President's
Scientific Research Board, October 18, 1947.

56. *Health Inquiry,* Hearings before the Committee on
Interstate and Foreign Commerce, House of Representatives, 83d Cong., October 7, 8 and 9, 1953, Part 4, p. 1050.
57. Raymond B. Allen, M.D., "Professional Education
in the Service of Health," *Annals of the American Academy of Political and Social Science*, January 1951, p. 12.

gists, for example, has led to a better appreciation of the importance of emotional factors in physical well-being. Medical science has also benefited from innumerable technological improvements. Examples, not necessarily listed in the order of their importance, are water fluoridation to reduce dental caries, development of new mechanical devices in the field of dental care, the production of synthetic blood, the development of rapid X-ray processes, new anesthetics, advances in surgical procedures, discoveries of new methods for relieving or controlling such conditions as arthritis and tuberculosis, and newer concepts of human nutritional requirements.

Atomic Energy

Great strides also have been taken in methods of diagnosis and treatment through developments in the field of atomic energy. For example, progress has been made in the study of the mechanism of digitalis in treating heart disease, in the treatment of thyroid cancer with radiations from radioiodine and of cancer of the bone marrow with radiophosphorus, in the use of "radiators" of radioactive cobalt in place of radium, and in the use of radioactive materials to strengthen antibodies to fight invading proteins. The acting chairman of the Atomic Energy Commission in 1950 estimated that over 40 per cent of all basic research in medicine and biology at that time was being done with the help of radioactive elements that had come from the Oak Ridge, Tennessee, project.

New Drugs

The federal Food, Drug, and Cosmetic Act of 1938 stimulated research in drugs by making it necessary for manufacturers to collect data on the use, safety and efficacy of their products. With the encouragement of the Council on Pharmacy and Chemistry of the American Medical Association, drug research and development has advanced rapidly in recent years, particularly since the beginning of World War II.

Recent discoveries and inventions in the sphere of drug therapy have been among the most dramatic medical achievements of our time. During the past fifteen years, according to one authority, drug therapy has contributed more to the happiness, well-being and health of humanity than has

any other advancement.[58] The development in this field has been so rapid that over 54 per cent of the drugs in use in 1947 had been unknown ten years before.

Antibiotics were first made available for clinical use in the United States in 1940 when penicillin was produced commercially. Aureomycin, terramycin, chloromycetin and others soon followed as the possibilities of antibiotic drugs to combat every infectious condition stimulated large-scale research projects. Some authorities believe that within the next ten or fifteen years there will be an antibiotic for every infectious condition, including the viral diseases. It is estimated that in the past five or six years the United States pharmaceutical industry alone has spent $20 million in the screening of soil samples, molds and yeasts for new and better antibiotic agents.[59]

National Institutes of Health

Development of new knowledge and its effective use require teamwork by scientists, industry, philanthropy and government. Industry, the large philanthropic foundations and voluntary health agencies have all developed large-scale research projects, and in recent years government also has taken an increasingly active role in scientific research related to health.

Today seven National Institutes of Health form a part of the Public Health Service — the Institutes of Mental Health, Cancer, Heart, Arthritis and Metabolic Diseases, Dental Research, Neurological Diseases and Blindness, and Microbiology. Through these Institutes, scientists in many fields are studying the major health problems of the day and valuable contributions are being made to scientific knowledge in medicine, in public health and in the biological, biochemical and biophysical processes. In addition, the Public Health Service gives grants-in-aid through the Institutes to thousands of research workers in universities and other institutions throughout the country. Facilities for clinical research were acquired recently with the opening of a new 500-

---

58. *Drug Research and Development,* edited by Austin Smith and Arthur D. Herrick, Revere Publishing Co., New York, 1948.

59. Robert Burlingham, *The Odyssey of Modern Drug Research,* Upjohn Co., Kalamazoo, Michigan, 1951, pp. 88, 96.

TABLE 147. NUMBER OF PEOPLE WITH VOLUNTARY HOSPITAL, SURGICAL AND
MEDICAL EXPENSE INSURANCE, END OF 1952
(*Thousands*)

Plan	Hospital	Surgical	Medical
Gross total	100,548	81,384	38,746
Less estimated duplication	8,881	8,223	2,949
Net total	91,667	73,161	35,797
Blue Cross, Blue Shield and other plans			
sponsored by medical societies	43,475	27,773	18,321
Personal	18,237	11,733	7,832
Dependents	25,238	16,040	10,489
Insurance company plans	51,709	48,817	15,275
Group insurance	29,455	29,621	10,157
Personal	12,982	13,639	5,388
Dependents	16,473	15,982	4,769
Individual insurance	22,254	19,196	5,118
Personal	10,090	7,710	2,411
Dependents	12,164	11,486	2,707
Independent plans	5,364	4,794	5,150
Industrial	3,630	3,450	3,246
Community	617	316	303
Consumer	312	308	281
Private group clinics	405	420	420
University health plans	400	300	900

Source: Annual Survey, Accident and Health Coverage in the United States as of December 31, 1952,
Health Insurance Council, New York, September 1953, p. 11.

bed clinical research center on the grounds of the National Institutes of Health at Bethesda, Maryland.

METHODS OF PAYING FOR MEDICAL CARE

Fee-for-Service

Traditionally, Americans have paid their medical bills on a fee-for-service basis. Hospital rates for room and board are related to the type of accommodation while the charges for most other items, such as nursing services, medications and appliances, are usually standard. Physicians' and dentists' charges, especially for surgical procedures, are usually influenced by such factors as the prevailing rates in the community, the individual doctor's experience and the patient's financial status.

Eighty-three per cent of all private expenditures for medical care in 1952 are estimated to have been direct fees for service. The percentage has dropped gradually during the last few years

— from 92 per cent in 1948 — as a result of the rapid growth of voluntary health insurance.[60]

Prepayment

The growth of voluntary health insurance [61] has been one of the most significant social developments of the last decade. By the end of 1952 an estimated 92 million persons, nearly 60 per cent of the total population of the United States, had some form of voluntary insurance protection against hospital or medical costs or both. (See Table 147.) Between 1940 and 1952 the number with insurance against all or some of the costs

60. "Voluntary Insurance Against Sickness: 1948–52 Estimates," Division of Research and Statistics, Office of the Commissioner, Social Security Administration, *Social Security Bulletin*, December 1953, pp. 7–13.

61. The term "voluntary health insurance" can be used to denote both disability insurance, which provides partial reimbursement for wage loss in the event of illness, and medical and hospital care insurance, which protects members against part or all of the direct cost of illness. It is used here to refer only to medical and hospital care insurance.

Millions of People

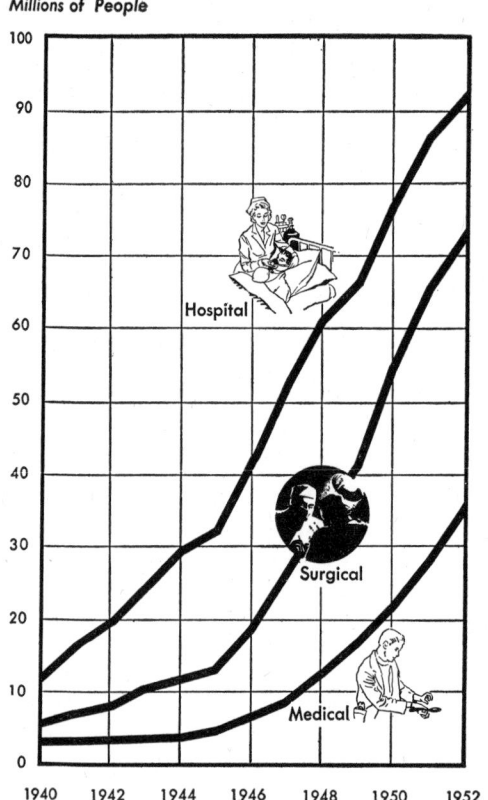

FIGURE 47. GROWTH IN NUMBER OF PEOPLE COV-
ERED BY HOSPITAL, SURGICAL AND MEDICAL PRO-
TECTION, 1940–1952

Source: Health Insurance Council, New York, N. Y.

of hospital care increased by more than 79 million, and surgical coverage increased from 5 million to 73 million. (See Figure 47.) Enrollment in 1952 showed the following increases over 1951: hospitalization, 7 per cent; surgery, 12 per cent; medical care, 29 per cent.[62]

Most voluntary health insurance programs now in operation provide protection chiefly against the costs of hospitalized illness. The hospital insurance programs have a large enrollment in urban areas but a comparatively small membership in rural areas. A recent survey of health insurance plans showed that 51 per cent of the population in urban states but only 27 per cent in rural states had hospital insurance. Moreover, 52 per cent of the people in high-income states had coverage in contrast to 26 per cent in low-income states.[63]

Voluntary health insurance payments in 1952 amounted to nearly $1.6 billion, or about 17 per cent of all consumer expenditures for medical care. They covered two fifths of all consumer expenditures for hospital services and about one fifth of all payments to physicians. For other types of medical services, insurance payments were negligible.[64] (See Figure 48.)

Blue Cross Hospital Plans

In December 1952, hospital plans approved by the Blue Cross Commission of the American Hospital Association were operating in every state except Nevada. At that time, more than 43 million persons (18.2 million subscribers and 25.2 million dependents) were eligible for hospital benefits through such plans, which then provided about 45 per cent of the total hospital insurance coverage.

The majority of Blue Cross subscribers have been enrolled on a group basis, but a number of the plans now permit individual enrollment. Members have free choice of hospitals participating in the plan, which usually means most of the hospitals in the area the plan is serving, and are protected against some of the costs of hospitalized illnesses while away from home.

---

62. A recent national study by the Health Information Foundation, covering the year July 1952 through June 1953, shows that 89.5 million people, or 58 per cent of the population, have one or more types of health insurance; about 87.4 million, or 57 per cent, have hospital insurance; 74.5 million, or 48 per cent, have some type of surgical or medical insurance, mostly in-hospital physicians' services for surgical and medical care, with 4.9 million of this total having substantially complete physicians' services. Odin W. Anderson, *National Family Survey of Medical Costs and Voluntary Health Insurance,* Preliminary Report, Health Information Foundation, New York, January 14, 1954, Table 1, pp. 16–17.

63. *Health Insurance Plans in the United States,* Report No. 359, U.S. Senate Committee on Labor and Public Welfare, 1951, Part 1, p. 8.

The Health Information Foundation study in 1952–1953 found the following coverage by area and by income: 70 per cent of families in urban areas, 57 per cent in rural nonfarm and 45 per cent in rural farm areas had some coverage; 80 per cent of families with annual incomes of $5,000 and over, 71 per cent of those with incomes of $3,000 to $5,000, and 41 per cent of those with incomes of less than $3,000 had some type of coverage. Each of the income groups represents about one third of the families in the United States. *National Family Survey of Medical Costs and Voluntary Health Insurance,* Preliminary Report, Tables 5 and 7, pp. 20 and 22.

64. The Health Information Foundation study found for the year July 1952 through June 1953 that consumers incurred a total cost of $10.2 billion for personal health services, with insurance benefits of $1.5 billion covering about 15 per cent of the total. About 50 per cent of hospital costs and about 13 per cent of physicians' services were covered by insurance benefits. *National Family Survey of Medical Costs and Voluntary Health Insurance,* Preliminary Report, Table 2, p. 34.

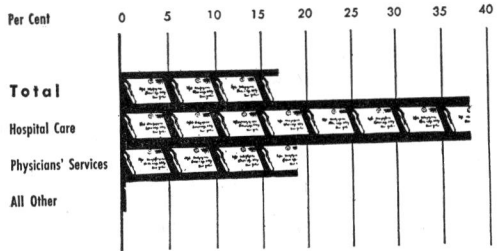

FIGURE 48. SHARE OF PRIVATE MEDICAL CARE EXPENDITURES COVERED BY VOLUNTARY INSURANCE BENEFITS, 1952

Source: "Voluntary Insurance Against Sickness: 1948–1952 Estimates," Social Security Bulletin, December 1953. Insurance benefits for "all other" items estimated from material in Health Insurance Plans in the United States, Report No. 359, U.S. Senate Committee on Labor and Public Welfare, 1951, Part 1, p. 3.

Typical Blue Cross benefits include up to thirty days' care in a semiprivate room per certificate year, plus partial benefits (usually half the full benefit) for an additional ninety days; general nursing care; special diets; operating room, anesthesia, laboratory service, routine medications and dressings; out-patient service for emergency accident cases within twenty-four hours after accident; maternity care under a family membership after a nine-month waiting period; and the use of the delivery room, and ordinary nursery care for the newborn. Basal metabolism tests, oxygen therapy, X-ray, and electrocardiograms are provided when called for by the conditions for which the patient is hospitalized.[65]

Most Blue Cross plans provide service rather than cash benefits. Under a service contract the plan specifies the amount and type of services it will provide and agrees to pay the cost of these services regardless of the rate charged by the hospital. Because of rising hospital costs, some plans now provide a specified dollar allowance for room and board but continue to provide service benefits for other types of hospital care. According to the Blue Cross Hospital Commission, 68 per cent of the persons enrolled in Blue Cross plans in 1951 were eligible for service benefits, about 19 per cent were eligible for cash benefits,

and the rest were members of plans offering either cash indemnity or service benefits.[66]

Subscription rates vary from plan to plan, according to local conditions, the extent of the benefits provided, and other factors. Monthly premium rates under group contracts reported in 1951 ranged as follows: 1 person, $0.75–$2.40; 2 persons, $2.00–$3.85; family, $1.60–$5.55. Average premiums for the three classifications were $1.53, $2.68 and $3.71.[67]

Subscription income of Blue Cross plans in 1952 amounted to about $640 million, of which more than $570 million, or 89 per cent, was returned in benefits.[68] Blue Cross payments represented about 50 per cent of all insurance payments for hospitalization and more than 20 per cent of all private expenditures for hospital care in that year.[69] The plans paid for 70 to 80 per cent of the average hospital bills of their subscribers in 1949. This proportion is a nationwide average, however, and does not represent the share of an individual's hospital bill for a particular illness.[70]

Blue Shield and Other Medical Society Plans

One or more prepayment plans sponsored by state or local medical societies are now operating in most states. The Blue Shield Commission, formed under the sponsorship of the American Medical Association, acts as a central coordinating agency for most of these programs. In December 1952, medical society plans had an enrollment of nearly 28 million persons (11.7 million subscribers and 16.0 million dependents) who were eligible for surgical benefits. More than 18 million of them were also eligible for some type of medical care, principally during hospitalized illnesses. (See Table 147.) Approximately one third of the total surgical and one half of the medical care enrollment under all types of voluntary health insurance is in the medical society plans. Members are permitted free choice of physicians participating in the plan, usually most of the physicians in the service area.

65. Helen Hollingsworth, Helen L. Johnston and Anna Mae Baney, *Health Programs Digest*, Publication No. 191, Division of Medical and Hospital Resources, U.S. Public Health Service, 1952, pp. 6–7.

66. *Building America's Health*, President's Commission on the Health Needs of the Nation, U.S. Government Printing Office, 1952, Vol. IV, p. 347.

67. *Blue Cross Guide*, Blue Cross Commission, Chicago, January 1952.

68. *Hospitals*, Administrator's Guide Issue, June 1953, p. 284.

69. "Voluntary Insurance Against Sickness: 1948–52 Estimates," *Social Security Bulletin*, December 1953, pp. 10–11.

70. *Health Insurance Plans in the United States*, Part 1, p. 4.

Although the principal benefits provided by most medical society plans are surgery, maternity care and, to a lesser extent, medical services in the hospital, a few of the plans include physicians' care in office, home and hospital. Most do not provide hospitalization but are coordinated with or administered by Blue Cross plans serving the same area.

Approximately 3 per cent of the members are in plans that provide service benefits to all members, about one third are in plans offering cash benefits, and almost two thirds in plans combining service with cash indemnity benefits.[71] When a plan combines service with cash benefits, the attending physician agrees to accept payments made according to a fee schedule as full reimbursement for his services to members whose annual incomes are below a specified sum (ranging from $1,500 for an individual to $6,000 for a family, the specifications varying considerably according to plan). If the member's income exceeds the specified amount, the plan pays the physician on the basis of the same fee schedule, but he may also bill the patient for an additional sum. In 1949 an estimated 25 to 33 per cent of Blue Shield subscribers were eligible for service benefits and the rest were "over-income" subscribers entitled to cash indemnities.[72]

Monthly premiums reported in 1951 by 57 Blue Shield plans, for contracts covering both surgical and medical benefits, ranged as follows: 1 person, $0.50–$2.50; 2 persons, $1.65–$3.20; family, $1.50–$5.15. Average premiums for these classifications were $1.18, $2.21 and $2.94.[73]

Insurance Company Contracts

Insurance companies during 1952 protected the largest number of people against hospital and medical care costs. Enrollment under both individual and group contracts was as follows: for hospitalization, 51.7 million; for surgery, 48.8 million; for medical care (principally in the hospital), 15.3 million. These figures represented, respectively, 51, 60 and 39 per cent of the total enrollment for such benefits under all types of voluntary health insurance.[74] (See Table 147.)

Insurance companies provide cash indemnity benefits only, but in 1952 at least one company considered the possibility of experimenting with a service contract.

Other Prepayment Programs

Approximately 5.4 million persons are enrolled in various other prepayment programs, sometimes referred to as "independent plans" because they are self-insuring and not associated with other similar programs. This category includes industrial plans that serve the employees of specific industries, plans established by consumer groups and by physicians in private group practice, and a few community programs. The largest enrollment is in the industrial plans, the oldest of which is the hospital department of the Southern Pacific Railroad, established in 1868. With few exceptions the members of these independent plans are eligible for some form of physicians' service in the home, office and hospital, and for hospitalization.

Independent plans were the first type of prepayment medical care plans to be established in the United States, and most of the present programs have been functioning for a number of years. Only a limited number have been set up within recent years. Outstanding examples of the more recently established plans are the Health Insurance Plan of Greater New York, New York City; the Group Health Association, Washington, D.C.; and the Group Health Cooperative of Puget Sound, Seattle, Washington.

Monthly premiums vary widely, since there is considerable difference in the amount of benefits for which members are eligible and in various other cost factors. A survey by the Social Security Administration of plans operating in 1949 shows that, for 57 plans reporting on monthly premiums, the monthly payment for a family of four ranged from $1 to $10; 22 of these plans, with a total membership of 261,000, charged from $1 to $3 a month, and 25, with a total of more than a million members, charged from $3 to $10.[75] In the same year, plans of this type paid out almost 90 per cent of premiums in benefits and paid

71. *Building America's Health*, Vol. IV, p. 347.

72. *Health Insurance Plans in the United States*, Part I, p. 41.

73. *Voluntary Prepayment Medical Care Plans*, Council on Medical Service, American Medical Association, Chicago, 1952.

74. The Health Information Foundation study (*op. cit.*) found as of July 1953 that group and individual enrollment in insurance companies represented slightly less than half of the total hospital coverage, and more than half the coverage for surgical or medical care.

75. Agnes W. Brewster, *Independent Plans Providing Medical Care and Hospitalization Insurance in 1949, in the United States*, Bureau Memorandum No. 72, Social Security Administration, 1952, p. 31.

more than 80 per cent of the average cost to members for services of physicians and hospitals.

Union Health Programs

By mid-1951 between 8 and 8.5 million workers were estimated to be eligible for health and welfare benefits under collective bargaining agreements, and by mid-1952 the number was thought to be as high as 10 million.

The medical services most commonly available to union members are hospitalization and medical care. In mid-1952 well over 7 million were estimated to have hospitalization coverage, and 6.5 million some form of medical protection. An unknown number of dependents were also eligible for similar benefits. These services are provided either through Blue Cross and Blue Shield or through insurance company group contracts. Although both the AFL and the CIO have expressed a desire for more comprehensive benefits than these programs usually offer, union groups have found it more practical to purchase available contracts than to initiate their own service programs.

A few unions, however, have established their own health centers, which provide diagnostic, preventive, and sometimes more extensive services. The Labor Health Institute of St. Louis, the health centers of the International Ladies' Garment Workers' Union in many parts of the country, and the Sidney Hillman Health Centers in New York City and Philadelphia are examples of such programs. Where prepayment programs offering comprehensive services through doctors practicing as groups are operating, unions often participate in these programs, but the small number of such plans limits their value to union groups. A few of the older-type industrial prepayment plans, for example the Consolidated Edison plan in New York City, have been brought under collective bargaining but continue to function as they formerly did.

Annual employer contributions to pension and health and welfare programs, both those collectively bargained for and others, increased from $200 million in 1941 to $2 billion in 1949, $3 billion in 1951 and over $34 billion in 1952.[76] About $1.3 billion of the $3.4 billion expenditure in 1952 was for health and welfare benefits, over

half (about $750 million) covering hospitalization and medical care.

EXPENDITURES FOR HEALTH AND MEDICAL CARE

About $14.4 billion was spent for civilian health and medical services and facilities in 1952 — an average of $94 per person. This was $10.4 billion more than the amount spent in 1929 and $9.5 billion over 1941 expenditures. In terms of 1935–1939 dollars the expenditures in 1952 were $7.6 billion, and the increases over 1929 and 1941 were $4.3 billion and $2.9 billion, respectively.

Consumers' direct payments accounted for 67 cents out of each health and medical dollar spent in 1952; governmental expenditures (excluding hospital construction), for 19 cents; expenditures by industry and philanthropy, for about 8 cents; and construction of hospitals, for the remaining 6 cents. The principal shift in these percentages since 1929 has been a decline in the share of consumers' direct expenditures and an increase in the share of expenditures by government. (See Table 148.)

Consumer Expenditures

Consumer expenditures for health and medical care include payments for services furnished by all categories of health personnel, for care in private hospitals and sanitariums, for drugs and other medical supplies, for prosthetic, orthopedic and other appliances, and net payments for health and accident insurance, for dues in voluntary prepayment plans, and for student fees for medical care — in other words, all expenditures for health that consumers pay for, either directly or through a third party, as individuals but not as taxpayers.

Medical Prices

Medical prices during the war and postwar years have lagged considerably behind prices in general. The price of all goods and services in 1950 was up 72 per cent from the 1935–1939 level, whereas the price of medical care and drugs had risen only 48 per cent; by 1952 the consumers' price index had risen 90 per cent and the medical care and drugs index 64 per cent over their 1935–1939 averages. Of all medical care items priced, hospital rates alone rose more rapidly than the price of all goods and services. (See Table 149.)

---

76. *National Income and Product of the United States, 1929–1950* (1951 National Income Supplement to the *Survey of Current Business*), p. 201, and *Survey of Current Business*, July 1953, p. 24.

TABLE 148. ESTIMATED TOTAL EXPENDITURES FOR CIVILIAN HEALTH AND MEDICAL SERVICES AND FACILITIES, BY SOURCE OF FUNDS, IN CURRENT AND 1935–1939 DOLLARS, FOR SELECTED YEARS, 1929–1952

Source of Funds	1929	1936	1941	1946	1949	1950	1951	1952
Current Dollars (Millions)								
Total expenditures	$3,944	$3,315	$4,869	$9,098	$11,711	$12,685	$13,572	$14,365
Consumer	3,023	2,539	3,401	6,165	7,831	8,441	8,986	9,634
Government (excluding hospital construction)	409	442	850	1,938	2,276	2,404	2,539	2,749
Philanthropy	82	43	230	300	365	370	400	400
Industry	225	200	300	525	560	630	700	715
Hospital construction	205	91	88	170	679	840	947	867
Publicly owned facilities	101	74	42	85	477	496	528	473
Privately owned facilities	104	17	46	85	202	344	419	394
1935–1939 Dollars[a] (Millions)								
Total expenditures	$3,220	$3,345	$4,628	$6,522	$6,881	$7,379	$7,312	$7,559
Consumer	2,468	2,562	3,233	4,420	4,601	4,910	4,842	5,076
Government (excluding hospital construction)	334	446	808	1,389	1,337	1,398	1,368	1,448
Philanthropy	67	43	218	215	215	215	215	211
Industry	184	202	285	376	329	367	377	377
Hospital construction	167	92	84	122	399	489	510	457
Publicly owned facilities	82	75	40	61	280	289	284	249
Privately owned facilities	85	17	44	61	119	200	226	208
Percentage Distribution								
Total expenditures	100.0	100.0	100.0	100.0	100.0	100.0	100.0	100.0
Consumer	76.6	76.6	69.8	67.8	66.9	66.5	66.4	67.1
Government (excluding hospital construction)	10.4	13.4	17.5	21.3	19.4	19.0	18.7	19.1
Philanthropy	2.1	1.3	4.7	3.3	3.1	2.9	2.9	2.8
Industry	5.7	6.0	6.2	5.8	4.8	5.0	5.2	5.0
Hospital construction	5.2	2.7	1.8	1.8	5.8	6.6	6.8	6.0
Publicly owned facilities	2.6	2.2	.9	.9	4.1	3.9	3.7	3.3
Privately owned facilities	2.6	.5	.9	.9	1.7	2.7	3.1	2.7

Sources: Building America's Health, President's Commission on the Health Needs of the Nation, U.S. Government Printing Office, 1952, Vol. IV, p. 151; Appendix 4–4; *Social Security Bulletin*, Annual Statistical Supplement, September 1953, p. 23; Louis S. Reed, "Hospital Construction Trends," *Modern Hospital*, March 1952, pp. 72–76; *Construction and Building Materials, Statistical Supplement*, U.S. Department of Commerce, May 1953, pp. 7–11.

a. Based on Bureau of Labor Statistics consumers' price index (all items).

TABLE 149. CONSUMERS' PRICE INDEX AND PRICE INDEXES FOR MEDICAL CARE
FOR MODERATE-INCOME FAMILIES IN LARGE CITIES, 1940–1952

(1935–1939 = 100)

	1940	1945	1949	1950	1951	1952
Consumers' price index (cost of living)	100.2	128.6	170.2	171.9	185.6	189.7[a]
Medical care and drugs	100.8	115.3	144.9	147.9	155.0	164.2
Medical care, excluding drugs	101.0	117.7	149.7	153.1	160.9	171.8
Physicians' fees (general practitioner, surgeon, specialist)	100.3	116.6	137.9	140.0	145.2	152.2
General practitioners' fees	100.4	116.6	137.7	139.8	145.2	152.4
Office visit	100.4	117.2	139.0	140.9	146.0	152.4
House visit	100.2	113.3	131.4	133.9	138.3	143.0
Obstetric case	101.3	126.1	155.6	157.3	167.3	185.6
Surgeons' and specialists' fees	99.5	116.9	138.4	140.6	144.3	150.4
Appendectomy, adult	100.3	118.2	134.2	137.4	141.6	148.0
Tonsillectomy, child	98.5	115.7	142.8	144.0	147.2	153.1
Dentists' fees	101.1	119.7	150.6	154.3	160.0	163.8
Fillings	101.8	118.8	150.9	154.5	159.5	164.1
Extractions	100.8	121.4	152.9	156.9	164.5	166.4
Optometrists' fees, eyeglasses	101.9	112.0	127.6	128.9	134.6	136.4
Hospital rates	103.5	132.3	226.8	235.3	260.7	288.8
Men's pay ward	104.2	136.0	253.5	265.5	297.2	331.8
Semiprivate room	103.7	133.3	221.7	229.6	253.6	278.7
Private room	103.3	128.9	207.7	213.7	233.7	257.4
Group hospitalization [b]	—	—	—	—	103.1	117.8
Prescriptions and drugs	99.9	105.6	123.3	124.8	128.4	129.7
Prescriptions	100.7	108.7	137.1	140.7	147.7	149.6

Sources: Frank G. Dickinson, "The Cost of Living and Medical Care Prices," *Journal of the American Medical Association,* July 19, 1952, p. 1157; and "Old and New Base Periods for Medical Care Price Indexes," *Journal of the American Medical Association,* August 1, 1953, p. 1365; *Consumer Prices in the United States, 1942–48,* Bulletin No. 96, U.S. Bureau of Labor Statistics, Table G.

a. All other indexes in this column computed by the author from Bureau of Labor Statistics quarterly indexes.

b. December 1950 = 100.

While medical care items have increased relatively little in price, average weekly earnings have mounted rapidly. As a consequence, just 54 per cent of a week's wages of production workers in manufacturing industries in 1952 was necessary to purchase the same amount of medical care and drugs as a whole week's wages in 1935–1939. The same amount of physicians' services could be bought with 50 per cent of a week's wages in 1952 as with a whole week's wages in 1935–1939. The amount of hospital services purchased with a week's wages in 1935–1939 would require 95 per cent of a week's wages in 1952.[77]

77. Frank G. Dickinson, *Expenditures for Medical Care in 1952,* American Medical Association, Bureau of Medical Economic Research, Miscellaneous Publication M-77, August 1953.

Trends in Consumer Expenditures

Total consumer expenditures for health and medical services almost quadrupled between 1936 and 1952 — increasing from $2.5 billion to $9.6 billion — according to Commerce Department data.[78] However, in terms of constant (1935–1939) dollars, expenditures scarcely more than doubled in the sixteen-year period, increasing from $2.5 billion to $5.1 billion.

The composition of the medical bill has

78. The health and medical totals in this series are derived from estimates of all items that go to make up health and medical expenditures, such as gross incomes which physicians, dentists, nurses and other health personnel in independent private practice derive from individual patients, income of hospitals and gross sales of drug stores.

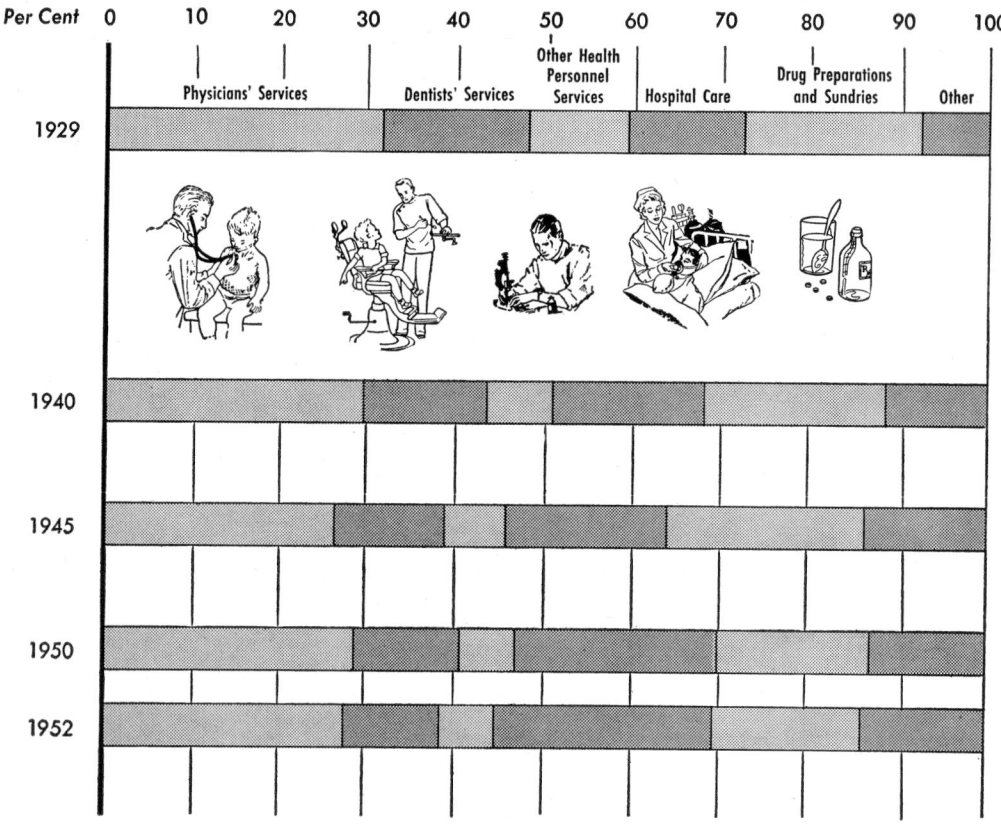

FIGURE 49. PERCENTAGE DISTRIBUTION OF CONSUMER EXPENDITURES FOR MEDICAL CARE, BY ITEM OF CARE, SELECTED YEARS, 1929–1952

Source: See Appendix 4–4.

changed considerably over the past twenty years. Expenditures for physicians' services, for example, dropped from 32 per cent of the total in 1929 to 30 per cent in 1940 and then to 26 per cent in 1945, when a large number of physicians were in the armed forces. By 1950 these costs had moved up to almost 29 per cent and in 1952 they were slightly less. In contrast, dentists have received a declining proportion of the total almost every year since 1929, when dental expenditures accounted for 16 per cent of the total, to 1950 and 1952 when they represented about 11 per cent. (See Figure 49.)

Payments to privately controlled hospitals and sanitariums (including payments by prepayment plans) took a much greater share of the consumer's medical dollar in 1952 than in 1929 — 25 per cent as against 13 per cent. This increase was due both to rapidly rising costs of hospital care and to the fact that voluntary prepaid hospital

plans have made hospital care more easily available to increasingly larger numbers of people — about 92 million at the end of 1952 as against about 12 million at the end of 1940 and 32 million at the end of 1945.[79]

79. In addition to these Commerce Department estimates, data on medical care expenditures are available also from surveys of family income and expenditures based on reports obtained through personal interviews with housewives. The Health Information Foundation study (*op. cit.*) includes data on family expenditures for medical care for the year July 1952 through June 1953 — a total of $10.2 billion in current dollars, or $5.4 billion in 1935–1939 dollars. This study, like similar studies, showed a higher percentage both of income and of total expenditures going for health and medical services than the Commerce series. The composition of the total medical bill as derived from these two sources also differed, with the family studies generally showing higher percentages used for services of physicians, dentists and nurses and lower percentages for drugs and appliances than the Commerce Department's estimates. Family expenditures were found to be distributed as follows in the Health Information Foundation study: physicians, 37 per cent of the total;

Expenditures and Earnings

Current information is not available on the distribution of total consumer expenditures for health and medical services among income classes. The last study of national scope, made in 1941 and 1942,[80] showed that the families and single consumers comprising the poorest 8 per cent of the nation accounted for less than 2.5 per cent of all medical expenditures while the 8 per cent of consumer units with the highest incomes accounted for more than 20 per cent. Although both incomes and expenditures are higher now than they were a decade ago, the general pattern of distribution probably remains the same.

The amount spent for health and medical care and the proportion of income or total expenditures used for such services vary widely among families in different income groups. Families with smaller incomes spend less in average absolute amount than families with higher incomes but their expenditures represent a larger fraction of their income or their total expenditures. For example, studies in ten cities in 1946–1949 showed that families and single individuals with incomes under $1,000 spent about 7 to 8 per cent of their income for health and medical care while those with incomes of $5,000 or more spent only about 4 to 5 per cent. Similar percentages were reported in earlier studies of family expenditures for medical care.[81]

The types of medical services and commodities purchased are also related to income. Expenditures for certain services, such as private-duty nursing care and X-ray examination and treatment, are virtually absent from the outlays of families with very small incomes; others, such as clinic services, are seldom reported by high-income families. Absence of expenditures, however, does not necessarily indicate that the particular service was not received, since some families, especially those in the lower income groups, get free services or pay only nominal fees.

In 1941, urban families with an annual money income of less than $500 spent only 7 cents of each medical dollar for dental care, while those with incomes of $5,000–$9,999 spent 19 cents. Hospital expenditures for the lowest income group represented less than 4 cents out of each medical dollar; families with intermediate incomes, on the other hand, spent 14 to 15 cents. The lowest-income families used a relatively large portion of their medical dollar for physicians' services — 42 cents as against a range of 26 to 36 cents in other income groups. Medicines and drugs accounted for at least as much as 10 cents of each dollar in all income groups, and tended to represent a larger proportion of the total medical dollar among the lower income groups.[82]

Other Variations in Costs

Aside from income, there are other family characteristics associated with the amount and percentage of income or total expenditures used by families for health care. Various studies have indicated that the size of the family and the age and sex composition of its members are such factors. Residence, whether in large cities, urban areas, or rural farm or rural nonfarm areas, is another differential factor. Family expenditures for health care also vary considerably in different regions of the country.

The costs of medical care cannot be predicted in advance, and they fall unevenly on families of all types. Few families go through a year without spending something for medical treatment. Expenditures of many families are moderate but a few pay large amounts in relation to their income.[83]

How unevenly these costs are distributed is indicated by the medical bills of 455 moderate-income wage-earning families in the San Francisco Bay area in 1947–1948, exclusive of costs covered by prepayment arrangements or by work-

hospitals, 20 per cent; prescriptions and other medicines, 15 per cent; dentists, 16 per cent; other medical goods and services, 13 per cent. Fifteen per cent of the total expenditures, or $1.5 billion, are estimated as payments made through insurance benefits. If these payments are excluded, the percentage distribution of the total "out-of-pocket" charges is as follows: physicians, 38; hospitals, 12; prescriptions and other medicines, 17; dentists, 18; and other medical goods and services, 15.

80. *Civilian Spending and Saving, 1941 and 1942*, U.S. Office of Price Administration, March 1, 1943.

81. *Family Income, Expenditures, and Savings in 10 Cities, 1946–1949*, Bulletin No. 1065, U.S. Bureau of Labor Statistics, 1952. See Appendix 10–2 for median gross charges and median net charges for medical care, by family income, for the year July 1952–June 1953 as found in the Health Information Foundation study.

82. *Family Spending and Saving in Wartime*, Bulletin No. 822, U.S. Bureau of Labor Statistics, 1945.

83. Helen Hollingsworth, Margaret C. Klem and Anna Mae Baney, *Medical Care and Costs in Relation to Family Income*, Bureau Memorandum No. 51, 2d ed., Bureau of Research and Statistics, Social Security Administration, 1947, pp. 169–170, 172–173, 175, 177–179; also Appendix 10–4.

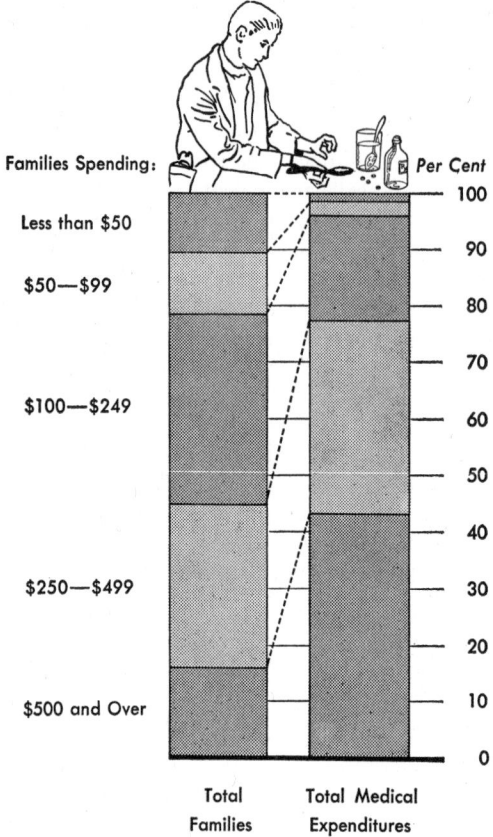

Families Spending:

Less than $50

$50—$99

$100—$249

$250—$499

$500 and Over

Per Cent
100
90
80
70
60
50
40
30
20
10
0

Total
Families

Total Medical
Expenditures

FIGURE 50. MEDICAL EXPENDITURES OF 455 FAMILIES IN THE SAN FRANCISCO BAY AREA, 1947–1948

Source: Emily H. Huntington, Cost of Medical Care: The Expenditures for Medical Care of 455 Families in the San Francisco Bay Area, 1947–1948, University of California Press, Berkeley and Los Angeles, 1951, p. 94.

care. All families spent something for drugs, the amounts ranging from 50 cents to $974.

More than 10 per cent of these families spent less than $50 during the year for all medical care, and the sum of their expenditures was equivalent to one per cent of the total expenditures of all the families in the group. At the other extreme, the 16 per cent of the families whose bills were $500 or more incurred total bills equivalent to 43 per cent of the total expenditures of the group. (See Figure 50.) This uneven distribution is the more striking since 60 per cent of the families were enrolled in some type of prepayment medical or hospital plan.

Further evidence of the uneven incidence of medical care costs is available from the records of medical and dental expenditures on federal income tax returns. The taxpayer may deduct his medical, dental, hospital and related expenses and those of his spouse or dependents that are not compensated by insurance or otherwise and that exceed a certain percentage of his income. In 1948 nearly 8 per cent of the 52 million persons filing income tax returns claimed such deductions. The proportion was highest — 10 per cent or more — among those reporting an adjusted gross income of $3,000 to $10,000. On the average, those who took advantage of the deduction reported using 13.4 per cent of their income for medical care — 5 per cent nondeductible and 8.4 per cent deductible. (See Table 150.) Recent unpublished estimates of the Bureau of Internal Revenue indicate that at current levels of income total deductions for medical care on income tax returns amount to $1.8 billion.

Outstanding Medical Bills and Loans

In spite of the fact that more than half the population had insurance against part or all of their hospital bills and a large proportion also had some degree of protection against the costs of physicians' services, at the beginning of 1952 about one fifth of the nation's spending units owed bills to doctors, dentists or hospitals, according to the Federal Reserve Board's 1952 survey of consumer finances. The proportion varied somewhat with the level of family income, being highest (22 per cent) among families with incomes of $2,000–$4,000 and lowest (14 per cent) in the income group $7,500 and over. A particularly large percentage of families with children under age 18 had outstanding bills — 30 per cent among families headed by persons between 18 and 44 years

men's compensation.[84] For physicians' services, more than 20 per cent of these families spent up to $25 a year, a similar proportion spent between $50 and $100, while over 10 per cent spent $250 or more. One family's doctor bill was $1,550. A few families received only free or prepaid care or services covered by workmen's compensation. Many more — over 15 per cent — received hospital service without direct payment. About 15 per cent of all families had hospital bills of less than $50, but three families paid $500 or more and one of these paid $813. Only 20 families had nursing services, but one paid $1,750 for such

84. Emily H. Huntington, *Cost of Medical Care: The Expenditures for Medical Care of 455 Families in the San Francisco Bay Area, 1947–1948,* University of California Press, Berkeley and Los Angeles, 1951, p. 29.

TABLE 150. NUMBER AND PER CENT OF INCOME TAX RETURNS WITH MEDICAL AND DENTAL DEDUCTIONS AND AMOUNT OF SUCH DEDUCTIONS COMPARED WITH ADJUSTED GROSS INCOME, BY INCOME CLASS, 1948

Adjusted Gross Income Class [a]	Number of Individual Tax Returns	With Medical and Dental Deductions		Adjusted Gross Income Reported on Returns with Medical Deductions	Returns with Medical and Dental Deductions [b]	
	Total	Number	Per Cent of Total [c]		Medical and Dental Deductions	
					Amount [d]	Per Cent of Adjusted Gross Income [d]
	(Thousands)			(Millions)		
Total	52,072 [e]	4,134	7.9	$15,486 [f]	$1,304	8.4
No adjusted gross income	326	8	2.5	−32 [g]	4	—
Under $1,000 [h]	7,711	137	1.8	108	28	26.0
1,000–1,999	11,145	607	5.4	947	147	15.5
2,000–2,999	12,459	1,041	8.4	2,628	278	10.6
3,000–3,999	9,397	1,059	11.3	3,684	299	8.1
4,000–4,999	5,095	628	12.3	2,803	210	7.5
5,000–6,999	3,473	428	12.3	2,463	167	6.8
7,000–9,999	1,193	124	10.4	1,007	71	7.1
10,000–14,999	600	55	9.2	657	44	6.7
15,000–24,999	359	31	8.6	567	31	5.6
25,000–49,999	185	13	6.9	421	18	4.2
50,000–99,999	53	3	4.8	164	5	2.9
100,000 or more	16	[i]	2.8	69	1	1.4

Source: Building America's Health, President's Commission on the Health Needs of the Nation, U.S. Government Printing Office, 1952, Vol. IV, p. 323.

a. Adjusted gross income means gross income minus allowable trade and business deductions, expenses of travel and lodging in connection with employment, reimbursed expenses in connection with employment, deductions attributable to rents and royalties, certain deductions of life tenants and income beneficiaries of property held in trust, and allowable losses from sales or exchange of property. Should these allowable deductions exceed the gross income, there is an adjusted gross deficit. The adjusted gross income classes are based on the amount of adjusted gross income, except that returns with adjusted gross deficit are designated "No adjusted gross income" without regard to the amount.

b. Medical and dental expenses, reported on returns with itemized deductions, paid for the care of the taxpayer, his spouse or dependents, not compensated by insurance or otherwise, which exceed 5 per cent of the adjusted gross income. The deduction cannot exceed $1,250 multiplied by the number of exemptions, other than those for age and blindness, with a maximum deduction of $2,500, except on a joint return of husband and wife, where the maximum is $5,000.

c. Percentages based on unrounded numbers of tax returns and dollar amounts in thousands.

d. Reported on returns with medical deductions. Does not include nondeductible medical expenses equal to 5 per cent of adjusted gross income.

e. Tax returns claimed 129,104,000 exemptions (other than age and blindness) for the taxpayer, his spouse (on a joint return) and each dependent.

f. Adjusted gross income less adjusted gross deficit.

g. Adjusted gross deficit.

h. Persons with gross incomes below $600 are not required to file returns. However, many such persons do file returns, chiefly for the purpose of claiming refunds of tax prepayments; and those returns are included in the tabulation.

i. 452 tax returns.

TABLE 151. PER CENT OF SPENDING UNITS[a] OWING MEDICAL BILLS BY AMOUNT OF DEBT[b] AND
BY INCOME, OCCUPATION, AGE OF HEAD OF HOUSEHOLD, AND FAMILY STATUS, EARLY 1952

| | | Per Cent Owing Medical Bills | | | | |
| | | | Amount of Debt | | | |
Group Characteristic	Number of Cases in Sample	Total	$1–$99	$100–$199	$200 and Over	Not Ascertained
All spending units	2,820	19	14	3	2	c
Income before taxes, 1951						
Under $1,000	278	17	14	2	1	c
$1,000–$1,999	359	18	13	1	3	1
$2,000–$2,999	454	22	17	2	3	c
$3,000–$3,999	482	22	17	2	3	c
$4,000–$4,999	424	19	12	4	3	c
$5,000–$7,499	490	18	12	4	2	c
$7,500 and over	333	14	10	2	2	c
Occupation [d, e]						
Professional and semiprofessional	273	12	9	2	1	c
Managerial	152	16	8	2	6	c
Self-employed	212	10	6	2	2	c
Clerical and sales	430	19	14	3	2	c
Skilled and semiskilled	780	23	16	4	3	c
Unskilled and service	280	21	14	2	4	1
Farm operator	215	23	18	2	3	c
Retired	178	13	10	c	1	2
Other [f]	266	21	17	1	2	1
Age [d, e]						
18–24	218	24	21	2	1	c
25–34	634	23	16	3	4	c
35–44	619	23	16	3	3	1
45–54	547	18	12	4	2	c
55–64	382	13	9	1	2	1
65 and over	362	13	11	c	1	1
Family status						
Single person						
Age 18–44	317	11	10	1	c	c
Age 45 or over	316	13	9	2	1	1
Married [g]						
Age 18–44, no children under 18	213	11	9	1	1	c
Age 18–44, children under 18	842	30	21	4	5	c
Age 45 or over, no children under 18	616	11	8	1	2	c
Age 45 or over, children under 18	302	24	18	4	2	c
Other [h]	122	27	23	1	3	c

Source: "1952 Survey of Consumer Finances, Part III, Income, Selected Investments and Short-Term Debt of Consumers," *Federal Reserve Bulletin,* September 1952, p. 991.

a. A spending unit is a group of persons living in the same dwelling and related by blood, marriage or adoption, who pool their incomes for their major items of expense. A family may include more than one spending unit because adult children, parents or other relatives living in one dwelling do not necessarily pool their incomes with that of the head of the family.

b. Includes debts at the beginning of 1952 to doctors, dentists and hospitals for medical and dental services.

c. No cases reported or less than 0.5 per cent.

d. Refers to person considered as the head of the spending unit.

e. Total number of cases exceeds sum of various groups because of inclusion of cases for which relevant characteristics were not ascertained.

f. Includes spending units headed by housewives, unemployed persons, or students.

g. Both husband and wife in spending unit.

h. Includes spending units with or without children from which husband or wife is absent.

TABLE 152. PERCENTAGE DISTRIBUTION OF SINGLE-PURPOSE LOANS MADE BY THE THREE LARGEST SMALL-LOAN COMPANIES, BY PURPOSE OF LOAN

Purpose	Company[a]		
	A	B	C
	Number of Loans		
Total	1,008,363	1,539,674	588,512
Consolidation of existing debts[b]	337,800	303,315	189,006
Single-purpose loans	670,563	1,236,359	399,506
	Percentage Distribution		
All single-purpose loans	100.0	100.0	100.0
Medical, hospital and dental	20.6	21.5	22.2
Clothing, food, fuel and rent	11.9	17.5	25.8
Repairs	12.8	9.5	10.5
Travel and education	12.0	9.3	10.7
Taxes, mortgages, interest, insurance	7.7	10.1	6.5
Home furnishings	2.0	7.5	10.5
Automobiles	4.2	3.6	3.8
All other	28.8	20.0	10.0

Source: *Building America's Health,* President's Commission on the Health Needs of the Nation, U.S. Government Printing Office, 1952, Vol. I, p. 321.

a. These data are for 1948, 1949 and 1951 for companies A, B and C, respectively. Loans of the three companies in the three different years aggregated $800 million. More recent data available on the amount of loans by companies A and B show loans of $1.1 billion for the three companies in 1951.

b. Represents consolidation of several small debts in a single obligation. The reasons for incurring the initial debts, and the percentages of these consolidated loans which are in part for medical bills, are not known.

of age and 24 per cent among those headed by persons aged 45 or over. (See Table 151.)

The average outstanding bill of these families was about $105 and the median was $50. The estimate of the aggregate medical indebtedness of all families based on this inquiry was $1.0 billion.[85]

Medical bills are responsible for more applications filed with small-loan companies than any other single type of expense, judging by the experience of the three largest companies, which did over 46 per cent of the small-loan business in

85. The Health Information Foundation study found 15 per cent of families with some medical indebtedness in June 1953. Of these, 9 per cent had debts of less than $95; 3 per cent, debts of $95 to $194; 2 per cent, $195 and over; 1 per cent, an unknown amount. The average debt per family was $121, amounting to a total national medical indebtedness of approximately $900 million. Insurance coverage had no appreciable effect on indebtedness. The percentage of families with some indebtedness was quite constant until the income group $5,000 and over was reached and dropped sharply thereafter. Families with children under 18 were more likely to have medical debts than families without children. *National Family Survey of Medical Costs and Voluntary Health Insurance,* Preliminary Report, pp. 67–68.

1951. Of the more than $1.1 billion these three companies loaned in that year, over 20 per cent was for medical, hospital and related expenses. (See Table 152.) All small-loan companies disbursed $2,437 million in loans in 1951, and had $1,268 million outstanding at the end of the year. If the experience of all companies is the same as the three largest, in lending over 20 per cent of the total for medical and related purposes, all small-loan companies may have loaned more than $480 million in 1951 for these purposes. Assuming that the average effective rate of interest is about 33 per cent on the principal amount of loans outstanding, the interest payments on loans outstanding for medical and related purposes amounted to $84 million or more during the year, in addition to repayments of principal.[86]

Government Expenditures for Civilian Health

In the fiscal year 1951–1952, government expenditures for civilian health and medical services and for the construction of facilities amounted to

86. *Building America's Health,* Vol. I, p. 321.

TABLE 153. LEVEL OF HEALTH AND HEALTH CARE OF INDIVIDUALS IN MICHIGAN FAMILIES, BY RESIDENCE AND GROSS INCOME OF FAMILY, 1948

Residence, Symptoms and Treatment	Gross Income of Family [a]					
	Under $1,000	$1,000– 1,999	$2,000– 2,999	$3,000– 3,999	$4,000– 4,999	$5,000 and Over
	Rural Families					
Number of individuals	159	309	528	357	166	94
Percentage distribution						
Total	100.0	100.0	100.0	100.0	100.0	100.0
No positive symptoms	32.7	50.4	59.5	58.0	66.3	65.9
All positive symptoms treated						
By M.D.	15.7	14.4	14.8	17.1	19.9	17.0
By non-M.D.	0.0	2.0	0.6	0.6	1.2	6.4
One or more untreated symptoms	51.6	33.2	25.1	24.3	12.6	10.7
	Urban Families [b]					
Number of individuals	92	241	418	323	167	140
Percentage distribution						
Total	100.0	100.0	100.0	100.0	100.0	100.0
No positive symptoms	45.7	62.7	51.7	71.5	61.6	70.1
All positive symptoms treated						
By M.D.	16.3	15.4	26.1	14.2	24.0	20.7
By non-M.D.	0.0	0.4	0.2	0.0	1.8	0.7
One or more untreated symptoms	38.0	21.5	22.0	14.3	12.6	8.5

Source: Charles R. Hoffer, Duane L. Gibson, Charles P. Loomis, Paul A. Miller, Edgar A. Schuler and John F. Thaden, *Health Needs and Health Care in Michigan,* Special Bulletin 365, Michigan State College Agricultural Experiment Station, East Lansing, 1950, pp. 82–83.

a. Individuals for whom income was not reported are excluded.

b. "Urban" is exclusive of Detroit and also of densely settled areas near a large city and designated by the 1940 Census as "metropolitan." A total of 153 households and 548 individuals residing in fringe areas are excluded from this table although tabulated in the survey.

$3.3 billion, of which the federal government contributed $1.1 billion, or about a third. In contrast, the total expenditures for 1946–1947 were $1.7 billion, of which federal contributions amounted to $678 million, or about 40 per cent.[87] State and local contributions for health purposes increased from 51 per cent of the total in 1946–1947 to 66 per cent in 1951–1952, rising in dollar amounts from $1.0 billion to $2.2 billion.

The following percentage distribution of total expenditures by type of program indicates the influence of the hospital construction program during the five-year period:

	1946–1947	1951–1952
Total	100.0	100.0
Hospital and medical care	62.7	58.7
Hospital construction	4.9	17.0
Other community and related health services	29.4	23.2
Maternal and child health care	3.0	1.1

87. *Social Security Bulletin,* Annual Statistical Supplement, September issues 1950, 1953.

STANDARDS AND NEEDS

A good many Americans fail to get proper medical and dental care — some because of ignorance or neglect, others because they find the cost prohibitive and do not have ready access to free services. Some recent information on the amount of unmet medical needs is available from surveys devised by the Department of Agriculture in cooperation with physicians attached to the Department.[88] The most comprehensive of several studies, that made in Michigan in 1949, covered 1,113 households containing 3,786 individuals, a sample considered representative of the state exclusive of metropolitan areas. Among the rural families in this survey, more than half

88. The technique used, based on a series of questions asked in a family interview, is described by Edgar A. Schuler, Selz C. Mayo and Henry B. Makover, M.D., in "Measuring Unmet Needs for Medical Care: An Experiment in Method," *Rural Sociology,* June 1946, pp. 152–158.

the individuals in the income group under $1,000 had one or more untreated symptoms in contrast to 11 per cent in the group with incomes of $5,000 and over. The corresponding rates among the urban families were 38 per cent and less than 9 per cent. In each income class the proportion of persons with untreated symptoms was greater in the rural group than in the urban. (See Table 153.)

Evidence that unmet needs increase with age comes from a study made in Greene County, North Carolina, in 1945, covering 1,394 individuals in 266 families.[89] In the surveyed population under 15 years of age, 37 per cent needed care that they were not receiving. The proportion increased to 50 per cent in the age group 15–44 and to 75 per cent in the group 45 years of age and over.

VITAL HEALTH PROBLEMS

Important problems which confront the nation in its effort to achieve the highest level of health for its people are the backlog of unmet dental needs, among the well-to-do as well as the poor; malnutrition; overweight; inadequate housing and sanitary facilities; high accident rates, especially in the home and among children. Probably the two foremost problems, however, are the prospective increase in long-term illness because of the aging of the population, and the high rate of mental illness.

Aging of the Population

The aging of our population has special implications for the future of medical services since it will materially affect the prevalence and types of disabling illness and will increase the need for services of health personnel and facilities.

According to recent projections by the Public Health Service [90] of the findings of the National Health Survey and the Baltimore study,[91] the number of disabling illnesses lasting seven consecutive days or longer is likely to be 25 to 30 per cent higher in 1960 and 40 to 50 per cent greater by 1975. The total annual days lost from such disability are expected to rise 30 to 40 per cent by 1960 and 60 to 70 per cent by 1975. By

1960, more than one fourth of this time loss will occur in the aged group; by 1975, the aged will account for almost a third of the total.

The aged will require increasing proportions of medical services, especially for chronic diseases. Physicians' calls for such cases in 1960, it is estimated, will be 10 per cent more than in 1940 as a result of the aging factor alone. When both the growth and the aging of the population are considered, the increase in physicians' calls over the 1940 figure is estimated at 35 per cent by 1960 and 62 per cent by 1975. (See Appendix 10–3.)

The prevention and control of disease among the aged must begin many years before they reach old age. From surveys of identical families in Hagerstown, Maryland, in 1923 and again twenty years later it has been estimated that out of every 1,000 persons who are well at age 45, approximately 100 will require medical attention during the next five years for the onset of a chronic disease or major impairment, and that nearly 250 of every 1,000 persons who are well at age 60 will develop within five years a chronic ailment for which they will probably seek or need medical attention, in many instances for the rest of their lives.[92] Perhaps the major conclusion from this investigation is that a substantial proportion of persons who are ill at age 65 have had the same or another chronic illness for at least twenty years and that the incidence of chronic illness increases rapidly after age 45.

Many communities have been giving serious consideration to the needs of the chronically ill, and this will be of direct benefit to the aged, since one fourth of the chronically ill are 65 years of age or older. The Chronic Illness Service Center of San Francisco, for example, after a two-year experience, has made the following recommendations for study and possible future action:

Evaluation of the present use of low-cost beds for prolonged illness in public and private institutions, to permit more flexible and appropriate use of beds and to promote an easy flow of patients into the facilities best suited to meet their needs.

Greater coordination of existing services to chronically ill persons, and the assurance of continuity in medical and nursing care as the patient's status changes.

Development and maintenance of standards for care in proprietary nursing homes, and the integration of these homes into the community program.

89. Selz C. Mayo and Kie Sebastian Fullerton, *Medical Care in Greene County*, Bulletin No. 363, North Carolina Agricultural Experiment Station, Raleigh, 1948.

90. Perrott, Goldstein and Collins, *op. cit.*

91. See p. 302.

92. Antonio Ciocco and Philip S. Lawrence, "Illness among Older People in Hagerstown, Maryland," in *Illness and Health Services in an Aging Population*, Publication No. 170, U.S. Public Health Service, 1952, pp. 26–37.

Maintenance of current and accurate information on resources and optimum methods of care or placement of chronically ill patients, to ensure maximum use of available resources.

Placing responsibility on public agencies and institutions for that section of the chronically ill group which is legally considered a public responsibility.

Broadening the concept of care to include emphasis on rehabilitation as an integral part of service, in order to prevent unnecessary deterioration.

Recognition of the need for a continuous resource to which the patient can turn for counselling, guidance, and understanding of the problems involved in prolonged illness.

Use of organized housekeeper service for chronically ill patients who require neither institutional nor nursing care, thereby postponing or eliminating the necessity for institutional care.

Development of hospital-based coordinated home care services, providing medical supervision, nursing services, and rehabilitative services in the home, as an extension of hospital service, with the objective of keeping the patient within the family wherever this is desirable.

Development and extension of a program of community education around the problem of the chronically ill so that a public conscience may be developed toward the needs of this group.[93]

Mental Illness

To attack the problem of mental disease effectively, the first great need is for more knowledge of its nature, cause, treatment and prevention. Yet research on mental disorders has lagged far behind research in such fields as tuberculosis, cancer and poliomyelitis.

More mental health clinics are greatly needed. In 1948 about 850 psychiatric clinics were in existence, most of them offering only limited services. At that time there was a need for 1,500 fully staffed and full-time clinics to meet the estimated basic requirement of one for every 100,000 persons.[94]

There is also a great need for a nationwide effective educational and preventive program, for more trained mental health personnel, and for community action against the problem. "The ultimate development of sound mental health programs," according to the Public Health Service, "depends on the local men and women who are closely in touch with the resources and needs of their community and who are deeply con-

cerned with bringing optimum mental health to all their neighbors." [95]

NEEDED FACILITIES AND PERSONNEL

In order to make the most of our health resources, we must have an effective, popular program of health education. A good beginning already has been made by governmental public health agencies — federal, state and local — in education for healthful living. Industry is furthering the effort through its health and safety campaigns. But there is need for a broader educational program, reaching every individual and teaching the value of periodic health examinations and early diagnostic and therapeutic measures.

Expansion of the Public Health Program

In recent years, experts in the public health field and in hospital administration have become increasingly aware of the necessity for bringing health departments and hospitals closer together if they are to make their full contribution to the health of the public. In 1948 the American Public Health Association and the American Hospital Association issued a joint statement stressing this need.[96] To demonstrate how the principle might be achieved, the Public Health Service in 1950 drew up a plan of local health service areas.[97]

In mapping out this plan, the Public Health Service gave primary consideration to two factors: first, there must be the highest possible degree of conformance between health service area plans and plans for existing or proposed general hospitals and health centers; and, second, the health service area must serve a population of at least 35,000. Other factors were also considered, such as the type and composition of local governmental units, transportation facilities, geographical location, existing health districts and existing medical service areas.

No area of the United States, under this proposal, would be without a planned health department. There would be 1,228 single-county and multicounty health units to serve the 3,069 counties of the continental United States and the Dis-

93. "Chronic Illness News Letter," Commission on Chronic Illness, Vol. 4, No. 2 (March-April 1953).

94. "The National Mental Health Program," Mental Health Series, No. 4, U.S. Public Health Service, June 1948.

95. *Ibid.*, p. 7.

96. American Hospital Association and American Public Health Association, "Coordination of Hospitals and Health Departments," *American Journal of Public Health*, May 1948, p. 702.

97. *Public Health Areas and Hospital Facilities: A Plan for Coordination*, Publication No. 42, U.S. Public Health Service, 1950.

TABLE 154. ESTIMATED NUMBER OF BASIC PERSONNEL NEEDED TO EXTEND MINIMUM SERVICES IN ORGANIZED HEALTH UNITS TO ENTIRE COUNTRY, 1951

Type of Personnel	Number Employed, Fiscal Year 1951 [a]	Additional Number Needed to Provide Minimum Services in 1951
Total	28,143	[b]
Physician	1,594	1,600
Nurse and supervisor	11,843	13,700
Sanitary personnel	7,186	4,000
Clerical worker	7,520	[b]

Sources: U.S. Public Health Service; W. P. Shepard, "Manpower Shortages in Official Health Agencies," *Public Health Reports,* August 1952, pp. 709–724.

a. Based on reports from 1,193 full-time local health units out of a total of 1,293.

b. Not available.

trict of Columbia. Somewhat more than two thirds of the proposed units would be of the multicounty type. Wherever feasible, existing local health department headquarters would be used as headquarters for the proposed units.

In its estimates of the personnel required to staff the units, the study emphasized the point that "modern, comprehensive health services require the skills of a wide variety of specialists in the medical, nursing, engineering, and scientific fields." The estimates were limited, however, to four types of workers needed to provide basic and minimum public health services, with minimum standards set as follows: one medically trained public health physician for every 50,000 persons; one public health nurse for every 5,000 persons, with a nurse of supervisory grade for every nine staff nurses; one sanitarian or sanitary engineer for every 15,000 persons; and one clerk for every 15,000 persons. On the basis of these standards, it was found that in the fiscal year 1946–1947 there was a deficiency of nearly 1,400 public health physicians, about 14,000 public health nurses, 4,000 sanitarians and nearly 3,500 clerical workers.[98] A more recent estimate based on identical standards showed a large unmet need for basic personnel in organized health

units. In 1951 less than half the number of physicians and nurses needed to provide minimum services were employed in the 1,193 full-time local health units reporting out of a total of 1,293 such units in existence in this country. (See Table 154.) In December 1950 only 24 per cent of the population lived in areas that had enough full-time public health physicians and less than 4 per cent lived in areas served by enough full-time public health nurses to meet the minimum staffing requirements.[99]

For several years, legislation has been introduced in Congress to enable the federal government to help states and localities meet the cost of providing organized local health services in areas without them. According to the hearings on the most recent proposals,[100] in 1950 it would have cost the federal government about $32 million with a matching payment from the states and localities of about $57 million for organized local health services which, during the initial period, would provide at least one health officer per 50,000 persons, one public health nurse per 15,000 persons, and one sanitarian or sanitary engineer per 50,000 persons. It was estimated that the federal share might reach $80 million a year when the nation was fully covered by participating health units.

98. *Ibid.,* p. 8. Many local health departments have staffs that exceed the minimum requirements in one or more categories. In determining personnel needs for the purposes of the study, it was assumed that personnel already employed in any of the proposed health units would be kept on, even though their employment meant that minimum requirements would be exceeded.

99. Greve and Campbell, *op. cit.*

100. *Local Public Health Units,* Hearings before the Committee on Interstate and Foreign Commerce on H.R. 274 and H.R. 913, House of Representatives, 1951, p. 115.

A plan such as that proposed by the Public Health Service in 1950, which would link local health units with community hospital facilities, would give opportunity to the local health unit to "perform the function of coordinator of community health and medical services. . . . It would give health departments and general hospitals the joint use of expensive and specialized diagnostic equipment. It would enable both agencies, through cooperative arrangements, to share the specialized professional personnel who make modern health services possible. It would form the basic framework for the establishment of local health programs in the control of cancer, diabetes, heart disease, and other chronic illnesses which are today's greatest challenge to public health." Moreover, through regional coordination, of both hospitals and health units, a natural flow of health services, preventive and curative, would be achieved—from the simple to the complex, the routine to the specialized, from the small local hospital and local health unit to the sizable and integrated medical center.

Hospital Bed Needs

Despite progress in hospital construction under the Hill-Burton Act of 1946, the nation is still far from having an adequate number of hospital beds. Projects approved under the program by December 1953 were sufficient to add nearly 106,000 beds to the nation's supply, but at the end of 1953 nearly 813,000 additional beds were needed to meet the minimum standards set by the Hill-Burton Act.

For general hospital beds, the standard was set at 4.5 to 5.5 beds per 1,000 population, depending on population density.[101] On this basis, which would call for a total of more than 700,000 beds, the supply at the end of 1953 would have had to be increased by more than 188,000 including replacements for beds in nonacceptable facilities. The need for additional mental hospital beds is even more acute. The Hill-Burton standard of 5 per 1,000 population would require a total of about 773,000. For hospital care of the tuberculous, more than 100,000 beds would be needed to meet the minimum standard of 2.5 beds per average annual deaths from tuberculosis for the latest

five-year period. The number available in acceptable facilities in 1953 fell short of this standard by almost 22,000.

Beds specifically designated for the chronically ill make up a relatively small share of the nation's hospital bed supply, but the deficiency in this group is large. By the end of 1953, acceptable chronic disease beds totaled more than 43,000. Yet, according to the Hill-Burton minimum standard of 2 per 1,000 population, a total of 309,000 should be available. (See Table 155.)

It is possible that these requirements will be diminished somewhat in the future because of changes in the incidence of various diseases and in concepts of prevention and treatment. As the President's Commission on the Health Needs of the Nation pointed out, "further decreases in the incidence of tuberculosis would free beds for use in the treatment of other diseases. The growing movement toward nursing homes for chronic illness will affect bed requirements in our mental and general hospitals. Development of organized home care and health and diagnostic centers outside hospitals will alter the need for hospital care."[102]

Personnel Needs

Before the second world war it was generally believed that our supply of physicians, dentists, nurses, technicians and other health personnel was quite adequate to meet the demands for medical care. In over-all numbers this may have been true, and in nearly every field of health there was actually an oversupply of personnel in some localities. However, in many places, and particularly in rural and low-income communities, shortages were severe. The war aggravated the problem in two ways. Heavy demands were made on the health professions for service in the armed forces, and at the same time civilian demands for health service increased steadily as the population became more "health minded." Since the war, the demand for more nearly complete health services has continued, and with it has come an increasing recognition of the need for more health personnel.

Physicians

Authorities differ as to whether there is at present a significant shortage of physicians. Ac-

101. "Hospital Construction under the Hill-Burton Program: Analysis of Projects Approved for Federal Aid," Division of Hospital Facilities, U.S. Public Health Service, December 31, 1953, mimeographed.

102. *Building America's Health*, Vol. I, p. 24.

TABLE 155. NONFEDERAL HOSPITAL BEDS IN THE UNITED STATES AND TERRITORIES,
JANUARY 1, 1954
(*Thousands*)

Type of Service	Existing Beds			Additional Beds Needed[b]	Total Beds Needed[c]
	Total	Acceptable	Non-acceptable[a]		
All categories	1,242	1,083	159	813	1,887
General	590	516	74	188	704
Mental	501	438	63	337	773
Tuberculosis	101	86	15	22	101
Chronic	50	43	7	266	309

Source: *Hospital Beds in the United States as of January 1, 1954*, Division of Hospital Facilities, U.S. Public Health Service, January 1954, mimeographed.

a. As classified by the state agencies on the basis of fire and health hazards.
b. As reported in the state plans for hospital construction.
c. According to ratios prescribed in the Public Health Service Act, as follows:
    General—4.5 beds per 1,000 population (except 5.0 and 5.5 where state population density is from 6 to 12 per square mile or below 6 per square mile)
    Mental—5 beds per 1,000 population
    Tuberculosis—2.5 beds per average annual deaths, for latest five-year period
    Chronic—2 beds per 1,000 population
Note: Individual items may not add to totals because of rounding.

cording to Dr. Frank Dickinson, Director of the Bureau of Medical Economic Research, American Medical Association, "1,000 physicians in 1950 could (and did) render at least one third more medical service than could 1,000 physicians in 1940." [103] He finds several factors working together to increase the "output" of physicians — expansion of service areas, the changes in medical practice brought about by the introduction of the wonder drugs, greater use of auxiliary personnel, and the decrease in home visits. The supply of physicians' services has been increasing at a reasonable rate, he believes — a rate favorable to the health of the American people and fast enough to meet the increasing demand for service. He finds that the distribution of specialists and of general practitioners (including part-time specialists) in relation to state populations was more even in 1949 than in 1938. He assumes, however, that imperfect geographic distribution can and will continue, since "there will always be attractive openings for physicians in some cities, towns and villages." His conclusion reached after examination of the facts relating to the supply and utilization of physicians' services is that "as a result of present trends we are

more likely to have more physicians than we need in the United States in the 1960s than we are to have fewer."

A contrasting opinion is expressed in the recent report of the President's Commission on the Health Needs of the Nation.[104] According to this report, the Commission's investigations showed an insistent indication of a shortage of physicians. Following a study of collected statistics and analysis of the testimony of medical experts, the Commission concluded:

There are not enough general physicians, and most of those we have are so busy that they cannot give the patient the time and sympathetic care the old family doctor used to give in a home visit. We need more pediatricians to assure children the optimum health protection that is their due. Our mental and tuberculosis hospitals are critically short of staff. Medical schools have many unfilled faculty positions. Physicians are needed to carry on research in many institutions and in many fields. In the expanding fields of public health, industrial medicine, and rehabilitation, physician shortages are holding up scores of dynamic programs. In fact, with the possible exception of surgery, there seems to be no area of specialization in which the supply of physicians meets even the present demand. On top of these many civilian demands lies the constant pressure to meet military requirements.

103. Frank G. Dickinson, "Supply of Physicians' Services," *Journal of the American Medical Association*, April 21, 1951, pp. 1260–1264.

104. *Building America's Health*, Vol. I, pp. 11-15.

The Commission further declared that "despite gains in the availability of physicians' services, the demand for service still far outruns the supply."

The Commission recognized that no exact determination of the future shortage of physicians can be made, but presented several estimates to give some indication of the size of the problem. As a minimum estimate, 22,000 more physicians than the predicted supply by 1960 would be needed to bring the regions of the country with the lowest ratios of physicians to population up to the national average. To provide reasonably comprehensive medical care to civilians [105] and to meet the additional needs of public health, industrial medicine, mental and tuberculosis hospital staffs, staffing of medical schools and schools of public health, and of the armed forces (assuming no change in mobilization rates), 30,000 more physicians would be needed in 1960 than the predicted supply by that time. A third estimate, based on bringing all regions of the country up to the average physician-population ratio of New England and the Central Atlantic states, indicated a need for 45,000 more physicians than the predicted supply in 1960. This last estimate, the Commission stated, "may be taken to represent a needed supply under present, but not necessarily under improved, methods of organization."

Nurses

The need for nurses in all fields of practice is critical. In public hearings conducted by the Commission, impressive evidence was given as to the nurse shortage in public health services, in hospitals of all types, in industrial health programs and in staffs of nursing schools.[106] In public health work alone, in which some 25,000 nurses were actively engaged in 1952, an additional 12,000 to 15,000 were needed.[107] Rural areas in more than 650 counties still had no full-time public health nurses, and thirteen towns of 10,000 or more population were without such service.

Enrollments in nursing schools are increasing, but not enough to catch up with the constantly growing demand. Although the ratio of nurses to population is expected to be somewhat higher in 1960 than in 1952, a severe shortage still is anticipated for that year. Estimates of authorities in the nursing field place the expected deficit in 1960 at more than 50,000.

Dentists

Until fairly recent years the nation has probably had as many dentists as could be used effectively, not because the need for dental services has been met adequately but because the demand for service has been relatively small. Yet studies have shown that dental care is one of the foremost health needs of the population. Less than 40 per cent of the American people, it has been estimated, receive any dental care during the course of a year.[108] Among school children, the rate of carious teeth is high; among older persons, "the prevalence of dental disease and defects is well-nigh universal."

In recent years, particularly since World War II, increased emphasis has been placed on dental health and its relation to general health. The spread of dental health education programs has helped create a greater demand for dental services. Consequently, a shortage of dentists is now recognized and the supply is expected to fall even further behind needs in the future.

By 1950 more than 82,500 dentists were in active practice in the United States — one for approximately every 1,800 persons. An additional 17,000 would be needed by 1960 to bring the regions of the country with the lowest dentist-population ratios up to this national average.[109] If all regions were raised to the 1950 ratios in New England and the Central Atlantic states, the ad-

---

105. The experience of group practice organizations in providing comprehensive medical care was used as the basis for estimating the number of physicians needed for this purpose.

106. *Ibid.*, pp. 18–19.

107. U.S. Public Health Service, press release FSA–E60, August 27, 1952.

108. *Building America's Health*, Vol. I, p. 60. The Health Information Foundation study, covering the year July 1952 through June 1953, found that only 34 per cent of the population received dental service during that twelve-month period. This study, like previous ones, found striking differences among income groups in the proportion of persons who visit a dentist during a year. In families with annual incomes of less than $2,000, 17 per cent sought service, while among families with incomes of $7,500 and over, 56 per cent received care. For other income groups the proportions of persons seeing a dentist during the year were as follows: $2,000–$3,499, 23 per cent; $3,500–$4,999, 33 per cent; $5,000–$7,499, 43 per cent. *National Family Survey of Medical Costs and Voluntary Health Insurance*, Preliminary Report, Table 7, p. 62.

109. *Ibid.*, p. 16.

TABLE 156. ESTIMATED NEEDS AND DEMAND FOR CIVILIAN HEALTH AND
MEDICAL CARE, 1950 AND 1960
(*Millions at 1950 Prices*)

Expenditure Group	1950		1960	
	Demand	*Needs*	*Demand*	*Needs*
Total	$12,315[a]	$18,300	$15,690	$22,900
Consumer expenditures	8,441	12,500	10,740	16,000
Personnel	3,916	—	4,850	—
Drugs and appliances	1,927	—	2,450	—
Hospitalization	1,963	—	2,420	—
Insurance—accident, health and pre-				
payment	635	—	1,020	—
Hospital facilities	840	1,300	1,200	1,800
Private	344	—	600	—
Public	496	—	600	—
Other	3,034	4,500	3,750	5,100
Government noncapital expenditures	2,404	—	2,750	—
Industrial expenditures	630	—	1,000	—

Sources: Table 148, Appendices 4–7 and 4–8, and discussion in text.

a. Total does not agree with total shown in Table 148, which includes philanthropic expenditures.

ditional number needed in 1960 would be twice as large — more than 34,000. These estimates, however, must be considered a minimum. To provide comprehensive care for current dental needs of the civilian population, without any attack on the great backlog of dental disease and defects, would require far more dentists than these estimates indicate.

Successful demonstrations in the control of dental disease and decay, such as the water fluoridation program, will unquestionably result in an eventual reduction in the need for dental services. So great is the current need, however, that such demonstrations would probably have little effect on the number of dentists required in the foreseeable future.

PROBABLE AND NEEDED EXPENDITURES

Although the costs of health and medical care have increased over the years, consumer expenditures for such services have represented a fairly steady share of total consumption expenditures — from 3 to 5 per cent. If the present spending pattern continues, consumers will spend about $11 billion (at 1950 prices) for health and medical services in 1960. However, there is some indication that the share of these services in the con-

sumer budget is growing slightly and may continue to do so, especially in view of the aging of the population. In that case consumer medical care outlays might run as high as $15 billion in 1960.

There is little basis for accurately estimating 1960 medical care expenditures by government — federal, state or local. A plausible assumption appears to be that present governmental expenditures, adjusted for population growth, will be maintained, although there may be some shifts in the source of governmental funds. This assumption implies governmental noncapital expenditures in 1960 of about $2.8 billion at 1950 prices. Expenditures for health and medical care by industry are expected to increase more substantially — to about $1 billion — because of the increasing awareness of the value of in-plant preventive health services by both management and employees and the growth of the labor force. On the basis of past relationships to total capital expenditures, outlays for hospital construction in 1960 are expected to increase to $1.2 billion at 1950 prices. Public expenditures for hospital facilities exceeded private in 1950, but it appears likely that private expenditures will rise more rapidly than public; an equal distribution is assumed for 1960. (See Table 156.)

Needs vs. Demand

So far as is known, no attempt has been made to ascertain the type, amount and cost of medical and health services required to provide adequate care on a national scale since the work of Drs. Lee and Jones and of Dr. Bradbury in the 1930s.[110] According to the Lee-Jones report, "adequate medical care . . . means a sufficient quantity of good medical care to supply the needs of the people according to the standards of good current practice." How such standards and needs may have changed in the past twenty years is difficult to determine. Little is known, for example, about the extent to which new techniques of treatment may have shortened the duration of certain cases. The development of psychosomatic medicine, the extension of chemotherapy, and the expansion of home care programs are but a few of the important factors that may have reduced the cost of adequate care. These, of course, may be partly offset by other factors, such as the aging of the population.

However, without making any allowance for the possible effects of such developments, it can be estimated very roughly that the cost of health and medical services needed by the civilian population in 1950 may have been in the neighborhood of $26 billion. This estimate assumes no changes in methods of providing and paying for services. Allowing for population increase only, the corresponding estimate for 1960 would approximate $30 billion in terms of 1950 dollars.[111]

Although it would appear from these estimates that the 1950 civilian population was spending approximately one third of the amount needed to secure adequate medical care, such an assumption should be made with caution and properly qualified, since the effects of new medical techniques and scientific developments on the costs of needed medical care are unknown. Moreover, in contrast to current expenditures, which apply only to persons who seek and pay for medical service, the estimate of dollar amounts needed for adequate medical care applies to all persons in the civilian population whether or not they would seek such care; it assumes that each person receives all needed services including periodic medical and dental examinations. (See Table 156.)

Adequate medical care might, however, be purchased at a substantially lower cost through widespread use of prepayment medical care plans providing service through group practice. One of the most comprehensive prepaid group plans currently in effect is the Labor Health Institute, which on June 30, 1952, covered about 13,700 union members and their families in St. Louis. The average annual cost for medical, dental and hospital benefits in 1951–1952 was about $50 per person eligible for care.[112]

Taking this figure as a minimum standard and making allowance for items not included in the prepayment plan, the average family would require about $190 worth of medical care per year.[113] According to the Health Information Foundation, about two thirds of all families surveyed spent less than this amount during 1952–1953. (See Appendix 10–4.) If medical outlays for these families were raised to $190 a year and if families spending more than that amount were assumed to continue at their established spending levels, average outlays for medical care among the surveyed families would have been increased by about 48 per cent.

If this increase of 48 per cent in expenditures is assumed to yield an outlay needed in all years to bring up to standard all families below the minimum standard, the resulting total cost would be $12.5 billion for 1950 and $16 billion (at 1950 prices) for 1960 (Table 156).

Needed expenditures for hospital facilities —

110. Roger I. Lee and Lewis Webster Jones, *The Fundamentals of Good Medical Care*, Publication No. 22, Committee on the Costs of Medical Care, University of Chicago Press, Chicago, 1933; Samuel Bradbury, *The Cost of Adequate Medical Care*, University of Chicago Press, Chicago, 1937.

111. The estimates of needed consumer expenditures are based on such assumptions as the civilian purchase, on a fee-for-service basis, of adequate medical care as defined in the Lee-Jones report and priced by Dr. Bradbury, with the costs converted to 1950 prices by means of the Dickinson index of medical costs. The consumer expenditure estimates also include allowances for annual maintenance dental care and drugs and medicines, not included in the Lee-Jones total.

112. Margaret C. Klem and Margaret F. McKiever, *Management and Union Health and Medical Programs*, U.S. Department of Health, Education and Welfare, June 1953, p. 182.

113. Family as used here includes families of one or more persons. The average family so defined contained 3.1 individuals in the period 1950–1952. (See *Current Population Reports: Population Characteristics*, U.S. Bureau of the Census, Series P–20, No. 33, Feb. 12, 1951, No. 38, April 29, 1952 and No. 44, September 6, 1953.) The additional allowance of $35 per family per year covers such items as additional days of hospital service beyond that provided in the contract, drugs and medicines, eyeglasses, appliances, care for drug addiction and alcoholism beyond the period allowed for diagnosis, private-duty nursing care, and dental plates and other materials used in dentistry.

private and public — are estimated at $1.3 billion in 1950 and $1.8 billion in 1960.[114] These amounts are about $500 million above actual 1950 and $600 million above probable 1960 outlays. Needed government noncapital and needed industrial expenditures for medical care are estimated at $4.5 billion for 1950 and $5.1 billion for 1960, roughly $1.4 billion above actual and projected outlays.

114. These estimates were derived from those prepared for public hospital facilities in Chapter 18.

The estimate for hospital construction assumes the completion of needed beds of all types — general, mental, tuberculosis and chronic disease — spread over the next fifteen years, with an adequate annual replacement of obsolete beds. Other assumptions include the provision of adequate public health services in all areas of the country, an expansion of health programs in industry, and more nearly adequate coverage and services in workmen's compensation cases.

## CHAPTER II

RECREATION

THE PURSUIT OF PLEASURE was frowned on by our forefathers. Idleness for them was indeed the thief of time — time needed to produce the necessities of life. Today, man's survival no longer depends on endless toil. Machines, while turning out untold commodities and appliances for his comfort and convenience, have also yielded him leisure hours undreamed of even fifty years ago.

American workers today put in an average of forty hours a week on the job. The five-day week is now almost universal. Vacations with pay are an established custom. Old-age insurance and pension plans permit many of the aged to retire.

The way these leisure hours are spent is of major social and economic concern. Recreation is recognized as necessary to individual and community well-being. Supplying the means to it is the job of hosts of federal, state and local officials, businessmen, promotion men, actors, musicians, artists, thousands of men, women, boys and girls who work in public and private places of amusement. Recreation is big business; it is an important item in the budget — both public and private.

SCOPE AND ECONOMIC IMPORTANCE

By its very nature, however, interwoven as it is in the daily lives of the people, recreation is difficult to define and harder still to measure. No rigid line can be drawn between work and play. What means drudgery to one as a means of livelihood may bring relaxation to another as a form of recreation. One need only remember the untold miles hiked for the exercise, the thousands of trees felled for the fun of it, the millions of fish caught for the pleasure of telling about the ones that got away.

Men and women have probably always spent the greater part of their leisure time in visiting

and entertaining friends, in storytelling and love-making, in walking and talking, or just plain loafing. But these simple pleasures are hidden in the obscurity of private lives and have no direct impact in the market place. Likewise hidden in obscurity are such illicit activities as dope peddling, prostitution, and many forms of gambling, which though unquestionably of no little economic importance defy accurate measurement.

We must, therefore, limit our discussion to leisure-time activities measurable in terms of their use of or consumption of goods and services. Even this limitation leaves the problem of defining the boundaries between recreation and various overlapping fields of human wants. The consumption of food and liquor, for example, has recreational as well as nutritional values, if one can accept the ancient advice to "eat, drink and be merry." Counting expenditures for such items as liquor, soft drinks, tobacco, candy and gum as part of the cost of recreation might easily be justified. For the purposes of this survey, however, it appears more reasonable to consider as a single group all those commodities that, like food, are taken to "sustain the inner man." (See Chapter 5.)

Purchase of certain articles of attire such as bathing suits and sports shoes might also properly be considered as recreational expenditures. In this survey, however, all purchases of clothing and related articles are grouped in a separate field of consumer expenditures. (See Chapter 6.)

It is also clear that a substantial share of what consumers pay for automobile upkeep and other forms of transportation is spent for recreational purposes. For this reason, some space is devoted in this chapter to recreational travel and transportation, although all consumer transportation is considered in this survey as another single field of consumer expenditures. (See Chapter 9.)

Obviously, recreation and education also overlap a good deal, not only in extracurricular activities, but increasingly in recent years within the classroom itself. Some consumer expendi-

By J. FREDERIC DEWHURST AND FRANCES KLAFTER, Research Associate of this study. Opinions and judgments expressed in this chapter are those of the authors and should not be attributed to the organization with which they are associated.

tures for recreational activities of educational institutions, such as college football admissions, are considered in this chapter as expenditures for recreation, but the major portion of such expenditures are counted as part of the cost of education. Some overlapping also exists between the field of recreation and some of the activities of religious and welfare organizations, and also to some extent perhaps between recreation and the field of health and personal care. Here again it is impossible to make wholly logical and consistent distinctions.

The American public in its quest for activities to fill its leisure time creates markets for goods and services, jobs for hundreds of thousands of citizens. Its patronage of public and private places of amusement supports large-scale investments, produces income and revenue for federal, state and local governments.

Amount Spent for Recreation

Because of difficulties and disagreements in defining the field and the great fluctuation in expenditures of this sort from prosperity to depression, estimates of the amount spent for recreation annually vary widely.[1]

The estimate of the Department of Commerce, upon which this chapter is based, sets total consumption expenditures for strictly recreational goods and services at $10.2 billion in 1950 and $10.5 billion in 1952. This is more than five times the depression total of $1.9 billion in 1933 and nearly twice as much as the $5.4 billion spent in 1945. Government expenditures for recreation added another $403 million in 1950, while expenditures of semipublic and private organizations raised the total still further. Thus, recreational activities account for close to $11 billion of expenditures, even when the field is narrowly defined. (See Table 157 and Table 163, page 371.)

As pointed out above, this total would be greatly increased by adding many other kinds of expenditures that might properly be included but

TABLE 157. CONSUMPTION EXPENDITURES FOR RECREATION, 1909–1952

| Year | Amount | | Per Cent of:[b] | |
	Current Dollars	1950 Dollars[a]	National Consumption Income	Total Expenditures
	(Millions)			
1909	$ 859	$ 2,982	3.0	3.0
1914	997	3,185	2.9	3.0
1919	2,157	4,093	3.2	3.6
1921	2,068	3,293	4.0	3.7
1923	2,624	4,323	3.8	3.9
1925	2,840	4,618	3.9	4.0
1927	3,141	5,058	4.1	4.2
1929	3,836	6,089	4.4	4.8
1931	2,873	4,589	4.9	4.6
1933	1,868	3,155	4.7	4.0
1935	2,254	3,820	4.0	4.0
1937	2,933	4,792	4.0	4.4
1939	2,994	4,745	4.1	4.4
1940	3,269	5,053	4.0	4.5
1941	3,720	5,602	3.6	4.5
1942	4,154	6,020	3.0	4.6
1943	4,180	5,664	2.5	4.1
1944	4,761	6,027	2.6	4.3
1945	5,423	6,597	3.0	4.4
1946	7,907	9,302	4.4	5.4
1947	8,651	9,475	4.4	5.2
1948	8,917	9,327	4.0	5.0
1949	9,154	9,237	4.2	5.1
1950	10,211	10,211	4.2	5.2
1951	10,180	9,893	3.7	4.9
1952	10,489	9,961	3.6	4.8

Sources: Appendices 4–2, 4–4 and 4–5; U.S. Bureau of Labor Statistics: *Consumers' Prices in the United States, 1942–1948,* Bulletin No. 966, 1949, p. 76; *Handbook of Labor Statistics,* 1950 edition, Bulletin No. 1016, 1951, p. 100; "Consumers' Price Index for Moderate-Income Families, Large Cities Combined," 1949, 1950, 1951 and 1952.

a. For 1909, carried back from 1914 by use of the Snyder-Tucker general price index as published in *Historical Statistics of the United States, 1789–1945,* U.S. Bureau of the Census, 1949, p. 231; for 1914–1933, carried back from 1935 by use of the Bureau of Labor Statistics "miscellaneous" price index; for 1935–1952, based on the BLS index for "recreation."

b. Based on income and expenditures in current dollars.

are treated separately in this report. Vacation travel expenditures in 1950 have been conservatively estimated at $12 billion,[2] while consumers

1. Harold D. Meyer and Charles K. Brightbill, in *Community Recreation, A Guide to Its Organization and Administration* (Heath, Boston, 1948, p. 36), say: "There is no way of accurately estimating how much is spent each year for recreation in America. Estimates depend upon what items are included. They vary from $8 billion to $20 billion. An excellent case can be made for the higher figure. If the purchase of books, radios, and alcoholic beverages is included the figures are astronomical."

2. Estimates varied from $12 billion (*Business Bulletin,* Cleveland Trust Company, May 15, 1950) to $14.9 billion for tourist travel within the United States alone with an additional $945 million for all foreign travel by United States citizens, both for business and pleasure (National Association of Travel Organizations, Washington). The National Association of Travel Organizations estimated

spent more than $8.1 billion for liquor and $4.4 billion for tobacco in that year. (See Appendix 4-4.)

Consumer spending for sports clothes, candy, soft drinks and chewing gum probably accounts for as much as $5 billion more. Hence an estimate of $40 billion for total expenditures for recreation could easily be supported. This is nearly five times what consumers spend for medical care and twice the amount paid for rent, including the rental value of owner-occupied dwellings. Even this total leaves out of account, however, the recreational activities of educational and religious organizations, and at the other extreme, such illicit activities as dope peddling and prostitution and the net cost of illegal betting and gambling.[3]

Recreational Goods and Services

Even the more restricted sense in which the field is considered here covers a wide variety of services, products and organized community activities for which consumers and governments spent a total of nearly $11 billion in 1950. Government expenditures go largely for the operation, maintenance and expansion of parks, playgrounds and other public recreational facilities and services. Consumers spend money to participate in golf and tennis, swimming, ice and roller skating, billiards, bowling and other indoor and outdoor sports. They pay admissions to football and baseball games, horse races, hockey and other spectator sports, to motion-picture and other theaters, amusement parks, circuses, etc. They pay dues and fees to social clubs and organizations.

Goods purchased for recreational purposes include television sets; radios, phonographs and other musical instruments; toys and games; supplies and equipment for sports and hobbies; and a considerable proportion of books, magazines and newspapers. Supplying the recreational needs of the American people thus involves a

vast variety of individual products and a multitude of personal and institutional services, alike only in that they are all competing for the consumer's time and money. Some idea of the wide range and importance of the industries and mercantile and service trades catering to the consumer's varied recreational requirements can be obtained from Table 158. These statistics provide no precise measure, but only a general indication, of the economic importance of recreation.

Jobs and Wages

Some of the manufacturing industries and retail and wholesale trades listed in the table — notably newspapers, periodicals and books — obviously cannot be regarded as catering exclusively to recreational needs. On the other hand, some industries and trades not included partially contribute to meeting such needs. On the whole it is reasonable to assume that in 1947 more than 600,000 workers were engaged in the manufacture and distribution of recreational products. In addition, the 1948 Census of Business showed more than 330,000 persons employed in commercial amusement establishments, which in that year numbered over 50,000, reported receipts of $2.7 billion, and paid over $581 million in salaries and wages. If government employees are added, it is probable that about a million workers gain their livelihood from the field of recreation. And this does not include operators of motels and roadside filling stations and others who profit from tourist travel.

Taxes and Revenues

Major federal and state revenues from recreational goods and services, and revenues from the largest cities (see Table 159, footnote a), totaled $822 million in 1950 and $915 million in 1952. Federal admissions taxes to theaters, concerts, etc., which amounted to more than $371 million in 1950 but had declined to $331 million by 1952, were the largest single source of revenue. (Revenues from this source were considerably reduced after April 1, 1954 by the Excise Tax Reduction Act of 1954, which lowered taxes on admissions to various places of amusement.) Next came the almost $103 million in 1950 and $138 million in 1952 in gross receipts taxes on pari mutuels collected by the states,

---

that by 1952 domestic tourist travel expenditures had risen to $16.6 billion. Estimated expenditures for foreign travel in that year were $1.2 billion.

3. About 50 million adults and "quite a number of minors" bet a total of close to $30 billion a year, according to the July 19, 1950, issue of *Life*. The net cost would of course be only a small fraction of this total, as most of what one bettor loses another wins. The same article estimates that 200,000 slot machines in the United States yield an average profit of $100 a week. This would mean a net cost for this form of gambling of about $1 billion yearly.

TABLE 158. RECREATION INDUSTRIES, 1947, AND TRADES AND BUSINESSES, 1948 [a]

Industry, Trade or Business	Number of Establishments	Number of Wage Earners [b]	Total Wages	Value of Products Shipped, Sales
				(Thousands)
Manufacturing (1947)				
Ammunition	8	6,748	$ 17,297	$ 77,660
Bicycles, motorcycles and parts	76	13,659	37,732	163,670
Boat building and repairing	809	17,315	43,535	117,991
Books, periodicals and newspapers	11,920	158,264	495,385	3,656,835 [c]
Firearms	34	9,249	25,876	57,067
Fireworks	73	2,982	5,706	15,219
Games, toys, dolls and children's vehicles	1,334	40,833	84,565	337,556
Motion pictures (not including projection in theaters)	277	25,977 [d]	243,165	460,143 [e]
Musical instruments — pianos, organs and parts	91	10,229	26,780	55,086 [f]
Musical instruments — other	169	4,585	11,418	31,366
Photographic apparatus and materials	366	36,273	101,765	440,134
Radios, tubes, phonographs and records	1,019	173,295	393,844	234,702 [g]
Sporting and athletic goods	864	26,395	53,785	202,462
Wholesale trade (1948)				
Amusement, sporting goods	2,799	23,999	76,915	1,138,457
Books, periodicals, newspapers	1,921	27,920	68,399	646,806
Radios, television sets	1,231	12,594	42,596	513,266
Retail trade (1948)				
Bicycle and motorcycle dealers	2,962	3,668	7,281	89,085
Boat dealers	1,037	2,211	6,126	66,265
Book stores, news dealers, newsstands	10,080	40,022	65,753	490,241
Camera, photographic supply stores	3,030	9,594	22,231	202,099
Music stores	6,120	19,249	45,380	337,338
Radio stores	7,231	14,399	33,286	384,057
Sporting goods stores	6,859	12,693	28,766	309,632
Service establishments (1948)				
Bicycle repair shops	1,283	365	549	7,390
Coin-operated machines, rental and repair	1,302	3,623	10,061	50,500
Musical instrument repair shops	789	598	1,188	5,534
Photographic and photo finishing	13,252	34,033	70,012	235,957
Radio repair shops	12,558	10,262	20,791	100,679
Taxidermists	211	191	353	1,570
Amusement places (1948)				
Amusement devices	1,604	1,096	4,703	24,400
Amusement parks	368	2,708	12,237	42,048
Bands, orchestras and entertainers	2,026	10,335	17,066	28,532
Bathing beaches (not including municipal)	261	200	1,014	4,078
Bicycle rentals	147	15	35	426
Billiard and pool parlors	9,661	9,766	12,413	65,927
Boat and canoe rentals	1,587	441	1,000	6,981
Bowling alleys	4,505	66,777	51,902	138,198
Clubs — baseball (professional)	357	3,066	28,394	77,183
Clubs — football (professional)	21	1,047	5,464	12,000
Coin-operated amusement device services	2,447	7,265	20,232	99,191
Dance halls, studios and schools	1,074	8,597	9,879	37,205
Golf courses	325	900	2,501	8,368
Race track operation — automobile	112	316	817	8,615

(Continued on page 350)

TABLE 158 (continued)

Industry, Trade or Business	Number of Establishments	Number of Wage Earners [b]	Total Wages	Value of Products Shipped, Sales
				(Thousands)
Amusement places (continued)				
Race track operation — dog	15	325	$ 3,523	$ 17,046
Race track operation — horse	71	6,974	31,198	162,244
Riding academies	709	698	1,145	5,197
Shooting galleries	181	139	339	1,586
Skating rinks (ice)	42	741	1,029	3,444
Skating rinks (roller)	1,382	4,042	4,254	18,475
Sports operators, not elsewhere classified	977	830	1,934	8,229
Stadiums, athletic fields, etc.	211	4,772	8,945	41,614
Swimming pools (not including municipal)	499	444	1,838	7,338
Theaters, motion pictures	18,631	187,031	302,511	1,614,282
Theaters and theatrical producers	1,426	13,288	56,803	144,283
Other amusements	1,708	10,118	28,858	96,107

Sources: Manufacturing industries, 1947 Census of Manufactures; trades and businesses, 1948 Census of Business.

a. Consumer expenditure estimates shown in Appendix 4–4 will not necessarily agree with sales data in this table, since results of the 1948 Census of Business had not been incorporated into the Commerce Department's consumer expenditure estimates shown in Appendix 4–4.

b. For manufacturing, average for the year; for all other trades and businesses, week ended November 15, 1948.

c. Value of products (receipts).

d. For pay period ending nearest October 15.

e. Cost of work done during year as index of production.

f. For pianos only. Others omitted because of duplication.

g. Tubes and records only. Others omitted because of duplication.

---

which also took in over $58 million in hunting and fishing licenses in 1950 and about $70 million in 1952. (See Table 159.)

Local revenues for the most part consist of fees for public recreational services to help defray the costs of operation and maintenance. More and more cities, however, are levying local admissions taxes on theaters and other amusements. At least 182 cities with populations of over 10,000 had adopted such taxes by 1950.

Tourist Trade

"Tourist trade," including vacation and holiday expenditures for travel, for food, drink and lodging and for souvenirs and incidental purchases, is of vast economic importance. Roadside stands, motels, souvenir and handicraft shops entirely dependent on vacation travelers, dot the nation. The tourist trade is particularly important in New England and the Rocky Mountain areas. Recreation produces about 22 per cent of the annual income of the State of New Hamp-

shire and, ranking next to manufacturing, brings in four times the revenue derived from agriculture.[4] More than half the states rate the tourist trade one of their three largest sources of income. New Jersey and New Mexico rank travel first.[5] Two thirds of Santa Fe's 30,000 residents draw their livelihood directly or indirectly from tourists' expenditures.[6]

GROWTH AND CHANGE [7]

Changes in the use of leisure time have accompanied basic alterations in our social and eco-

---

4. Recreation — A National Economic Asset, Division of Recreation, Office of Community War Services, Federal Security Agency, 1945, p. 6.

5. Americans on the Highway: A Report on Habits and Patterns in Vacation Travel, American Automobile Association, 1953.

6. Wall Street Journal, September 10, 1951.

7. Sources used in this section include: Foster Rhea Dulles, America Learns to Play, Appleton-Century, New York, 1940; Martin H. and Esther S. Neumeyer, Leisure and Recreation, Barnes, New York, 1949, Chapters 2 and 3; Meyer and Brightbill, op. cit., Chapter 1.

TABLE 159. GOVERNMENTAL REVENUE FROM RECREATION, FISCAL YEARS ENDED
JUNE 30, 1950 AND 1952

Type of Revenue, Tax Source	Amount Collected	
	1950	1952
	(Thousands)	
Total: federal, state, largest cities [a]	$821,612	$914,639
Federal	610,708	649,563
Internal Revenue collections:		
Playing cards	10,546	7,353
Radio sets, phonographs, components, etc.	42,085	118,244 [b]
Phonograph records	5,769	6,880
Musical instruments	8,865	9,412
Photographic apparatus	39,931	33,766
Sporting goods	18,969	13,644
Firearms, shells and cartridges	9,351	10,679
Pistols and revolvers	481	1,172
Fishing rods, creels, etc.	2,055 [c]	2,857
Admissions to theaters, concerts, etc.	371,244	330,817
Admissions to cabarets, roof gardens, etc.	41,453	45,489
Club dues and initiation fees	28,740	33,592
Bowling alleys, pool tables, etc.	3,608	3,597
Coin-operated devices	20,174	18,823
Wagering — occupational	—	973
Wagering — excise	—	4,372
Operation of national parks and recreational areas	3,528	3,557
Migratory waterfowl hunting stamp	3,909	4,336
State	186,915	236,474
Sales and gross receipts taxes:		
Pari mutuels	102,734	138,253
Admissions and amusements	14,228	13,944
License and privilege taxes:		
Hunting and fishing	58,346	69,891
Amusements	4,961	5,037
Operation of state parks	6,646	9,349
Largest cities [a]	23,989	28,602
Charges for current services:		
Golf	3,761	
Auditoriums and stadiums	4,329	} 20,629 [d]
Other	6,829	
Sales and gross receipts taxes:		
Admissions and amusements	9,070	7,973

Sources: Internal Revenue collections — *Statistical Abstract of the United States, 1951*, U.S. Bureau of the Census, p. 314, and the Accounts and Collections Unit, Internal Revenue Bureau; other federal figures from Information Service and National Park Service, U.S. Department of the Interior. State figures — *Compendium of State Government Finances in 1950*, U.S. Bureau of the Census, 1951, pp. 11, 12; *Compendium of State Government Finances in 1952*, 1953, pp. 12, 13; *State Park Statistics in 1950*, National Park Service, 1951, p. 7; and *State Park Statistics — 1952*, August 1953, p. 2. Local figures — *Large-City Finances in 1950*, U.S. Bureau of the Census, October 1951, pp. 12, 16; and *Compendium of City Government Finances in 1952*, 1953, pp. 38 and 41.

a. Covers 39 largest cities in 1940 and all cities of 250,000 or more population (41) in 1950.
b. Includes television sets and components.
c. Figure is for year ending June 30, 1951; June 30, 1950 not available.
d. Detailed breakdown shown for 1950 is not available for 1952.

nomic structure. Our transformation from a predominantly agrarian to a highly industrialized urban society brought about new opportunities for recreation and new attitudes toward it.

Quilting Bees and Housewarmings

The rules the early American settlers lived by were hard: "early to bed and early to rise" left little time for weekday leisure, and Sundays were devoted to worship. Social life in this stern atmosphere was largely confined to the merry-making at collective work-gatherings — quilting and corn-husking bees, barn-raising parties, hunting and fishing trips, and so on.

Many of the social patterns of colonial days were preserved as the frontier moved west, but in the wide-open spaces the rare social gatherings were much more lively and unrestrained. Weddings and housewarmings provided opportunities for hilarious festivities to break the loneliness of wilderness and prairie. Religious revivals and camp meetings were important recreational as well as religious events. To the sedate traditions of the family settlers were added the dangerous and daring diversions of the cowboys and prospectors. Combined, they made up social life in the "wild West."

With the growth of towns, new recreational patterns developed, many of which survive today in small towns and to some extent in suburban neighborhoods: neighborly visiting, Sunday school picnics, church suppers and lodge nights, Chautauquas, popular sports, fairs and bazaars, horse races, livestock and agricultural exhibits. This informal, easygoing social life was quite distinct from that typical of the developing industrial, urban society.

Industrialization and Urbanization

Recreation was not considered of great importance in our early nineteenth-century cities. Puritan repression, which had somewhat relaxed its grip during the eighteenth century, attempted to inculcate in the working man of the nineteenth century the necessity of elevating his soul and improving his mind.

But neither church nor lecture hall provided the needed relaxation from the long, arduous working day. Despite the strenuous efforts of the reformers, the saloon, the beer garden, the theater and horse races flourished in urban com-

munities. As the century advanced, the theater became the center of entertainment for all classes. Melodrama, burlesque, comedy, vaudeville and serious drama played to packed audiences. By the middle of the century, entertainment had already become big business. Barnum with his showmanship had captured the entertainment world.

Urban dwellers began to take an active interest in sports. Gymnasiums were opened and, despite the Victorian emphasis on feminine delicacy and decorum, women as well as men began to participate in both indoor and outdoor sports. Spectator sports also became popular, especially baseball, which after the Civil War emerged as a national sport. Trolleys, first horse-drawn and later electric, made it possible for city people to travel to near-by beaches.

The long work week was continuously shortened until the end of the 1920s brought the 48-hour week and widespread adoption of the summer vacation. The shortening of the work week since the turn of the century had more than doubled the amount of leisure time. By the second decade of the century, both church and saloon were losing ground to Sunday golf and baseball, to the movies and the automobile. Recreation was no longer regarded as a sinful waste of time.

THE PUBLIC RECREATION MOVEMENT [8]

Little attempt was made to provide recreational opportunities through public channels until the latter part of the nineteenth century. Commercial enterprises had long since begun offering every kind of diversion that promotional ingenuity could devise. Commercial recreation, because of its cost, excluded large parts of the population and failed to supply "the social contacts, cultural experiences and creative activities which have become especially necessary to supplement the limited opportunities for mental and spiritual growth that the daily work of many people now offers." [9] By and large, early efforts

---

8. For more detailed accounts of the development of public recreation see: *Recreation and Park Yearbook, Mid-century Edition, A Review of Local and County Recreation and Park Developments, 1900–1950*, National Recreation Association, New York, 1951; George D. Butler, *Introduction to Community Recreation*, McGraw-Hill, New York, 1949, Chapter 5; Neumeyer, *op. cit.*, pp. 63–77; Meyer and Brightbill, *op. cit.*, Chapter 1.

9. C. Gilbert Wrenn and D. L. Harley, *Time on Their Hands*, American Council on Education, Washington, 1941, p. 57.

in the field of public recreation were directed toward furnishing play facilities for children, particularly the children of the slums. Slower in developing was the concept of public recreation for all.

World War I

The first widespread interest in community recreation for adults came with World War I, when the War Camp Community Service, under the leadership of the Playground and Recreation Association (now the National Recreation Association), organized recreational programs in communities near military installations and in industrial centers.[10]

During the prosperous 1920s all types of recreation expanded rapidly. Municipal park acreage grew faster than in any other ten-year period. Marked expansion in the number and variety of facilities also characterized the decade.[11] The calling of the National Conference of Outdoor Recreation by President Coolidge in 1924 exemplified the recognition of the importance of recreation in the national life.

The Depression

The depression of the 1930s brought another great expansion of public recreation. Under the sponsorship of the relief programs of the federal government, thousands of recreation buildings, new parks, athletic fields, swimming pools, tennis courts, golf courses, ski trails, etc., were built.[12] In the more than 10,000 communities reached by WPA-sponsored recreation programs, the seeds were planted for future town and city systems, many of which have since been established.[13]

World War II

Because of its importance in maintaining morale, organized community recreation received marked attention during World War II. Varied leisure-time programs were inaugurated in about 2,500 war-swollen industrial centers and communities adjacent to military establishments. These activities were coordinated by the Recreation Division, Office of Community War Services, Federal Security Agency. Each of the armed services set up its own recreation program, supplemented by programs of private agencies, such as the Red Cross and the United Service Organizations. To meet the pressing needs of the overcrowded industrial communities, federal funds were allocated for building and maintaining recreational facilities.[14]

Postwar Development

Thus, American communities had at their disposal at the close of World War II the results of twenty-five years of intensive development in public recreation. Each year since the end of the war has seen a steady growth in facilities, trained leadership and public participation.[15]

State and National Services and Facilities

In addition to local governments, the state and federal governments maintain extensive public recreation services and facilities. State and national parks and forests today cover more than 200 million acres. They had a few hundred thousand visits in 1910, 210 million in 1952. (See Table 160.)

Besides maintaining park areas, the federal government carries on such services as the conservation of fish and wild life areas, the maintenance of museums and historic sites and monuments, the provision of recreational facilities in public housing projects. Federal agencies sharing in these and related services include: the Corps of Engineers of the Department of the Army; various bureaus of the Department of the Interior, the Department of Agriculture, the Federal Security Agency and the Federal Works Agency; the National Capital Parks and Planning Commission; and the Tennessee Valley Authority. The Federal Inter-Agency Committee on Recreation coordinates their activities.[16]

In the past, the states largely confined their recreational services to the maintenance of state parks. In the postwar years, however, state governments have assumed increasing responsibility

---

10. Neumeyer, *op. cit.*, p. 72.
11. Butler, *op. cit.*, pp. 69 and 70.
12. Meyer and Brightbill, *op. cit.*, pp. 14 and 16.
13. G. Ott Romney, *Off-the-Job-Living*, Barnes, New York, 1945, p. 72.

14. R. K. McNickle, "Recreation for Millions," *Editorial Research Reports*, July 13, 1949, p. 459.
15. For detailed figures, see yearbooks issued biennially by the National Recreation Association.
16. *The Role of the Federal Government in the Field of Public Recreation*, Federal Inter-Agency Committee on Recreation, June 1949.

TABLE 160. VISITORS AND ACREAGE, NATIONAL PARKS [a]
AND FORESTS AND STATE PARKS, 1910–1952

(*Thousands*)

Year and Type of Area	Visitors	Total Acreage
1910		
National parks	199	[b]
National forests	[b]	168,029 [e]
State parks	[b]	[b]
1920		
National parks	1,058	8,440
National forests	4,660 [d, e]	156,032 [e]
State parks	[b]	2,613 [f]
1930		
National parks	3,247	10,340
National forests	6,911 [e]	160,091 [e]
State parks	[b]	[b]
1940		
National parks	16,755	21,551
National forests	16,163 [e]	174,770 [e]
State parks [g]	93,393 [h]	4,261 [h]
1950		
National parks	32,782	21,855
National forests	27,368 [e]	179,685 [e]
State parks [g]	105,582	4,657
1952		
National parks	41,517	21,820
National forests	33,007 [e]	180,603 [e]
State parks [g]	135,762	4,928

Sources: National parks: visitors — Information Division, National Park Service, U.S. Department of the Interior; acreage — Lands Division. National forests: visitors — Division of Recreation and Lands, U.S. Forest Service, U.S. Department of Agriculture; acreage — Division of Land Acquisition. State park acreage for 1925, *State Parks and Recreational Uses of State Forests in the United States*, National Conference on State Parks, Washington, 1926, p. 17; 1941 data, *State Parks — 1941*, National Park Service, U.S. Department of the Interior, October 1943, Parts I and II; 1950, acreage, *State Parks, Areas, Acreages, and Accommodations*, December 31, 1950, and visitors, *State Park Statistics — 1950*, July 1951, both prepared by Recreation Planning Division, National Park Service; 1952, *State Park Statistics — 1952*, August 1953.

a. Acreage figures are for areas within the boundaries of national parks, monuments and historical areas; visitor figures are for all areas administered by the National Park Service, some of which are outside national parks. Visitor figures are for years ending September 30.

b. Not available.

c. Acreage for 1910 includes forest lands owned by the government but not included in boundaries of national forests. Acreage shown for subsequent years includes only total within the national forest boundaries.

d. 1924; 1920 not available.

e. Visitors to national forests include picnickers, campers, hotel and resort guests and summer residents; others using forest roads are excluded as total count includes people on business as well as tourists. Figures are for the calendar year.

in guiding local communities in the development of recreation programs.[17]

TECHNOLOGICAL DEVELOPMENTS

Just as technological developments have greatly increased the hours of leisure, the products of technology have had far-reaching effects on the use of that time. Though the greatest advances belong to the twentieth century, the fruits of science and invention were already enriching the recreational life of the nineteenth century.

The steamboat and the railroad, and toward the end of the century the electric trolley, made possible excursions and visits to friends and relatives. Bicycling was a popular outdoor sport for young and old, and in its heyday new and improved models were constantly appearing. In the 1870s, "talking machines" were placed on the market. Peep shows and "living pictures" attracted crowds to the penny arcades. The first "horseless carriages" were thrilling the populace with their daring speed in the late 1890s. Photography was becoming a popular hobby by the turn of the century. Thus science had already begun to affect recreational pursuits before the technological developments of the twentieth century radically transformed them.

The Automobile

Probably the most important of these developments was the automobile. A toy of the rich in the last years of the nineteenth and the early part of the twentieth century, the automobile had become a possession of the people by the 1920s.

The automobile made it possible to travel to beaches, golf courses, sports events and other places of amusement, to visit woodland picnicking and camping areas, and to take vacation trips to distant places. For example, in 1910, when there were only 500,000 automobiles registered, less than 200,000 persons visited National Park Service areas. By 1952, with automobile registrations at almost 44 million, about 42 million visi-

17. See Harold D. Meyer and Charles K. Brightbill, *State Recreation*, Barnes, New York, 1950; also *Recreation*, June 1950, p. 118.

f. 1925; 1920 not available. Definition of areas covered is "state parks or equivalent areas."

g. Includes state parks, historic sites and parkways. Data for state park areas for which reports were received in fiscal years ending June 30. Reports were not received for all areas in any of the years covered.

h. 1941; 1940 data not available.

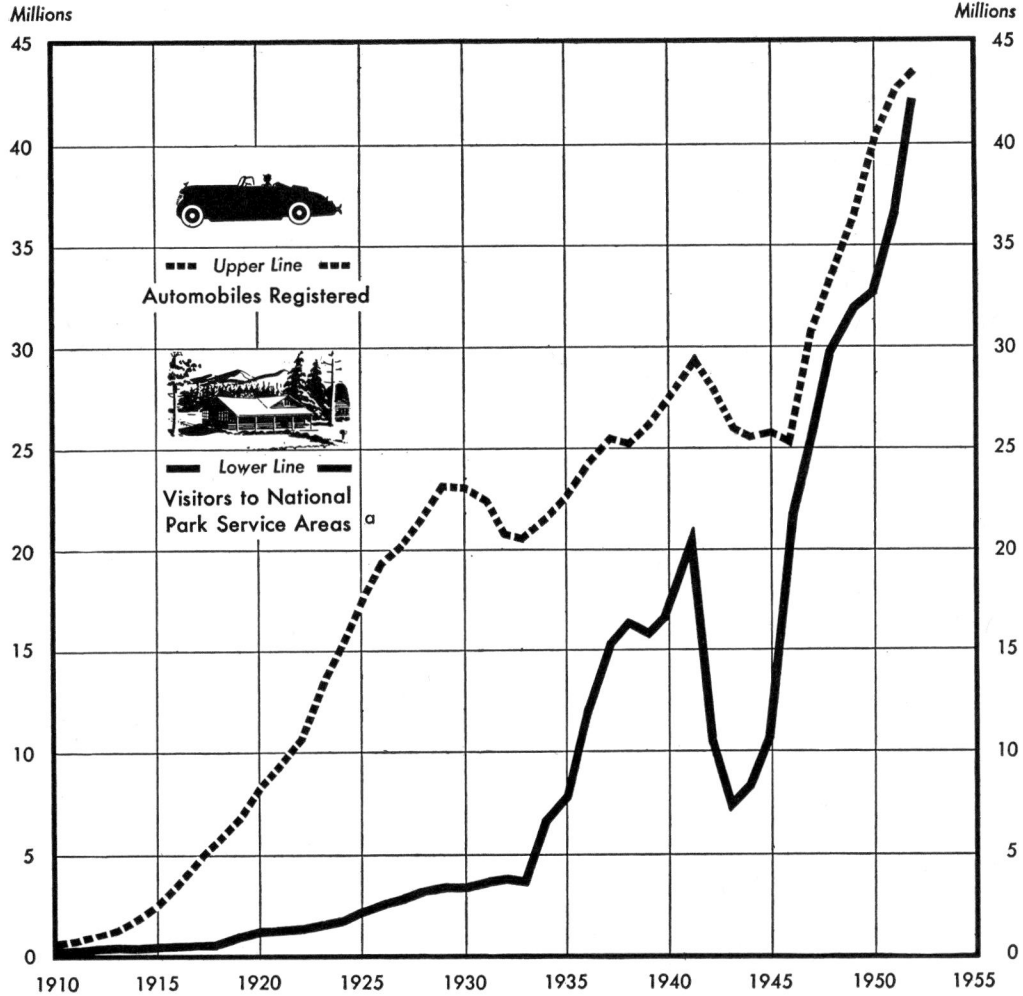

Millions

FIGURE 51. REGISTRATION OF AUTOMOBILES AND VISITORS TO NATIONAL PARK AREAS, 1910–1952

Source: Automobile Facts and Figures, 1953, Automobile Manufacturers Association, p. 24; National Park Service, U.S. Department of the Interior.

a. 1910–1940, for travel years ending September 30; 1941–1952, for calendar years.

tors to these areas were recorded. (See Figure 51.) Thus the automobile opened new vistas to the American family, broadening experience and increasing enjoyment. At the same time it created vast new economic opportunities in tourist trade.

It was automobile touring, the National Association of Travel Organizations points out, that sold the public on the automobile in the 1920s. " 'Touring' and use of the car to go to the golf course, football games, fishing, social events, the county fair, etc., etc., still comprises over one half of the use of all automobiles and still constitutes one of the most powerful urges that each individual has for owning an automobile." [18] Travel surveys indicate that about 85 per cent of vacation travel today is done by automobile. The American Automobile Association estimated in 1953 that 66 million people take automobile vacations annually.[19]

18. "Travel U.S.A.," National Association of Travel Organizations, Washington, August 1952, p. 2.

19. American Automobile Association, *op. cit.,* and *The American Magazine's Seventh Annual Travelogue,* 1951.

The Airplane

While airplane travel does not offer the same possibilities for cheap transportation to distant places as the automobile, it is today within the means of persons of moderate income. More than 3 per cent of the vacationists in 1950 traveled by plane, according to one survey.[20] The airplane has brought distant relatives and friends, sports and cultural events in faraway places, even vacation spots in other lands, within a few hours traveling time. Havana, Cuba, for example, which is an overnight trip from Miami by boat, is only an hour away by plane. In 1950 more than 80 per cent of the tourists arriving in Cuba came by plane, compared with about 35 per cent in 1937, the peak prewar year.[21] Airplane companies in Washington, D.C., advertise the convenience of their schedules for attending an evening's theater performance in New York City, though not many can afford such a trip. Helicopter taxi service is now available between New York airports and nearby cities and soon will begin in Los Angeles and other major centers.[22]

After World War I, air races and stunt flying enjoyed great popularity as sports. The National Air Races attracted 270,000 persons in 1938. Another very popular type of flying during the 1930s was gliding. In 1932 there were 1,360 gliders in the United States, but by 1940 the number had declined to 150.[23] Since World War II, aviation has become primarily commercial, though an estimated 341,000 persons held licenses as private noncommercial pilots in 1950.[24]

Motion Pictures

Simultaneously with the advent of the automobile as a means of mass transportation, another development was taking place that was to become the most popular of all the offerings of commercial recreation — the motion picture. By 1910 the nickelodeon had so captivated the public that 10,000 theaters were playing to total weekly audiences of 10 million. With the extravagant productions of the 1920s and the intro-

duction of sound, the motion-picture industry eclipsed all other forms of commercial amusement. Such simple small-town diversions as lodge night, the Grange meeting and the church social, although by no means extinguished, could not compete with the appeal of the movies.[25] By the end of the decade annual box-office receipts had reached $720 million. (See Appendix 4-4.)

During the depression, box-office receipts dropped to a low of $482 million in 1933. But by 1940, estimated attendance had jumped to over 54.3 million weekly [26] and receipts had returned almost to the 1929 level. Attendance continued to rise during the war years, when movies provided an easily accessible release from tension for civilians and for soldiers in camps at home and even abroad.

The years immediately following the war brought weekly movie attendance to its all-time peak of almost 81 million in 1946, with annual receipts of $1.5 billion. (See Appendix 4-4.) Attendance and box-office receipts slipped steadily thereafter, so that by 1950 weekly attendance had dropped slightly below the 1940 level to 54 million, and annual box-office intake to little better than $1.2 billion.

This steady decline in attendance gave rise to much speculation as to whether TV had put a permanent crimp in the motion-picture theater business or whether the competition from TV would diminish as the novelty wore off. A further dip of an estimated 9 million in weekly movie attendance by 1952, accompanied by a drop in annual receipts to $1.1 billion, did not give much encouragement to theater owners. In fact, one exhibitor reported that "most neighborhood houses couldn't stay open without popcorn and candy sales." [27]

Just as the motion-picture industry was able to meet the competition of radio in the 1920s by improvements in techniques — culminating in sound pictures toward the end of the decade — so it may withstand the competition of television. Interesting systems have been developed, for example, providing "depth perception" or a three-

---

20. *Americans on the Highway, a Report on Vacation Travel in 1950,* American Automobile Association.

21. *Wall Street Journal,* December 6, 1950.

22. Civil Aeronautics Administration.

23. William Fielding Ogburn, *The Social Effects of Aviation,* Houghton Mifflin, Boston, 1946, pp. 418–419.

24. *Statistical Abstract of the United States, 1951,* U.S. Bureau of the Census, p. 948.

25. Dulles, *op. cit.,* pp. 295 and 305.

26. Except where otherwise indicated, movie attendance figures cited are estimates of Audience Research, Inc., from a letter dated February 28, 1951 to the Twentieth Century Fund. Estimates published annually in the *Film Daily Yearbook* are considerably higher.

27. John T. Rule, "Movies and TV, Murder or Merger?," *Atlantic Monthly,* October 1953, pp. 55–58; *Wall Street Journal,* October 8, 1953.

dimensional effect. The most prominent of these are CinemaScope, VistaVision and Cinerama. Nearly 3,500 of the nation's theaters had converted to CinemaScope by the spring of 1954, but Cinerama, because of its conversion cost, appeared doomed to a limited market. Most critics seemed to believe, however, that it would take more than technical changes to keep the movie industry as big a business as it now is. Some pointed out that not only television but poor quality of films had brought about the box-office slump. Others predicted that the salvation of the movies would be television itself, through theater television or presentation of movies on home sets on some form of subscription basis.[28]

Radio

As the automobile and the movies were increasingly enticing the American family from the home, the radio arrived to draw it back into the living room once again. From 5,000 amateur radio fans in 1920, the audience grew rapidly. In 1924, 5 million homes had radios; by 1928, 10 million; by 1940, 28 million.[29]

The sale of radios took another upward turn in the postwar years. By 1947 it was estimated that more than 66 million radios were in use, including 36 million sets in homes (about 91 per cent of all homes had radios), over 8 million auto sets and about 22 million other sets.[30] By 1952, radios numbered over 100 million, including 27 million in automobiles. Almost 44 million, or about 95 per cent, of all homes had radios in January 1953.[31]

In the 1920s, the radio put the piano and the phonograph in almost total shadow.[32] In the late 1940s, television threatened to blot out radio. In a survey in November 1950, it was found that while 87 per cent of the people in homes without television sets listened to the radio daily, only 67 per cent of those in homes with television did so. The average radio-listening time in non-TV homes was estimated at 3 hours, 33 minutes; in TV homes, at 2 hours, 10 minutes.[33] It is still too early, however, to predict the ultimate effect of television on radio's popular appeal.

Television

Though television had been reported as being "just around the corner" all through the 1930s, large-scale production had to wait until the end of the war. The number of sets produced annually jumped from 7,500 in 1946 to 6.5 million by 1950.[34] As of January 1, 1951, an estimated 10.5 million TV sets were in use in 63 areas served by broadcasters. Almost 40 per cent of the families in these areas had sets.[35] By the end of 1951 it was estimated that 15 million sets were in use. Almost 20 million, or about 46 per cent, of all homes had television sets by January 1953. New Jersey had the highest proportion of set ownership — 88 per cent.[36]

Despite its rapid growth, the television industry was in some respects still in the pioneering stage in the early 1950s. By the end of 1951 there were only 107 stations, and these were largely concentrated in the East; the West had few and the North Central states almost none. With the Federal Communications Commission's lifting of its ban on new stations in 1952 and the opening of the ultra-high-frequency band, it was predicted that the number of stations would soon reach 1,400 to 2,000, covering the whole country. By the spring of 1954, however, there were still only 381 stations, 135 of which were ultra-high-frequency. Color television was in the offing and three-dimensional television had been publicly displayed.[37]

28. "Hollywood's Future Begins to Take Shape," *Business Week*, May 8, 1954, pp. 42–43; Rule, *op. cit.*; Jack Howard, "Hollywood and Television — Year of Decision," *Quarterly of Film, Radio and Television*, Summer 1953, pp. 359–369; Bosley Crowther, "The Three Dimensional Riddle," *New York Times Magazine*, March 29, 1953.

29. Dulles, *op. cit.*, pp. 320, 321 and 327; Table 78.

30. Neumeyer, *op. cit.*, pp. 278–279 and p. 280.

31. Letter from Broadcast Advertising Bureau, Inc., September 22, 1952; *Statistical Abstract of the United States, 1953*, p. 836.

32. In 1919, consumers spent $204 million for pianos. By 1929, when radio sales were at their pre-World War II peak, piano sales had dropped to $87 million, and in 1933 to $17 million. Sales of phonographs and records declined from $339 million in 1919 to $153 million in 1929 and by 1933 sank to $6 million. (Julius Weinberger, "Economic Aspects of Recreation," *Harvard Business Review*, Summer Number, 1937, p. 452.)

33. *What's Happening to Leisure Time in Television Homes? A Study of the Activities of 5,657 Persons in Urban America*, Batten, Barton, Durstine and Osborn, Inc., New York, 1951.

34. "Progress Report on Television," George J. Martin Co., 79 Wall Street, New York, 1951.

35. *Ibid.*

36. David Sarnoff, quoted in *U.S. News and World Report*, November 9, 1951, p. 39; *Statistical Abstract of the United States, 1953*, p. 836; *Sales Management*, March 15, 1954, p. 67.

37. *Life*, September 17, 1951, p. 63; *U.S. News and World Report*, November 9, 1951, p. 43; *Wall Street*

Because of the economic repercussions of television on other entertainment media, surveys comparing the leisure-time activities in homes with and without television sets have been legion. Almost unanimously they have arrived at the over-all conclusion that families with television sets stay at home more, go to movies, night clubs and other places of amusement less, devote less time to radio listening and to reading than families who are without TV.[38]

There are developing possibilities that both Hollywood producers and the television industry can benefit, financially and in quality of offerings, from a closer working relationship. Proposals have been made for broadcasting regular motion pictures by television on a subscription or "pay-as-you-see" basis, by "phonevision," "telemeter," "subscribervision" or other systems in an experimental stage.[39] Such proposals have met with enthusiastic response from some Hollywood producers, while others fear the effects on theater operators, "who have borne the brunt of what TV has done to box office receipts" and on whom the producers must still place their main reliance for a market for their pictures.[40]

With most major sports events shown on television, the drop in gate receipts at these events that began to be felt after 1948 and had become a definite trend by 1950 was also attributed to television. The inroads of television on sports from 1947 to 1953 (as well as the relative appeal of radio and TV) are suggested by the amounts sponsors paid for television and radio rights to the World Series games during the period. In 1947 radio rights sold for $175,000 and TV rights for $65,000; in 1948 the figures were almost even, $150,000 and $140,000; by 1949 radio was trailing with $150,000 to TV's $200,000; by 1950 radio had been left far behind: radio rights were back up to $175,000 but TV rights were $800,000. In 1953 both mounted further — radio rights to $200,000 and television to $925,000.[41]

Although most sports promoters are still concerned over the effects of television on their gate receipts, others are beginning to hope that television has stimulated an interest in sports and promises not fewer but more spectators for the future. A survey in 1950 on the effect of television on sports attendance indicated that after one or two years of TV ownership, television owners' rate of attendance at sports events was higher than that of nonowners.[42]

Hobbies

Mass-produced technical and mechanical equipment has opened new opportunities to millions of hobby enthusiasts, such as amateur photographers and radio amateurs, model builders, home carpenters, young "scientists" who experiment in chemistry, electricity and other fields of science. A few examples will serve to indicate the widespread popularity of some of these hobbies.

There are 34 million cameras in the hands of nonprofessional photographers, who spend $400 million a year on supplies and equipment. The more ambitious amateurs, 150,000 of them, belong to the 6,000 neighborhood camera clubs and regard their photography as an art. New techniques and equipment have greatly heightened interest in this popular hobby in recent years. This has been particularly true since World War

---

Journal, April 14, 1952 and March 30, 1953; *Radio and Television News*, May 1954, p. 110.

38. Estimates as to the extent of the effect of TV ownership on other recreational activities vary. A few examples serve to illustrate the radical changes it has brought about.

A Gallup survey early in 1949 indicated that television had cut movie attendance by one per cent. A study by the Paramount Company in the New York metropolitan area indicated that television ownership cuts motion-picture attendance by 20 to 30 per cent, and another survey in the Washington, D.C., area in 1950 concluded that television ownership cuts movie-going by 74 per cent. (*New York Times Magazine*, March 26, 1950, p. 17.)

From a survey conducted in November 1950, it was concluded that movie attendance suffered a 33 per cent loss when television came into the home; that 23 per cent of people in TV homes read books, compared with 32 per cent in non-TV homes; and that the average time spent in reading books also was greater in non-TV homes. Magazine reading was found to have suffered less through television ownership, and newspaper reading hardly at all. In the TV homes, 67 per cent listened to the radio daily, compared with 87 per cent in non-TV homes. (*What's Happening to Leisure Time in Television Homes?*)

In a survey in 1953, it was found that 73 per cent of the people in homes with television sets watch at some time during weekday evenings. Total viewing time for all people in homes with television was 12 hours, an increase of 30 minutes over 1952. Television did not seem to have affected newspaper or magazine reading. (*Sales Management*, November 20, 1953, p. 70.)

39. Samuel Goldwyn, "Television's Challenge to the Movies," *New York Times Magazine*, March 26, 1950; Rule, *op. cit.*; Howard, *op. cit.*

40. *Wall Street Journal*, April 13, 1951 and August 7, 1951.

41. Frank G. Menke, *The All-Sports Record Book*, Barnes, New York, 1950, pp. 45 and 319, and *The World Almanac*, 1951, p. 819, and 1954, pp. 800 and 809.

42. Jerry N. Jordan, *The Long-Range Effect of Television and Other Factors on Sports Attendance*, Radio-Television Manufacturers Association, Washington, 1950.

II, when photographic equipment developed for military use became available to amateur photographers. Developments have continued since the war. Cameras that will take and develop a picture in a minute, "three-dimensional" cameras, and cameras capable of taking pictures in semidarkness without the use of photoflash bulbs are now on the market. Interest in home movie cameras has also boomed since World War II. Though production of movie cameras for home use is the youngest branch of the photographic business, manufacturers say it is the fastest growing, with movie cameras already in 3 million homes by 1952.[43]

Woodworking, too, has boomed in recent years, largely owing to the availability of home-sized tools and equipment, such as electric drills, saws and lathes. It is estimated that more than 5 million builders-for-fun purchased about $60 million worth of home tools in 1952, compared with sales of about $6 million in 1947.[44]

Gardening, which is probably the nation's number one hobby, has also been encouraged, by the adaptation of seed, plants and fertilizers to the needs of amateur gardeners with limited space. Expenditures for flowers, seeds and potted plants increased from $211 million in 1940 to $689 million in 1950. (See Appendix 4-4.)

Model-plane building and flying absorbs the interest of perhaps 3 million Americans, who spend over $20 million a year for equipment. In 1950 more than 30,000 model-builders participated in contests recognized by the Academy of Model Aeronautics.[45]

Planes have not been alone in capturing the interest of the model-making fans. Model trains run a close second, and models of early types of automobiles are also very popular. Expenditures for the varied kits available for making models — including houses, ships, stage coaches, howitzers, circuses — total about $50 million annually.[46]

Amateur radio has fascinated technically inclined youth since 1903 when Marconi, who considered himself an amateur, succeeded in spanning the Atlantic Ocean by wireless. The hobby has attracted an increasing number of adults, the average age of amateurs having risen from 22 years in 1926 to 33 by 1950. Today there are approximately 100,000 amateur radio operators in the United States. Their average investment is $400, and operation and maintenance costs about $150 annually. They have combined to form the American Radio Relay League.[47]

Sports Equipment

Science has also vastly stimulated interest and participation in sports by making more durable materials available for various types of sports equipment and making sports events accessible to large numbers of people through improved transportation and communication. Advances in electric lighting have made night sports contests possible, thus enabling millions of people who work during the day to attend.

Auto racing is an outstanding example of a sport created by the products of technology. In 1951, auto races attracted 35 million spectators, who paid $61 million to watch the races — a 40 per cent gain in attendance and a 74 per cent gain in gate receipts over 1939.[48]

The experience of World War II resulted in many improvements in sports equipment. Materials used for war, such as improved firearms, waterproof clothing, portable boats, tents, cooking and heating equipment, have added greatly to the pleasures of fishermen, hunters and campers. New materials such as nylon and plastics have also found extensive use in sports equipment.

The introduction of a new item of sports equipment may stimulate interest in the sport itself. The glass fishing rod, for example, is credited with some of the responsibility for the greatly increased popularity of fishing since the end of World War II. The direct intervention of science in improving opportunities for sports may be seen also in the experimentation with cloud seeding at winter resorts to assure snow for skiing and bobsledding.[49]

43. "Crazy Over Pictures," *Saturday Evening Post*, February 3, 1951, pp. 32 ff.; *Wall Street Journal*, December 15, 1952.

44. *Wall Street Journal*, October 14, 1952.

45. "Don't Build Airplanes in the Bathtub," *Saturday Evening Post*, November 4, 1950, pp. 32 ff.

46. *Wall Street Journal*, February 11, 1952.

47. "Amateur Radio Data from the American Radio Relay League," West Hartford, Connecticut, 7 pp., mimeographed, no date; "All Ham and a World Wide," *Nation's Business*, September 1953.

48. *Wall Street Journal*, April 28, 1952.

49. *Ibid.*, December 20, 1950; January 25, 1952; August 14, 1953.

CURRENT RECREATIONAL TRENDS

Because of the almost universal appeal of the most spectacular American amusements — the movies, motoring, spectator sports, radio and television — Americans are often accused of standardization in their leisure-time pursuits.

It is true that many identical recreational activities are available to and enjoyed by the majority of the population. The American public goes to the movies, listens to the radio and watches television either at home or at a neighbor's, goes to baseball games in the spring and summer and to football games in the fall, bowls, plays softball, swims, reads, gardens, plays cards, goes to public parks and playgrounds, travels in the summer by car or public conveyance to near-by beaches and picnic areas.

All of these things most Americans do some of the time. The result has been a large degree of homogeneity: North and South, East and West, rich and poor, young and old, urban and rural — all today have a large area of recreational experience in common. But for each individual a wide, rich variety of activities compete for his leisure hours. In one evening, movies, radio and television programs, sports events, books and magazines offer almost unlimited choice — a far cry from the limited and much more standardized pursuits available to most of the population even half a century ago.

Americans engage also in many active sports and hobbies. One need only glance through a list of national associations for the advancement of various recreational activities: badminton, bowling, camping, contract bridge, motorcycling, stamp-collecting, amateur radio, billiards, boys' and girls' activities of various kinds, fishing, baseball, skiing, shuffleboard, boating, barber shop quartet singing, golf, tennis, paddle tennis, softball, rodeos, roleos, archery, snowshoe enthusiasts, homing pigeon fanciers, photography, button collectors, polo, soaring, coin collecting — to name but a few. Their combined membership runs into many millions.

The postwar years have seen many startling changes in leisure-time trends. Of these the influence of television in keeping people at home and away from the movies and other types of entertainment has been the most discussed. Less observed has been a sharply increased interest in more serious types of music. It is estimated that the number of classical music concerts held out-side of New York City increased by 130 per cent between 1940 and 1950. Today, sales of classical records account for 40 per cent of the total of all record sales — compared with 30 per cent in the prewar period. Attendance at concerts of serious music jumped 88 per cent between 1941 and 1951. The number of symphony orchestras increased from 111 to 200 and local opera companies from 2 to 13. Twice as many towns — more than 2,000 — now provide serious music regularly for the general public.[50]

In 1951 more than 30 million persons — nearly twice as many as in 1941 — paid admission to concerts, opera and ballet. Total box-office receipts for programs of this type were about $45 million. As one writer points out, this is "relatively small potatoes as U.S. industries go. A comparable business, for example, is the sale of popcorn in movie theaters, which also runs about $45 million annually. But it's more than the $40 million spent by the public at stadiums to see professional baseball games this year." [51]

While spectator sports still remain extremely popular, there has been a rising trend toward participation in sports during the last two decades. The depression-sponsored play areas and facilities of the 1930s and the war-sponsored recreational programs of the early 1940s taught millions of Americans to play. Today active-sports programs are considered a necessary part of community life. Newspaper sports pages, radio and television sports reviews stimulate wide interest in participant as well as spectator sports.

PARTICIPATION IN SPORTS

No exact figures can be given on either participants or spectators, and many of the estimates are provided in the first instance by organizations or individuals interested in promoting the particular activity. Such estimates are unlikely to err in the direction of understatement. A few recent estimates of participation in the more popular sports and games follow: [52]

---

50. Fenton B. Turck, "Science on the March: The American Explosion," *Scientific Monthly,* September 1952, pp. 188, 189.

51. *Wall Street Journal,* December 18, 1951.

52. Unless otherwise indicated, the figures on number of participants and spectators are from Frank G. Menke, *op. cit.* Most figures are for 1950, though some are for earlier years where 1950 figures are not available.

18 million fishermen bought licenses in 1953. The total number who go fishing is much greater, as licenses are not required for salt-water fishing or of children.

Nearly 18 million ride bicycles, though not all for pleasure, as bicycles are used in various occupations.

17 million men and women, boys and girls roller skate. (John R. Tunis says roller skating tops the list of participant sports.) [53]

16 million of all ages play softball.[54]

Almost 15 million hunters bought licenses in 1953, according to the Fish and Wildlife Service.

5 million play horseshoes.[55]

4 million play golf.[56]

6 million play shuffleboard.[57]

Millions play tennis. (Tunis reports that almost 2 million players utilize courts in the public parks.) [58]

2 to 3 million participate in the increasingly popular sport of skiing.[59]

5 million play volleyball, which Tunis [60] characterizes as a sport that isn't fashionable, just a sport for folks to play and enjoy.

Water sports have been increasingly popular in recent years. Untold millions swim. A Gallup poll survey in 1950 indicated that 52 per cent of adult Americans can swim. In addition, there has been a nationwide boom in boating since World War II, with an estimated half million sailboat owners and over 4 million power boat owners navigating both inland and coastal waters.[61]

Indoor sports attract tens of millions of fans. For the most popular, card games and checkers, no estimates of the total number of players exist. Menke calls checkers "one of the most popular indoor sports of the ages." In a survey of the adult readers of *Collier's* in 1948, 84 per cent of the men and 87 per cent of the women said they played cards.[62]

16 to 20 million people a year go bowling.[63]

10 to 15 million play table tennis.[64]

8 to 10 million play billiards.[65]

50 million people play coin-operated games (exclusive of slot machines and similar gambling devices).[66]

SPECTATORSHIP

Estimates of the numbers who annually attend various sports spectacles are as follows:

125 million turn out each spring and summer to see the softball games going on in every hamlet, town and city.[67]

105 million people see basketball games. 65 million watch high-school, college and professional football games.[68]

50 million attend horse races — saddle and harness.[69]

40 million attend auto speed races.[70]

25 million go to boxing matches.

63 million see major- and minor-league baseball games.

20 million attend roller-skating contests.

10 million attend ice-skating contests and carnivals.

7 million attend wrestling matches.

7 million see the races of the American Motorcycle Association.

6 million go to rodeos.

Record crowds in the history of sports during the past few decades are indicative of trends in public taste. In 1926 the Tunney-Dempsey boxing match drew almost 121,000 spectators; the

53. *Sport for the Fun of It,* Barnes, New York, 1950, p. 141.
54. According to the *Allsports Review,* November-December 1950.
55. Tunis, *op. cit.,* p. 113.
56. *Ibid.,* p. 72.
57. *Ibid.,* p. 148.
58. *Ibid.,* p. 222.
59. According to the National Ski Association in a letter of December 21, 1950.
60. *Op. cit.,* pp. 237, 238.
61. *Public Opinion News Service,* September 2, 1950; *Wall Street Journal,* February 25, 1952; *Time,* July 27, 1953.
62. "Leisure-Time Activities of Collier's Adult Readers," Crowell-Collier Publishing Company, February 1948, p. 26.
63. The higher estimate was made by the Brunswick-Balke-Collender Company in a letter of January 16, 1951.
64. According to the U.S. Table Tennis Association, letter, February 1951.
65. Letter, Brunswick-Balke-Collender Company, January 16, 1951.
66. According to the Coin Machine Institute, letter, January 19, 1951.
67. *Allsports Review,* November-December 1950.
68. According to Theodore Bank of the Athletic Institute, letter, January 8, 1951.
69. *Wall Street Journal,* May 12 and June 14, 1952.
70. *Ibid.,* April 28, 1952.

Louis-Conn fight in 1946 drew only slightly more than 45,000. An estimated 150,000 to 175,000, the largest crowd in sports history, attended the 500-mile auto race at Indianapolis on Memorial Day in 1950. Surprisingly, as of 1950, the next largest attendance, 150,000, was at a corn-husking contest near Davenport, Iowa, in 1940.

PASTIMES AND PETS

Figures on participation in hobbies are very sparse, but the widespread organization of hobby groups gives some indication of the popularity of such pastimes. The American Philatelic Society, for example, has 11,500 members, who represent only a fraction of the millions of stamp collectors the country over; [71] 30,000 members harmonize regularly in the 670 local chapters of the Society for the Preservation and Encouragement of Barber Shop Quartet Singing in America.[72] Garden clubs and sewing circles are found everywhere. It is estimated that in 1948, 11 per cent of the population 20 years of age and over, and 15 per cent of the children 19 and under, played musical instruments.[73] Social dancing, always popular, attracts new millions yearly. These activities, together with hobbies and amusements discussed in preceding sections, are but a few examples of the infinite number of pastimes that add diversity to daily living.

Despite these varied attractions, reading still holds high favor. In a 1946 survey made by the National Opinion Research Center,[74] 41 per cent of the people interviewed said reading was their favorite pastime. In Wisconsin in 1949, playing cards, reading and radio listening topped the list; attending movies followed as a poor fourth.[75] A public opinion poll in the State of Washington yielded the following results: 86 per cent of the people reported reading as one of their leisure-time pursuits, with an average of 471 hours annually spent in this way; 84 per cent reported that they participated in hobbies and spent an average

of 582 hours annually on them; and 83 per cent reported that they went to the movies, but spent an average of only 36 hours a year in this way.[76] A Gallup poll of September 2, 1950 showed that the reading of the American people is confined largely to newspapers and magazines: 97 per cent of the people questioned said they read newspapers, 89 per cent magazines, and only 21 per cent books.

A survey made in the State of Minnesota in 1949 showed variations in favorite leisure-time pursuits according to place of residence: "City residents' principal interests are reading, radio listening, and movie-going, in that order. Town residents name radio listening first, reading second, and listening to music and watching sports events, third. Farm people's replies show radio listening comes first, reading second, and movie-going third." [77] Two of the most popular of these diversions were unknown half a century ago.

Pets of all types offer pleasure and diversion to many American families. Dogs and cats outnumber all other pets in popularity. A survey in 1951 showed that about 17 million families owned dogs and that the nation's total dog population was about 22 million.[78] The number of cats undoubtedly equals or exceeds the number of dogs. When canaries, goldfish and other pets are taken into consideration, it is undoubtedly true that between half and two thirds of American families keep pets of some kind.

"GOLDEN AGE" CLUBS

An important development of recent years is the emphasis on recreational activities for older people. The proportion of the population 65 years and over has increased steadily, reaching 9.0 per cent in 1953. (See Table 21.) Not only their increased numbers but also many other factors have made it important to provide community activities for old people. With retirement systems widespread, more old people have leisure. More live in comparatively good health during their later years and thus are able to pursue recreational activities. More live in small,

71. Letter from the Society, January 2, 1951.

72. Letter from the Society, December 29, 1950.

73. Letter from the Philip Lesley Company, Chicago, January 3, 1951.

74. *What, Where, Why, Do People Read?*, Highlights of a Survey Made for the American Library Association and 17 Cooperating City Libraries, National Opinion Research Center, University of Denver, Denver, Colorado, 1946.

75. Marvin Rife, *Survey of Recreation in Metropolitan Madison, Wisconsin*, Community Welfare Council, Madison, Wisconsin, July 1950.

76. *Leisure Use Attitudes,* Washington Public Opinion Laboratory, Report No. 4, University of Washington, Seattle, and State College, Pullman, Washington.

77. *Recreational Resources of the People of Minnesota,* Report of the Governor's Advisory Committee on Recreation, St. Paul, Minnesota, January 1950.

78. Gaines Dog Research Center, New York City.

modern city dwellings with small families, so that they have little in the way of indoor and outdoor chores to occupy them.

The answer in many cities has been the formation of "golden age" clubs where old people can plan and participate in their own games, hobbies, arts and crafts, form friendships and find opportunities to develop lifelong interests and talents. Of the perhaps 300 such community clubs, one of the best known is the William Hodson Community Center in New York. Organized in 1943, it had 450 members by 1949, ranging in age from 60 to 90. A number of cities have opened day centers for the aged, where older people who would otherwise be left alone during the day can be cared for and find recreation. New York City alone has 12 day centers.[79]

Many old people have found pleasure in travel in their years of retirement. They represent a considerable proportion of the migration to the West and South, particularly Florida and California.

INDUSTRIAL RECREATION

Another important recreational trend is the rapid growth of industrial recreation — recreational programs attached to industrial enterprises and businesses. These programs became particularly important during World War II because of crowded and substandard living quarters, night shifts, long hours, increased employment of women, separation of workers from their families, and elimination of company playfields as a result of plant expansion. Many industrial firms established or expanded company recreation programs during the war and in the postwar years, on the theory that such programs improve morale, increase efficiency, and make for good relations between management and workers.

Interest in the field was great enough for 12 companies to join together in the Industrial Recreation Association in 1942; today the organization has 330 member companies and membership is increasing rapidly. In 1950, 20,000 firms were reported to have some type of employee recreation program. Their annual expenditure of $450 million exceeded the amount spent during any of the war years. It is estimated that about half the workers in the United States participate in these programs.[80]

Before World War II, many companies merely had athletic teams, which competed with teams of other industrial concerns. Today the emphasis is on activities for all employees, with athletic competitions within the plant predominating. Most popular are bowling, softball, basketball, picnicking, parties, horseshoes, baseball and social dancing. During the noon hour, table tennis, horseshoes, checkers, movies and chess are favorite pastimes. Activities for the whole family have become a vital part of industrial recreational programs. Day camps, junior baseball clinics, swimming, plant visits for families, picnics, outings, and excursions to near-by places of interest are an integral part of many plant programs.[81]

Employees help to pay the cost of the program in most companies, through dues, assessments, purchases in vending machines, admissions or in other ways. The median total annual cost per employee (company and employee contributions and receipts from other sources) is approximately $5.[82]

YOUTH PROGRAMS

Voluntary agencies, such as the YMCA, the YWCA, the Jewish Welfare Board, Boy Scouts, Girl Scouts, Boys' Clubs, Girls' Clubs, Camp Fire Girls, Catholic Youth Organizations, neighborhood centers, various church groups, have extensive recreation programs involving thousands of young people. The Boy Scouts, for example, have 541 local councils with almost 3 million members; the Camp Fire Girls' 281 local councils serve 400,000 members; the 325 Boys' Clubs have 310,000 members.[83]

TRENDS IN RECREATION EXPENDITURES

The years 1909–1952 saw an enormous increase in expenditures of both public and private funds for recreational purposes. National crises — war and economic depression — affected recreational expenditures during those years. Major technological advances in means of recreation

79. Harry A. Levine, "Community Programs for the Elderly," *Annals of the American Academy of Political and Social Science,* January 1952, p. 165.

80. *Wall Street Journal,* May 25, 1951 and May 22, 1952.
81. C. E. Brewer, "The Industrial Recreation Program," *Recreation,* June 1951, pp. 140–141.
82. *Ibid.*
83. Letters from the respective organizations, January 1951.

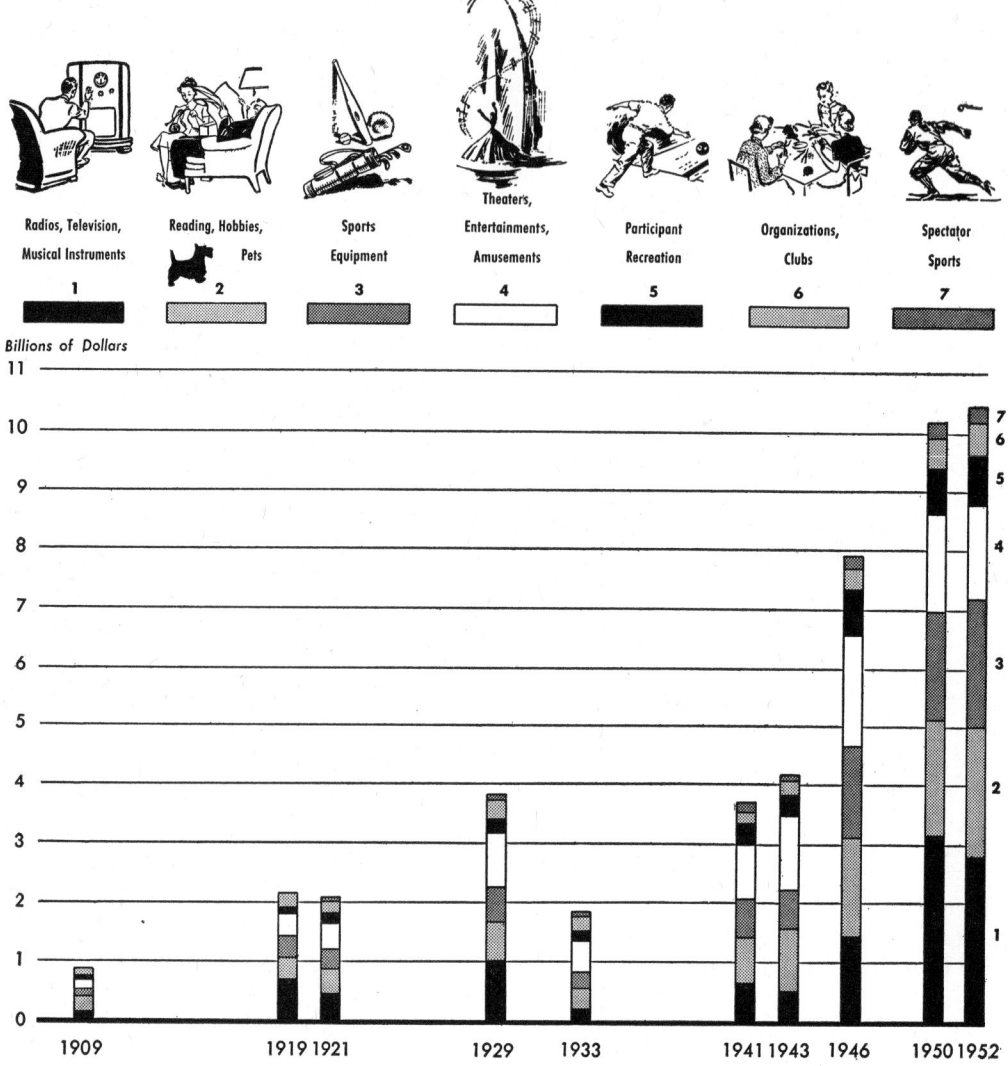

FIGURE 52. CONSUMPTION EXPENDITURES FOR RECREATIONAL GOODS AND SERVICES, BY CLASS OF EXPENDITURE, SELECTED YEARS, 1909–1952

Source: Appendix 4–4.

brought about upheavals in recreational spending patterns.

Consumer purchases of recreational goods and services were almost twelve times greater in 1950 than they were forty-one years earlier, while from 1940 to 1950 alone they more than tripled. Even when price fluctuations are taken into account, expenditures for recreation increased steadily over the period except in the depression years 1921 and 1931–1933 and in the war year 1943.

In terms of percentage of national income spent for recreation, the all-time peak, 4.9 per cent, came in 1931 and the 42-year low, 2.5 per cent, in 1943. The high for the decade of the 1940s was 4.4 per cent, in 1946 and 1947. (See Table 157.)

The trend in the percentage of total consumption expenditures devoted to recreation reveals even more clearly the developing importance of recreation as an item of personal expenditure, when viewed for the whole period 1909–1952.

The percentage rose steadily from 3.0 in 1909 to 4.8 in 1929. Only slowly was the proportion of the family budget allotted to recreation reduced. In 1933, the worst depression year, 4 per cent of consumption expenditures went for recreation, the same proportion as in the relatively prosperous year of 1925. By 1937, it had risen to 4.4 per cent, higher than in any previous year except 1929. (See Table 157.) The proportion continued to rise, to 4.6 per cent in 1942, but all-out war brought it down to 4.1 in 1943 — almost the depression level.

The upward trend began again with the end of the war, and in 1946 the proportion of consumption expenditures devoted to recreation reached its highest point, 5.4 per cent. Thereafter, through 1950, it fluctuated between 5 per cent and 5.2 per cent, but the percentage fell to 4.8 by 1952.

Although recreation is an item of family spending that responds sharply to changing economic conditions, it has become sufficiently accepted as a necessity so that even war and depression cannot return it to the low position in the family budget it occupied in the first quarter of the century.

CONSUMER EXPENDITURES

Not only have economic and social conditions, new inventions and periodic fads and crazes affected over-all expenditures but they have also caused shifts in the types of recreational goods and services for which consumers have spent their money. (See Figure 52.)

Particularly marked has been the depressing effect of business slumps on sales of durable home entertainment goods — pianos and phonographs in 1921 and radio sets, phonographs, radio tubes, sporting goods, books, toys and games in 1930–1933. Recreational services, representing frequent small expenditures, have weathered such storms better. (See Tables 157 and 161 and Appendices 4–4 and 4–5.) Even when recreational expenditures in two prosperous years, 1929 and 1950, are compared, marked differences in consumer tastes are apparent. (See Figure 53.)

1909–1929

The period 1909–1929 saw recreation emerge as an important economic factor. From 1909 to 1919 recreational expenditures rose from $859 million to almost $2.2 billion, owing in part to the price inflation of World War I. The mild economic depression that followed resulted in a sharp decline in consumer purchases of durable entertainment goods, particularly musical instruments, which dropped from $667 million in 1919 to $439 million in 1921. Total recreational expenditures, however, declined by only $89 million and expenditures for theaters, entertainments and amusements actually rose, from $380 to $433 million.

After 1921, in the boom period ending in 1929, spending for all types of entertainment soared. People had more leisure and more money than ever before. Radios, mammoth sports events, motion pictures, travel and other attractions helped empty their pockets and fill their time. Dance marathons, mah-jong, crossword puzzles and other fads swept the country.[84] Motion-picture receipts and sales of radios and musical instruments skyrocketed — the first from $301 million in 1921 to $720 million in 1929, the second from $439 million to over $1 billion.

Sports became big business during the twenty-year period from 1909 to 1929. Expenditures for participant sports increased from $23 million to $221 million; for spectator sports, from a negligible amount to $63 million; and for sports equipment, from $140 million to $542 million.

1929–1941

The span of years from 1929 until our entrance into the war affords a good opportunity to observe the impact of a severe and prolonged depression on recreational expenditures of different kinds, and to examine these trends in greater detail than is possible for the earlier period. Total recreational expenditures declined sharply from $3.8 billion in 1929 to $1.9 billion in 1933, then rose very gradually almost to the 1929 level by 1941. Consumer expenditures during the 1930s do not, however, give a complete picture of recreation during the depression. Many public recreation facilities were built with WPA and other emergency relief funds, and numbers of people participated in the various emergency recreational and cultural programs

84. For interesting descriptions of this period, see Walter S. Hiatt, "Billions — Just for Fun," *Collier's*, October 25, 1924, p. 31; and Dulles, *op. cit.*, Chapter 20.

TABLE 161. PERCENTAGE DISTRIBUTION OF CONSUMPTION EXPENDITURES FOR RECREATIONAL GOODS AND SERVICES, 1909–1950

Class	1909	1919	1921	1929	1933	1941	1943	1946	1950
Total	100.0	100.0	100.0	100.0	100.0	100.0	100.0	100.0	100.0
Theaters, entertainment and amusements	22.0	17.6	20.9	25.0	31.6	25.4	29.6	23.9	16.6
Motion-picture theaters	[a]	[a]	14.6	18.8	25.8	20.3	24.8	19.1	12.2
Legitimate theaters, opera and entertainments of nonprofit organizations (except athletics)	[a]	[a]	[a]	3.4	2.2	2.1	2.8	2.2	1.7
Other commercial amusements (except athletics)	[a]	[a]	[a]	2.8	3.5	2.9	2.4	2.6	2.7
Spectator sports	[a]	[a]	1.4	1.6	2.6	2.7	1.8	2.9	2.6
Professional baseball, football and hockey	[a]	[a]	[a]	.5	.7	.8	.5	.8	.7
Horse and dog race tracks	[a]	[a]	[a]	.1	.1	.3	.3	.5	.4
Amateur sports	[a]	[a]	[a]	1.0	1.8	1.6	1.1	1.5	1.6
Reading, hobbies and pets	24.1	19.3	21.1	17.7	20.7	20.5	25.4	20.9	19.0
Reading	12.1	9.4	11.6	9.3	12.8	9.8	12.2	9.4	8.1
Hobbies and pets	12.0	9.9	9.6	8.4	7.8	10.7	13.2	11.5	11.0
Organizations and clubs	15.6	12.4	13.0	8.7	12.4	6.3	5.8	4.9	5.0
Camp fees	[a]	[a]	[a]	.8	1.3	.8	.6	.4	.4
Clubs	[a]	[a]	[a]	7.9	11.1	5.5	5.2	4.5	4.6
Participant recreation	2.7	2.6	6.4	5.8	7.3	9.5	9.2	9.4	7.5
Pari-mutuel and nonvending coin machines (net receipts)	[a]	[a]	[a]	.4	.8	4.0	4.3	5.2	3.5
Billiard parlors and bowling alleys	[a]	[a]	[a]	1.5	1.8	2.2	2.0	1.4	1.2
Golf instruction, club rental and fees	[a]	[a]	[a]	2.4	2.8	1.7	1.5	1.4	1.4
Other participant recreation	[a]	[a]	[a]	1.5	1.8	1.6	1.4	1.4	1.4
Radio and television receivers and musical instruments	19.3	30.9	21.2	27.1	11.2	18.1	12.5	18.2	31.1
Radios, phonographs, parts and records	[a]	[a]	[a]	23.6	9.2	14.4	} 11.1	16.8	27.9
Pianos and other musical instruments	[a]	[a]	[a]	2.8	1.3	2.7			
Radio and television repair	[a]	[a]	[a]	.7	.7	1.0	1.4	1.4	3.2
Sports equipment	16.3	17.1	16.0	14.1	14.2	17.6	15.4	19.8	18.2

Source: Appendix 4–4.
a. Not available.

Note: Slight discrepancies in addition are due to rounding.

of the time. Similarly, expenditures for reading, which dropped from $356 million in 1929 to $240 million in 1933, obscure the great upsurge of interest in reading during this period through the public library.

A few items departed decidedly from the general trend of recreational expenditures from 1929 to 1941. (See Table 162 and Appendix 4–4.) Gambling and betting showed a particu-

larly sharp rise from depression low points, perhaps reflecting attempts to recoup income losses. After declining from $16 million in 1929 to $10 million in 1932, pari-mutuel and nonvending coin machine net receipts increased to $15 million by 1933 and skyrocketed to $147 million by 1941. Net receipts of nonvending coin machines alone actually increased from $8 million in 1929 to $9 million in 1933, and climbed fur-

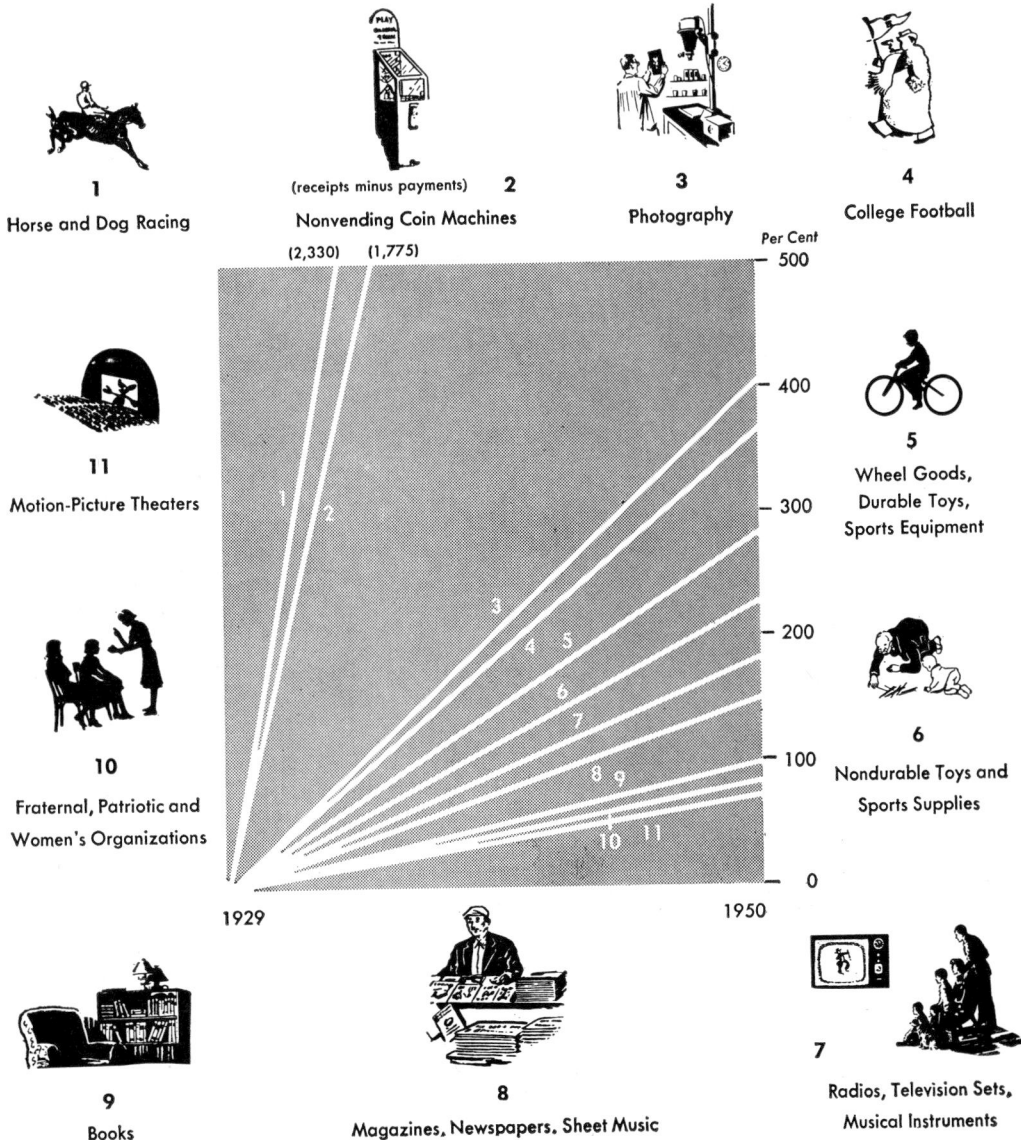

1
Horse and Dog Racing

(receipts minus payments) **2**
Nonvending Coin Machines

(2,330)   (1,775)

3
Photography

4
College Football

11
Motion-Picture Theaters

5
Wheel Goods,
Durable Toys,
Sports Equipment

6
Nondurable Toys and
Sports Supplies

10
Fraternal, Patriotic and
Women's Organizations

9
Books

8
Magazines, Newspapers, Sheet Music

7
Radios, Television Sets,
Musical Instruments

FIGURE 53. PERCENTAGE INCREASE IN SELECTED CONSUMPTION EXPENDITURES FOR RECREATION, 1929–1950
Source: Table 162.

ther to $82 million by 1941, resulting in a 1929–1941 increase of 925 per cent. Expenditures at horse and dog race tracks follow a somewhat similar pattern. Falling below the 1929 level of $2 million only in 1932 (to $1 million), they jumped to $6 million by 1934 and to $13 million by 1941.

The stock-market collapse had a disastrous ef-

fect on organizations and clubs. Expenditures in this category declined from $334 million in 1929 to a low of $224 million in 1935, and had recovered to only $233 million by 1941. Expenditures for dues and fees of school fraternities suffered very little, however, probably reflecting parental indulgence. They declined slightly in one year only — from $14 million in 1932 to $13 million

TABLE 162. INCREASES AND DECREASES IN CONSUMPTION EXPENDITURES FOR RECREATION, 1929–1950
(*Dollar Figures in Millions*)

Class	Expenditures			Increase, 1929–1950	
	1929	*1941*	*1950*	*Amount*	*Per Cent*
Horse and dog racing [a]	$ 10	$ 78	$ 243	$ 233	2,330
Nonvending coin machines — receipts minus payments	8	82	150	142	1,775
Professional football	1	3	9	8	800
Collectors' net acquisitions of stamps and coins	2	9	12	10	500
Photography	73	112	366	293	401
College football	22	39	103	81	368
Book rental and repairs [b]	2	4	9	7	350
Wheel goods, durable toys, sports equipment	182	254	695	513	282
Sightseeing buses and guides	3	6	10	7	233
Nondurable toys and sports supplies	336	371	1,102	766	228
Professional baseball	17	21	55	38	224
Luncheon clubs	6	9	19	13	217
Radios, television sets and musical instruments [c]	1,012	636	2,848	1,836	181
Dancing, riding, shooting, skating and swimming places	30	33	83	53	177
Boats and pleasure aircraft	24	30	64	40	167
Magazines, newspapers and sheet music [b]	538	619	1,338	800	149
Billiard parlors and bowling alleys	58	82	125	67	116
Entertainments of nonprofit organizations (except athletics) [d]	33	35	70	37	112
Veterinary service and purchase of pets	27	29	56	29	107
Amusement devices and parks	16	19	33	17	106
Professional hockey	3	4	6	3	100
Boat and bicycle rental, storage and repair	9	9	18	9	100
Books [b]	307	247	611	304	99
Fraternal, patriotic and women's organizations	134	102	241	107	80
School fraternities — dues and fees	14	18	25	11	79
Motion-picture theaters	720	756	1,247	527	73
Golf instruction, club rental and fees	91	64	143	52	58
Camp fees	32	30	44	12	38
Athletic and social clubs — dues and fees	148	74	182	34	23
Legitimate theaters and opera [d]	91	40	90	— 1	— 1
Private flying operations	9	6	8	— 1	— 11

Source: Appendix 4–4 and sources cited there.

a. Includes pari-mutuel net receipts.

b. Includes total consumer expenditures for these items. In Appendix 4–4, these expenditures are combined under "reading" and allocated partly to "recreation" and partly to "private education" in the ratio of 42 to 58.

c. Excludes expenditures for repairs.

d. Excludes ticket brokers' markup on admissions and purchase of programs.

in 1933; they were up to $16 million by 1936 and $18 million by 1941.

Like many other kinds of durable goods, radios and musical instruments suffered most drastically from depression economies. Purchases declined from $1 billion in 1929 to $195 million in 1933 and made only a partial recovery, to $636 million, by 1941. Sharp reductions in the prices of radios account for a large part of the decrease, of course, but not for all of it. Less than 11 per cent of the recreation dollar was spent for these

goods in 1933, compared with 26 per cent in 1929. (See Table 161.)

Also hard hit were legitimate theaters, operas and entertainments of nonprofit organizations, whose receipts (including ticket brokers' markup on admissions and purchase of programs) dropped from $130 million in 1929 to $42 million in 1933 and rose to only $79 million by 1941. Expenditures for hobbies and pets declined from $323 million in 1929 to $146 million in 1933, but had more than recovered by 1941 with expenditures of $397 million. Outlays for sports equipment dropped from $542 million in 1929 to $266 million in 1933, but had again reached the 1929 level by 1940.

1941–1945

Both incomes and prices rose steadily from 1941 to 1945, resulting in an increase in total recreational expenditures from $3.7 billion to $5.4 billion. Variations within the major categories of recreational spending, however, reveal the effects of wartime restrictions. (See Appendix 4-4.)

Through 1942, for example, dealers' inventories of radios and musical instruments were large enough to permit a continued upward trend in such purchases. Within a year, however, expenditures for these items dropped from $720 million to $463 million, and by the following year they were down to $364 million. By 1945, as restrictions on civilian production were beginning to be lifted, sales were improving slowly. Radio repairs meanwhile rose from $36 million to $84 million during the war years.

With the young men of the country in camps and on battle fronts around the world, expenditures for spectator sports dropped from $102 million in 1941 to $75 million in 1943. By 1945 they had increased to $128 million.

Though expenditures for organizations and clubs as a whole rose steadily during the war period, those organizations primarily dependent on youth for their dues and fees suffered. Receipts of athletic and social clubs dropped slightly — from $74 million in 1941 to $71 million in 1942. By 1945 they had jumped to $104 million. Dues and fees for school fraternities fell off from $18 million in 1941 to $11 million in 1944, and in 1945 they were still only $12 million.

The popularity of theaters, entertainments and amusements was very revealing of the times. People had money to spend, and they could not spend it on durable goods or travel. They needed escapist entertainment. Expenditures in this category rose from $944 million in 1941 to almost $1.7 billion in 1945. Motion-picture receipts alone accounted for more than $600 million of the increase.

1945–1950

With the end of the war, the American people were pleasure-bent. Working time was cut to about 40 hours a week; times were good and people had saved during the war. Postwar prosperity and increased leisure were reflected in heavier expenditures for recreation — most significantly for purchases of radios, television and musical instruments, which accounted for $2.4 billion, or half of the total increase from 1945 to 1950. In 1950 these products accounted for 28 per cent of all recreational expenditures, compared with 15.5 per cent in 1940.

Contributing to this phenomenal upsurge were pent-up demand for durable goods, accumulated savings, the appearance of television sets on the retail market, and improvements in radio and phonographic equipment. The 1949–1950 increase of over $850 million in expenditures for radios, television sets and musical instruments was no doubt due largely to scare buying after the outbreak of Korean hostilities in the summer of that year.

The only other major category of recreational expenditures to show a continuing rise from 1945 through 1950 was reading, hobbies and pets, which increased from $1.4 billion to $1.9 billion. An important factor in this increase has been the popularity of paper-covered books priced at 25 cents to a dollar. This type of publishing, which began in the 1930s, has boomed since the war. An estimated 200 million copies of the 25-cent pocket-size books alone were sold in 1950.[85]

The trend in expenditures for theaters, entertainments and amusements was quite different. This form of spending reached a peak of $1.9 billion in 1946, and dropped steadily thereafter to $1.7 billion by 1950. Motion-picture admissions, the largest item in the group, declined from $1.5 billion in 1946 to $1.2 billion in 1950. The group as a whole, which since 1909 had always taken more than 20 per cent and in some years more than 30 per cent of the recreation dollar, had declined in importance to less than 17 per cent by 1950. (See Table 161.)

Expenditures for spectator sports, which almost doubled (from $128 million to $230 million) between 1945 and 1946, continued to rise until 1949, when they reached $284 million, then dropped to $266 million in 1950. Amateur sports accounted for well over half the total increase, and it was primarily these, particularly college

---

85. *Wall Street Journal,* November 24, 1950.

football, that accounted for the postwar rise of the group.

Expenditures for participant recreation rose from $534 million in 1945 to a high of $777 million in 1948, dropping slightly to $763 million by 1950. Throughout the postwar years, about half the expenditures in this group were for pari-mutuel betting and nonvending coin machines.

Much more indicative of general interest in sports participation is the figure for sports equipment, purchases of which increased from $920 million in 1945 to almost $1.9 billion in 1950, despite a slight drop in 1949.

1950–1952

In general, postwar trends in recreational spending continued into the early 1950s with some modification probably due largely to effects of the Korean conflict.

Total expenditures increased by less than $300 million from 1950 to 1952, but this modest overall increase was accompanied by marked rises and declines in various types of expenditures.

Spectator amusements outside the home showed no tendency to regain their former preeminence. Motion-picture receipts were down another $100 million. Spectator sports held their own only by virtue of a $6 million increase in expenditures at horse and dog race tracks and a slight increase in gate receipts at both professional and college football games.

Consumers continued to spend an increasing amount on hobbies and pets. In the two years, the amount spent for reading increased by $66 million, for photography by $76 million, and for flowers, seeds and potted plants by almost $150 million.

The 1949–1950 decline in expenditures for participant recreation was reversed, with an increase of more than $100 million in spending for various sports in the two years. However, the category which showed the greatest increase ($62 million), pari-mutuel net receipts, could scarcely be classed as an active sport. The largest increase among active sports was the $26 million increase in expenditures for golf instruction, club rentals and fees.

Purchases of radios, television sets and musical instruments declined in these two years for the first time since the war, probably because so many families had rushed to buy these items after the outbreak of fighting in Korea. At the same time, repair bills on these instruments increased by $152 million.

As in the late 1940s, the increase in the number of children and a rising interest in active sports were accompanied by an increase of almost $300 million in expenditures for sports equipment and toys.

GOVERNMENT EXPENDITURES

Government expenditures for recreation were negligible at the beginning of this century and amounted to only $49 million just before World War I. Thereafter, and particularly during the prosperous 1920s, government rapidly expanded its promotion of recreation. By 1932, total government expenditures amounted to $220 million; federal and state expenditures had expanded more rapidly than local.

World War II brought a retrenchment. Federal, state and local governments combined spent only $157 million in 1942. With the end of the war, however, emphasis on public recreation services and facilities was renewed. Total public expenditures reached $403 million by 1950, with expenditures by the states more than four times as large and local expenditures more than twice as large as in 1942. (See Table 163.)

Since 1913, local government expenditures for operation of community recreation programs have increased much more rapidly than capital outlays for recreational facilities. In 1913, local expenditures were almost equally divided between capital outlay and current operation — $23 million and $22 million. By 1932, current operation was costing $99 million and capital outlay $82 million. In 1942 the figures were $110 million and $27 million; in 1950, $218 million and $109 million. The postwar period thus saw expenditures for organized community recreation programs and services almost doubled — largely because of higher wage and material costs. Rising land and construction costs have greatly deterred expansion of facilities since World War II. As a result of the sharp price increases, the local capital outlay of $109 million in 1950 bought far less than the $82 million spent for buildings and facilities in 1932. In 1950, government restrictions on construction caused modification of plans for new construction and area development.[86]

86. Arthur Williams, "Parks and Recreation — Developments in 1950," *Municipal Year Book*, 1951, pp. 455–458.

TABLE 163. GOVERNMENT EXPENDITURES FOR RECREATION, FISCAL YEARS ENDING 1913, 1932, 1942 AND 1950
(Millions)

Division	1913	1932	1942	1950
Total	$49	$220	$157	$403
Federal	1	15	8	24
State	3	24	12	52
Local	45	181	137	327
Capital outlay				
Federal	0	9	4	8
State	1	16	4	23
Local	23	82	27	109
Operation				
Federal	1	6	4	16
State	2	8	8	29
Local	22	99	110	218

Sources: Federal and local — unpublished estimates, Governments Division, U.S. Bureau of the Census; state — Wealth, Debt and Taxation, Vol. II, U.S. Bureau of the Census, 1913; Historical Statistics of the United States, 1789–1945, U.S. Bureau of the Census, 1949, Series P 210; unpublished tabulations, Governments Division, U.S. Bureau of the Census; Compendium of State Government Finances in 1942 and Compendium of State Government Finances in 1950, U.S. Bureau of the Census.

Note: Totals differ from totals shown in Chapter 18, in which various items classified here as recreation are classified elsewhere. For example, in that chapter state park expenditures are shown under "natural resources" and outlays for recreational facilities operated by school systems are classified under education. Both are included here as recreational expenditures.

An outstanding development of the postwar years is the new interest of the states in recreation.[87] Three states had established separate recreation commissions as of 1950: North Carolina, with a 1950-1951 budget of $45,000; Vermont, with a 1950 budget of $11,000; and California, with an estimated 1949–1950 budget of $88,000.

PRIVATE SPENDING FOR COMMUNITY RECREATION

No figures are available on total expenditures of private funds for community recreation, but indications are that the amount is impressive. According to reports to the National Recreation Association for 1950, 4 per cent of total expenditures for local recreation and park programs came from private sources, including community chests, contributions, memberships and gifts. Of the 1,880 cities that reported park and recreation

programs, 120 said these programs were supported entirely from private funds and 519 that public funds were supplemented by private funds.[88] In 1950, 38.1 per cent of community chest funds in 159 areas were appropriated to local agencies for leisure-time activities.[89]

A few examples suggest the enormous contribution of voluntary agencies to organized community recreation. In 1950, Boys' Clubs had local operating budgets of nearly $7 million; the Camp Fire Girls' local councils spent more than $3 million in 1949; the local councils of the Boy Scouts of America had a budget of about $18 million in 1950.[90] Walter F. Stone, in 1949, estimated that in urban communities, private agencies spent about one dollar per capita for recreation.[91]

PUBLIC RECREATION NEEDS IN 1950

Despite the great developments of the postwar period, local surveys throughout the country have indicated the need for continued expansion of public programs and facilities, to provide adequate recreational opportunities for all.

The California Recreation Commission, for example, reported in March 1950 that almost half of all communities of 2,500 population or over in the state were without year-round recreation programs.[92] In Minnesota, only 25 cities had year-round programs in 1949.[93] In Pennsylvania, there were 1,827 communities in 1950 with no organized recreation program whatever, 122 cities and towns with year-round programs, and 611 with part-time programs. Less than 5 per cent of the communities in the state had adequately provided for both outdoor and indoor areas and facilities.[94]

In a national survey made by the Institute of

87. "State Recreation Services," Recreation, June 1950, pp. 118–133.

88. Recreation and Park Yearbook, Midcentury Edition, pp. 12–22.

89. Community Chest Budgeting for 1950, Bulletin 149, Community Chests and Councils of America, Inc., June 1950.

90. Letters from the three organizations, January 1951.

91. The Field of Recreation, William-Frederick Press, New York, 1949, p. 16.

92. Recreation in California, Second Annual Report, State of California Recreation Commission, Sacramento, California, March 1950, p. 10.

93. Recreational Resources of the People of Minnesota, Report of Governor's Advisory Committee on Recreation, St. Paul, Minnesota, January 1950, pp. 17, 18.

94. "Recreation in the Commonwealth of Pennsylvania Has Recognized and Accepted the Challenge of Our Increasing Leisure," State Planning Board, Department of Commerce, mimeographed, no date.

Public Opinion in 1949, only 42 per cent of the voters questioned considered the public parks and playgrounds in their communities adequate.[95]

STANDARDS FOR PUBLIC FACILITIES AND SERVICES

In order to give communities some basis for estimating the adequacy of their recreational areas and facilities and for planning for expansion to meet present and future needs, standards have been established by such organizations as the National Recreation Association and the American Society of Planning Officials. Meyer and Brightbill in their book *Community Recreation* suggest standards that are a composite of the recommendations of these and other municipal, regional and national planning and operating organizations.[96]

Briefly, the standards arrived at by Meyer and Brightbill are as follows:

Facility	Suggested Standard	Unit of Population
Total recreation acreage	1 acre	100
Large recreation park	200 acres	40,000
Playfields	1 acre	800
Playgrounds	1 acre	800
Softball	1 field	3,000
Baseball	1 field	6,000
Tennis	1 court	2,000
Swimming (outdoor)	Pools to accommodate 3 per cent of the population at one time — 12 sq. ft. per swimmer.	
Swimming (indoor)	1 pool	50,000
Gymnasium (large)	1	10,000
Auditorium (large)	1	15,000
Recreation buildings	1	15,000
Clubrooms	1	5,000
Outdoor theater	1	100,000
Golf (public)	1 hole	3,000

Densely populated areas, according to these writers, should have playlots (simple play areas for small children) of from 1,500 to 10,000 square feet serving the population within a radius of an eighth of a mile; playlots serving a quarter-mile radius are adequate in less densely populated areas. Playgrounds (larger play areas with play equipment) should be located in such a way as to serve the surrounding area one-fourth to one-half mile distant, depending on population density. Playfields, which are usually utilized by the teen-agers and adults, can adequately serve the population within a radius of a mile or a mile and a half.

Services considered essential for a successful community program of recreation include: a full-time, trained recreation executive; a year-round program serving all the recreational interests of the people without restriction as to race, religion, age or sex; availability of all suitable city-owned property for recreational use; a segregated recreation budget; and a governing board or commission of responsible citizens. A final essential is interagency cooperation through recreation councils, committees of councils of social agencies or other groups.[97]

PROGRESS TOWARD ATTAINMENT

The standards outlined provide ready measures of the adequacy of recreational facilities in any given community. It is difficult, however, to apply them on a national basis as there is no complete centralized reporting on recreation. The best national figures available are those published biennially in the yearbooks of the National Recreation Association. These reports, submitted by localities on a voluntary basis and therefore incomplete, nevertheless furnish a yardstick of progress.

Reports made to the Association in 1940 and 1950 indicate that urban residents had only slightly more adequate space for recreation in 1950 than in 1940. In 1940, urban places averaged an estimated 133 persons per acre of park and recreation area; in 1950, 126 persons per acre.[98] (See Tables 27 and 164.)

Average population per acre of recreation space is, of course, only a rough measure of the extent to which the need is being met. Of great importance, and impossible to estimate on a national scale with the data available, is the distribution of the space.

An analysis of park and recreational areas in 22 large cities in 1946 showed that these cities averaged only one acre to every 242 people —

95. "Voters See Need for More Parks, Playgrounds," Public Opinion News Service release, July 2, 1949.

96. *Op. cit.*, pp. 454–456 and 474, 475.

97. Article on "Recreation" in 1943 *Social Work Year Book*, p. 427.

98. The urban population according to the old Census definition of urban areas is used here for comparability with 1940. Use of the urban population according to the new urban definition would raise the average to 137 persons per acre, but it would be misleading to compare this with the 1940 average. For an explanation of the difference in area covered under the 1940 and 1950 Census urban definitions, see Chapter 3, p. 72.—

TABLE 164. ESTIMATED PARK ACREAGE OF COMMUNITIES OF 2,500 POPULATION AND OVER, 1940 AND 1950

| Population Group | Acreage — 195 Cities [a] | | | Estimated Total Park Acreage | |
	1940	1950	Ratio 1950 to 1940	1940 [b]	1950 [c]
Total				557,653	704,330
1 million and over	26,901	31,490	117.0	48,718	57,000
500,000 to 1 million	36,099	44,398	122.9	51,443	63,223
250,000 to 500,000	33,195	44,503	134.0	66,010	88,453
100,000 to 250,000	58,129	67,055	115.3	79,915	92,142
50,000 to 100,000	15,260	22,353	146.4	75,007	109,810
25,000 to 50,000	7,361	9,225	125.3	57,704	68,544
10,000 to 25,000	6,092	7,512	123.3	97,637	120,386
5,000 to 10,000	1,098	1,354	123.3	53,760	66,286
2,500 to 5,000 [d]	—	—	—	30,459	38,486

a. A selected group of 195 cities of 5,000 population and over for which 1940 and 1950 figures are considered comparable by the National Recreation Association. Figures for 1940 are from *Municipal and County Parks in the United States, 1940*, National Park Service, U.S. Department of the Interior, in cooperation with the National Recreation Association and the American Institute of Park Executives, 1942; 1950 figures are from *Recreation and Park Yearbook*, National Recreation Association, 1951.

b. Based on reports received on park acreage in the 1940 survey cited in footnote *a* above. The estimate is computed on the assumption (1) that for all communities in each size class, the percentage with parks and without parks would be the same as for each size class in the cities reporting and (2) that the average park acreage for each size class in all cities having parks would be the same as for reporting cities having parks.

c. Computed on the assumption that the 1950 to 1940 ratio of park acreage for each size class in the 195-identical-cities sample would be the same for all cities in each size class.

d. No cities in this size group included in 195-cities sample; 1950 park acreage estimated on basis of percentage of total this group comprised in 1940.

less than half the minimum national standard. But the older, more congested sections of these cities — which accounted for nearly 5 million of the total population of 21 million — averaged only one acre of recreation and park space to 960 people.[99]

The expanding role of government in recreation during the past two or three decades has been reflected not only in a steady increase of recreational facilities but also in the greater number of cities able to provide paid supervisors. Particularly marked during the last decade has been the increased emphasis on organized recreation programs. Communities reporting to the National Recreation Association listed 58,029 paid leaders in 1950 compared with 24,533 in 1940. During the same period the number of volunteer leaders reported increased from 12,890 to 52,982. (See Table 165.)

CURRENT EXPENDITURES IN RELATION TO NEEDS

Local governments in 1950 spent $218 million, or less than $2.25 per capita, to provide recreational services to the urban population. (See Table 163.) Per capita expenditure for recreation programs and services for the 474 cities having more than 25,000 inhabitants in 1950 was $2.51.[100] For the nation's 39 largest cities, the per capita outlay was only slightly higher, $2.70. Of this group of cities, only two spent more than $5.00: San Francisco, $6.39 (the highest recorded for any city), and San Diego, $5.15.[101]

The National Recreation Association estimated before World War II that American cities should spend $3.00 per capita each year to provide adequate recreation service. A conservative adjustment to current prices would bring the standard to $5.00 per capita.

99. Testimony of Tam Deering, Planning Consultant, Hearings on H.R. 2026 before a Subcommittee of the Committee on Education and Labor, House of Representatives, 81st Cong., 1st sess., June 1, 1949, pp. 27–28.

100. *Compendium of City Government Finances in 1950*, U.S. Bureau of the Census, 1951, p. 5.

101. *Large-City Finances in 1950*, U.S. Bureau of the Census, 1951, p. 28.

TABLE 165. SELECTED FACILITIES AND PERSONNEL IN MUNICIPAL RECREATION, 1920–1950

Facility or Type of Personnel	1920	1930	1940	1950
Baseball diamonds	—	4,322	3,904	5,502
Bathing beaches	260	457	572	780
Golf courses	—	312	387	454
Handball courts	—	—	2,737	1,953
Ice-skating areas	—	—	2,912	3,274
Playgrounds — outdoor	4,293	7,316	9,921	14,747
Recreation buildings [a]	300	642	1,750	2,987
Recreation centers — indoor	—	1,963	3,986	6,630
Stadiums	—	—	261	504
Swimming pools	359	1,042	1,200	1,616
Tennis courts	—	8,422	12,075	13,085
Toboggan slides	—	221	314	268
Paid leaders	10,218	24,949	24,533 [b]	58,029
Volunteer leaders	—	8,216	12,890	52,982

Source: Yearbooks and reports of the National Recreation Association for 1920, 1930, 1940 and 1950. Figures are totals for all communities that sent reports to the National Recreation Association for the years cited, and are therefore not complete national totals. The numbers of communities reporting for each facility vary from year to year. In 1950, for example, the Census reported 4,270 communities of over 2,500 population, but the number of communities reporting to the National Recreation Association ranged from 209 to 2,277, according to the facility reported on.

a. Exclusive of schoolhouses.
b. Excluding leaders paid with emergency funds.

It is obvious that expenditures in 1950 fell far short of the National Recreation Association's standard, which presumably would have brought recreational services within the reach of every city dweller (assuming that facilities were available for such programs).

Needs, as expressed in this study, are based on a minimum standard of adequacy to meet the health needs of the population. On the basis of local budget requests examined, and taking into account the recommendations of the National Recreation Association, it is assumed that an increase of 25 per cent in urban spending for recreational programs and services in 1950 would have made it possible to extend the services to areas where such services were lacking or where expansion of public services was urgently needed because of inadequate private facilities.

An increase of 25 per cent would have brought local expenditures in 1950 to about $275 million, or roughly $2.80 per urban dweller.[102]

Although most of the gap between need and demand must be made up by local governments, which accounted for five sixths of all current outlays in 1950, state governments and the federal government would also have to increase outlays. If it is assumed that the relationship of actual current expenditures in 1950 to expenditures needed to provide adequate services is the same at the state level as for local governments, needed state expenditures for recreational services in 1950 would have amounted to roughly $36 million, compared with actual outlays of $29 million. Because of the vastly increased public use of federal recreational facilities over the past decade, assumption of a sharper rise between actual and needed federal outlays — in the neighborhood of 60 per cent — seems defensible. On this basis, needed federal outlays would have been about $25 million in 1950 compared with actual outlays of $16 million.

Thus, total governmental current operating expenditures of $336 million were probably needed in 1950 to provide minimum needs of the population for public recreation services, compared with the $263 million actually spent for this purpose.

CAPITAL EXPENDITURES AND NEEDS

According to the standard of one acre of park and recreation space for each 100 of the population, the 98 million inhabitants of our cities in 1950 [103] would have "needed" 980,000 acres of park and recreation space.

The actual acreage of municipal park and play areas is unknown, but a rough estimate can be derived from a survey covering the year 1940 conducted by the National Park Service in cooperation with the National Recreation Association and the American Institute of Park Executives, and reports made to the National Recreation Association for the *1950 Recreation and Park Yearbook.*

Estimates of total park acreage in 1950 were arrived at in the following way: Percentage increases in park acreage between 1940 and 1950 in a sample of 195 cities selected by the National Recreation Association for comparability of reporting were applied to estimates of park acreage in 1940 in various sizes of cities. According to this very rough estimate, the total for 1950

102. Based on the new Census definition. See Table 27.

103. New Census definition.

amounted to about 704,000 acres. (See Table 164.) This acreage fell short by 276,000 of the standard of one acre for each 100 urban residents.

In 1940 the total municipal park area of 1,021 cities reporting to the Association came to 353,-184 acres and the total value to $1.7 billion, or an average of $4,685 per acre. In all probability, considerably less than half of this sum represented the value of the "raw land," so that buildings and improvements may have averaged as much as $3,000 per acre. Adjusted to 1950 prices, the average would be about $6,800.[104]

On this basis, a total capital outlay of more than $1,850 million would have been required in 1950 for buildings and improvements on the 276,000 additional acres of municipal park land needed. It is, of course, unreasonable, and most unrealistic, to expect these "deficiencies" to be made good in a year's time. If this additional capital expenditure were made over a period of ten years, the annual outlay would approximate $186 million. Deficiencies will increase, of course, as population grows over the decade, so that an even larger annual capital expenditure would be required in future years. Actual local capital expenditures of about $109 million in 1950 seem small in contrast.

Despite the increased public use of state parks from 1940 to 1950, the expansion of park acreage did not keep pace with the growth of population, so that per capita acreage in these areas actually declined in this period. The high cost of labor and materials also deterred improvements on existing acreage. It is estimated that the 1950 expenditures of $23 million for expansion and improvement of state park facilities should have been increased about 25 per cent to meet the need, or to about $29 million in 1950.

The per capita decline in national park acreage from 1940 to 1950 was even greater than the decline in state parks. This was attended by almost doubled public use of these areas. It is estimated that the federal capital expenditures of $8 million in 1950 should have been increased by almost 100 per cent, or to roughly $15 million, to keep pace with need for expansion and improvement of national park facilities.

Thus, there was an estimated gap of $90 mil-

lion between actual and needed total public expenditures for capital improvement of recreational areas and facilities in 1950. (See Table 166.)

NEEDS AND DEMAND FOR PUBLIC RECREATION IN 1960

Over the past two decades, increases in spending for recreational services and facilities at the state and local levels have been largely accounted for by changes in the costs of goods and services. Therefore there is little basis for assuming that, measured in 1950 dollars, expenditures at these levels will be significantly higher in 1960 than in 1950.

PROBABLE EXPENDITURE

It is likely that current expenditures in 1960 by state governments will be $29 million and by local governments $218 million — the same amounts as in 1950. Because of the vastly increased public use of national park facilities, and the expected expansion of these facilities by 1960, the federal government is expected to increase its 1960 outlays for recreational services to about $29 million — about 80 per cent over 1950. On this basis, total public current outlays for recreation are expected to increase by about $13 million — from $263 million in 1950 to $276 million in 1960.

The projected increase in total capital outlays is expected to be somewhat greater — from $140 million in 1950 to $180 million in 1960. On the basis of recent trends, federal expenditures in 1960 for expansion and improvement of recreational facilities are expected to increase to $25 million by 1960, more than three times the 1950 capital outlay. The projected expenditure of about $25 million for capital improvements in state parks is based on recent trends in state expenditures in relation to total expenditures at all government levels.

At the local level, past trends would indicate that outlays (measured in constant dollars) for buildings and improvements in recreational areas would not increase by 1960. Because of the enormous increase in the number of school age children, however, an increase to $130 million is projected. This estimate is based largely on the expected increase in playgrounds and play areas, sports fields, stadiums, etc., that are built in con-

---

104. Price index for new construction, "National Income and Product of the United States, 1952," *Survey of Current Business*, July 1953, Table B, p. 27, adjusted to a 1950 base.

TABLE 166. ESTIMATED RECREATIONAL EXPENDITURES TO MEET DEMAND AND NEEDS
IN 1950 AND 1960

(Millions)

	1950		1960	
	Demand	*Needs*	*Demand*	*Needs*
Total	$10,861	$11,024	$13,466	$13,720
Current	10,474	10,547	12,946	13,070
Consumer	10,211	10,211	12,670	12,670
Government [a]	263	336	276	400
Capital	387	477	520	650
Private	247	247	340 [b]	340
Government [c]	140	230	180	310

Sources: Table 163, Appendices 4–4, 4–7 and 4–8 and discussion in text.

a. Figures differ from figures shown in Chapter 18. State park expenditures, classified here as recreational, are shown in that chapter under "natural resources."

b. Difference between total capital expenditures for recreation shown in Appendix 4–7 and government capital expenditures.

c. Figures differ from figures shown in Chapter 18 because of the inclusion here of state park expenditures, as noted above, and because some activities classified here as recreation are classified elsewhere in Chapter 18 — for example, capital expenditures for recreational facilities operated by school systems.

junction with expanding school facilities but for purposes of this chapter are classified as recreational facilities.

GAP BETWEEN EXPENDITURE AND NEED

By 1960, the disparity between actual and needed expenditure for current operation is expected to be even greater than in 1950. A total projected need of $400 million in expenditures for recreational programs and services will mean unmet need for current expenditure of $124 million. The expected gaps between current expenditure and need at the state and local levels are based on the projected increase in total population and urban population, respectively. Estimated local need of $305 million for recreational programs and services accounts for most of the total gap. Federal need also is expected to greatly exceed probable outlays. The use of national parks increased by almost 100 per cent from 1940 to 1950. The rate of increased use was much faster during the early 1950s. It is obvious, therefore, that the expected 80 per cent rise in federal current expenditures from 1950 to 1960 will not meet the need for expanded programs and services. Moreover, in view of the extremely rapid rise in the rate of use of these services in recent

years, need will undoubtedly rise at a faster rate than probable outlays. Since need exceeded demand by nearly 60 per cent in 1950, it probably will be almost double 1960 outlays, or about $55 million.

The backlog of need for capital improvements, as well as the need for continuing expansion because of growth in population, will call for a 1960 estimated needed capital expenditure of $310 million, or $130 million more than expected expenditures. Most of the gap between need and demand in 1960 is accounted for by the estimated local need of $240 million, $110 million higher than expected local capital expenditures. This estimate is based on the expected increase of about 16 per cent in the urban population with an additional much wider disparity between expenditure and need estimated for recreational facilities operated by school systems.

SUMMARY OF RECREATION EXPENDITURES AND NEEDS IN 1950 AND 1960

In 1950, total expenditures for recreation amounted to about $10.9 billion, of which current expenditures by consumers accounted for $10.2 billion, and by government for $263 million. Private and public capital expenditures amounted to $387 million. Total expenditures are expected to rise to $13.5 billion (at 1950 prices) in 1960, consisting of $12.7 billion in consumer expenditures, $276 million in government expenditures for current operation and $520 million in private and public capital outlays.

In order to meet the additional needs described above, government current expenditures would have had to rise from $263 million to $336 million in 1950 and would have to reach $400 million in 1960, some $124 million higher than is expected for that year. To meet these needs, government capital outlays would have had to be increased from $140 million to $230 million in 1950 and would have to reach $310 million in 1960, compared with an expected level of $180 million. (See Table 166.)

No attempt has been made to distinguish between "need" and "demand" in the case of the largest single item, consumer expenditures, or in the case of private capital expenditures. The reasons for this are obvious. Although recreation and relaxation are now recognized as necessities in the modern world, and the community has accepted responsibility for providing many public recreational facilities, nobody has yet had the temerity to establish "minimum standards of decency" for the use of leisure time, or a minimum budget for the purchase of the wide variety of recreational goods and services offered to consumers. How often, if at all, the consumer "should" be able to go to the movies or the horse races, how many mystery stories or decks of cards he "ought" to have the money to buy, what minimum of pool playing, bowling or skating is necessary to maintain mental and physical health, are questions on which there is unlikely to be any consensus among recreation authorities. Indeed, the nature and purpose of most kinds of recreational pursuits are such that their essential contribution to the individual's welfare would be lost once free choice was abandoned.

## CHAPTER 12

EDUCATION

"POPULAR GOVERNMENT without popular education," declared James Madison, "is a prologue to a farce or a tragedy." There has been great progress since this warning was written, but in the second half of the twentieth century we have still not fully achieved "popular education" adequate to the needs of popular government.

Until 1880 there was neither effective compulsory education nor child labor laws, little provision for adult and technical education and virtually none for the teaching of handicapped children. Few men had a secondary school education; women seldom were allowed to venture above the elementary level. Only a small percentage of public school teachers had any professional training for their work. School buildings and equipment often were primitive.

Today, popular education, although by no means equally available to all, is provided on a constantly expanding scale. It is one of the most widely available social services, often with special provision for handicapped children. Vocational and adult education opportunities are widely spread, especially in the cities. Boys and girls, in virtually every community, are on a par. Professionally trained teachers are the rule rather than the exception.

The resources and efficiency of the United States are sufficient to provide a high quality of schooling for all. Nevertheless, certain educational deprivations and inequalities are insistent reminders of our democratic shortcomings.

STATUS AND SCOPE OF AMERICAN EDUCATION

In 1950 the American people spent just over $10.5 billion for education in all categories. Of this total, schools and colleges spent $9.1 billion; individuals spent $1.1 billion for educational reading matter; and the rest was spent by li-

braries, educational and research foundations, and museums. There were about 170,000 schools of various levels, with a capital (land, buildings and equipment) value of $16.2 billion and endowments totaling $2.6 billion.[1] There were more than 1.2 million teachers. Enrollments in schools and colleges amounted to more than 31 million individuals — more than three quarters of the population between the ages of 5 and 21. Part-time and adult education reached at least another 30 million.

There are many ways of acquiring an education other than sitting before a teacher in a classroom. Libraries, museums and foundations, as well as schools and colleges, are educational institutions. Books, newspapers and periodicals and radio and television also play a major part in the educational process.

Museums attract more than 50 million visitors a year.[2] Public libraries in 1950 loaned about 360 million books to approximately 29 million registered borrowers.[3] Enough pamphlets are sold to supply every man, woman and child with almost three a year, and enough books are printed to supply every individual with more than three a year.[4] The circulation of periodicals per issue is more than double the total population.[5] The circulation of newspapers per issue, including daily, Sunday, weekly and others, is 120 million.[6]

---

1. Exclusive of the property and endowments of private elementary and secondary schools.

2. Museum visitors in 1939 were estimated at 50 million annually (Laurence Vail Coleman, *The Museum in America,* American Association of Museums, 1939, Vol. II, p. 278). How much higher the 1950 figure would be is unknown; no estimate seems to have been published.

3. Information supplied by the Library Service Section, U.S. Office of Education. This does not include the borrowers from libraries which accept credentials such as drivers' licenses in lieu of a library card; nor does it include books used within the library premises.

4. *1947 Census of Manufactures,* Vol. II, p. 358, reports 487 million books and 402 million pamphlets sold in 1947.

5. *Ibid.,* p. 357. The circulation of periodicals is given at 385 million.

6. *Ibid.,* p. 354.

By WILLIAM G. CARR, Executive Secretary, National Education Association. Opinions and judgments expressed in this chapter are those of the author and should not be attributed to the organization with which he is associated.

TABLE 167. PER CENT OF POPULATION 5–24 YEARS OF AGE ENROLLED IN SCHOOL, BY AGE, 1910–1950 [a]

Age	1910	1920	1930	1940	1950
Total, 5–24 years	b	b	58.2	57.7	62.5
5–19 years	62.6	67.4	73.4	74.8	78.7
5 and 6 years	34.6	41.0	43.2	43.0	55.7
7–13 years	86.1	90.6	95.3	95.0	95.7
14 and 15 years	75.0	79.9	88.8	90.0	92.9
16 and 17 years	43.1	42.9	57.3	68.7	74.4
18 and 19 years	18.7	17.8	25.4	28.9	32.2
20–24 years	b	b	7.4	6.6	12.9

Source: Seventeenth Census of Population (1950), Vol. II, *Characteristics of the Population,* Tables 42 and 43.

a. Kindergarten enrollment figures are included for 1950 but only partially included in the figures for earlier years.

b. Not available.

ORGANIZED EDUCATION [7]

An outstanding social achievement of this century has been the raising of the general educational level of the American people. During the past fifty years, school attendance has more than doubled. Approximately three fifths of the population 5 to 19 years of age attended school in 1910. By 1950 the proportion had increased to almost four fifths. The proportion of the population in school has increased in all age groups. (See Table 167.)

Compulsory school attendance laws have played an important role in this progress. However, such legislation, as a rule, has been the result, rather than the primary cause, of broad social and economic change.

Beyond the letter of the law, the developments of recent years have increased greatly the amount of schooling provided for Americans. Specialization of labor has increased the demand for both general and vocational education. Because of greater productivity, it has been possible to use more economic resources for the care and education of young people. Advancing technology has required not only longer periods of pre-employment training but also frequent retraining of those already employed. With the growing complexity of national and international prob-

lems, a successful democracy must provide more and better civic education for more of its population. Such influences as these have resulted in increased enrollments in schools and colleges beyond the years of compulsory schooling, and these same trends have forced changes in the content of education.

Other social forces, however, work in the opposite direction. Secondary school enrollments tend to decrease when jobs for adolescents are most plentiful. Deficiencies in family income cut short the education of many who otherwise might profit by added years in school or college. Lack of ingenuity in devising suitable school programs and lack of funds to provide specialized programs prevent full utilization of the capacities of the entire population. The failure or inability of many school systems to provide kindergarten and nursery schools limits the enrollment of preschool children, many of whom need this early group experience. A further limitation, however, is the parental fear of "institutionalizing" young children.

According to 1950 Census data, about 71 per cent of the adult population (25 years of age and over) have completed grade school. Half of all persons aged 25 and over in 1950 had completed 9.3 or more years of school. This median figure for the entire adult population, however, is less revealing than the medians for the subgroups. For persons 65 and over, who finished school around the turn of the century, the median was 8.2 years; and for those 45 to 54, the median

7. Data in this section, unless otherwise indicated, are from biennial surveys of education conducted by the U.S. Office of Education. See particularly *Statistical Summary of Education, 1949–50,* 1953, *Statistics of State School Systems, 1949–50,* 1952, and *Statistics of Higher Education, 1949–50,* 1952.

TABLE 168. YEARS OF SCHOOL COMPLETED BY PERSONS 25 YEARS OLD AND OVER, 1950

Age	Median School Years Completed	Per Cent Who Completed at Least: [a]			
		8 Years of Grade School	4 Years of High School	2 Years of College	4 Years of College
Total, 25 years and over	9.3	70.8	33.4	10.6	6.0
25–29 years	12.1	84.8	52.2	13.9	7.6
30–34 years	11.5	82.4	46.1	12.4	6.8
35–39 years	10.5	77.9	39.5	12.3	6.8
40–44 years	9.9	74.6	34.9	12.7	7.4
45–54 years	8.8	68.0	28.2	10.3	5.8
55–64 years	8.4	59.7	21.4	8.0	4.5
65 years and over	8.2	53.2	16.7	5.7	3.3

Source: 1950 Census of Population: Preliminary Reports, Series PC–7, No. 6, May 13, 1952, Table 1.

a. Excludes small percentage of cases (2.2 per cent of the total) for which years of schooling were not reported.

was 8.8 years. But for those between 25 and 29 years, who reflect more closely the *present* status of education, the median was 12.1 years. Thus the typical young adult today completes four years of high school, while the chances are that his father had less than a year in high school and that his grandfather did not go beyond grade school. (See Table 168.)

Educational Progress

The period between the two world wars saw striking advances in the educational level of the population. The proportion completing grade school increased by a third; twice as many graduated from high school; and there was a comparable expansion at the college level. But there is much room for improvement both in quality and quantity. More than one young person out of ten today fails to complete grade school; about one half of the young persons of appropriate age graduate from high school; and only about 14 per cent obtain education of the kind represented by the junior college and other institutions of college grade.

Another indication of educational progress during the past generation is that in 1917–1918 the typical (median) enlisted man in the army had completed 7 years of schooling, while in 1944 he had completed 10 years. Only 4.1 per cent of enlisted men in World War I had finished high school; in World War II, more than 23 per cent were high school graduates. The proportion of servicemen who were college grad-

uates trebled between the two wars, rising from 1.2 per cent in World War I to 3.6 per cent in World War II. (See Table 169.)

TABLE 169. DISTRIBUTION OF SAMPLINGS OF ENLISTED MEN IN THE ARMY, BY YEARS OF EDUCATION, WORLD WARS I AND II

Years of Schooling Completed	Per Cent of Enlisted Men in:	
	World War I [a]	World War II [b]
Total	100.0	100.0
Grade school (8 years or less)	76.7	30.9
High school		
1 year	6.3	7.8
2 years	4.8	10.9
3 years	2.7	11.2
4 years	4.1	23.3
College		
1 year	1.8	6.3
2 years	1.5	4.0
3 years	0.9	2.0
4 years	1.2	3.6

a. Data adapted by the U.S. Office of Education from *Memoirs,* National Academy of Sciences, 1921, Vol. XV, Chap. 10.

b. "Educational Level of Men and Women in the Armed Forces," U.S. Office of Education, mimeographed memorandum dated October 1, 1944.

Elementary and Secondary Schools

Public elementary and secondary schools are at the heart of organized education. In the 1949–1950 school year 8 per cent of all elementary and secondary schools were private schools. They accounted for almost 12 per cent of the total enrollment. This was a slight increase over 1940, when private schools enrolled 9 per cent of the total. Private schools are usually smaller than the public schools in the same locality; however, on the average, private schools are larger than public because of the many small public schools in sparsely settled rural areas.

School Plant

There are about 167,000 public and private elementary and secondary schools in the United States. A peak was reached sometime during World War I; the steady decline since then has been due mainly to the closing of many one-room, one-teacher schools. The number of one-teacher schools declined at the rate of about 3,900 a year during the 1920s, about 3,500 a year during the 1930s, and approximately 3,900 a year during the early 1940s. During the latter part of the 1940s the rate of decline was greatly accelerated. Between 1946 and 1950 the total dropped from 86,563 to 59,852. The number of schools has continued to decline since then, although at a slower rate, as the process of consolidation of schools and transportation of pupils reaches the limits set by geography and population dispersal.

The cost value of public secondary and elementary school property and the value of permanent school funds in 1950 totaled more than $12 billion, of which $11.4 billion represented land, buildings and equipment.[8] Since 1920 the cost value of public elementary and secondary school property has increased from $112 to $454 per pupil enrolled, but facilities are still far from adequate.

Enrollment and Attendance

Some 29 million pupils were enrolled in elementary and secondary schools in 1950. This total amounted to approximately 79 per cent of the population between the ages of 5 and 19, compared with 75 per cent in 1940 and 63 per cent in 1910.

Elementary school enrollments have increased steadily. More than one fifth of all 5-year-olds and all but 5 per cent of the 6-year-olds were in school in 1950. In 1910 less than 74 per cent

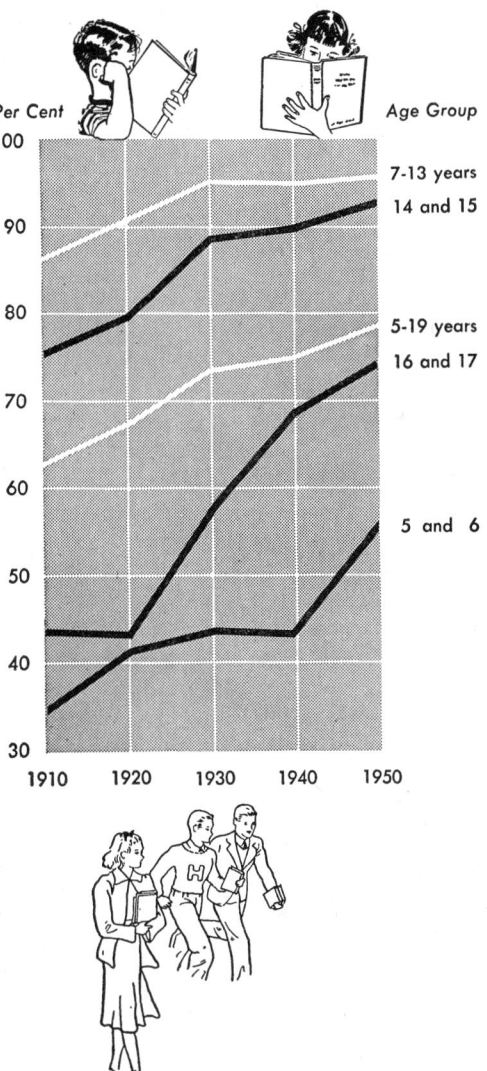

FIGURE 54. PER CENT OF POPULATION IN SELECTED AGE GROUPS ENROLLED IN SCHOOL, 1910–1950
Source: Table 167.

of children aged 5–13 were enrolled in elementary school; by 1950 the proportion of this age group enrolled had risen to 88 per cent. (See Table 167 and Figure 54.)

Secondary school enrollments, however, have increased at a much more striking rate. In 1890 these accounted for only 2.5 per cent of the total school enrollment. By 1950 and in 1953 this proportion reached 21.5 per cent.[9] However, the

8. This does not include state public-school lands, upon which it is difficult to set a value.

9. Schools and the 1950 Census, National Education Association, Research Bulletin, Vol. XXIX, No. 4, December 1951, p. 167.

proportion of all school enrollment in high school has decreased slightly in the past ten years because of the very rapid rise in elementary school enrollments, which accompanied the sharp increase in the number of children of elementary school age.

The rapidly expanding program of secondary education undoubtedly has been the major characteristic of this country's twentieth-century school system.

Another measure of increasing education is the extension of the school term. Public schools were in session an average of 135 days a year in 1890; in 1940 they were in session 175 days; in 1950 the figure was 178 days. During the same period the average number of days attended by each pupil enrolled increased from 86 to 152 and then to 158 days — an increase in the average rate of attendance from 64 per cent in 1890 to 89 per cent in 1950.

The average number of pupils per teacher in public schools declined from a peak of nearly 37 in 1900 to 29 by 1940, and to 28 in 1950. In many cities, however, class size has increased markedly in the last decade, and double "shifts" are increasingly common. The Research Division of the National Education Association has estimated that in 1952 at least a half million children were on half-day or similar part-time arrangements; the comparable number for 1953–1954 was almost certainly in excess of 600,000. A backlog of school construction needs has been built up by many years of relative neglect and by the recent birth rate increases. School construction is not in pace with current classroom needs. In 526 urban communities, one third of the children were in classes enrolling 35 or more.

Teachers

Public elementary and secondary schools employed 962,000 teachers (including principals and supervisors) and private schools employed an estimated 118,000 in 1950. The number of teachers more than doubled between 1900 and 1950, while the number of pupils enrolled increased by two thirds. The average salary of public school teachers was $325 in 1900; in 1920 it was $871.[10] It rose to $1,420 by 1930; in 1940 it was $1,441; in 1950, $3,010; and in 1953–1954, $3,725.

The educational level of teachers has also increased considerably. In the nineteenth century, many institutions which prepared elementary school teachers were little better than secondary schools. Today, teachers' colleges offer four-year post–high school courses leading to degrees. In addition, liberal arts colleges and state universities offer teacher-training programs. About 1,200 institutions give professional teacher training.

Since 1930 there have been substantial changes in the minimum qualifications for teaching. Twenty years ago, few states required more than one year of training beyond high school for elementary school teachers. Today, nineteen states require four years of college for the lowest-grade regular certificate for elementary school teaching, and only five states will accept persons with less than two years of such training.[11] For secondary school teachers, at least four years of college or the equivalent is the rule in all but one state, and four states require five years for teachers of academic subjects.

Curriculum Changes

Because the control of American education is highly decentralized, curriculum changes are uneven and difficult to summarize. Changes in the content and methods of education are usually gradual and experimental. Nevertheless, some important trends are apparent. At one time, the major function of our schools was the development of literacy. Now, much more is required of the schools to fit the pupil for life in the modern world. Once, education was regarded as complete at a certain age. Now education is seen as a continuous lifetime process and as an essential part of personal development.

In recent decades, there has been little change in the elementary school curriculum. By the early years of this century, most of the additions to the basic three R's, geography and history — hygiene, art, music and nature study — had been made. Subsequent changes have been not so much in new "subjects" as in enrichment of content and change of emphasis.

In secondary schools, there has been a decreased emphasis on mathematics and ancient languages. The major change in content has been

---

10. The figure for 1900 is for teachers only; for later years it includes principals and supervisors also.

11. *Teachers in the Public Schools,* National Education Association, Research Bulletin, Vol. XXVII, No. 4, December 1949, p. 131.

in the arts, social studies, commerce, science and vocational education.

The most recent development has been in the field of social studies. This has been a matter not only of increasing emphasis, but of new content and orientation. Society and its institutions are currently regarded as part of man's environment, and consequently of parallel importance to the physical world. This viewpoint is increasingly influential in the secondary and even the elementary schools.

Utility

Perhaps the chief long-range development in public education is the emphasis upon utility. Where we used to recite "pieces," we now practice ordinary polite conversation; where we used to study Latin, we now are more likely to study a modern language; where we used to learn the "drum-and-trumpet" history of successive wars, we now study current social problems in the light of their historical development; where we used to begin learning to read by memorizing the alphabet, we now begin to read by reading words; where we used to study physiology, we now study how to keep well.

Pupils as People

Another development of great and growing importance is the discovery of the individual. Although mass instruction has not vanished, schools today are far more aware of individual differences than were the schools of the nineteenth century. Tests to estimate individual capacities and interests are now in wide use. "Guidance" — systematic, personalized and professional advice and help in personal adjustment, vocational choice and planning for further education — is a recognized function of the teaching staff.

In most cities and larger towns, a wide variety of classes and services are available for those with special educational needs. In secondary schools, some subjects are required of all students. However, there remains a margin of time which, under guidance, the student may use for studying what appears to be of particular personal value or interest to him. Along with this elective system has come a diversification of secondary school courses in an endeavor to provide a program tailored to all, or nearly all, the youth of high school age.

New Methods

By the end of the last century, learning solely by means of memorized answers to the teacher's questions was losing favor. Although this method has not altogether disappeared, pupils today generally are expected to think about what they have read and observed rather than to reproduce what they have memorized. The main function of the modern teacher is to stimulate and assist the pupil to learn, think and understand, rather than to impart information by word of mouth. The school library supplants exclusive reliance on single textbooks. Students are given direct experience with their environment. In today's schools, there is more attention to constructive activities, and pupils observe in practice what they used to read about in books.

In elementary schools both content and methods reflect progress toward a unified and continuous process of education. Fewer secondary schools have shown the same success in eliminating sharp subject-matter lines and in integrating the various disciplines. The task has been complicated by the expansion of the curriculum, the rapid growth in enrollment and the wider variations in pupil requirements. A growing specialization of teachers and departmentalization in administration have retarded further the progress of secondary education toward a synthesis of subject matter. This also holds true in the colleges, where, despite some experimental deviations, highly departmentalized teaching still is the typical method of instruction.

Costs

Changes in curriculum and in methods have not been the principal cause for the increased total cost of education in the United States. Far more important have been the increasing numbers enrolled and the steadily decreasing purchasing power of the dollar. Nevertheless, part of the increased cost can be ascribed to curricular and pedagogical changes.

The enrichment of the curriculum, especially its adaptation to the needs of individuals of varying capacities, interests and backgrounds, necessarily means some increases in the cost of educational service. Effective use of modern methods of instruction requires teachers of greater ability, longer and more specialized preparation, and extended supervised experience.

TABLE 170. PUBLIC ELEMENTARY AND SECONDARY SCHOOL EXPENDITURES, 1900–1950 [a]

| Year | Total Expenditures | Current | | Capital | Total Expenditures per Pupil | |
		Salaries	Other		Enrolled	In Average Daily Attendance
			(Millions)			
1900	$ 215.0	$ 137.7	$ 41.8	$ 35.5	$ 13.87	$ 20.21
1910	426.3	253.9	102.4	70.0	23.93	33.23
1920	1,036.2	613.4	269.2	153.5	48.02	64.16
1930	2,316.8	1,295.2	650.7	370.9	90.22	108.49
1940	2,344.0	1,369.5	716.6	258.0	92.16	105.74
1950	5,837.6	2,999.9 [b]	1,823.5 [b]	1,014.2	232.47	258.85

Source: *Statistics of State School Systems, 1949–50,* U.S. Office of Education, 1952, Table 1, p. 28.

a. Does not include residential schools for exceptional children or federal schools for Indians.

b. Differs from 1950 figures shown in Table 182, which includes expenditures for residential schools for exceptional children.

The cost of school supplies and equipment has risen with the introduction of studies which require more elaborate equipment than a single textbook. A varied curriculum which relies on methods of learning other than direct study of the printed page is likely to attract more students for more years, resulting in higher costs for buildings, staff and equipment.

All public and private elementary and secondary schools combined spent $6.6 billion in 1950, of which more than $1 billion was capital expenditures. Of the total, almost 88 per cent was spent by publicly controlled schools. (See Tables 170 and 173.) Expenditures per pupil, when adjusted for price changes, were four times as great in 1950 as in 1900 — $259 compared with $62 in 1949–1950 dollars.

Institutions of Higher Education

In 1950 this country had 1,851 institutions of higher education. Almost two thirds were degree-granting colleges, universities and independent professional schools, while almost one third were junior colleges and normal schools. The total number of institutions has increased considerably since 1920, with the greatest expansion in junior colleges. Both publicly controlled and privately controlled institutions have grown in number; but the former constituted 39 per cent of the total number of higher institutions in 1920, and only 35 per cent in 1950. (See Table 171.) However, the public institutions of all types tend

to be larger. Ninety-four per cent of teachers' college enrollments, 77 per cent of junior college and normal school enrollments and 46 per cent of other higher education enrollments are in public institutions.

In 1950 the cost value of property and endowment of institutions of higher education was $7.9 billion, of which almost $5 billion consisted of land, buildings and equipment. Although the private institutions were almost twice as numerous as the public, their total physical property was worth less. However, private institutions accounted for the bulk of endowments. In 1950 total property and endowments of all institutions of higher learning were 75 per cent higher than in 1940 and about 130 per cent higher than in 1930. Expenditures by institutions of higher education in 1950 totaled $2.1 billion, of which $417 million was capital outlay. Expenditures by public institutions represented 55 per cent of the total.

The New Scene

In 1900 only 237,000 persons were enrolled in institutions of higher education — 4 per cent of the population 18 to 21 years of age. During the next fifty years, enrollments increased more than tenfold. By 1950 the number of students totaled 2.7 million, or about 30 per cent of the college-age group.[12]

12. Owing partly to the decrease in veteran student enrollments and partly to increasing military service require-

In 1950 the administrative and instructional staff numbered 210,349 compared with 131,552 in 1940. Thus, the administrators and the faculty had increased by almost 60 per cent, while students had increased 78 per cent during the same period.

In response to pressures of military manpower needs, about two hundred higher institutions have adopted, or have definite plans for, an accelerated program. One method is to divide the academic year into quarters instead of semesters, thus enabling students to earn some college credit during short periods of college residence. In addition, more classes are being scheduled for evenings and Saturdays and in some cases the maximum load of classwork that students are permitted to carry has been raised.

There are no complete nationwide data on the economic status of university and college teachers. Reports from 462 institutions for the school year 1950–1951 showed average salaries for nine months' service ranging from $3,052 for instructors to $4,805 for full professors.[13] Salaries had risen an average of 6 per cent since 1949–1950. Of the institutions reporting, 288 were private schools, which have considerably lower salary scales than state and municipal universities. The United States Office of Education, for example, reported that professors in 50 land-grant institutions received a median salary of $6,132 for nine months in 1949–1950 and that this had risen to $6,926 by 1951–1952. Instructors in these same schools received $3,202 in 1949–1950 and $3,656 in 1951–1952.[14]

Data on the preparation of college teachers are also scanty. Among institutions of higher learning belonging to the North Central Association of Colleges and Secondary Schools, the median number of months of graduate study completed by faculty members in 1946 was 26.4. The median per cent of the teachers holding doctoral degrees was 34.4 and the median per cent holding master's degrees was 77.3.[15]

The Changing College Curriculum

An expansion, and in some sense a revolution, in the college curriculum has resulted from the influx of new types of students and the growing complexity of modern American society. Educators have come to the conclusion that the high school curriculum fails to provide a complete general education. Simultaneously, there is an increasing emphasis on professional courses during the last two years of college. A significant response to these factors has been the rapid development of the junior college, indicating that more young people are likely to continue their formal education at least two years beyond high school.

Other Organized Education

Beyond the usual educational services are a wide variety of special schools for various groups of the population and for particular purposes, extensive programs of adult education, and educational services for children too young for the usual school program.

Special Schools

Data on these are scattered. In 1950 there were more than 1,000 schools of nursing not affiliated with colleges and universities. There were more than 325 federal schools for Indians, which employed more than 1,500 teachers. State and private residential schools for delinquent, blind, deaf and mentally deficient children numbered 444 (1945–1946), and employed almost 6,000 teachers. There were 37,000 full-time enrollments in federal schools for Indians, about 59,000 in residential schools for exceptional children and 78,000 in schools of nursing. Expenditures for federal schools for Indians totaled over $19 million; state and private residential schools for exceptional children spent more than $32 million. (See Tables 172 and 173.) In addition, there are a great variety of private commercial, vocational, trade, correspondence, religious, art, music, dancing and dramatic schools for which data on enrollment, teaching staff and expenditures are not fully available.

ments, college enrollments declined to about 2.23 million at the outset of the academic year 1951–1952. (U.S. Office of Education estimates as reported in *The College and University Bulletin,* September 1951, p. 3.)

13. Charles Hoff, "Trends in Fees, Salaries, and Enrollments in 497 Colleges and Universities," *School and Society,* September 1, 1951, pp. 135–137.

14. *Faculty Salaries in Land Grant Colleges and State Universities,* U.S. Office of Education, Circular No. 358, 1952.

15. John H. Russell and Norman Burns, "Faculty Status in Member Colleges and Universities of the North Central Association of Colleges and Secondary Schools, 1945–46,"

North Central Association Quarterly, April 1948, pp. 397–413.

TABLE 171. NUMBER OF PUBLIC AND PRIVATE INSTITUTIONS OF HIGHER EDUCATION, 1900–1950

Type of School	1900 Public and Private	1910 Public and Private	1920 Public	1920 Private	1930 Public	1930 Private	1940 Public	1940 Private	1950 Public	1950 Private
Total	969	866	414	627	519	890	610	1,141	641	1,210
Degree-granting universities, colleges and professional schools [a]	664 [b]	602 [b]	99	519	117	684	142	855	161	948
Junior colleges			10	42	129	148	217	239	297	227
Normal schools	305	264	266	60	139	52	87	30		
Teachers' colleges	—	—	39	6	134	6	164	17	183	35

Source: U.S. Office of Education biennial surveys.

a. Only independent professional schools not connected with other colleges or universities are counted.

b. Does not include professional schools.

TABLE 172. SCHOOLS, TEACHERS AND ENROLLMENT, BY TYPE OF SCHOOL, 1949–1950

Type of School	Schools	Teachers [a]	Enrollment
			(Thousands)
Total	169,833	1,235,578	31,402.1
Elementary [b]	138,600	665,665	22,152.6
Secondary	27,873	366,277	6,417.3
Higher institutions	1,851	190,353	2,659.0
Federal Indian	325 [c]	1,548 [d]	36.7
Residential schools for exceptional children [e]	444	5,919	58.7
Nursing (not affiliated with colleges and universities)	1,065	[f]	77.8

Source: Statistical Summary of Education, 1949–50, U.S. Office of Education, 1953.

a. Does not include principals, supervisors and administrative staff; excludes 5,816 elementary and secondary teachers in noncollegiate departments of colleges.

b. Kindergartens are excluded in the number of schools but are included in the number of teachers and enrollment.

c. U.S. Bureau of Indian Affairs.

d. Includes a small number of teachers in federal schools for Alaskans.

e. State and private schools for delinquent, blind, deaf and mentally deficient children; figures are for 1945–1946, the latest available.

f. Not available.

TABLE 173. EXPENDITURES FOR ORGANIZED EDUCATION, 1949–1950
(Millions)

Type of School	Total	Public	Private
Total	$8,795.7 [a]	$7,056.9	$1,738.8 [a]
Elementary	4,993.0	4,381.6	611.4
Secondary	1,627.6	1,456.1	171.5
Higher institutions	2,123.3	1,174.1	949.2
Federal Indian	19.4	19.4	—
Residential schools for exceptional children	32.4 [b]	25.7	6.7

Source: Statistical Summary of Education, 1949–50, U.S. Office of Education, 1953.

a. Excludes $352 million spent by commercial, trade and other specialized schools.

b. Estimated.

Adult Education

Data here are not complete. In 1950 federally aided vocational education, operated as part of the state public school systems, reached nearly 3.4 million students, and cost $129 million.[16]

It has been estimated that approximately 30 million adults belong to various informal educational groups and organized classes in the United States.[17] This equals the number of children and youth in all types of education.

Many kinds of institutions and organizations offer general or vocational education for adults: public school systems, colleges, technical institutes and universities, libraries and museums, prisons and hospitals, community centers,

16. Digest of Annual Reports for Vocational Education (fiscal year ended June 30, 1951), U.S. Office of Education, pp. 3 and 4.

17. International Directory of Adult Education, UNESCO, Ed. No. 69, Paris, 1950.

churches and other religious organizations, radio and television stations, business concerns and labor unions, settlement houses, consumer co-operatives, local clubs and societies, large voluntary organizations, and private vocational and correspondence schools.

Enrollment in university extension courses [18] varies from time to time between 300,000 and 500,000 adults. About 10,000 public schools in the United States reach some 666,000 adult farmers annually in programs of systematic education in agriculture and home economics. In the 1949–1950 school year there were 347,000 veterans enrolled in on-the-farm vocational training and 340,000 in other forms of on-the-job training programs of the public schools. Among the business and industrial concerns which employ more than 3,000 workers, about half provide various forms of adult education for their employees, including both vocational training and general education.

Approximately three fourths of all school districts with a population of 2,500 or more provide some kind of educational activities for adults and out-of-school youth.[19] The most widespread types are special daytime and evening classes, public exhibits, apprentice training, programs of educational films, training within industry, workshops, institutes, community centers, forums, concerts, lectures and adult educational guidance. About 2.6 million persons were reported enrolled in such activities in 1950, but this figure is certainly far less than the true enrollment, because of underreporting. The United States Office of Education estimates that public schools probably provide some type of organized and systematic education to approximately three million adults and out-of-school youth. The three states with the greatest adult education activity in the public schools relative to their population were California, Wisconsin and New York. The three states with the least were Mississippi, Louisiana and North Dakota.

In a national public opinion survey in 1947, more than two fifths of all adults questioned said they were interested in securing further education.[20] As the average educational level of the population increases, the demand for further adult education increases.

Preschool Education

The 1930s saw great impetus given to preschool education by the Works Progress Administration, which conducted about 1,500 nursery schools. These served both to provide education and care for small children and to give work to teachers and other school employees. Many of the WPA nursery schools were, in effect, continued in operation under the Federal Works Agency's program of community services in war-industry centers. By July 1945 approximately 60,000 children of wage-earning mothers were enrolled in nursery schools receiving federal funds. With the end of the war, many of these were closed, yet many parents who were interested in enrolling their children in nursery schools sought in vain for such facilities.[21]

Inequalities in Organized Education

For the country as a whole, educational facilities, accomplishments and expenditures are impressive. However, in opportunity and quality we still have far to go before we have adequate popular education. Education is universal now in the sense that most children get some kind and amount of schooling. It is still unequal both in quality and amount. Some communities have excellent schools which their children attend over a long period of years; others have poor schools attended briefly and intermittently. Local needs and standards vary, and local resources and efforts influence the quality of education. Standards of teachers' qualifications and curricular opportunities also vary widely.

Finally, the American school system is selective. Ability to profit by advanced education is, of course, one factor in the opportunity to secure it. But another factor is the individual's ability to finance a program of higher education. Many who are qualified for university or college work and could benefit from it cannot afford this training. Tuition fees are charged in all private colleges and — under one guise or another — in many public colleges as well. These increased

18. University extension refers to instruction offered, on or off campus, by mail or in classes, to persons unable to carry the usual program of full-time resident instruction.

19. *Adult Education Activities of the Public Schools,* U.S. Office of Education, Pamphlet No. 107, 1949.

20. George Gallup, American Institute of Public Opinion, March 17, 1950.

21. Gertrude E. Chittenden, Margaret Nesbitt, and Betsey Williams, "The Nursery School Today," *Education Digest,* January 1949, pp. 46–48.

60 per cent in the decade 1940–1950 and further increases are anticipated.[22]

Regional Differentials

Where a child happens to live is likely to be important in determining the quality of his education. In some areas, children are taught by meagerly qualified teachers in substandard schools with inadequate equipment. The money spent per pupil is below the accepted standard; the school session shorter and the school-leaving age lower than the national level. The generally low educational attainment of the adult population in some sections of the nation probably reflects these inferior educational opportunities.

The average length of the school session in 1950 in the various states ranged from 153 to 187 days. (See Table 174.) Thus a child in one state might have to attend school for 14 years to receive as much schooling as a child in another state would obtain in 12 years. The longest average session was 22 per cent greater than the shortest average session, while the average number of days attended by each pupil enrolled in the state with the highest average was 28 per cent greater than in the state with the lowest. Absenteeism ranged from less than one day per enrolled pupil in Nevada to 34 in New Mexico. Lost time is not necessarily a reflection on the school system since it often depends on weather, health and family income. However, truancy may be due, in part at least, to a lack of educational opportunities adapted to individual needs, abilities and interests.

The average value of school property per pupil in average daily attendance was $511 for the United States as a whole in 1950. But it ranged from $152 in Mississippi, $162 in Alabama and $171 in Tennessee to $768 in Illinois, $828 in the District of Columbia and $929 in New York. In general, low value of property indicates inferior school buildings and equipment. However, the differentials can be explained in part by the higher value of real estate in urban communities and the need for more costly buildings in cold areas.

Annual teachers' salaries averaged $3,010 in 1950, but the state averages ranged from $1,416 to $4,268, with five states falling below $2,000. Although variations in the cost of living may offset some of these differences, there obviously are differences in teachers' purchasing power.

In the same year, current expenditures in the states ranged from $80 to $295 per pupil in average daily attendance and averaged $209 for the country as a whole. Ten states spent under $150. (See Figure 55.) Current expenditure comprises the bulk of school costs and is a good general indication of the quality of instruction, equipment and services available.

Most states require school attendance to the sixteenth birthday, but all states permit exceptions. Loopholes exist in school attendance laws, and enforcement in some areas is lenient or entirely lacking. The states with the lowest school-leaving age, lowest teachers' salaries, substandard value of school property and lowest school expenditures also tend to be those with the lowest adult educational level.[23]

On the whole, the sole blame for deficiencies should not rest on the administration of the states concerned. An important cause of these inadequacies is the lack of financial resources. In fact, many of the states which are least able to support an adequate educational program make a greater *effort* to do so than is made by the states which have more economic resources and fewer children. Thus, of the 24 states with the lowest current school expenditure per pupil, 17 spent a larger percentage of income for schools in 1947–1948 than the national average. Of the 16 southern states which generally make the lowest per capita education expenditure, 12 exceeded the national average in proportion of income spent for education.[24]

Rural-Urban Differences

The one-room, one-teacher school, which has given many Americans their only chance to learn the three R's, is gradually disappearing. Although about 60,000 of our 128,000 public elementary schools were still in this category in 1950, their number had fallen to less than a third of the 212,000 that dotted the countryside

---

22. Hoff, *op. cit.*, pp. 135–137.

23. This conclusion is supported by the statistics on educational deficiencies collected by the Selective Service System and by the figures on the proportion of the population with less than five years of schooling, collected by the U.S. Bureau of the Census. These data are conveniently assembled for comparison with statistics on school expenditure in *Facts on Federal Aid for Schools,* National Education Association, Washington, revised September 1950. See particularly Tables 16, 17 and 18.

24. *Ibid.*

TABLE 174. COMPARISON OF PUBLIC ELEMENTARY AND SECONDARY EDUCATION IN THE 48 STATES, SELECTED MEASURES, 1949–1950

State	Average Number of Days in School Session	Average Number of Days Attended per Pupil Enrolled	Value of School Property per Pupil in Average Daily Attendance	Average Salary per Member of Instructional Staff	Current Expenditures per Pupil in Average Daily Attendance
United States	177.9	157.9	$511	$3,010	$208.83
The North					
Maine	180.0	164.9	353	2,115	157.47
New Hampshire	176.5	161.5	472	2,712	210.57
Vermont	170.1	156.6	399	2,348	192.87
Massachusetts	178.4	158.1	688	3,338	236.44
Rhode Island	180.0	156.6	747	3,294	240.40
Connecticut	180.7	162.3	644	3,558	254.62
New York	182.6	155.4	929	3,706	295.02
New Jersey	182.2	157.4	689	3,511	279.81
Pennsylvania	182.6	165.8	612	3,006	215.76
Ohio	178.0	164.2	552	3,088	202.12
Indiana	173.7	148.3	408	3,401	235.49
Illinois	186.6	166.9	768	3,458	258.46
Michigan	180.0	166.1	640	3,420	219.55
Wisconsin	181.9	165.6	676	3,007	230.01
Minnesota	171.5	154.6	553	3,013	242.24
Iowa	179.3	156.8	490	2,420	230.53
Missouri	179.1	155.1	458	2,581	173.57
North Dakota	172.7	155.5	548	2,324	226.27
South Dakota	175.0	158.2	486	2,064	230.34
Nebraska	177.4	158.5	553	2,292	217.07
Kansas	165.1[a]	142.9	684	2,628	218.57
The South					
Delaware	181.9	161.5	612	3,723	258.77
Maryland	184.1	164.1	493	3,594	213.39
District of Columbia	176.0	153.0	828	3,920	256.24
Virginia	180.0	161.6	381	2,328	145.56
West Virginia	175.0	159.2	363	2,425	149.86
North Carolina	179.9	162.2	290	2,688	140.82
South Carolina	177.4	148.5	219	1,891	122.39
Georgia	178.0	153.7	255	1,963	123.37
Florida	180.1	166.2	350	2,958	181.27
Kentucky	171.2	147.3	271	1,936	120.82
Tennessee	176.7	156.2	171	2,302	132.17
Alabama	176.3	154.2	162	2,111	117.09
Mississippi	152.5	136.5	152	1,416	79.69
Arkansas	173.9	151.7	278	1,801	111.71
Louisiana	179.0	155.8	332	2,983	214.08
Oklahoma	184.2	164.5	485	2,736	207.05
Texas	174.6	149.1	425	3,122	208.88
The West					
Montana	183.5	163.5	535	2,962	267.56
Idaho	175.8	159.6	418	2,481	186.00
Wyoming	175.0	143.7	581	2,798	262.77
Colorado	176.1	154.7	564	2,821	219.66
New Mexico	180.0	146.1	478	3,215	222.48
Arizona	170.9	155.2	489	3,556	240.70
Utah	175.3	162.3	456	3,103	178.56
Nevada	176.6	176.4	644	3,209	246.22

(Continued on page 391)

TABLE 174 (continued)

State	Average Number of Days in School Session	Average Number of Days Attended per Pupil Enrolled	Value of School Property per Pupil in Average Daily Attendance	Average Salary per Member of Instructional Staff	Current Expenditures per Pupil in Average Daily Attendance
The West (contd.)					
Washington	173.8	154.7	$721	$3,487	$247.63
Oregon	179.2	160.6	665	3,323	280.75
California	175.0	161.7	462	4,268	263.51

Sources: U.S. Office of Education: "State School Systems: Statistical Summary for 1949–50," Circular No. 344, June 1952, and Statistics of State School Systems, 1949–50, 1952, p. 90.
a. 1947–1948.

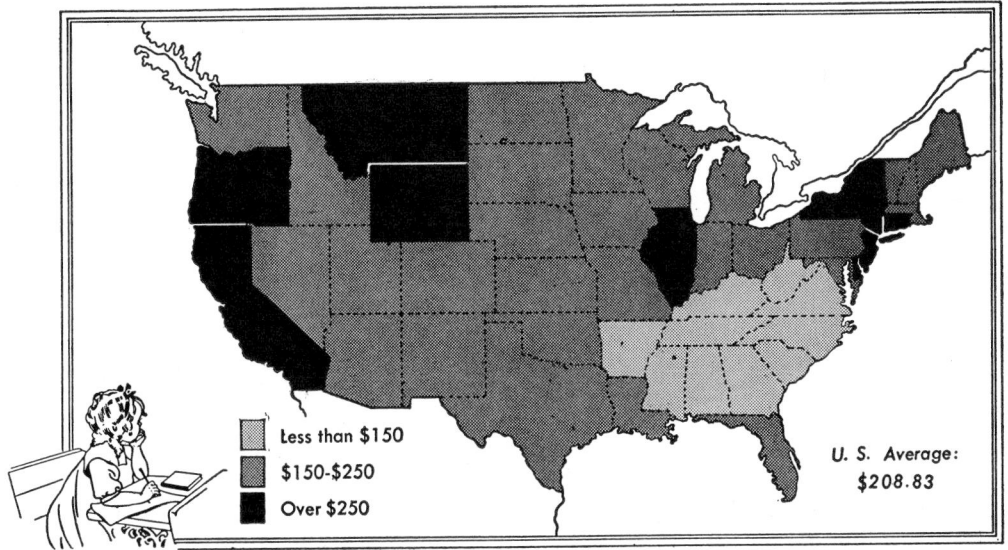

FIGURE 55. CURRENT EXPENDITURES PER PUPIL IN AVERAGE DAILY ATTENDANCE, PUBLIC ELEMENTARY AND SECONDARY SCHOOLS, BY STATE, 1949–1950
Source: Table 174.

in 1910. In 1950 they had an enrollment of about one million boys and girls, or about 5 per cent of all pupils in public elementary schools.[25]

These are low-cost schools, usually housed in poor buildings, with low-salaried, inexperienced teachers. The low quality of instruction is due not only to the inadequate teaching staff but to the impossibility of securing specialized services, including supervision, and to meager school supplies and equipment. Only if the school is part of a large administrative unit can adequate services and supplies be provided.

The most common type of one-room, one-teacher school has about 16 pupils. One young woman gives instruction for about eight months to pupils in all eight grades. She is the school nurse, librarian, dietitian, clerk, janitor, business agent and psychologist. She brings far less preparation and maturity to this complex task than her colleagues in urban areas who can call upon many types of specialized educational serv-

25. Walter H. Gaumnitz and David T. Blose, The One-Teacher School — Its Midcentury Status, U.S. Office of Education, Circular No. 318, 1950, p. 13; and Statistics of State School Systems, 1947–48, U.S. Office of Education, 1950, Table IX, p. 15.

TABLE 175. COMPARISON OF PUBLIC EDUCATION IN RURAL AND URBAN [a] AREAS,
SELECTED MEASURES, 1935–1936, 1941–1942 AND 1947–1948 [b]

	Average Salary of Instructional Staff	Total Current Expenditure per Pupil in Average Daily Attendance	Capital Outlay per Pupil in Average Daily Attendance	Average Length of School Term (Days)
1935–1936				
Rural	$ 844	$ 63	$ 9	166
Urban	1,874	93	6	182
1941–1942				
Rural	1,009	89	7	169
Urban	2,072	119	6	182
1947–1948				
Rural	2,086	173	19	172
Urban	3,174	206	12	183
1940 population–size:				
2,500–4,999	2,443	168	14	179
5,000–9,999	2,587	175	15	180
10,000–29,999	2,769	190	12	181
30,000–99,999	3,085	209	9	182
100,000 and over	3,803	230	12	186

Source: Education in Rural and City School Systems: Some Statistical Indices for 1947–48, U.S. Office of Education, Circular No. 329, November 1951, Table 1, p. 3 and Table 2, p. 6.

a. "Urban" includes cities and incorporated places with 2,500 or more inhabitants. "Rural" includes all other areas. Many rapidly growing suburban areas, which are more urban than rural in nature, are included with the rural statistics.

b. Based on data for 36 states; the 12 excluded states, generally more rural in character than the average, had average current expenditures per pupil in average daily attendance of $151 in 1948, compared with $179 for the United States as a whole.

ices for assistance. She will remain on the job only a year or two. If she is reasonably successful, she will be offered a better position in a near-by town or city. Or she may marry or enter some other occupation.

This is about how she spends her day. At nine o'clock the Pledge of Allegiance is recited, and if the weather is clear the flag is hoisted over the little school building. At 9:10 she starts the first of three successive 10-minute reading lessons to the first, second and third grades. Then will follow a half hour of silent reading, with some individual help, for all grades. At 10:10 the upper grades are taught spelling, and at 10:30 the entire school has a 15-minute recess. Beginning at 10:45, the arithmetic classes for the different grades follow at 10-minute intervals. At 11:45 the entire school has a writing lesson. Lunches are unpacked and eaten at noon. The teacher and some of the pupils may have found a few minutes to prepare a supplementary hot dish of soup or cocoa. In the afternoon there are classes in language, grammar, hygiene, civics, geography, history. If the teacher is ingenious, she will find opportunities for teaching through individual study and for combining classes and grades. At 4 o'clock, school closes and the teacher has nothing left to do but clear up the schoolroom, grade the day's papers, prepare the next day's lessons and fill out the reports required by law.

Education in rural areas is inferior to that in urban areas. Rural children, as a group, have a school term about 6 per cent shorter than urban children; their teachers are paid about 34 per cent less and current expenditures per pupil are 16 per cent lower. Furthermore, rural children have practically no opportunity to attend kindergarten. (See Table 175.)

In recent years rural areas have been spending more per pupil for land, buildings and equipment than urban areas. The value of rural school property per pupil enrolled, however, probably is still well below that of urban school property since as recently as 1940 rural school property had less than half the value of urban school property.[26]

The differences between rural and urban

26. Statistical Summary of Education, 1939–40, U.S. Office of Education, 1943.

TABLE 176. COMPARISON OF PUBLIC EDUCATION IN WHITE AND NEGRO SCHOOLS, 17 STATES AND THE DISTRICT OF COLUMBIA, SELECTED MEASURES, 1949–1950

State	Average Days in School Session		Average Days Attended by Each Pupil Enrolled		Enrollment per Teacher		Average Salary of Instructional Staff	
	White	Negro	White	Negro	White	Negro	White	Negro
17 states and the District of Columbia	177.1	173.4	157.0	147.9	27	32	$2,701[a]	$2,143[a]
Alabama	176.2	176.5	156.1	150.6	29	33	2,214	1,901
Arkansas	174.5	172.1	155.2	141.0	29	37	1,900[b]	1,416[b]
Delaware	181.8	182.8	161.9	159.5	23	28		
Florida	180.1	180.1	167.3	163.0	24	27	3,056	2,643
Georgia	179.0	176.0	158.4	144.9	27	34	2,080[b]	1,680[b]
Kentucky	171.1	174.0	147.3	147.3	29	27		
Louisiana	179.6	178.0	157.8	152.6	26	34	3,222	2,486
Maryland	184.2	183.9	165.0	160.9	28	30	3,600	3,575
Mississippi	162.9	141.3	152.2	120.9	28	40	1,884[b]	760[b]
Missouri	178.2	187.9	154.4	162.0	28	31		
North Carolina	179.9	179.9	164.5	157.0	29	34	2,675[b]	2,721[b]
Oklahoma	184.5	180.0	165.9	149.1	24	24		
South Carolina	180.0	174.0	155.6	139.7	27	32	2,149[b]	1,515[b]
Tennessee	176.7	177.0	156.2	156.1	29	32		
Texas	174.5	174.9	149.6	146.7	26	27	3,154[b]	2,934[b]
Virginia	180.0	180.0	163.0	157.9	27	31		
West Virginia	175.0	175.2	158.9	165.1	27	26	[b]	[b]
District of Columbia	178.5	173.5	152.2	154.0	25	30	3,963	3,863

Source: Statistics of State School Systems, 1949–50, U.S. Office of Education, 1952, Table 43, p. 105.

a. Ten states and the District of Columbia only.
b. Data not available.

schools become more marked as the size of the urban area increases. Salaries, current spending per pupil and length of school term all increase with the size of city. Cities of 100,000 and over paid their teachers 82 per cent more, spent 26 per cent more per pupil and had 8 per cent longer school terms than rural areas in 1949–1950.

Passage of time, however, appears to be narrowing the gap between rural and urban school systems. The average urban teacher's salary was more than double that of the average rural teacher in 1936; in 1948 it was little more than 50 per cent higher. Current expenditures per pupil were about 50 per cent higher in urban than in rural schools in 1936 but only 20 per cent higher in 1948. The average urban school term hardly changed between 1936 and 1948 (from 182 to 183 days), whereas the rural term increased from 166 to 172 days. The future, with the possible increased use of mechanical aids such as movies and television, should reduce still further the difference between urban and rural education.

Racial Differentials

In 1950, seventeen states and the District of Columbia provided separate schools for Negro and white children. With some exceptions, the quality of education in the Negro schools was somewhat inferior to that in the white schools. (See Table 176.) In recent years, however, spurred by developing public opinion and by a series of state and federal court decisions, the southern states have greatly improved the educational opportunities for Negro citizens. By a unanimous decision in June 1954, the Supreme Court ruled against racial segregation in public schools, but it is expected that it will be at least several years, or even a decade, before all the public schools of the South are open to Negro and white children on a nonsegregated basis.

In the seventeen southern states and the District of Columbia, the average attendance of Negro children enrolled increased from 80 days to 126 days between the school years 1919–1920 and 1939–1940. Between 1939–1940 and 1949–

TABLE 177. COMPARISON OF NEGRO AND ALL PUBLIC ELEMENTARY AND SECONDARY
SCHOOLS, SELECTED MEASURES, 1919–1920 TO 1949–1950

School Year	Negro Schools [a]	All Schools	Ratio: Negro Schools to All Schools
Average Number of Days Attended by Each Pupil Enrolled			
1919–1920	80	121	.66
1929–1930	97	143	.68
1939–1940	126	152	.83
1949–1950	148	158	.94
Average Length of School Term in Days			
1919–1920	119	162	.73
1929–1930	132	173	.76
1939–1940	156	175	.89
1949–1950	173	178	.97
Per Cent of Pupils in Secondary Grades			
1919–1920	2	10	.20
1929–1930	5	17	.29
1939–1940	10	26	.38
1949–1950	14	23	.61
Average Salary of Members of Instructional Staff			
1939–1940	$ 601	$1,441	.42
1949–1950	2,143	3,010	.71

Source: *Statistics of State School Systems, 1949–50,* U.S. Office of Education, 1952, Table 1,
pp. 28-29 and Table 36, p. 98.

a. In 17 southern states and the District of Columbia.

1950, the attendance figure rose still further to an average of 148 days per pupil enrolled. During the same periods the average school term for Negro schools rose from 119 days to 156 days, and then increased still further to 173 days by 1949–1950. The percentage of Negro pupils in the secondary schools increased sevenfold between 1919–1920 and 1949–1950. Teachers' salaries in Negro schools increased 257 per cent between 1939–1940 and 1949–1950, rising from $601 a year to $2,143. (See Table 177.)

These advances narrowed the gap between white and Negro schools. In 1919–1920 school attendance per pupil in Negro schools was two thirds that in all schools; by 1949–1950 attendance per pupil in Negro schools was more than nine tenths that in all schools. During the same period, the average length of the school term of Negro schools rose from less than three fourths that of all schools to within a few days of the average length of all schools. Between 1939–1940 and 1949–1950, average teachers' salaries in Negro schools rose from 42 to 71 per cent of salaries in all schools. (See Figure 56.)

Recent years have seen important changes in the higher education of Negroes. Until about twenty years ago, the general tendency was to try to develop an adequate program for the education of Negroes in separate institutions. More recently, anticipating the 1954 Supreme Court decision, the emphasis has been on the admission of qualified Negroes to all institutions.[27] The emphasis used to be on "separate but equal" education for Negroes. In earlier decisions the courts tended to support the viewpoint that segregation is a form of discrimination, as indicated by the Sweatt and McLaurin cases. In the first case,[28] the Supreme Court required the University of Texas Law School to admit a Negro although Texas had recently established a separate law school for Negroes. The Court held that the new school was not yet substantially equal to the Texas Law School in faculty, courses, library, size of student body, reputation or influence of

27. Charles H. Thompson, "The Courts and Racial Integration in Education," *Journal of Negro Education,* Winter 1952, pp. 1–7.
28. *Sweatt* v. *Painter,* 339 U.S. 629, June 5, 1950.

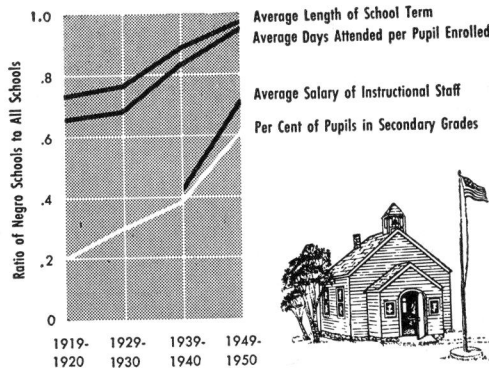

FIGURE 56. COMPARISON OF NEGRO AND ALL PUBLIC ELEMENTARY AND SECONDARY SCHOOLS: RATIOS OF SELECTED MEASURES, 1919–1920 TO 1949–1950

Source: Table 177.

the alumni. It also noted that "The law school to which Texas is willing to admit petitioner excludes from its student body members of the racial groups which include most of the lawyers, witnesses, jurors, judges, and other officials with whom petitioner will inevitably be dealing when he becomes a member of the Texas bar."

In the McLaurin case,[29] a previous court action had required the University of Oklahoma Graduate School to accept G. W. McLaurin, a Negro, as a graduate student in education. At first, the section of the classroom in which he sat was surrounded by a rail on which there was a sign stating "Reserved for Colored"; later he was seated in a row specified for colored students, and was assigned to a separate table in the library and cafeteria. The Supreme Court held that "Such restrictions impair and inhibit his ability to study, to engage in discussions and exchange views with other students, and, in general, to learn his profession. . . . State-imposed restrictions which produce such inequalities cannot be sustained. . . . Appellant . . . must receive the same treatment at the hands of the state as students of other races."

INFORMAL EDUCATION

Education is not limited to the organized school system. Books, magazines and newspapers contribute to education as well as to recreation. Similarly, lectures, motion pictures, radio and

television broadcasts help to fill both needs. Museums and foundations also perform educational functions.[30]

Total expenditures for printed materials can be readily estimated, but it is difficult to divide them between educational and recreational uses. Here it is assumed that 58 per cent are for education.[31] The contribution of radio, television and motion pictures to education cannot be measured, but because they are primarily devoted to entertainment, expenditures for these items have been allocated to recreation in this survey.

Though foundations are established for a variety of purposes, they are all treated here as educational and all their expenditures are similarly classified.

Expenditures for public libraries are partially for books and hence involve some duplication. Since not all public libraries are reported and since the proportion of books regarded as educational is arbitrary, the duplication is allowed to remain.

There are a number of institutes, unions, commissions, bureaus, boards, societies and associations with educational functions, for which no information is available. This omission is probably offset by the inclusion of all foundations.

Thus the total expenditure for informal education is roughly estimated at $1.3 billion in 1950. This comprises private expenditures for reading, and by foundations, museums and libraries, plus public expenditures for museums and libraries. (See Table 178.)

Reading [32]

The American people spent $1.1 billion for educational reading matter in 1950 and an additional $0.8 billion for recreational reading. Thus, total reading costs were $1.9 billion.

In 1947 there were 4,610 magazines and periodicals published, with a total circulation of almost 385 million copies per issue. Most of these were specialized trade journals. Monthlies accounted for over half the total circulation. The circulation of all periodicals combined, as well as

29. *McLaurin* v. *Oklahoma State Regents for Higher Education,* 339 U.S. 637, June 5, 1950.

30. *Moral and Spiritual Values in the Public Schools,* National Education Association, Washington, 1951, p. 92.
31. Julius Weinberger, "Economic Aspects of Recreation," *Harvard Business Review,* Summer 1937.
32. Data on consumption expenditures are from Appendix 4–4; all other data from Census of Manufactures, 1909, 1929, 1939, 1947.

TABLE 178. EXPENDITURES FOR SELECTED TYPES OF
INFORMAL EDUCATION, 1950
(*Millions*)

Type of Expenditure	Total	Public	Private
Total	$1,337	$114[a]	$1,223
Reading	1,136	—	1,136
Museums and libraries	133	114[a]	19
Foundations	66	—	66

Sources: Appendix 4–4 and Table 264.
a. Libraries only.

the average circulation of each, more than doubled in thirty years. This represented not only a total increase but a per capital increase as well, since the population grew by only 39 per cent during the same period.

Americans buy (and presumably read) more newspapers per capita than the people of any other country. In 1860 there were fewer than 400 dailies in the country; by 1900 the number had grown to 2,200, with a circulation of 15 million. Although the number of newspapers has decreased during the twentieth century, circulation has risen rapidly. By 1947 the number of daily newspapers had dropped to 1,854, with a combined circulation of more than 53 million. Sunday, weekly and other newspapers brought the total newspaper circulation to almost 120 million per issue.

Public Libraries [33]

There were 7,408 public libraries in the United States in 1945, the last year for which such statistics were compiled. Registered library book borrowers numbered around 29 million. Public libraries contained over 124 million books, or about half the total of all libraries combined. The circulation of books amounted to 360 million. Professional librarians and clerical staff employed by public libraries totaled 22,000 full-time and 15,000 part-time persons.

Expenditures for public libraries totaled $114 million in the fiscal year 1949–1950. This outlay was equivalent to about $.75 per capita of the population.

Public library resources and services are by no means nationwide. About one third of the population live in areas with no public libraries. To another third, the public library offers very limited service. Only to the remaining third are adequate facilities available. Deficiencies are greatest in rural areas, particularly in the South. As in the case of public schools, there is a correlation between economic resources and the adequacy of public libraries.

Private Libraries and Museums [34]

Current expenditures in 1950 by privately operated museums and libraries amounted to $19 million, a slight increase over the $16 million level of 1940. (See Table 178 and Appendix 4–4.)

In 1910 there were about 600 museums in the United States, housed in buildings worth $36 million. By 1939 the estimated number of museums had increased to 2,500 and the value of their buildings to $180 million. By 1950 there were about 3,000 museums. Though some are supported wholly or partially by public funds, most were set up by original gifts or bequests, and are maintained largely through income from endowment, current gifts or membership fees.

About half these institutions are history museums, of which a large number are historic houses. Science museums constitute a third of the total. Art museums are among the largest and most heavily endowed and they account for half the total expenditures for museums.

Foundations [35]

Foundation expenditures for education and research in 1950 totaled $66 million. After 1929, when expenditures were $91 million, there was a decline, but since the war, expenditures have risen. (Appendix 4–4.) In 1948 there were about 899 foundations (including community trusts) disbursing substantial sums to outside beneficiaries. Their assets totaled about $1.5 billion, largely in the form of endowment funds. Money grants for the support of projects in the fields of social welfare, health, education and religion led all others. Substantial sums, however, were distributed for the physical and biological sciences, government and public administration, eco-

33. *Public Library Statistics, 1944–45*, U.S. Office of Education, Bulletin No. 12, 1947.

34. Coleman, *op. cit.,* and F. Emerson Andrews, *Philanthropic Giving*, Russell Sage Foundation, New York, 1950, pp. 209–210.

35. Wilmer S. Rich and Neva R. Deardorff (Editors), *American Foundations and Their Fields*, Vol. VI, Raymond Rich Associates, New York, 1948.

nomics, the other social sciences, international relations, aesthetics, the humanities and child welfare.

Foundations have spent for education and research about three times as much as for other activities. From the viewpoint of education, the outstanding foundation activities of the past decade were the launching of the $250 million Ford Foundation and the assignment by the Kellogg Foundation of $3 million to improve the quality of school administration.

EDUCATIONAL TRENDS, 1940–1950

The conduct of education is in part a reflection of the changing social scene and in part one of the causes of such changes. It is not easy in these times of uncertainty to survey the varied scene of American education and to identify those trends which in later years may seem most significant. However, the following may be listed as among the educational trends which will probably appear in retrospect as the most important of the war decade.

IMPACT OF THE WAR

During World War I thousands of teachers left the schools for more remunerative occupations. As a result, some schools were closed and many others had to employ substandard teachers. Two years after the war the Commissioner of Education reported more than 18,000 schools closed for lack of teachers.[36] By 1923 one out of every seven rural teachers had less than one year of training beyond the eighth grade. Twenty years later, during World War II, 659,000 men were rejected by the Army on account of educational deficiencies; another 300,000 had to be taught to write simple sentences.

World War II resulted in another flight of teachers from the schools. In 1943, testimony before a Senate committee showed that teachers, weary of asking for reasonable salary adjustments, were simply leaving the profession. Meanwhile, the school building deficit, already serious because of reduced construction during the depression, has continued to grow worse because of wartime and cold-wartime restrictions on construction.[37]

The high birth rates of the 1940s produced a larger group of children than ever before in American history. The decade closed with an estimated 3.7 million registered live births in 1949, exceeding any other year except 1947, in which approximately 3.9 million live births were registered.[38] This development was soon to strain the already overburdened educational facilities of the nation.

Every year the elementary schools need new teachers to replace those who leave the profession. Further, because of the shortage of elementary school teachers, more than one out of every ten teachers today is serving on an emergency basis.[39] Most of these emergency teachers need to have additional training, or to be replaced. The demand for elementary school teachers will be further swollen in the next eight or ten years by the tide of war babies.

The present rate of replenishment from all training schools and colleges is wholly inadequate to meet the need for qualified elementary school teachers. To meet the needs of a growing school population and to replace teachers who leave the profession, more than 100,000 new teachers will be needed in elementary schools each year of the current decade. The number of qualified elementary school teachers graduating each year is slightly more than one fifth of this number. The implications of this fact for American education are serious enough to justify the use of the much-overworked word "crisis."

The war has had other effects, among them an expansion of adult education. As a result of shifts from wartime to peacetime production, millions required special vocational retraining. In addition, hundreds of thousands of war casualties needed vocational training and rehabilitation.

Disqualification of many by the armed services because of illiteracy focused attention on inequalities in educational opportunity. In 1950, there were more than 9.6 million adults who had had less than five years of elementary school.[40]

---

36. *Public Schools: A Top Priority,* Educational Policies Commission, 1951, pp. 3–4.
37. *Ibid.*

38. National Office of Vital Statistics: *Vital Statistics — Special Reports,* Vol. 33, No. 8, September 29, 1950, p. 141; and *Monthly Vital Statistics Bulletin,* March 31, 1950. The figures have been corrected for underregistration.
39. *Teachers in the Public Schools,* National Education Association, Research Bulletin, Vol. XXVII, No. 4, December 1949, p. 138.
40. *1950 Census of Population: Preliminary Reports,* Series PC–7, No. 6, May 13, 1952.

TABLE 179. VETERANS TRAINED UNDER THE G.I. BILL,[a]
BY TYPE OF TRAINING, 1945-1950 [b]
(*Annual Averages in Thousands*)

		School Training			On-the-Job Training	Institutional On-the-Farm Training
Year	Total	Total	Below College Level	College Level		
1945	79	61	17	44	15	3
1946	1,267	815	258	537	410	42
1947	2,413	1,539	561	978	691	183
1948	2,342	1,533	674	859	531	280
1949	2,238	1,518	776	741	386	334
1950 [c]	1,790	1,252	745	506	218	320

Source: *Report of the House Select Committee to Investigate Educational and Training Program under G.I. Bill,* H.Rept. No. 3253, 81st Cong., 2d sess., 1951, p. 6.

a. Specifically, Public Laws 16 and 346, Seventy-eighth Congress, as amended.
b. During last half of 1944 an average of 12,000 veterans were in training of all types.
c. Through November 30, 1950.

These for the most part are illiterate or nearly so, and their lack of education is a handicap not only to themselves but to society. Some of their educational needs are being met by the expanded adult education program of postwar years.

VETERANS EDUCATIONAL PROGRAM

The so-called "G.I. Bill" gave veterans of World War II extensive educational opportunities. The provisions for their rehabilitation, education and training are included primarily in three pieces of federal legislation.

Public Law 16, Seventy-eighth Congress, March 24, 1943, granted courses of vocational rehabilitation to all veterans with service-connected disabilities, with a time limit of four years on the training provided.

Public Law 346, Seventy-eighth Congress, June 22, 1944, made education and training available to practically all other veterans for periods up to one year. Additional training was made available for veterans whose education had been impaired, delayed or interrupted by military service. Veterans were free to choose their own courses in any training or educational institution willing to accept them and approved by the state in which it was located. The federal government paid up to $500 a year for tuition, plus subsistence allowances ranging from $75 to $120 a month, depending upon the number of dependents of the veteran. In addition, the federal government paid for textbooks and other necessary educational supplies and materials.

Public Law 208, Seventy-ninth Congress, December 28, 1945, allowed education and training beyond the one-year limit for all qualified veterans without regard to the educational interruption proviso of Public Law 346.

These laws were further amended in the Seventy-ninth, Eightieth and Eighty-first Congresses, but their basic provisions were not essentially changed.

Under Public Laws 16 and 346, as amended, in the seven years following their enactment, about eight million different veterans attended school or college under government subsidy. Of these, 2.3 million attended colleges, 3.4 million attended schools of less-than-college grade, 1.6 million took on-the-job training, and 0.8 million took on-the-farm training.[41] At the peak of the program, in 1947, nearly a million veterans crowded college campuses and 1.4 million others were enrolled in other training of various kinds. (See Table 179.)

The total cost of the two bills was $11.5 billion, distributed as follows: subsistence, $8.2 billion; tuition, $2.9 billion; equipment, $329 million; supplies and materials, $74 million; and counseling, $24 million. (See Table 180.)

---

41. *New York Times,* July 22, 1951.

TABLE 180. DIRECT EXPENDITURES FOR VETERANS VOCATIONAL REHABILITATION, EDUCATION AND TRAINING UNDER THE G.I. BILL,[a] JULY 1, 1943–NOVEMBER 30, 1950

(*Millions*)

Fiscal Year	Total	Subsistence	Tuition	Equipment	Supplies and Materials	Counseling
Total[b]	$11,515.4	$8,178.0	$2,910.8	$328.5	$74.3	$23.8
Vocational rehabilitation,[c] total	1,225.1	977.7	200.6	30.4	7.1	9.3
1943–1944	.7	.6	[d]	[d]	[d]	—
1944–1945	8.4	7.0	1.2	.1	[d]	.1
1945–1946	46.8	38.0	5.8	1.1	.2	1.7
1946–1947	223.8	190.9	24.4	4.9	.8	2.9
1947–1948	335.5	265.3	56.1	9.9	2.1	2.2
1948–1949	336.5	262.2	62.1	8.4	2.5	1.3
1949–1950[e]	273.4	213.6	51.1	6.1	1.5	1.1
Education and training,[f] total	10,290.3	7,200.3	2,710.2	298.1	67.2	14.5
1944–1945	9.5	7.8	1.5	.2	.1	[d]
1945–1946	350.6	317.9	25.3	5.2	1.6	.5
1946–1947	2,122.3	1,550.8	496.3	60.7	10.9	3.6
1947–1948	2,505.9	1,628.9	769.6	85.2	17.9	4.2
1948–1949	2,702.8	1,865.8	735.4	77.9	21.2	2.6
1949–1950[e]	2,599.2	1,824.1	682.0	68.9	15.6	3.5

Source: Report of the House Select Committee to Investigate Educational and Training Program under G.I. Bill, H.Rept. No. 3253, 81st Cong., 2d sess., 1951, p. 4.

a. Specifically, Public Laws 16 and 346, Seventy-eighth Congress, as amended.

b. Excludes $318.5 million in salaries of Vocational Rehabilitation and Education (VA) personnel and $17.3 million in appropriations to state approving agencies.

c. Vocational rehabilitation of veterans with service-connected disabilities under Public Law 16, as amended.

d. Less than $50,000.

e. To November 30, 1950.

f. Education and training for all qualified veterans under Public Law 346, as amended.

In spite of some waste and some outright dishonesty, the program has been a definite success. A sample postcard inquiry conducted by a congressional committee gives clear evidence on this point. Of the first 1,600 replies, 1,200 said that they secured a job or went into business for themselves as a direct result of their G.I. training. Practically all who replied said that they believed that the benefits derived from the course were worth the money which the government had spent.[42]

It now appears probable that veterans' educational benefits will become a relatively fixed and continuing aspect of national policy. Public Law 550, Eighty-second Congress, July 16, 1952, extended educational benefits to all veterans with 90 days' service in the armed forces after June 27, 1950.

42. See *Report of the House Select Committee to Investigate Educational and Training Program under G.I. Bill,* H.Rept. No. 3253, 81st Cong., 2d sess., 1951, p. 31.

PUBLIC REACTION TO EDUCATION

It is a curious paradox that the disasters which befell education during the war and the difficulties yet to come should occur in a country where public opinion generally insists on universal public education of high quality for all the people.

In general, the American people wish every child to have a good start in life, which means a good education. Why did a nation holding such a viewpoint permit a major crisis in education to develop and to continue to run its course? The answer seems to be that the people were not convinced that a real crisis was in the making. The public in general has simply assumed that somehow or other the public schools would continue to operate at a satisfactory level of efficiency. This assumption has proved incorrect.

Today there are many indications, however, that the public has begun to recognize and respond to the crisis in education. The 288,000 local school board members have formed a national organization of growing strength to support measures for the improvement of public education. There are 1,700 voluntary citizens' groups working with the National Citizens Commission for the Public Schools, composed of distinguished leaders of public opinion. The 6,500,000 members of the Parent-Teacher Associations have rallied to the support of the institutions in which they have such a direct interest. Local citizens' committees for the improvement of education have been formed in every part of the nation.

Although this reaction comes late, there is reason to hope that the awakening of public opinion will prevent further damage to the whole concept of free public education in this country.

Most of this civic interest in the schools has been useful and constructive. However, not all current public interest in education has been sympathetic. Some groups and individuals feel that the public schools receive too much money, that the whole concept of public secondary education should be re-examined, that elementary education is sufficient for the masses of the people, and that substantial reduction in the program with consequent reduction in costs is the proper procedure.

Adverse critics of the schools plead a variety of causes, bewildering and contradictory. The public schools are told on one hand that they fail to provide a broad liberal education and on the other hand that they do not meet the practical demands of vocational efficiency. Some say that school discipline is too soft and easy, while others reproach school administrations for allowing the schools to become soulless machines for mass production of literacy. Such conflicting pressures are normal enough, but their impact has been greatly increased during the past decade and probably will continue at least so long as high birth rates push up the cost of educational services.

What do the American people think of their schools? What are they asking schools to be and to do? These are not questions capable of a simple answer. Public opinion varies from one community to another and fluctuates with the changing fortunes of individuals and nations. However, a 1950 public opinion survey makes it possible to venture certain generalizations.[43]

For each person who thinks that today's school

43. Roper Survey of Public Opinion as reported in *Life,* October 16, 1950.

children are not taught as many worth-while and useful things as were children twenty years ago there are five who think the schools are better than they used to be.

For each person who is dissatisfied with the schools in his local community, there are four who are fairly well or very well satisfied.

Ninety per cent of the American people favor compulsory school attendance laws reaching to age 15 or higher.

More than half of them think that the law should require children to stay in school until the age of 17 or longer.

Over half the population think that the nation should provide some free college education for all who want it and can qualify for it.

Two thirds of the people think that grade school is more important than high school in influencing the kind of person a child will be when he grows up.

Almost half the people think the most important role of the high school is the development of personality and character; nearly as many believe its major function should be the teaching of vocational skills. Only 13 per cent think academic training its more important job.

Teachers are considered of more importance to the community than clergymen, public officials, merchants and lawyers.

About 20 per cent of the American public have no idea whether the teachers in their community are underpaid or overpaid. Of those who have an opinion, substantially more than half believe that teachers are underpaid, and less than 2 per cent believe that they are overpaid.

EDUCATIONAL TECHNIQUES

In spite of the publicity which naturally attaches to novelty, the basic techniques of education change very little over the years. Communication is still mainly a matter of words between teacher and learner and between a learner and a book. While this process will probably remain for a long time the heart of education, there have been some developments in educational technique which probably will be regarded as permanent ten years from now. One such development was the experience of the United States armed forces and other agencies in the wartime teaching of foreign languages. As a need arose for large numbers of persons who could speak foreign languages, it became necessary to arrange quick courses in French, German, Russian, Japanese, etc. The techniques used, involving chiefly immediate communication and methods of drill and practice, were not essentially new, but they were applied broadly for the first time and were refined.

It would be a great mistake to suppose that these techniques will make it easy for anyone to learn another language. The process remains a long and tedious one. There are degrees of difficulty, however, and the new techniques bid fair to make a substantial contribution to the efficiency of language teaching.

The use of mechanical aids to learning such as radio and motion pictures was substantially increased during the war years. The armed forces made extensive use of visual aids in teaching a variety of skills. These auditory and visual aids continue to find wider application in the public schools.

There has been preliminary experimentation with the use of television as a teaching instrument. Programs shown include such subjects as health problems, vocational guidance, safety, American history.[44]

In 1944 the Federal Communications Commission reserved certain channels for educational FM broadcasting stations and in 1950 similar action was taken for educational television. The use of motion pictures and radio in teaching has continued to grow. Wire and tape recorders are proving useful in many branches of education, particularly in the teaching of foreign languages and music. Here again, while the new developments are important and useful, it is necessary to avoid extremes. Neither radio nor television nor motion pictures can replace a skilled teacher. These new instruments can only supplement the work of teachers and in some instances make it more effective.

OTHER RECENT TRENDS

Among other events of the 1940s which served to establish major trends in American education were the following:

1. The assumption by the United States of definite responsibilities in international relations in education as revealed in Articles 55 and 56 of the Charter of the United Nations (1945), the establishment of the United Nations Educational, Scientific, and Cultural Organization (1945), and the establishment of many nongovernmental international educational and cultural organizations, such as the World Organization of the Teaching Profession (1946).

2. The establishment of the national school lunch program, which provides federal funds on a permanent basis for this purpose (1947).

3. The Smith-Mundt Act, the Fulbright Act and other legislation providing the financial and administrative basis for an extensive program of educational interchange between the schools and colleges of the United States and those of other countries (1948).

4. The Mid-Century Conference on Children and Youth held under the auspices of the President of the United States directed national attention to educational and associated problems (1950). The emphasis was on wholesome personal relationships and mental health.

5. The vocational education program in the public schools and colleges of the United States underwent rapid and effective expansion to meet a major national emergency for the training of specialized workers. For five years the war training program under the United States Office of Education trained approximately 12 million men and women for essential war jobs (1940–1945).

6. During the entire decade state school administration continued to develop. The staffs of state boards of education were enlarged and the share of all public school funds contributed by state governments was increased in many of the states.

7. The trend toward consolidation of small rural school districts into large districts capable of supporting modern, well-equipped school buildings was greatly accelerated during the war decade. In addition to the marked decline in the number of one-room schools already discussed, another index of the growing centralization of rural education is the increase in the number of school children transported at public expense. In 1949–1950, almost 7 million school children were furnished transportation at a cost of $215 million, compared with almost 2 million pupils transported at a cost of $55 million in 1929–1930, and 4 million pupils at a cost of $83 million in 1939–1940.[45]

44. Dr. Earl James McGrath, U.S. Commissioner of Education, "I Challenge TV . . . ," *Parade*, March 23, 1952.

45. U.S. Office of Education: *Statistical Summary of Education, 1947–48,* 1950, Table 5, p. 20, and *Statistics of State School Systems, 1949–50,* 1952, p. 62.

8. During the war the principle that secondary education in the United States must become a school for all rather than a selective school was clearly enunciated.[46] This decision is still imperfectly translated into action but its effects are gradually becoming evident.

9. Plans matured for cooperation among the states in higher education on a new basis, most definitely in the Southern Regional Education Program, a system of voluntary regional cooperation in higher education. Under an interstate compact drawn up in 1948, fourteen states are now cooperating in the program of assisting states and institutions and agencies concerned with higher education to advance knowledge and to improve the social and economic level of the South. More than one million dollars is invested in the program.

Some 850 students (583 whites and 267 Negroes) are crossing state lines to obtain education not available at home but provided in 19 colleges and universities under contract through the Southern Regional Education Board. The program now operates in the fields of medicine, dentistry, veterinary medicine, social work and forestry. A commission is at work to start a regional nursing education program.

The Rocky Mountain and Pacific Coast states have begun action to establish similar planning, and have used the South's experience for suggestions on organization and procedure.[47]

10. The education of women was profoundly affected by the war. This was in part due to the formation of various specialized units for women in the armed forces. The gainful employment of women in commerce and industry has also been responsible for change in the vocational preparation of women.

11. International relations also affected American education with the arrival of approximately 30,000 students annually from overseas and the inauguration of summer sessions abroad and other special training overseas by a great many American schools and colleges.

12. During the postwar years a new emphasis has been placed on the necessity for adequate

education for gifted children. A national society for the encouragement of better education for gifted children was formed (1948), and a number of important research and policy reports published. There is a growing feeling that, without surrendering the principle of universal secondary education, American schools must find ways and means of providing greater educational opportunity for gifted pupils.

13. Religious instruction on released time in public school buildings was declared unconstitutional by the United States Supreme Court in 1948, but such instruction on released time at other locations was approved in 1952.

14. Beginning with the interest in outdoor life engendered in part by the Civilian Conservation Corps and in part by concern for the conservation of natural resources, outdoor education through school and summer camps has become a matter of growing interest.

EDUCATIONAL NEEDS AND STANDARDS [48]

In an attempt "to summarize the best thinking of hundreds of educators and laymen," the National Education Association a decade ago set forth the public educational needs of the United States in terms which are as valid today as they were then.[49] An adaptation of this statement follows.

OBJECTIVES

An adequate educational program should enable the American people to live happily and usefully while contributing to the development and preservation of a democratic order. This means educational opportunity regardless of economic status, so oriented as to promote physical, mental and emotional health. It involves emphasis upon self-direction in study and learning, an opportunity to learn through doing, a chance to know and to practice democratic group living. It calls for methods of teaching, educational content and a length of schooling adapted to individual and social requirements.

Based as it ought to be on fundamental needs, the curriculum recognizes not only the present conditions of life throughout the world but the contributions of our social heritage and the

46. *Education for ALL American Youth* (National Education Association and American Association of School Administrators), Educational Policies Commission, Washington, 1944.

47. See "The Southern Regional Education Program," *School and Society,* March 8, 1952, p. 156; and William J. McGlothlin, "Toward More Effective Education — The South Plans across the Region," *Educational Forum,* March 1952, pp. 293–302.

48. All dollar estimates for 1960 in this section are expressed in 1950 prices.

49. See *Proposals for Public Education in Postwar America,* National Education Association, Washington, April 1944.

emerging future as well. It follows that the curriculum should be flexible — to embrace new needs, knowledge and skills. Along with the mastery of specific information and techniques should go realistic experience and a sense of the relationship of schoolwork to other aspects of life, and to youthful hopes and plans.

To make these general objectives more specific: The educational system should cultivate the child's natural curiosity about his world, and encourage and foster his desire to learn. It should further the use of language; develop the basic skills needed to read, listen, speak and write; and establish attitudes and habits required for their satisfactory use.

It should do the same with respect to the number system and the ability to interpret quantitative situations, including the ability to solve problems of technical interest to the individual.

In the field of natural phenomena it should enrich the individual's background of facts, concepts and principles; vitalize his understanding of these phenomena; enable him to use his knowledge of them in his daily life and apply scientific principles in areas of special interest to him.

The educational system should develop, broaden and intensify desirable understandings, attitudes, habits and skills in the field of human relations. This includes social amenities, moral and ethical practices, the spirit of service and good will, effective work and play with others, enjoyment of a rich and varied social life, participation in family and community life.

The educational system should perform a similar function with respect to the individual's civic responsibilities, including the development of a sensitivity to social injustice and a disposition to try to improve unsatisfactory conditions.

Similarly, the system should deal with the economic aspects of life: promote understanding of the ways in which economic needs are met; inculcate a sense of the importance of work, good workmanship, wise use of time, energy and money; develop productive skills or a general knowledge of several occupational fields.

An adequate educational program, moreover, should stimulate interest in fine arts, increase and extend the enjoyment of beauty in all its forms, and develop the skills needed in the creation of beauty through the arts. It should increase the range and skill of participation in congenial leisure-time activities.

IMPLEMENTATION

The attainment of these objectives requires an educational program adequate in nature and magnitude; a properly trained staff of sufficient size; school plant and equipment equal to the demands of the program.

As a first step, each state should provide school opportunities and services at public expense for all its residents who want or need them. Except where population is sparse, school attendance units should be large enough to provide a rich and varied school program at reasonable cost. School attendance for the ages 3–4 should not be required, but facilities should be available for those whose parents wish them to attend. All educable children in the 6–17 age group should be required to attend school by law, and all 5-year-olds, except in sparsely populated areas where travel time would be too great.

Every educable person should be encouraged to utilize college or other appropriate facilities of advanced education on a full-time basis for two years, and either on a full-time or part-time basis thereafter.

Helping each individual obtain the kind and amount of schooling he needs requires special attention beyond that ordinarily given in class instruction. Guidance and counseling services should be provided to assure the pupil's satisfactory progress in school, to deal with problems not only of emotional but of social maladjustment as well, and to help individuals plan their educational and occupational future.

Vocational and general education should be integrated in a single school, with each phase handled by different teachers. Outside work experience, camping activities and travel should be part of the educational program.

Rigid and uniform criteria for grade placement should give way to a more flexible system. While it is desirable to promote pupils regularly in accordance with their advancing maturity, no one should be permitted to take work for which he is not prepared. The length of the school term for persons of compulsory attendance age should be at least 40 weeks or 200 days each year.

The Staff

As to personnel requirements, there is need, first, for a broader cultural background coupled with greater technical knowledge and skill than is now generally the case. Principals should not have any teaching duties in schools with 12 or more teachers, and only half-time teaching duties in schools with 6 to 11 teachers. The number of pupils per qualified staff member should be no more than 25 at each age level from 6 through 19. This means 28 pupils per classroom teacher, 500 per school librarian, and from 500 per full-time pupil counselor for the younger children to 200 for the older ones. The maximum number of children for each teacher of 5-year-olds should be 20, and half that for 3- and 4-year-olds.

Classes for those older than 5 should be no larger than 25–30 pupils. At least one full-time graduate nurse is needed for every 1,000 children aged 3–5, every 1,500 aged 6–11, and every 2,000 aged 12–19.

Professional personnel should, at a minimum, have graduated from junior college and have at least an additional two years of professional preparation. A minimum salary for a 40-week (200-day) school year of approximately $2,900 [50] would be needed to attract personnel capable of putting the program into practice.

It is the duty of each state to provide for the preparation of all types of professional personnel needed in schools, to set up standards, and establish requirements for certification of teachers and others. In addition, a continuous and systematic program to encourage growth in service is necessary to enable teachers and others to cope with changing educational needs. In addition to the professional personnel, a full-time clerk is recommended for every 500 pupils, and a full-time janitor-engineer for every 16,000 square feet of floor area or for approximately every 250 pupils.

The Physical Setup

Schools should be located and built to serve as community educational and recreational centers. The entire plant, moreover, should be flexible enough to permit changes or additions. Each unit should be large enough to make possible a rich and varied school experience at reasonable building and operating costs; yet it should be small enough to encourage friendly and co-operative community living.

Elementary schools should be designed for a

---

50. The figure given in the NEA statement was $1,665 in 1940 prices. This was increased by 72 per cent, which is the increase in the consumers' price index between 1940 and 1950.

minimum of about 7 professional staff members and 175 pupils, while for secondary schools the corresponding figures are 12 and 300. Somewhat larger schools are greatly to be preferred, but not beyond a maximum of about 1,000 pupils for elementary and 1,500 for secondary schools. It is difficult to attain the optimum size in areas where population is sparse and transportation difficult. On the other hand, it is hard not to exceed this size where population is dense and school sites scarce.

In addition to regular classrooms, schools should include workshops for arts and crafts (and science laboratories in secondary schools), music rooms and a library, a gymnasium and game rooms, an auditorium for assembly and theatrical activities, space for social gatherings, a cafeteria, conference or study rooms for small groups, offices for staff members, rest rooms for children and adults. Ample outdoor space should be provided for games and sports, concerts and dramatics, gardening and nature study. At least 5 acres of ground should be provided for an elementary and 15 for a secondary school, with 25 acres or more desirable for the latter. Equipment should be based on minimum standards set up by the state department of education, including not only books, magazines, pamphlets, tools and materials for arts and crafts, but audio-visual aids as well.

Financial Assistance beyond High School

Tuition-free education through the fourteenth school grade should be available in public institutions just as high school education is now available. Because of inadequate family incomes and high living costs, financial assistance must be provided for worthy students who need it if they are to remain in school.

ELEMENTARY AND SECONDARY SCHOOL

According to the criteria of the previous section, enrollments under an "adequate program" of education should equal the population aged 6–17 and perhaps 85 per cent of the 5-year-olds. Had the standards of this "adequate program" been in effect in 1950, elementary and secondary school enrollments would have totaled 31.1 million, or 2.5 million above the level actually recorded. By 1960 an adequate program should mean enrollment of 43.7 million, or about 1.7 million higher than the level likely to be reached if past trends continue. (See Table 181.)

TABLE 181. POPULATION 5–17 YEARS OF AGE AND ELEMENTARY AND SECONDARY SCHOOL ENROLLMENT AND ENROLLMENT GOALS, BY AGE, 1950 AND 1960

(Thousands)

| | Population [a] | | Enrollment [b] | | | |
| | | | Existing Program | | Adequate Program | |
Age	1950	1960	1950	1960 [c]	1950	1960
Total, 5–17 years	31,517	44,235	28,629 [d]	42,009	31,092	43,693
5–6 years	5,756 [e]	7,343 [f]	3,207	6,259	5,331	6,801
7–13 years	17,275	25,700	16,530	25,700	17,275	25,700
14–15 years	4,360	5,483	4,050	5,483	4,360	5,483
16–17 years	4,126	5,709	3,068	4,567	4,126	5,709

Sources: Population: 1950 based on unpublished estimates of the U.S. Bureau of the Census; 1960 from Appendix 12–1. Enrollment under existing program: 1950 total from *Statistical Summary of Education, 1949–50*, U.S. Office of Education, 1953, with distribution by age based on enrollment rates as indicated in *1950 Population Census Report P-B1*, U.S. Bureau of the Census, 1952, Table 42, p. 1–95; 1960 derived as follows: 5–6-year group raised from 55 per cent in 1950 to 85 per cent in 1960 on assumption that school facilities and personnel will be sufficient to care for about two thirds of the 5-year-olds and that all 6-year-olds, practically all of whom were enrolled in 1950, would be in school in 1960; 7–15-year group, with close to 95 per cent enrollment in 1950, assumed to be fully enrolled in 1960; 16–17-year-olds raised from just under 75 per cent in 1950 to 80 per cent by 1960 on basis of past trend. Enrollment under adequate program: see discussion in text.

a. As of July 1: includes allowance for armed forces overseas and adjustment for underenumeration of population under 15 years of age.

b. For the 1960 estimates and for the "adequate program" in 1950 it is assumed that all elementary and secondary school pupils come from the 5–17-year age group; allowance is made for older students in the college enrollment figures in Table 184.

c. Probable enrollment under assumptions listed above.

d. Includes an estimated 1,774,000 students over 17 years of age.

e. Consists of 2,833,000 aged 5 years and 2,923,000 aged 6.

f. Consists of 3,612,000 aged 5 years and 3,731,000 aged 6.

Operating Expenditures

Operating expenditures comprise all expenditures except capital outlays and interest. By far the largest item is salary for the professional staff; professional salaries in public elementary and secondary schools, for example, amounted to 62 per cent of their total operating expenditures in 1949–1950. The remaining expenditures are for books and supplies, administration, plant operation and maintenance, auxiliary services and fixed charges.

The staff needed to handle the enlarged student bodies adequately — including teachers, counselors, librarians, nurses and clerks — would have totaled about 1.3 million in 1950, probably some 300,000 above the actual level.[51]

By 1960, 1.9 million staff members would be needed. Different types of personnel needed would be as follows:

	1950	1960
Professional staff	1,287,000	1,805,000
Teachers, counselors and librarians *	1,268,000	1,778,000
School nurses †	19,000	27,000
School clerks ‡	62,000	87,000
Total staff	1,349,000	1,892,000

* One per 20 pupils aged 5 and per 25 aged 6–17.

† One for each 1,000 pupils aged 5; one for each 1,500 aged 6–11 and one for each 2,000 aged 12–17.

‡ One for each 500 pupils.

Figures on the number of counselors and librarians were not available. In the public schools, there were 9,411 school clerks, of whom 1,953 were part time; 4,567 school nurses, of whom 619 were part time. Comparable data on clerks and nurses are not available for private schools. In all likelihood, the total school personnel in all these categories did not exceed 1.1 million in 1950.

---

51. There were 1,045,225 teachers in all types of public and private elementary and secondary schools in 1950.

TABLE 182. ESTIMATED OPERATING EXPENDITURES NEEDED FOR AN ADEQUATE PROGRAM
OF ELEMENTARY AND SECONDARY SCHOOL EDUCATION, 1950 AND 1960
(*Dollar Amounts at 1950 Prices*)

	1950		1960	
	Pupils Enrolled	Operating Expenditures	Pupils Enrolled	Operating Expenditures
	(*Thousands*)	(*Millions*)	(*Thousands*)	(*Millions*)
Demand	28,629	$5,433	42,009	$ 8,810
Public	25,210	4,862 [a]	36,548	7,660
Private	3,419	571	5,461	1,150
Deficiencies	—	2,375	—	2,560
Not enrolled	2,463	603	1,684	410
Inadequate program	24,966	1,772	32,598	2,150
Urban	13,142	783	18,198	1,000
Rural	11,824	989	14,400	1,150
Need [b]	31,092	7,808	43,693	11,370
Public	27,361	6,988	38,013	9,890
Private	3,731	820	5,680	1,480

Sources: Demand figures for 1950: enrollment and public expenditures from *Statistical Summary of Education, 1949–50*, U.S. Office of Education, 1953; private expenditures from Appendix 4–4. Demand figures for 1960: total enrollment from Table 181; total expenditures computed at $205 per pupil enrolled (see Appendix 12–2, footnote 9) plus an allowance of $200 million for interest and for expenditures for summer and part-time adult schools, residential schools for exceptional children and federal schools for Indians. Public enrollment and ex-penditures based on distribution in *School Life*, May 1950, Table 1, p. 116. Deficiencies for 1950 and 1960: from Appendix 12–2.

a. Includes $101 million interest, $36 million expenditures for summer and part-time adult schools and $38 million for residential schools for exceptional children and federal schools for Indians.

b. Distributed between public and private in same proportions as demand.

Total salaries at an adequate level for this staff are estimated at $5.7 billion in 1950 and $8.0 billion in 1960.[52]

These figures imply that an adequate education program of elementary and secondary schooling, including kindergarten, would have required $7.6 billion for operating expenditures in 1950 and would require $10.7 billion in 1960.[53] These aggregate figures, however, do not represent needed expenditures as the concept of need is used in this study. Here need is viewed not in terms of equalizing all expenditures to a uniform level, but rather as bringing those below up to the standard of adequacy while leaving those above undisturbed.

The standard of adequacy may be expressed in terms of expenditures per enrolled pupil, and, on the basis of the aggregate figures, annual operating expenditures of $245 per pupil could provide an adequate educational program for all. Since the rate of spending is above that level in some parts of the school system, needed expenditures would be made up of three parts:

(1) The amount now spent where expenditures exceed $245 per enrolled pupil;

(2) The amount to be spent for pupils now outside the school system who should be in it — the number of such pupils multiplied by $245; and

(3) The amount to be spent to bring the average expenditure level up to standard where it is now below — the number of pupils in those

52. Based on the NEA recommended average salaries in 1940 prices of $2,500 a year for professional personnel and $1,800 for clerks; adjusted upward by 72 per cent in line with the consumers' price index, these recommended averages are $4,300 and $3,100 respectively, in 1950 prices.

53. Assuming salaries constitute 75 per cent of total operating expenditures. Based on material in *Proposals for Public Education in Postwar America*, Table 1, p. 32; derived from an estimate of the cost of pupil transportation plus the average per pupil expenditure for the remainder of the school budget in ten cities in each of which the average teacher salary in 1940–1941 was the recommended average. These data agree rather well with similar data for 1950–1951 in *Expenditure per Pupil in City School Systems, 1950–51*, U.S. Office of Education, Circular No. 337, 1952, p. 13 and pp. 18–23.

parts of the school system with below-standard expenditure rates multiplied by the difference between the standard and the actual expenditure rate.

Operating expenditures under such a program would have been $7.8 billion in 1950, compared with actual expenditures of $5.4 billion; in 1960, needed operating expenditures would be $11.4 billion, compared with probable expenditures of $8.8 billion.

In addition to the 2.5 million children who should have been enrolled in school in 1950 but were not, about 25 million, or 87 per cent, of those enrolled were receiving an inadequate education which ranged all the way from minor to very serious deficiencies. By 1960, if past trends continue, the number remaining out of school should drop to 1.7 million and the proportion of those receiving inadequate education should decline to 78 per cent of the total enrolled. In view of the large increase in total enrollments expected, however, more than 30 million children would be receiving inadequate education. (See Table 182.)

Capital Expenditures

Constructing and equipping the school buildings needed to house the educational program constitutes a substantial economic task. The current dimensions of that task are increased by the formidable backlog of school shortages that has been accumulating for many years.

As a result of the depression, capital outlays for public elementary and secondary schools declined from $434 million in 1925 to a low of $59 million in 1934. They managed to climb to $258 million by 1940 only to fall, under the impact of the war, to a new low of $54 million in 1944. Not until 1949 did outlays exceed the 1925 level; even then, as a result of increased construction costs, the school plant added during the year was far below the level of the mid-1920s. Not until 1950 did the real volume of school construction return to that level. (See Table 183.) As a result, the public school system in the fall of 1952 needed about $10.7 billion in additional plant and equipment.[54] This need, expressed in 1950 prices and adjusted to include private elementary and secondary schools, may be estimated at approximately $11 billion.

54. *School Facilities Survey*, U.S. Office of Education, Second Progress Report, December 1952, p. 46.

TABLE 183. CAPITAL EXPENDITURES[a] FOR PUBLIC ELEMENTARY AND SECONDARY SCHOOLS, 1920–1951
(*Millions*)

School Year Ending June 30	At Current Prices	At 1950 Prices[b]
1920	$ 154	$ 312
1922	306	892
1924	388	928
1925	434	1,080
1926	411	1,012
1928	383	950
1930	371	944
1931	289	830
1932	211	692
1933	135	401
1934	59	152
1935	115	300
1936	171	422
1937	205	445
1938	239	521
1939	248	539
1940	258	545
1941	149	295
1942	138	255
1943	69	122
1944	54	93
1945	76	126
1946	111	162
1947	205	252
1948	412	456
1949	599	644
1950	1,014	1,014
1951	1,293	1,222

Source: The Sustaining Economic Forces Ahead, Materials Prepared for the Joint Committee on the Economic Report, 1952, Table 13, p. 43.

a. Including expenditures for land.

b. Price adjustment based on *Engineering News-Record* index of general construction costs as published in *Construction and Building Materials: Statistical Supplement, May 1952*, U.S. Department of Commerce, Table 10, p. 34.

In addition to these backlog needs are the needs due to arise from the huge increase in enrollments and from replacement of worn-out buildings and equipment. If enrollments were to reach the level of 44 million assumed desirable under an adequate education program, they would have to rise by about 13 million between 1952 and 1960. At a cost of about $1,200 per pupil,[55] capital outlays needed to house this group would total $16 billion. Normal replacement needs would be another $4 billion.[56]

55. *The Sustaining Economic Forces Ahead*, Materials Prepared for the Joint Committee on the Economic Report, 1952, p. 40. Based on allowance of $6 billion for enrollment increase of 5 million.

56. *Ibid.*

Between 1952 and 1960, therefore, a total capital outlay of about $31 billion would be needed to provide the buildings and equipment necessary to handle decently the number of elementary and secondary school children who might be enrolled under an adequate program. Such a building program spread over a ten-year period would mean annual expenditures at the rate of about $3 billion.

In 1950 capital expenditures for elementary and secondary schools amounted to $1.2 billion, some $1.8 billion below the needed level. Were these expenditures to expand at the same rate as projected for probable total educational construction, they would rise about 40 per cent to a level of $1.7 billion in 1960 [57] — well above the $1.4 billion spent in 1951.[58] In view of the excellent financial condition of most state governments and the vast amount of capital outlay needed to make our school system adequate, it seems safe to assume probable capital expenditures for 1960 somewhat above the most recent levels. This assumption still would leave an annual capital deficit of about $1.3 billion. (See Table 186.)

Needs and demands for elementary and secondary plant and equipment may be summarized as follows (in billions of 1950 dollars):

	Total	Public	Private
1950			
Demand	$1.2	$1.0	$0.2
Need	3.0	2.5	0.5
1960			
Demand	1.7	1.4	0.3
Need	3.0	2.5	0.5

HIGHER EDUCATION [59]

Who Should Go to College?

The President's Commission on Higher Education suggested in its 1947 report that college education should be available to all persons who have the mental ability to take advantage of it. It applied this criterion to the results of two similar tests of mental ability: the Army General Classification Test, which was given to al-

most 10 million men during World War II,[60] and the American Council of Education's Psychological Examination (1942 College Edition) taken by entering students in several hundred colleges.

These data, together with information on the number of years of college later completed by the students who began college in 1942, led to the conclusion that at least 49 per cent of our population have the mental ability to complete two years of college, and at least 32 per cent the mental ability to complete an advanced liberal or specialized professional education. Some of these should go on to graduate and professional school, the number being determined by the needs of society for people with such training. On the basis of these considerations 1950 college enrollments of 2,659,000 fell 1,468,000 short of the desired goal and 1960 enrollments are likely to fall 1,564,000 short of reaching the goal of 4,489,000. (See Table 184.)

The estimate of probable 1960 enrollment in higher education of 2,925,000 was derived from the trend in the ratio of total enrollment to population in the 18–21-year age group for the pre-depression, nonwar years 1915 and 1920–1928. During that period enrollments rose from 5.5 to 12.1 per cent of the population in this age group. A continuation of that trend to 1960 would imply an enrollment ratio of about 28 per cent.[61] Although enrollments reached almost 30 per cent of the population in the 18–21-year age group in 1950, they included veterans, most of whom were over 21 years of age and normally would have been in college in earlier years, if at all. The fact that many veterans did take advantage of G.I. educational benefits to go to college, however, is bound to spread the desire for higher education and to affect the long-run enrollment trend. Consequently, the projected 28 per cent ratio was raised to 30 per cent for 1960. The resultant enrollment figure is almost the same as the 1960 projection of the President's Commission on Higher Education,[62] and is 10 per cent higher than 1950 enrollment.

57. See Appendix 4–7, Table B.

58. See Table 183. The $1.2 billion expenditure rate for 1951 (in 1950 prices) was upped by $0.2 billion to allow for private schools and public schools outside the regular state school system.

59. The President's Commission on Higher Education, reporting in 1947, spelled out the needs and standards of the college age group of the population. (See *Higher Education for American Democracy*, Vol. I, *Establishing the Goals*, December 1947.) This section is based entirely on this report.

60. Although women were hardly represented and Navy personnel, those inducted as officers and those deferred because of engagement in essential activity were not covered, the test is considered "conservatively representative of the general population." (*Ibid.*, p. 40.)

61. *Statistics of Higher Education: Faculty, Students and Degrees, 1949–50*, U.S. Office of Education, 1952, Table II, p. 6.

62. See *Higher Education for American Democracy*, Vol. I, p. 43; the projection given there is 2,924,000.

TABLE 184. POPULATION 18–21 YEARS OF AGE, COLLEGE ENROLLMENT
AND ENROLLMENT GOALS, 1950 AND 1960
(Thousands)

Ages	Population [a]		Enrollment		Enrollment Goals	
	1950	*1960*	*1950*	*1960*	*1950*	*1960*
			(Actual)	*(Probable)*		
Total, 18–21	8,985	9,522	2,659	2,925	4,127 [b]	4,489 [b]
18–19	4,422	4,955	—	—	2,167	2,428
20–21	4,563	4,567	—	—	1,460	1,461

Sources: 1950 population based on unpublished estimates of the U.S. Bureau of the Census; 1960 population based on Appendix 12–1; 1950 actual enrollment from *Statistics of Higher Education: Faculty, Students and Degrees, 1949–50,* U.S. Office of Education, 1952, Table II, p. 6; for 1960 probable enrollment and 1950 and 1960 enrollment goals, see text.

a. Includes allowance for armed forces overseas.

b. Includes 500,000 graduate and professional school enrollments in 1950 and 600,000 in 1960, which are not included in components.

Operating Expenditures

The estimated 10 per cent increase in probable enrollment between 1950 and 1960 should result in at least a like increase over the $1.7 billion educational and general expenditure of 1950.[63] On a per pupil basis, these expenditures have shown a tendency to increase during the past twenty years in terms of constant prices.[64] A 10 per cent increase in enrollments plus a like increase in outlay per pupil could result in aggregate expenditures of $2.1 billion in 1960.

Past trends indicate that public institutions are likely to enroll a growing proportion of college students, perhaps as high as 55 per cent by 1960.[65] Since public expenditures in 1950 were slightly more proportionately than public enrollments, probable public expenditures in 1960 are estimated at 57 per cent of the total, or $1.2 billion. Probable expenditures by private schools and colleges would be about $900 million.

Turning to the cost of an adequate program of higher education, the President's Commission on Higher Education advocates 20 students per faculty member (teachers, researchers and counselors) in the first two years, 13 during the next two, 10 in graduate and professional schools, and recommends that administrative faculty should comprise 15 per cent of the total.[66] Application of these figures to the enrollment data in Table 184 shows a need of approximately 320,000 faculty members in 1950 and 350,000 in 1960.

Following the recommendation of "at least a 50 per cent increase" [67] in the salary level, the Commission arrives at a total faculty salary for 1960 which, when corrected from 1947 to 1950 prices, amounts to about $1.8 billion, or an average of $5,057 a year for each faculty member.[68] On this basis, total salaries for a faculty of 320,000 would have amounted to $1.6 billion in 1950 if instruction of the quality required for an adequate program of higher education had been provided.

On the basis of recent experience, expenditures for resident instruction needs would amount to about 45 per cent of total needed educational and general expenditures.[69] Hence total operating expenditures needed for an adequate program of higher education would have amounted to $3.6

63. *Statistics of Higher Education: Receipts, Expenditures and Property, 1949–50,* U.S. Office of Education, 1952, Table 7, p. 52.

64. From $490 in 1930, to $612 in 1940 and $642 in 1950, in 1950 prices. Derived from *Statistics of Higher Education: Faculty, Students and Degrees, 1949–50,* Table 1, p. 40.

65. See *ibid.,* pp. 14–17 for data for past years.

66. *Higher Education for American Democracy,* Vol. IV, pp. 9 and 11.

67. *Ibid.,* Vol. V, p. 14.

68. *Ibid.*

69. See, for example, *Statistics of Higher Education: Receipts, Expenditures and Property, 1949–50,* Table 7, p. 52.

TABLE 185. ESTIMATED OPERATING EXPENDITURES NEEDED FOR AN ADEQUATE PROGRAM
OF HIGHER EDUCATION,[a] 1950 AND 1960
(Dollar Amounts at 1950 Prices)

	1950		1960	
	Pupils Enrolled	*Operating Expenditures*	*Pupils Enrolled*	*Operating Expenditures*
	(Thousands)	*(Millions)*	*(Thousands)*	*(Millions)*
Demand	2,659	$1,706	2,925	$2,100
Public	1,355	898	1,609	1,200
Private	1,304	808 [b]	1,316	900
Deficiency	1,468	1,864	1,564	1,830
Need	4,127	3,570	4,489	3,930
Public	2,823	2,440	3,173	2,780
Private	1,304	1,130	1,316	1,150

Sources: Demand figures for 1950: from U.S. Office of Education, Circular No. 326, August 1951 and Circular No. 332, December 1951. Demand figures for 1960: total enrollment from Table 184; public and private enrollment and all expenditure figures based on discussion in text. Needed enrollment figures from Table 184. For other need and deficiency figures, see text.

a. Excludes expenditures for auxiliary and other noneducational expenditures.

b. Differs slightly from expenditure figure of $804 million in Appendix 4–4; the $808 million figure is for the school year 1949–1950, whereas the smaller figure is the U.S. Commerce Department estimate for the calendar year 1950.

billion in 1950 and should amount to $3.9 billion in 1960.[70]

Distribution of these needed expenditures between public and private schools should be related to their relative enrollments. The President's Commission on Higher Education felt that private enrollments under an adequate program of education should remain at the level of 900,000 reached during the 1946–1947 school year. This conclusion was based on consideration of the potential sources of income available to private colleges and universities.[71] Since that time, however, private enrollments have increased, reaching a total of 1,304,000 in 1949–1950. On the assumption that private institutions can somehow manage to provide adequately for approximately the level of enrollment already experienced, but — in line with the Commis-

sion's analysis — not for any higher level, private enrollments have been kept the same under the adequate program in 1950 as they actually were in that year. For 1960 they have been allowed to rise slightly to 1,316,000, the probable level projected under the present program.

Consequently, public enrollment under an adequate program would have been 2,823,000 in 1950 and would reach 3,173,000 in 1960. These enrollment figures imply needed expenditures of $2.4 billion for public institutions in 1950 and $2.8 billion in 1960, and between $1.1 and $1.2 billion for private institutions in both years. (See Table 185.)

Capital Expenditures

Institutions of higher learning spent some $417 million on physical property [72] in 1949–1950. This expenditure rate was the highest on record, yet it was less than one third the amount needed annually to bring the size and quality of our higher educational structures up to par within a decade.

70. These represent minimum estimates since they imply reducing expenditures to the level of adequacy in areas where spending is above that level. In the case of elementary and secondary school programs, needed expenditures were raised about 3 per cent in 1950 and 11 per cent in 1960 when allowance was made for keeping spending above the minimum adequate level in those areas where it already exceeded or is likely to exceed that level. Although data are not available for making a similar adjustment in the case of higher education, it is believed that the adjustment would be much smaller.

71. *Higher Education for American Democracy*, Vol. V, p. 11.

72. Including additional ground for educational or auxiliary purposes; new construction and remodeling; new equipment, etc. *Statistics of Higher Education: Receipts, Expenditures, and Property, 1949–50*, Table XII, p. 32.

According to the recommendations of the President's Commission on Higher Education, the desired 1960 enrollment of 4.5 million students would require about 700 million square feet of "educational plant" with a total value of $16.8 billion (in terms of replacement cost at 1950 prices).[73] In 1950 the value of the physical plant was approximately $5.3 billion.[74] To make up for deficiencies existing in 1950 and to provide for the additional enrollments that an adequate educational program would require by 1960, about $11.5 billion in new buildings and equipment should be added. Allowance for normal replacement of obsolete structures [75] would bring needed capital outlays during the decade up to $13.5 billion, or approximately $1.4 billion a year. Should capital outlays for higher education follow the historical trend indicated for educational expenditures (see Appendix 4–7, Table B), they may run in the neighborhood of $0.6 billion in 1960, or less than half the needed amount.

On the assumption that the expansion of enrollments will be concentrated in public institutions of higher education and that the value of buildings and equipment in 1960 should be distributed between public and private institutions roughly in proportion to the size of their respective student bodies, public institutions would need a school plant valued at about $11.9 billion and private institutions at about $4.9 billion (in 1950 prices). In contrast, public institutions had a 1950 value of $2.9 billion and private institutions $2.4 billion.[76] Whereas private schools would need only to double their value, public schools would have to more than quadruple theirs during the decade. To do this, public institutions would have to spend at the average rate of about $1.0 billion a year and private institutions at the rate of $0.4 billion a year between 1950 and 1960.

The needed and probable capital outlays for higher education may be summarized as follows (in billions of 1950 dollars):

	Total	Public	Private
1950			
Demand	$0.4	$0.3	$0.1
Need	1.4	1.0	0.4
1960			
Demand	0.6	0.4	0.2
Need	1.4	1.0	0.4

INFORMAL EDUCATION

Needs and probable expenditures for the less regular forms of education are more difficult to determine than those of the regular school systems. For most of these groups, the concept of need as used in this volume is hardly applicable.

Private

In expenditures for specialized private schools, individual spending for reading, and foundation giving for education, individual choice is so great that it seems best to assume that no more needs to be spent than actually was spent in 1950 or is likely to be spent in 1960. Needed expenditures of private museums and libraries also may be assumed equal to actual or probable expenditures, but for a different reason. In this case, it may be argued that any additional spending needed to meet higher standards should come from public rather than private bodies. Private libraries and museums, although highly valuable, may be viewed as supplementary to public educational institutions and should not be held responsible for bringing the general level of activity up to standard.

Should past relationships to disposable income continue, spending for courses in commercial, business, trade, correspondence and other specialized private schools would rise from about $350 million in 1950 to $400 million in 1960. Spending for private informal education — by individuals for reading and by foundations, museums and libraries — would rise from $1.2 to $1.6 billion.[77] Expenditures for new buildings and equipment by these specialized schools and private museums and libraries would probably remain in the neighborhood of $20 million a year.

Public

Information on public spending for informal education is incomplete. Data for public museums for recent years are unavailable and these

73. Recommendations in *Higher Education for American Democracy*, Vol. V, p. 20, with adjustment for price change from 1946–1947 to 1950; recommended construction cost of $18 per square foot upped by one third to $24.

74. *Statistics of Higher Education: Receipts, Expenditures, and Property, 1949–50*, p. 33; this figure includes land and also about $0.5 billion in funds allocated but not yet spent.

75. At a rate of 2 per cent per year on the assumption of a 50-year life span per building.

76. *Ibid.*, Table XII, p. 32.

77. Appendix 4–7, Table A.

TABLE 186. ESTIMATED DEMAND AND ADEQUATE EXPENDITURES FOR EDUCATION, 1950 AND 1960
(*Millions at 1950 Prices*)

Type of Expenditure	1950		1960	
	Demand	Adequate Program	Demand	Adequate Program
Total education expenditures	$10,505	$17,573	$15,340	$21,920
Private	3,334	4,445	4,550	5,530
Operating or consumption	2,954 [a]	3,525	4,030	4,610
Schools	1,731	2,302	2,450	3,030
Elementary and secondary	571	820	1,150	1,480
Higher	808	1,130	900	1,150
Other [b]	352	352	400	400
Informal	1,223	1,223	1,580	1,580
Reading	1,136	1,136	1,480	1,480
Foundations	67	67	70	70
Museums and libraries	20	20	30	30
Capital [c]	380	920	520	920
Schools	360	900	500	900
Elementary and secondary	219 [d]	500	300	500
Higher	141	400	200	400
Other [b] (including museums and libraries)	20 [e]	20	20	20
Government	7,171	13,128	10,790	16,390
Operating	5,856	9,578	8,970	12,840
Schools	5,760	9,428	8,860	12,670
Elementary and secondary	4,862	6,988	7,660	9,890
Higher	898	2,440	1,200	2,780
Libraries	96 [f]	150	110	170
Capital [c]	1,315	3,550	1,820	3,550
Schools	1,297	3,500	1,800	3,500
Elementary and secondary	1,021 [g]	2,500	1,400	2,500
Higher	276	1,000	400	1,000
Libraries	18 [f]	50	20	50

Sources: Demand figures for 1950: subtotals and total derived by addition. Except as otherwise noted, individual items are from other tables in this chapter; Appendix 4–4; *Statistical Summary of Education, 1949–50*, U.S. Office of Education, 1953, Table 33; and *Statistics of Higher Education: Receipts, Expenditures and Property, 1949–50*, U.S. Office of Education, 1952, Table XIII, p. 22. Estimates for adequate program and of demand in 1960 from other tables and text discussion in this chapter.

a. This total differs slightly from the figure for private education in Appendix 4–4 because of substitution here of $808 million operating expenditures for higher education from Table 185 in place of $804 million shown in Appendix 4–4. (See Table 185, footnote *b*.)

b. Commercial, business, trade, correspondence schools and other specialized instruction.

c. Comprises plant, equipment and land.

d. Total private elementary and secondary school expenditures of $790 million (*Statistical Summary of Education, 1949–50*, Table 33) less $571 million operating expenditures.

e. Assumed equal to 5 per cent of operating expenditures.

f. Unpublished estimates of the U.S. Bureau of the Census.

g. Includes $7 million estimated capital expenditures by residential schools for exceptional children and federal schools for Indians.

agencies have therefore had to be omitted. Public libraries, however, spent $114 million in 1950, $96 million on day-to-day operations and $18 million on new buildings and equipment.[78] If

78. Unpublished estimates of the U.S. Bureau of the Census.

past relationships continue, their operating expenditures are likely to be about $110 million and their capital outlays $20 million in 1960.

Standards of needs for library service to the community are difficult to set. A recent survey of librarians, however, indicates some of the more urgent needs.[79] Public library leaders considered that the 1950 public library bill needed increasing by 50 per cent. The most essential needs in their opinion were: a 12 per cent increase for salaries; a 15 per cent increase for materials; a 33 per cent increase for extension of library service to uncovered areas. This is a minimum program; many librarians would consider expenditures 100, 150 or 200 per cent above the current level as a sound social investment. The minimum program implies needed operating expenditures of $150 million for 1950 and $170 million for 1960. A needed capital outlay of about $50 million a year is based on the American Library Association's estimate that as of 1948 about $500 million was needed for public library buildings.[80] The estimate of $50 million (which is stated in 1950 prices) makes allowance for the price rise between 1948 and 1950 and assumes a building program spread over a ten-year period.

SUMMARY

Spending for education totaled $10.5 billion during the school year ending in 1950. More than two thirds ($7.2 billion) was for public education; about 87 per cent ($9.1 billion) was for formal schooling; and close to 85 per cent ($8.8 billion) was for operating, as opposed to capital, expenditures. (See Table 186.)

79. Robert D. Leigh, *The Public Library in the United States,* Columbia University Press, New York, 1950, pp. 145–147.

80. Andrews, *op. cit.,* p. 210.

These totals do not include indirect spending for education. For example, subsistence payments by the government to veterans, although not spent directly on education, enabled many veterans to return to school. Also, by careful tuning, radio and television audiences were able to benefit from a number of educational programs whose cost has not been included in the above figures. These and other indirect outlays probably added considerably to the total spent in one way or another on education.

By 1960 direct educational expenditures are expected to rise by almost 50 per cent, to $15.3 billion (in 1950 prices). If past trends continue, public spending probably will rise more sharply than private to a level of $10.8 billion, or 70 per cent of the total.

Total expenditures needed for an adequate educational program are estimated at $17.6 billion for 1950, $7.1 billion above actual expenditures, and $21.9 billion (in 1950 prices) for 1960, $6.6 billion above probable expenditures.[81] Most of the gap between needs and demand is in the public educational field — $6.0 billion in 1950 and $5.6 billion in 1960. It appears logical for public rather than private means to assume the major burden for eliminating any serious gaps in our educational system.

81. The decline in the gap between needs and demand results from the assumption that a needed program of capital expenditures must be spread over a period of time so that needed annual capital outlays are the same for 1950 and 1960.

## CHAPTER 13

RELIGION

ORGANIZED RELIGION represents a relatively small share of the economic life of the nation. But total contributions to churches constitute an important part — perhaps as much as one half — of all philanthropic giving by the people. Church members, who contribute these substantial sums, comprise more than half the national population.

Apart from the churches themselves, religious bodies have wide and varied interests, which they serve through a variety of institutions.[1] Prominent among these are agencies of religious education — Sunday schools, weekday classes, elementary and high schools, and church colleges. Other educational work is carried on through adult education programs and youth organizations. Administrative agencies and associations have been set up to supervise these activities and to promote the cause of religious education, and conferences are held from time to time to consider educational aims, plans and programs. Professional training is offered both in theological seminaries and in other specialized training schools.

Interests of evangelism, social welfare, fellowship and recreation, as well as education, are served by local church societies, by community centers and by youth associations such as the YMCA, B'nai B'rith, the Christian Endeavor Society and the Catholic Youth Organization. Religious bodies have organized for social action and for the promotion of common interests in local clubs and discussion groups, national councils and committees, periodic conferences and political lobbies. Magazines, newspapers, pamphlets and books of broad and varied content flow from the religious press.

Many of these institutions serve groups of churches or are means of interdenominational and interfaith cooperation, but local churches are still the center of most religious activity. Indeed, attendance at weekly services marks the limit of religious participation of many church members.

There are no complete, annual church statistics. The periodic compilations which are available are limited in coverage and based on no uniform system of reporting. The Bureau of the Census, under the law, may take a census of religious bodies, but is not required to do so. The Bureau has gathered data decennially since 1906, but the 1936 count was incomplete and the 1946 census was a failure. In 1936, about 20 per cent of the pastors and clerks of local congregations did not reply to urgent requests mailed to them by the Census Bureau, despite additional appeals from national officials of the religious bodies. In 1946, Congress voted initial funds for the usual decennial census, but when returns from about 60 per cent of the parishes were in hand, further grants were denied and the compilation was abandoned. Some degree of noncooperation on the part of the local churches was again experienced in this unsuccessful survey. No figures are available, broken down by states, cities, or rural and urban communities, after the federal Census of Religious Bodies for 1936.

THE CHURCHES TODAY [2]

In both the first and last half of the war decade the churches recorded more people on their rolls than at any previous time. All major faiths added many members, in spite of the adverse effect on local churches of the increased mobility of the population. The gains, which were accounted for largely by expansion of the membership of existing institutions rather than by organization of new local units, were due in part to the sharp rise in the birth rate during this

By BENSON Y. LANDIS, Associate Executive Director, Central Department of Research and Survey, National Council of the Churches of Christ in the United States of America. Opinions and judgments expressed in this chapter are those of the author and should not be attributed to the organization with which he is associated.

1. For a description and discussion of religious institutions see Herbert W. Schneider, *Religion in 20th Century America,* Harvard University Press, Cambridge, 1952.
2. Unless otherwise stated the sources of this section are the *Yearbook of American Churches, 1953 Edition,* and earlier volumes, published by the National Council of Churches, New York.

TABLE 187. CHURCH AND SUNDAY SCHOOL TRENDS, 1906–1950 [a]

	1906	1916	1926	1940	1950
Churches (*thousands*)	210	227	232	244	286
Value of buildings (*millions*)	$1,258	$1,677	$3,839	—	$5,235 [b]
Church members (*thousands*)	35,068	41,927	54,576	64,501	86,830
Membership as per cent of population	38	41	46	49	57
Sunday schools (*thousands*)	168	186	185	213 [e]	246
Sunday-school pupils (*thousands*)	14,686	19,936	21,039	22,777	27,775

Sources: *Religious Bodies,* U.S. Bureau of the Census, 1906, 1916 and 1926; *Yearbook of American Churches,* 1941, 1951 and 1953, National Council of Churches, New York.

a. Data from the 1936 Census of Religious Bodies not given, as the reporting was incomplete.
b. Value of all church property.
c. 1941–1942; 1940 not available.

period. But because of the critical nature of the times, people apparently turned to the churches for help to a far greater extent than in the 1920s or even in the depression years of the 1930s.

Enrollments in theological seminaries of all faiths grew steadily during and after World War II. The postwar years were marked by widespread resumption of church construction. Remodeling and expansion of many church buildings made it possible to broaden weekday social activities and to introduce more kinds of religious education.

Church Membership

Although the people of this country are probably offered a wider choice of religious worship in both form and substance than in any other country in the world, nearly three fourths of the churches and almost 90 per cent of church members are attached to the 19 largest denominations. On the other hand, about 200 denominations have only about 2 per cent of the church members. Official statisticians of the various religious bodies reported nearly 286,000 local churches or congregations in 1950, compared with some 244,000 in 1940. Total membership of the more than 250 religious bodies of the United States amounted to 86.8 million [3] in 1950 and 64.5 million in 1940 — a gain of over 22 million during the war decade. The previous decade added only about 5 million persons to church rolls. In 1952 over 92 million persons were reported to be church members.

About 49 per cent of the total population were church members in 1940, and about 59 per cent in 1952. This latest gain was unusually large, although the long-term membership trend has been upward. (See Table 187.) The latest measure of rural-urban distribution is furnished by the Census of Religious Bodies for 1936. In that year, more than two thirds of the local churches, but only about one third of the church members, were found in communities classified as rural (i.e., those with a total population, with some exceptions, up to 2,500).

Definitions of membership vary. The Roman Catholics and a small proportion of Protestant denominations count all baptized persons as members.[4] Most Protestant denominations count only those who have come into full membership through an expressed desire to do so, usually at age 13. The Eastern Orthodox bodies generally include all persons of the cultural or national group in the country.

Largest of the religious bodies in membership is the Roman Catholic Church; in 1952 it had more than 30 million members in 15,500 parishes and many additional missions. Next in line is the Methodist Church, with over 9 million members in 40,000 local churches. The Southern Baptist Convention, which follows with more than 7.5 million members in over 28,000 churches in Oregon and Washington as well as in the South, has recently been reported to be the "fastest-growing large denomination."

The Census of Religious Bodies, 1936, re-

3. This is a correction of the total of 87,548,021 published in the *Yearbook of American Churches, 1951.*

4. Some religious bodies baptize infants; others administer the rite only after a child reaches a certain age or becomes an "adult."

ported 4.6 million members in the Jewish congregations, on the basis of estimates by congregations of the number of Jews in their communities. There are eminent Jewish scholars who state that a person born in a Jewish family is regarded as in the synagogue unless he separates himself from it. On this basis a membership of 4.6 million was reported for 1940 in the *Yearbook of American Churches, 1941*. The *Yearbook's* 5 million figure for 1950 was an estimate by officials of Jewish agencies, based on the 1936 Census.[5]

The American Jewish Year Book, 1951 estimates that 1,735,000 persons, or less than 40 per cent of the estimated total Jewish population, were "associated with congregations in worship." Jewish congregations fall into three general groups: the Union of Orthodox Jewish Congregations, with a membership of 500 congregations comprising 100,000 families; the United Synagogue of America (Conservative), with 400 congregations totaling 150,000 families; and the (Reform) Union of American Hebrew Congregations, with over 400 congregations comprising 100,000 families.[6]

The only two large religious groups which are native to the United States are the Church of Christ, Scientist, and the Church of Jesus Christ of Latter-Day Saints (Mormons). The Church of Christ, Scientist, had 268,915 members in 1936, according to the Census of Religious Bodies of that year. No later membership figures are available, but the membership is undoubtedly large, since every city of any size in the United States has a Christian Science church and organization.[7] The Mormons have over a million members in more than 2,000 churches. (Table 190 shows membership figures for 1940 and 1950 under Latter-Day Saints.)

Among the smallest denominations are the Church of the Gospel, Inc., with three churches and a total membership of 50; the Latter House of the Lord (Apostolic Faith), with two churches and a membership of 29; the Church of Daniel's Band, with four churches and a membership of 131.

5. These are the figures used in Table 190, where all data are based on the most inclusive definitions of membership.

6. *The American Jewish Year Book, 1951*, American Jewish Committee, New York, p. 87; population estimate, p. 4.

7. William Seward Salisbury, *Religion in America*, Oxford Book Co., 1951, p. 39.

In 1952, when the Roman Catholic Church reported a membership of more than 30 million, more than 54 million members were officially reported by the churches commonly called Protestant. Of the Protestant membership, about 49 million were 13 years of age and over; of the Roman Catholic Church, about 23 million. Baptized children in the Protestant churches who have not been received into full membership probably number more than 10 million, so that there are actually about 62 million Protestants, including all baptized children.

Since 1906, the date of the first adequate Census of Religious Bodies, both Protestant and Roman Catholic churches have increased their membership at almost the same rate. In that year, about 60 per cent of all church members were classified as Protestant, and in 1950 the same proportion was so classified.

For the country as a whole and for all denominations, the relation of church membership to population was more favorable in 1950 than it had been for a long time. In 1926 about 53 per cent of the population aged 13 and over were counted as church members. The proportion varied little until the war years brought about a rise; by 1950 it had moved up to about 64 per cent. (See Table 188.)

Sunday Schools

More than 80 per cent of the local churches have Sunday schools, which are significant contributors to church growth. Enrollments in the 246,240 local Sunday and Sabbath schools in 1950 amounted to 27.8 million. (See Table 187.) Enrollment in church schools increased from 1900 to 1933 but then began to decline. The causes of the decline have not been studied thoroughly, but the lowered birth rate of the depression years and the disruption of social life are believed to have been important factors. Recovery did not become marked until 1947. The steady increase in the number of Sunday school pupils since then is obviously influenced by the rise in the birth rate during the 1940s. By 1952 the total enrollment was 32.6 million.

Local Church Budgets

Local church situations differ so widely that an average budget can be presented in only general terms. Since local churches outnumber ac-

TABLE 188. CHURCH MEMBERSHIP AND POPULATION
AGED 13 OR OVER, 1926–1950

Fiscal Year Ending in June	Church Members Aged 13 or Over	Estimated Population Aged 13 or Over	Members per 1,000 of Estimated Population Aged 13 or Over
	(Millions)		
1926	45.2	85.9	527
1930	48.9	91.5	534
1931	49.1	92.9	529
1932	49.4	94.1	524
1933	49.6	95.4	521
1934	50.5	96.8	522
1935	51.0	98.0	521
1936	51.7	99.1	522
1937–1938	52.4	101.0	519
1939–1940	52.4	103.2	507
1950	71.2	111.6	636

Sources: *Information Service,* Federal Council of the Churches of Christ in America, New York, June 19, 1943; *Christian Herald,* New York, various issues, 1932–1940; U.S. Bureau of the Census: *1940 Census of Population: Population Characteristics,* Series P–5, No. 1, January 30, 1941; and *Current Population Reports: Population Characteristics,* Series P–20, No. 32, December 4, 1950.

tive clergymen by almost two to one, many local churches have only part-time clergymen. At one extreme will be found a small "preaching point" or "mission" in an isolated neighborhood visited by a clergyman every few months. At the other are a few urban congregations with several thousand members and with paid staffs of several clergymen and fifty or more full-time workers. Since most local churches are Protestant, the following generalizations are largely drawn from their experience.

In general, and as might be expected, rural churches have fewer members and lower budgets than city churches. An increasing number of local churches base their budgets on systematic annual pledges from their members, instead of relying entirely on the older devices of passing the collection plate and running church suppers and special drives. The larger and better-supported churches of the big cities seem to have the most systematic and rigid budgets, while the informality of the country churches may enable them to react more spontaneously to special appeals and situations.

The typical local church receives each year about what it spends, except when it conducts a special campaign for a building fund, in which case it segregates the receipts in a special account until construction can be undertaken. The chief item in the local church budget is usually the minister's salary. The average church in 1950 had more than 300 members, and the average member contributed some thirty-five cents a week toward support of activities and benevolences. (In 1940 an average of about 270 members per church contributed twenty cents a week.) Thus in 1950 the annual budget of the typical local church was probably about $6,000 a year, of which less than half covered the salary of the clergyman. The remainder was spent for salaries of the part-time organist and the janitor, for fuel and light, for repairs to buildings, for home and foreign missions and for other benevolences.

The Clergyman

Professional leader and main administrator of the local church, the minister literally runs the organization, aided at times by his wife, who is not paid for her services. This holds true even when lay leaders have responsibility for raising money and for administering the building. It is the popularity of the minister which determines the size of the congregation on a Sunday. He is in a position to determine the driving power of his organization and its influence in the life of the community.

The minister may be paid $2,500 a year or less in cash, and he may receive an additional $300 a year for special services at baptisms, marriages and funerals. His cash salary is often, but not always, supplemented by the free use of a modest home, which may be known as parsonage, manse or rectory. Generally, the local minister must pay for and maintain his own car, without the benefit of an expense account for travel in connection with his work. There are recent reports that more churches are now including "car allowances" in their budgets, but the practice is not yet common.

In rural communities, the minister's salary is often closer to $2,000 than to $2,500, while in urban communities the average is probably over $4,000. In 1939 only about one per cent of the clergy received $5,000 a year or more, according to the Bureau of the Census. Since 1940 there has been a steady rise in the compensation of ministers, though this adjustment may not have entirely compensated for the increased cost of living. In 1949, 6 per cent of clergymen received salaries of $5,000 or more, according to a 20 per cent sample tabulated by the Census Bureau.[8]

The rural minister generally preaches at one church each Sunday morning, and at another in the afternoon or evening. In some city and suburban Protestant churches the sermon is repeated at a second Sunday morning service when the congregation is too large to be cared for at one sitting. Roman Catholic churches traditionally celebrate the Sunday morning mass at several hours.

A minister is expected to be preacher, pastor and teacher. He usually instructs one or two classes of adults or young people in Sunday school. He is a steady buyer of books, has a special interest in the public library, and encourages his church to maintain a literature table or a small library. He is identified with local civic organizations such as the Parent-Teacher Association. A good many Boy Scout troops are organized within local churches, and the minister must often find troop leaders, if not serve as scoutmaster or assistant himself. He is expected to be *en rapport* with both young and old. He often advises young people about their education and helps many to go to college. Increasingly, he is called upon for personal counsel, both by members of his congregation and by other people in the community. A small proportion of clergymen have been specially trained for this work, usually with emphasis on the technique of listening to people rather than preaching to them.

Of the more than 300,000 ordained clergy listed in official statistics in 1952, approximately 184,000 were reported to be actively in charge of local churches. Among the clergy were more than 3,700 women, of whom 2,400 were ministers in charge of local churches, the remainder being in religious education and other church vocations. Only thirty-eight religious bodies reported women among the clergy, but their number seems to be slowly increasing.

Training for the Ministry

Although in some religious bodies all, or practically all, clergymen have had professional training, many ministers of religion have never received any special training for their jobs. In 1926 a study of 105,000 clergymen in the Roman Catholic Church, in seventeen white Protestant bodies and in three Negro Protestant bodies showed that the typical Catholic priest had a better educational background for his professional duties than the typical Protestant minister. Over two thirds of the Roman Catholic clergy had graduated from both college and theological seminary, compared with only one third of the ministers in the sample of white Protestant denominations and fewer than one out of twelve ministers among the Negro denominations.

A more recent study of the training of ministers, dating from 1936, indicated some improvement.[9] Of all ministers in a national sample of 140 rural communities, 44 per cent in 1936 were trained in college and seminary, as against 33 per cent in 1930 and 35 per cent in 1924. More than three fifths in 1936 were college graduates or better, as against slightly over half in 1930 and a little less than half in 1924. Of the nearly two fifths with no college training, less than 8 per cent had graduated from so-called Bible Schools, where relatively short courses are given,

---

8. *1940 Census of Population: Characteristics of the Labor Force*, Series P–16, No. 6, December 14, 1942; *Characteristics of the Population*, 1950, Part I, U.S. Summary, Table 129.

9. Edmund de S. Brunner and Irving Lorge, *Rural Trends in Depression Years*, Columbia University Press, New York, 1937.

and 32 per cent had received no formal training whatever. The majority of those without formal training were serving either in the South or with churches of the more emotional sects. There is little doubt that the educational level of clergymen has advanced further in recent years.

Although some religious bodies forbid their clergymen to engage in other work, probably a significant proportion of clergymen combine their ministerial work with other occupations. Often low salaries plus the high cost of living have forced ministers to supplement their professional income. In many predominantly rural communities, a farmer or a lumberman or a railroad worker may serve as minister of a congregation. Many a sharecropper on a cotton plantation is also a preacher.

Reports to the national headquarters of the Selective Service System from 528 theological seminaries, a large majority of those in the nation, showed that the number of full-time ministerial students in these institutions increased from 46,273 in the academic year 1946–1947 to 53,378 in 1949–1950. In the interval, students in 280 Protestant seminaries increased from 23,475 to 29,316; in 234 Roman Catholic seminaries, from 20,866 to 21,837; in 14 Jewish institutions, from 1,932 to 2,225. The gains were most striking for Episcopal institutions (63 per cent) and Presbyterian seminaries (58.8 per cent). Reporting for earlier years, 458 schools listed 31,893 students in 1939–1940 and 36,531 in 1945–1946.

The following comments from a report of the Harvard Divinity School Endowment Fund [10] point to a need for expanding institutional training for the ministry:

Today there is great need of specialized facilities for the professional training of ministers, chaplains, student advisers and teachers of religion. This condition is due in part to the closing down of theological schools affiliated with the German universities, for many years the leading seats of advanced theological study and training. Today the flow is in the other direction. Students are coming from Europe and even from Asia to attend American university theological schools; scholarships are being made available to encourage them.

There is an acute shortage of ministers in this country. In the Episcopal Church a recent survey indicated unfilled positions for 2,000. The Methodist Church is reported to be facing a need for 4,000 new ministers within the next four years in addition to those normally supplied by the seminaries.

10. "A New Center of Religious Learning at Harvard," June 1952.

Church Buildings

The servicing and maintenance of the church building, which is generally still of frame construction, is an important item of expense for the typical church. The average seating capacity of the auditorium is about 300 persons. Possibly many of the seats are empty at the principal Sunday morning service in Protestant churches, but among Roman Catholics the practice of attending church appears to be more general.

In Protestant churches small rooms are typically provided for classes of the church school, which meets for an hour every Sunday morning under lay leadership. The church usually has a basement, large and sparsely furnished, with a well-equipped kitchen but ordinarily without facilities for indoor sports. This is a meeting place for classes of the younger children in the church school and for organizations and committees. It is used also for special occasions, such as church suppers, and for some recreational events.

Only about four out of five local church congregations have buildings of their own; the others rent halls or church buildings of neighboring congregations for their weekly services. Small congregations sometimes meet in members' homes until money is available to erect a church building. Because building costs are high, the basement is now often built first and temporarily roofed to serve while funds are accumulated for further construction. Probably most large religious bodies assist local congregations through building grants and loans from their national agencies. This is customary in the less-favored communities and may be done also to speed the establishment of a new church building in a wealthy and enterprising suburb.

The value of church edifices cannot be estimated with accuracy. The trustees of a local church often struggle with the problem of evaluating church property, particularly when seeking a loan secured by mortgage. It has been said that an ecclesiastical building, exclusive of the land, would be worth nothing if it were not used for a church, no matter how thriving the congregation. The cost of reproducing the building can be estimated, of course, but the ordinary bases for appraising real estate seldom apply to churches.

In 1936, according to the federal Census of Religious Bodies (which was incomplete), the total value of all church edifices owned by local churches was approximately $3.5 billion. In 1950 the value of all church property of 125 religious bodies, half the total number, amounted to more than $5.2 billion. (See Table 187.)

During World War II, many churches conducted campaigns for building funds, while wartime restrictions made it necessary for them to defer building activities. As supplies were released from controls at the end of the war, many building operations got under way; church structures and parish houses were remodeled or enlarged, and new structures appeared in considerable numbers.

Department of Commerce estimates reveal the sharp impact of the war on religious construction. From $59 million in 1940, expenditures for religious construction dropped to $6 million in 1943, but by 1946 they had risen well above the prewar level to $76 million. The outlay increased sharply each year thereafter until 1949, when it reached $360 million. Even when the demands of the Korean War began to limit the use of construction materials, religious construction continued to increase, but at a much slower rate. In 1950 the expenditure amounted to $409 million and in 1951 to $452 million. In 1952 it fell slightly to $399 million.[11]

Benevolences and Missions

The only annual reports of church finance which have been compiled are those for a group of relatively large Protestant bodies made by the United Stewardship Council, an interdenominational Protestant agency which in 1951 became the Joint Department of Stewardship of the National Council of Churches. Annual contributions reported for the group are not strictly comparable, because of variations in the number of bodies reporting from year to year. These compilations probably reflect general trends, however, for the contributions reported in both 1926 and 1936 equaled about one half the amounts reported to the Bureau of the Census for those years.

According to these reports, 46 Protestant bodies with more than 36 million members (over 70 per cent of all Protestants) received total contributions of $1.4 billion in 1950, of which $286.3 million, or about 20 per cent, was for all benevolences, including home and foreign missions.

The yearly gift per member for all purposes was $41.94. Of this amount, $8.57 was for benevolences and the remainder for local congregational expenses. Contributions for benevolences comprised a higher proportion of the total in 1952 than they had a decade earlier. In 1940, when only 19 religious bodies reported, total contributions amounted to $310 million, of which $48 million, or 16 per cent, was for benevolences. The per member gift for all purposes in that year was $13.18.

The *Yearbook of American Churches,* with a wider coverage than the report of the United Stewardship Council, shows total gifts of $1.14 billion to 125 religious bodies in 1950. A breakdown of this total allocates $115 million, or about 10 per cent, to home and foreign missions alone (not to all benevolences). Among the bodies reporting were many of the smaller denominations. No figures were included for Jewish congregations and Roman Catholic dioceses, which do not report annually.

An analysis of the financing of a number of Protestant foreign missions over the twenty-year period 1928–1948 [12] shows widely fluctuating receipts. From $41 million in 1928, the total dropped to $22.5 million in 1933. After rising 17 per cent, receipts slumped to a low of $22.4 million in 1942 as missionary appeals were confronted by more pressing local demands. Programs of relief and reconstruction began to show results in 1943, and by 1946 the receipts of 1942 had been doubled. But as uncertainties began to cloud the future the rapid increases immediately following the war were slowed. By 1948, total contributions to foreign missions had risen only slightly further, to $47 million.

Few studies have been made of the giving of families and individuals, such as might provide checks against the totals officially reported by church agencies. The National Resources Committee, on the basis of an investigation in 1935–1936, reported an average annual outlay for church support per family of $17, equal to 1.1 per cent of all annual expenditures per family.[13] With only about half the families of the nation

11. *Construction and Building Materials: Statistical Supplement, May 1953, Construction Volume and Costs, 1915–1952,* p. 7.

12. Thomas S. Donohugh, "A Study of Foreign Missions Financing," Foreign Missions Conference of North America, New York, 1950 (mimeographed). The number of member boards reporting varied slightly from year to year, but not enough to affect the trends significantly.

13. *Consumer Expenditures in the United States, Estimates for 1935–1936,* National Resources Committee, Washington, 1939.

TABLE 189. AVERAGE ANNUAL EXPENDITURES PER UNIT FOR GIFTS AND CONTRIBUTIONS, ALL FAMILIES AND SINGLE CONSUMERS, BY OBJECT, 1941

Object of Expenditure	Urban	Rural Nonfarm	Rural Farm
Gifts	$42.01	$20.26	$16.52
Support of relatives	26.61	11.76	5.81
Donations to others	2.55	1.40	.91
Community chests, etc.	5.79	1.10	.49
Religious organizations	28.42	18.59	15.56
Red Cross, U.S.O.	3.72	1.43	1.16
Other, including foreign relief	3.39	.56	.82

Source: *Family Spending and Saving in Wartime*, Bulletin No. 822, U.S. Bureau of Labor Statistics, 1945.

on the church rolls, and no evidence of systematic giving to churches by nonmembers, church contributions therefore must have represented about 2 per cent of the total expenditures of church members.

Differences between urban and rural farm families in contributions to religious organizations roughly paralleled their differences in income in 1941, according to a Department of Labor study. The rural nonfarm group, however, gave more per family than the rural farm, although average family income — including noncash items, such as food and fuel produced — was slightly higher for the farm group. (See Table 189.)

TRENDS IN ORGANIZED RELIGION

Data on past trends in expenditures by the people for religious purposes, church membership, church attendance, Sunday school growth and church program provide useful guides for estimating the future position of the churches in our economy.

Expenditures for Religious Purposes

"Consumption expenditures" for religious purposes increased from perhaps $300 million in 1909 to $1,125 million in 1950 and $1,296 million in 1952. The proportion of all consumption expenditures going for religious purposes dropped, however, from 1 per cent in 1909 to 0.6 per cent in 1950 and 1952. In dollar volume, the outlay increased steadily until 1930, when it amounted to $900 million. Then came a decline. By 1934, only $600 million was being spent for religious purposes. By 1944, expenditures were still $100

million under the 1930 figure, but they had reached $1 billion by 1948. (See Appendix 4-4.)

Total contributions to religious bodies have been estimated in two recent independent studies of philanthropy. "About fifty per cent of present voluntary giving," according to F. Emerson Andrews,[14] "still goes to religious agencies, though not all of it for direct church purposes." Andrews estimates total giving to religious bodies for all purposes at $1,582 million in 1948 and $1,894 million in 1949.[15] He apportions about 40 per cent of the total as going for salaries of employees. For three decades, Andrews points out, religious giving has not increased in proportion to the increase in the national income.

Estimates of total contributions to religious bodies by Edward C. Jenkins[16] run somewhat lower than Andrews' figures. Jenkins' estimate for 1948, for example, is $1,378 million. Examining the effects of higher rates of taxation during recent years, Jenkins concludes that high rates encourage certain people to give and discourage others, the two groups probably canceling each other out, leaving no noticeable effect on voluntary giving.

---

14. F. Emerson Andrews, *Philanthropic Giving*, Russell Sage Foundation, New York, 1950.

15. Total giving to churches for all purposes as estimated by Andrews is close to an unpublished figure of the Department of Commerce. Total gifts received by the churches, as measured by the Department of Commerce, far exceed "consumption expenditures" as defined by the Department. "Consumption expenditures" include pastors' salaries; salaries of other employees; other current expenses, including interest; missions and benevolences; depreciation. The series excludes payment on the church debt and expenditures for local relief and charity.

16. *Philanthropy in America*, Association Press, New York, 1950.

Per Cent

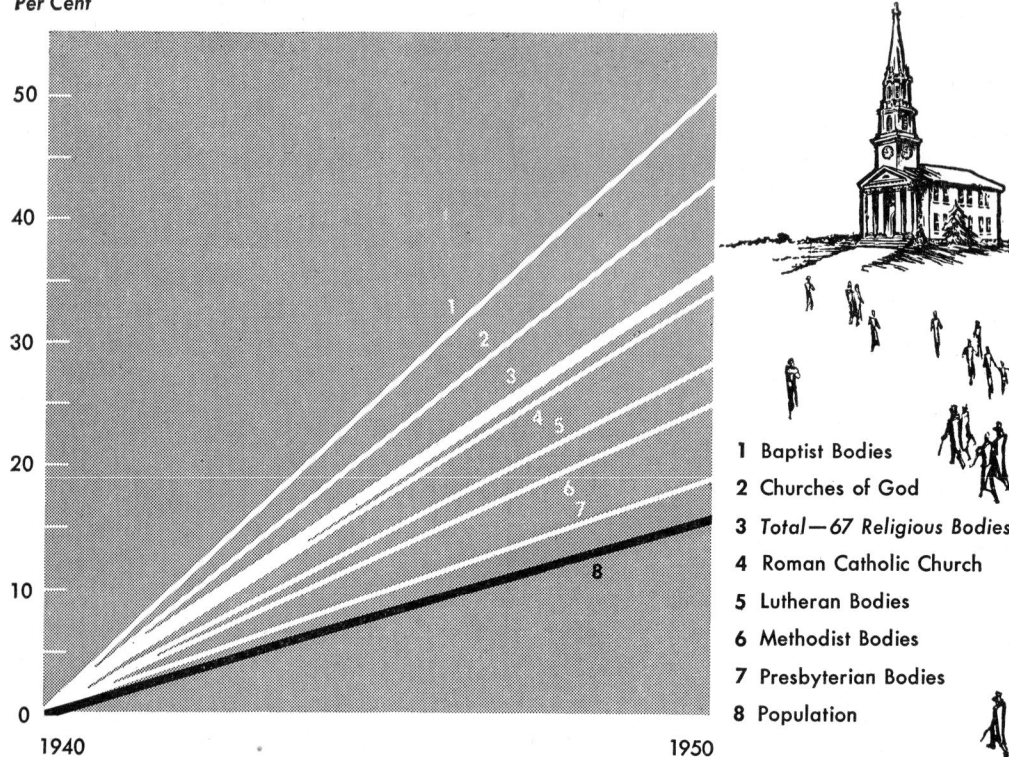

FIGURE 57. PERCENTAGE INCREASE IN MEMBERSHIP OF RELIGIOUS BODIES [a] AND IN POPULATION, 1940–1950

Sources: Table 190 and Appendix 3–6.

a. Jewish congregations and Eastern Orthodox are not shown separately because complete membership figures are not available. See discussion in text.

Membership Trends

Figures on church membership, considered alone, are somewhat unsatisfactory for estimating future needs for church services, since they reveal neither the proportion of church members who actually give money nor the extent to which members participate in the church program. Membership statistics are not closely comparable, moreover, because of the varied methods of keeping local records — the responsibility of pastors (who admit they are poor statisticians) and of volunteer clerks and secretaries. Usually a formal membership roll exists, but the figure for current members or living members may be an estimate or a guess, partly because of the practice of retaining people on the rolls after they have moved to other communities.

Many informed observers think that a good number of these "nonresident" members become inactive in church life. A cursory estimate made by the present writer indicates that about one sixth of the members of non-Catholic churches may be in the nonresident category. The large but unknown number of inactive persons on the rolls introduces a further element of uncertainty into already inexact figures. These limitations should be kept in mind in any attempt to interpret membership statistics for the future.

Officially reported memberships of the larger religious bodies in 1940 and 1950, covering 98 per cent of all the church members of the nation, give no evidence of a spectacular turn to religion or a widespread "revival." For the 67 largest bodies as a whole, however, membership increased more than population — 36 per cent compared with 16 per cent. (See Figure 57.) Of course, not all groups have gained members at the same rate, and some have barely held their ground. The impressive gain in total church membership indicates at least a continuation of "interest in religion." (See Table 190.)

TABLE 190. MEMBERSHIP OF RELIGIOUS BODIES WITH 1950 MEMBERSHIP
OF 50,000 OR MORE, 1940 AND 1950

Religious Body	1940	1950	Percentage Increase
	(Thousands)		
Total for 67 bodies	62,968	85,319	35
Adventists, Seventh Day	176	237	35
Assemblies of God	199	318	60
Baptist bodies			
American Baptist Convention	1,544	1,561	1
Southern Baptist Convention	4,949	7,080	43
National Baptist Convention, U.S.A., Inc.	} 4,047 [a]	4,446	} 75
National Baptist Convention of America		2,646	
American Baptist Association	115	240	109
Free Will Baptists	119	220	85
National Baptist Evangelical Life and Soul Saving Assembly of U.S.A.	56	71	27
National Primitive Baptist Convention of the U.S.A.	44 [b]	79	80
Primitive Baptists	69	72	4
United American Free Will Baptist Church	20 [b]	75	282
Buddhist Churches of America	35	70	100
Christian and Missionary Alliance	33	58	77
Church of the Brethren	177	186	5
Churches of God			
Church of God (Cleveland)	63	175	178
Church of God (Anderson, Ind.)	74	107	44
Church of God in Christ	32	317	903
Church of the Nazarene	166	227	37
Churches of Christ	310	1,000	223
Congregational Christian Churches [c]	1,050	1,205	15
Disciples of Christ	1,659	1,768	7
Eastern Orthodox churches			
Armenian Orthodox Church in America	19 [b]	100	432
Greek Orthodox Church (Hellenic)	425	1,000	135
Russian Orthodox Church	90	400	345
Serbian Orthodox Church	100	75	−25
Syrian Antiochan Orthodox Church	61	75	23
Evangelical and Reformed Church [d]	659	726	10
Evangelical United Brethren [e]	666	718	8
Federated Churches	88	88	0
Friends, Five Years Meeting	68	69	1
Independent Fundamental Churches of America	—	65	—
International Church of the Four Square Gospel	16	75	363
Jewish congregations [f]	4,641	5,000	8
Latter-Day Saints			
Church of Jesus Christ of Latter-Day Saints	724	1,111	53
Reorganized Church of Jesus Christ of Latter-Day Saints	107	125	17
Lutherans			
American Lutheran Conference			
American Lutheran Church	561	692	23
Evangelical Lutheran Augustana Synod of N.A.	340	440	29
Evangelical Lutheran Church of America	536	814	52
Lutheran Free Church	48	60	24
Lutheran Synodical Conference of North America			
Lutheran Church, Missouri Synod	1,277	1,675	31
Evangelical Lutheran Joint Synod of Wisconsin and Other States	256	307	20
Other Lutheran bodies			
United Lutheran Church in America	1,612	1,954	21

(Continued on page 424)

TABLE 190 (continued)

Religious Body	1940	1950	Percentage Increase
	(Thousands)		
Mennonite Church	51	56	10
Methodist bodies			
African Methodist Episcopal Church	650	1,166	79
African Methodist Episcopal Zion Church	414	530	28
Colored Methodist Episcopal Church	365	381	4
Free Methodist Church of N.A.	46	50	9
The Methodist Church	7,377	8,936	21
Pentecostal Assemblies			
Pentecostal Assemblies of the World, Inc.	6	50	775 g
Pentecostal Church of God of America	4	63	
Pentecostal Church, United	31	100	221
Polish National Catholic Church	63	250	295
Presbyterian bodies			
Cumberland Presbyterian Church	73	81	11
Presbyterian Church in the U.S.	532	678	27
Presbyterian Church in the U.S.A.	1,971	2,319	18
United Presbyterian Church of N.A.	187	214	14
Protestant Episcopal Church	1,996	2,541	27
Protestant Reformed bodies			
Christian Reformed Church	122	152	25
Reformed Church in America	163	183	12
Roman Catholic Church	21,284	28,635	35
Salvation Army	238	209	-12
Evangelical Mission Covenant Church of America	46	51	11
Spiritualists			
International General Assembly of Spiritualists	1	150	g
Christ Unity Spiritual Science Church	—	657	—
Unitarian churches	64	75	18
Universalist Church	51	65	26

Source: Yearbook of American Churches, New York, 1941 and 1951.

a. Negro Baptists in 1940 include both bodies reporting separately in 1950.
b. 1936.
c. Includes Congregational and General Convention of the Christian Church, merged in 1931.
d. Includes Reformed in the U.S. and Evangelical Synod of N.A., merged in 1934.
e. Includes Evangelical Church and the United Brethren in Christ, merged in 1946.
f. See discussion on p. 416.
g. Over 1,000 per cent.

Note: Percentages calculated before rounding.

Church Attendance

Information on church attendance might provide a better index of the "demand" for church services than membership figures, were it available, but few local churches keep attendance records. During World War II, even informed impressions were contradictory. On the one hand, the crisis of war was considered to have raised church attendance; on the other hand, gasoline rationing and restrictions on the use of motor cars were believed to have cut down church at-

tendance. But there is general agreement that attendance was relatively high from 1945 to 1950.

According to newspaper reports of a poll conducted by the American Institute of Public Opinion, 47 per cent of adults over 21 years of age attended church on a Sunday in February 1954. Sixty per cent of the Roman Catholics queried had gone to church, but only 40 per cent of the Protestants. Age seemed to affect churchgoing: 49 per cent of the people over 50 years of age reported attending church, compared with

43 per cent of those aged 21–29. Of the women queried, 50 per cent said they had gone to church; of the men, only 44 per cent.

An anlysis of several field studies of Protestant churches in large cities made between 1945 and 1949 states that:

In fifteen studies reporting on the subject, church attendance at the main Sunday service ranged from 33 per cent to 50 per cent of the church membership, with a median of 40 per cent. This means that with average memberships of 406, metropolitan churches get congregations of about 160. Half the cases closely approximate the median. Attendance relative to total membership is . . . larger in the Far West than elsewhere. Western cities get congregations more easily than they secure permanent members.

The rate of suburban church-going does not differ substantially from that of the total metropolitan district.

About one-third of the city churches maintain a second Sunday service, which adds approximately 15 per cent per Sunday to the attendance at the main service.

Sunday school attendance approximates 60 per cent of the enrolment in the median case. In twelve complete studies it ranges from 52.6 to 70.1 per cent. With average enrolments of 217, metropolitan Sunday schools have an average attendance of about 150. Over one-fourth of the Sunday schools have less than fifty in average attendance. With such small schools normal grading is difficult or even impossible.[17]

Trends in Religious Education

Sunday schools have always been regarded as of first importance in the Protestant churches, partly because of the basic interest in education which Protestants share with Jews and Catholics, but also because Protestants particularly look upon the Sunday school as a means of maintaining and increasing interest in the church.

Comparison of Sunday school enrollment in 1950 with that in 1942 (no data are available for 1940) reveals no significant trend. In 1942 the total enrollment was equal to 35 per cent of church membership, and in 1952 to 35 per cent. (See Table 187.) In the interval many persons moved out of the church school into active adult church membership, but evidently the substantial gain in church membership during the period came about largely through the enlistment of adults beyond age 13 or the re-enlistment of inactive adults. Nevertheless, the church

school seems to have contributed importantly to membership growth.

Certain Protestant bodies have recently shown increasing interest in organizing day schools where both religion and the secular subjects may be taught. Preston King Sheldon, on surveying Protestant parish schools in 1950, reported at least 2,500, mostly under Lutheran auspices, and enrollment in excess of 150,000 pupils. Lutherans had about 1,400 schools, of which the Missouri Synod had over 1,100. The Seventh Day Adventists had 942 schools.[18] Ten new parish schools, with 875 pupils, were organized among Baptists in Los Angeles between 1947 and 1950. In 1952 there were about 3,000 Protestant church-affiliated schools, with about 187,000 children enrolled in elementary grades, according to a study reported in *Information Service*, National Council of Churches, May 3, 1952.

According to the *Official Catholic Directory*, 7,914 Catholic parishes had elementary parochial schools in 1950 and students numbered nearly 2.5 million. In 1952 there were 8,488 schools with 2.8 million pupils. The comparable figures for 1940 were 7,660 schools and 2.0 million pupils. Roman Catholics also reported 1,577 high schools in 1952, with 361,852 students, and 839 private high schools with 216,008 students. These figures represented a marked increase over 1940: Catholic high schools of all types in 1940 numbered 1,442 and pupils, 493,754.

The total number of pupils enrolled in Jewish schools of various types in 1950 was 266,609. Of these, 49 per cent were enrolled in Sunday schools, 41.7 per cent attended weekday afternoon schools, 8 per cent attended all-day schools, and 1.3 per cent were enrolled in released-time classes.[19]

Attitudes toward Religion

Several studies of attitudes and opinions on religion have been made in the last decade. On January 10, 1948, the American Institute of Public Opinion reported the response of a sample of adults to the question, "Do you, personally, believe in God?" Ninety-four per cent replied "Yes"; 3 per cent, "No"; 3 per cent, "Don't know." To the question, "Do you believe in life after death?" 68 per cent of those queried answered "Yes"; 13 per cent, "No"; and 19 per

---

17. H. Paul Douglass, "Some Protestant Churches in Urban America," *Information Service*, Federal Council of the Churches of Christ in America, New York, January 21, 1950.

18. *New York Times*, January 7, 1951.
19. *American Jewish Year Book, 1951*, p. 98.

cent had no opinion. On December 26, 1949, the Institute reported on a series of questions about "the next fifty years." To the question, "Do you think people in this country will go to church more often or less often than they do now?" the replies were: more often, 39 per cent; less often, 32 per cent; no change, 21 per cent; no opinion, 8 per cent. The question, "Are you a member of a church?" drew the answer "Yes" from 79 per cent of a sample of persons over 21 years of age, the Institute reported in July 1954. This would be the equivalent of 81 million persons in the total population of that age range.

A study of changes in religious beliefs among 547 pupils in the sixth, ninth and twelfth grades showed some tendency among these adolescents to discard a number of specific beliefs with advance in grade.[20] Also with increasing age, a greater tolerance was noted. The authors concluded, however, that adolescence is not "a period of generally increased religious doubts and problems," although many of those questioned had "problems of a religious sort" and wanted help (which seemed to be difficult to get), and were "dissatisfied with conventional church services."

In a survey at Ripon College, Wisconsin,[21] freshmen showed "a greater inclination to believe the twenty-five religious propositions" put to them than did seniors. The investigator concluded, however, that "college freshmen and college seniors believe essentially the same religious propositions."

An opinion study of 3,758 students in 18 colleges and universities[22] indicated that the students were "definitely favorable toward the churches." Eighty-four per cent of the group professed "a belief in God." Sixty-one per cent felt that God was an influence on their daily conduct. Freshmen were more inclined to feel so than juniors and seniors, and women more than men. Another finding of the study was summed up as "the more religious, the more conservative."

The same investigator, pursuing much the same lines of inquiry, retested in 1950 close to

nine hundred persons whom he had tested as students fourteen years earlier.[23] He found them to have become more favorable toward the church and more inclined to believe in God. He attributed this shift toward the church to increased maturity, on the evidence that a control group of the new generation of college students in 1950 expressed belief in God less often than the retest group had in 1936. The change in religious attitudes over the years was not, as might have been expected, accompanied by increased conservatism. The group had, in fact, become more liberal in social-economic-political views and less favorable toward Sunday observance.

Program Trends

In the early 1940s, the churches took part, along with many other agencies, in a burst of "postwar planning," concerned with better ways by which people could, or should, live when the war was over. These published plans were, like those of many other organizations, simply restatements of long-time goals formulated long before the war.

Officials of churches of all faiths supported plans for organizing the United Nations. The Catholic Association for International Peace, the Federal Council's Department of International Justice and Goodwill, the Social Justice Commission of the Central Conference of American Rabbis, all poured forth literature on issues of peace and war, on the need for international cooperation, on the practical problems of food and health. Religious bodies acted promptly to ask the Senate's ratification of the United Nations Charter and appointed consultants to attend UN meetings and report to church constituencies.

Some of these new interests and activities resulted in a high degree of interfaith cooperation. The Commission on Displaced Persons of the United States called upon church agencies to assume heavy responsibilities in connection with the resettlement of the more than 339,000 displaced persons who came to our shores. For example, the National Lutheran Council, a federation of a number of Lutheran denominations, aided in the resettlement of some 30,000 families. Roman Catholic agencies were equally active,

20. Raymond G. Kuhlen and Martha Arnold, "Age Differences in Religious Beliefs and Problems During Adolescence," *Journal of Genetic Psychology*, 1944, pp. 291–300.

21. George J. Dudycha, "The Religious Beliefs of College Students," *Journal of Applied Psychology*, October 1933, pp. 585–603.

22. Erland Nelson, "Student Attitudes Toward Religion," *Genetic Psychology Monographs*, 1940, Vol. 22, pp. 323–425.

23. Erland Nelson, "Religious Attitude Shifts and Overt Behavior," a paper delivered before the American Association for the Advancement of Science at St. Louis, December 29, 1952.

but the most extensive activities were carried on by Jewish agencies. During 1946–1949, Jewish immigrants averaged more than 23,000 annually, most of them displaced persons who needed aid in resettlement.[24]

An organization named CROP (Christian Rural Overseas Program) grew out of the conviction of some rural church leaders that country people could contribute to the overseas relief work of churches more effectively "in kind" than in cash. Within a few years CROP, in which both Roman Catholic and Protestants were officially represented, sent 5,500 carloads of grain and cotton to the needy of 29 nations. Church agencies also took part in CARE projects and supported United States contributions to UNNRA.

New church offices sprang up in Washington from which reports on pending legislation went out to church constituencies. Information on housing, social security, health, the North Atlantic Treaty, military training and other public problems was thus made available for discussion at local meetings. Local churches, in turn, sent representatives to Washington for seminars on citizenship. Some forty farmers, members of the Society of Friends, paid their own expenses to attend a seminar on farm surpluses. Churches not only passed resolutions for social action — alert minorities of many denominations carried them out.

"Economic life" became a real concern of more churchmen, lay and professional, than ever before. Roman Catholic parishes continued their studies of the Papal encyclicals on the social order, and frequently advocated social and economic action. When the Federal Council of Churches organized a Department of the Church and Economic Life (now a department of the National Council of Churches), most of the voting members were laymen instead of clergymen — a big departure from precedent. These laymen were all identified with the churches of the Federal Council, but they were also persons who had some part in organizations representing management, labor, farmers, consumers and the professions; several were economists.

In 1950, after fifteen years of planning, the integration was completed of twelve interdenominational organizations — representing 28 Protestant and Eastern Orthodox denominations

with over 30 million members — in the National Council of the Churches of Christ in the U.S.A. Although the new National Council has no more power over its member denominations than any of its predecessors, and has no authority to unite the constituent denominations, it provides for closer coordination of activities and promises to become a means to more adequate expression of a spirit of unity.

Needs vs. Demand in 1950

A decade of international crisis had also been a period of relatively high church activity. Large numbers of people were preparing to enter the ministry. There were many efforts to expand programs — local, state and national. Like all other nonprofit agencies, the churches were feeling the effects of rising costs. Church employees, as comparatively low-paid professional workers, were vulnerable to the inflation which followed the Korean outbreak in June 1950. Continued international tension challenged the American churches to continue their relief work abroad at the highest possible level, in Western Europe especially, but also in India and Southeast Asia.

While inflation increased the problem of costs, the atmosphere of continuing crisis brought more people to the churches for aid. At the same time fund raising for churches seemed to be easier when there was a war than when there was none.

Religious bodies for a decade and a half had accounted for somewhat less than one per cent of all consumption expenditures. Church leaders informally questioned for this study felt that they needed 25 per cent more than the current outlays they were spending in 1950. For buildings, they felt that they needed 50 per cent more than the $409 million they spent in that year. Needed consumption expenditures in 1950, therefore, would have totaled about $1.4 billion and needed construction spending roughly $600 million.

NEEDS AND DEMAND IN 1960

As with other areas of human need, estimates of what consumers will actually pay for and effectively demand in the way of religious services do not measure the actual needs, nor do they measure the need for contributions as seen by churchmen. The estimates of needs and demand presented here are rough calculations made after

---

24. *American Jewish Year Book, 1951*, p. 142.

informal consultations with church officials. Understandably, nearly every church administrator feels he needs and could efficiently use much more money than he receives. The estimates here offered are certain to fall far short of overcoming what churchmen themselves consider to be the inadequacies of the churches.

Of late years, people have frequently expressed the need for more thorough personal counseling, an activity which is in line with the historic priestly or pastoral function of the church. Many of the ablest and busiest ministers, priests and rabbis devote a good deal of time to listening to and advising people in distress. The Roman Catholic Church has always emphasized the practice of confession. Other churches, while not precisely imitating the methods of the confessional, have been doing work in the tradition of that method. Clergymen have entered widely into the study of psychology, and many seminary students have been receiving special training for individual counseling. Although we have developed specialized agencies for personal and family counsel, a large proportion of people in trouble still go first to a minister for help or guidance.

Churches, too, have been very actively endeavoring to apply their teachings to the social order and to economic affairs. All of life has come to be regarded as in the scope of church influence. Ethics is not looked upon only as a subject for Sunday morning — it has to do with labor-management relations, with the way one participates in a farmers' cooperative, with contributions to an election campaign, with housing and health and immigration, with all the issues before the United Nations.

Goals of the Churches

Whether an adequate ministry to individuals or a more extensive participation in social and economic affairs is in question, the successful performance of church work is largely dependent upon improvement and increase of personnel. In these terms the goals of the churches may be broadly stated as follows:

1. More adequate compensation, including pensions, for clergymen and other professional religious workers. To make clergymen's salaries "adequate" would require increases of about 50 per cent in prevailing rates of compensation. Many of the church pension programs were inaugurated thirty years ago and have not been brought up to date in terms of purchasing power. It will probably be difficult to increase the pension provisions. The permissive inclusion of lay workers under federal old-age and survivors insurance in 1950 was a welcome step. Extension of voluntary insurance coverage to clergymen seemed likely in 1954.

2. Employment of large numbers of professional workers in religious education. Religious education is now carried on not only through Sunday schools, with their lay officers, but also through vacation schools, weekday instruction, summer camps, conferences, seminars, etc. Many of these require trained professional workers, who must know how to train volunteers as teachers and officers.

3. A more mobile ministry to follow and minister to a mobile population. Since 1940, population movements — from country to city, from the East to the Pacific Coast, from cities to suburbs, from all kinds of communities to various defense installations — have caused huge losses to many churches while bringing new constituencies and opportunities to others. Here and there, ministers have used trailers to serve a mobile church membership. More ministers-at-large are needed.

4. Retraining of the ministry. Many informed church officials feel that a large proportion of ministers have had no adequate training for their present tasks. They advocate in-service training on a broad scale — in summer schools and special institutions and through formal graduate study. This can only be accomplished with the cooperation of theological seminaries and other professional schools, some of which already offer in-service training.

5. Large-scale relief and rehabilitation operations. Despite all the relief and rehabilitation work of governmental and private agencies, people of other lands continue to need food, clothing and medicine. The general expectation is that needs for direct relief will continue extensive for some years to come, and the churches will want to carry forward the programs of assistance which they began in the 1940s.

6. Broad new programs of missions at home and abroad. In this country, for example, special missions are needed in rapidly growing communities of farm people in the Pacific Northwest, where funds for buildings are not available in the community. Churchmen hope to send to for-

TABLE 191. ESTIMATED NEEDED AND PROBABLE EXPENDITURES FOR RELIGION,
1950 AND 1960
(Millions of 1950 Dollars)

| | 1950 | | 1960 | |
	Reported	Needed	Probable	Needed
Total	$1,534	$2,000	$1,850	$2,200
Consumption expenditures	1,125	1,400	1,300	1,600
Construction expenditures	409	600	550	600

Sources: "Reported" and "probable" expenditures from Appendix 4–7, Tables A and B; "needed" expenditures from text.

eign lands many more physicians, nurses and teachers of agriculture. The intense communist opposition to missions has been cited as one reason for stepping up missionary work in areas where communist propaganda is at its height — as, for example, in India.

7. The development of cooperative work among churches. Many people believe that only by better local cooperation can the churches render their best services to the community. The process of achieving such cooperation is a very slow one. A large group of Protestant and Eastern Orthodox churches are committed to the organization of local and state councils of churches, in addition to the maintenance and expansion of the National Council. Numerous local councils exist, and they are found in most states. But many of them have only the most meager budgets, and they need trained and skilled leaders. The "profession of church cooperation" is said to be still in its infancy, with few centers of training available. Much needs to be done in interfaith cooperation, the cultivation of the common interests of all religious groups.

8. New buildings. The demand for new buildings is greater than in 1940, but costs are so high as to prevent much of the needed construction. By 1950 considerable progress had been made in meeting the demand deferred during the war years, particularly in thriving suburbs. But church officials predict that considerable construction will be required for some years to come. Many congregations have outgrown their buildings, and many are handicapped in expanding their programs of service, especially their weekday activities. Thus expenditures for religious construction may well continue for several years at close to the unusually high level of 1950.

Cost of Meeting Needs

Assuming that at 1950 prices national income will be $312.5 billion in 1960, and total consumption expenditures $241.5 billion, consumption expenditures for religion might be about $1.3 billion, 0.54 per cent of all consumption expenditures. This estimated outlay for religious purposes is 15.6 per cent above the 1950 figure of $1,125 million. Church administrators will probably "need" about 25 per cent more than this amount. For religious building, approximately $550 million might be spent, compared with $409 million in 1950 and the $600 million annual expenditure estimated as needed to provide adequate structures. (See Table 191.) Consumption expenditures are not to be confused with total contributions of individuals to religious organizations.

## CHAPTER 14

WELFARE

THE TAP ROOT of welfare always has been the concern for individuals in distress. In most civilizations, the family unit has been responsible for the well-being of its own members, but in complex societies responsibility for dependents also has been assumed by wealthy individuals, churches, private charitable organizations, and by local government to a greater or lesser degree. In this country, aid to needy individuals has been supplemented by programs directed toward eliminating the sources of distress and toward preparing in advance for the presumed needs of the future.

To separate welfare from other forms of organized community activity is difficult. Attempts to alleviate the distress of individuals often have been merged with public economic and population policy. To combat the depression of the 1930s, the federal government embarked on what was at the time the greatest peacetime spending program in history. Determination of the need of the individual or group often was secondary to the first requisite that funds be distributed and spent quickly. In other respects, too, ministering to individual economic need was made incidental to large-scale programs designed, on the one hand, to stimulate industrial activity or, on the other, to salvage skills and to preserve morale. Interest in the well-being of the farm population, for example, and in maintaining a balanced economy resulted in a system of subsidized income for farmers.

NATURE AND SCOPE OF THE FIELD

This chapter is limited to a discussion of those programs of financial aid or service designed especially for persons who are presently or potentially unable to provide themselves with a minimum standard of living, who need other assist-

ance in adjusting to the circumstances of modern life, or who can benefit from systematic character-building and health programs. Other parts of this volume consider separately education, health service, farm programs, waterways and electric power facilities, highway construction, and other public works which, when they gain a large measure of financial support from the government, often are likely to have a basic welfare purpose.[1]

Here an effort will be made to appraise the various undertakings which are distinctively welfare programs. These include: (1) private welfare, under which come private philanthropy and employee health and welfare; and (2) public welfare, which covers social insurance, including old-age and survivors insurance, public retirement systems, unemployment insurance, temporary disability benefits, workmen's compensation, and social insurance for railroad workers, together with veterans programs, public assistance, general relief and social welfare services.

THE CHANGING PATTERN OF WELFARE

The past thirty years have been years of rapid transition in welfare, marked especially by:

(1) The shifting of the financial burden of individual dependency (direct relief) from private agencies, local government, and religious groups to state and federal government;

(2) The devotion of professional skill and resources of the private agencies to personal and family adjustment, group recreation and education, experimental programs and research;

(3) The coordination and improved administrative efficiency of private and voluntary welfare agencies;

(4) The growth of the concept of systematic provision in advance for presumptive need through social insurance, planned public works and government fiscal policy;

(5) The assumption by industry of a major share of the financial responsibility for welfare and the increasing initiative exerted by both industry and unions in the development of private welfare.

BY JOHN W. McCONNELL, Professor of Industrial and Labor Relations, New York State School of Industrial and Labor Relations, Cornell University. Opinions and judgments expressed in this chapter are those of the author and should not be attributed to the organization with which he is associated.

1. Chapters 7, 9, 10, 12, 17 and 18 of this volume.

TABLE 192. ESTIMATES OF PUBLIC AND PRIVATE WELFARE EXPENDITURES, 1930, 1940 AND 1950

(Millions)

Item of Expenditure	1930	1940[a]	1950[a]
Total, including public health and medical services	$3,076.0	$7,708.1	$19,955.5
Public health and medical services	510.0[b]	860.3	3,045.0
Veterans program	—	83.5	716.5
Total, excluding public health and medical services	2,566.0	6,847.8	16,910.5
Private welfare	1,278.0	1,419.0	4,526.0
Charitable contributions of living donors and corporations, and bequests for welfare	1,154.0[c]	1,249.0[c]	1,722.0
Employers' contributions to private health, welfare and pensions[d]	124.0	170.0	2,804.0
Public welfare	1,288.0	5,428.8	12,384.5
Social insurance[e]	407.0	1,241.3	4,743.9
Veterans welfare programs[f]	695.0	451.9	4,544.9
Public aid (relief, work relief and assistance)	105.0	3,592.3	2,585.5
Other welfare[g]	81.0	143.3	510.2

Sources: Ida C. Merriam, "Social Welfare Programs in the United States," *Social Security Bulletin*, February 1953, p. 8, and *Social Security Bulletin*, October 1953, Table 1, p. 14, especially for public expenditures 1940 and 1950; 1951 National Income Supplement to the *Survey of Current Business*, Tables 34 and 36, pp. 201–202; *Survey of Current Business*, July 1953; and F. Emerson Andrews, *Philanthropic Giving*, Russell Sage Foundation, New York, 1950, p. 72.

a. 1940 and 1950 public expenditure figures represent calendar year figures derived by averaging data for fiscal years 1939–1940 and 1940–1941, and 1949–1950 and 1950–1951.

b. Based on data assembled by Committee on Costs of Medical Care and analyzed by I. S. Falk, *Millbank Memorial Fund Quarterly Bulletin*, April 1933.

c. Includes contributions to religion, corporate and private gifts for higher education, museums and libraries which were included in the table found in Andrews, *op. cit.*, p. 72.

d. A firm total of benefit payments and cost of services rendered to employees through private industry health, welfare and pension plans is not available. The contributions of employers to these plans provide a rough estimate of their magnitude. Derived from 1951 National Income Supplement to the *Survey of Current Business* and *Survey of Current Business*, July 1953.

e. For a more detailed analysis of social insurance payments, see Table 200.

f. Includes pension and compensation, readjustment allowances and welfare services such as vocational rehabilitation, homes and autos for disabled veterans, counseling, beneficiaries' travel, loan guarantee and domiciliary care. Subsistence allowances are included, but the cost of tuition, supplies and equipment for veterans in school is excluded. Dividend payments on National Service Life Insurance are also excluded.

g. Vocational rehabilitation (nonveteran), child welfare services, school lunch program and institutional care.

F. Emerson Andrews summarized the nature of these changes:

In broad generalization, public agencies undertake to meet, more or less adequately, basic economic, health, and educational needs; in some cases for the whole population, in others for only certain specific classes of the disadvantaged. To voluntary agencies remain the important tasks of filling in gaps and inadequacies in these fields, of establishing standards and checking the work of public agencies, of covering many additional needs not now met by government, and of doing most of the exploratory, experimental, and research work . . .[2]

Expenditures for public and private welfare

2. F. Emerson Andrews, *Philanthropic Giving*, Russell Sage Foundation, New York, 1950, p. 112.

increased from $3 billion in 1930 to $8 billion in 1940 and to $20 billion in 1950. (See Table 192.) In proportion to national income, however, the increases are less striking. Welfare expenditures were 4.1 per cent of the national income in 1930, 9.5 per cent in 1940, and 8.3 per cent in 1950.

The growth in public programs is largely responsible for the vast increase in welfare expenditures. From $1.8 billion in 1930, public expenditures rose to $15.4 billion in 1950. Though proportionately much smaller, the increases in private welfare spending have been substantial — from $1.3 billion in 1930 to over $4.5 billion in 1950. Despite this increase, however, private wel-

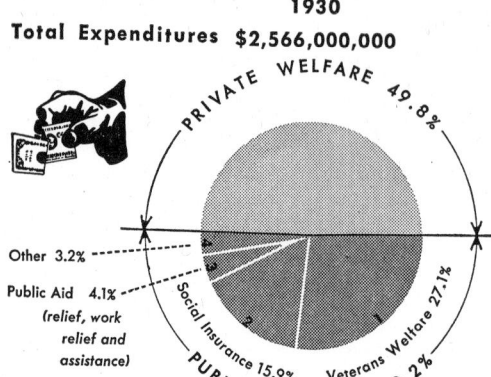

1930

Total Expenditures $2,566,000,000

PRIVATE WELFARE 49.8%

Other 3.2%

Public Aid 4.1%
(relief, work
relief and
assistance)

Social Insurance 15.9%   Veterans Welfare 27.1%

PUBLIC WELFARE 50.2%

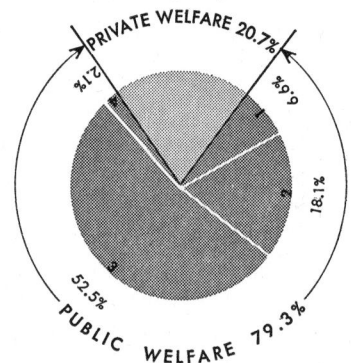

1940

Total Expenditures $6,848,000,000

PRIVATE WELFARE 20.7%

2.1%   6.9%

18.1%

52.5%

PUBLIC WELFARE 79.3%

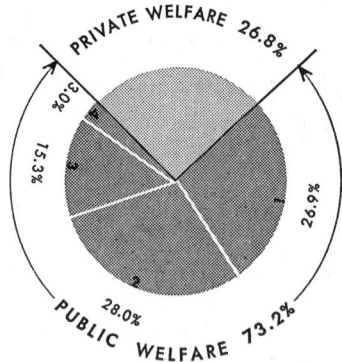

1950

Total Expenditures $16,910,000,000

PRIVATE WELFARE 26.8%

20.0%

15.3%

26.9%

28.0%

PUBLIC WELFARE 73.2%

FIGURE 58. TOTAL WELFARE EXPENDITURES [a] AND PERCENTAGE DISTRIBUTION BY TYPE, 1930, 1940 AND 1950

Source: Table 192.

a. Excluding public health and medical services.

fare declined from 50 per cent of total outlays (excluding public health and medical services) in 1930 to 27 per cent in 1950. (See Figure 58.)

On the side of public welfare spending, all forms of welfare have taken more money, but social insurance and veterans benefits have accounted for most of the increase. In private welfare, contributions have more than tripled, but the big new item is employer contributions to employee health, welfare and pension plans. In 1950 this item alone amounted to $2.8 billion as compared with $124 million in 1930.

As sources of revenues changed, so did program emphasis. The sums spent for economic assistance and social adjustment services increased from $3.32 per capita in 1924 to $45.13 in 1938. Expenditures for these functions dropped back to $15.26 per capita in 1948. Recreational and group work activities, of relatively little importance in 1924, now constitute a principal welfare field. Their major financial support comes from private contributions. Even in this activity, however, public money each year meets an increasingly larger share of the total cost. The shifting emphasis in private welfare expenditures is suggested by the changes in the distribution of community chest appropriations by type of service between 1935–1939 and 1953: [3]

Type of Service	1953 Chest Appropriations as Per Cent of 1935-1939 (27 Cities)	Percentage Distribution of Total Appropriations to Local Agencies by Type of Service, 1953
Care of the aged	210.0	1.25
Family service and general dependency	153.3	18.98
Care of children	244.9	17.64
Hospital care	147.8	6.47
Health other than hospital	190.8	13.91
Leisure time	359.1	40.41
Miscellaneous	*	1.34
Total for local agencies †	224.8	100.00

* Not available.
† Excludes planning, financing and common services.

THE RESURGENCE OF PRIVATE WELFARE

For a decade (1935–1946) there was general acceptance of government's dominant position in initiating and carrying through large-scale, long-

3. *Budgeting for 1953*, Bulletin No. 170, Community Chests and Councils of America, Inc., June 1953, pp. 2–4.

range welfare programs. Government alone, especially the federal government, was believed to have the funds and the power to deal with problems of unemployment, dependent old age, sickness, accident, child care and chronic disease. The illusion was widespread that the magic wand of government in the hand of those willing to use it could cause poverty and dependency to disappear from the land.

Emergence of Employee Benefit Plans

Experience soon revealed how far below the accepted standards of adequacy were the benefits paid under most public programs and how many gaps there were in the protective net of social insurance and public assistance established by the Social Security Act of 1935. Voluntary action by progressive employers and the collective bargaining demands of organized labor promoted a vast new program of welfare through the medium of employee benefit plans — supplementary to the minimum security provided under government sponsorship.

Industrial health, welfare and pension plans emphasize the renewed vigor of private initiative in welfare. Indeed, one author has seen in employee benefit plans, especially pensions, a golden opportunity for business to wrest from government the initiative in setting social policy and program, not merely in welfare matters, but in all areas of social concern.[4]

In 1950, industry spent $2.8 billion on contributions to private health, welfare and pension plans, exclusive of employer contributions to social insurance and workmen's compensation on behalf of their employees. In addition to supporting these plans for their own employees, business enterprises in 1950 contributed around $252 million to charitable undertakings according to the United States Department of Commerce.[5] In this traditional type of welfare — aid to individuals — corporations contributed more than private individuals. The National Industrial Conference Board found that the charitable contributions of 79 large manufacturing corporations in 1948 were distributed as follows: community chests, 31 per cent; hospitals, 17.5 per cent; education,

14 per cent; other philanthropies and charities, 37.5 per cent.[6]

Of the total $20 billion of public and private welfare expenditures in 1950, industry accounted for 14 per cent in payments to health, welfare and pension plans, and an additional 20 per cent by contributions to social insurance funds required by law. The role of industry in welfare is expanding rapidly and restoring to private organizations some responsibility for supplying money and services to those among whom economic need may at any time become reality.

WELFARE EXPENDITURES AS TRANSFER PAYMENTS

That the hand of government continues to dominate welfare expenditures in the United States is attested by the amount of transfer payments reported in 1950. The Department of Commerce defines a transfer payment as consisting of "monetary income receipts of individuals from government and business (other than government interest) for which no services are rendered currently, of government payments and corporate gifts to nonprofit institutions, and of individuals' bad debts to business."[7] Federal transfer payments in 1950 amounted to $10.9 billion, approximately 26.2 per cent of all federal expenditures. In addition, the state governments made transfer payments of $3.4 billion in 1950, some of which (about $2.3 billion) came from federal grants-in-aid to state governments for public assistance.[8] Federal, state and local government transfer payments, therefore, constituted nearly 70 per cent of all welfare payments in 1950. (See Table 193.) The decline in government transfer payments from $14.3 billion in 1950 to $12.0 billion in 1952 was due to the absence of any National Service Life Insurance dividend and a decline in veterans readjustment allowances in 1952.

About 50 per cent of all government transfer payments came from trust funds maintained by employer and employee contributions earmarked for social insurance. The federal, state and local governments collected $7 billion in social insur-

---

4. Russell Davenport, "Pensions — Not If, But How!," *Fortune*, February 1950.

5. *Survey of Current Business*, July 1953, pp. 24 and 25, as revised subsequently.

6. Andrews, *Philanthropic Giving*, p. 67; see also *idem*, *Corporation Giving*, Russell Sage Foundation, New York, 1952, Chapters 8 and 9. The latter volume contains a somewhat higher estimate for 1950.

7. 1951 National Income Supplement to the *Survey of Current Business*, p. 53. Bad debts to business amounted to $755 million in 1950, or three times the amount of corporate gifts to education and welfare.

8. *Ibid.*, pp. 136, 154–155.

TABLE 193. GOVERNMENT TRANSFER PAYMENTS FOR WELFARE PURPOSES, 1930, 1940, 1950 AND 1952

(Millions)

Item of Expenditure	1930	1940	1950	1952
Total government transfer payments for welfare purposes	$1,010	$2,688	$14,305	$11,960
Federal government	746	1,426	10,885	8,886
Benefits from social insurance funds	51	840	6,101	4,793
Old-age and survivors insurance benefits	—	40	955	2,177
State unemployment insurance benefits	—	518	1,367	992
Railroad retirement insurance benefits	—	118	337	481
Railroad unemployment insurance benefits	—	16	60	42
Federal civilian pensions	22	73	273	328
Government life insurance benefits	29	75	3,109[a]	773
Direct relief [b]	—	63	—	—
Military pension, disability and retirement payments	468	476	2,478	2,558
Adjusted veterans compensation benefits [c]	117	28	2	—
Mustering-out payments to discharged servicemen and terminal-leave benefits	—	—	116	396
Readjustment, self-employment and subsistence allowances to veterans	—	—	1,708	652
Other [d]	110	19	480	487
State and local government	264	1,262	3,420	3,074
Benefits from social insurance funds	78	163	398	527
Government pensions	78	163	360	485
Cash sickness compensation	—	—	38	42
Direct relief	105	1,013	2,345	2,297
Special types of public assistance	} 105	630	2,055	2,129
General assistance		383	290	168
Other [e]	81	86	677	250

Sources: 1951 National Income Supplement to the *Survey of Current Business,* Table 36, pp. 201–202, and *Survey of Current Business,* July 1953, Table 36, p. 25.

a. Includes $2.7 billion dividend payments to holders of National Service Life Insurance policies. *Annual Report,* 1950, U.S. Veterans Administration, p. 3.

b. Consists of Farm Security Administration grants and the value of free stamps issued under the surplus-food and cotton stamp programs.

c. Covers benefits under the World War Veterans Adjusted Compensation Act of May 19, 1924, as amended, and under the Adjusted Compensation Payment Act of January 27, 1936. For the period 1929 through May 1936 this series represents very largely net loans to veterans on the security of their adjusted service certificates from the U.S. Government Life Insurance Fund and the Adjusted Service Certificate Fund; for the period since June 1936 it consists almost entirely of cash redemptions by veterans of their adjusted service bonds. The series includes also (1) payments to beneficiaries on certificates matured by death of veterans; (2) "adjusted service dependent pay," which comprises cash payments (negligible in amount) to veterans and their beneficiaries where, under certain circumstances, no certificates were issued; (3) payments to veterans in settlement of adjusted service certificates not covered by issuance of bonds; and (4) payments to veterans holding certificates to maturity.

d. Consists of military and naval insurance payments, payments to nonprofit institutions, profits of military post exchanges and Navy exchanges and ships' stores, payments under the Panama Canal Construction Annuity Act, enemy alien and civilian war assistance, payments to U.S. military and civilian prisoners of war, and Atomic Energy Commission fellowships.

e. Consists of veterans' aid and bonuses; payments for the care of foster children in private family homes; and payments to nonprofit institutions.

ance contributions in 1950. Benefits paid from these funds amounted to $6.5 billion. (See Table 193.) When the income from investments of accumulated funds is added — $1 billion — and the amounts retained by government subtracted, the net income of social insurance funds for 1950 was $1.1 billion. If the operation of National Service Life Insurance is excluded from the calculations, the total accumulation amounts to nearly $3.5 billion.[9] Total reserve funds on June 30, 1951 of the Old-Age and Survivors Insurance Trust Fund ($14.7 billion), the Unemployment Insurance Trust Fund ($8 billion), the Railroad Retirement Account ($2.4 billion) and the Civil Service Retirement Fund ($4.4 billion) amounted to $29.5 billion.[10]

Decline of Personal Gifts

While the role of government and business in social welfare has been expanding, individual contributions out of personal income to private welfare have fallen. After sharp increases during World War II (to $1 billion in 1946), following the low level of contributions in the depression ($0.35 billion in 1934), gifts to private welfare remained close to the $1 billion level. Dollar amounts appear highly variable, but the percentage of all consumption expenditures devoted to private welfare has been steadily decreasing except for a brief resurgence during the war years 1942–1946. In 1909, 1.8 per cent of all consumption expenditures were for private welfare. In 1931 only 0.81 per cent went to this purpose, despite the vast need at the onset of the depression. In 1944, the percentage rose to 0.87, but in 1951 it was only 0.45 per cent, the lowest on record.[11] (See Appendices 4–4 and 4–5.)

PRIVATE SOCIAL WELFARE

Private, or voluntary, social welfare originated as the charitable work of religious groups. Though church benevolences are still part of this country's welfare picture, secular or non-denominational private agencies and public programs are responsible for the predominant share of welfare activity.

The three principal religious groups expended an estimated $565 million on welfare activity in 1949, divided as follows: Catholic, $200 million; Protestant, $200 million; Jewish, $165 million.[12] Most of the contribution to Jewish charities was spent to aid the needy abroad. Roman Catholic and Protestant philanthropy supported health, educational, child and family services in the United States. Information on welfare expenditures of religious bodies is incomplete and does not permit a clear separation of welfare outlays from sums spent for ecclesiastical activities. One authority [13] suggests that about 20 per cent of the total contributions to religious bodies goes for benevolences, including missions and miscellaneous purposes.[14]

CHURCH WELFARE

Church welfare expenditures were approximately 3.4 per cent of the total welfare expenditures of the United States in the years 1949 and 1950. They were about 13 per cent of all private welfare expenditures and 4.5 per cent of all public expenditures excluding public health and medical services. Reliable data on welfare expenditures of religious bodies are not available. Local church groups seldom keep systematic accounts, and there is no regular central collection of welfare statistics for church groups. All estimates therefore rest on a shaky base.

In 1949 an estimated $165 million was raised directly by Jewish charitable organizations for welfare activities, about two thirds of it allocated to overseas activity and the remainder for welfare services and administrative expenses in the United States.[15]

Jewish federations which solicit funds on a nationwide basis receive most of the Jewish welfare contributions. In 1949 the United Jewish Appeal raised $112 million — somewhat less than the 1948 total — for foreign aid. The Jewish Agency for Palestine and the Palestine Foundation took nearly 75 per cent of this amount for resettlement work in Palestine. The Joint Distribution Committee spent most of the remainder for re-

---

9. Cf. *Social Security Bulletin*, March 1952, Table 3, p. 20.

10. *Ibid.*

11. These data include personal remittances to foreign countries. This accounts for the high percentages in the years before 1924, when mass immigration ceased. The basic trend, however, in personal social welfare contributions, excluding personal remittances to foreign countries, has been consistently downward.

12. Figure for Jewish expenditures is derived from *Social Work Year Book, 1951*, American Association of Social Workers, New York, 1951, p. 267; Catholic from Andrews, *Philanthropic Giving*, pp. 179–180; and Protestant from *ibid.*, pp. 181–182.

13. Andrews, *Philanthropic Giving*, p. 184.

14. See Chapter 13 for further discussion of expenditures for religious activities.

15. *Social Work Year Book, 1951*, p. 267.

lief in Europe and the Near East. A very small proportion, about $1.5 million, was spent on the resettlement of Jewish immigrants in the United States.[16] Domestic expenditures provided new educational and hospital facilities, and paid current operating expenses of existing institutions.

The phenomenal rise in Jewish contributions from $15 million in 1939 to the present level can be attributed to the burning interest the world over in two significant developments: the plight of Jewish people in Central Europe, and the needs of the new state of Israel.

Complete information on the extent of Roman Catholic giving for welfare is not available. The extensive educational system, the great number of hospitals, the recognized charitable work of the many Catholic benevolent organizations, and the welfare activity in local parishes obviously require substantial sums of money for operating expenses in addition to the huge capital investment in buildings, grounds and equipment, but actual amounts are unknown. The New York diocese alone received contributions of $2.7 million in 1949.[17]

Benevolent giving among the Protestant denominations can be pictured only as scattered sources are pieced together. The United Stewardship Council has estimated that for 15 religious bodies general contributions per member were $17.53 in 1920, rose to $23.03 in 1924, dropped to $11.73 in 1936, and rose further to $28.29 in 1949. The rise in the 1940s did not keep pace with the depreciated value of the dollar, so that per member contributions represented a smaller proportion of income than in 1924. The Council also estimates that in 1949 some 75 per cent of the Protestant church membership gave about $971 million for religious purposes;[18] total Protestant giving for welfare may be estimated at about $200 million.

Originally, church-sponsored social work agencies hesitated to join in consolidated fundraising activities of any kind lest they lose their independence and, particularly, their right to keep a religious emphasis in their work. Despite such misgivings, most Protestant and Jewish agencies, and many Catholic as well — other than those officially connected with the various denominations — now are supported wholly or in part by funds received through coordinated community financial campaigns.

SECULAR PRIVATE WELFARE

The secular private or voluntary welfare agencies arose in the closing decades of the nineteenth century in the United States as a protest against inefficient, inhuman and politics-riddled public relief. Leaving to public authorities the hopeless cases and those for whom institutional care alone was necessary, private agencies sought through assistance to families in their own homes, by professionally trained personnel, to restore to normal life a large percentage of the dependent and maladjusted with whom they dealt. From 1870 to 1930, private charitable organizations, sometimes with public funds, set the pattern and provided leadership for local welfare programs.

Eventually private agencies became so numerous, competitive and overlapping that a more systematic approach was necessary. The coordination of various private welfare activities became a major function of integrated agencies (usually known as charity organization societies) in the latter part of the nineteenth century. These associations sought through study and investigation to ascertain the causes of dependency. Family and children's services were the chief focus of their activities, and case work became idealized as the symbol of professional competence in welfare.[19]

Another significant development in private welfare was the community chest. Although federations of social agencies had been known for decades, the community chest as we know it today dates from the founding of the Cleveland Federation for Charity and Philanthropy in 1913.

Effects of War and Depression

Wars have resulted in the coordination and expansion of private welfare activity. At the onset of World War I, joint community appeals were virtually unknown even in the larger cities. The unusual demands for funds by so many different agencies for welfare work among soldiers and in war-devastated areas forced cities and small

16. Ibid.
17. Andrews, Philanthropic Giving, pp. 179–180.
18. Ibid., pp. 181–182.

19. C. F. McNeil, "Community Organization for Social Welfare," Social Work Year Book, 1951, p. 122.

TABLE 194. CONTRIBUTIONS TO ALL RECORDED COMMUNITY CHESTS, 1925–1953

Chest Year	Number of Campaigns	Raised for Specified Year	
		Amount	Per Cent of Goal
		(Millions)	
1925	240	$ 58.0	94.0
1929	331	73.2	95.9
1930	353	75.9	95.5
1931	386	84.7	98.7
1932	397	101.3	96.8
1935	406	69.7	87.2
1940	561	86.2	95.3
1945	772	221.2	101.9
1950	1,318	192.9	93.1
1951	938	200.9	94.5
1952	1,500	240.9	93.8
1953	1,560	266.1	96.1

Sources: *Trends in Community Chest Giving, 1951,* Bulletin No. 157, Community Chests and Councils of America, Inc., July 1951, p. 14, and information provided directly by the Community Chests and Councils.

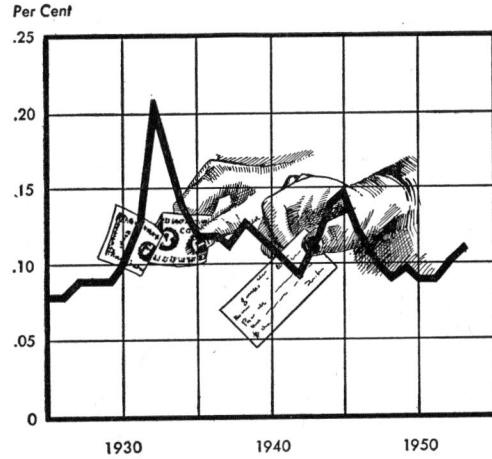

FIGURE 59. CONTRIBUTIONS TO COMMUNITY CHESTS AS PER CENT OF DISPOSABLE PERSONAL INCOME, 1925–1953

Sources: *Trends in Community Chest Giving, 1951,* Bulletin 157, Community Chests and Councils of America, Inc., July 1951, p. 14, and information provided directly by the Community Chests and Councils; Appendix 4–2, Table A; and *Survey of Current Business,* July 1953.

towns which never had raised a penny through community-wide appeals to coordinate their efforts. Over 400 communities initiated war chests, and some of these communities in 1918 formed the American Association for Community Organization, now known as Community Chests and Councils of America, Inc. The chest idea took root, and the period 1920–1924 was one of rapid growth.

With America's entrance into World War II new developments took place. Recreational and educational services to members of the armed forces as well as to areas at home dominated by war industries were coordinated in the United Service Organizations. The American Red Cross, supported by private funds, was officially integrated with the military organization to carry on welfare work, and to serve as a liaison agency between men in the service and their families at home. To support these additional activities community chests added substantial sums to their annual appeal budgets. In some instances U.S.O. drives were carried on independently of the normal welfare campaigns. Again, however, as after World War I, new community chests were formed to finance these coordinated efforts, and persisted even after the emergency appeals ceased. Community chest contributions reached an all-time peak of $266.1 mil-

lion in 1953. This was 0.11 per cent of personal disposable income in that year. (See Table 194 and Figure 59.)

Meeting the Korean Emergency

With the outbreak of hostilities in Korea, welfare organizations once again were asked to assume added financial burdens and new responsibilities. Local community agencies were requested to direct their attention to four problem areas: strengthening regular service to meet the added civilian needs of the emergency; civil defense welfare services; needs of members of the armed forces; and international programs for relief and rehabilitation. Coordination of voluntary activity was secured by the National Social Welfare Assembly and Community Chests and Councils of America, Inc.; on the government side, by the planning activity of the National Security Resources Board.[20] Financial campaigns for the defense welfare programs were made on a united basis as part of the regular community appeals. The United Defense Fund served as the coordinating organization for the United Service Organizations, the American Social Hygiene Association, the National Recreation Association,

20. John H. Moore, "Social Work and the National Emergency," *Social Work Year Book, 1951,* pp. 486–490.

the United Community Defense Services, the United Seamen's Service and American Relief for Korea. The United Defense Fund budget for 1954 was $20 million, or approximately 8 per cent of the total community chest contributions in 1953.

Changes Wrought by the Depression

The impact of the depression which intervened between the two world wars affected private welfare agencies in two directions. The initial decision by high government officials that welfare was essentially a private and local matter threw the full burden of the unemployed upon local agencies. The tremendous increase in private giving for relief between 1929 and 1932 indicates the degree to which individuals responded to the widespread need. Contributions to community chests, for example, were 0.21 per cent of disposable personal income in 1932, whereas in 1929 they were only 0.09 per cent. (See Figure 59.)

But the burden of providing a minimum income for millions of families made destitute by unemployment proved too heavy for private resources — no matter how willing. By the end of 1932, the Reconstruction Finance Corporation was ready to lend money to local governments for relief purposes, and in 1933, the Federal Emergency Relief Administration and the Civil Works Administration shifted the financial burden from local to federal budgets.

Private welfare contributions for all purposes declined sharply after 1932. In 1935 the contributions in 406 community appeals yielded less than 353 appeals received in 1930. (See Table 194.) A comparison of public and private expenditures for relief in 120 urban communities from 1929 to 1935 shows the changing responsibility very clearly. (See Table 195.)

In 120 urban communities, private relief expenditures rose from $10 million in 1929 to five times that level by 1932. Despite this increase, private relief funds in those centers, which had risen from 23.5 per cent of the total in 1929 to 28.6 per cent in 1931, fell to 18.5 per cent in 1932. By 1935, private funds totaled $11.6 million, still slightly above the 1929 level, but they constituted only 1.4 per cent of total relief expenditures.[21]

Despite the decline in private contributions during the three years 1933 to 1935, contributions to community chests increased from $58 million in 1925 to $266 million in 1953, and the number of community-wide appeals has grown from 240 to 1,560 in the last quarter century. (See Table 194.) Wartime giving for welfare among military personnel and for foreign relief brought contributions in 1944 and 1945 to more than double the amounts given in 1942. By 1947, contributions had declined about 25 per cent from the 1945 peak, only to rise sharply with the onset of the Korean conflict.

Private welfare has continued to grow. It has assumed new functions, set aside some old ones, and has become less important only by comparison with the astounding growth of public welfare programs.

Community Chests

Within the more traditional area of social welfare, the community service organizations financed by the community chest, eight types of activity predominate. These eight activities in 1953 received about 75 per cent of the community chest funds. Ranked in order from the activity receiving the most to the one receiving the least, they are: [22]

(1) Community-wide building-centered programs, Young Men's and Young Women's Christian and Hebrew Associations — 16.10 per cent
(2) Neighborhood non-building-centered programs (Boy and Girl Scouts, Campfire Girls) — 11.65 per cent
(3) Boys' clubs, settlements, and other neighborhood building-centered programs — 10.93 per cent
(4) Family service organizations, including Protestant, Catholic and Jewish, as well as nonsectarian — 10.88 per cent
(5) General case work services for children — 7.71 per cent
(6) Children's institutions — 6.73 per cent
(7) Hospital care — 6.47 per cent
(8) Nursing services — 5.45 per cent

Analysis of chest expenditures shows that in 1953 about 44 per cent was spent for leisure-time activities, 39 per cent for all types of financial and social adjustment services, 14 per cent for central

---

21. Public funds included in this comparison were direct relief grants only; wages paid on works programs were excluded.

22. *Budgeting for 1953*, Community Chests and Councils of America, Inc., 1953.

TABLE 195. EXPENDITURES FOR RELIEF FROM PUBLIC AND PRIVATE FUNDS IN
120 URBAN AREAS, 1929–1935

(Dollar Figures in Thousands)

| Year | Total | Public Funds | | Private Funds | |
		Amount	Per Cent	Amount	Per Cent
1929	$ 43,745	$ 33,449	76.5	$10,296	23.5
1930	71,425	54,754	76.7	16,671	23.3
1931	172,749	123,320	71.4	49,429	28.6
1932	308,185	251,104	81.5	57,081	18.5
1933	448,921 [a]	421,032 [a]	93.8	27,889	6.2
1934	667,153 [a]	652,467 [a]	97.8	14,686	2.2
1935	840,867 [b]	829,224 [b]	98.6	11,643	1.4

Source: Emma A. Winslow, *Trends in Different Types of Public and Private Relief in Urban Areas, 1929–1935,* Publication No. 237, Children's Bureau, U. S. Department of Labor, 1937.

a. Excludes Civil Works Administration expenditures.
b. Excludes Works Progress Administration expenditures.

service expenditures, cost of campaign planning and common service, and 3 per cent for out-of-area activities.

National Organizations

In addition to local agencies carrying on private welfare activities, there are several large national welfare organizations. Some of these operate as part of the community chest; others conduct their own campaigns.

The American National Red Cross is by all odds the largest national welfare organization. Local chapters of the Red Cross function independently of the national organization. Local budgets, therefore, are considered separately. Local and national expenditures of the Red Cross are approximately one third the figure for all community chests.

The greatest annual financial increases in recent years (as shown in Table 196) have been registered by such national health appeals as those of the American Heart Association and the National Foundation for Infantile Paralysis. These organizations have engaged in independent, high-powered fund raising, completely unrelated to federated community efforts. These independent campaigns have challenged the basic philosophy of modern private welfare financing. The objective of the community chest has been to relieve the contributor of numerous competitive appeals, by a single annual welfare drive. The protest on the part of employers and workers against the multiplication of special campaigns has led to united appeals in many industrial areas according to Community Chests and Councils of America. In 1953 the American National Red Cross participated in a united appeal in 227 cities. In about 500 cities at least one of the big six national health funds (Red Cross, Infantile Paralysis, Heart, Cancer, Tuberculosis, Crippled Children) joined in a single community welfare campaign.

The total expenditures of the organizations listed in Table 196 amounted to $177 million in 1953, compared with $19.4 million in 1938. Red Cross local chapters and national groups together spent about $85 million. Each of the organizations listed multiplied its expenditures more than three times between 1938 and 1948, except the Boy Scouts, the Child Welfare League, and the Family Service Association of America, which doubled their expenditures.

Contributions to private welfare (excluding nonwelfare contributions to religious bodies) probably ran at less than $2 billion a year during the early 1950s. The objects for which this money was contributed, judged by the activity of the organizations which received it, present an interesting pattern of private philanthropy in this country today. (See Table 197.)

TABLE 196. COMPARATIVE FINANCIAL DATA OF SEVERAL NATIONAL WELFARE
ORGANIZATIONS FOR 1938, 1943, 1948 AND 1953

Organization	1938		1943		1948		1953	
	Income	Expenditures	Income	Expenditures	Income	Expenditures	Income	Expenditures
Child Welfare League of America	$ 57,048	$ 56,200	$ 76,218	$ 72,796	$ 121,780	$ 120,165	$ 250,520	$ 232,060
American Heart Association	14,789	14,747	31,219	21,544	1,713,769	524,814	8,607,749	[a]
American National Red Cross	5,091,189	10,358,566	90,645,416	56,875,863	43,293,804	50,928,779	42,052,527	39,741,388
Red Cross local chapters	7,159,000	6,805,000	41,000,000	35,000,000	42,000,000	47,400,000	48,136,000	45,669,000
Boy Scouts of America	1,276,435	1,269,615	1,965,949	1,869,743	2,564,912	2,564,055	4,793,645	4,337,782
Family Service Association of America	122,277	122,153	147,328	143,218	274,658	279,614	382,234	378,637
National Foundation for Infantile Paralysis	1,613,985	525,240	2,712,798	1,336,163	9,945,494	14,167,339	36,491,000 [b]	42,694,000 [b]
National Tuberculosis Association	276,181	278,764	491,696	318,510	963,984	829,985	23,238,148	[a]
American Cancer Society	—	—	—	—	—	—	20,130,548	16,220,905

Sources: Adapted from separate financial statements for these associations and
information appearing in F. Emerson Andrews, *Philanthropic Giving*, Russell Sage
Foundation, New York, 1950, pp. 126–133, and 1953 annual reports of the
organizations.

a. Expenditures by the local offices and affiliates are not available.
b. 1952: gross income for the March of Dimes in 1953 was reported as $51.5
million. Expenditures for 1953 were not tabulated at time of writing.

TABLE 197. ESTIMATE OF CURRENT ANNUAL GIVING TO PRIVATE PHILANTHROPY, EXCLUDING CHURCHES AND EDUCATION, BY OBJECT [a]

(*Millions*)

Category	Amount
Total	$1,838
Religious welfare	565[b]
National health funds	177
Foundations	151
Charity rackets[c]	100
Community chests (1953)	266
Foreign relief, except religious	40
Miscellaneous and unallocated	539

Sources: Adapted from F. Emerson Andrews, *Philanthropic Giving,* Russell Sage Foundation, New York, 1950, pp. 72–73, 179–182; *Social Work Year Book, 1951,* American Association of Social Workers, New York, p. 267; annual reports of national health funds; and data provided directly by Community Chests and Councils of America.

a. These figures are generally for 1949–1953 when available. In some instances averages of several recent years are given, or projections made from the last published year.

b. United Jewish Appeal is included with other religious contributions even though its primary concern is with foreign relief and resettlement.

c. Charity rackets are appeals in which "the profit of the promoter is paramount and the cash receipts for a high sounding cause are negligible."

Note: These figures exclude annual contributions to educational organizations. Contributions to religion exclude contributions for ecclesiastical activities.

Andrews' figures are considerably higher than the sums reported for 1950 in the "Consumers' Expenditures" tabulations of the 1951 National Income Supplement to the *Survey of Current Business.* The total of $865 million for private welfare presented by the *Survey* consists principally of individual gifts exclusive of religious and educational contributions made out of personal disposable income. This sum is made up as follows (in millions):

Personal remittances to foreign countries (net)	$160
Social welfare and foreign relief agencies	670
Other private welfare	
Foundation expenditures	25
Political organizations	10

Outlays by religious bodies for all purposes, according to this source, amounted to $1,125 million.

Sources of Private Welfare Contributions

The slight evidence available as to the sources of welfare contributions indicates that gifts from individuals still predominate in private welfare financing. In recent years about three fourths of all receipts of private philanthropy, *including religious and educational activity,* came from individuals. Another productive source of private welfare funds was income received from the investment of funds and the rental of facilities. (See Table 198.)

TABLE 198. ESTIMATE OF RECENT ANNUAL RECEIPTS OF PRIVATE PHILANTHROPY IN THE UNITED STATES, BY SOURCE [a]

Source	Amount	Per Cent
	(*Millions*)	
Total [b]	$4,471	100
Contributions from individuals	3,304	74
Charitable bequests	182	4
Contributions from corporations	241	5
Foundations	133	3
Income from capital (except foundations)	611	14

Source: F. Emerson Andrews, *Philanthropic Giving,* Russell Sage Foundation, New York, 1950, p. 73. This total is somewhat larger than that reported in Table 197 since the figures here include all sources of income, such as income from endowment, rental of property, and sale of assets (Table 197 reports only contributions to philanthropy); they also include income received for educational and religious work.

a. Includes all religious, educational and health contributions and is based on estimates projected from last recorded year and averages of estimates for the past several years.

b. Excludes payments for services by those receiving them.

The day when philanthropy was the exclusive right of the well-to-do is now past, if in reality it ever existed. Large numbers of small contributions total considerably more than the very large gifts. The percentage of total income by size of gift received during the 1951 campaign by 176 community chests was as follows: [23]

Size of Gift	Per Cent of Total Income
$500 and over	38.8
$100-$499	17.8
$25-$99	11.3
Less than $25	32.1

By comparison with 1935–1939, there are as many large donors, but a great many more small givers. Losses in number of gifts and total volume of contributions have been sustained largely in the middle-size gift group.[24]

Business Contributions to Welfare

A new giver has sprung into prominence in America in the past few years. As a philanthropist he does not much resemble previous givers — neither the widow with her mite, nor the churchman, nor

23. *Trends in Community Chest Giving, 1951,* Bulletin No. 157, Community Chests and Councils of America, Inc., July 1951, p. 3.

24. *Ibid.,* p. 4.

Lady Bountiful. . . . This new giver is the corporation. It is estimated that in 1952 corporate contributions may have exceeded $300 million.[25]

Employers, especially corporate employers, are called upon to contribute to all forms of social welfare with increasing frequency and insistence. Between 1936, when the first records were made of such information, and 1950, corporate contributions increased from $30 million to about $252 million, as follows (figures in millions):[26]

1936	$30	1944	$234
1937	33	1945	266
1938	27	1946	214
1939	31	1947	241
1940	38	1948	239
1941	58	1949	223
1942	98	1950	252
1943	159		

Corporation gifts to the community chests constituted about 40 per cent of all chest contributions in 1950.

The welfare dollar contributed by corporations is allocated to a large number of welfare groups in the following percentages (1950):[27]

Welfare agencies	44.3
Health agencies	26.6
Education	21.2
Religious agencies	4.1
Unallocated	3.8

The demands by welfare and educational agencies upon business are increasing rapidly. Opinion is sharply divided among executives as to the obligation of the corporation to support philanthropies. Some feel the responsibility is wholly personal and no concern of the corporations. Others, just as emphatically, believe the corporation must be a substantial contributor to worthy community enterprises in terms of the local need.[28]

Although private philanthropic giving has increased substantially since 1940, personal gifts to welfare have not kept pace with the combined impact of increases in population and price nor with increases in disposable personal income. Contributions to community chests, for example, were 0.11 per cent of disposable personal income in 1940 and only 0.09 per cent in 1950.[29]

War-Born Employee Benefit Plans

World War II introduced a new element into the pattern of private welfare. Even yet, the full impact of this new influence cannot be appraised. Limitation on wage increases, and high corporate taxes during the war, promoted the development of health, welfare and pension plans in industry.

Here is a rough estimate of the coverage of employee benefit programs:[30]

	Per Cent of Firms with Plans	Per Cent of Employees Covered
Hospitalization	75.7	70.9
Life insurance	62.4	75.0
Surgical plan	46.7	49.1
Pension	29.7	40.7
Cash sickness	27.9	55.0
Medical care	12.7	8.4
Sick leave	40.9	24.3

It is clear that industry through voluntary programs has contributed tremendously to welfare by strengthening the insurance method of employee security. With these dikes holding back the floodwaters of poverty and dependency, the need for "charity" or direct relief has substantially decreased.

The exact cost of these programs is difficult to determine. The United States Chamber of Commerce[31] concluded that the average employer in 1951 paid 5 per cent of payroll, or 8.4 cents per man-hour, for pensions and health and welfare. This represents an annual cost of $171 per employee. Between 1949 and 1951 employer payments for health, welfare and pension plans increased approximately 14 per cent. The United States Department of Commerce estimates that

25. F. Emerson Andrews, *Atlantic Monthly*, February 1953, p. 63.

26. John H. Watson, "Corporate Donations in 1948," *Conference Board Business Record,* National Industrial Conference Board, New York, January 1950, pp. 18–19 (based on contributions in 1948); and Andrews, *Corporation Giving*, pp. 42–44. See also p. 433 above.

27. Andrews, *Corporation Giving*, p. 71.

28. Helen A. Winselman, "Postwar Trends in Corporate Giving," *Conference Board Business Record,* National Industrial Conference Board, New York, May 1947, p. 138.

29. See Figure 59.

30. *Employee Benefit Plans,* Publication No. 69, Research Council for Economic Security, Chicago, 1950, p. 11. The study from which these figures are derived embraced nonagricultural industry of all types, and firms of all sizes located in 12 metropolitan areas of the United States. The percentages are probably fairly representative of the distribution of these plans among firms in the nation as a whole.

31. *Fringe Benefits, 1951,* Chamber of Commerce of the United States, Washington, 1952, p. 9.

TABLE 199. EXTENT OF EMPLOYER AND EMPLOYEE FINANCING
OF EMPLOYEE BENEFIT PLANS

Type of Plan	Per Cent of Firms with Plans:			
	100 Per Cent Employer-Financed	50–99 Per Cent Employer-Financed	1–49 Per Cent Employer-Financed	100 Per Cent Employee-Financed
Prepaid hospitalization	19.7	18.8	9.5	52.0
Life insurance	35.7	42.4	17.9	3.9
Prepaid surgical benefits	25.9	29.0	12.0	33.1
Pension and retirement	54.4	41.5	3.5	0.6
Organized cash sickness	48.6	27.0	12.2	12.2
Paid sick leave	100.0	0.0	0.0	0.0
Prepaid medical care	38.2	27.0	0.6	25.2

Source: Employee Benefit Plans, Publication No. 69, Research Council for Economic Security, Chicago, 1950, p. 13.

employer contributions to private pension and welfare funds amounted to $2.8 billion in 1950 as compared with $2.1 billion in 1949 and only $170 million in 1940. In the ten years between 1940 and 1950, employers' contributions increased 16 times, while between 1930 and 1940 the increase was from $124 million to $170 million, or about 37 per cent. In 1952, employers reported contributions of $3.4 billion to health, welfare and pension plans, indicating a continuation of the sharp increase in the amount devoted to this form of employee benefit.[32] The amount contributed by business to employee benefit plans is more than half the total of all other private welfare expenditures in the country.[33]

The cost of employee benefit plans to employers was also estimated by the Research Council for Economic Security in 1948. Using a much smaller sample than the Chamber of Commerce study mentioned above, the Research Council arrived at a total cost of employee benefit plans (exclusive of public social insurance) of 8.95 per cent of payroll. The estimated share paid by the employer was 5.66 per cent of payroll.[34]

The trend in the financing of health, welfare and pension plans is toward the noncontributory

plan,[35] especially for pensions and among the larger companies. The employer's payment constitutes roughly three fourths of the total payment for employee benefit plans. Employers are paying the full cost of 54 per cent of all pensions and more than half the cost of almost all other plans. Employees pay all or most of the cost in only 4 per cent of all pension plans. Only in hospitalization programs do employees bear the full cost of more than half the plans. In all other programs, life insurance, temporary disability, surgical and medical care, employers pay all or more than 50 per cent of the cost in more than half the plans. (See Table 199.)

Attitude of Labor Unions

The active interest of business in welfare has been matched in the past by the interest of trade unions and employee mutual-benefit organizations. The railroad brotherhoods, for example, were founded initially because railroading was such a hazardous industry that private insurance companies would not insure railroad employees, or offered insurance at rates too high for the worker to pay. Welfare interests led to the founding of a number of other unions.

For many years unions objected to both public social insurance and employer-sponsored benefits. Union leaders believed, on the one hand, that the welfare aspect of union membership was necessary to a strong organization, and, on the

32. 1951 National Income Supplement to the *Survey of Current Business,* p. 201; and *Survey of Current Business,* July 1952, pp. 26–27, and July 1953, p. 24.

33. Employee contributions are not included in the tabulation above.

34. *Social Security in Industry,* Publication No. 46, Research Council for Economic Security, Chicago, 1948, p. 8.

35. A noncontributory plan is one into which employees make no payment.

other hand, that employer-sponsored benefits were designed to promote loyalty to the employer and undermine union affiliation.

Wartime restrictions on wage increases, wartime cost-plus contracts, the exhaustion of public patience with successive rounds of postwar wage increases, and a new type of labor leadership, all contributed to a changed union outlook upon health, welfare and pension plans. In 1950, about 5.1 million employees were covered by collectively bargained pension plans out of the total of 10 million employees in all plans. Of the 25 million employees in other types of employee benefit plans, about 7.1 million were in collectively bargained plans.[36]

GOALS OF PRIVATE WELFARE

The record of expenditures is probably the most tangible evidence of the avenues of interest along which voluntary welfare activity moves today. Needless to say, the goals of social welfare constantly outrun the resources available. In what direction would the voluntary agencies move if funds were available?

Identifying new community needs and planning for community organization to meet these needs have been accepted by voluntary agencies as a basic responsibility. Not only have funds been devoted to research and planning, but the development of community organization to meet welfare needs is of paramount importance to social workers. It is characteristic of social welfare planning, however, that there is not only an acceptance of the participation of public agencies, and to some extent the use of public funds, but there is in fact a dependence upon government participation in the initiation and expansion of programs. Ralph H. Blanchard says the general goals of social welfare are:

(1) Growth and development in health, welfare and recreational services needed by people.
(2) Balance and orderliness in this growth and development process.
(3) The highest possible quality and efficiency in the operation of these services.
(4) Coordination of effort and thus total community efficiency in the field of health and welfare.
(5) Making services readily available to people as and when they need them regardless of race, creed or economic status.

"These objectives hold true," he says, "regardless of auspices of the services, whether public

or private. In fact, they take for granted the existence of both kinds of services." [37]

In addition to general community needs, special groups of people often are singled out for special service or study. In 1950, for example, the welfare of children and youth and the aged became the focus of attention. The needs of these groups were defined in national conferences held in Washington during 1950.[38] Indeed, the defining of social welfare aims by means of national conferences of technical specialists, professional workers and public-spirited citizens seems to be an accepted procedure. Analysis of the aims for youth and for the aged reveals the character of social welfare today. The problems of these two groups were believed to be the outgrowth of new relationships, circumstances and practices in society; therefore, most recommendations had broader implications than the promotion of different or better services to the young and the old.

Suggested private welfare activity consisted principally of counseling and other personal aids to social adjustment. To organize the community for social welfare appeared to be the basic function of the private community welfare agencies. Fundamentally, the conferences made clear the impossibility of setting welfare goals for private agencies as distinct from public agencies, or divorced from public funds.

SUMMARY

Current activity in private social welfare is dynamic and expanding, and it is moving in new directions. The fresh emphases are community planning for social welfare and the realization that welfare means integrating and perhaps changing community practices. Aid to the individual through counseling service and group educational and recreational activity still bulks large as a field for voluntary welfare activity. There is a growing dependence upon industry to provide protective programs through group insurance, to finance services to its own employees and to support the private welfare work of its community. Finally, there is increasing depend-

---

36. *Monthly Labor Review*, February 1951, p. 160.

37. Ralph H. Blanchard, "Community Organization in Support of Public Welfare Programs," *Social Work in the Current Scene, 1950*, National Conference of Social Work, Columbia University Press, New York, 1950, p. 5.

38. Mid-Century White House Conference on Children and Youth, December 1950; National Conference on Aging, Washington, D.C., August 1950. Also, A Conference on Retirement of Older Workers, National Social Welfare Assembly, Arden House, January 1952.

ence upon public funds and public welfare programs. That welfare now requires a coordination of private philanthropy, industry and union welfare programs, and public money and personnel is evident.[39]

Public Welfare

Despite far larger expenditures, and the allocation of authority among federal, state and local governments, public welfare is less complex than is the organization and financing of private welfare. The total public expenditures for welfare, including veterans benefits and social insurance (excluding medical care and state and local education expenditures), amounted to $12.4 billion in 1950. (See Table 192.) This sum was 5.1 per cent of the 1950 national income ($241 billion), and 20.2 per cent of all government expenditures ($61.4 billion) in 1950. Federal payments amounted to $7.7 billion, and state and local governments spent $4.7 billion, whereas private expenditures for social welfare, including industry's contribution to health, welfare and pensions, amounted to $4.6 billion. Public expenditures, therefore, were two and a half times the amount of private welfare in 1950.

A year later (1951) public payments for welfare (excluding medical care and state and local education expenditures) amounted to $13.3 billion. Social insurance benefits increased, because of increases in old-age and survivors insurance payments, but unemployment compensation and veterans benefits, especially educational benefits, declined by more than $1 billion. Although there was an increase of 5.5 per cent in the dollar amount expended, the total expenditure in 1951 represented only 4.2 per cent of the gross national product as compared with 4.9 per cent in 1950.[40]

By way of historic comparison, federal, state and local government expenditures for welfare rose from about one quarter of a billion dollars in 1913 [41] to over $13 billion in 1951. Thus, in less than forty years the welfare expenditures of government were multiplied more than fifty times.

What is the reason for this astounding growth in government welfare payments? Before 1930, local government provided public relief for needy cases which private charity could not or would not accept. Private agencies assumed responsibility for cases with a high probability of return to self-support. The aged, the chronically ill, the hopelessly indigent, were left to public care. Public funds frequently were appropriated to private agencies for children's aid, and for help to other special groups. State governments took some of the burden from local shoulders by building, staffing and maintaining hospitals for incurables, and in general supervising the institutional work of the state.[42]

In large part, state efforts were confined to integrating the welfare work conducted by many public agencies. Some states created effective social welfare departments, but most of them continued a board of charities and correction which had general supervisory powers. States with workmen's compensation laws administered their provisions and provided funds for special education and rehabilitation.

The federal government financed vocational rehabilitation and veterans services and pensions; beyond that, it limited its activities to setting goals and acting as an information clearing house.

The years between 1930 and 1940 saw rapid and radical change in the country's welfare patterns. "While it is not too much to say that prior to 1930 no other industrial country had made so little provision for public aid, it is equally true that in no other country has so much been achieved in the course of 10 years."[43]

Three Major Changes

The revolutionary changes in social welfare arising out of the depression were of three types. First, there was the change in the role of the fed-

39. Reference to the needs, qualifications, salaries and training of social workers as one measure of the needs and resources in social welfare will be found in E. V. Hollis and A. L. Taylor, *Social Work Education in the United States,* Columbia University Press, New York, 1950, and Ellen J. Perkins and Charles C. Lopes, "Public Assistance Employees: Their Salaries," *Social Security Bulletin,* March 1952, p. 7.

40. *Social Security Bulletin,* February 1953, Table 1, p. 8, and October 1953, Table 1, p. 14. Figures used in these calculations differ from those in the *Bulletin* because expenditures for health and medical service and education are excluded. *Survey of Current Business,* July 1952, Table 9.

41. See Table 261.

42. Marietta Stevenson, "The States and a Federal Department of Welfare," *Proceedings of the National Conference of Social Work, Selected Papers, Seventy-third Annual Meeting, 1946,* Columbia University Press, New York, 1947.

43. *Security, Work, and Relief Policies,* National Resources Planning Board, 1942, p. 7.

eral government between 1933 and 1935. Washington not only provided funds on an emergency basis to meet the relief costs of states and local communities; it also initiated plans to reduce unemployment by providing work to the able-bodied unemployed. Initially, work programs were temporary. Before the end of the depression, there was widespread conviction that government had a continuing obligation to combat depression and unemployment by the creation of large-scale public works and by the use of fiscal powers to stimulate business activity. This policy was made explicit in the Full Employment Act of 1946.

The second far-reaching development was the social insurance program providing cash benefits as a right to those who suffered economic loss because of the hazards of industry.

Finally, in the creation of the assistance programs — for the aged, dependent children, the blind (and, since 1950, for the permanently and totally disabled) — the federal government established a partnership with the states to finance programs for persons in need. At the same time, the federal government, as a condition of making grants-in-aid for assistance, forced the states to abandon traditional concepts of need (based upon Elizabethan Poor Laws) and insisted upon state rather than local responsibility for the administration of assistance. This development is well summarized by an authority with long experience in public welfare administration.

I believe we can say that, by and large, the states have reorganized effective systems of administering public assistance, at least for the three [now four] major categories under the federal Social Security Act, though we still have a long way to go in general assistance. The states arrived at the present stage of development through a long process. We faced an emergency. We set up new agencies. We got permanent federal legislation. Then we reorganized, rewrote our laws, and re-established our agencies. It was a fifteen-year process.[44]

The Number Aided

The number of persons and households helped by the various programs gives some conception of the magnitude of the public welfare effort in the depression years 1933–1940. In June 1940, about 6.9 million households, containing 19.4 million persons, or 14 per cent of the total population, received public aid through a formal program. Two years earlier, 7.5 million households and 23 million persons (about 17 per cent of the population) were assisted.[45] In 1938 and 1939, when public aid reached its peak, the annual expenditure was nearly $5 billion, 27 per cent of all government expenditures.[46]

The major outlines of the present public programs of social welfare were formulated by 1941. Developments since then, with but one exception, have been concerned with adjustment to meet changing price and wage levels, and the closing of gaps in the program left in the enactment of the basic leglislation during the 1930s. The one exception is the elaborate program of veterans benefits enacted by Congress at the close of World War II.

SOCIAL INSURANCE

Social insurance may be defined as governmentally administered programs which, by systematic means set up in advance, pay, as a right, cash benefits in place of income lost to individuals as a result of old-age retirement, unemployment, illness, accident or death. Social insurance expanded tremendously between 1940 and 1950. During the ten-year period benefits rose from $1.5 billion to $6.4 billion, and by 1952 they reached $7.8 billion. The percentage increase was not distributed evenly among all phases of the program. Survivorship monthly benefits were almost six times as large in 1950 as in 1940, while unemployment benefits were less than three times the 1940 level. (See Table 200 and Figure 60.)

Contributions for social insurance increased in the same period from $2.2 billion to $6.3 billion. In 1952 they amounted to $8.2 billion. The increase was due principally to the rise in the contribution rate for old-age and survivors insurance, but was influenced also by increased wages. Employers and employees contribute equally for retirement and permanent disability benefits, but employers bear the entire cost of unemployment insurance in every state except Alabama and New Jersey. In 1950, employers' contributions amounted to $3.8 billion while employees contributed $2.4 billion. Of all the types of social insurance, retirement benefits are the most costly,

---

44. Robert T. Lansdale, "The Public Welfare Agency in an Insurance World," *Proceedings of the National Conference of Social Work, Selected Papers, Seventy-third Annual Meeting, 1946,* Columbia University Press, New York, 1947.

45. *Security, Work, and Relief Policies,* Appendix 9, pp. 557–599.
46. *Ibid.,* p. 8.

requiring $6.3 billion out of the total of $8.2 billion in contributions in 1952. (See Table 201.)

Old-Age and Survivors Insurance

The old-age insurance provision of the Social Security Act, administered by the Social Security Administration of the Department of Health, Education and Welfare, was designed to offer basic protection to all persons over 65 who retire from gainful employment.[47] The original program followed the lines of private pension systems. As a result of the threats of Townsendism and the dissatisfaction with private insurance concepts, the system was modified in 1939, in order to: (1) begin payments at an earlier date than planned initially; (2) pay benefits to the survivors of covered employees; (3) pay benefits on average monthly wages rather than lifetime earnings in order to pay higher benefits at the outset; (4) pay proportionately higher benefits to low-income workers than to high-income workers; (5) modify the full reserve to a contingency reserve.

The first benefits were paid in 1940. Within the first year of operation, the shortcomings of the system became clear. Coverage was narrow, benefits low, and improvement under the law would be slow. The clearest evidence of the failure of OASI to meet the need was the continued superiority of old-age assistance in number of recipients and level of benefits over old-age and survivors insurance. Revisions attempted in succeeding years failed except for minor changes in 1946 and 1948.

Just before major revisions in 1950, the old-age and survivors insurance system covered about 37 million workers (at any one time) and paid an average benefit of $26 a month to 1.4 million old-age beneficiaries. For a retired husband and wife the average monthly benefit was $41.

The 1950 amendments to old-age and survivors insurance brought striking changes not only in coverage but in underlying philosophy as well. The operation of the system as of January 1952 has been described as follows: [48]

1. In January 1940, 23 million persons were "fully" insured under the Federal Old-age and Survivors Insurance system. As of January 1952, there were 62.3 million insured — an increase of nearly 40 million persons.

2. In January 1952, there were 3.3 million workers, 65 years of age or over, who were fully insured under the Federal old-age insurance program and eligible to draw benefits. About 2.3 million workers had "retired" and were drawing benefits. In addition, over one million other persons aged 65 or over were receiving insurance benefits as wife, widow, or parent. A total of 3.3 million persons were drawing benefits in January 1952.

3. The number of aged persons drawing Federal old-age insurance benefits has exceeded the number drawing old-age assistance payments every month since February 1951. The number receiving insurance is increasing about 40,000 each month.

4. The number of persons receiving old-age assistance has dropped 120,000 from the high of 2,810,000 in September 1950 to 2,690,000 in January 1952 — a decrease averaging about 7,500 per month.

5. The average monthly old-age insurance payment for a retired worker in January 1952 was about $42; the average old-age assistance payment was about $44.50.[49]

6. The number of aged persons receiving an insurance, retirement or pension payment from any public agency (excluding old-age assistance) has increased from about 600,000 in December 1940 to about 4.5 million in December 1951. This number is expected to increase to about 5 million by the end of 1952.

7. By the end of 1952 over 7 million persons will be receiving some form of public old-age payment — more than the total number of aged persons in 1930.

Originally the old-age retirement system was to be financed through a reserve system fully capable of meeting all retirement claims in the future without additional taxes or a government contribution. From 1937, the contribution rate, under the Social Security Act, would increase periodically on wages up to $3,000 to reach 3 per cent on employers and employees in 1948. By successive legislation from 1939 throughout the 1940s, Congress prevented the rise in the contribution rate.

Varying reasons prompted this action. There was a belief that to take that sum from available consumer purchasing power would have a deflationary effect. Further, the reserve was to be invested in government bonds. A comparison of

---

47. Old-age and survivors insurance is designed to pay a benefit as a right to persons over 65 who have retired from the labor force. Old-age assistance is a needs test program which pays an allowance to persons 65 years of age and over whose total income from all sources is less than the welfare budget established by state and local governments.

48. Wilbur J. Cohen, Technical Assistant to the Commissioner, Social Security Administration, Washington,

D.C., 1952, mimeographed release. Mr. Cohen was appointed Director of Research, Social Security Administration in 1953.

49. OASI benefits were increased in June 1952 by $5 or 12.5 per cent a month, whichever was greater. Old-age assistance benefits were increased by $5. In December 1952 the average old-age insurance benefit (primary benefit) was $49.30.

TABLE 200. BENEFITS AND BENEFICIARIES UNDER SOCIAL INSURANCE
AND VETERANS PROGRAMS, 1940, 1950 AND 1952 [a]

(Thousands)

Risk and Program	Benefits			Beneficiaries [b]		
	1940	1950	1952	1940	1950	1952
Total	$1,545,380	$6,392,956	$7,834,195	—	—	—
Old-age retirement	330,277	1,469,291	2,637,144	—	—	—
Old-age and survivors insurance [e]	21,074	718,473	1,613,365	77.2	1,918.1	3,187.3
Railroad retirement	83,342	176,925	267,343	102.0	174.8	268.6
Federal civil service	49,069	135,267	175,616	47.4	111.0	128.3
Other federal contributory [d]	714	2,440	3,075	.6	2.0	2.3
Federal noncontributory [e]	53,308	148,600	190,525	32.2	68.8	84.7
State and local government retirement [f]	103,000	230,000	300,000	113.0	213.0	250.0
Veterans program [g]	19,770	57,586	87,220	29.2	53.5	78.4
Survivorship:						
Monthly benefits	162,928	924,544	1,377,658	—	—	—
Old-age and survivors insurance	7,784	299,672	615,604	35.7	1,093.9	1,484.6
Railroad retirement	1,448	43,884	74,085	3.0	136.3	149.9
Federal civil service	—	8,409	19,986	—	18.3	40.0
State and local government retirement [f]	16,000	26,000	30,000	25.0	40.0	44.0
Veterans program	105,696	491,579	572,983	323.2 [i]	991.7 [i]	1,044.2 [i]
Workmen's compensation [h]	32,000	55,000	65,000			
Lump-sum payments	36,659	86,693	131,019	—	—	—
Old-age and survivors insurance	11,736	32,740	63,298	—	—	—
Railroad retirement	2,497	12,722	13,745	—	—	—
Federal civil service	5,810	8,147	8,364	—	—	—
Other federal contributory	156	375	470	—	—	—
State and local government retirement [f]	12,500	20,000	30,000	—	—	—
Veterans program [g]	3,960	12,709	15,142	—	—	—
Disability	480,855	2,444,545	2,644,805	—	—	—
Workmen's compensation [h]	129,000	362,000	475,000	[i]	[i]	[i]
Veterans program [g]	298,081	1,674,622	1,635,005	580.9	2,301.8	2,343.9
Railroad retirement	30,824	77,315	93,857	39.3	76.0	80.3
Federal civil service	12,950	40,520	49,504	15.5	43.0	48.4
Federal noncontributory [e]	[e]	148,730	161,410	[e]	56.0	68.1
State and local government retirement [f]	10,000	24,000	30,000	14.3	32.0	38.0
State temporary disability insurance [j]	—	89,259	165,340	—	54.1	75.0
Railroad temporary disability insurance [k]	—	28,099	34,689	—	31.2	31.5
Unemployment	534,661	1,466,217	1,043,557	—	—	—
State unemployment insurance	518,700	1,373,426	998,237	982.4 [l]	1,305.0 [l]	873.6 [l]
Railroad unemployment insurance	15,961	59,804	41,793	41.5	76.8	42.6
Veterans unemployment allowances	—	32,987	3,527	—	32.1 [l]	15.1 [l]
Self-employment allowances to veterans	—	1,666	12	—	1.5	.1

(Notes on facing page)

the expected size of the reserve ($46 billion in 1980) with the then existing government debt ($29 billion in 1939) led to the natural conclusion that the government would not be able to absorb the reserve, which by law it was required to do. (This problem became purely academic as the national debt grew rapidly, reaching $266 billion by 1950.) Insurance company executives and actuaries joined in opposing the full reserve principle for the old-age insurance system.

Despite congressional action preventing the rise in the contribution rate for more than ten years, favorable employment records among older workers caused continued growth of the reserve to $13 billion just before the 1950 amendments. Realization of the magnitude of future costs of the new benefit levels and coverage encouraged a return to the full reserve system of financing. Consequently, increases in the contribution rate and the taxable wage base were prescribed by the 1950 amendments. Starting with 1951, wages up to $3,600 a year were taxed, and on January 1, 1954 the contribution rate rose to 2 per cent for employer and employee. The maximum contribution rate of 3.25 per cent was scheduled to be

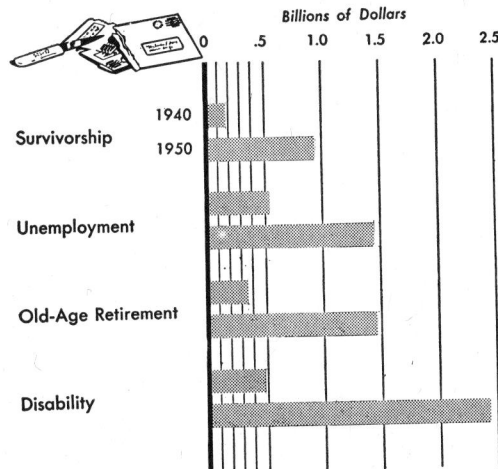

FIGURE 60. BENEFITS UNDER SOCIAL INSURANCE AND VETERANS PROGRAMS, 1940 AND 1950 [a]

Source: Table 200.

a. Excludes all lump-sum survivorship payments, and self-employment allowances to veterans.

reached in 1970. Amendments being considered in mid-1954 — which probably will be enacted — would raise the tax base to include wages up to

Source: Based on reports of administrative agencies. Social Security Bulletin, September 1953, Table 4, p. 24.

a. Partly estimated. Data for state and local governments and for federal civil service and other contributory retirement plans exclude refunds of employee contributions. National Service Life Insurance and subsistence allowances to veterans in schools are excluded, but benefits for all types of federal employees, in addition to civil service, have been included. Slight differences in totals in this table and Table 193 are due to the inclusion of some estimated totals here. Administrative costs of social insurance are excluded.

b. Average monthly number, except as otherwise noted.

c. Includes benefits paid to aged wives, to dependent husbands (first payable September 1950), and to dependent minor children of retired-worker beneficiaries; for aged wives and dependent husbands receiving benefits in 1952, the average number was 684,296; for children of retired-worker beneficiaries, 70,310; payments certified to these groups were $208,948,700 and $12,469,400 respectively.

d. Includes a small but unknown number and amount of disability and survivor beneficiaries and benefits.

e. In 1950 and 1952, identifiable disability benefits and beneficiaries shown separately and only a small but unknown number and amount of disability and survivor payments included with old-age retirement. For 1940, old-age retirement data include small amount of survivor and significant amount of disability payments.

f. Benefits for fiscal year (usually ending June 30); beneficiaries for last month of fiscal year. Data for 1952 preliminary.

g. Under Veterans Administration. Old-age retirement data are for veterans of the Spanish-American War, the Boxer Rebellion and the Philippine Insurrection; 1952 data include all service pensions. Disability data include pensions and compensation, and subsistence payments to disabled veterans undergoing training. Lump-sum payments are for burial of deceased veterans.

h. A small but unknown amount of lump-sum death payments included with monthly survivor payments. Disability benefits exclude payments for medical care. Data for 1952 preliminary.

i. Not available.

j. Benefits first payable in Rhode Island, April 1943; in California, December 1946; in New Jersey, January 1949; and in New York, July 1950. Includes maternity data for Rhode Island. Excludes hospital benefits in California and hospital, surgical and medical care benefits paid in lieu of cash benefits in New York. Number represents average weekly number of beneficiaries; excludes private plan beneficiaries in California and New Jersey.

k. Temporary disability benefits first payable July 1947; includes maternity data. Number represents average number of beneficiaries during 14-day registration period.

l. Average weekly number.

TABLE 201. CONTRIBUTIONS FOR SOCIAL INSURANCE BY EMPLOYERS AND EMPLOYEES, BY PROGRAM, 1940, 1950 AND 1952

(Millions)

Program	1940			1950			1952			
	Total	Employer	Employee	Total	Employer	Employee	Total	Employer	Employee	Self-Employed
Total	$2,201	$1,617	$584	$6,384	$3,853	$2,429	$8,213	$4,737	$3,107	$200
Retirement and survivors insurance [a]	1,176	635	540	4,796	2,424	2,372	6,333	3,089	3,044	200
Federal insurance contributions [b]	637	319	319	2,667	1,334	1,334	3,819	1,826	1,793	200
Taxes on carriers and their employees	130	65	65	546	273	273	636	318	318	—
Federal civil service contributions [c]	141	97	45	678	307	370	748	325	423	—
State and local government contributions [d]	267	155	112	905	510	395	1,130	620	510	—
Unemployment insurance	1,026	982	44	1,438	1,427	12	1,659	1,645	13	—
State unemployment contributions [e]	854	810	44	1,191	1,180	12	1,368	1,354	13	—
Federal unemployment taxes	105	105	—	224	224	—	266	266	—	—
Railroad unemployment insurance contributions [f]	67	67	—	23	23	—	25	25	—	—
State temporary disability insurance contributions [g]	—	—	—	149	2	46	221	2	50	—

Source: Social Security Bulletin, September 1951, Table 8, p. 27, and September 1953, Table 8, p. 27.

a. Permanent disability provisions included under railroad, federal civil service, and most state and local government retirement systems.

b. For 1952, on an estimated basis.

c. Under the Civil Service, Alaska Railroad, and Canal Zone Retirement Acts. Employer share represents government contributions, and employee share includes voluntary contributions.

d. Estimated by the Social Security Administration. Employer share represents government contributions.

e. Includes penalties and interest collected from employers. Allocation of contributions between employers and employees estimated.

f. For 1950 and 1952, covers also temporary disability insurance.

g. Beginning June 1942 in Rhode Island, May 1946 in California, June 1948 in New Jersey, and January 1950 in New York. Totals include state and private plans; data for New York and for private plans in California and New Jersey in totals only, not available separately.

$4,200 a year and would increase the maximum contribution rate to 4 per cent by 1975.

Future Costs

Estimates of the actual cost of old-age and survivors insurance vary, depending upon which assumptions are used as to future wage levels, size of the labor force, size of the population 65 and over, the number who retire and changes in mortality. The relative cost of the program — expressed as a percentage of payroll — depends, in addition, on general economic conditions, since contributions are more affected by changes in employment and payrolls than are benefits. Intermediate estimates prepared in 1950 and covering the law as amended in that year indicated that OASI benefits would cost 6.05 per cent of payroll on a level premium basis.[50] Estimates prepared in 1952 and covering the amendments enacted that year indicated an intermediate long-run benefit cost of 5.85 per cent of payroll. (Although the 1952 amendments liberalized the law, changes in the assumed interest rate and other basic factors reduced the cost estimate below that made for the 1950 law.) Allowance for administrative expenses brought the cost estimate up to 6 per cent of payroll. It is likely that the 1954 amendments will push the level premium cost up to between 7 and 8 per cent.

The long-run cost estimates vary too widely to support any definite conclusion about the self-sufficiency of the OASI program. There is little doubt, however, that the reserve will grow for many years; only under the most drastic set of assumptions would this not be true. Moreover, any lack of self-support showing up in the future can be remedied in advance by legislation.

Unresolved Issues

Despite the very sweeping nature of the recent revisions, several questions remain unanswered: (1) Is the reserve really a reserve? Even if it is a reserve, is it financially necessary and desirable? (2) Would not a flat-rate benefit to everyone at a certain age, say 65, be more equitable, easier to administer, and, in the long run, more economical? (3) What should be the ultimate relationship of government-sponsored pensions to the rapidly expanding private pension system in industry?

Discussion and experience in the next decade may serve to crystallize thinking about the reserve and the flat-rate benefit issue. The relationship of private to public old-age pensions appears to be settled for the present. To government goes the responsibility for the basic minimum protection against old-age dependency. It is conceded that government probably cannot provide more than a minimum benefit; therefore, comfort in old age can be provided only by private pensions or personal savings. In 1951 four and one half times as many people were covered by OASI as by private plans. The government system in 1951 paid eight times as much in benefits to ten times as many beneficiaries as did the private plans. (See Table 202.)

Proposals for further amendment of the old-age and survivors insurance program were presented to Congress in 1954. These included extension of coverage to about 10 million individuals (farmers and farm workers, self-employed professionals, additional domestic workers, civilian employees of the federal government not covered by a staff retirement plan, clergymen on a voluntary basis, and other small groups), liberalization of both benefit and retirement test provisions, protection of benefit rights of disabled persons, and raising the amount of annual earnings on which benefits and contributions are based from $3,600 to $4,200. There is little doubt that the proposed amendments will be enacted into law. The revisions called for reflect acceptance of the basic philosophy of old-age and survivors insurance as now embodied in the law. They are, however, only the immediate improvements desired by the Administration. Consequently, these proposals do not deal with the issues which involve the fundamental structure of the program.

Many other changes, major and minor, have been proposed by various individuals and groups. Four of them are:

(1) Permanent and total disability benefits to all persons covered under OASI at an estimated cost of from $200 million to $500 million a year or from 0.1 to 0.3 per cent of payroll.
(2) Hospitalization for all persons eligible for benefits under OASI at a cost of $200 to $300 million.

---

50. This is the long-run cost assuming equal payments during the lifetime of the plan into a reserve which is at all times large enough to meet liabilities when due. Contributions (premiums) may be level in terms of dollars or percentage of payroll. The "intermediate" estimate is merely the average of a "low" estimate and a "high" estimate, which is about one fourth above the "low"; it does not necessarily represent the most probable estimate.

TABLE 202. FINANCIAL POSITION OF PRIVATE PENSION PLANS AND
OLD-AGE AND SURVIVORS INSURANCE, 1950 AND 1951

	1950		1951	
	Private Pension Plans	OASI	Private Pension Plans	OASI
	(Billions)			
Contributions	$ 2.1	$ 2.7	$ 2.4	$ 3.4
Employer	1.7	1.3	1.9	1.7
Employee	.4	1.3	.5	1.7
Benefits paid	.2	1.0	.23	1.9
Persons over 65	a	.7	a	1.5
Dependents, widows	a	.3	a	.4
Pension reserves	10.2	13.7	11.8	15.5
	(Millions)			
Beneficiaries	.35	2.9	.4	4.0
65 and over	a	2.1	a	3.0
Under 65	a	.8	a	1.0
Number covered	8-9	35.0	9-10	45.0

Source: Bureau of Research and Statistics, Social Security Administration, 1952. Private pension plans include all formally established plans in industry, employer-initiated plans, and collectively bargained pension plans.   a. Not available.

(3) Added benefits (increment) to those who continue working beyond the age of 65.

(4) Extension of OASI protection to all persons at 65 regardless of their past employment history. The Chamber of Commerce of the United States recommended in 1953 (a) inclusion in old-age and survivors insurance of all persons 65 and over not already covered, at a minimum benefit of $25 a month, and (b) continuation of the then existing tax rate, despite the higher benefit outlay, in order to reduce the reserve and finance the program in the future on a pay-as-you-go basis. The Chamber also recommended complete withdrawal of the federal government from the public assistance program.[51]

Unemployment Insurance

Unemployment insurance is a state rather than a federal system. There are 51 different programs, including those of the District of Columbia and the territories. The basic law was passed by Congress as part of the Social Security Act in 1935. A federal tax of 3 per cent of payroll was levied on each employer with eight or more employees in certain industries, but the employer could offset up to 90 per cent of this tax by amounts paid in taxes to an acceptable state un-

51. "Federal Security Program for the Aged," Chamber of Commerce of the United States Referendum No. 93.

employment insurance program. By 1937, all the states had enacted acceptable laws. In addition to the offset device, the federal government exercises control over state plans by its financial control over the state administration. The tax of 0.3 per cent of payroll which cannot be offset goes directly into the United States Treasury as general revenue; it is not earmarked for any special purpose. In an entirely separate procedure, the state unemployment insurance agencies present their requests for administrative funds to the federal agency charged with supervising the program — currently the United States Department of Labor. This federal agency, after reviewing the state requests, and with the approval of the United States Bureau of the Budget, presents to Congress its estimate of the total administrative funds needed by the state agencies. Congress then appropriates annually the amount it deems sufficient and this total is distributed to the states by the United States Department of Labor in relation to the estimated needs of each state, without reference to the amounts of money raised by the 0.3 per cent tax from employers in the individual states.

The requirements of the federal law are not restrictive. So long as the states comply with

TABLE 203. SUMMARY DATA ON UNEMPLOYMENT INSURANCE OPERATIONS, 1950

Number of recipients (average weekly)	1,323,000
Number of claimants exhausting benefit rights	811,000[a]
Average potential duration of benefits	21 weeks[a]
Average actual duration of benefits	10 weeks
Average weekly benefit payment	$ 20.76
Total amount paid in benefits *(thousands)*	$1,373,426
Total taxes collected by states *(thousands)*	$1,191,438
Unemployment trust fund balance, December 1950 *(thousands)*	$6,972,295
Total taxes collected by federal government *(thousands)*	$ 226,000
Grants to states for state administration *(thousands)*	$ 177,671[a]
Salaries and expenses, Bureau of Employment Security *(thousands)*	$ 5,532[a]

Sources: *Social Security Bulletin,* September 1951, p. 29; *The Labor Market and Employment Security,* U.S. Department of Labor, February 1951, p. 32 and March 1951, p. 31; and *The Budget of the United States Government for the Fiscal Year Ending June 30, 1953.*

a. Fiscal year 1951.

these minimum requirements they are free to formulate their unemployment insurance laws as they choose. The state laws have much in common. Recent developments — experience rating [52] and increasingly critical examination of claims — reveal a definite trend toward private insurance concepts and tighter administration.

Since 1935, all 51 jurisdictions (the 48 states, the District of Columbia, Alaska and Hawaii) have adopted experience-rating provisions. High employment since 1940 and the rapid growth of the unemployment trust fund have encouraged the use of experience rating to reduce contribution rates and induce employers to stabilize employment. Opponents of experience rating continue to warn of the inherent danger of lowering the tax rate during prosperous years, and of placing the major share of the cost of unemployment upon the less stable industries.

Experience under Unemployment Insurance

In 1950 an average of 1.3 million unemployed persons each week received a total of $1.37 billion in benefits. The average beneficiary received just under $21 a week for about ten weeks. Benefits

exceeded taxes collected by the states by about $200 million, indicating the need of a reserve. Over 800,000 persons exhausted their benefits after an average of about 19 weeks and before finding other employment.[53] (See Table 203.) Between 1936 and June 1952, the states collected $16.4 billion in taxes. Interest credited to the reserve fund, from which all benefits are payable, amounted to $1.5 billion. In only two years did the fund decline — the fiscal years 1947 and 1948. Experience-rating laws throughout the United States limited actual tax collections by the states to 1.64 per cent of taxable payrolls in 1951. By 1952 the average weekly number of beneficiaries had declined to 874,000, while the average benefit rose to $22.79. Total benefit payments in that year amounted to $998 million. The Unemployment Insurance Trust Fund balance in June 1952 was $7.9 billion and by June 1953 had reached $8.6 billion.[54]

In addition to the portion of the payroll taxes retained by the states, the federal government collected $2.6 billion between 1936 and June 1952. During this period, the federal government distributed $1.7 billion to the states to administer

52. Experience rating refers to a method of varying the tax rate of individual employers above and below the standard rate specified in the state unemployment insurance law on the basis of some acceptable measure of the employer's experience with the risk of unemployment in his establishment. Employers in a state whose experience-rating provisions meet the rather simple requirements of the Social Security Act may be granted the full 90 per cent offset credit against the federal 3.0 per cent tax even though they are assigned a tax rate below 2.7 per cent under the state's experience-rating provisions.

53. The length of time during which benefits are paid varies from state to state. In some states, all eligible claimants are entitled to a uniform number of weeks of benefits, which varied from 12 weeks (Arizona) to 26 weeks in several states in 1950; in others the duration of benefits varies from claimant to claimant depending upon his previous employment record.

54. Ida C. Merriam, *Social Security Financing,* Bureau Report No. 17, Federal Security Agency, 1952, p. 61; *Social Security Bulletin,* September 1952, Table 4, p. 16, and September 1953, p. 2 and Table 5, p. 12.

their unemployment insurance programs [55] — leaving a net difference (or profit, as some states-rights protagonists insist) to the federal government of $900 million.

Proposals for liberalizing unemployment insurance laws, arising from diverse sources, may be summarized briefly:

(1) Federalize the entire unemployment insurance system to eliminate wide variation in costs, benefits, duration of benefits, and eligibility.

(2) Levy the federal tax on all employers having one or more employees (as under OASI).

(3) Increase benefits to re-establish the original standard of 50 per cent of average weekly wages. The recent average even on the $3,000 taxable base has been less than 40 per cent of wages.

(4) Extend the benefit period, which varies from state to state and among claimants within many states, to 26 weeks for all eligible claimants in all states. Over 20 per cent of claimants in 1950–1951 exhausted their benefits.

(5) Establish a basic minimum tax of 1.5 per cent, 0.3 per cent retained by the federal government as at present, the remaining 1.2 per cent retained by the state unemployment insurance reserve account. The purpose of this revision is to slow up the rapid accumulation of reserves, but at the same time to discourage all but a modest type of experience rating by limiting variations in taxes.

Railroad Social Insurance

Since its inception in 1937, social insurance for railroad workers has been an entirely separate system administered by the Railroad Retirement Board. It has become increasingly cumbersome and financially unwieldy as new types of benefits (unemployment, disability, survivors) have been added to the original retirement system.

In essential elements railroad social insurance is similar to the general social insurance program. Though railroad employees pay part of the cost, while unemployment insurance is noncontributory, benefits are related to the individual claimant's wages, and reserves are deposited with the United States Treasury.

Here, similarity ceases. In its details railroad social insurance differs markedly from the public program for people in other industries. While the average benefit under OASI in June 1953 was $45 a month, railroad retirement paid an average benefit of $81.[56] Wage and payroll taxes of 6.25 per cent levied upon both employer and

employee are paid into the United States Treasury, from which like amounts are appropriated to the Railroad Retirement Account. Hence a contribution rate of 12.5 per cent for railroad retirement must be compared to the 1954 rate of 4 per cent under OASI or to the proposed final rate of 8 per cent for OASI, effective in 1975. Railroad workers also have a permanent and total disability benefit, which OASI does not provide.

In 1950, total taxes paid under the railroad retirement system equaled $546 million; benefits amounted to $309 million. (See Tables 200 and 201.) Consequently, there was a net accumulation by the Railroad Retirement Account of $237 million plus interest during the year, bringing the total assets of this account to approximately $2,419 million at the end of the fiscal year. Beneficiaries receiving retirement and disability benefits in 1950 numbered 250,800; those receiving survivors benefits, 136,000.

The Railroad Retirement Act amendments of 1951, which raised existing benefits and provided payments to wives of retired railroaders, have created serious financial problems for the system. Whereas the benefit levels of the old law were within the level contribution of 12.5 per cent of payroll, the new benefit schedule would require a contribution rate of 14.43 per cent.

The railroad unemployment and temporary disability system is independent of both the railroad retirement system and the federal-state unemployment insurance system. By amendments in 1948, contributions to the Railroad Unemployment Insurance Account, then 3 per cent of annual wages up to $3,600, were placed on a sliding scale, rising or falling according to the amount in the reserve. When the account falls below $250 million the full tax of 3 per cent will be collected; when it exceeds $450 million the tax will be 0.5 per cent. The contribution rate has remained at the 0.5 per cent level, and interest payments have exceeded contributions.

Benefits of $60 million were paid to 77,000 unemployed railroad workers in 1950, as against 1940 figures of 41,500 beneficiaries receiving

---

55. Including administrative expenses of the state employment services but excluding administrative expenses of the federal government.

56. These averages are the amount of benefits per beneficiary; the figure for OASI covers retirement benefits—old-age, wife's and husband's benefits, and benefits to children of old-age beneficiaries; that for railroad retirement covers old-age and disability and includes spouse's annuities. The average old-age benefit alone under OASI was $50.42 in June 1953. *Social Security Bulletin,* September 1953, pp. 2 and 9.

TABLE 204. BENEFITS AND BENEFICIARIES UNDER STATE AND LOCAL
EMPLOYEE PENSION PLANS, 1940, 1950 AND 1952

(*Thousands*)

	1940		1950		1952	
	Benefits	*Benefi-ciaries*	*Benefits*	*Benefi-ciaries*	*Benefits*	*Benefi-ciaries*
Total	$141,500	—	$300,000	—	$390,000	—
Old-age retirement	103,000	113.0	230,000	213.0	300,000	250.0
Survivorship	16,000	25.0	26,000	40.0	30,000	44.0
Lump-sum payments	12,500	—	20,000	—	30,000	—
Disability	10,000	14.3	24,000	32.0	30,000	38.0

Source: Table 200 (see footnotes a and f).

$16 million. (See Table 200.) The reserve in the Railroad Unemployment Insurance Account in June 1951 was $766 million.

The most serious problem here is that raised by preferential treatment of the employees of one industry. Historical development explains the separate and more liberal social security program for railroad workers, but political expediency appears to be the only explanation for the continued separation of the railroad programs. From a financial viewpoint, the heavy contribution rate necessary to sustain the benefit structure adds materially to the cost of railroad operation and reacts unfavorably upon the competitive position of railroads as a means of transportation.

Other Social Insurance Systems

The social insurance systems for the employees of federal, state and local governments cover more than 5.4 million persons. For some years to come the number of beneficiaries receiving aid in disability and retirement will be larger than those aided by the programs of private employers.

State and Local Retirement Systems

Programs for policemen, firemen and school teachers were initiated by local governments. State retirement systems came later. By 1950, more than 64 per cent of the cities with populations of 10,000 or over either had retirement systems for their employees, or had their employees covered by a state-wide system.[57] At the outset,

most of the municipal social insurance systems were poorly financed. State systems frequently were designed as substitutes for bankrupt local programs.

Most state and local retirement systems are sound in structure, but dependent upon the consistency with which city and state legislative bodies vote the public contribution to the reserve. In the past, state and local governments have exhibited little enthusiasm for setting aside their own plans in favor of joining federal old-age and survivors insurance, since they have not been able to elect to join OASI so long as their employees are covered by or are eligible for membership in an existing system. This situation may change when the 1954 proposal to permit voluntary OASI coverage for such employees becomes effective. The lack of coordination between state and local plans and old-age and survivors insurance has created basic problems which can be dealt with only by fundamental changes in legislation.

During the decade between 1940 and 1950 the scope of state and local government pension plans nearly doubled. The amount of benefits in the form of old-age retirement, survivorship and disability pensions and lump-sum payments jumped from just over $140 million to $300 million. In 1952, $390 million was paid to an estimated 332,-000 monthly beneficiaries. (See Table 204.)

In 1940, employees of state and local governments formed the largest single group receiving retirement benefits. By 1950, this group was second only to the retired beneficiaries of the federal old-age and survivors insurance system.

---

57. Carl H. Chatters, "The Spread of Public Employee Retirement Plans," *Virginia Municipal Review,* September 1950.

TABLE 205. BENEFITS AND BENEFICIARIES UNDER FEDERAL EMPLOYEE
PENSION PLANS, 1940, 1950 AND 1952

(*Thousands*)

	1940		1950		1952	
	Benefits	Benefi-ciaries	Benefits	Benefi-ciaries	Benefits	Benefi-ciaries
Total	$122,007	95.7	$492,488	298.3	$608,950	371.8
Old-age retirement						
Federal civil service	49,069	47.4	135,267	111.0	175,616	128.3
Other federal contributory	714	.6	2,440	2.0	3,075	2.3
Federal noncontributory	53,308	32.2	148,600	68.0	190,525	84.7
Survivorship						
Federal civil service	—	—	8,409	18.3	19,986	40.0
Survivorship lump-sum payments						
Federal civil service	5,810	—	8,147	—	8,364	—
Other federal contributory	156	—	375	—	470	—
Disability						
Federal civil service	12,950	15.5	40,520	43.0	49,504	48.4
Federal noncontributory	—	—	148,730	56.0	161,410	68.1

Source: Table 200 (see footnotes a, b, d and e).

Federal Retirement Systems

The civil service retirement system and the nine other retirement systems for civilian employees of the federal government taken together were nearly as large in scope as the systems maintained by the state and local governments for their employees in 1940. Some of these federal retirement systems are contributory, others noncontributory. All the programs were established after World War I except the retirement system for the federal judiciary, which was organized in 1869. The civil service retirement system, a contributory pension plan, was inaugurated in 1920.

Federal civil service retirement, which covered 1.9 million employees as of January 1951, is comparable to a private industry pension plan in that the government participates as employer — not as sovereign. Many of the other federal retirement plans at the outset took the form of special incentives to promote employment in distant and dangerous places or occupations. Like other national retirement systems, the federal systems have grown substantially since 1940. Total outlays for retirement, survivorship and disability pensions and for lump-sum payments to survivors rose from $122 million in 1940 to nearly $500 mil-

lion in 1950, and the monthly number of beneficiaries rose from 96,000 to 298,300. By 1952 there were 371,800 beneficiaries a month and benefits totaled $609 million. (See Table 205.)

The most significant growth took place in the size of the civil service retirement system. In 1950, contributions to civil service retirement amounted to $678 million (over $307 million government, over $370 million employee), as compared with $141 million in 1940. (See Table 201.) But despite this tremendous increase, contributions to state and local retirement systems were considerably higher than in the federal systems for both 1940 and 1950 — $267 million in 1940 ($155 million government, $112 million employee) and $905 million in 1950 ($510 million government, $395 million employee).

Contributions to retirement systems of all governmental employees amounted to about three quarters of the sums paid by employers for private industry retirement plans. In terms of beneficiaries, however, retired public pensioners equaled retired private pensioners. If those receiving disability pensions are included, however, the number of public pensioners was perhaps 100,000 greater. The balance is expected to swing in favor of private industry pensioners as the newly organized systems mature.

Workmen's Compensation and Temporary Disability Systems

The oldest and the youngest social insurance programs — workmen's compensation and temporary disability — operate under state jurisdiction.

Workmen's compensation, providing cash benefits and medical care to employees disabled by accident or illness arising out of or in the course of employment, dates from the 1910–1914 period when the first state laws were tested for constitutionality. Today, all 48 states have workmen's compensation. But since these are state programs, there is wide variation as to financing, administration, coverage and benefit standards.[58] In 1951, workmen's compensation costs amounted to $710 million, including $233 million in medical care and $477 million in benefits paid to an untold number of injured workmen or their survivors. In 1952, benefit outlays totaled $787 million, including $260 million in medical payments.[59] There is no way to establish definitely the present coverage of workmen's compensation. Estimates range from 60 per cent to 90 per cent of the labor force. It is safe to say that not only is a substantial proportion of the work force not covered, but a large number of those presumably covered by law are not covered because of optional laws (in 28 states) and the ease of evasion.

Workmen's compensation laws are in a constant process of change,[60] usually in details rather than basic elements. Of state legislatures meeting in 1950–1951, 31 increased the level of benefits. Maximum benefits of $25 to $35 a week, in partial replacement of wages lost, are widespread. An increasing number of specific occupational diseases were added to the lists for which compensation would be paid, and new groups of employees were brought under several state laws.

The legislative program proposed by the National Association of Claimants Compensation Attorneys advocated as goals of future legislation: (1) increase of benefits to two thirds the average weekly wage without maximum limitation; (2) all-inclusive coverage, especially for occupational diseases, and extension to groups now excluded; (3) rights of the injured employees to third-party action [61] and action against the employer in cases of negligence without loss of rights to compensation; (4) adequate rehabilitation administered by the state but paid for by insurance companies.[62] Other proposals seek to tighten administration against fraud and against too liberal settlements for permanent partial disability.

The youngest social insurance program is temporary disability compensation. Loss of income due to illness generally has been accepted as one of the most serious economic risks. Only recently (1943) has public protection for income against loss from this source been available in the United States. Currently, four states maintain temporary disability programs: Rhode Island (1943), California (1946), New Jersey (1949) and New York (1950).[63] As with workmen's compensation, considerable variety exists in financing and administration. In general, benefits and eligibility parallel the standards set in the unemployment insurance laws of the separate states. Reports for the 1950 operation of disability compensation show that a weekly average of 51,400 persons got $89 million in benefits. In 1952, $165 million was paid to 75,000 weekly beneficiaries. Inclusion of the railroad temporary disability system in this calculation would increase benefits to $200 million and the average weekly number of beneficiaries to 106,000.[64]

PUBLIC ASSISTANCE

When the Social Security Law was enacted in 1935, there was full recognition of the gaps in coverage, the limited benefits, and the long period of time for a social insurance system, especially old-age insurance, to mature. To assure a meas-

---

58. There is no central fact-gathering or statistical agency for workmen's compensation. Indeed, many states are not fully aware of the extent of programs operating within their own borders. Statements, therefore, as to coverage, beneficiaries and total benefit payments are not very reliable.

59. *Social Security Bulletin*, December 1953, p. 22. These figures are more inclusive than those shown under social insurance benefits in Table 200.

60. *National Association of Claimants Compensation Attorneys Law Journal*, Vol. 8, 1951, pp. 251–257.

61. Legal action against a party, other than employer or employee, who is presumably at fault in the injury.

62. *National Association of Claimants Compensation Attorneys Law Journal*, pp. 248–249.

63. In these and in other states private industry health and welfare plans pay supplemental benefits, which are often higher than those required by state law.

64. Benefit estimates include maternity data for Rhode Island and exclude hospital benefits in California and hospital, surgical and medical benefits paid in lieu of cash in New York; estimates of number of beneficiaries exclude private plans in California and New Jersey.

TABLE 206. BENEFICIARIES AND EXPENDITURES UNDER PUBLIC
ASSISTANCE PROGRAMS, 1936, 1950 AND 1952

Program	Beneficiaries			Expenditures		
	1936	1950	1952	1936	1950	1952
	(Thousands)			(Millions)		
Total	1,655	5,026	4,669	$656.7	$2,369.4	$2,323.5
Old-age assistance	1,106	2,786	2,635	155.2	1,461.8	1,468.0
Aid to dependent children	404[a]	1,661[a]	1,495[a]	49.7	551.6	542.2
Aid to the blind	45	97	98	12.8	52.7	59.7
Aid to permanently and totally disabled	—	69	161	—	8.0	81.8
General assistance [b]	1,510	413	280	439.0	295.3	171.7

Source: *Social Security Bulletin*, September 1951, Table 37, p. 44, and September 1953, Table
41, p. 49.

a. Children only.

b. General assistance (or relief) is the locally administered needs-test program providing for
those who do not qualify for the special assistance programs. General assistance is financed
solely by local and state governments. The federal government participates in the special assistance
programs. Vendor payments for medical care excluded. Figures apply to cases, not to individual
recipients.

ure of economic security even for those who failed
to qualify for social insurance benefits, as well as
to plug the holes in the plans themselves, three
public assistance programs were formulated.
These covered special categories of needy persons
— the aged, dependent children and the blind.
In 1950, permanently and totally disabled persons
were added. These programs are financed jointly
by the federal and state governments according to
formulas which result in the federal government's paying an average of 45 per cent of the
whole; they are state-administered programs. Finally, to fill gaps left by these special assistance
programs is general assistance — the last defense
against destitution.

The common characteristic of all assistance
programs is the needs test. In order to qualify,
an individual must be in need according to
whatever definition of need a state adopts. In
general, need is defined as a budgetary deficiency,
that is, the individual or family income is insufficient to purchase a minimum subsistence
which is described in terms of articles and their
cost. The needs test is looked upon as a humiliat-
ing procedure to be avoided except as a last resort.

The development of the assistance programs
has exceeded estimates made in 1935, when assistance was considered a temporary program, certain to diminish as social insurance took hold.
Except for the general assistance program, the

number of beneficiaries and annual expenditures
rose sharply between 1936 and 1950. Payments to
5 million recipients in 1950 amounted to $2.4
billion — a marked increase over 1936, when 1.7
million recipients received $657 million. Al-
though the number of dollars paid remained
practically constant between 1950 and 1952, the
number of recipients declined by nearly 400,000,
despite substantial increases in aid to the permanently and totally disabled, which became
effective in 1950. (See Table 206.)

The most striking increases in assistance came
between 1936 and 1940, the years when general relief and work relief declined. Average
monthly benefit payments increased from about
$25 in 1936 to $45 in 1950 (with an average
of $71.44 per family in the programs of aid to
dependent children). As a consequence of the
1950 and 1952 revisions in old-age and survivors
insurance, in which coverage was extended and
benefits raised, the rise in the number of recipients and amount of benefit payments under old-
age assistance was checked. However, the change
has been small and, even though the 1954 revisions in OASI are likely to extend coverage to
about 10 million additional individuals, the
future course is uncertain.

Despite the rise in population and price increases since 1936, and the increases in the special assistance programs, relief and assistance of

all types, general and special, have declined since 1936. In 1936, there were 3.7 million provided for through works programs, who received $2.4 billion of benefits in the form of wages. From 1936 to 1950, owing to the decline in relief work, the total burden of relief, relief work and assistance fell 20 per cent, from $3.1 billion to $2.4 billion.[65]

Public assistance seems to be a necessary form of income maintenance in the social security structure. The maturing and extension of the social insurance program may gradually reduce the importance of the assistance programs. In magnitude, social insurance was in 1952 three times as important as assistance. Total expenditures through social insurance amounted to $7.8 billion. Public assistance, including general assistance and vendor payments for medical care, amounted to $2.6 billion.

Numerous issues continue to crop out in charting the course of public assistance. Should the federal government assume a greater share of public assistance payments by changing the formula to favor states with low per capita income? Should the federal government impose more rigid controls on the states, in order to establish greater equality throughout the nation, as the price of continued federal aid? Should the federal government get out of the assistance business altogether?[66]

MATERNAL AND CHILD HEALTH AND CHILD WELFARE SERVICES

A minor provision of the Social Security Act authorized the federal government to make grants-in-aid to states for maternal and child health and for child welfare services. These grants help pay for medical service to expectant mothers, hygiene service to infants, public health nursing service, immunizations, dental inspections, midwife supervision and services to crippled children. Expenditures for these services in the fiscal year 1949–1950 amounted to $28.8 million for maternal and child health care and $3.8 million for child welfare. Under the 1950 amendments, maximum federal grants for maternal and child health services were increased

from $11 million to $16.5 million, grants for services to crippled children from $7.5 million to $15 million, and grants for child welfare from $3.5 million to $10 million.[67]

MISCELLANEOUS PROGRAMS

Federal, state and local governments in 1950 spent about $510 million for grants-in-aid and services for vocational rehabilitation, institutional and other care, school lunch programs and child welfare. In the fiscal year 1951–1952 the total expenditure for these programs amounted to $679 million.[68]

These items for the most part are self-explanatory. Vocational rehabilitation is a state program supplemented by federal funds, designed to restore disabled persons to self-supporting employment. It received strong support following World Wars I and II, and now seems to have been established as an aid to injured employees and older workers. The 1950 expenditure was about $30 million.

Experience in the decades preceding 1930 brought public institutional care into disrepute. The Social Security Act, through the special assistance programs, sought to eliminate dependence upon institutional care. Nevertheless, both the federal and the several state governments have found certain types of institutional care indispensable. In 1950, about $349 million was spent on institutions such as (federal) the Columbia Institute for the Deaf, the United States Soldiers Home, the U.S. Naval Home and (state and local) institutions for chronic disease, for the handicapped and the aged. Domiciliary care of veterans also is included.

The school lunch program, which cost about $126 million in 1950, is a federal government program designed, on the one hand, to relieve farmers of surplus commodities at market prices and, on the other, to subsidize hot noonday meals for children in the public schools.

The Social Security Act authorized the federal government to make grants-in-aid to states to establish child welfare services for the protection of homeless, dependent and neglected children, and children in danger of becoming delinquent,

---

65. *Social Security Bulletin*, September 1951, p. 43. The figure cited for 1950 includes vendor payments for medical care, i.e., direct payments by relief agencies to doctors, hospitals, etc., for medical care of relief recipients.

66. The Chamber of Commerce of the United States so recommended in 1953. See p. 452.

67. A. J. Altmeyer, *Collier's Year Book, 1950*, New York, 1951, p. 582.

68. *Social Security Bulletin*, September 1953, Table 3, p. 23. The 1950 total and the figures for each program that follow are averages of expenditures during fiscal years 1949–1950 and 1950–1951.

TABLE 207. TOTAL BENEFITS PAID TO VETERANS BY JUNE 30, 1950, AND NUMBER OF VETERANS
AND DEPENDENTS PAID BENEFITS DURING YEAR ENDING JUNE 30, 1950

War	Cumulative Totals to June 30, 1950		Year Ending June 30, 1950	
	Benefits to Veterans	Benefits to Dependents	Living Veterans or Dependents	Deceased Veterans or Dependents
	(Millions)			
Total	$25,334.4 [a, b]		2,368,238	658,123
Revolutionary War	70.0 [a]		—	—
War of 1812	14.0	32.2	—	—
Mexican War	28.7	33.0	—	24
Indian Wars	57.6	47.6	530	1,799
Civil War	8,162.6 [a]		15	11,132
Spanish-American War	2,381.0	570.8	91,984	79,624
Regular establishment	353.0	113.2	53,765	17,470
World War I	6,042.0	1,769.5	520,925	284,110
World War II	4,610.1	1,032.6	1,701,019	263,964

Source: Annual Report, 1950, Administrator of Veterans Affairs, Table 45.
a. Total benefits paid to veterans and dependents.
b. Includes $16.5 million of unclassified payments.
Note: Benefits in this table do not include subsistence payments to veterans in school or readjustment allowances.

with special attention to rural children. About $5 million was spent on this program in 1950.

VETERANS BENEFITS

Veterans of American wars numbered about 19 million in 1950, or 40 per cent of the adult male population of the United States. With their dependents, they accounted for more than one third of the total population.

The Veterans Administration estimated in 1954 that there would be roughly 80 million veterans and persons in their families by 1960 — about 24 million veterans, 53.5 million wives, children and other dependents, and 2.5 million survivors of deceased veterans.[69] Thus in 1960 nearly half the total population appears likely to consist of veterans or dependents of veterans.

Even in 1950, the expenditure for veterans benefits of all types — pension and disability benefits, readjustment allowances, vocational rehabilitation, payments made to veterans from National Service Life Insurance, and educational benefits under the G.I. Bill — was $7.2 billion.[70]

69. Unpublished estimates of the Research Division, U.S. Veterans Administration.
70. Cf. Table 193, transfer payments — derived from 1951 National Income Supplement to the Survey of Cur-

This was equal to two thirds the total federal, state and local expenditures for education, somewhat greater than benefits paid under all social insurance, and almost three times as large as public assistance payments.

And this is just the beginning. History indicates that, as the average age of the veterans increases, public payments to them increase. Benefits and services provided because of service-connected disabilities are extended to nonservice disabilities. Furthermore, as benefits and services are made available not only to the veteran himself, but to his dependents, the program gradually spreads and provides a duplicate set of benefits and services to an increasing segment of the population. Finally, the patriotic fervor supporting veterans benefits apparently requires that veterans programs, even those based on need, provide a higher standard of benefit and service with milder eligibility requirements than do welfare programs for civilians.

Though current annual payments are huge, the cumulative totals of past wars are equally impressive. By June 30, 1950, over $25 billion had been paid out in benefits to veterans of past wars

rent Business, Table 36, p. 201, and Social Security Bulletin, February 1953, Table 1, p. 8.

TABLE 208. VETERANS BENEFITS PAYMENTS AND BENEFICIARIES, 1940 AND 1950 [a]

Type of Benefit	Benefits		Beneficiaries	
	1940	1950	1940	1950
	(Millions)		(Thousands)	
Total [a]	$424.5	$4,612.4	—	—
Pensions and compensation [b]	423.5	2,223.8	933.3	3,347.0
Readjustment allowances	—	34.7	—	33.6
Welfare and other [c]	1.0	359.6	[d]	[d]
Subsistence allowances	—	1,596.0	—	[d]
State veterans benefits	—	398.3	—	[d]

Sources: Pensions and compensation and readjustment allowances from Table 200. Other estimates are averages of successive fiscal year figures from *Social Security Bulletin,* February 1953, Table 1, p. 8, and October 1953, Table 1, p. 14; these estimates include some administrative costs.

a. Excludes health and medical services, tuition payments and dividends on National Service Life Insurance; includes some administrative costs. Beneficiaries are average monthly number.

b. Includes burial awards.

c. Vocational rehabilitation, specially adapted homes and autos for disabled veterans, counseling, beneficiaries' travel and domiciliary care.

d. Not available.

and their survivors. Civil War benefits amounted to $8.2 billion. (See Table 207.) By June 30, 1953, payments to World War I and World War II veterans and their survivors had substantially exceeded the total Civil War payments, reaching $9.8 billion and $9.4 billion respectively.[71]

During the year 1950, 3.4 million veterans or dependents a month drew benefits, designated as compensation, allowances or pensions. There were a million each month in 1940. Two thirds of these recipients in 1950 received payments for service-connected losses or disability; about 700,000 of them received benefits for non-service-connected permanent and total disability while in need. Disability payments amounted to $1.7 billion in 1950, but only $0.3 billion in 1940. Monthly benefits ranged from an average of $156.50 for Spanish-American War veterans to an average of $48 for World War II veterans. Unemployment and self-employment allowances, not available to World War I veterans, amounted to $34.5 million. Total veterans benefits of $4.6 billion in 1950 (exclusive of health and medical service and National Service Life Insurance) were more than ten times all benefits paid in 1940.[72] (See Table 208.)

71. *Annual Report, 1953,* Administrator of Veterans Affairs, pp. 191–195.

72. For a discussion of educational, hospital and medical benefits available to veterans and their dependents, see Chapters 10 and 12.

The important issues raised by the present veterans program are obvious. Should income-maintenance benefits be provided in excess of benefits under public programs available to civilians, especially if civilian benefits approximate minimum need? Can veteran and civilian programs be integrated into one comprehensive social security program? Should benefits and services be available for those with non-service-connected disabilities, and should dependents be eligible for benefits and services? Future costs of veterans benefits, subject to increase even under present rules, will to a large extent be determined by whether or not veterans programs can be integrated with the welfare programs established for the general population.

GOALS OF PUBLIC WELFARE

At the close of 1950, public welfare had four goals. First, and basic, was income maintenance for those whose income was cut off or reduced because of the hazards of industry. Second, the goal of economic assistance to special disadvantaged groups, such as the aged, dependent children, the blind and the disabled, and also to others who for unspecified reasons are in need. Third, the goal of providing income, medical services and loans to disabled veterans, veterans in need and veterans who could improve their status by education or financial assistance. Finally, the goal of exploring new needs, integrating diverse welfare programs, encouraging general consideration of special welfare problems of important elements in the population, for example, children, youth and the aged.

Implementing these goals in most instances has required action by federal and state legislatures. The degree to which these goals have been met can be appraised only by comparing concrete proposals with legislative action.

Social Insurance [73]

The goals of social insurance may be summarized as follows: (1) complete coverage of all workers as a means of (a) helping families to help themselves in times of economic stress and (b) preventing the loss of benefits because of job changes or fortuitous circumstances such as working for employers with too few employees or in noncovered industries; (2) increased benefit levels to maintain a stable relationship with wages and living costs.

Legislative action in 1950 and 1952, as well as the President's 1954 proposals, reaffirmed the belief in the value of social insurance. State and federal legislatures generally have acted to increase benefits for all types of social insurance. Except for old-age and survivors insurance, in which coverage was extended to 10 million more workers in 1952 (and probably will be extended to a like number by the 1954 amendments), little effort has been made to increase the coverage of social insurance. The flurry of interest in temporary disability insurance of the 1945–1950 period apparently died with the passage of the Disability Benefits Law in New York State in 1949. Widespread interest in permanent and total disability coverage produced numerous legislative proposals but no action. Increased appropriations were made by Congress and state legislatures for rehabilitation work among the aged and the disabled. Gaps in coverage, unmet risks, and benefits well below locally determined minimum subsistence levels of living characterized the social insurance systems of the United States at the beginning of the 1950–1960 decade.

The 1952 annual conference of the International Labor Organization in Geneva adopted a Convention on minimum standards of social security.[74] (See Table 209.) Though the Convention gives general guidance in the establishment of public welfare goals, the specific standards prescribed are *minimum* standards. Present American practices equal or exceed these standards, except that this country lacks a program of family allowances and benefits paid, when expressed as a percentage of average wages, fall below both the commonly accepted American standards and the minimum standards promulgated by the International Labor Organization. The failure of state governments to adjust maximum benefit limits as wage levels rise is responsible for the lag of practice behind standards. For example, workmen's compensation benefits in New York State are fixed by law at 66.6 per cent of average wages. However, in 1952, benefits were limited by law to a maximum of $32 a week for disability. Average weekly earnings of wage earners in New York State in manufacturing were $68.77 for September 1952.[75] Hence, benefits averaged about 47 per cent of the average weekly wage.

The International Labor Organization standards suggest minimum coverage of 50 per cent of all employees or 20 per cent of all residents; benefit standards average 45 per cent of the average weekly wage up to the average earnings of a skilled worker; standards for the duration of benefits vary, but specify 26 weeks for sickness and 13 weeks for unemployment. These, it must he emphasized, are minimum standards.

Public Assistance

Many proposals have been advanced for improving the public assistance program. The most commonly recommended are inclusion of new groups of dependents, adjustment of the federal program to meet medical care costs and family services costs, and adjustment of the grants-in-aid formula to aid low-income states. The trends toward state and federal financing of assistance and toward assistance for special groups rather than general assistance are well recognized.

In 1950 and again in 1952, Congress adjusted the public assistance program. An assistance program for the disabled was established similar to the programs for the aged, the blind and

---

73. These goals have been stated by the Advisory Council on Social Security in its Report to the Senate Committee on Finance, by spokesmen for the Social Security Administration.

74. Convention 102, Social Security (Minimum Standards Convention, 1952).

75. *Labor Market Review*, State of New York Department of Labor, October 1952, p. S-3.

TABLE 209. SUMMARY OF CONVENTION ON MINIMUM STANDARDS OF SOCIAL SECURITY OF THE INTERNATIONAL LABOR ORGANIZATION, 1952

Branch	Contingencies Provided For	Coverage [a]	Qualifying Conditions	Amount of Benefits [b]	Duration of Benefits
Medical care	For covered person and his wife and children, all morbid conditions and pregnancy.	50% of all employees, or 20% of all residents.[c]	Period of contributions, employment or residence.[d]	General practitioner care, specialist care at hospitals,[e] hospitalization and essential medicines; maternity care by midwife at least.	26 weeks in each case of morbid condition, or if longer during payment of sickness benefit (also longer for prescribed diseases requiring prolonged care).[f]
Sickness benefit	Incapacity for work due to sickness and resulting loss of earnings.	50% of all employees, or 20% of all residents.	Period of contributions, employment or residence.[d]	45% for man, wife and 2 children.	26 weeks in each case, with 3-day waiting period.[g]
Unemployment benefit	Loss of earnings due to unemployment if able to work.	50% of all employees.	Period of contributions, employment or residence.[d]	45% for man, wife and 2 children.	13 weeks in a 12-month period, with 7-day waiting period.[h]
Old-age benefit	Age 65[i] and retirement.	50% of all employees, or 20% of all residents.	A. 30 years of contributions or employment, 20 years of residence, or where all gainfully occupied are covered, yearly average of contributions.[j, k] B. 10 years of contributions or employment, or 5 years of residence.[k]	A. 40% for man and wife of pensionable age. B. 30% for man and wife of pensionable age.	For life, but may be subject to suspension on account of employment, and in a non-contributory system may be subject to a means test.

(Continued on page 464)

TABLE 209 (continued)

Branch	Contingencies Provided For	Coverage[a]	Qualifying Conditions	Amount of Benefits[b]	Duration of Benefits
Employment injury benefit	Morbid conditions resulting from employment, and resulting loss of earnings.	50% of all employees.	Employed at time of injury.	Complete medical care.[l] For both incapacity for work and invalidity, 50% for man, wife and 2 children; for survivors, 40% for widow and 2 children.[m]	Medical care as long as needed. For incapacity for work and invalidity, unlimited duration, with 3-day waiting period for incapacity for work; for survivor benefits, same duration as in that branch.
Family allowances	Responsibility for maintenance of children.	50% of all employees, or 20% of all residents.	3 months of contributions or employment, or 1 year of residence.	Cash payments and payments in kind.[n]	During childhood.[o]
Maternity benefit	Pregnancy and confinement for female workers and wives of male workers; in addition, for female workers, resulting loss of earnings.	50% of all employees, or 20% of all residents.	Period of contributions, employment or residence.[d]	45% for female worker; medical care same as in that branch.	Medical care as long as needed; cash benefits for 12 weeks.
Invalidity benefit	Presumably permanent invalidity, with inability to engage in any gainful activity to a prescribed extent.	50% of all employees, or 20% of all residents.	A. 15 years of contributions or employment, 10 years of residence, or where all gainfully occupied are covered, yearly average of contributions.[j,k] B. 5 years of contributions, employment or residence.[k]	A. 40% for man, wife and 2 children. B. 30% for man, wife and 2 children.	For duration of invalidity, but not when sickness or old-age benefit payable.

| Survivor benefit | Presumed incapacity of widow and orphan children for self-support. | 50% of all employees, or 20% of all residents. | A. 15 years of contributions or employment, 10 years of residence, or where all gainfully occupied are covered, yearly average of contributions.[j,k]

 B. 5 years of contributions, employment, or residence.[k] Additional requirements for widow without children.[p] | A. 40% for widow and 2 children.

 B. 30% for widow and 2 children. | For children, during childhood;[o] for widow until remarriage. Benefit may be subject to suspension, as in old-age branch. |

Source: Social Security Bulletin, October 1952, p. 6.

a. Percentages indicated are a measurement of the minimum coverage permissible. Where percentages relate to all residents, such coverage is to be obtained from selected classes of gainfully occupied persons (with benefits also available to their wives and children). Alternatively, for all branches except medical care, employment injury, and maternity, the system may cover all residents, subject to a means test. Underdeveloped countries may temporarily cover groups making up at least 50 per cent of employees in firms of 20 or more employees.

b. For cash benefits other than family allowances, percentages shown relate either (1) to individual average earnings (up to prescribed maximum of the earnings of a typical skilled male worker) or (2) to a flat benefit, based on the prescribed proportion of earnings of a typical unskilled male worker. As an alternative, for plans with a needs test, covering all residents, benefits must be determined from a fixed scale, but from such amount there may be deducted means of the family in excess of a substantial amount (but total of benefit and means taken into account must be sufficient to maintain in health and decency and must at least equal benefit under 2); however, lower individual benefits may be provided under the branches for sickness, old-age, invalidity or survivor benefits if aggregate paid is at least 30 per cent higher than would have been paid under system covering 20 per cent of the population and paying flat benefits as in 2.

c. As a further alternative, where based on selected classes of residents, total persons protected (including wives and children) must be 50 per cent of all residents.

d. Sufficiently long, considering the scope of the system, to prevent abuse.

e. Also specialist care outside hospitals if available.

f. As temporary exception for underdeveloped countries, 13 weeks in each case.

g. As temporary exception for underdeveloped countries, either 13 weeks with 3-day waiting period, or such period as will result in benefits paid for an average of 10 days per year per person covered.

h. Duration of 26 weeks required for systems covering all residents, subject to a means test. For systems covering employees under which duration of benefit varies with contributions and previous benefits, average duration must be 13 weeks. Special conditions are permitted in regard to seasonal workers.

i. Higher age is permitted if fixed by competent authority with due regard to working ability of elderly persons.

j. Reduced benefits must be available (1) when a yearly average of contributions is required, if half the requirement for full benefits is met; (2) for old-age branch, if there have been 15 years of contributions or employment; and (3) invalidity and survivor branches, if there have been 5 years of contributions or employment.

k. The conditions of paragraph A apply for the benefit rate of paragraph A of the next column. Likewise, the conditions of paragraph B apply for the benefit rate of paragraph B. For qualifying periods falling between those of paragraphs A and B, the benefit rate is determined proportionately.

l. As temporary exception, underdeveloped countries may provide same medical care as in medical care branch.

m. Provisions to be made for permanent partial disability at lower benefit rates. Lump-sum payments may be made in lieu of periodic benefits in certain cases.

n. Aggregate payments must be at least either (1) 3 per cent of the wage of an unskilled male worker times the number of children of persons protected or (2) 1 1/2 per cent of such wage times the number of children of all residents.

o. Children are defined as being under age 15, or under school-leaving age if that age is lower.

p. Specified length of marriage.

dependent children. The 1952 grants-in-aid formula requires the federal government to pay $20 of the first $25 and $15 of the next $30 a month paid to the recipient. The law was changed to permit the use of federal funds for persons confined to public as well as to private medical institutions.

Veterans Benefits

There is every indication that veterans will continue to be a favored group for welfare purposes. Not only do they receive general protection against dependency, but also special consideration is accorded their dependents and survivors. Veterans themselves are entitled to education at government expense, aid in purchasing homes or businesses, and life insurance at special rates. Although a few individuals foresee difficulties in the future when veterans in large numbers are entitled to differential benefits from welfare, in general the goal of special consideration is accepted.

Veterans legislation in 1952 extended World War II G.I. benefits to veterans of the Korean War. Korean veterans are eligible for service-connected disability compensation, for pensions (granted for non-service-connected disability if in need), for dependents allowances, for educational and unemployment benefits, and for loans for housing and business. There has been little interest in the social and economic problems inherent in this separate welfare system. In his veto message on Public Laws 356 and 357, President Truman summarized the dilemma of veterans benefits:

. . . our first obligation to our veterans is to care for those who have disabilities resulting directly from their service to their country. Financial assistance to veterans with non-service-connected disabilities, on the other hand, should be put as soon as possible on the same basis as financial assistance payable to the nonveterans of our population.

World War II left us with over 19 million veterans. World events since then mean that hundreds of thousands more will be added each year. At the same time, we have expanded and perfected our social security laws so that they now protect most of our people. The consequences are obvious. Thousands upon thousands of veterans and their families have entitlement to government payments under both laws. This is confusing, wasteful, and, to many people, hard to understand.[76]

76. *Conference Board Business Record,* National Industrial Conference Board, New York, September 1952, p. 359.

Summary

Many other proposals for the improvement of the public welfare structure are highly controversial. They could be described only as the goals of special groups — not as objectives of organized society as a whole. Other goals, while generally accepted, are recognized for many reasons only as distant possibilities. Consequently, stating public welfare goals raises peculiar problems not found in private welfare. The definition of private welfare goals can be stated clearly; their implementation is limited primarily by lack of money, professional personnel and facilities. Public welfare, on the other hand, is a victim of conflicting philosophies of government and of pressure politics. Nevertheless, as one looks toward the future, past trends outline the respective roles and the magnitude of public and private welfare.

In 1950, the roles of public and private welfare might be described in the following terms: Public welfare was allotted the primary income maintenance functions, to be performed so far as possible through social insurance. Assistance for special groups of dependents would be necessary until social insurance could be extended to cover all workers and risks. Perhaps special assistance would be required permanently. At the least, however, it was expected that general welfare (relief) soon would be unnecessary. The need for public welfare might be stated as the extension of social insurance to cover all wage and salary employees and the self-employed for all clearly definable risks, and the lifting of benefit levels to provide a reasonable proportion of wage loss.

To private welfare was allotted responsibility for counseling service, family adjustment, group work and the care of individuals and families whose problems were only partially economic. From private welfare was expected leadership, coordination of public and private activity, and experimentation.

It would be impossible to state the need for private welfare services in quantitative terms. How much counseling is necessary to prevent separations and divorce? How much group work is needed to prevent juvenile delinquency? How much coordination of private and public efforts is necessary to prevent wasted effort? How much research is needed to find better means of meeting the welfare needs of America?

Between the extremes of the public and private welfare functions, industrial welfare programs find a middle ground. Health, welfare and pension plans have grown up because of the absence or inadequacy of public social insurance and the need for greater flexibility in meeting needs arising from special circumstances. At present, private group insurance is supplementary to social insurance. Private plans also are adventuring into the provision of services in addition to their primary function of replacing wage loss.

NEEDS AND EXPENDITURES IN 1950 AND 1960

Welfare expenditures — as defined for this chapter — are likely to grow from $16.9 billion in 1950 to $23.0 billion in 1960 (at 1950 prices). The lion's share of the increase, $5.2 billion, is looked for in the social insurance programs, particularly old-age and survivors insurance. Welfare outlays in 1950 fell some $3.6 billion short of the amount deemed necessary to meet desired goals and are expected to be $1.8 billion below the "needed" level in 1960. (See Table 210.)

Private Welfare

Although private welfare outlays are expected to rise about one third, from $4.5 billion to $6.1 billion (at 1950 prices), health, welfare and pension plans of private industry seem likely to expand by about 50 per cent during the 1950–1960 decade. Trends in individual and private philanthropic giving since World War II, especially in contributions to community chests, indicate a probable increase of about 10 per cent in such expenditures during the decade.

Needs for private welfare have been set equal to actual and projected outlays. It seems reasonable to take as a welfare goal for the 1950–1960 decade the development as needed and wherever economically practicable of health, welfare and pension plans in private industry. These plans, however, may be considered as something more than a minimum-needs program, supplementing the basic protection afforded by the public social insurance program. Consequently, needed outlays for this purpose may be taken as equal to actual and projected outlays. In the case of private philanthropy, the goal of a minimum-needs program would include extension to towns and rural neighborhoods of counseling, family adjustment

services and group work now available in cities, and the development of leadership. Since any quantitative statement of such a goal would have to be arbitrary, no specific increase over actual and probable outlays could be chosen to express needs in dollar terms.

Public Welfare

Public welfare outlays are expected to rise from over $12 billion in 1950 to nearly $17 billion in 1960 (at 1950 prices). Increases in expenditures under all social insurance programs are likely to more than make up for declines in outlays for public assistance and veterans programs.

Except for the workmen's compensation and veterans programs, the estimates of probable and needed public welfare expenditures are based on the analysis in Chapter 18. Probable social insurance outlays for 1960 represent expenditures under systems existing in 1950, with allowance for the maturing of these systems, likely expansion of coverage, and increases in benefit levels sufficient to maintain their relation to wage levels. Allowance has also been made for the establishment of a permanent disability insurance program during the decade. Needed outlays differ from actual and probable only in that they are based on full coverage of the labor force. Probable 1960 outlays for workmen's compensation are estimated to rise 14 per cent over 1950 outlays, along with growth of the labor force; needed outlays, at a level equal to 66 per cent of average wages, would be about 25 per cent higher than actual 1950 expenditures and the same percentage above probable 1960 expenditures.

Expansion of some social insurance programs is bound to affect others. For example, probable 1960 outlays under old-age and survivors insurance are based on the assumption that 15 per cent of federal and 25 per cent of state and local employees would come under that program, while needed 1960 outlays are based on the assumption that state and local employee coverage would expand to 50 per cent. Under these assumptions government employees would be protected by old-age and survivors insurance as well as by their own independent systems and, consequently, needed 1950 and 1960 outlays under public retirement systems are estimated lower than they would be if these systems were to provide full coverage for government workers.

The decline projected for probable 1960 public

TABLE 210. ESTIMATED NEEDED WELFARE EXPENDITURES COMPARED WITH
ACTUAL 1950 AND PROBABLE 1960 EXPENDITURES [a]
(*Millions at 1950 Prices*)

Program	1950		1960	
	Actual	*Needed*	*Probable*	*Needed*
Total [b]	$16,911	$20,521	$22,950	$24,750
Private welfare	4,526	4,526	6,100	6,100
Philanthropy	1,722	1,722	1,900	1,900
Industry programs	2,804	2,804	4,200	4,200
Public welfare	12,385	15,995	16,850	18,650
Social insurance	4,744	8,950	9,950	11,850
Old-age and survivors insurance	1,176	3,000	4,400	4,800
Railroad retirement [c]	313	410	600	600
Public employee retirement [d]	833	1,120	1,400	1,200
Permanent disability insurance	—	500	500	800
Temporary disability insurance [e]	137	1,040	500	1,200
Unemployment insurance [f]	1,620	2,050	1,800	2,300
Workmen's compensation	665	830	750	950
Assistance	2,586	1,900	2,300	2,100
Veterans programs [g]	4,545	4,545	4,000	4,000
Other [h]	510	600	600	700

Sources: Actual expenditures for 1950: private welfare, Table 192; public welfare, average of outlays during fiscal years 1949–1950 and 1950–1951, *Social Security Bulletin,* October 1953, Table 1, p. 14. For other figures see text discussion.

a. Figures include administrative costs.
b. Excludes public health and medical services, allowance for which is made in Chapter 10.
c. Includes railroad permanent disability insurance.
d. Includes pensions to regular military personnel.
e. General and railroad programs combined; includes privately administered plans.
f. General and railroad programs combined; includes employment service administrative expenditures.
g. Includes subsistence allowances to veterans attending schools; excludes other payments for education and veterans life insurance payments.
h. Vocational rehabilitation (nonveteran), child welfare services, school lunch program and institutional care.

assistance outlays and the use of needs estimates below actual or probable expenditures for public assistance reflect the assumed expansion of social insurance programs. As the retirement and survivorship programs mature and expand, fewer individuals will need relief assistance and those who do should need lower amounts.

Welfare payments to veterans are expected to decline slightly between 1950 and 1960. Although pensions and compensation undoubtedly will rise — as a result of the growing and aging veteran population — federal readjustment allowances, educational subsistence payments, vocational rehabilitation and related services, and outlays by states and localities all are likely to be lower in 1960 than in 1950. By the 1951–1952 fiscal year they had already dropped appreciably below 1950 levels.[77]

77. See *Social Security Bulletin,* October 1953, Table 1, p. 14.

## PART III

CAPITAL REQUIREMENTS

## CHAPTER 15

PRIVATE PRODUCTIVE FACILITIES

PRODUCTIVE FACILITIES are the structures, plant, machinery and equipment used to produce goods and services. This basic nucleus of capital goods comprises mining and manufacturing facilities; construction machinery; plant and equipment for providing transportation, communication, electricity and gas services; and commercial and nonresidential agricultural structures and equipment. The term, as used here, excludes *developmental works,* such as highways and sewage disposal systems, and *consumer construction,* such as houses and schools. Private productive facilities, which make up the bulk of all productive facilities, include only those capital goods that are privately owned; excluded are, for example, publicly owned military and naval plant and equipment, transit lines and utilities. Private productive facilities in recent years accounted for about three fifths of annual expenditures for all capital goods, including military and naval.

FACTORS AFFECTING CAPITAL EXPENDITURES

Demand for productive facilities and most other kinds of capital goods is unlike that for consumption goods, which results from the pressure of continuing human wants supported by adequate purchasing power. Outlays for productive facilities can be postponed for a considerable time in a way that consumer expenditures for food, medical care and other necessities cannot. Moreover, outlays for productive facilities are usually made only after careful deliberation, and involve a formality of decision not usually present in day-to-day expenditures.

All of this accounts for the fact that the demand for productive facilities varies greatly from year to year, and bears a much more indirect relationship than consumption outlays to size of population, income and standard of living. Demand for facilities arises not so much as a reflection of steady sustained consumption as from changes in

TABLE 211. OUTLAYS FOR PRIVATE PRODUCTIVE FACILITIES AS PER CENT OF OUTLAYS FOR ALL CAPITAL GOODS[a] AND GROSS NATIONAL PRODUCT, 1920–1952

| Year | Per Cent of: | |
	All Capital Goods	Gross National Product
1920	71.0	10.4
1921	57.7	7.8
1922	50.5	7.8
1923	54.4	9.4
1924	49.6	8.9
1925	48.8	9.0
1926	51.4	9.5
1927	50.5	9.2
1928	52.6	9.4
1929	60.4	10.3
1930	59.1	9.0
1931	51.2	6.7
1932	49.6	4.8
1933	52.9	4.6
1934	53.5	5.3
1935	56.0	6.2
1936	52.4	7.3
1937	58.6	8.5
1938	49.2	6.6
1939	47.8	6.9
1940	54.6	8.1
1941	55.6	8.2
1942	45.7	4.1
1943	51.9	2.8
1944	69.0	3.5
1945	76.1	4.7
1946	70.9	8.4
1947	68.0	10.1
1948	64.4	10.7
1949	60.8	10.1
1950	57.8	10.6
1951	60.8	10.5
1952	60.4	10.2

Sources: Appendix 4–2, Table A, and Appendix 4–9.

a. Outlays for all capital goods exclude outlays for publicly owned military and naval plant and equipment and outlays of state governments for equipment.

consumer tastes, introduction of new products and changing technology. The incidence of demand for these goods depends on current and past profits, depreciation practices, interest rates

By THOMAS C. FICHANDLER, Associate Research Director of this study. Opinions and judgments expressed in this chapter are those of the author and should not be attributed to the organization with which he is associated.

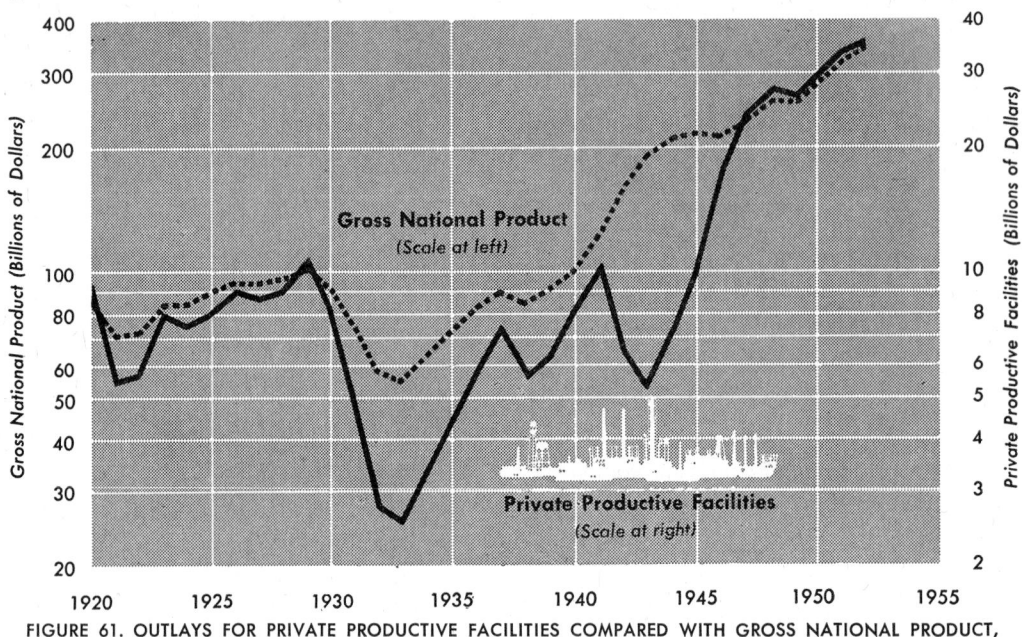

FIGURE 61. OUTLAYS FOR PRIVATE PRODUCTIVE FACILITIES COMPARED WITH GROSS NATIONAL PRODUCT, 1920–1952

Sources: Appendix 4–2, Table A, and Appendix 4–8.

and, perhaps most important of all, on prospects for future profits. In the long run, of course, capital expenditures are unquestionably related to population growth and income changes, but in the more immediate view the importance of these special factors just mentioned tends to obscure long-term relationships. This is true of individual enterprises, of entire industries and of productive enterprise as a whole.

Except for the World War II period, outlays for productive facilities followed closely the cyclical movement of gross national product during 1920–1952, but fluctuated much more sharply. This held true during such minor movements as the 1920–1921 and the 1937–1938 business recessions as well as during the long upswing from 1921 to 1929, the precipitous decline to 1933 and the recovery to 1937. (See Figure 61.) Expressed somewhat differently, output of private productive facilities, as well as of most other capital goods, constitutes a larger share of gross national product in boom than in depression. In 1929, for example, the proportion was more than double that in 1933 — 10.3 per cent compared with 4.6 per cent. During World War II private outlays for plant and equipment gave way to huge government expenditures aimed at quickly building up our war potential. Since these public

outlays contributed to the increase in gross national product, the ratio of private productive facilities investment to national output dropped off. Outlays for private facilities rose again after 1943, when the peak of the government's basic war production program was reached. By 1947 spending for private productive facilities exceeded 10 per cent of gross national product — a level reached earlier only in 1920 and 1929. (See Table 211.)

Although total outlays for private productive facilities have grown along with the gross national product over the years, outlays for equipment have risen at a more rapid pace. Between 1909 and 1952, for example, gross national product (measured in constant dollars) tripled but expenditures for private productive equipment increased fivefold. (See Figure 62.) This shift in demand — from plant to equipment — may have resulted from the growing complexity of our industrial technology. The relatively simple machines that once were manned by large numbers of workers have given way to increasingly complex engines of production turning out fabulously large numbers of units with little or no human supervision. Not only does this more complicated machinery cost more, but once the basic plant has been constructed expenditures are likely to

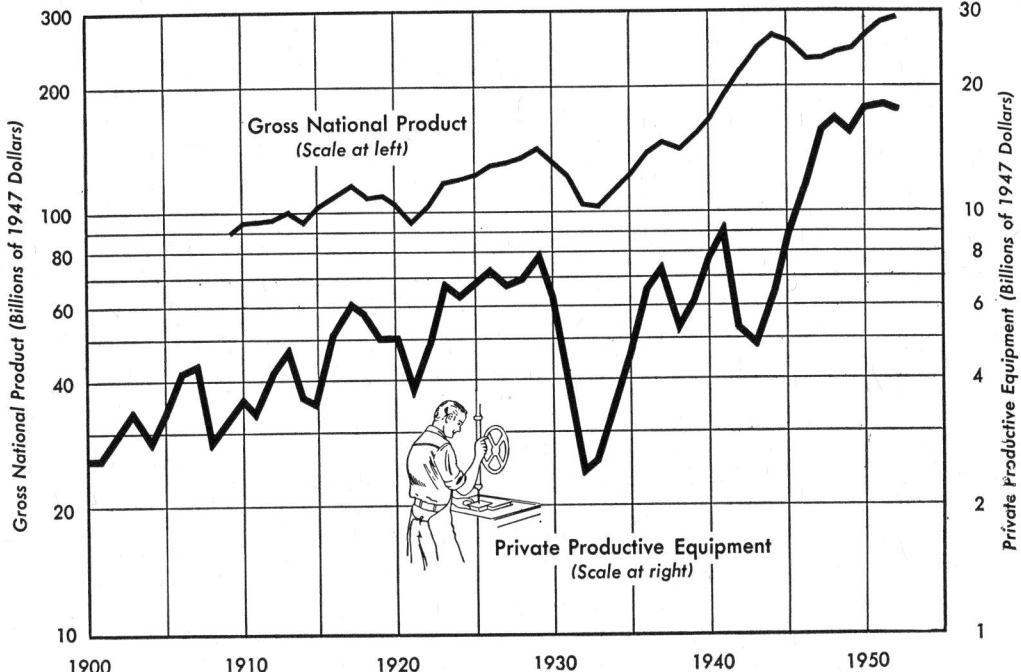

FIGURE 62. OUTLAYS FOR PRIVATE PRODUCTIVE EQUIPMENT, 1900–1952, COMPARED WITH GROSS NATIONAL PRODUCT, 1909–1952, IN CONSTANT (1947) DOLLARS

Sources: Appendix 4–2, Table B, and Robert C. Wasson, "Investment in Production Equipment, 1929–52," Survey of Current Business, November 1953, p. 14.

shift toward replacement of machines, which become physically and, what is more important, technologically obsolete at a much faster rate than the buildings that house them. A second possibility is that the shift of capital oulays from plant to equipment occurred because construction costs outran equipment costs. In 1952, for example, nonresidential construction costs were about 2.5 times their 1929 level, whereas equipment prices were only 1.8 times as great.[1]

Technological Changes

Although outlays for productive facilities are predominantly related to trends and variations in the economy as a whole, the magnitude and timing of expenditures in particular industries are significantly influenced also by changes in technology and tastes. Changes in the industrial arts or consumer habits may cause rapid obsolescence or expansion of productive facilities in one industry without affecting others. This fact may be illustrated by a number of examples.

1. Robert C. Wasson, "Investment in Production Equipment, 1929–52," Survey of Current Business, November 1953, p. 14.

The total consumption of wheat flour in the United States has changed very little, although the quantity consumed per capita has decreased over the years. The flour mills in operation at the end of World War I were adequate; with good care and maintenance they would probably have lasted for decades. Nevertheless, substantial capital expenditures were made for construction of improved mills in 1919 and 1920. These outlays were possible because of the large profits of the industry during the war, but they were actually made primarily because of important technical developments in the mechanization of flour milling.

In other food-processing industries, very large expenditures were made during the 1920s to provide facilities for the production of new types of prepared and packaged foods. Before World War I, most foods were retailed in bulk. Prepared salad dressings, precooked foods and dessert mixes, quite common twenty years later, were little known in 1915. The frozen-food industry, bringing with it deep-freezing units in the home and community locker plants, has had a similar effect. All of these new products required elaborate processing equipment and, in many instances, new factories.

Capital expansion for the production of new and improved products is clearly evident in many other industries: continuous mills to roll steel sheets; tools and dies for new models of automobiles; mills to weave synthetic fibers such as orlon and nylon; plants to manufacture airplanes and airplane motors; the whole range of "electronics" industries — television, electronic cooking, computing and measuring machines; and many others.

The important relation of technological change to capital expansion is clearly demonstrated in petroleum refining. In 1920 gasoline, kerosene and heavier fuels and lubricating oils were obtained by selective distillation of crude petroleum. Today, petroleum serves rather as a raw material to produce many new products — either not existing as such in crude petroleum, or contained in much smaller quantities than those ultimately derived. The chemical process of hydrogenation, for example, is now used to obtain a yield of more than one gallon of gasoline from each gallon of crude, with many other products left over. The average yield of gasoline from the distillation process used around 1920 was approximately one fourth of this amount. The petroleum industry, in fact, has become a complex chemical industry. Because of these and similar technical developments, heavy capital expenditures must be made by concerns in the industry to keep their productive facilities up to date. Obsolescence is rapid and many elaborate installations in this industry have a useful life of little more than five to ten years.

Other Factors

Large net earnings, as well as the availability of funds for investment, also facilitate capital expansion and frequently influence its timing. They are seldom the controlling factors in particular industries, however. Many profitable enterprises make relatively small capital expenditures even in good times; but many make substantial ones when profits are low. This does not mean that capital expenditures are unrelated — or are inversely related — to profit. Expenditures for new installations, such as a continuous sheet mill, are often made as a matter of competitive necessity only after more venturesome competitors have proved such investments to be profitable.

New capital expenditures do not rise and fall in direct proportion to previously realized profits. They are more often conditioned by the expectation of future profits from the introduction of new processes or new models, or by the appearance of types of products that require new facilities. In manufacturing, technological change appears to be an especially important influence in the determination of capital expenditures.[2] In mining, agriculture and other extractive industries, profitability seems to play a larger part.

Favorable interest rates tend to encourage capital expansion. Economists once placed great emphasis on the rate of interest, but in recent years they have attached less importance to this factor. In any case the influence of interest rates on capital expansion varies widely with the type of industry. According to John Maurice Clark:

A low rate of interest can be a material stimulus to investment in some important areas where maintenance and depreciation are low, risks are moderate and interest is a really substantial part of the cost incurred on account of an investment of capital. This is pre-eminently true of hydroelectric installations and is broadly true of housing. But in the general field of industry and trade, low interest rates cannot accomplish as much as many economic theorists give them credit for. Interest alone is a minor part of the total cost or sacrifice involved in a capital outlay, especially in a dynamic industry, where equipment gets obsolete long before it is worn out and the allowance for obsolescence alone dwarfs the element of interest.[3]

Reserves for obsolescence and depreciation are generally set aside by business firms according to a rigid, predetermined pattern. Capital expenditures may thus be limited by the reserve position of the enterprise, whereas actual obsolescence and the need for new facilities depend on the tempo of technological change, which often cannot be predicted.

Depreciation allowances for income tax purposes have an important bearing on business investment decisions since depreciation is a major source of business investment funds. Public policy recognized this in recent years by offering rapid write-off allowances as an incentive to private capital to expand defense facilities. There is some feeling that depreciation allowances are considerably smaller than they should be. One estimate is that "American industry is

2. See the preceding section on "Technological Changes" and "Manufacturing Industries" below.
3. John Maurice Clark, in *Financing American Prosperity*, Twentieth Century Fund, 1945, pp. 110–111.

receiving in depreciation allowances $7 billion a year less than it is realistically entitled to." [4] Any increase in the rate at which industry is allowed to write off its investment for tax purposes would tend to increase the rate of capital investment.

Despite rapid technological changes and satisfactory profits and reserves, however, expenditures by business firms for productive facilities may still remain low if confidence in the future is lacking. Whether justified by subsequent developments or not, business optimism or pessimism is the most powerful and pervasive influence on the volume and timing of business investment.

THREE DECADES OF EXPERIENCE

Between the end of World War I and the beginning of World War II, annual outlays for private productive capital facilities averaged $6.7 billion, or 8.1 per cent of gross national product — more than half of total outlays for capital goods. In 1940–1944, private outlays rose to an average of $7.6 billion, but because public capital investment was so great in this period they equaled less than 5 per cent of gross national product. After the end of World War II, expenditures for private productive facilities moved to an entirely new level — averaging $21 billion a year during 1945–1949 and exceeding $30 billion in each of the years 1950–1952. The 1952 peak of $35.6 billion was more than three times the prewar high of $10.7 billion reached in 1929. (See Table 212.)

Rising prices and a shift to more expensive equipment accounted for some of the vast difference between prewar and postwar outlays, but by far the major share came from the huge increase in the physical volume of productive facilities. For example, expenditures for private equipment, measured in dollars of constant purchasing power, more than doubled between 1929 and the early 1950s. (See Figure 62.)

THE PROSPEROUS 1920S AND THE DEPRESSED 1930S

In the first half of the 1920s, outlays for private productive facilities averaged $7.2 billion a year, and in the prosperous second half they increased to $9.2 billion. With the post-1929 collapse they decreased to an annual average of $4.4 billion

in 1930–1934, and with recovery increased to $6 billion in the second half of the 1930s. From the peak in 1929 to the low in 1933, they declined from nearly $11 billion to less than $3 billion. (See Table 212.)

Manufacturing Industries

Outlays for productive facilities by manufacturing industries attained a peak of more than $3 billion in 1920, not thereafter surpassed until 1941. Outlays by the automobile industry were at a high point of $187 million in 1920 because of the switch from war to peacetime production and the introduction of wartime technical innovations. Capital expenditures for the fabrication of textiles and related products averaged $238 million in the early 1920s, principally because of the rapid expansion of the cotton industry into the southeastern states. Subsequently, the textile industry's outlays declined markedly. Capital expenditures in the lumber and lumber products industries also reached a peak of $159 million in 1920 and thereafter declined sharply. The paper and pulp industry showed no clear trend during the two decades, although its capital expenditures varied extremely. A peak of $183 million was established in 1937 — mainly because of the construction of mills in several southern states as a result of new methods of manufacturing kraft paper and newsprint from southern yellow pine.

In the food industries, capital outlays reached a high point of $423 million in 1928, reflecting, among other influences, the especially rapid growth of processing: packaging, canning and quick freezing. Sharp peaks were established in expenditures to expand the blast furnace, steelworks and rolling mill industry during World War I (nearly $350 million went for this purpose in 1917). Expenditures declined precipitously immediately after the war, but they reached $300 million in 1930 and $316 million in 1937.

Expansion of facilities for manufacturing airplanes and airplane motors and parts was long relatively negligible. At the end of 1939, the total value of fixed capital investment in the airplane-manufacturing industry was only approximately $70 million. It was really not until the 1940s that the industry began its phenomenal growth.

Transportation and Utilities

The largest annual expenditures for railroad rolling stock and improvements to right of way

---

4. *Realistic Depreciation Policy — A Summary*, Machinery and Allied Products Institute, Chicago, 1953, p. 7.

TABLE 212. EXPENDITURES FOR PRIVATE PRODUCTIVE FACILITIES, 1920-1952

(Millions)

	Annual Average						1950	1951	1952	Peak[a]		Low[a]
	1920–1924	1925–1929	1930–1934	1935–1939	1940–1944	1945–1949				Prewar	All Time	
Total[b]	$7,232	$9,202	$4,444	$6,006	$7,582	$20,988	$30,263	$34,524	$35,617	$10,726	$35,617	$2,589
Agriculture	793	863	365	782	1,129	2,740	3,996	4,620	4,210	1,362	4,620	173
Nonresidential construction	183	172	37	91	137	585	872	875	860	300	875	13
Farm machinery and equipment	610	691	328	691	992	2,155	3,124	3,745	3,350	1,062	3,745	160
Mining	584	785	431	692	432	635	707	929	880	962	962	275
Manufacturing	1,971	2,294	1,041	1,640	3,070	7,152	7,491	10,852	11,994	3,165	11,994	574
Primary iron and steel	138	188	110	178	c	541	599	1,198	1,538	316	1,538	40
Motor vehicles and equipment	107	150	78	146	c	436	510	851	896	187	896	48
Stone, clay and glass products	154	228	61	80	c	223	280	397	318	283	397	28
Food and beverages	261	357	194	247	c	796	760	853	785	423	1,053	171
Paper and allied products	101	112	52	97	c	280	327	420	354	183	420	28
Rubber products	39	39	16	27	c	117	102	150	139	105	150	11
Other manufacturing	1,171	1,220	529	865	c	4,760	4,913	6,983	7,964	2,003	7,964	257
Transportation	904[d]	958[d]	458[d]	484[d]	974	1,923	2,308	2,964	2,754	1,302[d]	2,964[d]	153[d]
Railroads	718	775	342	304	514	938	1,111	1,474	1,391	1,077	1,474	101
Transit	145	128	88	103	83	185	168	e	e	180	281[f]	46
Oil pipeline	40	55	28	31	54	91	141	149	196	83	196	6
Other transportation	d	d	d	d	322	709	888	1,341[e]	1,167[e]	d	d	d
Communication	350	558	400	334	354	1,120	1,104	1,319	1,598	762	1,742	190
Utilities	713	1,015	488	470	561	1,701	3,309	3,664	3,838	1,112	3,838	196
Electric light and power	548	739	376	388	439	1,198	2,187	c	c	851	2,272[f]	151
Gas	165	276	112	82	122	503	1,122	c	c	330	1,122[f]	45
Commercial and miscellaneous[g]	1,918	2,729	1,261	1,604	1,061	5,717	11,348	10,176	10,343	h	h	h

Source: Appendix 4-8.

a. Totals may not equal sum of items since peaks (and low points) for individual items may have occurred in different years.

b. Total includes equipment charged to current account; these charges are not included in the detailed industry figures but are grouped with "Commercial and miscellaneous."

c. Not available.

d. For the years 1920-1938, "Other transportation" is included with "Commercial and miscellaneous."

e. "Transit" included in "Other transportation" for 1951 and 1952.

f. Excluding 1951 and 1952, for which no data were available.

g. Total includes, in addition to commercial buildings, facilities not allocable by industry division, equipment charged to current account and statistical discrepancies arising from use of varied sources.

h. Not determined because of changing composition of this group of expenditures.

were $1,077 million in 1923, and outlays were well maintained near this level through 1930. Transit expenditures decreased during these decades, the biggest year being 1923 with $180 million. Outlays for oil pipelines rose erratically from $35 million in 1920 to a peak of $83 million in 1929. Investment in this industry almost dried up during the subsequent depression, falling to $6 million in 1933. Capital outlays varied less in the telephone and telegraph industries than in many others. They grew steadily to a peak of more than $762 million in 1930, decreased to $208 million in 1933, and then increased to between $300 and $400 million in the last three years of the 1930s. Electric light and power expenditures reached high points beyond $800 million in 1924 and in 1930 and were well maintained in the intervening years. They declined sharply to $151 million in 1933 and, despite substantial recovery, thereafter failed to approach the level of the latter 1920s.

Extractive and Other Industries

Mining is the only industry group that had not surpassed its prewar peak capital outlay — $962 million, reached in 1937 — by 1952. The trend for mining was generally upward, with allowance for cyclical swings, until 1937, but after that a long-term decline appears to have set in.

Agriculture had a banner year in 1920, when $1.4 billion worth of capital facilities were paid for. This record was not exceeded until 1944. The larger share — more than $1 billion — went for farm machinery and equipment, and spending for this purpose did not reach such a level again until 1942. Expenditures for farm machinery and equipment averaged about the same during the second half of the 1920s and 1930s, when they were higher than during the early 1920s.

Although no separate estimates are available for commercial facilities — stores, theaters, banks, office buildings and their equipment — outlays for these purposes fell off sharply after 1929 and did not return to the levels of 1925–1929 until after World War II.

WARTIME AND POSTWAR YEARS

Expenditures for industrial and commercial facilities during the defense and war period of the 1940s greatly overshadowed those of any previous period of equal length, except the latter half of the 1920s, which witnessed a great boom in commercial building. Much of the new plant and equipment, however, was owned and paid for by the federal government and was so highly specialized that its use was limited largely to war production. Some was badly located with reference to a peacetime economy. Some was hurriedly made, of inferior design and quality. Nevertheless, the innovations and advancing technology of the war period had profound effects on our peacetime productive plant.

Expenditures for Productive Facilities

Out of a total of approximately $38 billion spent during 1940–1944 for private plant and equipment, about $15 billion, or 40 per cent, was for manufacturing facilities. In the immediately preceding five-year period, the proportion of total outlays going into manufacturing facilities was only 27 per cent. Public funds, naturally, were concentrated almost exclusively in the so-called "war matériel" industries. Wartime public expenditures in these industries averaged about $3.2 billion a year, more than private outlays for all manufacturing facilities in any single year during the 1920s and 1930s. Private outlays for productive facilities in the war manufacturing industries averaged very little more than during peacetime, as the following comparison with 1939 shows (figures in millions): [5]

	1939 (Private)	Wartime (Annual Rate)	
		Private	Public
War manufacturing, total	$1,146	$1,228	$3,186
Machinery and metals	392	506	1,008
Chemicals, petroleum and coal products	579	336	921
Transportation equipment	175	386	1,257

Public expenditures in the transportation equipment industry, for building up our capacity to produce planes, ships and tanks, were over seven times as great during the average war year as in 1939.

The new wartime capital plant and equipment consisted of four main types of facilities:

---

5. Appendix 4–8; *Facilities Expansion, July 1940–June 1945*, Civilian Production Administration, January 1946; and unpublished data of the Federal Reserve Board.

(1) Those of a highly specialized military character that were made necessary almost wholly by war, such as powder plants, shell-loading plants, tools and dies for the fabrication of guns and ammunition, armor plate mills and synthetic rubber plants.

(2) Those that fabricated peacetime products which were required in time of war in vast quantities — ten, twenty or fifty times their normal peacetime production — such as shipyards and airplane-manufacturing facilities.

(3) Those that had a brisk peacetime demand for their products and services but which were inadequate or were strained to meet wartime requirements, such as blast furnaces, steelworks and rolling mills, aluminum and other nonferrous reduction plants, machine-tool shops, railroad facilities, and electric generating and distribution systems.

(4) Those for which requirements in wartime were almost the same as, or less than, in peacetime, such as most food-processing industries; textile mills; stone, clay and glass products plants; office buildings, stores and other commercial structures.

Expenditures for facilities in the first two categories and in the manufacturing industries of the third group were far beyond peacetime rates. These so-called war industries spent $22 billion for capital facilities, or an average of $4.4 billion a year.

Wartime capital outlays of the nonmanufacturing industries in the third group — railroads and other public utilities and mining — were not extraordinary. Many were less than in 1939, when converted to comparable prices. Most of these industries strained capacity to the utmost to meet the intensified demand. Thus they prolonged the life of their capital facilities unduly, and reduced the quality of the service provided.

The industries in the fourth group were for the most part required to get along as best they could with new capital expenditures well below peacetime levels.

Hence, only in certain manufacturing industries — metal and metal products, chemicals, and petroleum and coal products — were wartime capital outlays phenomenal. Even in these industries outlays for some facilities were below peacetime rates — for example, specialized tools and dies for manufacturing automobiles and other consumer durables.

Most of the nonwar manufacturing industries and especially the nonmanufacturing fields, such as commercial structures, were left at the end of the war with vast needs to fill.

The relatively heavy wartime outlays for productive facilities were quickly dwarfed by the extraordinary expansion that followed V-J Day. In the five-year period 1945–1949, United States business spent over $100 billion to expand and modernize its plant and equipment. The annual rate of $21 billion was more than double that of the late 1920s. Annual outlays in the early 1950s exceeded $30 billion, reaching more than $35 billion in 1952. In contrast, the prewar (1929) peak was less than $11 billion. (See Table 212.) The record investment levels of the early 1950s were supported by consumer demand that had been building up during depression and war, by foreign demand created by wartime devastation and partly financed by United States government aid, and by government demand for military goods with which to fight the Korean War.

Most industries shared in this postwar expansion. The sharpest gains were made in manufacturing, where new industries (television, synthetics, antibiotics, home freezers) and old industries whose output of consumer goods (passenger automobiles and other consumer durables) had been practically eliminated during the war began a mad scramble to expand production in answer to tremendous consumer demand. Manufacturers also were anxious to apply wartime developments in the form of up-to-date plant layout and machinery and they had the reserves earned during the war with which to finance modernization. Commercial building, which had practically ceased during the war, expanded almost as much as manufacturing. On the other hand, postwar purchases of new capital goods by industries such as mining and transit ran at rates relatively little above prewar levels.

Regional Shifts of Industry

Many changes occurred in the regional distribution of industry during and after the war. Plants located in hitherto unindustrialized localities may provide the nucleus for more extensive industrial development, with far-reaching effects on capital expansion.

Industry, like population, has moved west and south from its first locale along the New England and Middle Atlantic coasts. Wartime and postwar industrial expansion followed in general the geographical pattern of prewar growth. There were, however, a number of major exceptions largely for military reasons. Airplane-manufac-

TABLE 213. PERCENTAGE DISTRIBUTION OF VALUE ADDED BY MANUFACTURE, BY REGION,
SELECTED YEARS, 1919–1952

Region [a]	1919	1929	1939	1947	1950	1952
United States total	100.00	100.00	100.00	100.00	100.00	100.00
New England	12.90	10.38	9.84	9.15	8.27	8.29
Middle Atlantic	33.67	32.08	29.79	27.94	26.19	26.31
East North Central	28.42	31.67	31.53	31.54	33.22	32.65
West North Central	5.63	5.72	5.52	5.53	5.74	5.73
South Atlantic	7.42	7.64	9.05	9.33	9.44	8.83
East South Central	2.65	2.82	3.36	3.86	3.85	3.57
West South Central	2.91	2.92	3.34	4.07	4.29	4.75
Mountain	1.25	1.09	1.11	1.13	1.16	1.17
Pacific	5.15	5.68	6.46	7.45	7.84	8.70

Sources: Based on Census of Manufactures, 1919, 1929, 1939 and 1947, and on Annual Survey of Manufactures, 1950 and 1952.

a. Regions consist of following states: New England—Maine, New Hampshire, Vermont, Massachusetts, Rhode Island and Connecticut; Middle Atlantic—New York, New Jersey and Pennsylvania; East North Central—Ohio, Indiana, Illinois, Michigan and Wisconsin; West North Central—Minnesota, Iowa, Missouri, North Dakota, South Dakota, Nebraska and Kansas; South Atlantic—Delaware, Maryland, District of Columbia, Virginia, West Virginia, North Carolina, South Carolina, Georgia and Florida; East South Central—Kentucky, Tennessee, Alabama and Mississippi; West South Central—Arkansas, Louisiana, Oklahoma and Texas; Mountain—Montana, Idaho, Wyoming, Colorado, New Mexico, Arizona, Utah and Nevada; Pacific—Washington, Oregon and California.

turing plants, aluminum and magnesium reduction plants, and powder and shell-loading plants were established in widely distributed areas, usually inland. Often such industries were new to these regions or else they had been relatively minor before the war.[6]

The West South Central states — Texas, Louisiana, Oklahoma and Arkansas — experienced more substantial industrial expansion during and just before the war than any other part of the country. In 1919, 1929 and 1939 these four states accounted for around 3 per cent of manufacturing capacity. New facilities installed in 1939 were nearly twice that proportion, and during the war they exceeded 10 per cent. (See Tables 213 and 214.)[7] Several industries, particularly in Texas, were responsible for this expansion: petroleum refining, new paper mills, magnesium-manufac-

6. For a discussion of the factors influencing the location of wartime industrial facilities see Glenn E. McLaughlin, "Wartime Expansion in Industrial Capacities," American Economic Review, Supplement, March 1943, pp. 108–118.

7. Tables 213 and 214 show some of the changes that occurred in the regional distribution of manufacturing industries between the two world wars and after. Capital outlays by manufacturing industries are available by regions and states only for 1939, the subsequent war period and after. Value added by manufacture gives a rough measure of manufacturing capacity, and capital expenditures measure the expansion of capacity.

turing and aircraft-manufacturing facilities. The rapid tempo of wartime growth fell off somewhat in early postwar years but in 1952 this region was absorbing 11.6 per cent of all new manufacturing facilities, even more than during the war. During the war and postwar periods this region enlarged its manufacturing output more rapidly than any other — from 3.34 per cent of total value added by manufacture its share jumped to 4.75 per cent.

The wartime rate of plant expansion in Missouri and Kansas was also notable. A large part, however, was in explosives, shell loading and aircraft manufacturing, all of which fell off sharply after the war.

The East South Central states, especially Alabama, experienced major expansion in basic industries, such as iron and steel, as well as in strictly war industries, such as shell loading.

In the Mountain and Pacific regions, Colorado, Utah, Washington, Nevada, Arizona and California acquired considerable new facilities in different industries during the war. Whereas the growth rate of manufacturing facilities in the Mountain states declined after the war, the Pacific Coast states went on to absorb an even greater share of the newly added facilities. By 1952, this area's output had risen to the point

TABLE 214. PERCENTAGE DISTRIBUTION OF EXPENDITURE FOR NEW MANUFACTURING PLANT AND EQUIPMENT, BY REGION, SELECTED PERIODS, 1939–1952

Region [a]	1939	Wartime: July 1940–May 1944	1947	1951	1952
United States total	100.0	100.0	100.0	100.0	100.0
New England	8.2	5.1	7.0	6.0	5.5
Middle Atlantic	24.6	18.8	22.2	21.7	22.8
East North Central	33.9	30.5	31.1	32.6	32.4
West North Central	4.5	6.9	5.7	4.9	4.2
South Atlantic	11.1	6.7	11.3	11.1	9.1
East South Central	3.9	6.1	4.3	4.3	4.1
West South Central	5.9	10.6	7.6	8.5	11.6
Mountain	1.3	3.4	1.6	1.5	1.6
Pacific	6.6	8.8	9.2	9.4	8.7
Undistributed	—	3.2	—	—	—

Sources: Based on Census of Manufactures, 1939 and 1947; *Annual Survey of Manufactures,* 1951 and 1952; *Geographic Distribution of Manufacturing Facilities Expansion, July 1940–May 1944,* War Production Board, June 1, 1945.

a. See Table 213, footnote *a* for states included in each region.

where it accounted for 8.70 per cent of total value added by manufacture compared with 6.46 per cent before the war.

The principal wartime expenditures in Utah were for iron and steel mills; in Washington, for aluminum and aircraft manufacturing; in Nevada, for magnesium; and in California, for aircraft, shipbuilding, and magnesium-manufacturing facilities. Aircraft manufacturing and shipbuilding have been well-established industries on the Pacific Coast for many years. But aluminum, iron and magnesium were for the most part newcomers.

Enlargement of industrial facilities in the New England and Middle Atlantic states during the war was less marked than in most other parts of the country. These states were, of course, already heavily industrialized when the war began.

The South Atlantic states expanded industrially from 1919 to 1939 somewhat more rapidly than the country as a whole, but they did not participate heavily in the wartime industrial capital expansion. This may have been partly because of considerations of military security. Probably more fundamental was the fact that the principal industries here — cotton textiles, tobacco manufactures, pulp and paper, and cottonseed oil — did not require any unusual expansion to meet wartime demands.

The relative decline of the East is portrayed by the fall in the proportion of total value added

by manufacture in the New England, Middle Atlantic and South Atlantic states from 48.7 per cent before the war to 43.4 per cent in 1952. These were the only regions that suffered a relative decline.

By far the largest wartime expenditures for industrial facilities in any region were made in the East North Central states — Ohio, Indiana, Illinois, Michigan and Wisconsin. The relative importance of these five states in the industrial life of the country, however, changed very little between 1929 and 1952. Although large expenditures were made in this region for specialized war facilities, the proportion convertible to peacetime purposes was greater than in many of the southern and western states.

This expansion of manufacturing brought other industries, businesses and services in its wake, and increased the demand for already existing ones. Transportation, utilities and commerce have all been stimulated. Insofar as industrial facilities were expanded during and after the war, especially in the less highly industrialized areas, they brought a higher standard of living, with the shifting of population from agricultural to urban pursuits. Extensive wartime population movements occurred from rural states and from some of the older industrial districts to the newer war-industry centers. This migration followed the long-term trends of the past. Likewise, the regional redistribution of industry during the

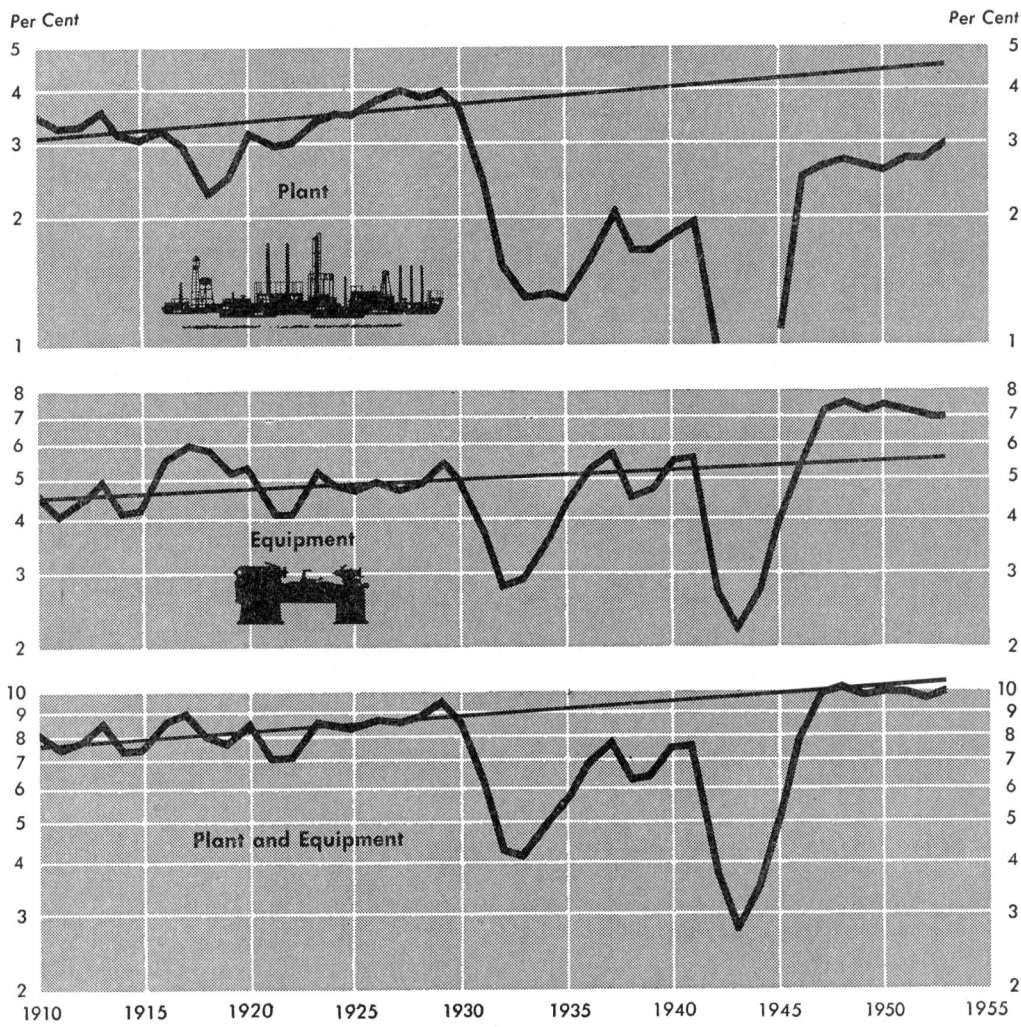

FIGURE 63. EXPENDITURES FOR PRIVATELY OWNED BUSINESS PLANT AND EQUIPMENT AS PER CENT OF PRIVATELY PRODUCED GROSS NATIONAL PRODUCT, 1910–1953 [a]

Source: Machinery and Allied Products Institute, *Capital Goods Review*, February 1954, p. 3.

a. Both the plant and the equipment series relate to capitalized outlays only, exclusive of items charged to current expense.

war was not a distortion, but largely an acceleration, of past trends. The continuation of both trends into the postwar period is proof of this fact.

PLANT AND EQUIPMENT TRENDS

Productive facilities consist of the basic structure — the plant — and the equipment which it houses. These two forms of capital can be combined in varying proportions. Some industries, such as airplane and automobile manufacturing, require specialized structures to house the complicated machine tools and handle the large units turned out; others require little investment in plant — apparel manufacturing, for example, can get along with just enough space in an ordinary loft building to take care of cutting, sewing and pressing machines. Manufacturing industries generally require a higher ratio of equipment to plant than wholesale and retail trade, where equipment may consist of a few typewriters but a relatively costly warehouse or store is essential.

Although the reasons are not entirely clear, a definite shift has occurred in the proportions of total business outlays going to equipment over the past forty-odd years. In 1910, equipment outlays were 33 per cent higher than plant outlays; in 1953 they were 133 per cent above plant outlays. This may be an extreme comparison since plant expenditures in 1910 were slightly above and in 1953 considerably below "normal," whereas equipment outlays were well above "normal" in 1953. (See Figure 63.) However, the so-called "normal" is merely an extension of the pre-depression trend and there is some reason to believe that the postwar shift in proportions represents a permanent change.[8] In that case, the ratio of equipment to plant outlays is likely to be considerably higher in the future than in prewar years, although not as high as the 1910–1953 comparison would imply.

Such a development would have important effects on business cycle swings in the United States. Plant expenditures historically have been more volatile than equipment outlays, as Figure 63 shows. At the depth of the depression in 1933 private expenditures for equipment fell to just under 30 per cent of the 1929 level but private expenditures for plant dropped to less than 20 per cent of 1929 outlays.[9] There are good reasons for this difference between plant and equipment outlays. Structures depreciate much more slowly than equipment and their replacement can be postponed much more easily. It is generally possible to make necessary adjustments within an old plant but much more difficult to go on using an obsolete piece of machinery. In addition, plant expansion normally calls for larger outlays than replacement of equipment. When the economic outlook is uncertain, management is more likely to refrain from committing itself to spend several million dollars for a new plant than it is to stop a planned equipment purchase of several thousand dollars.

Equipment Outlays

In recent years over 70 per cent of all expenditures for private productive facilities have gone for equipment.[10] During the five-year period

8. "Normal" represents straight-line projection of the ratios of expenditures for private productive facilities (plant and equipment) to private gross national product based on the years 1910–1930. Such a statistical measure of "normal," while helpful, is hardly definitive. It is less satisfactory for plant than for equipment expenditures, since in the case of plant outlays the trend line does not fit the base period data too well.
9. Based on Appendix 4–8.
10. Appendix 4–8.

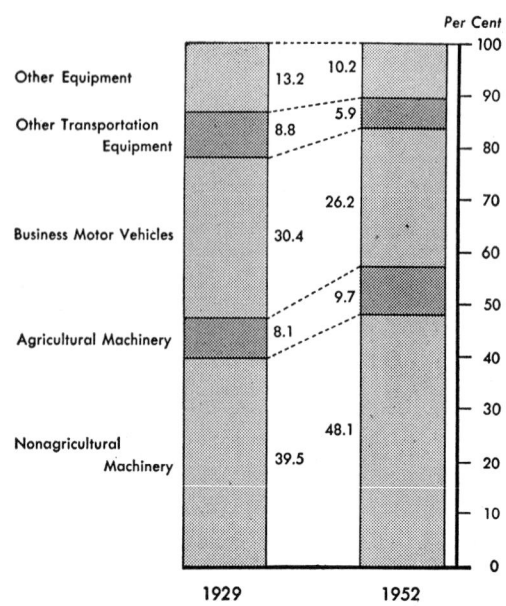

FIGURE 64. PERCENTAGE DISTRIBUTION OF PRIVATE PURCHASES OF PRODUCERS' DURABLE EQUIPMENT, 1929 AND 1952

Source: Robert C. Wasson, "Investment in Production Equipment, 1929–52," *Survey of Current Business*, November 1953, Table 1, pp. 16 and 17.

1948–1952, producers' durable equipment purchases ran 3 to 4 times as great as in 1929, in terms of current dollars. Adjusted for price changes, these postwar expenditures meant the addition annually of about twice the physical volume of equipment bought during 1929.[11] Since 1929, a growing proportion of this total has been spent for machinery while transportation equipment has been declining in importance. (See Figure 64.) The greatest relative increases have occurred in expenditures for agricultural, construction, electrical, mining and oil field, and metalworking machinery. Expenditures for practically all groups outside the machinery industries declined in relative importance. An outstanding exception was the instruments group, expenditures for which were over seven times as great in 1952 as in 1929 whereas total equipment purchases were just under four times as high.

Just as equipment outlays appear to be less

11. These and the following data on equipment purchases are from Wasson, *op. cit.* These estimates are a new series, which differ from those in Appendix 4–8. The equipment estimates in that appendix are consistent with the estimates incorporated in the Department of Commerce national income accounts at the time this survey was prepared.

TABLE 215. DECLINES FROM 1929 AND RECOVERY THROUGH 1936–1938 IN PRIVATE PRODUCTIVE EQUIPMENT EXPENDITURES, BY PRODUCT GROUP, AS PER CENT OF 1929

Product Group	Decline		Advance	
	Per Cent[a]	Rank	Per Cent[b]	Rank
Total productive equipment expenditures	−74	—	61	—
Aircraft	−98	1	44	17
Railroad equipment	−94	2	89	5
Construction machinery	−92	3	72	6
Metalworking machinery	−85	4	100	4
Ships and boats	−84	5	147	1
Tractors	−84	6	129	2
Electrical machinery	−82	7	71	7
Agricultural machinery (except tractors)	−82	8	68	8
Engines and turbines	−82	9	100	3
Mining and oil field machinery	−79	10	61	10
Passenger cars	−75	11	52	15
Trucks, buses and trailers	−74	12	60	11
Furniture and fixtures (nonresidential)	−73	13	38	19
General industrial machinery	−70	14	61	9
Fabricated metal products	−70	15	41	18
Special-industry machinery	−67	16	58	12
Service industry and household machines	−65	17	55	14
Instruments	−64	18	57	13
Office and store machinery	−64	19	49	16
Miscellaneous equipment	−54	20	23	20

Source: Robert C. Wasson, "Investment in Production Equipment, 1929–52," *Survey of Current Business,* November 1953, Table 2, p. 16.

a. Decline from 1929 to low year in cycle (1932 or 1933) expressed as per cent of 1929 figure for group.

b. Advance from low year (1932 or 1933) to next subsequent high year (1936, 1937 or 1938) expressed as per cent of 1929 figure for group.

---

volatile than plant outlays, expenditures for "heavy" equipment tend to have wider cyclical swings than expenditures for "light" equipment. The so-called "heavy" equipment is more costly and has a longer life span than the lighter equipment. In addition, it is often found in industries which themselves are subject to wide cyclical swings. Product groups which had the most violent swings down from 1929 to their depression lows in 1932 or 1933 and then up again during the following recovery period to 1936, 1937 or 1938 were ships and boats and railroad equipment, followed closely by metalworking machinery, construction machinery and engines and turbines. Product groups least disturbed by the business cycle between 1929 and 1937 were miscellaneous equipment, office and store machinery, fabricated metal products [12] and nonresidential furniture and fixtures. (See Table 215.)

12. Consisting largely of safes and vaults, stills, pressure and storage tanks (not including boilers), and fabricated plate steel for storage tanks.

The sharpest decline occurred in purchases of aircraft. The subsequent recovery for this product group was slow. Not until after the war, in 1946, did private purchases of aircraft surpass the 1929 level. By then all but three of the twenty separate product groups had surpassed their 1929 peaks. New records for nineteen groups were set in 1947 and for nearly all again in the early 1950s.

Relation to "Normal"

Private buying of productive equipment in the late 1940s and early 1950s has been substantially above the level indicated by projection of pre-depression trends. This is true whether outlays are expressed in current dollars, constant dollars or in relation to over-all economic activity.[13] One indicator of economic activity against which the relative importance of business capital expendi-

13. See *Capital Goods Review,* Machinery and Allied Products Institute, Nos. 13–17.

tures may be measured is the privately produced gross national product. Actual outlays for equipment have been running between 7 and 8 per cent of private gross national product, whereas a projection of the 1910–1930 trend would have put them between 5 and 6 per cent. On the other hand, outlays for plant have been between 2 and 3 per cent of private product whereas the trend projection reached between 4 and 5 per cent during the late 1940s and early 1950s. Interestingly enough, when plant and equipment are combined, actual outlays were just at about the level indicated by the trend projection. (See Figure 63.)

The full implications of these facts are far from clear. One surprising implication, however, is that despite the apparent huge volume of expenditures for private productive facilities during recent years, they do not appear to have been excessive by past standards. In fact, considering the backlog accumulated as a result of the low rate of combined private plant and equipment outlays during the depressed 1930s and the wartime 1940s, the postwar outlays would seem surprisingly low. At any rate, these figures do not imply either that the recent level of private capital outlays has been excessive or that it cannot be sustained in the future.[14]

NEEDS AND DEMAND: 1950 AND 1960

A basic assumption underlying the statistical framework of this study is that the future year that has been focused on, 1960, will be a relatively prosperous and relatively peaceful one. In such a year expenditures for private productive facilities would have to be high. While the projections that follow were influenced by this basic assumption, there are a number of additional reasons why private outlays for producers' goods at the close of the current decade should be relatively as high or higher than in the early 1950s.

BASIC DETERMINANTS OF FUTURE OUTLAYS

Three influences appear likely to affect productive capital expansion in the next decade or so: (1) changes in population, the standard of living and the volume of national income — all of which will be reflected in future consumption expenditures; (2) changes in techniques and products and in the location of industry; (3)

changes in public developmental, social and fiscal policies.

Changes in Population and Income

Population growth is not likely to exert the same pressure to expand productive capital facilities as in the distant past, but it is likely to be more important than in recent decades. Between 1840 and 1890 our population increased by 25 to 35 per cent each decade, and in the next two decades the rate of increase was about 20 per cent. The rate of growth dropped sharply after 1910 to a low of 7 per cent in the 1930s. Wartime influences altered the trend, pushing the 1940–1950 increases up to 15 per cent. Secondary effects of World War II plus the high employment levels of the early 1950s are expected to yield a 1950–1960 population growth of about 16 per cent. (See Tables 16 and 27.) Consequently, capital expansion for the mere purpose of providing for population growth should be greater than at any time since 1910.

If we enjoy a rising standard of living and a high level of income during the next several years, consumer expenditures will undoubtedly increase at a greater rate than population. This means that productive facilities must be expanded at a more rapid rate than would be required merely by continued population growth.[15]

Industrial Changes

Throughout the past two centuries, each generation believed it had reached the peak of human achievement. But each succeeding generation outstripped the achievements of its predecessors. History, much of it recent, suggests strongly that technological innovation is likely to be rapid for a long time to come. Although authorities may differ about the effect of the war on pure science, it is clear that the practical adaptation of scientific knowledge was greatly accelerated by the war and postwar defense programs.[16]

The outstanding wartime and postwar defense developments that have had and will continue to have special effects on the expansion of productive capital facilities are:

14. Cf. *Economic Report of the President*, January 1954, p. 61.

15. See Chapter 4 for a full statement of the basic assumptions as to population, national income, consumer expenditures, etc., used in this survey.

16. See Chapter 24 for discussion of recent technological developments.

(1) New communication devices, particularly wartime sonic developments, industrial electronics — computors and process controls — and television, new scientific instruments, heat- and corrosion-resistant metals and alloys, high-speed cutting tools and heavy forge presses.

(2) Improved internal-combustion engines and fuels.

(3) Advances in air transport, such as larger planes, higher speeds, jet propulsion, traffic-control devices, navigation aids, extensive terminal landing fields and many new air routes with frequent intermediate landing strips, as well as perfection of the helicopter.

(4) Chemical processes, such as the hydrogenation and controlled oxidization of coal and petroleum, biochemical processes, and many others that by industrial chemical methods produce substances with almost any desired molecular structure. Among the most notable of such products are plastics, synthetic rubber and synthetic fibers and fabrics of various kinds.

(5) New uses of plastic materials and of glass, plywood, magnesium and other materials with newly developed properties.

(6) New food products resulting from biochemical and physiological studies, and new methods of food processing, such as dehydration and quick freezing.

(7) New applications of atomic energy and fissionable products in medicine (radioisotopes) and power production.

The long-run effects of these technical developments should be enormous because many of the new techniques and processes are utilized in only recently industrialized parts of the country. Developments in communication and air transport are also likely to produce secondary effects, creating new tastes and consumption habits among people in the more remote and undeveloped parts of the country and bringing new employment opportunities.

Public Policy

In the past, government policies have influenced the expansion of productive facilities. The protective tariff from the earliest days encouraged American industrial growth. Local tax concessions to attract new industries were always important. Through canal and waterway development, land grants and other kinds of aid to railroads, and highway construction, the federal government encouraged huge investments in water, rail and motor transportation. It also subsidized shipbuilding, promoted electrical development and developed entire river valleys.

Government is already embarked on further expansion of our schools, hospitals, highways and airports, and additional river valley improvement may be undertaken. Government will directly or indirectly aid consumers through lower taxes, widened social security and possibly health insurance. Through these and other measures, government is likely to play an important role in promoting capital expansion.

Fiscal policy is likely to have a more powerful effect than hitherto on capital outlays, if for no other reason than because of the large public debt and heavier tax burden. During World War II and during the Korean conflict privately financed capital expansion was encouraged by allowing a high rate of depreciation and consequent lower taxes. A general revision of depreciation allowances designed to allow more rapid replacement of equipment is currently receiving widespread business support and is likely to find its way into income tax law. Such a change would be likely to induce greater capital outlays.

The President's January 1954 Economic Report gave a number of reasons for expecting new and enlarged investment opportunities: [17]

The emergence of a long-range outlook among business firms promises well for the future, the magnitude of industrial expenditures for research and development being merely one evidence of this outlook. Another is the long-range planning of investments, partly to assure growth, partly to meet the competition of other enterprising firms. The urge or need to cut costs is reflected in an active demand for automatic controls and materials-handling, inspection and office equipment. It also is accelerating outlays for the modernization of existing plant and equipment. Despite heavy postwar installations, a substantial volume of productive facilities is approaching "normal" retirement age or has become obsolete as a result of recent technological advances.

ESTIMATED DEMAND IN 1960

On the basis of past trends and relationship, it is estimated that outlays for private productive facilities in 1960 will total $42.3 billion (at 1950 prices). The long-run relationship upon which this projection was based is the ratio of private productive facilities to private gross national product. Extension of the trend line of Figure 63 to 1960 gives a "normal" projection of 11.0 per cent. The estimates of capital outlays used in constructing the trend line, however, differ from those used in the statistical framework for this study. They come from different sources and the

17. *Economic Report*, January 1954, p. 63.

estimates in Figure 63 exclude, for example, items charged to current expense, a fairly sizable amount of outlays that are included in the Department of Commerce national income estimates, which served as an important source of the basic statistics of this study. When adjusted for these differences and expressed in terms of gross national product (private plus public), the projected outlays for private productive facilities come to slightly over 11.4 per cent of gross national product in 1960.

The proportion of gross national product assigned to private productive facilities for 1960 is somewhat higher than at any time in the past for which we have reasonably reliable estimates. In 1920 the ratio was 10.4 per cent; in 1929, 10.3 per cent; and, after a peak of 10.7 per cent in 1947, it dropped to 10.2 per cent in 1952. (See Table 211.) However, the slight upward trend derived from the estimates in Figure 63 and the resulting estimate of $42.3 billion seem well justified by the factors mentioned in the previous section.

Estimated expenditures by each of the industry groups for private productive facilities in 1960 were made in most cases by determining the long-run relationship between the industry group's outlays and gross national product. In several instances where this approach was unsatisfactory, the projections were derived by determining the past trend in the relative importance of each group in total capital expenditures and extending the trend into the future.

With the exception of mining, all industry groups are expected to purchase a larger physical volume of plant and equipment in 1960 than in 1950. In addition, all except the mining, oil pipeline and gas industries are expected to account for a larger share of total capital expenditures in 1960 than in 1950. (See Appendix 4–7, Table B.)

Manufacturing industries spent $7.5 billion for plant and equipment in 1950, more than any other related group of industries, and probably will spend the highest amount, $11.0 billion (at 1950 prices), in 1960.[18] Many recent technological innovations should make their way into manufacturing industries. The probable increase in the rate of depreciation allowed for tax purposes should spark capital demand and should add to the rise in demand for equipment likely to come as the large volume recently purchased begins to need replacing.

Farm spending, particularly for machinery and equipment, is likely to continue second only to manufacturing. During 1950, farmers were spending for buildings and equipment at an annual rate of $4.0 billion. This high rate — high by historical standards — resulted from the need to eliminate backlogs built up during and immediately following World War II and was made possible by the availability of equipment and the average farmer's financial ability to buy what he needed. While a drop from this high level of outlays may be expected during the mid-1950s, the end of the decade should see a sharp rise in farm investment to about $5.7 billion a year (at 1950 prices) as demand for replacing large amounts of equipment bought during the recent postwar boom is added to normal growth.[19]

Public utilities, keeping step with growing industrial and domestic demands for light, heat and power, are likely to spend about $4.3 billion in 1960 (at 1950 prices), almost one third more than in 1950. In current dollars, these industries exceeded this expenditure in 1953; expressed in 1950 price levels, however, the 1953 outlays were in the neighborhood of $4 billion. Even so, expansion in these industries — especially in electric light and power — has been rapid since 1950 and is nearly certain to continue in order to meet the needs for electricity created by installation of new atomic energy facilities. If anything, capital outlays projected for the utility industries may fall short of actual 1960 expenditures.

Transportation, dominated by the railroads, has been having an investment spree while the roads have been replacing their coal burners with diesel engines. In 1951, for example, the railroads spent around $1.4 billion (at 1950 prices) for new capital goods. Although outlays declined in 1952 and 1953, it seems likely that the 1960 trend projection of $1.5 billion (at 1950 prices) will easily be reached. Outlays for airplanes, intercity buses and trucks, which dominate the "Other transportation" group, are expected to increase their volume of capital goods purchases by about one third between 1950 and 1960.

New developments in electronics, plus normal growth, should readily support the large increase

18. Although higher estimates are shown for "Commercial and miscellaneous," this is a catch-all group without statistical significance since it includes expenditures by other industries which could not be properly allocated.

19. See John W. Kendrick and Carl E. Jones, "Farm Capital Outlays and Stock," *Survey of Current Business,* August 1953, p. 16.

TABLE 216. ESTIMATED NEEDS AND DEMAND FOR PRIVATE PRODUCTIVE
FACILITIES IN 1950 AND 1960
(*Millions at 1950 Prices*)

Industry	1950		1960	
	Demand	Needs	Demand	Needs
Total private productive facilities[a]	$30,263	$34,800	$42,310	$44,800
Agriculture	3,996	4,590	5,700	6,040
Nonresidential construction	872	1,000	1,200	1,270
Farm equipment and machinery	3,124	3,590	4,500	4,770
Mining	707	810	700	740
Manufacturing	7,491	8,620	11,000	11,650
Transportation	2,308	2,650	3,150	3,330
Railroads	1,111	1,280	1,500	1,590
Transit	168	190	250	260
Oil pipeline	141	160	200	210
Other transportation	888	1,020	1,200	1,270
Communication	1,104	1,270	1,850	1,950
Utilities	3,309	3,810	4,300	4,550
Electric light and power	2,187	2,520	2,900	3,070
Gas	1,122	1,290	1,400	1,480
Commercial and miscellaneous[b]	11,348	13,050	15,610	16,540

Sources: Appendix 4–7 and discussion in text.

a. Total includes equipment charged to current account; these charges are not included in the detailed industry figures but are grouped with "Commercial and miscellaneous."

b. Includes facilities not allocable by industry division, equipment charged to current account and statistical discrepancies (1950 demand) arising from use of varied sources.

(nearly 70 per cent) indicated by past trends for the communication industries — telephone and telegraph. The mining industry, in a long-term decline, seems unlikely to spend more in 1960 than the $700 million it laid out in 1950.

Modernization

Capital expenditures in 1960 are likely to be considerably heavier for modernization than for expansion of facilities. A shift in this direction already has occurred. Taking manufacturing as an example, right after World War II most capital outlays were for expansion of plant and addition of equipment. By 1952, however, the split was about 50–50, and in 1953 more was spent in modernizing existing facilities than in expanding them. A McGraw-Hill survey taken early in 1954 revealed that manufacturing companies expected to devote about three fifths of their investment during 1955–1957 to modernization.[20]

20. *Business Week*, April 17, 1954, pp. 108–109.

An important incentive to modernization is the drive to cut unit costs in order to meet competition in the new market conditions, following disappearance of the lush sellers' markets of the war and early postwar years.

ESTIMATES OF NEEDS IN 1950 AND 1960

The concept of need as indicating a minimum level of expenditure is not generally applicable to productive capital facilities. The minimum need for food, housing, medical care, and all consumer and capital goods and services used directly by consumers, can be stated with some degree of exactness in terms of definite quantities, types and minimum standards as established by experts. This is also true to a limited extent of developmental works, used only partly by consumers. Productive facilities, however, are "intermediate goods" that are "used" by consumers only indirectly. The "need" for plant and equipment cannot be objectively measured; it is necessary only that they be adequate to supply the goods and services required to meet consumer and other needs.

Consequently, the need for productive facilities may be related to the estimated demand for such facilities in somewhat the same way as the need for other goods and services is related to the demand for them. In general, however, the volume of productive facilities should be more responsive to an increase in the demand for goods than to a rise in the demand for services. Allowance for this differential factor was made by weighting increases in expenditures for goods more heavily than increases for services. The estimated need for other goods and services — for consumer and government goods and services (primarily goods) and for capital goods other than productive facilities — totals 15 per cent greater than the estimated demand in 1950 and 6 per cent greater in 1960. (See Appendix 15–1.)

Hence, total needs for productive facilities in 1950 may be estimated at $34.8 billion, or 15 per cent in excess of estimated demand of $30.3 billion; for 1960, at $44.8 billion, or 6 per cent in excess of estimated demand of $42.3 billion (at 1950 prices). In the absence of specific estimates of need for the various individual categories of productive facilities, it has been assumed that the excess of needs over probable demand for each category would be proportional to the excess of needs over demand for productive facilities as a whole. (See Table 216.)

## CHAPTER 16

URBAN REDEVELOPMENT

WITHIN LITTLE MORE than a century, the United States has changed from a primarily agricultural economy into one of the most highly industrialized countries. Only 5 per cent of the nation's 4 million inhabitants lived in urban communities in 1790; in 1850, when the total population was 23 million, urban areas accounted for only 15 per cent; at the turn of the century the proportion was 39 per cent of a total of 76 million; by 1940 it had risen to nearly 57 per cent of 132 million; and by 1950 to 64 per cent of 151 million.[1]

The great majority of the urban population, 88 per cent, lived in the 168 standard metropolitan areas delineated by the Census in 1950. A standard metropolitan area, according to the Census, contains one or more cities of at least 50,000 population and generally includes the county containing the central city and any other contiguous counties which are deemed to be in close economic relation with that city. In a broad sense, the country's standard metropolitan areas include all the leading urban centers and all adjoining territory which is closely linked with the central cities.[2]

The rapidity with which this concentration of population came about has created serious problems, particularly in the larger metropolitan areas — problems with which our cities have so far been unable to cope. There was no time for planning; the cities just grew. And slums and blight grew with them. When ancient peoples fouled their communities, the population moved on and built anew. Today there is no chance of such a new start, even though in many cases it would probably be more efficient and economical. The only recourse is redevelopment of the existing city.

Estimates of housing needs presented in Chapter 7 are based solely on minimum physical standards of adequacy for individual dwelling units and are not concerned with the surrounding environment. This chapter goes beyond the needs for replacement of individual substandard dwelling units and considers the needs for redevelopment of larger areas within cities. "Urban redevelopment," for the purposes of this chapter, is defined as the rehabilitation where possible, or total elimination and rebuilding where necessary, of slums and blighted areas, including residential units and neighborhood commercial and service structures, according to accepted standards of health, livability and convenience.

In order to illustrate the relation between urban redevelopment and a program limited to the fulfillment of housing needs, let us assume a city of 40,000 dwellings with 10,000 of them below an acceptable minimum standard. Of these, let us say that 8,000 units must be replaced and 2,000 can be effectively repaired. The replacement or rehabilitation of these dwelling units would meet the physical need for adequate structures. Now suppose that, in addition, we removed completely all the slums and blighted areas in this city (and to do so we would have to remove some dwellings units which were *not* below minimum physical standards), replanned the streets, put in necessary utilities and provided new structures and all necessary neighborhood facilities. These activities would constitute urban redevelopment.

Phases of Redevelopment

The first phase of urban redevelopment consists in planning for livability in the widest

BY LAWRENCE N. BLOOMBERG, Chief Economist, Public Housing Administration; HOWARD G. BRUNSMAN, Chief, Population and Housing Division, Bureau of the Census; and A. BENJAMIN HANDLER, Associate Professor of Planning, University of Michigan. Opinions and judgments expressed in this chapter are those of the authors and should not be attributed to the organizations with which they are associated.

1. The Census definition of "urban" changed between the years 1940 and 1950. According to the 1940 definition, about 59 per cent of the population lived in urban areas in 1950. Thus, between 1940 and 1950 there was a 2.5 per cent increase in urban population based on a constant definition. There is no question that the 1950 definition more accurately reflects the commonly accepted view of what constitutes an urban area.

2. *1950 Census of Population,* Vol. I, *Number of Inhabitants,* p. xxxiii and Tables 13, p. 1–15, and 26, p. 1–66. See pp. 72–73 above.

sense of the term. This planning must take into account not only the particular area, or areas, to be redeveloped within the city but also the city as a whole — or, better still, the entire metropolitan area. Urban redevelopment is a second chance — this time to cure what we failed to prevent, and to do so in a manner that will not permit the evil to recur.

An essential part of the planning phase consists in studying the dislocation of families which the redevelopment program will cause and finding a workable way to provide these families with suitable housing within their means. Indeed, when urban redevelopment is undertaken with federal assistance the law has very rigid requirements for taking care of displaced families before redevelopment can start.

The relocation of displaced families is probably the most critical single problem in urban redevelopment. There can be no question that the elimination of a slum or blighted area works an unusual hardship on some families living in the area. The elimination of the blight is for the good of the community as a whole, or it would not be done. Every precaution must be taken, however, not to place an undue burden on the families directly affected. Nor can cities afford to continue evil conditions for fear of the problems their correction will entail. Either the cancer is inoperable and the patient will die, or bold surgery — which inevitably takes some living tissue along with the diseased — is attempted in order to preserve life.

Another phase of redevelopment is the acquisition of slum and blighted areas. Since the purchase of land and buildings is merely a transfer of funds, it does not add directly to national production and hence is not an element in capital formation. Although an estimate of acquisition cost is made later in this chapter, the sum does not enter into an accounting of possible future investment growing out of urban redevelopment.

However land is acquired for redevelopment, one thing is clear: substantial net losses must be absorbed in order to write down the cost of the land to a point where it can be utilized for the greatest good of the community. Undoubtedly there will be an actual increase in site values in certain redevelopment operations, but on balance there is almost certain to be a net loss. This represents payment for mistakes of the past. If urban redevelopment is to be successful in ac-

complishing its primary purpose, the new uses of the land must be determined by what is best for the community in the long run, not by what the land costs, nor by what new use will cause the minimum loss or perhaps even yield a profit.

After the slum or blighted area has been acquired, the next step is the preparation of the site for its planned use, whether it be residential, commercial, industrial, or for a park, playground or public building. This means razing buildings which do not fit into a proper rebuilding program, installing necessary utilities and providing adequate streets, sidewalks and off-street parking facilities. If the acquired land is to be used for parks and playgrounds, the appropriate facilities and equipment must be provided.

The final step is the construction of residences and commercial and other facilities, their number, location and design having been determined by the physical characteristics of the area and by the needs of the neighborhood and of the city as a whole. Some sites in redevelopment areas will be suitable for high-rent housing. Others will be adapted to moderate-rent dwellings. Still others will be appropriate for low-rent public housing, to take care of the many displaced families who cannot afford the lowest rents achievable by private enterprise for standard housing accommodations, even though the land cost would be written down to its value in use.

Nature and Extent of Slums and Blight

The slum is no new phenomenon. It has been with us many years, but slum conditions have been aggravated by the rapid industrialization and urbanization of our population. Much has already been written on the subject of slums, and none of us can fail to be aware of their existence.

For a brief and apt description we can turn to a 1931 report of the President's Conference on Home Building and Home Ownership: "We think of the slum as the abode of half-starved, filthily clothed children, of diseased and crippled individuals; a place of poverty, wretchedness, ignorance and vice. We think of it as a recession from the normal standards of a sound society." In short, "a slum is a residential area where the houses and conditions of life are of a squalid and wretched character and which hence has become a social liability to the community." [3]

---

3. *Slums, Large-Scale Housing and Decentralization,* President's Conference on Home Building and Home Ownership, 1931.

Although not yet a slum, a blighted area is on the verge of becoming one. A blighted area is any area which is not already a slum but in which, because of faulty planning, intrusion of inharmonious land uses, or economic or environmental changes, property owners are no longer able or willing to maintain, renew or reconstruct their holdings and to assure good neighborhood conditions.[4]

Slums and blight are a form of erosion, parallel to the depletion of soil when land is intensively cultivated without putting back the fertilizers necessary to growth. Unlike the land, however, eroded urban areas do not gather energy when left fallow, but pull down all that surrounds them to their level. Slums and blight flourish in the less desirable physical locations — often on the edges of swamps, in hollows, along industrial waterfronts, or along rivers into which refuse and sewage are dumped, or where factories and business and commercial establishments have taken hold. They thrive also in areas which, though not inherently disadvantageous, have become undesirable as a result of city growth.

Types of Slums and Blight

A substantial part of the housing in present slum areas was poorly planned and built. As examples we have the masses of tenements crowded on the land in our eastern cities when housing was in demand for newly arrived immigrants; the shantytowns built out of salvage from the city dump; the cheap, jerry-built, dense housing put up for workers in southern mill towns; the little more than shacks built for mine workers who were required to live in them as a condition of employment; the shoddy construction, in any town, motivated solely by a desire for obtaining maximum profits through exploiting land and the demand for shelter, and built without regard to sanitary facilities or even a thought for the people who would live there.

Other slums and blighted areas are the result of handing down originally good housing to successively lower income groups. This is particularly true of neighborhoods near urban business centers, where substantial old single-family houses have been split up into apartments or rooming houses and are interspersed with make-

shift offices, shops and occasional business or industrial buildings.

Different cities have characteristic slums. New York has its old-law tenements with windowless interior rooms and inadequate sanitary facilities. Typical of Chicago are two- or three-story frame structures built close together and two or three deep on long, narrow lots. In Philadelphia's courts and alleys are little brick houses (sometimes built back to back), old, neglected, with shared outdoor toilets and no indoor water supply. The alley dwellings of Washington are hidden by the façades of substantial brick structures. Boston also has its rear houses, houses fronting on courts and alleys, and dark, gloomy structures on ancient, narrow streets. In Los Angeles and many other western cities the slums consist largely of converted "hotels" and "apartments" into which are crowded thousands of families.

While not so obvious, because they are less concentrated, slum conditions in the smaller urban communities are often among the most vicious. The proportion of dilapidated housing alone is over two thirds greater in urban places outside metropolitan areas than in urban places inside such areas. Slums and blight in rural non-farm communities, which are not covered in this chapter, are also a grave problem.[5]

Of relatively recent origin are "suburban" slums — ribbon or strip developments along roads just outside the limits of cities, or small settlements adjoining cities, in which the dwellings were substandard when built. Much of this type of development is "shack building," largely by owners for their own use. Some of it was done under the stress of the depression of the 1930s, but much more is a recent attempt of lower-income families to solve their housing problem. Such construction is made possible by the absence of building or housing codes in many outlying areas. While these are already acknowledged conditions of slum and blight, many experts see future problems in much of the postwar flood of suburban building, a large part of which was flimsy and undertaken with complete disregard for normal and healthy community growth.

Extent of Slums and Blight

The extent of slums and blighted areas varies widely among cities of different size and in dif-

---

4. Alvin Hansen and Guy Greer, *Urban Redevelopment and Housing*, National Planning Association, Washington, 1942.

5. See Appendix 7-1.

TABLE 217. NUMBER AND PER CENT OF DWELLING UNITS IN
SLUMS AND BLIGHTED AREAS, SELECTED CITIES, 1950

City	Total Dwellings	In Slums and Blighted Areas	
		Number	Per Cent
Columbia, S. C.	22,989	10,150	44.2
Topeka, Kans.	26,231	5,946	22.7
Manchester, N. H.	25,547	5,618	22.0
Wilmington, Del.	32,280	5,554	17.2
Jersey City, N. J.	86,009	11,964	13.9
Hammond, Ind.	25,745	2,839	11.0
Lincoln, Neb.	31,467	3,276	10.4
Portland, Ore.	131,413	10,648	8.1
Salt Lake City, Utah	56,091	1,293	2.3

Source: Based on data from 1950 Census of Housing. For method of estimating number in slums and blighted areas, see Appendix 7–2.

ferent parts of the country. In nine illustrative cities the proportion of dwelling units in slums and blighted areas in 1950 ranged from 2.3 per cent (Salt Lake City, Utah) to 44.2 per cent (Columbia, South Carolina). More characteristic were Wilmington, Delaware, with 17.2 per cent, and Topeka, Kansas, with 22.7 per cent. (See Table 217.)

Of the 32.7 million dwelling units in standard metropolitan areas and other urban areas in 1950, 6.1 million, or 19 per cent, were located in concentrated slums and blighted areas, including isolated substandard blocks. In standard metropolitan areas alone, 5.0 million, or 20 per cent, of the 25.6 million dwelling units were in concentrated areas of slums and blight. In urban places outside standard metropolitan areas more than a million dwelling units were in such areas, or 15 per cent of the 7.1 million units.

The 6.1 million dwellings in concentrated slum areas do not include 3.8 million scattered substandard dwellings which taint their neighborhoods and form potential nuclei of blight and slums. Altogether, then, there are 9.9 million substandard urban units.[6] To put it another way, more than 30 million people live in urban houses which, either because of deficiencies in the structures themselves or because of their bad environment, are below reasonable minimum standards of health, safety, decency or convenience. This is the toll of neglect of our cities, and the challenge for the future.

6. See Appendix 7–2, Table B.

DEVELOPMENT OF SLUMS AND BLIGHTED AREAS

Nobody wants to live in the slums. People live there because they have no other choice — either they cannot afford adequate housing or, in the case of minority groups, they cannot obtain it at any price. If everyone had an adequate income and access to decent housing, slums and blighted areas would become empty relics, museum pieces of a benighted civilization — if they were allowed to remain at all.

UNPLANNED URBANIZATION

To many, the city is a vast, overcrowded network of streets, transportation lines and buildings. To others, the city means a main street with movies and shops, and perhaps seven or eight hundred houses scattered back for a quarter of a mile on either side. Our concept of the city, town or village depends on our individual experience, but there are few American cities, large or small, that do not belong to a type. The larger metropolitan areas repeat the same pattern over and over again.[7]

The pattern is one of unplanned growth. At the center is the main business district, often the

7. For exhaustive analyses of the structure of our cities, see Henry Wright, *Rehousing Urban America,* Columbia University Press, New York, 1935; *Our Cities,* National Resources Committee, Washington, 1937; James Ford, *Slums and Housing,* Harvard University Press, Cambridge, 1936; Homer Hoyt, *The Structure and Growth of Residential Neighborhoods in American Cities,* Federal Housing Administration, 1939.

TABLE 218. POPULATION CHANGES, INSIDE AND OUTSIDE THE CENTRAL CITIES,[a] SELECTED METROPOLITAN AREAS, 1940–1950

Standard Metropolitan Area	In the Central Cities		Outside the Central Cities	
	Number of Persons (Gain or Loss)	Per Cent	Number of Persons (Gain)	Per Cent
Atlanta, Ga.	29,026	9.6	124,671	57.8
Baltimore, Md.	90,608	10.5	163,465	72.9
Boston, Mass.	30,628	4.0	161,737	11.5
Cleveland, Ohio	36,472	4.2	161,769	41.6
Hartford, Conn.	11,130	6.7	51,338	39.7
Houston, Texas	211,649	55.0	66,091	45.8
New York–northeastern New Jersey	443,822	5.4	807,333	23.2
Philadelphia, Pa.	140,271	7.3	331,140	26.1
Portland, Ore.	68,234	22.3	135,320	69.1
Providence, R. I.	−4,830	−1.9	65,267	15.4
San Francisco-Oakland, Calif.	223,233	23.8	555,730	105.8
Seattle, Wash.	99,289	27.0	128,723	94.2
St. Louis, Mo.	40,748	5.0	208,445	33.8
Washington, D. C.	139,087	21.0	357,017	117.1
Wilmington, Dela.	−2,148	−1.9	48,699	44.5

Source: 1950 Census of Population, Vol. I, Number of Inhabitants, Table 27, p. 1–69.
a. For definition of "central city" see 1950 Census of Population, Vol. I, p. xxxiii.

site of the earliest settlement or very close to it. Surrounding the central business district are the warehouse and light manufacturing districts, interspersed with slums and blighted areas. Out from the center, the houses are a little better. Many of them were mansions fifty years ago but are now shabby multiple dwellings. Here and there are newer houses of poorer construction — tenements and workers' homes. Next are likely to be found thick clusters of apartment houses. Intensive residential areas ultimately thin out and merge with areas dominated by single-family homes with open space about. Finally, when the end of the built-up area seems to have been reached, there will probably be some open ground, where newer single-family homes and garden apartments begin to appear. Larger metropolitan areas repeat this pattern many times, so that parts of them reflect the convergence of a whole series of forces.

The rapidity of urban growth is one of the major factors contributing to the development of slums and blight. Another is the failure of housing technology to keep pace with needs for shelter. The slums should be technologically unemployed but are not; they are teeming with families who have no other place to go.

MOVEMENT TO SUBURBS

As the central cities became crowded and uncomfortable, people who could afford to do so moved outward. The well-to-do naturally sought the most desirable locations, and high-grade residential development therefore spread steadily away from the centers of cities and from "dead-end" sections limited by natural or artificial barriers to expansion.[8]

The escape, by those who could afford it, from the most objectionable features of city living was an entirely natural process, accelerated by the automobile and rapid transit lines. Developments in transportation have increased the radius of home-to-work travel from the 3 to 5 miles of twenty-five years ago to 10 to 15 miles and even more. This means that at least nine times as much land has been brought within the same time zone.[9]

The Census of 1950 shows that the trend toward the suburbanization of our population has continued. Between 1930 and 1940, for the 140

8. Hoyt, op. cit.
9. Since the area varies as the square of the radius; i.e., a circle with a radius of 5 miles would have an area of about 78.5 square miles, whereas one with a 15-mile radius would have an area of about 707 square miles.

metropolitan districts then defined by the Census, the population in the central cities increased by about 2.5 million, or 6 per cent, while the population outside the central cities increased by about 3.0 million, or approximately 17 per cent.[10] This was only a slightly larger absolute increase but a relative increase three times as great.[11]

For the decade 1940 to 1950, in the 168 standard metropolitan areas defined by the Census, the population increase in the central cities was only 6 million, or 14 per cent, while the increase outside the central cities was more than 9 million, or about 36 per cent. A strict comparison with the 1930–1940 period is not possible because of changes in definition, but it would appear that the absolute population increase in both the central city and the suburbs is considerably larger between 1940 and 1950 and that the relative increase in the suburbs over the central cities is only slightly less.

In contrast to the period 1930 to 1940, however, very few principal metropolitan areas suffered population declines in their central cities between 1940 and 1950. This was largely because of the expansion of city limits during the period. Another possible explanation is that during nearly half the decade there were restrictions on building and on utility extensions due to the war; these factors tended to keep population increases confined to the central cities. There is nothing to show that the trend to the suburbs has been reversed, or even that the rate has declined.

In the hundred largest metropolitan areas in 1950, only seven of the central cities lost population in the ten years preceding, and in only three of these cases did the central city lose while the suburban area gained. In four areas both the central city and the area outside had population declines. In nine instances (all southern cities except one) the central city grew more than the metropolitan area outside; this, however, was due to annexations to city limits.[12]

In three areas the central city increased while the surrounding area declined in population; for one of these the difference was due to changes in city limits. The other two — Stamford, Connecticut, and Duluth, Minnesota — appear to be the only ones among the hundred largest metropolitan areas where the city, without changes in limits, grew more rapidly than the suburbs.

In all but one of 15 widely scattered and more or less representative metropolitan areas, population outside the central city rose at a far greater rate than within the central city between 1940 and 1950. In two cases the number of suburbanites increased at the same time that the number of in-town dwellers declined. The population changes in these areas typify the nationwide trend to the suburbs. (See Table 218.)

DISPERSION OF BUSINESS AND INDUSTRY

The outward drift of population from the central city has been accompanied by a dispersion of the central business districts, a trend which was well established in the 1930 decade and continued at a greatly accelerated rate from 1940 to 1950. Retail business, moving closer to the sources of purchasing power, has spread into an ever-increasing number of shopping subcenters. Large department stores of the downtown districts have found it advantageous to establish branches in the suburbs. The almost intolerable traffic conditions in the downtown districts have made the outlying commercial centers, with their wide parking bays and greater convenience, increasingly popular.

There is a heavy investment in the central business districts of our cities. The central business district, although not specifically defined, is generally considered to be the area within which are located the principal office buildings and which ranks first in retail sales per unit of population.

The importance of the central business district in the economy of our cities is easily illustrated. In Philadelphia, for example, the main business district has less than .007 per cent of the total area of the city but contains 17.4 per cent of the entire city assessment.[13] In Milwaukee the central business district occupies 2.3 per cent of the land area but carries 13 per cent of the total assessed valuation,[14] an investment which is de-

10. Sixteenth Census (1940), *Population*, Vol. I, Table 18, p. 61.

11. The term "metropolitan district," used in the censuses of 1930 and 1940, is not the same as the term "standard metropolitan area" used in 1950. *1950 Census of Population*, Vol. I, p. xxxv.

12. In all of these cases there were annexations to the central city. In six cases the annexations definitely explain the larger increase in the central cities; in the remaining three cases the same explanation is probable.

13. *Proposals for Downtown Philadelphia*, Urban Land Institute, 1942, p. 38.

14. *Proposals for Downtown Milwaukee*, Urban Land Institute, 1941, p. 17.

preciating rapidly, owing primarily to obsolescence. The basic decline has been somewhat obscured in recent prosperous years by new office construction and investment in modernization. But the basic problem remains: intolerable traffic congestion, lack of adequate parking facilities, unsightly and largely outmoded business establishments.

Many groups are concerned with the long-term decline of central business districts. The Urban Land Institute has made a series of studies on the rebuilding of the central parts of cities. As one of these studies aptly says:

The central business district continues as the focal point of the disintegrating community, the locale of vast investment, the center of economic, public, and cultural life. If the old civilizing values of urban living are to become real again, replanning must transfer these centers into places of character, outstanding interest, and expressions of the city personality. They must be made accessible, and they must be stripped of the drabness, unsightliness, and shabbiness that mark them today.[15]

There have been many elaborate plans for central business district redevelopment but only a few have been put into operation.[16]

Industrial Migration

Not only has there been a dispersion of the business district, but industry as well has been moving to the suburbs and even entirely away from the large metropolitan areas.[17] Much of the new plant expansion during World War II occurred on the outskirts of cities. Even before that, industries located in cities were building additional plant facilities outside the central city.

This industrial migration is exerting a strong influence upon residential development. While people do not like to live close to the smoke, odors and noise of industry, neither do they like to travel long distances to work. Furthermore, the great technical advances in plant construction

and in the control of smoke and other nuisances have probably lifted some of the curse off living close to industry. The modern plants of light industries particularly have little or no bad effect upon the surrounding areas.

The possibility of atomic attack is a new stimulus to industrial decentralization. According to the National Security Resources Board, "There is no known military defense against the atomic bomb itself except space."[18] The major defense, the Board said in its report, is the dispersion of industry. "The scarcity of the essential materials for the manufacture of an atomic bomb makes production so costly that we may reasonably assume that no country in the foreseeable future will ever have enough to afford to use one on each city of as few as 50,000 people, or on a congested industrial area of less than five square miles."

The Board recognized that the maximum desired dispersion was economically impossible, but it urged that security factors be taken into account in new plant location or plant expansion. Industrial construction should be avoided within a three-mile radius of prime targets such as an industrial plant producing a large percentage of a highly critical item, power plants, railroad terminals, key establishments of the armed forces, dams and bridges.

LAND SPECULATION

Land speculation and the consequent artificial increase in land values have contributed heavily to the development of slums and the conditions which perpetuate them. Ironically, many of our efforts — in zoning, for example — aggravated the very conditions they were intended to alleviate.

In the second decade of this century, we began to take official notice of the fact that unbridled use of land by individuals sometimes reacts unfavorably upon the community as a whole. The introduction of zoning was bitterly fought as a transgression against the inalienable rights of pri-

---

15. *Ibid.*, p. 5.
16. Among the most notable is Pittsburgh's redevelopment of its Golden Triangle. See pp. 506–507.
17. "An intensive analysis of recent industrial decentralization and relocation in the Chicago area, conducted by the City Planning Commission, disclosed that during the ten years preceding 1935 there was a known exodus of 127 manufacturing concerns from corporate Chicago to various outside points within its industrial area. Within the past five years alone, over 4,000 net employment opportunities were transferred from the city to outlying areas as a result of the excess of industries leaving Chicago over new manufacturing concerns locating inside the city's boundaries." Leverett S. Lyon, "Economic Problems of American Cities," *American Economic Review Supplement*, March 1942.

18. "National Security Factors in Industrial Location," National Security Resources Board Doc. 66, revised July 22, 1948. The National Security Resources Board, established by the National Security Act of 1947, is part of the Executive Office of the President, and is charged with advising the President concerning the coordination of military, industrial and civilian mobilization, including "the strategic relocation of industries, services, government, and economic activities, the continued operation of which is essential to the Nation's security." *United States Government Organization Manual, 1951–52*, p. 65.

vate property. Property owners nearly always exerted their influence to maximize the area designated for intensive use, that is, use for apartment houses and other multi-family structures of high density and yielding a high return per acre. Largely as a matter of expediency, but partly out of ignorance, this pressure generally was yielded to in drafting zoning ordinances.[19]

As a result, American cities have in general been overzoned for commercial and intensive residential use. Owners of property in areas in which intensive use is permitted interpreted mere permission as a blueprint for the future. They rapidly began to build mental skyscrapers, department stores or apartment house blocks on their sites. And these visions began to be translated into dollars and cents. Astute appraisers called them values, and financial institutions made loans on these values.

Landowners adopted a policy of waiting until the projected intensive use of their land, and the consequent increase in value, would materialize. They neglected to make improvements and devised temporary uses of their land. High expectations led to a wild scramble for land; the holders, three or four times removed from the original purchasers, sat back patiently waiting. And many of them are still waiting.

In order to sustain their illusions, many of those who held the land for long-term increments were willing to pay taxes on valuations out of all proportion to the property's worth. Thus our system of general property taxes, with little or no relation to the earning power of the property, operated to sustain fictitious values.

High land values in the central sections of our cities are among the principal obstacles to making our cities attractive places in which to live. Even if a builder with great difficulty were able to assemble a sufficient plot of this land, he would be forced, because of its cost, to develop it at a density comparable to the crowded condition which originally contributed to its decay. Hence the paradox that the land which holds a large part of all that is mean and sordid in our cities is also among the most expensive.

INCREASED MUNICIPAL SERVICES

Many efforts to improve urban living conditions also accelerated the movement away from cities. Some cities widened main thoroughfares so that people from the newly created suburbs could more easily get downtown to do their shopping. But these through streets also made it easier for people to move out. Utilities and services were extended to the limits of cities — even though the land within the city had not been fully developed — and more and more land outside was opened up for development.

The movement away from the central city came at a time when the services and functions of city governments were increasing and calling for greatly increased expenditures. The availability of many of these services actually encouraged those who could best afford their higher cost to move away. But when industrial plants and commercial establishments moved to the suburbs the cities still had to provide services — or relief — for their workers, although the plants themselves were outside the cities' taxing jurisdiction. Left behind was an urban population with a greater concentration of low-income groups — potential inhabitants of blighted and slum areas who, at the same time, were less able to finance urban redevelopment.

ATTEMPTS TO COPE WITH SLUMS AND BLIGHT

If slums and blight are not new, neither are attempts to deal with them. Elaborate housing legislation made its first recorded appearance in the Code of Hammurabi about 2000 B.C. In ancient Rome, which became crowded with slums, Emperor Augustus found it necessary to limit the height of tenements as a protection against disastrous fires.[20]

In America, a city plan for New Netherland (New York City) as early as 1625 provided for the layout of the city and the control of lot size, height of buildings, space between buildings and size of kitchens. Intermittently, the city passed various laws to regulate housing, usually as a consequence of epidemics, fires or the collapse of buildings. The first extensive act dealing with tenements was passed in New York in 1867. Philadelphia enacted a tenement house law in 1895; Chicago in 1902; and Pittsburgh in 1903.[21]

Over the years, these cities changed, modified

---

19. Ernest M. Fisher, "Economic Aspects of Zoning, Blighted Areas, and Rehabilitation Laws," a paper before the annual meeting of the American Economic Association in New York City, December 29, 1941.

20. Arthur B. Gallion, *The Urban Pattern*, Van Nostrand, New York, 1950, p. 28.

21. Edith Elmer Wood, *Slums and Blighted Areas in the United States*, Bulletin No. 1, Housing Division, Federal Emergency Administration of Public Works, 1936.

and extended their laws and many other cities attempted to remove or improve slums by similar legislation. But all of these efforts were feeble. The intermittent crusades quickly foundered when enforcement officers discovered that if slum buildings were torn down, their occupants had no place to go; if owners were forced to make necessary improvements, many of them would close their structures; if the improvements were made, the capital investment was written off quickly in sharply increased rentals.

The testimony of the Solicitor of the City of Pittsburgh before the Joint Committee on Housing clearly illustrates the problems of the enforcement officer:

We have a problem of human beings who have nowhere to sleep. When a building gets into such condition that there is fear of killing the people in the building and killing the passersby in the street, we condemn the building and tear it down, but in any way where our inspectors find they can still stay another month, another 2 months, we cannot be so soulless as to forget the needs of our people and put them out on the street, just to penalize the landlord. We would be glad to padlock the houses and penalize the landlord, but we cannot penalize our citizens.[22]

In very recent years a number of localities have made real attempts to improve housing conditions through law enforcement. Law enforcement can be effective if it does not result in rental increases beyond the tenants' ability to pay or in the demolition of houses while no satisfactory alternative accommodations are available. Effective prosecution of local housing ordinances can succeed best when new or existing standard dwellings are being made available at reasonable rentals or prices.

The problem of bad housing is so large that it must be attacked on all fronts: through private housing; public housing for the very low income groups; rehabilitation; and enactment and enforcement of housing and sanitary codes. None of these alone can do the job that needs to be done. Each must be viewed in its proper perspective.

PUBLIC HOUSING

The first concentrated attack upon slums and blight in this country was made by the federal government, under the National Industrial Recovery Act of 1933. Before that, the only efforts were a few isolated projects by nonprofit organizations and a small number of loans to limited-dividend companies by the Reconstruction Finance Corporation; only one such project was built in a cleared slum.

The Public Works Administration Housing Division was set up to carry on a program of slum clearance and to build houses for low-income families. Under this program, 56 projects containing 24,600 units were constructed, of which 7 projects, with 3,100 units, were built with loans to limited-dividend corporations. The others were built by the government and were federally owned. As of December 31, 1953, 5 projects with 1,900 units were still being operated by the federal government, 27 projects with 14,750 units were leased to local housing authorities, and 17 projects with 4,900 units had been transferred to local authorities.[23] Even in this program the primary emphasis was upon alleviation of unemployment rather than elimination of bad housing.

This method of direct federal action was replaced, under the provisions of the United States Housing Act of 1937, by a system of loans and annual contributions to local housing authorities designed to enable localities to carry out their own slum clearance and building. The housing act, in the words of its preamble, was an act "for the elimination of unsafe and insanitary housing conditions, for the eradication of slums, for the provision of decent, safe, and sanitary dwellings for families of low income, and for the reduction of unemployment and the stimulation of business activity." New projects did not have to be placed on slum sites, but for every new unit built a substandard unit had to be eliminated or effectively repaired. Actually, about half the projects were built on slum sites.

About 170,000 units were provided under the Housing Act of 1937. During the war, 50,000 of these units were diverted from their intended use for low-income families to serve war workers. Practically all were returned to low-rent use by the end of 1946.

The Housing Act of 1949 amended the original legislation to permit the construction of an estimated 810,000 low-rent dwelling units over a six-year period, at a rate not exceeding 135,000

---

22. Testimony of Anne X. Alpern, Solicitor, City of Pittsburgh, Pennsylvania, Hearings before the Joint Committee on Housing, 80th Cong., 1st sess., 1947, Part 1, p. 175. At this point in her testimony the Solicitor was dealing only with extremely hazardous structures. She says later that enforcement officers were almost powerless to deal with less critical cases.

23. *Annual Report, 1953*, Public Housing Administration.

units a year.[24] The new act continued the requirement of equivalent elimination of substandard units, except where the project was being built in a rural nonfarm area or on the site of a slum cleared subsequent to July 15, 1949.

Throughout the course through Congress of the various bills which eventuated in the Housing Act of 1949 the entire consideration was for provision of decent housing for low-income families who could not otherwise afford it. The act set forth a housing policy for the nation:

The Congress hereby declares that the general welfare and security of the Nation and the health and living standards of its people require housing production and related community development sufficient to remedy the serious housing shortage, the elimination of substandard and other inadequate housing through the clearance of slums and blighted areas, and the realization as soon as feasible of the goal of a decent home and a suitable living environment for every American family, thus contributing to the development and redevelopment of communities and to the advancement of the growth, wealth, and security of the Nation.

Under this low-rent program, as of December 31, 1953, allocation had been made of 356,000 units in 1,115 localities in the United States, Hawaii, Alaska, Puerto Rico and the Virgin Islands; and 178,000 units were completed or under construction. Owing to the extreme housing shortages in most cities, the majority of the first projects were being built on vacant land, but about half of the 227,000 units for which definitive plans had been approved as of December 31, 1953 were to be built on slum sites. In the earlier program only 11 per cent of the units were on vacant sites; 47 per cent were on dense slum sites and 42 per cent on partially vacant sites, from which, however, a substantial number of substandard dwellings had to be removed.

LEGISLATION FOR PRIVATE REDEVELOPMENT

Following enactment of the public low-rent housing program, it was claimed that private industry, if given the same powers as public agencies, could successfully undertake compar-

able slum clearance and housing projects.[25] Ultimately 13 states passed laws authorizing the creation of private redevelopment corporations.

While these acts vary in detail, all are essentially enabling acts authorizing the creation of private redevelopment corporations for the purpose of acquiring land in slums and blighted areas and constructing and operating dwelling accommodations and auxiliary commercial facilities in such areas. Projects are authorized to be undertaken with the assistance of certain public powers, privileges and exemptions, but subject to certain limitations and regulations and to supervision by public bodies. All of the state laws provide assistance through the power of eminent domain, authorizing either the exercise of the power by the redevelopment corporations or by municipalities in their interest. Over half the laws authorize some form of tax exemption or exemption from increased assessment for tax purposes. Some of the laws also provide for public assistance in furnishing streets, parks, and other public works and facilities.[26]

Activity under the state private redevelopment corporation laws has been very limited. Probably the most noteworthy accomplishment to date has been the building of Stuyvesant Town in New York City by the Metropolitan Life Insurance Company.[27] It became apparent that the aids in the various state laws were insufficient to induce private corporations to carry out slum clearance and redevelopment projects. One of the principal difficulties was the fact that the cost of land in the central city slum areas and the costs of demolition were too great to permit redevelopment at rentals consistent with community plans.[28]

Furthermore, these laws provided only for residential redevelopment, which in some areas might not be in keeping with a community's long-range requirements.

FEDERAL LEGISLATION

As it became apparent that relatively little could be accomplished under state redevelop-

---

24. A limitation in the Independent Offices Appropriation Act for fiscal year 1952 placed this at 50,000 units for that fiscal year and the Appropriation Act for fiscal 1953 limited construction to 35,000 units in 1953 and in subsequent years unless increased by Congress. The 1954 Appropriation Act limited construction to 20,000 units out of those already under contract.

25. Philip H. Hill, "Recent Slum Clearance and Urban Redevelopment Laws," *Washington and Lee Law Review,* Vol. IX, No. 2, 1952.

26. Data for this paragraph were taken from *Comparative Analysis of the Principal Provisions of the State Urban Redevelopment Corporation Laws,* Office of the General Counsel, National Housing Agency (now the Housing and Home Finance Agency), as supplemented October 15, 1950.

27. Hill, *op. cit.*

28. *Ibid.*

ment laws, proposals began to be made for federal assistance to localities for the assembly and writing down of high-cost slum land.[29]

Legislative History

Two of these proposals resulted in specific legislation introduced in the first session of the Seventy-eighth Congress. The first of these was the Hansen-Greer proposal, which is found in the Thomas bill; the second was the Wagner bill, based on proposals of the Urban Land Institute.[30] These two bills represented a synthesis of informed opinion at the time; though differing in detail, they agreed on certain basic points:

(1) Federal loans to localities for the public purchase of land in slum and blighted areas, the granting of loans to be conditional upon a comprehensive master plan and effective local controls over land use;

(2) Revaluation of the purchased land through federal subsidy, the value of the land to be determined by its value in use and without regard to its cost;

(3) Lease or sale of the land to private and public agencies for redevelopment through large-scale neighborhood projects.

No hearings were held on either of the bills, nor were they reintroduced in the Seventy-ninth Congress.

In 1945, after extensive hearings, the Wagner-Ellender-Taft bill (S. 1592) was introduced in the Senate. Title VI of the bill provided for federal assistance to localities in the acquisition of slum areas, in their preparation for redevelopment, and in the writing down of the land cost to its value in appropriate use. The funds provided, $500 million in loans and $20 million yearly in contributions, were admittedly small

and would have made possible little more than a demonstration program. The bill passed the Senate with hardly a dissenting vote but failed to come to a vote in the House, when it adjourned before adequate hearings were held.

The Wagner-Ellender-Taft bill represented important changes from the earlier proposals. It was based on a narrower concept of urban redevelopment: the federal interest was conceived to extend only to the clearance of residential slums together with commercial buildings generally found in such neighborhoods. The second important change was the use of annual contributions by the federal government, rather than long-term federal loans, to finance the deficits involved in writing down land values. Finally, the bill forthrightly recognized the problem of rehousing families displaced from cleared sites. It required that before any redevelopment could take place there must be (1) a plan for the temporary relocation of displaced families, and (2) decent, safe and sanitary dwellings available or being provided at rents within the reasonable ability of the displaced families to pay.

When the political character of Congress changed in 1946, the Wagner-Ellender-Taft bill became the Taft-Ellender-Wagner bill (S. 866). The only notable change between the two bills was in the financing of losses. In the first, this was to be done by annual contributions from the federal government; in the second, by capital grants. The method of annual contributions had considerable merit, since the federal assistance each year was limited to just the amount necessary to make up the difference between income and expense, including amortization of the cost of acquisition. However, the difficulties of administration are manifest when the amount of property held is continually changing. The capital grant approach was probably the best solution in this case.

The Taft-Ellender-Wagner bill, like its predecessor, passed the Senate with hardly a dissent. Although there were extensive hearings in the House, the bill never came to a vote there.

Early in 1949, at the first session of the Eighty-first Congress, twenty-two senators, eleven Democrats and eleven Republicans, including among their number the authors of the two previous bills, introduced a new housing bill (S. 1070).[31]

---

29. See Hansen and Greer, *op. cit.; Handbook on Urban Redevelopment for Cities in the United States*, Federal Housing Administration, 1941; *Outline for a Legislative Program to Rebuild Our Cities*, Urban Land Institute, 1942; *A Proposal for Rebuilding Blighted City Areas*, National Association of Real Estate Boards, 1942; Charles Ascher, *Better Cities*, National Resources Planning Board, 1942; "Report of the Committee on Urban Redevelopment of the American Society of Planning Officials," in the proceedings of the National Conference on Planning, 1942; and "A Summary of Studies and Proposals in the U.S.A. on Assembly of Land for Urban Development and Redevelopment," Urban Development Division, National Housing Agency, September 1944 (mimeographed).

30. S. 953, introduced April 2, 1943 by Senator Thomas of Utah, cited as the "Federal Urban Redevelopment Act of 1943"; and S. 1163, introduced June 4, 1943 by Senator Wagner of New York, cited as the "Neighborhood Redevelopment Act."

31. There had previously been two bills: S. 138, introduced by a group of Democratic senators; and S. 709, sponsored by a group of Republican senators. There were

This bill passed the Senate by a record vote of 57 to 13. The House again held extensive hearings and finally passed what became the Housing Act of 1949 by a vote of 228 to 185.

While some groups opposed the redevelopment feature of the bill, it was not a major item of discussion either during the hearings or in floor debate. Generally speaking, there was overwhelming support. It was recognized that the amounts involved were small in comparison with the total need for urban redevelopment. The sponsors of the program said often: this is an overwhelming problem; let us get on with an experimental program and see what we can do.

The Housing Act of 1949

Title I of the Housing Act of 1949 provides for federal assistance to local public agencies for slum clearance and urban redevelopment. This Title is administered by the Slum Clearance and Urban Redevelopment Division of the Housing and Home Finance Agency. Assistance may be in the form of loans and capital grants. The act provides for a total of $1 billion in loan funds outstanding at any time and $500 million in capital grants.[32]

Two forms of loans are provided. First, the federal government may make loans to local public agencies for the assembly, clearance, preparation, and sale or lease of land for redevelopment. Such loans may not exceed a forty-year term and are to bear interest at not less than the applicable federal going rate at the time the loan is made. Before definitive loans are made, there may be temporary loans up to the time the full cost of the project is determined. At the time of definitive financing the local public agency issues its own bonds, which may be purchased by the federal government or sold in the private market.

Second, in connection with projects on land which is open or predominantly open, the federal government may make loans not exceeding a ten-year term to municipalities or other public bodies for the provision of public buildings or facilities necessary to serve or support the new uses of land in the project area.

In addition, the federal government may make advances for surveys and plans in connection with the preparation of projects. These advances are to be repaid out of any funds which may become available for the eventual undertaking of the particular project.

The federal government, except in the case of projects on open land, may also make capital grants to local public agencies to enable such agencies to make land in project areas available for redevelopment at its fair value for the uses specified in the redevelopment plans. The federal government may agree to bear two thirds of any loss, provided the locality agrees to bear one third. The capital grant is intended to make possible the most appropriate use of the land without regard to its original cost.

In extending financial assistance, the law requires that consideration be given to the extent to which (1) local public bodies have undertaken positive programs for encouraging reductions in housing costs through modernization of local building and other codes so as to permit the use of new materials, techniques and methods, and (2) there is local action to prevent the spread or recurrence of slums and blight through the adoption, improvement and modernization of local codes and regulations relating to land use and adequate standards of health, sanitation and safety for dwelling accommodations. The law also requires that encouragement be given to the operations of local public agencies established on a state or regional (within a state) or unified metropolitan basis.

During the course of this legislation through Congress consideration was given to making certain of the above conditions prerequisites to financial assistance. It was finally agreed, however, that the absolute requirement of all of these conditions might, in certain cases of conflicting political jurisdiction, delay urban redevelopment for years. Nonetheless, Congress announced as a matter of policy that these important matters are to be taken into account in determining whether to extend federal assistance.

Conditions of Federal Assistance

There are, however, certain conditions which must be met before financial assistance by the federal government is made available:

1. The redevelopment plan must be approved by the governing body of the locality, and this approval must include a finding that the financial aid is necessary for such redevelopment; that the plan for the

---

some differences in the bills, none affecting urban redevelopment, but these were reconciled and S. 1070 was introduced with bipartisan support.

32. These funds were made available in installments through 1953.

area will afford maximum opportunity, consistent with the needs of the locality as a whole, for redevelopment by private enterprise; and that the plan for the area conforms to a general plan for the redevelopment of the locality as a whole.

2. When land in the redevelopment area is sold or leased, the purchasers or lessees must agree to devote the land to the uses specified in the plan and to begin the building of these improvements within a reasonable time.

3. There must be a feasible plan for the temporary relocation of families displaced from the project area and, very importantly, assurance "that there are or are being provided, in the project area or in other areas not generally less desirable in regard to public utilities and public and commercial facilities and at rents or prices within the financial means of the families displaced from the project area, decent, safe, and sanitary dwellings equal in number to the number of and available to such displaced families and reasonably accessible to their places of employment." [33]

4. Finally, no land for any project may be acquired except after public hearing.

The definitions in the law also place conditions upon financial assistance. In defining "redevelopment plan" the law states that the plan must be sufficiently complete to indicate its relationship to definite local objectives as to appropriate land uses and improved traffic, public transportation, public utilities, recreational and community facilities and requires that in approving the plan steps must be taken to assure consistency between it and any highways or other public improvements for which the locality is receiving assistance from the Federal Works Agency.[34]

A "project" as defined in the law may include four types of land, all of them to be developed for predominantly residential use: a slum area or a deteriorated or deteriorating area which is predominantly residential in character; any other deteriorated or deteriorating area; land which is mostly open and which because of obsolete platting, diversity of ownership, or for other reasons substantially impairs or arrests the sound growth of the community; and open land necessary for sound community growth.[35]

While there are, and will be, some isolated instances of urban redevelopment carried on entirely by local government, it is probable that in the immediate future the far larger portion of urban redevelopment programs will be carried on with the assistance offered by the federal government. There are a few instances, and these may increase in the future, in which local appropriations are made to supplement the rather limited programs which can be undertaken in any one locality with the federal financial aid available.

Proposed Housing Act of 1954

In September 1953, the President appointed a twenty-two-man Advisory Committee on Government Housing Policies and Programs. The report of this committee, issued in December 1953, contained a number of recommendations on urban redevelopment which were ultimately embodied in proposed new housing legislation.[36]

Although utilizing the urban redevelopment provisions of Title I of the Housing Act of 1949 as the essential framework, the proposed amendments broaden the concept of urban redevelopment. In particular, the changes contemplated are: [37]

1. The definition of "project" is enlarged so that it may include not only areas requiring clearance but also other areas suitable for the application of rehabilitation and conservation measures.

2. More site improvement items are eligible for inclusion in project cost. Existing legislation permits the inclusion of streets, utilities and other site improvements essential to prepare sites for uses in accordance with the redevelopment plan. The proposed legislation would add parks, playgrounds and other improvements not only in a clearance area but in a rehabilitation or conservation area.

3. Permissible uses of loan funds are expanded to include the preparation of plans to carry out a program of voluntary repair and rehabilitation and plans for the preparation and enforcement of state and local laws, codes and regulations relating to the use of land and the use and occupancy of buildings and improvements, and to the compulsory repair, rehabilitation, demolition or removal of buildings and improvements.

4. A sum of $5 million is authorized to assist the development of pilot projects to demonstrate the possibilities of local action in eliminating slums and blight and preventing their spread.

The proposed legislation also requires as a condition of federal aid for redevelopment that there be in the locality a workable program "for utilizing appropriate private and public resources

---

33. Housing Act of 1949, Title I, Section 105(c).
34. *Ibid.*, Section 110(b).
35. *Ibid.*, Section 110(c).

36. H.R. 7839, 83d Cong., 2d sess., in the House of Representatives and a companion bill, S. 2938, 83d Cong., 2d sess., in the Senate.
37. Hearings before the Committee on Banking and Currency, U.S. Senate, 83d Cong., 2d sess., on the Housing Act of 1954, Part 1, pp. 216–218. There are, in addition, a number of technical amendments not covered in this section.

to eliminate, and prevent the development or spread of, slums and urban blight, to encourage needed urban rehabilitation, to provide for the redevelopment of blighted, deteriorated, or slum areas, or to undertake such of the aforesaid activities or other feasible community activities as may be suitably employed to achieve the objectives of such a program." [38] This proposal grew out of a strong belief that the federal government should assist only localities that undertake positive programs to prevent the recurrence of conditions which urban redevelopment is called upon to correct.

STATE LEGISLATION

Ability of localities to take advantage of the assistance offered by the federal government is derived from state laws. At the heart of urban redevelopment activity is legal authority to engage in planning.

A report on the park system in the District of Columbia in 1902 marked the beginning of community planning in the United States. The first official planning commission was not created until 1907, and the first modern city plan was not prepared and published until 1909.

Rapid strides have been made since. By 1951, the legislatures of 40 states had expressly authorized community planning. Twenty-seven of these states authorize planning on a county-wide basis and 22 authorize regional planning. The absence of state authorization does not necessarily preclude action under a local charter provision or under some general statutory authority.

The state enabling statutes vary widely in the powers they grant. For example, in 17 states, there is no express authority for extending planning activities beyond the corporate limits of cities; in 26 states, there is no express authority granted for final approval or adoption of a comprehensive plan by the city council or other local governing body; in 9 states there is no authority for including in the plans any recommendations with regard to such items as land use, population density, or location of streets, parks or similar facilities.[39]

Not only must a local public agency have legal authorization for planning, but under the federal law financial assistance may be extended only to those agencies which have the power to acquire land in slum and blighted areas by eminent domain or otherwise, to dispose of such land for redevelopment, to finance redevelopment projects through the issuance of bonds or other obligations, and to enter into contracts with the federal government for financial assistance.[40] By the end of 1953, these conditions were met by 32 states, 4 territories and the District of Columbia.[41] A specific public agency was designated to carry out redevelopment in 31 of the 37 laws. Sixteen laws named the local housing authority as the redevelopment agency; 7 set up a separate redevelopment agency; and in 8 laws the municipality was designated as the operating unit. Of the 6 laws giving an option as to the agency to be designated, 4 permitted a choice among a separate redevelopment agency, the local housing authority or the municipality, and 2 provided only for selection between the first two of these.

URBAN REDEVELOPMENT IN OPERATION

Something must be done about our cities. However, there are many different opinions as to what should be done. Some of these differences are largely in emphasis; others are basic.

Whatever the approach to urban redevelopment, these points are paramount:

1. There should be an effective plan for the relocation of displaced site occupants.

2. It is generally agreed that planning should be done on a broad scale, extending not only to the city's corporate limits but to the whole metropolitan area. Although tax rates and municipal services may change abruptly at artificial political boundaries, all the residents of a metropolitan district are part of a single urban organism, whether they occupy an apart-

---

38. H.R. 7839, 83d Cong., 2d sess., as passed by the House of Representatives, Title III, Section 303.

39. Data for this and the two preceding paragraphs were taken from *Comparative Digest of the Principal Provisions of State Planning Laws Relating to Housing, Slum Clearance, and Urban Redevelopment, as of January 1, 1951,* Office of the Administrator, Division of Law, Housing and Home Finance Agency.

40. See Hill, *op. cit.*

41. "State and Territorial Legislation Authorizing Local Public Agencies to Undertake Slum Clearance and Urban Redevelopment Projects," Division of Law, Housing and Home Finance Agency, December 31, 1951 (mimeographed) and the Annual Report of the Housing and Home Finance Agency, 1953. Although Texas had no enabling legislation, the city charter adopted by San Antonio on October 2, 1951 under home rule provisions of the state constitution expressly authorized the city to engage in redevelopment activities. In two states, Florida and Georgia, state supreme courts held redevelopment laws unconstitutional on the grounds that the condemnation of land for redevelopment for private use was not a public purpose. In a large number of states, redevelopment laws were upheld by the courts.

ment downtown or a house in the suburbs. Whatever is done anywhere in the metropolitan area affects all of its residents directly or indirectly. The principal job of planning falls upon local planning agencies, but broad citizen interest and participation are needed if we are eventually to have the kind of cities all of us want.

3. When an area is acquired, its redevelopment must be dictated by the best interests of the locality. Land use and density of development should be rigidly controlled. And, above all, adequate safeguards must be provided to prevent a recurrence of the conditions which brought about the need for urban redevelopment.

PROBLEMS OF REDEVELOPMENT

The problem of what to do about displaced site occupants dwarfs all other difficulties in an urban redevelopment program.

Occupants of slum and blighted areas by no means fall in a narrow band of income or of racial, social or cultural characteristics. Many families belonging to racial minority groups live in substandard areas neither through economic necessity nor by choice, but solely because decent housing is not available to them elsewhere in the community at any cost. Racial minority groups probably present the greatest relocation problem, but there are many others.

What is to be done with those individuals at the bottom of the economic scale — the occupants of flop houses and rooming houses? There is no housing program for them nor are they protected by the relocation provisions of the law. The public housing program as presently constituted is restricted to families of two or more persons. It is hardly conceivable that private enterprise will develop decent accommodations for the poor who live alone. Of the families displaced in New York City by slum clearance, public improvements and various forms of redevelopment over the period 1946–1953, nearly 30 per cent were one-person families, according to a report of the New York City Planning Commission on Relocation.

What, also, is to be done with those at the very lowest end of the social and moral scale? Along with families struggling to make a better life for themselves and their children, the slums also shelter the prostitutes, the thieves, the cripples and the mentally handicapped. Many of these need institutional care more than new housing. For them, however, the bulldozers only cause a scurrying for new holes and not a better life.

The relocation of homeowners who live in the redevelopment area is another difficult problem. Many of these hold only nominal title because of a very small equity. A good deal of this type of possession is reputed to have been forced within the past ten years by previous owners because of their desire to avoid rent control or payment for correction of violations. Even with a very small down payment the return in the form of debt service was greater than the rental. In a number of cases the courts have ruled against fictitious sales, and the Baltimore press has called attention to the practice.

The majority of owners in these areas, however, do have substantial equities, and a number of them own their homes free of encumbrance. It is a serious question whether these people will receive enough for their homes either in a negotiated sale or through a condemnation award to enable them to purchase elsewhere at equivalent monthly costs. The problem is particularly acute for Negro owners because of their limited opportunities for purchasing homes. In the early stages of redevelopment, therefore, it will be necessary to avoid areas where there are any substantial number of owners. Ultimately, however, it will be necessary to redevelop these areas if our cities are to be regenerated as places in which it is good to live.

The problems of relocation for many of these groups are aggravated by a shortage of decent low-rent housing. Although the federal urban redevelopment law sets up safeguards for families living in areas to be redeveloped, the lack of alternative accommodations is at present a major stumbling block. Except for those families who qualify for public low-rent housing — and this program has been greatly reduced — other dwellings have not been readily available.

Public Housing and Redevelopment

Throughout the legislative course of the Housing Act of 1949 it was brought out time and again that one of the reasons for the low-rent public housing program was to care for the families displaced by urban redevelopment. But the act stipulates that a family must be in the lowest income group to be eligible for admission to public housing. Although a major portion of the families in redevelopment areas are eligible on this basis, a substantial number are not.

Furthermore, the law requires that in any event

the maximum rent for admission to public housing must be at least 20 per cent below the lowest
rents at which private enterprise is making available a substantial supply of standard housing.
Since rent in public housing is fixed at 20 per
cent of income (less certain exemptions and deductions), a maximum limitation is placed upon
the income group which may be served. As a
result, some families have too much income for
public housing but too little to afford other
standard accommodations.

The difference in handling the cost of slum
clearance under public housing and in an urban
redevelopment program under Title I of the
Housing Act of 1949 creates a serious problem. In the case of public housing, slum clearance
may be achieved through the acquisition of a
slum site or through building on a vacant site
and clearing elsewhere. When public housing is
built on a slum site, the cost of clearance is part
of the cost of the project and is subsidized. But
when the building is on a vacant site any clearance that is done is not charged to the project.
Furthermore, when slums are cleared through
public housing there is no write-down of the
cost of the slum site; public housing bears the
entire cost. On the other hand, when land is
made available through urban redevelopment at
its value in the use to which it will be put, the
necessary loss is subsidized. Thus, under public
housing there is every incentive to increase the
densities of projects in order to hold down high
unit costs which result from the purchase of
expensive slum sites. A large part of the funds
which were primarily intended for housing are
used for slum clearance. This runs directly
counter to the urban redevelopment objective of
reducing density, one of the main causes of
slums.

It is generally recognized that public housing
is a necessary part of an urban redevelopment
program if residential slum and blighted areas
are to be reclaimed.[42] The amount of assistance it
can give, however, is limited by law. The major
burden of urban redevelopment therefore falls
upon private enterprise. Hence ways and means
must be found for reducing the cost of private
housing if urban redevelopment is to succeed. It
is important, however, that portions of redevelopment areas adapted to public housing develop-

ment be made available to local housing authorities at a cost which will enable them to rebuild at
densities permitting healthy and decent living.

Scope of Planning

Another problem of urban redevelopment is
the danger of inadequate planning.

The site must, first of all, be large enough for
an effective project. A redevelopment program
should not be used, for example, to clean out a
small group of very bad slum housing while leaving a deteriorated periphery untouched.

One of the primary purposes of urban redevelopment is to promote stability. Stability cannot be achieved unless the use to which land is
put is adequately protected both by regulation
and by good planning.

A redevelopment plan should be concerned
not only with the immediate project site but also
with the city and the metropolitan area as a
whole. So far as a site itself is concerned, the
principal danger is in piecemeal planning. The
plans for any one urban redevelopment site are
necessarily affected by the plans for others. The
entire program must mesh; particular programs
must conform to a general plan for the community as a whole, if assistance is sought from the
federal government.

A city plan alone, however, is in itself piecemeal planning. To be of maximum benefit now,
and to future generations, planning should not
be limited to the city proper, but should extend
to the entire metropolitan area. One of the early
redevelopment bills introduced in Congress required that there be a metropolitan plan as a
condition of federal assistance.[43] This proposal
was dropped from subsequent legislation because of the difficulty of forcing separate political
jurisdictions to act in unison. It was believed that
the provision would hold up urban redevelopment indefinitely.

Regardless of the difficulties, communities
must be planned on a metropolitan area basis and
redevelopment programs must be geared to such
plans if we are not again to repeat the mistakes
of the past. The answer may lie in easier annexa-
tion proceedings making it possible for an entire
area to be governed as an integrated unit. Or it
may lie in state legislation requiring large-area
planning. Even this, of course, would not solve

42. See Coleman Woodbury and Frederick A. Gutheim,
Rethinking Urban Redevelopment, Public Administration Service, 1949, p. 13.

43. The Thomas bill, S. 953, 78th Cong., 1st sess.

the problem for metropolitan areas which cross state lines.

REBUILDING CENTRAL CITIES

The rebuilding of central cities is an alternate approach to urban redevelopment. This is an attempt to halt the flight to the suburbs, to reconstitute the central city on a sound financial basis and to stabilize and protect central city realty values. The theory is that if we can again make city life attractive we can lure back many of the higher-income families from the suburbs.

This approach visualizes a renascence of cities as places in which to live and work. Old and dilapidated structures in slums and blighted areas would be ripped out, areas replanned, and the outmoded gridiron street pattern replaced with drives and service streets functionally designed and following the contours of the land. Many unneeded old streets would be vacated and turned into open space for playgrounds or gardens.

Many cities throughout the country, large and small, have prepared comprehensive redevelopment plans. These plans have a richness in variety of concept and planning which is brought about largely by the peculiar conditions faced in each locality.

Philadelphia

The City Council of Philadelphia is carrying out one of the most extensive redevelopment plans in the country. There are five project areas in various stages of planning and development, involving in all about eight square miles and containing a population of 22,600. City, state and federal funds will be used, with large-scale participation by private enterprise. The total cost of redevelopment from federal, state and city funds is estimated to exceed $30 million. This investment of public funds is expected to generate private investment of approximately $200 million.

Clearance and redevelopment northeast of the central business district is being combined with rehabilitation of three adjoining areas, known as East Poplar, Southwest Temple and North Allen, totaling 85 acres. Uses of the land will be principally residential, including private housing and state-assisted and federally-assisted low-rent housing. The rebuilding and rehabilitation of the area will provide also for a new junior high school, additional playgrounds, and improved institutional and commercial facilities. In the University Project, located near the University of Pennsylvania and the Drexel Institute of Technology, the city is planning a project of about 25 acres. A part will be sold to the University and Drexel Institute for institutional use and another part is allocated to new private housing. One of the nation's largest projects is expected to be the Eastwick Project in the southwest section of the city near the Municipal Airport. Here an area of 3,000 acres is being replanned to provide 12,600 new dwelling units of varied types together with related commercial and civic uses. Also being planned is the Triangle Project near the center of the city, which will eliminate a slum area and provide new apartment buildings.

Consideration is also being given to the Old City Area, containing numerous buildings of national historical importance — Independence Hall, Carpenters Hall, Old Customs House, and a number of churches and residences dating back to colonial days. The plan calls for selective clearance to provide a suitable setting for these historic shrines. To blend the new with the old and to retain as much of the feeling of the area as possible, the height and design of the new buildings will be determined after consultation with various civic and historical groups.

St. Louis

The City of St. Louis envisions an extensive long-range program for redevelopment by clearance, redevelopment and rehabilitation. Principal points in the city's plan include a central parkway linking Jefferson Memorial and Memorial Plaza with garages beneath; commercial expansion along Market and Chestnut Streets; and residential redevelopment of blighted central and outlying areas with related expansion of school and recreation facilities. The completion of the initial slum clearance and urban redevelopment proposals will result in clearance of a nine-block blighted nonresidential area at the edge of the central business district and construction of some 1,100 apartment units, together with extension of the Soldiers Memorial Park area. Other projects under preliminary consideration involve redevelopment for residential use in some areas and industrial expansion in others.

Nashville

The availability of federal assistance enabled Nashville, Tennessee, to coordinate three separate and unrelated construction projects which were in preliminary planning stages: enlargement of the state capitol grounds, with the construction of another office building and a library and archives building; erection of a new highway bridge across the Cumberland River; and possible construction of a new public auditorium. Any one of these projects would have imposed a new load on traffic facilities and created a new traffic pattern.

These projects have now been integrated with a plan for slum clearance and redevelopment for the city as a whole and will serve as supporting elements in the plans to rescue the capitol of Tennessee from some 65 acres of slums that now border it on three sides.

Norfolk

Norfolk, Virginia, an old city, has its slums tightly packed around its downtown business area. Experiencing an enormous population increase under the impetus of World War II, and faced with a critical situation, Norfolk became one of the first cities to plan a large-scale postwar redevelopment program. Besides cleaning up deplorable slum conditions, Norfolk wishes to give breathing space to its downtown area and to provide pleasanter access to the business district and the United States Naval Base.

The project of 127 acres is providing a site for a large low-rent housing development, an elementary school, a fire station and a police station, playgrounds and other public facilities to serve the area. It has also made available industrial and commercial sites for future development. An improved street pattern will provide a more direct east-west highway to serve the business district and commuters.

Birmingham

Birmingham has undertaken a slum clearance project comprising a blighted residential area of 60 acres near the central business district and adjoining the University of Alabama Medical School and the Veterans Hospital. Federal financial assistance is enabling the city to wage a three-pronged attack to better the city. First, one of the worst slum areas will be eliminated. Sec-

ond, traffic flow will be greatly improved by the widening of streets. Finally, the main asset to the city, and to the state, will be the opportunity to create one of the finest medical centers in the South. The area will provide sites for a concentration of hospitals, clinics and doctors' offices and for related business uses.

Pittsburgh

Pittsburgh has shown what can be done in a somewhat different field, the renewal of central business districts. The tip of the city's Golden Triangle, wedged between the Allegheny and Monongahela rivers, where they join to form the Ohio, has long been vulnerable to floods and had become an economically blighted area which required drastic action if it was to be reclaimed. This area was not only blighted, a determination upheld by the courts, but was also a traffic bottleneck into downtown Pittsburgh.

A campaign was launched in 1939 to develop plans for the area. Under the authority of Pennsylvania's urban redevelopment law, passed by the legislature in 1947, Pittsburgh's Urban Redevelopment Authority began to condemn and acquire property. By 1949 an agreement was reached with the Equitable Life Assurance Society of the United States to develop the 23-acre fringe of the park which was to replace the hodgepodge of structures at the tip of the "Point." In mid-1952 tenants began occupying the first three of a projected group of eight office buildings, 20 and 24 stories high.

The new office buildings are built in an area until recently covered with run-down business and industrial properties. Impressive Point Park, traversed by new roads, provides easier downtown access and additional off-street parking facilities. Flood control and new bridges have all been integrated into this plan for the rejuvenation of downtown Pittsburgh.[44]

Another redevelopment project in Pittsburgh, financed entirely by private funds, was undertaken for the purpose of industrial expansion. The Jones & Laughlin Steel Company, seeking room for vitally needed new installations, acquired a 120-acre blighted area on the south side, a residential pocket in the midst of heavy industry. Jones & Laughlin, with the Urban Redevel-

---

44. Data for this and the two preceding paragraphs were taken from *Engineering News-Record*, April 24, 1952, pp. 61–64.

opment Authority as representative, began acquisition in November 1949, and has since completed construction of new open-hearth furnaces on the cleared site.

The Urban Redevelopment Authority is now planning redevelopment of the Lower Hill District, a close-in residential slum covering 101 acres. Proposed redevelopment, to be undertaken with federal financial assistance, involves construction of a combination sports arena and opera house along with some allocation of land to residential use.

A DECENTRALIZED PROGRAM

Central city redevelopment is expensive because of the high land cost, including the cost of acquiring structures which will be demolished. Furthermore, it almost invariably involves the displacement of families, and most often, families that can least ably fend for themselves. An alternate proposal would be to emphasize decentralization rather than the rebuilding of central cities.

Such a proposal implies that deterioration of the central city is not really the principal cause of the flight to the suburbs. Might the exodus not "be partly attributable to a sense of freedom from the restraints formerly imposed by restricted modes and facilities of transport? Fashion and custom exert strong influence upon modes of living. It is fashionable to move on out." [45]

Moreover, supporters of such proposals question whether the trend toward decentralization is really undesirable:

It is interesting to point out that most of the evil conditions which urban rebuilding is expected to correct are attributed to decentralization — a phenomenon we have come to consider an automatic and inevitable feature of city growth and development. The enemy is identified as the hostile and sinister tendency of people to fly to the suburbs and the peripheral fringe areas. . . . We are told that the vicious public enemy who creates most of our urban problems is decentralization. But when we examine the listed social objectives of urban redevelopment — to be rid of noise, dirt and odors and to make life safe and healthful — we discover an interesting thing. We may use each and every one of them as arguments which support the idea that decentralization is beneficial. . . . In other words, the suburban trend does not appear to be the real enemy. The flight to the fringe is itself

a method of achieving, in part, many of the social objectives of urban rebuilding.[46]

This approach leads readily to a re-examination of the nature of the urban community, its organization and its functions. Why should we retain the existing, perhaps outmoded, form? The basic structure of our cities is obsolescent, and cannot be corrected by restoring or patching up. We must design and build anew. No good reason exists for concentrating so many urban functions at the center. They could be performed more efficiently and economically if spread over the whole metropolitan area. It is argued that we should stop thinking of the city and the suburbs as separate entities. The solution is to integrate the city with the countryside rather than attempt to lure suburbanites back to the central city.

The primary argument for decentralization is that with the continuation of suburban development the centers of cities ultimately will collapse. Then is the time, when the land can be bought cheaply, to consider an urban redevelopment program. A supplementary argument is that the scarcity of urban land is being converted rapidly to a surplus because of the greater quantity of land brought within the urban sphere by the automobile. This, too, will deflate central city land prices and make redevelopment cheaper in the future.

There are other reasons for opposition to central city redevelopment. They hinge on the difficulty of disrupting families living on project sites, and the desirability of lowering the density of the central city. These objections could be met by a redevelopment program which utilized close-in vacant land for housing development through aids to cities in extending utilities and streets, in land assembly, and in planning good subdivisions. Only when new housing is available to families living in the central city would a central city clearance program be initiated. This program would then probably provide for fewer houses than are now on the sites, and the remaining land could be used for parks, playgrounds, parking areas or public buildings.

This point of view does have advantages. One of the principal difficulties, however, is the narrowness of political jurisdictions. For full accomplishment a way must be found to encourage or force cooperation between, or consolidation of, the city and its environs.

Urban redevelopment may seem a visionary

45. Frederick M. Babcock, "The Objectives of Urban Redevelopment," a speech before the Mortgage Bankers Association, Chicago, October 1, 1942.

46. *Ibid.*

and hopeless proposal — one that could not reasonably be expected to be made effective in the foreseeable future. Acceptance of this view would suggest concentration on a few fundamental reforms to solve some of our most pressing needs: more realistic political subdivisions instead of our present artificial city limits; raising local revenues from some base other than real property; revising outmoded building codes; reducing financing costs of home purchase and rental housing construction; cutting building costs drastically through better construction methods and elimination of monopolistic practices and speculative wastes. These measures, however, would not provide the final answer; a complete metamorphosis of our whole urban structure would be desirable in the long run.

STATUS OF URBAN REDEVELOPMENT

By the end of 1953, federal capital grant funds for slum clearance and urban redevelopment under Title I of the Housing Act of 1949 were reserved or earmarked for 211 localities. Of these localities, 166 had actually initiated at least planning activities in connection with their local programs, and 154 projects had been delineated in 97 of the localities.

Sixty of the delineated projects had reached the execution stage by the end of 1953, with activities including land acquisition, relocation of families, site clearance, installation of site improvements, and, in some instances, disposition of land for redevelopment. In Baltimore, Chicago, Little Rock, Norfolk and Philadelphia redevelopment had progressed to the point where tenants were occupying units on land made available through Title I projects.

Slum clearance activity under Title I has been initiated not only in most of the larger cities but also in many smaller communities. About two thirds of the localities with capital grant reservations at the end of 1953 had populations in 1950 of less than 100,000.

Although Title I authorizes four types of projects, local public agencies are concentrating their programs on the clearance of slums and other built-up blighted residential areas. Almost 90 per cent of the delineated projects were of this type. Seven projects involved built-up areas of nonresidential blight, and nine were on predominantly open land which generally had been laid out as subdivisions but was undeveloped and

blighted. Title I permits a project exclusively on open land under certain circumstances. No such project had been finally approved by December 31, 1953 although some were in the planning stage. Predominantly residential redevelopment is mandatory under Title I unless the project, prior to clearance, consists of slums or other predominantly residential blighted areas.

Residential uses will prevail in most of the area in 84 projects, or over half the total, and will occupy some of the area in 11 additional projects. The land intended for residential use will be made available for private construction except in ten cases where part or all was scheduled for public housing as of December 31, 1953. Preliminary estimates indicate that some 50,000 private dwelling units, representing an investment of $500 million, will be built in these areas. Some nonresidential development, consisting typically of neighborhood shopping centers and public facilities such as highways and schools, is planned in most of the residential projects.

In 29 projects the area is planned mainly for industrial use; in 27, for commercial use; and in 14, for nonresidential public use.

A PROGRAM FOR THE FUTURE

An urban redevelopment program in the United States has been started, primarily under the impetus of the Housing Act of 1949. The pattern of federal financial aid is fairly well established, although it may be changed or modified as experience with the program progresses. To what extent state and local aid will be forthcoming to supplement the federal assistance program is problematical.

An urban redevelopment program aims at a satisfactory environment for family life. This means not only housing but also facilities for recreation, shopping, education and protection. The program for which costs are estimated here does not include facilities used by a number of neighborhoods or by the city as a whole, such as bridges, tunnels, interurban terminals, airports, hospitals, general public administration buildings and high schools. It is concerned solely with residential neighborhoods. Essentially an extension of the housing program outlined in Chapter 7, it supplements and completes the remedies suggested there with equally necessary site and other nonresidential improvements.

This neighborhood redevelopment program

leaves untouched the rural part of the housing program outlined in Chapter 7; it concentrates solely on the urban area as there defined, which include not only urban but all land within standard metropolitan areas. It would result in the elimination of all urban slums and blighted areas. But the rebuilding would not all be done on the old areas as contemplated by the extreme "centralizers," nor would it all be on vacant ground as urged by the extreme "decentralizers." An intermediate prospect is likely, perhaps in the ratio of two-thirds centralized and one third on vacant land. One third of the slums and blighted areas would then be turned into permanently open space or devoted to nonresidential use.

Each new neighborhood, whether on cleared or vacant land, would be planned as a unit. Local streets and sidewalks would be designed for maximum amenity and efficiency, and other utilities would be installed where they are not already present. Play areas, service buildings and other nonresidential facilities would be sufficient in number and properly situated. Existing facilities would be utilized as much as possible.

In estimating the extent of the program, it has been assumed that the total number of dwelling units built would equal the number torn down, although they would not necessarily be in the same location. Even where a like number of units were rebuilt on cleared sites and gross densities remained the same, net densities would be greatly improved through better land planning. Open space would be so arranged as to provide adequate light, air and recreation areas for the inhabitants.

In short, the program would provide every urban family with an acceptable standard dwelling in attractive, quiet and healthful surroundings. Schools and shops would be close at hand. Safe play areas for children and convenient recreation and communal facilities for all ages would be provided.

MAGNITUDE OF PROGRAM [47]

About 32.7 million dwelling units were located in urban areas in 1950. In estimating housing needs in Chapter 7, the more than 8.9 million

47. The estimates which follow do not attempt to forecast the volume of construction activity which might actually take place, but rather to sum up the possible capital outlays for urban redevelopment so that it can be cast in the balance sheet of future needs and resources.

of these that were substandard were classified as follows:

In substandard blocks—need to be replaced	5,566,000
Outside substandard blocks	3,365,000
Need to be replaced	1,369,000
Can be rehabilitated	1,996,000

Thus it was estimated that we would need to replace about 6.9 million dwelling units and rehabilitate about 2.0 million in order to bring our housing up to standard.

These estimates, however, were based on structural deficiencies, and did not take into account replacement needs arising out of environmental deficiencies. In order to eliminate slum and blighted areas, it would be necessary to replace all dwellings in such areas, whether or not the structures were physically substandard. A comprehensive urban redevelopment program would therefore call for a somewhat different classification of substandard dwellings and would include the replacement of some physically acceptable dwellings.

Under the housing program considered in Chapter 7, the existence of clusters of substandard housing was regarded as evidence of deterioration of the whole area; and when most of the dwelling units in a block were found to be substandard, it was assumed that all units should be replaced in order to bring the block up to standard.[48] Under the redevelopment plan considered here, large clusters of substandard houses are treated differently from small clusters. Where a number of substandard blocks are contiguous the whole neighborhood is judged to be in need of redevelopment, even though it may contain "islands" of above-standard blocks. Some of the houses in these islands may already have been classified as requiring replacement and others as needing rehabilitation, but many are physically acceptable. In redeveloping the neighborhood, all dwellings would be replaced, site improvements would be made, and neighborhood facilities provided.

In some cases, substandard blocks are "islands" in otherwise satisfactory neighborhoods. Both the good and bad dwellings in such blocks would, of course, be replaced under the redevelopment plan, but only a minimum of new nonresidential facilities would be needed since the neighborhood in general is satisfactory.

Of the 5.6 million dwelling units in substand-

48. See p. 221.

ard blocks, 3.8 million are in concentrated areas. A further 496,000 dwelling units in above-standard blocks are in these areas.[49] Thus 4.3 million dwelling units are found in our larger and more established slums and blighted areas and 1.8 million in smaller areas of deterioration. The entire 6.1 million units in both types of areas would be torn down and replaced under a redevelopment program.

All of the 5.6 million units in substandard blocks and some of the 496,000 in above-standard blocks were included in the program outlined in Chapter 7. It was estimated there that 3,365,000 substandard units outside substandard blocks were in need of replacement or rehabilitation. Of the 1,369,000 scheduled for replacement, it is estimated that 47,000 are in substandard neighborhoods and consequently would be included in the slum clearance program. The remaining 1,322,000 would be handled as scattered replacements. Similarly, of the 1,996,000 scheduled for rehabilitation, it is estimated that 85,000 are in substandard neighborhoods and consequently would be replaced under a development program. Only the remaining 1,911,000 would be left for rehabilitation.

The housing program as revised to take account of urban redevelopment needs would therefore be as follows:

Dwelling units to be replaced	7,384,000
Intensive area replacement	6,062,000
In concentrated areas	4,282,000
In isolated substandard blocks	1,780,000
Scattered replacement	1,322,000
Dwelling units to be rehabilitated	1,911,000

The housing program outlined in Chapter 7 contemplated replacing 6,935,000 units. An urban redevelopment program would add 449,000 to this number. On the other hand, such a revised program would reduce the number to be rehabilitated by 85,000 — from 1,996,000 to 1,911,000.

Thus, so far as replacement and rehabilitation of housing units are concerned, this program of urban redevelopment would not be much more extensive or costly than the program designed solely to eliminate structural deficiencies.

---

49. Thirty-one per cent of these units are substandard. The blocks are above-standard by definition, since less than 50 per cent of the units in them are substandard. See Appendix 7–2.

COST OF PROGRAM

The estimate of cost given here includes the meeting of all urban housing needs as outlined in Chapter 7 and, in addition, the fulfillment of the urban redevelopment program described above. A cost estimate is also given for the acquisition of slum and blighted areas, although this expenditure, while a prerequisite to the prosecution of the program, does not directly result in capital formation and is not part of the investment and employment-creating aspects of urban redevelopment. No attempt is made to allocate the various costs between private enterprise and government, federal or local.

Site Acquisition

It would cost an estimated $22 billion (at 1950 prices) to acquire all land and buildings in residential slum and blighted areas in the United States.[50] This estimate covers all residential structures together with such neighborhood commercial and light industrial units as are generally found in such areas. It would not include land and structures used for heavy industry, any part of central business districts or any publicly owned land or buildings.

The total acquisition costs consist of about $13.6 billion for large-scale redevelopment areas, $5 billion for individual slum blocks and nearly $3.3 billion for scattered units.

An urban redevelopment program would naturally concentrate on the first two categories. However, if the scattered units in the third category were not replaced eventually, they would remain as a constant threat to the neighborhoods in which they are located.

If it were decided to acquire all residential slum and blighted areas, but to replace only two thirds of the units on these sites and to replace the remaining third with new units on vacant ground, the $22 billion site acquisition cost would be increased by about $1.4 billion.

Site Improvements

The cost of site improvements in concentrated redevelopment areas is estimated at $1,200 per family. These improvements include local streets (i.e., two-way-traffic streets and local parking bays but no high-speed through-traffic arteries); sidewalks, sewer, gas, water, electricity and telephone connections outside building walls; architectural and engineering fees; and overhead. The estimate

---

50. See Appendix 16–1 for basis of this estimate.

assumes that 50 per cent of all subsurface utilities can be salvaged in redeveloping built-up sites.

As 4,282,000 of the housing units to be replaced are located in concentrated substandard areas, site improvements in such areas at $1,200 per unit would cost $5.1 billion.

The cost of site improvements in isolated deteriorated blocks is estimated at $900 per unit. Since 1,780,000 units stand in such blocks, replacement of these would involve an expenditure of $1.6 billion for site improvements.

For the 1,322,000 scattered substandard units outside the above areas no allowance is made for most of the site improvements described above because improvements would be confined almost solely to the structures themselves. A cost of $200 per unit is estimated, primarily within lot lines. This comes to a total of $264 million for the 1,322,000 units.

If one third of the new units were built on outlying vacant land, site improvement costs would increase because of the lessened possibility of using existing facilities. Moreover, some improvements would be required even on the portion of the close-in area that would be turned into open space. The additional cost under such a program is estimated at $2.1 billion. In making this estimate, it is assumed that all building on outlying vacant land would be in the form of large-scale developments.

Thus, site improvements would cost a total of $7 billion if all units were replaced on cleared sites and $9.1 billion if the program were partly decentralized by constructing one third of the new housing on outlying vacant land.

Nonresidential Facilities

Nonresidential facilities include all those customarily found in neighborhoods or sections of communities: post offices, employment offices, small banks, fire stations, police precinct stations, local shopping centers, and community and recreation buildings. Schools and health clinics are excluded because they have been covered elsewhere in this survey. No allowance is made for the cost of movie theaters because it is assumed that nearly all of those in existence could be salvaged and also because it is difficult to allocate the entire cost of such structures to particular neighborhoods.

For every 100 families in a neighborhood, 100 front feet of street space, 60 feet deep and two stories high, would probably be required to house these facilities if land were efficiently used and structures were well designed. Since the cost of these facilities is estimated to average approximately 80 cents a cubic foot, it would come to $1,000 per family. This assumes that no salvage of isolated commercial or service buildings would be possible, but that there would be a one-third salvage of shopping centers and of such public buildings as police stations, fire stations, etc. It is assumed also that schools of acceptable standard would not be torn down to conform to the neighborhood plan, but that the plan would be adapted to the location of such schools.

Thus, with 4,282,000 units to be replaced in concentrated redevelopment areas, the total cost of nonresidential facilities in these areas at $1,000 per family would be $4.3 billion.[51]

Where only individual blocks are redeveloped, there would naturally be less need for nonresidential facilities. Some commercial and service space would undoubtedly be provided, as well as a certain amount of play space. The cost of these items is estimated at $250 for each of the 1,780,000 dwelling units located in isolated substandard blocks, or a total of $445 million.

In a program that would replace one third of the slum dwellings with new units built on vacant ground, the total cost of nonresidential facilities would rise, because there would be little salvage of existing facilities on the outlying vacant sites. Furthermore, since it is assumed that the building on these sites would be large-scale development, all necessary facilities would be provided, whereas only a minimum would be provided in the case of individual block development in the central area, and none at all in the case of scattered replacement. In such a program, therefore, the cost of nonresidential facilities would probably be increased by $2.3 billion.

Thus the total cost of nonresidential facilities in a wholly centralized program would be $4.7 billion, as against $7 billion in a program that was only two-thirds centralized.

SUMMARY OF HOUSING AND DEVELOPMENT COSTS

The entire urban housing replacement, rehabilitation and redevelopment program can now be summarized. With a completely centralized redevelopment program, it would cost $85.5 billion

51. It is estimated that an additional $75 per family should be allocated for improvements and equipment necessary for neighborhood parks and playgrounds. Allowance for such improvements, however, is excluded here since Chapter 11 covers them.

TABLE 219. ESTIMATED COST OF PROGRAM FOR URBAN HOUSING REPLACEMENT,
REHABILITATION AND REDEVELOPMENT
(*Billions at 1950 Prices*)

	Total		Housing Needs [a]	Urban Redevelopment	
	Entirely Centralized	Two-Thirds Centralized		Entirely Centralized	Two-Thirds Centralized
Total	$85.5	$91.3	$49.1	$36.4	$42.2
Dwelling replacement	48.0[b]	48.0[b]	45.1	2.9	2.9
Dwelling rehabilitation	3.8	3.8	4.0	—0.2	—0.2
Site improvements	7.0	9.1	—	7.0	9.1
Nonresidential facilities	4.7	7.0	—	4.7	7.0
Site acquisition	22.0	23.4	—	22.0	23.4

a. See Chapter 7 for basis of estimate.

b. This assumes a minimum-standard house costing $7,500 to construct. Since redeveloped areas will contain housing for various income groups, the average house will undoubtedly be above the minimum.

to eliminate all our urban residential slums and blighted areas and to provide every family living in urban areas in 1950 with at least a minimum-standard dwelling in a satisfactory neighborhood. The total cost would be $91.3 billion, or $5.8 billion more, if only two thirds of the cleared areas were rebuilt and one third of the new building was on vacant land. (See Table 219.)

An urban redevelopment program would therefore add $36.4 billion or $42.2 billion to the housing program outlined in Chapter 7, depending on whether the redevelopment was entirely or only partly centralized. Of the added $36.4 billion, $22 billion represents the cost of acquiring all land and buildings in slum and blighted areas. An additional $1.4 billion expenditure is involved in the partly decentralized program for the purchase of vacant land. Since the cost of site acquisition is merely a transfer payment and does not enter directly into national income or production, the productive effort involved in urban redevelopment over and above that required to fulfill housing needs amounts to $14.4 billion for a completely centralized program and $18.8 billion for one only two-thirds centralized.

The estimates presented here are based on the provision of minimum-standard dwellings at a construction cost of $6,500 per unit (at 1950 prices).

OTHER URBAN REDEVELOPMENT NEEDS

Of course, the remaking of our cities need not stop with redeveloping residential neighborhoods. The job is much bigger and much more complex than that.

Our cities should have more through high-speed traffic arteries, bridges, tunnels and public rapid transit. Many of our interurban terminals are outmoded both in location and structure. Airports will be needed in increasing numbers. Costs of meeting these requirements are discussed in Chapter 9.

Large parts of our public utility systems require renovation and replacement, and many new or improved public administration buildings are needed. Rehabilitation, replacement and new construction of schools, hospitals and recreation centers are also essential. Costs of providing needed medical, recreational and educational facilities are discussed in Chapters 10, 11 and 12.

Many other improvements should be made. For example, Main Street needs to have its face lifted. There are, however, few demonstrations of real accomplishment in refurbishing central business districts. Pittsburgh and Chicago are two notable exceptions. Undoubtedly, our cities will eventually come to grips with the problem of the largely outmoded business core, but for the present, little action is in view beyond a general cleaning up and remodeling, relief of traffic congestion and provision of parking space. Elimination of smoke, noise and odors remains another unsolved problem.

Data are not available for estimating needs such as these, or for attempting an over-all estimate of how much should be done to remake our cities and what it would cost.

## CHAPTER 17

LAND AND WATER CONSERVATION
AND DEVELOPMENT

AMERICA'S GREATEST NATURAL assets originally were its fertile land, with the luxuriant cover of forest and grass, and its abundant water. These initially were the bases of the American economy. Without them, the nation even today would be weak despite the current tendency to regard industrial capacity and production as the cornerstone of America's strength as a world power.

In the beginning, these assets appeared limitless, and as a growing population rapidly put them to use, prosperous farms and cities spread westward over the continent from the Atlantic to the Pacific. The vision our forefathers held of a rich and powerful nation became a reality in less than a century and a half as human enterprise and ingenuity turned the wilderness into a promised land. Great as this accomplishment was, it was not without its costs. In the several generations of our existence as a nation, we have gouged and misused the land until almost one fifth of our crop and grazing lands have been badly damaged by soil washing and blowing. We have hacked away at our forest lands until one third of them are gone. We have allowed many of our rivers to get out of control until we suffer alternately from lack of water and from torrents of it.

The continuing availability of these natural resources in good quantity and quality is essential to the survival of our nation. They will make possible the provision of the ample and relatively low-cost food, clothing and housing supplies that will be needed for our busy and growing population. Their products will also furnish many of the raw materials and much of the power that will be needed in increasing amounts for supplying our expanding industries. Abundant and cheap water supplies will be absolutely indispensable to our highly industrialized, urban way of life, while at the same time that way of life will be peculiarly vulnerable to an overabundance of water in the form of destructive floods.

Properly managed and wisely used, our great natural resources can continue to aid us in maintaining prosperity for ourselves and for the rest of the free world. Poor management and misuse of them may well lead us to poverty. The choice between these alternatives is important not only to rural folk or to the people of our western regions. It is of *national* importance — both to city and to rural dwellers, both to industrial workers and to farmers.

All Americans are beginning to understand that providing for a larger population with a higher level of productivity will require us to exploit fully our great natural resources. But we shall also have to protect these resources and, where possible, to renew them. The emphasis of future conservation and management measures must be on expanding use of our natural assets rather than on withholding them from production. This will require investments on a national scale not only for the development of these resources but also for their rehabilitation, and the task must be a joint responsibility of private enterprise and government.

CONSERVATION AND DEVELOPMENT OF CROP AND GRAZING LANDS

The land area of the continental United States is about 1,904 million acres. Of this whole area, forest vegetation originally covered about 904 million acres, or 48 per cent; grass vegetation covered about 745 million acres, or 39 per cent; and shrub vegetation about 157 million acres, or 8 per cent. The remainder, about 98 million acres, or about 5 per cent, was barren, desert, rock and other land.[1]

By ROBERT W. HARTLEY, senior staff member, The Brookings Institution. Opinions and judgments expressed in this chapter are those of the author and should not be attributed to the organization with which he is associated.

1. The data in this and the following two paragraphs are from L. A. Reuss, H. H. Wooten and F. J. Marschner, *Inventory of Major Land Uses in the United States,* Miscellaneous Publication No. 663, U.S. Department of Agriculture, 1948, Table 15, p. 27, and H. H. Wooten, *Major Uses of Land in the United States,* Technical Bulletin

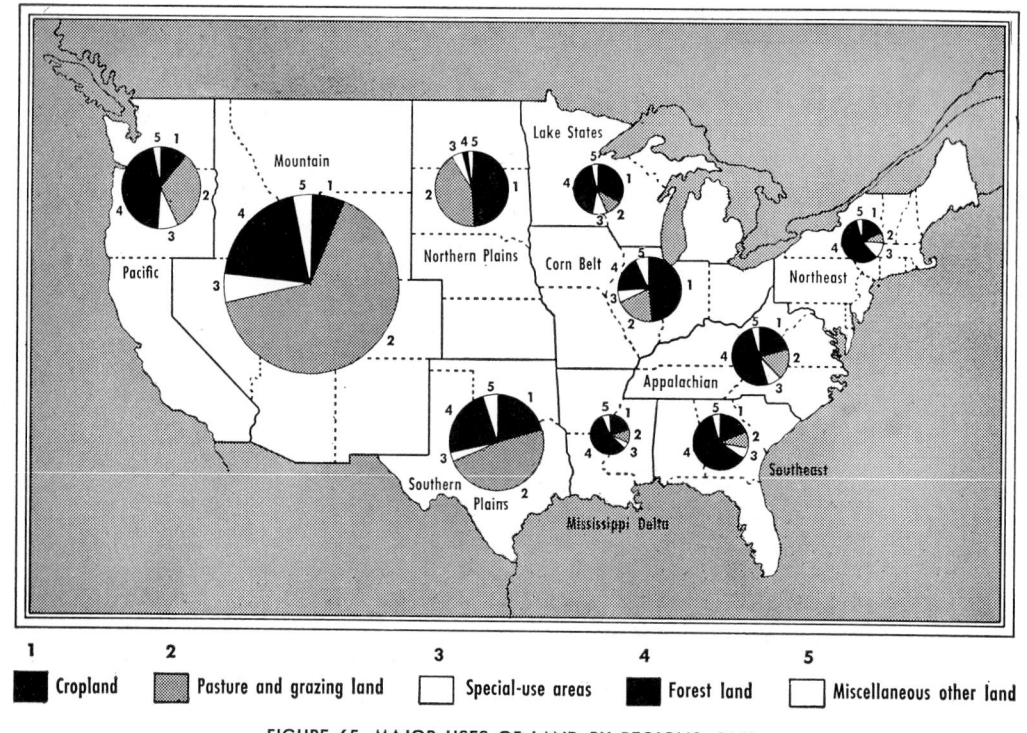

1 ■ Cropland   2 ▨ Pasture and grazing land   3 □ Special-use areas   4 ■ Forest land   5 □ Miscellaneous other land

FIGURE 65. MAJOR USES OF LAND BY REGIONS, 1950

Source: *Major Uses of Land in the United States*, Technical Bulletin No. 1082, U.S. Department of Agriculture, October 1953, pp. 13 and 15.

In the four and a half centuries that have passed since America was discovered, this picture has changed radically because of the uses to which we have put the land. By 1950, the area in forest and woodland amounted to only about 606 million acres, or approximately 32 per cent of our land area. Land used for crops, including land on which crops failed and fallow or idle cropland, comprised about 409 million acres, or roughly 21 per cent of the total area. Grassland available for pasture and range comprised about 700 million acres, or 37 per cent. The remainder, 189 million acres, or about 10 per cent of the total, was used for farmsteads, urban areas, highways and roads, parks, and military reservations and so on, or was unused barren or desert land.

The land used and available for crops and grazing in 1950 included not only the 409 million acres of cropland and the 700 million acres of grassland but also 320 million acres of the forest and woodland. The total of 1,429 million acres thus used and available for crops and grazing

was 75 per cent of our total land resources. (This percentage varies greatly among regions, as shown in Figure 65.) Of this land, 1,029 million acres were in farms: the cropland of 409 million acres plus 620 million acres of the land available for grazing. The rest of the land available for grazing —about 400 million acres — was in federal, state, railroad and other public and private ownership.

What lies ahead? When we look to the future, it is clear that estimates of the needs for rehabilitating and developing crop and grazing lands in the United States must be governed, in the final analysis, primarily by the required capacity of the national agricultural plant to provide adequate supplies of food, fiber and other raw materials for domestic and foreign consumption. That required capacity is discussed elsewhere in this survey.[2] The most that can be done here is to indicate some of the needs for rehabilitation and the possibilities for development that now exist — soil and range conservation work, the retire-

1082, U.S. Department of Agriculture, 1953, Table 3, p. 10, and Figure 3, p. 11.

2. See Chapter 22.

TABLE 220. LAND USED FOR CROPS AND GRAZING, 1900–1950
(*Millions of Acres*)

Year	Total	Land in Farms Used for Crops [a]	Land Available for Grazing [b]		
			Total	In Farms	Outside Farms
1900	1,450	319	1,131	363	768
1910	1,468	347	1,121	382	739
1920	1,468	402	1,066	405	661
1930	1,455	413	1,042	464	578
1940	1,464	399	1,065	561	504
1950	1,429	409	1,020	620	400

Sources: Data for 1900 to 1940 from L. A. Reuss, H. H. Wooten and F. J. Marschner, *Inventory of Major Land Uses in the United States,* Miscellaneous Publication No. 663, U.S. Department of Agriculture, 1948, pp. 30 and 32, Tables 16 and 17; data for 1950 from H. H. Wooten, *Major Uses of Land in the United States,* Technical Bulletin 1082, U.S. Department of Agriculture, 1953, Table 3, p. 10, and Figure 3, p. 11.

a. Includes cropland harvested, crop failure and cropland idle or fallow.
b. Includes both grassland and forest and woodland grazed.

ment of unproductive lands, and the opening of new lands — and that, if met, would tend to increase the productive capacity of the nation and the employment opportunities for our people.

CONSERVATION AND REHABILITATION NEEDS

The first need in any national program for rehabilitating and developing crop and grazing lands is to conserve and protect the lands already in use. Otherwise new lands must be developed merely to replace the acreage allowed to waste away. Such land replacement, which would be in addition to the requirements — whatever they might be — for new acreage to meet increased future demands for agricultural products, would be more expensive than the conservation and protection of existing crop and grazing lands.

Over the past fifty years the land used and available for crops and grazing has fluctuated around 1,455 million acres, or slightly more than three fourths of our total land area. (See Table 220.) But the proportion of the total that has been used for crops has increased with the growth of our population, and the corresponding rise in our national food requirements, and with the enormous export demands during and after the first and second world wars. Part of the increased acreage was obtained by shifting pasture and woodland already in farms to cropland, and part by developing new lands. Much of the new land was developed in the lower Mississippi Valley, through drainage, flood control and clearing, and in the western states through irrigation and clearing. While this new land was being developed, worn-out cropland in the eastern and southern states was being shifted to pasture and woodland.

The over-all result of these changes was that although land used for crops increased about 83 million acres in the first two decades of this century, it has increased relatively little since then and has hovered around slightly more than 400 million acres. At the same time, the land available for grazing has been slowly decreasing, and over the fifty-year period this decrease has resulted in a net loss of 111 million acres — a decrease of 368 million acres in grazing land outside farms and an increase of 257 million acres in farmland available for grazing.

Cropland

The 409 million acres of cropland (i.e., land harvested, land on which crops failed, and idle or fallow cropland) in 1950 did not, however, comprise all of the land in farms regarded as immediately available for crops. About 100 million acres of plowable pasture brought the total of land available for crops to about 509 million acres. The national total of land in farms available for crops has not varied much since the rapid increase in the cropland area during the first two decades of this century. Over the past thirty years, the total has averaged about 512

TABLE 221. LAND IN FARMS AVAILABLE FOR CROPS, 1900–1950
(*Millions of Acres*)

Year	Total	Cropland Harvested	Lands on Which Crops Failed and Cropland Idle or Fallow	Plowable Pasture
1900	409	295	24	90
1910	442	322	25	95
1920	507	362	40	105
1930	522	359	54	109
1940	510	321	78	111
1950	509	345	64	100

Source: *Agricultural Statistics, 1952*, U.S. Department of Agriculture, Table 635, p. 619.

million acres. (See Table 221.) There have been, however, considerable changes in the acreages available in particular regions. Some of these regional shifts have been caused by deterioration in the soil resources: erosion by wind or water, and depletion through cropping.

There once was a time when the people of the United States did not regard their soil resources as conservable. When the land wore out or eroded away, the individual farm operator moved to new lands, so long as they were available. Or he became a tenant on a better farm. Or he simply lapsed deeper into poverty as he tried to scratch a living from his dying acres. Or he gave up farming and turned to another occupation. Fortunately, this attitude no longer generally prevails. The modern concept, which is becoming more widely accepted as the understanding of it increases, is that our soil resources can be both protected and renewed.

Conservation of Croplands

Beginning in 1933, the nation took concerted action to reduce the ravages of soil erosion and depletion. The federal government first stimulated farmer interest in adopting soil conservation practices and then broadened the program in 1935 to provide technical assistance to groups of farmers in applying measures to save soil and water — planting of cover crops, terracing, contour furrowing, gully control through check dams and planting, building of drainage ways, etc. By 1950, a total of 2,253 soil conservation districts had been established in the continental United States under this program, covering more

than 4,712,000 farms with an area of nearly 840 million acres. Among the accomplishments of this program were: more than 22 million acres of contour farming, nearly 6 million acres of strip cropping, more than 13 million acres of cover cropping, 35 million acres of cropland mulched, over 700,000 miles of terraces built, nearly 180,000 farm ponds built, and about 5 million acres of farm drainage. In all, a total of more than 217 million acres were covered by active conservation plans under the program and a total of 120 million acres had received some treatment.[3]

Despite more than a decade of widespread soil conservation work and the increasing application of fertilizers, phosphate and lime, our cropland area as a whole still needs more attention. Losses to our soil resources continue to be heavy. About one fourth of the land now used for crops is being damaged by erosion at a critically severe rate. Another fourth is eroding at a less rapid but still serious rate.[4] Nor are our soil losses due to erosion alone. One authority estimates that the mineral elements removed annually from our soils under cultivation now total about 3 million tons of potash, nearly 2 million tons of phosphate, and over 3 million tons of nitrogen; and that, except for phosphate, not nearly these amounts are returned. The loss of organic matter, which is difficult to estimate, is believed to be even more

3. *Report of the Chief of the Soil Conservation Service, 1950*, U.S. Department of Agriculture, 1950, Table 2, pp. 12–13; Table 3, pp. 15–17; Table 4, p. 18.
4. H. H. Bennett, *Our American Land: The Story of Its Abuse and Conservation*, Miscellaneous Publication No. 596, U.S. Department of Agriculture (revised edition), 1950, p. 4.

serious.[5] To prevent further deterioration of our soil resources, much of the land now available for crops would have to be placed under continuous good soil conservation and rebuilding practices, and the remainder would have to be shifted permanently to pasture or reforested.

Experience gained under the present program and surveys made by the U.S. Soil Conservation Service [6] indicate that the productive capacity of about 110 million acres of land in farms now available for crops will be permanently impaired unless this acreage is placed under a sound conservation farming system within the next ten to fifteen years. Another 110 million acres of cropland will also be permanently impaired unless they are similarly placed under such a system within the next fifteen to thirty years. Furthermore, practically all of the acres available for crops in farms would — without soil rebuilding measures — lose productivity under cropping, some more rapidly than others depending on the soil types. The conservation measures to be used would comprise those already being employed under the present program. In addition to such protective measures, greater emphasis should also be given to steps that would rebuild soil productivity: a planned crop rotation system to include grasses and legumes that will offset soil losses; a greater use of chemical fertilizers; the liming of acid soils; and the return of crop residues, including animal manures, to the soil.[7]

Cost of Cropland Conservation

It has been estimated that failure to undertake appropriate soil conservation measures during the next twenty years would cost the country a minimum of $1 billion a year in direct and indirect losses and damages.[8] The amounts of public and private investments that would be required to prevent such losses are, however, difficult to calculate. It is estimated, for example, that technical assistance from the federal government over a twenty-year period would alone amount to about $1.4 billion.[9] The full program would require about 3.6 million man-years of skilled and unskilled labor, plus large amounts of equipment and materials.[10] In addition, greatly increased quantities of lime and chemical fertilizers would need to be applied to rebuild the productivity of the soil — perhaps two and a half times as much as in 1950, when consumption of lime was about 26.5 million tons and of chemical fertilizers about 19.7 million tons.[11]

Many of the soil conservation and rebuilding practices needed, such as good crop rotation, strip cropping, green manuring, cover crops, application of limes and fertilizers, are part of continuing good farm management. Whatever expenditures of labor or materials they would involve, therefore, would be properly chargeable to — and should be reflected in — the current costs of agricultural production. Beyond these, however, are the capital expenditures required for a well-rounded soil conservation and rebuilding program that would result in a permanent improvement of the land. For a program of the kind described, a total capital outlay of between $6.5 and $7 billion does not appear unreasonable. Add to this the technical assistance required, and the total investment by public agencies and private enterprise would become approximately $8 to $8.5 billion.

Currently, the U.S. Soil Conservation Service reports that about one fifth of the basic conservation job is completed on the nation's farmland and that at the present rate of progress in applying the needed measures, about thirty-five years would be required to complete the job. According to the Service, "There is a vital need for completing the application of basic measures to the land within less time — within the next 20 years if humanly possible." [12] If, therefore, the total capital outlays estimated above were to be made within a twenty-year period, an average annual outlay of between $400 and $425 million would be required. (See Table 222.)

Grazing Lands

The foregoing program for the conservation and rebuilding of our soil resources would cover

5. R. M. Salter, "Utilizing Our Soil Resources for Greater Production," *Annals of the American Academy of Political and Social Science*, November 1951, p. 182.

6. Bennett, *op. cit.*, p. 4.

7. Salter, *op. cit.*, pp. 182–186.

8. *Hearings before the Subcommittee of the Committee on Appropriations, House of Representatives . . . on the Department of Agriculture Appropriation Bill for 1948*, 80th Cong., 1st sess., 1947, Part 1, p. 980.

9. *Ibid.*, p. 986.

10. For the full details of the program, see *Soil and Water Conservation Needs Estimates for the United States*, Soil Conservation Service, U.S. Department of Agriculture, 1945, pp. 12–13.

11. *Resources for Freedom*, President's Materials Policy Commission, 1952, Vol. V, pp. 76–78. Also Salter, *op. cit.*, pp. 183, 185–186.

12. *Report of the Chief of the Soil Conservation Service, 1950*, pp. 6–7.

TABLE 222. ESTIMATED COSTS AND TIME REQUIRED FOR LAND
CONSERVATION AND DEVELOPMENT PROGRAMS
(*Dollar Figures in Millions, 1950 Prices*)

Type of Program	Total Cost	Years Required	Annual Cost
Total	$20,000		$795[a]
Conservation and rehabilitation needs	10,500		525
Cropland	8,500	20	425
Grazing lands	2,000	20	100
Land retirement	[b]	20	[b]
Developmental possibilities	9,500		270[c]
Clearing	3,250	50	65
Drainage	2,250	50	45
Irrigation	4,000	25	160

Source: See discussion in text.

a. Total for first 20 years only.
b. Transfer payments only.
c. Total for first 25 years only.

some pasture and grazing land in farms even though the program is focused primarily on the treatment of land available for crops. In order properly to check erosion on cropland, it is necessary also to treat other lands in the farm — pasture, woodland, and idle or waste land. A considerable portion of the lands available for grazing, however, would have to receive special attention and treatment in a separate program. It is important to protect and rebuild grazing lands because they provide more than one third of our livestock feed.

During the past fifty years, the acreage available for grazing has been decreasing, as noted earlier, and the proportion of this land in farms has been rapidly increasing. These trends become even more striking when the acreages involved are examined from the standpoint of their cover. The decline in the area of grassland available for grazing has been particularly marked. This area decreased about 131 million acres from 1900 to 1950, or almost 16 per cent. The increase during the same period of 20 million acres in the area of forest and woodland grazed was not nearly enough to offset the loss. (See Table 223.)

Roughly 50 per cent, or about 64 million acres, of the decrease in grassland occurred during the decade of World War I, when much grassland was plowed to meet the tremendously increased wartime demands for food production, especially

for export. This trend continued in the postwar agricultural boom, but under the impact of the agricultural depression during the late 1920s and early 1930s some of the plowed land reverted to grass and the total grassland area increased slightly. With the advent of World War II, however, the downward trend was resumed.

Nearly three quarters of our present grazing lands, or roughly 750 million acres, are in the 17 western and Great Plains states.[13] These lands form the largest and most important grazing area in the nation. About 700 million of these acres are range lands, large reaches of which have a low livestock-carrying capacity and do not provide year-long pasture. About one half of the range lands are publicly owned, and a little more than 300 million acres of these publicly owned lands are administered by the federal government.

Conservation Efforts of the Thirties

The original grazing capacity of the western range lands was greatly impaired by overgrazing during the agricultural boom of World War I and by recurring drought. By the early 1930s the

13. For the data in this paragraph, see H. H. Wooten and C. P. Barnes, "A Billion Acres of Grasslands," *Grass — The Yearbook of Agriculture, 1948,* U.S. Department of Agriculture, pp. 25–34; and Reuss, Wooten and Marschner, *op. cit.,* pp. 14–17.

TABLE 223. LAND AVAILABLE FOR PASTURE AND GRAZING, 1900–1950
(*Millions of Acres*)

Year	Grand Total	Grasslands					Forest and Woodland Grazed		
		Total	In Farms				Total	In Farms	Outside Farms
			Total in Farms	Plowable Pasture	Other Pasture	Outside Farms			
1900	1,131	831	276	90	186	555	300	87	213
1910	1,121	814	284	95	189	530	307	98	209
1920	1,066	750	328	105	223	422	316	77	239
1930	1,042	708	379	109	270	329	334	85	249
1940	1,065	723	461	111	350	262	342	100	242
1950	1,020	700	485	100	385	215	320	135	185

Sources: L. A. Reuss, H. H. Wooten and F. J. Marschner, *Inventory of Major Land Uses in the United States,* Miscellaneous Publication No. 663, U.S. Department of Agriculture, 1948, Tables 16 and 17, pp. 30 and 32; H. H. Wooten, *Major Uses of Land in the United States,* Technical Bulletin 1082, U.S. Department of Agriculture, 1953, Table 10, p. 31; and *Agricultural Statistics, 1952,* U.S. Department of Agriculture, Table 635, p. 619.

grazing capacity of these lands had been reduced nearly 50 per cent. Failure to adjust livestock numbers to the grazing capacity of the range lands had led to a deterioration of the plant cover; deterioration of the cover had laid the land open to erosion by wind and water; and loss of the topsoil had made it more difficult to maintain the cover. Reduced forage production meant less return from the livestock, and efforts to increase the return by expanding the numbers of livestock led to an even further deterioration of the plant cover through overgrazing, with subsequent erosion, further reduction in forage, etc.

To break this uneconomic cycle, the federal government inaugurated, in 1934, a program of management and control to preserve and increase the carrying capacity of the so-called "Federal Range," which comprises nearly one half of the western grazing lands under federal administration. Under the program, use of the Federal Range has been restricted to certain seasons of the year, improvements have been made to rebuild the lands, and livestock numbers have been reduced to correspond more closely with the safe carrying capacity of the range.[14] Federal leadership through this program and similar programs undertaken on other federally administered range lands, together with the provision of technical assistance, encouraged private enterprise to take steps to preserve and rebuild the range lands under private ownership.[15]

All these efforts, along with favorable weather, considerably slowed — even if they did not completely halt — the deterioration of the western grazing lands. During World War II, however, livestock numbers on these lands again became dangerously high, and in the future demands on them will grow with increasing population and a high level of national income. But it will be impossible to add appreciably to the acreage of grazing lands in the western states, because practically all of the range lands are already used for livestock.

Conservation and Rehabilitation Needs

It is difficult to estimate the total extent of the deterioration in our western range lands. But it is known that on the Federal Range alone, which comprises roughly one fifth of all the public and private western range lands, about 50 per cent — or nearly 90 million acres — is in a state of severe to critical erosion. Range fires, which destroy the cover and expose the soil to washing and blowing, burn over an average of about 250,000 acres annually. About 22 million acres are in need of some form of revegetation.[16]

14. *Rebuilding the Federal Range*, Bureau of Land Management, U.S. Department of the Interior, 1951, pp. 3–6.

15. See N. W. Johnson and C. W. Loomer, "The Help the Government Offers," *Grass — The Yearbook of Agriculture, 1948*, pp. 39–44.

16. *Rebuilding the Federal Range*, pp. 8–20.

There is a vital need not only for improved grazing management in order-to adjust livestock numbers to the present grazing capacity of both the public and private range lands, but also for a comprehensive program to conserve and rebuild these lands. Such a program would include soil and moisture conservation measures to prevent erosion and excessive runoff, artificial reseeding, control of noxious weeds and rodents, fire control, fencing, and stockwater developments. It would probably cost from $2 to $3 an acre in public and private funds,[17] and this would mean total outlays in the neighborhood of $1.5 to $2 billion for the more than 700 million acres of western range involved. If a program of this sort were to be carried out over a twenty-year period, which appears to be a reasonable goal,[18] the average annual outlays would be between $75 and $100 million. (See Table 222.) Even with such a program, and continuing careful management, it would be many, many years indeed before these lands could be restored to anything like their original grazing capacity.

Land Retirement

Programs for conserving and rehabilitating our crop and grazing lands, along the lines outlined above, would not be complete without a concomitant program of land retirement. Conservation and rehabilitation measures can often prevent further deterioration of reasonably productive land. But many crop and grazing lands — because of poor soil, rough topography, undependable rainfall, and other causes — will not respond to such efforts and frequently they must be retired from intensive use.

Recent Programs

Some lands now used for agriculture should never have been settled for that purpose, or at least not so intensively — lands, for instance, in the southern Appalachians, in the Ozark Mountains and their foothills, in the cutover regions of the Lake states, and in the semiarid portions of the Great Plains. Intensive settlement of some lands in these areas led to serious destruction of the soil and to the impoverishment of farm families. These agricultural areas became chronically depressed and large expenditures of public funds were required to maintain public services in them.[19]

Along with the soil and range conservation programs that it inaugurated in 1934, the federal government undertook to acquire lands no longer suitable for agriculture in order to shift them to other uses. Under this program the government purchased more than 11 million acres, 4 million of which it turned over to state and local government agencies for rehabilitation and management. The rest has been retained under federal control.[20]

Future Needs

Surveys of the U.S. Soil Conservation Service indicate that of the land now in farms, about 40 million acres currently regarded as cropland should be permanently retired to less intensive uses, such as grazing and woodland, and more than 10 million acres now used for grazing should be shifted to woodland or wildlife uses.[21] The retirement of a good part of this land by individual farmers probably could be accomplished during the course of a comprehensive national program stressing good farm management and soil conservation practices. Such a program would also encourage the consolidation of many small, uneconomic farm holdings into larger agricultural units in which the land would be put to its most beneficial use. This shifting of land-use patterns through consolidation of farms probably would effect the retirement of another portion of the acreage now deemed unsuitable for crop or grazing purposes. There would remain, however, some acreage which probably could not be retired except through acquisition by public agencies.

Combined with the twenty-year programs of crop and range land conservation and rehabilitation already outlined, it would probably be wise, therefore, to contemplate a modest program of land acquisition and retirement by public agencies. These lands would then be returned to range or forest, or used as parks and wildlife refuges,

---

17. *Resources for Freedom*, Vol. V, p. 68.
18. Cf. the program for the Federal Range in *Rebuilding the Federal Range*, p. 22.

19. For information in this and the preceding paragraph, see *Public Land Acquisition in a National Land-Use Program, Part I: Rural Lands*, National Resources Planning Board, 1940, pp. 1–5.
20. *Hearings before the Subcommittee of the Committee on Appropriations . . . on the Department of Agriculture Appropriation Bill for 1948*, Part I, p. 978 and *Agricultural Statistics, 1951*, Table 764, p. 679.
21. *Soil and Water Conservation Needs Estimates for the United States*, p. 12.

after such reseeding, replanting and other rehabilitation as might be required. Public expenditures for the purchase and rehabilitation of these poorer lands would be lessened, however, to the extent that these lands were abandoned, for then public agencies could acquire them through tax delinquency procedures.

DEVELOPMENTAL POSSIBILITIES

The gradual retirement of 40 to 50 million acres of land unsuitable for crops or grazing plus an increasing demand for farm products because of population growth and rising levels of income could create a future need for additional acreage of agricultural lands.[22] The additional acreage might be provided by shifting woodland and other land now in farms to crops and grazing and by developing new lands for agriculture through clearing, drainage and irrigation. The need for additional acreage would be lessened, however, in so far as we could increase the productivity of lands already in use.

Some authorities take the view that future needs and demands for increased acreage could be met primarily by combining an increase in the productivity of the lands now used for crops and grazing with a shift to those uses of other land already in farms.[23] But others believe that possible increases in productivity and the conversion of land now in farms will not be sufficient. They conclude, therefore, that the development of new land must proceed on a reasonable scale if the needs for increased acreage of agricultural lands are to be met.[24]

Because of these differing opinions, the best that can be done here is to indicate the *possibilities* during the next few decades for developing new land by clearing, drainage or irrigation. The precise needs and demands for new land in terms of the agricultural capacity and production of the nation that will be required in the future will be discussed later in this volume.[25]

Clearing

In the early days of the nation, the most common and rapid — and generally the most destructive — method of developing new land for agriculture was by clearing the forest from it. The timber was destroyed and burned merely to get at the soil. It has been estimated that from Colonial times down to 1850, when large-scale farm settlement was concentrated in the eastern part of the country, a region which included approximately three fourths of the original forest vegetation, about 113 million acres were cleared and improved for agriculture.[26] By 1880 the total had risen to about 150 million acres, equivalent to about 22 per cent of the original forest area of the eastern states.[27] In the years since then, land in both the eastern and western parts of the nation has been cut over for lumber more rapidly than it has been needed for agricultural purposes. It is estimated that between 350 and 375 million acres have been cleared, of which about 25 million acres are now used for urban areas, roads, etc., and between 50 and 75 million acres have reverted to forest or brush. The rest — between 275 and 300 million acres — either lies in farms or is idle.[28]

Land-Clearing Cycle

Now that much of the original forests have been logged, clearing land for agriculture generally involves the removal of brush, stumps or small-growth timber. Clearing of cutover land for agricultural use was greatly stimulated by the boom of World War I, but much of the land so cleared was of poor quality. When the agricultural boom ended in the late 1920s and early 1930s, large areas of this land reverted to brush as farms were abandoned. The failure of the settlement attempts served as a lesson that cutover lands should not be settled haphazardly, but only after careful consideration of their economic possibilities. It also pointed to the greater advantage of developing new lands by drainage and irrigation rather than by clearing.[29]

22. Another contributing factor will be the need to replace crop and grazing lands that will be transferred to nonagricultural uses, such as urban and industrial development. It is estimated that 15 million acres of crop and grazing lands might be lost by such transfers during the next twenty-five years. *Resources for Freedom*, Vol. V, p. 72.

23. *Resources for Freedom*, Vol. I, pp. 45–50 and Vol. V, pp. 63–75.

24. *A Water Policy for the American People*, Report of the President's Water Resources Policy Commission, 1950, Vol. I, pp. 154–166.

25. See Chapter 22.

26. O. E. Baker, "Rural-Urban Migration and the National Welfare," *Association of American Geographers Annals*, Vol. 23, 1933, p. 60.

27. *The Yearbook of Agriculture*, 1922, U.S. Department of Agriculture, pp. 85–86.

28. O. E. Baker, *A Graphic Summary of Physical Features and Land Utilization in the United States*, Miscellaneous Publication No. 260, U.S. Department of Agriculture, 1937, p. 21.

29. *Public Works and Rural Land Use*, National Resources Planning Board, 1942, p. 23.

TABLE 224. CHANGES IN AGRICULTURAL LANDS IN ORIGINALLY FORESTED AREAS
EAST OF THE GREAT PLAINS, 1910–1945
(*Millions of Acres*)

Year	Land in Farms	Cleared Agricultural Land in Farms [a]	Changes in Previous Decade in Cleared Agricultural Land in Farms		
			Gross Increase	Gross Decrease	Net Change
1910	421	275	[b]	[b]	[b]
1920	411	279	15	11	+4
1930	376	265	7	21	−14
1940	393	284	24	5	+19
1945	400	279	9	14	−5

Source: L. A. Reuss, H. H. Wooten and F. J. Marschner, *Inventory of Major Land Uses in the United States,* Miscellaneous Publication No. 663, U.S. Department of Agriculture, 1948, pp. 41–43, Tables 22–25, inclusive.

a. All land in farms minus woodland in farms.
b. Data not available.

But the cycle of clearing land, using it for crops and pasture, allowing it to revert to brush and saplings, and then reclearing it when more agricultural land is needed and farming appears profitable, is a familiar one in our national history. To reclear land that has once been used for farming is less expensive than to clear land for the first time. Because this cycle is constantly under way but is at various stages in different areas of the country, there appears to have been little if any net increase nationally in agricultural lands as a result of clearing during recent decades, even though there may have been considerable increases or decreases within particular regions. In the originally forested areas east of the Great Plains, where clearing has been concentrated, the net increase during the period 1910 to 1945 amounted to only about 4 million acres. (See Table 224.)

Land Available for Clearing

About 45 million acres of brush and woodland now in farms could be cleared and used for a rotation of crops and pasture. With good farm management and soil conservation practices, two thirds of this acreage when improved could be continuously cultivated and one third occasionally cultivated.[30] Outside farms, there are about 90 million acres that might be physically suitable

for crops after clearing,[31] but only about 10 million of these acres would be worth clearing at present costs.[32] About 135 million acres in all are thus available for clearing.

In recent years, land clearing has become an organized and mechanized operation, and it can be quite costly. In some parts of the South, where the land cover is not heavy, clearing may cost as little as $20 to $30 an acre, while in the Pacific Northwest, where the land cover is heavy, it may cost as much as $200 an acre.[33] It is likely that the costs of carrying out the clearing considered to be feasible at present would average about $25 an acre for the first 10 million acres; between $60 and $80 an acre for the next 50 million acres; and $200 and more an acre for the next 75 million acres.[34] Clearing the 45 million acres now in farms would thus probably involve an outlay of about $2.5 billion, and clearing the 10 million acres outside farms which are now regarded as economically feasible of clearing would require an additional outlay of not less than $750 million. The total outlay of about $3.25 billion would cover the removal of brush and timber and the improvements necessary for preparing the land

30. *Soil and Water Conservation Needs Estimates for the United States,* pp. 1, 2 and 12.

31. *Resources for Freedom,* Vol. V, p. 71.
32. *A Water Policy for the American People,* pp. 162 and 165–166.
33. Reuss, Wooten and Marschner, *op. cit.,* p. 39. Also *Public Works and Rural Land Use,* p. 24.
34. Cf. the unit-cost estimates, when translated into 1950 prices, in R. W. Hartley and Associates, *America's Capital Requirements,* Twentieth Century Fund, New York, 1950, p. 188.

for agricultural use, as undertaken by both individual farmers and organized commercial operations. (See Table 222.)

If we were to bring 55 million acres into agricultural use in this way over a fifty-year period, it would mean clearing an average of 11 million acres each decade — a record comparable to what we achieved from 1850 to 1880 [35] — and would require an average annual outlay of about $65 million.

Drainage

Development of crop and pasture lands through drainage began soon after the first Colonial settlements were made. But it was soon found that it was difficult to obtain the voluntary cooperation of all persons concerned in the successful operation of a particular drainage enterprise. Consequently, as drainage projects grew in size and complexity, the states passed laws authorizing the formation of public drainage districts. By this means, the costs of works and structures could be assessed against all landowners benefiting from them and adequate financing was ensured.[36]

Development of Drainage Programs

Before 1910, the most intensive development of drainage districts occurred in the Middle West, where relatively good agricultural lands and comparatively simple drainage problems made such enterprises very profitable. The agricultural boom accompanying World War I caused a more widespread and speculative development. During the period of high land prices, cutover and swamp lands were drained, particularly in the alluvial area of the lower Mississippi Valley. Poorly designed drainage systems, improper selection of land, and failure to allow for the costs of farm settlement and maintenance led to the bankruptcy of many of these drainage enterprises after the collapse of agricultural prices in the 1920s.

The generally low price level of agricultural products for a decade after World War I deterred new investments in drainage projects to some extent and led to inadequate maintenance of existing developments. This lack of maintenance resulted in reduced crop yields and income and made it even more difficult to raise funds. Early in the 1930s, therefore, the federal government began to assist many drainage districts. It refinanced outstanding obligations and, in connection with its new land conservation and rehabilitation programs, gave direct aid for repairs and maintenance. Later, many projected drainage improvements were deemed to be within the expanding authority of federal flood control programs. Now, new major drainage improvements are usually undertaken as a part of those programs.

During the decade of World War II, as demands for, and prices of, agricultural products increased, the acreage in drainage enterprises expanded once again. In the war years, this expansion was hampered somewhat by shortages of men and critical materials, but once the war was ended, men and materials were obtainable, and ample capital was available as well because of the growing prosperity of farmers.[37]

We have come a long way in developing land by drainage in the past fifty years. Between 1910 and 1920, nearly 40 million acres were added to the area in drainage enterprises. In the two decades thereafter, the increase was only a little more than 20 million acres, but in the past ten years the increase has been almost 16 million acres. In 1950 slightly more than 100 million acres were in drainage enterprises — almost a fourfold increase over 1910. (See Table 225 and Figure 66.) These data, however, do not include improvements on farms outside organized drainage enterprises. Although no exact figures are available, it appears that perhaps between 40 and 50 million acres have been improved through these individual undertakings.[38]

Drainage Possibilities

Substantial acreages of wet lands are still available for further development by drainage, but most of this land would require clearing in addition to drainage and would therefore be expensive to develop. Estimates indicate that a little more than 50 million acres are now economically

---

35. As noted above, by 1850 about 113 million acres in the eastern part of the country had been cleared and improved for agriculture, and by 1880 this had increased to 150 million acres, a net gain of 37 million acres for the three decades, or an average of about 12 million acres for each ten-year period.

36. For information in this and the next two paragraphs, see *Public Works and Rural Land Use*, pp. 20–21.

37. U.S. Bureau of the Census Press Release, Series DR50–1, No. 00, October 30, 1951.

38. Reuss, Wooten and Marschner, *op. cit.*, pp. 46–47.

TABLE 225. DEVELOPMENT OF LAND IN DRAINAGE ENTERPRISES, 1900–1950
(*Millions of Acres*)

| Year | Land Drained | Improved Land | Unimproved Land | | |
			Total	Timber and Cutover	Other
1900	7.3	a	a	a	a
1910	26.3	a	a	a	a
1920	65.5	44.3	21.2	11.3	9.9
1930	84.4	63.5	20.9	11.3	9.6
1940	86.9	67.4	19.5	11.0	8.5
1950	102.7 [b]	a	a	a	a

Sources: Data for 1900 and 1910 estimated from *Sixteenth Census of the United States* (1940), *Drainage of Agricultural Lands*, Table 11; data for 1920 to 1940 from same source, Table 1; data for 1950 from *1950 Census of Agriculture*, Vol. IV, *Drainage of Agricultural Lands*, Table 1, p. 2.

a. Data not available.
b. Excludes enterprises of less than 500 drained acres.

feasible of development by drainage. Much of this available acreage is in the lower Mississippi Valley states. About 30 million acres lie in farms and roughly 20 million acres outside farms. Nearly 25 million acres of the land in farms are already partly improved and under some cultivation, but further drainage improvements are needed to bring these acres under continuous cultivation. The remaining 5 million acres in farms are underdeveloped and would have to be improved in order to make them suitable for crops. Of the 20 million acres outside farms, more than 5 million have been partially developed.[39]

Expenditures Required

The costs of draining new lands and preparing them for agriculture (including the costs of both outlet and field drainage, clearing and flood protection if required, and access roads and bridges) vary considerably. Of the land in farms, rehabilitating 25 million acres might cost an average of $15 an acre; developing 5 million acres might cost an average of $70 an acre. Of the land outside farms, completing the development on more

than 5 million acres of partially improved land might cost an average of $40 an acre; developing the other 15 million or less acres of unimproved land outside farms might cost an average of $100 an acre.[40]

Rehabilitation and development of the entire 50 million acres might require a total capital expenditure of more than $2.25 billion. About $750 million of this amount would represent outlays for the 30 million acres of land in farms, and the remaining $1.5 billion would represent outlays for the 20 million acres outside farms. If the development were spread over a fifty-year period, so that an average of 10 million acres were improved during each decade, the average annual outlays would amount to $45 million. (See Table 222.)

Irrigation

The artificial supplying of water to arid and semiarid lands in our western states in order to make them suitable for general agriculture began in 1832 with the irrigation of garden tracts outside Fort Bent on the Arkansas River in Colorado. In 1848 the Mormons initiated larger-scale operations near Great Salt Lake, Utah. From these early undertakings the use of irrigation spread quite rapidly throughout the West as settlement proceeded. By the beginning of the

39. All data are adapted from: *A Water Policy for the American People*, pp. 161–162 and 165–166; Reuss, Wooten and Marschner, *op. cit.*, p. 56; *Construction of Drainage Works in the United States*, Hearings before a Subcommittee of the Committee on Agriculture and Forestry, U.S. Senate, 78th Cong., 2d sess., 1944, p. 14; and *Public Works and Rural Land Use*, p. 23.

40. Cf. the unit-cost estimates, in terms of 1950 prices, in *America's Capital Requirements*, p. 186.

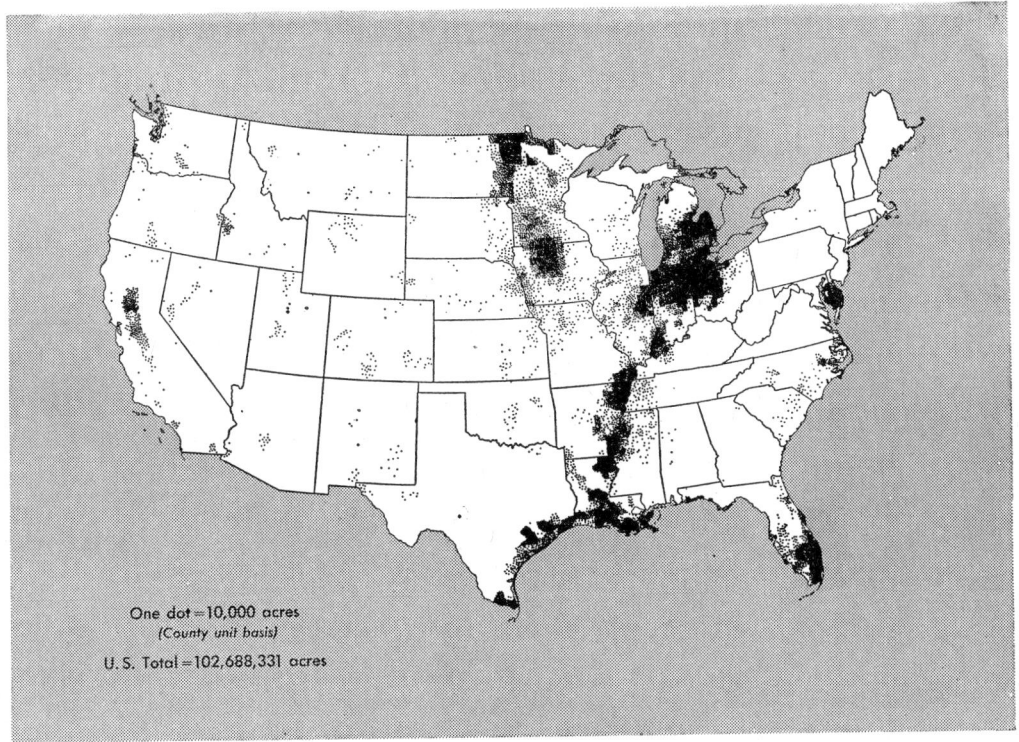

One dot = 10,000 acres
(County unit basis)

U. S. Total = 102,688,331 acres

FIGURE 66. AGRICULTURAL LAND IN DRAINAGE ENTERPRISES, JANUARY 1, 1950

Source: 1950 Census of Agriculture, Vol. IV, Drainage of Agricultural Lands.

twentieth century more than 7.5 million acres were under irrigation. But the turn of the century also marked a turning point in the development of land by irrigation.

The early developments had been comparatively simple, consisting of small diversion works, usually built by private capital for the single purpose of irrigating lands. By 1900, however, most of the stream flow that could easily be diverted had been tapped for irrigation use and most of the less costly projects had been constructed. Further development required capital investments and complicated engineering works beyond the capacity of private groups to finance and undertake. In 1902, therefore, the federal government began to assist in irrigation development by constructing the larger and more expensive projects. As federal development of irrigation progressed, projects became even more complex, until now most of them serve multiple purposes, providing not only for irrigation but also for power development, public water sup-

ply, flood control, navigation, fish and wildlife conservation, and recreation.[41]

Present Extent of Irrigation

By 1950, irrigation enterprises were serving nearly 24.9 million acres in the 17 western states. This represented an increase of more than 230 per cent over the acreage served in 1900. About 2.2 million acres, or nearly 9 per cent of the total in 1950, were in enterprises under the U.S. Bureau of Reclamation — more than a fivefold increase since 1910. (See Table 226.) Through its projects the Bureau was also furnishing supplemental water supplies to nearly 2.6 million acres, or about 11 per cent, of the other irrigated land in these states in 1950.[42]

Over the years, the practice of irrigation has spread beyond the 17 western states, and by 1950 about 1.5 million acres were under irrigation in

41. For information in this and the preceding paragraph, see *A Water Policy for the American People*, pp. 150–152.
42. *Annual Report of the Secretary of Interior for the Fiscal Year Ended June 30, 1950*, pp. 20–29, Table 7.

TABLE 226. IRRIGATED LAND IN IRRIGATION ENTERPRISES, 17 WESTERN STATES, 1900–1950
(*Millions of Acres*)

Year	Total	U.S. Bureau of Reclamation Projects	Private and Other Public Enterprises
1900	7.5	—	7.5
1910	14.0	0.4	13.6
1920	18.6	1.3	17.3
1930	18.9	1.5	17.4
1940	20.4	1.8	18.6
1950	24.9	2.2	22.7

Sources: Data for 1900 to 1940 from Sixteenth Census of the United States (1940), *Irrigation of Agricultural Lands;* data for total for 17 western states in 1950 from *1950 Census of Agriculture,* Vol. III, *Irrigation of Agricultural Lands,* Table 1, p. 34; data for U.S. Bureau of Reclamation for 1950 from *Annual Report of the Secretary of the Interior for . . . 1950,* pp. 20–29, Table 7; data for private and other public enterprises for 1950 estimated as the residual amount.

other sections of the country. About 90 per cent of this acreage lay in Arkansas, Louisiana and Florida, where supplemental water supplies are furnished to rice lands in the alluvial and coastal areas.[43]

In comparison with the entire land area now available in farms for crops, the acreage of irrigated land in the 17 western states is indeed small, being roughly about 5 per cent. But the productivity of irrigated land is high. Crop yields per acre average 50 per cent higher on irrigated land than on nonirrigated land, and the delivery of additional water supplies to already irrigated lands increases their yield an average of about one third.[44] Unfortunately, however, the further development of land by irrigation in the western states is likely to cost more per acre than the development of land by clearing or drainage elsewhere in the nation. Furthermore, the amount of additional land that can be brought under irrigation in the West is fixed by the amount of water available for this purpose.[45]

Possibilities for Further Irrigation

Based on present considerations of the economic feasibility of proposed irrigation projects and past experience in bringing land into use for general agriculture by irrigation, it appears pos-

sible over the next twenty-five years to develop about 6 million additional acres in our western states by irrigation and to provide additional water supplies to about 5 million acres now under irrigation.[46] At an estimated average cost of $425 an acre for bringing the new land under irrigation and $300 an acre for providing the supplemental water supplies, the total outlay required over the twenty-five-year period would approximate $4 billion.[47] This would amount to an average annual expenditure of about $160 million. (See Table 222.)

An outlay of this magnitude, however, would cover *more* than the works, structures and improvements necessary to bring water to land so that it could be used for agriculture. The expenditure would also cover the costs of multiple-purpose projects that would be properly chargeable to power, flood control and the other purposes of the projects. But desirable as it might be, it is not possible further to estimate precisely how large a proportion of the total estimated outlay ultimately should be charged to these other purposes, thus perhaps reducing considerably the given estimated average developmental costs per acre for irrigation. It must be borne in mind,

43. *1950 Census of Agriculture,* Vol. III, *Irrigation of Agricultural Lands,* Table 2, p. 35.
44. *A Water Policy for the American People,* pp. 160–161.
45. See the discussion, later in this chapter, of irrigation in connection with the conservation and development of our water resources.

46. *A Water Policy for the American People,* pp. 160–161 and *Resources for Freedom,* Vol. V, p. 72.
47. Cf. the cost estimates, when adjusted to 1950 prices, in "Land Available for Agriculture Through Reclamation," *Supplementary Report of the Land Planning Committee,* National Resources Board, 1936, Vol. I, Part 4, p. 5; *A Water Policy for the American People,* pp. 171–172; and a comparable advance construction program of the U.S. Bureau of Reclamation in *Annual Report of the Secretary of the Interior for . . . 1950,* pp. 66–68, Table 12.

however, that regardless of what might be the final division of costs among the various purposes of the individual projects, it would be necessary to make a rather large initial capital outlay in order to bring a relatively small acreage into agricultural use by means of irrigation.

Any attempt to estimate the future possibilities of developing land by irrigation must take into account also the further potentialities of supplemental irrigation in the humid regions of the eastern states. As a means of insurance against damage to crops by droughts occurring in the growing season, the practice of supplemental irrigation has been spreading rapidly in recent years in the New England, Middle Atlantic and South Atlantic states. Large increases in yields have resulted from its use, but in times of normal rainfall, land irrigated by this method has shown no particular gain in yield over nonirrigated land. Although the economic justification of supplemental irrigation in the East is still to be determined, it appears in general that the practice is likely to be rather costly, and the margin of profit rather low.[48]

It is estimated, however, that there are large areas in southeastern Texas and in Louisiana and Arkansas where supplemental irrigation for rice land is practical. These rice lands, usually in coastal or alluvial areas, now aggregate about 1.6 million acres, and perhaps 2.2 million more acres could be brought into production by a combination of flood protection, drainage and supplemental irrigation.[49] But data are not readily available for estimating the costs or time period required for developing this additional acreage.

Forest Conservation and Development

Our forests are among our richest natural resources. Originally they covered almost half the land area of the continental United States, but by 1950 slightly less than a third of the area was in forests and woodlands. This reduction resulted largely from the wasteful practices of the early settlers.

During the Colonial period, forests and woods were so abundant, and such an encumbrance to settlement, that the general feeling was to get rid of them as quickly as possible. This attitude persisted until after the Civil War. But heavy requirements for wood during the war, rapid lumbering of the forested areas in the Lake states, and widespread destruction by forest fires brought about a gradual change in the attitude of the American people toward their forest resources.

In the latter half of the nineteenth century, the federal government and the states began to take measures to protect and manage the remaining forests, in response to public recognition of the need. Public action was greatly strengthened by the conservation movement of the early 1900s, in which the federal government, under President Theodore Roosevelt, assumed a leading role. In 1905 the U.S. Forest Service was established and to it was assigned the management of the national forests. In the years since then, great strides have been made in private as well as public policies and practices of forest conservation and management.[50]

Even though only a little less than two thirds of our original forest land remains, government experts claim that *if properly used,* it will be plenty eventually to furnish again all the forest wealth required by a growing and prosperous nation.[51] From this land, we are extracting currently slightly more than 12 billion cubic feet of timber a year, including more than 52 billion board feet of saw timber.[52] This annual cut supplies lumber for building, furniture and boxes, and wood for many vital chemical products — pulp, paper, rayon and other textile fibers, plastics, and so on. But our forest lands are not a source of wood alone; they are also of great value for watershed protection, for forage crops, for wildlife habitat, and for recreation. And the same acreage may be used for several of these purposes simultaneously.

The forest cover on our hills and mountains preserves the soil and helps regulate the flow of rivers. At least three fourths of our present forest acreage is of some value in protecting our watersheds, although misuse of much of it has lessened

48. *A Water Policy for the American People,* pp. 164–165.

49. "Summary of Plans for Conservation and Development of the Water Resources of the United States," presented by the Chief of Engineers, U.S. Army, *Congressional Record,* Vol. 94, Part 8, 80th Cong., 2d sess., 1948, pp. 9944–9949. See especially p. 9946, paragraph 20 (b).

50. See W. N. Sparhawk, "The History of Forestry in America," *Trees — The Yearbook of Agriculture, 1949,* U.S. Department of Agriculture, pp. 702–714.

51. *Forests and National Prosperity — A Reappraisal of the Forest Situation in the United States,* Miscellaneous Publication No. 668, U.S. Forest Service, U.S. Department of Agriculture, 1948, p. 13.

52. *Resources for Freedom,* Vol. V, Table VII, p. 36.

its effectiveness in this respect. More than half of our forest lands are used for grazing, and with proper management, most of this range can continue to provide forage for millions of animals without interference with other uses of the land. Virtually all of our forest land supports and shelters some wildlife — fur-bearing animals, birds and big game. In many cases, such wildlife is one of the most valuable products of land which is incapable of producing commercial timber. Our forests are also places for camping, hunting, fishing and other outdoor sports. Millions of people seek recreation in our forests each year, and it is estimated that nearly two thirds of the forest land is of some recreational use.[53]

Important as these many other uses of our forests are, the major factor that will determine the future need for their conservation and development will be our future national requirements for timber. These requirements, which constitute the primary prospective drain on our forest resources, must be considered, however, in light of the prospective growth of those resources.

TIMBER RESOURCES AND REQUIREMENTS

Not all of the nearly 625 million acres in forest and woodland in the continental United States is available for timber cutting. Some of this acreage is reserved in national and state parks, game refuges, military reservations and other special land-use areas. Excluding these areas, the available forest land totals about 606 million acres, and this has not changed much over the past twenty years. (See Table 227.) Prior to 1900 and through the decade ending with 1910, the acreage of such lands had been decreasing.[54] Thereafter, it increased slightly, but since 1930 there has been little change, with the average staying around 605 million acres.

To a degree, the halt in the decline of, and the subsequent slow increase in, the acreage of forest land which occurred during the past fifty years reflected the changing American attitude toward our forest resources. But it is also true that most of the forest land that remains is unsuitable for agriculture or for other uses because of roughness, stoniness, poor soil, aridity, a short growing season or other shortcomings. It appears unlikely,

53. See *Forests and National Prosperity*, pp. 15–16.
54. For comparison with 1900, forest and woodland comprised 628 million acres in 1880 and 604 million acres in 1890. Reuss, Wooten and Marschner, *op. cit.*, Table 16, p. 30.

TABLE 227. AVAILABLE FOREST AND WOODLAND,
1900–1950
(*Millions of Acres*)

Year	Total [a]	Outside Farms [a]	In Farms
1900	579	388	191
1910	562	371	191
1920	567	399	168
1930	607	457	150
1940	602	445	157
1950	606	386	220

Sources: Data for 1900 to 1940 from L. A. Reuss, H. H. Wooten and F. J. Marschner, *Inventory of Major Land Uses in the United States,* Miscellaneous Publication No. 663, U.S. Department of Agriculture, 1948, Table 16 and Figure 9, pp. 30–31; data for 1950 from H. H. Wooten, *Major Uses of Land in the United States,* Technical Bulletin 1082, U.S. Department of Agriculture, 1953, Table 3 and Figure 3, pp. 10–11.

a. Does not include forest land in parks, game refuges, military reservations, etc., which is estimated to be about 14 million acres in 1950. See Wooten, *op. cit.,* Table 15, p. 51.

therefore, that the total acreage of the presently available forest land will change much in the future. Although some of the land, particularly on the Pacific Coast and in the South, is suitable for agriculture and may be cleared for that purpose, such decreases in the forest acreage would undoubtedly be offset by the reversion to forest use of poor agricultural land in the eastern and southern states.[55]

Forest Drain and Growth

Approximately 460 million acres, or roughly three fourths, of the present forest and woodland are capable of producing timber of commercial quantity and quality. More than 75 per cent, or about 350 million acres, of this land lies in the humid area east of the Great Plains, about half of it in the northern and half in the southern states. Only one fourth of the present commercial forest acreage is publicly owned, but the proportion varies greatly from region to region. In the West, for example, almost two thirds of the acreage is in public ownership. The size of private holdings also varies widely. Only one fourth of the private commercial forest land is in holdings of more than 5,000 acres. Three fourths of it (almost 260 million acres) is split among about 4.25 million small holdings averaging only 62 acres each. But private holdings supply about 90 per

55. *Forests and National Prosperity*, p. 13.

cent of the timber cut, and they will continue to be our main source of timber because much of the publicly owned commercial forest land is in rough, often remote back country and is therefore difficult to develop.[56]

The present stand of timber in our commercial forest lands is estimated at nearly 470 billion cubic feet, including more than 1.6 trillion board feet of saw timber.[57] In terms of total cubic volume, this would be enough timber to provide a layer of wood one foot deep over the land area of Massachusetts and New Hampshire. In terms of board feet of available saw timber, it would be enough lumber to lay a wood flooring one inch thick over the land area of New York, New Jersey and nearly half of Connecticut.

About 80 per cent of all timber products are cut from trees of saw-timber size. It is therefore important to consider our timber resources and future requirements primarily in terms of saw timber. About half of the available stand of 1.6 trillion board feet of saw timber is virgin timber, the rest representing growth which has occurred since the settlement of our continent. When that settlement began, the stand of saw timber probably amounted to about 8 trillion board feet. Thus we have used or destroyed about 90 per cent of the virgin timber stand — plus much of the later growth.[58]

The annual drain on our forests continues to be heavy. In 1950 it amounted to about 13.6 billion cubic feet of timber, including about 56.4 billion board feet of saw timber. Cutting accounted for about 12.1 billion cubic feet of the total drain and 52.2 billion board feet of the saw-timber drain. The rest of the drain was caused by losses from fire, insects, disease, storms, etc. The total annual growth in 1950 was estimated at about 13.4 billion cubic feet, and the saw-timber growth at 35.3 billion board feet. Thus, although the total annual growth almost equaled the total annual drain in terms of the total volume of tim-

ber, there was a heavy deficit with respect to saw timber.[59]

Meeting Future Timber Requirements

The time is obviously long past when timber could safely be viewed as a reserve to be drawn upon without regard for replenishment. It must now be thought of as a crop, to be tended and cared for year by year just like food crops, but with much more planning and forethought. Many of the trees we will need for timber next year must have had their start at least twenty-five years ago, and most of them, perhaps, not later than the turn of the century. If we are to start now taking steps to met our future timber requirements, we must try to estimate those requirements at least as far ahead as 1975, and better yet in the years 2000 or 2025.

Recent government estimates indicate that over the next fifty to seventy-five years timber requirements may increase to an annual average of from 18 to 20 billion cubic feet, including 65 to 72 billion board feet of saw timber.[60] These requirements would cover not only the estimated demands for timber for domestic commodity uses for which we now employ it and expected losses from fire, insects, etc., but also provide a margin for new uses of wood, national security and export. Present uses of wood will, in a future expanding economy, require a larger volume of timber than is now cut. In addition, the outlook for new uses of wood as a chemical raw material indicates a further increase in the demand for timber. (See Chapter 21.)

If annual growth is maintained at only the 1950 rate (i.e., 13.4 billion cubic feet for all timber and 35.3 billion board feet for saw timber), it may fall as much as 33 per cent short of meeting the future requirements for all timber, and 50 per cent short of meeting future saw-timber requirements. Clearly then, if we are to meet long-range future requirements we must increase the over-all growth by about 50 per cent and double the saw-timber growth. As things are going now, the U.S. Forest Service believes there is no prospect of doubling the saw-timber growth in the foreseeable future, but if positive measures to maintain and increase forest productivity were

---

56. See *Resources for Freedom*, Vol. V, pp. 37–38; and *Forests and National Prosperity*, pp. 14–16.

57. *Resources for Freedom*, Vol. V, Table XIII, p. 39. Forest statistics are usually given in terms of all material in trees not less than 5 inches in diameter, breast high, and in terms of board feet (a unit of lumber measurement one foot long, one foot wide, and one inch thick, or its equivalent) in trees suitable for saw logs. Trees deemed suitable for saw logs are usually not less than 9 inches in diameter, breast high, and depending on the species may be not less than 11, 15, and even 23 inches in diameter. See *Forests and National Prosperity*, p. 17, fn. 6 and 7.

58. *Forests and National Prosperity*, p. 17.

59. *Resources for Freedom*, Vol. V, pp. 36–37.

60. *Forests and National Prosperity*, pp. 33–39; and *Resources for Freedom*, Vol. V, pp. 33–37.

to be applied promptly throughout the nation, the goal could eventually be achieved.[61]

Sustained-Yield Management

To maintain an annual crop of merchantable timber, there must be a succession of age classes from seedlings up to full-grown timber so that new trees will be ready to take the place of those cut each year. If the age classes are properly balanced and the amount cut each year is equal to the annual growth, the volume of standing timber will remain constant. It can then be viewed as a growing stock of forest capital on which the annual crop accrues as interest.

The present growth classes of our timber resources are not well balanced, and much of the forest land is poorly stocked.[62] In the North almost half the commercial forest land bears only seedlings and saplings or is denuded. Large saw timber is scarce in the South; stands in which more than half the saw-timber trees are over 18 inches in diameter occupy only one per cent of the forest land. In the West, virgin timber stands now occupy less than two fifths of the commercial forest land, and one fourth of such land has been reduced to seedling or sapling growth or is denuded. About 35 per cent of all the commercial forest land in this country is deforested or has less than 40 per cent of the number of trees required for full stocking. Almost 90 per cent of the poorly stocked stands are in the North and the South, the southern forest lands being the most deficient, with almost half their area deforested or poorly stocked. Moreover, sustained-yield management — operation for continuous production — is at present practiced on slightly less than 60 per cent of the publicly owned commercial forest acreage and on only slightly more than 35 per cent of the private holdings of 5,000 acres or more.[63]

A Forest Management Program

In order to sustain a higher output of timber products in the future, we must not only maintain but also increase the volume of standing timber, which is our forest capital. Otherwise, we face the prospect that with increasing future de-

mands for timber steadily outdistancing the present annual growth, we will slowly liquidate our forest capital, and this will in turn gradually cut down the size of the annual crop that accrues as an interest on it. Eventually, our available timber resources would dwindle to nothing.

If we are to bring forest drain and growth into balance in the future, the U.S. Forest Service believes that we must undertake a program along the following lines on the 460 million acres of our commercial forest lands:

(1) About 100 million acres should be placed under intensive management that would result in yields consistent, in both quantity and quality, with the full productive capacity of the land.

(2) About 300 million acres should be placed under a less intensive type of management that would maintain growth in sufficient quantity for commercial utilization.

(3) The remaining 60 million acres could be operated under minimum management standards that would ensure protection against fire and provide some reforestation.[64]

To achieve this kind of forest management program will be difficult and will require extensive effort by both public agencies and private enterprise. Most of the publicly owned forest lands are now under good management, and those that are not are largely in remote localities in the West, where much developmental work would have to be done to bring them into full use.[65] But more than 80 per cent of our privately owned forest lands would have to be brought under good management, and this would mean at least a doubling of the area now under such management.[66] The growing stock in the forests in the eastern part of the country would have to be almost doubled, and the virgin timber remaining in our western forests would have to be carefully husbanded so that cutting would proceed on a sustained-yield basis.[67]

FOREST MANAGEMENT FOR TIMBER PRODUCTION

Good forest management for timber production requires a combination of two principal types of forestry practices. First, our existing forest resources must be protected from fire, insects and disease. Second, the cutting practices used on them must be directed toward achieving the best standards under which continuous natural re-

61. *Forests and National Prosperity*, p. 40.
62. For data on growth classes and stocking, see *ibid.*, pp. 22–23.
63. *Ibid.*, p. 49; and *Resources for Freedom*, Vol. V, pp. 41–42.

64. *Resources for Freedom*, Vol. V, p. 37.
65. *Forests and National Prosperity*, p. 49.
66. *Resources for Freedom*, Vol. V, p. 38.
67. *Forests and National Prosperity*, pp. 40–45.

forestation will occur. This means selective cutting, trimming of nonmerchantable timber, and other work necessary to improve the quality and growth rate. Planting of areas not fully stocked by natural regeneration will also be needed, and improvements must be undertaken that will make easier the access to all of our commercial forest lands, thus relieving the heavy drain on those now being used.

These practices and improvements will require heavy public and private investments in order to increase our forest capital. If such investments are made during the coming years, they will eventually be repaid with interest in the form of an increased annual growth that will meet our increasing requirements for timber.

Fire Protection

Fire is the most spectacular of the unnecessary drains on our forest resources, and some forest fires have been national disasters.[68] The Peshtigo fire in Wisconsin in 1871 burned nearly 1.3 million acres. Homes, towns and settlements were swept away and 1,500 persons perished. In 1910, raging fires in Idaho laid waste a strip of mountain country 20 to 35 miles wide and 120 miles long, wiped out several million acres of virgin timber in a few days, and killed 75 fire fighters. The Tillamook fire in Oregon during 1933 burned more than a quarter of a million acres of the finest virgin forests in the state, destroying timber equivalent to the entire lumber cut of the United States in 1932. In Maine during the autumn of 1947, small wildfires, fanned by strong winds, burned a quarter of a million acres, took 16 lives, forced some 3,500 people to flee Bar Harbor and destroyed 400 homes there.

When our country was young, fire was one of the means used to clear land. Many devastating fires also resulted from carelessness in early logging operations. Millions of acres were burned in these ways and the growth of new timber was held back. A half century ago, however, the American people, awakening to the seriousness of the destruction, began to institute systematic forest fire control as we now know it. Earlier, the chief concern in fighting forest fires had been to protect human life and property, but systematic forest fire control concentrated on protecting the forest itself. The states enacted laws designed to prevent fires and protect forest lands. National forests were created and their organized protection was undertaken. Responsible owners of timberland in the West established forest fire protective associations.[69]

Development of Organized Protection

Since the turn of the century, much of our forest land has been brought under fire protection. Organized fire control in the national forests, which began with their establishment in 1905, was greatly expanded after 1910. The area protected, which includes intermingled or adjacent lands in other ownership, averaged close to 165 million acres between 1916 and 1930 and has been around 185 million acres since 1940. Fire protection on other federally owned forest lands has also been extended, especially since the 1930s. In 1950, well over 200 million acres of federal forest lands, including the national forests, were under protection.[70]

Great progress has also been made in bringing state and privately owned forest lands under organized protection, as shown by the increases achieved from 1911, when the statistics were first collected, to 1950 (in millions of acres): [71]

Year	Area Protected
1911	61
1915	83
1920	135
1925	184
1930	228
1935	241
1940	279
1945	303
1950	360

About 85 per cent of the state and privately owned forest land needing protection is now receiving it.[72]

Despite this progress, about 23.5 million acres of our forest lands, both public and private, were burned over in 1950, and in recent years the average annual drain caused by fire has approached one half billion cubic feet of timber, including more than 800 million board feet of saw timber.[73] Government experts believe that our future goal

68. R. F. Hammatt, "Bad Business; Your Business," *Trees — The Yearbook of Agriculture, 1949*, pp. 479–84.

69. A. A. Brown, "Progress, But Still a Problem," *Trees — The Yearbook of Agriculture, 1949*, p. 478.

70. *Forests and National Prosperity*, p. 78.

71. *Forests and National Prosperity*, pp. 82–83; and *Agricultural Statistics, 1951*, Table 776, p. 689.

72. *Resources for Freedom*, Vol. V, p. 37.

73. *Forests and National Prosperity*, p. 28.

TABLE 228. ESTIMATED COSTS AND TIME REQUIRED FOR FOREST
CONSERVATION AND DEVELOPMENT PROGRAMS
(*Dollar Figures in Millions, 1950 Prices*)

Type of Program	Total Cost	Years Required	Annual Cost
Total	$7,800	—	$275 [a]
Forest management for timber production	4,200	—	140 [b]
Fire protection	625	25	25
Protection from insects and disease	325	25	15
Stand improvements	750	25	30
Planting	500	25	20
Roads and trails	1,500	50	30
Other improvements	500	25	20
Forest protection and development for nontimber uses	3,600	—	135 [a]
Watershed protection	750	50	15
Forage production	600	20	30
Wildlife habitat	250	25	10
Recreation	2,000	25	80

Source: See discussion in text.

a. For first 20 years only.
b. For first 25 years only.

should be to cut these timber losses at least in half.[74] This can be accomplished in part by a continuing program of public education. Nine out of every ten forest fires are caused by man; and of these nine, seven are due to negligence and carelessness.[75] In addition, however, some 66 million more acres of forest lands, mostly in the South, must be brought under organized protection, and more intensive protection must be provided in many other areas.[76]

Need for Increased Protection

To be prepared to suppress forest fires requires equipment, manpower and organization.[77] Capital outlays are needed for the construction of additional fire towers and communication systems to make possible prompt detection and reporting, for the removal of hazardous, inflammable materials, for the building of firebreaks as a means of checking the progress of fires, and for the construction of more truck trails and airplane landing fields to provide quick transportation of men and equipment. Other outlays are needed for additional fire-fighting equipment, fire crew barracks and headquarters, warehouses and tool caches, waterholes, etc.

It is probable that a capital outlay of about $625 million of public and private funds would be required over the next twenty-five years, or $25 million annually, in order to meet the need for increased fire protection on our public and private forest lands.[78] (See Table 228.) Besides these capital outlays, considerable increases would be needed in the current annual expenditures for manning and maintaining the necessary operating organization.

Protection from Insects and Disease

Although less spectacular than fire, insects and disease take a heavier toll in our forests. In recent years, they have caused average annual timber losses of about 600 million cubic feet, including 1.9 billion board feet of saw timber.[79] Except in parts of the West, disease generally causes greater damage than insects. A principal source of dis-

74. *Resources for Freedom,* Vol. V, p. 37.
75. Hammatt, *op. cit.,* p. 482.
76. *Resources for Freedom,* Vol. V, p. 43.
77. E. S. Pierce and C. A. Gustafson, "Building a Fire Organization," *Trees — The Yearbook of Agriculture, 1949,* pp. 485–493.

78. This estimate is based on data available in: *Public Works and Rural Land Use,* pp. 100–101; *Forests and National Prosperity,* pp. 9, 83–84; and *Resources for Freedom,* Vol. I, pp. 40–41, and Vol. V, p. 43.
79. *Forests and National Prosperity,* p. 28.

ease losses is heart rot, which occurs in practically every timber stand.[80]

The so-called "endemic" losses in our forests result from a great variety of insect and disease pests which are constantly at work on tree leaves and stems. These pests seldom kill trees outright, and may cause only minor damage in young, full-stocked forests, but in mature stands they often accumulate to destroy timber faster than it is replaced by current growth. These pests flourish especially in unmanaged forests.[81]

"Epidemic" losses in our forests result from outbreaks of insect and disease pests which injure trees rapidly and seriously and are frequently so destructive as to jeopardize lumbering investments and operations. As such outbreaks are usually unpredictable, little allowance can be made for them in long-range planning. There are several recent examples of these epidemics. The larch sawfly destroyed practically all mature stands of larch in the Lake states area about thirty-five years ago. Chestnut blight has wiped out our commercial chestnut trees. Numerous outbreaks of bark beetles in the pine forests of the West and the South have destroyed many billions of board feet of timber. A widespread outbreak of spruce budworm now threatens spruce and balsam in the Northeast. Blister rust has threatened our valuable commercial white pine forests wherever it has occurred.

Good forest management is generally the best way in which all of these losses can be prevented, for a vigorous, growing forest — the aim of such management — suffers comparatively little injury from insects and disease. Conversion of natural stands to fast-growing, managed forests will remove the trees most susceptible to attack. Good forest management also aids in keeping insects and disease from reaching the epidemic stage where control may be very expensive, if not impossible. Furthermore, much can be done to make some forests less susceptible through adjusting the mixture of the species or the density of the stand and by avoiding unnecessary wounding of trees in logging operations.

Until such time, however, as all of our forest lands are under good management practices, it will be necessary to undertake special control work in many areas in order to combat insects and disease pests. The outlays needed for such work should be regarded as further investments for the protection of a larger investment — our forest capital. Over the next twenty-five years, it appears that we might need to invest about $325 million — an annual average of about $15 million — from public and private funds for the detection and suppression of forest insects and disease.[82] (See Table 228.) Additional sums will be needed for research.

One example of the kind of control work needed is that to combat white pine blister rust.[83] This disease, which was introduced into the United States early in the present century, is a fungus that destroys white pine trees by girdling the limbs and trunk. It is spread by wild gooseberry and currant bushes commonly called ribes. It is controlled primarily by having small parties of men search out and remove by hand or mechanical methods — or kill with chemical sprays — the ribes in the vicinity of white pine. Areas that have been selected for control now total about 28 million acres and comprise the white pine areas of high productivity where expensive control work can be economically justified. About 23 million acres have been worked over, of which 11 million have received only initial treatment and will have to be worked over again. About 5 million acres remain to be given even initial treatment. The cost of treating the acreage to be controlled may vary from $1 to $10 per acre.

Stand Improvements

Protection of forests from fire and from insects and disease is only the beginning of good forest management. Such management also involves the improvement of existing stands so that the maximum timber crops can be grown in the shortest possible time. Forest stand improvements cover the work necessary to better the quality and growth rate of any forest stand, from the sapling to the saw-timber stage. Many such improvements can be made during the course of

---

80. G. H. Hepting and J. W. Kinney, "Heart Rot," *Trees — The Yearbook of Agriculture, 1949,* p. 462.

81. For this and the succeeding paragraphs in this section, see *Forests and National Prosperity,* pp. 85–86, and the several articles under the heading "Insects, Diseases, Parasites" in *Trees — The Yearbook of Agriculture, 1949,* pp. 407–476.

82. This estimate based on data in *Public Works and Rural Land Use,* pp. 121–123, and *Resources for Freedom,* Vol. I, p. 41.

83. For further details of this control work, see J. F. Martin and P. Spaulding, "Blister Rust on White Pine," *Trees — The Yearbook of Agriculture, 1949,* pp. 453–458.

commercial lumbering through proper timber-cutting practices. They will undoubtedly be taken care of increasingly in the future if the present forest management program is extended to national coverage.

Although progress has been encouraging, more than half of all recent timber cutting was rated in a nationwide survey as poor or destructive, and less than one fourth measured up to good forestry standards.[84] The widespread adoption of proper cutting practices will aid greatly in improving forest stands; not only can the quantity of the remaining stand be improved, by removing currently less volume than is added by growth, but also its quality can be improved by removing trees of poor form and vigor and reserving the better trees until they are ready to be cut. In addition, during the course of timber cutting, thinning and pruning operations and the removal of "forest weeds" — trees of low timber value that grow so rapidly as to overtop and suppress neighboring trees of greater value — can be undertaken to improve forest stands. Such improvements can yield sufficient marketable products — fuel wood, pulpwood, etc. — to offset practically all of the cost of the work. Thus, there is an ever-increasing opportunity for real forest stand improvement, on both public and private lands, through the extension of better cutting practices.

As a result of unsystematic cutting and abuse of our forest lands in the past, however, millions of acres of young timber stands now contain much material that should be removed because it is either too small or too poor to be marketable. In the South, for example, clear cutting and turpentining operations have resulted in areas of second growth that need thinning, others that need pruning. The Lake states area also has extensive second-growth cutover lands where the production rate will remain low for years unless aided by stand improvements. Furthermore, natural stands, like those in the Pacific Northwest, often become so dense that thinning is essential for satisfactory growth.[85]

Pending the coming into effect on a national scale of a management program under which the bulk of our commercial forest lands will have the continuing benefit of good timber-cutting practices, forest stand improvements should be undertaken in some areas. It has been estimated

that about 65 million acres are in need of such improvements, of which almost 50 million acres, or more than 75 per cent, are privately owned.[86] Nearly two thirds of the stands needing improvement lie in the Lake states area and the South. At a rough estimate, improvement of forest stands might require a total outlay of about $750 million of public and private funds over a twenty-five-year period, or an annual average of about $30 million. (See Table 228.) Future needs for additional outlays of this magnitude will be lessened to the extent that our forest lands are placed on a sustained-yield basis.

Planting

Proper forest management practices will enable most forest lands to regenerate themselves. In fact, natural reproduction is by far the cheapest and most successful method of reproducing a forest, and it can be easily and successfully achieved under high standards of silvicultural practice. Planting is desirable, however, where natural reproduction is sparse, irregular, slow or of poor species.

Forest planting was sporadic in the United States until recent years. Most of the early work was done on publicly owned land, but under the leadership and with the assistance of the federal government, extensive planting operations on privately owned land began during the 1920s. Planting did not reach a significant level, however, until the 1930s, when it averaged about 450,000 acres annually in the years toward the end of the decade. During World War II the annual average dropped below 150,000 acres.

Since the war, planting has rapidly accelerated, owing to the introduction of mechanical tree-planters, and it is currently proceeding at the rate of almost 500,000 acres a year, of which about four fifths are privately owned. Farmers and other owners of small forest lands planted 227 million trees in 1950, a record far surpassing their previous accomplishments. In the same year the forest industries, principally pulp and paper and large lumber companies, planted more than 150 million trees — more than one third of the total number they had planted in all previous years. This is perhaps our best assurance that large timber owners and operators are adopting timber growing as a permanent policy.[87]

84. *Forests and National Prosperity*, pp. 46–47.
85. *Public Works and Rural Land Use*, pp. 119–120.

86. *Ibid.*, p. 120.
87. For this and the preceding paragraph, see *Resources for Freedom*, Vol. V, pp. 40–41.

Despite the great progress during recent years, much remains to be done. The U.S. Forest Service estimates that about 75 million acres — or about 1 acre in every 6 — of the commercial forest land in the United States are poorly stocked or deforested; of this total more than 60 million acres — or roughly four fifths — are in private ownership. So long as this land remains idle, it will contribute nothing to an expanding American economy.[88]

The rehabilitation of these idle lands is the responsibility of both public agencies and private enterprise. The U.S. Forest Service has suggested an over-all planting goal, public and private, of 32 million acres in the next twenty-five years — over a billion trees a year — as a reasonably adequate attack on the reforestation job. About 25 million acres, or 80 per cent, would be on private lands; the rest, about 7 million acres, would be on public lands. Nearly 80 per cent of the acreage to be reforested lies east of the Great Plains.[89]

The total cost of such a program is somewhat uncertain. In the past hand-planting has been very costly, and even now sometimes costs as much as $35 an acre. The recent development of tree-planting machines and experiments in seeding large areas by airplane indicate, however, that the average cost per acre of reforestation will be considerably cheaper in the future. A planting program covering 32 million acres during the next twenty-five years might therefore require a total capital outlay of about $500 million, an average of $20 million a year. (See Table 228.)

If the acreage of the projected program were to be doubled, thus providing for planting on about 85 per cent of the present 75 million acres of poorly stocked or deforested land, and the time period were set at fifty years, the total outlay would approach $1 billion, but the average annual costs would remain about the same. This would probably be the maximum program required, for if a good forest management program is undertaken on a national scale, covering both public and private lands, it is reasonable to assume that the acreage of poorly stocked forest land will progressively decrease as a result of improved fire protection and better cutting practices. Surveys of forest land in the southern states

show, for example, that stocking in them is better now than it was ten years ago, because young growth is springing up on millions of acres now protected from fire. This is one of the hopeful signs for the future.[90]

Roads and Trails

Early logging operations in this country were limited largely to areas where water transportation was available. As the railroad network spread over the land in the latter half of the nineteenth century, logging became possible in many new areas. But only in the twentieth century did truck transportation provide the economy and flexibility of operation in rough and previously inaccessible forest lands that logging by water and rail had not been able to achieve.

Despite the rapid growth during the past three decades of truck logging — with its greater flexibility — the over-all pattern of logging operations since the earliest days of the industry has been such that our forest lands with the best timber and nearest to the market have largely been cut. Our remaining good timber resources, especially saw logs, are becoming increasingly difficult of access, and in the future the satisfactory management of our forest lands for timber production purposes will require the construction of additional forest development roads leading from the back areas to the main highways. Trails for horse and foot travel will also have to be built in order to reach areas beyond the range of forest development roads. Such trails are indispensable for fire protection and other forest management services.

Forest development roads and trails are needed primarily in the West, which has 65 per cent of the country's saw-timber stand. Nearly 40 per cent of the commercial forest land in the West is in virgin timber, and much of this is in remote country. Elsewhere in the country, particularly in the South, the construction of additional forest development roads would make it possible to spread the cut over a wider area and thus permit the better development of second-growth timber.[91]

It has been estimated that in order properly to serve our forest lands, we will need to construct about 100,000 miles of forest development roads,

88. *Forests and National Prosperity,* p. 23.

89. For further details of this planting program, see Lyle F. Watts, "A National Program for Forestry," *Trees — The Yearbook of Agriculture, 1949,* p. 759; and *Public Works and Rural Land Use,* pp. 117–118.

90. *Forests and National Prosperity,* pp. 23–24.

91. Data in this paragraph from *Forests and National Prosperity,* pp. 19, 22–23, and 43–44.

a 20 per cent increase in the existing mileage, and about 160,000 miles of foot and horse trails, a 33 per cent increase in the existing mileage.[92] Approximately three fifths of the new mileage would be on private forest lands, the rest on publicly owned lands. Most of the roads would be of fairly simple construction, primarily unsurfaced and of single-lane width with steep grades and sharp curves, but they would serve the purpose.

The total capital outlays from public and private funds needed to cover the construction of these roads and trails would probably be not less than $1.5 billion, of which about 90 per cent would be for roads. Spread over a fifty-year period, the outlay would average about $30 million a year. (See Table 228.) In addition, capital outlays would be required for the construction of high-speed and heavy-duty passenger and freight highways through our forest lands. But such highways are usually part of our national and state highway network, and estimates for them are therefore included within the over-all estimates of highway needs given elsewhere in this study.[93]

Other Improvements

The proper management of our public and private forest lands also requires many kinds of buildings, communication systems, shelters, water developments and similar improvements. These improvements would be apart from the saw mills, pulp mills and wood-using plants of various kinds that private firms will need to build to work the timber they take from the forests.

A rough estimate indicates that the capital outlays needed for improvements such as these might approach $500 million.[94] If these outlays were to be made over a twenty-five-year period, the annual average expenditure would amount to about $20 million. (See Table 228.) Almost 50 per cent of the outlays would be for improvements on privately owned forest land.

These improvements round out the picture of the capital investments needed during the coming years in order to ensure good forest management for timber production.

FOREST PROTECTION AND DEVELOPMENT FOR NONTIMBER USES

The several programs outlined in the preceding section, although designed primarily to increase timber production, would also be beneficial for other uses of our forest lands. Increased fire protection, for example, prevents the destruction of forage crops for livestock and saves wildlife. Protection of forests from fire and from insects and disease and restoration of forest growth by planting result in better watershed protection and thus help prevent floods and ensure water supplies. Stand improvements facilitate grazing and heighten the recreational value of forests. Roads and trails and other improvements make forest areas more accessible for recreational use.

There are, however, further improvements that should be undertaken primarily for the sake of the principal nontimber uses of our forest lands — watershed protection, forage production, wildlife habitat and recreation.

Watershed Protection

Apart from timber production, watershed protection is the paramount service rendered to our national economy by our forest lands, about 470 million acres of them having some value in this respect. By slowing the runoff of rain and melting snow, trees and their litter help greatly to maintain the underground reservoirs that are so important in supplying water for domestic, industrial and agricultural purposes. Surface water supplies are also ensured to a great extent by our forests, because in regulating water runoff on land they help control the flow of rivers. As regulators of stream flow, forests also reduce the danger of disastrous floods and facilitate the development and use of our rivers for hydroelectric power and navigation. Finally, by preventing the soil erosion caused by rapid runoff, forests reduce the sedimentation in our streams and rivers that hinders navigation, clogs irrigation ditches and canals, ruins fishing, impairs domestic and industrial water supplies, and backs up behind dams until reservoirs eventually become useless.[95]

---

92. These estimates are based on data in: *Resources for Freedom*, Vol. I, p. 44; *Statistical Supplement — Report of the Chief of the Forest Service, 1950*, U.S. Department of Agriculture, 1951, Table 2b, p. 4; and *Public Works and Rural Land Use*, pp. 108–109.

93. See Chapter 9.

94. See estimates, when converted into 1950 costs and prices, in *Public Works and Rural Land Use*, p. 114.

95. *Report of the Chief of the Forest Service, 1947 — Forests and the Nation's Water Resources*, U.S. Department of Agriculture, 1947, pp. 1–15.

The watershed protection services being performed by our forests are below par, however, in all parts of the country. We have lost entirely, and perhaps forever, the services previously rendered by the one third of our original forest lands that were cleared in the process of settling and building our nation. The remaining forest lands are not as useful as they might be for watershed protection, as a result of poor timber-cutting practices and our failure to prevent or control forest fires and insects and disease. Overgrazing has also damaged the cover and soil on perhaps 20 per cent of the forest land, especially in the western and northern states.[96]

The situation now confronting the nation is not, however, new. It has been worsening for decades, but until comparatively recent times little was done to correct it. A growing recognition of the value of forest lands in affording watershed protection was one of the forces motivating the forest conservation movement early in this century. During the 1930s, the federal government — in connection with its expanded flood control activities — also began to encourage the undertaking of large-scale measures for retarding waterflow and preventing soil erosion on watershed lands. These corrective measures have emphasized the restoration and proper management of watershed cover, including reforestation or revegetation, intensified fire control, and changes in land use.

Measures Needed

If we take the proper steps, most of the remaining forest lands will be able in the future to provide watershed protection at the same time as they are being used for timber production, livestock grazing and other purposes. Many of these steps have already been described as part of good forest management for timber production: adequate fire protection; maintenance of good forest growth; planting of poorly stocked or denuded areas. Others will be described below in connection with the improvements needed to maintain forage production. Several special measures, however, will be required for adequate protection of watersheds.

Much of the forest land that is important in watershed protection is in farm ownership, dispersed among more than 3 million farms. Most of these woodlands are understocked. The U.S. Forest Service estimates there are 44 million acres of farm lands that should be planted to trees.[97] One of the earliest returns from such a planting program would be more adequate protection of watersheds and a retardation of water and wind erosion.

On the watersheds in the Great Plains area, wind often causes as much soil erosion as water does in the more humid areas of the country. The Shelterbelt project, a special planting program inaugurated by the federal government in 1935, has as its central purpose the protection of fields in the prairie states against drying winds and the drifting of soil. Under this project, separate plantings of 5 to 10 rows of trees are placed so as to provide maximum protection for individual farms. Less than 10 per cent of the needed planting, however, has so far been done. It has been estimated [98] that, during the next fifty years, about 2 million additional acres, involving about 320,000 farms, should be planted in the Shelterbelt zone, which runs from North Dakota through eastern South Dakota, thence westward to central Nebraska, and then through middle Kansas into the Texas Panhandle. Each acre planted would protect about 20 acres of cropland, and if properly handled the shelter strips would renew themselves, thus perpetuating the protection they afford.

Other physical improvements and minor engineering work will be needed to supplement reforestation in the permanent control of watershed conditions on our forest lands. Such devices as terraces, contour trenches, water spreaders, diversion ditches and check dams must be installed in order to control erosion and encourage infiltration of water into the soil. These improvements form a temporary base from which reforestation can proceed to restore permanent watershed protection.

In all, it is probable that a total capital outlay of about $750 million would be required over the next fifty years to cover these special plantings and improvement operations for watershed protection. Annual capital outlays during the period would therefore average at least $15 million. (See Table 228.)

Forage Production

In 1950, about 320 million acres of forest and woodland were used for pasture and grazing.

---

96. *Forests and National Prosperity*, p. 69.

97. *Report of the Chief of the Forest Service*, 1947, p. 23.

98. *Public Works and Rural Land Use*, pp. 126–127.

TABLE 229. GRAZING USE OF FOREST AND WOODLAND, 1900–1950
(*Millions of Acres*)

Year	Total Forest and Woodland Area [a]	Grazed			Not Grazed		
		Total	In Farms	Outside Farms	Total	In Farms	Outside Farms
1900	579	300	87	213	279	104	175
1910	562	307	98	209	255	93	162
1920	567	316	77	239	251	91	160
1930	607	334	85	249	273	65	208
1940	602	342	100	242	260	57	203
1950	606	320	135	185	286	85	201

Sources: L. A. Reuss, H. H. Wooten and F. J. Marschner, *Inventory of Major Land Uses in the United States,* Miscellaneous Publication No. 663, U.S. Department of Agriculture, 1948, pp. 30–32, Tables 16 and 17 and Figure 9; *Agricultural Statistics, 1951,* U.S. Department of Agriculture, Table 607, p. 530; and H. H. Wooten, *Major Uses of Land in the United States,* Technical Bulletin 1082, U.S. Department of Agriculture, 1953, Table 3 and Figure 3, pp. 10–11.

a. Does not include forest land in parks, game refuges, military reservations, etc.

(See Table 223.) This acreage accounted for nearly one third of the country's available pasture and grazing land, and well over half of our forest land. The acreage of forest and woodland used as pasture and range for livestock has increased during the past fifty years, particularly in farms. The area of such farmland used for grazing increased by nearly 50 million acres from 1900 to 1950, although the total area of forest and woodland in farms increased slightly less than 30 million acres. (See Table 229.)

Forests and woodlands all over the country are in strong demand as pasture and range. In some regions forage is second only to timber as a source of revenue from these lands. But the use of forest land for grazing requires good management. Bad grazing practices not only reduce the available forage but also may impair the land for timber production, watershed protection or recreation.[99]

The forest acreage used for grazing is divided almost equally between the western and Great Plains states and the states east of the Great Plains. The bulk of the forest lands grazed east of the Great Plains lies in the South, much of it in piney woods. From the standpoint of forage production, these lands are in fairly good condition. The same cannot be said, however, of the forest lands in the western and Great Plains states. Rough estimates indicate that, primarily because of overgrazing, about two thirds of the western forest range is in an unsatisfactory condition.

Needed Improvements

An important task of good forest management is the rehabilitation of both public and private forest ranges, particularly in the West. More emphasis needs to be placed on grazing practices that will build up and maintain the forage — better seasonal use of the range, more efficient control and distribution of livestock, adjustments in kinds of animals using the range, rotation grazing, etc. Improvements such as soil and moisture conservation, artificial reseeding, fencing and stock-water developments must also be undertaken in order to rehabilitate millions of acres of badly depleted forest range.

The capital outlays covering the needed improvements on a good portion of the 135 million acres of pastured forest and woodland in farms have been included in the estimated outlays for the conservation and rehabilitation of our croplands.[100] Of the remaining 185 million acres of grazed forest land, more than 150 million acres are in the western forest ranges, and capital outlays for the improvement of these acres have also already been estimated.[101] Between 30 and 50 million acres of forest range lands remain, how-

99. For this and the next two paragraphs, see *Forests and National Prosperity,* pp. 71–73; and C. A. Connaughton, "Grass, Water and Trees," *Grass — The Yearbook of Agriculture, 1948,* pp. 239–243.

100. See estimates on p. 517.
101. See estimates on p. 520.

ever, and improvement of these might require capital outlays of $100 to $150 million. If this work were to be accomplished over a twenty-year period (which corresponds to the period set for the programs of conservation and rehabilitation improvements on crop and grazing lands projected earlier in this chapter), the average annual outlays would be between $5 and $7.5 million.

It would appear, therefore, that roughly $600 million of capital outlays would cover the grazing improvements needed on *all* forests and woodlands used for pasture and range, including those in and outside farms and eastern as well as western lands. Over a twenty-year period, then, an average annual outlay of $30 million would appear to be required if the capacity of our forests to produce forage is not only to be maintained but also to be increased in order to meet the needs of an expanding economy. (See Table 228.)

Wildlife Habitat

Next to watershed protection and forage production, probably the most valuable nontimber use of our forests is as a wildlife habitat. Although almost all of our land area sustains some wildlife, about 95 per cent of our big-game animals — deer, elk and moose, big-horn sheep, mountain goats and bear — and roughly one fourth of the lesser game and fur bearers live in forested areas.[102]

When the first white settlers arrived on this continent, they found a land abounding in wildlife of many varied and valuable kinds. They relentlessly pursued and killed the wild animals and birds in order to provide themselves with food and clothing and to obtain pelts for export to Europe in exchange for the manufactured goods they needed. By clearing the land for agriculture, by logging, and by failing to control forest fires, our forefathers also destroyed much of the wildlife habitat. But the wildlife resources appeared so limitless that they were used with little concern for the future.

A little less than fifty years ago, however, we suddenly became aware that there were left scarcely more than scattered remnants of what was once the richest resource of its kind in the world. In the eastern states, the elk were gone by 1870 and most of the white-tailed deer had disappeared by 1910. Even in many parts of the western states, the elk were killed off, and one

species had disappeared entirely by the end of the nineteenth century. Beavers were practically exterminated from large areas of the eastern states and even became scarce in the western states. The American bison was hardly to be found except in zoos. Many valuable species of wild fowl had disappeared and others were in danger of extinction.

Beginning early in this century, steps were taken to protect our diminishing wildlife resources. The states gradually enacted protective laws. During the 1920s and 1930s, refuges were set aside and restocking was undertaken on a large scale. These measures began to restore our wildlife; in some areas, in fact, surpluses developed in relation to the ranges available for feeding. Today, many big-game ranges in the Lake states area and the West are in serious danger of depletion.[103]

The American people derive several benefits from the protection and development of their wildlife resources.[104] Although the time is long past when our wildlife was a primary source of food, game still supplies annually an estimated one quarter of a billion pounds of meat to supplement the American diet, particularly that of low-income rural people. The annual take of wild furs averages better than $100 million, but the United States does not produce enough furs to meet more than half of its own demands. Hunting is a sport and recreation for millions of Americans, and each year about 13 million hunting licenses are issued.

Wildlife is a renewable natural resource. The principal requirements for maintaining it are the preservation, rehabilitation, development and protection of its habitat. If these requirements are met, and if hunting is held within reasonable bounds, wildlife will increase. So long as measures are taken to conserve an adequate seed stock, a surplus will be available for harvesting — on a sustained-yield basis — for food, furs and sport. At the same time, we must control the predatory animals and rodents that exact a heavy toll on

---

102. *Forests and National Prosperity*, pp. 75–76.

103. For this and the preceding two paragraphs, see L. W. Swift, "Forests as a Wildlife Habitat," *Trees — The Yearbook of Agriculture, 1949*, pp. 565–567.

104. Data in this paragraph from: J. P. Miller and B. B. Powell, *Game and Wild-Fur Production and Utilization on Agricultural Land*, Circular No. 636, U.S. Department of Agriculture, 1942, pp. 29–30; *Forests and National Prosperity*, p. 76; F. G. Ashbrook, *Fur — An Important Wildlife Crop*, Wildlife Leaflet 314, U.S. Department of the Interior, 1945, pp. 1–2; and *A Water Policy for the American People*, p. 259.

other game and on domestic livestock and agricultural crops.[105]

Future Wildlife Management

Good wildlife management for the future first of all involves adequate federal and state game laws, and proper enforcement of them. Next it requires the kind of skillful administration that will result in an increasing wildlife population without overstocking. Finally, improvements in habitat are needed to ensure food, water and cover. These improvements, and the capital outlays they will require, are of particular concern here.[106]

It has been estimated that about 1,150 million acres — or approximately 60 per cent of the land area in the continental United States — provide some food and cover for wildlife. Almost half this area, or about 523 million acres, is in forest and woodland.[107] In fact, more than 90 million acres — or nearly 5 per cent of the continental land area — are so rough, swampy, or otherwise unfitted for agriculture or forestry that they are considered suitable *only* for sustaining wildlife.[108]

It would not be economically feasible, however, to increase very much the total area that now supports wildlife. Only a little over 150 million acres could be added — an increase of about 13 per cent. Of this increase a little more than one sixth, or about 23 million acres, would be in forest and woodland.[109] To summarize, approximately two thirds of our continental land area either provides or could provide food and cover for wildlife, and about 546 million acres of this are in forest and woodland.

Improvement of forest lands for the benefit of wildlife can often be accomplished as part of other forest conservation, management or development activities.[110] Fire protection and control contribute greatly, of course, in preserving the forest environment. Certain kinds of timber cutting increase the food supply of animals and birds, yet leave plenty of dense cover for their protection. The needs of wildlife can be taken into account in improving timber stands, as they can in work undertaken for watershed protection. Use of forests for livestock grazing can be guided so as to complement and avoid conflict with wildlife management, and recreational use can be similarly guided. Some special improvements will be needed, however, to protect our wildlife resources: watering facilities, fencing, and some provision of supplementary food patches and shelters.

Beyond the forests and woodlands, there are about 675 million acres of crop, grazing and other agricultural lands which can be improved for the benefit of wildlife. Soil and water conservation practices and improvements on these lands, along the lines outlined in the first part of this chapter, will provide more food, water and cover for wildlife, and frequently can be carried out as part of regular farm operations. For example, in planting to prevent erosion in gullies, along stream and ditch banks, and on contour strips, plants can be used that produce seeds, berries or other food for game animals. Planting of hedgerows on contours also provides cover for game. Field and woodland borders can be planted in grasses useful for wildlife food and cover, as well as for weed and erosion control. These and similar measures on agricultural lands improve wildlife habitat.[111]

Parks, military reservations and other reserved lands in rural areas also support wildlife, but more special refuge areas are needed, especially for animals and birds which are now rare or threatened with extinction. In 1950 almost 8.9 million acres of publicly owned land in the continental United States were used primarily as wildlife refuges, and millions of acres in other public and private holdings were used or leased for this purpose.[112] The development of more refuges will require not only the acquisition or setting aside of land but also investment in shelter, nesting and feeding areas; water control structures; fire protection and fencing against

---

105. For this paragraph, see *Public Works and Rural Land Use*, p. 156.

106. Estimates of the additional capital outlays required for the conservation and development of our fish resources and for some kinds of wildlife closely associated with our water resources, like migratory waterfowl, are contained in a section later in this chapter on "Fish and Wildlife Conservation and Recreation" under "River Valley Development."

107. Miller and Powell, *op. cit.*, Table 3, pp. 27–28.

108. *Soil and Water Conservation Needs Estimates for the United States*, p. 12.

109. Miller and Powell, *op. cit.*, Table 4, pp. 29–30.

110. Swift, *op. cit.*, pp. 568–569; and *Forests and National Prosperity*, p. 76.

111. *Conservation of Wildlife*, Hearings before the Select Committee on Conservation of Wildlife Resources, House of Representatives, 79th Cong., 2d sess., 1946, pp. 225–233.

112. R. D. Davidson, *Federal and State Rural Lands, 1950*, Circular No. 909, U.S. Department of Agriculture, 1950, pp. 21, 51–52 and 67.

marauders; and trails, roads and other facilities necessary for administration.

Although no over-all estimates are readily available of the cost of the improvements needed specifically for good wildlife management, it appears that a total capital outlay of $250 million might be needed over the next twenty-five years, an annual average of about $10 million. (See Table 228.) This would be in addition to the outlays needed for forest management directed primarily toward other purposes, and expenditures for the conservation and rehabilitation of crop and grazing lands — many of which outlays would improve our wildlife resources.

Recreation

Each year, millions of people go to forests and woodlands to picnic, camp or enjoy the natural scenic beauty; to rest and relax in the summer; to ski and engage in other winter sports; or to hunt and fish. National parks and monuments, state parks, parkways and beaches also offer recreational opportunities in rural areas. The automobile — and improved public transportation — have made all these recreational facilities much more accessible to the average American than they were thirty years ago.[113]

With the use of rural recreational facilities increasing by leaps and bounds, a major question arises of what, if any, limits there are to using our land for recreational purposes. According to the National Park Service, about 300 million acres — or about one sixth of the continental area of the United States — could be used in this way.[114] This would be over and above our land requirements for agriculture, timber production and urban development, and would exclude lands that are of little use for mass recreation. In 1950 about 48 million acres of our publicly owned lands in rural areas were being used specifically for park and recreational purposes,[115] and many more millions of acres of public and private land had some recreational use. Therefore, it is apparent that for many, many decades to come, further development of rural lands for recreational purposes will be limited only by the amount we wish to invest for this purpose. The potentialities of private forest lands for recreational use, for example, are as yet far from being fully realized,

especially in New England, the Lake states and the Appalachians.[116]

Future requirements for recreational facilities must be considered, however, from several other standpoints. Generally, people must travel some distance to reach the outlying natural areas, but a good proportion of our population have neither the time nor the means for long-distance travel and must spend their leisure periods close to home. The development of recreational facilities in or near our urban centers should, therefore, have first priority, and the needs for such development are discussed elsewhere in this volume,[117] as are the needs for parkways.[118] Our foreseeable requirements for recreational facilities and improvements in forests, woodlands and other rural areas will be considered here primarily in terms of the national forests, national parks and state parks involved. Later in this chapter, consideration will be given to rural recreational developments that are more closely related to the use and control of our water resources.[119]

National Forests

There are more than 200 million acres of national forests in the continental United States, virtually all of which, except for fire hazard restrictions, are available for some form of recreation.[120] Recreational use of these forests has generally developed without serious conflicts with other uses, mainly because many forms of forest recreation — camping and picnicking, swimming, winter sports, and the like — do not require a large acreage even though they involve exclusive use of the land. Nearly 150,000 acres in our national forests are reserved exclusively for recreational use, an area which the U.S. Forest Service estimates should be doubled. The Forest Service also estimates that the private facilities which supplement and increase the recreational use of our national forests will have to be increased about two thirds in order to meet the rising demand.

National Parks

In 1950 the national park system of the federal government, and other recreational areas admin-

---

113. See Chapter 11.
114. *A Study of the Park and Recreational Problem of the United States,* National Park Service, U.S. Department of the Interior, 1941, p. 29.
115. Davidson, *op. cit.,* Table 4, p. 21 and pp. 50–51.

116. *Forests and National Prosperity,* p. 74.
117. See Chapter 11.
118. See Chapter 9.
119. See the section on "Fish and Wildlife Conservation and Recreation" under "River Valley Development."
120. For data in this paragraph, see *Forests and National Prosperity,* pp. 74–75.

istered by the National Park Service, comprised more than 16 million acres in the continental United States.[121] These park areas include some of the finest scenery and natural beauty in America — the Grand Canyon, the Great Smoky Mountains, the Yellowstone area, the Everglades and Yosemite Valley. The first national parks were established on lands already owned by the government on which there were striking natural phenomena — mountains, glaciers, waterfalls, lakes, geysers, hot springs, etc. Later, efforts were made to acquire sites with special attractions — a notable forest, a scenic lake, a national shrine or landmark.

Several hundreds of thousands of additional acres are needed to round out the presently planned national park system. Facilities in the present park areas will also have to be expanded to accommodate the steadily mounting number of visitors.

State Parks

State park areas may be considered as falling into two categories: outing and picnic areas near large cities and towns; and outlying areas with special natural features similar to the national parks.[122] In 1950 almost 2.4 million acres of land owned by the states were reserved for permanent use in state parks. Roughly 2 million acres of other state-owned land, principally state forests, were also used primarily for recreation. In all, there were nearly 3,400 state park units. Colorado was the only state with none; Arizona had only 2, and Texas, at the head of the list, had 570. Twelve states each had more than 100 separate park units in operation or in process of development.

In the past fifteen years, the total number of annual visitors to state parks increased by about one third. Because of the growing demand, it is estimated that the states should acquire, or set aside, and develop an additional 4 million acres for recreational purposes.

Other Possibilities

There are innumerable other possibilities for recreational development in rural areas.[123] Many federal, state and private lands could be developed for recreational use without interfering with the purposes which they are primarily intended to serve. For example, 14 million acres in our national forests have been set aside as wilderness areas, and another 1.5 million acres are reserved in roadside strips. There are about 17 million acres of state-owned forest land, more than half of which has no commercial forest value and might be developed for recreation. Trails and trailways, like the Appalachian Trail from Maine to Georgia; wayside and roadside picnic and outing sites; private resorts, hotels, dude ranches, camps, summer homes, hunting and sports clubs — these and many other developments like them offer opportunities for new capital investments, both public and private, in our rural areas.

All together, capital outlays of about $2 billion might be needed during the next twenty-five years — an annual average of about $80 million — to cover the kinds of rural recreational developments outlined. (See Table 228.) This estimate differs from those in Chapter 11 (Table 166), which include urban recreational areas and exclude national and state forest areas.

RIVER VALLEY DEVELOPMENT

The area of the continental United States comprises the basins of over 160 separate rivers with their tributaries, and the valleys of innumerable small streams that flow directly to the sea or to the Great Lakes. The use and control of the waters of these rivers and streams have played a dominant role in the development of the country. Rivers were highways leading to new lands. Their natural falls furnished an early source of power. Boats plying them carried the nation's commerce until the railway net spread over the land.

As the land became more fully occupied and cities grew, our rivers became even more useful. Today they provide drinking water for a good part of our population, carry away municipal sewage and industrial wastes, and once again transport an important share of our commerce.

---

121. For information in this paragraph see: *A Study of the Park and Recreational Problem of the United States*, pp. 51–52; *Public Works and Rural Land Use*, pp. 151–152; and *Annual Report of the Secretary of the Interior — Fiscal Year Ended June 30, 1950*, pp. 303–337.

122. For data in this and the following paragraph see: Davidson, *op. cit.*, pp. 50–51; *Public Works and Rural Land Use*, pp. 142–143 and 151; and *A Study of the Park and Recreational Problem of the United States*, p. 50.

123. For data in this paragraph see: *Forests and National Prosperity*, p. 74; Davidson, *op. cit.*, Table 12, p. 51; and *Public Works and Rural Land Use*, pp. 146–148.

They enable us to irrigate new lands for agriculture and are a vital source of power for the generation of electricity. But our rivers also have become a greater menace. The increased occupancy of their flood plains and the abuse of the lands in their drainage areas have caused flood damages to mount. Uncontrolled, the rivers rampage in flood, destroying lives and property. Many of them dwindle to a trickle in drought, leaving commerce stranded, cities and industries short of water, and the land parched.

Our success in using and controlling our water resources in the future will depend first of all on how we handle our land and forest resources — whether we will undertake the conservation and rehabilitation measures outlined earlier in this chapter. For the proper management of our water resources cannot be separated from that of our land and forest resources. Next will be the question of our willingness to continue making the increasingly large capital outlays for the works and structures required to regulate our river systems. The amounts involved will be very large, and many decades — perhaps fifty to seventy-five years — of constant effort will be needed before the task can be reasonably complete. Finally, there will be the question of how we will view the whole problem and whether we will act accordingly. River basins are the natural subdivisions of our water resources, and unless we approach their future use and control on this basis, trouble will certainly follow.

PRINCIPAL PURPOSES OF DEVELOPMENTAL WORKS

The American people have made large capital outlays to control and develop their water resources. It is estimated that by 1950 about $50 billion had been invested in structures and facilities, about one fourth of it by the federal government. Our principal technical contribution to the control and development of water — the most essential single material man uses, and the vital link of all living things — has been in the building of great dams and control works, the drilling of very deep wells, and the designing of huge pumps that can literally dry up a river.[124]

Fresh water is our primary self-renewing resource, and our supply of it is enormous. The total quantity in constant circulation, measured by the average annual precipitation over the United States in the form of rain and snow, amounts to about 4,300 billion gallons daily. About 3,000 billion gallons return to the atmosphere through evaporation and transpiration, and the rest runs off to the sea. But our use of fresh water is also enormous. We use about 170 billion gallons of fresh water daily for domestic, industrial and irrigation purposes — four times as much as we used for these purposes fifty years ago. Approximately seven times this amount passes through turbines to generate electricity. Furthermore, the capacity of our rivers and streams to dilute, purify and transport sewage and industrial wastes saves cities and industries millions of dollars.

The possibilities for the future are equally impressive. Proper control of stream flow will ensure navigation, prevent floods, provide more water for irrigation, domestic and industrial use, and make possible the generation of even larger amounts of hydroelectric power. The stopping of pollution will eliminate health hazards, aid in restoring wildlife, and facilitate recreational use of rivers.

River works and structures that would serve each of these purposes alone would be highly desirable, but the greatest benefits will be derived in the future from works designed to serve several of these purposes at the same time. Multiple-purpose projects will be the cornerstones of future river valley development programs.

Waterways and Port Development

In the early days, our rivers and harbors were used mostly in their natural state with limited improvements undertaken primarily by local private and public interests. From its beginning the federal government showed interest in marking harbors and waterways for safer navigation, but the first definite steps to improve our river systems were not taken until 1824, when the Supreme Court ruled that Congress had the power to legislate with respect to the navigable waters of the United States. In that year Congress authorized snagging and dredging work on the Ohio and Mississippi rivers. Nevertheless, for many years thereafter, private interests and state and local public agencies made the major capital outlays for canals and waterways — such as the Erie Canal and the Chesapeake and Ohio Canal.

124. For data in this and the next paragraph see *A Water Policy for the American People*, pp. 109–110, and *Resources for Freedom*, Vol. V, pp. 83–86.

With the rapid development of railroad transportation after 1850, the canal-building era came to an end, and since then the federal government has financed the majority of river and harbor improvements.[125]

As faster and more dependable rail transportation became available during the second half of the nineteenth century, commerce on our inland rivers and canals, which played such a great part in the early development of the interior of the nation, almost disappeared. Late in the century, however, dissatisfaction with rail rates gave rise to an insistent public demand for waterway improvements and a revival of domestic waterway commerce. Shortly after 1900 the development of inland waterways and canals was therefore resumed, and it has gradually expanded since then.

The major projects undertaken during the twentieth century include the conversion and extension of the Erie Canal into the New York State Barge Canal, the canalization of the Ohio, Tennessee and upper Mississippi rivers to 9-foot depth by means of locks and dams, and the deepening of the open-river channels of the lower Mississippi and Missouri rivers to 9 feet. Much work has also been done on the major coastal harbors and on the harbors and channels of the Great Lakes, and an intracoastal waterway has been constructed along the Atlantic and Gulf coasts. In recent years, navigation projects have been combined in multiple-purpose river development programs. The main river dams on the Tennessee River and the Bonneville Dam on the Columbia River, for example, serve navigation, power development, flood control and other purposes.

Past Outlays

By 1950, the federal government had spent about $2.4 billion for the improvement of rivers and harbors (excluding the costs of maintaining and operating the completed improvements). More than 90 per cent of this outlay had been made since 1910, when the government embarked on its modern improvement program.[126]

State and local governments had spent an estimated total of about $650 million by 1950. In all, public outlays for such improvements were probably not less than $3 billion. Inclusion of public investments in water terminals of all kinds would increase this figure by well over $1 billion. Reliable estimates are not available of private investments in port and dock developments, but they probably exceed federal expenditures. The total public and private investment in water transportation improvements and developments is therefore probably between $6.5 and $7 billion.[127]

Improved inland waterways, which are of particular concern in this chapter, now total about 28,600 miles, of which more than 12,000 miles lie in the Mississippi River system. About 60 per cent of the total federal expenditure of $2.4 billion for river and harbor improvements has been made on these waterways. Inland waterways, including the Great Lakes system, carry about 15 per cent of the total ton-miles of freight traffic in the United States. Traffic on inland waterways, exclusive of the Great Lakes system, increased about 500 per cent between 1929 and 1950. About 80 per cent of this traffic is now carried on 15 major waterways having an aggregate length of 7,100 miles, almost half of which are on the main streams of the Mississippi River and its principal tributaries, the Ohio and Missouri.[128]

Future Estimates

It is difficult for several reasons to estimate what we will need to spend in the future for navigation improvements, especially on inland waterways. The need for such outlays will be determined largely by the future national volume of freight traffic and the transport required to handle it, a question which is discussed elsewhere in this volume.[129] Depending on the volume and nature of that future traffic, present waterways might carry an even larger share than now without the necessity of additional outlays, except for

hand, some portions of the additional $1.1 billion which had been expended by the federal government up to 1950 for maintenance and operation were really for the replacement of obsolete improvements.

127. Data for this paragraph adapted from *Report of the Chief of Engineers, U.S. Army, 1951*, Part I, Vol. III, pp. 131, 264–265, 271–272; and *Transportation and National Policy*, National Resources Planning Board, 1942, pp. 434–435.

128. Data in this paragraph from *Report of the Chief of Engineers, U.S. Army, 1951*, Part I, Vol. III, pp. 267–268 and 278–284.

129. See Chapter 9.

125. For information in this and the next two paragraphs see *A Water Policy for the American People*, pp. 198–199, and *Report of the Chief of Engineers, U.S. Army, 1951*, 1952, Part I, Vol. III, pp. 261–268.

126. This total expenditure of $2.4 billion did not, however, represent the net federal investment in 1950 in river and harbor improvements, because nothing had been deducted for depreciation and obsolescence. On the other

TABLE 230. ESTIMATED COSTS AND TIME REQUIRED
FOR RIVER VALLEY DEVELOPMENT PROGRAMS
(*Dollar Figures in Millions, 1950 Prices*)

Type of Program	Total Cost	Years Required	Annual Cost
Total	$80,000		$1,685 [a]
Waterways and port development	7,500	50–75	125
Flood control	15,000	50–75	250
Irrigation	10,000	50–75	160
Hydroelectric power	30,000	50–75	480
Domestic and industrial water supply	6,250	25	250
Pollution abatement	10,000	25	400
Fish and wildlife conservation and recreation	1,250	50–75	20

Source: See discussion in text.   a. Total for first 25 years only.

maintenance and repair. On the other hand, waterways create their own traffic to a great degree, and a national river valley development program for the future which emphasizes navigation improvements may considerably increase the total ton-mileage of commodities transported by inland waterways. If the total traffic volume should remain about the same as it is now or grow very slowly, then increases in water-borne traffic might decrease the amount carried by other forms of transport.

The long-term trend of an increasing use of our waterways appears to presage a continuing public demand for the further improvement of existing waterways and the development of new waterways. In 1950, the federal program of authorized river and harbor improvement projects totaled about $4.1 billion, of which probably more than one third was for the completion of projects already under construction.[130] A large number of other improvements are being studied, among them such important and controversial waterway developments as the Lake Erie to Ohio River Canal and the deepening to a 12-foot channel of the Mississippi, Illinois and Ohio rivers.[131] Looking ahead fifty to seventy-five years, it appears possible that the need for river and harbor improvements might involve an outlay of perhaps $7.5 billion (see Table 230), of which more than one half would probably be for water-

way improvements on the Mississippi River system.[132] This would indicate a possible average annual outlay of around $125 million, with additional substantial public and private investments required for further port and terminal improvements.

Perhaps the most spectacular, and at the same time the most controversial, of the proposed waterway improvements is the St. Lawrence Seaway Project.[133] This joint American-Canadian project, which was recently authorized by Congress, is estimated to cost about $800 million. It will open an unobstructed 27-foot waterway well over 2,000 miles long from the entrance of the St. Lawrence River near Newfoundland to Duluth, Minnesota, thus enabling deep-draft ocean-going vessels to navigate into the heart of the North American continent. A multiple-purpose project, it involves the construction of dams, locks and canals above and below the International Rapids on the St. Lawrence and the installation of hydroelectric power facilities. The installed capacity of the generators will be more than 1.8 million kilowatts, and the average annual output of electricity will be nearly 13 billion kilowatt-hours, to be divided about equally between the United States and Canada.

130. *Report of the Chief of Engineers, U.S. Army, 1950,* 1951, Part I, Vol. I, p. 24.
131. *Report of the Chief of Engineers, U.S. Army, 1951,* Part I, Vol. III, p. 289.

132. "Summary of Plans for Conservation and Development of the Water Resources of the United States," Table 3, p. 9949, and *A Water Policy for the American People,* Table 4, p. 93.
133. *St. Lawrence Seaway and Power Project,* Hearings before the Committee on Foreign Relations, U.S. Senate, 82d Cong., 2d sess., 1952. The detailed project description and cost estimates (at 1950 prices) appear on pp. 524–530.

An important economic justification claimed for this project is that it will permit the American steel industry in the midcontinental area to tap the rich iron ore reserves of Labrador, now that the end can be foreseen of the higher-grade reserves in the great Mesabi range, upon which we have relied so heavily in the past.

Flood Control

Floods occurred on the rivers of North America even before the continent was discovered and settled, and our nation established. The first Spanish explorers of the Mississippi Valley during the sixteenth century encountered floods there, and efforts to control and protect against floods began when the French settled Louisiana. Levees were built at New Orleans and adjacent areas for protection against the great floods of the Mississippi River, and as settlement grew in the alluvial valley, the levees were strengthened and extended. These works were constructed and maintained by local public agencies, for the cost of flood protection in river areas was considered as a burden to be borne locally by those directly benefited. Because of the high cost of adequate flood protection, however, only the most valuable urban areas and farm lands actually enjoyed a reasonable degree of flood protection.[134]

Failure of local agencies to control floods on the Mississippi River led to the first federal action. In 1879 the federal government established the Mississippi River Commission for repairing and strengthening the levees, which had suffered greatly from neglect and from military operations during and after the Civil War. Later, the Commission — which still has jurisdiction over flood control and navigation work on the lower Mississippi — helped state and local levee districts to construct new levees. In 1917 the scope of federal activity in the Mississippi Valley was broadened to include federal construction of levees and related works according to rigid standards. In the same year, federal flood control operations were extended to the Sacramento River in California.

The disastrous flood on the lower Mississippi River in 1927 dramatically focused public attention on flood control as a national problem. A year later, Congress adopted for the first time a comprehensive program for flood control along the lower river, and a nationwide study was inaugurated of the control problems in other river valleys. Although state and local government agencies had been expending large sums for flood control, and had achieved notable results in some instances — as, for example, in the projects constructed by the Miami Valley (Ohio) Conservancy District after the great Ohio basin flood of 1913 — local works were largely ineffective because of the increasing magnitude and complexity of the flood problem. Therefore, soon after the federal government embarked early in the 1930s on its expanded program of land and water conservation and development, Congress broadened federal responsibility for flood control to cover the entire country. Great impetus was given to the carrying out of this expanded responsibility by the great flood on the Ohio River in 1937.

Past Outlays

Expenditures for flood control by the federal government alone in the years up to 1950 totaled about $2.4 billion, exclusive of expenditures for operation and maintenance of completed projects. Approximately 80 per cent of the outlay had been made since 1936, and about one quarter of it had been for works and structures in the lower Mississippi Valley. Expenditures by state and local agencies in cooperation with the federal program amounted to almost $200 million, and public agencies in the lower Mississippi Valley had spent about $300 million before 1928, when the present federal program was inaugurated in that area. In total, the public investment in flood control approached $3 billion. The completion of projects under construction in 1950 involved the additional outlay of more than $6 billion, about $5.8 billion of federal funds and $300 million of state and local funds.[135]

Despite these recent large expenditures, there is a growing public impression that floods seem to be increasing, and not decreasing, in frequency and destructiveness. To some extent, this impression is correct in that during the past few decades there has been an increased use by agriculture and industry of flood plain areas that lack

---

134. For information in this and the next two paragraphs, see *A Water Policy for the American People*, pp. 142–143 and *Report of the Chief of Engineers, U.S. Army, 1951*, Part I, Vol. III, pp. 331–334.

135. Data in this paragraph adapted from: *Report of the Chief of Engineers, U.S. Army, 1950*, Part I, Vol. I, p. 24; *A Water Policy for the American People*, p. 143; *Report of the Chief of Engineers, U.S. Army, 1951*, Part I, Vol. I, pp. 337, 339, 350.

adequate protection. But it is also true that small flash floods have been occurring more frequently on the headwater tributaries of many of our river systems, owing partly to the stripping of the original forest and other cover from the land. Because of the spectacular nature of the floods that still occur, the effectiveness of existing flood control works in preventing flood damages is, however, often overlooked. The alluvial valley of the lower Mississippi River, for example, has not suffered severe flooding since the undertaking of a comprehensive program of flood control along the lower river after the great flood of 1927. In fact, the U.S. Army Corps of Engineers estimates that all federal flood control works in operation in 1950 were preventing *average* annual flood damages of about $300 million.[136]

Future Estimates

A rough measure of the future capital outlays needed for flood control can be derived from estimates of the flood damages, both direct and indirect, that would occur if no additional control works were constructed. As of 1950 it was estimated that such damages would *average* about $500 million annually.[137] It would not be economically feasible, however, to construct all the works necessary to reduce these damages to zero. In order for new flood control works to be economically justified, the average annual charges for them (amortization of the original capital investment, interest on the investment, major repairs and replacements, etc.) must not exceed — and should, if possible, be considerably less than — the average annual flood damages that would be incurred if the works were not in existence. Assuming that annual charges for such works would vary between 3 and 4 per cent of the original capital outlay,[138] and that as a *maximum* control works that would prevent somewhere between 80 and 90 per cent, or roughly about $425 million, of the remaining $500 million of future

average annual flood damages could be economically justified, then an ultimate capital outlay of $10 to $14 billion for additional flood control might be contemplated.

In practice, of course, every effort is and should be made to ensure that individual flood control projects are so designed and located that their average annual costs will be very much less than the average annual flood damages they will prevent. To the extent that the planning of future projects is successful in this respect, the total capital outlays needed for flood control will be considerably less than what otherwise might be expected. On the other hand, some of the most difficult and expensive control work still remains to be undertaken, involving complex multiple-purpose projects that combine with flood control other features such as hydroelectric power, irrigation, drainage and navigation. It appears reasonable, therefore, to estimate that perhaps as much as $15 billion would be needed over the next fifty to seventy-five years to provide the nation with economically justified flood protection works.[139] (See Table 230.) The annual outlays for such a program, nearly two thirds of which would be undertaken in the valleys of the Mississippi River system, would average around $250 million.

To be completely effective, however, a national program of this kind, which covers the works, structures and improvements on and along rivers necessary to control and prevent floods, must be coupled with a program of watershed management covering soil and forest conservation and rehabilitation practices of the kind described earlier in this chapter. If by such practices the upper basins of many of our rivers could be made into vast sponges that would absorb brief deluges or continued rains, not only would soil erosion be prevented but downstream floods would be considerably alleviated. Even now, part of the storage capacity of flood control dams and reservoirs is provided to accommodate flood flows that formerly were retarded by the forests and other land cover. Without watershed management, future flood control programs will be more expensive than is now estimated.

Pending the completion of a national flood control program of the magnitude described

---

136. *Report of the Chief of Engineers, U.S. Army, 1951,* Part I, Vol. III, p. 335.

137. *Ibid.,* Table 1, p. 362.

138. This would cover amortization of the original capital outlay based on an average physical life of fifty to a hundred years for the works, structures and improvements involved, interest rates of 2 to 3 per cent a year on the original investment, and annual charges of 0.5 to 1.0 per cent for major repairs and replacements. *Economic Evaluation of Federal Water Resource Projects,* Report to the Committee on Public Works, House of Representatives, from the Subcommittee to Study Civil Works, 82d Cong., 2d sess., House Committee Print No. 24, Table 1, p. 9.

139. Cf. "Summary of Plans for Conservation and Development of the Water Resources of the United States," Table 3, p. 9949; and *A Water Policy for the American People,* Table 4, p. 93.

above, further consideration might be given to the possibility of establishing a national flood insurance system.[140] This possibility has recently aroused considerable interest because of the destructive Missouri River floods in 1951 and 1952, which paralyzed agriculture, industry and trade for weeks. Such an insurance system, however, would be more than an interim measure. As flood control works become more expensive to build, the adoption of the system might appear more attractive as an alternative. At some not too distant date, therefore, it may be deemed far less expensive from a national point of view to invest in a national system of flood insurance, and concurrently to place some limits on the use of flood plain areas through zoning restrictions, than to construct further flood control works.

Irrigation

Depending on our future needs for additional agricultural land, the use and control of our water resources for irrigation may be an important feature of future river valley development programs. Earlier in this chapter, some consideration was given to the possibilities of using irrigation — as well as clearing and drainage — to develop new crop and pasture lands.[141] Further consideration is given here, however, to these irrigation possibilities in light of the broader question of the availability of water in the western states for such purposes and of the longer-range aspects of the problem in a national river valley development program.

About 740 million acres of land in 17 western states — almost 40 per cent of the area of the continental United States — receive too little rainfall to ensure general agriculture. If they are to be so used, water must be supplied to them by irrigation. But not enough water is available in the right places to irrigate all these lands. Previously, it had been estimated that water could be conserved economically to irrigate a *maximum* of perhaps 50 million acres, or about 7 per cent of the area.[142] As additional engineering investiga-

tions have been completed, however, and with nearly 25 million acres of land now under irrigation in these states, it appears that more than one half of the acreage in these states for which water can be conserved economically is now under irrigation. In fact, it was estimated in 1950 that there is sufficient water available to irrigate only about 16.7 million additional acres with an adequate supply and to provide 8.7 million acres of presently irrigated lands with needed additional water.[143]

Conservation of our water resources for irrigation purposes, which has been growing steadily since the middle of the last century, is now one of the most important uses of our rivers west of the hundredth meridian — a line running north and south through the Dakotas, Nebraska, Kansas, Oklahoma and Texas. If it had not been for irrigation, the West as we know it today would not exist. The conservation of water alone makes possible not only agriculture but also life itself in this vast semiarid region of our nation. This has been a primary reason for the growing investment of public funds in irrigation enterprises during the past fifty years.[144]

Past Outlays

From 1900 to 1950, the total private and public investment in irrigation enterprises in the 17 western states rose from $68 million to more than $1.8 billion. The public share of this investment has increased steadily since the federal government began, in 1902, to assist in irrigation development. By 1950, 36 per cent of the capital invested was from funds provided through the U.S. Bureau of Reclamation. (See Table 231.) Furthermore, as irrigation projects have grown in size and complexity, the average investment per acre of irrigated land in both public and private enterprises has increased. Between 1900 and 1950 the average increased more than eightfold, from a little more than $9 an acre to nearly $74 an acre.[145]

---

140. For the general outlines of such a system see *National Flood Insurance,* Message from the President of the United States, H. Doc. 458, 82d Cong., 2d sess., May 5, 1952.

141. See "Developmental Possibilities — Irrigation" under "Conservation and Development of Crop and Grazing Lands."

142. "Land Available for Agriculture through Reclamation," p. 5; *National Irrigation Policy — Its Development and Significance,* S. Doc. 36, 76th Cong., 1st sess., pp. 34–35; *Public Works and Rural Land Use,* pp. 18–19.

143. *A Water Policy for the American People,* p. 160. These estimates, made by the U.S. Bureau of Reclamation, are based on recognized requirements for engineering feasibility and do not take into consideration the economic feasibility or justification of individual projects. Neither do they take into account the development that might be accomplished under unrestricted transbasin diversions of water, which are now being studied.

144. *A Water Policy for the American People,* p. 152.

145. These estimates are derived from the data in Tables 226 and 231.

TABLE 231. CAPITAL INVESTED IN IRRIGATION ENTERPRISES
IN THE 17 WESTERN STATES, 1900–1950
(*Millions*)

Year	Total	U.S. Bureau of Reclamation	Private and Other Public Enterprises
1900	$ 68	—	$ 68
1910	314	a	a
1920	676	$130	546
1930	870	194	576
1940	1,035	250	785
1950	1,833	661	1,172

Sources: Data for 1900 and 1910 from Sixteenth Census of the United States (1940), *Irrigation of Agricultural Lands;* data for 1920 to 1950 from *1950 Census of Agriculture,* Vol. III, *Irrigation of Agricultural Lands,* Table 66, p. 95.

a. Data not available.

When the future possibilities of conserving our water resources for irrigation are considered, however, it is clear that the projects involved will generally be even more complex and expensive than they have been in the past. For example, in 1950, the advance construction program of the Bureau of Reclamation, covering projects authorized as of that date, contemplated the development by irrigation of about 7.3 million acres of additional land and the provision of supplemental water supplies to nearly 4.4 million acres already irrigated. The Bureau estimated that to carry this program to completion would require a total outlay of more than $4.3 billion.[146]

Future Estimates

The ultimate cost of developing by irrigation the remaining acreage in the western states for which sufficient water is available would probably be more than double the amount of the presently authorized programs. In other words, the total cost (at 1950 prices) of constructing and bringing into operation the multiple-purpose projects that would use the presently estimated available water resources in our 17 western states for irrigating 16.7 million additional acres, for providing supplemental water supplies to 8.7

million acres of presently irrigated lands, and for extending related benefits in the form of hydroelectric power, flood control, etc., would probably approach $10 billion.[147] Such a program should probably extend over a period of fifty to seventy-five years, with annual outlays averaging around $160 million.[148] (See Table 230.)

It is highly debatable, as has already been pointed out (cf. p. 521), whether our future needs for additional agricultural land alone would justify a long-range irrigation program of this magnitude. But immense benefits for the West are claimed by the proponents of such a program: The stability of existing farm and business communities would be ensured and opportunities for their expansion would be opened. Cheaper and more abundant supplies of many agricultural commodities would be available to the eastern and midwestern states, which, in turn, could find larger markets for their manufactured products in the western states. The West would have many new industrial expansion pos-

146. *Annual Report of the Secretary of the Interior for . . . 1950,* pp. 63–68, Table 12. This estimated outlay would cover, however, not only the costs of irrigating new land and of providing supplemental water supplies to presently irrigated lands, but would also include the costs of the accompanying hydroelectric, flood control and other features involved in the multiple-purpose projects of which the program is largely comprised.

147. Cf. the cost estimates, in terms of 1950 prices, and after allowing for work completed before 1950, in "Summary of Plans for Conservation and Development of the Water Resources of the United States," Table 3, p. 9949; and "Status of Irrigation and Reclamation Development under the Bureau of Reclamation — 17 Western States, June 30, 1948," Report of the Senate National Resources Economic Committee, *Congressional Record,* Vol. 94, Part 8, 80th Cong., 2d sess., 1948, pp. 9950–9953. See also *A Water Policy for the American People,* Table 4, p. 93.

148. The annual outlays during the first twenty-five years of the period would, of course, be identical with estimates made earlier in this chapter in connection with "Developmental Possibilities — Irrigation" under "Conservation and Development of Crop and Grazing Lands."

TABLE 232. INSTALLED CAPACITY FOR AND ANNUAL PRODUCTION
OF ELECTRIC ENERGY, 1902–1950

Year	Installed Capacity			Annual Production		
	Total	Hydro	Steam and Other	Total	Hydro	Steam and Other
	(Millions of Kilowatts)			(Billions of Kilowatt-Hours)		
1902	2.9	1.1	1.8	5.9	a	a
1912	11.0	2.8	8.2	24.8	7.4	17.4
1922	20.4	5.2	15.2	61.2	21.3	39.9
1932	42.8	10.2	32.6	99.4	36.0	63.4
1940	50.9	12.3	38.6	179.9	51.7	128.2
1950	82.9	18.7	64.2	388.7	100.9	287.8

Sources: Data for 1902 to 1940 from *Historical Statistics of the United States, 1789–1945*, U.S. Bureau of the Census, 1949, Series G 171–4, p. 156, and Series G 205–8, p. 158; data for 1950 from *Statistical Abstract of the United States, 1952*, U.S. Bureau of the Census, Table 573, p. 479.

a. Data not available.

sibilities for developing its light-metal ores in conjunction with the electric power provided by multiple-purpose irrigation projects. In short, it is claimed that carrying to completion the ultimate development for irrigation, power and other related purposes of the water resources of the western states could materially assist in making the whole region, with its rapidly growing population, an even greater land of opportunity than it has been in the past.

Hydroelectric Power

The use of falling water as a source of power began early in the industrial history of our country. From Colonial times until late in the nineteenth century, however, the power could be used only at the site of the waterfall, and industries that used such power grew up around the water wheels of New England, New York, Pennsylvania and along the fall line southward. Beginning in the 1880s with the commercial use of electricity as a source of power, the energy of falling water became available anywhere within reach of electric transmission from the power site. Thereafter, national interest in the development of water power, which had lagged after the introduction of coal as a source of power, revived rapidly.

Over the past five decades, the installed generating capacity of hydroelectric plants has increased seventeen times, the largest increase occurring in the 1940–1950 decade. Similarly,

the annual production of hydroelectric plants has shown a striking increase over the years, particularly in the decade prior to 1950, when it almost doubled. The rapid growth in the use of hydroelectric power, however, was only one feature of the phenomenal increase in the use of electric energy during the past fifty years. From 1912 to 1950, the combined annual production of electric energy from both hydro and steam and other plants doubled in nearly every decade, and the trend in the total installed generating capacity was almost identical, although the rate of increase was slower during the last twenty years as the interconnection of utilities systems made possible a greater utilization of the capacity of existing plants. (See Table 232.) By 1950, 92 per cent of the urban homes and 83 per cent of the rural homes in the United States were using electricity, and electric motors were providing about 90 per cent of the mechanical power in industrial plants.[149]

Federal Activities

Of particular importance in the increasing development and use of hydroelectric power during recent years has been the role of the federal government. Because dams and related structures that make hydroelectric power available affect other uses of a river, the federal government as early as 1890 forbade their construction on navigable waters without its consent. By a series of

149. *Resources for Freedom*, Vol. III, p. 31.

TABLE 233. INSTALLED CAPACITY FOR AND ANNUAL PRODUCTION OF ELECTRIC ENERGY IN FACILITIES OWNED BY THE FEDERAL GOVERNMENT, 1927–1950

Year	Installed Capacity			Annual Production		
	Total in All Private and Public Plants	In Federal Plants	Per Cent of Total in Federal Plants	Total in All Private and Public Plants	In Federal Plants	Per Cent of Total in Federal Plants
	(Millions of Kilowatts)			(Billions of Kilowatt-Hours)		
1927	34.6	0.21	0.6	101.4	0.67	0.7
1932	42.8	0.23	0.5	99.4	0.44	0.4
1936	43.6	0.80	1.8	136.0	1.07	0.8
1940	50.9	1.94	3.8	179.9	8.58	4.8
1945	62.9	5.08	8.1	271.2	28.00	10.3
1950	82.9	6.92	8.4	388.7	40.39	10.4

Sources: Data for 1927 to 1945 from *Historical Statistics of the United States, 1789–1945,* U.S. Bureau of the Census, 1949, Series G 183 and 188, p. 156, Series G 217 and 222, p. 158; data for 1950 from *Statistical Abstract of the United States, 1952,* U.S. Bureau of the Census, Table 573, p. 479.

steps, it broadened its interest in water power development until in the Federal Water Power Act of 1920 it established a licensing procedure for encouraging private enterprise to undertake such projects but at the same time left the way open for possible ultimate public ownership of the projects. The act also required that water power development be undertaken as a part of comprehensive multiple-purpose plans for the improvement or development of the nation's river systems.[150]

Meanwhile, the federal government had started building hydroelectric plants in connection with irrigation projects of the Bureau of Reclamation. The enactment of the Boulder Canyon Project Act in 1928 for the construction of Hoover Dam (formerly Boulder Dam) launched the federal government on its present large-scale, multiple-purpose river development program, with the generation and distribution of large amounts of hydroelectric power as one of the major purposes. When, in the 1930s, the federal government expanded its land and water conservation and development activities, it also greatly increased its construction of hydroelectric power facilities.

From 1927 to 1950, federally owned generating capacity, of which more than 90 per cent is now in hydroelectric plants, increased more than thirty times, and the federal share of annual kilowatt-hours generated increased about sixty times. In 1950 more than 8 per cent of the installed capacity of all private and publicly owned generators was in federal plants, which generated more than 10 per cent of the electric energy produced. (See Table 233.)

Undeveloped Resources

Water power is unique as a source of energy in that it is wasted if not used, and we may continue to enjoy the use of it so long as the processes of nature continue to function as they do at present. Coal, oil and gas, on the other hand, must be considered as irreplaceable national assets, and the drain on our reserves of them can be lessened to the extent that we develop our water power resources. Therefore, it appears that in order to meet the growing needs and demands for energy in the future, the undeveloped hydroelectric power resources of the nation should be utilized as fully and as rapidly as possible.[151]

Government studies indicate that in 1950 less than 20 per cent of the potential hydroelectric power in the United States had been developed. Undeveloped hydroelectric power was estimated to be about 88 million kilowatts, nearly five times the installed capacity of existing developments. (See Figure 67.) The undeveloped sites were estimated to be capable of generating an annual average of about 390 billion kilowatt-hours, almost four times the annual output of existing developments. Fifty-five per cent of our undevel-

150. For information in this and the next paragraph see *A Water Policy for the American People,* pp. 220–228.

151. *Resources for Freedom,* Vol. I, pp. 117–122.

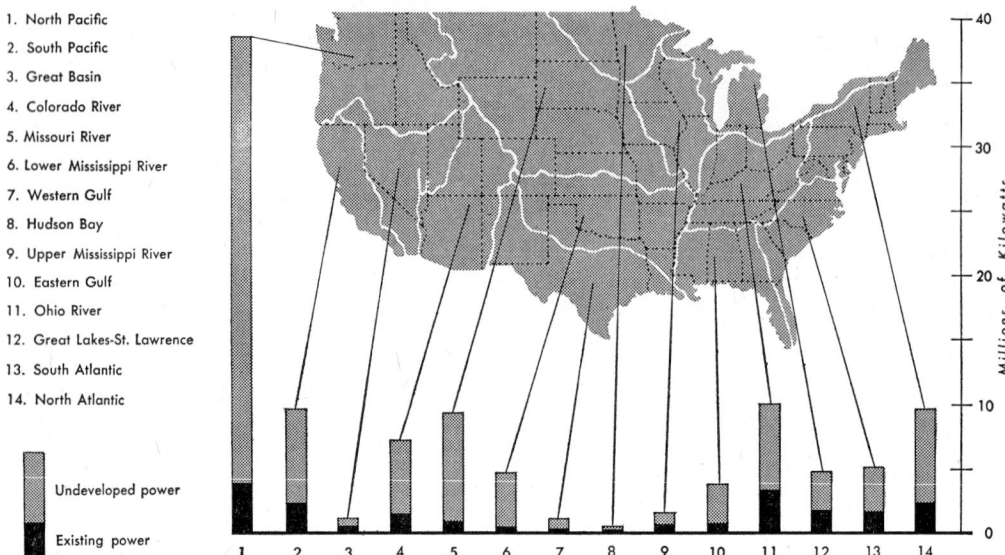

1. North Pacific
2. South Pacific
3. Great Basin
4. Colorado River
5. Missouri River
6. Lower Mississippi River
7. Western Gulf
8. Hudson Bay
9. Upper Mississippi River
10. Eastern Gulf
11. Ohio River
12. Great Lakes-St. Lawrence
13. South Atlantic
14. North Atlantic

Undeveloped power

Existing power

FIGURE 67. EXISTING AND UNDEVELOPED HYDROELECTRIC POWER, BY MAJOR DRAINAGE BASINS, DECEMBER 31, 1950

Source: Federal Power Commission.

oped water power is west of the Continental Divide, with about 31 million kilowatts — or 35 per cent — in the Columbia River basin alone. The Missouri River basin contains nearly 10 per cent of the undeveloped water power, while the largest concentration of undeveloped power east of the Mississippi River lies in our northeastern states, with Maine, New York and Pennsylvania in the lead.[152]

Future Estimates

Estimates of the future increases in the demand for electric energy are so large, however, that our resources of undeveloped water power alone could not be expected to meet them. For example, if our total national output of goods and services should double during the next twenty-five years, as it did during the past twenty-five years, it is estimated that the annual demand for electric energy would increase from the 389 billion kilowatt-hours generated in 1950 to about 1,400 billion kilowatt-hours in 1975.[153] Even if *all* of the undeveloped hydroelectric power resources in the United States in 1950 were to be developed by 1975, they would meet

only about 38 per cent of the estimated increase in the demand for electric energy. Clearly, then, we must continue to rely heavily on our fuel resources in the production of electric energy.

Hydroelectric power can reasonably be expected to meet about 400 billion kilowatt-hours of the estimated demand for electric energy in 1975. This would require a hydroelectric generating capacity of about 60 million kilowatts, an increase of roughly 41 million kilowatts over the installed hydro capacity in 1950.[154] Of the 88 million kilowatts of undeveloped hydroelectric power, it is estimated that more than 18 million kilowatts, or about 20 per cent, are in projects under construction, or authorized for construction, by the federal government.[155] If all these projects were to be completed by 1975, about 23 million more kilowatts would have to be developed by private enterprise and public agencies in order to provide the 60 million kilowatts of hydroelectric generating capacity that it is estimated will then be needed.

Given a growing national demand for electric energy, it appears that we might expect to approach the complete development of our hydro-

152. For data in this paragraph see *Thirty-first Annual Report of the Federal Power Commission, 1951*, 1952, pp. 72–75.
153. *Resources for Freedom*, Vol. III, Table III, p. 32.

154. *Ibid.*, Table VI, p. 36.
155. *Report of the Chief of Engineers, U.S. Army, 1951*, Part I, Vol. III, p. 70 as revised by *Annual Report of the Secretary of the Interior, Fiscal Year Ended June 30, 1951*, Table 8, pp. 57–59.

electric power resources during the next fifty to seventy-five years. Complete development of these resources may not be achieved, however, because it may not be economically feasible to utilize all of the available sites. Furthermore, as we approach complete development, the average construction cost per kilowatt of installed generating capacity will rise steadily because most of the cheaper sites will be developed first. For these reasons, it is difficult to estimate the total capital outlays that would be needed to provide for the ultimate development of our hydroelectric power resources.

As a rough estimate, however, it appears that we could probably regard somewhere between 65 and 75 per cent of our undeveloped hydroelectric power resources as economically feasible of development over the next fifty to seventy-five years. Part of the capital outlays needed to develop these resources have already been included in the estimated outlays for waterways, flood control and irrigation development, which also cover the costs of developing hydroelectric power on the many multiple-purpose river development projects that are involved. In addition, it is likely that about $30 billion would be required for hydroelectric development.[156] This would mean an average annual outlay of about $480 million by private enterprise and public agencies over a fifty- to seventy-five-year period. (See Table 230.)

Domestic and Industrial Water Supply

In the early days when the population of our nation was mostly rural and there was little industry, the amount of water used for domestic and industrial purposes was relatively small. As our nation grew, however, its original agrarian economy was transformed by the development of industry and our population became more concentrated in cities, with the result that domestic and industrial uses of water rapidly increased. Beginning with the first waterworks system in Boston in 1652, a century and a quarter before our nation came into being, the number of waterworks grew to 17 by 1800; to 4,000 by 1900; and by 1950 it was well over 15,000. Although at first waterworks systems generally were privately owned, the reverse is now true; 80 per cent are now publicly owned and 20 per cent privately owned.[157]

Today, adequate domestic and industrial water supplies are absolutely indispensable to the continued health and prosperity of our people. Over 60 per cent of our population lives in urban areas and depends on public water supply systems, many of which are vast, complex undertakings. Most of the manufacturing industries, which produce one third of our national income, could not operate without water supplies. A water shortage in a modern American metropolis can produce a crisis in our urban way of life, as the recent experiences in New York City have clearly showed.

Use of Water

Together, domestic and industrial uses of fresh water in 1950 averaged more than 80 billion gallons a day. Almost 70 billion gallons — or roughly 85 per cent of this total — were withdrawn from our rivers, streams and lakes, and the remainder came from wells. Most of this water was not actually consumed, but was returned to the streams and aquifers, later to be withdrawn and used over again. On the average, cities and industries probably return as waste between 90 and 95 per cent of the water they withdraw.[158]

Our modern large industries are heavy users of water. In 1950 they used an average of 80 billion gallons a day, of which about 15 billion gallons were taken from brackish or salty sources, which are unlimited, and about 65 billion gallons were from fresh water sources. Of the withdrawals from fresh water sources, nearly 60 billion gallons — or more than 90 per cent — were from rivers, streams and lakes, and the remainder was taken from wells. In addition, a part of the water distributed daily through municipal systems was purchased by many small industries located in or near urban areas.

Nearly 45 per cent of the water used by industry is used for cooling and condensing in the steam generation of electric energy. The steel industry takes the next largest share, more than 15 per cent of the total. A single large steel mill may require as much as 500 million gallons of water a day, enough to supply all normal daily requirements of a city of several million people.

156. Cf. "Summary of Plans for Conservation and Development of the Water Resources of the United States," Table 3, p. 9949; and *A Water Policy for the American People*, Table 4, p. 93.

157. *A Water Policy for the American People*, p. 176.
158. For data in this and the next three paragraphs, see *Resources for Freedom*, Vol. V, pp. 84–86.

Municipal systems in 1950 used about 13.5 billion gallons of water daily, taking 10 billion gallons — or about 75 per cent — from rivers, streams and lakes, and the remainder from wells. A large part of this water was used by small industries and commercial establishments and for fighting fires and flushing streets and sewers. Of the part that reached individual homes, a large proportion was probably used for washing and sanitation purposes and only a small amount for drinking. New appliances and equipment such as air-conditioning units and automatic washing machines are increasing the use of water in the home.

Many urban areas must import water from rural sources, and the problems involved tend to become greater and more complex. The initial capital outlays are large, now averaging from $100 to $125 for each person to be served, and the average daily requirement to be met is estimated at about 150 gallons per capita, although it may be as high as 300 to 500 gallons in some heavily industrialized cities.[159] Conflicts also frequently develop with other potential users of water in industry or agriculture, sometimes leading to long legal battles.

Future Estimates

Government studies indicate that the average daily need for water for domestic and industrial purposes over the next two or three decades might increase as much as 150 per cent, with industrial uses accounting for 95 per cent of the increase.[160] The capital outlays that many private industries will have to make for developing their individual water supplies are included in the estimates of total outlays for future industrial plant and equipment in this volume.[161] The need for some of these private outlays would be considerably reduced, however, if further regulation of stream flow could be achieved, through multiple-purpose river development programs of the kind outlined in this chapter.

Because of future urban population growth and the rise in domestic use of water, government experts estimate that the average daily municipal water requirements might rise to 20 billion gallons in 1975, as against 13.5 billion

gallons in 1950.[162] The capacity of many existing municipal systems would, of course, need to be expanded in order to meet such increased requirements, and many of them also would need to be modernized, improved and extended. In all, therefore, capital outlays ranging between $5 and $7.5 billion might be needed during the next twenty to thirty years for the expansion and improvement of municipal water supplies — an average annual outlay of about $250 million. (See Table 230.) The need thereafter will depend largely on how much and how rapidly our urban population increases.

Despite the large and rising cost of providing municipal water supplies, water is one of the least expensive of the essential commodities we buy. At present, water for domestic use costs an annual average of only $6 a person, less than 2 cents a day. In general, such water is procured, filtered, pumped and distributed at a cost *of less than 5 cents a ton*.[163] To the extent that we fail, however, to reduce the pollution of our rivers, streams and lakes, the costs of both our municipal and our industrial water supplies will increase, because it will be necessary either to spend more in purifying and protecting existing supplies or to seek new, and probably more costly, pollution-free sources.

Pollution Abatement

For many decades, the American people believed that water — like matter in general — was indestructible regardless of what was done with it. But we are beginning to learn that when pollution of our rivers, streams and lakes renders the water in them unfit for use, that water has been destroyed for all practical purposes. We must await the slow operation of the hydrologic cycle — the evaporation of water, perhaps not until after it has run to the sea, and its precipitation again in the form of rain or snow — before we can use it again.[164]

A century ago, when our population was still predominantly rural and our economy agrarian, water pollution was not a problem. Now, however, we depend on rivers and other surface waters — which are most subject to pollution — for more than 80 per cent of the fresh water we need daily for households, industry and agricul-

159. *A Water Policy for the American People,* Vol. I, pp. 176–177.
160. *Resources for Freedom,* Vol. V, Table X, p. 94.
161. See Chapter 15.
162. *Resources for Freedom,* Vol. V, Table X, p. 94.
163. *A Water Policy for the American People,* p. 176.
164. *Water Pollution in the United States,* Publication No. 64, U.S. Public Health Service, 1951, pp. 8–9.

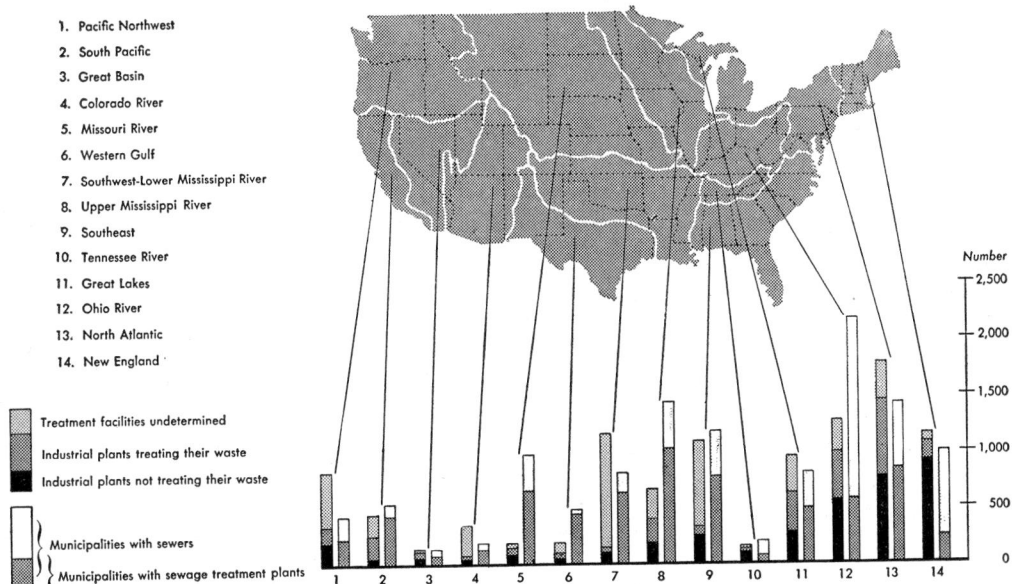

1. Pacific Northwest
2. South Pacific
3. Great Basin
4. Colorado River
5. Missouri River
6. Western Gulf
7. Southwest-Lower Mississippi River
8. Upper Mississippi River
9. Southeast
10. Tennessee River
11. Great Lakes
12. Ohio River
13. North Atlantic
14. New England

Treatment facilities undetermined
Industrial plants treating their waste
Industrial plants not treating their waste

Municipalities with sewers
Municipalities with sewage treatment plants

FIGURE 68. NUMBER OF CITIES AND INDUSTRIES THAT POLLUTE WATER, 1950

Source: *Water Pollution in the United States,* Publication No. 64, U.S. Public Health Service, 1951, pp. 16–19.

ture.[165] At the same time, our cities and industries and, to a lesser extent, our farms discharge obnoxious and harmful substances into our rivers and other surface waters — domestic wastes and sewage; industrial acids, oils, grease and chemicals; and the drainage of barn lots and farm lands. These may cause disease, produce offensive tastes, colors and odors, corrode structures, destroy aquatic life, or interfere with water sports. Water laden with such wastes may not only become unfit for use but even unfit to live near or look at. Many of our rivers have become merely waste carriers or — as they are sometimes bitterly called — "open sewers." [166]

Past Progress

The first steps to combat pollution were taken when filter plants had to be built in order to purify water and make it fit to drink. The first such plant was built in Poughkeepsie, New York, in 1875. By 1900 other cities had installed waterworks capable of supplying purified water to 2 million people, but this was only about 3 per cent of the population. As cities grew, the danger of typhoid fever made it necessary to in-

crease rapidly the number of waterworks systems providing for purification. Today, more than 15,000 waterworks supplying nearly 100 million people — about two thirds of our population — are playing a major part in virtually eliminating typhoid in the United States.

It was early recognized, however, that pollution abatement efforts had to go beyond purifying water at the intakes of municipal supply systems. Beginning in the 1880s, sewer systems were built to dispose of wastes in our urban areas in order to avoid disease and the danger of epidemics. Although sewer systems were not built as rapidly as waterworks systems, today there are about 11,800 public sewerage systems serving nearly 92 million people.[167] But the construction of sewer systems has outrun the provision of sewage treatment plants at the points where the wastes are discharged into our rivers, streams and lakes. Such plants extract the solid matter or sludge from the sewage and discharge the running waste water relatively free of impurities. Today, only 6,700 of our municipal sewer systems have these treatment plants, and the capacity of more than 2,500 of these plants is inadequate. (See Figure 68.)

165. *Resources for Freedom,* Vol. V, Table 2, p. 84.
166. For information in this and the next two paragraphs see *A Water Policy for the American People,* pp. 188–189.

167. For the current data in this paragraph regarding municipal sewer systems and sewage treatment plants, see *Water Pollution in the United States,* pp. 15–17 and 20–21.

The general attitude of the American public toward pollution caused by industrial wastes was similar in the beginning to its attitude toward municipal wastes.[168] With increasing industrial development, however, more factory owners and managers became alert to the need in the public interest for treating industrial wastes before discharging them into our rivers. In some cases, it was found possible to recover portions of the waste materials and convert them into valuable products. However, some industrial wastes, especially those of the chemical industry, have defied treatment, and even yet we do not know how to eliminate mine drainage acid, a long-time cause of stream pollution. Furthermore, our modern technology constantly develops new industrial processes and materials that produce wastes having as yet unknown effects on water, thus making uncertain the future requirements for their treatment.

Private enterprise nevertheless has made much progress during recent years in dealing with the pollution problem. About 2,600 industrial plants that have direct outlets to our rivers and other surface waters now treat their wastes before discharging them.[169] Much, however, needs to be done. About 3,600 plants are providing no treatment for their industrial wastes, and of the 2,600 plants providing treatment, less than one half have treatment facilities with adequate capacity. Furthermore, the treatment facilities, if any, provided by an estimated additional 4,100 industrial plants remain to be determined by future surveys.

Future Estimates

Despite the treatment facilities now being provided by public agencies and private enterprise, the U.S. Public Health Service estimates that the total pollution load now being carried by our rivers and other surface waters exceeds the raw untreated sewage from 150 million people, which by sheer coincidence happens to be almost our present population. If we did not have the present 9,300 treatment plants (6,700 municipal and 2,600 industrial), the pollution that would be pouring into our rivers, streams, lakes and bays would probably be twice what it is now.[170]

In order to attack the pollution problem on a broad scale, the U.S. Public Health Service has suggested national goals for public agencies and private enterprise.[171] It estimates that nearly 6,600 new municipal plants, replacements, additions or enlargements — involving a total capital outlay of nearly $2.5 billion — are now needed, and during the next decade the obsolescence of other plants, the needs of new communities, and population growth would require an additional $2 billion of capital outlays. To this foreseeable total cost of $4.5 billion for municipal pollution abatement must be added the capital outlays for industrial pollution abatement, which are estimated at somewhere between $4.5 and $7.5 billion.[172]

Over the next two or three decades, then, the total capital outlays needed would probably not be less than $10 billion. Over a twenty-five-year period this would imply an average annual outlay of about $400 million. (See Table 230.) But, as the President's Water Resources Policy Commission has pointed out, "Grave as it is now, the pollution problem is bound to deepen as population and industry grow." [173] What the future requirements for pollution abatement will be twenty-five years from now, even if in the interim we should make the capital outlays estimated above, is pretty much anyone's guess.

Fish and Wildlife Conservation and Recreation

Plans for the control and development of our rivers must take into account their valuable fish resources. The rivers and other fresh-water bodies in the continental United States yield annually a commercial catch of nearly 250 million pounds (including sea-run fishes).[174] The large fish-producing areas — the Great Lakes, the Mississippi River system and the rivers of the Pacific Northwest — and the numerous smaller lakes, ponds and streams are also fished for sport by millions — as indicated by the nearly 16 million fishing licenses held in 1948–1949.[175]

---

168. For information in this and the next paragraph, see *A Water Policy for the American People*, p. 189.
169. For the current data in this paragraph regarding facilities for disposing of industrial wastes, see *Water Pollution in the United States*, pp. 15 and 18–20.
170. *Ibid.*, p. 10.

171. *Ibid.*, pp. 28–29 and 37.
172. The bulk of such estimated outlays would not be included, however, within the estimates of total outlays for future industrial plant and equipment in Chapter 15.
173. *A Water Policy for the American People*, p. 194.
174. *Fishery Resources of the United States*, S. Doc. 51, 79th Cong., 1st sess., 1945, pp. 1–4.
175. *A Water Policy for the American People*, p. 259.

Effects of River Projects

Works and structures that radically change the natural flow and use of our rivers are bound to affect our fishery resources, and often very adversely. This is especially true in the Pacific Northwest, where indiscriminate damming of the rivers and streams could imperil the Pacific salmon, the nation's most valuable fishery resource. Exploitation of these salmon resources proceeded rapidly once the settlement of our nation reached the Pacific Coast, and by 1913 all the important Pacific salmon-producing areas were being intensively fished. Since then, the annual catch has not greatly increased.[176] But the construction of new dams and diversions could curtail the salmon catch materially, and perhaps even ruin it in some areas. Unless effective fish ladders or fish locks can be designed at dams, and their penstocks and spillways effectively screened, the salmon runs eventually could be destroyed, with disastrous consequences for both the regional and the national economy. In the Columbia River basin alone, for example, the salmon industry processes enough fish annually to provide every American household with a quarter-pound can.[177]

In planning the control and development of our rivers we must also remember that many of the important fur-bearing animals — the beaver, muskrat, mink, otter and raccoon — and many of the migratory wild fowl — principally ducks and geese — thrive only in or near rivers, streams, lakes, marshes and sloughs. Of particular concern in recent years has been the fate of the migratory waterfowl, which are hunted by more sportsmen than any other game bird. As a result of overhunting and steady destruction of their feeding and nesting grounds, the waterfowl — once one of the richest wildlife resources in the United States — were threatened with extinction in the early decades of the present century. By 1934 the continental population of these game birds had dropped to an estimated low of 27 million. A national program during the next ten years, under which hunting of waterfowl was curtailed and their habitat improved, brought about a gradual increase in their number to a high of about 125 million in 1944. Since the war, however, the total number has again declined, owing in part to increased hunting pressure.[178]

Flood control and drainage projects often destroy the habitat of waterfowl, and of many other species of wildlife dependent on our water resources, because low wet lands are the most productive of their food and cover. This has been the case especially in the upper and lower Mississippi Valley, where such projects have frequently been undertaken. In all, it has been estimated that about 120 million acres of the marsh and swamp lands that have been drained in the United States have represented a loss of waterfowl habitat and that less than 30 million acres of water habitat remain for waterfowl.[179] Consequently, it has been necessary to create refuge areas in order to prevent a severe decline of the species, or perhaps even their disappearance altogether in many regions.

Finally, development and control of our rivers in the future must take into account the extensive recreational use we make of our water resources. An estimated 120 million persons annually visit beaches in the United States. Near densely populated areas, therefore, or in regions where natural lakes are lacking, recreation may be a primary consideration in planning future water resource developments.[180] Conflicts frequently develop, however, between recreational and other uses of these resources. Reservoirs created by dams may often inundate natural park or scenic areas, and diversions or impoundments frequently deprive downstream areas of water for recreational use.

Many kinds of river control and developmental works greatly benefit fish and wildlife conservation and recreation. Structures and improvements on our rivers that regulate their flow in order to ensure a constant volume of water for navigation, irrigation or domestic and industrial use also ensure the water levels needed for fish and wildlife propagation and for recreation. Reservoirs built for flood control and power provide opportunities for swimming, boating and fishing.

Pollution control is probably one of the most important steps we could take to protect our fresh-water fishery resources, our waterfowl and other wildlife with a water habitat, and the

---

176. *Fishery Resources of the United States*, p. 3.
177. *A Water Policy for the American People*, pp. 259, 261–262.

178. *Conservation of Wildlife*, pp. 25–42, 67–75, 101–111.
179. *Public Works and Rural Land Use*, p. 159.
180. *A Water Policy for the American People*, p. 252.

use of our water resources for recreation. Nor would the benefits of this protection be confined to our inland waters. They would extend to those coastal bays, inlets and shores where the polluted discharges of our rivers create health hazards and destroy valuable shellfish.

Effects of Soil and Moisture Conservation Measures

Soil and moisture conservation measures on our crop and grazing lands, along the lines described earlier in this chapter, can also be adjusted to provide food and cover for wildlife, as has been previously noted.[181] Another boon to fish and wildlife conservation is the construction of small ponds on farms to aid in erosion control or to conserve water for livestock, irrigation and other farm use. More than 800,000 such ponds have been constructed under the soil and water conservation programs sponsored by the federal government since the 1930s.[182] When these ponds are stocked with fish, and the water is fertilized to provide food for them, the value of the edible fish that can be produced annually by each acre of inundated farmland frequently may be greater than the value of the beef that could be produced annually from an acre of good pasture.[183] Well-managed farm ponds also can provide swimming and boating for the landowner and his friends.

Special Projects Needed

In addition to these and other works and improvements already described, special kinds of projects should be undertaken in a future river control and development program in order specifically to aid in fish and wildlife conservation and recreational development.[184] These special undertakings would include improvements of the banks and bottoms of many of our rivers and streams in order to provide food and cover for land and water fur animals and aid in fish propagation. Many small marshes and swamp areas should be restored, and food patches planted and maintained. More than 4 million acres of carefully located land and water areas need to be set aside and developed for waterfowl

181. See p. 540.
182. *A Water Policy for the American People*, p. 253.
183. *Conservation of Wildlife*, pp. 219–220.
184. See: *A Water Policy for the American People*, pp. 252–253, 265; *Public Works and Rural Land Use*, pp. 159, 161; and *A Study of the Park and Recreational Problem of the United States*, pp. 125–126.

use in the southern wintering grounds, the northern nesting grounds and along the flyways. River frontage should be developed for parks, picnic areas, trails and parkways. Perhaps as much as 20 per cent of the national coast line and the shores of our major lakes and rivers should be acquired and developed for public use. Camping areas and stop-over and servicing facilities for small pleasure craft should be provided along inland and intracoastal waterways.

Taken all together, and excluding land acquisition costs, these special works and improvements for fish and wildlife conservation and for recreational development related to our water resources might involve capital outlays of between $1 and $1.5 billion during the next fifty to seventy-five years, or an average annual outlay of about $20 million. (See Table 230.)

PRINCIPAL VALLEYS WITH DEVELOPMENTAL POSSIBILITIES

River valleys, as the natural subdivisions of our water resources, are generally accepted as the best units for planning and developing the use and control of those resources. River valleys are not, however, the perfect units for such planning and development activities. The watershed boundaries of a particular river basin frequently overlap other natural regions — forest, soil or mineral areas — and often they cut directly across the political boundaries of states, counties and even of the nation. Furthermore, many unified industrial areas, such as the Cleveland-Pittsburgh steel district, lie in two or more river basins.

The use of the river valley as the unit for controlling and developing our water resources does *not* require, however, the establishment all over the nation of valley development agencies modeled after the Tennessee Valley Authority. Apart from the widely divergent political differences over the merits of such an approach, it is precluded by the tremendous variations in size and prevailing conditions among the 160 separate river basins in the country. But it is undeniable that coordinated and cooperative action of the various federal, state and local agencies and private groups and interests concerned in the development of a particular river valley promises the best returns for the outlays involved. Without such cooperative action, bitter conflicts are certain to arise regarding the best uses to which the available water resources should be put.

Practically every river valley in the country offers some possibilities for a coordinated development of its water resources, but attention will be focused here only on the principal valleys with developmental possibilities. For this purpose, a review is made of the drainage areas along the eastern seaboard, in the Mississippi Valley and on the Pacific Coast.

Eastern Seaboard

Water has always been an abundant resource along the eastern seaboard of our nation. In fact, so much of it has been available that, until recent years, there has been little need for comprehensive plans for control and development. Intensive urban and industrial growth, however, has increased the demands on our eastern rivers as carriers of commerce, producers of electric energy, suppliers of water for domestic and industrial use, and disposers of municipal and industrial wastes. To meet these several demands, multiple-purpose works and structures will be needed in many of the river valleys along our eastern seaboard.

The Great Lakes–St. Lawrence Basin

The Great Lakes–St. Lawrence basin probably has the greatest developmental possibilities of all the North American river valleys that drain into the Atlantic Ocean, and will require the cooperative action of both the United States and Canada to bring about the full utilization of its water resources.[185] The growth of industry and commerce in the Great Lakes area has hinged largely on the utilization of the lakes system as a waterway, and — as has been noted earlier[186] — enormous possibilities loom for even greater growth in the future through the improvement, recently authorized by Congress, of the St. Lawrence River link between the lakes and the ocean so that deep-draft sea-going vessels may pass between the two. An equally important feature of this waterway improvement is the hydroelectric power development that will be undertaken in the International Rapids section of the river. The development, which will provide an annual

output of nearly 13 billion kilowatt-hours to be divided between the United States and Canada, is one of the best opportunities still available in the nation for producing low-cost hydro power. Because of its low cost, St. Lawrence power can be transmitted over long distances and delivered to New York and New England markets at prices well below rates now prevailing in those areas.

These navigation and power improvements, which have been combined into the controversial St. Lawrence Seaway and Power Project, do not, however, constitute all of the developmental needs and possibilities in the Great Lakes–St. Lawrence basin. Harbor improvements and further port developments of various kinds are needed at many of the principal American lake ports — Duluth, Milwaukee, Chicago, Detroit, Cleveland and Buffalo — where traffic has tended to concentrate more and more in recent years. The redevelopment of Niagara Falls to use additional stream flow, released for power generation by a treaty between the United States and Canada in 1950, would provide this country with an annual net increase of almost 7.9 billion kilowatt-hours of low-cost electric energy, which, like the low-cost power from the St. Lawrence project, could be transmitted to distant markets in New York and New England.

Flood protection and control works are needed in many of the short and relatively flat valleys that drain into the Great Lakes, and there are numerous opportunities, especially in the rugged uplands of northern New York, for combining flood control reservoirs with hydroelectric power developments. The large metropolitan areas, such as Chicago, on the shores of the Great Lakes draw freely on them for domestic and industrial water supplies, but at the same time many of these areas indiscriminately dump municipal sewage and industrial wastes into the lakes. Sewage treatment plants are needed at many points to control pollution, and filtration and water treatment plants, along with extensions of water supply systems, are needed in several of the lake shore cities.

The Connecticut River Valley

In New England, the greatest river and the most extensive watershed is the Connecticut.[187]

185. See: *St. Lawrence Seaway and Power Project*, especially pp. 524–530; *Resources for Freedom*, Vol. III, pp. 37–58; *Possibilities for Redevelopment of Niagara Falls for Power*, Federal Power Commission, 1949; *Drainage Basin Problems and Programs*, National Resources Committee, 1937, pp. 41–46 and 244–269.
186. See pp. 545–546.

187. For data regarding the basin contained in this and the next two paragraphs, see *Ten Rivers in America's Future*, Report of the President's Water Resources Policy Commission, 1950, Vol. II, pp. 467–519.

The Connecticut Valley, which is one of the longest settled and most densely populated areas in the nation, is heavily dependent on manufacturing for its prosperity, although agriculture and lumbering — both once dominant in the valley — are still practiced there. But the second largest industry in the valley, as in all of New England, is the tourist and recreation trade, which is based on the large areas of forests and wildlands there, the rolling or mountainous landscape, the attractive lakes and streams, and the shoreline beaches.

In the lower reaches of the Connecticut Valley, where manufacturing and agriculture are concentrated, periodic floods are a hazard and threat to the regional economy. Additional flood protection and control works are needed, especially more reservoirs on the principal tributaries of the river. Improved watershed management practices would also aid in flood control because overuse of pasture lands, lack of conservation practices on many agricultural lands, and abuse of the forest lands have resulted in accelerated water runoff and erosion. Several of the projected flood control reservoirs combine hydroelectric power possibilities. The undeveloped hydroelectric power sources are believed capable of an average annual output of about 2.7 billion kilowatt-hours, almost double the production of the existing hydro facilities in the basin.

Many of the needed flood control and potential hydroelectric projects in the Connecticut Valley that would benefit urban areas are strongly opposed, however, by local interests in the rural areas because the reservoirs created by the projects would inundate good agricultural lands, which are scarce in the basin. But it is also true that such reservoirs would benefit the rural areas because they would provide new opportunities for recreational development, thus increasing the tourist and vacationer trade. Also, control of pollution, which is a serious problem locally at several points in the basin, coupled with improved stream flows resulting from flood control and hydroelectric projects, would make the Connecticut River suitable for recreational use through the greater part of its length.

From New England to Florida, the principal developmental needs in the river valleys that drain into the Atlantic arise from the primary requirements of finding additional domestic and industrial water supplies and of controlling pollution.[188] Here are many of the nation's great

and established metropolitan areas — New York, Philadelphia and Baltimore — and many of the growing industrial and manufacturing cities and towns of the new South. To all of them, assured water supplies are vital, and the importance of abating the health hazards and nuisances created by municipal and industrial wastes is being increasingly recognized. This is especially true in the Hudson and Delaware valleys, whose watersheds must furnish most of the water for the New York–Philadelphia urban region. Other developmental needs grow out of the continuing industrialization of many areas, especially in the South. Although rivers and streams of the Piedmont in Virginia and the Carolinas have been utilized extensively for hydroelectric power, large undeveloped power resources remain.

The Potomac River Valley

An example of the river valley developmental possibilities that are encountered along this section of the seaboard is offered by the Potomac.[189] Like many of the drainage basins along the southern Atlantic seaboard, the Potomac Valley — which contains the national capital — is small and contains three contrasting types of land: the broad and level coastal plain, the sloping and hilly terrain of the Piedmont Plateau, and the high ridges and steep slopes of the Appalachian Mountains where the river has its source. Again like many of the other Atlantic basins, the Potomac has a long and navigable tidal section, which stretches 117 miles from Washington to the Chesapeake Bay and supports a substantial seafood and fishing industry.

Almost two thirds of the Potomac Valley is in farms, but less than one third of the area is tilled cropland. About 50 per cent is in forest and woodland, but timber cutting over nearly two centuries has so depleted the stand that little marketable timber is left. Coal mining is an important industry in the western part of the basin, and some heavy manufacturing has developed around the coal fields, as at Cumberland, Maryland. Most of the manufacturing activity, however, is carried on by diversified small industries scattered among a number of localities in the valley.

So far, control and development of the waters of the Potomac River have been concerned pri-

---

188. *Drainage Basin Problems and Programs*, pp. 15–25.

189. For data in this and the next three paragraphs, see *Ten Rivers in America's Future*, pp. 527–624.

marily with navigation improvements in the tide-water section. Flood protection and control works are needed in the valley. Severe floods have occurred on an average of once every ten to twelve years, and as the shape and character of the valley favor rapid runoff, the Potomac and its tributaries are known for their frequent flash floods. Pollution also is a problem in the basin because it damages the fishery resources and adds to the cost of providing municipal and industrial water supplies, which are derived principally from surface sources. Depletion of the soil resources in the valley needs to be arrested. Three fourths of the cropland and one half of the grassland is in a serious or critical state of erosion and only about one third of the forest land is contributing adequately to the protection of the watershed.

Plans are now being studied for flood control projects in the valley, several of which would be of a multiple-purpose character. Some of these would produce hydroelectric power, which would encourage further industrial development. The hydroelectric power potential of the basin is still almost completely unused; undeveloped power resources are estimated to be capable of producing an annual average of 2.3 billion kilowatt-hours, or roughly a hundred times the output of existing hydro plants in the valley. Many of the proposed multiple-purpose projects, by regulating stream flow, would also increase the supply of water for households and industry and aid in pollution abatement. Control of pollution through the construction of treatment plants would protect the fisheries and also help ensure domestic and industrial water supplies. The undertaking of all these works and improvements plus the installation of the proper watershed management practices that are needed on the crop, pasture and forest lands could provide a clean, well-controlled, efficiently used and attractive river in the Potomac Valley.

Valleys of the Southeast

Between the Atlantic seaboard and the Mississippi River lie several rivers that drain into the Gulf of Mexico, such as the Suwannee, the Chattahoochee, the Alabama and the Tombigbee. The valleys of the last two, which flow into Mobile Bay, include the deposits of coal, iron ore and cement materials that are the basis of the economy of the Birmingham industrial area. The

Alabama, with its principal tributary, the Coosa, has attracted much attention recently because the valley, like so many others in the Southeast, is an area of low rural income, and would benefit greatly from further control and development of the river and its watershed.

Mississippi Valley

The valley of the Mississippi River system embraces more than 40 per cent of the area of the continental United States. Between the Rocky Mountains and the Appalachians, which constitute the western and eastern rims of the Mississippi basin, lies the broad, gently sloping lowland that is the floor of this great valley. This valley floor, which extends for more than 1,200 miles across the heart of the North American continent, is the largest, most populous and most productive temperate lowland in the New World.[190]

In the western part of the valley is the Great Plains area, where water is scarce and land must be irrigated if it is to be used for general agriculture. In the central and eastern parts of the valley, however, lies a vast expanse of fertile, rolling country where water is plentiful and generally sufficient for ordinary agriculture. It is in these parts that settlement has tended to concentrate and here are the most prosperous farms, the largest cities and the most important industries in the valley. These are the lands and the cities that are served by the great inland waterway system provided by the Mississippi and its tributaries, a system that now comprises more than 12,000 miles of improved waterways. But these lands and cities also are the ones most threatened by the frequent floods of the Mississippi and its tributaries.

Along the main stem of the Mississippi, which stretches more than 2,300 miles from its source in Lake Itasca in Minnesota to its mouth at the Gulf of Mexico, lie the corn belt lands of the upper valley and the rich alluvial lands of the lower valley. The use of these lands, especially those in the lower valley, has always been menaced by floods. The tremendous flood control program in the lower valley on which the federal government embarked after the great flood of 1927, and which is more than half completed, is opening new developmental possibilities on

190. For information in this and the next paragraph, see C. H. Paul, *Inventory of the Water Resources of the Mississippi River Drainage Area,* National Resources Board, 1935, pp. 1–6.

these agricultural lands. Further potentialities are appearing in the expansion of drainage activities. New industrial and commercial opportunities along the upper and lower river may also be opened by the proposed deepening to 12 feet of the navigation channel, which now extends from the Minneapolis–St. Paul area to New Orleans.[191]

The Southwestern Tributaries

The valleys of the southwestern tributaries of the lower Mississippi, especially the basins of the Arkansas, Red and White rivers, also possess several interesting developmental potentialities, similar in some respects to those of the Tennessee Valley. Farmland in the area, which supports about half the population, is seriously eroded. In the western parts of these valleys, water is precious and droughts are frequent, while the eastern parts suffer from recurring floods. Several water conservation and flood control works, combining hydroelectric developments that will encourage industrial expansion, are needed to bring about unified development of these valleys. Such works and structures, along with appropriate soil conservation and rehabilitation measures, would open up the potentialities of the area.[192]

Farther south and west of these Mississippi tributaries are the river valleys that drain across Texas directly into the Gulf of Mexico. In several of them flood control and protection works are needed, while in others water conservation for irrigation is necessary. An outstanding example of a basin needing such control and developmental work is the Rio Grande Valley, one of the oldest continuously settled regions in the United States. Agriculture — principally livestock production on extensive range lands and crop production on 2 million acres of irrigated land — is the most important element in the economy of the valley, but a precarious balance exists in man's adjustment to the water and land resources in the basin. The limited water resources available for irrigation, domestic and industrial use have been developed to the point where claims for the resources exceed the supply. The scarcity of water has forced intensive land use practices that have caused erosion and created heavy sedimentation in the river, which, in turn, threatens many of the irrigation projects. A comprehensive water and land program, requiring the cooperation of the United States and Mexico, is badly needed in order to stabilize and improve conditions in the valley.[193]

The Ohio River Basin

The two principal tributaries of the Mississippi River, the Ohio and the Missouri, which flank it on east and west at approximately its midpoint, account for nearly 60 per cent of the Mississippi's flow when it empties into the Gulf of Mexico.[194] These two tributaries, and more particularly the Ohio, have always contributed heavily to floods on the lower Mississippi. Control of their flood flows would do much to increase the protection of the alluvial lands in the lower Mississippi Valley. Furthermore, according to estimates made by the U.S. Army Corps of Engineers, more than one fifth of the capital outlays needed for the control and development of our rivers would be invested in the Ohio and Missouri valleys.[195]

In terms of volume of annual flow, the Ohio River is the largest tributary of the Mississippi.[196] The greater basin of the Ohio includes the Tennessee Valley, where the water resources have been controlled and developed as part of a unified program for the economic development of the region undertaken by the federal government through the establishment in 1933 of the Tennessee Valley Authority.[197] Under the program, the Tennessee River and its tributaries have been harnessed (1) to create a 9-foot navigation channel 630 miles long from Paducah, Kentucky, on the Ohio River to Knoxville, Tennessee; (2) to provide flood protection for both the Tennessee Valley and the lower Mississippi; and (3) to develop incidental hydroelectric power, which has resulted in new industrial developments in the valley. Along with these primary purposes, water control has also been undertaken to pre-

---

191. *Report of the Chief of Engineers, U.S. Army, 1951,* Part I, Vol. III, p. 289.

192. An extended review of the basic problems and developmental possibilities of this area appears in *Regional Planning, Part XII — Arkansas Valley,* National Resources Planning Board, 1943.

193. For a summary of the problems and needs in the valley, see *A Water Policy for the American People,* pp. 26–29. For a more detailed treatment see *Ten Rivers in America's Future,* pp. 285–351.

194. Paul, *op. cit.,* p. 13.

195. "Summary of Plans for Conservation and Development of the Water Resources of the United States," Table 3, p. 9949.

196. Paul, *op. cit.,* p. 13.

197. For a recent report on the status of the TVA program, see *Annual Report of the Tennessee Valley Authority for the Fiscal Year Ended June 30, 1953.*

vent and reduce malaria, to provide increased recreational opportunities, to reduce pollution, and to improve the habitat for fish and wildlife. To complement these water resource activities, there are valley-wide programs of erosion control, reforestation and rural rehabilitation. Although the economy of the valley is still predominantly rural and agricultural, significant changes have been taking place under the impact of the TVA program. Manufacturing enterprises employ a greater proportion of workers than they did in 1933, and per capita incomes of all workers in the valley have increased more than those in the rest of the country.

The Ohio basin — excluding the Tennessee Valley — covers approximately 100 million acres, only a little more than 5 per cent of the area of the United States, but its economy is one of the richest and perhaps the most diversified of any major river basin in the nation.[198] Although most of the Ohio Valley was originally covered by forests, much of these were cleared by the early settlers to make way for farms, which now occupy about three fourths of the land area. Some of the most productive agricultural land in the nation is in the valley, and farming is a major occupation in the area. The valley also contains rich mineral resources; it accounts for more than three fourths of the nation's annual production of bituminous coal. Because of its extensive coal fields and cheap water transportation, the Ohio Valley has become an outstanding industrial region, containing the important iron and steel producing area centering on Pittsburgh and several large manufacturing centers, such as Cincinnati.

Almost one ninth of the population of the United States lives in the Ohio Valley. To these people, the river serves as "a sewer, a source of water supply, an outlet for floods, and a highway."[199] To them, the future of the valley, from the standpoint of both its industry and agriculture, will be greatly influenced by the way in which the river and its tributaries are controlled and developed.

The pollution problem in the Ohio Valley is one of the most serious in the country.[200] Nearly 2,200 municipalities and 1,300 industrial plants discharge wastes into the rivers and streams in the valley, but only a little more than one fourth of the municipalities and one third of the industrial plants provide any treatment for their wastes. Although great progress has been made in recent years in controlling pollution on some of the tributaries of the river, treatment plants are lacking on the main stem and the major tributaries. The United States Public Health Service estimates that in the valley as a whole, more than 1,100 municipal and nearly 800 industrial treatment plants, replacements, additions or enlargements are needed.

The growing demand for domestic and industrial water supplies in face of increasing pollution also poses a major problem in the Ohio Valley, and especially affects such industrial centers as Pittsburgh, Charleston (West Virginia), Cincinnati and Indianapolis. About 6.5 million persons, or well over one third of the valley's population, are served by surface water supplies, and industrial water requirements — especially in the iron and steel producing areas — also place a heavy drain on those supplies. In some areas in the valley, future urban and industrial development will be restricted unless new sources of water supplies can be developed. Proper regulation of stream flow in the main river and many of its tributaries would help greatly to provide adequate future sources of such supplies. Many of the reservoirs so badly needed for flood control purposes will also aid in regulating flow for water supply. But special water supply reservoirs will need to be constructed in some cases.

Devastating floods have swept down the Ohio Valley frequently since it was settled, and protection works on a limited scale were taken in some areas beginning early in the nineteenth century. Local groups built levees and flood walls and later even a system of retarding reservoirs in the Miami River basin. After the disastrous flood of 1937, a comprehensive flood control plan for the entire valley was developed by the U.S. Army Corps of Engineers. The plan, which is now being carried out, provides for 80 reservoirs located on the tributaries and 240 local flood protection projects on the tributaries and along the main stem of the river. Many of the reservoirs will provide opportunities for hydroelectric power development. The potential undeveloped hydro power in the Ohio Valley would produce an annual average of almost 25 billion kilowatt-hours, nearly fourteen times the present output.

198. Except where otherwise noted, the data in this and the next several paragraphs regarding the Ohio Valley are from *Ten Rivers in America's Future*, pp. 627–701.

199. *Drainage Basin Problems and Programs*, p. 37.

200. For data in this paragraph, see *Water Pollution in the United States*, pp. 30–31.

Navigation on the Ohio will also benefit from the stream flow regulation to be provided by the flood control works. The greatest tonnage of river traffic in the country is carried on the Ohio and some of its tributaries, particularly the Monongahela. But the existing system of locks and dams on the main stem is inadequate for the demands of modern water transportation. Improvements are needed, including replacement of obsolete locks and dams and additional channel dredging. Furthermore, there is the possibility that the present channel, which provides a minimum navigable depth of 9 feet, may need to be deepened to 12 feet and perhaps even more if the Ohio waterway system should be directly linked to that of the Great Lakes by the proposed canalizing and connecting of the Beaver and Mahoning rivers.

The Missouri River Basin

Although the Ohio is the Mississippi's largest tributary in terms of volume of annual flow, the Missouri is the longest river in the nation and has the largest drainage area of the Mississippi tributaries.[201] This great basin, which covers one sixth of the area of the continental United States, is a land of extreme cold and intense heat; of deep, rich prairie soils, grassy plains and tall, bare mountains. In the upper western part of the valley, the land and the people suffer from a lack of water; in the lower eastern part, from recurring floods. The river itself is as variable as the climate and land of which it is a product, rising and falling swiftly and noted for the sudden, unexpected shifts of its channel.

Agriculture is the principal livelihood of the valley's 8 million inhabitants. The farms and ranches of the Missouri Valley account for one third of the bread grains produced in the nation, nearly one third of the wool, one fourth of the pork and mutton, and one fifth of the beef and butter. Manufacturing in the valley consists principally of processing crops and livestock into food products. Although there are important mineral deposits in the valley, many of them have lain virtually untapped for lack of power, of local demand for mineral products, or of adequate

methods of beneficiating the ores, some of which are low-grade.

Plans for the control and development of the waters of the Missouri River and its tributaries, which had been evolving for many years, were given great impetus during the 1930s by the prolonged drought in the Great Plains area of the valley. In a single decade, the capital investment and livelihood of thousands of families were destroyed. Overcultivation of the parched land led to serious wind erosion of the thin layer of topsoil, which turned much of the region into a "dust bowl" and threatened to make it a desert. New soil treatment practices and cover crops to hold the topsoil in place were developed and shelter belts were planted. Small water conservation projects were established and surveys begun for a great expansion of irrigation.[202]

During this same drought period, floods in the Missouri Valley took many lives and caused great property damage. Water which, if properly conserved and regulated, could have brought prosperity and stability to the western part of the valley was instead an instrument of destruction in the eastern part. Since 1935, seven major floods have occurred in the valley, taking a toll of nearly 300 lives and causing property damage mounting into hundreds of millions of dollars. The great flood of 1951, which alone inflicted damages of more than $1 billion, and the 1952 flood have recently spurred action on plans for control of the river.

Although there have been recurring proposals for the creation of a Missouri Valley Authority along the lines of the federal agency for the Tennessee Valley, so far these have been consistently rejected in favor of a cooperative approach on the part of the federal, state and local agencies and the private interests concerned. This approach has produced a multiple-purpose program for harnessing the river and its tributaries and for improving their watershed lands. The program, which is estimated to cost at least $9.4 billion, is one of the largest water and land resources undertakings of its kind in history.

A central feature of this Missouri River Basin Development Program is the construction on the river and its tributaries of a system of more than 100 multipurpose reservoirs. The plan for this system is based on the famous "Pick-Sloan Plan,"

201. Except where otherwise noted, data in this and the next several paragraphs regarding the Missouri Valley are from: *The Missouri River Basin Development Program,* Missouri Basin Inter-Agency Committee and Missouri River States Committee, June 1952.

202. For a summary of the steps that were taken and the surveys begun, see *Regional Planning, Part IX — The Northern Great Plains, A Progress Report,* National Resources Planning Board, 1939.

which represents a merging in 1944 of the two plans for river control and development that had been worked out by the principal federal agencies involved: the U.S. Army Corps of Engineers and the U.S. Bureau of Reclamation.[203] The reservoir system will serve three major purposes: flood control, irrigation and hydroelectric power. A key project in the system is Garrison Dam and Reservoir on the main stem of the Missouri about 75 miles northwest of Bismarck, North Dakota. This dam, which is under construction and scheduled for completion in 1956, will be the world's largest rolled-earth dam, and its reservoir will extend more than 200 miles upstream.

Control of floods through the storage capacity provided by the reservoir system on the Missouri and its tributaries will eliminate or reduce considerably flood damage on 5 million acres of rural and urban land in the valley. To supplement the protection provided by the upstream reservoirs, local flood protection works — earthen levees and concrete floodwalls — will be provided at numerous downstream locations in order further to safeguard the urban areas. Also about 1,500 miles of levees will be constructed in order further to protect about 1.5 million acres of agricultural lands.

The reservoirs in the headwaters of the Missouri and its tributaries will permit the irrigation of more than 5.3 million additional acres of land and will furnish supplemental water for approximately 2 million acres now receiving an inadequate supply. On the new lands to be irrigated, about 67,000 new farms can be created, supporting a farm population of more than a quarter of a million. All of these irrigated lands will be islands of stable production in future periods of drought and will thus help prevent another economic disaster like the one that struck the area during the 1930s.[204]

Hydroelectric plants proposed at the reservoirs will have an ultimate installed generating capacity of 3.2 million kilowatts and an average annual output of more than 13 billion kilowatt-hours. This would be nearly five times the present generating capacity of hydro plants in the valley and almost four times their present output. The increased supply of electric energy plus improved mining technology should make it economically feasible to develop many of the valley's untapped mineral resources, thus fostering industrial expansion in the area.

The controlled stream flow that will result from the reservoir system will also benefit navigation, improve domestic and industrial water supplies, and aid in alleviating pollution. The present program calls for a 9-foot navigation channel from the mouth of the river to Sioux City, Iowa, a distance of about 760 miles, and when completed it is expected to have a potential annual traffic load of about 5 million tons. Stabilization and maintenance of the navigation channel will also prevent erosion of valuable agricultural land and protect cities, roads and bridges along the riverbank. Nearly 1.5 million people in the lower valley depend on the Missouri for their drinking water, and studies indicate that the regulated water supply of the river will be adequate, except on rare occasions, for all purposes including both upstream irrigation and downstream domestic and industrial use. In addition to stream flow regulation, however, a comprehensive program of pollution control will have to be undertaken in the Missouri Valley. There are nearly 1,200 municipal and industrial sources of pollution on the river and its tributaries, and only 15 per cent of the urban population in the valley lives in localities that have adequate sewage treatment facilities.

All of these river control and development works in the Missouri Valley will have companion undertakings on the land, for it is a cardinal principle of the program that "conservation and use of land and water must be dealt with as inseparable." [205] Farmers and ranchers are expected to assume primary local responsibility for soil and moisture conservation on their 270 million acres of crop and grazing lands. Terracing is needed on 20 million acres, contour farming on 36 million acres, and strip cropping on 20 million acres. In addition, thousands of small erosion control structures are needed to reduce runoff and increase the water absorption of the land. Reseeding of more than 17 million acres of grazing lands, building of more than 400,000 ponds for livestock water, and waterspreading measures for over 2 million acres of range lands are also needed.

203. The Army Corps of Engineers plan appears in H. Doc. 475, 78th Cong., 2d sess.; the Bureau of Reclamation plan in S. Doc. 191, 78th Cong., 2d sess.; the merger of the two — the Pick-Sloan Plan — in H. Doc. 784, 78th Cong., 2d sess.

204. *The Missouri River Basin Project,* Bureau of Reclamation, U.S. Department of the Interior, May 1950, p. 3.

205. *The Missouri River Basin Development Program,* p. 26.

On the 45 million acres of forest and forest-range lands in the valley, more intensive management is needed to increase timber production, to improve range conditions, and to promote watershed protection. Tree planting is needed on about 5 million acres of public and private forest lands, and an additional 245,000 miles of shelter belts and 750,000 acres of windbreaks are proposed on farms and ranches.

The land of the Missouri is a beckoning empire, as it was to its first settlers. But it still confronts its people with great natural odds — drought, scarcity of water, blizzards and floods. As the President's Water Resources Policy Commission has put it: "Today, despite 150 years of settlement, the challenge of the Missouri still remains. We have largely taken over the basin, but we have yet to learn fully how to meet nature's requirements." [206]

Pacific Coast

As in the western part of the Mississippi Valley, water is a precious commodity in the three great river valleys of the Pacific Coast — the Columbia in the Pacific Northwest, the Central of California, and the Colorado in the Pacific Southwest. A major portion of the land in each of these valleys is arid or semiarid. Water not only must be stored for use during the dry seasons, but it must often be transported long distances from areas where it is in surplus to areas where it is in deficit. Careful and comprehensive planning is therefore needed in these valleys to ensure that the available water resources are controlled and developed for their best use.

For decades, a steady stream of migration has flowed from the east into these great western river valleys. Agriculture and industry in the area have expanded phenomenally and large sprawling cities have grown. Nevertheless, the valleys still offer enormous developmental possibilities. According to estimates made by the U.S. Army Corps of Engineers, the capital outlays needed for the control and development of water resources in the three valleys would comprise more than two fifths of the total required in the entire country.[207]

The Columbia River Valley

The valley of the Columbia River and the Snake, its largest tributary, has particularly great developmental possibilities. [208] Although the Columbia is exceeded in volume of flow by both the Mississippi and the St. Lawrence rivers, it is the largest present producer and the greatest potential source of hydroelectric power in the nation. Its waters are used to irrigate an area second in size only to that supplied from the Missouri River, and could serve twice the present irrigated area. It is the primary salmon-producing stream in the nation, and the forest lands it drains contain the largest reserve of standing saw timber in the United States. Within its drainage area are large deposits of mineral resources, many of which are as yet not fully exploited.

But the economy of the Columbia Valley is still relatively immature. The more than three million people who make their homes in the valley are dependent upon the production of raw materials — food, lumber and minerals — for their living. The greater part of the gainful employment in the valley can be traced, directly or indirectly, to agriculture. More than half of the harvested crop acreage is used for growing small grain, mostly by dry farming. Livestock ranching on large acreages is also an important agricultural activity. Forestry comprises, along with agriculture, a major segment of the regional economy. Each year the forest lands in the Columbia basin yield about 15 per cent of the nation's lumber output. Manufacturing is widely dispersed in the valley and largely devoted to processing raw materials, agricultural products and fish — saw mills and paper and pulp mills near the lumbering operations; mineral-processing plants near the mines; food-processing plants near the irrigated farms that produce vegetables and fruits; fish canning and processing near the fisheries.[209]

Expansion of economic opportunities in the Columbia Valley will rest fundamentally upon the further development of the waters of the river and its tributaries for hydroelectric power and irrigation. That development began in modern times with the construction during the 1930s

206. *Ten Rivers in America's Future*, p. 161.
207. "Summary of Plans for Conservation and Development of the Water Resources of the United States," Table 3, p. 9949.

208. Except where otherwise noted, data in this and the next several paragraphs regarding the Columbia River Valley are from *The Columbia River — A Comprehensive Report on the Development of the Water Resources of the Columbia River Basin . . .* , Bureau of Reclamation, U.S. Department of the Interior, 1947, pp. 15–90.
209. For information in this paragraph see *Ten Rivers in America's Future*, pp. 2–3.

of the Bonneville and Grand Coulee dams on the main stem of the river. These were the key multiple-purpose projects in an evolving plan to control and make full use of the river system, and the Bonneville Power Administration was established to transmit and distribute the hydroelectric power produced by these and other federal projects. Subsequently a Columbia Valley Authority has been frequently proposed as an agency for carrying out and operating an overall plan for the valley. Proposals along these lines have so far been rejected, however, and an approach to a coordinated plan for the valley has been sought through the cooperative action of the federal, state and local agencies and private interests involved, especially of the principal federal agencies.[210]

Potentially, the Columbia River is one of the greatest power-producing streams not only in the nation but also in the world. Existing hydroelectric installations in the valley comprise about one sixth of the developed hydro capacity in the United States, but they utilize less than 10 per cent of the potential water power in the valley. In 1950 the installed capacity of both public and private hydro plants in the basin was about 2.9 million kilowatts and their annual output approached 20 billion kilowatt-hours. According to estimates of the Federal Power Commission,[211] the hydroelectric potential in the valley was then more than 34 million kilowatts of installed capacity and the potential average annual output nearly 170 billion kilowatt-hours. The Commission estimated that there were more than 380 additional power sites in the basin, with a large part of the undeveloped power lying on the main stem of the Columbia and the lower courses of its principal tributaries. Slightly less than one third of the undeveloped power was in projects under construction or authorized for construction by the federal government.

Further development of hydroelectric power in the Columbia Valley would make it possible to expand and diversify the industrial base of the regional economy. During World War II there was a rapid growth of electrometallurgical industries in the Pacific Northwest, and increasing availability of low-cost power in the future would provide more opportunities for new specialized

electrometallurgical and electrochemical industries, many of which could utilize the undeveloped mineral resources. Additional expansion of forest products industries — pulp and pulp products and various kinds of woodworking — is also possible, and the growth of other types of special and light manufacturing would be fostered.

Equally great developmental possibilities exist through the further control and use of the waters of the Columbia and its tributaries for irrigation purposes. Irrigated lands in the valley now total about 3.7 million acres, and present developmental plans would not only provide supplemental water supplies for the more than 1.5 million acres of these lands that need it, but also irrigate about 3.8 million acres of new land. About one million acres of the lands to be newly irrigated lie in the Columbia Basin project, the principal features of which are still under construction by the federal government. The central structure of this project is, of course, the completed Grand Coulee, the largest concrete dam in the world.

Storage and controlled release of water for power and irrigation will also aid navigation, which is an important use of the main stem of the Columbia, and flood control. Although floods in the Columbia River system are not the recurring menace they are on the Mississippi and its tributaries, still they do much damage in the valley. The major flood of 1948 on the lower Columbia caused damages in excess of $100 million. The water storage projects in combination with levee and drainage projects will provide flood protection for almost 1.4 million acres of agricultural land and will increase the protection now provided to urban and industrial areas. Drainage undertaken in connection with flood control works in various parts of the valley would benefit an additional half million acres.

But the construction of additional multiple-purpose dams on the Columbia and its tributaries might threaten the valuable salmon fishery,[212] unless, as noted earlier, special facilities are constructed at the dams. Rehabilitation of former spawning grounds on the lower river and its tributaries also might help greatly in saving the fishery.

Along with all these improvements and structures, programs of improved watershed management must also be undertaken.[213] Although the

210. For the coordinated plans of the U.S. Bureau of Reclamation and the U.S. Army Corps of Engineers, see *The Columbia River*, H. Doc. 473, 81st Cong., 2d sess., 1950, Vol. I, pp. 23–32.

211. Reported in *Ten Rivers in America's Future*, p. 22.

212. See p. 557.

213. For data in this paragraph see *Ten Rivers in America's Future*, pp. 23–24.

needs for such programs are less critical in the Columbia Valley than in many other river valleys, a number of acute situations demand attention. The U.S. Forest Service estimates that about 4 million acres of private and public forest lands in the valley are in need of replanting and that large acreages of the private forest lands are subject to poor timber-cutting practices that add to erosion hazards. There is also need for additional fire control measures on both public and private forest lands. About 42 million acres of grazing lands are deteriorating rapidly and proper rehabilitation measures are badly needed on them. Further erosion control work is needed in the dry farming areas of the valley, for about 6 million acres in these areas are being damaged at a critical rate.

These watershed improvements would greatly aid in ensuring the livelihood of the more than three million inhabitants of the Columbia Valley. Extension of irrigation, drainage and flood control would enable the valley lands to support a population increase of at least 20 to 30 per cent. How much greater this increase could be by reason of industrial expansion based on hydroelectric power development cannot be precisely estimated. But the further possible increase would — from all indications — be substantial.

The Central Valley of California

In contrast to the Columbia Valley, where the initial purpose of the river control and developmental works was primarily to provide opportunities for expansion, the works in the Central Valley of California were initially intended to rehabilitate the existing regional economy.[214] Although the Central Valley is one of the most productive farm regions in the world, with prosperous cities and many food-processing industries, its agricultural economy began to sicken during the two decades after World War I because of a shortage of water for irrigation, on which it is heavily dependent. Thousands of acres of farmland were abandoned and many more thousands threatened to return to desert because of a maldistribution of the water re-

sources in the valley in relation to the needs for them.

The northern half of the Central Valley is drained by the Sacramento River, which flows southward into a delta region near the center of the state. Here it meets the San Joaquin River, which flows northward and drains two thirds of the southern half of the valley. Together the waters of the two rivers flow into San Francisco Bay. But the Sacramento Valley to the north, which has only about one third of the need for irrigation water supplies, receives two thirds of the rains and snows that fall in the whole Central Valley, while the San Joaquin Valley to the south, which has about two thirds of the irrigation need, receives only about one third of the precipitation. The rains and snows, moreover, come in the winter and spring, whereas the need for irrigation water supplies is greatest during the summer. The problem, therefore, was both to store water and to redistribute it.

To solve this problem, a State Water Plan was evolved. During the early 1930s, after the State of California had been unable to finance the undertaking, the federal government agreed to construct and operate the initial stages of it. As a result of this program, the winter flood waters of the Sacramento River are now stored at Shasta Dam, second largest and second highest dam in the world. A portion of the regulated flow thus achieved in the Sacramento River is transferred in the delta region by a series of canals and pumping plants southward up the San Joaquin Valley, where it is put into the San Joaquin River to replace the flow stored and diverted farther upstream at Friant Dam. The diversion at Friant Dam is carried farther southward to irrigate lands in the rich farming region that lies beyond the headwaters of the San Joaquin.

In its initial stages, the plan for the Central Valley will provide supplemental water for about a half million irrigated acres now insufficiently supplied and will provide a full irrigation supply for an additional half million acres. The projects involved will also improve flood control and navigation on the two rivers, supply cities and industries along them with water, and provide nearly one million additional kilowatts of installed generating capacity for electric power.

The next stages of the plan for the Central Valley involve the construction of a series of dams and other irrigation works on the tributaries of the Sacramento and San Joaquin rivers.

214. Data regarding the Central Valley of California are from: *Central Valley Basin — A Comprehensive Departmental Report on the Development of the Water and Related Resources of the Central Valley Basin . . . ,* Bureau of Reclamation, U.S. Department of the Interior, 1949, pp. 27–93; and *Working Water for California's Central Valley,* Bureau of Reclamation, U.S. Department of the Interior.

These works would conserve enough water to irrigate more than 750,000 acres. About 250,000 of these acres are now irrigated but need more water; the rest are now dry. Power installations to be made in connection with these projects would have a total capacity of about a half million kilowatts. Many of the dams would also help check floods.

Ultimately, the plan for the Central Valley might include a total of 38 major dams and reservoirs, many hydroelectric plants and thousands of miles of irrigation canals and laterals. They could provide water for more than 3 million acres not now irrigated and double the number of prosperous farms in the valley. They could also produce about 8 billion kilowatt-hours of electric energy a year, ensure supplies of domestic water, and provide a high measure of flood protection.

The Colorado River Valley

The third great western valley draining into the Pacific is that of the Colorado River.[215] The Colorado is the nation's second longest river outside the Mississippi River system. It rises high in the mountains of north central Colorado, flows nearly 1,400 miles southwest through many deep gorges and chasms — most spectacular of which is the world-famous, 200-mile-long Grand Canyon of Arizona — and empties into the Gulf of California in Mexico. Its drainage area comprises nearly 250,000 square miles and includes parts of seven states and a small portion of Mexico.

The Colorado Valley is a land of sharp contrasts — of tall, rugged, snow-capped mountains; of high, dry plateaus; of low, flat desert country; and of semitropical alluvial lands. The entire valley is, however, arid except in the high altitudes of the headwaters areas, and rainfall generally is insufficient for the profitable production of crops without irrigation. Nearly 2.7 million acres in the valley are under irrigation, and the waters of the Colorado irrigate an additional 0.4 million acres in the adjoining Imperial and Coachella valleys in southern California.

Because of the forbidding terrain and climate, settlement of the valley was slow and difficult,

and today it is still sparsely inhabited. Although the valley includes about 8 per cent of the area of the continental United States, it contains less than one per cent of the nation's total population, and this small population is largely concentrated in a few locations favorable for agriculture or mining. There are no very large cities, but the great Los Angeles urban area lies immediately west of the valley and is largely dependent on the Colorado River for electric power and water.

The Colorado Valley is rich in natural resources, however. It has vast range areas for livestock production, which is the principal agricultural pursuit in the valley, especially in its upper part. The alluvial lands in the lower valley can, with irrigation, produce citrus fruits and green vegetables in abundance the year around. There are extensive mineral resources both in the upper and lower valley, and mining is a principal industry in the area. Several of the most important natural recreational resources in the nation are to be found in the valley; five national parks — Rocky Mountain, Mesa Verde, Bryce Canyon, Zion and Grand Canyon — lie wholly or partly within it. Finally, there are the waters of the Colorado itself, which — in addition to their consumptive uses — now provide an annual average of more than 7 billion kilowatt-hours of hydroelectric energy and have an undeveloped potential of about four times that amount.[216]

But the aridity of the valley means that its prosperity will be dependent in the future, as in the past, on control and development of the waters of the Colorado River and its tributaries. Control of the river became especially vital in the lower valley during the early decades of this century because of frequent destructive floods along the main stem, resulting primarily from snow melts in the upper valley, which contributes roughly three fourths of the water in the lower river. This uneven distribution of the runoff in the valley also led to conflicting claims between users of the waters of the river and its tributaries in the upper and lower basin areas. Existing demands and further plans for the development of these waters rapidly increased these conflicts after the turn of the present century. Key to the full control and development of the river and its tributaries was the conclusion of the Colorado River Compact of 1922 — now commonly

215. Except where otherwise noted, data in this and the next several paragraphs regarding the Colorado Valley are from *The Colorado River — A Comprehensive Departmental Report on the Development of the Water Resources of the Colorado River Basin* . . . , Bureau of Reclamation, U.S. Department of the Interior, 1946, pp. 9–103.

216. Estimates of the Federal Power Commission in mid-1950 as reported in *Ten Rivers in America's Future*, pp. 369–374.

known as the "law of the river" — among the seven states involved that apportioned the waters in the valley between the upper and lower basin states.

The Colorado River Compact made it possible for the federal government to construct the Boulder Canyon Project in the lower valley. Central to this undertaking was Hoover Dam, which was completed in 1935 and is the highest in the world.[217] This dam, by completely regulating the flow of the lower Colorado, has protected the lower valley from floods and assured it of water for irrigation and for domestic and industrial use. Completion of Hoover Dam also made possible the construction of a whole series of river control and developmental works in the lower valley, among them the Parker and Davis dams and power plants; the All-American Canal, which provides water for irrigating lands in the Imperial and Coachella valleys of southern California; and the Colorado River Aqueduct, which transports water 240 miles into the Los Angeles and San Diego metropolitan districts.

A major development in the upper basin since the compact of 1922 has been the Colorado–Big Thompson project.[218] Begun in 1938, this spectacular and complex undertaking has as its central purpose the diversion of surplus water from the headwaters of the Colorado River on the western side of the Continental Divide to the eastern side, where it is needed for irrigation during the summer months. The more than one hundred separate engineering features of the project are integrated into a major irrigation and power system which spreads 250 miles over and through mountains and out into the plains area in northeastern Colorado.

The Upper Colorado River Basin Compact of 1948, which divides the upper basin waters among the states in that part of the valley, provides the framework for further integrated planning and development of the waters in the upper valley. According to the inventory made by the U.S. Bureau of Reclamation, there are about a hundred projects or units of projects, mostly multiple-purpose in character, for the control and use of these waters. These would bring more than

1.2 million acres of new land under irrigation and furnish supplemental water to about 0.5 million acres now irrigated. The hydroelectric power installations would produce an average annual energy output of about 9.2 billion kilowatt-hours. Beyond these projects, possibilities exist for additional transmountain diversions of water from the upper Colorado basin into adjoining watersheds.

In the lower valley, further development of the waters of the Colorado and its tributaries is greatly hampered by a continuing lack of agreement among the states concerned — particularly California and Arizona — over the division of the waters allocated to them under the compact of 1922. However, according to the inventory made by the U.S. Bureau of Reclamation, there are about 34 potential projects or units of projects, mostly multiple-purpose in character, for the control and use of waters in the valley. These would bring about 0.3 million acres of new land into cultivation by irrigation and supplement the water supply of more than 0.6 million acres now under irrigation. The hydroelectric power features of these projects would produce an average annual energy output of about 10.2 billion kilowatt-hours.

But the Bureau of Reclamation also reports that there is not enough water in the Colorado River system to permit construction of all the potential projects in both the upper and lower valleys and, at the same time, provide for full expansion of existing developments, given the present agreements — or lack thereof — among the states concerned. Even if new and comprehensive agreements were reached regarding the allocation of the water, and integrated plans were evolved for the full control and development of all the water in the valley, it seems clear that the available supplies could not meet the potential demands. Nor is there much hope for large-scale diversions of water from adjoining basins into the Colorado Valley. Not only might such diversions be tremendously expensive, but it is doubtful whether the adjoining basins are in a position to satisfy needs other than their own.[219]

Another difficulty in planning the future control and use of the Colorado River and its tributaries arises from the silt problem.[220] Large parts of the valley have been impaired by water and

217. For data in this paragraph regarding the Boulder Canyon Project, see *The Story of Hoover Dam*, Conservation Bulletin No. 9, Bureau of Reclamation, U.S. Department of the Interior, 1949.

218. For data in this paragraph regarding this project, see *Colorado–Big Thompson Project*, Bureau of Reclamation, U.S. Department of the Interior, no date.

219. *Ten Rivers in America's Future*, p. 443.

220. For information in this paragraph see *ibid.*, pp. 366–369 and 429–433.

wind erosion; it is estimated that about 50 per cent of the land area is in a state of severe to critical erosion. Such erosion in the upper valley apparently contributes heavily to the sediment in the lower portions of the river. At Hoover Dam, for example, 100,000 acre-feet of sediment are deposited annually in Lake Mead, the reservoir behind the dam. If sedimentation continues unchecked, the useful life of engineering works on the river will be greatly shortened, for silt-filled reservoirs would be useless in controlling the river. As an aid in checking this problem, extensive and continuous programs of watershed management, involving especially proper use and conservation of range land, reforestation and control of runoff, are badly needed on both private and public lands in the valley.

SUMMARY OF NEEDS AND POSSIBILITIES

An estimated total outlay of more than $103 billion — after allowing for duplication — would be required during the next several decades to meet the needs and possibilities for land, forest and water conservation and development as outlined in this chapter. Programs covering these needs and possibilities, which are summarized in the accompanying Table 234, would require from twenty to seventy-five years to complete and would involve average annual outlays of nearly $2.6 billion during their first two decades. Thereafter, their estimated average annual costs would gradually decline to about $1 billion during the first decade or so of the twenty-first century.

Land Conservation and Development

Slightly less than one fifth of the total estimated outlays would be required to meet the conservation and rehabilitation needs of the nation's agricultural land resources and to cover the possible needs for additional crop and pasture lands through the development — by clearing, drainage or irrigation — of land now inside and outside farms. All told, more than 1.1 billion acres, or not less than 60 per cent of our national land area, would be directly involved under the estimated outlays of about $20 billion for the conservation, rehabilitation and possible development of our crop and grazing lands.

About 220 million acres of the cropland in farms that is now in danger of serious erosion would be protected along with a sizable proportion of the intensive-use pasture lands now in farms. More than 700 million acres of the grazing lands that comprise the western range would be rehabilitated and restored to something like their original grazing capacity. Between 40 and 50 million acres of land now in farms that are unsuitable for crop and grazing purposes could be shifted to less intensive uses.

About 30 million acres of the cropland in farms could be further developed by means of improved drainage or additional irrigation in order greatly to increase their productivity. Another 50 million acres of the land now in farms that is not used for crops could be developed by clearing or drainage for use in a rotation of crops and pasture. Outside of farms, roughly 36 million acres could be developed by clearing, drainage or irrigation for use as cropland. Development and settlement of these additional acres of new lands could provide perhaps as many as 300,000 new farms.

Forest Conservation and Development

Of the $7.8 billion of capital outlays estimated to be needed for forest conservation and development, a little more than one half would be for improvements and facilities needed in connection with the management of our forests for timber production. Such management — if we are to meet our larger future requirements for timber — must seek to place practically all of the 460 million acres of our commercial forest land on a sustained-yield basis as rapidly as possible. To facilitate that kind of management, the estimated outlays would provide the improvements needed to extend organized fire protection to some 66 million acres of forest lands not now receiving it and to provide more intensive protection in many other areas. Increased protection also would be provided against insects and diseases that attack our forests. Stand improvements would be undertaken on about 65 million acres, and another 32 million acres of poorly stocked or deforested lands would be planted. In order to provide better access to and use of our forests, about 100,000 additional miles of forest-development roads would be constructed and about 160,000 additional miles of foot and horse trails. Other improvements, such as buildings, communication systems, shelters and similar facilities needed for forest management, would also be provided.

The remainder of the estimated outlays for

TABLE 234. ESTIMATED COSTS AND TIME REQUIRED FOR LAND, FOREST
AND WATER CONSERVATION AND DEVELOPMENT PROGRAMS
(Dollar Figures in Millions, 1950 Prices)

Type of Program	Total Cost	Years Required	Annual Cost
Land conservation and rehabilitation needs			
Cropland	$ 8,500	20	$ 425
Grazing lands	2,000	20	100
Land retirement	a	20	a
Subtotal, land conservation	$10,500		$ 525
Land development possibilities			
Clearing	$ 3,250	50	$ 65
Drainage	2,250	50	45
Irrigation	4,000	25	160
Subtotal, land development	$ 9,500		$ 270 [b]
Forest management for timber production			
Fire protection	$ 625	25	$ 25
Protection from insects and disease	325	25	15
Stand improvements	750	25	30
Planting	500	25	20
Roads and trails	1,500	50	30
Other improvements	500	25	20
Subtotal, timber production	$ 4,200		$ 140 [b]
Forest protection and development for nontimber uses			
Watershed protection	$ 750	50	$ 15
Forage production	600	20	30
Wildlife habitat	250	25	10
Recreation	2,000	25	80
Subtotal, nontimber uses	$ 3,600		$ 135 [c]
River valley development			
Waterways and port development	$ 7,500	50–75	$ 125
Flood control	15,000	50–75	250
Irrigation	10,000	50–75	160
Hydroelectric power	30,000	50–75	480
Domestic and industrial water supply	6,250	25	250
Pollution abatement	10,000	25	400
Fish and wildlife conservation and recreation	1,250	50–75	20
Subtotal, river valley development	$80,000		$1,685 [b]
Unadjusted total — land, forest and water conservation and development	$107,800		$2,755 [c]
Deduct for duplications between estimates	$ 4,460 [d]		$ 167 [c]
Adjusted total — land, forest and water conservation and development needs and possibilities	$103,340		$2,572 [c]

Source: See discussion in text.

a. Transfer payments only.
b. For only first 25 years.
c. For only first 20 years.
d. Principal duplications are between estimates of (1) "Land conservation and rehabilitation needs — Grazing lands," and "Forest protection and development for nontimber uses — Forage production," where the duplication is about $460 million; and (2) "Land development possibilities — Irrigation" and "River valley development — Irrigation," where the duplication is about $4,000 million.
e. For only first 20 years, or roughly 1951 to 1970. Average annual costs for period 1971 to 1975 are estimated at $2,040 million; from 1976 to 2000 at about $1,190 million; and for the first decade or so of the twenty-first century at about $1,035 million.

forest conservation and development would cover the additional improvements needed in the protection and development of our forest lands for nontimber uses. Special planting on 44 million acres of farm lands and other improvements needed to restore the watershed protection services that our forests can afford us would be undertaken. The forage production of 320 million acres of forest and woodland would be ensured by special soil and water conservation operations. Preservation and rehabilitation measures would be taken in the area needed for wildlife habitat, nearly half of which lies in our forests and woodlands. The development of recreational facilities would be speeded up to keep abreast of the increasing need for such facilities in rural areas, especially in our forests.

River Valley Development

Considerably more than three quarters of the total outlay estimated to be required for land, forest and water conservation and development would be for river valley development, and would cover the works and structures still needed for the regulation and use of our river systems. In light of the $50 billion that the nation has already invested in such works and structures, a total capital outlay of between $125 and $130 billion can be foreseen as the possible gross investment we may need to make in order to control and develop our water resources. Taking into account the differences between past and present price and cost levels, it appears that the over-all job of providing the principal works and structures needed on our rivers is approximately somewhere between one third and one half completed.

More than $60 billion, or the largest proportion, of the estimated capital outlays still needed for river valley development would go for waterways and port development, flood control, irrigation and hydroelectric power. An outlay of that magnitude would probably approach the ultimate control and development of our rivers now deemed economically feasible for those purposes, but in the end an outlay of such magnitude may not be needed. In the case of irrigation, for example, our future national needs for agricultural land may not require the expansion of crop and pasture acreage by developing through irrigation all of the new lands for which water can now be made available.

On the other hand, roughly one fifth — or about $16.25 billion — of the total estimated capital outlays still needed for river valley development would be for domestic and industrial water supply and pollution abatement, and the outlays that have been estimated for these purposes are undoubtedly less than what will be ultimately needed. As our urban population and industry grow, their needs for water supplies will also increase, as will the volume of municipal and industrial wastes. How much will ultimately be needed for works and facilities will depend, however, on the long-term trend in our population and industrial growth, which it is not yet possible to forecast with certainty.

About two thirds of the total estimated capital outlays still needed for the regulation and use of our water resources would be concentrated in just six of our great river valleys. Two of the six — the Great Lakes-St. Lawrence and the Ohio — lie in the humid eastern part of the nation where water is relatively plentiful, and because of its abundance the needs for works and structures to control it are generally greater than for those to conserve it. Three of the six — the Columbia, the Central of California and the Colorado — lie in the arid and semiarid western part of the nation where water is relatively scarce and carefully planned measures must be taken to meet the needs for conserving it. The remaining one, the Missouri, lies athwart the hundredth meridian, which roughly divides the humid eastern part of the nation from the dry western part, thus making difficult the development of a coordinated plan for the control and use of the waters of the river and its tributaries.

Conclusion

Although vast capital outlays — from both private and public funds — are estimated to be required over the next several decades in order to meet the needs and possibilities for land, forest and water conservation and development, the benefits that would accrue to the nation would be enormous. In terms of immediate dividends, the making of such outlays would contribute to the maintenance of the high level of national economic activity and the continuing expansion of business, investment and employment opportunities that are assumed for the future under the present survey of the Twentieth Century Fund. Beyond these immediate returns, however, are many long-term gains that would accrue. Ensuring the future productivity and better use of one of our most important national assets — our land — would be a primary benefit to every American. Ensuring the future timber supply through better forest management would be an incalculable benefit to the future well-being of the timber products industries, which annually pour lumber and other commodities worth billions of dollars into our national economy. In addition, through better forest management we would have increased watershed protection, more livestock products from the forest range, and greater wildlife and recreational values from our forest lands.

And large as they alone may seem, the private and public capital outlays needed to bring about the full control and development of our river systems would be only the beginning of other large private and public investments that would follow. The protection and further development of agriculture, industry and commerce that would be provided by river works and structures would mean greatly expanded business and employment opportunities and the possibilities of further increases in national and regional levels of living. This would be particularly true in some of our western river valleys, such as the Columbia, where great expansion possibilities still exist.

## PART IV

GOVERNMENT AND FOREIGN TRANSACTIONS

## CHAPTER 18

GOVERNMENT EXPENDITURES

ABOUT ONE OUT OF EIGHT persons employed in the United States in 1950 had a government job. In that year, almost 8 million public employees, including the armed forces, earned $22.1 billion in wages and salaries, roughly 15 per cent of all wages and salaries. By 1952, largely as a result of the defense program, government — federal, state and local — hired more than one out of seven employed Americans and paid $32.5 billion in annual public payrolls. How the public sector of the economy has grown over the past several decades is revealed by the rise in its share of total employment — from less than 5 per cent in 1910 to over 12 per cent in 1950 and over 15 per cent in 1952.

Relation to Gross National Product

The total output of government and private enterprise, represented by the gross national product, increased 176 per cent between 1929 and 1950. This expansion of the economy was the result of two upward trends of different magnitude. The larger proportional rise was in government purchases of goods and services, a growth of 396 per cent from $8.5 billion to $42 billion.[1] Outlays of the private sector rose only 157 per cent, although in absolute amount the increase in this sector was over four times that of the public sector. While the proportion of government purchases of goods and services to total product nearly doubled between these years, government accounted for less than 15 per cent of the 1950 total production. The governmental proportions are affected, of course, by depression and war. At the low point of the depression, the public sector sagged only slightly, while the total product fell to half the 1929 level. During World War II, government purchases of goods and services rose to 46 per cent of the gross

national product, accompanying a huge growth of the private sector. By 1952, after development of the Korean crisis, the government portion had risen again to 22 per cent of gross national product.

Purchases of goods and services alone understate the significance of the public sector of the economy, for they exclude government expenditure in the form of public-to-private transfers, which enter into private transactions reflected in the national product. Total government expenditure grew over fourfold from 1913 to 1929, largely as a result of increased state and local spending, but the proportion it equaled of gross national product increased only from 6 per cent to 10 per cent. In the next twenty-one years, however, the proportion more than doubled to 21 per cent in 1950. In amount, public spending expanded sixfold from 1929 to 1950. In the two years 1950 to 1952, government expenditure grew over 50 per cent. Growing federal expenditure accounted for the larger part of the increase during the last two decades. (See Table 235.)

In prosperous peacetime years the ratio of government revenue to national product moves correspondingly to the expenditure ratio, either being a useful measure of the economic importance of government. During depression and war the expenditure ratio exceeds the revenue ratio because borrowings supplement insufficient government revenue. The recent period of the Korean conflict was an exception; for the first time, huge expenditure was matched, or nearly so, by huge revenue.

International Comparisons

Of all nations, in fiscal 1951, the United States had by far the highest per capita gross national

By WYLIE KILPATRICK, Research Professor of the University of Florida, and ROBERT F. DRURY, Assistant Chief of the Governments Division, U.S. Bureau of the Census. Interpretations and conclusions are those of the authors and are not to be imputed to the Bureau of the Census or to other organizations with which the authors have been or are associated.

[1]. For consistency with wide usage, governmental finance figures in this section are derived from *National Income and Product of the United States, 1929–1950* (1951 National Income Supplement to the *Survey of Current Business*), and *Survey of Current Business*, July 1953. This source permits a consistent use of governmental finance figures, although they differ from the reclassified figures presented elsewhere in this chapter.

TABLE 235. GOVERNMENT EXPENDITURES AS PER CENT OF GROSS NATIONAL PRODUCT,
SELECTED CALENDAR YEARS, 1913–1952

	All Government Expenditures			Government Purchases of Goods and Services		
Year	Total	Federal	State and Local	Total	Federal	State and Local
1913	6.4	1.8	4.6	a	a	a
1919	29.8	26.0	3.8	a	a	a
1929	9.8	2.4	7.4	8.2	1.3	6.9
1932	18.1	5.2	12.9	13.8	2.5	11.3
1937	16.3	7.2	9.1	12.9	5.1	7.8
1942	39.6	34.2	5.4	37.0	32.2	4.8
1945	43.2	39.0	4.2	38.5	34.8	3.7
1950	21.4	14.3	7.1	14.7	7.7	7.0
1952	27.1	20.4	6.7	22.3	15.6	6.7

Sources: 1913 and 1919, W. I. King, *The National Income and Its Purchasing Power*, National Bureau of Economic Research, New York, 1930; 1929 to 1945, *National Income and Product of the United States, 1929–1950* (1951 National Income Supplement to the *Survey of Current Business*); 1950 and 1952, *Survey of Current Business*, July 1953.

a. Not available.

product ($2,023) and the highest per capita national government expenditure.[2] The ratio of national government expenditures to national product was lower in the United States at 15.1 per cent than in eleven of the fourteen other countries for which data were available. (See Table 236.) In general, per capita national product and per capita national government expenditure were correlated; the wealthier countries spent more per capita and the poorer countries less. The ratio of government expenditure to national product tended to be comparatively low in countries with limited armament programs — Denmark, Norway and Portugal, for example.

Exclusion of state and local funds understates government spending more in the United States than in other countries. This omission, however, does not vitiate the contrast. On a per capita basis, total taxes of all units of government were much larger in the United States than in other nations. On the basis of the ratio of taxes to the national product, which is a truer measure of tax weight, the American load was appreciably lower than the loads of Great Britain, France, West Germany, and several smaller nations. The relative tax load was less than the American only

in countries having either small defense expenditures or very meager wealth. Except for the top-heavy debt of Great Britain and the Netherlands, national debt loads were heavier in the United States than in other countries. This is not surprising, since these nations either escaped large war debts or reduced their weight by hyperinflation.

Before World War I, restricted military and welfare expenditure kept total per capita taxes materially lower in the United States than in European countries; and the ratio of American taxes to the national product was correspondingly low. The aftermath of that war raised American costs per capita above the corresponding costs of all other powers except Great Britain. Yet the ratio of taxes to product still continued much lower in the United States than in all but the smaller nations. Even though American tax loads more nearly approached European tax loads during the early 1950s, the principal foreign powers devoted a larger proportion of their economies to government operations than the United States.

MECHANISM OF PUBLIC FINANCING

The impact of government upon the economy can be understood better after outlining the com-

2. As used here, "national" refers to central government exclusive of regional and local units; in the United States, national expenditures are equivalent to federal expenditures.

TABLE 236. INTERNATIONAL COMPARISONS OF PUBLIC FINANCE AND GROSS NATIONAL PRODUCT, FISCAL YEAR 1951

| Country | Gross National Product Per Capita | Per Cent of Gross National Product | | | |
		Taxes of All Governments	National[a] Government Expenditure	Defense Expenditure	National[a] Government Gross Debt
United States	$2,023	22.3	15.1	7.1	83[c]
Canada	1,432	23.1	17.0[b]	4.7	
Denmark	800	19.7	12.4	1.6	42
Iceland	792	19.0[b]	14.9	—	21
Great Britain	779	34.4	27.3	6.7	188
Belgium	760	25.0	24.0	2.9	75
Norway	736	26.1	16.0	2.8	65
France	690	29.8	25.5	7.8	47
Netherlands	529	29.0	24.7	4.2	130
Germany	509	31.0	21.7	4.9	23
Italy	324	20.7	19.3	4.2	34
Austria	308	30.9	34.0	.9	31
Portugal	285	9.7	7.6	2.1	16
Greece	243	16.7	33.7	9.8	10
Turkey	161	17.9	20.1	6.5	18

Source: Division of Statistics and Reports, Mutual Security Administration.

a. "National" refers to the central governmental authority; in the United States it refers to the federal government.

b. Preliminary figure.

c. Not available.

plicated governmental mechanism through which income is collected from and expenditure paid to private business and individuals. In terms of organization, the number, size and functions of government units largely shape the volume and purpose of public spending.

UNITS OF GOVERNMENT

Newspaper headlines tend to identify the federal budget as "the government budget," when in fact government financing in the United States is the composite action of almost 117,000 units of government. The federal government, it is true, accounted for over three fifths, or $42 billion, of the total $69 billion spent by American governments in 1950, but the 48 states spent $11 billion, not counting the fiscal aid they gave to local government, and the 116,694 local units disbursed $16 billion. Thus state and local governments account for nearly two fifths of total public expenditure, and their share is much larger if military spending is eliminated. In 1952 the distribution of government expenditure was even more heavily weighted by the federal share. Of the 1952

total of $101 billion, the federal government accounted for $71 billion, the states for $11 billion and local units for $20 billion.

By far the most numerous of the units through which public expenditure flows are the local school districts. Despite a reduction of more than one third in the number of school districts during the 1940s, there were 67,346 in 1952. Second in number in 1952 were the 17,202 townships or

TABLE 237. NUMBER OF GOVERNMENT UNITS IN THE UNITED STATES, 1942 AND 1952

Type of Unit	1942	1952
Total	155,116	116,743
Federal government	1	1
States	48	48
Counties	3,050	3,049
Townships (or towns)	18,919	17,202
Municipalities	16,220	16,778
School districts	108,579	67,346
Special districts	8,299	12,319

Sources: U.S. Bureau of the Census: *Governmental Units in the United States, 1942,* and *Governments in the United States in 1952.*

TABLE 238. CONCENTRATION OF GOVERNMENT EXPENDITURES,
FISCAL YEARS 1932, 1942 AND 1950 [a]
(Dollar Amounts in Millions)

	1932		1942		1950	
Government Unit	Amount	Per Cent of Total	Amount	Per Cent of Total	Amount	Per Cent of Total
All governments	$13,246	100.0	$50,202	100.0	$69,480	100.0
10 largest spending units	5,723	43.2	41,182	82.0	49,145	70.7
Federal government	4,324	32.6	38,580	76.9	42,175	60.7
New York City	601	4.5	913	1.8	1,529	2.2
Pennsylvania	122	.9	386	.8	1,123	1.6
California	103	.8	200	.4	1,016	1.5
New York State	251	1.9	306	.6	992	1.4
Ohio	67	.5	210	.4	617	.9
Michigan	55	.4	205	.4	514	.7
Illinois	102	.8	182	.4	510	.7
Texas	72	.5	112	.2	344	.5
Washington	26	.2	88	.2	325	.5
All other spending units	7,523	56.8	9,020	18.0	20,335	29.3

Source: See Appendix 18–1.
a. Figures for individual spending units are expenditures for own purposes only; they exclude payments to other governments.

towns of the New England type. These, too, declined numerically during the past decade, chiefly through the withering away of Iowa townships. Almost as numerous but much more important financially were the municipalities, the number of which rose slightly in the 1940s. Special districts, of which there were 12,319 in 1952, have had the largest percentage increase in recent years, mainly because of the emergence of soil conservation districts. County organization, on the other hand, is almost static. During the 1940s the number of county governments decreased by one, to 3,049 — excluding 32 urban governments that perform both county and city functions. (See Table 237.)

Concentration

Although many units of government spend some money, a few spend most of it. Not a few city governments spend more annually than a number of the states. Indeed, New York City's expenditure of $1.5 billion in 1950 exceeded that of any state. Similarly, the transactions of a few large counties and major school and special districts account for a large proportion of the spending by these levels of government. The ten largest spending units accounted for 43 per cent

of all government expenditure in 1932 and for 71 per cent in 1950. (See Table 238.) The comparison, of course, includes the federal government, but even without this dominating entity, expenditure is highly concentrated. The nine largest state and local governments accounted for 16 per cent of state and local expenditure in 1932 and for 26 per cent in 1950. Such concentration parallels the concentration found in private industry; a small minority of large governments determine the trends of public expenditure just as a small minority of corporations shape industrial expenditure trends.

The federal government and the states accounted for 76 per cent of all public expenditure in 1950 and a few hundred local governments were responsible for the larger part of the remainder. This pattern of concentration is modified by the attempt of all three government levels to find suitable areas of administration. Federal and state functions are often decentralized into administrative districts, sometimes without regard to a norm for administrative areas. Small unit operations are frequently centralized either through the supervision of larger units or the transfer of functions to units having more ample resources.

Responsibility

The units that make up the public sector of our economy are more closely tied together financially than those in the private sector. Private organizations influence one another through credit extension, agency and marketing agreements, purchase of assets, interlocking directorates, and the tacit price leadership of big companies. In government, interlevel fiscal aid is the fulcrum by which the federal body exercises a degree of control over the states and the device by which the states make palatable extensive regulation of local units. This combination of aid and supervision makes the 67,346 school districts, in one sense, 48 state units; though not fully centralized, they operate under state control. The states exert similar control over local public assistance, public health and rural highways, but they exercise little or no administrative supervision over urban highways and other local functions. State statutory prescriptions and tax and debt limits, however, channelize and restrict local expenditures for all functions in a way which has no parallel in private enterprise except in credit limitation and chain store arrangements.

Within organization units, public bodies are less centralized than private corporations and companies. Except for a few states and cities, the federal government is the most integrated public organizaton. Even here, repeated efforts at reorganization, best illustrated by the Hoover survey, must be made to retain reasonable integration and control of the vast number of constituent units and activities.[3] Typically, states and counties and, to a lesser degree, cities operate through a number of separate funds and frequently through a composite of semiautonomous boards, comissions and authorities that make over-all budgeting either difficult or impossible. Administrative units at times are so separate as to be almost independent units of government only nominally connected with the parent bodies. Funds often float in a control vacuum, protected from administrative discretion by legislative prohibitions.

Public and private organizations alike have been growing to a size that depersonalizes them; public relations experts and mechanical media of mass communication take the place of personal contact and accountability. Proxy voting in private corporations and nonvoting in government have dulled official responsibility. The managerial class, although not always known by this name, has sprung to prominence in government as in industry. The city manager plan is an instance of successful adaptation of a private business concept to government. However, Robert Moses put his finger on some of the limits to government imitation of private corporations when he said:

I have learned that government is not just another business with the profit motive left out. The electorate is not exactly like a group of stockholders who choose directors to run a corporation, and the Mayor is expected to have qualities quite different from those of a bank president. . . . Capitalism, whose practices government is asked to imitate, has not always been internally healthy and without sin, and it has even been whispered that great corporations have their own diseases paralleling those of government, including politics, deadheads, nepotism, illusions of grandeur, and gout. It is senseless to foul our municipal personnel with unproved charges of general corruption and then demand that better people hurry into government service.[4]

TOOLS FOR ANALYSIS

This analysis aims at comprehensive coverage of all government transactions. In addition to those uniquely public expenditures normally viewed as "general government" activities, it covers social insurance, public debt redemption, public enterprises and public corporations, and the financial transactions of all other publicly created funds.

In determining total public expenditures and receipts, all transactions between governments and the private economy are shown fully so as to report total costs, but transactions between government units are excluded to avoid exaggeration of those costs. For example, interest on the debt of the Reconstruction Finance Corporation and other federal credit agencies is excluded if the debt concerned is owed to the United States Treasury, which concurrently pays interest to the public on the same debt. But if the debt is owed to private investors, the interest is shown as a government cost. Similarly, state aid to local school districts is shown only as a local expenditure and is not repeated as a state expenditure. These criteria correct the distortion of both receipts and disbursements that results from us-

---

3. See reports of the Commission on Organization of the Executive Branch of the (federal) Government (1949).

4. Robert Moses, "The Budget Must Go Up," *Atlantic Monthly*, November 1951, pp. 36-39.

ing net-basis reporting for commercial-type public agencies, and the inflation that would result from combining rather than consolidating transactions of separate government units.[5]

Analysis of government expenditure requires far more than the balance sheets and statements of income and expense used in private enterprise accounting. The classification used for government finance must report public expenditure in terms that at once permit comparison with private business and afford also a comprehensive view of those aspects of public financing that are nonexistent or entirely different in nature in private financing. These seemingly contradictory aims cannot be reconciled by forcing government transactions into a profit and loss framework but only by classifying public finance in different ways that simultaneously record the impact of government upon the economy and the performance of social functions.

Differentiation of Transactions

Consequently, while it is important to include all public financial transactions in a comprehensive analysis of government financing, it is also helpful to separate out those special activities not commonly considered part of "general government." One such activity is the social insurance program, which may be viewed as a distinct category since it is financed not from general taxes but from employer and employee contributions (though the contributors may regard their contributions as taxes). Another distinct category consists of government-run utilities and enterprises, which are financed from sales revenue — or some other price system — rather than taxes. A third group of transactions which may be treated separately is government credit operations. In the federal budget, loans extended and repaid either are obscured in separate corporate accounts or are included in revenue and expenditure on a net basis. Since a loan extended is not a cost but a recoverable asset and a loan repaid is not revenue but a recovered asset, credit transactions have been excluded from revenue and expenditure and shown in separate categories of receipts and disbursements.

5. Similar methods of public finance reporting have been urged by Morris Copeland in his *Concerning a New Federal Financial Statement*, Technical Paper No. 5, National Bureau of Economic Research, New York, December 1947.

Method of Classification

Two complementary methods of classification may be used to fully describe public financial transactions. One of these is a classification by character, which may be viewed as the form in which monies are paid out; the other is a classification by function, which is more closely related to the purpose for which funds are expended.

Character of Expenditure

Public expenditure takes the form of payrolls, current expenditure for materials, supplies and contractual services, expenditure for assistance and insurance benefits, subsidies, capital outlay and interest on debt. It also takes the form of nonexpenditure disbursements such as loans extended by governments to individuals and corporations and the net reduction of public debt, resulting in public-to-private transfers. Through these classes, the outflow of money from the public to the private sector can be traced. Conversely, the inflow of government funds from the private economy is traced by differentiating sources of funds — tax revenues, sales revenues, public borrowings from the private sector, and private repayments of public loans to individuals and corporations.

Classifications of this or a similar nature have long been discussed, but their application has been restricted to some of the more progressive state and local governments. Despite an abundance of detail on spending by character for certain agencies, federal budget classification along these lines generally has lagged behind. Capital outlay, for example, is shown only for public works construction. This analysis not only shows capital outlay for all government levels but also differentiates among types of outlay — new construction, equipment, and purchase of land and structures — that differ in their effect upon the economy.

The separation of one class of outlays — so-called "transfer payments" — from government purchases of goods and services has come into widespread use through national income analysis and is basic to an understanding of the part that governments play in generating or distributing income. Transfer and related payments are here defined as public assistance, pensions, subsistence payments and other cash benefits to veterans, social insurance benefits, subsidies of all types, and interest on war or unproductive debt. Public-to-private transfers are part of the costs of government, of course, and they are paid from taxes and borrowings as are other costs, or from insurance reserve funds. However, since they involve no governmental purchase of goods and services, transfers are merely the redistribution of income through the intermediary of governments. Other public outlays expended, for example, in employing labor, buying materials and equipment, undertaking construction and paying interest on productive debt, are "two-way transactions" in which governments pay money and receive goods and services in exchange. The distinction between the two categories is necessary in measuring income creation as well as the inflationary or deflationary effect of government financing.

Purposes of Expenditure

Governments do not maintain schools merely to pay teachers' salaries, erect buildings or buy chalk. These are simply the ways in which dollars are spent to provide for public education. Aside from social and citizenship objectives, education produces economic effects through increasing the productive capacity of the nation's labor force. Highways require the hiring of workers, purchase of materials, and construction contracts that affect the tempo of business activity, but their long-run economic result is to provide transportation facilities. Classification of public financial transactions in terms of their function is therefore of prime importance; it discloses the purposes for which governments spend money and permits evaluation of how well or indifferently these aims are attained. The functional classification has been designed to embrace the activities — both alike and unlike — of all government levels. Functional classes, it should be noted, comprise both current and capital expenditures for the purposes specified. No attempt has been made, however, to allocate interest expenditure according to the functions for which public debts have been incurred.

FINANCING GOVERNMENT: A SUMMARY PICTURE [6]

Growth is one of the most striking characteristics of government operations today — growth in scale, scope and cost. In four of the five key

6. In this and subsequent sections of this chapter, government expenditures are given for fiscal years ending in the year stated. Data in other chapters of this book generally refer to calendar years.

years reviewed here, government expenditures were obviously swollen by a particular set of emergency conditions — antidepression activities in 1932, "hot" wars in both 1942 and 1952, and a state of "cold war" in 1950. However, underlying the peaks of emergency activity, the role and scale of government has increased steadily through the years.

HISTORICAL TRENDS

Government expenditure for all levels, federal, state and local, was $3.1 billion back in 1913. By 1932, after World War I and a decade of expanding government services in the 1920s, the total was $13.2 billion. In 1942, even though the fiscal year overlapped only partly the beginning of World War II and much greater spending followed shortly after, the expenditure total reached $50.2 billion. The fiscal year 1950 represented a comparatively low period of national defense spending, coming prior to the outbreak of the Korean conflict. However, government expenditure was $69.5 billion in that year, 38 per cent higher than in 1942. Thus in the roughly four-decade period from 1913 to 1950 government expenditure multiplied more than twenty-two times. (See Table 239.) After 1950, expenditure again moved sharply upward, reaching $101.5 billion in 1952.

Sources of Funds

Except in war years, current revenue sources have supplied the bulk of resources for financing government expenditure. The 23-fold expenditure increase from 1913 to 1950 was matched by an increase from $2.9 billion to $67.9 billion in government revenues. By 1952 government revenue had risen still further to $101.1 billion.

New forms of taxation, higher tax rates and expanding tax bases combined to lift tax revenue from $2.2 billion in 1913 to $8.3 billion in 1932, $20.7 billion in 1942, $50.7 billion in 1950, and $79.1 billion in 1952. At the same time, the proportion of taxes yielded by various types of taxation shifted markedly; the percentage of total revenue coming from different sources was as follows:

	1913	1932	1950	1952
Income taxes	1.2	11.2	40.5	50.4
Sales taxes *	21.8	12.4	19.1	15.5
Property taxes	42.4	43.4	10.8	8.6
Other taxes	9.5	9.5	4.2	3.7
Nontax revenue	25.2	23.6	25.3	21.7

* Includes federal customs receipts.

TABLE 239. GOVERNMENT RECEIPTS AND DISBURSEMENTS, FISCAL YEARS
1913, 1932, 1942, 1950 AND 1952
(Millions)

Item	All Governments					Federal				
	1913	1932	1942	1950	1952	1913	1932	1942	1950	1952
Receipts[a]	$3,140	$14,649	$55,096	$80,371	$111,557	$979	$5,924	$43,285	$54,902	$80,018
From other governments	—	—	—	—	—	—	—	—	—	—
Net borrowings[b]	253	3,384	21,817	7,140	6,943	—	2,643	22,457	4,489	3,883
Loans recovered	—	472	3,119	5,338	3,509	—	472	3,119	5,338	3,509
Revenue from own sources	2,887	10,793	30,160	67,893	101,105	979	2,809	17,709	45,075	72,626
Taxes	2,159	8,250	20,677	50,723	79,067	667	1,892	12,150	34,795	59,744
Income	35	1,210	8,525	27,515	50,991	35	1,057	7,977	26,134	49,147
Sales	628	1,334	5,687	12,986	15,689	628	781	3,334	7,832	9,332
Property	1,223	4,681	4,544	7,363	8,652	—	—	—	—	—
Other	273	1,025	1,921	2,859	3,735	4	54	835	829	1,264
Sales of commodities and services	508	1,687	4,600	8,468	11,189	298	745	2,696	4,295	5,786
Social insurance contributions	2	158	3,845	6,310	8,710	—	100	2,540	4,718	5,986
Other revenue	218	698	1,038	2,392	2,139	14	72	323	1,267	1,110
Disbursements[a]	3,051	14,795	53,255	75,926	106,439	990	6,106	42,541	50,759	78,141
To other governments	—	—	—	—	—	14	233	908	2,137	2,585
Net debt reduction[b]	—	—	—	—	—	1	—	—	—	—
Loans extended	—	1,549	3,053	6,447	4,988	—	1,549	3,053	6,447	4,988
Expenditure for own purposes[d]	3,051	13,246	50,202	69,479	101,451	975	4,324	38,580	42,175	70,568

TABLE 239 (continued)

Item	State					Local				
	1913	1932	1942	1950	1952	1913	1932	1942	1950	1952
Receipts[a]	$399	$2,676	$6,929	$14,835	$17,316	$1,868	$7,052	$8,280	$17,258	$21,999
From other governments	3	228	886	2,325	2,485	102	775	1,872	4,299	5,281
Net borrowings[b]	31	241	—	1,178	501	223	500	—	1,473	2,569
Loans recovered	—	—	—	—	—	—	—	—	—	—
Revenue from own sources	365	2,207	6,043	11,330	14,330	1,543	5,777	6,408	11,486	14,149
Taxes	301	1,890	3,903	7,929	9,857	1,191	4,468	4,624	7,999	9,466
Income	c	153	518	1,310	1,751	—	—	30	71	93
Sales	140	553	2,220	4,670	5,730	—	—	133	484	627
Property	161	328	271	307	370	1,083	4,353	4,273	7,056	8,282
Other		856	894	1,642	2,006	108	115	188	388	465
Sales of commodities and services	35	165	687	1,449	1,652	175	777	1,217	2,724	3,751
Social insurance contributions	—	23	1,245	1,475	2,462	2	35	60	117	262
Other revenue	29	129	208	479	359	175	497	507	646	670
Disbursements[a]	381	2,765	5,530	15,133	15,834	1,786	6,927	8,582	16,658	20,249
To other governments	91	770	1,804	4,282	5,044	—	—	46	205	156
Net debt reduction[b]	—	—	195	—	—	—	—	445	—	—
Loans extended	—	—	—	—	—	—	—	—	—	—
Expenditure for own purposes[d]	290	1,995	3,531	10,851	10,790	1,786	6,927	8,091	16,453	20,093

Sources: See Appendix 18–1; 1952 statistics, however, are from *Summary of Governmental Finances in 1952*, U.S. Bureau of the Census.

a. Total receipts and total disbursements for all governments are less than the sum of the separate figures for federal, state and local governments for two reasons: (1) because of the elimination of transfers between levels of government from the "all governments" totals and (2) because net borrowing of particular government levels has been offset by net debt reduction of other government levels in arriving at net borrowing and net debt reduction for the "all governments" totals.

b. See (2) in footnote a above.
c. Included in "other taxes."
d. See Table 240.

These shifts reflect the association of various tax sources with particular levels of government. Thus they show the changing fiscal importance of the federal government (which relies heavily on income taxes) as against state and local governments more than they demonstrate the results of conscious changes in tax policy.

Government revenue from sources other than taxes has also risen to meet the demand of government expenditure growth. Revenue from sales of commodities and services by government rose from $0.5 billion in 1913 to $8.5 billion in 1950 and $11.2 billion in 1952. This growth was influenced by new government economic activities, such as commodity price support, retailing of alcoholic beverages, public housing and public power, expansion of metropolitan transportation, and by the fact that more consumers were paying higher rates for traditional services like the postal service, water supply and municipal electric light and power.

Social insurance revenue, amounting in 1913 to merely $0.2 billion from employee contributions received by retirement systems, grew in thirty-nine years to $8.7 billion received from employers and employees and through earnings on asset accumulation. By 1952, tens of millions of Americans were participating in a wide range of contributory insurance programs affording protection to public and private employees and veterans against the hazards of old age, sickness, accident, unemployment, disability and death.

Despite these increases in collections, government expenditure exceeded government revenue in all five of the years compared here, and borrowing made up the gap. Although the deficits or surpluses for particular levels of government — federal, state or local — partially offset one another in certain of these years, the over-all balance between revenue (excluding borrowing and loan repayments) and expenditure (excluding debt redemption and loan disbursement) was on the deficit side each year. (See Table 239.)

INTERLEVEL TRANSFERS IN 1950[7]

Intergovernmental transfers of funds, which totaled $6.6 billion in 1950, flow predominantly

from state to local governments, particularly since state-to-local flows include federal funds which state governments may, at their discretion, pass on to local governments. This happens when states fix the responsibility for performance of federally aided functions at the local level. Local governments received $4.3 billion in transfers from higher government levels in the 1950 fiscal year. Since $0.2 billion flowed upward to the states, a total gap of some $4.1 billion in local expenditure was financed from state-to-local transfers. State governments spent $12.8 billion from their own sources, but only $10.9 billion for their own functions. The difference represented the net difference between federal and local transfers to states and state aid to local governments. The federal government also spent for its own functions somewhat less than the yield from its own sources of income in 1950 — $42.2 billion compared with $44.3 billion. (See Table 240.)

The contrast between expenditure before and after intergovernmental transfers is especially striking for certain functions. Public welfare expenditure in 1950, excluding veterans pensions, was $1,219 million for the federal government before interlevel transfers, $1,184 million for the states and $292 million for local units. After interlevel transfers totaling $1,998 million were made, direct federal expenditure was merely a trickle of $6 million, while the states spent $1,611 million and the local governments $1,078 million. For transportation, expenditure before and after aid was as follows (in millions):

	Before Transfers	Transfers		After Transfers
		From	To	
Federal	$1,300	$465	—	$ 835
State	2,251	738	$501	2,014
Local	2,200	36	738	2,902

Education, social insurance, and health and community facilities services also were notably affected by intergovernmental transfers, as Table 240 shows. In these areas of governmental activity, the principle of state or local responsibility for administration, with federal or state sharing in responsibility for financing, has been widespread. Other functions are financed and admin-

---

7. Government is treated here as a single sector of the economy in describing over-all levels of government revenue and expenditure. Internal transfers between levels of government have been eliminated, so that the picture presented is of flows of revenue and expenditure from and to the public — i.e., all other sectors of the economy.

This procedure disguises complex flows and counterflows of resources between levels of government, which must be accounted for in analyzing the relative importance of the various levels. Intergovernmental transactions also affect the distribution between the levels of responsibility for financing, on the one hand, and performing, on the other, various public services.

TABLE 240. EFFECT OF INTERLEVEL TRANSFERS ON GOVERNMENT EXPENDITURES IN FISCAL YEAR 1950 BY FUNCTION

(Millions)

Function	Expenditures from Own Sources[a]			Interlevel Transfers			Expenditures for Own Purposes[b]		
	Federal	State[c]	Local[c]	Federal to State and Local[d]	State to Local[c]	Local to State	Federal	State	Local
All functions	$44,312	$12,809	$12,359	$2,137	$4,282	$205	$42,175	$10,852	$16,453
National defense	12,535	38	—	—	—	—	12,535	38	—
International affairs	4,618	—	—	—	—	—	4,618	—	—
Civilian public safety	107	351	1,050	—	39	—	107	312	1,089
Education	3,128	3,663	3,515	68	2,287	9	3,060	1,453	5,793
Public welfare and veterans pensions	3,482	1,649	321	1,213	808	22	2,269	2,076	1,107
Social insurance	4,918	2,090	304	208	22	98	4,710	2,374	228
Health and community facilities	1,311	998	3,158	82	281	29	1,229	828	3,410
Transportation	1,300	2,251	2,200	465	738	36	835	2,014	2,902
Agriculture and natural resources	3,901	382	131	62	7	2	3,839	439	136
Regulation and promotion of business and labor	133	105	33	—	1	—	133	104	34
Postal service	2,223	—	—	—	—	—	2,223	—	—
Liquor stores	—	652	15	—	—	—	—	652	15
Interest on debt	5,853	120	497	—	17	5	5,853	108	509
General control	688	328	683	—	26	—	688	302	709
Other	115	181	455	39	55	5	76	153	522

Source: See Appendix 18-1.

a. Includes expenditure for transfers to other levels but excludes expenditures financed from transfers from other levels.

b. Excludes expenditures for transfers to other levels but includes expenditures financed from transfers from other levels.

c. The sum of $546 million in shared taxes and grants distributed by states to local governments for general financial support without specification as to functional use has been prorated among functions in proportion to local expenditures "for own purposes." The $546 million is distributed functionally as follows (in millions): $37 for civilian public safety; $182 for education; $38 for public welfare and veterans pensions; $8 for social insurance; $117 for health and community facilities; $99 for transportation; $5 for natural resources; $1 for regulation and promotion, etc.; $17 for interest on debt; $26 for general control; and $18 for other.

d. Aside from $17 million paid to Washington, D.C., all federal transfers are treated as paid to state governments for purposes of this analysis.

istered exclusively, or almost exclusively, by a single level of government. Thus the federal government pays for and administers national defense, international affairs and the postal service. The local governments take almost exclusive responsibility for police and fire protection, water supply, sanitation and sewage disposal, metropolitan transit services and local utilities. Other broad public functions are distributed piecemeal among the three levels without any substantial degree of interlevel assistance in financing. This is true particularly of legislative, judicial and general administrative activities, correction activities, regulatory activities, veterans welfare and insurance programs, and recreation.

FEDERAL-STATE-LOCAL EXPENDITURE RELATIONS

The enormous size of federal expenditure for new or enlarged functions, such as national defense, international assistance and the various veterans programs, has obscured the importance of federal participation in financing state and local functions in the last decade. The proportion of federal expenditure devoted to direct aid to state and local government increased from 1.4 per cent in 1913 to 5.1 per cent in 1932. Then it dropped to 2.3 per cent in 1942 and was only 4.8 per cent in 1950. These percentages, all small, reflect changes in the expenditure total more than changes in the extent of federal aid to state and local governments.

Federal Aid

In dollar amounts involved and in the scope of programs, however, the growth of federal aid has been an extremely significant factor in financing state and local government operations. The $14 million of federal aid paid out in 1913 had increased to $2,137 million in 1950 and further to $2,585 million in 1952. Whole new functions of government grew up under the stimulus of federal financial assistance during this period. The miscellany of local and state public welfare programs early in the century changed to an organized srtucture of protection to economically weak classes of the public — the aged, the blind, children and the disabled. All forty-eight states and the District of Columbia established unemployment compensation insurance programs, state-administered but induced and partially financed by the federal government. National programs and national standards developed by state and local action have been achieved

through federal grants for highways, hospitals, health services, vocational education, airports, public works planning and promotion of agriculture.

The growing significance of federal aid to the states is shown by the rise in the ratio of their aid receipts to their gross expenditure from 0.8 per cent in 1913 to 8.2 per cent in 1932 and 15.4 per cent in 1950. On the outgo side, the states for decades have spent a significant proportion of their funds to aid their local units. During the thirty-seven-year period 1913–1950 the states regularly used from one fourth to one third of their gross expenditures for this purpose. The trend in dollar amounts has been from $91 million in 1913 to $4,282 million in 1950.

Effect of Aid on Local Government

Even more than the states, the local units have become increasingly dependent on other levels of government to finance functions they administer. In 1913 only $102 million, or 5.7 per cent, of gross local expenditure was derived from aid received from higher levels. In 1932 the figure was $775 million, or 11.2 per cent; in 1942, $1,872 million, or 23.0 per cent; and in 1950, $4,299 million, or 25.8 per cent. (See Table 241.)

Only the growth of intergovernmental fiscal aid has made it possible for local governments to meet the increased demands on them for services. Local revenue sources tend to be weak and inflexible. Efforts to develop local revenue sources other than the property tax have been successful only in isolated instances. Although adoption of local sales taxes and income or payroll taxes has provided substantial financial relief and additional resources for some local governments, the sum total of all such experience has been negligible. In the best of circumstances, such sources are probably open only to urban communities and can afford little benefit to governments in rural areas. Fiscal aid has kept the administration of such services as education, health and public welfare within the local communities, when otherwise centralization at the state or federal level would have been the only answer. Fiscal aid has been used not only to maintain decentralized responsibility for old functions but also to develop local responsibility for new functions, such as public housing, community redevelopment, public works planning and recently civil defense.

TABLE 241. INTERLEVEL FINANCING OF GOVERNMENT EXPENDITURES,
FISCAL YEARS 1913, 1932, 1942 AND 1950

Government Unit and Year	Expenditures from Own Sources	Plus Interlevel Transfers Received	Equals Gross Expenditures	Less Interlevel Transfers Paid	Equals Expenditures for Own Purposes
	Amount (*Millions*)				
Federal					
1913	$ 989	—	$ 989	$ 14	$ 975
1932	4,557	—	4,557	233	4,324
1942	39,488	—	39,488	908	38,580
1950	44,312	—	44,312	2,137	42,175
State					
1913	378	$ 3	381	91	290
1932	2,537	228	2,765	770	1,995
1942	4,449	886	5,335	1,804	3,531
1950	12,809	2,325	15,133	4,282	10,851
Local					
1913	1,684	102	1,786	—	1,786
1932	6,152	775	6,927	—	6,927
1942	6,265	1,872	8,137	46	8,091
1950	12,359	4,299	16,658	205	16,453
	Per Cent of Federal-State-Local Total				
Federal					
1913	32.4	—	31.3	13.3	32.0
1932	34.4	—	32.0	23.2	32.6
1942	78.7	—	74.6	32.9	76.8
1950	63.8	—	58.2	32.3	60.7
State					
1913	12.4	2.9	12.1	86.7	9.5
1932	19.2	22.7	19.4	76.8	15.1
1942	8.9	32.1	10.1	65.4	7.0
1950	18.4	35.1	19.9	64.6	15.6
Local					
1913	55.2	97.1	56.6	—	58.5
1932	46.4	77.3	48.6	—	52.3
1942	12.5	67.9	15.4	1.7	16.1
1950	17.8	64.9	21.9	3.1	23.6

Source: See Appendix 18–1.

These effective efforts to utilize and sustain the structure of local government and local responsibility tend to be overshadowed by increases in the functions performed at the federal and state levels — functions that cannot be administered at lower government levels, such as national defense and social insurance. Administration of certain older functions has also been shifted from small to large units. Notably, many states have assumed responsibility for additional portions of the highway system and many have taken over the administration of special welfare programs and even occasionally general relief activities.

Fiscal Aid Problems

Fiscal aid is now an integral part of American governmental structure. Without it the local governments particularly could not continue to render service in many important areas of public activity. Basic flaws nevertheless impair the operation of fiscal aid. No satisfactory solution has been found to the problem of separation of responsibility for spending from responsibility for taxing. Furthermore, present methods of distributing federal aid and many programs of state-to-local aid are more likely to favor the well-to-do areas and communities than to equalize aid among areas of varying resources. This results not from conscious discrimination but from disregard of relative need and capacity. Substantial proportions of both federal aid to states and state aid to local governments are distributed either on the basis of percentage matching grants or on the basis of population. Neither basis directly takes into account local need or fiscal capacity.

A second important defect in present patterns of aid distribution is their fragmentizing and haphazard effect on the goal of a balanced program of governmental services. A few states are now experimenting with outright grants to local governments for unrestricted purposes, and many shared tax distributions are of this nature. The bulk of interlevel grants-in-aid, however, is distributed for specific programs, and much of such distribution is on a basis which encourages disproportionate local spending for the aided purpose at the expense of locally financed functions and services. State and local governments have great difficulty in maintaining some degree of balance and proportion between aided and nonaided services and functions. The minor implications of this problem appear in differences in salary scale and other expenditure standards as between functions. Its major implications are reflected in the contrast in the last twenty years between expenditure trends for such unaided activities as police protection, fire protection, sanitation and recreation, on the one hand, and the aided public welfare, education and social insurance, on the other.

Causes of Expenditure Behavior

The rising trend of government expenditure stems from a multitude of interrelated causes. The factors causing expenditure change vary in relative importance from year to year and as between the federal, state and local levels of government. Localized or transitory factors may influence public expenditures in particular communities, but longer-run, more widespread expenditure changes arise from underlying economic, social and political causes of nationwide impact.

Changes in volume and kind of public services, changes in population or in the number of consumers of such services, and changes in the level of prices entering into the production of services are three of the most significant influences on government expenditure behavior. As these factors vary and interact, net increases or decreases in public costs result.

CHANGING PRICES, POPULATION AND SERVICES

Such measurement is applied in military budgeting; for example, hairline estimates of food expenditure requirements are made on the basis of the quantities of different kinds of food served at mess, the number of persons served daily, and the unit prices at which the food is purchased. Application of similar analysis to all functions of government and to total government expenditure requirements is not impossible but must be less exact.

Index of Prices Paid by Government

To measure the results of basic influences shaping expenditure, expenditure of different years must be expressed in dollars of constant buying power. Expression in constant dollars not only reveals the effect of fluctuating price levels on expenditure but also shows other influences without distortion from price changes.[8]

If 1950 prices paid by government are assumed to equal 100, the 1942 government price level equals 58.8, the 1932 level 48.9 and the 1913 level 31.5. Owing to decreases in the buying power of the dollar, a 1950 dollar would have

---

8. Use of any single general price index, however, would seriously distort any such adjustment for prices paid for goods and services by governments. As the Supreme Court observed in a utility rate case, the price index used must be related to the specific class to which it is applied, eliminating price changes unconnected with the category under examination. Therefore, governmental price and cost indexes are required that are specifically related to the kinds and quantities of goods and services purchased by governments, as distinct from the kinds of purchases made by households, manufacturers, farmers or other economic entities. Expenditure figures in constant dollars in this chapter are based on separately applied indexes for 26 distinct classes or items of government expenditure, ranging from four different types of government payrolls to separate classes for each of the various types of social insurance benefits and public assistance categories. The indexes have been separately applied to the various components of expenditure for each function of each government level. This differentiation resulted in separate price indexes for each function as well as a composite price index for aggregate government expenditure, as shown in Table 242. Special indexes used in this chapter were constructed by Owen C. Gretton, Assistant Chief, Industry Division, Bureau of the Census, in consultation with the authors. The component classes and the methodology employed are explained in Appendix 18-2.

TABLE 242. PRICE INDEXES OF GOVERNMENT EXPENDITURES, FISCAL
YEARS 1913, 1932, 1942 AND 1950

	1950 = 100			1913 = 100		
	1913	1932	1942	1932	1942	1950
By Function						
All functions	31.5	48.9	58.8	155.2	186.7	317.5
National defense	31.5	41.4	55.6	131.4	176.5	317.5
International affairs	26.3	43.2	58.5	164.3	222.4	380.2
Civilian public safety	43.5	47.7	57.9	109.7	133.1	229.9
Education	25.4	48.4	57.7	190.6	227.2	393.7
Public welfare and veterans pensions	34.1	50.3	56.0	147.5	164.2	293.3
Social insurance	71.4	93.7	73.2	131.2	102.6	140.1
Health and community facilities	28.9	40.2	56.8	139.1	196.5	346.0
Transportation	28.9	42.1	62.6	145.7	216.6	346.0
Agriculture and natural resources	30.4	41.3	66.2	135.9	217.7	328.9
Regulation and promotion of business and labor	42.9	49.5	55.6	115.4	129.6	233.1
Postal service	27.2	46.5	55.7	171.0	204.8 [a]	367.6 [a]
Liquor stores	—	—	60.9	—		
Interest on debt	116.1	139.6	117.4	120.2	101.1	86.1
General control	36.0	43.7	57.3	121.4	159.2	277.8
Other	32.2	41.0	57.9	127.3	179.8	310.6
By Character						
Total	31.5	48.9	58.8	155.2	186.7	317.5
Payrolls	31.0	53.8	51.6	173.5	166.5	322.6
Military	37.0	42.5	41.3	114.9	111.9	270.3
Other	30.5	54.5	55.7	178.7	182.6	327.9
Supplies, materials and contractual services	43.2	39.8	61.0	92.1	141.2	231.5
Assistance and insurance benefits to individuals	35.0	59.8	60.9	170.9	174.0	285.7
Agricultural, business and international subsidies	—	—	62.2	—	[a]	[a]
Capital outlay	22.5	35.3	57.5	156.9	255.6	444.4
Construction	21.2	35.4	57.7	167.0	272.2	471.7
Other	29.0	35.2	57.4	121.4	197.9	344.8
Interest on debt	116.1	139.6	117.4	120.2	101.1	86.1

Source: See Appendices 18–1 and 18–2.   a. Not computed.

bought for government only 58.8 cents worth of goods and services in 1942 and the cited amounts in 1932 and 1913. (See Table 242.) Essentially this price series, based on 1950 as 100, answers the question: What would the services rendered in 1913, 1932 and 1942 have cost at 1950 price levels? [9]

9. Since the earliest year is often used as the base for indexes, Table 242 also shows the governmental price indexes on a 1913 base. Roughly, this price series answers the question: What would the services rendered in 1932, 1942 and 1950 have cost at 1913 price levels? If 1913 prices equal 100, a 1913 government dollar would have bought $1.55 worth of goods and services in 1932, or $1.87 worth in 1942, or $3.18 worth in 1950. The index

Effect of Price and Cost Changes

The composite indexes of prices paid by governments vary widely in application to different public functions, owing to differences in the composition of government expenditure as between functions. A 1913 educational dollar would have

series based on 1950 is a closer fit to government prices than the series based on 1913 because generally the types of goods and services purchased by governments in 1913, 1932 and 1942 were also purchased in 1950. The index based on 1913, which is merely an arithmetic reversal of that based on 1950, makes no specific allowance for 1913 prices of kinds of expenditure not undertaken by government until 1932, 1942 or 1950.

bought $3.94 worth of service in 1950, but a 1913 dollar for interest on debt would have purchased only $0.86 worth in 1950. Stated conversely, a 1950 transportation dollar would have bought merely $0.29 of service in 1913, while a 1950 social insurance dollar would have bought $0.71 of service in that year. A 1913 construction dollar would have purchased $4.72 of construction in 1950, but a 1913 dollar for current supplies would have bought only $2.32 worth in 1950.

The effect of price fluctuation on government expenditure varies between federal, state and local governments because each level purchases different proportions of the various kinds of goods and services to perform the functions for which it is responsible. These differences are sufficiently important to affect the expenditure level materially. Looking backward, the buying power of the 1950 governmental dollar varied in 1932 from 45 cents for state government to 56 cents for federal civilian government and in 1913 from 37 cents for states to 27 cents for federal civilian functions. For the different levels of government, the buying power of the 1950 governmental dollar in three key years was as follows:

	1913	1932	1942
All governments	$ .32	$ .49	$ .59
Federal			
National defense	.32	.41	.56
Other functions	.27	.56	.63
State	.37	.45	.63
Local	.33	.48	.61

The influence of prices, population and services can be isolated for separate measurement only by assuming that the particular factor under consideration changes while the other two remain constant. In this manner dollar values can be allocated to the effect of each of the three causes alone without reference to other causes. Since, in fact, all three are changing simultaneously, part of the expenditure growth or decline results from the interaction of prices, population and services. That part represents the expenditure change remaining after the separate influence of each of the three factors is measured.

The effect of price changes was of less importance in earlier years and of more influence in recent years than is commonly appreciated. By 1932, rising price levels added $1,443 million to total governmental expenditures of $3,050 million in 1913. Although this represented a growth of nearly one half from price changes alone, other factors were more significant, so that price changes accounted for only 14 per cent of the total expenditure rise during this period. During the next ten years, 1932 to 1942, price changes added more in amount ($3,314 million) but less in proportion to the total growth in public cost (only 9 per cent).

Rising price levels were by far the most important reason for expenditure increases from 1942 to 1950 and affected all functions. If price changes had been the only influence at work in this period, total expenditure would have been higher by $35 billion in 1950 than in 1942. Only decreases in many services, particularly the cutbacks in national defense and foreign assistance programs, held down the actual expenditure growth to $19.3 billion. (See Table 243.)

Price changes do not, of course, affect all functions uniformly in each time period. Significant differences among functions are illustrated by national defense and other services. The decrease in defense spending after World War II more than compensated for price level increases from 1942 to 1950. What is apt to be overlooked is that the truncated defense program of 1950 cost 80 per cent more than the same program would have cost in 1942. In contrast, the social insurance program in 1950 cost less than 40 per cent more than a program of the same scale would have cost in 1942. During the 1930s the variation among functions was even more pronounced. In both periods, interest prices — that is, the interest rate — moved opposite to the general price trend; its decline exerted a negative influence on interest expenditure. The relatively small minus factor was, of course, overcome by the soaring public debt, so that interest expenditure mounted, though at a lesser rate than volume of debt.

Price changes over the entire 1913–1950 time span made government expenditures total $69 billion in 1950 instead of the $22 billion the same public services would have cost in 1913 dollars. In reverse, if paid for in 1950 dollars, the 1913 expenditure would have been nearly $10 billion instead of $3 billion. Expenditures during this thirty-seven-year span multiplied only sevenfold in constant dollars but over twenty-two times when measured in current dollars. When price changes are wiped out, the 1930s emerge as the decade of the most significant expenditure expansion. Indeed, expenditure in constant dollars declined materially from 1942 to 1950. (See Table 244.)

TABLE 243. ROLE OF PRICE CHANGES, POPULATION GROWTH AND EXPANSION OF SERVICES IN ACCOUNTING FOR GROWTH OF GOVERNMENT EXPENDITURE, SELECTED FISCAL PERIODS, 1913–1950

(Dollar Amounts in Millions)

Function and Time Period	Amount of Expenditure Change	Amount Resulting from:				Percentage Distribution			
		Price and Cost Changes	Population Changes	Expansion of Services	Interaction of Prices, Population and Services	Price and Cost Changes	Population Changes	Expansion of Services	Interaction of Prices, Population and Services
1913–1932									
All functions	$10,196	$1,443	$ 867	$ 4,176	$ 3,708	14.2	8.5	41.0	36.4
National defense	511	83	75	195	158	16.2	14.7	38.2	30.9
International affairs	14	3	1	4	6	21.4	7.1	28.6	42.9
Civilian public safety	552	19	55	336	142	3.4	10.0	60.9	25.7
Education	1,838	510	160	419	749	27.7	8.7	22.8	40.8
Public welfare and social insurance	1,273	119	72	571	511	9.3	5.7	44.9	40.1
Health and community facilities	1,030	144	105	415	366	14.0	10.2	40.3	35.5
Transportation	2,172	228	142	927	875	10.5	6.5	42.7	40.3
Agriculture and natural resources	268	22	18	127	101	8.2	6.7	47.4	37.7
Postal service	525	191	76	93	165	36.4	14.5	17.7	31.4
Interest on debt	1,308	38	53	782	435	2.9	4.1	59.8	33.3
Other functions	703	86	110	307	200	12.2	15.7	43.7	28.4
1932–1942									
All functions	36,956	3,314	937	22,960	9,745	9.0	2.5	62.1	26.4
National defense	23,804	266	55	16,185	7,298	1.1	.2	68.0	30.7
International affairs	5,038	7	1	3,420	1,610	.1	—	67.9	32.0
Civilian public safety	89	160	53	−108	−16	75.1[a]	24.9[a]	—	—
Education	299	461	170	−300	−32	73.1[a]	26.9[a]	—	—
Public welfare and social insurance	2,233	73	108	1,998	54	3.3	4.8	89.5	2.4
Health and community facilities	1,010	577	99	182	152	57.1	9.8	18.0	15.0

(Continued on page 594)

TABLE 243 (continued)

Function and Time Period	Amount of Expenditure Change	Amount Resulting from: Price and Cost Changes	Population Changes	Expansion of Services	Interaction of Prices, Population and Services	Percentage Distribution Price and Cost Changes	Population Changes	Expansion of Services	Interaction of Prices, Population and Services
1932–1942 (continued)									
Transportation	$ 714	$ 1,301	$ 189	$ −559	$ −217	87.3[a]	12.7[a]	—	—
Agriculture and natural resources	2,478	199	23	1,332	924	8.0	.9	53.8	37.3
Postal service	80	157	56	−122	−11	73.7[a]	26.3[a]	—	—
Interest on debt	696	−238	106	919	−91	—	10.3[a]	89.7[a]	—
Other functions	515	351	77	13	74	68.2	15.0	2.5	14.4
1942–1950									
All functions	19,277	35,120	6,126	−10,068	−11,901	85.1[a]	14.9[a]	—	—
National defense	−12,006	19,639	2,999	−18,356	−16,288	—	—	53.0[b]	47.0[b]
International affairs	−439	3,587	617	−2,652	−1,991	—	—	57.1[b]	42.9[b]
Civilian public safety	673	607	102	−57	21	83.2[a]	14.0[a]	—	2.9[a]
Education	7,665	1,979	329	2,340	2,957	26.0	4.3	30.8	38.9
Public welfare and social insurance	9,002	2,487	459	3,726	2,330	27.6	5.0	41.4	25.9
Health and community facilities	3,059	1,831	294	358	576	59.9	9.6	11.7	18.8
Transportation	2,365	2,021	413	−176	107	79.5[a]	16.3[a]	—	4.2[a]
Agriculture and natural resources	1,665	1,434	343	−205	33	79.2[a]	19.0[a]	—	1.8[a]
Postal service	1,349	695	107	228	319	51.5	7.9	16.9	23.6
Interest on debt	4,279	−324	267	4,577	−241	—	5.5[a]	94.5[a]	—
Other functions	1,785	1,164	196	149	276	65.2	11.0	8.3	15.5

Source: See Appendix 18-1.

a. Percentage distribution of increases only.
b. Percentage distribution of decreases only.

TABLE 244. GOVERNMENT EXPENDITURES IN CURRENT AND CONSTANT
DOLLARS, FISCAL YEARS 1913, 1932, 1942 AND 1950

| | Total | | | Index (1913=100) | |
| | Current Dollars | 1913 Dollars | 1950 Dollars | Current Dollars | Constant Dollars |
Year					
	(Billions)				
1913	$ 3.1	$ 3.1	$ 9.7	100	100
1932	13.2	8.5	27.1	426	280
1942	50.2	26.9	85.4	1,619	882
1950	69.5	21.9	69.5	2,242	717

Source: See Appendix 18–1.

Population Growth

A public or private business, even if it remains stationary in other respects, is affected by changes in the population it serves. Changes in the number of public or private consumers do not affect all public functions or all sales of private business alike. Thus internal shifts in the age distribution of the population may call for larger or smaller changes in expenditure for education of the young or care of the aged than are indicated by the growth of the total population.[10]

In the absence of separate measures of the effect of population upon each function, this analysis applies the percentage increase of total population uniformly to all functions.[11] Population growth had the least effect of the influences under examination. From 1932 to 1942, a period of relatively small population growth, the increase of population accounted for merely 2.5 per cent of the total expenditure rise. From 1913 to 1932, population expansion accounted for 8.5 per cent of total expenditure growth, while from 1942 to 1950 population increase was responsible for 14.9 per cent of the rise in government expenditure.

10. Population growth obviously is unrelated to the introduction of new functions like atomic energy production, or to the declaration and cessation of war, or to the invention of new transportation facilities like aircraft and the decline of old ones like canals, or to assistance to foreign nations having different populations and needs. Education provides a striking example: enrollment in elementary and secondary schools declined from 1930 to 1950, while collegiate enrollment rose at a much higher rate than population.

11. A serious error would result if population changes were a major influence on all government expenditure, as they are in rapidly changing communities; but in the United States as a whole, population change is a minor influence.

New and Expanded Services[12]

Growth in scope of services was the most important cause of government expenditure increases from 1913 to 1942. In contrast, total public services underwent a net decrease between 1942 and 1950; increases in some functions were more than balanced by decreases in others. Between 1913 and 1932 new and expanded services added $4.2 billion to the 1913 public spending of $3.1 billion. The amounts by which education, highways, interest on debt and other functions grew accounted for 41 per cent of the expenditure rise during this period.

An even larger proportion, or 62 per cent, of the rise from 1932 to 1942 can be attributed to expansion of services alone. This was a period of new kinds of spending of unprecedented magnitude for welfare, social insurance and natural resources, a period of conscious effort to counteract reduced private spending by larger public outlays. With the approach of World War II, national defense and foreign aid added further to governmental activities. However, several important services declined in magnitude or were relatively stationary from 1932 to 1942. Adjusted

12. The share of cost increase attributable to larger services may be derived from the total expenditure increase and the estimated rises in the price level and in population. For example, if expenditures had increased 98 per cent between two years and if prices had risen 50 per cent and population 10 per cent, then the increase attributable to new or expanded services (x) would be computed from the equation $(1.5)(1.1)(x) = 1.98$. This would yield a value of 1.2 for x and would imply that 20 per cent of the increase came from new or expanded services. The remaining 18 per cent would be attributable to the interaction of the three separate factors. (See p. 597.) The accuracy of the measure of change in service clearly depends upon the accuracy of the measures of price levels and population.

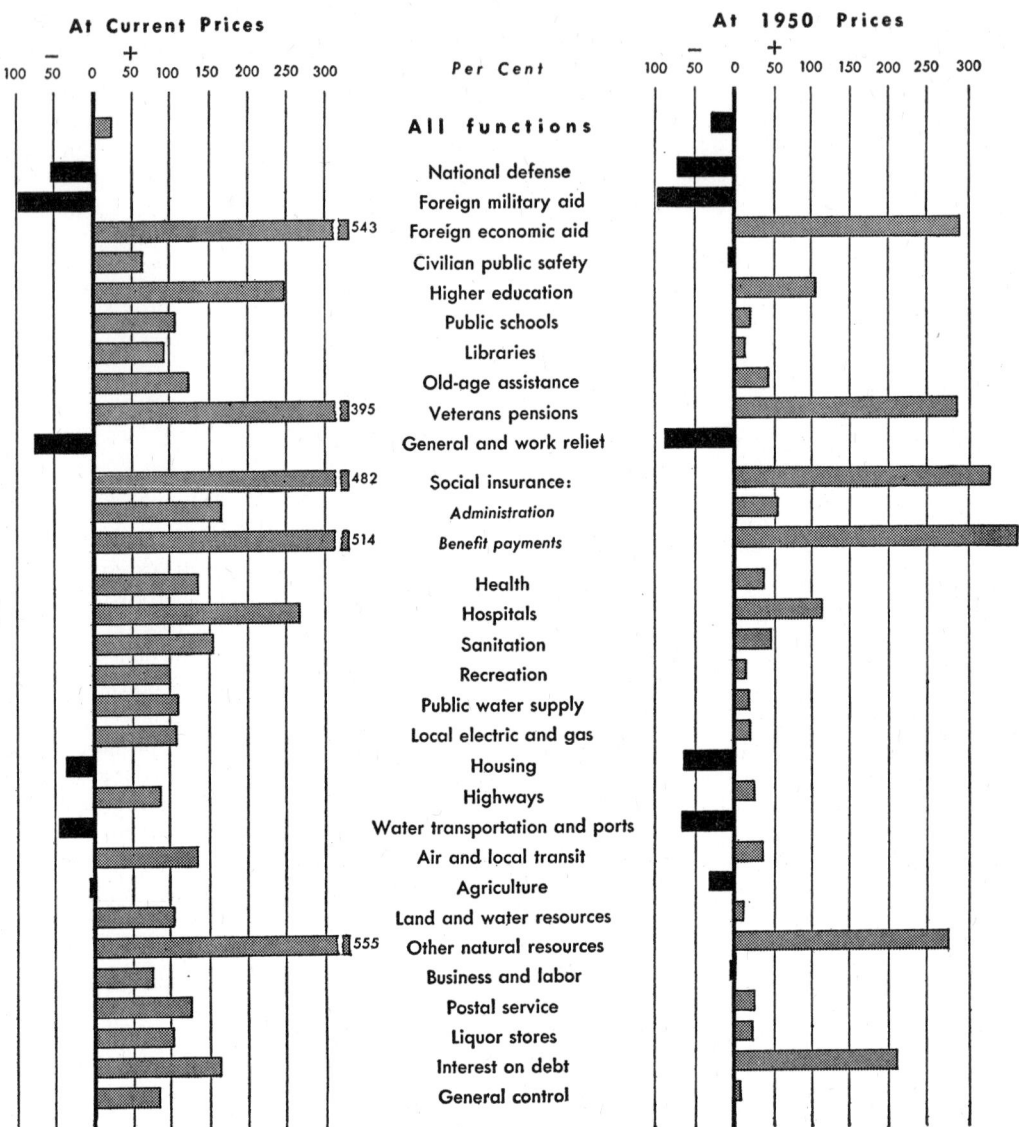

FIGURE 69. PERCENTAGE CHANGE IN PER CAPITA GOVERNMENT EXPENDITURES FOR SELECTED FUNCTIONS, 1942 TO 1950

Source: See Appendix 18–1.

to constant population and price levels, education, civilian public safety, transportation and postal services all dropped off. Only relatively small increases were registered for general control, health, hospitals and other community services.

None of the increase in total expenditure during the 1940s can be imputed to expansion of services. Even though expenditures for several important functions rose more than could be attributed to price and population increases, reductions in other services brought a decrease in total government expenditure in terms of constant dollars and constant population. In addition to the postwar decrease in activities connected with national defense and international affairs, declines occurred in the fields of civilian public safety, transportation and natural resources. Expansion of services was marked for welfare and social insurance, education and interest on debt; and the increase was not unimportant for health, hospitals and other community services, the postal service and general control.

The simplest way of expressing changes in the real volume of services is to state expenditures in per capita terms and in constant dollars. Comparison of costs per capita in current dollars eliminates the population factor, while comparison of costs per capita in constant dollars eliminates not only the population factor but also price fluctuations. In current dollars, changes in per capita expenditures during the 1940s ranged from a 481 per cent increase for social insurance to a 54 per cent decrease for national defense. In constant dollars, per capita expenditures of major categories ranged from a rise of 326 per cent for social insurance between 1942 and 1950 to a decline of 75 per cent for national defense.

In a number of functions, per capita cost increases in current dollars became decreases in constant dollars. Thus civilian public safety rose 61 per cent in current dollars but declined 7 per cent in constant dollars; transportation was up 51 per cent in current dollars but down 5 per cent in constant dollars; and natural resources, although rising 40 per cent in current dollars, shrank 7 per cent in constant dollars. (See Figure 69.) Swings were more extreme for individual functions than for major categories, thereby showing how unlike are the trends in functional components of total expenditure.

Prices-Population-Services Interaction

Prices, population and services do not act alone but, in fact, interact in such a manner as to account for an important part of expenditure changes. Price rises take place simultaneously with population growth and expansion of the volume of government services. Accordingly, the rise in price levels affects not only the cost of customary services but also the cost of performing new or enlarged services. Similarly, population growth calls not only for a broadening of old services but also for an expansion of new added services.

The interaction of prices, population and services was most important from 1913 to 1932. Over one third of the total expenditure growth in this period was due to this multiple cause. In the following ten years over one fourth of the total rise in spending can be assigned to the interaction of the three factors. For seven of the major functions, however, the result of interaction was negative or minor because decreases in service volume cancelled the effect of price increases. From 1942 to 1950, interaction was important in expenditure increase where service volume rose, as in education, welfare and social insurance, and negative in effect for national defense, foreign affairs and other functions for which service volume decreased. For total government expenditure, the effect of interaction was negative in this period. A negative effect measures the extent of saving over and above that resulting from curtailment of services, that is, the amount of price increase that would have applied to the eliminated services had they been continued.

Summary

Over the entire time span from 1913 to 1950, expansion of services was the number one influence on expenditure growth, accounting for two fifths of the total increase. Price change was number two, inducing three tenths of the growth. Interaction of service expansion, prices and population growth contributed one fifth of the expenditure increase, and population change alone accounted for 7 per cent. The effect of the four influences during the period from 1913 to 1950 is not represented by the sum of the changes during each of the three component periods set forth in Table 243. Because of problems of weighting, it is necessary to compute the changes directly over the entire period. Conceiving of the thirty-seven-year period as a whole, the dollar values attributable to each of these influences and the percentage distribution of responsibility for expenditure increase among the factors may be summarized as follows:

	Amount (Millions)	Percentage Distribution
1913 expenditure	$ 3,051	—
1950 expenditure	69,479	—
Expenditure increase	66,428	100.0
Higher prices alone	20,736	31.2
Increased population alone	4,602	6.9
Larger services alone	27,136	40.9
Three factors interacting	13,953	21.0

The causes of expenditure behavior may be examined not only in terms of dollars but also in terms of the physical volume of services back of the dollars. The costs of social insurance and public assistance have grown hugely, primarily because of the large increase in the number of beneficiaries of welfare programs. Growth of payments per beneficiary, although large in current dollars, has contributed little to the cost growth in constant dollars. In contrast, the number of pupils enrolled in public schools declined from 1932 to 1950, while school expenditure rose 143 per cent. For most functions, costs per unit of work (per beneficiary, per pupil, and the like), although materially larger in current dollars, have not risen sufficiently in constant dollars to account for more than a minor part of expenditure growth.

Nature of Measurements

Physical measurements are not as yet applicable to all public services, and for some the measures are experimental or nationwide data are not available. In some cases, however, a relatively simple single measure of service volume can cover all the service involved in a given major function. Pupils in school attendance, road mileage and welfare case loads, if classified by type, fairly represent such functions. Other services by nature can best be reported according to a number of work classes. Services of the Bureau of Internal Revenue, for example, involve the number of tax returns received and processed, the number of audits and investigations of tax returns, cases of interpreting revenue laws, extra efforts to collect delinquent taxes, conferences with and appeals from taxpayers, and field inspections to ferret out tax law violations. Similarly, the Forest Service performs multiple services in administering forest areas and in promoting state and private forestry.

Because of space limitations, however, some of these activities are only represented rather than covered exhaustively. The most significant single measure has been chosen in such instances rather than a wide range of alternative measures. Data for different years for a particular activity may be only approximately comparable by reason of changes in the character or quality of work performed. For example, the kind of highway miles constructed before the day of heavy-duty superhighways differs tremendously from the kind of highway miles constructed in recent years.[13]

Military Services

The few military trend series that can be constructed reveal the alternating expansion and contraction of military services better than dollar figures alone. In terms of the number of men and women in uniform, plus the number of civilians employed, the military forces expanded 553 per cent between 1932 and 1950 despite a drop of 84 per cent during the postwar demobilization period 1945–1950. (See Table 245.)

Years ago, before military equipment and operations became highly mechanized, this measure would have been sufficient to indicate changes in the scale of military services. With mechanization, other indexes must be sought, such as growth in the number of aircraft, especially of large expensive types, or rise in the number and tonnage of ships. Nevertheless, total payrolls and allowances had risen so sharply by 1950, as a result of increased pay per person in the service, as to account for a larger part of total military expenditure than during the war. Total military cost per member of the armed forces — including outlays for equipment and services — was slightly less in 1950 than during World War II, despite inflation in the price level. In constant (1950) dollars, this unit cost of 1950 was only 58 per cent of the cost in 1945, when spending on equipment was high.

Social Insurance and Public Assistance

More comprehensive measures are available for social insurance and public assistance than for

---

13. Cost units are often used in more or less successful attempts to measure efficiency, but measures of efficiency or inefficiency cannot be derived from the kind of service volume and unit-cost figures developed here. The engineering concept of efficiency originally contrasted energy input with energy output. As employed by economists, efficiency has stood for the ratio between production effort and production results. Applied to government services, efficiency means securing the greatest possible results from given costs or obtaining a given level of results at the lowest possible cost. Whichever way the cost-result ratio is stated, it involves reference to standards of cost and service against which to measure actual expenditure and performance. Such standards are outside the scope of this analysis. Even the question of relative efficiency from year to year, disregarding differences in performance standards, would not be answered on the basis of unit costs that do not cover all factors of input and output.

TABLE 245. PHYSICAL VOLUME AND COST OF MILITARY SERVICES,
FISCAL YEARS 1932, 1942, 1945 AND 1950

Item	1932	1942	1945	1950	Index (1942 = 100)		
					1932	1945	1950
Number in service (*thousands*)	348	4,745	14,416	2,272	7.3	303.8	47.9
Military	251	3,968	11,608	1,513	6.3	292.5	38.1
Civilian	97	777	2,808	759	12.5	361.4	97.7
Ships and craft of U.S. Navy							
Total number	598	2,673	10,120	4,297	22.4	378.6	160.8
Total tonnage (*thousands*)	2,052	2,694	11,817	8,413	76.2	438.6	312.3
Number of aircraft							
U.S. Navy	1,066	5,260	36,721	14,015	20.3	698.1	266.4
U.S. Air Force [a]	1,689	20,808	29,396	8,700	8.1	141.3	41.8
Expenditure (*millions*) [b]							
Pay and allowances	$ 392	$ 3,735	$27,692	$ 6,213	10.5	741.4	166.4
Total military purposes	756	24,545	84,569	12,535	3.1	344.6	51.1
Cost per member in service							
Pay and allowances							
Current dollars	1,126	787	1,921	2,735	143.1	244.1	347.5
Constant (1950) dollars	2,489	1,728	2,736	2,735	144.0	158.3	158.3
Total military purposes							
Current dollars	2,172	5,173	5,866	5,517	42.0	113.4	106.7
Constant (1950) dollars	5,256	9,304	9,405	5,517	56.5	101.1	59.3

Source: See Appendix 18–1.

a. Consists of first-line aircraft. Column for 1932 presents 1934 data and that for 1945 reports 1946 data.
b. Excludes military commissaries and exchanges.

military services. Units of performance here consist of numbers of program beneficiaries, that is, insurance beneficiaries, military pensioners, retired or disabled employees, or public assistance cases. Social insurance and public assistance are two of the principal areas of government expansion in the past two decades, owing largely to programs initiated in the depression of the 1930s. Begun in 1933, federal work relief programs reached a peak in 1938 when 4.1 million people were given employment, and ended in 1942 when under 1 million were employed. Emergency measures gave way to more permanent programs in the Social Security Act of 1935: federally aided public assistance, which was extended to 2.5 million cases in 1942 and to 3.5 million in 1950; old-age and survivors insurance, which was paid to 0.5 million persons in 1942 and to 3.1 million in 1950; and state unemployment compensation, which benefited 2.8 million persons in 1942 and 5.2 million in 1950. Two world wars raised veterans insurance benefits to their present substantial levels. Meanwhile governments came to recognize an obligation to provide their own employees with retirement, disability and survivors insurance. These changes are traced to 1950 in Table 246.[14]

For nearly all insurance and assistance programs, expenditure increases have exceeded increases in volume of services as measured by number of beneficiaries. Between 1942 and 1950, total benefits paid to retired federal civil service employees rose 152 per cent, while the number of beneficiaries increased 124 per cent. Similarly, living veterans received pensions of $420 million in 1932 and $1,524 million in 1950, but this cost increase of 266 per cent accompanied a rise of only 138 per cent in the number of pensioners (from 994,000 to 2,368,000). Huge as was the growth of service volume for social insurance

14. This table adjusts payments per beneficiary according to the Bureau of Labor Statistics consumers' price index in order to gauge the effect of rising price levels on the purchasing power of benefits. In contrast, the other tables expressing expenditure in constant dollars are based on indexes measuring the price level effect on costs to governments. (See Appendix 18–2.)

TABLE 246. BENEFICIARIES AND PAYMENTS PER BENEFICIARY OF SELECTED SOCIAL INSURANCE, PUBLIC ASSISTANCE AND WORK RELIEF PROGRAMS, CALENDAR YEARS 1932, 1942 AND 1950 (*Number of Beneficiaries in Thousands*)

Type of Program	Number of Beneficiaries			Payment per Beneficiary					Percentage Change, 1942–1950		
				Current Dollars			1950 Dollars			Cost per Beneficiary	
	1932	1942	1950	1932	1942	1950	1932	1942	Number of Beneficiaries	Current Dollars	1950 Dollars
	On Basis of Annual Benefits and Total Number of Beneficiaries during Year										
Federal civil service retirement system[a]	25.6	69.1	155.1	$ 920	$ 943	$1,060	$1,619	$1,391	124.5	12.4	−23.8
Military pensions to:											
Living veterans	994.4	623.7	2,368.2	424	514	644	746	757	279.7	25.3	−14.9
Dependents of deceased veterans	334.3	312.0	991.2	372	355	490	655	524	217.7	38.0	−6.5
Unemployment insurance											
State programs	b	2,815.1	5,211.9	b	122	264	b	180	85.1	116.4	46.7
Railroad	b	39.3	205.0	b	159	292	b	235	421.6	83.6	24.3
	On Basis of Annual Benefits and Average Monthly Number of Beneficiaries										
Retirement insurance											
Old-age and survivors	b	322.8	1,918.1	b	249	375	b	367	494.2	50.6	2.2
Railroad	b	114.1	174.8	b	803	1,012	b	1,183	53.2	26.0	−14.5
Federal civil service	b	51.1	111.0	b	1,041	1,219	b	1,535	117.2	17.1	−20.6
State and local government	b	126.7	213.0	b	911	1,033	b	1,343	68.1	13.4	−23.1
Disability insurance											
Veterans	b	581.1	2,301.8	b	510	728	b	752	296.1	42.7	−3.2
Railroad	b	39.7	76.0	b	787	1,017	b	1,160	91.4	29.2	−12.3
Federal civil service	b	18.0	43.0	b	828	942	b	1,220	138.9	13.8	−22.8
State and local government	b	16.3	32.0	b	699	750	b	1,031	96.3	7.3	−27.3
Survivorship insurance											
Old-age and survivors	b	217.4	1,093.9	b	192	274	b	283	403.2	42.7	−3.2
Railroad	b	3.7	136.3	b	433	322	b	639	3,583.8	−25.6	−49.6
State and local government	b	28.2	40.0	b	628	650	b	925	41.8	3.5	−29.7
Veterans	b	316.4	991.7	b	351	496	b	518	213.4	41.3	−4.2
Public assistance[e]											
Old-age assistance	107.0	2,227.0	2,786.0	244	267	525	429	394	25.1	96.6	33.2
Aid to dependent children (families)	112.0	348.0	651.0	362	455	847	636	671	87.1	86.2	26.2
Aid to the blind	25.0	79.0	97.0	234	312	543	411	460	22.8	74.0	18.0
General assistance	3,347.0	460.0	413.0	228	393	715	402	579	−10.2	81.9	23.5
Federal work relief[d]	787.0	601.0	—	971	965	—	1,743	1,423	−100.0	—	—

(*Notes on page 601*)

TABLE 247. PERCENTAGE CHANGE IN NUMBER OF BENEFICIARIES PER 1,000 POPULATION
UNDER PUBLIC INSURANCE AND ASSISTANCE PROGRAMS, 1942 TO 1950

Percentage Increase					
Over 300	200 to 300	100 to 200	50 to 100	Under 50	Percentage Decrease
Old-age and survivors insurance: retirement	Pensions for living veterans	Dependents of deceased veterans	Railroad disability	Railroad retirement	General assistance (19.6)
Old-age and survivors insurance: survivors	Veterans disability	Federal civil service disability	Unemployment insurance: state programs	State and local retirement	Federal work relief (100)
Railroad survivors		Survivors of veterans	Federal civil service retirement	State and local survivors	
Unemployment insurance: railroad			State and local disability	Old-age assistance	
			Aid to dependent children	Aid to blind	

Source: Table 246.

in the period 1942–1950, the size of benefit expenditure rose even faster; old-age and survivors insurance retirement grew 494 per cent in number of beneficiaries and 795 per cent in benefits paid.

The number of beneficiaries of insurance and welfare programs has grown more rapidly than the total population. Between 1932 and 1942, however, the number of beneficiaries per 1,000 population decreased in the case of veterans pensions, federal work relief and general assistance. In the 1940s, decreases were confined to general assistance and the elimination of work relief, although the volume of old-age assistance and aid to the blind rose by only one tenth. Otherwise, volume of services in relation to population expanded by large percentages, soaring by

Source: See Appendix 18–1. The Bureau of Labor Statistics index of consumers' prices (adjusted to a 1950 base) was used to adjust 1932 and 1942 payments to 1950 dollars.

a. Includes both retirement insurance and disability.

b. Programs nonexistent in 1932 or data not available.

c. Data in 1932 columns are for 1933. Numbers of beneficiaries are for December of reported years.

d. Data in 1932 columns are for 1934. Beneficiaries and payments are on a full-time equivalent basis.

433 per cent in the case of old-age and survivors insurance. (See Table 247.)

Government Enterprises

Utilities and other government business enterprises warrant separate attention because they are financed largely, although not necessarily always, from rates or fees charged the consumers of their services. Since enterprises constitute the governmental segment most nearly resembling private business, service and cost are likely to be measured as a basis for rate making and revenue collection.

The postal service is the oldest and one of the largest of government enterprises. The number of pieces of mail and other transactions handled by the postal service grew from under 25 billion in 1932 to 46 billion in 1950. This increase of 86 per cent in physical volume accompanied a rise of 178 per cent in expenditure. Differences in rates of increase in volume of various postal services were pronounced; the range was from 38 per cent for second-class mail to 859 per cent for domestic airmail.

TABLE 248. PHYSICAL VOLUME AND EXPENDITURE PER WORK UNIT FOR SELECTED

Type of Function	Physical Unit	Volume of Functions		
		1932	1942	1950
		(Thousands)		
U.S. postal service	Piece	24,768,967	30,787,550	45,961,168
First-class mail	Piece	14,598,192	16,972,321	24,500,072
Domestic airmail	Piece	88,993	463,235	853,183
Second-class mail	Piece	4,552,420	4,571,041	6,264,838
Third-class mail	Piece	3,640,939	5,434,559	10,342,921
Fourth-class mail	Piece	616,532	778,859	1,179,415
Other mail	Piece	809,667	1,897,618	1,923,309
Special services[a]	Transaction	462,224	669,917	897,430
State liquor stores[b]	Gallon	38,446	56,417	50,064
Housing and home finance				
Public housing started annually[c]	Family unit	12.1	192.9	43.8
HOLC loans outstanding[b]	Number	858	780	15
Federal Savings and Loan Insurance Corporation total insured associations	Number	—	2.4	2.9
FHA insurance yearly[b]				
Property loans	Number	382	433	1,449
Home mortgages	Number	109	218	341
Claims paid on property loans	Number	29.4	22.7	56.5
Electric power operation[d]				
Tennessee Valley Authority	Kilowatt-hour	699,000	5,983,000	14,166,000
Rural Electrification Administration	Mile energized	50.9	30.0	144.2
Columbia River[e]	Kilowatt-hour	—	2,425,000	13,042,000
Farm loan programs				
Commodity Credit Corporation				
Corn	Bushel	268,000	56,000	385,300
Cotton	Bale	1,930	3,140	3,200
Wheat	Bushel	—	408,100	382,800
Farm Credit Administration[f]	Loan	614.9	417.3	326.2
Farmers Home Administration[g]	Loan	399.2	532.1	142.3
Transportation services				
Inland Waterways Corporation	Ton	1,573	5,607	2,809
Alaska Railroad[e]	Ton per mile	14,570	63,559	141,261
Panama Canal	Ton	19,808	13,607	30,365

Source: See Appendix 18–1.

a. Comprises postal notes, special delivery, money orders, registry and other services.

b. Data in 1932 column are for 1938.

c. Data in 1932 column are for 1936. Figures repre-sent all publicly financed new nonfarm family dwelling units started in the United States in each year reported.

d. Transactions represent current operations, except loan payments by REA, and include both direct consump-

Utility and Enterprise Functions, Fiscal Years 1932, 1942 and 1950

Expenditure per Unit of Work					Percentage Change, 1942 to 1950	
Current Dollars			1950 Dollars		Physical Volume	Unit Cost in 1950 Dollars
1932	1942	1950	1932	1942		
$ .03	$ .03	$ .05	$ .07	$ .05	49.3	—
.02	.02	.03	.04	.03	44.4	—
.27	.08	.13	.57	.14	84.2	—7.1
.03	.02	.04	.06	.04	37.1	—
.02	.02	.03	.05	.03	90.3	—
.24	.22	.41	.51	.39	51.4	5.1
.07	.03	.10	.15	.05	1.4	100.0
.18	.14	.25	.38	.26	34.0	—3.8
5.31	5.11	13.02	10.91	8.39	—11.3	55.2
6,495.21	3,991.69	8,447.49	15,554.21	7,298.12	—77.3	15.7
2,526.81	2,008.94	639.47	5,493.06	3,652.61	—98.1	—82.5
—	1,521,666.67	4,693,448.28	—	2,766,666.67	20.8	69.6
394.53	326.01	483.25	857.66	592.75	234.6	—18.5
4,341.71	4,396.61	7,300.14	9,438.50	7,993.83	56.4	—8.7
204.63	314.19	321.56	444.83	571.23	148.9	—43.7
.004	.004	.002	.01	.01	136.8	—80.0
1,061.04	1,076.37	1,894.64	2,029.86	1,902.53	380.7	—.4
—	.002	.002	—	.004	437.8	—50.0
.45	.78	1.35	2.07	1.20	588.0	12.5
51.55	92.61	143.06	267.12	167.47	1.9	—14.6
—	1.15	1.99	—	2.07	—6.2	—3.9
290.57	3,074.51	8,211.45	944.36	5,675.54	—21.8	44.7
247.70	353.84	1,175.74	511.86	720.78	—73.3	63.1
2.09	1.49	3.75	4.81	2.55	—49.9	47.1
.08	.08	.07	.17	.13	122.3	—46.2
.64	1.43	.97	1.53	2.41	123.2	—59.8

tion and that through other organizations. Data in 1932 column are for 1938 for TVA.

e. Revenue data substituted for expenditure data to permit interyear comparisons.

f. Total loans annually extended, exclusive of those to cooperatives.

g. Number and amount of loans extended during year for farm ownership, production, and emergencies. Data in 1932 column are for 1938.

TABLE 249. PERCENTAGE CHANGE IN NUMBER OF WORK UNITS PER 1,000 POPULATION FOR SELECTED PUBLIC ENTERPRISES, 1942 TO 1950

Percentage Increase				Percentage Decrease	
Over 200	100 to 200	50 to 100	Under 50	Under 50	50 and Over
REA miles energized	TVA kilowatt-hours produced	Alaska Railroad ton-miles	Postal services	State liquor store sales	Farmers Home Administration loans
Columbia River system kilowatt-hours produced	FHA claims paid on property loans	Panama Canal tonnage City electric utility production [a]	FHA home mortgage insurance	CCC cotton and wheat loans	Inland Waterways Corporation tonnage
CCC corn loans	FHA property improvement loan insurance			Farm Credit Administration loans	HOLC loans outstanding Public housing started annually

Source: Table 248.

a. Based on data from the Federal Power Commission.

The over-all expenditure per work unit for the postal service rose 67 per cent from 1942 to 1950 in current dollars but was stationary when converted into constant (1950) dollars. Classified by type of postal service, expenditure per work unit in constant dollars underwent no change for several classes of mail, varied little for several classes, and rose sharply only for the one class of miscellaneous or "other mail." Increases from 1942 to 1950 in expenditures per work unit in current dollars were substantial for several functions, most notably state liquor stores, Rural Electrification Administration activities, Commodity Credit Corporation programs, and farm credit and home loan programs. But expenditures per work unit in current dollars actually decreased for the HOLC loan program, TVA, the Alaska Railroad and the Panama Canal. For most government business enterprises, expenditure per work unit in constant dollars either did not change or decreased between 1942 and 1950. Rising price levels have concealed decreases in the expenditure required to provide a given volume of services for most government utilities and business enterprises. (See Table 248.)

Trends in physical volume have varied widely as between different enterprises in the last decade. Increases were apt to be largest for electric power systems, while decreases occurred in several loan programs, liquor store sales and public housing. (See Table 249.)

Selected General Functions

The functions selected for examination comprise, in range of service and in size, a significant block of activities for analysis of government expenditure behavior. Over the eighteen-year span from 1932 to 1950, trends in physical volume of work varied enormously between functions. For example, the number of passenger-miles of flight supervised by the Civil Aeronautics Authority grew from 148 million to 10,558 million, or more than 7,000 per cent; visitors at national parks increased from 4 million to 33 million, nearly 800 per cent; and the number of tax returns processed by the Bureau of Internal Revenue rose from 5 million to 89 million, almost 1,700 per cent. On the other hand, the service volume decreased for patents, naturalization proceedings, airmail subsidies, forest roads, libraries and federal courts. In education, the number of pupils enrolled in elementary and secondary schools declined slightly, while the number of university students more than doubled. (See Table 250.)

In relation to population, work loads decreased for several functions and rose moderately for others. Increases of over 50 per cent in the ratio of work loads to population, however, prevailed for almost half of the selected functions. (See Table 251.)

For several public services — local parks, civil aeronautics, national park visitors, immigration inspection and national tax collection — the volume of work loads grew from 1932 to 1950 by a larger percentage than current dollar expenditure, and expenditure per work unit declined. In constant dollars, cost per work unit decreased not only in these services but also in state highway construction and maintenance, local recreation, airmail subsidies, national forest fire protection and national meat inspection. For the other general functions, cost per work unit underwent moderate to large increases in current dollars but much smaller increases in constant dollars. For example, operation cost per enrolled pupil in public schools rose 171 per cent between 1932 and 1950 in current dollars as against 41 per cent in constant dollars. (See Table 250.)

Summary of Unit-Cost Changes

Has government become more costly per unit of work performed? This question, which is separate from any growth of functions, can best be answered for the period 1942–1950, during which nearly all of the present-day functions were performed. In brief, service expansion and price rises — not increased unit cost — were primary causes of expenditure growth for public insurance and assistance programs and for public enterprises and utilities, while increases in unit costs were one of several important reasons for the expenditure rise in the more general functions.

Cost per beneficiary rose moderately in current dollars for half the insurance and assistance programs and considerably for the other half — unemployment insurance, old-age and survivors insurance retirement, old-age assistance and aid to dependent children. Even in constant dollars, these functions revealed fairly large unit-cost rises, while the other insurance and assistance functions either declined or increased moderately in unit cost. (See Figure 70.) For insurance and assistance programs as a whole, therefore, costs grew primarily from an increase in the volume of service, not in unit cost of service rendered.

Unit costs of utilities and enterprises disclosed larger growth in current dollars than in the case of insurance and assistance. Increases were over 100 per cent for state liquor stores, public housing, the Farm Credit Administration and the Inland Waterways Corporation. Nonetheless, decreases occurred in current dollars for the TVA, the Panama Canal, the Alaska Railroad and HOLC. The same enterprises showed even larger decreases, of course, in unit costs expressed in constant dollars. Most of the other functions in this category were performed at the same or a lower unit cost in constant dollars in 1950 than in 1942. The only important exceptions were liquor stores and public housing. Again it is evident that the expenditure growth was induced by the enlarged service volume, in conjunction with price inflation, rather than by an increase in the per unit cost of public service measured in constant dollars.

Rises in unit costs were greater for selected general functions than for the previously considered services. In current dollars, increases were over 100 per cent — and in a number of cases well over — for public schools, hospitals, rivers and harbors, airmail, forest roads and fire protection, animal disease and meat inspection, patents, immigration and naturalization, and state road maintenance. Although decreases of unit costs in constant dollars were frequent, increases of over 100 per cent were recorded for veterans hospitals, animal disease and meat inspection, and naturalization proceedings, and smaller but appreciable increases for all public hospitals, public schools, rivers and harbors, irrigation maintenance and immigration inspection. For several functions the rise of unit costs was so small, as with highway construction and maintenance, as to point to similar cost patterns in 1942 and 1950. Not much meaning needs to be read into the decline of military cost per member of the armed forces because the ebb of equipment expenditure abnormally lowered this 1950 unit cost. For the general-functional category as a whole, it appears that higher unit costs contributed appreciably to the total cost growth without being the dominating cause.

INCREASE IN GOVERNMENT RESPONSIBILITIES

The upward trend of government expenditure, and of its various components, reflects underlying economic and social forces that have affected both the public and the private sectors of the

TABLE 250. PHYSICAL VOLUME AND EXPENDITURE PER WORK UNIT OF

Type of Function	Physical Unit	Volume of Functions		
		1932	1942	1950
Education and community facilities[a]		*(Thousands)*		
Elementary and secondary schools	} Pupil	26,275	24,562	25,111
Colleges and universities	} enrolled	425	732	1,326
Public libraries[b]	Book issued	415,924	333,365	384,606
City and county recreation[c]	Attendance	238,931	389,935	499,462
City and county parks[c]	Acre	417.3	641.5	644.1
Hospitals (all governments)[d]	} Average	610.2	858.6	942.0
Veterans hospitals and homes	} patient-day	49.3	69.0	113.5
Neuropsychiatric	Same	12.7	32.0	48.2
Tuberculosis	Same	5.1	4.7	7.0
General	Same	14.9	18.0	41.5
Domiciliaries	Same	16.5	14.4	16.8
Transportation and natural resources				
Highways[e]				
State construction	Mile	29.6	17.0	42.5
State maintenance	Mile	266.6	468.1	545.1
County maintenance	Mile	613.0	998.5	1,168.7
Municipal maintenance	Mile	*f*	192.5	228.4
U.S. rivers, harbors, flood control[g]	Traffic ton	445,648	653,600	740,721
U.S. civil aeronautics[h]	Flight mile	148,187	1,741,593	10,558,166
Airmail pay and subsidy[i]	Voyage	1.5	0.8	1.4
National parks and recreation areas				
Visitors	Visitor	3,755	10,769	32,782
Acreage	Acre	12,592	21,686	23,910
U.S. forestry (selected services)				
Fire protection	Acre	158,000	184,000	208,000
Aid to state and private forest	Acre	222,000	291,092	363,543
Road maintenance	Mile	153.0	191.3	130.4
U.S. soil conservation[j]	Acre	—	19,835	96,316
U.S. animal industry[k]				
Animal disease inspection	Inspection	1,374,616	2,015,929	2,978,417
Meat inspection	Inspection	114,448	764,147	603,626
Drainage maintenance[l]	Acre	84,408	86,967	102,673
Irrigation maintenance[l]	Acre	18,690	21,174	26,259
Other specified services				
U.S. courts	Case filed	156.9	75.7	95.0
U.S. currency, stamps, checks	Piece	24,889,431	40,567,110	44,417,315
U.S. patents issued	Patent	49.1	39.3	43.4
U.S. prison operation Average no. of inmates		13.3	17.8	16.9
U.S. immigration and naturalization[k]				
Inspection for entry into U.S.	Inspection	2,815	18,670	12,198
Naturalization proceedings	Petition	243	501	162
U.S. tax collections	Tax return	5,070	44,752	89,132

Source: See Appendix 18–1.

a. Expenditure represents current operation except for the inclusion of capital outlay for recreation.

b. Data are for 1939, 1945 and 1950, respectively.

c. Data are for 1930, 1940 and 1950. Park acreages differ from those in Table 164, which were adjusted for changes in coverage.

d. Expenditure for operation as estimated by U.S. Bureau of the Census; patient-days as reported by the American Hospital Association.

e. Mileage comprises all surfaced highways.

f. Not available.

g. Volume of service is measured indirectly by tons of traffic carried on affected waterways.

SELECTED GENERAL GOVERNMENT FUNCTIONS, FISCAL YEARS 1932, 1942 AND 1950

| Expenditure per Unit of Work | | | | | Percentage Change 1942 to 1950 | |
| Current Dollars | | | 1950 Dollars | | | |
1932	1942	1950	1932	1942	Physical Volume	Unit Cost in 1950 Dollars
$ 66.88	$ 84.54	$ 186.52	$ 131.91	$ 143.77	2.2	29.7
595.09	504.00	851.31	1,248.49	871.97	81.1	—2.4
.12	.19	.29	.20	.27	15.4	7.4
.15	.15	.24	.39	.26	28.1	—7.7
287.00	149.18	231.33	747.40	261.26	.4	—11.5
493.28	585.84	1,874.13	1,062.03	1,003.15	9.7	86.8
752.41	1,217.58	4,492.11	1,605.68	2,191.94	64.5	104.9
897.80	848.06	2,932.59	1,909.61	1,525.34	50.6	92.3
1,777.25	1,792.55	5,815.00	3,786.27	3,222.34	48.9	80.5
979.53	2,341.00	7,415.73	2,096.33	4,219.33	130.6	75.8
123.21	438.26	1,193.21	265.03	787.50	16.7	51.5
19,493.24	25,647.06	36,541.18	45,011.62	34,033.65	150.0	7.4
663.92	452.89	926.44	1,396.88	774.18	16.4	19.7
‡	250.38	471.46	‡	425.89	17.0	10.7
‡	841.56	1,659.37	‡	1,431.49	18.6	15.9
.24	.31	.85	.65	.57	13.3	49.1
.07	.08	.02	1.59	.14	506.2	—85.7
14,840.00	10,942.50	28,420.00	34,370.67	23,085.00	75.0	23.1
.71	.48	.47	1.51	.85	204.4	—44.7
.21	.24	.65	.45	.42	10.3	54.8
.04	.04	.08	.10	.07	13.0	14.3
.01	.01	.03	.02	.02	24.9	50.0
12.16	17.03	76.46	26.80	29.78	—31.8	156.7
—	.87	.53	—	1.58	385.6	—66.5
.01	.01	.02	.02	.01	47.7	100.0
.13	.02	.09	.27	.04	—21.0	125.0
.09	.13	.24	.19	.22	18.1	9.1
2.77	2.19	4.89	5.76	3.74	24.0	30.7
57.40	148.48	273.51	117.65	272.22	25.5	.5
.0003	.0004	.001	.001	.001	9.5	—
103.56	118.60	250.51	220.37	214.30	10.4	16.9
431.05	756.01	1,299.94	937.37	1,328.20	—5.1	—2.1
4.33	1.12	2.55	9.15	2.01	—34.7	26.9
50.15	41.70	192.25	106.04	74.79	—67.7	157.0
6.68	1.64	2.59	13.77	2.98	99.2	—13.1

h. Federal civil aeronautic expenditure related to passenger-miles flown by all aviation companies.

i. Volume of service is the number of airplane voyages receiving mail pay and subsidy. Data for 1938 in lieu of 1932.

j. Volume of service is the acreage for conservation farm planning and treatment.

k. Each class covers unlike types of service that differently affect expenditure.

l. Data are for 1930, 1940 and 1950. Includes small amounts for private enterprise.

TABLE 251. PERCENTAGE CHANGE IN NUMBER OF WORK UNITS PER 1,000 POPULATION
IN SELECTED GENERAL GOVERNMENT FUNCTIONS, 1932 TO 1950

Percentage Increase				Percentage Decrease	
Over 200	100 to 200	50 to 100	Under 50	Under 25	Over 25
U.S. civil aeronautics	Colleges	Recreation	Hospitals	Public schools Libraries	
U.S. soil conservation		U.S. veterans hospitals	State road construction	Drainage	U.S. courts
U.S. park attendance		State road maintenance	County road maintenance		U.S. patents
U.S. meat inspection		U.S. park acreage	U.S. rivers and harbors		U.S. naturalization proceedings
U.S. immigration inspection		U.S. animal inspection	U.S. forestry		
U.S. tax collections			Local parks		
			U.S. prisons		
			U.S. currency		
			Irrigation		

Source: Table 250.

economy. The new role of the United States in world affairs, the increasing scale and complexity of economic organization, the extraordinary developments in technology and the utilization of resources, the urbanization of the population and its changing age distribution have all influenced importantly the responsibilities of government in our time.

Political and Economic Changes

The rise of the United States to a position of world leadership has increasingly molded the fiscal pattern of the nation. The present world leadership of the United States — military, economic and political — was foreshadowed at the turn of the century by a broadening of the American outlook after the war with Spain. This was expressed, for example, in expenditure to build the Panama Canal. The more significant but temporary American intervention in world affairs through World War I gave rise in the postwar years to then substantial allotments in federal budgets for defense, veterans benefits and war debt interest. As the United States shifted from a debtor to a creditor nation, it acquired a different stake in the economies of other nations. World War II, of course, exercised enormous influence on federal expenditure during hostilities and after. In addition, the postwar position of the United States as the balance wheel of the noncommunist world brought types and volume of government expenditure undreamed of in earlier decades. Military and economic assistance to other nations and the necessity for the United States to function as the military arsenal of democracy typify the influence of the nation's new world role on government expenditure.

Government activities to accomplish domestic economic objectives also had their origin around and shortly after the turn of the century, in regulation of various areas of economic activity, antitrust legislation, measures for the protection of labor interests and establishment of the Federal Reserve System. The economic cataclysm after

FIGURE 70. PERCENTAGE CHANGE IN UNIT COSTS OF SELECTED GOVERNMENT FUNCTIONS, 1942 TO 1950

Sources: Tables 246, 248 and 250.

1929 forced government into more positive action. Through work relief, assistance and social insurance programs, government assumed responsibility for individual economic security. Subsidies, loans and price support measures were developed to "shore up" segments of the economy that had sagged — most notably agriculture and the merchant marine. The RFC, farm credit agencies and home financing agencies supplied public capital or insurance where private capital was lacking. Public works expenditures were employed to prime the pump of private enterprise. By these and other devices, government units extended their early compensatory functions of caring for dependents, defectives and delinquents. Today government in the United States functions to compensate as well for the economically maladjusted or weak — the unemployed, the aged, the dependent, sick industries — and to provide the economic setting required to generate employment, production and profits.

Technological Changes

With the closing of the Great Frontier around the turn of the century, public funds began to be used more and more to develop resources and economic facilities, including agriculture, forestry, transportation and enterprises. In this intensive cultivation of resources — both material and human — government units participate increasingly in ways that cannot always be predicted. In the past few years, for example, atomic energy has been unlocked for a revolution that is only beginning. The vast resources of the oceans, to cite only one more example, have only begun to be tapped for tidelands oil, and other unpredictable crops may be added in the years to come. In the development of resources and facilities, government acts less as a welfare state than as a business state, promoting private enterprise and occasionally undertaking enterprises itself.

Controversy between exponents of "fat" and "lean" government has raged since the Industrial Revolution. The bringing of power to manufacturing, mining and trade and, more recently, agriculture raised the private standard of living and called for an accompanying rise in what may be called the "public standard of living," that is, the conception of what public functions are needed and the capacity to pay for public services. The progressive merging of mechanical power and technology both required governmental growth and provided the means to pay for it. For example, government has now come not only to regulate electric power but also — through the REA, the TVA and other federal, state and local activities — to produce and distribute an important volume of electrical energy.

Perhaps the most frequently cited example of the influence of technological changes on public expenditure is transportation. The digging of the Erie Canal and similar waterways was an early form of government participation in this field; public aid to private railroad construction followed; later, the motor vehicle required public development of modern highways; and the airplane similarly stimulated government expenditure. Each wave of transportation progress left a deposit of public expenditure programs, of which waterways, highways and air transport are sizable present-day functions.

Urbanization

Increasing urbanization of the population has accompanied technological progress and also has affected government expenditure. Less than one third of the nation's population before 1890 lived in urban places having populations over 2,500. The urban proportion for the first time exceeded one half in 1920, and rose to 56 per cent in the next ten years. Manufacturing and commerce have been spreading from the old industrial areas of the Northeast to the South and the West. So-called "industrial diffusion," the branching out of large corporations and the opening of small independent firms, is diffusing urbanism, calling for more expensive governments, and providing larger tax capacity. Mechanization of agriculture, by increasing farm output per worker, is stimulating the migration of rural people to cities, retarding the rise in rural public costs, and increasing rural tax capacity. Urban government is expensive government. As the 1942 Census of Governments demonstrated, city costs are correlated with population size; the larger the city, the higher the per capita cost of government. The decades leading up to 1930 were a period in which large-city costs contributed importantly to increasing public expenditure.

Urbanization has been a less significant factor in expenditure growth since 1930 as the population shift to urban areas has become less pronounced. By 1950 the urban population formed 59 per cent of the total,[15] or only a slightly larger proportion than two decades previously. Two reservations, however, may be attached to this leveling off. First, the old Census definition of

15. According to the "old" Census definition. See Chapter 3.

urbanism on which these percentages are based failed to reflect important kinds of urban growth. The new definition adopted in 1950, which included more of the built-up areas contiguous to urban centers, classified 64 per cent of the population as urban in that year. Second, under the old definition the nonurban population is made up of two quite different classes — rural farm and rural nonfarm. The rural farm population declined by over one fourth from 1930 to 1950, while the proportion of total population in this class shrank by almost one half (from 25 per cent to 15 per cent). The greatest proportionate increase during the two decades was in the rural nonfarm population, which rose from 19 per cent of the total to 26 per cent. The urban group, although it rose only from 56 to 59 per cent of the total, gained more people (20 million) than any of the others. The rural nonfarm group, consisting largely of municipalities of under 2,500 population and built-up unincorporated areas surrounding urban centers, is more urban than rural in its governmental needs.

The significant expansion of the rural nonfarm population indicates important changes in the population structure during the past generation — a growth of small cities, classified either as urban or rural nonfarm, and of suburban areas near the metropolitan centers. The outward movement from congested urban centers to their peripheries has implications for public expenditure patterns which are partly, though far from entirely, visible at this time. Satellite and other growing urban areas require physical facilities and functions that are expensive at present prices, although on the whole below metropolitan city costs. Big cities face rising costs with the increased transportation demands of a fluid population and expensive rehabilitation problems for blighted areas.

Property tax trends highlight rural and urban differences. Revenue from all local property taxes, rural and urban together, almost doubled between 1932 and 1950, but taxes levied on farm real estate stood at 64 cents per acre in 1950, only seven cents more than in 1930, and taxes on farm real estate per $100 of full valuation declined by 29 cents to $1.01 during this period. Not only are taxes higher on urban than on rural property, but the new or nonproperty taxes to which local governments have turned in recent years have provided revenue chiefly for urban communities.

Costs of rural government have not remained stationary, as tax trends might suggest, since fiscal aid often has made up the difference between expenditure and local revenue. Insofar as states adjust their distributions to the economic ability of local governments, state aid lessens the tax load on rural areas for school and other functions. The transfer of many thousands of miles of rural highways to state road systems illustrates the effect of functional transfers in giving tax relief to underaverage areas. Federal spending favors rural areas, especially through price support and other programs, although moderate federal funds are channeled to urban highways, airports and housing. In brief, the different urban and rural needs have induced larger expenditure. On the one hand, urbanization has resulted in a more expensive brand of local government; and, on the other hand, state and federal distributions have liberally supported rural areas.

Changing Age Distribution

Changes in the age distribution of the population also influence government expenditure. The percentage of the population 65 years of age and over nearly doubled between 1910 and 1950, when 12.3 million persons, or 8.1 per cent of the population, were in this age group. This increasing proportion of the aged obviously affects such services as old-age insurance.

A decline in the proportion of persons under 20 years of age from nearly 42 per cent of the population in 1910 to 34 per cent in 1950 was reflected in stationary enrollment in elementary and secondary schools during the last two decades of the period. Part of this group — children aged 10 to 19 years, and especially the older teenagers — declined in absolute numbers. As these children pass out of the public school system, they are being replaced by a larger number of children under 10 years of age. The under-10 group increased 39 per cent during the 1940s and is now crowding elementary schools. As more of its members enter and advance through school, the cost of education will rise. With enrollment stationary, cost per pupil doubled in the 1940s and the increased per pupil rate will be applied to a much larger enrollment during the 1950s.

National Income and Public Expenditure

Public standards of living, like private standards of living, depend upon economic ability and current income. Unlike the private individual, however, government may by fiscal and expenditure policies alter the income framework within which it operates and spend to increase the private income from which it derives revenue.

That national income and public expenditure grow simultaneously, though not by the same rates, is axiomatic. Significantly, taxes and expenditure grow not proportionately to income but progressively; that is, in the long run, the larger the national income, the larger the proportion going into taxes to pay for expenditure. Causal relations between income and expenditure can be drawn only cautiously. A rising income at once permits greater expenditure and itself partly results from greater expenditure. The effect of income variations among states and nations on public spending is apparent especially at the extremes of the income range. Poor areas are particularly repressed in public services by subnormal incomes, while rich areas are stimulated by abnormal incomes. Between the extremes, many influences modify the effect of economic ability upon spending.

Crisis expenditure, whether for war or depression, raises the ratio of expenditure to income; but this ratio varies widely among nations and states, depending upon their size and resources. Local governments are sensitive to economic barriers to taxation even if no legal limits restrain them. In a different way, an overextended Great Britain has been withdrawing from commitments in various parts of the world because she exceeded the capacity of her economy to sustain these responsibilities. Growing income, therefore, is not a magic gold mine to draw on for unlimited expenditure but a framework (alike permissive and restraining) within which income and other influences interact to shape expenditure.

The effects of government finance on the level of national income depend, in no small part, upon the degree to which public finance, especially expenditure, is flexible or rigid. Expenditure trends in this country show marked shifts in pattern chiefly under the duress of war and depression. Certain elements of flexibility have been "built in" to government financial policy — unemployment insurance, general relief, farm aid and some public works — which are reduced in prosperity or war and enlarged in depression or in peacetime. "Built-in" rigidity, however, results not only from interest on debt and insurance

or assistance for the aged and other groups but also from a large hard core of public services that must be performed regardless of the business cycle. Perhaps many "hard core" services could, accordion like, be made more expansible or contractable; but in practice most of this public expenditure has proved rigid. In the absence of anticyclical plans for administering intergovernmental aid and public works, flexible adjustment of expenditure to the business cycle depends upon emergency expansion of spending during depressions and, less reliably, contraction during prosperity.

Redistributive Role of Government

In earlier years, when taxes on consumption and property accounted for most tax revenue, the tax system tended to accentuate economic inequality. The emergence of progressive income and death transfer taxation resulted in a degree of governmental redistribution of income, although consumption and other taxes have not lost their importance. The area too much neglected by economists — although not by politicians — is governmental equalization of income, through the distribution of expenditure benefits.

As far as statistical evidence is available, government operates as an equalizer chiefly at the extremes of the income scale by reducing the income of the richest classes and increasing the income or services of the poorest.[16] Such a result is likely to occur in peacetime years, especially in depressions, when benefits to the poor increase; in years of prosperity and war, benefits to the poor decrease and public expenditure virtually guarantees large business profits after taxes. Middle-income groups are much less directly affected; government returns benefits broadly proportional to revenues collected from these groups.

Equalization occurs also among rich and poor areas within states, although less than is commonly believed, through school and public assistance programs. A very mild federal equalization among states results from social security and highway distributions. Redistribution of income through federal expenditure, however, is apt to be the fortuitous outcome of unrelated political decisions rather than the result of planning. Even the WPA and other relief distribu-

16. See Kenyon E. Poole, *Fiscal Policies and the American Economy,* Prentice-Hall, New York, 1951, pp. 359–409.

TABLE 252. GOVERNMENT EXPENDITURES BY NATURE OF FUNCTIONAL
RESPONSIBILITY, FISCAL YEAR 1950

Category of Expenditure	Total (Net)	Federal (Gross)	State (Gross)	Local (Gross)	Percentage Distribution[a]			
					Total	Federal	State	Local
	(Billions)							
Total expenditure	$69.5	$44.3	$15.1	$16.7	100.0	100.0	100.0	100.0
Old functions (1930 and before)	49.4	28.4	6.0	15.1	71.1	64.2	39.3	90.4
New functions (after 1930)	17.8	13.6	2.7	1.4	25.6	30.7	18.2	8.4
Taken over from other governments (after 1930)	2.3	.2	2.1	—	3.3	.3	14.2	—
Aid paid to other governments	—	2.1	4.3	.2	—	4.8	28.3	1.2
Exhibit of expenditure paid from aid received	6.6	—	2.3	4.3	9.5	—	15.4	25.8

Source: See Appendix 18–1.   a. Computed from unrounded figures.

tions in the 1930s had no correlation with the economic ability of the states. Equalization is more likely to occur on the tax side, since tax rates lend themselves to manipulation more readily than expenditure benefits. In combination, tax and expenditure redistribution increases consumer expenditure and decreases savings. Thus equalization provides an inflationary impetus but dampens investment.

Shifts in Responsibility

The ease with which income is tapped and debt is incurred nationally has contributed to an increasing federal share of total government expenditure. Between 1932 and 1950 the federal proportion rose from 32 per cent to 61 per cent. War-connected functions, however, account for the federal pre-eminence. Although the federal share of nonwar outlays grew from one fifth in 1932 to over one third (36.5 per cent) in 1950, state and local governments continue to lead in this sphere.

Social welfare and educational spending is predominantly state and local. In 1950, states and localities accounted for 88 per cent of such outlays. More is spent federally for economic development than for social welfare. The federal share of all economic development expenditure was 61 per cent in 1950. The much smaller expenditure for general control and other functions, despite a rise in the federal portion, continues to be predominantly state and local because of civilian public safety and interest on nonwar debt.

Although the last two decades seem to have witnessed a revolution in government financing, the 1950 expenditure pattern differed surprisingly little from the predepression pattern. As much as 71 per cent of the 1950 total expenditure was for functions performed in 1930 and earlier years. The remaining — and controversial — area consisted of 26 per cent for functions newly undertaken since 1930 and only 3.3 per cent for functions transferred from one level of government to another. (See Table 252.)

The role of new functions varies widely among government levels. Nearly 31 per cent of federal spending in 1950 was due to new functions, notably international aid, veterans education, old-age insurance, farm price support, atomic energy and housing. The state proportion of 18 per cent was a consequence chiefly of unemployment insurance and liquor stores, while the small local proportion of less than 9 per cent was a result largely of housing and categorical public assistance. State government has been most affected by the several methods of adjusting functional responsibility. Not only was more than 14 per cent of state expenditure in 1950 for functions taken over from localities after 1930 but 28 per cent also was in the form of aid paid to local governments.

Federal expansion particularly and state growth to a lesser degree have come about through the assumption of new functions without disturbing the services of other levels. Since most new functions have channeled through big governments, the small units have merely "held their own" and indeed receded relatively. States have simultaneously assumed new functions, taken over services from localities, and increased aid to local governments. Local governments not only lost functionally to states during the past two decades but they also gained by receiving increasing state aid, which in 1950 amounted to nearly 26 per cent of total local expenditure.

Growth of Government Enterprises

Just as income redistribution does not work out simply by prearranged design, the growth of government utilities and business enterprises has followed a confused pattern in which public competition with private business has gone side by side with public aid and encouragement to private business. The development of government enterprises is reflected in the figures on selected transactions for 1913, 1932, 1942 and 1950 shown in Appendix 18–3. Government enterprises grew importantly during the 1930s particularly. Their expansion during the 1940s was not so much in undertaking new enterprises as in administering a larger dollar volume of business at higher price levels for a larger population. Significantly, enterprise expenditure grew only in keeping with general-government functions; in 1932, enterprises accounted for 13 per cent of total public expenditure and in 1950 for 12 per cent. An outstanding development of the past two decades has been the creation of the RFC, the CCC and other federal credit corporations. Their operations are included in the following figures summarizing federal, state and local enterprise finances, exclusive of debt incurred and repaid and contributions to and from general government (in millions):

	1913	1932	1942	1950
Revenue	$ 411	$1,298	$ 4,029	$ 6,863
Liquidation of assets	—	459	3,101	5,324
Expenditure *	534	1,743	6,549	8,020
Loans extended	—	1,513	3,037	6,418
Debt outstanding	1,145	5,676	16,463	17,192

* Includes interest on federal obligations held by the Treasury, which is excluded elsewhere in this analysis.

A question always asked is whether government enterprises result in surpluses transferable to general funds, as do many city-owned utilities and state liquor stores, or in deficits that drain tax funds as has been true of the postal service and the New York City subways. An exact

answer would require cost accounting, based on depreciation, tax liabilities and other factors not applied to many government enterprises. In the absence of this information, an approximate answer is provided by the net cash results of enterprise operations in the extent to which they draw on or contribute to general funds. Instead of confining the measure to annual cash transfers, the net results may be broadened to include later transfers arising from each year's operations. The surpluses and deficits yielded by this procedure are as follows (in millions):

	1913	1932	1942	1950
General contributions to enterprises	$ 40	$547	$1,088	$ 966
Enterprise contributions to general funds	8	200	2,855	1,273
Net surplus (+) or deficit (−) of enterprises	−32	−347	+1,767	+307

The role of government enterprises in employment indicates that governments account for a slightly larger share of all business undertakings than they did two decades ago. Measured in terms of employment, government enterprises expanded 83 per cent between 1929 and 1950, from 409,000 to 747,000 employees. General-government employment grew more rapidly, 135 per cent, while private industry expanded at a rate of only 28 per cent. Consequently, enterprise employment was smaller in relation to general-government employment at the end than at the beginning of this period, but larger in relation to private employment. (See Table 253.)

Employment does not fully measure enterprise activity, however. The influence of RFC or other credit agencies on the economy is much greater than is indicated by the number of employees administering federal loans. Likewise, the economic influence of private credit institutions far exceeds the number of their employees.

CHARACTER OF GOVERNMENT EXPENDITURE

The great bulk of government spending in 1913 was for wages and salaries of employees, procurement of supplies, materials and contractual services, and capital outlay, the last class consisting chiefly of contract construction. Subsidies and other public-to-private transfer payments required a relatively small share of the

TABLE 253. ROLE OF PUBLIC ENTERPRISES IN EMPLOYMENT,
1929, 1932, 1942 AND 1950

| Year | Number of Full-Time Equivalent Employees | | | Enterprise Employment as Per Cent of: | |
	Private	General Government	Government Enterprises	Private	General Government
	(Thousands)				
1929	32,101	2,785	409	1.3	14.7
1932	23,289	2,883	401	1.7	13.9
1942	37,890	8,563	569	1.5	6.6
1950	40,930	6,554	747	1.8	11.4

Source: National Income and Product of the United States, 1929–1950 (1951 National Income Supplement to the Survey of Current Business).

total expenditure, and interest on debt comprised 6 per cent. By 1950 the character of government expenditure had greatly changed. Payrolls had dropped to 30 per cent of the total. Current procurement, even including price support purchases, required only 15 per cent, and capital outlays 17 per cent. Transfer payments,[17] requiring 29 per cent, had become a major item in the over-all total. Interest on debt had risen to 9 per cent of total expenditure. After 1950, the Korean crisis brought a sharp increase in the aggregate expenditure and a change in its distribution by character. The 1952 total of $101.5 billion spent was divided as follows: personal services — still almost 30 per cent of the total; current procurement — up to 26 per cent; capital outlay — 25 per cent; transfer payments — reduced to 14 per cent; and interest — cut to 6 per cent.

PAYROLLS

Although government payrolls more than trebled from 1913 to 1932, doubled again from 1932 to 1942, and more than redoubled from 1942 to 1950, their share of total government expenditure declined from 47 per cent in 1913 to 37 per cent in 1932 and 20 per cent in 1942, then rose to 30 per cent in 1950 (Table 254), remaining at about that proportion through 1952.

Government payroll trends reflect both the growing number of public employees and increased rates of pay. The higher rates of pay in

17. These include assistance and insurance benefits to individuals and agricultural, business and international subsidies. (See Table 254.)

turn reflect adjustments to rising prices and changes over the years in the economic status of such employees as teachers, military personnel and postal workers. Because of the rising earnings of public employees — their average earnings more than trebled between 1913 and 1950 — the increase in number of employees over the period has been considerably less spectacular than the growth of payroll costs. Government employees numbered 1.7 million in 1913, 3.6 million in 1932, 7.5 million in 1942 (including 2.4 million military personnel) and 7.9 million in 1950. (See Table 255.)

Between 1913 and 1932, the growth in government employment paralleled but did not equal the growth in scale of government as a whole. The states and the local governments both increased their personnel more than did the federal government during this period. In 1913 about one third of all public employees were on the rolls of the federal government; in 1932, only one fourth. Average salaries paid to federal and state and local employees were very similar both in 1913 and 1932.

From 1932 to 1942, federal employment and state and local employment trends diverged. The federal government increased its military personnel from 0.3 million to 2.4 million and its civilian employees from 0.6 million to 1.8 million. Although state and local government employment rose substantially, from 2.7 million to 3.3 million, the increase was not nearly as sharp as the federal expansion. Marked changes in the composition of public employment with the onset of World War II affected average earnings trends in this period. The large number of mili-

TABLE 254. CHARACTER OF GOVERNMENT EXPENDITURE, FISCAL YEARS
1913, 1932, 1942 AND 1950

Character Class	Amount				Percentage Distribution			
	1913	1932	1942	1950	1913	1932	1942	1950
	(Millions)							
Total	$3,050	$13,246	$50,202	$69,479	100.0	100.0	100.0	100.0
Payrolls	1,418	4,937	9,966	20,563	46.5	37.3	19.9	29.6
Materials, supplies and contractual services	534	2,819	9,386	10,675	17.5	21.3	18.7	15.4
Assistance and insurance benefits to individuals	215	1,330	3,381	14,827	7.0	10.0	6.7	21.4
Agricultural, business and international subsidies	—	—	5,778	5,048	—	—	11.5	7.3
Capital outlay	696	2,666	19,500	11,895	22.8	20.1	38.8	17.1
Interest on debt	187	1,495	2,191	6,470	6.1	11.3	4.4	9.3
General functions (including social insurance benefits)	2,516	11,505	43,657	61,560	100.0	100.0	100.0	100.0
Payrolls	1,191	4,210	8,734	17,762	47.3	36.6	20.0	28.8
Materials, supplies and contractual services	422	2,344	7,191	7,421	16.8	20.4	16.5	12.1
Assistance and insurance benefits to individuals	215	1,330	3,381	14,827	8.5	11.6	7.7	24.1
Agricultural, business and international subsidies	—	—	5,739	4,888	—	—	13.2	7.9
Capital outlay	541	2,356	16,846	10,445	21.5	20.5	38.6	17.0
Interest on debt	146	1,265	1,766	6,216	5.8	11.0	4.0	10.1
Enterprises	534	1,741	6,545	7,919	100.0	100.0	100.0	100.0
Payrolls	227	727	1,234	2,801	42.5	41.8	18.9	35.4
Materials, supplies and contractual services	112	475	2,195	3,254	21.0	27.3	33.5	41.1
Subsidies to business	—	—	39	160	—	—	0.6	2.0
Capital outlay	155	310	2,654	·1,450	29.0	17.8	40.6	18.3
Interest on debt	41	230	425	254	7.7	13.2	6.5	3.2
Exhibit of additional items								
Loans extended	—	1,549	3,053	6,447	—	—	—	—
General functions	—	36	16	29	—	—	—	—
Enterprises	—	1,513	3,037	6,418	—	—	—	—

Sources: See Appendix 18–1.

Note: 1952 figures on character of government expenditure, based on the Bureau of the Census Report, *Summary of Government Finances in 1952,* were as follows (in billions):

Total expenditures	$101.5
Payrolls	29.8
Materials, supplies and contractual services	26.4
Transfer payments	13.9
Capital outlay	24.9
Interest on debt	6.6

tary personnel on the rolls in 1942 depressed the over-all average of employee earnings, since many members of the armed forces have very low cash salaries and allowances because they are furnished subsistence and quarters in kind. Excluding military personnel, earnings of federal and state and local employees rose slightly over the ten years, but not as much as the cost of living. In terms of purchasing power, earnings of gov-ernment employees dropped materially between 1932 and 1942.

With the nation at war, federal employment rose to a sharp peak in 1945, and when the war was over both military and civilian federal employment dropped off to a fraction of the wartime level. By 1950, federal employment totaled 3.7 million as compared with 4.2 million in 1942. State and local employment declined somewhat

TABLE 255. GOVERNMENT PAYROLLS, FISCAL YEARS 1913, 1932, 1942 AND 1950

	1913	1932	1942	1950	Percentage Increase 1913–1932	1932–1942	1942–1950
Payrolls (*millions*)	$1,418	$4,937	$9,966	$20,563	248.2	101.5	106.3
Federal	474	1,311	5,483	10,524	176.6	318.2	91.9
National defense	170	392	3,735	6,213	130.6	852.8	66.3
Military	123	249	2,240	3,809	102.4	799.6	70.0
Civilian	47	143	1,495	2,404	204.3	945.5	60.8
Other	304	919	1,748	4,311	202.3	90.2	146.6
State	125	577	925	2,502	361.6	60.3	170.5
Local	819	3,049	3,558	7,538	272.3	16.7	111.9
Total in 1950 dollars							
At 1950 rates of pay	4,577	9,183	19,303	20,563	100.6	110.2	6.5
At 1950 purchasing power	3,450	8,692	14,699	20,563	151.9	69.1	39.9
Number of employees (*thousands*)	1,713	3,608	7,525	7,925	110.6	108.6	5.3
Federal	595	878	4,221	3,701	47.5	380.8	—12.3
National defense	210	347	3,261	2,425	65.2	839.8	—25.6
Military	150	264	2,440	1,714	76.0	824.2	—29.8
Civilian	60	83	821	711	38.3	889.2	—13.4
Other	385	531	960	1,276	37.9	80.8	32.9
State and local	1,118	2,730	3,304	4,224	144.2	21.0	27.8
Average annual pay per employee	$ 828	$1,368	$ 1,324	$2,594	65.2	—3.2	95.9
Federal	795	1,490	1,299	2,844	87.4	—12.8	118.9
Military	822	944	918	2,222	14.8	—2.8	142.0
Civilian	787	1,731	1,820	3,379	119.9	5.1	85.7
State and local	844	1,328	1,357	2,377	57.3	2.2	75.2
Average at 1950 purchasing power	2,014	2,409	1,953	2,594	19.6	—18.9	32.8

Source: See Appendix 18–1.

as the war progressed, but this trend was sharply reversed after the war. By 1950 there were more state and local employees than ever before — 4.2 million as compared with 3.3 million in 1942. In 1952 both federal and state and local employment were markedly higher than in 1950 owing to the influence of the Korean situation on federal activities and a continuing increase in the scale of state and local activities.

Average earnings of government employees doubled between the fiscal years 1942 and 1950, reflecting continuing adjustments of civilian wage and salary rates to cost-of-living increases, and even more marked changes in military pay scales. Average earnings increased 75 per cent for state and local and 86 per cent for federal civilian employees between 1942 and 1950.

Public and Private Employees

Of all the money paid in wages and salaries in calendar year 1950, approximately 15 per cent went for compensation of government employees. In 1913, 8 per cent of the combined public and private payroll was for public employees. From 1913 to 1929, public payrolls more than tripled but private payrolls expanded almost as much so that their relationship changed little. During the depression the public portion of payrolls exceeded 16 per cent; then later, at the peak of World

TABLE 256. COMPARATIVE PUBLIC AND PRIVATE PAYROLLS,
SELECTED CALENDAR YEARS, 1913–1950

Year	Public Payrolls as Per Cent of All Payrolls			Average Annual Pay per Employee			Index (1940 = 100)	
	Total	Federal	State and Local	Private	Federal	State and Local	Private Payrolls	Public Payrolls [a]
1913	8.4	2.5	5.9	$ 673	$ 795	$ 845	41.2	18.4
1918	16.7	12.1	4.6	1,039	1,022	986	64.1	62.3
1929	9.9	2.8	7.1	1,408	1,689	1,504	109.9	72.2
1932	16.2	4.6	11.6	1,086	1,620	1,445	61.5	71.3
1937	12.7	4.3	8.4	1,254	1,642	1,441	93.3	84.9
1942	18.9	13.4	5.5	1,736	1,745	1,594	160.0	225.9
1945	30.2	25.6	4.6	2,259	2,122	1,966	199.6	518.0
1950	15.2	8.2	7.0	3,015	3,221	2,837	300.5	323.9

Sources: 1913 and 1918, W. I. King, *The National Income and Its Purchasing Power*, National Bureau of Economic Research, New York, 1930, pp. 56, 60, 132, 138, 361 and 364; 1929–1950, *National Income and Product of the United States, 1929–1950* (1951 National Income Supplement to the *Survey of Current Business*), and *Survey of Current Business*, July 1953.

a. Excludes work relief.

War II, it topped 30 per cent, but by 1950 it had dropped off to about half this wartime high. (See Table 256.) Although public employment accounts for a slowly rising proportion of the peacetime total, it has not yet threatened to eclipse private employment. There were 41 million private employees (on a full-time equivalent basis) who earned $124 billion in 1950, as compared with 7 million public employees (full-time equivalent), including the armed forces, who earned $22 billion.

The public and private sectors of the economy have not differed significantly in recent years as to rates of pay for their employees; in 1950 the average annual pay in private employment (i.e., private wages and salaries divided by the number of full-time equivalent private employees) was $3,015 and in public employment $3,031. During prewar years, average public pay was usually significantly higher than private pay, the advantage being as much as 37 per cent in 1932. Private industry advanced wages materially beyond public rates during World War II, but in the last few years government pay rates have caught up.

The 1950 federal average of $3,221 per full-time equivalent employee was $206 above the private average, while the state and local average was $178 below the private level. Except for a few years, federal average pay has been superior to private since World War II. State and local pay did not lag behind federal pay until the depression of the 1930s or behind private pay until World War II. There are wide differences between military and civilian pay at the federal level and between school and nonschool pay at the state and local level.

MATERIALS, SUPPLIES AND CONTRACTUAL SERVICES

Government expenditure for procurement of materials, supplies and contractual services amounted to $534 million in fiscal 1913 — 18 per cent of total expenditure. By 1932 the proportion had increased to 21 per cent and the amount spent to $2,819 million. Between these two years, the price level of commodities dropped slightly, unlike price levels affecting other classes of government expenditure, so that the real increase in government expenditure for current procurement was even greater than the apparent fivefold expansion. (See Table 257.)

Between 1932 and 1942, expenditure for materials, supplies and services grew 233 per cent to $9,386 million. About half of this increase, however, was due to rising prices. In constant dollars, government purchases increased 117 per cent in the 1932-1942 period. Even though figures for 1942 include extensive purchases of goods for resale rather than use, such as price support purchases and purchase of liquor for sale by state liquor monopolies, the proportion of total ex-

TABLE 257. GOVERNMENT EXPENDITURES FOR SUPPLIES, MATERIALS AND CONTRACTUAL SERVICES, FISCAL YEARS 1913, 1932, 1942 AND 1950

	Amount				Percentage Change		
	1913	1932	1942	1950	1913–1932	1932–1942	1942–1950
	(Millions)						
Total, all governments	$ 534	$2,819	$ 9,386	$10,675	427.9	233.0	13.7
Federal	155	957	6,848	5,499	517.4	615.6	—19.7
National defense	43	248	4,840	2,638	476.7	1,851.6	—45.5
Other	112	709	2,008	2,861	533.0	183.2	42.5
State	88	429	876	2,021	387.5	104.2	130.7
Local	291	1,433	1,662	3,155	392.4	16.0	89.9
Total, all governments, in constant (1950) dollars	1,237	7,087	15,381	10,675	472.9	117.0	—30.6

Source: See Appendix 18–1.

penditure going for current procurement dropped to 19 per cent because of the more rapid increase of other kinds of government expenditure, particularly transfer payments. Despite an increase to $10,675 million by 1950, procurement continued to fall relative to total government expenditure between 1942 and 1950, dropping to 15 per cent. In adjusted cost terms, government procurement fell off 31 per cent between 1942 and 1950. However, the substantial rise in the price level in this period forced government to pay out 14 per cent more dollars in 1950 than in 1942 in return for a substantially smaller volume of commodities and contract services. Shortly after 1950 the downward trend was sharply reversed by the speedy expansion of federal military procurement made necessary by the Korean crisis. In 1952 current procurement expenditure totaled $26.4 billion — 26 per cent of total outlays.

PUBLIC-TO-PRIVATE TRANSFERS

Government transfer payments include cash public assistance grants, social insurance benefits, subsidies to agriculture and business, and other payments that represent merely transfers of purchasing power rather than expenditures for goods or services utilized in the performance of government activities. For a single governmental entity such transfers would include payments to other governments as well as payments to private individuals, but for this analysis in which

transactions of all levels of government have been consolidated, such amounts have been eliminated, except for assistance to foreign governments.

Transfer payments have come to loom large in the total of government expenditure because many of the expensive new functions that government has taken on in the past two decades consist of assistance to economically weak groups through transfer of purchasing power in the form of cash grants financed from taxation, or insurance benefits financed from accumulated contributions from employers, from the government itself, and, in some cases, from the prospective beneficiaries.

In 1913, transfer payments were a relatively minor item. Veterans pensions, a few employee retirement systems, and relatively small amounts for public welfare programs, then administered entirely by state and local governments, accounted for outlays of $215 million, about 7 per cent of government expenditure.

By 1932, employee retirement systems were more widespread; veterans of World War I had expanded the pension rolls; life insurance programs for veterans had been established; aid to the needy, at that time mostly general relief, had become an important governmental cost. These types of transfer payments totaled $1,330 million, or 10 per cent of government expenditure. Interest on nonproductive debt, that is, on the World War I debt of the federal government, which may be combined with transfer

TABLE 258. GOVERNMENT TRANSFER PAYMENTS AND RELATED EXPENDITURES,
FISCAL YEARS 1913, 1932, 1942 AND 1950
(*Dollar Amounts in Millions*)

Category	Amount				Percentage Change		
	1913	1932	1942	1950	1913–1932	1932–1942	1942–1950
	Expenditure in Current Dollars						
Total	$215	$1,837	$9,957	$25,128	754.4	442.0	152.4
Assistance and insurance benefits to individuals	215	1,330	3,381	14,827	518.6	154.2	338.5
Veterans and other educational benefits	—	—	—	2,864	—	—	a
Assistance to the needy except veterans	18	215	1,885	2,263	b	776.7	20.1
Veterans pensions and bonuses	183	829	476	2,658	353.0	−42.6	458.4
Social insurance benefits	15	282	1,016	7,000	b	260.3	589.0
Other assistance to individuals	—	4	4	42	a	—	950.0
Agricultural, business and international subsidies	—	—	5,778	5,048	—	a	−12.6
Agricultural subsidies	—	—	744	499	—	a	−32.9
Subsidies to business	—	—	44	37	—	a	−15.9
International assistance	—	—	4,990	4,512	—	a	−9.6
Interest on nonproductive debt[c]	—	507	798	5,253	a	57.4	558.3
	Expenditure in 1950 Dollars						
Assistance and insurance benefits to individuals							
At 1950 benefit levels[d]	$614	$2,224	$5,551	$14,827	262.2	149.6	167.1
At 1950 purchasing power	523	2,342	4,923	14,827	347.8	110.2	201.2
Agricultural, business and international subsidies							
At 1950 price levels	—	—	9,282	5,048	—	a	−45.6
Interest on nonproductive debt at 1950 interest rates[e]	—	380	680	5,253	a	78.9	672.5

Source: See Appendix 18–1.
a. Not computed.
b. Increase of more than 1,000 per cent.

c. War debt of the federal government.
d. Adjusted to the 1950 level of average payments per beneficiary for the programs concerned.

payments, amounted to $507 million. Thus assistance and insurance benefits to individuals and interest on war debt together aggregated $1,837 million, or 14 per cent of government expenditure, in 1932.

In the depression decade, the development of categorical public assistance, old-age and unemployment insurance, and subsidies to business and agriculture brought a substantial rise in government transfer payments. Veterans pensions dropped in amount, but wartime programs of international assistance added $5 billion to the 1942 expenditure total. Assistance, insurance benefits and subsidies cost government a total of

$9,159 million in that year, of which $3,381 million went to individuals and $5,778 million to agriculture, business and foreign governments. However, the enlarged amount of transfer payments called for only 7 per cent of government expenditure, the same ratio as in 1913, because military costs had so greatly increased total government outlays. Interest on war debt amounted to $798 million in 1942, and the total of transfer payments, plus nonproductive, or federal war, debt interest, came to $9,957 million.

The year 1950 was marked by large expenditure for subsidies to veterans for education, state bonuses to veterans, veterans life insurance dividends and other veterans transfers that aggregated over $8.5 billion. Total assistance and insurance benefits to individuals amounted to $14,827 million. Agricultural, business and international subsidies, all lower than in 1942, cost $5,048 million. The total of these categories, $19,875 million, required 29 per cent of government expenditure in 1950. Interest on war debt, reflecting World War II financing, increased six and a half times over the 1942 level to $5,253 million. Total transfer and federal war debt interest payments amounted to over 36 per cent of total expenditure in 1950, or $25,128 million, as compared with $44,351 million spent for all other classes of expenditure. (See Table 258.) By 1952, however, these payments had dropped substantially in relation to total government expenditure. Assistance, subsidies and insurance payments fell to $13.9 billion — only 14 per cent of aggregate outlays. Transfers plus interest on federal war debt totaled $19.1 billion in 1952, accounting for a much smaller share — under 19 per cent — of total expenditure than in 1950.

INTEREST ON DEBT

Interest expenditure is the current cost of financing government expenditures through issuance of debt obligations. The effect on interest costs of the fifty-fold increase in governmental debt outstanding between 1913 and 1950 was somewhat mitigated by a decrease in interest rates during the period. In 1913 the average interest rate on governmental debt was 43 per cent higher than in 1950. In 1932 interest rates were 61 per cent higher than in 1950. Interest expenditure, including interest on federal war debt described under transfer payments above, amounted to 6 per cent of total expenditure in 1913, 11 per cent in 1932, 4 per cent in 1942, 9 per cent in 1950 and 7 per cent in 1952. The relatively small change in this proportion indicates that the interest burden has increased only slightly more than the total of other kinds of government expenditure. (See Table 259.)

At the end of 1950, total public and private debt were about equal. Of the public portion, the federal government, of course, accounted for the greater share — some $219 billion on a net basis. As late as 1930, state and local debt was almost equal to the federal debt, but now state and local governments account for little more than one tenth of all public debt. The present virtual parity between net public and private debt marks a resurgence of private borrowing since 1945, when the private debt was $104 billion smaller and represented only 35 per cent of all public and private obligations. During the previous two decades private debt varied a little above or a little below the 1945 figure of $141 billion, while public debt rose steadily from 15.5 per cent of the public and private total in 1929 to 65.4 per cent in 1945.

Use of federal surpluses in several postwar years together with unexpended war-end balances permitted a reduction of net federal debt by $34 billion during the recent period of private debt resurgence. On a gross basis, federal debt reached a peak of $269 billion in 1946 when state and local debt had ebbed to $15.9 billion. By June 1951, federal gross debt was down by $14 billion and state and local debt was up by an almost equal amount to $27 billion, the highest figure on record to that date.

CAPITAL OUTLAY

Government expenditure for capital outlay is largely for contract construction of government facilities and, in wartime, for military equipment. It also includes purchase of land and existing structures and purchase of durable equipment. Purchases of military equipment and construction of military facilities are included in capital outlay for purposes of analysis of government expenditure, even though such equipment and facilities may be expendable in military operations.[18]

Capital outlay by all governments was $696 million in 1913, 23 per cent of total expenditure. This sum was used largely for construction of highway facilities and sanitation, water supply, recreation and other community facilities by local governments, water transportation facilities by federal, state and local governments, and military facilities by the federal government.

In the decade following World War I, government capital outlay expanded enormously, particularly for the state and local governments. The local governments went heavily into debt to finance new highways, community facilities and

---

18. In other chapters of this volume, however, military outlays are included in the goods and services classification, not in the capital goods classification. Capital outlay is defined here in terms of the kinds of things purchased rather than in terms of the effect of expenditure on governments' balance sheets.

TABLE 259. GOVERNMENT EXPENDITURE FOR INTEREST AND RELATED DEBT STATISTICS,
FISCAL YEARS 1913, 1932, 1942 AND 1950
(*Dollar Amounts in Millions*)

	All Governments				Federal				State and Local			
	1913	1932	1942	1950	1913	1932	1942	1950	1913	1932	1942	1950
Interest cost												
Total	$ 187	$ 1,495	$ 2,191	$ 6,470	$ 23	$ 655	$ 1,489	$ 5,853	$ 164	$ 840	$ 702	$ 617
On general debt	146	1,265	1,766	6,216	23	600	1,260	5,817	123	665	506	399
On utility and enterprise debt[a]	41	230	425	254	—	55	229	36	41	175	196	218
As per cent of 1950 cost	2.9%	23.1%	33.9%	100.0%	0.4%	11.2%	25.4%	100.0%	26.5%	136.1%	113.8%	100.0%
As per cent of debt outstanding	3.3%	3.7%	2.2%	2.3%	1.9%	3.2%	1.9%	2.3%	3.6%	4.3%	3.6%	2.6%
At 1950 cost level	161	1,070	1,866	6,470	28	491	1,269	5,853	133	580	597	617
Debt outstanding June 30												
Total	5,691	40,299	98,854	281,797	1,193	20,723	79,164	258,150	4,498	19,576	19,690	23,647
General	4,546	34,973	86,470	273,028	1,193	19,487	72,422	257,357	3,353	15,486	14,048	15,671
Utility and enterprise[b]	1,145	5,326	12,384	8,769	—	1,236	6,742	793	1,145	4,090	5,642	7,976
As per cent of 1950 level	2.0%	14.3%	35.1%	100.0%	0.5%	8.0%	30.7%	100.0%	19.0%	82.8%	83.3%	100.0%
Net increase or decrease during year	253	3,384	21,817	7,139	—1	2,643	22,457	4,489	254	741	—640	2,651
General debt	226	3,561	22,732	6,748	—1	2,686	23,461	4,587	227	875	—729	2,161
Utility and enterprise debt[c]	27	—177	—915	391	—	—43	—1,004	—98	27	—134	89	489

Source: See Appendix 18-1.

a. Excludes interest on federal agency debt held by U.S. Treasury amounting (in millions) to $2 in 1932; $4 in 1942; and $101 in 1950.

b. Excludes federal agency debt held by U.S. Treasury amounting (in millions) to $350 in 1932; $4,079 in 1942; and $8,423 in 1950.

c. Excludes changes in debt of federal agencies held by U.S. Treasury.

TABLE 260. GOVERNMENT CAPITAL OUTLAY, FISCAL YEARS 1913, 1932, 1942 AND 1950
(Dollar Amounts in Millions)

Type of Outlay	All Governments				Federal				State and Local			
	1913	1932	1942	1950	1913	1932	1942	1950	1913	1932	1942	1950
Total capital outlay												
Current dollars	$696	$2,666	$19,500	$11,895	$148	$411	$17,230	$5,655	$548	$2,255	$2,270	$6,240
At 1950 cost levels	3,093	7,544	33,931	11,895	677	1,289	30,354	5,655	2,416	6,255	3,577	6,240
Construction												
Current dollars	553	2,142	4,943	6,767	108	282	3,045	1,656	445	1,860	1,898	5,111
At 1950 cost levels	2,603	6,056	8,574	6,767	552	914	5,620	1,656	2,051	5,142	2,954	5,111
Purchase of land and structures												
Current dollars	58	213	3,037	578	9	31	2,855	64	49	182	182	514
At 1950 cost levels	271	618	5,558	578	45	99	5,267	64	226	519	291	514
Equipment												
Current dollars	84	310	11,519	4,550	31	98	11,330	3,935	53	212	189	615
At 1950 cost levels	219	869	19,799	4,550	80	276	19,467	3,935	139	593	332	615
Outlay in Current Dollars as Per Cent of 1950												
Total capital outlay	5.9	22.4	163.9	100.0	2.6	7.3	304.7	100.0	8.8	36.1	36.4	100.0
Construction	8.2	31.7	73.0	100.0	6.5	17.0	183.9	100.0	8.7	36.4	37.1	100.0

Source: See Appendix 18-1.

schools. By 1932, capital outlay by local governments still was substantial, despite the onset of the depression. In that year 20 per cent of total government expenditure, or $2,666 million, went for capital outlay, chiefly for construction of facilities. Federal capital outlay was three times and state and local outlay four times the 1913 level. The increase from 1913 to 1932 was marked even when allowance is made for the rise in construction costs and equipment prices. In constant prices, 1932 capital outlay was more than double the 1913 level. (See Table 260.)

By 1942, capital outlay had climbed to $19,500 million, 39 per cent of all government expenditures, and had changed radically in form. Three fifths of the total was accounted for by equipment, nearly all of it military. At the state and local level, capital outlay in current dollars was substantially the same as in 1932, but in constant costs it was little more than half the 1932 amount. Local housing authorities, nonexistent in 1932, were spending substantial sums for housing construction, so that state and local expenditure for traditional public improvements had decreased even more than these figures suggest. At the federal level, prosecution of the war was requiring large purchases of equipment; later in the war, military capital outlay rose to several times the 1942 amount.

After World War II the situation again changed sharply. Military requirement cutbacks helped to reduce the total government capital outlay from $19,500 million in 1942 to $11,895 million in 1950. Rapidly rising construction and equipment costs concealed a real reduction in capital outlay of much greater proportions; in terms of constant costs, the 1950 total was little more than one third of the amount spent in 1942. Capital outlay accounted for only 17 per cent of government expenditure in 1950, a smaller share than in any of the other years covered by this study. State and local governments spent three times as much for capital outlay in 1950 as in 1942. At constant cost levels, however, the increase was less than twofold and merely restored their spending for this purpose to approximately the 1932 level.

As in the case of current procurement spending, the Korean and post-Korean military build-up brought another upward swing. Capital outlay rose to $24.9 billion in 1952, of which no less than $11.2 billion was for military equip-

ment. All told, capital outlay accounted for one fourth of all public spending in fiscal 1952.

A breakdown of capital outlay by object of expenditure shows that the 1932-1942 trend was influenced chiefly by the military equipment purchases of the federal government and federal purchases of land and existing structures. Government construction expenditure increased somewhat between 1942 and 1950, but only because of rising costs; in terms of constant cost levels the volume of public construction declined. State and local construction expenditure rose from $1,898 million in 1942 to $5,111 million in 1950. State and local equipment and land and structure purchases also increased substantially between 1942 and 1950. State and local governments dominate the capital outlay trend, except for the important military equipment and war construction classes.

Public versus Private Construction Activity

Except during depression and war years, private enterprise has dominated the construction industry. In the prosperous peacetime years of 1929 and 1950 the private sector undertook three fourths of all construction. In contrast, the private proportion was only two fifths in 1934 and 1944.

The amount spent for all new construction, public and private, in 1950 — $29 billion — was over twice the wartime peak of 1952 and well over twice the previous peak of 1926. Aside from the wartime peak, public construction expenditure of $7.1 billion in 1950 was the highest on record, over twice the total for all but one year of the 1930s, when construction was expanded to induce a chain reaction of antidepression spending. Except in war years, construction of federal projects has been relatively minor. In addition to direct federal expenditure for construction, however, some federal aid to state and local governments has been used by them for construction projects. State and local governments spent $4.6 billion from their own funds and $0.5 billion from federal funds for construction in the 1950 fiscal year.

DISBURSEMENTS FOR DEBT
REDEMPTION AND LOANS

Expenditure does not, of course, reveal the complete picture of government outgo. Two other classes of disbursements can play an important part in the disposition of government funds. Debt redemption has been significant among the disbursements of different government levels during different time periods. However, in the four years covered intensively by this review, 1913, 1932, 1942 and 1950, there was no net decrease in governmental debt but rather a net increase. The effect of debt redemption by particular governments on the economy, and on government considered as a single sector, has been countered by simultaneous public borrowing of even greater amounts.

Governmental loan disbursement, however, has had a different history. Public loans were not a factor in the economy of 1913, but by 1932 important loan programs for agriculture and business enterprises had been instituted. In that year, when the Reconstruction Finance Corporation was organized, the federal government disbursed $1,549 million in loan payments, almost equally divided between agriculture and business. A relatively small amount was disbursed for loans to transportation activities. By 1942, the federal government's loan disbursements totaled $3,053 million annually. To agricultural loans of $1,798 million and business loans of $448 million in that year had been added housing loans, loans for electric power development and loans to foreign governments.

In 1950, federal loan programs, not included in the $69 billion of government expenditure for that year, had grown further to a level of $6,447 million in loan disbursements. Credit extension for housing accounted for $1,037 million, agricultural loans for $4,501 million, electric power loans for $379 million and business promotion loans for $503 million. Credit extension to foreign governments, such as the World War II loans and the postwar loan to Great Britain, had practically disappeared by 1950, and was replaced by grants of the Economic Cooperation Administration.

There are scattered state and local government loan programs for agriculture, housing, aid to veterans and miscellaneous purposes, but data concerning their operations were not available on a sufficiently comprehensive basis for inclusion in this analysis. Government loan disbursements discussed here relate only to the federal credit extension programs. (See Tables 239 and 254.)

FUNCTIONAL PATTERNS OF GOVERNMENT EXPENDITURE

The growth of government in the United States in the twentieth century is a composite of expansion in all of the separate areas of governmental responsibility and the addition of new areas of government action. Each area of government activity has its own pattern of development and contributes its influence to the change in nature and scale of government and to probable future trends in government expenditure.[19]

NATIONAL DEFENSE

National defense consists of military, air and naval activities of the federal government, and the civil defense, national guard and related activities of state and local governments. The costs of services for veterans, interest on war debt, and military assistance to foreign countries have not been classified as national defense expenditure, although some of these are in a sense current costs for past or present national defense activities.

National defense has been the principal determinant of government expenditure trends in recent years. Even when stripped of closely allied activities like veterans programs and economic and military assistance to foreign governments, national defense required almost as much government spending as all other functions combined in 1942. (See Table 261.) At the height of World War II, of course, a great deal more than half of all public spending went for national defense. In 1913 and 1932, only 9 per cent and 6 per cent, respectively, of government expenditure was for national defense. On the other hand, in 1950, the low point after World War II,

19. In the following analysis government revenue and expenditure include all revenue and expenditure of government utilities and business enterprises on a gross basis. Operating costs, capital outlay, interest on debt, and purchase of commodities for resale are treated as expenditure; receipts from sales of commodities are treated as revenue. Transactions between these enterprises and general government funds are eliminated to avoid duplication. A particular functional category, such as transportation, includes not only tax-supported activities — highways, for example — but also activities that are generally financed from service charges, such as toll roads and bridges, canals, railroads and transit systems. To make clear the extent of government utilities and enterprises, their transactions have been specified in various tables and have been brought together in Appendix 18-3, which shows the sources and disposition of enterprise funds.

TABLE 261. GOVERNMENT EXPENDITURE BY FUNCTION AND ACTIVITY, FISCAL YEARS 1913, 1932, 1942 AND 1950 [a]

(Millions)

Function	All Governments				Federal				State and Local			
	1913	1932	1942	1950	1913	1932	1942	1950	1913	1932	1942	1950
All functions (net expenditure) [b]	$3,050	$13,246	$50,202	$69,479	$975	$4,324	$38,580	$42,175	$2,075	$8,922	$11,622	$27,304
Expenditure by major category												
General government [e]	2,542	11,770	43,728	55,526	693	3,736	34,269	33,847	1,849	8,034	9,459	21,679
Functional services	2,502	11,223	42,640	54,560	653	3,189	33,286	32,986	1,849	8,034	9,354	21,574
Contributions to enterprises	40	547	1,088	966	40	547	983	861	[d]	[d]	105	105
Enterprises [e]	542	1,941	9,400	9,192	330	1,153	7,647	5,619	212	788	1,753	3,573
Functional services	534	1,741	6,545	7,919	322	953	4,903	4,614	212	788	1,642	3,305
Contributions to general government	8	200	2,855	1,273	8	200	2,744	1,005	[d]	[d]	111	268
Social insurance benefits	15	282	1,016	7,000	—	182	391	4,575	15	100	625	2,425
Expenditure by function												
National defense	264	775	24,579	12,573	253	756	24,545	12,535	11	19	34	38
International affairs	5	19	5,057	4,618	5	19	5,057	4,618	—	—	—	—
Military assistance	—	—	4,423	42	—	—	4,423	42	—	—	—	—
Economic and other	5	19	634	4,576	5	19	634	4,576	—	—	—	—
Civilian public safety	194	746	835	1,508	6	45	66	107	188	701	769	1,401
Police and crime control	88	374	438	725	1	21	37	68	87	353	401	657
Fire prevention	61	214	234	407	—	—	—	—	61	214	234	407
Correction	45	158	162	376	5	24	29	39	40	134	133	337
Education	563	2,401	2,700	10,305	7	23	36	3,060	556	2,378	2,664	7,245
Higher education	43	224	317	1,242	1	3	4	9	42	221	313	1,233
Elementary and secondary	502	2,096	2,281	5,794	3	8	8	12	498	2,088	2,273	5,782
Libraries	15	54	52	114	1	2	5	8	14	52	47	106
Other education	4	27	50	3,155 [e]	2	10	19	3,031 [e]	2	17	31	124

626

Public welfare and veterans pensions	$241	$1,234	$2,642	$5,452	$181	$829	$1,426	$2,269	$60	$405	$1,216	$3,183
Aid to aged	—	—	569	1,438	—	—	1	1	—	—	568	1,437
Veterans pensions and bonuses [f]	189	850	497	2,758	180	816	473	2,263	9	34	24	495
Other special classes	11	36	180	572	—	—	1	1	11	36	179	571
General and work relief	9	248	1,289	329	—	—	948	—	9	248	341	329
Institutional care	26	69	62	134	—	—	—	—	26	69	62	134
Other welfare	6	30	46	221	1	13	3	4	5	17	43	217
Social insurance	15	295	1,120	7,312	—	193	431	4,710	15	102	689	2,602
Administration	—	13	105	311	—	11	40	135	—	2	64	176
Benefit payments	15	282	1,016	7,000	—	182	391	4,575	15	100	625	2,425
Retirement and survivorship [g]	15	129	501	1,679	—	29	315	1,302	15	100	186	377
Unemployment [h]	—	—	380	1,991	—	—	9	143	—	—	371	1,848
Veterans life insurance [i]	—	148	56	3,108	—	148	56	3,108	—	—	—	—
Other [j]	—	5	80	222	—	5	11	22	—	—	69	200
Health and community facilities	368	1,398	2,408	5,467	9	109	553	1,229	359	1,289	1,855	4,238
Health	27	129	138	364	3	8	12	84	24	121	126	280
Hospitals	78	419	569	2,349	5	86	90	904	73	333	479	1,445
Sanitation	86	292	228	645	—	—	—	1	86	292	228	644
Recreation	46	196	145	326	1	15	8	24	45	181	137	302
Public water supply	123	291	354	832	—	—	—	—	123	291	354	832
Local electric and gas utilities	8	72	145	338	—	—	—	—	8	72	145	338
Housing and other	—	—	829	613	—	—	443	216	—	—	386	397
Transportation	499	2,671	3,385	5,750	97	426	1,157	835	402	2,245	2,228	4,915
Highways	368	2,025	2,023	4,200	—	6	10	65	368	2,019	2,013	4,135
Water transportation and ports	128	498	1,008	622	94	384	976	523	34	114	32	99
Air, local transit and other	3	148	353	928	3	36	171	247	—	112	182	681
Agriculture and natural resources	62	330	2,808	4,413	31	170	2,582	3,839	31	160	226	574
Promotion of agriculture [k]	26	133	2,225	2,440	13	79	2,146	2,213	13	54	79	227
Land and water resources	22	114	457	1,043	11	62	381	908	11	52	76	135
Other natural resources	14	83	126	931	7	29	55	718	7	54	71	213
Regulation and promotion of business and labor	30	94	138	271	3	26	57	133	27	68	81	138

TABLE 261 (continued)

Function	All Governments				Federal				State and Local			
	1913	1932	1942	1950	1913	1932	1942	1950	1913	1932	1942	1950
Postal service	$269	$794	$ 874	$2,223	$269	$794	$ 874	$2,223	—	—	—	—
Liquor stores [l]	—	—	293	667	—	—	—	—	—	—	$293	$667
Multipurpose functions	542	2,489	3,363	8,920	114	934	1,796	6,617	$428	$1,555	1,567	2,303
Interest on debt	187	1,495	2,191	6,470	23	655	1,489	5,853	164	840	702	617
General control	272	696	818	1,699	80	248	272	688	192	448	546	1,011
Unallocated	83	298	354	751	11	31	35	76	72	267	319	675

Source: See Appendix 18-1.

a. Total government expenditures shown here are generally higher than in other chapters mainly because no allowance is made here for offsetting income; for example, these figures include gross outlays of government enterprises and gross interest payments whereas Table 29 includes only net outlays. In addition, expenditures here include gross gifts to foreign countries (in public-to-private transfers) whereas other chapters include such gifts (on a net basis) in net foreign investment (see Table 29, for example).

Figures shown here also differ from government expenditures in other chapters because these figures are for fiscal years and in other chapters calendar years are generally used.

b. Excludes intragovernmental contributions between categories.
c. Includes intragovernmental contributions between categories.
d. Not available.
e. Includes veterans educational benefits.
f. Includes pensions to regular military personnel, which are combined with public employee retirement figures in Chapter 14. On the other hand, federal subsistence payments to veterans attending school, which are here grouped with outlays for education, are grouped in Chapter 14 with other welfare outlays for veterans.

g. Includes disability benefits associated with retirement and survivorship insurance.
h. Includes disability benefits associated with unemployment insurance.
i. Includes disability benefits associated with veterans life insurance.
j. Includes disability benefits associated with workmen's compensation insurance.
k. Includes purchases of commodities by Commodity Credit Corporation to the extent that such commodities are not used in the performance of other functions — e.g., foreign economic assistance.
l. Includes purchases of alcoholic beverages for resale.

Note: Expenditure is allocated to the level of government making final disbursement; interlevel transfers are excluded from expenditure of the transferring government.

national defense required 18 per cent of total government expenditure — 30 per cent of federal government expenditure.

In the years following 1950, the Korean War and the rebuilding of an adequate level of military preparedness called for unusually heavy military spending, considerably more than the anticipated recurring cost of national defense. Although this condition was temporary, the nation apparently must continue to devote a far greater portion of its peacetime public spending to military preparedness than it did before World War II or even in postwar 1950.

Demand and Needs: 1950 and 1960

Changes in technology, methods of warfare, foreign policy commitments and the international situation make any projection of defense needs and expenditure highly conjectural. The Department of Commerce has estimated that after the early 1950s the annual rate of defense spending might run between $40 billion and $50 billion.[20] Taking the midpoint of the range, applying a cost deflation factor for the difference between 1950 prices and the 1952 prices reflected in the Department of Commerce study, and making deductions for activities not classified here as national defense — atomic energy and foreign aid — gives a figure of $33.4 billion for 1960. In making this projection it is assumed that the cost of maintaining armed forces of nearly 3.5 million will be somewhat over $23 billion (in 1950 dollars) and that the recurring expenditure for military equipment and construction will total slightly less than $10 billion annually.

These estimates presuppose a continued atmosphere of international tension and continuing heavy commitments to defense of the free world. Needs for defense expenditure in 1960 are assumed to be the same as the forecast of probable expenditure for that year. On the other hand, the events of 1950 to 1953 clearly indicate that expenditure in the year ending June 30, 1950 was far below the amount needed at that point in history. It is assumed that a defense program in 1950 adequate to meet the nation's postwar commitments and assure a continuing strong position would have cost as much as such a program is expected to cost in 1960, i.e., $33.4 bil-

lion. In summary, expenditures and needs for defense purposes in 1950 and 1960 are estimated as follows (in millions at 1950 prices):

	1950	1960
Actual or projected expenditure	$12,573	$33,350
Needed expenditure	33,350	33,350

Obviously estimates of needs and expenditures for governmental activities in total are enormously influenced by assumptions as to the defense segment. The dominance of defense requirements should be kept in mind in considering the over-all magnitudes relating to government operations.

INTERNATIONAL AFFAIRS

The function of international affairs consists of military and economic assistance to foreign governments and conduct of the nation's foreign relations. Military assistance consists of military equipment and supplies furnished foreign nations in kind or credits or grants extended to enable foreign nations to purchase those items; it does not include the cost of maintaining United States troops abroad or other direct expenditure for United States military forces. In 1913 and 1932, government expenditure for international affairs was restricted to the Department of State; the cost was approximately $5 million in 1913 and $19 million in 1932. In 1942 the lend-lease program was in full swing and the nation was spending at an annual rate of $5.1 billion to conduct its foreign affairs and to support the war efforts of the allied nations. The vast bulk of this amount consisted of military equipment distributed abroad. Economic assistance was a relatively small part of the total. In 1950, almost as much was spent in total for foreign affairs, $4,618 million, but only $42 million was for military assistance, while economic grants totaled $4,471 million. Administration of foreign affairs, including administration of economic assistance, cost $105 million. (See Table 261.)

Expenditure trends, therefore, reflect clearly the change in the role of the United States in world affairs and the price of world leadership. Emergency assistance to foreign economies in war and in peace on a multi-billion-dollar scale constitutes a vast new function of the federal government that came into existence with World War II.

---

20. *Markets after the Defense Expansion*, U.S. Department of Commerce, 1952.

TABLE 262. GOVERNMENT EXPENDITURE AT 1950 PRICES, BY FUNCTION,
FISCAL YEARS 1913, 1932, 1942 AND 1950

Function	Amount				Percentage Change			
	1913	1932	1942	1950	1913– 1950	1913– 1932	1932– 1942	1942– 1950
	(Millions)							
All functions	$9,682	$27,109	$85,313	$69,479	617.6	180.0	214.7	−18.6
National defense	838	1,873	44,207	12,573	a	123.5	a	−71.6
International affairs	19	44	8,641	4,618	a	131.6	a	−46.6
Civilian public safety	446	1,563	1,442	1,508	238.1	250.4	−7.7	4.6
Education	2,216	4,961	4,681	10,305	365.0	123.9	−5.6	120.1
Public welfare and veterans pensions	706	2,452	4,721	5,452	672.2	247.3	92.5	15.5
Social insurance	21	315	1,530	7,312	a	a	385.7	377.9
Health and community facilities	1,274	3,474	4,243	5,467	329.1	172.7	22.1	28.8
Transportation	1,725	6,338	5,404	5,750	233.3	267.4	−14.7	6.4
Agriculture and natural resources	204	800	4,242	4,413	a	292.2	430.3	4.0
Regulation and promotion of business and labor	70	190	248	271	287.1	171.4	30.5	9.3
Postal service	989	1,708	1,569	2,223	124.8	72.7	−8.1	41.7
Liquor stores	—	—	481	667	—	—	—	38.7
Interest on debt	161	1,071	1,866	6,470	a	565.2	74.2	246.7
General control	755	1,593	1,428	1,699	125.0	111.0	−10.4	19.0
Other	258	727	611	751	191.1	181.8	−16.0	22.9

Source: See Appendix 18–1.   a. Increase of more than 1,000 per cent.

Demand and Needs: 1950 and 1960

Probably substantial sums will continue to be spent for international assistance throughout the 1950s. Military assistance, which was reinstituted in conjunction with the post-1950 defense expansion, can be expected to continue as an important requirement closely tied to the defense program. Economic assistance, however, should taper off as the free nations regain their economic health. In keeping with the assumption that defense expenditure should have been several times higher in 1950 than it actually was, needs for military assistance in 1950 are set at the level projected for 1960. However, if expenditure for military assistance had been this large, presumably less would have been needed for economic assistance than actually was spent. The amount requested by the President in the 1950 budget has been taken to equal the need for foreign aid expenditure in 1950. It has been assumed that if military assistance had been extended at the needed level in 1950, the difference between the total need and needed military assistance would equal needed economic assistance.

In projecting 1960 expenditures and needs, it has been assumed that military assistance needs, like direct defense needs, will be provided for, whereas funds needed for economic assistance will be approved for expenditure only to the extent that total needs for foreign assistance were met by actual expenditure in 1950.

On these assumptions, international affairs expenditures may be summarized as follows (in millions at 1950 prices):

	1950 (Fiscal Year)		1960	
	Actual	Needed	Probable	Needed
Total	$4,618	$6,709	$3,640	$4,260
Military assistance	42	2,400	2,400	2,400
Economic and other	4,576	4,309	1,240	1,860

CIVILIAN PUBLIC SAFETY

Police and crime control, fire protection and correction are the nonmilitary public safety activities of government. Of these, police and crime control is predominantly a function of local government; state and federal police activities are important, but they account for only a minor portion of the total expenditure for this function. Fire protection is almost exclusively a local government function. Correction activities are performed by all levels of government.

Governments in the United States spent $194 million in 1913 and $746 million in 1932 for civilian public safety. After dropping off during the depression, the annual rate rose again until by 1942 it was $835 million, only slightly higher than in 1932. In 1950, $1,508 million was spent for this function. (See Table 261.)

Although expenditure for public safety increased in absolute amount, the scale of public safety services decreased in the ten years 1932–1942 and in the period 1942–1950. When adjustment is made for price level changes, there was an 8 per cent decrease in the total amount spent between 1932 and 1942 and a 5 per cent increase between 1942 and 1950. The small increase from 1942 to 1950 was not enough to keep up with the 12 per cent population increase in this period, so that per capita expenditure in constant dollars dropped in spite of the near doubling of expenditure by 1950 in terms of current dollars. (See Tables 262 and 263.)

An increase in efficiency of service may also partly account for lower costs, however. Public safety expenditure trends may reflect either better organization and use of resources or lower standards of service.

Demand and Needs: 1950 and 1960

The problem of estimating needs for police protection, fire fighting and correction services in dollar terms is made difficult by the absence of data and the nature of these services. Mechanization of police forces, for example, can make it possible to fulfill additional needs without increasing payroll costs. Professionalization of fire fighting can provide better protection but probably would increase costs. Adequate fulfillment of needs in other fields — education, public welfare, housing and community redevelopment, and health and hospital services — might be expected to decrease materially the need for public safety expenditure.

For police and fire services, constant dollar expenditure has increased during the last five

years roughly in proportion to population growth. This trend has been projected to 1960 to estimate probable expenditure in that year. For correctional institutions and services, the stationary or slightly declining prisoner population over the last decade and recent trends in actual expenditure point to a very slight increase in expenditure between 1950 and 1960.

In the absence of direct measures of need for public safety services, analysis of the relation of departmental budget requests to actual expenditures for a group of selected local governments has been used to arrive at estimates. Since budget requests generally are made with an eye to what it may be practicable to attain in the short run, this technique probably understates the broader need for a better long-range program of services. It has been assumed that, since economic attitudes and pressures in 1960 are expected to be similar to those of 1950, expenditure will probably fall short of needs in 1960 in the same proportion as in 1950. Expenditures for public safety services are therefore estimated as follows (in millions at 1950 prices):

	1950 (Fiscal Year)		1960	
	Actual	Needed	Probable	Needed
Total	$1,508	$1,613	$1,697	$1,822
Police and crime control	725	791	850	925
Fire prevention	407	435	462	494
Correction	376	387	385	403

EDUCATION

Education is the largest single function of state and local governments. Approximately 27 per cent of their expenditure went for this purpose in 1950. At the federal level, national defense, international affairs, social insurance and natural resources overshadow education. Nevertheless, in total expenditure of all levels of government in 1950, the 15 per cent devoted to education was second only to the 18 per cent for national defense.

Government expenditure for education rose from $563 million in 1913 to $2,401 million in 1932. Large though this increase was, it was less proportionately than the growth in many other government functions, so that education commanded a slightly smaller share of total public expenditure in 1932 than in 1913. The depression setback had a marked effect on educational expenditure in the next ten years. Although cur-

TABLE 263. PER CAPITA GOVERNMENT EXPENDITURE, BY FUNCTION, FISCAL YEARS 1913, 1932, 1942 AND 1950

Function	Current Dollars				1950 Dollars			Percentage Change (1950 Dollars)			
	1913	1932	1942	1950	1913	1932	1942	1913–1950	1913–1932	1932–1942	1942–1950
All functions	$31.37	$106.10	$372.79	$459.74	$99.58	$217.15	$633.52	361.7	118.1	191.7	−27.4
National defense	2.72	6.21	182.52	83.19	8.62	15.00	328.27	865.1	74.0	a	−74.7
International affairs	.05	.15	37.55	30.56	.20	.35	64.17	a	75.0	a	−52.4
Civilian public safety	2.00	5.98	6.20	9.98	4.59	12.52	10.71	117.4	172.8	−14.5	−6.8
Education	5.79	19.23	20.05	68.19	22.79	39.74	34.76	199.2	74.4	−12.5	96.2
Public welfare and veterans pensions	2.48	9.88	19.62	36.07	7.26	19.64	35.06	396.8	170.5	78.5	2.9
Social insurance	.15	2.36	8.32	48.38	.22	2.52	11.36	a	a	350.8	325.9
Health and community facilities	3.78	11.20	17.88	36.17	13.10	27.83	31.51	176.1	112.4	13.2	14.8
Transportation	5.13	21.40	25.14	38.05	17.74	50.77	40.13	114.5	186.2	−21.0	−5.2
Agriculture and natural resources	.64	2.64	20.85	29.20	2.10	6.41	31.50	a	205.2	391.4	−7.3
Regulation and promotion of business and labor	.31	.75	1.02	1.79	.72	1.52	1.84	148.6	111.1	21.1	−2.7
Postal service	2.77	6.36	6.49	14.71	10.17	13.68	11.65	44.6	34.5	−14.8	26.3
Liquor stores	—	—	2.18	4.41	—	—	3.57	—	—	—	23.5
Interest on debt	1.92	11.98	16.27	42.81	1.66	8.58	13.86	a	416.9	61.5	208.9
General control	2.80	5.58	6.07	11.24	7.77	12.76	10.60	44.7	64.2	−16.9	6.0
Other	.85	2.39	2.63	4.97	2.65	5.82	4.54	87.5	119.6	−22.0	9.5

Source: See Appendix 18–1.
a. Increase of more than 1,000 per cent.

Note: Per capita computations based on U.S. Bureau of the Census population estimates as of July 1 of each year.

rent dollar costs increased to $2,700 million by 1942, expenditure in constant dollars was less in 1942 than in 1932. In 1950, educational benefits for veterans provided by the federal government accounted for a substantial share of total government expenditure for education. A new type of service, assistance to students, had been added to traditional educational functions. Altogether, public education cost $10,305 million in 1950. (See Table 261.)

Federal, state and local governments all participate in educational expenditure. Elementary and secondary education is administered largely on the local level and financed by property taxes, other local revenues and state aid. Total public expenditure for elementary and secondary education was $5,794 million in 1950, with local governments accounting for $5,692 million. Two fifths of this, $2,289 million, was paid for from state aid. A few states, such as North Carolina, finance the current operation of local schools through direct state payment of teachers' salaries. The federal government traditionally has not participated in providing elementary and secondary education on any significant scale.

Public expenditure for higher education, primarily a state government responsibility, amounted to $1,242 million in 1950. State and local expenditures for higher education rose from $313 million in 1942 to $1,233 million in 1950, under the stimulus of the veterans education program.

Federal participation in education in 1950 was limited chiefly to the $2,874 million expended in that year for educational benefits to veterans. The national government operates a few institutions of higher education and certain elementary and secondary schools. Until recently, federal aid to state and local programs was confined to special programs such as vocational training and agricultural education. New legislation, however, has opened the door to federal aid for construction of elementary and secondary school facilities. Federal expenditure for education also includes central research and statistical activities of the federal government.

Demand and Needs: 1950 and 1960

In estimating needs for education expenditure in 1950 and 1960, actual federal expenditure in 1950 and projected federal expenditure for 1960 for veterans education have been assumed to be equivalent to needed expenditure for this program. Educational benefits paid to World War II veterans have been declining since 1947 and will disappear before 1960 but will be followed by programs for servicemen of the Korean War period. Probably 4 million ex-servicemen of this period will be potential trainees, of whom less than one half will enroll in school programs. Vocational rehabilitation training will, on the pattern of earlier programs, enroll a total of 140,-000. Both types of program will be on the decline in 1960, as in 1950, and together may account for just over 1 million trainees. At a 1950 average cost of $1,331 per student, the 1960 benefits would be $1,342 million, or less than half the 1950 benefits.

State and local educational expenditures in 1950 and as projected for 1960 are far below what would be required to take care of potential students not now receiving any formal instruction and to bring existing educational services and plant up to an adequate level.[21] Major increases in both current expenditure and capital outlay are needed. (See Table 264.)

PUBLIC WELFARE AND VETERANS PENSIONS

Public welfare and veterans pensions is a currently large class of public expenditure which includes a variety of programs for assistance to or care of the needy and special aids to veterans (other than those associated with other public functions, such as educational benefits, insurance and hospital services). Responsibility for public welfare is shared by all three levels of government in substantial proportions, and involves large amounts of intergovernmental fiscal aid.

Total expenditure for public welfare and veterans pensions was $241 million in 1913, of which federal pensions to veterans accounted for $180 million. State and local governments bore all responsibility at that time for other assistance to the needy. By 1932, veterans pensions had increased to $850 million and the total to $1,234 million. General and work relief, costing $248 million, made up the bulk of state and local welfare costs. (See Table 261.)

Sharing of welfare financing among government levels was only beginning in 1932. When state and local governments became obviously

---

21. Projected 1960 expenditure and 1950 and 1960 needs for public higher education, elementary and secondary schools, libraries and other educational programs are based on the detailed analysis and estimates of Chapter 12.

TABLE 264. ESTIMATED NEEDED EXPENDITURES FOR PUBLIC EDUCATION IN 1950 AND 1960
COMPARED WITH ACTUAL 1950 AND PROBABLE 1960 EXPENDITURES [a]
(Millions at 1950 Prices)

	1950 (Fiscal Year)		1960	
	Actual	Needed	Probable	Needed
Total public education expenditure	$10,305	$16,255	$12,372	$17,652
Federal (chiefly veterans education)	3,060	3,075	1,507	1,517
State and local	7,246	13,180	10,865	16,135
Construction and equipment	1,231	3,361	1,595	3,372
Higher education	272	997	268	997
Elementary and secondary schools	934	2,300	1,288	2,300
Libraries and other	25	64	39	75
Current and other	6,015	9,819	9,270	12,763
Higher education	961	2,432	1,467	2,772
Elementary and secondary schools	4,848	7,043	7,522	9,590
Libraries and other	206	344	281	401

Sources: Table 261 and discussion in text.

a. The same basic assumptions as to needed and probable expenditure underlie this analysis and that in Chapter 12, but because of certain differences in concept somewhat different figures are used here. The principal differences are in the treatment of (1) interest on school debt, which is classified here as part of total government expenditure for interest but is treated as an education cost in Chapter 12; (2) expenditure for land purchases, which is included in capital outlay in Chapter 12 but is here included in the "current and other" expenditure class rather than under "construction and equipment"; and (3) federal subsistence payments to veterans attending school, classified here as educational expenditure, are not so considered in Chapter 12 (they are included in Chapter 14 as welfare expenditure). The division between public expenditure and private expenditure (only public expenditure is considered in this chapter) is projected on the basis of current experience. The needed annual expenditure for capital improvements to the school systems is computed on the basis of correcting existing deficiencies and providing for additional growth over a ten-year period of construction; the annual requirement is therefore one tenth of the deficiency existing at the time plus the additional need that will accumulate during the 1950–1960 decade.

unable to meet the burden of increased welfare costs brought by the depression, the federal government shouldered financial responsibility for work relief, and set up assistance programs for special categories of the needy for which federal and state or local governments have shared costs on a matching basis. Federal work relief programs reached their peak of cost in the late 1930s and then dropped off as economic conditions improved and emphasis shifted to other methods of aiding the needy.

By 1942, total expenditure for public welfare and veterans pensions was $2,642 million, of which approximately $1,426 million was spent directly by the federal government and $1,216 million by state and local governments with federal financial assistance. Federal veterans pensions had dropped to $473 million, but work relief and general relief still cost $1,289 million despite the improving state of the national economy and the new special assistance programs, which themselves required outlays of $569 million for the aged and $180 million for other special classes. Institutional care made up a relatively small portion of total welfare costs, the cash assistance programs having reduced the necessity for institutional care of the needy.

By 1950, despite a prosperous national economy, total public welfare and pension costs had risen to $5,452 million. Most of the increase was in cash assistance to veterans in the form of federal pensions and state bonuses. Assistance to veterans, excluding education, hospital and insurance benefits, made up one half of all public welfare expenditure in that year. Expenditure for general and work relief had dropped to a fraction of the 1942 level, but the cost of assistance to the needy aged, blind, dependent children and other special classes had almost trebled. Aid to the aged cost $1,438 million in 1950 and aid to other special classes $572 million.

Of the total expenditure for public welfare and veterans pensions in 1950, the federal government spent directly about two fifths and about

TABLE 265. ESTIMATED NEEDED EXPENDITURES FOR PUBLIC WELFARE AND VETERANS PENSIONS IN 1950 AND 1960 COMPARED WITH ACTUAL 1950 AND PROBABLE 1960 EXPENDITURES
(Millions at 1950 Prices)

	1950 (Fiscal Year)		1960	
	Actual	Needed	Probable	Needed
Total public welfare and veterans pensions	$5,452	$4,922	$5,745	$5,657
Aid to aged[a]	1,438	741	1,114	869
Veterans pensions and bonuses[b]	2,758	2,758	2,901	2,901
Aid to dependent children and the blind	572	660	772	847
General and work relief	329	385	371	420
Institutional care	134	134	215	215
Other welfare	221	244	372	405

Sources: Table 261 and discussion in text.

a. Probable expenditure for old-age assistance in 1960 estimated on basis of expanded coverage of old-age and survivors insurance and establishment of permanent disability insurance; needed expenditure in 1950 and 1960, on basis of full coverage but incomplete maturity of these insurance systems.

b. Includes pensions to regular military personnel, which are combined with public employee retirement figures in Chapter 14. On the other hand, federal subsistence payments to veterans attending school, which in this chapter are grouped with expenditures for education, are classified in Chapter 14 as welfare expenditures.

another fifth indirectly through grants to state and local governments. State and local governments financed two fifths from their own sources.

Demand and Needs: 1950 and 1960

While general and work relief expenditure rises and falls with economic conditions, the special public assistance programs have all steadily increased in cost since their inception.

Aid to the Aged

Old-age assistance, the largest of the special programs, has grown partly because of the increasing proportion of older age groups in the population and partly because average benefit payments have increased. The cost of the program therefore continues to rise even though the need for cash assistance to the aged might be expected to decline as more old people become eligible for payments under the companion program of old-age and survivors insurance. In 1950, 2.8 million persons, or 22.5 per cent of the population 65 years of age and over, received old-age assistance benefits. This same percentage would result in 3.5 million beneficiaries in 1960. The number of aged gainfully employed, since it has remained an almost constant proportion of the aged population, should not affect the number receiving assistance in 1960. Accordingly, the

1960 expenditure, at 1950 cost levels, would be $1.8 billion as against $1.4 billion in 1950 if the ratio of recipients to aged population remained unchanged.

However, this ratio will decline because the old-age and survivors insurance program is gradually taking over more of the burden of providing economic security in old age. The scope of the insurance program is broadened, and its effect on old-age assistance increased, in two ways: through legislative revisions enabling new groups of workers to participate and through the gradual maturing of the system as more of the insured reach retirement age. Even with full insurance coverage — all potential participants actually brought into the system — old-age assistance expenditures probably would not have been less than $0.7 billion in 1950, because many of the aged would not have participated in the insurance program during their working lives and so would not be eligible for retirement benefits. By 1960, full coverage but incomplete maturity of old-age and survivors insurance in conjunction with the increase in the number of aged might bring the needed expenditure for old-age assistance to $0.9 billion. Probable expenditure in that year, on the assumption that insurance coverage will be enlarged but incomplete, is estimated at $1.1 billion in 1950 dollars. (See Table 265.)

Veterans Pensions

Pensions to war veterans vary, of course, with the number and age of the veteran groups as well as with benefit levels. Benefit levels are assumed to be the same in 1950 and 1960. Pensions to living veterans of the Spanish-American War will continue to decrease, and payments to survivors of veterans of this war will increase. A decline in service-connected compensation to World War I veterans will be more than offset by the rise in non-service-connected compensation as this group advances in age. Service-connected pensions to World War II veterans are stabilized for the decade ahead, but non-service-connected compensation will rise moderately. Pensions for the regular military establishment must rise because of the larger size of the establishment after World War II and especially beginning with the Korean War. Federal payments of pensions for military service are accordingly expected to grow from $2.3 billion in 1950 to $2.9 billion in 1960.

State and local payments to veterans, amounting to $0.5 billion in 1950, were almost entirely in the form of state bonuses, which have been or will be received by 55 per cent of World War II veterans. Such payments will be reduced to a trickle by 1960, and the conjectural nature of a federal bonus forbids any 1960 estimate for this purpose. Veterans pensions and bonuses of under $2.8 billion paid by all levels of government in 1950 are therefore estimated at only $2.9 billion in 1960.

Children and the Blind

The number of children 19 years of age or under is expected to grow from 52.2 million in 1950 to 66.8 million in 1960. This rise of 27.8 per cent, if accompanied by a proportional increase in the number receiving assistance, would result in over 2.1 million recipients of aid to dependent children in 1960. Probable expenditure in that year, at 1950 benefit levels, would be $705 million; needed payments, at higher benefit levels, would total $770 million. For care of the blind, which cost $53 million in 1950, probable expenditure in 1960 is estimated at $65 million and needed outlay at $75 million (in 1950 dollars).

General Relief

With the disappearance of WPA and similar agencies, the remaining program of public assistance consists of general relief administered without federal aid. General relief costs of $329 million for fiscal 1950 (which included part of high 1949 costs) would probably not exceed $371 million in 1960. An outlay of $420 million in that year would represent reasonable needs to correct for substandard benefit rates.

Institutional Care

Institutional care of dependents, after declining from 1932 to 1942 with the development of public assistance and insurance, resumed an upward swing during the past decade. Even with social security programs, a hard core of dependency remains for institutional care at increasingly higher inmate costs. Expenditure of $134 million in 1950 will probably rise to $215 million in 1960, but neither year calls for additional expenditure for unmet needs. De-emphasis of institutional care is warranted when social security more completely satisfies welfare needs.

Other Welfare; Summary

The remaining class, other welfare, consists of state and local administrative costs and miscellaneous services such as charity care of patients in hospitals. Costs for this class have climbed so fast since World War II as to point to a probable increase of expenditure from $221 million in 1950 to $372 million in 1960. Needed expenditure would be only slightly larger to pay administrative costs and moderately larger to correct substandard services.

All public welfare and veterans pensions of $5.5 billion in 1950 would, by reason of offsetting increases and decreases, rise to little more than $5.7 billion in 1960.

SOCIAL INSURANCE

The social insurance function consists of government contributory insurance programs for protection against the hazards of old age, sickness, injury, disability, unemployment and death.

In 1913, social insurance was limited to retirement systems for employees of a relatively few state and local governments. Annual contributions of these employees totaled $2 million and benefit payments $15 million. By 1932, state and local employee retirement plans had increased manyfold and the federal government had instituted the U.S. Civil Service Retirement System for its employees. Benefit payments to ex-employees — federal, state and local — totaled $129 million. Federal life insurance had been established for veterans of World War I and paid $148 million in death and disability benefits and dividends to policyholders in 1932. The state governments had set up programs for workmen's compensation insurance. Total government expenditure for social insurance benefits was $282 million and an additional $13 million was spent for administrative costs.

The next ten years were a period of enormous expansion in publicly administered social insurance. Retirement systems for public employees grew in number and coverage. Federally administered old-age and survivors insurance, railroad retirement insurance and railroad unemployment insurance programs were established. Stimulated by federal legislation, all forty-eight states had enacted unemployment insurance plans. Total social insurance benefits were $1,016 million in 1942 and $105 million was spent for social insurance administration.

After 1942, the scope of social insurance continued to expand, particularly through wider coverage of existing plans and institution of new insurance plans for World War II veterans, but also through establishment of new types of insurance by some of the state governments. In 1950, social insurance benefits cost $7,312 million. A large part of this total, $2,687 million, was for dividends on federal veterans life insurance of various types, including special dividends on National Service Life Insurance policies distributing several years' surplus accumulations. Death and disability benefits for veterans accounted for $421 million. Benefits of insurance programs for nonveterans were as follows (in millions):

Old-age and survivors insurance	$727
Railroad retirement	302
State unemployment compensation	1,848
Railroad unemployment and sickness	143
Public employee retirement	650
Other	222

Administration of these social insurance programs cost $311 million.

Social insurance benefits are financed in large part from reserves built up by contributions from employers and covered employees. Some programs, such as the unemployment insurance system, usually have either large excesses of current contributions over current benefits or the reverse, depending upon the state of the economy. Plans such as retirement insurance, old-age insurance and veterans insurance, on the other hand, have large excesses of contributions over benefits in the early years of operation, as their reserves build up. Aside from veterans life insurance dividends, over-all contributions for publicly administered insurance plans exceeded benefit payments by over $2 billion in 1950.

Demand and Needs: 1950 and 1960

Even without any further increase in coverage beyond that authorized in the 1950 amendments to the Social Security Act, social insurance will necessarily grow with an expanding economy. Growth in the labor force from 64.6 million in 1950 to an estimated 72.5 million in 1960 is expected to be coupled with a rise in private national income per private man-hour from $1.93 to $2.40. In keeping with this expansion and the increased coverage authorized in 1950, existing public insurance systems are expected to cost $9.2 billion in 1960. This compares with a 1950 cost of $7.3 billion, which included $2.7 billion for abnormally high dividends on government life insurance. (See Table 266.)

Full coverage of the labor force and of risks in 1960 would cost $14.6 billion, or $7.3 billion more than was spent in 1950. With 1950 coverage, insurance systems now existing would cost $9.2 billion in 1960. Full coverage would therefore increase expenditure by $5.4 billion. Full coverage of risks would involve the establishment of a system of health insurance and considerable extension of permanent and temporary disability insurance beyond the present small coverage. No change in present regulations for eligibility to benefits is assumed, however, in full coverage as used here. To provide a minimum insurance benefit for all retired persons, for instance, would call for additional expenditure beyond these estimates.

Full coverage may be attained not only through government insurance programs but also through private insurance carriers and self-insurers. These estimates present the expenditures of public systems only and exclude the costs of private or cooperative plans for temporary disability, workmen's compensation, health insurance and the like. Large areas for private action remain in these and other fields, such as fire, marine, and

TABLE 266. ESTIMATED EXPENDITURES FOR SOCIAL INSURANCE UNDER EXISTING AND FULL COVERAGE, 1950 AND 1960

(Millions at 1950 Prices)

| Type of Program | 1950 (Fiscal Year) Expenditures | | Estimated 1960 Expenditure | | | |
| | | | Existing Coverage | | Full Coverage[a] | |
	Actual for Existing Programs	Estimated for Non-existent Programs	Amount	Excess over 1950 Actual Expenditure	Amount	Excess over 1950 Actual and Non-existent Programs
Total[b]	$7,312	$2,980	$9,165	$1,853	$14,606	$4,314
Administration	311	130	410	99	730	289
Benefits[b]	7,001	2,850	8,755	1,754	13,876	4,025
Retirement	1,680	750	6,040	4,360	6,946	4,516
Old-age and survivors	727	—	4,300	3,573	4,600	3,873
Permanent disability	—	500	—	—	800	300
Railroad[c]	302	—	566	264	566	264
Government (civilian)[c]	651	250	1,174	523	980	79
Veterans life insurance[d]	3,108[e]	—	712	−2,396	712	−2,396
Temporary disability	65	600	109	44	769	104
General system[f]	36	600	60	24	720	84
Railroad	29	—	49	20	49	20
Unemployment	1,962	—	1,674	−288	2,084	122
State system	1,848	—	1,600	−248	2,000	152
Railroad	114	—	74	−40	84	−30
Health (alternatives)						
National system	—	4,600	—	—	7,200	2,600
Federally aided state system[b]	—	1,500	—	—	3,120	1,620
Workmen's compensation[f]	186	—	220	34	245	59

Source: Prepared by the authors with the assistance of the technical staffs of the Department of Health, Education and Welfare, the Veterans Administration, the Railroad Retirement Board and the Bureau of Employment Security.

a. Assumes old-age and survivors insurance coverage for all workers except railroad workers and 85 per cent of federal and 50 per cent of state and local employees, with the exempted groups covered by separate retirement systems.

b. The health benefits included in totals are those under a federally aided state system.

c. Includes survivor benefits and permanent disability benefits.

d. Excludes veterans pensions and readjustment allowances, which are included in public welfare and veterans pensions. Veterans life insurance is excluded from the social insurance category in Chapter 14.

e. Includes abnormally large payment of $2,687 million for special dividends.

f. Excludes insurance paid by private carriers or self-insurers.

Note: "Existing Programs" and "Existing Coverage" refer to provisions of laws enacted as of end of 1950.

auto accident insurance, and in providing minimum security in the retirement area as well.

Probable expenditure for social insurance in 1960 represents the expenditure under systems now existing and under any new systems whose establishment is likely during the decade. For example, present trends indicate that substantially large but incomplete coverage for temporary and permanent disability and health insurance may be expected by 1960. Needed expenditure differs from probable only in that it is based on full coverage of all the labor force.

Essentially the basis of the projections is that benefit levels in 1960 will be as adequate in relation to wage levels as they were in 1950. That is, the benefit-wage relationship will remain unchanged between the two years. This means that the legal limit to taxable earnings and to benefits must be assumed to increase proportionately to the rise in wage levels during the 1950s. This

TABLE 267. ESTIMATED NEEDED RETIREMENT BENEFITS IN 1950 AND 1960 UNDER GOVERNMENT INSURANCE SYSTEMS COMPARED WITH ACTUAL 1950 AND PROBABLE 1960 BENEFITS
(*Millions at 1950 Prices*)

Type of Benefit	1950 (Fiscal Year)		1960	
	Actual	Needed	Probable	Needed
Total	$1,680	$4,795	$6,540	$6,946
Old-age and survivors	727	3,000	4,300	4,600
Permanent disability	—	500	500	800
Railroad[a]	302	395	566	566
Federal, state and local government employee retirement plans[a, b]	651	900	1,174	980

Sources: Table 266 and text discussion.

a. Includes survivor benefits and permanent disability benefits.

b. Excludes pensions to regular military personnel, which are combined with public employee retirement figures in Chapter 14.

increase would be expressed in a rise in the taxable earnings limit for old-age and survivors insurance to $4,500 in 1960 from the 1950 limit of $3,600. Accordingly, the growth of benefits between these years under "existing" insurance coverage represents not only the maturing of the systems (that is, a larger proportion of persons qualifying for benefits) but also an increase in benefit levels proportionately with wage levels.

Retirement Insurance

Retirement insurance accounts for about half the probable 1960 social insurance costs. It covers not only retirement but also survivor and permanent disability insurance for employees of railroads and of federal, state and local governments. For workers coming under the old-age and survivors insurance program it also covers these types of insurance, on the assumption that by 1960 the present retirement and survivorship benefits under this program will be coupled with benefits for permanent disability. Old-age and survivors insurance coverage of government employees is assumed, in estimating 1960 probable benefits, to be extended to 15 per cent of federal employees and 25 per cent of state and local employees, while needed benefits in 1950 and 1960 are predicated on the basis that this coverage would rise to 50 per cent for state and local employees and continue at 15 per cent for federal employees. Such a development implies that government employees would be protected by two systems — old-age and survivors insur-

ance and their own independent systems. For this reason, benefits needed in 1950 and 1960 for government employee retirement plans are estimated materially lower than they would be if these systems were to provide full coverage for federal, state and local employees. The bulk of the increase in retirement benefits between 1950 and 1960 on both the probable and needs bases will be in old-age and survivors insurance expenditure. (See Table 267.)

Health Insurance

The principal new social insurance program likely to be adopted in the 1950s is health insurance. What its exact form, coverage and cost will be is difficult to predict in the absence of American experience with social insurance of this type. By 1952, the earlier proposals for a national system of health insurance were displaced in public discussion by the proposals of the President's Health Commission for a federally aided state system. The cost of $1.5 billion was estimated as needed in 1950 for health insurance benefits, as distinct from other public health expenditure, while $2 billion to $3 billion might be required for such benefits in 1960. The plan for a federal-state system contemplates a substantial share of health coverage by private and cooperative systems.

Disability Insurance

Permanent disability insurance, now limited to workmen's compensation and benefits under the railroad and government employee systems, would cost in 1960 an additional $500 million if provided under old-age and survivors insurance with the 1950 coverage of that program, and $800 million with full coverage. Temporary disability, on which merely $65 million of public money was spent in 1950, is expected to grow apace. Benefits of $769 million would be needed for full coverage, but only $400 million will probably be spent because this insurance will be extended piecemeal by the states, and private carriers will pay part of the benefits.

Unemployment Insurance

Experience with unemployment insurance illustrates the fact that an insurance system providing current — rather than long-term — benefits may change little in cost if basic conditions and legal provisions are unaltered. Unemployment compensation outlays in 1960 are expected to be less than actual expenditure in 1950 — $1.7 billion as compared with $2 billion — since the fiscal year 1950 included part of 1949, when unemployment was higher than the level assumed for 1960. Indeed, needed expenditure of $2.5 billion for full coverage in 1950 would have been well above the comparable 1960 benefits of $2.1 billion. Although increased benefit rates accord with the strategy of moderating business cycles, it is assumed that benefits will be increased only in proportion to wages.

Veterans Life Insurance

Veterans life insurance depends on forces other than the behavior of the economy. The coverage of veterans who retained government insurance after the two world wars is already established, and indemnities for Korean War service are predictable. Benefits in 1960 are estimated on the basis of past experience and the changing age distribution of the veteran groups. Veterans insurance benefits, amounting in 1950 to $421 million exclusive of dividend payments of $2.7 billion, are expected to rise to $712 million in 1960. Veterans pensions are excluded here and included with public welfare.

Summary

In summary, social insurance expenditure in 1950 of $7.3 billion, including veterans dividends, contrasts to probable 1960 expenditure of $12.3 billion, while the rise in needed expenditure would be from $13.3 billion to $14.6 billion.

HEALTH AND COMMUNITY FACILITIES

Government community services — public health services, hospitals, sanitation, recreation, water supply, local electric and gas utilities, and public housing and community redevelopment — accounted for 12 per cent of all government spending in 1913. All these activities (except public housing, which was not yet in the picture) grew vastly between 1913 and 1932 — far more than the cost level or the population. Government expenditure for hospital services increased the most, rising from $78 million to $419 million. Total expenditure for health and community facilities reached $1,398 million in 1932 as compared with $368 million in 1913.

Between 1932 and 1942 the depression hit hard at government community services. Sanitation and recreation facilities particularly were cut back. Governments spent even less in 1942 than in 1932 for these services, despite increased population and costs. Except for public housing, none of the community services expanded between 1932 and 1942 in terms of per capita expenditures at comparable cost levels. Public housing, introduced in the late 1930s, accounted for $829 million, or one third, of the $2,408 million spent in 1942 for health and community facilities. Many local housing authorities were engaged in construction in 1942 to provide dwellings in war industry centers, and substantial expenditures were being made for initial capital outlays. Capital outlay for other community services was curtailed because of materials shortages. Hospitals, sanitation, recreation and water supply usually call for substantial new construction expenditure each year, but in 1942 construction of such facilities was largely deferred because of the war.

Between 1942 and 1950 government expenditure for health and community facilities rose rapidly. Although expenditure for housing, the big factor of increase between 1932 and 1942, dropped off, the total for health and community facilities rose by $3 billion to $5,467 million in 1950. Even in constant (1950) dollars, the effective increase in expenditure between 1942 and 1950 was about one and one quarter billion dollars. Larger hospital expenditure was the chief component in

TABLE 268. ESTIMATED NEEDED HEALTH AND COMMUNITY FACILITIES EXPENDITURES IN 1950 AND 1960 COMPARED WITH ACTUAL 1950 AND PROBABLE 1960 EXPENDITURES

(Millions at 1950 Prices)

Type of Expenditure	1950 (Fiscal Year)		1960	
	Actual	Needed	Probable	Needed
Total	$5,467	$7,381	$6,167	$8,405
Health	364	589	496	688
Hospitals	2,349	3,186	2,976	4,106
Sanitation and water supply	1,477	2,150	1,344	1,986
Recreation	326	418	356	517
Local electric and gas utility	338	338	382	382
Housing and community redevelopment	613	700	613	726

Sources: Table 261 and discussion in text.

the increase. Hospital operation and construction cost $569 million in 1942, $2,349 million in 1950. Hospital operation increased threefold and hospital construction tenfold during the eight-year period. Expanded veterans hospital facilities were important in the expenditure rise. Expenditure for other community facilities, except public housing, mounted also but less spectacularly. Although public housing expenditure declined with the cessation of wartime construction, loans disbursed by federal agencies to promote private housing increased from $176 million in 1942 to $1,034 million in 1950.

Demand and Needs: 1950 and 1960

The $5,467 million spent in 1950 for health and community facilities was far below the amount needed to provide adequate services. To meet all needs in that year, spending of $7,381 million would have been required. For 1960, an expenditure total of $6,167 million is projected in contrast to estimated needs of $8,405 million. (See Table 268.)

Public Health

Public health services, excluding hospital facilities and sanitation services, accounted for $364 million of government expenditure in 1950. The major specific programs that were needed but not available in 1950 were programs of federal aid for medical education, assistance to local health units, and assistance for school health services. Assuming that federal expenditures for adequate

programs in these areas would have called forth $1 of state and local money for every $2 of federal money, the total bill for government health services would have been $589 million in 1950. This understates the need for the whole program of health services since only specific additional programs that are needed have been considered.

Projection of constant dollar trends of the last decade would result in a probable expenditure level of $496 million by 1960. At the same time, health needs will have grown to $688 million. The deficiency will therefore have been reduced but not eliminated.

Hospitals

The disparity between available and needed hospital facilities in 1950 was also large. According to the U.S. Public Health Service, the nation needed almost twice as many hospital beds in 1950 as were then available.[22] Assuming that 45 per cent of the needed beds should be in public institutions (the ratio applying to hospital construction grants under the Hill-Burton Act) and allowing an average of $17,000 per bed for construction and $1,500 per bed for equipment, a program which would remove deficiencies over a fifteen-year period would require spending almost $1 billion a year for construction and equipment for public hospitals other than federal veterans hospitals. This rate of spending would eliminate the deficiency in acceptable beds, pro-

22. See *Hospital Beds in the United States, 1950*, U.S. Public Health Service.

vide for replacement of 2.5 per cent of existing beds annually, and take care of annual population growth. Additional construction on this scale would soon require substantially greater operating expenditure also — fairly small in the initial year of such a program but increasing as the number of hospital beds increased.

Expenditure requirements for federal veterans hospitals in 1960 would be slightly greater than a billion dollars. Veterans hospitals accounted for $812 million of the $904 million that the federal government spent for hospitals in 1950. Construction of veterans hospitals has been curtailed since then and at the rate now authorized would result in a moderate increase of hospital capacity to 131,000 beds and of domiciliary capacity to 18,000 beds by 1955. Resumption of construction at the 1950 rate is improbable during the years of peak military expenditure, but likely during the latter part of this decade. In consequence, the average number of veterans hospitalized in federal institutions will probably rise from the 134,900 under the authorized capacity to 151,000 in 1960, although the number whose needs are a federal responsibility would approximate 206,000. Expenditure for construction and equipment in 1960 would be $160 million at the 1950 rate. Needed expenditure for this purpose would be $200 million. At 1950 cost levels per patient, according to type of institution, operating expenditure would probably be $697 million in 1960, while $917 million would be needed. Total veterans hospital and domiciliary expenditure would be $857 million on a probable basis and $1,117 million on a needed basis.

Over half the $92 million federal hospital expenditures in 1950 (excluding veterans hospitals) was for grants for private hospital construction and equipment, exclusive of similar grants to state and local governments classified in nonfederal expenditure. Assuming a renewal of authority for these grants, as well as moderate increases for Indian and other federal hospitals, nonveteran hospital cost will probably be $112 million in 1960 as against $126 million needed expenditure. The aggregate of federal hospital expenditure in that year will probably be $969 million, while $1,243 million will be needed.

All told, the bill for public hospital services needed in 1950 and 1960 compares with actual and projected expenditures as follows (in millions at 1950 prices):

	1950 (Fiscal Year)		1960	
	Actual	Needed	Probable	Needed
Total	$2,349	$3,186	$2,976	$4,106
Construction and equipment	632	1,166	752	1,341
Current and other	1,717	2,020	2,224	2,765

The estimates of probable expenditure in 1960 are based on projection of present trends. For 1960 needs, the projection is based on population growth and on the effect on current costs of the level of construction activity postulated to satisfy hospital needs.

Sanitation and Water Supply

In the field of sanitation and water supply, governments spent $1,477 million in 1950. The U.S. Public Health Service's nationwide inventory of sanitation and water supply construction needs in 1947 serves as a starting point for estimating annual expenditure required to satisfy existing needs. The backlog of need existing in 1947, when adjusted to 1950 costs, would require for its elimination annual expenditure of $600 million over a fifteen-year period. These costs are in addition to a normal rate of capital expenditure (average annual expenditure in 1950 dollars for the period 1921–1940) of $545 million. This total of $1,145 million compares with $638 million of actual capital expenditure in 1950. Current expenditure needs for 1950 were more nearly met by actual expenditure — $1,005 million versus $838 million. In all, needed expenditure in 1950 was $2,150 million.

On the basis of trends of expenditure in current dollars, it is likely that public outlays for sanitation and water supply in 1960 will reach $1,344 million (in 1950 dollars). By 1960, capital expenditure at the projected rate will have reduced the backlog of needed expenditure by about one seventh but will still be far below the level required to wipe out the backlog in a reasonable length of time. Current expenditure in 1960 is expected to bear about the same relation to need as in 1950. Total needed expenditure in 1960 is therefore estimated at $1,986 million.

Recreation Facilities

Adequate public recreation facilities would have called for 1950 expenditure of $418 million, not including state parks and forests, which are classified here under conservation of resources. Governments actually spent $326 million for recreation in 1950. By 1960, the disparity between expenditure and needs is expected to be still greater — $356 million as against $517 million — if present expenditure trends continue. Little increase in spending can be foreseen, but needs will increase substantially owing to population growth and increasing urbanization.

In order to develop estimates of need, budgetary requests for recreation funds have been compared with actual expenditures and the National Recreation Association's recommended standards of per capita expenditure have been taken into account. On the federal level, although the National Park Service accounted for less than 10 per cent of recreation expenditure of all levels of government in 1950, use of the national parks and costs for this service are expected to almost double during this decade. Public recreation is primarily a responsibility of city governments and the needs cited, other than those for federal activities, pertain chiefly to the urban population.

Local Utilities

Local electric and gas utility services are public responsibilities only in a relatively few communities. Whether or not such facilities are to be publicly owned is largely a matter of local choice. Beyond this, the scale of local operation is determined by consumer demand at the prices established by the utility rather than by political decision as to how much to spend. Therefore, actual expenditure for operation and construction of local electric and gas utility services may be taken as equivalent to needed expenditure. Actual and needed expenditure was $338 million in 1950 and will probably rise to $382 million by 1960 if current trends continue.

Housing and Community Redevelopment

Like a number of other community services, housing and community redevelopment is carried out partly through governmental activities and partly by private enterprise. The dividing line is a matter of public policy as expressed in legislation and appropriations. During the period 1949–1951 about 4 per cent of all residential construction was publicly undertaken. An additional substantial percentage was stimulated by federal housing loan guarantees, but only this limited percentage was actually constructed under public auspices. It is impossible to predict the percentage, if any, of public responsibility for housing construction by 1960 or to specify what percentage of needed housing should be undertaken publicly. For purposes of this analysis, therefore, the actual proportion of 4 per cent that applied in the 1949–1951 period has been applied also to needs estimates for 1950 and 1960 — not because this represents an ideal percentage but only because it represents the actual distribution in a time period relevant to the analysis.

Public housing and community redevelopment expenditure was $613 million in 1950, mostly for construction of residential housing by local housing authorities. No change is projected in the total public expenditure for this purpose in 1960, although there will be a substantial shift in the ratio of construction to maintenance expenditure.

Needs for public housing and community redevelopment expenditure are estimated at $700 million in 1950 and $726 million in 1960. These figures are based, first, on an estimate of needed maintenance expenditure for public projects, which will increase between 1950 and 1960 because of the larger volume of housing to be maintained in the latter year. Then, to this cost will be added 4 per cent of the total need for housing and redevelopment construction as developed in Chapters 7 and 16, assuming a fifteen-year program for elimination of existing deficiencies in residential housing and redevelopment of existing blighted areas in urban communities.[23]

TRANSPORTATION

Transportation, like community facilities, comprises many different governmental activities. It includes provision and maintenance of highways, bridges and other facilities for land transportation. It includes facilities for water transportation, such as harbors, wharves and other port improvements, canals and other waterways, private water transportation subsidies and actual performance of water transportation services. It also includes airports and other public facilities for air transportation and private air transportation subsidies, provision of urban rapid transit services and a number of miscellaneous opera-

23. This analysis takes into account only urban redevelopment and urban housing needs since responsibility for public action to meet housing and redevelopment problems does not yet extend to rural needs.

tions facilitating or providing air, land and water transportation.

In 1913 government expenditure for transportation, then limited mostly to highways and water transportation facilities, amounted to $499 million, about 16 per cent of all public spending. By 1932, this proportion had increased to 20 per cent, owing to the large-scale development of highways and the expansion of public local transit services. Highway expenditure accounted for $2,025 million of the $2,671 million total government expenditure for transportation in that year.

Highway construction and maintenance were used to provide employment during the depression 1930s, but later cutbacks in highway services, plus the difficulty of obtaining construction materials, held 1942 spending for highways to the 1932 amount. Given the rise in price level, population and volume of highway use between the two years, the amount of highway services rendered in relation to need obviously dropped substantially. Growth of water transportation and extensive development of air transportation raised the total public outlay for transportation to $3,385 million in 1942. However, owing to greater growth of such competing functions as national defense, public welfare and social insurance, transportation dropped to 6.7 per cent of total government expenditure in that year.

By 1950, with the lifting of wartime restrictions and the stimulus of increased federal aid, highway expenditure had doubled, reaching $4,200 million. Facilities for air transportation expanded greatly between 1942 and 1950, but water transportation construction was down substantially. In Chicago, during this period, the metropolitan transit system was taken over by the Chicago Transit Authority for public operation. The net effect of these changes was to increase public expenditure for transportation to $5,750 million in 1950.

Demand and Needs: 1950 and 1960

Highways

Highway expenditure needs were carefully studied in 1948 by the Joint Committee on the Economic Report of the United States Congress. The Committee's report on "Highways and the Nation's Economy" revealed an enormous backlog of needed highway repair, improvement and construction. In terms of 1950 price levels, annual expenditure of $4.0 billion would have been re-quired for construction and equipment over a ten-year period to wipe out the accumulated deficit that existed in 1948, plus an additional $1.5 billion annually to cover new deficiencies expected to develop during the ten-year period. Additional needed maintenance expenditure plus maintenance actually carried on in 1950 would have called for $2.3 billion in 1950 spending. Actual spending in 1950 was $2.3 billion for construction and equipment and $1.9 billion for maintenance.

Highway expenditure is largely conditioned on the volume of highway-user revenue from gallonage taxes on gasoline, motor vehicle registration fees and tolls for self-liquidating projects. These sources do not, as do income and sales taxes based on money receipts, respond to increases in price levels or level of income except as increased economic activity results in greater sales of motor fuels and in the registration of larger numbers of motor vehicles. Unless methods of highway financing are drastically changed, expenditure growth during the 1950s will be more limited for highways than for functions financed from more volatile revenue sources. Expenditure of $3.7 billion for construction and equipment and $2.1 billion for maintenance are projected for 1960 in comparison with the $5.5 billion for construction and equipment and $2.3 billion for maintenance that will be needed in that year.

Federal Water Transportation

Public water transportation services are provided chiefly by the federal government, which spent $523 million for this purpose in 1950. Since national policy is stabilized for the Coast Guard and the Panama Canal, growth in expenditure for these services to 1960 would correspond to growth in the economy. Policy is less well settled for subsidies and other costs of the merchant marine, the navigation aspects of river valley development, and river and port improvement by the U.S. Army Corps of Engineers. Navigation aspects of TVA will be small. Requests for the navigation development of the Missouri River Valley and other areas will require careful screening to approve meritorious projects and to reject ones for which the service returns will not warrant the expenditure. If new river valley agencies are set up with state participation, the federal government will nevertheless bear a large share of the costs, perhaps as much as 70 per cent. Federal expenditure for water transportation will therefore probably reach $677 million in 1960, while it is estimated that $742 million would be needed.

Other Federal Transportation

Aviation, regulatory, scientific and enterprise services constitute other federal nonhighway transportation activities. These called for direct expenditure of $247 million in 1950, with aviation accounting for by far the largest part. Since federal civil aeronautics agencies are the "traffic cops" for all civilian aviation, as well as for certain military flights, their expenditure will rise as air traffic grows. The switch from radio to electronics patrol will be complete by 1960, when only small costs will be necessary for maintenance. Other types of aviation expenditure call for no departures in policy or large increases. No sharp change should occur in the expenditure by the Interstate Commerce Commission, the Coast and Geodetic Survey and the Panama and Alaskan railroads. Probable expenditure for the entire class of other federal transportation would, in keeping with the growth of the economy, be $276 million in 1960 (in 1950 dollars), as against needed expenditure of $295 million.

Federal transportation, as a whole, has already settled into a standardized pattern, except for river navigation. Exclusive of the federal grants included in state and local expenditure, aggregate costs of $835 million in 1950 will probably grow to no more than $1,039 million in 1960, when $1,136 million will be needed.

State and Local Air and Transit Services

State and local expenditure for air transportation and local transit services amounted to $681 million in 1950 and will probably rise to $935 million in 1960. Expected expenditure in 1960 represents a projection of current trends in terms of 1950 dollars.

Needed expenditure is estimated at $803 million in 1950 and at about the same amount as probable expenditure in 1960. Estimates of needed state and local expenditure for air transportation are based on ratios of budget requests of selected local governments to their actual expenditures. Needs for local transit services are estimated on the basis of the distribution of facilities between public and private operation that existed in 1950 and the proportion of the urban population that was served in 1930 — before transit systems began to lose substantial numbers of customers to other forms of transportation. It is assumed that more adequate mass transportation facilities would materially alleviate the almost overwhelming problems of urban traffic congestion.

Summary

Actual and probable government expenditures for transportation compare as follows with needs for such services (in millions at 1950 prices):

	1950 (Fiscal Year)		1960	
	Actual	Needed	Probable	Needed
Total	$5,749	$9,549	$7,801	$9,933
Highways	4,199	7,770	5,763	7,792
Water transportation and ports	622	706	827	910
Air, local transit and other	928	1,073	1,211	1,231

AGRICULTURE AND NATURAL RESOURCES

Natural resources activities associated with agriculture include agricultural research and extension services, agricultural marketing aids, credit facilities and subsidies for farmers, and support of agricultural prices through operations of the Commodity Credit Corporation.[24] In addition to agricultural activities, the natural resources function includes development of land and water resources through irrigation, reclamation, flood control, drainage, soil conservation and the like; development and conservation of forest resources, fish and wildlife, and mineral resources; development of public electric power resources; and development of atomic energy.

Government activities in the natural resources field have expanded markedly since 1913, both by the addition of new areas and types of activity and by the broadening of existing services. From $62 million, or 2 per cent of total government expenditure, in 1913, this function grew to $4,413 million, or 6 per cent of the total, in 1950.

---

24. Expenditure for purchase of agricultural commodities for price support purposes has been included, for this analysis, without offsetting these amounts by receipts realized from eventual sale or other disposition of such commodities. Receipts from sales are included in the figures on sources of funds for financing expenditure in Tables 239 and 269.

Between 1913 and 1932 both the federal and the state and local levels of government participated in enlarging services to agriculture and developing drainage, reclamation, forestry and other activities to conserve land, water and forest resources. Public spending for natural resources reached $330 million in 1932. Even adjusted for cost level changes, natural resources expenditure quadrupled between 1913 and 1932.

Between 1932 and 1942, major innovations took place in public power development and in depression-born aids for agriculture. The federal government shouldered responsibility for guaranteeing adequate farm income and adequate food production through direct subsidies, farm credit operations and price support programs. In 1942, $744 million was spent for farm subsidies and over $1 billion for operating the Commodity Credit Corporation (including commodity purchases), farm credit activities and other federal agricultural enterprises. These new activities and new kinds of expenditure raised total government spending for natural resources to $2,808 million in 1942. An additional sum of $1,798 million was disbursed by federal corporations in agricultural loans.

Between 1942 and 1950, subsidies to agriculture decreased but price support purchases of commodities increased. As a result, expenditure for agriculture changed little over the eight-year period. Not included in this expenditure, however, was $4,501 million disbursed in agricultural loans in 1950, two and a half times the 1942 amount. The relatively small change in outlay for promotion of agriculture contrasted with a doubling of expenditure for land and water resources. At the same time new activities for atomic energy development multiplied the amount spent for other natural resources, so that total government expenditure for natural resources reached $4,413 million in 1950.

Demand and Needs: 1950 and 1960

Government resources policy is so often identified with subsidies, price supports and electric power development that a restatement is necessary to clarify the objectives of public expenditure for natural resources. American policy seeks adequate supplies of food and fiber for improved levels of living; prices and returns to producers comparable to those obtained by others who make like contributions; improve-

ment in efficiency of both production and distribution; maintenance and improvement of our physical resources on a gradually increasing yield basis; parity in facilities and services between farm and nonfarm groups. To be effective, government efforts must mesh with productive enterprise and market demands by employing an arsenal of weapons, of which subsidies and price supports are only one type. Marketing organizations, crop insurance, credit programs, soil conservation and land development, reforestation and timber-cutting control, river basin development, flood control, rural housing, extension services and research programs are among the purposes of expenditures and loans whose importance is not always measured by their size.

Promotion of Agriculture (Federal)

Central to the problem of balanced resource development is the necessity for keeping agricultural production, as affected by technological progress, in adjustment with the demand of domestic and foreign markets. Production can be expected to keep pace with demand during the 1950s not because of larger crop acreage but because of better use of resources through mechanization, application of fertilizer, and other practices that may increase farm productivity. Ample production in 1960, however, hinges upon incentive fair prices, adequate credit, balanced resource conservation, aggressive marketing, farm returns sufficient to invest in machinery, electrical power and fertilizer, and application of extended research programs.

Governmental programs, consequently, will play perhaps an even more important role in 1960 and later years than they have in the past. Loans and price supports will continue to provide incentives to increase crops that are in short supply and to limit production of surplus crops. When the present price support program expires it will doubtless be renewed, though in revised form. As a phase of this program, purchases by the Commodity Credit Corporation (included in expenditure on a gross basis) are estimated for 1960 at the 1948–1951 average of $1.4 billion.

Ordinary commercial credit provided by the Farm Credit Administration and other agencies is more likely to decline than to rise. The backbone facilities of rural electrification will be completed by 1956, leaving to the Rural Electrification Administration loans for rural power extension in keeping with population growth and loans for rural telephone service. The reporting basis of this and other credit agencies, it should be noted, excludes all loans from expenditure. Nonetheless, payrolls and other expense can be expected to rise in correspondence with the larger volume of loans by the Farmers Home Administration for farm housing and ownership and of noncommercial loans by other agencies.

Greatly increased farm production in the future will result in more emphasis on soil and other conservation programs, marketing and distribution, extension services, nutritional and other education, and research. For example, the Soil Conservation Service, which cost $58 million in 1950, would under recent programing require nearly $90 million for 1960. The Production and Marketing Administration in 1950 spent $237 million on conservation of land resources, $39 million for marketing quotas and services, and $60 million for sugar subsidies. Except for subsidies, these expenditures are likely to be materially higher in 1960 — as are the expenditures for research and regulation, which cost $74 million in 1950.

Federal agricultural expenditure as a whole, after allowing for moderately lower purchases by the CCC and decreased outlays of some credit agencies, is expected to grow from $2.2 billion in 1950 to $2.5 billion in 1960 with the economy similar in high-level activity in both years. Backed by bipartisan support, government promotion of agriculture lacks a significant basis for differentiating between probable and needed expenditure.

Land and Water Resources (Federal)

The $908 million federal cost in 1950 for land and water resources included, as the largest component, $438 million spent by the Corps of Army Engineers for flood control. For the years 1954 to 1958, the Army Engineers estimate an average needed capital and current expenditure of $860 million annually. Although much of this expenditure is deferrable, and undoubtedly will be deferred during years of heavy military outlay, $500 to $600 million might be spent in 1960. What the Tennessee Valley Authority will spend depends both on the future scope of this agency, a debatable policy question, and on the timing of its projects. The decisions could result in a 1960 expenditure similar to the 1950 cost of $84 million for power and flood control or in higher costs.

Projects of the Bonneville Power Administration, costing $45 million in 1950, will be mostly completed during this decade, resulting in a lower 1960 outlay. Proposed power dams to be constructed by the Army Engineers, involving expenditure over a period of years, total $1.7 billion for twelve major projects. The Bureau of Reclamation in 1952 scheduled construction projects for the period 1953–1959 ranging from a low of $220 million in 1953 to a high of $413 million in 1956. Missouri River Basin projects of the same bureau for this period range from a low of $65 million in 1953 to a high of $237 million in 1956.

Revision of power policy in 1953, as exemplified by the substitution of private for public construction of the Hells Canyon dams, indicates that federal expenditure will be low in the near future and only moderately higher by 1960. Less subject to dispute than power projects are programs for reclamation and irrigation and land management, requiring inventories, soil conservation and development of the vast western acreage owned by the federal government.

All phases of federal land and water resources activity in 1960 will probably cost $1.2 billion as against needed expenditure of $1.5 billion.

Other Natural Resources (Federal)

Atomic energy accounted for $550 million of the $718 million spent by the federal government in 1950 for other resources. Running much higher now, the cost of atomic energy is subject to an unusually large margin of estimating error because both the military and civilian patterns of atomic development have yet to be worked out. Probable expenditure in 1960 is estimated at $1.5 billion, while potential needs would be much larger.

Next largest in size in 1950 was federal forestry expenditure of $78 million, which was shared by several agencies. The continuing excess of the annual drain upon forest products over timber growth points to the necessity of increasing annual growth and decreasing fire and other losses. Timber cut totaled 12.1 billion cubic feet in 1950, and will approach 13 billion in 1960. With annual growth running at 13 billion cubic feet and net imports at 1.3 billion, timber needs appear superficially to be met. Allowances for fire and other losses, new uses and exports, however, require a total growth of 18 billion cubic feet annually. Past substantial progress, therefore, calls for extension of public aids and services to private landowners through protection from forest fires, insects and diseases; rapid increase of tree planting; technical assistance to forest owners; educational campaigns; legislation to control timber cutting on private lands; and more funds for the development of public forests to full capacity. Federal forest expenditure in 1960 will probably be $115 million as against a need for $160 million.

Expenditure for the three services of mineral resources, fish and wildlife, and geological surveys totaled $79 million in 1950. Trends during the past decade and unmet service requirements suggest that spending in 1960 will be under $110 million on a probable basis and above that amount on a needed basis. TVA's program for chemicals and fertilizers, costing $28 million in 1950, should be only moderately larger in 1960.

Lumping together all federal expenditure for other resources, atomic energy primarily and other services secondarily will raise the total in 1960 probably to $1,754 million with the needed level at $2,318 million.

State and Local; Summary

State and local expenditures for the various categories of natural resources are very much more stable than those of the federal government. Constant dollar cost trends in recent years reveal only minor growth in state and local conservation services. With this dominance of federal programs, unmet needs are largely accounted for at that level. State and local natural resources expenditure was $575 million in 1950, only a little more than one eighth of the federal, state and local total. It is estimated that approximately $628 million was needed in that year. In 1960 the $828 million projected as probable expenditure for state and local governments is expected to fulfill needs for this type of expenditure.

The aggregate of federal, state and local expenditure for agriculture and natural resources in 1950 was only moderately under needs — $4.4 billion as compared with $5.3 billion. Nearly all the difference was accounted for by federal land and water resources and, especially, atomic energy cost. The same two categories account for the difference in 1960 between probable expenditure of $6.3 billion and needed expenditure of $7.2 billion.

REGULATION AND PROMOTION OF BUSINESS AND LABOR

Activities to regulate and promote business and labor form a function of government which has an effect on the private economy and on society far greater than the relatively small expenditure for this purpose would indicate. Increasing expenditure for this function from $30 million in 1913 to $94 million in 1932, $138 million in 1942, and $271 million in 1950 was supplemented by disbursements for loans to promote business activity totaling $760 million in 1932, $448 million in 1942, and $503 million in 1950. Regulatory activities included in this category range from local building inspection and state regulation of economic activities to the functions of the Federal Trade Commission and the Securities and Exchange Commission. Business promotional activities include those of the Reconstruction Finance Corporation and various other federal units which advise and assist the business community. Services to labor include both state and federal agencies with responsibility for protecting and promoting labor interests.

Of the $133 million spent by the federal government in 1950 for these purposes, $58 million was for the RFC, other credit corporations and the Housing Expeditor. This cost will probably be materially reduced before 1960. The remaining portion of the cost can be expected to increase in keeping with population growth but without the proliferation of services that marked the past two decades. For example, responsible officials of the National Labor Relations Board, the Federal Mediation and Conciliation Service, the Securities and Exchange Commission, the Tariff Commission and the Patent Office forecast a relatively stable expenditure trend, with only minor growth. In contrast, substantial growth is required for regulatory or service activities, according to officials of the Federal Communications Commission, the Food and Drug Administration, the Bureau of Foreign and Domestic Commerce, and other agencies that are likely to be broadened in scope. Expenditure for the entire category will probably increase only slightly to $144 million, while needed expenditure would be as much as $174 million to pay for more ample promotional and scientific programs.

State and local expenditure of $138 million in 1950 is expected to drop slightly to $135 million by 1960 on the basis of current trends. Actual and probable expenditures have been taken as equivalent to needed expenditure in this field of activity.

POSTAL SERVICE

Total postal service expenditure rose from $269 million in 1913 to $794 million in 1932. Adjusted for changes in cost level and for population growth, this increase still showed an expansion in services rendered.

After 1932 the depression materially affected postal service financing. Expenditure rose to $874 million in 1942, but if cost increases are taken into account, a substantial reduction in expenditure per capita took place in this period.

During and after World War II, mail volume grew enormously while operating costs were pushed up by the rising general price level and upward adjustments in salary scales for postal employees. Consequently, expenditure was over two and a half times as great in 1950 as in 1942. Postal revenue in 1950 was half a billion dollars short of covering the $2,223 million spent in that year.

Postal expenditure expressed in 1950 dollars was equivalent to $11.65 per capita in 1942 and $14.71 in 1950. If the same rate of increase should prevail during the present decade, the total cost of postal service for the larger 1960 population would be $3,452 million. In contrast, if per capita costs should be the same in 1960 as in 1950, the total would grow only with population to $2,538 million. Neither assumption is warranted. Costs follow not merely population but more particularly the volume of postal business. The number of items of mail or special services grew by one half between 1942 and 1950, from 30.1 billion to 46 billion. Rates of growth during the 1940s, however, were larger for the postal service, as well as for national income and other indexes, than are anticipated during the 1950s. Since the beginning of 1949 the postal service has experienced a consistent growth, a rate of physical increase of 3.63 per cent annually. Applied to the present decade, this rate of increase would result in a volume of 62.6 billion pieces of mail in 1960.

Cost per piece at 1950 prices was 5¢ in 1942 and 1950. Variation of costs by class of mail over this period indicates a possible reduction in unit costs by 1960, but since 1960 estimates in this study are in terms of 1950 price or cost levels, the 1950 unit cost is projected to 1960. On this basis the 1960 expenditure would be $3,132 million. Such an expenditure should be adequate for needs, except to pay for additional services. Re-institution of a second mail delivery, for example, would cost $130 million annually in 1950 dollars. Unit costs in relation to physical volume are a more reliable index for the postal service than for some functions because postal costs exclude variable capital outlay for construction of post offices, which are included, with other public buildings, in the category of general control. In terms of 1960 price levels, the total expenditure would be materially larger by reason of salary and other cost increases reflecting price inflation since 1950.

LIQUOR STORES

After repeal of the prohibition amendment, some of the states undertook to control the sale of alcoholic beverages by means of retail liquor monopolies. Sixteen states now operate such monopolies and three other states authorize their local governments to operate retail liquor stores. Expenditure for liquor stores, as defined for this study, consists of the costs of operating these state and local retail establishments plus the costs of liquor purchased for resale. The latter item, of course, accounts for the great bulk of the expenditure shown.[25] There was no expenditure for liquor stores in 1913 and 1932, but $293 million was spent in 1942 and $667 million in 1950. Increases in cost and population were largely responsible for the rise during the eight-year period.

Liquor store expenditure, since it is largely the cost of liquor purchased for resale, is determined by the level of demand at the established price levels. Therefore, expenditure has been assumed to be equivalent to need. By 1960, assuming there is no change in the number of states which provide for governmental ownership and operation of liquor stores, expenditure is expected to reach $715 million on the basis of present trends.

INTEREST ON DEBT

Government expenditure for interest on debt rose from $187 million, or 6 per cent of public

---

25. Revenue from sales is included in sources of funds available for government spending as shown in Tables 238 and 244.

expenditure, in 1913 to $1,495 million, or 11 per cent, in 1932. The increase was associated with an increase in outstanding debt from $5,691 million to $40,299 million in this period. Federal debt, which was minor before World War I, was multiplied many times by the financial burden of that war and, though reduced in the 1920s, still totaled $20,723 million in 1932. State and local debt more than doubled in the decade 1910–1920 and doubled again in the 1920s because of the large capital outlay undertaken by these governments during the postwar period. State and local debt reached $19,576 million by 1932. As these figures show, the federal government and state and local governments shared equally in the total public debt at that time.

By 1942, federal deficit financing during the depression and in the first year of World War II had raised the federal debt to $79,164 million. Overextension of credit and their limited resources prevented state and local governments from adequately caring for the unemployed and for necessary public works during the depression. Relief and capital needs, although resulting in more state and local expenditure than is commonly realized, were largely met by the federal government. State and local borrowing of $9.3 billion from 1932 to 1941 was nearly all offset by debt redemption, so that nonfederal public debt was about the same at the end as at the beginning of this period. Increases in the interest burden through the rise in federal debt were somewhat offset by substantial reductions in interest rates, so that government expenditure for interest rose less than 50 per cent to $2,191 million in 1942 although debt outstanding increased 145 per cent.

After 1942, the federal government's financing of war operations continued to determine public debt and interest trends. The tremendous growth of the federal debt during World War II was only slightly offset by debt redemption in postwar years. That the federal debt still stood at $258 billion in 1950 attests to the difficulty of reducing debts of national governments except by hyperinflation and repudiation. State and local governments cut their debt sharply during the war years as surpluses were built up and improvement programs postponed because of wartime shortages. After World War II, however, financing of delayed capital outlay, as well as state military bonuses, rapidly raised state and local debt above

the prewar total. By June 30, 1950 it was $23,647 million.

During this period state and local governments generally continued to benefit from lower interest rates. Since they retired or refunded their high-rate older debt obligations at new lower rates, their expenditure for interest actually declined despite the increase in outstanding debt. However, substantial amounts of state and local debt outstanding at the end of 1950 had been so recently issued that the annual interest cost was not fully reflected in interest expenditure for the 1950 fiscal year.

State and local debt has shifted significantly in its composition in the last twenty years. Whereas general debt of state and local governments was about the same in 1950 as in 1932, and slightly lower in 1942, debt for state and local utilities and enterprises almost doubled over the eighteen years, rising from $4,090 million in 1932 to $5,642 million in 1942 and $7,976 million in 1950.

Total government expenditure for interest was $6,470 million in 1950, three times the 1942 amount. Nine per cent of all government expenditure in 1950 was for interest on debt. Fourteen per cent of federal expenditure was for this purpose and 2 per cent of state and local expenditure.

Debt and Interest in 1960

The outstanding debt of the federal government requires adjustment to establish an accurate base for estimating future interest payments. As of June 31, 1953, the federal debt of over $279 billion comprised not only the United States government debt of $266 billion but also the guaranteed and nonguaranteed obligations of government corporations and other agencies, amounting to over $13 billion. Agency securities of $12 billion held by the United States must be subtracted from the total in order to prevent duplicate counting of the same debt. An additional deduction of $2 billion must be made for non-interest-bearing debt. Thus, the total federal debt calling for interest was $265 billion on June 30, 1953.[26]

The federal debt requiring interest in 1960 is estimated at $275 billion. Although the Eisenhower administration is committed to a balanced budget, some rise in the debt seems probable in view of the 1953–1954 business decline and pres-

---

26. Federal debt data for 1953 based on a communication from U.S. Treasury, September 4, 1953.

sures for reduced taxes. A serious depression during the 1950s, however, probably would push the federal debt over $300 billion, following an upward adjustment of the debt limit.

The Twentieth Century Fund Committee on the Federal Debt has recommended "the adoption of a regular program of extinguishing part of the federal debt whenever employment is at or below a frictional level and prices are stable or rising." [27] This might be a desirable policy, but the chances of debt retirement during the 1950s appear slight. In the decade after World War I, relatively small federal expenditure and rising national income simultaneously permitted debt retirement and tax reduction. Moreover, half of the $9 billion retirement in that period was not from budget surpluses but from sales of surplus war goods and from European repayments of war loans — sources now obviously dried up. In the 1950s, tax reductions are scheduled at a time when expenditures are necessarily high; and any expenditure decrease is likely to be offset by tax reductions, without provision for debt retirement. Only the levy of new and unlikely taxes to create surpluses would permit a substantial cut in debt.

This analysis assumes for all functions a price and cost level in 1960 similar to that in 1950. Therefore, federal interest costs in 1960, after allowing for bonds outstanding in 1950 and maturing after 1960, will reflect the interest rates prevailing in 1950 rather than the subsequent higher rates. The chief difference between the two years, aside from the slightly larger debt in 1960, will be that a much larger proportion of the 1960 debt will be in long-term bonds bearing higher rates of interest than the short-term securities that bulked so large in 1950. Consequently, federal interest in 1960 is estimated at $6,350 million as against $5,853 million in 1950. Like other prices, interest rates in all probability will be higher during the remaining years of this decade than in 1950. Federal interest may rise materially more by 1960 than the $0.5 billion increase based on 1950 price levels.

State and Local

State and local debt and interest payments are only a fraction of the federal government magni-

tudes. However, during 1947–1952, state debt increased at an average rate of $780 million a year. This rate of increase may be applied to the 1950–1960 decade if it is adjusted to exclude debt incurred to finance veterans bonuses, which are not likely to be paid on a large scale in the next few years. It is estimated, therefore, that state debt will grow at an average annual rate of $500 million between 1950 and 1960. This assumes continued high levels of state and local construction. In view of the enormous backlog of unmet needs and the assumed continuation of high-level economic activity, this seems a likely pattern for the decade. Similar calculation yields a corresponding prospective annual increase in local government debt of $1,750 million for the 1950–1960 decade. These trends in debt outstanding would raise state and local expenditure for interest from $617 million in 1950 to $1,334 million in 1960.

GENERAL CONTROL

Activities grouped under "general control" consist of the legislative, central executive, judicial and general administrative responsibilities of government. They include also administrative activities not allocable to particular functions. Government expenditure for general control, as for most other functions, grew significantly between 1913 and 1932, rising from $272 million annually to $696 million. Even adjusted for price level changes and population growth, general control services expanded markedly during this period.

After 1932, expenditure for general control increased to $818 million in 1942 and $1,699 million in 1950. When account is taken of price changes and population increases, however, the real extent of general control services apparently declined from 1932 to 1950. Per capita expenditure for general control at constant price levels fell 17 per cent between 1932 and 1942, and had climbed back only part of the way by 1950.

For the federal government, the rise in general control costs during the 1940s was largely concentrated in the Treasury and other fiscal management services, which accounted for two thirds of the 1950 expenditure of $688 million. A much larger volume of federal taxes was collected at lower unit costs in 1950 than in 1942. In the 1950s, therefore, financial administration costs may be expected to rise with national growth but

27. Charles Cortez Abbott, *The Federal Debt: Structure and Impact,* Twentieth Century Fund, New York, 1953, p. 220.

TABLE 269. VETERANS PROGRAMS, BY TYPE OF BENEFIT, SELECTED
FISCAL YEARS, 1913–1950 [a]

Type of Benefit	1913	1922	1932	1942	1950
Amount of Expenditures (*Millions*)					
Total	$189	[b]	$852	$629	$9,754
Federal	180	$744	818	605	9,259
Life insurance benefits	—	103	140	48	421
Life insurance dividends	—	2	7	8	2,687 [c]
Compensation and pensions					
Living veterans	127	253	421	320	1,524
Dependents of deceased veterans	48	124	124	111	485
Readjustment allowances [d]	—	—	—	—	138
Vocational rehabilitation	—	166	—	—	274
Education and training	—	—	—	—	2,600
Hospitals and domiciliaries	4	77	56	69	761
Current operation	4	76	43	65	601
Hospitals	—	69	32	59	581
Domiciliaries	4	7	11	6	20
Capital outlay	—	1	13	4	160
Loan guaranty or insurance	—	—	—	—	59
Administration and other	1	19	70	49	310
State and local pensions and bonuses	9	[b]	34	24	495
Number of Beneficiaries of Selected Types (*Thousands*)					
Life insurance benefits [e]	--	142	164	43	480
Life insurance dividends	—	345	582	389	15,628
Compensation and pensions [f]					
Living veterans	504	431	994	624	2,368
Dependents of deceased veterans	317	341	334	312	991
Annual Payment per Beneficiary of Selected Types					
Life insurance benefits	—	$724	$854	$1,116	$877
Life insurance dividends	—	6	13	21	172
Compensation and pensions					
Living veterans	$251	588	424	514	644
Dependents of deceased veterans	151	364	372	356	490

Sources: Federal data are from tabulations furnished by the Veterans Administration; state and local figures are from U.S. Bureau of the Census reports and estimates by the authors. Detail of figures differs slightly from Table 270 because of differences in method of allocation.

a. The figures shown here include veterans life insurance payments and medical care, both of which are excluded in the "veterans programs" classification in Chapter 14.

b. Not available.

c. Includes $2,635 million of National Service Life Insurance surplus earned from 1940 to 1948.

d. Unemployment and self-employment allowances.

e. Cases on which payments were being made on June 30, and cases on which lump-sum payments were completed during year.

f. Number of beneficiaries on June 30.

Note: Costs for veterans programs are allocated in other tables to the basic functional categories of government expenditure.

not from increased tax collection or addition of services. The historical core agencies of the legislative, judicial and executive branches have already undergone expansion and are not likely to be further enlarged during the 1950s. This category, it will be recalled, excludes functional or noncentral administration as well as the many regulatory and informational agencies elsewhere classified. Probable expenditure is estimated at $973 million in 1960 for requirements of the 1960 population at the 1950 cost level of $4.55 per capita. Moderate additional expenditure would be needed to carry out the so-called decentralization of federal offices and to substitute federal

TABLE 270. ESTIMATED NEEDED EXPENDITURE UNDER ALL VETERANS PROGRAMS IN 1950 AND 1960 COMPARED WITH ACTUAL 1950 AND PROBABLE 1960 EXPENDITURE[a]
(*Millions at 1950 Prices*)

Type of Expenditure	1950 (Fiscal Year)		1960	
	Actual	Needed	Probable	Needed
Total	$9,754	$9,909	$5,923	$6,183
Education	2,968	2,968	1,393	1,393
Hospitals	812	967	857	1,117
Pensions and bonuses[b]				
Federal	2,263	2,263	2,878	2,878
State and local	495	495	23	23
Life insurance	3,108	3,108	712	712
Loan guaranty and other	108	108	60	60

Sources: Table 261, same sources as shown for Table 269, and discussion in text.

a. The data shown here include veterans life insurance payments and medical care, both of which are excluded in Chapter 14.

b. Includes pensions to regular military personnel, which are combined with public employee retirement figures in Chapter 14. On the other hand, federal subsistence payments to veterans attending school, which are here grouped with outlays for education, are grouped in Chapter 14 with other welfare expenditures for veterans.

buildings for a portion of the now large office rentals.

State and local general control expenditure will probably change little between 1950 and 1960 if current trends continue. Budget requests indicate that needed expenditure was about 14 per cent above the actual level in 1950. The same relation has been assumed for 1960.

General control needs and expenditure for all levels of government may be summarized as follows (in millions at 1950 prices):

	1950 (Fiscal Year)		1960	
	Actual	Needed	Probable	Needed
Total	$1,699	$1,863	$2,048	$2,218
Federal	688	708	973	989
State and local	1,011	1,155	1,075	1,229

VETERANS SERVICES AND BENEFITS

The full import of services and benefits to veterans is lost when, as in the above analysis, outlays for veterans are split up into various functions. Veterans hospitals have been included with other public hospitals, veterans life insurance with other social insurance, veterans pensions and bonuses with other public assistance to special groups, and veterans educational benefits with other public education. The combined cost of all these and other programs for veterans rose

from $189 million, or 6 per cent of government expenditure, in 1913 to $852 million in 1932, also about 6 per cent of expenditure. In the next ten years these costs fell to $629 million, but by 1950 they had climbed to $9,764 million and accounted for 14 per cent of all public spending. (See Table 269.)

Certain expenditures for veterans programs that were large in 1950 probably will decline substantially or disappear entirely during this decade. Examples are educational benefits, state bonuses and the large special life insurance dividends paid in 1950, which represented several years' accumulation of dividend rights. On the other hand, costs of pensions, hospital service and other programs, and life insurance benefits will grow. Although their over-all cost is on the decline, veterans programs probably will continue indefinitely to require a substantial fraction of government expenditure.

Probable expenditure in 1960 is estimated at $5.9 billion, compared with the peak cost of $9.8 billion in 1950. Benefits for education, pensions and insurance are based on carefully devised plans that require no separation of needed expenditure from actual or probable costs. The one category in which needs outrun costs is veterans hospitals. Needed expenditure therefore does not greatly exceed actual or probable expenditure.

Actual expenditure of $9.8 billion in 1950 compares with needed expenditure of $9.9 billion, probable expenditure of $5.9 billion in 1960 with needed expenditure of $6.2 billion. Even if the abnormally large insurance dividends of $2.7 billion paid in 1950 are excluded from the comparison, veterans expenditure of $7.1 billion in 1950 would drop to $6 billion in 1960 — a little less on a probable basis and a bit more on a needed basis. (See Table 270.)

Summary

Government expenditure developed very differently in each of the three divisions of the historical period covered by this analysis. From 1913 to 1932, expenditure for virtually all public functions increased substantially, even when allowance is made for price increases. Total per capita costs of government grew in current dollars from $31.37 in 1913 to $106.10 in 1932, while in 1950 dollars the growth was from $99.58 to $217.15. (See Table 263.) For social insurance (chiefly employee pensions), agriculture and natural resources, and interest on debt, per capita costs in constant dollars were over three times higher in 1932 than in 1913. Increases for national defense, civilian public safety, education, public welfare, health and community facilities, transportation, regulation and business promotion, and general control were also large. Only the postal service showed a relatively small increase.

Expenditure behavior was strikingly different in the second period. In constant (1950) dollars, per capita costs rose from $217.15 in 1932 to $633.52 in 1942. Excluding national defense and foreign affairs expenditures, however, the increase was only from $201.80 to $241.08. Expenditure for public welfare, housing, social insurance and agricultural aids rose sharply in relation to population during the depression years. Per capita expenditure also rose for interest on debt and regulation and business promotion. Per capita costs for many other functions fell off as emphasis shifted from standard services to new relief, aid and insurance programs. Civilian public safety, education, community facilities other than housing, transportation, the postal service, general control and miscellaneous services were reduced in relation to population during this decade.

Expenditure patterns again changed significantly in the eight years from 1942 to 1950. Total per capita expenditure in 1950 dollars fell from $633.52 to $459.74, owing largely to reduced military and international affairs costs. Excluding these, public expenditure per capita rose during the period from $241.08 to $345.99. New veterans programs and enlarged operations of social insurance systems pushed up sharply per capita costs for education and social insurance. Interest costs increased threefold in relation to population as the federal government accumulated a huge war debt. Public welfare costs, on the other hand, remained almost stationary, despite large veterans pensions and bonuses. Postal service expenditure per person in the population rose only slightly even though there was a tremendous increase in mail volume. Per capita expenditure for general control and liquor stores also increased on an adjusted cost basis. Expenditure for civilian public safety, consisting chiefly of local police and fire protection, continued to decline on a per capita basis. Per capita expenditure for community facilities also declined, although costs of hospitals and certain other programs included in this category grew during the period. Transportation, natural resources, and regulation and business promotion all showed lower per capita expenditures on an adjusted cost basis in 1950 than in 1942.

DEMAND AND NEEDS: 1950 AND 1960

Government expenditure trends and needs for government services relate to a wide variety of fields of activity, some of which cut across other sections of the economy. The problem of expenditure estimation is complicated by potential changes in the division of effort in certain major areas between public and private action. This is true in particular for such functions as higher education, hospitals, housing, utilities, many forms of transportation, recreation, and the fields of operation of government business enterprises. Further problems arise from the variety of circumstances — legislative attitudes, conflicting pressures, differential priorities and the like — that set areas of governmental activity apart from the rest of the economy and from each other. These considerations have made it necessary to piece together the analysis of the government sector of the economy like a jigsaw puzzle, with each major function or kind of activity receiving separate attention.

TABLE 271. ESTIMATED PERCENTAGE DISTRIBUTION OF GOVERNMENT EXPENDITURE BY MAJOR CHARACTER CLASS, 1950 AND 1960

| Character Class | 1950 (Fiscal Year) | | 1960 | |
	Actual	Needed	Probable	Needed
All expenditure	100.0	100.0	100.0	100.0
Public-to-private transfers	28.6	22.4	18.8	18.6
Construction and equipment	16.3	24.0	21.6	23.6
Interest	9.3	5.8	7.4	6.5
Other	45.8	47.8	52.3	51.2

Sources: Table 254 and discussion in text.

When the separate components are all added up, the total amount spent for public services in 1950 comes to $69 billion and the total needed expenditure to almost $111 billion. About $21 billion of the deficiency was in national defense expenditure and represents the additional amount that would have been required to operate the kind of defense establishment now considered appropriate in a world of tension and cold war. The remaining $21 billion of deficiency represents needed schools, highways, sewers, waterworks, social insurance expansion, hospitals, health services, and a host of other facilities and services that are inadequate to the needs of the population. Much responsibility for these deficiencies rests with the economic distortions caused by World War II, which delayed needed improvements in the governmental plant. Rising standards and expectations in the way of education, health, transportation and other services also share in responsibility for the deficit.

By 1960, government expenditure is expected to grow to $104 billion annually (in terms of 1950 dollars), if present trends calculated in detail for each function continue. Meanwhile, needs for government services will have grown to $118 billion a year. The gap between accomplishment and need seems likely to be greatly reduced largely because of more adequate defense spending. For other functions, the government expenditure program probably will fall some $14 billion short of meeting calculated needs.

Expenditure by Character Class

Estimates of needed government expenditure in 1950 and of probable and needed outlays in 1960 differ significantly from actual 1950 expenditure in their distribution by character class — that is, in the forms in which they would be paid out. Public-to-private transfers, which represented nearly 29 per cent of the total 1950 expenditure, are expected to fall below 19 per cent in 1960. (See Table 271.) This sharp drop in proportion results from the expected leveling off of transfers in striking contrast to their huge increase during the period 1932–1950, when public assistance, social insurance, farm subsidies and international aid were added to greatly increased military pensions and allotments. In contrast to earlier pages (see Table 258), transfers here exclude the interest on war debt that is included in total interest cost set forth in Table 271.

Transfers in 1960 are expected to be lower than actual transfers in 1950 — $19.6 billion as compared with $19.9 billion — although the two years can be compared better after subtracting $2.7 billion in 1950 for abnormally large insurance dividends to veterans. A large increase is expected in social insurance, especially in old-age and survivors insurance and disability insurance, but this would be offset by decreases in veterans payments, old-age assistance and international aid. Even if social insurance needs were met by expanding old-age and survivors insurance to full coverage as well as increasing other insurance liberally, total transfers would be only $2.4 billion higher.

Since transfers represent merely a redistribution of national income through government, the tax and revenue load that does not add to national income should be smaller in 1960 than in 1950. The economy will more readily carry transfers because they are expected to decline from 7.2 per cent of gross national product in 1950 to 5.6 per cent in 1960. Even needed expenditure in

TABLE 272. ESTIMATED PER CAPITA GOVERNMENT EXPENDITURE AT 1950 PRICES, BY MAJOR CHARACTER CLASS, 1950 AND 1960

Character Class	1950 (Fiscal Year)		1960	
	Actual	Needed	Probable	Needed
All expenditure	$460	$733	$588	$668
Construction and equipment	75	176	127	158
Public-to-private transfers	131	165	110	124
Interest	43	43	43	43
Other	210	350	308	342
Federal	279	459	378	394
Construction and equipment	37	96	84	89
Public-to-private transfers	97	115	68	74
Interest	39	39	36	36
Other	106	209	190	196
State and local	181	275	210	274
Construction and equipment	38	80	43	69
Public-to-private transfers	34	50	42	51
Interest	4	4	8	8
Other	104	139	118	146

Sources: Tables 254, 255, 257, 259 and 260, Appendix 18–1 and discussion in text.

that year would call for transfers amounting only to 6.3 per cent of gross national product.

Public capital investment for construction and equipment, which ran to $11.3 billion in 1950, will probably double by 1960. As a proportion of total government expenditure, however, this category probably will rise only from 16.3 per cent in 1950 to 21.6 per cent in 1960. About two thirds of the dollar increase is expected to be for national defense, while the other one third would be largely for transportation and natural resources.

Interest on public debt, which soared during the 1940s, should grow only very moderately in the 1950s, probably declining from 9.3 per cent of total government outlays in 1950 to 7.4 per cent in 1960.

The remaining category of government outlays, which is composed primarily of salaries and wages and secondarily of supplies, materials and contractual services, should increase significantly by 1960 — from 46 to 52 per cent of all government spending. These current operating payments of government are largely expended by their recipients upon personal consumption, although private investment is also importantly affected. Spending for these purposes totaled $31.8 billion in 1950 and by 1960 will probably grow to $54.4 billion (at 1950 prices); needed

outlays in 1960 would be $60.5 billion. Per capita expenditure is expected to rise from $210 in 1950 to $308 in 1960. (See Table 272.)

The $13.9 billion deficiency between needed and probable government expenditure in 1960 is expected to consist of a $5.5 billion deficit for construction and equipment, to which a lag in education, hospitals, housing and transportation will contribute; a $2.4 billion deficit in transfers, mostly concentrated in public welfare and social insurance; and a $6 billion deficit for payrolls, supplies and related operating cost, of which education will account for over one half. (See Table 273.)

Expenditure by Function

In 1950, war-connected [28] costs of $27.6 billion represented not quite 40 per cent of American government spending, although almost 46 per cent would have been taken for war purposes if all functional needs had been satisfied. In 1960 about 45 per cent of probable outlays will be war-connected; however, were all needs met, the proportion would drop to two fifths. This will be due primarily to the leveling off of defense costs to $33.4 billion (in 1950 dollars), and inci-

28. "War-connected" is defined to embrace not only defense but also veterans payments of all types, interest on war debt, and military aid to other nations.

TABLE 273. ESTIMATED NEEDED GOVERNMENT EXPENDITURE IN 1950 AND 1960 COMPARED WITH ACTUAL 1950 AND PROBABLE 1960 EXPENDITURE, BY MAJOR FUNCTION AND CHARACTER
(*Millions at 1950 Prices*)

Function and Type of Expenditure	1950 (Fiscal Year)			1960		
	Actual	Needed	Deficiency	Probable	Needed	Deficiency
All expenditure [a]	$69,479	$110,851	$41,372	$104,091	$118,010	$13,919
Construction and equipment [b]	11,317	26,552	15,235	22,437	27,898	5,461
Public-to-private transfers	19,875	24,879	5,004	19,546	21,973	2,427
Other [b]	38,287	59,420	21,133	62,108	68,139	6,031
National defense	12,573	33,350	20,777	33,350	33,350	—
Construction and equipment	3,667	9,860	6,193	9,860	9,860	—
Other	8,906	23,490	14,584	23,490	23,490	—
International affairs	4,618	6,709	2,091	3,640	4,260	620
Construction and equipment	—	1,900	1,900	1,900	1,900	—
Public-to-private transfers	4,512	4,204	(−308)	750	1,125	375
Other	106	605	499	990	1,235	245
Civilian public safety	1,508	1,613	105	1,697	1,822	125
Construction and equipment	119	123	4	108	114	6
Other	1,389	1,490	101	1,589	1,708	119
Education [c]	10,306	16,255	5,949	12,372	17,652	5,280
Construction and equipment	1,235	3,368	2,133	1,602	3,379	1,777
Public-to-private transfers	2,864	2,868	4	1,362	1,369	7
Other	6,207	10,019	3,812	9,408	12,904	3,496
Public welfare and social insurance [d]	12,764	18,262	5,498	18,030	20,263	2,233
Construction and equipment	32	42	10	46	48	2
Public-to-private transfers	11,922	17,268	5,346	16,798	18,877	2,079
Other	810	952	142	1,186	1,338	152

(Continued on page 658)

dentally to a decline in veterans payments. (See Table 274.)

The most significant growth in nonwar functions is expected to occur in social welfare, which includes education, public welfare, social insurance, health, nonveteran hospitals, recreation and housing. Social welfare expenditure of $17.1 billion in 1950 will probably grow to $29.6 billion in 1960, and would reach $39.1 billion if needs were satisfied. Education and social insurance are expected to account for most of this growth; health, nonveteran hospitals and recreation for a minor part. Public welfare and housing should not contribute to the increase, because a decline in old-age assistance should offset increases in other welfare classes, while housing costs will be stationary unless needs are more fully recognized. The share of social welfare in total costs, which was one fourth in 1950, will probably rise to over 28 per cent in 1960. If all calculated needs were met in 1960, social welfare would account for one third of all government outlays.

Economic development undertaken by governments — which includes all forms of transportation, agriculture and natural resources, economic aid to other nations, the postal service, liquor stores, public utilities (water supply, electric power and gas), and the regulation and promotion of business and labor — cost $19.6 billion in 1950. Only $1 billion more will probably be expended in 1960 because of the moderateness of the increase in resources development, the stabilization of other programs, and the decline in foreign economic aid. The meeting of needs for this function would have added only about $4 billion to the 1950 outlay and would require nearly the same additional amount in 1960. Economic development is expected to drop from 28 per cent of total expenditure in 1950 to 20 per cent in 1960.

Expenditure for all other purposes — civilian public safety, general control, interest on nonwar debt, and unallocated — amounted to $5.2 billion in 1950. None of these items of cost is expected

TABLE 273 (continued)

Function and Type of Expenditure	1950 (Fiscal Year)			1960		
	Actual	Needed	Deficiency	Probable	Needed	Deficiency
Health and community facilities	$5,467	$7,381	$1,914	$6,167	$8,405	$2,238
Construction and equipment	1,820	2,863	1,044	1,831	2,929	1,098
Other	3,647	4,517	870	4,336	5,476	1,140
Transportation	5,749	9,549	3,800	7,801	9,933	2,132
Construction and equipment	2,890	6,146	3,256	4,397	6,302	1,905
Public-to-private transfers	37	37	—	53	57	4
Other	2,822	3,366	544	3,351	3,574	223
Agriculture and natural resources	4,414	5,255	841	6,316	7,180	864
Construction and equipment	1,353	1,984	631	2,418	3,048	630
Public-to-private transfers	502	502	—	545	545	—
Other	2,559	2,769	210	3,353	3,587	234
Postal service	2,223	2,365	142	3,132	3,282	150
Construction and equipment	5	5	—	7	7	—
Other	2,218	2,360	142	3,125	3,275	150
Other functions	9,858	10,112	254	11,586	11,863	277
Construction and equipment	196	260	64	268	311	43
Public-to-private transfers	38	—	—38	38	—	—38
Other	9,624	9,852	228	11,280	11,552	272

Sources: See Appendix 18–1 and discussion in text.

a. Total government expenditures shown here are generally higher than in other chapters mainly because no allowance is made here for offsetting income; for example, these figures include *gross* outlays of government enterprises and gross interest payments whereas Table 29 includes only *net* outlays. In addition, expenditures here include gross gifts to foreign countries (in public-to-private transfers) whereas other chapters include such gifts (on a net basis) in net foreign investment (see Table 29, for example).

Figures shown here also differ from government expenditures in other chapters because these figures are for fiscal years and in other chapters calendar years are generally used.

b. Expenditures for publicly owned military and naval plant and equipment and state expenditures for equipment are included in construction and equipment here, but in other chapters they are grouped with government expenditures for "other goods and services."

c. See Table 264 for explanation of conceptual differences between these figures and those in Chapter 12. In addition, these figures include and those in Chapter 12 exclude federal subsistence payments to veterans attending school.

d. Includes veterans life insurance and health insurance, both of which are excluded in Chapter 14.

---

to rise importantly during the 1950s, except interest on new borrowings. Accordingly, expenditure for these various purposes in 1960 will probably be $6.9 billion, accounting for only 6.6 per cent of total spending, a slightly smaller proportion than in 1950.

Expenditure by Level of Government

Division of expenditure between the federal government and state and local units affects not only administrative responsibility but also the sources of revenue to pay for functions. In the main, the 1960 projections follow the logic of the division of authority in 1950. Thus in social insurance the expansion of old-age retirement, including provision for permanent disability, would be made possible through federal expenditure,

while insurance for temporary disability and health would be provided through state expenditure. State and local governments would provide the funds for increased educational, hospital and highway spending to satisfy needs more adequately.

Such a projection will not modify significantly the 1950 revenue pattern by 1960. Social insurance benefits will be financed by employer or employee contributions, whether on the federal or state levels. Any future revision of the federal grant system, or the sloughing off of some federal excises for state use, would probably modify the revenue pattern without radically altering it. In general the division of expenditure between government levels in 1960 is expected to be similar to that in 1950, when the federal government accounted for two thirds and state and local

TABLE 274. ESTIMATED NEEDED GOVERNMENT EXPENDITURE FOR WAR AND NONWAR FUNCTIONS IN 1950 AND 1960 COMPARED WITH ACTUAL 1950 AND PROBABLE 1960 EXPENDITURE
(Billions at 1950 Prices)

Function	1950 (Fiscal Year)		1960	
	Actual	Needed	Probable	Needed
Total	$69.5	$110.9	$104.1	$118.0
War-connected	27.6	50.9	47.0	47.2
National defense	12.6	33.4	33.4	33.4
Veterans, interest, aid	15.1	17.6	13.6	13.9
Nonwar functions	41.9	59.9	57.1	70.8
Social welfare	17.1	30.9	29.6	39.1
Economic development	19.6	23.6	20.6	24.4
Other [a]	5.2	5.4	6.9	7.3

Source: See discussion in text.

a. Consists of police, fire control, correction, general control, interest on nonwar debt, and unallocated.

TABLE 275. ESTIMATED NEEDED FEDERAL AND STATE AND LOCAL EXPENDITURE IN 1950 AND 1960 COMPARED WITH ACTUAL 1950 AND PROBABLE 1960 EXPENDITURE, BY GOVERNMENT LEVEL
(Dollar Amounts in Millions at 1950 Prices)

Year	Amount			Per Cent of Total		
	Total	Federal	State and Local	Total	Federal	State and Local
	Total Expenditure					
1950 (fiscal year)						
Actual	$ 69,479	$42,175	$27,304	100.0	60.7	39.3
Needed	110,851	69,393	41,458	100.0	62.6	37.4
1960						
Probable	104,091	66,901	37,190	100.0	64.3	35.7
Needed	118,010	69,693	48,317	100.0	59.0	41.0
	Expenditure Exclusive of War-Connected Costs [a]					
1950 (fiscal year)						
Actual	$41,847	$15,076	$26,771	100.0	36.0	64.0
Needed	59,929	19,016	40,913	100.0	31.7	68.3
1960						
Probable	57,107	19,990	37,117	100.0	35.0	65.0
Needed	70,766	22,522	48,244	100.0	31.8	68.2

Sources: See Appendix 18–4 and discussion in text.

a. War-connected costs are defined as national defense, international military aid, veterans payments and interest on war debt.

governments for one third of total expenditure.[29] On the basis of probable cost, the scales would tilt a little more toward federal authority because their more limited resources would prevent state

29. For a more detailed breakdown of expenditure by government level, see Appendix 18–4.

and local bodies from closing as much of the gap between needed and probable outlays. (See Table 275.)

Since payment of war-connected cost, except for the National Guard and veterans bonuses, is exclusively a federal obligation, flexibility in al-

TABLE 276. ESTIMATED NEEDED GOVERNMENT EXPENDITURE IN 1950 AND 1960 COMPARED WITH
ACTUAL 1950 AND PROBABLE 1960 EXPENDITURE, BY FUNCTION
(*Millions at 1950 Prices*)

Function	1950 (Fiscal Year)			1960		
	Actual	Needed	Deficiency	Probable	Needed	Deficiency
All functions[a]	$69,479	$110,851	$41,372	$104,091	$118,010	$13,919
National defense	12,573	33,350	20,777	33,350	33,350	—
International affairs	4,618	6,709	2,091	3,640	4,260	620
Civilian public safety	1,508	1,613	105	1,697	1,822	125
Police and crime control	725	791	66	850	925	75
Fire prevention	407	435	28	462	494	32
Correction	376	387	11	385	403	18
Education[b]	10,306	16,255	5,949	12,372	17,652	5,280
Higher education	1,242	3,440	2,198	1,746	3,780	2,034
Elementary and secondary	5,794	9,356	3,562	8,826	11,907	3,081
Libraries	115	200	85	129	220	91
Other education	3,155	3,259	104	1,671	1,745	74
Public welfare and veterans pensions	5,452	4,922	—530	5,745	5,657	—88
Aid to aged	1,438	741	—697	1,114	869	—245
Veterans pensions and bonuses[c]	2,758	2,758	—	2,901	2,901	—
Other special classes	572	660	88	772	847	75
General and work relief	329	385	56	371	420	49
Institutional care	134	134	—	215	215	—
Other welfare	221	244	23	372	405	33
Social insurance[d]	7,312	13,340	6,028	12,285	14,606	2,321
Administration	311	550	239	600	730	130
Benefit payments	7,001	12,790	5,789	11,685	13,876	2,191
Retirement and survivorship[e]	1,680	4,795	3,115	6,540	6,946	406
Unemployment	1,962	2,537	575	1,684	2,084	400
Veterans life insurance	3,108	3,108	—	712	712	—
Health	—	1,500	1,500	2,080	3,120	1,040
Temporary disability and workmen's compensation	251	850	599	669	1,014	345
Health and community facilities	5,467	7,381	1,914	6,167	8,405	2,238
Health	364	589	225	496	688	192
Hospitals	2,349	3,186	837	2,976	4,106	1,130
Sanitation and water supply	1,477	2,150	673	1,344	1,986	642
Recreation	326	418	92	356	517	161
Local electric and gas utility	338	338	—	382	382	—
Housing and community re-development	613	700	87	613	726	113

(*Continued on page 661*)

locating responsibility between levels of government is confined to nonwar cost. Yet nonwar cost in 1950 accounted for 60 per cent of all expenditure and is expected in 1960 to represent 55 per cent of probable cost or 62 per cent of needed cost. The 1950 division for this category of 36 per cent federal and 64 per cent state and local is typical and probably will be repeated in 1960. If needed functions were performed, however, the division would tilt still more toward state and local, with these units accounting for 68.2 per cent of the total and the federal government for only 31.8 per cent. Underlying the entire allocation among government levels, therefore, are two basic questions: How large is war-connected cost, and what is the ability of states and localities to pay

TABLE 276 (continued)

Function	1950 (Fiscal Year)			1960		
	Actual	Needed	Deficiency	Probable	Needed	Deficiency
Transportation	$5,749	$9,549	$3,800	$7,801	$9,933	$2,132
Highways	4,199	7,770	3,571	5,763	7,792	2,029
Water transportation and ports	622	706	84	827	910	83
Air, local transit, and other	928	1,073	145	1,211	1,231	20
Agriculture and natural resources	4,414	5,255	841	6,316	7,180	864
Promotion of agriculture	2,440	2,440	—	2,818	2,818	—
Land and water resources	1,043	1,281	238	1,344	1,644	300
Other natural resources	931	1,534	603	2,154	2,718	564
Regulation and promotion of business and labor	271	303	32	279	309	30
Postal service	2,223	2,365	142	3,132	3,282	150
Liquor stores	667	667	—	715	715	—
Multipurpose functions	8,920	9,142	222	10,592	10,839	247
Interest on debt	6,470	6,470	—	7,684	7,684	—
General control	1,699	1,863	164	2,048	2,218	170
Unallocated	751	809	58	860	937	77

Sources: See Appendix 18–1 and discussion in text.

a. Total government expenditures shown here are higher than in Table 29 mainly because no allowance is made here for offsetting income; for example, these figures include gross outlays of government enterprises and gross interest payments whereas Table 29 includes only net outlays.

b. See Table 264 for explanation of conceptual differences between these figures and those in Chapter 12. In addition, these figures include and those in Chapter 12 exclude federal subsistence payments to veterans attending school.

c. Includes pensions to regular military personnel, which are combined with public employee retirement figures in Chapter 14. On the other hand, federal subsistence payments to veterans attending school, which are here grouped with outlays for education, are grouped in Chapter 14 with other welfare outlays for veterans.

d. Includes veterans life insurance and health insurance, both of which are excluded in Chapter 14; excludes pensions to regular military personnel, which are included under social insurance in Chapter 15.

e. Includes permanent disability insurance.

for needed functions from their own resources supplemented by federal aid?

Major Problem Areas

The largest continuing problem for government seems to be in the field of education, despite the recent high rate of spending for school buildings. Public expenditure for schooling and related activities was $5.9 billion under the estimated needs level in 1950 and is expected to fall $5.3 billion short in 1960. National defense showed a much larger gap between actual and needed outlays in 1950 but, under the assumed conditions, this deficit would vanish by 1960. Expenditure for social insurance, which fell short of needs by just about as much as educational spending in 1950, is likely to show a much smaller deficiency — $2.3 billion — in 1960. (See Table 276.)

The estimates for hospital construction and operation imply an increasingly serious situation. The 1950 deficiency of $0.8 billion in this expenditure is expected to increase to $1.1 billion in 1960. The outlook for recreation — a less critical area — appears even worse. Here, the deficit between needs and outlays seems likely to rise by 75 per cent, from $92 million to $161 million. Hospitals and recreation, together, account for most of the expected increase in the gap between needs and outlays for health and community facilities from $1.9 billion in 1950 to $2.2 billion in 1960.

Outlays for civilian public safety are also expected to fall further behind needed expenditure during the 1950–1960 decade. The gap of $105 million in 1950 is likely to widen to $125 million in 1960. Unless expenditure trends change, police and crime control, fire prevention and correction programs will all provide a smaller proportion of the services deemed necessary.

Other government activities that may fall short of reasonable goals by larger amounts in 1960 than in 1950 are land and water resource programs and the postal service, where deficiencies of $300 million and $150 million, respectively, are projected.

On the other hand, many areas, particularly transportation, may benefit considerably from increased government expenditure. A reduction from $3.8 billion to $2.1 billion in the deficiency between needs and expenditure for public transportation may be centered in the highway construction program. But outlays for highways would still fall far short of needed expenditure, and this would mean a worsening of our already critical highway problem. The large-scale highway construction program proposed by the President in 1954, however, would, if carried through, reduce the seriousness of this problem considerably.

## CHAPTER 19

FOREIGN TRADE AND FINANCE

EVERY GREAT WAR has wrought changes in the international position of the United States. The Civil War prepared the way for intensified industrialization in the next two decades. This transformed the United States from a raw-material-supplying country with an import surplus of goods to an industrialized nation with an export surplus. World War I brought a similar change in the American international financial position. Having entered the war with a net indebtedness to the rest of the world, this country emerged from it a net creditor. World War II worked a third transformation: the tremendous expansion of the country's industry and agriculture which the war stimulated left the rest of the world dependent on the American economy as never before. With the international "dollar shortage" came the end of American economic isolation.

From the point of view of future needs and resources, American international transactions command attention for several reasons. Imports add to, and exports subtract from, the sum total of resources at the disposal of our economy; hence the balance of trade is an important element in the balance of our resources and needs. But since, after World War II, imports amounted to no more than 3.5 per cent, and exports to less than 7 per cent, of our gross national product, international transactions play a far smaller part in our economy than in the economies of other countries, where the ratios are much higher.

Still, the balance of payments of the United States and its trade behavior are of world-wide concern. Expanding enormously in the 1940s and 1950s, the American economy became an almost indispensable reservoir of manufactured products and raw materials. Though foreign markets became less important to the United States, the American market acquired greater significance for the rest of the world. Moreover, although the United States has grown increasingly independent of foreign supplies, relatively small fluc-

By HERBERT K. ZASSENHAUS, Economist, Research Department, International Monetary Fund. Opinions and judgments expressed in this chapter are those of the author and should not be attributed to the organization with which he is associated.

tuations in its economy produce considerably larger variations in the absolute volume of its imports. These variations in turn have a marked influence not only on the resources available to the rest of the world but also on economic activity within foreign countries.

The dilemma created by the great significance of American resources to the rest of the world and the relative insignificance of the world's resources to the United States dominates our international economic relations. An appraisal of the available statistical facts concerning the international position of the United States is therefore essential to an evaluation of our foreign economic policy. Policies affecting our aid in the reconstruction and maintenance of "viable" western economies and the economic development of "underdeveloped" countries require special attention.

UNITED STATES BALANCE OF PAYMENTS, 1919–1952

The transactions of the United States with the rest of the world are recorded by a system of double-entry accounts. The first entry for any year records the receipts by Americans for goods exported. The second shows the payments made by Americans to foreigners for goods imported. The excess of merchandise exports or imports, as the case may be, is obtained by subtracting the smaller of these sums from the larger. Similar entries cover current receipts and current payments for services, or, as they are often called, "invisible items." Such items include payments for transportation, income on loans or investments, foreign travel and private donations. The excess of invisible exports or imports, taken together with the excess of merchandise exports or imports, constitutes the foreign "trade balance," also called the balance on current account, of the United States. (See Table 277.)

Unless annual payments for imports of goods and services exactly equal total exports there must be some other means of financing the difference. The second main part of the international account lists these means (see "Financing" in Table 277). There customarily is long-term lend-

TABLE 277. UNITED STATES INTERNATIONAL

	Merchandise [a]			Invisibles [c]			
							Total
							Trade
	Receipts	Payments		Receipts	Payments	Balance	Balance
Year	(Exports)	(Imports)	Balance				
(1)	(2)	(3)	(4)	(5)	(6)	(7)	(8)
1919	$ 8,159	$3,993	$ 4,166	$1,758	$2,794	$—1,036	$3,130
1920	8,342	5,366	2,976	1,846	2,063	—217	2,759
21	4,537	2,572	1,965	935	1,318	—383	1,582
22	3,895	3,184	711	954	1,150	—196	515
23	4,239	3,866	373	1,136	1,195	—59	314
24	4,701	3,684	1,017	1,075	1,289	—214	803
25	5,009	4,291	718	1,224	1,401	—177	541
26	4,901	4,500	401	1,350	1,475	—125	276
27	4,941	4,240	701	1,371	1,564	—193	508
28	5,215	4,159	1,056	1,493	1,720	—227	829
29	5,324	4,463	861	1,589	1,835	—246	615
1930	3,897	3,104	793	1,400	1,673	—273	520
31	2,451	2,120	331	1,083	1,324	—241	90
32	1,625	1,343	282	757	970	—213	69
33	1,694	1,510	184	663	754	—91	93
34	2,150	1,763	387	755	802	—47	340
35	2,302	2,462	—160	881	877	4	—156
36	2,465	2,546	—81	970	1,107	—137	—218
37	3,358	3,181	177	1,131	1,290	—159	18
38	3,101	2,173	928	1,129	1,073	56	984
39	3,171	2,409	762	1,141	1,155	—14	748
1940	4,124	2,713	1,411	1,267	1,060	207	1,618
41	5,343	3,486	1,857	1,385	1,049	336	2,193
42	9,187	3,965	5,222	1,219	773	446	5,668
43	15,115	5,427	9,688	1,181	907	274	9,962
44	16,969	5,589	11,380	1,266	1,095	171	11,551
45	12,473	5,666	6,807	3,847	5,086	—1,239	5,568
46	11,672	5,242	6,430	3,225	2,630	595	7,025
47	15,977	6,129	9,848	4,072	3,107	965	10,813
48	13,346	7,822	5,524	3,821	3,324	497	6,021
49	12,337	7,066	5,271	3,787	3,209	578	5,849
1950	10,658	9,315	1,343	3,789 [h]	—3,316 [h]	473	1,816
51	15,485	11,668	3,817			935	4,752
52	15,806	11,503	4,303	[h]	[h]	119	4,422

Sources: Publications of the U.S. Department of Commerce as follows:

1919–1939: *The United States in the World Economy,* 1943, Appendix Tables I and III.

1940–1944: *International Transactions of the United States During the War, 1940–1945,* 1948, Tables 1 (p. viii) and 21 (p. 93).

1945: *The Balance of International Payments of the United States, 1946–1948,* 1950, Tables A (p. 189), D (p. 196) and E (p. 197).

1946–1952: *The Balance of Payments of the United States, 1949–1951,* 1952, Appendix Tables 1, 20, 21 and 22; *Survey of Current Business,* June 1953.

a. Trade includes silver shipments in merchandise trade.

b. Net inflow of funds and gold outflow or net outflow of funds and gold inflow (—).

c. Includes transportation, travel, income on foreign investments, private donations, and miscellaneous private

ing — foreign investment either by Americans in foreign enterprises or by foreigners in the United States — and short-term financing —

short-term loans arising out of, for example, current goods and services transactions or speculative transfers of funds. In addition, a major item in

TRADE AND FINANCE, 1919-1952 *(Millions)*

| Private Long-Term Capital (Net) | | | U.S. Government Foreign Aid d (Net) | Gold Movement (Net) | Short-Term Financing e (Net) | Total Financing (Net) |
U.S. (9)	Foreign (9a)	Total (9b)	(10)	(11)	(12)	(13)
$ −169	$−215	$ −384	$ −1,632	$ 164	$−1,278	$ −3,130
−554	−278	−832	−72	50	−1,905	−2,759
−588	−4	−592	12	−686	−316	−1,582
−822	7	−815	127	−235	408	−515
−383 f	−338 f	−45 f	234	−295	−208	−314
−885 f	−185 f	−700 f	172	−216	−59	−803
−871 f	301 f	−570 f	168	102	−241	−541
−821	95	−726	179	−72	343	−276
−987	−50	−1,037	213	154	162	−508
−1,310	463	−847	198	272	−452	−829
−636	358	−278	171	−120	−388	−615
−364	66	−298	215	−278	−159	−520
128	66	194	85	176	−545	−90
251	−26	225	90	−11	−373	−69
−48	165	77 g	15	173	−358	−93
185	−15	200 g	1	−1,178	637	−340
116	320	436	—	−1,720	1,440	156
177	600	777	—	−1,147	152	218
276	245	521	−48	−1,271	780	−18
40	57	97	−17	−1,657	593	−984
113	−86	27	−16	−3,018	2,259	−748
68	−90	−22	−83	−4,243	2,730	−1,618
67	−327	−260	−1,348	−719	134	−2,193
−64	−84	−148	−6,478	23	935	−5,668
40	−63	−23	−12,767	757	2,071	−9,962
9	175	184	−14,133	1,350	1,048	−11,551
−350	−124	−474	−7,659	548	2,017	−5,568
−59	−347	−406	−5,231	−623	−765	−7,025
−810	−96	−906	−8,875	−2,162	1,130	−10,813
−748	−170	−918	−5,043	−1,530	1,470	−6,021
−796	144	−652	−5,968	−164	935	−5,849
−1,168	974	−194	−4,274	1,743	909	−1,816
−963	−543	−1,506	−4,664	−53	1,471	−4,752
−973	400	−573	−5,134	−379	1,664	−4,422

and government services. Donations received are estimated as the difference between total private unilateral transfers and the sum of identified private donations made to foreign recipients.

d. For 1919–1939, "government aid and settlements"; for 1940–1952, government unilateral transfers and net government long-term and short-term capital outflow.

e. Includes short-term United States capital, short-term foreign capital, and errors and omissions.

f. U.S. long-term capital excludes transactions in outstanding foreign securities and foreign direct investments in the United States, which are unavailable for 1923–1925. Only total net figures include these transactions.

g. Includes $40 million outflow (1933) and $30 million inflow (1934), which cannot be separated into domestic and foreign capital.

h. Not available.

recent years is United States government aid through grants and loans. Lastly, there is transfer of international reserves — mainly gold, although at least in recent postwar years also foreign hold- ings of American bank accounts and short- or long-term securities. Theoretically the total of all recorded means of financing ought to equal the trade balance, since all transfers of goods or serv-

Billions of Dollars   *Billions of Dollars*

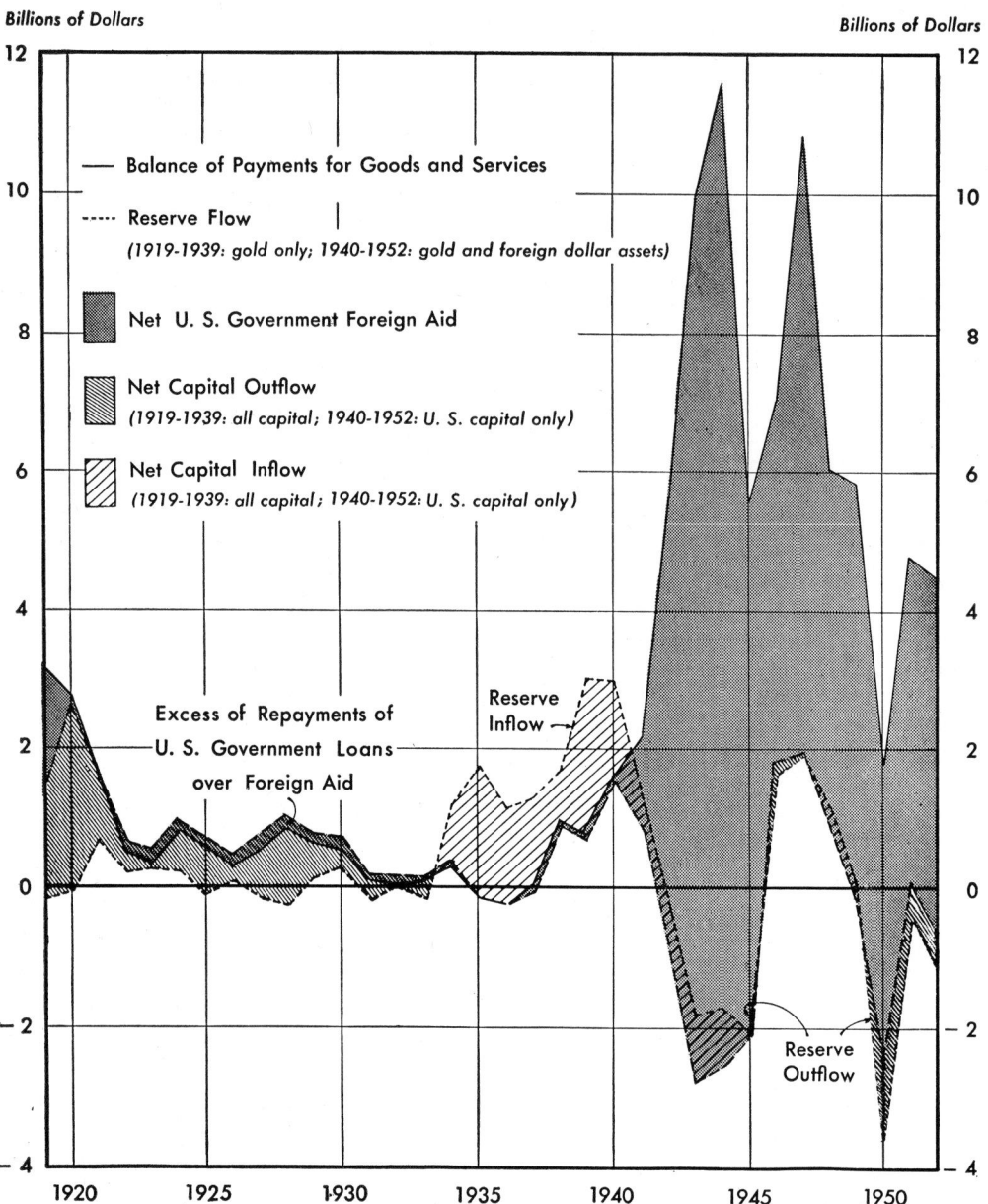

FIGURE 71. UNITED STATES BALANCE OF PAYMENTS, 1919–1952
(Trade, Aid, Capital and Reserves)

Sources: Publications of the U.S. Department of Commerce as follows:
   1919–1939: *The United States in the World Economy,* 1943, Appendix Tables.
   1940–1945: *International Transactions of the United States during the War, 1940–1945,* 1948, Tables 1 and 23
      (pp. viii and 104).
   1946–1951: *Balance of Payments of the United States, 1949–1951,* Table 1, pp. 118–126.
   1952: *Survey of Current Business,* June 1953.

Note: The lined areas (capital movements) include errors and omissions throughout.

666

ices must either be donated or paid for. But such large figures, gathered from so many sources, seldom if ever do exactly balance, and so an item for "errors and omissions" is included.[1]

With the exception of 1935 and 1936, merchandise exports exceeded imports in all years during the period 1919–1952. Between the wars, the export surplus was large enough to swamp the deficit in the invisibles account. During the war and afterwards the transactions in invisibles typically also yielded a surplus. Since lend-lease shipments were accounted for as merchandise exports (with an equivalent offset in the government aid column), the merchandise surplus expanded enormously beginning in 1942, and did not decline substantially until 1950.[2]

The large surplus of receipts over payments for total trade in goods and services was financed in the 1920s chiefly by net new long-term investments by Americans abroad. Short-term capital movements were relatively small, and foreigners had to make comparatively little use of their gold and dollar reserves to finance the remainder of their balance of payments with the United States. From a peak in 1928, however, American long-term investments declined rapidly. At the same time, the stock exchange boom attracted considerable foreign capital, and then during the mid-1930s, despite the vanishing American export surplus, the economic and political uncertainties caused foreigners to transfer short-term funds to the United States to the very considerable extent of more than $1 billion a year on the average. During the late 1930s this flight of "hot money" together with a reappearing United States trade

surplus, which exceeded even the levels of some years in the 1920s, brought large inflows of gold to the United States.

During the war years, foreign aid (given mainly to Europe) financed considerably more than the total trade surplus of the United States, and foreign nations (especially in South America) were able to accumulate considerable gold and dollar reserves. In the years immediately after the war, government foreign aid was too small to settle the American trade surplus. The outward capital movement revived, but was offset by short-term capital inflows in the crisis year 1947 and in 1949 before foreign currencies were devalued. Gold and dollar reserves again flowed into the United States. Then, as American long-term lending regained its level of the 1920s, and after the outward movement of short-term capital receded from the high levels preceding the 1949 currency devaluations, the improved trade balance of the rest of the world with the United States, together with continuing foreign aid, permitted foreign nations to add to their gold and dollar reserves. The outflow of these reserves reached a peak in 1950. The Korean disturbance reversed movements again, but by 1952 the improvement of the foreign position was resumed. (See Figure 71.)

The Significance of United States International Transactions

During the past seventy-five years the foreign trade of the United States has become smaller and smaller in comparison with its internal trade and production. One reason for this tendency is that the expansion of the United States economy has been extremely rapid. This country, with its great wealth of natural resources, could supply food for its growing population and many materials for its advancing industries without a correspondingly large increase in imports of raw products, while the output of its mills and factories fulfilled most of the growing domestic wants for manufactures.

Other industrial nations, which in earlier days had exchanged manufactured products for the food and raw materials they were accustomed to obtain from this country, needed increasing quantities of many of these materials, but found that the American market for their manufactures did not grow proportionately. On the contrary, they

1. This grouping is purely for statistical convenience and does not imply that any one of the subitems of the balance of payments is more dependent on the rest than any other; financing may follow trade, and trade may follow financing; capital movements may be induced by changes in the trade balance, or the other way around; and both may induce gold flows, or vice versa.

In reading Table 277, two further points should be noted. The distinction between short-term and long-term capital cannot be made statistically perfect. Sales or purchases of bonds and stocks, for example, are recorded as part of long-term capital movements because the instruments of indebtedness involved have a maturity from date of issue of more than one year, although such transactions are frequently of a short-term nature. Secondly, there is a difference between prewar and postwar financing. Widespread foreign exchange controls put transactions by foreigners in United States securities and bank deposits under the control of public authorities abroad. Therefore they acquire the nature of reserve movements rather than private transactions, and often are actually carried out by foreign government agencies.

2. For a discussion of developments after 1950, see pp. 706–711.

began to import more factory products from the United States.

For a while they paid for the excess of imports which they needed mainly by the earnings of their investments in the United States. These earnings were large enough at the beginning not only to buy their import excess but also to increase foreign capital holdings in this country. But gradually the trade discrepancy grew so large as to eat into the capital itself, and during World War I the debts of western Europeans to the United States jumped ahead of their American property holdings.

At this point the United States became in its turn a net exporter of capital. The capital outflow of the 1920s for a while supplied Europe with the extra dollars needed to pay for the American goods they could not buy with the net proceeds of trade, but this outflow began to diminish in 1928 and virtually ceased in the early 1930s. During this depression decade the trade gap was more than bridged by a tremendous net flow of gold from other nations to the United States. But World War II, during which western Europe simultaneously needed immensely increased quantities of American goods and suffered a further liquidation of its overseas investments, sharpened the problem and produced a crisis in international payments.

The pressure on resources abroad of postwar reconstruction and the general acceptance of full employment and economic development programs combined with the change in the relative international position of the United States to create the postwar problem of the "dollar gap." It led to almost universal restrictions abroad on imports from the United States. Considerable progress has been made, since 1946, in solving this problem. Increased capacity abroad to produce and to export, a series of alignments of the values of foreign currencies in terms of the dollar, and a more realistic appraisal of the inflationary consequences of overfull employment and too rapid development programs leading to their control have improved the position of foreign countries in relation to the United States. The "gap" began to be closed in 1950 and, after the disturbance created by the outbreak of the Korean War had been overcome, it appeared to be near the vanishing point in 1952–1953. However, all restrictions against imports from the United States have by no means been abolished.

American foreign trade policy frequently appears inconsistent to the world abroad. The United States has supported freedom of trade for the raw materials it needs to import and for the goods it wishes to export. At the same time it has historically hampered the import of manufactured goods and some agricultural products by protective tariffs and quotas, while it has stimulated the export of crops by subsidies. Although the protective policy has been greatly modified, many obstructions still remain.

The major policy adopted by the United States to meet this apparent impasse has been to extend grants and loans to bridge the dollar gap. But neither the recipients nor the donors wish to prolong this expedient indefinitely. If the development of American needs and resources is to be fully nourished by international trade, some other solution of the problem is desirable. A policy of "trade, not aid" has been called for, but it requires both an elimination of obstacles to American imports and a further increase in the competitiveness of foreign exports.

THE UNITED STATES AND WORLD TRADE

Up to the first world war, the share of United States foreign trade in world trade, both in imports and in exports, remained fairly constant. After a noticeable increase during the 1920s, the United States proportion of world trade dropped back seriously during the 1930s. But after World War II this country accounted for a larger share of the world's trade, especially of world exports, than ever before: the 32 per cent rise in its export share between 1926–1929 and 1952 was almost twice the 17 per cent increase in its import share. (See Table 278.)

Moreover, the effects of American industrialization plus those of its tariff policy and its raw materials position resulted in a change in the role which the United States played in the world's trade in manufactures and raw materials.

European experience suggests that as a nation becomes industrialized, its imports of raw materials expand and its exports of these crude products shrink, while its exports of manufactured goods expand more than its imports of manufactures. In one respect, the United States has behaved as one would expect a fairly rapidly industrialized nation to behave. The progress of industrialization created an export surplus of manufactured products rather early (in 1901–1905) and later, after the first world war, an import

TABLE 278. UNITED STATES TRADE AND WORLD TRADE, 1876–1952

| | U.S. Trade as Per Cent of World Trade | | | | | | U.S. Balance of Trade [a] | | |
| | Exports | | | Imports | | | | | |
Years	Total	Manu-factures	Primary Products	Total	Manu-factures	Primary Products	Total	Manu-factures	Primary Products
							(Millions)		
1876–1880	11.0	4.0	15.4	7.0	6.8	7.1	$ 171	$ —77	$ 248
1881–1885	11.5	4.2	16.0	8.7	8.4	8.5	108	—142	250
1886–1890	10.4	4.1	14.4	9.1	8.4	9.5	9	—134	143
1891–1895	11.9	4.7	16.1	9.4	8.1	10.0	91	—106	197
1896–1900	13.1	7.0	16.7	7.6	6.7	8.9	334	—1	335
1901–1905	13.1	8.0	16.0	8.1	6.7	8.9	455	41	414
1906–1910	12.2	8.2	14.7	8.6	6.9	9.5	406	53	353
1911–1913	12.2	9.2	13.8	8.4	6.1	9.7	539	196	343
1921–1925	16.8	13.8	16.0 [b]	12.4	7.5	16.2 [b]	330	615	—285
1926–1929	15.5	16.3	15.0	12.5	8.2	15.1	638	963	—325
1931–1936	12.0	12.3	11.8	9.6	6.4	11.5	194	287	—93
1936–1938	12.9	16.3	10.7	10.0	6.2	12.2	273	519	—246
1948–1950 [c]	21.1	13.4 [d]	7.7 [d]	14.1	4.0 [d]	10.1 [d]	3,264	5,004	—1,740
1952 [c]	20.5	13.6 [d]	6.9 [d]	14.6	3.9 [d]	10.7 [d]	3,545	6,579	—3,034

Sources:

1876–1938: *Industrialization and Foreign Trade*, League of Nations, Geneva, 1945, Tables VII–VIII (p. 157), IX (p. 158) and XIII (p. 166).

1948–1952: World trade: *International Financial Statistics*, International Monetary Fund, January 1952.
U.S. trade: estimated at c.i.f. (cost plus insurance and freight) values from that source and *Foreign Trade of the United States, 1936–1949*, U.S. Department of Commerce, 1951, as well as *Business Information Service, International Trade Statistics Series*, February 1952 and March 1953.

a. Exports less imports (recorded trade data; differ from data in Table 277).

b. Figures supplied; not contained in League of Nations source.

c. U.S. trade in manufactures: trade of finished manufactures and manufactured foodstuffs; U.S. trade in primary products: trade of all other categories.

d. Represents U.S. trade expressed as per cent of *total* world trade since data for world trade for manufactures and primary products are not available separately for postwar years. Comparative ratios of U.S. manufactures and primary products trade to *total* world trade for earlier years are as follows (per cent):

| | Exports | | Imports | |
	Manu-factures	Primary Products	Manu-factures	Primary Products
1926–1929	6.4	9.1	3.1	9.4
1936–1938	6.5	6.5	2.4	7.6

surplus of primary products. (See Table 278.) This development was accompanied by an increase in the United States share of world imports of primary products and exports of manufactures. Between the 1870s and the 1920s and 1930s, this country's share of world exports of manufactures increased fourfold, and its share of imports of primary products more than doubled. Further increases after World War II probably brought the United States proportion both of manufactured exports and of imports of primary products to about 25 per cent.

On the other hand, this country's share of the world's *exports* of primary commodities appears to have remained above that of the late 1930s (but apparently somewhat below that of the 1920s), while even after World War II its share of imports of manufactured articles may not have increased beyond the 6 to 8 per cent of the prewar years.[3]

Thus, while the United States increased its ex-

3. More precise estimates for the postwar years are impossible since no data for world trade in manufactures and primaries are available. The ratio of United States exports of manufactures to total world exports, however, rose considerably more than that of total American exports to world exports (Table 278) when comparison is made with either the 1920s or the 1930s. On the import side, manufactures rose more than the total relative to world trade, and primary materials held their own, while

ports of manufactures and its imports of primaries relative to the world as a whole, the persisting "dollar shortage" indicates that it may not have countered this "normal" development with a sufficiently large relative increase in manufactured imports and a relative decline in raw material exports.

Triangular Trade

This trade position brought about an especially strong dependence of foreign primary producers on the United States market, and of both the developing and the industrial nations on United States resources. It thus made the growth of a "triangular" trade of special importance. So long as this country serves as the supplier of both manufactures and raw materials to industrialized countries (and especially to western Europe), the latter will find it possible to pay for imports from the United States only by achieving a surplus of exports to other suppliers of raw materials. This will be difficult to the extent that the United States increases its exports of manufactures to the relatively underdeveloped areas as well as to the industrialized countries and diminishes its intake of raw materials from them. Thus, allied with the difficulty arising from the growing discrepancy between the diminishing over-all importance of United States trade to the home economy and its growing importance to the world, there is the threat of a special problem which may develop from the *direction* taken by this country's trade.

After World War II the increase in the American intake of raw materials was far greater in such products as tropical foods (coffee) and certain industrial materials for which domestic substitutes did not become available (mainly oil and certain nonferrous metals) than for such materials as wool, rubber and tin, for which synthetic substitutes were developed. "Triangular" trade was effective enough for at least some of the foreign suppliers of the first group of raw materials. But producers of the materials competitive with synthetics (especially the non-European countries of the sterling area) found themselves between the two grindstones of insecure American markets for their products and continued dependence on American supplies of manufactures.

United States Terms of Trade

What a country gains from its international trade depends on two things: how much it trades and at what relative prices it exchanges its exports for imports. As we saw above, the United States has almost always, since World War I, had an export surplus — it shipped more goods out than it took in from the rest of the world.

Like all countries which exported mainly industrial products and imported mainly raw materials during the interwar period, the United States was able to obtain an increasing number of units of imports for a unit of its exports, especially during the 1930s when raw materials prices collapsed internationally. This may be seen from an examination of the real terms [4] on which the United States has carried on its merchandise trade. By 1939–1941, the United States obtained 21 per cent more imports per unit of exports than in 1926–1930. In the depression years 1931–1935 it not only had a much smaller export surplus, but its gain in the terms of trade offset almost half of the loss in the total volume of its trade, which fell by almost 40 per cent.

After World War II this trend was sharply reversed. By 1950, and even more so after the Korean boom in 1951–1952, the rest of the world had recaptured all the advantage it held at the end of the 1920s, and considerably surpassed it, because of a relative rise in prices of crude materials. (See Table 279.)

The United States remains, however, an important supplier of raw materials. Moreover, the prices of several of its major raw materials exports fell no less severely in the prewar depression (wheat and cotton, for example), and rose more after the war, than the prices of its raw materials imports.[5] Vis-à-vis countries which imported

---

exports of primaries seem to have declined somewhat in importance relative to world trade.

Thus, so far as one can observe the development of the American trade pattern from these figures, its *direction* conformed to what may be called the "normal" one. The problem created for the rest of the world is rather whether the movements were of sufficient *magnitude* to promise an alleviation of the "dollar problem."

4. A country's "terms of trade" are computed by dividing the average unit value of its exports by the average unit value of its imports. They thus measure how many units of imports can be obtained for a unit of exports.

5. It took the early post-Korean boom to bring the prices of a number of important United States import commodities — coffee, wool, tin, rubber, for instance — up to levels at which these commodities regained the purchasing power over United States exports which they had had in the 1930s, to say nothing of that in the 1920s. *International Financial Statistics,* International Monetary Fund, July 1951.

TABLE 279. UNITED STATES EXPORT AND IMPORT PRICES (UNIT VALUES) AND TERMS OF TRADE,[a] 1921–1952

(*Indexes of Annual Averages, 1936–1938 = 100*)

Annual Average or Year	Unit Values of: Total Exports	Unit Values of: Total Imports	Total Terms of Trade	Unit Values of: Exports of Finished Manufactures	Unit Values of: Imports of Crude Materials	Unit Values of: Imports of Crude Foodstuffs	Partial Terms of Trade: Finished Manufactures Against: Crude Materials	Partial Terms of Trade: Finished Manufactures Against: Crude Foodstuffs	Unit Values of: Exports of Crude Materials and Foodstuffs	Unit Values of: Imports of Finished Manufactures and Semi-manufactures	Partial Terms of Trade: Crude Materials and Foodstuffs against Finished Manufactures and Semi-manufactures
1921–1925	148	168	88	158	182	155	87	102	174	160	109
1926–1930	128	160	80	135	174	185	78	73	151	151	100
1931–1935	87	86	101	95	73	96	130	99	88	95	93
1936–1938	100	100	100	100	100	100	100	100	100	100	100
1939–1941	102	105	97	106	111	94	95	113	95	109	87
1942–1945	153	144	106	162	149	160	109	101	155	142	109
1946	158	173	91	156	162	221	96	71	200	173	116
1947[b]	188	213	88	182	180	311	101	59	238	215	111
1948[b]	200	235	85	193	203	343	95	56	249	239	104
1949[b]	185	224	83	181	195	330	93	55	222	227	98
1950	180	243	74	179	214	454	84	39	202	218	93
1951	206	305	68	199	312	512	64	39	227	267	85
1952	205	289	71	200	256	516	78	39	237	268	88

Sources: Computed from *Foreign Trade of the United States, 1936–1949,* U.S. Department of Commerce, 1951, and *Business Information Service, International Trade Statistics Series,* 1952–1953, various issues.

a. Export unit values divided by import unit values.
b. Including civilian supplies by United States armed forces.

these raw materials from her against manufactures — such as Europe for instance — this country thus suffered the disadvantages of a raw materials supplier, and after the last war when raw product prices rose it participated in the corresponding advantage. Vis-à-vis the countries which in turn furnished the United States with its crude foodstuffs and industrial materials, such as Latin America and Asia, its position changed in the reverse direction. Nevertheless, on balance this country enjoyed *less* than the full advantage typical of a supplier of finished goods in the interwar years, and also less than the full advantage typical of a supplier exclusively of raw materials, especially food, after World War II.[6]

From the 1920s to the 1930s, when its over-all trade advantage increased, the United States gained as a trader of finished manufactures against crude materials and to a smaller extent against crude foods. But it lost ground insofar as it traded crude materials and foods against manufactures and semimanufactures. Almost the complete reverse happened when in the 1940s and 1950s there was a series of unprecedented export surpluses, and the country's over-all terms of trade worsened considerably. The terms of trade of finished manufactures against crude foods turned especially sharply against the United States, so that by 1952 it obtained only 39 per cent as much crude foods per unit of manufactures exports as in 1936–1938; and even the terms of trade of finished manufactures exports against crude materials imports moved against the United States, to 22 per cent below the 1936–1938 level in 1952. Moreover, the prices of United States exports of crude materials and foodstuffs had in 1952 risen by almost as much as the prices of its imports of crude materials (though much less than those of its food imports). Thus the terms of its trade in crude materials and foodstuffs against finished and semimanufactured imports moved adversely and by 1952 had fallen even below 1931–1935 levels. (See Table 279.)

The increased share of the United States in world trade after World War II brought with it a terms-of-trade benefit to other countries, which accrued mostly to the nations supplying crude foods (mainly Latin America), much less to suppliers of crude materials (mainly sterling area countries outside Europe) and of finished commodities (mainly Europe). These benefits were

of material assistance to the rest of the world in its attempts to combat the "dollar shortage" — quite apart from the benefit derived abroad from the large postwar government foreign aid which financed the overwhelming part of that shortage.

UNITED STATES TRADE AND THE DOMESTIC ECONOMY

In the decreasing importance of its aggregate international trade to its economy, the United States differs from other western industrialized nations. Even in the larger countries of western Europe, both exports and imports are at least two to three times larger in relation to gross national product than they are in this country.

The significance of foreign trade to the United States is not only small, but declining. The ratio between imports and gross national product, which stood at a level of 4.6 to 6.3 per cent before World War I, has declined persistently, though with significant interruptions. It dropped from about 4.5 per cent in the 1920s to between 2.4 and 3.4 per cent in the 1930s, perhaps in part because of the revival of a strong protective tariff. It remained at 3.1 per cent even in 1950 after imports had revived considerably, though the effects of the post-Korean boom brought the ratio up to 3.3 per cent in 1951.[7] The ratio of United States exports to domestically produced exportable goods, which rarely exceeded 10 per cent, also declined from the 1920s, but at a considerably slower rate than in the case of imports. (See Table 280.)

Fluctuations in American imports are more likely to lead to contractions or expansions of world trade (and thus of world economic activity) than fluctuations in the imports of other economies. This is true because American imports practically do not depend on United States exports, whereas imports of the rest of the world closely depend on exports *to* the United States, because of the dollar shortage. Between prewar and postwar years for which reasonably reliable data are available, the relevant sectors of the

---

6. *Ibid.*

7. When both imports and gross national product are measured at constant prices, the decline of the ratio between them is seen to begin only with the depression of the early 1930s. The ratio in the text above is, however, what matters when considering the "dollar problem" of the rest of the world. But it is important to realize that its decline has been to a large extent the result of the relative decline of prices of the world's exports to the United States — i.e., of a worsening of the world's terms of trade with the United States.

TABLE 280. RELATION OF EXPORTS TO PRODUCTION OF EXPORTABLE GOODS AND OF IMPORTS TO
GROSS NATIONAL PRODUCT, UNITED STATES, 1889-1952
(Dollar Amounts in Billions)

Year	Production of Exportable Goods	Exports of U.S. Merchandise	Exports as Per Cent of Production	Gross National Product	Recorded Merchandise Imports [a]	Imports as Per Cent of Gross National Product
1889–1898	—	—	—	$ 12.7	$ 0.8	6.3
1899–1908	—	—	—	21.6	1.0	4.6
1909–1918	—	—	—	40.1	2.0	5.0
1919	$ 47.5	$ 7.8	16.4	79.9	3.9	4.9
1921	33.9	4.4	13.0	71.5	2.5	3.5
1923	44.8	4.1	9.2	85.2	3.8	4.5
1925	47.1	4.8	10.2	90.2	4.2	4.7
1927	47.5	4.8	10.1	94.9	4.2	4.4
1929	52.8	5.2	9.8	103.8	4.4	4.2
1931	32.0	2.4	7.5	75.9	2.1	2.8
1933	25.2	1.6	6.3	55.8	1.4	2.5
1935	33.1	2.2	6.6	72.2	2.0	2.8
1937	43.5	3.3	7.6	90.2	3.1	3.4
1938	[b]	[b]	[b]	84.7	2.0	2.4
1939	41.4	3.1	7.5	91.3	2.3	2.5
1946	100.4	10.0	10.0	211.1	4.9	2.3
1947	126.1	15.2	12.1	233.3	5.8	2.5
1948	138.0	12.5	9.1	259.0	7.1	2.7
1949	126.1	11.9	9.4	258.2	6.6	2.6
1950	143.5	10.1	7.0	286.8	8.9	3.1
1951	163.3	14.9	9.1	329.8	11.0	3.3
1952	170.1	15.0	8.8	348.0	10.7	3.1

Sources: Trade: *Foreign Trade of the United States 1936–1949*, U.S. Department of Commerce, 1951, Table 35, p. 55; *Foreign Commerce Weekly*, July 27, 1953; *Report to the President on Foreign Economic Policies* ("Gray Report"), 1950, p. 124. Gross national product: 1889–1918, *Report to the President on Foreign Economic Policies*, p. 124; 1919–1952, based on Appendix 4–2.

a. Recorded trade data differ from those in Table 277 because they are not adjusted for imports (and exports) not recorded by U.S. Customs.

b. Not available.

American economy have decreased their absorption of imports. (See Table 281.) [8]

Comparing prewar relatively prosperous years (1929, 1937) with 1948 and 1950, the sharp drop in imports of crude materials in relation to domestic manufacturing output is especially noticeable. Imported finished products and imported foods fell to about 60 and 50 per cent, respectively, of their ratios to total consumption previous to 1938. While the decline of food imports may in part be a response to the postwar increase of food prices, the greater reduction of

8. The data in this table are expressed in values measured at constant (1929) prices and thus eliminate the effect of the considerable price movements between 1929 and 1950.

crude materials imports must have a cause other than price movements alone. For the increase in the import price of crude materials just kept in step with the rise in domestic prices, whereas prices of imported foods rose considerably more than domestic prices. Although United States imports, especially of manufactured materials, rose after World War II in relation to world trade, they declined in relation to domestic output while exports maintained their relationship to domestic output. This development is the nub of the postwar "dollar problem."

Moreover, ups and downs in the United States economy have a greatly magnified effect on other countries. Domestic depressions, or even slight

TABLE 281. UNITED STATES IMPORTS AND DOMESTIC DEMAND, SELECTED CATEGORIES OF COMMODITIES, 1929–1950

(Per Cent) [a]

	Ratio of:			
Year	Imports of Manufactures to Total Consumer Expenditures on Nonfood Items (Excluding Services)	Imports of Crude and Manufactured Foodstuffs to Total Consumer Expenditures on Food	Imports of Crude Materials to Total Manufacturing Production [b]	Imports of Semimanufactures to Total Manufacturing Production [b]
1929	3.70	4.88	7.12	4.13
1930–1933	3.27	4.88 [c]	8.57	4.10
1934–1936	3.12	4.71 [c]	7.02	3.73
1937	3.40	4.76	6.60	3.80
1938	2.73	3.73	5.81	3.31
1948	2.02	2.95	4.13	2.47
1949	1.88	3.16	3.81	2.43
1950 (first half)	1.99	3.03	3.10	2.90

Source: World Economic Report, 1949–1950, United Nations, New York, 1951, p. 146.

a. Underlying absolute values in 1929 prices.

b. As measured by total of net value added by manufacturing industries.

c. This figure is affected by the exceptionally heavy imports of food grains due to the drought in the United States, 1933–1935.

TABLE 282. AGRICULTURE AND TRADE, 1921–1952

(Per Cent)

	Ratio of:				
Period or Year	Agricultural Exports to Total Exports	Supplementary Agricultural Imports [a] to Total Imports	Agricultural Exports to Value of Agricultural Output [b]	Supplementary Agricultural Imports [a] to Value of Agricultural Output [b]	Agricultural Export Surplus [c] to Total Export Surplus
1921–1925	46.8	21.1	17.3	8.3	114.1
1926–1930	36.1	23.0	14.5	9.5	102.6
1931–1935	36.8	24.7	10.2	6.3	99.0
1936–1940	21.8	25.5	7.5	6.7	52.4
1941–1945	17.0	27.6	8.5	4.0	10.5
1946	33.4	24.8	11.5	4.1	41.2
1947	26.1	24.8	12.0	4.1	26.6
1948	27.7	22.8	10.4	4.6	33.6
1949	30.1	21.9	11.7	4.7	38.3
1950	28.3	20.7	9.5	5.9	79.6
1951	27.2	21.3	11.6	6.6	41.5
1952	22.8	17.8	9.7	5.4	34.9

Source: Compiled from data provided by the U.S. Departments of Agriculture and Commerce, and Foreign Agricultural Trade (Calendar Year 1952), May 1953.

a. Agricultural imports of commodities similar and therefore competitive to domestic agricultural products.

b. Total gross farm income, less value of seed, feed and waste.

c. Agricultural exports less supplementary agricultural imports.

TABLE 283. INDEXES[a] OF AGRICULTURAL PRODUCTION, EXPORTS AND IMPORTS,
SELECTED YEARS, 1929–1952

Period	Production for Sale and Home Consumption (1935–1939 = 100)	Exports of Agricultural Products (1924–1929 = 100)	Imports of Supplementary Agricultural Products (1924–1929 = 100)
1929	97	101	110
1936–1940	103	60	92
1947–1949	136	100	100
1950	137	90	107
1952	143	96	105

Sources: Statistical Abstract of the United States, 1950, and U.S. Department of Agriculture, Foreign Agricultural Trade (Calendar Year 1952), May 1953.

a. Quantity indexes based on series in constant prices.

recessions, appear to diminish United States imports more, sometimes considerably more, than the fall of the nation's gross national product. A decline in domestic business activity is thus intensified as it reaches the outside world. For example, a 27 per cent decline in gross national product between 1929 and 1931 was accompanied by a 52 per cent fall in imports; when gross national product fell a further 26 per cent in 1931–1933, imports dropped 33 per cent. (See Table 280.) Even during the small inventory recession of 1949, when gross national product fell less than 0.5 per cent, imports declined 7 per cent. Although tariffs and other barriers must have had their influence, the great sensitivity of United States imports to domestic fluctuations apparently arises from the peculiar marginal character of international trade to the economy of the United States, especially from its susceptibility to domestic fluctuations in inventories.

Agriculture and Trade

In contrast to the rest of the economy, American agriculture remained highly dependent on exports to foreign markets through the 1920s. At the same time, imports of directly competitive products were much greater in relation to domestic output in agriculture than in industry. This position changed rapidly from the 1930s onwards. (See Table 282.)

It is true that agricultural exports fell relative to domestic output (as well as in relation to total exports) during the 1920s and 1930s and that this decline has continued in the postwar years. The

drop was from 47 per cent in the early 1920s to about 36 per cent in 1926–1935 (and to 22 per cent in the dust-storm years) and continued to around 30 per cent in the immediate postwar years in spite of the large foreign aid programs.[9] Although after the war the volume of domestic agricultural production had risen almost 40 per cent above 1929, the exceptional postwar stimuli had no more than restored the 1929 volume of agricultural exports. (See Table 283.)

Nevertheless, the share of agricultural production exported in the postwar years exceeded the proportion of nonagricultural production exported, as it did during the 1920s and 1930s. (Compare Tables 280 and 282.) In 1952, 12 per cent of United States production of dry milk, 22 per cent of lard, 48 per cent of wheat and 58 per cent of rice were exported, and the export proportions for cotton, tobacco, and dried and condensed fruits were all above 25 per cent. Such high export ratios cannot be found among industrial products, except for a few special commodities.

On the other hand, supplementary agricultural imports — imports of products similar to home-produced commodities and therefore directly competitive with them — fell in relation to domestic output, in both monetary and real terms. Moreover, the ratio of supplementary agricultural imports to total imports has fallen from about 25 per cent prewar to below 20 per cent. (See Tables 282 and 283.)

---

9. It should be remembered, however, that substantial agricultural exports financed through aid programs were shipped at below-market prices.

TABLE 284. INTERNATIONAL INVESTMENT POSITION[a] OF THE UNITED STATES, 1914–1950
(*Billions; Creditor or Debtor* [−])

Year	Net Investment Position	Net Long-Term			Net Short-Term		
		Private	U.S. Government	Total	Private	U.S. Government	Total
1914	$−3.4	—	—	—	—	—	—
1919	3.7	—	—	$ 4.0	—	—	$−0.3
1930	8.8	—	—	9.5	—	—	−0.7
1945	−0.6	$ 5.6	$ 1.2	6.8	$−4.1	$−3.2[b]	−7.4
1946	4.2	6.6	4.6	11.2	−3.9	−3.1[b]	−7.0
1947	12.3	7.9	11.4	19.3	−3.8	−3.2[b]	−7.0
1948	14.1	9.3	12.3	21.6	−4.2	−3.3[b]	−7.5
1949	15.0	9.8	12.7	22.5	−4.5	−3.0[b]	−7.5
1950	14.5	10.9	12.0	22.9	−4.9	−3.5	−8.4

Sources: 1914 from Cleona Lewis, *America's Stake in International Investments,* Brookings Institution, Washington, 1938, p. 447. Data for other years from the following publications of the U.S. Department of Commerce: 1919 and 1930, *The United States in the World Economy,* 1943; 1945, *The Balance of International Payments of the United States, 1946–1948,* 1950, p. 162; 1946–1950,

The Balance of Payments of the United States, 1949–1951, 1952, Table 41.

a. Excluding World War I intergovernmental debts.

b. Including the following estimates of U.S. currency and coins held abroad (in millions): 1945, $572; 1946, $633; 1947, $704; 1948, $746; 1949, $812; 1950, $772.

Consequently, the part played by the relevant American *agricultural trade balance* — i.e., the difference between the values of agricultural exports and supplementary agricultural imports — in the total United States export surplus has been reduced to a marked degree. In the 1920s, the agricultural surplus, so measured, more than offset a net deficit of all other merchandise trade; by the end of the 1930s, it equaled only one half the total export surplus; ten years later it had been reduced to little more than one third. Only the large total imports during the Korean boom raised the proportion temporarily.

The partial postwar revival of agricultural exports has a double significance. On the one hand, it is only the American reflection of one part of the European dollar shortage. On the other hand, when considered in connection with the foreign aid program, it indicates one of the reasons why postwar United States foreign economic policy has tended to combine foreign aid with protection instead of combining reduction of aid with the liberalization of trade.

INTERNATIONAL FINANCING AND THE "DOLLAR GAP"

In 1914, Americans owed $3.4 billion more to foreigners than foreigners owed to them. In 1930, foreigners owed Americans (and their government) $8.8 billion more than the foreign debts of

Americans. Ever since World War I the United States has been a creditor rather than a debtor nation. The only year, 1945, for which this statement does not hold true was affected by exceptional circumstances. (See Table 284.) In the early 1950s the United States was a larger net creditor than ever before.

When foreigners have a net balance to pay to the United States for current and private capital transactions, they can do so only by receiving grants or loans from the United States government, or by dipping into their reserves of gold and dollar resources. The distinction between that part of financing which is carried out by private economic units and that part which is either directly financed by the public authorities (e.g., through the granting of foreign aid) or provided for from the officially held reserves of international currency (e.g., dollars) or gold is of interest because it leads to some statistical measurement of the "dollar gap." If this gap is defined as the sum of the loss, in any one year, of international reserves by the rest of the world to the United States *plus* foreign aid furnished by the United States, it may serve as a measure of that element in the United States balance of payments by which private foreign earnings of dollars fall short of private foreign expenditure to the United States.

It does not, however, show in any sense the excess of the "need" of foreign countries for dollars over their dollar earnings; rather, it simply measures the amounts by which United States foreign aid or foreign gold and dollar reserves were in fact used in financing the rest of the balance of payments. If, for instance, aid had been forthcoming less generously than it was, the "gap" would have been smaller. Nevertheless, the "gap," so defined, is a useful figure: It is the measure of that portion of the international transfer of United States resources made possible, in some fashion, by government action.[10]

10. These qualifications of the definition of the "dollar gap" should be carefully noted. In general, available data indicate the amounts of gold foreigners transfer to or acquire from Americans, but not whether those gold shipments take place to balance other international payments or whether these other transactions (such as the transfer of short-term funds) take place to balance gold shipments made for entirely different reasons. Consequently, occurrence of such transactions as gold shipments does not necessarily mean that the balance of payments is "not in equilibrium," i.e., that the domestic forces (incomes, prices, etc.) which determine trade and capital movements across national boundaries do not lead to balanced international payments. For years prior to World War II, when foreign aid was insignificant, the volume of gold transactions is known, but not what part, if any, of the movement of foreign capital represented transfer of reserves. In addition, "errors and omissions," which were quite sizable, may have concealed unrecorded capital transfers. Thus, for the years 1926–1939, the best available indicator is the gold flow, and the "dollar gap" so measured indicates the extent to which reserves were transferred from the rest of the world probably, but not necessarily, because private transactions failed to bring about a balance.

There is no satisfactory way to measure the dollar gap during the war years 1940–1945. Lend-lease transactions dominated American international payments, but they were largely gifts in kind. As such, they are clearly public transactions, but to record them once as exports and then to enter an offset on the other side of the balance sheet called government aid is simply a bookkeeping device, for this item would not in any way be a transfer of international reserves.

After 1945 the "dollar gap" acquired a novel and important characteristic. It was no longer simply the financing, through transfer of reserves, of a temporary and unavoidable balance of payments deficit. Rather, the American government adopted the specific policy of providing foreign aid in various forms to the rest of the world for military purposes, postwar reconstruction and development. The "dollar gap" no longer measured (as it might have in the 1930s) only the unplanned disequilibrium among private transactions, but mainly the planned volume of United States foreign assistance. Government aid acquired the balancing function previously performed to a large degree by private capital, because the transfer of goods and services which had been decided upon as a matter of policy had become unmanageable by private means. To put it another way: not to perform this resource transfer would have entailed an economically and politically intolerable reduction of consumption, employment or reconstruction and development abroad. That

The development of American international financing is seen to have consisted largely in a shift from private foreign investments to an increasing "dollar gap." The "gap" was small as long as American capital flowed out freely in the 1920s. It grew big when foreign capital — largely short-term "hot money" — flowed in during the later 1930s ("errors and omissions" also acquired a considerable size). After the war, the "gap" narrowed steadily to only $79 million in 1950, when the Korean boom produced a trade deficit and "errors and omissions" fell to $156 million. The spread of this boom abroad, raising the American trade surplus again, reversed this movement in 1951, but in 1952 and 1953 the narrowing of the "gap" was resumed. There is thus no evidence that the "gap" is inevitable or irreducible. To be sure, it is forced down in part by foreign restrictions on dollar payments, but in 1952 even these restrictions were being removed, and the world had come closer than at any other time after the war to a payments pattern which might permit currency convertibility — i.e., freedom in exchanging foreign currencies for dollars without fear of an unmanageable "dollar gap."[11] (See Table 285.)

is the essence of the postwar change in the character of United States international financing.

Several adjustments in the balance of payments figures appear desirable in measuring the postwar dollar gap. Since 1947 there has been a substantial volume of foreign military aid consisting of gifts in kind of military equipment and, like lend-lease during the war years, this aid should be deducted from the trade balance in Table 285. Some nonmilitary ("economic") aid was of the same nature, but a complete record of its extent is not available. Also, with widespread foreign exchange control, the net additions to, or inroads into, private foreign holdings of dollar assets were largely under the control of the public authorities. As a result, foreign capital movements acquired the nature of reserve transfers. Lastly, there was an extraordinarily large volume of unidentified transactions ("errors and omissions") of which a large part probably consisted of concealed foreign capital movements. Thus the postwar "dollar gap" is best described as the sum of nonmilitary aid plus gold and foreign capital movements, always keeping in mind that "errors and omissions" should, in part, be added in also.

11. A further caution should be added. After the war United States imports were swelled by large government purchases: partly of military goods for use by the American armed forces abroad, and for transfer to foreign countries under military aid programs (so-called offshore procurement purchases); partly of strategically important commodities for domestic government stockpiling. The first of these three totaled $602 million in 1950, $1,248 million in 1951, $1,943 million in 1952 and $1,880 million during the first nine months of 1953 (Survey of Current Business, December 1953, p. 6). Stockpiling added between $0.5 billion and $1 billion a year. If these very large sums — about $2 to $3 billion a year — were deducted from imports and included, instead, with aid,

TABLE 285. THE "DOLLAR GAP," 1926–1939 AND 1946–1952

(*Millions*)

Year	Balance of Trade, U.S. Capital and Government Settlements (Surplus or Deficit [—])	Unidentified Receipts or Payments (—) (Errors and Omissions)	Foreign Capital (Net) (Inflow or Outflow [—])	"Dollar Gap": Gold [a] (Outflow or Inflow [—])
1926	$—402	$—75	$ 549	$—72
1927	—615	—423	884	154
1928	—514	—104	346	272
1929	—50	—384	554	—120
1930	180	320	—222	—278
1931	931	92	—1,199	176
1932	637	73	—699	—11
1933	95	61	—329	173
1934	622	415	141	—1,178
1935	394	368	958	—1,720
1936	14	157	976	—1,147
1937	290	425	556	—1,271
1938	1,034	249	374	—1,657
1939	1,056	789	1,173	—3,018

	Balance of Nonmilitary Trade and U.S. Capital (Surplus or Deficit [—])	Unidentified Receipts or Payments (—) (Errors and Omissions)	Net Addition to Foreign Short- and Long-Term Assets (Foreign Capital)	Gold (Outflow or Inflow [—])	Nonmilitary Government Aid	"Dollar Gap" [b]
1946	$6,656	$ 179	$—981	$—623	$—5,231	$—6,835
1947	9,740	980	243	—2,162	—8,801	—10,720
1948	4,737	1,037	379	—1,530	—4,623	—5,774
1949	5,038	785	107	—164	—5,766	—5,823
1950	—75	156	1,888	1,743	—3,710	—79
1951	2,224	536	495	—53	—3,202	—2,760
1952	2,436	596	1,532	—379	—4,185	—3,032

Sources: Table 277 and sources there cited.

a. For discussion of extent to which gold movements may be taken to correspond to the "dollar gap," see footnote 10 and related text.

b. Algebraic sum of net additions to foreign short- and long-term assets, gold flow and nonmilitary government aid.

TRENDS IN FOREIGN TRADE, 1923–1952

Because of the great relative weight of the American economy in the world, American im-

the "dollar gap" would be sharply increased. To maintain the current annual volume of United States imports — about $11 billion — foreign nations would have to increase their private exports to us by fully 25 per cent to make up for present American government imports if and when total military expenditures of the United States declined. Thus the recent shrinkage of the "dollar gap" may be deceptive. But so long as these expenditures continue, and it is not likely that they will drop substantially for some time, the "gap" as computed in Table 285 is correct, provided it can be assumed that the military au-

ports are especially important as the vehicle through which booms and recessions spread to other countries. Under conditions of a nearly universal dollar shortage, American imports, rather than incomes and demand in the exporting countries, have set the limit to the volume of American exports which the rest of the world can acquire. It is true that there has been government

thorities buy what they need where it is cheapest. Their foreign purchases should then be considered as normal imports and not as concealed aid; as normal imports they decrease the "dollar gap" but as concealed aid they would increase it.

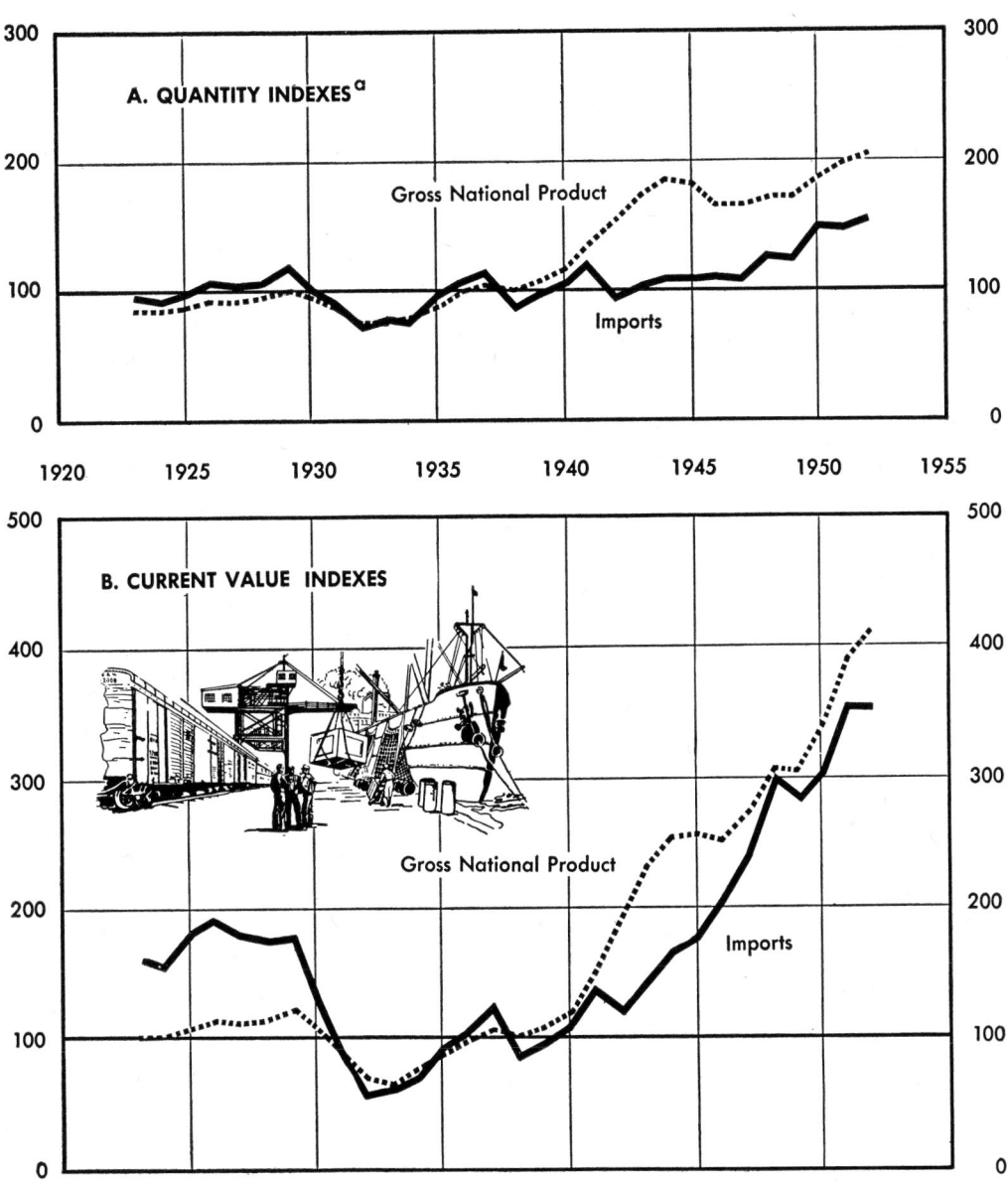

FIGURE 72. INDEXES OF UNITED STATES GROSS NATIONAL PRODUCT AND MERCHANDISE IMPORTS, 1923–1952
(1935–1939 = 100)

Sources: Appendix 4–2; J. H. Adler et al., The Pattern of United States Import Trade since 1923, Federal Reserve Bank of New York, 1952, Appendix D, pp. 80–82; and U.S. Department of Commerce, Business Information Service, International Trade Statistics Series, issue of March 1953.

a. Indexes based on series from which effects of price changes have been eliminated.

foreign aid and private foreign investment; but the one has clearly been an emergency device, adopted for special and limited purposes, and the other has been far from sufficient to finance the demand from abroad for American goods and services.

IMPORTS AND THEIR DOMESTIC ABSORPTION

The volume and nature of commodities which a country imports depend on three sets of factors: the country's volume of economic activity and thus its level of income and expenditure; its pro-

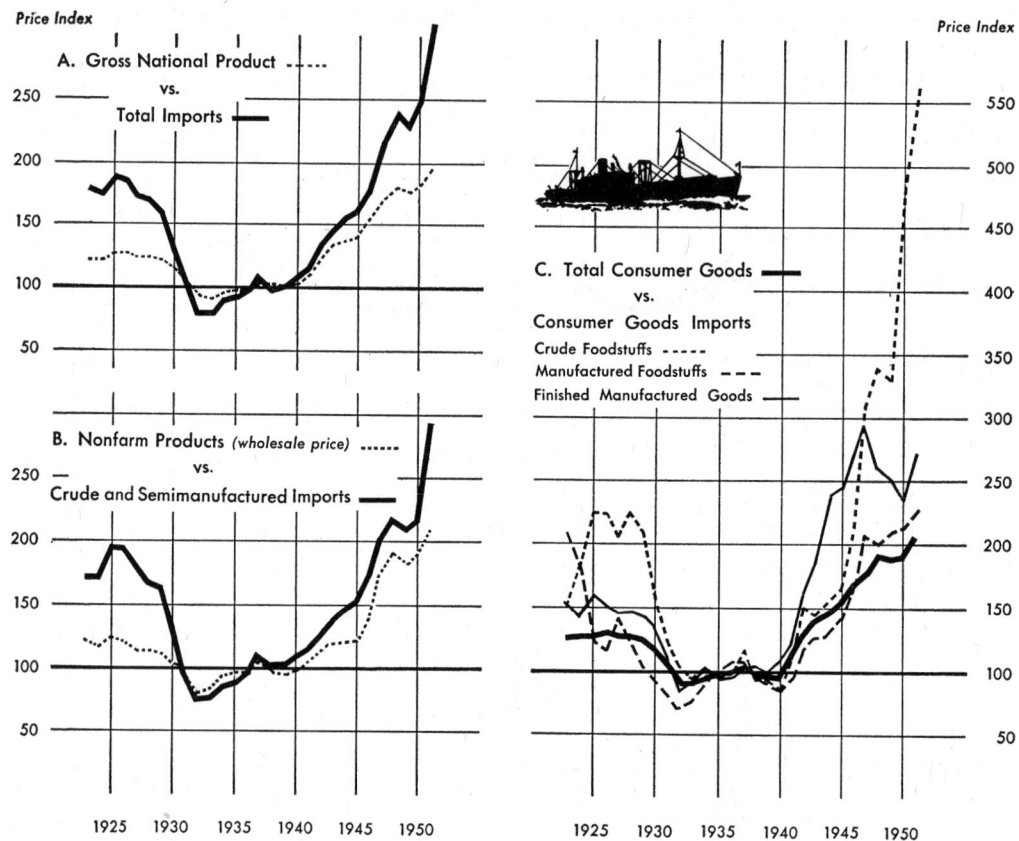

FIGURE 73. UNITED STATES DOMESTIC AND IMPORT PRICES: COMPARISON OF PRICE INDEXES, 1923–1951
(1935–1939 = 100)

Sources: Appendix 4–2; U.S. Department of Commerce, Business Statistics, 1953 (Supplement to Survey of Current Business); Survey of Current Business, July 1953; and J. H. Adler et al., The Pattern of United States Import Trade since 1923, Federal Reserve Bank of New York, 1952.

ductive efficiency relative to other nations — as reflected in the prices of its products compared with those abroad; and public policies adopted to influence the volume and composition of imports — such as tariffs, exchange restrictions, quotas and subsidies. For the United States, the volume of economic activity is the most important of these three factors.

The recent development of United States imports shows two important characteristics: (1) a decline, between prewar and postwar, in the ratio of imports to gross national product when both are measured in constant dollars; (2) an exaggerated reaction of imports to short-run fluctuations of United States gross national product when both are measured in current dollars. (See Figure 72.)

During the great depression and up to 1937

import quantities followed real gross national product fairly closely. But from that time onward, even if we neglect the abnormal war years, this close relationship ceased, and the volume of imports moved up much more slowly than real gross national product. There was a decided drop in the physical quantity of imports absorbed by the growing physical output of the United States economy. On the other hand, the exaggerated fluctuations of imports accompanying changes in the gross national product were chiefly a value phenomenon, due to the fact that import prices fluctuated more widely than domestic prices. Even quantitative reactions of imports, however, were larger than the changes in real national product which induced them. (See Figures 72 and 73.)

The significance of these two characteristics

may be found in the commodity composition and the patterns of geographical origin of United States imports.

Commodity Groups: Import Quantities

When quantities of imports are compared with the volume of domestic activity — total imports with real gross national product, consumer goods imports with all goods purchased by consumers, and raw material imports with the volume of domestic manufacturing production — it becomes apparent that the American economy has much reduced its relative intake in every category of imports. (See Figures 72, 74 and 75.)

This development is explained partly by the sharper rise of import prices than domestic prices since the depression. (See Figure 73.) But the statistical record of prices fails to disclose whether the import price movement was the *effect* or the *cause* of the decline in the volume of imports relative to domestic activity. Except for finished manufactures — in whose market the United States does not nearly carry the dominant weight as it does in the raw material and foodstuffs markets — there is good reason to believe that the first of these alternatives is the correct interpretation: the movement of import prices appears to have resulted from rather than caused the decline in import volume.

The tariff reduction which began with the Reciprocal Trade Agreements Act of 1934 seems to have had surprisingly slight effect in increasing imports. The lowering of duties affected particularly manufactured foodstuffs and finished manufactures. But the showing of these two import groups (Figure 75) indicates that the tariff reductions were far less effective in increasing imports than the size of the cut in rates on dutiable imports between 1934 and 1949 (from an average of 47 per cent to 13.3 per cent ad valorem) might lead one to expect. Moreover, even the strong rise in imports of finished manufactures after 1950 was due predominantly to the postwar recuperation of export capacities abroad — especially among European suppliers — although lowered rates of American duties probably played a part.

Much more important factors responsible for the import development in the United States were the apparently rising efficiency in the use of imported materials and a tendency to substitute domestic for foreign products, both raw materials and finished goods. Of the three import categories made up largely of consumer goods, only imports of crude foodstuffs for which domestic substitutes are not available — coffee, cocoa and bananas, for example — followed the rising trend of domestic food consumption.[12] Manufactured foodstuffs even by 1950 showed practically no rise over 1929, while finished manufactures, though recovering sharply in 1950 and 1951, were still 13 per cent below 1929. This is in pronounced contrast to the change in consumers' total expenditures on goods. (See Figure 75, A.) Substitution of domestic for imported products, which began in the prewar period, was a major factor in the continued relative decline of these imports.[13]

The most important group of imports — crude

---

12. For the three categories quantity indexes were as follows (1929 = 100):

	Personal Consumption Expenditure on Goods	Total Apparent Food Consumption *	Imports of Crude Foodstuffs	Imports of Manufactured Foodstuffs †	Imports of Finished Manufactures ‡
1929	100	100	100	(100)	100
1937	108	104	134	86	71
1948	168	130	142	93	55
1951	181	139	134	104	87

* Agricultural production for sale and farm home consumption *plus* agricultural imports, *less* agricultural exports.

† Excluding alcoholic beverages to allow for the effect of prohibition; 1928–1930 = 100.
‡ Excluding newsprint and jute burlaps.

From John H. Adler, Eugene R. Schlesinger and Evelyn Van Westerborg, *The Pattern of United States Import Trade Since 1923*, Federal Reserve Bank of New York, 1952, Appendix D, and *Resources for Freedom*, Vol. II, *The Outlook for Key Commodities*, President's Materials Policy Commission, June 1952, Table II, p. 180.

13. Cheese provides a classic example of domestic substitution among consumer goods. The United States Department of Agriculture stimulated the domestic production of foreign types of cheeses during the war. The result was that, in spite of the rise in United States incomes in the interval, cheese imports fell from 58 million pounds in 1936–1938 to 32 million pounds in 1949. The United States showed an export surplus after the war, while in 1936–1939 it was a net importer.

materials and semimanufactures — dropped far behind the rapid growth of United States domestic manufacturing production.[14] Since 60 to 65 per cent of United States imports after World War I consisted of crude and semimanufactured materials, their failure to keep up with rising domestic output had important implications for the entire import structure.

United States absorption of imported *materials* has, in fact, been subject to *two* opposing influences. On the one hand, increasing difficulties in the expansion of domestic output made the United States a net importer of such materials as zinc (from 1933), copper (from 1937), lumber (from 1940) and petroleum (from 1945), and together with a change in consumers' tastes, induced unexpectedly large postwar imports of raw wool. On the other hand, the increased prices of imported materials, plus the need for their unimpeded supply, reinforced a tendency to substitute domestic for imported materials. The dramatic prewar substitution of rayon for silk was followed by that of synthetic for natural rubber during the war, of synthetic fibers for wool, of paper and cotton cloth for jute burlap, of aluminum for copper;[15] and after the war, of plastics for leather. In addition, certain kinds of technological improvements designed to save materials, such as electrolytic tinplating, reduced the required input of imported materials per unit of output.

So far as the net effect of these two conflicting forces can be shown in the movement of very general indexes, two developments may be observed. Total consumption of industrial materials (both domestic and imported) did not keep step with manufacturing production, and industrial raw materials imports in turn lagged behind total consumption of industrial materials.[16] The sum of the substitution and the technological effects appears to have been stronger than the effect on imports of the relative exhaustion of domestic resources.

Commodity Groups: Import Values

The movement of import *prices* is responsible for the fact that the impression of import retardation found when examining *real* imports vanishes almost completely on inspecting the same data in terms of *current values*. (See Figures 72,B, 74,B and 75,B.) Some increases in import prices far exceeded increases in corresponding domestic prices; import values kept step with domestic output and consumption far more closely when measured in current rather than constant dollars.

To the outside world this means that foreign dollar receipts from shipments of goods to the United States in the 1930s and 1940s kept pace with the rise in American national product because foreign countries were able to obtain much better prices for their exports. But it does not mean that the 1940s compared favorably in this respect with the 1920s. Even the enormous American prosperity in the war decade failed to bring imports back to their position relative to gross national product in the prosperous predepression decade. (See Table 280 and Figure 72, B.)

The rise of import prices after World War II was manifest in all groups of imports. By 1950 the price of imported crude foods was four times its 1935–1939 level. Imports of manufactured food and finished manufactures showed rises of

---

14. Quantity indexes were as follows (1929 = 100):

	Industrial Production	Imports of Crude and Semimanufactured Materials
1929	100	100
1937	103	90
1948	180	118
1950	190	140

From Federal Reserve Board index of production and Adler *et al., loc. cit.*

15. See the diagrammatic presentation of this case on pp. 18–19, Vol. I, of the monumental report by the President's Materials Policy Commission (PMPC), *Resources for Freedom*, Washington, 1952. The PMPC report is a storehouse of invaluable material for this whole complex of questions.

16. Quantity indexes were as follows (1929 = 100):

	Industrial Production [*]	Apparent Consumption of Materials [†]	Imports of Crude and Semimanufactured Materials [‡]
1929	100	100	100
1937	103	107	96
1948	180	150	118
1949	176	136	110
1950	190	146	140

[*] Federal Reserve index.

[†] Excluding agricultural foods and gold. From *Resources for Freedom*, Vol. II, *The Outlook for Key Commodities*, President's Materials Policy Commission, June 1952, Table II, p. 180; production less exports plus imports.

[‡] The 1950 imports figure was pushed up by the impact of the first post-Korean developments beyond what it would otherwise have been, in part because of government strategic stockpiling purchases. From John H. Adler, Eugene R. Schlesinger, Evelyn Van Westerborg, *The Pattern of United States Import Trade Since 1923*, Federal Reserve Bank of New York, 1952, Appendix D.

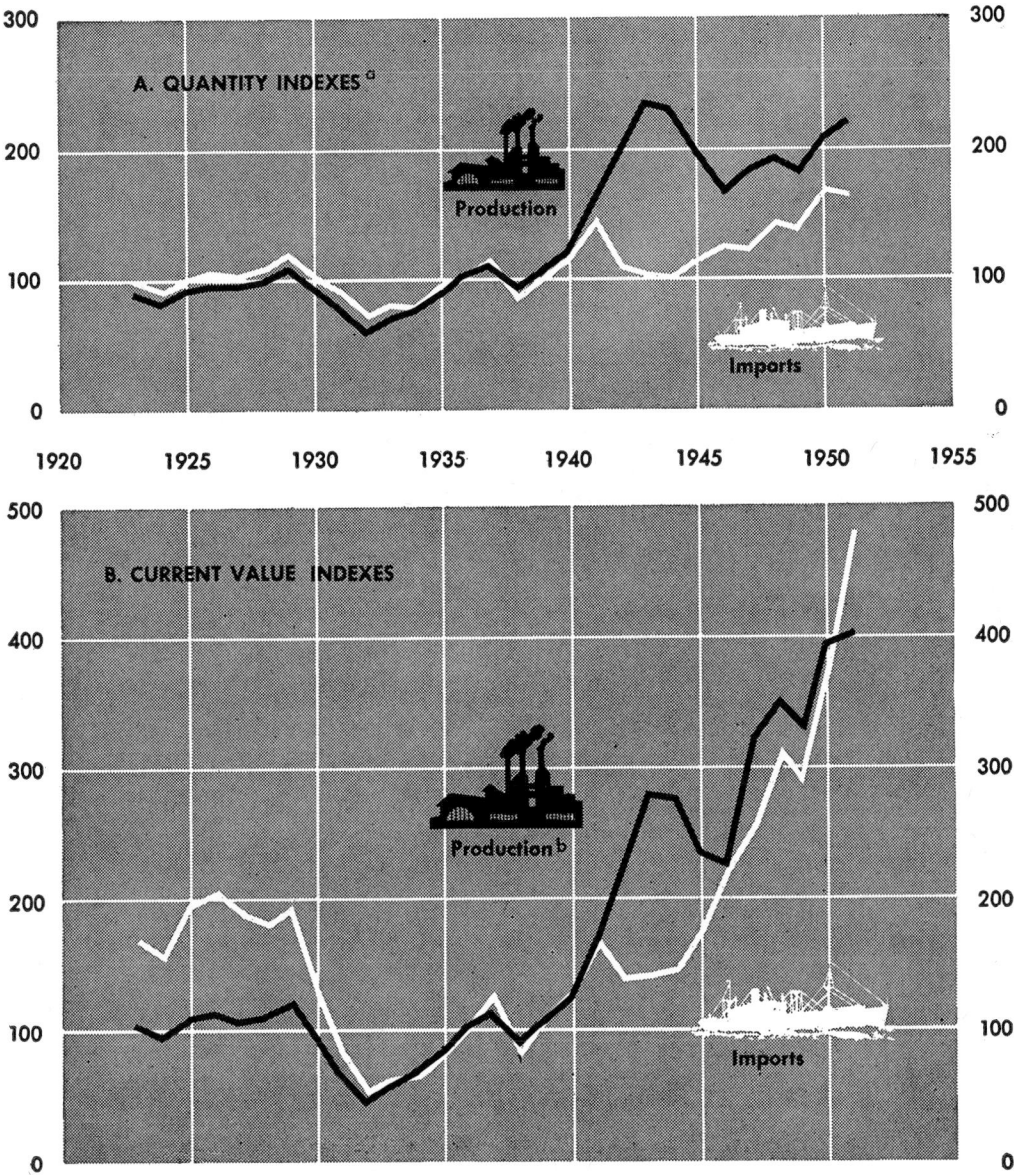

FIGURE 74. INDEXES OF UNITED STATES MANUFACTURING PRODUCTION AND IMPORTS OF CRUDE AND
SEMIMANUFACTURED MATERIALS, 1923–1951
(1935–1939 = 100)

Sources: Federal Reserve Board; U.S. Bureau of Labor Statistics; and J. H. Adler et al., The Pattern of United States
Import Trade since 1923, Federal Reserve Bank of New York, 1952, Appendix D.

a. Indexes based on series from which effects of price changes have been eliminated.
b. Valued at wholesale prices (Bureau of Labor Statistics wholesale price index).

150 and 100 per cent respectively. The noteworthy rise for finished manufactures, which came mainly from western Europe and Canada, shows that the benefit of high export prices was not restricted to the raw-materials-supplying areas. In fact, suppliers of crude and semimanufactured materials (largely countries of the British Commonwealth) experienced a smaller price rise for their exports than did the more industrialized countries. (See Figure 73.)

The divergence between value and quantity movements after World War II resulted in part from limitations of supply abroad. To the degree to which this is true, the greater rise of import prices than of import quantities indicates the extent to which the expanding United States demand pressed on the available supply of our import commodities. This pressure was felt most in raw materials markets, where United States demand is a dominant force.

United States import demand in the postwar years impinged upon insufficient supplies especially of crude foodstuffs. Prices rose 300 per cent above the high levels of the 1920s, although import quantities were only about 50 per cent higher. On the other hand, a similar increase in import quantities of crude and semimanufactured materials was accompanied by a price increase above the 1920s of only 10 to 20 per cent; supplies of these clearly were more adequate. The high prices of manufactured imports were due largely to high domestic price levels in the supplying countries, because of the inflationary consequences of overstrong home demand, quite independent of this country's increased import demand.

United States imports by value are concentrated in comparatively few crude foods and industrial raw materials. The following ten commodities accounted for 54 per cent of the total value of all United States imports in 1952: [17]

	Per Cent
Nonferrous metals and ores	12.8
Coffee	12.9
Newsprint	5.3
Sugar	3.9
Rubber, crude	5.8
Wool, raw	3.6
Petroleum, crude	4.1
Wood pulp	3.0
Cocoa	1.7
Burlaps	1.1
Total, 10 commodities	54.2

United States demand is a dominant force in the international markets of most of these commodities. Coffee, sugar, wool and rubber supplies are fixed each season and not easily varied except in the longer run; any variation in the output of the nonferrous metals (copper, tin, zinc, nickel) requires a considerable investment. Conse-

17. *Business Information Service, International Trade Statistics Series,* U.S. Department of Commerce, September 1953.

quently, small domestic changes lead to magnified fluctuations in demand for these imports and provoke very strong price reactions. This phenomenon was dramatically demonstrated during the Korean War. Along with the general tendency toward declining imports per unit of domestic product, there occurred particularly vigorous import responses to declines in domestic activity. Therefore it is no surprise to find that the very small recession of gross national product in the United States in 1938 and 1949 (6 per cent and less than 0.5 per cent, respectively, in current dollars) provoked drops in import values of 34 and 7 per cent respectively. The value of crude and semimanufactured materials fell by 43 per cent and crude foodstuffs by 37 per cent in the earlier of these recessions; in 1949, raw materials imports fell 11 per cent. This pattern of import behavior complicates the difficulties of foreign suppliers in balancing their accounts with this country.

Major Commodities

As a result of the concentration of United States imports, the behavior of a comparatively small number of commodities dominates import trends. Thus, coffee and cocoa make up two thirds of crude food imports (1948, by value), and sugar represents almost one half of manufactured food imports. The remaining commodities listed above (metals, wool, newsprint, wood pulp, crude oil and burlaps) account for almost 60 per cent of crude and semimanufactured materials imports.

Consumer Goods

Rising incomes in the United States have increased the demand for coffee sharply, while high prices have done little, until recently, to discourage consumption. Coffee imports rose from 12 pounds per capita in 1929 to 13 in 1939 and to 19 in 1948. The reaction of the coffee price, especially after 1949 when war-accumulated coffee stocks abroad were depleted by the smaller current crops, was the most important element in the spectacular rise in crude food import values. The failure of manufactured foodstuff imports to keep up with domestic consumers' expenditures is to be accounted for very largely by the drop in cane sugar imports from 9.8 billion pounds in 1929 to 6.4 billion in 1937 and 1948.

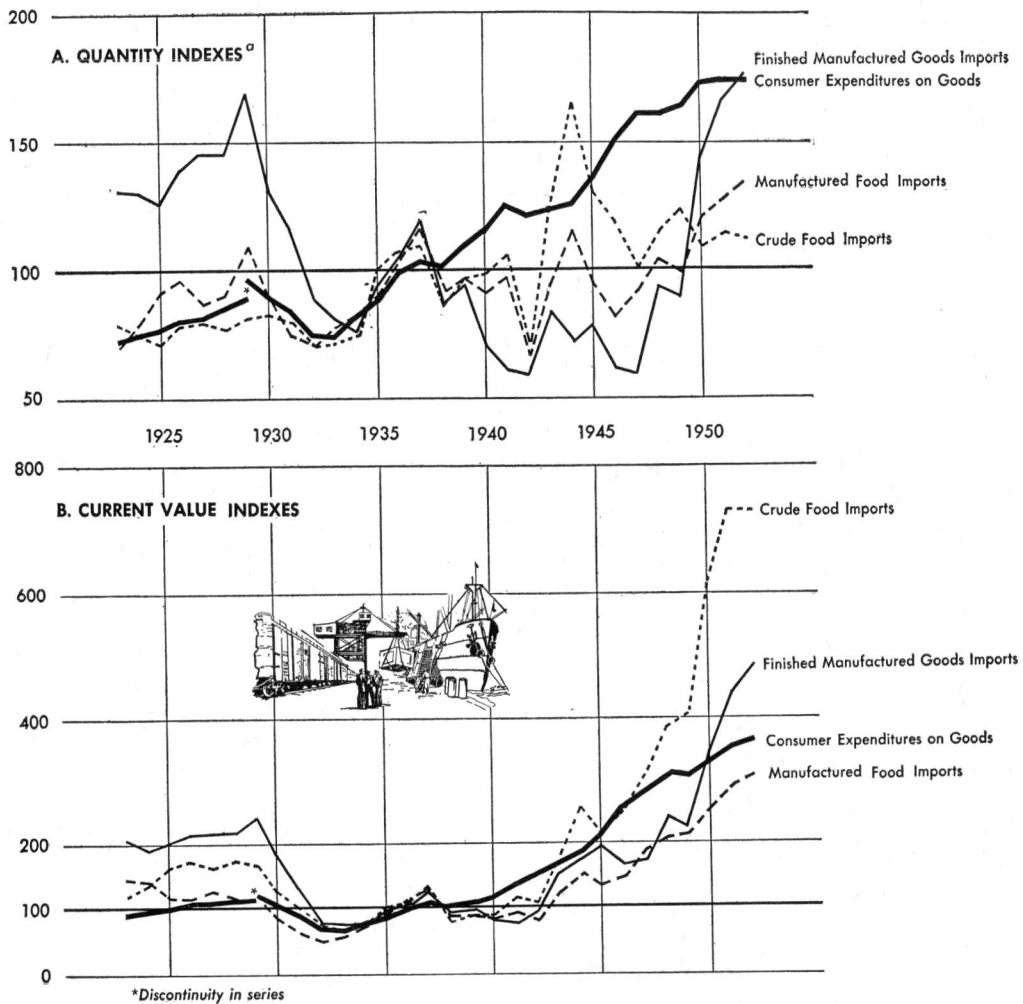

FIGURE 75. INDEXES OF TOTAL UNITED STATES CONSUMER GOODS PURCHASES AND CONSUMER
GOODS IMPORTS, 1923–1952
(1935–1939 = 100)

Sources: Survey of Current Business, July 1953 and U.S. Department of Commerce, Foreign Trade of the United
States, 1936–1949, Table 13.

a. Indexes based on series from which effects of price changes have been eliminated.

This was due first to the rise in the preferential duty under the Smoot-Hawley tariff and later to the introduction of the sugar import quota scheme under the Jones-Costigan Act (1934) and the various Sugar Acts (1937 to 1948).

The sharp increase in the quantity of finished manufactures imported during 1950 and 1951 — the largest since prewar days — indicates the sensitivity of this group of imports to price variations.[18] The first major break in the postwar rise of the unit values of these imports occurred be-

18. See Adler et al., op. cit., Table XV, p. 75.

tween 1949 and 1950, apparently connected at least in part with the 1949 devaluations when the price dropped 9 per cent. During the same period a price drop of 27 per cent for this group of imports from western Europe was accompanied by a 140 per cent rise in the volume of imports from that part of the world.

Raw Materials

Changes between prewar and postwar years in imports of crude and semimanufactured materials, comprising the bulk of United States imports, were by no means uniform. In some cases — petroleum, copper, lead and zinc, for example — the United States changed from a net exporter to a net importer, in terms of quantity as well as of value. In others — such as oils and fats and chemical fertilizers — the United States shifted in the opposite direction.

Perhaps the most interesting cases are in a third group: rubber, silk, tin, wool, jute burlaps, hides and skins. In this group, the United States maintained a net import position but gross imports showed a decline, either absolutely (silk and burlaps) or relative to the movement of total imports. The declining trend in import quantities of the group as a whole has been overshadowed at times by substantial price rises (tin, rubber), and at others by what since seems to have been a temporary rise (wool).

In all these cases import patterns are determined by a contest between domestic exhaustion of supplies and domestic substitution. These two processes take time to become fully effective, and the outcome is by no means clear. Thus the increased demand for some imported nonferrous metals (copper, tin, lead) is checked by the rise in domestic output of others (especially aluminum), by technological improvements (tinplating) or by nonmetallic substitutes (paint ingredients). The increased requirements of the United States for other nonferrous metals, however, has become so great that despite these substitutions the prewar United States trade surplus of crude and refined metals has been transformed into a substantial deficit. The increased domestic demand for rubber and textiles provoked an expansion in synthetic rubber and man-made fiber production, and domestic output of fats and oils and fertilizers took the place of corresponding imports.

Although price developments played a significant part in stimulating the absorption of domestic as against imported materials, other factors were no less important. Among these were strategic necessities and, especially, the assurance of steady supplies at prices free from seasonal and speculative fluctuations. Moreover, when investment has been made in the technological changes and in building markets for the substitute products it is in many cases difficult to return to imports even if import prices fall. The methods of using or producing synthetic rubber, rayon and other synthetic fibers, paper bags instead of burlap bagging, aluminum instead of copper, all illustrate this point. These technological changes reduce the prospects for re-establishing a large United States import dependence, and with it a large dollar supply to the rest of the world. Protectionist policies which have accompanied the exhaustion-substitution process, especially in agricultural products, intensify this whole development. (See Table 286.) [19]

Among textiles, synthetics have made rapid advances at the expense of all natural fibers but particularly silk, formerly a large import.

The growth of wool consumption, the result of a change in women's fashions, apparently has come to a halt. The shift to synthetic fibers, which up to 1950 formed only a small part of total fiber consumption, will not become fully evident until the plants for their manufacture now being constructed come into full production.[20] But the trend is clear enough — especially the marked rise in the use of synthetics for carpets and draperies and for industrial products, including tires. The wool price boom of 1950–1951 strongly reinforced this trend.

The growth in the use of synthetic rubber as against natural rubber — first supported by official synthetic-admixture regulations — now depends chiefly on relative price developments, since there has been marked improvement in the quality of the synthetic product. The state of the triangular jute-paper-cotton competition is similar. Between 1940 and 1948 the use of cotton bags declined 26 per cent, that of burlap bags rose 114 per cent and of paper bags 337 per cent. The Korean jute price boom supported this trend, and in both cases, technological reasons apparently impede its reversal.[21]

Comparable developments in the use of the major nonferrous metals have been completed only in part. The introduction of the electrolytic

19. For most of this table, as well as a considerable part of the statistical information on which these pages are based, the author is indebted to an unpublished manuscript of Howard K. Carlson of the International Monetary Fund.

20. Output of acrylic fibers is soon expected to equal domestic output of wool, and total noncellulose manmade fibers are expected to see an increase to more than 350 million pounds — almost three times the domestic wool production.

21. Apart from technical differences in the handling of paper instead of burlap bags, the spread of bulk handling (sugar, potatoes, grains) accounts for the relatively weak showing of burlap bag demand. There was a partial reversal of the paper-jute substitution with the fall of foreign burlap prices in 1952. But this reversal left dollar receipts of India — the main supplier — from burlap exports almost unchanged.

TABLE 286. PERCENTAGE CHANGE IN QUANTITIES OF DOMESTIC CONSUMPTION, PRODUCTION AND IMPORTS OF SELECTED RAW MATERIALS, 1929–1950

	Years	Consumption	Production	Imports		
Silk, raw	1929 to 1948	—91	—	—93		
Rayon (including acetate) filament yarn and staple	1929 to 1948	+762	+822	+146[a]		
Cotton, raw	1929 to 1948	+30	—	—57		
Rubber (including synthetic)	1929 to 1948	+130	(no production in 1929)	+30		
Wool	1929 to 1948	+88	—27	+173		
Jute burlaps	1940 to 1948	—	—	—21		
Use of burlap bags		+114	—	—		
Use of paper bags		+337	—	—		
Tin	1929 to 1950	+22[b]	+10	+25		
Tinplate production	1937 to 1948	—	+43	—		
Hides and skins	1929 to 1948	—	—	—50		
Shoe production	1929 to 1948	—	+28	—		
Fats and oils	1929 to 1949	+13	+43	—50		
Chemical fertilizers	1929 to 1949	+70	+150	—40		
				Net Imports (Short Tons)		
				1930	1948	
Copper	1929 to 1950	+32[b]	—1	—13	+448	
Lead	1930 to 1950	+75	+10	+28	+565	
Zinc	1930 to 1950	+70	+8	—14	+382	
Crude petroleum	1930 to 1950	+119	+125	—33[c]	+89[c]	

Sources: Computed from data furnished by the Departments of Agriculture and Commerce; Resources for Freedom, Vol. II, The Outlook for Key Commodities, President's Materials Policy Commission, June 1952; and Textile Organon, Textile Economics Bureau, January 1952.

a. Including waste.
b. Apparent consumption (production + imports − exports).
c. Millions of 42-gallon barrels.

process of tinplating since World War II and the substitution of frozen for canned foods have resulted in enormous savings in the use of this metal.[22] Tin consumption and imports therefore have risen far less than tinplate output. The consumption of copper, though much larger than before the war, is limited now by the growing competition of aluminum. The rise in United States aluminum production between 1930 and 1950 — over sixfold — gives an exaggerated impression of this substitution since the end uses of the two metals differ. But the 1951–1952 world copper shortage led to an increasing invasion of the electrical equipment field by the lighter metal, only to threaten a copper surplus.

In sum, semimanufactured and crude materials imports, the largest United States import group, when measured in quantitative terms and compared with domestic output, show an apparent retardation which is explained in large part by the domestic exhaustion-substitution process.

EXPORTS

Export developments have differed sharply from the record made by imports in three important respects. In contrast to imports, during the years after World War II exports rose markedly relative to gross national product, only to decline relatively after 1947. (See Table 280.) Price fluctuations for exports have been less sharp than for imports: between 1929 and 1933 total export unit values dropped only 38 per cent while import prices fell 50 per cent, and between 1933 and 1948 export unit values rose 150 per cent compared with a 170 per cent rise for imports. As a consequence, export trends measured in current

22. Tinplating absorbs better than 60 per cent of all tin consumed in the United States. While tinplate deliveries were 43 per cent larger in 1948 than in 1937, the quantity of tin consumed declined by 20 per cent. This development is still continuing.

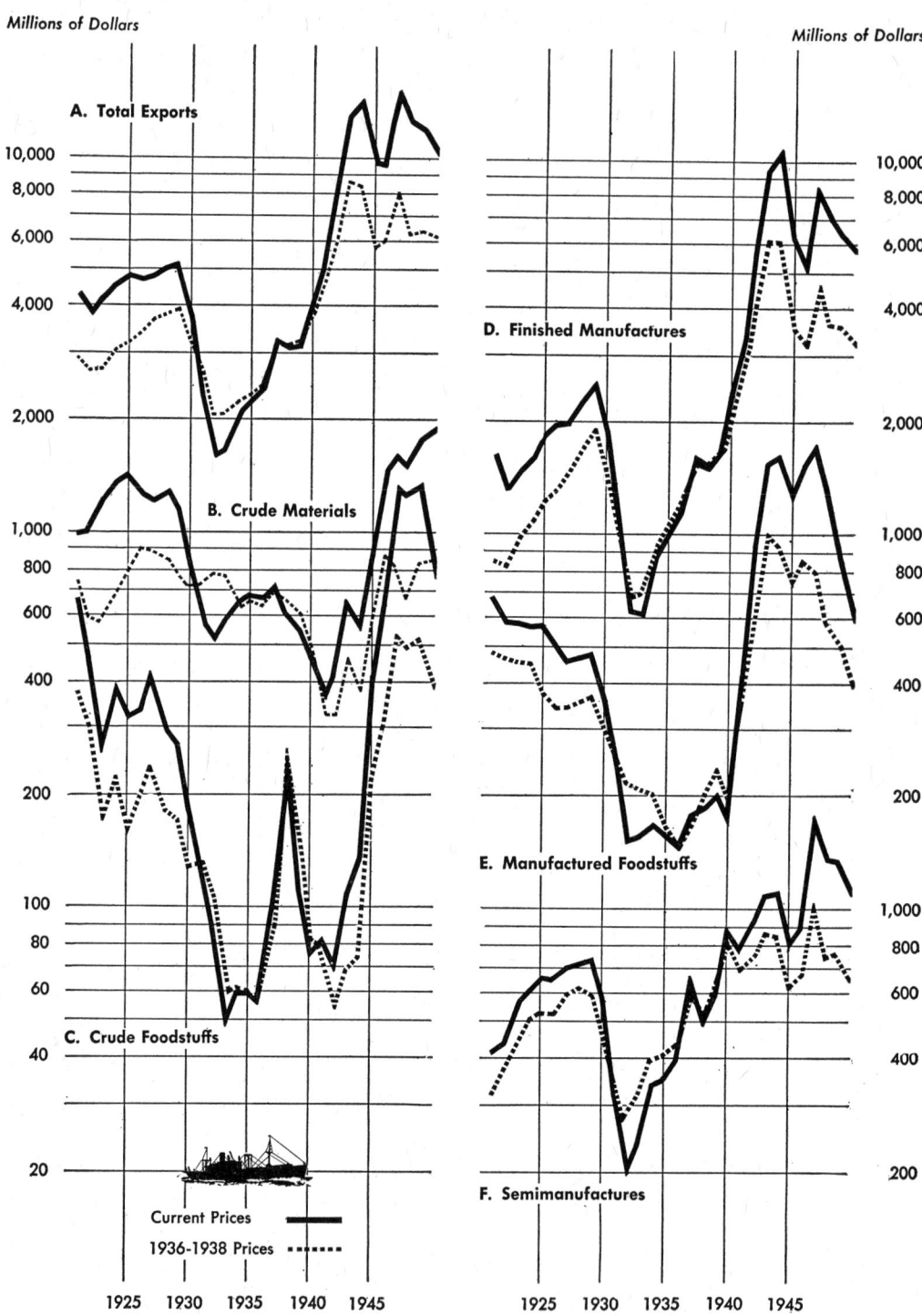

FIGURE 76. VALUE OF UNITED STATES MERCHANDISE EXPORTS, BY TYPE, 1921–1950 [a]

Sources: Computed from U.S. Department of Commerce, *Foreign Trade of the United States, 1936–1949,* Tables 6 and 10 and sources there mentioned, and *Business Information Service, International Trade Statistics Series,* February 1952.

a. General exports of domestic merchandise. Totals differ from those in Table 277 because of statistical discrepancies in the different sources used; subgroups do not necessarily add to totals in 1936–1938 dollars since separate price indexes were used in each case.

TABLE 287. UNITED STATES SURPLUS AND DEFICIT OF SELECTED RAW MATERIALS,
1929, 1937, 1948 AND 1950
(*Millions at Average 1935–1939 Prices*)

| Year | Agricultural | | Forest Products | Iron and Ferroalloys | Other Metals | Mineral Fuels |
	Foods	Nonfoods				
1929	$—168	$ 82	$—17	$—29	$—62	$100
1937	—365	—49	—46	1	—151	157
1948	225	—206	—94	—68	—225	50
1950	—25	—26	—116	—115	—316	—161

Source: *Resources for Freedom*, Vol. II, *The Outlook for Key Commodities*, President's Materials Policy Commission, June 1952, p. 183.

Note: Surplus equals net export, deficit equals net import (—).

and in constant prices have diverged from one another less than import trends. Lastly, exports are far less concentrated than imports. Although about two thirds of all exports usually have consisted of finished and semimanufactured commodities, the only export goods rivaling in relative importance the dozen major raw materials imports are wheat and cotton, and perhaps automobiles and trucks.

United States foreign aid (grants as well as loans) has been the dominant factor in the great rise of exports. In fact, when foreign aid is allowed for, the export surplus is turned into an import surplus both for the war years and for 1949, 1950 and 1952. (See Figure 71.) The use of a major part of foreign aid to finance agricultural exports as well as exports of textiles and textile manufactures points to one of the major postwar changes in the pattern of international trade. Political developments cut off European industrialized nations, in particular, from their prewar food supply areas, and increasingly rapid economic developments, especially in South America, led to rising demand for basic foods and textiles there, which in turn cut exportable surpluses and increased import demand. On the other hand, this same economic development generated demand in the less developed countries for the implements of economic advance, at a time when exportable European capital goods output was not only reduced but was needed desperately for domestic reconstruction. This situation gave a strong impetus to American exports of machinery and transportation equipment. Reduction of the postwar dollar shortage is related largely to the success of western European competition with the United States in third-area capital goods markets.

Commodities

In 1950, industrial semimanufactured and finished products accounted for two thirds of the value of all exports, manufactured foods for 6 per cent, agricultural crude materials and foodstuffs for another 20 per cent, and industrial raw materials for almost all of the remaining 8 per cent. The pattern was much the same as in the 1930s, except that industrial finished products and foods gained at the expense of crude nonfood materials, both agricultural and industrial. This change was the continuation of a tendency which began in the 1930s. Considering the increase in United States output, the increase of finished exports is not surprising. At the same time, it furnishes an explanation for the relatively small export price movement; value and quantity of this export group — as is typical for industrial manufactures in contrast to raw materials generally — moved very closely together. (See Figure 76.)

The rise in the value of food exports was solely a war and postwar phenomenon. Crude foods exports increased more than tenfold and manufactured foods sevenfold compared with the 1930s. The variation between value and quantity figures reflects the effects of this country's farm support policies.

Finally, exports of semimanufactures showed only a small relative rise, even after the war, and exports of crude materials showed a tendency to decline. (Crude materials include such agricultural products as cotton, which are mainly responsible for the upturn after World War II.) This reflects a growing deficit [23] of the United States in a number of basic raw materials (as Table 287 shows) and is only the reverse side of the coin of which the face is the shift from an export to an import surplus of some of the major metals and of petroleum and wood products. If it were not for the postwar increase of coal exports (54 million short tons in 1948, compared with an average of 14 million tons in 1936–1938), the decline would have been still larger. Export quantities for major commodities in 1948, as compared with the average for 1936–1938, had fallen as follows:

	Percentage Decline
Crude petroleum	40
Gasoline and fuel	9
Iron and steel (excluding scrap)	10
Copper	52
Lead	98

TRADE BY AREAS

An important shift in the geographical distribution of United States foreign trade took place between the prewar and postwar periods.[24] The proportion of United States international trade — exports and imports — carried on with the rest of the Western Hemisphere was substantially larger in 1952–1953 than before World War II, while the share of United States trade going to and coming from Europe and the rest of the Eastern Hemisphere declined substantially. (See Table 288.)

Canada and the Latin American republics, which accounted for only 30 to 35 per cent of United States foreign trade before the war, by 1952–1953 were involved in more than half of all United States imports and exports. The volume of trade between the United States and the rest of the Western Hemisphere increased even more — six to seven times over prewar years. The United States continued to export more to Canada than it imported from there and less to

Latin America than it imported from those countries. The export surplus with Canada rose from $111 million to $550 million; the export deficit with Latin America rose from only $51 million to $688 million.[25]

Member countries of the Organization for European Economic Cooperation took 24 per cent of United States exports and shipped 19 per cent of its imports in 1952–1953 whereas in the late 1930s these countries absorbed 37 per cent of United States exports and were the source of 24 per cent of its imports. However, inclusion of shipments to them under the Mutual Security Program, which totaled $2.8 billion in the period October 1952–September 1953 — practically the same amount as private shipments — would bring their postwar share of United States exports up to the prewar level.

Although imports from OEEC countries rose more rapidly than exports to them from the late 1930s to 1952–1953, they still fell short of matching United States exports. OEEC Europe's deficit with the United States was $690 million in 1952–1953, about $175 million larger than during the prewar period. In view of the war-inherited disturbances in the economies of Europe and the more rapid rise in United States export prices than in its import prices, to have kept the increase to that amount actually represents a considerable achievement.

United States trade with the overseas sterling area [26] and the "all other" group of countries [27] increased less than its trade with any other main area. Largely through the efforts of the United Kingdom to restrain its imports, and the large rise in United States imports from the outer sterling area, the $252 million prewar United States export surplus to the sterling area became a $255 million deficit in 1952–1953.

Changes in Commodity Pattern

These changes are linked to changes in the commodity pattern of United States trade. On the export side, typical commodities shipped to

23. Deficit = United States imports less exports for each commodity.

24. This comparison is based on the record for the years 1936–1938, which shows the typical prewar geographical structure of trade, and the period October 1952–September 1953, which is far enough removed from the immediate postwar disturbances and clear enough of the Korean War to serve as a fairly typical postwar year. The discussion here (and Table 288 as well) concerns privately financed trade only, exclusive of military shipments.

25. The net outflow of United States capital to Latin America did not cover the large return flow of interest and dividends on total United States investment in the Western Hemisphere. (See pp. 693–694.)

26. Including the United Kingdom, its colonies and the British Dominions, except Canada, plus Ireland, Iraq, Burma and Libya.

27. Mainly nonsterling independent countries in Asia and Africa plus dependencies of nonsterling European countries.

TABLE 288. AREA DISTRIBUTION OF UNITED STATES FOREIGN TRADE,[a] 1936-1938 AND OCTOBER 1952-SEPTEMBER 1953

(Dollar Amounts in Millions)

Area	1936-1938 Average				October 1952-September 1953					
	Exports		Imports		Exports[b]			Imports		
	Amount	Per Cent of Total	Amount	Per Cent of Total	Amount	Total	1936-1938	Amount	Total	1936-1938
						Per Cent of:			Per Cent of:	
Total	$2,967	100	$2,461	100	$11,590	100	390	$11,080	100	450
Canada	462	16	351	14	3,040	26	660	2,490	22	710
Latin American republics	484	17	535	22	2,895	25	600	3,583	32	670
OEEC Europe	1,113	37	598	24	2,828	24	255	2,137	19	355
Continental	614	21	424	17	2,243	19	365	1,592	14	375
United Kingdom	499	18	174	7	585	5	115	545	5	315
Other sterling area	283	9	356	14	898	8	315	1,193	11	335
All other areas	625	21	621	25	1,929	17	305	1,677	15	270

a. Reported exports including re-exports and reported general imports.
b. Excluding "Special Category" exports. Since special categories closely corresponded to shipments under the Mutual Security Program, exports in the table above in effect represent approximately privately financed exports.

Sources: John H. Adler, Eugene R. Schlesinger and Evelyn Van Westerborg, *The Pattern of United States Import Trade Since 1923,* Federal Reserve Bank of New York, 1952; *Foreign Commerce and Navigation of the U.S., 1940,* U.S. Department of Commerce, 1942, and *Business Information Service, International Trade Statistics Series,* January-September 1953, December 1953.

TABLE 289. UNITED STATES IMPORTS, BY COMMODITY GROUPS AND MAIN TRADE AREAS,
1936–1938 AND 1950
(*Dollar Amounts in Millions*)

	1936–1938 Average		1950		
	Amount	Per Cent of Total	Amount	Per Cent of Total	Per Cent of 1936–1938 Average
Finished manufactures[a]	$ 337	100	$1,108	100	330
OEEC Europe	200	60	569	51	285
Canada	29	9	286	26	980
All other areas	108	31	253	23	235
Crude and semimanufactured materials[b]	1,405	100	4,977	100	350
OEEC Europe	292	21	506	10	175
Canada	227	16	1,325	27	585
Latin America	194	14	1,239	25	640
Overseas sterling area	315	22	1,006	20	320
All other areas	377	27	901	18	240
Crude and manufactured foods[c]	604	100	2,485	100	410
OEEC Europe	106	18	173	7	165
Canada	71	12	303	12	425
Latin America	319	53	1,670	67	525
All other areas	108	17	339	14	315

Source: John H. Adler, Eugene R. Schlesinger and Evelyn Van Westerborg, *The Pattern of United States Import Trade Since 1923,* Federal Reserve Bank of New York, 1952, Appendix D.

a. Excluding jute burlaps and newsprint.
b. Including jute burlaps and newsprint.
c. Excluding drought-affected imports.

Europe — crude materials and crude and manufactured foods — slowly declined in importance. On the import side, there was an equally slow decline in the proportions of imports coming in the form of finished manufactures, largely from Europe. The smaller share of Asia in United States trade is linked to the decline in the proportion of United States exports in the form of crude materials and, on the import side, to the shift away from crude materials and toward semimanufactures.

These declines were accompanied by a relative growth of semimanufactures among exports and of crude foods as well as semimanufactures among imports. The growing importance of semimanufactured goods exports reflects increased United States shipments of commodities usually in demand in rapidly developing countries — Canada and several Latin American republics. The relative increase in imports of crude foods and semimanufactures, such as coffee and metals, chiefly benefits this same group of countries.

Europe and Asia suffered a decline as well in their share of trade in commodity groups in which they had been dominant before the war, particularly among United States imports. Canada's share in the imports of finished manufactures by the United States grew considerably at the expense of Europe, and the "all other" countries in Asia lost out to the American continent as a supplier of crude and semimanufactured materials.[28] (See Table 289.) In other words, after the swift loss of their share in United States imports during World War II, neither Europe nor Asia was able to regain its position

28. The reduced position of Europe as a supplier of semimanufactures as well as crude materials is in part due to the decline of the use of European countries (especially the United Kingdom, France and the Netherlands) as entrepôts for the shipment of such commodities as rubber, tin and tea. (See Adler *et al., op. cit.,* pp. 30 ff.) Another reason for this, however, is purely statistical. From 1937 onwards, United States imports are recorded by area of origin rather than by area of consignment. The transit trade with, for example, the United Kingdom from the middle 1930s onward is thus shown to have suffered a loss which appears as a gain by the outer sterling area.

even in those commodity classes where customarily they had been the most important source.

The bulk of the decline of Asian semimanufactures and crude materials imports — the major class of imports from that area — occurred almost completely outside the Asian sterling area countries. The overseas sterling area appears to have maintained almost its former share in United States imports. Quantities imported actually rose after the war by more than 40 per cent above their interwar levels.

The decline in imports from Europe and Asia relative to those from American areas, even in materials within the same economic class, appeared to result not from price differentials, but rather from a shift in the composition of United States import demand within commodity classes. There is very little competition between Asiatic and North or South American suppliers of raw materials. The main raw materials which the United States imports from Asia (rubber, tin, silk) either cannot be supplied at all by the Western Hemisphere (rubber, silk) or can be supplied only at noncompetitive prices (tin).

The picture on the export side is less clear, mainly because of the continuing volume of United States aid to Europe. Without this aid, Europe's role as a recipient of United States exports certainly would have been smaller, but continuing restrictions of dollar imports show that, given sufficient means of financing, her role would have been larger than it was in the early 1950s.

Foreign aid increased United States exports of dairy products, grains, fruits and vegetables, and solid fuels, and at the same time shifted them to Europe and Asia (Japan). In addition, areas undergoing rapid economic development, such as Canada, Latin America and Africa, demanded the very goods most readily furnished by the United States. Canada, and to a lesser extent Australia and South Africa, absorbed an increasing share of industrial equipment exports from the United States as they developed economically. Most of the Latin American countries and much of Africa, advancing rapidly through the early stages of development, increased their demand for basic foods and basic textile products to make up for the drop in farm output which characteristically accompanies a shift of labor from agriculture to industry. Accordingly, there have been extraordinary increases in United States exports of grains and other foods, machinery, chemicals (including fertilizers) and textiles to the rest of the Western Hemisphere and of grains, textile products and industrial shipments to Africa.

United States exports to Asiatic sterling area countries are small, compared with total exports; a change in their relative size would make little difference. But the share of total United States exports going to these countries seems, at least since 1936–1938, to have risen rather than declined.[29]

Surpluses and Deficits

The over-all balance of private trade was much the same in the period October 1952–September 1953 as the average of the years 1936–1938. In the postwar period United States private exports exceeded imports by $510 million and in the prewar period the excess averaged $506 million. Although exports rose 92 per cent and imports only 62 per cent, the gap remained constant because import prices rose more sharply than export prices: 177 per cent compared with 103 per cent.

The performance of the various trading areas in this respect was, however, very different, as shown in the following tabulation (in millions; surpluses [+], deficits [−]):[30]

	1936–1938 Average	October 1952– September 1953
Total	$+506	$+510
Canada	+111	+550
Latin American republics	−51	−688
OEEC Europe	+515	+691
Continental	+190	+651
United Kingdom	+325	+40
Overseas sterling area	−73	−295
All other areas	+4	+252

The large United States surplus with Canada in 1952–1953 and the large deficit with Latin America require some evaluation, as will be shown later, to avoid a possibly deceptive impression. While both areas enjoyed the benefit of considerable additions to American investments, payments of interest and dividends on previous in-

---

29. Development exports (machinery, chemicals, steel-mill products), and also cotton manufactures and grains, rose fourfold between the late 1930s and 1949–1950 — a little more than total United States exports. This is in contrast to the movement of American exports to the United Kingdom alone, which fell from 18 per cent of total exports in 1936–1938 to a mere 5 per cent in October 1952–September 1953. (See Table 288.)

30. Derived from Table 288. Data represent recorded trade, excluding "special category" exports, mainly military shipments.

vestments in Latin America more than offset new capital inflow there, whereas such an offset to capital movements did not exist in the case of Canada. Thus the American surplus with Canada was less of a threat to that country's dollar position and the deficit with Latin America was a smaller benefit to that area than the figures would imply.

Private capital movements were far less important to OEEC Europe, and the American trade surplus with respect to those countries indicates their continual difficulty in balancing accounts with the United States. On the other hand, through severe restrictions imposed on American exports to the United Kingdom and the overseas sterling area, a United States export surplus of $252 million in 1936–1938 was turned into a deficit of about the same magnitude in the 1952–1953 period covered.

Finally, the sharp rise in the American trade surplus with the countries of the "all other" group again indicates the increased pressure on the dollar position of such countries as Egypt, Japan and the Philippines, which are included in this group.

THE INVISIBLES

Between World Wars I and II, payments by the United States for the so-called invisibles — travel, transportation and other miscellaneous public and private services, plus foreign investment income and private donations — generally exceeded receipts from other countries, but from 1940 on the deficit became a surplus. (See Table 290.) The chief reason for the change was the substantial rise in receipts of income from American investments abroad and from transportation charges, and the rather small American tourist expenditures overseas. But the transportation surplus declined rapidly, the travel deficit grew, and the government services [31] surplus turned into a large deficit, so that the surplus of receipts for all invisibles had, by 1952, become relatively small — only $120 million — and in 1953 there was again a deficit of more than $300 million.

Actually, postwar investment income receipts are understated, since reinvested profits of subsidiaries of United States business abroad are not included in balance of payments records

after 1929.[32] The rapid rise after the war of the net private international creditor position of the United States and the concentration of foreign investment in direct investment, where returns are much higher than from portfolio investment (an average of 16 per cent as against 3 per cent), induced a return flow of investment income which in the 1950s became larger than the current net outflow of private capital.

The development of tourist expenditures was disappointing. Although personal disposable income (i.e., income after taxes) almost tripled between 1929 and 1952, expenditures on foreign travel rose by only 65 per cent. This was surprising since "luxury" expenditures generally increase faster than income.[33] Receipts from the expenditures of foreign travelers in the United States, on the other hand, quadrupled between the 1920s and 1930s and 1953. The result was that net payments for foreign travel to the rest of the world remained unchanged.

As a result of wartime developments the transport account had a sizable excess of receipts over payments after World War II, when the proportion of total ocean-going merchant ship tonnage carrying the American flag had temporarily increased to 50 per cent compared with 13.5 per cent in 1939. Even in 1948, when the proportion had receded again to one fifth, the "American Flag Rule" [34] and continued heavy subsidies to this country's merchant marine supported high United States transportation receipts.

However, in spite of these protective measures, American postwar shipping, except in the immediate post-Korean period, had to yield increasingly to foreign competition.[35] In this turn of

---

31. Government service payments include payments for services engaged abroad in the construction of American military facilities, such as airports (so-called "infrastructure" expenditures); they rose rapidly after the outbreak of hostilities in Korea.

32. They would have to appear on one side of the balance as investment income and on the other as capital outflows.

33. Expenditures on foreign travel apparently also depend on the proportion of the United States population which is foreign-born, and this proportion has declined steadily. See *Survey of Current Business*, May 1951.

34. Public Res. 17 (73d Cong., 1934) relating to goods acquired with funds lent by any agency of the United States, and Section III (a) of the Foreign Assistance Act of 1947 relating to Mutual Security aid.

35. *Survey of Current Business*, September 1953. Percentages carried in U.S. bottoms were as follows:

Dry Cargo:	Exports	Imports
1946	69	62
1950	40	48
1953 (1st Quarter)	22	44
Tanker Cargo:		
1946	44	91
1950	45	69
1953	28	63

Table 290. United States Invisible Trade, 1921–1953
(Annual Averages in Millions)

Years	Total Balance	Travel			Transport			Income from Foreign Investment			Private Donations (Net)	All Others (Net)
		Receipts	Payments	Balance	Receipts	Payments	Balance	Receipts	Payments	Balance		
1921–1925	$ −206	$ 74	$271	$ −197	$ 325	$ 352	$ −27	$ 596	$132	$ 464	$ −361	$ −85
1926–1930	−210	123	425	−302	363	456	−93	899	268	631	−338	−108
1931–1935	−117	93	252	−159	160	235	−75	502	152	350	−202	−31
1936–1938	−80	127	316	−189	220	305	−85	576	255	321	−168	−201
1940	207	95	190	−95	403	334	69	564	210	354	−178	57
1946	595	252	457	−205	1,420	599	821	810	216	594	−679	64
1948	497	308	600	−292	1,299	630	669	1,375	284	1,091	−678	−293
1950	473	377	727	−350	926	798	128	1,743	437	1,306	−481	−130
1952	119	524	822	−298	1,348	1,075	273	1,886	432	1,454	−433	−877
1953	−312	545	908	−363	1,287	1,117	170	1,899	448	1,451	−487	−1,083

Sources: 1921–1952, Table 277 and sources there cited; 1953, Survey of Current Business, March 1954, p. 22.

TABLE 291. UNITED STATES BALANCE OF PAYMENTS FOR SERVICES WITH WESTERN EUROPE,[a]
THE WESTERN HEMISPHERE[b] AND ALL OTHER AREAS, 1948 AND 1952
(*Millions; U.S. Surplus or U.S. Deficit* [−])

	1948			1952		
	Western Europe and Dependencies	Western Hemisphere	All Others	Western Europe and Dependencies	Western Hemisphere	All Others
Total	$−116	$710	$−97	$−660	$893	$−114
Travel	−82	−215	5	−251	−57	10
Transportation	412	42	215	78	46	149
Investment income	72	809	210	164	886	404
Private donations	−371	−42	−265	−227	−50	−156
Miscellaneous	−147	116	−262	−424	68	−521

Sources: *The Balance of Payments of the United States, 1949–1951*, U.S. Department of Commerce, 1952, and *Survey of Current Business*, June 1953.

a. 1948: OEEC Europe; 1952: western Europe (OEEC plus Yugoslavia, Finland and Spain).
b. Canada and Latin American republics.

events the attempt of foreign countries to conserve their dollar resources played an important part. The result was a reduction in the United States transportation surplus from $821 million in 1946 to $170 million in 1953.

These developments led to a spectacular shift in the United States balance of payments for services in favor of western Europe and its dependencies and against the Western Hemisphere and the rest of the world. The western European countries substantially increased their surplus and decreased their deficit with regard to travel and transportation respectively, lost through the decline of private donations and the increase of their interest payments, but gained considerably from the increase of United States payments for miscellaneous (especially government) services. The result was an increase in the American services deficit from $116 million in 1948 to fully $660 million in 1952. (See Table 291.)

The United States surplus with the Western Hemisphere rose from $710 million to $893 million, principally because of an increase in travel expenditures of residents of the Western Hemisphere, especially Canadians, in this country. There were also heavy increases of Canadian and Latin American payments of investment income to Americans.

The balance with the rest of the world shows two opposite movements: American net receipts of investment income — after the large postwar oil investments in the Near East — rose by almost $200 million. On the other hand, net miscellaneous service payments rose by $260 million, largely as the result of government service payments to the Far East, and the deficit in private donations fell about $100 million. On balance, the American deficit with these countries rose by about $20 million between 1948 and 1952.

TRENDS IN UNITED STATES FOREIGN FINANCING,
1919–1952

"Financing" transactions are set aside because they involve compensation in claims (securities), gold or, in the case of donations, nothing, while the immediate objects of trade are goods and services. They are by no means always the passive part of the balance of payments. In fact, with the exception of purely compensatory payments, such as — at least frequently — gold movements, financing is closely tied to, and often induces, commodity movements. As a form of dollar supply to the rest of the world, it is frequently more narrowly circumscribed than receipts from trade. United States imports and a gold outflow leave the foreign recipient completely free to dispose as he pleases of the dollars he thus obtains; capital movements are usually (though not necessarily and formally) "tied" to a movement of goods in the same direction, as is government foreign aid.

UNITED STATES LONG-TERM PRIVATE CAPITAL
MOVEMENTS

United States long-term private capital movements from 1919 to 1952 reveal three characteristics.

TABLE 292. NET OUTFLOW OF UNITED STATES PRIVATE LONG-TERM CAPITAL, 1921–1952
(*Millions*)

Annual Average or Year	Direct Investment[a]		Portfolio Investment[b]			Total Net Outflow[c]
	Net Outflow (Balance of Payments)	Reinvested Earnings	Outflow	Inflow	Net Outflow	
1921–1925	$172		$639[d]	e	e	$681
1926–1930	431		849	$457	$392	823
1931–1935	38	e	79	243	−164	−126
1936–1938	−13	e	38	189	−151	−164
1940	32	43	84	48	36	111
1946	183	303	335	459	−124	362
1947	724	387	487	401	86	1,197
1948	684	581	223	159	64	1,329
1949	786	436	206	196	10	1,232
1950	621	475	879	412	467	1,563
1951	528	752	597	236	361	1,641
1952	850	876	e	e	143	1,869

Sources: Publications of the U.S. Department of Commerce, as follows: for 1921–1938, *The United States in the World Economy*, 1943; for 1940, *International Transactions of the United States during the War, 1940–1945*, 1948, Table 21, p. 93; for 1946–1952, *The Balance of Payments of the United States, 1949–1951*, 1952, Table 34, p. 156, and *Survey of Current Business*, January 1954.

a. Investments in plant abroad. Since 1929, official United States balance of payments statistics on capital outflow do not include reinvested earnings of U.S. subsidiaries.

b. Purchases (outflow) or sales (inflow) of securities by U.S. residents.
c. Including reinvested earnings.
d. New issues on foreign account only for 1923–1925.
e. Not available.

Note: Capital outflows from the United States are shown as positive figures in this table and capital inflows with a minus (−) sign, in contrast to Table 277 and elsewhere. Figures for 1950–1952 are also revisions of those contained in Table 277.

First, United States private long-term foreign investment was even more sensitive to the depression of the 1930s than United States trade. With insignificant exceptions, there was no United States net capital outflow for a long time after 1931; for almost fifteen years after that crisis, the United States ceased to be a long-term foreign lender. The disappointing experiences of the 1920s as well as the particularly difficult international situation for postwar foreign investment prevented more than a limited revival after 1945. (See Table 292.)

Second, a very large part of United States foreign investment — in the postwar years, the predominant part — consisted of direct investment (i.e., additions to American-controlled foreign-located production facilities) rather than portfolio investment (acquisitions of foreign securities).[36] As early as 1930, almost half the total

value of United States investments abroad, $15.8 billion, is estimated to have consisted of direct investments; in 1940, after the "great liquidation" of the 1930s, the proportion was seven to four in favor of direct investments. In the five years 1946–1950 only $500 million of a total new investment of $5.7 billion (including reinvested earnings) was in portfolio form. The importance of this pattern is that United States exports of equipment, and even of personnel, accompany investment of the direct type. In return, since the predominant aim of United States foreign direct investment has been to develop raw materials for the American market, a substantial share of the product of United States foreign installations is shipped back to this country.

Finally, even in the interwar period, most United States foreign investment went to Canada and Latin America. Europe, which in 1945 ranked third, has become unimportant and is

36. The year 1950 was an exception. Purchases of Canadian securities in the expectation of a free exchange rate for the Canadian dollar were abnormally large. The corresponding inflow of funds depressed the figure for portfolio investment equally abnormally in 1952–1953.

outranked by the Middle East. This geographical pattern of capital movement is related to the trade pattern. To a large extent, in fact, United States investments of the 1920s prepared the ground for the shift especially of imports to the Western Hemisphere countries, which have remained among all developing countries those of most rapid economic growth.

Role in Financing the Trade Balance

Although the amount of long-term foreign lending was considerably larger in the 1946–1952 period than in 1926–1930, it no longer played its crucial earlier role of balancing the difference between exports and imports. That our private long-term financing remained so inadequate in relation to the trade balance after the war is another aspect of the postwar "dollar gap" problem.

Of the two types of foreign investment — portfolio and direct — only the figures on direct investment are sufficiently reliable to throw some light on this question. Portfolio investment data have two weaknesses. Net portfolio investments — mainly net purchases by Americans of foreign securities, new or outstanding — may indicate no more than an international redistribution of liquid holdings. Foreign borrowers may maintain their receipts in the United States in the form of short-term balances. The large inflow into the United States of short-term funds recorded during the middle and later 1920s appears to have originated partly in the concurrent United States long-term loans,[37] and a sizable part of the "uphill" flow [38] of long-term capital into the United States in 1924–1939 certainly contained "hot" money which, though taking the form of purchases of United States securities, had the economic nature of a movement of short-term funds. A direct consequence of this fact is the greater sensitivity of portfolio investments to business cycle fluctuations.

Another reason why direct investments were more significant than portfolio investment is that a considerable proportion of portfolio investment was used for armament expenditures, the covering of public budget deficits, the repayment of

public debts to the United States, the settlement of reparations and similar purposes rather than for the expansion of economic production.[39] While portfolio investment thus tends to be less closely tied to exports, it is not always safe to regard its total as a net dollar-supplying item in the balance of payments.

Redirection of U.S. Investment

As early as the 1920s, Western Hemisphere countries began to move toward the preferred position as debtors to the United States which they occupied after World War II. By 1930, 52 per cent of total investments and 72 per cent of all *direct* investments were in Canada and Latin America. This redirection of United States investment was accelerated in the following decade, paralleling the increased two-way trade brought on by the breakdown of the world economy after 1930.[40] With the disruption of triangular trade between Europe, the United States and the third areas, and the growth of trade and exchange restrictions in Europe after 1931, it became increasingly difficult and finally impossible for the relatively underdeveloped countries to maintain the service (payments for interest, dividends and amortization) on their foreign obligations except bilaterally by exports to their creditors. Continental Europe, which in the 1920s had played an important part as intermediary in trade and debt service between the large creditors and non-European debtors, was largely dealt out of this trade and investment process.

---

37. See on this point: *International Capital Movements during the Interwar Period,* United Nations, New York, 1949, p. 27.

38. That is, flow from high- to low-interest-rate countries. See Hal B. Lary and Associates, *The United States in the World Economy,* U.S. Department of Commerce, 1943, p. 90; and United Nations, *op. cit.,* pp. 40–41.

39. This is a debatable point; but see the various official attempts (mostly ineffective) of the United States government to arrive at a foreign investment control policy, which are the subject of the sober, if disillusioned, study by Herbert Feis, *The Diplomacy of the Dollar: First Era 1919–1932,* Johns Hopkins University Press, Baltimore, 1950. Fully one half of the interwar portfolio investment had been lending to foreign governments, and the disappointing default record of this "dollar diplomacy" episode (see Ilse Mintz, *Deterioration in the Quality of Foreign Bonds Issued in the United States, 1920–1930,* National Bureau of Economic Research, New York, 1951) finally led to the Johnson Act of 1934, which prohibited new loans to public authorities of countries which had defaulted on their war debt obligations to the United States — precisely at a time when such loans might have been important instruments of a defensible "dollar diplomacy." See also Cleona Lewis, *America's Stake in International Investments* and *The United States and Foreign Investment Problems,* Brookings Institution, Washington, 1938 and 1948 respectively.

40. A similar process may be observed to have taken place between the United Kingdom and its "investment empire," the sterling area. See *International Capital Movements during the Interwar Period,* pp. 38 and 46.

TABLE 293. NET OUTFLOW OF UNITED STATES PRIVATE LONG-TERM CAPITAL, BY TYPE, INCLUDING REINVESTED EARNINGS, 1946–1952

(*Millions*)

Area and Type	1946	1947	1948	1949	1950	1952
Total	$362	$1,197	$1,329	$1,232	$1,542	$1,869
Direct (net)	183	724	684	786	621	850
Reinvested earnings	303	387	581	436	475	876
Portfolio (net)	−124	86	64	10	446	143
Canada	134	−24	394	277	678	649
Direct (net)	38	13	77	119	287	420
Reinvested earnings	98	131	213	144	146	199
Portfolio (net)	−2	−168	104	14	245	30
Latin American republics	13	504	481	557	123	546
Direct (net)	59	442	321	429	40	277
Reinvested earnings	89	117	209	147	109	303
Portfolio (net)	−135	−55	−49	−19	−26	−34
Europe [a]	62	230	155	136	429	185
Direct (net)	17	49	53	44	119	−8
Reinvested earnings	64	75	88	83	151	174
Portfolio (net)	−19	106	14	9	159	19
All others [b]	153	487	299	262	312	489
Direct (net)	69	220	233	194	175	161
Reinvested earnings	52	64	71	62	69	200
Portfolio (net)	32	203	−5	6	68	128

Sources: The Balance of Payments of the United States, 1949–1951, U.S. Department of Commerce, 1952, Tables 29 and 34, pp. 154 and 156, and *Survey of Current Business*, January 1954. 1950 and 1952 data are from revised series and do not necessarily agree with (unrevised) balance of payments data used elsewhere in this chapter.

a. 1950 and 1952; western Europe only.

b. Includes international institutions (especially International Bank for Reconstruction and Development).

The countries that managed to remain net creditors were the ones with the largest relatively accessible markets for raw materials and crude foods exported by the debtor areas. The United States became the predominant creditor of Western Hemisphere countries, and the United Kingdom of the overseas sterling area. Direct investments, especially in branches of industry and agriculture which produced raw materials for the creditor countries, survived the international economic warfare of the 1930s considerably better than did portfolio investments. Between 1930 and 1940, direct investments decreased from $8 billion to $7 billion, while portfolio investments (at par value) fell from $7.8 billion to $4.1 billion.[41]

By 1950, after the postwar revival of private American foreign lending, direct investment constituted 70 per cent of the total; only Canadian investment, favored by the similarity of capital markets and legal institutions and the absence of serious capital transfer restrictions, retained about one half the portfolio form. (See Table 293.) The concentration of investment in the Western Hemisphere — $12.5 billion out of the total of $19.3 billion, as against $9.2 billion out of $15.8 billion in 1930 — had increased only a little, but Europe was being replaced by the "all other" countries — mainly the Middle East.

Small Net Outflow

Compared with the 1920s, when total net long-term capital outflow (including reinvestment of earnings) was $750 million annually, the figures for 1946–1952 are impressive enough. But when allowance is made for the 62 per cent rise in export prices it is found that the net outflow was only a little larger in 1952 than the average of

41. Portfolio investments, at market values, amounted to only $2.8 billion (see *Foreign Investment Experience of the United States, 1920–1940*, U.S. Department of Commerce, 1945, p. 1, mimeographed).

1926–1930. In any event, it did not keep pace with gross private domestic investment, which increased threefold (measured at constant prices it increased by two thirds). Moreover, the geographical pattern was clearly inadequate for the financing of the regional export surpluses of the United States after World War II. (See Table 293.)

The major reasons for this situation are well known. "Development consciousness" abroad, especially in underdeveloped countries, and the growing conviction, rightly or wrongly, that postwar economic development must be accompanied by economic and political independence from foreign investors and their governments, led to a series of restrictions imposed by underdeveloped countries on the foreign ownership of basic industries, the transfer of net earnings and capital abroad and the proportion of foreign personnel. All this made foreign investment less attractive to American investors. These obstacles operate with greater force against portfolio investments, and at the same time make for a significant increase in the financing of foreign investment from reinvested earnings of the foreign-incorporated enterprises controlled by American interests. (See Table 293.)

Concentration of Direct Investment

Postwar direct investment showed an increasing concentration in manufacturing industries and in petroleum production. (See Table 294.) Direct investment in manufacturing occurred mainly in Canada, but also in the OEEC countries of western Europe and even in Latin America. In petroleum production, direct investment was connected with the considerable Latin American developments, especially in Venezuela, with developments in the Near East and in European dependencies and, from 1949 on, with the new oil developments in Canada. The increased interest of American investors in manufacturing industries, apart from the rapid Canadian industrial development, arises from the profitable branch plants set up in countries whose markets would otherwise be inaccessible to United States producers because of the postwar restrictions abroad on dollar imports.

The postwar growth of United States private foreign investment, and more especially its geographical distribution, determined the flow of foreign investment income. Total earnings on United States private investments abroad, including undistributed earnings, were (in millions): [42]

	Direct (Including Reinvested Earnings)	Portfolio	Total
Total, 1946–1952	$11,708	$1,192	$12,900
1946	939	153	1,092
1947	1,211	156	1,367
1948	1,692	162	1,854
1949	1,584	159	1,743
1950	1,766	181	1,947
1951	2,236	185	2,421
1952	2,280	196	2,476

Of these total investment earnings, almost two thirds came from two regions, Latin America (40 per cent) and Canada (25 per cent), and the earnings from investments in manufacturing and petroleum industries were each equal to about one third.

The significance for the United States balance of payments of direct foreign investment is that it is part of a twin set of bilateral transactions: the original investments are accompanied by exports of investment goods, and the operation of the resulting capital installations abroad causes a return flow both of investment income and newly produced commodities to the United States. The net dollar earnings of foreign countries generally are small since they equal only the excess of new imports over induced exports less the excess of United States income from foreign investments over new current capital outflow.

UNITED STATES FOREIGN AID

The increased self-sufficiency of the United States was perhaps the most important and lasting consequence of World War II for the trade pattern of United States foreign transactions. Similarly, the enormously increased international economic role of the United States government in the form of increased foreign aid was by all odds the most significant, though not the most permanent, development on the financing side of the United States balance of payments. The invention of lend-lease during the war, and of the Marshall Plan afterwards — to say nothing of such other instruments as UNRRA and the Export-Import Bank — gave a completely new

42. Data for 1946–1949 from *The Balance of Payments of the United States, 1949–1951*, U.S. Department of Commerce, 1952, Tables 25 and 30; for 1950–1952, from *Survey of Current Business*, December 1953, Table 1, p. 9.

TABLE 294. VALUE OF UNITED STATES PRIVATE FOREIGN DIRECT INVESTMENTS BY INDUSTRIES AT END OF SELECTED YEARS, 1929-1952

(Millions)

Industry	1929	1940		1946		1950		1952	
		Amount	Change from 1929	Amount	Change from 1940	Amount	Change from 1946	Amount	Change from 1950
Total	$7,528	$7,000	$-528	$8,854	$+1,854	$11,788	$+2,934	$14,819	$+3,031
Manufacturing	1,535	1,618	+83	2,854	+1,236	3,831	+977	4,920	+1,089
Distribution	368	522	+154	740	+218	762	+22	966	+204
Agriculture	875	432	-443	545	+113	589	+44	662	+73
Mining and smelting	1,185	782	-403	1,062	+280	1,129	+67	1,642	+513
Petroleum	1,117	1,277	+160	1,769	+492	3,390	+1,621	4,291	+901
Public utilities	1,609	1,514	-95	1,277	-237	1,425	+148	1,469	+44
All other [a]	839	855	+16	607	-248	662	+55	869	+207

Sources: 1929, 1940: U.S. Department of Commerce presentation at Hearings on Bretton Woods Agreements Act, April-May 1945, p. 304; 1946, 1950, 1952: Survey of Current Business, January 1954, Table 1, p. 6. Classification is not necessarily completely consistent between years.

a. Includes negligible amounts of investments in distribution, mining and smelting, manufacturing, agriculture and public utilities in 1929 and 1940.

TABLE 295. DESTINATION AND COMPOSITION BY COMMODITIES OF UNITED STATES GROSS[a] LEND-LEASE AID, MARCH 1941 TO OCTOBER 1945

	Amount	Percentage Distribution
	(Billions)	
Total	$46.05	100
Destination:		
British Empire	30.27	66
USSR	10.80	23
Continental Europe[b]	1.78	4
China	0.63	1
American republics	0.42	1
All other countries	0.04	—
Aid not charged to foreign governments	2.09	5
Commodity composition:		
Munitions (including ships)	22.10	48
Petroleum products	2.32	5
Industrial materials and products	9.69	21
Agricultural products	6.09	13
Shipping and other services	3.76	8
Other lend-lease charges	2.09	5

Source: Twenty-first Report to Congress on Lend-Lease Operations, Lend-Lease Administration, Washington, 1946, pp. 11 and 14.

a. Reverse lend-lease not deducted.
b. France, Netherlands, Greece, Belgium, Norway, Turkey, Yugoslavia.

complexion to the international transactions of the United States.

Of the $42.4 billion of foreign aid in 1941–1945, more than three quarters was net lend-lease (United States lend-lease, less $6 billion reverse lend-lease), and of the $39.2 billion net outflow of aid funds under the various postwar aid schemes in 1946–1952, between one third and one half was accounted for by the European Recovery Program. The two sums together — $82 billion — amounted to more than 50 per cent of all United States exports between 1941 and 1952.

The twelve years 1941–1952 in which United States foreign aid was given in substantial amounts — before that it was inconsiderable — may be subdivided into five periods:

(1) The first was the war years, when foreign aid took the form of lend-lease. It is questionable whether lend-lease really should be considered a form of foreign aid financing. Its distinguishing characteristic and its originality lay precisely in the fact that *no* financial transactions were involved; the entry which identifies lend-lease in the balance of payments is no more than a bookkeeping offset to the export entry recording the delivery of goods and services. It was foreign aid in kind, just as military aid after the inauguration of the Mutual Defense Assistance Program (MDAP) in 1949 was aid in kind. There is virtually no difference between this form of aid, however, and those European Recovery Program grants which are closely tied to shipments of goods and services (or for that matter Export-Import Bank loans, which are explicitly tied to corresponding commodity shipments). (See Table 295.)

(2) The second phase of foreign aid covered the period from July 1945 to June 1946, when UNRRA and transfers of military-civilian supplies were the chief methods of aid.

(3) From July 1946 to March 1948, loans made up the bulk of foreign aid — the loan to the United Kingdom and extensive Export-Import Bank reconstruction loans, as well as credits extended for the disposal of surplus property.

(4) With congressional approval of the Foreign Assistance Act of 1948 on April 3, 1948, postwar foreign aid entered its last phase before the Korean invasion, the predominance of the European Recovery Program (ERP), which again furnished aid mainly in the form of grants.

(5) The institution of MDAP in October 1949 actually initiated a separate phase. By 1953, military aid had become dominant, and with the disappearance of the "dollar gap," economic aid was cut back to one third of the total. Loans,

TABLE 296. UNITED STATES GOVERNMENT FOREIGN AID, SECOND HALF OF 1945 TO 1948 [a]

Program	Amount
	(Millions)
Total grants and loans	$16,184
Long-term government loans (net)	8,332
Lend-lease	1,434
UNRRA surplus property credits	1,388
Export-Import Bank loans	2,230
British loan	3,750
All other credits (less repayments)	— 470
Government grants (net)	7,852
Lend-lease (less reverse lend-lease and lend-lease settlements)	— 62
Interim aid [b]	558
UNRRA (incl. post-UNRRA)	2,370
Military-civilian supplies [c]	2,799
European Recovery Program (less counterpart funds)	1,363
Greek-Turkey program	423
Philippine reconstruction	286
International Refugee Organization and Children's Emergency Fund	148
Aid to China (1946–1948)	183
All other grants (less reverse grants)	— 216

Source: The Balance of International Payments of the United States, 1946–1948, U.S. Department of Commerce, 1950, Tables 28 and 29.

a. Subscriptions of capital to the International Monetary Fund and the International Bank for Reconstruction and Development are not included.

b. Aid to ERP countries previous to ERP.

c. Supplies distributed by United States military authorities in occupied areas.

Note: The difference of about $10 billion between the total of this table and total aid shown for 1945–1948 in Table 277 is accounted for by the exclusion above of the first half of 1945, ERP aid for 1948 and lend-lease grants for 1945.

as compared to grants, had become almost insignificant — $804 million of a total of $14 billion, in the years 1950–1952. Military aid, which amounted to only $200 million in 1949, was increased to $2.6 billion in the three following years and in 1953 was running at an annual rate of $4.25 billion.

Early Phases: Lend-Lease and Loans

As a result of lend-lease operations, total United States exports reached unprecedented levels. (See Figure 76.) In 1942–1945, exports of finished manufactures and semimanufactures rose from a prewar level of 20–25 per cent of total exports to 80 per cent, and exports of manufactured foodstuffs increased from 6 per cent in the late 1930s to 12 per cent during the war. Exports to Europe rose from 50–60 per cent of the total to a wartime peak of 72 per cent.

During the next two phases of postwar foreign aid (July 1945–June 1946 and July 1946–1948), the composition of aid changed radically from grants to loans. (See Table 296.) Grants, though smaller than loans for the three-and-one-half-year period, still were larger during the fiscal year 1945–1946, but loans predominated for the remainder of the period. The bulk of the grants through UNRRA and GARIOA [43] were made immediately after the war, while the major loans — by the Export-Import Bank for reconstruction purposes and by the Treasury Department for the disposal of surplus property, and to the British government — came in the years 1946–1948.

The area and commodity composition of the aid in these two periods is difficult to establish in detail. Speaking generally, however, UNRRA aid

43. Government and Relief in Occupied Areas, which furnished the largest part of military-civilian supplies.

TABLE 297. UNITED STATES GOVERNMENT FOREIGN AID, SECOND QUARTER 1948
TO SECOND QUARTER 1950, BY AID PROGRAM

Program	Amount	Percentage Distribution
	(Millions)	
All aid (net)	$11,708	100.0
Grants (net)	10,506[a]	89.7[b]
Military aid (Greece, Turkey, China)	592	5.1
Economic aid (net)	9,914[a]	84.7[b]
ERP	6,987	59.7
Army civilian supplies	2,425	20.7
Point IV assistance	2	0.02
Post-UNRRA	273	2.3
Philippine reconstruction	388	3.3
Grants to U.N. organizations[c]	234	2.0
Miscellaneous	62	0.5
Government pensions, etc.[d]	57	0.5
Loans (net)	1,202[e]	10.2[f]
Long-term loans (net)	1,025[e]	8.7[f]
ECA	989	8.4
Export-Import Bank loans	555	4.7
Surplus property credits (including ships)	79	0.7
All others	115	1.0
Short-term loans (net)	177	1.5

Source: Survey of Current Business, June 1951.
a. Gross total less $514 million in revenue economic aid grants.
b. Gross total less 4.4 per cent in reverse economic aid grants.
c. International Refugee Organization and International Children's Emergency Fund.
d. The items included here are shown in official statistics as unilateral government transfers, though they are not foreign aid, strictly speaking.
e. Gross total less $713 million in repayments.
f. Gross total less 6.1 per cent in repayments.

and military-civilian supplies went mainly to European countries, Japan and China, in that order of importance, chiefly in the form of food and clothing. Loans by the Export-Import Bank went, in order of importance, to continental Europe (especially France), Latin America, the British Commonwealth and China, financing mainly shipments of industrial equipment and raw materials. Lend-lease pipeline loans were similar in composition to lend-lease shipments during the war, and the British loan was used for a wide variety of commodities among which foods and raw materials were the most important.[44]

44. See U.S. Department of Commerce: *Foreign Transactions of the United States Government* (basic data through June 30, 1950), September 1950; and *The Balance of International Payments of the United States, 1946–1948,* 1950, pp. 114 ff.

The Fourth Phase: Grants

In the fourth phase of United States postwar aid — extending from the second quarter of 1948 through the second quarter of 1950 — the immediate postwar emergency and relief needs had already been met. But the dollar shortage crisis of 1947 indicated that major problems of postwar reconstruction remained to be solved. Total foreign aid in this period amounted to $11.7 billion (Table 297); the proportion of grants to loans was nine to one. By type of program, about 68 per cent (60 per cent in grants, 8 per cent in loans) was ERP aid; military-civilian supplies still constituted about 20 per cent of the total; and Export-Import Bank loans were about 5 per cent (less some repayments). Military aid (5 per

TABLE 298. UNITED STATES FOREIGN AID, 1948, 1949 AND FIRST HALF OF 1950,
BY RECIPIENT AREA

(Dollar Amounts in Millions)

Recipient Area	1948		1949		First Half of 1950	
	Amount	Per Cent	Amount	Per Cent	Amount	Per Cent
Total	$5,127	100	$5,968	100	$2,275	100
ERP countries	4,057	79	4,712	79	1,823	80
ERP dependencies	20	a	32	1	5	a
Other European countries	92	2	1	a	16	1
Canada	5	a	11	a	4	a
Latin America	−33	−1	75	1	15	1
All other countries	867	17	1,013	17	349	15
International institutions [b]	119	2	124	2	63	3
Sterling area	947	18	1,117	19	456	20

Source: *Survey of Current Business,* June 1951.
a. Less than 0.5 per cent.

b. International Monetary Fund and International Bank for Reconstruction and Development.

cent of the total) made its reappearance at this time.

The proportion of aid going to the main recipient areas remained approximately constant. (See Table 298.) Western (ERP) Europe received 80 per cent, even though the total includes all forms of aid, not only ERP aid; the "all other" group of countries (mainly the Far East, and the independent members of the British Commonwealth except Canada and the United Kingdom), 15–17 per cent of the total; and the sterling area (which overlaps with ERP Europe and its dependencies), 18 to 20 per cent.

A substantial part — 34 per cent — of ERP aid during these years was not spent on American exports but used for the offshore procurement of aid shipments. This proportion, however, was very different for different commodities. All coffee (the only commodity completely procured abroad), 90 per cent of the sugar, 85 per cent of all meat and paper and pulp, 75 per cent of the nonferrous metals and petroleum and its products, as well as more than half of all lumber, hides and skins and leather, were obtained from such dollar countries as Canada, Latin America and the Near East (petroleum).

Offshore procurements affected mainly commodities of which the United States was a net importer. Therefore the importance of ERP-financed exports from the United States was considerable in the case of several major products which the United States normally exports in large quantities.

The $904 million ERP shipments of raw cotton represented more than half the total United States exports of this commodity during the two-and-one-fourth-year period. More than one third of all United States wheat exports during 1948–1950 were included in the $810 million shipment under the ERP. About two fifths of American exports of tobacco and its products and over one fifth of all coal exports were covered by ERP aid. Clearly, at least at the beginning, ERP aid was of considerable assistance to United States agricultural exports.

With the rebuilding of the European economies, however, the commodity composition of total aid shipments shifted away from foods and fuel, at first toward industrial raw materials, and later toward machinery and vehicles. The extent of this shift may be seen in the decline of the food, feed and fertilizer group from almost 50 per cent of the total in 1948 to about 20 per cent by 1950, and of fuel shipments from 27 per cent to about 18 per cent.[45] On the other hand, the machinery and vehicles share rose from almost nothing in 1948 to more than 25 per cent in 1950; and although raw and semimanufactured materials fell from a 1949 peak of nearly 40 per cent, they still accounted for about 30 per cent of the total in 1950. Thus, with the exception of raw cotton, the support which ERP aid gave to

45. Fuel shipments had dropped to 10 per cent of the total in 1949 but rose in response to the increased fuel needs of expanding European manufacturing industries.

TABLE 299. UNITED STATES GOVERNMENT FOREIGN AID, 1950–1953
(*Millions*)

	1950, Second Half	1951	1952	1953
Total	$2,018	$4,664	$5,042	$6,400
Type of aid				
Nonmilitary				
Grants, net	1,489	2,969	1,959	794
Loans, net	43	163	402	1,235 [a]
Military [b]	486	1,532	2,681	4,371
Destination				
Western Europe and				
dependencies [c]	1,591	3,216	3,789 [d]	4,497 [d]
Canada	5	12		
Latin American republics	10	171	127	400
All other countries [e]	412	1,265	1,126	1,503

Sources: *The Balance of Payments of the United States, 1949–1951*, U.S. Department of Commerce, 1952; and *Survey of Current Business*, June 1953 and April 1954.

a. Includes $1,000 million of prior grants to Germany converted into credits.

b. Grants; less reverse grants and returns including "other unilateral transfers."

c. OEEC Europe and dependencies and other Europe for 1950–1951; western Europe and dependencies for 1952–1953.

d. Not available.

e. Includes grants and loans to international institutions of $50 million in 1950, $252 million in 1951, $85 million in 1952, and $70 million in 1953.

United States exports of agricultural commodities was concentrated in its earlier phases. The subsequent shift toward support of industrial exports is likely to continue as military aid, begun in 1949, increases in importance.

The Fifth Phase: Military Aid

The outbreak of hostilities in Korea in June 1950 opened the fifth postwar phase of American foreign aid. Military aid increased sharply — both to western Europe to provide equipment for the North Atlantic Treaty Organization and to the Far East to equip United Nations armed forces there. At the same time, as the improvement of the economic position of western European countries reduced their need for American assistance, economic aid tapered off. On the other hand, during 1950–1953, the increased apportionment of economic activity to the production of military goods began to show an effect on the import side of the American balance of payments also. United States expenditures abroad for the acquisition of such goods and services — to be used both for American armed forces abroad and for the armed forces of foreign countries — assumed the following considerable proportions (in millions):

	Western Europe and Dependencies	Other Countries	Total
1950	$198	$ 404	$ 602
1951	387	861	1,248
1952	815	1,128	1,963

Part of these expenditures were financed from funds of the various military aid programs (and are thus included in the military aid figures of Table 299), but part came from ordinary defense appropriation ("offshore procurement"). If to these military imports are added foreign expenditures made to acquire materials for the government's strategic stockpile (the amounts involved are not published but may have been above $500 million), approximately 20 to 25 per cent of American imports in 1952–1953 consisted of military or quasi-military imports, and almost 20 per cent of total exports were financed by military aid.

GOLD MOVEMENTS AND OTHER FINANCING

In spite of the large long-term capital movements of the interwar period, total financing showed an uneasy stability. The international creditor position of the United States was by no means so reliable an element in international financing as that of the United Kingdom in the nineteenth century. For example, short-term capital and gold movements appear to have been genuine "balancing" items only in twelve out of the thirty-two years from 1919 through 1950. For the remaining twenty years, the two balance of payments items, "gold movement" and "other financing," [46] carry opposite signs. (See Table 277.) This means that a negative gold entry (i.e., an American gold purchase) usually was accompanied by a positive "other financing" entry, i.e., an inflow of short-term capital. What happened in these cases was that the rest of the world as well as American residents exchanged a holding of foreign assets for short-term dollar assets, and an inward movement of gold accompanied this exchange. One of the two movements (in the 1930s clearly the short-term capital movement) appears to have induced the other, instead of both having a common source in a foreign deficit in the rest of the balance of payments with the United States.

The years 1931, 1933, 1934–1936 and 1939–1940 are examples of such "hot money" movements, that is, of autonomous short-term fund flows or capital flight from and to the United States.[47] Even long-term United States funds (mainly portfolio investments) flowed inward in the late 1930s. But the considerable excess of the gold inflow over that of other financing in 1940 suggests that at least part of it was a genuine balancing flow, to settle the large United States

trade surplus before lend-lease became operative.

On the other hand, the war and immediate postwar years saw a huge flow, first outward and then inward, of gold and other financing which was in both cases largely a genuine balancing movement, though there was some capital flight to the United States especially in the earlier war years. But the more than $6 billion increase in the foreign acquisition from the United States of gold and dollar assets was brought about by the fact that United States exports not financed by lend-lease fell increasingly short of United States imports unsupported by reverse lend-lease. The resulting "cash" deficit of the United States trade balance induced the outward flow of reserves.

Not all foreign areas, however, shared in this outward flow. Rather, the United States "cash" trade balances with the sterling area showed a surplus except in 1943 and 1944, and this area lost gold and dollar assets to the United States in 1940–1945. In contrast, the large United States "cash" trade deficits with the Latin American countries, beginning in 1942, produced a flow of gold and dollar assets to them which by 1945 had increased their holdings by almost $2.5 billion.

From 1946 through 1948 these war-accumulated funds were used by foreigners to finance imports from the United States. This liquidation amounted to almost $3.5 billion.[48] (See Table 277.) After 1949 — interrupted only in 1951 — the "dollar gap" diminished sharply (as Table 285 shows), and foreigners acquired considerable net gold and dollar assets from the United States.

RECENT BALANCE OF PAYMENTS DEVELOPMENTS

In 1950, the "dollar gap" had diminished to about $79 million (Table 285). The outbreak of hostilities in Korea in June of that year, however, initiated a series of abrupt changes in the United States balance of payments.

During the first period of the Korean conflict, which lasted to about mid–1951, the sudden American and, later, foreign demand for raw

---

46. This item (see note to Table 277) includes errors and omissions — that is, the unexplained residual of the official balance of payments statement. To assume that these unknown transactions cover unrecorded short-term capital movements is debatable, but not implausible. In any case, that assumption is the justification for combining errors and omissions with the rest of the short-term capital and long-term foreign capital items, as has been done in Table 277.

47. It is surprising to find also 1947 and 1948 in this category. In each of these two years, errors and omissions were in excess of $1 billion, and the conclusion must be that (if the interpretation of errors and omissions is correct), though there was a large-scale liquidation of foreign-held dollar assets and gold — Marshall Plan funds became available in volume only at the end of 1948 — there was an even larger unrecorded inflow of foreign funds.

48. This figure would have to be increased by almost $2.2 billion if the large errors and omissions, of approximately this amount, are not deducted. Foreign gold losses to the United States were $4,315 million, and the loss of dollar assets was $1,406 million (allowing for a net outflow of United States short-term capital of $222 million); losses of gold and dollar assets together totaled $5,721 million. But errors and omissions show a net inflow of $2,401 million for the three years. The net loss to foreigners of gold and dollar assets by the United States was thus $3,320 million (Table 277).

TABLE 300. UNITED STATES BALANCE OF PAYMENTS, BY HALF-YEARS, 1950–1953
(Billions of Dollars; Receipts [+], Payments [−])

	1950 I	1950 II	1951 I	1951 II	1952 I	1952 II	1953 I	1953 II
I. Private transactions								
1. Imports, merchandise[a]	−3.8	−5.0	−6.0	−5.0	−5.4	−5.3	−5.6	−5.2
Services and donations (excluding investment income)	−1.0	−1.3	−1.0	−1.2	−1.3	−1.3	−1.4	−1.4
Total	−4.8	−6.3	−7.0	−6.2	−6.7	−6.6	−7.0	−6.6
2. Exports, merchandise and services[b]	+5.8	+6.1	+8.1	+8.8	+8.7	+7.3	+7.4	+7.3
3. Balance on goods and services (excluding investment income) (Surplus [+], Deficit [−])	+1.0	−0.2	+1.1	+2.6	+2.0	+0.7	+0.4	+0.7
4. Balance on U.S. capital and income on foreign investments	+0.3	−0.5	+0.1	+0.3	−0.1	+0.4	+0.5	+0.4
5. Errors and omissions	+0.1	+0.1	+0.3	+0.2	+0.6	+0.1	+0.1	+0.1
6. Total private balance	+1.4	−0.6	+1.5	+3.1	+2.5	+1.2	+1.0	+1.2
II. Government transactions								
1. Imports, goods and services[c] (excluding investment income)	−0.5	−0.6	−0.8	−1.0	−1.1	−1.4	−1.4	−1.7
2. Exports, military goods and services (including miscellaneous services)	+0.2	+0.5	+0.7	+0.8	+1.1	+1.7	+2.9	+1.8
Balance, goods and services	−0.3	−0.1	−0.1	−0.2	—	+0.3	+1.5	+0.1
3. Total aid (grants and loans less net income on government loans) Military	} −2.2	−1.8	−2.4	−2.3 {	−1.0	−1.6	−2.7	−1.6
Other					−1.5	−1.1	−1.0	−0.8
4. Total government balance	−2.5	−1.9	−2.5	−2.5	−2.5	−2.4	−2.2	−2.3
III. Net foreign earnings of gold and dollar assets (+)[d]	+1.1	+2.5	+1.0	−0.6	—	+1.2	+1.2	+1.1

Sources: The Balance of Payments of the United States, 1949–1951, U.S. Department of Commerce, 1952; *Survey of Current Business,* June 1953, December 1953 and March 1954, and *Business Information Service, International Trade Statistics Series,* 1953 and 1954.

a. Recorded general merchandise imports (Census includes stockpile imports and some unidentifiable military imports).

b. Exports of merchandise (balance of payments adjusted), *less* military aid, *plus* private services, excluding investment income.

c. Difference between imports, balance of payments adjusted, and recorded general imports, *plus* government miscellaneous services imports. Excludes stockpile imports and includes private imports of $100–$150 million a year which cannot be separated.

d. U.S. gold sales *plus* net foreign capital (long- and short-term) inflow.

materials and other strategically important imports drove prices of these commodities sharply up and induced a steep rise in American imports: private imports (including government stockpile imports which cannot be separately identified) rose from $3.8 billion in the first half of 1950 to $6 billion a year later. (See Table 300.)

At the same time, the Canadian government, faced with the threat of domestic inflationary consequences of rapid economic development and a growing inflow of capital from the United States, abandoned the fixed parity of the Canadian dollar in September 1950. Transfers of funds, partly speculative, to Canada in anticipation of this move swelled American capital outflow, so that in the second half of 1950 this outflow exceeded the receipts of incomes from investment by $0.5 billion. The result was that the rest of the world succeeded in acquiring as much as $2.5 billion of gold and dollar assets from the United States. The "dollar gap" in private transactions [49] actually became negative to the extent of more than $1 billion.

But this was clearly an abnormal occurrence of short duration. Beginning in 1951, the boom spread abroad. The greatly increased availability of dollars, especially in raw-materials-exporting countries, such as the overseas sterling area and Latin America, induced governments to relax their restrictions on dollar imports and, their incomes growing, foreign nationals began to increase their purchases in the United States. American private exports, which had totaled $5.8 billion in the first half of 1950, were pushed up to $8.8 billion by the second half of 1951; at the same time imports began to fall from their abnormally high level of $7 billion in the first half of 1951. By the end of 1951, the earlier position had been completely reversed, foreign countries were losing gold and dollars to the United States at an annual rate of more than $1 billion, and the private transactions "dollar gap" expanded to almost $2 billion again.

Foreign countries reacted to these rapidly changing events in two ways. They re-intensified their restrictions on dollar imports, but they also adopted a series of domestic measures, such as disinflationary monetary policies and the generation of government budget surpluses, in an attempt to right their balance of payments position. These measures, supported by the consistent improvement in volume and efficiency of their home output, proved successful. In the second half of 1952, the American balance of payments again showed an increase in foreign holdings of gold and dollar assets of $1.2 billion, and the "dollar gap" had disappeared completely. This development was supported by strongly rising American government imports, which by the last half of 1952 had reached almost $1.5 billion (excluding stockpile imports).

The increased provision for military equipment and materials strongly affected both sides of the American balance of payments (Table

300). Government exports of military goods and services were on the way to the phenomenal annual rate of $5 billion; and government imports both for the provision of American and friendly foreign armed forces abroad and for the strategic stockpile may have exceeded $2 billion in 1952. Increases in military aid more than offset the substantial decline in economic aid. As a result, total aid rose to $3.7 billion in the first half of 1953.

The position reached in the year ending in mid-1953 showed evidence of stability. By then, the "dollar gap" had been reduced to a negative figure; United States private merchandise imports had stabilized at around $5-$5.5 billion; and exports, after abnormally large agricultural shipments due to special factors had ceased, were down to below $7.5 billion, thus leaving a private merchandise surplus of about $2 billion. Mainly as a result of United States deficits on services payments (excluding income on private investments) and on government transactions, the rest of the world was earning roughly $2.5 billion a year in gold and dollar assets.

Although the non-U.S. world as a whole had practically succeeded in eliminating the "dollar gap," its disapearance depended on two factors: foreign restrictions on dollar imports, and large imports by the United States government. It is impossible to tell how large foreign imports would be if dollar import restrictions were abandoned — that is, if the full convertibility of foreign currencies into one another and into dollars were re-established. Such restoration of convertibility would do two things: it would free whatever suppressed demand for dollar goods still existed abroad, and it would subject foreign exporters to full competition — both in their home markets and in non-U.S. third markets — from American exports. The combined result of these two influences cannot be ascertained with precision.

Although the rest of the world as a whole had increased its reserves of gold and dollars after 1948 by about $6 billion, reaching about $18 billion in December 1953, different areas and countries did not by any means share equally in this improvement. Total reserves and, even more, gold and dollar reserves, when measured against imports, were even then considerably less adequate for the sterling area than for continental Europe, Latin America and Canada. (See Table 301.)

---

49. Measured by nonmilitary aid, less foreign accumulation of gold and dollar assets, so as to eliminate military aid and the corresponding military exports.

TABLE 301. WORLD GOLD AND DOLLAR RESERVES AND TRADE, EXCLUSIVE OF THE
UNITED STATES, 1952-1953

(Dollar Amounts in Millions)

| | Official Reserves as of December 1953[a] | | Increase since December 1952 | | | Imports (c.i.f.) 1953 | | Reserves as Per Cent of Total Imports 1953 | |
| | | | | Gold and Dollars | | | From U.S. and Canada[c] | | |
	Total	Gold and Dollars	Total	Total	From U.S.[b]	Total		Total	Gold and Dollars
Non-U.S. world	$25.8	$17.9	$2.7	$2.5	$2.0	$64.3	$15.0	40.1	27.8
Canada	1.8	1.8	-0.1	-0.1	-0.6	4.8	3.5	37.5	37.5
Latin America	3.5	2.9	0.4	0.2	0.2	6.4	3.8	54.7	45.3
Continental OEEC Europe[d]	10.0	7.7	1.7	1.5	1.3[e]	25.2	2.8	39.7	30.6
Sterling area	7.4	3.4	1.0	0.8	0.7	20.0	2.8	37.0	17.0
United Kingdom	2.5	2.5	0.6	0.7	0.4	9.4	1.6	26.6	26.6
Rest of the world	3.1	2.1	-0.3	0.1	0.4	7.9	2.1	39.2	26.6

Sources: International Financial Statistics, International Monetary Fund, June
1954, and *Survey of Current Business,* March 1954.

a. Estimates of International Monetary Fund, excluding international institutions.

b. Earned in direct transactions with the United States; i.e., excluding multilateral dollar transfers (including errors and omissions). These figures therefore differ from those in Table 300.

c. Excluding military-aid-financed imports.

d. Including continental European dependencies.

e. Including Finland, Spain and Yugoslavia; not included in rest of this line.

710

Much will depend on the trend of United States imports; and this, in turn, will depend on domestic developments in the United States and on the outcome of proposed efforts to reduce American import duties and other import impediments, such as the current practices of customs classification, import quotas and export subsidies.[50]

PROSPECTS FOR 1960

With the help of the report of the President's Materials Policy Commission,[51] it is possible to make an informed guess about United States imports a few years hence. The main task is to estimate United States trade, in particular, imports, for a year such as 1960. This is hazardous enough; the invisibles and especially capital and foreign aid transactions may be assumed to lie in even wider ranges of plausible but largely arbitrary limits.

At 1950 prices, the trade balance in 1960 may show a deficit of $1.5 billion, excluding exports financed by government aid. United States private capital outflow is estimated at $2.2 billion, offset in part by a small inflow for foreign direct investment [52] in the United States. On the other hand, there are estimated to be net receipts of fully $2.5 billion of income on United States foreign investments. Most of these are in the form of direct investment in foreign plants and carry a very high rate of return — averaging 14 to 16 per cent. Even on as optimistic an assumption as is here made, long-term net capital outflow will be insufficient to finance net inflow of dividends and interest. The excess of payments over receipts on merchandise trade and combined capital and investment income account is estimated at about $0.9 billion. This and net payments on travel, private donations and transportation accounts may result in a foreign accumulation of about $2.5 billion of United States gold and dollars (a highly speculative projection).

IMPORTS

Total recorded imports for consumption may be expected to rise from $8.7 billion in 1950 to $11.0 billion by 1960 (at 1950 prices). This increase (26 per cent) is less than that estimated for the gross national product (29 per cent). (See Tables 302 and 303.) Imports of industrial raw materials are estimated to rise somewhat more than total imports, and consumer goods, both foods and nonfoods, are expected to do less well. In the case of finished manufactures — a group which contains a relatively large proportion of "luxury" commodities — this comparative deficiency of imports should be rather smaller than for foods. With a rising standard of living, the quantity of imports per capita is expected to increase by approximately 7 per cent from 1950 to 1960.

Though recorded imports per capita can be expected to rise (from $57 to $62), they will drop as a proportion of gross national product, from about 3.0 per cent to 2.98 per cent. This implies a "marginal propensity to import" [53] of about 0.027 and a gross income elasticity of imports [54] of about 0.90. Both figures appear to be reasonable, to judge from past experience.

Three very general points must be carefully noted in interpreting these projections.

First, all value data for 1960 are expressed in terms of 1950 prices. That is, the possible effect on 1960 import values of a changed supply situation for imports, especially in the international

---

50. The reports of two United States government commissions — the report of the Public Advisory Board for Mutual Security and that of the Commission on Foreign Economic Policy (the Bell Commission and the Randall Commission) — have set the relevant issues out in public. For example, the successive tariff reductions under the Reciprocal Trade Agreements Program succeeded in lowering the average rate of duty from 59 per cent in 1932 to 12.5 per cent in 1951. The figures are not unequivocal for statistical reasons and, among other reasons, because of the effect of rising import prices on the ad valorem equivalent of specific duties. Even apart from these difficulties, it was found that this reduction was to a large extent ineffectual. For instance, imports have been "classified out" of the classes to which duty reductions were applied while remaining rates continued their restrictive effects, and such factors as the uncertainties created for foreign exporters by American customs classification practices and the threat of protective measures on agricultural imports under existent agricultural legislation were found to maintain American imports at levels below what they could otherwise be. Estimates of the amount by which imports might be raised if suitable measures of tariff and trade policy were taken range from $1 billion to $2.6 billion. But this whole subject is fraught with analytical and statistical difficulties which cannot be covered here. See *A Trade and Tariff Policy in the National Interest,* a report to the President by the Public Advisory Board for Mutual Security, Washington, 1953, and also the optimistic estimates in Howard S. Piquet, *Aid, Trade and the Tariff,* Crowell, New York, 1953.

51. *Resources for Freedom,* Washington, 1952, 5 vols.

52. As explained above (p. 667), inflow of foreign portfolio capital is best treated as movements of reserves.

53. The increase in imports per unit increase in gross national product.

54. The proportionate increase in imports per unit proportionate increase in gross national product.

TABLE 302. UNITED STATES GROSS NATIONAL PRODUCT AND CONSUMER EXPENDITURES
IN RELATION TO IMPORTS, 1950 AND ESTIMATE FOR 1960
(*Billions at 1950 Prices*)

	Actual 1950	Estimated 1960	Percentage Change
Gross national product	$286.8	$370.0	+29.0
Consumption expenditures, total	194.6	241.5	+24.1
On goods	131.8	164.4	+24.7
Imports, total [a]	8.7	11.0	+26.0
Crude and semimanufactured materials	5.1	6.5	+26.9
Foodstuffs	2.65	3.30	+24.5
Finished manufactures	0.96	1.20	+25.0

Sources: Tables 37 and 303 and Appendix 4–7.

a. Figures are somewhat smaller than imports shown in Table 304. The latter are recorded imports plus adjustments for unrecorded imports for 1950, projected to 1960.

food and raw materials markets, has been neglected. Because of obvious difficulties, no price projections have been made. The same procedure has been applied to the domestic determinants of imports.

Second, it should be understood that imports in 1950 already showed the effects of the commodity boom which set in immediately after the outbreak of hostilities in Korea late in June of that year. Imports, therefore, were larger than they would have been without that boom. While quantities rose between the second and fourth quarters of 1950 by roughly only 15 per cent, values rose by 30 per cent. Consequently, the projected increases in import values between 1950 and 1960 are smaller than they would have been if 1950 import values had not been raised for essentially transitory reasons.

Third, the major import-deterrent factors, especially the substitution of domestic for imported materials, strongly affect the changes between 1950 magnitudes and 1960 estimates. Perhaps the most important aftereffect of the import boom caused by the Korean War was the acceleration of domestic substitution. The ratio between imports and gross national product, therefore, is likely to drop between 1950 and 1960, despite increasing exhaustion of domestic materials supplies, especially of nonferrous metals, iron ore and crude oil. The ratio would have a tendency to decline in any case; but the decline is likely to be sharper since 1950 imports were abnormally large. In fact, the 1960 proportion — 2.98 per

cent, compared with 3.0 per cent for 1950 — appears on this score to be rather conservatively high.

Foods and Manufactures

The relatively bad showing of foodstuff imports results from the fact that the assumed increases in the per capita consumption of the two main imported foods, coffee and sugar (in all forms) — from 16 and 97 pounds, respectively, in 1950, to 18 and 103 pounds in 1960 — are below the expected rise in consumers' expenditures on foods. Cocoa imports, used for a "luxury" (chocolates), however, are projected to increase by 32 per cent.[55] These quantities have been derived by assuming a declining rate of increase in consumption, based on data for the period 1925 to 1950 (assuming no change in sugar import quota arrangements). Imports of other foodstuffs (meat, fish, beverages) are expected also to rise more than total consumers' expenditures on goods (and more than food expenditures), as they are largely in the semiluxury class. The increase has been assumed at 26 per cent for this import group. (See Table 303.)

Imports of finished manufactures also have been assumed to rise in proportion to con-

55. The projected cocoa consumption, while still smaller than in 1940, may not materialize if cocoa output in the African supplying areas continues to fall short of expectations because of the severe incidence there of the "swollen shoot" disease.

TABLE 303. PROJECTION OF UNITED STATES IMPORTS FOR 1960
(*Dollar Amounts at 1950 Prices; in Millions, except for Per Capita*)

	Unit of Measurement for Quantity	1950		Percentage Increase 1950 to 1960 [a]	1960 Value
		Quantity	Value		
Domestic determinants					
Gross national product	—	—	$286,800	29.0	$370,000
Consumption expenditures	—	—	194,600	24.1	241,500
Gross national product per capita	—	—	1,881	11.1	2,091
Imports (for consumption)	—	—	8,743	26.0	11,013
Foodstuffs	—	—	2,648	24.5	3,296
Coffee	Million lbs.	2,439	1,092	26.4	1,380
Sugar	"	7,361	381	11.5	425
Cocoa and beans	"	670	167	31.7	220
All other	—	—	1,008	26.0	1,270
Crude and semimanufactured materials [b]	—	—	5,135	26.9	6,516
Rubber, crude	Thousand long tons	801	458	10.9	508
Wool, processed	Million lbs. (clean)	477	428	—10.0	385
Crude petroleum	Million barrels	174	369	103.0	750
Residual fuel oil	"	123	198	56.6	310
Burlaps	Million lbs.	419	91	10.0	100
Copper (crude and semi-manufactured)	Thousand short tons	606	243	31.7	320
Lead (crude and semi-manufactured)	"	568	136	20.0	163
Zinc (crude and semi-manufactured)	"	406	65	30.8	85
Tin (metal and metal content of ore)	Thousand long tons	108	200	—5.0	190
Aluminum	Thousand short tons	245	62.5	77.6	111
Bauxite	Million long tons	2.5	15.7	97.5	31
Nickel	Thousand short tons	97	77.9	30.9	102
Manganese ore	"	888	40.6	28.1	52
Other nonferrous metals and ores	—	—	127	19.7	152
Iron ore	Million long tons	8	44	300.0	132
Industrial diamonds	Million carats	11	12	50.0	18
Wood pulp	Thousand short tons	2,379	240	20.0	288
Newsprint	Million lbs.	9,726	453	28.0	580
Sawmill products	Million board ft.	3,423	264	20.1	317
Oilseeds	Million lbs.	1,281	105	10.0	115
All others	—	—	1,506	20.0	1,807
Finished manufactures [c]	—	—	960	25.0	1,200
Imports per capita	—	—	57	7.0	62

Sources: "Domestic determinants" and population from Table 37. Imports: data for 1950 from *Foreign Commerce Weekly,* March 10, 1952; for 1960 estimates, see discussion in text.

a. Minus sign indicates decrease.
b. Including newsprint and burlaps.
c. Excluding newsprint and burlaps.
Note: Data do not include unrecorded imports.

sumers' expenditures. This assumption implies that domestic resistance to these imports, both because of domestic substitution (textiles) and because of the possible stiffening of the protectionist attitude in the United States, will not diminish in the future. This perhaps is too pessimistic.

Raw Materials and Semimanufactures

Among raw materials, the most spectacular increase is projected in crude petroleum. The expected deficit of domestic output in the face of an extremely rapid rise in domestic consumption (the President's Materials Policy Commission report projects a fivefold rise by 1975) will lead to a doubling of imports. Iron ore imports (the PMPC report projects imports of 65 million tons for 1975) are expected to triple. For the major nonferrous metals — tin, copper, lead, zinc, nickel, manganese — as well as residual fuel oil, the projections of the PMPC report have been accepted with some modifications.[56] A progressively rising efficiency in the use of tin will lead to an actual decline in new tin imports. The PMPC estimates 84,000 tons for 1975. In the wood and paper group, imports have been derived by assuming a continuation of the rate of increase since 1925 (along a linear logarithmic trend), except that the sawmill products estimate was based on the PMPC estimate of residential construction with some allowance for increased dependence on imports.

This implies an income elasticity to import raw materials of about 0.93, the proportion of these imports to gross national product falling from 1.79 to 1.76 per cent. It appears that the use of new domestic substitute materials will about offset the simultaneous process of exhaustion of domestic supplies of old raw materials.

Rubber, wool, oilseeds and burlaps were assumed to show marked effects of domestic substitution. The President's Materials Policy Commission report [57] projects per capita wool consumption in 1975 at 2.2 pounds. Consumption in 1960 is estimated here at 3.3 pounds per capita and total domestic output at 125,000 pounds (clean). This yields the $385 million import

figure (1950 prices), a 10 per cent decline from the 1950 level. The major reason for this decline is the expected steady rise in per capita consumption of rayon and other synthetic fibers from 9.8 pounds in 1950 to 16.6 by 1975. In view of the rapid rise of nonrayon synthetics consumption from 0.04 pounds per capita in 1940 to 1.35 pounds in 1951, and the probable substantial increase in the next two years, there seems to be no reason to contradict the PMPC estimate for nonrayon synthetics output of 1.25 billion pounds in 1975. Rubber consumption in 1960 is expected to rise by 35 per cent over 1950 — to 1.8 million tons, of which 50 per cent has been assumed to be supplied in the form of synthetic rubber. It is expected that burlap and oilseed imports will be kept close to 1950 levels as a result of the substitution of cotton and paper for burlap bagging and of synthetic detergents for soap, as well as the rise in domestic oilseed output.

The increase of crude and semimanufactured materials imports which results from these assumptions — 26.9 per cent — falls short of the estimated increase in gross national product (29 per cent).

INVISIBLES

In what must also be very rough estimates, the invisibles in the balance of payments can be projected as follows:

Assume the annual gross outflow of private long-term capital in 1960 to increase to $1.5 billion for direct and $0.7 billion for portfolio investments, in each case net of amortizations and repatriation. These figures represent almost a doubling of those for 1950, and thus are very optimistic. The value of United States direct investments abroad then will have been increased, in 1960, by about $6 billion derived from current outflow plus, say, $3 billion (an average of $500 million a year) from current reinvestments, or $9 billion in all. To this is added an estimated $4.2 billion for portfolio investments. Since total American foreign investments were $13.5 billion for direct and $5.8 billion for portfolio investments in 1950, we arrive at a total of $32.5 billion for 1960.

Assume that the income earned on this investment will be somewhat lower than the rate obtaining after the war — i.e., about 12.5 per cent on direct investment (excluding reinvestment) and 3 per cent on portfolio investment.

56. These projections assume a doubling of *net* imports between 1950 and 1975. Computed at a constant compound rate of increase, this implies a 35 per cent increase to 1960. This was applied to total imports, since increases in domestic production are not expected to be material. The PMPC copper projection makes allowance for the substitution of aluminum for copper.

But the PMPC report is based on a gross national product projection corresponding also to a 35 per cent increase by 1960. Since the present projection leads to only a 29 per cent rise of gross national product by 1960, the import projections have been reduced to under 30 per cent, with a further reduction for lead since foreign supplies do not seem to warrant as large an increase for lead as for the other metals. These assumptions are more likely to err on the generous than on the deficient side.

57. Vol. II, p. 105.

TABLE 304. UNITED STATES BALANCE OF PAYMENTS, ACTUAL 1950
AND ESTIMATED 1960
(*Billions at 1950 Prices*)

	1950	Estimated 1960
Supply of dollar funds	$12.75	$17.05
Merchandise imports [a]	9.30	11.60
Private long-term capital outflow		
Direct	0.70	1.50
Portfolio	0.45	0.70
Income on investments	0.40	0.50
Transport	0.80	1.35
Travel	0.70	1.00
Donations (net)	0.50	0.40
Miscellaneous services (net)	— 0.10	—
Use of dollar funds	12.75	17.05
Merchandise exports (unaided) [a]	6.40	10.15
Private long-term capital inflow (direct investment only)	— 0.05	0.10
Income on investments		
Private	1.60	3.00
Government	0.10	0.20
Transport	0.90	0.70
Travel	0.40	0.40
Balance [b]	3.40	2.50

Sources: Data for 1950 based on *The Balance of Payments of the United States, 1949–1951,* U.S. Department of Commerce, 1952. For 1960 estimates, see discussion in text.

a. Adjusted for unrecorded trade (by the same proportionate additions in 1960 as in 1950).

b. Accumulation of gold and dollar assets except direct investments; U.S. short-term capital; errors and omissions.

Receipts from income on foreign investment in 1960 will then be $3.0 billion as against $1.6 billion in 1950. A similar computation for direct long-term investment [58] of foreign nationals in the United States, on the assumption that the recent rate of addition to such investment, $0.1 billion, will apply in 1960, and that the average rate of return will be 6 per cent, yields an increase in the value of foreign direct investment in the United States from $3.3 billion in 1950 to $4.0 billion in 1960. The income from this investment then will rise from $0.4 billion to $0.5 billion. Income on government foreign investment (such as the 1946 loan to the United Kingdom) has been projected as $200 million a year on the average.

These computations show that, unless one assumes very large capital outflows for the future,

the United States will remain a country with a net investment income exceeding net capital outflow. This net receipt on private investment and investment income accounts combined was $0.1 billion in 1950. The present projection will raise it to about $0.4 billion despite the doubling of United States gross outflow that has been assumed.

The projected increase in both imports and exports will raise the bill for international transportation. If it remains at about 8–10 per cent of total trade (i.e., of imports plus exports), and its distribution shifts further in favor of the rest of the world than it was in 1950 — both assumptions have been made — transport receipts in 1960 will be $0.7 billion and transport payments $1.35 billion. Assuming further that United States travel expenditure abroad will rise by 40 to 50 per cent with the expected 29 per cent increase in gross national product, thus catching up with its role as a "luxury" consumers' expenditure, and

58. For reasons mentioned above, foreign portfolio investments are treated together with the balancing items — i.e., short-term capital movements and gold.

TABLE 305. UNITED STATES TRADE[a] BY AREAS, 1950 AND PROJECTED 1960
(Dollar Amounts in Millions at 1950 Prices)

| | 1950 | | | | 1960 | | | |
| | Exports | | Imports | | Exports | | Imports | |
Area	Amount	Per Cent	Amount	Per Cent	Amount	Per Cent	Amount	Per Cent
Total	$10,084	100	$9,315	100	$10,150	100	$11,600	100
Continental OEEC Europe	2,409	24	953	10	2,030	20	1,276	11
Canada	2,010	20	1,951	21	2,131	21	2,668	23
Latin America	2,717	27	3,090	33	2,842	28	3,596	31
Sterling area	1,341	13	1,617	18	1,421	14	1,740	15
All others	1,607	16	1,704	18	1,726	17	2,320	20

Sources: *The Balance of Payments of the United States, 1949–1951,* U.S. Department of Commerce, 1952, and discussion in text.

a. Adjusted exports excluding military-aid-financed shipments.

assuming that foreign travel expenditure here will not change, we arrive at an American foreign travel deficit of $0.6 billion, compared with $0.3 billion in 1950. Finally, it is assumed that private donations will drop from $0.5 to $0.4 billion and that miscellaneous services will balance out.

EXPORTS

Exports may be assumed, as in past postwar years, to depend on the supply of dollar funds made available to the non-U.S. world, *minus* (or *plus*) the increase (or decrease) in gold and dollar reserves on which the monetary authorities of foreign countries decide. If foreign aid in 1960 is nil, and assuming that the change in foreign gold and dollar holdings through transactions with the United States is decided to be nil as well, the assumptions concerning the 1960 balance of payments made so far would permit United States exports of a value (at 1950 prices) of $12.65 billion. If, on the other hand — and this may be the more likely alternative — an amount of, say, $2.5 billion is to be added to foreign gold and dollar reserves, exports of only $10.15 billion could be financed. These figures have been entered in Table 304. United States government aid would have to be added — added, that is, to exports as well as to the supply of dollars. While it is impossible even to guess the magnitude of this aid, it is approximated at $3.5 billion and may consist primarily of military assistance.

AREAS

Only a few tentative conclusions can be hazarded about the probable area distribution of United States imports in 1960.

Of the commodities imports which have been projected as increasing most from 1950 to 1960, some — iron ore, crude oil, aluminum, residual fuel oil — originated in 1950 predominantly in Canada and Latin America, though a few others (bauxite and crude oil) may be supplied in the future in increasing proportions by dependencies of OEEC European nations (Surinam, Jamaica) or the Middle East (Arabia). The tendency of the Western Hemisphere to grow in its role of major raw material supplier is, however, offset to some extent by the retardation in the growth of imports of wool, tin and sugar. Since imports of other nonferrous metals, wool and paper products as projected will show a rise only moderately above total imports, it may be expected that Canada will increase its share in American imports while the proportion coming from Latin American countries is likely to decline from the high level reached in 1950.

Major sterling area raw materials — rubber, tin, wool, jute and burlaps, but not cocoa and industrial diamonds — are likely either to fall below 1950 or to rise less than imports as a whole. Therefore, the share of the sterling area in United States imports is almost certain to decline.

The "all others" group of countries (including

nonsterling OEEC dependencies and countries in the Near and Far East) rely for a rise in their share in imports on oil and its products, copper and bauxite, a relatively minor commodity by value. About imports from OEEC Europe it is difficult to generalize; it is reasonable to suppose that by 1960 these countries will supply a somewhat larger proportion of total United States imports than in 1950.

The geographic distribution of United States trade in 1960 can be roughly calculated on the basis of these very general assumptions. (See Table 305.) If exports are not augmented by government aid, exports in 1960 at 1950 prices are estimated at $10.15 billion. This represents a small decline from actual 1950 exports, which included government economic and military aid. It has been assumed that by 1960 the proportion of United States exports going to continental Europe will drop from 24 to 20 per cent as a result of the reduction of shipments of grain and other raw materials as well as capital equipment. On the other hand, Canada and Latin America are expected to receive an increased percentage of United States exports, in part the result of projected increases in private investments there. Some increase in the proportion of exports to the European dependencies, the Far East and the Near East also has been assumed, to account for the increase in shipments which is likely to follow both capital movements to those areas and increased imports from them.

As a result, the deficit of continental Europe with the United States, as here shown, is reduced from about $1,500 million to about $800 million; Canada acquires a surplus of between $500 and $525 million; the sterling area surplus is increased to over $300 million, and that of the "all others" group increased to about $600 million. The Latin American trade surplus with the United States rises to over $700 million.

These figures are expressed in 1950 prices. A change in the terms of trade in favor of the raw materials countries — that is, a rise in the prices of their exports relative to the prices of United States exports — would further improve their position by an equal proportion. What the movement of prices will be, however, depends not only on the conditions of supply confronting United States demand in 1960, but also on possible official interference in the major markets by government stockpiling, either for strategic purposes or for straightforward price support. It is impossible to project the patterns of trade any distance into the future with assurance that the projections will prove reasonably accurate, but it is important nevertheless to try to foresee future problems and prospects.

PART V

RESOURCES AND CAPACITIES

## CHAPTER 20

THE LABOR FORCE

PRECEDING CHAPTERS of this report have included estimates of the demand and needs for various kinds of consumer goods and services, capital goods and government services — all at high levels of employment, production and income in 1950 and 1960. In this and the following five chapters an attempt is made to assess the capacity of our labor force, our natural resources, our agricultural land and equipment, our industrial and commercial facilities, and our "intangible" resources — technology and productivity — to meet these requirements. This chapter is concerned with the probable size and character of the labor force as a factor in our capacity to produce during the 1950 decade.

CHARACTERISTICS OF THE LABOR FORCE

The labor force includes a great variety of different kinds of workers engaged in a wide range of jobs. Although the majority are employees working for wages or salaries at regular full-time jobs, in 1950 some 11 million members of the labor force — or not quite one out of five — were self-employed as businessmen, farmers, professional men, retail merchants, independent craftsmen or unpaid family workers. The welfare of such workers does not depend upon whether they have jobs or not; rather the success of their operations determines whether jobs are available for others.

Among the employee group are many who neither have nor want full-time jobs: summer farm workers, extra help during the Christmas season, students working after school, waitresses working two or three hours a day and domestic servants working two or three days a week. Some, on the other hand, fill two or more jobs during the course of a year — for example, the schoolteacher with a vacation job in a children's camp — while a few hold down two jobs concurrently.

The labor force includes those seeking jobs as well as those actually at work. In addition to the unemployed, members of the armed forces are counted in the labor force unless the civilian labor force alone is being considered.

Seasonal Movements

The size of the labor force varies from month to month and even from day to day. There is a definite seasonal rhythm, with an influx of new workers after the closing of schools and colleges, at harvesttime and during the spring season, and in retail stores during the Christmas rush. Between the high point in July and the low point in January, the variation in the number at work or seeking work is at least 4 million, while the number who belong to the labor force in certain seasons and withdraw from it at other times of the year is probably twice as large.[1] (See Appendix 20-1.)

Relation to Business Cycle

Although the labor force has moved up and down with the changing seasons, its response to shifts in the economic climate has been much less clear. Some analysts believe that the number of job seekers increases in boom times under the pressure of heavy demand for labor and the consequent lure of high wages. Others argue that it rises during depressions when lowered wages and unemployment of the usual breadwinner prompt other members of the household to look for jobs in an attempt to augment the family income. The thesis that the labor force expands both in boom times and in depressions also has its supporters.

By THOMAS C. FICHANDLER. Opinions and judgments expressed in this chapter are those of the author and should not be attributed to the organization with which he is associated.

1. "The work force is not a fixed group of people. Indeed, there is constant movement into and out of the work force. Usually there are three or four million more job seekers in July than in January. In a year there are usually about ten million persons who have been in the work force only part of the year. Thus if the work force averages 55 million persons, it will have had during the course of a year 65 million or more different persons in it." Sumner H. Slichter, "More Job Givers Wanted," *Fortune*, October 1945.

Wives and children of some underemployed or unemployed family heads certainly enter the labor market during depressions. But some young people who normally would be working continue in school when no jobs are to be found. Depressions prolong the working life of many young women who in better times would marry and become housewives. At the same time, older workers and marginal workers, confronted with increasing competition for fewer and fewer jobs, accept the inevitable and retire from the labor force. It is impossible to say on purely theoretical grounds whether the in or out movements are greater during depressions. Nor do the fragmentary data that are available help. All that can be concluded from these "inconclusive and contradictory" figures is that statistical evidence gives no support to the thesis of a depression-inflated labor force.[2]

Boom times, like depressions, witness migrations into and out of the labor force. Labor shortages, rising wages and a better selection of jobs undoubtedly draw some oldsters, housewives and students into the labor market. The inflationary tendencies that frequently accompany a boom probably induce some secondary workers to increase family income. On the other hand, better earnings for the family head make it easier to keep children in school longer. Favorable economic conditions normally bring higher marriage and birth rates with the consequent withdrawal of women from employment.

In the past these opposite trends seem to have balanced each other, but data for recent years point to a possible net increase in the labor force during boom times. Occasional measurements indicate a remarkably steady over-all rate of participation in the labor force up to 1940, if the effects of changing age and sex composition of the population are eliminated.[3] The figures are:[4]

	Per Cent
1890	50.9
1900	52.1
1920	52.7
1930	52.5
1940	52.7

Between 1940 and 1950, however, the standardized labor force participation rate jumped from 52.7 to 55.3 per cent.[5]

Factors other than booming business suggest themselves as possible causes of this rise in the proportion of the population in the labor force. Conceivably, the growth of the armed services from 300,000 to 1,300,000 between 1940 and 1950 may have contributed to the rise. It may also have been only a temporary phenomenon lingering on after the war or a permanent, long-run adjustment speeded up by the war.

If the armed forces in 1950 had been made up largely of draftees, the one million increase in service personnel over 1940 would have been attributable to the special ability of the government to draw into the labor force individuals who would prefer to remain outside it. Since, however, the armed forces in 1950 consisted almost entirely of voluntary enlistees rather than draftees, the increase over 1940 was similar to the opening up of new jobs during business expansion. Any enlargement of the labor force in response to such an intensification of demand for labor would give support to the thesis that the labor force expands in boom times. It may be argued, however, that growth of the armed forces differs from expanding civilian employment in its impact on the labor force and that 1950 should not be compared with previous years

2. John D. Durand, *The Labor Force in the United States, 1890–1960,* Social Science Research Council, New York, 1948, p. 104. W. S. Woytinsky (*Three Aspects of Labor Dynamics,* Social Science Research Council, New York, 1942, Part III) finds statistical support for the theory that "additional workers" inflate the labor force during depressions; Clarence D. Long ("The Labor Force and Economic Change," in Richard A. Lester and Joseph Shister, Eds., *Insights into Labor Issues,* Macmillan, New York, 1948, p. 351) finds that the labor force tends to decline slightly in depression, but he cautions against accepting this conclusion with great confidence. Durand (*op. cit.*) is close to Long's position but stresses the inconclusiveness of the data somewhat more.

3. The labor force participation rate for a standardized population is used in order to rule out the growth of the labor force that accompanies population increases as well as changes in the composition of the population. The labor force participation rate is the proportion of a specific age-sex population group that is in the labor force; consequently it is automatically adjusted for changes in the size of the population. Use of a standardized population adjusts for changing composition of the population. In this instance, the population was standardized for age and sex only, i.e., the population was assumed to be distributed by age and sex each year in the same way as in 1940. Hence, the average participation rate for each year was computed by weighting the participation rates for each age and sex class for that year by the 1940 population. The individual participation rates were derived from Durand, *op. cit.,* Table A–6, pp. 208–209. The rates used here, and below for 1950, are based on 1940 Census concepts, which differ slightly from those which the Bureau of the Census now uses to measure the size of the labor force.

4. Data for 1910 omitted because of their unreliability (see Durand, *op. cit.,* pp. 192–197).

5. During the war the rate was much higher, but from 1946 on it was at about the 1950 level. (This 1950 rate is consistent with 1940 Census concepts.)

without adjustment for changes in the size of the armed forces. Yet, even if all the one million servicemen added between 1940 and 1950 were excluded, the 1950 labor force participation rate would have been 54.4 per cent — still an appreciable increase over the 1940 rate of 52.7 per cent. Clearly, then, neither the increase in the size of the armed forces nor any special attraction that such an increase might have for those normally outside the labor force caused the jump between 1940 and 1950.

Sufficient time had elapsed between the end of the war and 1950 to rule out the possibility that the increase in the labor force participation rate was simply a temporary war-induced phenomenon. If anything, the war's aftereffect was in the opposite direction. Largely because of the wartime interruption of schooling and the educational benefits provided for servicemen, about three quarters of a million World War II veterans were still in school in 1950. Moreover, the war-induced marriage and baby booms kept many younger women from work outside the home. Consequently, a smaller proportion of both men and women between the ages of 30 and 34 were in the labor force in 1950 than in 1940. The increase in the over-all participation rate despite these strong adverse currents points to the power of rising employment and wages to lure people into the labor force.

If it were only the older age groups who were working or seeking work to a greater extent than in 1940, natural inertia following the patriotic pull of the war years might explain the expansion. But a higher proportion of both men and women under 20 years of age, none of whom were old enough to work during wartime, were in the labor force in 1950 than in 1940. This age group's increased participation, which runs counter to prewar trends, seems also to point to the power of job openings and higher wages to draw additional workers into the labor force. At the same time, it was true that some of the 1940–1950 increase was attributable to the continued presence in the labor force of older workers drawn in during the war. However, even if the participation rates for these older workers had exactly followed prewar trends, the standardized rate for the entire labor force would have been 54.8 per cent, well above the 1940 level.[6]

The war's tendency to speed up some long-run trends probably accounted for part of the labor force growth between 1940 and 1950. Although up until 1940 the labor force as a whole exhibited no apparent long-run trend, women between the ages of 20 and 65 had been entering it in ever greater numbers since 1890. The war appears to have accelerated this movement for women between 45 and 64. They came into the labor market to a much greater extent between 1940 and 1950 than prewar trends indicated. However, if women between 45 and 64 had joined the labor force only to the extent indicated by prewar trends, 54.5 per cent of the population would have been in the labor force in 1950 — a significantly higher proportion than the 52.7 per cent in 1940.

As was indicated above, any increase in the labor force that accompanied the growth in the size of the armed forces between 1940 and 1950 is consistent with the theory that additional workers become available during good times. Any increase caused by temporary wartime factors or a speeding up of long-run trends, on the other hand, has nothing to do with the effect of good times on the supply of labor. Elimination of above-normal labor force participation rates for workers 65 and over and for women between 45 and 64, therefore, should yield an over-all rate free of all but the cyclical factor. Assumption of prewar trends for these groups yields a total labor force participation rate of 54.0 per cent for 1950. This estimate probably is too low since it makes no allowance for the impact of the cyclical factor on these groups. If the cycle affected other population groups, it undoubtedly induced some of those 65 and over and some women of 45 to 64 to enter the labor force. Thus the healthier 1950 economy appears to have raised the over-all participation rate at least 1.3 percentage points above the 1940 level. While this may seem to be a small increase, it represents an increment of almost 1.5 million workers. Furthermore, it occurred despite withdrawal from the labor force of veterans completing their schooling and of the unusually large number of women who became wives and mothers after the war ended.

This postwar development does not justify the generalization that the labor force necessarily expands during the prosperity phase of the business cycle. For example, would just as many people have sought work in the postwar years if prices had risen less sharply? This or some other

---

6. This estimate is based on Bureau of the Census projections of the "normal" labor force from 1940 to 1950. These projections assumed continuation of prewar trends.

nonrecurring factor, rather than the enlarged demand for labor, may have caused the increase. Unfortunately, the early 1950s and the years ahead, which promise at least a partially mobilized economy, are not likely to clarify the nature of labor force fluctuations during peacetime. Perhaps the best summary of our current knowledge of how the labor supply reacts is presented in two statements by John D. Durand in his authoritative work on the labor force. He concludes that

. . . wartime trends must be considered as giving some support to the hypothesis that increasing demand for labor during boom periods results in the addition of extra workers to the available supply.[7]

but that

. . . it would be rash to try to predict, on the basis of present information, how the labor force will be affected by depressions or booms in the future.[8]

This position is not at variance with the tentative conclusion of Clarence D. Long, another careful student of labor force trends, that "the over-all labor force may remain a fairly invariable proportion of the standard working-age population, at least relative to fluctuations in other important economic magnitudes."[9] The observed variation is small indeed when compared with fluctuations in almost any other economic series.

Long-Term Trends

The labor force in the United States has expanded in the past with population growth — but at a faster rate. From about one third in 1870 the proportion of the population in the labor force increased to more than two fifths in 1950. (See Figure 77.)

This long-term trend in the size of the working force has been accompanied by changes in its composition and its occupational and industrial distribution. Child labor has become less and less important; there has been a trend toward earlier retirement from work; but the proportion of women in the labor force has steadily increased. Agricultural occupations have diminished in importance as commerce and industry, and more recently the service trades, have shown rapid relative gains. Another marked trend has been toward clerical and professional work and away from the more arduous manual occupations.

7. *Op. cit.*, p. 103.
8. *Ibid.*, p. 104.
9. *Op. cit.*, p. 353.

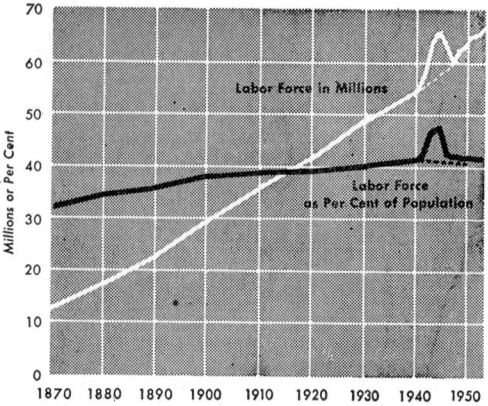

FIGURE 77. GROWTH OF THE LABOR FORCE, 1870–1953

Sources: Table 306, Appendix 20–1 and *Current Population Reports: Population Estimates,* U.S. Bureau of the Census, Series P–25, No. 71, Table 2, p. 5.

Note: Dashed lines between 1940 and 1950 indicate expected "normal" labor force based on projection of prewar trends.

SIZE AND GROWTH

At the time of the last census in April 1950, 63.5 million persons were members of the labor force.[10] This was the total number of persons who were at work for pay or profit in the week ending April 8 (including members of the armed forces), or working without pay in a family enterprise, or with a job but temporarily absent from work, or unemployed and seeking work. The 1950 labor force was equal to 42.0 per cent of the total population and 52.1 per cent of the population 10 years of age and over. Except for the war years, these percentages were unmatched in any earlier period. During the early 1950s the labor force continued to grow but at a slightly slower rate than the total population. The population growth, however, reflected the addition of the bumper postwar crop of babies; consequently, the labor force rose faster than the population 10 years of age and over, reaching about 52.5 per cent of that group by 1951. (See Table 306.)

While the labor force increased relative to total population every decade from 1870 on, it remained almost a constant proportion of the population 10 years of age and over from the

10. This is not the estimate of the 1950 Census of Population but comes from the special sample survey taken every month by the Census Bureau for its current population reports series. There are good reasons to believe that the monthly survey, carried out by regularly employed field personnel, yields more accurate results than the decennial census in this instance.

TABLE 306. GROWTH OF THE LABOR FORCE, 1870–1953 [a]

| Year | Population | | Labor Force | | |
	Total	10 Years of Age and Over	Number	Per Cent of Population	Per Cent of Population 10 Years and Over
	(Millions)		(Millions)		
1870	39.8	29.1	12.9 [a]	32.5	44.4
1880	50.2	36.8	17.4 [a]	34.7	47.3
1890	62.6	47.4	22.8	36.4	48.1
1900	76.0	58.0	29.2	38.4	50.3
1910	92.0	71.6	36.0	39.1	50.3
1920	105.7	82.7	41.7	39.5	50.4
1930	122.8	98.7	49.3	40.1	49.9
1940	131.7	110.4	54.7	41.5	49.5
1950	151.1	121.8	63.5	42.0	52.1
1951	153.7	123.1	64.6	42.0	52.5
1952	156.4	124.6	65.3	41.7	52.4
1953	159.0	126.2	66.3	41.7	52.5

Sources: Population 1870–1930, and labor force (i.e., gainful workers) 1870–1880, *Comparative Occupation Statistics for the United States, 1870–1940,* U.S. Bureau of the Census, 1940, Table XIV, p. 91; population 1940 and 1950–1953, *Current Population Reports: Population Estimates,* U.S. Bureau of the Census, Series P–25, Nos. 43, 90 and 93; labor force 1890–1900 and 1920–1930, adjusted for comparability with current Bureau of the Census concept of "labor force" on basis of figures in John D. Durand, *The Labor Force in the United States, 1890–1960,* Social Science Research Council, New York, 1948, Table A–5, p. 207, and Table A–6, pp. 208-209; labor force 1910, computed from figure on labor force as percentage of total population, which was derived by straight-line interpolation between 1900 and 1920 (see Durand, *op. cit.,* pp. 192-197, for weakness in census figure for 1910); labor force 1940–1953, Appendix 20–1.

a. Figures for 1870 and 1880 represent those "gainfully employed," a somewhat broader concept than "labor force"; all figures at date census for particular year was taken.

turn of the century to 1940. Between 1940 and 1950, however, it rose much more sharply than the population aged 10 and over, whose growth was retarded by the low birth rates of the 1930s.

These trends reflect diverse influences. The gradual rise in the average age of the population as life expectancy has increased has meant a smaller proportion of children and a larger proportion in the working ages; the adult population has grown faster than the total population. Child labor increased steadily from 1870 through the last decade of the nineteenth century, but has declined continuously since then, and was almost at the vanishing point by 1940. The proportion of women in the labor force has risen substantially during the past several decades. In fact, the most important influences on the size and growth of the labor force over the past several decades have been changes in its age and sex composition.

SEX AND AGE COMPOSITION

A large part of the growth in the labor force and the proportion of the population gainfully occupied has been due to the rapid expansion of female employment. Over nine times as many women were engaged in gainful work in 1950 as in 1870, whereas the number of male workers barely quadrupled. The proportion of women with gainful occupations has more than doubled since 1870 — from 13 per cent of all females 10 years of age and over to 29 per cent in 1950. In contrast, the proportion of males in the labor force has remained around 75 to 80 per cent of all those 10 years old and over, with a moderate increase between 1870 and 1910, a roughly comparable decline until 1940, and a slight rise since then. These shifts appear to have been due chiefly to the changes in the proportion of young males employed, the drop resulting from curtailment of child labor and the rise from the large-scale movement of young men into the armed forces, which are considered part of the labor force. (See Table 307.)

With more than one worker out of four a woman in 1950, as compared with one out of five in 1920 and only one out of seven in 1870,

TABLE 307. NUMBER AND PROPORTION OF MALES AND FEMALES IN THE LABOR FORCE, 1870–1953 [a]

Year	Number		Per Cent of Labor Force		Per Cent of Respective Population 10 Years of Age and Over	
	Male	Female	Male	Female	Male	Female
	(Millions)					
1870[a]	11.0	1.9	85.2	14.8	74.9	13.3
1880[a]	14.7	2.6	84.8	15.2	78.7	14.7
1890	18.8	4.1	82.1	17.9	77.0	17.7
1900	23.7	5.5	81.2	18.8	79.8	19.5
1910[b]	28.8	7.2	80.1	19.9	77.8	20.8
1920	32.9	8.9	78.7	21.3	77.8	22.0
1930	38.2	11.1	77.5	22.5	76.6	22.7
1940	40.9	13.8	74.8	25.2	74.0	25.1
1950	45.4	18.1	71.5	28.5	75.3	29.4
1951	45.9	18.6	71.2	28.8	75.4	29.9
1952	46.4	18.8	71.2	28.8	75.3	29.8
1953	47.4	19.0	71.4	28.6	76.1	29.7

Sources: *Comparative Occupation Statistics for the United States, 1870–1940*, U.S. Bureau of the Census, 1940, Table XIV, p. 91; *Current Population Reports: Population Estimates*, Series P–25, No. 93; *Current Population Reports: Labor Force*, Series P–50, No. 31; and unpublished estimates.

a. Figures for 1870 and 1880 are in terms of "gainfully employed," a somewhat broader concept than "labor force"; all figures at census date level.

b. Labor force estimates for 1910 derived by applying male-female distribution indicated in *Comparative Occupation Statistics for the United States, 1870–1940*, p. 91, to total shown in Table 306.

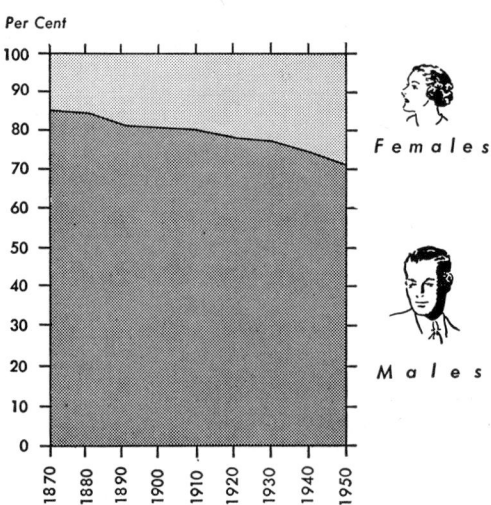

FIGURE 78. COMPOSITION OF THE LABOR FORCE, BY SEX, 1870–1950

Source: Table 307.

the movement of women into work outside the home is clearly a long-term trend which may be expected to continue in the future. (See Figure 78.) It is attributed by the Census Bureau not only to lessened resistance to employment of women and increased opportunities for them to secure vocational and professional training, but also to decreasing family responsibilities. A Census report states:

This trend of women into gainful pursuits outside the home doubtless is closely associated with a number of other changes, such as smaller families, the transfer to the factory of much productive work formerly done in the home, the increase in labor-saving equipment and conveniences in the home, and the increasing desire of women for economic independence. Increased opportunity for women to secure work outside the home came with the increased openings for women in the professions and in clerical, sales, and kindred pursuits.[11]

World War II further increased the number of jobs open to women. Continued reduction in the length of the work week has helped make it possible for women to take outside jobs and still perform many home duties.

Increased participation by women in the labor force is largely a mere shift from "nongainful" work inside the home to gainful employment outside. Indeed, it is probable that women as a group have always worked just as hard as men,

11. *Comparative Occupation Statistics for the United States, 1870–1940*, U.S. Bureau of the Census, 1940, p. 90.

TABLE 308. PER CENT OF BOYS AND GIRLS 10–15
YEARS OF AGE GAINFULLY OCCUPIED, 1870–1930

Year	Boys	Girls
1870	19.3	7.0
1880	24.4	9.0
1890	25.9	10.0
1900	26.1	10.2
1910	21.7	8.1
1920	16.8	5.8
1930	6.4	2.9

Source: Comparative Occupation Statistics for the United States, 1870–1940, U.S. Bureau of the Census, 1940, Table XV, p. 92.

even though they have not received statistical recognition of their efforts since homemakers, in census terminology, are "nongainful females." The Census report cited above points out that "The proportion of men who are gainful workers is roughly the same as the proportion of women who are gainful workers plus the proportion who are home-makers."

Age Composition

The most striking changes in the age composition of the working force have been among the youngest and the oldest age groups. Child labor, both male and female, expanded steadily from 1870 to 1900, when 26 per cent of all boys 10 to 15 years old, and 10 per cent of girls of this age group, were gainfully occupied. After 1900 the proportion of gainfully occupied fell steadily for both sexes, dropping abruptly after 1920. (See Table 308.) Gainful employment of younger children had virtually ceased by 1940. Although the 1940 Census failed to enumerate the 10-to-13-year-olds, only 35 per cent of boys and 19 per cent of girls in the group 14 to 19 years old were members of the labor force, as compared with 40 per cent and 23 per cent respectively in 1930.[12]

Throughout the entire period after 1870, more than twice as many boys as girls were gainfully occupied, and over two thirds of the boys were engaged in agricultural pursuits. At the peak of child labor in 1900, some 18 per cent of boys aged 10 to 15 were farm workers and less than 8 per cent were in nonagricultural pursuits, while only 4.4 per cent of girls of this age range were in agriculture, as compared with 5.8 per cent in other occupations. With the widespread senti-

ment against child labor these proportions have since fallen sharply, particularly in nonfarm occupations. In 1930 — and doubtless also in 1950 — the *relative* importance of agriculture as a children's occupation had increased.[13]

At the other end of the age scale, there has been a marked decline — though less pronounced than in the case of children — in the proportion of men 65 years of age and over working or seeking work. This long-term trend is related to the changing character and declining importance of farming, which is an occupation adapted to the capacities of both young and old, the decrease in self-employment and the substitution of semi-skilled for skilled labor. The old-age security program may also have encouraged earlier retirement in the last two decades. More than two thirds of all men 65 and over were in the labor force in 1890, as compared with less than half in 1940 and 1950. A rise occurred between 1940 and 1950 but this appears to be only a temporary interruption in the downward trend — partly a carry-over from the huge wartime labor force expansion and partly in response to the heavy demand for labor in 1950. (See Table 309.)

In the 20-to-64 age group a slight decline has occurred in the case of men — due largely to increased college attendance on the part of younger members of the group, particularly after World War II when veterans' educational benefits were available. Women between the ages of 20 and 64, on the other hand, have greatly increased their participation in the labor force. Between 1890 and 1950 the proportion of 20-to-34-year-old women in the labor force rose from less than one fourth to well over one third, and the proportion of 35-to-64-year-old women from less than one seventh to more than one third. The decline between 1940 and 1950 among the 20-to-34-year-olds followed the extraordinary postwar baby boom and is unlikely to alter the long-run upward trend. (See Figure 79.)

With the progressive aging of the population, the labor force has come to consist more largely of those in the upper age groups — from 35 to 64 years old. The median age of male workers increased from 33.0 years in 1890 to 38.4 years in

---

12. *Ibid.,* Table II, p. 13.

13. *Ibid.,* Table XVIII, p. 97. In 1950 employment data were not reported for children under 14 years of age; however, the proportion of employed workers in agricultural jobs was higher for 14- and 15-year-olds than for any other age group. 1950 Census of Population, Vol. II, Part 1, Table 122, pp. 286–287.

TABLE 309. PER CENT OF POPULATION IN THE LABOR FORCE, BY SEX AND AGE, 1890–1950 [a]

	Male				Female			
Year	14–19 Years	20–34 Years	35–64 Years	65 Years and Over	14–19 Years	20–34 Years	35–64 Years	65 Years and Over
1890	54.2	94.7	94.9	70.1	25.6	23.3	13.3	8.6
1900	67.2	93.9	93.4	64.9	28.0	25.5	15.3	9.4
1920	55.8	94.3	93.9	57.1	29.6	30.1	19.1	8.2
1930	43.5	94.0	94.2	55.5	23.9	34.2	21.1	8.2
1940	38.4	93.8	93.0	43.4	19.8	39.8	24.8	6.8
1950	47.9	91.6	92.8	45.1	26.4	37.0	34.8	9.5

Sources: 1890–1930, John D. Durand, *The Labor Force in the United States, 1890–1960*, Social Science Research Council, New York, 1948, Table A–6, pp. 208–209; 1940–1950, unpublished estimates of the Bureau of the Census.

Durand's published figures for 1890–1930 were adjusted for comparability with the Census estimates on the basis of comparison of the two sets of estimates for 1940.

a. Estimates for 1910 not available.

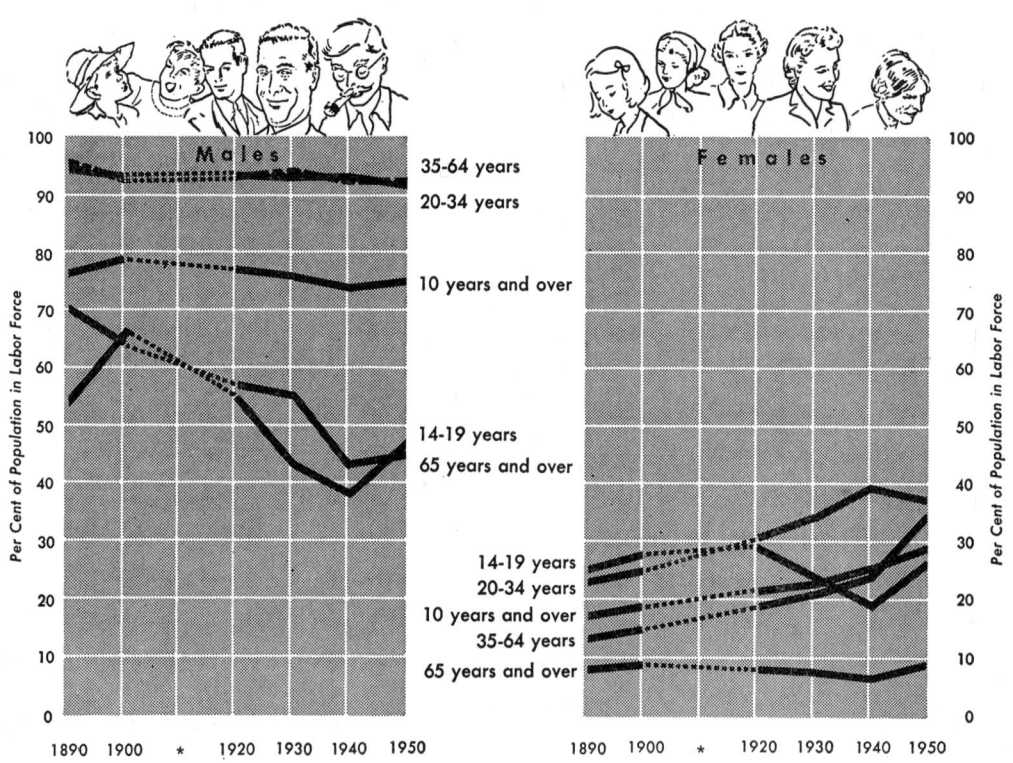

*Estimates for 1910 not available

FIGURE 79. RATE OF PARTICIPATION OF POPULATION IN THE LABOR FORCE, BY SEX AND AGE, 1890–1950
Sources: Tables 307 and 309.

1950. For females the median increased even more sharply, from 24.0 years in 1890 to 36.7 in 1950. Durand estimates that "during the half-century from 1890 to 1940 the average age of entrance to the labor force probably rose by about 3 years." [14]

_____

14. *Op. cit.*, p. 31.

TABLE 310. EDUCATION AND INCOME OF OCCUPATIONAL GROUPS, 1950

Occupational Group	Median School Years Completed[a]		Median Income[b]	
	Male	Female	Male	Female
Professional, technical and kindred workers	16+	15.8	$3,958	$2,262
Farmers and farm managers	8.3	8.1	1,455	759
Nonfarm managers, officials and proprietors	12.2	12.1	3,944	2,122
Clerical and kindred workers	12.2	12.4	3,010	2,042
Sales workers	12.3	11.6	3,028	1,244
Craftsmen, foremen and kindred workers	9.3	9.9	3,125	1,999
Operatives and kindred workers	8.7	8.7	2,607	1,541
Private household workers	8.1	7.9	1,176	652
Service workers, except private household	8.7	9.1	2,195	1,054
Farm laborers: unpaid family workers	7.9	8.4	} 863	576
Farm laborers, except unpaid, and farm foremen	7.1	6.5		
Laborers, except farm and mine	8.0	8.6	1,961	1,425

Sources: 1950 Census of Population, Vol. II, *Characteristics of the Population*, Part 1, United States Summary, 1953, Table 129, pp. 279 ff., and Volume IV, *Special Reports*, Part 5, Chapter B, Education, 1953, Table 11, pp. 88 and 92.

a. Based on population 14 years and over reporting some occupation in April 1950.

b. 1949 income of the April 1950 "experienced civilian labor force"; i.e., employed workers and the unemployed with previous work experience. Income excludes the value of income in kind, such as food produced and consumed in the home and free living quarters; inclusion of such income would increase the medians for those in farm and private household occupations.

CHARACTER AND QUALITY OF THE LABOR FORCE

The Census classification of workers into "social-economic groups," indicative of the character and quality of the labor force, gives a significant picture of the shifts in the nature of gainful work during the past few decades. This classification aims at dividing all members of the working force into homogeneous groups based not only on skill and earnings but also on intellectual, educational and social characteristics.[15]

These groups vary widely in their economic and educational characteristics as measured by income and years of schooling. Occupational groupings for 1950 corresponding roughly to the social-economic groups as defined by the Census

15. "The workers in each group have been included partly because of their social and partly because of their economic status. The standard — if it be a standard — is thus a hybrid — partly social and partly economic. And the weight of the social factor varies from one group to another, and from one occupation to another, as does, also, the weight of the economic factor. Thus, the social factor is of greater weight in the clerical group than in the skilled group, but the reverse is true as to the economic factor. 'Stenographers, typists, and secretaries,' as a group, outrank plumbers socially, but not economically. Education is a very large factor in the social status of workers, and wage or salary income is a very large factor in their economic status." *Comparative Occupation Statistics for the United States, 1870–1940*, p. 180.

show that professional, technical and kindred workers were at the highest level — followed closely by nonfarm managers, officials and proprietors — and farm laborers were at the lowest level, both in terms of cash income and educational attainment. The relationship between education and earnings was not consistent, however; craftsmen, foremen and kindred workers had about three years less schooling on the average than clerical and sales workers but their 1949 income was slightly higher. Operatives and kindred workers, largely semiskilled labor, had about the same schooling as service workers but substantially higher earnings than nonhousehold service workers and about two and a half times the cash income of domestic service workers. Domestic service workers were at a lower social-economic status than any other group except farm laborers. In educational attainment and cash income, however, farmers and farm managers were very little higher than either of these groups. (See Table 310.) Cash income does not, of course, give the full measure of the earnings of workers in farm and private household occupations, since it ignores the value of food produced and consumed in the home, free living quarters and other types of income in kind.

TABLE 311. SOCIAL-ECONOMIC STATUS OF GAINFUL WORKERS AND PERSONS
IN THE LABOR FORCE, 1910–1940[a]

	Percentage Distribution				Number in Labor Force 1940
	Gainful Workers			Labor Force	
Group	1910	1920	1930	1940	
					(Millions)
Total	100.0	100.0	100.0	100.0	52.0
Professional persons	4.4	5.0	6.1	6.5	3.4
Proprietors, managers and officials	23.0	22.3	19.9	17.8	9.2
Farmers and farm managers	16.5	15.5	12.4	10.1	5.3
Others	6.5	6.8	7.5	7.6	3.9
Clerks and kindred workers	10.2	13.8	16.3	17.2	8.9
Skilled workers and foremen	11.7	13.5	12.9	11.7	6.1
Semiskilled workers	14.7	16.1	16.4	21.0	10.9
Unskilled workers	36.0	29.4	28.4	25.9	13.5
Farm laborers	14.5	9.4	8.6	7.1	3.7
Other laborers	14.7	14.6	12.9	10.7	5.6
Servants	6.8	5.4	6.9	8.0	4.2

Source: Comparative Occupation Statistics for the United States, 1870–1940, U.S. Bureau of the Census, 1940, Table XXVII p. 187.

a. Excluding workers under 14 years of age in all years and new workers in 1940.
Note: Discrepancies in addition are due to rounding.

Trend away from Unskilled Work

What changes have been taking place in the social-economic composition of the working force over the past decades, and what factors account for these changes? The Census Bureau observed that "the social-economic status of the nation's labor force was rising rather rapidly from 1910 to 1940. The trend was definitely upward — definitely away from heavy, arduous, unskilled manual labor, and definitely toward more highly skilled manual pursuits and intellectual pursuits."[16] Technological advances, which have made physical toil easier and contributed to the shift from production to distribution and service activities, the drift of women into gainful work and the spread of education all help to account for this upward trend in the social-economic composition of the labor force.

Unskilled workers, including farm hands, industrial workers and domestic servants, numbered less than 14 million out of the 52 million persons in the labor force in 1940. This was less than 26 per cent of the total, against 36 per cent

16. *Ibid.,* p. 184.

in 1910. The second largest group in 1940 was the 11 million semiskilled workers, but here the trend, reflecting the spread of automatic machinery and mass production, was steeply upward — from less than 15 per cent of the total in 1910 to 21 per cent in 1940. White-collar occupations, comprising professional persons and clerks and kindred workers, grew from less than 15 per cent in 1910 to nearly 24 per cent in 1940. (See Table 311.)

Although "proprietors, managers and officials" declined from 23 per cent of the working force in 1910 to 18 per cent in 1940, the decline was more than accounted for by the smaller proportion of farmers. Wholesale and retail dealers and other proprietors and officials, who together with independent professional persons are not "jobholders" but usually "job-givers," were a more important part of the labor force in 1940 than they were thirty years before.

The trend away from heavy, unskilled labor and toward higher-skilled work continued during the 1940s. Although Census data on the social-economic status of workers are not available after 1940, estimates of the occupational distribution

TABLE 312. OCCUPATIONAL DISTRIBUTION OF THE EXPERIENCED CIVILIAN LABOR FORCE, 1940, 1950 AND 1953

Major Occupation Group	Percentage Distribution		
	1940	1950	1953[a]
Total	100.0	100.0	100.0
Professional and semiprofessional workers	7.0	7.3	8.7
Proprietors, managers and officials	18.0	17.4	16.2
Farmers and farm managers	10.4	7.0	5.9
Others	7.6	10.4	10.3
Clerical and kindred workers and salespeople	16.3	18.9	18.9
Craftsmen, foremen and kindred workers	11.7	13.0	14.0
Operatives and kindred workers	18.7	20.8	20.9
Farm laborers and foremen	7.0	5.1	3.8
Laborers, except farm and mine	9.1	6.4	6.2
Domestic service workers	4.6	3.2	3.0
Service workers, except domestic	7.6	8.0	8.4

Sources: Current Population Reports: Labor Force, U.S. Bureau of the Census, Series P–20, No. 19, Table III, p. 4; Series P–50, No. 40, Table D, p. 4; and additional data supplied by the Bureau of the Census.

a. Annual average based on data collected for months representing three calendar quarters: January, April and October.

of experienced labor force members provide an adequate substitute.[17]

Between 1940 and the early 1950s the proportions of the labor force occupied as nonfarm proprietors and managers, clerical workers and salespeople, skilled and semiskilled workers continued to rise while the proportions engaged as farmers, laborers and domestic service workers followed their long-run declines. The proportion of the civilian labor force engaged in agricultural occupations — farmers and farm managers, foremen and laborers — dropped precipitously, from 17.4 per cent in 1940 to 12.1 per cent in 1950 and 9.7 per cent in 1953. A sharp increase in the

17. The main differences between the two classifications are between the "servants" and "service workers." Only servants and laundresses in private families are "domestic service workers" in the occupational classification and "servants" in the social-economic classification. Housekeepers in private families are viewed as "domestic service workers" in the occupational classification but as semiskilled workers in the social-economic scale. The occupational class "service workers, except domestic or protective," is split between "servant classes" and "semiskilled workers" in the social-economic classification. Several types of "protective service" workers — firemen, policemen, sheriffs and marshalls — are even found in the "skilled workers and foremen" group in the social-economic scale.

relative number of nonfarm proprietors, managers and officials — from 7.6 per cent in 1940 to 10.4 per cent in 1950 and 10.3 per cent in 1953 — practically offset the decline in the proportion of farm owners and managers in the labor force. The professional and semiprofessional group grew only slightly in relative size between 1940 and 1950 — from 7.0 to 7.3 per cent of the total. The smallness of the increase probably reflected the temporary absence from the labor force of veterans attending college under the "G.I. Bill." Most of these, whose entry into civilian jobs was delayed by the war, undoubtedly elected to follow professional or semiprofessional occupations upon graduation. By 1953 those occupations accounted for 8.7 per cent of the total. (See Table 312.)

INDUSTRIAL TRENDS

Marked changes have also occurred in the industrial composition of the labor force since 1870, largely reflecting long-term trends that can be expected to continue in the future. Technological progress has made it possible for us to produce an ever-increasing quantity of physical goods per

TABLE 313. PERCENTAGE DISTRIBUTION OF MANPOWER BY INDUSTRY DIVISION, 1870-1950

Industry Division	Gainful Workers							Experienced Labor Force		
	1870	1880	1890	1900	1910	1920	1930	1930	1940	1950
Total	100.0	100.0	100.0	100.0	100.0	100.0	100.0	100.0	100.0	100.0
Agriculture	50.3	50.1	42.4	37.3	31.4	27.0	22.1	21.5	18.0	11.9
Forestry and fishing	0.5	0.5	0.8	0.7	0.7	0.7	0.6	0.3	0.3	0.2
Mining	1.6	1.8	2.0	2.6	2.9	3.0	2.4	2.5	2.2	1.4
Construction	5.9	4.8	6.1	5.8	6.4	5.3	6.4	6.4	7.0	6.2
Manufacturing	17.6	18.4	20.1	22.1	22.8	26.4	23.1	22.8	23.9	25.8
Transportation, communication and public utilities	4.8	4.7	6.3	7.1	8.4	9.7	9.6	9.6	7.7	8.6
Trade	6.1	6.7	7.7	8.6	9.3	9.9	12.7	13.1	14.4	18.0
Finance, insurance and real estate	0.3	0.4	0.7	1.1	1.4	1.9	3.0	3.1	3.1	3.2
Government, including postal service	2.0	2.3	2.5	2.8	3.6	4.5	5.1	5.3	6.1	7.9
Professional service (including amusement)	1.6	1.8	2.2	2.5	3.0	3.6	4.9	4.8	5.9	6.3
Personal and domestic service	9.3	8.4	9.1	9.4	10.2	8.1	10.1	10.7	11.4	10.6

Sources: 1870-1940, based on Daniel Carson, "Changes in the Industrial Composition of Manpower since the Civil War," *Studies in Income and Wealth*, Vol. 11, National Bureau of Economic Research, New York, 1949, Table 1, p. 47; 1950 based on unpublished estimates of the Bureau of the Census, derived from its current population sample for April 1950, and an independent estimate of the percentage of the labor force attached to "eating and drinking places" (3.4 per cent) which was shifted from "trade" to "personal and domestic service" for comparability with Carson's classification.

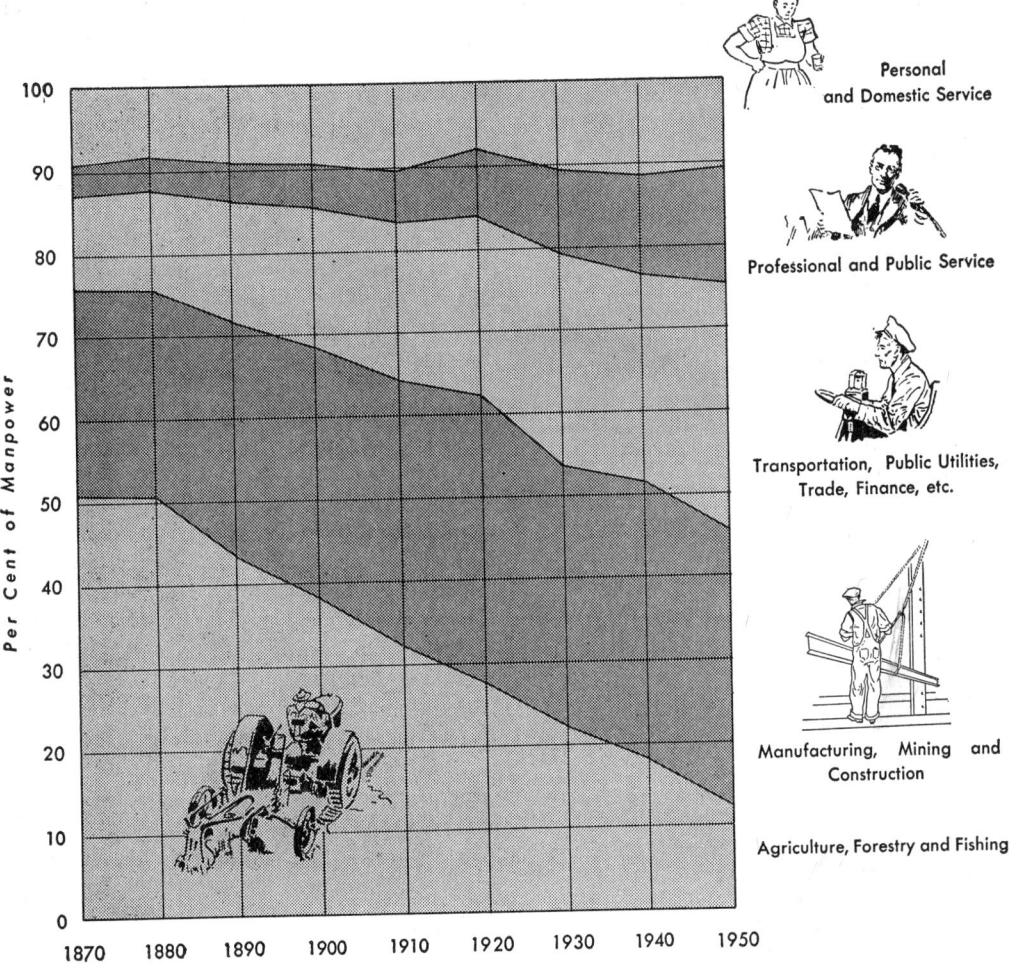

FIGURE 80. CHANGING INDUSTRIAL COMPOSITION OF AMERICAN MANPOWER, 1870–1950

Source: Table 313, using distribution of gainful workers, 1870–1920, and experienced labor force, 1930–1950.

person, with a decreasing proportion of the labor force. More than three fourths of the labor force were engaged in the production of physical goods — agriculture, forestry and fishing, extraction of minerals, construction and manufacturing — in 1870, with more than half in agriculture. By 1950 only 12 per cent were in farming and only 46 per cent in all phases of production. (See Table 313 and Figure 80.)

The shift away from agriculture, especially in recent decades, has been largely in the direction of trade, finance and related industries, government and professional service, all of which have absorbed a continuously greater share of available manpower over the years. Trade, which

accounted for 6 per cent of all gainful workers in 1870, had 18 per cent of the experienced labor force in 1950 and was second only to the manufacturing division. The proportion engaged in finance, insurance and real estate rose tenfold, from 0.3 per cent in 1870 to over 3 per cent in 1950. Government [18] took only 2 per cent of the

18. Government as used here is not representative of the public service. The decennial censuses classify many government workers in other industry divisions — government library and hospital workers in professional service, workers attached to arsenals, navy yards, municipal power plants and government printing offices in manufacturing, and so on — and it has not been feasible to shift these groups. However, employees of the postal and public school systems, which the censuses also coded elsewhere, have been shifted to the government division.

total in 1870 and nearly 8 per cent in 1950. Professional service, including the amusement and entertainment industries, rose from less than 2 per cent to more than 6 per cent in the same period.

Manufacturing and the transportation, communication and public utilities industries also have taken up some of agriculture's excess manpower, but neither of these groups has expanded its relative share of the working force in the last three decades. The proportion of the total attached to manufacturing industries rose from 18 per cent in 1870 to over 26 per cent by 1920. After a decline during the depression of the 1930s it was just about back to the 1920 level in 1950. The transportation, communication and public utilities division, which upped its proportionate share from about 5 to 10 per cent in the half-century from 1870 to 1920, has since declined slightly.

Construction and personal and domestic service, while fluctuating in the proportion of manpower used over the years, accounted in 1940 for about the same percentages as in 1870. Among the services, however, the relative growth of personal services, such as laundries, eating and drinking places, barbers and beauticians, hides the declining importance of domestic service as an occupation. Domestics dropped from 7 to 5 per cent while personal service workers rose from 2 to more than 6 per cent of the total between 1870 and 1940.[19] In general, the shift in labor force concentration away from production of goods to rendering of service (in the wide sense) has increased the proportion of "lighter" jobs. This has facilitated, and probably partly induced, the continuing increase in the proportion of women in the labor market.

UTILIZATION AND EFFICIENCY OF THE LABOR FORCE

The effectiveness of the labor force as a factor in production depends not only on its size, composition and quality, but also upon the extent and efficiency of its employment. In concrete terms, this means that it is the number of persons actually at work, the length of the work week and production per man-hour that determine the total national output of goods and services.

Unemployment

The labor force has probably never been fully employed in the sense that every person able and willing to work was actually at work on the same day or in the same week. There is always some unemployment, even in periods when heavy demand for labor expands the labor force far beyond its normal size.

During the long depression of the 1930s unemployment remained at record high levels. Nearly 13 million workers, or one fourth of the entire labor force, were out of work in 1933. Unemployment did not drop below 8 million, or about 14 per cent of the labor force, until 1937; and the minor boom of that year was followed by another slump and a rise in the number of unemployed to more than 10 million in 1938.[20] At no time during the decade, and indeed not until some months after we entered the war, did our utilization of the labor force remotely approach "full employment."

In spite of the rising tempo of the defense program after the summer of 1940, when more than 8 million were out of work, it was not until the spring of 1942 that unemployment dropped below 3 million, or to as little as 5 per cent of the labor force. By that time about 3 million emergency workers had already been drawn into the labor market. Even at the peak of activity in late 1944 and early 1945, when the labor force included some 8 million emergency workers, there were never less than 400,000 workers unemployed.[21]

Cessation of hostilities brought a quick rise in unemployment. But the 2.7 million peak reached during transition from war to peace was far below prewar levels. Several factors helped to avert the sizable amount of unemployment that might have arisen from the sharp cut in government spending and the extremely rapid demobilization of our armed forces, which dropped by almost 10 million in the year after V-J Day. Chief among these factors were the withdrawal from the labor market of many veterans and most of the emergency workers, whose numbers dropped from 8 million in early 1945 to just over one million during most of 1946, and the rapid

---

19. Based on estimates of Solomon Fabricant, "The Changing Industrial Distribution of Gainful Workers" in *Studies in Income and Wealth,* Volume 11, National Bureau of Economic Research, New York, 1949, Table 2, p. 42.

20. *Handbook of Labor Statistics,* 1950 edition, Bulletin No. 1016, U.S. Bureau of Labor Statistics, Table A-13, p. 35.

21. See Appendix 20-1 for monthly estimates of size and composition of the labor force during the defense and war periods.

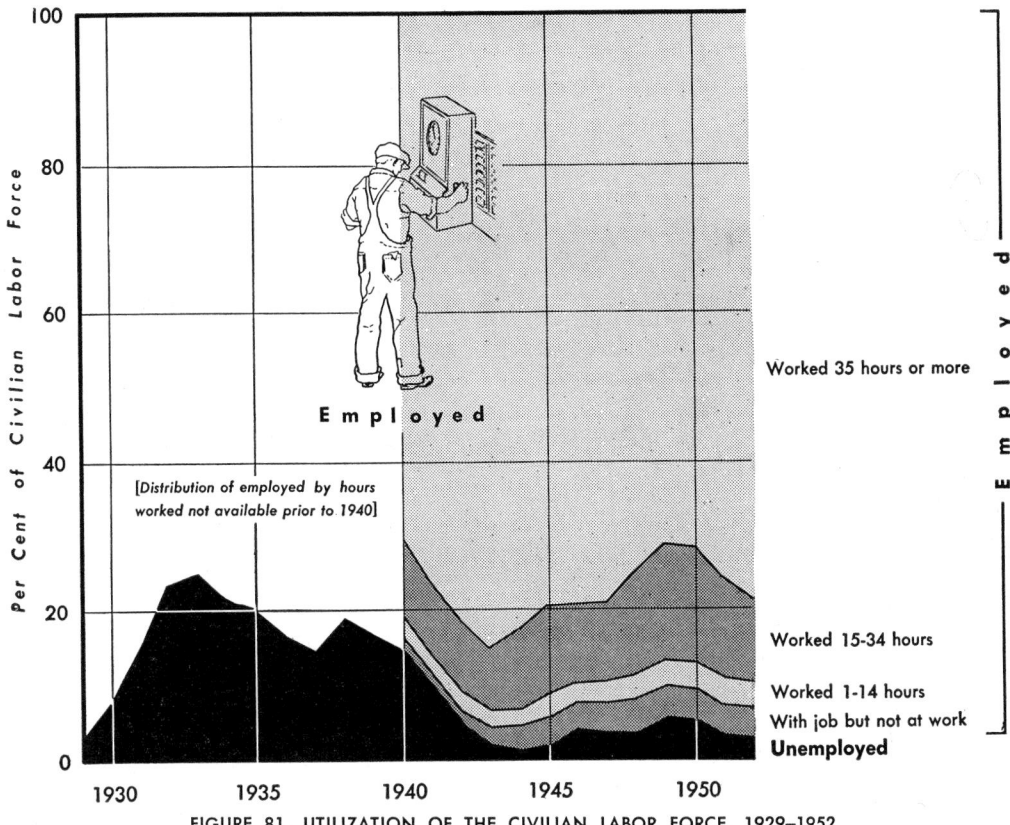

FIGURE 81. UTILIZATION OF THE CIVILIAN LABOR FORCE, 1929–1952

Sources: 1929–1939, Handbook of Labor Statistics, U.S. Bureau of Labor Statistics, 1950, Table A–13, p. 35; 1940–1952, Current Population Reports: Labor Force, U.S. Bureau of the Census, Series P–50, Nos. 2, 13, 19, 31, 40 and 45.

opening of peacetime jobs in response to the unleashing of pent-up demand for goods and services.

After the initial reconversion shock, unemployment declined slightly, but, despite boom conditions during the next three years, it remained between 1.5 and 2.5 million. The so-called "inventory" recession of 1949 once again began to raise the question of serious underutilization of the labor force. By early 1950 the number of jobless approached the 5 million mark but before any emergency measures were undertaken the tide turned and, with the start of the Korean War, the volume of unemployment began dropping toward its World War II level. After reaching a low point of just over one million toward the end of 1953, it rose again to about 3.5 million in early 1954 when the long postwar boom showed signs of tapering off.

Reliable unemployment records for earlier periods are almost nonexistent, but such estimates as have been made confirm the opinion that unemployment never disappears and rarely falls much below 5 per cent of the labor force. The best estimates for the prosperous 1920s are those prepared by Leo Wolman for the years 1920 to 1927.[22] Except for 1921 and 1922, these were years of prosperity and high-level employment. Yet the estimated "average minimum volume of unemployment" in nonagricultural pursuits, according to Wolman, ranged from about 1.5 million, or nearly 4 per cent of the total labor force, in prosperous 1920 and 1923, to 2.3 million, or more than 5 per cent, in the mild recession of 1924. In the depression year 1921 unemployment amounted to 4.3 million, or about 10 per cent of the labor force. For the entire 1920–1927 period, unemployment averaged 5.4 per cent; excluding 1921 and 1922, the average was about 4.2 per cent.

22. *Recent Economic Changes,* McGraw-Hill, New York, 1929, Vol. II, Table 37, p. 478, and Table 29, p. 469.

The estimates of Paul Douglas are of more limited industrial coverage than the more recent data, but they provide an interesting picture of the fluctuating level of employment from 1889 to 1926.[23] For the period from 1889 to 1896, his estimates show that unemployment in manufacturing and transportation fell below 5 per cent of the working force in these industries in only one year, 1892, and rose above 15 per cent in the depression year 1896. For the period from 1897 to 1926 the Douglas estimates covered manufacturing, transportation, building trades and mining. Only in 1906, 1917 and 1918 did unemployment fall as low as 6 per cent of the available labor supply in these industries; in twenty of the thirty years it amounted to more than 7 per cent, and in eleven to 10 per cent or more. These percentages cannot be taken as representative of total unemployment during this period, however, since the industries covered by the estimates are subject to wider employment fluctuations than most of those not represented. But the evidence does confirm the conclusion that although unemployment fluctuates widely from year to year, it persists in considerable volume even in years of prosperity. In other words, the labor force, viewed as an element in our productive capacity, apparently has rarely or never been completely utilized. This does not mean that "the irreducible minimum of unemployment" consists of a "hard core" of unemployed workers who never find jobs. On the contrary, unemployment in years of prosperity is largely "frictional" in nature, consisting of a shifting group of workers, most of them out of work only for short periods between jobs.

Underemployment

Estimates of total unemployment minimize the extent to which the labor force is underutilized. In addition to people who have no jobs, and who are counted as unemployed, there are those who have jobs but are either not working at all [24] or are working less than their usual number of hours and are viewed as employed. Some of these "employed" individuals have all the work they desire at the moment but others among them are definitely not occupied as fully as they would like to be. Any measure of the extent of underutilization of the labor force should include this last group.[25]

In recent years the proportion of the labor force employed but working less than full time or not at work has been on the increase. It dropped from 14.7 per cent in 1940 to 12.7 per cent in 1943 but increased fairly steadily after that and by 1950 had reached 23.3 per cent. The expansion of this group was so marked that, although the rate of unemployment dropped by two thirds between 1940 and 1950, the proportion of the labor force employed 35 hours or more changed hardly at all. After 1950, under the impact of the Korean War build-up, the proportion declined. In 1952, at 18.6 per cent it was still well above the 1940 level even though the percentage unemployed was less than one fifth as great as in 1940. (See Figure 81 and Appendix 20-2.) Although most of these individuals are not underemployed, in the sense that they want and can accept more work, those who are constitute a sizable addition to the unemployed in measuring the extent to which the labor force is underutilized.

During the years 1948–1950, when the economy had pretty well passed through the transition from war to peace and had not yet been affected by the Korean War, the great majority of people working part time or with jobs but not at work were without full-time work for what may be termed "noneconomic" reasons. They were people who were working part time out of preference or were away from work for part or all of the week because of illness, vacation, bad weather and the like. During the three-year period about three fourths of all those working part time did so because they did not wish or could not accept full-time work or because of illness, bad weather and other "noneconomic" factors. An even higher

---

23. Paul H. Douglas, *Real Wages in the United States, 1890–1926*, Houghton Mifflin, New York, 1930, Table 163, p. 440, and Table 172, p. 460.

24. Under the definitions now used by the Census Bureau people who have jobs but are temporarily not at work because of illness, bad weather, vacation, industrial dispute or short, definite layoff and those scheduled to report to new jobs within thirty days are classified as employed.

25. This is not meant as a criticism of the Bureau of the Census unemployment estimates. The Census objective in counting the unemployed is to measure pressure on the labor market. People, for example, who have definite jobs to which they expect to report within thirty days exert little or no pressure as job seekers — in this sense they are much closer to those at work than to the unemployed. Individuals who are employed less than full time but have all the work they want clearly exert no labor market pressure as job seekers and are well classified as employed; those who want more work, and are therefore both employed and unemployed at the same time, present a problem which in a dichotomous classification can be solved only in a somewhat arbitrary manner — the Census Bureau does so by calling them employed. We may accept this view but still consider them as underutilized.

TABLE 314. PER CENT OF INDIVIDUALS WORKING PART TIME AND PER CENT OF THOSE WITH JOBS BUT NOT AT WORK FOR ECONOMIC [a] AND NONECONOMIC [b] REASONS, SELECTED MONTHS, 1948–1950

Year and Month	Worked Part Time for:		With a Job but Not at Work for:	
	Economic Reasons	Noneconomic Reasons	Economic Reasons	Noneconomic Reasons
1948				
March	15.7	84.3	10.8	89.2
September	17.6 [e]	82.4 [e]	7.0	93.0
1949				
May	28.8	71.2	16.4	83.6
August	30.8	69.2	7.4	92.6
November	26.6 [d]	73.4 [d]	12.7	87.3
1950				
February	23.4	76.6	6.8 [e]	93.2 [e]
May	23.9	76.1	14.4	85.6
August	29.9	70.1	3.8	96.2
November	19.2 [f]	80.8 [f]	7.2	92.8

Sources: Appendix 20–3 and *Current Population Reports: Labor Force,* U.S. Bureau of the Census, Series P–50, No. 13, p. 30, No. 19, p. 22, No. 31, p. 24.

a. "Economic" reasons include slack work, layoff, material shortages, repairs to plant and equipment, and job turnover.

b. "Noneconomic" reasons include illness, vacation, industrial dispute, transportation difficulties and various personal reasons.

c. Excludes those working part time because of Labor Day holiday.

d. Excludes those working part time because of Armistice Day holiday.

e. Includes effect of sizable industrial dispute, which is considered a "noneconomic" factor for the purposes of this tabulation.

f. Excludes those working part time because of Armistice or Election Day holiday.

proportion — between 84 and 96 per cent, depending upon the time of the year — of those with a job but not at work were without work because of such "noneconomic" factors. (See Table 314.)

Although noneconomic factors caused most of the part-time employment and absence from jobs, the number not fully utilized for "economic" reasons averaged over three-fourths as high as total unemployment during 1948–1950. These individuals, who may be termed the underemployed, consist of part-time workers who prefer and can accept full-time work and those with jobs but working part time or not at all because of slack work, layoff, material shortages, repairs and job turnover. During the months for which the Bureau of the Census collected data on underemployment, total unemployment ran between 1.9 and 4.7 million while the underemployed numbered between 1.5 and 2.9 million. Total unemployment during these months ranged between 3.0 and 7.4 per cent and underemployment between 2.4 and 4.4 per cent of the labor force.

Together, the unemployed and the underemployed ranged from 5.4 per cent to as high as 11.0 per cent of the labor force — an indication of appreciable underutilization of the work force during a period of relatively good times. (See Table 315.)

Working Hours

The length of the work week varies widely from prosperity to depression. When business slackens and orders begin to fall off, factories have to curtail operations and put their workers on part time. As depression deepens, social pressure develops to spread the work and provide as many jobs as possible, in order to hold unemployment to a minimum. This happened during the early 1930s, and it means that to say 25 per cent of the labor force were unemployed at the bottom of the depression is considerably to understate the underutilization of the labor force.

At the other extreme, overtime work spreads widely at the peak of a boom, and average working hours of the labor force rise considerably

TABLE 315. UNDERUTILIZATION OF THE LABOR FORCE, SELECTED MONTHS, 1948–1950

	1948		1949			1950			
	March	September	May	August	November	February	May	August	November
Number (Thousands)									
Underutilized	3,899	3,445	6,022	6,580	5,974	6,921	5,461	5,028	4,161
Unemployed	2,440	1,899	3,289	3,689	3,409	4,684	3,057	2,500	2,240
Underemployed	1,459	1,546	2,733	2,891	2,565	2,237	2,404	2,528	1,921
With full-time job but worked part time because of economic factors[a]	712	814	1,571	1,474	1,387	1,095	1,087	1,245	986
With part-time job but prefer and could accept full-time job	511	546	886	1,081	965	988	1,068	1,112	821
With full- or part-time job but did not work because of economic factors[a]	236	186	276	336	213	154	249	171	114
Per Cent of Labor Force									
Underutilized	6.4	5.4	9.5	10.1	9.3	11.0	8.5	7.6	6.3
Unemployed	4.0	3.0	5.2	5.7	5.3	7.4	4.8	3.8	3.4
Underemployed	2.4	2.4	4.3	4.4	4.0	3.6	3.7	3.8	2.9
With full-time job but worked part time because of economic factors[a]	1.2	1.3	2.5	2.3	2.2	1.7	1.7	1.9	1.5
With part-time job but prefer and could accept full-time job	0.8	0.8	1.4	1.7	1.5	1.6	1.7	1.7	1.2
With full- or part-time job but did not work because of economic factors[a]	0.4	0.3	0.4	0.5	0.3	0.2	0.4	0.2	0.2

Source: Current Population Reports; Labor Force, U.S. Bureau of the Census, Series P–50, various numbers.

a. These factors include slack work, layoff, material shortages, repairs to plant or equipment, and job turnover (i.e., workers waiting to report to a new job or whose jobs were terminated during the survey week). Excluded from this count are persons with jobs but not at work for noneconomic reasons — own illness, vacation, bad weather, industrial dispute, illness or death in family, transportation difficulties and various personal reasons.

above normal. At the peak of the war effort, for example, average working time reached 49 hours a week, or 12 per cent above the 1940 average.

Apart from these cyclical variations, the long-run tendency has been toward a steady decline in the length of the working week, due partly to the shift of workers from agriculture, with its longer workday, to industrial and commercial pursuits. Largely, however, it reflects the shortening of working hours in industry and commerce from the 11 hours a day and 6 days a week of a century ago, first to the 10-hour day, then to the 48-hour week, later to the 5-day 40-hour week, and finally toward the recently stated goal of a 5-day week of 35 hours. Accompanying this downtrend has been the growing tendency to grant annual vacations with pay, further shortening the average number of weekly hours worked during the year.

Although data on hours of work, except for recent decades, are far from satisfactory, an attempt has been made in this survey to estimate hours of work for nonagricultural pursuits and for agriculture back to 1850. These estimates show that the length of the work week in nonagricultural activities declined decade by decade from 66 hours in 1850 to 41 hours in 1940 and that, despite a rise to 45 hours during World War II, it was down to about 39 hours during the early 1950s. Hours in agriculture fell from an estimated 72 a week in 1850 to 55 in 1940 and to around 48 hours in the early 1950s — a substantial decline, but smaller than that for nonagricultural pursuits. (See Appendix 20-4.)

Combining estimated hours worked in agriculture with nonagricultural activities (each weighted according to its importance in employment), there was a decline from an estimated 70 hours a week in 1850 to 44 hours in 1940 and 40 hours in 1950. On the average the drop in the estimated length of the work week over the entire 100-year period was 3 hours, or more than 5 per cent, per decade. However, the declines varied from 1.4 hours a week, or 2.2 per cent, from 1870 to 1880, to more than 5 hours, or almost 10 per cent, from 1910 to 1920. In general, the declines in the work week since the turn of the century were larger in terms of hours and percentages than during earlier decades.

Productivity

This persistent decline in working hours was made possible by steady gains in productivity and a rising standard of living. With increased output per worker and per man-hour, we have been able as a nation to consume an ever larger volume of goods and services, while producing and distributing them with less and less effort. Indeed, average working hours were cut so sharply after 1900 that, despite a more than two-fold increase in private employment during the next half century, total man-hours worked in private employment rose only 40 per cent. In other words, the increase in employment after 1900 was more than offset by the reduction in the length of the work week, but output per man-hour gained so rapidly that by 1950 total production was about three and a half times as great as in 1900.

Average productivity can be measured readily in physical terms for only a few industrial groups and then only for recent decades. Indexes of output per man-hour for manufacturing, mining, railroad operation, and electric light and power, and an index of output per worker in agriculture, all tell the same story of sharply rising productivity, at least between the early 1900s and the outbreak of World War II. Although the trend over the entire period was steeply upward for these industries, there were wide differences among them, and the year-to-year fluctuations were quite irregular. (See Table 316.)

During World War I (from 1914 to 1919), for example, output per man-hour in manufacturing showed no gain. Relatively moderate increases occurred in mining, in steam railroads and in output per worker in agriculture. During World War II (from 1940 to 1945), on the other hand, productivity rose rather sharply. For all private industry [26] and for railroads the rise was about one third; for private electric utilities it was 68 per cent; and in agriculture, output per worker rose 17 per cent. Mining had a relatively small increase of less than 4 per cent.

Output per man-hour in the production of such war materials as tanks, airplanes and ships increased dramatically. But these gains in most cases were not due so much to the development of new methods as to the application of well-known techniques to the new product, for example, the use of the automobile assembly line in the mass production of aircraft.

Other instances of great increases in average productivity of workers resulted from the full

---

26. Based on trend in private national income per man-hour in constant prices; see Table 14.

TABLE 316. INDEXES OF PRODUCTIVITY IN SELECTED INDUSTRIES, 1909–1950
(*1939 = 100*)

| | Output per Man-Hour | | | | Output per Worker |
Year	All Manufacturing	Mining	Steam Railroads[a]	Electric Light and Power[b]	Agriculture
1909	39.4	—	—	—	66.4
1914	45.5	—	—	—	79.4
1915	—	48.6	—	—	77.0
1916	—	48.1	51.6	—	73.4
1917	—	48.5	54.2	43.1	78.2
1918	—	49.4	53.5	—	81.3
1919	45.3	49.6	56.7	—	81.2
1920	48.0	51.8	57.6	—	86.5
1921	55.2	54.2	58.5	—	73.7
1922	60.5	57.5	60.9	46.0	79.7
1923	59.5	59.0	62.9	51.0	81.9
1924	63.4	60.7	64.6	49.1	83.8
1925	67.6	62.6	68.2	50.4	88.6
1926	69.5	63.4	70.4	53.1	91.3
1927	71.3	65.3	70.2	52.7	88.3
1928	75.1	68.0	73.7	—	91.8
1929	78.1	69.9	75.1	54.1	91.6
1930	80.0	72.9	75.1	50.1	89.8
1931	83.5	77.2	75.6	51.9	99.0
1932	77.8	77.6	73.7	58.3	93.4
1933	81.9	78.8	83.0	68.1	89.2
1934	85.9	81.4	83.7	77.4	76.6
1935	90.8	84.9	87.6	82.5	87.5
1936	91.0	86.6	93.5	87.8	81.6
1937	90.0	88.0	95.2	89.6	105.3
1938	91.6	90.1	94.7	89.0	97.8
1939	100.0	100.0	100.0	100.0	100.0
1940	—	102.1	105.2	108.6	102.5
1941	—	103.9	115.5	123.2	106.5
1942	—	104.0	139.6	145.8	117.8
1943	—	101.5	150.9	182.7	115.5
1944	—	104.7	148.1	191.1	122.6
1945	—	106.1	139.5	182.5	120.1
1946	—	107.2	129.1	160.7	120.2
1947	—	111.1	135.0	167.0	115.9
1948	—	110.9	133.2	171.0	130.1
1949	—	108.6	131.5	—	133.9
1950	—	117.4	149.9	—	131.0

Sources: Handbook of Labor Statistics, 1950 edition, Bulletin No. 1016, U.S. Bureau of Labor Statistics, Table F–1, p. 168, and 1951 supplement, 1952, p. 53.

a. Revenue traffic per man-hour for Class 1 steam line-haul railroads.

b. Privately owned electric utilities only.

and continuous utilization of productive capacity. After a decade of subnormal operations the railroads, for example, suddenly found both their freight and passenger facilities pushed far beyond normal capacity at a time of manpower shortage. Under these pressures and with highly efficient management, productivity per man increased greatly. However, both labor and the consumers, as well as the industry, would probably have been better off in terms of working conditions and quality of service, if traffic volume, and consequently output per worker, had been at lower levels.

In some other cases, too, what appeared statistically as increased productivity involved greater inconvenience and diminished service to customers. Notable examples were retail trade and personal service activities, where consumers had to perform for themselves many services normally performed for them.

There were also many examples of decreased per capita output and lowered efficiency arising directly from the fact that the peak demands of war "scraped the bottom of the labor barrel" and drew into the labor market many workers who would have been unable to hold down jobs in normal times. Some branches of manufacturing and retail trade, as well as filling stations and restaurants, illustrate this situation. Perhaps the most glaring example is domestic service, where efficiency, if measurable, would certainly have shown a sharp drop despite increased rates of pay.

After World War II, over-all productivity declined and even as late as 1949 it hardly exceeded the 1945 level. A jump in 1950 raised it to nearly 10 per cent above the 1945 rate. (See Table 14.) The pattern was much the same for railroads and agriculture; it appears to have been similar for private electric utilities, for which data are available only through 1948. Although productivity in mining did not drop below its 1945 rate, the increase between 1945 and 1950 was also in the area of 10 per cent.

Some of the year-to-year changes, particularly the declines from one year to the next, are hard to explain; they probably indicate that these indexes are at best very rough measures useful only in determining broad trends. Despite these inadequacies, however, the pronounced gains registered leave little doubt that productivity advanced greatly over the period as a whole.

This increase in labor productivity has come from two sources: improvements in technical and in economic efficiency.[27] Technical efficiency — or so-called "pure" productivity — refers to the efficiency with which man-hours are used to produce particular items which do not change over long periods of time. Gains in technical productivity come from improved methods of operation, more efficient machines and more skilled workers.

Economic efficiency is affected by the way in which manpower is allocated among industrial processes. Output per man-hour varies from industry to industry and from process to process within an industry. Shifting manpower from a process or industry with lower output per man-hour to one with higher output increases economic efficiency and hence over-all productivity even though there is no change in technical productivity.

Although the two types of productivity are different, both are important to the nation's welfare. Gains in economic productivity are no less real than gains in technical productivity. Increased productivity resulting from allocation of labor to the jobs in which it is most efficient benefits society just as much as technological improvements which raise output in particular processes.

An important difference between the two, however, is the accuracy with which they can be measured. Determining changing productivity for a single process is a relatively simple mechanical problem; the results have a reasonable degree of accuracy. Determining differences in productivity for different sections of the economy is much more difficult and considerably less accurate. It depends on the assumption that differences in market prices for different commodities truly reflect differences in economic worth. Prices, however, can be affected by factors which have little relation to the value of the product. Nevertheless, they should give a general guide to relative economic values, especially in the long run. The resulting measures of productivity reflecting changes in both technical and economic efficiency, while rough, are sufficiently accurate to support the conclusion that the efficiency of the economy has increased greatly during the past hundred years. The rate of increase has been far from steady but it appears to have been accelerating over the years. (See Figure 5.)

THE WAR DECADE

The war emergency brought great changes in the size and composition of the labor force, in hours of work and in productivity of labor.

GROWTH OF THE WAR LABOR FORCE

The mobilization of manpower in the United States was marked by two distinct phases: up to

27. See John W. Kendrick, "National Productivity and Its Long-Term Projection," paper presented before the Conference on Research in Income and Wealth, New York, 1951.

December 1941 the nation was preparing to defend itself; after Pearl Harbor it had to face the grim reality of war. During the first period, unemployed workers were reabsorbed by the gradual expansion in production of war materials and in the armed forces. At the outbreak of war we had less than 2 million men in the Army and Navy, while about 6 million workers were employed in munitions industries. Unemployment had dropped to 3.6 million, which might be regarded as not far from a normal level for midwinter. The labor force was somewhat "inflated" by the addition of some 1.8 million emergency workers.

The acceleration of the war effort after Pearl Harbor resulted in a rapid expansion of the labor force, chiefly because of the addition of several million emergency workers, and a rapid growth of the armed forces and of employment in munitions industries. By the fall of 1944 the war effort had reached its peak with close to 12 million in the armed forces and a total labor force of close to 67 million (exceeded only by the seasonal high of 68 million in midsummer). This represented an increase of 12 million over the labor force in the spring of 1940 — some 4 million normal accessions to the labor market and about 8 million emergency workers. In addition, nearly 8 million of the 1940 unemployed had been reabsorbed over the four-year period, so that approximately 20 million more persons were at work or in the armed forces at the peak of the war effort than the 46 million holding jobs in the spring of 1940.

The labor force expanded most rapidly during 1942 and 1943, and the winter of 1944–1945 marked the high plateau of the war effort. With the collapse of Germany, military discharges commenced, and these, as well as the withdrawal of emergency workers from the labor force, accelerated rapidly after the defeat of Japan. As a result, there was a rapid decline in total employment (inclusive of the armed forces) after the summer of 1945, a considerable rise in unemployment, and a substantial shrinkage in the size of the labor force due to the prompt withdrawal of the bulk of emergency workers. The seasonal peak of more than 68 million people in the labor force reached in July 1944 was not equaled again until 1953.

With the demobilization of the armed forces after V-J Day, however, the civilian labor force and civilian employment expanded rapidly, and soon reached the highest levels ever before attained.

SOURCES OF EMERGENCY LABOR SUPPLY

Essentially the emergency labor force of 8 million was drawn from three types of labor reserves: (1) Young people who would normally be attending school or college — mostly 14-to-19-year-olds and including those drafted into the armed forces — probably accounted for nearly half the total. (2) Married women apparently accounted for about a fourth of the emergency labor force. These consisted chiefly of the younger service wives and those of 35 to 64 years of age with lightened home responsibilities for younger children. (3) The remaining fourth was about equally divided between superannuated and retired workers and marginal workers who had little chance of finding jobs in the prewar economy.

Participation in the labor force of boys and girls from 14 to 19 years of age increased tremendously between March 1940 and April 1944, and these age groups alone accounted for about 50 per cent of the surplus workers in the labor market in early 1944. About 71 per cent of all boys 14 to 19 and 39 per cent of girls in this age range were in the labor force in April 1944, whereas the normal participation rates would have been about 37 per cent for boys and 19 per cent for girls. There was also a marked increase in the 20-to-24 age group on the part of both men and women, while considerable increases also occurred for men over 54 years of age and for women over 34. The smallest gains over normal participation occurred in the case of men in the 25-to-54 age groups, who are normally almost all in the labor force, and of 25-to-34-year-old women, whose responsibility for the care of younger children prevented their entrance into the labor market. (See Table 317.)

WARTIME INDUSTRIAL-OCCUPATIONAL CHANGES

The war brought at least a temporary reversal of many prewar industrial and occupational trends, as it did in the sex and age composition of the labor force. The great wartime emphasis on production, especially of munitions and durable goods, increased employment in manufacturing and mining enough to reverse the downward trend of recent decades. With the restriction

TABLE 317. PARTICIPATION IN LABOR FORCE OF PERSONS 14 YEARS OF AGE AND OVER BY SEX AND AGE GROUPS, 1940 AND 1944

| | Per Cent in Labor Force | | |
| | | April 1944 | |
Group	March 1940[a]	Normal	Actual
Total	54.1	54.6	61.7
Male	80.9	80.5	88.5
14–19	38.4	37.3	70.9
20–24	89.2	89.2	97.0
25–34	96.3	96.2	97.8
35–44	96.6	96.3	97.7
45–54	93.7	92.8	95.4
55–64	85.6	84.3	90.3
65 and over	43.3	40.7	48.8
Female	27.4	28.9	35.2
14–19	19.9	18.7	39.1
20–24	47.8	49.2	54.7
25–34	35.3	38.2	38.4
35–44	29.2	32.8	39.0
45–54	24.2	26.0	33.6
55–64	17.8	18.5	23.6
65 and over	6.7	6.4	7.5

Sources: March 1940 and actual April 1944 estimates from U.S. Bureau of the Census. "Normal" April 1944 estimates are based on the concepts and assumptions underlying the projections published in "A Projected Growth of the Labor Force in the United States under Conditions of High Employment: 1950 to 1975," Current Population Reports: Labor Force, U.S. Bureau of the Census, Series P–50, No. 42; these figures therefore reflect trends observed during the past several decades.

a. Figures refer to the last week in March, which was the period covered by the 1940 Census. The over-all labor force participation rate is a revision of that shown for 1940 on p. 722. The revision reflects primarily changes in techniques of measurement subsequently introduced by the Bureau of the Census.

of trade and service activities, and the curtailment of construction after completion of the war plants, employment in these branches drifted downward or failed to make relative gains.

It is true that employment increased in all large industrial divisions under the initial impact of the defense program, reflecting a general recovery stimulated and accelerated by government spending. As the program gained momentum, however, the character of economic activities changed rapidly. Employment gains were greatest between 1940 and 1941, amounting to about 4.2 million in all nonagricultural establishments. Between 1941 and 1942 the gain in the average number of nonagricultural employees was down to 3.5 million, and in the next year it dropped to 2.3 million. After 1943, when the war production program reached its peak, the number of nonagricultural employees began to fall off, and the average was down by more than half a million.

The expansion between 1940 and 1943 involved the addition of nearly 7 million workers in manufacturing and nearly 2 million in civilian government. Small gains occurred in all other industry divisions, except mining and finance, which were virtually at the same level in 1943 as in 1940. (See Table 318.)

Manufacturing showed widely varying employment trends. Durable goods added almost 6 million employees between 1940 and 1943 and nondurable goods less than one million. Machinery, transportation equipment, primary metal industries, and ordnance and accessories, in the durable goods group, and chemicals and allied products and rubber products in the nondurable group, made striking gains. On the other hand, printing, publishing and allied industries, and tobacco manufacturing employed fewer people in 1943 than before the war.

The monthly variations of employment in major industrial divisions from April 1943 to April 1944 suggest that the wartime plateau of civilian employment came some time toward the end of 1943. In early 1944 there was some decline in civilian employment, partly because demand for labor by munitions industries was slowly diminishing, and partly because labor reserves were becoming exhausted and the entrance of new workers could hardly offset the induction of men into the armed forces. Total employment continued to rise above the level of the same month the year before until V-J Day, largely because of the steady growth of the armed forces.

The decline in employment in war industries, which had started by the end of 1943, was accelerated after the German collapse. Cutbacks were made in shipbuilding, in aircraft plants and in the production of ordnance, but renewed production of some civilian goods partly offset these losses. After the surrender of Japan the war production program was drastically reduced; the sharp curtailment of war-industry employment tended, however, to be offset by expansion of civilian production.

WARTIME WORKING HOURS

At the time the defense program was inaugurated in the summer of 1940 we were still recovering from the depression of the 1930s. Because of

TABLE 318. NUMBER OF EMPLOYEES IN NONAGRICULTURAL ESTABLISHMENTS BY INDUSTRY DIVISION AND MAJOR MANUFACTURING INDUSTRY GROUP, 1940–1944 [a]

(*Thousands*)

Industry	1940	1941	1942	1943	1944
Total	32,031	36,164	39,697	42,042	41,480
Mining	916	947	983	917	883
Contract construction	1,294	1,790	2,170	1,567	1,094
Transportation and public utilities	3,013	3,248	3,433	3,619	3,798
Trade	6,940	7,416	7,333	7,189	7,260
Finance	1,419	1,462	1,440	1,401	1,374
Service	3,477	3,705	3,857	3,919	3,934
Government	4,192	4,622	5,431	6,049	6,026
Manufacturing	10,780	12,974	15,051	17,381	17,111
Durable goods	5,337	6,945	8,804	11,077	10,858
Ordnance and accessories	22	71	329	486	368
Lumber and wood products (including furniture and fixtures)	865	1,013	1,032	993	956
Stone, clay and glass products	366	430	432	422	395
Primary metal industries (including fabricated metal products) [b]	1,588	1,945	2,029	2,198	2,135
Machinery (except electrical)	779	1,053	1,365	1,628	1,588
Electrical machinery	442	598	744	968	1,043
Transportation equipment	834	1,297	2,259	3,666	3,682
Miscellaneous manufacturing industries	440	538	614	716	691
Nondurable goods	5,443	6,028	6,247	6,304	6,253
Food and kindred products	1,207	1,293	1,386	1,418	1,454
Tobacco manufactures	104	106	107	103	96
Textile mill products	1,212	1,372	1,375	1,326	1,225
Apparel and other finished textile products	904	1,024	1,063	1,084	1,058
Paper and allied products	333	372	376	389	388
Printing, publishing and allied industries	562	572	557	549	550
Chemicals and allied products	437	524	615	655	695
Products of petroleum and coal	159	169	176	176	189
Rubber products	153	184	183	226	242
Leather and leather products	371	412	410	378	356

Source: Handbook of Labor Statistics, 1950 edition, Bulletin No. 1016, U.S. Bureau of Labor Statistics, Table A–1, p. 5, and Table A–3, pp. 9 and 10.

a. Data include all full- and part-time employees in nonagricultural establishments who worked during, or received pay for, the pay period ending nearest the fifteenth of the month. These employment figures differ from those shown in Appendix 20–1. The figures in this table exclude proprietors, self-employed persons, domestic servants and personnel of the armed forces, but they may count the same individual in more than one job since they are based on establishment reports. The figures in Appendix 20–1 are all-inclusive, but they count an individual only once since they are based on household surveys.

b. Except ordnance, machinery and transportation equipment.

Note: Discrepancies in addition are due to rounding.

widespread unemployment and part-time work, actual average hours of work in nonagricultural pursuits were not much above what was coming to be regarded as the "normal 40 hours a week." Working hours increased gradually as the defense program got under way. Overtime work became quite common in 1942, when the average work week in nonagricultural activities had risen to around 43 hours and was lengthening steadily.

In manufacturing, average weekly hours of work advanced from 38.1 in 1940 to 40.6 in 1941, 42.9 in 1942 and 44.9 in 1943. In durable goods

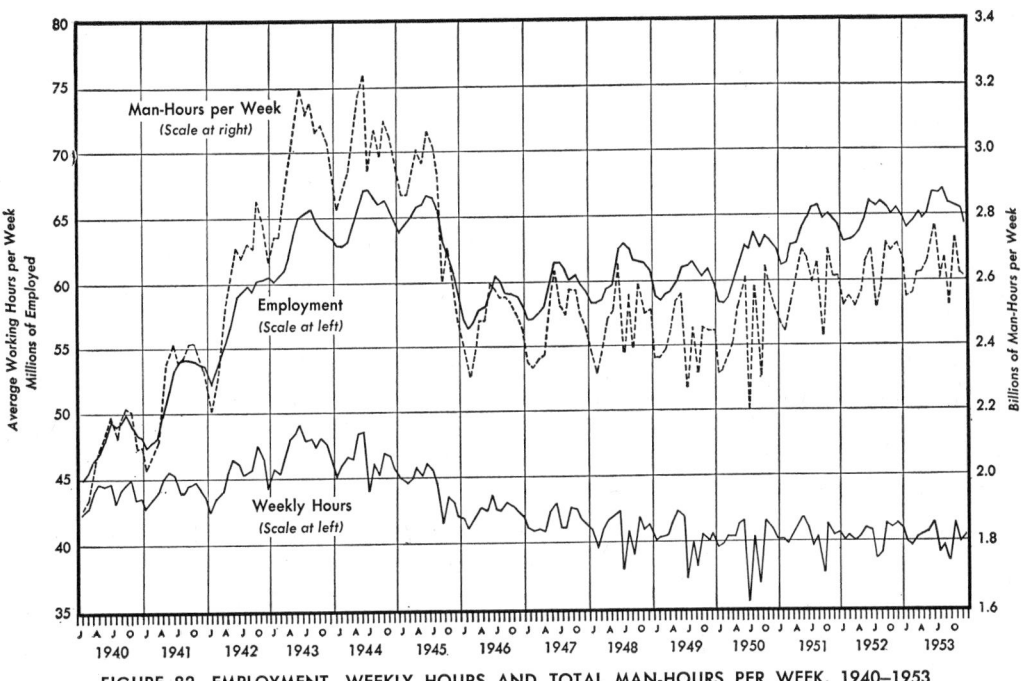

FIGURE 82. EMPLOYMENT, WEEKLY HOURS AND TOTAL MAN-HOURS PER WEEK, 1940–1953

Source: Appendix 20–1.

manufacturing, the average increased from 39.3 in 1940 to 46.6 in 1943, while nondurable goods showed a smaller gain over the four-year period — from 37.0 to 42.5 hours. Hours of work in bituminous coal mining moved irregularly upward after the war got under way, but did not rise much above 40 a week until the end of 1943 and early 1944. Only minor changes were recorded in retail trade, with an irregular downward trend until the spring of 1944, reflecting the closing of stores and shortage of goods.

On the whole it appears that average working time reached a peak of 49 hours a week in mid-1943, compared with an estimated average for the year of under 44 hours a week in 1940. This was an increase of about 12 per cent for agricultural and nonagricultural activities combined. Average working hours in nonagricultural employment reached a peak of over 46 a week in the fall of 1943, compared with about 41 in early 1940 before the defense program began. The agricultural work week reached a seasonal peak of more than 63 hours in the early summer of 1943 and averaged 58.5 hours for the year as a whole, compared with a seasonal peak of 59 hours and a monthly average for the year of 54.6 hours in 1940.

In mid-1944 the average work week began to decline below the levels reached during the same month of the year before. This was true of nonagricultural occupations as a whole, although bituminous coal mining showed fairly substantial increases and manufacturing and retail trade small gains. Beginning with June, each month of 1944 showed a decline from the corresponding month of the previous year in total average hours worked, and the average for the year was 46.2 hours a week, or about one hour less than the 1943 average of 47.3. In nonagricultural activities the 1944 average was 44.6 hours as compared with 45.1 in 1943. These declines continued in early 1945 and were sharply accelerated after the war ended.[28] It is apparent from these trends that the peak of the *industrial* war effort was passed in the winter of 1943–1944.

The monthly changes in employment and average weekly hours over the 1940–1945 period are shown in Figure 82, together with the fluctuations in total "labor effort," as measured by total man-hours per week. Total man-hours

---

28. See Appendix 20–1 for monthly data on hours of work in agricultural and nonagricultural activities; also Bureau of Labor Statistics publications for working hours in mining, manufacturing and retail trade.

worked rose from 1940 to 1943 but flattened out in 1944 because the continued rise in total employment (chiefly through expansion of the armed forces) was partially offset by the decline in the length of the work week.

POSTWAR ADJUSTMENTS

Readjustment of the war economy really began shortly after the peak of war production in the last months of 1943. Although the labor force did not stop rising above the corresponding month of the year before until mid-1945, the rise after mid-1943 was caused entirely by expansion of the armed forces. Between June 1943 and June 1945 the armed forces grew by 3.3 million while civilian employment was falling 1.7 million below its high point. Employment in war industries declined by about half a million in the first half of 1944 and continued downward, but at a somewhat slower pace, throughout the rest of the year. Working hours in the spring of 1944 also began to fall below the corresponding months of the previous year and this decline continued throughout the year.

The magnitude of the transition from war to peace can be visualized by considering the situation in April 1945. By that time close to a million munitions workers had already shifted to civilian activities, but the labor force had risen above 66 million with about half a million unemployed and about 8 million emergency workers in the labor market.[29] With close to 66 million at work, about 18 million were occupied in supplying the needs of the civilian population, about 25 million were employed in "mixed" war-civilian industries and 23 million were engaged in supplying war requirements. Of the latter, about 12 million were in the armed forces and 11 million in the "war" industries. On the face of it, this appeared to present the problem of finding peacetime jobs within a few years after the end of the war for a minimum of 23 million workers plus a good number of those in the "mixed" industries — in addition to providing work for normal accessions to the labor market.[30]

Reconversion of War Industry

Such an alarming picture of the difficulties of reconversion was of course wholly unrealistic.

29. See Appendix 20–1.
30. *The Labor Market and Employment Security*, U.S. Department of Labor, August 25, 1950, p. 39.

The fact that some of the 11 million "war"-industry workers and a large number of those in the mixed war-civilian industries were to go on working at the same jobs in the same factories was often overlooked in describing the difficulties of reconversion. Interestingly, in April 1950, before the Korea-induced expansion, nearly 9 million workers were still in "war"-industry jobs. In many other cases the shift to peacetime activities was made with little delay. Exactly the same products often serve both war and peacetime purposes, and plants turning out such products do not have to be converted to war or reconverted to peace. This is true of such raw material industries as coal mining, oil production, steel mills and lumber production, of foodstuffs, of many fabricated products such as machinery, and of transportation and utility services.

For some consumer goods, reconversion meant new product designs but no fundamental change in tools and techniques. This type of adjustment was possible in textiles, leather, rubber and chemical industries, as well as in the production of apparel, electrical machinery, optical goods, scientific, professional and photographic equipment, and the like. These enterprises were able to shift to peacetime production without interrupting operations for more than a few weeks. The short reconversion period gave enough time for deferred repairs of workshops and reshuffling of personnel, including replacement of emergency war workers by returning ex-servicemen.

Far-reaching reorganization and retooling were necessary in automobile and airplane factories, in shipyards, and in those machinery and chemical industries which had been converted to production of guns, munitions and explosives.

Transitional Unemployment

Although the demobilization of war personnel and reconversion of industry from war to peace proved a less formidable technical problem than was feared, it did involve some temporary unemployment, as well as the reduction and eventual elimination of overtime work.

Unemployment during the period of peak wartime activity dropped to the abnormally low level of about half a million. During the period of reconversion after the end of the war there was considerable turnover unemployment and temporary idleness while workers were returning to their prewar homes and jobs. Unemployment of this frictional kind rose to nearly 3 million in the early reconversion period and thereafter declined.

Curtailment of Working Hours

The average length of the work week reached its highest level of 49 hours in June 1943. Thereafter working time began to decline. For the year 1944 as a whole, the employed labor force worked about one hour less per week than in 1943. Curtailment of working hours continued in 1945 and was accelerated after the war's end, with the average for 1945 dropping two hours below the 1944 average.

However, certain industries continued to work more than 40 hours during the early part of the transition period. This was the case not only in the capital goods and construction industries, but also in many consumer goods industries, such as textiles.

Reduction of working hours from the wartime level to normal peacetime levels helped to ease the transition from a wartime to a peacetime economy by creating additional labor requirements for civilian production. For example, about 7 million fewer individuals would have been needed to supply the 130 billion man-hours worked in 1947 if average weekly hours had remained at the 1943 level of 47.3 instead of dropping to 41.7.

Deflation of the Labor Force

Re-employment of returning servicemen and of workers laid off by munitions industries was facilitated by the withdrawal of emergency war workers from the labor market. The labor force was expanded during the war at the price of temporary disorganization of the educational system and disruption of families and households, and by employment of the handicapped and superannuated.

The maximum of about 8 million emergency workers who were in the labor force in the winter of 1944–1945 consisted predominantly of those who expected to leave the labor market at the end of the war. True, not all the boys and girls who left school to enter the armed forces or to take office or factory jobs returned to school or college. Those who remained in the labor force, however, could no longer be considered a surplus group once they reached the age when they would normally have entered gainful work. This surplus, then, was progressively "liquidated" as the nation returned to the prewar pattern of school attendance.

Likewise most of the married women, especially service wives, were eager to return to their homes as soon as possible. This tendency was evident even at the peak of the war effort. After each layoff in war industries in early 1944, a large proportion of working women left the labor market — some temporarily, others for good. On the other hand, some of the married women who found jobs outside their homes during the war were inclined to stay in the labor force; but this again was in line with the long-range trend toward greater participation of women in the labor force. Most of the superannuated and handicapped workers were squeezed out of the labor market soon after the end of the war, although some remained to compete with one another for dwindling work opportunities. All but one million emergency workers had left the labor force within a year after the war's end.

THE LABOR FORCE AND FUTURE OUTPUT

The labor force, however, did not return to the level that would have been expected from a projection of prewar trends at any time during the 1940–1950 decade. As late as 1950, it was running about 2 million higher than "normal." (See Figure 77.)

Whether this was a permanent change that would have persisted during a period unmarked by hot- or cold-war demands on the labor force cannot be determined yet. The late 1940s were years of great economic activity during which we strove mightily to satisfy many of the wants left over from depression and war. Unemployment during most of these years was low by historical standards and jobs were plentiful, even for inexperienced and marginal workers. The 1949–1950 recession was too short-lived to exert much pressure in the direction of pushing people out of the labor force. The early 1950s were also years of extraordinary economic activity. First, the briefly interrupted postwar boom got under way again. Then on top of this came the impact of the rearmament program sparked by the Korean outbreak and kept alive by the uncertainties of the cold war. Thus our entire experience after the immediate postwar transition period and up until late 1953 was one of heavy pressures on the labor force — hardly a period conducive to a return to prewar "normality" in labor force trends!

Even in April 1954, after half a year of declining business activity during which unemployment rose from just over one million to almost 3.5 million, a higher proportion of the population was in the labor force than would normally have been expected after allowance for changing patterns during the war and immediate postwar years. Of all those 14 years of age and over, 58.1 per cent were in the labor force whereas in 1952 the Bureau of the Census, following 1920–1951 trends and assuming "a prosperous peace-time economy," projected a labor force participation rate of only 57.0 per cent for 1955 (no projection was shown for 1954). Not until 1975 was the over-all participation rate expected to exceed 58 per cent, and the increase was expected to come about primarily as a result of growth in the proportion of women in the labor force. Even though the Census Bureau projected a steadily rising rate of participation for women, it did not expect that rate to reach the 33.4 per cent observed in April 1954 until about 1960; the projection for 1955 was only 32.6 per cent.[31]

SIZE OF THE LABOR FORCE IN 1960

Although the labor force in the first half of this decade has remained somewhat larger than trends in labor force participation rates during the preceding three decades appeared to indicate, the projections chosen for 1960 in this study are based on those trends. This choice was made primarily because a basic assumption underlying all projections for this study is that the year 1960, although a very good one, would not be quite such a boom year as, say, 1951 or 1952. By 1960, therefore, any temporary inflation of the labor force should have disappeared and the long-term trends reflected in the Census Bureau's projections should be the best indicators of labor force participation rates. The projected rates imply that participation by women in the labor force will continue to increase, but at a decelerated pace; that child labor will continue its rapid decline until it has all but disappeared; and that the proportion of gainful workers among persons over 65 years of age will continue to fall, with the decline among older men more than offsetting

a continued increase in the percentage of older women in the labor force. The drop expected among men 65 and over reflects such trends as continued migration from farms to urban centers; reduced mortality rates, with the resultant increase in the number of old people in the population; and earlier retirement induced by the spread of public and private pension plans.

A further extension in the average period of formal education is expected to cut the rate of labor force participation for teen-agers of both sexes and for men in the early twenties. However, little change is foreseen for men between 25 and 64, the traditional core of the full-time labor force. They are expected to be in the labor force to the same extent that they have been during the past several decades.

The population projections with which the participation rates were combined to yield labor force estimates for 1960 are considerably more reliable than projections of total population for 1960. At present, the greatest variable in projecting population is the birth rate. But the population group considered for potential labor force membership in 1960 — those who will have reached their fourteenth birthday — is unaffected by future birth rates since all were alive at the time the projections were made. Changes in the size of this group can come only from deaths and migration. Although some uncertainty is involved in both these factors, they may be forecast with far greater certainty than birth rates, which have fluctuated sharply in the past.

The labor force estimated for 1960 from the application of participation rates to population by sex and age class came to 71.9 million. (See Table 319.) The participation rates upon which this estimate is based, however, reflect the April level of activity, which is about one per cent below the annual average. Consequently, the average labor force for 1960 was projected as 72.5 million, 10 per cent higher than the 1944 average of 65.9 million (the World War II peak) and 8 per cent above the 1953 average of 67.0 million.

During the 1950s the increase would average about 800,000, or 1.2 per cent, a year. This projection thus implies a slower rate of labor force growth during the present decade than during the 1940s — 12 per cent compared with 15 per cent. After 1960, however, as the large crop of babies born during and shortly after World War II reaches working age, the labor force should grow at a considerably more rapid rate — prob-

31. *Current Population Reports: Labor Force,* U.S. Bureau of the Census, Series P–50, No. 42, December 10, 1952, Table 1, p. 7.

TABLE 319. ESTIMATED LABOR FORCE BY AGE AND SEX, 1960 [a]

(*Number in Thousands*)

Age	Population			Per Cent of Population in Labor Force			Labor Force		
	Total	*Male*	*Female*	*Total*	*Male*	*Female*	*Total*	*Male*	*Female*
Total, 14 and over	126,317	61,640	64,677	56.9	81.2	33.8	71,919	50,081	21,838
14–19	16,147	8,207	7,940	37.0	46.7	27.0	5,977	3,833	2,144
20–24	11,282	5,697	5,585	68.3	88.0	48.2	7,705	5,013	2,692
25–34	22,650	11,232	11,418	66.6	96.5	37.2	15,086	10,839	4,247
35–44	23,948	11,710	12,238	69.4	96.9	43.0	16,609	11,347	5,262
45–54	20,908	10,198	10,710	66.6	94.2	40.3	13,923	9,607	4,316
55–64	15,681	7,517	8,164	56.8	86.8	29.2	8,909	6,525	2,384
65 and over	15,701	7,079	8,622	23.6	41.2	9.2	3,710	2,917	793

Sources: Population — Appendices 3–6 and 12–1. Participation rates — *Current Population Reports: Labor Force*, U.S. Bureau of the Census, Series P–50, No. 42, December 10, 1952, Table 1, p. 7. Labor force — derived from population and participation rate estimates.

a. Trends on which these labor force estimates are based reflect the April level of activity, which is about one per cent below the annual average. The average number in the total labor force in 1960 is estimated at 72.5 million.

ably by 1.2 million, or 1.5 per cent, a year — about the same rate as during the 1940s.[32]

UTILIZATION AND PRODUCTIVITY OF LABOR IN 1960 [33]

What we can produce with a labor force of 72.5 million in 1960 will depend on the extent to which the labor force is utilized and on its productivity at high levels of activity. The number of persons actually at work, the average length of the work week and the amount produced per man-hour will determine the total output of goods and services.

Employment

How much unemployment is consistent with "high-level employment" of the labor force is essentially a matter of definition about which there are honest differences of opinion among competent investigators. Certainly all of them would agree that complete "full employment" can never be achieved. Even at the peak of the war effort, when demand for labor was strong enough to have drawn 8 million emergency workers into the labor market, between half a million and a million job seekers were out of work.

For the purposes of this survey it seemed realistic to assume that an attainable high level of activity for the future would be roughly comparable to what was actually maintained during the prosperous last half of the 1920s, rather than to a theoretical maximum of "full employment" and "capacity operation of the economy." In view of the volume of unemployment in past periods of prosperity, and especially during the 1920s, an assumption that high levels of activity in the future would involve average unemployment amounting to about 5 per cent of the labor force appeared to be reasonable.

On this basis, approximately 3.5 million of the 1960 labor force of 72.5 million would be unemployed, and 69 million would be at work. These assumptions compare with an actual labor force numbering 64.6 million in 1950, when an average of 3.1 million were out of work and 61.5 million

were employed. Allowing for government employment of 10.5 million in 1960, private employment would be 58.5 million. (See Appendix 20-4.)

Hours of Work

The trend of working hours both in agriculture and in nonagricultural activities has been steadily downward over the past century, and this trend appears to have been accelerated in recent decades. The estimated average work week in agriculture fell from about 72 hours in the 1850–1860 decade to between 54 and 55 hours in 1940, and then dropped rapidly to just over 47 hours in 1950. In nonagricultural activities the average work week declined by more than a third from 1850 to 1930 — from an average of 65.7 hours a week to 43.2. By 1950 an additional 4.4 hours had been transferred to leisure time. This has meant an average decline in the length of the work week over the entire period of about 3 hours a decade.[34]

There is every reason to believe that this long-term decline in working hours did not end abruptly in 1950, even though the Korean emergency kept the average work week close to the 1950 level of 40 hours during 1951–1953. The goal of the 40-hour week had been attained by 1950, but the goal has changed. Talk of a 35-hour week is now heard.

It has been assumed (as explained in Chapter 2) that the average work week in nonagricultural pursuits would fall from 38.8 hours in 1950 to 36.5 hours in 1960, and that average hours in agriculture would decline from slightly above 47 a week in 1950 to 44 in 1960. This would mean that at high levels of economic activity in 1960 the work week for agricultural and nonagricultural pursuits combined would average 37.5 hours. Since the estimated average work week in 1950 was 40 hours, this would mean a decline of 2.5 hours in the present decade. Part of this decline is expected to come about from further extension of paid vacations.[35]

---

32. See *Current Population Reports: Labor Force*, U.S. Bureau of the Census, Series P–50, No. 42, December 10, 1952, p. 2.

33. See Chapter 2 for a discussion of the assumptions regarding employment and unemployment, as well as hours of work and productivity.

34. See Appendix 20–4 for estimates of the average work week for 1850 and every tenth year thereafter to 1940, and Chapter 2 for a discussion of these trends.

35. The average weekly hours used here for recent years are based on estimates in *Current Population Reports: Labor Force*, U.S. Bureau of the Census, Series P–50. The Census estimates, however, were adjusted by including in computation of the average those employed workers classified by the Census as with a job but not at work. Since these individuals had zero hours of work during

Productivity

Labor productivity, or output per man-hour, of those employed in 1960 is the third factor determining the productive capacity of the labor force. Recent changes in labor productivity have been discussed earlier in this chapter, and the long-term trend in average output per man-hour in Chapter 2.

Over the 100-year period from 1850 to 1950, output per man-hour, as measured by private national income [36] in constant prices, multiplied almost sixfold. The average rate of increase in productivity has been about 18.4 per cent a decade. The rate, however, appears to have been accelerating slowly over the years and long-term trends indicate a probable rise of about 25 per cent during the present decade.[37] This would mean that net output per man-hour — as measured by private national income at 1950 prices — would increase to about $2.40 in 1960.

PRODUCTIVE CAPACITY OF THE LABOR FORCE IN 1960

The productive capacity of the future labor force, or the output of goods and services that would be produced at high levels of activity, can of course be readily determined — granting the assumptions stated above. These assumptions, it must be remembered, contemplate "normal" conditions of high-level activity rather than the operation of our economy under "forced draft" as at the peak of the war effort in 1943–1945. The war emergency demonstrated our ability to increase substantially our capacity to produce by expanding the labor force and employing a larger proportion of it, and by lengthening the workday and the work week.

Under "Normal" Conditions

With 58.5 million persons in private employment working an average of 37.5 hours a week in 1960, total private man-hours for the 52-week year would amount to 114 billion. Private national income, on the basis of a net output of $2.40 per man-hour, would amount to about $275 billion at 1950 prices. This would imply a total national income of $312.5 billion and a gross

national product of about $370 billion (at 1950 prices).

Under "Emergency" Conditions

Under the pressure of war's imperative, we were able to produce a much larger volume of goods and services than would have been possible at the hours of work prevailing at the time the defense program began — even if we had had relatively full employment of the normal labor force. This great expansion of output was made possible largely by (1) employing most of the unemployed workers, (2) adding millions of emergency workers to the labor force, and (3) increasing hours of work. These three methods of expanding our capacity to produce would be available to us in any future emergency.

To begin with, a future emergency might be expected to reduce the number of unemployed to about one per cent of the labor force — as at the peak of the recent war effort. This would mean that about 2.5 million out of 3.5 million who would be unemployed under normal conditions would be added to the force actually at work in 1960. The number of emergency workers that might be added to the labor force during a national emergency in 1960 is more difficult to foretell. One guide is the extent to which different population groups participated in the labor force during World War II. Although the overall peak was reached in 1945, when 62.3 per cent of those 14 years of age and over were in the labor force compared with 54.1 per cent in 1940, not all groups reached their peaks at the same time. Men between the ages of 14 and 44 reached their highest rates of participation in 1944, but older men and all women regardless of age reached their highest participation rates only in 1945.

The World War II peak rates for men in all age classes were considerably higher than the projected rates for 1960 under nonemergency conditions. (See Table 319.) As a result of the rapidly rising trend in labor force participation of women, however, World War II peaks are likely to be exceeded even under normal conditions in 1960 for women aged 35 and over. In a wartime emergency these rates probably would be pushed up further but, because of the reduced "slack" between 1944 and 1960, the increase above "normal" probably would be relatively smaller in a future emergency. A reasonable set of assumptions for participation in the 1960 labor force under emergency conditions, therefore,

---

the week, the adjusted averages are lower than those published by the Census Bureau. However, they automatically make allowance for people on vacation, who are counted as with a job but not at work.

36. Private national income excludes compensation of government employees.

37. See Figure 5 and related discussion in Chapter 2.

would seem to be the following: (1) rates equal to World War II peaks for men in all age classes and for women between 14 and 34 years of age; and (2) rates equal to the "normal" projections for 1960 plus half the difference between April 1945 normal and actual rates for women 35 years of age and over. These assumptions would yield the following "emergency" labor force participation rates for 1960: [38]

Age Class	Male	Female
	(Per Cent)	
14–19 years	70.9	39.6
20–24 years	97.0	55.6
25–34 years	97.8	40.5
35–44 years	97.7	46.0
45–54 years	95.8	45.3
55–64 years	90.5	33.6
65 years and over	50.0	10.7

The size of the labor force in 1960 indicated by these ratios would be about 79 million at the April level, which would mean an average labor force of 80 million for the year, or the addition of about 7.5 million emergency workers. These 7.5 million workers plus the 2.5 million unemployed who would be put to work would add 10 million to the employment rolls.

If these admittedly speculative — but not extravagant — assumptions are correct, it would be possible to expand employment from the assumed normal of 69 million to 79 million under the stress of an emergency in 1960. This is by no means the absolute maximum. It would be very possible to draw still more workers into the labor force if the national emergency required it. Even at the height of World War II, we had not begun to exhaust available means of inducing workers into the labor force and we had, of course, done relatively little — the military draft excepted — in the way of forcing people into work. In a dire emergency additional measures surely would be taken. The 80-million-member "emergency" labor force projected for 1960 merely indicates the level we could reach under emergency conditions essentially similar to those of World War II.

Speculation about the maximum length of the work week that could be achieved under emergency pressures in 1960 is surrounded with even greater uncertainties than an attempt to estimate how many additional workers could be drawn into the labor market. With the extension of overtime work and the progressive elimination of

vacations, the length of the work week increased from an estimated average of 43.8 hours for the year 1940 to 47.3 hours for 1943, or 8 per cent.

It would probably be a mistake to assume that the 1943 average could be maintained under comparable conditions in 1960. The downward trend of working hours over the past several decades has been partly a matter of choice because increased productivity made it possible to enjoy more leisure as well as more goods, but also partly a matter of necessity because the increased tempo of work in modern industry makes a shorter workday essential. With continuing increase in productivity over the next decade, it is more reasonable to assume a maximum work week shorter than at the peak of World War II. On the other hand, it seems logical to conclude that the progressive shortening of the work week assumed in this survey for the 1950 decade will provide sufficiently greater "elasticity" to permit much more than an 8 per cent expansion under emergency conditions. What the effect of these conflicting influences will be can only be a matter of judgment, but it may not be out of line to conclude that the maximum work week under emergency conditions in 1960 would be at least 45 hours.

During World War II productivity (measured in terms of private national income per private man-hour) rose considerably. Between the last substantially prewar year, 1941, and the peak war year, 1944, the rise was about 18 per cent.[39] Although this experience is hardly conclusive, it furnishes some evidence that productivity for the private part of the economy can be increased under emergency conditions — perhaps by as much as one fifth over a three-year period. Such an assumption would raise private national income per man-hour to about $2.70 (expressed in 1950 prices) under "emergency" conditions in 1960.[40]

---

38. Based on data supplied by U.S. Bureau of the Census.

39. The economic meaning of the increase in productivity measured in this fashion is not clear. The difficulty of pricing many special wartime products raises serious questions about the accurate measurement of national income — and productivity estimates derived therefrom — during wartime. Clarence D. Long concluded that "It may be impossible to tell whether aggregate output per man-hour . . . went up or down." (*Manpower Needs and the Labor Supply*, American Enterprise Association, New York, 1951, p. 29.) However, in order to estimate the gross national product in terms of the statistical framework of this volume, it seems desirable to follow patterns revealed by estimates for the World War II period.

40. This is 20 per cent above the $2.25 level which would be reached three years earlier (in 1957) in line with the assumptions underlying the projection of $2.40 for 1960 under "normal" conditions (see Figure 5).

If the 79 million workers who would be employed under such conditions in that year were distributed between private and public employment as they were at the height of World War II, about 59 million would be in private jobs and 20 million in government service — as civilian employees and members of the armed forces. With 59 million people in private employment working an average of 45 hours a week, total private man-hours would amount to 138 billion. At $2.70 per man-hour, private national income would come to $373 billion (at 1950 prices). Past relationships between public national income [41] as a percentage of total national income and government employment as a percentage of total employment indicate that 20 million public employees in 1960 would account for about 18 per cent of total national income. On this basis, total national income would be estimated at roughly $450 billion (at 1950 prices). If indirect taxes and capital consumption allowances equal 12 per cent of gross national product, as they did in 1944, the gross national product under emergency conditions in 1960 would reach slightly more than $500 billion (at 1950 prices). Thus, the labor force working at maximum capacity in

1960 would be able to turn out over a third more in goods and services than under "normal" conditions, and about three fourths again as much as in 1944, the peak World War II year, when gross national product equaled $288 billion at 1950 prices.

These rough estimates make it clear that we can greatly surpass normal output under the pressure of necessity, as we did during the last war. But experience during the war also makes it clear that, although the labor supply constitutes the ultimate ceiling on production, it is only one of the determinants of our productive capacity. Almost four years passed after the defense program began in the summer of 1940 before we were able to mobilize and coordinate all the material and human resources needed to achieve capacity operation of our economy in turning out a gross national product more than 40 per cent of which was devoted to war purposes. Whether or not as much time would be required to meet a comparable future emergency, it is clear that the "reserve labor capacity" — that is, the difference between the normal volume of employment and length of the work week and those under emergency conditions — can be drawn into use only gradually and by means of increasing incentives and pressures.

41. Defined as equal to government wages and salaries plus supplements to wages and salaries (see Chapter 2).

## CHAPTER 21

NATURAL RESOURCES

OUR NATION, looking toward a future of continuing economic progress, is well-advised to take stock of its natural resources. Industry can expand only so far as raw materials are available. Their supply and nature may be such as to dictate new directions of development, permit advancement along established channels, or block further growth.

The United States, with 6 per cent of the world's population and 7 per cent of the land area, already produces an almost incredible share of the world's industrial goods — about 40 per cent of the total.

In 1950, the American economy consumed 2.5 billion tons of industrial raw materials and foods, or about 18 tons per capita. Fuel consumption alone amounted to 7 tons per capita. The next bulkiest group was nonmetallic building materials — lumber, stone, sand, gravel, etc.— which amounted to 5 tons per capita. About 2.5 tons of ores per capita were required to yield four tenths of a ton of metals. To these amounts of materials must be added a little less than half a ton of miscellaneous nonmetallic minerals, such as lime, fertilizers and chemical raw materials.

Among replenishable raw materials, pulpwood and agricultural products other than foods — mostly cotton, wool, other fibers and industrial oils — were consumed at the rate of a little more than 2 tons per capita. Finally, each person consumed 1,600 pounds of food, or almost 4.5 pounds a day, including all wastage and losses.

The value of the individual materials consumed, of course, varied greatly. Nevertheless, their sheer bulk gives some idea of the tremendous amount of handling, processing and transportation required to satisfy our standard of living.[1]

Of many raw materials the United States consumes as much as all the rest of the world combined. It accounts for about half the world's steel capacity, for example, now that the post-Korean expansion has been completed. It consumes more than half of the world's crude petroleum and nine tenths of the world's natural gas. It is the leading consumer of nearly every industrial raw material, and, with some notable exceptions, is also the leading producer. In the postwar period of vigorous industrial activity, the United States has been the world's largest consumer of every major metal and of fuels (except peat), sulfur, phosphates, cement, feldspar, bromine, fluorspar, mica, gypsum and asbestos. In the same period, it has ranked first as a producer of iron ore, copper, aluminum, lead, zinc, molybdenum, vanadium, coal, petroleum, natural gas, sulfur, phosphates, cement, feldspar, bromine, fluorspar, mica and gypsum.[2]

THE PROBLEM OF NATURAL RESOURCES

Some observers of this remarkable performance point with alarm to the denuding of the soil and the depletion of key minerals. They foresee for the United States — and not far off — the fate of those Old World nations which retrogressed after gaining first rank. Before accepting such a dire prediction (or even the thesis that the goal of full and increasingly efficient employment cannot be met), we should note that the depletion of some resources is avoidable, and depletion in any case is significant only if what remains cannot be used advantageously. Despite man's seemingly devastating exploitation, he has merely scratched a small segment of this gigantic ball of resources on which he lives. Our power to use the materials in nature is growing

BY WILBERT G. FRITZ, Consultant on Materials, Office of Defense Mobilization. Opinions and judgments expressed in this chapter are those of the author and should not be attributed to the organization with which he is associated.

1. Data are taken from *Resources for Freedom*, President's Materials Policy Commission, June 1952, Vol. I, p. 4.
2. See data in *Minerals Yearbook, 1950*, U.S. Bureau of Mines, and preprints for 1951; *Statistical Yearbook, 1952*, United Nations, New York; *Statistical Summary of the Mineral Industry, 1942–1948*, Colonial Geological Survey, His Majesty's Stationery Office, London, 1950; and Office of Defense Mobilization announcements of expansion goals of the United States.

rather than diminishing, through favorable technology and economic organization.

As a springboard for assessing the future, we need answers to two basic questions: How much effort is now being applied to supplying raw materials in the United States? How large and versatile is our usable stock of natural resources?

EFFORTS APPLIED TO MATERIALS

The answer to the first question is simple. The United States has progressed to the point where it devotes only a small share of its efforts to producing raw materials. It no longer faces the plight of underdeveloped areas, which must work incessantly — and with varying success — to produce enough food and other bare essentials to ward off starvation. The United States has a large reserve of manpower which it applies to a multitude of other pursuits. A small part of this reserve occupies itself with exploring, studying and experimenting to discover resources and to devise more thorough and efficient uses of them.

Supplying materials other than foods in crude form, from farms, forests, mines and marine sources, is estimated to occupy 4.5 per cent of the total manpower engaged in all gainful pursuits in the United States. Even after allowing for converting the materials into usable form, such as processing crude ores into refined metals, and for transporting the materials to centers of consumption, the supply of materials appears to require less than 10 per cent of the total national manpower. Mining and forestry together account for about 2 per cent of total employment. Fishing accounts for less than one fifth of one per cent and agriculture for about 15 per cent of the total. But about 80 per cent of the value of agricultural production and a large share of the fish caught are used as foods, which are not counted as raw materials in this discussion. Thus despite its prodigious consumption, our economy is not primarily a raw materials economy, thanks to a favorable combination of resources and methods of using the resources.[3]

---

3. Estimates in this paragraph have been prepared from data on persons employed in occupations and industry groups in 1940 and 1950 and in manufacturing in 1947 as reported in *Statistical Abstract of the United States, 1951,* U.S. Bureau of the Census, pp. 173–177, 182–185 and 747–758, supplemented by estimates of the value of agricultural output in President's Materials Policy Commission, *op. cit.,* Vol. V, p. 64, Table III.

DETERMINANTS OF RESOURCE ADEQUACY

The extent of usable resources is much more difficult to estimate than the effort required to supply them. It cannot be determined by a routine recording of physical quantities, for the quality and utility of resources are almost infinitely variable. The volume of commercially accessible reserves, economies in use, the discovery of new sources, the discovery of new materials, the use of a wider variety of materials — all these, and other considerations, determine the usable supply.

Gross Supply of Resources

We are not yet able to exploit fully any of the more abundant elements, though we are making headway in that direction. We are beginning to take advantage of more "dilute" resources. Where once only highly concentrated mineral deposits were used, now deposits of low concentration are worked on a large scale. In obtaining magnesium from sea water, for example, we are making use of a source in which the metal occurs in less than its *average* concentration at the earth's surface. Taking inventory of the elements in the earth's crust is no longer merely of interest to academic geologists. It suggests the direction of our materialistic development.

Most minerals appear in nature in combination with other minerals not regarded as immediately useful. Physical scientists and engineers are developing ways to discover resources, to break them up more readily into usable elements, to separate wanted from unwanted substances and to find uses for those minerals formerly discarded. More and more, science is going back to the atom as the building block of materials, working out ingenious combinations to meet our complex needs.

Some chemical elements are so rare that they are most difficult to isolate and identify; others are abundant. Almost half of the earth's crust (defined to include terrestrial matter to a depth of ten miles and the earth's enveloping atmosphere) consists of oxygen, mostly in combination with other elements. Silicon constitutes about a fourth of the total.

Other elements are much less plentiful. Aluminum, at 7.5 per cent of the earth's crust, ranks ahead of iron (4.7 per cent). In fifth place is calcium (3.4 per cent); sixth, sodium (2.6 per cent); seventh, potassium (2.4 per cent); and eighth, magnesium (1.9 per cent). The next two elements run considerably far behind but nevertheless are relatively abundant: hydrogen (0.9 per cent) and titanium (0.6 per cent). Difficult though it is to believe, all the other elements combined amount to only a little more than one per cent of the total. Each of the commonly used metals — copper, lead, zinc, tungsten, cobalt, tin, antimony, cadmium and mercury — forms less than 0.02 per cent of the earth's crust, or less than one half of one per cent as much as aluminum or iron.[4]

How these elements are distributed over the earth is not known for certain. A plausible guess is that the United States, with its diverse geological structure, has a share of the more plentiful elements about proportional to its area, but not of the scarcer ones, such as nickel, tin and chromium.

Exhaustibility

Despite our scientific and technological progress in using more "dilute" sources, the economic availability of materials still depends heavily on favorable combinations and concentrations of chemical elements. Thus we must face the possibility of practical exhaustion of certain materials — copper, lead, zinc, silver and so on — even though our total supply of each may be thousands of times as great as the amount we use yearly.

The degree of exhaustibility, of course, varies immensely. Some readily usable resources occur in such abundance that exhaustion is no threat. This happy situation prevails for nitrogen from the atmosphere and magnesium from sea water, as well as for many of the bulky building materials — stone, sand, gravel and clays. Other resources, though not available in unlimited quantities, are renewable. Probably the best example is solar energy, supplied daily in varying amounts according to the length of the day and atmospheric conditions. Supplies of fresh water are renewed continually, thanks to the sun, and can be stored and regulated in their flow by man. Forests will renew themselves if protected from destruction, but require a long time to complete the cycle. Even the soil and some minerals are at least partially renewable, but the waiting period is too long to meet our needs.

4. Data from Paul M. Tyler, *From the Ground Up,* McGraw-Hill, New York, 1948, p. 153.

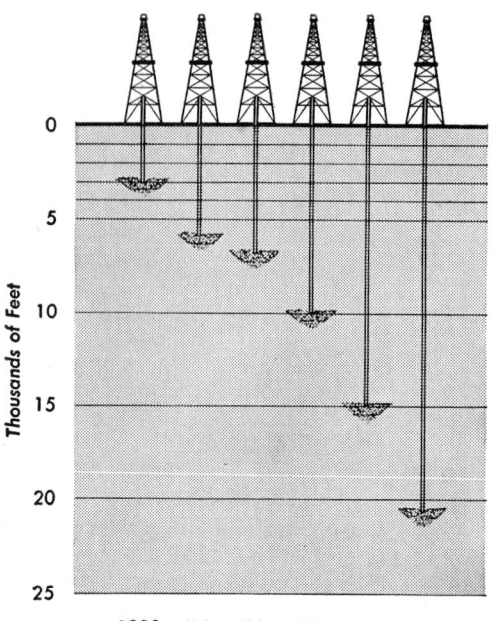

FIGURE 83. MAXIMUM DEPTH OF OIL WELLS DRILLED IN THE UNITED STATES, 1900–1950

Source: *Petroleum Productive Capacity,* National Petroleum Council, Washington, 1952, chart on p. 49.

At the opposite extreme are those resources which, once used or destroyed, are gone forever. For all practical purposes, coal, oil, natural gas and all metals are irreplaceable. Metals and other durable materials, however, are in part merely stored for a time when used in products, and can be returned for further use in the form of scrap. A portion continues in service until lost by abrasion, corrosion or conversion to a form in which recovery is uneconomical.[5]

The supply of some of our most valuable resources is diminishing rapidly. Reserves of high-grade bauxite in Arkansas, formerly the nation's main source of aluminum, are approaching an end. Domestic lead reserves are so meager that production is lower than in the 1920s even though the demand is large. Steel companies, un-

5. The extent to which scrap can be a source of materials in the future is a matter of dispute. The case for substantial recovery is well illustrated by R. M. Weidenhammer in "Two Methods of Estimating the U.S. Demand of Copper, Lead and Zinc, 1947–1960," *Mining Year Book,* 1947, pp. 13–20. On the other hand, Donald M. Liddell states, in a communication discussing the subject, that the idea is vastly overdone. He points out that Germany with its immense copper imports over two generations did not have enough copper for its war needs, despite all possible salvage both in its own and conquered areas.

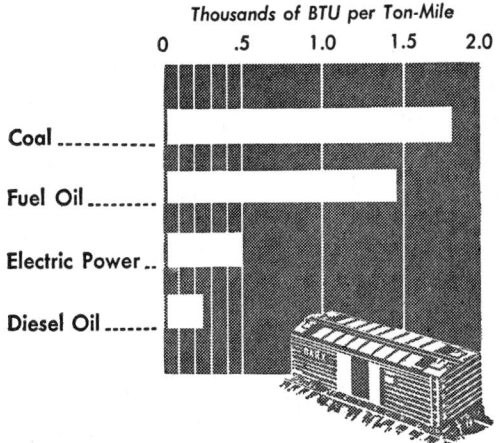

Thousands of BTU per Ton-Mile

0   .5   1.0   1.5   2.0

Coal ....

Fuel Oil ....

Electric Power ..

Diesel Oil ....

FIGURE 84. FUEL EFFICIENCY IN RAILROAD FREIGHT SERVICE, 1949

Source: Interstate Commerce Commission, *Study of Railroad Motive Power,* File No. 66–A–11, Statement No. 5025, May 1950, Appendix G, for quantity of fuels per ton-mile. The following conversion factors were used: coal, 13,100 BTU per pound; fuel oil, 149,000 BTU per gallon; diesel oil, 138,000 BTU per gallon; electric power, 1.22 pounds of coal per kilowatt-hour.

certain of a continuing supply of iron ore in the Lake Superior district, are turning to lower-grade domestic ores and to high-grade foreign resources. Many of the most accessible coal beds have been mined out completely. The National Petroleum Council estimates, in a recent report, that the domestic production of crude petroleum is likely to register only a small gain after 1955.[6]

Depletion may become a serious problem if flagrant waste is not sharply reduced and if techniques of using lower-grade resources fail to keep abreast of needs. Thus far, technology has more than kept pace. Sixty years ago copper deposits of less than 3 per cent metal content would have been considered poor; now the average grade is less than one per cent. A few decades ago aluminum was so difficult to extract and so costly that it was scarcely used at all; now it ranks second only to steel in terms of metal volume. Coal was strip-mined only if under a shallow cover; now as much as a hundred feet of cover is removed. The search for oil, particularly, has pushed us to greater efforts. The deepest oil well drilled in 1900 was about 3,000 feet; by 1950 the world's deepest well went down more than 20,000 feet — about four miles. (See Figure 83.)

6. *Petroleum Productive Capacity,* National Petroleum Council, Washington, D.C., 1952, pp. 25–28.

At least part of the materials problem of the future, nevertheless, has been solved or is close to solution. Unlimited supplies of nitrogen and magnesium can now be drawn from the atmosphere and sea water, respectively, as long as power and facilities can be provided. We are approaching the same mastery of production of aluminum and iron from low-grade resources, again provided power and facilities are available. The main roadblocks to the future are possible shortages of power itself and of certain materials essential to construct facilities for extracting materials which occur in nature in ample quantities.

Economy in Use

The urge to reduce costs, and imminent exhaustion of some vital raw materials, have encouraged economy in consumption. Railroads, for example, have effected substantial economies through more efficient use of fuel. The coal-consuming "iron horse" is being replaced by diesel locomotives, which are about seven times as efficient as steam locomotives in the use of fuel in freight service and twice as efficient as electrified lines. (See Figure 84.) Diesels, in fact, could have replaced all of the 38,000 steam locomotives in use in 1948 and would still have consumed less oil than the 6,000 oil-burning steam locomotives then in service.[7]

Striking economies have also been achieved in the use of tin. Electroplating as a replacement of the hot-dip method of producing tin plate saves 60 per cent of this scarce metal.[8] When the supply of tin from the Far East was cut off during World War II, the electrolytic process relieved much of the shortage. Other ways to save tin were found: reducing the amount of solder used for various purposes; reducing the tin content of solder; replacing tin plate by glass, plastics, lacquered metal and other materials.

Reductions in size and weight of end products are saving vast quantities of materials. "Miniaturization" is reducing the need for scarce materials in the rapidly growing electronics industry. Light-weight aggregates, light-metal components, curtain walls and other innovations are enabling us to construct less massive buildings. Engines are doing more work per pound

7. Press release of Electro-Motive Division, General Motors Corporation, LaGrange, Illinois, September 26, 1948.
8. Douglas A. Fisher, *Steel Making in America,* United States Steel Corporation, New York, 1949, p. 81.

of weight, jet engines most particularly. One modern jet fighter plane has enough power to pull 360 freight cars, fully loaded. The six diesel locomotives which would normally be required for the job weigh ninety times as much as the plane.[9]

Laurels for the ultimate in work per unit of material go to atomic energy, which, even at low efficiency, releases 20,000 times as much energy as nitroglycerin. The smashing of the hydrogen atom (which has no known peacetime application) has stepped up the energy output per unit of material many times over.

Such multiplication of work by given quantities of materials does not necessarily solve the materials problem. Atomic energy requires resources that are relatively scarce. Savings of iron may depend heavily on the use of scarce alloying metals — in jet engines, for example. But small quantities of boron and rare earths can replace large amounts of the scarce additive alloys used in making steel. Progress along these lines taxes our ingenuity to find new fissionable materials to smash and new materials to save materials.

Use of Wider Variety of Resources

We are expanding the capacity of our resources by drawing on a wider variety and using them in new and more complex ways. A few decades ago gasoline, aluminum, magnesium, chromium, molybdenum and tungsten, to cite a few examples, were rarely used. Yet today they are so important that a shortage of supply is cause for serious concern. We have learned during the past several decades, and particularly during World War II, that substitutes and varied combinations can play an extremely important part in expanding our supply of materials. Synthetic rubber takes its place beside natural rubber and even crowds it out for many uses. The basic products obtained by refining and purifying crude materials may be shaped into myriad forms the complexity of which is limited only by our state of technological advancement.

The innovations in the field of plastics have been among the most spectacular. Before World War II, plastics were used mainly for such simple items as novelties, ornaments, radio and electrical appliance parts, and decorative buttons. The demands of the war period brought forth

new varieties of plastic materials, many of them stronger, able to withstand wide and sudden temperature changes, and resistant to chemicals and salt water. Largely because of these improvements, we discovered countless new ways of using plastics. Not only have they proved acceptable as substitutes for scarce metals where high tensile and impact strength is required, but they have proved to be superior in many applications, even in products which must stand such stress as machinery bearings.[10]

Thousands of products, including some of the modern wonder drugs, are produced from coal tar, a by-product of coke manufacture. The petroleum industry has discovered that it can reproduce almost any hydrocarbon material — at a cost, but sometimes more cheaply than from any other source. In petrochemicals a whole new field is developing.[11]

Hundreds of forest research projects are concerned with new uses for wood, especially with using more of the tree and with finding ways to use "inferior" species. Wood waste has become a source of plastics, rayon, molasses for cattle feed, and alcohol for industry; compressed with binders, it forms construction materials. Many logging operations are reported to be taking 20 per cent more usable material from the same type of forest than before World War II.[12]

New Resources and Sources of Supply

Discovery will continue to play an important part in making more resources available to us — through disclosing new sources of materials, new techniques of recovering materials, and more economical ways of using them.

Mineral Exploration

Supplies of minerals which occur in widespread deposits — clays, limestone, coal, granite and so on — are already comparatively well known. Information is spotty, in contrast, for those minerals which occur only in small, scat-

9. *Planes*, Aircraft Industries Association of America, May 1952, p. 4.

10. See Herbert R. Simonds, Archie J. Weith and M. H. Bigelow, *Handbook of Plastics*, Van Nostrand, New York, 1949, and article on "Plastic Bearings," *South African Mining and Engineering Journal*, March 22, 1952, p. 143.
11. See W. E. Kuhn, "Petrochemistry Comes of Age," *Texaco Star*, The Texas Company, New York, Petrochemical Number, 1952, pp. 3–8.
12. "The Nation's Wood Supply," American Forest Products Industries, Inc., Washington, D.C., 1951, pp. 19–21.

tered deposits, notably petroleum, natural gas, sulfur, and nearly all high-grade metallic ores. But the chances of finding further supplies of these are decreasing, because we have already explored many frontiers and exhausted many possibilities. We will be forced, therefore, to give more attention to low-grade and less accessible resources.

The pick-and-shovel prospector will soon strike pay dirt only in western movies. From now on, discovery of really new sources of minerals will generally require both a knowledge of geology and use of special instruments and equipment designed to detect hidden ore bodies. Geological information provides general guidance, but usually must be supported by other investigation.

Extensive use is being made of geophysical records of the electrical, seismic and thermal characteristics of rock formations. The location and density of underground strata, for example, can be determined at the surface with surprising accuracy by measuring the rate at which sound travels through various media. This method of exploration has been especially successful in the petroleum industry. Geochemistry — the chemical analysis of soils, rocks, surface or ground water, or plants — sometimes discloses mineral concentrations. Recently, for example, the leaves and twigs of trees in the mineralized area of the Nigerian lead-zinc belt have been found to contain up to 270 times as much lead as those in the unmineralized area.[13]

One of the most significant contributions to mineral exploration in recent years has been the development of methods of scanning wide areas by air. Airborne magnetometers, measuring the variations in the earth's magnetic field caused by magnetic rocks, are being used to map petroleum, natural gas, magnetite and other mineral deposits. The scintillometer, based on the fact that all minerals are more or less radioactive, detects deposits from the air by counting the number of gamma rays emanating from the earth's surface. A still more recent device, the electromagnetic surveyor, sets up a secondary current in ore bodies and then registers the magnetic field by highly sensitive receivers.

All these quick surveys by air, however, give only general indications of mineral occurrences. As a rule, no kind of surface exploration can

provide positive proof of concealed ore bodies. Drilling is necessary to yield samples for assaying, cores of the formations, or the valuable information of well logs.

Mining

In mining, as in prospecting, pick-and-shovel methods have all but disappeared. Power drills and cutting machines, mechanical loaders and electrical rail haulage or continuous conveyor belts have greatly increased the productivity of mining labor. Continuous mining machines dislodge and load minerals in a single operation. Cumbersome timbering to support the mine roof is being displaced by bolting to solid rock above to prevent cave-ins. Tougher bits and tools have speeded up mining, and now some of the hardest rocks, such as the taconites in Minnesota, are being pierced with ease by applying heat in jets. New systems for undercutting and caving minerals from the deposit are being applied. Block caving has been a boon in low-grade, underground copper mines, facilitating the large-scale removal of ores which is required for economical recovery of the contained copper.

The necessity for sending workers underground is sometimes avoided entirely. Hot water is pumped into deposits of native sulfur to dissolve the sulfur and bring it to the surface. Solution mining might be feasible also for potash and certain other soluble minerals. Controlled burning of coal beds to produce manufactured gas, as undertaken experimentally in Alabama, is another application of the principle of surface recovery of underground minerals.

The availability of machinery capable of moving bulk tonnages has brought about a conspicuous shift to the large-scale working of surface deposits, especially of coal and copper. Coal is now being mined in open pits under as much as a hundred feet of cover. The Bingham Canyon copper mine in Utah is probably the largest man-made excavation on earth. The recovery of magnesium and bromine from sea water and of nitrogen from the atmosphere also exemplifies this trend away from underground operations.

Recovery and Use

Despite the need for finding new deposits, discovery of new techniques for using resources will probably be more important than discoveries

13. "Review of Geochemistry," *Mining Journal* (London). May 1952, p. 73.

of the resources themselves, except possibly for petroleum and natural gas. Most of the metalliferous ore deposits being mined today were known long before World War I, but output has been expanded as a result of improved methods of recovery and use. We can be reasonably certain of further development along these lines; the crude materials as mined will be less concentrated and accessible but they will undergo much greater chemical transformation.

Improvements in milling, separating, concentrating, smelting and refining ores will make it economical to use deposits that were previously passed over. This has happened with copper, is now occurring with iron, and is likely to occur in the distant future with aluminum.

Hand panning and sorting of minerals have been mostly supplanted by mechanized equipment that takes advantage of every sort of difference in properties to separate wanted from unwanted material — specific gravity, shape, size, magnetism, melting temperature, cohesion and so on. Chemical methods of producing metals from ores are gaining rapidly on thermal and electrolytic methods, showing special promise in the recovery of such metals as nickel and cobalt. Steady reduction of losses, fuller use of by-products, and multiple recovery of products are making it possible to use more resources profitably.

The most dazzling of all recent discoveries has been the finding of a way to split the atom. Uranium has been used for years as a colorant in ceramics and glass, but not until World War II did man learn how to control the reactions in order to derive a net output of energy from the atom. Atomic power plants may eventually be built for some purposes, most logically for areas remote from other power supplies and for such mobile equipment as ships and aircraft. But it is doubtful that atomic energy will displace most of the power derived from coal, oil, natural gas and water, unless uranium 235 resources surpass expectations or fissionable material can be bred efficiently from more plentiful nonfissionable material.[14]

CONSUMPTION VERSUS PRODUCTION

In 1952 we consumed about $10.5 billion of industrial crude materials in terms of 1935–1939

14. See discussion of Eugene Ayres and Charles A. Scarlott, *Energy Sources—The Wealth of the World*, McGraw-Hill, New York, 1952, pp. 168–176.

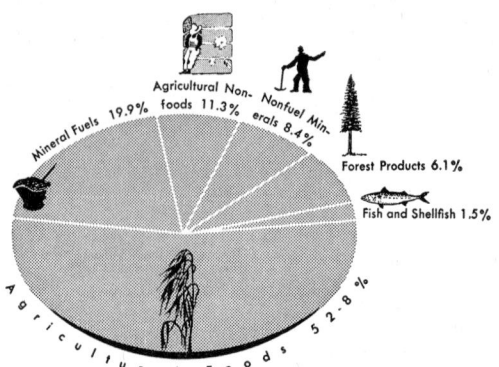

FIGURE 85. RELATIVE VALUE OF CRUDE MATERIALS CONSUMED BY THE AMERICAN ECONOMY, 1950
(Per Cent of U.S. Total)

Source: Resources for Freedom, President's Materials Policy Commission, June 1952, Vol. II, pp. 176–182. Percentages are based on the value of crude, or unprocessed, materials at or near the point of production.

prices — about one half more than in 1940. This total excludes one large group of crude materials — agricultural foods. If we were to include the outlay for agricultural foods at the crude stage, the figure would have to be doubled.

Of the industrial crude materials, mineral fuels lead in value of both consumption and production, and bulk larger than nonfuel minerals and forest products combined. Agricultural nonfoods rank next to mineral fuels. Together these two groups of industrial crude materials overshadow all others, accounting for approximately two thirds of the value of all industrial crude materials. (See Figure 85 and Table 320.)

The value of industrial materials at the crude stage, of course, does not fully measure the role of these materials in our economy. As supplied at the farm, mine, forest or other source, these products are only in part consumable. They have had only enough effort applied to them to bring them into being, ready for refining, processing or, possibly, direct consumption. As a rule, values magnify enormously after the crude stage is passed. The market or sales value of crude materials does, however, indicate roughly how much effort and cost are involved in supplying them.

Deficiency of Production

The United States is no longer mainly a supplier of raw materials; it imports more than it exports. Among the few materials it produced in

TABLE 320. PRODUCTION AND CONSUMPTION OF INDUSTRIAL RAW MATERIALS:
AMOUNT IN 1950 AND RELATION TO 1940 [a]
(*Amounts in Millions of 1935–1939 Dollars*)

Material	Production		Consumption	
	Amount in 1950	Per Cent of 1940 Volume	Amount in 1950	Per Cent of 1940 Volume
Grand total raw materials	$8,635	129	$9,496	132
Agricultural nonfoods	2,184	119	2,210	109
Fishery and wildlife products	169	102	281	110
Forest products	1,104	115	1,220	122
Saw logs	516	122	555	132
Pulpwood	158	167	245	181
Other forest products	430	98	419	96
Minerals	5,179	138	5,785	149
Mineral fuels	3,731	135	3,892	146
Bituminous coal	957	112	911	111
Anthracite	173	86	158	82
Crude petroleum	2,128	148	2,361	166
Natural gas	327	229	318	233
Natural gasoline	147	152	145	155
Metals	572	113	1,002	138
Iron and ferroalloys	299	123	414	162
Iron	265	129	264	188
Ferroalloy ores				
Chromite	[b]	—	16.4	176
Cobalt	0.8	800	9.7	225
Manganese	9.1	91	56.5	130
Molybdenum	19.4	83	14.6	77
Nickel	[b]	—	29.2	115
Tungsten	4.9	92	23.3	186
Other metals	272.4	104	588.3	125
Silver	20.7	60	71.3	64
Copper	148.7	103	227.8	148
Lead	24.9	94	57.6	177
Zinc	39.8	93	64.4	145
Antimony	1.3	217	5.9	118
Bauxite	9.0	310	29.9	467
Cadmium	7.0 [c]	149 [c]	7.0 [c]	155 [c]
Magnesium	7.4	255	7.4	296
Mercury	0.4	13	4.9	196
Platinum	1.2	240	10.5	318
Tin	0.0	—	85.3	85
Titanium	12.0 [c]	2,000 [c]	16.5 [c]	275 [c]
Nonmetallic minerals other than fuel	876	177	891	178
Construction materials	528	163	553	165
Other nonmetals	348	202	338	200

Source: Resources for Freedom, President's Materials Policy Commission, June 1952, Vol. II, pp. 176–182.

a. Excludes agricultural foods and gold.
b. Less than $50,000.
c. Estimate by the author. Data for 1950 not published.
Note: Components will not necessarily add to totals because of rounding.

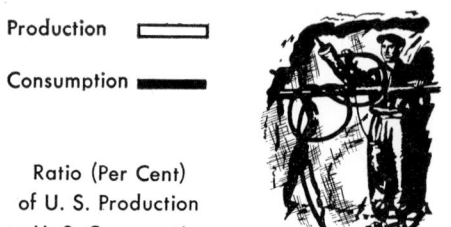

Production ▭

Consumption ▬

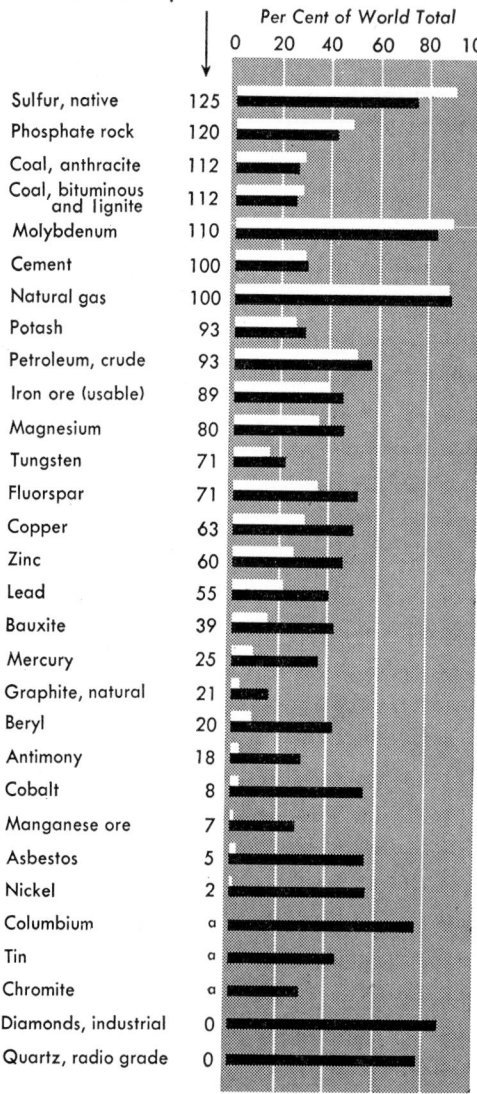

Ratio (Per Cent)
of U. S. Production
to U. S. Consumption

Per Cent of World Total

	Ratio	0	20	40	60	80	100
Sulfur, native	125						
Phosphate rock	120						
Coal, anthracite	112						
Coal, bituminous and lignite	112						
Molybdenum	110						
Cement	100						
Natural gas	100						
Potash	93						
Petroleum, crude	93						
Iron ore (usable)	89						
Magnesium	80						
Tungsten	71						
Fluorspar	71						
Copper	63						
Zinc	60						
Lead	55						
Bauxite	39						
Mercury	25						
Graphite, natural	21						
Beryl	20						
Antimony	18						
Cobalt	8						
Manganese ore	7						
Asbestos	5						
Nickel	2						
Columbium	a						
Tin	a						
Chromite	a						
Diamonds, industrial	0						
Quartz, radio grade	0						

FIGURE 86. SHARE OF THE WORLD'S OUTPUT OF MINERALS PRODUCED AND CONSUMED IN THE UNITED STATES, 1950

Source: Appendix 21–1.
a. Less than 0.5 per cent.

surplus in 1950 were native sulfur, phosphate rock, anthracite, molybdenum and bituminous

coal; and the surplus for export was not large. Production and consumption of natural gas and cement were about in balance. On the other hand, antimony, graphite, cobalt, manganese, asbestos, beryllium, nickel, tin, chromite, columbium, diamonds and radio-grade quartz — rather an imposing list — were produced domestically only in minor quantities or not at all. (See Figure 86.)

Before the late 1930s the United States produced slightly more raw materials in most years than it consumed; it had an export balance. Since that time, the reverse has been true, and the deficit has tended to grow. Indeed, total materials requirements have gone to new heights since V-J Day, contrary to expectations that they would fall off after the war. (See Figure 87.)

The deficiency of domestic production in recent years is especially pronounced in pulpwood, wool, copper, lead, zinc, most of the ferroalloys, and bauxite, among the major materials. Although we are much more nearly self-sufficient in crude petroleum and iron ore — two of our really heavyweight requirements — we have become net importers of these materials also.

Trends in Consumption and Supply

United States consumption of raw materials, excluding agricultural foods and gold, grew 75 per cent in the period from 1923, after the World War I readjustment, to 1952, following World War II, while the gross national product (adjusted for price changes) increased 143 per cent. Consumption of mineral fuels, industrial metals and construction materials as groups increased about two thirds as much as the gross national product over the twenty-nine years; the agricultural nonfoods group increased one half as much; and forest products remained unchanged. (See Table 321.)

The fastest growth in the consumption of the more common raw materials since 1923 has occurred in pulpwood, crude petroleum, natural gas, natural gasoline, chromium, cobalt, molybdenum, nickel, tungsten, bauxite, cadmium, magnesium, platinum and titanium. Consumption of anthracite, bituminous coal and saw logs declined in absolute amount.

The trends of materials consumption reflect the changing needs of our economy. Exceptionally rapid has been the growth of demand for the ferroalloys and the light metals, aluminum and magnesium — metals which are strong, able to

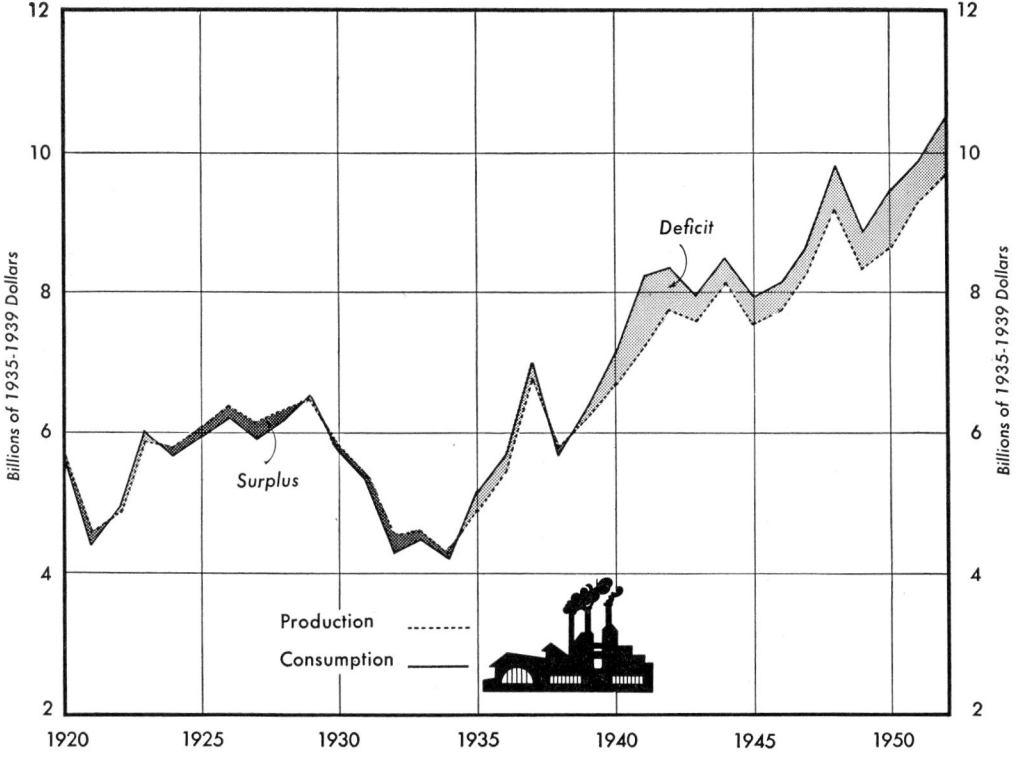

FIGURE 87. UNITED STATES PRODUCTION AND PRIMARY CONSUMPTION OF ALL RAW MATERIALS EXCEPT AGRICULTURAL FOODS AND GOLD, 1920–1952

Source: Raw Materials in the United States Economy: 1900–1952, U.S. Bureau of the Census, Working Paper No. 1 (preliminary), 1954.

withstand high temperatures, resistant to corrosion, compact, and light in weight. Growth of consumption of the older, bulkier metals and nonmetallic minerals, on the other hand, has been slackening as a result of the growing depletion of some of our best reserves, economies in the use of materials, the shift to substitutes, and the rising importance of old scrap as a source of supply.

Although ours is becoming more and more a power-driven civilization, the total consumption of fuels has risen only enough to roughly parallel the increase of the gross national product. Fuel consumption doubtless has been held back by spectacular improvements in the efficiency of use, in which nearly all types have shown marked gains. The liquid and gaseous fuels have moved deeply into the territory of the solid fuels, usually with a notable rise in efficiency. Coal, however, gaining strength from continuous mining and flow methods, is battling for the market and

in the long pull its advantage of more plentiful reserves is likely to be decisive.

ENERGY SUPPLY

Of the resources needed to maintain our industrial civilization, the energy-providing ones are the most vital, because they are required constantly in huge volume to supply heat, light and motive power. The extraordinary gains in American productivity and levels of living have been due largely to our possession of coal, petroleum, natural gas and water power and to our use of these resources, more than any other nation, to reduce human toil and multiply its effectiveness. Each person in the United States has scores of energy "slaves" working for him.

Our tremendous increases in output per worker and per man-hour have been made possible largely by drawing upon inanimate energy in place of human energy. Since 1900 we have

TABLE 321. APPARENT CONSUMPTION OF INDUSTRIAL RAW MATERIALS IN THE UNITED STATES, 1923–1952 [a]

(*Millions of 1935–1939 Dollars*)

Year	Total	Agricultural Nonfoods	Fishery, Wildlife Products	Forest Products	Total Minerals	Iron and Ferroalloys	Other Metals	Mineral Fuels	Other Nonmetallic Minerals
1923	$6,001	$1,552	$143	$1,220	$3,085	$217	$282	$2,235	$350
1924	5,680	1,528	157	1,179	2,815	176	246	2,044	349
1925	5,953	1,680	154	1,195	2,924	213	267	2,063	382
1926	6,220	1,708	167	1,177	3,168	228	302	2,225	413
1927	5,928	1,438	172	1,137	3,181	205	272	2,276	428
1928	6,133	1,645	190	1,117	3,180	199	296	2,246	440
1929	6,487	1,611	213	1,148	3,515	242	328	2,467	478
1930	5,739	1,456	206	1,016	3,060	193	217	2,219	421
1931	5,380	1,704	195	861	2,620	105	219	1,962	332
1932	4,282	1,270	172	747	2,093	36	111	1,716	230
1933	4,481	1,160	163	794	2,363	66	199	1,846	251
1934	4,272	798	164	802	2,509	81	206	1,939	284
1935	5,159	1,206	199	850	2,903	107	452	2,043	301
1936	5,708	1,256	233	931	3,288	185	376	2,307	420
1937	6,954	2,194	234	967	3,558	232	396	2,476	455
1938	5,686	1,601	196	889	3,000	96	323	2,178	403
1939	6,316	1,815	218	952	3,331	180	321	2,360	470
1940	7,145	2,028	234	991	3,892	253	453	2,675	510
1941	8,223	2,380	243	1,092	4,508	355	640	2,890	623
1942	8,326	2,439	185	1,100	4,602	400	588	2,940	674
1943	7,948	1,987	210	1,042	4,709	402	596	3,097	615
1944	8,451	2,399	236	1,033	4,783	358	499	3,349	577
1945	7,936	1,977	248	977	4,734	335	466	3,361	573
1946	8,123	2,130	296	1,083	4,615	274	338	3,347	656
1947	8,601	2,142	238	1,117	5,104	300	422	3,630	752
1948	9,788	2,786	270	1,175	5,558	376	477	3,893	812
1949	8,821	2,392	256	1,074	5,100	329	502	3,489	780
1950	9,488	2,166	256	1,212	5,853	415	578	3,944	916
1951	9,848	2,148	241	1,220	6,239	472	504	4,238	1,024
1952	10,514	2,638	237	1,242	6,398	431	641	4,256	1,070

Source: Vivian E. Spencer and Charles A. R. Wardwell, *Raw Materials in the United States Economy, 1900–1952*, U.S. Bureau of the Census, Working Paper No. 1, Preliminary, 1954, pp. 78–79.

a. Apparent consumption is defined as primary production plus imports minus exports. Agricultural foods and gold are excluded. Components will not necessarily add to totals because of rounding.

increased our supply of inanimate energy almost fourfold. Per capita we consumed almost twice as much energy in 1950 as in 1900. Most of the increase in the first two decades of this century came from coal. Since then the use of natural gas and petroleum has grown rapidly and coal use has declined somewhat. Liquid and gaseous fuels now supply a larger share of the total than the solid fuels. Use of water power, although increasing, still accounts for only about one per cent of the total energy supply. (See Chapter 25 and Appendix 25–3, Table J.)

Mineral Fuels

The outstanding advantage of petroleum products and natural gas is their ease of handling.

Fluids and gases are particularly well suited to modern technology, and petroleum products, in common with coal, have the further attractions of compactness and portability. The most important use of petroleum is in transportation, which seems to grow endlessly. Although many people believed that the automotive market was approaching saturation before the war, the number of passenger cars increased from 29.5 million at the end of 1941 to 45 million at the end of 1953 and motor truck registrations more than doubled, from 4.9 million to 9.5 million. The rate of growth of these mobile users of petroleum was exceeded by the increase in stationary oil burners for home heating, from 2.4 million to 7 million in the twelve years.

TABLE 322. MINERAL FUEL RESERVES OF THE UNITED STATES, JANUARY 1, 1950
(Amounts in Quadrillions of BTU)

Fuel Source	Ultimately Recoverable Reserves		Assured Recoverable Reserves	
	Amount	Per Cent of Total	Amount	Per Cent of Total
All fuel sources	29,060.8	100.00	9,177.6	100.00
Coal	25,409.3	87.43	7,623.0	83.06
Bituminous coal	16,024.3	55.14	4,807.4	52.38
Subbituminous coal	4,443.2	15.29	1,333.0	14.53
Lignite	4,766.8	16.40	1,430.0	15.58
Anthracite and semi-anthracite	175.0	0.60	52.6	0.57
Petroleum	366.4	1.26	170.3	1.86
Bituminous sandstone	7.5	0.03	3.9	0.04
Oil shale	3,000.0	10.32	1,200.0	13.08
Natural gas	277.6	0.96	180.4	1.96

Source: Paul Averitt and Louise R. Berryhill, Coal Resources of the United States, Geological Survey Circular 94, U.S. Department of the Interior, December 1950, pp. 30–31.

In spite of heavy consumption, proven reserves of mineral fuels have been maintained remarkably well and the outlook for the future is at least moderately satisfactory. In the early 1920s a decline in the rate of discovery led to a fear that domestic crude oil supplies were fast approaching exhaustion. In the next twenty years, however, discoveries in the United States kept pace with the rapidly rising demand. Since World War II, discoveries have again lagged somewhat. As a result, imports of crude petroleum and petroleum products increased from 377,000 barrels daily in 1946 to 1,050,000 barrels daily in 1953 while exports showed almost no change from 419,000 barrels daily. Proven reserves of natural gas have increased more than those of petroleum since 1938, and since 1944 have represented a larger content of energy than petroleum reserves, although the current rate of consumption has been lower.[15]

The quantities of petroleum and natural gas in the ground are not definitely known, and estimates change as the processes of discovery and depletion continue. Recent estimates of the Geological Survey place the assured reserves of petroleum at 16 times, and of natural gas at 38 times, the 1940–1950 annual production; ultimately recoverable reserves are figured at about 34 years for petroleum and about 59 years for natural gas. Rising production will shorten these life expectancies, of course, unless the estimates of reserves are revised upward.[16] (Cf. Table 322.)

The picture for coal resources is very different. Coal reserves as a whole are comparatively well known and have been since 1908. No large additions or reductions in the estimates are probable. Assured reserves are figured at 484 times the 1940–1950 annual production (a rate which the industry is apparently failing to sustain), and ultimately recoverable reserves at 1,612 times.[17]

Coal resources, like most resources, vary in geographical location, depth, thickness, and grade or rank. Obviously, not all deposits are equally susceptible of exploitation; the amount of material that is commercially recoverable depends upon the cost of mining. The Bureau of Mines and the Geological Survey estimated for the President's Materials Policy Commission that only about 30 billion tons of coal are recoverable at costs prevailing early in 1951. This is about equivalent to the amount of coal mined in the

15. Basic Data Relating to Energy Resources, S.Doc. 8, 82d Cong., 1st sess., 1951, pp. 172–173, and Oil and Gas Journal, January 28, 1952, pp. 218–227.

16. Paul Averitt and Louise R. Berryhill, Coal Resources of the United States, Geological Survey Circular 94, U.S. Department of the Interior, December 1950, pp. 30–31.
17. Ibid.

United States from the earliest days up to January 1, 1950. A rise of 50 per cent in prices and costs, however, would mean a 20-fold increase in estimated recoverable reserves.[18] Technological improvements may permit such an increase in commercial reserves with an even smaller increase in price.

Less Used Energy Sources

The outlook for energy supply fortunately is not narrowly restricted to coal, petroleum and natural gas. Falling water provides a continuous source of energy which, though limited by the volume and steadiness of the flow and the height of the headwaters above sea level, is capable of some further development.[19]

Synthetic liquid fuels also offer possibilities. Conversion of coal to oil or gas merely changes an abundant form of energy to a less abundant one, but production of oil from shale adds a new source of supply, equal to roughly four times the petroleum and natural gas reserves combined. (See Table 322.) Whether oil from shale can be produced as cheaply as crude petroleum is a subject of hot debate. The fact that the experts continue to argue the question is probably good evidence that the costs are coming within close range of each other. One barrier to the development of oil-shale deposits — the location of the bulk of them in Utah, Colorado and Wyoming — is definitely surmountable. If enough oil is produced, large-diameter pipelines can deliver it to distant markets at low cost.

Another source of fuel is bituminous tar sands. The United States, in sharp contrast to neighboring Canada, has only a minor resource of fuel in this form.

Vegetation can be burned directly as a fuel or can be converted to alcohol for use in internal combustion engines and other equipment. High costs and limited possibilities of production, however, stand in the way of large-scale development along these lines. The calorific value of all lumber and wood products, fuel wood and vegetation, wood pulp, food and other forest and agricultural products in 1947 totaled far less than the calorific value of either coal or petroleum in recent years. Fast-growing plants, such as sugar cane, might multiply the output several times.

But the drain on soil resources would be burdensome, and it is doubtful that the end product could compete with imports of petroleum and other sources of liquid fuels. Experiments with the single-celled plant Chlorella indicate that it or some other means of rapid photosynthesis might enable us to capture more of the sunlight falling upon the earth and convert it into usable energy.[20]

Why not capture solar energy directly? This is already being done by design in "solar houses" and incidentally in many homes of conventional design where windows, roofs or other features happen to lend themselves to absorption of heat from the sun. Solar energy is relatively diffuse, however, and would require high expenditures for equipment to concentrate it. It has possibilities for the distant future — probably many decades ahead.[21]

Atomic Energy

Progress is being made toward employing atomic fission for productive purposes. The British government announced in November 1951 that it would use waste heat from its Harwell reactor to warm an eighty-room office building. The United States Atomic Energy Commission followed a month later with an announcement that a small electric-power-generating unit had been operated successfully at Arco, Idaho. By January 21, 1954, the United States launched the first atomic-powered submarine, the engine of which had been developed at Arco.[22]

Certain applications of atomic energy are almost assured, but whether atomic fission will become the chief source of energy for mass use remains problematical. Fissionable materials are relatively scarce, and the cost of obtaining them may remain high. Shielding against the lethal rays is a continuing problem. Disposal of atomic wastes, which appeared to set limitations, however, seems to be nearly solved; in fact, "atomic garbage" might even prove useful.[23]

---

18. President's Materials Policy Commission, op. cit., Vol. II, pp. 164–165.

19. See pp. 775–776.

20. See Ayres and Scarlott, op. cit., various pages, but especially pp. 98, 225, 226 and 241.

21. Ibid., pp. 279–283.

22. New York Times, January 22, 1954, p. 1.

23. Reported by Eugene Holman, President of Standard Oil Company (New Jersey), "Our Inexhaustible Resources," speech before the American Association of Petroleum Geologists, Los Angeles, March 25, 1952. See also Jacob Sacks, "Useful Power the Ultimate Goal," The Atom at Work, Ronald Press, New York, 1951, pp. 308–319.

Atomic fission might offer more possibilities for nonenergy applications than for power — especially in such ways as killing micro-organisms, inducing chemical reactions, penetrating otherwise inaccessible areas of solids, ionizing gases and making materials glow. The possibility of artificially inducing radioactivity in minerals is especially interesting, since it might be a means of separating desired from undesired material.[24]

IRON AND STEEL

Steel is our most widely used and versatile metal. In 1950, before restrictions on consumption were applied, the automotive industry used 22 per cent of the steel produced in the United States; the construction industry, 17 per cent; the oil, gas, water and mining industries, a little more than 9 per cent; containers, a little less than 9 per cent; machinery and tools, 8 per cent; and railroads, 7 per cent. About 11 per cent went into agricultural uses, aircraft, ships, and the pressing and stamping industries. Miscellaneous uses accounted for 13 per cent of the steel output and 4 per cent was exported.[25]

About 90 per cent of our iron ore requirements are met from domestic reserves; the remainder we import from Chile, Cuba, Canada, Brazil, Venezuela, Sweden and minor sources. The Lake Superior district accounts for about 85 per cent of the domestic supply. This percentage is expected to decline gradually because of increasing depletion of the high-grade reserves.

The hard, low-grade taconites of the Lake Superior area are being developed as a new source of iron. These ores may be more expensive to use at first than the high-grade ores, but eventually they may become cheaper, for several reasons. First, the taconites are almost at the surface. Second, they can be mined cheaply by the new jet-piercing method. Third, beneficiation (concentration) of the ore at the mine, though costly, produces pellets with 65 per cent iron content (30 per cent higher than Mesabi iron ore). This saves transportation costs, increases blast furnace output and conserves coke. Further savings will be achieved if it should develop that the pellets can be used directly in the open-hearth furnace in place of some iron and steel scrap.

Processes for reducing taconites, magnetites, brown ores and other low-grade domestic iron ores are now being studied. One of these is the Humboldt, or low-shaft, process developed in Germany before the end of the war and now to be introduced on a fairly large scale in East Germany. Another process uses hydrogen from natural gas to reduce low-grade ores to iron suitable as a charge for electric furnaces.

Meanwhile, iron and steel producers in the United States are developing or helping to develop high-grade iron ore deposits in Canada's Steep Rock Lake area north of the Lake Superior district and in the eastern Quebec–western Labrador area, and the exceptionally rich deposits in Venezuela.

Iron ore consumption increased from 75 million long tons in 1940 to 105 million in 1952. The government's industrial expansion program is intended to increase the production of high-grade iron ore 49 million long tons annually by 1955 and of taconites 15 million long tons annually by 1956, over the pre-Korean level.[26]

FERROALLOYS

Production of alloy steels — which are made by combining steel with tungsten, nickel, chromium, manganese, vanadium, molybdenum and other metals — grew from 3.9 million net tons in 1929 to 5.0 million in 1940 and 9.1 million in 1952. In 1943, a peak of 13.1 million tons was reached — evidence of the extreme demand for these materials in wartime. Production of stainless steels, which require large amounts of such alloys as nickel and chromium, increased from 250,000 tons in 1940 to 930,000 in 1952. So little stainless steel was produced before 1934 that the output was not reported systematically.

The alloy steels are far better for many special purposes than ordinary carbon steel. They may also achieve a considerable saving in iron consumption, by permitting lighter-weight construction or extending the life of the product.

Manganese

Manganese, indispensable as a scavenger of impurities in the production of open-hearth steel by present methods, is used also to some extent in special-purpose alloys. The United States has

---

24. Antoine M. Gaudin, Frank E. Senftle and Wilfred L. Freyberger, "Beneficiation of Ores by Nuclear Methods," *Technology Review*, January 1952, pp. 143–144.

25. American Iron and Steel Institute, as reported in *Iron Age*, January 3, 1952, p. 390.

26. Press releases of Defense Production Administration, December 5, 1951 and July 1, 1952.

only minor reserves of high-grade manganese ore, and ordinarily produces very little. Domestic output amounted to less than 10 per cent of the requirements in 1953.

Since the start of the Korean War, efforts have been made to expand production, with indifferent success. Although the country has extensive low-grade deposits, these are far from economical to use. Recovery of manganese from open-hearth slags appears to be feasible by at least two processes. If the cost of recovery from slags proves competitive with the cost of production from ore, the new source could meet about half the total domestic manganese requirements and would be a boon in conserving manganese resources.

Nickel

Among the steel alloys, nickel is probably the most essential. Of the nickel used in the United States in 1951, 48 per cent went into the manufacture of iron and steel, 31 per cent into nonferrous metals, 9 per cent into high-temperature alloys and 7 per cent into electroplating.

Nickel substantially increases the strength and corrosion resistance of iron, steel and other alloys. It resists loss of strength at high temperatures, improves magnetic properties, and is much favored as a plating metal and as a base for other plating materials.

The United States usually accounts for less than one per cent of the world output of nickel, even though it now consumes about 50 per cent of the world supply. Canada is, and probably will continue to be, our major supplier, although new methods for treating low-grade ores offer promise of new sources in Cuba, Venezuela, the Philippines, New Caledonia and even in the United States.

Tungsten

Tungsten is essential in high-speed tools for cutting metal, in certain projectiles and, in small quantities, in filaments for electric lights and radio tubes. Loss of access to China, source of much of the world's tungsten, was a serious blow in World War II and is again a problem, making a substantial strategic stockpile necessary. Domestic production has increased so rapidly, however, as a result of a favorable market and government assistance to expand supplies that by 1953 the production exceeded the current consumption.

Molybdenum

Molybdenum is used chiefly as an alloy in the production of high-speed tools, in alloy steels for engines, as a catalyst in the production of dyes, and as a metal in the electronics industry. Before World War I, only 13 per cent of the world's small output was produced in the United States. By 1950, however, we accounted for 90 per cent of the world production and 82 per cent of the world consumption. We achieved this tremendous gain by exploiting the Climax deposit in Colorado and by recovering molybdenum as a by-product of copper mined from the Bingham Canyon of Utah.

Vanadium

Vanadium as an alloy imparts extreme strength and toughness to steels. It was first produced in the United States as a by-product of radium plants in southwestern Colorado and southeastern Utah. Production as a radium by-product has increased, and now the metal is produced also as a by-product of uranium recovery. Phosphate deposits in Idaho yield a small supply and are a large potential source. Although we continue to import vanadium concentrates from Peru, we could be practically self-sufficient in the metal.

Chromium

Chromium is a leading alloy used in making stainless steels and in plating steels to prevent rust. The United States consumes about a third of the world's chrome but produces almost none itself and must therefore stockpile the metal against possible interruption of imports. The principal sources of supply are Turkey, the Philippines, the Union of South Africa, Southern Rhodesia, Cuba and New Caledonia — mostly in the eastern hemisphere.

Boron

Boron occupies a special place among the alloy materials, for the use of small quantities as a hardening agent in steel can save large quantities of nickel, chromium and molybdenum. An ounce of boron may save as much as twenty pounds of these critical metals. The raw material, borax, is an abundant source of boron in the United States.

TABLE 323. PHYSICAL PROPERTIES OF SELECTED METALS
(*Aluminum Taken as 100*)

Metal	Weight	Electrical Resistance	Hardness	Tensile Strength per Unit of Size	Tensile Strength per Unit of Weight
Aluminum	100	100	100	100	100
Aluminum alloy [a]	103	170	456	476	440
Magnesium	64	165	130	108	160
Magnesium alloy [b]	65	536	347	382	560
Iron	290	351	291	292	100
Steel (carbon)	290	370	761	691	220
Copper	329	65	182	246	80
Nickel	329	228	369	354	100
Zinc	264	222	152	177	60

Source: Calculated from W. H. Gross, *The Story of Magnesium,* American Society for Metals, Cleveland, Ohio, 1949.

a. Alcoa 17S–T.
b. Dowmetal O–1 containing 8.5 per cent aluminum and 0.5 per cent zinc.

LIGHT METALS

In contrast to the ferroalloys, the light metals — aluminum, magnesium and titanium — can be produced indefinitely in large amounts, being among the most abundant elements.

Aluminum

The assertion that aluminum is abundant may seem rash, since our reserves of high-grade bauxite, from which aluminum is obtained, are on the verge of exhaustion. Since 1937, we have imported more bauxite than we have mined within our borders. This shift to imports, however, is due more to the availability of abundant high-grade ore in the Guianas and Jamaica than to a lack of usable ore in the United States. Pressure to reduce costs even slightly leads producers to use the cheapest source first.

The United States has low-grade bauxite, high-alumina clays and anorthosite almost without limit, and these could be employed at a small additional cost. About sixty processes have been developed for deriving alumina from these materials. Some medium-grade ores are now being used in Arkansas, and necessity eventually will prod us into further development of our extensive resources. But we shall continue for many years to rely heavily on imports of bauxite, unless barriers are erected against foreign supplies or by-products considerably reduce the cost of processing domestic ores.

The spectacular growth of aluminum consumption appears to be an established trend, owing to the abundance of the resources and a belated recognition of what aluminum can do in the modern world. Major current and prospective uses are in aircraft, guided missiles, cartridge cases, military equipment of various types, transportation equipment, industrial machinery, building materials, electric power transmission lines, utensils and food containers.

Production of primary aluminum in the United States increased from 206,000 short tons in 1940 to 1,250,000 in 1953, and the federal government's goal in early 1954 was a domestic capacity of about 1.7 million tons.

The price of aluminum is declining relative to the prices of most competitive metals. Until the latter part of 1946, aluminum sold continually at a higher price per pound than electrolytic copper, its principal competitor; since then it has been selling for less. Comparative prices per unit of weight, moreover, conceal many of the advantages of aluminum over other metals. A pound of aluminum will go more than three times as far as a pound of copper in a sheet of a given thickness and will conduct twice as much electric energy in a wire of a given weight. Pure aluminum is not especially hard or strong, but when aluminum is combined with small quantities of alloys its hardness and strength may increase more than four times, reaching about two thirds that of carbon steel. Per pound, aluminum alloys may have double the strength of carbon steel. These alloys are generally much cheaper than stainless or high-alloy steel. (See Table 323.)

Magnesium

Magnesium looks like aluminum and has 60 per cent more strength per pound, but it is about one third lighter and one third harder. It is alloyed principally with aluminum, manganese and zinc to form light and tough forgings, castings, sheets and shapes for aircraft and other industries.

The chief problem in the production and use of magnesium is its affinity for oxygen at critical temperatures. In powder or foil form, it is highly inflammable and thus excellent for flares and incendiary bombs. In bulky forms, a heat of more than 800 degrees Fahrenheit is usually required to ignite it. It can be machined safely, except that not even small amounts of magnesium dust may be allowed to accumulate because of the danger of explosion.

Before World War II, magnesium was used mostly in such products as sewing machines, textile machinery and vacuum cleaners. In the future the metal will probably be used in thousands of products, but especially in aircraft, buses, trucks and other mobile equipment in which both lightness and strength are at a premium.

Because of its lighter weight, magnesium at the recent price of 28 cents a pound is cheaper on a volume basis than aluminum at 21.5 cents a pound. It is not used as widely, however, for it is more difficult to refine and to "work," and is less resistant to corrosion. The metal is especially corrosive when in contact with steel, tending to protect steel at a sacrifice to itself. For this reason, it is commonly attached at intervals to pipelines to lessen rusting.

Our magnesium supply is not limited by any dearth of resources. In 1929, magnesium was extracted from only one source — Michigan's brine wells — by only one producer and by only one method. Now sea water is the most economical source. One cubic mile of the ocean contains more than 12 billion pounds of magnesium, and one tenth of a cubic mile could have supplied all the magnesium that has ever been produced in the United States. The water is pumped into huge settling tanks and the magnesium is precipitated in the form of magnesium hydroxide by mixing with lime, which is produced by roasting oyster shells; refined metal is recovered in electrolytic cells. This method of production can meet all our magnesium needs indefinitely.[27]

27. See W. H. Gross, *The Story of Magnesium*, American Society for Metals, Cleveland, Ohio, 1949.

Titanium

Titanium is the fourth most plentiful structural metal in the earth's crust, following after aluminum, iron and magnesium. It has been the most neglected metal, but a sudden appreciation of its possibilities in aircraft, guided missiles, weapons, corrosion-resistant equipment, and generally in uses which place a premium on a combination of lightness, strength and durability, is making it the fastest-growing metal in American history. The federal government's industrial expansion goal called for increasing the supply seventy-five times in a five-year period up to 1956.

The silvery-gray metal is classified as a light or middle-weight metal, being 60 per cent heavier than aluminum but about 40 per cent lighter than steel. Titanium alloys are far stronger than aluminum alloys and stronger even than most alloy steels. They are superior to all the usual engineering metals and alloys in ratio of strength to weight. Titanium is highly resistant to corrosion and is almost immune to deterioration from salt water.[28]

Titanium metal was little more than a laboratory curiosity until 1946, when the Bureau of Mines announced the success of the Kroll process. This requires twice as much electric power per pound as aluminum, and the use of one pound of magnesium to produce each pound of titanium. Metal so produced, of course, will be relatively costly. Titanium sponge metal sells for $5 a pound, forgings for $6, and sheets and strip for $15.

Although new production processes are not being publicized, it is likely that mass-production, electrolytic or iodide processes are not far off. One process, in the laboratory stage, eliminates the need for using magnesium and is held capable of producing titanium for less than $2 a pound.[29]

COPPER

Our economy is still heavily dependent on copper even though this metal is one of the oldest in existence, dating back to the Bronze Age. One half of the United States supply of refined copper in 1953 was consumed in the production of

28. "Titanium Metal," Titanium Metals Corporation of America, New York, 1952, pp. 3 and 4.

29. See Philip O'Keefe, Jr., "Future Materials Supply," *Ordnance*, March-April 1952, pp. 758–760, and *Engineering and Mining Journal*, February 1952, p. 154.

copper wire and cable. Forty-seven per cent was consumed in the production of copper and brass sheets, rod, bar, tube and pipe. The remaining 3 per cent was used in the production of castings, chemicals and a variety of other miscellaneous products.

At prewar rates of consumption, known economic copper supplies of the United States would last about thirty years. Mine production of copper, however, increased from 728,000 short tons in 1939 to 925,000 in 1953. At the peak wartime rate of consumption, our reported copper reserves of commercial grade would not have lasted more than twelve years.

Major discoveries of copper reserves or such spectacular advances in technology as those which made possible the use of low-grade porphyry ores are unlikely to be made again. Nevertheless, supplies are being extended by several means. Scrap metal is being recovered intensively. Higher prices for copper and government assistance for the development of ore bodies are leading to the working of reserves formerly considered uneconomic. Aluminum and other substitutes are curtailing the demand; power transmission lines are being built of aluminum, for example, and steel is replacing copper in ammunition, the largest form of consumption in wartime.

Despite these efforts to balance domestic supplies and requirements, we are becoming more dependent on foreign sources of copper. Domestic mine production changed only slightly between 1940 and 1953, but imports increased from 491,000 to 678,000 short tons and exports decreased from 435,000 to 110,000 tons. Although the United States exported more copper than it imported throughout the 1920s and most of the 1930s, an increasing import balance seems probable in the future.

LEAD AND ZINC

Zinc is used largely for coating iron and steel products and in alloys with copper and other metals. Of the 978,000 short tons of slab zinc consumed in the United States in 1953, about 42 per cent was used in galvanizing iron and steel, 31 per cent in zinc-base alloys, 18 per cent in making brass, 5 per cent in rolled zinc for such products as photoengraving plates and glass-jar tops, and 4 per cent in zinc oxide and miscellaneous products.

Storage batteries accounted for 31 per cent of the 1.2 million short tons of lead consumed in 1953, paint pigments for 10 per cent, cable covering for about 12 per cent, tetraethyl lead for 14 per cent, and solder for 6 per cent. No other single use — calking lead, pipe, ammunition, bearing metals, sheet lead, type metal, brass and bronze castings, collapsible tubes and so on — accounted for as much as 5 per cent of the total consumption.

Both lead and zinc production in the United States have declined since the late 1920s, reflecting a weakness of reserves. Lead production dropped from 654,000 short tons in 1929 to 335,000 in 1953; zinc production somewhat less, from 724,000 tons to 535,000 tons in the same years. Demand for each of the metals increased meanwhile by more than a third.

Although new techniques for recovering these metals, especially in the Rocky Mountain region, have added materially to domestic reserves, discouraging results of recent exploration offer little hope that extensive new ore bodies will be found. Any increases in output, such as are now occurring under the defense program, are almost certain to be bought only at a rise in cost. Despite some decline in requirements after government stockpile objectives have been met, progressive depletion of our supply will remain a critical problem. Imports, which exceeded domestic primary production of both lead and zinc in 1953, are likely to be further encouraged by this deficiency of reserves.

We are trying now, and will redouble our efforts, to find substitutes for these metals. Plastic-and-aluminum sheathing is being substituted for lead as a covering for cables. Titanium dioxide is taking the place of lead and zinc pigments in paints. We can expect extensive substitutions of steel, glass and plastics for rolled zinc and of aluminum for zinc castings and brass. Substitutions for lead appear at the present time to be more difficult for the most part. This firmness of lead requirements, coupled with the extreme deficiency of domestic reserves, will cause us to turn more than ever to Canada, Mexico, Peru and other outside sources. A bright spot for domestic supply is the high recovery of lead from scrap, which in some recent years has exceeded production from domestic mines.

TIN

We are most certainly a "have not" nation as to tin. Although the United States normally consumes about half of all the tin produced in the world, it produces almost none and must obtain its supply from Asia and South America. About 60 per cent of the tin used in the United States in 1953 went into tinplate and solder. The remainder was used in babbitt, bronze, collapsible tubes, type metal, chemicals, tin oxide and other products.

Exploration in recent years has confirmed the long-standing belief that the United States has no significant deposits capable of supplying tin even at several times the normal price. Wider use of electroplating in place of hot dipping, and the substitution of readily available materials, notably aluminum, magnesium, glass and plastics, are the main hope for avoiding excessive dependence on this metal in the future.

SULFUR

Sulfur, the cheapest source of the most important industrial acid, has been one of the most critical materials in the program for mobilizing the free world. The United States normally produces a surplus for export, but many of the salt domes in Texas and Louisiana, which have yielded most of the supplies, are approaching exhaustion. Recent discovery and development of further salt domes have improved the outlook.

At higher cost, sulfur could be obtained in great quantity from pyrites and from fumes blown into the air through thousands of industrial smokestacks. At still higher cost, almost unlimited quantities could be obtained from calcined gypsum, which contains about 23 per cent sulfur. Then, too, a cheap process for producing nitric acid from the atmosphere could readily provide the hydrogen ion now supplied by sulfuric acid. One of the most interesting speculations for the future is the possibility of putting to work micro-organisms which thrive on a diet of sulfur from diffuse sources and deposit it in concentrated form.[30]

CERAMICS

Some observers believe that the limits for improving metals by alloying have almost been reached. Although it is too early to pass judgment, ceramic products may be a better answer to the problem of high temperatures such as are required in gas turbines. Technologists are taking a careful look at this possibility.[31]

OXYGEN

The earth's most abundant surface element, oxygen, is one of our valuable resources. We are beginning to realize the potential usefulness of low-cost, pure oxygen in numerous chemical reactions, especially in the production of materials from petroleum and coal tar and in the new field of chemical metallurgy. As we move more and more into mass production of materials by these processes, this "unsung" material will come into its own.

SILICON

Silicon, the second most abundant element, is also being "discovered." Silicon, of course, is the principal ingredient of glass, some of the unique properties of which have been known for centuries. Only recently, however, has it been found that glass can be spun, woven or cast into serviceable forms little resembling windows or bottles. Silicones are now even made into artificial rubber, plastics and superior protective coatings. During World War II, silicon carbide proved so satisfactory a substitute for alloy steel in some applications that it displaced the metals permanently. Notably satisfactory has been its ability to withstand the hot blast in the throats of rocket motors.[32]

Pure silicon looks and acts much like a metal. Some authorities consider it a metal; others challenge this classification. It has the silvery luster of metal but is exceedingly brittle. If a process could be developed for alloying silicon so as to make it ductile, a most useful and abundant material would be added to our supply.

GERMANIUM

Besides discovering more of the earth's major assets and exploiting them more wisely, technology is finding uses for relatively scarce materials. For example, germanium, a minor but magic material, was long recognized, along with silicon, as a semimetal but considered of scarcely any utility. Germanium crystals of positive and

---

30. One of the best short discussions is presented in "Sulfur," *Chemical Engineering,* January 1952, pp. 165–176.

31. O'Keefe, *op. cit.,* pp. 759–760.
32. John L. Everhart, "Silicon Carbide as Alternative to Special Service Alloys," *Metallurgia,* March 1952, p. 150.

negative types can now be produced to take the place of vacuum tubes in electronic equipment. The minute crystals require only one thousandth to one millionth as much power as a vacuum-tube circuit. The revolution made possible by these "transistors" is just beginning.[33]

TIMBER RESOURCES

One third of the total land area of the United States is useful primarily as forest land. More than two thirds of the total forest land (including parks, game refuges, etc.) is capable of producing timber of commercial quantity and quality and is available now or prospectively for commercial use. The remainder consists of mountain tops, desert fringes or other scrub forests, mostly in the West. (See Table 324.)

Of the 461 million acres of commercial forest land, 205 million bear saw timber, timber large enough and dense enough for commercial harvesting. Nearly all the saw timber in the South and most of that in the North is second growth; the West accounts for more than 90 per cent of the country's virgin timber acreage.[34] On the remaining 246 million acres of commercial forest land the trees are too small or too scattered for profitable production of saw logs.

Acreage provides only a rough indication of timber resources, because the amount of timber which is readily usable varies greatly from area to area. Nearly two thirds of the volume of saw-timber stand is in the West, a region which contains about one fourth of the commercial forest land of the country; but the South, with heavy rainfall, a long growing season and generally favorable soil, accounts for more than half of the annual volume of saw-timber growth.

Consumption of Wood

Our forest problem would not be a difficult one if trees of any variety and size could be used, for over-all growth and drain (both through cutting and losses) on the commercial forest land of the country are about in balance. The main requirement, however, is for trees of saw-timber size — 9 to 11 inches in diameter or larger. The problem of sustaining the timber supply, therefore, centers largely on the rates of growth and depletion of the saw-timber growing stock. Growth of the smaller trees can have only a small effect on the supply of saw logs in as short a time as ten or fifteen years. The reserve of 1,600 billion board feet of standing saw timber on commercial forest land could be cut at a faster rate, but this would increase the drain, and drain on saw timber already has exceeded growth by more than 50 per cent during and since World War II.

Most of the drain on timber results from cutting. Fire losses have been declining steadily and now usually represent less than 2 per cent of the annual drain. Insects, disease and windstorms in recent years have caused 5 or 6 per cent of the drain. The total removal of wood, including losses, from standing timber in the United States amounted to about 12.5 billion cubic feet in 1953 — enough to build a "causeway" one foot thick and at least 700 feet wide between New York and San Francisco. Such a large requirement for wood cannot be met easily by other materials, should our forests become depleted.[35]

Almost half of the timber used in 1953 represented saw logs to be cut into lumber; about one fourth was used as fuel wood and about one fifth as pulpwood. The remainder was divided among veneer logs, mine timbers, railroad ties, poles, fence posts and miscellaneous items. Of the domestic consumption of lumber in 1953, about 75 per cent went into construction, maintenance and repair, about 10 per cent into factory products, and most of the remaining 15 per cent into crates, dunnage and other shipping uses.

Trends in the consumption of forest products are diverse. Production of lumber, and probably consumption also, reached its highest point in 1907. Consumption of timber for railroad ties, shingles, cooperage stock and wood lath also has declined since the first decade of this century. Consumption of fuel wood has dropped since 1870–1880, although one tenth of the dwellings in the United States, according to the 1950 Census of Housing, depend primarily on wood as fuel for heating and cooking. These declines occurred not only because of substitutions of other materials but also because of improved fire protection and the use of wood preservatives and fireproofing.

In sharp contrast with these declines, the use

33. *Engineering and Mining Journal,* February 1952, p. 154.

34. As used here, the North comprises the New England, Middle Atlantic, Lake Central and Plains states; the South includes the South Atlantic, Southeast and West Gulf states; the West represents the Mountain and Pacific states.

35. See report of the President's Materials Policy Commission, *op. cit.,* Vol. I, Chapter 8, and Vol. V, Report 5.

TABLE 324. LAND USE AND TIMBER RESOURCES OF THE UNITED STATES, 1945 [a]

Item	Total U.S.	North [b]	South [c]	West [d]
	(Millions of Acres)			
Land area	1,905.4	821.7	326.0	757.6
Forest land (including parks, etc.)	623.8	211.8	186.8	225.3
Commercial [e]	461.0	170.3	183.3	107.5
Noncommercial	162.8	41.4	3.5	117.8
Cropland in farms	525.1	364.5	91.5	69.1
Pasture and range	609.5	185.9	11.4	412.1
Other	146.9	59.5	36.3	51.2
All timber on commercial forest land	(Billions of Cubic Feet)			
Stand	470.0	99.9	130.9	239.3
Saw-timber trees [f]	316.5	54.3	76.8	185.4
Pole-timber trees [g]	153.6	45.6	54.0	53.9
Growth	13.4	4.7	6.4	2.3
Drain	13.7	3.7	6.5	3.5
Lumber	6.7	1.3	2.8	2.6
Fuel wood	2.2	1.0	1.2	0.1
Pulpwood	1.3	0.4	0.6	0.3
Other use	2.0	0.7	1.0	0.3
Fire	0.5	0.1	0.3	0.1
Insects, disease, etc.	1.0	0.3	0.6	0.2
Saw timber on commercial forest land	(Billions of Board Feet)			
Stand	1,601.0	220.4	338.0	1,042.6
Growth	35.3	8.4	19.9	7.0
Drain	53.9	9.0	24.9	20.0
Lumber	34.4	4.9	14.2	15.3
Fuel wood	3.9	0.9	2.7	0.3
Pulpwood	4.8	1.2	1.8	1.8
Other use	6.6	1.3	3.9	1.4
Fire	0.9	0.1	0.4	0.3
Insects, disease, etc.	3.4	0.6	1.8	0.9

Source: *Gaging the Timber Resource of the United States*, U.S. Forest Service, December 1946 (revised July 1947), various tables.

a. Status data are for the beginning of 1945, growth and drain for 1944. Land-use data shown here for 1945 are not strictly comparable with data shown in Chapters 17 and 22 for 1950, because of differences in classification. The principal difference is that cropland used only for pasture is classified as pasture in those chapters and as cropland in this chapter.

b. North Dakota, South Dakota, Nebraska, Kansas, the portions of Oklahoma and Texas west of the one hundredth meridian, Minnesota, Iowa, Missouri, Wisconsin, Illinois, Michigan, Indiana, Kentucky, Ohio, New York, Pennsylvania, West Virginia, Maryland, New Jersey, Delaware, Vermont, Maine, New Hampshire, Washington, Connecticut, Rhode Island.

c. The portions of Oklahoma and Texas east of the one hundredth meridian, Arkansas, Louisiana, Tennessee, Mississippi, Alabama, Georgia, Florida, District of Columbia, Virginia, North Carolina, South Carolina.

d. Washington, Oregon, California, Montana, Idaho, Nevada, Wyoming, Utah, Arizona, Colorado, New Mexico.

e. Land capable of producing timber of commercial quantity and quality and available for commercial use.

f. Trees 9 inches to 11 inches or more in diameter at breast height, depending on area and species.

g. Trees between 5 inches in diameter at breast height and minimum saw-timber size.

of pulpwood and veneer logs has been rising faster than the national income. Wood waste is being used in rapidly growing quantities in the production of fiber board and synthetics.

Demand for timber is unevenly distributed among tree species and grades. Lumber free from knots and blemishes is becoming exceptionally scarce and high priced. The market for such tree species as Douglas fir, red gum and tupelo has grown as a result of their suitability for use in veneers and plywoods. As new ways of using wood are found, species now considered inferior may come into their own.

Need for Conservation

The era of abundant timber available for practically the cost of cutting is drawing to a close. We shall have to extend forest management and research if we are to assure a continuing timber supply for the future. Because of the long growth cycle, we should emphasize protection and selective cutting of forests, but denuded areas will need to be replanted. Some improvement can be accomplished by constructing access roads to permit the cutting and protection of timber in the mature stands of the national forests.

Any extensive forestry program will have to enlist the cooperation of the owners of small woodlots, who hold three fourths of the private commercial forest acreage. In the larger holdings, the progress of scientific forestry and other improvements has been relatively good in recent years. Prospects of tree farming generally are favorable in the humid climates of the Southeast and the Northwest coastal area, where the growth of trees is exceptionally rapid.

WATER RESOURCES

Water is perhaps our most widely used resource. The water withdrawn for use from surface and underground sources in the United States outweighs all other materials combined more than a hundredfold. The daily take in 1950 is estimated by the President's Materials Policy Commission at 185 billion gallons, of which 170 billion gallons were fresh water and 15 billion gallons were salt water. Of this quantity, 48 per cent was used in irrigation, 43 per cent directly by industry, and 9 per cent by industry, households and others through municipal or rural water systems.

These estimates are on a gross basis and include a large reuse. About three fifths of the water withdrawn is returned to the streams or the ground to be used again. The remainder is evaporated or consumed, more than three quarters of this disappearance occurring in the irrigation of land in the western states.

Lack of water and water pollution are becoming serious problems in many localities and particularly in two major regions of the country. Pollution is becoming a menace in the manufacturing belt from Chicago and St. Louis eastward to the Atlantic Coast. A shortage threatens in the face of growing industrial needs in the area from the Great Plains to the Pacific Coast, except the Pacific Northwest. In this shortage area, precipitation is so small that a large proportion of the rainfall evaporates or transpires to the atmosphere. Many streams are dried up, and underground water tables generally are falling.[36]

States, local governments and industrial establishments are making some progress in pollution abatement, but the rate of improvement is hardly enough to keep up with the increased pollution attending population and industrial growth. Stronger regulatory measures may therefore be needed.

In the seventeen most westerly states, about 90 per cent of the water is used for irrigation. Although supplies may be increased somewhat further through costly projects, the chief question is one of priority of use. The needs of both industry and agriculture have to be considered, and the enterprises using the most water per dollar of output may have to move to more favorably endowed areas.

Falling water is a replenishable source of energy. Where stream gradients are steep and favorable dam sites exist, it may provide the cheapest power. Since water power can be turned on instantaneously and requires no outlays for fuel, it is a convenient complement to fuel-generated power. But it can never serve as a substitute for a large proportion of our fuel supply. If all the rain and snow falling on the United States were transformed into power at the existing stream gradients (an obvious impossibility), the energy produced would not equal that derived from coal in good years. Water power has usually accounted for only 3 or 4 per cent of the total supply of inanimate energy, and about one fourth of the water power at feasible dam sites has been developed.

Water resources are especially susceptible of development for multiple ends. A given develop-

36. These water resource problems were discussed at length by the President's Water Resources Policy Commission, and more recently industrial water was discussed by the President's Materials Policy Commission. See, respectively, *A Water Policy for the American People,* President's Water Resources Policy Commission, 1950, and President's Materials Policy Commission, *op. cit.,* Vol. I, Chapter 10, and Vol. V, Report 9.

TABLE 325. ANNOUNCED SUPPLY EXPANSION GOALS UNDER THE MOBILIZATION PROGRAM

Material	Unit	Domestic Production Plus Imports 1950	Goal Year	Goal Amount	Percentage Increase
Electric power	Million kilowatts	65	1957	117[a]	80
Crude-oil, refining	Million bbls. daily	6.9	1956	8.7[b]	26
Iron ore, excluding taconites	Million gross tons	98[e]	1955	147[e]	50
Iron ore, taconites	Million gross tons	0	1956	15[b]	—
Aluminum	Thousand net tons	719	1955	1,746	143
Cobalt	Million pounds	10	1955	27	170
Chromite, metallurgical grade	Thousand long tons	641	1953	800	25
Copper	Thousand net tons	2,031	1955	2,270	12
Fluorspar, acid grade	Thousand net tons	145	1953	300	107
Lead	Thousand net tons	1,207[d]	1955	1,342	11
Manganese ore, metallurgical grade	Thousand long tons	1,870	1954	2,500	34
Molybdenum	Million pounds	28.5	1954	70	146
Nickel	Thousand net tons	101	1955	190	88
Phosphate rock (P₂O₅ content)	Million long tons	3.5[e]	1954	5.0[f]	43
Potash	Million net tons	1.4[g]	1954	2.0[f]	43
Sulfur	Thousand long tons	6,082	1955	7,700	27
Titanium	Thousand net tons	0.5[h]	1956	37.5[b]	7,400
Tungsten	Million pounds	9	1954	40	344
Zinc	Thousand net tons	1,084	1956	1,245	15

Source: Defense Production Administration and Office of Defense Mobilization announcements of goals up to February 10, 1954.

a. Annual capacity, beginning of 1957.
b. Annual capacity, beginning of 1956.
c. Annual capacity for year specified.
d. Domestic production plus imports in 1949.
e. Annual rate of production, 1950–1951.
f. Annual capacity, middle of 1954.
g. Annual capacity, end of 1950.
h. Domestic production plus imports in 1951, the second year of commercial production.

ment program may provide water power, aid navigation, prevent floods, reduce pollution in periods of low stream flow, provide irrigation, and regularize the water supply. Multiple-purpose projects are especially suitable to headwaters areas, where soil also may be conserved.

FUTURE REQUIREMENTS FOR MATERIALS

Estimates of requirements for materials in 1960 should give heavy weight to the federal government's mobilization program. Accelerated tax amortization, loans, purchase contracts, government-subsidized purchase and sale, and other inducements to production largely invalidate past relationships as a basis for projections into the future. We are witnessing in this period of "partial mobilization" a situation which is akin to neither past peacetime periods nor full-scale war. Never before, short of a major war, has the government exerted so much influence on the trend of productive capacity nor engaged on such a vast scale in the stockpiling of materials.

Requirements for materials as projected for this study take into account the government's expansion programs, but introduce modifications as required by long-term trends basic to the general projections and assumptions of this report or where needed to extend the data to 1960. The projections also draw heavily on those of the President's Materials Policy Commission for 1975.

The government's expansion programs for materials usually extend ahead for a period of four to six years, but some of them go up to 1962. The more pertinent of those goals which have been publicly announced, all of relatively short term, are shown in Table 325. These expansions range from 11 per cent for lead to a 75-fold

TABLE 326. GROSS NATIONAL PRODUCT AND MATERIALS CONSUMPTION,
SELECTED YEARS AND ESTIMATE FOR 1960
(*Index Numbers, 1950 = 100*)

| Item | 1929 | 1940 | Wartime Peak | | 1950 | 1960 Estimate [a] |
			Year	Index		
Gross national product at 1950 prices	56	64	1944	100	100	129
All industrial materials [b]	68	76	1944	89	100	122
Agricultural nonfoods	78	92	1942	110	100	115
Fishery and wildlife products	73	91	1945	95	100	111
Forest products	94	81	1942	90	100	109
Saw logs	91	74	1942	91	100	101
Pulpwood	43	55	1945	70	100	132
Other forest products	129	104	1942	102	100	99
Total minerals [c]	61	67	1944	82	100	128
Iron and ferroalloys	58	61	1942	98	100	136
Other metals [c]	59	80	1943	101	100	135
Mineral fuels	63	69	1945	86	100	127
Other nonmetallics	53	56	1942	79	100	122
Electric power production for public use	28	43	1944	69	100	190

Sources: Gross national product data for 1929–1950 from Appendix 4–2. Industrial materials indexes are based on those of the President's Materials Policy Commission, *Resources for Freedom*, June 1952, Vol. II, p. 180. Electric power for public use is based on data of the Federal Power Commission as reported in *Historical Statistics of the United States, 1789–1945*, U.S. Bureau of the Census, 1949, p. 156, and *Annual Report of the Federal Power Commission.*

a. Gross national product figure is the one provided in the basic assumptions for this study; other projections are explained in the accompanying text.
b. Excludes agricultural foods and gold.
c. Excludes gold.

increase for titanium within six years. These increases, of course, represent goals which, for various reasons, may or may not be met.

Although the government "balance sheets" show details for individual materials, these do not provide a dependable basis for projections to 1960, nor is it necessary or feasible for this study to attempt projections for individual commodities. The real problem is the availability of classes of commodities — agricultural nonfoods, mineral fuels, and so on. Substitutions can be made within these classes to meet the underlying needs.

Despite the current mobilization program, total industrial materials requirements are expected to increase only 22 per cent between 1950 and 1960 as compared with 29 per cent for the gross national product. (See Table 326.) The

principal reasons for this smaller increase are the continued rapid growth of service industries, which use only small quantities of materials, and continued pressure to make materials go further. Much of the expansion for national defense is a speed-up process to build stockpiles of materials for an expanded mobilization base. Within several years most of the stockpiling will have been completed and thereafter the mobilization base will grow more slowly, barring a full-scale war.

Minerals

Requirements for minerals are expected to increase in the same manner as the gross national product. The largest increases are expected to occur among metals used in high-temperature, high-strength and corrosion-resistant alloys.

These metals, required in jet engines, high-speed equipment of various types, and equipment for the chemical processing industries — all fast-growing sources of demand — are in the main channel of technology. Requirements for other metals are expected to grow at almost the same rate. Although this group includes the light metals — aluminum, magnesium and titanium — it also includes such metals as copper, lead and zinc, which will show a slower growth and which have a heavy influence on the total.

Consumption of the mineral fuels — coal, petroleum and natural gas — is expected to grow at almost the same rate as the gross national product. Actually, the useful supply of energy will increase much faster, but progressive efficiency in the use of fuels will retard the drain on these resources. We can be fairly certain that inanimate energy will be further substituted for human and animal energy — to the extent that opportunities for such substitution still exist.

Use of nonmetallic minerals other than fuels in the past has closely followed changes in expenditures (at constant prices) for construction and capital equipment, since these materials are used mostly in construction. Rather large shifts in demand take place within the group, as in timber products, but the group as a whole keeps pace with construction activity. An increase of 22 per cent is expected between 1950 and 1960. This is equal to the estimated increase in civilian outlays for construction and capital equipment included among the general assumptions of this study. Military construction and capital equipment are not expected to affect the relationship by 1960.

Other Industrial Materials

Requirements for agricultural, aquatic and forest materials for industrial use have grown more slowly than the gross national product over the past two decades, or have declined. They are expected to show about the same relative trends up to 1960. A gain of 15 per cent over 1950 is expected in agricultural nonfoods — slightly better than past performance because of anticipated large gains in productivity and emphasis on new uses, including some defense uses of oils and fibers. In fishery and wildlife products, public protection and conservation appear to have more influence in determining consumption than does the level of national income. An increase of

11 per cent is expected between 1950 and 1960, continuing the trend of the previous decade.

Requirements for forest products are expected to increase only 9 per cent from 1950 to 1960. This estimate is proportionately considerably higher than the twenty-five-year increase of 12 per cent estimated by the President's Materials Policy Commission. It assumes a higher increase in pulpwood consumption but less consumption of saw logs. The principal reasons for the expected sag in saw-log consumption are: (1) the expected high price for lumber, which will encourage economies in the use of wood and shifts to substitutes; (2) the decline being shown in the marriage rate, which will mean less demand for new houses; and (3) the fact that the increase in the birth rate that began in 1946 will not affect formation of new households until after 1960.

All these estimates of materials requirements in 1960 pertain to materials in crude form, following the classification of the Bureau of the Census. If refined and intermediate materials were included, the upward trend doubtless would be stronger. The more costly refined materials are growing faster than the cheaper crude materials, reflecting the trend toward more processing. Chemical industries, for example, are expanding with exceptional speed. Electric power, it is believed, will continue to grow rapidly in relation to the gross national product, as is shown in Table 326.

LABOR REQUIREMENTS AND PRODUCTIVITY

The larger requirements for minerals in 1960 than in 1950 probably will call for about 7 per cent more production workers in the mining industries, reversing the long-term decline. The percentage gain, however, will be less than that of the employed civilian labor force; the ratio of employees in mining to the employed civilian labor force is expected to remain at 1.5 per cent for the decade. (See Table 327.)

The reluctance of workers to enter the mining industries is likely to mean less prospect of a shortening of weekly hours in mining than in industry generally. In 1950, working time in all mining averaged about 38 hours a week as against a general average of 39 for all industry. Although the nonagricultural work week is expected to decline from 39 hours to 36.5 hours by 1960, workers in mining will probably also spend a little more than 36 hours a week at their jobs

TABLE 327. LABOR REQUIREMENTS AND PRODUCTIVITY IN MINING,
SELECTED YEARS AND ESTIMATE FOR 1960

Item	1929	1940	Wartime Peak Year	Wartime Peak Amount	1950	1960 Estimate
Labor Employed (*Number in Millions*)						
Employed civilian labor force	47.6	47.5	1943	54.5	60.0	65.5
Employees in mining	1.08	0.92	1942	0.98	0.90	0.96
Per cent in mining	2.3	2.0	1942	1.8[a]	1.5	1.5
Indexes of Labor Use and Productivity in Mining						
Production workers	127[b]	108	1942	112	100	107
Man-hours	152	97	1944	122	100	103
Output						
Per production worker	71[c]	78	1945	107	100	112
Per man-hour	59	87	1945	90	100	117

Sources: Data for 1929–1950 obtained as follows: data on labor employed from *Statistical Abstract of the United States, 1950,* U.S. Bureau of the Census, pp. 173 and 175; labor use and productivity data from *Productivity Trends in Selected Industries, Indexes through 1950,* Bulletin No. 1046, U.S. Bureau of Labor Statistics, October 1951, pp. 16 and 17.

The data on mining employment may contain some duplications because they are based on the number of jobs, and one man may appear on more than one payroll. This duplication is believed to be negligible in the mining industries as a whole.

The estimates for 1960 assume: (1) labor force changes from 1950 consistent with the general assumptions of this volume, (2) an increase in mine production of 20 per cent over 1950 as against a 24 per cent increase in consumption, (3) an increase in output per man-hour at a rate less than that in the five years after the war but more than that in the decade 1940 to 1950, when the war retarded productivity increases, and (4) a small decrease in working time per week. The other estimates for 1960 are derived.

a. Based on the employed civilian labor force of 53.8 million in 1942.

b. Computed from the change in employees in mining between 1929 and 1940 as given above in the table.

c. Derived index using output as reported in the Bureau of Labor Statistics bulletin mentioned above.

in 1960. This equalization of hours in mining and other industries would partly reverse the trends of the 1940–1950 decade, when weekly hours in mining increased from 33 to 38 while those in industry generally declined from 41 to 39. Rising consumption of minerals in that decade was met partly by increased productivity per man-hour and partly by more working time. Less extreme tightness of mine labor supply in the 1950–1960 decade would tend to lower the hours of work even if the total national income rises as expected.

Productivity in Mining

Output per man-hour in the mining industries is expected to increase 17 per cent from 1950 to 1960, an improvement over the preceding decade, when the increase was about 15 per cent, or 1.4 per cent a year, but below the rate of earlier decades and the five-year period after the war. The gain from 1940 to 1950 was abnormally low because of interruptions of new methods during World War II. Since the war, productivity has resumed a faster rate of improvement, but depletion of reserves is expected to retard the rise of productivity increasingly. (See Table 328 and Figure 88.)

The gains in output per man-hour were largest in bituminous coal mining, where resources are still good. The anthracite industry, with poorer reserves and less progressive production policies, showed a decline in productivity from 1940 to 1951. The lead and zinc industries, which have a weak resource position, also showed a decline of productivity. Copper and iron ore mining, with somewhat better resources, recorded increases in output per man-hour but not as much as the bituminous coal industry.

Problem of Depletion

A sustained high level of mineral production is likely to retard productivity gains more than a lower level of production. Mining, unlike manufacturing, is subject to depletion which increases as output rises. Writers on natural resources commonly make much of the drain on

TABLE 328. PRODUCTIVITY IN MINING INDUSTRIES, 1935–1951

(Indexes of Output per Man-Hour, 1939 = 100)

Year	Mining Industries Group [a]	Anthracite Industry	Bituminous Coal and Lignite Industries	Copper Mining Industry [b]	Iron Ores Mining Industry [c]	Lead and Zinc Ores Industry [b]
1935	84.9	79.3	82.4	97.5	87.7	99.5
1936	86.6	86.2	86.3	101.7	98.8	93.7
1937	88.0	87.4	88.1	94.0	105.9	90.1
1938	90.1	97.9	92.9	93.0	70.2	97.6
1939	100.0	100.0	100.0	100.0	100.0	100.0
1940	102.1	98.5	104.0	103.2	117.4	96.4
1941	103.9	100.5	104.4	99.3	117.3	98.3
1942	104.0	92.1	102.9	101.6	107.8	90.4
1943	101.5	87.5	98.7	103.6	96.9	75.3
1944	104.7	92.0	102.5	113.1	99.7	78.8
1945	106.1	89.2	105.7	114.1	110.5	78.7
1946	107.2	93.5	109.7	99.4	104.9	70.5
1947	111.1	90.5	112.1	110.8	106.0	76.5
1948	110.9	90.5	111.7	106.2	105.5	82.3
1949	108.6	90.6	109.9	104.4	101.9	85.3
1950	117.4 [d]	86.3	124.4	116.5	108.8	94.7
1951		93.4	125.5	117.7	117.4	89.6

Source: Productivity Trends in Selected Industries, Indexes through 1950, Bulletin No. 1046, U.S. Bureau of Labor Statistics, October 1951, and unpublished data for 1951.

a. Includes production of petroleum, natural gas and natural gasoline.
b. Based on mine production of recoverable metal.
c. Based on usable ore produced.
d. Not available.

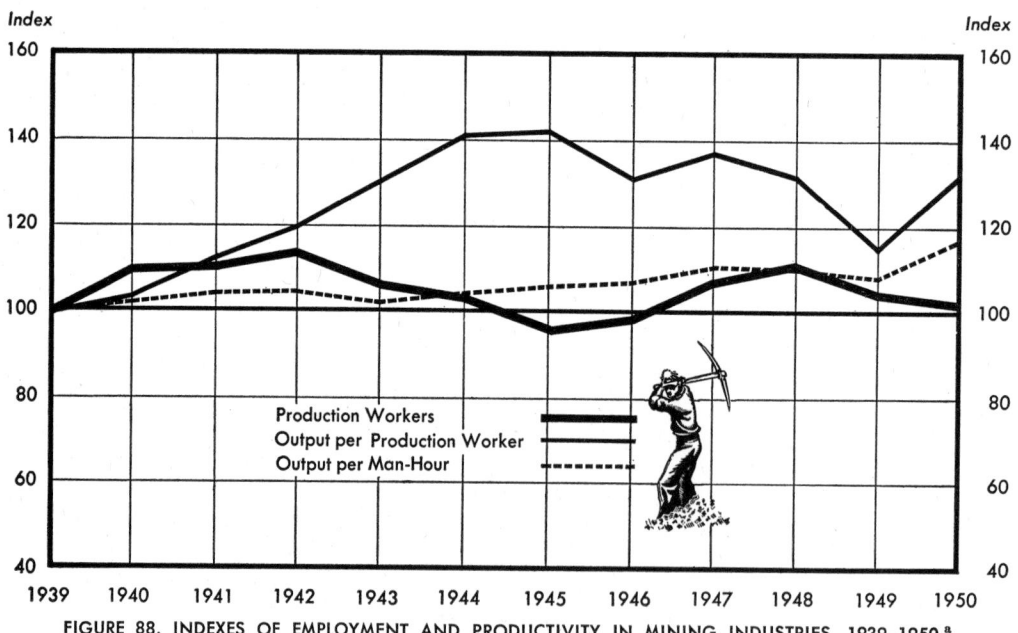

FIGURE 88. INDEXES OF EMPLOYMENT AND PRODUCTIVITY IN MINING INDUSTRIES, 1939–1950 [a]

(1939 = 100)

Source: Productivity Trends in Selected Industries, Indexes Through 1950, Bulletin No. 1046, U.S. Bureau of Labor Statistics, October 1951, p. 17.

a. Based on six principal mining industries: bituminous coal; anthracite; copper; iron; lead and zinc; and crude petroleum, natural gas and natural gasoline.

reserves during World War II, yet the demand for minerals projected to 1960 exceeds even the peak year of demand during the war and will require even a larger work force. (See Tables 326 and 327.)

Optimism about our ability to maintain productivity in these wasting assets requires faith in technological advancement through which we may be able to use lower-grade resources and to shift the burden of meeting requirements from scarce to abundant materials.

In the event of serious depletion of mineral resources combined with restrictions on imports and public subsidies to increase domestic production, a concentration of effort on minerals would be required, at an economic disadvantage, and the number of workers would increase at least temporarily. On the other hand, if minerals are imported to meet deficiencies in our resources, a smaller domestic labor force would be devoted to mining, but could be sustained over a longer period of time. Perhaps the most plausible assumption is that mining will be increasingly handicapped by depletion, which will retard the rise of productivity and tend to stabilize the trend of employment. At the same time, imports of certain minerals will probably increase markedly but imports of minerals as a group only moderately.

SUMMARY AND CONCLUSIONS

The United States, with its high standard of material well-being, has long made exacting demands on its natural resources. During and after World War II, these demands were intensified and they are now rapidly changing in emphasis.

Although we have imported certain raw materials for many decades — tin, chromite, manganese, nickel, tungsten and rubber, for example — we were self-sufficient in raw materials as a whole or had an exportable surplus until about 1940. Since then our demands for raw materials generally have exceeded domestic supplies. We have gone far afield to meet the deficit.

Vast resources in foreign areas — with the notable exception of western Europe — remain almost untouched. The occurrence of many favorable mineral resources throughout the world is already known even though many areas have never been explored. We know, for example, that Venezuela has extraordinarily good deposits of iron ore, Brazil of manganese, the Middle East of petroleum and China of tungsten and coal which await only the development of production facilities and transportation. The list could be greatly enlarged.

Despite our general efficiency and economy in using our resources, we have often been guilty of extravagance, and the best grades of many of our raw materials are now approaching depletion. Most of the basic materials for which concern is shown at present, however, can be obtained within our borders from low-grade deposits or can be replaced by substitutes — although rapid depletion of valuable resources unfortunately is encouraged where the cost of alternative materials is high.

We may need to apply relatively more effort to supply materials in the future than we have in the past. The additional work may place resource industries at a handicap, especially in competition with foreign supplies of higher grade. The effect on our economy as a whole, however, is likely to be small. Only a minor share of the total labor force in the United States is engaged in supplying raw materials. Even at twice the cost, supplying raw materials would still require only a small part of the total national effort.

Marked shifts of emphasis may be expected — toward materials for organic chemicals; light metals and light nonmetallic construction materials; high-temperature, high-strength and corrosion-resistant metals; liquid fuels; and natural gas. Most of these shifts were already under way before World War II. The war emphasized the trend and unveiled some spectacular new developments — most particularly, jet propulsion and the practicability of using atomic energy.

Ways to Meet Needs

Although technological changes, and rising consumption accompanying full employment, have created serious problems of raw materials supply, further technological changes can probably solve these problems in the longer pull to 1960 even on a full-employment basis. There are strong reasons for this optimism:

(1) The development and application of improved methods of discovering mineral deposits. Deep drilling for oil, for example, is locating new, large supplies.

(2) The introduction of more thorough methods of extraction.

(3) The substitution of less scarce for more scarce resources. We are learning how to

make better use of the more abundant elements of the earth.

(4) The trend toward economy in the use of materials, which permits the standard of living to rise more than the requirements for materials.

(5) The increasing use of by-products formerly discarded, and the discovery that by-products can aid in the economical production of primary products.

(6) The spreading of the resource base of industry by using a wider variety of resources.

(7) The discovery of techniques for using basic materials which previously were considered unusable. Titanium metal is a newcomer and zirconium metal shows promise, but the outstanding example is the splitting of the atom.

Three lines of action need especially to be pursued to assure a sufficient supply of materials for all future requirements. We should (1) promote intensive research into low-cost techniques for utilizing more abundant resources to relieve the demands on scarcer resources, (2) freely rely on imports to the extent necessary to compensate for deficiencies of domestic resources, and (3) stockpile materials which would be vital in case of war and can be stored without excessive deterioration.

Most Serious Problems

Petroleum, copper, lead and zinc are likely to present the most serious problems for the future from the standpoint of value and volume and the wide variety of their uses. The most intense and acute deficiencies threaten in the additive alloys for steel which are relatively scarce the world over — nickel, cobalt, columbium, tantalum, tungsten, molybdenum and vanadium. Although World War II hastened, and the current mobilization program continues to hasten, the depletion of our best reserves of many important industrial raw materials, the effect is most evident, and increasingly so, in the scarce alloys. The growing problem threatens to tax our ingenuity for a long time to come.

Iron and aluminum ores probably will be imported in increasing quantities, but fundamentally these materials are exceedingly plentiful. At most, only a slight sacrifice of cost may be necessary to permit the use of lower-grade reserves of these two materials.

Continuing depletion and uneven geographical distribution of resources appear to be inevitable. Advancing technology may be able to keep abreast of depletion and even to reduce costs. At least, productivity per man-hour seems still to be rising. But technology probably can never make an area self-sufficient without some sacrifice in standards of living. The United States is no exception. It has an abundance of resources, and depletion is hardly so extensive as to become a serious barrier to expanding production. Nevertheless, it does not possess all the varied kinds of materials needed for its complex civilization. Its further industrial growth depends more than ever on free access to the world's resources to supplement its own wherever deficiencies exist.

## CHAPTER 22

AGRICULTURAL CAPACITY

WHAT ACCOUNTS FOR agriculture's contribution to the high level of prosperity following World War II? Can it make the same kind of contribution in the years ahead, as we approach the 1960s?

The outstanding feature of agriculture today is the accentuated progress in productivity — more output per farm, per acre, per man-hour, per animal. The rapid technological advance of the 1930s and 1940s now makes it possible for fewer farmers operating larger farms to meet the greatly expanded agricultural requirements for domestic and foreign markets and for foreign aid. Further progress in productivity will make it possible for still fewer farms and farmers to meet the still greater requirements of the 1950s and 1960s. We are nowhere near the end of technological advance in agriculture, or of potential expansion of land under cultivation if that should become necessary.

Looking toward 1960, we can expect a demand for farm products about 20 per cent greater than in 1950, chiefly as a result of the expected rise in population and only partly as a result of a further increase in per capita consumption. There appears to be nothing among any of the elements in agriculture's capacity to produce — whether land, labor, livestock, technology, industrial products for farm production, or farmers' purchasing power — that would prevent agricultural production from expanding 20 per cent during the 1950s. In fact, the most recent and comprehensive official survey of capacity, published in 1952, indicated that such an increase in production could be attained by 1955 instead of 1960 if necessary.[1]

OUR AGRICULTURAL BASE

Normally the "farm plant" is capable not only of producing the food and fiber needed for our own population but of supplying foreign markets as well. In the 1920s about 85 per cent of the annual agricultural output went into domestic markets and 15 per cent for export. Imports of certain foods, feeds and fibers supplemented the domestic supply, but these imports amounted to only about 60 per cent of the value of agricultural exports. Thus we have normally produced more farm products than we have consumed. However, if we exclude cotton and tobacco from our foreign trade figures the result is a net import balance of food products to supplement our own production. There is also a small volume of imports of items we do not produce — rubber, coffee, silk, bananas, tea and spices. But the net import balance has been so small that we may be said to be virtually self-sufficient in food as well as in cotton and tobacco.

The farm plant, made up chiefly of land, buildings, crops, livestock and machinery, was valued at $44 billion in January 1940 and, largely as a result of the rise in land values, at $135 billion as of January 1, 1953. At constant prices the 1953 value of the farm plant would not exceed the 1940 value by more than about 10 per cent, reflecting the increase in physical inventories of machinery, livestock and crops. About 64 per cent of this inventory value consisted of the value of land and buildings, 15 per cent of livestock and poultry, and the remainder, 21 per cent, of machinery and motor equipment and of crops held for sale.[2]

The important elements in the agricultural plant are revealed by the 1950 Census. In that year all land in farms, a relatively fixed total, amounted to 1,159 million acres, of which about one third was used for crops. Land actually used to grow crops in 1950 amounted to 345 million acres, and land available for crops (harvested,

By LOUIS H. BEAN, Consulting Economist; formerly, Office of the Secretary of Agriculture. Opinions and judgments expressed in this chapter are those of the author and should not be attributed to the organization with which he has been associated.

1. *Agriculture's Capacity to Produce — Possibilities under Specified Conditions*, Agriculture Information Bulletin No. 88, U.S. Bureau of Agricultural Economics, June 1952, prepared under the auspices of the Land Grant College, U.S. Department of Agriculture Joint Committee on Agricultural Productive Capacity.

2. U.S. Department of Agriculture.

TABLE 329. LAND USED FOR AGRICULTURE,
1940 AND 1950 [a]

(*Millions of Acres*)

Type of Use	1940	1950
Total land used for agriculture	1,565	1,559
Total land in farms	1,061	1,159
Cropland	399	409
Harvested	321	345
Crop failure, idle or fallow	78	64
Pasture	461	485
Plowable	111	100
Not plowable	350	385
Forest and woodland	157	220
Pastured	100	135
Not pastured	57	85
Other land in farms [b]	44	45
Pasture and grazing land, not in farms [c]	504	400

Sources: U.S. Department of Agriculture: *Agricultural Statistics, 1952,* Table 635, p. 620; *Inventory of Major Land Uses in the United States,* Miscellaneous Publication No. 663, 1948, pp. 30 and 32; *Major Uses of Land in the United States,* Technical Bulletin No. 1082, 1953.

a. Excludes forests not grazed and not in farms.
b. Includes farmsteads, roads, wastelands and other land in farms.
c. Includes grassland and noncommercial brushland and woodland pastured and commercial forest and woodland grazed.

crop failure, idle and fallow and plowable pasture) amounted to 509 million acres. (See Table 329.) Thus, nearly half of all the land in farms was available for crops and 68 per cent of this actually was planted to crops. More than this was planted in the peak year of the war.

In April 1950, 25.1 million persons lived on farms. (This is an adjusted estimate which runs somewhat higher than the Census count.) The farm labor force of that date is estimated at 7.4 million. This working force is annually augmented during the planting and harvesting period by 3 million or more seasonal laborers, chiefly from schools and farm homes.

The third major element in agricultural capacity is equipment and supplies required for production. Here the most conspicuous development during the 1940s was a sharp drop in the number of work animals and a great increase in the number of trucks and tractors and specialized equipment. By 1950 there were on farms 4.2 million automobiles used for both business and household purposes, 3.6 million tractors and

2.2 million trucks. The number of tractors increased 134 per cent between 1940 and 1950 and the number of trucks 111 per cent. Other mechanical equipment such as corn pickers and milking machines was adopted at an even faster rate. By 1953 the number of tractors had risen to 4.4 million and the number of trucks to 2.5 million, while other machines continued to make greater gains.

Electric power, an important part of farm equipment, now is available to about nine tenths of all farms, compared with 30 per cent in 1940. Consumption of fertilizer and lime in 1950 amounted to 34 million tons, more than twice as much as in 1940.

REQUIREMENTS FOR DOMESTIC CONSUMPTION AND EXPORT

Total domestic requirements for agricultural products are fairly simple to estimate for the next decade or two. The major question is the number of bodies to be fed and clothed; the amount required for each is not subject to much variation.

STABLE PER CAPITA FOOD CONSUMPTION

In spite of our varied tastes and eating habits and changes in our individual diets, the national per capita consumption of food — measured in pounds and not in terms of quality or value — tends to be quite stable from year to year and to increase moderately from decade to decade. The per capita consumption of tobacco has been rising, but tobacco occupies a relatively minor place both in the national expenditure for farm products and in acreage requirements. While our per capita consumption of fiber crops — chiefly cotton and wool — varies substantially from year to year with industrial conditions, it changes little from decade to decade.

In good years we purchase food at retail on an average of about 1,550 pounds per capita, and in depression years not much less. During the period of great unemployment from 1932 to 1934, the average fell to about 1,500 pounds per capita, less than 5 per cent below 1929. This resistance of consumption to the downward pull of greatly reduced purchasing power is possible because food needs are primary needs, because retail food prices decline with earnings, and because farmers in general continue to produce re-

TABLE 330. DAILY PER CAPITA FOOD CONSUMPTION, 1909–1952
(*Retail Weights*)

Year	Total	Proteins	Fats	Carbohydrates	Calories.
	(*Pounds*)	(*Grams*)	(*Grams*)	(*Grams*)	(*Number*)
1909	4.42	103	126	499	3,530
1919	4.22	96	128	480	3,430
1929	4.32	93	136	476	3,470
1939	4.27	91	138	445	3,350
1950	4.17	95	144	401	3,250
1951	4.18	94	140	402	3,210
1952	4.19	96	145	398	3,240

Source: Consumption of Food in the United States, 1909–52, Agriculture Handbook No. 62, U.S. Department of Agriculture, 1953, pp. 144 and 162. (These figures include wastage only in the home.)

gardless of the condition of the markets. There is of course considerable shifting from one commodity to another, but total acreage in production remains about the same.

These constants simplify the problem of making projections for a growing population. Given the rate of population increase to 1960, our main problem in projecting acreage requirements is to determine the extent to which consumption of food and fibers may be increased by improving the substandard diets and living conditions of the lower income groups.

SHIFTS IN CONSUMPTION OF FOODS

The composition of the national diet has undergone striking changes. In 1909 the average person consumed 4.42 pounds of food a day (weight at the retail store). The average was about the same, 4.32 pounds, twenty years later, and after a span of another two decades it had dropped to 4.17 pounds. The content of the diet changed in favor of foods containing more fats and less proteins and carbohydrates, and the calorie count declined. Over the entire span of 43 years from 1909 to 1952, the per capita diet showed a 5 per cent drop in poundage but a decline of almost 9 per cent in proteins, 20 per cent in carbohydrates, and 8 per cent in calories, while the fat content increased by 15 per cent. (See Table 330.)

More Protective Foods

In general, these shifts reflect the growing consumer awareness of the need for protective foods, such as dairy and poultry products and fruits and vegetables. We now consume about half the amount of potatoes and sweet potatoes that we consumed in 1909. Meat, poultry and fish consumption today is about the same as in 1909 (having recovered from a decline in the 1920s and 1930s). Consumption of eggs and dairy products, and of fruits and vegetables, has increased substantially. Sugar consumption has increased since 1909, but after a decline during World War II has not since reached the prewar level. The greatest changes have been a threefold increase in consumption of canned vegetables over the forty-three years, and an enormous increase in consumption of canned fruit juices. (See Table 331.)

More Expensive Foods

If the individual items in our diet are added together (combining them on the basis of their relative importance in recent years, as reflected in average prices per unit), we find that from 1909 to 1952 total food consumption increased about 13 per cent, or a third of one per cent a year. This consumption index reflects the shift toward more expensive foods.

While the price-weighted index of per capita consumption rose 12 points from an index of 89 in 1909 to 101 in 1952, 6 points of that advance occurred between 1929 and 1941. There was only a 2 point rise in the twenty years between 1909 and 1929, and a 4 point rise in the eleven years between 1941 and 1952.

Per capita food consumption on a weight basis

TABLE 331. INDEXES OF PER CAPITA CONSUMPTION OF FOODS BY MAJOR
GROUPS IN SELECTED PROSPERITY YEARS [a]

$(1947-1949 = 100)$

Food Group [b]	1909	1919	1929	1941	1944	1948	1952 [c]
Total foods							
Pounds	103	99	101	101	107	99	98
Pounds, weighted by average prices	89	88	91	97	101	99	101
Potatoes and sweet potatoes	176	154	147	118	128	92	85
Cereal products	131	118	115	106	108	100	97
Meats, poultry, fish	100	92	88	96	105	98	103
Dairy products	86	86	94	97	99	98	97
Beans, peas, nuts	82	95	93	108	107	103	100
Fruits, total	79	80	90	102	92	99	100
Vegetables, total	73	75	84	96	107	101	101
Coffee, tea, cocoa	60	69	73	93	86	101	93
Eggs	75	78	86	80	90	101	110
Sugar and sirups	58	71	84	102	92	101	101
Canned vegetables	39	56	67	92	86	96	108
Canned fruit juices	4	2	2	53	58	106	92

Source: Consumption of Food in the United States, 1909–52, Agriculture Handbook No. 62,
U.S. Department of Agriculture, 1953, pp. 144 and 146–147.

a. Indexes for individual food groups, and for total weighted by prices, weighted by average
retail prices for the base period 1947–1949.

b. Items of greatest decrease appear at the top and items of largest increase at the bottom.

c. Preliminary.

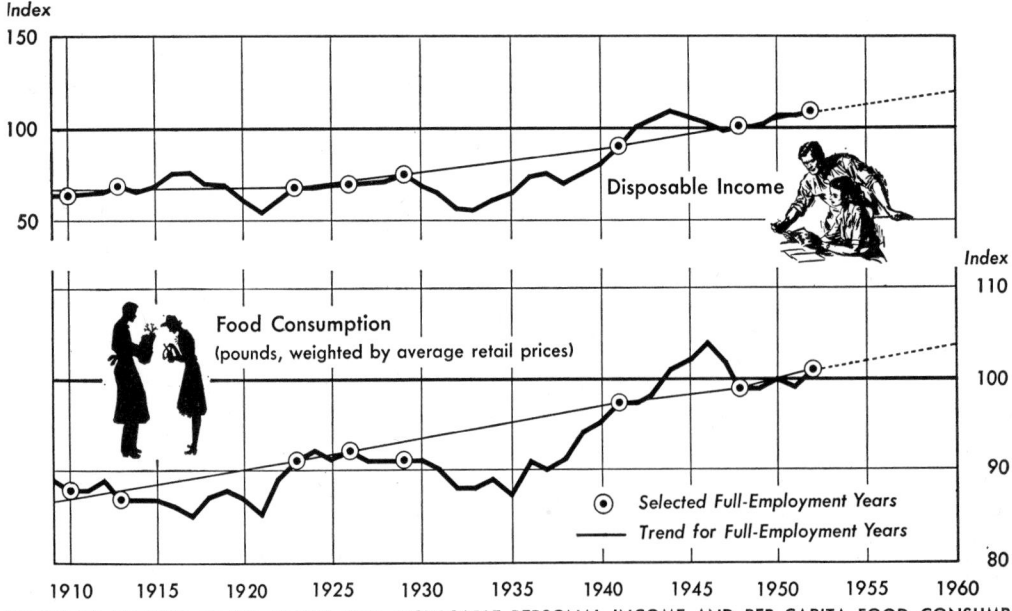

FIGURE 89. INDEXES OF PER CAPITA REAL DISPOSABLE PERSONAL INCOME AND PER CAPITA FOOD CONSUMP-
TION, 1909–1952, WITH ESTIMATED TRENDS TO 1960 BASED ON SELECTED FULL-EMPLOYMENT YEARS
$(1947-1949 = 100)$

Sources: Appendix 22–1; 1960, discussion in text.

TABLE 332. PER CAPITA CONSUMPTION OF FIBERS, 1913–1952

(Pounds)

Year	Total	Cotton	Wool	Flax	Silk	Synthetics
1913	30.4	27.5	2.3	0.3	0.3	a
1919	30.6	26.9	3.1	0.1	0.5	0.1
1929	32.7	27.7	3.0	0.1	0.8	1.1
1941	47.9	38.4	4.8	0.1	0.2	4.5
1948	43.0	30.0	4.7	a	0.1	8.2
1951	43.7	31.0	3.1	0.1	0.1	9.5
1952	40.5	28.2	2.9	a	0.1	9.3

Sources: U.S. Bureau of Agricultural Economics: *The Cotton Situation*, January-March 1953, p. 11, and *Agricultural Outlook Charts, 1954*, October 1953, p. 67.

a. Less than 0.05 pounds.

shows only a fraction of the increase recorded by the consumption index reflecting shifts in diet composition. If real income at full employment levels continues during the 1950s to follow the trend of 1924–1952 (see Figure 89), the corresponding trend in food consumption per capita might rise, on a price-weighted basis, 3 or 4 per cent between 1950 and 1960. This is also about what might be expected according to the trend of the price-weighted index from 1941 to 1952, or over the longer span from 1909 to 1952.

For the nation as a whole, therefore, the expected 16 per cent rise in population by 1960 will be about five times as important a factor in determining future agricultural requirements as this moderate increase in per capita consumption, unless further real progress is made in improving the incomes and diets of the low-income part of the population.

IMPACT OF WORLD WAR II ON FOOD CONSUMPTION

The war brought about a marked and almost immediate increase in per capita consumption of food. Between 1940 and 1944, per capita consumption on a poundage basis increased about 7 per cent and on a price-weighted basis about 6 per cent. This resulted from a rise in the purchasing power of the lower income groups in 1941 and 1942 and from increased food purchases by persons drawn into physical war work. Taking the 1947–1949 average as 100, consumption of all foods on a price-weighted basis rose from 95 in 1940 to 100 in 1950, with no material change between 1950 and 1952.

Wartime civilian per capita consumption exceeded the average of the five prewar years, and was indeed about 10 per cent above the consumption of such prosperity years as 1909, 1923 and 1929. The price-weighted index rose to 102 in 1945 and to a peak of 104 in 1946 and then declined to 102 in 1947 and 99 in 1948. It is not clear how much of the postwar rise was due to wasteful consumption and hoarding, how much to the fact that more people were able to afford better diets, and how much to the return of service men and women to civilian life. In any case, there is some reason to regard the 1946 peak as abnormal, the result of peculiar temporary conditions in the demand for certain dairy products, fats and oils, and canned goods probably related to the sharp inflation following the removal of price controls.

During the war years 1942 to 1945 much attention was given to Victory gardens. The American Institute of Public Opinion estimated that about 20 million families planned to have gardens in the spring of 1943 and 1944, as compared with 15 million in 1940. These were about equally divided among farm, rural nonfarm and urban areas. It was also estimated that 25.5 million families planned to can fruits, vegetables and other preserves. How much food noncommercial sources supplied is not definitely known, but they contributed very little permanent increase to the national diet. The Department of Agriculture estimates roughly that these gardens added only about 2 per cent to the national diet in 1944 and only about one per cent in 1940 and 1948.

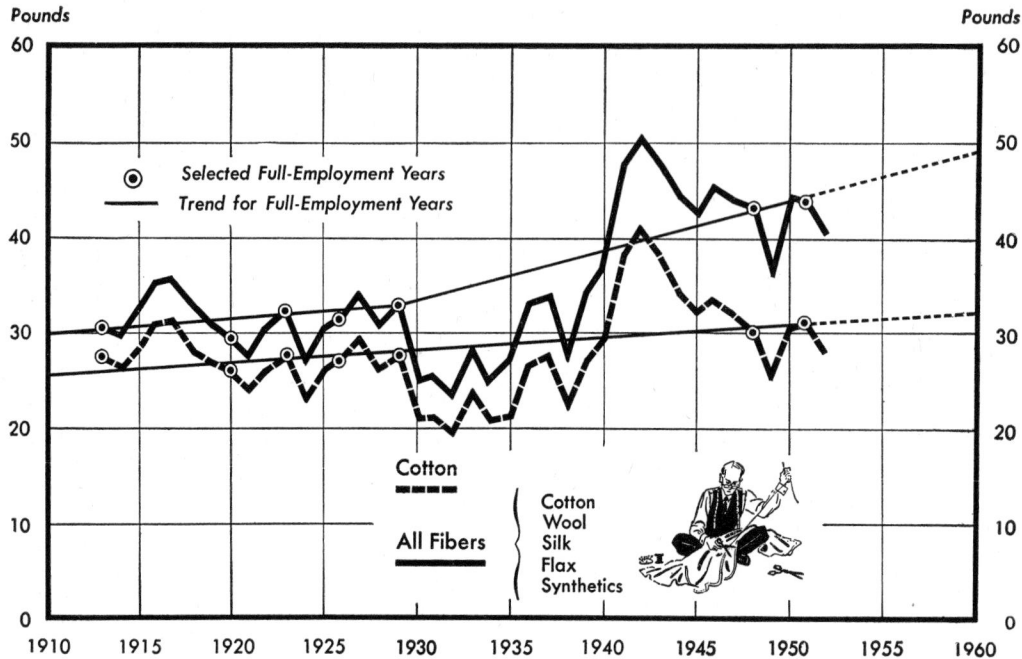

FIGURE 90. PER CAPITA CONSUMPTION OF COTTON AND ALL FIBERS, 1913–1952, WITH ESTIMATED TRENDS TO 1960 BASED ON SELECTED FULL-EMPLOYMENT YEARS

Sources: Appendix 22–2; 1960, discussion in text.

STABLE PER CAPITA CONSUMPTION OF FIBERS

The major fiber, cotton, still supplies nearly three fourths of all fiber consumption, with wool and synthetics accounting for more than a fourth. Per capita mill consumption of cotton totaled 27 pounds in 1913 and 28 in 1952. Consumption of rayon and other synthetics, which amounted to only about a pound per capita in the late 1920s, has increased to more than 9 pounds per capita. The rise in the use of synthetic fibers has not reduced the per capita consumption of cotton and wool, but it may have deprived these natural fibers of their full potential expansion. (See Table 332.)

Consumption of cotton and wool by textile mills varies from year to year in response to fluctuations in consumer spending and industrial activity. But in years of prosperity the consumption of cotton — like the per capita consumption of food — has tended to be relatively constant. (See Figure 90.)

After World War II, as after World War I, the war-stimulated demand for fibers subsided. A higher level of postwar industrial activity has, however, supported a moderately increased per capita consumption over the prewar. Compared with 30 pounds per capita in 1948, a projection of cotton consumption to 1960 would show only a moderate increase to 32 pounds. The consumption of synthetic fibers might increase to 14 pounds per capita by 1960, compared with 9.7 pounds in 1950 and 9.3 in 1952. Production and acreage requirements for domestic use of cotton and wool, as for food, thus may be projected chiefly on the basis of population growth, but with an eye to the extent to which synthetic fibers might displace these natural fibers.

TOBACCO CONSUMPTION

Next to fibers, tobacco is of chief importance among the nonfood crops. It takes at most only about 2 million acres, or less than two thirds of one per cent of the total acreage for harvested crops. However, as labor requirements per acre are relatively large, tobacco absorbs nearly 3 per cent of the total man-hour requirements for all crops.

The long-time rising demand for cigarette tobacco, accentuated by the war, has been accompanied by a reduction in other uses of tobacco.

The net result is that per capita tobacco consumption increased at an average rate of less than one per cent a year during the twenty years before the war and at about the same rate once the war was over. We may, therefore, expect acreage requirements for tobacco production to continue to expand slowly and to represent a negligible share of total acreage.

ADDITIONAL REQUIREMENTS FOR BEST-ADAPTED DIET

How much will food consumption increase in 1960 over 1950 if conditions of high employment make possible further improvements in the diets of the low income groups?

In the early days of World War II, the National Research Council recommended certain standards for low-income diets, and the Bureau of Agricultural Economics estimated the additional production required to meet those standards. These estimates indicated that to supply the entire population (in 1943) with an adequate diet at moderate cost, assuming an even distribution of consumption, would have required substantial increases in the production of truck crops and hay (to permit a marked increase in dairy products), and moderate increases in the production of hogs, sheep and lambs, and poultry. But the adequate, moderate-cost diet would have involved reductions in grains for food and in other minor crops which would have about offset the increase in livestock production. On balance, production would have had to be very little greater than in 1936–1940.

Even higher goals would have affected production only slightly. To supply the nation with the best-adapted low-cost diet for families of moderate income, and with a liberal diet for all high-income families, assuming an even distribution of consumption among families in each group, it was estimated, would have required a total volume of foodstuffs not much larger than that of 1936–1940. The Department of Agriculture suggested that 10 per cent additional production would permit those consuming above the average in their income groups to continue to do so.[3]

A number of more recent estimates are now available.[4] The greatest required increase[5] is that indicated by estimates of "potential human consumption." This attempts to measure what people really want, not what they can afford to eat, as "demand" estimates do, nor what they need, as estimates based on the idea of adequacy do. On this basis the nation could consume 20 per cent more food. Estimates which the Bureau of Agricultural Economics prepared for the Council of Economic Advisors were lower, limiting the goal to supplementing the national diet so as to bring low-income families up to an adequate diet. The BAE found that the nation as a whole, on this basis, could consume about 10 per cent more.

During the 1940s some progress was made toward a more even distribution of income, which may in part explain the increase in per capita food consumption during that period. For the 1950s it would be reasonable to assume that the same tendencies in income distribution could favor a further increase in national per capita food consumption of the order of 3 to 4 per cent, in line with the trend associated with conditions of full employment.

EXPORT REQUIREMENTS

How much of our agricultural capacity we shall need for foreign markets cannot be determined with any certainty. Before World War I, farmers obtained 15 per cent or more of their gross income from exports of all farm products combined. But exports supplied less than 10 per cent of their total income from food production. During 1916–1920, shipments abroad increased

3. Some authorities pointed out that the National Research Council's standards were admittedly liberal and subject to revision, and held the view that optimum nutrition could be ensured without an increase in acreage. The assumption that there would be no reduction in the standard of those above the recommended dietary level tended, of course, to overstate acreage requirements. However, if general education and income and food distribution should be such as to permit the low income groups to lift their diets up to standard, some of those who, for various reasons of taste, income or wasteful consumption habits, consume above standard would be expected to adjust their diets down to standard, and an increase of something less than 10 per cent over the 1936–1940 production for domestic use would have sufficed to meet the best-adapted-diet standard.

For a discussion of later revisions in the National Research Council's standards see Chapter 5, particularly Table 52, footnote a.

4. These have been summarized by Marguerite C. Burk in an article entitled "An Analysis of Estimates of Food Requirements and Demand" in Agricultural Economics Research, January 1951.

5. Contained in Testimony Proposing Long-Range Agricultural Policy and Programs before congressional committees on agriculture, April and October 1947, presented by Assistant Secretary Brannan of the U.S. Department of Agriculture.

TABLE 333. GROSS FARM INCOME AND VALUE OF AGRICULTURAL
EXPORTS FOR SELECTED YEARS, 1910–1952

(*Dollar Amounts in Millions*)

Crop Year Beginning in:	Farm Income	Agricultural Exports	Exports as Per Cent of Income
1910	$ 7,349	$1,029	14
1914	7,633	1,474	19
1919	17,681	3,850	22
1928	13,468	1,847	14
1932	6,400	590	9
1937	11,185	891	8
1944	24,113	2,191	9
1951	36,961	4,053	11
1952	36,526	2,816	8

Sources: U.S. Department of Agriculture: *Agricultural Statistics, 1952*, p. 698, and *Agricultural Outlook Charts, 1954*, October 1953, pp. 14 and 18.

somewhat. Food exports accounted for 14 per cent of farm income from food production, and all exports, including cotton, accounted for nearly 18 per cent of income from all farm products. Toward the end of the 1920s the export outlet contracted to its prewar proportion, and with the greatly reduced foreign trade of the 1930s it shrank further. During 1935–1937, only 8 per cent of farm production was exported — the output, it is estimated, of 24 million acres. (See Appendix 22–3.)

Food Exports and Lend-Lease

Under the lend-lease program of World War II, food exports increased sharply. By 1943, $2 billion of food was exported under the program, accounting for about 12 per cent of gross income from farm production. Other food exports brought the total to $2.5 billion, or 14 per cent of our large food output at the time. This about equaled the share of our food production that was shipped out in 1916–1920 and exceeded that of the 1920s.

At the height of World War II, in 1944, the civilian population consumed about 80 per cent of our food supply. The other 20 per cent went into these channels: 13 per cent was distributed by the military, chiefly abroad; 6 per cent was distributed by the Department of Agriculture for lend-lease, relief and purchases for foreign governments; and one per cent represented commercial exports.

Postwar Exports

After the war we continued to export a relatively large share of our food output. Liberated areas needed much in the way of foods, feeds and seeds, although of course the requirements fell off as production in these areas was restored. Our food exports were chiefly in grains. Cotton was the principal nonfood export. Various foreign aid programs aimed at restoring normal economic life in Europe and Asia provided funds for the export of farm products in quantities greater than would otherwise have been the case. Exports in the 1951–1952 crop year reached the equivalent of 11 per cent of gross farm income. In 1952–1953 the ratio fell to 8 per cent, as against 14 per cent in 1928–1929. Allowing for a freight differential between farm and port values of approximately 10 per cent, the 1952–1953 ratio indicates that the export market was then about 7 per cent of the total market for farm products. (See Table 333.)

Wheat exports were also subsidized under the International Wheat Agreement in effect for the five-year period 1948 to 1952. The United States obligated itself to sell as much as 280 million bushels of wheat for prices ranging from $1.80 in the initial year to $1.30 in the fifth, on the expectation that the United States would have ample supplies and that world prices would drift downward, which they in general failed to do. Our annual deliveries under the wheat agreement averaged about 250 million bushels

Index   *Index*

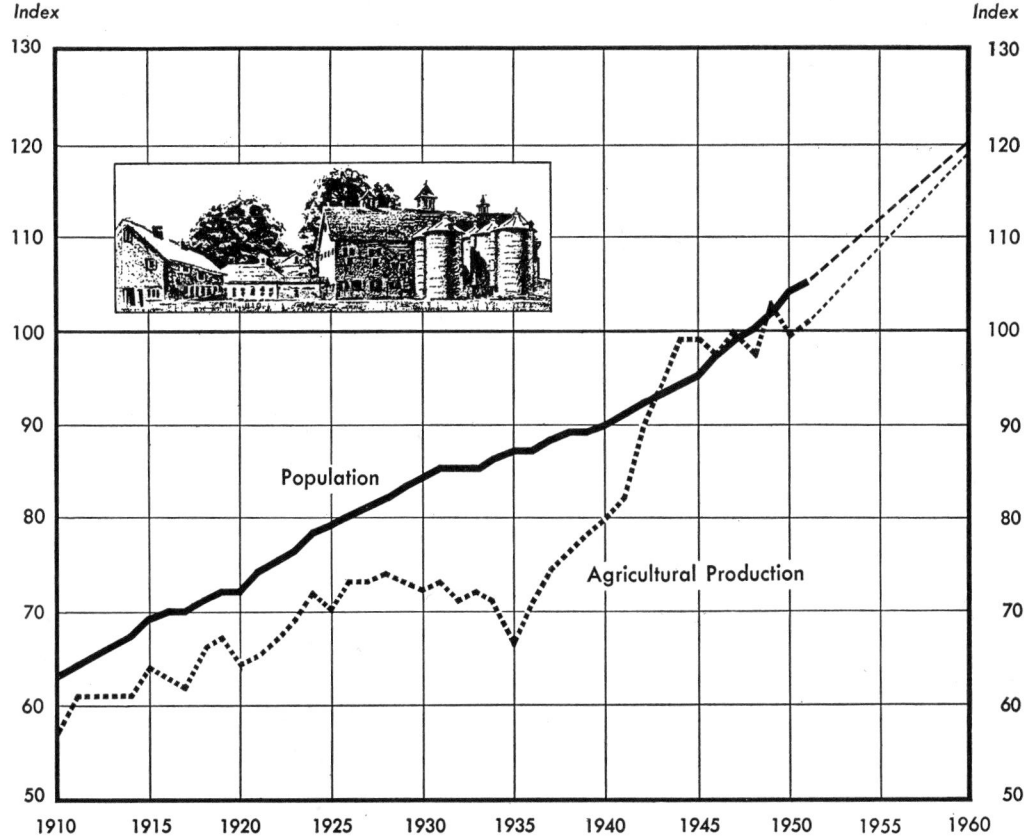

FIGURE 91. INDEXES OF AGRICULTURAL PRODUCTION AND POPULATION, 1910–1951, WITH ESTIMATED TRENDS TO 1960
(1947–1949 = 100)

Sources: Appendix 22–4; 1960, discussion in text.

a year for the 1950, 1951 and 1952 crop years, with prices substantially below the domestically supported price level. Cotton exports, too, have averaged well above expectations, amounting to 5 million bales in 1951–1952.

In 1952, 91 per cent of our total food supply was used by the civilian population at home and only 9 per cent was exported: relief shipments amounted to only one per cent; commercial exports to 4.5 per cent; and military requirements to 4 per cent. It is estimated that for these export purposes, the product of about 40 million acres was required.

Future Exports

The volume of exports of grains and cotton is as difficult to predict for the 1950s as it was for the late 1940s. A great deal depends on United States government foreign aid programs. In 1949 and 1950, when annual agricultural exports surpassed $3 billion, about 60 per cent of the total was financed with relief and ECA funds. In 1951, when agricultural exports amounted to $4 billion, these funds financed only 24 per cent. More than half of these exports were bread grains and cotton.

In 1952, negotiations were started for renewing the International Wheat Agreement, with higher price provisions and some flexibility to permit adjustment to changes in general economic conditions. This agreement, ratified by Congress in 1953, will affect our wheat exports, and so will unforeseen foreign relief needs, such as the loan of $190 million to India in 1951 for grain purchases in the United States.

For present purposes we may assume an intermediate prospect between the two extremes of liberal or restricted foreign outlets. If other countries, as well as the United States, maintain high industrial employment, and if certain European countries gradually shift from agriculture to industry, our exports might be restored to about the level of the late 1920s. They would then represent nearly 15 per cent of our total farm production. These speculations would indicate greater rather than smaller future acreage requirements for export demand. If, however, exports of grains and cotton should fall off during the 1950s, the effect would be to stimulate diversion of land used for these crops to grass and pasture in order to meet expanded domestic consumption of livestock and livestock products.

Such a volume would provide the average person in the 1960 population of 177 million with about 1,580 pounds of food, including the usual imports of sugar, coffee, etc., plus 32 pounds of cotton and 3 pounds of wool for apparel; and it would leave 15 per cent of the total production available for export.

This projected trend of production takes into account the changing importance of certain products. Based on past trends, it implies a continuation of the gradual shifts that have been taking place in composition of demand and in acreage requirements. These same considerations apply to the projections that follow of labor requirements per acre and per unit of output.

PRODUCTION REQUIREMENTS FOR 1960

On the basis of the record of fairly constant per capita consumption of food and nonfood crops, and the assumed population growth, we may now project the volume of production required for domestic consumption and for export, assuming that per capita domestic consumption (1) remains unchanged or (2) increases 3 to 4 per cent by 1960 in line with the 1940–1950 trend.

The course of our net agricultural production (for domestic consumption and export) roughly parallels our population growth. (See Figure 91.) For both food crops and livestock products the parallel was particularly close up to about 1930. Following the relatively low per capita production of the mid-1930s, a new level of output in relation to population was attained. A good part of the increase occurred under the stimulus of World War II, which shows up not only in increased takings for military purposes and export but also in increased per capita consumption of the civilian population. As previously indicated, per capita food consumption has already been placed on a permanently higher level.

To meet this level of per capita domestic consumption and to maintain the present share of production destined for foreign consumption, an increase of about 16 per cent by 1960 over the 1950 output will be required to meet the increase in population. Another 4 per cent will be needed if continuing prosperity and better distribution of income bring further shifts in consumption, approximating the moderate rise in per capita consumption from 1941 to 1951. The total increase, then, would be about 20 per cent.

ACRES REQUIRED IN 1960

The acreage needed to meet the required 20 per cent increase in production will depend upon the productivity of the acres harvested and on the "efficiency" of feed-consuming animals in producing meats and dairy and poultry products. The long-term record of per acre production of "finished goods" — both crops and livestock, including livestock products marketed and those consumed on farms where produced — shows a marked increase in productivity after World War I and an even more striking gain after 1935.[6] (See Figure 92.)

Various assumptions may be made as to the future course of productivity. Common practice would be to assume that the average yields of 1948–1952 will prevail in 1960. But the technological basis of the sharp increase in productivity during the past two decades and the prospect of further, more widely applied technological advances warrant the assumption of further increases in yields. The index of net production per harvested acre in 1960 could thus be as much as 10 to 15 per cent greater than in 1950.

The increase in production required between 1950 and 1960 could be obtained partly by an increase in acreage harvested. Since the reduction in harvested acreage that took place in the 1930s due to abandonment in years of poor growing conditions and to acreage curtailment programs, there has been a gradual expansion. The total of harvested acreage in 1949 was practically equal

---

6. The measure of production per acre used here is not the usual index of crop yields per acre. It was obtained by dividing the index of net production of crops and livestock by the index of acreage in harvested crops as shown in Appendix 22–5.

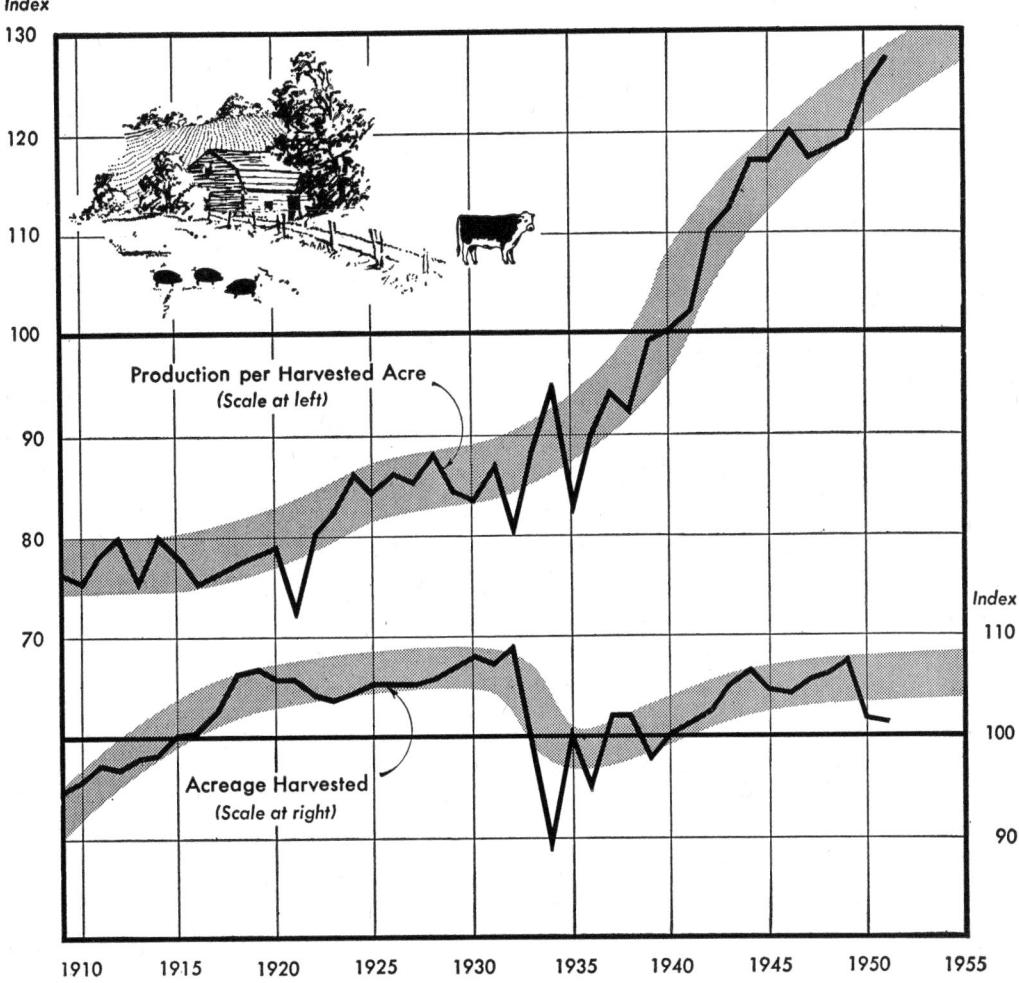

FIGURE 92. INDEXES OF ACREAGE HARVESTED AND PRODUCTION OF CROPS AND LIVESTOCK (FOR SALE OR HOME CONSUMPTION) PER ACRE, 1909–1951

(1940 = 100)

Source: Appendix 22–5.

to that of 1930–1932. Both types of reduction held the total down again in 1950 and 1951. In 1950 we had a planned curtailment in cotton acreage; in 1951, and again in 1953, abandonment of grain acreage due to unfavorable weather practically offset the restoration of cotton acreage. By 1960, therefore, acreage harvested may be expected to be at least equal to that of 1949, and possibly 2 or 3 per cent greater if we assume a slightly rising trend in line with recent experience. (See Figure 92.)

This would mean an 8 per cent increase in output over 1950 if production per acre were no

greater than in that year. If, in addition, production per acre increased 12 per cent in line with past experience, the total increase would amount to 21 per cent. This would be just about enough to meet the probable demand arising from the growth in population and from a moderate improvement in per capita consumption and total exports.

PHYSICAL RESOURCES FOR EXPANDED PRODUCTION

Will we have ample physical and material resources — land, machinery, electric power, livestock, fertilizer, other production supplies —

with which to provide the food, feed and fiber needed during the 1950s? [7]

LAND RESOURCES

The tremendous wartime demand for food for domestic civilian consumption, for the armed forces and for our allies converted our agricultural restriction programs into expansion programs. Under the war food program, 364 million acres were planted to crops. This exceeded the 342 million acres planted in 1940 by less than 7 per cent, and fell 10 million acres short of the record plantings of 1932, before the AAA curtailment programs were adopted to reduce export surpluses. In 1932, for various reasons, about 15 million of the acres planted were abandoned. In subsequent years, particularly in the record drought years 1934 and 1936, about 50 million acres were abandoned. In 1944 only 12 million acres were abandoned and 352 million were harvested. This is 68 million acres less than the projected maximum requirement for 1960 of about 420 million acres and only slightly less than the projected minimum of about 370 million acres.

Under the 1944–1945 food program, almost all of the wheatland and cornland that had been kept out of cultivation because of a weak export market and below-parity prices was returned to cultivation, while idle cotton land was planted largely to peanuts, soybeans and corn. A large stock of American cotton, together with much higher yields per acre, made it possible to keep cotton acreage down to less than half of what it used to be before the AAA cotton programs were adopted in 1933.

The fair certainty that the additional land required for food production in 1960 will be available springs from two sources: the long-time record of expansion of our land resources, and the potentialities for greatly increasing harvested cropland under a well-directed soil conservation program.

Projection on the Basis of Past Trends

The amount of land in farms shown by census records from 1850 to date is as follows (in millions of acres):

1850	293
1860	407
1870	408
1880	536
1890	623
1900	839
1910	879
1920	956
1930	987
1940	1,061
1950	1,159
1960 (est.)	(1,250)

On the basis of the increases from decade to decade one might have expected all land in farms, amounting to 1,061 million acres in 1940, to reach 1,100 million acres by 1950 and 1,130 million acres by 1960. But the total reported had already risen to 1,159 million acres by 1950. At this rate of increase we may expect to have 1,250 million acres of land in farms by 1960.

Within this total, at least a 10 per cent increase in cropland could be expected. The 879 million acres of farmland recorded in 1910 provided 347 million acres of cropland (harvested, failure and fallow), or 39.5 per cent of the total. The 987 million acres of total land in farms recorded in 1930 provided 413 million acres of cropland, or 41.8 per cent of the total. Of the 1,061 million acres recorded in 1940, 35 per cent was cropland. (See Table 334.) On the basis of these percentages we should expect an increase of at least 35 million acres of cropland between 1950 and 1960, raising the total to about 445 million acres, if the total land in farms should be expanded to 1,250 million acres.

Because of increased productivity per acre, however, we may not need this much of an increase in land in farms and land in crops. In 1910, cropland per capita averaged 3.77 acres; in 1920, 3.80 acres; in 1930, 3.37 acres; and in 1940, 3.03 acres. (See Table 334.) At this rate of decline we would need about 2.40 acres of cropland per capita by 1960, or a total of about 425 million acres — only 16 million acres more than we had in 1950. Such a requirement is well within the realm of potential expansion.

Potential Increase through Conservation

The future is likely to see substantially greater potentialities for land use than the requirements suggested by past trends.[8] Acreage planted to

---

7. We are not concerned here with the ability of farmers to pay for these additional production facilities; that is taken for granted by assuming conditions of high employment and agricultural prosperity.

8. The following are the views of Hugh Bennett, former Chief of the Soil Conservation Service.

TABLE 334. CROPLAND IN RELATION TO POPULATION, 1900–1950

Year	Cropland, Harvested, Failure, Idle or Fallow	Population [a]	Cropland Per Capita
	(Millions of Acres)	(Millions)	(Acres)
1900	319	76.0	4.20
1910	347	92.0	3.77
1920	402	105.7	3.80
1930	413	122.7	3.37
1940	399	131.8	3.03
1950	409	151.2	2.71

Sources: *Agricultural Statistics, 1952*, U.S. Department of Agriculture, p. 620; *Statistical Abstract of the United States, 1952*, U.S. Bureau of the Census, pp. 5 and 6.

a. Figures for 1900 through 1930 are for continental United States; 1940 and 1950 include armed forces and civilians stationed outside continental United States.

crops could be greatly increased through a program of improved land use, including sound practices of soil and water conservation. We could expand our harvested cropland by 135 million acres or more if the following objectives were immediately adopted and vigorously pursued:

(1) Putting some idle and fallow farmland into use (40 million acres or more).
(2) Reducing crop failures to a minimum by adopting soil and water conservation practices and other methods of good land use (15 million acres).
(3) Utilizing plowable farm pasture for cropland (40 million acres or more).
(4) Draining and irrigating suitable land not now in farms (20 million acres).
(5) Breaking up cutover upland forest areas not in farms (10 million acres).
(6) Leasing and selling to farmers western land owned by states or private corporations (10 million acres).

These measures would provide the country with a total of about 480 million acres for harvesting crops, compared with the 345 million in 1950. Even without increased yields per acre, it would thus be possible to expand production by about 40 per cent. However, if lands were used according to their capacity under this rounded land program, and if soil management, erosion control and conservation were stressed, it is estimated that yields per acre would also increase, perhaps enough for a 50 per cent gain in production.

PRODUCTIVITY PER ACRE

Part of the increased production required in the 1950s can be expected to come from continuing improvement in yields per acre. Since 1936, yields of the most important crops and fruits have risen phenomenally. Favorable weather has played its part, but hybrid seed and improved soil care, retirement of poor land, greatly expanded use of lime and fertilizer, and many technological improvements in plant breeding, planting, cultivating and harvesting have all contributed greatly. Hundreds of thousands of farmers under the agricultural adjustment programs of the late 1930s were taught and encouraged to use these and other means of achieving greater productivity of land and livestock. All of this progress is likely to perpetuate a substantial part of the remarkable gains into future years.

Corn Yields

One of the most striking achievements in crop yields is the advance in the yield of corn, associated in recent years with the adoption of hybrid corn in place of open-pollinated varieties. Indeed, this is perhaps the most important of such developments, for corn occupies around 100 million acres, or about 30 per cent of the total of harvested crops.

For sixty years, from 1879 to 1939, from decade to decade, the yield per acre averaged between 25.9 and 27.3 bushels. The dry weather of the 1930s, particularly the record droughts of 1934 and 1936, lowered the average level for that decade to 23.5 bushels. As the use of hybrid seed spread throughout the corn belt, however, and as other farming practices improved, per acre

TABLE 335. INDEXES OF FIELD AND FRUIT CROP YIELDS PER ACRE, 1909–1953
(1923–1932 = 100)

Year	18 Field Crops	10 Fruit Crops	Year	18 Field Crops	10 Fruit Crops
1909	101	66	1931	102	114
1910	102	70	1932	100	97
1911	98	82	1933	95	94
1912	113	83	1934	80	99
1913	98	77	1935	101	112
1914	109	102	1936	87	99
1915	110	97	1937	118	135
1916	97	90	1938	113	129
1917	101	75	1939	114	135
1918	98	85	1940	120	129
1919	100	88	1941	121	139
1920	109	102	1942	135	140
1921	94	65	1943	124	132
1922	99	103	1944	136	153
1923	99	103	1945	129	142
1924	99	89	1946	133	169
1925	101	91	1947	127	164
1926	102	116	1948	152	146
1927	103	83	1949	141	169
1928	104	116	1950	142	168
1929	99	85	1951	141	181
1930	92	111	1952	148	172
			1953	151	169

Sources: U.S. Bureau of Agricultural Economics: Crops & Markets, 1952 edition, p. 4, and Crop Production, December 1953, p. 35.

yields went to a record of 42.5 bushels in 1948, a substantial part of which must be attributed to favorable weather. The average yield for the four years 1949–1952 was 38 bushels per acre, an increase of 40 per cent over the best previous decade average.

Hybrid seed is now being used in most of the corn belt, where more than half the crop is produced. Extensive distribution of hybrids is going forward in the South as well. The United States Department of Agriculture estimates that adoption of hybrids for 80 per cent of the corn acreage in the corn belt and for 40 per cent of that in other states would result in a 10 per cent larger crop. This estimate appears conservative, for recent records suggest that the 15 to 30 per cent increase in per acre yields on which it is premised has already been exceeded where hybrids have been introduced. A normal United States average yield of 50 bushels is not unlikely in another decade. In the corn belt proper the next impetus to greater production per acre is likely to come from much wider use of fertilizers.

Cotton

Experience in cotton yields per acre duplicates that with corn. In all the decades from 1870 to 1930, the ten-year average yield per acre of cotton ranged between 162 and 192 pounds. The record annual yield in that long period was about 220 pounds. But this record has been surpassed in every season since 1936. The annual yield per acre reached a new high of 270 pounds in 1937, and another of 311 pounds in 1948. These recent record yields, which may be attributed in large part to use of fertilizer, abandonment of low-yielding lands, soil conservation practices and use of higher-yielding seeds, have apparently established a new "normal" nearly twice that of the 1920s.

Other Crops

Yields per acre of 28 crops were 42 to 52 per cent greater in 1948–1951 than in the ten-year period 1923–1932. Fruit crops, as well as feed grains, vegetable crops and cotton, have shown

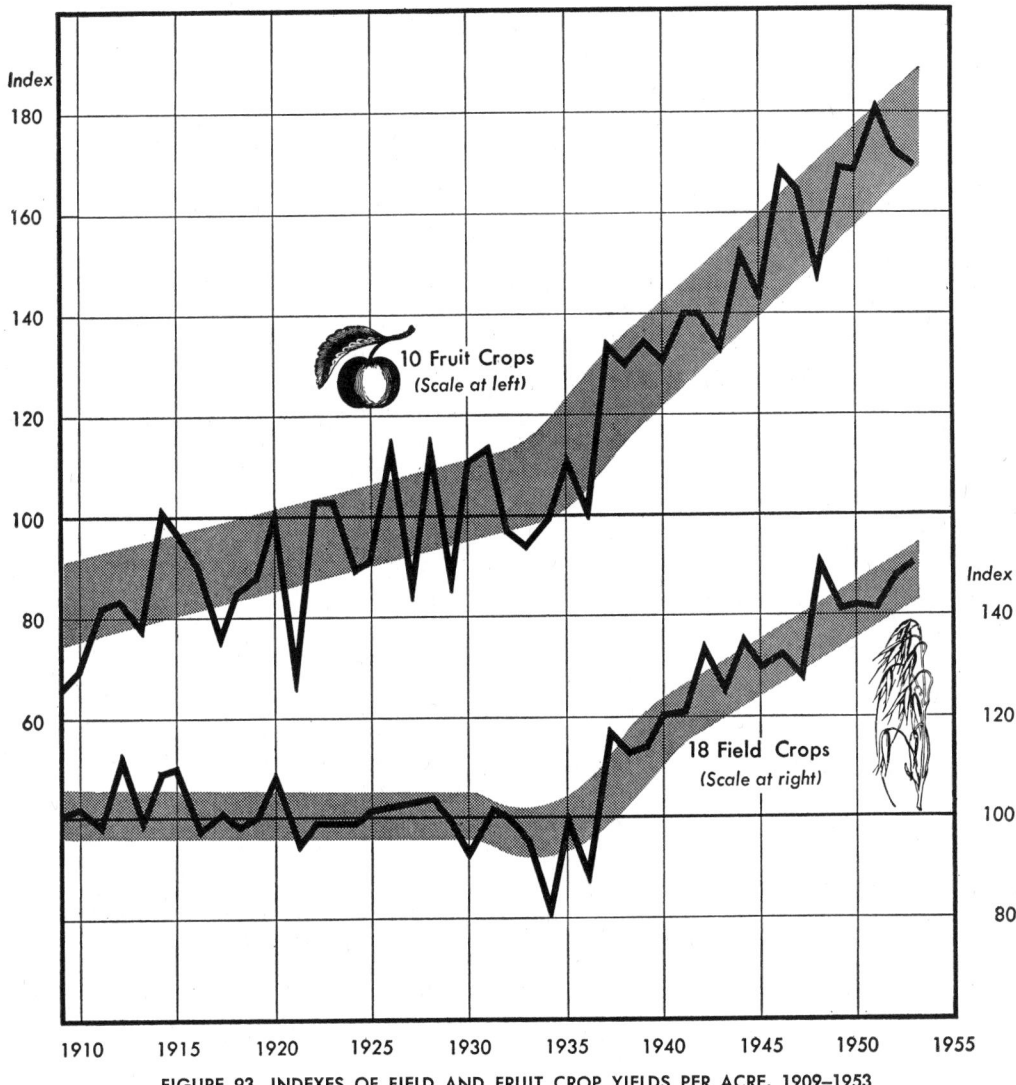

FIGURE 93. INDEXES OF FIELD AND FRUIT CROP YIELDS PER ACRE, 1909–1953
(1923–1932 = 100)

Source: Table 335.

a remarkable rise in yields since 1936. Ten important fruits had average yields per acre 50 per cent higher during 1948–1951 than their 1923–1932 average. This is a greater improvement than occurred in the 18 field crops included in the group of 28. (See Table 335 and Figure 93.)

This marked upward trend in per acre yields, which characterized most crops, contrasts sharply with the long-time record. Average yields of major crops varied little from decade to decade in the past. Part of the trend alteration appears to be a direct parallel and effect of increased

applications of lime and fertilizer. Beginning with the recovery in agricultural prices and income after 1932 and the launching of government programs to stimulate conservation efforts, the use of lime and fertilizer began to mount and crop yields improved. Over the twenty years from 1930 to 1950, average crop yields per acre for these 28 crops increased by 55 per cent (Figure 94), and over the twenty-three-year span from 1930 to 1953 they increased by more than 60 per cent.

The same technological, educational and eco-

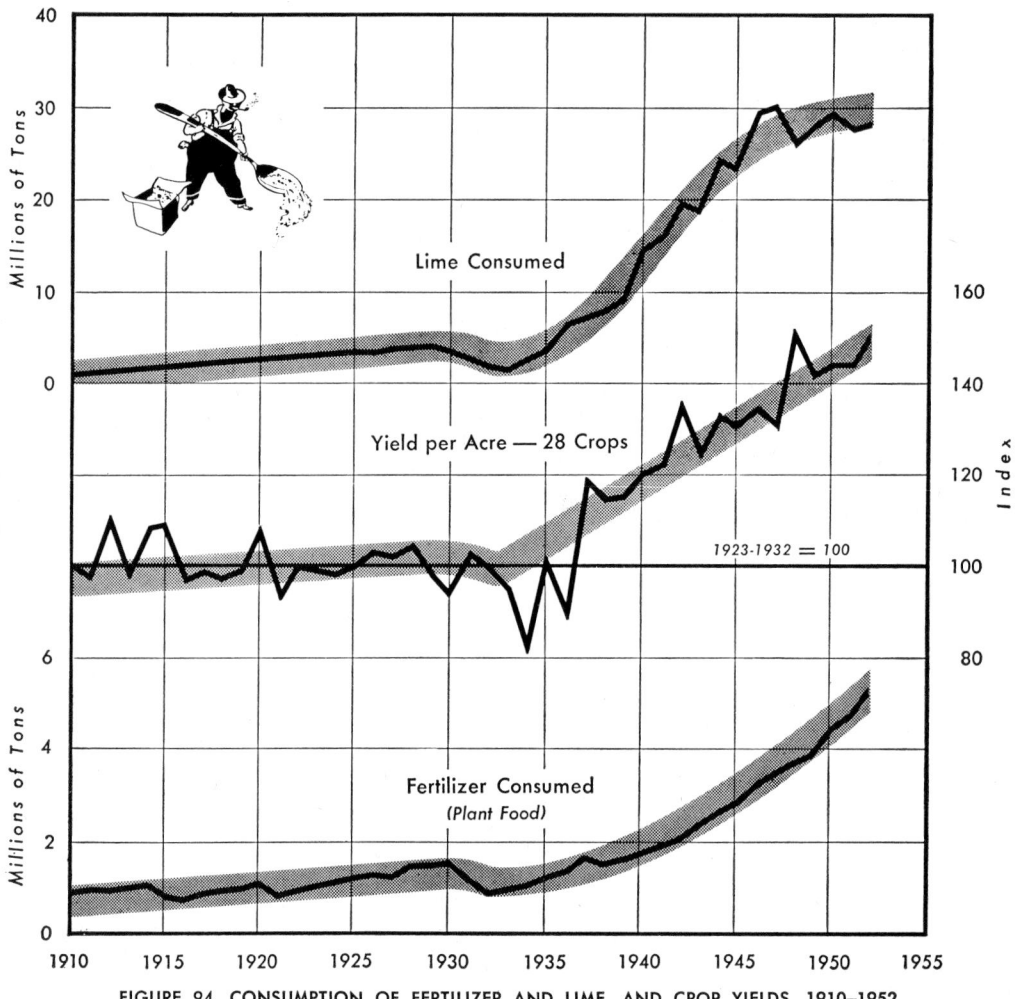

FIGURE 94. CONSUMPTION OF FERTILIZER AND LIME, AND CROP YIELDS, 1910–1952

Sources: Data on lime consumed: 1910–1945, Historical Statistics of the United States, 1790–1945, U.S. Bureau of the Census; 1946–1952, U.S. Department of Agriculture, Production and Marketing Administration. Data on yield per acre, Crops and Markets, 1952 edition, Bureau of Agricultural Economics, U.S. Department of Agriculture. Data on fertilizer consumed, U.S. Department of Agriculture, Production and Marketing Administration.

nomic forces that were responsible for the increase in per acre yields during the 1930s and 1940s are still operative. A large part of the improvement in the yield of corn, wheat, oats, cotton, potatoes, tobacco and other crops will therefore probably continue, and yields per acre in 1960 could easily be about 15 per cent greater than in 1950.

Livestock

Improvement in the production of livestock and livestock products per unit of feed consumed and per animal unit was apparent in the 1920s,

before crop productivity began its sharp upward climb. Meat production increased 30 per cent between 1929 and 1951, whereas feed grain production increased only 15 per cent. The output of milk per dairy cow has been rising slowly over the years. It reached a peak of 4,579 pounds in 1929 and, after a decline in the 1930s, rose to a new peak of 5,314 pounds in 1950 and 5,323 in 1953, an increase of 16 per cent over 1929. Although the number of basic livestock on farms in 1940 was about the same as in 1920, the production of livestock and livestock products was more than 30 per cent greater.

The number of livestock on farms started a

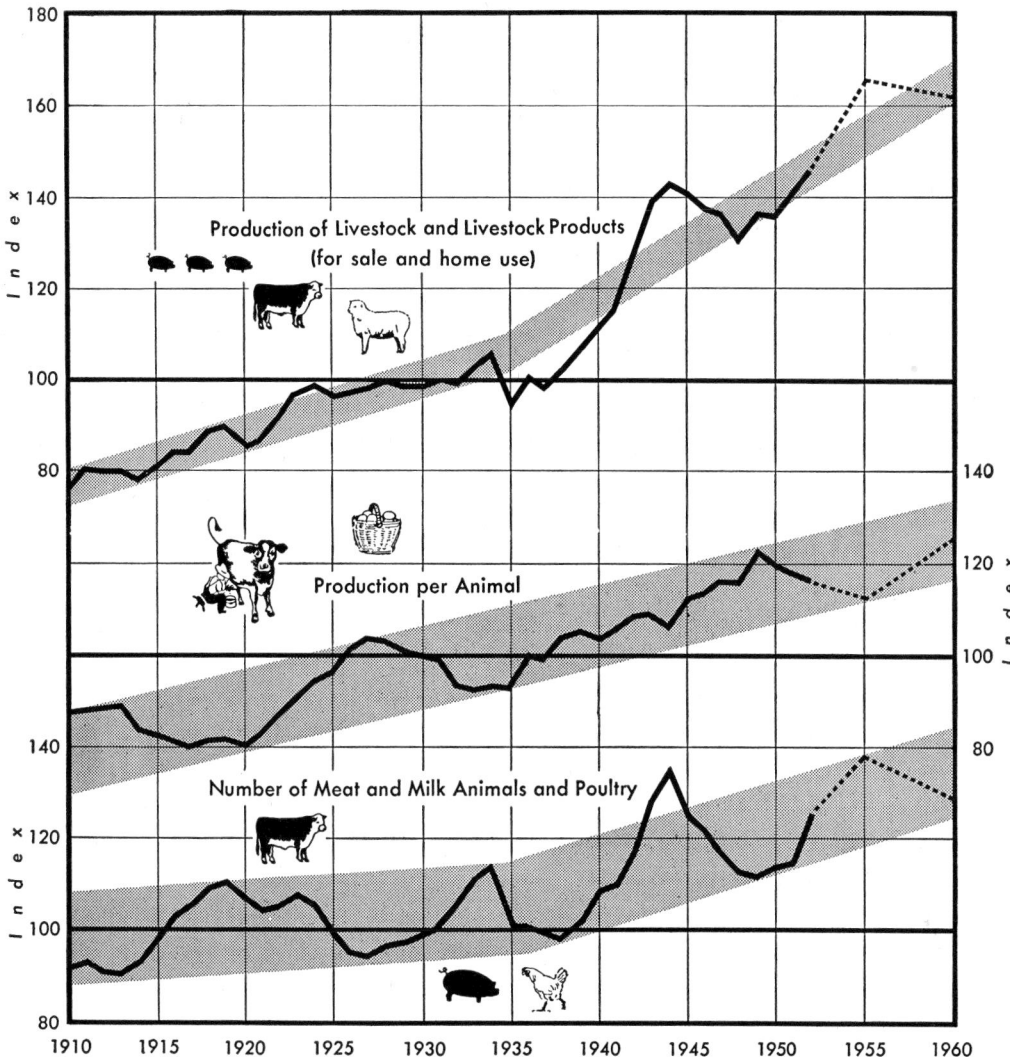

FIGURE 95. INDEXES OF PRODUCTION OF LIVESTOCK AND LIVESTOCK PRODUCTS, NUMBER OF ANIMALS ON FARMS AND PRODUCTION PER UNIT, 1910–1952, WITH ESTIMATES TO 1960
(1935–1939 = 100)

Sources: Appendix 22–6; 1960, discussion in text.

new cycle of increase in 1950 which may attain its peak by the mid-1950s and then give way to a decline. Production per animal unit, however, tends to fluctuate inversely with the cycle of animal numbers on farms. When profitable prices are expected and numbers of animals on farms are being expanded, marketings for slaughter and consumption are checked or curtailed. This inverse relation is likely to mean a moderate decline in production per unit by the mid-1950s and a moderate rise by 1960. The net result

may be a volume of production or marketings in 1960 about 20 per cent greater than in 1950. (See Figure 95.)

Further Technological Developments

More actively than ever before, the Department of Agriculture and the Extension Service are fostering technological developments which can be expected to increase production per harvested acre. Further increases and progress are being advocated particularly in the following: (1) the adoption and use of smaller tractors; (2) the productive efficiency of livestock; (3) the adoption of hybrid corn outside the corn belt, and of high-yielding hays; (4) the adoption of new disease-resistant varieties of plants, particularly of wheat and oats; and (5) cultural and soil-engineering practices.

The most important way of increasing per acre productivity, according to the Soil Conservation Service, will be through wider adoption of modern soil-engineering practices and through better use of land. Much can be achieved, for example, by measures to hold the soil in the field and on the range and to conserve rainfall. Wherever conservation efforts have been undertaken, per acre yields have generally increased. One of the most promising possibilities of all is the potential rehabilitation of 30 million acres now included in soil drainage districts. This land, while generally good, is not producing to capacity, or at all, because drainage ditches have silted up or have become obstructed with vegetation.

The President's Materials Policy Commission has summarized other possibilities in its report of June 1952. Looking toward our requirements and supplies for the 1970s, with the benefit of advice from federal and state agricultural experts, the Commission gives "examples of what can be done" and points specifically to the following possibilities:

(1) Raising the national average corn yield of 40 bushels per acre to around 80 bushels through proper use of fertilizer, high-yielding hybrid seeds, closer and more uniform spacing, and adequate pest control;
(2) Improving deteriorated farm pastures to support two or three times the number of dairy and beef animals by liming, fertilizing, and reseeding with improved types of grasses and legumes;
(3) Increasing the carrying capacity of the more than 300 million acres of publicly owned or managed grazing lands by 30 per cent or more through various types of range improvements and pest control;
(4) Increasing milk production per cow still further, from 5,314 pounds in 1950 to 8,000 pounds, by improving feeding and by wider use of artificial insemination and other breeding improvements, such as the development of hot-weather milk-producers in the South; and
(5) Nearly doubling egg production per hen by 1975 and increasing the productive efficiency of chickens in general and of hogs by extending the use of antibiotics in their feeding.

FERTILIZER

Fertilizer consumption will undoubtedly continue to expand and help to sustain and improve the yields of such crops as cotton, tobacco, wheat and potatoes. Between 1880 and 1926, the tonnage of all commercial fertilizers (excluding limestone) consumed in the United States increased tenfold — from 753,000 tons to 7.5 million tons. In 1930, total consumption reached 8.4 million tons. Following curtailment during the 1930s, consumption again rose; in 1950 the total was over 18 million tons, and in 1952, over 20 million tons.

Fertilizers now in use contain a larger proportion of plant food, and farmers have learned how to apply them more effectively than in the past. While the tonnage of fertilizer used in agriculture doubled between 1930 and 1950, its plant food content trebled: from 1.5 million tons in 1930 it rose to 4.4 million in 1950; by 1952 it had reached 5.2 million. (See Figure 94.) As a result of the defense program, stimulated by the outbreak in Korea in 1950, the fertilizer industry has expanded its production facilities. Another doubling of production during the 1950s is therefore fairly certain, especially since the Department of Agriculture and private interests have also been stimulating the demand. This increasing use of fertilizer is bound to show up in a further rise in yields per acre.

FARM MACHINERY AND WORK STOCK

The war prosperity of 1918–1919 set off a wave of agricultural mechanization. Another wave in the 1920s reached its crest in 1929 and then abruptly receded. Farmers emerged from the depression of the 1930s financially equipped to resume their acquisition of machinery. A third high point of purchases followed in 1937 and still another during the 1940s.

Just as the machinery they had bought in 1928–1929 enabled farmers to maintain their acreage and total production during the hard times when they had to curtail their buying, so the record purchases of 1941–1942 made it possible for farmers to meet the demands of war, even though at least 40 per cent less farm machinery was produced in 1943 than in 1940. After World War II the mechanization trend was resumed with vigor.

There need be little concern over the avail-

TABLE 336. PRINCIPAL MACHINES ON FARMS, 1910–1953

(Thousands)

Year	Tractors	Autos	Motor Trucks	Grain Combines	Field Corn Pickers	Farms with Milking Machines
1910	1	50	—	1	—	—
1920	246	2,146	139	4	10	12
1930	920	4,135	900	61	50	55
1940	1,545	4,144	1,047	190	110	100
1950	3,616	4,208	2,209	714	456	636
1951	3,940	4,280 [a]	2,310	810	522	655
1952	4,170	4,350 [a]	2,410	887	588	686
1953	4,400	4,400 [a]	2,500	940	635	700

Sources: U.S. Department of Agriculture: *The Agricultural Situation,* February 1952; *Agricultural Outlook Charts, 1954,* October 1953; and *Agricultural Statistics, 1953.*

a. Preliminary.

ability of industrial resources for further mechanization during the 1950s. Our capacity for producing iron and steel is much greater than ever before and should easily provide the metal required for farm machinery and equipment, which amounts to only 3 to 4 per cent of the total iron and steel output.

The momentum of the trend toward mechanization and its possibilities may be seen from the figures. At the peak of the 1920s cycle of purchases of farm machinery, 123,000 tractor moldboard plows were produced; at the 1937 peak, 149,000; and in 1950, 342,000. For these same years, the output of corn pickers was 12,000, 16,700 and 88,000, respectively; of combines (harvester-threshers), 37,000, 48,000 and 116,000; and of tractor cultivators, 56,000, 127,000 and 248,000. The record for tractors is especially significant.

Tractors

The tractor, the most important agricultural machine, has recently been adapted to new tasks and to small farms. Through these improvements and its wider use it will continue to reduce the need for horses and to release farm labor. At the beginning of World War II there were 1.5 million tractors on farms, compared with less than a million in 1930, about a quarter of a million in 1920, and practically none in 1910. By 1950 there were 3.6 million; by 1953, 4.4 million. (See Table 336.)

When a quarter of a million tractors appeared on farms — about 1920 — the number of horses began to decline. (See Figure 96.) Between 1920 and 1930 the number of horses and mules 2 years old and over on farms fell from 22 to 18 million; by 1940 there were only 13 million, and by 1951 half as many — 6.8 million. The Department of Agriculture estimates that the decrease in horses and mules has been offset by the increase in tractors. Taking one tractor as equivalent to five work animals, the Department estimates the number of "equivalent work-animal units" (the number of horses and mules 2 years old and over plus five times the number of tractors) at 6.5 per 100 harvested acres in 1920 and 1940, and 7.4 in 1950 and 1951. (See Table 337.)

The use of manpower and horsepower on farms is still on the downtrend, and the mechanical revolution promises to gain further momentum during the 1950s and 1960s. Programs under United Nations sponsorship for mechanizing agriculture in areas of low productivity foreshadow a greatly expanded foreign market for farm machinery and tractors. This large-scale demand would make it possible to produce new-model tractors to sell at considerably lower prices, thus opening up a wider market among our own smaller farming units.

LIVESTOCK RESOURCES

The basic herds of dairy and beef cattle and the hogs, sheep and poultry on farms are — like

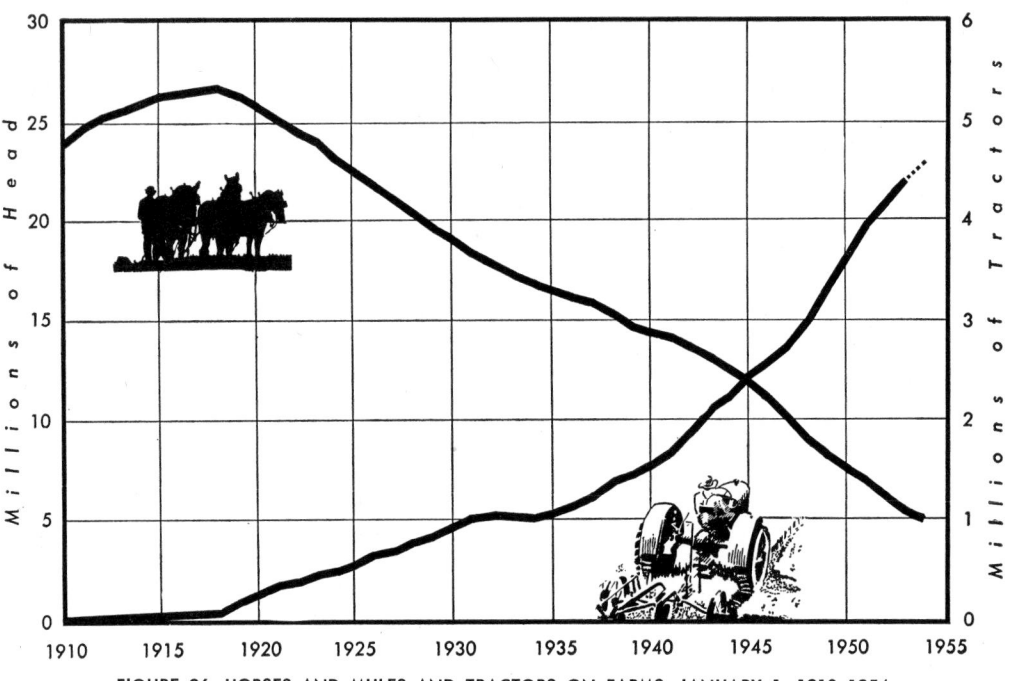

FIGURE 96. HORSES AND MULES AND TRACTORS ON FARMS, JANUARY 1, 1910–1954

Sources: Agricultural Outlook Charts, 1953, Bureau of Agricultural Economics, U.S. Department of Agriculture. Data for 1953 and 1954 from *Livestock and Poultry on Farms and Ranches, January 1,* Crop Reporting Board, U.S. Department of Agriculture.

the work stock — part of the physical resources required for expanding food production. The number of animal units on farms — considering all livestock together as feed-consumers — reached a high point, around the year 1890, of approximately 100 million. At the next peak, in 1905, the total reached 116 million, and in 1919, the peak year of the World War I period, it rose

TABLE 337. NUMBER OF TRACTORS, HORSES AND MULES TWO YEARS OLD AND OVER, AND EQUIVALENT WORK-ANIMAL UNITS ON FARMS, 1920–1951

Year	Tractors on Farms	Horses and Mules 2 Years Old and Over on Farms	Total Equivalent Work-Animal Units[a]	Acres Harvested	Equivalent Work-Animal Units per 100 Acres of Harvested Cropland
	(Thousands)			(Millions)	(Number)
1920	246	22,386	23,616	362	6.5
1930	920	17,981	22,581	359	6.3
1935	1,048	15,473	20,713	296	7.0
1940	1,545	13,000	20,725	321	6.5
1945	2,422	11,116	23,226	353	6.6
1950	3,619	7,415	25,510	345	7.4
1951	3,940	6,763	24,963	337	7.4

Sources: U.S. Department of Agriculture: *The Agricultural Situation,* February 1952, and *Agricultural Statistics, 1952,* pp. 459 and 620.

a. One tractor considered equivalent to five work animals.

to 142 million. During the next fifteen years the increase in livestock numbers was less pronounced, because of the decline in horses on farms; in 1934 all animal units on farms numbered only 144 million.

Wartime demand expanded these resources. Hog production, in fact, increased so much that, in spite of record-breaking feed supplies, the production and feeding of hogs had to be reduced in order to assure an ample supply of feed grains for 1944 and 1945. Wheat stocks were also drawn upon for feed. After 1948, hog numbers increased again as feed supplies improved.

Since World War II we have had unusually large grain crops, part of which have been used for foreign aid, but most for domestic feed supplies. Ample consumer purchasing power for meats after the war, and the expansion of grassland farming, also helped increase livestock numbers and production. The increase occurred chiefly in cattle. From the record high of 86 million head on farms in 1945, numbers fell off about 10 per cent by 1949, but another increase brought a new peak of 95 million head by January 1954. The long-term trend points to adequate livestock for the increase in consumption of dairy, poultry and meat products estimated to be required between 1950 and 1960.

Livestock Population

The composition of our basic "livestock population" has been changing in response to increased demand for dairy and poultry products. Work stock, we have noted, rose to a peak before 1920 and declined after that, with the advent of the tractor. However, trends in cattle, sheep, hogs and poultry are quite different; generally they are in the direction of yielding more of the protective foods.

The number of cattle other than milk cows has tended to run in long-term cycles, reaching successively greater peaks about every fifteen years. Since this expansion has been slower than the growth of population, the number of these cattle per capita has declined. At the cyclical high point in 1904, there were 49 million cattle other than milk cows on farms. At the peak in 1918, there were 52 million. At the 1934 peak, cut short by the record drought of that year, the number was 47 million. Following the record of the past, the cycle that began after 1938 reached

a peak of 58 million in the mid-1940s, and after an unexpected brief decline reached a new record of nearly 70 million in 1953. A still higher mark in beef cattle numbers will probably be set later in the 1950s.

Dairy Cattle

Dairy cattle numbers were at a peak of 26.9 million in January 1934. Following a cutback due to the droughts of the 1930s and relatively high feed costs, the number went up again and by January 1945 was at 27.8 million. As a result of the greatly expanded wartime demand, and because of the emphasis placed on dairy products as protective foods, it was expected that the long-time rate of expansion would continue. The basis for continuing expansion was seen in the increasing proportion of one- and two-year-olds in the milk cow population.

By 1950 the number of milk cows should have been close to 28 million. Instead, a downward trend set in, undoubtedly induced by an accentuation of the cityward drift of the farm population and by the greater profitability of other types of livestock production. By 1952 the number of cows 2 years old and over kept for milk was actually reduced to 23.4 million, or about 5 million below expectations based on the long-time trend. Most of the decline was offset by an increase in milk production per cow, leaving milk production in 1952 approximately 5 per cent above 1940.

Poultry

Output of poultry products, like dairy production, is also expanding as national nutritional needs rise. In 1940 the number of hens and pullets fell short of the 1930 inventory, but by 1944 it had risen to a peak of 524 million. Since then numbers have been cut back (to about 406 million in 1953), but this reduction has been more than offset by increased productivity per layer. As a result of better feeding and improved varieties in poultry flocks, egg production per laying hen increased noticeably during the 1920s and even faster during the 1930s and 1940s. Between 1930 and 1940 the number of eggs produced per layer rose from 93 to 101. By 1952 it had increased to 145.

With numbers maintained and expanded, and with continued improvement in egg production per layer, the per capita production and consumption of poultry products should readily meet the national nutritional requirements of the 1950s.

BUILDINGS

There is little direct information about the condition of farm buildings. Estimates of expenditures and prices made by the Department of Agriculture point to considerable construction activity in 1939–1941, following a very low volume of construction during the depression of the 1930s. The 1941 expenditure for service buildings — all farm buildings except operators' dwellings, fences, windmills and wells — surpassed that of any previous year except in the period 1917–1920.

Allowing for the decline in construction costs, annual expenditures during 1939–1941 were above those of any year in the 1920s. During that decade, expenditures for service buildings amounted to 5 to 7 per cent of the inventory value of all service buildings on farms, but in 1939–1941 they were the equivalent of 8 to 9 per cent of inventory value. At this rate, farm building exceeded mere replacement needs and presented no real problem in sustaining postwar agricultural productivity. The same may be said for the 1950s. By 1950, capital expenditures for building (repairs and maintenance as well as new construction and improvements of farm dwellings, service buildings and other structures) amounted to $2.25 billion — nearly twice the normal depreciation allowance — compared with $600 million in 1940.

As with farm machinery, the relatively large expenditures for farm buildings during the late 1920s made it possible for farmers to maintain production throughout the financial setback of the 1930s. The sharp increase in outlays during 1939–1941, together with substantial outlays during the war and postwar years, have put farm buildings in better condition to contribute to the maintenance of the present and prospective large volume of farm production.

There need be no concern over the adequacy of farm buildings in the 1950s. If farmers continue to have ample income, as they would have under the assumed condition of a high level of economic activity, and if supplies of lumber and other building materials are ample, as there is every reason to expect, any serious deficiencies due to undermaintenance will be corrected and new construction will be undertaken.

RURAL ELECTRIFICATION

Electricity is used in some 250 ways on farms. About 40 to 50 per cent of farm electric power is used for irrigation, 30 per cent for household appliances, and 20 to 30 per cent mainly for lighting barns and operating small equipment, such as pumps and milking machines. Extension of rural electrification during the 1930s and 1940s contributed to the increase of agricultural productivity. Only 178,000 farms in the entire country had electric power in 1923; in 1941, about 2.4 million, or nearly 40 per cent of all farms, had electric power; in 1952, 4.7 million, or 88 per cent of all farms.[9]

This expansion has gone hand in hand with lower average costs per kilowatt-hour and increased use per farm, particularly in the eastern half of the country. Farms east of the one hundredth meridian used 672 kilowatt-hours of energy per farm in 1929, at an average cost of 7.5 cents an hour. By 1950, with ten times as many farms electrified in this area, using on the average over three times as many kilowatt-hours per farm as in 1929, the rate was down to 3.2 cents. By 1960 practically all farms will have electricity.

HUMAN RESOURCES FOR EXPANDED CAPACITY

World War II demonstrated that the productivity of human, as well as of physical, resources can be greatly increased. When the normal working population in agriculture was reduced by the draft and by the competition of more attractive pay in war industries, more women, children and older men were employed and hours of work were lengthened. In 1944 a total agricultural working force only 94 per cent as large as in 1940 harvested about 6 per cent more acres and produced about 25 per cent more crops and livestock products. Most of this increase was achieved by those farms — about half the total number — which normally produce about 90 per cent of the total production for market.

The return of farm labor from industry and the armed services released women and older men from farm work and thus permitted a return to, and even a reduction of, the prewar hours of labor on farms. However, the defense program launched in connection with the Korean outbreak in 1950 again stimulated a transfer of workers from farming to industrial occupations. Will the increased production required for the

9. Rural Electrification Administration.

TABLE 338. WORKING FORCE IN AGRICULTURAL AND
NONAGRICULTURAL PURSUITS, 1820–1950 [a]

(Number in Thousands)

Year	All Occupations	Agricultural Pursuits		Nonagricultural Pursuits	
		Number	Per Cent [b]	Number	Per Cent
1820	2,881	2,069	71.8	812	28.2
1830	3,932	2,772	70.5	1,159	29.5
1840	5,420	3,720	68.6	1,700	31.4
1850	7,697	4,902	63.7	2,795	36.3
1860	10,533	6,208	58.9	4,325	41.1
1870	12,925	6,850	53.0	6,075	47.0
1880	17,392	8,585	49.4	8,807	50.6
1890	23,318	9,938	42.6	13,380	57.4
1900	29,073	10,912	37.5	18,161	62.5
1910	37,371	11,592	31.0	25,779	69.0
1920	42,434	11,449	27.0	30,985	73.0
1930	48,830	10,472	21.4	38,358	78.6
1940	52,148 [c]	9,163	17.6	42,986	82.4
1950	62,012	7,369	11.9	54,643	88.1

Sources: Historical Statistics of the United States, 1789–1945, U.S. Bureau of the Census, 1949, Series D2-7, p. 63; 1950 from unpublished census data.

a. Includes persons 10 years old and over. For years after 1880, figures differ slightly from those shown in Table 306 and Appendices 20–1 and 20–4, where the data have been made consistent with current Bureau of the Census labor force concepts.

b. These percentages differ slightly from those in Table 313, where adjustments have been made to achieve comparability with estimates for other industries.

c. Includes persons on public emergency work previously in agricultural pursuits.

1950 decade be possible with a permanently reduced labor force? With the fair certainty of further progress in mechanization, is there reason to expect a continuing rise in the number of acres handled per agricultural worker and in the volume of production per worker?

As has already been pointed out, comprehensive soil conservation and land development programs could increase national production by 50 per cent, or far beyond our projected future requirements. Similarly, greater output could be obtained from the many thousands of bona fide farmers now operating on an unproductive, self-subsistence basis if they were educated in farm management and given financial aid and if some of them shifted to more productive land. These measures would increase the average productivity of agricultural workers and permit a continuation of the decline in the total agricultural working population.

IMPACT OF WAR ON LABOR SUPPLY

In April 1940, over 9 million persons were in agricultural pursuits. According to estimates of the Census Bureau, this total decreased over half a million by April 1942 and another million by April 1944, as farm workers were absorbed into the armed services and into industrial activities. Farm family labor and 10 to 20 per cent longer working hours in the summer months of the war years partly made up for the loss of hired labor, and women, youths and older men helped fill the ranks.

This shift in the composition of the farm labor force was only temporary, and some of the reduction in the total was restored with the closing of war plants and the return of men and women from the armed services. The farm labor supply for the 1950s was expected to decrease in line with the long-term trend in the agricultural population, a trend which the war in Korea accentuated.

DECLINE IN LABOR FORCE

The long-term change in the balance between agricultural and industrial employment has been remarkably regular and persistent. The maxi-

TABLE 339. PER CENT OF WORKING FORCE IN AGRICULTURE, 1860–1950

| Year | Per Cent in Agriculture | Change in Decade of: | |
		Prosperity	Depression
1860	58.9		
1870	53.0	−5.9	
1880	49.4		−3.6
1890	42.6	−6.8	
1900	37.5		−5.1
1910	31.0	−6.5	
1920	27.0		−4.0
1930	21.4	−5.6	
1940	17.6		−3.8
1950	11.9	−5.7	
Average		−6.1	−4.2

Source: Table 338.

mum number engaged in agricultural pursuits was reached in 1910, with a total of nearly 11.6 million, exclusive of summer seasonal labor. By 1920 there was a reduction of 140,000; by 1930, another reduction of nearly a million; and by 1940, a further reduction of nearly 1.5 million. (See Table 338.)

While the total number engaged in agricultural pursuits declined from 11.6 million in 1910 to 9.2 million in 1940, the total of experienced workers in all industries expanded from 37.4 million to 52.1 million. Persons engaged in agriculture constituted only 17.6 per cent of the nation's working force in 1940, as compared with 31 per cent in 1910, 37.5 per cent in 1900, 53 per cent in 1870, and 71.8 per cent in 1820. The rate of decline has averaged roughly half a percentage point a year. In line with past experience in decades of industrial prosperity, the decline between 1940 and 1950 was somewhat greater than average.

With the total number engaged in all occupations in 1960 estimated at about 70 million,[10] how large is the agricultural working force likely to be? We have a choice of several assumptions. If the agricultural portion of the total working force had continued to decline at the average rate characteristic of the past eighty years (5.2 points a decade), we would have expected only about 12 per cent of the working population to be engaged in agriculture in 1950, compared with over 17.6

10. This figure is based on the projected national labor force of 72.5 million for 1960, adjusted for consistency with the totals in Table 338.

per cent in 1940. The 1950 proportion — 11.9 per cent — was actually somewhat lower. Projection of the long-term trend to 1960 points to a proportion of only 7 per cent in that year — about as small as the proportion in the United Kingdom in recent decades. On this assumption, the total number of agricultural workers would be about 4.9 million in 1960. A reduction to such a low figure would mean cutting the agricultural working force to little more than half the 1940 level. Though not necessarily impossible, this would require greater increases in the size of farms, in the number of acres per worker, and in productivity per worker than past experience would suggest as probable.

The proportion of the national working force engaged in agriculture may also be projected on the basis of shifts that have taken place in previous decades of relatively full employment, such as we are assuming for 1950–1960. This procedure also leads to results that seem improbable, though not impossible. In the decades of industrial prosperity ending in 1870, 1890, 1910 and 1930, the percentage of the working force in agricultural pursuits fell relatively more (an average decline of 6.1 points) than in the decades of industrial depression ending in 1880, 1900 and 1940 (an average decline of 4.3 points). During the decade ending in 1920 and embracing World War I, the decline was also only 4 percentage points — probably because of the rise in demand for farm labor during World War I. During the war and postwar prosperity decade ending with 1950, the decline was 5.7 points, or about the

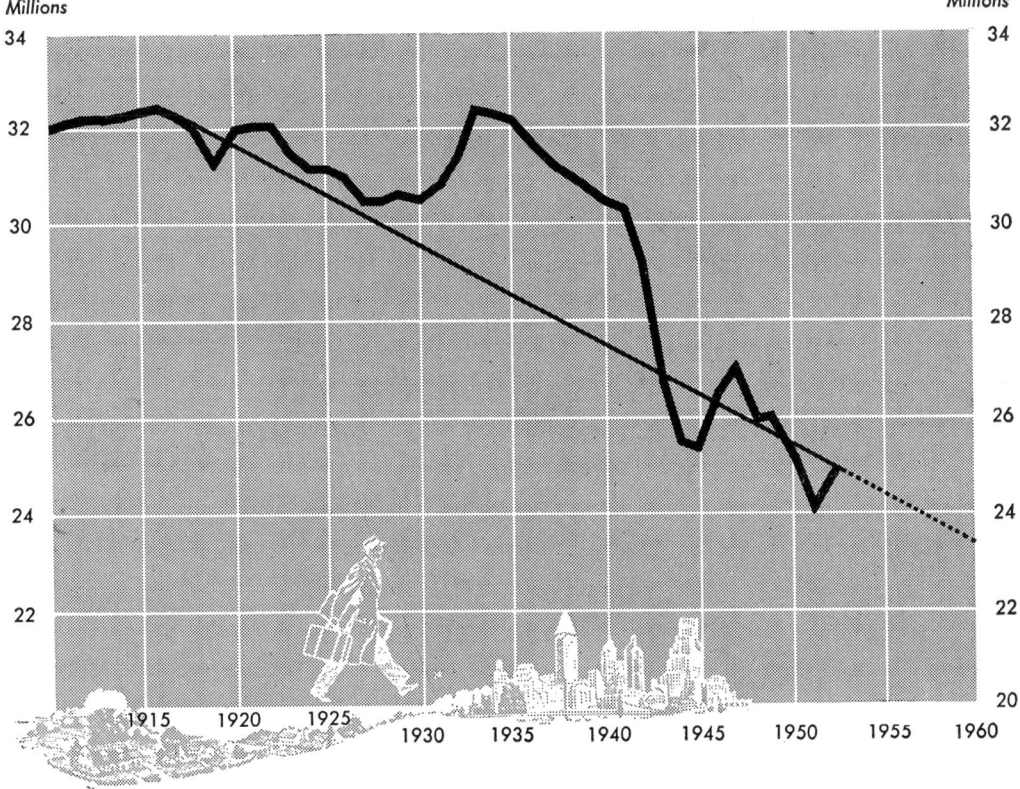

Millions

Millions

FIGURE 97. DECLINE IN FARM POPULATION, 1910–1952, PROJECTED TO 1960 [a]

Source: Agricultural Outlook Charts, 1954, Bureau of Agricultural Economics, U.S. Department of Agriculture, October 1953, p. 28. These are adjusted estimates which run higher than the Census counts shown in Table 37.

a. Estimates for the years 1910–1949 have been revised to be comparable with the new definition of farm population. Projections for 1955 and 1960 are based on the assumption that the farm population will continue the average annual rate of decline that prevailed between 1916 and 1952, an average decrease of 0.75 per cent a year.

average for prosperity decades. Another reduction of 5 to 6 points during the decade of relatively full employment ending in 1960 would mean that 6 to 7 per cent of the total working force would be engaged in agriculture in 1960, or only about 4.5 million persons, as against over 17.6 per cent in 1940. (See Table 339.) Obviously this kind of arithmetical projection would soon bring the agricultural labor force down to the vanishing point.

A somewhat larger number occupied in agriculture in 1960 is suggested by a projection on the basis of farm population estimates. The number of persons living on farms in 1950 was down to 25.1 million, compared with 30.5 million in 1940 and 32.5 million at the peak in 1916. (See Figure 97.) It is estimated that a more moderate downtrend will continue to 1960 and 1975. The proportion of total farm population occupied

in agriculture was 36 per cent in 1910 and 1920, but dropped to 34 per cent in 1930 and to about 30 per cent in 1940 and 1950. If the proportion remains at 30 per cent in 1960, or even if it is somewhat lower, it would be the equivalent of something under 7 million persons engaged in agriculture. The production requirements of 1960 could be met with this amount of agricultural manpower, provided the 1930 to 1950 trend in output per man-hour is maintained.

PRODUCTION PER MAN-HOUR

The expansion of agricultural production required in the 1950s will undoubtedly be achieved very largely by the same means that produced the increase in output between 1940 and 1950. Rising output per man-hour is the key.

The Department of Agriculture estimates that

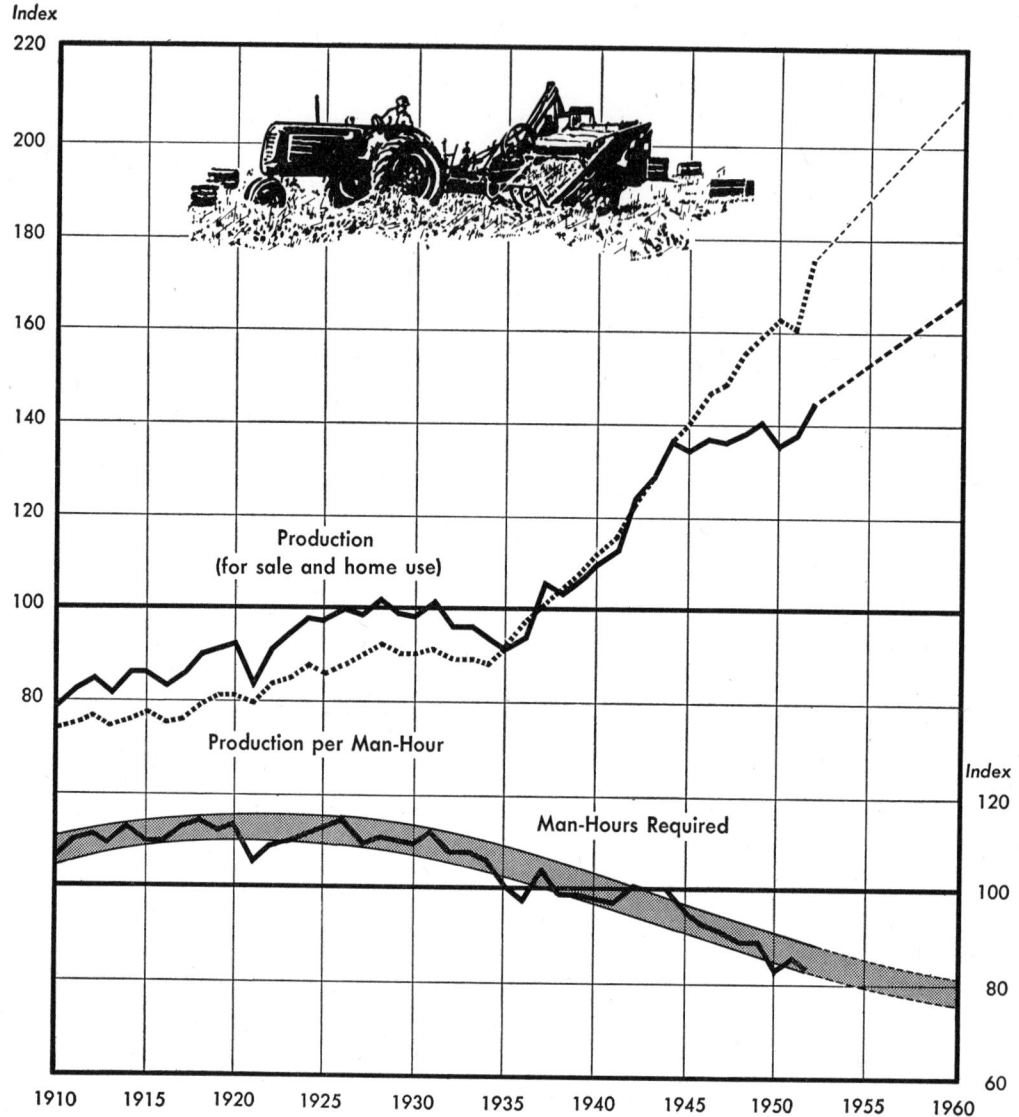

FIGURE 98. INDEXES OF AGRICULTURAL PRODUCTION, MAN-HOURS REQUIRED AND PRODUCTION PER MAN-HOUR, 1910–1952, WITH PROJECTIONS TO 1960
(1935–1939 = 100)

Sources: Appendix 22–7; 1960, discussion in text.

production (for market and home use) increased about a fourth between 1940 and 1949–1951. This was accomplished with an 11 per cent decrease in the number of hours (adult male equivalent) of labor. Production per man-hour thus increased by about 44 per cent, in line with the uptrend that started after 1934. (See Figure 98.) If productivity were to continue to expand at this pace, a 20 per cent increase in output by 1960 could be achieved with a further

moderate decline (about 10 per cent) in the number of man-hours. And if hours worked per year were to remain unchanged, the number of persons engaged in agricultural occupations could decline from 7.4 million in 1950 to about 6.7 million in 1960, or slightly less than 10 per cent of the total number of persons in all occupations.

A working force of this size would call for a further increase in acreage per worker. Such

TABLE 340. HARVESTED ACRES, WORKERS IN AGRICULTURE AND ACRES PER WORKER, 1880–1950 AND ESTIMATES FOR 1960

Year	Harvested Acres	Workers in Agriculture	Acres per Worker
	(Millions)	(Thousands)	
1880	178	8,585	20.7
1890	233	9,938	23.4
1900	295	10,912	27.0
1910	322	11,592	27.8
1920	362	11,449	31.6
1930	359	10,472	34.3
1940	321	9,163	35.0
1950	345	7,369	46.8
1960 (proj.)	375	6,700	56.0

Sources: U.S. Department of Agriculture: *Agricultural Statistics, 1951*, p. 530, and *Agricultural Statistics, 1952*, p. 620; and Table 338 above.

an increase, however, would not be out of line with the long-term trend in acres harvested per agricultural worker or with the increase of average farm size.

Farm Size

The average size of farm enterprises has been expanding ever since the land adjustments after the Civil War broke up the southern plantations. The 1850 and 1860 Censuses reported about 200 acres per farm, but as a result of the postwar adjustments, the 1880 Census reported only 134 acres per farm. Since then there has been a trend toward larger farms, the average increase per decade being a little over 10 acres. The typical farm in 1940 comprised 174 acres; by 1950 the average size had grown to 215 acres. With continuing expansion in the use of electric power and mechanical equipment, the average farm could, in line with this trend, consist of almost 220 acres in 1960, and acreage harvested per worker could increase accordingly.

Acreage per Worker

Acreage harvested per worker increased from nearly 21 in 1880 to about 32 in 1920, 34 in 1930 and 35 in 1940. By 1950 the average had risen sharply to nearly 47 acres, and its trend potential for 1960 is a further increase to 56 acres. Supposing that we have in 1960 a total of 375 million acres in harvested crops (in line with the in-

crease from 1940 to 1950, or with the long-term trend), the increased acreage would thus require only about 6.7 million persons working in agriculture. (See Table 340.)

Where these trends in production per manhour, acreage per worker, and the number of workers in agriculture will actually lead by 1960 is of course not certain. Their directions are clear, but the exact combination and permutation will depend on various other developments. One of these is the number and productivity of low-income farmers as these may be influenced by vigorous programs of financial and technical aid in a decade which is likely to see more and more emphasis placed on both foreign and domestic rural rehabilitation.

UNDEREMPLOYMENT OF LOW-INCOME FARMERS

The difficulties of getting more production from the fully utilized large farms have focused attention on those resources, both human and physical, which are not yet fully utilized. The 1940 and 1950 Censuses of Agriculture provide a fairly clear picture of the manpower and productive capacity of our farms. It is now possible to examine the actual and potential productive capacity of the 5.4 million farms listed in the 1950 Census in contrast with the capacity of the 6.1 million farms recorded in the 1940 Census. Only a small part of the reduction in the total number of farms is due to the different definitions of farms in the two counts. Essentially the same

TABLE 341. NUMBER OF FARMS, BY ECONOMIC CLASS AND BY
MAJOR GEOGRAPHIC DIVISION, 1950[a]

(Number in Thousands)

Economic Class	Class Interval (Value of Products Sold)	United States		North	South	West
		Number	Per Cent			
All farms		5,382.1	100.0	2,268.0	2,652.5	461.7
Commercial farms						
Class I	$25,000 and over	105.5	2.0	44.8	29.1	31.6
Class II	$10,000 to $24,999	386.1	7.2	247.3	79.8	59.0
Class III	$5,000 to $9,999	725.6	13.5	497.7	153.3	74.5
Class IV	$2,500 to $4,999	882.3	16.4	484.5	326.0	71.9
Class V	$1,200 to $2,499	895.9	16.6	327.2	509.2	59.5
Class VI	$250 to $1,199[b]	707.7	13.1	168.4	513.3	26.0
Other farms						
Part-time farms	$250 to $1,199[c]	642.1	11.9	220.4	364.0	57.8
Residential farms	Under $250	1,032.4	19.2	275.7	676.3	80.3
Abnormal farms[d]		4.5	.1	2.0	1.5	1.0

Source: The Agricultural Situation, U.S. Bureau of Agricultural Economics, March 1952.

a. Preliminary census data; totals obtained by adding state or county census releases.

b. With the operator working off the farm less than 100 days and farm sales greater than other family income.

c. With the operator working off the farm 100 or more days and/or other family income exceeding farm sales.

d. Chiefly public and private institutional farms.

---

concentration of agricultural capacity on relatively few farms shows up in both cases, and the general analysis of the 1940 production figures in relation to size and class of farms is applicable today.

The 1940 Census listed about 40,000 unclassified farms, 88,000 farms reporting no income, 760,000 farms with the operator working off the farm for more than 150 days, and 414,000 retired operators, of whom half were over 65 years old. In other words, there were 1,302,000 farms that were not actually bona fide farms. The remaining 4,795,000 farms were capable of providing full employment, but over half of the operators of these bona fide farms may be said to have been underemployed, since their low-income enterprises did not fully utilize their time and potential managerial ability. Fully two thirds of these were in the South.

With the 1950 Census of Agriculture we now have a division of farms into "commercial" and "other," the latter consisting of farms with less than $1,200 of production for sale on which the operator is not dependent as a primary source of income. The six classes of commercial farms (see Table 341) represent 69 per cent of all farms. The other 31 per cent are either part-time farms producing $250 to $1,200 of products for sale or residential farms with less than $250 of products for sale.

Classes V and VI, the small-scale commercial farms, offer the main possibilities for potential increases in production through better management. More than 1.6 million farms, or 30 per cent of all farms, are in these two economic groups. These could be made more efficient producing units if their operators were educated in farm management and given financial aid. If the output of these farms doubled, national output would be increased by $2 billion — about 7 per cent of the total cash income from marketings in 1951. Two thirds of this potential increase would be provided by farms in the South.

SUMMARY

No material obstacle appears to stand in the way of our producing enough food and fiber in 1960 for both domestic and foreign markets, for civilian consumption, for our armed forces here and abroad, and for regular and foreign aid exports. We have new lands that can be brought into production; lands already in cultivation can be made more productive through better management and better soil and water conservation practices; and continuing progress can be expected in the production of better-yielding plants and animals. Recent advances in the agricultural sciences point toward even greater productivity during the next decade.

Under the stress of war in the 1940s and the Korean War in the early 1950s, farm plant and farm labor were made much more productive. These gains will be retained. Cropland was made more productive through wider use of higher-yielding seeds and through improved planting, cultivating and harvesting practices. The conversion of feed crops into livestock and livestock products became more efficient. Mechanical power continued to displace horses and hired labor, especially when farm labor moved into the armed services and nonagricultural war industries. Work stock will continue to be displaced by tractors, but other livestock will probably increase in number as demand for their products grows. Under the stress of the war production programs, hours of labor on farms were substantially increased, and women — as well as old and young people — were drawn into farm work. These abnormal shifts were readjusted only in part as regular farm workers returned from the armed services and from industry.

Farm machinery will be in greater demand than ever before, partly because higher wages will stimulate mechanization and partly because many more farmers and farm youths have acquired mechanical skills. Our industrial capacity will readily supply all the necessary farm machinery and equipment, all the building materials and commercial fertilizer, and all the rural electric power needed to keep an expanded agricultural plant in full operation in the 1950 decade.

Acreage Requirements

For our own domestic requirements, assuming an adequate national diet and increasing productivity per acre, we shall need about 400 million acres in harvested crops by 1960. For export, assuming that we can maintain a reasonable share of international trade in farm products, we may need an additional 40 million acres. Our projected requirements for 1960 thus total 440 million acres in harvested crops, as compared with about 321 million in 1940 and 345 million in 1950. This estimate assumes that recent gains in

productivity per acre and per animal feed-consuming unit will be retained.

These requirements for harvested cropland appear to be attainable. Soil experts estimate that, if necessary, the amount of land in crops could be expanded by about 40 per cent over the 1950 acreage — to about 480 million acres — and that production could be increased by 50 per cent. This would be accomplished chiefly by bringing certain idle land into cultivation, converting plowable pasture into cropland for harvest, clearing some forest land, bringing new lands under irrigation, and applying immediately on a national basis the soil erosion and soil conservation measures which have been found beneficial and profitable so far. Prices, of course, would have to be favorable in order for these measures to be undertaken. Thus, our land resources can be expanded substantially beyond domestic requirements under conditions of high employment, and they could also be made to contribute substantially to world needs.

Manpower Needed

The labor force for cultivating and harvesting this expanded acreage will be adequate, even though the number of persons following agricultural pursuits may be smaller than in 1950. With the aid of mechanical power, the average operator or farm tenant has been able to handle a larger and larger crop acreage. The 9.2 million persons engaged in farming in 1940 handled about 35 acres per person compared with 34 acres per worker in 1930 and 32 in 1920. In 1950 each of the 7.4 million workers in agriculture handled nearly 47 acres. This increase and the expansion of the agricultural production program indicate that by 1960 the average could even increase to 56 acres. This would undoubtedly mean a continuation of the trend toward larger and better-managed farms.

Just as there is ample opportunity to expand the total of land in harvested crops under a vigorous scientific soil management program, so there is a great opportunity to make lower-income farmers more efficient. Of the 5.4 million farms in 1950, 1.6 million were low-income commercial operations with only limited land and financial resources, incapable of providing full-time employment. Almost two thirds of these farms were in the South, producing single crops of cotton or tobacco. With moderate managerial and financial assistance, more than half of all these relatively unproductive farms could contribute substantially to the nation's food production by diversifying their operations to include poultry or hogs or truck crops.

The resources of many other low-income farms are so inadequate that efforts at rehabilitation would not be fruitful. By and large, these farms supply merely part-time work and the productive contribution of their operators could best be made in nonagricultural employment. This shift to other occupations is likely to continue, for it is in line with the long-term change in the agricultural-industrial balance and with the rapid progress in agricultural productivity and mechanization in recent years.

## CHAPTER 23

INDUSTRIAL AND COMMERCIAL CAPACITY

AMERICA's industrial development dates back to the year 1648, when iron works situated at what is now Saugus, Massachusetts, were credited with an annual capacity of 465 tons of pig iron and iron products. In the next 250 years this country acquired vast territories rich in natural resources and grew industrially into the world's most powerful nation. Since 1900 we have grown little in area and our expansion has been in the technological development at which America excels.

Two successive waves of expansion in a single decade — the forced-draft wartime installations of 1940–1945, followed by the impressive postwar additions — brought the United States by 1950 to an unprecedented high of industrial capacity and consumer-products output. In that decade we doubled the aggregate manufacturing capacity of 1939–1940, which had taken nearly three centuries to develop and build. Finding even the national industrial plant of 1950 insufficient for the defense program and expected civilian demand, we undertook another enlargement in a program which is due to be completed in the second half of this decade.

Size of Capital Plant

Strange as it may seem, although we pride ourselves on our industrial might, we have no exact knowledge of the size or value of our productive capital plant. A complete inventory of our productive and distributive facilities has never been made. It would be of extraordinary statistical scope and complexity, covering in 1950–1952, for example, the equipment used in the 10,000 coal mines and 20,000 other mines and quarries, 475,000 oil wells and 65,000 gas wells; the 4,000,000 tractors and 22,000,000 implements and machines on the 5,380,000 farms; the 58,000

fishing vessels and motor boats; the 63,000 lumber sawmills; the 360,000 construction outfits; the 4,000 central utility electric power stations; the 560 gas utility plants and stations; the 20,000 telephone exchanges; the 4,000 radio and television stations; the 7,700 powered and 14,000 nonpropelled (barges, etc.) passenger and cargo vessels operating on 28,400 miles of navigable inland waterways and 4,840 miles of coastline; the 42,000 locomotives, 1,800,000 freight cars and 36,000 passenger cars operating on 400,000 miles of railway track; the 9,000,000 trucks operating on 3,322,000 miles of highways and streets; the 570,000 miles of oil and gas pipelines; the 1,100 airliners operating on 78,000 miles of airline routes; the 228,000 factories, mills and refineries; and the 240,000 wholesale establishments and 1,800,000 retail stores.

One recent estimate puts the value of our nonfarm productive and commercial facilities at about $275 billion in 1949. About two thirds of this was in the form of buildings, mines, roads, river and harbor installations, and other structures and about one third was in the form of producers' durable equipment — machinery, ships and boats, railway and transit equipment, aircraft, business automobiles, trucks, and nonresidential furniture and equipment.[1] At the rate at which nonfarm structures and equipment were expanding in the early postwar years, their total value almost certainly exceeded $300 billion by 1950, and further large gains were made in the early 1950s. Valued at constant prices, our nonfarm capital facilities more than tripled in the first half of this century. (See Table 342.)

Operating our enviable array of productive plant and equipment is an unparalleled staff of trained men and women. Their organized "know-how" in engineering, design, production, technical and scientific research is directed by

---

By THOMAS C. FICHANDLER, with the research assistance of JOHN A. WARING, JR., research writer on technology and resources. Opinions and judgments expressed in this chapter are those of the author and should not be attributed to the organization with which he is associated.

[1]. See Raymond W. Goldsmith, "A Perpetual Inventory of Wealth," *Studies in Income and Wealth*, Vol. 14, National Bureau of Economic Research, New York, 1951, Table 1, p. 18.

TABLE 342. ESTIMATED VALUE OF INDUSTRIAL AND COMMERCIAL
FACILITIES, 1850–1949 [a]

Year	Current Prices	Constant (1929) Prices		
		Total Value		Value Per Capita
		Amount	Index (1900 lower figure = 100)	
	(Billions)	(Billions)		
1850	$ 1.3	$ 3.3	7	$ 142
1880	9.0	18.6	42	370
1890	16.8	36.6	82	580
1900 [b]	24.9	56.0	126	736
1900 [c]	21.3	44.6	100	586
1910	39.2	72.1	162	780
1920	106.3	93.3	209	876
1929	122.6	125.7	282	1,032
1930	119.1	129.8	291	1,054
1940	131.1	127.7	286	967
1949	275.6	152.4	342	1,022

Sources: Total values based on estimates of Raymond W. Goldsmith Associates, Washington, D.C. Per capita figures based on population estimates as of July 1 of each year from *Historical Statistics of the United States, 1789–1945,* U.S. Bureau of the Census, 1949, Series B–31, p. 26, and *Statistical Abstract, 1952,* Table 9, p. 10.

a. Includes all government facilities, except military, and those of nonprofit institutions; excludes agriculture.

b. Consistent with estimates for earlier years, especially 1880 and 1890.

c. Consistent with estimates for later years.

specialists in business, financial and personnel fields, professional managerial control having supplanted control by the owners or "captains" of industry.

We have more than enough industrial facilities to maintain our present standard of living, and to provide full employment of our labor force. During World War II our output so far surpassed any other country's that we became the "arsenal of democracy," helping feed and supply our allies while practically maintaining our standard of living at home. All the while we never reached our maximum possible productive capacity. Indeed, before the war our economy was in a depressed state, with idle plants and idle men. Furthermore, there is no evidence that our industrial machine was incapable of meeting the demands made upon it in the years of great prosperity during the 1920s. Even on the prevailing one-shift basis, we could have produced about one fourth more than we did.[2]

2. See Edwin G. Nourse and Associates, *America's Capacity to Produce,* Brookings Institution, Washington, 1934, Chapter 20.

NATURE OF CAPACITY

Potential output can be measured either in terms of equipment — the installed and available machinery — or in terms of rated or actual capacity, that is, the maximum attainable productivity of the machinery as rated or proved. Although the amount of machinery is a relatively poor measure of capacity, it is the only one available in some industries. The number of cotton spindles and the number of machine tools, for example, serve as capacity indicators for their respective industries.

In most industries only *rated capacity to produce* the industry's product is known. Although not always so stated, capacity is usually rated on the basis of an industry's normal or standard working hours per week — working hours for the machinery and equipment, that is. In but few instances is productive capacity rated at the intrinsic capacity of the machinery itself regardless of the time element, for example, electric utility generating capacity.

Rated capacity is far less than the total quantity

of goods and services that could conceivably be produced with all existing productive facilities. The latter concept, essentially an engineering view of capacity, assumes the fullest and most continuous utilization of all existing plant and equipment that would be technically possible. The engineering capacity of an industry would be the combined production of all plants — efficient and obsolete, active and idle — working 24 hours a day 365 days a year, less the time needed for repairs, cleaning, breakdowns and other technical purposes. Such a concept of capacity really implies that what is technically feasible is economically possible. But so long as living and working habits and costs and prices are relevant, they limit the full use of existing capital facilities.

At the other extreme, a strictly utilitarian view might regard as submarginal and therefore not part of an industry's capacity all plant and equipment that is idle at the price and market conditions of the moment. According to this view, capacity would never be excessive, for it would change with every fluctuation in prices and costs and would thus always be equal to production. Such a definition of capacity would be meaningless.

Neither of these extreme views can be accepted. The first is too absolute in its complete independence of anything but the physical capacity of existing facilities and its complete disregard of costs. With demand at high levels (or under monopoly conditions) the high price of a product might temporarily permit the use of obsolete facilities. But demand cannot be sustained if costs are disregarded for long, and any nationwide attempt to use all our obsolete facilities alongside our efficient ones would impose an impossible drain on our resources. No sooner would simultaneous use of all of them be attempted than forces leading to their partial disuse would be set in motion. In the real world, as soon as we even begin to approach capacity in the "engineering sense," acquisition of additional efficient machinery increases capacity. Considerations of cost or resource utilization have a way of either keeping obsolete plants idle or replacing them with more efficient ones. The engineering view of capacity as the sum total of all existing physical facilities cannot apply in a dynamic world of changing costs and prices.

Any realistic view of capacity lies somewhere between these extremes. It must recognize on the one hand that only plant and equipment that can be used economically should be included in reckoning capacity, and on the other that only permanently uneconomic plant and equipment should be excluded. Idle facilities range all the way from those so costly to operate that they can never be run profitably again to those that will come into operation with the slightest increase in price.

Because the question of whether a plant is permanently or only temporarily idle cannot always be answered, the precise measurement of capacity is difficult if not impossible. The problem is further complicated in industries where capacity is variable, as in electric light and power, where it may change with stream flow. Moreover, in continuous-operation industries capacity is easier to measure than in automobile manufacturing, where it is customary to work only one shift a day and where demand is highly seasonal. Furthermore, if the efficiency of an industry depends greatly on the volume of business, surprising results may be achieved; in wartime railway traffic, for example, swollen demands were met to a large extent through fuller utilization of equipment and use of marginal rolling stock. In some industries, measurement is impossible because of the flexibility of capacity in relation to hours, shifts and working conditions. The capacity of an industry is rarely static; it can expand and contract with no change in physical facilities.

Output, which is the real measure of our national productivity and living standards, however, is much more volatile than capacity. Output moves rapidly up or down for many reasons which do not necessarily affect capacity — seasonality, good and poor managerial and financial practices, strikes, changes in raw material supplies, prosperity or lack of demand, and endless others. Productive capacity is more directly related to the available plant and equipment, both of which require considerable amounts of time for expansion.

Prewar Industrial Capacity

Our industrial and commercial capacity was greater than ever just before World War II. With few exceptions, capacity had increased over the decades as the United States grew and developed its industrial sinews. (See Table 343 and Figure 99.)

In some basic industries the rise was both rapid and steady. In manufacturing, aluminum

TABLE 343. GROWTH OF BASIC INDUSTRIAL RATED CAPACITY, 1900–1952

(Data as of January 1 of Each Year)

Item	Unit	1900	1910	1920	1930	1940	1945	1950	1952
Manufacturing									
1. Flour milling	Thousand barrels	470,788[a]	n.a.	634,815	554,000	443,000	414,500	n.a.	394,000[b]
2. Cotton spindles	Thousands in place	19,472	28,929	35,834	34,025	24,750	23,128	22,995	23,152
3. Wool spindles	" " "	2,226[c]	n.a.	2,401	2,295	1,777	1,632	1,439	1,197
4. Worsted spindles	" " "	995	n.a.	2,356	2,557	2,083	1,943	1,835	1,786
5. Cotton looms	" " "	451	633	763	693	498	460	n.a.	396
6. Worsted combs	Number	1,450	n.a.	2,382	2,744	2,592	2,609	2,715	2,761
7. Aluminum ingots	Thousand tons	n.a.	n.a.	76[d]	125	245	767[e]	721	871
8. Steel ingots	" "	21,168	39,424	62,314	72,985	81,620	95,505	99,393	108,588
9. Pig iron	" "	27,780[f]	39,014[g]	56,249	57,855	55,724	67,314	71,498	73,782
10. Copper refining	" "	n.a.	644	1,384	1,627	1,572	1,595[e]	1,557	1,599
11. Petroleum refining	Million barrels	n.a.	n.a.	559	1,374	1,687	1,935	2,444	2,686
12. Coke ovens	Thousand tons	n.a.	67,700	87,000	76,900	n.a.	n.a.	82,382	88,087
13. Portland cement	" barrels	n.a.	93,500	134,093	258,917	253,759	241,631[e]	258,948	281,532
14. Phenol	" tons	n.a.	2[h]	7[i]	7[i]	45[j]	n.a.	172[b]	192[k]
15. Paper, all types	" "	2,782	n.a.	8,540	13,704	16,557	20,282	24,425	25,346
Mining									
16. Bituminous coal	Million tons	255	538	725	700	639	620	790	749
Transportation									
17. Surfaced rural roads	Thousand miles	128	204	369	694	1,340	1,461	1,865	2,070
18. Railroad miles operated	" "	193	241	253[m]	249	235	227	225	223
19. Petroleum pipelines	" "	18[f]	40[l]	53[m]	107	122	135	152	162
20. Trucks	Thousands	n.a.	6	898	3,408	4,407	4,513	7,693	9,036
21. Railroad locomotives	Number	37,665	60,020	68,980	61,260	45,170	46,300	43,270	42,420
22. Railroad freight cars	Thousands	1,196	2,149	2,427	1,731	1,681	1,797	1,778	1,776
23. Merchant vessels, documented	Thousand gross tons	5,165	7,508	16,324	16,068	14,018	32,813	31,215	30,416
Utilities									
24. Electric power	Thousand kilowatts	894	2,709[n]	13,094	29,839	38,863	49,189	63,100	75,775
25. Telephones in use	Thousands	1,356[f]	7,635[l]	12,668	20,068	20,831	26,859	40,709	45,636

Sources: Line 1. *Northwestern Miller* magazine; U.S. Bureau of the Census.

Lines 2–4. U.S. Bureau of the Census.

Line 5. 1900–1920 from *The Cotton Manufacturing Industry*, Copeland, and U.S. Bureau of the Census; 1930–1952 from *Davison's Textile Blue Book*, used by permission.

Line 6. U.S. Bureau of the Census.

Line 7. 1919–1940, Aluminum Corporation of America; since 1950, from *Chemical Facts and Figures, 1950*, and from Defense Production Administration.

Lines 8–9. American Iron and Steel Institute.

Line 10. American Bureau of Metal Statistics.

Lines 11–13. U.S. Bureau of Mines.

Line 14. 1914, 1928, 1939 from *Chemical and Engineering News*, August 2, 1948; 1951, from Defense Production Administration; 1953, from Office of Defense Mobilization.

Line 15. American Paper and Pulp Association.

Line 16. 1900–1950, U.S. Bureau of Mines; 1952, based on computation from rated capacity data given in *Keystone Coal Buyer's Manual*, 1952.

Line 17. U.S. Bureau of Roads.

Line 18. Interstate Commerce Commission, Association of American Railroads.

Line 19. U.S. Bureau of Mines, Interstate Commerce Commission, American Petroleum Institute.

Line 20. U.S. Bureau of Public Roads.

Line 21. Interstate Commerce Commission, Association of American Railroads.

Line 22. Interstate Commerce Commission, Association of American Railroads.

Line 23. U.S. Department of Commerce, Treasury Department.

Line 24. Federal Power Commission, U.S. Geological Survey, Edison Electric Institute. (Excludes capacity in industrial establishments.)

Line 25. American Telephone and Telegraph, Federal Communications Commission, U.S. Independent Telephone Association.

a. 1898. b. 1951. c. 1899. d. 1919. e. 1946. f. 1901. g. 1907. h. 1914. i. 1928. j. 1939. k. 1953. l. 1911. m. 1921. n. 1908.

n.a. Not available.

Note: In certain industries — notably textile spindles and looms, and railroad rolling stock — the number of units of equipment has been declining since reaching an all-time peak around 1919–1920. This does not indicate a decline in capacity, inasmuch as the mechanical efficiency and *productive* capacity per unit of equipment, i.e., per spindle or per railroad locomotive or freight car, has been gradually increasing since then, thereby maintaining aggregate capacity in these industries at levels about as high as in 1919–1920.

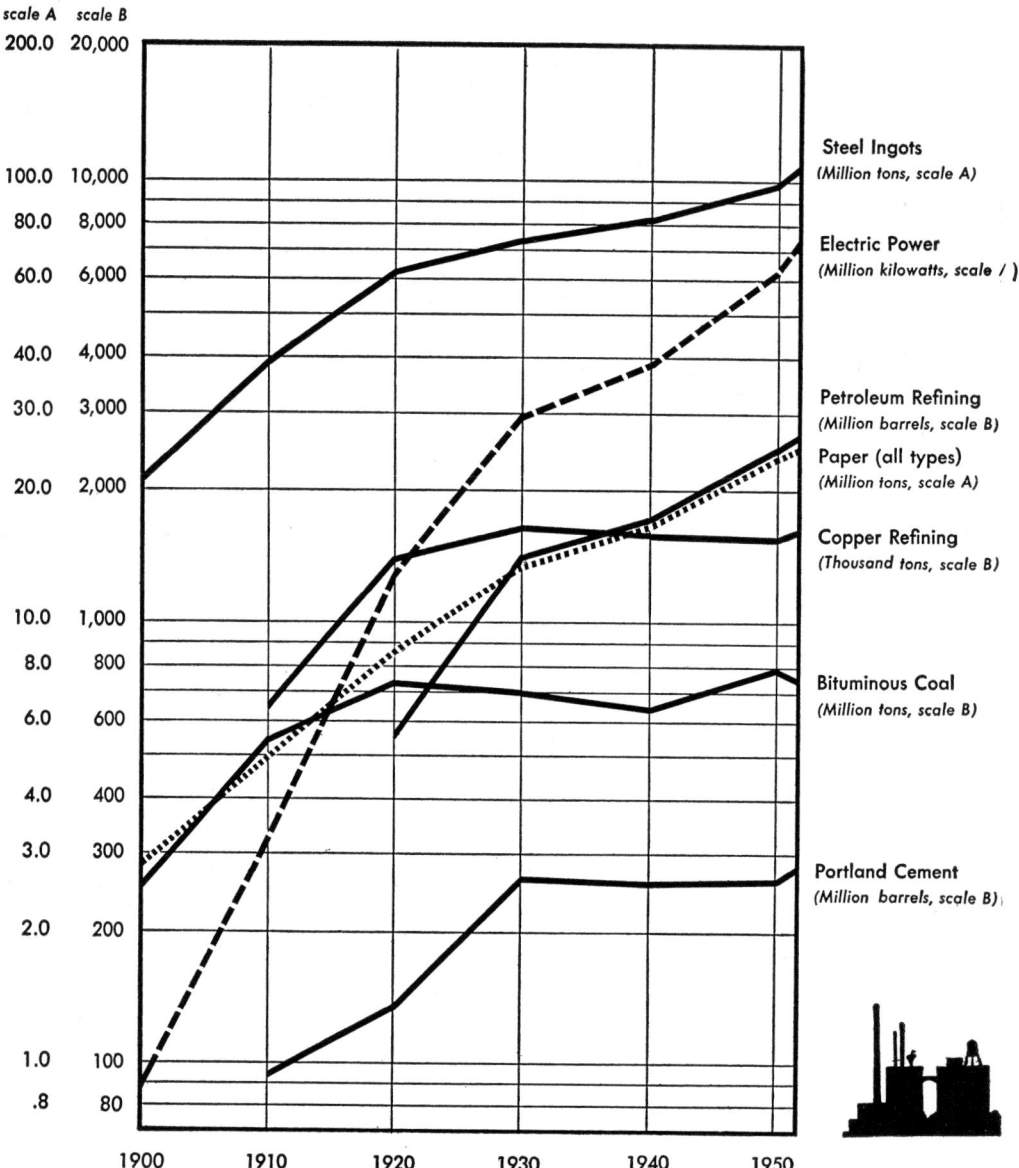

FIGURE 99. GROWTH OF BASIC INDUSTRIAL RATED CAPACITY, 1900–1952

Source: Table 343.

ingot capacity jumped from a mere 182.5 tons in 1890 to 245,000 tons in 1940, and steel ingot capacity, which had reached a sizable 21-million-ton level by 1900, continued upward to 82 million tons in 1940. In transportation, petroleum pipelines increased their mileage from 18,000 in 1901 to 122,000 in 1940, and the number of trucks on the road climbed from 6,000 in 1910 to 4.4 million in 1940. Among the utilities, electric power had

a phenomenal rise from 894,000 kilowatts in 1900 to 38.9 million in 1940, while the number of telephones in use rose from 1.4 million in 1901 to 20.1 million in 1930.

In a number of basic manufacturing industries — pig iron, copper refining, Portland cement, for example — and in railroad mileage, the depression of the 1930s put a stop to expansion. While the 1940 capacities of these industries were far

TABLE 344. HORSEPOWER RATING OF IMPORTANT
PRIME-MOVER ENGINES,[a] 1849–1952
(*Millions*)

Year	Including Automotive Vehicles	Excluding Automotive Vehicles
1849	1.9	1.9
1859	4.2	4.2
1869	7.4	7.4
1879	13.1	13.1
1889	26.2	26.2
1899	41.4	41.3
1909	94.3	86.6
1919	373.9	143.5
1929	1,641.0	216.0
1939	2,627.8	227.8
1950	4,740.8	337.1
1952	5,720.8	359.4

Source: Based on Appendix 25–4.

a. Steam, hydro-turbine or internal combustion engines. In addition to engines in automotive vehicles, totals include engines installed in factories (electric motors not included), mines, railroads, merchant ships (powered only), farms (horses and other work animals not included), electric central stations and aircraft (including private planes and commercial aircraft).

above the levels at the turn of the century, they were slightly below predepression peaks.

In several manufacturing industries — notably textiles — and in the railroad industry, the amount of equipment declined after reaching an all-time peak around 1920. Capacity in these industries, however, has been maintained since the mechanical efficiency and *productive* capacity per unit of equipment increased. On the other hand, bituminous coal mining, affected by competition from other fields as well as the depression, suffered a 12 per cent drop between 1920 and 1940.

In the two decades from 1920 to 1940, rated capacity almost doubled for the following basic manufacturing industries taken as a group: pig iron; aluminum; copper, petroleum and steel refining; cement; and paper.

An indirect but potent indicator of the rise in potential output of the American economy has been the rapid growth of the amount of horsepower harnessed to important prime-mover engines. Exclusive of automotive vehicles (the largest source of horsepower in recent years) installed prime-mover horsepower rose more than fivefold in the first four decades of this century — from 41 million in 1899 to 228 million in 1939. Including automotive vehicles, installed prime-mover horsepower in 1939 was over sixty times as great as in 1899. The available machine energy

in mines, merchant ships, electric central stations and on farms has increased steadily decade after decade. In factories, there was relatively little increase between 1919 and 1939, and actually a slight drop in the first half of that period. On railroads, available power increased rapidly until 1929 and then dropped about 20 per cent by 1939. (See Table 344 and Appendix 25–4.)

Output of every nondurable manufacturing industry, as well as of telephone service, electric light and power and retail trade, had reached new peaks by 1939. New high levels were attained by mining and by every durable manufacturing industry except lumber by 1940. Transportation reached a new high level a year later. Yet these records were attained despite mass unemployment and considerable underutilization of available facilities. In 1940, a year of high production, about one fifth of the nonagricultural labor force was unemployed. And in the recession year 1938, consumer income was only about two thirds of what could have been achieved with full employment.[3]

Underutilization of Facilities

During the 1930s marked and widespread increases occurred in the efficiency of labor. Output per man-hour in manufacturing was 28 per cent higher in 1939 than in 1929. In railway transportation the increase in productivity was equally striking. Output per man-hour on steam railroads increased about a third between 1919 and 1929 and by another third during the 1930s. In mining output per man-hour increased more than 40 per cent between 1929 and 1939; in the electric light and power industry, almost 85 per cent.[4] In the telephone industry output per employee, whether measured by number of calls or number of telephones, increased by about 40 per cent,[5] and the increase in output per man-hour was probably greater.

Because of these large increases in productivity, the total volume of output in 1939 was achieved with less labor than would have been required a decade earlier. In manufacturing the number of man-hours worked in 1939 was 25 per cent less than in 1929 but total output increased slightly;

3. *Patterns of Resource Use*, National Resources Committee, Washington, 1938.
4. See Table 316.
5. Output (from *Statistical Abstract, 1943*, Tables 450 and 453) divided by employment (from *Survey of Current Business*, 1942 Supplement, p. 46).

on steam railroads man-hours declined by 43 per cent but traffic by only a quarter; in mining man-hours declined by 49 per cent and output by only a quarter.[6] In the electric light and power industry employment was 11 per cent less than in 1929, while production was about 40 per cent greater; and in the telephone industry employment fell by 24 per cent, while production rose slightly.[7] Since the number of hours in the work week declined during the decade, the number of man-hours worked in these two industries declined even more than employment fell off.

Not only was a given unit of output in 1939 turned out with less labor than in 1929, but in the railroad industry with less equipment as well. The numbers of locomotives, freight cars and passenger cars in service were each reduced by more than a quarter.[8] In the interwar period technological changes, together with administrative and control measures, increased the load per train and its speed of movement. Rails became heavier; double-tracking was increased; automatic signal systems were improved. Locomotives were able to travel half as far again in a day with loads half again as heavy. Lightweight steel boxcars could carry 25 per cent more freight than the old wooden cars. Freight handling at terminals was speeded up. Operating methods were improved and the idle time of freight cars reduced.[9] These improvements in efficiency were not confined to the 1920s, but continued during the 1930s, despite the fact that capital expenditures by the railroads dropped to an average of $322 million a year from $747 million in the 1920s.

In manufacturing, depreciation charges during the 1930s exceeded capital expenditures by about $3 billion.[10] If this is taken as a rough measure of the "consumption" of manufacturing fixed capital assets, available facilities declined by about 5 per cent. Furthermore, manufacturing plant and equipment increased in age and obsolescence during the 1930s; for only $13 billion worth of capital expenditures were made in that decade compared with $21 billion in the 1920s.[11] Thus, with a replacement value of $55 billion just before World War II, three quarters of the facilities were more than ten years old, compared with well under two thirds in 1929.

In the electric light and power industry, however, total installed capacity of generating plants increased about 30 per cent,[12] while in the telephone industry miles of wire and investment both increased by about a quarter.[13] Thus in these two industries 1939 per unit output was achieved with less labor but with more facilities than a decade earlier.

Everywhere productivity was increased and employment reduced, while available capital facilities either increased or were not reduced commensurately. Consequently, there was everywhere more idle plant and equipment than a decade earlier. If this unused or excess capacity had been put into operation, substantial increases in output could have been achieved. On the basis of the same level of employment and hours of work and the same degree of utilization of equipment as in 1929, and *with productivity per man-hour at the 1939 level,* manufacturing production in 1939 could have increased by about 22 per cent.[14] In bituminous coal mining the Bureau of Mines has estimated that, merely by utilizing the existing supply of labor full time, output could have been increased by 47 per cent in 1939.[15]

Problem of Excess Capacity

The conclusion that we had considerable excess capacity before the war is, of course, inescapable. Excess capacity was not merely a depression phenomenon, however. The report of the Brookings Institution on *America's Capacity to Produce,*[16] the most elaborate statistical study of capacity undertaken prior to 1950, shows that

6. Witt Bowden, "Wages, Hours and Productivity of Industrial Labor, 1909–1939," *Monthly Labor Review,* September 1940.

7. *Survey of Current Business, loc. cit.*

8. *Statistical Abstract, 1943,* Table 504, p. 453.

9. See *Monthly Letter of the National City Bank of New York,* October 1943.

10. See the article by Lowell J. Chawner entitled "Capital Expenditures for Manufacturing Plant and Equipment — 1915 to 1940," *Survey of Current Business,* March 1941, p. 12.

11. Based on *ibid.,* p. 9, where the replacement value of productive facilities in existence shortly before World War II was estimated to be in the neighborhood of $55 billion.

12. Table 343.

13. *Statistical Abstract, 1943,* Table 455, p. 416.

14. Productivity multiplied by facilities. Manufacturing productivity or output per man-hour increased to 128 per cent, while facilities declined to 95 per cent of the 1929 level; 128% × 95% = 122%, which is the level to which output could have been raised in comparison with 1929.

15. W. H. Young, R. L. Anderson and L. H. Isaac, "Bituminous Coal and Lignite," a chapter from *Minerals Yearbook, 1944,* Table 13, p. 22.

16. See footnote 2.

nearly every industry was operating below capacity during the prosperous 1920s and had been doing so since the beginning of the century. Even in 1929, at the end of five years of high employment and prosperity, it was found that only the steel and machine tool industries were producing near their rated capacity, that few mining industries were operating near capacity, and that transportation could have doubled the tonnage carried. Production was generally below 1929 levels in 1939, while total plant capacity had been increased appreciably in the later 1930s. In short, the problem remained unsolved.

As early as 1886 Carroll Wright, in a famous work,[17] pointed out that "the means of production were far in excess of the needs of consumption" (i.e., effective demand) and that "this overproduction has been a growth nourished by permanent and not transitory phases of the industrial development of the last half century," i.e., the development of laborsaving machinery.[18]

During the 1930s rated capacity was never attained in any industry, but the defense expansion program initiated in 1940 anticipated the demands that hit heavy industry after Pearl Harbor. Again, after the war, nondurable and consumer goods industries had to be enlarged to take advantage of the potential demand of a public that had waited fifteen years for any substantial enhancement of its standard of living.

So successful have we been in keeping capacity a jump ahead of production that we would seem to have built to the hilt by 1950. The Korean War, however, provided an impetus that extended the expansion still further — almost as much in the consumer products industries as in the heavy industries and defense plants.

According to one student of the problem, unused capacity is inevitable when an area under price system controls becomes highly industrialized:

Existing capacity is forced into idleness not only because of age and technological obsolescence, but because for innumerable other reasons its owners are unable to obtain a large enough share of the market to keep it busy. The unused capacity may be technically and mechanically good, but the product it turns out may lack market appeal, or the owners may be poor salesmen, or may be inadequately supplied with outlets, or may be insufficiently financed. Idle capacity in this condition is seldom scrapped, partly because it is not physically ready for the junk pile, partly because its idleness is likely to be only partial. . . . Since the operation of competition spreads idleness thin, instead of concentrating it, as a monopoly usually tries to do, the affected capacity tends to hang on in the industry. . . . In the great majority of cases it requires a sizable amount of unused and partially used facilities before additions to capacity by expanding producers are held down sufficiently to prevent a further growth in the under-used plant. . . . The full utilization of the mechanical capacity of an industry must be regarded as a temporary and self-limiting condition. It will ordinarily set in motion responses calculated to restore a margin of unused capacity.[19]

The Brookings study [20] cites the case of the automobile industry, where, until after World War I, capacity was deficient because of the rapidly growing demand for cars and trucks. Thereafter, expansion of productive facilities took on "a slightly speculative character," and this "tendency to build up fully to or even beyond current demands of the market" continued until 1929.

This illustrates what has happened to the economy as a whole. In the early stages of industrialization, plant and equipment could not be expanded rapidly enough to take care of mounting demands. Then, as demand ceased to grow so rapidly, or leveled off or declined, the urge for quick profits, coupled with inability properly to analyze their markets, caused producers to continue accumulating facilities for production beyond what the foreseeable future could actually purchase. Of course, in most industries this excess disappeared in time either because it was taken out of use by dismantling or by an indefinite shutdown, or because it was converted to the production of other products for which demand happened to be rising. This process continuously occurring and recurring throughout the economy results in a constant condition of excess capacity.

Some industries are able, by means of well-integrated financial management plus cost reductions through mechanization, to keep this excess capacity and still show a profit, as most Class I railroads have done. Other industries, such as the telegraph industry and coal mining, had long been operating in the red but in recent years have turned to mechanization to cut operating costs.

17. *The First Annual Report of the Commissioner of Labor;* see especially pp. 254–263 *passim.*

18. ". . . this wonderful introduction and extension of power machinery is one of the prime causes, if not the prime cause, of the novel industrial condition in which the manufacturing nations find themselves." *Ibid.,* p. 89. See also pp. 80 and 257.

19. From an unpublished memorandum by George Terborgh, "The Problem of Manufacturing Capacity," April 20, 1940.

20. Nourse *et al., op. cit.,* pp. 228–230.

Bituminous coal mines, too, were designed to produce far more than has ever been required of them. Increased demand and the doubling of coal prices during World War I resulted in the opening of 3,500 new mines in addition to the 5,500 already in operation in 1915. With the failure of demand for coal to increase after 1918, largely because of competition from other fuels, the number of idle mines grew, "diminished only by the reluctant decision of the owners to abandon them entirely." After a loss of a thousand mines following the severe 1921 depression, when coal demand dropped by 150 million tons, the number quickly rose to 9,330 by 1923, bringing capacity (as rated by the U.S. Bureau of Mines) to its all-time peak: 885 million tons a year, on the 280-day standard basis. Soft-coal mines steadily declined in number and capacity through the remaining prosperous years and the depression years, the count falling to 5,427 and annual capacity to 594 million tons in 1933, both below the levels of 1915. Thereafter both the number of mines and capacity grew slowly to 1946.

Soft-coal production reached an all-time high in 1947, but the subsequent output has leveled off considerably under that, and rated capacity continues to be several hundred million tons annually above demand despite the recent decline in the over-all number of mines from a high of 9,430 in 1950 to 7,275 in 1952.[21]

Among the factors influencing the changes in the number of coal mines and total capacity are invasion of the industry's market by competitive fuels, increases in the efficiency with which coal is burned, and depletion of coal deposits, and, on the other hand, the steady increase in coal-using steam-powered turbo-generators for supplying electric power and technological changes within the coal-mining industry which have led to more and more mechanization and fewer mines each having greater capacity.

Apparently, the existence of some excess capacity is unavoidable in an industrial society organized for profit and dependent on the inevitable fluctuations of monetary value and demand. Unused capacity is costly primarily to those who have invested in it, and although overcapitalization often reflects a misuse of resources and may lead to higher prices, it is not in itself harmful. Only when it reflects a widespread deficiency in demand is it a cause for alarm, for

then it reflects unemployment and a lowered standard of living.

RECENT GROWTH OF CAPACITY

Installed rated capacity in basic manufacturing industries increased at an average rate of 3.9 per cent a year during the prosperous 1920s — based on the over-all change between the 1919–1920 average capacity and the 1930 capacity in pig iron, steel, copper refining, aluminum refining, oil refining, cement and paper.

In the depressed 1930s, basic capacity (in essentially the same industries) also increased, despite widely held views to the contrary, but at an annual rate of only 1.8 per cent. This also was approximately the over-all yearly rate of increase in all manufacturing production over the period.

The rate of capacity increase between 1940 and 1950 for 25 basic nonchemical and 15 chemical manufacturing industries averaged 9 per cent annually — or 132 per cent for the decade.[22] The 25 nonchemical industries, as a group, doubled their capacity, but the chemical group nearly tripled its potential output! Incidentally, the average annual rate of increase in rated capacity for all industries during the five years 1940–1945 was almost precisely the same as in the five following postwar years. Of course, in all these periods since World War I, changes in capacity varied widely from one industry to another.

EXPANSION DURING THE 1940s

The problem of unused capacity and idle men that had been the dilemma of the depression years vanished very soon after the start of World War II. In place of the perennial problem was a new one of insufficient capacity. Idle or partially used plant was rapidly converted to munitions production, and new productive facilities were built both in basic industries and in direct fighting-equipment industries. The expansion was at the greatest rate in the nation's history in terms of the amount of new machinery and other equipment installed as well as in percentage increases over existing capacity.

21. The numbers of mines used here refer to those with annual output of 1,000 tons or more.

22. These are unweighted arithmetic means of percentage increases for the individual industries; however, industries and products with extremely high rates of increase — such as alumina, secondary aluminum, magnesium refining and synthetic rubber — and those in which capacity declined were omitted in computing the average rate of increase.

Additions to Facilities

During the first half of the war decade, from 1940 through 1944, we installed more than $50 billion worth of new plant and equipment in privately owned manufacturing, mining, transportation, communications, gas and electric, and commercial enterprises, and in publicly owned military, naval, commercial and industrial operations. This was a very substantial addition to our prewar productive plant, especially in manufacturing. Wartime additions of over $15 billion in privately owned manufacturing facilities were nearly a third as great as the estimated total value of our prewar manufacturing facilities. If allowance is made for the publicly owned manufacturing plants, it is probable that we increased our manufacturing capacity by about one half. Meanwhile we expanded private nonmanufacturing productive capacity by an investment of $2.2 billion in mining, nearly $5 billion in transportation, $2.8 billion in gas and electricity, and $1.8 billion in telephone and telegraph facilities.

Construction of new plant and installation of new equipment not only kept pace with military demands made upon industry, but went ahead of it so far and so fast that in a number of instances entire plants had to be shut down at the peak of the fighting. Even a global war proved insufficient to absorb this nation's new total of capacity. Certain large ammunition, aluminum and other plants first cut back production and then closed, until the accumulated stock could be shot away by the armed forces of the Allies. Some of these plants were never needed again and did not reopen. This was not true of all war industries, but it was by no means a rare occurrence.

Private Nonagricultural Facilities

Investment in private nonagricultural facilities, which amounted to about $34 billion during the period 1941–1945, jumped to approximately $109 billion during the postwar years 1946–1950.[23] The pressure of expansion needs pent up first by depression and then by war exploded into the highest half decade of spending for capital facilities in our history. No earlier five-year period approached the capital expenditure rate of 1946–

1950; perhaps the closest was the last half of the 1920s, when some $42 billion was put into new industrial and commercial facilities. (See Appendix 4–8.)

The percentage distribution by industry of the $109 billion invested in the five years after World War II (1946–1950) compared as follows with the distribution of 1939 investment:

	1939	1946–1950
Mining	5.9	3.2
Manufacturing	35.3	36.0
Durable	13.7	14.4
Nondurable	21.6	21.6
Transportation	11.7	10.8
Railroads	5.1	4.8
Other	6.6	6.0
Communication	5.5	5.9
Utilities	9.5	10.3
Commercial and miscellaneous	32.1	33.8
Total	100.0	100.0

The other industrial divisions gained relatively at the expense of mining and transportation. Except in the case of mining, which dropped by nearly half in relative importance as an outlet for capital investment and thereby fell below the communications industry, intervention of the most capital-costly war in our history did not alter the order of rank of the industrial divisions.

Production Records

Production records achieved during World War II provide a rough indication of how we were able to expand capacity to meet wartime needs. Increases to the wartime peak over the 1939 level of output in manufacturing varied from 22 per cent for the printing and publishing industry group to 662 per cent for the transportation equipment group. (See Table 345.)

Even more spectacular increases were recorded by individual industries within the more inclusive groups. For example, production of synthetic rubber — practically nonexistent before the war — reached over three quarters of a million long tons by 1944. Output of airplanes increased over fifteen times, from 5,856 in 1939 to 96,318 in 1944, the wartime peak year. Gross tonnage of merchant ships produced increased over twenty-six times, from 422,000 in 1939 to 11.6 million in 1943. (See Appendix 23–1.)

---

23. Excluded from these and the figures that follow are expenditures for publicly owned facilities, including all publicly owned military and naval plant and equipment.

TABLE 345. PEAK INDUSTRIAL AND COMMERCIAL ACTIVITY DURING WORLD WAR II [a]
(*Percentage Increase over 1939*)

Type of Activity	Individual Peak [b]		November 1943 [c]
	Date	Per Cent	
Mining	June 1945	36	25
Manufacturing			
Durable			
Iron and steel	October 1943	88	83
Machinery	November 1943	345	345
Transportation equipment	November 1943	662	663
Nonferrous metals and products	November 1943	165	165
Lumber and products	December 1943	29	28
Stone, clay and glass products	January 1943	58	47
Nondurable			
Textiles and products	February 1943	45	36 [d]
Leather and products	April 1942	26	
Manufactured food products	March 1945	48	38
Alcoholic beverages	January 1945	117	44
Tobacco products	August 1945	42	40
Paper and products	March 1942	43	23
Printing and publishing	January 1942	22	[e]
Petroleum and coal products	February 1945	151	94
Chemicals	August 1943	261	248
Rubber products	January 1945	119	113
Transportation	March 1945	120	107
Communications			
Telegrams	1944	20	19
Telephones	1944	29	27
Electric light and power	1944	79	71
Construction	1942	43	[d]

Sources: Mining and manufacturing — *Federal Reserve Bulletin*, October 1943, pp. 964–984, February 1944, pp. 180–181, February 1945, pp. 168–169, and January 1946, p. 69.
Transportation — *Survey of Current Business*, May 1943, pp. 26–27, and June 1944, p. S–21.
Communications — Federal Communications Commission.
Electric light and power — *Statistical Abstract of the United States, 1948*, U.S. Bureau of the Census, Table 534.
Construction — *Construction and Building Materials, Statistical Supplement*, May 1953, p. 39.
a. Between January 1942 and August 1945.
b. Based on seasonally adjusted monthly indexes of production, except for communications, electric power and construction, where peak year was used.
c. Based on seasonally adjusted November 1943 indexes of production, except for communications, electric power and construction, where the whole year 1943 was used.
d. Decrease.
e. No change.

These records show how readily we could expand our capacity to produce a large number of individual items. But they do not indicate what we achieved in the way of simultaneous production of *each* at the peak of our total economic effort. Total *industrial* production was at a peak in November 1943, when the Federal Reserve index stood at 247 as compared with an average of 122 for 1940. In that month such war industries as iron and steel, machinery, transportation equipment, nonferrous metals and products, lumber and products, chemicals and rubber products were operating at or very close to their peak production levels. At the other extreme, the leather products and construction industries had fallen from their wartime peaks to below their 1939 levels.

With some significant exceptions — tobacco

products and communications — the other industries not directly connected with the war were operating at appreciably lower levels in November 1943 than at other times during the war. Mining output, for example, was only 25 per cent above 1939 in November 1943; it had been higher earlier and did not reach its wartime peak of 36 per cent above 1939 until June 1945. Output of alcoholic beverages was about two and a half times as great in January 1945 as in November 1943. Petroleum and coal products and transportation also reached their wartime peaks during 1945, and electric light and power reached its high point in 1944. Stone, clay and glass products and textiles, on the other hand, were at their World War II peaks early in 1943, while paper and products as well as printing and publishing declined after the early months of 1942. On the whole, however, the output of the nonwar industries was remarkably high at the peak of the industrial war effort in November 1943. (See Table 345.)

Postwar Production Trends

High as the wartime production peaks were, many of them were soon surpassed during the postwar boom. The transportation industries and the utilities made new records during the postwar years. The 1946–1952 production peaks for trucks and buses, tractors, locomotives and freight cars ran from nearly double to almost triple their wartime highs. In 1952 nearly six times as many revenue passenger-miles were flown within the United States as in 1944. Telephones in use, which had risen less than a third between 1939 and 1944, jumped to well over double the 1939 number in 1952. Total electric energy generated, which had almost doubled between 1939 and 1944, nearly doubled again by 1952.

Output of cement, which had reached a peak of 185 million barrels during the basic expansion program early in the war, shot up to 253 million barrels in 1952 under the impetus of the postwar housing and commercial building boom. Sharp increases over wartime peaks occurred during 1946–1952 in the production of nondurables such as wheat, margarine, pulp and paper, newsprint, gasoline and coke. In the case of newsprint and coke there had been practically no increase in output during the war, but the other items had made substantial gains over their 1939 levels even before the postwar jump.

Peacetime production of most of the nonferrous metals was sharply below maximum wartime achievements. Although aluminum output was slightly higher in the early 1950s than during the war, domestic bauxite production was about 70 per cent under its wartime peak. Airplane production and shipbuilding, as would be expected, fell far below their wartime high points but both remained well above prewar, with civilian airplane output in 1946 seven times as high as in 1939. (See Appendix 23–1.)

Wartime and Postwar Capacity Changes

Among industries for which data on wartime and immediate postwar capacity changes are available, a number of newcomers registered phenomenal growth during the war. Capacity to turn out synthetic rubber, for example, rose more than 8,000 per cent; magnesium ingot capacity jumped more than 3,000 per cent; floor space available for the manufacture of aircraft expanded nearly 300 per cent; and aluminum ingot capacity increased more than 200 per cent. (See Table 346.)

Among older, more established industries comparatively modest percentage increases masked tremendous additions to the amount of available capacity. The 21 per cent rise in pig iron capacity meant an addition of 11 million tons of potential annual output; the 17 per cent rise for steel ingots meant that 14 million more tons could be produced each year. The 23 per cent increase in potential output of glass containers between 1939 and 1945 was equivalent to 2.5 billion more units annually. About 1.5 million more tons of wood pulp and 1.5 million more tons of paper (all types except newsprint) could be produced after the war than before. Some 8 million more tons were haulable by railroad freight cars and about 12,500 additional miles of petroleum pipelines were available. Six million more telephones were in use and electric generating capacity had increased by 10 million kilowatts.

Many industries, flushed with wartime profits and contemplating huge demands from a war-depleted world, continued to expand capacity rapidly during the last half of the decade. The pace was somewhat more rapid than during the war for glass containers, wood pulp, paper (all types except newsprint), crude-oil refining, carbon black, both petroleum and gas pipelines, telephones and electric generating capacity. In

TABLE 346. CHANGES IN RATED CAPACITY IN SELECTED INDUSTRIES, 1940–1945 AND 1945–1950

Industry	Unit	Capacity (as of January 1)			Percentage Increase[a]	
		1940	1945	1950	1940–1945	1945–1950
Manufacturing						
Ferrous metals						
Pig iron	Thousand tons	55,724	67,314	71,498	20.8	6.2
Steel ingots	"	81,620	95,505	99,393	17.0	4.1
Ferroalloys (blast furnace)	"	922	993	1,108	7.7	11.6
Nonferrous metals						
Copper smelter	"	10,722	10,909[b]	9,748[c]	1.7[d]	−10.6[e]
Copper refinery	"	1,572	1,595[b]	1,557	1.5[d]	−2.4[f]
Lead smelter	"	2,500	2,078[b]	1,858[c]	−16.9[d]	−10.6[e]
Lead refinery	"	1,168	975[b]	866[c]	−16.5[d]	−11.2[e]
Zinc refinery	"	223	365[b]	373[c]	63.7[d]	2.2[e]
Aluminum ingots	"	245	767[b]	721	213.1[d]	−6.0[f]
Magnesium ingots	"	9[g]	293	127[c]	3,155.5[h]	−56.7[i]
Stone, clay and glass products						
Portland cement	Thousand barrels	253,759	241,631[b]	258,948	−4.8[d]	7.2[f]
Glass containers	Million units	10,973[j]	13,522	18,829	23.2[k]	39.2
Transportation equipment						
Aircraft mfg. floorspace	Thousand sq. ft.	44,200[g]	171,400[l]	120,000[c]	287.8[m]	−30.0[n]
Manufactured food products						
Flour mills	Thousand barrels	443,000	414,500	394,000[c]	−6.4	−4.9[l]
Paper						
Wood pulp	Thousand tons	10,421	11,994	16,167	15.1	34.8
Paper, all types exc. newsprint	"	7,951	9,543[b]	11,739	20.0[d]	23.0[f]
Paperboard	"	7,531	9,900[b]	11,762	31.4[d]	18.8[f]
Newsprint	"	1,075	981	924	−8.7	−5.8
Textiles and products						
Cotton ginning	Thousand bales per day	1,043	905[b]	744[c] (est.)	−13.2[d]	−17.8[l]
Rayon and acetate fiber	Thousand tons	270	446[b]	625	65.2[d]	40.1[z]
Petroleum and coal products						
Crude oil refining	Million barrels	1,687	1,935	2,444	14.7	26.3
Catalytic cracked gasoline	Thousand "	381,800	543,120	664,300	42.2	22.3
Cycling plant	"	2,190	42,000[b]	57,700	1,817.8[d]	37.4[f]
Natural gasoline	"	100,000	114,000[b]	178,800	14.0[d]	56.8[f]
Industrial chemicals						
Methanol	Thousand gallons	73,500[j]	82,500[o]	157,000	12.2[p]	90.3[q]
Ethylene oxide	Tons	74,000[j]	100,500	220,000	35.8[k]	118.9

Item	Unit					
Explosives						
Permissible and high explosives	Thousand tons	311	376	414	20.9	10.1
Black powder	"	82	69	23	−15.9	−66.7
Fertilizers						
Synthetic nitrogen	"	625	1,028	1,639[c]	64.5	59.4[l]
Synthetic rubber and materials						
Synthetic rubber	Tons	11,200[j]	932,300[o]	1,002,400[o]	8,224.1[p]	7.5[r]
Carbon black	"	312,805	471,835[o]	743,724	50.8[s]	57.6[q]
Nonmanufacturing						
Mining: fuels						
Bituminous coal	Thousand tons	639,000	620,000	790,000	−3.0	27.4
Anthracite coal	"	84,000	62,000	63,400	−26.2	2.2
Crude petroleum	Thousand barrels (capacity at wells)	1,715,500	1,679,000[b]	2,226,500	−2.1[d]	32.6[f]
Transportation						
Locomotive tractive effort	Thousand tons	1,060	1,159	1,159	9.3	0
Freightcar carrying capacity	"	82,002	89,960	90,465	9.7	0.6
Trucks in use (nonfarm)	units	3,360	3,023	5,819	−10.0	92.5
Petroleum pipelines	Miles	122,500	135,240	152,500	10.4	12.8
Gas pipelines	"	282,300	307,900	364,080	9.1	18.2
Communications						
Telephones in use	Thousand units	20,831	26,859	40,709	28.9	51.6
Utility power						
Electric generating capacity	" kilowatts	38,863	49,189	63,100	26.6	28.3
Agriculture						
Tractors on farms	" units	1,545	2,422	3,616	56.8	49.3
Grain combines	" "	190	375	714	97.4	90.4
Corn-picking machines	" "	110	168	456	52.7	171.4
Motor trucks on farms	" "	1,047	1,490	2,209	42.3	48.2
Storage						
Refrigerated warehouse (cold storage) space	" cubic feet	433,378	511,377	613,000[e]	18.0	19.9[l]

Source: Appendix 23–2 and its sources. a. Minus sign denotes decrease. b. 1946. c. 1951. d. 1940–1946. e. 1946–1951. f. 1946–1950. g. 1941. h. 1941–1945. i. 1945–1951. j. 1939. k. 1939–1945. l. 1943. m. 1941–1943. n. 1943–1951. o. 1944. p. 1939–1944. q. 1944–1950. r. 1944–1951. s. 1940–1944.

Note: These figures represent installed capacity as rated by the appropriate authority for industry statistics, whether industrial trade association, government bureau, or trade or technical publication. All figures are in terms of capacity per year, unless otherwise indicated. For uniformity, this applies even to industries where capacity (and output) are ordinarily given daily, such as petroleum products.

some instances the postwar rate of expansion was many times the wartime rate. Capacity for natural gasoline and the industrial chemicals methanol and ethylene oxide rose from three to seven times as fast. In other instances — notably coal mining and nonfarm trucks — wartime declines gave way to postwar growth.

Potential output in agriculture rose sharply both during and after the war as a result of the addition of much new equipment. By the end of the war the nation's farms had roughly half again as many tractors, corn-picking machines and motor trucks as in 1940 and nearly double the number of grain combines. These wartime rates of expansion were maintained between 1945 and 1950; in the case of corn-picking machines, in fact, the rate more than tripled.

EXPANSION DURING THE EARLY 1950S

When the cold war flamed into battle in Korea in mid-1950, the need for quick additional capacity in certain munitions industries was apparent. This meant in turn expansion of finished-steel, copper, aluminum and other metals industries, the machine tool industry, the transportation equipment industry, and additional primary raw materials and power — electric and gas.

These changes had to be largely superimposed on the existing pattern of industrial and consumer production, for the Controlled Materials Plan (or CMP) of allocations, though it limited normal usage to some extent, was by no means so restrictive as to require civilian rationing or the closing down of any basic consumer production industries as in World Wars I and II. The problem facing the government in 1950 has been summed up as follows:

There was no idle productive capacity we could set at the task [of producing war machines]. There wasn't enough, even in our rich country, to make huge quantities of munitions fast, while continuing to turn out record numbers of civilian products. Something had to give way; we had a choice to make. (a) We could start making arms at a rate so high that we would stop the production of many civilian goods, as we did in World War II; (b) we could build up munitions production slowly and cut down on civilian goods gradually, to fit our existing capacity; or, (c) we could expand our basic production machinery as quickly as possible, so that we would have more industrial capacity to divide between defense and civilian production, to meet our military needs without crippling peacetime enterprise.

We chose the third way, expansion . . . We are making weapons — but we are also building new steel mills and power plants, digging new mines, sinking new oil wells, doing all the things necessary to augment the flow of raw materials and speed their conversion into the vital end-products we need. At the same time we are preparing our economic structure to sustain, *for as long a time as necessary*, both a military effort and a high level of civilian production.[24]

Implementing this program, the Revenue Act of 1950 provided for an accelerated tax amortization plan to stimulate profitable private expansion of industry. In contrast to World War II practice, government ownership of industrial facilities was held to a minimum.

On the average, about 60 per cent of the construction and machinery cost of a proposed plant receiving a "certificate of necessity" was made subject to depreciation at the rapid rate. The exact percentage eligible for rapid depreciation depended, according to the Office of Defense Mobilization, "on the type of facility, the amount of expansion required for the emergency, the probable usefulness of the plant for other than defense purposes after the emergency, and the degree of financial aid necessary as an incentive to encourage the expansion." The period of time during which the eligible capital facilities could be written off was reduced to five years from the normal period, which varies up to twenty-five years.

By the end of September 1953 the ODM and other federal agencies had issued over 17,000 certificates. These covered capital facilities costing $27.6 billion, of which almost two thirds went for machinery and equipment and slightly more than one third for construction, land and overhead expenses. More than half the total was centered in six main industries, distributed as follows:[25]

	Amount (Millions)	Per Cent of Total
Electric power utilities	$4,167	15.1
Railroads, line haul	3,464	12.5
Steel works and rolling mills	2,568	9.3
Petroleum refining	1,739	6.3
Iron ores	985	3.6
Blast furnaces	924	3.3
Total, six industries	$13,847	50.1

24. *Expanding Our Industrial Might*, Defense Production Administration, Washington, 1952.

25. *Expansion Progress: Projects Under Certificates of Necessity*, Office of Defense Mobilization, January 22, 1954, Table IV.

Additional certificates granted after September 1953 brought the cumulative total at the end of June 1954 to $28.9 billion. Of this sum, $17.3 billion was eligible for rapid depreciation.[26]

The "certificates of necessity" were only supplementary to over-all expenditures for industrial expansion by private business enterprises. The $28.9 billion covered by these certificates was less than the amount spent by business for new plant and equipment during any single year from 1950 on. By far the greatest share of investment by business in new facilities during the early 1950s was without benefit of rapid tax amortization, regardless of whether it was in the defense and munitions category or in production of consumer goods and services. Whether these capital expenditures were allowed the rapid tax amortization or not, they all represented private capital — almost entirely corporate investment. Limited direct government defense loans, in the post-Korea program, have been made "only when the tax amortization incentive alone is not sufficient to accomplish the necessary industrial expansion."

Stimulated by the rapid write-off program, productive capacity by the end of 1952 had expanded tremendously over the levels reached at the end of World War II. During the years 1946–1952 corporations invested in fixed capital $124 billion, an amount almost equal to the book value of their gross capital assets ($140 billion) at the end of the war. Actual capacity was considerably less than doubled during these seven postwar years, however, since some obsolete facilities were retired and rising prices continuously reduced the amount of productive capacity that could be purchased for each dollar spent. Book values in 1945 reflected largely original cost (undepreciated) of plant and equipment, which was well below replacement cost at that time; in addition, postwar outlays were made at prices that were well above those at the end of the war.

Manufacturing, which by the end of 1952 accounted for about half the total postwar capital outlay, had also increased its capacity by 50 per cent. Within manufacturing the largest relative gains were in electrical machinery, nonelectrical machinery and chemicals, all of which just about doubled their capacity between the end of 1945 and the end of 1952. Extremely rapid expansion of capacity took place in plants turning out some of the new postwar products such as television sets, electronic devices, plastics, the newer synthetic fibers and antibiotics.[27]

Some important nonmanufacturing segments, such as the utilities, expanded capacity at least as rapidly as manufacturing. Private electric utilities, for example, increased their generating capacity by about three fourths in the first seven postwar years.

CAPACITY AND REQUIREMENTS

During World War II the nation's requirements for goods and services exceeded our capacity to supply them. Consequently, we had to choose among the various demands on our limited industrial and commercial capacity, which probably would not have been so restricted if capital outlays had not dropped so low during the depressed 1930s. The decision, quite naturally, was in favor of expanding capacity needed to prosecute the war, and government controls were set up to reduce or eliminate capital expenditure not directed toward that end.

After World War II we shifted gears and concentrated on expanding capacity to meet peacetime civilian needs. The tremendous capital outlays between 1945 and 1950 brought our over-all industrial capacity a long way toward meeting the needs of a prosperous peacetime economy.

The Korean War, however, brought us face to face again with the question of how to meet the requirements of an enlarged national defense program at a time when our industrial machinery was already working at top speed to supply civilian needs. We could not meet the new defense needs merely by turning to the magnificent industrial machine we had created during World War II. That machine no longer existed since we had rapidly demobilized our war industry after the fighting was over. Moreover, advances in military technology required expansion of some industrial capacity far beyond the levels reached during World War II and creation of some types of capacity not even in existence during that war.

World War II Experience

A significant lesson learned from our World War II experience was that insufficient capacity in the form of plant and equipment imposes no real limitation on rapid expansion in the produc-

---

26. Press Release, Office of Defense Mobilization, July 12, 1954.

27. *Survey of Current Business*, April 1952, pp. 3 and 4.

tion of needed goods and services. Not only did we greatly increase output by more continuous and intensive use of existing capacity, but we made vast additions to our productive facilities.

The wartime expansion of facilities was for the single purpose of winning the war as soon as possible. Sometimes this goal coincided with postwar needs and we expanded capacity far beyond our previous peacetime requirements. In other instances, facilities to meet the special needs of war were of little use in supplying civilian requirements and had to be written off as one of the necessary costs of winning the war. Moreover, wartime restrictions delayed or prevented expansion of facilities for many goods and services not essential to prosecuting the war. At the end of World War II American industry and commerce thus found itself with surplus capacity in some directions and serious deficiencies in others.

Closing the Postwar Gap

The shortages were largely overcome during the immediate postwar and Korean War booms of the late 1940s and early 1950s. The National Industrial Conference Board reported, on the basis of a survey of 159 manufacturing firms in 1953, that in a healthy proportion of American industries capacity to produce had caught up with demand for goods. About 17 per cent of the reporting firms said that capacity in their industries had outrun demand; three out of four said production potential for their goods had caught up with demand; and only 7 per cent said demand exceeded capacity.[28]

By early 1954, over-all capacity was quite sufficient to handle over-all civilian demand, as evidenced by the so-called "inventory liquidation" at that time. In fact, if it had not been for the national defense program, we would have had the industrial and commercial capacity easily to close the gap between needs and demand indicated in other chapters of this study.

Even in the area of national defense most of the needed additional industrial capacity had been provided for by 1954. Needs in this area were expressed in terms of "expansion goals," set by the Office of Defense Mobilization (with the help of other federal agencies). These goals served to identify and measure deficiencies in productive capacity and supply required for national defense. In March 1953 the ODM announced that of the

28. *Wall Street Journal*, September 22, 1953.

242 expansion goals it had set, 150 had been closed; that is, no additional accelerated tax amortization certificates would be issued for capacity expansion in these 150 industries, in view of the amount of expansion already completed or planned.

In addition, some items remaining on the "open" list, in which rapid amortization was still available, had sufficient capacity when allowance was made for foreign sources of supply[29] and others had expansion programs under way, or planned, sufficient to meet most of the estimated defense needs. By the end of 1953, for example, inclusion of foreign sources would have made it possible to supply all mobilization needs for antimony, barite, bauxite, chromite (metallurgical and refractory grades), metallurgical coal for by-product coke, columbite and tantalite ores, copper, fluorspar (acid grade), iron ore, lead, manganese ore (metallurgical grade), mercury, molybdenum, rare earths, rutile, tungsten ore and zinc. At that time also, expansion goals had been at least 90 per cent subscribed for commercial aircraft, aluminum sheet and plate-producing facilities, casting steel, by-product coke, electrolytic tin plate, grain-oriented steel sheets, and tires (specific types). In total, it was estimated that the end of 1954 would see the completion of approximately 90 per cent of all facilities expansion granted "certificates of necessity" through September 30, 1953 under the rapid amortization program.[30]

Recent Expansion Goals

The expansion goals deemed necessary for some of our basic industries to meet military needs and to supply a high level of civilian demand dwarfed anything we had before the war. Although we had already added tremendously to our capacity by 1950, expansion goals in late 1953 called for adding one fourth to our 1950 steel capacity, almost doubling 1950 electric power generating capacity and nearly tripling 1950 domestic primary aluminum capacity. Our

29. Even though the goal was fully subscribed from a combination of foreign and domestic sources, it was left "open" in order to encourage increased domestic production where necessary.

30. *Expansion Progress: Projects Under Certificates of Necessity*, Office of Defense Mobilization, January 22, 1954, pp. 2 and 3. The ODM thought this estimate probably would turn out to be too high since completions had fallen about a fifth short of the amount estimated for the end of 1953 nine months earlier.

steel capacity, about 100 million tons in 1950, reached 120 million tons by September 1953, with a future goal as of that date of 124.3 million tons. Aluminum capacity, 650,000 tons in 1950, reached 1.4 million tons in September 1953, compared with an annual goal of 1.7 million tons. We could generate 63 million kilowatts of electric power in 1950 and 91 million in September 1953 and had set a 1955 goal of 116 million.[31]

Expansion was also planned in many other industries, as indicated by goals set early in 1954.[32] The Office of Defense Mobilization set the goal for domestic nitrogen production at an annual capacity of 3.5 million short tons (contained nitrogen) by January 1957, or 1.8 million higher than the industry's 1950 capacity.[33] The domestic titanium industry, with a melting capacity of 7,680 short tons a year in early 1954, was scheduled for expansion to 37,500 tons by 1956. Some 1,250 new railroad passenger cars were to be added, to make up for some of the decline over the past ten years; between 1944 and 1954, the number of cars owned by Class I railroads and the Pullman Company decreased from about 29,000 to 22,300 and seating capacity fell from 1.7 million to 1.3 million — a decrease of nearly 25 per cent.

Capacity and National Output

These recently established expansion goals are important as indicators of the fact that, despite the tremendous capital growth during the 1940s and early 1950s, industrial capacity in this country is still not excessive. Another and more inclusive indication that capacity is not too high is supplied by a comparison of the size of the stock of all privately owned plant and equipment with the privately produced gross national product over the years 1910–1953.[34] On the basis of such a comparison, the Machinery and Allied Products Institute concluded, with qualifying reservations, that the over-all relation between capacity and output in 1953 was near normal as judged by predepression standards.[35]

This conclusion is based primarily on the trend in the value of the stock of equipment, the ratio of which to private gross national product ran very close to the 1910–1930 average during the years 1949–1953. The value of the stock of plant and the value of all facilities — equipment plus plant — when compared with gross private product have run below predepression standards in recent years. (See Figure 100.) However, these low ratios, which would appear to mean that current capacity is insufficient, may be discounted. There appears to have been a drastic change in the amount of plant necessary to produce a given level of output. In recent decades expenditures for new equipment have taken an ever-increasing share of total outlays for productive facilities. Consequently, the stock of equipment, which had less than half the value of the plant existing in 1910, was just about equal in value to the stock of plant in 1953.[36] Apparently, "a number of forces have been at work, some fairly apparent, some obscure, to make it possible to use more and more equipment with a given amount of plant."[37]

Although the equipment ratio may be more significant than the plant ratio as an indicator of our capacity to meet needed output, nevertheless it seems reasonable to infer that the difference between the two suggests a somewhat more intensive utilization of facilities than normal. Despite the heavy capital installations in recent decades, therefore, we do not appear to have developed generally excessive industrial and commercial capacity for the long run.

Flexibility of Capacity

As for any deficiencies that exist, the war experience demonstrated how quickly these can

31. *Defense Mobilization,* Report to the President by the Director of the Office of Defense Mobilization, October 1, 1953, pp. 10 and 11.

32. The following data on existing and future goal capacities are from various press releases of the Office of Defense Mobilization during the first half of 1954.

33. By April 1954 this goal was assured; rated capacity for producing nitrogen in the form of synthetic ammonia was 2.9 million tons — either in production or under construction — and the estimated supply from by-product and organic wastes was 265,000 tons. In addition, construction was scheduled to start on an additional 190,000 tons of capacity under outstanding "certificates of necessity" and applications covering the remaining 163,000 tons had been received.

34. The estimated stock of privately owned plant and equipment provides a measure of the country's productive capacity which may be compared with the privately produced gross national product, a measure of national output. Government-owned facilities and government production are excluded from this comparison. One excellent reason for this exclusion is that the measure of government production is extremely weak since, in the absence of market prices for its product, it is measured by government wages and salaries plus supplements.

35. *Capital Goods Review,* Machinery and Allied Products Institute, August 1953, p. 4.

36. Both valued in constant prices; data supplied by Machinery and Allied Products Institute.

37. *Capital Goods Review,* August 1953, p. 3.

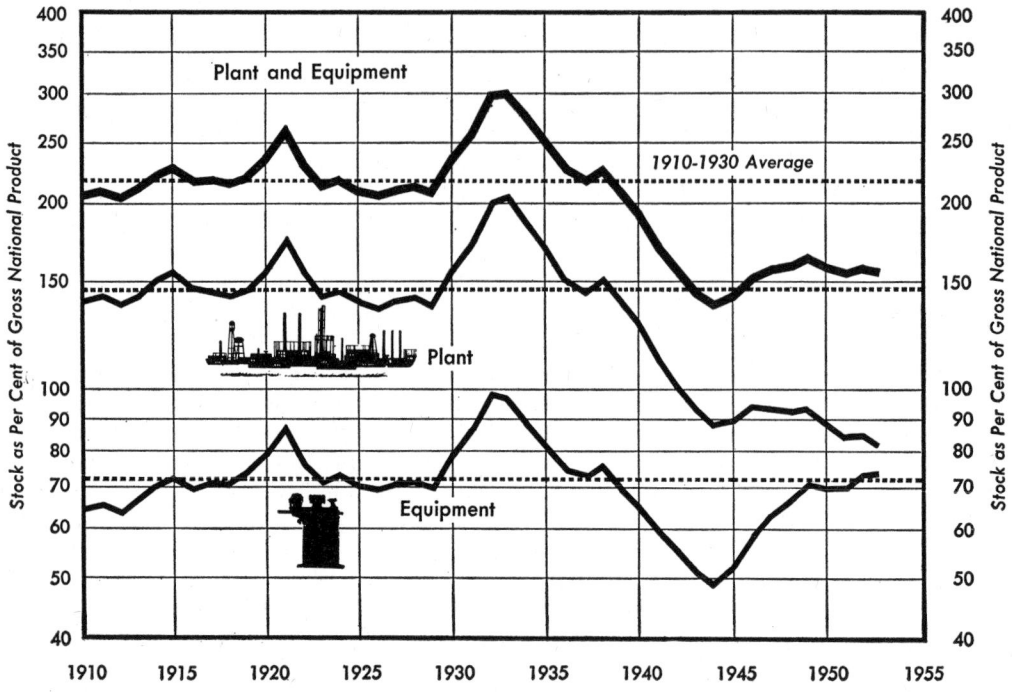

FIGURE 100. RATIOS OF STOCKS OF PRIVATELY OWNED PLANT AND EQUIPMENT TO PRIVATE GROSS NATIONAL PRODUCT, 1910–1953 [a]

Source: Based on *Capital Goods Review*, Machinery and Allied Products Institute, Chicago, August 1953, p. 2.

a. Ratios of values of stock at midyear to annual product both measured at constant (1953) prices; private gross national product, as used here, excludes production by general government and government enterprises.

be remedied. In spite of the draft of millions of workers into military service and munitions production, we were able to maintain our civilian standard of living at high levels, and at the same time to construct more new plants and facilities than ever before in a comparable period.

Given time, any country can make tremendous increases in its productive capacity. But, of course, the more backward a country is technologically, the smaller is its surplus after it has fed, clothed and sheltered its population, and the more time it will need to create new facilities. The United States has reached such a high stage of industrial development that great quantities of facilities can be added in a short time — if there is a demand for their products. Indeed, in such industries as shipbuilding it requires no longer to construct the facilities than to build the product. During the war we increased our manufacturing facilities — though in a distorted fashion — by roughly 50 per cent. We were able to expand our productive capacity enormously and rapidly, devote almost half our economic effort to produc-

tion for war, and still maintain a high living standard for the civilian population.

There were problems, of course. Lack of raw materials, labor shortages and transportation difficulties each played a part in slowing up the expansion of production. In peacetime these same factors may make it difficult to expand rapidly the supply of goods and services available for certain regions or localities. There may be enough facilities to meet requirements on a national basis, but capacity may be inflexible in a particular region or locality. Similarly, bottlenecks can occur in individual industries. During the war they occurred in certain types of turbines, in electrical and chemical equipment, in metals and various other products. Sometimes a lag in the supply of one product has serious repercussions on other industries. If steel capacity can be expanded only slowly, a host of other industries are rendered inflexible simply because they lack an essential material. The war, however, proved that bottlenecks of this kind can be quickly overcome.

Often capacity could be increased without building new equipment. Small adjustments in existing machinery made it possible to shift rapidly from one product to another. Shifts of this sort were made from food machinery to amphibious tanks, from typewriters to small parts for guns, from printing presses to machine tools, from refrigerators to marine engines and helicopters. In peacetime, too, similar substitutions can be made if required by rapid shifts in demand.

We have reached a stage of economic development and technical competence where inadequate industrial and commercial capacity can be quickly overcome through the construction of new facilities. We have more than enough manpower and potential productive facilities to fulfill our requirements under every conceivable circumstance. Fears of excess capacity need not trouble us unduly. The only real dangers for the future are an inadequate level of income and a low standard of living.

CHAPTER 24

TECHNOLOGY: PRIMARY RESOURCE

ALL THE material resources discussed in these chapters, whether natural or man-made, are the fruits of technology. Technology, in fact, can be thought of as the primary resource; without it all other resources would be economically nonexistent. This is clearly true of industrial and commercial facilities and of improved agricultural land. But it is also true of coal and oil, of iron ore, and of all the raw materials we obtain from the earth, the forests and the oceans. These are potential resources; they become actual resources only as technology makes it possible to extract them and convert them into useful products.

After all, the territory of what is now the continental United States was occupied without threat of foreign enemies for more than a thousand years by tribes of American Indians whose total number never approached a million. They possessed all of the natural riches we have today — and indeed much more, for we have used up many of our best.

Yet, as Wesley Mitchell has said:

[These] aboriginal inhabitants of what is now the United States lived in a poverty-stricken environment. For them no coal existed, no petroleum, no metals beyond nuggets of pure copper. Of electrical energy they had no inkling. Their agriculture was so crude that they could use only tiny patches of soil. Their rudimentary social organization combined with their ineffective production to keep their groups small and mutually hostile. Division of labor went scarcely beyond a traditional recognition of what was man's and what was woman's work. Trading was feebly developed. A precarious food supply, flimsy housing, mystical medicine, and chronic warfare limited the increase in numbers.[1]

Because their technology was primitive and static, this scanty population was never able to achieve a standard of living remotely approaching that enjoyed by the 160-odd million people who today live in the same territory. Even the

English technology — itself the product of less than a thousand years' development from crude Saxon beginnings — had little influence on the natives' way of life. Gunpowder made the Indian more efficient as a hunter and fighter. So did the horse, but the Indian made little use of the horse to improve his farming. Textiles, hardware, and other products of the white man's technology found a ready market among the natives, but the industrial techniques used by the white settlers, such as steam and water power, though freely available, found little acceptance. Living in the midst of natural plenty, but lacking superior technology, the American Indian was unable to achieve an advanced standard of living.

As technology consists of accumulated knowledge, techniques and skills, and their application in creating useful goods and services, the ultimate fruits of a country's technology are found in the standard of living its people are able to enjoy. This statement is subject to important qualifications. Living standards suffer in time of war or intensive preparation for war, not through failure of technology, but because human and material resources must be diverted to armament. In the Soviet Union and other dictatorships the interests of consumers may be sacrificed indefinitely, even in time of peace, to permit rapid formation of capital and expansion of military power. Under such conditions the standard of living of the people fails to reflect the nation's technology.

TECHNOLOGY AND CONSUMPTION STANDARDS

In countries enjoying political and economic freedom, however, technological progress reflects itself in the kinds and amounts, and the cost, of the goods and services available to consumers. Measured by these evidences American technology today far surpasses that of any other country. And technological progress during the past century, especially since 1900, appears to have been

---

By J. FREDERIC DEWHURST, with the assistance of JOHN A. WARING, JR., research writer on technology and resources, in assembling some of the material. Opinions and judgments expressed in this chapter are those of the author and should not be attributed to the organization with which he is associated.

1. Wesley C. Mitchell, article on "Conservation, Liberty and Economics" in *The Foundation of Conservation Education,* National Wildlife Federation, Washington, 1941, p. 1.

more rapid in the United States than anywhere else in the world.

Income Gains

The material welfare of the American people and our progress during recent decades can be suggested by such measures as national income per capita and per family, output per worker or per man-hour, average hours of work and hours of leisure, and the quantities of various articles produced or consumed. National income per capita in the United States, for example, amounted to $1,585 in 1950; per family, or household, to $5,535. (By 1953 these averages had risen to $1,925 and $6,635, respectively.) Income per capita in this country in 1950 exceeded that of any other country and was probably five times the average for the world as a whole — ample evidence that the typical American was very "well off" in the things that money could buy. Per capita income, measured in 1950 dollars, was nearly twice as high in that year as in 1900 and almost four times the 1850 average.

The great majority of American workers today normally work a five-day week of 40 hours or less. This is a shorter work week than now prevails in most countries of the world. A 60-hour week was the rule in the United States in 1900 and a 70-hour week a century ago. Our high and rising living standards have thus been achieved with less and less human effort, and this has meant more and more leisure to consume the additional goods and services that our larger incomes can buy. These statistical averages are only rough approximations, but they provide an indication of how a dynamic technology has enabled the American people to increase their productivity and material well-being.

Qualitative Changes

Such quantitative measures, however, fail to suggest the tremendous qualitative alteration that technology has brought in the way we live and work today compared with half a century ago. No period of comparable length in human history has brought such great changes in the variety, quality and quantity of goods and services available for consumption. In many ways those of us now passing middle age have within our lifetime experienced a greater advance in our material standard of living and a more pervasive change

in our way of life than occurred in all the previous centuries of Western history. The mass of the people, it is important to emphasize, have been the chief beneficiaries of this great material progress. In every past age and civilization only the favored few were able to enjoy a high standard of living, because they alone could command the lavish personal service to make it possible.

Increasingly progressive income taxes in the United States, especially since the beginning of World War II, have greatly lowered the "take-home pay" of those at the upper income levels, and heavy inheritance taxes have had a similar effect on the transmission of wealth from one generation to the next. Those with the least income, on the other hand, have profited from application of a "regressive" principle in the payment of relief and social security benefits. An increasing share of the national income has been taxed away from those who receive it and given to those who need it. These and other influences have greatly narrowed the money income gap between rich and poor. But even more striking has been the trend toward equalization of living standards, particularly in the new and improved products that technology has created and that mass production and mass distribution have made available for mass consumption.

The banker or well-to-do businessman of the 1890s dressed and acted the part. He rode in his own carriage, driven by a hired coachman. The man of modest income, whether farmer or mechanic, also dressed and acted the part. Although the farmer drove to town with his own horse and buggy, the bicycle was the only form of personal transportation the city worker could afford — as it is today even in the more advanced European countries. Today American farmers and city dwellers, those well off and those in modest circumstances, drive their own cars. The debutante of half a century ago was distinguishable at a distance from her unfortunate sister who had to work for a living. Today they both wear nylon stockings and fur coats and although there may still be a big difference in the cost of their wardrobes, it takes a discerning feminine eye to tell them apart.

Changing Consumption Patterns

As to the typical products that have transformed the household during the past half century, the upper and lower income groups both use the same vacuum cleaners, refrigerators, deep-freezers, oil burners, gas and electric stoves, radios and television sets. Their homes may have much the same kind of bathroom equipment and plumbing and lighting fixtures. They read the same newspapers and magazines, go to the same movies, listen to the same radio and television programs. They smoke the same brands of cigarettes, drink the same frozen orange juice, eat the same canned, frozen or out-of-season fresh food, bought at the same supermarket.

This democratization of our way of life has been only recently and to a limited extent the result of an organized program to "equalize welfare" and "redistribute wealth more equitably." On the contrary, it is the inevitable outcome of a progressive technology applied to production. It is the outcome, to use Frederick Lewis Allen's words, of:

> . . . the logic of mass production—which is that the more goods you can produce, the less it costs to produce them; and that the more people are well off, the more they can buy; thus making this lavish and economic production possible . . . that it pays better to produce the same sort of food, clothing, and equipment for everybody, of all income levels, than to produce luxury goods for a few, and second- and third-rate goods for the rest; and that therefore one can make money by lowering class barriers. Thus is Marxism confounded — not by dogma, but by the logic of advanced industrialism itself; or, to put it another way, by capitalism turned to democratic ends.[2]

Worth mentioning is the fact that this momentous development has been taking place not in communist Russia but in capitalist America. Of all the great industrial nations, the one that clings most tenaciously to private capitalism has come closest to the socialist goal of providing abundance for all in a classless society.

Underlying many of the changes in technology that have helped to raise and equalize living standards since the turn of the century has been the technological revolution in agriculture. This has greatly increased the production of foods and textile fibers and lessened labor requirements. With fewer people needed in farming, the nation has become highly urbanized and industrialized. Even though the farm-to-city drift had been under way for several decades, at the turn of the century nearly 38 per cent of the

gainfully employed were still engaged in farming and 60 per cent of the population lived on farms and in rural territory. Today only 12 per cent of the labor force are engaged in agriculture, while nearly two thirds of the population live in cities and towns and other urban areas. This drift to the cities, which still continues, is thus itself a result of technological change. It has contributed to many changes in the life of the family and the operation of the home.

HOUSEHOLD OPERATION

The typical family housing unit of half a century ago, whether in town or country, was more commodious than it is today — but a good deal less convenient and comfortable. Although some central heating was in use, most dwellings were still heated by stoves and fireplaces. Gas for cooking was not unusual, but the typical kitchen still had a coal or wood range. The well-to-do could afford gas lights and Welsbach mantles, and electricity was coming into use, but most families still depended on kerosene lamps, and even on candles to some extent. No man whose boyhood did not include the chores of cleaning out ashes, splitting kindling, filling coal scuttles, lugging in wood, filling lamps, trimming wicks, and starting fires on cold winter mornings can really appreciate the technological revolution in this single phase of household operation.

New Materials

Today's new dwellings are typically prefabricated to a much greater extent than they were half a century ago, although the complete factory-made house still accounts for only one out of twenty homes built each year. Indeed, more automobile trailers are produced each year than factory-fabricated houses. *Time* has estimated that 1,750,000 owners and their families were living in trailers in 1952.[3]

Although the traditional brick, stone and wood still predominate in house construction, "new" materials — poured concrete, plywood, metal lath, copper tubing, metal sash windows, gypsum wallboard, glass bricks, aluminum, linoleum and composites of various kinds — are being used much more widely. Houses today are built more tightly and compactly, and are thus easier to keep clean. They are easier to heat be-

---

2. *Harper's Magazine,* Centennial Issue, 1850–1950, October 1950, p. 156.

3. November 17, 1952.

cause they are insulated with rockwool, glass fiber or other materials unknown or not used fifty years ago.

Even the least expensive new houses are equipped with thermostatically controlled heating plants burning convenient oil or gas instead of coal. Where coal is still being used, automatic household stokers are available. In the kitchen the modern gas or electric stove, with accurate heat control, has displaced the old coal range. Household electric lighting is now almost universal and of course vastly superior to gas lights and oil lamps. These new fuels have vastly improved the quality and range of heat and light, and are used without effort or inconvenience.

Electrical Equipment

Electric energy has brought many other changes in household equipment and operation. The ubiquitous sewing machine, manually operated in 1900, today is run by electricity — and is less prevalent. In place of the old-fashioned icebox — and not all homes had even this at the turn of the century — about nine out of every ten homes now have mechanical refrigerators, and many have deep-freeze units as well. The electric toaster has been a commonplace for so long that it is hard to imagine toasting bread in any other way; yet it was a curiosity in 1900, as was the electric iron. Today nearly three out of four American homes have electric toasters, and more than 90 per cent electric irons. Some 60 per cent use vacuum cleaners and nearly 80 per cent have electric washers.[4]

A multitude of new machines and devices are helping to save labor in the kitchen and to make it a much more efficient workshop. To such stand-bys as electric refrigerators, dishwashers, toasters, juicers and mixing machines, are now being added such new devices as timing mechanisms to prevent food from burning or overcooking, automatic ice cream freezers, automatic "disposers" to get rid of the garbage can, refrigerators requiring no defrosting and equipped with germ-killing lamps to destroy bacteria and odors, completely engineered "packaged kitchens," frozen-food units, and electric deep-friers and roasters.

With the perfection of the electronic range a

major frustration of the American housewife, the meal spoiled by her husband's lateness, will have disappeared. Since the cave man, food has always been cooked from the outside in — whether over a wood fire or by an electric coil. With the Radarange the food is cooked *internally* by high-frequency radio waves — in a matter of seconds instead of minutes or hours.

In household cleaning, the broom and the carpet sweeper still have a place, but the vacuum cleaner — in three out of five homes — has taken over the heavy work and does it much more thoroughly. In the laundry, the washing machine (in three out of four households), together with detergents and other new cleaning materials, has displaced the legendary washboard and tub. Automatic wringer-washers, dryers, and now even an automatic ironer, are further lightening the housewife's tasks.

To the frugal American housewife of half a century ago, paper was a relatively costly product to be carefully folded and put away for future use. Today, thanks to inexpensive wood pulp as a raw material, the typical household is supplied with such conveniences as oiled and waxed paper, paper napkins and towels, cleansing tissues, paper cups and plates, and other specialized products which can be used once and thrown away.

Another new household aid is a pressurized "push-button" aerosol can, now used to dispense more than forty different products — from whipped cream to shaving soap — in a fine spray or foam. The aerosol can sprays a transparent plastic bandage on a burned or injured area of the body; it acts the same as gauze bandages or dressings while the progress of healing may be seen through it without removal. Plastic squeeze bottles are another new device introduced soon after World War II. While most of the scores of products dispensed in them are consumer and household items, the bottles are also in everyday industrial use, holding as much as 12 gallons. They weigh only a third as much as glass and are so strong they will resist a 30-foot drop on concrete.[5]

Air Conditioning

Electric blankets, a novelty just before World War II, are becoming increasingly popular. New

---

4. *Electrical Merchandising,* Statistical and Marketing Issue, January 1954.

5. "Genie in a (Squeeze) Bottle," article in *Investor's Reader* (Merrill Lynch, Pierce, Fenner, & Beane), June 18, 1952.

methods of room heating, such as concealed radiators and panel heating, are coming into wide use. Air conditioning, almost unheard of a generation ago, is now standard equipment in trains, theaters, stores, hotels and many other types of commercial structures. Although few dwellings are now completely air conditioned, room-size units are meeting with a steeply rising demand, and another decade may well find air conditioning as common as central heating. Even today new houses provided with complete all-weather air conditioning are being built in the $12,000–$15,000 price class.

Radiant heat has been used to some extent for years, and complete radiant heating installation for the typical household may come in the not-distant future. Almost any kind of substance in walls or ceiling can be used as a panel, and heat can be provided through pipes or as warm air within the panel. Such an installation permits heat to be turned on or off as needed in different rooms, and the system can also be designed to provide cooling in the summer time. Radiant heat, in contrast to all conventional systems, keeps the people in a room warm without heating the air. Since the heat radiates from the panel directly to the body, as the sun's warmth is radiated through a hundred million miles of cold space, a person in ordinary summer clothes will be comfortable with the air temperature of the room as low as 50°.

Another device with great future promise is the heat pump — technically, reverse-cycle heating and cooling. In summer, it operates like a modern refrigerator, extracting the heat, by means of a small compressor and pump motor, from inside the house and transferring it outside. The effectiveness of this principle is obvious whenever a person touches the warm condenser usually located behind or on top of the kitchen refrigerator. This same principle in the heat pump cools the inside of the house to a comfortable, controlled temperature and circulates filtered dehumidified air. By flipping a switch to change a valve, the whole mechanism operates in reverse during the winter, sending filtered and humidified warm air through the dwelling. In this case the inside of the house is warmed by heat "pumped in" from outdoors just as the condenser on the refrigerator is warmed by the heat pumped out of its interior.

The heat pump operates without fuel of any kind, thus eliminating chimneys, flames, fuel bins, tanks and other fire hazards. For cooling it does not require water or cooling towers. A two- or three-horsepower unit encased in a metal cabinet suffices for the average small home. The householder has only to plug it into the nearest electric outlet, set the thermostat and humidity control to the desired range or levels and operation is automatic. Present installation costs are high, but a survey by the Edison Electric Institute in early 1953 shows more than a thousand heat pump installations in the United States, half in residences and the rest in stores and other buildings; in 1945 there were only fifty installations in the country.[6]

Household Lighting

Household electric lighting has been vastly improved since Edison's first "wire in a bottle." The long-lived tungsten-filament lamp is now universal, with three quarters of a billion lamp bulbs lighting more than 42 million homes. Fluorescent lighting promises substantial development of indirect home lighting and the possibility of automatic control of light intensity. Even more efficient is the cold cathode lamp, which gives the most light (lumens) per watt of electricity consumed, and has the longest life of any present commercial lighting equipment. Still more sensational developments, among them tinted light "adjusted to the mood" of the consumer, germicidal and odor-killing lamps, a fluorescent light generating vitamins in the body, and invisible or "black light" to detect false gems and bad teeth, are all available even today, according to one leading lighting authority.[7]

Electroluminescence is the lengthy name for the newest source of light. Operating without bulbs or tubes, it gives off a soft glow from a flat surface of glass. The glass is coated with a transparent film, over which is a layer of phosphor powder and, on top of that, metallic foil. When connected with regular household current, the glass glows. Different colored phosphors will give different colored light. Among the first uses of "electrolume" light to be made available

6. W. F. Friend, article on "Progress Report on the Heat Pump," *Refrigerating Engineer*, January 1951; also Norris Willatt, article on "The Heat Pump," *Barron's*, January 5, 1953.
7. Letter of December 1, 1953 from Samuel G. Hibben, Director of Applied Lighting, Westinghouse Electric Corporation.

for the home are luminescent light-switch plates and clock dials.

Technological progress has made life easier for the man of the house as well as the housewife. In the garden, muscle power is being supplanted by such laborsavers as gasoline-driven lawn mowers, electric hedge clippers and electric and gasoline-driven chain saws.

For the more ambitious gardener, a hand-operated power plow and cultivator with various gardening attachments is available. And when physical effort can't be avoided, even a child is strong enough to push a rubber-tired aluminum wheelbarrow and put the plastic hose away. Electricity has transformed the home workshop with a multitude of laborsaving tools unthought of a generation ago. Paint can be mixed and sprayed electrically — and science has now produced a smooth-flowing "one-coat" variety that is odorless. Portable hand-operated electric tools are available, with attachments for drilling, sawing, buffing, grinding, sanding, waxing and polishing. Home workshops, nearly all of them equipped with at least one power tool, are used by 11 million families in about one quarter of the nation's homes.[8]

The scarcity and high cost of building labor is making it profitable for every man to become a household craftsman, and electricity and easily applied materials are making it possible. Even the housewife can paint a set of furniture, paper a room, or lay a tile floor — and do it with a smile, if the advertisements are to be believed.

FOOD PREPARATION

Among the most significant technological changes affecting the household during the past half century has been the increasing "commercialization" of many of the functions formerly performed in the home. The household of 1900, especially in the country, was still warehouse and factory, as well as home. The housewife bought potatoes, apples, flour, sugar and other staples in bulk, in larger quantities than today, and stored them in the pantry or cellar. Packaged and trade-marked goods were a rarity in the primitive grocery store of that period. Molasses came in barrels, as did sugar, flour — and crackers.

Fresh fruits and vegetables were not available out of season, although the store carried

dried prunes, apples and apricots, as well as dried and salted fish. Canned goods were still uncommon, limited in variety, and believed by the more conservative to be not quite safe to eat. Frozen foods were far in the future, although the butcher shop offered refrigerated meat in all seasons. The typical home functioned as bakery and cannery, producing bread, cakes and pies from raw materials purchased from the grocer, and "putting up" fruits and vegetables in season to carry the family through the winter.

Today the modern supermarket offers almost every foodstuff in small, sanitary packages and all sorts of canned goods — for infants and pets as well as adults. Ready-mixed and semicooked bakery products are canned or packaged. The quick-freezing process, so effective in preserving the taste of fresh fruits, fruit juices, vegetables, fish and meats, is now applied to prepared biscuits, cakes, pies, waffles, and other semicooked and uncooked bakery products. Such fresh vegetables as lettuce, tomatoes, cabbage and celery, and potatoes, are likely to be the only foods sold in bulk in modern chain stores, and even these are often packaged in the ubiquitous plastics.

Within the next few years a revolutionary development — cold sterilization — may further simplify the housewife's task and profoundly influence present methods of food preservation and distribution. For several years General Electric and other companies have engaged in research on the use of cathode rays to sterilize foods and drugs. If successful this "ideal food preservation method" will make possible the retention of the original taste and quality of fresh foods and may reduce or eliminate the need for freezing, canning and other methods of preservation.[9]

One relatively new product is concentrated milk — not condensed milk, which has been used for generations. It is available in liquid or powdered form, and — after water is added — tastes like fresh milk. Widespread consumer acceptance of this new product in place of fresh milk will result in revolutionary economies of shipment and delivery. Another recent development is the successful canning of whole milk to preserve its quality and natural flavor for weeks or months before use.

These developments provide the family, in and

8. *Esso Magazine*, March 1953.

9. Advertisement of General Electric, in *Scientific American*, December 1953, p. 85.

out of season, with foods of such quality and variety as to have been beyond the imagination of the consumer of 1900. They have greatly reduced the necessity of food storage in the home and simplified the task of preparing meals. Where once the housewife went to the grocer's to buy the raw materials for a meal, today she can buy the meal, packaged, precooked, frozen and ready to be heated. The time has arrived when anyone able to read a label and turn on the gas can cook a meal — though perhaps not a gourmet's delight.

Thus, while technological improvements have been making the household, and especially the kitchen, a more efficient and pleasant operating unit, the factory and the marketing system have been taking over more and more of the household's former production and storage functions.

CLOTHING AND FABRICS

Technology has had important direct and indirect effects on clothing and on textile products used in the home. The shift from rural to urban life and work, entrance of women into the labor market, and better heating of homes and offices account for the trends toward lighter-weight clothing and toward simplicity and uniformity in apparel. Mass production economies have moved production of women's and children's garments from the home, and of men's clothing from the custom tailor shop, to the factory. Because of low-cost factory products and increased incomes, the typical wardrobe is much more extensive and varied than it was fifty years ago, but the amount of clothing worn at any one time, especially by women, is a mere fraction of what it was then.

The technology of shoe manufacture has not changed greatly, as shoes were largely factory-made in 1900, but as a result of better heating and paved streets, the "high shoe" is now only a memory. Leather is still the standard raw material for shoe uppers, but in shoe soles synthetics such as Neolite and Solite are now more important than leather.[10] Perhaps invasion of plastics into the field of luggage, furniture coverings, upholstery and belts presages the arrival of an all-plastic shoe.

Described as the first basic change in the shoe since Julius Caesar invented the hard heel, the "ripple sole" consists of an extra sole of corru-

gated rubber permanently affixed to the bottom of the shoe. It gives a spring to the foot, cuts the shock of ground contact, lengthens the stride and greatly reduces fatigue.[11]

The most striking technological change in textiles has of course been the widespread displacement of natural fibers by synthetics. At the turn of the century cotton, wool, silk and linen were the standard textiles for clothing and household fabrics, as they had been for centuries. Although "artificial silk," or cellulose rayon, was first exhibited at the Paris World's Fair in 1889, it was not widely used until well into the twentieth century, when it and acetate rayon began to displace silk and even cotton for some uses. More recently, newer organic fibers have been produced, such as lanital, made from casein, and vicara, made from corn protein.

Synthetics

It was not until the development of nylon by du Pont just before World War II that the possibilities of "true synthetics" made from such mundane inorganic materials as coal and air and water were recognized. Nylon has already virtually supplanted silk and rayon for women's stockings. Its strength and easy washability have brought it into widespread use for dresses, shirtwaists, shirts, underclothing, sweaters and socks, and for curtains, upholstery and other soft goods in the home — not to mention its many industrial uses.

Du Pont's development of nylon has been followed by Orlon and Dacron. Other synthetic fibers, designed as substitutes, supplements and improvements of natural fibers, are marketed under such names as Acrilan, Dynel, Vinyon, Reevon, Vicara, Velon and Saran. Indeed, the new synthetics are finding wide use in combination not only with such natural fibers as wool, but with each other and with the older cellulose synthetics, such as viscose, acetate and cuprammonium, marketed under a number of trade names, which have been greatly improved in quality since the war. Along with the chemical synthetics, one of the oldest materials, glass, is finding new uses as an incombustible fiber in draperies and curtains and for a great variety of industrial purposes.

---

10. *Wall Street Journal*, May 15, 1952, p. 1.

11. David O. Woodbury, "Shoes That Walk for You," *Technology Review* (Massachusetts Institute of Technology), January 1952.

With the new synthetic fibers and plastics, man was able for the first time to combine the atoms into new molecules with exactly the characteristics desired. These are therefore truly "new" products with a wide range of qualities not possessed by natural fibers. Most of the synthetics are light in weight, resilient, wash and dry easily, and resist moths and insects. For instance, Saran, a "plastic fiber," is almost incombustible, sheds water, and will not rot or mildew — thus being ideal as a hard fabric for automobile seats and as a fiber for window screens. Dynel is warmer than some wools but has poor heat resistance, which makes it unsuitable for ironing; hence, it is being used in blankets, socks and underwear, or as a blend. Nylon is strong and resilient and dries quickly.

Men's suits of Dacron hold their crease after being worn scores of times with repeated dry cleanings and even after being washed in a home laundry. Dacron does have one serious drawback, susceptibility to flame, but the chemists are working on that, as they are on Dynel's low heat resistance. Orlon's remarkable resistance to sunshine and weathering makes it ideal for awnings, and in lighter fabric form it makes excellent summer suits and taffeta-like evening dresses. Vicara has a cashmere-like softness for blending. Acrilan weighs very little, will not shrink, is flame resistant, very warm, and blends well.

In 1952, about 40 per cent of women's suits, 50 per cent of skirts and much larger proportions of dresses and blouses were made of rayon or other synthetic fibers and blends,[12] and the proportion was still higher in 1953. The consumption of apparel wool in men's summer suits dropped from 49 per cent of the total in 1950 to 27 per cent in 1952, another indication of the rapid displacement of natural fibers by synthetics.[13] Although the all-synthetic suit is still a rarity, blends of the newer fibers with wool and rayon and with each other are becoming more and more common.

In 1950 less than 10 per cent of carpets and rugs were made with rayon and acetate blended with wool; the next year this increased to 28 per cent, and in 1952 fully 40 per cent of the floor coverings had synthetics in them. One of the leading manufacturers was using synthetic fibers in 75 per cent of its line.[14]

Only 10 per cent of all textile fibers used in the United States in 1940 were rayon and acetate, while other synthetics were negligible. By 1952, some 18 per cent of the total was rayon and acetate, with nylon and the other newer synthetic fibers providing a full 3 per cent.[15]

What the future will bring is anybody's guess, but it seems certain that use of the newer synthetics in fabrics of all kinds will expand greatly. The President's Materials Policy Commission, reporting in June 1952, predicted a 1950–1960 production growth for:

Nylon	from	100 million pounds	to	300 million	"
Orlon	"	6.5	"	"	"	125	"
Dynel	"	5	"	"	"	100	"
Acrilan	"	none		"	100	"
Dacron	"	negligible amounts	"	150	"

Chemical Methods

Chemical technology is also contributing to the improvement of the older fibers. More recently cotton has been cyanoethylated, or treated with acrylonitrile, which is the basic ingredient of the wool-like synthetic fibers, Acrilan, Orlon and Dynel. This treatment, it is claimed, gives the cotton permanent resistance to mildew and bacteria, greater strength and elasticity and resistance to abrasion and heat, and better dyeing qualities.[16]

The du Pont company has introduced a metallic salts mixture that makes rayon and cotton flame resistant as well as more capable of withstanding laundering and dry cleaning. Woolen clothing may now be made shrink-proof by a process similar to the sanforizing of cotton. By chemical treatment, cotton can be partially "acetylated," making it mildew resistant; this same process makes cotton more heat resistant for electrical insulation. Nearly 600 different chemicals are available for improving and treating the finish of both natural and synthetic fibers, in

12. Data from Burlington Mills Corporation, quoted in the *New York Herald Tribune*, June 4, 1952.

13. *Textile World*, Annual Review and Forecast Edition, February 1953.

14. Advertisement of Celanese Corporation of America, in *Time*, May 12, 1952.

15. J. Paul Sanderson, "The Synthetic Fibers Industry," address at University of Pennsylvania, June 23, 1952, reprinted in "The Technology behind Investment," a brochure published by Arthur D. Little, Inc., Cambridge, Massachusetts.

16. " 'New Fibre Family,' Seen from Effect of Chemical on Cotton," *Wall Street Journal*, October 13, 1953.

some thirty different ways, in order to make them resistant to water, flame, shrinkage, etc.[17]

Synthetic furs have been developed by treating cheap hides like sheepskins with a plastic chemical through the Calva process. This transforms the wool into a fur that is hard to distinguish from mink, or sable, or sealskin, or Persian lamb, or ermine — only a slight alteration in the formula being necessary to obtain whatever is wanted. The furs have the same warmth as the natural, and last as long or longer; they can be made in any bright color or to simulate the appropriate animal fur color.[18]

Chemistry is making it possible, for the first time, to alter the nature of natural fibers and to design new fibers or blends of natural and synthetic fibers to perform particular functions, instead of having to adjust human needs to the qualities and limitations of natural fibers, such as wool and cotton. Special advantages of fabrics made from synthetic fibers are their ease of care and serviceability. Most synthetics, however, are inferior to natural fibers in moisture absorption, and therefore less comfortable to wear. Many require new dyeing techniques and, of course, are much more expensive than most natural fibers.

Despite the virtual disappearance of natural silk because of the competition of nylon, and the threat that some of the newer fibers offer to wool, it would be rash to predict that natural fibers will soon, or ever, completely disappear as textile raw materials. But it seems likely that their importance will greatly diminish with the development of a wider range of tailor-made blends, designed to perform exactly the functions required of them.[19]

TRAVEL AND COMMUNICATION

Few changes in the way of life of the average American during the past half century have been as striking as those in the field of transportation

and communication. In the country, where 60 per cent of the people still lived in 1900, the horse and buggy — or the horse alone — was the only means of transportation to visit town or call on a neighbor. Farm produce was hauled to market by wagon over roads which in most of the country were virtually impassable in spring and fall. Communication was effected by mail on the RFD route, in person, or — in great emergencies — by telegraph. Telephones were still newfangled gadgets, not yet widely used in rural areas.

Horses and Railroads

In the cities — smaller and less populous than they are now — most people walked to work, although the bicycle had ceased to be a fad and was becoming a utilitarian vehicle. The horse-car was a standard form of urban transportation, and cable cars dependent on steam power had been operating for several years in some of the larger cities. Electric trolleys were displacing both horsecars and cable cars, and interurban electric trains were beginning to provide speedy transport between near-by cities and cities and suburbs. For those who could afford them, horse-drawn cabs were the taxis of that day. In the transportation of goods, even more than of people, the horse and wagon was in universal use in the cities as well as in farm-to-town traffic. In the city, as in the country, people living at a distance from one another communicated mostly by mail, although the telephone was beginning to prove its worth, particularly for commercial use.

The nation was crisscrossed by a coal-powered steam railroad network, reaching all the cities and most of the small towns and offering frequent service for freight and passengers. For those towns distant from the "depot," especially in the West, the stagecoach still functioned, as it had for a century.

Since the turn of the century all this has changed. The horse-drawn vehicle is almost a curiosity on city streets and has disappeared from country roads, except in a few rural backwaters. The cable car has all but disappeared, except in San Francisco where it will be retained as a permanent curiosity. The electric streetcar, which first displaced the cable car, is in turn losing out to the motor bus and to the hybrid electric trolley coach. The number of these coaches in operation more than doubled during the war decade.

---

17. Georg Mann, "Pick Your Own Clothing Formula," *Science Digest,* November 1952.

18. *National Geographic Magazine,* March 1948; also *Coronet,* March 1946. At present, until production and marketing arrangements are worked out, women's coats are not yet on the market, although some 2,000,000 skins are so processed annually for use in toys, slippers, men's stormcoat collars, and similar pieces. (Personal communication from Dr. Jose B. Calva, chemical technologist, who discovered the process.)

19. Some of the material on synthetics is from "Wool's Battle with the Synthetics," *Fortune,* May 1952.

By 1951 not a single city or town was served exclusively by streetcar,[20] while in 1,535 cities the bus was the only form of public transportation.[21]

Motor Trucks and Planes

Together with the motor truck, the bus is taking over much of the work of the railroads in the country. Indeed, more than 40,000 communities are solely dependent on motor vehicles for all their transportation needs, three fourths of all passenger travel between cities, towns and farms goes by car or bus, and two thirds of all freight is shipped by truck during some part of its journey.[22]

On the railroads, still the dominant long-haul carriers for freight and passengers, the coal-powered locomotive, first losing ground to the oil-burner engine, is now being rapidly displaced by diesel power. On the oceans, the coal-burning steamships of the nineteenth century are increasingly giving way to oil burners and more recently, in the case of smaller craft, to diesel power. Joseph Conrad's "black gang" and the fireman of the Casey Jones era have all but disappeared.

Meanwhile the airplane, first demonstrated by the Wright brothers in 1903, has developed to the point where it competes with the railroad for passenger travel on land and with the steamship for travel across the ocean. At mid-century, airplanes handled half or more of the transatlantic passenger travel from and to the United States, and as much of the total intercity passenger travel as was carried first-class by the railroads. Its advantage of speed has already made the airplane the most important intercity carrier of first-class mail as well.

Automobiles and Good Roads

Most important of all the transport developments of the past half century in the life of the average family, however, has been the coming of the automobile. A playboy's toy in 1900, it is now a necessity for most of the nation's households. More than anything else, it is responsible for the fact that the typical American today travels an average of 2,400 miles a year outside of cities, compared with 400 miles in 1916.

Partly cause and partly effect of the wide use of automobiles has been the paving of city streets and country roads. At the turn of the century, in the typical American city only the most traveled streets were hard-surfaced, usually with brick or cobblestones laid by hand. The pavement ended at the city limits. Today, thanks to the coming of the automobile, every street is paved in all but the smallest villages.

Fifty years ago there was nothing approaching a national highway system. Cities and towns were linked together by the railroad network, and the roads, such as they were, radiated out a few miles from the cities to the near-by communities and farms. At the turn of the century there were less than 150,000 miles of hard-surfaced highway in the entire country, and until 1909 concrete was only in experimental use.[23] Today nearly 2 million miles of hard-surfaced highways blanket the nation, reaching all but the most inaccessible points. Toll roads and thruways are under construction to form a new network for modern high-speed traffic.

Communications

The first telegraph line crossed the United States in 1861, but the spanning of the continent by telephone, radio and television has occurred during the present generation. The first cross-country telephone circuit was established in 1915, the first nationwide radio network in 1924 — three years after the first radio broadcast — and the first transcontinental television network went into service in August 1951.

The telephone was just emerging from the gadget class at the turn of the century, with less than 2 million in use. Today more than 50 million instruments are in operation—about as many phones as there are private automobiles, or not far from one to every three persons. Until recent years nearly all calls were made through an operator at the central switchboard; more than three fourths of all telephones are now dial-equipped, and the dial system is being extended to long-distance service.

20. The last streetcar operated in Manhattan in June 1947 — just 30 years after the horsecar disappeared from New York streets — but three short trolley lines continued to operate in Brooklyn. In London, the last streetcar, a "doubledecker," completed its final trip on July 6, 1952. (*New York Times,* July 7, 1952, p. C23.)

21. Leon F. Banigan, Editor, *Bus Transportation,* in an address at the Centennial of Engineering, Chicago, September 3–13, 1952.

22. Talk by Harvey S. Firestone, Jr., Voice of Firestone, Radio and Television Program, N.B.C., October 26, 1953.

23. Letter of December 1, 1953 from J. E. Dunn, Portland Cement Association, Washington. D.C.; and Bulletin No. 249, U.S. Department of Agriculture, July 26, 1915.

One of the most interesting recent developments was the revelation by scientists at the Bell Telephone Laboratories in January 1953 that they had built an electronic device which recognizes and responds, by flashing an appropriate light, to *ten specific sounds spoken to it in plain English by the human voice* — the numbers from one to ten. "Audrey," automatic digit recognizer, it is said, "could equally well control . . . operations such as dialing mechanisms." Here, in the near future perhaps, will be the automatic telephone operating without even the dial! [24]

Radio-telephone service to the principal cities of the world has become a reality, as has wirephoto transmission of documents and photographs — all unthought of fifty years ago. Mobile radio-telephone service is already in use in several thousand private automobiles and taxis, fishing boats and yachts, as well as on trains and airplanes. A device for automatic message recording during the subscriber's absence is now on the market. A television attachment making it possible to see as well as hear the person at the other end of the line may not be too long arriving.

Miniature radio receiving sets are now made so small that they can be held in the hand. Likewise, a "micro-talkie" radio transmitter, with an operating range up to five miles, has been put on the market for use by patrolmen on foot, watchmen, firemen at the scene of a fire, in on-the-spot news reporting, railroad car checking, materials handling in factories, and in sports and recreation. To do your own "broadcasting" it is only necessary to press a button. The total weight of this portable radio station is less than two pounds.[25]

Future Developments

Some of the future technological developments in the field of transportation are already in sight. Jet propulsion, already a commonplace for military planes, will soon be providing vibrationless high-altitude transportation at close to double the present speed of existing long-distance transport planes, which in turn travel twice as fast as the 150-mile-an-hour cruising speed before World War II. Now on the drawing boards of American aircraft designers are jet-propelled commercial airliners that will bring New York and Los Angeles within four hours of each other.[26] Hawker-Siddeley, British plane builders, have plans for a delta-wing jet transport that may be able to cross the ocean almost as fast as the sun [27] — thus making it possible to eat breakfast at 8 A.M. in London and be ready for a second one at 9 A.M. in New York. Now that the sound barrier has been pierced, nobody can safely predict what ultimate speeds may be with new methods of propulsion.

Likewise the helicopter, which has long since arrived militarily (in the Korean War, rescue helicopters were credited with saving almost as many lives as penicillin), is already finding use in short-haul transfer of mail in large urban areas and is now being used for short hops between terminals in passenger operations. The development of helicopters with larger passenger capacity is well on its way and before long may permit passenger transportation between cities 100 to 200 miles apart. At present, air travel between such cities is not practical because of the time required for ground travel between airport and city center. It is not too much to expect, as Charles H. Kaman has suggested, that the four- or five-passenger "family helicopter" will begin to supplement the family automobile within a decade. Such craft may soon be available at the price of an expensive automobile.

The private automobile will probably continue to evolve in the direction of greater power, speed and comfort, with human effort all but eliminated. It used to be said that the automobile of the future would do everything but drive itself, but that day has already nearly arrived. At least electronic devices may soon be available to aid in bad-weather steering and collision prevention.[28]

One of the most significant contributions to the safety of night driving is fully automatic control of headlight intensity. As a car approaches from the opposite direction, a device automatically lowers the light beam, and it reverses the operation when the car has passed.

For the automobile engine one can expect greater power, higher compression, compactness, lighter weight, greater speed and acceleration,

---

24. Press release, Bell Telephone Laboratories, January 5, 1953.

25. *Dun's Review*, January 1953, p. 87.

26. Aircraft Industries Association of America, General James H. Doolittle, in press release, January 30, 1953.

27. John G. Norris, "New Look in Jets," *Washington Post*, October 12, 1953.

28. "RCA's Midget Auto Steers Itself Along the Road by Electronics," *Wall Street Journal*, July 23, 1953.

and, it is to be hoped, more economical fuel consumption. The trend toward fuels with higher octane ratings seems likely to continue. Rear-engine cars and diesel power are still planned for the future.

Automobile models of the late 1950s will differ as much from those we have been riding since World War II as today's cars do from those of the 1920s. As a single measure of the popularity of such new devices as directional signals, defrosting fans, windshield wipers, dual horns and radios, electricity demand in the modern car is three times what the storage battery supplied to autos twenty-five years ago, and five times the ampere capacity of cars of forty years ago.[29]

Automatic transmission and overdrive, introduced shortly after the war, and now optional on most cars, save both driver effort and fuel. Power steering and power braking are relieving the driver of practically all work and fatigue. One automotive engineer [30] predicts that within a decade or less, one out of every ten new cars will be air conditioned. Even in 1953 four or five manufacturers offered optional air conditioning in their more expensive models.

Today's automobile tire is a miracle of comfort, durability and safety compared with the early tires, which cost three times as much and lasted 5,000 miles instead of 40,000 or more — and it is constantly being improved. Puncture-proof, self-sealing tires are already freeing the motorist of his fear of a blowout or a flat tire miles from the nearest service station. Improved types of inner tubes have been developed; now tires requiring no inner tubes are in wide use. Science has not yet produced a tire that will change itself, but it has gone far toward providing one that doesn't have to be changed. At least one manufacturer guarantees his product, without time or mileage limits, against blowouts, bruises and rim cuts.

HEALTH AND MEDICAL CARE

Technological developments in the field of sanitation, public health and medicine, along with better nutrition and rising standards of living, have added twenty years to life expectancy since 1900. This has come about chiefly through radical reduction of mortality rates for such infectious diseases of childhood as diphtheria, measles, typhoid fever and scarlet fever. Diphtheria deaths dropped from 40 per 100,000 of the population in 1900 to 0.3 per 100,000 in 1950; measles, from 13 per 100,000 to 0.3 per 100,000; typhoid and paratyphoid, from 31 to 0.1; and scarlet fever, from 9.6 to practically none. The mortality rate for the population as a whole fell from 17.2 per thousand in 1900 to 9.6 in 1950, and the infant mortality rate from 162 per thousand to 33. As further evidence of how far we have come in the past half century, the average hospital stay per patient has dropped since 1900 from 30 days to 8 days, largely because of improved surgical science and modern chemotherapy.[31]

Much of this great progress in health and mortality experience has been due to the development of smallpox vaccination and other immunization procedures, and much to protective measures such as sterilization, refrigeration and sanitary packaging. It is hard to realize that window screens, and pure water and milk, which we in the United States take for granted, are really elements of a very high standard of living that most of the rest of the world has never been able to enjoy.

Therapeutic Progress

The science of therapeutics has probably made greater progress since 1900, and perhaps even since the 1920s, than in all previous medical history. Immunology, with its most important example the use of diphtheria antitoxin to virtually eliminate this dreaded disease, is a virtually new branch of medicine since the turn of the century.

Chemotherapy — the development of synthetic specifics for individual diseases — is also a product of twentieth century research. Its first great success was Ehrlich's development of salvarsan in 1909 as a specific against syphilis. This was followed in the 1920s by the new synthetics for treating malaria. The treatment of this disease, which for three hundred years depended on plant quinine, has been greatly advanced by the development of synthetic quinines — plasmochin, which first came out in 1924, then atabrine (1930), aralen (1944), and later primaquin. The

29. *New York Journal of Commerce,* April 3, 1952; also *Dun's Review,* January 1953, p. 86.

30. P. J. Kent of the Chrysler Corporation, speaking before the Society of Automotive Engineers, and quoted in *New York Herald Tribune,* March 6, 1953.

31. *Monsanto Magazine,* March 1952, and National Office of Vital Statistics, U.S. Public Health Service. The infant mortality rates in this paragraph are averages for the nation as a whole and are slightly higher than those for birth-registration areas only, discussed in Chapter 10.

latter is both preventive and cure; it destroys the malaria parasite in the tissues and reduces the relapse rate from about 30 per cent to less than 1 per cent. The newest malaria preventive is daraprim, which is tasteless and does not discolor the skin. Malaria is almost extinct in the United States today, largely because of these new synthetics and the more than 6 million sprayings with DDT in malarial areas during the six years after World War II. Some 63,000 cases were reported in the nation in 1945, but only about 2,000 in 1950.[32]

In the 1930s came the great transformation in the treatment of bacterial infections from the discovery and application of sulfanilamide and its many derivatives. Discovery of the sulfa drugs was followed in 1939 by one of the most revolutionary developments in the history of medicine. This was the purification of penicillin, which had been accidentally discovered ten years before. Penicillin and such other antibiotics as streptomycin, aureomycin, terramycin and chloromycetin have saved countless lives and are finding new uses in all kinds of disease. It has been estimated that from a third to a half of physicians' patients receive some type of antibiotics.

Pneumonia mortality rates per 100,000 of the population fell from 55 in 1940 to less than 30 in 1950, chiefly through the use of penicillin. The same antibiotic has cut the scourge of syphilis from 14.4 in 1940 (after a slight decline from 16.5 in 1920) to only 8.0 in 1948, and 5.0 two years later. Magnamycin, a still newer antibiotic which acts against pneumonia, is reported to be effective in certain cases where penicillin does not help.

The search for these "wonder drugs" goes on; new antibiotics, of which more than a hundred have already been isolated and identified, have been discovered in soils and among molds, fungi and many other kinds of plant growth. Among recent discoveries are neomycin, for diseases of the skin and infections of the eye, ear, nose and throat and the gastrointestinal tract; bacitracin, for dysentery and sore throat; polymixin, used for eye infections and infected burns; and ilotycin, which is effective for a variety of diseases, including typhus, undulant fever and Rocky Mountain spotted fever.[33]

Early in 1952 came the dramatic announce-

32. *Think*, November 1951.
33. "Wonder Drugs," *Barron's*, June 30, 1952, p. 9.

ment of the first successful antituberculosis specifics, new triumphs of chemotherapy. Called isoniazides, they are prepared under a number of trade names: Rimifon, Ditubin, Marsilid, Nydrazid. These specifics should still further reduce the tuberculosis death rate, which with the help of streptomycin had already fallen from 36 per 100,000 in 1946 to under 20 in 1951.

Identification and separation of the vitamins and, in the 1930s, their artificial synthesis have brought us new knowledge of nutrition and transformed practice in this field. Today we know enough — if we can apply our knowledge — virtually to eliminate nutritional disorders. Endocrinology is another twentieth century science, which began with the discovery of secretin, the first of the hormones, in 1902. Growing knowledge of the importance of the hormones in the functioning of the endocrine glands is altering our understanding of the nature of disease and our physico-chemical methods of diagnosis and treatment.

The vast accomplishments of the past half century and the promise of the future have been ably described by Sir Henry H. Dale, the distinguished British medical leader, as follows:

Look back, those who can do so, to the beginning of this century, and recall again the state of medicinal treatment fifty years ago. Heart tonics, purgatives, diaphoretics, analgesics — such, indeed, were in use, and could be reasonably credited with the promotion of a natural function, or the relief of a distressing symptom; but there was a wide range of remedies then still current for which nothing more definite than a generally "tonic" or even "alterative" action could even be suggested. The idea that a remedy could directly remove or neutralize the cause of an illness was still a startling innovation, and neither physician nor patient had yet learned to expect a medication which would go thus to the root of the trouble. Compare such a position with that to-day, when we have become so accustomed to the effective and radical treatment, or prevention, of diseases which till recently were beyond the reach of remedy that there is a tendency to regard the existence of others as a reproach, as well as an incentive, to medical science. Rickets, scurvy, myxoedema, diabetes, pernicious anaemia, syphilis, pneumonia, coccal meningitis, dysentery, typhus — these are no more than a sample from a list which could be made of diseases now brought under such rational and effective treatment that the whole attitude to them, of the public as well as the profession, has been radically changed. It can hardly be doubted that this aspect of medicine, at least, has been the subject of a greater advance since this century began than in all the centuries which went before it. Members of the public who remember the position even thirty years ago, and recognize the contrast between the prospects of sufferers from diabetes, say, or pneumonia, then and now, not unnaturally inquire when anything similarly effective is to be expected for cancer or poliomyelitis or the common cold. The proper reply is surely that, though therapeutics as an experimental science is now on the march, it has only begun to get into its stride. We who have been able to watch the beginning of this great movement may be glad and proud to have lived through such a time, and confident that an even wider and more majestic advance will be seen by those who live on through the fifty years now opening.[34]

Chemical technology has not only developed vaccines, antibiotics, hormones and other new substances for preventing and curing diseases, but has applied mass-production methods to the manufacture of these products once their effectiveness is proved and accepted. Penicillin, as a simple example, sold for $20 per 100,000 units in 1942, but through tremendous volume fell in price to a mere two cents for the same quantity by 1952. Manufacturing costs, according to one authority, had been reduced "so far that in some packages the cost of the penicillin in a bottle is less than the combined cost of the bottle, stopper, label, and carton!" [35] The price of streptomycin dropped 97 per cent in the five years ending in the spring of 1952.

In addition to progress in the field of therapeutic medicine, chemistry has developed drugs to quiet nerves and kill pain, to induce sleep or to keep one awake, and many new and better antiseptics and anesthetics. Among the latter are the barbiturates and novocain and other synthetic substitutes for cocaine. Now there is Demerol, a synthetic morphine with lower addiction properties and no "withdrawal pains" when its use is stopped. Methadone, with no more aftereffects than novocain and similar anesthetics, has been tried with great success in the last few years on hospital patients and on wounded soldiers in Korea.

In the field of dentistry perhaps one of the most significant chemical developments of the past generation has been the discovery that an infinitesimal amount of fluoride — one millionth part per gallon of city drinking water — effectively reduces dental decay in children. The nation's dentists through their professional associations have urged the adoption of fluoridation, and many municipal water systems are now employing this chemical treatment.

Blood transfusions having become common practice in serious operations, the supply of whole, natural blood is insufficient to meet civilian and military needs. Synthetic blood plasma substitutes are now available to fill this need, among them PVP, made from acetylene and other chemicals, and Expandex, fermented from dextran, a sucrose. These two synthetic plasmas, costing about one seventh as much as natural blood plasma, can be sterilized, stored without refrigeration, and made in "practically unlimited quantities" once production facilities are built.[36] The Korean War made the "blood bank" familiar to everyone. More recently, the U.S. Naval Medical School at Bethesda, Maryland, has developed skin, bone and artery banks, available for instant use by surgeons in restoring tissue and bone to injured patients.[37]

Medical Equipment

Chemistry's contribution to the advancement of medical technology has been rivaled by the contributions of mechanics and electricity to the improvement of the equipment and techniques used in diagnosis and treatment.

The X-ray, which was just coming into use at the turn of the century, has enormously facilitated diagnosis in surgery and other branches of medicine, as well as in dentistry. The use of radioisotopes, though still in the experimental stage, promises great further progress in the diagnosis of disease. Although radiodiagnosis has long been well established, constant improvements are taking place. For example, an X-ray viewer recently announced by Westinghouse enlarges the view of internal organs two hundred times and does not require a completely darkened room.[38] The use of the X-ray in treatment of many disorders has launched the new science of radiotherapy. The science of physics has contributed a great variety of new and improved mechanical, electrical and electronic devices useful in diagnosis and treatment, in medicine and in dentistry.

Medical technology has also developed a multitude of mechanical and physical aids to prevent

34. "Advances in Medicinal Therapeutics," *British Medical Journal*, January 7, 1950, p. 7.

35. Dr. Ernest H. Volwiler, President of Abbott Laboratories, quoted in *Financial World*, April 2, 1952.

36. Leon G. Davis, "Synthetic Blood Substitutes," *Think*, May 1952.

37. *Today's Science*, May 1952, p. 94.

38. Press release, December 6, 1952, Westinghouse Electric Corporation, Pittsburgh, Pennsylvania.

pain, remedy incapacity and improve techniques. Illustrative of these developments is the electronically controlled mechanical heart-lung,[39] developed by Dr. John H. Gibbon, Jr., and first used at Philadelphia's Jefferson Hospital in 1953; the mechanical heart at Cincinnati Children's Hospital, a relatively simple device made of glass and plastic tubes and costing only $60 to build; and the mechanical kidney, which has already been used successfully in hundreds of cases.[40]

Several ingenious devices have been developed for the handicapped. International Business Machines engineers have designed an electrically operated arm and nylon-molded hand with almost natural-looking fingers that can write, typewrite, pick up a telephone, unlock doors, squeeze toothpaste on a toothbrush, and perform smoothly other commonplace acts which heretofore were beyond the capacity of amputees. Chromovox, an electronic seeing-hearing machine, is used in teaching deaf children, improving the speech of children who have had cerebral palsy or are mentally retarded, and helping adults overcome speech defects and language difficulties.[41] A short-distance radar enables the blind to detect obstructions a few feet away, and a manual device for scanning and translating a printed page by means of an "electronic eye" will eventually replace the slow, painstaking, bulky and costly braille system.

Among the many uses of plastics in medical technology is a white powdered plastic for tooth fillings which is far more permanent than the crumbly plasters formerly used, and a heart valve made of plastic which has already proved successful.[42]

Future Progress

What directions medical progress will take in the development of new devices and techniques and of new drugs and treatments in the years ahead is impossible to predict. But it is safe to expect that the brilliant successes of medical science during the past generation will be equaled or surpassed in the future.

Medical research today is directed toward such unsolved problems as the common cold and diseases of old age, with every prospect that new victories will be won. Indeed, what is described as "the first successful attack on hardening of the arteries and resulting paralytic strokes" may ultimately add another twenty years to life expectancy. A new drug consisting of thyroid gland hormone and a concentration of B vitamins has apparently been successful in preventing the deposit of cholesterol, which causes hardening of the arteries. The drug, given to one group of over a thousand persons by Dr. William B. Kountz of Washington University Medical School, caused the symptoms of most of the patients to disappear.[43]

One distinguished research scientist predicts great further progress in these directions. He says:

Great strides will be made in the fields of biochemistry and neurophysiology. Today the scientist is gaining insight into control of the degenerative diseases . . . Brilliant researches in steroid chemistry and allied fields, with their applications to body functions, will continue, resulting in healthier, longer lives.

Hormones, those complex, powerful chemicals secreted by the endocrine glands, which so influence man's feeling of well-being, will be further synthesized and more cogently applied. The virus, and such virus-caused diseases as the common cold and infantile paralysis, will be successfully checked. Cancer will be controlled. The heart will pump longer. Neuropsychologists will learn how the mind functions during sleep and will solve the mystery of memory. All this adds up to the fact that we will have not only an older population, but one that is more robust with advancing age.[44]

RECREATION

The effects of technology have nowhere been more spectacular during the past half century than in recreational activities. In the first place, steady advancement of productivity in the factory and home has shortened working hours and greatly increased leisure time. Allowing for the necessities of eating and sleeping, and the drop in the work week since 1900, the average American adult now has close to twice as much time for recreation as he had then. On the whole we probably spend as much time enjoying ourselves as we do at work.

In the second place, technology has given us many new and different — if not better — ways

39. *Time*, May 18, 1953, p. 70.
40. "A Stainless Kidney for Your Blood," *Steel Horizons*, Fall 1951.
41. "Color Magic Teaches the Deaf to Speak," *Steel Horizons*, Spring 1952.
42. *Think*, November 1952.

43. *Population Bulletin*, Population Reference Bureau, Washington, August 1952, p. 27.
44. Dr. Charles Allen Thomas, President, Monsanto Chemical Company, in the *Monsanto Magazine*, December 1951, p. 35.

to spend our leisure time. Around the turn of the century two products of technology were finding mass acceptance. Bicycling, which, like golf and tennis, was first a rich man's diversion, was becoming a mass craze for both sexes and all ages — and later a utilitarian means of transportation. In the household the phonograph, available on the partial-payment plan at $2 a month, was on its way to fulfilling Thomas Edison's widely advertised desire to see one "In Every American Home." Motion pictures and automobiles were both mechanical curiosities of which not much was expected.

The half century since then has seen the silent "flicker" developed from its nickelodeon beginnings to the color-sound 3-D films of today, with weekly audiences at one time passing the 80 million mark. The automobile, first a plaything for the few and now a necessity for the masses, today meets the recreational and utilitarian needs of two thirds of the nation's families.

Amateur photography has been greatly stimulated by technological advances since 1900, when daylight-loading film was still relatively new. Since that time the development of faster and more sensitive film and paper, color photography, amateur motion-picture film and apparatus, greatly improved cameras and equipment, and such sensational innovations as the polaroid one-minute camera and the "three-dimensional" stereopticon camera, have greatly increased the popularity of this hobby.

Radio and Television

The radio is another technological triumph, undreamed of until World War I but now found in virtually every household. And television, which was still "just around the corner" until World War II, has in the past few years been supplied to a majority of the nation's homes. With the expansion of the television broadcasting network and the arrival of color transmission, television is proving a real threat not only to radio but to motion pictures.

How much these new recreational devices have affected the people exposed to them — and whether for good or bad — is something about which there is much argument and little agreement. The automobile has reduced provincialism by increasing personal mobility and contact. The movies, radio and television are having much the same effect in promoting uniformity of speech, dress and behavior. But whether the American consumer, exposed as he is to a wide range of mass-produced diversions and amusements, is any more standardized than his great-grandfather of Civil War days seems highly questionable. In spite of the standardization of modern products, the variety of choice in literature, entertainment and enlightenment enjoyed today is vastly greater than it was then.

Technological developments of the more distant future in the field of recreation are probably as difficult to foresee as radio and television were in 1900. It seems safe to predict, however, that the next few years will bring further improvements in the quality and reception of television programs and wider use of that medium. Before long television service of some sort will be available to virtually the entire population. With larger screens and color transmission, better television-film programs seem inevitable. Whether wired television providing feature films on a pay-as-you-see basis will prove economically feasible is still uncertain. Such a development would obviously have further profound effects on the radio and motion-picture industries.

An event of revolutionary importance not only for television but possibly for photography and motion pictures was the "photographing" on *magnetic tape* of a color television program broadcast from New York to Princeton, New Jersey. This method of "electronic photography," when perfected, will eliminate the need for developing and processing film and will greatly reduce costs since the tape can be used over and over again.[45]

Movies, Photography and Music

The movies are trying to meet television competition in various ways. One possibility is the exhibition in theaters of color television on large screens. Wired home television, or "phonevision," on a fee basis for presentation of current film features is another possibility. The quality of films will be further improved; wider use of color can be expected and exhibition of "three-dimensional" films is now commonplace. Cinerama, CinemaScope and VistaVision, through the use of large, curved screens and several projectors, give a "3-D effect" without the aid of special

---

45. "Magnetic Tape Used by RCA to Photograph Television Program," *Wall Street Journal*, December 2, 1953, p. 1.

polarized glasses. But glasses are required for true three-dimensional films, and judging from audience reception people don't like to wear glasses.

An inexpensive, practical system for receiving television programs in natural color has been invented by Ernest O. Lawrence of the University of California, Nobel prize winner for his development of the cyclotron. This tube, which is compatible (i.e., can be synchronized) with the CBS, NBC-RCA, or other TV systems, is being developed by the Chromatic Television Laboratories in association with the Paramount Pictures Corporation.

A simple attachment devised by Major Robert V. Bernier, U.S. Air Force photographic officer, converts a conventional 16mm. movie camera or projector into a three-dimension machine, using full color.[46]

The number of amateur photographers has doubled since the end of World War II, and it is estimated that about 26 million families in the United States take one and a half billion still-pictures every year, using everything from inexpensive box cameras to f/1.9 Kiné-Exacta's and Contax's. About 3 million home-movie cameras are in use. It is estimated that eight or nine out of every ten feet of home-movie films are color. Now it is even possible for the amateur to make natural color movies with sound.

Although Thomas Edison invented the phonograph (which he deemed the most useful of all his inventions) many years before the twentieth century, there were still only 8 million phonographs in the United States by 1946. Owing largely to the perfection of micro-groove long-playing phonograph records, inexpensive phonograph attachments for any radio, and radio-phonograph combination sets, the total number of phonographs in use rose to nearly 27 million by the end of 1953 [47] — another contribution of technology to musical recreation in the home. The availability of high-quality electronic components has led to the rapid development of a new hobby, "hi-fi," or the design, construction and operation of high-fidelity phonographic and sound reproduction equipment. Tape and wire recorders, another contribution of electronics since World War II, are finding widespread use for home recreation, as well as in education, news reporting and other fields.

TECHNOLOGICAL GAINS IN AGRICULTURE

Technology's contribution to American living standards has not been limited to the creation of new and different consumer products. Revolutionary advances in techniques have improved the quality of existing products and greatly increased efficiency in producing and distributing both old and new products. Technological progress has enabled us to improve the quality, widen the variety, and enlarge the quantity of goods available to American consumers — and all with less and less expenditure of human effort.

Technological progress in American agriculture has resulted in a virtual doubling of labor productivity during the past half century. "In 1900 one farm worker produced enough for himself and seven others; now he produces enough for himself and 14 others." [48] And the farm worker at the turn of the century worked harder, and much longer hours, than his successor does today. Besides bringing these economies of human effort, technology has substantially increased the average output of livestock products per animal and average crop production per acre, the latter by more than half since the turn of the century.

These gains have been accompanied by the introduction of new products and the breeding of new varieties of crops and livestock better adapted to environmental conditions and consumer needs. These and other changes still under way constitute an agricultural revolution comparable to that of the last half of the nineteenth century, which was marked by the development of steel plows, mowers, reapers, "combines" and other machinery designed for use with animal power.

MECHANIZATION

World War I gave the first real stimulus to this second mechanical revolution in farming, with a sharp increase in the number of tractors on farms. After the war, the introduction of the general-purpose tractor and other improvements in design led to a further rapid extension of their use and a steady decline in the number of horses

---

46. R. L. McIntyre, "Grandma's Stereoscope Is Back," article in *Today's Science*, May 1952.

47. Letter of January 5, 1954 from Kenyon Kilbon, Radio Corporation of America.

48. *Research and Related Services in the United States Department of Agriculture*, Vol. I, prepared for the Committee on Agriculture of the House of Representatives, 81st Cong., 2d sess., December 21, 1950, p. 1.

and mules on farms. This upward trend was only briefly slowed during the early depression years. The operating economies and advantages resulting from the adaptation of rubber tires to tractors in the 1930s, and the development of planting, cultivating and harvesting machines specially designed for tractor use, led to a further great expansion in the use of tractors and other kinds of farm machinery.

Today more than 4 million tractors are used on American farms, while the number of horses and mules has dropped to around 5 million from nearly 27 million at their peak in World War I. One of the most striking effects of this reduction of the farm animal population has been the release of some 63 million acres of farmland, formerly needed to grow animal feed, for the production of marketable farm products.[49] A partial offset to this gain is the reduction in the supply of animal fertilizer, which necessitates the use of chemical substitutes.

The chief effect of the shift from animate to inanimate energy has been to lessen the drudgery of farm labor and greatly increase the output of the farm worker and the speed with which he can work. Because much of farm work must be accomplished while weather is favorable, mechanization can have an important bearing on the timeliness of agricultural operations. "With a tractor and power equipment 3 acres of land can be prepared and planted to corn during the time that 1 acre is planted with work animals. If the tractor is put on a 24-hour schedule, which is not feasible with work animals, the preparation and planting job can be done seven times as fast as with animal power." [50] Specialized machinery designed for use with tractors has contributed greatly to a lessening of toil and to higher productivity on farms. These trends can be expected to continue until mechanical energy has virtually supplanted animal power, just as the earlier revolution largely substituted the horse for the human worker.

Smaller tractors adapted to hilly terrain will find wider use on small farms. Plowing, planting and cultivating are now largely mechanized on big farms, as is the harvesting and processing of grains and hay. With the introduction of "baby" and "midget" combines, grain harvesting can be mechanized on even the smallest farms.

Specialized Machines

Combines are now available not only for wheat but for beans, barley, maize, flax, timothy and oats. Stimulated by war and postwar agricultural prosperity and by the much steeper rise in farm labor rates than in machinery costs, the use of corn pickers, hay balers, milking machines, grain combines, and other laborsaving equipment is spreading rapidly. New machines have been devised for harvesting beets and removing leaves, for digging, cleaning and loading potatoes, for chopping forage, for high-speed corn planting, and for planting beets, beans and potatoes, for cultivating slopes and curves to aid in erosion control, and for many other tasks formerly done by hand, or by horse. Today one can travel for hundreds of miles through mixed farming country without finding a horse in harness.

One of the most back-breaking tasks has been conquered by the cotton picker, use of which is spreading fast. It will do as much work in a day as 40 men. In Texas the machine-harvested portion of the cotton crop rose from one per cent in 1946 to an estimated 20 per cent in 1952 and 30 per cent in 1953.[51] Even such crops as tobacco, sweet potatoes and tomatoes may soon yield to the machine. Conveyor belts have been used successfully to save labor in harvesting tomatoes in California. Agricultural engineers at the University of California are working toward complete mechanization of tomato harvesting, which will involve breeding of new varieties adapted to mechanical harvesting.[52] Such laborsaving processes as power spraying and the use of flame in weed control are also finding wide acceptance, as is use of the airplane for seeding, spraying and fertilizing — as well as for transport. Indeed, the nation's farmers use several times as many planes as the airlines, though much smaller ones. The Air Transport Mobilization Survey of the National Security Resources Board revealed that in May 1951, 11,715 planes were used in agriculture, compared with 1,377 operated by commercial air carriers.[53]

Rural electrification is also easing the burden

49. *Changes in Farming*, U.S. Bureau of Agricultural Economics, June 1948, p. 12.

50. *Ibid.*, pp. 12–13.

51. Letter of January 19, 1954 from H. P. Smith, Professor of Agricultural Engineering, Agricultural and Mechanical College of Texas.

52. Letter of January 7, 1954 from Roy Bainer, Chairman, Department of Agricultural Engineering, College of Agriculture, University of California.

53. Lecture by Joseph T. Geuting, Jr., Aircraft Industries Association of America, at American University, Washington, D.C., November 13, 1952.

of farm and household labors. Though fairly recent, electrification is spreading rapidly and nearly nine out of ten of the nation's farms are already electrified.

Irrigation, which helps to increase yields in normal seasons and save crops in drought years, is spreading rapidly throughout farming lands. The irrigated area of the 17 western states has more than tripled since 1900. By 1950, in addition to the 25 million acres under irrigation in these states, there were 1.5 million irrigated acres in other sections of the country, chiefly in Arkansas, Louisiana and Florida. In Texas the 10 per cent of the state's cotton acreage grown on irrigated land yields 25 per cent of the crop.

SOIL USE AND CHEMICALS

Better use and management of the soil and greater consumption of lime, fertilizers and other chemicals have been among the important technological developments contributing to increased agricultural productivity since the turn of the century. These developments, like mechanization, have taken place chiefly since World War I, and on an accelerated basis since the 1930s.

During most of America's agricultural history little attention was paid to soil and water conservation. As a result, output per acre showed no great improvement until the 1930s, probably because soil deterioration was offsetting the many advances in farming methods. Although the soil is still being "mined" in some regions, the past two decades have witnessed great improvement. Contour plowing and better tillage and terracing, together with the practice of summer fallowing, are helping to conserve both soil and water. Crop rotation is more widely understood and applied; legumes and green manures have been utilized for replenishing nitrogen and soil humus.

These and other improved techniques of soil and water management have checked the trend toward soil deterioration, and on many farms, especially in the East, the soil is more fertile and productive than it ever was. There is still room for improvement, but all signs point to a continuance of the present trend toward widespread use of better methods in soil management and water conservation. Much has also been learned about drainage methods and about control of salinity and soil management under irrigation.

Lime and Fertilizer

Along with better soil and water management has come much more extensive application of lime and commercial fertilizers and a wide variety of insecticides and other chemicals. Although lime and chemical fertilizers have long been used in agriculture, their use has increased greatly since the late 1930s. After a dip during the early depression years, lime consumption in 1937 was double the predepression volume and is now more than three times the 1937 figure. During the first half of the century, consumption of all agricultural fertilizers in the United States increased over 1,000 per cent, and fertilizer consumption in 1950 was three times what it was only fifteen years before.

These changes have contributed directly to increased crop yields, and have also been essential to the development of better soil management practices. Applications of both lime and phosphate are required to provide the legumes and grasses needed for successful crop rotation and soil maintenance.

Given favorable economic conditions, there is every prospect of still wider use of lime and fertilizer. Continuing spread of soil maintenance practices will create a need for more of both materials; a much larger use of fertilizer for small grains (other than wheat) and for legumes, hay and pastures would be profitable. New methods of applying fertilizers, in granular, liquid and gaseous forms, are being developed, and the importance of such minor plant nutrients as cobalt, zinc and iron is becoming better understood. These "trace elements" of scarce minerals have been found to be vital. For example, application of adequate amounts of them has doubled yields on New Jersey tomato farms. Prizes used to be given to farmers who raised as much as 10 tons of tomatoes to the acre; now the mark is set at 20 tons.[54] One of the most significant recent developments was the announcement by Monsanto Chemical Company on December 29, 1951 of Krilium, a powdered plastic soil conditioner. This product and numerous other soil conditioners now on the market aid poor soils, reduce erosion and, though not fertilizers, increase crop yields. They are said to be a hundred times as efficient in improving soil structure as compost, manure or peat moss.

54. *Weekly Market Letter,* Goodbody & Co., New York, December 10, 1952.

Pest Control

Chemical technology has made other significant contributions to agriculture. Particularly important have been the control of harmful insects and plant and animal diseases and the betterment of feeding practices. Among the important chemical aids for agriculture developed during the past half century have been: successful hog-cholera serum, fungicide to control brown rot of peaches, calcium arsenate to eliminate the boll weevil, carbon tetrachloride to control hookworm, vitamin D in cod liver oil to prevent rickets in chicks, vitamin D added to milk by irradiation, copper and iron combination in feeds to save baby pigs, vitamin A to improve the diet of farm animals, use of "fixed coppers" to eliminate fungus diseases of vegetables, eradication of the Mediterranean fruit fly from Florida, soil fumigation to destroy nematodes, development of effective insecticides against the European corn borer, control of the Mexican bean beetle by rotenone, oil insecticide to kill the corn earworm, feeding of copper and iron to correct "salt sick" in Florida cattle, use of DDT against livestock and crop and household pests to prevent insect-borne diseases, sodium fluoride to combat swine roundworms, phenothiazine to remove internal livestock parasites, chemical weed killers, chlordane and taxaphene to control grasshoppers, and bactericidal radiation to increase egg production.

One acre out of every ten planted in the United States is still lost annually to insect damage. The Department of Agriculture estimates that adequate use of insecticides could add a billion pounds of meat and several billion pounds of milk to our annual output.

A new approach to insect control is to apply toxic agents which the plant can absorb in its growth. One such systemic plant insecticide has already been approved by the Department of Agriculture. Systox, made by the Pittsburgh Coke and Chemical Company, is not sprayed like other chemicals to cover cotton plants and protect them from the outside, but is absorbed by the plant through its foliage and roots to make the entire plant toxic to any insects attacking it. A similar technique is used to protect cattle from deerflies, mosquitos, hornflies and other biting insects. In this case an insecticide — lindane — is injected under the hide.

Herbicides — output of which now exceeds more than 10,000 tons a year — are cutting down the annual loss of crops to weeds. These chemical "weedicides" are tremendous laborsavers; they can do in minutes what would require hours with a hoe.

Among the promising possibilities of the future are dual-purpose chemicals to kill both weeds and insects in one application. Substantial economies would be realized from equipment designed for dual-purpose chemicals, as well as from new types of high-pressure spraying and dusting equipment.

Beyond such direct aids, chemical research is helping agriculture indirectly by developing new uses for farm products. Examples are the recent development for industrial use of a filament spun from milk casein, production of a new textile fiber from corn protein and of a synthetic rubber with high heat resistance from milk sugar.[55] The large amount of research being carried on by private corporations, universities and government agencies gives assurance that there will be further rapid progress in the use of chemicals for advancing agricultural practices and products.

NEW AND IMPROVED VARIETIES

Technology has contributed products new to American agriculture and well-adapted to the soil and climate. Soybeans are an example of such a "new product"; insignificant until the 1930s, they have since risen to major importance. Soybean acreage, which was only half a million in 1930, shot up to more than 10 million during World War II and this legume now ranks sixth in acreage among all our crops. Soybean oil content and yields per acre have been moving upward, and the development of new higher-yielding varieties gives promise that soybean production will remain high.

Among other products introduced into the United States during the past half century are Egyptian cotton, now grown extensively on irrigated western acreage, crested wheat grass as a forage crop for the Great Plains, Ladino clover, Korean lespedeza, the Rutgers tomato and a nematode-resistant grape. Development of a new strain of cotton — Acala 4–42 — has already made California the second cotton-growing state in the Union. Average yields in the San Joaquin

55. *Research and Related Services in the United States Department of Agriculture*, Vol. I, pp. 38–43.

Valley are better than 800 pounds per acre, compared with a national average of under 300.[56]

Hybrids

The breeding of plants for yield and of animals for weight, strength and other qualities by simple selection is centuries old. With the application of the science of genetics during the past half century, however, the possibilities of selective breeding have been vastly enhanced.

One of the most important agricultural discoveries of this period was that crossing inbred lines of corn resulted in increased vigor and larger yields. This was followed by development of special hybrids adapted to different parts of the country. Since 1933, planting of hybrid corn, giving a 30 per cent higher yield, has spread from a tiny fraction of the total corn acreage to more than 80 per cent. Hybrid seed corn brought the national average corn yield from slightly over 20 bushels an acre in 1930 to nearly 40 bushels in the years 1948–1950, while the corn-picking machine has reduced the man-hours of work per hundred bushels from 135 some forty years ago to an average of 67 today.

Hybrid onions, with a 50 per cent higher yield and greater ability to withstand disease, soon followed hybrid corn. More recently, agricultural research has been able to apply the profoundly significant principle of hybridization to alfalfa, sugar beets, tomatoes, cucumbers and other crops, as well as to such livestock as hogs and chickens. And the great results achieved thus far will probably be surpassed in the future.

Polyploids, plants having three or more (instead of only two) chromosomes in the somatic cells, may prove to be as revolutionary as hybrids. Polyploidal varieties of raspberries, strawberries, blackberries and grapes are already being developed, with highly favorable effects on the flavor and size of the fruit. "Giant-fruited" apples, pears and peaches, enabling breeders to obtain new desired crosses, are also on the way to practical application.

Crossbreeding has also resulted in strains and varieties with greater resistance to insects and disease. Examples include "varieties of corn resistant to the corn borer, corn earworm, or chinch bug; wheat resistant to Hessian fly; barley resistant to greenbug; sugar beets resistant to leaf-hoppers; and alfalfa resistant to aphids." [57] Other examples are the development of Thatchen wheat, resistant to stem rust; Vigo disease-resistant wheat; the Katahdin disease-resistant potato; bees resistant to American foulbrood; varieties of sugar beets resistant to curly top disease; and new wilt-resistant varieties of tomatoes, alfalfa, tobacco and flax. Although the idea of using the principles of natural selection in breeding for resistance to disease is only half a century old, it now appears that "We can breed almost any character we want in a plant if we work at it long enough and hard enough." [58]

Breeding and Feeding of Livestock

Selective breeding of livestock, better feeding practices and other measures have brought spectacular gains in the amount of livestock products obtained per unit of breeding stock, comparable to the increases in crop yields per acre. For instance, average egg production per laying hen has increased more than 75 per cent since 1909, with the sharpest gains occurring since the 1930s.[59] These gains and comparable gains in broiler output have been achieved in spite of considerable economies in feed consumption. For example, with the addition of the recently discovered vitamin B_{12} to soybean meal in poultry feeds it is possible to produce three-pound broilers on about two pounds less feed and in two weeks less time than with the more expensive animal-protein diet.[60]

Soon after antibiotics had been proved effective against human illnesses, veterinarians discovered that these potent microscopic chemicals could save livestock and poultry. Unexpected, however, was the discovery that *one tenth to one twentieth* the amount of antibiotic used for animal disease treatment would make amazing and consistent changes in the rate of growth of healthy animals. Piglets fed Terralac (synthetic sow's milk made with terramycin) weigh 10 to 35 per cent more than animals fed natural sow's milk. Relieved of her family early, the sow can produce two and a half to three litters a year, instead of one or two — which means more pork at lower

---

56. "Away Out *West* in the Land of Cotton," *Collier's*, June 23, 1951; also *Fortune*, May 1949.

57. *Research and Related Services in the United States Department of Agriculture*, Vol. I, p. 16.

58. *Ibid.*, p. 4.

59. *Agricultural Statistics, 1952*, U.S. Department of Agriculture, pp. 538–539.

60. *Research and Related Services in the United States Department of Agriculture*, Vol. I, p. 13.

prices. In addition, piglets raised on Terralac are safer from disease and from accidental crushing by sows. From a fifth to a third of all the pigs born each year die without going to market.

With separate and adequate weaning the death rate is reduced to about 5 per cent. If the feeding methods used at one experimental farm — Arenel Farms, near Shoemakersville, Pennsylvania — were applied to all hogs, "there would be a reduction in corn requirements for hog feeding by 100 million bushels. Assuming an average yield of 50 bushels of corn per acre, the savings due to antibiotics-fortified feed could thus reduce the planting average by 2 million acres." [61]

Of equal or even greater significance are the effects of better feeding practices, selective breeding and artificial insemination on the milk production of dairy cows. Although "test-tube breeding" did not begin in the United States until 1936, a total of 4 million of the nation's 24 million dairy cows had been bred artificially at the beginning of 1952,[62] and the number is increasing rapidly each year. Since artificial insemination enables a bull to father 2,000 calves a year, instead of the normal 40, it permits a more intensive use of well-proven sires and thus a more rapid improvement of herds and milk production.

One authority contends that "through the upgrading of herds by artificial insemination, present milk production could be maintained with about 4 million fewer cows — and this would free more grain for other purposes." [63] As a result of better breeding and feeding practices as well as artificial insemination, annual output of milk has increased from about 3,800 pounds per cow prior to 1920 to about 5,000 pounds today, with a sharp interruption to the trend due to the drought and depression of the early 1930s.[64]

Recent experiments suggest that hormones offer promising possibilities for livestock breeding as they do for human health. Injection of hormones by trained veterinarians at one livestock experiment station caused a group of five heifers and sterile cows to give milk, without having had calves. This technique could add to the milk supply by saving thousands of sterile cows that are sent to slaughter annually. Another new chemical hormone known as ECP (estradiol cyclopentylpropionate) when given to ewes causes them to lamb twice a year instead of the usual once, a development which could add appreciably to the supply of mutton and wool.

New Varieties

The desire to meet changes in consumer demand has been responsible for the crossing of American hogs with the Danish Landrace breed. The new strains yield more lean meat, and less fat and more meat in the choice cuts; at the same time they retain the ability to produce large and fast-growing litters. After years of experimentation several such strains are now in commercial production. Another example of breeding a "tailor-made" product is the Beltsville white turkey, developed to meet the demand for smaller, more compact turkeys, suitable for small kitchens, small ovens and small families.

The Columbia sheep, a cross of the Rambouillet and Lincoln breeds developed for the intermountain area, yields more good wool and more meat than any other breed in that area. Demand for dairy cattle able to withstand the hot summer climate of the South led to the introduction of the Red Sindhi breed from India and its crossing with Jerseys. This experiment, being carried on at the Department of Agriculture farm at Beltsville, has already demonstrated the possibility of breeding heat resistance into dairy cattle. Introduction of Brahman cattle several years ago has permitted successful beef cattle production in the South and, together with improved fattening practices, has helped make Florida the fastest-growing beef-cattle-producing state in the Union.[65]

ADVANCING INDUSTRIAL TECHNOLOGY

American industry, like the home and the farm, has been transformed during the past half century. Mining and manufacturing, construction, transportation and marketing — all have been profoundly affected by new materials and techniques, improved products and more efficient methods. The technological triumphs of this period have been numerous and important, di-

61. John L. Davenport, "Antibiotics Perform Modern Miracles," *General Electric Review*, March 1952.

62. *Farm Journal*, February 1953, p. 64.

63. C. B. Bender, Professor and Research Specialist in Dairy Husbandry, New Jersey State Experimental Station, Rutgers University, in "Dairy Farming Faces Nation's Crisis with Special Assets," *Sperryscope*, Sperry Gyroscope Corp., Spring 1951.

64. *Changes in Farming*, p. 101.

65. "Florida's Cowpokes," *Wall Street Journal*, June 30, 1952, p. 1.

verse in tneir nature, interrelated and far-reaching in their application. It is possible only to indicate some of the more important developments.

Two of the most significant and pervasive technological changes affecting industry since the turn of the century have been the widespread electrification of productive operations and the large and growing use of the internal combustion engine in agriculture and construction and nearly all branches of transportation. Although both the electric motor and the gasoline engine were first used industrially in the latter part of the nineteenth century, their full impact is only now being felt. The nineteenth was the century of coal, the steam engine and the horse. The twentieth has been the century of electricity, petroleum and the automotive vehicle.

ELECTRIFICATION

Invisible and immaterial, electricity is an infinitely mobile, flexible and divisible form of energy. Since it can be delivered instantaneously anywhere in any quantity, the factory is no longer chained to a waterfall or to a site where coal can be cheaply delivered. As electricity can be supplied as needed to a motor at the workbench, cumbersome overhead shafts and belts have all but disappeared from the factory. As a result factories today are much more efficient producing units. What is just as important, they are cleaner, brighter, and more pleasant working places.[66]

The substitution of this readily controllable form of energy for the crude line shaft opened the way to the development on a tremendous scale of every kind of automatic machinery to replace and multiply human effort and greatly speed up mechanical operations in the factory. With the application of electronic discoveries in recent years, vast new possibilities are in view — for communication, for high-precision instrumentation, for automatic inspection and industrial

66. Typical of the changes of the past half century are these figures on equipment installed at the South Bend plant of the Studebaker Corporation, which between 1902 and 1952 increased the number of production workers from 2,500 to 14,526:

	1902	1952
Capacity of plant electric generators	2,500 h.p.	16,000 kw.
Incandescent and fluorescent lamps	1,250	26,420
Metalworking machines	312	2,539
Combined length of belting and shafting (*miles*)	10	—
Combined length of electric wiring and cables (*miles*)	—	5,338

(Letter from W. R. Walton, The Studebaker Corp., January 12, 1954.)

control, and for mental laborsaving in high-speed computation.

Electric Heat

Electricity is finding wide and increasing industrial use in heating processes. The electric furnace was first developed in the nineteenth century to provide much higher temperatures and much "cleaner heat" than could be obtained through combustion of any fuel. It was greatly improved about thirty years ago by the application of the induction principle, whereby the current is induced in the metal to be melted rather than applied externally, the better to control temperatures and operations.

Because of its better quality, electric steel has virtually supplanted crucible steel, and indeed both furnace and crucible are eliminated in a new process worked out by Westinghouse, whereby the metal is actually held in an electromagnetic field floating in space while it is being melted.[67] The electric furnace is also widely used in the production of ferroalloys, fused silica and fused quartz, and a variety of metallic compounds and alloys. Aluminum is another metal produced electrolytically that would not be available in quantity at today's low prices were it not for cheap and plentiful electricity. Electric welding and electroplating are other important industrial processes made possible by electricity, while dielectric heating to bond wood and plastics is one of the outstanding recent developments. In many low-temperature industrial processes such as enameling, firing of glassware, annealing, carbonizing and hardening, electricity is finding wide use. The electromagnet has long had important industrial uses, notably in traveling cranes for bulk moving of iron and steel scrap and other products.

Electricity is just as necessary for cooling and refrigeration, which are vital in many industrial operations as well as in the storage and transportation of fresh, frozen and processed foodstuffs. Air conditioning on the scale available today would, of course, be impossible without electricity, which is also needed to operate ventilating and heating systems as well as the multitude of recording and control devices so essential in factories today.

Finally, it is hard to imagine the operation of

67. Press Release, January 1, 1952, Westinghouse Electric Corporation, Pittsburgh, Pa.

a modern factory with the inadequate industrial lighting available before the advent of electricity. The electric arc light and gaslight have both long since been displaced by the tungsten-filament lamp for domestic, industrial and commercial lighting. The fluorescent light, in turn, is displacing the filament lamp for overhead lighting in offices, factories, hotels, and even in homes.

Electricity found one of its first applications, before the turn of the century, in the electric trolley and the high-speed interurban car. Although these are now losing out to the gasoline-driven bus and the trolley coach, the cleanliness and economy of electricity have led to the electrification of many former steam railroad lines, particularly in the densely settled regions of the East.

Electricity and Mechanization

There is every reason to expect further expansion in the industrial, as in the domestic, use of electricity. Mechanization of industry is going forward rapidly. Electrically operated hand tools are providing great economies over manually operated ones. New and improved machines are continually being installed in the most progressive establishments, while many of the more backward enterprises are being forced by competition to install laborsaving machines that have been available for a generation. Machine operating speeds are being greatly increased. Such improvements mean greater productivity and over-all economy of operation, and they often involve more than proportional increases in electric power consumption.

Techniques are changing so rapidly, and opportunities for profitable mechanization appearing so frequently, however, that even the most advanced industrial establishments will probably find both need and opportunity to increase greatly their use of electricity. One would expect that the leading manufacturers of electrical equipment in the United States would, if anything, be "overelectrified." Yet the president of the Westinghouse Electric Corporation, one of the two leading firms, stated in 1948: "When our plant-planning engineers made a survey of our operations, they found that if we added all the new processes and machines which are justified for present production, our electric-power consumption would increase by 35 per cent." [68] If

this was the postwar situation in one of the most progressive establishments, it seems reasonable to conclude that American industry as a whole could profit by a much larger increase.

Total utility output of electricity, which was 142 billion kilowatt-hours in 1940 and 400 billion in 1952, is expected by the General Electric Company to reach 600 billion kilowatt-hours annually by 1960; and if the same expansion of generating capacity continues, General Electric engineers predict 1 trillion kilowatt-hours a year by 1970.

There will be a continuing rapid growth in the industrial use of electricity, though hardly so rapid a percentage increase as during the past half century. The total electric-generating capacity in the United States in 1900 was less than one million kilowatts; in 1950 it was 63 million kilowatts.[69] Figures of the Census Bureau show that the capacity of all the power equipment of manufacturing industries in 1899 amounted to 9.6 million horsepower, of which electric motors accounted for less than 500,000 horsepower, or under 5 per cent of the total. By 1950, total capacity had increased to 128 million horsepower, while the capacity of electric motors had increased to about 100 million horsepower and accounted for 80 per cent of the total.

The proportion of power purchased from the electric utility industry has now risen to more than 70 per cent of the total. This is another illustration of the economies and advantages arising from specialization, not only in jobs, machines and establishments, but of entire industries. This tendency to carry specialization to the plant and industry level is peculiarly American and helps account for the high productivity of American industry.

Electric Power Industry

The electric power industry not only has been able to meet a vastly expanded demand but has greatly improved its own technology during the past half century. During a period of generally rising commodity prices, which has included two drastic wartime inflations, the industry has been able to achieve sufficient economy of operation to sell its product at progressively lower prices.[70]

---

68. Address by Gwilym A. Price, President, Westinghouse Electric Corporation, at convention of the Edison Electric Institute, Atlantic City, June 2, 1948.

69. Table 343. These data include only utility power available for public use, exclusive of capacity in industrial plants, which amounted to 13.5 million kilowatts on January 1, 1950.

70. On January 1, 1952, the average cost was 5.0 cents per kilowatt-hour for consumers of 25 kilowatt-hours a month, compared with 6.8 cents in 1931; 3.6 cents for

Among the technological developments that have made this possible have been astonishing improvements in fuel consumption and generating efficiency. In 1900 more than seven pounds of coal were required to generate one kilowatt-hour of electricity. By 1950 an average of only 1.19 pounds was needed and one of the most modern plants consumed less than three quarters of a pound per kilowatt-hour. Nor has the limit yet been reached, although future fuel savings clearly cannot approach those of the past: it will hardly be possible to get something for nothing.

These economies have been gained through constant improvement of turbines and generators and the use of such fuel-saving devices as superheaters, air preheaters, hydrogen cooling and coal pulverizers. Generating equipment has been revolutionized. The "last word" in electric-generating equipment in 1904 was the 7,500-horsepower reciprocating engines installed in the New York subway powerhouse. The largest stationary engines ever built, these cumbersome pieces of machinery operated under only 175 pounds of steam pressure and made 75 revolutions a minute. Today the system uses 65,000-horsepower turbogenerators operating at 3,600 revolutions a minute. Each has the power equivalent of nine of the 1904 engines, and is far more efficient.[71]

Among the latest innovations in generating equipment are reheat turbines to increase thermal efficiency, gas turbines burning natural gas, and the use of a liquid and, in one case, hydrogen gas to cool generators. Motors are also much more compact and efficient; today a 30-horsepower motor is about as big as a 5-horsepower motor of half a century ago.

In another direction, scientists are producing electricity directly from heat, long a goal of science and engineering. Although industrial application is not yet practicable, in tests at the laboratories of the Pittsburgh Consolidation Coal Company electricity has been generated by a chemical reaction involving water-gas made from coal, in the presence of electrodes. Efficiency is said to be as high as 75 per cent.[72]

Great advances have also been achieved during the past half century in the transmission and distribution of electricity. It was considered a great triumph in 1896 when alternating current was transmitted at 2,000 volts over the 13 miles from Niagara Falls to Buffalo. Today current from Boulder Dam is delivered at 287,000 volts to Los Angeles, 278 miles away. Even higher transmission voltages are being installed, and voltages of 500,000 will probably be used before long. These developments have been made possible by great improvements in the quality and capacity of insulators, transformers, high-tension cables, and other kinds of transmission and control equipment.

INTERNAL COMBUSTION ENGINES

Although the internal combustion principle dates from the nineteenth century, the original crude and heavy engines bore about as little resemblance to the modern automobile engine or diesel as the ponderous Corliss steam engine proudly exhibited at the Philadelphia Centennial of 1876 bears to the modern turbogenerator. The first internal combustion engines, fueled by manufactured gas instead of gasoline, and operating at 200 revolutions a minute, weighed close to 1,100 pounds per horsepower [73] — about as much as a horse!

After fifty years of steady improvement in design, the lightweight high-compression gasoline engine today weighs only 5 or 6 pounds per horsepower. Higher compression ratios, higher-octane gasoline and lighter steel alloys have brought especially rapid improvement since 1925. In that year a six-cylinder automobile engine developing 40 to 45 horsepower weighed over 900 pounds; with a compression ratio of $4\frac{1}{2}$ to 1, maximum speed was 60 to 70 miles an hour. A V-8 engine of the 1950s generates 135 horsepower but weighs only 745 pounds. It has a compression ratio of $7\frac{1}{2}$ to 1 and a top speed approaching 100 miles an hour. Petroleum technology has kept pace by increasing the octane rating of automotive gasoline from 57 to the present 90, thus conserving petroleum resources. Continuation of this trend to a goal of a 12 to 1 compression ratio will save another 10 billion gallons of gasoline annually.[74]

consumers of 100 kilowatt-hours, compared with 4.7 cents; and 2.7 cents for consumers of 250 kilowatt-hours, compared with 3.8 cents. *Statistical Abstract of the United States, 1952,* Table 346, p. 313 and *ibid., 1951,* Table 336, p. 288.

71. "A Century of Engineering Progress: 1852–1952," *Scientific Monthly,* August 1952.

72. Reported in *Natural Resources Notes.* U.S. Chamber of Commerce, July 1952.

73. *Encyclopædia Britannica,* Vol. 12 (1946), p. 505.

74. Charles L. McCuen, General Motors Research Laboratories Division, in *1900 to 19xx, A Report on Auto-*

Similar improvement is taking place in other kinds of internal combustion engines. Packard recently developed for the Navy an all aluminum diesel weighing only 5 pounds per horsepower instead of the usual 15 or 20. The turbojet offers fantastically greater savings in weight. In the early Korean War period jet engines weighing 3,000 pounds developed 7,500 pounds of thrust; by 1955 the industry expected to produce even lighter engines developing 20,000 pounds of thrust.[75] In some of the recent fighter aircraft, the pilot has 50,000 horsepower at his command — more than 12 times the power of the World War II fighter and over 100 times the power of the primitive fighter craft used in World War I. Although engines and planes are heavier than they were then, weight increases have been only a minute fraction of the gain in power.[76]

Such developments as greater horsepower, greater efficiency of fuel consumption and lighter weight have revolutionized land transport and agriculture, made air travel possible, and mechanized a multitude of heavy operations in mining and quarrying, in logging and lumbering, and in land clearing and construction.

Transportation Techniques

Those modern beasts of burden, the motor truck and the automobile, together haul a volume of traffic over distances and at speeds that would have been unimaginable even a generation ago. When the horse was in its heyday, in 1918, there were nearly 27 million work animals in the country — about one to every four human beings. By 1951 we had close to a one to three ratio of motor vehicles to our much larger population, and the internal combustion engines of our 52 million cars and trucks could deliver nearly two hundred times 27 million horsepower. And this leaves out of account the 4 million farm tractors which were doing vastly more work on the farm, and doing it faster and better, than horse-drawn equipment ever could.[77] Horses have not yet disappeared from farms, but most of those that are left are taking it easy in the pas-

ture. Here again the efficient and easy to operate internal combustion engine has relieved the workhorse, as the horse relieved the human worker, of back-breaking toil.

On the railroads the greatly improved diesel-electric locomotive, first developed in improved form by General Motors, is proving far more economical and efficient than either the coal-burning steam locomotive or the oil burner. The President of the Erie Railroad, for example, reported that an investment of $18 million in diesel locomotives would result in savings, compared with steam operation, of $6 million in the single year 1948.[78] Such large savings may not be typical, but the economies of diesel operation are so great that this decade will probably see virtually complete dieselization of all railway mileage except that already operated by electricity.

Diesel-electric power has many advantages, of which a thermal efficiency three times that of modern steam engines is perhaps the greatest. It takes only one gallon of diesel fuel to haul a ton of freight the 625 miles from New York City to Cleveland.[79] Maintenance costs and time lost for repairs are also much less for diesels than for steam locomotives, and diesels do not have to carry and replenish the water supply required for steam generation.

New applications of diesels as well as improvements in design are likely to make them even more useful in the future. For example, a "self-propelled railcar" is replacing the old suburban electric car on hitherto unprofitable branch lines and short runs. Air conditioned and smooth-running, these "one-car trains," with two diesel engines and a two-man crew, achieve a running speed of 70 miles an hour on a fuel oil consumption of only 2.7 gallons per mile.[80]

The opposed-piston diesel, said to be the first basic change in the diesel since its invention, is being developed for both ships and locomotives. Employing two pistons forced apart by central combustion instead of the conventional single piston, the new engine packs nearly twice the power in the same space, has no valves or cylinder heads, and has 40 per cent fewer moving parts.

Like the diesel-electric, the gas turbine is a

mobile Engine Progress, General Motors Corp., Detroit, 1951; also "Power for Modern Motors," article in Bulletin of the Standard Oil Company of California, April 1951.

75. Letter of June 17, 1954, from J. S. McFeaters, Westinghouse Electric Corporation.

76. Planes, Aircraft Industries Association of America, November 1952.

77. See pages 800 ff.

78. Erie Railroad Company, Report at Annual Meeting of Stockholders, April 13, 1948.

79. Letter of January 18, 1954 from Volney B. Fowler, Electro-Motive Division, General Motors Corporation.

80. Charles F. Kettering, "Transportation," Journal of the Franklin Institute, January 1951.

prime mover which drives an electric generator, which in turn operates a motor connected to the drive shafts turning the locomotive's wheels. The gas turbine, used also for stationary (utility) power generation, is of simpler design, and lighter weight and smaller size per horsepower, though its fuel consumption is high. A 175-horsepower gas turbine engine designed by the Boeing Aircraft Corporation for use in trucks and buses, for example, weighs only 200 pounds, whereas a diesel engine of the same horsepower, of the type now used in big intercity trucks, weighs fifteen times as much. On the railroads, the gas turbine locomotive has already passed the experimental stage and is now being used regularly by several lines for hauling both passenger and freight trains.

The free-piston engine, a prime mover combining features of both the gas turbine and the diesel, shows interesting possibilities although still in the experimental stage. Two free pistons slide back and forth in a horizontal cylinder compressing air at the center into which fuel (oil, kerosene, natural gas, etc.) is injected. Burning fuel pushes the pistons apart and compresses air on the opposite sides of the pistons. This compressed air is used to supercharge the combustion chamber between the pistons. The product of this cylinder is exhaust gas at relatively high pressure and temperatures and this gas is used to drive a turbine which provides the sole power output from the unit. The free-piston engine has an efficiency as good as or slightly better than the diesel engine and, having no crank shaft or bearings, it overcomes some limitations of the conventional diesel engine. Because of its balanced construction, the free-piston engine is essentially vibrationless. Its efficiency is considerably higher than that of a simple gas turbine and surpasses even that of the more complex gas turbine cycles.[81]

Thus, the internal combustion engine in one form or another will soon virtually monopolize land transport, both road and rail. Sea transport is still largely steam-powered by oil burners, although the marine diesel is predominant in tugboats, inland towboats, fishing vessels and other smaller craft.

The evolution of the gasoline engine toward greater speed and power, and lighter weight, has nowhere been more conspicuous than in aircraft motors. The speed, dependability and lifting capacity of today's propeller-driven planes were undreamed of as recently as twenty years ago. But today's best conventional aircraft engines are even now being outmoded by jet and turbojet engines, the latest and most spectacular developments of the internal combustion principle.

The jet engine is providing great increases in speed and capacity and great economies in engine weight, although at the expense of much heavier fuel consumption. A modern four-engine propeller-type airliner burns a gallon of high-test gasoline every six seconds. A jet liner of the type to be expected on our airways in a few years burns lower-cost kerosene and will travel twice as fast as existing types, but it consumes a gallon every 3.6 seconds.[82] Developed thus far primarily in military aircraft, the jet engine will unquestionably find wide commercial application in long-distance flights. One modification, the turboprop, involving use of part of the jet power to turn propellers, offers great promise.

Improvements in aircraft design as well as in engines will contribute to higher speeds and more economical operation. Aerodynamically there is a trend toward the delta-type all-wing craft, the first basic change in design since the Wright brothers' first plane. This flying wing design is considered by some aeronautical engineers to be the most efficient airfoil since it eliminates the dead weight and air drag of the fuselage. This means more speed and greater range or carrying capacity for the same size and power. The flying wing also has greater maneuverability and can be powered by reciprocating engines or turboprops or jets. Northrop flying wing bombers have proved their efficiency and Convair is producing supersonic speed delta-wing fighters for military service.

Heavy Equipment

Among the most significant applications of the automotive engine, especially the modern diesel, is its use in various types of heavy "outdoor" equipment. The diesel engine has taken over the heavy work in road building. The steam donkey-engine familiar to an older generation of loggers has been displaced by the much more powerful caterpillar tractor. This powerful and versatile vehicle is used for all kinds of heavy hauling over

81. Letter from L. N. Rowley, Executive Editor, *Power* (McGraw-Hill), June 11, 1954.

82. Wilfred Owen, "Plane Facts," *The Lamp,* Standard Oil Co. (N.J.), June 1952.

rough terrain. In the winter of 1951–1952, for example, the Sherritt-Gordon Company used these "cats" to haul an entire village and the structures and equipment of a mining enterprise from Sherridon 165 miles north over frozen lakes and rivers to a new mining location at Lynn Lake, Manitoba.

Although the steamroller will probably survive in political metaphor, it has long since ceased to symbolize road building, where it has been succeeded by the more powerful petroleum-fueled power roller. Likewise, the traditional steamshovel has given way to a wide range of diesel-driven power shovels and excavators of greater flexibility and capacity. These digging and lifting machines are used extensively in building and even more in quarrying; it is only through them that the great economies of strip mining are possible.

The bulldozer, ranging in size from one small enough to attach to a garden tractor to a 45-ton monster with a 16-foot blade, is probably the most spectacular demonstration of how technology has displaced muscle power and vastly multiplied human effort. A generation ago three men, sweating away with pick and shovel and with the help of a team of horses and a metal scoop, required eighteen days to remove the 125 cubic yards of earth in the excavation of a typical house cellar. The cost of the job — in the days when common labor earned $4 a day — came to $360. Without the horses, using hand labor alone, the job would have cost twice as much and taken four times as long. In recent years the same job could be done with a 60-horsepower bulldozer in a single day and, despite a much higher price level, at less than one third of $360. Still more recently General Motors has announced a diesel road scraper that can dig, haul and spread the earth from eight or ten average home basements in one eight-hour day.[83]

The road scraper is only one among many specialized types of diesel-powered equipment developed in recent years for heavy construction work. Others include ditch-digging machines doing the work of 30 or 40 men and a wide variety of equipment for laying roads, loading and moving earth, and clearing land. Much of this equipment, originally designed for track-type tractors, now operates with four-wheel drive on massive rubber tires, gaining greatly in speed and flexibility thereby.

To say that motorized equipment has displaced the horse and vastly augmented the effectiveness of human effort is to tell only half the story, for much of the newly designed equipment performs tasks that would be economically if not physically impossible with muscle power. Dragline excavators, for example, with buckets capable of taking 50 tons in a single bite, can perform stripping and loading operations that would be so costly as to be economically out of reach with horse-drawn or steam-driven equipment.

Another diesel-powered machine, the Bushwacker, clears land of underbrush and trees up to six or eight inches in diameter. Uprooting the smaller trees and felling the larger ones, it literally pounds them to pieces, returning the fibers to the soil as a mulch. Moving forward at a steady pace of a mile and a half an hour, it will clear four or five acres a day.[84] It is hard to visualize the crew needed to do this job by hand.

In city and country large trucks with automatic equipment remove the heaviest snowfalls promptly, though it was virtually impossible before the days of the automotive vehicle to clear any but the busiest streets all winter long. Modern motorized fire-fighting equipment far excels in power and efficiency the horse-drawn steam equipment of a generation ago. Examples of such specialized equipment powered by internal combustion engines could be listed almost endlessly.

Meanwhile, the many-purposed motor truck has been attaining greater capacity, more power, higher speeds and better control. Trucks are now turned out in sizes ranging up to 30 tons or more, but even larger models are on their way. The Heil Company has announced a new dump-truck, believed to be the biggest of this type available, having a body capacity of 25 cubic yards and equipped with an automatic hoist capable of handling a 45-ton payload.[85] Powered by two engines delivering a total of 700 horsepower is the world's largest truck, a 60-ton off-the-highway ore carrier.[86] Of possibly great significance for the future is the 55,000-pound truck designed by Boeing Aircraft Corporation, capable of carrying a load of 68,000 pounds and powered, on an experimental basis, by a gas tur-

---

83. General Motors advertisement in *Saturday Evening Post*, September 27, 1952.

84. Letter of November 17, 1952 from Vernon G. Mandt, American Steel Dredge Company, Inc.
85. Letter from the Heil Company, October 6, 1952.
86. Advertisement of the U.S. Steel Corporation.

bine. With the development of General Motors' "Twin Hydra-Matic" for heavy-duty trucks, announced in March 1954, automatic transmissions became available on all sizes of trucks from small to large. It is claimed that elimination of gear shifting, which on one 300-mile stretch of highway may involve 600 shift sequences averaging as many as 8 to 13 individual shifts per sequence, should mean greater economy of operation, less driver fatigue, greater safety, less maintenance and faster service.[87]

Portable Tools

At the other extreme from such heavy equipment, the internal combustion engine has been adapted in recent years to a wide range of light equipment and portable tools. The portable chain saw, driven by a one-cylinder gas engine weighing less than 20 pounds, eases the tasks of tree cutting and brush clearing. The small gasoline-powered lawn mower, a rarity before World War II, is commonplace today. As if it were not enough to take the sweat out of mowing the lawn, Fairbanks-Morse has now announced an automatic mower which actually seeks out the grass and mows it while the operator sits on the porch.[88]

One of the most versatile laborsavers, the tiny garden tractor, comes close to making gardening a pleasure even for those who dislike work. Weighing less than 200 pounds and costing less than a dollar a pound, it is powered by a two-horsepower engine which will drive it as fast as a man can walk. Attachments available include plow, shovel cultivator, spike-tooth harrow, sickle bar, lawn mower, disc seeder with fertilizer attachment, bulldozer and snow-plow blade, and a rotary weed-cutter which can be converted into a brush and log saw.

Future Progress

Today's internal combustion engine is the product of steady improvement over more than half a century, and there is no evidence that those responsible for these technological gains are satisfied with their accomplishments. Not only are spectacular new types being developed, such as the jet engine and turboprop for airplanes and

the gas turbine for possible use in road vehicles, but conventional types are being steadily improved and more widely applied. New metals and improved design are making possible still lower weights per horsepower. Compression ratios are being raised, with resultant gains in power and economy of operation. The carrying capacity of trucks and buses is being increased steadily, as is the power and capacity of heavy land-clearing and earth-moving equipment. At the other extreme, very lightweight portable engines are being adapted to a growing variety of uses. The sensational progress in the design and operation of the internal combustion engine is not at an end.

MECHANICAL METHODS

Although the mechanization of industry through the use of inanimate energy began two thousand years ago with the first water mill and advanced rapidly following the invention of the steam engine, greater progress has probably been made during the past fifty years than in all previous history. Just as the internal combustion engine has made it possible and profitable to mechanize "outdoor" activities, the electric motor has greatly speeded the mechanization of "indoor" operations.

Present trends point toward: the application of mechanical methods to more and more operations formerly done by hand; the development of new and improved machines with much greater power and speed; and the design of appliances and controls to make machines much more automatic in operation.

American management has discovered that any repetitive task that can be done by human hands can be done as well or better by a machine — and usually far more economically. With common labor getting $1.25 an hour, human energy costs more than $30 per kilowatt-hour, while electric energy is available for two or three pennies. It is a failure to appreciate how costly muscle power really is that accounts for the wonderment of foreign visitors to our shores that we "waste everything else to save human labor."

Materials Handling

The rapid spread of mechanical methods to the field of materials handling is largely a postwar development. The fork-lift truck and the

87. Press release by Philip J. Monaghan, Vice-President, General Motors Corporation, March 8, 1954.

88. *Farm Journal*, February 1953, p. 182.

conveyor belt (and various adaptations of these machines) promise to have an effect on the movement of materials within the factory or warehouse comparable to that of the motor truck on their distribution throughout the nation. Since they make horizontal transportation speedy and economical, these devices have already contributed a powerful influence to the trend from multistory city factory buildings to the single-story building located in the country.

The fork-lift truck is a compact little vehicle, powered by electric batteries, gasoline or diesel fuel and controlled by a single operator. Its flat forks can be shoved under a heavy load placed on a pallet and it can then carry the burden rapidly to the place desired and hoist and stack it to a height of twelve feet or more. Other attachments enable it to manipulate a load weighing several tons almost as easily as a human hand can handle a can of beans. Scoops can be attached to carry coal or loose materials; pitchforks to lift straw; and clamps and other devices to handle barrels and kegs, rolls of paper, bales of cotton and other odd-shaped products. These devices speed up loading and unloading, save warehouse space because loads can be stacked higher, and reduce breakage losses.

Striking economies are reported from use of fork trucks and other materials-handling equipment. By means of portable conveyors, two fork trucks and hydraulic jacks, one unit of the Radio Corporation of America reported that it could handle 97 million pounds of material in 44 per cent less space than was required for 36 million pounds before — and with a smaller number of workers.[89] While neither this nor any other single example can be considered typical, manufacturers of fork trucks and similar equipment are able to demonstrate economies of 50 per cent or more where three or more men are now handling, moving and stacking manually. Under such conditions it is claimed that an investment in mechanical equipment of $25,000 or more per employee may be justified.

More powerful versions of lift trucks — some capable of hoisting and moving 40 or 50 tons in a single load — are used in railroad yards and terminals. One gasoline-powered pusher-truck with retractable rubber tires can haul two loaded boxcars or eight empty ones.[90] One of the most versatile and powerful automotive vehicles is a four-wheel-drive tractor developed by the Frank G. Hough Company for use as a "switcher" of railroad cars. Operating on big rubber tires, it can travel on any surface and move right across rails to its next task. More powerful than rail-mounted switchers of the same weight, it can push or pull loaded freight cars at speeds up to 24 miles an hour.

Another powerful automotive vehicle, produced by Salem-Brosius, Inc., reaches into a steel furnace, removes a red-hot forging billet, carries it to hammer or press and manipulates it in almost any desired way, thus replacing much cumbersome stationary handling equipment. A "straddle truck" on high wheels can roll over a load of lumber weighing several tons, pick it up, and carry it away.

Vehicles for pushing, pulling, lifting and transporting materials in factories, terminals and warehouses achieve their great economies not merely by performing identical tasks more quickly and cheaply than men. The big savings, as in the case of earth-moving equipment, come not only from substituting cheap mechanical power for costly muscle power but from handling materials in much larger units or batches. One soft-drink distributor, for example, reduced the loading time of delivery trucks from two hours to five minutes by substituting fork trucks handling cases in batches of fifty for human workers loading one case at a time.[91]

Conveyor Belts

Even larger savings are realized when conditions warrant complete continuity of movement. The conveyor belt in transporting solid and bulk materials is beginning to play the role of the factory pipeline in the movement of gases and liquids. Small portable and adjustable conveyor belts are being used more and more for loading and moving goods in factories and at warehouses and freight terminals, for loading trucks with earth in road-building, for handling crops in harvesting, and in many other operations.

Permanently installed conveyor belts, bucket hoists and other similar equipment find wide and increasing use throughout industry, especially in mines, smelters, collieries, cement mills, chem-

89. H. L. Bock, Radio Corporation of America, Address before National Materials Handling Exposition, 1951.

90. *Ibid.*
91. *Wall Street Journal*, July 25, 1950.

ical plants, pulp and paper mills, canneries and other establishments dealing with large amounts of bulky materials. These installations, operating continuously and automatically, surpass the economies obtainable by operating with batches, however large they may be. Automatization is carried to new heights by a recently announced conveyor belt that has the built-in "electronic intelligence" to measure and continuously record the exact weight of its load, including quantities added or subtracted anywhere along the line.[92] Pneumatic tubes for carrying small parts from one floor or department to another are now operated by dials and push-button controls.

In construction, mining and industry these "rubber railroads" are providing great savings in moving enormous masses of materials. A ten-mile-long conveyor belt installed several years ago by Goodyear, for example, supplied the cement, sand and other materials for construction of Shasta Dam at the rate of 8,500 tons an hour and at a small fraction of the cost of moving the same tonnage by truck. Another conveyor belt in an open-pit iron mine in Minnesota carries 900 tons of ore an hour up a 1,100-foot slope. It is estimated that a thousand or more such heavy conveyor belts are now in use in coal mines alone.[93] Although conveyor belts were first installed in mines in the late 1920s, it is estimated that by 1949 there were more than a thousand miles of underground belts in operation.

While legal obstacles still stand in the way of extensive development of cross-country conveyor belts, one of the most ambitious ideas contemplates a rubber railroad stretching from Lake Erie to the steel centers of southern Ohio to carry coal in one direction and ore and limestone in the other. In fact, the world's first passenger conveyor belt was recently installed in a tunnel connecting two railroad stations in Jersey City. Proposals have also been made to replace the shuttle trains between Times Square and Grand Central Station with conveyor belts — perhaps on the assumption that any change would be for the better.

Mining Methods

Mining machines and methods have made rapid progress since the end of the war. Open-pit mining of coal, which had been expanding steadily for several years before World War II, has been greatly stimulated since its end, as already pointed out, by the development of much more powerful dump-trucks, dragline excavators and power shovels.

Recent changes in underground mining methods and equipment have been even more striking. At the end of World War II the "continuous miner" was still only an idea; by the end of 1950 a dozen companies were turning out these machines and 152 continuous miners were operating in coal mines as well as in a number of potash and other mines. In 1950 about 4 million tons of coal were produced by continuous miners; by 1952 the tonnage had risen to 8.2 million, with every prospect of further rapid rise in the years ahead.

These rugged electrically driven machines chew into the mine face, rip out the coal, and load it continuously, eliminating the need for drilling and blasting. They triple the productivity of the miner at the face, cut costs up to 50 per cent, and work so fast that they have created a problem of getting the coal out of the mine with equal speed. Automatic loading machines have been greatly improved since the end of the war, and this helps explain why four out of every five tons of coal mined underground are now loaded by machine, compared with one out of three before World War II.[94]

Traditional types of mining machinery such as cutters, drills, shuttle cars and dump-trucks, as well as equipment for preparing, cleaning and sizing coal, have also been improved. All of this brings coal mining and other types of underground mining a long distance from the days of the pick and shovel and mule and mine-car.

The use of mechanical laborsavers in underground mining is being greatly facilitated by the new "pin-up method" of supporting mine roofs. Steel rods driven every few feet at angles into the roof eliminate the need for timber supports, permit better ventilation, and provide clear space for operating new types of mining equipment. The Bureau of Mines expects wide and rapid extension of roof bolting in all types of underground mining during the next few years.

A new method for piercing hard rock formations first applied on taconite deposits in upper

---

92. "Smart Conveyor Belt Finds Out Just How Big a Load It Carries," *Wall Street Journal*, November 8, 1952.
93. *Wall Street Journal*, July 25, 1952.

94. *Minerals Yearbook, 1952*, and *Weekly Coal Report*, No. 1902, February 26, 1954, U.S. Bureau of Mines.

Minnesota has been developed by Union Carbide and Carbon engineers. This jet-piercing "drill" is a sort of enormous blowtorch burning petroleum fuel and oxygen and developing a heat of 4,300° F. It will accomplish in a day what the metal churn drill does in a week, burning through and disintegrating the hardest rock at a speed of 60 feet an hour.[95] Metals are also extracted from their ores today far more rapidly and efficiently than with old-time washer, rocker and sieve methods. Among newer methods are the Dorr continuous flotation process, Humphrey spirals, the Mobil-Mill separator and, more recently, hydro-oxygen metallurgy [96] and heat-chemical metallurgy.[97]

In prospecting for minerals the geologist, geophysicist and chemist, with seismographs, gravity meters, magnetometers and other devices, have displaced the wandering prospector with his pick and shovel. More scientific methods of oil well exploration have reduced the proportion of dry holes in wildcat drilling from 24 out of 25 to 7 out of 8.[98]

Before the end of World War II the electronic magnetometer was in use only on the ground. Now it is towed by survey planes at the end of an electric cable which continuously conveys to recording instruments in the plane the magnetic intensity of underground rocks and ore. The "magnetic eye" thereby shows up pools of oil and gas, as well as iron, copper, lead, zinc, etc. Developed by the Gulf Oil Company, the airborne magnetometer has discovered a number of important mineral deposits, and at a cost of a few cents a mile compared with several dollars for ground prospecting.[99]

Processing Foodstuffs

The processing of foodstuffs provides endless examples of the substitution of mechanical for manual methods. Canneries have become almost completely automatic. Crops move along conveyor belts while they are washed, graded and sterilized. They are then packed into cans, which are sealed and carried through a continuous cooker. After this they go through a cooling bath and are carried in a steady stream through labeling machines and into cases in the warehouse, ready for shipment.

Special machines are capable of even more complicated operations. Robert Froman gave the following examples in an article in *Collier's:*

> . . . a machine . . . grasps an ear of corn, cuts the butt end slickly off and brushes off the silk in a final flourish. After a thorough washing, the ear races through another machine where whirling knives separate the kernels from the cob at exactly the right depth—all at the rate of a few seconds per cob. . . . [Another] machine . . . removes the stems from gooseberries. The berries fall through a series of light chains which revolve like skipping ropes and neatly pull loose the stems without bruising the fruit.[100]

Cocktail olives can be pitted and stuffed automatically at a rate of three a second. Still another automatic machine — designed to make life easy for the drinker of Manhattans — removes the stones from cocktail cherries but leaves the stems in, ready for use. A mechanical dough-mixer recently introduced shapes, fills and decorates Danish pastries as well — and saves half the manpower required with existing equipment. Even the intricacies of "pretzel tying" have been solved by a machine produced by the American Machine & Foundry Company which mechanically ties the knot in the same way human hands did in the past.

Butter for the first time is being made without churning. An automatic butter-maker turns it out in one continuous step from cream to wrapped one-pound packages at a rate of 2,000 pounds an hour.[101]

Technology is revolutionizing the catch-as-catch-can fishing industry. The unhappy whale is now spotted from a helicopter flown from the whaling vessel — and harpooned with an electric charge. Deepwater schools of fish are detected by the electronic Fathometer, ordinarily used by navigators to measure the depth of water under their vessels.

Diesel-powered trawlers now come back to port with their catch frozen and, in some cases,

95. D. H. Fleming and J. J. Calaman, "Production Jet-Piercing of Blastholes in Magnetic Taconite," *Mining Engineering*, American Institute of Mining Engineering, July 1951.

96. Described in address by R. W. Diamond and B. P. Sutherland, of the Consolidated Mining & Smelting Co. of Canada, Ltd., at Centennial of Engineering, Chicago, September 1952.

97. Described in *Esso Oilways*, September 1952; also *Barron's*, June 9, 1952.

98. "Synergism Between Engineering and Petroleum," address by Robert E. Wilson, Centennial of Engineering, Chicago, September 1952.

99. *Engineering & Mining Journal*, August 1951

100. "We Can and the Reds Can Not," *Collier's*, November 15, 1952.

101. *Industrial Bulletin*, Arthur D. Little, Inc., April 1950.

filleted, ready for shipment. Shore fish canneries are highly mechanized, and automatic filleting machines have been perfected for extracting bones from different species.

On Long Island Sound a diesel vessel with a seven-man crew sucks up oysters through a rubber hose at the rate of 1,000 bushels an hour.[102] The individual oysterman patiently pulled in a rowboat-load a day.

These examples, trivial in themselves, illustrate what is going on in nearly all fields of industrial activity not already fully mechanized. Even the most difficult and intricate manual operations are now surrendering to the machine. This is being accomplished only rarely by Rube Goldberg contraptions that duplicate the movements of human hands and arms, but rather through redesign of products and adaptation of operations to the requirements of the machine. There is no longer the technical question of whether an operation can be mechanized, but only the economic question of whether and how quickly mechanization will pay for itself.

MACHINE POWER AND SPEED

While new machines are being developed and machine methods applied in new ways, the speed, power and capacity of traditional equipment are being steadily increased. These changes have been spectacular in the automotive field, as pointed out above, conspicuously in the strength and carrying capacity of road and rail vehicles, in the power of heavy equipment used in clearing land and construction, and in the size and speed of aircraft.

Less visible to the layman are the constant improvements in machinery and mechanical methods behind factory walls, which are making it possible to get more work done in less time and at lower costs than formerly. One of the most significant and pervasive improvements has been the increased cutting speed of machine tools.

"High speed" tools of tungsten alloy made their appearance around the turn of the century. Capable of removing metal at cutting speeds of 60 to 100 feet a minute, depending on the type of metal and depth of cut, they were a great advance over carbon steel cutting tools, which could not operate at red heat. About thirty years later the use of tungsten carbide — a cemented

alloy made of powdered carbon, tungsten and cobalt — raised cutting speeds to between 200 and 800 feet a minute on the same types of metals. These carbide tools, which can operate at white heat without deteriorating, together with heavier equipment, now make it possible to turn out work two or three times faster than with typical prewar models. This is only one of many advances in the metalworking industries.

Faster Operation

All kinds of continuous industrial processes have been speeded up since prewar years. At the Irwin plant of U.S. Steel the electrolytic tinning line operated at 600 feet a minute; when the Fairless plant was opened fifteen years later, in December 1952, the speed was 1,200 feet a minute. A new strip mill of National Steel, said to be the fastest in operation, rolls thin-gauge strip steel at the rate of a mile a minute, producing enough for 5 million cans in an 8-hour day. A still newer design calls for a speed of 10,000 feet a minute — or 100 miles of steel sheet 14 feet wide every hour — with only eight men operating the plant from a control room three stories above the automatic machines. Yet it was little more than a quarter of a century ago that the first continuous strip mills began to displace the slow-moving hand mills.

Methods employing high-frequency current have greatly speeded up the rate at which large spur gears can be hardened.[103]

New processes make it possible to freeze fruits and ice cream in minutes rather than hours, to cut the time of cooking canned creamed corn from 70 minutes to 17, to roast coffee in a few minutes instead of more than an hour. A new machine for checking the weight of canned vegetables increases the speed of operation from 250 cans a minute to 450.[104]

The speed of conveyor belts before World War II seldom exceeded 300 feet a minute. In many cases speeds have since doubled, and some belts now move at more than 1,000 feet a minute.

All kinds of packaging machinery also operate much faster than before World War II. One machine recently introduced wraps 65 loaves of bread a minute, compared with a limit of 45 to

---

102. "Ever Catch Oysters with a Vacuum Cleaner?", *Steel Horizons*, Winter 1950–1951.

103. *Metal Progress*, July 1943, p. 78.
104. Food Machinery and Chemical Corporation, *Wall Street Journal*, November 15, 1950.

48 loaves a few years ago.[105] On display at the first postwar Packaging Exposition were a cigarette-wrapping machine handling 400 packs a minute compared with 200; a machine that automatically counts and bottles pills and other small items at the rate of 120 bottles of 25 items a minute; a machine to wrap irregularly shaped products such as chickens and vegetables; and a host of other packaging time-savers. All this is a far cry from the practices at the turn of the century, when "packaging" of most products was done for the consumer at the retail counter. Today virtually all foods and drugs, as well as many other products, ranging from nylon stockings to hardware, come from the factory hermetically sealed in bottles or cans or securely wrapped in cellophane or other plastics.

Paper and Printing Machines

The operating speeds, and therefore the capacities, of paper-making and printing machines have also been greatly increased. In the 1920s the fastest machine for manufacturing newsprint could turn out 900 feet a minute; today the best machines run twice as fast and some attain a speed of 2,500 feet a minute. Before World War II the fastest tissue machines operated at 1,800 feet a minute, while postwar speeds are up to 2,800 feet a minute.

Magazine-printing speeds have doubled and trebled. Postwar photogravure presses make 20,000 cylinder revolutions a minute, compared with 9,000 in the 1930s. Color-offset presses turned over at 4,500 revolutions a minute then, and are capable of 8,000 revolutions today. The best newspaper presses now produce 1,200 or more standard newspapers a minute, which is faster than bullets come out of a Browning machine gun and twice the best speed of such presses in the late 1930s. These gains have come not from any single spectacular development but from steady improvement in quality of paper and methods of operation as well as in the machines themselves.

Thanks largely to electronics, printing and the transmission of graphic material have undergone greater technical changes since World War II began than in all the years since the first linotype and the first telegraph. All phases — transmission, composition and actual printing — are being revolutionized. Facsimile transmission of photographs and drawings by wire and radio came into use in the 1930s. The teletype machine spelling out words over telephone or telegraph wires is taking the place of the old hand dash-dot system. Now the teletype-setter is becoming commonplace. With this device type can be set on a linotype machine in a distant printing plant by remote control — and at twice the speed of manual operation.

But the teletype's transmission of 300 words a minute is already a horse-and-buggy speed compared with the latest achievements. Western Union's High Speed Fax, using microwave radio beams, transmits over any distance any written, pictured or printed matter at the rate of 3,000 words of newsprint a minute.[106] The "Flying Typewriter," an electronic printer produced by the Potter Instrument Company for use with punchcard sorting systems and electronic automatic computers, prints 24,000 characters a minute, or five lines of type a second.[107] A few months after this machine was introduced, another electronic device, the Synchroprinter, was announced as capable of printing 36,000 characters a minute.[108] Fastest of all is Ultrafax, a sensational recent development of the Radio Corporation of America which unifies in one process television, radio facsimile relaying and high-speed motion-picture photography.[109] At its first official demonstration at the Library of Congress, every page of the novel *Gone With the Wind* was transmitted *and reproduced* in less than three minutes — a rate of a million words a minute. The day may be near when "radio mail" moving across the continent at the speed of light will make even the fastest airmail — which is still less than the speed of sound — seem hopelessly slow.

Printing and engraving developments are keeping pace with those in transmission. The time-consuming processing of zinc and copper photoengraving plates is rapidly being replaced by electronic processing of inexpensive plastic plates with such automatic devices as the Scan-a-Graver made by Fairchild Camera and Instrument Corporation. Entirely new printing techniques are

105. Letter from E. F. Mertis, American Machine and Foundry Company, January 27, 1954.

106. Letter from George P. Oslin, Western Union Telegraph Company, April 28, 1954.

107. "High-Speed Printer for Computers and Communications," by John J. Wild, *Electronics,* May 1952.

108. *Wall Street Journal,* June 19, 1952.

109. *Ultrafax,* pamphlet published by Radio Corporation of America.

being brought close to general application. The Battelle Memorial Institute has developed Xeroprinting, an electrostatic method of reproducing words and pictures at high speed from photographed material. The method, which works equally well on paper, wood, glass or metals, uses a dry iron powder and plastic mixture instead of wet ink, and requires no rollers or presses and no chemical solutions. General Electric has developed a method of high-speed impression printing called Ferromagnetography, capable of printing 6,000 figures a minute.[110]

Easily the most revolutionary device ready for immediate use is the Photon, a "typeless typesetter" developed by the Graphic Arts Research Foundation of Cambridge, Massachusetts, and being produced by the Lithomat Corporation. The Photon looks like a standard electric typewriter fitted into a streamlined cabinet about the size of an office desk. Glass discs are inserted into the machine for the reproduction of various type faces. Each disc bears sixteen type alphabets in a dozen type sizes, or a total of 192 different alphabets of type and over 17,000 characters. All this is controlled and actuated by the typewriter keyboard with 46 keys. As type characters are selected, they are recorded on photographic film, rather than cast in metal, and from this film an ordinary letterpress or lithographic plate is processed. Each one-and-a-half-pound disc replaces two *tons* of mats, which would cost $25,000 in conventional typesetting. The Photon, moreover, completely eliminates the need for metal type and for the bulky equipment now used in setting and casting type. This technological triumph thus not only saves time and labor, but also materials, power and capital investment.[111]

AUTOMATION AND ELECTRONICS

Along with greater mechanization and the development of faster and more powerful machines has come a rapidly widening use of automatic controls in all kinds of industrial operations. Although a few simple self-regulating control systems employing the "feed-back principle" actually antedate the primitive fly-ball governor invented by James Watt in 1788, the develop-

ment of electronics during the past decade is ushering in a new and revolutionary era of "automation." Self-correcting feed-back controls are no longer limited to a few situations but can now be applied throughout industry.

Development of the passenger elevator provides an interesting example of increased speed and flexibility made possible by greater automation. Early elevators crept upward at a stately 40 feet a minute. This soon increased to 200 feet a minute and thereafter speeds increased so rapidly that shortly after the turn of the century city regulations imposed a "speed limit" of 700 feet a minute because the problem of smooth control had not been solved. The passenger in the early elevator was entirely at the mercy of the operator, as he is in a taxicab today.

With the adoption of a variety of automatic controls to avoid jerky starting and stopping and to provide smooth acceleration, however, speeds increased to 1,000 feet a minute before World War II and to 1,400 feet or more today. Electronic controls have just recently made possible for the first time a fully automatic office building elevator flexibly adjusted to rush-hour needs. Electronic devices replace the human operator in avoiding overloading and starting the car ahead of schedule when fully loaded during the rush hour, in returning the car promptly to pick up a new load when the last passenger has been discharged, and even in gently nudging a dilatory passenger out of the car. This is only one illustration of how the application of electronics is stimulating the widespread adoption of automatic controls throughout industry. The new elevators not only pay for themselves in operating economies, but are fully as speedy and serviceable as conventional ones, if not more so.

And it is typical rather than unusual for the inanimate controls not only to do what the human operator does, but to do it better. The household thermostat is a familiar illustration of man's capacity to devise equipment far excelling his own observational powers, just as he has developed machines that far surpass his physical powers. Economy is only one, and often the least important, of the advantages of automatic controls. In most cases such controls are essential to produce goods of uniformly high quality which must "be processed under conditions of speed, temperature, pressure and chemical exchange which make human control impossible, or at least impracticable, on an extensive scale.

---

110. "Ferromagnetography — High-Speed Printing with Shaped Magnetic Fields," *General Electric Review,* July 1952, p. 21.

111. *The Higonnet-Moyroud or Photon Photographic Type-Composing Machine,* pamphlet published by Graphic Arts Research Foundation, Cambridge, Massachusetts.

... beyond certain limits the discrimination and control of qualitative differences elude human capacity." [112]

Push-Button Operation

A good example of the superiority of inanimate controls is the modern petroleum refinery, which could not function at all if these controls had to be replaced by human operators. As graphically described by Eugene Ayres:

It is a bewildering kind of factory, with metallic towers rising 20 stories high, hundreds of miles of pipe, and only an occasional modest building. A few lonely men wander about the spectral monster doing supervisory or maintenance tasks here and there. The plant is almost noiseless, all but devoid of visible moving parts. Despite its apparent inertness, however, the plant is throbbing with internal heat and motion. Every day a quarter of a million barrels of oil flow unobtrusively into its maw, and about as many flow out in the form of dozens of finished petroleum products — all profoundly and specifically altered by processing. Forty tons of catalyst are being circulated every minute of the day and night. Great volumes of chemicals are being consumed in processing, and greater volumes of chemical intermediates are being manufactured. Scores of unit processes are interlocked, with a meticulous balance of energy distribution.

The nerve center of this mechanical organism is the control room with its control panel. Here are ensconced the human operators . . . [who] watch, . . . sometimes help or correct the instruments. . . . Barring emergencies, they take over completely only when the plant is starting up or shutting down— normally only about once a year in a catalytic cracking plant.[113]

In spite of the great improvements in quality of products and the economies in design and in consumption of raw materials already made possible by automatic controls, further rapid progress can be expected. The final triumph, which would make the refinery — and probably many other continuous-process chemical plants — an almost fully "automatic factory" will come with the perfection of end-point control. This will employ such delicate methods as infrared spectroscopy, mass spectrometry and X-ray photometry to analyze the flow of final products, "compute what changes must be made in the process conditions, and signal instructions back to appropriate points." [114] With such a feed-back control system, deviation from normal operations or quality would be detected immediately and corrected automatically.

Even today certain continuous-flow manufacturing industries, small hydroelectric power stations, small-town telephone exchanges, pipelines and long-distance conveyor belts have virtually reached the goal of complete automatism. Pipelines with their pumping stations can be operated by remote control through a dial-equipped teletype system run by technicians at a switchboard hundreds of miles distant. The Girdler Corporation describes its "Hygirtol" plant built for Wilson & Company and used to produce high-purity hydrogen:

Instruments control the operations and the plant is practically automatic. One man keeps this sizable plant in operation, furnishing hydrogen at any desired rate. For fuel and process materials, Hygirtol plants use natural gas, propane or butane.[115]

Generally speaking the so-called processing industries, such as chemicals, paints, plastics, rubber and paper, are best adapted to instrumentation and automatic controls. Automation of processes involving the continuous flow of liquids, gases or electric energy presents much simpler problems than automatic control in such industries as steel, where the product is turned out in batches, or in the cutting and machining of solid metals, or in radios or automobiles, where discrete solid parts are first produced and then assembled into the final product. Highly automatic packaging and bottling procedures have been developed for solid products of uniform dimensions, it is true, and the textile industry has also achieved almost complete automation of separate phases of operations, such as spinning and weaving. Single-purpose automatic machine tools have long been used in the metalworking industry for the mass production of simple standardized parts. Such highly specialized tools, however, lack flexibility and are uneconomical except in machining very large quantities of identical units.

Today, thanks to the development of electronic controls capable of issuing "instructions" to a more versatile general-purpose machine tool, it is possible to automatize the production of relatively small quantities of a variety of products. William Pease has described a milling machine in operation at the Massachusetts Institute

112. Ernest Nagel, "Automatic Control," *Scientific American*, September 1952, p. 44.

113. Eugene Ayres, "An Automatic Chemical Plant," *Scientific American*, September 1952, pp. 85–86.

114. *Ibid.*, p. 95.

115. Advertisement of the Girdler Corporation in *Business Week*, April 7, 1951.

of Technology "that converts information on punched tape into the contours of a finished part." [116] Through a complex series of electrical and electronic devices the initial instructions recorded on the tape activate servo-mechanisms that control the operation of the tool. A feedback mechanism assures accurate execution of the instructions.

The successful performance of this model attests the practicability of "versatile machine tools which will perform any kind of work without the guidance of a human hand. The possible economic effects of such machines, on many industries besides metal-cutting, are beyond prediction. Automatized general-purpose machine tools, combined with high-production special-purpose tools, would make possible the automatic metals-fabricating factory. Nor are we restricted to metals. With digital machines in control we can conceive of factories which will process, assemble and finish any article of manufacture." [117]

The Automatic Factory

Thus all of the elements of the automatic factory are present today. Along with the controls described above, which make short machine runs feasible, automatic and flexible handling of materials and loading of machines is made possible by electronically controlled "transfer machines." These devices transport the semifinished part from one machine and automatically load it into the next one, thus integrating and connecting many separate operations. By tying together a series of separate operations, these transfer machines speed up the entire process, with resultant increased output and lower costs.

. . . An example is the 32-station machine in use by one manufacturer. It performs 198 fully automatic operations while machining all the holes in the top and both cylinder head faces of a V-8 engine block. It loads raw blocks, machines them, rolls them into position, automatically gages the holes and sends them on to the next phase of manufacture.[118]

The Rockford Ordnance Plant, described by John Diebold,[119] which manufactures 155–mm.

steel shell casings from six-inch steel bars, comes close to being completely automatic. After the long bars are cut into one-foot blocks, all subsequent operations, including numerous transfers and repeated loading and unloading of the blocks, heating them to 2,000° F., de-scaling, forging, cooling, rough machining and final drilling and threading, are handled by machines requiring a minimum of human attention. Here again the devices for loading and unloading the semifinished parts and for automatically transferring them from machine to machine are the key to the automation of the entire series of operations, each one of which has long been done automatically.

The even more difficult task of automatizing an assembly operation will soon be possible; several of the automobile companies are already experimenting with pilot plants for completely automatic subassembly,[120] and automatic assembly of automobile frames has long been a reality at the plant of the A. O. Smith Company.

One of the most significant developments has resulted from joint efforts of the Navy and the Bureau of Standards. Known as "Project Tinkertoy," it is a completely automatic factory for the production of electronic modules consisting of a vacuum tube with resistors and capacitators attached. Groups of these modules can then be assembled to make various types of finished electronic devices. Radically new procedures and designs were developed, involving the use of ceramic wafers stencilled with silver to provide electric conductance in place of all the coils and wiring and soldering in the conventional radio set. Groups of these wafers properly assembled provide a wide variety of circuits to be used in all kinds of electronic products, military and civilian. The entire operation from raw material to the final assembled module, including rigorous inspection at every stage of the process, is automatic.[121] But even this completely automatic factory is not able to operate without workers. Trouble shooters are needed when something goes wrong, as well as maintenance workers to keep equipment in operating condition. Automatic equipment will always require a great deal of human attention to ensure its proper functioning and for its repair and replacement.

116. William Pease, "An Automatic Machine Tool," *Scientific American*, September 1952, p. 101.

117. *Ibid.*, pp. 114–115.

118. "Electronic Marvels Speed Automotive Progress," *Automobile Facts*, Automobile Manufacturers Association, March 1953, p. 6.

119. John Diebold, *Automation: The Advent of the Automatic Factory*, Van Nostrand, New York, 1952, pp. 74–80.

120. John Kord Logeman, "If Robots Run the Works," *Nation's Business*, March 1951.

121. Waldemar Kaempffert, "A New Tinkertoy Speeds Production," *New York Times*, September 20, 1953.

Increasing numbers of inspection, repair and maintenance workers will be required as automatic equipment becomes more complex and its use more widespread.

But automation will help to relieve the worker of monotony and mental boredom just as mechanization relieved him of heavy work and physical fatigue. Automatic instruments and controls, like power-driven machinery, are laborsaving devices — the first for the brain, the second for the muscles. Electronics is the new tool which enables us to do things "electrically that require the use of the human senses, such as hearing, seeing, speaking and smelling, and also need a muscular response but not the thinking part of the brain." [122]

And these mental labor savers not only do what the human being does, but like the muscle labor savers, do it more rapidly, more accurately and more dependably. Devices that are more perceptive and reliable than our own senses are taking over the monotonous routine jobs of industry and freeing the human workers for creative intellectual effort.

Electronic Computers

Electronic digital computers are key elements in modern automatic control systems, but they have a far broader application. First developed at the end of World War II, these "electronic brains," though of course not able to think creatively, are indeed capable of something closely resembling the reasoning process.[123] When properly "instructed" they can solve complex and infinitely tedious problems with incredible speed. Information and instructions are fed into one end of the computer on punched cards or tape; solutions come out the other end on magnetic tape or recorded on cards or a roll of paper. Thus far these machines are extremely bulky and costly and have been used chiefly for engineering, military and scientific computations that would otherwise be enormously time-consuming or even impossible of accomplishment.

These computers are many thousands of times more efficient than the human brain in perform-

ing routine arithmetic operations; in minutes and hours they solve problems that would require months or years with ordinary methods. In two weeks, during which it actually operated only two hours, ENIAC — the primitive prototype of today's electronic computers, which was built in 1945 — obtained the solution to a problem that would have required a hundred years of work by a trained human computer.[124]

Computation speeds have increased greatly in later models. Multiplying 6,834,872 by 1,488,639 takes a man five minutes or more using pencil and paper, but an electronic computer completed at the University of Toronto in 1952 could multiply 500 pairs of such numbers in two seconds. This seems like fast work, but only a year later the Argonne Laboratory of the Atomic Energy Commission completed a new model, the Oracle, able to multiply 683,487,243,834 by 438,342,784,-386 about 2,000 times in one second. A mathematical problem which would take two mathematicians working with ordinary electric calculating machines five or six years to complete can be done by this new machine in half an hour or less.[125]

These complex machines are costly to build, but they result in great economies. A computer designed by RCA for the Navy, for example, made more than two thousand "test runs" of proposed guided missiles for the Navy at an estimated saving of more than $250 million.[126] Such complicated engineering tasks as developing a gear design table required up to four years' work on the part of a staff of mathematicians; electronic computers do the job in two hundred hours, with substantial savings in cost.[127]

Experience gained in designing these large-scale "scientific" computers has led to the development of simpler, less expensive and much more compact machines for business and industrial use. These machines are suitable for the mass processing and analysis of all kinds of operating and accounting data: sales, cost, price and production figures; material and inventory control; quality control; accounting of receivables and payables; handling of personnel and

---

122. Address by W. C. White of the General Electric Company before the Institute of Radio Engineers, New York City, February 1, 1950.

123. Sufficient reasoning capacity "to play a fairly strong game of chess," according to Claude E. Shannon. See his article, "A Chess-Playing Machine," in *Scientific American*, February 1950.

124. "Practical Electronics," article in *Systems for Modern Management Magazine*, Remington Rand, Inc., May 1950.

125. *Wall Street Journal*, August 4, 1953, p. 4.

126. David Sarnoff, "This Amazing Electron," *Challenge Magazine*, February 1953.

127. "Electronic Marvels Speed Automotive Progress," *loc. cit.*

financial records, etc. Electronic computers are already displacing mechanical computation methods and are beginning to revolutionize the clerical operations of business and government — just as power-driven machines have taken over the manual tasks of industry.

One such machine, with a single operator, in a few days computes records for a firm's retirement system that would otherwise take four people three months to do. Another electronic calculator used by an insurance company takes information about individual policyholders, computes premiums due and types out premium statements at the rate of a hundred a minute. Consolidated Edison of New York uses three "electronic calculating punches" to perform all the arithmetic operations involved in preparing bills for 1,800,000 customers.[128] Police departments of Los Angeles and several other cities use an electronic machine to track down criminal suspects from their records of the characteristics of crimes committed.[129] American Airlines' "magnetronic reservisor" automatically records, for ten days in advance, reservations and cancellations and keeps a running inventory of space on most of the flights originating on the eastern seaboard; in addition it keeps track of space on all flights regardless of origin.[130] One electronic computer, with proper "instructions," can handle all accounting of receivables, payables, purchases and stock controls for a large department store. These are but a few illustrations of the wide application of electronic computers in industry and commerce.[131] The day is probably near when no large firm with large masses of operating data to process can afford to be without one.

In addition to the digital computers, analogue machines are used not only to guide the servomechanisms which control actual operations, as in the automatic machine tool discussed above, but also for the construction of models and for pretesting industrial processes and machines. For instance, differential analyzers are used in the automotive industry to test brake and engine

efficiency, riding qualities and other characteristics of new designs of cars long before the experimental models have been built.[132] In the same way, the effects of hypothetical wave and wind conditions on the hulls of hypothetical ships and of air resistance on airplane wings can be ascertained by electronic analyzers in advance of the construction of actual models. Thus "an analogue of a water pipe network can be built by plugging together the correct electrical units, and the effect of varying operating conditions and loads studied easily, quickly, and with little cost or danger." [133]

TV and Other Electronic Devices

These fabulous "thinking machines" are perhaps the most intriguing of electronic devices, but it is not certain that they are the most significant application of the science of electronics, which promises to penetrate into almost every phase of economic activity.

Until World War II the word "electronics" was hardly to be found in the dictionary, although as early as the turn of the century, physicists had begun to accept the existence of the electron and the concept of the electrical constitution of matter, and Marconi's wireless was in operation even earlier. With the development of the triode tube by De Forest in 1906, the electronic era was on its way, but until 1940, radio, wireless communication, X-rays, fluorescent lamps and the "electric eye" for opening doors and automatic counting were about the only important developments.

The speed-up of production during the defense and war periods led to the use of large numbers of induction and dielectric heating machines for setting plastics and for heating and sealing with high-frequency electronics, as well as electronic tubes for controlling the electric current used in electroplating and in producing aluminum, magnesium, chlorine and other materials. X-ray apparatus became more widely used for industrial inspection purposes. Combat needs also led to the extensive development of new electronic detection and control devices, of which radar in its various applications was the most important.

Since the end of World War II, however,

128. Letter from K. F. Bellows, Consolidated Edison Company of New York, April 29, 1954.

129. Keith Monroe, "The Detective Who Never Sleeps," *Saturday Evening Post*, October 10, 1953.

130. Letter from Charles E. Amman, American Airlines, April 22, 1954.

131. "Electronic Brains: Calculating Machines Help Lighten Industry's Record-Keeping Chores," *Wall Street Journal*, July 29, 1953, p. 1.

132. "Electronic Marvels Speed Automotive Progress," p. 6.

133. Diebold, *op. cit.*, p. 25.

there has been a veritable flood of new military and civilian developments and applications which have made electronics the most rapidly growing American industry, with some $4 billion production in 1952, or twenty times the 1940 output.[134] Television, like prosperity, was always "just around the corner" during the 1930s, but it finally arrived after the war and today is the most important civilian electronic product. The number of sets in use jumped from less than 17,000 at the end of 1946 to 10 million at the end of 1951, and was well over 30 million by the middle of 1954. The end of the decade may well see as many sets in use as there are households, with the entire population a potential audience.[135]

Utilities, steel mills and other industries are already applying wired television to observe dangerous or distant operations. TV cameras connected to a screen at the control tower are used in railroading to note freight car numbers, inspect passing cars for mechanical defects, watch for hotboxes, etc. Department stores are beginning to place television screens on sales floors to display and advertise goods. Such uses promise to increase rapidly, as does the use of television in training and education, for example, in enabling medical students to get a close-up view of surgical operations. Another "medical use" of the television camera is in conjunction with a microscope in observing at low light levels microbes which would be destroyed by intense light.[136] And, of course, the electron microscope, capable of magnifying to more than 300,000 diameters, has made it possible to observe hitherto invisible viruses, bacteria and blood corpuscles. Industrial X-ray machines and other electronic inspection devices are available for checking the cleanliness and purity of drugs and foods, and for a multitude of sensitive inspection and measuring operations throughout industry. This kind of apparatus, capable of such diverse tasks as detecting tiny flaws buried deep in metal slabs or accurately gauging the thickness of cellophane, is being used more and more extensively.

One important development with vast future possibilities for electronics was the discovery in 1948 by Bell Telephone scientists that a tiny particle of the "semimetal" germanium is capable of performing the functions of most vacuum tubes. This speck of metal with three tiny "cat's whiskers" terminals not only has an advantage in size over vacuum tubes but is also extremely rugged and long-lived, does not heat up in use and is not subject to warm-up delay, and operates with high efficiency on minute amounts of electric current.

Already the transistor is finding uses in dial telephone apparatus, in the manufacture of better and much smaller hearing aids and in the miniaturization of much delicate electronic equipment. One engineer predicts for the near future "a really personal radio of hearing-aid size running indefinitely on one set of batteries." [137] As evidence of the practical possibilities of the transistor, technologists of the Radio Corporation of America, in November 1952, exhibited experimental portable television receivers, loudspeaker systems, miniature radio transmitters, an automobile radio (minus the high-voltage power supply usually needed) operating directly off a six-volt auto battery, a transformerless power amplifier, and automatic computer components — all using transistors instead of vacuum tubes.

Among a multitude of such devices developed since the war are spectroscopes using microwaves for chemical analysis of gases and liquids; magnetometers for use in aerial prospecting for oil and mineral deposits; the use of cathode rays in cold sterilization of blood plasma, foods and drugs, and in converting liquid materials into solid plastics; an electronic instrument that can play music beyond the capacity of conventional instruments; techniques employing radar in taking high-speed X-ray motion pictures; an electronic leak detector for detecting leakages of extremely small quantities of chlorine, bromine and other gases; extremely sensitive instruments for measuring camera shutter speeds, projectile velocities, power line frequencies, nuclear radiation, as well as weight, pressure, temperature and acceleration, and for detecting defects and irregularities in materials, controlling motor speeds and chemical operations and counting and measuring products; an electronic clock with much greater accuracy; a wide variety of dictating machines, wire and tape recorders and other sound recording and reproduction devices; the use of radar in making contour maps at a rate of 1,000 square miles per flying hour; an arrangement of phototubes and light filters to determine the ex-

134. *U.S. News and World Report,* June 27, 1952.
135. Based in part on article by Sarnoff, *op. cit.*
136. *Ibid.*

137. I. J. Karr, Manager, Electronics Division, General Electric Company, in *Scientific American,* July 1952.

act ripeness of tomatoes; a shore-based radio system for guiding ships into harbors in dense fog and a multitude of sensitive aids to air and water navigation; an "electronic selector" which automatically sifts through data and selects needed data; a "teleplotter" for automatically charting data; a device for measuring the water content of snow on mountain slopes and reporting by radio to a central station; pasteurization of cheese by radio waves; use of high-frequency radio waves to improve germination of carrot, beet, onion and tomato seeds; an infrared telescope for seeing "invisible" objects in the dark; and a device for translating printed words into spoken words for the benefit of the blind.[138]

Telephone experts are already hinting that the subscriber may soon be able to get a number directly, without dialing and without human intervention, merely by asking for it. More remarkable still is the rumor of a "voice typewriter," which would translate speech directly into typescript.[139] It is hard to believe, however, that even electronics would be capable of mastering the inconsistencies of English spelling and pronunciation.

Ultrasonics

High-frequency sound waves have also been put to industrial use for a variety of purposes since World War II. Sonar, indeed, preceded radar in airplane detection during the war, while depth-sounding devices have long been used in water navigation. More recently Minneapolis-Honeywell has demonstrated the Sea Scanar, which employs sound waves to "look around" in all directions under water and detect schools of fish or other objects.[140]

Industrial uses of ultrasonics include a sound device for detecting flaws in solid steel, equipment for speedy degreasing and cleaning of metals and for clearing the air by "lumping" dust and smoke particles, and a sound generator using high frequencies to mix and homogenize paints, chemicals, medicinals and food preparations. Oil and water can be mixed so thoroughly that they will not separate for years, thus contradicting the wisdom of the ages. At the other

extreme low-frequency sound waves are being used in an infrasonic oil well pump, which increases yields by vibrating more oil out of the sand and rock strata in which it lodges.[141] (And between high and low frequencies "normal" sound waves created by a dynamite explosion are used in reflection-seismographic prospecting to locate oil-bearing strata.)[142]

But these are only a few of the potential uses of this strange new form of energy. Milk can be homogenized by ultrasonic waves without raising the temperature, fruit and vegetable juices can be sterilized in the can without changing their taste or quality, dissolved gases can be driven out of liquids, solid substances can be shattered or heated hot enough to decompose or burn, and germination and growth of seeds and plants can be speeded up.[143]

Doctors are using an ultrasonic echoing device to locate gallstones, shell fragments and other foreign objects in the human body and have even used it to shatter gallstones in dogs and rabbits. Although still a long way from commercial development, engineers of Bell Telephone Laboratories have patented an echo-sounding instrument to enable the blind to detect obstructions in their path,[144] an adaptation of the method which bats are believed to have used since time immemorial to avoid collisions when flying in the dark.

Among the promising applications of sound waves is their use in cleaning fabrics. They are effective in removing spots in dry cleaning, while ultrasonic washing machines have already had limited commercial use. Experiments at Pennsylvania State College indicate that sonic energy, which vibrates the dirt off the textile fibers, can launder clothes in a small fraction of the time required by conventional household washers and with no appreciable wear on the fabric.[145] That supersonic sound waves might sometimes be used to extinguish fires and might even be substituted for existing sprinkler systems has been suggested as a future possibility by

---

138. *Productionwise* Magazine, Colton Press, New York, July 1953, p. 97.

139. Reported to have been experimentally constructed in Japan.

140. "Putting Sound to Work for Fishermen," *Business Week*, October 17, 1953, p. 86.

141. Ross L. Holman, "Harnessing Sound," *Barron's*, March 16, 1953, p. 15.

142. *The Story of Seismograph*, pamphlet published by Seismograph Service Corporation, Tulsa, Oklahoma.

143. Holman, *op. cit.* Also, "Selected Issues," Samuel S. Cadwell Co., Westport, Connecticut, January 6, 1951.

144. Letter from Ken Brigham, Bell Telephone Laboratories, April 27, 1954.

145. H. K. Schilling, *et al.*, "Sonic Laundering," *Journal of the Acoustical Society of America*, January 1949.

Dale K. Auck of the Federation of Mutual Fire Insurance Companies.[146]

Sonic energy is a new and promising tool that is peculiarly a product of technology. As long as the earth has possessed an atmosphere sound waves have existed; without them there could be no speech or music, and no hearing. But until science discovered and technology harnessed frequencies of less than 20 vibrations per second and of more than 20,000 — the narrow band audible to the human ear — this new force was economically nonexistent.

RAW MATERIALS AND CHEMISTRY [147]

The significance of technology as *the* primary resource is nowhere more evident than in the way new chemical and engineering methods have increased the supply, widened the variety, and enhanced the utility of the raw materials out of which finished goods and services are created. Such natural substances as coal and iron ore are usually thought of as gifts of Nature, fixed in amount and therefore exhaustible. In a limited sense this is true, for the ton of coal burned today is gone forever, thus reducing by that amount the reserve remaining for future use.

But this view overlooks the fact that without an advanced technology the world's coal deposits would not be known to exist, and if known to exist could not be mined successfully, and if mined successfully could not be burned efficiently to produce useful heat and power. Without technology our coal would be as useless as the earth's solid core of iron and nickel is today, or indeed as coal itself was until a few hundred years ago.

As for the exhaustion of coal reserves, technological progress has in effect increased our supply far more rapidly than we have used it up. During the first half of the twentieth century we burned up and lost forever some 23 billion tons of bituminous coal, or about 2 per cent of our reserves.[148] But every ton of coal we burn for power today yields about six times as much delivered energy as we were able to extract in 1900.[149] In spite of heavy consumption,

therefore, the energy content of our bituminous reserves today is vastly larger than that of our "larger" reserve in 1900.

Beyond this, improved technology enables us to mine coal more economically and efficiently, to exploit deeper and thinner seams, and to bring more of the deposit to the surface. Still more important, technology has discovered and developed new fuels and sources of energy some of which are superior to coal, and all of which reduce the drain on coal reserves. Just as coal displaced wood, which for thousands of years had been the only fuel, as it is today in many parts of the world, coal is now being supplemented and displaced by natural gas, petroleum and hydroelectricity, and tomorrow perhaps will give way to atomic and solar energy.

Thus, although modern technology is burning or "chewing up" our natural resources, especially minerals, at a breathtaking rate, it is constantly adding to the effective supply by means of a variety of methods of which only a few illustrations can be cited.

Better Prospecting

The grizzled prospector has long since gone the way of the village shoemaker. His faithful burro has been displaced by the vastly more efficient airplane and helicopter in transporting equipment and men to remote regions, in aerial mapping and photography, and with the "flying magnetometer" in aerial prospecting. Instead of his pick and shovel, today's prospector employs that indispensable tool in modern mineral exploration, the diamond core drill. Science has brought to his aid techniques virtually unknown a generation ago — colorimetric, spectrochemical, radiometric and geochemical methods; photogeology in studying land structure and color photography to detect minerals on the basis of the color and nature of surface vegetation; and a variety of geophysical methods and equipment.[150]

The contribution of geophysics is graphically described by one writer as follows:

. . . the exploration geophysicist, equipped with new and more powerful instruments for the detection of broad types of mineral deposits . . . will

---

146. Letter from Dale K. Auck, June 3, 1954.

147. Part of the analysis and some of the illustrations in this section are based on Chapter 21.

148. The U.S. Geographical Survey estimated bituminous coal reserves in 1950 at 1,281 billion tons, which would indicate reserves of 1,304 billion tons in 1900.

149. Efficiency of energy conversion for bituminous coal used for work performance is estimated to have increased

from 3 per cent in 1900 to 18.5 per cent in 1950. See Appendix 25–3, Table E.

150. *Resources for Freedom,* Vol. IV, *The Promise of Technology,* President's Materials Policy Commission, June 1952, pp. 25–30.

be using methods that are the logical outgrowth of the physical techniques, old and new, for identifying minerals and aggregates of minerals. From the identifying of mineral specimens in thin section by their effect upon light rays, according to the laws of refraction, we have proceeded to the identification of mineral bodies (rocks) by their effect on seismic waves, according to the laws of refraction. From the ancient use of the magnet to identify magnetic minerals such as pyrrhotite and magnetite, we have developed the sensitive magnetometer to identify rock bodies containing minute percentages of magnetic minerals. From the Jolly balance and its measurement of specific gravity of small specimens, we have graduated to the unbelievably sensitive gravimeter, with which to measure the specific gravity of great hidden bodies of mineral aggregates. From the laboratory knowledge of electrical phenomena, we have learned how to measure and define the electrical reactions of hidden minerals and rocks in the field.[151]

How much new techniques will enlarge our known reserves of needed minerals it is impossible to predict, but such developments as the discovery and exploitation of new iron ore deposits at Steep Rock and in Venezuela and Newfoundland, of petroleum in the Williston Basin, on the Continental Shelf, and at greater drilling depths in older fields, and of a wide variety of new ore deposits in the United States, as well as Canada and Africa, give ample evidence that we have not yet approached the end of our resources.

It is significant that the National Research Council panel reporting to the President's Materials Policy Commission in 1952 expressed the opinion that "abundant reserves of undiscovered minerals lie within economically accessible depths below the surface" and further that, "with adequate research and development, exploration techniques capable of locating a large part of these reserves can be made available." [152]

More Efficient Extraction and Use

Technology has also helped to expand the effective supply of raw materials through development of more effective methods of extraction and use. Technological improvements thus make possible larger yields from existing mineral deposits and the exploitation of more dilute and inaccessible deposits, as well as economies in the industrial use of the raw material.

The technology of fuels and energy materials, especially coal and petroleum, provides striking illustrations of all these economies. Mechanization of underground coal mining, coupled with the "pin-up system" which eliminates the obstruction of supporting coal pillars, and the development of strip mining have lowered costs and increased yields. In petroleum extraction a variety of techniques make it possible to obtain a much larger proportion of oil from the strata in which it is lodged, once the oil-sand has been pierced. Wells can now be drilled to a depth of more than four miles, compared with half a mile at the turn of the century, thus bringing into economic existence vast quantities of oil that were hitherto inaccessible.

Once the oil has been brought to the surface the triumph of chemical technology in the catalytic cracking plant produces a much higher yield of gasoline and other desired derivatives of the crude petroleum, while the improvement of the diesel and other internal combustion engines provides greater economies of use. In the use of mineral fuels in generating steam for electric power, as pointed out above, technology has multiplied our reserves several times in the past half century.

Improved mining techniques, such as block-caving of low-grade ores, stripping and other methods, have also increased the efficiency and completeness of extraction of metallic ores, while advances of chemical technology in ore beneficiation enable us to use much "leaner" ores than was formerly possible. Copper ore with less than one per cent metal content is now being used, whereas ore of 3 per cent concentration was considered low grade fifty years ago. Similar progress has been made in the treatment of lead, zinc, copper, nickel, cobalt and other metallic ores. Chemical metallurgy employing acids or ammonia as leaching agents may displace fire metallurgy for certain types of metallic ore. These new advances in chemical technology not only promise great economies in cost and time, but will make possible the exploitation of lower-grade ore deposits formerly considered submarginal.[153]

One of the most interesting recent achievements in mining has been the use of jet-piercing as a substitute for drilling in the extraction of taconite. This is a low-grade refractory iron ore which will be used increasingly with the exhaustion of the high-grade Mesabi ore. Iron ore re-

151. Sherwin F. Kelly, "Science on the March," *Scientific Monthly,* August 1952, p. 122.
152. *Resources for Freedom,* Vol. IV, p. 25.

153. William F. Boericke, "Chemical Metallurgy," *Barron's,* June 9, 1952.

serves are also being "stretched out" by better smelting practices. For example, Arthur D. Little, Inc., has developed a "high top pressure" method of blast furnace operation that cuts costs and increases output up to 30 per cent.[154]

Two of the most remarkable contributions of chemical technology to raw material supply in the past half century have been the development of processes for fixation of atmospheric nitrogen and for the commercial extraction of magnesium from sea water. Since for all practical purposes there are unlimited amounts of nitrogen in the air and of magnesium salts in the ocean, technology has thus "created" inexhaustible reserves of these two formerly scarce materials.

New methods that eliminate waste and loss in cutting, shaping and application also have the effect of increasing the useful supply of metallic reserves. Much iron is saved in making special steels by the use of small quantities of such alloy metals as tungsten and chromium, while the latter in turn can be economized by the use of minute quantities of boron and the rare earths. Electroplating requires only 40 per cent of the tin formerly used in making tin plate with the old hot-dip method. Shaping of steel by the hot and cold extrusion processes reduces wastage to negligible proportions, compared with the large losses involved in the forging process.[155] Powder metallurgy, though still a costly process, almost eliminates scrap loss, which may vary from 30 to 70 per cent in casting and machining operations. This method, by which fine metal powder is compacted under heavy pressure in a steel die and later sintered in a furnace, has other advantages for small metal parts besides saving material; it can be used with iron, copper, brass, bronze and other metals.

These and many other economies of extraction and use, by making every ton of raw material "go farther" in accomplishing the purposes for which it is intended, are fully as effective as the discovery of new deposits in adding to our reserves of mineral resources.

New Materials and New Uses

Technology is also constantly adding to our supply of basic resources by discovering new materials and ways to put them to use and new uses for existing materials. Chemical elements that were no more than laboratory curiosities a few years ago have become industrial necessities today; products limited to a few simple uses a generation ago have acquired a much wider versatility and utility. The increase in variety and substitutability of raw materials is, in fact, a good index of technological progress.

Energy Materials. The history of fuels and sources of power is a conspicuous example of an accelerated increase in variety and versatility. For many thousands of years man had only wood for fuel and his own muscles for power. A few thousand years ago work animals began to be used and much later, and only to a limited extent, water and wind were harnessed. Coal and the steam engine ushered in the Industrial Revolution less than two hundred years ago, but long before its exhaustion, coal is now being supplemented and displaced as a heating fuel and source of power by new energy materials and new devices to utilize them. And petroleum, natural gas and hydroelectricity may in turn be supplemented or displaced, as they were created, by the advance of technology.

The mineral fuels particularly illustrate the way in which technology finds new uses for old materials. Originally used only as a heating fuel, coal was later distilled by chemical methods to provide gas for lighting streets and buildings and coke for smelting ore. Coal tar, first a troublesome by-product of the distillation process, now provides the base of a vast organic chemical industry, supplying a range of primary products from which dyestuffs, perfumes, drugs, antiseptics, detergents, food flavors, solvents, photographic chemicals, and scores of other everyday products are obtained.

The most revolutionary advance in coal technology, however, is the recent development by Union Carbide and Carbon Corporation of a practicable method for obtaining the raw materials for such products, as well as plastics, synthetic rubbers and textiles, solvents, dyes and explosives, by the liquefaction of coal. In addition to relieving the coal tar industry from dependence on a by-product of coke manufacture, which in turn depends on the rate of steel activity, the new process gives much higher yields per ton of coal and provides large amounts of rare and costly chemicals only small quantities of which are present in coal tar. The new plant, which is almost completely automatic, processes

154. *Wall Street Journal,* November 5, 1951.
155. "Chemical Blueprint," *Barron's,* October 9, 1950.

several hundred tons each day by grinding the coal into a fine powder, converting it to a paste with oils derived from earlier cycles of the process and then mixing it with hydrogen gas in huge converters, where it is subjected to moderate heat and huge pressures. The whole process takes only four minutes and the resulting product comes out in three grades of oil which are then distilled to obtain desired chemicals.[156]

Petroleum is another natural resource for which technology has been constantly developing new processes and end-products and finding new uses. Indian Rock Oil was "good for what ails you," it was claimed, but it was not good for much else. Then chemistry discovered how to drive off the then useless volatile fractions and separate the kerosene to save the world from the "threat of darkness" arising from the critical shortage of whale oil. The heavier residues proved a satisfactory substitute for the organic lubricants then in use.

With the coming of the internal combustion engine, and of household lighting by gas and electricity, demand shifted away from kerosene and heavier fractions to gasoline. The "cracking" process was then developed to break up the surplus heavier oils and get a larger yield of the needed lighter fractions. With further technological progress the modern catalytic cracking plant, operating silently and automatically, pours out in an endless stream scores of refined products.

Petroleum derivatives, with natural gas, also furnish the base for an extensive petrolochemical industry, which is concentrated along the Texas-Louisiana Gulf Coast. Beginning in 1925 on an even smaller scale than coal hydrogenation, with a 75-ton annual output, production of chemicals from oil and gas has increased to more than 8 million tons. Though the petrolochemical industry consumes no more than one per cent of the annual output of oil and gas, it supplies 40 per cent of all synthetic organic chemicals produced today — 70 per cent of "grain" alcohol, 75 per cent of acetic acid, and 95 to 100 per cent of acetone, synthetic rubber and detergents.[157]

Natural gas — once a waste product and cheap illuminant near the oil fields — has now become an important industrial and household fuel available to almost the entire country, the source of carbon black and of "natural gas gasoline" as well as an important raw material for the petrolochemical industry. Moreover, the Carthage Hydrocal plant near Brownsville, Texas, which began operation in 1950, has successfully converted natural gas into liquid fuels. With the use of huge amounts of water, oxygen, compressed air and a special catalyst, some 90 million cubic feet of natural gas are converted daily into about 6,000 barrels of gasoline, 900 barrels of diesel oil, 200 barrels of fuel oil, as well as 300,000 pounds of twenty petrochemical compounds.[158]

In spite of all that technology can do, however, petroleum and natural gas are rapidly wasting resources and it may be necessary before long to supplement them with liquid fuels obtained from the much more plentiful reserves of coal and oil shale or from renewable vegetable resources. All of these sources are technically — though not yet economically — feasible. Union Carbide's coal hydrogenation plant could produce gasoline instead of more valuable and scarcer chemicals. The Bureau of Mines and a number of other private concerns have experimented successfully in converting coal, or gases derived from coal, into liquid fuels, and in distilling oil shale to produce motor fuel. A chemical process to produce petroleum from weeds and noxious plants has been reported from Australia,[159] while the Institut Pasteur de Tunisie claims to have produced an oil similar to petroleum from a wide range of organic waste products by a process utilizing a common bacillus in the presence of a catalyst.[160]

Whether or not these particular experiments prove economically feasible, it seems likely that technology will eventually have to harness our replenishable energy sources to replace our rapidly wasting reserves of mineral fuels. Since the Industrial Revolution we have been living on our "energy capital" at an accelerating rate. Half of all the coal ever used in the United States has been consumed since 1920 and about the same proportion of the oil and gas ever consumed has been burned since 1940.[161]

156. "Coal Chemicals," *Wall Street Journal*, May 8, 1952.

157. Survey by Frank J. Soday, Chemstrand Corporation, in *The Analysts Journal*, New York Society of Security Analysts, Third Quarter 1951.

158. *Oil and Gas Journal*, March 4, 1949.

159. *New York Times*, June 5, 1952. S. P. Belov developed a process demonstrated at the Queensland Industries Fair at Brisbane, Australia.

160. *Oil and Gas Journal*, November 15, 1951.

161. *Energy in the Future*, by Palmer Cosslett Putnam, Consultant to the U.S. Atomic Energy Commission, Van Nostrand, New York, 1953, p. 221.

With the discovery of nuclear energy — unquestionably the most revolutionary technological accomplishment of the century — and the successful application of "breeding," the world's energy capital has been vastly increased. Uranium is a common element in the earth's crust. On the basis of incomplete 1953 data, Palmer Putnam estimates a world reserve "on the order of 25 million tons of uranium and 1 million tons of thorium" with a recoverable heat content over 25 times as large as that of the world's coal reserves and 100 times that of oil and gas.

How soon and to what extent atomic energy will contribute to our rapidly growing energy needs would depend upon relative costs even if security and safety considerations were not involved. Several experimental reactors will probably be generating electric power before the end of the decade, although it seems unlikely that the costs of such operations will be competitive with conventional central stations using coal as a fuel. What the possibilities of the more distant future may be is a matter on which qualified experts differ widely. Putnam is of the opinion that, in spite of the vast reserves of fissionable materials in the United States, the fission of uranium and thorium is unlikely in the foreseeable future to supply more than 10 to 20 per cent of our energy needs, although he believes that with high though not "prohibitive" costs nuclear fuels could supply as much as 60 per cent of our requirements.

Irrespective of its long-range possibilities the great utility of atomic energy for special needs will soon be demonstrated. The first of what will be a number of atomic-powered submarines is already in experimental operation. The success of this experiment will probably be followed by use of atomic power in aircraft carriers and possibly in large commercial vessels and in locomotives. Because of the negligible weight of the fuel, atomic energy power plants also offer great promise in meeting special power needs, such as those of mining operations in mountainous and other remote and inaccessible places.

The possibility of using hydrogen fusion to create useful energy can no longer be considered completely fantastic now that the H-bomb is a reality. If the seemingly insoluble difficulties of controlling this reaction, involving temperatures of several million degrees, could be surmounted, a virtually inexhaustible source of energy would be available. Hydrogen is not costly to produce,

and Ayres and Scarlott have estimated that "the energy realized even at only 10-percent efficiency in converting the hydrogen in 1 cubic mile of sea water into helium would be ... enough to satisfy our energy wants at the 1950 rate for about 300 centuries." [162]

Barring some such spectacular accomplishment, we shall probably have to look to replenishable sources for our energy supplies in the more distant future. In the last analysis this means solar energy, which is the basic source of water and wind power, of food crops, vegetation and forest growth, and as a legacy from the past, of all the mineral fuels which we are burning up at such a rapid rate. Although man has not yet been able to harness, or even understand, photosynthesis, nature uses this method of converting and storing the sun's heat so successfully that the world's annual growth of vegetation amounts to around 100 billion tons (of which 90 per cent is marine vegetation) — equivalent in energy content to nearly 100 times that produced by the annual combustion of coal.[163]

Although it is technically feasible to produce alcohol or gasoline from almost any type of vegetation, it is not economically profitable to do so; the vast bulk of the world's vegetation must be used for food, fuel, animal feed or lumber or be returned to the soil. "Those who know most about vegetation are inclined to believe that the best that technology will be able to do in the decades ahead will be to provide a sufficient amount of food for the $2\frac{1}{3}$ billion people of the earth. ... For energy we shall have to be content with the 'scraps' unless, indeed, photosynthesis can be industrialized." [164]

Aside from the possibilities of photosynthesis, which has immediate promise only in producing algae for food, rather than energy supplies, solar energy will probably be used increasingly as a direct source of heat and energy. Technology has already demonstrated that solar energy can now be used successfully in heating household water supplies, in domestic space heating, and in operation of the heat pump. As more is learned about heat storage, architectural design for effective use of solar heat, and possibly about photogalvanism, solar energy will probably take over an

162. Eugene Ayres and Charles A. Scarlott, *Energy Sources — The Wealth of the World,* McGraw-Hill, New York, 1952, p. 185.

163. *Ibid.,* p. 194.

164. *Ibid.,* p. 243.

increasing share of the energy requirements of the country.

One recent development with great future promise is the announcement by Bell Telephone Laboratories of the first successful solar battery capable of converting the sun's energy directly and efficiently into useful amounts of electricity. In an experimental demonstration the battery, made of specially prepared thin strips of silicon wired in series, delivered enough energy to power a transistor radio transmitter carrying both speech and music. This revolutionary device is made from one of the earth's most abundant materials, has no moving parts and suffers no wear in operation, and should therefore last indefinitely. It can deliver power from the sun at the rate of 50 watts per square yard of surface and with an efficiency of energy conversion comparable with steam and gasoline engines.[165] Actual use of the silicon solar battery to meet certain low-power requirements in telephone system operation may not be far away. To what extent the almost limitless flow of energy from the sun, all but a minute fraction of which is now being "wasted," can be put to work in the more distant future is of course wholly speculative. With the solar battery a reality, however, the question is no longer a technical but solely an economic one.

Metals. Modern life without steel and other metals would be unimaginable. Yet our Stone Age ancestors for many thousands of years had only wood and stone, bone and horn, out of which to fashion their weapons and tools. Man had no useful metal until technology brought copper into existence some six thousand years ago. Another thousand years passed before the copper-tin alloy, bronze, was discovered, and perhaps another thousand before lead came into common use.

Iron was first smelted a thousand years before the Christian Era began. From that time until the middle of the nineteenth century iron was the dominant industrial metal. Though fine steel for tools and weapons had long been manufactured at high cost and in small quantities, it was not until advancing technology developed the Bessemer and open-hearth furnaces less than a century ago that steel became abundant and cheap. These two processes for the first time made possible the mass production of steel and made what was still a

scarce and costly metal a century ago the great industrial and structural material it is today. World production in recent years has been in excess of 200 million tons, the United States producing and using half the total.

The rapid progress of metallography, especially the use of the microscope and later the X-ray in studying the crystalline structure of metals, led to the development of a host of new alloy steels — tungsten, chromium, nickel, manganese, vanadium — each with unique qualities for special applications. Introduction of the electric furnace toward the end of the nineteenth century, and later the application of induction heating, greatly facilitated manufacture of the newer alloy steels. Today we have not just steel but a wide variety of steels each "tailor-made" to meet special needs. Alloying can greatly raise the tensile strength of steel, increase ductility, toughness, surface hardness and hardenability, add antiscaling and acid-resisting qualities and enhance or lessen the magnetic qualities. One of the most significant and pervasive inventions was high-speed steel, an alloy of tungsten, chromium, cobalt and vanadium, with cutting qualities far superior to the best carbon tool steel. Cutting speeds have been further increased by the use of tools tipped with extremely hard and heat-resistant carbides of tungsten, tantalum, molybdenum and other metals.

Thus in less than a century technology has made a scarce and costly metal plentiful and cheap, thereby opening up to it hundreds of new uses. At the same time scores of special steels have been developed — in reality new materials with new properties and new uses.

Aluminum is another "new material" created by technology in recent decades. Though one of the most abundant of the metallic elements, it was still precious "silver from clay" when used to cap the Washington monument in 1884. Today, either pure or alloyed with copper or magnesium, it is not only an increasingly important structural metal in aircraft, ships and automotive vehicles but is also used widely in the manufacture of cooking utensils, electrical equipment, screens, paints, foil, roofing, ladders, furniture and other products. And so with magnesium. Although magnesium salts have long been important in medicine and industry, the metal itself until recently was important only in flash powder and fireworks. With the development of new production methods using sea water as a raw material, magnesium, which is even lighter than aluminum,

165. News Release, Bell Telephone Laboratories, April 25, 1954.

is competing with that metal in many structural and other uses.

A more recent product of technology is titanium, which has become useful as a metal only since World War II. Heavier than aluminum but much lighter than alloy steel, titanium alloys are stronger than most alloy steels, have excellent ductility, are nearly as hard as alloy steel, and have high resistance to corrosion and heat. Because of these latter qualities and its light weight, titanium is in great demand for jet engines and many other uses. Although titanium ores are plentiful, extraction of the metal is difficult and costly, with the result that titanium is still a precious metal selling for $5.00 a pound. Even at this price demand is expanding, and with lower costs titanium will have great promise as an industrial metal.

Zirconium is another new and still costly metal, though technology has already brought its price down from $300 a pound to less than $30 with the likelihood of further substantial reductions. All of the present output is used in nuclear energy installations, but its high degree of corrosion and acid resistance promise greatly expanded usefulness as an alloy with steel, magnesium and other metals. Nuclear technology has also found new and critically important uses for uranium and thorium — two metals whose existence has been known for a century and whose compounds have long been used industrially.

Silicon, the most abundant metal in the earth's crust and one of the most easily recovered, is one of the cheapest of the "new" metals, selling for 20 cents a pound. It is now used largely for protective coatings on steel, molybdenum and other metals and as a raw material in the manufacture of silicone plastics. In spite of its brittleness, its resistance to heat and corrosion and its property as an electrical semiconductor eventually "should make it one of our most useful metals." [166]

Many other metals that were formerly only laboratory curiosities or were used in minute quantities in steel alloys are now or may soon be applied in their own right. Among these are the rare earth, cerium, which makes the spark in lighters; beryllium, the second lightest metal known but hard enough to scratch glass, which produces a very light and malleable alloy when combined with copper; molybdenum, which can substitute for scarcer tungsten in hardening steel; boron, a superlative hardening agent which re-

places several hundred times its own weight of such other alloy metals as manganese and chromium; lithium, the lightest of all metals, used as an atomic bomb ingredient and in castings, porcelain and drugs. Gallium, indium, germanium, columbium, selenium, rhenium, tantalum, tellurium, strontium and cobalt are further examples of metals that have come into industrial use for the first time in most cases in the past decade.

Wood. Along with the discovery of new sources of energy and the "creation" of new metals, technology has given new properties and new versatility and utility to some of the oldest materials, particularly wood, glass and composite materials of various kinds.

Wood is not only man's oldest fuel but also his oldest structural material for buildings and furniture and many other products. It can be readily cut, sawed and planed into shape, and nailed, screwed or glued into place, and until recent decades that is about all that could be done with it.

Less than a century ago chemical technology discovered how to remove the impurities so that the cellulose of softwood could be used in the manufacture of paper, thus relieving a critical shortage of raw material for newsprint. With this cheap and plentiful raw material, the quality, variety and utility of paper products have been greatly increased. Paperboard, having proved itself as a strong and durable packaging material, is finding new uses because of its insulating qualities, strength and lightness. Formed into a honeycomb structure, impregnated with resin and sometimes sandwiched between thin sheets of metal or fiber glass, it is being used in partitions, bulkheads and floors of planes and for insulation in refrigerator cars and house walls and partitions.[167] Wood pulp has also long been the principal raw material in the manufacture of rayon and other cellulose fibers.

Under the spur of higher costs of timber since World War II, technology is finding uses for the waste products of paper and lumber manufacture. Crown Zellerbach Corporation, for example, is now using the waste fluid from pulp manufacture as a source for a product that can serve as a fuel, a fertilizer, a glue, and a soil conditioner to stimulate plant growth.[168] Lumber and plywood mills have installed chipping machines to cut wood scraps to uniform size for use in making hard-

166. *Resources for Freedom,* Vol. IV, p. 111.

167. *Wall Street Journal,* November 28, 1950.
168. "Wood Saving," *ibid.,* October 4, 1952, p. 1.

board, paperboard and Kraft paper. These formerly wasted wood chips may be able to serve also as a fuel in smelting metals, while experiments in using sawdust as a fuel to operate gas turbines promise success.[169] In one way or another virtually all of the fir log is used today whereas it is estimated that half was wasted before World War II.

Lumber itself is also becoming more and more of a synthetic product. Pressed wood is being made from chips and scraps, and the now old-fashioned plywood is being supplanted by a wide variety of "densified woods" produced under tremendous heat and pressure and with the use of synthetic resin binders.[170] Softwoods treated in this way are made as durable as oak or mahogany and suitable for fine furniture. One interesting development is the "Unicel," a glued wood box-car using twenty tons less steel than an all-steel car, which its manufacturer, the Pressed Steel Car Company, claims is more rugged and stronger and will be more economical to produce in quantity than a steel car.[171]

Cement and Concrete. Compared with wood, cement and concrete are comparatively new. Although clay and other natural adhesives have been used since earliest times, modern Portland cement dates back little more than a century. This new material, reinforced with steel, released engineers from the design limitations of timber, brick and stone, and in the United States at least has become the all-but-universal building material for highways, streets, bridges, tunnels and aqueducts, foundations and heavy structures of all kinds.

While today's Portland cement for most uses has about the same composition and character as when first perfected, a number of specialized cements have lately been developed. One new cement composite, containing in addition to sand a lightweight mineral known as vermiculite, has a resiliency similar to wood flooring. Other lightweight concretes made with such ingredients as sawdust and volcanic ash, or aerated by the use of soaps or detergents, are being used increasingly for roof, wall and floor slabs with light loading requirements. Although these new composites

lack compressive strength, some of them weigh only one fifth as much as ordinary concrete and conduct less than one tenth as much heat.[172]

Precast concrete panels consisting of a sheet of insulating glass fiber sandwiched between two thin layers of wire-reinforced concrete are being turned out on the assembly line and trucked to building sites to be used for the outer walls of new plants. They result in great savings in construction time and in labor and material costs. "Vacuum concrete," produced by a technique which removes excess water from the concrete immediately after pouring, is now being used in many industrial plants. It requires less cement, reduces construction time and saves up to 90 per cent of the steel usually needed in building.[173]

One of the most remarkable new structural materials is prestressed concrete, which is already being used in the construction of short bridges. In one bridge built near Los Angeles it was found that the conventional design would have required 88 cubic yards of concrete and 40,000 pounds of steel, whereas the prestressed design, put up in less time, required only 50 cubic yards of concrete, 5,000 pounds of high-tensile-strength steel wire and 7,000 pounds of reinforcing steel.[174]

Technology is also finding ways to correct unsatisfactory qualities of ordinary sand and gravel. Cornell University engineers have developed a "synthetic gravel" strong enough to support trucks by mixing plain mud with small amounts of lignin (from waste sulfite liquor from pulp mills) and a chromium compound to form small waterproof briquettes.[175] Vibroflotation, a new process for ramming and packing sand into permanently hardened form, is used to provide better foundations in sandy areas and in building earth dams, levees and airports.[176] Asphalts containing additives that permit effective mixing with wet aggregates and thus make it possible for roads to be laid in damp weather have been developed by one of the oil companies.[177]

169. "Waste-Wood-Fired Gas-Turbine Power Unit," paper by G. A. Atherton and S. E. Corder, Spring Meeting, American Society of Mechanical Engineers, Seattle, Washington, March 24–26, 1952.
170. *Industrial Bulletin,* Arthur D. Little, Inc., June 1952.
171. "Wood Wonders," *Wall Street Journal,* September 5, 1951.

172. *Industrial Bulletin,* Arthur D. Little, Inc., September 1950.
173. "Construction Speeded in New Concrete Set-Up," *New York Herald Tribune,* March 23, 1952.
174. "Prestressed Concrete," by Arnold Neidle, in *Vector,* March 1951, School of Technology, College of the City of New York.
175. "New Slant on Solidifying Mud," *Chemical Engineering* (McGraw-Hill), January 1952.
176. *Wall Street Journal,* November 24, 1952.
177. "Synergism Between Engineering and Petroleum," address by Robert W. Wilson, Chairman of the Board, Standard Oil Co. (Indiana), Centennial of Engineering, Transactions, Paper No. 2654, 1953, p. 1226.

Glass. Glass, which may be considered the oldest man-made plastic, for thousands of years served only a decorative function. With the development of glass-blowing just before the Christian Era began, it found new usefulness as a container for liquids, but only during the past two or three centuries has it been inexpensive enough to use for the windows of ordinary buildings. And it was not until the present century, when Michael J. Owens' invention of the automatic bottle-blowing machine in 1903 transformed the industry from a handicraft to a mass-production basis, that glass became a universal "packaging material."

In spite of its unique quality of transparency, the brittleness and fragility of ordinary glass and its low resistance to heat have limited its usefulness until recently. Within the past generation, however, a revolution in glass technology has created hundreds of new types of glass with widely varying physical characteristics, and hundreds of new uses for this ancient material. Glass blocks, first introduced in this country by Owens-Illinois Glass Company at the Chicago World's Fair in 1933,[178] are being used more and more widely for decorative and structural purposes and for light transmission and diffusion.

Thirty-five years ago the Corning Glass Works introduced borosilicate heat-resistant glasses which have found widespread use in science, industry and the home in many types of products marketed under the trade name "Pyrex." Just before World War II the same company developed an unusual glass containing 96 per cent silica which has extremely high heat resistance. Articles made of this glass can be heated with a blowtorch while resting on a cake of ice without breaking.

Glass is now produced with precise control of purity, color and transparency. The best optical glass today absorbs so little of the visible light rays that the absorption can hardly be measured; a bar of optical glass ten feet long is so clear that a book at one end can be read from the other. Another type of glass is opaque to the visible rays, while transmitting much of the invisible ultra-violet rays. Still another type transmits much of the infrared light, but absorbs the visible wave lengths. "Anti-glare" glass lies between these two extremes for it absorbs most of both the infrared and ultraviolet rays, but transmits more than 70 per cent of the visible rays.[179] Polaroid glass permits full visibility but eliminates glare. "One-way" glass can be seen through from one side but not from the other, thus providing privacy without serious loss of light. These special types of glass are used in a number of ways: in sun glasses, goggles for furnace workers, germicidal lamps, fluorescent lighting, "electric eye" burglar alarms, car windshields, infrared cooking, lamps, etc.

Not all glass is the fragile, brittle substance used for windows and bottles. It can be made as light as aluminum, or as heavy as iron, and as strong as steel. A hollow cylinder of one type of glass is hard enough to hammer a spike into a heavy plank.[180] Although ordinary glass will break but not bend, one company turns out glass ribbons as thin and flexible as cellophane to be used for electrical insulation. One type of glass can be melted by a match, while another resists furnace heat. Although itself a nonconductor, glass can be coated with metallic film conductors, some of which are practically invisible. This method is already being used for de-icing windshields and for radiant heaters for offices and homes.

One of the oddest recent accomplishments of glass technology is a method developed by the Corning Glass Works for including photo-sensitive constituents in a glass and thus permitting photographic reproduction in the material. This technique was used, for example, in making the simulated marble panels in the United Nations General Assembly building, which are in reality a three-dimensional reproduction of marble patterns imbedded in a thin glass sheet. A basic new use of Corning's photo-sensitive glass now seems possible through the perfection of a photo-chemical engraving process. By exposure to ultra-violet light, a heat treatment and acid etching, any image recorded on a photo-negative may be photoengraved on a glass plate which can be used in standard printing processes.[181]

Glass fiber has been known for generations, but it has only been since the 1930s when Owens-Illinois Glass Company and Corning Glass Works began to make it by drawing it from molten glass with steam that fibrous glass has

178. Letter from Joseph M. McGarry, Owens-Illinois Glass Company, May 4, 1954.

179. "Visibility Unlimited," *Wall Street Journal*, September 23, 1953.
180. *Ibid.*, September 28, 1949.
181. Letter from J. T. Lanahan, Corning Glass Works, June 28, 1954.

been used industrially. Today its use is expanding rapidly, chiefly as a substitute for other products. Glass fiber will not rot or burn, is much stronger than steel, much lighter than wool, and superior to silk as an insulating material. It is being used as insulation for refrigerators and for buildings, instead of kapok in life preservers, in place of peat moss in packing asparagus, in electrical insulation and so on. It is spun into yarn and woven into fabrics, mixed with asphalt to substitute for felt, and impregnated with plastic to form a solid substance.[182]

This last use may turn out to be the most important. Impregnating fibrous glass with polyester resins or other plastics makes a substance which is stronger than steel but more resilient and much lighter. Aside from military uses for such things as body armor, housing for radar equipment and fuel tanks, civilian uses are expanding. Glass plastics are being used as interior building partition panels; for luminous ceilings; as housings for washing machines and refrigerators; for automobile bodies; for the hulls of canoes and sail and motor boats; in molded sheets for porch furniture, kitchenette tables and chairs; for awnings; for movable oil storage tanks; and even for lightweight bathtubs to be used in auto trailers.[183]

Glass — or the many "glasses" created by technology — is a remarkable engineering material with enormous potentialities. In addition to its unique transparency, its corrosion resistance and tremendous tensile strength in fiber form, it can be given a wide range of physical properties that enable it to compete successfully with metals and other materials for many uses. In the long run perhaps its chief advantage is that sand and the other glass-making materials are so plentiful as to be almost inexhaustible.

The ceramics industry also has the advantage that it rests on an inexhaustible supply of clays and minerals. Ceramics, like glass-making, is one of the oldest industrial arts, but the industry needs scientific research and experimentation to develop its full potentialities. Experiments show, for example, that ceramic coating on steel and alloys enhances their resistance to high temperatures, and that ceramic materials may in some cases be suitable substitutes for metals under high temperature conditions.[184] One illustration of the

possibilities of ceramics is Fiberfax, a fluffy white fiber developed by the Carborundum Company. Made by subjecting a stream of molten aluminum oxide and silicate to an air blast, it is a substitute for asbestos and can be used as an industrial filter and in fireproofing and insulating materials. Available now in bulk and in block form, it may soon prove useful as a textile material.[185]

Plastics. Plastics are genuinely new materials, endowed by man with what one producer describes as the "properties nature forgot." [186] They constitute the latest and greatest contribution of chemical technology to human well-being.[187] As one distinguished chemist has explained:

The science of chemistry started out as the groping empirical manipulation of almost completely misunderstood materials found in nature. It proceeded to the refinement and duplication of materials found in nature. Over the past few decades, it has started the creation of a variety of improvements on nature, and herein lies the most profound promise, the most dignified and humanitarian significance of applied chemistry.[188]

Although celluloid, made from nitrocellulose and camphor, "doyen of synthetic plastics," is almost as old as Bessemer steel, and bakelite, a composite of phenol and formaldehyde, dates back to the first decade of the present century, most of the great plastic developments have come during the past two decades. Today this group of technologically created substances is the most versatile, widely used and rapidly growing of raw materials.

In the field of plastics and resins, a whole new department of creative chemistry is unfolding. Polymerization and condensation reactions have already

182. *Wall Street Journal,* May 31, 1951.
183. "'Glass' Plastics," *ibid.,* October 2, 1952.
184. "Research the Keynote in Ceramics and Glass," *Chemical Engineering,* July 1952, p. 200.
185. "An Introduction to Fiberfax," circular of the Carborundum Company, Perth Amboy, New Jersey.
186. Advertisement of Monsanto Chemical Company, *Time,* August 31, 1953, p. 63.
187. The terms "plastics" and "synthetic resins" are both inexact in meaning. Plastics could be defined so widely as to include glass, as a man-made plastic, and wood, as a natural plastic (because of its resinous nature); while synthetic resins are not similar in composition and structure to natural resins, but are new resinous substances produced by synthetic methods. As used here plastics are synthetic organic products of two main types: "thermosetting plastics, which become soft and plastic under the influence of heat (and generally pressure) and on continued heating become hard and infusible; and thermoplastics, which soften under heat and can be pressed to shape but require cooling to set." C. A. Redfarn, "Synthetic Resins and Plastics," in *What Industry Owes to Chemical Science,* Chemical Publishing Company, New York, 1946, p. 173.
188. Carroll A. Hochwalt, "The Impact of Chemistry on the World of Science," *Scientific Monthly,* July 1953.

produced three dozen commercially important polymers, copolymers, and resins. These materials run the gamut of properties which were formerly possessed only by diverse materials found in nature. They offer transparency, lightness, insulating properties, controlled flexural strength, and impact strength. They can be hard, they can be flexible, they can be elastomeric. Plastics have put at man's disposal new methods of manufacture: molding, extruding, and laminating. As little as fifteen years ago, plastic materials were unimportant in the lives of average people. Today they touch many of the sciences and contribute to work-a-day living almost every hour of the day.[189]

Until just before World War II, consumers looked upon most plastic articles as flimsy substitutes for something better. Today plastics are not only proving superior to glass, wood and metal for many purposes, but they are performing new functions for which no other materials are suitable. Most plastics, however, are still more expensive than wood, glass, rubber and the cheaper metals; and total production of all plastics has only recently exceeded one million tons,[190] compared with one and a quarter million tons of aluminum, for example. In the long run, plastics have the great advantage that they are derived from light, cheap and abundant materials. Their main constituents are hydrogen, carbon, often chlorine, and sometimes silicon and fluorine. Basic raw materials, besides air and water, are coal tar, coal, petroleum, and any number of organic substances such as furfural obtained from corn cobs. These considerations, coupled with the extraordinary versatility and ease of application of plastics, account for the rapid expansion in their use.

The average consumer thinks of plastics primarily in terms of household products — dishes, kitchenware, curtains, slip-covers, aprons, bathroom and kitchen floor coverings, garden hose, phonograph records, toys, raincoats, refrigerator trays, squeeze bottles and other containers of all kinds, toilet seats, electrical fixtures and equipment, and so on. But industrial uses of plastics are multiplying rapidly. Polyester glass-fiber laminates, as indicated above, are valuable structural materials. Because of their light weight, tremendous strength, and resistance to heat, chemicals,

corrosion and decay, as well as the ease with which they can be shaped and worked, these composites have a promising future in spite of their present relatively high cost. Synthetic resins are also used as a binding material in the production of other types of laminates, such as plywood and paper and wood composites of various kinds. In addition to the laminates, some plastics used alone have considerable structural strength. Lockheed has developed a porous plastic which can be poured like molasses into the cavities of airplane wings and which then solidifies to provide greater structural strength.[191]

Another rapidly growing use for plastics, especially for polyethylene and polystyrene, is in the manufacture of extruded plastic pipe and in the lining of metal pipes. Because of its light weight, its flexibility which enables it to follow uneven ground, and its ease of installation and resistance to corrosion, plastic pipe is being used for handling corrosive coal mine water and brines and sour crude oil, and in food and chemical plants. When high temperatures and pressures are involved, the more expensive plastic-lined metal pipes are used. However, plastic pipe has been used successfully on an experimental basis to carry gas and water, in concrete floors for radiant heating and for various other purposes for which metal pipe is now used. When it is considered that some 8 million tons of steel pipe and tubing [192] and additional tonnages of copper tubing are used each year, it seems highly probable that plastic pipe will find many new uses. But even on the basis of the limited existing uses, the President's Materials Policy Commission estimates that the market for plastic pipe will expand from little more than 5 million pounds in 1950 to 75 million pounds by 1960.[193]

Improvement of the injection technique for molding thermo-setting plastics is making possible the production of much larger articles:

Thus, possible future applications, now being considered by the plastics industry, include such items as one-piece kitchen cabinets complete with molded-in racks, handles, and shelves, one-piece refrigerator interiors with molded-in shelf supports, colorful and light weight wash basins, colorful covers for hot and cold water inlet controls for basins and sinks, and so on.[194]

189. *Ibid.*, p. 50.
190. Estimated total plastic consumption in 1952 was 2,198 million pounds, of which 1,234 million pounds consisted of vinyls, polystyrene, polyethylene and other thermo-plastics, and 944 million of alkyd, phenolic, urea and other thermo-setting plastics. *Monthly Letter,* Goodbody & Co., New York, November 1953.

191. *Wall Street Journal,* October 4, 1952.
192. *Weekly Market Letter,* Goodbody & Co., New York, March 25, 1953.
193. *Resources for Freedom,* Vol. IV, p. 148,
194. *Ibid*, p. 149.

New plastics and new uses for plastics spring up almost overnight; it is impossible to predict future uses, or even to catalog present ones. A recent technological development has been the introduction of polyvinyl chloride resin as a base for resilient floor covering. Although higher priced than other linoleums, the vinyl product has a much harder surface and therefore costs less to maintain and is remarkably durable. A vinyl-asbestos floor covering which was walked on by 20 million people at the Chicago World's Fair in 1933 was still giving service at Bakelite's New York offices nearly two decades later with little sign of wear.[195] These floor coverings will probably find a market in schools, hospitals and restaurants, and eventually in homes.

Synthetics, such as the alkyd resins, are also being used in paints, even in the newer water emulsion paints. Synthetic resins have all but displaced animal glue and other traditional adhesives for both domestic and industrial purposes. Plastic sprays — du Pont's resin called Teflon, for example — can be applied by paint-spraying equipment to the inside of metal tanks and thus provide a lining which is highly resistant to heat and impervious to chemical corrosion. The same material can be used to coat glass fabrics and applied as an enamel to insulate fine wire.

Among the most interesting and significant of the newer synthetics are the silicones, first produced by Dow Corning Corporation and actively developed by a number of chemical companies since World War II. These organo-silicon-oxide polymers, as they are scientifically described, are "a chemical hybrid, a cross between organic and inorganic materials"[196] with a most extraordinary combination of properties not possessed by any other materials, natural or synthetic. Silicones are water repellent, and little affected by wide temperature changes. They will not mix with other materials or conduct electricity, and they are highly resistant to oxidation. They are available in the form of fluids and oils, greases and compounds, resins, varnishes and rubbers.

The first significant consumer use of silicones was in the form of remarkably effective, long-lasting and easy-to-apply polishes for glassware, furniture and automobiles. As water repellents, silicones have been applied to a wide variety of surfaces from apparel and upholstery fabrics woven of wool, synthetics and blends, to glass and the above-grade masonry walls of buildings. Silicone fluids are widely used as damping media in devices ranging from overload relays to torsional vibration dampers for crankshafts because they will not thicken at low temperatures or thin out and evaporate at high temperatures. This quality plus oxidation resistance and heat stability account for the remarkable success of silicone lubricants.

"Silastic," a silicone rubber produced by Dow Corning, retains its rubbery quality at temperatures ranging from —100° F. to over 500° F., and is therefore far superior to either natural or synthetic organic rubbers for gaskets, seals, insulation and other special uses where extreme temperatures are involved. Silicone resins are used to multiply by ten the life of electric machines and to make paints that protect metal surfaces at temperatures up to 1000° F. Modified silicone resins are blended with alkyd or phenolic resins to increase the heat- and weather-resistance of organic paints. Silicones are also valuable as defoamers in many industrial processes. Incompatibility with most organic materials plus resistance to heat and oxidation account for the almost universal use of silicone "release agents" to prevent sticking in the commercial baking of bread, the molding of rubber products and the making of sand shells in which metals are cast.

Synthetic exchange resins are large polymeric molecules which are finding extensive use in ion-exchange processes, which are so essential in the purification of water, in sugar refining and in many other industrial processes requiring the removal or recovery of small quantities of dissolved substances. One of the most significant applications of ion-exchange techniques involving the use of a synthetic resin membrane makes possible the continuous delivery of potable water from brackish or salt water. Although the costs of the electric energy needed are still high, this process offers great promise for irrigation in regions where the natural water table has been steadily declining.[197]

Epoxies are another new synthetic resin. Their high gloss and high resistance to abrasion, heat and corrosion make them valuable for lining tanks, drums and chemicals containers and for heavy-duty protective coatings for metal, concrete

195. *Wall Street Journal,* July 30, 1952.

196. "what's a silicone?" Dow Corning Corporation, 1952. The description of silicone properties and products which follows is based on this informative and authoritative pamphlet.

197. William L. Laurence, "New Process Desalts Sea Water," *New York Times,* February 21, 1952.

and wood. Unlike silicones, epoxies have strong adhesive qualities and will bind metals, plastics, glass, rubber and wood, all without special pressure or temperature.[198] Fluorcarbons are still another of the newer plastics with special qualities of durability and resistance to corrosive agents and solvents which are proving useful in industry. And, of course, the synthetic fibers discussed earlier in the chapter in their chemical nature are also plastics. Nylon, in fact, finds wide industrial use as a molded plastic in such articles as small gears and zippers where great resistance to abrasion is required.

New Materials from Chemistry

Plastics and synthetic resins are only one of many groups of new materials which chemical technology has created by using the elemental atoms and molecules as "building blocks." Originally mere substitutes for superior natural products, these newly created materials have come to surpass the natural ones in the variety and versatility of their properties. Thus plastics can perform most of the functions of the older natural materials, and many more as well. Synthetic resin adhesives are not mere substitutes, but are far superior to animal glue and starch. Synthetic fibers have also been given many of the "properties that nature forgot" — though not yet all of those that nature remembered.

Artificial dyestuffs, the first contribution of applied organic chemistry, were originally developed as a substitute for indigo, madder, cochineal and a few more of the mere score or so of dyes then obtainable from vegetable and animal sources. Before long chemists had not only accomplished their original purpose, but were obtaining from coal tar a thousand or more chemically different dyestuffs — and the number is growing year by year. Not only that, but coal tar, the unpleasant by-product of gasworks, was soon yielding perfumes, food essences, drugs, benzene, fertilizers, paints, solvents, and scores of other groups of products of which plastics are only one.

When World War II began, natural rubber was one of the most critical raw materials. Today most of our rubber requirements are met by artificial rubbers — buna, neoprene and a number of others. These synthetic rubbers are hydrocarbon products similar to plastics, derived by complex processes from such raw materials as coal, petroleum and alcohol. Most of the synthetics have all the elastic qualities of the natural product, but are more resistant to abrasion and to the destructive action of oil and organic solvents, as well as having better insulating qualities.

Materials which in one way or another add to the supply of foodstuffs and other agricultural products are among the most useful contributions of modern chemistry. Since the first successful fixation of atmospheric nitrogen the chemical industry has been helping solve the problem of maintaining soil fertility with mechanized agriculture. The recent development of synthetic soil conditioners not only offers the possibility of adding further to farm productivity but promises to improve our understanding of soils, fertilization and plant growth.

Chemical technology also adds constantly to the American farmer's arsenal of insecticides in his endless struggle with the hordes of insect pests which attack his crops and livestock.[199] Among the most promising of the new and still experimental products are the systemic insecticides, which are absorbed by the plant thus making the whole plant resistant to insect attack. Fungicides and other chemicals help prevent or overcome the appalling variety of diseases from which plants suffer even more than animals and humans.

Weeds are another of the farmer's — and city gardener's — enemies which chemistry is helping to conquer. Although such chemicals as rock salt and chlorates had long been used to burn above-ground weed growth, the first of the hormone-type herbicides, 2, 4-D, was not used until after World War II. This product kills broadleafed plants by causing them to "grow themselves to death," but is harmless to grassy plants, which include the cereals. Herbicides having a selective effect on other types of plants are being developed with still greater promise for the future.

Milk and meat yields have been increased by the use of insecticides to control the insect pests which afflict cattle. Of even greater importance for future livestock and poultry production is the use of antibiotics, vitamins, choline chloride, phos-

---

198. "Epoxies — Too Good to Be True?" reprinted in *McGraw-Hill Digest*, December 1952, from *Modern Plastics.*

199. Of an estimated 686,000 species of insects in the world, some 82,000 flourish in the United States, and of these, 7,000 are injurious to crops. The number of different ticks and mites in this country is estimated at 2,600. *The Story of Farm Chemicals,* E. I. du Pont de Nemours & Company, Wilmington, Delaware, pp. 14 and 16.

phate mineral supplements and other chemicals in fortified feeds. As a single illustration, a three-pound frying chicken can be produced in nine weeks with nine pounds of fortified feed, compared with the former requirement of twelve pounds of feed and twelve to fourteen weeks.[200]

Working with the elemental atoms and molecules, applied chemistry is turning out a steady stream of new and different products. At the turn of the century chemicals in regular production, such as soda ash, sulfuric acid, borax, tar distillates, numbered only a few score. Today the number of different chemicals produced and marketed in the United States runs to several thousand. More than 500,000 distinct organic compounds are already known, and with industrial research teams constantly preparing new ones, the total will soon approach a million.[201] Nobody yet knows what most of these new compounds can do. Many of them may never prove useful. But others, like "bouncing putty," which appear first as strange oddities later acquire a versatile utility.

Radioisotopes, described by one scientist as "without question the most spectacular of the materials on which chemistry has presumed to make an improvement on nature," [202] are by-products of nuclear fission that are serving many fields of science and research. These radioactive compounds are being used in medical diagnosis and treatment, experimentally in cold sterilization of packaged foods, in strengthening plastics, in the construction of delicate gauges and measuring instruments, and in research in a number of fields — for example, photosynthesis, plant growth and fertilizer use, structure of metals, and industrial materials and processes.

Aside from these innumerable products of the chemical industry itself, chemical techniques have replaced the old rule-of-thumb traditions throughout the entire range of industry. The smelting and refining of metals, sugar refining, laundering, textile dyeing and finishing, pulp and paper manufacture, leather and rubber processing, photography, ceramic and glass manufacture, water purification, the brewing, fermenting and distilling of alcoholic beverages and the processing and preservation of foodstuffs have all become, in some measure at least, chemical industries.

200. Hochwalt, *op. cit.*, p. 53.
201. *Ibid.*, p. 53.
202. *Ibid.*, p. 50.

TECHNOLOGY IN DISTRIBUTION

Technology is usually defined as embracing the "industrial arts," i.e., the chemical, mechanical and electrical processes used in extracting, transporting, processing and fabricating physical goods and services. In its broadest sense, however, technology can be thought of as encompassing all of the organized policies and procedures and all of the public and private institutions involved in the creation and consumption of useful goods and services. This would mean that such social inventions as the modern corporation, the Federal Reserve System, the industrial union, the trade association and the mutual fund are technological developments. The technology of the factory would thus include not only mechanical and chemical processes but also incentive wage and bonus systems, procedures for selection, training and management of personnel, and systems of cost accounting and inventory control.

This broader concept of American technology would obviously also include our system of universal education with its great emphasis on the vocational and practical, our governmental system, especially its research and regulatory agencies, American methods of advertising and selling, and indeed the habits and attitudes of American consumers. Although such a broad definition of technology might be justified on philosophical grounds, it would make the term almost identical with the national culture. This chapter has therefore been limited thus far to consideration of what appear to be some of the more significant developments in American technology in the narrow, rather than the broadest, meaning of the term.

However, because of the close interdependence in the American economy between producing goods and selling them, certain of the intangible aspects of what might be called the "technology of distribution" merit brief consideration. The high degree of specialization in American industry, simplification of design, and the lavish use of automatic power-driven machinery in turning out low-cost standardized goods would be impossible without the means for assuring mass consumption in a mass market. In a scarcity economy the consumer needs no conditioning to make him want enough food to keep alive, sufficient clothing and shelter to keep warm. But in an economy of luxury and plenty, the consumer has to be persuaded to want, for example, an electric blanket with a separate thermostatic control for each side of the bed, or an air-conditioned automobile with a 250-horsepower motor, power steering and a hydramatic drive. This constant "education" of consumers to desire products never heard of before is just as essential to the smooth functioning of an economy which is geared to turn out a steady flood of new and different products as are an adequate supply of electric energy and plentiful raw materials. The American standard of living is thus the cause no less than the result of American creativeness and productivity.

This essential relationship is often overlooked by foreign observers who leave American shores lavish in praise of our industrial efficiency but unsparing in condemnation of our "wasteful" selling and advertising methods. It implies neither praise nor criticism of such methods to recognize that only by their use can the great advantages and economies of mass production be achieved. The distribution institutions and methods which make this possible — the mail order house, the chain store, the supermarket, instalment buying, market analysis, national advertising and, whether we like it or not, even the singing commercial — are just as much part of American technology as are radioisotopes and fork-lift trucks.

Most of the significant changes in the physical aspects of distribution have come in response to changes in transportation techniques and in the geographic distribution of population. Both the general store and the mail order house were American inventions because our large and growing population once lived so largely on scattered farms and in small communities with poor access to urban shopping centers. The chain store expanded with growing urbanization, better roads and the automobile. With the movement of our now highly urbanized population to the suburbs, itself a result of the concrete highway and the automobile, have come the suburban shopping center and the self-service supermarket.

Self-Service

Perhaps the most striking contrast to the turn-of-the-century grocery and butcher shop offering its customers — and the flies — a few staple commodities in open bins and barrels is the modern supermarket, which displays a vast variety of fresh, frozen and preserved foods, all in sanitary packages. This retail counterpart of the factory assembly line, where the consumer does everything for himself but add up his bill, is a technological advance made possible not so much by the simple mechanical devices involved in its operation as by consumer acceptance of standardized factory-packaged products requiring no personal selling.

A significant and often overlooked factor accounting for the growth of self-service retailing, and indeed for the whole do-it-yourself trend in the American mode of life, is the high cost of individualized custom service, i.e., painters, plumbers, paperhangers, domestic servants, tailors, chauffeurs, etc. Service wages are high in the United States because the general wage level is high, and the wage level is high because our technology has given us the highest productivity in the world. Because mass-produced goods are efficiently produced, they are inexpensive in spite of high wages; but paying comparable wages for domestic service or for custom-made goods makes these seem to cost more than they are worth.

It is thus *because* we have the highest standard of living in the world that the middle-class American "does his own work" to a much greater extent than his counterpart in countries with lower living standards. The American housewife drives the family car, but she carries the groceries home, cooks the family's meals, and her husband helps with the dishes and cuts the grass. Together they paint the woodwork, paper the walls and tile the kitchen floor. The comparable European family may have at least one domestic servant, but it lives in more crowded quarters, with less light and heat, with no family car or TV set, and with little or none of the electrical household equipment which simplifies work and life in the typical American household. Because productivity is lower than in the United States, wages are lower and manufactured goods are more expensive, which means that the standard of living is lower. However, because labor is cheap, the relatively small number in the European middle class can afford domestic servants and custom-made goods. In the United States, on the other hand, labor is costly and we do our own work to the extent that we are unable to get what we need from the factory — and at a substantial saving.

Retail self-service, whose economies are most fully realized in the distribution of foodstuffs, drugs and other packaged household products, is thus only one manifestation of the effects of technological progress in raising both productivity and wage levels in American industry. Techniques of retail distribution for clothing, furniture, house furnishings, household equipment and other more costly products do not, for obvious reasons, involve self-service. However, national advertising and brand identification of these products have diminished the need for and cost of personal selling. This is particularly evident in the discount house, where goods are not displayed and demonstrated but sold to the customer in the unopened factory package.

Extensive changes have also taken place in the intermediate stages of distribution. The design and operation of warehouses have been greatly improved during the past generation, in their physical aspects most recently by the movable conveyor belt and the fork-lift truck. Wholesale warehouses and factories, alike, have adopted better systems of inventory control. This has enabled them to achieve a more flexible basis of operation in spite of the greater burden thrust upon them by the fact that retailers no longer carry heavy stocks of goods and therefore expect prompt and frequent delivery of orders.

The railroads, which carried almost everything moving between inland cities at the turn of the century, still haul the great bulk commodities; but the motor truck has taken over an increasing share of the intercity traffic in finished consumer goods and has revolutionized transport within the great metropolitan areas. With daily, and in some cases twice-daily, replenishment of supplies, a retail store is no longer what it was originally — a "store" of goods patiently awaiting buyers — but is more like a pumping station speeding the steady flow of goods from factories through warehouses and distribution channels to consumers.

Pricing

These changes in the physical movement of goods from producers to consumers would not have come about, however, without significant advances in credit and pricing practices and sales techniques. The old-fashioned art of personal salesmanship has been elaborated into modern advertising, brand identification and promotion, market analysis and "creative selling."

One of the most significant advances in retailing — almost forgotten today because it is all but universal in the United States — was the adoption of the "one-price system" by the Wanamaker store in Philadelphia a century ago. This substitution of an administered price for individual bargaining between merchant and customer over every transaction was the counterpart in retailing of the standardization of product which came with the shift from handicraft to mass production in manufacturing. Not only did this new pricing system — unknown even today in many parts of the world — ensure fair treatment of customers and lessen dishonesty among sales personnel, but the elimination of higgling over every sale was a laborsaving measure of vast importance. Without it modern mass distribution would be quite impossible.

Along with the one-price system, however, American retail distribution — notably through mail order houses, chain store and supermarket systems, and department stores — is characterized by a high degree of price competition and flexibility. In mass distribution, profits come from rapid turnover and volume sales more than from high mark-ups, and the appeal of low prices coupled with large-scale advertising of price savings is the most constantly used selling technique. The use of price-cutting as a technique for clearing stocks reaches a peak in the "bargain basement," where goods not sold at the normal speed are disposed of at successive drastic price reductions, to the point where those remaining are eventually given away to charitable organizations.

Visiting merchants from parts of the world where a store is still a "store" and a storekeeper would rather keep an article forever than sell it at a loss find the obsessive preoccupation of the American retailer with turnover hard to understand, or even mildly amusing. What is not so readily realized is that American methods of selling and distribution are an essential counterpart of our system of mass production, which commands so much admiration abroad.

Sales Techniques

Instalment buying is another modern development in the technology of retail distribution in the United States. Although selling goods on credit is probably as old as retail trade, organized instalment credit on a large scale did not become important until the automobile came into common use. Today not only automobiles but also mechanical refrigerators, freezers, gas and electric stoves, washing machines, clothes dryers and ironers, and many other expensive consumer goods are sold "on time." Aside from unanswerable philosophical questions as to whether consumer credit is good or bad for the individual, there can be little doubt that instalment buying has been a tremendous stimulant to the sale of costly consumer durables, most of which are bought on the partial-payment plan. Human nature being what it is, it seems highly probable that the vast majority of buyers of such products who are now able to make the required down payment and meet the subsequent payments would go without if they had to save enough money in advance to pay cash. Thus this system of what Paul Mazur has called "fractional selling" is a method of making articles of high unit cost as easy to pay for as those of low unit cost.

Other significant advances in the techniques of advertising and selling are sales and cost analysis in terms of types of buyers, size of orders, etc.; market research on the basis of demographic and other statistical data; and sample surveys of consumer attitudes and responses. Decisions as to the design and pricing of new products are no longer made without pretesting consumer reactions. More scientific methods of measuring consumer motivation are helping to make advertising and promotional methods more productive.

About half of the total cost of distributing goods in the United States appears to be accounted for by these selling and promotional activities, in contrast to the physical task of handling, storing and delivering goods.[203] This function of demand creation, of conditioning and educating the customer and persuading him to buy, is unquestionably a more costly one in the United States than in countries with lower standards of living. That the high-pressure methods of persuasion so characteristic of American marketing are costly, and often wasteful and offensive, is as undeniable as the fact that their use is essential in creating the mass demand without which the low costs of mass production could not be realized.

The true significance of technology in raising the American standard of living is apparent only when production and distribution are viewed as a unified process. Then it is clear that technological progress has brought over the years and decades a steady lowering of the real costs of supplying the consumer with an ever wider range of useful goods and services.

203. Paul W. Stewart and J. Frederic Dewhurst, *Does Distribution Cost Too Much?*, Twentieth Century Fund, New York, 1939, p. 298.

## CHAPTER 25

PRODUCTIVITY: KEY TO WELFARE

AMERICAN TECHNOLOGY finds its visible manifestations in a constant stream of innovations and improvements in consumer goods and services and of new and better materials, machines and methods in industry and commerce. But the final and most significant fruits of our technological progress are the high productivity of the American economy and the correspondingly high standard of living the American people are able to enjoy. What this means in material terms is epitomized in the fact that with little more than 6 per cent of the world's population and less than 7 per cent of the world's land area, we produce and consume well over one third of the world's goods and services. In factory goods alone, we turn out close to one half of the global total. As measured by national income, the most comprehensive indicator of the net output of all goods and services, the American proportion of the world total is roughly 40 per cent.

NATIONAL INCOME AND EARNINGS

The aggregate national income of all the nations of the world has been estimated at about 260 billion "American dollars" in 1938, and at nearly $550 billion in 1948, when the United States price level was some 75 per cent higher. The United States share of this total increased from about 26 per cent in 1938 to almost 41 per cent in 1948.[1] Because European countries had not fully recovered from the effects of World War II by 1948, while the United States was enjoying a full-fledged boom in civilian products, the American share may have declined slightly since that year. But it has probably not dropped far below 40 per cent of the total.

Obviously this means that the typical American enjoys a standard of living several times higher than the average of the 2.5 billion people of the world, and of course many times that of the hundreds of millions who keep the world

average as low as it is. The aggregate real income of the more than 160 million Americans today probably exceeds the combined income of the 600 million people living in Europe and Russia and far surpasses the total income of the more than one billion inhabitants of Asia.

In 1948, per capita income in the United States exceeded $1,500, whereas the average for the world as a whole was not much above $200. In many of the underdeveloped countries, per capita income averaged less than $100, and in some the average was less than $50. Income estimates for the latter countries are notably unreliable, and comparisons between subsistence economies and advanced industrial economies fail to reflect real differences in well-being.

Comparisons of the United States with other urban-industrial countries are more valid and relevant. Even here, disparities are striking. Only in Canada, Australia, New Zealand, Switzerland, Sweden, Denmark and the United Kingdom did per capita income in 1948 approach 60 per cent of the American average. In most of the other European countries as well as in the more advanced South American countries the average was considerably less than half what it was in the United States. In the Soviet Union, Poland, Hungary, Spain and several other European countries, indeed, per capita income was less than the world average of $200.[2]

Natural Resources

The economic supremacy of the United States is often attributed to our possession of a disproportionately large share of the world's natural riches. The United States does possess large reserves of mineral fuels and many other minerals, but one reason our known reserves

---

BY J. FREDERIC DEWHURST. Opinions and judgments expressed in this chapter are those of the author and should not be attributed to the organization with which he is associated.

1. W. S. Woytinsky and E. S. Woytinsky, *World Population and Production,* Twentieth Century Fund, New York, 1953, pp. 393-394. These estimates, which the authors admit are very rough, make allowance for the fact that published data on the money incomes of countries with subsistence economies understate the real incomes of such countries.

2. *Ibid.,* p. 393.

are so large is that our natural resources have been more fully explored and exploited than those of most other parts of the world. Even so, we have always had to import many important raw materials, and our reliance on imports has increased substantially since World War II because of the exhaustion of many of our high-grade mineral reserves. On the whole, there is little evidence that, when the world's resources have been fully mapped and measured, it will be found that we possess within our borders more than "our share" of the world's natural wealth in terms of population or land area.

In any event, America's economic supremacy cannot be explained simply by favorable climate, fertile land and abundant natural resources. These are clearly significant, but they are not of controlling importance. If they were, it would be hard to explain how Switzerland, with meager resources, has been able to achieve a high standard of living; or why Rumania, with large oil reserves, makes little use of automotive power; or why the steam engine is a rarity in China in spite of her extensive coal deposits.

If natural wealth were the sole or principal source of productivity and prosperity, we would expect a country like Bulgaria to have a higher standard of living than Denmark, Poland to be more prosperous than Holland, and Yugoslavia to be more productive than Sweden, whereas the opposite is true in each case. Russia, as another example, has a population larger than our own, a land area more than twice as extensive, and rivals or surpasses us in the quantity and variety of minerals and other natural resources. Yet Russia, throughout the centuries of her existence, has remained a country with low labor productivity and a low standard of living.

Productive Efficiency

The fact that we produce so much of the world's goods with such a small share of the world's manpower reflects an outstanding ability to apply efficient and productive methods in converting virgin resources into useful products. Technology has enabled this country to raise labor productivity, or output per man-hour, more rapidly and to a much higher point than anywhere else in the world.

The higher productivity of American industry and the consequent higher earnings of American workers were measured a generation ago by

Colin Clark,[3] who found that the purchasing power of American workers' wages in 1925-1934 was nearly one third more than that of British workers' wages, more than twice as much as that of French and German wages, and about four times that of wages received by Italian, Japanese or Russian workers. And this was during a period that included five years of a depression that was especially severe in the United States.

In a later survey [4] Clark found that the "real national product per man-hour" in the United States in 1940 was over 75 per cent higher than in Great Britain, more than twice as high as in Germany, around three times that of Switzerland, Denmark, Norway and France, and over five times that of Japan, the USSR and Hungary. By 1947 the United States had increased its lead over Great Britain and other European countries, while New Zealand and Canada showed even sharper gains and followed closely after the United States.

Clark's comparisons were in terms of entire national economies; the American lead in productivity is undoubtedly especially large in mass-production manufacturing industries. In a careful comparison of output and employment in 31 manufacturing industries for the 1935-1939 period, Lássló Rostas found that average output per man-hour in the United States was about 2.8 times what it was in Great Britain, where productivity was approximately the same as in Germany and Sweden and probably as high as anywhere else in the world.[5]

Because occupational and industrial patterns vary widely from one country to another, comparisons of money wages for a single industry may be more significant. One such comparison for the relatively prosperous prewar year 1937 [6] showed American steel workers earning 82 cents an hour, British and French steel workers earning 40 cents, German 35 cents, Swedish 32 cents, Italian 20 cents, Belgian 17 cents, and Japanese 10 cents. Thus the American steel

---

3. Colin Clark, *The Conditions of Economic Progress,* Macmillan, London, 1940, p. 41.

4. "Review of Economic Progress," Vol. I, No. 4, Queensland Bureau of Industry, Brisbane, Australia, April 1949 (a leaflet).

5. Lássló Rostas, *Comparative Productivity in British and American Industry,* National Institute of Economic and Social Research, London, 1948, pp. 27 and 34–35.

6. A study by the American Iron and Steel Institute, based largely on data from the 1937 Year Book of the International Labor Office, reported in *Steel Facts,* April 1945, p. 3.

industry, because of its greater productivity, was able to pay its workers more than twice as much as the British or French, nearly two and a half times as much as the German and Swedish, four times as much as the Italian, five times as much as the Belgian and eight times as much as the Japanese.

PURCHASING POWER IN DIFFERENT COUNTRIES

However, comparisons of money wages in different countries expressed in terms of a single monetary unit, like the dollar, are subject to serious errors. This is true not only because controlled foreign exchange rates fail to reflect differences in the domestic purchasing power of various currencies, but also because consumption habits and costs of living vary widely from one country to another. A better measure of the real international differences in the purchasing power of wages is the amount of working time required in different countries to earn enough to purchase various articles of common consumption.

COMPARISONS REPORTED BY GERARD SWOPE

Recovery from the effects of World War II was long delayed in most belligerent and occupied countries whose factories and homes were heavily damaged. For that reason, comparisons of conditions just before the war probably reflect more nearly normal relationships than comparisons made even some years after its end.

European Countries

A series of such comparisons between the United States and various countries in Europe, South America and Asia have been made by Gerard Swope, former President of the General Electric Company.[7] In his first report, published on his return from Europe, Swope compared the time required in 1937 for typical industrial workers to earn enough to buy various items used by consumers in the United States and in eight European countries: Austria, Belgium, England, France, Germany, Holland, Hungary and Italy. There were striking differences in the

7. Gerard Swope, "Standards of Living," *Atlantic Monthly*, March 1938; "The Cost of Living in South America," *ibid.*, June 1940; "Standards of Living in Asia," *ibid.*, December 1950. The identity of the countries studied in 1938 and 1940, not indicated in the articles cited, was supplied by Mr. Swope.

purchasing power of wages, especially between the United States and Europe, but also among the European countries studied. Generally speaking, the productivity of English, French and German workers, as measured by what they could obtain with the proceeds of their labor, was much higher than that of workers in the other five countries, while the wages of Italian and Hungarian workers had the lowest purchasing power.

American workers, according to Swope's estimate, had to work 2.2 months to earn enough to pay a year's rent, while their opposite numbers in the eight European countries had to work an average of 2.8 months, or nearly 30 per cent longer. The shortest period, for Austria, was 2.1 months, while the longest, for the Netherlands, was 3.9 months. Although there were smaller variations here than for other items of expenditure, the differences in quality obtained were probably greater, for the typical family dwelling in the United States provides about twice the floor space of the European, and superior heating and lighting facilities.

A comparison of the working time required to purchase a "food basket" consisting of one quart of milk, a dozen eggs and one pound each of bread, butter and beef showed the American worker enjoying a marked advantage. To obtain these items he had to work only 1.7 hours, compared with the English worker's 4.2 hours, the Italian's 7.3 hours and an average of 5.7 hours for all eight European countries.

To earn enough to buy an automobile, the American had to work only 4.5 months; the average European, 16.3 months—nearly four times as long. In Hungary two years were required, in Italy nearly as long, and even in England, which was closest to the American level, 8.5 months were needed. These figures help explain why European workers ride bicycles to work, while the provision of adequate parking space for factory workers' cars has become an important problem for American industry.

To buy an electric refrigerator, the worker in the United States had to spend one month's wages, while the average for the eight European countries was 3.7 months. A radio cost less than five days' wages in the United States and more than three weeks' wages, on the average, in the eight European countries. The American worker earned enough in 3.6 minutes to pay for a kilowatt-hour of electricity; the European worker had to put in 24 minutes. To purchase an incandescent lamp only 12 minutes' working time was required in the United States. It required six times as long in England, slightly more time in France and Germany, and *3.4 hours* in Hungary. No wonder homes, streets, factories and hotels in the United States are lighted with a lavishness that would be considered scandalously wasteful almost anywhere else in the world.

South America and Asia

A comparison of working time required to purchase various items of consumption in Argentina, Brazil, Chile and Uruguay and the United States which Swope made in the early part of 1940 showed the American worker enjoying a similar advantage. To obtain the food basket of milk, eggs, bread, butter and meat, 5 to 6 hours of work were required in Argentina and Uruguay, compared with 13 to 14 hours in Brazil and Chile—and only 2.25 hours in the United States. To buy one kilowatt-hour of electricity, the South American worker had to work seven or eight times as long as the American worker; to purchase an incandescent lamp, the worker in Argentina had to work about seven times as long as his American counterpart, and the worker in Chile almost sixteen times as long. To buy a newspaper required 3 minutes of work in the United States, 12 minutes in Argentina and Uruguay, 16 minutes in Chile and 24 minutes in Brazil. And this is only part of the story, for whether or not the United States has the best newspapers in the world, it certainly has the biggest ones.

Swope's comparison of the purchasing power of wages in the United States and eight countries in the Near East and Far East was made in 1950. It showed even more striking disparities than the prewar comparisons with Europe and South America, especially in the case of Pakistan and Indonesia, where workers' purchasing power appeared to be incredibly low. Outstanding exceptions were Israel, where productivity and purchasing power were relatively high, though much lower than in the United States, and, to a lesser extent, Japan, which had not yet regained its industrial strength.

The time required to purchase a food basket of four items, which was about 1.5 hours in the United States, was 2.75 hours in Israel, but rose to nearly 38 hours in Indonesia and more than

48 hours in Pakistan. Electricity, gasoline and newspapers showed similar or greater disparities.

POSTWAR RELATIONSHIPS

Most of the studies summarized above relate to conditions before World War II. Disparities today are probably greater, for the gains in productivity and living standards in the United States since World War II have not been equaled in many other countries, while living conditions behind the Iron Curtain are often worse than they were before the war. Indeed, such recovery as had occurred in most European countries by 1948 failed to lift real income and purchasing power up to prewar levels.

For Europe as a whole (exclusive of the Soviet Union) the purchasing power of per capita income declined 12 per cent between 1938 and 1948, in contrast to a rise of 31 per cent in the United States. Apparently the only substantial gains not affected by territorial changes occurred in the neutral countries, Ireland, Sweden and Switzerland. Other western European countries, with the exception of the Netherlands, held close to prewar levels, while most countries in southern and central Europe suffered considerable declines. (See Table 347.) Economic recovery was rapid in Europe after 1948, but not enough so to bring much, if any, reduction in the disparity between European countries and the United States.

So far as productivity is concerned, the Economic Commission for Europe reported that even in 1950 the average output per man-hour in 15 European countries was only 6 per cent above the 1935–1938 average.[8] In Austria, Belgium, Germany, the Netherlands and Norway, productivity still remained below the prewar level, while the largest gain—28 per cent for Ireland—was appreciably less than the advance in American productivity during the same period. In the United States, output per man-hour in 1950, according to the estimates used in the present survey, was about 47 per cent above the 1940 average.

The Organization for European Economic Cooperation has recently published a study by Milton Gilbert and Irving B. Kravis (*An International Comparison of National Products and the Purchasing Power of Currencies*) which

8. *Economic Survey of Europe in 1950*, Economic Commission for Europe, United Nations, Geneva, 1951, Table 26, p. 57.

TABLE 347. PER CAPITA INCOME IN THE UNITED STATES AND VARIOUS EUROPEAN
COUNTRIES IN DOLLARS OF 1938 PURCHASING POWER, IN 1938 AND 1948

	1938	1948	Percentage Change, 1938–1948
United States	$521	$683	31.1
Europe (excluding USSR)	207	182	−12.1
Austria	179	130	−27.4
Belgium-Luxembourg	275	278	1.1
Bulgaria	68	66	−2.9
Czechoslovakia	176	195	10.8
Denmark	316	307	−2.8
Finland	178	173	−2.8
France	236	228	−3.4
Germany	337	160	−52.5
Greece	80	62	−22.5
Hungary	112	98	−12.5
Ireland	252	287	13.9
Italy	127	105	−17.3
Netherlands	323	250	−22.6
Norway	255	253	−0.8
Poland	104	141	35.6
Sweden	367	413	12.5
Switzerland	367	441	20.2
United Kingdom	378	401	6.1

Source: Economic Survey of Europe in 1948, Economic Commission for Europe, United Nations, Geneva, 1949, from Table E, p. 235.

gives a rough indication of international differences in productivity by comparing per capita consumption in leading European countries and the United States. Because retail margins to cover indirect taxes and transportation and distribution costs vary widely among countries, this study presents indexes of per capita consumption valued both by United States prices and by average European prices. The results of this comparison (for 1950) confirm the wide lead held by the United States even over the industrially advanced western European countries. Per capita indexes were as follows:

	U.S. Prices	European Prices
United States	100	100
United Kingdom	66	53
France	53	40
Germany	42	32
Italy	31	22

Purchasing Power for Foods

A detailed study made by the United States Department of Labor of the comparative purchas-

ing power for typical foodstuffs in 1950 shows not only that the American worker was far ahead of workers in other countries, but that the "degree of superiority in the power of United States earnings to buy food" had increased since 1937.[9] This survey, made in 19 foreign countries and the United States, covered about 40 commodities, of which 8 were staples consumed in nearly all countries.

The working time required for an American worker to buy a unit of each of these commodities was far less than the average for workers in the 19 foreign countries. To purchase a dozen eggs and a pound each of wheat flour, bread, butter, cheese, potatoes, lard and sugar required only 98 minutes' working time in the United States, compared with an average of 356 minutes, or more than three and a half times as long, for the other 19 countries. Only in Australia, Canada, Great Britain, Israel, Norway and Sweden was less than 200 minutes' working time needed to acquire this package, while more than 500 min-

9. "Work Time Required to Buy Food, 1937–50," Monthly Labor Review, February 1951.

TABLE 348. MINUTES OF WORKING TIME REQUIRED TO BUY VARIOUS STAPLE FOODS IN THE UNITED STATES AND 19 FOREIGN COUNTRIES, 1950[a]

Country	Total[b]	Wheat Flour	Bread	Butter	Cheese	Eggs	Potatoes	Lard	Sugar
		(Lb.)	(Lb.)	(Lb.)	(Lb.)	(Doz.)	(Lb.)	(Lb.)	(Lb.)
United States	98	4	6	31	22	22	2	7	4
Average for 19 foreign countries	356	12	10	116	56	94	5	42	22
Australia	123	4	5	30	23	52	3	—	6
Austria	561	12	13	148	136	124	6	94	28
Canada	133	4	6	39	35	29	2	12	6
Chile	522	13	14[e]	167	96	105	6	108	13
Czechoslovakia[d]	346	8	6	93	58	92	2	70	17
Denmark	219	7	10	57	43	61	2	35	4
Finland	349	12	14[e]	106	74	74	3	49	17
France	560	17	9	169	164	96	9	71	25
Germany	285	11	10	129	—	105	4	—	26
Great Britain	168	7	6	37	18	66	3	22	9
Hungary	471	17	11	160	—	106	4	133	40
Ireland	291	6	7	76	61	94	4	33	10
Israel	147	8	4	40	20	64	3	—	8
Italy	567	17	15	183	133	102	8	66	43
Netherlands	515	14	12	163	105	128	4	66	23
Norway	180	6	5	58	25	75	3	—	8
Sweden	171	7	10[e]	60	28	54	3	—	9
Switzerland	310	19	7	117	35	76	5	39	12
USSR	852	36	19	373	—	291	11	—	122

Source: "Work Time Required to Buy Food, 1937–50," Monthly Labor Review, February 1951.

a. Prices obtained in January-May 1950 period in all countries except Chile, Czechoslovakia, Denmark and Norway, where prices apply to latter part of 1949.

b. Figures shown are simple totals of the minutes required to buy stated units of staple foods and do not attempt to reflect differences in consumption habits in different countries.

c. French bread.

d. Ration prices; free-market prices much higher for most items.

e. Average.

utes were required in Austria, Chile, France, Italy and the Netherlands, and 852 minutes in the Soviet Union. (See Table 348.)

That the contrast in the purchasing power of workers' wages is even more striking for manufactured products than for foods is revealed in an unpublished study by the distinguished French economist Jean Fourastié, of l'Ecole Pratique des Hautes Etudes. This survey, made in December 1950 in 29 countries, showed the number of hours a common laborer would have to work to buy each of 14 products or services, including 10 nonfood items. To buy a radio set, for example, required the earnings of 20 hours' work in the United States, but as much as 500 hours in Portugal and Indonesia. Even in such advanced European countries as France, Germany, the United Kingdom and the Netherlands,

the cost in working time was from four and a half to six and a half times what it was in the United States. Blue denim overalls cost as little as 3.5 hours of work in Canada and 4 hours in the United States, compared with 50 hours or more in Spain, Hungary, Indonesia and Turkey, and with 30 hours or more in France, East Germany, Austria, the Philippines, Syria and Trieste. The cost of gas and electricity showed a similar or greater range among the countries covered in Professor Fourastié's survey.

It is significant, however, that there was a much narrower range in the cost of personal services such as haircuts and maid service, which are little affected by mechanization and in which, therefore, productivity shows small variations from one country to another. For example, the cost of a man's haircut was identical in the

United States, Italy, Switzerland and Uruguay — the equivalent of one hour's earnings. But the purchase of a pair of shoes, which required 4 hours' work in the United States, cost three times as much in Uruguay, four and one half times as much in Switzerland, and eight times as much in Italy. Clearly, mechanization and inanimate energy, rather than manual skill and "labor efficiency," are the predominant causes of high productivity, low prices and a high standard of living.

These comparisons of the purchasing power of workers' wages in different countries are affected by other factors as well as productivity. Price differences may arise from the fact that certain foodstuffs are especially plentiful and cheap in some countries, e.g., beef in Argentina (before the Peron regime) and Australia and dairy products in New Zealand and Denmark. In certain cases, as in Great Britain and to a much greater extent in Czechoslovakia, prices of food staples have been held down, and the supply limited, by rationing and subsidies. At the other extreme, imposition of heavy sales taxes distorts price relationships. The tremendous difference between the purchasing power of wages in the United States and in the Soviet Union,[10] for example, is due partly to the much higher productivity of American industry and partly to the steeply regressive tax system of the Soviet Union, which, in contrast to the United States, relies so heavily on a retail sales tax.

Purchasing power disparities between countries may also be affected by differences in the distribution of income between wages, on the

one hand, and the return to property in the form of profits, rent and interest, on the other. The existence of these and other factors means that the relative purchasing power of workers' wages in different countries provides no exact measure, but only a general indication, of actual differences in output per worker or per man-hour.

Whatever the precise differences in average productivity, purchasing power and per capita income may be, there can be no doubt that they have all reached a much higher level in the United States than anywhere else in the world. The advantage enjoyed by the average American cannot be expressed in exact terms, but probably varies from some 50 or 60 per cent in the case of a few industrially advanced countries, like Canada and Sweden, to several hundred per cent for the relatively underdeveloped countries of Europe. In most parts of the Middle East, Africa and Asia, living conditions for the mass of the people are so wretched, and industrial and agricultural methods so primitive, as to defy comparison with the United States. The typical American today takes for granted a level of material well-being which is beyond even the comprehension of the vast majority of the world's people.

PURCHASING POWER GAINS

The economic position of the American worker today is also far superior to that of his own parents only a generation ago. A detailed study published by the National Industrial Conference Board in 1950 provides striking evidence of how technological progress has shortened working hours and increased the purchasing power of hourly wages.[11]

Between 1914 and 1948, average working time in the 25 manufacturing industries surveyed declined from 51.5 hours a week to 39.7 hours, or by 23 per cent, while the purchasing value of an hour's work, in terms of the goods and services required to meet family needs, increased by 134 per cent. The typical factory worker in these 25 industries was unable in 1914 to meet his family's needs for food, housing, clothing and other items without working overtime or supplementing the family resources in some other way. The worker of 1948, on the other hand, in

---

10. "Few persons in the United States realize how hard a Russian already had to work for the little he received, and what a great strain was put upon his physical and mental resources in being forced to increase the duration and speed of his labor. At the time the currency was changed [December 1947], we calculated that a Soviet worker had to work 4 hours and 57 minutes for a dozen eggs, 14 hours and 5 minutes for one pound of coffee, 1 hour and 10 minutes for one pound of wheat bread, 2 hours and 34 minutes for one pound of sugar, 2 hours and 4 minutes for a package of cigarettes, 104 hours and 30 minutes for a pair of men's shoes, 107 hours and 30 minutes for a pair of women's shoes, 580 hours and 15 minutes for a man's wool suit, and 252 hours for a woman's wool dress. His counterpart in the United States worked 38 minutes for the dozen eggs, 22 minutes for the coffee, 6 minutes for the bread, 5 minutes for the sugar, 9 minutes for the cigarettes, 7 hours and 15 minutes for the men's shoes, 5 hours and 32 minutes for the women's shoes, 28 hours and 4 minutes for a man's wool suit, and 12 hours and 52 minutes for a woman's wool suit." Walter Bedell Smith, *My Three Years in Moscow*, Lippincott, Philadelphia, 1950, p. 139.

11. *What an Hour's Work Would Buy, 1914–1948*, Studies in Labor Statistics, No. 3, National Industrial Conference Board, New York, March 1950.

spite of his shorter work week and higher standard of living, earned enough to meet his family's
requirements and to save part of his weekly
paycheck.

INDIVIDUAL PRODUCTS

Prices of nearly all articles used or consumed
by the worker's family increased over the 34-
year period, of course, but average factory wages
rose much more than commodity prices. Hence
the purchasing power of an hour's pay increased
greatly. Of the several scores of products and
services surveyed by the Conference Board, all
but seven—aspirin, cleaning powder, milk of
magnesia, razor blades, kerosene, automobile
tires and electricity—sold at a higher dollar price
in 1948 than in 1914, but none sold at a higher
"working-hour price." (See Table 349.)

The advantage in purchasing power possessed
by the 1948 worker over his predecessor varied
widely among different products. He had to
work almost as long to buy a davenport—nearly
75 hours, compared with 80 hours for the worker
of 1914; but an automobile tire, which required
the proceeds of 96 hours' work in 1914, cost the
1948 worker less than 11 hours' wages and actually required a smaller cash outlay. Moreover, this nine-to-one gain would be multiplied
several times if the greatly increased mileage of
today's tire were taken into account.[12] The spectacular impact of technology in lowering costs and
improving performance is also illustrated by the
decline in the price of electricity during this 34-
year period, which included two major price
inflations.

Of course, neither tires nor electricity—nor
razor blades, which also declined in price—are
typical of what has happened to productivity and
prices in American industry. However, there
were many family necessities— ranging from eggs
to anthracite and from silk stockings and men's
hats to washing machines and automobiles—
whose real cost, in terms of the hours of work
required to earn enough to buy them, was from
two to five times as great in 1914 as it was in 1948.

The 134 per cent increase over the 34-year
period in the purchasing power of factory workers' average hourly wages for all the goods and

services covered in the Conference Board's survey
represents an average gain of 2.5 per cent a
year. Inasmuch as the productivity of the American economy as a whole appears to have risen
about 100 per cent between 1914 and 1948, or
at an annual rate of only 2.1 per cent, it appears
that factory workers considerably improved their
relative position over this period.

FACTORY WORKERS' BUDGETS

Changes in family size and consumption
habits, in the quality and variety of products
available, and in the prices of individual goods
and services all complicate the task of comparing
family budgets in years as widely separated as
1914 and 1948. It is as difficult to make such
comparisons for widely separated time periods
in the same country as it is to compare workers'
family budgets in France or Belgium today with
those in the United States. The Conference
Board's study attempts to overcome some of
these difficulties, first, by comparing the costs of
the actual family budget of the 1914 factory
worker in that year with the costs of a substantially identical family budget in 1948, and, second,
by comparing the costs of the actual budget
of the 1948 factory worker in that year with the
costs of a substantially identical family budget
in 1914. (See Figure 101 and Appendix 25–1.)

For both budgets food was the most important
item in both years, whether the cost is measured
in dollars or in working hours. Although the
dollar cost of the family's weekly food supply
virtually trebled between 1914 and 1948, the
working time required to purchase it was cut
to less than half. In all other categories as well,
dollar costs increased, and hourly costs decreased
—with the single exception of income taxes, which
did not appear in the 1914 budget.

The 1948 budget showed spectacular gains.
Actually amounting to $49.51 a week in 1948,
it would have cost only $23.81, or less than half as
much, in 1914. However, that dollar cost would
have been completely out of reach for the typical
factory worker of 1914, whose average weekly
wages were only $12.72. By 1948, average weekly
earnings had risen to $58.52 and were thus $9
in excess of the weekly budget. In terms of working time, the 1948 factory worker's budget required less than 34 hours, compared with an
actual work week of 39.7 hours in that year. But
the wages earned by the factory worker in 1914

---

12. Henry Hazlitt reported in the June 30, 1952 issue
of *Newsweek* that the 1947 automobile tire was good for
34,000 miles on the average, compared with a 3,500-mile
life for the 1910 tire.

TABLE 349. PRICES OF SELECTED HOUSEHOLD PRODUCTS AND SERVICES AND HOURS
OF WORK REQUIRED TO PURCHASE EACH, 1914 AND 1948

	Price		Hours of Work	
Product or Service	1914	1948	1914	1948
Food				
Rib roast, lb.	$ .20	$ .70	.81	.47
Pork chops, lb.	.21	.73	.87	.50
Bacon, lb.	.27	.76	1.08	.52
Butter, lb.	.35	.91	1.42	.62
Milk, qt.	.09	.20	.36	.14
Eggs, doz.	.32	.67	1.29	.45
Bread, lb.	.06	.14	.25	.09
Sugar, lb.	.05	.10	.21	.06
Clothing				
Women's wool suit	9.17	16.82	37.13	11.41
Cotton dress	1.05	4.48	4.25	3.04
Rayon slip	1.00	1.79	4.05	1.21
Silk hose	.58	1.32	2.35	.90
Women's pumps	2.70	4.44	10.93	3.01
Women's wool coat	12.63	30.65	51.13	20.79
Men's suit	16.75	34.85	67.81	23.64
Men's overcoat	12.75	32.48	51.62	22.04
Cotton shirt	.86	3.49	3.48	2.37
Men's felt hat	4.00	4.79	16.19	3.25
Men's wool hose	.24	.67	.97	.45
Household equipment and operation				
Carpet, 9 x 12	19.85	49.73	80.36	33.74
Linoleum, sq. yd.	1.10	1.87	4.45	1.27
Living room suite, 2 pc.	38.13	171.23	154.37	116.17
Davenport	19.65	109.95	79.55	74.59
Mattress	6.47	16.90	26.19	11.47
Sheets, pair	.80	2.51	3.24	1.70
Vacuum cleaner	19.65	64.95	79.55	44.06
Washing machine	54.35	93.95	220.04	63.74
Anthracite, stove, ton	7.70	18.74	31.2	12.7
Fuel oil, gal.	.11	.13	.4	.1
Kerosene, gal.	.17	.15	.7	.1
Gas, 1,000 cu. ft.	.85	1.16	3.4	.8 [a]
Electricity, kwh.	.09	.05	.4	
Transportation				
Trolley fare	.05	.09	.2	.1
Automobile	682.50	1,405.50	2,763.2	953.5
Gasoline, gal.	.17	.24	.7	.2
Tires	23.70	15.90	96.0	10.8
Miscellaneous				
Aspirin tablets, 100	.78	.59	3.2	.4
Castor oil, 4 oz.	.10	.36	.4	.2
Milk of magnesia, 16 oz.	.38	.36	1.5	.2
Cleaning powder, lb.	.18	.11	.7	.1
Men's haircut	.30	.93	1.2	.6
Motion pictures	.22	.60	.9	.4
Newspapers, yearly	5.41	14.63	21.9	9.9
Razor blades, doz.	.78	.31	3.2	.2
Soap, bar	.04	.10	.2	.1
Toothpaste, tube	.17	.21	.7	.1

Source: *What an Hour's Work Would Buy, 1914–1948*, Studies in Labor Statistics, No. 3,
National Industrial Conference Board, New York, March 1950.

a. Less than 0.1 hours' work.

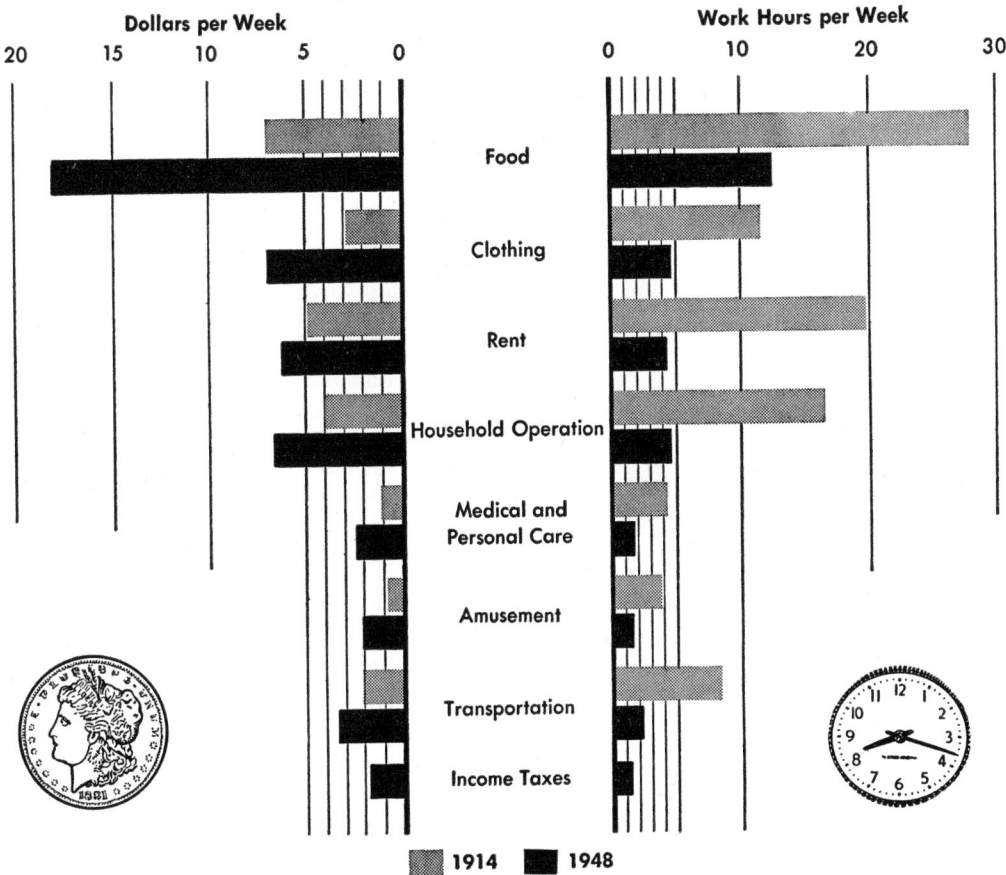

FIGURE 101. DOLLAR COST AND HOURLY WORK EQUIVALENT OF TYPICAL UNITED STATES FACTORY WORKER'S 1948 WEEKLY BUDGET IN 1914 AND 1948

Source: Appendix 25–1.

were so low that he would have had to work almost three times as long to supply himself with the articles in the 1948 budget.

The much more modest 1914 budget, which cost $16 a week in 1914, would have cost nearly $41 in 1948. But the working time required to provide it dropped from 64.7 hours for the 1914 worker to 27.6 hours for the 1948 worker. Wages earned during the actual 51.5-hour work week of 1914 fell short of family requirements, whereas the 1948 worker would have had "surplus" equal to the proceeds of 12 hours' work.

ENERGY USE AND PRODUCTIVITY

These changes in living standards and productivity can be expressed more compactly—though less concretely—in terms of averages for the national economy as a whole. Thus our 1950 national income of $241 billion meant that average per capita income in that year was $1,580 and average income per household, $5,530. This represented almost a fourfold rise over 1850, when per capita income, in dollars of 1950 purchasing power, was $405. This means that if the national income were divided among the nation's breadwinners, it would have provided each of them with an average weekly income of about $24 in 1850; by 1950, despite the decline in the length of the work week, the average would have jumped to roughly $75, or more than three times what it was a century before. (See Tables 14 and 37.)

Output Up and Hours Down

Since this great advance in material well-being accompanied a steady decline in working hours, it reflects even larger gains in productivity, or output per man-hour. The 1850 worker, putting in nearly 70 hours a week, turned out in each hour of work less than 34 cents worth of goods—in terms of what money would buy in 1950. By 1900, productivity had more than doubled, rising to 75.5 cents per man-hour, while the next fifty years saw an even larger increase to an average of $1.94 per man-hour. Today's worker can enjoy a 40-hour week, and his family a high standard of living, because with modern power-driven tools and equipment he can produce almost as much in ten minutes as his 1850 ancestor could in an hour.

It is this fabulous gain in productivity that enabled us in 1950 to turn out twenty-five times the volume of goods and services produced a century before, while the total "input of labor," as measured by the aggregate of man-hours worked, was less than five times as large — 127 billion man-hours compared with 27 billion. Employment during this period increased a little over eight times and working time dropped more than 40 per cent — from 70 hours a week to 40.

That less than five times as much effort can produce twenty-five times the volume of goods and services means that output per man-hour in 1950 was almost six times what it was in 1850. This rapid increase in productivity, far surpassing that of any other great industrial nation, explains the vast material progress of the United States in the past. Productivity is the key to welfare — in America as in the rest of the world.

Causes of Productivity Differences

For an individual factory or farm or for the economy as a whole, productivity can be most conveniently measured—as it usually is—in terms of output per man-hour or per worker. But productivity is only to a limited degree either the result, or the measure, of labor efficiency. As every industrial manager knows, some workers are more efficient than others, because of better aptitude for the job or greater skill or intelligence. Other things being equal, an industrious, efficient worker will produce more in a given time than one who is lazy and incompetent. But if the first man is working with a shovel and wheelbarrow and the second with a bulldozer, the inferior worker will be far more productive than the superior one.

It is also true that the productivity or efficiency of a specific business enterprise can vary within wide limits, depending upon the energy, ability and loyalty of the working force, the experience and competence of the management, and the morale of the organization as a whole. On the basis of various productivity studies made by the United States Department of Labor, it is obvious that in some American industries the best plants are as much as three times more efficient than the worst.

Obviously, too, as we found out in the depths of the depression, and again when the war boom got under way, unit operating costs are lower—which means that productivity is higher—when an individual plant or an entire industry is operating close to capacity than when it is using only a small fraction of its capacity.

All of these factors are responsible for wide variations in productivity, among individual workers and individual enterprises at any given time, and for the economy as a whole between a year of depression like 1932, a year of moderate prosperity like 1941, and a boom year like 1951. If the least efficient workers and enterprises in an industry could operate as efficiently even as the average, and if we could avoid both severe depressions and excessive booms, the average productivity of American industry could be greatly increased.

Important as these factors are, however, they are chiefly short-run influences. Taken together, they fall far short of accounting for the sixfold increase in the productivity of the American economy as a whole over the past century.

Both the competence of the management and the skill, intelligence and energy of the individual worker have been minor elements in the steep upward trend of American productivity over the past several decades. The most energetic and skillful shoemaker working long hours under the ablest supervision, but with the hand tools of a century ago, did not remotely approach the productivity of today's semiskilled operator, working with the aid of power-driven machinery. The fabulous increase in output per man-hour over the past century and the marked lead which the United States holds over the rest of the world have not been achieved by working harder or more skillfully. The causes have been the steady expansion of our productive plant, and our technological progress in devising superior techniques and processes and more and better machinery to multiply human effort through the use of vast amounts of inanimate energy.

INTERNATIONAL DIFFERENCES

Our high productivity and standard of living are in large part the fruits of a "high-energy civilization." It is no accident that the United States leads the world in the per capita consumption of inanimate energy, as it does in per capita income.

Energy Consumption and Per Capita Income

Americans consumed a per capita amount of mineral energy (including water power) equivalent to nearly 8 tons of coal in 1949, when per capita income stood at $1,453.[13] At the other extreme, the teeming population of Burma, largely dependent on subsistence agriculture, consumed only 570 *pounds* of "coal equivalent" per capita and had average income per head of only $36. Not far from the Burmese level, in terms of energy consumption and per capita income, are Egypt, Pakistan and India and many other smaller underdeveloped countries. At upper income levels are such high-standard countries as Canada, the United Kingdom, New Zealand, Sweden, Switzerland, Denmark and Australia. (See Figure 102.)

Because of climatic and occupational differences between countries, the relation between energy consumption and income is by no means close and consistent, however. The high energy consumption of Canada reflects the cold climate as well as the fact that such important Canadian industries as mining and paper pulp manufacture are especially heavy consumers of energy. In Switzerland, on the other hand, the tourist trade and precision manufactures, though not heavy energy consumers, provide a high standard of living. In Norway abundant water power provides cheaper and therefore more plentiful energy than in some countries with higher income. New Zealand and Denmark provide a relatively generous livelihood to their people from dairying and other kinds of agriculture not dependent on mechanical power.

In spite of the exceptions, however, the high-energy civilizations are generally those with high productivity and a high standard of living, while extremely low energy consumption is characteristic of subsistence economies, of poverty, and of low productivity. To some extent this contrast

13. This figure differs slightly from the per capita estimate implied by Table 14, which includes a later, revised national income estimate for the United States.

arises from the fact that the rich community can afford more plentiful heat and light and more extensive use of power-driven family equipment, such as automobiles and vacuum cleaners. But the stronger causation is in the opposite direction: heavy consumption of inanimate energy means the use of power-driven, instead of animal- or human-powered, equipment in agriculture and transportation, and the multiplication of human effort through the use of laborsaving machinery and techniques in all branches of industry and commerce.

Other Causes of Productivity Differences

It is by no means true, however, that international differences in productivity even between comparable industrial countries can always be attributed exclusively to differences in energy consumption. Specialization of tasks and division of labor appear to be carried much further in the mass-production industries of the United States than in other countries. The efficiencies of mass production in the United States in turn rest on the existence of a mass market supported by high wages and consumer acceptance of standardized products. This simplification and standardization of products, coupled with specialization of tasks, could account for higher productivity in American establishments, even against foreign establishments using similar mechanical equipment.

Differences in plant layout and operation, in lighting and ventilation, and in the effectiveness of managerial supervision undoubtedly help to account for international differences in productivity, just as they are responsible for the often great differentials among plants in the same industry in the United States.

Foreign observers of American industrial methods have sometimes remarked that the tempo of work is more rapid here than abroad, that American workers work harder and faster than their opposite numbers in European industries. Whether this is true or not, and if so whether it is due to the better nutrition enjoyed by American workers, to their greater physical energy, to the "competitive spirit" of American economic life, or to other more subtle psychological or social influences, cannot be determined without a good deal of further study, and perhaps can never be known.

Whatever all the causes of the higher produc-

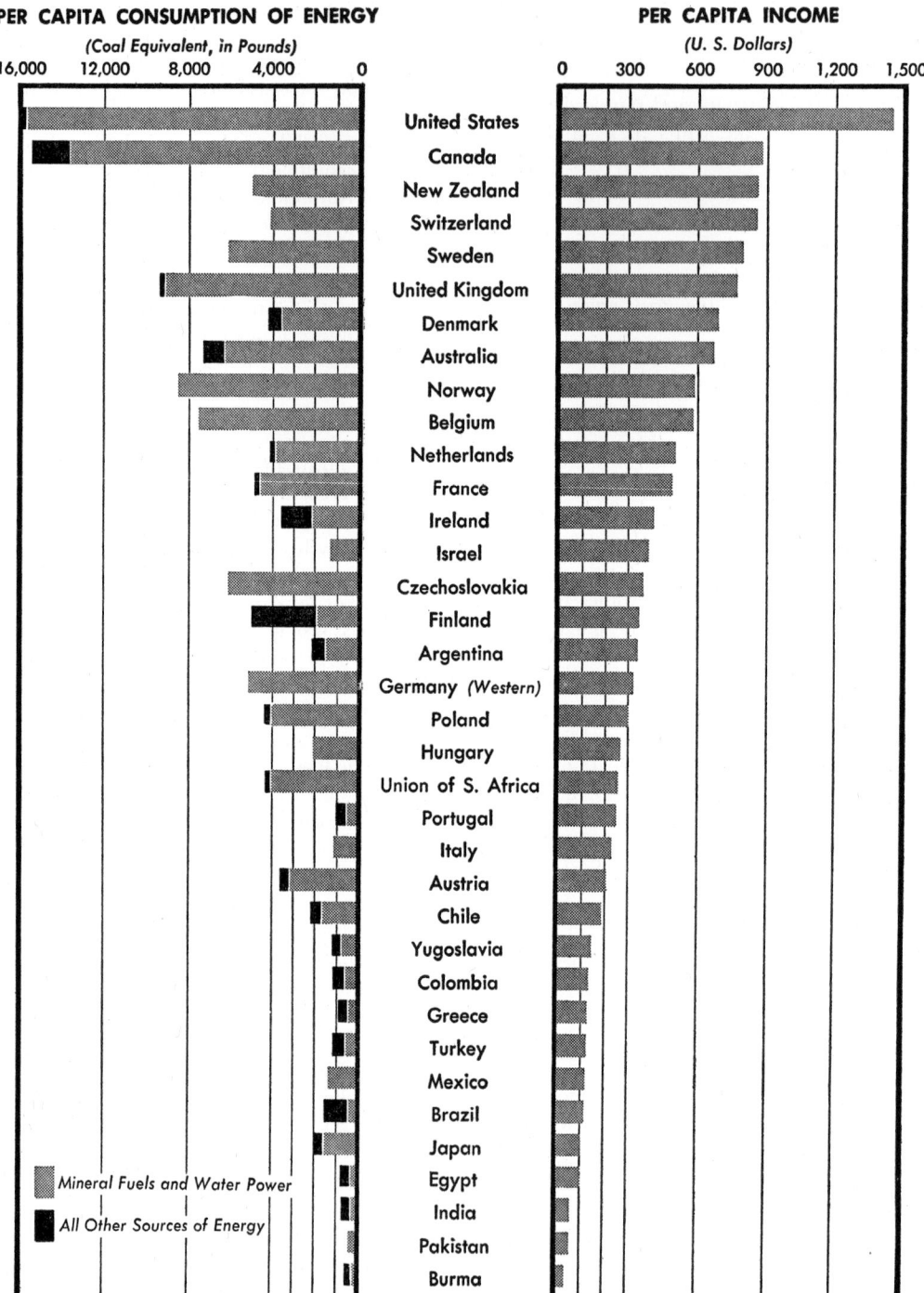

PER CAPITA CONSUMPTION OF ENERGY
(Coal Equivalent, in Pounds)

PER CAPITA INCOME
(U. S. Dollars)

Mineral Fuels and Water Power

All Other Sources of Energy

FIGURE 102. PER CAPITA INCOME AND ENERGY CONSUMPTION,[a] SELECTED COUNTRIES, 1949

Source: Appendix 25–2.

a. Per capita consumption of energy from sources other than mineral fuels and water power is not available for some of the countries listed (see Appendix 25–2). However, mineral fuels and water power constitute virtually the only important sources of inanimate energy in these countries, except in Sweden, where considerable fuel wood is used, and in Hungary, Italy, Mexico and Pakistan.

tivity of industry in the United States may be, however, statistical evidence merely confirms common observation that in all phases of economic life the American worker has the use of far more numerous and powerful tools and equipment than his colleague in Europe or other parts of the world. It is hard to believe that this lavish use of inanimate energy is not a primary, or even the primary, factor responsible for the high productivity of American industry.

HISTORICAL CHANGES IN THE UNITED STATES

In the United States the relation between labor productivity and the kinds and amounts of energy consumed can be traced on a roughly estimated basis over the past century. Our total energy supply a hundred years ago was obtained, as it is today, almost exclusively from the muscular effort of human workers and work animals, from wind and water power, and from the combustion of fuel wood and mineral fuels.

Trends in Energy Use

For purposes of comparison, the energy derived from each of these diverse sources can be reduced to the common denominator of a standard unit of heat, such as the British Thermal Unit, or a ton of typical bituminous coal (with a heat content of 13,100 BTUs per pound). Thus measured, the relative importance of these six energy sources has changed radically during the past century. In 1850, fuel wood, the vast bulk of which, then as now, was burned inefficiently in household fireplaces, contributed 90 per cent of our total energy, and mineral fuels, wind and water power, 9 per cent. Fuel wood had dropped to 21 per cent of this total by 1900, and to less than 3 per cent by 1950, when mineral fuels and water power accounted for nearly all of the remaining 97 per cent. Animate sources contributed a negligible proportion of our total energy supply in 1950, as they did in 1850 and throughout the entire century. (See Figure 103.)

Total Energy Input

The total consumption of energy in 1850 amounted to the equivalent of about 4 tons of coal per capita; in 1950, to about 8 tons per capita. (See Table 16 and Appendix 25–3, Table J.)

This mere doubling of the per capita input of energy, in the face of a more than threefold increase in the per capita output of goods and services (as measured by national income expressed in constant prices), appears to furnish no very striking confirmation of the existence of a "high-energy civilization."

These long-term trends in total energy supply, however, fail to reveal some very significant changes that have been taking place throughout the century. In the first place, as pointed out above, the least efficient source of energy, fuel wood, predominated a century ago but now accounts for only a negligible share of the total supply. Second, technological advances have brought steady and spectacular gains in the efficiency of fuel combustion, especially for mineral fuels. We have thus been able to obtain in useful form, whether for heat or power generation, an increasingly larger proportion of the original input of energy. A third factor affecting the significance of historical trends in total energy input is the fact that a much larger proportion of the much more efficiently converted 1950 energy supply than of the 1850 input was used to provide motive power for "work performance," i.e., the production of agricultural, mineral and industrial products and the transportation of goods and people. An estimated 13 per cent of total energy input was used for work performance in 1850, compared with close to 40 per cent in recent decades. (See Appendix 25–3, Tables J and K.) It is this fraction of total energy input, and the "work output" obtained from it, that is of special significance in accounting for the volume of national production and the level of labor productivity.

Energy Used to Perform Work

"Work" as defined here includes only such operations as have been, or could be, performed (however inadequately) by the muscle power of animals and men.[14] Muscular energy can be

14. So far as human beings are concerned, of course, their work today usually requires more brain power than muscle power. Very few people — in the United States, at least — have to work like a horse any more. Pushing buttons, punching typewriters, selling goods, driving taxicabs, answering telephone calls, dictating letters, thinking up bright ideas — all of these jobs require more mental than physical effort. There is an obvious anachronism, therefore, in comparing and "combining" manpower with other kinds of energy in the United States under present conditions. However, any error aris-

used for such activities as pulling, pushing, lifting, cutting and digging, but not for smelting metals or cooking food, or to provide heat, light and refrigeration.

Some of the basic components of our energy supply have always been used exclusively for performing work as defined above. These would include human and animal muscle power, wind power to operate windmills and sailing vessels, and water wheels (before the advent of hydroelectric power). Fuel wood and anthracite coal, on the other hand, have been used predominantly for space heating and only to a limited extent to provide motive power for work performance. The most important of today's energy sources—bituminous coal, petroleum, natural gas and hydroelectricity—have always been used for heating, lighting and a variety of other end purposes, of which performance of work is only one, though usually among the more important ones.

In the aggregate, the *energy input used for work performance* in 1950 amounted to the equivalent of 468 million tons of coal. This was 38 times the 12.2 million tons of coal equivalent used for the same purposes in 1850. This compares with a 14-fold increase in *total energy consumption*—from 91 million tons of coal equivalent in 1850 to almost 1.3 billion tons in 1950. The difference in these gains reflects the substantial increase in the proportion of the total energy supply used for work performance. (See Appendix 25-3, Tables J and K.)

There were marked differences in the trends for different types of energy. Animate energy, all of which is used to perform work, increased 51 per cent during the century; that obtained from wind and fuel wood declined sharply; water power increased steeply; while there was seventy-three times as much mineral energy devoted to work performance in 1950 as in 1850—461 million tons of coal equivalent compared with 6.3 million tons.

Efficiency of Energy Conversion

The most relevant measure of the significance of energy use in the economy, however, is not what goes in as coal under the boiler but rather what comes out as work performed by the

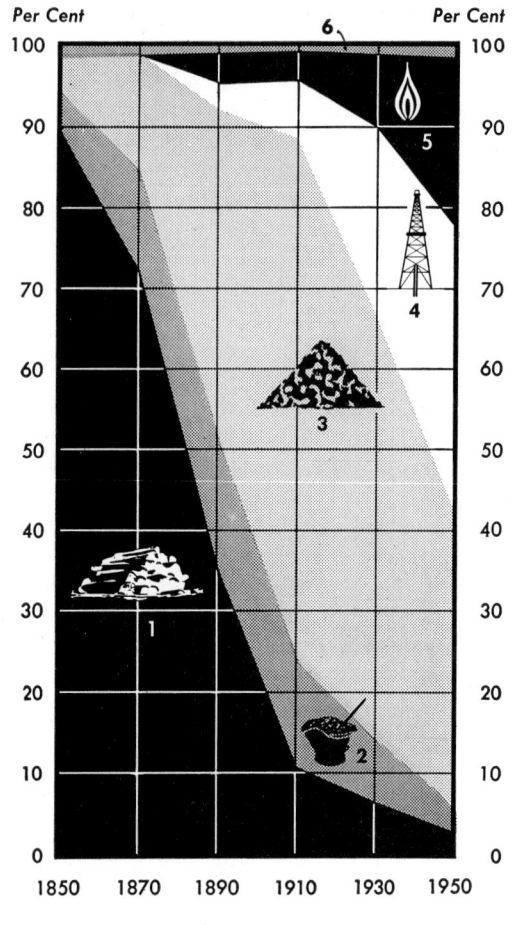

| 1 Fuel Wood | 3 Bituminous Coal | 5 Natural Gas |
| 2 Anthracite | 4 Petroleum | 6 All Others |

FIGURE 103. PERCENTAGE DISTRIBUTION OF TOTAL ENERGY SUPPLY IN THE UNITED STATES, 1850–1950

Source: Appendix 25–3, Table J.

lathe or drill press in a machine shop, by the wheels of a locomotive or a ship's propeller, or by a bulldozer or power shovel. Work output (as this concept in its limited form is defined above) can be measured in terms of the kilowatt-hour, or the horsepower-hour. Traditionally, this latter term represents roughly the amount of work a horse can do in an hour,[15] and this has long been regarded as eight or ten times what a man can do. Recent studies, however, indicate that human workers are not capable of sustained effort at anything like such a rate, and that a

___

ing from this is of little consequence, because human workers today account for only an extremely small fraction of total work output, whereas a century ago, when their contribution was much larger, human effort was more largely physical than mental.

___

15. Accurately defined, the horsepower-hour (the equivalent of 0.746 kilowatt-hours) is the amount of work performed in lifting a 550-pound weight one foot per second for an hour.

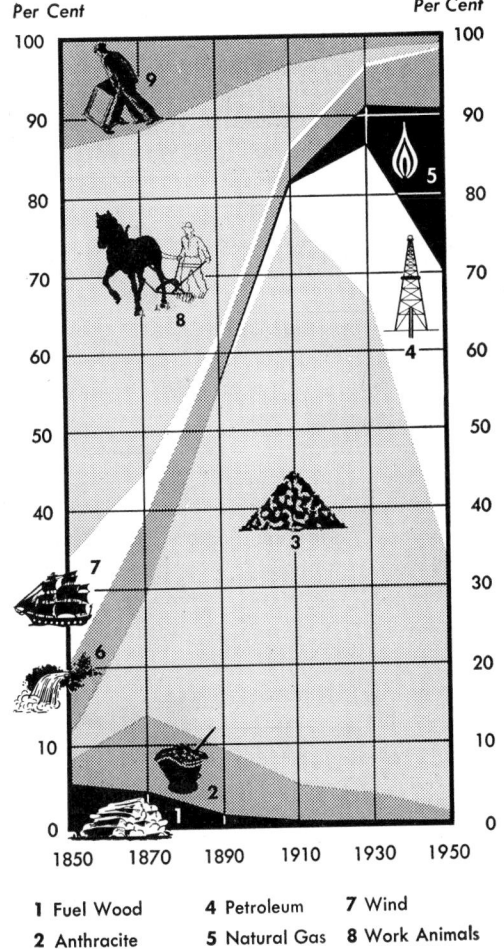

Per Cent   Per Cent

FIGURE 104. PERCENTAGE DISTRIBUTION OF WORK
OUTPUT OBTAINED FROM DIFFERENT ENERGY SOURCES
IN THE UNITED STATES, 1850–1950

Source: Appendix 25–3, Table L.

1 Fuel Wood	4 Petroleum	7 Wind
2 Anthracite	5 Natural Gas	8 Work Animals
3 Bituminous Coal	6 Water	9 Human Workers

ratio of 20 manpower to one horsepower is much more realistic.[16]

Not only has an increasing share of our total energy input been devoted to work performance, but there have been steady and substantial gains in the ultimate work output derived from each unit of energy originally consumed. Anything approaching precise measurement of the efficiency with which energy has been converted to work over the past century is impossible, and estimates, especially for earlier periods, can be little better than guesses. That there have been vast gains,

especially in combustion efficiency for fuels, however, is undeniable.

Electric central stations today are getting as many kilowatt-hours of delivered energy out of one pound of coal as they got out of seven pounds at the turn of the century. The estimate used in this survey is more conservative in that a sixfold rise in the combustion efficiency of bituminous coal is assumed to have taken place since 1900—from 3 per cent efficiency in that year to 18.5 per cent in 1950. Other energy fuels are also being burned much more efficiently than when first used to generate power.

Since anthracite and fuel wood, as well as natural gas, are also burned under boilers to generate steam, the improvement in conversion efficiency for these fuels is assumed to have been the same as for bituminous coal. Petroleum, used so extensively in inefficiently operated private motor vehicles, is estimated to have shown a smaller gain than solid fuels—from 3 per cent efficiency in 1900 to 9 per cent in 1950. In hydroelectric generation it is estimated that more than 85 per cent of the energy of the falling water is delivered in work output at the factory lathe or household vacuum cleaner. This compares with about 70 per cent in 1900, and a rise from 64 per cent efficiency in that year for direct-drive waterwheels to 77 per cent in 1950. Windmill efficiency has also increased slightly since 1900. (See Appendix 25–3, Tables B–H.)

Although there was steady improvement during the last half of the nineteenth century, most of these truly spectacular gains have come with the spreading use of electricity in the past fifty years. The gain in efficiency for all fuels and water power combined[17] (weighted in accordance with their relative importance in each year) was from 1.8 per cent in 1850 to 3.2 per cent in 1900 and to 13.6 per cent in 1950. If these figures are even roughly correct they indicate that we have been able to increase the "productivity" of our inanimate energy supply over the past century somewhat more rapidly than we have increased the productivity of human labor. One hour of human labor in 1950 produced as much as two and a half hours did in 1900 and nearly as much as six hours produced in 1850.

16. "Twenty Men Equal One Horse, Says C. M. Ripley," *Power* (McGraw-Hill), March 1947.

17. Since wind power used to propel sailing vessels, manpower and animal power are all expressed in terms of delivered energy, or work output, no question of the efficiency of energy conversion arises for these sources. Expressed differently, it is only practicable to assume 100 per cent efficiency for these sources throughout the century.

(See Table 14.) One ton of coal equivalent of inanimate energy (exclusive of wind power) in 1950 resulted in as much delivered work output as four tons produced in 1900 and as seven tons did in 1850.[18] In the case of fuels used in steam generation (anthracite, bituminous coal, natural gas and fuel wood) the gains were even larger — from 1.1 per cent efficiency in 1850 to 3 per cent in 1900 and 18.5 per cent in 1950. (See Appendix 25–3, Table I.)

Thus we have not only been greatly increasing the amount of energy used for motive power (i.e., for work performance) but have been getting more and more work done with every unit of inanimate energy consumed. Measured in terms of energy delivered at the point of use (i.e., work performed), the total work output of the American economy — obtained from human workers, work animals, wind, water, mineral fuels and fuel wood — increased from an estimated 10.3 billion horsepower-hours in 1850 to 78.3 billion in 1900 and to 673 billion in 1950. Thus the rate of increase was actually greater during the first half of the twentieth century than during the last half of the nineteenth. And the 65-fold increase in the work output measured in energy terms over the entire century was far greater than the 25-fold increase in the net output of goods and services, as measured by national income at constant prices.

_____

18. These estimates, it should be noted, are not the usual measures of fuel efficiency for they attempt to take into account, in addition to combustion losses, the subsequent losses in the transmission and application of energy at the point of use. A special difficulty arises in defining and attempting to estimate "work output." In terms of ultimate economic results, the "work done" by the fuel used in the diesel engine of a power shovel is measured by the amount of earth and rock lifted, and that of a steam locomotive by the weight of the goods and passengers carried. As a practical matter, however, the work done has to be defined in terms of the entire weight of material moved, i.e., of the shovel itself as well as its contents, and of the train as well as its load. This introduces an additional source of error into a task which involves many other probable errors. Insofar as the weight of equipment has been increasing over the years (and there is reason to believe that it has), the estimate of "total work output" of the economy tends to overstate the amount of "work done" in the economic sense. This might help to explain the fact that these estimates of "work output" show a much steeper upward trend than the estimates of national income at constant prices, which might be regarded as an economic measure of work output. In the first edition of the present volume and in a paper presented before the December 1947 meeting of the American Association for the Advancement of Science, the author of this chapter attempted an estimate of _economic_ "work output," which showed a much smaller rise over the past century than the estimates given here.

Shifting Sources of Work Output

Even more striking changes have taken place in the relative importance of the energy sources accounting for total work output. In the middle of the nineteenth century more than one eighth of all the work was done by human beings and more than half by horses, mules and oxen. Animate energy — muscle power — thus accounted for slightly less than two thirds of the work, and inanimate sources for a little more than one third. By 1900 the work-animal share had dropped to 22 per cent of the total and that of human workers to 5 per cent. Fifty years later muscle power was all but eliminated, and inanimate energy accounted for nearly 99 per cent of our much larger work output. (See Figure 104.)

More precisely, these changes in the percentage share of animate and inanimate sources of energy in total work output, at fifty-year intervals during the past hundred years, are as follows (based on Appendix 25–3, Table L):

	1850	1900	1950
Human	13.0	5.3	0.9
Animal	52.4	21.5	0.6
Inanimate	34.6	73.2	98.5

The relative importance of the inanimate work-energy sources has also changed radically during the century. During the golden era of the clipper ships in the 1850s, when some 3 million tons of shipping were operating under sail, wind accounted for close to 40 per cent of the work output obtained from inanimate energy and for nearly 14 per cent of the total. After the Civil War, wind power dropped off rapidly, falling to one per cent of the total in 1900 and virtually disappearing thereafter.

Water, like wind, is one of the oldest inanimate energy sources used for motive power. The primitive water wheels in use in 1850 accounted for about one fourth of the work output from inanimate sources and for close to 9 per cent of the total. With the spreading use of steam, water power development lagged during the latter part of the nineteenth century, but after hydroelectric generation began it increased rapidly, until today it accounts for close to 8 per cent of the total.[19]

_____

19. In view of the many extravagant predictions about atomic fission as a virtually "free" source of energy in the future, it is interesting to observe that we have never got far in the exploitation of water power and wind power, both of which have been free, and the latter almost unlimited in amount, since there has been life on this

Fuels in 1850 accounted for more than 12 per cent of total work output — less than wind power and about as much as human workers contributed. Anthracite and bituminous coal together accounted for a little more than fuel wood, which — though predominantly a space-heating fuel — was also used extensively on railroads and in river and lake transport, as well as industrially for power generation. By 1900, fuel wood, like wind, had dropped to insignificance as a source of power for work performance although it was still of some importance in household heating.

Dominance of Mineral Energy

The most spectacular and significant development during the past century has of course been the virtual displacement of most of the other work-energy sources by water power, coal, oil and natural gas and the tremendous advance in harnessing the energy obtained from minerals to supplement and vastly multiply the work performed by human beings. Mineral fuels and water power together accounted for less than 16 per cent of our total work output in 1850, for more than 70 per cent in 1900, and for more than 98 per cent of a vastly larger total in 1950. Bituminous coal was the dominant energy mineral until recent years; it steadily increased its share from less than 4 per cent of total work output in 1850 to a peak of 72 per cent in 1910. After that, with the growing importance of the internal combustion engine on highways and farms and later the rapid rise in the use of natural gas, the contribution of bituminous coal dropped to 32 per cent in 1950. Petroleum accounted for 37 per cent of the total work output in that year, and natural gas for 20 per cent.

This great shift to mineral, or "mechanical," energy and the vast expansion in its use are the essence of technological progress. Every new laborsaving device means a substitution of mineral energy for human energy and an augmentation of human effort. Our net output of goods and services in 1950 was twenty-five times what it was in 1850, and we did the job with only eight times as many workers. Allowing for the shorter work week of 1950, we used less than five times

as large an actual input of human effort — which means a nearly sixfold increase in productivity.

But we used 74 times as much nonhuman energy, 186 times as much inanimate energy, and 863 times as much mineral energy, as we used in 1850. With productivity at the 1850 level and working hours at the 1950 level, we would have required in 1950 a working force of some 340 million — about five and a half times the number actually employed — to produce what we did in that year. Even with the long work week of 1850, more than three times as many workers would have been required in 1950 if their productivity had been no greater than it was a century earlier. In other words, one man with today's power-driven mechanical equipment can do as much work in 40 hours as three men working 70 hours a week with the primitive tools of a century ago. (See Table 14.)

Technological Displacement

These vast gains in productivity have involved the decline and disappearance of old industries and products, the growth of new ones and the consequent redistribution of capital and labor on an enormous scale. Yet throughout this period of rapid technological displacement, technological unemployment has never appeared as a persistent and cumulative phenomenon.

Resistance to the introduction of laborsaving machinery is understandable, for it sometimes results in personal tragedy to the workers who are displaced. Over the long run, however, it is *only through technological disemployment* that material progress is possible. If all the men operating canal boats in 1830, and livery stables in 1900, and other dying industries, had stayed in the business, and their sons had followed them, railroad travel would still be a luxury that few people could afford and the private automobile a plaything of the idle rich. If the capital, labor and entrepreneurial talent released by technological progress had failed to enter and create new industries, we would have been unable to raise our standard of living by producing more of existing goods and a fabulous variety of new, better and cheaper products.

Instead of technological unemployment, we have enjoyed not only a vast increase in the amount and variety of goods available and a marked advance in our labor productivity, but also a steady rise in the number and proportion

---

planet. So long as atomic energy is used to generate electricity, the costs of transmission and distribution of electricity will be inescapable — and these costs, in the case of central stations, amount to around 80 per cent of what the user has to pay.

of the population in gainful occupations and a steady shortening of the work week. With some costly and painful interruptions, we have had our cake in the form of expanding employment, and eaten it in the form of increased leisure and an ever higher standard of living.

The immediate reasons for this vast increase in the use of inanimate energy, and the displacement of work animals and multiplication of human effort by power-driven machinery, are not hard to find. Whether delivered as electricity to farm or factory, produced under the hood of an automobile, or generated in the hold of the S.S. United States, mineral energy provides a greater concentration of power in more convenient, compact, mobile and controllable form than would be possible with the most ingenious and efficient application of unlimited amounts of human and animal effort.

The almost legendary "Borax 20-Mule Team," with a speed of six or eight miles an hour, was probably the largest aggregation of animal power ever brought under the control of a single driver — outside of the circus. But the frailest of women drives around today with ten times as much horsepower and a potential hundred miles an hour under the hood. In a single day the Consolidated Edison System in New York delivers enough electricity to do the work of four million draft horses or twenty times as many hard-working men. In 1953 the Consolidated System turned out 18 billion horsepower-hours — almost twice as much as the total work-energy output from fuels, muscles, water and wind for the entire nation in 1850. And electric energy is delivered cleanly, instantaneously, and in just the right amount needed to drill a tooth or beat an egg — or to operate an electric crane or a subway train in the rush hour.

Mineral energy has many advantages over muscle power in doing the work of the world, but its chief advantage is its extremely low cost. Electric energy is delivered at a cost of a penny or two per horsepower-hour; a draft horse — if one can be found — can be hired for $10 a day; while the present rate of $1.25 an hour for common labor means that the least expensive human energy (on the basis of one horsepower equivalent to 20 manpower) costs $25 per horsepower-hour. On the whole, animal power probably costs from fifty to a hundred times as much as "mechanical" power, and manpower more than

a thousand times as much. Only the most backward nations can afford to use even slave labor on a bare subsistence basis for tasks that machines can perform.

Capital Investment and Productivity

Have we, then, crossed the threshold into a workless Utopia where all we have to do to increase productivity is to dig more coal and build more power plants? Obviously not, for the consumption of mineral energy is in a sense merely an index of the state of our technology. It reflects the extent to which we have designed, acquired and put to use the elaborate, complicated and costly machines and equipment without which mineral energy could not be translated into useful work.

The inanimate energy that is taking over the work of the world would not be so fabulously cheap, or indeed usable at all, were it not for the heavy investment in capital facilities needed to make it available. A construction worker with a diesel-powered road-scraper is hundreds of times more productive than one with a pick and shovel and a wheelbarrow, but the former investment is many thousands of dollars and the latter amounts to only a few dollars. A farm tractor and gang-plow can do more work in a day than horse-drawn equipment can do in a week, but it is a more complex piece of machinery and a far more costly investment. A modern turbogenerator is simple to operate and much more efficient in converting the energy of fuel into useful work than the primitive reciprocating engine of the nineteenth century, but it costs a great deal more to build and install. In factory operations, individual motors at the workbench deliver power as needed far more quietly and efficiently than the clanking shafts and flapping belts of a generation ago, but they involve a much bigger capital investment.

Of course, not every gain in labor productivity entails a corresponding increase in investment. An improved rate of output may come from changes in plant layout or management practices, or in the kind of raw materials used, or in other ways involving no new capital investment. Conversely, capital investment may often be designed to save materials rather than labor, or to improve quality even at the expense of losses in labor productivity or in the use of materials.

On the whole, however, the great advances

during the past half century toward greater productivity have involved an accelerated "mechanization of the economy" in harnessing, transmitting and applying inanimate energy to the creation of useful goods and services. Where we stand today is the result, on the one hand, of ceaseless experimentation, invention, and adaptation over past decades and, on the other, of continuous saving and capital investment.

Capital Investment per Worker

There is, unfortunately, no very satisfactory statistical evidence of the trend of capital formation over a sufficiently long period to permit valid conclusions as to the exact relation between capital investment and output. The limited data available, however, confirm common observation that the United States today is not only the heaviest consumer of mechanical energy and the most productive country in the world, but also the most highly capitalized. It is equally evident that the steep upward trend in the productivity of American labor over the past several decades has been accompanied by an even sharper rise in the use of mechanical energy [20] and by a steeply rising level of capital investment per worker.

A significant figure is the average investment per employee, although any such average is obviously subject to qualifications. The National City Bank's annual tabulation of the assets of the 100 largest nonfinancial corporations in the United States showed an average investment (including plant and equipment and current assets of cash, government securities, receivables and inventories) per employee in 1952 of over $15,000.[21] The average capital per worker for the major kinds of business ranged from $52,000 for electric and gas utilities to $8,000 for trade. Railroads averaged $24,000, and manufacturing as a whole had an average of $14,000, but this average also concealed wide variations among individual manufacturing industries.[22] These averages can hardly be considered representative, because the largest firms are probably also the most highly capitalized and mechanized.

A much more comprehensive and representative analysis of investment per worker was made in 1950 by the Machinery and Allied Products Institute.[23] Covering all nonfinancial business enterprises in the United States, this survey showed estimated total assets of $560 billion, or $11,200 per worker; of this, $350 billion, or $7,000 per worker, consisted of buildings, land and other fixed assets. When farms are eliminated the averages, curiously enough, are reduced to $10,800 per worker for total assets and to $6,700 for fixed assets — which would seem to indicate that American agriculture is more "capitalistic" than American business.

About $9,000 of this $10,800 total for nonfarm business is a long-term capital requirement, i.e., financed by equity investment and funded debt. However, since this figure was arrived at "by valuing fixed assets at estimated current reproduction cost, less depreciation," an even larger investment would be required if a new enterprise purchased new structures and facilities. Under such circumstances — which are obviously most relevant in providing employment for a steadily growing labor force — an average investment of $14,000 per worker would be necessary, of which $12,000 would require long-term financing.

Capital requirements to provide jobs for a labor force growing at the rate of 500,000 a year would thus amount to about $7 billion annually, of which $6 billion would be long-term capital. In order to maintain the stock of existing physical capital, assuming an average depreciation rate of 4 per cent, nonfarm business alone would have to invest an additional sum of close to $15 billion a year.[24] According to these estimates, therefore, an annual long-term capital investment of $21 billion would be required to provide tools and working facilities "for the annual increment in the labor force and to offset the consumption of existing productive facilities."

Beyond this, the Institute's analysis points out that even a one per cent annual increase in the

---

20. Estimated work output from inanimate energy sources increased from 3.6 billion horsepower-hours in 1850 to 664.7 billion in 1950. (See Appendix 25–3, Table L.)

21. *Monthly Letter on Economic Conditions, Government Finance*, National City Bank, New York, July 1953, p. 82.

22. Average investment per job in manufacturing ranged from $4,000 for the aircraft industry and $8,000 for food, automobiles, tires and electrical equipment to $38,000 for petroleum refining and distilling and $46,000 for tobacco products.

23. *Capital Goods Review*, No. 3, Machinery and Allied Products Institute, Chicago, August 1950.

24. The Institute estimated that the depreciated reproduction cost of all existing nonfarm buildings, structures and equipment was $230 billion and that the estimated reproduction cost new (on which depreciation would be figured) was $370 billion.

amount of investment per worker would mean an additional yearly investment of $4 billion in long-term capital alone, thus bringing total long-term capital requirements to about $25 billion a year. Since the labor force appears to be growing at an annual rate of close to 800,000 rather than the "normal" 500,000 assumed by the Institute, the long-term capital requirements would come to about $28.5 billion.

Horsepower and Productivity

Actually, average investment per worker probably must increase more than this modest one per cent a year if we are to continue increasing labor productivity at the rate maintained in the past. Past trends in productivity, according to the estimates used in the present survey, indicate for the near future an average annual rise of about 2.3 per cent in output per man-hour, or approximately 1.7 per cent in output per worker. The long-run rise in output per worker has been accompanied by, and can undoubtedly be attributed chiefly to, a steady increase in the amount of capital facilities per worker.

One physical indicator of the increase in capital equipment is the rated horsepower of prime movers in the United States. In 1850 there were 6 million work animals — prime movers in agriculture and transportation. Waterwheels and steam engines in factories and mines, and steam engines on railroads and merchant ships, accounted for about 2.1 million "mechanical" horsepower; while sailing vessels can be estimated as the equivalent of 400,000 additional horsepower. Since there were about 7.4 million people at work in 1850, the "average" worker had the help of a little more than one horsepower. By 1950, horses and sailing vessels had virtually disappeared while mechanical horsepower had grown tremendously, and the average available per worker was about five and one half horsepower.[25] This fivefold increase in horsepower per worker was slightly less than the increase in output per man-hour, but was considerably more than the increase in output per worker,

which, measured in terms of national income in 1950 dollars per employed worker, rose from $1,270 in 1850 to $3,912 in 1950. (See Figure 105.)

On the face of it, this comparison (as well as the evidence presented earlier indicating that horsepower-hours of "work output" have been increasing more rapidly than the net output of goods and services) might suggest that the increasing productivity of the economy must be supported by a more-than-proportional increase in the rated horsepower of the prime movers used. Whether this in turn would mean a more-than-proportional increase in investment per worker is impossible to answer. There is no clear evidence as to whether, on the average, the cost per horsepower of prime movers and all the equipment needed to transmit, deliver and apply energy at the point of use has been increasing or decreasing over recent years.

In the absence of evidence to the contrary, it might be reasonable to assume that average investment per worker should rise a little faster than output per worker, say about 2 per cent a year.[26] If this were true, an average investment of $8 billion per year (instead of $4 billion) would be required to facilitate rising productivity. The total annual long-term capital requirement of the nonfarm economy would thus amount to about $32.5 billion at 1950 prices, and in view of the rise in prices since 1950, to somewhere between $35 and $40 billion on the basis of today's prices. And, of course, as our productive capital stock increases from year to year the annual investment needed to maintain and improve it will grow steadily larger. By 1960 the long-term capital requirements of the nonfarm economy will probably rise by another $5 billion to a total of $37.5 billion in terms of 1950 prices, or to somewhere between $40 and $45 billion on the basis of current prices.

Such computations are of course hypothetical and speculative. Furthermore, whatever the average relation between productivity and invest-

---

25. Because work animals constituted 60 per cent of the horsepower in 1850 and a negligible proportion in 1950, this comparison understates the improvement that has taken place. Actually the horse is not a very satisfactory source of horsepower, for though he is "burning fuel" the year around he is able to work only a small fraction of the time. Mechanical horsepower, on the other hand, can be delivered almost uninterruptedly.

26. Raymond W. Goldsmith's revised unpublished estimates of the value of industrial, commercial and agricultural facilities (exclusive of livestock) in the United States, when compared with the growth of employment, indicate approximately a fivefold increase since 1850 — or about the same as the increase in horsepower per worker. See paper in *Income and Wealth of the United States: Trends and Structure*, Income and Wealth Series II, International Association for Research in Income and Wealth, Bowes & Bowes, Cambridge, 1952, for Goldsmith's earlier estimates.

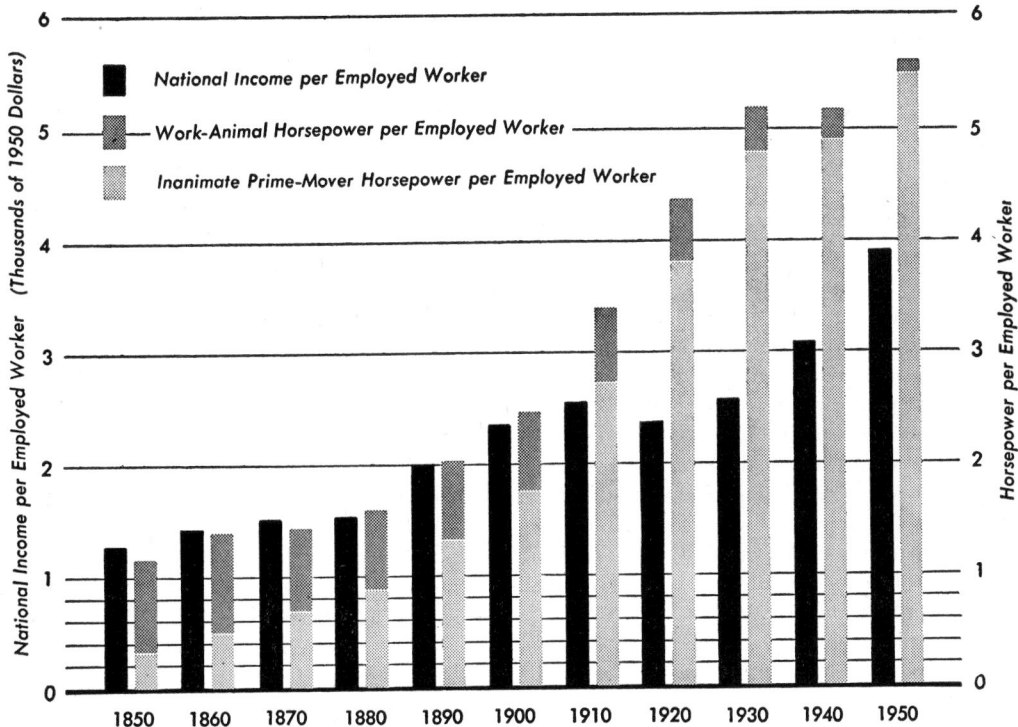

FIGURE 105. HORSEPOWER OF NONAUTOMOTIVE PRIME MOVERS AND NATIONAL INCOME PER EMPLOYED WORKER IN THE UNITED STATES, 1850–1950

Sources: Table 14 and Appendix 25–4.

ment may be, there is obviously no close year-to-year correspondence between the two. Productivity may increase from one year to another, or even over a period of several years, as it did during the 1930s, while the stock of productive capital in existence remains unchanged, or diminishes. At other times capital expansion may go ahead rapidly for a year, or for several years, before it has much effect on average productivity.

HUMAN AND INTANGIBLE FACTORS

Heavy capital investment in productive facilities and lavish use of mechanical power are unquestionably the most important immediate causes of the high and rising level of American productivity. Although climate, soil and resources have also played a part, such geographic and environmental factors are not originating causes. They fail to explain why American industry makes greater use of power and machinery, invests more capital per worker and has developed a more dynamic technology than the industries of other western capitalist countries, which in

turn are industrially far ahead of the rest of the world.

Here again an immediate explanation for technological progress can be found in the fact that American industry attaches great and growing importance to scientific and industrial research in a constant search for new and improved products, techniques, materials and methods. Corporation research laboratories in 1952 accounted for almost two thirds of the nation's total outlay of $3.5 billion for research and development work.[27] Indeed there is general recognition throughout American industry, especially in the newer industries and among the largest establishments throughout industry, that an aggressive program of research and development is essential to profitable operation and even to survival.

Whether this widespread attitude on the part of corporate managements in the United States can be attributed to "competition" in the highly

27. Estimate of the Research and Development Board of the Defense Department reported in the *Wall Street Journal*, February 3, 1953.

restricted sense in which this word is used in formal economic analysis or to "market rivalry" is less important than the fact that it exists and that it keeps industry technologically alert and redounds to the benefit of both workers and consumers. Foreign observers of American business, to be sure, are in no doubt about the existence of competition in American industry as a most powerful force working toward greater productivity. The French productivity teams brought to the United States under the auspices of ECA, for example, found the American economy much more competitive than their own and observed that a "truly competitive state of mind" made the American businessman "more ready to seek ways of lowering his costs, and less ready to seek ways of restricting competition." [28]

One of the British teams which visited the United States under the auspices of the Anglo-American Council on Productivity attributed "American cost-consciousness" to the "constant and unremitting force of competition," and another stated that "In the comparatively free economy of America there is no single factor which has a more important bearing on productivity than competition — and competition, not only in industry but in all walks of life, is intense." [29]

In his thoughtful analysis of the findings and observations of the Council's sixty-six productivity teams, Graham Hutton reported a "much greater degree of competitiveness in American business" than in British, and asserted that this "leads to a much higher average of productive efficiency, through a much higher degree of managerial competence." He concluded that in the United States "Competitiveness still rules the roost, whether the competing units are few and huge or many and small." [30]

Whatever the causes, it is unquestionably true that American industrial managements have an eagerly receptive attitude toward experimentation and change, toward the substitution of new products and methods for old ones, toward progress and expansion, even at the risk of loss. It may be, as the French Association for the Improvement of Productivity suggests, that "Productivity is above all a state of mind. It is the mentality of progress, of constantly improving what there is. It is the willingness not to be content with the present situation, however good it may be. It is continuous effort to apply new techniques and new methods. It is faith in human progress." [31]

One of the most thoughtful English journals expressed much the same thought in commenting on British and American productivity:

It begins to look as if we have been dealing with the surface symptoms of poor productivity and that the real causes lie deeper. Slowly, the conviction has been growing that the essential element has been missing. That element is the human will. Unless the ordinary man or woman sees the virtue, or at least the necessity, of producing more, more will not be produced.

The real secret of American productivity is that American society is imbued through and through with the desirability, the rightness, the morality of production.[32]

Ultimately, of course, the dynamic form which capitalism has taken in the United States, like the special character of any other political or social institution, must be traced back to the people who created it. America was settled by people of almost every European strain, though immigration during most of the nineteenth century was predominantly from western and northern Europe. These immigrants came from varied economic and political backgrounds, but most of them had in common a dissatisfaction with the traditions and institutions of their homelands, a willingness to experiment with change that promised improvement, and the courage and resourcefulness required to buy a one-way ticket to an unknown land. Though immigration was unrestricted, the new arrivals were a highly selected group, because they were *self-selected*. Since most of the immigrants were of middle-class origin and arrived not in large cohesive masses but as individuals and families, wave after wave of them were quickly absorbed into a rapidly growing population.

Thus nineteenth century American capitalism always had a broad middle-class base. Despite its many faults, it was always free from the feudal and manorial tradition so evident even today in European business enterprise. And nepotism, far from being characteristic of American business,

28. "American Productivity and Full Employment," *Monthly Labor Review*, February 1952, pp. 126–127.

29. "Fruit and Vegetable Utilisation," Productivity Team Report, Anglo-American Council on Productivity, May 1952, p. 6; "Food Canning," *ibid.*, p. 5.

30. *We Too Can Prosper*, George Allen & Unwin, Ltd., London, 1953, pp. 98, 189, 194.

31. "Productivity, Source of Well-Being," The French Association for the Improvement of Productivity, 41 Quai Branly, Paris 7, France, p. 11.

32. "The Riddle of Prosperity," *The Economist*, London, July 11, 1953, p. 80.

has been almost nonexistent so far as the large publicly owned corporations are concerned. In Europe the long-standing family enterprise is still quite common today, and even in the largest enterprises the corporate directorship, usually a well-paid sinecure, is often regarded as private property to be passed on from father to son.

The relative "classlessness" and fluidity of American society, the absence of an aristocratic attitude toward trade as an occupation, together with abundant opportunities for business success, created an atmosphere that attracted into business the gifted and superior youths who in the older countries might have chosen careers in the army, the law or the ministry. In the United States, to a much greater extent than in other countries, business success was generously rewarded, not only in material terms but in the coin of social approval and public esteem.

These ideas and attitudes, developing within a "hybrid population" that was spreading rapidly over a new continent, created a political and social climate favorable to invention and innovation, to the growth of individual enterprise, to the willingness to take risks and invest capital. America's unique industrial achievements are the result not only of favorable climate, soil and resources but to an indeterminable extent of these more subjective factors. A skilled, vigorous population — an individualistic, aggressive people with an extroverted approach toward themselves and their environment — has probably been more crucial to our technical development than the objective factors of climate and resources. In the last analysis it is the attributes — and the attitudes and ideals — of the American people which account for the dynamic character of the American economic system.

PART VI

SUMMARY

## CHAPTER 26

NEEDS VS. RESOURCES

THE HUMAN and material resources at our command, and — still more important — the requisite technical knowledge and skill to use them effectively, are the fundamental elements in our capacity as a nation to provide the goods and services we require. That there is nothing automatic and inevitable in the functioning of these basic resources is clear from our experience during the Great Depression, when national output fell to less than half of what we were capable of producing and consuming. That the normal capacity of our economy to provide needed goods and services can be radically modified and rapidly expanded is clear from our experience during the decade and a half since we emerged from that depression.

WAR AND POSTWAR

World War II furnished dramatic evidence of our ability to transfer labor and resources from one use to another, to convert facilities to new and different productive ends and to call forth potential and idle resources and thus greatly expand total productive capacity. When the defense program began in 1940, there was much slack in the economy. We had a good deal of idle plant capacity, and one man out of seven of our normal labor force was out of work. But as war production gained momentum and military forces expanded, we soon absorbed idle manpower and facilities and began to draw on our human and material reserves.

THE WAR POTENTIAL

By the winter of 1944–1945 we had achieved our war potential with some 65 million at work in civilian and military occupations, compared with less than 48 million in 1940. There were almost 12 million in military service, nearly 8 million

By J. FREDERIC DEWHURST. Opinions and judgments expressed in this chapter, which is based largely on data presented in preceding chapters of this report, are those of the author and should not be attributed to the organization with which he is associated.

emergency workers in the labor force, and unemployment was close to the vanishing point. In the peak year of the war effort gross national product was more than twice as large as in fairly prosperous 1940 — almost $214 billion compared with less than $102 billion. Allowing for a rise in prices and costs of about one third during this four-year period, we turned out nearly 60 per cent more goods and services in 1944 than in 1940. And, in spite of the unprecedented postwar boom, it was not until 1951 that this wartime production record was surpassed.

This, in bare statistical detail, was the "miracle of war production" that enabled the United States to become the arsenal of democracy for half the world while maintaining home civilian consumption close to the highest peacetime levels. This magnificent wartime accomplishment was a tribute to American technical ingenuity and organizing genius in both the military and industrial spheres; to the health, energy, intelligence and skill of American workers and soldiers; and to the willingness of American consumers to accept the inconveniences and sacrifices essential in fighting a war. The war experience proved that we can greatly alter and expand our capacity to produce, given time and sufficiently powerful pressures and incentives. But it did not — as was sometimes said at the time — demonstrate that our productive capacity was unlimited or that we had "solved the problem of production," whatever that expression may mean.

On the contrary, all but a small part of the increase of $112 billion in the dollar volume of output during the defense and war period can be accounted for by higher prices, more workers and longer working hours. Prices rose by an average of 34 per cent between 1940 and 1944, the number at work increased by 36 per cent, while the work week lengthened by almost 6 per cent. Taken together these three factors accounted for $94 billion of the total increase in gross national product. The remaining $18 billion could be accounted for by a 3 to 4 per cent annual increase in average productivity — which does not appear unreasonable for the war period. During the four-year period we moved rapidly from the quasi-prosperity of 1940, with much slack in the economy, to a condition of forced-draft operation at considerably above normal "full-employment" levels.

POSTWAR PROSPERITY

Perhaps the best evidence that production and employment were both abnormally high during the war is what happened when demobilization took place. Government war spending dropped precipitously from an annual rate of $90 billion just before V-J Day to $16 billion by the end of 1946, and total employment fell by 8 million during that period. But unemployment — despite dire predictions at the time — never rose to even a "normal" level, for some 6 million emergency workers promptly withdrew from the labor force.

In spite of the tremendous task of reconverting the economy to peacetime requirements, the physical volume of gross national product for the year 1946 was only 11 per cent less than for 1945. By the end of 1946 the postwar boom, which was to continue with only minor interruptions for more than seven years, was already gathering momentum.

The long boom after World War II has been unique in a number of respects. That there was no immediate speculative collapse after the war — in contrast to what happened after every other major war — was due to the fact that most of the inflation came after the war rather than during it. While the burst of inflation from 1946 to 1948 and again in 1950–1952 had a disastrous effect on the purchasing power of prewar and wartime savings, it was a powerful stimulus to production and employment. The price level rose by 35 per cent between 1946 and 1953 while gross national product measured in current dollars increased from $211 billion to $367 billion, or by 74 per cent. Thus the physical volume of total national output increased by 29 per cent. (For some basic 1954 data see Appendix 26–1.)

Another factor helping to support the postwar boom was the unprecedented payments to veterans for educational and other purposes. Through the 1953 fiscal year these amounted to nearly $40 billion. Added to this was a huge accumulation of some $228 billion of liquid assets in the hands of consumers and business firms at the end of the war.

Population Growth

Another powerful influence was the spurt in the marriage rate immediately after the war and the sharp and sustained rise in births and population growth. Whether measured by the annual increase in the number of people or the number of households, the consumer market has been growing more than twice as fast since World War II as during the depressed 1930s. The stimulus of population growth has been especially marked in the South Atlantic, Mountain and Pacific states.

Technical Progress

The postwar years have also been marked by a burst of technological progress resulting in aggressive development of new materials and products, new industrial methods, and new and fast-growing industries. Consumers have benefited from new products such as synthetic fibers and television sets. Industry has been transformed by faster and more powerful machines, new structural materials, new types of automatic equipment, and particularly by the adoption of electronic instruments and controls which promise to usher in the automatic age. Improvement of industrial techniques has brought unusually rapid gains in productivity. From 1947 to 1952 output per man-hour for the private economy as a whole rose 3.5 per cent a year — almost twice as fast as the 2.0 per cent average for 1910–1952.

Savings and Debt

Both public and private buyers at the end of the war were in a strong financial position to make pent-up demands effective. Consumers had an unprecedented accumulation of liquid assets, both in actual amount and in relation to disposable income and consumer indebtedness. Personal debt was close to an all-time low in relation to income and savings. Finally, consumers enjoyed large and rising incomes during the postwar years, and they spent more of their earnings and saved less than during the war.

Consumers were thus able to finance their expanding purchases by spending more freely from larger incomes, by using accumulated savings, and by going into debt more heavily. Thus, while personal consumption expenditures rose from $147 billion in 1946 to $230 billion in 1953 (at 1950 prices the rise was from $171 to $207 billion), total consumer indebtedness at the end of

1953 was more than three times what it was at the end of the war and the ratio of individuals' liquid assets to the sum of mortgage and consumer credit dropped from 6.33 in 1946 to 2.70 in 1952.

Government and Business Spending

Although consumer spending was the chief element in the postwar boom, heavy spending by government, and investment expenditures by business, were also important factors. Corporations during the war retained more than half of their earnings after taxes, and their $40 billion of liquid asset holdings at the end of the war was supplemented during the seven-year postwar period by $82 billion of additional borrowing, which raised corporate debt outstanding to $167 billion by the end of 1952. These sources of funds, together with ample earnings during most of the postwar years, resulted in a steady rise of spending for investment purposes from $33 billion in 1946 to a peak of nearly $59 billion in 1951, followed by a decline to just over $52 billion in 1952 and 1953. Investment spending for construction and capital facilities rose even more sharply — from $23 billion in 1946 to slightly under $52 billion in 1953.

Although federal government expenditures were cut sharply at the war's end, they remained far above prewar levels, while state and local government outlays, no longer checked by war shortages, soon doubled. Federal expenditures jumped sharply again after the outbreak of Korean hostilities. Total government expenditures, after dropping to a postwar low point of $44 billion in 1947, rose to $61 billion in 1950 and to $103 billion in 1953. Government purchases of goods and services advanced from a 1947 low point of $28.6 billion to a 1953 peak of $84.9 billion.

Superimposed upon domestic demand were substantial foreign demands for American goods. Heavy backlog demand from abroad supported in part by foreign dollar balances accumulated during the war accounted for an export surplus of $45 billion during 1946–1952. Over two thirds of this was given away as government aid or private gifts.

Phases of the Boom

The postwar boom came in two phases. The years from 1946 to 1949 were a "catching-up period" when defense spending fell off to low levels and most wartime shortages of civilian goods were made good to the accompaniment of an inflationary price rise. This phase ended with a minor inventory readjustment in 1949, but was followed after the outbreak of the Korean War by another rearmament effort and another sharp price advance.

This second phase of the postwar boom reached a crest in the second quarter of 1953, from which moderate declines have occurred in government defense spending and in spending by industry for construction and capital facilities. In the first quarter of 1954 federal government spending had declined to an annual rate of $55 billion, compared with nearly $61 billion in the second quarter of 1953. Gross national product during the same period declined from an annual rate of $371 billion to less than $358 billion. Unemployment by March 1954 had risen to 3.7 million, but was still less than the high mark of 4.7 million reached in the 1949–1950 recession. Consumer spending, because of tax cuts in 1954, held at virtually the same level in the first quarter of 1954 as in the preceding three quarters.

BASIC GROWTH TRENDS

The extent of the rather mild and apparently short-lived recession which began in the second half of 1953 is, however, of little significance in determining the long-run progress of the American economy, compared with the basic trends in the growth of population and in the size and productivity of the labor force.

POPULATION

Population trends are obviously of basic importance in measuring both needs and resources. The size and character of the population and its rate of growth are important determinants of the market for goods and services and of the labor force required to produce them.

Although population growth has been rapid throughout the history of the United States, the trend in the *rate* of growth has been generally downward. Thus, our population more than trebled between 1850 and 1900, reflecting heavy immigration as well as a large surplus of births over deaths, but merely doubled during the next fifty years. The slackening rate of growth became most pronounced in the 1930s, when the numerical increase was little more than half what it was in the preceding decade and the percentage gain of 7 per cent was smaller than in any previous decade in history.

The long decline in marriage and birth rates was sharply reversed, however, after we entered the war. Immediately after the end of the war (in 1946) the marriage rate established a high record which had probably never before been equaled, while the 1947 birth rate of 26.6 per thousand was higher than in any year since 1921, which followed the postwar marriage peak in 1920. Although some decline has occurred since 1947, the birth rate has continued to hover above 24 per thousand — a higher rate than at any time since just after World War I.

This radical change in population trends can undoubtedly be attributed in part to the effects of World War II and the Korean War and to the accompanying economic prosperity (although the birth rate slowly declined during the prosperous 1920s), but it appears also to reflect a changed attitude on the part of young married people toward family size. Apparently there will be fewer families with one child or none at all, and more with two or three children. But there is no evidence yet of a return of the very large family, which was quite common in the nineteenth century.

These population developments since the end of World War II were wholly unexpected by most population students, and even in the late 1940s many "projections" contemplated an ultimate population peak for the United States at a level not far above our present population of some 160 million. It goes without saying, therefore, that the projection of 177 million for 1960 population used in this study (which is slightly higher than the Bureau of Census medium projection issued in August 1953) may prove to be wide of the mark. This population total would mean an increase of nearly 25 million, or 16 per cent, over the 1950 figure of 152 million. This would be the largest numerical increase of any decade in American history and a larger percentage gain than in any decade since 1900–1910. It would compare with an increase of about 20 million, or 15 per cent, in the 1940–1950 decade.

WORK INPUT AND PRODUCTIVITY

The output of the national economy in any year is obviously determined by the "work input," or total man-hours worked, and the productivity of labor, or average output per man-hour. Total man-hours worked during the year in turn depend upon the size of the labor force and the number actually at work, and average hours of work.

Labor Force

Although the labor force had been growing more rapidly than the population for several decades prior to 1910, since that year the proportion of population in the labor force has shown little change — rising from 39 per cent to 42 per cent in 1950. Because the proportion of younger children in the population will probably be larger in 1960 than in 1950 and because the 1950 labor force still had a considerable number of "emergency workers" retained through the postwar boom, this study estimates that the labor force in 1960 will constitute 41 per cent of the population, or 72.5 million. This estimate of the size of the 1960 labor force is, of course, speculative, but there are fewer uncertainties in projecting the population of working age than in estimating total population, for all of the adults who will constitute the 1960 labor force were already living in 1950.

"Full employment" of the labor force, in the sense that every member is at work at the same time, has of course never been achieved. Even at the peak of the war effort, when several million emergency temporary workers had been recruited, unemployment never fell much below half a million and rarely below a million. During the "super boom" that has continued almost without interruption since the end of World War II unemployment has exceeded 3 million on only two occasions: in 1949–1950 and after January 1954.

Past experience shows, however, that even in periods of prosperity, such as the 1920s, an average of close to 5 per cent of the labor force is out of work. Such a proportion does not imply a hard core of unemployed, but rather a shifting group unemployed for temporary periods between jobs. The assumption made in this study that unemployment at a high level of activity in 1960 would amount to slightly less than 5 per cent of the labor force would indicate 3.5 million unemployed, and an average of 69 million at work.

Working Hours

Hours of work have been dropping steadily for many decades, even more rapidly since the turn of the century than before. The six-day week and the 12-hour day were common a century ago, and estimates of this study showed an average work week of about 70 hours in 1850. The work week dropped to 60 hours by 1900, to 44 hours by 1940, and to 40 hours in 1950. Since the peak of the rearmament effort has passed, average weekly hours, which increased slightly in 1951 and 1952, have declined, and recently they dipped below 40. There is certainly no reason to believe that the long downtrend in working time will not continue with further gains in productivity. Since 1910 it appears that less than two thirds of the *potential* gains attributable to increasing productivity have been taken in the form of additional goods and services, while more than one third has been in the form of shorter working hours and increased leisure.

This survey has made the assumption of a further moderate decline in working hours to an average of 37.5 hours per week in 1960.

Labor Input

Labor input of the private sector of the economy,[1] on the assumption that 58.5 million of the 69 million total employed workers in 1960 will be engaged in private activities, is estimated at 114 billion man-hours. This aggregate of labor input is only slightly larger than the 1950 work input and some 5 per cent above the 1929 total. Labor input increased steeply from 26 billion man-hours in 1850 to 92 billion in 1910, but thereafter rose much more gradually to the wartime peak of 119.8 billion man-hours in 1943. From that all-time high point the total declined to 112.3 billion in 1950, but rose again to 115.3 billion in 1953. That these modest long-range increases in labor input have produced so much larger gains in national output of course reflects substantial advances in productivity, or output per man-hour.

Productivity, as measured by private national income per man-hour, amounted to $1.93 in 1950. In terms of dollars of 1950 purchasing power this represented close to a sixfold increase over the

33.7 cents per man-hour net output of 1850. Gains in productivity have varied widely from one decade to another and have been larger in recent decades than in earlier ones. This study assumes a 25 per cent increase in productivity between 1950 and 1960, which is over half the increase realized during the 1940s and exceeds that in many earlier decades. Such a gain would result in net output, or average private national income, per man-hour of about $2.40 in 1960.

NATIONAL OUTPUT

Private net output, or the national income produced by the private sector of the economy, on the basis of 114 billion man-hours of labor input and average productivity of $2.40 per man-hour, would thus amount to roughly $275 billion (at 1950 prices) in 1960. This is a gain of 27 per cent over 1950 and 37 per cent over private national income in 1944, at the peak of the war. The 1960 total would be thirty-one times the $8.8 billion of private national income produced in 1850. And this tremendous gain would have been achieved with a labor input of only four and a half times as many man-hours as in 1850 — thus reflecting a sevenfold gain in productivity.

Since goods purchased by government are produced by the private economy, the value of the government share of total national income is usually considered to be equal to total payments for the services of government employees. This study has assumed that 10.5 million persons, including armed service personnel, would be in government employment in 1960 and that the government share of total national income would amount to 12 per cent. This would mean total national income of $312.5 billion. Assumption that indirect business taxes would amount to $29.5 billion in 1960, and capital consumption allowances to 7.5 per cent of gross national product, would indicate gross national product of $370 billion [2] at 1950 prices, or about $415 billion in terms of the 12 per cent higher price level prevailing in 1953.

It is obvious that this projection and the assumptions on which it is based are surrounded with so many uncertainties that they are certain to be wrong in some respects. Although a single figure was needed to provide a base line for other projections in this study, it is much more realistic

---

1. The government share of national income is estimated by a different method. See Chapter 2, Table 14.

2. These estimates are explained in Chapter 2 and shown in Table 15.

in attempting to view the future to project a range of likely possibilities. If hours of work remain at 1950 levels instead of declining moderately as assumed in the "medium projection" above, if the labor force should be larger and unemployment smaller, if productivity increases more rapidly and if intensification of the cold war leads to heavier government armament spending, gross national product could easily rise to $440 billion at 1950 prices, or about $495 billion at 1953 prices.

On the other hand, with smaller growth of the labor force, more unemployment, a smaller increase in productivity, a shorter work week and less government activity than were assumed for the medium estimate, gross national product in 1960 would be no more than $315 billion at 1950 prices, or about $355 billion at 1953 prices.

DEMAND AND NEEDS

The preceding section, summarizing briefly the data presented in greater detail in earlier chapters, showed the trends and projections of the basic factors determining the size of the national output. Since gross national product is identical with gross national expenditure, these terms measure the demand for, as well as the supply of, goods and services in the American economy. The identity between total labor input and productivity, on the one hand, and total output, on the other, is purely a matter of arithmetic. Hence the projection of gross national product for 1960 will be correct only to the extent that assumptions regarding employment, hours and productivity in that year prove correct.

Future Demand

Estimates of the composition of 1960 gross national product, or the way in which total demand will be distributed among consumption goods and services, public and private capital goods, and government noncapital goods and services, are subject to even greater likelihood of error. Although such estimates of future *demand* necessarily employ statistical techniques to analyze and project past trends and relationships, in the last analysis they rest on an exercise of judgment as to how the American people are *likely* to spend and invest their money — including what they pay in taxes and spend collectively through government. Obviously uncertainties are

still greater when an attempt is made, as in the present chapter, to project the future demand for various groups of goods and services included within each of these three major categories.

Estimating Needs

An attempt to estimate future *needs* is an even more uncertain and difficult undertaking, which involves a different order of judgment. In the final analysis, an estimate of the kinds and quantities of various goods and services needed to provide a "standard of living at a health and decency level" for the entire population must rest on someone's opinion as to what constitutes health and decency in twentieth-century America. A statement of what we need — whether in terms of food, clothing or housing, of parks and playgrounds, or of railway equipment and public buildings — requires first of all an opinion as to how much of these necessities is required to provide an adequate standard of living for everyone. Beyond this the concept of need also implies an opinion as to how the substandard income groups *ought* to spend their money (assuming that they could be provided with enough income to buy what they need) rather than a judgment as to how they would *want* to spend it.

Perhaps the best evidence that the pattern of need, as defined above, is not identical with that of demand is the attitude of consumers who have adequate incomes to meet either needs or demand. Witness the American male, who prefers steak and potatoes and apple pie to a better-balanced diet; the American female, who prefers nylons to more adequate leg covering in the depth of winter; the American family, which sometimes prefers housing below the decency level to the indecency of getting along without a car. We put off going to the dentist — a disagreeable service that we need — but are careful to avoid running out of cigarettes, which we want but do not need. We are apt to drink milk dutifully, but highballs gladly. As a nation we spend more than half again as much for liquor and tobacco as for medical care; about the same on movies as in support of churches; almost as much for beauty parlor services as for private social welfare. Whether wise or unwise, however, these decisions on the part of individuals as to how they will spend their money represent their own opinions, expressed within the limits of their incomes, as to what they need. In a system dedi-

TABLE 350. MAJOR COMPONENTS OF GROSS NATIONAL PRODUCT: NEEDS AND DEMAND
IN 1950 AND 1960
(*Billions at 1950 Prices*)

	1950		1960	
	Demand	Needs	Demand	Needs
Gross national product	$286.8	$336.1	$370.0	$396.4
Personal consumption expenditures	194.6	206.4	241.5	251.9
Inventory change and net foreign investment	5.2	5.2[a]	—	—
Capital goods expenditures[b]	52.3	66.7	66.5	78.3
Private	45.0	51.7	56.0	62.1
Government[b]	7.3	15.0	10.5	16.2
Government noncapital expenditures for goods and services[c]	34.7	57.8[d]	62.0	66.2[d]
Government expenditures for goods and services	42.0	72.8[e]	72.5	82.4[e]
Other government expenditures[f]	19.4	23.8[d]	22.0	24.0[d]
Government expenditures, total	61.4	96.6[g]	94.5	106.4[g]

Sources: Demand estimates from Table 29. Needs estimates for personal consumption and capital goods expenditures from Tables 34 and 36; other needs estimates derived as indicated in footnotes.

   a. Assumed equal to demand.

   b. Excludes expenditures for publicly owned military and naval plant and equipment and expenditures by state governments for equipment; these expenditures are included with government noncapital expenditures for goods and services.

   c. Includes expenditures for publicly owned military and naval plant and equipment and expenditures by state governments for equipment.

   d. Derived by subtraction.

   e. Demand estimate increased by same percentage as gross government expenditures for goods and services in Table 273.

   f. Includes transfer payments, net interest and subsidies less current surplus of government enterprises.

   g. Demand estimate increased by same percentage as gross government expenditures in Table 273 (adjusted to exclude outlays for health insurance as shown in Table 276).

cated to free consumer choice, it is the sum total of these decisions that determines the actual pattern of demand and production.

Needs vs. Demand

This survey, therefore, makes no attempt to resolve this dilemma of needs vs. demand with regard to those families and individuals who have enough money to supply their minimum needs. However, even at the high average level of personal income in 1950 and the still higher level assumed for 1960, there were and will be some American families with inadequate income to buy enough of the necessities of life to maintain themselves at a health and decency level. What this survey attempts, as explained in preceding chapters, is to estimate for the years 1950 and 1960: (1) the value of the additional quantities of consumption necessities — food, clothing, housing, medical care, etc. — required to bring the substandard consumers up to a health and decency level, (2) the additional investment in public and private capital goods necessary to bring about this result as well as to meet other capital deficiencies, and (3) the costs of supplying additional government services to provide satisfactory community living standards for the entire population. These estimates are made without "disturbing" the consumption patterns of those consumers (who are the vast majority) with adequate incomes to meet their needs. In other words, these estimates of needs are intended to show the cost of establishing a floor for consumption without in any way disturbing the ceiling established by free choice within the economy.

CONSUMPTION GOODS AND SERVICES

Of the three major components of gross national product, consumption goods and services is by far the most important, normally accounting for two thirds or more of the total. In 1950, expenditures for this category amounted to nearly $195 billion, or about 68 per cent of the $287 billion total. Projections for 1960 indicate that because of the large increase in government expenditures consumption goods and services will constitute a somewhat smaller share of the larger total: $241.5 billion, or 65 per cent of the $370 billion gross product in that year.[3] (See Table 350.)

With the growth of population over the years, and the rise in the standard of living — and in the price level — personal expenditures for all classes of consumption goods and services have greatly increased; and further increases have been assumed for 1960. Past experience, together with common observation, shows, however, that the "income-elasticity of demand" varies widely for different consumer products. As family incomes rise, a smaller proportion of the increased income goes for necessities such as housing and utilities, and a larger share for such luxuries as recreation and vacation travel. Over the past several decades, for example, the proportion of total consumption expenditures paid for consumer transportation has more than doubled, while the percentage devoted to housing and utilities has dropped sharply. A larger share of the consumer dollar is being paid for medical care and insurance, for household equipment and operation, for recreation and private education; a smaller proportion for the purchase of clothing and accessories and for religion and private welfare. Food, liquor and tobacco, which is the most important consumption group, has accounted for roughly one third of the consumer budget in recent years — about the same proportion as before World War I. (See Table 351.)

Food, Liquor and Tobacco

Expenditures for this group of commodities amounted to $65.6 billion in 1950, and 1960 expenditures are estimated at $81.8 billion, or slightly more than one third of total consumption expenditures, as in 1950.

How do these estimates of actual demand in 1950 and of probable consumption in 1960 compare with estimated consumer needs for this group of products? About $12.5 billion of the

1950 total for this group, and $15.9 billion of the estimated total for 1960, consists of expenditures for alcoholic beverages and tobacco products and smoking supplies. It is obvious that the concept of need is not relevant for these products — though this view might be contested by those addicted to their use! In any event, no attempt has been made to develop standards and estimate needs for these and other products not considered necessary to "maintain health and decency."

Physiological requirements of the human body for essential nutrients can be established more accurately than most human needs. The National Research Council's Food and Nutrition Board has developed and revised from time to time a set of "recommended dietary allowances" for ten nutrients needed by people of different sex, age groups and types of occupation. These recommendations allow a generous margin above the "minimal requirements of average individuals" to take care of "substantially all variations in the requirements of normal people" who may use specific nutrients somewhat less efficiently than the average.

These chemical requirements have been translated by the Bureau of Human Nutrition and Home Economics of the Department of Agriculture into a list of foodstuffs for moderate- and low-cost meals prepared at home. On this basis it is possible to estimate the cost of providing nutritionally adequate diets for those families and individuals who do not enjoy them.

To provide nutritionally adequate meals for those not getting enough of all the required nutrients in 1950 would have cost less than $800 million beyond the $53.1 billion actually spent for food and nonalcoholic beverages in that year. In 1960 the difference between estimated consumption and need would drop to $500 million. Since these estimates contemplate no change in the dietary habits of those with adequate incomes, it is clear that the American people are very well fed, or at least that they can afford to be. Indeed, Dr. Sebrell of the Public Health Service is authority for the statement that one out of four adult Americans is overweight and that obesity has become the "Number One nutrition problem" in the United States. Actually most of us would be better off nutritionally if we ate smaller amounts of sugar, fats and oils, and starchy foods and more milk, fruit, tomatoes and leafy, green and yellow vegetables.

---

3. These and all subsequent figures for 1960 are expressed in 1950 dollars, unless otherwise indicated.

TABLE 351. ESTIMATED NEEDS AND DEMAND FOR CONSUMPTION GOODS AND SERVICES, 1950 AND 1960, AND PERCENTAGE DISTRIBUTION OF CONSUMPTION EXPENDITURES, SELECTED YEARS, 1909–1960

| | Percentage Distribution of Demand | | | | | | | | Expenditures | | | |
| | | | | | | | | | 1950 | | 1960 | |
	1909	1914	1919	1929	1940	1950	1952	1960	Demand	Needs	Demand	Needs
									(Billions at 1950 Prices)			
Total	100.0	100.0	100.0	100.0	100.0	100.0	100.0	100.0	$194.6	$206.4	$241.5	$251.9
Food, liquor and tobacco	34.0	35.0	36.3	28.9	31.4	33.7	35.6	33.9	65.6	66.4	81.8	82.3
Clothing, accessories and personal care	14.9	14.1	15.8	14.8	13.5	12.8	12.5	13.3	25.0	27.4	32.1	34.4
Housing and utilities	24.0	23.6	16.9	18.0	17.6	14.0	14.6	13.8	27.2	30.7	33.2	34.4
Household equipment and operation[a]	11.8	11.1	12.1	16.4	15.4	14.9	14.2	14.6	29.1	29.3	35.4	35.5
Consumer transportation	5.2	6.4	8.1	9.9	9.9	12.1	11.0	11.8	23.5	23.5	28.5	28.5
Medical care and insurance[b]	2.8	2.7	3.4	3.7	4.3	4.3	4.4	4.4	8.4	12.5	10.7	16.0
Recreation	3.0	3.0	3.6	4.8	4.5	5.2	4.8	5.2	10.2	10.2	12.7	12.7
Private education	1.4	1.5	1.2	1.5	1.6	1.5	1.6	1.7	3.0	3.5	4.0	4.6
Religion	1.0	.9	1.0	1.1	.9	.6	.6	.5	1.1	1.4	1.3	1.6
Private welfare	1.8	1.6	1.4	.7	.6	.5	.5	.5	.9	.9	1.1	1.1
Occupational and miscellaneous expenses	.2	.2	.2	.2	.4	.3	.3	.3	.6	.6	.7	.7

Sources: Appendix 4–5 and Table 34.

a. Includes financial, legal, insurance (except accident, health and prepayment medical insurance) and death expenses.

b. Accident, health and prepayment medical insurance only.

Note: Discrepancies in addition are due to rounding.

927

Clothing, Accessories and Personal Care

Expenditures for clothing and personal care, which amounted to $25 billion in 1950 and are estimated at $32 billion for 1960, have experienced a moderate decline in relative importance over the past few decades. This group of goods and services approached 16 per cent of the consumer budget in 1919 but has since declined to around 13 per cent.

The amount and kind of clothing and personal care needed to maintain a health and decency standard of living depends far more on social and psychological considerations than on purely physiological ones. Decency is fully as important as health. This means that criteria of adequacy are hard to establish and must inevitably rest on someone's subjective judgment, rather than on objective determination.

Family budget and expenditure studies made by the Bureau of Labor Statistics and other government agencies in recent years indicate that in 1950 about 7 million urban families and a slightly larger number living in country districts were spending less than enough for clothing to provide for "health, efficiency, the nurture of children and for participation in community activities." Similar inadequacies were evident in the field of personal care. In most cases, of course, the deficiencies were not large. An additional expenditure of $2.4 billion in 1950, or about 10 per cent of actual expenditures, would have been sufficient to bring the entire population up to a level of adequacy in clothing and personal care. In 1960 the disparity between needs and demand would be even smaller — $2.3 billion, or 7 per cent of the total estimated expenditures of $32.1 billion.

These estimates, it must be remembered, are on a replacement basis, and make no allowance for the fact that families at the lowest income levels have inadequate inventories of clothing. To provide them with enough would of course be a nonrecurring cost, but it could easily amount to more than twice the annual cost of maintaining clothing standards at a health and decency level.

Housing and Utilities

Expenditures for housing and household utilities (water, heat and light) have been declining in relative magnitude for almost half a century. Before World War I they accounted for close to one dollar out of every four spent for consumption goods and services. In 1950 and again in 1960 they are estimated at about 14 per cent of the total. Expenditures in 1960 are estimated at $33.2 billion, compared with $27.2 billion in 1950.

Although housing inadequacies have long been recognized, the cost of meeting needs is difficult to estimate. Any realistic standard of adequacy must recognize that running water and modern sewerage facilities may be desirable in the small village or open country but are vital to city living. Fuel, heating equipment and insulation are obviously more important housing costs in Minnesota than in Mississippi; refrigeration is less essential in Maine than in Florida; and costly fireproof construction is an essential safety requirement in a crowded city but much less necessary in a small town.

In spite of these difficulties in establishing precise measures of need, the information collected in the 1950 Housing Census on dilapidation and plumbing equipment shows clearly that a large proportion of our existing housing is unsatisfactory by any reasonable definition of adequacy. In 1950, it is estimated, close to 15 million dwelling units in the United States, because of dilapidation, lack of running water or lack of satisfactory plumbing, or for other reasons, failed to provide fully adequate living quarters. The capital cost of bringing these units up to satisfactory standards either by rehabilitation or replacement was estimated at $67 billion.

A construction program of this magnitude could not be fulfilled except over a period of many years (as explained in the section on capital goods below). For that reason an estimate of the current cost, in terms of "rent and imputed rent," of meeting housing deficiencies lacks reality for 1950, and to only a slightly less extent for 1960. If the impossible had been achieved, however, and the capital expenditures needed to bring the 1950 stock of substandard housing up to standard had been made, about $2.4 billion would have been added to the actual 1950 shelter bill of $20.2 billion. Since it probably would take about fifteen years to handle such a housing job, roughly two thirds might be accomplished during the 1950–1960 decade. If we accept elimination of two thirds of the 1950 substandard housing as the goal for the decade and apply that standard to 1950, the shelter bill would have been upped by $1.6 billion instead of $2.4 billion. Close to 7 million subfamilies, secondary families and individuals were living with other families in 1950. Assuming a need for about 2 million additional households to accommodate a modest amount of "undoubling" of this group, an additional $1.2 billion of rental cost would have been involved.

More than a fourth of all housing costs consist of expenditures for household utilities — fuel, ice, lighting supplies, gas, electricity and water. On the basis of a standard that would provide every household with electricity and with central heat, the additional cost of meeting these needs in 1950 would have amounted to $700 million.

Thus the current cost of providing the entire population with adequate shelter (i.e., rent and imputed rent) and with heat, light and refrigeration would have come to $30.7 billion in 1950, or about 13 per cent more than the $27.2 billion actually spent in that year.

By 1960 a substantial part of our housing needs will have been filled through the normal operations of the market, thus narrowing the gap between needs and demand. The rental value of the stock of housing needed to provide adequate shelter in 1960 is estimated at $25.7 billion, or only 4 per cent more than the actual rent and imputed rent of $24.7 billion estimated for that year. This rental bill would pay for a stock of housing which included new or rehabilitated units in place of two thirds of the substandard units existing in 1950 plus dwellings for the additional households arising from desirable "undoubling" and population growth. All but about $200 million of the estimated needs for fuel and utilities will be met through the market, so that the current cost of meeting all housing needs in 1960 will exceed actual expenditures by less than 4 per cent — $34.4 billion compared with $33.2 billion.

Household Operation

The cost of household operation, which includes purchases of furniture, furnishings and equipment, payments for domestic service, telephone and communications, for cleaning, repair and maintenance, and for financial, legal, insurance and death expenses, was larger in 1950 than the cost of housing and utilities. Exclusive of financial, legal, insurance and death expenses, consumers paid almost as much to operate their households as they paid for rent and imputed rent. Over the past few decades, however, the share of the family budget going for household operation has risen considerably while housing costs have dropped sharply in relative importance. The $29.1 billion paid for household operation in 1950 was nearly 15 per cent of total consumption expenditures in that year, compared with 11 per cent in 1914.

What amount "ought" to be spent for household operation in order to maintain a health and decency standard for all is a question about which there are bound to be wide differences of opinion, for health could be maintained under conditions that decency would forbid. A minimum standard for household operation — even more than for housing or clothing — depends very heavily on social and psychological considerations. The City Worker's Family Budget, developed by the Bureau of Labor Statistics, is neither a subsistence nor a luxury budget, but "an attempt to describe and measure a modest but adequate American standard of living." This standard provides for needed articles of moderate-priced furniture and furnishings, miscellaneous household articles and supplies, and for a gas or electric cookstove, an electric iron, a mechanical refrigerator and a washing machine, all expressed in terms of customary replacement rates. No attempt is made to estimate "need" for domestic service, for cleaning and repair, for telephone and telegraph service and for financial and legal service; in other words, need for these items is regarded as being measured by demand.

For 1950, the cost of meeting the needs specified above for the families with inadequate incomes would have added to the $29.1 billion of actual expenditures in that year only $200 million, or less than one per cent. Estimated needs in 1960 would again exceed demand, estimated at $35.4 billion, by less than $200 million. These estimates on an annual replacement basis make no provision for supplying substandard families with their original inventories of durable equipment. For electric irons, refrigerators, gas or electric stoves and washing machines this initial investment would have cost $2.6 billion in 1950.

Consumer Transportation

Consumer expenditures for transportation, which amounted to $23.5 billion in 1950 and are estimated at $28.5 billion for 1960, have risen steeply over the past several decades. Only 5.2 per cent of the family budget went for transportation in 1909 but with the advent of the family automobile the share rose steeply to more than 12 per cent in 1950, and is estimated at slightly less for 1960.

Although it is undoubtedly true that an automobile is sometimes an unmet necessity, no basis exists for establishing a standard of health and decency in the field of personal transportation and for that reason need is considered equivalent to actual demand in this field of expenditure.

Medical Care and Insurance

Vast advances in the field of medical care during the past few decades have gone far toward eliminating many diseases. They have reduced infant and maternal mortality, lowered death rates, and in general brought health in the United States to a higher average level than ever before.

One authority, Dr. Raymond B. Allen, believes that greater progress was made in medical science in the first half of the twentieth century than in the previous five thousand years. Nevertheless, great deficiencies remain. Many physicians are handicapped by lack of modern technical facilities, many of the more remote areas are out of reach of adequate personnel and facilities, and, finally, large groups of the population cannot afford adequate medical care. This last is true in spite of the fact that medical care and insurance account for a larger share of total consumption expenditures than they did a few decades ago. In 1914 these items took only 2.7 per cent of the consumer dollar; by 1952 the proportion had risen to 4.4 per cent. The estimated expenditure of $10.7 billion in 1960 will amount to 4.4 per cent of total consumer spending.

Some of the deficiencies in the field of medical care require additional capital expenditures for hospital and other facilities, and an expanded government program is also necessary. These needs are referred to later in this chapter. However, the biggest gaps between demand and needs exist in the services of medical personnel and facilities ordinarily bought and paid for by consumers. Here the failure to obtain adequate care has been found to be evident at all income levels, but to be most serious among families and individuals who cannot afford adequate care.

Even if "educational barriers" to better medical care could be overcome, however, the cost of providing adequate care on the traditional fee-for-service basis would be prohibitive for the lowest income groups and far beyond what the middle income groups have been willing to pay in the past. Widespread use of prepayment medical care plans providing service through group practice could make adequate care available at a great saving over present costs. But even with such economies, the cost of providing adequate care for the entire population would require substantially larger consumer expenditures than have been made in the past. In 1950, even with such economies, adequate medical care at the consumer level (i.e., exclusive of capital and government costs) would have cost $12.5 billion instead of the $8.4 billion actually spent in that year. The gap of almost 50 per cent between estimated demand and needs would imply needed expenditures in 1960 of $16 billion compared with probable outlays of $10.7 billion.

Recreation

Recreation is another field of consumption expenditure which has been growing substantially in relative importance. About 3 per cent of total consumption expenditures went for recreational goods and services in 1909 and in 1914, while the $10.2 billion spent in 1950 represented 5.2 per cent of the total. The estimated $12.7 billion expenditures for 1960 would constitute just about the same share.

Although recreation is now regarded as necessary to human well-being, nobody has attempted to establish minimum standards of health and decency for the use of leisure time, or a minimum budget for the consumer's recreational expenditures. For this reason no attempt has been made to measure needs for recreation, as distinct from demand, as measured by actual or probable consumption expenditures. Estimates of need for government capital expenditures in the field of recreation have been made, however.

Private Education

Private education, financed through direct consumer payments, has long been insignificant by comparison with public education financed by taxpayers. Government now disburses almost 90 per cent of the operating costs of primary and secondary schools and about half of the higher education costs. Expenditures for private education in 1950 amounted to approximately $3 billion, or about 1.5 per cent of total consumption expenditures — about the same proportion as before World War I.

If the costs of the higher standards advocated by thoughtful and experienced educational leaders are to be met, it is obvious that the American people will have to pay for them largely in their role as taxpayers rather than as consumers. The minimum standard advocated by educators involves ten years of schooling for all children, which means the completion of the second year of high school in most cases, graduation from high school and completion of two years of college for half of all youths, and graduation from college or university for all young people who are mentally qualified. To meet these needs would require a great expansion of total educational expenditures — mostly on the part of government — over the amounts spent in 1950 and likely to be spent in 1960. For privately financed education, however, additional consumption expenditures of about $500 million over the roughly $3 billion spent in 1950, and of about $600 million over the estimated $4 billion demand in 1960, would be sufficient to meet educational needs in those years.

Religion

The support of religious institutions and activities is another minor and shrinking field of consumer expenditure. The $1.1 billion spent for current operations in 1950 and the $1.3 billion estimated for 1960 account for less than a penny out of every dollar spent by consumers — and the proportion is about half of what it was twenty-five years ago.

It is not surprising, therefore, that thoughtful church leaders believe that the "demand" for religious activities, as measured by consumer payments for them, falls short of need. To meet current operating needs — for more, better-trained and better-paid personnel, and for expanded services — expenditures of $1.4 billion, or 25 per cent more than the amount actually spent, were believed necessary for 1950. In 1960 probable expenditures are estimated at $1.3 billion and needs at $1.6 billion. Capital expenditures needed to provide additional buildings are considered later in this chapter.

Private Welfare

Individual giving for private social welfare purposes has always constituted a small share of the total costs of welfare, which includes in addition to relief expenditures the costs of unemployment and old-age insurance, old-age assistance, veterans programs, public and corporate retirement systems, etc. (i.e. all transfer payments to individuals). Since the onset of the Great Depression, government has assumed more and more of the existing welfare functions, as well as many new ones, while corporations have also become a far more important source of support for welfare.

Consumer expenditures for private welfare have declined in relative importance even more sharply than personal contributions to religious organizations. The $900 million contributed in 1950 and the estimated $1.1 billion for 1960 constitute only half of one per cent of total consumption expenditures, compared with 1.8 per cent going for welfare in 1909 and .7 per cent just before the depression in 1929.

No attempt has been made to estimate "need" for private welfare, as distinct from actual or estimated consumer expenditures. To do so would involve duplication with other categories of need previously estimated.

Summary

Total expenditures for consumption goods and services amounted to $194.6 billion in 1950 and are estimated at $241.5 billion for 1960. On the basis of the estimates of need summarized above and presented more fully in preceding chapters, expenditures of $206.4 billion in 1950, or 6 per cent more than the amount actually spent in that year, would have permitted the small minority of substandard families and individuals to achieve a "health and decency" standard of living without any modification in the living standards of the vast majority whose incomes were more than adequate to maintain such standards. In 1960, with the estimated cost of meeting total needs amounting to $251.9 billion (at 1950 prices), the margin between demand and needs would be reduced to 4 per cent.

CAPITAL GOODS

Capital goods constitute a small but critical fraction of gross national product. Although the aggregate expenditures of individuals, corporations and business firms, and government agencies for capital goods rarely exceed one sixth of total gross product, these expenditures are crucial

TABLE 352. ESTIMATED NEEDS AND DEMAND FOR CAPITAL GOODS[a] IN 1950 AND 1960 COMPARED WITH ESTIMATED EXPENDITURES IN SELECTED EARLIER YEARS

	Annual Average						1929	1933	1940	1950		1960	
	1920–1939	1920–1924	1925–1929	1930–1934	1935–1939	1945–1949				Demand	Needs	Demand	Needs
	(Billions at Current Prices)									(Billions at 1950 Prices)			
Total[a,b]	$12.5	$12.8	$17.4	$8.2	$11.4	$31.7	$17.7	$4.9	$15.0	$52.4	$66.7	$66.5	$78.3
Private[b]	10.1	11.2	15.0	5.9	8.1	27.8	15.1	3.2	11.6	45.0	51.7	56.0	62.1
Public[b]	2.4	1.6	2.4	2.3	3.3	3.9	2.6	1.7	3.4	7.3	15.0	10.5	16.2
Private productive facilities	6.7	7.2	9.2	4.4	6.0	21.0	10.7	2.6	8.2	30.3	34.8	42.3	44.8
Manufacturing	1.7	2.0	2.3	1.0	1.6	7.2	2.7	.7	2.7	7.5	8.6	11.0	11.7
Transportation,[c] communication and utilities	1.8	2.0	2.5	1.3	1.3	4.7	2.8	.6	2.0	6.7	7.7	9.3	9.8
Other[d]	3.2	3.2	4.4	2.1	3.1	9.1	5.2	1.3	3.5	16.1	18.5	22.0	23.3
Developmental and public enterprise construction	2.0	1.3	1.9	2.0	2.7	2.8	2.0	1.5	2.8	4.8	10.7	7.3	11.4
Highways[e]	1.1	.8	1.2	1.1	1.2	1.3	1.3	.8	1.3	2.3	5.5	3.5	5.5
Other[e]	.9	.5	.7	.9	1.5	1.5	.7	.7	1.5	2.5	5.2	3.8	5.9
Consumer construction	3.7	4.2	6.2	1.7	2.6	7.6	4.8	.7	3.8	16.8	20.7	16.2	21.4
Residential	2.9	3.5	5.1	1.1	2.0	6.4	3.8	.5	3.3	13.7	14.6	12.0	14.6
Other[f]	.8	.7	1.1	.6	.6	1.2	1.0	.2	.5	3.1	6.1	4.2	6.8
	Per Cent of Total												
Total[a,b]	100.0	100.0	100.0	100.0	100.0	100.0	100.0	100.0	100.0	100.0	100.0	100.0	100.0
Private[b]	80.6	87.3	86.0	71.7	71.1	87.8	85.3	65.7	77.0	86.0	77.5	84.2	79.3
Public[b]	19.4	12.7	14.0	28.3	28.9	12.2	14.7	34.3	23.0	14.0	22.5	15.8	20.7
Private productive facilities	53.9	56.4	52.8	54.3	52.6	66.2	60.4	52.9	54.6	57.8	52.2	63.6	57.2
Developmental and public enterprise construction	15.8	10.1	11.0	24.0	23.6	8.8	11.5	31.6	18.9	9.2	16.0	11.0	14.6
Consumer construction	29.4	33.0	35.5	20.4	22.6	24.1	27.3	14.1	25.2	32.0	31.0	24.4	27.3

Sources: Appendix 4–8 and Tables 36 and 215.

a. These estimates cover all expenditures for plant and equipment except (1) expenditures for publicly owned military and naval plant and equipment and (2) expenditures by state governments for equipment.

b. Includes expenditures for public equipment (except state government); these expenditures are not distributed by type of capital expenditure.

c. Prior to 1939 includes only railroads, transit and oil pipeline; remaining transportation included with other private productive facilities.

d. Agriculture, mining, commercial and miscellaneous.

e. Conservation and development; sewage disposal; water supply; urban redevelopment; private road, bridge, park and playground construction; and public industrial, commercial, administrative and miscellaneous construction.

f. Religious, educational, recreational and hospital construction.

Note: Slight discrepancies in addition are due to rounding; percentages computed from unrounded figures.

to the functioning of the economy because their volume swings widely from prosperity to depression. As with consumer durables, purchase of capital goods can be postponed when the outlook for jobs and profits is dark and correspondingly accelerated when income is rising and investors are optimistic. In 1929, for example, public and private expenditures for capital goods together totaled $17.7 billion, or 18 per cent of gross national product; by 1933 they had dropped to $4.9 billion, or 9 per cent of the much smaller gross product of that year. The recovery from the bottom of the depression was also pronounced. By 1940 capital goods expenditures were over three times, and by 1950, more than ten times, what they were in 1933. (See Table 352.)

The impact of depression, recovery and prosperity on various classes of capital goods also differs widely. Outlays for private productive facilities, which usually account for 50–70 per cent of the total, dropped from an average of $9.2 billion in 1925–1929 to a low point of $2.6 billion in 1933. Recovery brought the total to $8.2 billion in 1940 and, with rising prices, to more than $30 billion by 1950. The post-Korea boom lifted the total to nearly $36 billion by 1952.

Consumer construction, and especially its chief component, residential construction, showed the most violent cyclical fluctuations. Expenditures for this group as a whole averaged $6.2 billion a year in 1925–1929 and residential construction averaged $5.1 billion. By 1933 residential building volume had dropped to $500 million, or less than 10 per cent of its prosperity average. Recovery brought residential construction to nearly seven times its depression low point, while the dollar volume in 1950 was more than twenty-seven times what it was in 1933. The price rise, it must be remembered, probably accounts for at least half of this increase in dollar volume.

Developmental works, consisting predominantly of highways, and the least important of the three categories, showed much more cyclical stability, owing chiefly to the federal works program during the 1930s. Although there was a considerable recovery after the depression it was less pronounced than in the case of residential construction and productive facilities.

Demand and Needs in 1950 and 1960

Because of the extreme volatility of capital expenditures during the contrasting periods of boom and depression that have characterized the past generation, it is difficult to project future outlays with any assurance. As for need, whether in the past or future, this concept is obviously much more elusive in its application to capital goods than to such consumer necessities as food and clothing. The consumption needs summarized earlier could not, of course, be supplied without a considerable expansion of capital facilities. Higher standards for housing, education and medical care obviously necessitate the construction of more and better houses, schools and hospitals, not only to replace those that have outlived their usefulness, but to provide expanded facilities. The additional amounts of food, clothing, household equipment and other products needed to provide an adequate standard of living for the population would probably require an increase in factory capacity and other productive facilities used to produce and distribute these products. Beyond this will be needs for such forms of community capital as highways and streets, conservation and development projects, and sewer and water-supply systems. (See Table 352.)

Consumer Construction

Although consumer construction is not the most important category of capital goods, it is the most closely related to the consumption needs discussed in the preceding section. Actual expenditures for this class of goods amounted to $16.8 billion in 1950, of which $13.7 billion was used for residential structures. Estimated needs for consumer construction in that year would have been met by a total expenditure of $20.7 billion. Housing accounts for less than one billion of the $3.9 billion "deficiency" and schools and hospitals for most of the remainder. In 1960 about half of the estimated $5.2 billion gap between demand and needs is attributable to the housing deficiency. These estimates of needs are based on a construction program stretching over a period of years — generally ten or fifteen — for making up deficiencies, *not* on the *actual* difference between expenditures and total existing needs in 1950.

Private Productive Facilities

Outlays for private productive facilities — the structures, machinery, equipment and other facilities used to produce, transport and market economic goods and services — amounted to $30.3

billion in 1950, or close to 60 per cent of total capital expenditures. In 1960, expenditures for productive facilities are estimated to amount to $42.3 billion. In both years facilities for manufacturing, transportation, communication and utilities account for nearly half of total expenditures for productive facilities.

Since productive facilities are only used indirectly, the need for such goods can only be measured in terms of the need for the goods they supply. On the basis of the difference between demand and needs for consumption goods, for government noncapital goods and for developmental works and consumer construction, expenditures to meet the needs for private productive facilities are estimated at $34.8 billion for 1950 and at $44.8 billion for 1960. Thus the gap between demand and needs is $4.5 billion, or 15 per cent, for 1950, and $2.5 billion, or 6 per cent, for 1960.

Developmental Works

Although developmental works and public enterprise construction normally account for only a small fraction of total expenditures for capital goods, the gap between estimates of needs and demand in this field is much larger than in the case of either consumer construction or productive facilities. Expenditures for developmental works are estimated at $4.8 billion in 1950 and probable expenditures at $7.3 billion in 1960. In both years highway construction accounts for close to half of the total and conservation and development projects for the bulk of the remainder.

In order to meet capital needs in this field, expenditures at the average rate of $10.7 billion a year were estimated for 1950 and $11.4 billion for 1960. Filling the need for highway construction, costing $5.5 billion in each year, would provide us with a superlative interregional highway system and with rebuilt and improved state highways, rural roads, and city and town streets.

The estimate of needs for conservation and development and other projects, amounting to $5.2 billion in 1950 and $5.9 billion in 1960, would result in equally impressive accomplishments. Expenditures of this magnitude would vastly improve and restore our agricultural land, protect our forest and watersheds, reduce the danger of floods, improve our waterways and develop our potential water-power resources, in addition to providing parks, shore frontage and other needed recreational facilities.

The standards of need on which these estimates for developmental works are based obviously have been on a more generous scale than those for, say, food and clothing. In many ways they represent a program that, though highly desirable, is not absolutely essential. The full and prompt satisfaction of these needs therefore does not merit as high an order of priority as achieving a minimum standard of living for such urgent necessities as food, clothing, shelter, education and medical care. It must be remembered, however, that many types of developmental works — highways and conservation, for example — contribute to increased productivity, upon which a higher standard of living depends.

Summary

Total investment in capital goods by individuals, business and government in 1950 amounted to $52.4 billion — three and a half times the dollar amount spent in 1940. In 1960, expenditures for capital goods are estimated at $66.5 billion, an increase of nearly 27 per cent over the 1950 total. The estimates of needs summarized above indicate that an outlay of $66.7 billion for capital goods would have been required in 1950 and $78.3 billion in 1960 to supply the other goods and services required to provide a fully adequate standard of living for all. It is important to emphasize again, however, that the figure for total needs for capital goods is not a very dependable one.

GOVERNMENT EXPENDITURES

Every great war in American history has accelerated the long-term uptrend in government expenditures. World War II was no exception, and the Korean War brought another upward surge in government costs. By 1952 one out of every seven employed Americans was working for some governmental unit; the aggregate payrolls of federal, state and local governments in that year amounted to $32.5 billion. How the government role as an employer has grown can be seen from the rise in the government share of total employment from less than 5 per cent in 1910 to over 12 per cent in 1950 — with the further rise to more than 15 per cent after Korean hostilities began.

Although it is common practice to speak of "the Government" as if it were a single unified agency, it would be almost as accurate to speak of "the Church," when referring to the 286,000 local churches and congregations in the United

States, or "Industry," when speaking of the 260,-000 manufacturing establishments. There are some 117,000 units of government in the United States, ranging in size and importance from little school and water districts and thinly populated townships and counties at one extreme, to the federal government, New York City and the largest states at the other.

There is considerable concentration, it is true, just as there is in religion and industry, and the economic importance of the federal government has vastly increased, largely through the effects of two world wars and the Great Depression. Out of gross government expenditures (exclusive of intergovernmental transfers) of more than $101 billion in the 1952 fiscal year, the federal government accounted for more than $70 billion, the states for nearly $11 billion and the numerous local government units for about $20 billion.

The picture was far different before World War I. In 1913, local governments accounted for nearly 60 per cent of the tiny $3 billion total. The federal government spent less than one third of the total and the states less than 10 per cent. By 1932 the share of the states had increased to about 15 per cent, the share of local governments had dropped to 52 per cent, while the federal government, in spite of higher costs as an aftermath of World War I, still accounted for roughly one third of the $13.2 billion total.

The big change in the role of government, in the cost of government services, and in the relative importance of the federal government has come in the past twenty years. Total government expenditures in 1952 were almost eight times as large as in 1932, but federal expenditures had multiplied sixteen times.

Prices and Population Growth

A considerable part of the increase in the cost of government, of course, is due to the great rise of prices, which affects public no less than private activities. An index of the price of government goods and services shows that 1950 prices were 218 per cent above 1913, while a further rise of about 10 per cent or more had occurred by 1952. This means that today we would have to pay close to $11 billion for the same volume of government services that we bought for $3 billion in 1913.

Another factor responsible for expansion of government functions and costs is the growth of population. Population since 1913 has increased from about 97 million to some 160 million, or by 65 per cent. If government services expanded proportionately, the "1913 kind of government" would have cost around $18 billion if supplied to today's population at today's costs.

Per Capita Costs in 1950 Dollars

The influence of these two factors can be "eliminated" by measuring expenditures in terms of dollars of constant purchasing power and on a per capita basis. Per capita government expenditures were about $460 in 1950. Though less than the wartime expenditure, this was more than four and a half times the 1913 per capita cost of $100 and well over twice the 1932 average of $217, all measured in dollars of 1950 purchasing power.

The biggest increases were in international affairs (chiefly relief and aid to foreign countries) and social security, both of which were virtually nonexistent in 1913, but which cost nearly $31 and more than $48 per capita, respectively, in 1950. Other large increases were interest on debt, which rose from $1.66 per capita in 1913 to $42.81 in 1950; payment for agriculture and natural resources (chiefly farm aid), which rose from $2.10 to $29.20 during the same period; and national defense, which cost almost ten times as much in 1950 as in 1913 — $83.19 per capita compared with $8.62.

Among the other government costs of considerable importance in 1950, per capita expenditures of $68.19 for education were three times as large as in 1913, public welfare and veterans pensions, at $36.07, cost five times as much, health and community facilities, at $36.17, cost almost three times as much, and transportation, at $38.05, cost more than twice as much.

It is evident that government has been costing more not only because of larger population and higher costs and prices, but because government agencies have been providing new and expanded services. Some of these, like social security and improved education, have come in response to public demand; others, like foreign relief and national defense, have been imposed on the United States by world developments.

Relative Cost of Government

The rise in the relative economic importance of government can be measured by comparing government expenditures with gross national product. In 1913, government expenditures (including transfer payments, which are *not* a part of gross national product) equaled 6.4 per cent of gross national product. After a sharp rise in World War I, they dropped to less than 10 per cent of gross national product in 1929, rose to 18 per cent in 1932, to about 40 per cent in 1942, dropped to 21 per cent in 1950, and rose again to 27 per cent in 1952.

Needs and Demand for Government Services

In spite of the great rise in government expenditures over the past four decades, there is good reason to believe that the government services actually supplied in 1950 fell considerably short of the "need" for them. Total government expenditures amounted to $61.4 billion in calendar year 1950, of which $42 billion consisted of purchases of goods and services and about $19 billion of transfer and interest payments, etc. Civilian capital goods required $7.3 billion of expenditure, and other goods and services $34.7 billion.

Estimated needs for 1950 amount to $97 billion, which would indicate a deficiency of some $35 billion. In the neighborhood of $20 billion, or roughly two thirds of the total gap between actual and necessary expenditures in that year, is attributable to deficiencies in the national defense program — which became so evident after the summer of 1950. Most of the remaining deficiency is distributed between education and public welfare (including social insurance) and highway construction.

Of the total 1950 deficiency, capital goods, chiefly for transportation and education, account for $7.7 billion. Noncapital goods and services, which are defined to include expenditures for publicly owned military and naval plant, account for $23.1 billion of the total and national defense is responsible for almost the entire amount. A $4.4 billion gap in transfer and other payments is attributable almost exclusively to public welfare and social security.

Government expenditures in 1960 are expected to rise by more than half over the 1950 level to $94.5 billion, owing chiefly to increased national defense costs. Substantial rises in public welfare and social insurance costs and highway construction account for most of the remainder of the increase. The estimated gap between probable and needed expenditures shrinks to $12 billion in

1960, little more than one third the size of the 1950 deficiency. The largest 1960 deficiencies are likely to be in the fields of education, public welfare (including social insurance) and highway construction.

Of the total deficiency in 1960, capital goods, chiefly for schools and roads, account for $5.7 billion. Noncapital deficiencies amount to approximately $4.2 billion and transfer and other payments to $2 billion.

INVENTORIES AND TRADE BALANCE

Consumption goods and services, private and public capital goods, and government services and noncapital goods normally account for all but a very small fraction of gross national product. The two remaining items — inventory change and export balance — together accounted for slightly over 2 per cent of gross national product in prosperous 1929 and for less than 2 per cent in 1950. However, both these items are extremely volatile in periods of rapid economic change, and unlike the three major components they may fall below zero.

In periods of rising prices and expanding demand, business firms are likely to accumulate inventories at an abnormally rapid rate, as they did during the immediate postwar period, while they liquidate inventories rapidly in periods of declining business. In periods of stable prices and moderately rising activity, however, inventories usually increase steadily in accordance with an expanding volume of business, while the export balance under such conditions should change only gradually.

Foreign Trade

With the exception of a very few years since World War I, the United States has had an excess of exports over imports. This positive trade balance until World War II was accompanied by a small but consistent net outflow of payments for services: tourist expenditures, merchant marine costs, immigrant remittances and interest and dividends. The negative balance on services, however, was not large enough to offset the positive merchandise balance.

Our positive balance in current transactions with the rest of the world was reflected during the 1920s in a heavy outflow of investment capital to other countries. This outflow ended abruptly with the onset of the depression, and some net return flow took place during the 1930s. This continued until after World War II, when American investment abroad was resumed on a substantial scale, notably in the form of direct investment in raw material development and manufacturing.

World War II also brought sharp changes in our merchandise trade. Largely because of lend-lease, both the volume of exports and our positive balance of merchandise trade were maintained at very high levels. Merchandise exports averaged $10.5 billion during 1940–1945 and our positive balance averaged $6.1 billion. In the postwar period exports continued at close to peak wartime levels, largely as a result of our program of economic and military assistance to our allies. Imports rose to record high levels in the postwar years, reflecting the high level of domestic prosperity and stockpiling program. Our positive balance accordingly dropped below wartime levels.

The erratic course of our foreign transactions in the past coupled with the uncertainties of the cold war make any judgments about the future highly conjectural. This study assumes a rise of about one third from 1950 to 1960 in total international transactions of the United States. Both exports and imports are expected to increase in actual amount but imports will decline slightly in relative size, compared with gross national product. Exports seem likely to increase more than imports so that the positive merchandise balance will be larger than in 1950. Exports will of course be affected importantly by the government foreign aid program as well as by the annual flow of funds into foreign investment, which is expected to double by 1960. Even with this rise, income from our growing total of private foreign investment may exceed annual fresh capital outflow by as much as 35 per cent.

On balance, the excess of receipts from foreigners over payments to foreigners resulting from merchandise trade and capital investment and income, which may approximate $2 billion, will be just about offset by net American payments for travel abroad, private remittances and donations and merchant marine services — hence, a balance is assumed.

Inventories

Business inventories are likely to undergo substantial fluctuations during periods of actual or expected change in business volume and in prices. Thus inventories increased steadily during the price inflation after World War II, but contracted sharply with the minor recession in 1949 and early 1950. Again inventories expanded rapidly in 1950–1952, while a slight decline followed after the crest of the boom was reached in 1953. The assumptions of this study of a stable level of high activity in 1960, however, would suggest neither rise nor decline in the volume of inventories but their maintenance at a steady level.

SUMMARY OF DEMAND AND NEEDS

Under the assumptions of this study gross national product, which amounted to approximately $287 billion in 1950, would rise to $370 billion in 1960. This rise of 29 per cent in national output compares with estimated increases of 16 per cent in population and 12 per cent in the labor force. It would thus involve a rise in the amount of goods available per capita of the population and a substantially larger output per worker.

The aggregate of needs in 1950 is estimated at $336 billion — about $49 billion, or 17 per cent, in excess of the actual demand, or output, in that year. Consumption expenditures, though constituting more than two thirds of the 1950 gross national product, account for less than $12 billion, or only one fourth, of the total "deficiency." Actual expenditures for capital goods amounted to $52.3 billion in 1950, or $14.4 billion less than estimated needs. Although government expenditures for capital goods in 1950 amounted to only $7.3 billion, as compared with $45 billion for private, the public category accounts for more than half of the estimated deficiency for capital goods. Government expenditures for noncapital goods and services,[4] amounting to $34.7 billion in 1950, fell short of estimated needs by $23 billion, which means that government goods and services accounted for nearly $31 billion, or 62 per cent, of the $49 billion deficiency in 1950. This is attributable preponderantly to our failure to spend as much as we should have spent for national defense in that year — which became shockingly evident after the communist attack in Korea.

The disparity between total needs and demand, as measured by estimated gross national product, would drop to a little more than $26 billion,

---

4. Defined here to include outlays for publicly owned military and naval plant and equipment.

or 7 per cent of estimated demand, in 1960, under the assumptions of this study. This sharp decline is due very largely to the estimate of a reduction in the deficiency for government goods and services to about $10 billion, or one third of the 1950 disparity. Government expenditures for goods and services in 1960 are expected to rise by $30 billion over the 1950 level to a total of $72.5 billion.

With an expected rise in total expenditures for capital goods to $66.5 billion in 1960, needs are estimated at $78.3 billion, indicating a deficiency of less than $12 billion (about equally divided between government and private capital goods) — a smaller dollar amount than in 1950 and a considerably smaller percentage deficiency.

Consumption expenditures in 1960 are estimated at $241.5 billion, or only about $10 billion less than estimated needs of $251.9 billion. Thus the estimated actual demand in 1960 would have to be increased by only about 4 per cent to meet aggregate needs, compared with 6 per cent in 1950. (See Table 350.)

RESOURCES AND CAPACITIES

To satisfy the total needs outlined in the preceding section — for consumption goods and services, public and private capital goods and government services — would have required in 1950 a gross national product 17 per cent larger than was actually produced in that year. In 1960 the estimated deficiency would be reduced to 7 per cent. Is the capacity of our agricultural land and equipment, the supply of our natural resources, the capacity of our industrial and other productive facilities and of our labor force, and the level of our technology adequate to supply these needs?

FOOD AND AGRICULTURE

American agriculture has always been more than equal to the task of supplying us with an abundant and varied diet, an ample supply of natural fibers, and plenty of tobacco, as well as producing a surplus for export. In recent years, indeed, the major problem of American agriculture has not been that of meeting needs, but of solving the problem of excess supply — witness the farm surpluses piling up in government warehouses.

During World War II, in spite of serious labor shortages, we were able to meet vastly expanded requirements for civilian, military and lend-lease needs by quickly expanding acreage under cultivation and by achieving further gains in output per acre and per worker. In 1944 agricultural production reached an all-time peak almost one fourth above the 1940 volume. This was only partly because more land was brought under cultivation, for harvested acreage increased by only 6 per cent. The major factor was a continued rise in productivity, further accelerated during the war. Production of crops and livestock per harvested acre in 1944 was 17 per cent larger than in 1940 — and almost half again as large as just before World War I. Even more spectacular was the gain in agricultural production per man-hour — 22 per cent from 1940 to 1944. In the latter year productivity was almost twice as large as in the year before World War I began.

More than enough agricultural products to supply our 1950 population were produced by a labor force of 7.4 million, working on 345 million acres of harvested cropland (plus 485 million acres of pasture) with the aid of 3.6 million tractors, more than 6 million automobiles and trucks, and much other mechanical and electrical equipment. This was about the same agricultural output as in 1944, the peak war year, but it was achieved in 1950 with a much smaller labor input, which reflects a substantial gain in productivity per acre and per man-hour.

With our larger 1960 population, even without much increase in per capita consumption of foodstuffs, which has remained almost stationary for several decades, we can expect a demand for farm products, for domestic consumption and for export, about 20 per cent larger than in 1950. Meeting estimated need for foodstuffs in that year would increase this percentage only slightly.

Continued increases in the size of farms and in the use of fertilizer and mechanical equipment, as well as further development of better-yielding varieties of crops, will mean increased crop yields per acre and increased acreage and output per worker and per man-hour. If prewar gains in productivity continue in the future, we can expect to meet our 1960 domestic requirements with 400 million harvested acres and with another 40 million acres for exports. All of this, moreover, can probably be achieved with a smaller labor force than the number actually engaged in agricultural pursuits in 1950.

There will be no difficulty in meeting either

acreage or labor requirements in the future. So far as acreage is concerned, soil experts estimate that cropland could be expanded by 40 per cent, to 480 million acres, and that production could be augmented by 50 per cent, or by two and a half times the increase required. Therefore, even in the unlikely event that the long-term upward productivity trends fail to continue, we would still have more than enough acreage to meet requirements. Labor presents no problem, for there is every prospect that the long uptrend in productivity — in terms of acres per worker and output per man-hour — will continue. The larger future acreage and agricultural production can undoubtedly be handled by a smaller proportion of our larger future labor force.

NATURAL RESOURCES

In the process of turning out close to 40 per cent of the world's goods, the American economy burns and "chews up" an enormous quantity of raw materials every year. In 1950, for every man, woman and child of the population, we consumed an average of 7 tons of fuel and more than 11 tons of other materials, exclusive of vast quantities of water and air, which are important raw materials in many industrial processes. The United States is the world's largest consumer of all of the major metals, the mineral fuels and the principal nonmetallic minerals, and with certain significant exceptions is also the leading producer.

However, the war brought home to the American people the fact that, although within our own borders we are blessed with a wider variety and greater abundance of natural resources than any other industrial nation (with the possible exception of the Soviet Union), we are far from self-sufficient in many essential industrial raw materials. In 1950 we produced more than we consumed, and exported the surplus, of anthracite and bituminous coal, sulphur, phosphate rock and molybdenum. We just about met our own needs for natural gas and cement. But we were wholly or almost wholly dependent on foreign countries for tin, nickel, asbestos, graphite, antimony, manganese, chromite, columbium, beryl, cobalt, diamonds and quartz. Between half and three quarters of our total consumption of bauxite, lead and mercury was supplied by imports. And foreign countries supplied us with a fifth to half of our requirements for magnesium, tung-

sten, fluorspar, copper and zinc. Among other "unfavorable balance" minerals, we depended on foreign supplies for part of our total requirements for iron ore, crude petroleum and potash.

Heavy consumption of iron and nonferrous metals and petroleum during the war and postwar periods has brought us closer to a critical situation so far as some essential minerals are concerned. Petroleum, copper, lead and zinc — and the ferroalloy metals, such as nickel, cobalt and tungsten — present the most important and critical scarcity problems.

However, the exhaustion of some of our high-grade mineral reserves and the depletion of our supply of essential natural resources should present no serious problems so far as 1960 is concerned. To produce the estimated gross national product for that year would require about 22 per cent more industrial raw materials than were consumed in 1950; to meet the estimated needs for 1960 would involve a rise of less than 30 per cent over 1950 use of raw materials. Such an increase, or even a much larger one, would be easily within our reach.

With free trade throughout the noncommunist world, we will be able to obtain all the raw materials we need to maintain a high and rising standard of living. Denied free access to world raw materials, the United States would have to meet its future requirements for essential industrial materials by drawing further on its own dwindling reserves of high-grade resources, by using its abundant low-grade reserves, at higher cost, and by developing substitutes and new combinations of existing materials to satisfy existing and new demands.

What this would entail, in the final analysis, is devoting a larger proportion of our human and material effort to meeting our raw material needs. At present only 4.5 per cent of our total manpower is needed to produce all of our crude materials, other than food. If we were unable to obtain mineral raw materials from abroad we might have to increase this proportion substantially. This would present problems of readjustment for the mining industries, but would not have much effect on the economy as a whole. On the whole, it seems clear that we shall not be hampered in meeting future needs by a shortage of raw materials.

Although there are sound reasons for optimism, there are many uncertainties regarding the future. It would seem wise policy, therefore, (1) to promote intensive research designed to develop new techniques for utilizing our abundant reserves of low-grade resources, (2) to rely on imports as much as possible in order to maintain our domestic reserves of critical minerals, and (3) to maintain a stockpiling program for materials that can be stored without deterioration and would be vital necessities in the event of another war.

INDUSTRIAL CAPACITY

Our wartime experience demonstrated that deficiencies in the productive capacity of our physical plant can be quickly overcome. In spite of a multitude of difficulties that do not exist in time of peace, we were able to maintain our civilian standard of living, fight a global war and at the same time vastly expand our total capacity to produce the kinds of goods we needed to win the war. Inadequate capacity, in terms of specialized industrial and commercial structures and equipment, was no more than a temporary hindrance to the fulfillment of war requirements.

So fast was our creation of needed plant, indeed, that the actual deficiencies soon gave way to fear of a postwar surplus of capacity. During the five years after the defense program began we invested more than $50 billion in new productive facilities. Out of a total of $38 billion spent for privately owned productive facilities during the war period about $15 billion, or 40 per cent, was for manufacturing facilities. This outlay represented something like a one-third expansion of our prewar private manufacturing plant. The fear of excess capacity proved to be ill-founded, not only because some of the wartime plant was abandoned as unsuitable for peacetime purposes, but because postwar demand for new plant so far exceeded expectations.

Instead of surplus capacity, the end of the war was followed by an explosive expansion of industrial capacity. Approximately $109 billion, or three times the dollar total invested during the five-year war period, was spent for private nonagricultural plant and equipment during the second half of the war decade. These vast additions brought the total value of our industrial and commercial facilities to some $300 billion by 1950.[5] Measured in constant prices, the value of our civilian nonfarm capital facilities at the end of the war decade was about one fourth greater

5. Exclusive of agricultural and government military facilities.

than at the beginning and three and a half times what it was in 1900. Because of the extraordinary advances in the efficiency with which these facilities are used, however, our national productive capacity increased far more.

More than a third of the record-breaking 1946–1950 investment was in manufacturing facilities, another third in commercial and miscellaneous facilities, a little more than 10 per cent each in utilities and transportation, and the remaining 9 per cent in communication and mining facilities. The distribution of postwar investment among the major industrial fields was closely similar to what it was in 1939.

During the war decade our total manufacturing capacity roughly doubled. Some of the largest gains in individual industries during the decade occurred in synthetic rubber and nitrogen and industrial chemicals, in aluminum, magnesium, zinc refining, aircraft manufactures, glass containers, wood pulp and paper, petroleum refining and gas and petroleum pipelines, in communications and electric utilities, in rayon and acetate fiber and in iron and steel.

Agricultural capacity was also greatly expanded by substantial increases in the number of tractors, motor trucks, and specialized equipment for harvesting and cultivating. However, in many declining industries, such as copper and lead smelting and refining, flour milling, cotton ginning and anthracite mining, capacity actually fell during the decade.

In spite of these vast additions to our productive capacity, the requirements of the Korean War brought another sharp expansion of facilities. Although the tax provisions permitting five-year depreciation for facilities covered by "certificates of necessity" were a decided stimulus to the post-Korea expansion, most of the new investment was in facilities not favored by these provisions. The $29 billion covered by these certificates through June 30, 1954 was less than the amount spent by business for new plant and equipment during any single year from 1950 on. This new expansion brought total corporate investment in fixed capital to $124 billion for the 1946–1952 period — almost as much as the book value of corporate capital assets at the end of the war. Because of the higher prices of the postwar period, of course, this does not mean anything like a doubling of total industrial and commercial capacity. However, manufacturing, which accounted for half of the postwar capital investment, expanded capacity by 50 per cent during these seven postwar years while electric utilities expanded their generating capacity even more.

The tremendous expansion of our productive plant that has occurred since the summer of 1940 would have been a remarkable accomplishment under normal peacetime conditions. The ability of American industry to add so lavishly to its own productive facilities while meeting the urgent necessities of a great world war followed by cold war and renewed hostilities, and at the same time to provide the basis for a boom in consumer goods of unprecedented duration and magnitude, had to be seen to be believed. It leaves no question that whatever our industrial and commercial capacity may be at any one time, it can be expanded with great rapidity to meet any demands that are likely to be made on it. Our vast productive plant is a flexible man-made resource which, barring atomic devastation, will prove equal to any imaginable need.

LABOR FORCE

The size, quality and productivity of the labor force set the ultimate limit on a nation's capacity to produce. In a modern industrial society, however, the size of the normal labor force can be quickly expanded by drawing on the labor reserve: youths who would ordinarily be attending school or college; wives without younger children who might be playing bridge or sitting around at home; and older men and women who have retired. We drew on these labor reserves during World War II, with the result that at the manpower peak in the winter of 1944–1945 there were about 8 million "emergency workers" in the labor force out of a total of approximately 66 million.

While we never quite reached our "labor ceiling" during the war, there are obvious limits to the size of the emergency labor force in any industrial nation. Physical strength and mental capacity set upper and lower age limits, while participation in the labor force by women with young children is obviously inadvisable, and usually difficult or impossible.

"Labor input," or total work done by the labor force, can also be increased by working longer hours. During the war the length of the work week in the United States increased by 8 per cent between 1940 and 1943, but dropped again to its prewar level by 1945. Here again experience during both world wars showed that there are upper limits to the length of the work week beyond which diminishing returns set in because of cumulative fatigue and lessened productivity.

By absorbing the unemployed and the normal accessions to the labor force and employing emergency workers, and by increasing working hours for this expanding body of workers, total civilian and military "labor input" was increased by 44 per cent between 1940 and 1944. This increase in labor input, together with higher prices, accounted for nearly all of the wartime rise in gross national product.

Quality of the Labor Force

Quality is probably just as important as quantity as a factor in the capacity of the labor force, but it is much more difficult to define and explain. It has its roots partly in inherited traits, about which there is much disagreement, but even more in the "institutional" atmosphere into which the individual is born and grows to maturity.

On the physiological side, inherited physique, nutrition, living conditions and the quality of family and medical care determine health, vigor and energy. On the intellectual side, the quality of the labor force is most significantly related not so much to inherited intelligence as to acquired knowledge and understanding about the tasks to be performed. Part of this knowledge comes from formal education, which is carried further for more young people in the United States than in any other country of the world, but part also comes from everyday contact with the devices and practices of an industrial civilization. "Know-how" in today's world includes a whole complex of social attitudes, specialized skills and accumulated knowledge, plus imagination and initiative linked with an aptitude for cooperation and teamwork in discharging the complicated tasks of a modern industrial society.

The quality and the size of the labor force are obviously important elements in productive capacity, but the most significant determinant of our ability to meet the expanded requirements of the future will be productivity. This is conveniently measured in terms of output per man-hour, but is in no sense a measure of "labor efficiency." Over the long run, the "efficiency" of the individual worker is a minor element in the productivity of the labor force. The most efficient shoemaker working long hours with the hand tools of a century ago could not remotely approach the productivity of today's semiskilled operative, working with the aid of automatic power-driven machinery. Over the past century we have achieved a fabulous increase in output per man-hour, not by working harder or more skillfully, but by constantly devising new and better machinery to augment human effort by the use of vast amounts of inanimate energy.

What our labor force will be able to turn out in 1960 depends on its size and on future trends in working hours, but more than anything else, on the extent of further gains in productivity.

Output of the Labor Force

This survey's estimate of a normal gross output for 1960 of $370 billion (at 1950 prices), or $26 billion less than estimated total needs of $396 billion, is based upon a number of assumptions about which there can be no certainty. For example, if the average work week does not decline further as assumed in this survey, but remains at the 1950 level, gross output would be increased by $25 billion more, which would be enough to practically close the gap between needs and demand. If, in addition to keeping the average work week at 40 hours, the labor force were to reach 74 million with only 3 million unemployed and productivity were to rise 35 per cent (instead of 25 per cent) during the decade, we could produce a gross product of $440 billion instead of $370 billion. In this event, we could meet the stated needs with a handsome margin to spare.

Under emergency conditions similar to those of World War II, the 1960 labor force could be expanded from 72.5 to 80 million. Unemployment in such a national emergency could be reduced from 3.5 million to about one million. As a result, employment would rise from 69 million under "normal" conditions to 79 million, with 59 million in private jobs and 20 million in government civilian jobs and the armed services. Hours of work probably could be upped from an average of 37.5 to 45 per week and output per man-hour (i.e., private national income per private man-hour) from $2.40 to $2.70. These assumptions would imply an increase in the gross national product from $370 billion to just over $500 billion (at 1950 prices). In other words, under emergency conditions in 1960, the labor force could conceivably turn out over a third more goods and services than under normal conditions, and about

three fourths again as much as in 1944, the peak World War II year, when the gross national product amounted to $288 billion, measured in 1950 dollars.

TECHNOLOGY AND PRODUCTIVITY

Technology is an intangible factor in production, but it is in a very real sense the *primary* resource, for it determines the productivity of our tangible resources, or the efficiency with which they are used in creating useful goods and services.

American technology has always been dynamic, for our ways of doing things in factories and farms and in the home have never been controlled by custom and tradition. Most of American history has been characterized, on the one hand, by an abundance of fertile land and rich resources awaiting exploitation and, on the other, by a sparse population and a chronic shortage of labor. This low ratio of labor supply to natural resources is responsible not only for our free immigration policy throughout the nineteenth and into the twentieth century, but also for the fact that American agriculture and industry have always excelled in the application of laborsaving methods and machinery. Denied an abundance of muscle power, we have used mechanical substitutes and supplements to human labor on a scale never equaled in any other country of the world.

Mechanization has been taking place at an accelerating rate, and productivity has been making parallel gains during the past century. Today we produce more than three times as much per worker in a 40-hour week as our grandparents did working 70 hours a week a century ago. This means that average output per man-hour for the economy as a whole is six times what it was in the middle of the nineteenth century. But productivity little more than doubled during the second half of the nineteenth century while it has almost trebled since 1900, and the increase during the 1940s seems to have been greater than in any earlier decade. But even the average rate of increase over the past century would yield fabulous results if long continued. By 2050 we would be able to produce and earn as much in one 7-hour day as we do now in a 40-hour week, and as we did in 1850 working for more than three weeks at 70 hours a week.

These great advances have been achieved by

harnessing inanimate energy on a lavish scale to displace animal power and multiply human effort. Gasoline-powered trucks and buses have long since displaced the horse in transportation, and the tractor is fast displacing him in agriculture. Coal-generated steam power long ago became the dominant source of energy in industry, as in rail and water transportation, but technological progress is now fast displacing coal by fuel oil in ocean transport, by diesel power on the railroads, and by central-station electricity in industry. In the home a widening variety of mechanical devices and electrical equipment is easing housework and making life more pleasant. All of these technological changes involve heavy and expanding capital investment and growing use of mechanical power.

Since 1850, the average number of horsepower per worker used by prime movers in agriculture, industry and commerce and the average value of productive capital facilities per worker have both experienced about a fivefold increase — considerably more than the increase in output per worker, but slightly less than the sixfold gain in output per man-hour. It is reasonable to assume that fixed capital investment, which averaged about $7,000 per worker (for nonfinancial business enterprises) in 1950, must continue to parallel or exceed future advances in productivity. In view of the remarkable expansion of industrial capacity during the war and postwar periods, such a rate of growth can be easily maintained.

Nearly all the back-breaking tasks of industry have already been taken over by mechanical power. Mass production has become increasingly automatic, since any repetitive operation can be done better by machines than by men. Electronic controls are now opening a new era of "automation," which has already brought the automatic factory in such processing industries as petroleum refining and promises soon to automatize machining and even assembly operations. These new electronic laborsavers relieve the worker of routine mental tasks just as power-driven machinery has taken over physical tasks. And just as machines are more efficient than muscles, electronic computers and controls are more sensitive and dependable and far speedier in performing routine mental tasks than the human brain. The various industrial applications of electronics in computers, industrial TV, and instruments for measurement, communication, inspection and control open a revolutionary new field for further enhancement of labor productivity.

Technology has also made great contributions to the productivity of agricultural land and equipment and to the availability and utility of our natural resources. In farming as in manufacturing, mechanization — especially the advent of tractors and specialized planting, cultivating and harvesting machines since World War I — has lessened toil and advanced labor productivity. These gains have been accompanied by expanded use of improved fertilizers and other chemical aids to production and the development of new varieties of improved and higher-yielding crops and livestock.

Because of these technological gains, the farm worker today produces twice as much as his harder-working predecessor of 1900, while crop production per acre has increased by more than half since the turn of the century. Recent developments in disease, insect and weed control, in the development of higher-yielding hybrids, in the use of antibiotics in stimulating livestock growth and in the breeding of plants and animals for higher yields hold promise of continued progress in the future.

"Natural" resources are valuable only because technology has made them available and useful, and technology is constantly increasing the supply, widening the variety and enhancing the utility of raw materials. For example, in the case of energy sources, which are the key to all other resources, technology has enabled us to shift from wood as a fuel and from water, wind and work animals, first to coal and steam power, then to petroleum and the internal combustion engine, to natural gas, and perhaps tomorrow to atomic and solar energy. Technology is contributing to the supply of raw materials through better techniques of prospecting and discovery, improved methods of mining and extraction, discovery of new sources of supply, and economies in application and use. As a single example of the latter, we now get more than six times as much delivered energy by burning a ton of coal as we did in 1900.

Thus technical progress has had the same effect as if our actual reserves had been correspondingly increased through new discoveries. Today we obtain nitrogen from air and magnesium from sea water — for all practical purposes technology has unlocked an unlimited supply of each.

Perhaps the most striking contribution of chemical technology is the creation of synthetic raw materials: dyes, pharmaceuticals, paints, perfumes, insecticides, detergents, herbicides and notably synthetic resins and plastics. These latter are not mere imitations of natural products but genuinely new materials endowed by man with the "properties nature forgot." These tailor-made raw materials, familiar to consumers in a variety of household articles ranging from automobile tires and squeeze bottles to dishware and floor coverings, are finding wide and increasing usefulness in industry. Since plastics can be produced from cheap and plentiful raw materials such as coal, air and water, their potential supply is almost unlimited.

Besides creating new materials, technology is giving new properties to some of the oldest and finding new uses for them. Glass is no longer merely something breakable and transparent, but a versatile raw material used in products ranging from draperies to automobile bodies. Concrete is being made in many new forms, some light and resilient, others stronger than the traditional product. Wood is being torn apart and put together again as a more useful "synthetic."

Aside from these and literally thousands of other new and different products created by the chemical industry itself, chemical technology has replaced old rule-of-thumb methods throughout the entire range of industry. Smelting and refining, pulp and paper manufacture, leather and rubber processing, sugar refining, laundering, and a score of other industries, have all become, in some measure at least, chemical industries.

What directions technological change will take is highly uncertain but that progress in the foreseeable future will be rapid — perhaps more rapid than in the past — seems beyond any reasonable doubt. Technology involves the application of the discoveries of science to everyday life, and we have made no more than a beginning in exploiting the developments growing out of World War II. New discoveries are already on their way, for industry, government and universities are devoting more effort to pure and applied research than ever before. Barring the devastation of World War III, technology will continue to keep the American people supplied with a steady stream of new and improved consumer goods and services and American industry with new and better materials, machines and methods. Technology is our primary and inexhaustible resource.

APPENDICES

APPENDIX I-I. FACTORS CONTRIBUTING TO INCREASE IN GROSS NATIONAL PRODUCT ABOVE 1940 LEVEL, 1941-1952

	1941	1942	1943	1944	1945	1946	1947	1948	1949	1950	1951	1952
Percentage increase from 1940:												
In prices	7.8	22.8	31.5	34.2	38.2	50.3	65.8	77.9	76.7	80.8	94.6	99.3
In employment	8.2	20.2	32.2	36.1	33.8	22.2	24.2	26.6	25.6	28.3	33.4	35.2
From decline in unemployment	5.3	11.4	14.7	15.5	14.8	12.2	12.5	12.6	9.9	10.4	13.0	13.5
From normal additions to labor force	1.1	2.4	4.2	5.6	6.8	8.3	9.8	11.2	12.9	14.7	16.4	18.2
From addition of extra workers to labor force	1.8	6.4	13.3	15.0	12.2	1.7	1.9	2.8	2.8	3.2	4.0	3.5
In length of work week[a]	.9	3.2	8.0	5.5	1.1	—3.2	—4.8	—6.8	—8.2	—8.9	—7.8	—7.5
Due to interaction of increases in prices, employment and length of work week	.8	6.1	16.1	16.9	13.8	8.5	10.8	12.2	9.6	11.1	19.1	22.2
Total due to above factors	17.7	52.3	87.8	92.7	86.9	77.8	96.0	109.9	103.7	111.3	139.3	149.2
Additions to 1940 GNP[b] (billions of dollars) due to:												
Increase in prices	7.9	23.1	31.9	34.7	38.7	51.0	66.7	79.0	77.8	81.9	95.9	100.7
Increase in employment	8.3	20.5	32.7	36.6	34.3	22.5	24.5	27.0	25.9	28.7	33.9	35.7
From decline in unemployment	5.4	11.6	14.9	15.7	15.0	12.4	12.7	12.8	10.0	10.5	13.2	13.7
From normal additions to labor force	1.1	2.4	4.3	5.7	6.9	8.4	9.9	11.4	13.1	14.9	16.6	18.5
From addition of extra workers to labor force	1.8	6.5	13.5	15.2	12.4	1.7	1.9	2.8	2.8	3.3	4.1	3.5
Increase in length of work week[a]	.9	3.2	8.1	5.6	1.1	—3.2	—4.9	—6.9	—8.3	—9.0	—7.9	—7.6
Interaction of increases in prices, employment and length of work week	.8	6.2	16.3	17.1	14.0	8.6	11.0	12.4	9.7	11.3	19.4	22.5
Total due to above factors	17.9	53.0	89.0	94.0	88.1	78.9	97.3	111.5	105.1	112.9	141.3	151.3
1940 GNP[b] plus additions due to above factors (billions of dollars)	119.3	154.4	190.4	195.4	189.5	180.3	198.7	212.9	206.5	214.3	242.7	252.7
Total GNP as reported (billions of dollars)	126.4	161.6	194.3	213.7	215.2	211.1	233.3	259.0	258.2	286.8	329.8	348.0
Additions to 1940 GNP due to other factors:[c]												
Amount (billions of dollars)	7.1	7.2	3.9	18.3	25.7	30.8	34.6	46.1	51.7	72.5	87.1	95.3
As per cent of reported GNP each year	5.6	4.5	2.0	8.6	11.9	14.6	14.8	17.8	20.0	25.3	26.4	27.4

a. Minus sign denotes decrease.
b. 1940 gross national product was $101.4 billion.
c. Includes increased productivity.

Sources: Price increases from Appendix 4–2, Table B; employment increases and changes in length of work week from Appendix 20–1; reported gross national product from Appendix 4–2, Table A.

947

APPENDIX 3-1. IMMIGRATION FROM PRINCIPAL COUNTRIES, BY DECADES, 1851-1950

Country	1851–1860	1861–1870	1871–1880	1881–1890	1891–1900	1901–1910	1911–1920	1921–1930	1931–1940	1941–1950
	Number (*Thousands*)									
Total	2,598	2,315	2,812	5,247	3,688	8,795	5,736	4,107	528	1,035
Austria-Hungary	—	8	73	354	593	2,145	896	64	125	255
Germany	952	787	718	1,453	505	341	144	412	—	—
Great Britain (United Kingdom)	424	607	548	807	272	526	341	330	29	132
Ireland (Eire)	914	436	437	655	388	339	146	221	13	27
Italy	9	12	56	307	652	2,046	1,110	455	68	58
Scandinavia (Denmark, Norway, Sweden)	25	126	243	656	372	505	203	198	11	26
Poland [a]	1	2	13	52	97	—	5	228	17	8
Russia (USSR)	[b]	2	39	213	505	1,597	921	62	1	1
Canada and Newfoundland [c]	59	154	384	393	3	179	742	925	109	172
Mexico	3	2	5	2	1	50	219	459	22	60
All other countries	211	178	296	353	300	1,066	1,008	754	132	297
	Per Cent of Total									
Total	100.0	100.0	100.0	100.0	100.0	100.0	100.0	100.0	100.0	100.0
Austria-Hungary	—	.35	2.60	6.75	16.08	24.39	15.62	1.56	23.67	24.64
Germany	36.64	34.00	25.53	27.69	13.69	3.88	2.51	10.03	—	—
Great Britain (United Kingdom)	16.32	26.22	19.49	15.38	7.38	5.98	5.94	8.04	5.49	12.75
Ireland (Eire)	35.18	18.83	15.54	12.48	10.52	3.85	2.55	5.38	2.46	2.61
Italy	.35	.52	1.99	5.85	17.68	23.26	19.35	11.08	12.88	5.60
Scandinavia (Denmark, Norway, Sweden)	.96	5.44	8.64	12.50	10.09	5.74	3.54	4.82	2.08	2.51
Poland [a]	.04	.09	.46	.99	2.63	—	.09	5.55	3.22	.77
Russia (USSR)	[b]	.09	1.39	4.06	13.69	18.16	16.06	1.51	.19	.10
Canada and Newfoundland [c]	2.27	6.65	13.66	7.49	.08	2.04	12.94	22.52	20.64	16.62
Mexico	.12	.09	.18	.04	.03	.57	3.82	11.18	4.17	5.80
All other countries	8.12	7.69	10.53	6.73	8.13	12.12	17.57	18.36	25.00	28.70

Sources: 1851–1900, *Statistical Abstract of the United States, 1948*, U.S. Bureau of the Census, Table 120, p. 107; 1901–1950, *Statistical Abstract, 1951*, Table 107, p. 94.

a. From 1899 to 1919 Poland is included with Austria-Hungary, Germany and Russia.

b. Less than 500.

c. Immigrants from Canada, Newfoundland and Mexico not reported from 1886 to 1893, inclusive.

Note: Slight discrepancies in addition are due to rounding.

(*Thousands*)

Year	Admitted			Departing			Excess of Admissions over Departures [a]	
	Total	Immigrant	Nonimmigrant	Total	Emigrant	Nonemigrant	Total	Immigrant over Emigrant
1931	281	97	184	291	62	229	− 10	35
1932	175	36	139	288	103	184	− 113	− 68
1933	151	23	128	244	80	164	− 93	− 57
1934	164	29	134	177	40	137	− 13	− 10
1935	180	35	145	189	39	150	− 9	− 4
1936	191	36	155	193	36	157	− 2	1
1937	232	50	182	225	27	198	7	24
1938	253	68	185	223	25	197	30	43
1939	268	83	185	201	27	175	67	56
1940	209	71	138	166	21	145	43	49
1941	152	52	100	88	17	71	63	35
1942	111	29	82	75	7	67	37	21
1943	105	24	81	59	5	54	46	19
1944	142	29	114	84	6	79	58	23
1945	202	38	164	93	7	86	109	31
1946	312	109	203	204	18	186	108	91
1947	514	147	366	323	23	301	190	125
1948	647	171	476	448	21	427	198	150
1949	636	188	447	430	25	406	206	164
1950	676	249	427	457	28	429	219	222
1951	671	206	465	473	23	447	198	180
1952	782	266	516	509	22	488	272	244
1953	656	170	486	544	24	520	112	146

Sources: Statistical Abstract of the United States: 1948 and 1953, U.S. Bureau of the Census, and Immigration and Naturalization Service, U.S. Department of Justice.

a. Excess of departures indicated by a minus sign.
Note: Discrepancies in addition are due to rounding.

(*Thousands*)

Year	Number of Women 17–29, Mid-point of Each Year	Number of Marriages
1940	15,274	1,596
1941	15,380	1,696
1942	15,450	1,772
1943	15,493	1,577
1944	15,499	1,452
1945	15,499	1,613
1946	15,537	2,291
1947	15,514	1,992
1948	15,471	1,811
1949	15,385	1,580
1950	15,333	1,667
1951	15,174 [a]	1,595
1952	15,021 [a]	1,531 [b]

Sources: U.S. Bureau of the Census and National Office of Vital Statistics.

a. Estimate, based on age distribution shown in *Current Population Reports: Population Estimates,* U.S. Bureau of the Census, Series P–25, No. 93, April 26, 1954.
b. Estimate, based on marriage licenses issued in 1952.

APPENDIX 3–4. POPULATION OF CONTINENTAL UNITED STATES, DENSITY PER SQUARE MILE, AND CIVILIAN MIGRATION, BY DIVISION AND STATE, 1940–1950

Division and State	Population		Population per Square Mile		Net Change through Civilian Migration	
	1940	1950[a]	1940	1950	Number	Per Cent
	(Thousands)				(Thousands)	
Continental United States	131,669	150,697	44.2	50.7	1,611	1.2
New England	8,437	9,314	133.5	147.5	158	1.9
Maine	847	914	27.3	29.4	− 16	− 1.9
New Hampshire	492	533	54.5	59.1	5	1.0
Vermont	359	378	38.7	40.7	− 15	− 4.2
Massachusetts	4,317	4,691	545.9	596.2	55	1.3
Rhode Island	713	792	674.2	748.5	1	0.1
Connecticut	1,709	2,007	348.9	409.7	128	7.5
Middle Atlantic	27,539	30,164	274.0	300.1	448	1.6
New York	13,479	14,830	281.2	309.3	376	2.8
New Jersey	4,160	4,835	553.1	642.8	314	7.5
Pennsylvania	9,900	10,498	219.8	233.1	− 242	− 2.4
East North Central	26,626	30,399	108.7	241.1	900	3.4
Ohio	6,908	7,947	168.0	193.8	306	3.9
Indiana	3,428	3,934	94.7	108.7	133	3.4
Illinois	7,897	8,712	141.2	155.8	120	1.5
Michigan	5,256	6,372	92.2	111.7	392	7.5
Wisconsin	3,138	3,435	57.3	62.8	− 51	− 1.6
West North Central	13,517	14,061	26.5	27.5	− 891	− 6.6
Minnesota	2,792	2,982	34.9	37.3	− 143	− 5.1
Iowa	2,538	2,621	45.3	46.8	− 176	− 6.9
Missouri	3,785	3,955	54.6	57.1	− 168	− 4.4
North Dakota	642	620	9.2	8.8	− 115	− 18.0
South Dakota	643	653	8.4	8.5	− 76	− 11.8
Nebraska	1,316	1,326	17.2	17.3	− 126	− 9.6
Kansas	1,801	1,905	21.9	23.2	− 87	− 4.8

APPENDIX 3-4 (continued)

Division and State	Population		Population per Square Mile		Net Change through Civilian Migration	
	1940	1950 [a]	1940	1950	Number	Per Cent
	(Thousands)				(Thousands)	
South Atlantic	17,823	21,182	66.4	79.0	− 134	− 0.8
Delaware	267	318	134.7	160.8	24	9.0
Maryland	1,821	2,343	184.2	237.1	261	14.3
District of Columbia	663	802	10,870.3	13,150.5	16	2.4
Virginia	2,678	3,319	67.1	83.2	106	4.0
West Virginia	1,902	2,006	79.0	83.3	− 217	− 11.4
North Carolina	3,572	4,062	72.7	82.7	− 296	− 15.6
South Carolina	1,900	2,117	62.1	69.9	− 261	− 13.7
Georgia	3,124	3,445	53.4	58.9	− 326	− 10.4
Florida	1,897	2,771	35.0	51.1	559	29.5
East South Central	10,778	11,477	59.7	63.8	− 1,325	− 12.3
Kentucky	2,846	2,945	70.9	73.9	− 372	− 13.1
Tennessee	2,916	3,292	69.5	78.8	− 160	− 5.5
Alabama	2,833	3,062	55.5	59.9	− 343	− 12.1
Mississippi	2,184	2,179	46.1	46.1	− 451	− 20.7
West South Central	13,065	14,538	30.3	33.8	− 988	− 7.6
Arkansas	1,949	1,910	37.0	36.3	− 413	− 21.2
Louisiana	2,364	2,684	52.3	59.4	− 141	− 6.0
Oklahoma	2,336	2,233	33.7	32.4	− 431	− 18.5
Texas	6,415	7,711	24.3	29.3	− 3	− 0.1
Mountain	4,150	5,075	4.8	5.9	172	4.1
Montana	559	591	3.8	4.1	− 35	− 6.3
Idaho	525	589	6.3	7.1	− 21	− 4.0
Wyoming	251	291	2.6	3.0	− 7	− 2.8
Colorado	1,123	1,325	10.8	12.8	40	3.6
New Mexico	532	681	4.4	5.6	7	1.3
Arizona	499	750	4.4	6.6	142	28.5
Utah	550	689	6.7	8.4	13	2.4
Nevada	110	160	1.0	1.5	33	30.0
Pacific	9,733	14,487	30.4	45.3	3,272	33.6
Washington	1,736	2,379	25.9	35.6	353	20.3
Oregon	1,090	1,521	11.3	15.8	303	27.8
California	6,907	10,586	44.1	67.5	2,615	37.9

Sources: Seventeenth Census of Population (1950), Vol. I, *Number of Inhabitants,* pp. 1–8 and 1–12; *Current Population Reports: Population Estimates,* U.S. Bureau of the Census, Series P–25, No. 47, March 9, 1951, p. 6.

a. Figures differ from those shown in Table 28, since figures in that table are estimates as of July 1950 and include armed forces overseas and corrections for under-enumeration of children.

APPENDIX 3–5. PERCENTAGE DISTRIBUTION OF POPULATION BY TYPE AND SIZE OF COMMUNITY, 1900–1950

Type and Size of Community	1900	1910	1920	1930	1940	1950 New Urban Definition	1950 Old Urban Definition
Total population	100.0	100.0	100.0	100.0	100.0	100.0	100.0
Urban territory	39.7	45.7	51.2	56.2	56.5	64.0	59.0
1,000,000 or more persons	8.5	9.2	9.6	12.3	12.1	11.5	11.5
500,000–1,000,000	2.2	3.3	5.9	4.7	4.9	6.1	6.1
250,000–500,000	3.8	4.3	4.3	6.5	5.9	5.5	5.5
100,000–250,000	4.3	5.3	6.2	6.1	5.9	6.3	6.4
50,000–100,000	3.6	4.5	5.0	5.3	5.6	5.9	6.0
25,000–50,000	3.7	4.4	4.8	5.2	5.6	5.8	6.3
10,000–25,000	5.7	6.0	6.7	7.4	7.6	7.9	8.3
5,000–10,000	4.2	4.6	4.7	4.8	5.1	5.4	5.2
2,500–5,000	3.8	4.1	4.1	3.8	3.8	4.3	3.7
Other urban territory	—	—	—	—	—	5.3	—
Rural territory	60.3	54.3	48.8	43.8	43.5	36.0	41.0

Source: Seventeenth Census of Population (1950), Vol. I, *Number of Inhabitants,* Chapter 1, "U.S. Summary," p. 1–6.

Appendix 3-6. Population by Age Class, April 1940 and July 1950, and by Sex and Age Class, July 1960[a]

(Thousands)

Age	April 1940[b]	July 1950	July 1960[c] Total	July 1960[c] Male	July 1960[c] Female
All ages	132,532	152,479	176,928	87,512	89,416
Under 5	11,404	17,114	17,568	8,989	8,579
5 to 9	10,685	13,300	18,624	9,518	9,106
10 to 14	11,746	11,144	17,183	8,776	8,407
15 to 19	12,334	10,680	13,383	6,796	6,587
20 to 24	11,588	11,621	11,282	5,697	5,585
25 to 29	11,097	12,314	10,875	5,426	5,449
30 to 34	10,242	11,612	11,775	5,806	5,969
35 to 39	9,545	11,298	12,379	6,055	6,324
40 to 44	8,788	10,271	11,569	5,655	5,914
45 to 49	8,255	9,115	11,083	5,401	5,682
50 to 54	7,257	8,298	9,825	4,797	5,028
55 to 59	5,868	7,266	8,402	4,061	4,341
60 to 64	4,760	6,082	7,279	3,456	3,823
65 to 69	3,748	5,025	5,867	2,743	3,124
70 and over	5,216	7,339	9,834	4,336	5,498
"Dependent" age groups	42,799	53,922	69,076	34,362	34,714
Working age group (15-64)	89,733	98,557	107,852	53,150	54,702

Sources: U.S. Bureau of the Census, *Current Population Reports: Population Estimates,* Series P–25, No. 43, August 10, 1950, p. 11 (for 1940 data), and Series P–25, No. 78, August 21, 1953, pp. 5 and 6 (for 1950 and 1960 data).

a. Adjusted for underenumeration of children under 5 years of age. Figures for 1950 and 1960 include armed forces overseas. Figures for 1940 and 1950 differ from those in Table 21, which is based on unadjusted Census figures and excludes armed forces overseas.

b. Population 55 years of age and over adjusted for age biases in the nonwhite population as enumerated in 1940.

c. Based on Census population projections for 1960 in Series P–25, No. 78, under Assumption "C," which allows for a slow decline in age-specific birth rates from 1950–1953 average levels after 1953.

Note: Slight discrepancies in addition are due to rounding.

APPENDIX 4-1. INCOME AND EXPENDITURE RELATIONSHIPS, 1929–1952
(*Billions*)

	1929	1930	1931	1932	1933	1934
Gross National Product, National Income and Consumption Expenditures						
1. Gross national product	$103.8	$ 90.9	$ 75.9	$ 58.3	$ 55.8	$ 64.9
2. Less capital consumption	8.8	8.7	8.3	7.7	7.2	7.2
3. Net national product	95.0	82.1	67.6	50.7	48.5	57.7
4. Less indirect business taxes	7.0	7.2	6.9	6.8	7.1	7.8
5. Less miscellaneous [a]	.7	—.1	1.9	2.2	1.9	1.2
6. National income	87.4	75.0	58.9	41.7	39.6	48.6
7. Less corporate savings	2.6	—3.0	—5.4	—6.0	—2.4	—1.6
8. Less corporate profits taxes	1.4	.8	.5	.4	.5	.7
9. Less social insurance contributions	.2	.3	.3	.3	.3	.3
10. Plus net interest paid by government	1.0	1.0	1.1	1.1	1.2	1.2
11. Plus government transfer payments	.9	1.0	2.0	1.4	1.5	1.6
12. Plus miscellaneous [b]	.1	—2.7	—1.8	—.3	2.8	1.3
13. Personal income	85.1	76.2	64.8	49.3	46.6	53.2
14. Less personal taxes	2.6	2.5	1.9	1.5	1.5	1.6
15. Disposable personal income	82.5	73.7	63.0	47.8	45.2	51.6
16. Less personal consumption expenditures [c]	78.8	70.8	61.2	49.2	46.3	51.9
17. Personal saving	3.7	2.9	1.8	—1.4	—1.2	—.2
Government Receipts and Expenditures						
18. Government receipts, total	11.3	10.8	9.5	8.9	9.3	10.5
19. Business taxes	8.4	8.0	7.4	7.2	7.6	8.6
20. Personal taxes	2.6	2.5	1.9	1.5	1.5	1.6
21. Social insurance contributions	.2	.3	.3	.3	.3	.3
22. Government expenditures, total [d]	10.2	11.0	12.3	10.6	10.6	12.8
23. Purchases of goods and services	8.5	9.2	9.2	8.1	8.0	9.8
24. Construction and capital equipment (civilian) [e]	2.6	3.0	2.8	1.9	1.7	2.2
25. Other goods and services	5.9	6.2	6.4	6.2	6.3	7.6
26. Transfer payments	.9	1.0	2.0	1.4	1.5	1.6
27. Net interest paid	1.0	1.0	1.1	1.1	1.2	1.2
28. Subsidies less current surplus of government enterprises	—.1	—.1	—	—	—	.3
29. Government surplus (+) or deficit (—)	1.1	—.3	—2.8	—1.7	—1.3	—2.4
Private Savings and Capital Formation						
30. Gross private savings	15.5	11.2	8.4	2.8	2.7	5.6
31. Personal saving	3.7	2.9	1.8	—1.4	—1.2	—.2
32. Corporate saving	2.6	—3.0	—5.4	—6.0	—2.4	—1.6
33. Capital consumption allowances	8.8	8.7	8.3	7.7	7.2	7.2
34. Miscellaneous [f]	.4	2.6	3.6	2.5	—.9	.2
35. Gross investment [g, h]	16.6	10.9	5.6	1.1	1.5	3.2
36. Construction and capital equipment [g]	14.3	10.5	6.7	3.4	2.9	4.0
37. Inventory change and net foreign investment [h]	2.3	.4	—1.2	—2.4	—1.5	—.7
38. Savings minus investment	—1.1	.3	2.8	1.7	1.3	2.4
Private and Public Expenditures for Construction and Capital Equipment [i]						
39. Total [e, g]	16.9	13.5	9.5	5.3	4.6	6.2
40. Private capital facilities [g]	14.3	10.5	6.7	3.4	2.9	4.0
41. Government capital facilities (civilian) [e]	2.6	3.0	2.8	1.9	1.7	2.2

APPENDIX 4-1 (continued)

	1935	1936	1937	1938	1939	1940
Gross National Product, National Income and Consumption Expenditures						
1. Gross national product	$ 72.2	$ 82.5	$ 90.2	$ 84.7	$ 91.3	$101.4
2. Less capital consumption	7.4	7.7	8.0	8.0	8.1	8.4
3. Net national product	64.8	74.8	82.2	76.7	83.2	93.0
4. Less indirect business taxes	8.2	8.7	9.2	9.2	9.4	10.0
5. Less miscellaneous [a]	—.2	1.4	—.5	.2	1.3	1.6
6. National income	56.8	64.7	73.6	67.4	72.5	81.3
7. Less corporate savings	—.6	—.3	—	—.9	1.2	2.4
8. Less corporate profits taxes	1.0	1.4	1.5	1.0	1.5	2.9
9. Less social insurance contributions	.3	.6	1.8	2.0	2.1	2.3
10. Plus net interest paid by government	1.1	1.1	1.2	1.2	1.2	1.3
11. Plus government transfer payments	1.8	2.9	1.9	2.4	2.5	2.7
12. Plus miscellaneous [b]	.8	1.3	.6	—.5	1.2	.6
13. Personal income	59.9	68.4	74.0	68.3	72.6	78.3
14. Less personal taxes	1.9	2.3	2.9	2.9	2.4	2.6
15. Disposable personal income	58.0	66.1	71.1	65.5	70.2	75.7
16. Less personal consumption expenditures	56.2	62.5	67.1	64.5	67.5	72.1
17. Personal saving	1.8	3.6	3.9	1.0	2.7	3.7
Government Receipts and Expenditures						
18. Government receipts, total	11.4	12.9	15.4	15.0	15.4	17.8
19. Business taxes	9.2	10.1	10.7	10.2	10.8	12.9
20. Personal taxes	1.9	2.3	2.9	2.9	2.4	2.6
21. Social insurance contributions	.3	.6	1.8	2.0	2.1	2.3
22. Government expenditures, total [d]	13.2	15.8	14.7	16.5	17.3	18.3
23. Purchases of goods and services	9.9	11.7	11.6	12.8	13.1	13.9
24. Construction and capital equipment (civilian) [e]	2.3	3.6	3.2	3.5	3.8	3.4
25. Other goods and services	7.6	8.1	8.4	9.3	9.3	10.5
26. Transfer payments	1.8	2.9	1.9	2.4	2.5	2.7
27. Net interest paid	1.1	1.1	1.2	1.2	1.2	1.3
28. Subsidies less current surplus of government enterprises	.4	—	.1	.2	.5	.4
29. Government surplus (+) or deficit (—)	—1.8	—2.9	.7	—1.5	—1.9	—.5
Private Savings and Capital Formation						
30. Gross private savings	7.9	11.1	10.8	8.9	12.7	16.0
31. Personal saving	1.8	3.6	3.9	1.0	2.7	3.7
32. Corporate saving	—.6	—.3	—	—.9	1.2	2.4
33. Capital consumption allowances	7.4	7.7	8.0	8.0	8.1	8.4
34. Miscellaneous [f]	—.6	.1	—1.1	.9	.7	1.5
35. Gross investment [g, h]	6.1	8.2	11.5	7.4	10.8	15.5
36. Construction and capital equipment [g]	5.2	7.3	9.1	7.3	9.5	11.7
37. Inventory change and net foreign investment [h]	.9	.9	2.4	.1	1.3	3.8
38. Savings minus investment	1.8	2.9	—.7	1.5	1.9	.5
Private and Public Expenditures for Construction and Capital Equipment [i]						
39. Total [e, g]	7.5	10.9	12.3	10.8	13.3	15.1
40. Private capital facilities [g]	5.2	7.3	9.1	7.3	9.5	11.7
41. Government capital facilities (civilian) [e]	2.3	3.6	3.2	3.5	3.8	3.4

	1941	1942	1943	1944	1945	1946
Gross National Product, National Income and Consumption Expenditures						
1. Gross national product	$126.4	$161.6	$194.3	$213.7	$215.2	$211.1
2. Less capital consumption	9.3	10.0	10.7	11.9	12.4	12.2
3. Net national product	117.1	151.6	183.7	201.8	202.8	198.9
4. Less indirect business taxes	11.3	11.8	12.7	14.1	15.5	17.3
5. Less miscellaneous [a]	2.0	2.7	1.2	3.8	4.6	1.3
6. National income	103.8	137.1	169.7	183.8	182.7	180.3
7. Less corporate savings	4.9	5.1	6.2	6.1	3.8	8.1
8. Less corporate profits taxes	7.8	11.7	14.4	13.5	11.2	9.6
9. Less social insurance contributions	2.8	3.5	4.5	5.2	6.1	6.0
10. Plus net interest paid by government	1.3	1.5	2.1	2.8	3.7	4.4
11. Plus government transfer payments	2.6	2.7	2.5	3.1	5.6	10.9
12. Plus miscellaneous [b]	3.1	1.7	1.1	1.0	1.1	5.8
13. Personal income	95.3	122.7	150.3	165.9	171.9	177.7
14. Less personal taxes	3.3	6.0	17.8	18.9	20.9	18.8
15. Disposable personal income	92.0	116.7	132.4	147.0	151.1	158.9
16. Less personal consumption expenditures	82.3	91.2	102.2	111.6	123.1	146.9
17. Personal saving	9.8	25.6	30.2	35.4	28.0	12.0
Government Receipts and Expenditures						
18. Government receipts, total	25.2	32.9	49.5	51.8	53.7	51.7
19. Business taxes	19.1	23.4	27.1	27.7	26.7	26.9
20. Personal taxes	3.3	6.0	17.8	18.9	20.9	18.8
21. Social insurance contributions	2.8	3.5	4.5	5.2	6.1	6.0
22. Government expenditures, total [d]	28.7	64.0	93.4	103.1	93.0	47.1
23. Purchases of goods and services	24.7	59.7	88.6	96.5	82.8	30.9
24. Construction and capital equipment (civilian) [e]	4.3	5.8	3.9	2.3	1.8	2.4
25. Other goods and services	20.4	53.9	84.7	94.2	81.0	28.5
26. Transfer payments	2.6	2.7	2.5	3.1	5.6	10.9
27. Net interest paid	1.3	1.5	2.1	2.8	3.7	4.4
28. Subsidies less current surplus of government enterprises	.1	.2	.2	.7	.8	.9
29. Government surplus (+) or deficit (−)	−3.5	−31.2	−43.9	−51.4	−39.2	4.6
Private Savings and Capital Formation						
30. Gross private savings	23.0	41.8	47.4	57.0	48.5	28.7
31. Personal saving	9.8	25.6	30.2	35.4	28.0	12.0
32. Corporate saving	4.9	5.1	6.2	6.1	3.8	8.1
33. Capital consumption allowances	9.3	10.0	10.7	11.9	12.4	12.2
34. Miscellaneous [f]	−1.0	1.1	.4	3.6	4.3	−3.5
35. Gross investment [g, h]	19.5	10.7	3.5	5.6	9.3	33.3
36. Construction and capital equipment [g]	14.5	8.8	6.6	8.5	11.5	22.6
37. Inventory change and net foreign investment [h]	5.0	1.9	−3.2	−2.9	−2.2	10.7
38. Savings minus investment	3.5	31.2	43.9	51.4	39.2	−4.6
Private and Public Expenditures for Construction and Capital Equipment [i]						
39. Total [e, g]	18.8	14.6	10.5	10.8	13.3	25.0
40. Private capital facilities [g]	14.5	8.8	6.6	8.5	11.5	22.6
41. Government capital facilities (civilian) [e]	4.3	5.8	3.9	2.3	1.8	2.4

Sources: *National Income and Product of the United States, 1929–1950* (1951 National Income Supplement to the *Survey of Current Business*), and *Survey of Current Business,* July 1952 and July 1953.

a. Business transfer payments, statistical discrepancy and current surplus of government enterprises minus subsidies.

b. Business transfer payments minus corporate inventory valuation adjustment minus excess of wage accruals over disbursements.

c. For 1929–1932, personal consumption expenditures do not agree with totals used in Appendix 4–4, which include estimates for alcoholic beverages during prohibition years.

d. Government expenditures shown here differ from figures shown in Chapter 18. The figures in Chapter 18 are for *fiscal* years rather than *calendar* years and are *gross* rather than *net* expenditures. (See footnote a, Table 261.)

	1947	1948	1949	1950	1951	1952
Gross National Product, National Income and Consumption Expenditures						
1. Gross national product	$233.3	$259.0	$258.2	$286.8	$329.8	$348.0
2. Less capital consumption	14.8	17.6	19.4	21.6	24.2	27.0
3. Net national product	218.4	241.4	238.9	265.2	305.6	321.0
4. Less indirect business taxes	18.7	20.4	21.6	23.7	25.7	28.1
5. Less miscellaneous [a]	1.1	−2.4	1.0	.9	1.6	1.3
6. National income	198.7	223.5	216.3	240.6	278.4	291.6
7. Less corporate savings	12.0	13.5	8.8	13.6	10.9	9.5
8. Less corporate profits taxes	11.9	13.0	10.8	18.2	23.6	20.6
9. Less social insurance contributions	5.7	5.2	5.7	6.9	8.2	8.6
10. Plus net interest paid by government	4.4	4.5	4.6	4.7	4.8	4.9
11. Plus government transfer payments	11.1	10.5	11.6	14.3	11.6	12.0
12. Plus miscellaneous [b]	6.4	2.8	−1.3	5.8	2.2	—
13. Personal income	191.0	209.5	205.9	226.7	254.3	269.7
14. Less personal taxes	21.5	21.1	18.6	20.9	29.3	34.6
15. Disposable personal income	169.5	188.4	187.2	205.8	225.0	235.0
16. Less personal consumption expenditures	165.6	177.9	180.6	194.6	208.1	218.1
17. Personal saving	3.9	10.5	6.7	11.3	16.9	16.9
Government Receipts and Expenditures						
18. Government receipts, total	57.8	59.8	56.8	69.7	86.8	92.0
19. Business taxes	30.6	33.4	32.5	42.0	49.3	48.7
20. Personal taxes	21.5	21.1	18.6	20.9	29.3	34.6
21. Social insurance contributions	5.7	5.2	5.7	6.9	8.2	8.6
22. Government expenditures, total [d]	44.0	51.6	59.9	61.4	79.7	94.4
23. Purchases of goods and services	28.6	36.6	43.6	42.0	62.9	77.5
24. Construction and capital equipment (civilian) [e]	3.5	5.1	6.7	7.3	9.0	10.1
25. Other goods and services	25.1	31.5	36.9	34.7	53.9	67.4
26. Transfer payments	11.1	10.5	11.6	14.3	11.6	12.0
27. Net interest paid	4.4	4.5	4.6	4.7	4.8	4.9
28. Subsidies less current surplus of government enterprises	−.1	—	—	.4	.4	.1
29. Government surplus (+) or deficit (−)	13.7	8.2	−3.1	8.3	7.1	−2.4
Private Savings and Capital Formation						
30. Gross private savings	25.3	36.4	37.0	42.0	51.8	54.7
31. Personal saving	3.9	10.5	6.7	11.3	16.9	16.9
32. Corporate saving	12.0	13.5	8.8	13.6	10.9	9.5
33. Capital consumption allowances	14.8	17.6	19.4	21.6	24.2	27.0
34. Miscellaneous [f]	−5.4	−5.2	2.2	−4.5	−.2	1.4
35. Gross investment [g, h]	39.1	44.6	34.0	50.2	58.8	52.3
36. Construction and capital equipment [g]	31.0	37.7	35.9	45.0	47.7	48.8
37. Inventory change and net foreign investment [h]	8.1	6.9	−2.0	5.2	11.1	3.5
38. Savings minus investment	−13.7	−8.2	3.1	−8.3	−7.1	2.4
Private and Public Expenditures for Construction and Capital Equipment [i]						
39. Total [e, g]	34.5	42.8	42.6	52.3	56.7	58.9
40. Private capital facilities [g]	31.0	37.7	35.9	45.0	47.7	48.8
41. Government capital facilities (civilian) [e]	3.5	5.1	6.7	7.3	9.0	10.1

e. Excludes expenditures for publicly owned military plant and equipment and expenditures by state governments for equipment; such expenditures are included with "Other goods and services" purchased by government.

f. Miscellaneous includes corporate inventory valuation adjustment, excess of wage accruals over disbursements and statistical discrepancy.

g. 1939 and later years include expenditures for drilling oil and natural gas wells.

h. Includes government net foreign investment.

i. Slight differences between these data and the estimates in Appendix 4–8 are due to use of different sources and rounding.

Note: Slight discrepancies in additions and subtractions are due to rounding.

APPENDIX 4-2. GROSS NATIONAL PRODUCT AND NATIONAL INCOME AT CURRENT AND CONSTANT PRICES, 1909–1953

TABLE A. NATIONAL INCOME AND NATIONAL PRODUCT, 1909–1953, AT CURRENT PRICES
(Dollar Amounts in Billions)

Year	Gross National Product	National Income	Personal Income	Personal Taxes	Disposable Personal Income	Personal Savings	Personal Consumption Expenditures [a]	Personal Taxes and Savings as Per Cent of Personal Income	Personal Savings as Per Cent of Disposable Income
1909	$ 34.0	$ 28.7	$ 27.9	$ .6	$ 27.3	$ 1.8	$ 25.5	8.6	6.6
1910	36.7	30.4	29.6	.6	29.0	2.0	27.0	8.8	6.9
1911	36.8	30.5	30.1	.6	29.5	2.5	27.0	10.3	8.5
1912	38.5	32.9	32.2	.6	31.6	1.6	30.0	6.8	5.1
1913	40.0	34.8	33.9	.6	33.3	2.3	31.0	8.6	6.9
1914	38.5	33.9	33.8	.6	33.2	3.4	29.8	11.8	10.2
1915	42.1	37.0	36.0	.6	35.4	6.9	28.5	20.8	19.5
1916	47.8	44.8	42.4	.8	41.6	6.8	34.8	17.9	16.3
1917	59.5	53.7	50.9	.9	50.0	9.6	40.4	20.6	19.2
1918	65.5	58.3	57.5	1.6	55.9	11.5	44.4	22.8	20.6
1919	76.5	68.2	65.5	2.0	63.5	10.8	52.7	19.5	17.0
1920	85.0	69.5	68.9	2.1	66.8	9.0	57.8	16.1	13.5
1921	68.5	51.7	54.9	2.1	52.8	2.3	50.5	8.0	4.4
1922	69.9	59.5	58.9	1.9	57.0	5.0	52.0	11.7	8.8
1923	81.6	69.5	68.3	2.4	65.9	8.1	57.8	15.4	12.3
1924	82.0	69.1	68.8	2.1	66.7	5.8	60.9	11.5	8.7
1925	86.4	73.7	72.8	2.2	70.6	7.6	63.0	13.5	10.8
1926	92.3	76.6	75.6	2.4	73.2	6.9	66.3	12.3	9.4
1927	90.9	75.9	76.0	2.5	73.5	7.5	66.0	13.2	10.2
1928	93.7	78.7	78.1	2.7	75.4	6.6	68.8	11.9	8.8
1929	99.4	83.3	82.6	3.0	79.6	8.8	70.8	14.3	11.1
1929	103.8	87.4	85.1	2.6	82.5	3.7	78.8	7.4	4.5
1930	90.9	75.0	76.2	2.5	73.7	2.9	70.8	7.1	3.9
1931	75.9	58.9	64.8	1.9	63.0	1.8	61.2	5.7	2.9
1932	58.3	41.7	49.3	1.5	47.8	—1.4	49.2	.2	—2.9
1933	55.8	39.6	46.6	1.5	45.2	—1.2	46.3	.6	—2.7
1934	64.9	48.6	53.2	1.6	51.6	—.2	51.9	2.6	—.4
1935	72.2	56.8	59.9	1.9	58.0	1.8	56.2	6.2	3.1
1936	82.5	64.7	68.4	2.3	66.1	3.6	62.5	8.6	5.4
1937	90.2	73.6	74.0	2.9	71.1	3.9	67.1	9.2	5.5
1938	84.7	67.4	68.3	2.9	65.5	1.0	64.5	5.7	1.5
1939	91.3	72.5	72.6	2.4	70.2	2.7	67.5	7.0	3.8
1940	101.4	81.3	78.3	2.6	75.7	3.7	72.1	8.0	4.9
1941	126.4	103.8	95.3	3.3	92.0	9.8	82.3	13.7	10.7
1942	161.6	137.1	122.7	6.0	116.7	25.6	91.2	25.8	21.9
1943	194.3	169.7	150.3	17.8	132.4	30.2	102.2	31.9	22.8
1944	213.7	183.8	165.9	18.9	147.0	35.4	111.6	32.7	24.1
1945	215.2	182.7	171.9	20.9	151.1	28.0	123.1	28.4	18.5
1946	211.1	180.3	177.7	18.8	158.9	12.0	146.9	17.3	7.6
1947	233.3	198.7	191.0	21.5	169.5	3.9	165.6	13.3	2.3
1948	259.0	223.5	209.5	21.1	188.4	10.5	177.9	15.1	5.6
1949	258.2	216.3	205.9	18.6	187.2	6.7	180.6	12.3	3.6

APPENDIX 4–2. TABLE A (continued)

Year	Gross National Product	National Income	Personal Income	Personal Taxes	Disposable Personal Income	Personal Savings	Personal Consumption Expenditures[a]	Personal Taxes and Savings as Per Cent of Personal Income	Personal Savings as Per Cent of Disposable Income
1950	$286.8	$240.6	$226.7	$20.9	$205.8	$11.3	$194.6	14.2	5.5
1951	329.8	278.4	254.3	29.3	225.0	16.9	208.1	18.2	7.5
1952	348.0	291.6	269.7	34.6	235.0	16.9	218.1	19.1	7.2
1953	367.2	307.7	284.5	36.6	247.9	18.1	229.8	19.2	7.3

Sources: 1909–1928—National income, personal income and disposable personal income are unpublished data of Bureau of Foreign and Domestic Commerce; gross national product and personal consumption expenditures (Commerce) are based on unpublished data from Simon Kuznets; personal taxes derived by subtracting "disposable personal income" from "personal income"; personal savings derived by subtracting "personal consumption expenditures" from "disposable personal income."

1929 (upper figures)—*Survey of Current Business,* May 1942, p. 12.

1929 (lower figures) through 1952—*Survey of Current Business,* July 1953, Tables 1–4, pp. 10–13; 1953, *Survey of Current Business,* February 1954, Table 4, p. 12.

a. For 1909–1932, personal consumption expenditures do not agree with those used in Appendix 4–4; unlike the estimates in Appendix 4–4, the estimates in this table for 1909–1928 and the upper figures for 1929 are not consistent with those for later years, nor do they include expenditures for alcoholic beverages during prohibition years.

Note: There is a break in the continuity of these series in 1929; the series for 1909–1929 in the upper part of the table differ both statistically and conceptually from those for 1929–1953 in the lower part. Both old and current estimates for 1929 are shown in order to give a very rough indication of the size of the difference. Slight discrepancies in additions and subtractions are due to rounding.

TABLE B. NATIONAL INCOME AND NATIONAL PRODUCT, 1909–1953, AT 1950 PRICES
(*Dollar Amounts in Billions*)

Year	Gross National Product[a]	National Income[a]	Personal Income[b]	Disposable Personal Income[b]	Personal Consumption Expenditures[b]	Price Level Index (1950 = 100) Gross National Product[c]	Price Level Index (1950 = 100) Personal Consumption Expenditures[d]
1909	$ 94.4	$ 79.7	$ 73.4	$ 71.8	$ 67.1	36.0	38.0
1910	99.2	82.2	74.0	72.5	67.5	37.0	40.0
1911	99.5	82.4	77.2	75.6	69.2	37.0	39.0
1912	101.3	86.6	78.5	77.1	73.2	38.0	41.0
1913	105.3	91.6	82.9	81.8	75.8	38.0	40.9
1914	99.7	87.8	81.4	80.2	71.8	38.6	41.5
1915	108.2	95.1	85.9	84.7	68.0	38.9	41.9
1916	114.4	107.2	94.2	92.7	77.3	41.8	45.0
1917	120.9	109.1	96.2	94.7	76.4	49.2	52.9
1918	113.5	101.0	92.6	90.3	71.5	57.7	62.1
1919	115.0	102.6	91.5	89.1	73.6	66.5	71.6
1920	110.5	90.4	83.2	81.0	69.8	76.9	82.8
1921	99.9	75.4	74.4	71.7	68.4	68.6	73.8
1922	108.7	92.5	85.1	82.7	75.1	64.3	69.2
1923	124.6	106.1	96.9	93.9	82.0	65.5	70.5
1924	125.0	105.3	97.5	94.7	86.3	65.6	70.6
1925	128.4	109.5	100.4	97.8	86.9	67.3	72.5
1926	135.9	112.8	103.4	100.5	90.7	67.9	73.1
1927	136.5	114.0	106.0	102.9	92.1	66.6	71.7
1928	142.4	119.6	110.2	106.8	97.0	65.8	70.9
1929	151.1	126.6	116.7	112.7	100.0	65.8	70.8

APPENDIX 4-2. TABLE B (continued)

Year	Gross National Product [a]	National Income [a]	Personal Income [b]	Disposable Personal Income [b]	Personal Consumption Expenditures [b]	Price Level Index (1950 = 100)	
						Gross National Product [e]	Personal Consumption Expenditures [d]
1929	$157.8	$132.8	$120.2	$116.9	$111.3	65.8	70.8
1930	143.6	118.5	112.9	109.2	104.9	63.3	67.5
1931	132.7	103.0	107.3	104.3	101.3	57.2	60.4
1932	113.6	81.3	92.8	90.0	92.7	51.3	53.1
1933	113.0	80.2	91.9	89.2	91.3	49.4	50.7
1934	124.8	93.5	99.1	96.1	96.6	52.0	53.7
1935	135.7	106.8	108.9	105.5	102.2	53.2	55.0
1936	154.2	120.9	122.8	118.7	112.2	53.5	55.7
1937	161.4	131.7	128.0	123.0	116.1	55.9	57.8
1938	154.0	122.5	120.9	115.9	114.2	55.0	56.5
1939	167.5	133.0	129.6	125.4	120.5	54.5	56.0
1940	183.4	147.0	138.3	133.7	127.4	55.3	56.6
1941	212.1	174.2	158.6	153.1	136.9	59.6	60.1
1942	238.0	201.9	182.3	173.4	135.5	67.9	67.3
1943	267.3	233.4	204.8	180.4	139.2	72.7	73.4
1944	288.0	247.7	215.7	191.2	145.1	74.2	76.9
1945	281.7	239.1	215.4	189.3	154.3	76.4	79.8
1946	254.0	217.0	206.9	185.0	171.0	83.1	85.9
1947	254.4	216.7	202.8	179.9	175.8	91.7	94.2
1948	263.2	227.1	211.0	189.7	179.2	98.4	99.3
1949	264.3	221.4	210.1	191.0	184.3	97.7	98.0
1950	286.8	240.6	226.7	205.8	194.6	100.0	100.0
1951	306.5	258.7	237.0	209.7	193.9	107.6	107.3
1952	315.8	264.6	246.1	214.4	199.0	110.2	109.6
1953	327.9	274.7	254.0	221.3	207.0	112.0	111.0

a. Adjusted gross national product and national income derived by dividing estimates of Table A by price level index for gross national product.

b. Adjusted personal income, disposable personal income and personal consumption expenditures derived by dividing estimates of Table A by price level index for personal consumption expenditures.

c. 1909–1912, carried back from 1913 by use of Carl Snyder–Rufus J. Tucker general price index as published in *Historical Statistics of the United States, 1789–1945,* U.S. Bureau of the Census, 1949, Series L–1, p. 231. 1913–1928, carried back from 1929 by use of consumers' price index, *Handbook of Labor Statistics,* U.S. Bureau of Labor Statistics, 1950, Table D–1, p. 100; 1929–1952 are the implicit price indexes for gross national product from *Survey of Current Business,* July 1953, Table B, p. 26,

shifted to a 1950 base; 1953, derived from data in current and 1939 prices in *Survey of Current Business,* February 1954.

d. 1909–1928, same procedure as described in footnote c; 1929–1952 are implicit price indexes for personal consumption expenditures in *Survey of Current Business,* July 1953, Table B, p. 26, shifted to a 1950 base; 1953, derived from data in current and 1939 prices in *Survey of Current Business,* February 1954.

Note: There is a break in the continuity of these series in 1929; the series for 1909–1929 in the first part of the table differ both statistically and conceptually from those for 1929–1953 in the second part. Both old and current estimates for 1929 are shown in order to give a very rough indication of the size of the difference.

APPENDIX 4-3. DERIVATION OF ESTIMATED DISTRIBUTIONS OF CONSUMER UNITS BY AMOUNT OF CONSUMER MONEY INCOME AFTER PERSONAL TAXES, IN THE URBAN, RURAL NONFARM AND RURAL FARM RESIDENCE AREAS, 1950 AND 1960

Control Frequencies and Aggregate Income

The numbers of families and of single individuals for the accompanying income distributions were based on Table 22 and projections prepared in connection with Table 27. However, subfamilies were not counted separately as in those tabulations but were combined with main families as in U. S. Bureau of the Census publications Series P–60, Nos. 7 and 9. The number of unrelated individuals is slightly less than in Tables 22 and 27; it corresponds to data in the Census Series P–60 while the figures in those tables were derived from the Census Series P–20. These data were adjusted to represent the civilian populations as of December 31, 1950 and 1960. The 1950 totals for the urban, rural nonfarm and rural farm residence groups were based on Series P–60, Nos. 7 and 9. Corresponding 1960 figures were obtained by applying the ratios of change for the separate residence groups implicit in Table 37, and adjusting the resulting data to meet the over-all totals for all residence groups already estimated.

The aggregate amounts of consumer money income were derived from the personal income totals in Table 29. The concept of consumer money income used here corresponds closely to that used in the Census P–60 series and in U.S. Bureau of Labor Statistics surveys of consumer expenditures. It differs from personal income as used in the Commerce Department's national income estimates and in this report (see, for example, Table 29) in two major respects. It does not include personal income received by members of the armed forces not living with their families, by inmates of institutions and by nonprofit institutions, or income retained by private trust, pension and welfare funds. (Personal income less these items is equivalent to what is known as family personal income.) It also does not include nonmoney items such as imputed rent of owner-occupied homes, food and lodging received as wages, imputed interest, food and fuel produced and consumed by farm operator families, etc.[1]

In order to assign the income aggregates to the separate residence groups for 1950 and 1960, the over-all total was divided into four parts: salaries and wages, nonfarm entrepreneurial income, farm entrepreneurial income, and other income. Estimates of the relative amounts in these categories for each residence group were available from unpublished data of the 1950 Census Current Population Survey. Each category amount within a residence group was raised by a ratio which would bring the category

BY HYMAN B. KAITZ, formerly on the staff of the U.S. Department of Commerce, National Income Division.

total for all residence groups to the correct figure. The four adjusted category amounts within a given residence group were then added to yield the consumer money income for that group.

The amounts derived above were allocated between families and individuals by using a ratio of average family income to average income for unrelated individuals by residence group from Census release P–60, No. 9, Table 1.

For 1960 the same procedure was followed. The control aggregates in each source category were moved from 1950 to 1960 by approximately the same ratios as the corresponding categories in personal income and then adjusted for the proper totals. Income aggregates were allocated among families and unrelated individuals as before.

Distributions by Amount of Income before Tax

The consumer money income distributions of families and unrelated individuals for 1950 were based on an unpublished distribution constructed from 1947 income tax return information supplemented by Census Survey data. The Census data, estimated for 1947, were moved to 1950 by assuming the same Lorenz curve[2] for each of the two distributions. In order to break each of these two distributions into three separate distributions for the individual residence groups, a relationship from Census release P–60, No. 9, Table 1, between cumulative percentages of the total distribution and that of any given residence group by income level was used. This was done separately for families and for unrelated individuals.

The six 1960 distributions by size of consumer money income (in 1950 dollars) were obtained, each from the corresponding 1950 distribution, by keeping the Lorenz curve of the latter and meeting the control aggregate income and population total already determined.

Distributions of Tax Liabilities by Income Level before Tax

The personal tax aggregates used in connection with the consumer money income distributions include federal income taxes and state and local

1. A detailed reconciliation of personal income, family personal income and family (or consumer) money income is given in *Income Distribution in the United States by Size, 1944–1950*, U.S. Department of Commerce, 1953, Exhibit 16, p. 67.

2. See *Income Distribution in the United States*, a Supplement to the *Survey of Current Business*, 1953, footnote 12, p. 38.

TABLE A. ESTIMATED DISTRIBUTION OF URBAN AND RURAL
(*At 1950*

	Urban					
	Families of 2 or More Persons			Single Individuals		
Year and Income	Number of Families	Income per Family	Aggregate Income	Number of Individuals	Income per Individual	Aggregate Income
	(*Thousands*)		(*Millions*)	(*Thousands*)		(*Millions*)
1950						
Total	25,725.0	$ 4,726	$121,586.8	6,859.0	$ 1,981	$13,589.1
Under $1,000	1,102.0	317	349.2	1,807.0	477	861.5
$1,000–$1,999	2,422.0	1,544	3,739.6	2,210.9	1,500	3,316.0
$2,000–$2,999	3,721.7	2,531	9,419.6	1,663.8	2,463	4,097.2
$3,000–$3,999	5,242.7	3,508	18,391.4	718.6	3,419	2,456.6
$4,000–$4,999	4,723.5	4,493	21,221.2	228.4	4,390	1,002.5
$5,000–$5,999	2,984.1	5,460	16,293.2	95.8	5,422	519.3
$6,000–$7,499	2,457.6	6,660	16,367.6	62.7	6,590	413.2
$7,500–$9,999	1,793.8	8,455	15,165.9	37.6	8,300	312.1
$10,000 and over	1,277.6	16,155	20,639.1	34.2	17,857	610.7
1960						
Total	29,140.0	4,977	145,033.9	7,845.0	2,100	16,474.6
Under $1,000	1,182.1	313	369.5	1,954.2	475	927.9
$1,000–$1,999	2,537.8	1,542	3,913.3	2,388.4	1,503	3,589.1
$2,000–$2,999	3,740.7	2,534	9,478.9	1,922.3	2,469	4,746.5
$3,000–$3,999	5,574.5	3,520	19,622.2	935.3	3,433	3,210.9
$4,000–$4,999	5,359.5	4,490	24,064.2	327.9	4,397	1,441.8
$5,000–$5,999	3,549.4	5,460	19,379.7	133.5	5,420	723.6
$6,000–$7,499	3,302.6	6,660	21,995.3	95.1	6,590	626.7
$7,500–$9,999	2,208.4	8,450	18,661.0	43.8	8,350	365.7
$10,000 and over	1,685.0	16,350	27,549.8	44.5	18,930	842.4

a. Consumer units include family units and individuals who consume as single units. "Consumer unit" as used here differs slightly from the term as used in Tables 22 and 27; here, subfamilies (i.e., family units related to the head of the main family in multifamily households) are not counted as separate consumer units but are included with the main family. Also, the number of units shown here represents the estimated number at the end of the calendar year.

CONSUMER UNITS [a] BY MONEY INCOME AFTER TAXES,[b] 1950 AND 1960
Prices)

Rural Nonfarm			Rural Farm		
Number of Units	Income per Unit	Aggregate Income	Number of Units	Income per Unit	Aggregate Income
(*Thousands*)		(*Millions*)	(*Thousands*)		(*Millions*)
9,850.0	$ 3,570	$35,164.7	6,354.0	$ 2,731	$17,352.4
1,301.0	383	498.3	1,442.7	273	394.1
1,701.2	1,517	2,580.3	1,551.6	1,497	2,323.5
1,892.7	2,501	4,733.0	1,219.9	2,480	3,025.4
1,753.7	3,483	6,108.1	926.0	3,468	3,211.8
1,229.3	4,476	5,502.9	492.3	4,448	2,190.0
714.4	5,459	3,900.1	228.9	5,440	1,245.2
573.1	6,649	3,810.5	186.3	6,649	1,238.8
395.1	8,447	3,337.5	162.5	8,497	1,380.7
289.5	16,214	4,694.0	143.8	16,293	2,342.9
12,496.0	3,775	47,175.6	5,454.0	3,161	17,240.9
1,561.2	378	590.5	1,059.3	229	242.6
2,015.8	1,516	3,056.4	1,143.1	1,500	1,714.6
2,254.6	2,505	5,647.7	1,008.8	2,487	2,509.1
2,194.3	3,488	7,654.5	822.5	3,477	2,860.0
1,650.4	4,469	7,374.9	557.9	4,460	2,488.2
946.3	5,459	5,166.1	287.9	5,459	1,571.7
883.1	6,649	5,871.9	216.7	6,649	1,440.9
556.6	8,449	4,702.5	176.1	8,449	1,487.9
433.7	16,396	7,111.1	181.7	16,103	2,925.9

b. Money income excludes noncash items such as the imputed rent of owner-occupied homes and food and lodging received as wages. The taxes deducted are personal taxes such as federal and state income taxes and state and local personal property (not real estate) and poll taxes.

963

income, poll and personal property taxes mainly due for the year rather than collected during the year. For that reason and because of the exclusion of some minor items, these figures do not agree exactly with those in Table 29.

For the 1950 consumer money income distributions of families and of individuals, distributions of aggregate federal income tax liabilities were obtained from unpublished estimates based primarily on Census data. A pattern of relationship between federal income tax aggregates and state and local taxes was taken from an article by Musgrave and Frane.[3] Adjusted for the correct over-all control aggregates in 1950, this pattern was applied to the final distribution of federal income taxes by consumer money income level to obtain the state and local taxes at these levels. State and local taxes were split between families and unrelated individuals at each consumer money income level in proportion to the federal income taxes.

Variation in family size was used as a basis for allocating aggregate taxes by consumer money income level among the three residence groups. BLS data for three cities in 1948,[4] which offered average family personal taxes and average money income for families of different sizes by level of money income after taxes, were used for this purpose. By combining information from Census releases P–60, Nos. 7 and 9 (Table 4), and P–20, No. 30, distributions of families by size for the various residence groups and consumer money income levels were estimated and related to the tax rates by family size from the BLS data for three cities. Three sets of weighted tax aggregates were then obtained for the separate residence groups at each consumer money income level, and then adjusted proportionately to meet the previously calculated total at that level for all residence groups combined.

Among the unrelated individuals in the three

residence groups, the personal taxes were allocated by consumer money income level in proportion to the separate amounts of aggregate consumer money income at these levels.

In order to estimate the starting tax rates for 1960, it was first assumed that the price level structure in 1960 would be more like that of 1951 than 1950. The distributions by size of consumer money income already calculated for 1960 were in 1950 dollars. The 1950 tax rates previously estimated were first adjusted to tie in with a 1951 income level some 7 per cent above that of 1950.[5] The aggregate personal taxes computed on this basis were adjusted proportionately for families and unrelated individuals at all income levels and for all residence groups to meet the totals already set for 1960 in 1950 dollars.

Distributions by Level of Income after Tax

The same procedure was used to move each of these twelve estimated distributions from levels of consumer money income to consumer money income after personal taxes. It was assumed that in each distribution all of the units (families or unrelated individuals) at a particular income point were subject to the same tax rate. Average consumer money income in each income class was plotted against average consumer money income after personal taxes in each income class. From this relationship, values of income after taxes corresponding to the original consumer money income class limits were obtained by interpolation. Interpolation for frequencies, aggregate income and taxes lying between the conventional class limit values and the interpolated values of consumer money income after tax then followed. The frequencies and aggregates were finally recombined within the conventional class limits of consumer money income after personal taxes.

---

3. R. A. Musgrave and L. Frane, "Rejoinder to Dr. Tucker," *National Tax Journal*, March 1952, Table 5, p. 25.

4. *Monthly Labor Review*, December 1949.

5. Based on national income implicit price deflators for personal consumption expenditures in *Survey of Current Business*, July 1952, Table B, p. 28.

(Millions)

Class of Expenditure	1909	1914	1919	1921	1923	1925	1927	1929	1930	1931	1932
TOTAL CONSUMPTION EXPENDITURES [a]	$28,814	$33,395	$60,573	$55,766	$66,594	$71,750	$74,569	$80,761	$72,389	$62,453	$50,108
A. FOOD, LIQUOR AND TOBACCO	9,796	11,686	21,983	16,789	19,114	21,140	21,735	23,374	21,119	17,572	13,619
FOOD AND BEVERAGES	9,169	10,954	20,554	15,308	17,638	19,619	20,118	21,674	19,665	16,079	12,294
Consumed inside the home [b]	—	—	—	—	—	—	—	16,105	14,683	11,791	8,948
Purchased for off-premise consumption	—	—	—	—	—	—	—	14,520	13,255	10,633	8,033
Produced and consumed on farms	—	—	—	—	—	—	—	1,585	1,428	1,158	915
Consumed outside the home [b]	—	—	—	—	—	—	—	3,569	3,382	2,988	2,446
Purchased meals and beverages [e]	—	—	—	—	—	—	—	3,055	2,892	2,590	2,116
Hotels, restaurants, dining cars (inc. tips)	—	—	—	—	—	—	—	2,698	2,560	2,328	1,920
Schools, institutions, clubs, etc.	—	—	—	—	—	—	—	357	332	262	196
Food furnished government (including military) and commercial employees, and withdrawn by nonfarm proprietors	—	—	—	—	—	—	—	514	490	398	330
Food and nonalcoholic beverages [d]	7,369	8,954	18,554	13,908	16,138	17,919	18,318	19,674	18,065	14,779	11,394
Alcoholic beverages [e]	1,800	2,000	2,000	1,400	1,500	1,700	1,800	2,000	1,600	1,300	900
TOBACCO PRODUCTS AND SMOKING SUPPLIES [d]	627	732	1,429	1,481	1,476	1,521	1,617	1,700	1,454	1,493	1,325
B. CLOTHING, ACCESSORIES AND PERSONAL CARE [d]	4,277	4,708	9,567	9,336	11,120	11,059	11,787	11,913	10,400	8,911	6,646
CLOTHING AND RELATED PRODUCTS	4,016	4,403	8,952	8,734	10,247	10,156	10,745	10,797	9,361	7,932	5,829
Clothes and accessories	2,715	2,926	5,803	6,127	7,223	7,186	7,609	7,597	6,600	5,674	4,003
Clothing and accessories except footwear	—	—	—	—	—	—	—	7,502	6,516	5,606	3,948
Standard clothing issued to military personnel	—	—	—	—	—	—	—	12	11	9	10
Dressmakers and seamstresses (not in shops)	—	—	—	—	—	—	—	58	50	38	27
Net purchases and rentals of secondhand clothing and accessories	—	—	—	—	—	—	—	25	23	21	18
Shoes and other footwear	778	874	1,942	1,504	1,803	1,661	1,715	1,675	1,375	1,207	1,022
Jewelry and watches	242	259	668	531	549	575	570	560	513	328	252
Cleaning, repair and maintenance	281	344	539	572	672	734	851	965	873	723	552
Cleaning, repair and storage of garments, furs and shoes	—	—	—	—	—	—	—	637	561	466	352
Laundering (in establishments) [f]	—	—	—	—	—	—	—	237	229	196	155
Watch, clock and jewelry repair and miscellaneous personal services	—	—	—	—	—	—	—	91	83	61	45
PERSONAL CARE	261	305	615	602	873	903	1,042	1,116	1,039	979	817
Toilet articles and preparations	117	141	344	329	517	478	542	591	515	504	420
Barber shop, beauty parlor, and related services	144	164	271	273	356	425	500	525	524	475	397
Barber shop services	—	—	—	—	—	—	—	350	349	310	253
Beauty parlor services	—	—	—	—	—	—	—	167	167	158	138
Baths and masseurs	—	—	—	—	—	—	—	8	8	7	6

965

Appendix 4-4 (continued)

Class of Expenditure	1933	1934	1935	1936	1937	1938	1939	1940	1941	1942
TOTAL CONSUMPTION EXPENDITURES[a]	$46,346	$51,882	$56,215	$62,515	$67,121	$64,513	$67,466	$72,052	$82,255	$91,161
A. FOOD, LIQUOR AND TOBACCO	12,777	15,636	17,693	20,030	21,629	20,662	21,072	22,600	26,476	32,793
FOOD AND BEVERAGES	11,541	14,266	16,255	18,490	19,950	18,959	19,299	20,725	24,403	30,464
Consumed inside the home[b]	9,383	11,568	13,177	15,005	15,893	15,073	15,110	16,156	18,735	22,990
Purchased for off-premise consumption	8,457	10,576	11,960	13,734	14,589	13,889	13,976	15,029	17,441	21,320
Produced and consumed on farms	926	992	1,217	1,271	1,304	1,184	1,134	1,127	1,294	1,670
Consumed outside the home[b]	2,158	2,698	3,078	3,485	4,057	3,886	4,189	4,569	5,668	7,474
Purchased meals and beverages[e]	1,834	2,332	2,674	3,054	3,583	3,446	3,748	4,094	4,983	6,306
Hotels, restaurants, dining cars (inc. tips)	1,667	2,151	2,473	2,836	3,341	3,218	3,525	3,860	4,722	6,001
Schools, institutions, clubs, etc.	167	181	201	218	242	228	223	234	261	305
Food furnished government (including military) and commercial employees, and withdrawn by nonfarm proprietors	324	366	404	431	474	440	441	475	685	1,168
Food and nonalcoholic beverages[d]	10,915	12,263	13,702	15,326	16,508	15,722	15,874	17,091	20,165	25,254
Alcoholic beverages[e]	626	2,003	2,553	3,164	3,442	3,237	3,425	3,634	4,238	5,210
TOBACCO PRODUCTS AND SMOKING SUPPLIES[d]	1,236	1,370	1,438	1,540	1,679	1,703	1,773	1,875	2,073	2,329
B. CLOTHING, ACCESSORIES AND PERSONAL CARE[d]	5,908	7,117	7,603	8,279	8,773	8,684	9,159	9,746	11,518	14,327
CLOTHING AND RELATED PRODUCTS	5,248	6,357	6,801	7,415	7,812	7,733	8,155	8,639	10,310	12,926
Clothes and accessories	3,704	4,547	4,948	5,355	5,480	5,438	5,850	6,170	7,352	9,249
Clothing and accessories except footwear	3,653	4,497	4,896	5,296	5,414	5,376	5,776	6,061	7,085	8,439
Standard clothing issued to military personnel	11	7	9	12	13	14	22	54	210	745
Dressmakers and seamstresses (not in shops)	24	27	28	31	36	30	33	35	36	41
Net purchases and rentals of secondhand clothing and accessories	16	16	15	16	17	18	19	20	21	24
Shoes and other footwear	887	1,072	1,031	1,145	1,279	1,257	1,226	1,270	1,486	1,858
Jewelry and watches	172	198	233	265	333	323	355	406	547	715
Cleaning, repair and maintenance	485	540	589	650	720	715	724	793	925	1,104
Cleaning, repair and storage of garments, furs and shoes	328	367	408	452	505	509	511	564	657	787
Laundering (in establishments)[f]	126	131	136	152	161	154	156	164	187	224
Watch, clock and jewelry repair and miscellaneous personal services	31	42	45	46	54	52	57	65	81	93
PERSONAL CARE	660	760	802	864	961	951	1,004	1,107	1,208	1,401
Toilet articles and preparations	320	377	374	395	428	442	486	510	592	711
Barber shop, beauty parlor and related services	340	383	428	469	533	509	518	597	616	690
Barber shop services	213	221	230	245	272	254	252	289	295	332
Beauty parlor services	122	157	192	217	253	248	258	299	312	347
Baths and masseurs	5	5	6	7	8	7	8	9	9	11

Class of Expenditure	1943	1944	1945	1946	1947	1948	1949	1950	1951	1952
TOTAL CONSUMPTION EXPENDITURES [a]	$102,244	$111,550	$123,079	$146,907	$165,570	$177,890	$180,588	$194,550	$208,108	$218,130
A. FOOD, LIQUOR AND TOBACCO	37,893	41,461	45,924	53,738	60,483	63,884	63,145	65,606	73,715	77,750
FOOD AND BEVERAGES	35,314	38,894	42,994	50,285	56,609	59,737	58,879	61,208	69,012	72,595
Consumed inside the home [b]	25,538	27,414	29,571	37,133	43,364	46,334	45,769	47,816	53,879	56,707
Purchased for off-premise consumption	23,508	25,348	27,436	34,640	40,455	43,528	43,376	45,726	51,579	54,527
Produced and consumed on farms	2,030	2,066	2,135	2,493	2,909	2,806	2,393	2,090	2,300	2,180
Consumed outside the home [b]	9,776	11,480	13,423	13,152	13,245	13,403	13,110	13,392	15,133	15,888
Purchased meals and beverages [c]	7,862	8,854	10,427	11,514	11,863	11,933	11,679	11,859	12,984	13,545
Hotels, restaurants, dining cars (inc. tips)	7,512	8,507	10,035	10,973	11,155	11,124	10,885	11,044	12,047	12,541
Schools, institutions, clubs, etc.	350	347	392	541	708	809	794	815	937	1,004
Food furnished government (including military) and commercial employees, and withdrawn by nonfarm proprietors	1,914	2,626	2,996	1,638	1,382	1,470	1,431	1,533	2,149	2,343
Food and nonalcoholic beverages [d]	29,324	31,879	35,229	41,615	47,739	51,587	50,959	53,108	60,562	63,725
Alcoholic beverages [e]	5,990	7,015	7,765	8,670	8,870	8,150	7,920	8,100	8,450	8,870
TOBACCO PRODUCTS AND SMOKING SUPPLIES [d]	2,579	2,567	2,930	3,453	3,874	4,147	4,266	4,398	4,703	5,155
B. CLOTHING, ACCESSORIES AND PERSONAL CARE [d]	17,753	19,676	22,039	24,259	25,000	26,043	24,823	24,961	26,631	27,301
CLOTHING AND RELATED PRODUCTS	16,051	17,799	19,962	22,073	22,739	23,798	22,607	22,658	24,210	24,786
Clothes and accessories	11,877	13,359	14,906	15,898	16,234	17,176	16,135	15,975	17,112	17,561
Clothing and accessories except footwear	10,488	11,567	13,074	15,299	15,903	16,877	15,813	15,582	16,565	17,096
Standard clothing issued to military personnel	1,318	1,712	1,744	508	230	191	213	274	418	336
Dressmakers and seamstresses (not in shops)	46	54	60	60	68	72	72	81	88	88
Net purchases and rentals of secondhand clothing and accessories	25	26	28	31	33	36	37	38	41	41
Shoes and other footwear	1,914	2,009	2,281	2,808	2,975	3,023	2,958	3,080	3,295	3,300
Jewelry and watches	931	1,010	1,203	1,419	1,348	1,324	1,273	1,312	1,385	1,424
Cleaning, repair and maintenance	1,329	1,421	1,572	1,948	2,182	2,275	2,241	2,291	2,418	2,501
Cleaning, repair and storage of garments, furs and shoes	961	1,025	1,134	1,428	1,609	1,694	1,675	1,714	1,821	1,891
Laundering (in establishments) [f]	251	276	303	364	425	436	422	427	435	437
Watch, clock and jewelry repair and miscellaneous personal services	117	120	135	156	148	145	144	150	162	173
PERSONAL CARE	1,702	1,877	2,077	2,186	2,261	2,245	2,216	2,303	2,421	2,515
Toilet articles and preparations	853	965	1,088	1,130	1,208	1,226	1,193	1,245	1,312	1,352
Barber shop, beauty parlor and related services	849	912	989	1,056	1,053	1,019	1,023	1,058	1,109	1,163
Barber shop services	405	421	451	503	504	508	521	549	592	1,163
Beauty parlor services	431	477	523	536	532	495	486	492	499	
Baths and masseurs	13	14	15	17	17	16	16	17	18	

Class of Expenditure	1909	1914	1919	1921	1923	1925	1927	1929	1930	1931	1932
C. HOUSING AND UTILITIES											
RENT AND IMPUTED RENT[g]	6,910	7,872	10,244	12,327	13,777	14,237	14,431	14,512	14,085	13,108	11,611
Owner-occupied nonfarm dwellings—space-rental value	5,563	6,222	8,045	9,682	10,613	11,454	11,319	11,421	10,992	10,235	8,964
Tenant-occupied nonfarm dwellings (including lodging houses)—space rent	—	—	—	—	—	—	—	5,898	5,581	5,127	4,440
Rental value of farmhouses	—	—	—	—	—	—	—	4,445	4,346	4,139	3,691
Transient accommodations—clubs, schools and institutions	—	—	—	—	—	—	—	829	830	754	655
	—	—	—	—	—	—	—	249	235	215	178
FUEL, ICE AND LIGHTING SUPPLIES[d]	985	1,190	1,492	1,817	2,160	1,646	1,882	1,694	1,618	1,389	1,208
HOUSEHOLD UTILITIES	362	460	707	828	1,004	1,137	1,230	1,397	1,475	1,484	1,439
Electricity[g]	83	132	265	306	389	462	509	616	660	674	662
Gas[g]	139	173	272	342	425	470	506	548	567	562	544
Water[h]	140	155	170	180	190	205	215	233	248	248	233
D. HOUSEHOLD EQUIPMENT AND OPERATION											
FURNITURE AND FURNISHINGS[d]	3,389	3,695	7,333	6,722	8,986	10,031	10,971	13,277	11,030	9,521	7,615
Furniture—new and secondhand	1,229	1,333	2,841	2,474	3,589	3,668	3,630	3,698	2,893	2,527	1,872
Floor coverings	294	344	728	690	983	1,100	1,123	1,201	937	796	509
China, glassware, tableware and utensils	173	170	367	321	526	559	517	485	356	338	232
Miscellaneous furnishings	233	229	480	405	628	628	624	628	442	429	406
	529	590	1,266	1,058	1,452	1,381	1,366	1,384	1,158	964	725
MECHANICAL APPLIANCES[d]	145	167	400	294	511	548	667	768	671	565	344
Refrigerators, and washing and sewing machines	—	—	—	—	—	—	—	348	309	268	171
Miscellaneous electrical appliances (exc. radios)	—	—	—	—	—	—	—	132	121	103	55
Cooking and portable heating equipment	—	—	—	—	—	—	—	288	241	194	118
DOMESTIC SERVICE (exc. practical nurses)[g]	712	697	967	1,005	1,191	1,327	1,429	1,501	1,299	1,003	731
COMMUNICATION	174	214	427	466	557	641	721	860	839	770	677
Stationery, writing supplies and postage[d]	92	102	225	211	254	270	276	301	274	222	178
Telephone, telegraph, cable and wireless[g]	82	112	202	255	303	371	445	559	565	548	499
CLEANING, REPAIR AND MAINTENANCE[d]	259	307	625	535	656	681	754	805	792	706	546
Cleaning and polishing preparations	—	—	—	—	—	—	—	359	356	309	227
Services	—	—	—	—	—	—	—	446	436	397	319
Laundering (in establishments)[f]	—	—	—	—	—	—	—	238	229	196	155
Furniture, furnishings, electrical equipment (exc. radios) repair, and miscellaneous services	—	—	—	—	—	—	—	90	85	81	71
Moving, storage and express	—	—	—	—	—	—	—	118	122	120	93

Class of Expenditure	1933	1934	1935	1936	1937	1938	1939	1940	1941	1942
C. HOUSING AND UTILITIES	10,451	10,314	10,439	10,910	11,466	11,736	12,104	12,652	13,544	14,631
RENT AND IMPUTED RENT [g]	7,849	7,538	7,597	7,882	8,378	8,733	8,940	9,217	9,863	10,594
Owner-occupied nonfarm dwellings—space-rental value	3,865	3,662	3,665	3,778	3,969	4,124	4,200	4,326	4,655	5,109
Tenant-occupied nonfarm dwellings (including lodging houses)—space rent	3,244	3,099	3,142	3,295	3,560	3,773	3,898	4,039	4,312	4,544
Rental value of farmhouses	587	616	616	615	638	620	619	624	658	688
Transient accommodations—clubs, schools and institutions	153	161	174	194	211	216	223	228	238	253
FUEL, ICE AND LIGHTING SUPPLIES [d]	1,228	1,349	1,374	1,509	1,514	1,391	1,484	1,650	1,830	2,075
HOUSEHOLD UTILITIES	1,374	1,427	1,468	1,519	1,574	1,612	1,680	1,785	1,851	1,962
Electricity [g]	645	671	697	726	766	810	849	910	965	1,017
Gas [g]	504	504	511	520	531	528	544	584	587	633
Water [h]	225	252	260	273	277	274	287	291	299	312
D. HOUSEHOLD EQUIPMENT AND OPERATION	7,272	7,843	8,478	9,674	10,534	9,766	10,411	11,089	12,558	12,728
FURNITURE AND FURNISHINGS [d]	1,733	1,993	2,211	2,771	3,021	2,723	3,083	3,369	4,069	4,356
Furniture—new and secondhand	462	514	666	848	923	827	949	1,062	1,314	1,279
Floor coverings	186	238	273	385	382	321	383	417	513	536
China, glassware, tableware and utensils	364	404	407	456	515	472	475	517	633	674
Miscellaneous furnishings	721	837	865	1,082	1,201	1,103	1,276	1,373	1,609	1,867
MECHANICAL APPLIANCES [d]	408	518	614	733	845	711	774	884	1,165	705
Refrigerators, and washing and sewing machines	230	280	319	373	439	321	362	422	557	705
Miscellaneous electrical appliances (exc. radios)	74	99	113	137	154	167	174	197	254	
Cooking and portable heating equipment	104	139	182	223	252	223	238	265	354	
DOMESTIC SERVICE (EXC. PRACTICAL NURSES) [g]	644	749	806	897	1,048	910	995	1,081	1,118	1,285
COMMUNICATION	628	639	678	733	782	803	848	913	1,028	1,189
Stationery, writing supplies and postage [d]	175	201	225	255	284	281	303	332	398	414
Telephone, telegraph, cable and wireless [g]	453	438	453	478	498	522	545	581	630	775
CLEANING, REPAIR AND MAINTENANCE [d]	492	545	569	631	695	716	731	750	822	952
Cleaning and polishing preparations	222	260	265	299	334	353	359	353	378	419
Services	270	285	304	332	361	363	372	397	444	533
Laundering (in establishments) [f]	126	131	136	152	162	154	156	165	187	225
Furniture, furnishings, electrical equipment (exc. radios) repair, and miscellaneous services	67	79	92	100	111	117	125	135	148	175
Moving, storage and express	77	75	76	80	88	92	91	97	109	133

(The three items under MECHANICAL APPLIANCES are bracketed together for 1942, totaling 705.)

969

Class of Expenditure	1943	1944	1945	1946	1947	1948	1949	1950	1951	1952
C. HOUSING AND UTILITIES	15,383	16,092	16,835	18,003	20,401	22,892	24,413	27,184	29,335	31,732
RENT AND IMPUTED RENT g	11,125	11,702	12,205	13,047	14,603	16,466	18,080	20,210	21,874	24,014
Owner-occupied nonfarm dwellings—space-rental value	5,507	5,998	6,470	7,174	8,324	9,586	10,757	12,195	13,430	14,818
Tenant-occupied nonfarm dwellings (including lodging houses)—space rent	4,599	4,615	4,531	4,488	4,618	5,059	5,517	6,002	6,223	6,811
Rental value of farmhouses	731	784	863	995	1,220	1,334	1,294	1,468	1,623	1,740
Transient accommodations—clubs, schools and institutions	288	305	341	390	441	487	512	545	598	645
FUEL, ICE AND LIGHTING SUPPLIES d	2,236	2,256	2,376	2,559	3,136	3,500	3,133	3,392	3,465	3,350
HOUSEHOLD UTILITIES	2,022	2,134	2,254	2,397	2,662	2,926	3,200	3,582	3,996	4,368
Electricity g	1,045	1,125	1,194	1,270	1,406	1,564	1,746	1,955	2,190	2,418
Gas g	656	673	713	767	869	958	1,031	1,177	1,336	1,448
Water h	321	336	347	360	387	404	423	450	470	502
D. HOUSEHOLD EQUIPMENT AND OPERATION	13,029	14,127	15,655	20,345	23,956	25,922	25,695	29,060	30,047	30,875
FURNITURE AND FURNISHINGS d	4,530	4,778	5,317	7,627	8,453	9,012	8,536	9,513	9,808	9,667
Furniture—new and secondhand	1,241	1,315	1,561	2,339	2,721	2,957	2,843	3,311	3,375	3,487
Floor coverings	591	556	543	844	1,049	1,131	964	1,128	1,140	1,071
China, glassware, tableware and utensils	631	670	841	1,339	1,442	1,504	1,422	1,500	1,548	1,484
Miscellaneous furnishings	2,067	2,237	2,372	3,105	3,241	3,420	3,307	3,574	3,745	3,625
MECHANICAL APPLIANCES d	254	150	317	1,587	2,791	2,927	2,403	3,021	2,516	2,433
Refrigerators, and washing and sewing machines / Miscellaneous electrical appliances (exc. radios) / Cooking and portable heating equipment	254	150	317	1,587	2,791	2,927	2,403	3,021	2,516	2,433
DOMESTIC SERVICE (exc. practical nurses) g	1,416	1,669	1,861	1,872	2,116	2,187	2,238	2,525	2,751	2,734
COMMUNICATION	1,426	1,657	1,888	2,033	2,208	2,462	2,635	2,892	3,188	3,459
Stationery, writing supplies and postage d	491	605	711	738	814	794	779	821	890	924
Telephone, telegraph, cable and wireless g	935	1,052	1,177	1,295	1,394	1,668	1,856	2,071	2,298	2,535
CLEANING, REPAIR AND MAINTENANCE d	1,054	1,127	1,124	1,260	1,723	1,814	1,751	1,844	1,953	1,946
Cleaning and polishing preparations	451	455	380	368	708	736	670	718	748	692
Services	603	672	744	892	1,015	1,078	1,081	1,126	1,205	1,254
Laundering (in establishments) f	252	276	303	365	425	436	422	427	435	437
Furniture, furnishings, electrical equipment (exc. radios) repair, and miscellaneous services	195	212	234	284	332	372	392	413	440	453
Moving, storage and express	156	184	207	243	258	270	267	286	330	364

Class of Expenditure	1909	1914	1919	1921	1923	1925	1927	1929	1930	1931	1932
FINANCIAL, LEGAL, INSURANCE AND DEATH EXPENSES											
Financial expenses [l]	870	977	2,073	1,948	2,482	3,166	3,770	5,645	4,536	3,950	3,445
Brokerage charges and interest, and investment counseling [j]	459	482	1,036	844	1,186	1,615	2,054	3,710	2,636	2,122	1,758
Bank service charges, money order fees and other financial services	—	34	181	77	133	329	555	1,739	764	424	277
Fire and theft insurance on personal property (net payments) and vault rental [k]	—	—	—	—	—	—	—	1,346	1,211	1,087	941
Interest on personal debt [l]	10	11	20	17	25	25	25	48	44	40	37
Legal services [d]	—	—	—	122	265	360	431	577	617	571	503
Legal services [d]	97	100	257	254	305	334	365	402	397	410	348
Life insurance handling expenses [g]	157	219	376	488	598	740	836	936	965	947	932
Death expenses [d]	157	176	404	362	393	477	515	597	538	471	407
Funeral and burial services	—	—	—	—	—	—	—	323	291	254	228
Cemeteries and crematories	—	—	—	—	—	—	—	163	150	137	128
Monuments and tombstones	—	—	—	—	—	—	—	111	97	80	51
E. CONSUMER TRANSPORTATION	1,489	2,132	4,883	4,808	6,514	7,578	7,190	8,007	6,560	5,295	4,209
PRIVATE TRANSPORTATION [m]	660	1,090	3,472	3,129	4,695	5,625	5,109	5,804	4,533	3,627	2,835
New cars and net purchases of used cars [d]	167	417	1,300	1,157	2,289	2,411	1,995	2,588	1,642	1,144	635
Automobile parts, repair and maintenance	90	183	768	606	892	1,278	1,403	1,306	1,064	888	685
Tires and tubes [d]	50	101	485	322	419	601	694	419	320	264	189
Parts and accessories [d]	3	7	94	53	137	205	150	221	196	162	118
Automobile repair, greasing, washing, parking, storage and rental [g]	32	64	160	192	287	415	479	572	467	386	296
Automobile insurance—net payments [g]	5	11	29	39	49	57	80	94	81	76	82
Gasoline and oil [d]	123	233	1,226	1,256	1,386	1,819	1,595	1,814	1,749	1,540	1,476
Luggage [d]	42	41	96	78	93	92	94	96	78	55	39
PUBLIC CARRIER TRANSPORTATION	829	1,042	1,411	1,679	1,819	1,953	2,081	2,203	2,027	1,668	1,374
Local [g]	463	608	813	932	1,004	1,057	1,125	1,131	1,063	932	794
Streetcar, electric railway and local bus	—	—	—	—	—	—	—	820	772	705	624
Taxicabs—fares and tips	—	—	—	—	—	—	—	220	208	152	109
Steam railways (commutation) and ferries (foot passengers)	—	—	—	—	—	—	—	91	83	75	61
Intercity [n]	269	330	568	560	584	573	568	561	465	369	295
Steam railways, sleeping and parlor cars (exc. commutation)	—	—	—	—	—	—	—	413	333	247	170
Bus	—	—	—	—	—	—	—	52	53	50	48
Airline	—	—	—	—	—	—	—	3	2	2	3
Other intercity	—	—	—	—	—	—	—	93	77	70	74
Foreign travel [g]	97	104	30	187	231	323	388	511	499	367	285
Payments to U.S. vessels	—	—	—	—	—	—	—	34	33	25	16
Other foreign travel expenditures—net payments [o]	—	—	—	—	—	—	—	477	466	342	269

APPENDIX 4-4 (continued)

Class of Expenditure	1933	1934	1935	1936	1937	1938	1939	1940	1941	1942
FINANCIAL, LEGAL, INSURANCE AND DEATH EXPENSES	3,367	3,399	3,600	3,909	4,143	3,903	3,980	4,092	4,356	4,241
Financial expenses [i]	1,711	1,649	1,700	1,934	2,047	1,856	1,883	1,916	2,075	1,908
Brokerage charges and interest, and investment counseling [j]	378	248	245	322	313	207	195	154	131	118
Bank service charges, money order fees and other financial services	828	879	895	960	1,004	951	954	937	1,009	1,066
Fire and theft insurance on personal property (net payments) and vault rental [k]	39	42	40	38	42	38	41	44	48	54
Interest on personal debt [l]	466	480	520	614	688	660	693	781	887	670
Legal services [d]	334	359	371	383	402	392	407	423	450	478
Life insurance handling expenses [g]	942	981	1,095	1,113	1,192	1,177	1,197	1,238	1,271	1,264
Death expenses [d]	380	410	434	479	502	478	493	515	560	591
Funeral and burial services	214	225	241	259	272	263	272	284	316	340
Cemeteries and crematories	120	128	133	146	151	147	152	159	158	161
Monuments and tombstones	46	57	60	74	79	68	69	72	86	90
E. CONSUMER TRANSPORTATION	4,126	4,721	5,396	6,308	6,743	5,811	6,459	7,101	8,413	5,644
PRIVATE TRANSPORTATION [m]	2,926	3,459	4,093	4,827	5,161	4,333	4,974	5,691	6,790	3,422
New cars and net purchases of used cars [d]	779	1,024	1,508	1,921	1,988	1,228	1,679	2,228	2,708	423
Automobile parts, repair and maintenance	653	767	809	915	972	904	1,061	1,144	1,384	1,001
Tires and tubes [d]	154	182	175	167	176	193	237	257	318	{ 265
Parts and accessories [d]	117	153	181	220	238	185	220	243	316	}
Automobile repair, greasing, washing, parking, storage and rental [g]	306	346	354	404	421	402	462	489	577	600
Automobile insurance—net payments [g]	76	86	99	124	137	124	142	155	173	136
Gasoline and oil [d]	1,466	1,640	1,743	1,945	2,143	2,145	2,181	2,264	2,628	1,908
Luggage [d]	28	28	33	46	58	56	53	55	70	90
PUBLIC CARRIER TRANSPORTATION	1,200	1,262	1,303	1,481	1,582	1,478	1,485	1,410	1,623	2,222
Local [g]	728	769	799	855	882	848	885	913	985	1,298
Streetcar, electric railway and local bus	578	605	626	674	684	660	684	714	760	980
Taxicabs—fares and tips	96	111	119	127	145	141	153	153	177	261
Steam railways (commutation) and ferries (foot passengers)	54	53	54	54	53	47	48	46	48	57
Intercity [n]	266	286	287	362	389	368	391	403	466	667
Steam railway, sleeping and parlor cars (exc. commutation)	154	169	153	210	232	209	216	214	232	364
Bus	46	44	62	72	78	84	92	97	126	213
Airline	3	4	6	8	8	8	11	18	23	22
Other intercity	63	69	66	72	71	67	72	74	85	68
Foreign travel [g]	206	207	217	264	311	262	209	94	172	257
Payments to U.S. vessels	16	17	18	24	23	23	20	13	13	4
Other foreign travel expenditures—net payments [o]	190	190	199	240	288	239	189	81	159	253

Class of Expenditure	1943	1944	1945	1946	1947	1948	1949	1950	1951	1952
FINANCIAL, LEGAL, INSURANCE AND DEATH EXPENSES	4,349	4,746	5,148	5,966	6,665	7,520	8,132	9,265	9,831	10,636
Financial expenses [i]	1,873	2,107	2,365	2,711	2,928	3,428	3,807	4,552	4,949	5,447
Brokerage charges and interest, and investment counseling [j]	206	211	303	299	213	269	241	436	424	349
Bank service charges, money order fees and other financial services	1,128	1,383	1,526	1,720	1,777	1,992	2,190	2,372	2,607	2,958
Fire and theft insurance on personal property (net payments) and vault rental [k]	59	64	70	84	98	106	115	118	129	136
Interest on personal debt [l]	480	449	466	608	840	1,061	1,261	1,626	1,789	2,004
Legal services [d]	496	554	620	744	825	951	1,003	1,081	1,124	1,156
Life insurance handling expenses [g]	1,319	1,377	1,408	1,661	1,966	2,127	2,268	2,555	2,589	2,815
Death expenses [d]	661	708	755	850	946	1,014	1,054	1,077	1,169	1,218
Funeral and burial services	380	414	450	502	571	619	663	677	754	790
Cemeteries and crematories	178	176	177	185	201	204	203	206	211	212
Monuments and tombstones	103	118	128	163	174	191	188	194	204	216
E. CONSUMER TRANSPORTATION	6,053	6,731	8,152	12,148	15,511	17,605	20,243	23,546	23,280	23,968
PRIVATE TRANSPORTATION [m]	2,922	3,054	3,786	8,532	11,750	13,589	16,097	19,456	18,796	19,049
New cars and net purchases of used cars [d]	463	440	484	2,794	4,934	5,925	7,878	10,285	8,900	8,342
Automobile parts, repair and maintenance	1,149	1,288	1,548	2,600	3,094	3,312	3,415	4,070	4,307	4,630
Tires and tubes [d] / Parts and accessories [d]	334	418	603	1,414	1,626	1,590	1,511	2,030	1,967	2,072
Automobile repair, greasing, washing, parking, storage and rental [g]	660	710	770	926	1,087	1,246	1,369	1,478	1,670	1,770
Automobile insurance—net payments [g]	155	160	175	260	381	476	535	562	670	788
Gasoline and oil [d]	1,198	1,206	1,616	2,950	3,528	4,166	4,635	4,928	5,405	5,887
Luggage [d]	112	120	138	188	194	186	169	173	184	190
PUBLIC CARRIER TRANSPORTATION	3,131	3,677	4,366	3,616	3,761	4,016	4,146	4,090	4,484	4,919
Local [g]	1,653	1,732	1,753	1,957	2,000	2,123	2,094	2,084	2,134	2,187
Streetcar, electric railway and local bus	1,237	1,299	1,316	1,334	1,313	1,419	1,422	1,390	1,413	1,451
Taxicabs—fares and tips	353	370	372	554	614	621	586	608	632	641
Steam railways (commutation) and ferries (foot passengers)	63	63	65	69	73	83	86	86	89	95
Intercity [n]	1,058	1,117	1,155	1,159	1,126	1,155	1,083	1,030	1,174	1,273
Steam railway, sleeping and parlor cars (exc. commutation)	664	671	678	616	580	577	513	446	500	536
Bus	307	344	347	344	327	343	318	310	336	335
Airline	24	32	54	106	119	133	151	174	231	272
Other intercity	63	70	76	93	100	102	101	100	107	130
Foreign travel [g]	420	828	1,458	500	635	738	969	976	1,176	1,459
Payments to U.S. vessels	3	3	21	45	71	97	107	107	124	158
Other foreign travel expenditures—net payments [o]	417	825	1,437	455	564	641	862	869	1,052	1,301

APPENDIX 4-4 (continued)

Class of Expenditure	1909	1914	1919	1921	1923	1925	1927	1929	1930	1931	1932
F. MEDICAL CARE AND INSURANCE	799	905	2,060	1,536	2,195	2,491	2,690	3,023	2,909	2,605	2,168
MEDICAL CARE	782	881	2,019	1,483	2,130	2,411	2,599	2,915	2,799	2,513	2,096
Drugs and appliances [d]	211	258	593	457	586	603	673	735	701	634	542
Drug preparations and sundries	—	—	—	—	—	—	—	604	568	517	449
Ophthalmic products and orthopedic appliances	—	—	—	—	—	—	—	131	133	117	93
Personnel	434	452	1,152	850	1,310	1,533	1,596	1,777	1,694	1,484	1,168
Physicians [g]	293	297	718	520	800	890	928	959	924	819	661
Dentists [g]	82	94	277	186	305	378	386	482	463	408	312
Private-duty trained nurses [d]	20	22	59	60	68	91	100	113	104	88	67
Other personnel [g]	39	39	98	84	137	174	182	223	203	169	128
Osteopathic physicians	—	—	—	—	—	—	—	41	38	34	27
Chiropractors	—	—	—	—	—	—	—	49	46	40	30
Chiropodists and podiatrists	—	—	—	—	—	—	—	20	19	17	14
Practical nurses and midwives	—	—	—	—	—	—	—	86	74	56	41
Miscellaneous curative and healing professions	—	—	—	—	—	—	—	27	26	22	16
Privately controlled hospitals and sanitariums [g]	137	171	274	176	234	275	330	403	404	395	386
INSURANCE—ACCIDENT, HEALTH AND PREPAYMENT [p]	17	24	41	53	65	80	91	108	110	92	72
Net prepayments for hospitalization and medical care	—	—	—	—	—	—	—	2	2	2	2
Accident and health insurance—net payments	—	—	—	—	—	—	—	86	90	77	60
Mutual accident and sick-benefit associations—net payments	—	—	—	—	—	—	—	20	18	13	10
G. RECREATION	859	997	2,157	2,068	2,624	2,840	3,141	3,836	3,536	2,873	2,102
THEATERS, ENTERTAINMENTS AND AMUSEMENTS [q]	189	216	380	433	546	612	816	959	937	889	652
Motion picture theaters	—	—	—	301	336	367	526	720	732	719	527
Legitimate theaters, opera and entertainments of nonprofit organizations (exc. athletics)	—	—	—	—	—	—	—	130	97	80	58
Other commercial amusements (exc. athletics)	—	—	—	—	—	—	—	109	108	90	67
SPECTATOR SPORTS [q]	—	—	—	29	44	45	46	63	63	55	46
Professional baseball, football and hockey	—	—	—	—	—	—	—	21	21	18	15
Horse and dog race tracks	—	—	—	—	—	—	—	2	2	2	1
Amateur sports	—	—	—	—	—	—	—	40	40	35	30

Class of Expenditure	1933	1934	1935	1936	1937	1938	1939	1940	1941	1942
F. MEDICAL CARE AND INSURANCE	2,017	2,203	2,328	2,539	2,724	2,731	2,893	3,076	3,401	3,879
MEDICAL CARE	1,947	2,118	2,235	2,433	2,601	2,597	2,740	2,910	3,206	3,650
Drugs and appliances [d]	519	592	605	649	723	735	784	827	951	1,113
Drug preparations and sundries	427	468	474	509	558	578	612	640	725	858
Ophthalmic products and orthopedic appliances	92	124	131	140	165	157	172	187	226	255
Personnel	1,065	1,157	1,224	1,362	1,424	1,395	1,464	1,556	1,700	1,888
Physicians [g]	617	678	731	820	854	833	866	913	991	1,072
Dentists [g]	276	295	302	331	350	356	386	419	468	545
Private-duty trained nurses [d]	59	63	64	68	67	61	59	58	58	62
Other personnel [g]	113	121	127	143	153	145	153	166	183	209
Osteopathic physicians	26	28	30	33	36	40	43	47	57	61
Chiropractors	26	26	28	32	33	33	34	36	39	46
Chiropodists and podiatrists	13	13	14	15	15	14	15	17	18	22
Practical nurses and midwives	34	39	40	46	52	43	45	48	50	57
Miscellaneous curative and healing professions	14	15	15	17	17	15	16	18	19	23
Privately controlled hospitals and sanitariums [g]	363	369	406	422	454	467	492	527	555	649
INSURANCE—ACCIDENT, HEALTH AND PREPAYMENT [p]	70	85	93	106	123	134	153	166	195	229
Net prepayments for hospitalization and medical care	2	2	2	3	5	8	12	18	29	32
Accident and health insurance—net payments	56	71	78	87	99	104	115	126	141	164
Mutual accident and sick-benefit associations—net payments	12	12	13	16	19	22	26	22	25	33
G. RECREATION	1,868	2,086	2,254	2,609	2,933	2,809	2,994	3,269	3,720	4,154
THEATERS, ENTERTAINMENTS AND AMUSEMENTS [q]	590	639	683	772	841	802	813	873	944	1,155
Motion picture theaters	482	518	556	626	676	663	659	709	756	961
Legitimate theaters, opera and entertainments of nonprofit organizations (exc. athletics)	42	44	46	52	55	60	66	72	79	91
Other commercial amusements (exc. athletics)	66	77	81	94	110	79	88	92	109	103
SPECTATOR SPORTS [q]	49	63	70	81	87	93	96	95	102	87
Professional baseball, football and hockey	14	16	20	23	24	25	28	26	28	24
Horse and dog race tracks	2	6	7	8	9	12	11	12	13	12
Amateur sports	33	41	43	50	54	56	57	57	61	51

APPENDIX 4-4 (continued)

Class of Expenditure	1943	1944	1945	1946	1947	1948	1949	1950	1951	1952
F. MEDICAL CARE AND INSURANCE	4,367	4,852	5,147	6,165	6,866	7,482	7,831	8,441	8,986	9,634
MEDICAL CARE	4,092	4,521	4,774	5,716	6,362	6,915	7,240	7,806	8,335	8,834
Drugs and appliances a	1,331	1,414	1,507	1,690	1,744	1,822	1,829	1,927	2,111	2,177
Drug preparations and sundries	1,030	1,091	1,167	1,305	1,358	1,406	1,398	1,450	1,570	1,623
Ophthalmic products and orthopedic appliances	301	323	340	385	386	416	431	477	541	554
Personnel	2,009	2,261	2,342	2,863	3,224	3,508	3,688	3,916	4,068	4,268
Physicians g	1,112	1,289	1,342	1,658	1,946	2,141	2,267	2,435	2,529	2,676
Dentists g	606	643	648	821	837	895	931	959	989	1,028
Private-duty trained nurses d	67	75	79	87	97	104	109	114	117	125
Other personnel g	224	254	273	297	344	368	381	408	433	439
Osteopathic physicians	64	74	79	87	102	109	113	119	124	128
Chiropractors	49	53	56	64	76	84	88	93	96	98
Chiropodists and podiatrists	23	25	27	30	36	40	42	44	47	48
Practical nurses and midwives	63	74	82	83	94	96	98	111	122	120
Miscellaneous curative and healing professions	25	28	29	33	36	39	40	41	44	45
Privately controlled hospitals and sanitariums g	752	846	925	1,163	1,394	1,585	1,723	1,963	2,156	2,389
INSURANCE—ACCIDENT, HEALTH AND PREPAYMENT p	275	331	373	449	504	567	591	635	651	800
Net prepayments for hospitalization and medical care	37	46	47	65	82	110	126	139	145	189
Accident and health insurance—net payments	200	244	278	336	362	402	408	437	446	548
Mutual accident and sick-benefit associations—net payments	38	41	48	48	60	55	57	59	60	63
G. RECREATION	4,180	4,761	5,423	7,907	8,651	8,917	9,154	10,211	10,180	10,489
THEATERS, ENTERTAINMENTS AND AMUSEMENTS q	1,252	1,523	1,654	1,892	1,828	1,800	1,783	1,693	1,656	1,608
Motion picture theaters	1,038	1,253	1,359	1,512	1,407	1,364	1,342	1,247	1,193	1,134
Legitimate theaters, opera and entertainments of nonprofit organizations (exc. athletics)	115	138	144	171	184	180	176	171	177	175
Other commercial amusements (exc. athletics)	99	132	151	209	237	256	265	275	286	299
SPECTATOR SPORTS q	75	89	128	230	265	276	284	266	263	268
Professional baseball, football and hockey	19	24	32	69	83	86	82	70	66	65
Horse and dog race tracks	11	14	22	40	41	39	37	36	38	42
Amateur sports	45	51	74	121	141	151	165	160	159	161

Class of Expenditure	1909	1914	1919	1921	1923	1925	1927	1929	1930	1931	1932
READING, HOBBIES AND PETS q, r	207	225	417	437	533	590	631	679	608	522	399
Reading d	104	131	204	239	270	318	349	356	326	307	244
Hobbies and pets d	103	94	213	198	263	272	282	323	282	215	155
Photography	—	—	—	—	—	—	—	73	64	57	47
Photo developing and printing	—	—	—	—	—	—	—	13	11	10	8
Photographic studios	—	—	—	—	—	—	—	60	53	47	39
Collectors' net acquisitions of stamps and coins	—	—	—	—	—	—	—	2	2	2	1
Veterinary service and purchase of pets	—	—	—	—	—	—	—	27	26	22	18
Flowers, seeds and potted plants	70	56	135	128	176	182	183	221	190	134	89
ORGANIZATIONS AND CLUBS d	134	155	268	268	268	304	313	334	326	305	267
Camp fees	—	—	—	—	—	—	—	32	32	28	25
Clubs	—	—	—	—	—	—	—	302	294	277	242
Athletic, social and luncheon clubs, and school fraternities—dues and fees	—	—	—	—	—	—	—	168	164	147	114
Fraternal, patriotic and women's organizations (exc. school and insurance) net payments	—	—	—	—	—	—	—	134	130	130	128
PARTICIPANT RECREATION q	23	26	57	132	152	149	163	221	214	187	143
Pari-mutuel and nonvending coin machines—net receipts	—	—	—	—	—	—	—	16	13	12	10
Billiard parlors and bowling alleys	—	—	—	—	—	—	—	58	57	48	35
Golf instruction, club rental and fees	—	—	—	—	—	—	—	91	89	80	63
Other participant recreation	—	—	—	—	—	—	—	56	55	47	35
RADIOS, TELEVISION AND MUSICAL INSTRUMENTS q	166	193	667	439	637	739	713	1,038	948	502	287
Radio and television receivers, phonographs, parts and records	—	—	—	—	—	—	—	905	840	418	232
Pianos and other musical instruments	—	—	—	—	—	—	—	107	81	60	36
Radio and television repairs	—	—	—	—	—	—	—	26	27	24	19
SPORTS EQUIPMENT q	140	182	368	330	444	401	459	542	440	413	308
Nondurable toys and sports supplies	—	—	—	—	—	—	—	336	281	266	207
Wheel goods, durable toys and sports equipment	—	—	—	—	—	—	—	182	145	136	97
Boats and pleasure aircraft	—	—	—	—	—	—	—	24	14	11	4

Class of Expenditure	1933	1934	1935	1936	1937	1938	1939	1940	1941	1942
READING, HOBBIES AND PETS	386	438	481	551	621	598	631	678	762	873
Reading q, r	240	255	268	293	320	309	328	341	365	418
Hobbies and pets d	146	183	213	258	301	289	303	337	397	455
Photography	38	47	57	68	77	79	79	91	112	149
Photo developing and printing	7	8	10	13	15	17	18	21	26	35
Photographic studios	31	39	47	55	62	62	61	70	86	114
Collectors' net acquisitions of stamps and coins	1	2	4	7	12	9	8	9	9	9
Veterinary service and purchase of pets	17	18	22	24	26	25	25	26	29	33
Flowers, seeds and potted plants	90	116	130	159	186	176	191	211	247	264
ORGANIZATIONS AND CLUBS d	232	225	224	227	234	226	227	231	233	235
Camp fees	24	26	27	29	31	26	28	28	30	30
Clubs	208	199	197	198	203	200	199	203	203	205
Athletic, social and luncheon clubs, and school fraternities—dues and fees	91	91	91	96	102	99	100	103	101	95
Fraternal, patriotic and women's organizations (exc. school and insurance) net payments	117	108	106	102	101	101	99	100	102	110
PARTICIPANT RECREATION q	136	167	187	225	278	262	280	311	352	353
Pari-mutuel and nonvending coin machines—net receipts	15	33	48	63	90	99	99	124	147	154
Billiard parlors and bowling alleys	34	41	44	57	73	57	70	70	82	79
Golf instruction, club rental and fees	53	54	55	57	61	60	60	64	64	62
Other participant recreation	34	39	40	48	54	46	51	53	59	58
RADIOS, TELEVISION AND MUSICAL INSTRUMENTS q	209	246	269	354	408	364	448	539	672	766
Radio and television receivers, phonographs, parts and records	171	198	206	278	322	278	356	429	535 }	720
Pianos and other musical instruments	24	31	42	55	63	61	64	78	101 }	
Radio and television repairs	14	17	21	21	23	25	28	32	36	46
SPORTS EQUIPMENT q	266	308	340	399	464	464	499	542	655	685
Nondurable toys and sports supplies	181	200	216	242	269	268	285	309	371	419
Wheel goods, durable toys and sports equipment	81	102	115	144	179	186	195	210	254	252
Boats and pleasure aircraft	4	6	9	13	16	10	19	23	30	14

Class of Expenditure	1943	1944	1945	1946	1947	1948	1949	1950	1951	1952
READING, HOBBIES AND PETS [q, r]	1,062	1,229	1,395	1,651	1,751	1,842	1,879	1,945	2,088	2,237
Reading [q, r]	510	572	646	744	783	806	812	822	845	888
Hobbies and pets [d]	552	657	749	907	968	1,036	1,067	1,123	1,243	1,349
Photography	197	231	254	305	306	341	343	366	415	442
Photo developing and printing	46	54	59	74	86	97	98	110	127	141
Photographic studios	151	177	195	231	220	244	245	256	288	301
Collectors' net acquisitions of stamps and coins	9	10	10	10	10	11	11	12	12	12
Veterinary service and purchase of pets	35	37	39	44	52	54	55	56	58	59
Flowers, seeds and potted plants	311	379	446	548	600	630	658	689	758	836
ORGANIZATIONS AND CLUBS [d]	243	259	309	390	433	478	502	511	529	556
Camp fees	26	23	28	31	35	39	42	44	47	49
Clubs	217	236	281	359	398	439	460	467	482	507
Athletic, social and luncheon clubs, and school fraternities—dues and fees	95	99	127	170	189	209	220	226	240	265
Fraternal, patriotic and women's organizations (exc. school and insurance) net payments	122	137	154	189	209	230	240	241	242	242
PARTICIPANT RECREATION [q]	384	472	534	742	763	777	782	763	796	867
Pari-mutuel and nonvending coin machines—net receipts	181	252	281	410	402	398	385	357	374	419
Billiard parlors and bowling alleys	83	83	87	112	121	124	128	125	126	129
Golf instruction, club rental and fees	63	68	83	110	119	131	137	143	153	169
Other participant recreation	57	69	83	110	121	124	132	138	143	150
RADIOS, TELEVISION AND MUSICAL INSTRUMENTS [q]	522	434	483	1,440	1,859	1,925	2,205	3,172	2,841	2,800
Radio and television receivers, phonographs, parts and records / Pianos and other musical instruments	463	364	399	1,326	1,724	1,753	1,992	2,848	2,421	2,324
Radio and television repairs	59	70	84	114	135	172	213	324	420	476
SPORTS EQUIPMENT [q]	642	755	920	1,562	1,752	1,819	1,719	1,861	2,007	2,153
Nondurable toys and sports supplies	413	488	595	919	1,006	1,041	1,017	1,102	1,197	1,284
Wheel goods, durable toys and sports equipment	220	258	313	580	680	718	651	695	742	790
Boats and pleasure aircraft	9	9	12	63	66	60	51	64	68	79

Class of Expenditure	1909	1914	1919	1921	1923	1925	1927	1929	1930	1931	1932
H. EDUCATION (PRIVATE)	416	493	751	746	813	894	1,007	1,170	1,148	1,105	922
ORGANIZED EDUCATION g	174	204	352	291	360	399	460	573	592	596	510
Higher education	132	145	263	211	260	286	333	219	242	251	227
Secondary and elementary schools								162	170	185	158
Other schools and instruction	42	59	89	80	100	113	127	192	180	160	125
Commercial, business and trade schools—fees	—	—	—	—	—	—	—	27	27	25	19
Correspondence schools—fees	—	—	—	—	—	—	—	32	24	20	18
Other instruction (exc. athletics)—fees	—	—	—	—	—	—	—	133	129	115	88
UNORGANIZED EDUCATION d	242	289	399	455	453	495	547	597	556	509	412
Reading r	201	239	331	378	375	410	452	491	450	425	337
Foundations, museums and libraries	41	50	68	77	78	85	95	106	106	84	75
Foundation expenditures for education and research	—	—	—	—	—	—	—	91	91	69	61
Museums and libraries	—	—	—	—	—	—	—	15	15	15	14
I. RELIGION g	300	300	613	613	684	778	833	912	893	837	743
J. WELFARE (PRIVATE) s	519	537	842	751	607	532	614	557	558	507	398
PERSONAL REMITTANCES TO FOREIGN COUNTRIES—NET s, t	354	372	532	310	261	299	291	288	257	234	182
SOCIAL WELFARE AND FOREIGN-RELIEF AGENCIES	—	—	—	—	—	—	—	230	253	244	166
OTHER PRIVATE WELFARE	—	—	—	—	—	—	—	39	48	29	50
Foundation expenditures (exc. education and research)	—	—	—	—	—	—	—	30	30	23	20
Political organizations	—	—	—	—	—	—	—	9	18	6	30
K. OCCUPATIONAL AND MISCELLANEOUS EXPENSES u	60	70	140	70	160	170	170	180	151	119	75
WORKING EQUIPMENT	—	—	—	—	—	—	—	63	50	34	23
EMPLOYMENT AGENCIES AND PROFESSIONAL ASSOCIATIONS—FEES AND DUES	—	—	—	—	—	—	—	29	24	20	15
NET PAYMENTS TO LABOR UNIONS	—	—	—	—	—	—	—	38	33	26	6
CLASSIFIED ADVERTISEMENTS AND PERSONAL BUSINESS SERVICES, N.E.C.	—	—	—	—	—	—	—	50	44	39	31

Class of Expenditure	1933	1934	1935	1936	1937	1938	1939	1940	1941	1942
H. EDUCATION (PRIVATE)	825	847	892	965	1,056	1,061	1,096	1,126	1,213	1,409
ORGANIZED EDUCATION [g]	428	438	460	497	549	571	582	595	645	766
Higher education	205	213	228	242	249	256	267	277	283	316
Secondary and elementary schools	121	121	122	140	174	192	195	198	202	215
Other schools and instruction	102	104	110	115	126	123	120	120	160	235
Commercial, business and trade schools—fees	16	18	22	25	28	28	26	24	54	132
Correspondence schools—fees	16	17	18	18	20	20	20	21	22	22
Other instruction (exc. athletics)—fees	70	69	70	72	78	75	74	75	84	81
UNORGANIZED EDUCATION [d]	397	409	432	468	507	490	514	531	568	643
Reading [r]	331	351	371	405	441	426	452	471	505	578
Foundations, museums and libraries	66	58	61	63	66	64	62	60	63	65
Foundation expenditures for education and research	53	45	47	49	51	48	46	44	47	49
Museums and libraries	13	13	14	14	15	16	16	16	16	16
I. RELIGION [g]	665	641	627	621	638	651	659	662	652	662
J. WELFARE (PRIVATE) [s]	355	348	356	412	388	370	371	451	443	566
PERSONAL REMITTANCES TO FOREIGN COUNTRIES—NET [s, t]	161	132	135	148	141	114	108	129	97	59
SOCIAL WELFARE AND FOREIGN-RELIEF AGENCIES	168	182	195	204	219	219	237	268	321	472
OTHER PRIVATE WELFARE	26	34	26	60	28	37	26	54	25	35
Foundation expenditures (exc. education and research)	18	15	16	16	17	16	16	15	16	16
Political organizations	8	19	10	44	11	21	10	39	9	19
K. OCCUPATIONAL AND MISCELLANEOUS EXPENSES [u]	82	126	149	168	237	232	248	280	317	368
WORKING EQUIPMENT	25	34	38	44	53	41	45	53	65	72
EMPLOYMENT AGENCIES AND PROFESSIONAL ASSOCIATIONS—FEES AND DUES	14	17	20	25	28	23	24	25	29	34
NET PAYMENTS TO LABOR UNIONS	15	44	56	60	114	129	140	160	178	211
CLASSIFIED ADVERTISEMENTS AND PERSONAL BUSINESS SERVICES, N.E.C.	28	31	35	39	42	39	39	42	45	51

Class of Expenditure	1943	1944	1945	1946	1947	1948	1949	1950	1951	1952
H. EDUCATION (PRIVATE)	1,683	1,716	1,778	2,077	2,415	2,647	2,804	2,950	3,189	3,447
Organized Education [g]	911	857	817	978	1,257	1,452	1,598	1,727	1,909	2,082
Higher education	363	356	365	430	606	702	774	804	871	930
Secondary and elementary schools	237	244	246	304	385	453	498	571	652	734
Other schools and instruction	311	257	206	244	266	297	326	352	386	418
Commercial, business and trade schools——fees	206	151	75	74	82	101	118	134	151	156
Correspondence schools—fees	22	22	22	25	27	28	28	29	29	30
Other instruction (exc. athletics)—fees	83	84	109	145	157	168	180	189	206	232
Unorganized Education [d]	772	859	961	1,099	1,158	1,195	1,206	1,223	1,280	1,365
Reading [r]	704	789	891	1,027	1,082	1,114	1,122	1,136	1,167	1,227
Foundations, museums and libraries	68	70	70	72	76	81	84	87	113	138
Foundation expenditures for education and research	52	54	54	55	59	63	65	67	93	117
Museums and libraries	16	16	16	17	17	18	19	20	20	21
I. RELIGION [g]	695	750	783	818	891	975	1,053	1,125	1,206	1,296
J. WELFARE (PRIVATE) [s]	786	972	936	1,004	850	968	885	901	934	1,038
Personal Remittances to Foreign Countries—Net [g, t]	135	176	163	234	169	216	195	187	197	207
Social Welfare and Foreign-Relief Agencies	625	743	746	730	649	686	655	666	692	735
Other Private Welfare	26	53	27	40	32	66	35	48	45	96
Foundation expenditures (exc. education and research)	17	18	18	20	22	24	25	26	34	37
Political organizations	9	35	9	20	10	42	10	22	11	59
K. OCCUPATIONAL AND MISCELLANEOUS EXPENSES [u]	422	412	407	443	546	555	542	565	600	600
Working Equipment	63	68	76	114	139	147	137	153	165	157
Employment Agencies and Professional Associations—Fees and dues	35	35	38	54	56	55	53	55	57	57
Net Payments to Labor Unions	265	250	229	199	265	260	260	263	281	279
Classified Advertisements and Personal Business Services, n.e.c.	59	59	64	76	86	93	92	94	102	107

Sources: Estimates for 1909–1927 based on William H. Lough, *High-Level Consumption*, McGraw-Hill, New York, 1935; Harold Barger, *Outlay and Income in the United States, 1921–1938*, National Bureau of Economic Research, New York, 1942; and Julius Weinberger, "Economic Aspects of Recreation," *Harvard Business Review*, Summer 1937.

Estimates for 1929–1952 based on *National Income and Product of the United States, 1929–1950* (1951 National Income Supplement to the *Survey of Current Business*), Table 30, and *Survey of Current Business*, July 1953, Table 30, except 1942–1952 estimates for "Cleaning and polishing preparations" and 1949–1952 estimates for "Museums and libraries," "Foundation expenditures (excluding education and research)" and "Political organizations," which were prepared by the staff of this study.

a. For 1929–1932, total consumption expenditures exceed the Commerce totals, which exclude expenditures for alcoholic beverages, except *Food, Liquor and Tobacco* after 1932, do not correspond to the Commerce main category totals for 1929–1952 owing to a different arrangement of expenditure items.

b. From 1929 to 1932, does not include alcoholic beverages.

c. Excludes nonconsumer purchased meals and beverages.

d. From 1909 to 1927, based on Lough linked to Commerce.

e. Estimates for 1909 to 1932 based on Lough.

f. From 1929 to 1952, 50 per cent of Commerce estimates for "laundering (in establishments)" are included under *Clothing, Accessories and Personal Care* and 50 per cent under *Household Equipment and Operation.*

g. From 1909 to 1927, Barger linked to Commerce, and Lough linked to Barger-Commerce.

h. From 1909 to 1927, extrapolated on basis of $10 per nonfarm family. (No data in Lough or Barger.)

i. From 1909 to 1927, estimated on basis of relationship between total financial expenses and sum of legal services, brokerage charges, etc., and interest on personal debt for subsequent years.

j. From 1909 to 1927, based on sales of the New York Stock Exchange multiplied by combined price index of 402 stocks, linked to Commerce.

k. From 1909 to 1927, estimated on basis of relationship to furniture and furnishings for subsequent years.

l. From 1909 to 1927, based on total consumer credit outstanding in 1929 carried back on basis of net annual changes (Mordecai Ezekiel in *American Economic Review*, March 1942, p. 27), linked to Commerce.

m. From 1909 to 1927, includes expenditures for horse-drawn vehicles and equipment and for blacksmiths' services roughly estimated (in millions) at $238 in 1909, $216 in 1914, $82 in 1919, $32 in 1921, $35 in 1923, $25 in 1925, and $22 in 1927.

n. From 1909 to 1927, equal to sum of railway intercity estimates based on Barger linked to Commerce, and Lough linked to Barger-Commerce, and all other intercity based on Lough linked to Commerce.

o. "Other foreign travel expenditures," plus "expenditures by United States government personnel (military and civilian)," minus "expenditures by foreigners in the United States."

p. For 1909–1927, estimated at 11 per cent of life insurance expenditures.

q. From 1909 to 1927, based on Weinberger linked to Commerce.

r. From 1929 to 1952, 42 per cent of Commerce estimates for "books and maps; magazines, newspapers and sheet music; and book rental and repair" are included under *Recreation* and 58 per cent under *Private Education.*

s. From 1909 to 1927, derived by subtracting estimates for "religion" from estimates for "religion and private welfare" based on Lough linked to Commerce.

t. "Personal cash remittances by Americans to foreign countries" minus "personal cash remittances by foreigners to the United States."

u. From 1909 to 1927, based on relationship to changes in total employment.

APPENDIX 4–5. PERCENTAGE DISTRIBUTION OF SELECTED CLASSES OF CONSUMPTION EXPENDITURES, 1909–1952

Class of Expenditure	1909	1914	1919	1921	1923	1925	1927	1929	1930	1931	1932
TOTAL CONSUMPTION EXPENDITURES											
Amount (*Millions*)	$28,814	$33,395	$60,573	$55,766	$66,594	$71,750	$74,569	$80,761	$72,389	$62,453	$50,108
Per Cent	100.00	100.00	100.00	100.00	100.00	100.00	100.00	100.00	100.00	100.00	100.00
A. FOOD, LIQUOR AND TOBACCO	34.00	34.99	36.29	30.11	28.70	29.46	29.15	28.94	29.17	28.14	27.18
FOOD AND BEVERAGES	31.82	32.80	33.93	27.45	26.48	27.34	26.98	26.84	27.16	25.75	24.54
Consumed inside the home	—	—	—	—	—	—	—	19.94	20.28	18.88	17.86
Consumed outside the home	—	—	—	—	—	—	—	4.42	4.67	4.79	4.88
Purchased meals and beverages	—	—	—	—	—	—	—	3.78	3.99	4.15	4.22
Hotels, restaurants, dining cars (inc. tips)	—	—	—	—	—	—	—	3.34	3.53	3.73	3.83
Schools, institutions, clubs, etc.	—	—	—	—	—	—	—	.44	.46	.42	.39
Food furnished government (including military) and commercial employees, and withdrawn by nonfarm proprietors	—	—	—	—	—	—	—	.64	.68	.64	.66
Food and nonalcoholic beverages	25.57	26.81	30.63	24.94	24.23	24.97	24.57	24.36	24.95	23.67	22.74
Alcoholic beverages	6.25	5.99	3.30	2.51	2.25	2.37	2.41	2.48	2.21	2.08	1.80
TOBACCO PRODUCTS AND SMOKING SUPPLIES	2.18	2.19	2.36	2.66	2.22	2.12	2.17	2.10	2.01	2.39	2.64
B. CLOTHING, ACCESSORIES AND PERSONAL CARE	14.85	14.10	15.80	16.74	16.70	15.41	15.81	14.75	14.37	14.27	13.26
CLOTHING AND RELATED PRODUCTS	13.94	13.19	14.78	15.66	15.39	14.15	14.41	13.37	12.93	12.70	11.63
Clothes and accessories	9.42	8.76	9.58	10.99	10.85	10.02	10.20	9.41	9.12	9.09	7.99
Shoes and other footwear	2.70	2.62	3.21	2.70	2.71	2.31	2.30	2.08	1.90	1.93	2.04
Jewelry and watches	.84	.78	1.10	.95	.82	.80	.77	.69	.71	.52	.50
Cleaning, repair and maintenance	.98	1.03	.89	1.02	1.01	1.02	1.14	1.19	1.20	1.16	1.10
Cleaning, repair and storage of garments, furs and shoes	—	—	—	—	—	—	—	.79	.77	.75	.70
Laundering (in establishments)	—	—	—	—	—	—	—	.29	.32	.31	.31
Watch, clock and jewelry repair and miscellaneous personal services	—	—	—	—	—	—	—	.11	.11	.10	.09
PERSONAL CARE	.91	.91	1.02	1.08	1.31	1.26	1.40	1.38	1.44	1.57	1.63
Toilet articles and preparations	.41	.42	.57	.59	.78	.67	.73	.73	.71	.81	.84
Barber shop, beauty parlor and related services	.50	.49	.45	.49	.53	.59	.67	.65	.72	.76	.79

984

Class of Expenditure	1933	1934	1935	1936	1937	1938	1939	1940	1941	1942
TOTAL CONSUMPTION EXPENDITURES										
Amount (*Millions*)	$46,346	$51,882	$56,215	$62,515	$67,121	$64,513	$67,466	$72,052	$82,255	$91,161
Per Cent	100.00	100.00	100.00	100.00	100.00	100.00	100.00	100.00	100.00	100.00
A. FOOD, LIQUOR AND TOBACCO	27.57	30.14	31.47	32.04	32.22	32.03	31.23	31.37	32.19	35.97
FOOD AND BEVERAGES	24.90	27.50	28.91	29.58	29.72	29.39	28.60	28.77	29.67	33.42
Consumed inside the home	20.24	22.30	23.44	24.00	23.68	23.37	22.39	22.43	22.78	25.22
Consumed outside the home	4.66	5.20	5.47	5.58	6.04	6.02	6.21	6.34	6.89	8.20
Purchased meals and beverages	3.96	4.49	4.75	4.89	5.34	5.34	5.56	5.68	6.06	6.92
Hotels, restaurants, dining cars (inc. tips)	3.60	4.14	4.40	4.54	4.98	4.99	5.23	5.36	5.74	6.58
Schools, institutions, clubs, etc.	.36	.35	.35	.35	.36	.35	.33	.32	.32	.34
Food furnished government (including military) and commercial employees, and withdrawn by nonfarm proprietors	.70	.71	.72	.69	.70	.68	.65	.66	.83	1.28
Food and nonalcoholic beverages	23.55	23.64	24.37	24.52	24.59	24.37	23.53	23.72	24.52	27.70
Alcoholic beverages	1.35	3.86	4.54	5.06	5.13	5.02	5.07	5.05	5.15	5.72
TOBACCO PRODUCTS AND SMOKING SUPPLIES	2.67	2.64	2.56	2.46	2.50	2.64	2.63	2.60	2.52	2.55
B. CLOTHING, ACCESSORIES AND PERSONAL CARE	12.75	13.72	13.52	13.25	13.07	13.46	13.58	13.53	14.00	15.72
CLOTHING AND RELATED PRODUCTS	11.32	12.25	12.10	11.87	11.64	11.99	12.09	11.99	12.53	14.18
Clothes and accessories	7.99	8.76	8.80	8.57	8.16	8.43	8.67	8.57	8.94	10.15
Shoes and other footwear	1.91	2.07	1.84	1.83	1.91	1.95	1.82	1.76	1.81	2.04
Jewelry and watches	.37	.38	.41	.43	.50	.50	.53	.56	.66	.78
Cleaning, repair and maintenance	1.05	1.04	1.05	1.04	1.07	1.11	1.07	1.10	1.12	1.21
Cleaning, repair and storage of garments, furs and shoes	.71	.71	.73	.73	.75	.79	.76	.78	.80	.86
Laundering (in establishments)	.27	.25	.24	.24	.24	.24	.23	.23	.22	.25
Watch, clock and jewelry repair and miscellaneous personal services	.07	.08	.08	.07	.08	.08	.08	.09	.10	.10
PERSONAL CARE	1.43	1.47	1.42	1.38	1.43	1.47	1.49	1.54	1.47	1.54
Toilet articles and preparations	.69	.73	.66	.63	.64	.68	.72	.71	.72	.78
Barber shop, beauty parlor and related services	.74	.74	.76	.75	.79	.79	.77	.83	.75	.76

Class of Expenditure	1943	1944	1945	1946	1947	1948	1949	1950	1951	1952
TOTAL CONSUMPTION EXPENDITURES										
Amount (*Millions*)	$102,244	$111,550	$123,079	$146,907	$165,570	$177,890	$180,588	$194,550	$208,108	$218,130
Per Cent	100.00	100.00	100.00	100.00	100.00	100.00	100.00	100.00	100.00	100.00
A. FOOD, LIQUOR AND TOBACCO	37.06	37.17	37.31	36.58	36.53	35.91	34.97	33.72	35.42	35.64
FOOD AND BEVERAGES	34.54	34.87	34.93	34.23	34.19	33.58	32.61	31.46	33.16	33.28
Consumed inside the home	24.98	24.58	24.03	25.28	26.19	26.05	25.35	24.58	25.89	26.00
Consumed outside the home	9.56	10.29	10.90	8.95	8.00	7.53	7.26	6.88	7.27	7.28
Purchased meals and beverages	7.69	7.94	8.47	7.84	7.17	6.71	6.47	6.09	6.24	6.21
Hotels, restaurants, dining cars (inc. tips)	7.35	7.63	8.15	7.47	6.74	6.25	6.03	5.67	5.79	5.75
Schools, institutions, clubs, etc.	.34	.31	.32	.37	.43	.46	.44	.42	.45	.46
Food furnished government (including military) and commercial employees, and withdrawn by nonfarm proprietors	1.87	2.35	2.43	1.11	.83	.82	.79	.79	1.03	1.07
Food and nonalcoholic beverages	28.68	28.58	28.62	28.33	28.83	29.00	28.22	27.30	29.10	29.21
Alcoholic beverages	5.86	6.29	6.31	5.90	5.36	4.58	4.39	4.16	4.06	4.07
TOBACCO PRODUCTS AND SMOKING SUPPLIES	2.52	2.30	2.38	2.35	2.34	2.33	2.36	2.26	2.26	2.36
B. CLOTHING, ACCESSORIES AND PERSONAL CARE	17.36	17.64	17.91	16.51	15.10	14.64	13.74	12.83	12.80	12.52
CLOTHING AND RELATED PRODUCTS	15.70	15.96	16.22	15.02	13.73	13.38	12.52	11.65	11.64	11.37
Clothes and accessories	11.62	11.98	12.11	10.82	9.80	9.66	8.94	8.21	8.22	8.05
Shoes and other footwear	1.87	1.80	1.85	1.91	1.80	1.70	1.64	1.58	1.59	1.51
Jewelry and watches	.91	.91	.98	.96	.81	.74	.70	.68	.67	.66
Cleaning, repair and maintenance	1.30	1.27	1.28	1.33	1.32	1.28	1.24	1.18	1.16	1.15
Cleaning, repair and storage of garments, furs and shoes	.94	.92	.92	.97	.97	.95	.93	.88	.87	.87
Laundering (in establishments)	.25	.25	.25	.25	.26	.25	.23	.22	.21	.20
Watch, clock and jewelry repair and miscellaneous personal services	.11	.10	.11	.11	.09	.08	.08	.08	.08	.08
PERSONAL CARE	1.66	1.68	1.69	1.49	1.37	1.26	1.22	1.18	1.16	1.15
Toilet articles and preparations	.83	.86	.89	.77	.73	.69	.66	.64	.63	.62
Barber shop, beauty parlor and related services	.83	.82	.80	.72	.64	.57	.56	.54	.53	.53

Class of Expenditure	1909	1914	1919	1921	1923	1925	1927	1929	1930	1931	1932
C. HOUSING AND UTILITIES	23.98	23.57	16.91	22.10	20.69	19.84	19.35	17.97	19.46	20.99	23.17
RENT AND IMPUTED RENT	19.31	18.63	13.28	17.36	15.94	15.96	15.18	14.14	15.18	16.39	17.89
Owner-occupied nonfarm dwellings—space-rental value	—	—	—	—	—	—	—	7.30	7.71	8.21	8.86
Tenant-occupied nonfarm dwellings (including lodging houses)—space rent	—	—	—	—	—	—	—	5.50	6.00	6.63	7.37
Rental value of farmhouses	—	—	—	—	—	—	—	1.03	1.15	1.21	1.31
Transient accommodations—clubs, schools and institutions	—	—	—	—	—	—	—	.31	.32	.34	.35
FUEL, ICE AND LIGHTING SUPPLIES	3.42	3.56	2.46	3.26	3.24	2.30	2.52	2.10	2.24	2.22	2.41
HOUSEHOLD UTILITIES	1.25	1.38	1.17	1.48	1.51	1.58	1.65	1.73	2.04	2.38	2.87
D. HOUSEHOLD EQUIPMENT AND OPERATION	11.76	11.06	12.11	12.05	13.49	13.98	14.71	16.44	15.24	15.24	15.20
FURNITURE AND FURNISHINGS	4.27	3.99	4.69	4.44	5.39	5.11	4.87	4.58	4.00	4.05	3.73
Furniture—new and secondhand	1.02	1.03	1.20	1.24	1.48	1.53	1.51	1.49	1.30	1.28	1.01
Floor coverings	.60	.51	.61	.57	.79	.78	.69	.60	.49	.54	.46
China, glassware, tableware and utensils	.81	.68	.79	.73	.94	.88	.84	.78	.61	.69	.81
Miscellaneous furnishings	1.84	1.77	2.09	1.90	2.18	1.92	1.83	1.71	1.60	1.54	1.45
MECHANICAL APPLIANCES	.50	.50	.66	.53	.77	.76	.89	.95	.93	.90	.69
DOMESTIC SERVICE (EXC. PRACTICAL NURSES)	2.47	2.09	1.60	1.80	1.79	1.85	1.92	1.86	1.79	1.61	1.46
COMMUNICATION	.60	.64	.71	.83	.83	.90	.97	1.06	1.16	1.23	1.35
Stationery, writing supplies and postage	.32	.30	.37	.38	.38	.38	.37	.37	.38	.35	.35
Telephone, telegraph, cable and wireless	.28	.34	.34	.45	.45	.52	.60	.69	.78	.88	1.00
CLEANING, REPAIR AND MAINTENANCE	.90	.92	1.03	.96	.98	.95	1.01	1.00	1.09	1.13	1.09
Cleaning and polishing preparations	—	—	—	—	—	—	—	.45	.49	.49	.45
Services	—	—	—	—	—	—	—	.55	.60	.64	.64
FINANCIAL, LEGAL, INSURANCE AND DEATH EXPENSES	3.02	2.92	3.42	3.49	3.73	4.41	5.05	6.99	6.27	6.32	6.88
Financial expenses	1.59	1.44	1.71	1.51	1.78	2.25	2.75	4.59	3.64	3.40	3.51
Legal services	.34	.30	.42	.45	.46	.47	.49	.50	.55	.65	.70
Life insurance handling expenses	.55	.65	.62	.88	.90	1.03	1.12	1.16	1.34	1.52	1.86
Death expenses	.54	.53	.67	.65	.59	.66	.69	.74	.74	.75	.81

APPENDIX 4-5 (continued)

Class of Expenditure	1933	1934	1935	1936	1937	1938	1939	1940	1941	1942
C. HOUSING AND UTILITIES	22.55	19.88	18.57	17.45	17.08	18.19	17.94	17.56	16.47	16.05
RENT AND IMPUTED RENT	16.94	14.53	13.52	12.61	12.48	13.54	13.25	12.79	11.99	11.62
Owner-occupied nonfarm dwellings—space-rental value	8.34	7.06	6.52	6.05	5.91	6.39	6.22	6.00	5.66	5.61
Tenant-occupied nonfarm dwellings (including lodging houses)—space rent	7.00	5.97	5.59	5.27	5.30	5.85	5.78	5.60	5.24	4.98
Rental value of farmhouses	1.27	1.19	1.10	.98	.95	.96	.92	.87	.80	.75
Transient accommodations—clubs, schools and institutions	.33	.31	.31	.31	.32	.34	.33	.32	.29	.28
FUEL, ICE AND LIGHTING SUPPLIES	2.65	2.60	2.44	2.41	2.26	2.15	2.20	2.29	2.23	2.28
HOUSEHOLD UTILITIES	2.96	2.75	2.61	2.43	2.34	2.50	2.49	2.48	2.25	2.15
D. HOUSEHOLD EQUIPMENT AND OPERATION	15.69	15.12	15.08	15.48	15.70	15.14	15.43	15.40	15.27	13.96
FURNITURE AND FURNISHINGS	3.74	3.84	3.94	4.43	4.50	4.22	4.57	4.68	4.95	4.78
Furniture—new and secondhand	1.00	.99	1.19	1.36	1.37	1.28	1.41	1.47	1.60	1.40
Floor coverings	.40	.46	.49	.61	.57	.50	.57	.58	.62	.59
China, glassware, tableware and utensils	.78	.78	.72	.73	.77	.73	.70	.72	.77	.74
Miscellaneous furnishings	1.56	1.61	1.54	1.73	1.79	1.71	1.89	1.91	1.96	2.05
MECHANICAL APPLIANCES	.88	1.00	1.09	1.17	1.26	1.10	1.15	1.23	1.42	.77
DOMESTIC SERVICE (EXC. PRACTICAL NURSES)	1.39	1.45	1.43	1.44	1.56	1.41	1.47	1.50	1.36	1.41
COMMUNICATION	1.36	1.23	1.21	1.17	1.17	1.25	1.26	1.27	1.25	1.31
Stationery, writing supplies and postage	.38	.39	.40	.41	.43	.44	.45	.46	.48	.46
Telephone, telegraph, cable and wireless	.98	.84	.81	.76	.74	.81	.81	.81	.77	.85
CLEANING, REPAIR AND MAINTENANCE	1.06	1.05	1.01	1.01	1.04	1.11	1.08	1.04	1.00	1.04
Cleaning and polishing preparations	.48	.50	.47	.48	.50	.55	.53	.49	.46	.46
Services	.58	.55	.54	.53	.54	.56	.55	.55	.54	.58
FINANCIAL, LEGAL, INSURANCE AND DEATH EXPENSES	7.26	6.55	6.40	6.26	6.17	6.05	5.90	5.68	5.29	4.65
Financial expenses	3.69	3.18	3.02	3.10	3.05	2.88	2.79	2.66	2.52	2.09
Legal services	.72	.69	.66	.61	.60	.61	.60	.59	.55	.52
Life insurance handling expenses	2.03	1.89	1.95	1.78	1.77	1.82	1.78	1.72	1.54	1.39
Death expenses	.82	.79	.77	.77	.75	.74	.73	.71	.68	.65

Class of Expenditure	1943	1944	1945	1946	1947	1948	1949	1950	1951	1952
C. HOUSING AND UTILITIES	15.04	14.43	13.68	12.26	12.32	12.87	13.52	13.97	14.10	14.55
RENT AND IMPUTED RENT	10.88	10.49	9.92	8.89	8.82	9.26	10.01	10.39	10.51	11.01
Owner-occupied nonfarm dwellings—space-rental value	5.39	5.38	5.26	4.88	5.03	5.39	5.96	6.27	6.45	6.79
Tenant-occupied nonfarm dwellings (including lodging houses)—space rent	4.50	4.14	3.68	3.06	2.79	2.85	3.05	3.09	2.99	3.12
Rental value of farmhouses	.71	.70	.70	.68	.74	.75	.72	.75	.78	.80
Transient accommodations—clubs, schools and institutions	.28	.27	.28	.27	.26	.27	.28	.28	.29	.30
FUEL, ICE AND LIGHTING SUPPLIES	2.18	2.02	1.93	1.74	1.89	1.97	1.74	1.74	1.67	1.54
HOUSEHOLD UTILITIES	1.98	1.92	1.83	1.63	1.61	1.64	1.77	1.84	1.92	2.00
D. HOUSEHOLD EQUIPMENT AND OPERATION	12.75	12.66	12.72	13.85	14.47	14.57	14.23	14.94	14.44	14.15
FURNITURE AND FURNISHINGS	4.43	4.28	4.32	5.19	5.11	5.07	4.73	4.89	4.71	4.43
Furniture—new and secondhand	1.22	1.18	1.27	1.59	1.65	1.66	1.58	1.70	1.62	1.60
Floor coverings	.58	.50	.44	.58	.63	.64	.53	.58	.55	.49
China, glassware, tableware and utensils	.61	.60	.68	.91	.87	.85	.79	.77	.74	.68
Miscellaneous furnishings	2.02	2.00	1.93	2.11	1.96	1.92	1.83	1.84	1.80	1.66
MECHANICAL APPLIANCES	.25	.13	.26	1.08	1.68	1.64	1.33	1.55	1.21	1.11
DOMESTIC SERVICE (EXC. PRACTICAL NURSES)	1.38	1.50	1.51	1.28	1.28	1.23	1.24	1.30	1.32	1.25
COMMUNICATION	1.40	1.49	1.54	1.38	1.33	1.38	1.46	1.49	1.53	1.59
Stationery, writing supplies and postage	.48	.54	.58	.50	.49	.44	.43	.42	.43	.43
Telephone, telegraph, cable and wireless	.92	.95	.96	.88	.84	.94	1.03	1.07	1.10	1.16
CLEANING, REPAIR AND MAINTENANCE	1.03	1.01	.91	.86	1.04	1.02	.97	.95	.94	.89
Cleaning and polishing preparations	.44	.41	.31	.25	.43	.41	.37	.37	.36	.32
Services	.59	.60	.60	.61	.61	.61	.60	.58	.58	.57
FINANCIAL, LEGAL, INSURANCE AND DEATH EXPENSES	4.26	4.25	4.18	4.06	4.03	4.23	4.50	4.76	4.73	4.88
Financial expenses	1.83	1.89	1.92	1.84	1.77	1.93	2.11	2.34	2.38	2.50
Legal services	.49	.50	.50	.51	.50	.53	.55	.56	.54	.53
Life insurance handling expenses	1.29	1.23	1.15	1.13	1.19	1.20	1.26	1.31	1.25	1.29
Death expenses	.65	.63	.61	.58	.57	.57	.58	.55	.56	.56

APPENDIX 4–5 (continued)

Class of Expenditure	1909	1914	1919	1921	1923	1925	1927	1929	1930	1931	1932
E. CONSUMER TRANSPORTATION	5.17	6.38	8.06	8.62	9.78	10.56	9.64	9.92	9.06	8.48	8.40
PRIVATE TRANSPORTATION	2.29	3.26	5.73	5.61	7.05	7.84	6.85	7.19	6.26	5.81	5.66
New cars and net purchases of used cars	.58	1.25	2.15	2.07	3.44	3.36	2.67	3.20	2.27	1.83	1.27
Automobile parts, repair and maintenance	.31	.55	1.27	1.09	1.34	1.78	1.88	1.62	1.47	1.42	1.37
Gasoline and oil	.43	.70	2.02	2.25	2.08	2.54	2.14	2.25	2.41	2.47	2.94
Luggage	.14	.12	.16	.14	.14	.13	.13	.12	.11	.09	.08
PUBLIC CARRIER TRANSPORTATION	2.88	3.12	2.33	3.01	2.73	2.72	2.79	2.73	2.80	2.67	2.74
Local	1.61	1.82	1.34	1.67	1.51	1.47	1.51	1.40	1.47	1.49	1.58
Streetcar and electric railway and local bus	—	—	—	—	—	—	—	1.02	1.07	1.13	1.24
Taxicabs—fares and tips	—	—	—	—	—	—	—	.27	.29	.24	.22
Steam railways (commutation) and ferries (foot passengers)	—	—	—	—	—	—	—	.11	.11	.12	.12
Intercity	.93	.99	.94	1.00	.88	.80	.76	.70	.64	.59	.59
Steam railway, sleeping and parlor cars (exc. commutation)	—	—	—	—	—	—	—	.51	.46	.40	.34
Bus	—	—	—	—	—	—	—	.07	.07	.08	.10
Airline	—	—	—	—	—	—	—	—	—	—	—
Other intercity	—	—	—	—	—	—	—	.12	.11	.11	.15
Foreign travel	.34	.31	.05	.34	.34	.45	.52	.63	.69	.59	.57
F. MEDICAL CARE AND INSURANCE	2.77	2.71	3.40	2.75	3.30	3.47	3.61	3.74	4.02	4.17	4.33
MEDICAL CARE	2.71	2.64	3.33	2.66	3.20	3.36	3.49	3.61	3.87	4.02	4.18
Drugs and appliances	.73	.77	.98	.82	.88	.84	.91	.91	.97	1.01	1.08
Personnel	1.51	1.36	1.90	1.52	1.97	2.14	2.14	2.20	2.34	2.38	2.33
Physicians	1.02	.89	1.18	.93	1.20	1.24	1.25	1.19	1.28	1.31	1.32
Dentists	.28	.28	.46	.33	.46	.53	.52	.60	.64	.66	.62
Private-duty trained nurses	.07	.07	.10	.11	.10	.13	.13	.14	.14	.14	.13
Other personnel	.14	.12	.16	.15	.21	.24	.24	.27	.28	.27	.26
Privately controlled hospitals and sanitariums	.47	.51	.45	.32	.35	.38	.44	.50	.56	.63	.77
INSURANCE—ACCIDENT, HEALTH AND PREPAYMENT	.06	.07	.07	.09	.10	.11	.12	.13	.15	.15	.15

Class of Expenditure	1933	1934	1935	1936	1937	1938	1939	1940	1941	1942
E. CONSUMER TRANSPORTATION	8.90	9.10	9.60	10.09	10.05	9.01	9.57	9.85	10.23	6.19
PRIVATE TRANSPORTATION	6.31	6.67	7.28	7.72	7.69	6.72	7.37	7.90	8.26	3.75
New cars and net purchases of used cars	1.68	1.98	2.68	3.07	2.96	1.90	2.49	3.09	3.29	.46
Automobile parts, repair and maintenance	1.41	1.48	1.44	1.47	1.45	1.40	1.57	1.59	1.68	1.10
Gasoline and oil	3.16	3.16	3.10	3.11	3.19	3.33	3.23	3.14	3.20	2.09
Luggage	.06	.05	.06	.07	.09	.09	.08	.08	.09	.10
PUBLIC CARRIER TRANSPORTATION	2.59	2.43	2.32	2.37	2.36	2.29	2.20	1.95	1.97	2.44
Local	1.57	1.48	1.42	1.36	1.32	1.31	1.31	1.26	1.19	1.43
Streetcar and electric railway and local bus	1.25	1.17	1.11	1.08	1.02	1.02	1.01	.99	.92	1.08
Taxicabs—fares and tips	.21	.21	.21	.20	.22	.22	.23	.21	.21	.29
Steam railways (commutation) and ferries (foot passengers)	.11	.10	.10	.08	.08	.07	.07	.06	.06	.06
Intercity	.58	.55	.51	.58	.58	.57	.58	.56	.57	.73
Steam railway, sleeping and parlor cars (exc. commutation)	.33	.33	.27	.34	.35	.33	.32	.30	.28	.40
Bus	.10	.08	.11	.12	.12	.13	.14	.14	.16	.23
Airline	.01	.01	.01	.01	.01	.01	.01	.02	.03	.02
Other intercity	.14	.13	.12	.11	.10	.10	.11	.10	.10	.08
Foreign travel	.44	.40	.39	.43	.46	.41	.31	.13	.21	.28
F. MEDICAL CARE AND INSURANCE	4.35	4.25	4.14	4.06	4.06	4.23	4.29	4.27	4.14	4.26
MEDICAL CARE	4.20	4.08	3.98	3.89	3.88	4.02	4.06	4.04	3.90	4.01
Drugs and appliances	1.12	1.14	1.08	1.04	1.08	1.14	1.16	1.15	1.16	1.22
Personnel	2.30	2.23	2.18	2.18	2.12	2.16	2.17	2.16	2.07	2.08
Physicians	1.33	1.31	1.30	1.31	1.27	1.29	1.28	1.27	1.21	1.18
Dentists	.60	.57	.54	.53	.52	.55	.57	.58	.57	.60
Private-duty trained nurses	.13	.12	.11	.11	.10	.09	.09	.08	.07	.07
Other personnel	.24	.23	.23	.23	.23	.23	.23	.23	.22	.23
Privately controlled hospitals and sanitariums	.78	.71	.72	.67	.68	.72	.73	.73	.67	.71
INSURANCE—ACCIDENT, HEALTH AND PREPAYMENT	.15	.17	.16	.17	.18	.21	.23	.23	.24	.25

Class of Expenditure	1943	1944	1945	1946	1947	1948	1949	1950	1951	1952
E. CONSUMER TRANSPORTATION	5.92	6.03	6.62	8.27	9.37	9.90	11.21	12.10	11.18	10.99
PRIVATE TRANSPORTATION	2.86	2.74	3.07	5.81	7.10	7.64	8.91	10.00	9.03	8.73
New cars and net purchases of used cars	.45	.39	.39	1.90	2.98	3.33	4.36	5.29	4.27	3.82
Automobile parts, repair and maintenance	1.13	1.16	1.26	1.77	1.87	1.86	1.89	2.09	2.07	2.12
Gasoline and oil	1.17	1.08	1.31	2.01	2.13	2.34	2.57	2.53	2.60	2.70
Luggage	.11	.11	.11	.13	.12	.11	.09	.09	.09	.09
PUBLIC CARRIER TRANSPORTATION	3.06	3.29	3.55	2.46	2.27	2.26	2.30	2.10	2.15	2.26
Local	1.62	1.55	1.42	1.33	1.21	1.19	1.16	1.07	1.03	1.00
Streetcar and electric railway and local bus	1.21	1.16	1.07	.91	.79	.80	.79	.72	.68	.67
Taxicabs—fares and tips	.35	.33	.30	.38	.37	.35	.32	.31	.31	.29
Steam railways (commutation) and ferries (foot passengers)	.06	.06	.05	.04	.05	.04	.05	.04	.04	.04
Intercity	1.03	1.00	.94	.79	.68	.65	.60	.53	.56	.59
Steam railway, sleeping and parlor cars (exc. commutation)	.65	.60	.55	.42	.35	.33	.28	.23	.24	.25
Bus	.30	.31	.28	.24	.20	.19	.18	.16	.16	.15
Airline	.02	.03	.05	.07	.07	.07	.08	.09	.11	.13
Other intercity	.06	.06	.06	.06	.06	.06	.06	.05	.05	.06
Foreign travel	.41	.74	1.19	.34	.38	.42	.54	.50	.56	.67
F. MEDICAL CARE AND INSURANCE	4.27	4.35	4.18	4.20	4.15	4.21	4.34	4.34	4.32	4.42
MEDICAL CARE	4.00	4.05	3.88	3.89	3.84	3.89	4.01	4.01	4.01	4.05
Drugs and appliances	1.30	1.27	1.23	1.15	1.05	1.03	1.01	.99	1.01	1.00
Personnel	1.96	2.02	1.90	1.95	1.95	1.97	2.04	2.01	1.96	1.96
Physicians	1.09	1.15	1.09	1.13	1.18	1.20	1.26	1.25	1.22	1.23
Dentists	.59	.57	.53	.56	.50	.50	.51	.49	.47	.47
Private-duty trained nurses	.06	.07	.06	.06	.06	.06	.06	.06	.06	.06
Other personnel	.22	.23	.22	.20	.21	.21	.21	.21	.21	.20
Privately controlled hospitals and sanitariums	.74	.76	.75	.79	.84	.89	.96	1.01	1.04	1.09
INSURANCE—ACCIDENT, HEALTH AND PREPAYMENT	.27	.30	.30	.31	.31	.32	.33	.33	.31	.37

Class of Expenditure	1909	1914	1919	1921	1923	1925	1927	1929	1930	1931	1932
G. RECREATION	2.98	2.99	3.56	3.71	3.94	3.96	4.21	4.75	4.88	4.60	4.20
THEATERS, ENTERTAINMENTS AND AMUSEMENTS	.66	.65	.63	.78	.82	.85	1.09	1.19	1.29	1.42	1.30
Motion picture theaters	—	—	—	.54	.50	.51	.70	.89	1.01	1.15	1.05
Legitimate theaters, opera and entertainments of non-profit organizations (exc. athletics)	—	—	—	—	—	—	—	.16	.13	.13	.12
Other commercial amusements (exc. athletics)	—	—	—	—	—	—	—	.14	.15	.14	.13
SPECTATOR SPORTS	—	—	—	.05	.06	.06	.06	.08	.09	.09	.09
READING, HOBBIES AND PETS	.72	.67	.69	.78	.80	.82	.85	.84	.84	.84	.80
Reading	.36	.39	.34	.43	.41	.44	.47	.44	.45	.49	.49
Hobbies and pets	.36	.28	.35	.35	.39	.38	.38	.40	.39	.35	.31
ORGANIZATIONS AND CLUBS	.46	.46	.44	.48	.40	.43	.42	.41	.45	.49	.53
PARTICIPANT RECREATION	.08	.08	.09	.24	.23	.21	.22	.27	.29	.30	.29
Pari-mutuel and nonvending coin machines—net receipts	—	—	—	—	—	—	—	.02	.02	.02	.02
Billiard parlors and bowling alleys	—	—	—	—	—	—	—	.07	.08	.08	.07
Golf instruction, club rental and fees	—	—	—	—	—	—	—	.11	.12	.13	.13
Other participant recreation	—	—	—	—	—	—	—	.07	.07	.07	.07
RADIOS, TELEVISION AND MUSICAL INSTRUMENTS	.58	.58	1.10	.79	.96	1.03	.96	1.29	1.31	.80	.57
SPORTS EQUIPMENT	.48	.55	.61	.59	.67	.56	.61	.67	.61	.66	.62
H. EDUCATION (PRIVATE)	1.44	1.48	1.24	1.34	1.22	1.25	1.35	1.45	1.59	1.77	1.84
ORGANIZED EDUCATION	.60	.61	.58	.52	.54	.56	.62	.71	.82	.95	1.02
Higher education	.46	.43	.43	.38	.39	.40	.45	.27	.34	.40	.45
Secondary and elementary schools	.14	.18	.15	.14	.15	.16	.17	.20	.23	.30	.32
Other schools and instruction	—	—	—	—	—	—	—	.24	.25	.25	.25
UNORGANIZED EDUCATION	.84	.87	.66	.82	.68	.69	.73	.74	.77	.82	.82
Reading	.70	.72	.55	.68	.56	.57	.60	.61	.62	.68	.67
Foundations, museums and libraries	.14	.15	.11	.14	.12	.12	.13	.13	.15	.14	.15
I. RELIGION	1.04	.90	1.01	1.10	1.03	1.09	1.12	1.13	1.23	1.34	1.48

APPENDIX 4-5 (continued)

Class of Expenditure	1933	1934	1935	1936	1937	1938	1939	1940	1941	1942
G. RECREATION	4.03	4.02	4.01	4.17	4.37	4.36	4.44	4.54	4.52	4.56
THEATERS, ENTERTAINMENTS AND AMUSEMENTS	1.27	1.23	1.22	1.23	1.25	1.24	1.21	1.21	1.15	1.27
Motion picture theaters	1.04	1.00	.99	1.00	1.01	1.03	.98	.98	.92	1.06
Legitimate theaters, opera and entertainments of non-profit organizations (exc. athletics)	.09	.08	.08	.08	.08	.09	.10	.10	.10	.10
Other commercial amusements (exc. athletics)	.14	.15	.15	.15	.16	.12	.13	.13	.13	.11
SPECTATOR SPORTS	.11	.12	.12	.13	.13	.14	.14	.13	.12	.09
READING, HOBBIES AND PETS	.83	.85	.86	.88	.93	.93	.93	.94	.92	.96
Reading	.52	.49	.48	.47	.48	.48	.48	.47	.44	.46
Hobbies and pets	.31	.36	.38	.41	.45	.45	.45	.47	.48	.50
ORGANIZATIONS AND CLUBS	.50	.43	.40	.36	.35	.35	.34	.32	.28	.26
PARTICIPANT RECREATION	.29	.32	.33	.36	.41	.41	.42	.43	.43	.39
Pari-mutuel and nonvending coin machines—net receipts	.03	.06	.08	.10	.13	.16	.15	.17	.18	.17
Billiard parlors and bowling alleys	.07	.08	.08	.09	.11	.09	.10	.10	.10	.09
Golf instruction, club rental and fees	.12	.10	.10	.09	.09	.09	.09	.09	.08	.07
Other participant recreation	.07	.08	.07	.08	.08	.07	.08	.07	.07	.06
RADIOS, TELEVISION AND MUSICAL INSTRUMENTS	.45	.48	.48	.57	.61	.57	.66	.75	.82	.84
SPORTS EQUIPMENT	.58	.59	.60	.64	.69	.72	.74	.76	.80	.75
H. EDUCATION (PRIVATE)	1.78	1.63	1.59	1.54	1.57	1.64	1.62	1.56	1.47	1.54
ORGANIZED EDUCATION	.92	.84	.82	.79	.82	.88	.86	.82	.78	.84
Higher education	.44	.41	.40	.39	.37	.39	.39	.38	.34	.35
Secondary and elementary schools	.26	.23	.22	.22	.26	.30	.29	.27	.25	.23
Other schools and instruction	.22	.20	.20	.18	.19	.19	.18	.17	.19	.26
UNORGANIZED EDUCATION	.86	.79	.77	.75	.75	.76	.76	.74	.69	.70
Reading	.72	.68	.66	.65	.65	.66	.67	.66	.61	.63
Foundations, museums and libraries	.14	.11	.11	.10	.10	.10	.09	.08	.08	.07
I. RELIGION	1.43	1.23	1.12	.99	.95	1.01	.98	.92	.79	.73

Class of Expenditure	1943	1944	1945	1946	1947	1948	1949	1950	1951	1952
G. RECREATION	4.09	4.27	4.41	5.38	5.22	5.01	5.07	5.25	4.89	4.81
THEATERS, ENTERTAINMENTS AND AMUSEMENTS	1.22	1.37	1.35	1.29	1.10	1.01	.99	.87	.80	.74
Motion picture theaters	1.01	1.13	1.11	1.03	.85	.77	.74	.64	.57	.52
Legitimate theaters, opera and entertainments of non-profit organizations (exc. athletics)	.11	.12	.12	.12	.11	.10	.10	.09	.09	.08
Other commercial amusements (exc. athletics)	.10	.12	.12	.14	.14	.14	.15	.14	.14	.14
SPECTATOR SPORTS	.07	.08	.10	.16	.16	.16	.16	.14	.13	.12
READING, HOBBIES AND PETS	1.04	1.10	1.14	1.12	1.06	1.04	1.04	1.00	1.00	1.03
Reading	.50	.51	.53	.50	.47	.46	.45	.42	.40	.41
Hobbies and pets	.54	.59	.61	.62	.59	.58	.59	.58	.60	.62
ORGANIZATIONS AND CLUBS	.24	.23	.25	.26	.26	.27	.28	.26	.25	.25
PARTICIPANT RECREATION	.38	.42	.43	.51	.46	.44	.43	.39	.38	.40
Pari-mutuel and nonvending coin machines—net receipts	.18	.23	.23	.28	.24	.23	.21	.18	.18	.19
Billiard parlors and bowling alleys	.08	.07	.07	.08	.08	.07	.07	.07	.06	.06
Golf instruction, club rental and fees	.06	.06	.07	.08	.07	.07	.08	.07	.07	.08
Other participant recreation	.06	.06	.06	.07	.07	.07	.07	.07	.07	.07
RADIOS, TELEVISION AND MUSICAL INSTRUMENTS	.51	.39	.39	.98	1.12	1.08	1.22	1.63	1.37	1.28
SPORTS EQUIPMENT	.63	.68	.75	1.06	1.06	1.02	.95	.96	.96	.99
H. EDUCATION (PRIVATE)	1.65	1.54	1.44	1.41	1.46	1.49	1.55	1.52	1.53	1.58
ORGANIZED EDUCATION	.89	.77	.66	.66	.76	.82	.88	.89	.92	.95
Higher education	.36	.32	.29	.29	.37	.40	.43	.42	.42	.43
Secondary and elementary schools	.23	.22	.20	.21	.23	.25	.27	.29	.31	.33
Other schools and instruction	.30	.23	.17	.16	.16	.17	.18	.18	.19	.19
UNORGANIZED EDUCATION	.76	.77	.78	.75	.70	.67	.67	.63	.61	.63
Reading	.69	.71	.72	.70	.65	.63	.62	.58	.56	.56
Foundations, museums and libraries	.07	.06	.06	.05	.05	.04	.05	.05	.05	.07
I. RELIGION	.68	.67	.64	.56	.54	.55	.58	.58	.58	.59

Class of Expenditure	1909	1914	1919	1921	1923	1925	1927	1929	1930	1931	1932
J. WELFARE (PRIVATE)	1.80	1.61	1.39	1.35	.91	.74	.82	.69	.77	.81	.79
PERSONAL REMITTANCES TO FOREIGN COUNTRIES—NET	1.23	1.11	.88	.56	.39	.42	.39	.36	.35	.37	.36
SOCIAL WELFARE AND FOREIGN-RELIEF AGENCIES	—	—	—	—	—	—	—	.28	.35	.39	.33
OTHER PRIVATE WELFARE	—	—	—	—	—	—	—	.05	.07	.05	.10
K. OCCUPATIONAL AND MISCELLANEOUS EXPENSES	.21	.21	.23	.13	.24	.24	.23	.22	.21	.19	.15

Class of Expenditure	1933	1934	1935	1936	1937	1938	1939	1940	1941	1942
J. WELFARE (PRIVATE)	.77	.67	.63	.66	.58	.57	.55	.62	.54	.62
PERSONAL REMITTANCES TO FOREIGN COUNTRIES—NET	.35	.25	.24	.24	.21	.17	.16	.18	.12	.06
SOCIAL WELFARE AND FOREIGN-RELIEF AGENCIES	.36	.35	.35	.33	.33	.34	.35	.37	.39	.52
OTHER PRIVATE WELFARE	.06	.07	.04	.09	.04	.06	.04	.07	.03	.04
K. OCCUPATIONAL AND MISCELLANEOUS EXPENSES	.18	.24	.27	.27	.35	.36	.37	.38	.38	.40

Class of Expenditure	1943	1944	1945	1946	1947	1948	1949	1950	1951	1952
J. WELFARE (PRIVATE)	.77	.87	.76	.68	.51	.54	.49	.46	.45	.48
PERSONAL REMITTANCES TO FOREIGN COUNTRIES—NET	.13	.16	.13	.16	.10	.12	.11	.10	.10	.10
SOCIAL WELFARE AND FOREIGN-RELIEF AGENCIES	.61	.66	.61	.49	.39	.38	.36	.34	.33	.34
OTHER PRIVATE WELFARE	.03	.05	.02	.03	.02	.04	.02	.02	.02	.04
K. OCCUPATIONAL AND MISCELLANEOUS EXPENSES	.41	.37	.33	.30	.33	.31	.30	.29	.29	.27

Sources: See Appendix 4–4 and footnotes.

APPENDIX 4–6. CONSUMPTION EXPENDITURES IN 1952 CLASSIFIED ACCORDING TO SENSITIVITY TO CHANGES IN DISPOSABLE PERSONAL INCOME, 1929–1940

(Millions)

Commodities and Services	Total	Insensitive (Less than 8% change in expenditures with 10% change in disposable income)	Somewhat Sensitive (Between 8% and 12% change in expenditures with 10% change in disposable income)	Sensitive (More than 12% change in expenditures with 10% change in disposable income)
TOTAL CONSUMPTION EXPENDITURES	$218,130	$75,189	$108,369	$34,572
A. FOOD, LIQUOR AND TOBACCO [a]	77,750	5,474	71,592	684
FOOD AND BEVERAGES				
Food purchased for off-premise consumption	54,527	—	54,527	—
Food produced and consumed on farms	2,180	—	2,180	—
Purchased meals and beverages [b]				
Retail, service and amusement establishments	11,909	—	11,909	—
Hotels	1,223	—	1,223	—
Dining and buffet cars	84	—	—	84
Schools and school fraternities	346	346	—	—
Institutions, clubs and industrial lunchrooms	658	—	—	658
Tips	473	—	473	—
Food furnished government (including military) and commercial employees, and withdrawn by nonfarm proprietors	2,343	—	2,343	—
TOBACCO PRODUCTS AND SMOKING SUPPLIES	5,155	5,155	—	—
B. CLOTHING, ACCESSORIES AND PERSONAL CARE [c]	27,301	1,751	22,216	3,334
CLOTHING AND RELATED PRODUCTS				
Clothing and accessories except footwear	17,096	—	17,096	—
Standard clothing issued to military personnel [d]	336	336	—	—
Dressmakers and seamstresses (not in shops)	88	—	—	88
Costume and dress suit rental	7	—	7	—
Net purchases from secondhand clothing dealers	10	10	—	—
Net purchases from pawnbrokers and miscellaneous secondhand stores	24	—	24	—
Shoes and other footwear	3,300	—	3,300	—
Jewelry and watches	1,424	—	—	1,424
Shoe cleaning and repair	242	242	—	—
Fur storage and repair	97	—	—	97
Cleaning, dyeing, pressing, alteration, storage and repair of garments, n.e.c. (in shops)	1,552	—	—	1,552
Laundering in establishments [e]	437	—	437	—
Miscellaneous personal services	26	—	—	26
Watch, clock and jewelry repairs	147	—	—	147
PERSONAL CARE				
Toilet articles and preparations	1,352	—	1,352	—
Barber shop services / Beauty parlor services / Baths and masseurs	1,163	1,163	—	—

APPENDIX 4–6 (continued)

Commodities and Services	Total	Insensitive	Somewhat Sensitive	Sensitive
C. HOUSING AND UTILITIES	31,732	31,349	383	—
RENT AND IMPUTED RENT				
Owner-occupied nonfarm dwellings— space-rental value	14,818	14,818	—	—
Tenant-occupied nonfarm dwellings— space rent	6,811	6,811	—	—
Rental value of farmhouses	1,740	1,740	—	—
Transient hotels and tourist cabins	383	—	383	—
Clubs, schools and institutions	262	262	—	—
FUEL, ICE AND LIGHTING SUPPLIES	3,350	3,350	—	—
HOUSEHOLD UTILITIES				
Electricity	2,418	2,418	—	—
Gas	1,448	1,448	—	—
Water	502	502	—	—
D. HOUSEHOLD EQUIPMENT AND OPERATION [e]	30,875	15,097	3,517	12,261
FURNITURE AND FURNISHINGS				
Furniture	3,461	—	—	3,461
Net purchases from secondhand furniture and antique dealers	26	26	—	—
Floor coverings, durable house furnishings, n.e.c., and products of custom establishments, n.e.c.	2,341	—	—	2,341
China, glassware, tableware and utensils, and miscellaneous household paper products	1,782	1,782	—	—
Semidurable housefurnishings	2,057	—	2,057	—
MECHANICAL APPLIANCES				
Refrigerators, and washing and sewing machines ⎫ Miscellaneous electrical appliances (exc. radios) ⎬ Cooking and portable heating equipment ⎭	2,433	—	—	2,433
DOMESTIC SERVICE (EXC. PRACTICAL NURSES)	2,734	—	—	2,734
COMMUNICATION				
Writing equipment, stationery, etc.	641	—	—	641
Postage	283	283	—	—
Telephone	2,509	2,509	—	—
Telegraph, cable and wireless	26	—	26	—
CLEANING, REPAIR AND MAINTENANCE				
Cleaning and polishing preparations	692	—	692	—
Services				
Laundering in establishments [e]	437	—	437	—
Upholstery and furniture repair	146	146	—	—
Rug, drapery and mattress cleaning and repair	86	—	—	86
Care of electrical equipment (exc. radios) and stoves	188	—	188	—
Miscellaneous household operation services	33	33	—	—
Express charges	36	—	36	—
Moving expenses and warehousing	328	328	—	—

Commodities and Services	Total	Insensitive	Somewhat Sensitive	Sensitive
FINANCIAL, LEGAL, INSURANCE AND DEATH EXPENSES				
Financial expenses				
Brokerage charges and interest, and investment counseling	349	—	—	349
Trust services of banks	102	102	—	—
Bank service charges for deposit accounts, check collection and foreign exchange	230	230	—	—
Money order fees	68	68	—	—
Other financial services furnished	2,558	2,558	—	—
Fire and theft insurance on personal property (net payments)	81	—	81	—
Safety deposit box rental	55	55	—	—
Interest on personal debt	2,004	2,004	—	—
Legal services	1,156	1,156	—	—
Expense of handling life insurance— life insurance companies	2,675	2,675	—	—
Fraternal and assessment associations	140	140	—	—
Death expenses				
Funeral and burial services	790	790	—	—
Cemeteries and crematories	212	212	—	—
Monuments and tombstones	216	—	—	216
E. CONSUMER TRANSPORTATION	23,968	9,979	2,042	11,947
PRIVATE TRANSPORTATION				
New cars and net purchases of used cars	8,342	—	—	8,342
Tires and tubes ⎫ Parts and accessories ⎬	2,072	—	—	2,072
Automobile repair, greasing, washing, parking, storage and rental	1,770	—	1,770	—
Automobile insurance—net payments	788	788	—	—
Gasoline and oil	5,887	5,887	—	—
Luggage	190	—	—	190
PUBLIC CARRIER TRANSPORTATION				
Street car, electric railway and local bus	1,451	1,451	—	—
Taxicabs—fares and tips	641	—	—	641
Steam railways (commutation)	89	89	—	—
Ferries (foot passengers)	6	6	—	—
Steam railway (exc. commutation)	489	—	—	489
Sleeping and parlor cars—fares and tips	47	—	—	47
Intercity bus	335	335	—	—
Airline	272	—	272	—
Baggage transfer, carriage, storage and excise charges	8	—	—	8
Coastal and inland waterway	22	22	—	—
Bridge, tunnel, ferry and road tolls	100	100	—	—
Foreign travel				
Payments to U.S. vessels	158	—	—	158
Other foreign travel expenditures—net payments	1,301	1,301	—	—

Commodities and Services	Total	Insensitive	Somewhat Sensitive	Sensitive
F. MEDICAL CARE AND INSURANCE	9,634	4,190	5,077	367
MEDICAL CARE				
Drug preparations and sundries	1,623	1,623	—	—
Ophthalmic products and orthopedic appliances	554	—	554	—
Physicians	2,676	—	2,676	—
Dentists	1,028	—	1,028	—
Private-duty trained nurses	125	125	—	—
Osteopathic physicians	128	—	128	—
Chiropractors	98	—	98	—
Chiropodists and podiatrists	48	48	—	—
Practical nurses and midwives	120	—	—	120
Miscellaneous curative and healing professions	45	—	45	—
Privately controlled hospitals and sanitariums	2,389	2,389	—	—
INSURANCE				
Net payments to group hospitalization and health associations	184	—	—	184
Student fees for medical care	5	5	—	—
Accident and health insurance—net payments	548	—	548	—
Mutual accident and sick benefit associations—net payments	63	—	—	63
G. RECREATION	10,489	2,383	3,005	5,101
THEATERS, ENTERTAINMENTS AND AMUSEMENTS				
Motion picture theaters	1,134	1,134	—	—
Legitimate theaters and opera	87	—	—	87
Entertainments of nonprofit organizations (exc. athletics)	73	—	73	—
Ticket brokers' markup on admissions	7	—	—	7
Purchase of programs	8	8	—	—
Amusement devices and parks	36	—	36	—
Sightseeing buses and guides	13	—	13	—
Commercial amusements, n.e.c.	250	—	250	—
SPECTATOR SPORTS				
Professional baseball	49	—	49	—
Professional football	10	10	—	—
Professional hockey	6	6	—	—
Horse and dog race tracks	42	42	—	—
College football	105	105	—	—
Other amateur spectator sports	56	56	—	—
READING, HOBBIES AND PETS				
Reading [e]	888	620 [f]	—	268 [g]
Photo developing and printing	141	—	—	141
Photographic studios	301	—	301	—
Collectors' net acquisitions of stamps and coins	12	—	—	12
Veterinary service and purchase of pets	59	—	59	—
Flowers, seed and potted plants	836	—	—	836

Commodities and Services	Total	Insensitive	Somewhat Sensitive	Sensitive
ORGANIZATIONS AND CLUBS				
Camp fees	49	49	—	—
Athletic and social clubs—dues and fees	222	—	222	—
School fraternities—dues and fees	23	23	—	—
Luncheon clubs	20	20	—	—
Fraternal, patriotic and women's organizations (exc. school and insurance)—net payments	242	242	—	—
PARTICIPANT RECREATION				
Pari-mutuel net receipts	269	—	—	269
Nonvending coin machines — receipts minus payments	150	—	—	150
Billiard parlors and bowling alleys	129	—	—	129
Daily-fee golf courses—greens fees	38	38	—	—
Golf instruction, club rental and caddy fees	131	—	131	—
Dancing, riding, shooting, skating and swimming places	92	—	92	—
Private flying operations	9	—	—	9
Boat and bicycle rental, storage and repair	19	—	19	—
Hunting dog purchase and training, and sports guide service	30	30	—	—
RADIOS, TELEVISION AND MUSICAL INSTRUMENTS				
Radios, phonographs, parts and records } Pianos and other musical instruments }	2,324	—	—	2,324
Radio repair	476	—	476	—
SPORTS EQUIPMENT				
Nondurable toys and sports supplies	1,284	—	1,284	—
Wheel goods, durable toys and sports equipment	790	—	—	790
Boats and pleasure aircraft	79	—	—	79
H. PRIVATE EDUCATION [h]	3,447	2,659	418	370
ORGANIZED EDUCATION				
Higher education	930	930	—	—
Secondary and elementary schools	734	734	—	—
Commercial, business and trade schools—fees	156	—	156	—
Correspondence schools—fees	30	—	30	—
Other instruction (exc. athletics)—fees	232	—	232	—
UNORGANIZED EDUCATION				
Reading	1,227	857 [1]	—	370 [g]
Foundation expenditures for education and research	117	117	—	—
Museums and libraries	21	21	—	—
I. RELIGION	1,296	1,296	—	—
J. PRIVATE WELFARE	1,038	979	—	59
Personal Remittances to Foreign Countries—net	207	207	—	—
Social Welfare and Foreign-Relief Agencies	735	735	—	—
Foundation Expenditures (exc. education and research)	37	37	—	—
Political Organizations	59	—	—	59

APPENDIX 4–6 (continued)

Commodities and Services	Total	Insensitive	Somewhat Sensitive	Sensitive
K. OCCUPATIONAL AND MISCELLA-NEOUS EXPENSES	600	32	119	449
WORKING EQUIPMENT				
Tools	145	—	—	145
Miners' expenditures for explosives, lamps and smithing	12	—	12	—
EMPLOYMENT AGENCIES AND PROFESSIONAL ASSOCIATIONS—FEES AND DUES				
Theatrical employment agency fees	22	22	—	—
Nontheatrical employment agency fees	25	—	—	25
Employees dues and fees to professional associations	10	10	—	—
NET PAYMENTS TO LABOR UNIONS	279	—	—	279
CLASSIFIED ADVERTISEMENTS AND PERSONAL BUSINESS SERVICES, N.E.C.				
Classified advertisements	66	—	66	—
Personal business services, n.e.c.	41	—	41	—

Sources: Survey of Current Business, following issues: July 1953, Table 30, p. 22; January 1945, Louis J. Paradiso, "Classification of Consumer Expenditures by Income Elasticity," Table 3, p. 10; January 1950, Clement Winston and Mabel A. Smith, "Income Sensitivity of Consumption Expenditures," Table 1, p. 18.

a. Excludes $1,148 million of nonconsumer purchases included in the detailed figures under "Purchased meals and beverages."

b. Includes alcoholic beverages.

c. Includes one half of $874 million for laundering listed by Department of Commerce.

d. Standard clothing issued to military personnel assumed to be insensitive.

e. Includes 42 per cent of total expenditures for magazines, newspapers and sheet music; books and maps; book rental and repair.

f. Includes $617 million for magazines, newspapers and sheet music and $3 million for book rental and repair.

g. Books and maps.

h. Includes 58 per cent of total expenditures for items listed under footnote e.

i. Includes $851 million for magazines, newspapers and sheet music and $6 million for book rental and repair.

Appendix 4–7. Methods Used to Estimate Probable Expenditures for Consumption Goods and Services and for Capital Goods in 1960

Estimates of effective demand, or probable expenditures, for categories of consumption goods and services and capital goods, presented in Chapters 4 to 15, are based on the assumption of high levels of employment and income presented in Chapters 2 and 4. Probable expenditures for consumption goods and services and capital goods are estimated in dollars of 1950 purchasing power.

These estimates for 1960—like all estimates of future quantities—are based on the analysis and projection of past trends and relationships. In general, three methods are available for estimating future consumption or production on the basis of past experience:

(1) Extension of long-term (secular) trends for individual categories of expenditure or production

(2) Projection of past relationships between individual production or consumption categories, on the one hand, and (for example) gross national product or disposable income, on the other, to the assumed higher future levels for the latter

(3) (For consumption expenditures) Calculation of expenditures for assumed future patterns of income distribution on the basis of past consumption expenditures by income groups

1. *Extension of long-term trends.* This technique aims to discover a persistent and steady trend in the data under examination through the elimination or smoothing out of random and cyclical fluctuations and the extension of the resulting secular trends into the future. The trend may be measured in terms of physical volumes or quantities (e.g., steel production) or dollar amounts at current or constant prices (e.g., consumption expenditures for shoes), either on a total or per capita basis; or it may be measured in terms of the relative importance of a component within a larger class (e.g., expenditures for food as percentage of total consumption expenditures). In any event, a computed trend, to be significant, should reveal year-to-year changes in amounts or percentages that are either of the same magnitude or change in magnitude in a regular manner. In the estimates prepared for this survey, the data were analyzed to discover trends in the *relative importance* of the various components, as such trends appeared to move with the greatest regularity of change.

2. *Correlation of relationships.* This method estimates the future volume of production or consumption of various goods and services on the basis of past relationships between such production or consumption volumes, on the one hand, and gross national product, national income or disposable income, on the other. The method is based on a measurement of the extent to which one variable (e.g., consumption expenditures for food) increases or decreases with increases or decreases in the other (e.g., disposable income). As all of the statistical series with which this survey is concerned are time series characterized by both cyclical fluctuations and secular trends, the correlation of past relationships is partly a comparison of the fluctuations of functionally related variables and partly a comparison of their secular trends. To the extent that they reveal trend relationships and to the extent that trend and cyclical relationships correspond, the results obtained by this type of analysis should be substantially the same as those obtained by the simple extension of past trends (as in (1) above).

Wherever possible, correlation analysis was used as well as trend analysis, each supplementing and acting as a check on the other. Frequently when one method led to alternative possible estimates, the other indicated the most valid one. In either case, the validity of the results is questionable unless the time series covers a period sufficiently long for a secular trend to be observed, or for a correlation demonstrably to measure more than a relation peculiar to only one cycle or one phase of it. The more violent the fluctuations, the more important it is for the time series to cover a long period and the more questionable the results obtained from data covering only a short period. In some instances—particularly where past relationships were not clearly ascertainable, where the period of observation was too short or where rapid technological changes were likely to upset past trends—the "mechanical results" obtained by a projection of past trends or by correlation analysis were modified by judgment as to future probabilities.

3. *Patterns of expenditure by income groups.* This technique is applicable only to consumption expenditures, and cannot be used for estimating capital outlays. This method requires (a) an estimate of the future pattern of the distribution of consumer income by income groups and (b) a knowledge of the proportions of income spent at different income levels for various kinds of consumption goods and services. Although this survey presents estimates of cash income distribution in 1960 (see Chapter 4) and some information is available as to expenditures by income groups for past years, this method was not used for estimating future consumption expenditures in the present survey. Implied in the extension of past trends is the assumption that such long-term changes as have occurred in income distribution and savings and expenditure patterns will be projected into the future.

CONSUMPTION EXPENDITURE ESTIMATES

The process of estimating expenditures for the consumption goods and services involved the following steps: (1) estimates for 1960 of each of the individual items were obtained through correlation with disposable income (as separately estimated in Chapter 4), certain items being adjusted upward to allow for increased consumption due to technological advances; (2) these items were grouped into major categories, and the resulting items and groups compared with estimates obtained through extending the secular trend in the proportion of each of these items and groups to total consumption expenditures; (3) discrepancies between the two sets of estimates were adjusted by re-examining the secular trend and the line of regression, except that the upward adjustments due to technological advances were accepted; (4) finally, to make the aggregate of the items thus arrived at equal to total consumption expenditures, as independently estimated in Chapter 4, further slight adjustments were made within the "tolerances" allowed by the trend and regression lines.

The correlation of the consumption items with disposable income was performed graphically, not mathematically. It is true that the latter method would have meant greater accuracy, but such accuracy would have been largely spurious. It was frequently impossible to fit a satisfactory line to the data for the whole period; it was then necessary to choose from among lines fitted to parts of the period the one believed to represent a long-term rather than a short-term relationship. Furthermore, fitting a straight or curved line to the data also involved the exercise of judgment. These considerations, added to the necessity of making subsequent adjustments as indicated above, meant that the mechanical accuracy of mathematical computation would have been largely dissipated in subsequent modifications of the estimates, and might even have been worthless if followed blindly without the exercise of prior judgment in choosing the time period for the correlation.

Data on consumer expenditures were available for varying periods of time. For some items data went back as far as 1909, but for others 1929 was the earliest available year (see Appendix 4-4). Moreover, data for the depression years 1930-1934 and the war years 1941-1945 could not be used in many instances. Also, data for the postwar years had to be used with great care to avoid the special impacts of, for example, heavy consumer durable purchases after the outbreak of the Korean War.

The projected expenditures for consumption goods and services in 1960 are shown in Table A.

CAPITAL EXPENDITURE ESTIMATES

Expenditures for capital facilities tend to fluctuate much more widely than other types of expenditure. This makes it difficult to derive estimates based on past trends and relationships. In addition, data were available for a shorter period than in the case of consumption outlays. For the most part, the capital expenditure data covered the years 1920-1952 but, as in the case of consumption expenditures, data for the depression years 1930-1934 and the war years 1941-1945 generally were not used. In addition, the data for the post-World War II years had to be used carefully since in some instances they were unduly affected by temporary backlogs and Korean War demands.

Total capital outlays were determined by the basic assumptions underlying the 1960 projections in Chapter 4: as the sum of private capital outlays, which were set by the total of private savings, and public capital outlays, which were estimated on the basis of their long-run relationship to other capital outlays. The total was then distributed among three components — private productive facilities, developmental and public enterprise construction, and consumer construction. An estimate for public equipment was also prepared but not shown separately.

The major component of capital expenditure — private productive facilities — was projected on the basis of the long-run relationship between private productive facilities and private gross national product (see Chapter 15). Individual items within the private productive facilities group were estimated either from correlations with gross national product or on the basis of secular trends in the ratio of outlays for each item to total capital outlays. In some instances, both methods gave much the same results. The "Commercial and miscellaneous" item was a residual derived from the total for private productive facilities and the sum of the other items.

Both the totals for developmental and public enterprise construction and consumer construction and the individual items within these components, except for highway and residential construction and one residual item, were estimated either by correlation with gross national product or from secular trends of ratios to total capital outlays. Capital outlays for residential construction in 1960 were estimated on the basis of rent-capital ratios as explained in Chapter 7. The projection for highway construction is discussed in Chapter 9. Minor adjustments were made in the totals for these two components to achieve consistency with the over-all total.

The estimates for all the capital facilities items are shown in Table B.

APPENDIX 4–7 (continued)

TABLE A. ESTIMATED CONSUMPTION EXPENDITURES, 1960

Item	Amount		Percentage Distribution		Percentage Increase over
	1950	*1960*	*1950*[a]	*1960*[a]	*1950*[a]
	(Millions at 1950 Prices)				
TOTAL CONSUMPTION EXPENDITURES	$194,550	$241,500	100.00	100.00	24.1
A. FOOD, LIQUOR AND TOBACCO	65,606	81,800	33.72	33.87	24.7
FOOD AND BEVERAGES	61,208	76,300	31.46	31.59	24.7
Consumed inside the home	47,816	59,200	24.58	24.51	23.8
Consumed outside the home	13,392	17,100	6.88	7.08	27.7
Food and nonalcoholic beverages	53,108	65,900	27.30	27.29	24.1
Alcoholic beverages	8,100	10,400	4.16	4.30	28.4
TOBACCO PRODUCTS AND SMOKING SUPPLIES	4,398	5,500	2.26	2.28	25.1
B. CLOTHING, ACCESSORIES AND PERSONAL CARE	24,961	32,050	12.83	13.27	28.4
CLOTHING AND RELATED PRODUCTS	22,658	29,300	11.65	12.13	29.3
Clothes and accessories	15,975	20,700	8.21	8.57	29.6
Shoes and other footwear	3,080	3,800	1.58	1.57	23.4
Jewelry and watches	1,312	1,800	.68	.75	37.2
Cleaning, repair and maintenance	2,291	3,000	1.18	1.24	30.9
Cleaning, repair and storage of garments, furs and shoes	1,714	2,260	.88	.93	31.9
Laundering (in establishments)	427	550	.22	.23	28.8
Watch, clock and jewelry repair and miscellaneous personal services	150	190	.08	.08	26.7
PERSONAL CARE	2,303	2,750	1.18	1.14	19.4
Toilet articles and preparations	1,245	1,580	.64	.66	26.9
Services	1,058	1,170	.54	.48	10.6
C. HOUSING AND UTILITIES	27,184	32,220	13.97	13.76	22.2
RENT AND IMPUTED RENT	20,210	24,700	10.39	10.23	22.2
Owner-occupied nonfarm dwellings—space-rental value	12,195	15,050	6.27	6.23	23.4
Tenant-occupied nonfarm dwellings (inc. lodging houses)—space rent	6,002	7,150	3.09	2.96	19.1
Other	2,013	2,500	1.03	1.04	24.2
FUEL, ICE AND LIGHTING SUPPLIES	3,392	4,280	1.74	1.77	26.2
HOUSEHOLD UTILITIES	3,582	4,240	1.84	1.76	18.4
Electricity	1,955	2,350	1.01	.98	20.2
Gas	1,177	1,380	.60	.57	17.2
Water	450	510	.23	.21	13.3
D. HOUSEHOLD EQUIPMENT AND OPERATION	29,060	35,350	14.94	14.64	21.6
FURNITURE AND FURNISHINGS	9,513	11,850	4.89	4.91	24.6
Furniture—new and secondhand	3,311	4,090	1.70	1.69	23.5
Floor coverings	1,128	1,300	.58	.54	15.2

Item	Amount		Percentage Distribution		Percentage Increase over
	1950	1960	1950[a]	1960[a]	1950[a]

(Millions at 1950 Prices)

Item	1950	1960	1950[a]	1960[a]	1950[a]
FURNITURE AND FURNISHINGS (contd.)					
China, glassware, tableware and utensils	$ 1,500	$ 1,920	.77	.80	28.0
Miscellaneous furnishings	3,574	4,540	1.84	1.88	27.0
MECHANICAL APPLIANCES	3,021	3,830	1.55	1.59	26.8
DOMESTIC SERVICE (EXC. PRACTICAL NURSES)	2,525	2,910	1.30	1.20	15.2
COMMUNICATION	2,892	3,610	1.49	1.50	24.8
Stationery, writing supplies and postage	821	1,040	.42	.43	26.7
Telephone, telegraph, cable and wireless	2,071	2,570	1.07	1.07	24.1
CLEANING, REPAIR AND MAINTENANCE	1,844	2,330	.95	.96	26.4
Cleaning and polishing preparations	718	890	.37	.36	24.0
Services	1,126	1,440	.58	.60	27.9
FINANCIAL, LEGAL, INSURANCE AND DEATH EXPENSES	9,265	10,820	4.76	4.48	16.8
Financial expenses	4,552	5,200	2.34	2.15	14.2
Legal services	1,081	1,330	.56	.55	23.0
Life insurance handling expense	2,555	2,960	1.31	1.23	15.9
Death expenses	1,077	1,330	.55	.55	23.5
E. CONSUMER TRANSPORTATION	23,546	28,510	12.10	11.80	21.1
PRIVATE TRANSPORTATION	19,456	22,950	10.00	9.50	18.0
New cars and net purchases of used cars	10,285	10,760	5.29	4.46	4.6
Auto parts, repair and maintenance	4,070	5,070	2.09	2.10	24.6
Gasoline and oil	4,928	6,900	2.53	2.86	29.5
Luggage	173	220	.09	.09	27.2
PUBLIC CARRIER TRANSPORTATION	4,090	5,560	2.10	2.30	35.9
Local	2,084	2,650	1.07	1.10	27.2
Street car, electric railway and bus	1,390	1,760	.72	.73	26.6
Taxicabs—fares and tips	608	815	.31	.34	34.0
Steam railways (commutations) and ferries (foot passengers)	86	75	.04	.03	—12.8
Intercity	1,030	1,410	.53	.58	36.9
Railway	446	440	.23	.18	—1.3
Bus	310	350	.16	.14	12.9
Airline	174	500	.09	.21	187.4
Other intercity	100	120	.05	.05	20.0
Foreign travel	976	1,500	.50	.62	53.7
F. MEDICAL CARE AND INSURANCE	8,441	10,740	4.34	4.45	27.2
MEDICAL CARE	7,806	9,720	4.01	4.03	24.5
Drugs and appliances	1,927	2,450	.99	1.02	27.1
Personnel	3,916	4,850	2.01	2.01	23.9
Physicians	2,435	2,960	1.25	1.23	21.6
Dentists	959	1,230	.49	.51	28.3
Private-duty trained nurses	114	150	.06	.06	31.6
Other personnel	408	510	.21	.21	25.0
Privately controlled hospitals and sanitariums	1,963	2,420	1.01	1.00	23.3

Item	Amount		Percentage Distribution		Percentage Increase over
	1950	1960	1950[a]	1960[a]	1950[a]
	(Millions at 1950 Prices)				
INSURANCE—ACCIDENT, HEALTH AND PREPAYMENT	$ 635	$ 1,020	.33	.42	60.6
G. RECREATION	10,211	12,670	5.25	5.25	24.1
THEATERS, ENTERTAINMENTS AND AMUSEMENTS	1,693	2,090	.87	.87	23.4
Motion picture theaters	1,247	1,530	.64	.64	22.7
Legitimate theaters, opera and entertainments of nonprofit organizations (exc. athletics)	171	200	.09	.08	17.0
Other commercial amusements (exc. athletics)	275	360	.14	.15	30.9
SPECTATOR SPORTS	266	330	.14	.14	24.1
READING, HOBBIES AND PETS	1,945	2,540	1.00	1.05	30.6
Reading	822	1,090	.42	.45	32.6
Hobbies and pets	1,123	1,450	.58	.60	29.1
ORGANIZATIONS AND CLUBS	511	610	.26	.25	19.4
PARTICIPANT RECREATION	763	1,040	.39	.43	36.3
RADIOS, TELEVISION AND MUSICAL INSTRUMENTS	3,172	3,570	1.63	1.48	12.5
SPORTS EQUIPMENT	1,861	2,490	.96	1.03	33.8
H. PRIVATE EDUCATION	2,950	4,030	1.52	1.67	36.6
ORGANIZED EDUCATION	1,727	2,450	.89	1.02	41.9
Higher education	804	900	.42	.37	11.9
Secondary and elementary schools	571	1,150	.29	.48	101.4
Other schools and instruction	352	400	.18	.17	13.6
UNORGANIZED EDUCATION	1,223	1,580	.63	.65	29.2
Reading	1,136	1,480	.58	.61	30.3
Foundations, museums and libraries	87	100	.05	.04	14.9
I. RELIGION	1,125	1,300	.58	.54	15.6
J. PRIVATE WELFARE	901	1,140	.46	.47	26.5
NET PERSONAL REMITTANCES TO FOREIGN COUNTRIES	187	230	.10	.09	23.0
SOCIAL WELFARE AND FOREIGN RELIEF AGENCIES	666	840	.34	.35	26.1
POLITICAL ORGANIZATIONS AND FOUNDATION EXPENDITURES (EXC. EDUCATIONAL AND RESEARCH)	48	70[b]	.02	.03	45.8
K. OCCUPATIONAL AND MISCELLANEOUS EXPENSES	565	690	.29	.28	22.1

Sources: 1950, Appendix 4–4; 1960, see text.

a. The start of the Korean War in 1950 was accompanied by relatively heavy spending for such items as automobiles, refrigerators and television sets and, consequently, by relatively light spending for such items as food and clothing. Comparisons of 1950 and 1960 expenditures should be made with this fact in mind.

b. Based on trend of expenditures in presidential election years, when spending for political organizations is particularly high.

Note: Minus sign denotes decrease.

APPENDIX 4–7 (continued)

TABLE B. ESTIMATED EXPENDITURES FOR CAPITAL GOODS, 1950 AND 1960 [a]

Item	Amount		Percentage Distribution	
	1950	1960	1950	1960
	(Millions at 1950 Prices)			
Total expenditures[a]	$52,355	$66,500	100.0	100.0
Private productive facilities[b]	30,263	42,310	57.8	63.6
Agriculture	3,996	5,700	7.6	8.6
Nonresidential construction	872	1,200	1.7	1.8
Farm equipment and machinery	3,124	4,500	6.0	6.8
Mining	707	700	1.4	1.1
Manufacturing	7,491	11,000	14.3	16.5
Transportation	2,308	3,150	4.4	4.7
Railroads	1,111	1,500	2.1	2.3
Transit	168	250	.3	.4
Oil pipeline	141	200	.3	.3
Other transportation	888	1,200	1.7	1.8
Communication	1,104	1,850	2.1	2.8
Utilities	3,309	4,300	6.3	6.5
Electric light and power	2,187	2,900	4.2	4.4
Gas	1,122	1,400	2.1	2.1
Commercial and miscellaneous[c]	11,348	15,610	21.7	23.5
Developmental and public enterprise construction	4,821	7,300	9.2	11.0
Highways	2,272	3,500	4.3	5.3
Conservation and development	881	1,250	1.7	1.9
Sewage disposal	383	500	.7	.8
Water supply	276	300	.5	.5
Other[d]	1,009	1,750	1.9	2.6
Consumer construction	16,771	16,240	32.0	24.4
Residential	13,708	12,000	26.2	18.0
Religious	409	550	.8	.8
Educational	1,427	1,970	2.7	3.7
Recreational	387	520	.7	.8
Hospital	840	1,200	1.6	1.8

Sources: Appendix 4–8 and text discussion.

a. Total includes public equipment, not shown separately. These estimates cover all expenditures for publicly and privately owned plant and equipment except (a) expenditures for publicly owned military and naval plant and equipment and (b) expenditures by state governments for equipment.

b. Including equipment charged to current account; these charges are not included in the detailed industry figures but are grouped with commercial and miscellaneous expenditures.

c. Includes facilities not allocable by industry, equipment charged to current account and statistical discrepancies arising from use of varied sources.

d. Includes (a) public industrial and commercial and public administration construction and public construction, not elsewhere classified, and (b) private sewer, water, road and bridge construction and miscellaneous nonstructural items such as parks and playgrounds.

APPENDIX 4–8. EXPENDITURES FOR CAPITAL GOODS, 1920–1952 [a] (Millions)

Class	1920	1921	1922	1923	1924	1925	1926	1927	1928	1929	1930
Total expenditures [a]	$13,042	$9,637	$11,364	$14,718	$15,327	$16,712	$17,898	$17,396	$17,395	$17,748	$14,096
Private	11,833	8,102	9,654	13,039	13,322	14,469	15,677	14,867	14,790	15,145	11,109
Public [b]	1,209	1,535	1,710	1,679	2,005	2,243	2,221	2,529	2,605	2,603	2,987
Construction	6,988	6,255	7,922	9,616	10,698	11,731	12,471	12,322	11,926	11,174	9,012
Private	5,797	4,740	6,263	8,010	8,806	9,601	10,338	9,925	9,456	8,707	6,183
Public	1,191	1,515	1,659	1,606	1,892	2,130	2,133	2,397	2,470	2,467	2,829
Equipment	6,054	3,382	3,442	5,102	4,629	4,981	5,427	5,074	5,469	6,574	5,084
Private	6,036	3,362	3,391	5,029	4,516	4,868	5,339	4,942	5,334	6,438	4,926
Public [b]	18	20	51	73	113	113	88	132	135	136	158
Private productive facilities [c]	9,260	5,559	5,736	8,007	7,597	8,149	9,204	8,778	9,155	10,726	8,332
Agriculture	1,362	522	597	780	705	812	839	849	871	943	699
Nonresidential construction	300	125	150	175	165	170	160	195	175	160	86
Farm machinery and equipment	1,062	397	447	605	540	642	679	654	696	783	613
Mining	373	667	627	630	621	757	819	746	746	857	633
Manufacturing	3,165	1,367	1,542	2,050	1,731	1,969	2,350	2,108	2,306	2,739	1,908
Durable goods industries											
Primary iron and steel	190	100	100	120	180	200	230	160	200	150	300
Primary nonferrous metals	—	—	—	—	—	—	—	—	—	—	—
Fabricated metal products	—	—	—	—	—	—	—	—	—	—	—
Electrical machinery and equipment	—	—	—	—	—	—	—	—	—	—	—
Nonelectrical machinery	—	—	—	—	—	—	—	—	—	—	—
Motor vehicles and equipment	187	64	59	105	118	116	140	160	149	186	118
Transportation equip. (exc. motor vehicles)	—	—	—	—	—	—	—	—	—	—	—
Stone, clay and glass products	168	115	130	198	157	181	234	202	283	241	120
Lumber and lumber products	159	71	110	118	105	120	143	94	89	104	50
Other durable goods [e]	—	—	—	—	—	—	—	—	—	—	—
Nondurable goods industries											
Food and kindred products / Beverages }	354	214	257	248	234	272	371	343	423	378	267
Textile mill products	300	183	209	260	182	203	198	212	212	235	130
Apparel and related products / Paper and allied products }	158	89	63	102	93	85	92	116	129	137	110
Chemicals and allied products	—	—	—	—	—	—	—	—	—	—	—
Petroleum and coal products											
Petroleum refining	100	55	65	65	65	65	85	80	120	125	85
Rubber products	105	25	23	22	21	29	32	41	38	54	22
Printing and publishing	113	85	107	124	114	130	129	114	102	119	81
Other nondurable goods [g]	—	—	—	—	—	—	—	—	—	—	—
Unallocated	1,331	366	419	688	462	568	696	586	561	1,010	625

APPENDIX 4-8 (continued)

Class	1931	1932	1933	1934	1935	1936	1937	1938	1939	1940	1941
Total expenditures [a]	$9,886	$5,588	$4,895	$6,479	$7,960	$11,445	$13,048	$11,415	$13,182	$15,009	$18,587
Private	7,130	3,657	3,214	4,240	5,650	7,812	9,847	7,935	9,334	11,560	14,305
Public [b]	2,756	1,931	1,681	2,239	2,310	3,633	3,201	3,480	3,848	3,449	4,282
Construction	6,587	3,704	3,043	3,873	4,495	6,768	7,462	7,318	8,441	8,695	10,760
Private	3,968	1,876	1,431	1,709	2,299	3,281	4,403	3,960	4,757	5,452	6,629
Public	2,619	1,828	1,612	2,164	2,196	3,487	3,059	3,358	3,684	3,243	4,131
Equipment	3,299	1,884	1,852	2,606	3,465	4,677	5,586	4,097	4,741	6,314	7,827
Private	3,162	1,781	1,783	2,531	3,351	4,531	5,444	3,975	4,577	6,108	7,676
Public [b]	137	103	69	75	114	146	142	122	164	206	151
Private productive facilities [c]	5,064	2,771	2,589	3,466	4,462	6,002	7,651	5,613	6,302	8,188	10,343
Agriculture	371	173	203	381	597	786	956	771	800	901	1,184
Nonresidential construction	38	13	20	30	65	85	107	92	106	95	128
Farm machinery and equipment	333	160	183	351	532	701	849	679	694	806	1,056
Mining	381	356	275	510	650	858	962	664	326	480	584
Manufacturing	1,054	574	717	950	1,157	1,545	2,160	1,393	1,943	2,723	3,672
Durable goods industries	—	—	—	—	—	—	—	—	756	—	—
Primary iron and steel	120	40	50	40	122	200	316	132	122	—	—
Primary nonferrous metals	—	—	—	—	—	—	—	—	30	—	—
Fabricated metal products	—	—	—	—	—	—	—	—	91	—	—
Electrical machinery and equipment	—	—	—	—	—	—	—	—	49	—	—
Nonelectrical machinery	—	—	—	—	—	—	—	—	100	—	—
Motor vehicles and equipment	77	69	48	78	130	153	159	155	133	—	—
Transportation equip. (exc. motor vehicles)	—	—	—	—	—	—	—	—	42	—	—
Stone, clay and glass products	76	38	28	43	65	99	99	68	71	—	—
Lumber and lumber products	30	15	20	22	32	47	62	43	[a]	—	—
Other durable goods [e]	—	—	—	—	—	—	—	—	118	—	—
Nondurable goods industries	—	—	—	—	—	—	—	—	1,187	—	—
Food and kindred products	171	131	207	195	185	268	320	217	205	—	—
Beverages									38	—	—
Textile mill products	93	56	79	101	89	116	157	91	136 [f]	—	—
Apparel and related products	54	28	29	40	66	98	183	70	[f]	—	—
Paper and allied products	—	—	—	—	—	—	—	—	67	—	—
Chemicals and allied products	65	55	65	70	55	90	144	132	176	—	—
Petroleum and coal products	—	—	—	—	—	—	—	—		—	—
Petroleum refining									403	—	—
Rubber products	17	11	13	16	15	22	32	27	38	—	—
Printing and publishing	52	30	27	41	54	75	82	57	[f]	—	—
Other nondurable goods [g]	—	—	—	—	—	—	—	—		—	—
Unallocated	299	101	151	304	344	377	606	401	124	2,723	3,672

Class	1942	1943	1944	1945	1946	1947	1948	1949	1950	1951	1952
Total expenditures [a]	$14,427	$10,342	$10,753	$13,190	$25,001	$34,589	$42,897	$42,828	$52,355	$56,756	$58,959
Private	8,578	6,408	8,418	11,378	22,619	31,109	37,852	36,150	45,032	47,712	48,821
Public [b]	5,849	3,934	2,335	1,812	2,382	3,480	5,045	6,678	7,333	9,044	10,138
Construction	9,365	6,098	4,948	5,541	12,465	17,258	22,571	23,721	29,556	31,576	32,866
Private	3,721	2,326	2,712	3,833	10,291	14,029	17,904	17,453	22,733	23,132	23,428
Public	5,644	3,772	2,236	1,708	2,174	3,229	4,667	6,268	6,823	8,444	9,438
Equipment	5,062	4,244	5,805	7,649	12,536	17,331	20,326	19,107	22,799	25,180	26,093
Private	4,857	4,082	5,706	7,545	12,328	17,080	19,948	18,697	22,299	24,580	25,393
Public [b]	205	162	99	104	208	251	378	410	500	600	700
Private productive facilities [c]	6,595	5,365	7,418	10,036	17,734	23,538	27,615	26,017	30,263	34,524	35,617
Agriculture	1,187	1,017	1,357	1,362	1,850	2,926	3,716	3,848	3,996	4,620	4,210
Nonresidential construction	125	163	175	167	447	714	806	793	872	875	860
Farm machinery and equipment	1,062	854	1,182	1,195	1,403	2,212	2,910	3,055	3,124	3,745	3,350
Mining	354	311	431	383	427	691	882	792	707	929	880
Manufacturing	3,154	2,768	3,034	3,983	6,790	8,703	9,134	7,149	7,491	10,852	11,994
Durable goods industries	—	—	—	1,590	3,112	3,407	3,483	2,593	3,135	5,168	5,784
Primary iron and steel	—	—	—	198	500	638	772	596	599	1,198	1,538
Primary nonferrous metals	—	—	—	54	93	178	193	151	134	310	595
Fabricated metal products	—	—	—	216	356	370	343	271	350	433	355
Electrical machinery and equipment	—	—	—	123	282	304	289	216	245	373	376
Nonelectrical machinery	—	—	—	316	511	519	527	383	411	683	772
Motor vehicles and equipment	—	—	—	262	591	504	474	348	510	851	896
Transportation equip. (exc. motor vehicles)	—	—	—	56	109	95	106	87	82	219	253
Stone, clay and glass products	—	—	—	100	241	326	269	181	280	397	318
Lumber and lumber products	—	—	—	d	d	d	d	d	d	d	d
Other durable goods [e]	—	—	—	265	429	473	510	360	524	704	682
Nondurable goods industries	—	—	—	2,393	3,678	5,296	5,651	4,555	4,356	5,684	6,210
Food and kindred products	—	—	—	337	513	669	721	626	523	579	540
Beverages	—	—	—	97	157	277	332	249	237	274	245
Textile mill products	—	—	—	209	342	510	618	471	450	531	400
Apparel and related products	—	—	—	f	f	f	f	f	f	f	f
Paper and allied products	—	—	—	116	232	371	383	298	327	420	354
Chemicals and allied products	—	—	—	376	800	1,060	941	670	771	1,247	1,451
Petroleum and coal products	—	—	—	879	1,087	1,736	2,100	1,789	1,587	2,102	2,596
Petroleum refining	—	—	—	—	—	—	—	—	—	—	—
Rubber products	—	—	—	118	139	143	102	81	102	150	139
Printing and publishing	—	—	—	f	f	f	f	f	f	f	f
Other nondurable goods [g]	—	—	—	261	408	530	454	371	359	382	484
Unallocated	3,154	2,768	3,034	—	—	—	—	—	—	—	—

Class	1920	1921	1922	1923	1924	1925	1926	1927	1928	1929	1930
Private productive facilities (continued)											
Transportation	$827[h]	$676[h]	$620[h]	$1,302[h]	$1,094[h]	$898[h]	$1,030[h]	$949[h]	$853[h]	$1,058[h]	$1,015[h]
Railroads	630	550	434	1,077	901	728	883	751	673	840	865
Local transit	162	100	151	180	133	123	116	130	135	135	124
Oil pipeline	35	26	35	45	60	47	31	68	45	83	26
Other transportation	1	1	1	1	1	1	1	1	1	1	1
Communication	261	287	325	396	480	478	504	488	563	758	762
Utilities	568	379	588	916	1,112	1,012	1,037	1,059	974	995	1,040
Electric light and power	448	289	406	744	851	789	717	729	702	757	814
Gas	120	90	182	172	261	223	320	330	272	238	226
Commercial and miscellaneous [k]	2,704	1,661	1,437	1,933	1,854	2,223	2,625	2,579	2,842	3,376	2,270
Developmental and public enterprise construction	1,037	1,261	1,332	1,290	1,574	1,745	1,732	2,028	2,044	2,042	2,404
Private [m]	81	74	90	105	117	113	113	126	110	103	85
Public	956	1,187	1,242	1,185	1,457	1,632	1,619	1,902	1,934	1,939	2,319
Highways	656	853	876	805	987	1,082	1,067	1,222	1,289	1,266	1,516
Conservation and development	55	52	48	65	79	73	61	63	72	115	137
Sewage disposal	67	78	88	90	108	133	145	174	183	127	142
Water supply	86	100	113	113	155	145	140	138	117	126	201
Industrial and commercial	n	n	n	n	n	n	n	n	n	n	n
Public administration	38	51	55	44	39	56	70	84	85	109	128
Public construction, n.e.c.	54	53	62	68	89	143	136	221	188	196	195
Consumer construction	2,727	2,797	4,245	5,348	6,043	6,705	6,874	6,458	6,061	4,844	3,202
Private	2,492	2,469	3,828	4,927	5,608	6,207	6,360	5,963	5,525	4,316	2,692
Residential	2,281	2,203	3,479	4,542	5,193	5,656	5,737	5,320	4,926	3,772	2,182
Religious	55	71	103	117	130	165	177	179	168	147	135
Educational	22	32	61	83	91	108	108	106	107	120	118
Recreational	104	119	132	128	131	199	255	252	224	173	148
Hospital	30	44	53	57	63	79	83	106	100	104	109
Public	235	328	417	421	435	498	514	495	536	528	510
Residential	n	—	—	—	—	—	—	—	—	—	—
Educational	190	274	342	346	353	400	399	367	378	389	364
Recreational	12	14	15	20	22	37	47	48	50	38	28
Hospital	33	40	60	55	60	61	68	80	108	101	118

Class	1931	1932	1933	1934	1935	1936	1937	1938	1939	1940	1941
Private productive facilities (continued)											
Transportation	$ 558[h]	$ 257[h]	$ 153[h]	$ 306[h]	$ 302[h]	$ 452[h]	$ 682[h]	$ 341[h]	$ 645	$ 976	$1,054
Railroads	360	164	101	218	168	308	524	240	280	439	559
Local transit	132	61	46	78	117	109	101	83	107	113	105
Oil pipeline	66	32	6	10	17	35	57	18	30	26	51
Other transportation	—	—	—	—	—	—	—	1	228	398	339
Communication	496	308	208	225	250	316	419	383	302	370	540
Utilities	650	345	196	209	273	428	601	530	520	693	775
Electric light and power	501	259	151	155	211	336	501	449	444	574	632
Gas	149	86	45	54	62	92	100	81	76	119	143
Commercial and miscellaneous[k]	1,554	758	837	885	1,233	1,617	1,871	1,531	1,766	2,045	2,534
Developmental and public enterprise construction	2,266	1,639	1,549	1,963	1,997	2,947	2,627	2,896	2,994	2,840	3,511
Private[m]	61	40	45	36	28	24	31	30	28	33	32
Public	2,205	1,599	1,504	1,927	1,969	2,923	2,596	2,866	2,966	2,807	3,479
Highways	1,355	958	847	1,000	845	1,362	1,226	1,421	1,381	1,302	1,066
Conservation and development	156	150	359	518	700	658	605	551	570	528	500
Sewage disposal	114	69	45	102	101	230	209	235	243	184	118
Water supply	156	87	50	71	74	112	102	120	128	154	134
Industrial and commercial	n	n	6	24	9	18	24	30	55	198	1,301
Public administration	183	183	109	87	90	161	143	165	234	149	105
Public construction, n.e.c.	241	152	88	125	150	382	287	344	355	292	255
Consumer construction	2,419	1,075	688	975	1,387	2,350	2,628	2,784	3,722	3,775	4,582
Private	2,005	846	580	738	1,160	1,786	2,165	2,292	3,004	3,339	3,930
Residential	1,624	654	499	661	1,071	1,641	1,975	2,069	2,786	3,130	3,692
Religious	87	45	22	21	28	34	44	51	48	59	62
Educational	100	53	15	14	17	40	42	40	39	50	58
Recreational	123	60	34	33	34	54	73	97	100	67	72
Hospital	71	34	10	9	10	17	31	35	31	33	46
Public	414	229	108	237	227	564	463	492	718	436	652
Residential	—	—	—	1	9	61	93	35	65	200	430
Educational	285	130	52	148	153	366	253	311	468	156	158
Recreational	19	16	7	37	27	63	44	49	58	26	22
Hospital	110	83	49	51	38	74	73	97	127	54	42

Appendix 4-8 (continued)

Class	1942	1943	1944	1945	1946	1947	1948	1949	1950	1951	1952
Private productive facilities (continued)											
Transportation	$956	$812	$1,072	$1,122	$1,506	$2,187	$2,604	$2,197	$2,308	$2,964	$2,754
Railroads	539	458	577	548	583	889	1,319	1,352	1,111	1,474	1,391
Local transit	91	40	65	83	144	281	236	179	168	149	196
Oil pipeline	68	66	61	36	54	103	128	134	141		
Other transportation	258	248	369	455	725	914	921	532	888	1,341[l]	1,167[l]
Communication	450	190	220	321	817	1,399	1,742	1,320	1,104	1,319	1,598
Utilities	584	339	416	505	792	1,539	2,543	3,125	3,309	3,664	3,838
Electric light and power	471	264	254	360	565	925	1,866	2,272	2,187	—	—
Gas	113	75	162	145	227	614	677	853	1,122	—	—
Commercial and miscellaneous[k]	−90[l]	−72[l]	888	2,360	5,552	6,093	6,994	7,586	11,348	10,176	10,343
Developmental and public enterprise construction	4,946	2,925	1,931	1,496	1,655	2,708	3,668	4,468	4,821	5,765	6,726
Private[m]	19	7	12	21	52	69	65	78	112	64	85
Public	4,927	2,918	1,919	1,475	1,603	2,639	3,603	4,390	4,709	5,701	6,641
Highways	734	446	362	398	895	1,451	1,774	2,131	2,272	2,518	2,860
Conservation and development	357	285	163	130	240	394	629	793	881	853	854
Sewage disposal	76	37	26	37	97	188	300	354	383	425	413
Water supply	93	70	53	60	97	163	235	265	276	291	279
Industrial and commercial	3,443	1,874	1,234	759	117	96	196	177	224	946	1,667
Public administration	56	15	11	15	16	26	74	121	171	179	123
Public construction, n.e.c.	168	191	70	76	141	321	395	549	502	489	445
Consumer construction	2,681	1,890	1,305	1,554	5,404	8,092	11,236	11,933	16,771	15,867	15,916
Private	1,964	1,036	988	1,321	4,833	7,502	10,172	10,055	14,657	13,124	13,119
Residential	1,850	1,006	923	1,200	4,424	6,993	9,318	8,962	13,363	11,744	11,850
Religious	31	6	11	26	76	126	251	360	409	452	399
Educational	24	6	11	31	123	174	253	269	294	345	351
Recreational	30	7	17	27	125	99	224	262	247	164	125
Hospital	29	11	26	37	85	110	126	202	344	419	394
Public	717	854	317	233	571	590	1,064	1,878	2,114	2,743	2,797
Residential	545	739	211	80	374	200	156	359	345	595	654
Educational	128	63	41	59	101	287	618	934	1,133	1,513	1,619
Recreational	9	8	7	9	11	18	67	108	140	107	51
Hospital	35	44	58	85	85	85	223	477	496	528	473

Sources and methods: Construction expenditures are from Construction and Building Materials, Statistical Supplement, May 1952 and May 1953, U.S. Department of Commerce, except that Private construction expenditures also include expenditures for drilling petroleum and natural gas wells estimated for 1920–1928 on the basis of the number of wells drilled as reported in Twentieth Century Petroleum Statistics, DeGolyer and MacNaughton, Dallas, 1951, p. 25, and as reported for 1929–1951 in National Income and Product of the United States, 1929–1952, U.S. Department of Commerce, 1951, Table 31, footnote 8, and Survey of Current Business, July 1952 and July 1953, Table 31. Public expenditures exclude military and naval construction.

Private equipment expenditures for 1929–1952 are from National Income and Product of the United States, Table 2, p. 150, and Survey of Current Business, July 1952 and July 1953, Table 2; for 1920–1928 they were derived by linking to this series at the year 1929 estimates in W. H. Shaw, Value of Commodity Output Since 1869, National Bureau of Economic Research, New York, 1947, p. 69. Public equipment expenditures for 1920–1949 are estimates of Raymond W. Goldsmith, Associates, Washington; for 1950–1952 the estimates were based on relationship to government construction expenditures. Public equipment expenditures exclude expenditures by state governments for equipment.

Private productive facilities are the sum of Private equipment and producers' plant, which includes industrial buildings, warehouses, offices, lofts, stores, restaurants, garages, public utility buildings, farm service buildings and miscellaneous nonresidential buildings, as reported in Construction and Building Materials, and petroleum and gas well drilling, derived as indicated above.

Industry estimates under Private productive facilities came from the following sources:

Agriculture: Nonresidential construction from Construction and Building Materials; Farm machinery and equipment from unpublished estimates of the U.S. Department of Agriculture.

Mining and Manufacturing (Total): 1920–1938 from George Terborgh, "Estimated Expenditures for Durable Goods," Federal Reserve Bulletin, September 1939, p. 732 (Manufacturing and mining combined), and Lowell J. Chawner, "Capital Expenditures for Manufacturing Plant and Equipment, 1915 to 1940," Survey of Current Business, March 1941, p. 10 (Manufacturing alone); 1939 and 1945–1952 from Lawrence Bridge and Vito Natrella, "Capital Expenditures by Nonmanufacturing Industries," Survey of Current Business, August 1952, p. 20 and SCB, December 1953; 1940–1944 interpolated between 1939 and 1945 by use of trends indicated in Business Statistics: Statistical Supplement to the Survey of Current Business, 1951, p. 9.

Manufacturing detail: 1920–1938 from Chawner, "Capital Expenditures in Selected Manufacturing Industries," Survey of Current Business, December 1941, p. 20, and May 1942, p. 15; 1939 and 1945–1950 from Lawrence Bridge, "Capital Expenditures by Manufacturing Industries in the Postwar Period," Survey of Current Business, December 1951, p. 17; 1951 and 1952 from Survey of Current Business, December 1952 and December 1953; Unallocated is a residual.

Transportation detail: Railroads—1920–1934, Terborgh, loc. cit.; 1935–1938, Business Statistics, loc. cit.; 1940–1944 interpolated using trends in ibid.; 1939 and 1945–1952, Bridge and Natrella, loc. cit., and Survey of Current Business, December 1953. Transit—1920–1938, Terborgh, loc. cit.; 1939–1952, construction figures from Construction and Building Materials and equipment figures from unpublished estimates of the American Transit Association (1939–1948) and of the U.S. Department of Com-

merce (1949–1952). Oil pipeline—1948 from Bridge and Natrella, op. cit., p. 22; other years based on trend from Construction and Building Materials linked to the 1948 figures. Other transportation—1939 and 1945–1952 from Bridge and Natrella, op. cit., and SCB, December 1953, and Transit and Oil pipeline estimates; 1940–1944 interpolated as indicated above.

Communication: 1939 and 1945–1952, Bridge and Natrella, loc. cit., and SCB, December 1953; 1920–1938, trend for Telephone (Terborgh, loc. cit.) plus Telegraph (Chawner, Construction Activity in the United States, 1915–1937, U.S. Department of Commerce, 1938, Table 33) linked to 1939 figure; 1940–1944 unpublished estimates of Securities and Exchange Commission.

Utilities detail: Electric light and power derived from Statistical Bulletin, Edison Electrical Institute, No. 15, 1947, and No. 18, 1950, Table 11, adjusted by subtraction of estimates, based on data of the U.S. Bureau of the Census, of municipal expenditures. Gas, 1920–1931 from Chawner, op. cit., Table 31; 1932–1950 from Gas Facts, American Gas Association, 1950, Table 175, p. 235. Both Electric and Gas expenditures for 1939–1950 were adjusted so that their sum was consistent with the total for Utilities in Bridge and Natrella, loc. cit., for 1939 and 1945–1951; the estimates for 1920–1938 were made consistent with the corrected 1939 figures.

Commercial and miscellaneous is a residual.

Developmental and public enterprise construction detail from Construction and Building Materials.

a. Comprises all expenditures for publicly and privately owned capital goods, except expenditures for publicly owned military and naval plant and equipment and expenditures by state governments for equipment.

b. Excludes expenditures by state governments for equipment.

c. Total includes equipment charged to current account; these charges are not included in the detailed industry figures but are grouped with "Commercial and miscellaneous."

d. Included in "Other durable goods."

e. Starting with 1939, includes lumber, furniture and fixtures, instruments, ordnance and miscellaneous manufactures.

f. Included in "Other nondurable goods."

g. Starting with 1939, includes apparel and related products, tobacco, leather and leather products, and printing and publishing.

h. Railroads, transit and oil pipelines only. (See footnote i.)

i. Included in "Commercial and miscellaneous."

j. In 1951–1952, "Transit" included in "Other transportation."

k. Includes facilities not allocable by industry division, equipment charged to current account and statistical discrepancies arising from use of varied sources.

l. Statistical discrepancy.

m. Developmental construction only.

n. Not segregable from private industrial and commercial facilities. Amount believed negligible.

Note: Sum of expenditures for "Private Productive Facilities," "Developmental and Public Enterprise Construction," and "Consumer Construction" differs from "Total Expenditures" by amount equal to expenditures for "Public Equipment," which are not distributed in the body of the table. Also those estimates differ slightly from those in Appendix 4-I and Table 29 because of use of different sources and rounding.

Class	1920	1921	1922	1923	1924	1925	1926	1927	1928	1929	1930
1. Total expenditures [a]	100.00	100.00	100.00	100.00	100.00	100.00	100.00	100.00	100.00	100.00	100.00
2. Private	90.73	84.07	84.95	88.59	86.92	86.58	87.59	85.46	85.02	85.33	78.81
3. Public [b]	9.27	15.93	15.05	11.41	13.08	13.42	12.41	14.54	14.98	14.67	21.19
4. Construction	53.58	64.91	69.71	65.33	69.80	70.19	69.68	70.83	68.56	62.96	63.93
5. Private	44.45	49.19	55.11	54.42	57.45	57.45	57.76	57.05	54.36	49.06	43.86
6. Public	9.13	15.72	14.60	10.91	12.35	12.74	11.92	13.78	14.20	13.90	20.07
7. Equipment	46.42	35.09	30.29	34.67	30.20	29.81	30.32	29.17	31.44	37.04	36.07
8. Private	46.28	34.89	29.84	34.17	29.46	29.13	29.83	28.41	30.66	36.27	34.95
9. Public [b]	.14	.20	.45	.50	.74	.68	.49	.76	.78	.77	1.12
10. Private productive facilities [c]	71.00	57.68	50.47	54.40	49.57	48.76	51.42	50.46	52.63	60.43	59.11
11. Agriculture	10.44	5.42	5.25	5.30	4.60	4.86	4.69	4.88	5.01	5.31	4.96
12. Nonresidential construction	2.30	1.30	1.32	1.19	1.08	1.02	.90	1.12	1.01	.90	.61
13. Farm machinery and equipment	8.14	4.12	3.93	4.11	3.52	3.84	3.79	3.76	4.00	4.41	4.35
14. Mining	2.86	6.92	5.52	4.28	4.05	4.53	4.57	4.29	4.29	4.83	4.49
15. Manufacturing	24.27	14.18	13.57	13.93	11.29	11.78	13.13	12.12	13.26	15.43	13.54
16. Durable goods industries											
17. Primary iron and steel	1.46	1.04	.88	.82	1.17	1.20	1.29	.92	1.15	.85	2.13
18. Primary nonferrous metals	—	—	—	—	—	—	—	—	—	—	—
19. Fabricated metal products	—	—	—	—	—	—	—	—	—	—	—
20. Electrical machinery and equipment	—	—	—	—	—	—	—	—	—	—	—
21. Nonelectrical machinery	—	—	—	—	—	—	—	—	—	—	—
22. Motor vehicles and equipment	1.43	.66	.52	.71	.77	.69	.78	.92	.86	1.05	.84
23. Transportation equip. (exc. mo. veh.)	—	—	—	—	—	—	—	—	—	—	—
24. Stone, clay and glass products	1.29	1.19	1.14	1.35	1.02	1.08	1.31	1.16	1.63	1.36	.85
25. Lumber and lumber products	1.22	.74	.97	.80	.69	.72	.80	.54	.51	.59	.35
26. Other durable goods [e]	—	—	—	—	—	—	—	—	—	—	—
27. Nondurable goods industries											
28. Food and kindred products	2.71	2.22	2.26	1.69	1.53	1.63	2.07	1.97	2.43	2.13	1.89
29. Beverages	—	—	—	—	—	—	—	—	—	—	—
30. Textile mill products	2.30	1.90	1.84	1.77	1.19	1.21	1.11	1.22	1.22	1.32	.92
31. Apparel and related products	—	—	—	—	—	—	—	—	—	—	—
32. Paper and allied products	1.21	.92	.56	.69	.61	.51	.51	.67	.74	.77	.78
33. Chemicals and allied products	—	—	—	—	—	—	—	—	—	—	—
34. Petroleum and coal products	—	—	—	—	—	—	—	—	—	—	—
35. Petroleum refining	.77	.57	.57	.44	.42	.39	.47	.46	.69	.70	.60
36. Rubber products	.80	.26	.20	.15	.14	.17	.18	.24	.22	.30	.16
37. Printing and publishing	.87	.88	.94	.84	.74	.78	.72	.65	.59	.67	.57

Class	1931	1932	1933	1934	1935	1936	1937	1938	1939	1940	1941
1. Total expenditures [a]	100.00	100.00	100.00	100.00	100.00	100.00	100.00	100.00	100.00	100.00	100.00
2. Private	72.12	65.44	65.66	65.44	70.98	68.26	75.47	69.51	70.81	77.02	76.96
3. Public [b]	27.88	34.56	34.34	34.56	29.02	31.74	24.53	30.49	29.19	22.98	23.04
4. Construction	66.63	66.28	62.17	59.78	56.47	59.13	57.19	64.11	64.03	57.93	57.89
5. Private	40.14	33.57	29.24	26.38	28.88	28.67	33.75	34.69	36.08	36.32	35.66
6. Public	26.49	32.71	32.93	33.40	27.59	30.47	23.44	29.42	27.95	21.61	22.23
7. Equipment	33.37	33.72	37.83	40.22	43.53	40.86	42.81	35.89	35.97	42.07	42.11
8. Private	31.98	31.87	36.42	39.06	42.10	39.59	41.72	34.82	34.72	40.70	41.30
9. Public [b]	1.39	1.85	1.41	1.16	1.43	1.27	1.09	1.07	1.25	1.37	.81
10. Private productive facilities [c]	51.22	49.59	52.89	53.50	56.05	52.44	58.64	49.17	47.81	54.55	55.65
11. Agriculture	3.75	3.10	4.15	5.88	7.50	6.87	7.33	6.75	6.07	6.00	6.37
12. Nonresidential construction	.38	.23	.41	.46	.82	.74	.82	.80	.80	.63	.69
13. Farm machinery and equipment	3.37	2.87	3.74	5.42	6.68	6.13	6.51	5.95	5.27	5.37	5.68
14. Mining	3.85	6.37	5.62	7.87	8.17	7.50	7.37	5.82	2.47	3.20	3.14
15. Manufacturing	10.66	10.27	14.65	14.66	14.53	13.50	16.55	12.20	14.74	18.14	19.76
16. Durable goods industries	—	—	—	—	—	—	—	—	5.74	—	—
17. Primary iron and steel	1.21	.72	1.02	.62	1.53	1.75	2.42	1.16	.93	—	—
18. Primary nonferrous metals	—	—	—	—	—	—	—	—	.23	—	—
19. Fabricated metal products	—	—	—	—	—	—	—	—	.69	—	—
20. Electrical machinery and equipment	—	—	—	—	—	—	—	—	.37	—	—
21. Nonelectrical machinery	—	—	—	—	—	—	—	—	.76	—	—
22. Motor vehicles and equipment	.78	1.23	.98	1.20	1.63	1.34	1.22	1.36	1.01	—	—
23. Transportation equip. (exc. mo. veh.)	—	—	—	—	—	—	—	—	.32	—	—
24. Stone, clay and glass products	.77	.68	.57	.66	.82	.86	.76	.59	.54 [d]	—	—
25. Lumber and lumber products	.30	.27	.41	.34	.40	.41	.48	.38	—	—	—
26. Other durable goods [e]	—	—	—	—	—	—	—	—	.89	—	—
27. Nondurable goods industries	—	—	—	—	—	—	—	—	9.00	—	—
28. Food and kindred products	1.73	2.34	4.23	3.01	2.32	2.34	2.45	1.90	{ 1.55	—	—
29. Beverages									.29		
30. Textile mill products	.94	1.00	1.61	1.56	1.12	1.01	1.20	.80	{ 1.03	—	—
31. Apparel and related products									[f]		
32. Paper and allied products	.55	.50	.59	.62	.83	.86	1.40	.61	.51	—	—
33. Chemicals and allied products	—	—	—	—	—	—	—	—	1.33	—	—
34. Petroleum and coal products	—	—	—	—	—	—	—	—	3.06	—	—
35. Petroleum refining	.66	.98	1.33	1.08	.69	.79	1.10	1.15	—	—	—
36. Rubber products	.17	.20	.27	.25	.19	.19	.25	.24	.29	—	—
37. Printing and publishing	.53	.54	.55	.63	.68	.66	.63	.50	[f]	—	—

Class	1942	1943	1944	1945	1946	1947	1948	1949	1950	1951	1952
1. Total expenditures [a]	100.00	100.00	100.00	100.00	100.00	100.00	100.00	100.00	100.00	100.00	100.00
2. Private	59.46	61.96	78.29	86.26	90.47	89.94	88.24	84.41	86.01	84.07	82.81
3. Public [b]	40.54	38.04	21.71	13.74	9.53	10.06	11.76	15.59	13.99	15.93	17.19
4. Construction	64.91	58.96	46.02	42.01	49.86	49.89	52.62	55.39	56.45	55.63	55.74
5. Private	25.79	22.49	25.22	29.06	41.16	40.56	41.74	40.75	43.42	40.76	39.74
6. Public	39.12	36.47	20.79	12.95	8.70	9.33	10.88	14.64	13.03	14.88	16.01
7. Equipment	35.09	41.04	53.98	57.99	50.14	50.11	47.38	44.61	43.55	44.37	44.26
8. Private	33.67	39.47	53.06	57.20	49.31	49.38	46.50	43.65	42.59	43.31	43.07
9. Public [b]	1.42	1.57	.92	.79	.83	.73	.88	.96	.96	1.06	1.19
10. Private productive facilities [c]	45.71	51.87	68.99	76.09	70.93	68.05	64.37	60.75	57.80	60.83	60.41
11. Agriculture	8.23	9.83	12.62	10.33	7.40	8.46	8.66	8.99	7.63	8.14	7.14
12. Nonresidential construction	.87	1.58	1.63	1.27	1.79	2.06	1.88	1.85	1.66	1.54	1.46
13. Farm machinery and equipment	7.36	8.26	10.99	9.06	5.61	6.40	6.78	7.14	5.97	6.60	5.68
14. Mining	2.45	3.01	4.01	2.90	1.71	2.00	2.06	1.85	1.35	1.64	1.49
15. Manufacturing	21.86	26.76	28.22	30.20	27.16	25.16	21.29	16.69	14.31	19.12	20.34
16. Durable goods industries	—	—	—	12.06	12.45	9.85	8.12	6.05	5.99	9.11	9.81
17. Primary iron and steel	—	—	—	1.50	2.00	1.84	1.80	1.39	1.14	2.11	2.61
18. Primary nonferrous metals	—	—	—	.41	.37	.51	.45	.35	.25	.55	1.01
19. Fabricated metal products	—	—	—	1.64	1.42	1.07	.80	.63	.67	.76	.60
20. Electrical machinery and equipment	—	—	—	.93	1.13	.88	.67	.51	.47	.66	.64
21. Nonelectrical machinery	—	—	—	2.40	2.04	1.50	1.23	.90	.79	1.20	1.31
22. Motor vehicles and equipment	—	—	—	1.99	2.36	1.46	1.10	.81	.97	1.50	1.52
23. Transportation equip. (exc. mo. veh.)	—	—	—	.42	.44	.28	.25	.20	.16	.39	.43
24. Stone, clay and glass products	—	—	—	.76 [d]	.97 [d]	.94 [d]	.63 [d]	.42 [d]	.53 [d]	.70 [d]	.54 [d]
25. Lumber and lumber products	—	—	—								
26. Other durable goods [e]	—	—	—	2.01	1.72	1.37	1.19	.84	1.00	1.24	1.16
27. Nondurable goods industries	—	—	—	18.14	14.71	15.31	13.17	10.64	8.32	10.01	10.53
28. Food and kindred products	—	—	—	2.56	2.05	1.93	1.68	1.46	1.00	1.02	.92
29. Beverages	—	—	—	.74	.63	.80	.77	.58	.45	.48	.42
30. Textile mill products	—	—	—	1.58 [f]	1.37	1.48	1.44	1.10 [f]	.86 [f]	.94	.68 [f]
31. Apparel and related products	—	—	—								
32. Paper and allied products	—	—	—	.88	.93	1.07	.89	.70	.63	.74	.60
33. Chemicals and allied products	—	—	—	2.85	3.20	3.07	2.19	1.56	1.47	2.20	2.46
34. Petroleum and coal products	—	—	—	6.66	4.35	5.02	4.90	4.18	3.03	3.70	4.40
35. Petroleum refining	—	—	—								
36. Rubber products	—	—	—	.89 [f]	.55 [f]	.41 [f]	.24 [f]	.19 [f]	.19 [f]	.26	.24 [f]
37. Printing and publishing	—	—	—								

	Class	1920	1921	1922	1923	1924	1925	1926	1927	1928	1929	1930
	Manufacturing (continued)											
38.	Other nondurable goods[g]	—	—	—	—	—	—	—	—	—	—	—
39.	Unallocated	10.21[h]	3.80[h]	3.69[h]	4.67[h]	3.01[h]	3.40[h]	3.89[h]	3.37[h]	3.22[h]	5.69[h]	4.43[h]
40.	Transportation											
41.	Railroads	4.83	5.71	3.82	7.32	5.88	4.36	4.93	4.32	3.87	4.73	6.14
42.	Transit	1.24	1.04	1.33	1.22	.87	.74	.65	.75	.77	.76	.88
43.	Oil pipeline	.27[i]	.27[i]	.31[i]	.31[i]	.39[i]	.28[i]	.17[i]	.39[i]	.26[i]	.47[i]	.18[i]
44.	Other transportation											
45.	Communication	2.00	2.98	2.86	2.69	3.13	2.86	2.82	2.80	3.23	4.27	5.41
46.	Utilities	4.36	3.93	5.17	6.22	7.26	6.05	5.79	6.09	5.60	5.61	7.38
47.	Electric light and power	3.44	3.00	3.57	5.05	5.55	4.72	4.00	4.19	4.04	4.27	5.77
48.	Gas	.92	.93	1.60	1.17	1.71	1.33	1.79	1.90	1.56	1.34	1.60
49.	Commercial and miscellaneous[k]	20.73	17.23	12.64	13.13	12.10	13.30	14.67	14.82	16.34	19.02	16.10
50.	Developmental and public enterprise construction											
51.	Private[m]	7.95	13.08	11.72	8.76	10.27	10.44	9.68	11.66	11.75	11.51	17.05
52.	Public	7.33	12.32	10.93	8.05	9.51	9.76	9.05	10.93	11.12	10.93	16.45
53.	Highways	5.03	8.85	7.71	5.47	6.44	6.47	5.96	7.03	7.41	7.13	10.75
54.	Conservation and development	.42	.54	.42	.44	.52	.44	.34	.36	.42	.65	.97
55.	Sewage disposal	.51	.81	.78	.61	.71	.80	.81	1.00	1.05	.72	1.01
56.	Water supply	.66[n]	1.04[n]	.99[n]	.77[n]	1.01[n]	.87[n]	.79[n]	.79[n]	.67[n]	.71[n]	1.43[n]
57.	Industrial and commercial	.62	.76	.79	.71	.76	.68	.63	.73	.63	.58	.60
58.	Public administration	.29	.53	.48	.30	.25	.33	.39	.48	.49	.61	.91
59.	Public construction, n.e.c.	.42	.55	.55	.46	.58	.85	.76	1.27	1.08	1.11	1.38
60.	Consumer construction	20.91	29.02	37.35	36.34	39.43	40.12	38.41	37.12	34.84	27.29	22.72
61.	Private	19.11	25.62	33.68	33.48	36.59	37.14	35.54	34.28	31.76	24.32	19.10
62.	Residential	17.49	22.86	30.61	30.86	33.88	33.84	32.06	30.58	28.32	21.25	15.48
63.	Religious	.42	.74	.90	.80	.85	.99	.99	1.03	.97	.83	.96
64.	Educational	.17	.33	.54	.56	.59	.65	.60	.61	.61	.68	.84
65.	Recreational	.80	1.23	1.16	.87	.86	1.19	1.43	1.45	1.29	.97	1.05
66.	Hospital	.23	.46	.47	.39	.41	.47	.46	.61	.57	.59	.77
67.	Public	1.80	3.40	3.67	2.86	2.84	2.98	2.87	2.84	3.08	2.97	3.62
68.	Residential	1.46	2.84	3.01	2.35	2.30	2.39	2.23	2.11	2.17	2.19	2.58
69.	Educational	.09	.14	.13	.14	.15	.22	.26	.27	.29	.21	.20
70.	Recreational	.25	.42	.53	.37	.39	.37	.38	.46	.62	.57	.84
71.	Hospital											

Appendix 4-9 (continued)

#	Class	1931	1932	1933	1934	1935	1936	1937	1938	1939	1940	1941
	Manufacturing (continued)											
38.	Other nondurable goods[g]	—	—	—	—	—	—	—	—	.94	—	—
39.	Unallocated	3.02[h]	1.81[h]	3.09[h]	4.69[h]	4.32[h]	3.29[h]	4.64[h]	3.51[h]	—	18.14	19.76
40.	Transportation	5.65	4.60	3.12	4.73	3.79	3.94	5.23	2.99	4.89	6.50	5.67
41.	Railroads	3.64	2.94	2.06	3.37	2.11	2.69	4.02	2.10	2.12	2.93	3.01
42.	Transit	1.34	1.09	.94	1.20	1.47	.95	.77	.73	.81	.75	.57
43.	Oil pipeline	.67	.57	.12	.16	.21	.30	.44	.16	.23	.17	.27
44.	Other transportation	[l]	[l]	[l]	[l]	[l]	[l]	[l]	[l]	1.73	2.65	1.82
45.	Communication	5.02	5.51	4.25	3.47	3.14	2.76	3.21	3.36	2.29	2.47	2.91
46.	Utilities	6.57	6.17	4.00	3.23	3.43	3.74	4.61	4.64	3.95	4.62	4.17
47.	Electric light and power	5.07	4.63	3.08	2.39	2.65	2.94	3.84	3.93	3.37	3.83	3.40
48.	Gas	1.50	1.54	.92	.84	.78	.80	.77	.71	.58	.79	.77
49.	Commercial and miscellaneous[k]	15.72	13.57	17.10	13.66	15.49	14.13	14.34	13.41	13.40	13.62	13.63
50.	Developmental and public enterprise construction	22.92	29.33	31.64	30.30	25.09	25.75	20.13	25.37	22.71	18.92	18.89
51.	Private[m]	.62	.72	.92	.56	.35	.21	.24	.26	.21	.22	.17
52.	Public	22.30	28.61	30.72	29.74	24.74	25.54	19.89	25.11	22.50	18.70	18.72
53.	Highways	13.70	17.14	17.30	15.43	10.62	11.90	9.40	12.45	10.48	8.67	5.74
54.	Conservation and development	1.58	2.68	7.33	8.00	8.79	5.75	4.64	4.83	4.32	3.52	2.69
55.	Sewage disposal	1.15	1.23	.92	1.57	1.27	2.01	1.60	2.06	1.84	1.23	.63
56.	Water supply	1.58[n]	1.56[n]	1.02	1.10	.93	.98	.78	1.05	.97	1.03	.72
57.	Industrial and commercial	—	—	.12	.37	.11	.16	.18	.26	.42	1.32	7.00
58.	Public administration	1.85	3.28	2.23	1.34	1.13	1.40	1.09	1.45	1.78	.99	.57
59.	Public construction, n.e.c.	2.44	2.72	1.80	1.93	1.89	3.34	2.20	3.01	2.69	1.94	1.37
60.	Consumer construction	24.47	19.24	14.05	15.05	17.42	20.53	20.14	24.39	28.24	25.15	24.65
61.	Private	20.28	15.14	11.85	11.39	14.57	15.60	16.59	20.08	22.79	22.25	21.14
62.	Residential	16.43	11.70	10.19	10.20	13.45	14.34	15.13	18.12	21.13	20.86	19.86
63.	Religious	.88	.81	.45	.32	.35	.29	.34	.45	.36	.39	.33
64.	Educational	1.01	.95	.31	.22	.21	.35	.32	.35	.30	.33	.31
65.	Recreational	1.24	1.07	.70	.51	.43	.47	.56	.85	.76	.45	.39
66.	Hospital	.72	.61	.20	.14	.13	.15	.24	.31	.24	.22	.25
67.	Public	4.19	4.10	2.20	3.66	2.85	4.93	3.55	4.31	5.45	2.90	3.51
68.	Residential	—	—	—	.02	.11	.53	.71	.31	.49	1.33	2.31
69.	Educational	2.89	2.33	1.06	2.28	1.92	3.20	1.94	2.72	3.55	1.04	.85
70.	Recreational	.19	.29	.14	.57	.34	.55	.34	.43	.44	.17	.12
71.	Hospital	1.11	1.48	1.00	.79	.48	.65	.56	.85	.97	.36	.23

	Class	1942	1943	1944	1945	1946	1947	1948	1949	1950	1951	1952
	Manufacturing (continued)											
38.	Other nondurable goods [g]	—	—	—	1.98	1.63	1.53	1.06	.87	.69	.67	.82
39.	Unallocated	21.86	26.76	28.22	—	—	—	—	—	—	—	—
40.	Transportation	6.63	7.85	9.97	8.51	6.02	6.32	6.07	5.13	4.41	5.22	4.67
41.	Railroads	3.74	4.43	5.37	4.16	2.33	2.57	3.07	3.16	2.12	2.60 [j]	2.36 [j]
42.	Transit	.63	.38	.60	.63	.57	.81	.55	.42	.32	—	—
43.	Oil pipeline	.47	.64	.57	.27	.22	.30	.30	.31	.27	.26	.33
44.	Other transportation	1.79	2.40	3.43	3.45	2.90	2.64	2.15	1.24	1.70	2.36 [1]	1.98 [1]
45.	Communication	3.12	1.84	2.04	2.43	3.27	4.04	4.06	3.08	2.11	2.32	2.71
46.	Utilities	4.05	3.28	3.87	3.83	3.17	4.45	5.93	7.30	6.32	6.46	6.51
47.	Electric light and power	3.27	2.55	2.36	2.73	2.26	2.67	4.35	5.31	4.18	—	—
48.	Gas	.78 [1]	.73 [1]	1.51	1.10	.91	1.78	1.58	1.99	2.14	—	—
49.	Commercial and miscellaneous [k]	—	—	8.26	17.89	22.20	17.62	16.30	17.71	21.68	17.93	17.54
50.	Developmental and public enterprise construction	34.28	28.28	17.96	11.34	6.62	7.83	8.55	10.43	9.21	10.16	11.41
51.	Private [m]	.13	.07	.11	.16	.21	.20	.15	.18	.21	.11	.14
52.	Public	34.15	28.21	17.85	11.18	6.41	7.63	8.40	10.25	8.99	10.04	11.26
53.	Highways	5.09	4.31	3.37	3.02	3.58	4.19	4.13	4.98	4.34	4.44	4.85
54.	Conservation and development	2.47	2.75	1.52	.99	.96	1.14	1.47	1.85	1.68	1.50	1.45
55.	Sewage disposal	.53	.36	.24	.28	.39	.54	.70	.83	.73	.75	.70
56.	Water supply	.65	.68	.49	.45	.39	.47	.55	.62	.53	.51	.47
57.	Industrial and commercial	23.86	18.12	11.48	5.75	.47	.28	.46	.41	.43	1.67	2.83
58.	Public administration	.39	.14	.10	.11	.06	.08	.17	.28	.33	.32	.21
59.	Public construction, n.e.c.	1.16	1.85	.65	.58	.56	.93	.92	1.28	.96	.86	.75
60.	Consumer construction	18.58	18.27	12.14	11.78	21.61	23.39	26.19	27.86	32.03	27.96	27.00
61.	Private	13.61	10.01	9.19	10.01	19.33	21.69	23.71	23.48	28.00	23.12	22.25
62.	Residential	12.82	9.72	8.59	9.10	17.70	20.22	21.72	20.93	25.52	20.69	20.10
63.	Religious	.21	.06	.10	.20	.30	.36	.59	.84	.78	.80	.68
64.	Educational	.17	.06	.10	.23	.49	.50	.59	.63	.56	.61	.60
65.	Recreational	.21	.07	.16	.20	.50	.29	.52	.61	.47	.29	.21
66.	Hospital	.20	.10	.24	.28	.34	.32	.29	.47	.66	.74	.67
67.	Public	4.97	8.26	2.95	1.77	2.28	1.70	2.48	4.38	4.04	4.83	4.74
68.	Residential	3.78	7.15	1.96	.61	1.50	.58	.36	.84	.66	1.05	1.11
69.	Educational	.89	.61	.38	.45	.40	.83	1.44	2.18	2.16	2.67	2.75
70.	Recreational	.06	.08	.07	.07	.04	.05	.16	.25	.27	.19	.09
71.	Hospital	.24	.42	.54	.64	.34	.24	.52	1.11	.95	.93	.80

Sources and notes: See Appendix 4–8.

APPENDIX 5–1. METHOD OF ESTIMATING EFFECT OF MAY 1953 CHANGES IN NATIONAL
RESEARCH COUNCIL DIETARY STANDARDS

The following approach, described in detail for calcium, was used to estimate the effects of the changes in the National Research Council standards for protein and riboflavin as well. The quantity of calcium in diets is reported as so much per nutrition unit, "need" of an adult male being equal to one nutrition unit. This method of reporting makes it impossible to apply a new standard of need directly to the available data, which relate to 1948 diets, the adequacy of which was appraised by the 1948 NRC calcium allowance. (U.S. Department of Agriculture: *Nutritive Value of Diets of Urban Families, United States, Spring 1948, and Comparison with Diets in 1942*, 1948 Food Consumption Surveys, Preliminary Report No. 12, Table 15; and *Nutritive Value of Family Diets, Farm Cities, Part II, Distribution of Families Classified by Nutritive Content of Diets*, Preliminary Report No. 13, Table 2.)

The revision of 1953 in the allowance changed the interrelations of the age and sex groups as well as the over-all level of need. For example, it lowered the calcium allowance for most adults but did not lower it for children. As a result, for families with children the number of nutrition units per family is greater when the 1953 allowance is used than when the 1948 allowance is used.

The method of estimating the percentage of families having adequate diets in 1948 in terms of the 1953 calcium allowance was as follows:

(1) The NRC dietary allowances for calcium in age classes in 1948 and 1953 were averaged using as weights the age groups as reported in the 1950 Census of Population for urban communities with adjustments for number of unrelated individuals since these were not important in the population reporting diets. (See *1950 Census of Population*, Vol. II, *Characteristics of the Population*, Pt. 1, U.S. Summary, Chap. B, 1952, Tables 38 and 57.) It was assumed that all families ate enough meals at home to be classed as housekeeping families, that half the unrelated individuals were eating meals with housekeeping families and that they were all 21 years of age or over. It was also assumed that one half of the number of children under one year of age indicated the number of pregnant women in the population for the year during the stage of pregnancy when a relatively high calcium allowance is needed. This assumption is based on the notion that births occurred throughout the year and that the average mother of a child under one year of age was pregnant for about half the year, or — in equivalent terms for this purpose — that the mothers of half these babies were pregnant for a whole year. No account was taken of the number of lactating women; instead, the calcium need of children under one year of age was included. The average per capita need of the population was found to be 1.053 grams with the 1948 allowance and 0.9287 with the 1953 allowance. In other words, although the calcium allowance of an adult male was reduced by 20 per cent, the average need for the population as a whole was reduced by about 12 per cent.

(2) Per person need in terms of the 1953 standard was expressed as a ratio of per person need in terms of the 1948 standard.

(3) This ratio (0.88) was multiplied by 1.0 gram (the 1948 allowance per adult male, in which the nutrition units are expressed). The result, 0.88 grams, was the yardstick to be applied to the 1948 family dietary data in order to appraise adequacy in terms of the 1953 standard.

(4) Cumulative distributions were plotted of the percentage of families with diets providing at least a given level of calcium per nutrition unit measured in terms of the 1948 NRC recommended dietary allowance. These were found to be very smooth. The percentage of families having diets providing at least 0.88 grams per nutrition unit was interpolated from the curves.

APPENDIX 5–2. METHOD OF ESTIMATING AMOUNT OF ADDITIONAL FOODS NEEDED TO BRING ALL
FAMILIES UP TO STANDARD OF ADEQUACY FOR CALCIUM AND ASCORBIC ACID

The methods of estimating the additional milk products and the additional citrus fruits, tomatoes and leafy, green and yellow vegetables needed to bring up to standard the families consuming less than the amounts of calcium and ascorbic acid recommended by the National Research Council are similar in over-all approach. They differ largely in their adaptation to the available data.

CALCIUM

The estimate of additional milk products needed to make the calcium supply adequate was based on the following data:

(1) Amount of milk included in the low-cost food budget prepared by the U.S. Bureau of Home Nutrition and Home Economics, portions of which are shown in Table 53. (The low-cost and the moderate-cost budgets are about the same in quantity of milk recommended.) A downward adjustment was made to take account of the 1953 revision of the NRC dietary allowance for calcium. (See Tables 52 and 53.) An over-all per capita yardstick of need for milk was secured by weighting the amounts of milk per person for the various age and activity groups by appropriate population weights.

(2) Food consumption reported by income class in the following family dietary studies: (a) *Food Consumption of Urban Families (68 Cities) in the U.S., Spring 1948*, 1948 Food Consumption Surveys, Preliminary Report No. 5, U.S. Department of Agriculture, Table 3; (b) *Rural Levels of Living in Lee and Jones Counties, Mississippi, 1946*, Agriculture Information Bulletin No. 41, U.S. Department of Agriculture, 1951, Tables 36, 37 and 46; (c) Southern Cooperative Series, Bulletin No. 20, S. Carolina Agricultural Experiment Station, November 1951, Table 19; (d) *Family Food Consumption in the United States, Spring 1942*, Miscellaneous Publication No. 550, U.S. Department of Agriculture, 1944, text tables 2 and 3 and appendix table 34, and supplementary data in *Family Spending and Saving in Wartime*, Bulletin No. 822, U.S. Bureau of Labor Statistics, 1945, text table 10.

The dietary data in 2(a) relate to urban housekeeping families in the United States during the spring of 1948. These were assumed to describe food consumption during the entire year. Data in 2(b) relate to rural households in two counties in Mississippi during the late spring and early summer of 1946. These were assumed to represent rural nonfarm diets in the United States during the entire year and rural farm diets during the late spring, summer and fall, that is, the two thirds of the year when milk supplies on farms seem likely to be at a relatively high level. The Mississippi families surveyed had incomes appreciably below the average for rural families in the United States as a whole, so that in so far as income is directly related to quantity of milk consumed, the manner of using the data tends to overstate the additional milk needed to provide the amount in the low-cost food budget. This bias in the estimate is probably important for the rural nonfarm group. Milk consumption on farms, however, is greatly influenced by the extent of home production of milk; and the percentage of farms in these two counties having cows and heifers was close to the national average — 82 and 78 per cent, respectively, in 1940. (See *1940 Census of Agriculture*, Vol. I, county tables I and IV, and Vol. III.)

Data in 2(c) relate to diets of selected farm families during the winter and early spring of 1948 in five southern states. These were taken as typical of farm family diets in the United States as a whole during this season, even though it was recognized that the consumption of these families was probably too low for such purposes because of their relatively low income, but even more because in the counties surveyed the percentage of farms reporting cows and heifers was appreciably below the national average — 61 per cent compared with 78 per cent. (*Op. cit.*)

Data in 2(d) relate to households in the United States as a whole during the spring of 1942 and are given separately for urban, rural nonfarm and farm groups. These data were used as a check on the estimates made with the later data. The check indicated that 10 per cent additional milk would have made up the deficiencies between consumption and the low-cost food budget, and data on the national food supply indicated an increase from 1942 to 1948 of 3 per cent in the total supply of dairy products apart from butter. (See *Consumption of Food in the United States, 1909–48*, Miscellaneous Publication No. 691, U.S. Department of Agriculture, Table 38, and later supplements.)

Estimating Steps

The method of estimation was as follows: Per capita consumption of milk, including that in the form of processed products such as cheese, was determined for the various income classes in each set of data. For each income class the difference between average consumption and "need" was determined. Then average consumption and the additional amount needed per person were determined for each group of families. Estimates for the urban, rural nonfarm and farm families were averaged using as weights the population for 1950 as reported in *1950 Census of Population*, Vol. II, *Characteristics of the Population*, Pt. 1, U.S. Summary, Chap. B, 1952.

The additional amount of milk needed was expressed as a percentage of the average consumption reported by families. The per capita supply for 1948 and 1950, as reported by the U.S. Department of Agriculture, indicated that family dietary data for 1948 should be quite suitable for indicating dietary deficiencies within the population during 1950.

In estimating the gap in 1960 between probable demand and "need" for calcium the following procedures were used. (1) For each income class of the urban families reporting diets in 1948 the consumption in 1960 was estimated using the method described in Appendix 5-3. It was assumed that the rate of increase in food expenditures and in the consumption of foods with increases in food expenditures was the same at every income level. Family dietary data provide some support for this assumption, and any evidence to the contrary indicates that when real income of a country rises, consumption of food increases more among low- than among high-income families. Hence the procedure used probably leads to some understatement of the increase between 1950 and 1960 in the consumption of families most likely to have deficient diets in 1950, and thus it leads to an overstatement of the size of the gap remaining in 1960 between demand and "need." (2) The increase in the per capita demand for dairy products other than milk thus estimated was divided by the additional amount found to be "needed" in 1950. This division provided a ratio that expressed the extent to which the 1950 "gap" had been closed. This ratio was multiplied by the percentage increase in dairy products, excluding butter, estimated to be needed in 1950, which in turn yielded an estimate of the percentage by which "need" in 1960 exceeded probable demand. Since the additional per capita "need" for dairy products tends to be higher for urban than for rural families, it seems probable that this method of estimation may lead to some overstatement of the "gap" for the total population. The gap is too small and the data are too meager to warrant attempts at more refined methods of estimation.

Additional Assumptions

Other important assumptions were:

(1) That errors by families in reporting consumption did not introduce an important bias. (To the extent that there is more underreporting than overreporting, the data tend to overstate the deficiencies. Underreporting seems likely to be more common.)
(2) That the distribution of milk among members of the households was on the basis of "need." Because this undoubtedly does not occur, the estimate tends to understate "need."
(3) That no over-all error occurs if average need per person for a cross-section of the population is applied to the consumption of persons in various income categories.
(4) That deficiencies greater than the average for a given income class are insignificant when family consumption over a period of time is considered, perhaps for three or four weeks. (See discussion on p. 166 above.) It seems likely, however, that "deficiencies" of some families are overlooked by this method.
(5) That high consumption during a peak season does not make good the deficiency of a low season. For example, two out of three of the farm groups whose winter and late spring diets were used in estimating the quantity of additional milk "needed" (see reference (c) above) had very low milk consumption; whereas milk consumption was very high in the farm group whose diets during late spring and early summer are reported in reference (b). Part of the difference is probably geographical, but part is undoubtedly due to the season of the year covered. In so far as excess calcium of one season tends to be stored in the body and used in seasons when intake is below optimum, over a long period of time the method used in estimating deficiencies tends to overstate deficiencies.

Tendencies to an upward bias were in some measure offset by tendencies to a downward bias. The estimate should be looked upon only as a crude indication of the gap between consumption and need using one type of yardstick.

ASCORBIC ACID

Since no revision was made by the NRC in the allowance for ascorbic acid in 1953, the quantities of various fruits and vegetables recommended in the low-cost food budget provided the yardstick of need. The family dietary data used were as follows: (a) 1948 Food Consumption Surveys, Preliminary Report No. 5, U.S. Department of Agriculture, Tables 3, 4 and 5; (b) Agriculture Information Bulletin No. 41, U.S. Department of Agriculture, Tables 36, 40, 41 and 46; (c) Southern Cooperative Bulletin No. 20, South Carolina Agricultural Experiment Station, November 1951, Table 19; (d) Miscellaneous Publication No. 550, U.S. Department of Agriculture, 1944, and Bulletin No. 822, U.S. Bureau of Labor Statistics, 1945.

In using the family dietary data to represent various groups in the population one difference in assumptions was made, namely, that during one third of the year when local supplies of fruits and vegetables are likely to be lowest, the consumption of rural nonfarm people was halfway between that of the rural nonfarm group described in source (b) and the farm group described in source (c). This interpretation of the data yields a higher estimate of need than the assumption used in the case of calcium.

Estimating Steps

The method of estimation was as follows: Per capita consumption of three groups of fruits and vegetables — citrus fruits and tomatoes; leafy, green and yellow vegetables; and potatoes and other fruits and vegetables — was determined for each income class.

For each income class the difference between average consumption and "need" in terms of the low-cost budget was determined. In view of the marked increase which has been occurring in the consumption of citrus fruits and tomatoes and of leafy, green and yellow vegetables and the fact that these are the more important sources of ascorbic acid, over-all "deficiencies" in the consumption of the three groups of fruits and vegetables have been expressed as deficiencies in these two. Consumption below the level recommended in the low-cost food budget in one type was assumed to be compensated for by excess consumption in the other two. Because the three food groups differed appreciably as sources of ascorbic acid, the substitution or offset took into account the ascorbic acid content per pound. Ratios of ascorbic acid per pound were assumed to be as follows: potatoes and other fruits and vegetables, one; leafy, green and yellow vegetables, two; and citrus fruits and tomatoes, three. These ratios were based on average ascorbic acid content of these food groups reported in 1948 Food Consumption Surveys, Preliminary Report No. 12, U.S. Department of Agri-culture, Tables 1, 2 and 13. In addition, a rough adjustment was made for cooking losses.

In balancing deficiencies in one group against excesses in another in order to get a net figure, deficiencies in leafy, green and yellow vegetables were first adjusted if there were excesses of potatoes and other fruits and vegetables in the income classes. Only residual excesses in the other groups were deducted from citrus fruit and tomato deficiencies because of the importance of these foods as sources of ascorbic acid and their position of favor with consumers as indicated by consumption trends.

In estimating the probable gap in 1960 between demand and "need" for ascorbic acid, estimates of demand by income level for urban data were made using the procedure described above for calcium. Since foods rich in ascorbic acid tend to have a high coefficient of elasticity in relation to food expenditures, it is not surprising that the increase in demand estimated between 1950 and 1960 reduced the gap to zero for the urban families. With what is known about dietary patterns in general of rural compared to urban families and with the likelihood that markets by 1960 will probably have increased greatly the fresh fruits and vegetables available in rural areas, it seems likely that the gap between demand for foods that provide ascorbic acid and the "need" for these will be very small. It was decided quite arbitrarily to assume a gap of 2 per cent in excess of demand for both citrus fruits and tomatoes and for leafy, green and yellow vegetables.

APPENDIX 5–3. METHOD OF ESTIMATING DEMAND FOR MAJOR FOODS IN 1960

The estimated demand for major foods in 1960 was based on data in the following sources: (a) *Consumption of Food in the United States, 1909–52,* Agriculture Handbook No. 62, U.S. Department of Agriculture, September 1953; (b) *Food Consumption of Urban Families (68 Cities) in the U.S., Spring 1948,* 1948 Food Consumption Surveys, Preliminary Report No. 5, U.S. Department of Agriculture, May 1949, Table 3; and (c) other family dietary studies (see Appendix 5–2).

Estimating Procedure

The procedure was as follows:

(1) Average per capita expenditures for food consumed at home and the amount purchased in each of the major food groups were determined for the dietary data in source (b).

(2) Amount of food purchased was plotted against food expenditure. In general the relationship was found to be linear on a logarithmic scale.

(3) Regression coefficients were determined for each of the food groups using the equation $\log y = a + b \log x$, where x is per capita expenditure for food consumed at home and y is the quantity of a food purchased. Such regression coefficients are a measure of the coefficient of elasticity of quantity of food purchased in relation to food expenditure.

(4) Examination of data reported in other dietary studies indicated that urban households in the spring of 1948 could be taken as representative of families in all types of communities in the United States.

(5) The coefficient of elasticity for sugar and sweets was −0.1. In view of the sugar in bakery products and canned fruits, which were not included in the quantity of "sugar and sweets" reported by families, a coefficient of elasticity of zero was assumed for this food group. The dietary data also yielded a coefficient of elasticity of quantity of "fat" (excluding fat in bakery products) in relation to expenditures of −0.6. To omit the fat in bakery products, however, would tend to understate fat consumption at higher expenditure levels. A superficial examination of the dietary data led to an adjustment of the coefficient to −0.3.

(6) The adjusted coefficients of elasticity of purchases in relation to expenditures were used in conjunction with the estimate of change between 1950 and 1960 in per capita expenditure for food consumed at home (see p. 167) and per capita demand for selected foods in 1950. (See column 1 in Table 60.) In other words, the percentage change in the demand for a specific food from 1950 to 1960 had to be such in relation to the percentage change in food expenditures as to yield the coefficient of elasticity derived from the family dietary data.

Additional Assumptions

Some additional assumptions were: (a) that differences in methods of measuring foods between the family dietary data and the national aggregates did not introduce important biases, for example, the measuring of milk purchases in terms of "milk equivalent" in the family dietary data and in terms of pounds of food as purchased in the aggregate data; and (b) that changes in relative prices did not introduce important biases.

APPENDIX 6–1. PERSONAL CARE, CLOTHING AND RELATED INDUSTRIES, TRADES AND BUSINESSES, 1947–1948

Kind of Business	Number of Establishments	Number of Wage Earners [a]	Wages [b]	Value of Products, Sales or Receipts
				(Thousands)
Manufacturing — 1947	45,143	2,501,814	$5,310,613	$25,922,945
Textiles and fibers	7,603	1,074,811	2,272,464	10,296,403
Woolen and worsted	828	166,947	394,655	1,924,309
Yarn and thread mills	658	117,356	215,171	1,000,339
Cotton broad-woven	602	342,360	699,871	3,294,623
Rayon and related broad-woven	507	91,174	204,991	1,002,923
Narrow fabric mills	479	24,917	51,604	210,908
Knitting mills	3,126	212,962	414,036	1,721,314
Finishing textiles (except wool)	641	69,035	176,094	531,400
Hats	271	18,864	43,362	199,564
Miscellaneous textile goods [c]	491	31,196	72,680	411,023
Apparel and related products	29,730	959,734	2,017,234	9,632,411
Men's and boys' suits and coats	1,969	136,136	337,972	1,449,982
Men's and boys' furnishings	4,026	234,476	374,850	1,934,472
Women's and misses' outerwear	10,085	279,029	671,342	3,221,103
Women's and children's undergarments	2,051	83,895	145,208	857,582
Millinery	932	18,076	46,812	177,495
Children's outerwear	1,687	43,358	79,351	402,818
Fur goods	2,229	13,745	57,636	357,013
Miscellaneous apparel, accessories and notions [d]	4,100	117,979	238,173	976,821
Embroideries and trimmings	2,651	33,040	65,890	255,125
Leather and rubber products	4,606	360,553	758,713	3,753,661
Leather	561	48,627	130,586	1,070,085
Footwear — cut stock	606	19,706	38,468	294,309
Footwear	1,500	220,654	438,894	1,793,997
Gloves and mittens	341	10,464	17,040	62,838
Handbags and small leather goods	980	23,246	44,122	199,568
Luggage	592	13,904	31,141	134,173
Rubber footwear	26	23,952	58,462	198,691
Jewelry [e]	2,237	69,136	167,886	782,789
Soap, glycerin, perfumes, cosmetics and other toilet preparations	967	37,580	94,316	1,457,681
Wholesale trade — 1948	28,489	182,755	770,288	22,908,096
Clothing and furnishings	7,485	42,676	173,140	4,051,885
General line	624	5,183	18,692	698,793
Men's and boys'	2,015	12,100	51,482	997,783
Women's and children's	2,452	12,304	50,682	1,333,864
Furs, dressed, and fur clothing	638	1,949	7,797	211,679
Millinery and millinery supplies	610	3,044	10,554	160,290
Shoes and other footwear	891	6,589	26,815	474,503
Work clothing	218	1,007	3,964	113,082
Clothing not elsewhere classified	37	500	3,154	61,891
Dry goods	7,435	54,907	250,040	8,384,487
General line	574	11,018	41,020	1,082,833
Hosiery and lingerie	1,035	5,644	24,855	629,514
Notions and other dry goods	2,389	16,460	67,081	931,019
Piece goods jobbers	3,437	21,785	117,084	5,741,121
Piece goods converters	1,134	12,246	81,975	1,764,143
Raw materials	3,689	17,010	62,552	5,407,334
Cotton	1,925	9,218	27,691	3,524,250
Hides, skins and raw fur	1,240	5,007	19,365	900,437
Wool and mohair	524	2,785	15,496	982,647
Jewelry	3,853	18,226	71,285	1,016,911

APPENDIX 6-1 (continued)

Kind of Business	Number of Establish-ments	Number of Wage Earners [a]	Wages [b]	Value of Products, Sales or Receipts
			(Thousands)	
Leather and shoe findings	1,365	6,083	$ 23,418	$ 484,364
Leather goods	115	677	1,897	17,302
Textiles and materials	706	6,289	19,945	491,547
Yarns (industrial)	267	1,302	6,488	540,524
Toiletries	939	12,663	44,911	483,868
Barber and beauty supplies	1,063	6,257	16,956	100,228
Laundry and dry cleaning supplies	438	4,419	17,681	165,503
Retail trade — 1948	226,984	1,119,633	2,119,835	17,972,091
Apparel stores	115,246	585,703	1,178,820	9,803,218
Men's and boys' clothing, furnishings, hat stores	23,730	93,554	243,781	2,165,953
Family clothing stores	12,533	114,083	217,854	1,791,317
Women's ready-to-wear stores	30,677	228,881	404,012	3,305,162
Millinery, hosiery, accessories stores	13,481	31,135	49,858	436,867
Shoe stores	19,551	73,849	165,843	1,467,307
Children's and infants' and other apparel stores	15,274	44,201	97,472	636,612
Dry goods and general merchandise stores	29,754	175,029	281,578	2,823,869
Jewelry stores	21,269	68,898	178,306	1,224,878
Secondhand clothing and shoe stores	3,731	3,391	4,240	38,067
Luggage stores	1,188	3,721	8,406	68,828
Drugstores	55,796	282,891	468,485	4,013,231
Service establishments — 1948	328,655	742,867	1,604,667	3,467,323
Laundries and laundry services	26,529	300,230	541,433	1,085,193
Power laundries	6,783	272,495	501,646	913,036
Laundries — not power	10,839	12,671	17,751	80,861
Diaper service	384	4,685	10,061	25,887
Self-service laundries	8,523	10,379	11,975	65,409
Cleaning, dyeing, repair, etc.	116,056	268,660	489,268	1,392,134
Cleaning and dyeing (excluding rugs)	24,017	203,867	385,155	807,673
Pressing, alteration, garment repair (excluding fur)	45,554	37,488	59,197	320,148
Fur storage and repair	2,334	4,405	8,507	45,513
Hat cleaning	1,426	2,019	2,532	9,956
Shoe repair	39,763	19,191	32,711	202,176
Shoe shine	2,962	1,690	1,166	6,668
Barber and beauty services	170,704	159,202	282,434	856,205
Barber shops	91,993	64,509	126,012	404,441
Beauty shops	74,497	87,290	143,274	417,570
Barber and beauty shops combined	2,591	5,365	9,696	22,987
Turkish baths, massage, electrolysis, etc.	1,623	2,038	3,452	11,207
Miscellaneous personal services	15,366	14,775	29,532	133,791
Costume and dress suit rental	510	1,216	2,845	10,117
Watch, clock, jewelry repair	12,750	6,214	13,404	86,401
Personal services not elsewhere classified	2,106	7,345	13,283	37,273

Source: U.S. Bureau of the Census, volumes on Manufactures, Wholesale Trade, Retail Trade and Service Establishments, 1947–1948.

a. Employees in wholesale and retail trade, and service establishments.

b. Payrolls in wholesale and retail trade, and service establishments.

c. Felt goods, wool, hair and jute; lace goods; processed waste and recovered wool fibers; artificial leather and oilcloth; linen goods; jute goods.

d. Belts; gloves and mittens; handkerchiefs; suspenders, garters and other elastic goods; robes and dressing gowns; raincoats; leather and sheep-lined clothing; buttons, needles, pins, hooks, eyes and fasteners; umbrellas and canes; costume jewelry and novelties; dyed and dressed furs.

e. Clocks and watches; jewelry, jewelers' findings and lapidary work; watch, jewelry and instrument cases.

APPENDIX 6–2. INDEXES OF THE PHYSICAL VOLUME OF PRODUCTION OF TEXTILE AND LEATHER PRODUCTS, 1899–1937

(*1929 = 100*)

Year	Cotton Goods	Woolen and Worsted Goods			Silk and Rayon Goods	Knit Goods	Linen Goods	Leather Shoes
		Total	Woolen Goods	Worsted Goods				
1899	49	71	—	—	22	19	137	60
1904	54	86	—	—	30	24	—	68
1909	68	103	78	123	40	33	200	78
1914	73	102	83	118	49	45	192	81
1919	78	98	92	104	64	55	86	89
1921	70	93	80	105	58	59	72	76
1923	93	120	115	130	73	75	125	93
1925	93	108	112	106	86	77	117	84
1927	104	103	105	103	92	83	120	96
1929	100	100	100	100	100	100	100	100
1931	78	81	70	88	92	92	68	84
1933	87	87	—	—	84	100	72	94
1935	78	116	—	—	133	111	73	103
1937	99	114	—	—	135	116	77	112

Source: Data from Solomon Fabricant, *The Output of Manufacturing Industries, 1899–1937*, National Bureau of Economic Research, New York, 1940, pp. 169–171, and p. 192. Indexes calculated on basis of data from Census volumes on Manufactures over this period.

APPENDIX 6–3. FAMILY CLOTHING INVENTORIES AND PURCHASES,
MINNEAPOLIS–ST. PAUL, MINNESOTA, 1948–1949

(Families without Children or with One or Two Children Aged 2–15 Years)

Item	Husbands' Clothing (Number of Husbands — 514)					Boys' (2–15 Yrs.) Clothing (Number of Boys — 140)				
	Average Number Owned	Per Cent Owning	Average Number Purchased	Per Cent Purchasing	Average Expenditure	Average Number Owned	Per Cent Owning	Average Number Purchased	Per Cent Purchasing	Average Expenditure
All items	—	—	—	—	$128.94	—	—	—	—	$80.14
Overcoats, heavy storm coats	1.2	87	.17	17	10.44	.4	31	.10	10	1.74
Topcoats with heavy linings	.3	27	.05	5	2.28	.1	11	.03	3	.57
Topcoats with light linings	.7	66	.09	9	4.01	.4	41	.14	13	2.18
Raincoats, jackets, slickers	.6	53	.05	5	.72	.4	39	.11	11	.57
Heavy jackets	1.5	82	.20	19	2.78	1.0	59	.33	28	3.48
Light jackets	.8	62	.13	12	1.17	.8	59	.24	22	1.25
Snow suits, ski suits, etc.	a	3	a	a	.01	.7	54	.27	27	3.45
Ski pants, separate leggings	a	3				.3	24	.04	4	.23
Caps, beanies, helmets, stocking caps, etc.	1.0	62	.27	19	.54	2.3	99	.96	60	1.57
Hats for business or dress	2.1	93	.57	43	4.83	.2	16	.04	4	.06
Other hats	.4	20	.20	7	.21	.1	5	.03	3	.05
Shirt-pants outfits, slack suits, etc.	.3	16	.04	3	.35	1.2	36	.32	13	1.11
Year-round and winter suits	2.7	99	.50	40	31.61	.5	37	.13	13	2.10
Summer suits	.5	30	.08	7	4.66	.1	6	.04	4	.18
Dress suits	.1	8	.01	1	.54					—
Separate suit coats, sport jackets	.6	39	.10	9	2.30	.5	36	.08	8	.88
Separate trousers and slacks for dress	2.4	84	.55	37	6.44	3.5	86	1.62	64	8.33
Work trousers	2.4	68	.63	25	2.62	.3	6	.21	6	.43
Overalls, coveralls	1.3	51	.58	20	1.89	4.3[a]	91	1.99	69	4.62
Shop coats, work jackets, aprons	.4	14	.10	4	.30		1			—
Sportswear, sunsuits, shorts, bathing shorts	.7	47	.08	7	.34	2.6[a]	89	.54	36	1.14
Riding, fishing, hunting outfits	.2	18	.03	2	.28		1			—
Athletic uniforms	a	3	—	—	—	.1	5	.03	2	.05
Lodge and club uniforms, costumes		3				.2	14	.02	2	.16
Knit shirts	3.5	59	1.15	27	1.42	8.2[a]	99	3.37	69	4.10
Work shirts	3.2	67	.91	29	2.40		2			—

Woven sport shirts	2.6	69	.46	24	$2.63	3.7	81	.99	38	$2.55
Woven dress shirts	9.4	100	1.73	51	6.97	2.1	56	.59	24	1.58
Pull-over sweaters	1.4	52	.11	8	.50	2.0	79	.45	27	1.29
Coat-style sweaters, vests	.8	54	.08	8	.63	1.2	69	.21	18	.82
Knit briefs or shorts	3.0	45	1.07	25	1.00	6.2	91	3.61	68	2.22
Undershorts, woven	3.5	48	.92	22	1.03	.5	11	.22	7	.21
Separate drawers	.7	24	.19	8	.40	.6	22	.56	20	.86
Undershirts	4.6	65	1.31	32	1.19	4.4	81	2.26	52	1.48
Union suits, knit	2.1	53	.45	20	1.66	.9	31	.38	16	.61
Union suits, woven	.4	9	.09	3	.21	a	1	—	—	—
Pajamas	2.8	83	.32	21	1.37	3.5	94	.89	44	1.83
Night shirts	.3	10	.02	1	.05	a	1	.01	1	.03
Other sleeping garments	.1	2	—	—	—	.2	5	.07	3	.12
Bathrobes and lounging robes	.9	77	.05	5	.52	.8	75	.06	6	.21
Heavy athletic or work socks	4.7	63	2.42	30	1.39	1.2	29	.69	12	.38
Other socks — dress or general purpose	13.5	99	6.00	65	3.93	10.4	98	9.29	85	3.95
Canvas-rubber shoes, athletic, etc.	.3	23	.03	3	.19	.5	39	.26	20	.95
Boots — rubber, leather, felt	.4	31	.03	2	.22	.4	31	.14	14	.81
Heavy-duty work shoes	.7	46	.21	16	1.52	a	4	.04	3	.22
Shoes for street, dress, sport	3.1	100	.81	57	8.84	1.6	100	2.48	97	14.22
Bedroom, house slippers	1.1	90	.16	15	.65	.9	81	.34	30	.71
Rubbers, galoshes, arctics	1.7	93	.33	29	1.11	1.4	96	.77	65	2.55
Handkerchiefs	19.9	100	1.48	20	.63	4.5	59	.58	8	.17
Work gloves, mittens	1.5	60	3.27	33	1.61	.2	8	.44	6	.26
Dress or business gloves	1.8	93	.24	20	.98	2.7	94	1.09	51	1.23
Mufflers, scarfs	2.0	86	.07	6	.20	1.4	80	.11	9	.15
Ties	18.5	99	1.59	41	3.32	1.8	46	.21	12	.18
Jewelry — rings, watches, cuff links	—	—	—	18	2.93	—	—	—	16	1.47
Belts, wallets, misc. accessories	—	—	—	31	1.15	—	—	—	41	.83

APPENDIX 6–3 (continued)

Item	Wives' Clothing (Number of Wives — 514)					Girls' (2–15 years) Clothing (Number of Girls — 126)				
	Average Number Owned	Per Cent Owning	Average Number Purchased	Per Cent Purchasing	Average Expenditure	Average Number Owned	Per Cent Owning	Average Number Purchased	Per Cent Purchasing	Average Expenditure
All items	—	—	—	—	$181.66	—	—	—	—	$84.01
Heavy coats without fur	.7	54	.16	15	8.42	.5	46	.22	21	4.90
Heavy coats with fur trim	.4	34	.09	9	7.64	.1	14	.10	10	2.81
Lightweight coats, capes, etc.	1.4	93	.35	32	11.66	1.0	76	.25	25	3.40
Fur coats, jackets, capes	.7	62	.07	6	17.38	a	2	—	—	—
Fur scarfs, muffs, etc.	.2	18	.01	1	1.64	.1	11	.01	1	.02
Raincoats and capes	.3	26	.07	7	.99	.5	39	.09	9	.55
Heavy sport jackets	.3	26	.03	3	.33	.6	44	.09	9	.69
Snow suits, ski suits, etc.	.2	16	a	a	.08	1.1	71	.27	25	4.24
Ski pants, separate leggings	.1	5	—	—	—	.3	31	.10	10	.58
Hats, caps, hoods, berets, etc.	3.8	97	1.31	72	8.94	2.3	90	.70	54	1.69
Scarfs, mufflers, kerchiefs	2.9	95	.55	37	1.14	2.7	85	.50	33	.61
House dresses	4.8	94	1.23	48	5.40					
Other dresses — street, evening	6.3	99	1.87	70	26.50	9.1	97	1.74	63	8.27
Suits	1.4	68	.30	25	13.01	.5	37	.07	7	.78
Separate suit coats, jackets	.3	21	.03	2	.35	.4	27	.04	4	.09
Separate skirts	1.3	54	.38	24	2.63	3.2	94	.57	32	2.52
Blouses, shirts	4.4	82	.96	44	4.57	5.2	98	1.33	55	2.47
Pull-over sweaters, shirts	1.1	38	.22	13	.94	2.3	68	.83	35	2.12
Coat sweaters	1.2	71	.21	18	1.07	2.3	94	.59	36	1.91
Aprons, smocks	6.2	96	.22	12	.27	1.4	53	.06	6	.05
Slack suits	.3	20	.02	2	.33	.1	5	.02	2	.09
Slacks	1.0	54	.20	16	1.55	1.6	73	.49	32	2.10
Overalls, coveralls, jeans	.3	23	.09	7	.26	2.7	92	1.10	56	2.51
Play, sun, bathing suits	1.2	49	.19	15	1.21	3.6	90	.78	34	2.21
Gym suits and athletic uniforms	a	2	.01	1	.03	.1	10	.06	6	.21
Lodge, club uniforms, costumes	a	2	.01	a	.08	.1	8	.04	4	.21
Slips and petticoats	5.4	100	1.31	57	5.14	3.4	96	.73	40	1.55
Vests and undershirts	.5	16	.10	4	.12	3.6	78	1.75	50	1.17
Panties, step-ins, snuggies, drawers	7.2	97	2.55	61	2.41	10.5	100	4.83	87	2.76
Union suits	.2	8	.07	3	.16	.3	10	.18	8	.25

Brassieres	3.5	83	1.34	56	$2.95	.5	13	.34	13	$ .52
Corsets and girdles	1.7	85	.61	43	4.21	.1	9	.09	6	.23
Garter belts	.4	29	.14	11	.27	.3	24	.10	9	.11
Night gowns	3.4	89	.37	22	1.56	.7	40	.18	11	.45
Pajamas	1.4	52	.19	12	.69	3.1	93	.79	37	1.73
Other sleeping garments	a	1	.01	a	.01	.2	5	.06	2	.12
Bed jackets, shoulderettes	.6	34	.01	1	.03	a	3	—	—	—
Robes, housecoats, negligees	2.0	95	.18	16	1.81	1.3	90	.12	12	.56
Long hose	5.8	100	8.21	93	11.67	1.9	49	2.02	37	1.66
Anklets	3.6	65	1.99	37	.84	10.4	100	9.00	90	3.64
Boot socks	.1	6	.01	1	.01	.3	15	.08	4	.07
Footlets	.2	9	.03	2	.01	a	1	—	—	—
Special athletic shoes, tennis, etc.	.2	18	.02	2	.12	.6	37	.29	24	1.11
Street shoes	5.5	100	1.97	83	16.06	2.4	100	2.93	98	14.89
Leather boots	.1	10	a	a	.04	a	3	.02	2	.06
Bedroom and house slippers	1.2	85	.32	25	.85	1.2	91	.38	33	.77
Rubbers, galoshes, boots	1.8	97	.40	36	1.87	1.4	98	.75	63	2.97
Handkerchiefs	21.8	98	.64	11	.35	8.8	79	.21	3	.06
Gloves and mittens	4.7	100	.76	48	2.05	3.0	100	.71	47	.95
Handbags and purses	2.8	100	.64	47	4.45	1.9	87	.39	29	.77
Umbrellas	.9	75	.09	9	.39	.3	26	.06	6	.19
Necklaces, earrings, pins, watches, etc.	—	—	—	42	5.98	—	—	—	18	1.22
Belts, ribbons, flowers, etc.	—	—	—	26	.93	—	—	—	45	1.00
Headbands, veilings, shower caps	—	—	—	13	.26	—	—	—	12	.17

a. Not significant.

Note: Average expenditure for total family clothing purchases was $353.05.

Source: Compiled from U.S. Department of Agriculture *Studies of Family Clothing Supplies*, Preliminary Report No. 1, *Family Clothing Inventories by Income*, and Preliminary Report No. 2, *Family Clothing Purchases by Income*, Minneapolis–St. Paul, Minn., 1948–1949.

APPENDIX 6–4. ANNUAL CLOTHING REPLACEMENT RATES FOR CITY WORKER'S FAMILY AND FARM FAMILY BUDGETS COMPARED WITH PREVIOUSLY PUBLISHED STANDARDS

(Number of Garments to Be Purchased Each Year)

Clothing Item	WPA Maintenance Budget (Urban)	Heller Committee Wage-Earner Budget (San Francisco)	Standard Used in First Edition of America's Needs and Resources		City Worker's Family Budget	Farm Family Budget
			Nonfarm	Farm		
Allowance for a Man						
Coats and raincoats	.33	.17	.20	.10	.33	.10
Sweaters and jackets	.50	.66	.50	.75	.64	.90
Suits	.66	.50	.50	.35	.89	.38
Trousers, slacks, overalls	5.50	3.00	3.50	6.00	1.82	4.06
Shirts	5.00	5.00	4.50	4.25	5.12	5.04
Sportswear (slack suits, bathing shorts, etc.)	—	—	—	—	.47	.30
Underwear	3.50[a]	8.00[b]	5.00[b]	5.00[b]	7.52[b]	4.99[b]
Nightwear and bathrobes	1.50	1.13	1.00	1.00	.92	.20
Socks	10.00	9.00	12.00	12.00	13.52	10.76
Shoes and house slippers	3.33	2.25	2.25	2.00	2.30	2.40
Rubbers and arctics	.33	—	.33	.86	.37	.67
Hats and caps	1.66	1.50	1.08	1.25	1.26	2.15
Gloves	10.00	11.00	10.00	10.00	4.56	7.96
Ties	3.00	6.00	3.00	1.00	3.05	.51
Allowance for a Woman						
Coats and raincoats	.66	.66	.50	.35	.52	.45
Sweaters and jackets	.50	.25	.50	.50	.41	.39
Suits	—	—	—	—	.11	.14
Dresses	6.00	3.50	4.00	3.75	4.17	4.21
Skirts	—	—	.50	.34	.22	.16
Blouses	—	—	2.00	2.00	.48	.38
Housewear and sportswear	2.00	—	1.00	1.00	1.30	1.39
Underwear	10.00	7.00	8.75	8.40	7.44	7.16
Nightwear and bathrobes	1.80	1.67	1.20	1.20	1.39	1.17
Hosiery, including anklets	8.00	10.00	13.00	12.00	12.88	9.65
Shoes and house slippers	2.50	2.33	2.65	2.65	3.02	2.82
Rubbers, galoshes, arctics	.33	.33	.33	.57	.22	.53
Hats	1.50	2.00	1.75	.90	2.03	1.40

Sources: Compiled from Table 51, pp. 138–139, Chapter 7, "Clothing, Accessories and Personal Care," *America's Needs and Resources,* 1947 edition, and Table 73 of the current survey.

a. Union suits only.
b. Union suits, undershirts and shorts.

APPENDIX 6–5. METHOD OF ESTIMATING CLOTHING NEEDS

Estimates of the distribution of families and individuals by income class and by place of residence (urban, rural nonfarm and rural farm) for 1950 and 1960 were prepared from data furnished by the United States Department of Commerce. Expenditures for clothing and personal care were then estimated through an analysis of the relationships of expenditures for these items to disposable income, at various levels of income and for the different places of residence. The expenditure estimates for urban consumers were derived from data published in U.S. Bureau of Labor Statistics, Bulletin No. 1097 (revised), *Family Income, Expenditures, and Savings in 1950,* and in Bulletin No. 1065, *Family Income, Expenditures and Savings in Ten Cities in 1946–49.* Estimates for the rural farm and rural nonfarm areas were derived from data for earlier years, adjusted for changes in expenditures which might be expected to result from known changes in income and population in these areas.

The costs of the clothing standards for particular types of consumers (families or individuals; under 65 years or over 65 years) were weighted together by the relative proportion of consumers of each type at a specific income level to obtain the estimated need for clothing at each level of income in each place of residence. This average need at each income level was then compared with the estimated expenditure for clothing at that income level. If the amount spent by the average family in an income class was less than the estimated cost of the standard for that class, the need for the class was estimated to be the product of the total number of families in the class times the amount by which the standard cost exceeded the average expenditure. The sum of the estimated needs for each class where expenditures were less than the budget costs represented the total need for the year. For example, in 1950 there were an estimated 1,102,000 urban families of two or more persons with less than $1,000 of disposable income. These families had an estimated average expenditure for clothing of $49. When the $358 budget cost for urban families of two or more headed by persons less than 65 years old was weighted together with the $100 cost for families with heads 65 years of age or over, the average cost of the clothing budget at this income level was estimated at $275. The clothing need for this income class, therefore, was 1,102,000 times the difference between $275, the budget cost, and $49, the estimated expenditure.

APPENDIX 7–1. CONDITION AND PLUMBING EQUIPMENT OF DWELLING UNITS INSIDE AND OUTSIDE STANDARD METROPOLITAN AREAS, 1950[a]

(Thousands)

Location	Total	Not Dilapidated					Dilapidated		
		Total	With Hot Water, Private Toilet and Bath	With Private Toilet and Bath, No Hot Water	With Running Water, No Private Toilet or Bath	No Running Water	Total	With Hot Water, Private Toilet and Bath	Lacking Private Toilet, Bath, or Hot Water
Total	45,983	41,488	28,985	1,483	5,683	5,337	4,495	648	3,847
Urban	29,569	27,664	22,998	961	3,120	585	1,905	525	1,380
Rural nonfarm	10,056	8,704	4,503	390	1,608	2,203	1,352	91	1,261
Rural farm	6,358	5,120	1,484	132	955	2,549	1,238	32	1,206
Inside standard metropolitan areas	25,627	24,078	19,882	797	2,616	783	1,549	442	1,107
Urban	22,505	21,268	18,212	673	2,134	249	1,237	410	827
Places of less than 50,000	6,194	5,941	5,183	151	479	128	253	81	172
Cities of 50,000 to 100,000	2,723	2,554	2,117	105	295	37	169	41	128
Cities of 100,000 or more	13,588	12,773	10,912	417	1,360	84	815	288	527
Rural nonfarm	2,386	2,165	1,346	99	358	362	221	24	197
Rural farm	736	645	324	25	124	172	91	8	83
Urban places of less than 50,000 and rural	9,316	8,751	6,853	275	961	662	565	113	452
Outside standard metropolitan areas	20,356	17,410	9,103	686	3,067	4,554	2,946	206	2,740
Urban	7,064	6,396	4,786	288	986	336	668	115	553
Rural nonfarm	7,670	6,539	3,157	291	1,250	1,841	1,131	67	1,064
Rural farm	5,622	4,475	1,160	107	831	2,377	1,147	24	1,123
Standard metropolitan areas and urban outside	32,691	30,474	24,668	1,085	3,602	1,119	2,217	557	1,660

Source: 1950 Census of Housing.

a. Units not reporting on condition or plumbing equipment have been distributed in the same proportions as reporting units.

Appendix 7–2. Statistical Methods Used in Estimating Housing Needs

The estimates of housing needs in Chapter 7 and of urban redevelopment in Chapter 16 are based on city block data from the 1940 Census of Housing (the supplement to the First Series Housing Bulletin) and on a special analysis of data from the 1950 Census of Housing — in particular, a special tabulation of statistics by city blocks for the following nine cities, which contain a total of 437,772 dwelling units: Portland, Oregon; Jersey City, New Jersey; Salt Lake City, Utah; Wilmington, Delaware; Lincoln, Nebraska; Topeka, Kansas; Hammond, Indiana; Manchester, New Hampshire; and Columbia, South Carolina.

The 1950 statistics by blocks were tabulated to obtain the distribution by state of repair and plumbing equipment for all "substandard" blocks, that is, blocks in which 50 per cent or more of the dwelling units were dilapidated or lacked any of the following: hot running water in the structure, bathtub or shower in the structure for the exclusive use of the occupants of the unit, and a flush toilet in the structure for the exclusive use of the occupants of the unit. These substandard blocks were identified on maps, and contiguous blocks of this type in clusters of five or more were classified as in "concentrated areas." Blocks which were not substandard but were surrounded on three or more sides by substandard blocks in concentrated areas were classified as "surrounded blocks."

For each of the nine cities the number of dwelling units in substandard blocks as a percentage of the city total was computed for each of the following types of dwelling units:

(a) Dilapidated or lacking running water in structure;

(b) Not dilapidated, with running water, but lacking a private flush toilet or private bath;

(c) Not dilapidated, with private flush toilet and bath, but lacking hot running water in structure.

The composite percentage of each type was obtained by averaging the percentages for the nine cities in order to avoid giving undue weight to the larger cities in the group. To obtain factors to apply to data for all cities of 50,000 or more, the average 1950 factors for the nine selected cities were adjusted by the relationship of the corresponding average 1940 factor for these nine cities to the average 1940 factor for a representative sample of 42 cities of 50,000 or more. The factors for areas inside standard metropolitan areas but outside cities of 50,000 or more were obtained by assuming that these factors should bear the same relationship to those for the larger cities indicated by the 1940 data.

It was assumed that the factors for urban areas outside standard metropolitan areas should be one half of the corresponding factors for the portion of the standard metropolitan areas outside the larger cities. This procedure produced the percentages shown in lines 4, 12 and 20 of Table A.

The percentages shown on lines 6, 9, 14, 17, 22 and 25 represent the average of the corresponding percentages for the nine selected cities.

The relationship of the number of dwelling units which were dilapidated or lacked hot water, toilet or bath to all dwelling units was computed for the three types of blocks in each of the nine cities. The average percentage for the nine cities was adjusted on the basis of the 1940 relationship of the nine cities to the total. It was assumed that the factors for urban areas outside standard metropolitan areas would be the same as those for areas inside standard metropolitan areas but outside the larger cities. These factors are shown on lines 28, 32 and 36.

The figures on lines 1, 2, 10 and 18 of Table A were obtained from a special tabulation of the returns of the 1950 Census of Housing. The remaining figures in Table A were computed by the method indicated in the stub of the table in the following sequence: line 3, 5, 7, 8, 11, 13, 15, 16, 19, 21, 23, 24, 27, 26, 29, 31, 30, 33, 35, 34, 37.

The assumptions used in making these computations were based on the belief that the role of environmental factors in the determination of bad housing declines as the size of the locality declines and that the significance of the factors themselves varies with their degree of concentration. For example, the absence of hot water was used together with dilapidation and absence of other plumbing facilities to determine substandard blocks. This was done because the absence of hot water, when occurring alone in concentrations or in combination with other deficiencies, is a significant index in determining clusters of bad housing. As an index, however, the lack of hot water becomes less important when it occurs outside of substandard blocks within standard metropolitan areas and declines in importance in determining concentrations of bad housing as the size of the locality decreases.

TABLE A. ESTIMATED URBAN REDEVELOPMENT PROGRAM AND HOUSING NEEDS IN URBAN PLACES, 1950
(*Thousands of Dwelling Units*)

Line Number	Item	Total	Inside Standard Metropolitan Areas [a]		Urban Outside Standard Metropolitan Areas
			Outside Urban Places of 50,000 or More	*Urban Places of 50,000 or More*	
1.	Total	32,691	9,316	16,311	7,064
2.	Dilapidated or no running water	3,336	1,227	1,105	1,004
3.	In substandard blocks (2 × 4)	1,967	871	740	356
4.	Per cent	—	71.0	67.0	35.5
5.	In concentrated areas (3 × 6)	1,414	626	532	256
6.	Per cent of all substandard blocks	71.9	71.9	71.9	71.9
7.	Not in concentrated areas (3 − 5)	553	245	208	100
8.	Surrounded standard blocks (5 × 9)	47	21	18	8
9.	Per cent of concentrated substandard blocks	3.3	3.3	3.3	3.3
10.	Not dilapidated, with running water, no private toilet or bath	3,602	961	1,655	986
11.	In substandard blocks (10 × 12)	1,606	521	818	267
12.	Per cent	—	54.2	49.4	27.1
13.	In concentrated areas (11 × 14)	1,121	364	571	186
14.	Per cent of concentrated substandard blocks	69.8	69.8	69.8	69.8
15.	Not in concentrated areas (11 − 13)	485	157	247	81
16.	Surrounded standard blocks (13 × 17)	85	28	43	14
17.	Per cent of concentrated substandard blocks	7.6	7.6	7.6	7.6
18.	Not dilapidated, with private toilet and bath, no hot water	1,085	275	522	288
19.	In substandard blocks (18 × 20)	423	130	225	68
20.	Per cent	—	47.3	43.1	23.6
21.	In concentrated areas (19 × 22)	263	81	140	42
22.	Per cent of all substandard blocks	62.0	62.0	62.0	62.0
23.	Not in concentrated areas (19 − 21)	160	49	85	26
24.	Surrounded standard blocks (21 × 25)	32	10	17	5
25.	Per cent of concentrated substandard blocks	12.2	12.2	12.2	12.2
26.	In concentrated substandard blocks (27 ÷ 28)	3,786	1,450	1,681	655
27.	Dilapidated, or no hot water, toilet or bath (5 + 13 + 21)	2,798	1,071	1,243	484
28.	Per cent	—	73.9	73.9	73.9
29.	Not dilapidated, with hot water, toilet and bath (26 − 27)	988	379	438	171
30.	In substandard blocks not in concentrated areas (31 ÷ 32)	1,780	671	801	308
31.	Dilapidated, or no hot water, toilet or bath (7 + 15 + 23)	1,198	451	540	207
32.	Per cent	—	67.2	67.4	67.2
33.	Not dilapidated, with hot water, toilet and bath (30 − 31)	582	220	261	101
34.	In surrounded standard blocks (35 ÷ 36)	496	179	235	82
35.	Dilapidated, or no hot water, toilet or bath (8 + 16 + 24)	164	59	78	27
36.	Per cent	—	33.0	33.2	33.0
37.	Not dilapidated, with hot water, toilet and bath (34 − 35)	332	120	157	55

Source: See discussion in text.

a. Includes urban, rural nonfarm and rural farm units inside standard metropolitan areas.

TABLE B. SUMMARY OF ESTIMATES OF URBAN REDEVELOPMENT AND HOUSING NEED, 1950
(*Thousands of Dwelling Units*)

Location	Total	Dilapidated or No Running Water	Not Dilapidated		
			With Running Water, No Private Toilet or Bath	With Private Toilet and Bath, No Hot Water	With Hot Water, Private Toilet and Bath
Total urban [a]	32,691	3,336	3,602	1,085	24,668
Concentrated redevelopment areas	4,282	1,461	1,206	295	1,320
Substandard blocks	3,786	1,414	1,121	263	988
Other blocks	496	47	85	32	332
Outside redevelopment areas	28,409	1,875	2,396	790	23,348
Substandard blocks	1,780	553	485	160	582
Other blocks	26,629	1,322	1,911	630	22,766
Total inside standard metropolitan areas	25,627	2,332	2,616	797	19,882
Concentrated redevelopment areas	3,545	1,197	1,006	248	1,094
Substandard blocks	3,131	1,158	935	221	817
Other blocks	414	39	71	27	277
Outside redevelopment areas	22,082	1,135	1,610	549	18,788
Substandard blocks	1,472	453	404	134	481
Other blocks	20,610	682	1,206	415	18,307
Total urban outside standard metropolitan areas	7,064	1,004	986	288	4,786
Concentrated redevelopment areas	737	264	200	47	226
Substandard blocks	655	256	186	42	171
Other blocks	82	8	14	5	55
Outside redevelopment areas	6,327	740	786	241	4,560
Substandard blocks	308	100	81	26	101
Other blocks	6,019	640	705	215	4,459

Source: See discussion in text.

a. Includes all urban units plus rural nonfarm and farm units inside standard metropolitan areas.

APPENDIX 7–3. ESTIMATED AVERAGE RENT OR RENTAL VALUE OF SUBSTANDARD
DWELLING UNITS IN 1950

The series HB summaries of the 1950 Census of Housing give a distribution of nonfarm renter-occupied units by state of repair and plumbing, by contract rent, and of nonfarm owner-occupied units in single-family structures by state of repair and value of property, by condition and plumbing. These data may be used to obtain a figure on average rent or rental value of substandard dwelling units in 1950 utilizing the following assumptions: (1) that the average rent of all units in a renter group was at the mid-point of the interval and the average was about $125 for units renting at $100 or more; (2) that the average value of owner-occupied units in each value group was at the mid-point of the group and the average value of units worth $20,000 or more was $22,500; and (3) that the annual rental value of owner-occupied units represented 10 per cent of their value. The computation has been made separately for all urban units, including rural-nonfarm units in standard metropolitan areas, and for rural-nonfarm units outside standard metropolitan areas, as shown in Table A.

TABLE A. CONTRACT RENT AND VALUE OF NONFARM DWELLING UNITS — DILAPIDATED
OR LACKING PRIVATE FLUSH TOILET OR PRIVATE BATH, 1950

	Number Reporting	Average
Contract Monthly Rent of Renter-Occupied Units		
Urban (including all standard metropolitan areas)	3,482,415	$ 26.66
Rural nonfarm outside standard metropolitan areas	982,775	16.87
Total nonfarm	4,465,190	24.51
Value of Owner-Occupied One-Dwelling-Unit Structures		
Urban (including all standard metropolitan areas)	1,366,475	3,444.00
Rural nonfarm outside standard metropolitan areas	1,255,740	2,742.00
Total nonfarm	2,622,215	3,108.00
10 Per Cent of Value of Owner-Occupied One-Dwelling-Unit Structures plus 12 Times Contract Monthly Rent		
Urban (including all standard metropolitan areas)	4,848,890	327
Rural nonfarm outside standard metropolitan areas	2,238,515	243
Total nonfarm	7,087,405	300

Source: Based on U.S. Census of Housing, 1950, Vol. II, Pt. 1.

APPENDIX 8–1. DOMESTIC UTILIZATION OF SELECTED ELECTRICAL APPLIANCES, 1925–1952

End of Year	Number of Wired Homes	Per Cent of Wired Homes Owning:			
		Mechanical Refrigerators	Washing Machines	Vacuum Cleaners	Electric Ranges
	(*Thousands*)				
1925	14,965	a	21	31	3
1926	16,458	2	27	37	—
1927	17,951	4	28	39	3
1928	19,090	6	30	41	4
1929	19,967	9	33	44	4
1930	20,332	13	35	44	5
1931	20,151	17	41	45	5
1932	19,850	22	39	47	6
1933	20,004	25	44	49	6
1934	20,694	29	46	48	6
1935	21,235	34	49	48	7
1936	22,030	41	53	49	8
1937	22,939	49	56	49	9
1938	23,517	52	58	49	10
1939	24,599	57	60	51	11
1940	25,638	64	63	52	12
1941	27,012	73	65	53	13
1942	27,716	72	63	51	13
1943	28,000	71	62	49	13
1944	28,436	70	61	48	12
1945	29,215	67	59	47	12
1946	31,015	69	61	49	13
1947	33,050	71	63	49	14
1948	35,205	77	67	52	17
1949	37,244	79	69	53	18
1950	39,044	86	72	56	21
1951	40,967	87	74	58	23
1952	42,307	89	76	59	24

Sources: 1925–1938, Saul Nelson and Walter G. Klein, *Price Behavior and Business Policy,* TNEC Monograph No. 1, 1940, p. 262. Primary source, *Electrical Merchandising;* 1939–1950, *Electrical Merchandising,* mimeographed sheets dated January 1943 and regular January issues for subsequent years.

a. Less than one per cent.

APPENDIX 8–2

TABLE A. PER CENT OF FARMS WITH CENTRAL STATION ELECTRIC SERVICE, JUNE 30, 1951, AND WITH TELEPHONES, APRIL 1, 1950, BY REGION AND STATE

Region and State	Farms with Central Station Electric Service, June 30, 1951	Farms Having Telephones, April 1, 1950	Region and State	Farms with Central Station Electric Service, June 30, 1951	Farms Having Telephones, April 1, 1950
New England	91	73	South Atlantic — Cont'd		
Maine	87	64	Virginia	87	24
New Hampshire	95	75	West Virginia	82	27
Vermont	93	70	North Carolina	84	8
Massachusetts	92	78	South Carolina	76	8
Rhode Island	93	77	Georgia	81	9
Connecticut	93	84	Florida	75	18
Middle Atlantic	94	62	East South Central	74	14
New York	95	71	Kentucky	76	21
New Jersey	95	72	Tennessee	82	19
Pennsylvania	93	52	Alabama	76	8
			Mississippi	63	6
East North Central	94	60	West South Central	79	20
Ohio	94	60	Arkansas	77	11
Indiana	96	62	Louisiana	79	12
Illinois	91	65	Oklahoma	73	33
Michigan	98	53	Texas	82	24
Wisconsin	94	59	Mountain	80	44
West North Central	86	61	Montana	74	28
Minnesota	90	60	Idaho	95	55
Iowa	96	82	Wyoming	76	38
Missouri	81	46	Colorado	78	59
North Dakota	74	42	New Mexico	61	15
South Dakota	74	56	Arizona	87	43
Nebraska	87	65	Utah	91	52
Kansas	85	68	Nevada	61	50
South Atlantic	82	15	Pacific	92	56
Delaware	87	67	Washington	94	58
Maryland	88	54	Oregon	92	50
District of Columbia	64	61	California	92	57

TABLE B. PER CENT OF FARMS WITH CENTRAL STATION ELECTRIC SERVICE AND WITH TELEPHONES, 1920 AND 1935–1953

Year	Farms with Central Station Electric Service	Farms Having Telephones	Year	Farms with Central Station Electric Service	Farms Having Telephones
1920	7	39	1944	42	a
1935	11	a	1945	46	a
1936	12	a	1946	54	a
1937	16	a	1947	61	a
1938	19	a	1948	69	a
1939	22	a	1949	a	a
1940	30	25	1950	77	38
1941	35	a	1951	84	a
1942	38	a	1952	88	a
1943	40	a	1953	91	a

Source: Graphic Summary of the Rural Electrification and Rural Telephone Programs, Rural Electrification Administration, U.S. Department of Agriculture, May 1952, Figures 5 and 25 (processed), and releases, October 1952 and September 1953.

a. Not available.

APPENDIX 8–3. CITY WORKER'S FAMILY BUDGET FOR HOUSEHOLD OPERATION

A. HOUSEFURNISHINGS BUDGET

(Annual Replacement Rates)

Group	Item	Quantity per Family
Furniture		
Living room	Upholstered davenport, chair (set)	.058
	Upholstered davenport	.039
	Chair, upholstered seat	.068
	Chair, other	.077
	Table, occasional	.116
	Desk	.029
	Bookcase	.019
Bedroom	Bed, chest, dresser (set)	.048
	Chest	.048
	Bed	.106
	Bedspring	.150
	Cot	.048
Dining room and kitchen........	Dinette set	.020
	Kitchen table	.048
	Kitchen cabinet	.019
	Kitchen chair	.309
Other	Porch furniture, other unspecified items	a
Equipment, appliances, tableware and housewares		
Electrical equipment and appliances	Cook stove	.06 [b]
	Refrigerator	.06 [b]
	Washing machine	.07
	Ironing machine	.01
	Sewing machine	.01
	Vacuum cleaner	.06
	Lamp	.20
	Fan	.03
	Toaster	.04
	Iron	.09
	Waffle iron	.03
Tableware and housewares.......	Dishes, dinner set	.15
	Water glasses	6.00
	Pressure cooker	.01
	Pots, pans	.79
	Garbage pail	.50
	Carpet sweeper	.03
	Broom	1.40
	Floor mop	.40
	Ironing board	.10
	Clothespins, box of 2 dozen	1.00
	Clock	.13
	Electric light bulbs	8.00
	Flat silver, kitchen utensils, insurance on furnishings, other unspecified items	c
Textile housefurnishings		
Rugs	Axminster, 9′ x 12′	.06
	Wool, scatter, 27″ x 45″	.25
	Cotton, scatter, 24″ x 48″	.50
Blankets	Wool, 50 per cent or more	.24
	Wool, less than 50 per cent	.15
	Cotton	.20

APPENDIX 8–3 (continued)

Group	Item	Quantity per Family
Textile housefurnishings (continued)		
Other bedding	Sheets	2.16
	Pillowcases	1.98
	Pillow	.03
	Bedspread	.29
	Mattress	.21
	Mattress pad	.20
Bathroom linen	Bath towel	3.17
	Hand towel	1.29
	Face cloth	2.00
Dining room and kitchen linen....	Luncheon set (cloth, napkins)	.64
	Kitchen towel	1.58
	Dish cloth	1.00
	Pot holder	2.00
Window curtains	Pair	1.66
Other	Slip covers, yard goods, other unspecified furnishings	d

B. HOUSEHOLD OPERATION BUDGET

Group	Item	Unit	Quantity per Year
Laundry supplies	Laundry soap, bar	Bar	72.7
	Laundry soap, flakes, powder	24-ounce package	30.5
	Laundry starch	Pound	8.3
	Bluing	Box	4.9
Cleaning supplies	Scouring powder	Can	26.3
	Scouring balls, copper	Ball	3.4
	Polish, furniture	14-ounce bottle	.7
	Ammonia, household	Quart	1.5
	Moth preventative	Cake	2.6
Household paper	Toilet paper	Roll—650 sheets	51.0
	Wax paper	Roll—125 feet	3.7
	Shelf lining	Roll	.4
	Napkins	Package of 80	4.1
Matches	Matches	Box	37.5
Other	Refuse disposal (Depends on city)		—

Source: Workers' Budgets in the United States: City Families and Single Persons, 1946 and 1947, Bulletin No. 927, U.S. Bureau of Labor Statistics, pp. 33 and 34.

a. Porch furniture and other unspecified items: Cost of this group of items is 9 per cent of annual allowance for the itemized furniture items.

b. Included in rent if furnished by landlord.

c. Flat silver, kitchen utensils, etc.: Cost of this group of items is 15 per cent of annual allowance for the itemized equipment, appliances, tableware and housewares.

d. Slip covers, yard goods, etc.: Cost of this group of items is 9 per cent of annual allowance for the itemized textile housefurnishings.

APPENDIX 9–1. PERCENTAGE DISTRIBUTION OF PASSENGER-MILES OF INTERCITY
COMMON CARRIER TRANSPORTATION, 1929–1953

Year	Total	Rail	Air	Bus
1929	100.0	78.0	.1	21.9
1930	100.0	73.7	.3	26.0
1931	100.0	70.0	.4	29.6
1932	100.0	64.4	.6	35.0
1933	100.0	62.4	.8	36.8
1934	100.0	62.4	.7	36.9
1935	100.0	59.8	1.2	39.0
1936	100.0	62.6	1.3	36.1
1937	100.0	63.5	1.3	35.2
1938	100.0	60.9	1.7	37.4
1939	100.0	60.1	2.2	36.7
1940	100.0	61.0	3.2	35.8
1941	100.0	62.7	3.4	33.9
1942	100.0	68.0	2.0	30.0
1943	100.0	74.0	1.5	24.5
1944	100.0	75.9	1.8	22.3
1945	100.0	74.0	2.9	23.1
1946	100.0	65.1	6.6	28.3
1947	100.0	57.6	8.7	33.7
1948	100.0	55.0	9.2	35.8
1949	100.0	51.2	11.5	37.3
1950	100.0	45.0	15.0	40.0
1951	100.0	48.3	16.7	34.9
1952	100.0	47.1	19.6	33.3
1953	100.0	46.0	24.0	30.0

Source: Computed from passenger traffic data of the Interstate Commerce Commission.

APPENDIX 10–I. NUMBER OF REGISTERED HOSPITALS AND HOSPITAL BEDS
BY TYPE OF HOSPITAL AND TYPE OF CONTROL, 1952

Type of Control	All Hospitals		General		Special		Nervous & Mental		Tuberculosis		Department of Institutions	
	Number	Beds	Number	Beds	Number	Beds	Number	Beds	Number	Beds	Number	Beds
Total	6,665	1,541,615	4,924	640,923	548	57,622	585	732,929	428	89,571	180	20,570
Government	2,078	1,099,623	1,173	264,921	78	23,663	358	713,056	327	79,838	142	18,145
Federal	386	211,510	292	132,798	2	800	39	64,215	28	11,172	25	2,525
State	549	691,408	54	21,541	26	4,848	281	626,111	92	30,230	96	8,678
County	688	111,663	451	52,762	17	8,050	37	22,068	169	25,750	14	3,033
City	374	72,493	308	48,018	31	8,965	1	662	27	10,939	7	3,909
City-county	81	12,549	68	9,802	2	1,000	—	—	11	1,747	—	—
Church	1,136	158,389	1,017	148,145	78	5,266	23	3,115	13	1,647	5	216
Nonprofit	2,146	232,598	1,742	192,659	259	23,942	45	6,845	67	6,943	33	2,209
Individual and partnership	903	26,183	718	19,010	102	2,941	69	3,639	14	593	—	—
Corporations	402	24,822	274	16,188	31	1,810	90	6,274	7	550	—	—

Source: F. H. Arestad, M.D., and Mary A. McGovern, "Hospital Service in the United States: The 1952 Census of Hospitals," reprinted from *Journal of the American Medical Association*, May 9, 1953, pp. 4–5, 11.

APPENDIX 10-2. MEDIAN GROSS AND NET CHARGES FOR HOSPITAL, MEDICAL AND DENTAL SERVICES AND GOODS, BY FAMILY INCOME, FAMILIES WITH AND WITHOUT VOLUNTARY HEALTH INSURANCE, JULY 1952–JUNE 1953

Family Income	Number of Families			Median Gross Charges[a]			Median Net Charges[b]		
	All Families	With Insurance[e]	With No Insurance[c]	All Families	Families with Insurance	Families with No Insurance	All Families	Families with Insurance	Families with No Insurance[d]
Total	2,809	1,780	1,029	$110	$145	$63	$98	$117	$63
0–$1,999	560	176	384	54	82	43	53	77	42
2,000–3,499	617	347	270	82	103	54	74	88	54
3,500–4,999	693	514	179	119	134	83	105	112	79
5,000–7,499	577	466	111	176	187	105	144	151	105
7,500 and over	343	272	71	238	255	185	197	198	185
Income unknown	19	5	14	—	—	—	—	—	—

Source: Odin W. Anderson, *National Family Survey of Medical Costs and Voluntary Health Insurance,* Preliminary Report, Health Information Foundation, January 1954, Tables 4 and 5, pp. 35 and 36.

a. Gross charges are all charges incurred by the family unit for its own members for hospital, medical and dental services and goods. They do not include the cost of voluntary health insurance. The "cost" of free care is, of course, excluded. However, the cost of services received under a hospital service plan or a comprehensive medical care plan is included.

b. Net charges are gross charges incurred less voluntary health insurance benefits received. That is, net costs are the costs to the family itself. In the case of hospital service plans or comprehensive medical care plans, the cost of service benefits is not included here. In the case of indemnity plans or insurance, the amount which the insurance paid either to the hospital, physician, etc., or to the family is excluded. A small part of the difference in median net costs for families with insurance and

families with no insurance is accounted for by the fact that the average size of families with insurance (3.26 persons) is somewhat higher than the average size of families with no insurance (2.95 persons). This difference is less marked within specific income groups. In almost all instances this family size difference is too small to account for any substantial proportion of the difference in medians.

c. These are families with or without some voluntary health insurance at the end of the survey year.

d. Median net costs for families with insurance are, of course, substantially lower than median gross costs. However, median net costs and median gross costs are substantially the same in families with no insurance. Wherever median net costs are lower than median gross costs for families with no insurance at the end of the survey year, it is because at some time during the survey year one or more family members had been covered and received benefits.

APPENDIX 10–3. PHYSICIANS' CALLS PER 1,000 POPULATION, 1940
AND ESTIMATES FOR 1950, 1960 AND 1975

Year	Annual Physicians' Calls per 1,000 Persons, All Ages (Age Adjusted)[a]	Index (1940 = 100) of Annual Physicians' Calls Based on:		
		Aging of Population and Population Increase[b]	Aging of Population Only[c]	Increase in Population Only[d]
		Total Cases		
1940	2,539	100.0	100.0	100.0
1950	2,622	118.2	103.3	114.5
1960	2,602	126.1	102.5	123.0
1975	2,644	146.4	104.2	140.6
		Acute Cases		
1940	1,654	100.0	100.0	100.0
1950	1,703	117.8	103.0	114.5
1960	1,631	121.3	98.6	123.0
1975	1,625	138.1	98.3	140.6
		Chronic Cases		
1940	885	100.0	100.0	100.0
1950	919	119.0	103.9	114.5
1960	971	135.0	109.7	123.0
1975	1,019	161.9	115.2	140.6

Source: Based on annual rates as found in the Eastern Health District of Baltimore study, 1938–1943. G. St. J. Perrott, Marcus S. Goldstein and Selwyn D. Collins, "Health Status and Health Requirements of an Aging Population," in *Illness and Health Services in an Aging Population*, Publication No. 170, U.S. Public Health Service, 1952, p. 17.

a. The rate per 1,000 persons for each age interval was multiplied by the Census population in the respective age interval; the numbers for each age period were then summed, giving the total number of physicians' calls; these were divided by the total Census population to give the age-adjusted rate for all ages.

b. Total number of physicians' calls in 1950, 1960 and 1975 divided by the number of calls made in 1940.

c. Found by dividing the rate per 1,000 persons for 1940 into the rate for the dates specified.

d. Census population in 1950 (excluding armed forces overseas and not adjusted for underenumeration) and estimated population for 1960 and 1975 divided by that of 1940. The population increase between 1950 and 1960 used in the above source is smaller than that used elsewhere in this book. (See Appendix 3–6.)

APPENDIX 10-4. PERCENTAGE DISTRIBUTION OF FAMILIES WITH AND WITHOUT HEALTH INSURANCE, BY NET CHARGES INCURRED FOR HOSPITAL AND MEDICAL SERVICES AND GOODS AND BY FAMILY INCOME, JULY 1952–JUNE 1953

Net Charges[a]	Total	Family Income				
		$0–$1,999	$2,000–$3,499	$3,500–$4,999	$5,000–$7,499	$7,500 and Over
Families with and without Insurance						
All Families						
Number	2,809[b]	560	617	693	577	343
Per Cent	100	100	100	100	100	100
No net costs	9	16	11	6	5	3
Under $45	22	31	27	20	17	10
45–94	17	18	19	19	16	15
95–194	21	17	21	23	23	21
195–294	12	8	9	14	14	15
295–394	7	4	5	7	7	13
395–494	4	2	2	4	6	6
495–994	6	4	4	5	10	12
995 and over	1	1	1	1	1	4
Net costs unknown	1	1	1	1	1	1
Families with Insurance						
All Families						
Number	1,780[b]	176	347	514	466	272
Per Cent	100	100	100	100	100	100
No net costs	6	10	11	6	3	4
Under $45	18	29	22	17	18	9
45–94	17	19	20	20	14	15
95–194	24	23	25	25	24	22
195–294	14	9	11	15	15	16
295–394	8	4	5	8	7	13
395–494	4	2	2	3	7	6
495–994	6	3	3	4	10	11
995 and over	1	1	1	1	1	4
Net costs unknown	1	1	1	[c]	1	1
Families without Insurance						
All Families						
Number	1,029[b]	384	270	179	111	71
Per Cent	100	100	100	100	100	100
No net costs	12	18	11	6	10	3
Under $45	30	33	35	31	14	15
45–94	18	17	19	17	22	14
95–194	15	14	16	17	18	18
195–294	8	8	7	11	7	10
295–394	5	3	5	5	8	10
395–494	3	2	2	5	5	8
495–994	6	4	5	7	12	15
995 and over	1	1	1	1	2	4
Net costs unknown	1	[c]	1	1	2	1

Source: Odin W. Anderson, *National Family Survey of Medical Costs and Voluntary Health Insurance,* Preliminary Report, Health Information Foundation, January 1954, Tables 6, 7 and 8, pp. 37–39.

a. For definition see Appendix 10–2, footnote b.
b. Total includes 19 families whose income was unknown, 5 families with insurance and 14 families without insurance.
c. Less than one half of one per cent.

APPENDIX 12–1. ESTIMATED POPULATION 3 TO 21 YEARS OF AGE, 1960[a]

Age	Population (Thousands)
Total, all ages	176,928
Under 3	10,463
3	3,539
4	3,566
5	3,612
6	3,731
7	3,853
8	3,753
9	3,675
10	3,476
11	3,576
12	3,543
13	3,824
14	2,764
15	2,719
16	2,766
17	2,943
18	2,568
19	2,387
20	2,245
21	2,322
22 and over	105,603

Sources: Derived from birth and population projections in U.S. Bureau of the Census, *Current Population Reports, Population Estimates,* Series P–25, No. 43, August 10, 1950, and Series P–25, No. 78, August 21, 1953; U.S. Office of Vital Statistics birth estimates for fiscal years 1949–1950 through 1952–1953; and unpublished Census population projections for 1960 by single years of age consistent with projections in Series P–25, No. 43. The derived population estimates are consistent with the mortality assumptions underlying the Census "medium" population projections in Series P–25, No. 43 and with the 1960 Census totals for five-year age groups as projected in Series P–25, No. 78 under assumption "C," which allows for a slow decline in age-specific birth rates from 1950–1953 average levels after 1953.

a. Including armed forces overseas and consistent with estimates for earlier years adjusted to include those children under 15 not enumerated by the Census.

APPENDIX 12–2. ESTIMATED NEEDED EXPENDITURES FOR CURRENT OPERATION OF ADEQUATE ELEMENTARY AND SECONDARY SCHOOL SYSTEM

NEW ENROLLMENTS

In 1950 enrollments were 28,629,000 pupils against a calculated 31,092,000 "adequate program" enrollment; hence, there was a gap of 2,463,000 children who needed but did not receive any schooling. In 1960 the gap between probable enrollment of 42,009,-000 and needed enrollment of 43,693,000 would be 1,684,000. At an average current cost of $245 per pupil, it would have cost $603 million in 1950 and it would cost $410 million in 1960 to provide adequate schooling for those without any.[1]

INADEQUATE PROGRAMS: 1950

Data are available for 1950 on annual current expenditures per pupil in average daily attendance in city school systems, by expenditure groups.[2] Of the

1. See Chapter 12, p. 406.
2. *Expenditure per Pupil in City School Systems, 1950–51,* U.S. Office of Education, Circular No. 337,

cities studied, 21.8 per cent had average current expenditures of $275 or more per pupil in average daily attendance.[3] The others go all the way down to $80, with the number in each $10 class interval shown. It is estimated that 16,805,000 of the pupils enrolled in school in 1950 were in cities.[4] This is equivalent to 14,956,000 urban pupils in average daily

1952, Table B, p. 6. The study covers 259 cities, almost equally distributed among all city size groups.
3. The adequate expenditure standard of $245 per pupil enrolled may be translated into $275 per pupil in average daily attendance since the number of pupils in average daily attendance in 1950 equaled 89 per cent of the number enrolled. (See U.S. Office of Education, Circular No. 344, June 1952.)
4. *Statistical Abstract of the United States, 1951,* U.S. Bureau of the Census, p. 13, Table 14. The figure of 58.7 per cent of the population was used. This checks closely with the approximate rural-urban distribution of enrollment as derived from *Current Population Reports,* U.S. Bureau of the Census, Series P–20, No. 4, Tables 2 and 3.

TABLE A. Urban Secondary and Elementary School Pupils below Standard of Adequacy and Expenditures Needed to Bring Them up to Standard, 1950

Expenditure Group	Pupils in Average Daily Attendance		Average Amount Spent below $275 Standard	Additional Expenditures Needed [a]
	Number	Per Cent		
	(Thousands)			(Millions)
Total urban	14,956	100.0	—	$783.1
Standard or above	3,260	21.8	—	—
Below standard	11,696	78.2	$67	783.1
$260–269	658	4.4	10	6.6
250–259	1,241	8.3	20	24.8
240–249	972	6.5	30	29.2
230–239	1,047	7.0	40	41.9
220–229	1,301	8.7	50	65.0
210–219	972	6.5	60	58.3
200–209	838	5.6	70	58.7
190–199	912	6.1	80	73.0
180–189	1,167	7.8	90	105.0
170–179	568	3.8	100	56.8
160–169	479	3.2	110	52.7
150–159	598	4.0	120	71.8
140–149	329	2.2	130	42.8
130–139	239	1.6	140	33.5
120–129	—	—	—	—
110–119	194	1.3	160	31.0
100–109	105	.7	170	17.8
90–99	—	—	—	—
80–89	75	.5	190	14.2

Source: Number of pupils from *Expenditure per Pupil in City School Systems, 1950–51,* U.S. Office of Education, Circular No. 337, 1952, Tables B and C, pp. 6 and 8; percentage in each expenditure group was obtained by weighting each city size group by the proportion of population in that group. Resulting percentage distribution applied to total number of children below standard.

a. Number of pupils in average daily attendance multiplied by average amount spent below $275 standard.

attendance. On the assumption that the distribution of urban pupils by expenditure classes is the same as the distribution of urban public schools, 78.2 per cent of this number, or 11,696,000, fall below the $275 standard of adequacy. (Table A.)

The estimated cost of bringing outlays for these urban children up to the standard expenditure level would have been $783 million, or an average of $67 per pupil over and above what was spent for their education in 1950.

Rural School Program

According to the above calculations, 11,824,000 children outside urban places were enrolled in school in 1950. This is equal to 10,523,000 in average daily attendance. Average current expenditures for the schooling of these children amounted to $181 per pupil in 1950.[5]

5. This was obtained as follows: The percentage distribution of the expenditure groups used in the previous

No data are available to indicate how educational expenditures were distributed among different groups of rural pupils in 1950. However, data on average expenditures per rural school pupil for each of 36 states are available for 1947–1948.[6] These show only one state (Nevada) spending more than $250 per rural pupil in average daily attendance; only three states (Indiana, New York and Washington) between $230 and $250, and no state above the $275

table was used to obtain a weighted average current expenditure per city pupil in average daily attendance. This figure was $229. U.S. Office of Education, Circular No. 344, June 1952, shows a figure of $209 average current expenditures per pupil for all public elementary and secondary schools. Total pupils in average daily attendance (25,479,000) × $209, minus total urban pupils (14,956,000) × $229 = total expenditures for rural pupils enrolled ($1,900,000,000) ÷ rural pupils in average daily attendance (10,523,000) = average expenditure per rural pupil in average daily attendance ($181).

6. *Education in Rural and City School Systems,* U.S. Office of Education, Circular No. 329, November 1951.

standard of adequacy. Therefore, it may safely be assumed that spending for all groups of the rural elementary and secondary school population was below standard in 1950. At an average additional expenditure of $94 per pupil ($275–$181), the total cost of bringing them up to standard would have been $989 million.[7]

INADEQUATE PROGRAMS: 1960

Inadequacies among those likely to be attending school may be approached through an estimate of probable current expenditures per pupil in average daily attendance in 1960.

In 1950 current expenditures per pupil in average daily attendance in public elementary and secondary schools amounted to $209. The trend in this rate of expenditure has been as follows in the last four decades: [8]

	Current Prices	1950 Prices
1910	$ 28	$110
1920	54	105
1930	87	176
1932	81	182
1934	67	158
1936	74	165
1938	84	180
1940	88	183
1942	98	183
1944	117	196
1946	136	198
1948	179	194
1950	209	209

The time trend since 1910 of the series in 1950 prices and the relationship of this series and gross national product estimates in 1950 prices since 1930 both indicate a probable rate of expenditure of $230 (in 1950 prices) for 1960.[9]

Although the probable rate of increase in expenditures for all public schools therefore seems likely to be about 10 per cent for the decade, the expenditures for urban schools are almost certain to rise at a slower rate and for rural schools at a faster rate. Current expenditures per pupil in average daily attendance were $105 for urban schools and $70 for

rural schools in 1940.[10] These expenditures were equivalent to $218 and $145 in 1950 prices. Since in 1950 urban expenditures were $229 and rural expenditures were $181,[11] urban expenditures rose by 5 per cent and rural by 25 per cent between 1940 and 1950. On the assumption that rural expenditures per pupil would continue to rise about five times as rapidly as urban expenditures, it is estimated that in 1960 current expenditures per pupil in average daily attendance probably would be $238 in urban schools and $218 in rural schools.

Urban School Programs

The following estimate of the number of pupils receiving an inadequate education and the cost of bringing them up to standard is based on the assumption that each city school system will increase its expenditures by the same proportion (4 per cent) as the average increase for urban areas of the country as a whole. [12] This means that those cities spending approximately $265 per pupil in average daily attendance in 1950 will by 1960 equal or exceed the $275 standard of adequacy. Consequently 26.2 per cent of city school children are then likely to receive a satisfactory education, compared with 21.8 per cent in 1950. Assuming the same ratio of urban to rural children as in 1950, total urban enrollment in 1960 would be 24,659,000 and rural enrollment 17,350,000 pupils.[13] The corresponding average daily attendance figures would be 21,947,000 and 15,442,000, respectively.[14] Of the total urban children in average daily attendance, 5,750,000 would be receiving satisfactory education.

The same method of computation as in Table A, following an upward adjustment of 4 per cent applied to the expenditure rate classes, yields an estimate of $1.0 billion as the amount needed to bring current expenditures up to the standard for the 16.2 million urban school pupils in average daily attendance who are likely to be below the standard in 1960. This amounts to an average of $62 per pupil over and above what is likely to be spent on their education in the form of current operating outlays in 1960.

Rural School Program

Of the 15,442,000 rural children in average daily attendance, how many are likely to be inadequately educated in 1960 and how much would it cost to

---

7. Insofar as there are rural school systems within individual states spending above the standard of adequacy, the deficiency is overstated. On the other hand, their exclusion from the inadequate schools would reduce the average per pupil outlay of the remainder.

8. Data in current prices from U.S. Office of Education; data in 1950 prices derived from series in current prices by use of price index consisting of an index of average annual salaries of instructional staff and the U.S. Bureau of Labor Statistics wholesale price index, combined with weights in the ratio of 2 to 1.

9. On this basis, the average expenditure per pupil enrolled would be $205 (89 per cent of $230, the expenditure per pupil in average daily attendance).

10. *Statistical Summary of Education, 1939–40,* U.S. Office of Education, 1943.

11. See footnote 5.

12. And on the further assumption that the school population distribution among cities of different sizes will remain unchanged between 1950 and 1960.

13. The estimate of urban-rural population distribution in Table 37 shows no change between 1950 and 1960, despite a significant shift between farm and rural nonfarm areas.

14. Multiplying by 89 per cent. (See footnote 5.)

bring them up to standard? If it is assumed that each state will increase its current expenditures per rural pupil at the same rate (20 per cent per decade, or about 1.8 per cent per year) as the average increase for the country as a whole, then all states spending an average of $220 or more per rural pupil in 1948 are likely to reach the $275 standard by 1960. On the assumption either that there are no variations within states or that intrastate variations will offset each other, it is estimated that current operating expenditures for 83 per cent of the rural pupils in average daily attendance, or a total of 12,817,000, are likely to be inadequate in 1960.[15] On the basis of a

calculation similar to that in Table A, it is estimated that the cost of bringing these pupils up to the $275 standard would be $1,150 million, or an average of $90 per pupil.[16]

TOTAL NEEDED EXPENDITURES

Expenditures for current operation of the elementary and secondary school program were $5,433 million in 1950 and probably will total $8,810 million in 1960. (See Table 182.) Adding to these totals the estimated deficiencies would have brought needed expenditures to $7,808 million in 1950 and would bring them to $11,370 million in 1960.

---

15. U.S. Office of Education, Circular No. 329, gives total rural pupils in average daily attendance for 1948 in 36 states. *Statistics of State School Systems, 1947–48,* U.S. Office of Education, 1950, gives totals for urban and rural combined for the remaining 12 states. For each of these states an estimate of rural alone was made using the ratio of rural population to total from the 1950 Census of Population. Of these states, California and Montana were assumed to be likely to attain a level of adequacy by 1960. The remaining states consist of nine southern states and Utah, where the present level of expenditures per pupil is so low as to make it unlikely that at the 20 per cent per decade rate of growth the average expenditure per rural pupil will be adequate by 1960. To these were added 29 additional states where the current annual expenditures per pupil, as shown in Circular No. 329, were below $220 in 1948. The estimated number of rural pupils in these 39 states combined was 83 per cent of total rural pupils in the United States. It was assumed that the distribution by states would remain unchanged in 1960.

16. The 12,817,000 inadequately educated rural pupils were distributed among the 39 states according to the percentage distribution of rural enrollment by states in 1948. The current amount likely to be spent per rural pupil by each of these states was the figure shown for 1948 in U.S. Office of Education, Circular No. 329, multiplied by 125 (i.e., at the rate of 20 per cent increase per decade). The ten states not covered in this study were assumed to be equal to the average in the ten lowest of those covered. The difference between each of these figures and $275 was then multiplied by the number inadequately educated, and the products summed.

APPENDIX 15–1. METHOD OF ESTIMATING NEEDED EXPENDITURES FOR PRIVATE PRODUCTIVE FACILITIES

The gap between needs and demand for private productive facilities was determined by estimating the combined percentage increase of needs over demand for the following items in 1950 and 1960:

a. Private consumption expenditures (primarily for goods).
b. Government expenditures for noncapital goods.
c. Expenditures for developmental works and consumer construction.

PRIVATE CONSUMPTION EXPENDITURES

On the assumption that the needed additional productive facilities would be more closely related to expanded requirements for goods than for services, needs and demand estimates were compared for the following consumer expenditure groups, which accounted for 69 per cent of all consumer outlays in 1950:

Food, liquor and tobacco.
Clothing and related products.
Fuel, ice and lighting supplies and household utilities.
Furniture and furnishings and mechanical appliances.
Private transportation.
Reading, hobbies and pets; radios, television and musical instruments; and sports equipment.

Expenditures in these areas cover some services but are primarily for goods.

Among the consumer expenditure groups omitted in computing the gap between needs and demand for private productive facilities were the following, which provide services predominantly:

Personal care.
Rent and imputed rent.
Domestic service.

Cleaning, repair and maintenance.
Financial, legal, insurance and death expenses.
Medical care and insurance.
Private education.
Religion.

Although consumer expenditures for medical care and private education were not considered in this computation, the gap between needs and demand for hospital construction and school building are included in the section following on expenditures for developmental works and consumer construction.

GOVERNMENT EXPENDITURES FOR NONCAPITAL GOODS

Government outlays for noncapital goods, like private consumer expenditures, purchase both goods and services. Of the total noncapital goods outlays of $57.6 billion in the fiscal year 1949–1950, the major share — $46.9 billion — went for payrolls; assistance and insurance benefits to individuals; agriculture, business and international subsidies; and interest on debt. Only the remaining $10.7 billion, which was spent for materials, supplies and contractual services, was predominantly for direct purchase of goods. (See Table 254.) Since the $46.9 billion was in the form of transfer payments or payment for services, its impact on the need for productive facilities would be included for the most part in the consumer expenditure items covered in the preceding section.

Consequently, $10.7 billion was taken as actual government outlays for noncapital goods in 1950. In the absence of more detailed estimates, needed government outlays for 1950 and 1960 and probable demand for 1960 were estimated by applying to the $10.7 billion estimate the percentage changes between 1950 actual demand and 1950 and 1960 needs

TABLE A. SUMMARY OF DEMAND AND NEEDS ESTIMATES USED TO ESTIMATE NEEDS
FOR PRIVATE PRODUCTIVE FACILITIES

(Billions at 1950 Prices)

	1950		1960	
	Demand	*Needs*	*Demand*	*Needs*
Private consumption expenditures (primarily for goods)	$134.2	$138.0	$166.9	$169.7
Government expenditures for noncapital goods	10.7	16.6	17.4	19.0
Expenditures for developmental works and consumer construction				
Private	14.8	16.9	13.7	17.3
Public	11.8	26.6	22.4	27.9
Total	$171.5	$198.1	$220.4	$233.9

and between 1950 actual and 1960 probable demand for all government outlays, except construction and equipment and public to private transfers. (See Table 273.)

EXPENDITURES FOR DEVELOPMENTAL WORKS AND CONSUMER CONSTRUCTION

Outlays for private productive facilities were assumed to be directly related to all outlays for developmental works and consumer construction — private and public.

Private expenditures — on a demand and need basis — for developmental and consumer construction, as estimated in the various chapters of this volume, are summarized in Table 36. Public expenditures, also summarized in that table, were not used for this computation since they exclude total government outlays for publicly owned military and naval plant and equipment and state outlays for equipment. Instead, the all-inclusive demand and need estimates presented in Table 273 of the Government Expenditures chapter were used. Although these estimates are for fiscal rather than calendar years, the error introduced is far less than would be the case if outlays for military and naval plant and equipment, for example, were omitted.

SUMMARY

The demand and needs estimates used in computing needed outlays for productive facilities are summarized in Table A.

On the basis of the totals, it is estimated that needed private productive facilities outlays would have been 15 per cent higher than the amount spent in 1950 and would be 6 per cent higher than probable outlays in 1960.

APPENDIX 16–1. ESTIMATED COST OF ACQUIRING LAND AND BUILDINGS IN RESIDENTIAL SLUM AND BLIGHTED AREAS

Estimates of acquisition costs were based principally on the experience of local authorities in purchasing built-up slum sites for low-rent housing projects under the United States Housing Act of 1937, as amended. A sample of 75 projects with sites acquired in 1950–1951 was selected, stratified by size of locality and geographic area. These projects contained a total of nearly 7,400 dwelling units. It is believed that the sample is adequate for the purpose of estimating a national average.

On a national average, the acquisition cost was $2,513 ($2,500) per slum dwelling — $649 for land and $1,864 for the structure. This cost covers only residential structures and the land allocated to them. It does not include land and structures with industrial or commercial uses, any part of central business districts, publicly owned land and buildings, or vacant parcels.

It was estimated that physically standard units in slum areas would cost approximately one third more than substandard units, or $3,333 ($3,350) per unit.

The cost of acquiring neighborhood commercial space was estimated at $200 per front foot, and the amount of such space was estimated at two front feet per family in slum areas.

The above unit costs were applied to the distribution of units given in Chapter 16 to arrive at an estimate of total acquisition cost. This came to $22 billion. (See Table A.)

The additional cost that would be incurred if one third of the 7.4 million units to be replaced were relocated on vacant land was estimated as follows: It was assumed that land cost in outlying areas would be two thirds that in the central city. One third more land per dwelling would be acquired, however, thus reducing density by 25 per cent. The cost of land per dwelling unit was therefore estimated at $577 (66.7 per cent of $649 times one and one third). Accordingly, the relocation of about 2.5 million dwelling units (one third of 7.4 million) would involve an added cost of approximately $1.4 billion.

TABLE A. ESTIMATED SITE ACQUISITION COST: RESIDENTIAL SLUM AND BLIGHTED AREAS, 1950

	Number of Units	Unit Cost	Total Cost
	(Millions)		(Millions)
Total	7.4	—	$21,835
Intensive area replacement	—	—	18,585
Concentrated areas	—	—	13,575
Residential units	4.3	—	11,855
Physically substandard units	3.0	$2,500	7,500
Other units	1.3	3,350	4,355
Commercial (front feet)	8.6	200	1,720
Isolated substandard blocks	1.8	—	5,010
Physically substandard units	1.2	2,500	3,000
Other units	.6	3,350	2,010
Scattered replacement—physically substandard units	1.3	2,500	3,250

APPENDIX 18–1. SOURCES OF INFORMATION FOR CHAPTER 18

The basic data on government expenditure for 1913, 1932, 1942 and 1950, classified by government function and by character of expenditure, and the summary figures on governmental revenue were developed in the following way.

Federal Expenditure

The primary source of federal expenditure figures was the *Budget of the United States Government*. The editions for the fiscal years ended June 30, 1934, 1944 and 1952 reported actual expenditures for the fiscal years 1932, 1942 and 1950 respectively. Supplementary data for these years were drawn from the U.S. Treasury's *Combined Statement of Receipts, Expenditures, and Balances of the United States Government* for the fiscal years concerned. In the absence of a federal budget in 1913, the source employed was the *Annual Report of the Secretary of the Treasury on the State of the Finances* for that year.

In covering all governmental transactions Chapter 18 is broader in scope than the federal budget document, particularly in the area of business enterprise, corporate and trust fund operations. For certain data it was necessary to refer to individual financial statements of such agencies as the Postal Service, the Reconstruction Finance Corporation, the Commodity Credit Corporation, the Rural Electrification Corporation, the Tennessee Valley Authority, the Housing and Home Finance Agency and other federal corporations. It was necessary also to supplement the basic sources with certain social insurance statistics obtained from the Social Security Administration, the Railroad Retirement Board, the Veterans Administration, the Civil Service Commission and the Treasury Department.

These data were reviewed intensively and recast in the functional classification pattern selected for the presentation of expenditure data, which is outlined briefly in the section discussing functional patterns of expenditure. The resulting pattern of federal expenditure often varies from the admirable functional classification of the U.S. Bureau of the Budget. One significant reason for such variation lies in the need for using in this review a classification appropriate to all three levels of government — federal, state and local — while the Budget Bureau's classification needs only to be appropriate for the federal government's operations. A further difference results from the consolidation of general, enterprise and trust fund accounts, which are segregated in federal budgeting. A significant difference also arises from the treatment in this analysis of loan extensions and repayments. The Budget Bureau handles loan activities on a net basis, reporting loans made as expenditure to the extent that they exceed loans repaid. Chapter 18 excludes loan transactions entirely from "revenue" and "expenditure" but shows gross loans extended and gross loans repaid as exhibit disbursements and exhibit receipts. Perhaps the most significant departure from the federal budget's functional classification is in the reporting of expenditure for veterans services. Such expenditures are grouped in the federal budget under a single category for payments to and on behalf of veterans. In Chapter 18, veterans services expenditure is broken down and classified by function — veterans educational benefits under "education"; veterans pensions under "public welfare"; veterans insurance under "social insurance"; veterans hospitals under "hospitals," etc. Numerous other departures from the budget classification were made.

The character and object classification of federal expenditure applied in this analysis required a great deal of supplementation of budget materials and considerable estimation of breakdowns of data. Although an object classification of expenditure is applied in the detail of the budget document to data for individual agencies, no such classification is applied to federal expenditure as a whole. Certain classes, such as interest on debt and public-to-private transfer payments, were identified from Budget Bureau and Treasury Department reports and the social insurance sources cited earlier. Detailed payroll figures were furnished for 1942 and 1950 by the Civil Service Commission; budget and other sources were drawn upon for 1913 and 1932 payroll data. The category of capital outlay required the separate assembly of statistics for new construction, equipment and purchase of land and existing structures. Here the sources were the Budget Bureau's figures for public works and investments, the U.S. Department of Commerce's *Construction and Building Materials* (edition of May 1951), R. W. Goldsmith's *Saving and Capital Market Study,* and the reports of numerous federal agencies. The category of supplies, materials and contractual services was derived as a residual class, subject to review for consistency in the light of the nature of each agency's activities.

Physical Volume Statistics

Data on the physical volume of selected government services and on unit costs were obtained from publications issued or special tabulations prepared by the agency responsible for the services measured (e.g., U.S. Postal Service), agencies administering fiscal aid for the purpose concerned (e.g., U.S. Bureau of Public Roads), agencies maintaining statistical services covering particular functional areas (e.g., U.S. Office of Education) or private associations concerned with individual functions (e.g., National Recreation Association). Because these data were derived from many separate agencies in accordance with varying definitions, time periods and reporting methods, no attempt was made to reconcile performance data with basic financial data gathered for this analysis. In analyzing performance data, comparisons of physical volume with dollars expended have been made only when both sets of data were obtainable from the same source.

State and Local Expenditure

The primary sources of the basic expenditure statistics for state and local governments were the publications of the U.S. Bureau of the Census on the subject of state and local government finances. For the key years 1913, 1932 and 1942, data were assembled primarily from Census reports resulting from censuses of governments conducted for those years. The 1913 and 1932 censuses were known as censuses of *Wealth, Debt, and Taxation*. The 1942 enumeration was called the *Census of Governments*. Data for 1950 were developed by utilizing annual Census Bureau reports on state government finances, city finances, and governmental revenue and debt. Projections were required to develop data for the smaller local governments not covered by annual Census Bureau series.

As with federal expenditure data, it was necessary to revise extensively and reclassify state and local statistics obtained from these sources. This reclassification involved application of the uniform functional classification of Chapter 18 to census data classified originally in different ways in successive time periods, development of several important elements of an object classification, and a considerable amount of estimation of particular breakdowns of data.

Statistical publications of the U.S. Office of Education were utilized heavily for certain types of educational expenditure statistics. Special studies of the Bureau of the Census and the more detailed annual reports on finances of states and large local governments published by that Bureau were employed to estimate detailed breakdowns of summary financial data published in the basic governmental census reports.

The Census Bureau reports used for this analysis generally identified certain broad character classes of government expenditure — current operation, interest on debt, capital outlay. It was necessary to make extensive use of supplementary sources to obtain estimates for a more detailed breakdown of these data. Payroll expenditure statistics for 1942 and 1950 were developed from the Census Bureau's quarterly reports of state and local government employment and payrolls. For 1932, such data were developed from the Bureau of Labor Statistics report *Employment and Payrolls of State and Local Governments, 1929–1939*. For 1913, payroll data were developed from Wilford I. King's study, *The National Income and Its Purchasing Power*, National Bureau of Economic Research, 1930. Extensive use was made of Department of Commerce and Bureau of Labor Statistics estimates of construction expenditure to develop from Census data the figures on state and local government expenditures for construction. Detail in unpublished tabulations and worksheets of the Bureau of the Census relating to state and local government finances also was of considerable assistance in permitting the interpolations, projections and refinements of data needed to fit the pattern of presentation called for in this chapter.

Population

Population figures used are the following estimates of the Bureau of the Census for July of each year indicated:

1913	97,226,814
1932	124,840,471
1942	134,664,924
1950	151,132,000

and the July 1960 estimate of 176,928,000 shown in Appendix 3–6 of this volume.

APPENDIX 18–2. GOVERNMENT PRICE INDEX

Expenditure comparisons from year to year are of more value in understanding past trends and future prospects if the differences in the buying power of the dollar are eliminated. To use a general price index applicable to all kinds of prices for this purpose, however, would be almost as misleading as if public costs were stated merely in terms of current dollars. As the Supreme Court observed in a utility rate case, the price index used must be related to the specific class to which the index is applied. For this study, public expenditures were grouped into 27 principal categories, for each of which a separate price or cost index was computed.

The indexes were derived for the years 1913, 1932, 1942 and 1950, using 1950 as the base year in the compilations. This year was selected as the base period inasmuch as it represents the frame of reference of this study of public expenditure trends during the past four decades and the factors responsible for them. Most of the price or cost indexes are on a calendar year basis but are applied to fiscal year data in "inflating" 1913, 1932 and 1942 federal, state and local expenditures to 1950 dollars. Whenever feasible, as for example in the derivation of the 1942 and 1950 average pay to federal civilian employees, the index was calculated on a fiscal year basis identical with the actual expenditure data. In the other instances, however, it is felt that the relationship between the fiscal and calendar year periods is sufficiently stable to prevent the introduction of any significant error in the "conversion" of actual government expenditures into dollars of a constant buying power.

Whereas the government price index published in the 1947 edition of *America's Needs and Resources* was not entirely consistent in this respect, the component indexes in the present study are uniformly constructed in terms of changes in the price of the function or service to the federal, state and local governments rather than in terms of changes in the relative value of the service to the recipients. For example, the price index for deflating federal civilian payroll data is based on the average rates of pay to federal employees rather than on the purchasing power of the dollars paid the employees. The revised government price index shown in this study contains more than twice as many individual series as the index used in 1947 — 27 component indexes as compared with 10. For several expenditure functions, separate price series were computed for "deflating" state and local expenditures as distinct from indexes applicable to federal government items. This increase in number of series enhances the accuracy of the "deflation" technique inasmuch as it relates the price indexes more closely to the specified class

Constructed by OWEN C. GRETTON in consultation with WYLIE KILPATRICK and ROBERT F. DRURY.

or group of expenditures to which they are applied.

The individual price or cost indexes, using 1950 as a base year, were derived as follows:

(1) *Military payroll and cash allowances:* based on the percentage differences in the average annual payroll and cash allowance received by military personnel between 1950, on the one hand, and 1913, 1932 and 1942, on the other.

(2) *Federal civilian employee payrolls:* based on the percentage differences in the average monthly pay of federal civilian employees between 1950, on the one hand, and 1913, 1932 and 1942, on the other.

(3) *State and local employee payrolls, except educational employees:* based on the percentage differences in the average annual pay of state and local employees, except educational employees, between 1950, on the one hand, and 1913, 1932 and 1942, on the other.

(4) *State and local educational employee payrolls:* based on the percentage differences in the average annual pay of state and local educational employees between 1950, on the one hand, and 1913, 1932 and 1942, on the other.

(5) *Wholesale commodity prices:* based on the Bureau of Labor Statistics wholesale price index, which measures average price changes of about 850 commodities at the point at which the items initially enter the commercial market.

(6) *Consumers' prices:* based on the Bureau of Labor Statistics consumers' price index, which measures average changes in the retail prices of approximately 190 goods, rents and services purchased by moderate-income families of wage earners and clerical workers in large cities.

(7) *Interest payments on the federal debt:* based on percentage changes in the rate of interest paid on the federal debt, which is calculated by dividing interest payments during the year by the federal debt outstanding at the beginning of the year.

(8) *Interest payments on state and local government debt:* based on percentage changes in the rate of interest paid on state and local government debt, which is calculated by dividing interest payments during the year by the state and local debt outstanding at the beginning of the year.

(9) *Construction cost index:* based on the *Engineering News Record's* construction cost index, which measures the movement of construction costs in general.

(10) *Highway construction cost index:* based on the U.S. Bureau of Public Roads index of the cost of construction of a composite standard mile of highway, derived from aggregate bid prices for excavation and surfacing work, re-

inforced steel, structural steel and structural concrete.

(11) *Producers' goods prices:* based on the National Bureau of Economic Research index of producers' goods prices, representing weighted arithmetic means for 680 price series.

(12) *Federal veterans pension payments:* based on the percentage differences in the average payment per beneficiary of federal veterans pensions between 1950, on the one hand, and 1913, 1932 and 1942, on the other.

(13) *Federal retirement benefits:* based on the percentage differences in the average benefit paid federal retirement beneficiaries between January 1950, on the one hand, and January 1932 and 1942, on the other.

(14) *Old-age and survivors insurance benefits:* based on the percentage differences in the average benefit paid beneficiaries in the old-age and survivors insurance program between January 1950 and January 1942.

(15) *Railroad retirement benefits:* based on the percentage differences in average benefit paid beneficiaries in the railroad retirement program between January 1950 and January 1942.

(16) *Railroad unemployment benefits:* based on the percentage differences in the average benefit paid to recipients of railroad unemployment insurance benefits between January 1950 and January 1942.

(17) *Ratio of prices received to prices paid by farmers:* based on changes in relationship of Bureau of Agricultural Economics index of prices received by farmers, measuring the general level of farm prices, to the BAE index of prices paid for items farmers buy, including interest, taxes and wage rates.

(18) *Assistance payments to aged persons:* based on the percentage differences in the average assistance payment to aged persons between January 1950 and January 1942.

(19) *Assistance payments of aid to children:* based on the percentage differences in the average payment to a recipient of aid for children between January 1950 and January 1942.

(20) *Assistance payments to blind persons:* based on the percentage differences in the average payment to recipients of assistance for the blind between January 1950 and January 1942.

(21) *Assistance payments to general relief cases:* based on the percentage differences in the average assistance payment to individuals on general relief between January 1950, on the one hand, and January 1913, 1932 and 1942, on the other.

(22) *Benefit payments to state and local retirement beneficiaries:* based on the percentage differences in the average benefit payment to beneficiaries of state and local government retirement programs between 1950, on the one hand, and 1913, 1932 and 1942, on the other.

(23) *Unemployment compensation benefits:* based on the percentage changes in the average benefit paid to beneficiaries of unemployment compensation insurance between January 1950 and January 1942.

(24) *U.S. government life insurance dividends:* based on the percentage changes in the rate of dividends paid on U.S. government life insurance policies between 1950, on the one hand, and 1932 and 1942, on the other, calculated by dividing the amount of dividends during each year by the value of the life insurance policies outstanding during that year.

(25) *Death and disability benefits paid under the U.S. government life insurance program:* based on the percentage differences in the average benefit payment to beneficiaries of death and disability benefits from U.S. government life insurance policies between 1950, on the one hand, and 1932 and 1942, on the other.

(26) *National Service Life Insurance death benefits:* based on the percentage differences in the average benefit paid recipients of death benefits under the National Service Life Insurance program between the years 1950 and 1942.

(27) *Other veterans insurance benefits:* based on the percentage differences in the average benefit paid to beneficiaries of veterans insurance programs other than U.S. government life insurance and National Service Life Insurance between 1950, on the one hand, and 1932 and 1942, on the other.

Appendix 18-3. Selected Transactions of Government Utilities and Enterprises, Fiscal Years 1913, 1932, 1942 and 1950

(Dollar Figures in Millions)

Item	Federal Government				State and Local Governments				Percentage Increase, 1942–1950	
	1913	1932	1942	1950	1913	1932	1942	1950	Federal	State and Local
Specified sources of funds										
Total	$332	$2,678	$11,918	$15,925	$314	$547	$1,692	$3,697	33.6	118.3
Contributions from general government[a]	40	547	983	861	[b]	[b]	105	105	−12.4	0.0
Borrowings[c]	3	904	5,170	5,739	192	17[b]	222[b]	730[b]	11.0	228.8[b]
Liquidation of assets	—	459	3,101	5,324					71.7	
Revenue from sales of goods and services	289	764	2,557	3,852	122[b]	530[b]	1,296	2,754	50.6	112.5
Other revenue	—	4	107	149			69	108	39.3	56.5
Specified disbursements										
Contributions to general government	8	200	2,744	1,005	[b]	[b]	111	268	−63.4	141.4
Debt redemption[e]	2	10	1,230	3,787	165	151	133	241	207.9	81.2
Interest on debt[d]	—	55	229	36	41	175	196	218	−84.3	11.2
Operation and capital outlay	322	898	4,674	4,578	171	613	1,446	3,087	−2.1	113.5
National defense[e]	7	11	2,122	125					−94.1	—
Community facilities	—	—	86	144	131	363	885	1,545	67.4	74.6
Public water supply	—	—	—	—	123	291	354	832	—	135.0
Local electric and gas utilities	—	—	—	—	8	72	145	338	—	133.1
Housing	—	—	86	144	—	—	386	375	67.4	−2.8
Transportation	42	69	179	163	34	237	237	824	−8.9	247.7
Highways	—	—	—	—	7	18	23	56	—	143.5
Water transportation and ports	42	56	157	69	27	107	32	87	−56.1	171.9
Air, local transit and other	—	13	22	94	—	112	182	681	327.3	274.2

APPENDIX 18-3 (continued)

Item	Federal Government				State and Local Governments				Percentage Increase, 1942–1950	
	1913	1932	1942	1950	1913	1932	1942	1950	Federal	State and Local
Specified disbursements (contd.)										
Natural resources	—	6	1,375	1,852	—	—	14	12	34.7	−14.3
Promotion of agriculture	—	6	1,157	1,603	—	—	—	—	38.5	—
Electric power	—	—	174	215	—	—	14	12	23.6	−14.3
Other resources	—	—	44	34	—	—	—	—	−22.7	—
Promotion of business	—	1	16	37	—	—	—	—	131.3	—
Postal service	269	794	874	2,223	—	—	—	—	154.3	—
Liquor stores	—	—	—	—	—	—	293	667	—	127.6
Other functions	4	17	22	34	6	14	18	39	54.5	116.7
Payments for loans and investments										
Housing	—	1,513	3,037	6,418	—	—	—	—	111.3	—
Transportation	—	—	176	1,034	—	—	—	—	487.5	—
Promotion of agriculture	—	51	1,798	4,501	—	—	—	—	150.3	—
Electric power	—	702	168	379	—	—	—	—	125.6	—
Promotion of business	—	760	448	503	—	—	—	—	12.3	—
Foreign governments and other	—	—	447	1	—	—	—	—	−99.8	—
Debt outstanding										
Privately held	—	1,236	6,742	793	1,145	4,090	5,642	7,976	−88.2	41.4
Held by U.S. Treasury	—	350	4,079	8,423	—	—	—	—	106.5	—

Source: See Appendix 18-1.

a. Consists of the sum of contributions for individual enterprises; represents extent to which enterprises immediately or ultimately draw upon general government for financial support or contribute to general government as a result of the year's operations.

b. Not available.

c. Includes transactions between enterprises and general government; segregation not available.

d. Does not include interest on enterprise obligations held by U.S. Treasury as follows (in millions): $2 in 1932; $4 in 1942; and $101 in 1950.

e. Includes military exchanges and commissaries in all years and the subsidiary defense corporations in 1942.

Note: Data for these activities, including federal credit corporations, are merged in figures of other tables covering all government transactions.

APPENDIX 18-4. ESTIMATED NEEDED FEDERAL AND STATE AND LOCAL EXPENDITURE IN 1950 AND 1960 COMPARED WITH ACTUAL 1950 AND PROBABLE 1960 EXPENDITURE, BY MAJOR FUNCTION

(Millions at 1950 Prices)

| Major Function | 1950 (Fiscal Year) | | | | 1960 | | | |
| | Actual | | Needed | | Probable | | Needed | |
	Federal	State and Local	Federal	State and Local	Federal	State and Local	Federal	State and Local
All expenditure	$42,175	$27,304	$69,393	$41,458	$66,901	$37,190	$69,693	$48,317
National defense	12,535	38	33,300	50	33,300	50	33,300	50
International affairs	4,618	—	6,709	—	3,640	—	4,260	—
Civilian public safety	107	1,401	108	1,505	144	1,553	144	1,678
Education	3,060	7,246	3,075	13,180	1,507	10,865	1,517	16,135
Public welfare and social insurance	6,979	5,785	9,978	8,283	9,770	8,260	10,365	9,898
Health and community facilities	1,229	4,238	1,495	5,886	1,319	4,848	1,719	6,686
Transportation	835	4,914	934	8,615	1,039	6,762	1,136	8,797
Agriculture and natural resources	3,839	575	4,627	628	5,488	828	6,352	828
Postal service	2,223	—	2,365	—	3,132	—	3,282	—
Interest	5,853	617	5,853	617	6,350	1,334	6,350	1,334
Other functions	897	2,491	949	2,693	1,212	2,690	1,268	2,911

Source: See Appendix 18-1 and text discussion in Chapter 18.

APPENDIX 20-I. LABOR FORCE, EMPLOYMENT, UNEMPLOYMENT AND WORKING HOURS, BY MONTHS, 1940–1953

(Thousands of Persons 14 Years of Age and Over)

Year and Month	Labor Force							Employed			Average Hours Worked per Week			Average Total Man-Hours per Week
	Total (1)	Normal (2)	Additional (3)	Civilian (4)	Unemployed (5)	Total (6)	Military (7)	Civilian (8)	Nonagricultural (9)	Agricultural (10)	Total (Weighted) (11)	Nonagricultural (12)	Agricultural (13)	(Millions) (14)
1940														
J	54,310	54,310	—	54,010	9,220	45,090	300	44,790	37,020	7,770	42.3	40.7	50.0	1,907
F	54,480	54,480	—	54,170	9,180	45,300	310	44,990	37,160	7,830	42.6	40.6	52.0	1,930
M	54,740	54,740	—	54,460	8,360	46,380	280	46,100	37,350	8,750	44.0	40.7	58.0	2,041
A	55,140	54,760	380	54,870	8,230	46,910	270	46,640	37,230	9,410	44.5	40.8	59.0	2,087
M	55,880	55,530	350	55,590	7,990	47,890	290	47,600	37,150	10,450	44.4	40.9	57.0	2,126
J	57,640	57,290	350	57,330	8,310	49,330	310	49,020	37,500	11,520	44.5	41.0	56.0	2,195
J	58,310	57,620	690	58,000	9,150	49,160	310	48,850	37,870	10,980	43.2	40.9	51.0	2,124
A	58,010	57,080	930	57,670	8,740	49,270	340	48,930	38,610	10,320	44.1	41.5	54.0	2,173
S	56,780	56,150	630	56,330	6,850	49,930	450	49,480	38,690	10,790	44.3	41.6	54.0	2,212
O	56,350	55,830	520	55,830	7,240	49,110	520	48,590	38,570	10,020	44.9	41.8	57.0	2,205
N	55,570	55,450	120	54,960	7,260	48,310	610	47,700	39,210	8,490	43.4	41.1	54.0	2,097
D	55,150	54,910	240	54,460	6,910	48,240	690	47,550	39,400	8,150	43.5	41.8	52.0	2,098
Average	56,030	55,680	350	55,640	8,120	47,910	390	47,520	37,980	9,540	43.8	41.1	54.6	2,098
1941														
J	54,730	54,360	370	53,990	7,410	47,320	740	46,940	39,250	7,690	43.4	41.9	51.0	2,075
F	54,740	54,520	220	53,870	6,930	47,810	870	46,580	38,860	7,720	42.7	41.4	49.0	2,021
M	54,790	54,790	—	53,660	6,500	48,200	1,040	47,160	39,270	7,890	43.8	42.1	52.0	2,111
A	56,240	55,450	790	54,980	6,380	49,860	1,260	48,600	39,650	8,950	45.0	41.8	59.0	2,244
M	57,420	56,220	1,200	55,970	5,660	51,760	1,450	50,310	40,340	9,970	45.4	42.3	58.0	2,350
J	59,660	57,990	1,670	58,120	6,190	53,470	1,540	51,930	41,150	10,780	45.2	42.7	54.7	2,417
J	59,910	58,320	1,590	58,260	6,000	53,910	1,650	52,260	41,920	10,340	43.8	41.7	52.1	2,361
A	59,860	57,760	2,100	58,130	5,620	54,240	1,730	52,510	42,670	9,840	43.8	41.7	53.1	2,376
S	58,770	56,810	1,960	56,950	4,680	54,090	1,820	52,270	42,370	9,900	44.5	42.5	53.2	2,407
O	57,790	56,460	1,330	55,950	3,840	53,950	1,840	52,110	42,660	9,450	44.7	42.8	53.3	2,412
N	57,540	56,060	1,480	55,650	3,800	53,740	1,890	51,850	43,030	8,820	44.0	42.4	51.7	2,365
D	57,260	55,490	1,770	55,330	3,620	53,640	1,930	51,710	43,900	7,810	43.6	42.7	48.9	2,339
Average	57,380	56,190	1,190	55,910	5,560	51,820	1,470	50,350	41,250	9,100	44.2	42.2	53.2	2,290
1942														
J	56,510	54,910	1,600	54,540	4,320	52,190	1,970	50,220	42,630	7,590	42.3	42.0	43.9	2,208
F	57,140	55,060	2,080	54,880	4,040	53,100	2,260	50,840	43,000	7,840	43.5	42.5	48.9	2,310
M	57,820	55,330	2,490	55,260	3,580	54,240	2,560	51,680	43,570	8,110	43.9	42.5	51.6	2,381
A	58,740	56,000	2,740	55,880	3,050	55,660	2,860	52,830	43,700	9,130	45.4	43.2	56.0	2,528
M	59,670	56,790	2,880	56,500	2,590	57,080	3,170	53,910	44,010	9,900	46.4	43.8	57.8	2,649

Month														
J	61,820	58,590	3,230	58,340	2,890	58,930	3,480	55,450	44,300	11,150	46.1	43.5	56.5	2,717
J	62,180	58,950	3,230	58,400	2,830	59,350	3,780	55,570	45,060	10,510	45.3	41.6	61.3	2,689
A	62,110	58,430	3,680	57,900	2,190	59,920	4,210	55,710	45,450	10,260	45.4	42.7	57.2	2,720
S	61,110	57,500	3,610	56,500	1,680	59,430	4,610	54,820	45,320	9,500	45.6	42.8	58.8	2,710
O	61,820	57,190	4,630	56,800	1,610	60,210	5,020	55,190	45,020	10,170	47.4	44.8	58.9	2,854
N	61,900	56,820	5,080	56,240	1,630	60,270	5,660	54,610	45,730	8,880	46.4	44.5	55.9	2,797
D	61,970	56,270	5,700	55,680	1,520	60,450	6,290	54,160	46,250	7,910	44.2	43.2	50.2	2,672
Average	60,230	56,820	3,410	56,410	2,660	57,570	3,820	53,750	44,500	9,250	45.2	43.1	55.3	2,602
1943														
J	61,630	55,720	5,910	54,700	1,480	60,150	6,930	53,220	45,540	7,680	45.6	44.5	51.9	2,743
F	61,990	55,920	6,070	54,560	1,420	60,570	7,430	53,140	45,460	7,680	45.3	44.1	52.3	2,744
M	62,170	56,210	5,960	54,340	1,120	61,050	7,830	53,220	45,330	7,890	46.3	44.9	54.3	2,827
A	63,160	56,910	6,250	54,860	1,010	62,150	8,300	53,850	45,070	8,780	48.0	45.7	59.7	2,983
M	64,680	57,720	6,960	56,080	950	63,730	8,600	55,130	45,040	10,090	48.3	45.5	61.0	3,078
J	66,410	59,550	6,860	57,580	1,300	65,110	8,830	56,280	45,310	10,970	49.0	45.6	63.1	3,190
J	66,850	59,900	6,950	57,680	1,390	65,460	9,170	56,290	45,910	10,380	47.8	44.4	62.8	3,129
A	66,690	59,330	7,360	57,160	1,050	65,640	9,530	56,110	45,690	10,420	48.0	45.0	61.4	3,151
S	65,730	58,370	7,360	56,030	870	64,860	9,700	55,160	45,140	10,020	47.3	44.3	60.8	3,068
O	64,980	58,030	6,950	55,110	780	64,200	9,870	54,330	45,120	9,210	48.1	45.7	59.6	3,088
N	64,600	57,630	6,970	54,550	710	63,890	10,050	53,840	45,390	8,450	47.7	46.1	56.1	3,048
D	64,000	57,060	6,940	53,770	690	63,310	10,230	53,080	45,630	7,450	46.4	45.4	52.5	2,938
Average	64,410	57,700	6,710	55,540	1,070	63,340	8,870	54470	45,390	9,080	47.3	45.1	58.5	2,996
1944														
J	63,680	56,470	7,210	53,370	810	62,870	10,310	52,560	45,260	7,300	45.0	45.0	45.1	2,829
F	63,530	56,640	6,890	53,010	690	62,840	10,520	52,320	45,010	7,310	45.9	45.3	49.3	2,884
M	63,900	56,930	6,970	53,210	690	63,210	10,690	52,520	44,910	7,610	46.5	45.4	52.9	2,939
A	65,150	57,620	7,530	54,220	630	64,520	10,930	53,590	45,250	8,340	46.4	45.0	54.3	2,994
M	66,430	58,420	8,010	55,270	730	65,700	11,160	54,540	44,710	9,830	48.3	45.8	59.4	3,173
J	67,970	60,240	7,730	56,640	880	67,090	11,330	55,760	44,960	10,800	48.4	45.5	60.5	3,247
J	68,140	60,570	7,570	56,660	890	67,250	11,480	55,770	45,230	10,540	43.9	40.6	58.0	2,952
A	67,260	59,980	7,280	55,640	680	66,580	11,620	54,960	45,650	9,310	46.0	43.9	56.1	3,063
S	66,790	58,980	7,810	55,090	600	66,190	11,700	54,490	44,820	9,670	45.2	43.0	55.2	2,992
O	66,740	58,620	8,120	54,970	440	66,300	11,770	54,530	44,680	9,850	46.8	45.1	54.5	3,103
N	66,060	58,200	7,860	54,270	500	65,560	11,790	53,770	44,650	9,120	46.6	45.2	53.3	3,055
D	65,030	57,610	7,420	53,210	500	64,530	11,820	52,710	44,950	7,760	45.7	45.3	47.7	2,949
Average	65,890	58,360	7,530	54,630	670	65,220	11,260	53,960	45,010	8,950	46.2	44.6	54.4	3,013

Appendix 20-I (continued)

Year and Month	Labor Force					Employed					Average Hours Worked per Week			Average Total Man-Hours per Week (14)
	Total (1)	Normal (2)	Additional (3)	Civilian (4)	Unemployed (5)	Total (6)	Military (7)	Civilian (8)	Nonagricultural (9)	Agricultural (10)	Total (Weighted) (11)	Nonagricultural (12)	Agricultural (13)	(Millions)
1945					(Thousands of Persons 14 Years of Age and Over)									
J	64,600	57,020	7,580	52,770	630	63,970	11,830	52,140	44,890	7,250	45.0	44.8	46.2	2,879
F	65,240	57,190	8,050	53,340	640	64,600	11,900	52,700	45,270	7,430	44.5	44.2	46.1	2,875
M	65,790	57,470	8,320	53,820	590	65,200	11,970	53,230	45,130	8,100	44.9	44.3	48.4	2,927
A	66,250	58,160	8,090	54,180	530	65,720	12,070	53,650	44,950	8,700	45.7	44.4	52.6	3,003
M	66,500	58,980	7,520	54,370	530	65,970	12,130	53,840	44,880	8,960	45.1	43.9	51.4	2,975
J	67,590	60,840	6,750	55,460	890	66,700	12,130	54,570	44,350	10,220	45.9	44.4	52.3	3,062
J	67,450	61,180	6,270	55,350	950	66,500	12,100	54,400	44,500	9,900	45.5	43.2	55.7	3,026
A	66,470	60,600	5,870	54,460	830	65,640	12,010	53,630	44,540	9,090	44.5	42.6	53.6	2,921
S	64,770	59,610	5,160	53,050	1,650	63,120	11,720	51,400	42,560	8,840	41.3	39.2	51.2	2,607
O	63,770	59,260	4,510	53,170	1,560	62,210	10,660	51,610	42,800	8,810	43.5	41.9	51.5	2,706
N	62,410	58,850	3,560	53,190	1,740	60,670	9,220	51,450	43,070	8,380	43.1	41.9	49.1	2,615
D	60,920	58,270	2,650	53,130	1,970	58,950	7,790	51,160	44,000	7,160	42.1	41.6	45.5	2,482
Average	65,140	58,950	6,190	53,860	1,040	64,100	11,280	52,820	44,240	8,580	44.3	43.1	50.6	2,840
1946														
J	59,490	57,680	1,810	53,320	2,300	57,190	6,170	51,020	44,300	6,720	42.0	41.8	43.1	2,402
F	59,130	57,860	1,270	53,890	2,650	56,480	5,240	51,240	44,300	6,940	41.0	40.6	43.8	2,316
M	59,630	58,150	1,480	55,160	2,700	56,930	4,470	52,460	44,930	7,530	42.0	41.1	47.5	2,391
A	60,300	58,880	1,450	56,450	2,330	57,970	3,850	54,120	45,950	8,170	42.7	41.1	51.4	2,475
M	60,570	59,660	910	57,160	2,310	58,260	3,410	54,850	45,970	8,880	42.5	40.9	50.5	2,476
J	62,000	61,550	450	58,930	2,570	59,430	3,070	56,360	46,350	10,010	43.7	41.2	55.2	2,597
J	62,820	61,900	920	60,110	2,270	60,550	2,710	57,840	47,870	9,970	42.6	40.2	53.9	2,579
A	62,200	61,320	880	59,750	2,060	60,140	2,450	57,690	48,550	9,140	42.5	40.6	52.3	2,556
S	61,340	60,320	1,020	59,120	2,070	59,270	2,220	57,050	48,300	8,750	43.1	41.5	51.9	2,555
O	61,160	59,960	1,200	58,990	1,960	59,200	2,170	57,030	48,410	8,620	42.8	41.5	50.2	2,534
N	60,980	59,550	1,430	58,970	1,930	59,050	2,010	57,040	49,140	7,900	42.4	41.4	48.8	2,504
D	60,320	58,970	1,350	58,430	2,120	58,200	1,890	56,310	49,100	7,210	42.2	41.6	46.1	2,456
Average	66,820	59,650	1,170	57,520	2,270	58,550	3,300	55,250	46,930	8,320	42.4	41.1	50.0	2,483

1947														
J	59,510	58,370	1,140	57,790	2,400	57,110	1,720	55,390	48,890	6,500	41.2	41.1	41.6	2,353
F	59,630	58,550	1,080	58,010	2,490	57,140	1,620	55,520	48,600	6,920	40.8	40.7	41.5	2,331
M	59,960	58,840	1,120	58,390	2,330	57,630	1,570	56,060	48,820	7,240	41.0	40.7	43.1	2,363
A	60,650	59,550	1,100	59,120	2,420	58,230	1,530	56,700	48,840	7,860	40.8	40.0	45.5	2,536
M	61,760	60,380	1,380	60,290	1,960	59,800	1,470	58,330	49,370	8,960	42.4	40.7	52.0	2,630
J	64,007	62,290	1,717	62,609	2,555	61,452	1,398	60,055	49,678	10,377	42.8	40.6	53.3	2,526
J	64,035	62,648	1,387	62,664	2,584	61,451	1,371	60,079	50,013	10,066	41.1	38.5	53.9	2,504
A	63,017	62,053	964	61,665	2,096	60,921	1,352	59,569	50,594	8,975	41.1	39.3	51.0	2,571
S	62,130	61,041	1,089	60,784	1,912	60,218	1,346	58,872	50,145	8,727	42.7	40.9	53.2	2,579
O	62,219	60,674	1,545	60,892	1,687	60,532	1,327	59,204	50,583	8,622	42.6	41.1	51.7	2,503
N	61,510	60,248	1,262	60,216	1,621	59,889	1,294	58,595	50,609	7,985	41.8	40.9	47.4	2,452
D	60,870	59,643	1,227	59,590	1,643	59,227	1,280	57,947	50,985	6,962	41.4	41.0	44.2	
Average	61,668	60,357	1,251	60,168	2,142	59,466	1,440	58,027	49,761	8,266	41.7	40.5	48.8	2,480
1948														
J	60,455	59,026	1,429	59,214	2,065	58,390	1,241	57,149	50,089	7,060	41.0	40.7	43.4	2,394
F	61,004	59,197	1,807	59,778	2,639	58,365	1,226	57,139	50,368	6,771	39.6	39.7	38.5	2,311
M	61,005	59,488	1,517	59,769	2,440	58,565	1,236	57,329	50,482	6,847	40.9	40.5	43.5	2,395
A	61,760	60,210	1,550	60,524	2,193	59,567	1,236	58,330	50,883	7,448	41.7	40.4	50.4	2,484
M	61,660	61,063	597	60,422	1,761	59,899	1,238	58,660	50,800	7,861	42.0	40.6	51.1	2,516
J	64,740	62,999	1,741	63,479	2,184	62,556	1,261	61,296	51,899	9,396	42.4	40.4	53.5	2,052
J	65,135	63,370	1,765	63,842	2,227	62,908	1,293	61,615	52,452	9,163	37.9	35.3	52.6	2,384
A	64,511	62,778	1,733	63,186	1,941	62,570	1,325	61,245	52,801	8,444	40.8	39.2	50.9	2,553
S	63,578	61,764	1,814	62,212	1,899	61,679	1,366	60,312	51,590	8,723	39.0	37.0	50.9	2,405
O	63,166	61,413	1,753	61,775	1,642	61,524	1,391	60,134	51,506	8,627	42.1	40.6	51.3	2,590
N	63,138	61,001	2,137	61,724	1,831	61,307	1,414	59,893	51,932	7,961	40.8	40.0	46.1	2,501
D	62,828	60,399	2,429	61,375	1,941	60,887	1,453	59,434	52,059	7,375	41.3	40.7	45.3	2,515
Average	62,748	61,059	1,689	61,442	2,064	60,684	1,306	59,378	51,405	7,973	40.8	39.6	48.5	2,476
1949														
J	61,546	59,783	1,763	60,078	2,664	58,882	1,468	57,414	50,651	6,763	40.1	39.9	41.2	2,361
F	61,896	59,965	1,931	60,388	3,221	58,675	1,508	57,168	50,174	6,993	40.3	40.1	41.9	2,365
M	62,305	60,279	2,026	60,814	3,167	59,138	1,491	57,647	50,254	7,393	40.5	40.0	44.1	2,395
A	62,327	61,024	1,303	60,835	3,016	59,311	1,492	57,819	49,999	7,820	41.4	40.3	48.7	2,455
M	63,452	61,873	1,579	61,983	3,289	60,163	1,469	58,694	49,720	8,974	42.3	40.4	52.5	2,545
J	64,866	63,835	1,031	63,398	3,778	61,088	1,468	59,619	49,924	9,696	42.0	40.1	51.9	2,566
J	65,278	64,210	1,068	63,815	4,095	61,183	1,463	59,720	50,073	9,647	37.1	34.3	51.9	2,270
A	65,105	63,609	1,496	63,637	3,689	61,416	1,468	59,947	51,441	8,507	40.0	38.3	50.3	2,457
S	64,222	62,580	1,642	62,763	3,351	60,871	1,459	59,411	51,254	8,158	38.1	36.2	50.2	2,319
O	64,021	62,223	1,798	62,576	3,576	60,445	1,445	59,001	51,290	7,710	40.6	39.8	46.2	2,454

| Year and Month | Labor Force | | | | Unemployed (5) | Total (6) | Employed | | | | Average Hours Worked per Week | | | Average Total Man-Hours per Week (14) |
	Total (1)	Normal (2)	Additional (3)	Civilian (4)			Military (7)	Civilian (8)	Nonagricultural (9)	Agricultural (10)	Total (Weighted) (11)	Nonagricultural (12)	Agricultural (13)	(Millions)
					(Thousands of Persons 14 Years of Age and Over)									
1949 (contd.)														
N	64,363	61,805	2,558	62,927	3,409	60,954	1,436	59,518	51,640	7,878	40.1	38.8	48.9	2,444
D	63,475	61,204	2,271	62,045	3,489	59,986	1,430	58,556	51,783	6,773	40.7	40.2	44.5	2,441
Average	63,571	61,866	1,705	62,105	3,395	60,176	1,466	58,710	50,684	8,026	40.2	39.0	48.1	2,419
1950														
J	62,835	60,589	2,246	61,427	4,480	58,355	1,408	56,947	50,749	6,198	39.6	39.5	40.8	2,311
F	63,003	60,782	2,221	61,637	4,684	58,319	1,366	56,953	50,730	6,223	39.9	39.5	43.1	2,327
M	63,021	61,100	1,921	61,675	4,123	58,898	1,346	57,551	50,877	6,675	40.3	39.8	44.0	2,374
A	63,513	61,837	1,676	62,183	3,515	59,998	1,330	58,668	51,473	7,195	40.3	39.5	46.0	2,418
M	64,108	62,714	1,394	62,788	3,057	61,051	1,320	59,731	51,669	8,062	41.3	40.1	48.9	2,521
J	66,177	64,701	1,476	64,866	3,384	62,793	1,311	61,482	52,436	9,046	41.7	39.9	52.2	2,618
J	65,742	65,080	662	64,427	3,213	62,529	1,315	61,214	52,774	8,440	35.3	32.8	51.1	2,207
A	66,204	64,470	1,734	64,867	2,500	63,704	1,337	62,367	54,207	8,160	40.4	39.0	49.9	2,574
S	65,020	63,427	1,593	63,567	2,341	62,679	1,453	61,226	53,415	7,811	36.8	35.3	47.2	2,307
O	65,438	63,064	2,374	63,704	1,940	63,498	1,734	61,764	53,273	8,491	41.6	40.3	49.8	2,642
N	65,453	62,639	2,814	63,512	2,240	63,213	1,941	61,271	53,721	9,551	40.8	40.0	46.6	2,579
D	64,674	62,029	2,645	62,538	2,229	62,445	2,136	60,308	54,075	6,234	40.2	40.0	41.8	2,510
Average	64,599	62,703	1,896	63,099	3,142	61,457	1,500	59,957	52,450	7,597	39.9	38.8	47.2	2,452
1951														
J	63,759	a	a	61,514	2,503	61,256	2,245	59,010	52,993	6,018	40.2	40.0	42.1	2,462
F	63,868	a	a	61,313	2,407	61,461	2,555	58,905	52,976	5,930	39.8	39.6	41.3	2,446
M	64,956	a	a	62,325	2,147	62,809	2,631	60,179	53,785	6,393	40.3	39.8	44.5	2,531
A	64,577	a	a	61,789	1,744	62,833	2,788	60,044	53,400	6,645	41.1	40.3	47.5	2,582
M	65,728	a	a	62,803	1,609	64,119	2,925	61,193	53,753	7,440	42.0	40.6	52.0	2,693
J	66,800	a	a	63,783	1,980	64,820	3,017	61,803	53,768	8,035	41.1	39.7	50.5	2,664
J	67,477	a	a	64,382	1,856	65,621	3,095	62,526	54,618	7,908	39.7	37.8	52.5	2,605
A	67,371	a	a	64,208	1,578	65,793	3,163	62,630	54,942	7,688	40.3	38.8	50.7	2,651
S	66,396	a	a	63,186	1,666	64,790	3,210	61,580	54,054	7,526	37.6	36.0	49.5	2,436
O	66,662	a	a	63,452	1,616	65,046	3,210	61,836	54,168	7,668	41.4	40.1	50.6	2,693
N	66,422	a	a	63,164	1,828	64,594	3,258	61,336	54,314	7,022	40.4	39.9	44.3	2,610
D	65,973	a	a	62,688	1,674	64,299	3,285	61,014	54,636	6,378	40.7	40.3	44.4	2,617
Average	65,832	a	a	62,884	1,879	63,953	2,948	61,005	53,951	7,054	40.4	39.4	47.9	2,584

1952													
J	65,091	a	61,780	2,054	63,037	3,311	59,726	53,540	6,186	40.1	39.9	42.2	2,528
F	65,228	a	61,838	2,086	63,142	3,390	59,752	53,688	6,064	40.4	39.9	44.7	2,551
M	65,006	a	61,518	1,804	63,202	3,488	59,714	53,702	6,012	40.0	39.6	44.0	2,528
A	65,260	a	61,744	1,612	63,648	3,516	60,132	53,720	6,412	40.3	39.5	47.3	2,565
M	66,298	a	62,778	1,602	64,696	3,520	61,176	54,216	6,960	41.0	39.9	50.0	2,653
J	67,884	a	64,390	1,818	66,066	3,494	62,572	54,402	8,170	40.8	39.1	52.3	2,695
J	67,642	a	64,176	1,942	65,700	3,466	62,234	54,636	7,598	38.5	37.0	49.3	2,529
A	67,419	a	63,958	1,604	65,815	3,461	62,354	55,390	6,964	39.2	38.0	48.7	2,580
S	67,166	a	63,698	1,438	65,728	3,468	62,260	54,712	7,548	41.3	40.2	48.9	2,715
O	66,566	a	63,146	1,284	65,282	3,420	61,862	54,588	7,274	41.2	40.4	46.9	2,690
N	67,047	a	63,646	1,418	65,629	3,401	62,228	55,454	6,774	41.3	40.5	47.5	2,710
D	66,309	a	62,921	1,412	64,897	3,388	61,509	55,812	5,697	41.1	40.8	43.5	2,667
Average	66,410	a	62,966	1,673	64,737	3,444	61,293	54,488	6,805	40.5	39.6	47.4	2,622

1953													
J	65,959	a	62,416	1,892	64,067	3,543	60,524	55,072	5,452	39.9	39.8	40.9	2,556
F	66,255	a	62,712	1,788	64,467	3,543	60,924	55,558	5,366	39.7	39.5	42.0	2,559
M	66,679	a	63,134	1,674	65,005	3,545	61,460	55,740	5,720	40.3	39.9	44.0	2,620
A	66,338	a	62,810	1,582	64,756	3,528	61,228	55,158	6,070	40.5	39.7	47.7	2,623
M	66,497	a	62,964	1,306	65,191	3,533	61,658	55,268	6,390	40.7	39.9	47.9	2,653
J	68,290	a	64,734	1,562	66,722	3,556	63,172	55,246	7,926	41.5	39.9	52.8	2,769
J	68,258	a	64,668	1,548	66,710	3,590	63,120	55,492	7,628	39.1	37.3	52.3	2,608
A	68,238	a	64,648	1,240	66,998	3,590	63,408	56,134	7,274	39.7	38.4	50.0	2,660
S	67,127	a	63,552	1,246	65,881	3,575	62,306	55,044	7,262	38.3	36.6	51.2	2,523
O	66,954	a	63,404	1,162	65,792	3,550	62,242	55,083	7,159	41.4	40.3	49.8	2,724
N	66,874	a	63,353	1,428	65,446	3,521	61,925	55,274	6,651	40.0	39.2	46.7	2,618
D	66,106	a	62,614	1,850	64,256	3,492	60,764	55,326	5,438	40.5	40.1	44.3	2,602
Average	66,965	a	63,417	1,523	65,441	3,547	61,894	55,366	6,528	40.1	39.2	48.0	2,624

Sources: U.S. Bureau of the Census, *Current Population Reports: Labor Force*, Series P-50, Nos. 2, 13, 19, 31, 40 and 45, and Series P-57, Nos. 103 ff, with the following exceptions:

Col. 1: January and February 1940 derived from projection of trend corrected by unpublished Census seasonal indexes and adjusted to agree with two-month total implied by Census estimates for remainder of year and the annual average, which makes allowance for the two missing months.

Col. 2: January and February 1940 assumed identical with "Total labor force"; March 1940–December 1950 derived from unpublished Census estimates of the "Normal labor force" in the last week of March 1940 and in mid-April of each succeeding year and unpublished Census seasonal indexes.

Col. 3: Col. 1 minus Col. 2.

Col. 4: January and February 1940 assumed to follow same trend as "Total labor force" and adjusted to agree with two-month total implied by Census estimates for remainder of year and the annual average, which makes allowance for the two missing months.

Col. 5: January and February 1940, col. 1 minus col. 6.

Col. 6: January and February 1940 derived from estimates of the National Industrial Conference Board of 43,107,000 for January 1940 and 43,316,000 for February 1940 (*The Economic Almanac for 1950*, p. 164), adjusted to agree with two-month total implied by Census estimates for remainder of year and the annual average, which makes allowance for the two missing months. March 1940 and later, col. 1 minus col. 5.

Col. 7: Col. 1 minus col. 4.

Col. 8: January and February 1940, col. 6 minus col. 7.

Col. 9: January and February 1940, col. 8 minus col. 10.

Col. 10: January and February 1940, derived from application of unpublished

Census seasonal indexes to annual average agricultural employment with the results adjusted to agree with two-month total implied by Census estimates for the remainder of the year and the annual average, which makes allowance for the two missing months.

Col. 11: Weighted average of col. 12 and col. 13 using col. 9 and col. 10 as weights.

Col. 12: January 1940–May 1941 based on the weighted averages of weekly hours worked by production or nonsupervisory employees in the following industries for which Bureau of Labor Statistics estimates are available—Mining, Construction (represented by General Contractors and Special-Trade Contractors), Manufacturing, Wholesale Trade, Retail Trade, Transportation (represented by Class I Railroads and Street Railways and Buses), Communication and Public Utilities (represented by Telephone and Electric Light and Power), and Service (represented by Hotels, Power Laundries, and Cleaning and Dyeing Establishments); the weights used are for average employment for 1940 and represent a combination of B.L.S. estimates for individual major industry groups and Department of Commerce estimates for industry divisions (from *National Income Supplement to Survey of Current Business*, July 1947, Table 25, p. 37). The weighted averages were linked at June 1941 to the adjusted Census estimate (see below).

June 1941–February 1943 are estimates from Bureau of the Census *Labor Force Bulletin*, No. 6, July 1945, p. 24, adjusted for consistency with current Census esti-mates, which in turn were adjusted to reflect zero hours of work for those "with a job but not at work."

March 1943 and later are Census estimates adjusted to reflect zero hours of work for those "with a job but not at work."

Annual averages are weighted averages with data of col. 9 used as weights.

Col. 13: January and February 1940 derived by inspection and comparison with seasonals for other years.

March 1940–May 1941 estimated on the basis of a linear relationship between average weekly hours worked and the proportion of agricultural employees working 35 hours or more a week; the relationship was derived separately for each month of the year using Census estimates for the respective month for the years 1941–1950.

June 1941 and later derived in same way as estimates in col. 12 for that period.

Annual averages are weighted averages with data of col. 10 used as weights.

Col. 14: Col. 6 multiplied by col. 11. This assumes that average hours for military forces (for which no specific data are available) are equal to average for civilian workers.

a. Not available.

Note: Slight discrepancies in addition are due to rounding.

APPENDIX 20–2. PERCENTAGE DISTRIBUTION OF THE CIVILIAN LABOR FORCE BY EMPLOYMENT STATUS, 1940–1952

Employment Status	1940	1941	1942	1943	1944	1945	1946	1947	1948	1949	1950	1951	1952
Civilian labor force	100.0	100.0	100.0	100.0	100.0	100.0	100.0	100.0	100.0	100.0	100.0	100.0	100.0
Employed	85.4	90.1	95.3	98.1	98.8	98.1	96.1	96.4	96.6	94.5	95.0	97.0	97.3
35 hours or more	70.7	76.3	81.4	85.4	82.4	79.6	79.5	79.2	75.2	71.4	71.7	75.8	78.7
15–34 hours	10.0	9.8	9.6	8.4	10.7	11.8	10.2	10.4	13.9	15.6	15.5	13.3	10.9
1–14 hours	2.6	2.2	2.3	2.1	2.4	3.0	2.5	2.7	3.1	3.4	3.6	3.6	3.2
With a job but not at work	2.1	1.8	2.0	2.2	3.2	3.7	3.9	4.1	4.5	4.1	4.2	4.3	4.5
Unemployed	14.6	9.9	4.7	1.9	1.2	1.9	3.9	3.6	3.4	5.5	5.0	3.0	2.7

Source: Current Population Reports: Labor Force, U.S. Bureau of the Census, Series P–50, Nos. 2, 13, 19, 31, 40 and 45.

APPENDIX 20-3. PERSONS WORKING PART TIME FOR ECONOMIC AND NONECONOMIC REASONS, SELECTED MONTHS, 1948-1950

	1948		1949			1950			
	March	September[a]	May	August	November[b]	February	May	August	November[e]
Number (Thousands)									
Total working part time	7,813	7,724	8,536	8,293	8,854	8,926	9,003	7,898	9,434
Economic reasons	1,223	1,360	2,457	2,555	2,352	2,083	2,155	2,357	1,807
With full-time job but worked part time because of economic factors[d]	712	814	1,571	1,474	1,387	1,095	1,087	1,245	986
With part-time job but prefer and could accept full-time job	511	546	886	1,081	965	988	1,068	1,112	821
Noneconomic reasons	6,590	6,364	6,079	5,738	6,503	6,845	6,850	5,540	7,629
With full-time job but worked part time because of noneconomic factors[e]	2,408	1,934	1,022	1,744	1,492	2,217	1,816	1,329	2,024
With part-time job and do not prefer or could not accept full-time job	4,182	4,430	5,057	3,994	5,011	4,628	5,034	4,211	5,605
Percentage Distribution									
Total working part time	100.0	100.0	100.0	100.0	100.0	100.0	100.0	100.0	100.0
Economic reasons	15.7	17.6	28.8	30.8	26.6	23.4	23.9	29.9	19.2
With full-time job but worked part time because of economic factors[d]	9.1	10.5	18.4	17.8	15.7	12.3	12.1	15.8	10.5
With part-time job but prefer and could accept full-time job	6.6	7.1	10.4	13.0	10.9	11.1	11.8	14.1	8.7
Noneconomic reasons	84.3	82.4	71.2	69.2	73.4	76.6	76.1	70.1	80.8
With full-time job but worked part time because of noneconomic factors[e]	30.8	25.0	12.0	21.0	16.8	24.8	20.2	16.8	21.4
With part-time job and do not prefer or could not accept full-time job	53.5	57.4	59.2	48.2	56.6	51.8	55.9	53.3	59.4

Source: Current Population Reports: Labor Force, U.S. Bureau of the Census, Series P–50, Nos. 7, 12, 17, 18, 21, 25, 26, 28 and 33.

a. Excludes 12,875,000 working part time because of Labor Day holiday.
b. Excludes 6,033,000 working part time because of Armistice Day holiday.
c. Excludes 1,213,000 working part time because of Armistice or Election Day holiday.
d. These factors include slack work, layoff, material shortages, repairs to plant and equipment and job turnover.
e. These factors include illness, vacation, industrial dispute, transportation difficulties and various personal reasons.

Year	Gainfully Occupied or Labor Force[a] (1)	Unemployed[a] (2)	Employed Total[a] (3)	Employed Private[a] (4)	Average Weekly Hours		
					Weighted Average (5)	Nonagriculture (6)	Agriculture (7)
		(Millions)					
1850	7.7	0.3	7.4	7.2	69.8	65.7	72.0
1860	10.5	0.4	10.1	9.8	68.0	63.3	71.0
1870	12.9	0.5	12.4	12.0	65.4	60.0	70.0
1880	17.4	0.7	16.7	16.1	64.0	58.8	69.0
1890	22.8	0.9	21.9	21.0	61.9	57.1	68.0
1900	29.2	2.5	26.7	25.4	60.2	55.9	67.0
1910	36.0	2.0	34.0	32.1	55.1	50.3	65.0
1920	41.7	2.0	39.7	36.8	49.7	45.5	60.0
1929	49.4	1.6	47.8	44.4	47.0	44.5	55.5
1930	50.1	4.3	45.8	42.4	45.9	43.2	55.0
1940	56.0	8.1	47.9	43.3	44.0	41.1	54.6
1941	57.4	5.6	51.8	45.7	44.4	42.2	53.2
1942	60.2	2.7	57.6	48.4	45.4	43.1	55.3
1943	64.4	1.1	63.3	48.4	47.6	45.1	58.5
1944	65.9	0.7	65.2	47.9	46.4	44.6	54.4
1945	65.1	1.0	64.1	46.8	44.5	43.1	50.6
1946	60.8	2.3	58.5	49.6	42.6	41.1	50.0
1947	61.6	2.1	59.5	52.6	41.8	40.5	48.8
1948	62.7	2.1	60.7	53.8	40.9	39.6	48.5
1949	63.6	3.4	60.2	52.9	40.3	39.0	48.1
1950	64.6	3.1	61.5	54.0	40.0	38.8	47.2
1951	65.8	1.9	63.9	54.7	40.5	39.4	47.9
1952	66.4	1.7	64.7	54.7	40.5	39.6	47.4
1953	67.0	1.5	65.4	55.3	40.1	39.2	48.0
1960	72.5	3.5	69.0	58.5	37.5	36.5	44.0

Sources: Col. 1—1850–1880, *Historical Statistics of the United States, 1789–1945*, U.S. Bureau of the Census, 1949, Series D–2, p. 63; 1890–1920, Table 306; 1929–1930, *Handbook of Labor Statistics, 1950*, U.S. Bureau of Labor Statistics, 1951, Table A–13, p. 35; 1940–1953, Appendix 20–1.

Col. 2—1850–1890, unemployment assumed at approximately 4 per cent of the gainfully occupied since these were years of high business activity (see *Studies in Enterprise and Social Progress*, National Industrial Conference Board, New York, 1939, Part IV, A, p. 82; *Business Annals*, National Bureau of Economic Research, New York, 1926; "Index of Production and Trade in the United States from 1830," Board of Governors, Federal Reserve System, 1940; and Colin Clark, *The Conditions of Economic Progress*, Macmillan, London, 1951, pp. 46 and 51); 1900–1920, unemployment estimates in *The Economic Almanac for 1950*, National Industrial Conference Board, New York, 1950, p. 163, adjusted upward on basis of relationship during 1929–1941 between NICB unemployment rates (*The Economic Almanac, 1950*, pp. 163–164) and unemployment estimates in *Handbook of Labor Statistics, 1950*, Table A–13, p. 35; 1929–1953, same sources as col. 1.

Col. 3—1850–1930, col. 1 minus col. 2; 1940–1953, Appendix 20–1.

Col. 4—Derived from col. 1 and estimates of public military and civilian employment computed from estimates of the Office of Secretary of Defense and data in *Historical Statistics of the United States, 1789–1945*, Series P–62, p. 294; Solomon Fabricant, "The Changing Industrial Distribution of Gainful Workers," *Studies in Income and Wealth*, Vol. XI, National Bureau of Economic Research, New York, 1949, Table 2, p. 42; *The*

Economic Almanac, 1950, p. 160; *Employment and Earnings*, May 1954, U.S. Bureau of Labor Statistics; and Appendix 20–1.

Col. 5—1850–1930, average of col. 6 and col. 7 weighted on the basis of percentage of gainfully occupied in agriculture and in nonagriculture as shown in *Historical Statistics of the United States, 1789–1945*, Series D–6–7, p. 63, adjusted to exclude government employment (1930 weights used for 1929); 1940–1953, average of col. 6 and col. 7 weighted on the basis of percentage employed in agriculture and nonagriculture derived from Appendix 20–1, adjusted to exclude government employment.

Col. 6—1850–1900 based on trend in manufacturing hours as shown in National Association of Manufacturers, *The American Individual Enterprise System*, McGraw-Hill, New York, 1946, Vol. I, Table 6, p. 203; 1910–1930 based on trend in private nonagricultural hours indicated by estimates of John W. Kendrick in "National Productivity and Its Long-Term Projection," paper presented at the National Bureau of Economic Research Conference on Research in Income and Wealth, May 1951; 1940–1953 from Appendix 20–1.

Col. 7—1850 based on assumption of 12-hour day; 1860–1900 from approximate straight-line interpolation between 1850 and 1910; 1910–1930 based on data in Harold Barger and Hans H. Landsberg, *American Agriculture, 1899–1939*, National Bureau of Economic Research, New York, 1942, Table 43, p. 270; 1940–1953, from Appendix 20–1.

For 1960 projections, see text.

a. 1850–1880 in terms of gainful workers at census date level; 1890–1920, labor force at census date level; 1929–1953, labor force annual averages.

APPENDIX 21–1. Share of the World's Output of Minerals Produced and Consumed in the United States, 1950

Minerals in Order of U.S. Production-Consumption Ratio	U.S. Production as Per Cent of World Production	U.S. Consumption as Per Cent of World Production	Ratio (Per Cent) of U.S. Production to U.S. Consumption
Sulfur, native	91	73	125
Phosphate rock	49	41	120
Coal, anthracite	29	26	112
Coal, bituminous and lignite	28	25	112
Molybdenum	90	82	110
Cement	30	30	100
Natural gas [a]	89	89	100
Potash	27	29	93
Petroleum, crude	52	56	93
Iron ore (usable)	39	44	89
Magnesium	36	45	80
Tungsten	15	21	71
Fluorspar	36	51	71
Copper	31	49	63
Zinc	27	45	60
Lead	22	40	55
Bauxite	16	41	39
Mercury	9	36	25
Graphite, natural [b]	3	14	21
Beryl [b]	8	41	20
Antimony	5	28	18
Cobalt	4	53	8
Manganese ore	2	27	7
Asbestos	3	55	5
Nickel	1	56	2
Columbium [a]	c	75	c
Tin	c	43	c
Chromite	c	29	c
Diamonds, industrial	0	86	0
Quartz, radio grade [a]	0	78	0

Source: Minerals Yearbook, 1950, U.S. Bureau of Mines, various pages.

a. Estimated by the author.
b. Exclusive of the U.S.S.R.
c. Less than 0.5 per cent.

APPENDIX 22-1. INDEXES OF PER CAPITA REAL DISPOSABLE PERSONAL INCOME AND FOOD CONSUMPTION, 1909-1952

(1947-1949 = 100)

Year	Disposable Income	Food Consumption	
		Pounds	Pounds, Weighted by Average Retail Prices
1909	64	103	89
1910	64	102	88
1911	65	100	88
1912	66	103	89
1913	68	101	87
1914	66	100	87
1915	68	100	87
1916	74	97	86
1917	75	97	85
1918	71	100	87
1919	69	99	88
1920	62	99	87
1921	54	96	85
1922	61	100	89
1923	68	101	91
1924	68	101	92
1925	69	100	91
1926	70	100	92
1927	71	99	91
1928	72	100	91
1929	75	101	91
1930	70	99	91
1931	66	99	90
1932	57	97	88
1933	56	96	88
1934	60	96	89
1935	65	97	87
1936	73	97	91
1937	75	98	90
1938	70	98	91
1939	75	100	94
1940	79	99	95
1941	90	101	97
1942	101	102	97
1943	104	103	98
1944	108	107	101
1945	106	107	102
1946	103	106	104
1947	98	103	102
1948	101	99	99
1949	101	98	99
1950	107	97	100
1951	107	98	99
1952	108	98	101

Sources: Appendix 4-2, Table B; Statistical Abstract of the United States, 1953, U.S. Bureau of the Census, Table 7, p. 13; and Consumption of Food in the United States, 1909-52, U.S. Department of Agriculture, Agriculture Handbook No. 62, 1953, pp. 144 and 147.

APPENDIX 22-2. PER CAPITA CONSUMPTION OF COTTON AND OF ALL FIBERS, 1913-1952

(Pounds)

Year	Cotton	All Fibers
1913	27.48	30.44
1914	26.27	29.55
1915	28.55	32.37
1916	30.92	35.02
1917	31.28	35.21
1918	28.07	32.52
1919	26.85	30.64
1920	26.14	29.61
1921	23.62	27.47
1922	26.09	30.58
1923	27.51	32.20
1924	22.79	26.70
1925	26.17	30.41
1926	27.00	31.18
1927	29.74	34.29
1928	26.08	30.44
1929	27.74	32.69
1930	20.97	24.81
1931	21.10	25.59
1932	19.46	23.16
1933	23.96	28.79
1934	20.76	24.65
1935	21.36	27.26
1936	26.74	32.97
1937	27.92	33.77
1938	22.18	27.30
1939	27.34	34.32
1940	29.55	36.68
1941	38.37	47.88
1942	41.21	50.52
1943	38.03	47.72
1944	34.14	44.01
1945	31.85	42.25
1946	33.54	45.36
1947	31.93	43.89
1948	30.02	42.98
1949	25.37	35.93
1950	30.45	44.43
1951	30.99	43.66
1952	28.16	40.46

Sources: U.S. Bureau of Agricultural Economics: The Cotton Situation, January-March 1953, p. 11, and Agricultural Outlook Charts, 1954, October 1953, p. 67.

APPENDIX 22–3. PERCENTAGE CONTRIBUTION OF EXPORTS TO
GROSS FARM INCOME, 1869–1937

Period	All Agricultural Exports as Per Cent of Total Gross Farm Income	Exports, Excluding Cotton, as Per Cent of Total Gross Farm Income, Excluding Cotton
1869–1875	16.6	8.7
1876–1880	16.8	11.3
1881–1885	19.3	14.1
1886–1890	15.3	9.8
1891–1895	17.6	11.9
1896–1900	19.2	13.7
1901–1905	18.4	13.0
1906–1910	16.7	9.9
1911–1915	14.9	7.6
1916–1920	17.6	14.0
1921–1925	17.8	12.9
1926–1930	14.7	8.7
1931–1934	9.6	5.2
1935–1937	8.4	4.7

Source: Frederic Strauss and Louis H. Bean, *Gross Farm Income and Indices of Farm Production and Prices in the United States, 1869–1937,* Technical Bulletin No. 703, U.S. Department of Agriculture, 1940.

APPENDIX 22–4. INDEXES OF AGRICULTURAL PRODUCTION AND POPULATION, 1910–1951

(1947–$1949 = 100$)

Year	Population[a]	Agricultural Production	Crops	Livestock	Total Crops and Livestock	Nonfood Products
1910	63	57	50	58	56	63
1911	64	61	51	61	58	70
1912	65	61	56	60	59	70
1913	66	61	54	60	59	70
1914	67	61	61	59	60	64
1915	69	64	62	61	62	71
1916	70	63	58	63	62	68
1917	70	62	56	63	62	63
1918	71	66	63	68	66	67
1919	72	67	62	68	66	68
1920	72	64	62	66	65	59
1921	74	65	62	65	64	70
1922	75	67	64	69	68	62
1923	76	69	63	73	71	62
1924	78	72	66	74	72	72
1925	79	70	61	72	69	74
1926	80	73	66	73	71	78
1927	81	73	68	74	72	74
1928	82	74	70	75	74	73
1929	83	73	69	74	73	75
1930	84	72	67	74	72	71
1931	85	73	69	75	74	69
1932	85	71	65	75	72	68
1933	85	72	63	77	73	65
1934	86	71	61	79	74	59
1935	87	66	67	70	69	56
1936	87	71	65	75	73	63
1937	88	74	72	74	73	75
1938	89	76	77	76	77	74
1939	89	78	76	80	79	76
1940	90	80	74	84	81	75
1941	91	82	81	86	85	72
1942	92	90	88	95	93	79
1943	93	94	84	103	98	79
1944	94	99	91	107	103	84
1945	95	99	94	106	103	85
1946	97	97	96	104	102	79
1947	99	100	101	103	102	92
1948	100	97	102	97	98	95
1949	102	103	98	101	100	113
1950	104	99	92	102	100	99
1951	105	101	91	105	102	97

Source: U.S. Bureau of Agricultural Economics.

a. Based on estimates for April 1 of each year; estimates include armed forces overseas for 1917–1919 and for 1940–1952.

APPENDIX 22–5. INDEXES OF ACREAGE OF CROPS HARVESTED, AGRICULTURAL PRODUCTION
AND PRODUCTION PER HARVESTED ACRE, 1909–1951

(*1940 = 100*)

Year	Acreage Harvested [a]	Agricultural Production	Production per Harvested Acre [b]
1909	94.4	71.8	76
1910	95.4	71.8	75
1911	97.2	75.4	78
1912	96.6	77.3	80
1913	97.8	73.6	75
1914	98.1	78.2	80
1915	100.0	78.2	78
1916	100.3	75.4	75
1917	102.7	78.2	76
1918	106.3	81.8	77
1919	106.6	82.7	78
1920	105.4	83.6	79
1921	105.4	75.4	72
1922	103.9	82.7	80
1923	103.6	85.4	82
1924	104.2	89.1	86
1925	105.4	88.2	84
1926	105.1	90.9	86
1927	105.1	89.1	85
1928	105.7	92.7	88
1929	106.9	90.0	84
1930	108.0	89.1	83
1931	106.9	92.7	87
1932	108.9	87.3	80
1933	99.4	87.3	88
1934	88.6	84.5	95
1935	100.6	82.7	82
1936	94.5	85.4	90
1937	102.1	96.4	94
1938	102.1	93.6	92
1939	97.5	96.4	99
1940	100.0	100.0	100
1941	101.1	102.7	102
1942	102.4	112.7	110
1943	104.9	117.3	112
1944	106.3	124.5	117
1945	104.5	121.8	117
1946	104.1	124.5	120
1947	105.3	123.6	117
1948	106.0	125.5	118
1949	107.6	128.2	119
1950	101.5	125.5	124
1951	101.3	128.2	127

Source: U.S. Bureau of Agricultural Economics.

a. Based on 52 crops 1943–1951 adjusted to 46 crops, 1919–1942; 1909–1918—17 crops adjusted to 46 crops by adding 14 million acres annually.

b. This should not be confused with "crop production per acre," because it includes livestock marketed during a given year but fed in part from crops produced on the acreage of previous years. The distinction is particularly significant for the years 1934–1936.

APPENDIX 22–6. INDEXES OF NUMBER OF ANIMALS ON FARMS AND PRODUCTION OF
LIVESTOCK AND LIVESTOCK PRODUCTS, 1910–1952

(*1935–1939* = *100*)

Year	Meat and Milk Animals and Poultry on Farms	Production of Livestock and Livestock Products for Sale and Home Use	Ratio of Production to Animals on Farms
1910	91.5	77	84.2
1911	92.9	81	87.2
1912	90.9	80	88.0
1913	90.8	80	88.1
1914	93.1	78	83.8
1915	98.6	81	82.2
1916	103.5	84	81.2
1917	105.7	84	79.5
1918	109.0	89	81.0
1919	110.1	90	81.7
1920	106.7	85	79.9
1921	104.3	86	82.5
1922	104.8	91	86.8
1923	107.5	97	90.2
1924	105.3	99	94.0
1925	99.1	96	96.9
1926	95.3	97	101.8
1927	94.7	98	103.5
1928	96.8	100	103.3
1929	97.7	99	101.3
1930	99.3	99	99.7
1931	100.8	100	99.2
1932	105.4	99	93.9
1933	111.1	103	92.7
1934	113.9	106	93.1
1935	100.3	93	92.7
1936	100.6	101	100.4
1937	99.1	98	98.9
1938	98.3	102	103.8
1939	101.6	107	105.3
1940	108.4	112	103.3
1941	109.3	115	105.2
1942	117.0	127	108.5
1943	127.8	139	108.8
1944	135.5	143	105.5
1945	125.4	141	112.4
1946	122.1	138	113.0
1947	117.2	137	116.9
1948	112.0	130	116.1
1949	111.4	137	123.0
1950	113.7	136	119.6
1951	113.9	141	118.6
1952	125.3	146	116.5

Source: U.S. Bureau of Agricultural Economics.

APPENDIX 22-7. INDEXES OF AGRICULTURAL PRODUCTION, MAN-HOUR REQUIREMENTS
AND PRODUCTIVITY, 1910-1952

(1935-1939 = 100)

Year	Agricultural Production [a]	Man-Hour Requirements	Production per Man-Hour
1910	79	107	74
1911	83	110	75
1912	85	111	77
1913	81	109	74
1914	86	113	76
1915	86	110	78
1916	83	110	75
1917	86	113	76
1918	90	114	79
1919	91	112	81
1920	92	114	81
1921	83	105	79
1922	91	109	84
1923	94	110	85
1924	98	111	88
1925	97	113	86
1926	100	114	88
1927	98	109	90
1928	102	111	92
1929	99	110	90
1930	98	109	90
1931	102	112	91
1932	96	108	89
1933	96	108	89
1934	93	106	88
1935	91	100	91
1936	94	97	97
1937	106	105	101
1938	103	99	104
1939	107	99	108
1940	110	98	112
1941	113	97	116
1942	124	101	123
1943	129	100	129
1944	137	100	137
1945	134	95	141
1946	137	93	147
1947	136	91	149
1948	138	89	155
1949	141	89	159
1950	135	83	163
1951	138	86	160
1952	145	83	175

Source: U.S. Bureau of Agricultural Economics.

a. For sale and home use.

APPENDIX 23–I. WARTIME AND POSTWAR PEAK ACTIVITY OF SELECTED INDUSTRIES COMPARED WITH 1939

Item	Unit	1939 Rate of Production or Activity	Wartime Peak [a]			Postwar Peak [a]		
			Annual Rate of Production or Activity	Percentage Increase over 1939	Year	Annual Rate of Production or Activity	Percentage Increase over 1939	Year
Mining industries								
Bituminous coal	1,000 short tons	394,855	619,576	57	1944	630,624	60	1947
Anthracite	1,000 short tons	51,487	63,701	24	1944	60,507	18	1946
Petroleum	1,000,000 barrels	1,265	1,678	33	1944	2,292	81	1952
Iron ore	1,000 long tons	51,732	105,526	104	1942	116,505	125	1951
Bauxite (domestic only)	1,000 long dry tons	375	6,233	1,562	1943	1,849	393	1951
Manufacturing								
Durable								
Iron and steel								
Pig iron	1,000 short tons	34,805	61,007	75	1944	70,278	102	1951
Ingot steel	1,000 short tons	52,799	89,642	70	1944	105,200	99	1951
Bessemer	1,000 short tons	3,359	5,625	67	1943	4,891	46	1951
Open-hearth	1,000 short tons	48,410	80,364	66	1944	93,167	92	1951
Electric	1,000 short tons	1,029	4,589	346	1943	7,142	594	1951
Machinery	Index of industrial production	100	426	326	1943	342	242	1952
Transportation equipment								
Trucks and buses	1,000 units	710	819	15	1942	1,430	101	1951
Tractors	1,000 units	215	311	45	1944	794	269	1951
Airplanes (total)	Number	5,856	96,318	1,545	1944	n.a.	—	—
Airplanes (civilian)	Number	4,935	n.a.	—	—	35,001	609	1946
Locomotives	New units installed	298	1,245	318	1944	3,514	1,079	1951
Freight cars	New units installed	23,236	58,595	152	1942	95,979	313	1948
Merchant vessels launched	1,000 gross tons	422	11,580	2,644	1943	633	50	1949
Nonferrous metals and products								
Aluminum—primary and secondary	1,000,000 pounds	435	2,468	467	1943	2,489	472	1952
Magnesium	Short tons	3,350	183,584	5,380	1943	105,821	3,059	1952
Copper (refineries)	1,000 short tons	1,010	1,415	40	1942	1,240	23	1950
Lead (smelters)	1,000 short tons	484	567	17	1942	508	5	1950
Lumber (mills)	1,000,000 bd. feet	25,148	36,332	44	1942	38,682	51	1950
Stone, clay and glass products								
Cement	1,000 barrels	124,698	185,342	48	1942	252,658	103	1952
Glass containers	1,000 gross	52,535	n.a.	—	—	117,692	124	1951

APPENDIX 23-I (continued)

Item	Unit	1939 Rate of Production or Activity	Wartime Peak [a]			Postwar Peak [a]		
			Annual Rate of Production or Activity	Percentage Increase over 1939	Year	Annual Rate of Production or Activity	Percentage Increase over 1939	Year
Manufacturing (contd.)								
Nondurable								
Textiles and products								
Cotton consumption	1,000 bales	6,858	11,170	63	1942	10,654	55	1951
Woolen consumption	1,000,000 pounds	397	636	60	1943	738	86	1946
Rayon and acetate (mill consumption)	1,000,000 pounds	459	705	54	1944	1,276	178	1951
Nylon, dacron, orlon, etc. (mill consumption)	1,000,000 pounds	5 [b]	49	880	1944	260	5,100	1952
Leather and products								
Boots, shoes and slippers (exc. rubbers)	1,000 pairs	435,259	483,870	11	1942	528,962	22	1946
Manufactured food products								
Meat	1,000,000 pounds	17,534	25,178	44	1944	23,430	34	1947
Wheat	1,000,000 bushels	741	1,060	43	1944	1,367	84	1947
Evaporated milk	1,000,000 pounds	2,171	3,519	62	1942	3,383	56	1948
Cheese	1,000,000 pounds	709	1,112	57	1942	1,199	69	1949
Butter	1,000,000 pounds	1,782	1,764	-1	1942	1,412	-21	1949
Margarine	1,000,000 pounds	333	609	83	1944	1,286	286	1952
Tomatoes	1,000,000 cases	25	42	68	1942	32	28	1951
Peas	1,000,000 cases	16	37	131	1942	34	113	1951
Paper and products								
Wood pulp	1,000 short tons	6,993	10,783	54	1942	16,524	136	1951
Paper and paper board	1,000 short tons	13,510	17,183	27	1944	26,048	93	1951
Printing and publishing								
Newsprint	1,000 short tons	939	953	1	1942	1,147	22	1952
Printing paper	1,000 short tons	2,102	2,326	11	1942	3,514	67	1951
Petroleum and coal products								
Gasoline	1,000,000 of 42 gallon barrels	597	773	30	1944	1,156	94	1952
Coke	1,000 of 42 gallon barrels	8,330	9,014	8	1944	18,977	128	1951
Rubber—synthetic	Number of long tons	1,750	762,630	43,000	1944	845,155	48,000	1951
Transportation								
Railroad								
Car loadings	1,000 cars	33,911	43,408	28	1944	44,502	31	1947
Locomotives in service [c]	Number	45,172	46,305	3	1944	45,511	1	1946
Steam	Number	43,604	41,983	-4	1943	39,592	-9	1946

Item	Unit							
Diesel	Number	639	3,432	437	1944	22,118	3,361	1952
Electric	Number	879	907	3	1943	867	—1	1946
Freight cars in service	1,000 units	1,681	1,797	7	1944	1,792	7	1952
Passenger cars in service	Number	38,977	38,446	—1	1942	39,406	1	1948
Commodity traffic	1,000,000 ton-miles	333,375	740,586	122	1944	657,878	97	1947
Passenger traffic	1,000,000 passenger-miles	22,713	95,663	321	1944	64,754	185	1946
Air (domestic only)								
Miles of established air routes	Miles	39,782	62,937	58	1944	165,777	317	1952
Revenue passenger-miles flown	1,000,000 miles	683	2,265	219	1944	12,121	1,734	1952
Ton-miles of express freight and mail flown	1,000 ton-miles	11,324	68,132	502	1944	230,169	19,000	1952
Transit lines	1,000,000 passengers	10,252	18,735	83	1944	19,119	86	1946
Communications								
Telegraph	1,000 messages	207,780	249,978	20	1944	248,047	19	1947
Telephone								
Number of telephones in service	1,000 units	20,831	26,859	29	1944	48,056	131	1952
Miles of wire	1,000 miles	95,150	109,000	15	1944	176,000	85	1952
Electric light and power[d]								
Peak generating capacity	1,000 kilowatts	38,863	49,189	27	1944	82,117	111	1952
Total energy generated	1,000,000 kilowatt-hours	127,642	228,189	79	1944	398,924	213	1952
Gas								
Natural (marketed production)	Billions of cubic feet	2,477	3,711	50	1944	8,013	223	1952
Manufactured	1,000 millions of therms	1,834	2,604	42	1944	2,874	57	1947

c. Includes a few locomotives other than steam, diesel, electric, e.g., gasoline-driven.

d. Includes only electricity generated by electric utilities for public use.

n.a. Not available.

Note: Totals do not necessarily agree with sum of individual items since peak years may differ. Figures on equipment in this table are for end of year indicated, whereas those in Tables 343 and 346 and in Appendix 23–2 are for beginning of year.

Sources: Statistical Abstract of the United States, various issues; U.S. Bureau of the Census, Bureau of Mines, Interstate Commerce Commission, and various other official and private agencies.

a. Wartime period defined to include years 1942–1944 and postwar period the years 1946–1952; the year 1945 could not reasonably be assigned to either period and data for years after 1952 were not generally available at the time this tabulation was prepared.

b. 1940.

APPENDIX 23–2. TOTAL ANNUAL RATED CAPACITY AND EQUIPMENT OF THE BASIC INDUSTRIES OF THE UNITED STATES, SELECTED YEARS, 1920–1952 [a]

(Data as of January 1 of Each Year)

Industry and Item	Unit	1920	1930	1940	1945	1950	1952
DURABLE MANUFACTURES							
Metals—Ferrous							
1. Pig iron	Thousand tons	56,249	57,855	55,724	67,314	71,498	73,782 [b]
2. Foundries	"	—	—	27,270	—	—	22,045 [e]
3. Steel ingots	"	62,314	72,985	81,620	95,505	99,393	108,588 [e]
4. Structural shapes	"	—	—	5,670 [d]	—	—	6,768 [b]
5. Strip, cold rolled	"	—	—	1,610 [d]	—	—	2,826 [b]
6. Strip, hot rolled	"	—	—	4,799 [d]	—	—	4,908 [b]
7. Sheets, cold rolled	"	—	—	5,760 [d]	—	—	11,498 [b]
8. Sheets, hot rolled	"	—	—	12,267 [d]	—	—	24,890 [b]
9. Sheets, galvanized	"	—	—	2,282 [d]	—	—	3,183 [b]
10. Bars, concrete reinforcing, etc.	"	—	—	12,081 [d]	—	—	13,593 [b]
11. Bars, cold finished	"	—	—	1,722 [d]	—	—	2,968 [b]
12. Wire and wire products	"	—	—	7,872 [d]	—	—	10,789 [b]
13. Plates	"	—	—	6,164 [d]	—	—	8,261 [b]
14. Tubes	"	—	—	3,305 [d]	—	—	3,938 [b]
15. Rails	"	—	—	3,352 [d]	—	—	2,707 [b]
16. Bolts, nuts, rivets	"	—	—	830 [d]	—	—	349
17. Tinplate, electrolytic	"	—	—	0 [d]	—	—	3,253 [b]
18. Tinplate, hot dipped	"	—	—	4,089 [d]	—	—	3,201 [b]
19. Castings	"	—	1,400	1,740	—	2,500	—
20. Malleable iron foundries	"	—	—	—	—	1,368	—
21. Steel foundries	"	—	—	—	—	—	2,479 [b]
22. Ferroalloys, blast furnace	"	—	824	922	993	1,108	1,081
23. Ferroalloys, electric furnace (E)	Kilowatts	—	—	—	—	—	764,000 [b]
Metals—Nonferrous							
24. Copper smelter	Thousand tons	23,733	13,787	10,722	10,909 [e]	9,748 [b]	9,850
25. Copper refinery	"	1,384	1,627	1,572	1,595 [e]	1,557	1,599
26. Lead smelter	"	5,559	3,510	2,500	2,078 [e]	—	1,858
27. Lead refinery	"	—	1,178	1,168	975 [e]	866 [b]	866
28. Zinc refinery	"	—	226	223	365 [e]	373 [b]	375
29. Alumina	"	—	—	420 [f]	—	—	2,448 [b]
30. Aluminum ingots	"	76 [g]	125	245	767 [e]	721	871
31. Secondary aluminum	Thousand tons	—	—	71.6 [d]	—	358 [h]	—

No.	Item	Unit					
32.	Aluminum sheet	"	—	414[1]	—	954	—
33.	Aluminum sheet, heat-treated	"	—	—	—	351[b]	—
34.	Magnesium ingots	"	—	9.0[1]	293	127[b]	138
35.	Magnesium sheet	"	—	—	—	2.5	20
36.	Titanium metal	Tons	—	—	—	150	5,527[1]
37.	Molybdenum metal	Thousand tons	—	—	—	—	32.5
38.	Tin smelter	"	—	—	—	—	53.3
39.	Detinning plants	"	—	—	—	—	5.0
40.	Nickel refinery	"	—	—	—	8	—
41.	Antimony smelter	"	—	—	—	—	12.2
42.	Cadmium metal	"	—	—	—	—	5.1[b]
43.	Zirconium metal	Tons	—	—	—	—	31[b]
44.	Beryllium copper alloy	Thousand tons	—	—	—	—	1.8
45.	Beryllium copper fabricating	"	—	—	—	—	3.0
	Lumber and Products						
46.	Lumber, sawmill (est.)	Million bd. ft.	51,200	77,000[k]	—	—	—
47.	Timber fabricating	"	—	—	—	—	400[b]
48.	Insulating wallboard	Million sq. ft.	—	1,000	—	2,275[b]	2,500
49.	Plywood, all types	" " " (⅜ in., 3 ply)	—	—	—	—	—
50.	Hardboard	Million sq. ft. (¼ in.)	—	—	2,552[2]	—	4577
51.	Veneer	" " " (⅛ in.)	—	—	—	—	357
52.	Prefabricated houses	Standard units	—	—	—	92,880	2,532.5
53.	Red cedar shingles	Thousand "squares"	—	6,019	3,340[e]	—	3,237
	Machinery						
54.	Hydroelectric generators	Thousand kw.	—	} 3,500	—	—	2,600[b]
55.	Steam-electric generators	"	—		—	—	12,400[b]
56.	Hydroturbines	Thousand hp.	—	—	—	—	3,000[b]
57.	Steam boilers	Thousand lbs./hr.	—	—	—	—	175,000[b]
58.	Transformers, power and distribution	Thousand kw. amps.	—	—	—	—	63,500[b]
59.	Condensers	Thousand sq. ft. of condensing surface	—	—	—	—	8,000[b]
60.	Tubular heat exchangers	Thousand sq. ft. of surface	—	—	—	—	38,500[b]
61.	Machine tools (d.c.)	Standard units	—	—	—	—	219,000
62.	Ball and roller bearings (d.c.)	Thousand standard units	—	—	—	—	400,000[b]
63.	Power cranes and shovels	Units	—	—	—	—	14,500[b]
64.	Diesel engines	Thousand hp.	—	—	—	—	40,000
65.	Steel strapping	Tons	—	—	—	—	400,000[b]

Industry and Item	Unit	1920	1930	1940	1945	1950	1952
DURABLE MANUFACTURES							
Machinery (contd.)							
66. Metal tanks	Thousand tons	—	—	—	—	1,250 [b]	1,500
Steel containers:							
67. Heavy drums	Thousand units	—	—	35,000	—	—	52,500
68. Light drums	"	—	—	10,000	—	—	15,000
69. Pails	"	—	—	75,000	—	—	110,000
70. Metal cans	Thousand tons	—	—	—	—	—	4,100 [b]
71. Compressed-gas cylinders	Tons	—	—	—	—	260,000	—
72. Wire-braided hose, high pressure	Thousand ft.	—	—	—	—	—	25,000 [b]
73. Farm implements	Index of manufacturing capacity	—	—	100 [t]	—	200 [l]	—
Stone, Clay and Glass Products							
74. Portland cement	Thousand bbls.	134,093	258,917	253,759	241,631 [e]	258,948	281,532 [b]
75. Gypsum, kettles and kilns (E)	Units of equipment	—	—	195	—	221	225 [b]
76. Glass melting	Thousand tons	—	—	6,522 [k]	8,000 [m]	—	—
77. Optical glass	Tons	—	—	—	—	—	—
78. Glass fiber(s)	"	—	—	—	—	—	2,075 [b]
79. Glass containers	Million units (bottles and jars, etc.)	—	—	10,973 [f]	13,522 [m]	18,829	12,400 [b]
80. Structural clay products (inc. brick)	Thousand tons	—	—	—	10,000 [m]	—	20,995
Transportation Equipment							
81. Railroad locomotives, diesel powered	Units	—	—	—	2,000 [m]	—	4,300
82. Railroad steam locomotives	"	—	—	—	2,300 [m]	—	—
83. Railroad freight cars	"	—	—	160,800 [l]	204,000 [m]	—	150,000
84. Railroad passenger cars	"	—	—	—	4,000 [m]	—	—
85. Industrial locomotives	"	—	—	—	530 [m]	—	700
86. Automotive vehicles (d.c.)	Thousand cars and trucks	2,600	8,352 [n]	—	—	10,354 [h]	—
87. Shipbuilding ways (E)	Number of ways	—	—	156 [t]	—	227 [h]	—
88. Aircraft manufacturing floor space (E)	Thousand sq. ft.	—	—	44,200 [l]	171,400 [o]	—	120,000 [b]
NONDURABLE MANUFACTURES							
Alcoholic Beverages							
89. Distilleries, beverage	Thousand gal.	—	—	—	—	—	317,000 [b]
90. Breweries	Million gal.	—	—	—	—	—	129,733

	Unit							
Manufactured Food Products								
91. Flour mills	Thousand bbls.	634,815	554,000	443,000	414,500	—	—	394,000[b]
92. Ice cream freezing	Million gal.	—	—	—	—	—	—	4,250[b]
93. Sugar beet slicing	Tons per 24 hours	—	—	8,042[d]	—	—	150,000[h]	159,750
94. Sugar refining	Thousand tons	—	—	—	—	—	—	8,802
95. Meat packing (d.c.)	"	—	—	—	—	—	—	11,862
96. Soybean oil and meal crushing	Thousand bushels	172,000[p]	—	—	—	—	225,000[h]	—
97. Cotton seed oil milling	Thousand tons	—	—	—	—	—	6,382[h]	—
Paper								
98. Wood pulp	"	6,245[g]	7,322[q]	10,421	11,994	—	16,167	18,407
99. Paper, all types except newsprint	"	6,245[g]	6,295	7,951	9,543[e]	—	11,739	11,998
100. Paperboard	"	6,245[g]	5,697	7,531	9,900[e]	—	11,762	12,296
101. Newsprint	"	1,426[g]	1,712	1,075	981	—	924	1,052
Printing and Publishing								
102. Newspaper printing presses (E)	Units *in use* in publishing plants	—	—	—	2,261	—	7,320	—
103. Magazine printing presses (E)	(same)	—	—	—	1,824	—	—	—
104. Book printing presses (E)	(same)	—	—	—	—	—	—	—
105. Offset presses (E)	(same)	—	—	—	—	—	—	7,000[b]
Leather Products								
106. Shoes, all types	Million pairs	—	—	500	650	—	—	700
Textiles and Products								
107. Cotton ginning	Thousand bales per day	—	—	—	1,043	905	—	744[b](est.)
108. Cotton mill spindles (E)	Thousand spindles in place	—	35,834	34,025	24,750	23,128	22,995	23,152
109. Cotton mill looms (E)	Thousand looms in place	—	763	693	498	460	—	396
110. Woolen mill spindles (E)	Thousand spindles in place	—	2,401	2,295	1,777	1,632	1,439	1,197
111. Worsted mill spindles (E)	Thousand spindles in place	—	2,356	2,557	2,083	1,943	1,835	1,786
112. Worsted mill combs (E)	Combs in place	—	2,382	2,744	2,592	2,609	2,715	2,761
113. Woolen and worsted looms	Looms in place	—	81,700[g]	72,000	47,800	40,140	37,600	34,140
114. Carpet and rug looms (E)	" " "	—	9,550	9,940	6,884[f]	6,570	5,200	4,440
115. Rayon-synthetics—silk spindles (E)	Thousand spindles in place	—	—	—	4,097	3,217	3,376	4,223
116. Rayon-synthetics—silk looms (E)	Thousand looms in place	—	—	—	108	109	117	134

Industry and Item	Unit	1920	1930	1940	1945	1950	1952
NONDURABLE MANUFACTURES							
Textiles and Products (contd.)							
117. Rayon and acetate fiber	Thousand tons	—	—	270	446[e]	625	740
118. Synthetic fibers	"	—	—	—	—	—	158[b]
118a. Nylon alone	"	—	—	10	—	—	48[b]
119. Hosiery, women's full fashioned	Million pairs	—	—	—	—	—	1,030
120. Men's suits	Thousand units	—	—	—	—	—	27,300
121. Pyroxylin-coated spread	Thousand lbs.	—	—	—	178,800	230,213[h]	—
Tobacco Products							
122. Cigarettes (based on estimated number of machines)	Billion units	—	—	—	—	—	1,080[b]
Rubber Products							
123. Rubber tires	Thousand tires	45,645[s]	91,600[n]	—	—	—	108,000
124. Rubber reclaiming	Tons	—	—	—	362,880	—	459,000
Petroleum and Coal Products							
125. Crude oil refinery	Million bbls.	559	1,374	1,687	1,935	2,444	2,686
126. Catalytic cracked gasoline	Thousand bbls.	—	—	381,800	543,120	664,300	726,987
127. Catalytic reforming for gasoline	"	—	—	—	—	—	29,339
128. Cycling plant	"	—	—	2,190	42,000[e]	57,700	66,200
129. Natural gasoline	"	—	91,250	100,000	114,000[e]	178,800	231,000
130. Lubricating oil	Bbls.	—	—	—	—	64,809[b]	66,970
131. Lubricating oil additives	"	—	—	—	—	—	193,460
132. Lubricating oil detergents	"	—	—	—	—	—	46,260
133. Catalytic reforming for chemicals	Thousand bbls.	—	—	—	—	—	12,850
134. Propylene	"	—	—	—	—	—	25,365
135. Butylene	"	—	—	—	—	—	46,542
136. Isobutane	"	—	—	—	—	—	47,307
137. Naphthenic acid	Tons	—	—	—	—	—	33,050
138. Fuel briquettes	Thousand tons	—	—	—	4,533[e]	4,455	4,407[b]
139. Packaged fuel	"	—	—	—	534	294	277
140. Coke	"	87,000	76,900	—	—	82,382	88,087
Miscellaneous Products							
141. Radio receiving sets	Thousand sets	—	—	12,000	—	35,000[h]	55,000[b]
142. Television sets (d.c.)	"	—	—	—	—	—	10,440[b]
143. Electronic glass envelopes	Million units	—	—	—	—	—	2,400[b]
144. Technicolor film	Million ft.	—	—	—	—	—	400,000[b]
145. Filament tape	Thousand sq. yds.	—	—	—	—	—	1,250[b]
146. Acetate tape	"	—	—	—	—	—	5,750[b]

Chemicals—Industrial

#	Item	Unit						
147.	Sulfuric acid	Thousand tons	13,400[b]	13,000	9,500[e]	—	—	—
148.	Soda ash	"	5,700[b]	5,320[h]	4,722[e]	3,535[f]	—	—
149.	Caustic soda	"	2,100[b]	1,862[l]	—	767	302	—
150.	Chlorine	"	—	2,200	—	—	9,000	—
151.	Methanol	Thousand gal.	174,000[b]	157,000	82,500[u]	73,500[f]	—	—
152.	Ethanol	"	—	111,000[l]	—	—	—	—
153.	Benzene	"	215,000[b]	—	—	—	—	—
154.	Phosphorus, elemental	Thousand tons	161[b]	159	—	95[f]	65[q]	—
155.	Formaldehyde	"	663[b]	394[l]	—	2	—	—
156.	Maleic anhydride	"	14[b]	10[l]	—	168	—	—
157.	Naphthalene	"	205[j]	176	—	—	—	—
158.	Ethyl alcohol	Thousand gal.	398,000[b]	—	—	—	—	—
159.	Hydrofluoric acid	Thousand tons	47[b]	—	100	74[f]	—	—
160.	Ethylene oxide	"	273[b]	220	—	32[f]	—	—
161.	Phthalic anhydride	"	114[b]	102[l]	—	—	—	—
162.	Glycerine	"	113[b]	—	—	82[f]	—	—
163.	Ethylene glycol	"	262[b]	220[h]	—	—	—	—
164.	Sodium chlorate	"	34[b]	—	—	—	—	—
165.	Sulfur	"	—	6,080	—	—	—	—

Explosives

#	Item	Unit						
166.	Permissible and high explosives	Thousand tons	412[b]	414	376	311	312	271
167.	Black powder	"	26[b]	23	69	82	154	200

Fertilizers

#	Item	Unit						
168.	Nitrogen, synthetic	Thousand tons	1,639[b]	1,550[h]	1,028	625[l]	161	—
169.	Superphosphate, normal	"	16,538[b]	14,000[l]	—	8,429[l]	—	—
170.	Superphosphate, triple	"	793[b]	—	—	—	—	—
171.	Phosphoric acid	"	1,282[b]	—	—	—	—	—
172.	Potash	"	1,575[b]	—	—	—	—	—

Insecticides

#	Item	Unit						
173.	"DDT"	Thousand tons	51[b]	—	—	—	—	—
174.	Benzene hexachloride	"	9[b]	—	—	—	—	—
175.	Lindane	Tons	350[b]	—	—	—	—	—

Dyes

#	Item	Unit						
176.	Aniline	Thousand tons	53[b]	—	—	—	—	—
177.	Iron oxide, yellow	"	13[b]	—	—	—	—	20
178.	Titanium dioxide pigment	"	282[b]	—	—	—	—	—
179.	Anthraquinone vat dyes	"	18[b]	—	—	—	—	—

Industry and Item	Unit	1920	1930	1940	1945	1950	1952
NONDURABLE MANUFACTURES (contd.)							
Gases							
180. Oxygen	Tons	—	—	24,000[t]	—	—	922,150[b]
181. Helium	Thousand cu. ft.	—	—	—	—	192,000[i]	—
Plastic Machinery, in Place							
182. Injection machines (E)	Number	—	—	1,000[t]	1,400	3,966	5,035
183. Extrusion machines (E)	"	—	—	—	650	1,987	2,660
184. Compression machines (E)	"	—	—	8,000[i]	12,400[e]	—	13,700
Plastic Materials							
185. Phenol	Thousand tons	2[p]	7[t]	45[t]	—	172[b]	192[j]
186. Polystyrene	"	—	—	—	—	—	200[b]
187. Styrene monomer	"	—	—	—	—	—	313[b]
188. Vinyl resin	"	—	—	—	—	—	175[b]
189. Vinyl chloride	"	—	—	—	—	—	212[b]
190. Vinyl acetate	"	—	—	—	—	—	25[b]
191. Vinylidene chloride	"	—	—	—	—	—	18[b]
192. Acrylate monomer	"	—	—	—	—	—	25[b]
193. Butadiene (for plastics)	"	—	—	—	—	—	30[b]
194. Polyester resin	"	—	—	—	—	—	12[b]
Synthetic Rubber and Materials							
195. Synthetic rubber	Thousand tons	—	—	11[t]	932[u]	1,002[b]	1,165
196. Carbon black	"	—	263	313	472[u]	744	942
197. Furfural	"	—	—	—	—	—	500[b]
Abrasives							
198. Silicon carbide	Thousand tons	—	—	—	72[u]	84	107[b]
199. Aluminum oxide	"	—	—	—	233[u]	239	249[b]
200. Metallic abrasives	"	—	—	—	209[u]	210	244[b]
Special Chemicals							
201. Toluene	Thousand gal.	—	—	110[i]	—	—	83,000[b]
202. Tetraethyl lead	Thousand tons	—	—	—	148	175	262
203. Benzene, petroleum	Thousand gal.	—	—	—	—	—	40,000
204. Quinoline	Tons	—	—	—	—	—	850[b]
205. Chlorophyll, commercial	"	—	—	—	—	—	45
206. Hydrogen peroxide	Thousand tons	—	—	—	—	—	10[b]

No.	Item	Unit					
207.	Pentaerythretol	"	—	—	—	—	20 [b]
208.	Methylene chloride	"	—	—	—	—	20 [b]
209.	Acetone	"	—	—	—	—	312 [b]
210.	Methyl ethyl ketone	"	—	—	—	—	75 [b]
211.	Methyl isobutyl ketone	"	—	—	—	—	68 [b]
212.	Sodium bichromate	"	—	—	—	—	132 [b]
213.	Hexamethylene tetramine	"	—	—	—	—	9 [b]
214.	Ethylene dichloride	"	—	—	—	—	200 [b]
215.	Octyl alcohols	"	—	—	—	—	53 [b]
216.	Ethylene dibromide	"	—	—	—	—	60 [b]
217.	Ethyl chloride	"	—	—	—	—	215 [b]
218.	Lithium compounds	"	—	—	—	—	2 [b]
219.	Ammonia	Thousand gal.	—	—	—	—	2,000 [b]
220.	Resorcinol	Thousand tons	—	—	—	—	3 [b]
221.	Methyl alcohol	"	—	—	—	—	174,000 [b]
222.	Acetic acid	"	—	—	—	—	316 [b]

Chlorinated Solvents

No.	Item	Unit					
223.	Carbon tetrachloride	Thousand tons	—	—	—	—	112 [b]
224.	Perchlorethylene	"	—	—	—	—	52 [b]
225.	Trichlorethylene	"	—	—	—	—	138 [b]
226.	Methyl chloride	"	—	—	—	—	17 [b]

Bases for Polyamide Fibers (nylon types)

No.	Item	Unit					
227.	Adiponitrile	Thousand tons	—	—	—	—	30 [b]
228.	Adipic acid	"	—	—	—	—	78 [b]
229.	Cyclohexane	"	—	—	—	—	58 [b]
230.	Hexamethylenediamine	"	—	—	—	—	31 [b]

Other Chemical Products

No.	Item	Unit					
231.	Calcium carbide	Thousand tons	—	—	—	—	780 [b]
232.	Synthetic cryolite	"	—	—	—	—	22 [b]
233.	Artificial graphite	Thousand tons	—	—	—	—	101 [b]
234.	Activated carbon	"	—	—	—	—	38 [b]
235.	Vulcanized fiber	"	—	—	—	—	30 [b]
236.	Penicillin	Billion Oxford units	—	—	—	—	250,000 [b]

Ceramics

No.	Item	Unit					
237.	Vitrified chinaware and dinnerware	Million pieces	159 [h]	—	—	—	—
238.	Earthenware and semi-porcelain potteries and dinnerware	"	328 [h]	—	—	—	—
239.	Whiteware pottery	"	2,023 [h]	—	—	—	—
240.	Stoneware pottery	"	17 [h]	—	—	—	—

APPENDIX 23-2 (continued)

Industry and Item	Unit	1920	1930	1940	1945	1950	1952
NONDURABLE MANUFACTURES							
Ceramics (contd.)							
241. Electrical porcelain products	"	—	—	—	—	674[h]	—
242. Bathware fixtures	"	—	—	—	—	10[h]	—
243. Floor and wall tiles	Million sq. ft.	—	—	—	—	54[h]	—
244. Basic refractory brick (nine-inch equivalent)	Million units	—	—	—	—	75[b]	—
245. Fire-brick refractories (insulating) (nine-inch equivalent)	"	—	—	—	—	43[b]	—
MINING							
Fuels							
246. Bituminous coal	Thousand tons	725,000	700,000	639,000	620,000	790,000	749,935[b]
247. Anthracite	"	101,000	90,000	84,000	62,000	63,400	62,300[b]
248. Coal cleaning and preparation plants	"						350,000
249. Crude petroleum producing (capacity at wells)	Million bbls.			1,716	1,679[e]	2,226	2,628
250. Rotary drilling rigs (E)	Units				2,365	—	3,850[b]
251. Natural gas producing (capacity at wells)	Billion cu. ft.					9,547[b]	10,212
252. Natural gas liquids producing (capacity at wells)	Million bbls.					210[b]	246
253. Petroleum storage capacity	"					886	958
254. Underground gas storage reservoirs	Billion cu. ft.				135[u]	774	916[b]
TRANSPORTATION							
Railroads							
255. Total locomotive tractive effort (E)	Thousand tons	1,235	1,373	1,060	1,159	1,159	1,168
256. Total freight-car carrying capacity	"	97,350	105,411	82,002	89,960	90,465	92,671
257. Total road miles operated (E)	Miles	253,200	249,430	235,060	227,335	224,510	223,427
Trucks							
258. Trucks in use (except those on farms) (E)	Thousand units	759	2,508	3,360	3,023	5,819	6,626
259. Total surfaced highways and roads (E)	Thousand miles	369	694	1,340	1,461	1,865	2,070
Airlines							
260. Total freight-carrying capacity	Tons		—	154	—	1,455	—

	Unit						
Marine							
261. Inland waterway vessels, cargo capacity	Thousand tons	—	—	4,486[u]	4,911[e]	5,727	6,647
262. Great Lakes vessels, cargo capacity	"	—	—	4,208[u]	3,665[e]	4,142	4,249
262a. Great Lakes oreboats only, trip cargo capacity	"	3,073[g]	2,838[n]	2,836[t]	2,783	2,672[b]	2,881
263. Ocean-going vessels, cargo capacity	"	—	—	14,270[u]	23,389[e]	21,143	27,378
264. Coal-loading piers, Atlantic coast	Tons per 24 hrs.	—	—	—	—	—	950,000
Pipelines							
265. Petroleum, crude and all products (E)	Thousand miles	53[s]	107	122	135	152	162
266. Petroleum, full capacity	Thousand bbls.	—	—	24,550[q]	—	46,836	—
267. All gas pipelines (E)	Thousand miles	—	254[v]	282	308	364	406
COMMUNICATIONS							
Telephone							
268. Telephones in use (E)	Thousand units	12,668	20,068	20,831	26,859	40,709	45,636
269. Miles of wire (E)	Thousand miles	30,400	76,460	95,150	109,000	156,700[b]	165,100
270. Central offices (E)	Number	21,300[w]	—	—	—	—	19,690
Radio							
271. Radio broadcasting stations (AM & FM) (E)	Number	30[x]	612	764	1,500[e]	—	3,369
272. Radio transmitting stations, other (E)	"	400[x]	—	—	70,000[e]	—	537,650
273. Radio receiving sets (E)	Thousand units	—	10,500	45,300	57,000	81,000	99,000
274. Television stations (E)	Number	—	—	—	—	51[l]	107
275. Television receiving sets (E)	Thousand units	—	—	—	—	1,000[l]	15,000
Telegraph							
276. Message capacity	Index basis	—	—	—	100	—	200[b]
UTILITY POWER							
277. Electric utility generating capacity	Thousand kw.	13,094	29,839	38,863	49,189	63,100	75,775
278. Natural gas pipeline pumping	Billion cu. ft.	—	—	—	—	2,448[l]	4,020
279. Manufactured gas	Million cu. ft.	—	—	2,064	2,746[l]	—	—
AGRICULTURE							
280. Farm cropland available (E)	Million acres	507	522	510	512	509	—
281. Tractors on farms (E)	Thousand units	246	920	1,545	2,422	3,616	4,170
282. Grain combines (E)	"	4	61	190	375	714	887
283. Corn picking machines (E)	"	10	50	110	168	456	588
284. Trucks on farms (E)	"	139	900	1,047	1,490	2,209	2,410

Industry and Item	Unit	1920	1930	1940	1945	1950	1952
AGRICULTURE (contd.)							
285. Fisheries, coastal and inland (inc. Alaska)							
Vessels and motor boats (E)	"	—	—	37	—	—	58[b]
Equipment (E) (lines and gill nets)	"	—	—	13,071	—	8,664[1]	—
STORAGE							
286. Warehouse and storage space (exc. refrig.) (E)	Million sq. ft. of area	—	—	138[1]	—	—	130[b]
287. Refrigerated warehouse (cold storage) space (E)	Million cu. ft.	—	—	433	511	613[b]	701[b]
288. Frozen-food locker plants (B)	Thousand lockers	—	—	947	4,012[e]	—	5,719[b]
289. Grain elevators	Thousand bushels	—	—	—	—	—	677,426[b]
OFFICES							
290. Office buildings (E)	Million sq. ft. of total usable floor space	—	—	—	—	—	400[b]
CONSTRUCTING AND BUILDING EQUIPMENT AND MACHINES							
291. Bulldozers (E)	Number	—	—	—	—	—	130,000
292. Compressors, mobile (E)	"	—	—	—	—	—	42,000
293. Dredges, floating (E)	"	—	—	—	—	—	650
294. Graders, motor (E)	"	—	—	—	—	—	78,000
295. Mixers, concrete (E)	"	—	—	—	—	—	107,875
296. Scrapers, carrying (E)	"	—	—	—	—	—	36,000
297. Power shovels, cranes, draglines (E)	"	—	—	—	—	—	58,000
298. Trench and ditch-digging machines (E)	"	—	—	—	—	—	6,500
299. Electric welding machines (E)	"	—	—	—	—	—	40,000

Sources: The sources for each line are as follows:

1. 3–18, 22, 23. American Iron and Steel Institute.
2. *Foundry* magazine. Note that the figure for 1940 given in table is for U.S. and Canada combined total (separate data unavailable); figure given for 1951 is for U.S. only—the combined U.S. and Canada total in 1951 is 23,885,800 tons annual capacity.
19. U.S. Bureau of the Census.
20. *Business Week*, October 14, 1950, quoting Malleable Iron Founders Society.
21. Steel Founders Society of America.

24–28. American Bureau of Metal Statistics, *Annual Year Book*.
29. *Economics of American Manufacturing*, Holt, New York, 1952.
30. Aluminum Corporation of America; Manufacturing Chemists Association, *Chemical Facts & Figures*, 1950 ed.; Defense Production Administration.
31. *Modern Metals* magazine.
32. Memorandum dated December 23, 1941, of Aluminum and Magnesium Branch, Defense Plant Administration; Defense Production Administration.
33. Defense Production Administration.
34. American Bureau of Metal Statistics; Dow Chemical Co.

35. *Light Metals* magazine; *Modern Metals* magazine; *Wall Street Journal*, March 20, 1952.
36. *Chemical Engineering* magazine; *Quebec Miner*, August 20, 1948; U.S. Bureau of Mines.
37. U.S. Bureau of Mines.
38. *World's Non-Ferrous Smelters and Refiners, 1950*, a directory (London); U.S. Bureau of Mines.
39. U.S. Bureau of Mines. This 5,000-ton annual yield capacity is based on processing of 325,000 tons of tinplate scrap.
40. *World's Non-Ferrous Smelters and Refiners, 1950.*
41, 42. U.S. Bureau of Mines.
43. *Chemical & Engineering News*, January 1, 1951; U.S. Bureau of Mines.
44, 45. Defense Production Administration.
46. The 1930 capacity estimated in *America's Capacity to Produce*, Brookings Institution, Washington, 1934; 1942 in *Forests and National Prosperity: A Reappraisal of the Forest Situation in the United States*, Misc. Pub. No. 668, U.S. Forest Service, 1948. There are no later estimates, although the total number of sawmills in the U.S. is now three times the 1930 figure.
47. National Lumber Manufacturers Association.
48. *Dow Diamond* magazine, October 1952, published by Dow Chemical Co.
49. *The Timberman* magazine, January 1945 and January 1952.
50, 51. *The Timberman*, January 1952.
52. U.S. Housing and Home Finance Agency; Prefabricated Home Manufacturers Institute.
53. U.S. Tariff Commission; U.S. Bureau of the Census. A "square" of shingles provides enough to cover 100 square feet of roof surface.
54–60. Edison Electric Institute; Defense Production Administration.
61. Estimated from indexes of the National Machine Tool Builders Association and actual production totals of U.S. Bureau of the Census.
62. Estimated from unofficial maximum production data.
63. Defense Production Administration.
64. *Diesel Progress* magazine, quoted in *Industrial Marketing Data Book*, 1952–1953.
65. Defense Production Administration.
66. Defense Production Administration.
67, 68, 69. Steel Shipping Container Institute.
70, 71, 72. Defense Production Administration.
73. U.S. Department of Commerce.
74, 75. U.S. Bureau of Mines.
76. 1942, from U.S. Bureau of the Census; 1947, from Battelle Memorial Institute.
77, 78. Defense Production Administration.
79. Glass Container Manufacturers Association; Containers and Packaging Division, National Production Authority.
80. John D. Sullivan, assistant director, Battelle Memorial Institute, in *Bulletin of American Society of Testing Materials*, January 1949.
81, 85. 1947, U.S. Department of the Interior; 1952, from Railroad Equipment Division, National Production Authority.

82. U.S. Department of the Interior. This portion of the locomotive manufacturers' plant capacity has by now been largely dismantled, as steam locomotives are being superseded to a large extent by diesel-electric units.
83, 84. 1941, *Fortune* (1948); 1947, U.S. Department of the Interior; 1952, American Railway Car Institute.
86. Prewar figures from *Automotive Industries* magazine and the late Col. Leonard Ayres; 1948, from *Iron Age*, May 18, 1948; 1950, estimated from maximum weekly production data in *Automotive News* magazine, June and July 1950.
87. Shipbuilders Council of America. Ways capable of building vessels 200 feet long and over.
88. Aircraft Industries Association.
89. Licensed Beverage Industries, Inc.
90. *Brewer's Journal Directory, 1952; Modern Brewery Age Blue Book, 1952.*
91. U.S. Bureau of the Census; *Northwestern Miller* magazine.
92. *Ice Cream Review* magazine. Note that capacity given is for the 2,020 largest ice cream plants in the nation (wholesale); there are 5,100 (other) small wholesale ice cream plants not reporting capacity. The large plants have the bulk of the total capacity.
93, 94. *The Development of American Industries*, by Glover and Cornell, 1951; *Farr's Manual of Sugar Companies*, annual.
95. U.S. Department of Agriculture reports, based on maximum weekly outputs.
96. *New York Journal of Commerce*, November 20, 1952.
97. *The International Green Book of Cottonseed and Other Vegetable Oil Products*, 1948. Cottonseed oil capacity is given for the 186 largest mills in the U.S.; the remaining 192 small mills do not report capacity.
98. U.S. Wood Pulp Producers Association, Inc.
99, 100. American Paper and Pulp Association.
101. American Paper and Pulp Association; American Newspaper Publishers Association; Newsprint Service Bureau.
102. *Editor and Publisher* magazine, September 1952.
103, 104. U.S. Bureau of the Census. No other tabulations have been made.
105. National Production Authority.
106. National Shoe Manufacturers Association; *Chicago Sun*, October 26, 1948, p. 48.
107. U.S. Bureau of the Census; 1951, estimated from Census trends.
108. U.S. Bureau of the Census.
109. *The Cotton Manufacturing Industry*, Copeland; U.S. Bureau of the Census; *Davison's Textile Blue Book*, copyrighted; used by permission.
110–114. U.S. Bureau of the Census.
115, 116. *Davison's Rayon, Silk & Synthetic Textile Guide*; used by permission.
117. *Rayon Organon*. Note: In the year 1911 the total rayon capacity in the U.S. was 500 tons. (*New York Times*, September 2, 1951, special Chemistry section.)
118. *Rayon Organon*.
118a. *Textile World* magazine; Defense Production Administration.
119. National Association of Hosiery Manufacturers.
120. Clothing Manufacturers Association of the United States of America.
121. Plastic Coatings and Film Association, U.S. Bureau of the Census.

122. Based on estimated number of machines in the industry—6,000—and their known rated capacity, per machine.

123. Commercial Research Department, U.S. Rubber Co. Note that the 1952 tire capacity includes types of casings which were not made in large quantities before 1929, such as farm tractor and implement tires (steel wheels being predominant then), industrial plant truck and tractor tires, construction machinery tires (even wheelbarrows now use them, as well as bulldozers, etc.) and airplane tires.

124. *United Nations Statistical Yearbook.*

125-140. U.S. Bureau of Mines; Petroleum Administration for Defense; American Petroleum Institute; *Oil & Gas Journal; New York Journal of Commerce,* April 22, 1952.

141. Paul Galvin, President of Motorola, Inc.

142. Based on maximum monthly production figures supplied by Statistical Department, Radio-Television Manufacturers Association.

143. Defense Production Administration.

144. Technicolor, Inc.

145, 146. Defense Production Administration.

147. 1951, National Production Authority; 1950, 1946, *Chemical Engineering,* February 1950 and February 1949.

148. Defense Production Administration; *Chemical and Engineering News,* May 17, 1948.

149-165. Defense Production Administration; *Chemical and Engineering News; New York Journal of Commerce,* June 23, 1952.

166, 167, 181. U.S. Bureau of Mines.

168, 169, 200. U.S. Bureau of Mines. Note that 198 and 199 are combined totals for U.S. and Canada (separate figures not available).

201-236. *New York Journal of Commerce,* June 27, 1952; *New York Herald Tribune,* July 13, 1952; *Chemical Engineering,* February 1953; Defense Production Administration; *New York Journal of Commerce,* June 23, 1952; *The Analysts Journal,* June 23, 1952; Dr. Graham Edgar, in *Oil and Gas Journal,* September 21, 1950; *Chemical Industries,* August 1950.

237-243. *Ceramic Trade Directory,* 1947-1948 edition (latest).

244, 245. Defense Production Administration.

246. Data up to and including 1951, from U.S. Bureau of Mines (whose rating of "capacity"—average output per working day in each particular year, multiplied by 280—is compiled annually according to this definition formulated by the coal committee of the American Institute of Mining and Metallurgical Engineers);

1952, based on computation from rated capacity data given in *Keystone Coal Buyer's Manual,* 1952.

247. U.S. Bureau of Mines.

248. Computed from data in *Keystone Coal Buyer's Manual,* 1952.

249. Data from Subcommittee on Long-Term Availability of National Oil Policy Committee, American Petroleum Institute, published in *Petroleum Productive Capacity,* report of National Petroleum Council, 1952; *Oil and Gas Journal.*

250. *Oil and Gas Journal,* September 29, 1952.

251-252. Same as 249.

253. Petroleum Administration for Defense.

254. American Gas Association.

255, 256, 257. Interstate Commerce Commission; Association of American Railroads.

258. U.S. Bureau of Public Roads; American Trucking Association; Automobile Manufacturers Association.

259. U.S. Bureau of Public Roads.

260. *American Aviation Daily;* Dun & Bradstreet, Inc.

261, 262, 263. Water-Borne Commerce Branch, Board of Engineers for Rivers and Harbors, Corps of Engineers, U.S. Army.

262a. Lake Carriers Association.

264. Computed from data in *Keystone Coal Buyer's Manual,* 1952. Figure is for total capacity per 24-hour loading sequence.

265. U.S. Bureau of Mines; Interstate Commerce Commission; American Petroleum Institute.

266. U.S. Bureau of Mines.

267. U.S. Bureau of Mines; American Gas Association.

268, 269, 270. American Telephone & Telegraph Co; Federal Communications Commission; U.S. Independent Telephone Association.

271, 272. Federal Communications Commission. Radio transmitting stations (other) include marine, aeronautical, police and fire departments, forestry, railroad, city transit and bus and taxi, electric utilities, pipelines, disaster and safety, and amateurs (hams).

273. *World Almanac,* 1952, quoting *Radio & Television Retailing* magazine.

274. Federal Communications Commission.

275. Same as 272; also National Broadcasting Company.

276. Western Union Telegraph Company.

277. Federal Power Commission; U.S. Geological Survey.

278. Figures given are for capacities per year of identical company pipeline systems. However, more complete data plus new companies in the natural gas industry provide a greater coverage for January 1, 1952, at which date the grand total natural gas pumping capacity amounted to 9,590 billion cu. ft. per year. These figures correspond roughly to natural gas potential utility capacity per year.

279. American Gas Association. Figures not compiled since 1949.

280-284. Bureau of Agricultural Economics, U.S. Department of Agriculture.

285. Fish and Wildlife Service, U.S. Department of the Interior.

286. Warehouse and Storage Division, Defense Transport Administration.

287. Production and Marketing Administration, U.S. Department of Agriculture.
288. U.S. Department of Agriculture.
289. *Northwestern Miller* magazine.
290. *Industrial Marketing Data Book, 1952–1953.* Floor space in 6,500 principal office buildings in U.S.
291–299. "This Is Construction," brochure published by *Engineering News Record* and *Construction Methods & Equipment*, 1953 (McGraw-Hill).

a. Prepared for this volume by John A. Waring, Jr., research writer on technology and resources.

b. Figure is for 1951.

c. On January 1, 1954, rated capacity 124,330,410 tons annually (*Daily Metal Reporter*, January 5, 1954, from American Iron and Steel Institute).

d. 1938	o. 1943
e. 1946	p. 1914
f. 1939	q. 1936
g. 1919	r. 1945
h. 1948	s. 1921
i. 1941	t. 1928
j. 1953	u. 1944
k. 1942	v. 1933
l. 1949	w. 1915
m. 1947	x. 1922
n. 1929	

Note: These figures represent installed capacity as rated by the appropriate authority for industry statistics, whether industrial trade association, government bureau, or trade or technical publication. No output or production figures are given here, excepting in a very few (5) industries (see below).

All figures are in terms of capacity per year, unless otherwise indicated. For uniformity, this applies even to such industries where capacity (and output) are ordinarily given daily, such as petroleum products.

(d.c.) alongside an industry title indicates "demonstrated capability" used for a few industries which are included because of their importance despite the lack of any actual capacity statistics or even estimates of capacity. In these cases, the maximum monthly production attained in recent years is given. Applies only to Machine tools, Ball and roller bearings, Automotive vehicles (1950 figure), Meat packing and Television receiving set manufacturing (line 142).

(E) alongside industry title indicates the use of an indirect measure of capacity; i.e., the number of machines or installed equipment in use in all known plants of the particular industry. In all other instances some direct measure of capacity to produce was available.

APPENDIX 25-1. COST OF TYPICAL FACTORY WORKER'S BUDGET, 1914 AND 1948

Budget Group [b]	Cost of Typical 1914 Factory Worker's Budget in 1914 and 1948 [a]				Cost of Typical 1948 Factory Worker's Budget in 1914 and 1948 [a]			
	Dollars per Week		Equivalent Work Hours per Week		Dollars per Week		Equivalent Work Hours per Week	
	1914	1948	1914	1948	1914	1948	1914	1948
Food	$ 7.26	$20.34	29.4	13.8	$ 6.97	$18.28	28.2	12.4
Clothing	2.30	6.15	9.3	4.2	2.88	6.90	11.6	4.7
Rent	2.02	2.57	8.2	1.7	4.91	6.25	19.9	4.2
Household operation	1.83	4.00	7.3	2.7	4.09	6.68	16.6	4.6
Medical and personal care	1.09	2.71	4.4	1.8	1.02	2.36	4.2	1.6
Amusement	1.11	2.47	4.5	1.7	.94	2.04	3.8	1.4
Transportation	.41	.77	1.6	.5	2.08	3.31	8.4	2.2
Income taxes	—	1.79	—	1.2	—	1.79	—	1.2
Miscellaneous	—	—	—	—	.92	1.90	3.7	1.3
Total expenditures	16.02	40.80	64.7	27.6	23.81	49.51	96.4	33.6
Total average earnings [c]	12.72	58.52 [d]	51.5	39.7	12.72 [e]	58.52	51.5	39.7

Source: Laurence D. De Trude and Wistaria Nishimura, *What an Hour's Work Would Buy, 1914–1948,* Studies in Labor Statistics, No. 3, National Industrial Conference Board, New York, 1950, p. 5. In the source, consumption in 1914 was estimated from 1901 expenditures study by the Commissioner of Labor, and 1918–1919 expenditures study by the Bureau of Labor Statistics, U.S. Department of Labor. Consumption in 1948 was estimated from 1934–1936 expenditures study by the Bureau of Labor Statistics. The dollar figures were derived by dividing the annual figures in the source by 52.

a. Assuming that the manufacturing wage earner in 1914 and 1948 could each purchase the budget items available to the other.

b. Two of the budget groups shown here were derived by combining groups in the source, as follows: Household operation is the sum of House furnishings, Household operation and Fuel and light; Medical and personal care is the sum of Personal care and Medical care and drugs.

Food includes meat, dairy products, hens and eggs, flour, corn meal, rice, bread, potatoes, sugar, coffee and lard.

Clothing includes suits, skirts, blouses, dresses, underwear, nightgowns, stockings, shoes, coats and hats for women; suits, overcoats, sweaters, overalls, shirts, underwear, shoes, socks, pajamas, caps and gloves for men.

Household operation includes floor covering, living, dining and bedroom furniture, household linens, stove, dishes, vacuum cleaner, refrigerator, washing machine, sewing machine, soap, starch, matches, postage, cleaning powder, coal, fuel oil, kerosene, gas and electricity.

Medical and personal care includes doctor and dental care, medicines, haircuts, soap, toothpaste, shaving cream, cleansing cream, face powder and razor blades.

Amusement includes motion pictures, magazines and newspapers.

Transportation includes gasoline, tires, trolley fares and automobiles.

Income taxes calculated for 1948 for 3.61 persons, using standard deductions.

c. Based on average weekly earnings in twenty-five manufacturing industries for July of each year; compiled by the National Industrial Conference Board.

d. Average earnings of worker in 1948.

e. Average earnings of worker in 1914.

APPENDIX 25–2. PER CAPITA INCOME AND CONSUMPTION OF ENERGY FROM MINERAL FUELS AND WATER POWER AND FROM ALL SOURCES, SELECTED COUNTRIES, 1949 AND 1950

Country	Per Capita Income, 1949	Per Capita Consumption of Mineral Fuels and Water Power		Per Capita Consumption of Energy from All Sources
		1949	1950	1949
	(U.S. Dollars)	(Coal Equivalent in Pounds)		
Argentina	$ 346	1,560	1,695	2,110
Australia	679	6,405	7,000	7,330
Austria	216	3,235	3,390	3,670 [a]
Belgium	582	7,590	7,700	[a]
Bolivia	55	155	175	
Brazil	112	440	485	1,540
Burma	36	45	45	570
Canada	870	13,840	13,865	15,600
Ceylon	67	175	175	700
Chile	188	1,740	1,670	2,160
Colombia	132	660	680	1,120
Costa Rica	125	485	530	[a]
Cuba	296	1,055	1,210	[a]
Czechoslovakia	371	6,160	6,515	[a]
Denmark	689	3,740	4,600	4,290
Ecuador	40	330	440	730
Egypt	100	310	330	700
Finland	348	2,135	2,575	5,170
France	482	4,885	4,755	4,970 [a]
Germany (Western zone)	320	5,325	5,785	
Greece	128	460	485	880
Guatemala	77	310	350 [a]	880
Haiti	40	45		550
Honduras	83	330	330	[a]
Hungary	269	2,070	2,155 [a]	[a]
Iceland	476	6,580		[a]
India	57	220	240	770 [a]
Indonesia	25	90	130	
Iraq	85	350	420	810
Ireland	420	2,110	2,330	3,670
Israel	389	1,385	1,760	[a]
Italy	235	1,275	1,385	[a]
Japan	100	1,670	1,670	1,960 [a]
Mexico	121	1,340	1,340	
Netherlands	502	4,025	4,315	4,160 [a]
New Zealand	856	5,195	5,195 [a]	[a]
Nicaragua	89	155		[a]
Norway	587	8,650	9,460	[a]
Pakistan	51	90	65	[a]
Panama	183	680	660	[a]
Peru	100	460	440	1,030
Poland	300	4,270	4,600	4,400
Portugal	250	550	570	1,080
Southern Rhodesia	101	1,410	1,540	[a]
Sweden	780	6,205	7,175	[a]
Switzerland	849	4,160	4,685	[a]
Thailand	36	20	45	640
Turkey	125	595	570	1,120
Union of South Africa	264	4,115	4,115	4,220
United Kingdom	773	9,460	9,680	9,500

APPENDIX 25-2 (continued)

Country	Per Capita Income, 1949	Per Capita Consumption of Mineral Fuels and Water Power		Per Capita Consumption of Energy from All Sources
		1949	1950	1949
	(U.S. Dollars)	(Coal Equivalent in Pounds)		
United States	1,453[b]	15,975	17,515	16,100
Uruguay	331	1,300	1,365	1,690
Yugoslavia	146	790	880	1,230

Sources: 1949 per capita income, *National and Per Capita Incomes of Seventy Countries in 1949 Expressed in United States Dollars,* Statistical Papers, Series E, No. 1, Statistical Office of the United Nations, New York, 1950, Table 1, p. 14; per capita consumption of mineral fuels and energy from all sources, W. S. and E. S. Woytinsky, *World Population and Production,* Twentieth Century Fund, New York, 1953, Tables 399 and 400, pp. 941–942.

a. Not available.

b. This figure differs slightly from the per capita estimate implied by Table 14, which includes a later, revised national income estimate.

APPENDIX 25-3. EXPLANATORY NOTES TO TABLES A–L, ESTIMATES OF TOTAL ENERGY SUPPLY, ENERGY USED FOR WORK PERFORMANCE, EFFICIENCY OF CONVERSION, AND WORK OUTPUT IN THE UNITED STATES, 1850–1950

Energy Sources

The energy supply of the United States during the past century has been obtained almost exclusively from the following six sources, which have varied widely in their relative importance and in the uses to which they have been put:

(1) Human workers, supplying motive power used exclusively for work performance.
(2) Work animals (horses, mules and oxen), supplying motive power used exclusively for work performance, chiefly in agriculture and transportation.
(3) Wind power, used exclusively to supply motive power for work performance in the operation of windmills and sailing vessels.
(4) Water power, formerly harnessed directly for work performance in the operation of mill and factory machinery but now used almost exclusively to generate electricity, which in turn provides heat and light as well as motive power for work performance.
(5) Mineral fuels (anthracite, bituminous coal, petroleum and natural gas), used directly to provide heat and light and for various chemical-industrial purposes, as well as to generate power used for work performance.
(6) Fuel wood, used predominantly for space heating, also to supply charcoal for chemical-industrial uses and to generate power used for work performance.

There are, of course, many minor and insignificant sources of energy. Whale oil and other animal and vegetable oils have been used in lamps and candles to provide light. Waste substances of various kinds are burned to provide heat. The force of gravity is still used to slide logs downhill and to float log rafts to sawmills. A charge of dynamite is an effective motive force in quarrying and construction operations. A wide variety of chemicals, not ordinarily thought of as energy materials, can be used to provide heat and other forms of chemical energy; use of calcium carbide and water to generate acetylene gas is only one example.

The above classification also leaves out of account, at one extreme, the primary and basic and most abundant source of all energy, the heat of the sun, without which all other sources would be non-existent and life itself would be impossible. Not only is solar energy indirectly responsible for the existence of wind power and water power, but it is also the basic energy source in agricultural production and hence, through food and feed, of human and animal energy. At the other extreme the list omits atomic energy, which, however great its future promise may be, probably will not contribute appreciably to our supply of energy for productive purposes for several years to come.

Common Denominators for Measuring Energy

All forms of energy can be measured in terms of the common denominator of a standard unit of work, such as the horsepower-hour (the work involved in raising 550 pounds one foot a second for an hour against the force of gravity), or the kilowatt-hour (equivalent to 1.34 horsepower-hours), commonly used to measure electrical energy. Whatever its origin, energy can also be measured and compared in terms of a standard unit of heat, such as the British Thermal Unit (BTU), the amount of heat required to raise the temperature of one pound of water one degree Fahrenheit. Or energy from various sources can be compared in terms of pounds or tons of "coal equivalent," i.e., a standard bituminous coal with a heat value of 13,100 BTU's per pound. One horsepower-hour is theoretically equivalent to 2,544.5 BTU's, or to a little less than one fifth (19.4 per cent) of a pound of such coal. Thus, one ton of coal with a heat value of 26,200,000 BTU's is the theoretical equivalent of 10,297 horsepower-hours.

As a practical matter, however, the actual conversion of heat energy into work, as in the combustion of mineral fuels used to generate power, or the conversion of mechanical energy into heat, rarely even approaches the theoretical equivalence of the two units.

Since all of the most important sources of energy in the United States have always been used to provide heat and light as well as motive power for physical work, it is appropriate to show the supply of energy from each of the six principal sources in terms of a standard unit of heat, such as a ton of "coal equivalent." By using this common denominator it is possible to "add up" the energy obtained from such diverse sources as work animals, wind, coal and oil and thus to estimate the total supply of energy.

Energy Used for Work Performance

However, these estimates of our total energy supply and of the amounts of energy obtained from various sources are of limited value in measuring the productive power of the American economy. While there is an equivalence in physical terms between human effort exerted chopping wood, animal energy expended hauling a wagon, fuel wood burning in an open fireplace, wind power turning a windmill to pump water or propelling a sailing vessel, coke produced from bituminous coal used in a blast furnace to smelt iron, kerosene from petroleum providing light in an oil lamp, natural gas burned to provide carbon black for use as a coloring material, and gasoline exploding in an internal combustion engine to drive a truck, these varied forms in which energy appears and is used differ widely in their economic significance.

Of special significance for the economy are the amounts and kinds of energy devoted to the *performance of work* and the amounts of work performed. In this sense, "work" includes a multitude of operations in farming, construction, mining, manufacturing, transportation and household operation, such as digging, plowing, hauling, lifting, cutting, drilling, hammering, crushing, pumping and blowing. It includes only those operations which have been or could be done (however inadequately) by the muscle power of animals and men. Human energy can be used to row a boat, to lift a weight, to hammer metal, to saw a log or to beat a rug, but not to smelt metal or directly to produce heat, light or refrigeration.

Some of the six energy sources listed above, such as human workers, work animals, water wheels (or direct water power) and wind power in propelling sailing vessels, have always been used exclusively to supply motive force, i.e., in the performance of work. With minor exceptions this has also been true of windmills, which are used almost entirely for pumping water. Fuel wood and anthracite, on the other hand, are used predominantly for space heating, and only to a limited extent to generate power for work performance. The most important energy materials — bituminous coal, petroleum, natural gas and "hydroelectricity" — have always been used for heating, lighting and other end purposes, of which the performance of "mechanical" work is only one, though usually an important one. No accurate measures of the proportion of the total supply of energy from different sources used for work performance are available, and only very rough estimates can be made.

Efficiency of Energy Conversion

Another important factor affecting the significance of the total energy supply or of the energy input used for work performance is the efficiency of energy conversion, or the percentage of energy which is not lost in the various operations occurring before the final energy is delivered as work done at the point of use. Muscle power and wind power used in propelling sailing vessels are measured at the point of use and are therefore assumed to have 100 per cent conversion efficiency. Hydroelectric generation is also carried on at a high efficiency — more than 80 per cent of the energy of the falling water is delivered as work output.

For all of the fuels, however, only a small fraction of the energy input is delivered as work output at the point of use. Thus while the "heat content" of a pound of coal, or the energy it contains, is 13,100 BTU's and the theoretical heat equivalent of one horsepower-hour is only 2,544.5 BTU's, one pound of coal may have to be burned in a steam power plant to deliver one horsepower-hour of actual work performance. The efficiency of the energy conversion process is less than 20 per cent, inasmuch as more than 80 per cent of the energy content of the coal is lost.

The efficiency of fuel conversion is greater today than it was a decade ago and much greater than it was fifty or a hundred years ago. This is true not only of coal but of all the fuels. There have also been gains, though more modest ones, in the efficiency of energy conversion of water wheels and windmills.

Work Output

From these estimates of the efficiency of conversion of individual sources of energy used for work performance it is possible to derive estimates of the work output obtained from each. Expressed in terms of a common denominator such as the horsepower-hour, these can be summed to arrive at a measure of total work output, in the same way as total energy input can be measured in tons of coal equivalent.

The basis for estimates of energy input, energy used for work performance, efficiency of energy conversion, and work output for each energy source is shown below.

ANIMATE ENERGY: HUMAN WORKERS

Estimated Total Energy Supply

Table J, Line 3. Estimates of total human labor energy input were obtained by converting total man-hours worked (Table 14, page 40) to coal equivalent on the basis of 205,940 man-hours per ton of coal equivalent (since one man-hour is equal to .05 horsepower-hours and one ton of coal equivalent equals 10,297 horsepower-hours, assuming 26,200,000 BTU's per ton of standard bituminous coal and 2,544.5 BTU's per horsepower-hour).

Energy Input for Work Performance

Table K, Line 3. All human labor energy input is obviously used for work performance, since none of it can be used to provide heat and light or for chemical-industrial purposes; hence Table K, Line 3, is identical with Table J, Line 3.

Efficiency of Conversion

Since the energy input of human workers is measured at the point of use, the efficiency of energy conversion is 100 per cent.

Work Output

Table L, Line 3. Under these assumptions, work output is identical with energy input. It is shown in horsepower-hours in Table L, Line 3.

ANIMATE ENERGY: WORK ANIMALS

Energy Supply

Table A, Col. 1. The total number of horses and mules on farms was, in millions, 4.90 in 1850, 7.40 in 1860, 8.27 in 1870, 12.17 in 1880, 17.52 in 1890, and 21.53 in 1900; and the total number of working oxen on farms was, in millions, 1.70 in 1850, 2.26 in 1860, 1.32 in 1870, 0.99 in 1880, 1.12 in 1890, 0.55 in 1900, and negligible thereafter (according to a letter dated January 9, 1947 from C. L. Harlan, Division of Livestock and Poultry Statistics, Bureau of Agricultural Economics, U.S. Department of Agriculture, to J. Frederic Dewhurst).

Comparison of the number of horses and mules 3 years old and over (i.e., work stock) on farms since 1910 (from dittoed table transmitted by E .M. Dieffenbach, Division of Farm Machinery, U.S. Department of Agriculture, to J. Frederic Dewhurst, December 31, 1951) with the total number of horses and mules indicates that work stock constituted 74 per cent of all horses and mules in 1910, 79 per cent in 1920, 84 per cent in 1930, 84 per cent in 1940, and 92 per cent in 1950. In view of this upward trend in the average age of farm work animals, it was assumed that in 1850–1900, 70 per cent of all horses and mules were work stock.

The total number of work animals on farms in 1850–1900 was obtained by adding the number of working horses and mules thus estimated to the number of working oxen given above; the number of horses and mules 3 years old and over was used for the 1910–1950 totals.

Table A, Col. 2. Bulletin No. 1348, U.S. Department of Agriculture, July 1925, and advice of farm management experts indicate that farm work animals average about 500 hours of work a year. Energy input in horsepower-hours was therefore obtained by multiplying the figures in Col. 1 by 500.

Table A, Col. 3. The total number of nonfarm horses and mules, all of them assumed to be work animals, was, in millions, 1.19 in 1860, 1.55 in 1870, 3.11 in 1900, 3.45 in 1910, 2.13 in 1920, and 0.38 in 1925 (according to the letter from C. L. Harlan cited above). Assuming that the 1850–1860 increase was equal to the 1860–1870 increase and that there was a straight-line increase from 1870 to 1900, the number was estimated at 0.83 million in 1850, 2.07 million in 1880, and 2.59 million in 1890. Assuming a further sharp decline after 1925 and virtual disappearance by 1960, the number was estimated at 0.33 million in 1930, 0.30 million in 1940, and 0.20 million in 1950.

Table A, Col. 4. It was assumed that nonfarm work animals average the same number of work hours annually as nonfarm human workers. Therefore, to obtain the annual energy input of nonfarm work animals in horsepower-hours, average weekly hours worked by persons employed in nonagricultural pursuits (as shown in Appendix 20–4) were multiplied by 52 and then by the figures in Col. 3.

Table J, Line 4. The energy input of work animals in tons of coal equivalent was obtained by dividing the sum of Col. 2 plus Col. 4 (same as Table L, Line 4) by 10,297 (since one ton of coal is the energy equivalent of 10,297 horsepower-hours).

Energy Used for Work Performance

Table K, Line 4. This is identical with Table J, Line 4, since all work-animal energy input is used for work performance.

Efficiency of Conversion

Since the energy input of work animals is measured at the point of use, the efficiency of energy conversion is 100 per cent.

Work Output

Table L, Line 4. Under these assumptions, work output is identical with energy input. It is shown in horsepower-hours in Table L, Line 4.

INANIMATE ENERGY

WIND: WINDMILLS

Energy Supply

Table B, Col. 1. Estimates of the total number of windmills in the United States from 1880 to 1940 are from a letter from R. B. Gray, Division of Farm Machinery, U.S. Department of Agriculture, to J. Frederic Dewhurst, December 2, 1947. Estimates for earlier years are based on these trends and on the judgment of experts that the most rapid growth followed the settlement of the West after 1870.

No estimates of the number of windmills are available after 1940, but *Facts for Industry: Farm Pumps, Summary for 1950,* U.S. Bureau of the Census, Series M31B-00, April 11, 1951, Table 2, reports shipments of windmill heads, which paralleled the trend in the number of mills for 1930–1940. On this basis, the number of windmills in 1945 and 1950 was assumed to bear the same percentage relation to the number in 1940 as shipments of heads in 1945 and 1950 bear to shipments in 1940.

Table B, Col. 2. Windmill experts advise that the most common type of mill, rated at 0.33 horsepower, has an effective rating under typical operating conditions of 0.2 horsepower and operates an average of about 7 hours a day during the year, thus providing an energy input of about 500 horsepower-hours a year. Total wind energy input was therefore obtained by multiplying the number of windmills by 500.

Table J, Line 7. The energy input of windmills in tons of coal equivalent was obtained by dividing figures in Table B, Col. 2, by 10,297 (horsepower-hour equivalent of one ton of coal).

Energy Used for Work Performance

Table K, Line 7. Since windmills are used almost entirely for pumping water, 100 per cent of wind energy input is assumed to be used for work performance. The figures shown are therefore identical with those in Table J, Line 7.

Efficiency of Energy Conversion

Table B, Col. 3. Average efficiency was estimated on the basis of various tests showing that the work output of today's mills is about 36 per cent of the energy input and on the judgment of windmill experts that efficiency approximately doubled between 1850 and the first decade of the present century and has remained constant since 1910.

Work Output

Table L, Line 7. Work output of windmills in horsepower-hours was obtained by multiplying figures in Table B, Col. 2, by figures in Col. 3.

WIND: SAILING VESSELS

Energy Supply

Table B, Col. 4. Gross tonnage of sailing vessels operating under the American flag is from *Statistical Abstract of the United States, 1951,* U.S. Bureau of the Census, Table 629, p. 532.

Table B, Col. 5. Examination of records and judgment of shipping experts indicate that sailing vessels operated about 40 per cent of the time, or roughly 3,500 hours a year, and that their average speed while in operation was 6 miles an hour. Total ton-miles were estimated by multiplying the estimated gross tonnage by the indicated average mileage of 21,000.

Experience on English canals with horse-drawn barges indicates that one horsepower is required to pull a 60-ton barge at the standard rate of 3 miles an hour (according to article on "Canals and Canalized Rivers" in the Fourteenth Edition of *Encyclopaedia Britannica*); i.e., one horsepower-hour is the equivalent of 180 ton-miles. Since the power required increases approximately as the square of the speed, the estimated speed of 6 miles an hour for sailing vessels would require one horsepower-hour of work for 45 ton-miles (i.e., one fourth of 180 ton-miles, as work required per ton-mile would increase in ratio of the square of 3 to the square of 6, or 9 to 36). Figures in Table B, Col. 5, were therefore divided by 45 to obtain estimates of energy input in horsepower-

hours, which are identical with work output shown in Table L, Line 8.

Table J, Line 8. Wind energy input in tons of coal equivalent was obtained by dividing figures in Table L, Line 8, by 10,297 (horsepower-hour equivalent of one ton of coal).

Energy Used for Work Performance

Table K, Line 8. All wind energy used to propel sailing vessels is obviously used for work performance, since none of it is used to provide heat or light or for other purposes; hence energy used for work performance is identical with total energy input shown in Table J, Line 8.

Efficiency of Conversion

Since the input of wind energy used to propel sailing vessels is measured at the point of use, the efficiency of energy conversion is 100 per cent.

Work Output

Table L, Line 8. Under these assumptions, work output is identical with energy input. It is shown in horsepower-hours in Table L, Line 8.

WATER: WATER WHEELS — DIRECT DRIVE

Energy Supply

Table C, Col. 1. Figures for 1850 and for each ten-year interval to 1890 are based on kilowatt-hour production figures, supplied by L. D. Jennings of the Federal Power Commission for 1849 and for each ten-year interval through 1899, on the assumption of a straight-line increase or decrease for each decade. Production figures for 1900–1950 are from a special tabulation supplied by Mr. Jennings.

Table C, Col. 2. Figures on production shown in Table C, Col. 1, converted to horsepower-hours (on the basis of one kwh. equal to 1.34 horsepower-hours).

Table C, Col. 3. The estimated loss of energy from the fall of water on the wheel to the water-wheel shaft, according to power experts, is about 10 per cent today, compared with about 20 per cent in 1900. To obtain estimates of conversion efficiency for earlier years the 80 per cent efficiency figure for 1900 was "projected backwards" (on the basis of interpolation of trends shown in Figure 18, Statistical Supplement to *Electric Light and Power Industry in the U.S.,* revised to January 1, 1931, National Electric Light Association, N. Y.).

Table C, Col. 4. Total energy input (in terms of fall of water on wheel) in horsepower-hours was obtained by dividing production data (Table C, Col. 2) by efficiency rates (Table C, Col. 3).

Table J, Line 10. Figures in Table C, Col. 4, converted to energy input in tons of coal equivalent (on the basis of 10,297 horsepower-hours equal to one ton of coal equivalent).

Energy Used for Work Performance

Table K, Line 10. All direct-drive water-wheel energy input is used for work performance. Therefore energy used for work performance is identical with total energy input shown in Table J, Line 10.

Table C, Col. 5. The efficiency of energy transmission and delivery from the water-wheel shaft to the work bench or point of use, on the basis of consultation with power experts, is estimated to have risen from about 65 per cent in 1850, by 3 percentage points per decade, to 80 per cent in 1900, to 84 per cent in 1940 and 1945, to 85 per cent by 1950.

Table C, Col. 6. Over-all efficiency of energy conversion was obtained by multiplying figures in Table C, Col. 3, by figures in Col. 5.

Work Output

Table L, Line 10. Percentages of conversion efficiency given in Table C, Col. 6, multiplied by energy input (Table C, Col. 4).

WATER: HYDROELECTRIC

Energy Supply

Table D, Col. 1. No appreciable amount of hydroelectric energy was produced prior to 1890. A special tabulation furnished by L. D. Jennings shows production of 250,000 kwh. for 1889. It was assumed that the same amount was produced in 1890. Production figures for 1900–1950 were supplied by Jennings.

Table D, Col. 2. Figures shown in Table D, Col. 1, converted to horsepower-hours (on the basis of one kwh. equal to 1.34 horsepower-hours).

Table D, Col. 3. Estimated conversion efficiency of energy from fall of water on turbine to turbine shaft (on the basis of interpolation of trends shown in Figure 18, Statistical Supplement to *Electric Light and Power Industry in the U.S.*, revised to January 1, 1931, National Light Association, N. Y.).

Table D, Col. 4. Total energy input (in terms of fall of water on wheel) in horsepower-hours was obtained by dividing production data (Table D, Col. 2) by efficiency rates (Table D, Col. 3).

Table J, Line 11. Figures in Table D, Col. 4, converted to energy input in tons of coal equivalent (on the basis of 10,297 horsepower-hours equal to one ton of coal equivalent).

Energy Used for Work Performance

Table D, Col. 7. On the basis of early Census records and consultation with power experts it was roughly estimated that the proportion of energy used for work performance declined from about 70 per cent in 1890 and 1900 to about 42 per cent in recent years. These percentages are based on ultimate, rather than intermediate, use of electricity; in other words, all electricity used to provide industrial or space heat, for refrigeration, cooking, lighting or chemical use is excluded.

Table K, Line 11. Percentages shown in Table D, Col. 7, multiplied by energy input (Table J, Line 11).

Efficiency of Energy Conversion

Table D, Col. 5. The efficiency of energy transmission and delivery from turbine shaft to work bench or point of use, on the basis of consultation with experts, was estimated to have risen from 77 per cent in 1890 to 80 per cent in 1900 (as in the case of direct-drive water wheels), to 84 per cent in 1910 and by 2 percentage points per decade to 90 per cent in 1940 and thereafter.

Table D, Col. 8. Over-all efficiency of energy conversion (Table D, Col. 3, multiplied by Col. 5).

Work Output

Table D, Col. 6. Energy input (Table D, Col. 4) multiplied by the percentages of over-all conversion efficiency (Table D, Col. 8).

Table L, Line 11. Total energy output (Table D, Col. 6) multiplied by the percentages of output used for work (Table D, Col. 7).

MINERAL FUELS: BITUMINOUS COAL

Energy Supply

Table J, Line 14. For bituminous coal, consumption (energy input) in thousands of tons is identical with coal equivalent.

Consumption figures for 1920–1950 are from *1951 Bituminous Coal Annual*, Bituminous Coal Institute, Washington, 1951, Table 40, p. 98. Figures for 1850–1910 are apparent consumption (production plus imports minus exports).

H. N. Eavenson (*The First Century and a Quarter of the American Coal Industry*, Pittsburgh, 1942, Table 20) gives the following production figures: 1850, 4,028,770 tons; 1860, 9,056,887 tons; 1870, 20,471,006 tons; 1880, 50,757,119 tons. Production in 1890 was 111,302,322 tons; 1900, 212,316,112 tons; and 1910, 417,111,142 tons (*Historical Statistics of the United States, 1789–1945*, U.S. Bureau of the Census, 1949, Series G 13, G 16, p. 142).

Eavenson (*op. cit.*, Table 21, pp. 436–438) gives imports for bituminous coal and anthracite combined for 1850 and 1860, but since other sources (see Anthracite, below) indicate there were no imports of anthracite in 1870, it was assumed that the 202,092 tons imported in 1850 and the 269,581 tons in 1860 were all bituminous coal. Imports for 1870–1900 were as follows: 1870, 465,616 tons; 1880, 528,436 tons; 1890, 918,368 tons; 1900, 2,138,369 tons (*Mineral Resources of the United States, 1901*, U. S. Geological Survey, 1902, p. 310. Gross tons [2,240 lbs.] given in the source have been converted to net tons [2,000 lbs.]). Imports in 1910 were 1,819,760 tons (unpublished figure from the U.S. Bureau of Mines).

Eavenson (*op. cit.*, Table 21, pp. 436–438) gives

combined exports for bituminous coal and anthracite for 1850 and 1860. On the basis of trends in later years it was assumed that bituminous coal constituted 18 per cent of the total, or 8,000 tons, in 1850 and 32 per cent, or 67,000 tons, in 1860. The U.S. Geological Survey (*op. cit.,* p. 309) gives exports for 1870–1900 as follows: 1870, 119,638 tons; 1880, 249,350 tons; 1890, 1,434,642 tons; 1900, 7,014,458 tons. (Gross tons have been converted to net tons.) Exports in 1910 were 11,663,052 tons (unpublished figure of the U.S. Bureau of Mines).

Energy Used for Work Performance

Table E, Col. 1. Bituminous coal was originally used predominantly to generate power for work performance, when wood provided the bulk of fuel for space heating. Judgment of experts and consultation of literature indicate a steady shrinkage in the proportion used for work performance, as shown in the estimated percentages given.

Table K, Line 14. Total energy input (Table J, Line 14) multiplied by percentages used for work performance (Table E, Col. 1).

Efficiency of Conversion

Table E, Col. 6. U.S. Geological Survey records indicate that the average consumption of coal by electric central stations in 1900 was 6.85 pounds per kwh. delivered at the turbine, or 5.11 pounds per horsepower-hour. Data for subsequent years show declines to 3.56 pounds per horsepower-hour in 1910, 2.28 pounds in 1920, 1.19 pounds in 1930, 1.00 pounds in 1940, 0.97 pounds in 1945, and 0.89 pounds in 1950. These consumption figures "projected backwards" from 1900 (on the basis of interpolation of trends shown in Figure 17, Statistical Supplement to "Electric Light and Power Industry in the U.S.," revised to January 1, 1931, National Electric Light Association, N. Y.) give the following results: 11.43 pounds per horsepower-hour in 1850, 9.82 pounds in 1860, 7.67 pounds in 1880, and 6.29 pounds in 1890.

These data refer to the efficiency of energy delivery at the shaft of the steam turbine and do not take account of further losses in transmission and delivery of energy at the point of use. Consultation with power experts led to the conclusion that the efficiency of transmission from steam engine to work place was about 65 per cent in 1850, rose by 3 percentage points per decade to 80 per cent in 1900, advanced to 84 per cent in 1940 and in 1945, and to 85 per cent by 1950. When these percentages are applied to the data above it appears that 17.58 pounds of coal were required to deliver one horsepower-hour to the point of use in 1850. On the basis of a heat content of 13,100 BTU's per pound of coal and 2,544.5 BTU's per horsepower-hour, this represents an over-all efficiency of 1.1 per cent. The same method yielded data shown in Table E, Col. 6.

Work Output

Table E, Col. 2. Energy input for work expressed in coal equivalent (Table K, Line 14) multiplied by 10,297 (the horsepower-hour value of one ton of coal equivalent).

Table L, Line 14. Table E, Col. 2, multiplied by the percentages of efficiency of conversion shown in Table E, Col. 6.

MINERAL FUELS: ANTHRACITE

Energy Supply

Table E, Col. 3. Consumption figures (energy input) by ten-year intervals from 1850 to 1950 are based on the following sources: 1890–1945 — *1949 Minerals Yearbook,* U.S. Bureau of Mines, 1951, p. 364; 1950 — *Statistical Abstract of the United States, 1952,* p. 698. Figures for 1850–1880 are apparent consumption (production plus imports minus exports).

Production for these years was: 1850, 8,355,739 tons; 1860, 20,040,859 tons; 1870, 40,429,070 tons; 1880, 79,406,931 tons (according to H. N. Eavenson, *The First Century and a Quarter of the American Coal Industry,* Pittsburgh, 1942, Table 20).

Mineral Resources of the United States, 1901 (U.S. Geological Survey, 1902, p. 310) gives imports for 1870 as none and for 1880 as 9 tons (gross tons have been converted to net tons). It is therefore assumed that no anthracite was imported in 1850 and 1860.

Eavenson (*op. cit.,* Table 21, pp. 436–438) gives exports for these years for bituminous coal and anthracite combined. On the basis of trends in later years, it was assumed that anthracite constituted 72 per cent of the exports in 1850, or 35,390 tons, and 68 per cent, or 142,506 tons, in 1860. *Mineral Resources of the United States, 1901* (p. 309) shows exports of 135,630 tons for 1870 and 439,741 tons for 1880. (Gross tons have been converted to net tons.)

Table J, Line 15. Energy input (anthracite tons consumed, converted to coal equivalent on the basis of 25.4 million BTU's per ton of anthracite and 26.2 million BTU's per ton of coal equivalent).

Energy Used for Work Performance

Table E, Col. 4. Like bituminous coal, anthracite was originally used primarily to generate power for work performance. Judgment of experts indicates a steady shrinkage in the proportion used for work, from 70 per cent in 1850 to 25 per cent in 1900 and 10 per cent in 1950. Estimates of the percentages used for work in the intervening years were based on a straight-line interpolation of these figures.

Table K, Line 15. Total energy input (Table J, Line 15) multiplied by percentages used for work (Table E, Col. 4).

Efficiency of Conversion

Table E, Col. 6. The conversion efficiency of anthracite is assumed to be the same as that of bituminous coal, since anthracite, like bituminous coal, is used for steam generation.

Work Output

Table E, Col. 5. Energy input for work expressed in coal equivalent (Table K, Line 15) multiplied by 10,297 (the horsepower-hour value of one ton of coal equivalent).

Table L, Line 15. Table E, Col. 5, multiplied by the percentages of conversion efficiency shown in Table E, Col. 6.

MINERAL FUELS: PETROLEUM

Energy Supply

Table F, Col. 4. An insignificant amount of petroleum was used prior to 1870. Apparent net consumption (energy input) for 1870–1950 is based on production, import and export figures shown in Table F, Cols. 1, 2 and 3.

Table F, Col. 1. The estimate for 1870 is derived from the figure for 1869 in *Historical Statistics of the United States, 1789–1945,* Series G 168, p. 155; data for 1880–1900 are from *ibid.,* Series G 57, p. 146; for 1910–1950, from *Statistical Abstract of the United States, 1952,* Table 857, p. 704.

Table F, Col. 2. No data are available on imports prior to 1910. Data for 1910–1950 are from *Statistical Abstract of the United States, 1952,* Table 857, p. 704.

Table F, Col. 3. No data are available on exports prior to 1871. The figure for 1880 is the average of the ten-year period 1871–1880; that for 1890, the average of the period 1881–1890; and that for 1900, the average of the period 1896–1905, as given in *Statistical Abstract of the United States, 1948,* Table 862, p. 771; data for 1910–1950 are from the same source as figures in Col. 2.

Table J, Line 16. Apparent net consumption in barrels (Table F, Col. 4) converted to coal equivalent on the basis of 5.8 million BTU's per barrel of petroleum and 26.2 million BTU's per ton of coal equivalent.

Energy Used for Work Performance

Table F, Col. 5. Prior to 1900, petroleum was used exclusively for lighting. Since 1900, when an estimated 15 per cent was used for work performance, the rapid expansion of automotive transport, the development of the diesel engine and the growing use of fuel oil in power generation have had the effect of raising the percentage of petroleum used for work output rapidly to 51 per cent in 1930 and more slowly to 58 per cent in 1950.

Table K, Line 16. Total energy input (Table J, Line 16) multiplied by percentages in Table F, Col. 5.

Efficiency of Conversion

Table F, Col. 7. Consultation with power experts leads to the conclusion that the efficiency of energy conversion for petroleum in 1900 was about the same as for other fuels — 3 per cent. With the improvement of gasoline and diesel engines and the increased efficiency of fuel oil combustion in steam generation, the average efficiency of conversion has increased steadily. The 1950 estimated efficiency of 9 per cent, however, is only half the estimate for fuels used in steam generation, because a large proportion of petroleum is used inefficiently in the operation of private automobiles.

Work Output

Table F, Col. 6. Energy input for work expressed in coal equivalent (Table K, Line 16) multiplied by 10,297 (the horsepower-hour value of one ton of coal equivalent).

Table L, Line 16. Table F, Col. 6, multiplied by the percentages of conversion efficiency shown in Table F, Col. 7.

MINERAL FUELS: NATURAL GAS

Energy Supply

Table G, Col. 1. Estimates of production in cubic feet for 1880–1900 were supplied by L. D. Jennings, Federal Power Commission, in a memorandum of June 8, 1953; production figures for 1900–1920 are from *Historical Statistics of the United States, 1789–1945,* Series G 59; for 1930–1950, from *Statistical Abstract of the United States, 1952,* Table 854.

Table J, Line 17. Production in cubic feet (Table G, Col. 1) converted to tons of coal equivalent (on the basis of 1,075 BTU's per cubic foot of natural gas and 26,200,000 BTU's per ton of coal equivalent).

Energy Used for Work Performance

Table G, Col. 2. Natural gas was used almost exclusively for heating and lighting prior to 1900. Advice of power experts and examination of literature indicate a steady rise in the proportion used for work performance from 2 per cent in 1900 to 24 per cent in the early 1940s and to 28 per cent in 1950.

Table K, Line 17. Percentages in Table G, Col. 2, multiplied by total energy input (Table J, Line 17).

Efficiency of Conversion

Table G, Col. 4. Conversion efficiency is assumed to be the same as for bituminous coal and anthracite, since natural gas which is devoted to work output is also used predominantly for steam generation.

Work Output

Table G, Col. 3. Energy input for work expressed in coal equivalent (Table K, Line 17) converted to horsepower-hours (on the basis of 10,297 horsepower-hours per ton of coal equivalent).

Table J, Line 17. Table G, Col. 3, multiplied by the percentages of conversion efficiency shown in Table G, Col. 4.

FUEL WOOD

Energy Supply

Table H, Col. 1. Rough estimates of fuel wood consumption for end-of-decade years, 1850–1930, were obtained by averaging data for the preceding decade and the following decade from *Fuel Wood Used in the United States, 1630–1930*, Table 2 (U.S. Forest Service, U.S. Department of Agriculture, Circular 641, February 1942). Estimates for 1940 and 1950 were furnished by H. R. Josephson, Chief of the Forest Economics Division, U.S. Department of Agriculture. The 1945 estimate is based on an assumed straight-line decrease for each year from 1940 to 1950.

Table J, Line 18. H. R. Josephson, in a letter to J. Frederic Dewhurst, November 5, 1947, suggested that prior to 1900 a ratio of 1.25 cords of fuel wood to one ton of coal equivalent should be used in converting fuel wood to coal equivalent, and after 1900 (because of the larger proportion of soft wood used) a ratio of 1.35 cords. For 1900 a ratio of 1.30 cords was used. Figures in Table H, Col. 1, were converted into tons of coal equivalent on the basis of these ratios.

Energy Used for Work Performance

Table H, Col. 2. Data on the consumption of fuel wood for various uses are scanty, but there is general agreement that most of the total supply has been used to provide heat, predominantly in households. On the basis of a Census report for 1879 (Charles S. Sargent, "The Forests of the United States in Their Economic Aspects," *Census of Manu-*

factures, 1879, Vol. 9, p. 489), which indicated that nearly 4 per cent of the total supply in that year was used by manufacturing, mining and other industrial and transportation enterprises, it was assumed that in 1880 about 3 per cent was used to generate power for performing work. Prior to that year the proportion was undoubtedly larger, and later, because of the inroads of coal, there was a further decline. Today about the only use of fuel wood as a source of power for work is in a few small lumbering operations. In the absence of statistical records, the percentages of fuel wood energy used for work performance were estimated on the basis of scattered indications in the literature. Though arbitrary, they are believed to be reasonable.

Table K, Line 18. Percentages in Table H, Col. 2, multiplied by the figures for total energy input in Table J, Line 18.

Efficiency of Energy Conversion

Table H, Col. 4. Conversion efficiency is assumed to be the same as for bituminous coal, anthracite and natural gas, since fuel wood is also used for steam generation.

Work Output

Table H, Col. 3. Energy input for work expressed in coal equivalent (Table K, Line 18) converted to horsepower-hours (on the basis of 10,297 horsepower-hours per ton of coal equivalent).

Table L, Line 18. Table H, Col. 3, multiplied by percentages of conversion efficiency shown in Table H, Col. 4.

TABLE A. WORK ANIMALS: NUMBER, ENERGY INPUT AND WORK OUTPUT, 1850–1950

Year	Number of Farm Work Animals (1)	Farm Work Animals, Energy Input and Work Output (2)	Number of Nonfarm Work Animals (3)	Nonfarm Work Animals, Energy Input and Work Output (4)
	(Millions)	(Billions of Horsepower-Hours)	(Millions)	(Billions of Horsepower-Hours)
1850	5.1	2.6	0.8	2.8
1860	7.4	3.7	1.2	3.9
1870	7.1	3.6	1.6	4.8
1880	9.5	4.8	2.1	6.3
1890	13.4	6.7	2.6	7.7
1900	15.6	7.8	3.1	9.0
1910	18.0	9.0	3.5	9.0
1920	20.3	10.2	2.1	5.0
1930	17.3	8.7	0.3	0.7
1940	12.2	6.1	0.3	0.6
1945	10.6	5.3	0.3	0.6
1950	6.8	3.4	0.2	0.4

Sources: See accompanying text, *Animate Energy: Work Animals.*

APPENDIX 25-3 (continued)

TABLE B. WIND: NUMBER, ESTIMATED ENERGY INPUT AND EFFICIENCY OF ENERGY CONVERSION OF WINDMILLS; GROSS TONNAGE AND TON-MILES OF SAILING VESSELS, 1850-1950

| Year | Windmills | | | Sailing Vessels | |
	Number (1)	Wind Energy Input (2)	Efficiency of Energy Conversion (3)	Gross Tons (4)	Ton-Miles (5)
	(Thousands)	(Millions of Horsepower-Hours)	(Per Cent)	(Thousands)	(Billions)
1850	70	35	18	3,010	63.2
1860	100	50	20	4,486	94.2
1870	150	75	22	2,363	49.6
1880	200	100	25	2,366	49.7
1890	400	200	30	2,109	44.3
1900	600	300	35	1,885	39.6
1910	900	450	36	1,655	34.8
1920	1,000	500	36	1,272	26.7
1930	1,000	500	36	757	15.9
1940	650	325	36	200	4.2
1945	593	297	36	115	2.4
1950	294	147	36	82	1.7

Sources: See accompanying text, *Wind: Windmills* and *Wind: Sailing Vessels.*

TABLE C. WATER WHEELS — DIRECT DRIVE: ESTIMATED ENERGY INPUT AND EFFICIENCY OF ENERGY CONVERSION, 1850-1950

| Year | Production | | Efficiency Input to Shaft (3) | Energy Input (4) | Efficiency to Work Bench (5) | Efficiency of Energy Conversion (6) |
	Kilowatt-Hours (1)	Horsepower-Hours (2)				
	(Millions)		(Per Cent)	(Millions of Horsepower-Hours)	(Per Cent)	(Per Cent)
1850	1,033	1,384	60	2,307	65	39.0
1860	1,436	1,924	64	3,006	68	43.5
1870	1,830	2,452	68	3,606	71	48.3
1880	2,025	2,714	72	3,769	74	53.3
1890	1,961	2,628	76	3,458	77	58.5
1900	1,950	2,613	80	3,266	80	64.0
1910	2,220	2,948	84	3,510	81	68.0
1920	3,150	4,221	87	4,852	82	71.3
1930	1,100	1,474	88	1,675	83	73.0
1940	650	871	89	979	84	74.8
1945	620	831	90	923	84	75.6
1950	500	670	90	744	85	76.6

Sources: See accompanying text, *Water: Water Wheels — Direct Drive.*

TABLE D. HYDROELECTRIC: ESTIMATED ENERGY INPUT, EFFICIENCY OF ENERGY CONVERSION, TOTAL ENERGY OUTPUT AND PER CENT OF OUTPUT USED FOR WORK PERFORMANCE, 1850–1950

Year	Production Kilowatt-Hours (1) (Millions)	Production Horsepower-Hours (2) (Millions)	Efficiency Input to Shaft (3) (Per Cent)	Energy Input (4) (Millions of Horsepower-Hours)	Efficiency to Work Bench (5) (Per Cent)	Total Energy Output (6) (Millions of Horsepower-Hours)	Per Cent of Output Used for Work Performance (7)	Efficiency of Energy Conversion (8) (Per Cent)
1850	—	—	—	—	—	—	—	—
1860	—	—	—	—	—	—	—	—
1870	—	—	—	—	—	—	—	—
1880	—	—	—	—	—	—	—	—
1890	250	335	85	394	77	258	70	65.5
1900	1,600	2,144	88	2,436	80	1,715	70	70.4
1910	5,750	7,705	91	8,467	84	6,472	64	76.4
1920	20,311	27,217	93	29,266	86	23,407	58	80.0
1930	34,874	46,731	94	49,714	88	41,123	52	82.7
1940	51,659	69,223	95	72,866	90	62,301	47	85.5
1945	84,747	113,561	95	119,538	90	102,205	44	85.5
1950	100,885	135,186	95	142,301	90	121,667	42	85.5

Sources: See accompanying text, *Water: Hydroelectric.*

APPENDIX 25-3 (continued)

TABLE E. BITUMINOUS COAL AND ANTHRACITE: ESTIMATED ENERGY USED FOR WORK PERFORMANCE
AND EFFICIENCY OF ENERGY CONVERSION, 1850–1950

	Bituminous Coal		Anthracite			Bituminous Coal and Anthracite
Year	Energy Used for Work Performance (1)	(2)	Consumption (3)	Energy Used for Work Performance (4)	(5)	Efficiency of Energy Conversion (6)
	(Per Cent of Total)	(Billions of Horsepower-Hours)	(Thousands of Tons)	(Per Cent of Total)	(Billions of Horsepower-Hours)	(Per Cent)
1850	80	34.8	4,292	70	30.0	1.1
1860	79	75.4	10,841	61	66.0	1.3
1870	78	167.1	19,822	52	102.9	1.8
1880	77	404.7	28,210	43	121.1	2.3
1890	76	867.0	45,596	34	154.8	2.6
1900	75	1,602.0	55,515	25	138.6	3.0
1910	65	2,725.9	81,110	22	178.1	4.4
1920	55	2,877.8	85,786	19	162.7	7.0
1930	44	2,050.8	67,628	16	108.0	13.6
1940	35	1,583.1	49,000	13	63.6	16.3
1945	30	1,740.1	51,600	12	61.8	16.9
1950	25	1,168.1	39,900	10	39.8	18.5

Sources: See accompanying text, Mineral Fuels: Bituminous Coal and Mineral Fuels: Anthracite.

TABLE F. PETROLEUM: APPARENT CONSUMPTION, ESTIMATED ENERGY USED FOR WORK
PERFORMANCE AND EFFICIENCY OF ENERGY CONVERSION, 1850–1950

Year	Production [a] (1)	Imports [a] (2)	Exports [a] (3)	Apparent Net Consumption [a] (4)	Energy Used for Work Performance (5)	(6)	Efficiency of Energy Conversion (7)
	(Thousands of Barrels)	(Thousands of Barrels)	(Thousands of Barrels)	(Thousands of Barrels)	(Per Cent of Total)	(Billions of Horsepower-Hours)	(Per Cent)
1850	—	—	—	—	—	—	—
1860	—	—	—	—	—	—	—
1870	4,167	—	—	4,167	—	—	—
1880	26,286	—	53	26,233	—	—	—
1890	45,824	—	172	45,652	—	—	—
1900 [b]	63,621	—	594	63,027	15	21.5	3.0
1910	209,557	571	4,288	205,840	27	126.7	5.0
1920	442,929	106,175	9,295	539,809	39	479.9	7.0
1930	898,011	62,129	23,705	936,435	51	1,088.6	8.0
1940	1,353,214	42,662	51,496	1,344,380	55	1,685.5	8.5
1945	1,713,655	74,337	32,998	1,754,994	56	2,240.3	8.7
1950	1,973,574	177,714	34,823	2,116,465	58	2,798.2	9.0

Sources: See accompanying text, Mineral Fuels: Petroleum.   a. Crude oil only.
b. Prior to 1900, used exclusively for lighting.

APPENDIX 25–3 (continued)

TABLE G. NATURAL GAS: PRODUCTION, ESTIMATED ENERGY USED FOR WORK PERFORMANCE
AND EFFICIENCY OF ENERGY CONVERSION, 1850–1950

Year	Production (1)	Energy Used for Work Performance		Efficiency of Energy Conversion (4)
		(2)	(3)	
	(Millions of Cubic Feet)	(Per Cent of Total)	(Billions of Horsepower-Hours)	(Per Cent)
1850	—	—	—	—
1860	—	—	—	—
1870	—	—	—	—
1880	7,073	—	—	—
1890	250,000	—	—	—
1900	236,585	2.0	2.0	3.0
1910	509,155	10.0	21.5	4.4
1920	798,210	14.5	48.9	7.0
1930	1,943,421	19.0	156.0	13.6
1940	2,660,222	23.5	264.1	16.3
1945	3,918,686	25.8	427.1	16.9
1950	6,282,060	28.0	743.1	18.5

Sources: See accompanying text, *Mineral Fuels: Natural Gas*.

TABLE H. FUEL WOOD: CONSUMPTION, ESTIMATED ENERGY USED FOR WORK PERFORMANCE
AND EFFICIENCY OF ENERGY CONVERSION, 1850–1950

Year	Consumption (1)	Energy Used for Work Performance		Efficiency of Energy Conversion (4)
		(2)	(3)	
	(Millions of Cords)	(Per Cent of Total)	(Billions of Horsepower-Hours)	(Per Cent)
1850	102	6.0	50.5	1.1
1860	126	5.0	51.9	1.3
1870	138	4.0	45.5	1.8
1880	136	3.0	33.6	2.3
1890	120	2.0	19.8	2.6
1900	100	1.3	10.3	3.0
1910	91	1.0	6.9	4.4
1920	83	0.7	4.4	7.0
1930	75	0.5	2.9	13.6
1940	75	0.3	1.8	16.3
1945	62	0.3	1.4	16.9
1950	50	0.2	0.7	18.5

Sources: See accompanying text, *Fuel Wood*.

APPENDIX 25–3 (continued)

TABLE I. ESTIMATED EFFICIENCY OF ENERGY CONVERSION, BY SOURCE OF ENERGY, 1850–1950

(*Per Cent*)

Year	All Sources	Inanimate Energy				
		All Sources	Fuels and Water Power	Minerals and Water Power	Minerals	Bituminous Coal, Anthracite, Natural Gas and Fuel Wood
1850	8.2	3.0	1.8	2.4	1.1	1.1
1860	7.4	3.0	2.0	2.2	1.3	1.3
1870	5.8	2.7	2.3	2.4	1.8	1.8
1880	5.2	2.8	2.6	2.7	2.3	2.3
1890	4.5	2.9	2.8	2.8	2.6	2.6
1900	4.4	3.2	3.2	3.2	3.0	3.0
1910	5.4	4.7	4.7	4.6	4.4	4.4
1920	7.9	7.4	7.4	7.4	7.0	7.0
1930	12.7	12.3	12.3	12.3	11.8	13.6
1940	13.5	13.2	13.2	13.2	12.6	16.3
1945	13.7	13.5	13.5	12.5	12.8	16.9
1950	13.8	13.6	13.6	13.6	12.9	18.5

Sources: Based on energy input and work output as shown in Tables A–H and J–L.

APPENDIX 25-3 (continued)

TABLE J. ESTIMATED TOTAL ENERGY SUPPLY, BY SOURCE, 1850–1950

(Thousands of Tons of Coal Equivalent)

Source of Energy	1850	1860	1870	1880	1890	1900	1910	1920	1930	1940	1945	1950
1. Total	90,999	121,985	152,834	195,129	273,607	364,539	623,274	810,438	867,315	957,465	1,221,570	1,270,665
2. Animate	656	915	1,020	1,346	1,738	2,041	2,223	1,970	1,442	1,185	1,283	990
3. Human workers	130	173	204	269	341	405	471	495	528	530	714	619
4. Work animals	525	742	816	1,077	1,397	1,636	1,752	1,475	914	656	569	371
5. Inanimate	90,343	121,070	151,814	193,783	271,869	362,499	621,051	808,468	865,873	956,279	1,220,287	1,269,675
6. Wind	139	208	114	117	115	115	118	106	83	40	34	18
7. Windmills	3	5	7	10	19	29	44	49	49	32	29	14
8. Sailing vessels	136	203	107	107	95	85	75	57	34	9	5	4
9. Water	224	292	350	366	374	554	1,163	3,312	4,990	7,169	11,696	13,888
10. Water wheels (direct drive)	224	292	350	366	336	317	341	471	163	95	90	72
11. Hydroelectric	—	—	—	—	38	237	822	2,841	4,827	7,074	11,606	13,816
12. Fuel	89,980	120,570	151,350	193,300	271,380	361,830	619,770	805,050	860,800	949,070	1,208,557	1,255,769
13. Minerals	8,380	19,770	40,950	84,500	175,380	284,910	552,360	743,570	805,240	893,510	1,162,627	1,218,729
14. Bituminous	4,220	9,260	20,810	51,040	110,790	207,440	407,270	508,150	452,640	439,250	563,307	453,760
15. Anthracite	4,160	10,510	19,220	27,350	44,200	53,820	78,630	83,170	65,560	47,500	50,020	38,679
16. Petroleum	—	—	920	5,820	10,140	13,950	45,570	119,500	207,300	297,610	388,510	468,530
17. Natural gas	—	—	—	290	10,250	9,700	20,890	32,750	79,740	109,150	160,790	257,760
18. Fuel wood	81,600	100,800	110,400	108,800	96,000	76,920	67,410	61,480	55,560	55,560	45,930	37,040

Sources: Tables A through H and accompanying text.

Note: Slight discrepancies in addition are due to rounding.

TABLE K. Estimated Energy Input Used for Work Performance, by Source, 1850–1950

(Thousands of Tons of Coal Equivalent)

Source of Energy	1850	1860	1870	1880	1890	1900	1910	1920	1930	1940	1945	1950
1. Total	12,209	20,185	32,124	56,149	103,366	174,978	300,328	351,265	334,998	354,176	440,694	468,181
2. Animate	656	915	1,020	1,346	1,738	2,041	2,223	1,970	1,442	1,185	1,283	990
3. Human workers	130	173	204	269	341	405	471	495	528	530	714	619
4. Work animals	525	742	816	1,077	1,397	1,636	1,752	1,475	914	656	569	371
5. Inanimate	11,553	19,270	31,104	54,803	101,628	172,938	298,105	349,295	333,556	352,990	439,411	467,191
6. Wind	139	208	114	117	115	115	118	106	83	40	34	18
7. Windmills	3	5	7	10	19	29	44	49	49	32	29	14
8. Sailing vessels	136	203	107	107	95	85	75	57	34	9	5	4
9. Water	224	292	350	366	363	483	867	2,119	2,673	3,420	5,197	5,875
10. Water wheels (direct drive)	224	292	350	366	336	317	341	471	163	95	90	72
11. Hydroelectric	—	—	—	—	27	116	526	1,648	2,510	3,325	5,107	5,803
12. Fuel	11,190	18,770	30,640	54,320	101,150	172,320	297,120	347,070	330,800	349,530	434,180	461,298
13. Minerals	6,290	13,730	26,220	51,060	99,230	171,320	296,450	346,640	330,520	349,360	434,040	461,228
14. Bituminous	3,380	7,320	16,230	39,300	84,200	155,580	264,730	279,480	199,160	153,740	168,990	113,440
15. Anthracite	2,910	6,410	9,990	11,760	15,030	13,460	17,300	15,800	10,490	6,180	6,000	3,868
16. Petroleum	—	—	—	—	—	2,090	12,300	46,610	105,720	163,690	217,570	271,750
17. Natural gas	—	—	—	—	—	190	2,090	4,750	15,150	25,650	41,480	72,170
18. Fuel wood	4,900	5,040	4,420	3,260	1,920	1,000	670	430	280	170	140	70

Note: Slight discrepancies in addition are due to rounding.

Sources: Tables A through H and accompanying text.

APPENDIX 25-3 (continued)

TABLE L. ESTIMATED WORK OUTPUT, BY SOURCE OF ENERGY, 1850–1950

(*Billions of Horsepower-Hours*)

Source of Energy	1850	1860	1870	1880	1890	1900	1910	1920	1930	1940	1945	1950
1. Total	10.3	15.4	19.0	29.9	48.2	78.5	165.7	288.4	440.3	497.4	630.9	674.9
2. Animate	6.8	9.4	10.5	13.9	17.9	21.0	22.9	20.3	14.9	12.2	13.2	10.2
3. Human workers	1.3	1.8	2.1	2.8	3.5	4.2	4.9	5.1	5.4	5.5	7.4	6.4
4. Work animals	5.4	7.6	8.4	11.1	14.4	16.9	18.0	15.2	9.4	6.8	5.9	3.8
5. Inanimate	3.6	5.9	8.5	16.0	30.3	57.6	142.8	268.1	425.4	485.2	617.7	664.7
6. Wind	1.4	2.1	1.1	1.1	1.0	1.0	.9	.8	.5	.2	.2	.1
7. Windmills	a	a	a	a	.1	.1	.2	.2	.2	.1	.1	.1
8. Sailing vessels	1.4	2.1	1.1	1.1	1.0	.9	.8	.6	.4	.1	.1	a
9. Water	.9	1.3	1.7	2.0	2.2	3.3	6.5	17.0	22.6	30.0	45.7	51.7
10. Water wheels (direct drive)	.9	1.3	1.7	2.0	2.0	2.1	2.4	3.5	1.2	.7	.7	.6
11. Hydroelectric	—	—	—	—	.2	1.2	4.1	13.6	21.4	29.3	45.0	51.1
12. Fuel	1.3	2.6	5.7	12.9	27.1	53.2	135.4	250.3	402.3	455.0	571.9	612.9
13. Minerals	.7	1.8	4.9	12.1	26.6	52.9	135.1	250.0	401.9	454.7	571.6	612.8
14. Bituminous	.4	1.0	3.0	9.3	22.5	48.1	119.9	201.5	278.9	258.0	294.1	216.1
15. Anthracite	.3	.9	1.9	2.8	4.0	4.2	7.8	11.4	14.7	10.4	10.4	7.4
16. Petroleum	—	—	—	—	—	.7	6.3	33.7	87.1	143.3	194.9	251.8
17. Natural gas	—	—	—	—	—	.1	1.0	3.4	21.2	43.1	72.2	137.5
18. Fuel wood	.6	.7	.8	.8	.5	.3	.3	.3	.4	.3	.2	.1

Sources: Tables A through H and accompanying text.

a. Less than .05.

Note: Slight discrepancies in addition are due to rounding.

Appendix 25-4. Estimated Total Horsepower of All Prime Movers, United States, 1849-1952

(Thousands)

Year	Total	Automotive[a]	Nonautomotive Total	Work Animals	Inanimate Total	Factories[b]	Mines	Railroads	Merchant Ships—Powered	Sailing Vessels	Farms[c]	Wind-mills	Electric Central Stations	Air-craft[d]
1849	—	—	—	—	—	1,100	50	435	305	—	—	—	—	—
1850	8,495	—	8,495	5,960	2,535	1,150	60	586	325	400	—	14	—	—
1859	—	—	—	—	—	1,600	150	1,940	503	—	—	—	—	—
1860	13,763	—	13,763	8,630	5,133	1,675	170	2,156	515	597	—	20	—	—
1869	—	—	—	—	—	2,346	350	4,100	624	—	—	—	—	—
1870	16,931	—	16,931	8,660	8,271	2,453	380	4,462	632	314	—	30	—	—
1879	—	—	—	—	—	3,411	650	7,720	703	—	605	—	—	—
1880	26,314	—	26,314	11,580	14,734	3,664	715	8,592	741	314	668	40	—	—
1889	—	—	—	—	—	5,939	1,300	16,440	1,078	—	1,233	—	260	—
1890	44,086	—	44,086	15,970	28,116	6,308	1,445	16,980	1,124	280	1,452	80	447	—
1899	—	32	—	—	—	9,633	2,754	21,835	1,542	—	3,420	—	2,134	—
1900	65,045	100	64,945	18,730	46,215	10,309	2,919	24,501	1,663	251	4,009	120	2,443	—
1909	—	7,714	—	—	—	16,393	4,401	48,491	2,750	—	9,311	—	5,225	—
1910	138,810	24,686	114,124	21,460	92,664	16,697	4,473	51,308	3,098	220	10,460	180	6,228	—
1919	—	230,432	—	—	—	19,432	5,112	76,660	6,229	—	20,796	—	15,250	—
1920	453,450	280,900	172,550	22,430	150,120	19,422	5,146	80,182	6,508	169	21,443	200	17,050	—
1929	—	1,424,980	—	—	—	19,328	5,450	111,881	9,017	—	27,261	—	40,014	3,091
1930	1,663,944	1,426,568	237,376	17,660	219,716	19,519	5,620	109,743	9,115	100	28,610	200	43,427	3,382
1939	—	2,400,000	—	—	—	21,239	7,149	90,500	10,000	—	40,750	—	52,115	6,000
1940	2,759,018	2,511,312	247,706	12,510	235,196	21,768	7,332	92,361	10,094	26	42,488	130	53,542	7,455
1950	4,747,871	4,403,617	344,254	7,040	337,214	32,921	9,167	110,969	11,032	11	63,090	59	87,965	22,000
1952[e]	5,726,886	5,361,386	365,500	5,980	359,520	35,045	9,523	101,690	13,207	9	73,590	62	103,453	22,941

Sources: Data for work animals, sailing vessels (horsepower-hours, Table L, Line 8, divided by annual hours of operation, shown in Explanatory Notes, Sailing Vessels) and windmills based on Appendix 25-3. All other data for years 1849 through 1919 from C. R. Daugherty, A. H. Horton and R. W. Davenport, *Power Capacity and Production in the United States*, U.S. Geological Survey, Water Supply Paper No. 579, 1928. The original data from this source were for years 1849 and subsequent ten-year intervals through 1919; estimates for 1850 and subsequent ten-year intervals through 1940 are based on straight-line interpolation of original data. All data for years 1929, 1939, 1950 and 1952 supplied by John A. Waring, Jr., who prepared them for *Steelways* magazine (American Iron and Steel Institute).

a. Includes passenger cars, trucks, buses and motorcycles.

b. Electric motors not included.

c. Horses and other work animals not included.

d. Includes private planes and commercial airliners.

e. In addition to the above classifications, the installed mechanical horsepower in a number of special industries were also calculated by Waring, as follows: municipal service electric power stations, 431,200; government nonutility power plants, 463,400; gas utility stations, 2,875,000; motor boats and yachts, 9,675,000; outboard-powered boats, 10,000,000; petroleum pipeline pumping stations, 1,730,900; natural gas pipeline pumping stations, 3,411,500; interurban rail and bus lines, 1,177,000; underground gas storage pools, 211,500; warehouses and trucking terminals, 8,400; construction and contractors' building equipment, 78,421,250. These total 108,405,550 hp, which when added to the 1952 total shown above, result in an aggregate total of 5,835,-332,550 hp.

APPENDIX 26–1. SELECTED DATA AND PROJECTIONS AT 1954 PRICE LEVEL

TABLE A. BASIC DATA FOR 1940, 1950, 1954, AND PROJECTIONS FOR 1960

(*Dollar Amounts at 1954 Price Level*)

Table and Page Reference	Item	Unit	1940[a]	1950[a]	1954[b]	1960[a]
	Basic Assumptions of the Survey					
Table 37, p. 118	Population	Millions	132.5	152.5	163.2	177.0
	Urban	"	74.8[e]	97.6	104.4	113.0
	Rural nonfarm	"	27.2[e]	31.6	35.9	43.0
	Rural farm	"	30.4	23.3	22.9	21.0
	Consumer units	"	n.a.	50.4	54.5[d]	58.0
	Households	"	34.9	43.5	48.0[d]	51.0
	Primary families	"	31.6	38.7	41.5[d]	44.0
	One-person households and households of unrelated individuals	"	3.4	4.7	6.5[d]	7.0
	Lodgers and resident employees	"	n.a.	6.9	6.5[d]	7.0
	Labor force	"	56.0	64.6	67.8	72.5
	Unemployed	"	8.1	3.1	3.2	3.5
	Employed, total	"	47.9	61.5	64.6	69.0
	Private	"	43.3	54.0	54.5	58.5
	Average weekly hours	Number	44.0	40.0	38.9	37.5
	Private man-hours per year	Billions	99.1	112.3	110.2	114.1
	Private national income per man-hour	Cents	149.9	216.1	240.7	268.0
	Private national income	Billions	$148.6	$242.7	$265.3[e]	$307.0
	Total national income	"	166.4	268.8	300.2	349.0
	Disposable personal income	"	155.0	229.9	253.6	285.5
	Gross national product or expenditure	"	207.6	320.4	357.1	413.5[f]
	Personal consumption expenditures	"	147.6	217.4	234.0	270.0
	Government expenditures for goods and services	"	28.4	46.9	77.5	81.0
	Private gross capital formation[g]	"	31.7	56.1	45.5	62.5
	Per Capita and Per Household Income					
Table 30, p. 89	Personal income	Billions	$ 160.3	$ 253.2	$ 286.5	$ 315.0
	Per capita[h]	Dollars	1,210	1,670	1,760	1,780
	Per household	"	4,590	5,820	6,020[i]	6,180
	Disposable personal income	Billions	155.0	229.9	253.6	285.5
	Per capita[h]	Dollars	1,170	1,520	1,560	1,610
	Per household	"	4,440	5,290	5,330[i]	5,600

Appendix 26-1. Table A (continued)

Table and Page Reference	Item	Unit	1940 [a]	1950 [a]	1954 [b]	1960 [a]
	Government Receipts and Expenditures [j]					
Table 29, p. 82	Government receipts, total	Billions	$36.4	$77.9	$90.1	$105.6
	Business taxes	"	26.4	46.9	47.5	59.8
	Personal taxes	"	5.3	23.3	32.9	29.6
	Social insurance contributions	"	4.7	7.7	9.7	16.2
	Government expenditures, total	"	37.5	68.6	97.4	105.6
	Purchases of goods and services	"	28.4	46.9	77.5	81.0
	Transfer payments	"	5.5	16.0	14.8	19.0
	Net interest paid	"	2.7	5.2	5.4	5.6
	Subsidies less current surplus of government enterprises	"	.8	.5	−0.3	—
	Government surplus or deficit (−)	"	−1.1	9.3	−7.3	
	Private Savings and Capital Formation [j]					
Table 29, p. 82	Gross private savings	Billions	$32.8	$46.9	$52.8	$62.5
	Personal saving	"	7.6	12.6	19.6	15.6
	Corporate saving	"	4.9	15.2	8.0	15.6
	Capital consumption allowances	"	17.2	24.1	29.4	31.3
	Miscellaneous [k]	"	3.1	−5.0	−4.1	—
	Gross investment	"	31.7	56.1	45.5	62.5
	Construction and capital equipment	"	23.9	50.3	49.7	62.5
	Inventory change and net foreign investment	"	7.8	5.8	−4.2	—
	Savings minus investment	"	+1.1	−9.2	+7.3	—
	Marriage, Birth and Death Rates					
Table 17, p. 56	Marriages per 1,000 women aged 17-29	Number	105	110	100 [l]	—
	Births per 1,000 population	"	19.4	24.0	25.0	—
	Deaths per 1,000 population [m]	"	10.7	9.6	9.2	—

Sources: 1954 — U.S. Bureau of the Census, U.S. Office of Business Economics, U.S. Bureau of Labor Statistics, National Office of Vital Statistics and *Economic Report of the President,* January 1955. For other years, see table references.

a. Dollar estimates adjusted to 1954 price level on basis of implicit price deflator for gross national product in the *Economic Report of the President,* January 1955, Tables D–1 and D–2, pp. 137-138.

b. The 1954 labor force and income and expenditure figures are not exactly comparable with figures for other years since they are based on recently revised series. The income and expenditure figures are preliminary estimates of the Council of Economic Advisers.

c. These estimates are not comparable with those for later years; 1950 estimates comparable with 1940 are: urban, 90.0 million; rural nonfarm, 39.2 million.

d. Derived from U.S. Bureau of the Census estimates for 1953.

e. Derived from preliminary estimates of the national income in the *Economic Report of the President,* January 1955.

f. Medium projection of the survey. The gross national product (at 1954 prices) might be as low as $350 billion or as high as $490 billion (see Table 15, p. 46); under wartime emergency conditions it could rise to nearly $600 billion (see p. 753).

g. Includes government net foreign investment.

h. Based on population estimates not adjusted for underenumeration; population figures shown above have been so adjusted.

i. Based on household estimate of 47.6 million, which is consistent with figures used for other years.

j. Based on concepts used by U.S. Department of Commerce in national income analysis.

k. Includes corporate inventory valuation adjustment, excess of wage accruals over disbursements and statistical discrepancy.

l. Based on U.S. Bureau of the Census projections of number of women aged 18-29 adjusted to include the estimated number 17 years of age.

m. Excludes armed forces overseas.

n.a. Not available.

Note: Slight discrepancies in addition are due to rounding.

APPENDIX 26–1 (continued)

TABLE B. SELECTED NEEDS AND DEMAND ESTIMATES FOR 1950 AND 1960

(Billions at 1954 Price Level^a*)*

Table and Page Reference	Item	1950 Demand	1950 Needs	1960 Demand	1960 Needs
Table 350, p. 925	Gross national product	$320.4	$375.4	$413.5	$442.8
	Personal consumption expenditures	217.4	230.5	270.0	281.4
	Government expenditures for goods and services	46.9	81.3	81.0	92.0
	Private gross capital formation[b]	56.1	63.6	62.5	69.4
Table 34, p. 107	Personal consumption expenditures[c]	217.4	230.5	270.0	281.4
	Food, liquor and tobacco	73.0	73.9	91.0	91.6
	Clothing, accessories and personal care	26.7	29.3	34.2	36.7
	Housing and utilities	31.5	35.5	38.4	39.8
	Household equipment and operation	32.3	32.5	39.3	39.5
	Consumer transportation	27.1	27.1	32.8	32.8
	Medical care and insurance	10.1	14.8	12.7	18.9
	Recreation	10.6	10.6	13.1	13.1
	Private education	3.3	3.9	4.5	5.1
	Religion	1.3	1.6	1.5	1.8
	Private welfare	1.0	1.0	1.3	1.3
Table 36, p. 114	Expenditures for capital goods[d]	58.5	74.5	74.3	87.4

a. Gross national product and capital goods expenditures shifted from 1950 to 1954 price level on basis of implicit price deflator for gross national product in *Economic Report of the President,* January 1955, Tables D–1 and D–2, pp. 137-138. Individual personal consumption expenditure groups shifted by use of U.S. Bureau of Labor Statistics consumers' price indexes for related groups.

b. Includes government net foreign investment.

c. Total includes occupational and miscellaneous expenses, not shown separately.

d. These estimates cover all expenditures for plant and equipment except expenditures for publicly owned military and naval plant and equipment and expenditures by state governments for equipment.

Note: Slight discrepancies in addition are due to rounding.

TABLE C. ESTIMATED ENERGY SUPPLY, ENERGY INPUT USED FOR WORK PERFORMANCE, AND WORK OUTPUT, BY SOURCE, 1940, 1950 AND 1954[a]

Table and Page Reference	Source of Energy	Energy Supply			Energy Input Used for Work Performance			Work Output		
		(Thousands of Tons of Coal Equivalent)			(Thousands of Tons of Coal Equivalent)			(Billions of Horsepower-Hours)		
		1940	1950	1954	1940	1950	1954	1940	1950	1954
Appendix 25–3, Tables J, K and L, pp. 1114–1116	Total	957,465	1,270,665	1,360,028	354,176	468,181	548,961	497.4	674.9	759.6
	Animate	1,185	990	925	1,185	990	925	12.2	10.2	9.5
	Human workers	530	619	635	530	619	635	5.5	6.4	6.6
	Work animals	656	371	290	656	371	290	6.8	3.8	2.9
	Inanimate	956,279	1,269,675	1,359,103	352,990	467,191	548,036	485.2	664.7	750.1
	Wind	40	18	14	40	18	14	.2	.1	.1
	Windmills	32	14	12	32	14	12	.1	.1	.1
	Sailing vessels	9	4	2	9	4	2	.1	b	b
	Water	7,169	13,888	15,826	3,420	5,875	6,686	30.0	51.7	58.1
	Water wheels (direct drive)	95	72	67	95	72	67	.7	.6	.5
	Hydroelectric	7,074	13,816	15,759	3,335	5,803	6,619	29.3	51.1	57.6
	Fuel	949,070	1,255,769	1,343,263	349,530	461,298	541,336	455.0	612.9	691.9
	Minerals	893,510	1,218,729	1,306,223	349,360	461,228	541,280	454.7	612.8	691.8
	Bituminous	439,250	453,760	363,000	153,740	113,440	90,750	258.0	216.1	172.4
	Anthracite	47,500	38,679	25,000	6,180	3,868	2,250	10.4	7.4	4.3
	Petroleum	297,610	468,530	568,633	163,690	271,750	341,180	143.3	251.8	307.1
	Natural gas	109,150	257,760	357,000	25,650	72,170	107,100	43.1	137.5	208.0
	Fuel wood	55,560	37,040	29,630	170	70	56	.3	.1	.1

a. Estimates for 1954 based on same sources as estimates for 1940 and 1950; see reference tables.

b. Less than .05.

Note: Slight discrepancies in addition are due to rounding.

INDEX

INDEX

The designation (t) after a page number indicates that the reference is to a table; (f) that the reference is to a chart or figure; (n) that the reference is to a note.

528(t), 538(t), 784(t); outside farms, 528(t); grazed, 519(t)

Forest conservation and development, 527–42; needs, cost and time required, 532(t), 571–73; planting, 532(t), 534–35, 572(t); protection against forest fires, 531–32, 572(t); protection against insects and disease, 532–33, 572(t); for recreational use, 532(t), 541–42, 572(t); roads and trails needed in, 532(t), 535–36, 572(t); stand improvements, 532(t), 533–34, 572(t); for timber production, 530–36; for wildlife habitat, 532(t), 539–41

Forest products: consumption, 760(f), 761(t), 764(t), 777(t); foreign trade balance in, 689(f); production, 761(t); see also Saw logs; Sawmill products; Timber; Wood; Wood pulp

Forest services, federal: demand and needs for, 1950, 1960, 647–48

Forestry and fishing: employment in, 733(t)

Foundations: consumption expenditure trends, 980–82(t), 1001(t); contributions to, 441(t); expenditures, 396–97, 412(t); number, 396–97

Fourastié, Jean, cited, 897

France: energy consumption and income per capita, 904(f); income per capita, 1938, 1948, 896(t); public finance and gross national product, 579(t); working time required to buy staple foods in, 897(t)

Freight cars, see Railroad freight service

French Association for the Improvement of Productivity, quoted, 914

Friends, Five Years Meeting: membership, 423(t)

Froman, Robert, quoted, 865

Frozen-food locker plants: number, 1094(t)

Frozen foods, 134, 139–40, 142, 147

Fruit juices: canned, per capita consumption trends, 786(t)

Fruits: per capita consumption trends, 786(t)

Fruits and vegetables: consumption per capita, 131(t), 133(f), 134, 141(t); consumption and family size, 143(f); demand per capita, 1950, 1960, 167(t); home-grown, consumption, 137, 138(t); home preservation of, 139(t), 140; recommended diets, 153(t); see also Citrus fruits and tomatoes; Fruit juices; Fruits; Vegetables

Fuel, ice and lighting supplies: consumption expenditures, 206(t), 207(f); demand and needs, 1950, 1960, 227(t), 231(t)

Fuel oil: efficiency in railroad freight service, 757(f)

Fuel wood: consumption, 1112(t); as source of energy, 1850–1950, 906(f), 907(f), 1108, 1112(t), 1114(t), 1115(t), 1116(t); as source of energy, 1940, 1950, 1954, 1121

Fuels: comparative efficiency in railroad freight service, 757; consumption per capita, 754; see also Fuel wood; Mineral fuels

Fulbright Act, 401

Full Employment Act of 1946, 446

Furniture and furnishings: demand and needs, 1950, 1960, 252–53, 258(t); expenditure trends, 232, 244(f), 245(t), 247–48, 968–70(t), 987–89(t), 998(t), 1005–06(t); farm family expenditures, 247(t), 250–52; production, 236(t); synthetic fibers used in, 237–39; trends in design and character, 234–39; see also Floor coverings; Household mechanical appliances

Gambling: consumption expenditures for, 366; see also Pari-mutuel betting and nonvending coin machines

Games, see Sports and specific games

Gardening: as a hobby, 359; as source of food, 137, 138(f)

Garrison Dam and Reservoir, 565

Gas, manufactured: prewar, World War II and postwar production compared, 1083(t); see also Gas utilities; Natural gas; Pipelines, gas

Gas turbine engines, 859–60

Gas utilities: consumption expenditures for, 206(t), 968–

70(t), 998(t), 1005(t); number of households using, 200–01(t), 202–03(t); productive facilities expenditure trends and projections, 487(t), 1008(t), 1012–14(t), 1019–21(t); rated capacity, 1093(t); see also Gas, manufactured; Natural gas

Gasoline, see Petroleum

Gasoline industries: rated capacity, 826(t)

Gastroenteritic diseases: mortality rate, 300(t)

General assistance: beneficiaries and expenditures, 458(t); beneficiaries and payments per beneficiary, 600(t); definition, 458(t)n; demand and needs, 1950, 1960, 636, 660(t); government transfer payments for, 434(t); see also Relief; Work relief

General Electric Co., cited, 839, 857, 868

General Motors Corporation, cited, 859, 861, 862

Germanium: industrial uses, 772–73, 873

Germany: immigration from, 50(f), 52, 948(t); immigration quotas, 53; income per capita, 1938, 1948, 896(t); public finance and gross national product, 579(t); working time required to buy staple foods in, 897(t)

Germany (Western): energy consumption and income per capita, 904(f)

Gibbon, Dr. John H., Jr., cited, 848

G.I. Bill: and the marriage rate, 55; provisions extended to Korean war veterans, 466; vocational rehabilitation, education and training under, 399(t); see also Veterans programs

Gilbert, Milton, cited, 895

Girdler Corporation, quoted, 869

Girl Scouts, 363, 438

Girls' Clubs, 363

Glass: new uses, 883–84

Glass containers manufacturing: rated capacity, 826(t)

Glass fibers, 184, 884

Gold: movement in international finance, 665(t)

Gold and dollar reserves: excluding United States, 710(t)

"Golden age" clubs, 363

Golf: consumption expenditures, club rental and fees, 977–79(t), 993–95(t), 1001(t); number of players, 361

Goodyear Tire and Rubber Company, 184, 864

Government borrowing, net, 584–85(t)

Government debt, 621, 622(t); see also Federal government, debt; Government expenditures, interest on debt

Government employee retirement programs: benefits, 1950, 637; demand and needs, 1950, 1960, 638(t), 639(t); government and employee contributions, 450(t); see also under Federal government; State and local governments

Government employment: trends and projections, 45, 46(t), 615(t), 617(t), 733(t), 744(t), 923

Government enterprises: employment in, 614, 615(t); expenditures and financing, 614, 616(t), 622(t), 626(t), 1061–62(t); volume of services and expenditures per work unit, 601–04

Government expenditures, 115–16, 577–662, 934–36; per capita, 596(f), 935; for capital goods, 621, 623(t), 624, 925(t), 954–57(t); causes of rising trend in, 590–614; character of, 614–25; components, 115; concentration in large spending units, 580; in current and constant dollars, 595(t); demand and needs, 1950, 1960, 82(t), 117, 654–62, 925(t), 936, 1063(t); federal-state-local relations in, 588–90, 613–14; by function, 587(t), 625–54, 1063(t); for general control, 587(t), 628(t), 630(t), 632(t), 651–53, 661(t); and gross national product, 87, 577, 578(t), 935–36; and growth in services, 593–94(t), 595–97; and increased government responsibilities, 605–14; interest on debt, 587(t), 591(t), 621, 622(t), 628(t), 630(t), 632(t), 649–51, 954–57(t); interest on debt, 1954, 1119; and interlevel transfers, 586–90; for land and structures, 623(t); and national income, 611–12; in 1954, 1119; and political and economic changes, 608–10; and population growth, 593–

migration to suburbs, 495; regional shifts, World War II, 478–81; and technology, 855–91; welfare expenditures of, 433, 468(t)

Infant mortality, 60, 300–01, 845

Inflation: and the Korean war, 3, 15, 24, 81, 85; postwar, 15–16, 23, 30, 81, 84, 920

Influenza and pneumonia: mortality rate, 300(t)

Information Service, National Council of Churches, cited, 425

Insecticides manufacturing: rated capacity, 1920–1952, 1089(t)

Insects and insecticides, 532–33, 846, 853

Instalment buying, 890–91; *see also* Consumer credit; Consumer debt

Institute of Public Opinion, cited, 372

Institutional care of dependents: government expenditure demand and needs for, 1950, 1960, 636, 660(t)

Insurance: accident, health and prepayment, consumption expenditure demand and needs, 1950, 1960, 343(t); life, industrial programs, 442, 443(t); voluntary health, 323–27; voluntary health, and family health and medical costs, 1047(t), 1049(t); *see also* Health and medical care, insurance and prepayment plans; National Service Life Insurance; Social insurance; Veterans life insurance

Interest on government debt, *see under* Government expenditures

Interest rates: and capital expansion, 474; on government debt, 621

Internal combustion engines, 858–62

International affairs: demand and needs for, 1950, 1960, 630, 657(t), 660(t), 1063(t); government expenditures for, 587(t), 626(t), 629–30; government expenditures per capita, 632(t); price indexes of government expenditures for, 591(t); *see also* Economic Cooperation Administration loans; European Recovery Program; Foreign aid; Foreign trade and finance; Lend-lease; Organization for European Economic Cooperation

International Labor Office: housing statistics, 205

International Labor Organization: convention on minimum standards of social security of, 462, 463–65(t)

International Ladies' Garment Workers' Union, 327

International trade, *see* Foreign trade and finance

International Wheat Agreement, 790, 791

Interstate Highway System, 289

Inventories, *see* Business inventories

Investment, gross private: definition, 83; demand and needs, 1950, 1960, at 1954 prices, 1120; differentiated from "capital goods," 108n; at 1953 prices, 88; in 1954, 1119; trends to 1960, 82(t), 954–57(t); World War II, 5(t), 10(t); *see also* Business inventories; Capital expenditures; Capital formation; Capital investment; Construction and capital equipment; Foreign investment, net; Productive facilities, private

Ireland: energy consumption and income per capita, 904(f); immigration from, 50(f), 52, 948(t); income per capita, 1938, 1948, 896(t); working time required to buy staple foods in, 897(t); *see also* Eire; Northern Ireland

Iron: consumption and supply, 767; physical properties, 769(t); production and consumption, 761(t); *see also* Iron ore

Iron (nutrient), *see* Nutrients

Iron and ferroalloys: consumption, 764(t), 777(t); trade balance in, 689(t)

Iron and steel industry: peak activity, World War II, 824(t); rated capacity, 1900–1952, 816(t)

Iron (pig) industry: rated capacity, 826(t), 1084(t)

Iron ore: imports, 1950, 1960, 713(t); production, consumption and world output, 762(f), 1074(t); scarcity of, 757; supply expansion goal for, 776(t); *see also* Iron

Irrigation: of agricultural land, 524–26; conservation of

water resources for, 548–49; needs for, cost and time required, 518(t), 526–27, 545(t), 549–50, 572(t)

Irrigation enterprises, 526(t), 549(t)

Irrigation maintenance: acreage served and government expenditure per acre, 606–07(t)

Israel: energy consumption and income per capita, 904(f); working time required to buy staple foods in, 897(t)

Italy: energy consumption and income per capita, 904(f); housing conditions, 205(t); immigration from, 50(f), 52, 948(t); income per capita, 1938, 1948, 896(t); public finance and gross national product, 579(t); working time required to buy staple foods in, 897(t)

Japan: energy consumption and income per capita, 904(f)

Jenkins, Edward C., cited, 421

Jet engines, 278, 859, 860

Jewelry: consumption expenditures for, 172(t)

Jewish agencies: aid in resettlement of displaced persons, 427; welfare expenditures of, 435–36

Jewish congregations: membership, 416, 423(t); schools operated by, 425

Jones, Dr. Lewis Webster, quoted, 344

Kaman, Charles H., cited, 844

Kellogg (W. K.) Foundation, 320, 397

Kelly, Sherwin F., quoted, 875–76

Korean war: defense expenditures in, compared with World War II, 3; G.I. benefits extended to veterans of, 466; inflationary effect, 3, 15, 24, 81, 85; and private productive facilities expansion, 940; and welfare activities, 437–38

Kountz, Dr. William B., cited, 848

Kravis, Irving B., cited, 895

Kuznets, Simon, cited, 111

Labor, human: as source of energy, 1850–1950, 907(f), 1102–03, 1114(t), 1115(t), 1116(t); as source of energy, 1940, 1950, 1954, 1121

Labor force, 721–53, 941–42; age composition, 727–28; agricultural, 784, 804–07; and the business cycle, 721–24; characteristics of, 721–24; children in, 1870–1930, 727; civilian, 1071(t); definition of, 721; industrial distribution, 731–34; median age of men and women in, 727–28; occupational distribution, 731(t); participation rate for standardized population, 722n; and population, 724(f), 725(t); postwar adjustments in, 746–47, 922; and productivity, 941–42; projections, 1960, 37, 46(t), 118(t), 748–50, 751–53, 922, 942; seasonal movements in, 721; sex composition, 725–27; size, 1954, 1118; size, trends in, 37, 46(t), 118(t), 724–25, 1064–70(t), 1073(t); social-economic distribution, 729–31; under-utilization of, 738(t); utilization of, 734–39; and World War II, 12, 741–46; *see also* Employment; Unemployment; Wages and salaries; Work week

Labor Health Institute, 327, 344

Labor productivity, 739–41, 751; *see also* Productivity

Labor unions: consumption expenditures for, 980–82(t), 1002(t); and employee health, welfare and pension plans, 327, 443–44

Laborers: education and income, 729(t); number in labor force, 730(t), 731(t)

Land and water resources: government expenditure demand and needs for, 1950, 1960, 647, 661(t)

Land conservation and development, 513–27; drainage for, 523–24; irrigation for, 524–27; land clearing for, 521–23; land retirement for, 520–21; needs for, cost and time required, 518(t), 519–20, 571, 572(t); programs of the 1930s, 518–19; *see also* conservation and development *under* Cropland; Grazing lands

Land retirement: programs and needs for, 518(t), 520–21, 572(t)